BRITISH and AMERICAN

HIT

Singles

| 51 YEARS OF TRANSATLANTIC HITS | 1946–1997 |

Chris Davies

BRITISH and AMERICAN HIT SINGLES
1946–1997
Chris Davies

Printed by The Bath Press, Bath

for the publishers
BT Batsford
583 Fulham Road
London
SW6 5BY

ISBN 0 7134 8275 3

A catalogue record for this book is available from the British Library

ACKNOWLEDGMENTS

I extend my most heartfelt thanks to the following people and organisations that have made this book possible.

Frank Bacon (Radio Luxembourg) for supplying a valuable source of data and for his professionalism when faced with what must have seemed an endless barrage of questions!

Messrs Ian Chamberlain and **Stuart Butler-Mitchell** for their understanding, patience and courage in putting up with being asked to provide that I thought I wanted and for providing what I really needed.

The British Library whose staff could not have been more helpful countrywide

RIAA, Recording Industry Association of America, for helping to clarify the million sellers in the USA.

Keith Sivyer for providing much of the last-minute research literally days prior to delivery to the publisher.

Ivor Webber for supporting this project until the end (and who now knows more about pop music than he ever wanted to).

My wife and family – at last I have put my record ledgers to bed so you can now have your tables back!

Chris Davies 1997

PREFACE

This book lists those titles which appeared in the top 75 singles charts in the UK and the top 45 singles in the USA covering the years 1946 to 1977. Titles are listed in alphabetical order by the **first** name of the artist/s and these entries are sublisted to show the first dates of release. I have considered this necessary because for some titles as much as 20 years elapsed time exists between appearance as a hit in the USA and entry to the UK chart. As an example, Bing Crosby's *White Christmas* first appeared in the US charts in 1942 (see Bing Crosby entry number 231) but appeared in the UK charts in 1977 (entry number 333).

Those titles which sold one million copies or more as a single title are also included (see Legend) and these may precede 1946 (having taken many years to reach one million sales). Where this applies I have also included other 'well known' titles by that artist and have added notes giving a brief background to the artist (see Legend). Some entries do not include all hits simply because the finished volume would then have been far too long.

One of the difficulties encountered is that of US and UK spellings and we have tried to keep these as they appear on the records.

LEGEND

+   Chart position confirmed by US Rhythm and Blues charts

!   Chart position confirmed by US Country and Western Charts

*   Worldwide one million seller

B: date of birth

D: date of demise

FOREWORD

Chris Davies has been interested in popular music for as long as he can remember (and he's not prepared to say how long that is). He put his interest to good use running three mobile discos called 'The Music Machine' during the 1970s and 1980s which were well known around London and the Home Counties (DJs Chris Allan Gauci and Keith Sivyer. Allan and Keith have now gone on to do other things). Driven by the need to be well informed, as a hobby Chris started to keep handwritten lists of how singles titles were performing in the UK and the USA, which he maintained even while serving with HM Forces in various stations around the world.

From a personal collection of over 20,0000 singles, others belonging to associates and from documented records which he has traced, Chris has fulfilled a long-term ambition to create from his notes an authoritative book which lists singles that made it into the top 75 in the UK and the top 40 in the US between 1940 and 1997. His creation represents over 20 years of work and investigation, much of which was conducted in dusty back rooms of antique shops searching out old records in the interests of accuracy of information and in public libraries.

I am sure that Chris's long-suffering wife Jane, his two children Robert and Jennifer (who have had to get used to Daddy locking himself away for long periods) and the many people who have put up with his thirst for information will applaud his efforts and dedication which have culminated in the book you have before you.

His friend and partner

Ivor Webber

A

ISSUE	TITLE	UK LBL	UK POS	UK YEAR	US POS	US YEAR	US LBL
A Certain Ratio Vocal/Instrumental Group from the UK							
1	Won't Stop Loving You	(A&M ACR 540)	55	1990	0	1990	
A Guy Called Gerald Name: Gerald Simpson, Male Artist from the UK							
1	Voodoo Ray	(Rham! RS 804	55	1989	0	1989	
2	Voodoo Ray (Re-Entry)	(Rham! RS 804)	12	1989	0	1989	
3	Fx / Eyes Of Sorrow	(Subscape AG CG 1)	52	1989	0	1989	
A Homeboy, A Hippy & A Funki Dredd Vocal/Instrumental Group from the UK							
1	Total Confusion	(Tam Tam 7ttt 031)	56	1990	0	1990	
2	Freedom	(Tam Tam 7ttt 039)	68	1990	0	1990	
3	Here We Go Again	(Polydor Pzcd 302)	57	1994	0	1994	
A House Vocal/Instrumental Group from Ireland							
1	Endless Art	(Setanta Ahou 1)	46	1992	0	1992	
2	Take It Easy On Me	(Setanta Ahou 2)	55	1992	0	1992	
3	Why Me	(Setanta Cdahou 4)	52	1994	0	1994	
4	Here Comes The Good Times	(Setanta Cdhous 5)	37	1994	0	1994	
A Man Called Adam Vocal/Instrumental Group from the UK							
1	Barefoot In The Head	(Big Life Blr 28	70	1990	0	1990	
2	Barefoot In The Head (Re-Entry)	(Big Life Blr 28)	60	1990	0	1990	
A Split Second Production Group from Belgium and Italy							
1	Flesh	(Ffrr Fx 178)	68	1991	0	1991	
A Taste Of Honey Mixed Vocal Group from the USA Names: Janice Marie Johnson, Perry Kimble, Hazel Payne & Donald Johnson							
* 1	Boogie Oogie Oogie	(Capitol Cl 15988)	3	1978	1	1978	(Capitol 4565)
* 2	Sukiyaki		0	1981	3	1981	(Capitol 4953)
3	Boogie Oogie Oogie (Re-Mix)	(Capitol Cl 357)	59	1985	0	1985	
A Tribe Called Quest Male Rap Band from the USA							
1	Bonita Applebum	(Jive Jive 256)	47	1990	0	1990	
2	Can I Kick It	(Jive Jive 265)	15	1991	0	1991	
3	Oh My God	(Jive JiveCD 355)	68	1994	0	1994	
4	1nce Again	(Jive JiveCD 399)	34	1996	0	1996	
5	Stressed Out	(Jive JiveCD 404)	33	1996	0	1996	
6	The Jam (EP)	(Jive JiveCD 427)	61	1997	0	1997	
HIT 5 IS CREDITED TO A TRIBE CALLED QUEST FEATURING FAITH EVANS & RAPHAEL SAAGIQ							
A Way Of Life Vocal/Instrumental Group From the USA							
1	Trippin' On Your Love	(Eternal YZ 464)	55	1990	0	1990	
A'me Lorain Female Vocalist, B: 1978 And Hails from California							
1	Whole Wide World		0	1990	9	1990	(RCA 9098)
A-Ha Vocal/Instrumental Group from Norway Names: Morten Harket, Pal Waaktaar And Mags Furuholem							
1	Take On Me	(Warner Bros W 9006)	2	1985	1	1985	(Warner Bros 29011)
2	The Sun Always Shines On TV	(Warner Bros W 8846)	1	1985	20	1986	(Warner Bros 28846)
3	Train Of Thought	(Warner Bros W 8736)	8	1986	0	1986	
4	Hunting High And Low	(Warner Bros W 6663)	5	1986	0	1986	
5	I've Been Losing You	(Warner Bros W 8594)	8	1986	0	1986	
6	Cry Wolf	(Warner Bros W 8500)	5	1986	0	1986	
7	Manhattan Skyline	(Warner Bros W 8405)	13	1987	0	1987	
8	The Living Daylights	(Warner Bros W 8305)	5	1987	0	1987	
9	Stay On These Roads	(Warner Bros W 7936)	5	1988	0	1988	
10	The Blood That Moves The Body	(Warner Bros W 7840)	25	1988	0	1988	
11	Touchy	(Warner Bros W 7749)	11	1988	0	1988	

	ISSUE	TITLE	UK LBL	UK POS	UK YEAR	US POS	US YEAR	US LBL
	12	You Are The One	(Warner Bros W 7636)	13	1988	0	1988	
	13	Crying In The Rain	(Warner Bros W 9547)	13	1990	0	1990	
	14	I Call Your Name	(Warner Bros W 9462)	44	1990	0	1990	
	15	Move To Memphis	(Warner Bros W 0070)	47	1991	0	1991	
	16	Dark Is The Night	(Warner Bros W 0175cd)	19	1993	0	1993	
	17	Angel	(Warner Bros W 0195cd)	41	1993	0	1993	
	18	Shapes That Go Together	(Warner Bros W 0236cd)	27	1994	0	1994	

A.D.A.M. (Featuring) Amy Mixed Vocal/Instrumental Duo from France

	ISSUE	TITLE	UK LBL	UK POS	UK YEAR	US POS	US YEAR	US LBL
	1	Zombie	(Eternal YZ 951cd)	16	1995	0	1995	

Aaliyah Female Vocalist, Aaliyah (Al-Lee-Yah) Haughton from Detroit

	ISSUE	TITLE	UK LBL	UK POS	UK YEAR	US POS	US YEAR	US LBL
*	1	Back And Forth	(Jive Jivecd 359)	16	1994	5	1994	(Jive 42174)
*	2	(At Your Best) You Are Love	(Jive Jivecd 357)	27	1994	6	1994	(Jive 42239)
	3	Age Ain't Nothing But A Number	(Jive Jivecd 369)	32	1995	0	1995	
	4	Down With The Clique	(Jive Jivecd 377)	33	1995	0	1995	
	5	The Thing I Like	(Jive Jivecd 382)	33	1995	0	1995	
	6	I Need You Tonight	(Big Beat A 8130cd)	66	1996	0	1996	
	7	If Your Girl Only Knew	(Atlantic A 5669cd)	21	1996	11	1996	(Atlantic 98067)
	8	Got To Give It Up	(Atlantic A 5632cd)	37	1996	0	1996	
	9	If Your Girl Only Knew / One In A Million	(Atlantic A 5610cd)	15	1997	0	1997	
	10	4 Page Letter	(Atlantic At 0010cd1)	24	1997	0	1997	

HIT 6 IS CREDITED TO JUNIOR M.A.F.I.A. FEATURING AALIYAH

Aaron Hall Male Vocalist from the USA

	ISSUE	TITLE	UK LBL	UK POS	UK YEAR	US POS	US YEAR	US LBL
	1	Don't Be Afraid	(MCA Mcs 1632)	56	1992	0	1992	
	2	Get A Little Freaky With Me	(MCA Mcstd 1936)	66	1993	0	1993	
*	3	I Miss You		0	1994	14	1994	(Silas/MCA 54847)
	4	Dangerous Minds (EP)	(MCA Mcstd 48007)	35	1996	0	1996	

Aaron Neville Male Vocalist, B: 24 Jan 1941 New Orleans

	ISSUE	TITLE	UK LBL	UK POS	UK YEAR	US POS	US YEAR	US LBL
+	1	Over You		0	1960	21	1960	(Minit 612)
*	2	Tell It Like It Is		0	1966	2	1966	(Parlophone 101)
*	3	Don't Know Much	(Elektra Ekr 100)	2	1989	2	1989	(Elektra 69261)
	4	All My Life	(Elektra Ekr 105)	0	1990	11	1990	(Elektra 64987)
	5	Everybody Plays The Fool		0	1991	8	1991	(A&M 1563)
!	6	The Grand Tour		0	1993	38	1993	(A&M 580312)

Abba Group from Sweden/Norway

	ISSUE	TITLE	UK LBL	UK POS	UK YEAR	US POS	US YEAR	US LBL
*	1	Waterloo	(Epic Epc 2240)	1	1974	6	1974	(Atlantic 3035)
	2	Ring Ring	(Epic Epc 2452)	32	1974	0	1974	
*	3	So Long	(Polar, Sweden)	0	1974	0	1974	
*	4	Honey Honey	(Polar, Sweden)	0	1974	27	1974	(Atlantic 3209)
*	5	I Do, I Do, I Do, I Do, I Do	(Epic Epc 3229)	38	1975	15	1975	(Atlantic 3310)
*	6	S.O.S	(Epic Epc 3576)	6	1975	15	1975	(Atlantic 3265)
*	7	Mamma Mia	(Epic Epc 3790)	1	1975	32	1975	(Atlantic 3315)
	8	Fernando	(Epic Epc 4036)	1	1976	13	1976	(Atlantic 3346)
*	9	Dancing Queen	(Epic Epc 4499)	1	1976	1	1977	(Atlantic 3372)
	10	Money Money Money	(Epic Epc 4713)	3	1976	0	1976	
	11	Knowing Me Knowing You	(Epic Epc 4955)	1	1977	14	1977	(Atlantic 3387)
	12	The Name Of The Game	(Epic Epc 5750)	1	1977	12	1978	(Atlantic 3449)
	13	Take A Chance On Me	(Epic Epc 5950)	1	1978	3	1978	(Atlantic 3457)
	14	Summer Night City	(Epic Epc 6595)	5	1978	0	1978	
	15	Chiquitita	(Epic Epc 7030)	2	1979	29	1979	(Atlantic 3629)
	16	Does Your Mother Know	(Epic Epc 7316)	4	1979	19	1979	(Atlantic 3574)
	17	Angeleyes / Voulez-Vous	(Epic Epc 7499)	3	1979	0	1979	
	18	Gimme Gimme Gimme (A Man After Midnight)	(Epic Epc 7914)	3	1979	0	1979	
	19	I Have A Dream	(Epic Epc 8088)	2	1979	0	1979	
	20	The Winner Takes It All	(Epic Epc 8835)	1	1980	8	1981	(Atlantic 3776)
	21	Super Trouper	(Epic Epc 9089)	1	1980	0	1980	
	22	Lay All Your Love On Me	(Epic Epc A 1314)	7	1981	0	1981	
	23	One Of Us	(Epic Epc A 1740)	3	1981	0	1981	
	24	Head Over Heels	(Epic Epc A 2037)	25	1982	0	1982	
	25	The Day Before You Came	(Epic Epc A 2847)	32	1982	0	1982	
	26	When All Is Said And Done		0	1982	27	1982	(Atlantic 3889)
	27	Under Attack	(Epic Epc A 2971)	26	1982	0	1982	
	28	Thank You For The Music	(Epic Epc A 3894)	33	1983	0	1983	
	29	Dancing Queen (Re-Issue)	(Polydor Po 231)	16	1992	0	1992	

ISSUE	TITLE	UK LBL	UK POS	UK YEAR	US POS	US YEAR	US LBL
Abbacadabra Female Vocal/Instrumental Group from the UK							
1	Dancing Queen	(PWL International Pwl 246)	57	1992	0	1992	
ABC Names: Stephen Singleton, Mark White, Martin Fry & Mark Lickley.							
1	Tears Are Not Enough	(Neutron Nt 101)	19	1981	0	1981	
2	Poison Arrow	(Neutron Nt 102)	6	1982	25	1982	(Mercury 810340)
3	The Look Of Love (Part 1)	(Neutron Nt 103)	4	1982	18	1982	(Mercury 76168)
4	All Of My Heart	(Neutron Nt 104)	5	1982	0	1982	
5	The Look Of Love (Re-Entry)	(Neutron Nt 103)	71	1983	0	1983	
6	That Was Then But This Is Now	(Neutron Nt 105)	18	1983	0	1983	
7	S.O.S.	(Neutron Nt 106)	39	1984	0	1984	
8	How To Be A Millionaire	(Neutron Nt 107)	49	1984	20	1984	(Mercury 884382)
9	Be Near Me	(Neutron Nt 108)	26	1985	9	1985	(Mercury 880626)
10	Vanity Kills	(Neutron Nt 109)	70	1985	0	1985	
11	Ocean Blue	(Neutron Nt 110)	51	1986	0	1986	
12	When Smokey Sing	(Neutron Nt 111)	11	1987	5	1987	(Mercury 888604)
13	The Night You Murdered Love	(Neutron Nt 112)	30	1987	0	1987	
14	King Without A Crown	(Neutron Nt 113)	44	1987	0	1987	
15	One Better World	(Neutron Nt 114)	32	1989	0	1989	
16	The Real Thing	(Neutron Nt 115)	68	1989	0	1989	
17	The Look Of Love (Re-Mix)	(Neutron Nt 116)	68	1990	0	1990	
18	Love Conquers All	(Parlophone R6292)	47	1991	0	1991	
19	Say It	(Parlophone R6298)	42	1992	0	1992	
20	Stranger Things	(Deconstruction 74321453632)	57	1997	0	1997	
Abigail Female Vocalist from the UK							
1	Smells Like Team Spirit	(Klone Cdklone 25)	29	1994	0	1994	
Abigail Mead & Nigel Goulding Mixed Producer Duo from the UK/USA							
1	Full Metal Jacket (I Wanna Be Your Drill Instructor)	(Warner Bros W 8187)	2	1987	0	1987	
Absolute							
1	I Believe	(Am:Pm 5820752)	38	1997	0	1997	
AC/DC Names: Malcolm Young, Ron Belford Scott, Phil Rudd, Cliff Williams & Mark Evans							
1	Rock 'N' Roll Damnation	(Atlantic K 11142)	24	1978	0	1978	
2	Highway To Hell	(Atlantic K 11321)	56	1979	0	1979	
3	Touch Too Much	(Atlantic K 11435)	29	1980	0	1980	
4	Dirty Deeds Done Dirt Cheap	(Atlantic Hm 2)	47	1980	0	1980	
5	High Voltage (Live Version)	(Atlantic Hm 1)	48	1980	0	1980	
6	It's A Long Way To The Top	(Atlantic Hm 3)	55	1980	0	1980	
7	Whole Lotta Rosie	(Atlantic Hm 4)	36	1980	0	1980	
8	You Shook Me All Night Long	(Atlantic K 11600)	38	1980	35	1980	(Atlantic 3761)
9	Rock And Roll Ain't Noise Pollution	Atlantic K 11630	15	1980	0	1980	
10	Back In Black		0	1980	37	1980	(Atlantic 3787)
11	Let's Get It Up	(Atlantic K 11706)	13	1982	0	1982	
12	For Those About To Rock (We Salute You)	(Atlantic K 11721)	15	1982	0	1982	
13	Guns For Hire	(Atlantic A 9774)	37	1983	0	1983	
14	Nervous Shakedown	(Atlantic A 9651)	35	1984	0	1984	
15	Danger	(Atlantic A 9532)	48	1985	0	1985	
16	Shake Your Foundations	(Atlantic A 9474)	24	1986	0	1986	
17	Who Made Who	(Atlantic A 9425)	16	1986	0	1986	
18	You Shook Me All Night Long (Re-Issue)	(Atlantic A 9377)	46	1986	0	1986	
19	Heatseeker	(Atlantic A 9136)	12	1988	0	1988	
20	That's The Way I Wanna Rock 'N' Roll	L(Atlantic A 9098	22	1988	0	1988	
21	Thunderstruck	(Atlantic B 8907)	13	1990	0	1990	
22	Moneytalks	(Atco B 8886)	36	1990	23	1990	(Atco 98881)
23	Are You Ready	(Atco B 8830)	34	1991	0	1991	
24	Highway To Hell (Live)	(Atco B 8479)	14	1992	0	1992	
25	Dirty Deeds Done Dirt Cheap (Live)	(Atco B 6073cd)	68	1993	0	1993	
26	Big Gun	(Atco B 8396cd)	23	1993	0	1993	
27	Hard As A Rock	(Atlantic A 368cd)	33	1995	0	1995	
28	Hail Caesar	(East West 7559660512)	56	1996	0	1996	
Ace Rock Quintet, Disbanded In 1977							
1	How Long	(Anchor Anc 1002)	20	1974	3	1975	(Anchor 21000)
Ace Cannon Male Saxophonist, B: 5 May 1934 Mississippi							
1	Tuff		0	1961	17	1961	(Hi 2040)
2	Blues (Stay Away From Me)		0	1962	36	1962	(Hi 2051)

ISSUE	TITLE	UK LBL	UK POS	UK YEAR	US POS	US YEAR	US LBL
Ace Frehley B: 27 Apr 1951 Bronx, Formerly Lead Guitarist With Kiss							
1	New York Groove		0	1979	13	1979	(Casablanca 941)
Ace Of Base Vocal/Instrumental Quartet from Gothenburg, Sweden							
* 1	All That She Wants	(London 8612702)	1	1993	2	1993	(Arista 12614)
2	Wheel Of Fortune	(London 8615452)	20	1993	0	1993	
3	Happy Nation	(London 8619272)	42	1993	0	1993	
* 4	The Sign	(London Acecd 1)	2	1994	1	1994	(Arista 12653)
* 5	Don't Turn Around	(London Acecd 2)	5	1994	4	1994	(Arista 12691)
6	Happy Nation (Re-Issue)	(London 8610972)	40	1994	0	1994	
7	Living In Danger	(London Acecd 3)	18	1995	20	1994	(Arista 12754)
8	Lucky Love	(London Acecd 4)	20	1995	30	1996	
9	It's A Beautiful Life	(London Acecd 5)	15	1996	15	1995	(Arista 12889)
Acen Male Producer from the UK							
1	Trip Ii The Moon	(Production House Pnt 042)38		1992	0	1992	
2	Trip II The Moon (Re-Mix)	(Production House Pnt 042rx)71		1992	0	1992	
Acker Bilk Name Bernard Stanley Bilk B: 28 Jan 1929 Somerset, England							
1	Summer Set	(Columbia Db 4382)	5	1960	0	1960	
2	Goodnight Sweet Prince	(Melodisc Mel 1547)	50	1960	0	1960	
3	White Cliffs Of Dover	(Columbia Db 4492)	30	1960	0	1960	
4	Buona Sera	(Columbia Db 4544)	7	1960	0	1960	
5	That's My Home	(Columbia Db 4673)	7	1961	0	1961	
6	Stars And Stripes For Ever / Creole Jazz	(Columbia Scd 2155)	22	1961	0	1961	
* 7	Stranger On The Shore	(Columbia Db 4750)	2	1961	1	1962	(Atco 6217)
8	Frankie And Johnny	(Columbia Db 4795)	42	1962	0	1962	
9	Gotta See Baby Tonight	(Columbia Scd 2176)	24	1962	0	1962	
10	Lonely	(Columbia Db 4897)	14	1962	0	1962	
11	A Taste Of Honey	(Columbia Db 4949)	70	1963	0	1963	
12	Aria	(Pye 7n 45607)	5	1976	0	1976	
Act Mixed Vocal/Instrumental Group from Germany							
1	Snobbery And Decay	(Ztt Ztas 28)	60	1987	0	1987	
Act One Mixed Vocal/Instrumental Group from the USA							
1	Tom The Peeper	(Mercury 6008 005)	40	1974	0	1974	
Ad Libs Names: Mary Ann Thomas, Hugh Harris, Danny Austin, Norman Donegan & Dave Watt							
1	The Boy From New York City		0	1965	8	1965	(Blue Cat 102)
Adam & The Ants Names: Adam Ant, Andy Warren, Lester Square & Paul Flanagan							
1	Kings Of The Wild Frontier	(CBS8877)	48	1980	0	1980	
2	Dog Eat Dog	(CBS9039)	4	1980	0	1980	(CBS 9039)
3	Antmusic	(CBS9352)	2	1980	0	1980	
4	Young Parisians	(Decca F 13803)	9	1980	0	1980	
5	Cartrouble	(Do It Dun 10)	33	1981	0	1981	
6	Zerox	(Do It Dun 8)	45	1981	0	1981	
7	Kings Of The Wild Frontier (Re-Entry)	(CBS8877)	2	1981	0	1981	
8	Stand And Deliver	(CBSA 1065)	1	1981	0	1981	
9	Prince Charming	(CBSA 1408)	1	1981	0	1981	
10	Ant Rap	(CBSA 1738)	3	1981	0	1981	
11	Deutscher Girls	(Ego 5)	13	1982	0	1982	
12	The Antmusic '(EP) (The B-Sides)	(Do It Dun 20	46	1982	0	1982	
13	Goody Two Shoes	(CBSA 2367)	1	1982	12	1983	(Epic 03367)
14	Friend Or Foe	(CBSA 2736)	9	1982	0	1982	
15	Desperate But Not Serious	(CBSA 2892)	33	1982	0	1982	
16	Puss 'N' Boots	(CBSA 3614)	5	1983	0	1983	
17	Strip	(CBSA 3589)	41	1983	0	1983	
18	Apollo 9	(CBSA 4719)	1	1984	0	1984	
19	Vive Le Rock	(CBSA 6367)	50	1985	0	1985	
Adam Ant Real Name Stuart Goddard, B: 3 Nov 1954 London, England							
1	Room At The Top	(MCA 1387)	13	1990	17	1990	(Mca 53679)
2	Can't Set Rules About Love	(MCA 1404)	47	1990	0	1990	
3	Wonderful	(EMI Cdems 366)	32	1995	39	1995	(Capitol 58239)
4	Gotta Be A Sin	(EMI Cdem 379)	48	1995	0	1995	
Adam Clayton & Larry Mullen Male Instrumental Duo from Ireland							
1	Theme From Mission Impossible	(Mother Mumcd 75)	7	1996	7	1996	(Island 576670)

ISSUE	TITLE	UK LBL	UK POS	UK YEAR	US POS	US YEAR	US LBL
Adam Faith	Male Vocalist, Real Name Terence Nelhams B: 23 June 1940 London, England						
1	What Do You Want	(Parlophone R 4591)	1	1959	0	1959	
2	Poor Me	(Parlophone R 4623)	1	1960	0	1960	
3	Someone Else's Baby	(Parlophone R 4643)	2	1960	0	1960	
4	When Johnny Comes Marching Home /Made You	(Parlophone R 4665)	5	1960	0	1960	
5	How About That	(Parlophone R 4689)	4	1960	0	1960	
6	Lonely Pup (In A Christmas Shop)	(Parlophone R 4708)	4	1960	0	1960	
7	Who Am I / This Is It	(Parlophone R 4735)	50	1960	0	1961	
8	Easy Going Me	(Parlophone R 4766)	12	1961	0	1961	
9	Don't You Know It	(Parlophone R 4807)	12	1961	0	1961	
10	The Time Has Come	(Parlophone R 4837)	4	1961	0	1961	
11	Lonesome	(Parlophone R 4864)	12	1962	0	1962	
12	As You Like It	(Parlophone R 4896)	5	1962	0	1962	
13	Don't That Beat All	(Parlophone R 4930)	8	1962	0	1962	
14	Baby Take A Bow	(Parlophone R 4964)	22	1962	0	1962	
15	What Now	(Parlophone R 4990)	31	1963	0	1963	
16	Walkin' Tall	(Parlophone R 5039)	23	1963	0	1963	
17	The First Time	(Parlophone R 5061)	5	1963	0	1963	
18	We Are In Love	(Parlophone R 5091)	11	1963	0	1963	
19	If He Tells You	(Parlophone R 5109)	25	1964	0	1964	
20	I Love Being In Love With You	(Parlophone R 5138)	33	1964	0	1964	
21	Message To Martha (Kentucky Bluebird)	(Parlophone R 5201)	12	1964	0	1964	
22	It's Alright		0	1965	31	1965	(Amy 913)
23	Stop Feeling Sorry For Yourself	(Parlophone R 5235)	23	1965	0	1965	
24	Someone's Taken Maria Away	(Parlophone R 5289)	34	1965	0	1965	
25	Cheryl's Goin' Home	(Parlophone R 5516)	46	1966	0	1966	
Adam Wade	Male Vocalist, B: 17 Mar 1937 Pittsburgh						
1	Take Good Care Of Her	(HMV Pop 843)	38	1961	7	1961	(Coed 546)
2	The Writing On The Wall		0	1961	5	1961	(Coed 550)
3	Take Good Care Of Her (Re-Entry)	(HMV Pop 843)	38	1961	0	1961	
4	As If I Didn't Know		0	1961	10	1961	(Coed 553)
	Adamo Real Name Salvatore Adamo B: 1944 in Belgium						
* 1	Petit Bonheur		0	1969	0	1969	
Adamski	Male Producer/Instrumentalist from the UK						
1	N-R-G	(MCA MCA 1386)	12	1990	0	1990	
2	Killer	(MCA MCA 1400)	1	1990	0	1990	
3	The Space Jungle	(MCA MCA 1435)	7	1990	0	1990	
4	Flashback Jack	(MCA MCA 1459)	46	1990	0	1990	
5	Never Goin' Down / Born To Be Alive	(MCA MCS 1578)	51	1991	0	1991	
6	Get Your Body	(MCA MCS1613)	68	1992	0	1992	
7	Back To Front	(MCA CS1644)	63	1992	0	1992	
Addams & Gee	Male Vocal from the USA						
1	Chung Kuo (Revisited)	(Debut Debt 3108)	72	1991	0	1991	
Addis Black Widow	Male Rap Duo from the USA						
1	Innocent	(Mercury Black Vinyl MBVcd 1)	42	1996	0	1996	
Addrisi Brothers	Real Names Don And Dick Addrisi from the USA						
1	We've Got To Get It On Again		0	1972	25	1972	(Columbia 45521)
2	Slow Dancin' Don't Turn Me On		0	1977	20	1977	(Buddah 566)
3	Ghost Dancer	(Scotti Brothers K 11361)	57	1979	0	1979	
Adeva	Female Singer from the USA						
1	Respect	(Cooltempo Cool 179)	17	1989	0	1989	
2	Musical Freedom (Moving On Up)	(Cooltempo Cool 182)	22	1989	0	1989	
3	Warning	(Cooltempo Cool 185)	17	1989	0	1989	
4	I Thank You	(Cooltempo Cool 192)	17	1989	0	1989	
5	Beautiful Love	(Cooltempo Cool 195)	57	1989	0	1989	
6	Treat Me Right	(Cooltempo Cool 200)	62	1990	0	1990	
7	Ring My Bell	(Cooltempo Cool 224)	20	1991	0	1991	
8	It Should've Been Me	(Cooltempo Cool 236)	48	1991	0	1991	
9	Don't Let It Show On Your Face	(Cooltempo Cool 248)	34	1992	0	1992	
10	Until You Come Back To Me	(Cooltempo Cool 254)	45	1992	0	1992	
11	I'm The One For You	(Cooltempo Cool 264)	51	1992	0	1992	
12	Respect (Re-Mix)	(Network Nwkcd 79)	65	1993	0	1993	
13	Too Many Fish	(Virgin American Vuscd 89)	34	1995	0	1995	

ISSUE	TITLE	UK LBL	UK POS	UK YEAR	US POS	US YEAR	US LBL
14	Whadda U Want (From Me)	(Virgin American Vuscd 98)	36	1995	0	1995	
15	Do Watcha Do	(Avex Uk Avexcd 24)	54	1996	0	1996	
16	I Thank You (Re-Mix)	(Cooltempo Cdcools 318)	37	1996	0	1996	
17	Where Is The Love? /The Way That You Feel	(Distinctive Disncd 31)	54	1997	0	1997	
Adicts Male Vocal/Instrumental Group from the UK							
1	Bad Boy	(Razor Rzs 104)	75	1983	0	1983	
Adiemus Male Instrumental Duo from the UK							
1	Adiemus	(Virgin Ven 4)	48	1995	0	1995	
Adina Howard Female R&B Vocalist, B: 14 Nov 1974 Grand Rapids, Michigan							
1	Freak Like Me	(Atlantic A 4473cd)	67	1995	2	1995	(Mecca Don/Ew 64484)
2	Freak Like Me (Re-Entry)	(East West A 4473cd)	33	1995	0	1995	
3	What's Love Got To Do With It	(Interscope Ind 97008)	2	1996	0	1996	
Adonis Vocal/Instrumental Group from the USA							
1	Do It Properly (No Way Back)	(London Lon 136)	47	1987	0	1987	
Adrenalin M.O.D. Male Vocal/Instrumental Group from the USA							
1	0-0-0	(MCA Ragat 2)	49	1988	0	1988	
Adrian Baker Male Vocal/Instrumentalist from the UK See Also Gidea Park							
1	Sherry	(Magnet Mag 34)	10	1975	0	1975	
Adrian Gurvitz 3 Male Vocalist from the UK							
1	Classic	(RAK 339)	8	1982	0	1982	
2	Your Dream	(Rak 343)	61	1982	0	1982	
Adrian Kimberly Is A Don Everly Studio Production							
1	The Graduation Song...Pomp And Circumstance		0	1961	34	1961	(Calliope 6501)
Adriano Celentano Male Vocalist, B: 1938, Milan, Italy							
* 1	La Coppia Piu' Bella Del Mondo		0	1967	0	1967	
Adult Net Mixed Vocal/Instrumental Group from the USA/Uk							
1	Where Were You	(Fontana Brx 2)	66	1989	0	1989	
Adventures Male Vocal/Instrumental Group from the UK							
1	Another Silent Day	(Chrysalis Chs 2000)	71	1984	0	1984	
2	Send My Heart	(Chrysalis Chs 2001)	62	1984	0	1984	
3	Feel The Raindrops	(Chrysalis AD 1)	58	1985	0	1985	
4	Broken Land	(Elektra 69)	20	1988	0	1988	
5	Drowning In A Sea Of Love	(Elektra 76)	44	1988	0	1988	
6	Raining All Over The World	(Polydor Po 211)	68	1992	0	1992	
Adventures Of Stevie V Real Name Stevie Vincent Bedfordshire, England							
1	Dirty Cash (Money Talks)	(Mercury Mer 311)	2	1990	25	1990	(Mercury 875802#)
2	Body Language	(Mercury Mer 331)	29	1990	0	1990	
3	Jealousy	(Mercury Mer 337)	58	1991	0	1991	
Adverts Mixed Vocal/Instrumental Group from the UK							
1	Garry Gilmores Eyes	(Anchor ANC 1043)	19	1977	0	1977	
2	No Time To Be 21	(Bright BR1)	38	1978	0	1978	
Aerosmith Hard Rock Band From Sunapee, New Hampshire, Names Steven Tyler, Joe Perry & Brad Whitford							
1	Dream On		0	1973	59	1973	(Columbia 10278)
2	Sweet Emotion		0	1975	36	1975	(Columbia 10155)
3	Dream On (Re-Entry)		0	1976	6	1976	(Columbia 10278)
4	Last Child		0	1976	21	1976	(Columbia 10359)
5	Walk This Way		0	1977	10	1977	(Columbia 10449)
6	Back On The Saddle		0	1977	38	1977	(Columbia 10516)
7	Come Together		0	1978	23	1978	(Columbia 10802)
8	Dude (Looks Like A Lady)	(Geffen Gef 29)	45	1987	23	1987	(Geffen 28240)
9	Angel	(Geffen Gef 34)	69	1988	14	1988	(Geffen 28249)
10	Rag Doll	(Geffen Gef 70)	42	1990	17	1988	(Geffen 27915)
11	Love In An Elevator	Geffen Gef 63)	13	1989	5	1989	(Geffen 22845)
12	Janie's Got A Gun		0	1989	4	1989	(Geffen 22727#)
13	What It Takes		0	1990	9	1990	(Geffen 19944)
14	Dude(Looks Like A Lady) (Re-Issue)	(Geffen Gef 72)	20	1990	0	1990	
15	The Other Side	(Geffen Gef 79)	46	1990	22	1990	(Geffen 19927)
16	Livin' On The Edge	(Geffen Gfstd 35)	19	1993	18	1993	(Geffen 19149)
17	Eat The Rich	(Geffen Gfstd 46)	34	1993	0	1993	
* 18	Cryin'	(Geffen Gfstd 56)	17	1993	12	1993	(Geffen 19256)
19	Amazing	(Geffen Gfstd 63)	57	1993	24	1993	(Geffen 19264)
20	Shut Up And Dance	(Geffen Gfstd 75)	24	1994	0	1994	

ISSUE	TITLE	UK LBL	UK POS	UK YEAR	US POS	US YEAR	US LBL
21	Sweet Emotion	(Columbia 6604492)	74	1994	0	1994	
22	Crazy / Blind Man	(Geffen Gfstd 80)	23	1994	17	1994	(Geffen 19267)
23	Falling In Love (Is Hard On The Knees)	(Columbia 6640752)	22	1997	35	1997	(Columbia 78499)
24	Hole In My Soul	(Columbia 6645012)	29	1997	0	1997	

African Business Male Vocal/Instrumental Group from Italy

1	In Zaire (Urban Urb 64)		73	1990	0	1990	

Afrika Bambaataa Male Vocalist from the USA

1	Planet Rock	(EMI Em 41)	53	1982	0	1982	
2	Renegades Of Funk	(Tommy Boy Afr 1)	30	1984	0	1984	
3	Unity (Part 1 The Third Coming)	(Tommy Boy Afr 2)	49	1984	0	1984	
4	Reckless	(EMI USA Mt 100)	17	1988	0	1988	
5	Just Get Up And Dance	(Polydor Posp 497)	45	1991	0	1991	

After 7 Male R&B Vocal Trio, Names Keith Mitchell, Kevin & Melvin Edmonds

1	Heat Of The Moment		0	1989	74	1989	(Virgin 99204)
* 2	Ready Or Not		0	1990	7	1990	(Virgin 98995)
* 3	Can't Stop	(Virgin America Vus 31)	54	1990	6	1990	(Virgin 98961)
4	Heat Of The Moment (Re-Entry)		0	1991	19	1991	(Virgin 99204)
5	Nights Like This (From *The Five Heartbeats*)		0	1991	24	1991	(Virgin 98798)
6	'Il You Do Me Right		0	1995	31	1995	(Virgin 38494)

After The Fire Male Vocal/Instrumental Group from the UK

1	One Rule For You	(CBS 7025)	40	1979	0	1979	
2	Laser Love	(CBS 7769)	62	1979	0	1979	
3	Der Kommissar	(CBS A 2399)	47	1983	5	1983	(Epic 03559)

Afternoon Delights Female Studio Quartet from Boston

1	General Hospi-Tale		0	1981	33	1981	(Mca 51148)

Aftershock Male Vocal/Instrumental Duo from the USA

1	Slave To The Vibe	(Virgin America Vuscd 75)	11	1993	0	1993	

Agent Provocataur

1	Agent Dan	(Epic Agent 3cd)	49	1997	0	1997	

Age Of Chance Mixed Vocal/Instrumental Group from the UK

1	Kiss	(Fon Age 5)	50	1987	0	1987	
2	Who's Afraid Of The Big Bad Noise	(Fon Vs 962)	65	1987	0	1987	
3	Higher Than Heaven	(Virgin Vs 1228)	53	1990	0	1990	

Age Of Love

1	The Age Of Love – The Remixes	(React Cdreact 100)	17	1997	0	1997	

Agnetha Faltskog Female Vocalist, B: 5 Apr 1950 Sweden

1	The Heat Is On	(Epic A 3436)	35	1983	0	1983	
2	Wrap Your Arms Around Me	(Epic A 3622)	44	1983	0	1983	
3	Can't Shake Loose To Love	(Epic A 3812)	63	1983	29	1983	(Polydor 815230)

Ahmad Male Rapper, Real Name Al Lewis From Los Angeles

1	Back In The Day	(Giant 74321211042)	64	1994	26	1994	(Giant 18217)

Aimee Mann Female Vocalist from the USA

1	Time Stand Still	(Imago Rush 13)	42	1987	0	1987	
2	I Should've Known	(Imago 72787250432)	55	1993	0	1993	
3	Stupid Thing	(Imago 72787250522)	47	1993	0	1993	
4	I Should've Known (Re-Issue)	(Imago 72787250602)	45	1994	0	1994	

Air Lane Trio

1	My Guitar Is My Sweetheart		0	1947	23	1947	(Deluxe 1120)

Air Supply Names: Russell Hitchcock B: 15 Jun 1949, & Graham Russell B: 1 Jun 1950

1	Lost In Love		0	1980	3	1980	(Arista 0479)
2	All Out Of Love	(Arista Arist 362)	11	1980	2	1980	(Arista 0520)
3	Every Woman In The World		0	1980	5	1980	(Arista 0564)
4	The One That You Love		0	1981	1	1981	(Arista 0604)
5	Here I Am (Just When You Thought I Was Over You)		0	1981	5	1981	(Arista 0626)
6	Sweet Dreams		0	1982	5	1982	(Arista 0655)
7	Even The Nights Are Better	(Arista Arist 474)	44	1982	5	1982	(Arista 0692)
8	Young Love		0	1982	38	1982	(Arista 1005)
9	Two Less Lonely People In The World		0	1982	38	1982	(Arista 1004)
10	Making Love Out Of Nothing At All		0	1983	2	1983	(Arista 9056)
11	Just As I Am		0	1985	19	1985	(Arista 9353)
12	Goodbye	(Giant 74321153462)	66	1993	0	1993	

ISSUE	TITLE	UK LBL	UK POS	UK YEAR	US POS	US YEAR	US LBL
Airhead Male Vocal/Instrumental Group from the UK							
1	Funny How	(Korova Kow 47)	57	1991	0	1991	
2	Counting Sheep	(Korova Kow 48)	35	1991	0	1991	
3	Right Now	(Korova Kow 49)	50	1992	0	1992	
Airscape							
1	Pacific Melody	(Edel 0091165 Ext)	27	1997	0	1997	
Aka Male Vocal Group from the UK							
1	Warning	(RCA 74321360662)	43	1996	0	1996	
Akin							
1	Stay Right Here	(Wea Wea 117cd)	60	1997	0	1997	
Al B. Sure! Male Vocalist, Real Name Al Brown from Boston							
1	Nite And Day	(Uptown W 8192)	44	1988	7	1988	(Warner Bros 28192)
2	Off On Your Own (Girl)	(Uptown W 7870)	70	1988	0	1988	
3	If I'm Not Your Lover	(Warner Bros W 2908)	54	1989	0	1989	
4	Secret Garden (Sweet Seduction Suite)	(Qwest W 9992)	67	1990	31	1990	(Qwest 19992
5	Black Tie White Noise	(Arista 74321148682)	36	1993	0	1993	
Al Bano Real Name Albano Carrisi B: 1943, Italy							
* 1	Nel Sole (In The Sun)		0	1967	0	1967	
Al Brown('s) Tunetoppers Al Brown Was B: In 1930 Faimont, West Virginia formed in 1953							
1	The Madison		0	1960	23	1960	(Amy 804)
Al Caiola Male Orchestra Leader, B: 7 Sep 1920 Jersey City, New Jersey							
1	The Magnificent Seven	(HMV Pop 889)	34	1961	35	1961	(United Artists 261)
2	Bonanza		0	1961	19	1961	(United Artists 302)
Al Casey							
1	Surfin' Hootenanny		0	1963	48	1963	(Stacy 962)
Al Collins Male DJ/Vocalist, His Nickname is Jazzbo from the USA							
1	Little Red Riding Hood		0	1953	22	1953	(Brunswick 86001)
2	The Three Little Pigs		0	1953	22	1953	(Brunswick 86001)
Al Green Male Vocalist, B: 13 Apr 1946 Forrest City, Arkansas							
1	Back Up Train		0	1967	41	1967	(Hot Line 15000)
+ 2	You Say It		0	1970	28	1970	(Hi 2172)
+ 3	Right Now, Right Now		0	1970	23	1970	(Hi 2177)
4	I Can't Get Next To You		0	1970	60	1970	(Hi 2182)
+ 5	Driving Wheel		0	1971	46	1971	(Hi 2188)
* 6	Tired Of Being Alone	(London HI 10337)	4	1971	11	1971	(Hi 2194)
* 7	Let's Stay Together	(London HI 10348)	7	1972	1	1972	(Hi 2202)
* 8	Look What You Done For Me	(London HI 10369)	44	1972	4	1972	(Hi 2211)
* 9	I'm Still In Love With You	(London HI 10382)	35	1972	3	1972	(Hi 2216)
* 10	You Ought To Be With Me		0	1972	3	1972	(Hi 2227)
11	Guilty		0	1972	69	1972	(Bell 45-258)
12	Hot Wire		0	1973	71	1973	(Bell 45-305)
* 13	Call Me (Come Back Home)		0	1973	10	1973	(Hi 2235)
* 14	Here I Am (Come And Take Me)		0	1973	10	1973	(Hi 2247)
15	Livin' For You		0	1973	19	1973	(Hi 2257)
16	Let's Get Married		0	1974	32	1974	(Hi 2262)
* 17	Sha-La-La (Make Me Happy)	(London HI 10470)	20	1974	7	1974	(Hi 2274)
* 18	L.O.V.E. (Love)	(London HI 10482)	24	1975	13	1975	(Hi 2282)
19	Oh Me, Oh My (Dreams In My Arms)		0	1975	48	1975	(Hi 2288)
20	Full Of Fire		0	1975	28	1975	(Hi 2300)
21	Keep Me Cryin'		0	1976	37	1976	(Hi 2319)
22	Put A Little Love In Your Heart	(A&M Am 484)	28	1988	9	1988	(A&M 1255)
23	The Message Is Love	(Breakout USA 668)	38	1989	0	1989	
24	Love Is A Beautiful Thing	(Arista 74321162697)	56	1993	0	1993	
Al Hibbler Male Vocalist, B: 16 Aug 1915 Little Rock, Arkansas Al Was Blind From Birth							
* 1	Unchained Melody	(Brunswick 05420)	2	1955	3	1955	(Decca 29441)
2	He		0	1955	4	1955	(Decca 29660)
3	11th Hour Melody		0	1956	21	1956	(Decca 29789)
4	Never Turn Back		0	1956	22	1956	(Decca 29950)
5	After The Lights Go Down Low		0	1956	10	1956	(Decca 29982)
Al Hirt Real Name Alois Maxwell Hirt B: 7 Nov 1922 New Orleans							
* 1	Java		0	1964	4	1964	(RCA 8280)

ISSUE	TITLE	UK LBL	UK POS	UK YEAR	US POS	US YEAR	US LBL
Al Hudson Male Vocalist from the USA							
1	Dance, Get Down/How Do You Do	(ABC 4222)	57	1978	0	1978	
2	You Can Do It	(MCA 511)	15	1979	0	1979	
3	Music	(MCA 542)	56	1979	0	1979	
4	Let's Talk	(MCA 972)	64	1985	0	1985	
Al Jarreau							
1	We're In This Love Together	(Warner Bros K 17849)	55	1981	15	1981	(Warner Bros 49746)
2	Mornin'	(Wea U 9929)	28	1983	21	1983	(Warner Bros 29720)
3	Trouble In Paradise	(Wea International U 9871)	36	1983	0	1983	
4	Boogie Down	(Wea U 9814)	63	1983	0	1983	
5	Day By Day	(Polydor Posp 770)	53	1985	0	1985	
6	The Music Of Goodbye (From *Out Of Africa*)	(MCA MACCA038)	75	1986	0	1986	
7	*Moonlighting* Theme	(Wea U 8407)	8	1987	23	1987	(MCA 53124)
Al Jolson Male Vocalist, Real Name Asa Joelson B: 26 Mar 1886 St. Petersburg, Russia							
1	That Haunting Melody (From *Vera Violetta*)		0	1912	1	1912	(Victor 17037)
* 2	Ragging The Baby To Sleep		0	1912	1	1912	(Victor 17081)
3	Snap Your Fingers		0	1912	6	1912	(Victor 17075)
* 4	The Spaniard That Blighted My Life (From *The Honeymoon Express*)		0	1913	1	1913	(Victor 17318)
* 5	You Made Me Love You, I Didn't Want To Do It		0	1913	1	1913	(Columbia 1374)
* 33	Swanee (From *Sinbad*)		0	1920	1	1920	(Columbia 2884)
* 39	April Showers (From *Bombo*)		0	1922	1	1922	(Columbia 3500)
* 76	Sonny Boy (From *The Singing Fool*)		0	1928	1	1928	(Brunswick 4033)
* 87	The Anniversary Song (From *The Jolson Story*)		0	1947	2	1947	(Decca 23714)
* 88	My Mammy		0	1947	18	1947	(Decca 23614)
* 89	April Showers (From *The Jolson Story*)		0	1947	15	1947	(Decca 23470)
* 90	Alexander's Ragtime Band		0	1947	20	1947	(Decca 40038)
91	The Spaniard That Blighted My Life		0	1947	20	1947	(Decca 40038)
92	If I Only Had A Match		0	1948	26	1948	(Decca 24296)
	HITS 90-91 ARE CREDITED TO AL JOLSON AND BING CROSBY						
Al Martino Real Name Alfred Cini B: 7 Oct 1927 South Philadelphia							
* 1	Here In My Hear t	(Capitol Cl 13779)	1	1952	1	1952	(B.B.S. 101)
2	Take My Heart	(Capitol Cl 13769)	9	1952	12	1952	(Capitol 2122)
3	Now	(Capitol Cl 13835)	3	1953	0	1953	
4	Rachel	(Capitol Cl 13879)	10	1953	30	1953	(Capitol 2353)
5	Rachel (Re-Entry)	(Capitol Cl 13879)	12	1953	0	1953	
5	When You're Mine		0	1953	27	1953	(Capitol 2480)
6	Wanted	(Capitol Cl 14128)	12	1954	0	1954	
7	Wanted (Re-Entry)	(Capitol Cl 14128)	4	1954	0	1954	
8	The Story Of Tina	(Capitol Cl 14163)	10	1954	0	1954	
9	Wanted (2nd Re-Entry)	(Capitol Cl 14128)	17	1954	0	1954	
10	The Man From Laramie	(Capitol Cl 14343)	19	1955	0	1955	
11	The Man From Laramie (Re-Entry)	(Capitol Cl 14343)	20	1955	0	1955	
12	Summertime	(Top Rank Jar 312)	49	1960	0	1960	
13	I Love You Because	(Capitol Cl 15300)	48	1963	3	1963	(Capitol 4930)
14	Painted, Tainted Rose		0	1963	15	1963	(Capitol 5000)
15	Living A Lie		0	1963	22	1963	(Capitol 5060)
16	I Love You More And More Every Day		0	1964	9	1964	(Capitol 5108)
17	Tears And Roses		0	1964	20	1964	(Capitol 5183)
18	Always Together		0	1964	33	1964	(Capitol 5239)
* 19	Spanish Eyes	(Capitol Cl 15430)	49	1970	15	1965	(Capitol 5542)
20	Think I'll Go Somewhere And Cry Myself To Sleep		0	1966	30	1966	(Capitol 5598)
21	Mary In The Morning		0	1967	27	1967	(Capitol 5904)
22	Spanish Eyes (Re-Entry)	(Capitol Cl 15430)	5	1973	0	1973	
23	To The Door Of The Sun (Alle Porte Del Sole)		0	1975	17	1975	(Capitol 3987)
24	Volare		0	1975	33	1975	(Capitol 4134)
Al Matthews Male Vocalist from tThe USA							
1	Fool	(CBS 3429)	16	1975	0	1975	
Al Morgan Male Pianist from Chicago							
1	Jealous Heart		0	1949	4	1949	(London 500)
2	Half A Heart Is All You Left Me (When You Broke My Heart In Two)		0	1950	26	1950	(London 571)
3	The Place Where I Worship (Is The Wide Open Spaces)		0	1950	29	1950	(London 784)
4	My Heart Cries For You		0	1951	24	1951	(London 877)
Al Saxon Male Vocalist from the UK							
1	You're The Top Cha	(Fontana H 164)	17	1959	0	1959	

ISSUE	TITLE	UK LBL	UK POS	UK YEAR	US POS	US YEAR	US LBL
2	Only Sixteen	(Fontana H 205)	24	1959	0	1959	
3	Blue Eyed Boy	(Fontana H 278)	39	1960	0	1960	
4	There I've Said It Again	(Piccadilly 7n 35011)	48	1961	0	1961	

Al Stewart Male Vocalist, B: 5 Sep 1945 Glasgow, Scotland

1	Year Of The Cat (About The Comedian Tony Hancock)	(RCA 2771)	31	1977	8	1977	(Janus 266)
2	Time Passages		0	1978	7	1978	(Arista 0362)
3	Song On The Radio		0	1979	29	1979	(Arista 0389)
4	Midnight Rocks		0	1980	24	1980	(Arista 0552)

Al Trace Male Band leader/Composer from the USA

1	Mairzy Doast		0	1944	7	1944	(Hit 8079)
2	You Call Everybody Darlin'		0	1948	1	1948	(Regent 117)
3	You Call Everybody Darlin' (Re-Recording)		0	1948	31	1948	(Sterling 3023)
4	Pretty Eyed Baby		0	1951	26	1951	(Mercury 5609)
5	Hitsity Hotsity		0	1951	24	1951	(Mercury 5675)

Al Wilson Male Vocalist, B: 19 Jun 1939 Meridian, Mississippi

1	The Snake	(Bell 1436)	41	1975	27	1968	(Soul City 767)
* 2	Show And Tell		0	1973	1	1973	(Rocky Road 30073)
3	La La Peace Song		0	1974	30	1974	(Rocky Road 30200)
4	I've Got A Feeling (We'll Be Seeing Each Other Again)		0	1976	29	1976	(Playboy 6062)

Alabama Formed In Fort Payne, Alabama, Randy Owen, Jeff Cook, Teddy Gentry & Mark Herndon

1	I Wanna Be With You Tonight		0	1977	78!	1977	(Grt 129)
2	I Wanna Come OVer		0	1979	33	1979	(MDJ 7906)
3	My Home's Alabama		0	1980	17	1980	(MDJ 1002)
4	Tennessee River		0	1980	1	1998	(RCA 12018)
5	Why Lady Why		0	1980	1	1980	(RCA 12091)
6	Old Flame		0	1981	1	1981	(RCA 12169)
7	Feels So Right		0	1981	20	1981	(RCA 12236)
8	Love In The First Degree		0	1982	15	1982	(RCA 12288)
9	Mountain Music		0	1982	1	1982	(RCA 13019)
10	Take Me Down		0	1982	18	1982	(RCA 13210)
11	CLose Enough to Perfect		0	1982	65	1982	(RCA13294)
! 12	Christmas In Dixie		0	1982	35	1982	(RCA 13358)
! 13	Dixieland Delight		0	1983	1	1983	(RCA 13446)
14	The Closer You Get		0	1983	3	1983	(RCA 13524)
15	Lady Down On Love		0	1983	76	1983	(RCA 13590)
! 16	Roll On (Eighteen Wheeler)		0	1984	1	1984	(RCA 13716)
17	When We Make Love		0	1984	72	1984	(RCA 13763)
26	Deep River Woman		0	1986	10	1986	(Motown 1873)
	REST ARE C/W HITS						

Alan Dale Male Vocalist, Real Name Aldo Sigiamundi B: 9 Jun 1925 Brooklyn

1	At The Darktown Strutters' Ball		0	1948	— 29	1948	(Signature 15197)
2	Heart Of My Heart		0	1953	10	1953	(Coral 61076)
3	East Side, West Side (From *Underwater*)		0	1954	28	1954	(Coral 61176)
* 4	Cherry Pink And Apple Blosson White		0	1956	14	1956	(Coral 61373)
x 5	Sweet And Gentle		0	1955	10	1955	(Coral 61435)

Alan Dean Male Vocalist With The Joe Lipman Orchestra

1	Luna Rossa (Blushing Moon)		0	1952	26	1952	(MGM 11269)

Alan Drew Male Vocalist from the UK

1	Always The Lonely One	(Columbia DB 7090)	48	1963	0	1963	

Alan Jackson Male Vocalist Alan Eugene Jackson. B: 17 Oct 1958 In Newman, Georgia

* 14	Chattahoochee		0	1993	46	1993	(Arista 12573)
19	Little Bitty		0	1996	60	1996	(Arista 13048)
	OTHER HITS ARE C/W						

Alan O'Day Male Vocalist, B: 3 Oct 1940 Hollywood

* 1	Undercover Angel	(Atlantic K 10926)	43	1977	1	1977	(Pacific 001)

Alan Parsons Project Male Vocal/Instrumental Duo from the UK   Names Are Alan Parsons And Eric Woolfson

1	(The System Of) Doctor Tarr And Professor Fether		0	1976	37	1976	(20th Century 2297)
2	I Wouldn't Want To Be Like You		0	1977	36	1977	(Arista 0260)
3	Damned If I Do		0	1979	27	1979	(Arista 0454)
4	Games People Play		0	1981	16	1981	(Arista 0573)
5	Time		0	1981	15	1981	(Arista 0598)
6	Eye In The Sky		0	1982	3	1982	(Arista 0696)
7	Old And Wise	(Arista Arist 494)	74	1983	0	1983	

ISSUE	TITLE	UK LBL	UK POS	UK YEAR	US POS	US YEAR	US LBL
8	Don't Answer Me	(Arista Arist 553)	58	1984	15	1984	(Arista 9160)
9	Prime Time		0	1984	34	1984	(Arista 9208)

Alan Price Male Vocal/Instrumentalist (Keyboards) from the UK

ISSUE	TITLE	UK LBL	UK POS	UK YEAR	US POS	US YEAR	US LBL
1	I Put A Spell On You	(Decca F 12367)	9	1966	0	1966	
2	Hi Lili Hi Lo	(Decca F 12442)	11	1966	0	1966	
3	Simon Smith And His Amazing Dancing Bear	(Decca F 12570)	4	1967	0	1967	
4	The House That Jack Built	(Decca F 12641)	4	1967	0	1967	
5	Shame	(Decca F 12691)	45	1967	0	1967	
6	Don't Stop The Carnival	(Decca F 12731)	13	1968	0	1968	
7	Rosetta	(CBS 7108)	11	1971	0	1971	
8	Jarrow Song	(Warner Bros K 16372)	6	1974	0	1974	
9	Just For You	(Jet Up 36358)	43	1978	0	1978	
10	Baby Of Mine / Just For You (Re-Issue)	(Jet 135)	32	1979	0	1979	
11	Changes	(Ariola 109911)	54	1988	0	1988	

Alanis Morissette

ISSUE	TITLE	UK LBL	UK POS	UK YEAR	US POS	US YEAR	US LBL
1	You Oughta Know	(Maverick W 0307cd)	22	1995	6	1996	(Reprise 17644)
2	Hand In My Pocket	(Maverick W 0312cd)	26	1995	0	1995	
3	You Learn	(Maverick W 0334cd)	24	1996	0	1996	
4	Ironic	(Maverick W 0343cd)	11	1996	4	1996	(Reprise 17698)
5	Head Over Feet	(Maverick W 0355cd)	7	1996	0	1996	
6	All I Really Want	(Maverick W 0382cd)	59	1996	0	1996	

Alannah Myles Female Vocalist, B: Toronto, Canada

ISSUE	TITLE	UK LBL	UK POS	UK YEAR	US POS	US YEAR	US LBL
* 1	Black Velvet	(East West A 8742)	2	1990	1	1990	(Atlantic 88742)
2	Love Is	(East West A 8918)	61	1990	36	1990	(Atlantic 87945)

Alarm Male Vocal/Instrumental Group from the UK

ISSUE	TITLE	UK LBL	UK POS	UK YEAR	US POS	US YEAR	US LBL
1	68 Guns	(Irs Pfp 1023)	17	1983	0	1983	
2	Where Were You Hiding When The Storm Broke	(Irs Irs 101)	22	1984	0	1984	
3	The Deceiver	(Irs Irs 103)	51	1984	0	1984	
4	The Chant Has Just Begun	(Irs Irs 104)	48	1984	0	1984	
5	Absolute Reality	(Irs Alarm 1)	35	1985	0	1985	
6	Strength	(Irs Irm 104)	40	1985	0	1985	
7	Spirit Of 76	(Irs Irm 109)	22	1986	0	1986	
8	Knife Edge	(Irs Irm 112)	43	1986	0	1986	
9	Rain In The Summertime	(Irs Irm 144)	18	1987	0	1987	
10	Rescue Me	(Irs Irm 150)	48	1987	0	1987	
11	Presence Of Love (Laugherne)	(Irs Irm 155)	44	1988	0	1988	
12	Sold Me Down The River	(Irs Eirs 123)	43	1989	0	1989	
13	A New South Wales / The Rock	(Irs Eirs 129)	31	1989	0	1989	
14	Love Don't Come Easy	(Irs Eirs 134)	48	1990	0	1990	
15	Unsafe Building 1990	(Irs Alarme 2)	54	1990	0	1990	
16	Raw	(Irs Alarm 3)	51	1991	0	1991	

Albert Hammond Male Vocalist, B: 18 May 1942 London, England

ISSUE	TITLE	UK LBL	UK POS	UK YEAR	US POS	US YEAR	US LBL
* 1	It Never Rains In Southern California		0	1972	5	1972	(Mums 6011)
2	The Free Electric Band	(Mums 1494)	19	1973	0	1973	
3	I'm A Train		0	1974	31	1974	(Mums 6026)

Albert King Male Vocalist from the USA

ISSUE	TITLE	UK LBL	UK POS	UK YEAR	US POS	US YEAR	US LBL
+ 1	Cold Feet		0	1968	20	1968	(Stax 241)

Alberto Y Lost Trios Paranoias Male Vocal/Instrumental group from the UK

ISSUE	TITLE	UK LBL	UK POS	UK YEAR	US POS	US YEAR	US LBL
1	Head Down No Nonsense Mindlesss Boogie	(Logo Go 323)	47	1978	01978		

Alcatraz Male Production/Instrumental Duo from the USA

ISSUE	TITLE	UK LBL	UK POS	UK YEAR	US POS	US YEAR	US LBL
1	Giv Me Luv	(Am:Pm 5814332)	12	1996	0	1996	

Aldo Nova Male Vocal/Instrumentalist. Real Name Aldo Scarporuscio. B: Montreal

ISSUE	TITLE	UK LBL	UK POS	UK YEAR	US POS	US YEAR	US LBL
1	Fantasy		0	1982	23	1982	(Portrait 02799)

Aled Jones Male Vocalist from the UK

ISSUE	TITLE	UK LBL	UK POS	UK YEAR	US POS	US YEAR	US LBL
1	Memory	(BBC Resl 175)	42	1985	0	1985	
2	Walking In The Air	(HMV Aled 1)	5	1985	0	1985	
3	Pictures In The Dark	(Virgin Vs 836)	50	1985	0	1985	
4	A Winter Story	(HMV Aled 2)	51	1986	0	1986	

Alessi Male Vocal Duo

ISSUE	TITLE	UK LBL	UK POS	UK YEAR	US POS	US YEAR	US LBL
1	Oh Lori	(A&M Ams 7289)	8	1977	0	1977	

Alex Party

ISSUE	TITLE	UK LBL	UK POS	UK YEAR	US POS	US YEAR	US LBL
1	Saturday Night Party	(C.C.I. Ccicd 17000)	49	1993		1993	

ISSUE	TITLE	UK LBL	UK POS	UK YEAR	US POS	US YEAR	US LBL
2	Saturday Night Party (Read My Lips) (Re-Entry)	(C.C.I. Ccicd 17000)	29	1994	0	1994	
3	Don't Give Me Your Life	(Systematic Syscd 7)	2	1995	0	1995	
4	Wrap Me Up	(Systematic Sycd 22)	17	1995	0	1995	
5	Read My Lips (Re-Mix)	(Systematic Sycd 30)	28	1996	0	1996	

Alex Reece Male Producer from the UK

ISSUE	TITLE	UK LBL	UK POS	UK YEAR	US POS	US YEAR	US LBL
1	Feel The Sunshine	(Blunted Vinyl Blncd 016)	69	1995	0	1995	
2	Feel The Sunshine (Re-Mix)	(Fourth & Broadway Brcd 332)	26	1996	0	1996	
3	Candles	(Fourth & Broadway Brcd 333)	33	1996	0	1996	
4	Acid Lab	(Fourth & Broadway Brcd 344)	64	1996	0	1996	

Alex Welsh Male Instrumentalist (Trumpet) from the UK

ISSUE	TITLE	UK LBL	UK POS	UK YEAR	US POS	US YEAR	US LBL
1	Tansy	(Columbia DB 4686)	45	1961	0	1961	

Alexander O'Neal Male Vocalist, B: 15 Nov 1953 Natchez, Mississippi

ISSUE	TITLE	UK LBL	UK POS	UK YEAR	US POS	US YEAR	US LBL
1	Saturday Love	(Tabu A 6829)	6	1985	26	1986	(Tabu 05767)
2	If you Were Here Tonight	(Tabu A 6391)	13	1996	0	1986	
3	A Broken Heart Can Mend	(Tabu 6244)	53	1986	0	1986	
4	Fake	(Tabu 6508917)	53	1987	25	1987	(Tabu 07646)
5	Criticize	(Tabu 6512117)	4	1987	0	1987	
6	Never Knew Love Like This	(Tabu 65651382 7)	26	1988	28	1988	(Tabu 07646)
7	The Lovers	(Tabu 65651595 7)	28	1987	0	1987	
8	(What Can I Say) To Make You Love Me	(Tabu 652852 7)	27	1988	0	1988	
9	Fake '88 (re-mix)	(Tabu 652852)	55	1990	0	1990	
10	Christmas Song/Thank You for A Good Year	(Tabu 653182 7)	30	1988	0	1988	
11	Hearsay '89	(Tabu 654466 7)	56	1989	0	1989	
12	Sunshine	(Tabu 655191 7)	72	1989	0	1989	
13	Hitmix (Official Bootleg Mega-mix)	(Tabu 655504 7)	19	1989	0	1989	
14	Saturday Love (re-mix)	(Tabu 655680 7)	55	1990	0	1990	
15	All True Man	(Tabu 6565717)	18	1991	0	1991	
16	What Is This Thing Called Love	(Tabu 6567317)	53	1991	0	1991	
17	Shame On Me	(Tabu 6568737)	71	1991	0	1991	
18	Sentimental	(Tabu 6580147)	53	1992	0	1992	
19	Love Makes No Sense	(Tabu Amcd 7708)	26	1993	0	1993	
20	In the Middle	(Tabu 55877152)	32	1993	0	1993	
21	All That Matters to Me	(Tabu 55877232)	67	1993	0	1993	
22	Let's Get Together	(EMI Premier Prescd 11)	38	1996	0	1996	
23	Baby Come to Me	(One World ENt Owecd 1)	56	1997	0	1997	

Alexander Brothers

ISSUE	TITLE	UK LBL	UK POS	UK YEAR	US POS	US YEAR	US LBL
1	Goodnight Irene		0	1950	26	1950	(Mercury 5465)
20	In The Middle	(Tabu 55877152)	32	1993	0	1993	
21	All That Matters To Me	(Tabu 55877232)	67	1993	0	1993	
22	Let's Get Together	(EMI Premier Prescd 11)	38	1996	0	1996	

Alexei Sayle Male Comedian/Vocalist from the UK

ISSUE	TITLE	UK LBL	UK POS	UK YEAR	US POS	US YEAR	US LBL
1	'Ullo John Gotta New Motor	(Island IS 162)	15	1984	0	1984	

Alfi & Harry Alfi & Harry Is (And See Also David Seville)

ISSUE	TITLE	UK LBL	UK POS	UK YEAR	US POS	US YEAR	US LBL
1	The Trouble With Harry	(London HLU 8242)	15	1956	0	1956	

Alfonzo

ISSUE	TITLE	UK LBL	UK POS	UK YEAR	US POS	US YEAR	US LBL
1	Just The Way	(Cooltempo Cdcool 326)	38	1997	0	1997	

Alfred Drake Male Comedian/Vocalist, Real Name Alfred Capurro from the USA

ISSUE	TITLE	UK LBL	UK POS	UK YEAR	US POS	US YEAR	US LBL
1	The Surrey With The Fringe On Top (From *Oklahoma!*)		0	1944	22	1944	(Decca 23284)

Ali & Frazier Female Vocal Duo from the UK

ISSUE	TITLE	UK LBL	UK POS	UK YEAR	US POS	US YEAR	US LBL
1	Uptown Top Ranking	(Arista 74321158842)	33	1993	0	1993	

Ali & Kibbi

ISSUE	TITLE	UK LBL	UK POS	UK YEAR	US POS	US YEAR	US LBL
1	Somethin' Stupid		30	1995	0	1995	

Ali Campbell See Also Pato Banton

ISSUE	TITLE	UK LBL	UK POS	UK YEAR	US POS	US YEAR	US LBL
1	That Look In Your Eye	(Kuff Kuffdg 1)	5	1995	0	1995	
2	Let Your Yeah Be Yeah	(Kuff Kuffd 2)	25	1995	0	1995	
3	Somethin' Stupid	(Kuff Kuffdg 5)	30	1995	0	1995	

Ali Thomson Singer/Songwriter From Glasgow, Scotland

ISSUE	TITLE	UK LBL	UK POS	UK YEAR	US POS	US YEAR	US LBL
1	Take A Little Rhythm		0	1980	15	1980	(A&M 2243)

Alias Rock Quintet, Formed In Los Angeles By Freddy Curci & Steve Demarchi

ISSUE	TITLE	UK LBL	UK POS	UK YEAR	US POS	US YEAR	US LBL
1	More Than Words Can Say		0	1990	2	1990	(EMI 50324#)
2	Waiting For Love		0	1991	13	1991	(EMI 50337#)

ISSUE	TITLE	UK LBL	UK POS	UK YEAR	US POS	US YEAR	US LBL
3	Somethin' Stupid	(Kuff Kuffdg 5)	30	1995	0	1995	

Alibi

1	I'm Not To Blame	(Urgent 74321434762)	51	1997	0	1997	

Alice Babs Female Vocalist from Sweden

1	After You've Gone	(Fontana Tf 409)	43	1963	0	1963	

Alice Cooper Male Vocalist from the USA

1	Eighteen		0	1971	21	1971	(Warner Bros 7449)
2	School's Out	(Warner Bros K 16188)	1	1972	7	1973	(Warner Bros 7596)
3	Elected	(Warner Bros K 16214)	4	1972	26	1972	(Warner Bros 7631)
4	Hello Hurray	(Warner Bros K 16248)	6	1973	35	1973	(Warner Bros 7673)
5	No More Mr. Nice Guy	(Warner Bros K 16262)	10	1973	25	1973	(Warner Bros 7691)
6	Teenage Lament '74	(Warner Bros K 16345)	12	1974	0	1974	
7	Only Women		0	1975	12	1975	(Warner Bros 3254)
8	I Never Cry		0	1976	12	1976	(Warner Bros 8228)
9	No More Love At Your Convenience	(Warner Bros K 16935)	44	1977	0	1977	
10	You And Me		0	1977	9	1977	(Warner Bros 8349)
11	How You Gonna See Me Now	(Warner Bros K 17270)	61	1978	12	1978	(Warner Bros 8695)
12	Clones (We're All)		0	1980	40	1980	(Warner Bros 49204)
13	Seven And Seven Is (Live Version)	(Warner Bros K 17924)	62	1982	0	1982	
14	For Britain Only / Under My Wheels	(Warner Bros K 17940)	66	1982	0	1982	
15	He's Back (The Man Behind The Mask)	(MCA Mca 1090)	61	1986	0		1986
16	Freedom	(MCA Mca 1241)	50	1988	0	1988	
17	Poison	(Epic 655061 7)	2	1989	7	1989	(Epic 68958)
18	Bed Of Nails	(Epic Alice 3)	38	1989	0	1989	
19	House Of Fire	(Epic Alice 4)	65	1989	0	1989	
20	Hey Stoopid	(Epic 6569837)	21	1991	0	1991	
21	Love's A Loaded Gun	(Epic 6574387)	38	1991	0	1991	
22	Feed My Frankenstein	(Epic 6580927)	27	1992	0	1992	
23	Lost In America	(Epic 6603472)	22	1994	0	1994	
24	It's Me	(Epic 6605632)	34	1994	0	1994	

Alice in Chains Male Vocal/Instumental Group from the USA

1	Would	(Columbia 6588882)	19	1993	0	1993	
2	Them Bones	(Columbia 6590902)	26	1993	0	1993	
3	Angry Chair	(Columbia 6593652)	33	1993	0	1993	
4	Down In A Hole	(Columbia 6597512)	36	1993	0	1993	
5	Grind	(Columbia 6626232)	23	1995	0	1995	
6	Heaven Beside You	(Columbia 6628935)	35	1996	0	1996	

Alicia Bridges Female Vocalist from the USA Hails from Lawndale, North Carolina

*	1	I Love The Nightlife (Disco Round)	(Polydor 2066 936)	32	1978	5	978	(Polydor 14483)
	2	I Love The Nightlife (Re-Mix)	(Mother Mumcd 57)	61	1994	0	1994	

Alicia Myers Female Vocalist from the USA

1	You Get The Best From Me (Say Say Say)	(MCA MCA 914)	58	1984	0	1984	

Alisha Female Vocalist from the USA

1	Baby Talk	(Total Control Toco 6)	67	1986	0	1986	

Alisha's Attic Female Vocal Duo from the UK

1	I Am, I Feel	(Mercury Aatcd 1)	14	1996	0	1996	
2	Alisha Rules The World	(Mercury Aatcd 2)	12	1996	0	1996	
3	Indestructible	(Mercury Aatcd 3)	12	1997	0	1997	
4	Air we Breathe	(Mercury Aatcd 4)	12	1997	0	1997	

Alison Jordan Female Vocalist from the UK

1	Boy From New York City	(Arista 74321100427)	23	1992	0	1992	

Alison Limerick Female Vocalist from the UK

1	Where Love Lives	(Arista 144208)	27	1991	0	1991	
2	Come Back (For Real Love)	(Arista 114530)	53	1991	0	1991	
3	Magic's Back (The Ghosts Of Oxford Street)	(RCA Pb 45223)	42	1991	0	1991	
4	Make It On My Own	(Arista 114996)	16	1992	0	1992	
5	Gettin' It Right	(Arista 74321102867)	57	1992	0	1992	
6	Hear My Call	(Arista 115337)	73	1992	0	1992	
7	Time Of Our Lives	(Arista 74321180332)	36	1994	0	1994	
8	Love Come Down	(Arista 74321191952)	36	1994	0	1994	
9	Love Will Keep Us Together	(Acid Jazz Jazid 112cd)	63	1995	0	1995	
10	Where Love Lives (remix)	(Arista 74321381592)	9	1996	0	1996	
11	Make It On My Own (remix)	(Arista 74321407812)	30	1996	0	1996	
12	Put Your Faith In Me	(Mba Xes 9001)	42	1997	0	1997	

ISSUE	TITLE	UK LBL	UK POS	UK YEAR	US POS	US YEAR	US LBL
Alison Moyet	Female Vocalist, Full Name Genevieve Alison-Jane Moyet B: 18 Jun 1961 Basildon, Essex, England						
1	Love Resurrection	(CBS 4497)	10	1984	0	1984	
2	All Cried Out	(CBS A 4757)	8	1984	0	1984	
3	Invisible	(CBS A 4930)	21	1984	31	1984	(Columbia 04781)
4	The Ole Devil Called Love	(CBS A 6044)	2	1985	0	1985	
5	Is This Love	(CBSMoyet 1)	3	1986	0	1986	
6	Weak In The Presence Of Beauty	(CBS Moyet 2)	6	1987	0	1987	
7	Ordinary Girl	(CBS Moyet 3)	43	1987	0	1987	
8	Love Letters	(CBS Moyet 5)	4	1987	0	1987	
9	It Won't Be Long	(Columbia 6567577)	50	1991	0	1991	
10	Wishing You Were Here	(Columbia 6569397)	72	1991	0	1991	
11	This House	(Columbia 6575157)	40	1991	0	1991	
12	Whispering Your Name	(Columbia 6601622)	18	1994	0	1994	
13	Falling	(Columbia 595962)	42	1993	0	1993	
14	Getting Into Something	(Columbia 6603565)	51	1994	0	1994	
15	Ode To Boy	(Columbia 6607952)	59	1994	0	1994	
16	Solid Wood	(Columbia 6623265)	44	1995	0	1995	
Alive 'N Kickin'	American Sextet Consisted Of One Woman And Five Men						
* 1	Tighter, Tighter		0	1970	7	1970	(Roulette 7078)
All About Eve	Mixed Vocal/Instrumental Group from the UK						
1	In The Clouds	(Mercury Even 5)	47	1987	0	1987	
2	Wild Hearted Woman	(Mercury Even 6)	33	1988	0	1988	
3	Every Angel	(Mercury Even 7)	30	1988	0	1988	
4	Martha's Harbour	(Mercury Even 8)	10	1988	0	1988	
5	What Kind Of Fool	(Mercury Even 9)	29	1988	0	1988	
6	Road To Your Soul	(Mercury Even 10)	37	1989	0	1989	
7	December	(Mercury Even 11)	34	1989	0	1989	
8	Scarlet	(Mercury Even 12)	34	1990	0	1990	
9	Farewell Mr.Sorrow	(Mercury Even 14)	36	1991	0	1991	
10	Strange Way	(Vertigo Even 15)	50	1991	0	1991	
11	The Dreamer	(Vertigo Even 16)	41	1991	0	1991	
12	Phased (EP)	(MCA MCS 1688)	38	1992	0	1992	
13	Some Finer Day	(MCA MCS 1706)	57	1992	0	1992	
Allen Miller & His Orchestra							
1	It Can't Be Wrong		0	1943	3	1943	(Hit 7045)
All Systems Go	Male Vocal/Instrumental Group from the UK						
1	Pop Muzik	(Unique Niq 03)	63	1988	0	1988	
All-4-One	Male Vocal Quartet Group from the USA						
* 1	So Much In Love	(Atlantic A 7261cd)	60	1994	5	1994	(Blitzz/Atlantic 87271)
* 2	I Swear	(Atlantic A 7255cd)	2	1994	1	1994	(Blitzz/Atlantic 87243)
3	So Much In Love (Re-Mix)	(Atlantic A 7216cd)	49	1994	0	1994	
* 4	I Can't Love You Like That	(Atlantic A 8193cd)	33	1995	5	1995	(Blitzz/Atlantic 87134)
5	Someday (From *The Hunchback Of Notre Dame*)		0	1996	30	1996	(Hollywood 64011)
Allan Sherman	Male Vocalist, Real Name Allan Copeion. B: 30 Nov 1924 Chicago						
* 1	Hello Muddah Hello Faddah	(Warner Bros Wb 106)	14	1963	2	1963	(Warner Bros 5378)
2	Crazy Downtown		0	1965	40	1965	(Warner Bros 5614)
Alley Cats							
1	Puddin' N'Tain		0	1963	43	1963	(Philles 108)
Allisons	Real Names John Brian Alford B: 31 Dec 1942, Bob Colin Day B: 21 Feb 1942						
* 1	Are You Sure	(Fontana H 294)	2	1961	0	1961	
2	Words	(Fontana H 304)	34	1961	0	1961	
3	Lessons In Love	(Fontana H 362)	30	1962	0	1962	
Allman Brothers Band	Names Duane & Gregg Allman, Dickey Betts, Berry Oakley, Butch Trucks & Johnny Johanson						
* 1	Ramblln' Man		0	1973	2	1973	(Capricorn 0027)
2	Crazy Love		0	1979	29	1979	(Capricorn 0320)
3	Straight From The Heart		0	1981	39	1981	(Arista 0618)
Allnight Band	Male Instrumental Group from the UK						
1	The Joker (The Wigan Joker)	(Casino Classics Cc6)	50	1979	0	1979	
Alma Cogan	Female Vocalist from the UK						
1	Bell Bottom Blues	(HMV B 10653)	4	1954	0	1954	
2	Little Things Mean A Lot	(HMV B 10717)	11	1954	0	1954	
3	Little Things Mean A Lot (Re-Entry)	(HMV B 10717)	19	1954	0	1954	

ISSUE	TITLE	UK LBL	UK POS	UK YEAR	US POS	US YEAR	US LBL
4	Little Things Mean A Lot (2nd Re-Entry)	(HMV B 10717)	18	1954	0	1954	
5	I Can't Tell A Waltz From A Tango	(HMV B 10786)	6	1954	0	1954	
6	Dreamboat	(HMV B 10872)	1	1955	0	1955	
7	Banjo's Back In Town	(HMV B 10917)	17	1955	0	1955	
8	Go On By	(HMV B 10917)	16	1955	0	1955	
9	Twenty Tiny Fingers	(HMV Pop 129)	17	1955	0	1955	
10	Never Do A Tango With An Eskimo	(HMV Pop 129)	6	1955	0	1955	
11	Willie Can	(HMV Pop 187)	13	1956	0	1956	
12	The Birds And The Bees	(HMV Pop 223)	25	1956	0	1956	
13	Why Do Fools Fall In Love	(HMV Pop 223)	22	1956	0	1956	
14	In The Middle Of The House	(HMV Pop 261)	20	1956	0	1956	
15	You Me And Us	(HMV Pop 284)	18	1957	0	1957	
16	Whatever Lola Wants	(HMV Pop 317)	26	1957	0	1957	
17	The Story Of My Life	(HMV Pop 433)	25	1958	0	1958	
18	Sugartime	(HMV Pop 450)	16	1958	0	1958	
19	Sugartime (Re-Entry)	(HMV Pop 450)	30	1958	0	1958	
20	Last Night On The Back Porch	(HMV Pop 573)	27	1959	0	1959	
21	We Got Love	(HMV Pop 670)	26	1959	0	1959	
22	Dream Talk	(HMV Pop 728)	48	1960	0	1960	
23	Train Of Love	(HMV Pop 760)	27	1960	0	1960	
24	Cowboy Jimmy Joe	(Columbia Db 4607)	37	1961	0	1961	

Almighty   Vocal/Instrumental Group from the UK

ISSUE	TITLE	UK LBL	UK POS	UK YEAR	US POS	US YEAR	US LBL
1	Wild And Wonderful	(Polydor Po 75)	50	1990	0	1990	
2	Free 'N' Easy	(Polydor Po 127)	35	1991	0	1991	
3	Devil's Toy	(Polydor Po 144)	36	1991	0	1991	
4	Little Lost Sometimes	(Polydor Po 151)	42	1991	0	1991	
5	Addiction	(Polydor Pzcd 161)	38	1993	0	1993	
6	Out Of Season	(Polydor Pzcd 266)	41	1993	0	1993	
7	Over The Edge	(Polydor Pzcd 298)	38	1993	0	1993	
8	Wrench	(Chrysalis Cdchs 5014)	26	1994	0	1994	
9	Jonestown Mind	(Chrysalis Cdchs 5017)	26	1995	0	1995	
10	All Sussed Out	(Chrysalis Cdchs 5030)	28	1996	0	1996	
11	Do You Understand	(Raw Power Rawx 1022)	38	1996	0	1996	

Aloof   Male Vocal/Instrumental Group from the UK

ISSUE	TITLE	UK LBL	UK POS	UK YEAR	US POS	US YEAR	US LBL
1	On A Mission	(Cowboy Rodeo 5)	64	1992	0	1992	
2	Wish You Were Here.	(East West Ew 38cd)	61	1996	0	1996	
3	One Night Stand	(East West Ew 067cd)	30	1996	0	1996	
4	Wish You Were Here	(East West Ew 083cd1)	43	1997	0	1997	

Alphaville   Male Vocal/Instrumental Group From Germany

ISSUE	TITLE	UK LBL	UK POS	UK YEAR	US POS	US YEAR	US LBL
1	Big In Japan	(WEA Int X9505)	8	1984	0	1984	

Arab Strap

ISSUE	TITLE	UK LBL	UK POS	UK YEAR	US POS	US YEAR	US LBL
1	The Girls Of Summer (EP) (Chemikal Underground Chem 017cd)		74	1997	0	1997	

All Saints

ISSUE	TITLE	UK LBL	UK POS	UK YEAR	US POS	US YEAR	US LBL
1	I Know Where It's At	(London Loncd 398)	4	1997	0	1997	

Altered Images   Mixed Vocal/Instrumental Group from the UK

ISSUE	TITLE	UK LBL	UK POS	UK YEAR	US POS	US YEAR	US LBL
1	Dead Pop Stars	(Epic Epc A 1023)	67	1981	0	1981	
2	Happy Birthday	(Epic Epc A 1522)	2	1981	0	1981	
3	I Could Be Happy	(Epic Epc A 1834)	7	1981	0	1981	
4	See Those Eyes	(Epic Epc A 2198)	11	1992	0	1992	
5	Pinky Blue	(Epic Epc A 2426)	35	1982	0	1982	
6	Don't Talk To Me About Love	(Epic Epc A 3083)	7	1983	0	1983	
7	Bring Me Closer	(Epic Epc A 3398)	29	1983	0	1983	
8	Love To Stay	(Epic Epc A 3582)	46	1983	0	1983	

Altern 8   Male Instrumental/Production Duo from the UK

ISSUE	TITLE	UK LBL	UK POS	UK YEAR	US POS	US YEAR	US LBL
1	Infiltrate 202	(Network Nwk 24)	28	1991	0	1991	
2	Activ 8 (Come With Me)	(Network Nwk 34)	3	1991	0	1991	
3	Frequency	(Network Nwkt 37)	41	1992	0	1992	
4	Evapor 8	(Network Nwk 38)	6	1992	0	1992	
5	Hynotic St-8	(Network Nwk 49)	16	1992	0	1992	
6	Shame	(Network Nwkten 56)	74	1992	0	1992	
7	Brutal-8-E	(Network Nwk 59)	43	1992	0	1992	
8	Everybody	(Network Nwkcd 73)	58	1993	0	1993	

Althia & Donna   Female Vocal Duo From Jamaica

ISSUE	TITLE	UK LBL	UK POS	UK YEAR	US POS	US YEAR	US LBL
1	Uptown Top Ranking	(Lightning Lig 506)	1	1977	0	1977	

ISSUE	TITLE	UK LBL	UK POS	UK YEAR	US POS	US YEAR	US LBL
Alton & Destiny Mcclain Female Vocal Trio from the USA							
1	It Must Be Love		0	1979	32	1979	(Polydor 14532)
Alton Edwards Male Vocalist from South Africa							
1	I Just Wanna (Spend Some Time With You) Streetwave Stra 1897)		20	1982	0	1982	
Alvin Cash & The Crawlers Male Singer/Dancer, B: 15 Feb 1939 St Louis							
	The Crawlers Were Formed In 1960 With Brothers Robert, Albert And George, Although They Never Sang On Any Of His Hits						
1	Twine Time		0	1965	14	1965	(Mar-V-Lus 6002)
Allure							
1	Head Over Heals	(Epic 6645942)	18	1997	35	1997	(Track Masters 78522)
Alvin Robinson							
1	Something You Got		0	1964	52	1964	(Tiger 104)
Alvin Stardust Male Vocalist from the UK							
1	My Coo Ca Choo	(Magnet Mag 1)	2	1973	0	1973	
2	Jealous Mind	(Magnet Mag 5)	1	1974	0	1974	
3	Red Dress	(Magnet Mag 8)	7	1974	0	1974	
4	You You You	(Magnet Mag 13)	6	1974	0	1974	
5	Tell Me Why	(Magnet Mag 19)	16	1974	0	1974	
6	Good Love Can Never Die	(Magnet Mag 21)	11	1975	0	1975	
7	Sweet Cheatin' Rita	(Magnet Mag 32)	37	1975	0	1975	
8	Pretend	(Stiff Buy 124)	4	1981	0	1981	
9	A Wonderful Time Up There	(Stiff Buy 132)	56	1981	0	1981	
10	I Feel Like Buddy Holly	(Chrysalis Chs 2784)	7	1984	0	1984	
11	I Won't Run Away	(Chrysalis Chs 2829)	7	1984	0	1984	
12	So Near To Christmas	(Chrysalis Chs 2835)	29	1984	0	1984	
13	Got A Little Heartache	(Chrysalis Chs 2856)	55	1985	0	1985	
Alvino Rey & His Orchestra Male Bandleader/Instrumentalist (Guitar) from the USA							
10	Cement Mixer (Put-Ti, Put-Ti)		0	1946	5	1946	(Capitol 248)
11	Bloop-Bleep		0	1947	13	1947	(Capitol428)
12	Near You		0	1947	3	1947	(Capitol 452)
13	I'm Looking Over A Four-Leaf Clover		0	1948	6	1948	(Capitol 491)
Aly-Us Male Vocal/Instrumental Group from the USA							
1	Follow Me	(Cooltempo Cool 266)	43	1992	0	1992	
Alysha Warren Female Vocalist from the UK							
1	I'm So In Love	(Wild Card Cardd 10)	61	1994	0	1994	
2	I Thought I Meant The World To You	(Wild Card Cardd 16)	40	1995	0	1995	
3	Keep On Pushing Our Love	(Arista 74321390422)	30	1996	0	1996	
Alyson Williams Female Vocalist from The USA							
1	Sleep Talk	(Def Jam 6546567)	17	1989	0	1989	
2	My Love Is So Raw	(Def Jam 6548987)	34	1989	0	1989	
3	I Need Your Lovin'	(Def Jam 6551437)	8	1989	0	1989	
4	I Second That Emotion	(Def Jam 6554567)	44	1989	0	1989	
Amanda Barrie & Johnny Briggs Mixed Vocal Duo from the UK							
1	Something Stupid	(FMI Premier Cdems 411)	35	1995	0	1995	
Amanda Marshall							
1	Birmingham		0	1996	43	1996	(Epic 78385)
Amazing Rhythm Aces Names: Russell Smith, Barry Burton, Billy Earhart, Jeff Davis & Butch McDade							
1	Third Rate Romance		0	1975	14	1975	(ABC 12078)
2	Amazing Grace (Used To Be Her Favourite Song)		0	1975	72	1975	(ABC 12142)
3	The End Is Not In Sight (The Cowboy Tune)		0	1976	42	1976	(ABC12202)
! 4	Ashes Of Love		0	1978	99	1978	(ABC 12369)
! 5	Lipstick Traces (On A Cigarette)		0	1979	88	1979	(ABC 12454)
! 6	I Musta Died And Gone To Texas		0	1980	77	1980	(Warner Bros 49600)
Amazulu Mixed Vocal/Instrumental Group from the UK							
1	Excitable	(Island Is 201)	12	1985	0	1985	
2	Don't You Just Know It	(Island Is 233)	15	1985	0	1985	
3	The Things The Lonely Do	(Island Is 267)	43	1986	0	1986	
4	Too Good To Be Forgotten	(Island Is 284)	5	1986	0	1986	
5	Montego Bay		0	1935	20	1935	(Decca 360)
Ambrose & His Orchestra							
3	I'm On A See-Saw		0	1935	3	1935	(Decca 467)
4	Hors D'Oeurves		0	1935	6	1935	(Decca 5009
5	Embassy Stomp		0	1935	18	1935	(Decca 551)

ISSUE	TITLE	UK LBL	UK POS	UK YEAR	US POS	US YEAR	US LBL
6	I'm In A Dancing Mood (From *This'll Make You Whistle*)		0	1936	16	1936	(Decca 971)
7	South Of The Border (Down Mexico Way)		0	1939	8	1939	(Decca 2732)
Ambrosia Names David Pack, David Puerta, Burleigh Drummond & Christopher North							
1	Holdin' On To Yesterday		0	1975	17	1975	(20th Century 2207)
2	Magical Mystery Tour		0	1977	39	1977	(20th Century 2327)
3	How Much I Feel		0	1978	3	1978	(Warner Bros 8640)
4	Biggest Part Of Me		0	1980	3	1980	(Warner Bros 49925)
5	You're The Only Woman (You And I)		0	1980	13	1980	(Warner Bros 49508)
	CHRIS HAS SINCE LEFT THE BAND						
Amen Corner Vocal/Instrumental Group from Cardiff, Wales							
1	Gin House Blues	(Deram Dm 136)	12	1967	0	1967	
2	World Of Broken Hearts	(Deram Dm 151)	26	1967	0	1967	
3	Bend Me Shape Me	(Deram Dm 172)	3	1968	0	1968	
4	High In The Sky	(Deram Dm 197)	6	1968	0	1968	
5	(If Paradise Is) Half As Nice	(Immediate Im 073)	1	1969	0	1969	
6	Hello Susie	(Immediate Im 081)	4	1969	0	1969	
7	(If Paradise Is) Half A Nice (Re-Issue)	(Immediate Ims 103)	34	1976	0	1976	
Amen! UK							
1	Passion	(Feverpitch Cdfvr 1015)	15	1997	0	1997	
2	People Of Love	(Feverpitch Cdfvr 18)	36	1997	0	1997	
America Male Vocal/Instrumental Group from the USA Names: Gerry Beckley, Dewey Bunnell & Dan Peek							
1	Horse With No Name	(Warner Bros K 16128)	49	1971	0	1971	
* 2	Horse With No Name (Re-Entry)	(Warner Bros K 16128)	3	1972	1	1972	(Warner Bros 7555)
3	I Need You		0	1972	9	1972	(Warner Bros 7580)
4	Ventura Highway	(Warner Bros K 16219)	43	1972	8	1972	(Warner Bros 7641)
5	Don't Cross The River		0	1973	35	1973	(Warner Bros 7670)
6	Tin Man		0	1974	4	1974	(Warner Bros 7839)
7	Lonely People		0	1975	5	1975	(Warner Bros 8048)
8	Sister Golden Hair		0	1975	1	1975	(Warner Bros 8086)
9	Daisy Jane		0	1975	20	1975	(Warner Bros 8118)
10	Today's The Day		0	1976	23	1976	(Capitol 5142)
11	You Can Do Magic	(Capitol Cl 264)	59	1982	9	1982	(Capitol 5236)
12	The Border		0	1983	33	1983	(Capitol 5236)
American Breed Names: Gary Loizzo, Charles Colbert, Alan Ciner & Lee Anthony Graziano							
1	Step Out Of Your Mind		0	1967	24	1967	(Acta 804)
* 2	Bend Me Shape Me	(Stateside Ss 2078)	24	1968	5	1967	(Acta 811)
3	Green Light		0	1968	39	1968	(Acta 821)
American Music Club Male Vocal/Instrumental Group from the USA							
1	Johnny Mathis' Feet	(Virgin Vscdg 1445)	58	1993	0	1993	
2	Wish The World Away	(Virgin Vscdx 1512)	46	1994	0	1994	
American Quartet Vocal Group Lead By Billy Murray from The USA							
* 2	Casey Jones		0	1910	1	1910	(Victor 16483)
Ames Brothers Names: Joe, Gene, Vic & Ed B: Massachusetts							
1	A Tree In The Meadow		0	1948	21	1948	(Decca 24411)
2	You, You, You Are The One		0	1949	23	1949	(Coral 60015)
3	Cruising Down The River		0	1949	29	1949	(Coral 60035)
* 4	Rag Mop		0	1950	1	1950	(Coral 60140)
5	Sentimental Me		0	1950	1	1950	(Coral 60140)
6	Music, Music, Music (Put Another Nickel In)		0	1950	14	1950	(Coral 60153)
7	Stars Are The Windows Of Heaven		0	1950	17	1950	(Coral 60209)
8	Can Anyone Explain? (No, No, No!)		0	1950	5	1950	(Coral 60253)
9	Thirsty For Your Kisses		0	1950	26	1950	(Coral 60300)
10	Oh Babe!		0	1950	20	1950	(Coral 60327)
11	The Thing		0	1950	29	1950	(Coral 60333)
12	Wang Wang Blues		0	1951	16	1951	(Coral 60489)
13	Hawaiian War Chant (Ta-Hu-Wa-Hu-Wai)		0	1951	21	1951	(Coral 60510)
* 14	Undecided		0	1951	2	1951	(Coral 60566)
15	I Wanna Love You / I'll Still Love You		0	1952	19	1952	(Coral 60566)
16	Auf Wiederseh'n Sweetheart		0	1952	13	1952	(Coral 60773)
17	String Along		0	1952	18	1952	(Coral 60804)
18	My Favorite Song		0	1952	15	1952	(Coral 608469)
19	No Moon At All		0	1953	21	1953	(Coral 60870)
20	Can't I		0	1953	23	1953	(Coral 60926)

ISSUE	TITLE	UK LBL	UK POS	UK YEAR	US POS	US YEAR	US LBL
* 21	You, You, You		0	1953	1	1953	(RCA Victor 5325)
22	My Love, My Life, My Happiness		0	1953	29	1953	(RCA Victor 5404)
23	I Can't Believe That You're In Love With Me		0	1953	22	1953	(RCA Victor 5530)
24	The Man With The Banjo / Man, Man Is For Woman Made		0	1954	6	1954	(RCA Victor 5644)
25	Leave It To Your Heart		0	1954	29	1954	(RCA Victor 5764)
26	Hopelessly		0	1954	25	1954	(RCA Victor 5840)
* 27	Naughty Lady Of Shady Lane	(HMV B 10800)	6	1955	3	1954	(RCA 5897)
28	My Bonnie Lassie		0	1955	11	1955	(RCA 6208)
29	Forever Darling		0	1956	35	1956	(RCA 6400)
30	It Only Hurts For A Little While		0	1956	11	1956	(RCA 6481)
31	Tammy		0	1957	5	1957	(RCA 6930)
32	Melodie D'amour		0	1957	5	1957	(RCA 7046)
33	A Very Precious Love		0	1958	23	1958	(RCA 7167)
34	Pussy Cat		0	1958	17	1958	(RCA 7315)
35	Red River Rose		0	1959	37	1959	(RCA 7413)
36	China Doll		0	1960	38	1960	(RCA 7655)

Amii Stewart Female Vocalist, B: 1956 Washington D.C.

	TITLE	UK LBL	UK POS	UK YEAR	US POS	US YEAR	US LBL
* 1	Knock On Wood	(Atlantic/Hansa K 11214)	6	1979	1	1979	(Ariola 1922)
2	Light My Fire / 137 Disco Heaven (Medley)	(Atlantic/Hansa K 11278)	5	1979	0	1979	
3	Jealousy	(Atlantic/Hansa K 11386)	58	1979	0	1979	
4	The Letter / Paradise Bird	(Atlantic/Hansa K 1424)	39	1980	0	1980	
5	My Guy - My Girl (Medley)	(Atlantic/Hansa K 11550)	39	1980	0	1980	
7	Knock On Wood /Light My Fire (Re-Mix)	(Sedition Edit 3303)	70	1985	0	1985	
8	My Guy - My Girl (Medley)	(Sedition Edit 3310)	63	1986	0	1986	

Amnesia See Frank'O Moiraghi

Amos Male Vocalist from the Uk

	TITLE	UK LBL	UK POS	UK YEAR	US POS	US YEAR	US LBL
1	Only Saw Today / Instant Karma	(Positiva Cdtiv 16)	48	1994	0	1994	
2	Let Love Shine	(Positiva Cdtiv 24)	31	1995	0	1995	
3	Church Of Freedom	(Positiva Cdtiv 38)	54	1995	0	1995	
4	Stamp	(Positiva Cdtiv 65)	11	1996	0	1996	
5	Argentina	(Positive Cdtiv 74)	30	1997	0	1997	

Amos Milburn Male R&B Vocalist from the USA

	TITLE	UK LBL	UK POS	UK YEAR	US POS	US YEAR	US LBL
+* 1	Bad, Bad Whiskey		0	1950	1	1950	(Abcde 0000)

Amps Mixed Vocal/Instrumental Group from the USA

	TITLE	UK LBL	UK POS	UK YEAR	US POS	US YEAR	US LBL
1	Tipp City	(4ad Bad 5015cd)	61	1995	0	1995	

Amy Grant Female Vocalist, B: 25 Nov 1960 Augusta, Georgia

	TITLE	UK LBL	UK POS	UK YEAR	US POS	US YEAR	US LBL
1	Find A Way		0	1985	29	1985	(A&M 2734)
2	The Next Time I Fall		0	1986	1	1986	(Full Moon 28597)
3	Baby Baby	(A&M Am 727)	2	1991	1	1991	(A&M 1549)
4	Every Heartbeat	(A&M Am 783)	25	1991	2	1991	(A&M 1557)
5	That's What Love Is For	(A&M Am 666)	60	1991	7	1991	(A&M 1566)
6	Good For Me	(A&M Am 810)	60	1992	8	1992	(A&M 1573)
7	I Will Remember You		0	1992	20	1992	(A&M 1600)
8	Lucky One	(A&M 5807322)	60	1994	18	1994	(A&M 0724)
9	Say You'll Be Mine	(A&M 5808292)	41	1994	0	1994	
10	House Of Love	(A&M 5812312)	46	1995	37	1995	(A&M 0802)
11	Big Yellow Taxi	(A&M 5809972)	20	1995	0	1995	

Amy Holland Female Vocalist from the USA

	TITLE	UK LBL	UK POS	UK YEAR	US POS	US YEAR	US LBL
1	How Do I Survive		0	1980	22	1980	(Capitol 4884)

An Emotional Fish Male Vocal/Instrumental Group from the Uk

	TITLE	UK LBL	UK POS	UK YEAR	US POS	US YEAR	US LBL
1	Celebrate	(East West YZ 489)	46	1990	0	1990	

And Why Not? Male Vocal/Instrumental Group from The UK

	TITLE	UK LBL	UK POS	UK YEAR	US POS	US YEAR	US LBL
1	Restless Days (She Cries Out Loud)	(Island Is 426)	38	1989	0	1989	
2	The Face	(Island Is 444)	13	1990	0	1990	
3	Something Got You	(Island Is 452)	39	1990	0	1990	

Anderson Bruford Wakeman Howe Male Vocal/Instrumental Group from the UK

	TITLE	UK LBL	UK POS	UK YEAR	US POS	US YEAR	US LBL
1	Brother Of Mine	(Arista 112379)	63	1989	0	1989	
2	Bring Me Love	(Am:Pm 5817872)	44	1996	0	1996	

Andrea True Connection Female Vocalist, B: Andrea True In Nashville

	TITLE	UK LBL	UK POS	UK YEAR	US POS	US YEAR	US LBL
1	More More More (Part 1)	(Buddah Bds 442)	5	1976	4	1976	(Buddah 515)
2	N.Y., You Got Me Dancing		0	1977	27	1977	(Buddah 564)
3	What's Your Name What's Your Number	(Buddah Bds 467)	34	1978	0	1978	

A

ISSUE	TITLE	UK LBL	UK POS	UK YEAR	US POS	US YEAR	US LBL
Andrew Gold Male Vocal/Pianist, B: 2 Aug 1951 Burbank, California							
1	Lonely Boy	(Asylum K 13076)	11	1977	7	1977	(Asylum 45384)
2	Never Let Her Slip Away	(Asylum K 13112)	5	1978	0	1978	
3	How Can This Be Love	(Asylum K 13126)	19	1978	0	1978	
4	Thank You For Being A Friend	(Asylum K 13135)	42	1978	25	1978	(Asylum 45456)
Andrew Ridgeley Male Vocalist from the UK							
1	Shake	(Epic Ajr 1)	58	1990	0	1990	
Andrew Sisters Female Vocalists, Names Patti B:16 Feb 1920, Maxine B: 3 Feb 1918 & Lavern B: 6 Jul 1915							
* 1	Bei Mir Bist Du Schon		0	1938	1	1938	(Decca 1562)
* 48	Rum And Coca-Cola		0	1945	1	1945	(Decca 18636)
* 58	Winter Wonderland		0	1946	22	1946	(Decca 23722)
* 59	Christmas Island		0	1946	7	1946	(Decca 23722)
* 82	I Can Dream Can't I		0	1949	1	1949	(Decca 24705)
83	The Wedding Of Lili Marlene		0	1949	20	1949	(Decca 24705)
84	Charley My Boy		0	1949	15	1949	(Decca 24812)
85	Merry Christmas Polka		0	1950	18	1950	(Decca 24748)
86	The Wedding Samba		0	1950	23	1950	(Decca 24841)
87	I Wanna Be Loved		0	1950	1	1950	(Decca 27007)
88	Can't We Talk It Over?		0	1950	22	1950	(Decca 27115)
89	A Bushel And A Peck		0	1950	22	1950	(Decca 27252)
90	A Penny A Kiss - A Penny A Hug		0	1951	17	1951	(Decca 27414)
Andru Donalds Male Reggae Vocalist from Kingston, Jamaica							
1	Mishale		0	1995	38	1995	(Metro Blue 58256)
Andy & David Williams Male Vocal Duo from the USA. Andy Is The Nephew Of Another Andy Williams							
1	I Don't Know Why (I Just Do)	(MCA Mus 1183)	37	1973	0	1973	
Andy Cameron Male Vocalist from the UK							
1	Ally's Tartan Army	(KLUB 03)	6	1978	0	1978	
Andy Fairweather-Low Male Vocalist From The UK							
1	Reggae Tune	(A&M Ams 7129)	10	1974	0	1974	
2	Wide Eyed And Legless	(A&M Ams 7202)	6	1975	0	1975	
	SEE ALSO FAIR WEATHER						
Andy Gibb Male Vocalist, Real Name Andrew Roy Gibb B: 5 Mar 1958							
* 1	I Just Wanna Be Your Everything	(RSO 2090 237)	26	1977	1	1977	(RSO 872)
* 2	(Love Is) Thicker Than Water		0	1977	1	1977	(RSO 883)
* 3	Shadow Dancing	(RSO 001)	42	1978	1	1978	(RSO 893)
* 4	An Ever Lasting Love	(RSO 015)	10	1978	5	1978	(RSO 904)
* 5	(Our Love) Don't Throw It All Away	(RSO 26)	32	1979	9	1978	(RSO 991)
6	Desire		0	1980	4	1980	(RSO 1019)
7	I Can't Help It		0	1980	12	1980	(RSO 1026)
8	Time Is Time		0	1981	15	1981	(RSO 1059)
9	Me (Without You)		0	1981	40	1981	(RSO 1056)
	OBITUARY: D: 10 MAR 1988 HEART VIRUS						
Andy Griffith Male Comedian/Vocalist, B: 1 Jun 1926 Mount Airy, North Carolina							
1	What Is Was, Was Football		0	1954	9	1954	(Capitol 2693)
2	Romeo And Juliet		0	1954	27	1954	(Capitol 2698)
3	Make Yourself Comfortable		0	1955	26	1955	(Capitol 3057)
Andy Kim Male Vocalist, Real Name Andrew Joachim B: 5 Dec 1946 Montreal, Canada							
1	How'd We Ever Get This Way		0	1968	21	1968	(Steed 707)
2	Shoot'em Up, Baby		0	1968	31	1968	(Steed 710)
* 3	Baby, I Love You		0	1969	9	1969	(Steed 716)
4	So Good Together		0	1969	36	1969	(Steed 720)
5	Be My Baby		0	1970	17	1970	(Steed 729)
* 6	Rock Me Gently	(Capitol CI 15787)	2	1974	1	1974	(Capitol 3895)
7	Fire, Baby I'm On Fire		0	1974	28	1974	(Capitol 3962) Andy
Russell Male Vocalist, Real Name Andy Rabajos from the USA							
6	Laughing On The Outside (Crying On The Inside)		0	1946	4	1946	(Capitol 252)
7	They Say It's Wonderful (From *Annie Get Your Gun*)		0	1946	10	1946	(Capitol 252)
8	Pretending		0	1946	10	1946	(Capitol 271)
9	Anniversary Song		0	1947	4	1947	(Capitol 368)
10	I'll Close My Eyes		0	1947	15	1947	(Capitol 342)
11	Je Vous Aime		0	1947	22	1947	(Capitol 417)
12	Underneath The Arches		0	1948	13	1948	(Capitol 15183)

ISSUE	TITLE	UK LBL	UK POS	UK YEAR	US POS	US YEAR	US LBL
Andy Stewart Male Vocalist from Scotland							
1	Donald Where's Your Troosers	(Top Rank Jar 427)	37	1960	0	1960	
2	A Scottish Soldier	(Top Rank Jar 512)	19	1961	0	1961	
3	The Battles O'er	(Top Rank Jar 565)	28	1961	0	1961	
4	A Scottish Soldier (Re-Entry)	(Top Rank Jar 512)	43	1961	0	1961	
5	Dr Finlay	(HMV Pop 1454)	50	1965	0	1965	
6	Dr Finlay (Re-Entry)	(HMV Pop 1454)	43	1965	0	1965	
7	Donald Where's Your Troosers (Re-Issue)	(Stone Son 2353)	4	1989	0	1989	
Andy Taylor Male Vocalist, B: 16 Feb 1961 Wolverhampton, England							
1	Take It Easy		0	1986	24	1986	(Atlantic 89414)
2	Lola	(A&M Am 596)	60	1990	0	1990	
Andy Williams Male Vocalist, Real Name Harold Andrew Williams B: 3 Dec 1928 Wall Lake, Iowa							
1	Canadian Sunset		0	1956	7	1956	(Cadence 1297)
2	Baby Doll		0	1956	33	1956	(Cadence 303)
* 3	Butterfly	(London Hla 8399)	1	1957	1	1957	(Cadence 308)
4	I Like Your Kind Of Love	(London Hla 8437)	16	1957	8	1957	(Cadence 1323)
5	Butterfly (Re-Entry)	(London Hla 8399)	29	1957	0	1957	
6	Lips Of Wine		0	1957	17	1957	(Cadence 1336)
7	Are You Sincere		0	1958	3	1958	(Cadence 1340)
8	Promise Me Love		0	1958	17	1958	(Cadence 351)
* 9	Hawaiian Wedding Song / House Of Bamboo		0	1959	11	1959	(Cadence 1358)
10	Lonely Street		0	1959	5	1959	(Cadence 370)
11	Village Of St Bernadette		0	1960	7	1960	(Cadence 1374)
12	The Bilbao Song		0	1961	37	1961	(Cadence 1398)
13	Stranger On The Shore	(CBS Aag 103)	30	1962	38	1962	(Columbia 42451)
14	Don't You Believe It		0	1962	39	1962	(Columbia 42523)
* 15	Can't Get Used To Losing You	(CBS Aag 138)	2	1963	2	1963	(Columbia 42674)
16	Days Of Wine And Roses		0	1963	26	1963	(Columbia 42674)
17	Hopeless		0	1963	13	1963	(Columbia 42784)
18	A Fool Never Learns	(CBS Aag 182)	40	1964	13	1964	(Columbia 42950)
19	Wrong For Each Other		0	1964	34	1964	(Columbia 43015)
20	On The Street Where You Live		0	1964	28	1964	(Columbia 43128)
21	Dear Heart		0	1964	24	1964	(Columbia 43180)
22	And Roses And Roses		0	1965	36	1965	(Columbia 43257)
23	Almost There	(CBS 201813)	2	1965	0	1965	
24	Ain't It True		0	1965	40	1965	(Columbia 43358)
25	May Each Day	(CBS 202042)	19	1966	0	1966	
26	In The Arms Of Love	(CBS 202300)	33	1966	0	1966	
27	Music To Watch Girls By	(CBS 2675)	33	1967	34	1967	(Columbia 44065)
28	More And More	(CBS 2886)	45	1967	0	1967	
29	Can't Take My Eyes Of You	(CBS 3298)	5	1968	0	1968	
30	Battle Hymn Of The Republic		0	1968	33	1968	(Columbia 44650)
31	Happy Heart	(CBS 4062)	47	1969	22	1969	(Columbia 44818)
32	Happy Heart (Re-Entry)	(CBS 4062)	19	1969	0	1969	
33	Can't Help Falling In Love	(CBS 4818)	3	1970	0	1970	
34	It's So Easy	(CBS 5113)	13	1970	0	1970	
35	It's So Easy (Re-Entry)	(CBS 5113)	49	1970	0	1970	
36	Home Lovin' Man	(CBS 5267)	7	1970	0	1970	
* 37	(Where Do I Begin) Love Story	(CBS 7020)	4	1971	9	1971	(Columbia 45317)
38	(Where Do I Begin) Love Story (Re-Entry)	(CBS 7020)	49	1971	0	1971	
39	Love Theme (From *The Godfather*)	(CBS 8166)	50	1972	34	1972	(Columbia 45579)
40	Love Theme "(Re-Entry)	(CBS 8166)	44	1972	0	1972	
41	Love Theme " (2nd Re-Entry)	(CBS 8166)	42	1972	0	1972	
42	Solitaire	(CBS 1824)	4	1973	0	1973	
43	Getting Over You	(CBS 2181)	35	1974	0	1974	
44	You Lay So Easy On My Mind	(CBS 3167)	32	1975	0	1975	
45	The Other Side Of Me	(CBS 3903)	42	1976	0	1976	
Aneka Female Vocalist from the UK							
1	Japanese Boy	(Hansa 5)	1	1981	0	1981	
2	Little Lady	(Hansa 8)	50	1981	0	1981	
Angel Moraes Male Producer from the USA							
1	Heaven Knows / Deep Deep Down	(Ffrr Fcd 282)	72	1996	0	1996	
2	I Like It	(Am:Pm 5821792)	70	1997	0	1997	

ISSUE	TITLE	UK LBL	UK POS	UK YEAR	US POS	US YEAR	US LBL
Angelettes Female Vocal Group from the UK							
1	Don't Let Him Touch You	(Decca F 13284)	35	1972	0	1972	
1	Come Back To Me	(Hi-Life/Polydor 5776312)	68	1996	0	1996	
Angelic Upstarts Male Vocal/Instrumental from the UK							
1	I'm An Upstart	(Warner Bros K 17354)	31	1979	0	1979	
2	Teenage Warning	(Warner Bros K 17426)	29	1979	0	1979	
3	Never 'Ad Nothin'	(Warner Bros K 17476)	52	1979	0	1979	
4	Out Of Control	(Warner Bros K 17558)	58	1980	0	1980	
5	We've Gotta Get Out Of This Place	(Warner Bros K 17576)	65	1980	0	1980	
6	Last Night Another Soldier	(Angelic Upstarts Z 7)	51	1980	0	1980	
7	Kids On The Streets	(Angelic Upstarts Z 16)	57	1981	0	1981	
Angels Originally Formed As The Starlets And Disbanded In 1967							
1	Till		0	1961	14	1961	(Caprice 107)
2	Cry Baby Cry		0	1962	38	1962	(Caprice 112)
* 3	My Boyfriend's Back	(Mercury Amt 1211)	50	1963	1	1963	(Smash 1834)
4	I Adore Him		0	1963	25	1963	(Smash 1854)
Angelheart Female Vocal/Instrumental Duo from the UK							
1	Come Back To Me	(HiLife/Polydor 5776312)	68	1996	0	1996	
2	I'm Still Waiting	(Hi-Life 5735452)	74	1997	0	1997	
Angelwitch Male Vocal/Instrumental group from the UK							
1	Sweet Danger	(EMI 5064)	75	1980	0	1980	
Angie Brown							
1	I'm Gonna Get You	(Vinyl Solution Storm 46s)	3	1992	0	1992	
2	I'm Gonna Get You (Re-Entry)	(Vinyl Solution Storm 46s)	72	1993	0	1993	
3	Too My Love	(Vinyl Solution Storm 60cd)	19	1993	0	1993	
4	Rockin' For Myself	(Nuff Respect Nuff 002cd)	67	1993	0	1993	
Animal Nightlife							
1	Native Boy (Uptown)	(Innervision A 3584)	60	1983	0	1983	
2	Mr. Solitaire	(Island Is 193)	25	1984	0	1984	
3	Love Is Just The Great Prentender	(Island Is 200)	28	1985	0	1985	
4	Preacher Preacher	(Island Is 245)	67	1985	0	1985	
Animal A puppet from the USA							
1	Wipe Out	(Bmg Kidz 74321219532)	38	1994	0	1994	
Animals Names: Eric Burdon, Alan Price, Bryan Chandler, Hilton Valentine & John Steel							
1	Baby Let Me Take You Home	(Columbia Db 7247)	21	1964	0	1964	
* 2	House Of The Rising Sun	(Columbia Db 7301)	1	1964	1	1964	(MGM 13264)
3	I'm Crying	(Columbia Db 7354)	8	1964	19	1964	(MGM 13274)
4	Don't Let Me Be Misunderstood	(Columbia Db 7445)	3	1965	15	1965	(MGM 1311)
5	Bring It On Home To Me	(Columbia Db 7539)	7	1965	32	1965	(MGM 13339)
6	We've Gotta Get Out Of This Place	(Columbia Db 7639)	2	1965	13	1965	(MGM 13382)
7	It's My Life	(Columbia Db 7741)	7	1965	23	1965	(MGM 13414)
8	Inside – Looking Out	(Decca F 12332)	12	1966	34	1966	(MGM 13468)
9	Don't Bring Me Down	(Decca F 12407)	6	1966	12	1966	(MGM 13514)
10	Help Me Girl	(Decca F 12502)	14	1966	29	1966	(MGM 13636)
11	When I Was Young	(MGM 1340)	45	1967	15	1967	(MGM 13721)
12	San Franciscan Nights	(MGM 1359)	7	1967	9	1967	(MGM 13769)
13	Good Times	(MGM 1344)	20	1967	0	1967	
14	Monterey		0	1967	15	1967	(MGM 13868)
15	Sky Pilot	(Mgm 1373)	40	1968	14	1968	(MGM 13939)
16	Ring Of Fire	(MGM 1461)	35	1969	0	1969	
* 17	Spill The Wine		0	1970	3	1970	(MGM 14118)
18	House Of The Rising Sun (Re-Issue)	(Rak Rr 1)	25	1972	0	1972	
19	House Of The Rising Sun (Re-Issue) (Re-Entry)	(Rak Rr 1)	11	1982	0	1982	
	Hit 2 Was Based On A Negro Folk Song						
Animotion Mixed Vocal/Instrumental Quintet from the USA/Uk Led By Astrid Plane & Bill Wadhams							
1	Obsession	(Mercury Ph 34)	5	1985	6	1985	(Mercury 880266)
2	Let Him Go		0	1985	39	1985	(Mercury 880737)
3	Room To Move		0	1989	9	1989	(Polydor 871418)
Anita Baker Female Vocalist B: 20 Dec 1957 Memphis, Was Also With Chapter 8							
1	Sweet Love	(Elektra Ekr 44)	13	1986	8	1986	(Elektra 69557)
2	Caught Up In The Rapture	(Elektra Ekr 49)	51	1987	37	1987	(Elektra 69511)
3	Giving You The Best That I Got	(Elektra Ekr 79)	55	1988	3	1988	(Elektra 69371)
4	Just Because		0	1989	14	1989	(Elektra 69327)

ISSUE	TITLE	UK LBL	UK POS	UK YEAR	US POS	US YEAR	US LBL
5	Talk To Me	(Elektra Ekr 111)	68	1990	0	1990	
6	Body & Soul	(Elektra Ekr 190cd)	48	1994	36	1994	(Elektra 64520)

Anita Bryant Female Vocalist, B: 25 Mar 1940 Barnsdale, Oklahoma

* 1	Till There Was You		0	1960	30	1960	(Carlton 512)
2	Paper Roses	(London Hll 9144)	49	1960	5	1960	(Carlton 528)
3	Paper Roses (Re-Entry)	(London Hll 9144)	45	1960	0	1960	
4	Paper Roses (2nd Re-Entry)	(London Hll 9144)	24	1960	0	1960	
* 5	In My Little Corner Of The World	(London Hll 9171)	48	1960	10	1960	(Carlton 530)
6	Wonderland By Night		0	1960	18	1960	(Carlton 537)
	SHE WAS SECOND RUNNER-UP TO MISS AMERICA IN 1958						

Anita Dobson Female Actress/Vocalist from the UK

1	Anyone Can Fall In Love	(BBC Resl 191)	4	1986	0	1986	
2	Talking Of Love	(Parlophone R 6159)	43	1987	0	1987	

Anita Harris Female Vocalist, Real Name Anita Madeleine Harris. B: 3 Jun 1944 Somerset, England

* 1	Just Loving You	(CBS 2724)	6	1967	0	1967	
2	Playground	(CBS 2991)	46	1967	0	1967	
3	Anniversary Waltz	(CBS 3211)	21	1967	0	1967	
4	Dream A Little Dream Of Me	(CBS 3637)	33	1968	0	1968	

Anita O'Day Female Jazz Vocalist from the USA

1	Hi Ho Trailus Boot Whip		0	1947	24	1947	(Signature 15162)
2	Tennessee Waltz		0	1951	24	1951	(London 867)

Anita Ward Female Vocalist, B: 20 Dec 1957 Memphis

1	Ring My Bell	(TK Tkr 7543)	1	1979	1	1979	(Juana 3422)

Ann Breen Female Vocalist From Ireland

1	Pal Of My Cradle Days	(Homespun Hs 052)	69	1983	0	1983	
2	Pal Of My Cradle Days (Re-Entry)	(Homespun Hs 052)	74	1984	0	1984	

Ann Consuelo See Subterrania

Anne Murray Female Vocalist, Real Name Moma Anne Murray. B: 20 Jun 1945 Springhill, Nova Scotia

* 1	Snowbird	(Capitol Cl 15654)	23	1970	8	1970	(Capitol 2738)
2	Destiny	(Capitol Cl 15734)	41	1972	0	1972	
3	Sing High - Sing Low		0	1971	53	1971	(Capitol 2988)
4	A Stranger In My Place		0	1971	27!	1971	(Capitol 3059)
5	Put Your Hand In The Hand		0	1971	67!	1971	(Capitol 3082)
6	I Say A Little Prayer/By The Time I Get To Phoenix		0	1971	40!	1971	(Capitol 3200)
7	Cotton Jenny		0	1972	11!	1972	(Capitol 3260)
8	Danny's Song		0	1973	7	1973	(Capitol 3481)
9	What About Me		0	1973	64	1973	(Capitol 3600)
10	Send A Little Love My Way		0	1973	72	1973	(Capitol 3648)
11	Love Song		0	1974	12	1974	(Capitol 3776)
! 12	He Thinks I Still Care		0	1974	1	1974	(Capitol 3867)
13	You Won't See Me		0	1974	8	1974	(Capitol 3867)
! 14	Son Of A Rotten Gambler		0	1974	5	1974	(Capitol 3955)
! 15	Uproar		0	1975	2	1975	(Capitol 4025)
! 16	A Stranger In My Place (Re-Issue)		0	1975	79	1975	(Capitol 4072)
! 17	Sunday Sunrise		0	1975	49	1975	(Capitol 4142)
! 18	The Call		0	1976	19	1976	(Capitol 4207)
! 19	Golden Oldie		0	1976	41	1976	(Capitol 4265)
! 20	Things		0	1976	22	1976	(Capitol 4329)
! 21	Sunday School To Broadway		0	1977	57	1977	(Capitol 4375)
! 22	Walk Right Back		0	1978	4 !	1978	(Capitol 4527)
* 23	You Needed Me	(Capitol Cl 16011)	22	1978	1	1978	(Capitol 4574)
24	I Just Fall In Love Again	(Capitol Cl 16069)	58	1979	12	1979	(Capitol 4675)
25	Shadows In The Moonlight		0	1979	25	1979	(Capitol 4716)
26	Broken Hearted Me		0	1979	12	1979	(Capitol 4773)
27	Daydream Believer	(Capitol 161123)	61	1980	12	1980	(Capitol 4813)
28	Lucky Me		0	1980	42	1980	(Capitol 4848)
29	I'm Just Happy Just To Dance With You		0	1980	64	1980	(Capitol 4878)
30	Could I Have This Dance		0	1980	33	1980	(Capitol 4920)
31	Blessed are the Believers		0	1981	34	1981	(Capitol 4987)
32	We Don't Have To Hold Out		0	1981	16	1981	(Capitol 5013)
33	It's All I Can Do		0	1981	53	1981	(Capitol 5023)
34	Another Sleepless Night		0	1982	44	1982	(Capitol 5083)
54	Feed this Fire		0	1990	5	1990	Capitol 94102)

ISSUE	TITLE	UK LBL	UK POS	UK YEAR	US POS	US YEAR	US LBL
55	Bluebird		0	1990	39	1990	Capitol 94102)
56	Everyday		0	1991	56	1991	(Capitol 96310)
	HITS 35-54 WERE C/W						

Ann Nesby Female Vocalist from the USA

1	Witness (EP)	(Am:Pm 5875612)	42	1996	0	1996	
2	Hold On (EP)	(Am:Pm 5822332)	75	1997	0	1997	

Ann-Marie Smith Female Vocalist from the UK

1	Music	(Synthetic Cdr 6334)	34	1993	0	1993	

Ann Peebles Female Vocalist, B: 27 Apr 1947 St. Louis

1	I Pity The Fool		0	1971	45	1971	(Hi2186)
2	I Can't Stand The Rain	(London HI 10428)	50	1974	38	1973	(Hi 2248)
3	I Can't Stand The Rain (Re-Entry)	(London HI 10428)	41	1974	0	1974	

Ann Wilson Female Vocalist, B: 19 Jun 1951 San Diego

1	Almost Paradise... Love Theme From *Footloose*		0	1984	7	1984	(Columbia 04418)
2	Surrender To Me		0	1989	6	1989	(Columbia 44288)

Ann-Margret Real Name Ann-Margret Olsson B: 28 Apr 1941 Stockholm, Sweden

1	I Just Don't Understand		0	1961	17	1961	(RCA 7894)

Ann-Marie Smith Femal Vocalist from the UK

1	Music		34	1993	0	1993	(Synthetic CDR 6334)
2	Rockin' My Body		31	1995	0	1995	
3	(You're My One And Only) True Love	(MCA Mcstd 2060)	46	1995	0	1995	

Annabel Lamb Female Vocalist from the UK

1	Riders On The Storm	(A&M Am 131)	27	1983	0	1983	

Annabella Lwin Female Vocalist from the UK

1	Do What You Do	(Sony S2 6611235)	61	1995	0	1995	

Anne Shelton Female Vocalist from the UK

1	Be Mine		0	1949	25	1949	(London 239)
2	Galway Bay		0	1949	27	1949	(London 287)
3	Arriverderci Darling	(HMV Pop 146)	17	1955	0	1955	
4	Seven Days	(Philips PB 567)	20	1956	0	1956	
5	Lay Down Your Arms	(Philips PB 616)	1	1956	0	1956	
6	Village of St Bernadette	(Philips PB 969)	27	1959	0	1959	
7	Sailor	(Philips PB 1096)	10	1961	0	1961	

Anne-Marie David Female Vocalist From France

1	Wonderful Dream	(Epic Epc 1446)	13	1973	0	1973	

Anne Vincent Female Vocalist from the USA

1	You Call Everybody Darlin'		0	1948	6	1948	(Mercury 5155)

Annette With The Afterbeats Real Name Annettee Funicello B: 22 Oct 1942 Utica, New York

1	Tall Paul		0	1959	7	1959	(Disneyland 118)
2	First Name Initial		0	1959	20	1959	(Vista 349)
3	O Dio Mio		0	1960	10	1960	(Vista 354)
4	Train Of Love		0	1960	36	1960	(Vista 359)
5	Pineapple Princess		0	1960	11	1960	(Vista 362)
	HIT 3 IS CREDITED TO ANNETTE						

Annie Laurie Female R&B Vocalist from the USA

1	It Hurts To Be In Love		0	1957	61	1957	(Deluxe 6107)

Annie Lennox Female Vocalist, B: 25 Dec 1954 Aberdeen, Scotland

1	Put A Little Love In Your Heart	(A&M Am 484)	28	1988	9	1989	(A&M 1255)
2	Why	(RCA Pb 45317)	5	1992	34	1992	(Arista 12419)
3	Precious	(RCA 74321100257)	23	1992	0	1992	
4	Walking On Broken Glass	(RCA 74321107227)	8	1992	14	1992	(Arista 12452)
5	Cold	(RCA 74321116902)	26	1992	0	1992	
6	Little Bird / Love Song For A Vampire	(RCA 743211233832)	3	1993	0	1993	
7	No More I Love You's	(RCA 74321257162)	2	1995	23	1995	(Arista 12804)
8	A Whiter Shade Of Pale	(RCA 74321284832)	16	1995	0	1995	
9	Waiting In Vain	(RCA 74321316132)	31	1995	0	1995	
10	Something So Right	(RCA 74321332392)	44	1995	0	1995	

Another Bad Creation Names: Dave Shelton, Chris Sellers, Marliss & Demetrious Pugh With Romell Chapman

* 1	Alesha		0	1991	9	1991	(Motown 2070)
2	Playground		0	1991	10	1991	(Motown 2088)

ISSUE	TITLE	UK LBL	UK POS	UK YEAR	US POS	US YEAR	US LBL
Anthony Hopkins Male Vocalist from the UK							
1	Distant Star	(Juice Aa 5)	75	1986	0	1986	
Anthony Newley Male Actor/Vocalist From The UK							
1	I've Waited So Long	(Decca F 11127)	3	1959	0	1959	
2	Idle On Parade (EP)	(Decca Dfe 6566)	13	1959	0	1959	
3	Personality	(Decca F 11142)	6	1959	0	1959	
4	Why	(Decca F 11194)	1	1960	0	1960	
5	Do You Mind	(Decca F 11220)	1	1960	0	1960	
6	If She Should Come To You	(Decca F 11254)	6	1960	0	1960	
7	Strawberry Fair	(Decca F 11295)	3	1960	0	1960	
8	And The Heavens Cried	(Decca F 11331)	6	1961	0	1961	
9	Pop Goes The Weasel	(Decca F 11362)	12	1961	0	1961	
10	Bee Bom	(Decca F 11362)	15	1961	0	1961	
11	What Kind Of Fool Am I	(Decca F 11376)	36	1961	0	1961	
12	D-Darling	(Decca F 11419)	25	1962	0	1962	
13	That Noise	(Decca F 11486)	34	1962	0	1962	
Anthony Steel & The Radio Revellers Male Vocalist And Male Instrumental Group from the UK							
1	West Of Zanzibar	(Polygram P 1114)	11	1954	0	1954	
Anthony Way Male Vocalist (Choirboy) from the UK							
1	Panis Angelicus	(Decca 4481642)	55	1995	0	1995	
Anthrax Male Vocal/Instrumental Group from the USA							
1	I Am The Law	(Island Is Law 1)	32	1987	0	1987	
2	Indians	(Island Is 325)	44	1987	0	1987	
3	I'm The Man	(Island Is 338)	20	1987	0	1987	
4	Make Me Laugh	(Island Is 379)	26	1988	0	1988	
5	Anti-Social	(Island Is 409)	44	1989	0	1989	
6	In My World	(Island Is 470)	29	1990	0	1990	
7	Got The Time	(Island Is 476)	16	1991	0	1991	
8	Bring The Noise	(Island Is 490)	14	1991	0	1991	
9	Only	(Elektra Ekr 166cd)	36	1993	0	1993	
10	Black Lodge	(Elektra Ekr 171cd)	53	1993	0	1993	
Anti-Nowhere League Male Vocal/Instrumental Group from the UK							
1	Streets Of London	(Wxyz Abcd 1)	48	1982	0	1982	
2	I Hate...People	(Wxyz Abcd 2)	46	1982	0	1982	
3	Woman	(Wxyz Abcd 4)	72	1982	0	1982	
Anticappella Mixed Vocal/Instrumental Group from the UK/Italy							
1	2 231	(PWL International L Pwl 205)	24	1991	0	1991	
2	Every Day	(PWL Continental Pwl 220)	45	1992	0	1992	
3	Move Your Body	(Media Mcstd 1980)	21	1994	0	1994	
4	Express Your Freedom	(MCA Mcstd 2048)	31	1995	0	1995	
5	2 231 (Re-Mix) / Move Your Body THE 1994 HIT FEATURED MC FIXX IT	(Media Mcstd 40037)	54	1996	0	1996	
Antoine							
* 1	La Tramontana (The Bearings) Hit Was Number 1 In Italy		0	1968	0	1968	
Antoinette Roberson							
1	The Lover That You Are	(Ffrr Fcd 278)	22	1996	0	1996	
Anton Karas Male Zither Player, B: 7 Jul 1906 Vienna							
* 1	*The Third Man* Theme		0	1950	1	1950	(London 536)
Apache Indian Male Vocalist from the UK							
1	Fe' Real	(Ten 416)	33	1992	0	1992	
2	Arranged Marriage	(Island Cid 544)	16	1993	0	1993	
3	Chok There	(Island Cid 555)	30	1993	0	1993	
4	Nuff Vibes	(Island Cid 560)	5	1993	0	1993	
5	Movin' On	(Island Cid 580)	48	1993	0	1993	
6	Wreckx Shop	(MCA MCS 1725)	26	1994	0	1994	
7	Make Way For The Indian	(Island Cid 8016)	29	1995	0	1995	
8	Raggamuffin Girl	(Island Cid 606)	31	1995	0	1995	
9	Lovin' (Let Me Love You)	(Coalition Cola 002cd)	53	1997	0	1997	
Apollo 11 Astronauts & Hugh Downs							
* 1	First Man On The Moon		0	1969	0	1969	

ISSUE	TITLE	UK LBL	UK POS	UK YEAR	US POS	US YEAR	US LBL
Apollo 440	Male Production/Instrumental Group from the UK						
1	Astral America	(Stealth Sonic Ssxcd 2)	36	1994	0	1994	
2	Liquid Cool	(Stealth Sonic Ssxcd 3)	35	1994	0	1994	
3	(Don't Fear) The Reaper	(Stealth Sonic Ssxcd 4)	35	1995	0	1995	
4	Krupa	(Stealth Sonic Ssxcd 5)	23	1996	0	1996	
5	Krupa (Re-Entry)	(Stealth Sonic Ssxcd 5)	24	1996	0	1996	
6	Ain't Talking 'Bout Dub	(Stealth Sonic Ssxcd 6)	7	1997	0	1997	
7	Raw Power	(Stealth Sonic Ssxcd 7)	32	1997	0	1997	
Applejacks (1)	Mixed Vocal/Instrumental Group from the UK						
1	Tell Me When	(Decca F 11833)	7	1964	0	1964	
2	Like Dreamers Do	(Decca F 11916)	20	1964	0	1964	
3	Three Little Words	(Decca F 11981)	23	1964	0	1964	
Applejacks (2)	Studio Band From Philadelphia Led By Dave Appell						
1	Mexican Hat Rock		0	1958	16	1958	(Cameo 149)
2	Rocka-Conga		0	1959	38	1959	(Cameo 155)
Apples	Male Vocal/Instrumental Group from the UK						
1	Eye Wonder	(Epic 6566717)	75	1991	0	1991	
April Stevens	Female Vocalist From The USA						
1	I'm In Love Again		0	1951	6	1951	(RCA Victor 4148)
2	Gimme A Little Kiss, Will Ya, Huh?		0	1951	10	1951	(RCA Victor 4208)
3	And So To Sleep Again		0	1951	27	1951	(RCA Victor 4283)
April Wine	Male Vocal/Instrumental Group from Canada Names: Gerry Beckley, Dewey Bunnell & Dan Peek						
1	You Could Have Been A Lady		0	1972	32	1972	(Big Tree 133)
2	Roller		0	1979	34	1979	(Capitol 4660)
3	I Like To Rock	(Capitol Cl 16121)	41	1980	0	1980	
4	Just Between You And Me	(Capitol Cl 16184)	52	1981	21	1981	(Capitol 4975)
Aquarian Dream	Mixed Vocal/Instrumental Group from the USA						
1	You're A Star	(Elektra Lv 7)	67	1979	0	1979	
Aquatones	Names: Lynn Nixon, Larry Vannata, David Goddard & Eugene McCarthy						
1	You		0	1958	21	1958	(Fargo 1001)
Arbors	Names: Edward & Fred Farran With Scott & Tom Herrick						
1	The Letter		0	1969	20	1969	(Date 1638)
Arcadia	Male Vocal/Instrumental Group from the UK Names: Simon LeBon, Nick Rhodes & Roger Taylor						
1	Election Day	(Odeon Nsr 1)	7	1985	6	1985	(Capitol 5501)
2	The Promise	(Odeon Nsr 2)	37	1986	0	1986	
3	Goodbye Is Forever		0	1986	33	1986	(Capitol 5542)
4	The Flame	(Odeon Nsr 3)	58	1986	0	1986	
Archibald							
+ 1	Stack-A-Lee		0	1950	10	1950	(Imperial 5068)
Archie Bell & The Drells	Male Vocal/Instrumental Group From The Usa, B: 1 Sep 1944 Henderson, Texas						
* 1	Tighten Up		0	1968	1	1968	(Atlantic 2478)
2	I Can't Stop Dancing		0	1968	9	1968	(Atlantic 2534)
3	Do The Choo Choo		0	1968	44	1968	(Atlantic 2559)
4	There's Gonna Be A Showdown	(Atlantic K 10263)	36	1973	21	1969	(Atlantic 2583)
+ 5	Girl, You're Too Young		0	1969	13	1969	(Atlantic 2644)
6	Here I Go Again	(Atlantic K 10210)	11	1972	0	1972	
7	Soul City Walk	(Parlophone Int Pir 4250)	13	1976	0	1976	
8	Everybody Having A Good Time	(Parlophone Int Pir 5179)	43	1977	0	1977	
9	Don't Let Love Get You Down	(Portrait A 7254)	49	1986	0	1986	
Archie Bleyer	Male Music Arranger/Director, B: 12 Jun 1909 Corona, New York						
1	Hernando's Hideaway (From *The Pajama Game*)		0	1954	6	1954	(Cadence 1241)
2	Naughty Lady Of Shady Lane		0	1954	17	1954	(Cadence 1254)
Archies	Studio Group Created By Don Kirshner, Based On A Tv Series/Comic *Archie* from the USA						
1	Bang-Shang-A-Lang		0	1968	22	1968	(Calendar 1006)
* 2	Sugar Sugar	(RCA 1872)	1	1969	1	1969	(Calendar 1008)
* 3	Jingle Jangle		0	1970	10	1970	(Kirshner 5002)
4	Who's Your Baby		0	1970	40	1970	(Kirshner 5003)
Aretha Franklin	Female Vocalist, B: 25 Mar 1942 In Memphis, Raised In Buffalo						
+ 1	Today I Sing The Blues		0	1960	10	1960	(Columbia 41793)
+ 2	Won't Be Long		0	1961	7	1961	(Columbia 41923)
3	Rock-A-Bye Your Baby (With A Dixie Melody)		0	1961	37	1961	(Columbia 42157)
4	Runnin' Out Of Fools		0	1964	57	1964	(Columbia 43113)

ISSUE	TITLE	UK LBL	UK POS	UK YEAR	US POS	US YEAR	US LBL
+ 5	One Step Ahead		0	1965	18	1965	(Columbia 43241)
+ 6	Cry Like A Baby		0	1966	27	1966	(Columbia 43827)
* 7	I Never Loved A Man (The Way I Love You)		0	1967	9	1967	(Atlantic 2386)
* 8	Respect	(Atlantic 584 115)	10	1967	1	1967	(Atlantic 2403)
+ 9	Lee Cross		0	1967	31	1967	(Columbia 44181)
* 10	Baby I Love You	(Atlantic 584 127)	39	1967	4	1967	(Atlantic 2427)
+ 11	Take A Look		0	1967	28	1967	(Columbia 44270)
12	A Natural Woman (You Make Me Feel Like)		0	1967	8	1967	(Atlantic 2441)
* 13	Chain Of Fools / Satisfaction	(Atlantic 584 157)	43	1967	2	1968	(Atlantic 2464)
14	Satisfaction (Re-Entry)	(Atlantic 584 157)	37	1968	0	1968	
* 15	(Sweet Sweet Baby) Since You've Been Gone	(Atlantic 584 172)	47	1968	5	1968	(Atlantic 2486)
16	Ain't No Way		0	1968	16	1968	(Atlantic 2486)
* 17	Think	(Atlantic 584 186)	26	1968	7	1968	(Atlantic 2518)
* 18	I Say A Little Prayer	(Atlantic 584 206)	4	1968	10	1968	(Atlantic 2546)
19	The House That Jack Built		0	1968	6	1968	(Atlantic 2546)
* 20	See Saw		0	1968	14	1968	(Atlantic 2547)
21	My Song		0	1968	31	1968	(Atlantic 2574)
22	The Weight		0	1969	19	1969	(Atlantic 2603)
23	I Can't See Myself Leaving You		0	1969	28	1969	(Atlantic 2619)
24	Share Your Love With Me		0	1969	13	1969	(Atlantic 2650)
25	Eleanor Rigby		0	1969	17	1969	(Atlantic 2683)
26	Call Me		0	1970	13	1970	(Atlantic 2706)
27	Spirit In The Dark		0	1970	23	1970	(Atlantic 2731)
* 28	Don't Play That Song	(Atlantic 2091 027)	13	1970	11	1970	(Atlantic 2751)
29	Border Song (Holy Moses)		0	1970	37	1970	(Atlantic 2772)
30	You're All I Need To Get By		0	1971	19	1971	(Atlantic 2787)
31	Bridge Over Troubled Water		0	1971	6	1971	(ATLANTIC 2796)
32	Spanish Harlem	(Alantic 2091 138)	14	1971	2	1971	(Atlantic 2817)
33	Rock Steady		0	1971	9	1971	(Atlantic 2838)
34	Day Dreaming		0	1972	5	1972	(Atlantic 2866)
35	All the Kings Horses		0	1972	26	1972	(Atlantic 2883)
36	Master of Eyes (the Deepness of Your Eyes)		0	1973	33	1973	(Atlantic 2941)
37	Angel	(Atlantic K 10346)	37	1973	20	1973	(Atlantic 2969)
* 38	Until You Come Back To Me	(Atlantic K 10399)	26	1974	3	1974	(Atlantic 2995)
39	I'm In Love		0	1974	19	1974	(Atlantic 2999)
40	Ain't Nothing Like The Real Thing		0	1974	47	1974	(Atlantic 3200)
41	Without Love		0	1974	45	1974	(Atlantic 3224)
+ 42	With Everything I Feel In Me		0	1975	20	1975	(Atlantic 3249)
+ 43	Mr. DJ (5 For The DJ)		0	1975	13	1975	(Atlantic 3289)
44	Something He Can Feel		0	1976	28	1976	(Atlantic 3326)
45	What A Fool Believes	(Arista Arist 377)	46	1980	0	1980	
46	Love All The Hurt Away	(Arista Arist 428)	49	1981	0	1981	
47	Jump To It	(Arista Arist 479)	42	1982	24	1982	(Arista 0699)
48	Get It Right	(Arista Arist 537)	74	1983	0	1983	
49	Freeway Of Love	(Arista Arist 624)	68	1985	3	1985	(Arista 9354)
50	Who's Zoomin' Who	(RCA Pb 633)	11	1985	7	1985	(Arista 9410)
51	Sisters Are Doin' It For Themselves	(RCA Pb 40339)	9	1985	18	1985	(RCA 14214)
52	Another Night	(RCA Pb 657)	58	1986	22	1986	(ARISTA 9453)
53	Freeway of Love (Re-entry)	(Arista Aris 624)	51	1986	0	1986	
54	Jumpin' Jack Flash	(Arista Arist 678)	58	1986	21	1986	(Arista 9528)
55	Jimmy Lee	(Arista Ris 6)	46	1987	28	1987	(Arista 9546)
56	I Knew You Were Waiting (For Me)	(Epic Duet 1)	1	1987	1	1987	(Arista 9559)
57	Through The Storm	(Arista 112185)	41	1989	16	1989	(Arista 9809)
58	It Isn't, It Wasn't, It Ain't Never Gonna Be	(Arista 112545)	29	1989	0	1989	
59	Think	(East West A 7951)	31	1990	0	1990	
60	Everyday People	(Arista 114420)	69	1991	0	1991	
61	A Deeper Love	(Arista 74321187022)	5	1994	0	1994	
62	Willing To Forgive	(Arista 74321213342)	17	1994	26	1994	(Arista 12680)
Argen	Male Vocal/Instrumental Group From The UK						
1	Hold Your Head Up	(Epic Epc 7786)	5	1972	5	1972	(Epic 10852)
2	Tragedy	(Epic Epc 8115)	34	1972	0	1972	
3	God Gave Rock And Roll To You	(Epic Epc 1243)	18	1973	0	1973	
Ariel	Mixed Vocal/Instrumental Group From The UK						
1	Let It Slide	(Deconstruction 74321134512)	57	1993	0	1993	
2	Deep (I'm Falling Deeper)	(A&M Wboyd 005)	47	1997	0	1997	

ISSUE	TITLE	UK LBL	UK POS	UK YEAR	US POS	US YEAR	US LBL
Ario Guthrie	Male Vocalist, B: 10 Jul 1947 Coney Island, New York						
1	The City Of New Orleans		0	1972	18	1972	(Reprise 1103)
Arkarna							
1	House On Fire	(Wea Wea 088cd1)	33	1997	0	1997	
2	So Little Time	(Wea Wea 108cd1)	46	1997	0	1997	
Armand Van Helden							
1	The Funl Phenomena	(Zyx Zyx 8523u8)	38	1997	0	1997	
Armoury Show	Male Vocal/Instrumental Group from the UK						
1	Castles In Spain	(Parlophone R 6079)	69	1984	0	1984	
2	We Can Be Brave Again	(Parlophone R 6087)	66	1985	0	1985	
3	Love In Anger	(Parlophone R 6149)	63	1987	0	1987	
Army Of Lovers	Mixed Vocal Group From France/Sweden						
1	Crucified	(Ton Son Ton Wok 2007)	47	1991	0	1991	
2	Obsession	(Ton Son Ton Wok 2009)	67	1991	0	1991	
3	Crucified (Re-Issue)	(Ton Son Ton Wok 2017)	31	1992	0	1992	
4	Ride The Bullet	(Ton Son Ton Wok 2018)	67	1992	0	1992	
Arnee & The Terminaters	Male Vocal/Instrumental Group from the UK						
1	I'll Be Back	(Epic 6574177)	5	1991	0	1991	
Arnie's Love	Mixed Vocal/Instrumental Group from the USA						
1	I'm Out Of Your Life	(Streetwave Wave 9)	67	1983	0	1983	
Arpeggio	Mixed Vocal Group from the USA						
1	Love And Desire (Part 1)	(Polydor Posp 40)	63	1979	0	1979	
Arrested Development	Mixed Rap/Instrumental Group From The USA						
* 1	Tennessee	(Cooltempo Cool 253)	46	1992	6	1992	(Chrysalis 23829)
2	Tennessee (Re-Entry)	(Cooltempo Cool 253)	54	1992	0	1992	
* 3	People Everyday	(Cooltempo Cool 265)	2	1992	8	1992	(Chrysalis 50397)
* 4	Mr. Wendal / Revolution	(Cooltempo Cdcool 268)	4	1993	6	1993	(Chrysalis 24810)
5	Tennessee (Re-Issue)	(Cooltempo Cdcool 270)	18	1993	0	1993	
6	Ease My Mind	(Cooltempo Cdcool 293)	33	1994	0	1994	
Arrival	Mixed Vocal/Instrumental Group From The UK						
1	Friends	(Decca F 12986)	8	1970	0	1970	
2	I Will Survive	(Decca F 13026)	16	1970	0	1970	
Arrow	Male Vocalist From Montserrat						
1	Hot Hot Hot	(Cooltempo Arrow 1)	59	1984	0	1984	
2	Long Time	(London Lon 70)	30	1985	0	1985	
3	Hot Hot Hot (Re-Issue)	(The Hit Label Hlc 7)	38	1994	0	1994	
Arrows	Male Vocal/Instrumental Group from the USA/UK						
1	A Touch Too Much	(Rak 171)	8	1974	0	1974	
2	My Last Night With You	(Rak 189)	25	1975	0	1975	
Arsenal F.C.	Male Vocal Soccer Team from North London, England						
1	Good Old Arsenal	(Pye 7n 45067)	16	1971	0	1971	
2	Shouting For The Gunners	(London Loncd 342)	34	1993	0	1993	
Art & Dotty Todd	Mixed Vocal Duo from the USA						
1	Broken Wings	(HMV B 10399)	6	1953	0	1953	
2	Chanson D'amour (Song Of Love)		0	1958	6	1958	(Era 1064)
Art Carney	Male Actor/Vocalist from The USA						
1	Santa And The Doole-Li-Boop		0	1954	24	1954	(Columbia 40400)
Art Company	Male Vocal/Instrumental Group from Holland						
1	Susanna	(Epic A 4174)	12	1984	0	1984	
Art Garfunkel	Male Vocalist, B: 13 Oct 1942, New York City						
1	All I Know		0	1973	9	1973	(Columbia 45926)
2	I Shall Sing		0	1974	28	1974	(Columbia 45983)
3	Second Avenue		0	1974	34	1974	(Columbia 10020)
4	I Only Have Eyes For You	(CBS 3575)	1	1975	18	1975	(Columbia 10190)
5	Break Away		0	1976	39	1976	(Columbia 10273)
6	(What A) Wonderful World		0	1978	17	1978	(Columbia 10676)
7	Bright Eyes	(CBS 6947)	1	1979	0	1979	
8	Since I Don't Have You	(CBS 7371)	38	1979	0	1979	
Art Landry & His Orchestra	Male Bandleader/Instrumentalist (Violin) B: 1900						
* 1	Dreamy Melody		0	1923	1	1923	(Gennett 5255)

ISSUE	TITLE	UK LBL	UK POS	UK YEAR	US POS	US YEAR	US LBL
* 1	Mam'selle (From *The Razor Edge*)		0	1947	1	1947	(MGM 10011)
2	Peg O' My Heart (From *Ziegfeld Follies* Of 1913)		0	1947	4	1947	(MGM 10037)
3	And Mimi		0	1947	14	1947	(MGM 10082)
4	But Beautiful (From *The Road To Rio*)		0	1948	25	1948	(MGM 10126)
5	Love Is So Terrific		0	1948	24	1948	(MGM 10126)
6	Hair Of Gold (From *Silver Spurs*)		0	1948	20	1948	(MGM 10258)
7	You Call Everyone Darlin'		0	1948	22	1948	(MGM 10258)
8	On A Slow Boat To China		0	1948	12	1948	(MGM 10269)
9	I've Got My Love To Keep Me Warm (From *On The Avenue*)		0	1949	22	1949	(MGM 10348)
10	Mona Lisa (From Captain Carey, U.S.A.)		0	1950	14	1950	(MGM 10689)
11	Cincinatti Ding Dong		0	1952	27	1952	(Coral 60834)
12	Crying In The Chapel		0	1953	23	1953	(MGM 61018)

Art Mooney Orchestra Male Bandleader B: Lowell, Massachusetts, USA

ISSUE	TITLE	UK LBL	UK POS	UK YEAR	US POS	US YEAR	US LBL
* 1	I'm Looking Over A Four Leaf Clover		0	1948	1	1948	(MGM 10119)
* 2	Baby Face		0	1948	3	1948	(MGM 10156)
* 3	Bluebird Of Happiness		0	1948	5	1948	(MGM 10207)
4	Beautiful Eyes		0	1949	18	1949	(MGM 10357)
5	Doo De Ddo On An Old Kazoo		0	1949	21	1949	(MGM 10357)
6	Again (From Road House)		0	1949	7	1949	(MGM 10398)
7	Marry-Go-Round Waltz		0	1949	29	1949	(MGM 10405)
8	Twenty-Four Hours Of Sunshine		0	1949	13	1949	(MGM 10446)
9	Hop-Scotch Polka (Scotch Hot)		0	1949	16	1949	(MGM 10500)
10	Toot Toot Toosie (Good-Bye) (From Jolson Story)		0	1949	19	1949	(MGM 10548)
11	I Never See Maggie Alone		0	1949	21	1949	(MGM 10548)
12	If I Knew You Were Coming' I'd've Baked A Cake		0	1950	28	1950	(MGM 10660)
13	M-I-S-S-I-S-S-I-P-P-I		0	1950	23	1950	(MGM 10721)
14	Lazy River		0	1952	29	1952	(MGM 11347)
15	Heartbreaker		0	1952	24	1952	(MGM 11386)
* 16	Honey-Babe (From Battle Cry)		0	1955	6	1955	(MGM 11900)
17	Nuttin' For Christmas		0	1955	6	1955	(MGM 12092)

Art Of Noise Mixed Production/Instrumental Group from the UK

ISSUE	TITLE	UK LBL	UK POS	UK YEAR	US POS	US YEAR	US LBL
1	Close (To The Edit)	(Ztt Ztps 01)	8	1984	0	1984	
2	Moments In Love - Beat Box	(ZTT Ztps 01)	51	1985	0	1985	
3	Legs	(China Wok 5)	69	1985	0	1985	
4	Peter Gunn	(China Wok 6)	8	1986	0	1986	
5	Paranoimia	(China Wok 9)	12	1986	34	1986	(China Wok43002)
6	Dragnet	(China Wok 14)	60	1987	0	1987	
7	Kiss	(China China 11)	5	1988	31	1988	(China 871038)
8	Yebo	(China China 18)	63	1989	0	1989	
9	Art Of Love	(China China 23)	67	1990	0	1990	
10	Instruments Of Darkness	(China Wok 2012)	45	1992	0	1992	
11	Shades Of Paranoimia	(China Wok 2014)	53	1992	0	1992	

Artemesia Male Producer Patrick Prinz from Holland

ISSUE	TITLE	UK LBL	UK POS	UK YEAR	US POS	US YEAR	US LBL
1	Bits + Pieces	(Hooj Choons Hooj 31cd)	46	1995	0	1995	
2	Bits + Pieces (Re-Entry)	(Hooj Choons Hooj 31cd)	75	1995	0	1995	

Arthur Adams Male Vocalist from the USA

ISSUE	TITLE	UK LBL	UK POS	UK YEAR	US POS	US YEAR	US LBL
1	You Got The Floor	(RCA 146)	38	1981	0	1981	

Arthur Alexander Male Vocalist, B: 10 May 1940 Florence, Alabama

ISSUE	TITLE	UK LBL	UK POS	UK YEAR	US POS	US YEAR	US LBL
1	Every Day I Have to Cry Some		0	1975	45	1975	(Dot)
2	You Better Move On		0	1962	24	1962	(Dot 16309)

Arthur Baker Male Producer/Instrumentalist from the USA

ISSUE	TITLE	UK LBL	UK POS	UK YEAR	US POS	US YEAR	US LBL
1	It's Your Time	(Breakout USA 654)	64	1989	0	1989	
2	The Message Is Love	(Breakout USA 668)	38	1989	0	1989	

Arthur Collins Male Comedy Singer, B: 7 Feb 1864 In Philadelphia

ISSUE	TITLE	UK LBL	UK POS	UK YEAR	US POS	US YEAR	US LBL
* 22	A Preacher And The Bear		0	1905	1	1905	(Edison 9000)

Arthur Conley Male Vocalist, B: 4 Jan 1746 Atlanta, USA Arthur Was Discovered By Otis Redding

ISSUE	TITLE	UK LBL	UK POS	UK YEAR	US POS	US YEAR	US LBL
* 1	Sweet Soul Music	(Atlantic 584 083)	7	1967	2	1967	(Atco 6463)
2	Shake, Rattle And Roll		0	1967	31	1967	(Atco 6494)
3	Funky Street	(Atlantic 583 175)	46	1968	14	1968	(Atco 6563)
4	People Sure Act Funny		0	1968	58	1968	(Atco 6588)

Arthur Fiedler & The Boston Pops Orchestra Male Violinist/Conductor, B: 17 Dec 1894 Boston

ISSUE	TITLE	UK LBL	UK POS	UK YEAR	US POS	US YEAR	US LBL
* 1	Jalousie		0	1938	0	1938	(Victor)

ISSUE	TITLE	UK LBL	UK POS	UK YEAR	US POS	US YEAR	US LBL
Arthur Godfrey Male DJ/Banjoist, B: 31 Aug 1903 New York							
* 1	Too Fat Polka (I Don't Want Her-You Can Have Her - She's Too Fat For Me)		0	1947	2	1947	(Columbia 37921)
2	Slap 'Er Down Again Paw		0	1948	7	1948	(Columbia 38066)
3	The Thousand Island Song		0	1948	14	1948	(Columbia 38081)
4	I'm Looking Over A Four-Leaf Clover		0	1948	14	1948	(Columbia 38081)
5	Candy And Cake		0	1950	16	1950	(Columbia 38721)
6	Go To Sleep, Go To Sleep, Go To Sleep		0	1950	8	1950	(Columbia 38744)
7	The Thing		0	1950	24	1950	(Columbia 919)
8	I Like Wide Open Spaces		0	1951	13	1951	(Columbia 39404)
9	What Is A Boy		0	1951	27	1951	(Columbia 39487)
10	Dance Me Loose		0	1951	6	1951	(Columbia 29632)
11	Slow-Poke		0	1952	12	1952	(Columbia 39632)
12	I Love Girls		0	1952	17	1952	(Columbia 39792)
Arthur Lyman Group Male Instrumentalist, B: 1934, Kauak, Hawaii							
1	Yellow Bird		0	1961	4	1961	(Hi Fi 5024)
Arthur Smith & His Cracker-Jacks Male Guitarist, B: 1 Apr 1921 Clinton, South Carolina							
* 1	Guitar Boogie		0	1948	25	1948	(Mgm 10293)
Artie Shaw Orchestra Male Bandleader/Clarinetist, Real Name Arthur Arshawsky B: 23 May 1910 New York.							
* 9	Begin The Beguine		0	1938	1	1938	(Bluebird 7746)
* 10	Back Bay Shuffle		0	1938	8	1938	(Bluebird 7759)
* 11	Nightmare		0	1938	7	1938	(Bluebird 7875)
* 29	Traffic Jam		0	1939	9	1939	(Bluebird 10385)
* 37	Summit Ridge Drive		0	1940	10	1940	(Victor 26863)
* 38	Star Dust		0	1940	2	1940	(Victor 27230)
* 40	Dancing In The Dark (From *Band Wagon*)		0	1941	9	1941	(Victor 27335)
Artie Wayne Male Vocalist, Former Singer With Freddy Martin & His Orchestra							
1	Rachel		0	1953	21	1953	(Kem 2718)
2	My Hymn (To Her)		0	1953	21	1953	(Kem 2718)
3	Watermelon In December		0	1954	23	1954	(Mercury 70241)
Artists United Against Apartheid Mixed Vocal/Instrumental Charity Group from the UK							
1	Sun City	(Manhattan Mt 7)	21	1985	38	1985	(Manhattan 50017)
Asap Male Vocal/Instrumental Group from the UK							
1	Silver And Gold	(EMI Em 107)	60	1989	0	1989	
2	Down The Wire	(EMI Em 131)	67	1990	0	1990	
Ascension							
1	Someone	(Perfecto Perf 141cd)	55	1997	0	1997	
Ash Male Vocal/Instrumental Group from the UK							
1	Kung Fu	(Infectious Infect 21cd)	57	1995	0	1995	
2	Girl From Mars	(Infectious Infect 24cd)	11	1995	0	1995	
3	Angel Interceptor	(Infectious Infect 27cd)	14	1995	0	1995	
4	Goldfinger	(Infectious Infect 39cd)	5	1996	0	1996	
5	Oh Yeah	(Infectious Infect 41cd)	6	1996	0	1996	
6	Oh Yeah (Re-Entry)	(Infectious Infect 41cd)	69	1996	0	1996	
Asha Female Vocalist from Italy							
1	J.J. Tribute	(Ffrr Rabcd 228)	38	1995	0	1995	
Ashaye Male Vocalist from the UK							
1	Michael Jackson Medley	(Record Shack Soho 10)	45	1983	0	1983	
Ashford & Simpson Mixed Vocal Duo from the USA							
1	It Seems To Hang On	(Warner Bros K 17237)	48	1978	0	1978	
2	Found A Cure		0	1979	36	1979	(Warner Bros 8870)
3	Solid	(Capitol Cl 345)	3	1985	12	1985	(Capitol 5397)
4	Babies	(Capitol Cl 355)	56	1985	0	1985	
Ashton, Gardner & Dyke Male Vocal/Instrumental Group from the UK							
1	The Resurrection Shuffle	(Capitol Cl 15665)	3	1971	40	1971	(Capitol 3060)
Asia Male Vocal/Instrumental Group from the UK							
1	Heat Of The Moment	(Geffen Gef A2494)	46	1982	4	1982	(Geffen 50040)
2	Only Time Will Tell	(Geffen Gef A2228)	54	1982	17	1982	(Geffen 29970)
3	Don't Cry	(Geffen Gef A3580)	33	1983	10	1983	(Geffen 29571)
4	The Smile Has Left Your Eyes		0	1983	34	1983	(Geffen 29475)
Asia Blue Female Vocal Group from the UK							
1	Escaping	(Atomic Wnr 882)	50	1992	0	1992	

ISSUE	TITLE	UK LBL	UK POS	UK YEAR	US POS	US YEAR	US LBL
Assembled Multitude Studio Group from Philadelphia							
1	Overture From Tommy (Rock Opera)		0	1970	16	1970	(Atlantic 2737)
	CONDUCTED BY TOM SELLERS B: 1938 WAYNE, PENNSYLVANIA OBITUARY : TOM D: 9 MAR 1988 IN A FIRE.						
Assembly Male Vocal/Instrumental Group from the UK							
1	Never Never	(Mute Tiny 1)	4	1983	0	1983	
Associates Male Vocal/Instrumental Group from the UK							
1	Party Fears Two	(Associates Asc 1)	9	1982	0	1982	
2	Club Country	(Associates Asc 2)	13	1982	0	1982	
3	Eighteen Carat Love Affair - Love Hangover	(Associates Asc 3)	21	1982	0	1982	
4	Those First Impressions	(Wea Yz 6)	43	1984	0	1984	
5	Waiting For The Loveboat	(Wea Yz 16)	53	1984	0	1984	
6	Breakfast	(Wea Yz 28)	49	1985	0	1985	
7	Heart Of Glass	(Wea Yz 310)	56	1988	0	1988	
Association Male Vocal/Instrumental Group from the USA							
1	Along Comes Mary		0	1966	7	1966	(Valiant 741)
* 2	Cherish		0	1966	1	1966	(Valiant 747)
3	Pandora's Golden Heebie Jeebies		0	1966	35	1966	(Valiant 755)
* 4	Windy		0	1967	1	1967	(Warner Bros 7041)
* 5	Never My Love		0	1967	2	1967	(Warner Bros 7074)
6	Everything That Touches You		0	1968	10	1968	(Warner Bros 7163)
7	Time For Livin'	(Warner Bros Wb 7195)	23	1968	39	1968	(Warner Bros 7195)
	NAMES TERRY KIRKMAN, GARY ALEXANDER, BRIAN COLE, JIM YESTER, TED BLUECHEL JR. & LARRY RAMOS OBITUARY : BRIAN D: 2 AUG 1973 DRUG OVERDOSE.						
Astors							
+ 1	Candy		0	1965	12	1965	(Stax 170)
Aswad Male Vocal/Instrumental Group from the UK							
1	Chasing For The Breeze	(Island Is 160)	51	1984	0	1984	
2	54-46 (Was My Number)	(Island Is 170)	70	1984	0	1984	
3	Don't Turn Around	(Mango Is 341)	1	1988	0	1988	
4	Give A Little Love	(Mango Is 358)	11	1988	0	1988	
5	Set Them Free	(Mango Is 383)	70	1988	0	1988	
6	Beauty's Only Skin Deep	(Mango Mng 105)	31	1989	0	1989	
7	On And On	(Mango Mng 708)	25	1989	0	1989	
8	Next To You	(Mango Mng 753)	24	1990	0	1990	
9	Smile	(Mango Mng 767)	53	1990	0	1990	
10	Too Wicked (EP)	(Mango Mng 771)	61	1991	0	1991	
11	How Long	(Polydor Pzcd 252)	31	1993	0	1993	
12	Dance Hall Mood	(Bubblin' Cdbubb 1)	48	1993	0	1993	
Atlanta Rhythm Section Male Vocal/Instrumental Group From The USA							
1	Doraville		0	1974	35	1974	(Polydor 14248)
2	So In To You		0	1977	7	1977	(Polydor 14373)
3	Imaginary Lover		0	1978	7	1978	(Polydor 14459)
4	I'm Not Gonna Let It Bother Me Tonight		0	1978	14	1978	(Polydor 14484)
5	Do It Or Die		0	1979	19	1979	(Polydor 14568)
6	Spooky	(Polydor Posp 74)	48	1979	17	1979	(Polydor 2001)
7	Silver Eagle		0	1980	75	1980	(Polydor 2142)
8	Alien		0	1981	29	1981	(Columbia 02471)
Atlantic Ocean Male/Instrumental Duo fom Holland							
1	Waterfall	(Eastern Bloc Bloccdx 001)	22	1994	0	1994	
2	Body In Motion	(Eastern Bloc Bloccdx 009)	15	1994	0	1994	
3	Music Is A Passion	(Eastern Bloc Bloccdx 017)	59	1994	0	1994	
4	Waterfall (Re-Mix)	(Eastern Bloc Bloc 104cd)	21	1996	0	1996	
Atlantic Starr Mixed Vocal/Instrumental Group from the USA							
1	Gimme Your Lovin'	(A&M Ams 7380)	66	1978	0	1978	
2	Circles		0	1982	38	1982	(A&M 2392)
3	Silver Shadow	(A&M Ams 260)	41	1985	0	1985	
4	Only Love	(A&M Ams 273)	58	1985	0	1985	
5	Secret Lovers	(A&M Ams 307)	10	1986	3	1986	(A&M 2788)
6	If Your Heart Isn't In It	(A&M Ams 319)	48	1986	0	1986	
7	Always	(Warner Bors W 8455)	3	1987	1	1987	(Warner Bros 28455)
8	One Lover At A Time	(Warner Bors W 8327)	57	1987	0	1987	
* 9	Masterpiece		0	1992	3	1992	(Reprise 19076)
10	Everybody's Got Summer	(Arista 74321228072)	36	1994	0	1994	

ISSUE	TITLE	UK LBL	UK POS	UK YEAR	US POS	US YEAR	US LBL
Atmosfear	Male Vocal/Instrumental Group from the UK						
1	Dancing In Outer Space	(MCA 543)	46	1979	0	1979	
Atomic Rooster	Male Vocal/Instrumental Group from the UK						
1	Tomorrow Night	(B&C Cb 131)	11	1971	0	1971	
2	Devil's Answer	(B&C Cb 157)	4	1971	0	1971	
Audioweb							
1	Sleeper	(Mother Mumcd 69)	74	1995	0	1995	
2	Yeh? – Tha Mother	(Mother MumCD 72)	73	1996	0	1996	
3	Into My World	(Mother MumCD 76)	42	1996	0	1996	
4	Yeh? - Tha Mother	(Mother Mumcd 72)	73	1996	0	1996	
5	Into My World	(Mother Mumcd 76)	42	1996	0	1996	
6	Sleeper (Re-Mix)	(Mother Mumcd 78)	50	1996	0	1996	
7	Bankrobber	(Mother MumCD 85)	19	1997	0	1997	
8	Faker	(Mother Mumcd 91)	70	1997	0	1997	
Audrey Hall	Female Vocalist From Jamaica						
1	One Dance Won't Do	(Germain Dg7-1985)	20	1986	0	1986	
2	Smile	(Germain Dg 15)	14	1986	0	1986	
Aurra	Mixed Vocal Duo from the USA						
1	Like I Like It	(10 Ten 45)	51	1985	0	1985	
2	You And Me Tonight	(10 Ten 71)	12	1986	0	1986	
3	Like I Like It (Re-Issue)	(10 Ten 126)	43	1986	0	1986	
Austin Roberts	Male Vocalist, B: 19 Sep 1945 Virginia						
1	Something's Wrong With Me		0	1972	12	1972	(Chelsea 0101)
2	Rocky	(Private Stock Pvt 33)	22	1975	9	1975	(Private Stock 45020)
Autechre	Male Instrumental Duo from the UK						
1	Basscad	(Warp Wap 44cd)	56	1994	0	1994	
Auteurs	Mixed Vocal/Instrumental Group from the UK						
1	Lenny Valentino	(Hut Hutcd 36)	41	1993	0	1993	
2	Chinese Bakery	(Hut Hutdx 41)	42	1994	0	1994	
3	Back With The Killer (EP)	(Hut Hutcd 65)	45	1996	0	1996	
4	Light Aircraft On Fire	(Hut Hutcd 66)	58	1996	0	1996	
Autograph	Group Are A Rock Quintet from Los Angeles						
1	Turn Up The Radio	(RCA 483)	0	1985	29	1985	(RCA 13953)
Autumn	Male Vocal/Instrumental Group from the UK						
1	My Little Girl	(Pye 7n 45090)	37	1971	0	1971	
Avant-Garde	The Hit Was Written By Chuck Woolery, Who Is A Game-Show Host						
1	Naturally Stoned		0	1968	40	1968	(Columbia 44590)
Average White Band	Male Vocal/Instrumental Group from the UK						
* 1	Pick Up The Pieces	(Atlantic K 10489)	6	1975	1	1974	(Atlantic 3229)
2	Cut The Cake	(Atlantic K 10605)	31	1975	10	1975	(Atlantic 3261)
3	If I Ever Lose This Heaven		0	1975	39	1975	(Atlantic 3285)
4	School Boy Crush		0	1975	33	1975	(Atlantic 3304)
5	Queen Of My Soul	(Atlantic K 10825)	23	1976	40	1976	(Atlantic 3354)
6	Walk On By	RCA Xc 1087)	46	1979	0	1979	
7	When Will You Be Mine	(RCA Xb 1096)	49	1979	0	1979	
8	Let's Go Round Again (Part 1)	(RCA Awb 1)	12	1980	0	1980	
9	For You For Love	(RCA Awb 2)	46	1980	0	1980	
10	Let's Go Round Again (Re-Mix)	(The Hit Lable Hlc 5)	56	1994	0	1994	
	NAMES: ALLEN GORRIE, HAMISH STUART, ONNIE MCINTYRE, STEVE FERRONE, ROGER BALL & MALCOLM DUNCAN THE GROUP IS ALSO KNOWN AS AWB						
Avons	Mixed Vocal Group from the UK						
1	Seven Little Girls Sitting In The Back Seat	(Columbia Db 4363)	3	1959	0	1959	
2	We're Only Young Once	(Columbia Db 4461)	49	1960	0	1960	
3	We're Only Young Once (Re-Entry)	(Columbia Db 4461)	45	1960	0	1960	
4	Four Little Heels	(Columbia Db 4522)	45	1960	0	1960	
5	Four Little Heels (Re-Entry)	(Columbia Db 4522)	49	1960	0	1960	
6	Rubber Ball	(Columbia Db 4569)	30	1961	0	1961	
Awesome 3	Mixed Vocal/Instrumental Group from the UK						
1	Hard Up	(A&M Am 591)	55	1990	0	1990	
2	Don't Go	(Citybeat Cbe 1271)	75	1992	0	1992	
3	Don't Go (Re-Mix)	(Citybeat Cbx 771cd)	45	1994	0	1994	
4	Don't Go (2nd Re-Mix)	(XL XLS 78CD)	27	1996	0	1999	

ISSUE	TITLE	UK LBL	UK POS	UK YEAR	US POS	US YEAR	US LBL
Az the Visualiza Male Rapper, real name Anthony Cruz, from the USA							
1	Sugarhill	(Cooltempo CDCool 315)	67	1996	25	1995	(EMI 58407)
Aztec Camera Male Vocal/Instrumental Group from the UK							
1	Oblivious	(Rough Trade RT122)	47	1983	0	1983	
2	Walk Out To Winter	(Rough Trade Rt 132)	64	1983	0	1983	
3	Oblivious (Re-Issue)	(Wea Aztec 1)	18	1983	0	1983	
4	All I Need Is Everything	(Wea Ac 1)	34	1984	0	1984	
5	How Men Are	(Wea Yz 168	25	1988	0	1988	
6	Somewhere In My Heart	(Wea Yz 181)	3	1988	0	1988	
7	Working In A Goldmine	(Wea Yz 199)	31	1988	0	1988	
8	Deep And Wide And Tall	(Wea YZ 154)	55	1988	0	1988	
9	The Crying Scene	(Wea Yz 154)	70	1990	0	1990	
10	Good Morning Britain	(Wea Yz 521)	19	1990	0	1990	
11	Spanish Horses	(Wea Yz 688)	52	1992	0	1992	
12	Dream Sweet Dreams	(Wea Yz 740cd1)	67	1993	0	1993	
Azymuth Male Instrumental Group from Brazil							
1	Jazz Carnival	(Milestone Mrc 101)	19	1980	0	1980	

B

ISSUE	TITLE	UK LBL	UK POS	UK YEAR	US POS	US YEAR	US LBL
B B & Q Band Male Vocal/Instrumental Group from the USA							
1	On The Beat	(Capitol CL 202)	41	1981	0	1981	
2	Genie	(Cooltempo Cool 110)	40	1985	0	1985	
3	(I'm A) Dreamer	(Cooltempo Cool 132)	35	1986	0	1986	
4	Riccochet	(Cooltempo Cool 154)	71	1987	0	1987	
	HIT 2 WAS RECORDED BY BROOKLYN BRONX AND QUEENS						
B Bumble & The Stingers Male Instrumental Group from the USA							
1	Bumble Boogie		0	1961	21	1961	(Rendezvous 140)
2	Nut Rocker	(TOP RANK JAR 611)	1	1962	23	1962	(Rendezvous 166)
3	Nut Rocker (Re-Issue)	(Stateside SS 2203)	19	1972	0	1972	
B-52's Mixed Vocal/Instrumental Group from the USA							
1	Rock Lobster	(Island WIP 6506)	37	1979	0	1979	
2	Give Me Back My Man	(Island WIP 6579)	61	1980	0	1980	
3	Future Generation	(Island IS 107)	63	1983	0	1983	
4	Rock Lobster (Re-Issue) - Planet Claire	(Island BFT 1)	12	1986	0	1986	
* 5	Love Shack	(Reprise W 9917)	2	1990	3	1989	(Reprise 22817)
* 6	Roam	(Reprise E W 9827)	17	1990	3	1990	(Reprise 22667)
7	Deadbeat Club		0	1990	30	1990	(Reprise 19938)
8	Channel Z	(Reprise W 9737)	61	1990	0	1990	
9	Good Stuff	(Reprise W 0109)	21	1992	28	1992	(Reprise 18895)
10	Tell It Like It T-I-Is	(Reprise W 0130)	61	1992	0	1992	
11	(Meet) The Flintstones	(MCA MCSTD	3	1994	33	1994	(MCA 54839)
	NAMES: KEITH STRICKLAND, KATE PIESON, FRED SCHNEIDER, CINDY WILSON & RICKY WILSON • HIT 11 IS CREDITED TO B.C.52'S						
B-Movie Male Vocal/Instrumental Group from the UK							
1	Remembrance Day	(DERAM DM 437)	61	1981	0	1981	
2	Nowhere Girl	(SOME BIZZARE BZZ 8)	67	1982	0	1982	
B-Tribe Mixed Vocal/Instrumental Group from Spain							
1	Fiesta Fatal!	(EAST WEST YZ	64	1993	0	1993	(770CD)
B.A. Robertson Male Vocalist from the UK							
1	Bang Bang	(Asylum K 13152)	2	1979	0	1979	
2	Knocked It Off	(Asylum K 12396)	8	1979	0	1979	
3	Kool In The Kaftan	(Asylum K 12427)	17	1980	0	1980	
4	To Be Or Not To Be	(Asylum K 12449)	9	1980	0	1980	
5	Hold Me	(SWANSONG BAM 1)	11	1981	0	1981	
6	Time	(EPIC A 3983)	45	1983	0	1983	
B.B. King Male Vocal/Guitarist, Real Name Riley B King. B: 16 Sep 1925 Mississippi							
*+ 1	3 O'Clock Blues		0	1951	1	1951	(RPM 339)
+ 2	You Know I Love You		0	1952	1	1952	(RPM 363)
+ 3	Story From My Heart And Soul		0	1952	9	1952	(RPM 374)
+ 4	Woke Up This Morning		0	1953	5	1953	(RPM 380)
+ 5	Please Love Me		0	1953	2	1953	(RPM 386)
+ 6	Please Hurry Home		0	1953	8	1953	(RPM 391)
+ 7	You Upset Me Baby / Whole Lotta Love		0	1954	2	1954	(RPM 416)
23	Paying The Cost To The Boss		0	1968	39	1968	(BLUESWAY 61015)
* 26	The Thrill Is Gone		0	1970	15	1970	(BLUESWAY 61032)
+ 27	So Excited		0	1970	14	1970	(BLUESWAY 61035)
28	Hummingbird		0	1970	48	1970	(ABC 11268)
29	Chains And Things		0	1970	45	1970	(ABC 11280)
30	Ask Me No Questions		0	1971	40	1971	(ABC 11290)
31	Ain't Nobody Home		0	1971	46	1971	(ABC 11316)

ISSUE	TITLE	UK LBL	UK POS	UK YEAR	US POS	US YEAR	US LBL
32	To Know You Is To Love You		0	1973	38	1973	(ABC 11373)
33	I Like To Live The Love		0	1974	28	1974	(ABC 11406)
34	When Love Comes To Town	(ISLAND IS 411)	6	1989	0	1989	
35	Since I Met You Baby	(VIRGIN VS 1423)	59	1992	0	1992	

MANY OF THE HITS UNLISTED ARE R & B • HE WAS KNOWN AS THE BEALE ST BLUES BOY. NAME WAS THEN SHORTENED TO B.B. KING

B.J. Thomas   Male Vocalist, B: Billy Joe Thomas B: 7 Aug 1942, Hugo, Oklahoma

	ISSUE	TITLE	UK LBL	UK POS	UK YEAR	US POS	US YEAR	US LBL
*	1	I'm So Lonesome I Could Cry		0	1966	8	1966	(Scepter 12129)
	2	Mama		0	1966	22	1966	(Scepter 12139)
	3	Billy And Sue		0	1966	34	1966	(HICKORY 1395)
	4	The Eyes Of A New York Woman		0	1968	28	1968	(Scepter 12219)
*	5	Hooked On A Feeling		0	1968	5	1968	(Scepter 12230)
*	6	Raindrops Keep Falling On My Head	(WAND WN1)	38	1970	1	1969	(Scepter 12265)
	7	Everybody's Out Of Town		0	1970	26	1970	(Scepter 12277)
	8	Raindrops Keep Falling On My Head (Re-Entry)	(WAND WN1)	49	1970	0	1970	
	9	I Just Can't Help Believing		0	1970	9	1970	(Scepter 12283)
	10	Most Of All		0	1971	38	1971	(Scepter 12299)
	11	No Love At All		0	1971	16	1971	(Scepter 12307)
	12	Mighty Clouds Of Joy		0	1971	34	1971	(Scepter 12320)
	13	Rock And Roll Lullaby		0	1972	15	1972	(Scepter 12344)
*	14	(Hey Won't You Play) Another Somebody Done Something Wrong Song		0	1975	1	1975	(ABC 12054)
!	15	Help Me Make It (To My Rockin' Chair)		0	1975	37	1975	(ABC 12121)
!	16	Home Where I Belong		0	1977	98	1977	(MYRRH 166)
	17	Don't Worry Baby		0	1977	17	1977	(MCA 40735)
	18	Everybody Loves A Rain Song		0	1978	43	1978	(MCA 40854)
!	19	We Could Have Been The Closest Of Friends		0	1979	86	1979	(MCA 40986)
!	20	Some Love Songs Never Die		0	1981	27	1981	(MCA 51087)
!	21	I Recall A Gypsy Woman		0	1981	22	1981	(MCA 51151)
!	22	Whatever Happened To Old Fashioned Love		0	1983	1	1983	(Cleveland INT 03492)
!	23	New Looks From An Old Lover		0	1983	1	1983	(Columbia 03985)
!	24	Two Car Garage		0	1983	3	1983	(CLEVELAND INT 04237)
!	25	The Whole World's In Love When You're Lonely		0	1984	10	1984	(CLEVELAND INT 04431)
!	26	Rock And Roll Shoes		0	1984	14	1984	(Columbia 04531)
!	27	The Girl Most Likely To		0	1984	17	1984	Cleveland INT 04608)
!	28	The Part Of Me That Needs You Most		0	1985	61	1985	(Columbia 05647)
!	29	America Is		0	1986	62	1986	(Columbia 05771)
!	30	Night Life		0	1986	59	1986	(Columbia 06314)

B.M.U. (Black Men United)   Collection Of Top R&B Vocalists from the UK/USA

	ISSUE	TITLE	UK LBL	UK POS	UK YEAR	US POS	US YEAR	US LBL
	1	U Will Know	(Mercury	23	1995	28	1994	(Mercury MERCD 420856200)

B.T.   Male Producer Brian Transeau from the USA

	ISSUE	TITLE	UK LBL	UK POS	UK YEAR	US POS	US YEAR	US LBL
	1	Embracing The Sunshine	(EAST WEST YZ 895CD)	34	1995	0	1995	
	2	Loving You More	(Perfecto PERF 110CD)	28	1995	0	1995	
	3	Loving You More (Re-Mix)	(Perfecto PERF 117CD)	14	1996	0	1996	
	4	Blue Skies	(Perfecto PERF 130CD1)	26	1996	0	1996	
	5	Flaming June	(Perfecto PERF 145CD1)	19	1997	0	1997	

B.T. Express   Male Vocal/Instrumental Group from the USA

	ISSUE	TITLE	UK LBL	UK POS	UK YEAR	US POS	US YEAR	US LBL
*	1	Do It ('Til Your Satisfied)		0	1974	2	1974	(Roadshow 12395)
*	2	Express	(PYE 7N 25674)	34	1975	4	1975	(Roadshow International 7001)
	3	Give It What You've Got		0	1975	31	1975	(Roadshow 7003)
	4	Peace Pipe		0	1975	31	1975	(Roadshow 7003)
	5	Does It Feel Good	(CALIBRE CAB 503)	52	1980	0	1971	
	6	Express (Re-Mix)	(PWL International PWCD 285)	67	994	0	1994	

B.V.S.M.P.   Male Vocal Group from the USA

	ISSUE	TITLE	UK LBL	UK POS	UK YEAR	US POS	US YEAR	US LBL
	1	I Need You	(FOURTH & BROADWAY BRW102)	3	1988	0	1988	

B.W. Stevenson   Real Name Louis Stevenson B: 5 Oct 1949 Dallas

	ISSUE	TITLE	UK LBL	UK POS	UK YEAR	US POS	US YEAR	US LBL
	1	My Maria		0	1973	9	1973	(RCA 0030)

Babbity Blue   Female Vocalist from the UK

	ISSUE	TITLE	UK LBL	UK POS	UK YEAR	US POS	US YEAR	US LBL
	1	Don't Make Me	(Decca F 12053)	48	1965	0	1965	

Baby D   Mixed Vocal/Instrumental Group from the UK

	ISSUE	TITLE	UK LBL	UK POS	UK YEAR	US POS	US YEAR	US LBL
	1	Destiny	(Production House PNC 057)	69	1993	0	1993	
	2	Casanova	(Production House PNC 065)	67	1994	0	1994	
	3	Let Me Be Your Fantasy	(SYSTEMATIC SYSCD 4)	1	1994	0	1994	
	4	I Need Your Loving (Everybody's Got To Learn Sometime)	(SYSTEMATIC SYSCD 11)	3	1995	0	1995	

ISSUE	TITLE	UK LBL	UK POS	UK YEAR	US POS	US YEAR	US LBL
5	So Pure	(SYSTEMATIC SYSCD 21)	3	1996	0	1996	
6	Take Me To Heaven	(STSTEMCATIC SYSCD 26)	15	1996	0	1996	

Baby Ford   Male Instrumentalist (Keyboards) from the UK

1	Oochy Koochy	(Rhythm King 7BFORD 1)	58	1988	0	1988	
2	Chikki Chikki Ahh Ahh	(Rhythm King 7BFORD 2)	75	1988	0	1988	
3	Chikki Chikki Ahh Ahh (Re-Entry)	(RHYTHM 7BFORD 2)KING	54	1989	0	1989	
4	Children Of The Revolution	(Rhythm King 7BFORD 4)	53	1989	0	1989	
5	Beach Bump	(Rhythm King7BFORD 6)	68	1990	0	1990	

Baby June   Real Name Tim Hegarty Male Vocalist from the UK

1	Hey! What's Your Name	(ARISTA 115271)	75	1992	0	1992	

Baby O   Mixed Vocal/Instrumental Group from the USA

1	In The Forest	(CALIBRE CAB 505)	46	1980	0	1980	

Baby Roots   Male Vocalist from the UK

1	Rock Me Baby	(ZYX 68027)	71	1992	0	1992	

Baby Washington   Female Vocalist, Real Name Justine Washington B: 13 Nov 1940 Bamberg, South Carolina

1	That's How Heartaches Are Made		0	1963	40	1963	(SUE 783)

Babybird   Male Vocal/Instrumental Group from the UK

1	Goodnight	(ECHO ECSCD 24)	28	1996	0	1996	
2	You're Gorgeous	(ECHO ECSD 26)	3	1996	0	1996	
3	Candy Girl	(ECHO ECSCD 31)	14	1997	0	1997	
4	Cornershop	(ECHO ECSCD 33)	37	1997	0	1997	

Babyface   Male Vocalist from the USA

1	It's No Crime		0	1989	7	1989	(SOLAR 68966)
2	Tender Lover		0	1989	14	1989	(SOLAR 74003)
3	Whip Appeal		0	1990	6	1990	(SOLAR 74007)
4	My Kinda Girl		0	1990	30	1990	(SOLAR 74515)
5	Give U My Heart		0	1992	29	1992	(LAFACE 24026)
6	Never Keeping Secrets		0	1993	15	1993	(Epic 77264)
7	And Our Feelings		0	1994	21	1994	(Epic 77394)
8	Rock Bottom	(Epic 6601832)	50	1994	0	1994	
* 9	When Can I See You	(Epic 6606592)	35	1994	4	1994	(Epic 77550)
10	Someone To Love		0	1995	10	1995	(YAB YUM 77895)
11	This Is For The Lover In You	(Epic 6639352)	12	1996	6	1996	(Epic 78443)
12	Everytime I Close My Eyes	(Epic 6642492)	13	1997	6	1997	(Epic 78485)
13	How Come, How Long	(Epic 6646202)	10	1997	0	1997	

HIT 5 IS CREDITED TO BABYFACE FEATURING TONI BRAXTON · HIT 7 IS CREDITED TO BABYFACE FEATURING LL COOL J, H. HEWETT, J. WATLEY & J. DANIELS
HIT 10 IS CREDITED TO JON B. FEATURING BABYFACE

Babylon Zoo   Male Vocal/Multi-Instrumentalist Jas Mann from the UK

1	Spaceman	(EMI CDEM 416)	1	1996	0	1996	
2	Animal Army	(EMI CDEM 425)	17	1996	0	1996	
3	The Boy With The X-Ray Eyes	(EMI CDEMS 440)	32	1996	0	1996	

Babys   Male Vocal/Instrumental Group from the USA/UK

1	Isn't It Time	(Chrysalis CHS 2173)	45	1978	13	1977	(Chrysalis 2173)
2	Every Time I Think Of You		0	1979	13	1979	(Chrysalis 2279)
3	Back On My Feet Again		0	1980	33	1980	(Chrysalis 2398)

Baccara   Vocal Duo from Spain

1	Yes Sir I Can Boogie	(RCA PB 5526)	1	1977	0	1977	
2	Sorry I'm A Lady	(RCA PB 5555)	8	1978	0	1978	

Bachelors   Male Vocal Trio from Ireland

1	Charmaine	(Decca F 11559)	6	1963	0	1963	
2	Faraway Places	(Decca F 11666)	36	1963	0	1963	
3	Whispering	(Decca F 11712)	18	1963	0	1963	
* 4	Diane	(Decca F 11799)	1	1964	10	1964	(London 9639)
* 5	I Believe	(Decca F 11857)	2	1964	33	1964	(London 9672)
6	Ramona	(Decca F 11910)	4	1964	0	1964	
7	I Wouldn't Trade You For The World	(Decca F 11949)	4	1964	0	1964	
8	No Arms Could Ever Hold You	(Decca F 12034)	7	1964	27	1964	(London 9724)
9	True Love For Ever More	(Decca F 12108)	34	1965	0	1965	
10	Marie	(Decca F 12156)	9	1965	15	1965	(London 9762)
11	In The Chapel In The Moonlight	(Decca F 12256)	27	1965	32	1964	(London 9793)
12	Hello Dolly	(Decca F 12309)	38	1966	0	1966	
13	The Sound Of Silence	(Decca F 12351)	3	1966	0	1966	
14	Love Me With All Your Heart		0	1966	38	1966	(London 9828)

ISSUE	TITLE	UK LBL	UK POS	UK YEAR	US POS	US YEAR	US LBL
15	Can I Trust You	(Decca F 12417)	26	1966	0	1966	
16	Walk With Faith In Your Heart	(Decca F 22523)	22	1966	0	1966	
17	Oh How I Miss You	(Decca F 22592)	30	1967	0	1967	
18	Marta	(Decca F 22634)	20	1967	0	1967	

Bachman-Turner Overdrive Male Vocal/Instrumental Group from Vancouver, Canada

1	Let It Ride		0	1974	23	1974	(Mercury 73457)
2	Takin' Care Of The Business		0	1974	12	1974	(Mercury 73487)
* 3	You Ain't Seen Nothin' Yet	(Mercury 6167 025)	2	1974	1	1974	(Mercury 73622)
4	Free Wheelin'		0	1974	1	1974	(Mercury 73622)
5	Roll On Down The Highway	(Mercury 6167 071)	22	1975	14	1975	(Mercury 73656)
6	Hey You		0	1975	21	1975	(Mercury 73683)
7	Take It Like A Man		0	1976	33	1976	(Mercury 73766)

Randy B: 27 Sep 1943, Tim & Robbie Bachman With Fred Turner • Originally Known As Brave Belt

Back To The Planet Mixed Vocal/Instrumental Group from the UK

1	Teenage Turtles	(Parallel LLLCD3)	52	1993	0	1993	
2	Daydream	(Parallel LLLCD 8)	52	1993	0	1993	

Backbeat Band Male Vocal/Instrumental Group from the USA

1	Money	(Virgin VSCDX 1489)	48	1994	0	1994	
2	Money (Re-Entry)	(Virgin VSCDX 1489)	73	1994	0	1994	
3	Please Mr.Postman	(Virgin VSCDX 1502)	69	1994	0	1994	

Backstreet Boys Male Vocal Group from the USA

1	We've Got It Goin' On	(JIVE JIVECD 386)	54	1995	0	1995	
2	I'll Never Break Your Heart	(JIVE JIVECD 389)	42	1995	0	1995	
3	Get Down (You're The One For Me)	(JIVE JIVECD 394)	14	1996	0	1996	
4	We've Got It Goin' On (Re-Issue)	(JIVE JIVECD 400)	3	1996		1996	
5	I'll Never Break Your Heart (Re-Issue)	(JIVE JIVECD 406)	8	1996	0	1996	
6	Anywhere For You	(JIVE JIVECD 416)	4	1997	0	1997	
7	Anywhere For You (Re-Entry)	(JIVE JIVECD 416)	72	1997	0	1997	
8	Anywhere For You (2nd Re-Entry)	(JIVE JIVECD 416)	70	1997	0	1997	
9	Everybody (Backstreet's Back)	(JIVE JIVECD 426)	3	1997	0	1997	

Bad Boys Inc Male Vocal Group from the UK

1	Don't Talk About Love	(A&M 5803412)	19	1993	0	1993	
2	Whenever You Need Someone	(A&M 5804032)	26	1993	0	1993	
3	Walking On Air	(A&M 5804692)	24	1993	0	1993	
4	More To This World	(A&M 5806072)	8	1994	0	1994	
5	Take Me Away (I'll Follow You)	(A&M 5806912)	15	1994	0	1994	
6	Love Here I Come	(A&M 5807752)	26	1994	0	1994	

Bad Company Male Vocal/Instrumental Group from the UK

1	Can't Get Enough	(Island WIP 6191)	15	1974	5	1974	(SWAN SONG 70015)
2	Good Lovin' Gone Bad	(Island WIP 6223)	31	1975	36	1975	(SWAN SONG 70103)
3	Movin' On		0	1974	19	1974	(SWAN SONG 70101)
4	Feel Like Makin' Love	(Island WIP 6242)	20	1975	10	1975	(SWAN SONG 70106)
5	Young Blood		0	1976	10	1976	(SWAN SONG 70108)
* 6	Rock 'N' Roll Fantasy		0	1979	13	1979	(SWAN SONG 70119)
7	If You Needed Somebody		0	1991	16	1991	(ATCO 98914)
8	How About That		0	1992	38	1992	(ATCO 98509)

NAMES: PAUL RODGERS, MICK RALPHS, SIMON KIRKEM & BOZ BURRELL • THE GROUP DISBANDED IN 1982

Bad English Male Vocal/Instrumental Group from the USA/UK

1	When I See You Smile	(Epic 6553471)	61	1989	1	1989	(Epic 69082)
2	Price Of Love		0	1990	5	1990	(Epic 73094)
3	Possession		0	1990	21	1990	(Epic 73398)

Bad Manners Male Vocal/Instrumental Group from the UK

1	Ne - Ne Na - Na Na - Na Nu - Nu	(Magnet MAG 164)	28	1980	0	1980	
2	Lip Up Fattie	(Magnet MAG 175)	15	1980	0	1980	
3	Special Brew	(Magnet MAG 180)	3	1980	0	1980	
4	Lorraine	(Magnet MAG 181)	21	1980	0	1980	
5	Just A Feeling	(Magnet MAG 187)	13	1981	0	1981	
6	Can Can	(Magnet MAG 190)	3	1981	0	1981	
7	Walking In The Sunshine	(Magnet MAG 197)	10	1981	0	1981	
8	Buona Sera	(Magnet MAG211)	34	1981	0	1981	
9	Got No Brains	(Magnet MAG 216)	44	1982	0	1982	
10	My Girl Lollipop (My Boy Lollipop)	(Magnet MAG 232)	9	1982	0	1982	
11	Samson And Delilah	(Magnet MAG 236)	58	1982	0	1982	

ISSUE	TITLE	UK LBL	UK POS	UK YEAR	US POS	US YEAR	US LBL
12	That'll Do Nicely	(Magnet MAG 243)	49	1983	0	1983	

Bad News Male Vocal Group from the UK

1	Bohemian Rhapsody	(EMI EM 24)	43	1987	0	1987	

Bad Religion Male Vocal/Instrumental Group from the USA

1	21st Century (Digital Boy)	(Columbia 6611435)	41	1995	0	1995	

Baddiel & Skinner Male Comedian/Vocal Duo & The Lightning Seeds

1	Three Lions	(Epic 6632732)	1	1996	0	1996	

Hit Was The Official Song Of The England Soccer Team 1996

Badfinger Welsh Quartet Originally Known As The Iveys, Disbanded In 1982

* 1	Come And Get It	(Apple20)	4	1970	7	1970	(Apple1815)
* 2	No Matter What	(Apple31)	5	1971	8	1970	(Apple1822)
* 3	Day After Day	(Apple40)	10	1972	4	1972	(Apple1841)
4	Baby Blue		0	1972	14	1972	(Apple1844)

LEAD SINGER PETE HAM B: 27 APR 1947 WITH BASS PLAYER TOM EVANS & TONY KAYE UNTIL 1978
OBITUARY : PETE, D: 23 APR 1975 COMMITTED SUICIDE.   TOM   D: 23 NOV 1983 COMMITTED SUICIDE.

Badman Real Name Julian Brettle – A Producer from the UK

1	Magic Style	(Citybeat CBE 759)	61	1991	0	1991	

Balaam & The Angel Male Vocal/Instrumental Group from the UK

1	She Knows	(Virgin VS 842)	70	1986	0	1986	

Balance Rock Trio from New York

1	Breaking Away		0	1981	22	1981	(PORTRAIT 02177)

Balloon Farm Pop Quintet from New York

1	A Question Of Temperature		0	1968	37	1968	(LAURIE 3405)

Bally Sagoo Female Vocalist from India

1	Chura Liya	(Columbia 6607092)	64	1994	0	1994	
2	Cholike Ke Peeche	(Columbia6613352)	45	1995	0	1995	
3	Dil Cheez (My Heart...)	(Higher Ground 6634882)	12	1996	0	1996	
4	Tum Bin Jiya	(Higher Ground 6641372)	21	1997	0	1997	

Baltimora Real Name Jimmy McShane from Londonderry, Northern Ireland

1	Tarzan Boy	(Columbia DB 9102)	3	1985	13	1985	(Manhattan 50018)

Bam Bam Male Vocal/Instrumentalist from the UK

1	Give It To Me	(SERIOUS 7OUS 10)	65	1988	0	1988	

Bananarama Female Vocal Group from the UK

1	It Ain't What You Do It's The Way That You Do It	(Chrysalis CHS 2570)	4	1982	0	1982	
2	Really Saying Something	(DERAM NANA 1)	5	1982	0	1982	
3	Shy Boy	(London NANA 2)	4	1982	0	1982	
4	Cheers Then	(London NANA 3)	45	1982	0	1982	
5	Na Na Hey Hey Kiss Him Goodbye	(London NANA 4)	5	1983	0	1983	
6	Cruel Summer	(London NANA 5)	8	1983	9	1984	(London 810127)
7	Robert De Niro's Waiting	(London NANA 6)	3	1984	0	1984	
8	Rough Justice	(London NANA 7)	23	1984	0	1984	
9	Hotline To Heaven	(London NANA 8)	58	1984	0	1984	
10	Do Not Disturb	(London NANA 9)	31	1985	0	1985	
11	Venus	(London NANA 10)	8	1986	1	1986	(London 886056)
12	More Than Physical	(London NANA 11)	41	1986	0	1986	
13	Trick Of The Night	(London NANA 12)	32	1987	0	1987	
14	I Heard A Rumour	(London NANA 13)	14	1987	4	1987	(London 886165)
15	Love In The First Degree	(London NANA 14)	3	1987	0	1987	
16	I Can't Help It	(London NANA 15)	20	1988	0	1988	
17	I Want You Back	(London NANA 16)	5	1988	0	1988	
18	Love, Truth And Honesty	(London NANA 17)	23	1988	0	1988	
19	Nathan Jones	(London NANA18)	15	1988	0	1988	
20	Help	(London LON 222)	3	1989	0	1989	
21	Cruel Summer (Re-Mix)	(London NANA 19)	19	1989	0	1989	
22	Only Your Love	(London NANA 21)	27	1990	0	1990	
23	Preacher Man	(London NANA 23)	20	1991	0	1991	
24	Long Train Running	(London NANA 24)	30	1991	0	1991	
25	Movin' On	(London NANA 25)	24	1992	0	1992	
26	Last Thing On My Mind	(London NANA 26)	71	1992	0	1992	
27	More More More	(London NANA 27)	24	1993	0	1993	

THEIR NAME IS A COMBINATION OF BANANA SPLITS (A CHILDREN'S PROGRAMME) AND PYJAMARAMA (TAKEN FROM A ROXY MUSIC HIT)

ISSUE	TITLE	UK LBL	UK POS	UK YEAR	US POS	US YEAR	US LBL
Band	Male Vocal/Instrumental Group from Canada/USA						
1	The Weight	(Capitol CL 15559)	21	1968	0	1968	
2	Up On Cripple Creek		0	1969	25	1969	(Capitol 2635)
3	Rag Mama Rag	(Capitol CL 15629)	16	1970	0	1970	
4	Don't Do It		0	1972	34	1972	(Capitol 3433)
	OBITUARY RICHARD, D: 4 MAR 1976 COMMITTED SUICIDE.						
Band Aid	Multi National Mixed Vocal/Instrumental Group						
1	Do They Know It's Christmas?	(Mercury FEED 1)	1	1984	13	1985	(Columbia 04749)
2	Do They Know It's Christmas? (Re-Entry)	(Mercury FEED 1)	3	1985	0	1985	
3	Do They Know It's Christmas?	(PWL/POLYDOR FEED 2)	1	1989	0	1989	
	GROUP WAS PUT TOGETHER TO HELP RAISE MONEY FOR FAMINE RELIEF IN ETHIOPIA						
Band AKA	Male Vocal/Instrumental Group from the USA						
1	Grace	(Epic EPC A 2376)	41	1982	0	1982	
2	Joy	(Epic EPC A 3145)	24	1983	0	1983	
Band Of Gold	Mixed Vocal/Instrumental Group from Holland						
1	Love Songs Are Back Again	(RCA 428)	24	1984	0	1984	
Band Of The Black Watch	Male Military Band from the UK						
1	Scotch On The Rocks	(SPARK SRL 1128)	8	1975	0	1975	
2	Dance Of The Cuckoos	(SPARK SRL 1135)	37	1975	0	1975	
Banderas	Female Vocal/Instrumental Duo from the UK						
1	This Is Your Life	(London LON 290)	16	1991	0	1991	
2	She Sells	(London LON 298)	41	1991	0	1991	
Bandwagon	See Johnny Johnson & The Bandwagon						
Bang	Male Vocal Duo from the UK						
1	You're The One	(RCA PB 42715)	74	1989	0	1989	
Bangles	Female Vocal/Instrumental Group from the USA						
1	Manic Monday	(CBS A 6796)	2	1986	2	1986	(Columbia 05757)
2	If She Knew What She Wants	(CBS A 7062)	31	1986	29	1986	(Columbia 05886)
3	Going Down To Liverpool	(CBS A 7255)	56	1986	0	1986	
4	Walk Like An Egyptian	(CBS 650071 7)	3	1986	1	1986	
5	Walking Down Your Street	(CBS BANGS 1)	16	1987	11	1987	(Columbia 06674)
6	Following	(CBS BANGS 2)	55	1987	0	1987	
7	Hazy Shade Of Winter	(DEF JAM BANGS 3)	11	1988	2	1987	(DEF JAM 07630)
8	In Your Room	(CBS BANGS 4)	35	1988	5	1988	(Columbia 08090)
9	Eternal Flame	(CBS BANGS 5)	1	1989	1	1989	(Columbia 68533)
10	Be With You	(CBS BANGS 6)	23	1989	30	1989	(Columbia 68744)
11	I'll Set You Free	(CBS BANGS 7)	74	1989	0	1989	
12	Walk Like An Egyptian (Re-Issue)	(CBS BANGS 8)	73	1990	0	1990	
Banned	Male Vocal/Instrumental Group from the UK						
1	Little Girl	(HARVEST HAR 5145)	36	1977	0	1977	
Bar Code	Mixes Vocal Group from the UK						
1	Supermarket Sweep	(BLANCA CASA BC 101CD)	72	1994	0	1994	
Bar-Kays	Male Vocal/Instrumental Group from the USA						
1	Soul Finger	(STAX 601 014)	33	1967	17	1967	(VOLT 148)
2	Shake Your Rump To The Funk	(Mercury 617)	41	1977	23	1977	(Mercury 417)
3	Sexomatic	(CLUB JAB 10)	51	1985	0	1985	
	OBITUARY: CARL, JIMMY, PHALON AND RONNIE D: 10 DEC 1967 PLANE CRASH WITH OTIS REDDING						
Barbara Acklin	Female Singer/Songwriter, B: 28 Apr 1944 Chicago						
1	Love Makes A Woman		0	1968	15	1968	(Brunswick 55379)
Barbara Dickson	Female Vocalist from the UK						
1	Answer Me	(RSO 2090 174)	9	1976	0	1976	
2	Another Suitcase Another Hall	(MCA 266)	28	1977	0	1977	
3	Caravan Song	(Epic EPC 8103)	41	1980	0	1980	
4	January February	(Epic EPC 8115)	11	1980	0	1980	
5	In The Night	(Epic EPC 8593)	48	1980	0	1980	
6	I Know Him So Well	(RCA CHESS 3)	1	1985	0	1985	
Barbara Fairchild	Female Vocalist, B: 12 Nov. 1950 Arkansas, Now Lives In Nashville						
11	Teddy Bear Song		0	1973	32	1973	(Columbia 45743)
	ALL HER OTHER HITS WERE C/W						

ISSUE	TITLE	UK LBL	UK POS	UK YEAR	US POS	US YEAR	US LBL
Barbara George Female R&B Singer/Songwriter, B: 16 Aug. 1942 New Orleans							
1	I Know (You Don't Love Me No More)		0	1962	3	1962	(AFO 302)
2	You Talk About Love		0	1962	46	1962	(AFO 304)
Barbara Jones Female Vocalist From Jamaica							
1	Just When I Needed You Most	(SONET SON 2221)	31	1981	0	1981	
Barbara Lewis Female Singer/Songwriter, B: 9 Feb 1943, South Lyon, Michigan							
1	Hello Stranger		0	1963	3	1963	(ATLANTIC 2184)
2	Puppy Love		0	1964	38	1964	(ATLANTIC 2214)
* 3	Baby, I'm Yours		0	1965	11	1965	(ATLANTIC 2283)
4	Make Me Your Baby		0	1965	11	1965	(ATLANTIC 2300)
5	Make Me Belong To You		0	1966	28	1966	(ATLANTIC 2346)
Barbara Lynn Female Vocalist, Real Name Barbara Lynn Ozen B: 16 Jan 1942 In Beaumont, Texas							
1	You'll Lose A Good Thing		0	1962	8	1962	(JAMIE 1220)
2	You're Gonna Need Me		0	1962	65	1962	(JAMIE 1240)
3	Oh Baby		0	1964	69	1964	(JAMIE 1277)
Barbara Lyon Female Vocalist from the USA							
1	Stowaway	(Columbia DB 3619)	12	1955	0	1955	
2	Letter To A Soldier	(Columbia DB 3865)	27	1956	0	1956	
Barbara Mason Female Vocalist, B: 9 Aug. 1947 Philadelphia							
1	Yes, I'm Ready		0	1965	5	1965	(ARTIC 105)
2	Sad, Sad Girl		0	1965	27	1965	(ARTIC 108)
+ 3	Oh, How It Hurts		0	1968	11	1968	(ARCTIC 137)
+ 4	Bed And Board		0	1972	24	1972	(BUDDAH 296)
5	Give Me Your Love		0	1973	31	1973	(BUDDAH 331)
6	From His Woman To You		0	1974	28	1974	(BUDDAH 441)
7	Another Man	(STREETWAVE KHAN 3)	45	1984	0	1984	
Barbara Pennington Female Vocalist from the USA							
1	Fan The Flame	(Record Shack Soho 37)	62	1985	0	1985	
2	On A Crowded Street	(Record Shack Soho 49)	57	1985	0	1985	
Barbara Tucker Female Vocalist from the USA							
1	Beautiful People	(Positiva CDTIV11)	23	1994	0	1994	
2	I Get Lifted	(Positiva CDTIV 23)	33	1994	0	1994	
3	Stay Together	(Positiva CDTIV 39)	46	1995	0	1995	
Barbra Streisand Female Vocalist, Full Name Barbara Joan Streisand B: 24 Apr. 1942 Brooklyn							
1	People		0	1964	5	1964	(Columbia 42965)
2	Second Hand Rose	(CBS 202025)	14	1966	32	1966	(Columbia 43469)
3	Stoney End	(CBS 5321)	46	1971	6	1970	(Columbia 45236)
4	Stoney End (Re-Entry)	(CBS 5321)	27	1971	0	1971	
5	Where You Lead		0	1971	40	1971	(Columbia 45414)
6	Sweet Inspiration / Where You Lead		0	1972	37	1972	(Columbia 45626)
* 7	The Way We Were	(CBS 1915)	31	1974	1	1973	(Columbia 45944)
* 8	Love Theme From A Star Is Born (Evergreen)	(CBS 4855)	3	1977	1	1977	(Columbia 10450)
9	My Heart Belongs To Me		0	1977	4	1977	(Columbia 10555)
10	Songbird		0	1978	25	1978	(Columbia 10756)
11	Love Theme From Eyes Of Laura Mars (Prisoner)		0	1978	21	1978	(Columbia 10777)
* 12	You Don't Bring Me Flowers	(CBS 6803)	5	1978	1	1978	(Columbia 10840)
* 13	The Main Event / Fight		0	1979	3	1979	(Columbia 11008)
* 14	No More Tears (Enough Is Enough)	(Casablanca CAN 174/CBS	3	1979	1	1979	(Columbia 11125)
15	Kiss Me In The Rain		0	1980	37	1980	(Columbia 11179)
16	Woman In Love	(CBS 8966)	1	1980	1	1980	(Columbia 11364)
* 17	Guilty	(CBS 9315)	34	1980	3	1980	(Columbia 11390)
18	What Kind Of Fool		0	1981	10	1981	(Columbia 11430)
19	Comin' In And Out Of Your Life	(CBS A 1789)	66	1982	11	1981	(Columbia 02621)
20	Memory	(CBS A 1903)	34	1982	0	1982	
21	The Way He Makes Me Feel		0	1983	40	1983	(Columbia 04177)
22	Till I Loved You (Love Theme From *Goya*)	(CBS BARB 2)	16	1988	25	1988	(Columbia 08062)
23	Places That Belong To You	(Columbia 6577947)	17	1992	0	1992	
24	With One Look	(Columbia 6593422)	30	1993	0	1993	
25	The Music Of The Night	(Columbia 6597382)	54	1994	0	1994	
26	As If We Never Said Goodbye	(Columbia 6603572)	20	1994	0	1994	
27	I Finally Found Someone (From *The Mirror Has Two Faces*)	(A&M 5820832)	10	1997	8	1996	(Columbia 78480)

ISSUE	TITLE	UK LBL	UK POS	UK YEAR	US POS	US YEAR	US LBL
Barclay James Harvest	Male Vocal/Instrumental Group from the UK						
1	Live (EP)	(Polydor 2229 198)	49	1977	0	1977	
2	Live (EP) (Re-Entry)	(Polydor 2229 198)	49	1977	0	1977	
3	Love On The Line	(Polydor POSP 97)	63	1980	0	1980	
4	Life Is For Living	(Polydor POSP 195)	61	1980	0	1980	
5	Just A Day Away	(Polydor POSP 585)	68	1983	0	1983	
Bardeux	Female Dance Duo, Stacy Smith & Melanie Taylor from Los Angeles						
1	When We Kiss		0	1988	36	1988	(SYNTHICIDE 75018)
Bardo	Mixed Vocal Duo from the UK						
1	One Step Further	(Epic EPC A2265)	2	1982	0	1982	
Barnbrack	Male Vocal/Instrumental Group from the UK						
1	Belfast	(HOMESPUN HS 092)	45	1985	0	1985	
Barracudas	Male Vocal/Instrumental Group from the USA/UK						
1	Summer Fun	(EMI-WIPE OUT Z 5)	37	1980	0	1980	
Barrett Strong	Male Vocalist, B: 5 Feb 1941 Mississippi						
1	Money (That's What I Want)		0	1960	23	1960	(ANNA 1111)
Barrington Levy	Male Vocalist from Jamaica						
1	Here I Come	(London LON 62)	41	1985	0	1985	
2	Tribal Base	(DESIRE WANT 44)	20	1991	0	1991	
3	Work	(MCA MCSTD 2003)	65	1994	0	1994	
Barrington Pheloung	Male Composer from Australia						
1	*Inspector Morse* Theme	(Virgin VSCDT 1458)	61	1993	0	1993	
Barron Knights	Male Vocal/Instrumental Group from the UK						
1	Call Up The Groups	(Columbia DB 7317)	3	1964	0	1964	
2	Come To The Dance	(Columbia DB 7375)	42	1964	0	1964	
3	Pop Goes The Workers	(Columbia DB 7525)	5	1965	0	1965	
4	Merry Gentle Pops	(Columbia DB 7780)	9	1965	0	1965	
5	Under New Management	(Columbia DB 8071)	15	1966	0	1966	
6	An Olympic Record	(Columbia DB 8485)	35	1968	0	1968	
7	Live In Trouble	(Epic EPC 5752)	7	1977	0	1977	
8	A Taste Of Aggro	(Epic EPC 6829)	3	1978	0	1978	
9	Food For Thought	(Epic EPC 8011)	46	1979	0	1979	
10	The Sit Song	(Epic EPC 8994)	44	1980	0	1980	
11	Never Mind The Presents	(Epic EPC 9070)	17	1980	0	1980	
12	Blackboard Jumble	(Epic EPC 1795)	52	1981	0	1981	
13	Buffalo Bill's Last Scratch	(CBS A 1795)	49	1983	0	1983	
Barry & The Tamberlanes	Male Vocal/Instrumental Group from California						
1	I Wonder What She's Doing Tonight		0	1963	21	1963	(VALIANT 6034)
Barry Biggs	Male Vocalist from Jamaica						
1	Work All Day	(DYNAMIC DYN 101)	38	1976	0	1976	
2	Side Show	(DYNAMIC DYN 118)	3	1976	0	1976	
3	You're My Life	(DYNAMIC DYN 127)	36	1977	0	1977	
4	Three Ring Circus	(DYNAMIC DYN 128)	22	1977	0	1977	
5	What's Your Sign Girl	(DYNAMIC DYN 150)	55	1979	0	1979	
6	Wide Awake In A Dream	(DYNAMIC DYN	44	1981	0	1981	
Barry Blue	Male Vocalist from the UK						
1	Dancin' On A Saturday Night	(Bell 1295)	2	1973	0	1973	
2	Do You Wanna Dance	(Bell 1336)	7	1973	0	1973	
3	School Love	(Bell 1345)	11	1974	0	1974	
4	Miss Hit And Run	(Bell 1364)	26	1974	0	1974	
5	Hot Shot	(Bell 1379)	23	1974	0	1974	
	See Also Cry Sisco						
Barry Devorzon & Perry Botkin	Barry B: 31 Jul. 1934, Perry B: 16 Apr. 1933 from California						
1	The Young And The Restless ('Nadia's Theme')		0	1976	8	1976	(A&M 1856)
	The Hit Was Originally Called 'Cotton's Dream'						
Barry Gibb	Male Vocalist, B: 1 Sep 1946 Manchester, England						
* 1	Guilty	(CBS 9315)	34	1980	3	1980	(Columbia 11390)
2	What Kind Of Fool		0	1981	10	1981	(Columbia 11430)
3	Shine Shine		0	1984	37	1984	(MCA 52443)
Barry Gordon	See Art Mooney & His Orchestra						

ISSUE	TITLE	UK LBL	UK POS	UK YEAR	US POS	US YEAR	US LBL
Barry Gray & His Orchestra Male Orchestra Leader from the UK							
1	Thunderbirds	(PRT 7P 216)	61	1981	0	1981	
2	Joe 90 / Captain Scarlet Theme	((PRT 7PX 345)	53	1986	0	1986	
Barry Green Male Vocalist from the USA							
1	Brush Those Tears From Your Eyes		0	1948	16	1948	(RAINBOW 10090)
Barry Manilow Male Vocalist, Real Name Barry Alan Pincus B: 17 Jul. 1946 From Brooklyn, New York							
* 1	Mandy	(Arista 1)	11	1975	1	1974	(Bell 45613)
2	It's A Miracle		0	1975	12	1975	(Arista 0108)
3	Could It Be Magic	(Arista ARIST 229)	25	1978	6	1975	(Arista 0126)
* 4	I Write The Songs		0	1975	1	1975	(Arista 0157)
5	Tryin' To Get The Feeling Again		0	1976	10	1976	(Arista 0172)
6	This One's For You		0	1976	29	1976	(Arista 0206)
7	Weekend In New England		0	1977	10	1977	(Arista 0212)
* 8	Looks Like We Made It		0	1977	1	1977	(Arista 0244)
9	Daybreak		0	1977	23	1977	(Arista 0273)
* 10	Can't Smile Without You	(Arista 176)	43	1978	3	1978	(Arista 0305)
11	Even Now		0	1978	19	1978	(Arista 0330)
* 12	Copacabana (At The Copa) (From *Foul Play*)		0	1978	8	1978	(Arista 0339)
13	Ready To Take A Chance Again (From *Foul Play*)		0	1978	11	1978	(Arista 0357)
14	Somewhere In The Night	(Arista 196)	42	1978	9	1978	(Arista 0382)
15	Ships		0	1979	11	1979	(Arista 0464)
16	When I Wanted You		0	1980	20	1980	(Arista 0481)
17	I Don't Want To Walk Without You		0	1980	36	1980	(Arista 0501)
18	Lonely Together	(Arista ARIST 373)	21	1980	0	1980	
19	I Made It Through The Rain	(Arista ARIST 384)	37	1981	10	1981	(Arista 0566)
20	Bermuda Triangle	(Arista ARIST 406)	15	1981	0	1981	
21	Let's Hang On	(Arista ARIST 429)	12	1981	32	1982	(Arista 0675)
22	The Old Songs	(Arista ARIST 443)	48	1981	15	1981	(Arista 0633)
23	Somewhere Down The Road		0	1982	21	1982	(Arista 0658)
24	If I Should Love Again	(Arista ARIST 453)	48	1982	0	1982	
25	Stay	(Arista ARIST 464)	23	1982	0	1982	
26	Oh Julie		0	1982	38	1982	(Arista 0698)
27	I Wanna Do It With You	(Arista ARIST 495)	8	1982	0	1982	
28	I'm Gonna Sit Right Down And Write Myself A Letter	(Arista ARIST 503)	36	1982	0	1982	
29	Memory		0	1983	39	1983	(Arista 1025)
30	Some Kind Of Friend	(Arista ARIST 516)	48	1983	26	1983	(Arista 9003)
31	You're Looking Hot Tonight	(Arista ARIST 542)	47	1983	0	1983	
32	Read 'Em And Weep	(Arista ARIST 551)	17	1983	18	1983	(Arista 9101)
33	Please Don't Be Scared	(Arista 112186)	35	1989	0	1989	
34	Copacabana (At The Copa) (Re-Mix)	(Arista 74321136912)	22	1993	7	1978	
35	Could It Be Magic (Re-Mix)	(Arista 74321174882)	36	1993	0	1993	
36	Let Me Be Your Wings	(EMI CDEM 336)	73	1994	0	1994	
Barry Mann Male Vocalist, Real Name Barry Iberman B: 9 Feb 1939 Brooklyn							
1	Who Put The Bomp		0	1961	7	1961	(ABC-PARAMOUNT 10237)
Barry Mcguire Male Vocalist, B: 15 Oct 1937, Oklahoma City							
* 1	Eve Of Destruction	(RCA 1469)	3	1965	1	1965	(DUNHILL 4009)
Barry Ryan Male Vocalist, Real Name Barry Stevens from the UK							
* 1	Eloise	(MGM 1442)	2	1968	50	1968	(MGM)
* 2	Love Is Love	(MGM 1464)	25	1969	0	1969	
3	The Hunt	(Polydor 56 348)	34	1969	0	1969	
4	Magical Spiel	(Polydor 56 370)	49	1970	0	1970	
5	Kitsch	(Polydor 2001 035)	37	1970	0	1970	
6	Can't Let You Go	(Polydor 2001 256)	32	1972	0	1972	
	See Also Paul And Barry Ryan						
Barry St. John Female Vocalist from the UK							
1	Come Away Melinda	(Columbia DB 7783)	47	1965	0	1965	
Barry White Male Vocalist, B: 12 Sep 1944 Galveston, Texas See Also Love Unlimited, Love Unlimited Orchestra							
* 1	I'm Gonna Love You Just A Little More Baby	(Pye International 7N 25610)	23	1973	3	1973	(20th Century 2018)
2	I've Got So Much To Give		0	1973	32	1973	(20th Century 2042)
* 3	Never Never Gonna Give Ya Up	(Pye International 7N 256339)	14	1974	1	1973	(20th Century 2058)
* 4	Can't Get Enough Of Your Love Babe	(Pye International 7N 25661)	8	1974	1	1974	(20th Century 2120)
* 5	You're The First The Last My Everything	(20th Century BTC 2133)	1	1974	2	1974	(20th Century 2133)
6	What Am I Going To Do With You	(20th Century BTC 2177)	5	1975	8	1975	(20th Century 2177)

ISSUE	TITLE	UK LBL	UK POS	UK YEAR	US POS	US YEAR	US LBL
7	I'll Do For You Anything You Want Me To	(20th Century BTC 2208)	20	1975	40	1975	(20th Century 2208)
8	Let The Music Play	(20th Century BTC 2265)	9	1975	32	1975	(20th Century 2265)
9	You See The Trouble With Me	(20th Century BTC 2277)	2	1976	0	1976	
10	Baby We Better Try And Get It Together	(20th Century BTC 2298)	15	1976	0	1976	
11	Don't Make Me Wait Too Long	(20th Century BTC 2309)	17	1976	0	1976	
* 12	It's Ecstasy When You Lay Down Next To Me	(20th Century BTC 2350)	40	1977	4	1977	(20th Century 2350)
13	I'm Qualified To Satisfy	(20th Century BTC 2328)	44	1977	0	1977	
14	Oh What A Night For Dancing		0	1978	24	1978	(20th Century 2365)
15	Just The Way You Are	(20th Century BTC 2380)	12	1978	0	1978	
16	Sha La La Means I Love You	(20th Century BTC 1041)	55	1979	0	1979	
17	Sho' You Right	(BREAKOUT USA 614)	14	1987	0	1987	
18	Never Never Gonna Give Ya Up (Re-Mix)	(CLUB JAB 59)	63	1988	0	1988	
19	Secret Garden (Sweet Seduction Suite)	(QWEST W 9992)	67	1990	31	1990	(QWEST 19992)
20	Practice What You Preach	(A&M 5808992)	20	1995	18	1994	(A&M 0778)
21	I Only Want To Be With You	(A&M 5810252)	36	1995	0	1995	
22	In Your Wildest Dreams	(Parlophone CDR 6451)	32	1996	0	1996	

Barry Young Male Vocalist from the USA

1	One Has My Name (The Other Has My Heart)		0	1965	13	1965	(DOT 16756)

Bas Noir Female Vocal Duo from the USA

1	My Love Is Magic	(10 TEN 257)	73	1989	0	1989	

Basia Female Vocalist from Poland

1	Promises	(Epic BASH 4)	48	1988	0	1988	
2	Time And Tide	(Epic BASH 5)	61	1988	26	1988	(Epic 07730)
3	Cruising For Bruising		0	1990	29	1990	(Epic 73239)
4	Drunk On Love	(Epic 6611582)	41	1995	0	1995	

Bass Boyz Male Producer James Salmon from the UK

1	Gunz And Pianoz	(Polydor 5753432)	74	1996	0	1996	

Bass Bumpers Mixed Vocal/Instrumental Group from the UK/Germany

1	Runnin'	(VERTIGO VERCD 78)	68	1993	0	1993	
2	The Music's Got Me	(VERTIGO VERCD 84)	25	1994	0	1994	

Bass-O-Matic Male Multi/Instrumentalist from the UK

1	In The Realm Of The Senses	(Virgin VS 1265)	66	1990	0	1990	
2	Fascination Rhythm	(Virgin VS 1274)	9	1990	0	1990	
3	Ease On By	(Virgin VS 1295)	61	1990	0	1990	
4	Funky Love Vibrations	(Virgin VS 1355)	71	1991	0	1991	

Bassheads Mixed Vocal/Instrumental Group from the UK

1	Is There Anybody Out There	(Deconstruction R 6303)	3	1991	0	1991	
2	Back To The Old School	(Deconstruction R 6310)	12	1992	0	1992	
3	Who Can Make Me Feel Good	(Deconstruction R 6326)	28	1992	0	1992	
4	Start A Brand New Life (Save Me)	(Deconstruction R 6353)	49	1993	0	1993	
5	Is There Anybody Out There (Re-Mix)	(Deconstruction 74321293882)	24	1995	0	1995	

Bates Male Vocal/Instrumental Group from Germany

1	Billie Jean	(Virgin International D INSD 151)	67	1996	0	1996	

Bauhaus Male Vocal/Instrumental Group from the UK

1	Kick In The Eye	(Beggars Banquet BEG 54)	45	1981	0	1981	
2	The Passion Of Lovers	(Beggars Banquet BEG 59)	51	1981	0	1981	
3	Kick In The Eye (EP)	(Beggars Banquet BEG 74)	45	1983	0	1981	
4	Spirit	(Beggars Banquet BEG 79)	42	1982	0	1982	
5	Ziggy Stardust	(Beggars Banquet BEG 83)	15	1983	0	1983	
6	Lagartija Nick	(Beggars Banquet BEG 88)	44	1983	0	1983	
7	She's In Parties	(Beggars Banquet BEG 91)	26	1983	0	1983	
8	The Singles 1981-93	(Beggars Banquet BEG 100E)	52	1983	0	1983	

Bay City Rollers Male Vocal/Instrumental Group from the UK

1	Keep On Dancing	(Bell 1164)	9	1971	0	1971	
2	Remember (Sha-La-La-La)	(Bell 1338)	6	1974	0	1974	
3	Shang-A-Lang	(Bell 1355)	2	1974	0	1974	
4	Summerlove Sensation	(Bell 1369)	3	1974	0	1974	
5	All Of Me Loves All Of You	(Bell 1382)	4	1974	0	1974	
* 6	Bye Bye Baby	(Bell 1409)	1	1975	0	1975	
7	Give A Little Love	(Bell 1425)	1	1975	0	1975	
8	Money Honey	(Bell 1461)	3	1975	9	1976	(Arista 0170)
* 9	Saturday Night		0	1975	1	1975	(Arista 0149)
10	Love Me Like I Love You	(Bell 1477)	4	1976	0	1976	

ISSUE	TITLE	UK LBL	UK POS	UK YEAR	US POS	US YEAR	US LBL
11	Rock And Roll Love Letter		0	1976	28	1976	(Arista 0185)
12	I Only Wanna Be With You	(Bell 1493)	4	1976	12	1976	(Arista 0205)
13	It's A Game	(Arista 108)	16	1977	0	1977	
14	You Made Me Believe In Magic	(Arista 127)	34	1977	10	1977	(Arista 0256)
15	The Way I Feel Tonight		0	1977	24	1977	(Arista 0272)

NAMES: DEREK & ALAN LONGMUIR, ERIC FAULKNER, NOBBY CLARK & STUART WOOD • THEY WERE ORIGINALLY CALLED THE SAXONS IN 1967

Bazuka   Instrumental Studio Group Assembled By Tony Camillo from the USA

1	Dynomite (Part 1)		0	1975	10	1975	(A&M 1666)

THE HIT WAS CREDITED TO TONY CAMILLO'S BAZUKA

BBC Concert Orchestra & BBC Symphony Chorus   Orchestra And Chorus Conducted By Stephen Jackson from the UK

1	Ode To Joy (From Beethoven's Symphony Number 9)	(Virgin VSCDT 1591)	36	1996	0	1996	

BBD   See Bell Biv Devoe

BBE   Male Instrumental Group from Italy/France

1	Seven Days And One Week	(POSITIVA CDTIV 67)	3	1996	0	1996	
2	Flash	(POSITIVA CDTIV 73)	5	1997	0	1997	

BBG   Male Vocal/Instrumental Group from the UK

1	Snappiness	(URBAN URB 54)	28	1990	0	1990	
2	Some Kind Of Heaven	(URBAN URB 59)	65	1990	0	1990	
3	Let The Music Play	(MCA MCSTD 40029)	46	1996	0	1996	
4	Snappiness (Re-Mix)	(Polydor 5762972)	50	1996	0	1996	
5	Just Be Tonight	(Polydor 2738972)	45	1997	0	1997	

BBM   Male Vocal/Instrumental Group from the UK

1	Where In The World	(Virgin VSCDG 1495)	57	1994	0	1994	

Be Bop Deluxe   Male Vocal/Instrumental Group from the UK

1	Ship's In The Night	(HARVEST HAR 5104)	23	1976	0	1976	
2	Hot Valves (EP)	(HARVEST HAR 5117)	26	1976	0	1976	

Bea Wain   Female Vocalist from the USA

1	I'm Nobody's Baby		0	1940	11	1940	(VICTOR 26603)
2	Do I Worry?		0	1941	23	1941	(VICTOR 27353)
3	My Sister And I		0	1941	15	1941	(VICTOR 27363)
4	Kiss The Boys Goodbye		0	1941	8	1941	(VICTOR 27445)

Beach Boys   Male Vocal/Instrumental Group from the USA

	ISSUE	TITLE	UK LBL	UK POS	UK YEAR	US POS	US YEAR	US LBL
	1	Surfin'		0	1962	75	1962	(CANDIX 331)
	2	Ten Little Indians		0	1962	49	1962	(Capitol 4880)
	3	Shut Down		0	1963	23	1963	(Capitol 4932)
	4	Surfin' Safari		0	1963	14	1963	(Capitol 4777)
*	5	Surfin' USA	(Capitol CL 15305)	34	1963	3	1963	(Capitol 4932)
*	6	Surfer Girl - Little Deuce Coupe		0	1963	7	1963	(Capitol 5009)
*	7	Be True To Your School - In My Room		0	1963	6	1963	(Capitol 5069)
*	8	Fun Fun Fun		0	1964	5	1964	(Capitol 5118)
*	9	I Get Around	(Capitol CL 15350)	7	1964	1	1964	(Capitol 5174)
	10	When I Grow Up (To Be A Man)	(Capitol CL 15361)	44	1964	9	1964	(Capitol 5245)
	11	Don't Worry Baby		0	1964	24	1964	(Capitol 5174)
	12	Wendy		0	1964	44	1964	(Capitol E.P. 5267)
	13	When I Grow Up (To Be A Man) (Re-Entry)	(Capitol CL 15361)	27	1964	0	1964	
	14	Dance, Dance, Dance	(Capitol CL 15370)	24	1965	8	1964	(Capitol 5306)
	15	Do You Wanna Dance		0	1965	12	1965	(Capitol 5372)
*	16	Help Me Rhonda	(Capitol CL15392)	27	1965	1	1965	(Capitol 5395)
	17	California Girls	(Capitol CL 15409)	26	1965	3	1965	(Capitol 5464)
	18	The Little Girl I Once Knew		0	1965	20	1965	(Capitol 5540)
*	19	Barbara Ann	(Capitol CL 15432)	3	1966	2	1965	(Capitol 5561)
*	20	Sloop John B	(Capitol CL 15441)	2	1966	3	1966	(Capitol 5602)
	21	God Only Knows / Wouldn't It Be Nice	(Capitol CL 15459)	2	1966	8	1966	(Capitol 5706)
*	22	Good Vibrations	(Capitol CL 15475)	1	1966	1	1966	(Capitol 5676)
	23	Then I Kissed Her	(Capitol CL 15502)	4	1967	0	1967	
	24	Heroes And Villains	(Capitol CL 5510)	8	1967	12	1967	(Brother 1001)
	25	Wild Honey	(Capitol CL 15521)	29	1967	31	1967	(Capitol 2028)
	26	Darlin'	(Capitol CL 15527)	11	1968	19	1967	(Capitol 2068)
	27	Friends	(Capitol CL 15545)	25	1968	47	1968	
	28	Do It Again	(Capitol CL 15554)	1	1968	20	1968	(Capitol 2239)
	29	Bluebirds Over The Mountain	(Capitol CL 15572)	33	1968	0	1968	
	30	I Can Here Music	(Capitol CL 15584)	10	1969	24	1969	(Capitol 2432)

ISSUE	TITLE	UK LBL	UK POS	UK YEAR	US POS	US YEAR	US LBL
31	Break Away	(Capitol CL 15598)	6	1969	63	1969	(Capitol 2530)
32	Add Some Music To Your Day		0	1970	64	1970	(Reprise 0894)
33	Cotton Fields	(Capitol CL 15640)	5	1970	0	1970	
34	Long Promised Road		0	1971	89	1971	(Reprise 4047)
35	California Saga - California	(Reprise K	37	1973	0	1973	
36	Sail On Sailer		0	1973	79	1973	(Brother 1138)
37	Surfin' USA (Re-Issue)		0	1974	36	1974	(Capitol 3924)
38	Good Vibrations (Re-Issue)	(Capitol CL 15875)	18	1976	0	1976	
39	Rock And Roll Music	(Reprise K	36	1976	5	1976	(Brother 1354)
40	It's OK		0	1976	5	1976	(Brother 1368)
41	Here Comes The Night	(Caribou CRB 7204)	37	1979	0	1979	
42	Good Timin'		0	1979	40	1979	(Caribou 9029)
43	Lady Lynda	(Caribou CRB 7427)	6	1979	0	1979	
44	Sumahama	(Caribou CRB 7846)	45	1979	0	1979	
45	Beach Boys Medley	(Capitol CL 213)	47	1981	12	1981	(Capitol 5030)
46	Wipeout	(URBAN URB 5)	2	1987	12	1987	(TIN PAN 885960)
47	Come Go With Me		0	1981	18	1981	(Caribou 02633)
48	Getcha Back		0	1985	26	1985	(Caribou 04913)
49	Kokomo	(ELEKTRA EKR	25	1988	1	1988	(ELEKTRA 69385)
50	Wouldn't It Be Nice	(Capitol CL 579)	58	1990	0	1966	
51	Do It Again (Re-Issue)	(Capitol EMCT	61	1991	0	1991	
52	Fun Fun Fun	(Polygram TV 5762632)	24	1996	0	1996	
	OBITUARY : WILSON D: 28 DEC 1983 DROWNED.						

Beastie Boys Male Rap Group from the USA

ISSUE	TITLE	UK LBL	UK POS	UK YEAR	US POS	US YEAR	US LBL
1	(You Gotta) Fight For You Right (To Party)	(DEF JAM 650418 7)	11	1987	7	1987	(DEF JAM 06595)
2	No Sleep Till Brooklyn	(DEF JAM BEAST 1)	14	1987	0	1987	
3	She's On It	(DEF JAM BEAST 2)	10	1987	0	1987	
4	Girls / She's Crafty	(DEF JAM BEAST 3)	34	1987	0	1987	
5	Hey Ladies		0	1989	36	1989	(Capitol 44454)
6	Pass The Mic	(Capitol 12CL 653)	47	1992	0	1992	
7	Frozen Metal Head (Ep)	(Capitol 12CL 665)	55	1992	0	1992	
8	Get It Together / Sabotage	(Capitol CDCL 716)	19	1994	0	1994	
9	Sure Shot	(Capitol CDCLS 726)	27	1994	0	1994	

Beat Male Vocal/Instrumental Group from the UK

ISSUE	TITLE	UK LBL	UK POS	UK YEAR	US POS	US YEAR	US LBL
1	Tears Of A Clown - Ranking Full Stop	(2 TONE CHS TT	6	1979	0	1979	
2	Hands Off She's Mine	(GO FEET FEET	9	1980	0	1980	
3	Mirror In The Bathroom	(GO FEET FEET	4	1980	0	1980	
4	Best Friend - Stand Down Margaret (Dub)	(GO FEET FEET	22	1980	0	1980	
5	Too Nice To Talk To	(GO FEET FEET	7	1980	0	1980	
6	Drowning / All Out To Get Out	(GO FEET FEET	22	1981	0	1981	
7	Doors Of Your Heart	(GO FEET FEET	33	1981	0	1981	
8	Hit It	(GO FEET FEET 11)	70	1981	0	1981	
9	Save It For Later	(GO FEET FEET 333)	47	1982	0	1982	
10	Jeanette	(GO FEET FEET15)	45	1982	0	1982	
11	I Confess	(GO FEET FEET 16)	54	1982	0	1982	
12	Can't Get Use To Losing You	(GO FEET FEET 17)	3	1983	0	1983	
13	Ackee 1-2-3	(GO FEET FEET 18)	54	1983	0	1983	
14	Mirror In The Bathroom (Re-Mix)	(GO FEET74321232062)	44	1996	0	1996	
	SEE ALSO THE TWO TONE (EP), VARIOUS ARTISTS (EP, LP, 78S)						

Beat System Male Vocal/Instrumental Group from the UK

ISSUE	TITLE	UK LBL	UK POS	UK YEAR	US POS	US YEAR	US LBL
1	Walk On The Wild Side	(Fourth & Broadway BRW 163)	63	1990	0	1990	
2	To A Brighter Day	(FFRR FCD 217)	70	1993	0	1993	

Beatles Male Vocal/Instrumental Group from Liverpool, UK

	ISSUE	TITLE	UK LBL	UK POS	UK YEAR	US POS	US YEAR	US LBL
*	1	Love Me Do	(Parlophone R 4949)	17	1962	1	1964	(TOLLIE 9008)
*	2	Please Please Me	(Parlophone R 4983)	2	1963	3	1964	(VEE JAY 581)
	3	From Me To You	(Parlophone R 5015)	1	1963	0	1963	
*	4	My Bonnie - When The Saints Go Marching In	(Polydor NH 66833)	48	1963	26	1964	(MGM 13213)
*	5	She Loves You	(Parlophone R 5055)	1	1963	0	1963	
*	6	I Want To Hold Your Hand	(Parlophone R 5084)	1	1963	0	1963	
*	7	Twist And Shout		0	1964	2	1964	(TOLLIE 9001)
*	8	Can't Buy Me Love	(Parlophone R 5114)	1	1964	1	1964	(Capitol 5150)
	9	I Saw Her Standing There		0	1964	14	1964	(Capitol 5112)
	10	She Loves You (Re-Entry)	(Parlophone R 5055)	42	1964	2	1964	(SWAN 4152)
*	11	Do You Want To Know A Secret		0	1964	2	1964	(VEE-JAY 587
	12	I Want To Hold Your Hand (Re-Entry)	(Parlophone R 5084)	48	1964	1	1964	(Capitol 5112)

ISSUE	TITLE	UK LBL	UK POS	UK YEAR	US POS	US YEAR	US LBL
13	Thank You Girl		0	1964	35	1964	(VEE-JAY 587)
14	Ps I Love You		0	1964	10	1964	(TOLLIE 9008)
15	Ain't She Sweet	(Polydor 52 317)	29	1964	19	1964	ATCO 6308)
* 16	A Hard Day's Night	(Parlophone R 5160)	1	1964	1	1964	(Capitol 5222)
17	Can't Buy Me Love (Re-Entry)	(Parlophone R 5114)	47	1964	0	1964	
* 18	I Feel Fine	(Parlophone R 5200)	1	1964	1	1964	(Capitol 5237)
19	And I Love Her		0	1964	12	1964	(Capitol 5235)
20	She's A Woman		0	1964	4	1964	(Capitol 5237)
21	I'll Cry Instead		0	1964	5	1964	(Capitol 5234)
22	Matchbox		0	1964	17	1964	(Capitol 5255)
23	Slow Down		0	1964	25	1964	(Capitol 5255)
* 24	Eight Days A Week		0	1965	1	1965	(Capitol 5371)
* 25	Ticket To Ride	(Parlophone R 5265)	1	1965	1	1965	(Capitol 5407)
26	I Don't Want To Spoil The Party		0	1965	39	1965	(Capitol 5407)
* 27	Help	(Parlophone R 5305)	1	1965	1	1965	(Capitol 5476)
* 28	Day Tripper	(Parlophone R 5389)	1	1965	5	1966	(Capitol 5555)
29	Yes It Is		0	1965	46	1965	(Capitol 5407)
* 30	We Can Work It Out	(Parlophone R 5389)	1	1965	1	1965	(Capitol 5555)
* 31	Nowhere Man		0	1966	3	1966	(Capitol 5587)
* 32	Paperback Writer	(Parlophone R 5452)	1	1966	1	1966	(Capitol 5651)
33	Rain		0	1966	23	1966	(Capitol 5651)
* 34	Yellow Submarine	(Parlophone R 5493)	1	1966	2	1966	(Capitol 5715)
* 35	Eleanor Rigby	(Parlophone R 5493)	1	1966	11	1966	(Capitol 5715)
* 36	Penny Lane - Strawberry Fields Forever	(Parlophone R 5570)	2	1967	1	1967	(Capitol 5810)
* 37	All You Need Is Love	(Parlophone R 5620)	1	1967	1	1967	(Capitol 5964)
38	Baby You're A Rich Man		0	1967	34	1967	(Capitol 5964)
* 39	Hello Goodbye	(Parlophone R 5655)	1	1967	1	1967	(Capitol 2056)
40	Magical Mystery Tour	(Parlophone SMMT/MMT1)	2	1967	0	1967	
* 41	Lady Madonna	(Parlophone R 5675)	1	1968	4	1968	(Capitol 2138)
* 42	Hey Jude	(Apple R 5722)	1	1968	1	1968	(Apple2276)
* 43	Get Back	(Apple R 5777)	1	1969	1	1969	(Apple2490)
44	Don't Let Me Down		0	1969	35	1969	(Apple2490)
* 44	Revolution		0	1968	12	1968	(Apple2276)
* 45	Ballad Of John And Yoko	(Apple R 5786)	1	1969	8	1969	(Apple2531)
* 46	Come Together		0	1969	3	1969	(Apple2654)
* 47	Something	(Apple R 5814)	4	1969	3	1969	(Apple2654)
* 48	Let It Be	(Apple R 5833)	2	1970	1	1970	(Apple2764)
* 49	The Long And Winding Road		0	1970	1	1970	(Apple2832)
50	Let It Be (Re-Entry)	(Apple R 5833)	43	1970	0	1970	
* 51	Yesterday	(Apple R 6013)	8	1976	1	1965	(Capitol 5498)
52	Hey Jude (Re-Entry)	(Apple R 5722)	12	1976	0	1976	
53	Paperback Writer (Re-Entry)	(Parlophone R 5452)	23	1976	0	1976	
54	Get Back (Re-Entry)	(Apple R 5777)	28	1976	0	1976	
55	Strawberry Fields Forever (Re-Entry)	(Parlophone R 5770)	32	1976	0	1976	
56	Help (Re-Entry)	(Parlophone R 5305)	37	1976	0	1976	
57	Back In The U.S.S.R.	(Parlophone R 6016)	19	1976	0	1976	
58	Got To Get You Into My Life		0	1976	7	1976	(Capitol 4274)
59	Sgt Peppers Lonely Hearts Club Band	(Parlophone R 6022)	63	1978	0	1978	
60	Beatles Movie Medley	(Parlophone R 6055)	10	1982	12	1982	(Capitol 5107)
61	Love Me Do (Re-Entry)	(Parlophone R 4949)	4	1982	0	1982	
62	Please Please Me (Re-Entry)	(Parlophone R 4983)	29	1983	0	1983	
63	From Me To You (Re-Entry)	(Parlophone R5015)	40	1983	0	1983	
64	She Loves You (2nd Re-Entry)	(Parlophone R 5055)	45	1983	0	1983	
65	I Want To Hold Your Hand (2nd Re-Entry)	(Parlophone R 5084)	62	1983	0	1983	
66	Can't Buy Me Love (2nd Re-Entry)	(Parlophone R 5114)	53	1984	0	1984	
67	A Hard Day's Night (Re-Entry)	(Parlophone R 5160)	52	1984	0	1984	
68	I Feel Fine (Re-Entry)	(Parlophone R 5200)	65	1984	0	1965	
69	Ticket To Ride (Re-Entry)	(Parlophone R 5265)	70	1985	0	1985	
70	Twist And Shout (Re-Entry)		0	1986	23	1986	(Capitol 5624)
71	Eleanor Rigby - Yellow Submarine (Re-Entry)	(Parlophone R 5493)	63	1986	0	1986	
72	Penny Lane (2nd Re-Entry)	(Parlophone R 5570)	65	1987	0	1987	
73	All You Need Is Love (Re-Entry)	(Parlophone R 5620)	47	1987	0	1987	
74	Hello Goodbye (Re-Entry)	(Parlophone R 5655)	63	1987	0	1987	
75	Lady Madonna (Re-Entry)	(Parlophone R 5675)	67	1988	0	1988	
77	Get Back (2nd Re-Entry)	(AppleR 5777)	74	1989	0	1989	
77	Hey Jude (2nd Re-Entry)	(AppleR 5722)	52	1988	0	1988	

B
49

ISSUE	TITLE	UK LBL	UK POS	UK YEAR	US POS	US YEAR	US LBL
79	Love Me Do (2nd Re-Entry)	(Parlophone R 4949)	53	1992	0	1992	
80	Baby It's You	(AppleCDR 6406)	7	1995	0	1995	
81	Baby It's You (Re-Entry)	(AppleCDR 6406)	71	1995	0	1995	
82	Free As A Bird	(AppleCDR 6422)	2	1995	6	1995	(Apple58497)
83	Real Love (Ep)	(AppleCDR 6425)	4	1996	11	1996	(Apple)

SUTCLIFFE LEFT IN 1961, PETE BEST REPLACED BY RINGO STARR IN 1962 • PREVIOUS NAMES: QUARRYMEN JOHNNY & THE MOONDOGS, THE RAINBOWS & THE SILVER BEATLES
OBITUARY : JOHN D: 8 DEC 1980 MURDERED (SHOT) • STU D: 10 APR 1962 BRAIN HAEMORRHAGE.

Beatmasters   Mixed Instrumental Group from the UK

1	Rok Da House	(Rhythm King LEFT 11)	5	1988	0	1988	
2	Burn It Up	(Rhythm King LEFT 27)	14	1988	0	1988	
3	Who's In The House	(Rhythm King LEFT 31)	8	1989	0	1989	
4	Hey Dj I Can't Dance To That Music You're Playing	(Rhythm King LEFT 34)	7	1989	0	1989	
5	Warm Love	(Rhythm King LEFT 7)	51	1989	0	1989	
6	Boulevard Of Broken Dreams	(Rhythm King 6573617)	62	1991	0	1991	
7	Dunno What It Is (About You)	(Rhythm King 6580017)	43	1992	0	1992	

Beatrice Kay   Female Vocalist from the USA

1	I've Been Waitin' For Your Phone Call For Eighteen Years		0	1949	21	1949	(Columbia 38373)

Beats International   Mixed Vocal/Instrumental Group from the UK

1	Dub Be Good To Me	(GO.BEAT GOD 39)	1	1990	76	1990	(ELEKTRA 64970)
2	Won't Talk About It	(GO.BEAT GOD 43)	9	1990	0	1990	
3	Burundi Blues	(GO.BEAT GOD 45)	51	1990	0	1990	
4	Echo Chamber	(GO.BEAT GOD 51)	60	1991	0	1991	
5	The Sun Doesn't Shine	(GO.BEAT GOD 59)	66	1991	0	1991	
6	In The Ghetto	(GO.BEAT GOD 64)	44	1991	0	1991	

Beau Brummels   Male Vocal Duo, With Ron Elliott (Guitar) B: 21 Oct 1943 California

1	Laugh, Laugh		0	1965	15	1965	(AUTUMN 8)
2	Just A Little		0	1965	8	1965	(AUTUMN 10)
3	You Tell Me Why		0	1965	38	1965	(AUTUMN 16)

Beautiful People   Male Instrumental Group from the UK

1	If 60s Were 90s	(ESSENTIAL ESSX	74	1994	0	1994	2037)

Beautiful South   Mixed Vocal/Instrumental Group from the UK

1	Song For Whoever	(Go! Disc God 32)	2	1989	0	1989	
2	You Keep It All In	(Go! Disc God 35)	8	1989	0	1989	
3	I'll Sail This Ship Alone	(Go! Disc God 38)	31	1989	0	1989	
4	A Little Time	(Go! Disc God 47)	1	1990	0	1990	
5	My Book	(Go! Disc God 48)	43	1990	0	1990	
6	Let Love Speak Up Itself	(Go! Disc God 53)	51	1991	0	1991	
7	Old Red Eyes Is Back	(Go! Disc God 66)	22	1992	0	1992	
8	We Are Each Other	(Go! Disc God 71)	30	1992	0	1992	
9	Bell Bottomed Tear	(Go! Disc God 78)	16	1992	0	1992	
10	36D	(Go! Disc God 88)	46	1992	0	1992	
11	Good As Gold	(Go! Disc GodCD 110)	23	1994	0	1994	
12	Everybody's Talkin'	(Go! Disc GodCD113)	12	1994	0	1994	
13	Prettiest Eyes	(Go! Disc GodCD	31	1994	0	1994	
14	One Last Love Song	(Go! Disc GodCD 122)	14	1994	0	1994	
15	Pretenders To The Throne	(Go! Discs Go DCD 134)	18	1995	0	1995	
16	Rotterdam	(Go! Discs GoDCD 155)	5	1996	0	1996	
17	Don't Marry Her	(Go! Discs Go LCD 158)	8	1996	0	1996	
18	Blackbird On The Wire	(GO! DISCS 5821252)	23	1997	0	1997	
19	Liar's Bar	(GO! DISCS 5822492)	43	1997	0	1997	

Beavis   See Cher

Beck   Male Vocalist, Real Name Beck Hansen From Kansas City

* 1	Loser	(GEFFEN GFSTD 67)	15	1994	10	1994	(DGC 19270)
2	Where It's At	(GEFFEN GFSTD 2156)	35	1996	61	1996	(GEFFEN 22214)
3	Devil's Haircut	(GEFFEN GFSTD 22183)	22	1996	94	1996	(GEFFEN 22222)
4	The New Pollution	(GEFFEN GFSTD 22205)	14	1997	78	1997	(GEFFEN 22300)
5	Sissyneck	(GEFFEN GFSTD 22253)	30	1997	0	1997	

Bedazzled   Male Vocal/Instrumental Group from the UK

1	Summer Song	(Columbia 6581627)	73	1992	0	1992	

Bedrock   Mixed Vocal/Instrumental Group from the UK

1	For What You Dream Of	(STRESS CSTR	25	1996	0	1996	
2	Set In Stone / Forbidden Zone	(STRESS CDSTR 80)	71	1997	0	1997	

	ISSUE	TITLE	UK LBL	UK POS	UK YEAR	US POS	US YEAR	US LBL
	Bedrocks	Male Vocal/Instrumental Group from the UK						
	1	Ob-La-Di Ob-La-Da	(Columbia DB 8516)	20	1968	0	1968	
	Bee Gees	Male Vocal Trio, Real Names Maurice, Barry & Robin Gibb						
*	1	New York Mining Disaster 1941	(Polydor 56 178)	12	1967	14	1967	(ATCO 6487)
	2	To Love Somebody	(Polydor 56 178)	50	1967	17	1967	(ATCO 6503)
	3	To Love Somebody (Re-Entry)	(Polydor 56 178)	41	1967	0	1967	
*	4	Massachusetts	(Polydor 56 192)	1	1967	11	1967	(ATCO 6532)
	5	Holiday		0	1967	16	1967	(ATCO 6521)
*	6	World	(Polydor 56 220)	9	1967	0	1967	
*	7	Words	(Polydor 56 229)	8	1968	15	1968	(ATCO 6548)
	8	The Singer Sang His Song - Jumbo	(Polydor 56 242)	25	1968	0	1968	
*	9	I've Gotta Get A Message To You	(Polydor 56 273)	1	1968	8	1968	(ATCO 6603)
	10	I Started A Joke		0	1969	6	1969	(ATCO 6639)
	11	First Of May	(Polydor 56 304)	6	1969	37	1969	(ATCO 6657)
	12	Tomorrow Tomorrow	(Polydor 56 331)	23	1968	0	1968	
	13	Don't Forget To Remember	(Polydor 56 343)	2	1969	0	1969	
	14	I.O.I.O.	(Polydor 56 377)	49	1970	0	1970	
*	15	Lonely Days	(Polydor 2001 104)	33	1970	3	1971	(ATCO 6795)
	16	My World	(Polydor 2058 185)	16	1972	16	1972	(ATCO 6871)
*	17	How Can You Mend A Broken Heart		0	1971	1	1971	(ATCO 6824)
	18	Run To Me	(Polydor 2058 255)	9	1972	16	1972	(ATCO 6896)
	19	Alive		0	1972	34	1972	(ATCO 6909)
*	20	Jive Talkin'	(RSO 2090 160)	5	1975	1	1975	(RSO 510)
	21	Nights On Broadway		0	1975	7	1975	(RSO 515)
	22	Fanny (Be Tender With My Love)		0	1976	12	1976	(RSO 519)
	23	You Should Be Dancing	(RSO 2090 195)	5	1976	1	1976	(RSO 853)
	24	Love So Right	(RSO 2090 207)	41	1976	3	1976	(RSO 859)
	25	Boogie Child		0	1987	12	1987	(RSO 867)
	26	Edge Of The Universe		0	1977	26	1977	(RSO 880)
	27	How Deep Is Your Love	(RSO 2090 259)	3	1977	1	1977	(RSO 882)
	28	Stayin' Alive	(RSO 2090 267)	4	1978	1	1978	(RSO 885)
	29	Night Fever	(RSO 002)	1	1978	1	1978	(RSO 889)
	30	Stayin' Alive (Re-Entry)	(RSO 2090 267)	63	1978	0	1978	
	31	Too Much Heaven	(RSO 25)	3	1978	1	1978	(RSO 913)
	32	Tragedy	(RSO 27)	1	1979	1	1979	(RSO 918)
	33	Love You Inside Out	(RSO 31)	13	1979	1	1979	(RSO 925)
	34	Spirits Having Flown	(RSO 52)	16	1980	0	1980	
	35	He's A Liar		0	1981	30	1981	(RSO 1066)
	36	The Woman In You		0	1983	24	1983	(RSO 813173)
	37	Someone Belonging To Someone	(RSO 96)	49	1983	0	1983	
	38	You Win Again	(Warner Bros. W 8351)	1	1987	0	1987	
	39	E.S.P.	(Warner Bros. W 8139)	51	1987	0	1987	
	40	Ordinary Lives	(Warner Bros. W 7523)	54	1989	0	1989	
	41	One	(Warner Bros. W 2916)	71	1989	7	1989	(Warner Bros. 22899)
	42	Secret Love	(Warner Bros. W 0014)	5	1991	0	1991	
	43	Paying The Price Of Love	(Polydor PZCD 284)	23	1993	0	1993	
	44	For Whom The Bell Tolls	(Polydor PZCD 299)	4	1993	0	1993	
	45	How To Fall In Love (Part 1)	(Polydor PZDD 311)	30	1994	0	1994	
	46	Alone	(Polydor 5735272)	5	1997	0	1997	
	47	I Could Not Love You More	(Polydor 5712232)	14	1997	0	1997	
	Beggar & Co	Male Vocal/Instrumental Group from the UK						
	1	Somebody Help Me Out	(ENSIGN ENY 201)	15	1981	0	1981	
	2	Mule (Chant No. 2)	(RCA 130)	37	1981	0	1981	
	Beginning Of The End	Male Vocal/Instrumental Group from the USA						
	1	Funky Nassau (Part 1)	(ATLANTIC K 10021)	31	1974	15	1971	(ALSTON 4595)
	Beijing Spring	Female Vocal Duo from the UK						
	1	I Wanna Be In Love Again	(MCA MCSTD	43	1993	0	1993	
	2	Summerlands	(MCA MCSTD	53	1993	0	1993	
	Bel Canto	Male Vocal/Instrumental Group from the UK						
	1	We've Got To Work It Out	(GOOD GROOVE CDGG 2)	65	1995	0	1995	
	Belinda Carlisle	Female Vocalist B: 17 Aug 1958 Hollywood						
	1	Mad About You	(IRS IRM 118)	67	1988	3	1986	(I.R.S. 52815)
	2	Heaven Is A Place On Earth	(Virgin VS 1036)	1	1987	1	1987	(MCA 53181)

ISSUE	TITLE	UK LBL	UK POS	UK YEAR	US POS	US YEAR	US LBL
3	I Get Weak	(Virgin VS 1046)	10	1988	2	1988	(MCA 53242)
4	Circle In The Sand	(Virgin VS 1074)	4	1988	7	1988	(MCA 53308)
5	World Without You	(Virgin VS 1114)	34	1988	0	1988	
6	Love Never Dies	(Virgin VS 1150)	54	1988	0	1988	
7	Leave A Light On	(Virgin VS 1210)	4	1989	11	1989	(MCA 53706)
8	La Luna	(Virgin VS 1230)	38	1989	0	1989	
9	Summer Rain	(Virgin VS 1323)	23	1990	30	1990	(MCA 53783)
10	Runaway Horses	(Virgin VS 1244)	40	1990	0	1990	
11	Vision Of You	(Virgin VS 1264)	41	1990	0	1990	
12	(We Want) The Same Thing	(Virgin VS 1219)	6	1990	0	1990	
13	Visions Of You (Re-Entry)	(Virgin VS 1264)	71	1991	0	1991	
14	Live Your Life Be Free	(Virgin VS 1370)	12	1991	0	1991	
15	Do You Feel Like I Feel	(Virgin VS 1383)	29	1991	0	1991	
16	Half The World	(Virgin VS 1388)	35	1992	0	1992	
17	Little Black Book	(Virgin VS 1428)	28	1992	0	1992	
18	Big Scary Animal	(Virgin VSCDT 1472)	12	1993	0	1993	
19	Lay Down Your Arms	(Virgin VSCDG 1476)	27	1993	0	1993	
20	In Too Deep	(Chrysalis CDCHS 5033)	6	1996	0	1996	
21	Always Breaking My Heart	(Chrysalis CDCHS 5037)	8	1996	0	1996	
22	Love In The Key Of C	(Chrysalis CDCHS 5044)	20	1996	0	1996	
23	California	(Chrysalis CDCHSS 5047)	31	1997	0	1997	
	SEE ALSO THE GO-GO'S						

Bell & James Male Vocal Duo, Leroy Bell & Casey James from the USA

1	Livin' It Up (Friday Night)	(A&M AMS 7424)	68	1979	15	1979	(A&M 2069)
2	Livin' It Up (Friday Night) (Re-Entry)	(A&M AMS 7424)	59	1979	0	1979	
3	B.B.D. (I Thought It Was Me?)		0	1990	26	1990	(MCA 53897)

Bell Biv Devoe Male Vocal Group from the USA

1	Poison	(MCA MCA 1414)	19	1990	3	1990	(MCA 53772)
2	Do Me!	(MCA MCA 1440)	56	1990	3	1990	(MCA 79045)
3	B.B.D. (I Thought It Was Me)?		0	1990	26	1990	(MCA 53897)
4	When Will I See You Smile Again ?		0	1990	63	1990	(MCA 53976)
+ 5	She's Dope!		0	1991	9	1991	(MCA 54064)
6	The Best Things In Life Are Free	(PERSS 7400)	2	1992	10	1992	PERSPECTIVE 0010)
7	Gangsta		0	1992	21	1992	(MCA 54555)
8	Above The Rim		0	1993	81	1993	(MCA 54620)
+ 9	Something In Your Eyes	(MCA MCSTD	60	1993	38	1993	(MCA 54725)
	HIT 6 IS CREDITED TO LUTHER VANDROSS AND JANET JACKSON WITH SPECIAL GUESTS BBD & RALPH TRESVANT						

Bell Notes Names Carl Bonura, Ray Ceroni, Lenny Glamblavo, Peter Kane And John Casey

1	I've Had It		0	1959	6	1959	(TIME 1004)

Bell Sisters Female Vocal Duo, Cynthia And Kay from the USA

1	Bermuda		0	1952	7	1952	(RCA VICTOR 4422)
2	Wheel Of Fortune		0	1952	10	1952	(RCA VICTOR 4520)
3	Hambone		0	1952	19	1952	(RCA VICTOR 4584)

Bellamy Brothers Male Vocal Duo from Darby, Florida

I	Let Your Love Flow	(Warner Bros. K 16690)	7	1976	1	1976	(Warner Bros. 8169)
2	Satin Sheets	(Warner Bros. K 16775)	43	1976	0	1976	
	MANY OTHER HITS MADE THE US C/W CHARTS • NAMES: HOWARD B: 2 FEB 1946 & DAVID B: 16 SEP 1950 FLORIDA						
	HIT 28 IS CREDITED TO BELLAMY BROTHERS WITH THE FORESTER SISTERS						

Belle & The Devotions Female Vocal Group from the UK

1	Love Games	(CBS A 4332)	11	1984	0	1984	

Belle Stars Formed As The Bodysnatchers, Became The Belle Stars In 1983

1	Iko Iko	(STIFF BUY 150)	35	1982	14	1989	(Capitol 44343)
2	Clapping Song	(STIFF BUY 155)	11	1982	0	1982	
3	Mockingbird	(STIFF BUY 159)	51	1982	0	1982	
4	Sign Of The Times	(STIFF BUY 167)	3	1983	0	1983	
5	Sweet Memory	(STIFF BUY 174)	22	1983	0	1983	
6	Indian Summer	(STIFF BUY 185)	52	1983	0	1983	
7	80's Romance	(STIFF BUY 200)	71	1984	0	1984	

Bells Names Jacki Ralph, Cliff Edwards, Doug Gravelle, Charlie Clarke, Mike Wayne & Denny Will

* 1	Stay Awhile		0	1971	7	1971	(Polydor 15023)

Belltones Male Vocal Group from the USA

1	Way Up In North Carolina		0	1951	30	1951	(Mercury 5692)

ISSUE	TITLE	UK LBL	UK POS	UK YEAR	US POS	US YEAR	US LBL
Belly Mixed Vocal/Instrumental Group from the USA							
1	Feed The Tree	(4AD BAD 3001CD)	32	1993	0	1993	
2	Gepetto	(4AD BAD 2018CD)	49	1993	0	1993	
3	Now They'll Sleep	(4AD BAD 5003CD)	28	1995	0	1995	
4	Seal My Fate	(4AD BAD 5008CD)	35	1995	0	1995	
Belmonts Names Angelo D'Aleo, Fred Milano & Carlo Mastrangelo, Frankie Lyndon Replaced carlo In 1962							
1	Tell Me Why		0	1961	18	1961	(SABRINA 500)
2	Come On Little Angel		0	1962	28	1962	(SABRINA 505)
	GROUP PERFORMED WITH DION FROM 1957, SEE ALSO DION & THE BELMONTS						
Belouis Some Male Vocalist from the UK							
1	Imagination	(Parlophone R 6097)	50	1985	0	1985	
2	Imagination (Re-Issue)	(Parlophone R 1986)	17	1986	0	1986	
3	Some People	(Parlophone R 6130)	33	1986	0	1986	
4	Let It Be With You	(Parlophone R 6154)	53	1987	0	1987	
Beloved Mixed Vocal/Instrumental Duo from the UK							
1	The Sun Rising	(WEA YZ 414)	26	1989	0	1989	
2	Hello	(WEA YZ 426)	19	1990	0	1990	
3	You're Love Takes Me Higher	(EAST WEST YZ 463)	39	1990	0	1990	
4	Time After Time	(EAST WEST YZ 482)	46	1990	0	1990	
5	It's Alright Now	(EAST WEST YZ 541)	48	1990	0	1990	
6	Sweet Harmony	(EAST WEST YZ 709CD)	8	1993	0	1993	
7	You've Got Me Thinking	(EAST WEST YZ 738CD)	23	1993	0	1993	
8	Outer Space Girl	(EAST WEST YZ 726CD)	38	1993	0	1993	
9	Satellite	(EAST WEST EW 034CD)	19	1996	0	1996	
10	Ease The Pressure	(EAST WEST EW 058CD)	43	1996	0	1996	
11	The Sun Rising	(EAST WEST EW 122CD1)	31	1997	0	1997	
	PRE 1993 HITS THE DUO WAS MALE						
Beltram Real Name Joey Beltram Producer from the UK							
1	Energy Flash (Ep)	(R&S RSUK 3)	52	1991	0	1991	
2	The Omen	(R&S RSUK 7)	53	1991	0	1991	
	HIT 2 IS CREDITED TO PROGRAM 2 BELTRAM						
Ben E. King Male Vocalist, Real Name Benjamin Earl Nelson B: 23 Sep 1938 From Henderson, North Carolina							
1	Spanish Harlem		0	1961	10	1961	(ATCO 6185)
2	First Taste Of Love	(London HLK 9258)	27	1961	0	1961	
3	Stand By Me	(London HLK 9358)	50	1961	4	1961	(ATCO 6194)
4	Stand By Me (Re-Entry)	(London HLK 9358)	27	1961	0	1961	
5	Amor Amor	(London HLK 9416)	38	1961	18	1961	(ATCO 6203)
6	Don't Play That Song (You Lied)		0	1962	11	1962	(ATCO 6222)
7	I (Who Have Nothing)		0	1963	29	1963	(ATCO 6267)
8	Supernatural Thing (Part 1)		0	1975	5	1975	(ATLANTIC 3241)
9	Stand By Me (Re-Issue)	(ATLANTIC A	1	1986	9	1986	(ATLANTIC 89361)
10	Save The Last Dance For Me	(MANHATTAN MT 25)	69	1987	0	1987	
	HE JOINED FIVE CROWNS IN 1957 WHO BECAME THE NEW DRIFTERS, LATER THE DRIFTERS						
Ben Folds Five Male Vocal/Instrumental Group from the USA							
1	Underground	(CAROLINE CDCAR 008)	37	1996	0	1996	
2	Battle Of Who Could Care Less	(Epic 6642302)	26	1997	0	1997	
3	Kate	(Epic 6645365)	39	1997	0	1997	
Ben Liebrand Male Producer/Multi-Instrumentalist From Holland							
1	Puls(T)ar	(Epic LIEB 1)	68	1990	0	1990	
Ben Selvin Orchestra Male Vocalist/Orchestra Leader, B: 1898 from the USA							
* 3	Dardanella		0	1920	1	1920	(VICTOR 18633)
	Obituary : D: 15 Jul 1980, Aged 82.						
Benelux & Nancy Dee Female Vocal Group from Belgium, Holland And Luxembourg							
1	Switch	(SCOPE SC 4)	52	1979	0	1979	
Benjamin Orr Real Name Benjamin Orzechowski from Cleveland, Was Also With The Cars							
1	Stay The Night		0	1987	24	1987	(ELEKTRA 69506)
Benny Bell Jewish Risque Songwriter from New York City							
1	Shaving Cream		0	1975	30	1975	(VANGUARD 35183)
Benny Goodman Orchestra Male Orchestra Leader/Instrumentalist (Clarinet), Real Name Benjamin David Goodman, B: 30 May 1909 In							
149	Give Me The Simple Life (From Wake Up And Dream)		0	1946	13	1946	(Columbia 36908)
150	Don't Be A Baby, Baby		0	1946	11	1946	(Columbia 36967)
151	I Don't Know Enough About You		0	1946	12	1946	(Columbia 37053)

ISSUE	TITLE	UK LBL	UK POS	UK YEAR	US POS	US YEAR	US LBL
152	Blue Skies (From Betsy)		0	1946	9	1946	(Columbia 37053)
153	A Gal In Calico (From The Time, The Place,And The Girl)		0	1947	6	1947	(Columbia 37187)
154	Moon-Faced, Starry-Eyed		0	1947	21	1947	(Capitol 376)
155	I Want To Be Loved		0	1947	21	1947	(Capitol 416)
156	For Every Man There's A Woman (From Casbah)		0	1948	25	1948	(Capitol 15030)
157	La Mer (Beyond The Sea)		0	1948	26	1948	(Capitol 15030)
158	Give Me The Good Old Days		0	1948	24	1948	(Capitol 15044)
159	Somebody Else Is Taking My Place (Re-Issue)		0	1948	30	1948	(Columbia 38198)
160	On A Slow Boat To China		0	1948	7	1948	(Capitol 15208)
161	It Isn't Fair		0	1950	13	1950	(Capitol 860)
162	Oh, Babe!		0	1950	25	1950	(Columbia 39045)
163	Wang Wang Blues		0	1951	28	1951	(Columbia 39478)
164	I'll Never Say 'Never Again' Again		0	1953	30	1953	(Columbia 39976)
	OBITUARY: D: 13 JUNE 1986, (AGED 77).						
Benny Hill Male Comedian/Vocalist from the UK							
1	Gather In The Mushrooms	(PYE 7N 15327)	12	1961	0	1961	
2	Transistor Radio	(PYE 7N 15359)	24	1961	0	1961	
3	The Harvest Of Love	(PYE 7N 15520)	20	1963	0	1963	
4	Ernie (The Fastest Milkman In The West)	(Columbia DB 8833)	1	1971	0	1971	
5	Ernie (Re-Issue)	(EMI ERN 1)	29	1992	0	1992	
Benny Mardones Male Vocalist, from Maryland							
1	Into The Night		0	1980	11	1980	(Polydor 2091)
2	Into The Night (Re-Recording)		0	1989	20	1989	(Polydor 889368)
Benny Strong & His Orchestra Male Bandleader/Vocalist from Chicago							
1	That Certain Party		0	1948	9	1948	(TOWER 1271)
2	Five Foot Two, Eyes Of Blue		0	1949	30	1949	(TOWER 1456)
3	Dear Hearts And Gentle People		0	1950	19	1950	(Capitol 757)
4	If I Knew You Were Coming I'd've Baked A Cake		0	1950	11	1950	(Capitol 915)
Bent Fabric Real Name Bent Fabricius Bjerre B: 7 Dec 1944, Copenhagen, Denmark							
* 1	Alley Cat		0	1962	7	1962	(ATCO 6226)
Benz Male Rap/Vocal Group from the UK							
1	Boom Rock Soul	(HACKTOWN 74321329652)	62	1995	0	1995	
2	Urban City Girl	(HACKTOWN 74321348732)	31	1996	0	1996	
3	Miss Parker	(HACKTOWN 74321377292)	35	1996	0	1996	
4	If I Remember	(HENDRICKS CDBENZ 1)	59	1997	0	1997	
5	On A Sun-Day	(HENDRICKS CDBENZ 2)	73	1997	0	1997	
Berlin Vocal/Instrumental Trio from the USA							
1	No More Words		0	1984	23	1984	(GEFFEN 29360)
2	Take My Breath Away	(CBS A 7320)	1	1986	1	1986	(Columbia 05903)
3	You Don't Know	(Mercury MER 237)	39	1987	0	1987	
4	Like Flames	(Mercury MER 240)	47	1987	0	1987	
5	Take My Breath Away (Re-Entry)	(CBS A 7320)	52	1988	0	1988	
6	Take My Breath Away (Re-Issue)	(CBS 656361)	3	1990	0	1990	
	ORIGINALLY A SEXTET, NOW A TRIO, TERRI NUNN, JOHN CRAWFORD & ROB BRILL • HITS 2, 5, 6 ARE THE LOVE THEME FROM *TOP GUN*							
Bern Elliot & The Fenmen Male Vocalist/Male Vocal/Instrumental Group from the UK							
1	Money	(Decca F 11770)	14	1963	0	1963	
2	New Orleans	(Decca F 11852)	24	1964	0	1964	
Bernadette Peters Real Name Bernadette Lazzara B: 28 Feb 1944 Queens, New York							
1	Gee Whiz		0	1980	31	1980	(MCA 41210)
Bernard Bresslaw Male Actor/Vocalist from the UK							
1	Mad Passionate Love	(HMV POP 522)	6	1958	0	1958	
	SEE ALSO MICHAEL MEDWIN - BERNARD BRESSLAW - ALFIE BASS							
Bernard Cribbins Male Actor/Vocalist from the UK							
1	The Hole In The Ground	(Parlophone R 4869)	9	1962	0	1962	
2	Right Said Fred	(Parlophone R 4923)	10	1962	0	1962	
3	Gossip Calypso	(Parlophone R 4961)	25	1962	0	1962	
Berni Flint Male Vocalist from the UK							
1	I Don't Want To Put A Hold On You	(EMI 2599)	3	1977	0	1977	
2	Southern Comfort	(EMI 2621)	48	1977	0	1977	
Bernie Wayne Male Vocal/Pianist from the USA							
1	Zsa-Zsa		0	1953	29	1953	(CORAL 61085)

ISSUE	TITLE	UK LBL	UK POS	UK YEAR	US POS	US YEAR	US LBL

Berri   Female Vocalist from the UK

	1	The Sunshine After The Rain	(FFRREEDOM TABCD 223)	26	1994	0	1994	
	2	Sunshine After The Rain (Re-Mix)	(FFRREEDOM TABCD 223)	4	1994	0	1994	
	3	Shine Like A Star	(FFRREEDOM TABCD 239)	20	1995	0	1995	

HIT 1 IS CREDITED TO NEW ATLANTIC/U4EA FEATURING BERRI

Bert Kaempfert   Male Orchestra Leader, B: 16 Oct 1923 Hamburg, Germany   Obituary : D: 21 Jun 1980.

*	1	Wonderland By Night		0	1960	1	1960	(Decca 31141)
	2	Tenderly		0	1961	31	1961	(Decca 31236)
*	3	Red Roses For A Blue Lady		0	1965	11	1965	(Decca 31722)
	4	Three O'clock In The Morning		0	1965	33	1965	(Decca 31778)
	5	Bye Bye Blues	(Polydor BM 56 504)	24	1965	0	1965	

Bert Weedon   Male Instrumentalist (Guitarist) from the UK

	1	Guitar Boogie Shuffle	(TOP RANK JAR 117)	10	1959	0	1959	
	2	Nashville Boogie	(TOP RANK JAR 221)	29	1959	0	1959	
	3	Big Beat Boogie	(TOP RANK JAR 300)	37	1960	0	1960	
	4	Big Beat Boogie (Re-Entry)	(TOP RANK JAR 300)	49	1960	0	1960	
	5	Twelfth Street Rag	(TOP RANK JAR 360)	47	1960	0	1960	
	6	Apache	(TOP RANK JAR 415)	44	1960	0	1960	
	8	Sorry Robbie	(TOP RANK JAR 517)	28	1960	0	1960	
	9	Ginchy	(TOP RANK JAR 537)	35	1961	0	1961	
	10	Mr. Guitar	(TOP RANK JAR 559)	47	1961	0	1961	

Bertie Higgins   Male Singer/Songwriter Elbert Higgins B: 1946 Tarpon Spring, Florida

| | 1 | Key Largo | (Epic EPC A 2168) | 60 | 1982 | 8 | 1982 | (KAT FAMILY 02524) |
| | 2 | Just Another Day In Paradise | | 0 | 1982 | 46 | 1982 | (KAT FAMILY 02839) |

WORKED AS A DRUMMER IN THE ROEMANS IN THE 1960S

Bessie Smith   Female Blues Singer, B: 15 Apr 1895 Chattanooga, Tennessee

| * | 1 | Down Hearted Blues | | 0 | 1923 | 1 | 1923 | (Columbia 3844) |

OBITUARY: D: 26 SEP 1937 CAR ACCIDENT

Best Company   Male Vocal Duo from the UK

| | 1 | Don't You Forget About Me | (ZYX ZYX 69468) | 65 | 1993 | 0 | 1993 | |

Best Shot   Male Rap Group from the UK

| | 1 | United Colours | (EAST WEST YZ 795CD) | 64 | 1994 | 0 | 1994 | |

Bette Bright   Female Vocalist from the UK

| | 1 | Hello I Am Your Heart | (KOROVA KOW 3) | 50 | 1978 | 0 | 1978 | |

Bette McLaurin   Female Jazz/Type Vocalist from the USA

| | 1 | I May Hate Myself In The Morning | | 0 | 1952 | 23 | 1952 | (DERBY 790) |
| | 2 | Only A Rose | | 0 | 1953 | 25 | 1953 | (CORAL 61026) |

Bette Midler   Female Vocalist, B: 1 Dec 1945 Paterson, New Jersey

	1	Do You Want To Dance?		0	1973	17	1973	(ATLANTIC 2928)
	2	Boogie Woogie Bugle Boy		0	1973	8	1973	(ATLANTIC 2964)
	3	Friends		0	1973	40	1973	(ATLANTIC 2980)
	4	Married Men		0	1979	40	1979	(ATLANTIC 3592)
	5	When A Man Loves A Woman		0	1980	35	1980	(ATLANTIC 3643)
*	6	The Rose		0	1980	3	1980	(ATLANTIC 3656)
	7	My Mother's Eyes		0	1981	39	1981	(ATLANTIC 3771)
*	8	Wind Beneath My Wings	(ATLANTIC A 8972)	5	1989	1	1989	(ATLANTIC 88972)
*	9	From A Distance	(ATLANTIC A 7820)	45	1990	2	1990	(ATLANTIC 87820)
	10	From A Distance (Re-Entry)	(ATLANTIC A 7820)	6	1991	0	1991	

Better Than Ezra   Rock Trio from Louisiana With Kevin Griffin Lead Vocals

| | 1 | Good | | 0 | 1995 | 30 | 1995 | (ELEKTRA 64428) |
| | 2 | Desperately Wanting | | 0 | 1997 | 48 | 1997 | (ELEKTRA 64228) |

Betty Boo   Female Rapper from the UK

	1	Hey Dj I Can't Dance To That Music You're Playing	(Rhythm King LEFT 34)	7	1989	0	1989	
	2	Doin' The Do	(Rhythm King LEFT 39)	7	1990	0	1990	
	3	Where Are You Baby	(Rhythm King LEFT 43)	3	1990	0	1990	
	4	24 Hours	(Rhythm King LEFT 45)	25	1990	0	1990	
	5	Let Me Take You There	(WEA YZ 677)	12	1992	0	1992	
	6	I'm On My Way	(WEA YZ 693)	44	1992	0	1992	
	7	Hangover	(WEA YZ 719CD)	50	1993	0	1993	

HIT 1 IS CREDITED TO BEATMASTERS FEATURING BETTY BOO

ISSUE	TITLE	UK LBL	UK POS	UK YEAR	US POS	US YEAR	US LBL
Betty Clooney Female Vocalist, Older Sister Is Rosemary Clooney from the USA							
1	Sisters (From *White Christmas*)		0	1954	30	1954	(Columbia 40305)
Betty Everett Female Vocalist, B: 23 Nov 1939 Mississippi							
1	You're No Good		0	1963	51	1963	(VEE-JAY 566)
2	Let It Be Me		0	1964	5	1964	(VEE-JAY 613)
3	Getting Mighty Crowded	(FONTANA TF 520)	29	1965	0	1965	
4	It's In His Kiss (The Shoop Shoop Song)	(PRESIDENT PT 215)	34	1968	6	1964	(VEE-JAY 585)
5	There'll Come A Time		0	1969	26	1969	(UNI 55100)
Betty Garrett Female Actress/Vocalist from the USA							
1	Buttons And Bows (From Paleface)		0	1948	8	1948	(MGM 10244)
Betty Grable Female Actress/Vocalist from the USA							
1	I Can't Begin To Tell You (From Dolly Sisters)		0	1945	5	1945	(Columbia 36867)
	HIT IS CREDITED TO HARRY JAMES ORCHESTRA WITH VOCALS BY RUTH HAAG (PSEUDONYM)						
	OBITUARY : D: 2 JUL 1973, (AGED 56).						
Betty Harris Female Vocalist, B: 1943 Orlando, Florida							
1	Cry To Me		0	1963	23	1963	(JUBILEE 5456)
Betty Hutton Female Vocalist, Real Name Elizabeth June Thornburg B:26 Feb 1921 From Battle Creek, Michigan							
6	My Fickle Eye		0	1946	21	1946	(VICTOR 1915)
* 7	I Wish I Didn't Love You So (From *'The Perils Of Pauline'*)		0	1947	5	1947	(Capitol 409)
8	A Bushel And A Peck (From *Guys And Dolls*)		0	1950	3	1950	(RCA VICTOR 3930)
9	Orange Coloured Sky		0	1950	24	1950	(RCA VICTOR 3908)
10	The Musicians		0	1951	24	1951	(RCA VICTOR 4225)
11	Goin' Steady		0	1953	21	1953	(Capitol 2522)
Betty Jane Rhodes Female Actress/Vocalist from the USA							
1	Rumours Are Flying		0	1946	5	1946	(RCA VICTOR 1944)
2	Tonight Be Tender To Me		0	1947	21	1947	(RCA VICTOR 2227)
3	Buttons And Bows		0	1948	9	1948	(RCA VICTOR 3078)
Betty Johnson Female Vocalist, B: 16 Mar 1932 Charlotte, North Carolina							
1	I Want Eddie Fisher For Christmas		0	1954	22	1954	(NEW DISC 10013)
2	Dreamed		0	1956	9	1956	(BALLY 1020)
3	Little White Lies		0	1957	25	1957	(BALLY 1033)
4	The Little Blue Man		0	1958	17	1958	(ATLANTIC 1169)
5	Dream		0	1958	19	1958	(ATLANTIC 1186)
Betty Madigan Female Vocalist From Washington D.C.							
1	Joey		0	1954	12	1954	(MGM 11716)
2	Always You		0	1954	21	1954	(MGM 11812)
3	Dance Everyone Dance		0	1958	31	1958	(CORAL 62007)
Betty Wright Female Vocalist, B: 21 Dec 1953 Miami, Florida							
1	Girl's Can't Do What The Guys Do		0	1968	33	1968	(ALSTON 4569)
* 2	Clean Up Woman		0	1971	6	1971	(ALSTON 4601)
+ 3	Shoorah Shoorah	(RCA 2491)	27	1975	28	1974	(ALSTON 3711)
+ 4	Where Is The Love	(RCA 2548)	25	1975	15	1975	(ALSTON 3713)
+ 5	Is It You Girl		0	1972	10	1972	(ALSTON 4611)
6	Baby Sitter		0	1972	46	1972	(ALSTON 4614)
7	It's Hard To Stop (Doing Something When It's To You)		0	1973	72	1973	(ALSTON 4617)
8	Let Me Be Your Lovemaker		0	1973	55	1973	(ALSTON 4619)
9	Secretary		0	1974	62	1974	(ALSTON 4622)
10	Dance With Me		0	1978	8	1978	(DRIVE 6269)
11	Pain	(COOLTEMPO COOL 117)	42	1986	0	1986	
12	Keep Love New	(SURE DELIGHT SD 11)	71	1989	0	1989	
Betty Swann Real Name Betty Jean Champion B: 24 Oct 1944 Shreveport, LouisianaBetty Was Also In The Group The Fawns							
1	Make Me Yours		0	1967	21	1967	(MONEY 126)
2	Don't Touch Me		0	1969	38	1969	(Capitol 2382)
Beverley Craven Female Vocalist from the UK							
1	Promise Me	(Epic 6559437)	3	1991	0	1991	
2	Holding On	(Epic 6565507)	32	1991	0	1991	
3	Woman To Woman	(Epic 6574647)	68	1991	0	1991	
4	Memories	(Epic 6576617)	34	1991	0	1991	
5	Love Scenes	(Epic 6595952)	34	1993	0	1993	
6	Mollie's Song	(Epic 6598132)	61	1993	0	1993	

B

56

ISSUE	TITLE	UK LBL	UK POS	UK YEAR	US POS	US YEAR	US LBL
Beverley Knight Female Vocalist from the UK							
1	Flavour Of The Old School	(DOME CDDOME 101)	33	1995	0	1995	
2	Down For The One	(DOME CDDOME 102)	55	1995	0	1995	
3	Flavour Of The Old School (Re-Mix)	(DOME CDDOME 105)	33	1995	0	1995	
4	Moving On Up (On The Right Side)	(DOME CDDOME 107)	42	1996	0	1996	
Beverley Sisters Female Vocal Trio from the UK							
1	I Saw Mommy Kissing Santa Claus	(Philips PB 188)	11	1953	0	1953	
2	I Saw Mommy Kissing Santa Claus (Re-Entry)	(Philips PB 188)	6	1953	0	1953	
3	Willie Can	(Decca F 10705)	23	1956	0	1956	
4	I Dreamed	(Decca F 10832)	24	1957	0	1957	
5	Little Drummer Boy	(Decca F 11107)	6	1959	0	1959	
6	Little Donkey	(Decca F 11172)	14	1959	0	1959	
7	Green Fields	(Columbia DB 4444)	48	1960	0	1960	
8	Green Fields (Re-Entry)	(Columbia DB 4444)	29	1960	0	1960	
	SEE ALSO ALL STAR HIT PARADE, VARIOUS ARTISTS (EP, LP, 78S)						
Beverly Bremers Female Actress/Vocalist, B: Chicago							
1	Don't Say You Don't Remember		0	1972	15	1972	(Scepter 12315)
2	We're Free		0	1972	40	1972	(Scepter 12348)
Beyond Male Vocal/Instrumental Group from the UK							
1	Raging (Ep)	(HARVEST HARS 530)	68	1991	0	1991	
BG The Prince Of Rap Male Rapper Bernard Green from Washington D.C.							
1	Take Control Of The Party	(Columbia 6576330)	71	1992	0	1992	
Bianca Kinane Female Vocalist from Ireland							
1	All The Lover I Need	(COLISEUM TOGA 003CD)	59	1996	0	1996	
2	The Woman In Me	(COLISEUM TOGA007CD)	73	1996	0	1996	
Bible Male Vocal/Instrumental Group from the UK							
1	Graceland	(Chrysalis BIB	51	1989	0	1989	
2	Honey Be Good	(Chrysalis BIB	54	1989	0	1989	
Biddu Orchestra Orchestra from the UK							
1	Summer Of 42	(Epic EPC 3318)	14	1975	57	1975	(Epic 50139)
2	Rain Forest	(Epic EPC 4084)	39	1976	0	1976	
3	Journey To The Moon	(Epic EPC 5910)	41	1978	0	1978	
Big Audio Dynamite Male Vocal/Instrumental Group from the USA/UK							
1	E = Mc Squared	(CBS A 6963)	11	1986	0	1986	
2	Medicine Show	(CBS A 7181)	29	1986	0	1986	
3	C'mon Every Beatbox	(CBS 650147)	51	1986	0	1986	
4	V Thirteen	(CBS BADD 2)	51	1987	0	1987	
5	Just Play Music	(CBS BADD 4)	51	1988	0	1988	
6	Looking For A Song	(Columbia 6610182)	68	1994	0	1994	
	HIT 6 IS CREDITED TO BIG AUDIO						
Big Bam Boo Male Vocal/Instrumental Duo from the UK/Canada							
1	Shooting From The Heart	(MCA MCA 1281)	61	1989	0	1989	
Big Ben Banjo Band Instrumental Group from the UK							
1	Let's Get Together No 1	(Columbia DB 3549)	6	1954	0	1954	
2	Let's Get Together Again	(Columbia DB 3676)	19	1955	0	1955	
3	Let's Get Together Again (Re-Entry)	(Columbia DB 3676)	18	1955	0	1955	
Big Bopper Male Vocalist, Real Name Jiles Perry Richardson B: 14 Oct 1930 from Sabine Pass, Texas							
1	Chantilly Lace	(Mercury AMT 1002)	30	1958	6	1958	(Mercury 71343)
2	Big Bopper's Wedding		0	1958	38	1958	(Mercury 71375)
3	Chantilly Lace (Re-Entry)	(Mercury AMT 1002)	12	1959	0	1959	
	OBITUARY : D: 3 FEB 1959 PLANE CRASH • RITCHIE VALENS AND BUDDY HOLLY WERE ON THE SAME AEROPLANE						
Big Brother & The Holding Company Names: Peter Albin, James Gurley, Sam Andrew, Dave Getz Together With Janis Joplin Who Joined In 1966							
1	Piece Of My Heart		0	1968	12	1968	(Columbia 44626)
Big Country Male Vocalist/Instrumental Group from the UK							
1	Fields Of Fire (400 Miles)	(Mercury COUNT 2)	10	1983	0	1983	
2	In A Big Country	(Mercury 814467)	17	1983	17	1983	(Mercury COUNT 3)
3	Chance	(Mercury COUNT 4)	9	1983	0	1983	
4	Wonderland	(Mercury COUNT 5)	8	1984	0	1984	
5	East Of Eden	(Mercury MER 175)	17	1984	0	1984	
6	Where The Rose Is Sown	(Mercury MER 185)	29	1984	0	1984	
7	Just A Shadow	(Mercury BCO 8)	26	1985	0	1985	

ISSUE	TITLE	UK LBL	UK POS	UK YEAR	US POS	US YEAR	US LBL
8	Look Away	(Mercury BIG 1)	7	1986	0	1986	
9	The Teacher	(Mercury BIG 2)	28	1986	0	1986	
10	One Great Thing	(Mercury BIG 3)	19	1986	0	1986	
11	Hold The Heart	(Mercury BIG 4)	55	1986	0	1986	
12	King Of Emotion	(Mercury BIG 5)	16	1988	0	1988	
13	King Of Emotion (Re-Entry)	(Mercury BIG 5)	74	1988	0	1988	
14	Broken Heart (Thirteen Valleys)	(Mercury BIGC 6)	47	1988	0	1988	
15	Peace In Our Time	(Mercury BIGC 7)	39	1989	0	1989	
16	Save Me	(Mercury BIGC 8)	41	1990	0	1990	
17	Heart Of The World	(Mercury BIGC 9)	50	1990	0	1990	
18	Republican Party Reptile (Ep)	(VERTIGO BIC 1)	37	1991	0	1991	
19	Beautiful People	(VERTIGO BIC 2)	72	1991	0	1991	
20	Alone	(COMPULSION CDPULSS 4)	24	1993	0	1993	
21	Ships (Where Were You)	(COMPULSION CDPULSS 6)	29	1993	0	1993	
22	I'm Not Ashamed	(TRANSATLANTIC TRAX 1009)	69	1995	0	1995	
23	You Dreamer	(TRANSATLANTIC TRAX 1012)	68	1995	0	1995	

Big Daddy Male Vocal/Instrumental Group from the USA

1	Dancing In The Dark (EP)	(MAKING WAVES SURF 1033)	21	1985	0	1985	

Big Daddy Kane Male Vocalist, Real Name Antonio M. Hardy from Brooklyn

1	Rap Summary - Wrath Of Kane	(COLD CHILLIN' W 2973)	52	1989	0	1989	
2	Smooth Operator	(COLD CHILLIN' W 2804)	65	1989	0	1989	
3	Very Special		0	1993	31	1993	(COLD CHILLIN' 18437)

Big Dee Irwin Male Vocalist, Real Name Defosca Ervin from the USA

1	Swinging On A Star	(COLPIX PX 11010)	7	1963	38	1963	(DIMENSION 1010)
	See Also Little Eva						

Big Dish Male Vocal/Instrumental Group from the UK

1	Miss America	(EAST WEST YZ 529)	37	1991	0	1991	

Big Fun Male Vocal Group from the UK

1	Blame It On The Boogie	(JIVE JIVE 217)	4	1989	0	1989	
2	Can't Shake The Feeling	(JIVE JIVE 234)	8	1989	0	1989	
3	Handful Of Promises	(JIVE JIVE 243)	21	1990	0	1990	
4	You've Got A Friend	(JIVE CHILD 90)	14	1990	0	1990	
5	Hey There Lonely Girl	(JIVE JIVE 251)	62	1990	0	1990	

Big Mountain Mixed Vocal/Instrumental Group from the USA

* 1	Baby I Love Your Way	(RCA	2	1994	6	1994	(RCA 62780)
2	Sweet Sensual Love	(GIANT 74321234642)	51	1994			

Big Sound Authority Mixed Vocal/Instrumental Group from the UK

1	This House (Is Where Your Love Stands)	(SOURCE BSA 1)	21	1985	0	1985	
2	A Bad Town	(SOURCE BSA 2)	54	1985	0	1985	

Big Supreme Male Vocal Group from the UK

1	Don't Walk	(Polydor POSP 809)	58	1986	0	1986	
2	Please Yourself	(Polydor POSP 840)	64	1987	0	1987	

Big Three Vocal/Instrumental Group from the UK

1	Some Other Guy	(Decca F 11614)	37	1963	0	1963	
2	By The Way	(Decca F 11689)	22	1963	0	1963	

Bilbo Male Vocal/Instrumental Group from the UK

1	She's Gonna Win	(LIGHTNING LIG 548)	42	1978	0	1978	

Bill Male Vocalist from the UK

1	Car Boot Sale	(Mercury MINCD 1)	73	1993	0	1993	

Bill Anderson Real Name James William Anderson III B: 1 Nov 1937 Columbia, South Carolina

8	Mama Sang A Song		0	1962	89	1962	(Decca 31404)
9	Still		0	1963	8	1963	(Decca 31458)
10	8 X 10		0	1963	53	1963	(Decca 31521)
51	I Can't Wait Any Longer		0	1978	80	1978	(MCA 40893)
	(The Devil Made Me Fall)		0	1981	76	1981	(MCA 51204)
	HE ALSO HAD MANY US C/W HITS						

Bill Black's Combo Male Guitarist, B: 17 Sep 1926 Memphis

1	Smokie Part 1-2		0	1959	17	1959	(HI 2018)
* 2	White Silver Sands	(London HLU 9090)	50	1960	9	1960	(HI 2021)
3	Josephine		0	1960	18	1960	(HI 2022)
4	Don't Be Cruel	(London HLU 9212)	32	1960	11	1960	(HI 2026)
5	Blue Tango		0	1960	16	1960	(HI 2027)

ISSUE	TITLE	UK LBL	UK POS	UK YEAR	US POS	US YEAR	US LBL
6	Hearts Of Stone		0	1961	20	1961	(HI 2028)
7	Ole Buttermilk Sky		0	1961	25	1961	(HI 2036)
8	Twist-Her		0	1962	26	1962	(HI 2042)
	OBITUARY : D: 21 OCT 1965 BRAIN TUMOUR.						
Bill Conti Male Composer/Conductor, B: 13 Mar 1942 Providence, Rhode Island							
1	Gonna Fly Now (Theme From *Rocky*)		0	1977	1	1977	(United Artists 940)
Bill Cosby Male Comedian, B: 12 Jul 1938 Philadelphia							
* 1	Little Ole Man (Uptight-Everything's Alright)		0	1967	4	1967	(Warner Bros. 7072)
Bill Darnel Male Vocalist from the USA							
1	Chattanoogie Shoe-Shine Boy		0	1950	18	1950	(CORAL 60147)
2	M-I-S-S-I-S-S-I-P-P-I		0	1950	26	1950	(CORAL 60220)
3	Tonight, Love		0	1953	21	1953	(Decca 28706)
Bill Deal & The Rhondels Eight-Man Band From New York							
1	May I		0	1969	39	1969	(HERITAGE 803)
2	I've Been Hurt		0	1969	35	1969	(HERITAGE 812)
3	What Kind Of Fool Do You Think I Am		0	1969	23	1969	(HERITAGE 817)
Bill Doggett Male Organ/Pianist, B: 16 Feb 1916 Philadelphia							
* 1	Honky Tonk (Part 1-2)		0	1956	2	1956	(KING 4950)
2	Slow Walk		0	1956	26	1956	(KING 5000)
3	Soft		0	1957	35	1957	(KING 5080)
	JAZZ ORGANIST PLAYED WITH LUCKY MILLINDER, THE INK SPOTS AND OTHERS						
Bill Farrell Male Vocalist, Real Name William Fiorelli from the USA							
1	Circus		0	1949	26	1949	(MGM 10488)
2	It Isn't Fair		0	1950	20	1950	(MGM 10637)
3	My Heart Cries For You		0	1951	18	1951	(MGM 10868)
Bill Forbes Male Vocalist from the UK							
1	Too Young	(Columbia DB 4386)	29	1960	0	1960	
Bill Haley & His Comets Real Name William John Clifton Haley Jr, B: 6 Jul 1925 Michigan							
1	Crazy Man, Crazy		0	1953	12	1953	(ESSEX 321)
2	Fractured		0	1953	24	1953	(ESSEX 327)
3	Live It Up		0	1953	25	1953	(ESSEX 332)
* 4	Rock Around The Clock	(Brunswick 05317)	0	1954	23	1954	(Decca 29124)
* 5	Shake Rattle And Roll	(Brunswick 05338)	4	1954	7	1954	(Decca 29204)
6	Dim, Dim The Lights (I Want Some Atmosphere)		0	1954	11	1954	(Decca 29317)
* 7	Rock Around The Clock (USA Re-Issue)	(Brunswick 05317)	17	1955	1	1955	(Decca 29124)
8	Mambo Rock	(Brunswick 05405)	14	1955	17	1955	(Decca 29418)
9	Birth Of The Boogie		0	1955	17	1955	(Decca 29418)
10	Rock Around The Clock (Re-Entry)	(Brunswick 05317)	1	1955	1	1955	(Decca 29124)
11	Razzle-Dazzle	(Brunswick 05453)	13	1955	15	1955	(Decca 29552)
12	Burn That Candle		0	1955	9	1955	(Decca 19713)
13	Rock-A-Beatin' Boogie	(Brunswick 05509)	4	1955	23	1955	(Decca 29713)
14	See You Later Alligator	(Brunswick 05530)	7	1956	6	1956	(Decca 29791)
15	R-O-C-K		0	1956	16	1956	(Decca 29870)
16	The Saints Rock 'N Roll	(Brunswick 05565)	5	1956	18	1956	(Decca 29870)
17	Rockin' Though The Rye	(Brunswick 05582)	3	1956	0	1956	
18	Rip It Up	(Brunswick 05615)	4	1956	25	1956	(Decca 30028)
19	Rock Around The Clock (2nd Re-Entry)	(Brunswick 05317)	5	1956	0	1956	
20	See You Later Alligator (Re-Entry)	(Brunswick 05530)	12	1956	0	1956	
21	Rock 'N Roll Stage Show (Ep)	(Brunswick LAT 8139)	30	1956	0	1956	
22	Rudy's Rock	(Brunswick 05616)	30	1956	34	1956	(Decca 30085)
23	Rock Around The Clock (3rd Re-Entry)	(Brunswick 05317)	24	1956	0	1956	
24	Rudy's Rock (Re-Entry)	(Brunswick 05616)	26	1956	0	1956	
25	Rock Around The Clock (4th Re-Entry)	(Brunswick 05317)	25	1957	0	1957	
26	Rockin' Through The Rye (Re-Entry)	(Brunswick 05582)	19	1957	0	1957	
27	Rock Around The Clock (5th Re-Entry)	(Brunswick 05317)	22	1957	0	1957	
28	Rock The Joint	(London HLF 8371)	20	1957	0	1957	
29	Don't Knock The Rock	(Brunswick 05640)	7	1957	0	1957	
30	Skinny Minnie		0	1958	22	1958	(Decca 30592)
31	Rock Around The Clock (Re-Issue)	(MCA MU 1013)	20	1968	0	1920	
32	Rock Around The Clock (2nd Re-Issue)	(MCA 128)	12	1974	0	1974	
33	Rock Around The Clock (Re-Issue)		0	1974	39	1974	(MCA 60025)
34	Haley's Golden Medley	(MCA 694)	50	1981	0	1981	
	FIRST STARTED SINGING WITH THE DOWN HOMERS THEN FORMED THE FOUR ACES OF WESTERN SWING IN 1948.						
	LATER THE NEXT YEAR HE FORMED THE SADDLEMEN WHICH BECAME BILL HALEY & THE COMETS • OBITUARY : BILL D: 8 FEB 1981 HEART ATTACK.						

ISSUE	TITLE	UK LBL	UK POS	UK YEAR	US POS	US YEAR	US LBL
Bill Johnson Male Vocalist from the USA							
1	A Tree In The Meadow		0	1948	27	1948	(Columbia 38279)
Bill Hayes Male Vocalist, B: 5 Jun 1926 Harvey, Illinois							
* 1	Ballad Of Davy Crockett	(London HLA 8220)	2	1956	1	1955	(CADENCE 1256)
2	Wringle Wrangle		0	1957	33	1957	(ABC-PARAMOUNT 9785)
Bill Justis Male Saxophonist, B: 14 Oct 1946 Birmingham, Alabama							
1	Raunchy	(London HLS 8517)	24	1958	2	1957	(PHILLIPS 3519)
2	Raunchy (Re-Entry)	(London HLS 8517)	11	1958	0	1958	
	OBITUARY: D: 15 JUL 1982.						
Bill Kenny Male Vocalist, Former Lead Singer With The Ink Spots							
1	It Is No Secret		0	1951	18	1951	(Decca 27326)
2	(That's Just My Way Of) Forgetting You		0	1952	23	1952	(Decca 28462)
	HIT 1 IS WITH THE SONG SPINNERS						
Bill Lovelady Male Vocalist from the UK							
1	Reggae For It Now	(CHARISMA CB 337)	12	1979	0	1979	
Bill Medley Male Vocalist, B: 19 Sep 1940 Santa Ana, California							
* 7	(I've Had) The Time Of My Life	(RCA PB 49625)	6	1987	1	1987	(RCA 5224)
8	He Ain't Heavy He's My Brother	(SCOTTI BROTHERS PO 10)	25	1988	0	1988	
9	(I've Had) The Time Of My Life (Re-Entry)	(RCA PB 49625)	8	1990	0	1990	
	HITS 1-7 ARE C/W • HIT 7 IS CREDITED TO BILL MEDLEY AND JENNIFER WARNES • BILL ALSO SANG WITH THE RIGHTEOUS BROTHERS						
Bill Nelson Male Vocal/Instrumentalist (Guitar And Synthesizer) from the UK							
1	Furniture Music	(HARVEST HAR 5176)	59	1979	0	1979	
2	Revolt Into Style	(HARVEST HAR 5183)	69	1979	0	1979	
3	Do You Dream In Colour	(COCTEAU COQ 1)	52	1980	0	1980	
4	Youth Of Nation On Fire	(Mercury WILL 2)	73	1981	0	1981	
Bill Parsons Male Vocalist from the USA							
1	The All American Boy	(London HL 8798)	22	1959	2	1959	(FRATERNITY 835)
Bill Pursell Male Pianist From Tulare, California							
1	Our Winter Love		0	1963	9	1963	(Columbia 42619)
Bill Snyder Orchestra Male pianist/orchestra leader, B: 11 Jul 1916 Park Ridge, Illinois							
* 1	Bewitched, Bothered And Bewildered (From Pal Joey)		0	1950	3	1950	(TOWER 1473)
Bill Tarmey Male Vocalist from the UK							
1	One Voice	(Arista 74321140852)	16	1993	0	1993	
2	Wind Beneath My Wings	(EMI CDEM 304)	40	1994	0	1994	
3	IOU	(EMI CDEM 361)	55	1994	0	1994	
Bill Whelan (Featuring) Anuna & Male Composer With Mixed Choir And Orchestra from Ireland							
1	Riverdance	(SON RTEBUACD 1)	9	1994	0	1994	
Bill Withers Male Vocalist, B: 4 Jul 1938 Slab Fork, West Virginia							
* 1	Ain't No Sunshine		0	1971	3	1971	(SUSSEX 219)
* 2	Lean On Me	(A&M AMS 7004)	18	1972	1	1972	(SUSSEX 235)
* 3	Use Me		0	1972	2	1972	(SUSSEX 241)
4	Kissing My Love		0	1973	31	1973	(SUSSEX 250)
5	Lovely Day	(CBS 5773)	7	1978	30	1978	(Columbia 10627)
6	Just The Two Of Us	(ELEKTRA K)	34	1981	2	1981	(ELEKTRA 47103)
7	Oh Yeah	(CBS A6154)	60	1985	0	1985	
8	Lovely Day (Re-Mix)	(CBS 6530017)	4	1988	0	1988	
	HIT 6 IS CREDITED TO GROVER WASHINGTON JR., WITH UNCREDITED VOCALS BY BILL WITHERS						
Bill Wyman Male Vocalist from the UK							
1	Si Si Je Suis Un Rock Star	(A&M AMS 8144)	14	1981	0	1981	
2	A New Fashion	(A&M AMS 5209)	37	1982	0	1982	
	SEE ALSO THE ROLLING STONES						
Billie Anthony Female Vocalist from the UK							
1	This Ole House	(Columbia DB 3519)	4	1954	0	1954	
Billie Davis Female Vocalist from the UK							
1	Will I What	(Parlophone R 4932)	18	1962	0	1962	
2	Tell Him	(Decca F 11572)	10	1963	0	1963	
3	He's The One	(Decca F 11658)	40	1963	0	1963	
4	I Want You To Be My Baby	(Decca F 12823)	33	1968	0	1968	
	HIT 1 IS CREDITED TO MIKE SARNE WITH BILLIE DAVIS						

ISSUE	TITLE	UK LBL	UK POS	UK YEAR	US POS	US YEAR	US LBL
Billie Jo Spears	Female Vocalist, Billie Jean Spears, B: 14 Jan 1937 In Beaumont, Texas						
18	Sing Me An Old Fashioned Song	(United Artists UP 36179)	34	1976	0	1976	
	MANY HITS REACHED THE US C/W CHARTS						
Billie Ray Martin	Female Vocalist From Germany						
1	Your Loving Arms	(Magnet MAG 1028CD)	38	1994	46	1996	
2	Your Loving Arms (Re-Mix)	(Magnet MAG 1031CD)	6	1995	0	1995	
3	Running Around Town	(Magnet MAG 1035CD)	29	1995	0	1995	
4	Imitation Of Life	(Magnet MAG 1040CD)	29	1996	0	1996	
5	Space Oasis	(Magnet MAG 1042CD)	66	1996	0	1996	
Billy & Lillie	Names Billy Ford B: 9 Mar 1925 Bloomfield, New Jersey & lillie Bryant B: 14 Feb 1940 from Newburg,						
1	La Dee Dah		0	1957	9	1957	(SWAN 4002)
2	Lucky Ladybug		0	1959	14	1959	(SWAN 4020)
Billy 'Crash' Craddock	Male Vocalist B: 16 Jun 1939 North Carolina						
11	Rub It In		0	1974	16	1974	ABC 12013)
12	Ruby, Baby		0	1974	33	1974	ABC 12036)
15	Easy As Pie		0	1975	54	1975	(ABC/DOT 17584)
	(And Cry Myself To Sleep)		0	1978	50	1978	(ABC 12357)
	41 HITS. UNLISTED ONES WERE C/W						
Billy Bland	Male Vocalist, B: 5 Apr 1932 Wilmington, North Carolina						
1	Let The Little Girl Dance		0	1960	7	1960	(OLD TOWN 1076)
Billy Bragg	Male Vocalist from the UK						
1	Between The Wars	(GO! DISCS AGOEP 1)	15	1985	0	1985	
2	Days Like These	(Go! Discs GoD 8)	43	1985	0	1985	
3	Levi Stubbs Tears	(Go! Discs GoD 12)	29	1986	0	1986	
4	Greetings To The New Brunette	(Go! Discs GoD 15)	58	1986	0	1986	
5	She's Leaving Home	(Childline CHILD 1)	1	1988	0	1988	
6	Waiting For The Great Leap Forwards	(Go! Discs GoD 23)	52	1988	0	1988	
7	Won't Talk About It	(GO.BEAT GOD	29	1989	0	1989	
8	Sexuality	(Go! Discs GoD 56)	27	1991	0	1991	
9	You Woke Up My Neighbourhood	(Go! Discs GoD 60)	54	1991	0	1991	
10	Accident Waiting To Happen (Ep)	(Go! Discs GoD 67)	33	1992	0	1992	
11	Upfield	(Cooking Viny FRYCD 051)	46	1996	0	1996	
12	The Boy Done Good	(Cooking Vinyl FRYCD 064)	55	1997	0	1997	
Billy Butterfield Orchestra	Male Orchestra Leader/Instrumentalist (Trumpet) from the USA						
1	My Ideal (From Playboy On Paris)		0	1943	12	1943	(Capitol 134)
2	There Goes That Song Again		0	1945	10	1945	(Capitol 182)
* 3	Moonlight In Vermont		0	1945	15	1945	(Capitol 182)
4	Rumors Are Flying		0	1946	6	1946	(Capitol 282)
Billy Connolly	Male Comedian/Vocalist from Scotland						
1	D.I.V.O.R.C.E.	(Polydor 2058 652)	1	1975	0	1975	
2	No Chance (No Charge)	(Polydor 2058 748)	24	1976	0	1976	
3	In The Brownies	(Polydor 2059 160)	38	1979	0	1979	
4	Super Gran	(STIFF BUY 218)	32	1985	0	1985	
Billy Cotton & His Band	Male Bandleader/Vocalist/Band And Chorus from the UK						
1	In A Golden Coach	(Decca F 10058)	3	1953	0	1953	
2	I Saw Mommy Kissing Santa Claus	(Decca F 10206)	11	1953	0	1953	
3	Friends And Neighbours	(Decca F 10299)	12	1954	0	1954	
4	Friends And Neighbours (Re-Entry)	(Decca F 10299)	3	1954	0	1954	
Billy Eckstine	Male Vocalist, B: 8 Jul 1913 Pittsburgh, Pennsylvania & Raised In Washington D.C.						
* 1	Cottage For Sale		0	1945	8	1945	(NATIONAL 9014)
2	I'm In The Mood For Love	(From Every Night At Eight)	0	1946	12	1946	(NATIONAL 9016)
* 3	Prisoner Of Love		0	1946	10	1946	(NATIONAL 9017)
4	You Call It Madness (But I Call It Love)		0	1946	13	1946	(NATIONAL 9019)
5	The Wildest Gal In Town		0	1947	22	1947	(MGM 10069)
6	True		0	1948	22	1948	(MGM 10123)
7	Intrigue (Movie Title Song)		0	1948	27	1948	(MGM 10154)
8	Sophisticated Lady		0	1948	24	1948	(NATIONAL 9049)
* 9	Everything I Have Is Yours (From Dancing Lady)		0	1948	30	1948	(MGM 10259)
* 10	Blue Moon		0	1949	21	1949	(MGM 10311)
11	Bewildered		0	1949	27	1949	(MGM 10340)
* 12	Caravan		0	1949	27	1949	(MGM 10368)
13	Crying		0	1949	27	1949	(MGM 10458)
14	Somehow		0	1949	25	1949	(MGM 10383)

ISSUE	TITLE	UK LBL	UK POS	UK YEAR	US POS	US YEAR	US LBL
15	Body And Soul (From Three's A Crowd)		0	1949	27	1949	(MGM 10501)
16	Fool's Paradise		0	1949	24	1949	(MGM 10562)
17	Sitting By The Window		0	1950	23	1950	(MGM 10602)
* 18	My Foolish Heart		0	1950	6	1950	(MGM 10623)
19	I Wanna Be Loved		0	1950	7	1950	(MGM 10716)
20	If		0	1951	10	1951	(MGM 10896)
* 21	I Apologise		0	1951	6	1951	(MGM 10903)
22	Be My Love (From The Toast Of New Orleans)		0	1951	26	1951	(MGM 10799)
23	Kiss Of Fire (From El Chocio)		0	1952	16	1952	(MGM 11225)
24	Coquette		0	1953	26	1953	(MGM 11439)
25	Send My Baby Back To Me		0	1953	25	1953	(MGM 11511)
26	St.Louis Blues		0	1953	24	1953	(MGM 11573)
27	Lost In Loveliness (From The Girl In Pink Tights)		0	1954	24	1954	(MGM 11694)
28	No One But You	(MGM 763)	3	1954	0	1954	
29	Passing Strangers	(Mercury MT 164)	22	1957	0	1957	
30	Gigi	(Mercury AMT 1018)	8	1965	0	1965	
31	Passing Strangers (Re-Issue)	(Mercury MF 1082)	20	1969	0	1969	

Billy Falcon Male Singer/Songwriter, B: 13 Jul 1956 Valley Stream, New York

1	Power Windows		0	1991	35	1991	(JAMBCO 868672)

Billy Field Male Vocalist from Australia

1	You Weren't In Love With Me	(CBS A 2344)	67	1982	0	1982	

Billy Fury Male Vocalist, Real Name Ronald Wycherley from Liverpool, England

1	Maybe Tomorrow	(Decca F 11102)	22	1959	0	1959	
2	Maybe Tomorrow (Re-Entry)	(Decca F 11102)	18	1959	0	1959	
3	Margot	(Decca F 11128)	28	1959	0	1959	
4	Colette	(Decca F 11200)	9	1960	0	1960	
5	That's Love	(Decca F 11237)	19	1960	0	1960	
6	Wondrous Place	(Decca F 11267)	25	1960	0	1960	
7	A Thousands Stars	(Decca F 11311)	14	1961	0	1961	
8	Don't Worry	(Decca F 11334)	40	1961	0	1961	
9	Halfway To Paradise	(Decca F 11349)	3	1961	0	1961	
10	Jealousy	(Decca F 11384)	2	1961	0	1961	
11	I'd Never Find Another You	(Decca F 11409)	5	1961	0	1961	
12	Letter Full Of Tears	(Decca F 11437)	32	1962	0	1962	
13	Last Night Was Made For Love	(Decca F 11458)	4	1962	0	1962	
14	Once Upon A Dream	(Decca F 11485)	7	1962	0	1962	
15	Because Of Love	(Decca F 11508)	18	1962	0	1962	
16	Like I've Never Been Gone	(Decca F 11582)	3	1963	0	1963	
17	When Will You Say I Love You	(Decca F 11655)	3	1963	0	1963	
18	In Summer	(Decca F 11701)	5	1963	0	1963	
19	Somebody Else's Girl	(Decca F 11744)	18	1963	0	1963	
20	Do You Really Love Me Too	(Decca F 11792)	13	1964	0	1964	
21	I Will	(Decca F 11888)	14	1964	0	1964	
22	It's Only Make Believe	(Decca F 11939)	10	1964	0	1964	
23	I'm Lost Without You	(Decca F 12048)	16	1965	0	1965	
24	In Thoughts Of You	(Decca F 12178)	9	1965	0	1965	
25	Run To My Lovin' Arms	(Decca F 12230)	25	1965	0	1965	
26	I'll Never Quite Get Over You	(Decca F 12325)	35	1966	0	1966	
27	Give Me Your Word	(Decca F 12459)	27	1966	0	1966	
28	Love Or Money	(Polydor POSP 488)	57	1982	0	1982	
29	Devil Or Angel	(Polydor POSP 528)	58	1982	0	1982	
30	Forget Him	(Polydor POSP 558)	59	1983	0	1983	

OBITUARY: D: 1983 HEART FAILURE, AGED 42.

Billy Grammer Male Guitarist, B: 28 Aug 1925 Benton, Illinois

* 1	Gotta Travel On		0	1958	4	1958	(MONUMENT 400)
! 2	I Wanna Go Home		0	1963	18	1963	(Decca 31449)
! 3	I'll Leave The Porch Light A-Burning		0	1964	43	1964	(Decca 31562)
! 4	Bottles		0	1965	35	1965	(Epic 10052)
! 5	The Real Thing		0	1966	30	1966	(Epic 10103)
! 6	Mable (You Have Been A Friend To Me)		0	1967	48	1967	(RICE 5025)
! 7	The Ballad Of John Dillinger		0	1968	70	1968	(Mercury
! 8	Jesus Is A Soul Man		0	1969	66	1969	(STOP 321)

HE IS FOUNDER OF THE FAMOUS GRAMMER GUITAR

ISSUE	TITLE	UK LBL	UK POS	UK YEAR	US POS	US YEAR	US LBL
Billy Griffin Male Vocalist from the USA							
1	Hold Me Tighter In The Rain	(CBS A 2935)	17	1983	0	1983	
2	Serious	(CBS A 4053)	64	1984	0	1984	
Billy Howard Male Vocalist from the UK							
1	King Of The Cops	(Penny Farthing Pen 892)	6	1975	0	1975	
Billy Idol Male Vocalist, Real Name Willem Wolfe Broad B: 30 Nov 1955 London, England							
1	Hot In The City	(Chrysalis CHS 2625)	58	1982	23	1982	(Chrysalis 2605)
2	White Wedding	(Chrysalis IDOL 2605)	6	1985	36	1983	(Chrysalis 42697)
3	Rebel Yell	(Chrysalis IDOL 2)	6	1984	0	1984	
4	Eyes Without A Face	(Chrysalis IDOL 3)	18	1984	4	1984	(Chrysalis 42786)
5	Flesh For Fantasy	(Chrysalis IDOL 4)	54	1984	29	1984	(Chrysalis 42809)
6	Rebel Yell (Re-Issue)	(Chrysalis IDOL 6)	6	1985	0	1985	
7	To Be A Lover	(Chrysalis IDOL 8)	22	1986	6	1986	(Chrysalis 43024)
8	Don't Need A Gun	(Chrysalis IDOL9)	26	1987	37	1987	(Chrysalis 43087)
9	Sweet Sixteen	(Chrysalis IDOL 10)	17	1987	20	1987	(Chrysalis 43114)
10	Mony Mony	(Chrysalis IDOL 11)	7	1987	1	1987	(Chrysalis 43161)
11	Hot In The City (Re-Mix)	(Chrysalis IDOL 12)	13	1988	0	1988	
12	Catch My Fall	(Chrysalis IDOL 13)	63	1988	0	1988	
* 13	Cradle Of Love	(Chrysalis IDOL 14)	34	1990	2	1990	(Chrysalis 23509)
14	L.A. Woman	(Chrysalis IDOL 15)	70	1990	0	1990	
15	Prodical Blues	(Chrysalis IDOL 16)	47	1990	0	1990	
16	Shock To The System	(Chrysalis CDCHS 3994)	30	1993	0	1993	
17	Speed	(FOX	47	1994	0	1994	
	HE WAS A FORMER LEADER OF GENERATION X						
Billy J. Kramer & The Dakotas Male Vocal And Male Instrumental Backing Group from the UK							
1	Do You Want To Know A Secret?	(Parlophone R 5023)	2	1963	0	1963	
* 2	Bad To Me	(Parlophone R 5049)	1	1963	9	1964	(IMPERIAL 66027)
3	I'll Keep You Satisfied	(Parlophone R 5073)	4	1963	30	1964	(IMPERIAL 66048)
* 4	Little Children	(Parlophone R 5105)	1	1964	7	1964	(IMPERIAL 66027)
5	From A Window	(Parlophone R 5156)	10	1964	23	1964	(IMPERIAL 66051)
6	Trains And Boats And Planes	(Parlophone R 5285)	12	1965	0	1965	
	REAL NAME WILLIAM ASHTON B: 19 AUG 1943, BOOTLE, LIVERPOOL, ENGLAND • SEE ALSO DAKOTAS						
Billy Joe & The Checkmates Real Name Louis Bideu B: 21 Mar 1919 El Paso, Texas							
1	Percolator (Twist)		0	1962	10	1962	(DORE 620)
	Billy Was A Comedian, In the early 60s called himself Billy Joe Hunter						
Billy Joe Royal Male Vocalist/Multi-Instrumentalist, B: 3 Apr 1942 Valdosta, Georgia							
1	Down On The Boondocks	(CBS 201802)	38	1965	9	1965	(Columbia 43305)
2	I Knew You When		0	1965	14	1965	(Columbia 43390)
3	I've Got To Be Somebody		0	1966	38	1966	(Columbia 43465)
4	Cherry Hill Park		0	1969	15	1969	(Columbia 44902)
Billy Joel Male Vocal/Pianist, Real Name William Martin Joel B: 9 May 1949 Long Island, New York							
1	Piano Man		0	1974	25	1974	(Columbia 45963)
2	The Entertainer		0	1974	34	1974	(Columbia 10064)
* 3	Just The Way You Are	(CBS 5872)	19	1978	3	1977	(Columbia 10646)
4	Movin' Out (Anthony's Song)	(CBS 6412)	35	1978	17	1978	(Columbia 10708)
5	Only The Good Die Young		0	1978	24	1978	(Columbia 10750)
6	She's Always A Woman / Just The Way You Are (Re-Issue)	(CBS A 6862)	53	1986	17	1986	(Columbia 10788)
* 7	My Life	(CBS 6821)	12	1978	3	1978	(Columbia 10857)
8	Big Shot		0	1979	14	1979	(Columbia 10913)
9	Honesty		0	1979	24	1979	(Columbia 10959)
10	Until The Night	(CBS 7242)	50	1979	0	1979	
11	You May Be Right		0	1980	7	1980	(Columbia 11231)
12	All For Leyna	(CBS 8325)	40	1980	0	1980	
* 13	It's Still Rock And Roll To Me	(CBS 8753)	14	1980	1	1980	(Columbia 11276)
14	Don't Ask Me Why		0	1980	19	1980	(Columbia 11331)
15	Sometimes A Fantasy		0	1980	36	1980	(Columbia 11379)
16	Say Goodbye To Hollywood		0	1981	17	1981	(Columbia 02518)
17	She's Got A Way		0	1981	23	1981	(Columbia 02628)
18	Pressure		0	1982	20	1982	(Columbia 03244)
19	Allentown		0	1983	17	1983	(Columbia 03413)
20	Tell Her About It	(CBS A 3655)	4	1983	1	1983	(Columbia 04012)
* 21	Uptown Girl	(CBS A 3775)	1	1983	3	1983	(Columbia 04149)
22	An Innocent Man	(CBS A 4142)	8	1984	10	1984	(Columbia 04259)

ISSUE	TITLE	UK LBL	UK POS	UK YEAR	US POS	US YEAR	US LBL
23	The Longest Time	(CBS A 4280)	25	1984	14	1984	(Columbia 04400)
24	Leave A Tender Moment Alone	(CBS A 4521)	29	1984	27	1984	(Columbia 04514)
25	Keeping The Faith		0	1985	18	1985	(Columbia 04681)
26	You're Only Human (Second Wind)		0	1985	9	1985	(Columbia 05417)
27	The Night Is Still Young		0	1985	34	1985	(Columbia 05657)
28	She's Always A Woman (Re-Issue)	(CBS A 6862)	53	1986	0	1986	
29	Modern Woman (From Ruthless People)		0	1986	10	1986	(Epic 06118)
30	A Matter Of Trust	(CBS 650057 7)	52	1986	10	1986	(Columbia 06108)
31	This Is The Time		0	1986	18	1986	(Columbia 06526)
* 32	We Didn't Start The Fire	(CBS JOEL 1)	7	1989	1	1989	(Columbia 73021)
33	Leningrad	(CBS JOEL 3)	53	1989	0	1989	
34	I Go To Extremes	(CBS JOEL 2)	70	1990	6	1990	(Columbia 73091)
35	And So It Goes		0	1990	37	1990	(Columbia 73602)
36	All Shook Up	(CBS 6583437)	27	1992	0	1992	
37	The River Of Dreams	(Columbia 6595432)	3	1993	3	1993	(Columbia 77086)
38	All About Soul	(Columbia 6597362)	32	1993	29	1993	(Columbia 77254)
39	No Man's Land	(Columbia 6599202)	50	1994	0	1994	

HIS FIRST BAND WAS THE ECHOES WHICH BECAME THE LOST SOULS • IN THE LATE 60S WAS IN THE GROUP THE HASSLES THEN HE AND JON SMALL FORMED ATTILA

Billy May & His Orchestra   Male Orchestra Leader/Instrumentalist (Trumpet) from the USA

1	Charmaine		0	1952	17	1952	(Capitol 1919)
2	Main Title Theme From 'The Man With The Golden Arm'	(Capitol CL 14551)	9	1956	0	1956	

Billy Myles   Male Singer/Songwriter from New York

1	The Joker (That's What They Call Me)		0	1957	25	1957	(EMBER 1026)

Billy Ocean   Male Vocalist, Real Name Leslie Sebastian Charles B: 21 Jan 1950 from Trinidad

1	Love Really Hurts Without You	(GTO GT 52)	2	1976	22	1976	(ARIOLA 7621)
2	L.O.D. (Love On Delivery)	(GTO GT 62)	19	1976	0	1976	
3	Stop Me (If You've Heard It All Before)	(GTO GT 72)	12	1976	0	1976	
4	Red Light Spells Danger	(GTO GT 85)	2	1977	0	1977	
5	American Heart	(GTO GT 244)	54	1979	0	1979	
6	Are You Ready	(GTO GT 259)	42	1980	0	1980	
* 7	Caribean Queen (No More Love On The Run)	(JIVE JIVE 77)	6	1984	1	1984	(JIVE 9199)
8	Loverboy	(JIVE JIVE 80)	15	1985	2	1985	(JIVE 9284)
9	Suddenly	(JIVE JIVE 90)	4	1985	4	1985	(JIVE 9323)
10	Mystery Lady	(JIVE JIVE 98)	49	1985	24	1985	(JIVE 9374)
11	When The Going Gets Tough, The Tough Get Going	(JIVE JIVE 114)	1	1986	2	1986	(JIVE 9432)
12	There'll Be Sad Songs (To Make You Cry)	(JIVE JIVE 117)	12	1986	1	1986	(JIVE 9465)
13	Love Zone	(JIVE JIVE 124)	49	1986	10	1986	(JIVE 9510)
14	Bittersweet	(JIVE JIVE 133)	44	1986	0	1986	
15	Love Is Forever	(JIVE JIVE 134)	34	1987	16	1986	(JIVE 9540)
16	Get Outta My Dreams Get Into My Car	(JIVE BOS 1)	3	1988	1	1988	(JIVE 9678)
17	Calypso Crazy	(JIVE BOS 2)	35	1988	0	1988	
18	The Colour Of Love	(JIVE BOS 3)	65	1988	17	1988	(JIVE 9707)
19	Licence To Chill		0	1989	32	1989	(JIVE 1283)
20	Pressure	(JIVE BOSCD 6)	55	1993	0	1993	

Billy Paul   Male Vocalist, Real Name Paul Williams B: 1 Dec 1934 In North Philadelphia Billy First Recorded In 1952

1	Me And Mrs. Jones	(Epic EPC 1055)	12	1973	1	1972	(PHIL/INTER 3521)
2	Thanks For Saving My Life	(PHIL/INTER PIR 1928)	33	1974	37	1974	(PHIL/INTER 3538)
3	Let's Make A Baby	(PHIL/INTER PIR 4144)	30	1976	0	1976	
4	Let 'Em In	(PHIL/INTER PIR 5143)	26	1977	0	1977	
5	Your Song	(PHIL/INTER PIR 5391)	37	1977	0	1977	
6	Only The Strong Survive	(PHIL/INTER PIR 5699)	33	1977	0	1977	
7	Bring The Family Back	(PHIL/INTER PIR 7456)	51	1979	0	1979	

Billy Preston   Male Vocal/Instrumentalist (Keyboards), B: 9 Sep 1946 Houston

* 1	Get Back	(ApplcR 5777)	1	1969	1	1969	(Apple2490)
2	Don't Let Me Down	(AppleR 5777)	0	1969	35	1969	(Apple2490)
3	Thats The Way God Planned It	(Apple12)	11	1969	0	1969	
* 4	Outa-Space	(A&M AMS 7007)	44	1972	2	1972	(A&M 1320)
* 5	Will It Go Round In Circles		0	1973	1	1973	(A&M 1411)
* 6	Space Race		0	1973	4	1973	(A&M 1463)
* 7	Nothing From Nothing		0	1974	1	1974	(A&M 1544)
8	Struttin'		0	1975	22	1975	(A&M 1644)
9	Get Back (Re-Entry)	(AppleR 5777)	28	1976	0	1976	
10	With You I'm Born Again	(MOTOWN TMG 1159)	2	1979	4	1980	(MOTOWN 1477)

ISSUE	TITLE	UK LBL	UK POS	UK YEAR	US POS	US YEAR	US LBL
11	It Will Come In Time	(MOTOWN TMG 1175)	47	1980	0	1980	
12	Get Back (2nd Re-Entry)	(AppleR 5777)	74	1989	0	1989	

HITS 1, 2, 9, 12 ARE CREDITED TO BEATLES WITH BILLY PRESTON • HIT 10 IS CREDITED TO BILLY PRESTON AND SYREETA
SEE ALSO THE APPLE (EP), VARIOUS ARTISTS (EP, LP, 78S)

Billy Ray Cyrus Male Country Vocalist, B: 25 Aug 1961 Flatwoods, Kentucky

ISSUE	TITLE	UK LBL	UK POS	UK YEAR	US POS	US YEAR	US LBL
* 1	Achy Breaky Heart	(Mercury MER 373)	3	1992	46	1992	(Mercury 866522)
2	Could've Been Me	(Mercury MER 378)	24	1992	72	1992	(Mercury 866998)
! 3	Some Gave All		0	1992	52	1992	(Mercury 862094)
4	She's Not Crying Anymore		0	1992	70	1992	(Mercury 864778)
! 5	Wher'm I Gonna Live?		0	1992	23	1992	(Mercury 864502)
6	These Boots Are Made For Walkin'	(Mercury MER 384)	63	1992	0	1992	
7	Achy Breaky Heart	(Epic 6588837)	53	1992	0	1992	
8	In The Heart Of A Woman		0	1993	76	1993	(Mercury 862448)
! 9	Somebody New		0	1993	9	1993	(Mercury 862754)

SEE ALSO DAVID SEVILLE, & THE CHIPMUNKS

Billy Squire Male Vocalist, B: 12 May 1950 Wellesley Hills, Massachusetts

ISSUE	TITLE	UK LBL	UK POS	UK YEAR	US POS	US YEAR	US LBL
1	The Stroke	(Capitol CL 214)	52	1981	17	1981	(Capitol 5005)
2	In The Dark		0	1981	35	1981	(Capitol 5040)
3	Everybody Wants You		0	1982	32	1982	(Capitol 5163)
4	Rock Me Tonight		0	1984	15	1984	(Capitol 5370)

Billy Stewart Male Vocalist, B: 24 Mar 1937 Washington D.C.

ISSUE	TITLE	UK LBL	UK POS	UK YEAR	US POS	US YEAR	US LBL
1	I Do Love You		0	1965	26	1965	(CHESS 1922)
2	Sitting In The Park		0	1965	24	1965	(CHESS 1932)
3	Summertime	(CHESS CRS	39	1966	10	1966	(CHESS 1966)
4	Secret Love		0	1966	29	1966	(CHESS 1978)

OBITUARY : D: 17 JAN 1970 CAR ACCIDENT.

Billy Storm Male Vocalist, B: 29 Jun 1938 Dayton, Ohio

ISSUE	TITLE	UK LBL	UK POS	UK YEAR	US POS	US YEAR	US LBL
1	I've Come Of Age		0	1959	28	1959	(Columbia 41356)

Billy Swan Male Vocalist, B: 12 May 1942 Cape Girardeau, Missouri

ISSUE	TITLE	UK LBL	UK POS	UK YEAR	US POS	US YEAR	US LBL
* 1	I Can Help	(MONUMENT MNT 2752)	6	1974	1	1974	(MONUMENT 8621)
2	Don't Be Cruel	(MONUMENT MNT 3244)	42	1975	0	1975	
! 3	Everything's The Same (Ain't Nothing Changed)		0	1975	17	1975	(MONUMENT 8661)
! 4	Just Want To Taste Your Wine		0	1976	45	1976	(MONUMENT 8682)
! 5	You're The One		0	1976	75	1976	(MONUMENT 8706)
! 6	Shake, Rattle And Roll		0	1976	95	1976	(Columbia 10443)
! 7	Hello! Remember Me		0	1978	30	1978	(A&M 2046)
! 8	No Way Around It (It's Love)		0	1978	97	1978	(A&M 2103)
! 9	Do I Have To Draw A Picture		0	1981	18	1981	(Epic 51000)
! 10	I'm Into Lovin' You		0	1981	18	1981	(Epic 02196)
! 11	Stuck Right In The Middle Of Your Love		0	1981	19	1981	(Epic 02601)
! 12	With Their Kind Of Money And Our Kind Of Love		0	1982	32	1982	(Epic 02841)
! 13	Your Picture Still Loves Me (And I Still Love You)		0	1982	56	1982	(Epic 03226)
! 14	Rainbows And Butterflies		0	1983	39	1983	(Epic 03505)
! 15	Yes		0	1983	67	1983	(Epic 03917)
! 16	You Must Be Lookin' For Me		0	1986	45	1986	(Mercury 884668)
! 17	I'm Gonna Get You		0	1987	63	1987	(Mercury 888320)

HIT 1 REACHED NUMBER 1 IN THE US C/W CHARTS • HIT 3 REACHED NUMBER 91 IN THE US NATIONAL CHARTS

Billy Vaughn Orchestra Male Orchestra Leader, Real Name Richard Vaughn B: 12 Apr 1919 Glasgow, Kentucky

ISSUE	TITLE	UK LBL	UK POS	UK YEAR	US POS	US YEAR	US LBL
* 1	Melody Of Love		0	1955	2	1955	(DOT 15247)
2	Shifting Whispering Sands	(London HLD 8205)	20	1956	5	1955	(DOT 15409)
3	Theme From The Threepenny Opera (Moritat)	(London HLD 8238)	12	1956	37	1956	(DOT 15444)
4	When The White Lilacs Bloom Again		0	1956	18	1956	(DOT 15491)
5	Raunchy		0	1957	10	1957	(DOT 15661)
* 6	Sail Along Silvery Moon		0	1958	5	1957	(DOT 15661)
7	Tumbling Tumbleweeds		0	1958	30	1958	(DOT 15701)
8	La Paloma		0	1958	20	1958	(DOT 15795)
9	Blue Hawaii		0	1959	37	1959	(DOT 15879)
10	Dutchman's Gold		0	1960	30	1960	(DOT 16066)
11	Look For A Star		0	1960	19	1960	(DOT 16106)
* 12	Wheels		0	1961	28	1961	(DOT 16174)
13	A Swingin' Safari		0	1962	13	1962	(DOT 16374)

OBITUARY : D: 26 SEP 1991 CANCER.

ISSUE	TITLE	UK LBL	UK POS	UK YEAR	US POS	US YEAR	US LBL
Billy Vera	Real Name William Mccord Jr B: 28 May 1944 Riverside, California						
1	Country Girl-City Man		0	1968	36	1968	(Atlantic 2480)
2	I Can Take Care Of Myself		0	1981	39	1981	(ALFA 7002)
3	At This Moment		0	1981	79	1981	(ALFA 7005)
* 4	At This Moment (Re-Issue)		0	1986	1	1986	(RHINO 74403)
! 5	She Ain't Johnnie (Re-Recording)		0	1987	93	1987	(MACOLA 9812)
Billy Ward & His Dominoes	Male Vocalist, B: 19 Sep 1921 Los Angeles						
+ 1	I'd Be Satisfied		0	1952	8	1952	(FEDERAL 12105)
+ 2	Rags To Riches		0	1953	3	1953	(KING 1280)
+ 3	The Bells		0	1953	6	1953	(FEDERAL 12114)
+ 4	These Foolish Things Remind Me Of You		0	1953	5	1953	(FEDERAL 12129)
5	St.Therese Of The Roses		0	1956	13	1956	(Decca 29933)
6	Stardust	(London HLU 8465)	13	1957	12	1957	(LIBERTY 55071)
7	Deep Purple	(London HLU 8502)	20	1957	20	1957	(LIBERTY 55099)
8	Stardust (Re-Entry)	(London HLU 8465)	26	1958	0	1958	

FORMED IN 1950 AS THE DOMINOES. LEAD SINGER ON HIT 5 IS JACKIE WILSON • SEE ALSO THE DOMINOES

ISSUE	TITLE	UK LBL	UK POS	UK YEAR	US POS	US YEAR	US LBL
Billy Williams	Male Vocalist, B: 28 Dec 1910 From Waco, Texas						
* 1	My Adobe Hacienda		0	1947	12	1947	(RCA VICTOR 2150)
2	Shanghai		0	1951	20	1951	(MGM 10998)
3	Sin		0	1951	28	1951	(MGM 11066)
4	Pour Me A Glass Of Teardrops		0	1953	30	1953	(Mercury)
5	Sh-Boom (Life Could Be A Dream)		0	1954	21	1954	(CORAL 61212)
* 6	I'm Gonna Sit Right Down And Write Myself A Letter	(VOGUE/CORAL Q 72266)	22	1957	3	1957	(CORAL 61830)
7	I'm Gonna Sit Right Down And Write Myself Aletter (Re-Entry)	(VOGUE/CORAL Q 72266)	28	1957	0	1957	
8	Nola		0	1959	39	1959	(CORAL 62069)

WAS LEAD SINGER WITH THE CHARIOTEERS IN THE 30S AND 40S
FORMED THE BILLY WILLIAMS QUARTET WITH CLAUDE RIDDICK, EUGENE DIXON & JOHN BALL IN 1950
OBITUARY : D: 12 OCT 1972 IN A CHICAGO HOSPITAL

ISSUE	TITLE	UK LBL	UK POS	UK YEAR	US POS	US YEAR	US LBL
Bimbo Jet	Mixed Vocal/Instrumental Group from France						
* 1	El Bimbo	(EMI 2317)	12	1975	0	1975	
Bing Crosby	Male Vocalist, Real Name Harry Lillis Crosby B: 2 May 1901 In Washington						
1	Just A Gigolo		0	1931	12	1931	(VICTOR 22701)
2	Wrap Your Troubles In Dreams		0	1931	4	1931	(VICTOR 22701)
3	Out Of Nowhere (From *Dude Ranch*)		0	1931	1	1931	(Brunswick 6090)
4	Just One More Chance		0	1931	1	1931	(Brunswick 6120)
5	Were You Sincere?		0	1931	12	1931	(Brunswick 6120)
6	I Found A Million-Dollar Baby (From *Crazy Quilt*)		0	1931	2	1931	(Brunswick 6140)
7	I'm Through With Love		0	1931	3	1931	(Brunswick 6140)
8	At Your Command		0	1931	1	1931	(Brunswick 6145)
9	Many Happy Returns Of The Day		0	1931	3	1931	(Brunswick 6145)
10	Star Dust (From *The Band Wagon*)		0	1931	5	1931	(Brunswick 6159)
11	Dancing In The Dark (From *The Band Wagon*)		0	1931	3	1931	(Rrunswick 6159)
12	I Apologize		0	1931	3	1931	(Brunswick 6179)
13	Sweet And Lovely		0	1931	9	1931	(Brunswick 6179)
14	Good Night, Sweetheart (From *Earl Carroll's Vanities* Of 1931)		0	1931	5	1931	(Brunswick 6203)
15	A Faded Summer Love		0	1931	8	1931	(Brunswick 6200)
16	Gems From *George White's Scandals*		0	1931	3	1930	(Brunswick 20102)
17	Dinah		0	1932	1	1932	(Brunswick 6240)
18	Can't We Talk It Over?		0	1932	10	1932	(Brunswick 6240)
19	Where The Blue Of The Night (Meets The Goldof The Day)		0	1932	4	1932	(Brunswick 6226)
20	Snuggled On Your Shoulder (Cuddled In Your Arms)		0	1932	11	1932	(Brunswick 6248)
21	Paradise		0	1932	7	1932	(Brunswick 6285)
22	Shine		0	1932	7	1932	(Brunswick 6276)
23	Lazy Day		0	1932	4	1932	(Brunswick 6306)
24	Sweet Georgia Brown		0	1932	2	1932	(Brunswick 6320)
25	Cabin In The Cotton		0	1932	11	1932	(Brunswick 6329)
26	Love Me Tonight		0	1932	4	1932	(Brunswick 6351)
27	Some Of These Days		0	1932	16	1932	(Brunswick 6351)
28	Please		0	1932	1	1932	(Brunswick 6394)

ISSUE	TITLE	UK LBL	UK POS	UK YEAR	US POS	US YEAR	US LBL
29	Waltzing In A Dream		0	1932	6	1932	(Brunswick 6394)
30	Here Lies Love		0	1932	11	1932	(Brunswick 6394)
31	Brother, Can You Spare A Dime? (From *Americana*)		0	1932	1	1932	(Brunswick 6414)
32	Just An Echo In The Valley (From *Going Hollywood*)		0	1933	2	1933	(Brunswick 6454)
33	(I Don't Stand) A Ghost Of A Chance With You		0	1933	5	1933	(Brunswick 6454)
34	Street Of Dreams		0	1933	13	1933	(Brunswick 6464)
35	You're Getting A To Be A Habit With Me		0	1933	1	1933	(Brunswick 6472)
36	Young And Healthy (From *Forty-Second Street*)		0	1933	2	1933	(Brunswick 6472)
37	You're Beautiful Tonight, My Dear		0	1933	12	1933	(Brunswick 6477)
38	I've Got The World On A String		0	1933	19	1933	(Brunswick 6491)
39	You've Got Me Crying Again		0	1933	12	1933	(Brunswick 6515)
40	Shadow Waltz		0	1933	1	1933	(Brunswick 6599)
41	I've Got To Sing A Torch Song (From *Gold Diggers* Of 1933)		0	1933	9	1933	(Brunswick 6599)
42	Learn To Croon		0	1933	3	1933	(Brunswick 6594)
43	Down The Old Ox Road (College Humor)		0	1933	8	1933	(Brunswick 6601)
44	Blue Prelude		0	1933	10	1933	(Brunswick 6601)
45	My Love		0	1933	4	1933	(Brunswick 6623)
46	Thanks		0	1933	2	1933	(Brunswick 6643)
47	The Day You Came Along (From *Too Much Harmon'*)		0	1933	3	1933	(Brunswick 6644)
48	The Last Round-Up From *Ziegfeld Follies* Of 1934)		0	1933	2	1933	(Brunswick 6663)
49	Home On The Range		0	1933	18	1933	(Brunswick 6663)
50	Beautiful Girl (From *Going Hollywood*)		0	1933	11	1933	(Brunswick 6694)
51	Temptation (From *Going Hollywood*)		0	1933	3	1933	(Brunswick 6695)
52	We'll Make Hay While The Sun Shines (From *Going Hollywood*)		0	1934	8	1934	(Brunswick 6695)
53	Did You Ever See A Dream Walking (From *Sitting Pretty*)		0	1933	5	1933	(Brunswick 6724)
54	Little Dutch Mill		0	1934	1	1934	(Brunswick 6794)
55	Good Night, Lovely Little Lady (From *We're Not Dressing*)		0	1934	2	1934	(Brunswick 6854)
56	Once In A Blue Moon (From *We're Not Dressing*)		0	1934	11	1934	(Brunswick 6854)
57	Love Thy Neighbor (From *We're Not Dressing*)		0	1934	2	1934	(Brunswick 6852)
58	Ridin' Around In The Rain		0	1934	13	1934	(Brunswick 6852)
59	May I? (From *We're Not Dressing*)		0	1934	4	1934	(Brunswick 6853)
60	She Reminds Me Of You (From *We're Not Dressing*)		0	1934	10	1934	(Brunswick6853)
61	Love In Bloom (From *She Loves Me Not*)		0	1934	1	1934	(Brunswick 6936)
62	Straight From The Shoulder (From *She Loves Me Not*)		0	1934	16	1934	(Brunswick 6936)
63	Give Me A Heart To Sing To		0	1934	12	1934	(Brunswick 6953)
64	Two Cigarettes In The Dark (From *Kill That Story*)		0	1934	5	1934	(Decca 245)
65	The Very Thought Of You		0	1934	11	1934	(Decca 179)
66	The Moon Was Yellow (And The Night Was Young)		0	1934	13	1934	(Decca 179)
67	June In January (From *Here Is My Heart*)		0	1934	1	1934	(Decca 310)
68	Love Is Just Around The Corner (From *Here Is My Heart*)		0	1934	8	1934	(Decca 310)
69	With Every Breath I Take (From *Here Is My Heart*)		0	1934	4	1934	(Decca 309)
70	Maybe I'm Wrong Again		0	1934	14	1934	(Decca 309)
71	Soon (From *Mississippi*)		0	1935	1	1935	(Decca 392)
72	Down By The River (From *Mississippi*)		0	1935	17	1935	(Decca 392)
73	It's Easy To Remember (From *Mississippi*)		0	1935	1	1935	(Decca 391)
74	I Wished On The Moon (From *The Big Broadcast* Of 1936)		0	1935	2	1935	(Decca 543)
75	Without A Word Of Warning (From *Two For Tonight*)		0	1935	5	1935	(Decca 548)
76	I Wish I Were Aladdin		0	1935	7	1935	(Decca 547)
77	From The Top Of Your Head		0	1935	10	1935	(Decca 547)
78	Red Sails In The Sunset (From *Provincetown Follies*)		0	1935	1	1935	(Decca 616)
* 79	Silent Night		0	1935	7	1935	(Decca 621)
80	On Treasure Island		0	1935	8	1935	(Decca 617)
81	Would You? (From *San Francisco*)		0	1936	20	1936	(Decca 756)
82	The Touch Of Your Lips		0	1936	4	1936	(Decca 757)
83	Robins And Roses		0	1936	2	1936	(Decca 791)
84	It Ain't Necessarily So (From *Porgy And Bess*)		0	1936	18	1936	(Decca 806)
85	I'm An Old Cowhand (From *Rhythm On The Range*)		0	1936	2	1936	(Decca 871)
86	I Can't Escape From You (From *Rhythm On The Range*)		0	1936	7	1936	(Decca 871)
87	Empty Saddles (From *Rhythm On The Range*)		0	1936	8	1936	(Decca 870)
88	Song Of The Islands		0	1936	14	1936	(Decca 880)
89	South Sea Island Magic		0	1936	3	1936	(Decca 886)
90	Me And The Moon		0	1936	9	1936	(Decca 912)
91	Pennies From Heaven (From*Pennies From Heaven*)		0	1936	1	1936	(Decca 947)
92	Let's Call A Heart A Heart (From *Pennies From Heaven*)		0	1936	10	1936	(Decca 947)
93	So Do I (From *Pennies From Heaven*)		0	1936	18	1936	(Decca 948)

ISSUE	TITLE	UK LBL	UK POS	UK YEAR	US POS	US YEAR	US LBL
94	One, Two, Button Your Shoe (From *Pennies From Heaven*)		0	1937	19	1937	(Decca 948)
* 95	Blue Leilani		0	1937	1	1937	(Decca 1175)
96	Blue Hawaii		0	1937	5	1937	(Decca 1175)
97	Too Marvelous For Words (From *Ready, Willing And Able*)		0	1937	1	1937	(Decca 1185)
98	What Will I Tell My Heart? (From *Ready, Willing And Able*)		0	1937	5	1935	(Decca 1185)
99	Sweet Is The Word For You (From W*akiki Wedding*)		0	1937	8	1937	(Decca 1184)
100	Never In A Million Years (From *Wake Up And Live*)		0	1937	2	1937	(Decca 1210)
101	Moonlight And Shadows		0	1937	10	1937	(Decca 1186)
102	My Little Buckaroo		0	1937	19	1937	(Decca 1234)
103	Peckin' (From *New Faces* Of 1937)		0	1937	9	1937	(Decca 1301)
104	The Moon Got In My Eyes (From *Double Or Nothing*)		0	1937	1	1937	(Decca 1375)
105	(You Know It All) Smarty (From *Double Or Nothing*)		0	1937	18	1937	(Decca 1375)
106	It's The Natural Thing To Do (From *Double Or Nothing*)		0	1937	2	1937	(Decca 1376)
107	Remember Me? (From Mr.*Dodd Takes The Air*)		0	1937	1	1937	(Decca 1451)
108	I Still Love To Kiss You Goodnight (From *Fifty-Second Street*)		0	1937	6	1937	(Decca 1451)
109	Can I Forget You? (From *High, Wide And Handsome*)		0	1937	8	1937	(Decca 1462)
110	Bob White (Whatcha Gonna Swing Tonight?)		0	1937	1	1937	(Decca 1483)
111	Basin Street Blues		0	1937	12	1937	(Decca 1483)
112	The One Rose (That's Left In My Heart)		0	1937	8	1937	(Decca 1201)
113	Sail Along, Silvery Moon		0	1937	4	1937	(Decca 1518)
114	When The Organ Played Oh Promise Me		0	1938	5	1938	(Decca 1554)
115	There's A Gold Mine In The Sky		0	1938	6	1938	(Decca 1565)
116	On The Sentimental Side (From *Doctor Rhythm*)		0	1938	4	1938	(Decca 1648)
117	Moon Of Manakoora (From *The Hurricane*)		0	1938	10	1938	(Decca 1649)
118	Let Me Whisper I Love You		0	1980	7	1938	(Decca 1819)
119	When Mother Nature Sings Her Lullaby		0	1938	3	1938	(Decca 1874)
120	Now It Can Be Told (From *Alexander's Ragtime Band*)		0	1938	7	1938	(Decca 1888)
121	I've Got A Pocket Of Dreams (From *Sing, You Sinners*)		0	1938	1	1938	(Decca 1933)
122	Small Fry		0	1938	3	1938	(Decca 1960)
123	Mr.Gallagher And Mr.Shean		0	1938	7	1938	(Decca 1960)
124	Alexander's Ragtime Band (From *Alexander's Ragtime Band*)		0	1938	1	1938	(Decca 1887)
125	Don't Let That Moon Get Away		0	1938	19	1938	(Decca 1934)
126	Mexicali Rose		0	1938	3	1938	(Decca 2001)
127	My Reverie		0	1938	3	1938	(Decca 2123)
128	You Must Have Been A Beautiful Baby (From *Hard To Get*)		0	1938	1	1938	(Decca 2147)
129	Silent Night (Re-Entry)		0	1938	10	1938	(Decca 621)
130	You're A Sweet Little Headache (From *Paris Honeymoon*)		0	1939	3	1939	(Decca 2200)
131	I Have Eyes (From *Paris Honeymoon*)		0	1939	4	1939	(Decca 2201)
132	The Funny Old Hills (From *Paris Honeymoon*)		0	1939	5	1939	(Decca 2201)
133	Someone Stole Gabriel's Horn		0	1939	14	1939	(Brunswick 6533)
134	It's A Lonely Trail 'When You're Travelin' All Alone		0	1939	17	1939	(Decca 2237)
135	The Lonsome Road		0	1939	12	1939	(Decca 2257)
136	I Cried For You		0	1939	13	1939	(Decca 2273)
137	Between A Kiss And A Sigh		0	1939	15	1939	(Decca 2289)
138	My Melancholy Baby		0	1939	14	1939	(Decca 2289)
139	Ah! Sweet Mystery Of Life Naughty Marletta)		0	1939	12	1939	(Decca 2315)
140	East Side Of Heaven (From *East Side Of Heaven*)		0	1939	6	1939	(Decca 2359)
141	Sing A Song Of Sunbeams (From *East Side Of Heaven*)		0	1939	8	1939	(Decca 2359)
142	Deep Purple		0	1939	14	1939	(Decca 2374)
143	God Bless America		0	1939	17	1939	(Decca 2400)
144	That Sly Old Gentleman (From Featherbed Lane)		0	1939	10	1939	(Decca 2360)
145	Little Sir Echo		0	1939	3	1939	(Decca 2385)
146	And The Angels Sing		0	1939	10	1939	(Decca 2413)
147	Alla En El Rancho Grande		0	1939	6	1939	(Decca 2494)
148	Whistling In The Wildwood		0	1939	14	1939	(Decca 2448)
149	An Apple For The Teacher (From *The Star Maker*)		0	1939	2	1939	(Decca 2640)
150	Go Fly A Kite (From *The Star Maker*)		0	1939	10	1939	(Decca 2641)
151	A Man And His Dream (From *The Star Maker*)		0	1939	4	1939	(Decca 2641)
152	(Ho-Die-Ay) Start The Day Right		0	1939	12	1939	(Decca 2626)
153	What's New?		0	1939	2	1939	(Decca 2671)
154	My Isle Of Golden Dreams		0	1939	18	1939	(Decca 2775)
155	Between 18th And 19th On Chestnut Street		0	1940	12	1940	(Decca 2948)
156	Sweet Potato Piper (From *The Road To Singapore*)		0	1940	11	1940	(Decca 2999)
157	Just One More Chance (Re-Recording)		0	1940	16	1940	(Decca 2999)
158	I'm Too Romantic (From *The Road To Singapore*)		0	1940	3	1940	(Decca 2998)

ISSUE	TITLE	UK LBL	UK POS	UK YEAR	US POS	US YEAR	US LBL
159	The Singing Hills		0	1940	3	1940	(Decca 3064)
160	Tumbling Tumbleweeds		0	1940	12	1940	(Decca 3024)
161	April Played The Fiddle (From *If I Had My Way*)		0	1940	10	1940	(Decca 3161)
162	I Haven't Time To Be A Millionare (From *If I Had My Way*)		0	1940	13	1940	(Decca 3161)
163	Meet The Sun Half-Way (From *If I Had My Way*)		0	1940	15	1940	(Decca 3162)
164	Sierra Sue		0	1940	1	1940	(Decca 3133)
165	Mister Meadowlark		0	1940	18	1940	(Decca 3182)
166	Trade Winds		0	1940	1	1940	(Decca 3299)
167	Can't Get Indiana Off My Mind		0	1940	8	1940	(Decca 3321)
168	That's For Me (From *Rhythm Of The River*)		0	1940	9	1940	(Decca 3309)
169	Only Forever (From *Rhythm Of The River*)		0	1940	1	1940	(Decca 3300)
170	When The Moon Comes Over Madison Square (From *Rhythm Of The River*)		0	1940	27	1940	(Decca 3300)
171	Where The Blue Of The Night (Meets The Gold of The Day) (Re-Recording)		0	1940	27	1940	(Decca 2254)
172	You Made Me Love You		0	1940	25	1940	(Decca 3423)
173	Please (Re-Recording)		0	1941	24	1941	(Decca 3450)
174	Along The Santa Fe Trail		0	1941	4	1941	(Decca 3565)
175	Lone Star Trail		0	1941	23	1941	(Decca 3584)
176	New San Antonio Rose		0	1941	7	1941	(Decca 3590)
177	It Makes No Difference Now		0	1941	23	1941	(Decca 3590)
178	Does Your Mother Come From Ireland?		0	1941	22	1941	(Decca 3609)
179	Dolores (From *Las Vegas Nights*)		0	1941	2	1941	(Decca 3644)
180	Paradise Isle		0	1941	23	1941	(Decca 3797)
181	You And I		0	1941	5	1941	(Decca 3840)
182	Brahms' Lullaby (Cradle Song)		0	1941	20	1941	(Decca 3840)
183	'Til Reveille		0	1941	6	1941	(Decca 3886)
184	Be Honest With Me		0	1941	19	1941	(Decca 3856)
185	You Are My Sunshine		0	1941	19	1941	(Decca 3852)
186	The Whistler's Mother-In-Law		0	1941	9	1941	(Decca 3971)
187	The Waiter And The Porter And The Upstairs Maid		0	1941	23	1941	(Decca 3970)
188	Clementine		0	1941	20	1941	(Decca 4033)
189	Shepherd Serenade		0	1941	4	1941	(Decca 4065)
190	The Anniversary Waltz		0	1941	24	1941	(Decca 4065)
191	Silent Night (2nd Re-Entry)		0	1941	11	1941	(Decca 621)
192	Deep In The Heart Of Texas		0	1942	3	1942	(Decca 4162)
193	I Don't Want To Walk Without You (From *Sweater Girl*)		0	1942	9	1942	(Decca 4184)
194	Sing Me A Song Of The Islands (From *Song Of The Islands*)		0	1942	22	1942	(Decca 4173)
195	Miss You (From *Strictly In The Groove*)		0	1942	9	1942	(Decca 4193)
196	The Lamplighter's Serenade		0	1942	23	1942	(Decca 4249)
197	When The White Azaleas Start Blooming		0	1942	21	1942	(Decca 18391)
198	Skylark		0	1942	14	1942	(Decca 4193)
199	The Bombardier Song		0	1942	19	1942	(Decca 18432)
200	Be Careful, It's My Heart		0	1942	2	1942	(Decca 18424)
* 201	White Christmas (From *Holiday Inn*)		0	1942	1	1942	(Decca 18429)
202	Moonlight Becomes You (From *The Road To Morocco*)		0	1942	1	1942	(Decca 18513)
203	Constantly (From *The Road To Morocco*)		0	1943	13	1943	(Decca 18513)
* 204	Sunday, Monday, Or Always (From *Dixie*)		0	1943	1	1943	(Decca 18561)
205	If You Please (From *Dixie*)		0	1943	5	1943	(Decca 18561)
206	Mary's A Grand Old Name (From *Forty-Five Minutes*)		0	1943	20	1943	(Decca 18360)
207	People Will Say We're In Love (From *Oklahoma!*)		0	1943	2	1943	(Decca 18564)
208	Oh, What A Beautiful Mornin' (From *Oklahoma!*)		0	1943	4	1943	(Decca 18564)
* 209	I'll Be Home For Christmas		0	1943	3	1943	(Decca 18570)
210	White Christmas (Re-Entry)		0	1943	6	1943	(Decca 18429)
211	Let's Start The New Year Right (From *Holiday Inn*)		0	1943	18	1943	(Decca 18429)
212	San Fernando Valley		0	1944	1	1944	(Decca 18586)
213	Poinciana		0	1944	3	1944	(Decca 18586)
214	I Love You (From *Mexican Hayride*)		0	1944	1	1944	(Decca 18595)
215	I'll Be Seeing You (From *Right This Way*)		0	1944	1	1944	(Decca 18595)
* 216	Swinging On A Star		0	1944	1	1944	(Decca 18597)
* 217	Going My Way		0	1944	1	1944	(Decca 18597)
218	Amor (From *Broadway Rhythm*)		0	1944	2	1944	(Decca 18608)
219	Long Ago (And Far Away) (From *Cover Girl*)		0	1944	5	1944	(Decca 18608)
220	The Day After Forever		0	1944	15	1944	(Decca 18580)
221	It Could Happen To You (From *And The Angels Sing*)		0	1944	18	1944	(Decca 18580)
* 222	Too-Ra-Loo-Ra-Loo-Ral (From *Shameen Dhu*)		0	1944	4	1944	(Decca 18621)
223	Sweet And Lovely (Re-Issue)		0	1944	27	1944	(Brunswick 80057)
224	White Christmas (2nd Re-Entry)		0	1944	5	1944	(Decca 18570)

ISSUE	TITLE	UK LBL	UK POS	UK YEAR	US POS	US YEAR	US LBL
225	I'll Be Home For Christmas (Re-Entry)		0	1944	16	1944	(Decca 18570)
226	Evelina (From *Bloomer Girl*)		0	1945	9	1945	(Decca 18635)
227	Sleigh Ride In July (From *Belle Of The Yukon*)		0	1945	14	1945	(Decca 18640)
228	Like Someone In Love (From *Belle Of The Yukon*)		0	1945	15	1945	(Decca 18640)
229	Just A Prayer Away		0	1945	4	1945	(Decca 18658)
230	All Of My Life		0	1950	12	1945	(Decca 18658)
231	Yah-Ta-Ta, Yah-Ta-Ta (Talk, Talk, Talk)		0	1945	5	1945	(Decca 23410)
232	You Belong To My Heart (From *The Three Caballeros*)		0	1945	3	1945	(Decca 23413)
233	Baia (From The Three Caballeros)		0	1945	6	1945	(Decca 23413)
234	My Baby Said Yes		0	1945	14	1945	(Decca 23417)
235	On The Atchison, Topeka And The Santa Fe (From *The Harvey Girls*)		0	1945	3	1945	(Decca 18690)
236	If I Loved You (From *Carousel*)		0	1945	8	1945	(Decca 18686)
237	It's Been A Long, Long Time		0	1945	1	1945	(Decca 18708)
238	The Road To Morocco (From the same film)		0	1945	21	1945	(Decca 40000)
* 239	I Can't Begin To Tell You (From *Dolly Sisters*)		0	1945	1	1945	(Decca 23457)
240	White Christmas (3rd Re-Entry)		0	1945	1	1945	(Decca 18429)
241	Aren't You Glad You're You(From *The Bells of St. Mary's*)		0	1945	8	1945	(Decca 18720)
242	In The Land Of Beginning Again (From *The Bells Of St Mary's*)		0	1946	18	1946	(Decca 18720)
243	Symphony		0	1946	3	1946	(Decca 18735)
244	Give Me The Simple Life (From *Wake Up And Dream*)		0	1946	16	1946	(Decca 23469)
245	The Bells Of St.Mary's (From the same movie)		0	1946	21	1946	(Decca 18721)
* 246	Mcnamara's Band		0	1946	10	1946	(Decca 23405)
247	Day By Day		0	1946	15	1946	(Decca 18746)
248	Sioux City Sue		0	1946	3	1946	(Decca 23508)
249	Personality (From *The Road To Utopia*)		0	1946	9	1946	(Decca 18790)
250	They Say It's Wonderful (From *Annie Get Your Gun*)		0	1946	12	1946	(Decca 18829)
251	Night And Day (From *Gay Divorce*)		0	1946	21	1946	(Decca 18887)
252	You Keep Coming Back Like A Song (From *Blue Skies*)		0	1946	12	1946	(Decca 23647)
253	White Christmas (Re-Issue)		0	1946	1	1946	(Decca 23778)
254	A Gal In Calico (From *The Time, The Place, And The Girl*)		0	1947	8	1947	(Decca 23739)
255	Easter Parade (From *As Thousands Cheer*)		0	1947	22	1947	(Decca 23819)
256	That's How Much I Love You		0	1947	17	1947	(Decca 23840)
* 257	Alexander's Ragtime Band		0	1947	20	1947	(Decca 40038)
258	Feudin' And Fightin' (From *Laffing Room Only*)		0	1947	9	1947	(Decca 23975)
259	You Do (From *Mother Wore Tights*)		0	1947	8	1947	(Decca 24101)
260	How Soon (Will I Be Seeing You)		0	1947	6	1947	(Decca 24101)
* 261	Whiffenpoof Song		0	1947	7	1947	(Decca 23990)
262	White Christmas (Re-Isue) (Re-Entry)		0	1947	3	1947	(Decca 23778)
263	Silent Night (Re-Issue)		0	1947	22	1947	(Decca 23777)
264	Ballerina		0	1948	10	1948	(Decca 24278)
* 265	Now Is The Hour		0	1948	1	1948	(Decca 24279)
266	Pass That Peace Pipe (From *Good News*)		0	1948	21	1948	(Decca 24269)
267	But Beautiful (From *The Road To Rio*)		0	1948	20	1948	(Decca 24283)
268	Easter Parade (Re-Entry)		0	1948	22	1948	(Decca 23819)
269	Blue Shadows On The Trail		0	1948	23	1948	(Decca 24433)
270	A Fella WIth An Umbrella (From *Easter Parade*)		0	1948	23	1948	(Decca 24433)
271	White Christmas (Re-Issue) (2nd Re-Entry)		0	1948	6	1948	(Decca 23778)
272	Far Away Places		0	1949	2	1949	(Decca 24532)
* 273	Galway Bay		0	1949	3	1949	(Decca 24295)
274	If You Stub Your Toe On The Moon		0	1949	27	1949	(Decca 24524)
275	Careless Hands		0	1949	12	1949	(Decca 24616)
276	Riders In The Sky (Movie Title Theme)		0	1949	14	1949	(Decca 24618)
277	Some Enchanted Everning (From South Pacific)		0	1949	3	1949	(Decca 24609)
278	Bali Ha'i (From South Pacific)		0	1949	12	1949	(Decca 24609)
* 279	Dear Hearts And Gentle People		0	1949	2	1949	(Decca 24798)
280	Mule Train		0	1949	4	1949	(Decca 24798)
281	Way Back Home		0	1949	21	1949	(Decca 24800)
282	White Christmas (Re-Issue) (3rd Re-Entry)		0	1949	5	1949	(Decca 23778)
283	Chattanoogie Shoe-Shine Boy		0	1950	4	1950	(Decca 24863)
284	I Didn't Slip - I Wasn't Pushed – I Fell		0	1950	22	1950	(Decca 27018)
* 285	Play A Simple Melody (From *Watch Your Step*)		0	1950	2	1950	(Decca 27112)
286	Sam's Song		0	1950	3	1950	(Decca 27112)
287	La Vie En Rose		0	1950	13	1950	(Decca 27111)
288	I Cross My Fingers		0	1950	18	1950	(Decca 27111)
289	All My Love		0	1950	11	1950	(Decca 27117)
290	Beyond The Reef		0	1950	26	1950	(Decca 27219)

ISSUE	TITLE	UK LBL	UK POS	UK YEAR	US POS	US YEAR	US LBL
291	Harbour Lights		0	1950	8	1950	(Decca 27219)
292	White Christmas (Re-Issue) (4th Re-Entry)		0	1950	13	1950	(Decca 23778)
293	Rudolph, The Red-Nosed Reindeer		0	1950	14	1950	(Decca 27159)
294	A Crosby Christmas		0	1950	22	1950	(Decca 40181)
295	A Marshmellow World		0	1951	24	1951	(Decca 27230)
296	When You And I Were Young, Maggie, Blues		0	1951	8	1951	(Decca 27577)
297	Moonlight Bay		0	1951	14	1951	(Decca 27577)
298	Gone Fishin'		0	1951	19	1951	(Decca 27623)
299	In The Cool, Cool Of The Evening (From *Here Comes The Groom*)		0	1951	11	1951	(Decca 27678)
300	Shanghai		0	1951	21	1951	(Decca 27653)
301	Domino		0	1951	15	1951	(Decca 27830)
302	White Christmas (Re-Issue) 5th Re-Entry)		0	1951	13	1951	(Decca 23778)
303	Watermelon Weather		0	1952	28	1952	(Decca 28238)
304	Till The End Of The World		0	1952	16	1952	(Decca 28265)
305	Zing A Little Zong	(Brunswick 04981)	11	1952	18	1952	(Decca 28255)
306	Isle Of Innisfree	(Brunswick 04900)	3	1952	0	1952	
* 307	Silent Night - Adeste Fideles	(Brunswick 03929)	8	1952	0	1942	
308	Silver Bells (From *The Lemon Drop Kid*)		0	1952	20	1952	(Decca 27229)
309	Keep It A Secret		0	1952	28	1952	(Decca 28511)
310	You Don't Know What Lonesome Is		0	1953	23	1953	(Decca 28470)
311	Open Up Your Heart		0	1953	22	1953	(Decca 28470)
312	Hush-A-Bye		0	1953	24	1953	(Decca 28581)
313	White Christmas (Re-Issue) (6th Re-Entry)		0	1953	21	1953	(Decca 23778)
314	Changing Partners	(Brunswick 05244)	10	1954	13	1954	(Decca 28969)
315	Y'all Come		0	1954	20	1954	(Decca 28969)
316	Down By The Riverside		0	1954	28	1954	(Decca 28955)
317	Changing Partners (Re-Entry)	(Brunswick 05244)	9	1954	0	1954	
318	Changing Partners (2nd Re-Entry)	(Brunswick 05244)	11	1954	0	1954	
319	Young At Heart		0	1954	24	1954	(Decca 29054)
320	Count Your Blessings (Instead Of Sheep)	(Brunswick 05339)	18	1955	1	1955	(Decca 29251)
321	Count Your Blessings (Re-Entry)	(Brunswick 05339)	11	1955	0	1955	
322	White Christmas (Re-Issue) (7th Re-Entry)		0	1954	21	1954	(Decca 23778)
323	Stranger In Paradise	(Brunswick05410)	17	1955	0	1955	
324	White Christmas (Re-Issue) (8th Re-Entry)		0	1955	7	1955	(Decca 23778)
325	In A Little Spanish Town	(Brunswick 05543)	22	1956	0	1956	
* 326	True Love	(Capitol CL 14645)	4	1956	3	1956	(Capitol 3507)
327	Around The World	(Brunswick 05674)	5	1957	25	1957	(Decca 30262)
328	White Christmas (Re-Issue) (9th Re-Entry)		0	1957	34	1957	(Decca 23778)
329	White Christmas (Re-Issue) (10th Re-Entry)		0	1960	26	1960	(Decca 23778)
330	White Christmas (Re-Issue) (11th Re-Entry)		0	1961	12	1961	(Decca 23778)
331	White Christmas (Re-Issue) (12th Re-Entry)		0	1962	38	1962	(Decca 23778)
332	That's What Life Is All About	(United Artists UP	41	1975	0	1975	
333	White Christmas	(MCA 111)	5	1977	0	1977	
334	Peace On Earth - Little Drummer Boy	(RCA BOW 12)	3	1982	0	1982	
335	True Love (Re-Entry)	(Capitol CL 315)	70	1983	0	1983	
336	White Christmas (Re-Issue)	(MCA BING 1)	69	1985	0	1985	

THE HIT 'WHITE CHRISTMAS' HAS SOLD OVER 30 MILLION WORLDWIDE • OBITUARY: BING D: 14 OCT 1977 HEART ATTACK.

Bing Crosby & Andrew Sisters   See Also Separate Entries

* 3	Pistol Packin' Mama		0	1943	2	1943	(Decca 23277)
* 5	Jingle Bells		0	1943	19	1943	(Decca 23281)
* 8	Don't Fence Me In (From *Hollywood Canteen*)		0	1944	1	1944	(Decca 23364)
9	Ac-Cent-Tchu-Ate The Positive (From *Here Come The Waves*)		0	1945	2	1945	(Decca 23379)
* 12	South America, Take It Away (From *Call Me Mister*)		0	1946	2	1946	(Decca 23569)
13	Get Your Kicks On Route 66		0	1946	14	1946	(Decca 23569)
14	Tallahassee (From *Variety Girl*)		0	1947	10	1947	(Decca 23885)
15	There's No Business Like Show Business (From *Annie Get Your Gun*)		0	1947	25	1947	(Decca 40039)
16	The Freedom Train		0	1947	21	1947	(Decca 23999)
17	Jingle Bells (Re-Entry)		0	1947	21	1947	(Decca 23281)
18	Santa Claus Is Comin' To Town		0	1947	22	1947	(Decca 23281)
19	You Don't Have To Know The Language (From *The Road To Rio*)		0	1948	21	1948	(Decca 24282)
20	160 Acres		0	1948	23	1948	(Decca 24481)
21	Have I Told You Lately That I Love You?		0	1950	24	1950	(Decca 24827)
22	Quicksilver		0	1950	6	1950	(Decca 24827)
23	Sparrow In The Tree Top		0	1951	8	1951	(Decca 27477)

HIT 15 IS CREDITED TO BING CROSBY, ANDREW SISTERS & DICK HAYMES

ISSUE	TITLE	UK LBL	UK POS	UK YEAR	US POS	US YEAR	US LBL
Bingoboys	Male Dance DJ Trio From Vienna, Austria						
1	How To Dance		0	1991	25	1991	(Atlantic 87756)
Biohazard	Male Vocal/Instrumental Group from the UK						
1	Tales From The Hard Side	(Warner Bros. W 0254CD)	47	1994	0	1994	
2	How It Is	(Warner Bros. W 0259CD)	62	1994	0	1994	
Biosphere	Male Instrumentalist (Keyboards) Ger Jenssen From Norway						
1	Novelty Waves	(Apollo Apollo 020CDX)	51	1995	0	1995	
Birdland	Male Vocal/Instrumental Group from the UK						
1	Hollow Heart	(LAZY LAZY 13)	70	1989	0	1989	
2	Paradise	(LAZY LAZY 14)	70	1989	0	1989	
3	Sleep With Me	(LAZY LAZY 17)	32	1990	0	1990	
4	Rock And Roll Nigger	(LAZY LAZY 20)	47	1990	0	1990	
5	Everybody Needs Somebody	(LAZY LAZY 24)	44	1991	0	1991	
Birds	Male Vocal/Instrumental Group from the UK						
1	Leaving Here	(Decca F 12140)	45	1965	0	1965	
Bis	Mix Vocal/Instrumental Group from the UK						
1	Secret Vampire Soundtrack (EP)	(Chemikal Underground CHEM 003CD)	25	1996	0	1996	
2	Bis Vs The D.I.Y. Corps	(TEEN-C SKETCH 001CD)	45	1996	0	1996	
3	Atom Powered Action (EP)	(WIIIJA WIJ 55CD)	54	1996	0	1996	
4	Sweet Shop Avengerz	(WIIIJA WIJ 67CD)	46	1997	0	1997	
5	Everybody Thinks That They're Going To Get Theirs	(WIIIJA WIJ 69CD)	64	1997	0	1997	
Bitty McLean	Male Vocalist from the UK						
1	It Keeps Rainin' (Tears From My Eyes)	(Brilliant CDBRIL 1)	2	1993	0	1993	
2	Pass It On	(Brilliant CDBRIL 2)	35	1993	0	1993	
3	Here I Stand	(Brilliant CDBRIL 3)	10	1994	0	1994	(Columbia 44797)
4	Dedicated To The One I Love	(Brilliant CDBRIL 4)	6	1994	0	1994	
5	What Goes Around	(Brilliant CDBRIL 5)	36	1994	0	1994	
6	Over The River	(Brilliant CDBRIL 9)	27	1995	0	1995	
7	We've Only Just Begun	(Brilliant CDBRIL 10)	23	1995	0	1995	
8	Nothing Can Change This Love	(Brilliant CDBRIL 11)	55	1995	0	1995	
9	Natural High	(Brilliant CDBRIL 12)	63	1996	0	1996	
10	She's Alright	(KUFF KUFFD 9)	53	1996	0	1996	
Biz Markie	Male Rapper, Real Name Marce Hall B: 8 Apr 1964 Harlem						
1	Just A Friend	(COOL CHILLIN' W 9823)	55	1990	9	1990	(COLD CHILL 22784)
Bizarre Inc	Male Production/Instrumental Group from the UK						
1	Playing With Knives	(Vinyl Solution Storm 25R)	43	1991	0	1991	
2	Such A Feeling	(Vinyl Solution Storm 325)	13	1991	0	1991	
3	Playing With Knives (Re-Issue)	(Vinyl Solution Storm 25R)	4	1991	0	1991	
4	I'm Gonna Get You	(Vinyl Solution Storm 46S)	3	1992	0	1992	
5	I'm Gonna Get You (Re-Entry)	(Vinyl Solution Storm 46S)	72	1993	0	1993	
6	Took My Love	(Vinyl Solution Storm 60CD)	19	1993	0	1993	
7	Keep The Music Strong	(SOME BIZARRE MERCD 451)	33	1996	0	1996	
8	Surprise	(SOME BIZARRE MERCD 462)	21	1996	0	1996	
9	Get Up Sunshine Street	(SOME BIZARRE MERCD 471)	45	1996	0	1996	
Bizz Nizz	Mixed Vocal/Instrumental Group from the USA/Belgium						
1	Don't Miss The Party Line	(COOLTEMPO COOL 203)	7	1990	0	1990	
Bjork	Female Vocalist from Iceland						
1	Ooops	(ZTT ZANG 19)	42	1991	0	1991	
2	Human Behaviour	(One Little Indian 112 TP7CD)	36	1993	0	1993	
3	Venus As A Boy	(One Little Indian 122 TP7CD)	29	1993	0	1993	
4	Play Dead	(Island CID 573)	12	1993	0	1993	
5	Big Time Sensuality	(One Little Indian 132 TP7CD)	17	1993	0	1993	
6	Violently Happy	(One Little Indian 142 TP7CD)	13	1994	0	1994	
7	Army Of Me	(One Little Indian TP7CD)162	10	1995	0	1995	
8	Isobel	(One Little Indian 172 TP7CD)	23	1995	0	1995	
9	It's Oh So Quiet	(One Little Indian 182 TP7CD)	4	1995	0	1995	
10	Hyperballad	(One Little Indian 192 TP7CD)	8	1996	0	1996	
11	Possibly Maybe	(One Little Indian 193 TP7CD)	13	1996	0	1996	
12	Step By Step	(Arista 74321449332)	37	1997	0	1997	
13	I Miss You	(One Little Indian 194 TP7CD)	40	1997	0	1997	

ISSUE	TITLE	UK LBL	UK POS	UK YEAR	US POS	US YEAR	US LBL
Bjorn Again Mixed Vocal/Instrumental Group from Australia							
1	Erasure-Ish (A Little Respect)	(M&G MAGS 32)	25	1992	0	1992	
2	Santa Claus Is Coming To Town	(M&G MAGS 35)	55	1992	0	1992	
3	Flashdance	(M&G MAGCD 50)	65	1993	0	1993	
Black Male Vocalist Colin Vearncombe from the UK							
1	Wonderful Life	(UGLY MAN JACK71)	72	1986	0	1986	
2	Sweetest Smile	(A&M AM 394)	8	1987	0	1987	
3	Wonderful Life (Re-Recording)	(A&M AM 402)	8	1987	0	1987	
4	Paradise	(A&M AM 422)	38	1988	0	1988	
5	The Big One	(A&M AM 468)	54	1988	0	1988	
6	Now You're Gone	(A&M AM 491)	66	1989	0	1989	
7	Feel Like Change	(A&M AM 780)	56	1991	0	1991	
8	Here It Comes Again	(A&M AM 753)	70	1991	0	1991	
9	Wonderful Life (Re-Recording) (Re-Issue)	(Polygram TV 5805552)	42	1994	0	1994	
Black Box Dance Trio from Italy with Mirko Limoni & Valerio Semplici							
1	Ride On Time	(Deconstruction PB 43055)	1	1989	0	1989	
2	Everybody Everybody	(Deconstruction PB 43715)	16	1990	8	1990	(RCA 2628)
3	I Don't Know Anybody Else	(Deconstruction PB 43479)	4	1990	23	1990	(RCA 2735)
4	Fantasy	(Deconstruction PB 43895)	5	1990	0	1990	
5	The Total Mix	(Deconstruction PB 44235)	12	1990	0	1990	
6	Strike It Up		0	1991	8	1991	(RCA 2794)
7	Strike It Up / Ride On Time (Re-Mix)	(Deconstruction PB 44459)	16	1991	6	1991	(Not Known)
8	Open Your Eyes	(Deconstruction PB 45053)	48	1991	0	1991	
9	Rockin' To The Music	(Deconstruction 74321158122)	39	1993	0	1993	
10	Not Anyone	(Mercury MERCD 434)	31	1995	0	1995	
11	I Got The Vibration / Positive Vibration	(MAIFESTO MERCD 459)	21	1996	0	1996	
	THERE IS SOME CONFUSION AS TO WHO IS THE LEAD SINGER, KATRIN QUINOL (FRENCH MODEL) OR MARTHA WASH OF THE WEATHER GIRLS						
Black Crowes Male Vocal/Instrumental Group from the USA							
1	Hard To Handle	(DEF AMER DEFA 6)	45	1990	45	1990	(DEF AMER 19245)
2	Jealous Again - She Talks To Angels	(DEF AMER DEFA 8)	70	1991	30	1991	(DEF AMER 19403)
3	Twice As Hard	(DEF AMER DEFA 7)	47	1991	0	1991	
4	Hard To Handle (Re-Issue)	(DEF AMER DEFA 10)	39	1991	26	1991	(DEF AMER 19245)
5	Seeing Things	(DEF AMER DEFA13)	72	1991	0	1991	
6	Remedy	(DEF AMER DEFA 16)	24	1992	0	1992	
7	Sting Me	(DEF AMER DEFA 21)	42	1992	0	1992	
8	Hotel Illness	(DEF AMER DEFA23)	47	1992	0	1992	
9	High Head Blues / A Conspiracy	(AMERICAN 74321258492)	25	1995	0	1995	
10	Wiser Time	(AMERICAN 74321298272)	34	1995	0	1995	
11	One Mirror Too Many	(AMERICAN 74321398572)	51	1996	0	1996	
	NAMES: CHRIS & RICH ROBINSON, JEFF CEASE, STEVE GORMAN & JOHNNY COLT						
Black Diamond Male Vocalist from the USA							
1	Let Me Be	(SYSTEMATIC SYSCD 1)	56	1994	0	1994	
Black Duck Male Rapper from the UK							
1	Wiggle In Line	(FLYING SOUTH CDDUCK 1)	33	1994	0	1994	
Black Gorilla Mixed Vocal/Instrumental Group from the UK							
1	Gimme Dat Banana	(RESPONCE SR 502)	29	1977	0	1977	
Black Lace Male Vocal/Instrumental Group from the UK							
1	Mary Ann	(FLAIR 2919)	42	1979	0	1979	
2	Superman (Gioca Jouer)	(FLAIR FLA 105)	9	1983	0	1983	
3	Agadoo	(FLAIR FLA 107)	2	1984	0	1984	
4	Do The Conga	(FLAIR FLA 108)	10	1984	0	1984	
5	El Vino Collapso	(FLAIR LACE 1)	42	1985	0	1985	
6	I Speak Da Lingo	(FLAIR LACE 2)	49	1985	0	1985	
7	Hokey Cokey	(FLAIR LACE 3)	31	1985	0	1985	
8	Wig Wam Bam	(FLAIR LACE 5)	63	1986	0	1986	
9	I Am The Music Man	(FLAIR LACE 10)	52	1989	0	1989	
Black Machine Male Vocal Duo from France/Nigeria							
1	How Gee	(London LONCD 348)	17	1994	0	1994	
Black Oak Arkansas Rock Sextet Led By Jim Mangrum from the USA							
1	Jim Dandy		0	1974	25	1974	(ATCO 6948)
	Their Name Is Taken From Their Home Town						
Black Riot Male Producer from the USA							
1	Warlock - A Day In The Life	(CHAMPION CHAMP 75)	68	1988	0	1988	

ISSUE	TITLE	UK LBL	UK POS	UK YEAR	US POS	US YEAR	US LBL
Blackout Allstars							
1	I Like It		0	1997	25	1997	(Columbia 78455)
Black Sabbath Male Vocal/Instrumental Group from the USA/UK							
1	Paranoid	(VERTIGO 6059 010)	4	1970	0	1970	
2	Never Say Die	(VERTIGO SAB 001)	21	1978	0	1978	
3	Hard Road	(VERTIGO SAB 002)	33	1978	0	1978	
4	Neon Knights	(VERTIGO SAB 3)	22	1980	0	1980	
5	Paranoid (Re-Issue)	(NEMS BSS 101)	14	1980	0	1980	
6	Die Young	(VERTIGO SAB 4)	41	1980	0	1980	
7	Mob Rules	(VERTIGO SAB 5)	46	1981	0	1981	
8	Turn Up The Night	(VERTIGO SAB 6)	37	1982	0	1982	
9	Headless Cross	(IRS EIRS 107)	62	1989	0	1989	
10	TV Crimes	(IRS EIRS 178)	33	1992	0	1992	
	THE GROUP WAS A UK BAND ONLY FOR THE FIRST THREE HITS AND THE RE-ISSUE						
Black Sheep Male Rap Duo from the USA							
1	Without A Doubt	(Mercury MERCD 417)	60	1994	0	1994	
Black Slate Male Vocal/Instrumental Group from the UK/Jmaica							
1	Amigo	(ENSIGN ENY 42)	9	1980	0	1980	
2	Boom Boom	(ENSIGN ENY 47)	51	1980	0	1980	
Black Uhuru Male Vocal/Instrumental Group from Jamaica							
1	What Is Life	(Island IS 150)	56	1984	0	1984	
2	The Great Train Robbery	(Real Authentic Sound RAS7018)	69	1986	0	1986	
Blackbyrds Male Vocal/Instrumental Group from the USA							
* 1	Walking In Rhythm	(FANTASY FTC 114)	23	1975	6	1975	(FANTASY 736)
2	Happy Music		0	1976	19	1976	(FANTASY 762)
Blackfoot Male Vocal/Instrumental Group from the USA							
1	Highway Song		0	1979	26	1979	(ATCO 7104)
2	Train Train		0	1979	38	1979	(ATCO 7207)
3	Dry Country	(ATCO K 11686)	43	1982	0	1982	
4	Send Me An Angel	(ATCO B 9880)	66	1983	0	1983	
	LEAD SINGER IS RICK MEDLOCKE						
Blackfoot Sue Male Vocal/Instrumental Group from the UK							
1	Standing In The Road	(JAM 13)	4	1972	0	1972	
2	Sing Don't Speak	(JAM 29)	36	1972	0	1972	
Blackgirl Female Vocal Group from the USA							
1	90s Girl	(RCA	23	1994	0	1994	
Blackstreet Male Vocal Group from the USA							
1	Baby Be Mine	(MCA MCSTD	37	1993	0	1993	
2	Booti Call	(IInterscope A 8250CD)	56	1994	34	1994	(Interscope 98255)
3	Before I Let You Go		0	1994	7	1994	(Interscope 98211)
4	U Blow My Mind	(Interscope A 8222cd)	39	1995	0	1995	
5	Joy	(Interscope A 8195cd)	56	1995	0	1995	
6	No Diggity	(Interscope IND 95003)	9	1996	1	1996	(Interscope 97007)
Blackwells Male Vocal Group from the USA							
1	Love Or Money	(London HLW 9334)	46	1961	0	1961	
Blaggers I.T.A. Male Vocal/Instrumental Group from the UK							
1	Stress	(Parlophone CDITA 1)	56	1993	0	1993	
2	Oxygen	(Parlophone CDITA 2)	51	1993	0	1993	
3	Abandon Ship	(Parlophone CDITA 3)	48	1994	0	1994	
Blame Male Production/Instrumental Duo from the UK							
1	Music Takes You	(MOVING SHADOW SHADOW11)	48	1992	0	1992	
Blancmange Male Vocal/Instrumental Group from the UK							
1	God's Kitchen - I've Seen The Word	(London BLANC 1)	65	1982	0	1982	
2	Feel Me	(London BLANC 2)	46	1982	0	1982	
3	Living On The Ceiling	(London BLANC 3)	7	1982	0	1982	
4	Waves	(London BLANC 4)	19	1983	0	1983	
5	Blind Vision	(London BLANC 5)	10	1983	0	1983	
6	That's Love That It Is	(London BLANC 6)	33	1983	0	1983	
7	Don't Tell Me	(London BLANC 7)	8	1984	0	1984	
8	The Day Before You Came	(London BLANC 8)	22	1984	0	1984	
9	What's Your Problem?	(London BLANC 9)	40	1985	0	1985	
10	I Can See It	(London BLANC 11)	71	1986	0	1986	

ISSUE	TITLE	UK LBL	UK POS	UK YEAR	US POS	US YEAR	US LBL
Blast	Mixed Vocal/Instrumental Group from Italy						
1	Crayzy Man	(UMM MCSTD 1982)	22	1994	0	1994	
2	Princess Of The Night	(UMM MCSTD 2011)	40	1994	0	1994	
	HITS ARE CREDITED TO BLAST FEATURING VDC						
Blessid Union Of Souls	Male Vocal Group: Eliot Sloan, Eddie Hedges, C.P. Roth & Jeff Pence from Cincinnati						
1	I Believe	(EMI CDEM 374)	29	1995	8	1995	(EMI 58320)
2	Let Me Be The One	(EMI CDEM 378)	74	1996	29	1995	(EMI 58443)
3	All Along		0	1996	70	1996	(EMI 58576)
4	I Wanna Be There		0	1997	51	1997	(EMI 58643)
Blessing	Male Vocal/Instrumental Group from the UK						
1	Highway 5	(MCA MCS 1509)	42	1991	0	1991	
2	Highway 5 (Re-Mix)	(MCA MCS 1603)	30	1992	0	1992	
3	Soul Love	(MCA MCSTD	73	1994	0	1994	
Blind Melon	Male Vocal/Instrumental Group from Los Angeles						
1	Tones Of Home	(Capitol CDCL 687)	62	1993	0	1993	
2	No Rain	(Capitol CDCL 699)	17	1993	20	1993	(Capitol 44939)
3	Change	(Capitol CDCL717)	35	1994	0	1994	
4	Galaxie	(Capitol CDCL 755)	37	1995	0	1995	
Blink	Male Vocal/Instrumental Group from Ireland						
1	Happy Day	(LIME CDR 6385)	57	1994	0	1994	
Blondie	Mixed Vocal/Instrumental Group from the USA/UK						
1	Denis	(Chrysalis CHS 2204)	2	1978	0	1978	
2	I'm Always Touched By Your Presence	(Chrysalis CHS 2217)	10	1978	0	1978	
3	Picture This	(Chrysalis CHS 2242)	12	1978	0	1978	
4	Hanging On The Telephone	(Chrysalis CHS 2266)	5	1978	0	1978	
5	Heart Of Glass	(Chrysalis CHS 2275)	1	1979	1	1979	(Chrysalis 2295)
6	Sunday Girl	(Chrysalis CHS 2320)	1	1979	0	1979	
7	One Way Or Another		0	1979	24	1979	(Chrysalis 2336)
8	Dreaming	(Chrysalis CHS 2350)	2	1979	27	1979	(Chrysalis 2379)
9	Union City Blues	(Chrysalis CHS 2400)	13	1979	0	1979	
10	Atomic	(Chrysalis CHS 2410)	1	1980	39	1980	(Chrysalis 2410)
11	Call Me	(Chrysalis CHS 2414)	1	1980	1	1980	(Chrysalis 2414)
12	The Tide Is High	(Chrysalis CHS 2465)	1	1980	1	1980	(Chrysalis 2465)
13	Rapture	(Chrysalis CHS 2485)	5	1981	1	1981	(Chrysalis 2485)
14	Island Of Lost Souls	(Chrysalis CHS 2608)	11	1982	37	1982	(Chrysalis 2603)
15	War Child	(Chrysalis CHS 2624)	39	1982	0	1982	
16	Denis (Re-Mix)	(Chrysalis CHS 3328)	50	1988	0	1988	
17	Call Me (Re-Mix)	(Chrysalis CHS 3342)	61	1989	0	1989	
18	Atomic (Re-Mix)	(Chrysalis CDCHS 5013)	19	1994	0	1994	
20	Union City Blues (Re-Mix)	(Chrysalis CDCHS 5027)	31	1995	0	1995	
	NAMES: DEBBIE HARRY, CHRIS STEIN, FRANK INFANTE, JIMMY DESTRI, GARY VALENTINE & CLEM BURKE • DEBBIE ALSO RECORDED UNDER THE NAME OF NEW YORK BLONDES						
Blood, Sweat & Tears	Male Vocal/Instrumental Group From USA/Canada						
* 1	You've Made Me So Very Happy	(CBS 4116)	35	1969	2	1969	(Columbia 44776)
* 2	Spinning Wheel		0	1969	2	1969	(Columbia 44871)
* 3	And When I Die		0	1969	2	1969	(Columbia 45008)
4	Hi-De-Ho		0	1970	14	1970	(Columbia 45204)
5	Lucretia Mac Evil		0	1970	29	1970	(Columbia 45235)
6	Go Down Gamblin'		0	1971	32	1971	(Columbia 45427)
Bloodrock	Group Originating from Fort Worth, Texas						
1	D.O.A.		0	1971	36	1971	(Capitol 3009)
Bloodstone	Male Vocal/Instrumental Group from the USA Names: Charles McCormick, Willis Draffen, Charles Love, Roger Durham & Henry Williams						
* 1	Natural High	(Decca F 13382)	40	1973	10	1973	(London 1046)
2	Outside Woman		0	1974	34	1974	(London 1052)
	Originally Formed As The Sinceres In 1962 Obituary: Roger D: 1973.						
Bloomsbury Set	Male Vocal/Instrumental Group from the UK						
1	Hanging Around With The Big Boys	(STILETTO STL	56	1983	0	1983	
Blow Monkeys	Male Vocal/Instrumental Group from the UK Names: Robert Howard, Mick Anker, Neville Henry & Tony Kiley						
1	Digging Your Scene	(RCA PB 40599)	12	1986	14	1986	(RCA 14325)
2	Wicked Ways	(RCA MONK 2)	60	1986	0	1986	
3	It Doesn't Have To Be This Way	(RCA MONK 4)	5	1987	0	1987	
4	Out With Her	(RCA MONK 5)	30	1987	0	1987	
5	(Celebrate) The Day After You	(RCA MONK 6)	52	1987	0	1987	

ISSUE	TITLE	UK LBL	UK POS	UK YEAR	US POS	US YEAR	US LBL
6	Some Kind Of Wonderful	(RCA MONK 7)	67	1987	0	1987	
7	This Is Your Life	(RCA PB 42149)	70	1988	0	1988	
8	This Is Your Life (Re-Mix)	(RCA PB 42695)	32	1989	0	1989	
9	Choice	(RCA PB 42885)	22	1989	0	1989	
10	Slaves No More	(RCA PB 43201)	73	1989	0	1989	
11	Springtime For The World	(RCA PB 43623)	69	1990	0	1990	
Blue Male Vocal/Instrumental Group from the UK							
1	Gonna Capture Your Heart	(ROCKET ROKN 522)	18	1977	0	1977	
Blue Aeroplanes Mixed Vocal/Instrumental Group from the UK							
1	Jacket Hangs	(ENSIGN ENY 628)	72	1989	0	1989	
Blue Bamboo Male Producer Johan Gielen From Belgium							
1	Abc And D..	(ESCAPADE CDJAPE 6)	23	1994	0	1994	
Blue Barron Orchestra Orchestra Leader B: 22 Mar 1911 Cleveland, Ohio							
4	Chi-Baba, Chi-Baba		0	1947	14	1947	(MGM 10027)
5	You Were Only Fooling		0	1948	9	1948	(MGM 10185)
6	A Strawberry Moon (In A Blueberry Sky)		0	1948	20	1948	(MGM 10297)
* 7	Cruising Down The River		0	1949	1	1949	(MGM 10346)
8	Powder Your Face With Sunshine		0	1949	18	1949	(MGM 10346)
9	Whose Girl Are You		0	1949	25	1949	(MGM 10412)
10	Re You Lonesome Tonight?		0	1950	19	1950	(MGM 10628)
11	Let Me In		0	1951	26	1951	(MGM 10923)
Blue Cheer Hard-Rock Group, Led By Dickie Peterson From San Francisco							
1	Summertime Blues		0	1968	14	1968	(PHILIPS 40516)
Blue Diamonds Names Rudi & Riem De Wolff from Indonesia							
* 1	Ramona		0	1960	72	1960	(FONTANA)
	The Hit Sold Over A Million In Europe						
Blue Feather Male Vocal/Instrumental Group from Holland							
1	Let's Funk Tonight	(Mercury MER 109)	50	1982	0	1982	
Blue Haze Male Vocal/Instrumental Group from the UK							
1	Smoke Gets In Your Eyes	(A&M AMS 891)	32	1972	27	1972	(A&M 1357)
Blue Jays R&B Group, Led By Leon Peels from Los Angeles							
1	Lover's Island		0	1961	31	1961	(MILESTONE 2008)
Blue Lu Barker Female R&B Vocalist, Real Name Louisa Barker from the USA							
1	Don't You Make Me High		0	1938	15	1938	(Decca 7506)
2	A Little Bird Told Me		0	1948	4	1948	(Capitol 15308)
Blue Magic Names Vernon Sawyer, Keith Beaton, Wendell Sawyer, Richard Pratt & Ted Mills							
* 1	Sideshow		0	1974	8	1974	(ATCO 6961)
2	Three Ring Circus		0	1974	36	1974	(ATCO 7004)
Blue Mercedes Male Vocal/Instrumental Duo from the UK							
1	I Want To Be Your Property	(MCA BONA 1)	23	1987	0	1987	
2	See Want Must Have	(MCA BONA 2)	57	1988	0	1988	
3	Love Is The Gun	(MCA BONA 3)	46	1988	0	1988	
Blue Mink Mixed Vocal/Instrumental Group from the USA/UK							
1	Melting Pot	(Philips BF 1818)	3	1969	0	1969	
2	Good Morning Freedom	(Philips BF 1838)	10	1970	0	1970	
3	Our World	(Philips 6006 042)	17	1970	0	1970	
4	Banner Man	(Regal Zonophone RZ 3034)	3	1971	0	1971	
5	Stay With Me	(Regal Zonophone RZ 3064)	11	1972	0	1972	
6	Stay With Me (Re-Entry)	(Regal Zonophone RZ 3064)	43	1973	0	1973	
7	By The Devil (I Was Tempted)	(EMI 2007)	26	1973	0	1973	
8	Randy	(EMI 2028)	9	1973	0	1973	
Blue Nile Male Vocal/Instrumental Group from the UK							
1	The Downtown Lights	(LINN LKS 3)	67	1989	0	1989	
2	Headlights On The Parade	(LINN LKS 4)	72	1990	0	1990	
3	Saturday Night	(LINN LKS 5)	50	1991	0	1991	
Blue Oyster Cult Male Vocal/Instrumental Group from the USANames: Donald Dharma, Allen Lanier, Joe & Albert Bouchard And Eric Bloom							
1	Don't Fear The Reaper	(CBS 6333)	16	1978	12	1976	(Columbia 10384)
2	Burnin' For You		0	1981	40	1981	(Columbia 02415)
Blue Pearl Mixed Vocal/Instrumental Group from the USA/UK							
1	Naked In The Rain	(BIG LIFE BLR 23)	4	1990	0	1990	
2	Little Brother	(BIG LIFE BLR 32)	31	1990	0	1990	
3	(Can You) Feel The Passion	(BIG LIFE BLR 67)	14	1992	0	1992	

ISSUE	TITLE	UK LBL	UK POS	UK YEAR	US POS	US YEAR	US LBL
4	Mother Dawn	(BIG LIFE BLR 73)	50	1992	0	1992	
5	Fire Of Love	(LOGIC 74321170292)	71	1993	0	1993	

HIT 5 IS CREDITED TO JUNGLE HIGH WITH BLUE PEARL • SEE ALSO GIMME SHELTER (EP), VARIOUS ARTISTS (EP, LP, 78S)

Blue Ridge Rangers Male Vocal/Instrumentalist Real Name John Fogerty from the USA

1	Jambalaya (On The Bayou)		0	1973	16	1973	(FANTASY 689)
2	Rockin' All Over The World		0	1975	27	1975	(Asylum 45274)
3	The Old Man Down The Road		0	1985	10	1985	(Warner Bros. 29100)
4	Rock And Roll Girls		0	1985	20	1985	(Warner Bros. 29053)

Blue Rondo A La Turk Male Vocal/Instrumental Group from the UK

1	Me And Mr.Sanchez	(Virgin VS 463)	40	1981	0	1981	
2	Klactoveesedstein	(Diable Noir VS 476)	50	1982	0	1982	

Blue Stars Mixed Pop-Jazz Group Led By Blossom Dearie

1	Lullaby Of Birdland		0	1956	16	1956	(Mercury 70742)

Blue Swede Pop Sextet, Led By Bjorn Skifs From Sweden

* 1	Hooked On A Feeling		0	1973	1	1973	(EMI 3627)
2	Never My Love		0	1974	7	1974	(EMI 3938)

GROUP FORMED IN 1973, HIT 1 WAS ALSO NUMBER 1 IN GERMANY & CANADA

Blue Zoo Male Vocal/Instrumental Group from the UK

1	I'm Your Man	(Magnet MAG 224)	55	1982	0	1982	
2	Cry Boy Cry	(Magnet MAG 234)	13	1982	0	1982	
3	I Just Can't (Forgive And Forget)	(Magnet MAG 241)	60	1983	0	1983	

Blue-Belles See Starlets

Bluebells Male Vocal/Instrumental Group from the UK

1	Cath	(London LON 20)	62	1983	0	1983	
2	Sugar Bridge (It Will Stand)	(London LON 27)	72	1983	0	1983	
3	I'm Falling	(London LON 45)	11	1984	0	1984	
4	Young At Heart	(London LON 49)	8	1984	0	1984	
5	Cath (Re-Issue)	(London LON 54)	38	1984	0	1984	
6	All I Am (Is Loving You)	(London LON 58)	58	1985	0	1985	
7	Young At Heart (Re-Issue)	(London LONCD 338)	1	1993	0	1993	

Blues Band Male Vocal/Instrumental Group from the UK

1	Blues Band (EP)	(Arista BOOT 2)	68	1980	0	1980	

Blues Brothers Male Vocal Duo

1	Soul Man		0	1979	14	1979	(Atlantic 3545)
2	Rubber Biscuit		0	1979	37	1979	(Atlantic 3564)
3	Gimme Some Lovin'		0	1980	18	1980	(Atlantic 3666)
4	Who's Making Love		0	1981	39	1981	(Atlantic 3785)
5	Everybody Needs Somebody To Love	(EAST WEST A7591)	12	1989	0	1989	

JOHN BELUSHI B: 24 JAN 1949 WHEATON, ILLINOIS & DAN AYKROYD B: 1 JUL 1952 OTTAWA, ONTARIO • OBITUARY :JOHN D: 5 MAR 1982.

Blues Image Rock Quintet Led By Mike Pinera From Tampa, Florida

* 1	Ride Captain Ride		0	1970	4	1970	(ATCO 6746)

Blues Magoos Rock Quintet From New York, Originally Known As The Bloos Magoos

1	(We Ain't Got) Nothin' Yet		0	1967	5	1967	(Mercury 72622)

Blur Male Vocal/Instrumental Group from the UK

1	She's So High	(FOOD FOOD 26)	48	1990	0	1990	
2	There's No Other Way	(FOOD FOOD 29)	8	1991	0	1991	
3	Bang	(FOOD FOOD 31)	24	1991	0	1991	
4	Popscene	(FOOD FOOD 37)	32	1992	0	1992	
5	For Tomorrow	(FOOD CDFOODS 40)	28	1993	0	1993	
6	Chemical World	(FOOD CDFOODS 45)	28	1993	0	1993	
7	Sunday Sunday	(FOOD CDFOODS 46)	26	1993	0	1993	
8	Girls And Boys	(FOOD CDFOODS 47)	5	1994	0	1994	
9	To The End	(FOOD CDFOODS 50)	16	1994	0	1994	
10	Parklife	(FOOD CDFOODS 53)	10	1994	0	1994	
11	End Of A Century	(FOOD CDFOODS 56)	19	1994	0	1994	
12	Country House	(FOOD CDFOODS 63)	1	1995	0	1995	
13	Country House (4th Format)	(FOOD CDFOODS 63)	57	1995	0	1995	
14	The Universal	(FOOD CDFOODS 69)	5	1995	0	1995	
15	Stereotypes	(FOOD CDFOOD 73)	7	1996	0	1996	
16	Charmless Man	(FOOD CDFOOD 77)	5	1996	0	1996	
17	Beetlebum	(FOOD CDFOODS 89)	1	1997	0	1997	
18	On Your Own	(FOOD CDFOODS 98)	5	1997	0	1997	

ISSUE	TITLE	UK LBL	UK POS	UK YEAR	US POS	US YEAR	US LBL
Bo Diddley Male Vocal/Guitarist, Real Name Otha Elias Bates Mcdaniel B: 30 Dec 1928 Mississippi							
1	Say Man		0	1959	20	1959	(CHECKER 931)
2	Pretty Thing	(Pye International 7N 25217)	34	1963	0	1963	
3	Hey Good Lookin'	(Chess 8000)	39	1965	0	1965	
Bo Donaldson & The Heywoods Male Septet from Cincinnati							
* 1	Billy, Don't Be A Hero		0	1974	1	1974	(ABC 11435)
2	Who Do You Think You Are		0	1974	15	1974	(ABC 12006)
3	The Heartbreak Kid		0	1974	39	1974	(ABC 12039)
Bo Kirkland & Ruth Davis Mixed Vocal Duo from the USA							
1	You're Gonna Get Next To Me	(EMI International INT 532)	12	1977	0	1977	
Bob & Dor McFadden Bob Hails from Ohio And Dor Is Actor Rod McKuen							
1	The Mummy		0	1959	39	1959	(Brunswick 55140)
Bob & Doug Mckenzie Names Rick Moanis And Dave Thomas							
1	Take Off		0	1982	16	1982	(Mercury 76134)
Bob & Earl Male Vocal Duo from the USA							
1	Harlem Shuffle	(Island WIP 6053)	7	1969	0	1969	
Bob & Jeanne Mixed Vocal Duo from the USA							
1	Careless Hands		0	1949	21	1949	(Decca 24563)
Bob & Marcia Mixed Vocal Duo from Jamaica							
1	(To Be) Young Gifted And Black	(Harry J HJ 6605)	5	1970	0	1970	
2	Pied Piper	(Trojan TR 7818)	11	1971	0	1971	
Bob Azzam With His Singing Orchestra from Egypt							
1	Mustapha	(Decca F 21235)	23	1960	0	1960	
Bob B. Soxx & The Blue Jeans Mixed Vocal Group from the USAOriginal Group Names Were Darlene Love, Bobby Sheen & Fanita James							
1	Zip-A-Dee-Doo-Dah	(London HLU 9646)	45	1963	8	1962	(PHILLES 107)
2	Why Do Lovers Break Each Others Hearts		0	1963	38	1963	(PHILLES 110)
3	Not Too Young To Get Married		0	1963	63	1963	(PHILLES 113)
Bob Bachelder Orchestra Male Orchestra Leader from Boston, USA							
1	TV Rhumba		0	1953	22	1953	(MOOD 1011)
Bob Beckham Male Vocalist From Stratford, Oklahoma Now Lives In Nashville							
1	Just A Much As Ever		0	1959	32	1959	(Decca 30861)
2	Crazy Arms		0	1960	36	1960	(Decca 31029)
Bob Braun Real Name Robert Earl Brown B: 20 Apr 1929 Ludlow, Kentucky							
1	Till Death Do Us Part		0	1962	26	1962	(Decca 31355)
Bob Carlisle Male Vocalist							
1	Butterfly Kisses	(JIVE JIVECD 249)	56	1997	0	1997	
Bob Carroll Male Vocalist (Baritone) from the USA.							
1	Say It With Your Heart		0	1953	14	1953	(DERBY 814)
2	A Little Love		0	1953	28	1953	(DERBY 821)
	PREVIOUSLY SANG WITH JIMMY DORSEY, KAY KYSER, AND OTHERS						
Bob Crewe Male Vocalist/Songwriter, B: 12 Nov 1937 New Jersey							
* 1	Music To Watch Girls By\		0	1966	15	1966	(DYNO VOICE 229)
	HE FORMED THE BOB CREWE GENERATION FROM STUDIO MUSICIANS						
Bob Crosby Orchestra Bing Crosby's Younger Brother,							
36	Let It Snow! Let It Snow! Let It Snow!		0	1946	14	1946	(ARA 129)
37	Five Minutes More (From Sweetheart Of Sigma Chi)		0	1946	12	1946	(Decca 18909)
38	The Pussy Cat Song (Nyow! Nyot! Nyow!)		0	1949	12	1949	(Decca 24533)
39	Maybe It's Because		0	1949	22	1949	(Columbia 38504)
40	Play A Simple Melody (From Watch Your Step)		0	1950	25	1950	(CORAL 60227)
41	Shanghai		0	1951	22	1951	(Capitol 1525)
Bob Dini Male Vocalist From Boston, USA							
1	Too Long		0	1953	22	1953	(DERBY 826)
2	Goodbye My Love		0	1953	22	1953	(DERBY 833)
Bob Dylan Male Vocalist, Real Name Robert Allen Zimmerman B: 24 May 1941 From Duluth, Minnesota.							
1	The Times They Are A Changin'	(CBS 201751)	9	1965	0	1965	
2	Subterranean Homesick Blues	(CBS 201753)	9	1965	39	1965	(Columbia 43242)
3	Maggie's Farm	(CBS 201781)	22	1965	0	1965	
* 4	Like A Rolling Stone	(CBS 201811)	4	1965	2	1965	(Columbia 43346)
* 5	Positively 4th Street	(CBS 201824)	8	1965	7	1965	(Columbia 43389)

ISSUE	TITLE	UK LBL	UK POS	UK YEAR	US POS	US YEAR	US LBL
6	Can You Please Crawl Out Of Your Window	(CBS 201900)	17	1966	58	1966	(Columbia 43477)
7	One Of Us Must Know (Sooner Or Later)	(CBS 202053)	33	1966	0	1966	
8	Rainy Day Woman Nos 12 And 35	(CBS 202307)	7	1966	2	1966	(Columbia 43592)
9	I Want You	(CBS 202258)	16	1966	20	1966	(Columbia 43683)
10	Just Like A Woman		0	1966	33	1966	(Columbia 43792)
11	Leopard-Skin Pill-Box Hat		0	1967	81	1967	(Columbia 44069)
12	I Threw It All Away	(CBS 4219)	30	1969	85	1969	(Columbia 44826)
13	Lay Lady Lay	(CBS 4434)	5	1969	7	1969	(Columbia 44926)
14	Tonight I'll Be Staying Here With You		0	1969	50	1969	(Columbia 45004)
15	Wigwam		0	1970	41	1970	(Columbia 45199)
16	Watching The River Flow	(CBS 7329)	24	1971	41	1971	(Columbia 45409)
17	George Jackson		0	1971	33	1971	(Columbia 45516)
18	Knockin' On Heaven's Door	(CBS 1762)	14	1973	12	1973	(Columbia 45913)
19	A Fool Such As I		0	1973	55	1973	(Columbia 45982)
20	On A Night Like This		0	1974	44	1974	(Asylum 11033)
21	Most Likely To Go Your Way (And I'll Go Mine)		0	1974	55	1974	(Asylum 11043)
22	Tangled Up In Blue		0	1974	31	1974	(Columbia 3-10106)
23	Hurricane (Part 1)	(CBS 3878)	43	1976	33	1976	(Columbia 3-10245)
24	Baby Stop Crying	(CBS 6499)	13	1978	0	1978	
25	Is Your Love In Vain	(CBS 6718)	56	1978	0	1978	
26	Gotta Serve Somebody		0	1979	24	1979	(Columbia 11072)
27	Dignity	(Columbia 6620762)	33	1995	0	1995	

HIT 17 WAS DEDICATED TO RUBIN CARTER, A CONVICTED MURDERER • HE RETIRED FOR A LONG TIME AFTER HAVING A MOTORCYCLE ACCIDENT ON 29 JUL 1966

Bob Eberly   Male Vocalist, Real Name Robert Eberie from New York

1	Hair Of Gold (Eyes Of Blue) (From *Singin' Spurs*)		0	1948	25	1948	(Decca 24491)
3	When I Dream		0	1952	30	1952	(Capitol 2239)
4	You Are Too Beautiful (From Hallelujah I'ma Bum)		0	1953	30	1953	(Capitol 2525)

PREVIOUSLY SANG WITH THE JIMMY DORSEY ORCHESTRA AND THE DORSEY BROTHERS ORCHESTRA • OBITUARY : D: 17 DEC 1981, AGED 65.

Bob Geldof   Male Vocalist from Ireland   Former Lead Singer With The Boomtown Rats

1	This Is The World Calling	(Mercury BOB 101)	25	1986	0	1986	
2	Love Like A Rocket	(Mercury BOB 102)	61	1987	0	1987	
3	The Great Song Of Indifference	(Mercury BOB 104)	15	1990	0	1990	
4	Crazy	(VERTIGO VERCX85)	65	1994	0	1994	

Bob Hope   Male Comedian/Vocalist B: 29 May 1903 In London, UK

1	Two Sleepy People (From Thanks For The Memories)		0	1939	15	1939	(Decca 2219)
2	The Road To Moroco (Movie Title Theme)		0	1945	21	1945	(Decca 40000)
3	Blind Date		0	1950	16	1950	(Capitol 1042)

Bob Houston   Male Vocalist from the USA

1	A Tune For Humming		0	1947	26	1947	(MGM 10091)
2	That Lucky Old Sun		0	1949	27	1949	(MGM 10509)

Bob Kuban & The In-Men   Eight Man Pop-Rock Band From St. Louis

1	The Cheater		0	1966	12	1966	(MUSICLAND 20001)

LEAD SINGER WALTER SCOTT REAL NAME WALTER NOTHEIS JR.• OBITUARY : WALTER D: 27 DEC 1983 MURDERED (SHOT IN THE BACK).

Bob Lind   Male Vocalist, B: 25 Nov 1944 Baltimore

1	Elusive Butterfly	(Fontana TF 670)	5	1966	5	1966	(WORLD PAC. 77808)
2	Remember The Rain	(Fontana TF 702)	46	1966	0	1966	

Bob Luman   Country-Rockabilly/Vocalist, B: 15 Apr 1937 Nacogdoches, Texas

1	Let's Think About Livin'	(Warner Bros. WB 18)	6	1960	7	1960	(Warner Bros. 5172)
2	Why Why Bye Bye	(Warner Bros. WB 28)	46	1960	0	1960	
3	The Great Snowman	(Warner Bros.WB 37)	49	1961	0	1961	

ALSO HAD MANY C/W HITS • OBITUARY : D: 27 DEC 1978.

Bob Marley & The Wailers   Male Vocal/Instrumental Group From Jamaica

1	No Woman No Cry	(Island WIP 6244)	22	1975	0	1975	
2	Exodus	(Island WIP 6390)	14	1977	0	1977	
3	Waiting In Vain	(Island WIP 6402)	27	1977	0	1977	
4	Jamming / Punky Reggae Party	(Island WIP 6410)	9	1977	0	1977	
5	Is This Love	(Island WIP 6420)	9	1978	0	1978	
6	Satisfy My Soul	(Island WIP 6440)	21	1978	0	1978	
7	So Much Trouble In The World	(Island WIP 6510)	56	1979	0	1979	
8	Could You Be Loved	(Island WIP 6610)	5	1980	0	1980	
9	Three Little Birds	(Island WIP 6641)	17	1980	0	1980	
10	No Woman No Cry (Re-Entry)	(Island WIP 6244)	8	1981	0	1981	
11	Buffalo Soldier	(Island/TUFF 1S 108)	4	1983	0	1983	
12	One Love / People Get Ready	(Island IS 169)	5	1984	0	1984	

ISSUE	TITLE	UK LBL	UK POS	UK YEAR	US POS	US YEAR	US LBL
13	Waiting In Vain (Re-Issue)	(Island IS 180)	31	1984	0	1984	
14	Could You Be Loved (Re-Issue)	(Island IS 210)	71	1984	0	1984	
15	One Love / People Get Ready (Re-Issue)	(TUFF GING TGX1)	42	1991	0	1991	
16	Iron Lion Zion	(TUFF GONG TGX 2)	5	1992	0	1992	
17	Why Should I / Exodus	(TUFF GONG TGX 3)	42	1992	0	1992	
18	Why Should I / Exodus (Re-Entry)	(TUFF GONG TGX 3)	75	1993	0	1993	
19	Keep On Moving	(TUGG GONG TGXCD 4)	17	1995	0	1995	
20	What Goes Around Comes Around	(ANANSI ANACS 002)	42	1996	0	1996	

HIT 18 IS A DIFFERENT RECORDING TO HIT 2 • OBITUARY : D: 11 MAY 1981 CANCER.

Bob Moore   Male Guitarist, B: 30 Nov 1932 Nashville, Tennessee

* 1	Mexico		0	1961	7	1961	(MONUMENT 446)

Bob Roberts   Male Vocalist (Baritone) from the USA

* 22	Ragtime Cowboy Joe		0	1912	1	1912	(VICTOR 16909)

Bob Seger   Male Singer/Songwriter, B: 6 May 1945 Dearborn, Mitchigan

1	Ramblin' Gamblin' Man		0	1969	17	1969	(Capitol 2297)
2	Night Movies		0	1977	4	1977	(Capitol 4369)
3	Mainstreet		0	1977	24	1977	(Capitol 4422)
4	Still The Same		0	1978	4	1978	(Capitol 4581)
5	Hollywood Nights	(Capitol CL16004)	42	1978	12	1978	(Capitol 4618)
6	We've Got Tonight	(Capitol CL16028)	41	1979	13	1979	(Capitol 4653)
7	Old Time Rock And Roll		0	1979	28	1979	(Capitol 4702)
8	Fire Lake		0	1980	6	1980	(Capitol 4836)
9	Against The Wind		0	1980	5	1980	(Capitol 4863)
10	You'll Accomp'ny Me		0	1980	14	1980	(Capitol 4904)
11	Tryin' To Live My Life Without You		0	1981	5	1981	(Capitol 5042)
12	Hollywood Nights (Live)	(Capitol CL 223)	49	1981	0	1981	
13	We've Got Tonight (Live)	(Capitol CL 235)	60	1982	0	1982	
14	Shame On The Moon		0	1983	2	1983	(Capitol 5187)
15	Even Now	(Capitol CL 284)	73	1983	12	1983	(Capitol 5213)
16	Roll Me Away		0	1983	27	1983	(Capitol 5235)
17	Understanding		0	1984	17	1984	(Capitol 5413)
18	American Storm		0	1986	13	1986	(Capitol 5532)
19	Like A Rock		0	1986	12	1986	(Capitol 5592)
20	Shakedown		0	1987	1	1987	(MCA 53094)
21	The Real Love		0	1991	24	1991	(Capitol 44743)
22	We've Got Tonight (Re-Issue)	(EMI CDCL 734)	22	1995	0	1995	
23	Night Movies	(EMI CDCL 741)	45	1995	0	1995	
25	Lock And Load	(EMI CDCLS 765)	57	1996	0	1996	

THE SILVER BULLET BAND ARE MALE VOCAL/INSTRUMENTAL GROUP FROM THE USA

Bob Wallis & His Storyville Jazz Band   Male Instrumentalist (Trumpet) With Male Jazz Band from the UK

1	I'm Shy Mary Ellen I'm Shy	(PYE JAZZ 7NJ 2043)	44	1961	0	1961	
2	Come Along Please	(PYE JAZZ 7NJ 2048)	33	1962	0	1962	

Bob Welch   Male Vocal/Guitarist, B: 31 Jul 1946 Los Angeles

1	Sentimental Lady		0	1977	8	1977	(Capitol 4479)
2	Ebony Eyes		0	1978	14	1978	(Capitol 4543)
3	Hot Love, Cold World		0	1978	31	1978	(Capitol 4588)
4	Precious Love		0	1979	19	1979	(Capitol 4685)

SEE ALSO FLEETWOOD MAC

Bob Wills & His Texas Playboys   Male Country & Western Artist, B: James Robert Wills, 6 Mar 1905 Groesbeck, Texas

1	San Antonio Rose		0	1939	15	1939	(VOCALION 4755)
* 2	New San Antonio Rose		0	1940	11	1940	(OKEH 5694)
16	New Spanish Two-Step		0	1946	20	1946	(Columbia 36966)

OBITUARY : BOB D: 13 MAY 1975 FORT WORTH, TEXAS (AGED 70).

Bobbi Martin   Female Vocalist, Real Name Barbara Anne Martin B: 29 Nov 1943 In Brooklyn, USA

1	Don't Forget I Still Love You		0	1965	19	1965	(CORAL 62426)
2	For The Love Of Him		0	1970	13	1970	(United Artists 50602)

Bobbie Gentry   Female Vocalist, Real Name Roberta Streeter B: 27 Jul 1944 Chickasaw County, Mississippi

* 1	Ode To Billy Joe	(Capitol CL 15511)	13	1967	1	1967	(Capitol 5950)
! 2	Louisiana Man		0	1968	72	1968	(Capitol 2147)
! 3	Less of Me		0	1968	44	1968	(Capitol 2314)
! 4	Mornin' Glory		0	1968	74	1968	(Capitol 2314)
5	Let It Be Me		0	1969	36	1969	(Capitol 2387)
6	I'll Never Fall In Love Again	(Capitol CL 15606)	1	1969	0	1969	

ISSUE	TITLE	UK LBL	UK POS	UK YEAR	US POS	US YEAR	US LBL
7	All I Have To Do Is Dream	(Capitol CL 15619)	3	1969	27	1970	(Capitol 2745)
* 8	Fancy		0	1969	31	1969	(Capitol 2675)
9	Raindrops Keep Falling On My Head	(Capitol CL 15626)	40	1970	0	1970	

Bobby 'Boris' Pickett & The Crypt Kickers Male Vocalist, B: 11 Feb 1940 Somerville, Massachusetts

* 1	Monster Mash	(London HL10320)	3	1973	1	1962	(CARPAX 44167)
2	Monster's Holiday		0	1962	30	1962	(CARPAX 44171)
3	Monster Mash (Re-Issue)		0	1973	10	1973	(PARROT 348)

FORMED A QUINTET CALLED THE CORDIALS AROUND 1960

Bobby Angelo & The Tuxedos Male Vocal/Instrumental Group from the UK

1	Baby Sittin'	(HMV POP 892)	30	1961	0	1961	

Bobby Bare Male Actor/Vocalist, Real Name Robert Joseph Bare B: 17 Apr 1935 Ohio

1	All American Boy	(London HL 8798)	0	1959	2	1959	(FRATERNITY 835)
2	Shame On Me		0	1962	23	1962	(RCA 8032)
* 3	Detroit City		0	1963	16	1963	(RCA 8183)
* 4	500 Miles Away From Home		0	1963	10	1963	(RCA 8238)
5	Miller's Cave		0	1964	33	1964	(RCA 8294)

HIT 1 IS CREDITED TO BILL PARSONS

Bobby Bland Male R & B Vocalist, Real Name Robert Calvin Bland B: 5 Apr 1932 Rosemark, Tennessee

+ 1	Lead Me On		0	1960	9	1960	(DUKE 318)
+ 2	Cry, Cry, Cry		0	1960	9	1960	(DUKE 327)
3	I Pity The Fool		0	1961	46	1961	(DUKE 332)
+ 4	Don't Cry No More		0	1961	2	1961	(DUKE 340)
5	Turn On Your Love Light		0	1961	28	1961	(DUKE 344)
+ 6	Ain't That Loving You		0	1962	9	1962	(DUKE 338)
7	Stormy Monday Blues		0	1962	43	1962	(DUKE 355)
* 8	That's The Way Love Is / Call On Me		0	1963	22	1963	(DUKE 360)
9	Ain't Nothing You Can Do		0	1964	20	1964	(DUKE 375)
10	Share Your Love With Me		0	1964	42	1964	(DUKE 377)
11	Ain't Doing Too Bad		0	1964	49	1964	(DUKE 383)

NEXT FOUR HITS ARE R&B • HE WAS ONCE B.B. KING'S DRIVER AND PERSONAL VALET

Bobby Bloom Male Singer/Songwriter, B: 21 May 1944 from the USA

1	Montego Bay	(Polydor 2058 051)	3	1970	8	1970	(L&R/MGM 157)
2	Montego Bay (Re-Entry)	(Polydor 2058 051)	42	1970	0	1970	
3	Heavy Makes You Happy	(Polydor 2001122)	31	1971	0	1971	
4	Montego Bay (2nd Re-Entry)	(Polydor 2058 051)	47	1971	0	1971	

OBITUARY : D: 28 FEB 1974 ACCIDENTAL SHOOTING.

Bobby Brown Male Vocalist, B: 5 Feb 1969 Boston. He Was A Member Of The New Edition

* 1	Don't Be Cruel	(MCA MCA 1268)	42	1988	8	1988	(MCA 53327)
* 2	My Perogative	(MCA MCA 1299)	51	1988	1	1988	(MCA 53383)
3	Roni	(MCA MCA 1384)	21	1989	3	1989	(MCA 53463)
4	Don't Be Cruel (Re-Issue)	(MCA MCA 1310)	13	1989	0	1989	
5	Every Little Step	(MCA MCA 1338)	6	1989	3	1989	(MCA 53618)
* 6	On Our Own (From Ghostbusters II)	(MCA MCA 1350)	4	1989	2	1989	(MCA 53662)
* 7	Rock Wit'cha	(MCA MCA 1367)	33	1989	7	1989	(MCA 53652)
8	The Free Style Mega-Mix	(MCA MCA 1421)	14	1990	0	1990	
* 9	She Ain't Worth It	(London LON 265)	12	1990	1	1990	(MCA 79047)
* 10	Humpin' Around	(MCA MCA 1680)	19	1992	3	1992	(MCA 54342)
* 11	Good Enough	(MCA MCA 1704)	41	1992	7	1992	(MCA 54517)
12	Get Away		0	1993	14	1993	(MCA 54511)
13	That's The Way Love Is	(MCA MCSTD 1783)	56	1993	0	1993	
14	Something In Common	(MCA MCSTD 1957)	16	1994	0	1994	
15	Two Can Play That Game	(MCA MCSTD 1973)	38	1994	0	1994	
16	Two Can Play That Game (Re-Entry)	(MCA MCSTD 1973)	3	1995	0	1995	
17	Humpin' Around (Re-Mix)	(MCA MCSCD 2073)	8	1995	0	1995	
18	My Prerogative (Re-Mix)	(MCA MCSTD 2094)	17	1995	0	1995	
19	Every Little Step (Re-Mix)	(MCA MCSTD 48004)	25	1996	0	1996	

HIT 9 IS CREDITED TO THE GLENN MEREIROS FEATURING BOBBY BROWN • HIT 14 IS CREDITED TO THE BOBBY BROWN AND WHITNEY HOUSTON

Bobby Caldwell Male Vocal/Multi-Instrumentalist, B: 15 Aug 1951 New York City

1	What You Won't Do For Love		0	1979	9	1979	(CLOUDS 11)

Bobby Crush Male Pianist from the UK · Bobby Got His Big Break After Winning A TV Talent Show

1	Borsalino	(PHILIPS 6006 248)	37	1972	0	1972	

Bobby Darin Male Vocalist/Instrumentalist, Real Name walden Robert Cassotto, B: 14 May 1946 Bronx, New York

* 1	Splish Splash	(London HLE 8666)	28	1958	3	1958	(ATCO 6117)

ISSUE	TITLE	UK LBL	UK POS	UK YEAR	US POS	US YEAR	US LBL
2	Early In The Morning		0	1958	24	1958	(ATCO 6121)
3	Splish Splash (Re-Entry)	(London HLE 8666)	18	1958	0	1958	
* 4	Queen Of The Hop	(London HLE 8737)	24	1959	9	1958	(ATCO 6127)
5	Plain Jane		0	1959	38	1959	(ATCO 6133)
* 6	Dream Lover	(London HLE 8867)	1	1959	2	1959	(ATCO 6140)
* 7	Mack The Knife	(London HLE 8939)	1	1959	1	1959	(ATCO 6147)
8	Mack The Knife (Re-Entry)	(London HLE 8939)	30	1960	0	1960	
* 9	La Mer (Beyond The Sea)	(London HLK 9034)	8	1960	6	1960	(ATCO 6158)
10	Mack The Knife (2nd Re-Entry)	(London HLE 8939)	50	1960	0	1960	
11	Clementine	(London HLK 9086)	8	1960	21	1960	(ATCO 6161)
12	La Mer (Beyond The Sea) (Re-Entry)	(London HLK 9034)	40	1960	0	1960	
13	Bill Bailey	(London HLK 9142)	36	1960	19	1960	(ATCO 6167)
14	Bill Bailey (Re-Entry)	(London HLK 9142)	34	1960	0	1960	
15	Artificial Flowers		0	1960	20	1960	(ATCO 6179)
16	Lazy River	(London HLK 9303)	2	1961	14	1961	(ATCO 6188)
17	Nature Boy	(London HLK	4	1961	40	1961	(ATCO 6196)
18	You Must Have Been A Beautiful Baby	(London HLK 9429)	10	1961	5	1961	(ATCO 6206)
19	Come September	(London HLK 9407)	50	1961	0	1961	
20	Irresistible You		0	1962	15	1962	(ATCO 6214)
21	Multiplication	(London HLK 9474)	5	1961	30	1961	(ATCO 6214)
22	What'd I Say (Part 1)		0	1962	24	1962	(ATCO 6221)
* 23	Things	(London HLK 9575)	2	1962	3	1962	(ATCO 6229)
24	If A Man Answers	(Capitol CL 15272)	24	1962	32	1962	(Capitol 4837)
25	Baby Face	(London HLK 9624)	40	1962	0	1962	
26	You're The Reason I'm Living		0	1963	3	1963	(Capitol 4897)
27	Eighteen Yellow Roses	(Capitol CL15306)	37	1963	10	1963	(Capitol 4970)
28	If I Were A Carpenter	(Atlantic 584 051)	9	1966	8	1966	(Atlantic 2350)
29	Lovin' You		0	1967	32	1967	(ATLANTIV 2376)
30	Dream Lover / Mack The Knife (Re-Issue)	(LightningIG 9017)	64	1979	0	1979	

HIT 2 ORIGINALLY RECORDED AS BY THE DING DONGS • HIT 19 IS CREDITED TO BOBBY DARIN ORCHESTRA • OBITUARY : D: 20 DEC 1973 HEART FAILURE.

Bobby Day Male Vocalist, Real Name Robert Byrd B: 1 Jul 1930 Texas

* 1	Rockin' Robin	(London HL 8726)	29	1958	2	1958	(CLASS 229)

He Formed The Hollywood Flames In 1950   Obituary : D: 15 Jul 1990 Cancer.

Bobby Edwards Male Country Singer, Real Name Robert Moncrief Alabama

1	You're The Reason		0	1961	11	1961	(CREST 1075)

Bobby Freeman Male R&B Vocalist, B: 13 Jun 1940 San Francisco

1	Do You Want To Dance		0	1958	5	1958	(JOSIE 835)
2	Betty Lou Got A New Pair Of Shoes		0	1958	37	1958	(JOSIE 841)
3	(I Do The) Shimmy Shimmy		0	1960	37	1960	(KING 5373)
4	C'mon And Swim		0	1964	5	1964	(AUTUMN 2)

IN HIS EARLY TEEN HE FORMED THE VOCAL GROUP THE ROMANCERS • HE LATER FORMED THE R&B GROUP THE VOCALEERS

Bobby Fuller Four Male Vocal/Instrumental Group from El Paso, With His Brother Randy

1	I Fought The Law	(London HL 10030)	33	1966	9	1966	(MUSTANG 3014)
2	Love's Made A Fool Of You		0	1966	26	1966	(MUSTANG 3016)

DODDY D: 22 OCT 1943 BAYTOWN, TEXAS • OBITUARY. BOBBY D. 18 JUL 1966 ASPHYXIATION.

Bobby G Male Vocalist from the UK

1	Big Deal	(BBC RESL 151)	75	1984	0	1984	
2	Big Deal (Re-Entry)	(BBC RESL 151)	65	1984	0	1984	
3	Big Deal (2nd Re-Entry)	(BBC RESL 151)	46	1985	0	1985	

Bobby Goldsboro Male Vocalist/Songwriter/Guitarist, B: 18 Jan 1941, Maryanna, Florida

* 1	See The Funny Little Clown		0	1964	9	1964	(United Artists 671)
2	Whenever He Holds You		0	1964	39	1964	(United Artists 710)
* 3	Little Things		0	1965	13	1965	(United Artists 810)
4	Voodoo Woman		0	1965	27	1965	(United Artists 862)
* 5	It's Too Late		0	1966	23	1966	(United Artists 980)
6	Blue Autumn		0	1967	35	1967	(United Artists 50087)
! 7	I Just Wanted The Rest		0	1968	56	1968	(United Artists 50243)
* 8	Honey	(United Artists UP 2215)	2	1968	1	1968	(United Artists 50283)
9	Autumn Of My Life		0	1968	19	1968	(United Artists 50318)
10	The Straight Life		0	1968	36	1968	(United Artists 50461)
11	Glad She's A Woman		0	1969	61	1969	(United Artists 50497)
12	I'm A Drifter		0	1969	46	1969	(United Artists 50525)
13	Muddy Mississippi Line		0	1969	53	1969	(United Artists 50565)
! 14	Take a Little Goodwill Home		0	1969	31	1969	(United Artists 50591)

ISSUE	TITLE	UK LBL	UK POS	UK YEAR	US POS	US YEAR	US LBL
15	Mornin Mornin		0	1969	78	1969	(United Artists 50614)
16	Can You Feel It		0	1970	75	1970	(United Artists 50650)
* 17	Watching Scotty Grow		0	1971	11	1971	(United Artists 50727)
18	And So I Love You So		0	1971	83	1971	(United Artists 50776)
19	Summer (The First Time)	(United Artists UP 35558)	9	1973	21	1973	(United Artists 251)
! 20	Marlene		0	1974	52	1974	(United Artists 371)
! 21	I Believe The South Is Gonna Rise Again		0	1974	62	1974	(United Artists 422)
! 22	Hello Summertime	(United Artists UP 35705)	14	1974	79	1974	(United Artists 529)
23	Honey (Re-Issue)	(United Artists UP 35633)	2	1975	0	1975	

IN 1962 HE JOINED ROY ORBISON AS A GUITARIST

Bobby Gregg & His Friends Male Jazz Drummer, Real Name Robert Grego from Philadelphia

	TITLE	UK LBL	UK POS	UK YEAR	US POS	US YEAR	US LBL
1	The Jam (Part 1)		0	1962	29	1962	(COTTON 1003)

BOBBY WAS WITH STEVE GIBSON AND THE RED CAPS FROM 1955-1960

Bobby Hamilton Real Name Robert Caristo from Long Island, New York

	TITLE	UK LBL	UK POS	UK YEAR	US POS	US YEAR	US LBL
1	Crazy Eyes For You		0	1958	40	1958	(APT 25002)

Bobby Hart See Tommy Boyce & Bobby Hart

Bobby Hebb Male Vocalist, B: 26 Jul 1941, Nashville

	TITLE	UK LBL	UK POS	UK YEAR	US POS	US YEAR	US LBL
* 1	Sunny	(PHILIPS BF 1503)	12	1966	2	1966	(PHILIPS 40365)
2	A Satisfied Mind		0	1966	39	1966	(PHILIPS 40400)
3	Love Love Love	(PHILIPS 6051 023)	32	1972	0	1972	

BOBBY'S BROTHER HAL WAS A MEMBER OF THE GROUP MARIGOLDS

Bobby Helms Male Vocalist, B: 15 Aug 1933 Bloomington, Indiana

	TITLE	UK LBL	UK POS	UK YEAR	US POS	US YEAR	US LBL
1	Fraulein		0	1957	36	1957	(Decca 30194)
* 2	My Special Angel	(Brunswick 05721)	22	1957	7	1957	(Decca 30423)
3	Jingle Bell Rock		0	1957	6	1957	(Decca 30513)
4	No Other Baby	(Brunswick 05730)	30	1958	0	1958	
5	Jacqueline	(Brunswick05748)	20	1958	63	1958	(Decca 30619)
6	Jingle Bell Rock (Re-Entry)		0	1958	35	1958	(Decca 30513)
7	Jingle Bell Rock (2nd Re-Entry)		0	1960	36	1960	(Decca 30513)

Bobby Hendricks Male R&B Vocalist, B: 22 Feb 1938 Columbus, Ohio

	TITLE	UK LBL	UK POS	UK YEAR	US POS	US YEAR	US LBL
1	Itchy Twitchy Feeling		0	1958	25	1958	(SUE 706)

BACKING VOCALS ON HIT ARE BY THE COASTERS • BOBBY ALSO SANG WITH THE SWALLOWS IN 1956, THE FLYERS IN 1957 AND THE DRIFTERS IN 1958

Bobby Lewis Male R&B Vocalist, B: 17 Feb 1933 Indianapolis

	TITLE	UK LBL	UK POS	UK YEAR	US POS	US YEAR	US LBL
* 1	Tossin' And Turnin'		0	1961	1	1961	(BELTONE 1002)
2	One Track Mind		0	1961	9	1961	(BELTONE 1012)

HE FIRST RECORDED IN 1952

Bobby M Mixed Vocal/Instrumental Duo from the USA

	TITLE	UK LBL	UK POS	UK YEAR	US POS	US YEAR	US LBL
1	Let's Stay Together	(GORDY TMG 1288)	53	1980	0	1980	

HIT IS CREDITED TO BOBBY M FEATURING JEAN CARN

Bobby Marchan Male Vocalist, B: 30 Apr 1930 Youngstown, Ohio

	TITLE	UK LBL	UK POS	UK YEAR	US POS	US YEAR	US LBL
1	There's Something On Your Mind (Part 2)		0	1960	31	1960	(FIRE 1022)

BOBBY WAS A SINGER WITH HUEY 'PIANO' SMITH & THE CLOWNS

Bobby McFerrin Male Vocalist, B: 11 Mar 1950 New York

	TITLE	UK LBL	UK POS	UK YEAR	US POS	US YEAR	US LBL
* 1	Don't Worry Be Happy	(Manahattan MT 50146)	2	1988	1	1988	(EMI-MANHATTAN 56)
2	Thinkin' About Your Body	(Manahattan Blue 6)	46	1988	0	1988	

Bobby Moore & The Rhythm Male Vocalist/Saxophonist From Montgomery, USA

	TITLE	UK LBL	UK POS	UK YEAR	US POS	US YEAR	US LBL
1	Searching For My Love		0	1966	27	1966	(CHECKER 1129)

FORMED IN ALABAMA IN 1946 WITH BOBBY MOORE & CHICO JENKINS

Bobby Nunn Male Vocal/Multi-Instrumentalist from the USA

	TITLE	UK LBL	UK POS	UK YEAR	US POS	US YEAR	US LBL
1	Don't Knock It (Until You Try It)	(Motown TMG 1323)	65	1984	0	1984	

Bobby Russell Male Singer/Songwriter, B: 19 Apr 1941 Nashville

	TITLE	UK LBL	UK POS	UK YEAR	US POS	US YEAR	US LBL
1	1432 Franklin Pike Circle Hero		0	1968	36	1968	(ELF 90020)
! 2	Carlie		0	1969	66	1969	(ELF 90023)
! 3	Better Homes And Gardens		0	1969	34	1969	(ELF 90031)
4	Saturday Morning Confusion		0	1971	28	1971	(United Artists 50788)
! 5	Mid American Manufacturing Tycoon		0	1973	93	1973	(Columbia 45901)

Bobby Rydell Male Vocalist, Real Name Robert Ridarelli B: 2 Apr 1941 In Lawton, Oklahoma.

	TITLE	UK LBL	UK POS	UK YEAR	US POS	US YEAR	US LBL
1	Kissin' Time		0	1959	11	1959	(CAMEO 167)
2	We've Got Love		0	1959	6	1959	(CAMEO 169)
3	Wild One	(Columbia DB 4429)	7	1960	2	1960	(CAMEO 171)
4	Little Bitty Girl		0	1960	19	1960	(CAMEO 171)
5	Swingin' School	(Columbia DB 4471)	44	1960	5	1960	(CAMEO 175)

ISSUE	TITLE	UK LBL	UK POS	UK YEAR	US POS	US YEAR	US LBL
6	Ding-A-Ling		0	1960	18	1960	(CAMEO 175)
7	Wild One (Re-Entry)	(Columbia DB 4429)	47	1960	0	1960	
8	Volare	(Columbia DB 4495)	46	1960	4	1960	(CAMEO 179)
9	Volare (Re-Entry)	(Columbia DB 4495)	22	1960	0	1960	
10	Sway	(Columbia DB 4545)	12	1960	14	1960	(CAMEO 182)
11	Good Time Baby	(Columbia DB 4600)	42	1961	11	1961	(CAMEO 186)
12	That Old Black Magic		0	1961	21	1961	(CAMEO 190)
13	The Fish		0	1961	25	1961	(CAMEO 192)
14	I Wanna Thank You		0	1961	21	1961	(CAMEO 201)
15	Jingle Bell Rock	(Cameo Parkway C 205)	40	1962	21	1962	(CAMEO 205)
16	I've Got Bonnie		0	1962	18	1962	(CAMEO 205)
17	Teach Me To Twist	(Columbia DB 4802)	45	1962	0	1962	
18	I'll Never Dance Again		0	1962	14	1962	(CAMEO 217)
19	The Cha Cha Cha		0	1962	10	1962	(CAMEO 228)
20	Butterfly Baby		0	1963	23	1963	(CAMEO 242)
* 21	Forget Him	(Cameo Parkway C 108)	13	1963	4	1963	(CAMEO 280)
22	Wildwood Days		0	1963	17	1963	(CAMEO 252)
	SEE ALSO CHUBBY CHECKER						

Bobby Scott Male Vocal/Pianist/Composer, B: 29 Jan 1937 Mount Pleasant, New York

* 1	Chain Gang		0	1956	13	1956	(ABC-PARAMOUNT 9658)
	BOBBY TOURED WITH THE FAMOUS GENE KRUPA ORCHESTRA IN THE 50S • OBITUARY: D: 5 NOV 1990 LUNG CANCER.						

Bobby Setter & His Cash and Carry

* 1	Tchip Tchip	(CANNON)	0	1974	0	1974	(TARA)
	THE HIT SOLD A MILLION IN EUROPE						

Bobby Sherman Male Vocalist, B: 18 Jul 1943 Santa Monica, California

* 1	Little Woman		0	1969	3	1969	(METROMEDIA 121)
* 2	La La La (If I Had You)		0	1969	9	1969	(METROMEDIA 150)
* 3	Easy Come Easy Go		0	1970	9	1970	(METROMEDIA 177)
4	Hey, Mister Sun		0	1970	24	1970	(METROMEDIA 188)
* 5	Julie Do Ya Love Me	(CBS 5144)	28	1970	5	1970	(METROMEDIA194)
6	Cried Like A Baby		0	1971	16	1971	(METROMEDIA 206)
7	The Drum		0	1971	29	1971	(METROMEDIA 217)

Bobby Solo Male Vocalist, B: 1946 Now Lives In Rome.

* 1	Una Lacrima Sul Viso (A Tear On Your Face)	(RICORDI)	0	1964	0	1964	
	THE HIT WAS NUMBER 1 IN ITALY FOR NINE WEEKS • THE HIT WAS WITH THE GIANNI MARCHETTI CORCHESTRA						

Bobby Taylor & The Vancouvers Male Vocal/Instrumental Sextet from Canada

1	Does Your Mama Know About Me		0	1968	29	1968	(GORDY 7069)
2	Malinda		0	1968	48	1968	(GORDY 7079)
	NAMES: TOMMY CHONG, WES HENDERSON, ROBBIE KING, TED LEWIS & EDDIE PATTERSON						

Bobby Thurston Male Vocalist from the USA

1	Check Out The Groove	(Epic EPC 8348)	10	1980	0	1980	

Bobby Vee Male Vocalist, Real Name Robert Velline B: 30 Apr 1943 Fargo, North Dakota

* 1	Devil Or Angel		0	1960	6	1960	(LIBERTY 55270)
* 2	Rubber Ball	(London HLG 9255)	4	1961	6	1960	(LIBERTY 55287)
3	More Than I Can Say	(London HLG 9316)	4	1961	0	1961	
4	Stayin' In	(London HLG 9316)	4	1961	33	1961	(LIBERTY 55296)
5	How Many Tears	(London HLG 9389)	10	1961	0	1961	
* 6	Take Good Care Of My Baby	(London HLG 9438)	3	1961	1	1961	(LIBERTY 55354)
* 7	Run To Him	(London HLG 9470)	6	1961	2	1961	(Liberty 55388)
8	Please Don't Ask About Barbara	(Liberty LIB 55419)	29	1962	15	1962	(Liberty 55419)
9	Sharing You	(Liberty LIB 55451)	10	1962	15	1962	(Liberty 55451)
10	Punish Her		0	1962	20	1962	(Liberty 55479)
11	A Forever Kind Of Love	(Liberty LIB 10046)	13	1962	0	1962	
* 12	The Night Has A Thousand Eyes	(Liberty LIB 10069)	3	1963	3	1962	(Liberty 55521)
13	Charms		0	1963	13	1963	(Liberty 55530)
14	Be True To Yourself		0	1963	34	1963	(Liberty 55581)
15	Bobby Tomorrow	(Liberty LIB 55530)	21	1963	0	1963	
* 16	Come Back When You Grow Up		0	1967	3	1967	(Liberty 55964)
17	Beautiful People		0	1967	37	1967	(Liberty 56009)
18	My Girl / Hey Girl		0	1968	25	1968	(Liberty 56033)
	BOBBY'S FIRST DISC WAS 'SUSIE BABY' • HITS 16,17 ARE CREDITED TO BOBBY VEE & THE STRANGERS						
	IN 1959 BOBBY SANG WITH HIS BROTHERS 15-PIECE BAND THE SHADOWS WHO FILLED IN FOR BUDDY HOLLY AT THE NEXT VENUE FOLLOWING THE PLANE CRASH.						

Bobby Vinton Male Vocalist, Real Name Stanley Robert Vinton B: 16 Apr 1935 Cannonsburg, Pennsylvania.

* 1	Roses Are Red (My Love)	(Columbia DB 4878)	15	1962	1	1962	(Epic 9509)

	ISSUE	TITLE	UK LBL	UK POS	UK YEAR	US POS	US YEAR	US LBL
	2	Rain Rain Go Away		0	1962	12	1962	(Epic 9532)
	3	I Love The Way You Are		0	1962	38	1962	(DIAMOND 121)
	4	Trouble Is My Middle Name		0	1963	33	1963	(Epic 9561)
	5	Let's Kiss And Make Up		0	1963	38	1963	(Epic 9561)
	6	Over The Mountain (Across The Sea)		0	1963	21	1963	(Epic 9577)
	7	Blue On Blue		0	1963	3	1963	(Epic 9593)
*	8	Blue Velvet	(Epic 6505240)	2	1990	1	1963	(Epic 9614)
*	9	There I've Said It Again	(Columbia DB 7179)	34	1963	1	1963	(Epic 9638)
	10	My Heart Belongs To Only You		0	1964	9	1964	(Epic 9662)
	11	Tell Me Why		0	1964	13	1964	(Epic 9687)
	12	Clinging Vine		0	1964	17	1964	(Epic 9705)
*	13	Mr. Lonely		0	1964	1	1964	(Epic 9730)
	14	Long Lonely Nights		0	1965	17	1965	(Epic 9768)
	15	L-O-N-E-L-Y		0	1965	22	1965	(Epic 9791)
	16	What Colour (Is A Man)		0	1965	38	1965	(Epic 9846)
	17	Satin Pillows		0	1965	23	1965	(Epic 9869)
	18	Dum-De-Da		0	1966	40	1966	(Epic 10014)
	19	Coming Home Soldier		0	1967	11	1967	(Epic 10090)
	20	Please Love Me Forever		0	1967	6	1967	(Epic 10228)
	21	Just As Much As Ever		0	1968	24	1968	(Epic 10266)
	22	Take Good Care Of My Baby		0	1968	33	1968	(Epic 10305)
	23	Halfway To Paradise		0	1968	23	1968	(Epic 10350)
*	24	I Love How You Love Me		0	1968	9	1968	(Epic 10397)
	25	To Know You Is To Love You		0	1969	34	1969	(Epic 10461)
	26	The Days Of Sand And Showels		0	1969	34	1969	(Epic 10485)
	27	My Elusive Dreams		0	1970	46	1970	(Epic 10576)
	28	Every Day Of My Life		0	1972	24	1972	(Epic 10822)
	29	Sealed With A Kiss		0	1972	19	1972	(Epic 10861)
*	30	My Melody Of Love		0	1974	3	1974	(ABC 12022)
	31	Beer Barrel Polka		0	1975	33	1975	(ABC 12056)
	32	Make Believe It's Your First Time		0	1979	78	1979	(TAPESTRY 002)
	38	Roses Are Red (My Love) (Re-Issue)	(Epic 6564677)	71	1990	0	1990	

HIT 18 IS ALSO KNOWN AS 'SHE UNDERSTANDS ME' • UNLISTED HITS 33-37 ARE C/W

Bobby Womack   Male Vocalist, B: 4 Mar 1944 Cleveland, Ohio

	ISSUE	TITLE	UK LBL	UK POS	UK YEAR	US POS	US YEAR	US LBL
	1	That's The Way I Feel About Cha		0	1972	27	1972	(United Artists 50847)
*	2	Harry Hippie		0	1972	31	1972	(United Artists 50946)
	3	Nobody Wants You When You're Down And Out		0	1973	29	1973	(United Artists 255)
*	4	Lookin' For A Love		0	1974	10	1974	(United Artists 375)
	5	Tell Me Why	(MOTOWN TMG 1339)	60	1984	0	1984	
	6	I Wish He Didn't Trust Me So Much	(MCA MCA 994)	64	1985	0	1985	
	7	So The Story Goes	(Chrysalis LIB 3)	34	1987	0	1987	
	8	Living In A Box	(MCA MCA 1210)	70	1987	0	1987	
	9	I'm Back For More	(DOME CDDOME 1002)	27	1993	0	1993	
	10	It's A Man's Man's Man's World	(PULSE 8 CDLOSE 89)	73	1995	0	1995	

HIS NICKNAME IS THE PREACHER. BOBBY WAS WITH THE WOMACK BROTHERS WHO WERE VALENTINOS & THE LOVERS

Bobbysocks   Female Vocal Duo from Norway/Sweden

	ISSUE	TITLE	UK LBL	UK POS	UK YEAR	US POS	US YEAR	US LBL
	1	Let It Swing	(RCA PB 40127)	44	1985	0	1985	

Body Count   Male Vocal/Instrumental Group from the USA

	ISSUE	TITLE	UK LBL	UK POS	UK YEAR	US POS	US YEAR	US LBL
	1	Born Dead	(Rhyme Syndicate SYNDG 4)	28	1994	0	1994	
	2	Necessary Evil	(Virgin VSCDX 1529)	45	1994	0	1994	

Bodysnatchers   Female Vocal/Instrumental Group from the UK

	ISSUE	TITLE	UK LBL	UK POS	UK YEAR	US POS	US YEAR	US LBL
	1	Let's Do Rock Steady	(2 TONE CHS TT 9)	22	1980	0	1980	
	2	Easy Life	(2 TONE CHS TT 12)	50	1980	0	1980	

SEE ALSO BELLE STARS

Boiling Point   Male Vocal/Instrumental Group from the USA

	ISSUE	TITLE	UK LBL	UK POS	UK YEAR	US POS	US YEAR	US LBL
	1	Let's Get Funktified	(Bang Bang 1312)	41	1978	0	1978	

Bomb The Bass   Male Producer Tim Simenon from the UK

	ISSUE	TITLE	UK LBL	UK POS	UK YEAR	US POS	US YEAR	US LBL
	1	Beat Dis	(Mister-Ron DOOD 1)	2	1988	0	1988	
	2	Megablast - Don't Make Me Wait	(Mister-Ron DOOD 2)	6	1988	0	1988	
	3	Say A Little Prayer	(Rhythm King DOOD 3)	10	1988	0	1988	
	4	Winter In July	(Rhythm King 6572757)	7	1991	0	1991	
	5	The Air You Breathe	(Rhythm King 6575387)	52	1991	0	1991	
	6	Keep Giving Me Love	(Rhythm King 6579887)	62	1992	0	1992	
	7	Bug Powder Dust	(Stoned Heights BRCD 300)	24	1994	0	1994	

ISSUE	TITLE	UK LBL	UK POS	UK YEAR	US POS	US YEAR	US LBL
8	Darkheart	(Stoned Heights BRCD 305)	35	1994	0	1994	
9	1 To 1 Religion	(Stoned Heights BRCD 313)	53	1995	0	1995	
10	Sandcastles	(Stoned Heights BRCD 324)	54	1995	0	1995	

Bombalurina Mixed Vocal Group from the UK

1	Itsy Bitsy Teeny Weeny Yellow Polka Dot Bikini	(Carpet CRPT 1)	1	1990	0	1990	
2	Seven Little Girls Sitting In The Back Seat	(Carpet CRPT 2)	18	1990	0	1990	

HIT 2 IS CREDITED TO BOMBALURINA FEATURING TIMMY MALLETT

Bombers Mixed Vocal/Instrumental Group From Canada

1	(Everybody) Get Dancin'	(Flamingo FM 1)	37	1979	0	1979	
2	Let's Dance	(Flamingo FM 4)	58	1979	0	1979	

Bon Jovi Names Jon Bon Jovi, Dave Bryan, Richie Sambora, Alec Such & Tick Torres

1	Runaway		0	1984	39	1984	(Mercury 818309)
2	Hardest Part Is The Night	(Vertigo VER 22)	68	1985	0	1985	
3	You Give Love A Bad Name	(Vertigo VER 26)	14	1986	1	1986	(Mercury 884953)
4	Livin' On A Prayer	(Vertigo VER 28)	4	1986	1	1987	(Mercury 888184)
5	Wanted Dead Or Alive	(Vertigo JOV 1)	13	1987	7	1987	(Mercury 888467)
6	Never Say Goodbye	(Vertigo JOV 2)	21	1987	0	1987	
7	Bad Medicine	(Vertigo JOV 3)	17	1988	1	1988	(Mercury 870657)
8	Born To Be My Baby	(Vertigo JOV 4)	22	1988	3	1989	(Mercury 872156)
9	I'll Be There For You	(Vertigo JOV 5)	18	1989	1	1989	(Mercury 872564)
10	Lay Your Hands On Me	(Vertigo JOV 6)	18	1989	7	1989	(Mercury 874452)
11	Living In Sin	(Vertigo JOV 7)	35	1989	9	1989	(Mercury 876070)
12	Keep The Faith	(Vertigo JOV 8)	5	1992	29	1992	(JAMBCO 864432)
13	Bed Of Roses	(Vertigo JOVCD 9)	13	1993	10	1993	(JAMBCO 864852)
14	In These Arms	(v JOVCD 10)	9	1993	27	1993	(JAMBCO 862088)
15	I'll Sleep When I'm Dead	(Vertigo JOVCD 11)	17	1993	0	1993	
16	I Believe	(Vertigo JOVCD 12)	11	1993	0	1993	
17	Dry County	(Vertigo JOVCD 13)	9	1994	0	1994	
* 18	Always	(Vertigo JOVCD 14)	2	1994	4	1994	(Mercury 856227)
19	Please Come Home For Christmas	(Vertigo JOVCD 16)	4	1994	0	1994	
20	Someday I'll Be Saturday Night	(Mercury JOVDD 15)	7	1995	0	1995	
21	Please Come Home For Christmas (Re-Entry)	(Vertigo JOVCD 16)	46	1995	0	1995	
22	This Ain't A Love Song	(Mercury JOVCD 17)	6	1995	14	1995	(Mercury 856824)
23	Something For The Pain	(Mercury JOVMD 18)	8	1995	0	1995	
24	Lie To Me	(Mercury JOVCD 19)	10	1995	0	1995	
25	These Days / 634-5789	(Mercury JOVCD 20)	7	1996	0	1996	
26	Hey God	(Mercury JOVCD 21)	13	1996	0	1996	

SEE ALSO JON BON JOVI

Bone Male Vocal/Instrumental Duo from the UK

1	Wings Of Love	(Deconstruction 74321176282)	55	1994	0	1994	

Bone Thugs-N-Harmony Male Rap Quintet from Cleveland, USA

1	Thuggish-Ruggish-Bone		0	1994	22	1994	(RUTHLESS 5527)
+ 2	Foe Tha Love Of $		0	1995	33	1995	(RUTHLESS 5540)
3	1st Of Tha Month	(Epic 6625172)	32	1995	14	1995	(RUTHLESS 6331)
4	East 1999		0	1995	62	1995	(RUTHLESS 6332)
* 5	Tha Crossroads	(Epic 6635502)	8	1996	1	1996	(RELATIVITY 6335)
6	1st Of Tha Month (Re-Issue)	(Epic 6638505)	15	1996	0	1996	
7	Look Into My Eyes	(Epic 6647862)	16	1997	0	1997	

HIT 2 IS CREDITED TO BONE THUGS-N-HARMONY FEATURING 'AZY-E
GROUP CONSISTING OF KRAYZIE BONE, BIZZY BONE, LAYZIE BONE, WISH BONE, FLESH-N-BONE • FORMER NAME WAS BONE ENTERPRISE

Boney M Mixed Vocal Group from Jamaica/Antilles/MontserratNames Are Marcia Barrett, Liz Mitchell, Maizie Williams And Bobby Farrell

1	Daddy Cool	(Atlantic K 10827)	6	1976	0	1976	
2	Sunny	(Atlantic K 10892)	3	1977	0	1977	
3	Ma Baker	(Atlantic K 10965)	2	1977	0	1977	
4	Belfast	(Atlantic K 10965)	8	1977	0	1977	
5	Rivers Of Babylon / Brown Girl In The Ring	(Atlantic K 11120)	1	1978	30	1978	(SIRE 1027)
6	Rasputin	(Atlantic/HANSA K 11192)	2	1978	0	1978	
8	Mary's Boy Child - Oh My Lord	(Atlantic/HANS A K 11221)	1	1978	0	1978	
9	Painter Man	(Atlantic/HANS A K 11255)	10	1979	0	1979	
10	Hooray Hooray It's A Holi-Holiday	(Atlantic/HANS A K 11279)	3	1979	0	1979	
11	Gotta Go Home / El Lute	(Atlantic/HANS A K 1351)	12	1979	0	1979	
12	I'm Born Again	(Atlantic/HANS A K 11410)	35	1979	0	1979	
13	My Friend Jack	(Atlantic/HANS A K 11463)	57	1980	0	1980	
14	Children Of Paradise	(Atlantic/HANS A K 11637)	66	1981	0	1981	

ISSUE	TITLE	UK LBL	UK POS	UK YEAR	US POS	US YEAR	US LBL
15	We Kill The World (Don't Kill The World)	(Atlantic/HANS A K 11689)	39	1981	0	1981	
16	Megamix - Mary's Boy Child (Re-Mix)	(ARIOLA 111947)	52	1988	0	1988	
17	Boney M Megamix	(Arista 74321125127)	7	1992	0	1992	
18	Brown Girl In The Ring (Re-Mix)	(Arista 74321137052)	38	1993	0	1993	

Bonnie Guitar   Real Name Bonnie Buckingham B: 25 Mar 1924 Seattle

1	Dark Moon		0	1957	6	1957	(DOT 15550)

Bonnie Lou   Female Vocalist, Real Name Bonnie Lou KathB: 27 Oct 1924 Bloomington, Illinois

1	Tennessee Wig Walk	(Parlophone R 3730)	4	1954	0	1954	
2	Daddy-O		0	1955	14	1955	(KING 4835)

Bonnie Pointer   Female Vocalist, B: 11 Jul 1951 East Oakland, CaliforniaFormer Member Of The Pointer Sisters 1971-78

1	Heaven Must Have Sent You		0	1979	11	1979	(MOTOWN 1459)
2	I Can't Help Myself		0	1980	40	1980	(MOTOWN 1478)

Bonnie Raitt   Female Blues-Rock Singer/Guitarist, B: 8 Nov 1949 From Burbank, California

!	1	Don't It Make Ya Wanna Dance		0	1980	42	1980	(FULL MOON 47033)
	2	Something To Talk About		0	1991	5	1991	(Capitol 44724)
	3	I Can't Make You Love Me	(Capitol CL 639)	50	1991	10	1992	(Capitol 44729)
	4	Not The Only One		0	1992	34	1992	(Capitol 44764)
	5	Love Sneakin' Up On You	(Capitol CDCL 713)	69	1994	19	1994	(Capitol 58125)
	6	You	(Capitol CDCLS 718)	31	1994	0	1994	
	7	You Got It		0	1995	33	1995	(Arista 12795)
	8	Rock Steady	(Capitol CDCL 763)	50	1995	0	1995	with Bryan Adams

Bonnie Sisters   Names Sylvia, Jean And Pat Bonnie From New York

1	Cry Baby		0	1956	18	1956	(RAINBOW 328)

Bonnie Tyler   Female Vocalist, Real Name Gaynor HopkinsB: 8 Jun 1953 Swansea, Wales.

	1	Lost In France	(RCA 2734)	9	1976	0	1976	
	2	More Than A Lover	(RCA PB 5008)	28	1977	0	1977	
*	3	It's A Heartache	(RCA PB 5057)	4	1977	3	1978	(RCA 11249)
!	4	My Guns Are Loaded		0	1979	86	1979	(RCA 11468)
	5	Married Men	(RCA PB 5164)	35	1979	0	1979	
*	6	Total Eclipse Of The Heart	(CBS TYLER 1)	1	1983	1	1983	(Columbia 03906)
	7	Faster Than The Speed Of Night	(CBS A 3338)	43	1983	0	1983	
	8	Have You Ever Seen The Rain	(CBS A 3517)	47	1983	0	1983	
	9	A Rockin' Good Way	(Epic A 4071)	5	1984	0	1984	
	10	Holding Out For A Hero (From Footloose)	(CBS A 4251)	2	1985	34	1984	(Columbia 04370)
	11	Loving You's A Dirty Job But Somebody's Gotta Do It	(CBS A 6662)	73	1985	0	1985	
	12	Holding Out For A Hero (Re-Issue)	(TOTAL TYLER	69	1991	0	1991	
	13	Making Love (Out Of Nothing At All)	(EAST WEST EW 010CD)	45	1996	0	1996	

HIT 9 IS CREDITED TO SHAKY AND BONNIE • HIT 11 IS CREDITED TO BONNIE TYLER GUEST VOCALIST TODD RUNDGREN

Bono   Male Vocalist from Ireland

1	In A Lifetime	(RCA PB 40535)	20	1986	0	1986	
2	In A Lifetime (Re-Issue)	(RCA PB 42873)	17	1989	0	1989	
3	I've Got You Under My Skin	(Island CID 578)	4	1993	0	1993	
4	In The Name Of The Father	(Island CID 593)	46	1994	0	1994	

Bonzo Dog Doo-Dah Band   Male Vocal/Instrumental Group from the UK

1	I'm The Urban Spaceman	(Liberty LBF 15144)	5	1968	0	1968	

NAMES: VIVIAN STANSHALL, NEIL INNES, VERNON DUDLEY BOWHAY-NOWELL, LARRY SMITH, ROGER RUSKIN SPEAR, RODNEY SLATER & SAM

Boo Radleys   Male Vocal/Instrumental Group from the UK

1	Does This Hurt / Boo! Forever	(CREATION CRESCD 128)	43	1990	0	1990	
2	Wish I Was Skinny	(CREATION CRESCD 169)	75	1993	0	1993	
3	Barney (...& Me)	(CREATION CRESCD 178)	48	1994	0	1994	
4	Lazarus	(CREATION CRESCD 187)	50	1994	0	1994	
5	Wake Up Boo!	(CREATION CRESCD 191)	9	1995	0	1995	
6	Find The Answer Within	(CREATION CRESCD 202)	37	1995	0	1995	
7	It's Lulu	(CREATION CRESCD 211)	25	1995	0	1995	
8	From The Bench At Belvidere	(CREATION CRESCD 214)	24	1995	0	1995	
9	What's In The Box? (See Whatcha Got)	(CREATION CRESCD 220)	25	1996	0	1996	
10	C'mon Kids	(CREATION CRESCD 236)	18	1996	0	1996	
11	Ride The Tiger	(CREATION CRESCD 248)	38	1997	0	1997	

Boo-Yaa T.R.I.B.E.   Male Rap Group from the USA

1	Psyko Funk	(Fourth & Broadway BRW 179)	43	1990	0	1990	
2	Another Boy Murdered	(Epic 6597842)	36	1993	0	1993 and To Faith No More

Boogie Box High   Male Vocal/Instrumental Duo from the UK

1	Jive Talkin'	(HARDBACK 7BOSS 4)	7	1987	0	1987	

ISSUE	TITLE	UK LBL	UK POS	UK YEAR	US POS	US YEAR	US LBL
Boogie Down Productions	Male Scratch/Rap Duo from the USA						
1	My Philosophy	(JIVE JIVEX 170)	69	1988	0	1988	
Booker Newbury III	Male Vocalist from the USA						
1	Love Town	(Polydor POSP 613)	6	1983	0	1983	
2	Teddy Bear	(Polydor POSP 637)	44	1983	0	1983	
Booker T. & The M.G.'S	Male Instrumental Group from the USA The MG Stands For Memphis Group						
* 1	Green Onions	(Atlantic K 10109)	7	1979	3	1962	(STAX 127)
2	Boot-Leg		0	1965	58	1965	(STAX 169)
+ 3	My Sweet Potato		0	1966	18	1966	(STAX 196)
4	Hip Hug-Her		0	1967	37	1967	(STAX 211)
5	Groovin'		0	1967	21	1967	(STAX 224)
6	Soul Limbo	(STAX 102)	30	1968	17	1968	(STAX 0001)
7	Hang Em' High		0	1968	9	1968	(STAX 0013)
8	Time Is Tight	(STAX 119)	4	1969	6	1969	(STAX 0028)
9	Mrs Robinson		0	1969	37	1969	(STAX 0037)
10	Soul Clap '69	(STAX 127)	35	1969	0	1969	
	REAL NAME BOOKER T JONES B: 12 NOV 1944 MEMPHIS • OTHER MEMBERS ARE STEVE CROPPER (GUITAR), LEWIS STEINBERG (BASS) & AL JACKSON (DRUMS)						
Boom Boom Boom	Male Vocal/Instrumental Group from the UK						
1	Here Comes The Man	(FUN AFTER ALL FUN 101)	74	1986	0	1986	
Boomer Castleman	Male Vocalist, Real Name Owen Clark from Texas						
1	Judy Mae		0	1975	33	1975	(MUMS 6038)
Boomtown Rats	Male Vocal/Instrumental Group from Ireland Lead Singer Is (And See Also) Bob Geldof						
1	Lookin' After No.1	(ENSIGN ENY 4)	11	1977	0	1977	
2	Mary Of The 4th Form	(ENSIGN ENY 9)	15	1977	0	1977	
3	She's So Modern	(ENSIGN ENY 13)	12	1978	0	1978	
4	Like Clockwork	(ENSIGN ENY 14)	6	1978	0	1978	
5	Rat Trap	(ENSIGN ENY 16)	1	1978	0	1978	
6	I Don't Like Mondays	(ENSIGN ENY 30)	1	1979	0	1979	
7	Diamond Smiles	(ENSIGN ENY 33)	13	1979	0	1979	
8	Someone's Looking At You	(ENSIGN ENY 34)	4	1979	0	1979	
9	Banana Republic	(ENSIGN BONGO 1)	3	1980	0	1980	
10	The Elephants Graveyard (Guilty)	(ENSIGN BONGO 2)	26	1981	0	1981	
11	Never In A Million Years	(Mercury MER 87)	62	1981	0	1981	
12	House On Fire	(Mercury MER 91)	24	1982	0	1982	
13	Tonight	(Mercury MER 154)	73	1984	0	1984	
14	Drag Me Down	(Mercury MER 163)	50	1984	0	1984	
15	I Don't Like Mondays (Re-Issue)	(VERTIGO VERCD 87)	38	1994	0	1994	
Boothill Foot-Tappers	Mixed Vocal/Instrumental Group from the UK						
1	Get Your Feet Out Of My Shoes	(GO! DISCS TAP1)	64	1984	0	1984	
Boots Brown & His Blockbusters	Real Name Milton 'Shorty' Rogers B: 14 Apr 1924 Massachusetts						
1	Cerveza		0	1958	23	1958	(RCA 7269)
Boots Randolph Combo	Real Name Holmer Louis Randolph Iii B: Paducah, Kentucky						
1	Yakety Sax		0	1963	35	1963	(MONUMENT 804)
Bootsy's Rubber Band	Male Vocal/Instrumental Group from the USA						
1	Bootzilla	(Warner Bros. K 17196)	43	1978	0	1978	
Boris Gardiner	Male Vocal/Instrumentalist from Jamaica						
1	Elizabethan Reggae	(DUKE DU 39)	48	1970	0	1970	
2	Elizabethan Reggae (Re-Entry)	(DUKE DU 39)	14	1970	0	1970	
3	I Wanna Wake Up With You	(REVUE REV 733)	1	1986	0	1986	
4	You're Everything To Me	(REVUE REV 735)	11	1986	0	1986	
5	The Meaning Of Christmas	(REVUE REV 740)	69	1986	0	1986	
Boss	Male Producer David Morales from the USA See Also David Morales - Bad Yard Club						
1	Congo	(COOLTEMPO CDCOOL 296)	54	1994	0	1994	
Boston	Male Vocal/Instrumental Duo from the USA Names Tom Scholz & Brad Delp, Was Originally A Quintet						
1	More Than A Feeling	(Epic EPC 4658)	22	1977	5	1976	(Epic 50266)
2	Long Time		0	1977	22	1977	(Epic 50329)
3	Peace Of Mind		0	1977	38	1977	(Epic 50381)
4	Don't Look Back	(Epic EPC 6653)	43	1978	4	1978	(Epic 50590)
5	A Man I'll Never Be		0	1978	31	1978	(Epic 50638)
6	Amanda		0	1986	1	1986	(MCA 52756)
7	Were Ready		0	1987	9	1987	(MCA 52985)
8	Can'tcha Say (You Believe In Me) / Still In love		0	1987	20	1987	(MCA 53029)

ISSUE	TITLE	UK LBL	UK POS	UK YEAR	US POS	US YEAR	US LBL
Boston Pops Orchestra Arthur Fiedler, Male Viola Player/Orchestra Director from the USA, Obituary: D: 10 Jul 1979, Aged 85.							
* 1	Jalousie		0	1938	13	1938	(VICTOR 12160)
2	Sleigh Ride		0	1949	24	1949	(RCA VICTOR 78-1484)
3	Syncopated Clock		0	1951	28	1951	(RCA VICTOR 3044)
Bouncing Czecks Male Vocal/Instrumental Group from the UK							
1	I'm A Little Christmas Cracker	(RCA 463)	72	1984	0	1984	
Bourgeois Tagg Male Vocal/Instrumental Duo from the USAThe Group Was Formed In 1984 Led By, & See Also Brent Bourgeois							
1	I Don't Mind At All	(Island IS 353)	35	1988	38	1988	(Island 99409)
Bourgie Bourgie Male Vocal/instrumental Group from the UK							
1	Breaking Point	(MCA BOU 1)	48	1984	0	1984	
Bow Wow Wow Mixed Vocal/Instrumental Group from the UK Names: Annabella Lwin, Matthew Ashman, Leigh Gorman & David Barbarossa							
1	C30-C60-C90 Go	(EMI 5088)	34	1980	0	1980	
2	Your Cassette Pet	(EMI WOW 1)	58	1980	0	1980	
3	W.O.R.K. (N.O. Nah No No My Daddy Don't)	(EMI 5153)	62	1981	0	1981	
4	Prince Of Darkness	(RCA 100)	58	1981	0	1981	
5	Chihuahua	(RCA 144)	51	1981	0	1981	
6	Go Wild In The County	(RCA 175)	7	1982	0	1982	
7	See Jungle (Jungle Boy) / Tv Savage	(RCA 220)	45	1982	0	1982	
8	I Want Candy	(RCA 238)	9	1982	0	1982	
9	Louis Quatorze	(RCA 263)	66	1982	0	1982	
10	Do You Wanna Hold Me	(RCA 314)	47	1983	0	1983	
Bowa Male/ Female Vocal/Instrumental Duo from the USA							
1	Different Story	(DEAD DEAD GOOD GOOD 8)	64	1991	0	1991	
Box Tops Male Vocal/Instrumental Group from the USA							
* 1	The Letter	(STATESIDE SS 2044)	5	1967	1	1967	(MALA 565)
2	Neon Rainbow		0	1967	24	1967	(MALA 580)
* 3	Cry Like A Baby	(Bell 1001)	15	1968	2	1968	(MALA 593)
4	Choo Choo Train		0	1968	26	1968	(MALA 12005)
5	I Met Her In Church		0	1968	37	1968	(MALA 12017)
6	Sweet Cream Ladies, Forward March		0	1969	28	1969	(MALA 12035)
7	Soul Deep	(Bell 1068)	22	1969	18	1969	(MALA 12040)
	NAMES: ALEX CHILTON, BILL CUNNINGHAM & GARY TALLEY FORMED IN 1966 • RICK ALLEN & TOM BOGGS JOINED THE GROUP AFTER THEIR FIRST HIT							
Boy George Male Vocalist, Real Name George O'Dowd B: 14 Jun 1961 Bexleyheath, England							
1	Everything I Own	(Virgin BOY 100)	1	1987	0	1987	
2	Keep Me In Mind	(Virgin BOY 101)	29	1987	0	1987	
3	Sold	(Virgin BOY 102)	24	1987	0	1987	
4	To Be Reborn	(Virgin BOY 103)	13	1987	0	1987	
5	Live My Life	(Virgin BOY 105)	62	1988	40	1988	(Virgin 99390)
6	No Clause 28	(Virgin BOY 106)	57	1988	0	1988	
7	Don't Cry	(Virgin BOY 107)	60	1988	0	1988	
8	Don't Take My Mind On A Trip	(Virgin BOY 108)	68	1989	0	1989	
9	The Crying Game	(SPAGHETTI CIAO 6)	22	1992	15	1993	(SBK 50437)
10	More Than Likely	(GEE STREET GESCD 49)	40	1993	0	1993	
11	Funtime	(Virgin VST 1538)	45	1995	0	1995	
12	I'l Adore	(Virgin VSCDD 1543)	50	1995	0	1995	
13	Same Thing In Reverse	(Virgin VSCDT 1561)	56	1995	0	1995	
	HIT 10 IS CREDITED TO PM DAWN FEATURING BOY GEORGE • SEE ALSO CULTURE CLUB AND JESUS LOVES YOU							
Boy Meets Girl Mixed Vocal Duo from the USA Names: Shannon Rubicam & George Merill							
1	Oh Girl		0	1985	39	1985	(A&M 2713)
2	Waiting For A Star To Fall	(RCA PB 49519)	39	1988	5	1988	(RCA 8691)
Boyd Bennett & His Rockets Male Vocal/Instrumental Group from the USA							
1	Seventeen	(Parlophone R 4063)	16	1955	5	1955	(KING 1470)
Boys Male Vocal Group from the USA Names: Tajh & Baial Samad With Khiry Hakeem							
1	Dial My Heart	(MOTOWN ZB 42245)	61	1988	13	1989	(MOTOWN 53301)
2	Crazy	(MOTOWN ZB 44037)	57	1990	29	1990	(MOTOWN 924)
Boys Club Male Vocal Duo, Joe Pasquale & Eugene Wolfgramm							
1	I Remember Holding You		0	1988	8	1988	(MCA 53430)
Boys Don't Cry Male Vocal/Instrumental Group With Lead Singer Nick Richards from the UK							
1	I Wanna Be A Cowboy		0	1986	12	1986	(PROFILE 5084)
Boystown Gang Male Vocal Group from the USA							
1	Ain't No Mountain High Enough	(WEA DICK 1)	46	1981	0	1981	
2	Can't Take My Eyes Off You	(ERC 101)	4	1982	0	1982	

ISSUE	TITLE	UK LBL	UK POS	UK YEAR	US POS	US YEAR	US LBL
3	Signed, Sealed, Delivered (I'm Yours)	(ERC 102)	50	1982	0	1982	

HIT 1 IS A MEDLEY WITH 'REMEMBER ME'

Boyz II Men Male Vocal Group from the USA

	ISSUE	TITLE	UK LBL	UK POS	UK YEAR	US POS	US YEAR	US LBL
*	1	Motownphilly	(MOTOWN TMG 1402)	23	1992	3	1991	(MOTOWN 2090)
*	2	It's So Hard To Say Goodbye To Yesterday		0	1991	2	1991	(MOTOWN 2136)
*	3	End Of The Road	(MOTOWN TMG 1411)	1	1992	8	1992	(MOTOWN 2178)
	4	Uhh Ahh		0	1992	16	1992	(MOTOWN 2141)
*	5	End Of The Road		0	1992	1	1992	(MOTOWN 2178)
*	6	In The Still Of The Nite (I'll Remember)	(MOTOWN TMGCD 1415)	27	1993	3	1992	(MOTOWN 2193)
	7	Let It Snow		0	1994	32	1994	(MOTOWN 2218)
*	8	I'll Make Love To You	(MOTOWN TMGCD 1431)	5	1994	1	1994	(MOTOWN 2257)
*	9	On Bended Knee	(MOTOWN TMGCD 1433)	20	1994	1	1994	(MOTOWN 0244)
	10	I'll Make Love To You (Re-Entry)	(MOTOWN TMGCD 1431)	68	1994	0	1994	
	11	Thank You	(MOTOWN TMGCD 1438)	26	1995	21	1995	(MOTOWN 0274)
*	12	Water Runs Dry	(MOTOWN TMGCD 1443)	24	1995	2	1995	(MOTOWN 0358)
*	13	One Sweet Day	(Columbia 6626035)	6	1995	1	1995	(Columbia 78074)
	14	Hey Lover	(DEF JAM DEFCD 14)	17	1995	0	1996	

HIT 13 IS CREDITED TO MARIAH CAREY AND BOYZ II MEN • HIT 14 IS CREDITED TO L.L. COOL J FEATURING BOYZ II MEN
GROUP MEMBER ARE WANYA MORRIS, MICHAEL MCCARY, SHAWN STOCKMAN & NATHAN MORRIS

Boyzone Male Vocal Group from Ireland

ISSUE	TITLE	UK LBL	UK POS	UK YEAR	US POS	US YEAR	US LBL
1	Love Me For A Reason	(Polydor 8512802)	2	1994	0	1994	
2	Key To My Life	(Polydor PZCD 342)	3	1995	0	1995	
3	So Good	(Polydor 5797732)	3	1995	0	1995	
4	Father And Son	(Polydor 5775762)	2	1995	0	1995	
5	Coming Home Now	(Polydor 5775702)	4	1996	0	1996	
6	Words	(Polydor 5755372)	1	1996	0	1996	
7	A Different Beat	(Polydor 5732052)	1	1996	0	1996	
8	Isn't It A Wonder	(Polydor 5735472)	44	1997	0	1997	
9	Picture Of You	(Polydor 5713112)	2	1997	0	1997	

Boz Scaggs Male Vocalist William Royce Scaggs, B: 8 Jun 1944 In Ohio

	ISSUE	TITLE	UK LBL	UK POS	UK YEAR	US POS	US YEAR	US LBL
	1	It's Over		0	1976	38	1976	(Columbia 10319)
*	2	Lowdown	(CBS 4563)	28	1976	3	1976	(Columbia 10367)
	3	What Can I Say	(CBS 4869)	10	1977	0	1977	
	4	Lido Shuffle	(CBS 5136)	13	1977	11	1977	(Columbia 10491)
	5	Hollywood	(CBS 5836)	33	1977	0	1977	
	6	Breakdown Dead Ahead		0	1980	15	1980	(Columbia 11241)
	7	Jojo		0	1980	17	1980	(Columbia 11281)
	8	Look What You've Done To Me		0	1980	14	1980	(Columbia 11349)
	9	Miss Sun		0	1981	14	1981	(Columbia 11406)
	10	Heart Of Mine		0	1988	35	1988	(Columbia 07780)

BACKING VOCALS ON HIT 9 ARE BY LISA DAL BELLO • PREVIOUS GROUP WERE STEVE MILLER BAND, MARKSMEN & THE FABULOUS NIGHT TRAINS

Brad Male Vocal/Instrumental Group from the USA

ISSUE	TITLE	UK LBL	UK POS	UK YEAR	US POS	US YEAR	US LBL
1	20th Century	(Epic 6592482)	64	1993	0	1993	

Brad Newman Male Vocalist from the UK

ISSUE	TITLE	UK LBL	UK POS	UK YEAR	US POS	US YEAR	US LBL
1	Somebody To Love	(Fontana H 357)	47	1962	0	1962	

Bradford & Romano Male Vocal Duo from the USA

ISSUE	TITLE	UK LBL	UK POS	UK YEAR	US POS	US YEAR	US LBL
1	Chattanoogie Shoe-Shine Boy		0	1950	17	1950	(RCA VICTOR 3208)

Braids Female Vocal Group from the USA

ISSUE	TITLE	UK LBL	UK POS	UK YEAR	US POS	US YEAR	US LBL
1	Bohemian Rhapsody (From High School High)	(Atlantic A 5640CD)	21	1996	42	1996	(Atlantic 98055)

Bram Tchaikovsky Real Name Peter Bramall

ISSUE	TITLE	UK LBL	UK POS	UK YEAR	US POS	US YEAR	US LBL
1	Girl Of My Dreams		0	1979	37	1979	(Polydor 14575)

Brand New Heavies Mixed Vocal/Instrumental Group from the USA/UK

ISSUE	TITLE	UK LBL	UK POS	UK YEAR	US POS	US YEAR	US LBL
1	Never Stop	(FFRR F 165)	43	1991	0	1991	
2	Dream Come True	(FFRR F 180)	24	1992	0	1992	
3	Ultimate Trunk Kunk (Ep)	(FFRR F 185)	19	1992	0	1992	
4	Don't Let It Go To Your Head	(FFRR BNH 1)	24	1992	0	1992	
6	Stay This Way	(FFRR BNH 2)	40	1992	0	1992	
7	Dream On Dreamer	(FFRR BNHCD 3)	15	1994	0	1994	
8	Back To Love	(FFRR BNHCD 4)	23	1994	0	1994	
9	Midnight At The Oasis	(FFRR BNCDP 5)	13	1994	0	1994	
10	Spend Some Time	(FFRR BNHCD 6)	26	1994	0	1994	
11	Close To You	(FFRR BNHCD 7)	38	1995	0	1995	
12	Sometimes	(FFRR BNHCD 8)	11	1997	91	1997	(RED ANT 4009)

	ISSUE	TITLE	UK LBL	UK POS	UK YEAR	US POS	US YEAR	US LBL
	13	You Are The Universe	(FFRR BNHCD 9)	21	1997	0	1997	

Brandi Wells Female Vocalist from the USA

	ISSUE	TITLE	UK LBL	UK POS	UK YEAR	US POS	US YEAR	US LBL
	1	Watch Out	(Virgin VS 479)	74	1982	0	1982	

Brandy Female Vocalist from the USA

	ISSUE	TITLE	UK LBL	UK POS	UK YEAR	US POS	US YEAR	US LBL
*	1	I Wanna Be Down	(Atlantic A 7186CD)	44	1994	6	1994	(Atlantic 87225)
*	2	Baby		0	1995	4	1995	(Atlantic 87173)
	3	Best Friend		0	1995	34	1995	(Atlantic 87148)
	4	I Wanna Be Down (Re-Mix)	(Atlantic A 7186CD)	36	1995	0	1995	
*	5	Brokenhearted		0	1995	9	1995	(Atlantic 87150)
	6	Sittin' Up In My Room	(Arista 74321344012)	30	1996	2	1996	
	7	Missing You		0	1996	25	1996	(EASTWEST 64262)

HIT 4 IS CREDITED TO BRANDY, TAMIA, GLADY'S KNIGHT & CHAKA KHAN

Brass Construction Male Vocal/Instrumental Group from the USANine-Man Group Formed In Brooklyn In 1968 As The Dynamic Soul

	ISSUE	TITLE	UK LBL	UK POS	UK YEAR	US POS	US YEAR	US LBL
	1	Movin'	(United Artists UP 36090)	23	1976	14	1976	(United Artists 775)
	2	Ha Cha Cha	(United Artists UP 36205)	37	1977	0	1977	
	3	Music Makes Me Feel Like Dancing	(United Artists UP 615)	39	1980	0	1980	
	4	Walkin' The Line	(Capitol CL 292)	47	1983	0	1983	
	5	We Can Work It Out	(Capitol CL 299)	70	1983	0	1983	
	6	Party Line	(Capitol CL 335)	56	1984	0	1984	
	7	International	(Capitol CL 341)	70	1984	0	1984	
	8	Give And Take	(Capitol CL 377)	62	1985	0	1985	
	9	Movin' 1988 (Re-Mix)	(SYNCOPATE SY 11)	24	1988	0	1988	

Brass Ring Studio Group With Phil Bodner From New York

	ISSUE	TITLE	UK LBL	UK POS	UK YEAR	US POS	US YEAR	US LBL
	1	The Phoenix Love Theme		0	1966	32	1966	(DUNHILL 4023)
	2	The Dis-Advantages Of You		0	1967	36	1967	(DUNHILL 4065)

Brat Real Name Roger Kitter Male Vocalist from the UK

	ISSUE	TITLE	UK LBL	UK POS	UK YEAR	US POS	US YEAR	US LBL
	1	Chalk Dust / The Umpire Strikes Back	(HANSA SMASH 1)	19	1982	0	1982	

Brat Pack Names Patrick Donovan & Ray Frazier From New Jersey

	ISSUE	TITLE	UK LBL	UK POS	UK YEAR	US POS	US YEAR	US LBL
	1	You're The Only Woman		0	1990	36	1990	(VENDETTA 1447)

Bravado Male/Female Vocal/Instrumental Group from the UK

	ISSUE	TITLE	UK LBL	UK POS	UK YEAR	US POS	US YEAR	US LBL
	1	Harmonica Man	(PEACH PEACHCD 5)	37	1994	0	1994	

Bread Male Vocal/Instrumental Group from the USA

	ISSUE	TITLE	UK LBL	UK POS	UK YEAR	US POS	US YEAR	US LBL
*	1	Make It With You	(Elektra 2101 010)	5	1970	1	1970	(ELEKTRA 45686)
	2	It Don't Matter To Me		0	1970	10	1970	(ELEKTRA 45701)
	3	Let Your Love Go		0	1971	28	1971	(ELEKTRA 45711)
*	4	If		0	1971	4	1971	(ELEKTRA 45720)
	5	Mother Freedom		0	1971	37	1971	(ELEKTRA 45740)
*	6	Baby I'm A Want You	(Elektra K 12033)	14	1972	3	1971	(ELEKTRA 45751)
*	7	Everything I Own	(Elektra K 12041)	32	1972	5	1972	(ELEKTRA 45765)
	8	Diary		0	1972	15	1972	(ELEKTRA 45784)
	9	Guitar Man	(Elektra K 12066)	16	1972	11	1972	(ELEKTRA 45803)
	10	Sweet Surrender		0	1972	15	1972	(ELEKTRA 45818)
	11	Aubrey		0	1973	15	1973	(ELEKTRA 45832)
	12	Lost Without Your Love	(Elektra K 12241)	27	1976	9	1976	(ELEKTRA 45365)

NAMES: DAVID GATES, JAMES GRIFFIN, ROBB ROYER & JIM GORDON • GROUP WAS ORIGINALLY CALLED PLEASURE FAIRE IN 1969

Break Machine Male Vocal/Dance Group from the USA

	ISSUE	TITLE	UK LBL	UK POS	UK YEAR	US POS	US YEAR	US LBL
	1	Street Dance	(Record Shack Soho 13)	3	1984	0	1984	
	2	Breakdance Party	(Record Shack Soho 20)	9	1984	0	1984	
	3	Breakdance Party (Re-Entry)	(Record Shack Soho 20)	65	1984	0	1984	
	4	Are You Ready	(Record Shack Soho 24)	27	1984	0	1984	

Breakfast Club Male Vocal/Instrumental Group from the USAQuartet Based In New York. Madonna Was A Member Of The Group In The 80s

	ISSUE	TITLE	UK LBL	UK POS	UK YEAR	US POS	US YEAR	US LBL
	1	Right On Track	(MCA MCA 1146)	54	1987	7	1987	(MCA 52954)

Breathe Male Vocal/Instrumental Group from the UK

	ISSUE	TITLE	UK LBL	UK POS	UK YEAR	US POS	US YEAR	US LBL
	1	Hands To Heaven	(Siren SRN 68)	4	1988	2	1988	(A&M 2991)
	2	Jonah	(Siren SRN 95)	60	1988	0	1988	
	3	How Can I Fall?	(Siren SRN 102)	48	1988	3	1988	(A&M 1224)
	4	Don't Tell Me Lies	(Siren SRN 109)	45	1989	10	1989	(A&M 1267)
	5	Say A Prayer		0	1990	21	1990	(A&M 1519)
	6	Does She Love That Man?		0	1991	34	1991	(A&M 1535)

NAMES: DAVID GLASPER, MARCUS LILLINGTON, MICHAEL DELAHUNTY & IAN SPICE • MICHAEL DELAHUNTY LEFT THE GROUP IN 1988

Brecker Brothers Male Vocal/Instrumental Group from the USA

	ISSUE	TITLE	UK LBL	UK POS	UK YEAR	US POS	US YEAR	US LBL
	1	East River	(Arista ARIST 211)	34	1978	0	1978	

ISSUE	TITLE	UK LBL	UK POS	UK YEAR	US POS	US YEAR	US LBL
Breeders	Female/Male Vocal/Instrumental Group from the USA/UK						
1	Safari (EP)	(4AD BAD 2003)	69	1992	0	1992	
2	Cannonball (EP)	(4AD BAD 3011CD)	40	1993	0	1993	
3	Devine Hammer	(4AD BAD 3017CD)	59	1993	0	1993	
4	Head To Toe (EP)	(4AD BADD 4012)	68	1994	0	1994	
Breekout Krew	Male Vocal Duo from the USA						
1	Matt's Mood	(London LON 59)	51	1984	0	1984	
Brenda & The Tabulations	R&B Group from Philadelphia Original Names Brenda Payton, Jerry Jones, Eddie Jackson & Maurice Coates						
1	Dry Your Eyes		0	1967	20	1967	(DIONN 500)
2	Right On The Tip Of My Tongue		0	1971	23	1971	(TOP & BOTTOM 407)
Brenda Holloway	Female Vocalist, B: 21 Jun 1946 Atascadero, California						
1	Every Little Bit Hurts		0	1964	13	1964	(Tamla 54094)
2	I'll Always Love You		0	1964	60	1964	(Tamla 54099)
3	When I'm Gone		0	1965	25	1965	(Tamla 54111)
+ 4	Just Look What You've Done		0	1967	21	1967	(Tamla 54148)
5	You Made Me So Very Happy		0	1967	39	1967	(Tamla 54155)
Brenda K. Starr	Female Vocalist, Real Name Brenda Kaplan B: 15 Oct 1966 Manhattan						
1	I Still Believe		0	1988	13	1988	(MCA 53288)
2	What You See Is What You Get		0	1988	24	1988	(MCA 53367)
Brenda Lee	Female Vocalist, Real Name Brenda Mae Tarpley B: 11 Dec 1944 Lithonia, Georgia						
1	One Step At A Time		0	1957	43	1957	(Decca 30198)
* 2	Sweet Nothin's	(Brunswick 05819)	45	1960	4	1960	(Decca 30967)
3	Sweet Nothin's (Re-Entry)	(Brunswick 05819)	4	1960	0	1960	
* 4	I'm Sorry	(Brunswick 05833)	12	1960	1	1960	(Decca 31093)
5	That's All You Gotta Do		0	1960	6	1960	(Decca 31093)
6	I Want To Be Wanted	(Brunswick 05839)	31	1960	1	1960	(Decca 31149)
7	Just A Little		0	1960	40	1960	(Decca 31149)
8	Rockin' Around The Chrismas Tree	(Brunswick 05880)	6	1962	14	1960	(Decca 30776)
9	Emotions	(Brunswick 05847)	45	1961	7	1961	(Decca 31195)
10	I'm Learning About Love		0	1961	33	1961	(Decca 31195)
11	Let's Jump The Broomstick	(Brunswick 05823)	12	1961	0	1961	
12	You Can Depend On Me		0	1961	6	1961	(Decca 31231)
13	Dum Dum	(Brunswick 05854)	62	1961	4	1961	(Decca 31272)
14	Fool Number One	(Brunswick 5860)	38	1961	3	1961	(Decca 31309)
15	Anybody But Me		0	1961	31	1961	(Decca 31309)
16	Break It To Me Gently	(Brunswick 05864)	46	1962	4	1962	(Decca 31348)
17	Speak To Me Pretty	(Brunswick 05867)	3	1962	0	1962	
18	Everybody Loves Me But You		0	1962	6	1962	(Decca 31379)
19	Here Comes That Feeling	(Brunswick 05871)	5	1962	0	1962	
20	Heart In Hand		0	1962	15	1962	(Decca 31407)
21	It's Started All Over Again	(Brunswick 05876)	15	1962	29	1962	(Decca 31407)
* 22	All Alone Am I	(Brunswick 05882)	7	1963	3	1962	(Decca 31424)
23	Your Used To Be		0	1963	32	1963	(Decca 31454)
* 24	Losing You	(Brunswick 05886)	10	1963	6	1963	(Decca 31478)
25	My Whole World Is Falling Down		0	1963	24	1963	(Decca 31510)
26	I Wonder	(Brunswick 5891)	14	1963	25	1963	(Decca 31510)
27	The Grass Is Greener		0	1963	17	1963	(Decca 31539)
28	Sweet Impossible You	(Brunswick 05896)	28	1963	0	1963	
29	As Usual	(Brunswick 05899)	5	1964	12	1963	(Decca 31570)
30	Think	(Brunswick 05903)	26	1964	25	1964	(Decca 31599)
31	Is It True	(Brunswick 05915)	17	1964	17	1964	(Decca 31690)
32	Christmas Will Be Just Another Lonely Day	(Brunswick 05921)	29	1964	0	1964	
33	Thanks A Lot	(Brunswick 05927)	41	1965	0	1965	
34	Too Many Rivers	(Brunswick 05936)	22	1965	13	1965	(Decca 31792)
35	Rusty Bells		0	1965	33	1965	(Decca 31849)
36	Coming On Strong		0	1966	11	1966	(Decca 32018)
37	Ride, Ride, Ride		0	1967	37	1967	(Decca 32079)
38	Johnny One Time		0	1969	41	1969	(Decca 32428)
42	Nobody Wins		0	1973	70	1973	(MCA 40003)

THE OTHER HITS ARE C/W • SHE IS KNOWN AS LITTLE MISS DYNAMITE AND AS OF 1997 SHE IS STILL GOING STRONG

| **Brenda Lee Eager** | See Jerry Butler | | | | | | |

ISSUE	TITLE	UK LBL	UK POS	UK YEAR	US POS	US YEAR	US LBL
Brenda Russell	Female Vocalist, Real Name Brenda Gordon fom Brooklyn						
1	So Good So Right / In The Thick Of It	(A&M AM 7515)	51	1980	30	1979	(HORIZON 123)
2	Piano In The Dark	(Breakout USA 623)	23	1988	6	1988	(A&M 30039)
	FEATURING VOCALS ON HIT 2 BY JOE ESPOSITO						
	SHE RECORDED WITH HER THEN HUSBAND BRIAN RUSSELL AS BRIAN AND BRENDA						
Brendon	Male Vocalist from the UK						
1	Gimme Some	(Magnet MAG 80)	14	1977	0	1977	
Brent Bourgeois	B: New York, Lead Singer With Bourgeois Tagg						
1	Dare To Fall In Love		0	1990	32	1990	(CHARISMA 98971)
Brenton Wood	Male Vocalist, Real Name Alfred Smith B: 26 Jul 1941 Shreveport, Louisiana.						
1	The Oogum Boogum Song		0	1967	34	1967	(DOUBLE SHOT 111)
* 2	Gimme Little Sign	(Liberty LBF15021)	8	1967	9	1967	(DOUBLE SHOT 116)
3	Baby You Got It		0	1967	34	1967	(DOUBLE SHOT 121)
	FIRST RECORDED WITH LITTLE FREDDY & THE ROCKETS IN 1958						
Brewer & Shipley	Folk-Rock Duo, Names Mike Brewer & Tom Shipley						
1	One Toke Over The Line		0	1971	10	1971	(KAMA SUTRA 516)
Brian & Michael	Male Vocal Duo from the UK						
1	Matchstalk Men And Matchstalk Cats And Dogs	(PYE 7N 46035)	1	1978	0	1978	
Brian Hyland	Male Vocalist, B: 12 Nov 1943 Woodhaven, New York						
* 1	Itsy Bitsy Teeny Weeny Yellow Polka Dot Bikini	(London HLR 6161)	8	1960	1	1960	(KAPP 342)
2	Four Little Heels	(London HLR 9203)	29	1960	0	1960	
3	Let Me Belong To You		0	1961	20	1961	(ABC-PARAMOUNT 10236)
4	Ginny Come Lately	(HMV POP 1013)	5	1962	21	1962	(ABC-PARAMOUNT 10294)
* 5	Sealed With A Kiss	(HMV POP 1051)	3	1962	3	1962	(ABC-PARAMOUNT 10336)
6	Warmed Over Kisses (Left Over Love)	(HMV POP 1079)	28	1962	25	1962	(ABC-PARAMOUNT 10359)
7	The Joker Went Wild		0	1966	20	1966	(PHILIPS 40377)
8	Run, Run, Look And See		0	1966	25	1966	(PHILIPS 40405)
* 9	Gypsy Woman	(UNI UN 530)	45	1971	3	1970	(UNI 55240)
10	Gypsy Woman (Re-Entry)	(UNI UN 530)	42	1971	0	1971	
11	Sealed With A Kiss (Re-Issue)	(ABC 4059)	7	1975	0	1975	
	BRIAN HAD HIS OWN GROUP THE DELPHIS AT THE AGE OF 12						
Brian Kennedy	Male Vocalist from the UK						
1	A Better Man	(RCA	28	1996	0	1996	
2	Life, Love And Happiness	(RCA	27	1996	0	1996	
3	Put The Message In The Box	(RCA	37	1997	0	1997	
Brian May	Male Vocal/Guitarist from the UK						
1	Star Fleet	(EMI 5436)	65	1983	0	1983	
2	Driven By You	(Parlophone R 6304)	6	1991	0	1991	
3	Too Much Love Will Kill You	(Parlophone R 6320)	5	1992	0	1992	
4	We Are The Champions	(POLYGRAM TV TV PO 229)	66	1992	0	1992	
5	Back To The Light	(Parlophone R 6329)	19	1992	0	1992	
6	Resurrection	(Parlophone CDRS 6351)	23	1993	0	1993	
7	Last Horizon	(Parlophone CDR 6371)	51	1993	0	1993	
	HE WAS LEAD GUITARIST WITH QUEEN						
Brian Mcknight	Male Singer/Composer, B: 5 Jun 1969 From Buffalo, New York						
1	Love Is		0	1993	3	1993	(GIANT 19630)
2	One Last Cry		0	1993	13	1993	(Mercury 862404)
	HIT 1 IS CREDITED TO BRIAN MCKNIGHT AND VANESSA WILLIAMS						
Brian Poole & The Tremeloes	Male Vocalist, B: 3 Nov 1941 England, See Also The Tremeloes						
1	Twist And Shout	(Decca F 11694)	4	1963	0	1963	
2	Do You Love Me	(Decca F 11739)	1	1963	0	1963	
3	I Can Dance	(Decca F 11771)	31	1963	0	1963	
4	Candy Man	(Decca F 11823)	6	1964	0	1964	
5	Someone Someone	(Decca F 11893)	2	1964	0	1964	
6	Twelve Steps To Love	(Decca F 11951)	32	1964	0	1964	
7	Three Bells	(Decca F 12037)	17	1965	0	1965	
8	I Want Candy	(Decca F 12197)	25	1965	0	1965	
Brian Protheroe	Male Vocalist from the UK						
1	Pinball	(Chrysalis CHS 2043)	22	1974	0	1974	
Brian Wilson	Male Vocalist, B: 20 Jun 1942 Hawthorne, California						
1	Caroline, No		0	1966	32	1966	(Capitol 5610)
	SEE ALSO THE BEACH BOYS						

ISSUE	TITLE	UK LBL	UK POS	UK YEAR	US POS	US YEAR	US LBL
Briana Corrigan Female Vocalist from the UK							
1	Love Me Now	(EAST WEST EW 041CD1)	48	1996	0	1996	
Brick Male Vocal/Instrumental Group Formed In Atlanta							
1	Dazz	(BANG 004)	36	1977	3	1976	(BANG 727)
2	Dusic		0	1977	18	1977	(BANG 734)
Brighouse & Rastrick Brass Band Male Brass Band from Yorkshire, England							
1	The Floral Dance	(TRANSATLANTIC BIG 548)	2	1977	0	1977	
Brighter Side Of Darkness R&B Group, Names Darryl Lamont, Larry Washington, Randolph Murphy & Ralph Eskridge, Formed In							
1	Love Jones		0	1972	8	1972	(20th Century 2002)
Brighton & Hove Albion F.C. Male Soccer Team Vocalist from the UK							
1	The Boys In The Old Brighton Blue	(ENERGY NRG 2)	65	1983	0	1983	
Brilliant Male/Female Vocal/Instrumental Group from the UK							
1	It's A Man's Man's Man's World	(FOOD FOOD 5)	58	1985	0	1985	
2	Love Is War	(FOOD FOOD 6)	64	1986	0	1986	
3	Somebody	(FOOD FOOD 7)	67	1986	0	1986	
Broken English Male Vocal/Instrumental Group from the UK							
1	Comin' On Strong	(EMI EM 5)	18	1987	0	1987	
2	Love On The Side	(EMI EM 55)	69	1987	0	1987	
Bronski Beat Male Vocal/Instrumental Group from the UK							
1	Smalltown Boy	(Forbidden Fruit Bite 1)	3	1984	0	1984	
2	Why	(Forbidden Fruit Bite 2)	6	1984	0	1984	
3	It Ain't Necessarily So	(Forbidden Fruit Bite 3)	16	1984	0	1984	
4	I Feel Love (Medley)	(Forbidden Fruit Bite 4)	3	1985	0	1985	
5	Hit That Perfect Beat	(Forbidden Fruit Bite 6)	3	1985	0	1985	
6	Come On, Come On	(Forbidden Fruit Bite 7)	20	1986	0	1986	
7	Cha Cha Heels	(Arista 112331)	32	1989	0	1989	
8	Smalltown Boy (Re-Mix)	(London LON 287)	32	1991	0	1991	
	HIT 4 IS CREDITED TO BRONSKI BEAT AND MARK ALMOND • HIT 7 IS CREDITED TO EARTHA KITT AND BRONSKI BEAT • HIT 8 JIMMY SOMERVILLE WITH BRONSKI BEAT							
Brook Benton Male Singer/Songwriter, Real Name Benjamin Franklin Peay, B: 19 Sep 1931 Camden, South Carolina							
* 1	It's Just A Matter Of Time		0	1959	3	1959	(Mercury 71394)
2	Endlessly	(Mercury AMT 1043)	28	1959	12	1959	(Mercury 71443)
3	So Close		0	1959	38	1959	(Mercury 71443)
4	Thank You Pretty Baby		0	1959	16	1959	(Mercury 71478)
5	So Many Ways		0	1959	6	1959	(Mercury 71512)
* 6	Baby (You Got What It Takes)		0	1960	5	1960	(Mercury 71565)
7	The Ties That Bind		0	1960	37	1960	(Mercury 71566)
8	A Rockin' Good Way (To Mess Around And Fallin Love)		0	1960	7	1960	(Mercury 71629)
9	Kiddio	(Mercury AMT 1109)	42	1960	7	1960	(Mercury 71652)
10	The Same One		0	1960	16	1960	(Mercury 71652)
11	Kiddio (Re-Entry)	(Mercury AMT 1109)	41	1960	0	1960	
12	Fools Rush In (Where Angels Fear To Tread)	((Mercury AMT1121)	50	1961	24	1961	(Mercury 71722)
13	Think Twice		0	1961	11	1961	(Mercury 71774)
14	For My Baby		0	1961	28	1961	(Mercury 71774)
* 15	Boll Weevil Song	(Mercury AMT 1148)	30	1961	2	1961	(Mercury 71820)
16	Frankie And Johnny		0	1961	20	1961	(Mercury 71859)
17	Revenge		0	1961	15	1961	(Mercury 71903)
18	Shadrack		0	1962	19	1962	(Mercury 71912)
19	Lie To Me		0	1962	13	1962	(Mercury 73024)
20	Hotel Happiness		0	1962	3	1962	(Mercury 72055)
21	I Got What I Wanted		0	1963	28	1963	(Mercury 72099)
22	My True Confession		0	1963	22	1963	(Mercury 72135)
23	Two Tickets To Paradise		0	1963	32	1963	(Mercury 72117)
24	Going Going Gone		0	1964	35	1964	(Mercury 72230)
* 25	Rainy Night In Georgia		0	1969	4	1969	(COTILLION 44057)
	HITS 6,8 ARE CREDITED TO DINAH WASHINGTON AND BROOK BENTON • FIRST RECORDED UNDER HIS OWN NAME IN 1953							
	OBITUARY : D: 9 APR 1988 SPINAL MENINGITIS.							
Brook Brothers Male Vocal Duo from the UK							
1	Warpaint	(PYE 7N 15333)	5	1961	0	1961	
2	Ain't Gonna Wash For A Week	(PYE 7N 15369)	13	1961	0	1961	
3	He's Old Enough To Know Better	(PYE 7N 15409)	37	1962	0	1962	
4	Welcome Home Baby	(PYE 7N 15453)	33	1962	0	1962	
5	Trouble Is My Middle Name	(PYE 7N 15498)	38	1963	0	1963	

ISSUE	TITLE	UK LBL	UK POS	UK YEAR	US POS	US YEAR	US LBL
Brooklyn Bridge							
* 1	Worst That Could Happen		0	1969	3	1969	(BUDDAH 75)
	GROUP MADE UP OF VARIOUS OTHER GROUPS, CRESTS, DEL-SATINS, RHYTHM METHOD UNTIL THEY FORMED THE PRESENT SET-UP IN 1967						
Brooklyn Dreams Names Joe Esposito, Eddie Hokenson & Donna Summer's husband, Bruce Sudano							
* 1	Heaven Knows		0	1979	4	1979	(CASABLANCA 959)
	HIT IS CREDITED TO DONNA SUMMER WITH BROOKLYN DREAMS						
Bros Male Vocal/Instrumental Trio, Matt & Luke Goss And Craig Logan From 1989 The Act Became A Duo. They Were First Known As Caviar							
1	When Will I Be Famous	(CBS ATOM 2)	62	1987	0	1987	
2	When Will I Be Famous (Re-Entry)	(CBS ATOM 2)	2	1988	0	1988	
3	Drop The Boy	(CBS ATOM 3)	2	1988	0	1988	
4	I Owe You Nothing	(CBS ATOM 4)	1	1988	0	1988	
5	I Quit	(CBS ATOM 5)	4	1988	0	1988	
6	Cat Among The Pigeons / Silent Night	(CBS ATOM 6)	2	1988	0	1988	
7	Too Much	(CBS ATOM 7)	2	1989	0	1989	
8	Chocolate Box	(CBS ATOM 8)	9	1989	0	1989	
9	Sister	(CBS ATOM 9)	10	1989	0	1989	
10	Madly In Love	(CBS ATOM 10)	14	1990	0	1990	
11	Are You Mine	(Columbia 6569707)	12	1991	0	1991	
12	Try	(Columbia 6574047)	27	1991	0	1991	
Brother Beyond Male Vocal/Instrumental Group from the UK Names Nathan Moore, Carl Fysh, Steve Alexander & David White							
1	How Many Times	(EMI EMI 5591)	62	1987	0	1987	
2	Chain-Gang Smile	(Parlophone R 6160)	57	1987	0	1987	
3	Can You Keep A Secret	(Parlophone R6174)	56	1988	0	1988	
4	The Harder I Try	(Parlophone R 6184)	2	1988	0	1988	
5	He Ain't No Competition	(Parlophone R 6193)	6	1988	0	1988	
6	Be My Twin	(Parlophone R 6195)	14	1989	0	1989	
7	Can You Keep A Secret (Re-Mix)	(Parlophone R 6197)	22	1989	0	1989	
8	Drive On	(Parlophone R 6233)	39	1989	0	1989	
9	When Will I See You Again	(Parlophone R 6239)	43	1989	0	1989	
10	Trust	(Parlophone R 6245)	53	1990	0	1990	
11	The Girl I Used To Know	(Parlophone R 6265)	48	1991	27	1991	(EMI 50287)
Brother Bones Male Whistler/Knuckle Bones from the USA							
1	Sweet Georgia Brown		0	1948	10	1948	(TEMPO 652)
	HIT IS CREDITED TO BROTHER BONES & HIS SHADOWS						
Brotherhood Male Rap Group from the UK							
1	One Shot / Nothing In Particular	(BITE IT BHOODD 3)	55	1996	0	1996	
Brotherhood Of Man Mixed Vocal Group from the UK Names Tony Burrows, Johnny Goddison & Sunny (Female)							
1	United We Stand	(DERAM DM 284)	10	1970	13	1970	(DERAM 85059)
2	Where Are You Goin' To My Love	(DERAM DM 298)	22	1970	0	1970	
3	Save Your Kisses For Me	(PYE 7N 45569)	1	1976	27	1976	(PYE 71066)
4	My Sweet Rosalie	(PYE 7N 45602)	30	1976	0	1976	
5	Oh Boy (The Mood I'm In)	(PYE 7N 45656)	8	1977	0	1977	
6	Angelo	(PYE 7N 45699)	1	1977	0	1977	
7	Figaro	(PYE 7N 46037)	1	1978	0	1978	
8	Beautiful Lover	(PYE 7N 46071)	15	1978	0	1978	
9	Middle Of The Night	(PYE 7N 46117)	41	1978	0	1978	
10	Lightning Flash	(EMI 5309)	67	1982	0	1982	
	THE GROUP HAD NEW MEMBERS ON THE HIT 3 TONY'S PREVIOUS GROUPS HAVE BEEN EDISON LIGHTHOUSE, FIRST CLASS, PIPKINS & WHITE PLAINS							
Brothers Male Vocal Group from the UK							
1	Sing Me	(BUS STOP BUS 1054)	8	1977	0	1977	
Brothers Four Male Vocal Group from the USA Names Bob Flick, Mike Kirkland, John Paine & Richard (Dick) Foley							
* 1	Greenfields	(PHILIPS PB 1009)	49	1960	2	1960	(Columbia 41571)
2	Greenfields (Re-Entry)	(PHILIPS PB 1009)	40	1960	0	1960	
3	Frogg		0	1961	32	1961	(Columbia 41958)
Brothers In Rhythm Male Instrumental/Production Duo from the UK							
1	Such A Good Feeling	(FOURTH & BROADWAY BRW 228)	64	1991	0	1991	
2	Such A Good Feeling (Re-Entry)	(FOURTH & BROADWAY BRW228)	14	1991	0	1991	
3	Forever And A Day	(STRESS CDSTR 36)	51	1994	0	1994	
Brothers Johnson Male Vocal/Instrumental Duo, George B: 17 May 1953 & Louis B: 13 Apr 1955 from the USA							
1	I'll Be Good To You		0	1976	3	1976	(A&M 1806)
2	Get The Funk Out Of Ma Face		0	1976	30	1976	(A&M 1851)
3	Strawberry Letter 23	(A&M AMS 7297)	35	1977	5	1977	(A&M 1949)

ISSUE	TITLE	UK LBL	UK POS	UK YEAR	US POS	US YEAR	US LBL
4	Ain't We Funkin' Now	(A&M AMS 7379)	43	1978	0	1978	
5	Ride-O-Rocket	(A&M AMS 7400)	50	1978	0	1978	
6	Stomp	(A&M AMS 7509)	6	1980	7	1980	(A&M 2216)
7	Light Up The Night	(A&M AMS 7526)	47	1980	0	1980	
8	The Real Thing	(A&M AMS 8149)	50	1981	0	1981	

THE BROTHERS WERE MEMBERS OF JOHNSON THREE+ 1 WITH BROTHER TOMMY AND COUSIN ALEX WEIR UNTIL 1975

Brothers Like Outlaw (Featuring) Mixed Vocal Group from the UK Alison Evelyn

1	Good Vibrations	(GEE STREETGESCD 44)	74	1993	0	1993	

Brown Sauce Mixed Vocal Group from the UK

1	I Wanna Be A Winner	(BBC RESL 101)	15	1981	0	1981	

Browns Mixed Vocal Group Jim Brown And His Sisters Maxine & Bobby from Arkansas

*	1	The Three Bells	(RCA 1140)	6	1959	1	1959	(RCA 7555)
	2	Scarlet Ribbons		0	1959	13	1959	(RCA 7614)
	3	The Old Lamplighter		0	1960	5	1960	(RCA 7700)

THE THREE BELLS IS ALSO KNOWN AS THE JIMMY BROWN SONG • JIM & MAXINE STARTED AS A DUO AND WAS JOINED BY BONNIE IN 1952

Brownstone Female Vocal Trio from Los Angeles

*	1	If You Love Me	(MJJ MUSIC	8	1995	8	1995	(MJJ MUSIC 6614135)
	2	Grapevyne	(MJJ MUSIC 6620942)	16	1995	0	1995	
	3	I Can't Tell You Why	(MJJ MUSIC6623775)	27	1995	0	1995	
	4	5 Miles To Empty	(MJJ MUSIC 6640962)	12	1997	52	1997	(MJJ 78496)

Brownsville Station Male Vocal/Instrumental Group from the USA

*	1	Smokin' In The Boys Room	(PHILIPS 6073 834)	27	1974	3	1973	(BIG TREE 16011)
	2	Kings Of The Party		0	1974	31	1974	(BIG TREE 16001)

NAMES CUB KODA, MICHAEL LUTZ & HENRY WECK

Bruce Channel Male Vocalist B: 28 Nov 1940, Jacksonville, Texas

*	1	Hey Baby	(Mercury AMT 1171)	2	1962	1	1962	(SMASH 1731)
	2	Keep On	(Bell 1010)	12	1968	0	1968	

Bruce Cockburn Male Singer/Songwriter, B: 27 May 1945 Canada

1	Wondering Where The Lions Are		0	1980	21	1980	(MILLENNIUM 11786)

Bruce Dickinson Male Vocalist from the UK

1	Tattooed Millionaire	(EMI EM 138)	18	1990	0	1990	
2	All The Young Dudes	(EMI EM 142)	23	1990	0	1990	
3	Dive! Dive! Dive!	(EMI EM 151)	45	1990	0	1990	
4	(I Want To Be) Elected	(London LON 319)	9	1992	0	1992	
5	Tears Of The Dragon	(EMI CDEM 322)	28	1994	0	1994	
6	Shoot All The Clowns	(EMI CDEMS 341)	37	1994	0	1994	
7	Back From The Edge	(RAW POWER PAWX 1012)	68	1996	0	1996	
8	Accident Of Birth	(RAW POWER RAWX 1042)	54	1997	0	1997	

HIT 4 IS CREDITED TO MR BEAN & SMEAR CAMPAIGN FEATURING BRUCE DICKINSON

Bruce Foxton Male Vocalist from the UK

1	Freak	(Arista BFOX 1)	23	1983	0	1983	
2	This Is The Way	(Arista BFOX 2)	56	1983	0	1983	
3	It Makes Me Wonder	(Arista BFOX 3)	74	1984	0	1984	

Bruce Hornsby & The Range Male Vocalist, B: 23 Nov 1954 Williamburg, Virginia   The Range Are An Instrumental Group from the USA

1	The Way It Is	(RCA PB 49804)	15	1986	1	1986	(RCA 5023)
2	Mandolin Rain	(RCA PB 49769)	70	1987	4	1987	(RCA 5087)
3	Every Little Kiss (Re-Mix)		0	1987	14	1987	(RCA 5165)
4	The Valley Road	(RCA PB 49561)	44	1988	5	1988	(RCA 7645)
5	Look Out Any Window		0	1988	35	1988	(RCA 8678)
6	Across The River		0	1990	18	1990	(RCA 2621)

Bruce Johnson Male Instrumentalist (Keyboards) from the USA

1	Pipeline	(CBS 5514)	33	1977	0	1977	

Bruce Ruffin Male Vocalist from Jamaica

1	Rain	(TROJAN TR 7814)	19	1971	0	1971	
2	Mad About You	(RHINO RNO 101)	9	1972	0	1972	

Bruce Springsteen Male Vocalist, B: 23 Sep 1949 Freehold, New Jersey

1	Born To Run	(CBS BRUCE 2)	16	1987	23	1975	(Columbia 10209)
2	Prove It All Night		0	1978	33	1978	(Columbia 10763)
3	Hungry Heart	(CBS 9309)	28	1980	5	1980	(Columbia 11391)
4	Fade Away		0	1981	20	1981	(Columbia 11431)
5	The River	(CBS A 1179)	35	1981	0	1981	
6	Dancing In The Dark	(CBS A 4436)	28	1984	2	1984	(Columbia 004463)

ISSUE	TITLE	UK LBL	UK POS	UK YEAR	US POS	US YEAR	US LBL
7	Cover Me	(CBS 4662)	38	1984	7	1984	(Columbia 04561)
8	Born In The U.S.A.	(CBS A 6342)	5	1985	9	1984	(Columbia 04680)
9	I'm On Fire	(CBS A 6342)	5	1985	6	1985	(Columbia 04772)
10	Dancing In The Dark (Re-Entry)	(CBS A 4436)	4	1985	0	1985	
11	Cover Me (Re-Entry)	(CBS A 4662)	16	1985	0	1985	
12	Glory Days	(CBS A 6375)	17	1985	5	1985	(Columbia 04924)
13	I'm Going Down		0	1985	9	1985	(Columbia 05603)
14	Santa Claus Is Coming To Town - My Hometown	(CBS A 6773)	9	1985	6	1985	(Columbia 05728)
15	War	(Columbia 650193 7)	18	1986	8	1986	(Columbia 06432)
16	Fire	(Columbia 650381 7)	54	1987	0	1987	
17	Brilliant Disguise	(Columbia 651141 7)	20	1987	5	1987	(Columbia 07595)
18	Tunnel Of Love	(Columbia 651295 7)	45	1987	9	1987	(Columbia 07663)
19	One Step Up		0	1988	13	1988	(Columbia 07726)
20	Tougher Than The Rest	(CBS BRUCE 2)	13	1988	0	1988	
21	Spare Parts	(CBS BRUCE 4)	32	1988	0	1988	
22	Human Touch	(Columbia 6578727)	11	1992	16	1992	(Columbia 74273)
23	Better Days	(Columbia 6578907)	34	1992	16	1992	(Columbia 74273)
24	57 Channels (And Nothin' On)	(Columbia 6581387)	32	1992	0	1992	
25	Leap Of Faith	(Columbia 6583697)	46	1992	0	1992	
26	Lucky Town (Live)	(Columbia 65092282)	48	1993	0	1993	
* 27	Streets Of Philadelphia	(Columbia 6600652)	2	1994	9	1994	(Columbia 77384)
28	Secret Garden	(Columbia 6612955)	44	1995	0	1995	
29	Hungry Heart (Re-Issue)	(Columbia 6626252)	28	1995	0	1995	
30	The Ghost Of Tom Joad	(Columbia 6630315)	26	1996	0	1996	
31	Secret Garden (Re-Issue)	(Columbia 6643245)	17	1997	22	1997	(Columbia 77847)

HIT 19 IS CREDITED TO BRUCE SPRINGSTEEN AND E STREET BAND

Bruce Willis Male Actor/Vocalist, B: 19 Mar 1955 Penns Grove, New Jersey

1	Respect Yourself	(Motown ZB 41117)	7	1987	5	1987	(MOTOWN 1876)
2	Under The Boardwalk	(Motown ZB 41349)	2	1987	0	1987	
3	Secret Agent Man / James Bond Is Back	(Motown ZB 41437)	42	1987	0	1987	
4	Comin' Right Up	(Motown ZB 41453)	73	1988	0	1988	

Brucie Weil Small Boy Vocalist from the USA

1	God Bless Us All		0	1953	18	1953	(BARBOUR 451)

Bryan Adams Male Vocalist, B: 5 Nov 1959 Ontario, Canada

1	Straight From The Heart	(A&M AM 322)	51	1986	10	1983	(A&M 2536)
2	Cuts Like A Knife		0	1983	15	1983	(A&M 2553)
3	This Time	(A&M AM 295)	41	1986	24	1983	(A&M 2574)
4	Run To You	(A&M AM 224)	11	1985	12	1984	(A&M 2686)
5	Somebody	(A&M AM 236)	35	1985	11	1985	(A&M 2701)
6	Heaven	(A&M AM 256)	38	1985	1	1985	(A&M 2729)
7	Summer Of '69	(A&M AM 267)	42	1985	5	1985	(A&M 2739)
8	One Night Love Affair		0	1985	13	1985	(A&M 2770)
9	It's Only Love	(A&M AM 285)	29	1985	15	1986	(A&M 2791)
10	Christmas Time	(A&M AM 297)	42	1985	0	1985	
11	Heat Of The Night	(A&M ADAM 2)	50	1987	6	1987	(A&M 2921)
12	Hearts Of Fire	(A&M ADAM 3)	57	1987	26	1987	(A&M 2948)
13	Victim Of Love	(A&M AM 407)	68	1987	32	1987	(A&M 2964)
14	(Everything I Do) I Do It For You	(A&M AM 789)	1	1991	1	1991	(A&M 1567)
* 15	Can't Stop This Thing We Started	(A&M AM 612)	12	1991	2	1991	(A&M 1576)
16	There Will Never Be Another Tonight	(A&M AM 838)	32	1991	31	1992	(A&M 1588)
17	(Everything I Do) I Do It For You (Re-Entry)	(A&M AM 789)	73	1991	0	1991	
18	Thought I'd Died And Gone To Heaven	(A&M AM 848)	8	1992	13	1992	(A&M 1592)
19	All I Want Is You	(A&M AM 879)	22	1992	0	1992	
20	Do I Have To Say The Words?	(A&M AM 0068)	30	1992	11	1992	(A&M 1611)
22	Please Forgive Me	(A&M 5804262)	3	1993	7	1993	(A&M 0422)
* 23	All For Love	(A&M 5804772)	2	1994	1	1993	(A&M 0476)
24	Have You Ever Really Loved A Woman	(A&M 5810282)	4	1995	1	1995	(A&M 1028)
25	Rock Steady	(Capitol CDCL 763)	50	1995	0	1995	
26	Let's Make A Night To Remember	(A&M 5818672)	10	1996	24	1996	(A&M 581862)
27	The Only Thing That Looks Good On Me Is You	(A&M 5816392)	6	1996	0	1996	
28	I Finally Found Someone (From The Mirror Has Two Faces)		0	1996	8	1996	(Columbia 78480)
29	Star	(A&M 5820252)	13	1996	0	1996	
30	18 Til I Die	(A&M 5821852)	22	1997	0	1997	

FORMER LEAD SINGER WITH SWEENEY TODD IN 1976

ISSUE	TITLE	UK LBL	UK POS	UK YEAR	US POS	US YEAR	US LBL
Bryan Ferry	See Also Roxy Music						
1	A Hard Rain's Gonna Fall	(Island WIP 6170)	10	1973	0	1973	
2	The In Crowd	(Island WIP 6196)	13	1974	0	1974	
3	Smoke Gets In Your Eyes	(Island WIP 6205)	17	1974	0	1974	
4	You Go To My Head	(Island WIP 6234)	33	1975	0	1975	
5	Let's Stick Together	(Island WIP 6307)	4	1988	0	1988	
6	Extended Play (Ep)	(Island IEP 1)	7	1976	0	1976	
7	This Is Tomorrow	(Polydor 2001 704)	9	1977	0	1977	
8	Tokyo Joe	(Polydor 2001 711)	15	1977	0	1977	
9	What Goes On	(Polydor POSP 3)	67	1978	0	1978	
10	Sign Of The Times	(Polydor 2001 798)	37	1978	0	1978	
11	Slave To Love	(EG FERRY 1)	10	1985	0	1985	
12	Don't Stop The Dance	(EG FERRY 2)	21	1985	0	1985	
13	Windswept	(EG FERRY 3)	46	1985	0	1985	
14	Is Your Love Strong Enough	(EG FERRY 4)	22	1986	0	1986	
15	The Right Stuff	(Virgin VS 940)	37	1987	0	1987	
16	Kiss And Tell	(Virgin VS 1034)	41	1988	31	1988	(Reprise 28117)
17	Let's Stick Together (Re-Mix)	(EG EGO 44)	12	1988	0	1988	
18	The Price Of Love (Re-Mix)	(EG EGO 46)	49	1989	0	1989	
19	He'll Have To Go	(EG EGO 48)	63	1989	0	1989	
20	I Put A Spell On You	(Virgin VSCDG 1400)	18	1993	0	1993	
21	Will You Love Me Tomorrow	(Virgin VSCDG 1455)	23	1993	0	1993	
22	Girl Of My Best Friend	(Virgin VSCDG1488)	57	1993	0	1993	
23	Your Painted Smile	(Virgin VSCDG 1508)	52	1994	0	1994	
24	Mamouna	(VIFGIN VSCDG 1528)	57	1995	0	1995	
Bryan Johnson	Male Vocalist from the UK						
1	Looking High High High	(Decca F 11213)	20	1960	0	1960	
Bryan Powell	Male Vocalist from the UK						
1	It's Alright	(Talkin Loud TLKCD 34)	73	1993	0	1993	
2	I Think Of You	(Talkin Loud TLKCD 38)	61	1993	0	1993	
3	Natural	(Talkin Loud TLKCD 41)	73	1993	0	1993	
Bubble Puppy	Group Also Recorded As Demian						
1	Hot Smoke And Sasafrass		0	1969	14	1969	(INT ARTISTS)
Buchanan & Goodman	Names Bill Buchanan & Richard Goodman from the USA						
* 1	Flying Saucer (Part 1-2)		0	1956	3	1956	(LUNIVERSE 101)
2	Flying Saucer The 2nd		0	1957	18	1957	(LUNIVERSE 105)
3	Santa And The Satellite (Part 1-2)		0	1957	32	1957	(LUNIVERSE 107)
	HIT 1 WAS ORIGINALLY TITLED 'BACK TO EARTH'						
Buchanan Brothers	Male Producers Terry Cashman, Tommy West & Gene Pistilli						
1	Medicine Man (Part 1)		0	1969	22	1969	(EVENT 3302)
	SEE ALSO CASHMAN & WEST						
Bucketheads	Male Producer Kenny Gonzales from the USA						
1	The Bomb (These Sounds Fall Into My Mind)	(POSITIVA CDTIV 33)	5	1995	0	1995	
2	Got Myself Together	(POSITIVA CDTIV 48)	12	1996	0	1996	
Buckinghams	Rock Quintet from Chicago						
* 1	Kind Of A Drag		0	1967	1	1967	(U.S.A. 860)
2	Don't You Care		0	1967	6	1967	(Columbia 44053)
3	Mercy, Mercy, Mercy		0	1967	5	1967	(Columbia 44182)
4	Hey Baby (They're Playing Our Song)		0	1967	12	1967	(Columbia 44254)
5	Susan		0	1968	11	1968	(Columbia 44378)
	NAMES: DENNIS TUFANO, CARL GIAMMARESE, NICK FORTUNE, JON PAULOS & DENNIS MICCOLI WHO WAS REPLACED BY MARTIN GREBB IN 1967						
	OBITUARY : JON PAULOS D: 26 MAR 1980 DRUG OVERDOSE.						
Buckner & Garcia	Names Jerry Buckner & Gary Garcis From Atlanta						
1	Pac-Man Fever		0	1982	9	1982	(Columbia 02673)
Bucks Fizz	Mixed Vocal Group, Mike Nolan, Robert Gubby (Bobby G), Jay Aston & Cheryl Baker from the UK						
1	Making Your Mind Up	(RCA 56)	1	1981	0	1981	
2	Piece Of The Action	(RCA 88)	12	1981	0	1981	
3	One Of Those Nights	(RCA 114)	20	1981	0	1981	
4	The Land Of Make Believe	(RCA 163)	1	1981	0	1981	
5	My Camera Never Lies	(RCA 202)	1	1982	0	1982	
6	Now Those Days Are Gone	(RCA 241)	8	1982	0	1982	
7	If You Can't Stand The Heat	(RCA 300)	10	1982	0	1982	

ISSUE	TITLE	UK LBL	UK POS	UK YEAR	US POS	US YEAR	US LBL
8	Run For Your Life	(RCA FIZ 1)	14	1983	0	1983	
9	When We Were Young	(RCA 342)	10	1983	0	1983	
10	London Town	(RCA 363)	34	1983	0	1983	
11	Rules Of The Game	(RCA 380)	57	1983	0	1983	
12	Talking In Your Sleep	(RCA FIZ 2)	15	1984	0	1984	
13	Golden Days	(RCA FIZ 3)	42	1984	0	1984	
14	I Hear Talk	(RCA FIZ 4)	34	1984	0	1984	
15	You And Your Heart So Blue	(RCA PB 40233)	43	1985	0	1985	
16	Magical	(RCA PB 40367)	57	1985	0	1985	
17	New Begining (Mamba Seyra)	(Polydor POSP 794)	8	1986	0	1986	
18	Love The One You're With	(Polydor POSP 813)	47	1986	0	1986	
19	Keep Each Other Warm	(Polydor POSP 835)	45	1986	0	1986	
20	Heart Of Stone	(RCA PB 42035)	50	1988	0	1988	

Buddy Clark Male Vocalist, Real Name Samuel Goldberg from the USA

ISSUE	TITLE	UK LBL	UK POS	UK YEAR	US POS	US YEAR	US LBL
1	Spring Is Here		0	1938	19	1938	(VOCALION 4191)
2	Linda		0	1947	1	1947	(Columbia 37215)
3	How Are Things In Glocca Mora (From *Finian's Rainbow*)		0	1947	6	1947	(Columbia 372239)
4	Peg O' My Heart (From *Ziegfeld Follies* Of 1913)		0	1947	1	1947	(Columbia 37392)
5	An Apple Blossom Wedding		0	1947	14	1947	(Columbia 37488)
6	Don't You Love Me Anymore?		0	1947	22	1947	(Columbia 37920)
7	I'll Dance At Your Wedding		0	1947	3	1947	(Columbia 37967)
8	Those Things Money Can't Buy		0	1947	21	1947	(Columbia 37967)
9	You Are Never Away (From *Allegro*)		0	1948	26	1948	(Columbia 37985)
10	Ballerina		0	1948	5	1948	(Columbia 38040)
11	(The Treasure Of) Sierra Madre		0	1948	23	1948	(Columbia 38026)
12	Matinee		0	1948	22	1948	(Columbia 38083)
13	Serenade (Music Played On A Heartstring)		0	1948	23	1948	(Columbia 38091)
14	Now Is The Hour (Maori Farewell Song)		0	1948	6	1948	(Columbia 38115)
15	Love Somebody		0	1948	1	1948	(Columbia 38174)
16	Confess		0	1948	16	1948	(Columbia 38174)
17	Where The Apple Blossoms Fall		0	1948	23	1948	(Columbia 38241)
18	My Darling, My Darling (From *Where's Charley*?)		0	1948	7	1948	(Columbia 38353)
19	Powder Your Face With Sunshine (Smile! Smile! Smile!)		0	1949	16	1949	(Columbia 38394)
20	I Love You So Much It Hurts		0	1949	24	1949	(Columbia 38406)
21	It's Big, Wide, Wonderful World (From *All In Fun*)		0	1949	25	1949	(Columbia 38370)
22	Baby, It's Cold Outside (From *Neptune's Daughter*)		0	1949	4	1949	(Columbia 38463)
23	You're Breaking My Heart		0	1949	4	1949	(Columbia 38546)
24	A Dreamer's Holiday		0	1949	12	1949	(Columbia 38599)

OBITUARY : D: 1 OCT 1949, PLANE CRASH.

Buddy Greco Male Jazz Pianist/Vocalist, B: 14 Aug 1927 PhiladelphiaHe Was With The Benny Goodman Orchestra From 1949-51

ISSUE	TITLE	UK LBL	UK POS	UK YEAR	US POS	US YEAR	US LBL
* 1	Ooh Look-A There, Ain't She Pretty?		0	1947	15	1947	(MUSICRAFT 515)
2	I Ran All The Way Home		0	1951	30	1951	(CORAL 60573)
3	I'll Always Love You Some		0	1953	27	1953	(CORAL 60904)
4	You're Driving Me Crazy (What Did I Do)		0	1953	26	1953	(CORAL 60979)
5	Don't Say Goodbye		0	1953	29	1953	(CORAL 61038)
6	East Side, West Side		0	1954	28	1954	(CORAL 61176)
7	Lady Is A Tramp	(Fontana H 225)	26	1960	0	1960	

HIT 1 WAS WITH THE THREE SHARPS • HIT 2, 3, 4 ARE WITH THE HEATHERTONES • HIT 6 IS CREDITED TO JOHNNY DESMOND, ALAN DALE & BUDDY GRECO

Buddy Hackett Male Comedian/Vocalist from the USA

ISSUE	TITLE	UK LBL	UK POS	UK YEAR	US POS	US YEAR	US LBL
1	The Chinese Waiter		0	1953	29	1953	(CORAL 61105)

Buddy Holly Male Vocal/Instrumentalist (Guitar), Real Name charles Hardin Holley B: 7 Sep 1936 Lubbock, Texas)

ISSUE	TITLE	UK LBL	UK POS	UK YEAR	US POS	US YEAR	US LBL
* 1	Peggy Sue	(CORAL Q 72293)	6	1957	3	1957	(CORAL 61885)
2	Listen To Me	(CORAL Q 72288)	16	1958	0	1958	
3	Rave On	(CORAL Q 72325)	5	1958	37	1958	(CORAL 61985)
4	Early In The Morning	(CORAL Q 72333)	17	1958	32	1958	(CORAL 62006)
5	Heartbeat	(CORAL Q 72346)	30	1959	82	1959	(CORAL 62051)
6	It Doesn't Matter Anymore	(CORAL Q 72360)	1	1959	13	1959	(CORAL 62074)
7	Midnight Shift	(Brunswick 05800)	26	1959	0	1959	
8	Peggy Sue Got Married	(CORAL Q 72376)	13	1959	0	1959	
9	Heartbeat (Re-Issue)	(CORAL Q 72392)	30	1960	0	1960	
10	True Love Ways	(CORAL Q 72397)	25	1960	0	1960	
11	Learning The Game	(CORAL Q 72411)	36	1960	0	1960	
12	What To Do	(CORAL Q 72469)	27	1961	0	1961	
13	Baby I Don't Care / Valley Of Tears	(CORAL Q 72432)	12	1961	0	1961	
14	Listen To Me (Re-Issue)	(CORAL Q 72449)	48	1962	0	1962	

ISSUE	TITLE	UK LBL	UK POS	UK YEAR	US POS	US YEAR	US LBL
15	Reminising	(CORAL Q 72455)	17	1962	0	1962	
16	Brown Eyed Handsome Man	(CORAL Q 72459)	3	1963	0	1956	
17	Bo Diddley	(CORAL Q 72463)	4	1963	0	1963	
18	Wishing	(CORAL Q 72466)	10	1963	0	1963	
19	What To Do (Re-Issue)	(CORAL Q 72469)	27	1963	0	1963	
20	You've Got Love	(CORAL Q 72472)	40	1964	0	1964	
21	Love's Made A Fool Of You	(CORAL Q 72475)	39	1964	0	1964	
22	Peggy Sue / Rave On (Re-Issue)	(MCA MU 1012)	32	1968	0	1968	
23	True Love Ways (Re-Issue)	(MCA MCA 1302)	65	1988	0	1988	

HIT 1 WAS FIRST KNOWN AS CINDY LOU • HIT 20 IS CREDITED TO BUDDY HOLLY & THE CRICKETS
BECAUSE OF CONTRACT PROBLEMS ALL CRICKETS RECORDINGS WERE ON THE 'BRUNSWICK' LABEL, WHILST BUDDY HOLLY WAS ON 'CORAL'
BUDDY BROKE UP WITH THE CRICKETS IN THE AUTUMN OF 1958 • OBITUARY : D: 3 FEB 1959 PLANE CRASH, NEAR MASON CITY, IOWA.

Buddy Johnson Orchestra Male Composer/Blues Bandleader from the USA

ISSUE	TITLE	UK LBL	UK POS	UK YEAR	US POS	US YEAR	US LBL
1	When My Man Comes Home		0	1944	23	1944	(Decca 8655)
2	That's The Stuff You Gotta Watch		0	1945	14	1945	(Decca 8671)
3	Far Cry		0	1948	28	1948	(Decca 48076)
4	Did You See Jackie Robinson Hit That Ball?		0	1949	17	1949	(Decca 24675)

Buddy Kaye Quintet Male Vocalist/Saxophonist from the USA

ISSUE	TITLE	UK LBL	UK POS	UK YEAR	US POS	US YEAR	US LBL
1	Thoughtless		0	1948	22	1948	(MGM 10137)
2	A Your Adorable		0	1949	27	1949	(MGM 10310)

VOCALS ON HIT 1 ARE BY THE TUNE TIMERS • VOCALS ON HIT 2 ARE BY ARTIE MALVIN

Buddy Knox & The Rhythm Orchids Male Vocalist, Real Name Buddy Wayne Knox B: 20 Jul1933 Un Happy, Texas

ISSUE	TITLE	UK LBL	UK POS	UK YEAR	US POS	US YEAR	US LBL
1	Party Doll	(Columbia DB 3914)	29	1957	1	1957	(ROULETTE 4002)
2	Rock Your Baby To Sleep		0	1957	17	1957	(ROULETTE 4009)
3	Hula Love		0	1957	9	1957	(ROULETTE 4018)
4	Somebody Touched Me		0	1958	22	1958	(ROULETTE 4082)
5	Lovey Dovey		0	1961	25	1961	(Liberty 55290)
6	She's Gone	(Liberty LIB 55473)	45	1962	0	1962	
! 7	Gypsy Man		0	1968	64	1968	(United Artists 50301)

Buddy Morrow & His Orchestra Male Orchestra Leader/Instrumentalist (Trombone), Real Name Muni Zudekoff from the USA

ISSUE	TITLE	UK LBL	UK POS	UK YEAR	US POS	US YEAR	US LBL
1	Rose, Rose, I Love You		0	1951	8	1951	(RCA Victor 4135)
2	Night Train		0	1952	27	1952	(RCA Victor 4693)
3	One-Mint Julep		0	1952	30	1952	(RCA Victor 4868)
4	Greyhound		0	1952	19	1952	(RCA Victor 5041)
5	I Don't Know		0	1953	16	1953	(RCA Victor 5117)
6	Train, Train, Train		0	1953	28	1953	(RCA Victor 5212)
7	Re-Enlistment Blues		0	1953	27	1953	(RCA Victor 5466)
8	Mr. Sandman		0	1954	20	1954	(Mercury 70477)
9	Night Train	(HMV B 10347)	12	1953	0	1953	

Buddy Starcher Male Dj/Vocalist, Oby Edgar Starcher, B: 16 Mar 1910 Ripley, West Virginia

ISSUE	TITLE	UK LBL	UK POS	UK YEAR	US POS	US YEAR	US LBL
2	History Repeats Itself		0	1966	39	1966	(BOONE 1038)

Budgie Male Vocal/Instrumental Group from the UK

ISSUE	TITLE	UK LBL	UK POS	UK YEAR	US POS	US YEAR	US LBL
1	Keeping A Rendezvous	(RCA Budgie 3)	71	1981	0	1981	

Buffalo Springfield Names Stephen Stills, Neil Young, Richie Furay, Dewey Martin & Bruce Palmer, Who Was Replaced By Jim

ISSUE	TITLE	UK LBL	UK POS	UK YEAR	US POS	US YEAR	US LBL
* 1	For What It's Worth (Stop, Hey What's That Sound)		0	1967	7	1967	(ATCO 6459)

RICHIE FURAY WAS A FORMER MEMBER OF SOUTHER, HILLMAN, FURAY BAND IN 1974 • GROUP DISBANDED IN 1968, SEE ALSO CROSBY, STILLS, NASH AND YOUNG

Buffy Sainte-Marie Female Vocalist, B: 20 Feb 1941 Piapot Reservation, Canada

ISSUE	TITLE	UK LBL	UK POS	UK YEAR	US POS	US YEAR	US LBL
1	Soldier Blue	(RCA 2081)	7	1971	0	1971	
2	I'm Gonna Be A Contry Girl Again	(Vanguard VRS 35143)	34	1972	0	1972	
3	Mister Can't You See		0	1972	38	1972	(Vanguard 35151)
4	The Big Ones Get Away	(Ensign ENY 650)	39	1992	0	1992	
5	Fallen Angels	(Ensign ENY 655)	57	1992	0	1992	

Bug Kann & The Plastic Jam Mixed Vocal/Instrumental Group from the UK

ISSUE	TITLE	UK LBL	UK POS	UK YEAR	US POS	US YEAR	US LBL
1	Made In Two Minutes	(Optimum Dance BKPJ 1S)	70	1991	0	1991	
2	Made In 2 Minutes (Re-Mix)	(PWL International PWCD 286)	64	1994	0	1994	

HIT 1 FEATURED PATTI LOW AND DOOGIE

Buggles Male Vocal/Instrumental Duo from the UK   Names: Geoff Downes & Trevor Horn, Members Of Yes In 1980

ISSUE	TITLE	UK LBL	UK POS	UK YEAR	US POS	US YEAR	US LBL
1	Video Killed The Radio Star	(Island WIP 6524)	1	1979	40	1979	(Island 49114)
2	The Plastic Age	(Island WIP 6540)	16	1980	0	1980	
3	Clean Clean	(Island WIP 6584)	38	1980	0	1980	
4	Elstree	(Island WIP 6624)	55	1980	0	1980	

Buju Banton Male Vocalist from Jamaica

ISSUE	TITLE	UK LBL	UK POS	UK YEAR	US POS	US YEAR	US LBL
1	Make My Day	(Mercury BUJCD 2)	72	1993	0	1993	

ISSUE	TITLE	UK LBL	UK POS	UK YEAR	US POS	US YEAR	US LBL
Bulawayo Sweet Rhythms Band Male Band From South Africa							
1	Skokiaan		0	1954	17	1954	(London 1491)
Bull & The Matadors Names Jamell 'Bull' Parks, Hardy & James Otis Love							
1	The Funky Judge		0	1968	39	1968	(TODDLIN' TOWN 108)
Bull Moose Jackson Male R&B Singer, Real Name Benjamin Jackson from the USA							
1	I Love You, Yes I Do		0	1947	21	1947	(KING 4181)
Bullet John Cann & Paul Hammond from the USA Both Were Former Members Of Atomic Rooster							
1	White Lies, Blue Eyes		0	1971	28	1971	(BIG TREE 123)
Bump Male Production /Instrumental Duo from the UK							
1	I'm Rushin'	(GOOD BOY EDGE7 1)	40	1992	0	1992	
2	I'm Rushin' (Re-Mix)	(Deconstruction 74321320692)	45	1995	0	1995	
Bunker Hill Real Name David Walker B: 5 May 1941 Washington							
1	Hide And Go Seek (Part 1)		0	1962	33	1962	(MALA 451)
Bunny Paul Female Vocalist from the USA							
1	Magic Guitar		0	1953	23	1953	(DOT 15107)
2	Such A Night		0	1954	23	1954	(ESSEX 352)
3	Lovey Dovey		0	1954	24	1954	(ESSEX 359)
Bunny Sigler Real Name Walter Sigler B: 27 Mar 1941 Philadelphia							
1	Let The Good Times Roll-Feel So Good		0	1967	22	1967	(Parkway 153)
Buoys Rock Quintet From Pennsylvania, Lead Vocals From Bill Kelly							
1	Timothy		0	1971	17	1971	(Scepter 12275)
Burl Ives Male Folk Singer/Actor/Semi Pro Footballer/radio Host, B: 14 Jun 1909, Huntington Township, Illinois							
1	Blue Tail Fly		0	1948	24	1948	(Decca 24463)
2	Lavender Blue (Dilly Dilly) (From *So Dear To My Heart*)		0	1949	16	1949	(Decca 24547)
3	Riders In The Sky (Cowboy Legend)		0	1949	21	1949	(Columbia 38445)
4	On Top Of Old Smoky (From Valley Of Fire)		0	1951	10	1951	(Columbia 39328)
5	The Wild Side Of Life		0	1952	30	1952	(Decca 28055)
6	True Love Goes On And On		0	1954	23	1954	(Decca 29088)
7	A Little Bitty Tear	(Brunswick 05863)	9	1962	9	1962	(Decca 31330)
8	Funny Way Of Laughin'	(Brunswick 05868)	29	1962	10	1962	(Decca 31371)
9	Call Me Mr.In-Between		0	1962	19	1962	(Decca 31405)
10	Mary Ann Regrets		0	1962	39	1962	(Decca 31433)
	HIT 1 IS CREDITED TO BURL IVES AND THE ANDREW SISTERS • HIT 2 IS WITH CAPTAIN STUBBY & THE BUCCANEERS HIT 5 IS WITH GRADY MARTIN & HIS SLOW FOOT FIVE • OBITUARY : D: 14 APR 1995, AGED 85.						
Burt Bacharach Orchestra and chorus from the USA							
1	Trains And Boats And Planes	(London HL	4	1965	0	1965	
Burt Shepard Male Comedian B: in poverty on a Virginian plantation							
* 1	Laughing Song	(ZON-O-PHONE)	0	1910	0	1910	
	HE WENT ON TO STARDOM, BUT IN A DRUNKEN RAGE THREW HIS WIFE OUT OF A WINDOW, HE WAS HANGED FOR MURDER						
Burton Cummings B: 31 Dec 1947 Winnipeg, Canada. Lead Singer With Guess Who							
* 1	Stand Tall		0	1976	10	1976	(PORTRAIT 70001)
2	You Saved My Soul		0	1981	37	1981	(ALFA 7008)
Burundi Steiphenson Black Drummers/Chanters With Orchestra Led By Mike Stephenson from France							
1	Burundi Black	(BARCLAY BAR 3)	31	1971	0	1971	
Bush Male Rock Quintet From London, England							
1	Comedown		0	1995	30	1995	(TRAUMA/INTER. 98134)
2	Glycerine		0	1996	28	1996	
3	Machinehead	(Interscope IND95505)	48	1996	43	1996	(INTERSCOPE 98079)
4	Swallowed	(Interscope IND95528)	7	1997	0	1997	
5	Greedy Fly	(Interscope IND 95536)	22	1997	0	1997	
Busta Rhymes Male Rapper from the USA							
1	Woo-Nah! Got You All In Check	(Elektra EKR 220CD)	8	1996	8	1996	
2	It's A Party	(Elektra EKR 226CD)	23	1996	52	1996	(ELEKTRA 64268)
3	Hit 'Em High (The Monstars' Anthem)	(Atlantic A 5449CD)	8	1997	0	1997	
4	Do My Thing	(Elektra EKR 235CD)	39	1997	0	1997	
	HIS 2 IS CREDITED TO BUSTA RHYMES FEATURING ZHANE • HIT 3 IS CREDITED TO B REAL, BUSTA RHYMES, COOLIO, L.L. COOL J & METHOD MAN						
Buster Male Vocal/Instrumental Group from the UK							
1	Sunday	(RCA 2678)	49	1976	0	1976	
Buster Brown Male Harmonica/Vocalist, B: 15 Nov 1911 Cordele, Georgia							
1	Fannie Mae		0	1960	38	1960	(FIRE 1008)
	OBITUARY: D: 31 JAN 1976.						

ISSUE	TITLE	UK LBL	UK POS	UK YEAR	US POS	US YEAR	US LBL
Busters	Originally The Northern Lights, The Hit Was Also Known As Typhoid						
1	Bust Out		0	1963	25	1963	(ARLEN 735)
Butt-Head	See Cher						
Butterscotch	Male Vocal Group from the UK						
1	Don't You Know	(RCA 1937)	17	1970	0	1970	
Butthole Surfers	Male Vocal/Instrumental Group from the USA						
1	Pepper4	(Capitol CDCL 778)	59	1996	0	1996	
Buzz Clifford	Male Vocalist, Real Name Reese Francis Clifford III B: 8 Oct 1942 from Illinois						
1	Baby Sittin' Boogie	(Fontana H 297)	17	1961	6	1961	(Columbia 41876)
Buzzcocks	Male Vocal/Instrumental Group from the UK						
1	What Do I Get	(United Artists UP 36348)	37	1978	0	1978	
2	I Don't Mind	(United Artists UP 36386)	55	1978	0	1978	
3	Love Is More	(United Artists UP 36433)	34	1978	0	1978	
4	Ever Fallen In Love	(United Artists UP 36455)	12	1978	0	1978	
5	Promises	(United Artists UP 36471)	20	1978	0	1978	
6	Everybody's Happy Nowadays	(United Artists UP 36499)	29	1979	0	1979	
7	Harmony In My Head	(United Artists UP 36541)	32	1979	0	1979	
8	Spiral Scratch (Ep)	(New Hormones ORG 1)	31	1979	0	1979	
9	Are Everything	(United Artists BP 365)	61	1980	0	1980	
By All Means	Male Vocal Group from the USA						
1	I Surrender To Your Love	(Fourtht & Broadway BRW 102)	65	1988	0	1988	
Byker Groove!	Female Vocal Group from the UK						
1	Love You Sexy..!!	(Groove ROVD 01)	48	1994	0	1994	
Byrds	Male Vocal/Instrumental Group from the USA Names: James McQuinn, David Crosby, Gene Clark, Chris Hillman & Mike Clark						
* 1	Mr. Tambourine Man	(CBS 201765)	1	1965	1	1965	(Columbia 43271)
2	All I Really Want To Do	(CBS 201796)	4	1965	40	1965	(Columbia 43332)
* 3	Turn! Turn! Turn!	(CBS 202008)	26	1965	1	1965	(Columbia 43424)
4	It Won't Be Wrong / Set You Free This Time		0	1966	63	1966	(Columbia 42501)
5	Eight Miles High	(CBS 202067)	24	1966	14	1966	(Columbia 43578)
6	5D (Fifth Dimension)		0	1966	44	1966	(Columbia 43702)
7	Mr. Spaceman		0	1966	36	1966	(Columbia 43766)
8	So You Want To Be A Rock 'N' Roll Star		0	1967	29	1967	(Columbia 43987)
9	My Back Pages		0	1967	30	1967	(Columbia 44054)
10	Have You Seen Her Face		0	1967	74	1967	(Columbia 44157)
11	Goin' Back		0	1967	89	1967	(Columbia 44362)
12	You Ain't Goin' Nowhere	(CBS 3411)	45	1968	74	1968	(Columbia 44499)
13	Jesus Is Just Alright		0	1970	97	1970	(Columbia 45091)
14	Chestnut Mare	(CBS 5322)	19	1971	0	1971	
Byron MacGregor	News Director for CKLW-Detroit						
* 1	Americans		0	1974	4	1974	(Westbound 222)
Bystanders	Male Vocal/Instrumental Group from the UK						
1	98 6	(Piccadilly 7N 35363)	45	1967	0	1967	

C

ISSUE	TITLE	UK LBL	UK POS	UK YEAR	US POS	US YEAR	US LBL
C & C Music Factory Real Names David Cole & Robert Clivilles							
* 1	Gonna Make You Sweat (Everybody Dance Now)	(CBS 6564540)	3	1990	1	1991	(Columbia 73604)
* 2	Here We Go	(CBS 6567557)	20	1991	3	1991	(Columbia 73690)
* 3	Things That Make You Go Hmmm..	(CBS 6566907)	4	1991	4	1991	(Columbia 73698)
4	Just A Touch Of Love Everyday	(CBS 6575247)	31	1991	0	1991	
5	Pride (In The Name Of Love)	(CBS 6577017)	15	1992	0	1992	
6	A Deeper Love	(CBS 6578497)	15	1992	0	1992	
7	Keep It Comin'	(CBS 6584307)	34	1992	0	1992	
8	Do You Wanna Get Funky	(CBS 6584307)	27	1994	40	1994	(Columbia 77582)
9	I Found Love / Take A Toke	(Columbia 6612112)	26	1995	0	1995	
10	I'll Always Be Around	(MCA Mcstd 40001)	42	1995	0	1995	
C.B. Milton Male Vocalist From Holland							
1	It's A Loving Thing	(Logic 74321208062)	48	1994	0	1994	
2	It's A Loving Thing (Re-Mix)	(Logic 74321267212)	34	1995	0	1995	
3	Hold On	(Logic 74321292112)	62	1995	0	1995	
C.C.S. Male Vocal/Instrumental Group from the UK							
1	Whole Lotta Love	(Rak 104)	13	1970	0	1970	
2	Walkin'	(Rak 109)	7	1971	0	1971	
3	Tap Turns On The Water	(Rak 119)	5	1971	0	1971	
4	Brother	(Rak 126)	25	1972	0	1972	
5	The Band Played Boogie	(Rak 154)	36	1973	0	1973	
C.J. & Co Male Vocal/Instrumental Group from the USA							
1	Devil's Gun	(Atlantic K 10956)	43	1977	36	1977	(Westbound 55400)
C.J. Bolland Male Producer from the UK							
1	Sugar Is Sweeter	(Internal Liecd 35)	11	1996	0	1996	
2	The Prophet	(Ffrr Fcd 300)	19	1997	0	1997	
	See Also Ravesignal III						
C.J. Lewis Male Vocalist from the UK							
1	Sweets For My Sweet	(Black Market Bmitd 017)	3	1994	0	1994	
2	Everything Is Alright (Uptight)	(Black Market Bmitd 019)	10	1994	0	1994	
3	Best Of My Love	(Black Market Bmitd 021)	13	1994	0	1994	
4	Dollars	(Black Market Bmitd 023)	34	1994	0	1994	
5	R To The A	(Black Market Bmitd 030)	34	1995	0	1995	
C.O.D. Male Vocal/Instrumental Group from the USA							
1	In The Bottle	(Streetwave Wave 2)	54	1983	0	1983	
C.W. McCall Male Vocalist, Real Name Bill Fries. B: 15 Nov 1928 from Audulbon, Iowa							
1	Old Home Filler-up An' Keep On-a Truckin' Cafe		0	1974	54	1974	(MFGM 14738)
2	Wolf Creek Pass		0	1975	40	1975	(MGM 14764)
3	Classified		0	1975	13	1975	(MGM 14801)
4	Black Bear Road		0	1975	24	1975	(MGM 14825)
* 5	Convoy	(MGM 2006 560)	2	1976	1	1975	(MGM 14839)
6	There Won't Be No Country Music		0	1976	19	1975	(Polydor 14310)
7	Crispy Critters		0	1976	32	1976	(Polydor 14331)
8	Four-Wheel Cowboy		0	1976	88	1976	(Polydor 14352)
9	'round the World With the Rubber Duck		0	1976	40	1976	(Polydor 14365)
10	Audubon		0	1977	56	1977	(Polydor 14377)
11	Roses for Mama		0	1977	2	1977	(Polydor 14420)
12	Outlaws And Lone Star Beer		0	1979	81	1979	(Polydor 14527)
Ca Va Ca Va Male Vocal/Instrumental Group from the UK							
1	Where's Romeo	(Regard Rg 103)	49	1982	0	1982	
2	Brother Bright	(Regard Rg 105)	65	1983	0	1983	

ISSUE	TITLE	UK LBL	UK POS	UK YEAR	US POS	US YEAR	US LBL
Cab Calloway Orchestra Male Orchestra Leader, B: 25 Dec 1907 Rochester, New York							
* 35	(Hep-Hep!) Jumpin' Jive		0	1939	2	1939	(Vocalion 5005)
Cabana Mixed Vocal/Instrumental Duo from Brazil							
1	Bailando Con Lobos	(High Life 5792512)	65	1995	0	1995	
Cabaret Volatire Male Vocal/Instrumental Group from the UK							
1	Don't Argue	(Parlophone R 6157)	69	1987	0	1987	
2	Hypnotised	(Parlophone R 6157)	66	1989	0	1989	
3	Keep On	(Parlophone R 6157)	55	1990	0	1990	
4	Easy Life	(Parlophone R 6157)	61	1990	0	1990	
Cable							
1	Freeze The Atlantic	(Infectious Infect 38cd)	44	1997	0	1997	
Cacique							
1	Devoted to You	(Diamon Duel Disc 1)	69	1985	0	1985	
Cactus World News							
1	Years Later	(MCA MCA 1024)	59	1986	0	1986	
2	Worlds Apart	(MCA MCA 1040)	58	1986	0	1986	
3	The Bridge	(MCA MCA 1080)	74	1986	0	1986	
Cadets Also recorded as The Jacks							
1	Stranded in the Jungle		0	1956	15	1965	(Modern 994)
Cadsets with Eileen Read							
1	Jealous Heart		42	1965	0	1965	
Cadillacs Lead vocalist is Earl Speedo Carroll who joined The Coasters in 1958							
1	Spedo		0	1955	17	1955	(Josie 785)
2	Peek-a-boo		0	1958	28	1958	(Josie 846)
Cake							
1	The Distance	(Capricorn 5742212)	22	1997	0	1997	
2	I Will Survive	(Capricorn 5744712)	29	1997	0	1997	
California Sunshine							
1	Summer '89	(Perfecto Perf 143cd)	56	1997	0	1997	
Call Male vocal/instrumental group from the USA							
1	Let the Day Begin	(MCA MCA 1362)	42	1989	0	1989	
Calloway Names: Reggie & Vincent Calloway , see Also Midnight Starr							
1	I Wanna Be Rich		0	1990	2	1990	(CSloar 74005)
Camarata Orchestra Male orchestra leader/instrumentalist (trumpet) from the USA							
1	Veradero		0	1952	26	1952	(Decca 28376)
2	Return to Paradise		0	1953	27	1953	(Decca 28714)
Cameo Male vocal/instrumental group from the USA							
1	She's Strange	(Club Jab 2)	3	1984	0	1984	
2	Attack Me With Your Love	(Club Jab 16)	62	1985	0	1985	
3	Single Life	(Club Jab 21)	15	1985	0	1985	
4	She's Strange (re-issue)	(Club Jab 25)	22	1985	0	1985	
5	A Goodbye	(Club Jab 28)	65	1986	0	1986	
6	Word Up	(Club Jab 38)	3	1986	6	1986	(ATL ART 884933)
7	Candy	(Club Jab 43)	27	1986	11	1986	(ATL ART 888193)
8	Back and Forth	(Club Jab 49)	11	1987	0	1987	
9	She's Mine	(Club Jab 57)	79	1987	0	1987	
10	You Make Me Work	(Club Jab 70)	74	1988	0	1987	
Camouflage Mixed vocal/instrumental group from the UK							
1	Bee Sting	(State Stat 58)	48	1977	0	1977	
Camp Lo							
1	Luchini Aka (This Is It)	(Ffrr Fcd 305)	74	1997	50	1997	(Profile 5458)
Can Male vocalist/instrumental group from Germany							
1	I Want More	(Virgin VS 153)	26	1976	0	1976	
Candi Staton Female vocalist, B Hanceville, Alabama. Was married to Clarence Carter							
1	Stand By Your Man		0	1970	24	1970	(Fame 1472)
2	Young Hearts Run Free	(Warner Bros K 16730)	2	1976	20	1976	(Warner Bros 8181)
3	Destiny	(Warner Bros K 16806)	41	1976	0	1976	
4	Nights On Broadway	(Warner Bros K 16972)	6	1977	0	1977	
5	Honest I Do Love You	(Warner Bros K 17164)	48	1978	0	1978	

ISSUE	TITLE	UK LBL	UK POS	UK YEAR	US POS	US YEAR	US LBL
6	Suspicious Minds	(Sugarhill SH 112)	31	1982	0	1982	
7	Young Hearts Run Free (Re-Mix)	(Warner Bros W 8680)	47	1986	0	1986	
8	You Got The Love	(Truelove Tlove 7001)	4	1991	0	1991	
9	You Got The Love (Re-Issue)	(React Cdreact 89)	3	1997	0	1997	

HITS 8, 9 ARE CREDITED TO SOURCE FEATURING CANDI STATON

Candido Male Multi-Instrumentalist from the USA

1	Jingo	(Excaliber Exc 102)	55	1971	0	1971	

Candlebox Male rock band from Seattle

1	Far Behind		0	1994	18	1994	(Maverick/Sire 18118)

Candlewick Green Male Vocal/Instrumental Duo From The UK

1	Who Do You Think You Are	(Decca F 13480)	21	1974	0	1974	

Candy Dulfer Female Saxophonist from Holland

1	Lily Was Here	(RCA Zb 43045)	6	1990	11	1991	(Arista 2187)
2	Saxuality	(RCA Zb 43769)	60	1990	0	1990	

HIT 1 IS CREDITED TO DAVID A. STEWART FEATURING CANDY DULFER

Candy Flip Male Vocal/Instrumental Duo from the UK

1	Strawberry Fields Forever	(Debut Debt 3092)	3	1990	0	1990	
2	This Can Be Real	(Debut Debt 3099)	60	1990	0	1990	

Candy Girls Mixed Production Duo from the UK

1	Fee Fi Fo Fum	(Virgin Vcrd 1)	23	1995	0	1995	
2	Wham Bam	(VC Recordings Vcrd 6)	20	1996	0	1996	
3	I Want Candy	(Feverpitch Cdfvr 1013)	30	1996	0	1996	

Hit 2 Is Credited To Candy Girls Featuring Sweet Pussy Pauline

Candyland Male Vocal/Instrumental Group From The UK

1	Fountain O'Youth	(Non Fiction Yes 4)	72	1991	0	1991	

Candyman Male Rapper, B: 25 Jun 1968 Los Angeles

1	Knockin' Boots		0	1990	9	1990	(Epic 73450)

Candyskins Male Vocal/Instrumental Group from the UK

1	Mrs. Hoover	(Ultimate Topp 051cd)	65	1996	0	1996	
2	Monday Morning	(Ultimate Topp 055cd)	34	1997	0	1997	
3	Hang Myself On You	(Ultimate Topp 059cd)	65	1997	0	1997	

Canned Heat Male Vocal/Instrumental Group from The USA

1	On The Road Again	(Liberty Lbs 15090)	8	1968	16	1968	(Liberty 56038)
2	Going Up The Country	(Liberty Lbs 15169)	19	1969	11	1969	(Liberty 56077)
* 3	Let's Work Together	(Liberty Lbs 15302)	2	1970	26	1969	(Liberty 56151)
4	Sugar Bee	(Liberty Lbs 15350)	49	1970	0	1970	

NAMES BOB HITE, ALAN WILSON, HENRY VESTINE, LARRY TAYLOR & FRANK COOK • OBITUARY : BOB D: 6 APR 1981 HEART ATTACK

Cannibal & The Headhunters Quartet From Los Angeles Led By Frankie Garcia

1	Land Of A 1000 Dances		0	1965	30	1965	(Rampart 642)

Cannonball Adderley Real Name Julian Edwin Adderley. B: 15 Sep 1928 Tampa

1	Mercy, Mercy, Mercy		0	1967	11	1967	(Capitol 5798)

HE RECEIVED THE NICKNAME 'CANNONBALL' BECAUSE OF HIS LOVE FOR EATING (CANNIBAL) • OBITUARY : D: 8 AUG 1975 IN INDIANA

Capercaillie Mixed Vocal/Instrumental Group from the UK

1	A Prince Among Islands (EP)	(Survival Zb 45393)	39	1992	0	1992	
2	Dark Alan (Ailein Duinn)	(Survival Surcd 55)	65	1995	0	1995	

Capitols R&B Trio From Detroit, With Sam George, Donald Storball & Richard McDougall

1	Cool Jerk		0	1966	7	1966	(Karen 1524)

OBITUARY: SAM D: 17 MAR 1982 MURDERED

Cappella Male Producer Gianfranco Bortolotti from Italy

1	Push The Beat / Bauhaus	(Fast Globe Fgl 1)	60	1988	0	1988	
2	Helyom Halib	(Music Man Mmps 7004)	11	1989	0	1989	
3	House Energy Revenge	(Music Man Mmps 7009)	73	1989	0	1989	
4	Everybody	(Ffrr F158)	66	1991	0	1991	
5	Take Me Away	(Pwl Continental Pwl 210)	25	1992	0	1992	
6	U Got 2 Know	(Internal Dance Idc 1)	6	1993	0	1993	
7	U Got 2 Know Revisited (Re-Mix)	(Internal Dance Idcr 2)	43	1993	0	1993	
8	U Got 2 Let The Music	(Internal Dance Idc 3)	2	1993	0	1993	
9	Move On Baby	(Internal Dance Idc 4)	7	1994	0	1994	
10	U & Me	(Internal Dance Idcc 6)	10	1994	0	1994	
11	Move It Up / Big Beat	(Internal Dance Idc 7)	16	1994	0	1994	

ISSUE	TITLE	UK LBL	UK POS	UK YEAR	US POS	US YEAR	US LBL
12	Tell Me The Way	(Systematic Syscd 17)	17	1995	0	1995	
13	Be My Baby	(Nukleuz Psnc 0072)	53	1997	0	1997	
	HIT 5 IS CREDITED TO CAPPELLA FEATURING LOLEATTA HOLLOWAY. • SEE ALSO 49ERS						

Capris Group Disbanded In 1959, Reformed When Hit Was Re-Issued

1	There's A Moon Out Tonight		0	1961	3	1961	(Old Town 1094)

Captain & Tennille Male Instrumentalist and Female Vocalist from the USA   Names Captain Is Daryl Dragon, Tennille Is Toni Tennille

* 1	Love Will Keep Us Together	(A&M Ams 7165)	32	1975	1	1975	(A&M 1672)
* 2	The Way I Want To Touch You	(A&M Ams 7203)	28	1976	4	1975	(A&M 1725)
* 3	Lonely Night (Angel Face)		0	1976	3	1976	(A&M 1782)
* 4	Shop Around		0	1976	4	1976	(A&M 1817)
* 5	Muskrat Love		0	1976	4	1976	(A&M 1870)
6	Can't Stop Dancin'		0	1977	13	1977	(A&M 1912)
7	You Never Done It Like That	(A&M Ams 7384)	63	1978	10	1978	(A&M 2063)
8	You Need A Woman Tonight		0	1979	40	1979	(A&M 2106)
* 9	Do That To Me One More Time	(Casablanca Can 175)	7	1980	1	1979	(Casablanca 2215)

Captain Hollywood Project Mixed Vocal/Instrumental Group from the USA/Germany

1	I Can't Stand It	(Bcm Bcmr 395)	7	1990	0	1990	
2	Are You Dreaming	(Bcm Bcmr 07504)	17	1990	0	1990	
3	Only With You	(Pulse 8 Cdlose 40)	67	1993	0	1993	
4	More And More	(Pulse 8 Cdlose 50)	23	1993	17	1993	(Imago 25029)
5	Impossible	(Pulse 8 Cdlose 54)	29	1994	0	1994	
6	Only With You (Re-Issue)	(Pulse 8 Cdlose 62)	61	1994	0	1994	
7	Flying High	(Pulse 8 Cdlose 82)	58	1995	0	1995	

Captain Sensible Male Vocalist from the UK

1	Happy Talk	(A&M Cap 1)	1	1982	0	1982	
2	Wot	(A&M Cap 2)	26	1982	0	1982	
3	Glad It's All Over / Damned On 45	(A&M Cap 6)	6	1984	0	1984	
4	There Are More Snakes Than Ladders	(A&M Cap 7)	57	1984	0	1984	
5	The Hokey Cokey	(Have A Nice Day Cdhokey 1)	71	1994	0	1994	

Caramba Real Name Michael Tretow. Vocal/Instrumentalist from Sweden

1	Fedora (I'll Be Your Dawg)	(Billco Bill 101)	56	1983	0	1983	

Michael Is Also Known For His Dog Impersonations

Caravelles Female Vocal Duo from the UK   Names Andrea Simpson & Lois Wilkinson

1	You Don't Have To Be A Baby To Cry	(Decca F 11697)	6	1963	3	1963	(Smash 1852)

Cardigans Mixed Vocal/Instrumental Group from Sweden

1	Carnival	(Stockholm Pzcd 345)	35	1995	0	1995	
2	Sick And Tired	(Stockholm Pzcd 336)	34	1995	0	1995	
3	Carnival (Re-Entry)	(Trampolene Pzcd 345)	35	1995	0	1995	
4	Rise And Shine	(Trampolene 5778252)	29	1996	0	1996	
5	Lovefool	(Stockholm 5752952)	21	1996	0	1996	
6	Been It	(Stockholm 5759672)	56	1996	0	1996	
7	Lovefool (Re-Issue)	(Stockholm 5710502)	2	1997	0	1997	
8	Your New Cuckoo	(Stockholm 5716632)	35	1997	0	1997	

Care Male Vocal Duo from the UK

1	Flaming Sword	(Arista Kbird 2)	65	1983	0	1983	

Carefrees Vocal Group from the UK

1	We Love You Beatles		0	1964	39	1964	(London Int. 10614)

Carey Johnson Male Vocalist from Australia

1	Real Fashion Reggae Style	(Oval Ten 170)	19	1987	0	1987	

Carl Anderson Male Vocalist from the USA

1	Buttercup	(Streetwave Khan 45)	49	1985	0	1985	
2	Friends And Lovers		0	1986	2	1986	(USA Carrere 06122)
	HIT 2 IS CREDITED TO CARL ANDERSON AND GLORIA LORING						

Carl Carlton Male Vocalist B: 1952 Detroit

1	Everlasting Love		0	1974	6	1974	(Black Beat 27001)
2	She's A Bad Mama Jama	(20th Century Tc 2488)	34	1981	22	1981	(20th Century 2488)

Carl Dobkins Jr. Male Vocalist, Real Name Carl Edward Dobkins B: 13 Jan 1941 In Cincinnati

* 1	My Heart Is An Open Book		0	1959	3	1959	(Decca 30803)
2	Luck Devil	(Brunswick 05817)	44	1960	25	1960	(Decca 31020)

Carl Douglas Male Vocalist from Jamaica

* 1	Kung Fu Fighting	(Pye 7n 45377)	1	1974	1	1974	(20th Century 2140)
2	Dance The Kung Fu	(Pye 7n 45418)	35	1974	0	1974	

ISSUE	TITLE	UK LBL	UK POS	UK YEAR	US POS	US YEAR	US LBL
3	Run Back	(Pye 7n 46018)	25	1977	0	1977	

Carl Malcolm Male Vocalist from Jamaica

1	Fattie Bum Bum	(UK 108)	8	1975	0	1975	

Carl Mann Male Vocalist, B: 24 Aug 1942 Huntingdon, Tennessee

1	Mona Lisa		0	1959	25	1959	(Philips 3539)

Carl Perkins Male Singer/Songwriter/Guitarist, B: 4 Sep 1930 Tiptonville, Tennessee

* 1	Blue Suede Shoes	(London Hlu 8271)	10	1956	2	1956	(Sun 234)
2	Boppin' The Blues		0	1956	70	1956	(Sun 243)
5	Your True Love		0	1957	67	1957	(Sun 261)
	OTHERS HITS ARE C/W						

Carla Thomas Female Vocalist, B: 21 Dec 1942 Memphis, Daughter Of Rufus Thomas

1	Gee Whiz (Look At His Eyes)		0	1961	10	1961	(Atlantic 2086)
2	I'll Bring It Home To You		0	1962	41	1962	(Atlantic 2163)
3	Walking The Dog		0	1963	5	1963	
4	Let Me Be Good To You		0	1966	11	1966	(Stax 188)
5	Ba-b-y		0	1966	14	1966	(Stax 195)
6	Tramp		18	1967	26	1967	(Stax 216)
7	I'll Always Have Faith In You		0	1967	11	1967	(Stax 222)
8	Knock on Wood		35	1967	30	1967	(Stax 228)
9	I Like What You're Doing(To Me)		0	1969	49	1969	(Stax 0024)
	HITS 6, 8 ARE CREDITED TO OTIS REDDING AND CARLA THOMAS						

Carleen Anderson Female Vocalist from the USA

1	Nervous Breakdown	(Circa YRCD 112)	27	1994	0	1994	
2	Mama Said	(Circa Yrcd 114)	26	1994	0	1994	
3	True Spirit	(Circa Yrcd 118)	24	1994	0	1994	
4	Let It Last	(Circa Yrcd 119)	16	1995	0	1995	

Carleton Carpenter Male Singer/Dancer/Actor from the USA

* 1	Aba Daba Honeymoon		0	1951	3	1951	(MGM 30282)

Carlton Male Vocalist from the UK

1	Love And Pain	(Smith & Mighty Snm 4)	56	1991	0	1991	
2	1 To 1 Religion	(Stoned Heights Brcdx 313)	53	1995	0	1995	with Bomb The Bass

Carly Simon Female Vocalist, B: 25 Jun 1945 New York City

1	That's The Way I've Always Heard It Would Be		0	1971	10	1971	(Elektra 45724)
2	Anticipation		0	1972	13	1972	(Elektra 45759)
* 3	You're So Vain	(Elektra K 12077)	3	1972	1	1972	(Elektra 45824)
4	The Right Thing To Do	(Elektra K 12095)	17	1973	17	1973	(Elektra 45843)
* 5	Mockingbird	(Elektra K 12134)	34	1974	5	1974	(Elektra 45880)
6	Haven't Got Time For The Pain		0	1974	14	1974	(Elektra 45887)
7	Attitude Dancing		0	1975	21	1975	(Elektra 45246)
* 8	Nobody Does It Better	(Elektra K 12261)	7	1977	2	1977	(Elektra 45413)
9	You Belong To Me		0	1978	6	1978	(Elektra 45477)
10	Devoted To You		0	1978	36	1978	(Elektra 45506)
* 11	Jesse		0	1980	11	1980	(Warner Bros 49518)
12	Why	(Wea K 79300)	10	1982	0	1982	
13	Coming Around Again	(Arista Arist 687)	10	1987	18	1986	(Arista 9525)
14	Why (Re-Issue)	(Wea U 7501)	56	1989	0	1989	
15	You're So Vain (Re-Issue)	(Elektra Ekr 123)	41	1991	0	1991	
	MALE VOCALS ON HIT 3 ARE BY MICK JAGGER, • SEE ALSO WILL POWERS						
	HITS 5,10 ARE CREDITED TO CARLY SIMON AND JAMES TAYLOR • HIT 10 REACHED NUMBER 33 IN THE US C/W CHARTS						

Carmel Mixed Vocal/Instrumental Group from the UK

1	Bad Day	(London Lon 29)	15	1983	0	1983	
2	More, More, More	(London Lon 44)	23	1984	0	1984	
3	Sally	(London Lon 90)	60	1986	0	1986	

Carmen Cavallaro Orchestra Male Orchestra Leader/Pianist, B: 6 May 1913 New York City

* 1	Chopin's Polonaise		0	1945	3	1945	(Decca 18677)
2	There's Yes! Yes! In Your Eyes		0	1949	29	1949	(Decca 24678)
3	Music! Music! Music!		0	1950	5	1950	(Decca 24881)
4	Meet Mister Callaghan		0	1952	28	1952	(Decca 28373)
* 5	I Can't Begin To Tell You		0	1945	1	1945	(Decca 23457)

Carmen Miranda Female Actress/Vocalist

1	Mama Euquero (I Want My Mama)		0	1941	25	1941	(Decca 23132)
2	Cuanto La Gusta (From A Date With Judy)		0	1948	12	1948	(Decca 24479
3	The Wedding Samba		0	1950	23	1950	(Decca 24841)

ISSUE	TITLE	UK LBL	UK POS	UK YEAR	US POS	US YEAR	US LBL
	REAL NAME MARIA DO CARMO MIRANDA FROM BRAZIL. • OBITUARY: D: 5 AUG 1955 (AGED 46).						
Carol Bailey Female Vocalist From The UK							
1	Feel It	(Multiply Cdmulty 3)	41	1995	0	1995	
Carol Deene Female Vocalist from the UK							
1	Sad Movies	(HMV Pop 922)	44	1961	0	1961	
2	Norman	(HMV Pop 973)	24	1962	0	1962	
3	Johnny Get Angry	(HMV Pop 1027)	32	1962	0	1962	
4	Some People	(HMV Pop 1058)	25	1962	0	1962	
Carol Douglas Female Vocalist, B: 7 Apr 1948 Brooklyn							
1	Doctor's Orders		0	1975	1	1975	(Midland I. 10113)
2	Night Fever	(Gull Guls 61)	66	1978	0	1978	
Carol Hitchcock Female Vocalist from Australia							
1	Get Ready	(A&M Am 391)	56	1987	0	1987	
Carol Kay See Tommy Dee							
Carol Kenyon Female Vocalist from the UK							
1	Don't Waste My Time	(Chrysalis Paul 1)	8	1986	0	1986	
2	Here's My A	(Logiv 74321153092)	69	1993	0	1993	
	HIT 1 IS CREDITED TO PAUL HARDCASTLE AND CAROL KENYON • HIT 2 IS CREDITED TO RAPINATION FEATURING CAROL KENYON						
Carol Kidd (Featuring) Terry Waite Mixed Vocal Duo from the UK							
1	When I Dream	(The Hit Label Hls 1)	58	1992	0	1992	
Carol Lynn Townes Female Vocalist from the USA							
1	99 1/2 (Break Dance)	(Polydor Posp 693)	47	1984	0	1984	
2	Believe In The Beat	(Polydor Posp 720)	56	1985	0	1985	
Carole Bayer Sager Female Vocalist, B: 8 Mar 1946, New York City							
1	You're Moving Out Today	(Elektra K 12257)	6	1977	0	1977	
2	Stronger Than Before		0	1981	30	1981	(Broadwalk 02054)
Carole King Female Vocalist, Real Name Carole Klein. B: 9 Feb 1942 In New York City							
1	It Might As Well Rain Until September	(London Hlu 9591)	3	1962	22	1962	(Dimension 2000)
* 2	It's Too Late	(A&M Ams 849)	6	1971	1	1971	(Ode 66015)
3	I Feel The Earth Move		0	1971	1	1971	(Ode 66015)
4	So Far Away / Smack Water Jack		0	1971	14	971	(Ode 66019)
5	Sweet Seasons		0	1972	9	1972	(Ode 66022)
6	It Might As Well Rain Until September (Re-Issue) (London Hl 10391)		43	1972	0	1972	
7	Been To Canaan		0	1972	24	1972	(Ode 66031)
8	Believe In Humanity		0	1973	28	1973	(Ode 66035)
9	Carazon		0	1973	37	1973	(Ode 66039)
10	Jazzman		0	1974	2	1974	(Ode 66101)
11	Nightingale		0	1975	9	1975	(Ode 66106)
12	Only Love Is Real		0	1976	28	1976	(Ode 66119)
13	Hard Rock Cafe		0	1977	30	1977	(Capitol 4455)
14	One Fine Day		0	1980	12	1980	(Capitol 4864)
Carolyne Mas Female Vocalist from the USA							
1	Quote Goodbye Quote	(Mecury 6167 873)	71	1980	0	1980	
Caron Wheeler Female Vocalist from the UK							
1	Keep On Moving	(10 TEN 263)	5	1989	11	1989	(Virgin 99205)
2	Back to Life (However Do You Want Me)	(10 TEN 265	1	1989	4	1989)	(Virgin 99171)
3	Livin' In The Light	(RCA PB 43939)	14	1990	0	1990	
4	UK Blak	(RCA PB 44719)	40	1990	0	1990	
5	Don't Quit	(RCA PB 44259)	53	1991	0	1991	
6	I Adore You	(Perspective Perss 7407)	59	1992	0	1992	
7	Beach of the War Godess	(EMI CDEM 282)	75	1993	0	1993	
Carpenters Karen B 1950 and Richard B 1946. Brother & Sister vocal/instrumental duo from the USA							
1	(They Long To Be) Close To You	(A&M Ams 800)	6	1970	1	1970	(A&M 1183)
2	We've Only Just Begun	(A&M Ams 813)	28	1971	2	1970	(A&M 1217)
3	For All We Know	(A&M Ams 864)	18	1971	3	1971	(A&M 1243)
4	Rainy Days and Mondays	(A&M Amcd 0180)	63	1993	2	1971	(A&M 1260)
5	Superstar	(A&M Ams 864)	18	1971	2	1971	(A&M 1289)
6	Merry Christmas Darling	(A&M Ame 601)	45	1972	0	1972	
* 7	Hurting Each Other		0	1972	2	1972	(A&M 1322)
8	It's Going To Take Sometime		0	1972	12	1972	(A&M 1351)
9	Goodbye To Love	(A&M Ams 7023)	9	1972	7	1972	(A&M 1367)

ISSUE	TITLE	UK LBL	UK POS	UK YEAR	US POS	US YEAR	US LBL
10	I Won't Last A Day Without You	(A&M Ams 7023)	9	1973	11	1974	(A&M 1521)
* 11	Sing		0	1973	3	1973	(a&m 1413
* 12	Yesterday Once More	(A&M Ams 7073)	2	1973	2	1973	(A&M 1446)
* 13	Top Of The World	(A&M Ams 7086)	5	1973	1	1973	(A&M 1468)
14	Jambalaya (On The Bayou / Mr. Guder	(A&M Ams 7098)	12	1974	0	1974	
15	I Won't Last A Day Without You (Re-Issue)	(A&M Ams 7111)	32	1974	0	1974	
* 16	Please Mr. Postman	(A&M Ams 7141)	2	1975	1	1974	(A&M 1646)
17	Only Yesterday	(A&M Ams 7159)	7	1975	4	1975	(A&M 1677)
18	Solitaire	(A&M Ams 7187)	32	1975	17	1975	(A&M 1721)
19	Santa Claus Is Comin To Town	(A&M Ams 7144)	37	1975	0	1975	
20	There's A Kind Of Hush (All Over The World)	(A&M Ams 7219)	22	1976	12	1976	(A&M 1800)
21	I Need To Be In Love	(A&M Ams 7238)	36	1976	25	1976	(A&M 1828)
22	All You Get From Love Is A Love Song		0	1977	35	1977	(A&M 1940)
23	Calling Occupants Of Interplanetary Craft	(A&M Ams 7318)	9	1977	32	1977	(A&M 1978)
24	Sweet Sweet Smile	(A&M Ams 7327)	40	1978	0	1978	
25	Touch Me When We're Dancing		0	1981	16	1981	(A&M 2344)
26	Make Believe It's Your First Time	(A&M Am 147)	60	1983	0	1983	
27	Merry Christmas Darling	(A&M Am 716)	25	1990	0	1990	
28	(They Long To Be) Close To You (Re-Issue)	(A&M Am 716)	25	1990	0	1990	
29	Tryin' To Get The Feeling Again	(A&M 5807612)	44	1994	0	1994	

OBITUARY: KAREN. D: ANOREXIA-LINKED HEART ATTACK.

Carrie Lucas Female Vocalist from the USA

1	Dance With You	(Solar Fb 1482)	40	1979	0	1979	

Carrie McDowell Female Vocalist from the USA

1	Uh Uh No More Casual Sex	(Motown Zv 41501)	68	1987	0	1987	

Cars Male Vocal/Instrumental Group from the USA

1	Just What I Needed	(Elektra K 12312)	17	1979	27	1978	(Elektra 45491)
2	My Best Friend's Girl	(Elektra K 12301)	3	1978	35	1978	(Elektra 45537)
3	Let's Go	(Elektra K 12371)	51	1979	14	1979	(Elektra 46063)
4	Touch And Go		0	1980	37	1980	(Elektra 47039)
5	Shake It Up		0	1982	4	1982	(Elektra 47250)
6	Since You've Gone	(Elektra K 13177)	37	1982	0	1982	
7	You Might Think		0	1984	7	1984	(Elektra 69744)
8	Magic		0	1984	12	1984	(Elektra 69724)
9	Drive	(Elektra E 9706)	5	1984	3	1984	(Elektra 69706)
10	Hello Again		0	1984	20	1984	(Elektra 69681)
11	Why Can't I Have You		0	1985	33	1985	(Elektra 69657)
12	Drive (Re-Entry)	(Elektra E 9706)	4	1985	0	1985	
13	Tonight She Comes		0	1985	7	1985	(Elektra 69589)
14	I'm Not The One		0	1986	32	1986	(Elektra 69569)
15	You Are The Girl		0	1987	17	1987	(Elektra 69446)

NAMES: RIC OCASEK, ELLIOT EASTON, GREG HAWKES, BENJAMIN ORR & DAVID ROBINSON. • GROUP DISBANDED IN 1988

Carson Robison Male Singer/Songwriter, B: 4 Aug 1890 In Oswego, Kansas

11	Life Gits Tee-Jus, Don't It?		0	1948	14	1948	(MGM 10224)

OBITUARY : D: 24 MAR 1957 (AGED 66)

Carter - Unstoppable Sex Machine Vocal/Instrumental Duo from the UK

1	Bloodsports For All	(Rough Trade R 20112687)	48	1991	0	1991	
2	Sheriff Fatman	(Big Cat Usm 1)	23	1991	0	1991	
3	After The Watershed	(Big Cat Usm 2)	11	1991	0	1991	
4	Rubbish	(Big Cat Usm 3)	14	1992	0	1992	
5	The Only Living Boy In New Cross	(Big Cat Usm 4)	7	1992	0	1992	
6	Do Re Me So Far So Good	(Big Cat Usm 5)	22	1992	0	1992	
7	The Impossibe Dream	(Big Cat Usm 6)	21	1992	0	1992	
8	Lean On Me I Won't Fall Over	(Big Cat Cdusm 7)	16	1993	0	1993	
9	Lenny And Terence	(Big Cat Cdusm 8)	40	1993	0	1993	
10	Glam Rock Cops	(Big Cat Cdusms 10)	24	1994	0	1994	
11	Let's Get Tattoos	(Big Cat Cdusms 30)	30	1994	0	1994	
12	The Young Offender's Mum	(Chrysalis Cdusms 12)	34	1995	0	1995	
13	Born On The 5th November	(Chrysalis Usmcd 13)	35	1995	0	1995	

Carter Family Names Alvin Pleasant, His Wife Sarah & Alvin Carter From Virginia Together With Cousin Maybelle Carter

* 2	Wildwood Flower		0	1928	3	1928	(Victor 40000)
! 9	Busted		0	1963	13	1963	(Columbia 42665)
! 10	A Song To Mama		0	1971	37	1971	(Columbia 45428)

ISSUE	TITLE	UK LBL	UK POS	UK YEAR	US POS	US YEAR	US LBL
11	Travelin' Minstrel Band		0	1972	42!	1972	(Columbia 45581)
12	The World Needs A Melody		0	1975	35!	1972	(Columbia 45679)
13	Praise The Lord And Pass The Soup		0	1973	57!	1973	(Columbia 45890)

MAYBELLE'S DAUGHTER JUNE IS MARRIED TO JOHNNY CASH • MAYBELLE ALSO RECORDED WITH HER DAUGHTERS HELEN, JUNE & ANITA
HITS 9-13 ARE A REFORMED CARTER FAMILY WITH MAYBELLE AND HER DAUGHTERS & MOTHER MAYBELLE • OBITUARY: ALVIN D: 7 NOV 1960

Carter Twins

1	The Twelfth Of Never / Too Right To Be.	(RCA 74321453082)	61	1997	0	1997	

Carvells Male Vocalist, Real Name Alan Carvell from the UK

1	The L.A. Run	(Creole Cr 143)	31	1977	0	1977	

Cascades Male Vocal Group from the USA

* 1	Rhythm Of The Rain	(Warner Bros Wb 88)	5	1963	3	1963	(Valiant 6026)

NAMES: EDDIE SNYDER, DAVID STEVENS, JOHN GUMMOE, DAVID WILSON & DAVID ZABO

Case (Featuring) Foxxy Brown Male Instrumentalist And Female Vocalist from the USA

1	Touch Me, Tease Me (From The Nutty Professor)	(Def Jam Defcd 18)	26	1996	14	1996	(Mercury 854620)

Cashflow Male Vocal/Instrumental Group from the USA

1	Mine All Mine / Party Freak	(Club Jab 30)	15	1986	0	1986	

Cashman & West Names Dennis Terry Cashman Minogue & Thomas 'Tommy West Picardo Jr.

1	American City Suite		0	1972	27	1972	(Dunhill 4324)

Cashmere Male Vocal/Instrumental Group from the USA

1	Can I	(Fourth & Broadway Brw 19)	29	1985	0	1985	
2	We Need Love	Fourth & Broadway Brw 22)	52	1985	0	1985	

Casino

1	Sound Of Eden	(Worx Worxcd 005)	52	1997	0	1997	

Casinos Cincinnati Based Nine-Man Group Led By Gene Hughes

1	Then You Can Tell Me Goodbye	(President Pt 123)	28	1967	6	1967	(Fraternity 977)

Cass Daley Female Comedienne/Actress/Singer from the USA

1	The Old Piano Roll Blues		0	1950	11	1950	(Decca 24977)
2	The Aba Daba Honeymoon (From *Two Weeks In Love*)		0	1951	23	1951	(Decca 27474)

HITS ARE CREDITED TO HOAGY CARNICHAEL AND CASS DALEY

Cast Male Vocal/Instrumental Group from the UK

1	Finetime	(Polydor 5795072)	17	1995	0	1995	
2	Alright	(Polydor 5799272)	13	1995	0	1995	
3	Sandstorm	(Polydor 5778732)	8	1996	0	1996	
4	Walkaway	(Polydor 5762852)	9	1996	0	1996	
5	Flying	(Polydor 5754772)	4	1996	0	1996	
6	Free Me	(Polydor 5736512)	7	1997	0	1997	
7	Free Me (Re-Entry)	(Polydor 5736512)	64	1997	0	1997	
8	Guiding Star	(Polydor 5711732)	9	1997	0	1997	Charlatans
9	Live The Dream	(Polydor 5716852)	7	1997	0	1997	

Cast Of Coronation St. (Featuring) Bill Waddington Mixed Actor/Actress/Vocalists from The British TV Soap

1	Always Look On The Bright Side	(Premier/EMI Cdem 411)	35	1995	0	1995	

Castaways Three Members Of The Quintet Are Denny Craswell, Roy Hensley, Dick Roby

1	Liar, Liar		0	1965	12	1965	(Soma 1433)

Castells Names: Joe Kelly, Chuck Girard, Bob Ussery & Tom Hicks

1	Sacred		0	1961	20	1961	(Era 3048)
2	So This Is Love		0	1962	21	1962	(Era 3073)

Casuals Male Vocal/Instrumental Group from the UK

1	Jesamine	(Decca F 22784)	2	1968	0	1968	
2	Toy	(Decca F 22852)	30	1968	0	1968	

Cat Male Vocalist from the UK

1	Tongue Tied	(EMI Cdem 286)	17	1993	0	1993	

Cat Mother & The All Night News Boys Rock Quintet From New York

1	Good Old Rock 'N Roll (Medley)		0	1969	21	1969	(Polydor 14002)

Cat Stevens Male Vocalist, Real Name Steven Georgiou, (Yusef Islam) B: 21 Jul 1947 London, England

1	I Love My Dog	(Deram Dm 102)	28	1976	0	1976	
2	Matthew And Son	(Deram Dm 110)	2	1967	0	1967	
3	I'm Gonna Get Me A Gun	(Deram Dm 118)	6	1967	0	1967	
4	A Bad Night	(Deram Dm 140)	20	1967	0	1967	
5	Kitty	(Deram Dm 156)	47	1967	0	1967	
* 6	Lady D'Arbanville	(Island Wip 6086)	8	1970	0	1970	

C

110

ISSUE	TITLE	UK LBL	UK POS	UK YEAR	US POS	US YEAR	US LBL
7	Wild World		0	1971	11	1971	(A&M 1231)
8	Moon Shadow	(Island Wip 6092)	22	1971	30	1971	(A&M 1265)
9	Peace Train		0	1971	7	1971	(A&M 1291)
10	Morning Has Broken	(Island Wip 6121)	9	1972	6	1972	(A&M 1335)
11	Sitting		0	1972	16	1972	(A&M 1396)
* 12	Can't Keep It In	(Island Wip 6152)	13	1972	0	1972	
13	The Hurt		0	1973	31	1973	(A&M 1418)
14	Oh Very Young		0	1974	10	1974	(A&M 1503)
15	Another Saturday Night	(Island Wip 6206)	19	1974	6	1974	(A&M 1602)
16	Ready		0	1975	26	1975	(A&M 1645)
17	Two Fine People		0	1975	33	1975	(A&M 1700)
18	(Remember The Days Of The) Old School Yard	(Island Wip 6387)	44	1977	33	1977	(A&M 1948)

Catatonia Mixed Vocal/Instrumental Group From The UK

1	Sweet Catatonia	(Blanko Y Negro Neg 85cd)	61	1996	0	1996	
2	Lost Cat	(Blanco Y Negro Neg 88cd1)	41	1996	0	1996	
3	You've Got A Lot To Answer For	(Blanco Y Negro Neg 93cd1)	35	1996	0	1996	
4	Bleed	(Blanco Y Negro Neg 97cd1)	46	1996	0	1996	

Catch Male Vocal/Instrumental Group from the UK

1	Free (C'mon)	(Ffrr F 147)	70	1990	0	1990	

Cate Bros The Twins Names Are Ernie & Earl Cate B: 26 Dec 1942 Arkansas

1	Union Man		0	1976	24	1976	(Asylum 45294)

Caterina Valente Female Vocalist, B: 14 Jan 1931 Paris, France

* 1	The Breeze And I (Andalucia)	(Polydor Bm 6002)	5	1955	8	1955	(Decca 29467)

Catherine Stock Female Vocalist from the UK

1	To Have And To Hold	(Sierra Fed 29)	17	1986	0	1986	

Catherine Wheel Male Vocal/Instrumental Group from the UK

1	Black Metallic (EP)	(Fontana Cw 1)	68	1991	0	1991	
2	Balloon	(Fontana Cw 2)	59	1992	0	1992	
3	I Want To Touch You	(Fontana Cw 3)	35	1992	0	1992	
4	30 Century Man	(Fontana Cwcd 4)	47	1993	0	1993	
5	Crank	(Fontana Cwcd 5)	66	1993	0	1993	
6	Show Me Mary	(Fontana Cwcda 6)	62	1993	0	1993	
7	Waydown	(Fontana Cwcd 7)	67	1995	0	1995	

Catherine Zeta Jones Female Vocalist from the UK

1	For All Time	(Columbia 6583547)	36	1992	0	1992	
2	True Love Ways	(Polygram Tv Tlwcd 2)	38	1994	0	1994	with David Essex
3	In The Arms Of Love	(Wow! Wowcd 7101)	72	1995	0	1995	

Cathy Carr Female Vocalist, B: 28 Jun 1936 New York

1	Ivory Tower		0	1956	2	1956	(Fraternity 734)

Cathy Dennis Female Vocalist, B: 1970 Norwich, England   Former lead singer with D-mob

1	C'mon And Get My Love	(Ffrr F 117)	15	1989	10	1990	(Ffrr 996798#)
2	The Way Of The World	(Ffrr F 132)	48	1990	0	1990	
3	Touch Me (All Night Long)	(Polydor Cath 3)	5	1991	2	1991	
4	Just Another Dream	(Polydor Cath 2)	13	1991	9	1991	
5	Too Many Walls	(Polydor Cath 4)	17	1991	8	1991	
6	Everybody Move	(Polydor Cath 5)	25	1991	0	1991	
7	You Lied To Me	(Polydor Cath 6)	34	1992	32	1992	(Polydor 863452)
8	Irresistible	(Polydor Cath 7)	24	1992	0	1992	
9	Falling (The P.M. Dawn Version)	(Polydor Cathd 8)	32	1993	0	1993	
10	Why	(Ffrr fcd 227)	23	1994	0	1994	
11	West End Pad	(Polydor 5752812)	25	1996	0	1996	
12	Waterloo Sunset	(Polydor 5759612)	11	1997	0	1997	
13	When Dreams Turn To Dust	(Polydor 5711852)	43	1997	0	1997	

Cathy Jean & Her Roommates Female Vocalist, B: 8 Sep 1945 Brooklyn With Male Teenage Vocal Quartet from Queens, New York

1	Please Love Me Forever		0	1961	4	1961	(Valmor 007)

Cathy Troccoli Female Vocalist from New York City

1	Everything Changes		0	1992	14	1992	(Reunion 19118)

Cats Male Instrumental Group from the UK

1	Swan Lake	(Baf 1)	48	1969	0	1969	
2	Swan Lake (Re-Entry)	(Baf 1)	50	1969	0	1969	

Cats U.K. Female Vocal Group from the UK

1	Luton Airport	(Wea K 18075)	22	1979	0	1979	

ISSUE	TITLE	UK LBL	UK POS	UK YEAR	US POS	US YEAR	US LBL

Cause & Effect Male Duo, Sean Rowley And Robert Rowe Based In California

| 1 | You Think You Know Her | | 0 | 1992 | 38 | 1992 | (Src 14025) |

Caveman Male Rap Group from the UK

| 1 | I'm Ready | (Profile Prof 330) | 65 | 1991 | 0 | 1991 | |

Ce Ce Peniston Female Vocalist From Dayton, Ohio, Former Miss Black Arizona

*	1	Finally	(A&M Am 822)	29	1991	5	1991	(A&M 1586)
	2	We Got A Love Thang	(A&M Am 846)	6	1992	20	1992	(A&M 1594)
	3	I Like It	(A&M Am 847)	58	1992	0	1992	
	4	Finally (Re-Issue)	(A&M Am 858)	2	1992	0	1992	
	5	Keep On Walkin'	(A&M Am 878)	10	1992	15	1992	(A&M 1598)
	6	Crazy Love	(A&M Am 0060)	44	1992	0	1992	
	7	Inside That I Cried	(A&M Am 0121)	42	1992	0	1992	
	8	I'm In The Mood	(A&M 5804552)	16	1994	32	1994	(A&M 0460)
	9	Keep Givin' Me Your Love	(A&M 5805492)	36	1994	0	1994	
	10	Hit By Love	(A&M 5806932)	33	1994	0	1994	
	11	Movin' On		0	1996	83	1996	(A&M 581656)
	12	Finally	(Am:Pm 5823432)	26	1997	0	1997	

HIT 3 IS CREDITED TO OVERWEIGHT POOCH FEATURING CE CE PENISTON

Cece Winans

| 1 | Count On Me | (Arista 74321345842) | 12 | 1996 | 8 | 1996 | with Whitney Houston |

Celebration (Featuring) Mike Love Mike Love Is Also With The Beach Boys

| 1 | Almost Summer | | 0 | 1978 | 28 | 1978 | (MCA 40891) |

Celi Bee & The Buzzy Bunch Mixed Vocal/Instrumental Group from the USA

| 1 | Hold Your Horses Babe | (Tk Tkr 6032) | 72 | 1978 | 0 | 1978 | |

Celine Dion Female Vocalist, B: 30 Mar 1968 Quebec, Canada

	1	Where Does My Heart Beat Now	(Epic 6563265)	72	1993	4	1991(	Epic 73536)
	2	(If There Was) Any Other Way		0	1991	35	1991	(Epic 73665)
	3	Beauty And The Beast	(Epic 6576607)	9	1992	9	1992	(Epic 74090)
	4	If You Asked Me To	(Epic 6581927)	60	1992	4	1992	(Epic 74277)
	5	Nothing Broken But By Heart		0	1992	29	1992	(Epic 74336)
	6	Love Can Move Mountains	(Epic 6587787)	46	1992	36	1993	(Epic 74337)
	7	If You Asked Me To (Re-Entry)	(Epic 6581927)	57	1992	0	1992	
	8	When I Fall In Love		0	1993	23	1993	(Epic Sound. 77021)
	9	Misled	(Epic 6602922)	15	1994	23	1994	(550 Music 77344)
*	10	The Power Of Love	(Epic 6597992)	4	1994	1	1994	(550 Music 77230)
	11	Think Twice	(Epic 6606422)	5	1994	0	1994	
	12	Only One Road	(Epic 6613535)	8	1995	0	1995	
	13	Tu M'aimes Encore (To Love Me Again)	(Epic 6624255)	7	1995	0	1995	
	14	Misled (Re-Issue)	(Epic 6626495)	15	1995	0	1995	
	15	Falling Into You / If That's What It Takes	(Epic 6629795)	10	1996	0	1996	
*	16	Because You Loved Me (From Up Close & Personal)	(Epic 6632382)	5	1996	1	1996	(Music 78237)
*	17	It's All Coming Back To Me Now	(Epic 6637112)	3	1996	2	1996	(Music 78345)
	18	All By Myself	(Epic 6640622)	6	1996	0	1996	
	19	All By Myself (Re-Entry)	(Epic 6640622)	58	1997	4	1997	(Music 78529)
	20	Call The Man	(Epic 6646922)	11	1997	0	1997	

HIT 3 IS CREDITED TO CELINE DION AND PEABO BRYSON   HIT 8 IS CREDITED TO CELINE DION AND CLIVE GRIFFIN

Centory Male Rapper from the USA

| 1 | Point Of No Return | (EMICdem 354) | 67 | 1994 | 0 | 1994 | |

Central Band Of The Royal Air Force Military Band Conducted By W/Cdr A.E. Sims O.B.E. from the UK

| 1 | The Dambusters March | (HMV B 10877) | 18 | 1955 | 0 | 1955 | |

Central Line Male Vocal/Instrumental Group from the UK

1	(You Know) You Can Do It	(Mercury Line 7)	67	1981	0	1981	
2	Walking In To Sunshine	(Mercury Mcr 78)	42	1981	0	1981	
3	Don't Tell Me	(Mercury Mer 90)	55	1982	0	1982	
4	You've Said Enough	(Mercury Mer 117)	58	1982	0	1982	
5	Nature Boy	(Mercury Mer 131)	21	198	30	1983	
6	Surprise Surprise	(Mercury Mer 133)	8	1983	0	1983	

Cerrone Male Producer/Multi-Instrumentalist, Real Name Jean-Marc Cerrone B: 1952 France

1	Love In C Minor (Part 1)	(Atlantic K 10895)	31	1977	36	1977	(Cotillion 44215)
2	Supernature	(Atlantic K 11089)	8	1978	0	1978	
3	Je Suis Music	(CBS 6918)	39	1979	0	1979	
4	Supernature (Re-Mix)	(Encore Cdcor 013)	66	1996	0	1996	

C

112

ISSUE	TITLE	UK LBL	UK POS	UK YEAR	US POS	US YEAR	US LBL
Chad & Jeremy	Male Vocal Duo from England						
1	Yesterday's Gone	(Ember Emb S 180)	37	1963	21	1964	(World Artists 1021)
2	A Summer Song		0	1964	7	1964	(World Artists 1027)
3	Willow Weep For Me		0	1965	15	1965	(World Artists 1034)
4	If I Loved You		0	1965	23	1965	(World Artists 1041)
5	Before And After		0	1965	17	1965	(Columbia 43277)
6	I Don't Want To Lose You Baby		0	1965	35	1965	(Columbia 43339)
7	Distant Shores		0	1966	30	1966	(Columbia 43682)

CHAD STUART B: 10 DEC 1943, JEREMY CLYDE B: 22 MAR 1944 • HITS 1-2 ARE CREDITED TO CHAD STUART AND JEREMY CLYDE

Chad Jackson	Male Producer from the UK						
1	Hear The Drummer (Get Wicked)	(Big Wave Bwr 36)	3	1990	0	1990	

Chairmen Of The Board	Male Vocal Group from the USA	Names: Norman Johnson, Danny Woods, Harrison Kennedy & Eddie Curtis					
1	Give Me Just A Little More Time	(Invictus INV 501)	3	1970	3	1969	(Invictus 9074)
2	(You've Got Me) Dangling On A String	(Invictus Inv 504)	5	1970	38	1970	(Invictus 9078)
3	Everything's Tuesday	(Invictus Inv 507)	12	1971	38	1971	(Invictus 9079)
4	Pay To The Piper	(Invictus Inv 511)	34	1971	13	1971	(Invictus 9081)
5	Chairmen Of The Board	(Invictus Inv 516)	48	1971	0	1971	
6	Working On The Building Of Love	(Invictus Inv 519)	20	1972	0	1972	
7	Elmo James	(Invictus Inv 524)	21	1972	0	1972	
8	I'm On My Way To A Better Place	(Invictus Inv 527)	38	1972	0	1972	
9	I'm On My Way To A Better Place (Re-Entry)	(Invictus Inv 527)	30	1973	0	1973	
10	Finder's Keepers	(Invictus Inv 530)	21	1973	0	1973	
11	Loverboy	(EMI EMI 5585)	56	1986	0	1986	

HIT 3 IS CREDITED TO CHAIRMAN OF THE BOARD • HIT 11 IS CREDITED TO CHAIRMEN OF THE BOARD FEATURING GENERAL JOHNSON

Chaka Demus & Pliers	Male Vocal Duo from Jamaica						
1	Tease Me	(Mango Cidm 806)	3	1993	0	1993	
2	She Don't Let Nobody	(Mango Cidm 810)	4	1993	0	1993	
3	Twist And Shout	(Mango Cidm 814)	1	1993	0	1993	
4	Murder She Wrote	(Mango Cidm 812)	27	1994	0	1994	
5	I Wanna Be Your Man	(Mango Cidm 817)	19	1994	0	1994	
6	Gal Wine	(Mango Cidm 818)	20	1994	0	1994	
7	Twist And Shout (Re-Entry)	(Mango Cidm 814)	67	1995	0	1995	
8	Every Kinda People	(Island/Jamaica 1jcd 2005)	47	1996	0	1996	
9	Every Little Thing She Does is Magic	(Virgin VSCCDT 1654)	51	1997	0	1997	

Chaka Khan	Female Vocalist, Real Name Yvette Marie Stevens B: 23 Mar 1953 Great Lakes, Illinois						
* 1	Sweet Thing		0	1976	5	1976	(ABC 12149)
2	Stay		0	1978	38	1978	(ABC 12349)
3	I'm Every Woman	(Warner Bros K 17269)	11	1978	21	1978	(Warner Bros 8683)
4	Do You Love What You Feel		0	1980	30	1980	(MCA 41131)
5	Ain't Nobody	(Warner Bros Rck 1)	8	1984	22	1983	(Warner Bros 29555)
* 6	I Feel For You	(Warner Bros W9209)	1	1984	3	1984	(Warner Bros 29195)
7	This Is My Night	(Warner Bros W 9097)	14	1985	0	1985	
8	Eye To Eye	(Warner Bros W 9009)	16	1985	0	1985	
9	Love Of A Life Time	(Warner Bros W 8671)	52	1986	0	1986	
10	It's My Party	(Warner Bros W 7678)	71	1989	0	1989	
11	I'm Every Woman (Re-Mix)	(Warner Bros 2963)	8	1989	0	1989	
12	Ain't Nobody (Re-Mix)	(Warner Bros W 2880)	6	1989	0	1989	
13	I Feel For You (Re-Mix)	(Warner Bros W 2764)	45	1989	0	1989	
14	I'll Be Good To You	(Qwest W 2697)	21	1990	18	1989	(Qwest 22697
15	Love You All My Lifetime	(Warner Bros W 0087)	49	1992	0	1992	
16	Don't Look At Me That Way	(Warner Bros W 0192cd)	73	1993	0	1993	
17	Watch What You Say	(Cooltempo Cdcool 308)	28	1995	0	1995	
18	Never Miss the Water	(Reprise W 0393CD)	59	1997	0	1997	

HITS 1, 2, ARE CREDITED TO RUFUS FEATURING CHAKA KHAN HITS 5, 12 ARE CREDITED TO RUFUS AND CHAKA KHAN
HIT 14 IS CREDITED TO QUINCY JONES FEATURING RAY CHARLES AND CHAKA KHAN • HIT 17 IS CREDITED TO GURU FEATURING CHAKA KHAN

Chakachas	Mixed Vocal/Instrumental Group from Belgium	Lead Singer Gaston Boogaerts, B: 31 Jul 1921 Belgium					
1	Twist Twist	(RCA 1264)	48	1962	0	1962	
* 2	Jungle Fever	(Polydor 2121 064)	29	1972	8	1972	(Polydor 15030)

Chakka Boom Bang							
2	Home	(Wea Wea 116cd2)	46	1997	0	1997	
1	Tossing And Turning	(Hooj Choons Hoojcd 39)	57	1996	0	1996	

Chakra							
1	I Am	(Wea Wea 091)	24	1997	0	1997	
2	Home	(Wea Wea 116cd2)	46	1997	0	1997	

ISSUE	TITLE	UK LBL	UK POS	UK YEAR	US POS	US YEAR	US LBL
Chambers Brothers The Four Brothers Names Are Willie, Lester, George & Joe							
1	Time Has Come Today		0	1968	11	1968	(Columbia 44414)
Chambers Brothers							
2	I Can't Turn You Loose		0	1968	37	1968	(Columbia 44679)
Chameleon Male Vocal/Instrumental Group From The UK							
1	The Way It Is	(Stress Cdstr 65)	34	1996	0	1996	
Champ Butler							
1	I Apologize		0	1951	29	1951	(Columbia 39789)
2	Down Yonder		0	1951	17	1951	(Columbia 39533)
3	Be Anything (But Be Mine)		0	1952	26	1952	(Columbia 39690)
Champaign Mixed Vocal/Instrumental Sextet from Illinois Singers are Pauli Carman & Rena Jones							
1	How 'Bout Us	(CBS A 1046)	5	1981	12	1981	(Columbia 11433)
2	Try Again		0	1983	23	1983	(Columbia 03563) Lead
Champs Male Instrumental Group from the USA							
* 1	Tequila	(London Hlu 8580)	5	1958	1	1958	(Challenge 1016)
2	El Rancho Rock		0	1958	30	1958	(Challenge 59007)
3	Too Much Tequila	(London Hlh 9052)	49	1960	30	1960	(Challenge 59063)
4	Limbo Rock		0	1962	40	1962	(Challenge 9131)
Champs Boys Male Instrumental Group from France							
1	Tubular Bells	(Philips 6006 519)	41	1976	0	1976	
Chanelle Female Vocalist from the USA							
1	One Man	(Cooltempo Cool 183)	16	1989	0	1989	
2	One Man (Re-Mix)	(Deep Distraxion Oilycd 031)	50	1994	0	1994	
Change Mixed Vocal/Instrumental Group from the USA							
1	A Lover's Holiday	(Wea K 79141)	14	1980	40	1980	(RFC 49208)
2	Searching	(Wea K 79156)	11	1980	0	1980	
3	Change Of Heart	(Wea Yz 7)	17	1984	0	1984	
4	You Are My Melody	(Wea Yz 14)	48	1984	0	1984	
5	Let's To Together	(Cooltempo Cool 107)	37	1985	0	1985	
6	Oh What A Feeling	(Cooltempo Cool 109)	56	1985	0	1985	
7	Mutual Attraction	(Cooltempo Cool 111)	60	1985	0	1985	
Changing Faces Female Vocal Duo, Charisse Rose & Cassandra Lucas from the USA							
* 1	Stroke You Up	(Big Beat A 8251cd)	43	1994	3	1994	(Big Beat 98279)
2	Foolin' Around		0	1995	38	1995	(Big Beat 98207)
3	G.H.E.T.T.O.U.T.	(Atlantic At 0003cd)	10	1997	12	1997	(Atlantic 98026)
Channel X Mixed Vocal/Instrumental Group From Belgium							
1	Groove To Move	(Pwl Continental Pwl 209)	67	1991	0	1991	
Chanson Mixed Vocal Group from the USA							
1	Don't Hold Back	(Ariola Aro 140)	33	1979	21	1979	(Ariola 7717)
Chantal Curtis Female Vocalist from France							
1	Get Another Love	(Pye 7p 5003)	51	1979	0	1979	
Chantay Savage Female Vocalist from The USA							
1	I Will Survive	(RCA 74321377682)	12	1996	24	1996	
Chantay's Male Instrumental Group from the USA							
1	Pipeline	(London Hld 9696)	16	1963	4	1963	(Dot 16440)
Chante Moore Female Vocalist from the USA							
1	Love's Taken Over	(MCA Mcstd 1744)	54	1993	0	1993	
2	Free / Sail On	(MCA Mcstd 2042)	69	1995	0	1995	
Chantels Vocal Group From The Bronx, They formed when at high school and their name is taken from a rival school, St. Francis De Chantelle							
* 1	Maybe		0	1958	15	1958	(End 1005)
2	Every Night (I Pray)		0	1958	39	1958	(End 1015)
3	I Love You So		0	1958	42	1958	(End 1020)
4	Look In My Eyes		0	1961	14	1961	(Carlton 555)
5	Well, I Told You		0	1961	29	1961	(Carlton 564)
Chanter Sisters Female Vocal Group from the UK							
1	Side Show	(Polydor 2058 735)	43	1976	0	1976	
Chanters Vocal Group from the USA							
1	No, No, No		0	1961	41	1961	(Deluxe 6191)

ISSUE	TITLE	UK LBL	UK POS	UK YEAR	US POS	US YEAR	US LBL
Chaos Male Vocal Group from the UK							
1	Farewell My Summer Love	(Arista 74321116397)	5	1992	0	1992	
Chapterhouse Male Vocal/Instrumental Group from the UK							
1	Pearl	(Dedicated Stone 003)	67	1991	0	1991	
2	Mesmerise	(Dedicated Stone 001)	60	1991	0	1991	
Chaquito Real Name Johnny Gregory Male Producer/Arranger from the UK							
1	Never On Sunday	(Fontana H 265)	50	1960	0	1960	
Charioteers Male Vocal Group From Cincinnati, Led By William Williams							
1	So Long		0	1940	23	1940	(Columbia 35424)
2	On The Boardwalk In Atlantic City (From Three Little Girls In Blue)		0	1946	12	1946	(Columbia 37074)
3	Open The Door, Richard		0	1947	6	1947	(Columbia 37240)
4	Chi-Baba, Chi-Baba (My Bambina Go To Sleep)		0	1947	16	1947	(Columbia 37384)
5	What Did He Say?		0	1948	21	1948	(Columbia 38065)
6	Ooh! Look-A-There, Ain't She Pretty?		0	1948	20	1948	(Columbia 38065)
7	A Kiss And A Rose		0	1949	19	1949	(Columbia 38438)
Charlatans Male Vocal/Instrumental Group from the UK							
1	The Only One I Know	(Situation Two Sit 70t)	9	1990	0	1990	
2	Then	(Situation Two Sit 74t)	12	1990	0	1990	
3	Over Rising	(Situation Two Sit 76)	15	1991	0	1991	
4	Indian Rope	(Dead Dead Good Good 1t)	57	1991	0	1991	
5	Me. In Time	(Situation Two Sit 84)	28	1991	0	1991	
6	Weirdo	(Situation Two Sit 88)	19	1992	0	1992	
7	Tremelo Song (EP)	(Situation Two Sit 97t)	44	1992	0	1992	
8	Can't Get Out Of Bed	(Beggars Banquet Bbq 27cd)	24	1994	0	1994	
9	I Never Want An Easy Life If...	(BBQ 31cd)	38	1994	0	1994	
10	Jesus Hairdo	(Beggars Banquet Bbq 32cd1)	48	1994	0	1994	
11	Crashin' In	(Beggars Banquet Bbq 44cd)	31	1995	0	1995	
12	Just Lookin'/ Bullet Comes	(Beggars Banquet Bbq 55cd)	32	1995	0	1995	
13	Just When You're Thinkin' Things Over	(Beggars Banquet Bbq 60cd)	12	1995	0	1995	
14	One To Another	(Beggars Banquet Bbq 301cd)	3	1996	0	1996	
15	North Country Boy	(Beggars Banquet Bbq 309cd)	4	1997	0	1997	
16	How High	(Beggars Banquet Bbq 312cd)	6	1997	0	1997	
17	North Country Boy (Re-Entry)	(Beggars Banquet Bbq 309cd)	74	1997	0	1997	
Charlene Female Vocalist Real Name Charlene Duncan B: 1 Jun 1950 Hollywood							
1	I've Never Been To Me		0	1977	97	1977	(Motown 1611)
2	I've Never Been To Me (Re-Issue)	(Motown Tmg 1260)	1	1982	3	1982	(Motown 1611)
Charles & Eddie Male Vocal Duo from the USA							
1	Would I Lie To You	(Capitol Cl 673)	1	1992	13	1992	(Capitol 44809)
2	N.Y.C. (Can You Believe This City)	(Capitol Cdcl 681)	33	1993	0	1993	
3	House Is Not A Home	(Capitol Cdcls 688)	29	1993	0	1993	
4	24-7-365	(Capitol Cdcl 747)	25	1995	0	1995	
Charles Aznavour Male Vocalist B: 22 May 1924 Paris, France							
* 1	La Mama	(Various)	0	1963	0	1963	
2	The Old Fashioned Way	(Barclay Bar 20)	58	1973	0	1973	
3	The Old Fashioned Way (Re-Entry)	(Barclay Bar 20)	38	1973	0	1973	
* 4	She	(Barclay Bar 26)	1	1974	0	1974	
5	The Old Fashioned Way (2nd Re-Entry)	(Barclay Bar 20)	47	1974	0	1974	
	HIT 1 WAS NUMBER 1 IN FRANCE						
Charles Brown							
*+ 1	Black Night		0	1951	1	1951	
+ 2	Hard Times		0	1952	7	1952	(Aladdin 3116)
Charles Randolph Grean Sounde Former Director With RCA And Dot Records, B: 1 Oct 1913, New York City							
1	Quentin's Theme (from TV's Dark Shadow)		0	1969	13	1969	(Ranwood 840)
Charles Wright & The Watts 103rd Rhythm Band							
1	Do Your Thing		0	1969	11	1969	(Warner Bros 7250)
2	Love Land		0	1970	16	1970	(Warner Bros 7365)
3	Express Yourself		0	1970	12	1970	(Warner Bros 7417)
	THE BAND CONSISTS OF EIGHT MEN WHO WERE THE SOUL RUNNERS						
Charley Pride Male Vocalist, B: 18 Mar 1938 Sledge, Mississippi							
* 17	Kiss An Angel Good Mornin'		0	1971	21	1971	(RCA 0550)
26	Then Who Am I		0	1974	1	1974	(RCA 10126)
27	I Ain't All Bad		0	1975	6	1975	(RCA 10236)

ISSUE	TITLE	UK LBL	UK POS	UK YEAR	US POS	US YEAR	US LBL.
	Hope You're Feelin' Me (Like I'm Feelin' You)		0				(RCA 10374)
29	The Happiness Of Having You		0	1975	3	1975	(RCA 10455)
30	My Eyes Can Only See As Far As You		0	1976	1	1976	(RCA 10592)
31	A Whole Lotta Things To Sing About		0	1976	2	1976	(RCA 10757)
32	She's Just An Old Love Turned Memory		0	1977	1	1977	(RCA 10875)
33	I'll Be Leaving Alone		0	1977	1	1977	(RCA 10975)
	19-25 PLUS OTHER HITS WERE ALL C/W						

Charlie   Rock Quintet, Lead Singer Terry Thomas

1	It's Inevitable		0	1983	38	1983	(Mirage 99862)

Charlie Applewhite   Male Vocalist From the USA

1	Cabbages And Kings		0	1954	28	1954	(Decca 29001)
2	This Is You		0	1954	21	1954	(Decca 29055)
3	No One But You		0	1954	26	1954	(Decca 29125)
4	Blue Star (The Medic Theme)	(Brunswick 05416)	20	1955	0	1955	

Charlie Daniels Band   Male Vocal/Instrumental Group From the USA

1	Uneasy Rider		0	1973	9	1973	(Kama Sutra 576)
2	The South's Gonna Do It		0	1975	29	1975	(Kama Sutra 598)
4	Texas		0	1976	91	1976	(Kama Sutra 607)
* 8	The Devil Went Down To Georgia	(Epic Epc 7737)	14	1979	3	1979	(Epic 50700)
12	In America		0	1980	11	1980	(Epic 50888)
13	The Legend Of Wooley Swamp		0	1980	31	1980	(Epic 50921)
	OTHER HITS WERE C/W						

Charlie Dore   Female Vocalist from the UK

1	Pilot Of The Airwaves	(Island Wip 6526)	66	1979	13	1980	(Island 49166)

Charlie Drake   Male Actor/Vocalist, B: 19 Jun 1925 London, England

1	Splish Splash	(Parlophone R 4461)	7	1958	0	1958	
2	Volare	(Parlophone R 4478)	28	1958	0	1958	
3	Mr. Custer	(Parlophone R 4701)	12	1960	0	1960	
4	My Boomerang Won't Come Back	(Parlophone R 4824)	13	1961	21	1962	(United Artists 398)
5	Puckwudgie	(Columbia Db 8829)	47	1972	0	1972	

Charlie Gracie   Male Vocalist, Real Name Charles Graci B: 14 May 1936 In Philadelphia

* 1	Butterfly	(Parlophone R 4290)	12	1957	1	1957	(Cameo 105)
2	Fabulous	(Parlophone R 4313)	8	1957	16	1957	(Cameo 107)
3	I Love You So Much It Hurts	(London Hlu 8467)	20	1957	0	1957	
4	Wandering Eyes	(London Hlu 8467)	6	1957	0	1957	
5	Cool Baby	(London Hlu 8467)	26	1958	0	1958	

Charlie Harper   Male Vocalist from the UK

1	Barmy London Army	(Gem Gems 35)	68	1980	0	1980	

Charlie Kunz   Male Pianist from the USA

1	Piano Medley No 114	(Decca F 10419)	20	1954	0	1954	
2	Piano Medley No 114 (Re-Entry)	(Decca F 10419)	16	1955	0	1955	

Charlie Rich   Male Rockabilly-Country Singer/Pianist, B: 14 Dec 1932 Arkansas, He Is Known As The Silver Fox

* 1	Lonely Weekends		0	1960	22	1960	(Philips 3552)
2	Mohair Sam		0	1965	21	1965	(Smash 1993)
* 12	Behind Closed Doors	(Epic Epc 1539)	16	1974	15	1973	(Epic 10950)
* 14	The Most Beautiful Girl	(CBS 1897)	2	1974	1	1973	(Epic 11040)
15	There Won't Be Anymore		0	1974	18	1974	(RCA 0195)
16	A Very Special Love Song		0	1974	11	1974	(Epic 11091)
19	I Love My Friend		0	1974	24	1974	(Epic 20006)
23	We Love Each Other	(Epic Epc 2868)	37	1975	0	1975	
	OTHER HITS WERE C/W						

Charlie Sexton   Charlie Hails From Austin, Texas

1	Beat's So Lonely		0	1986	17	1986	(MCA 52715)

Charlie Spivak & His Orchestra   Male Bandleader/Instrumentalist (Trumpet) from the USA

12	Oh! What It Seemed To Be		0	1946	5	1946	(RCA Victor 1806)
13	(I Love You) For Sentimental Reasons		0	1946	5	1946	(RCA Victor 1981)
14	Linda		0	1947	5	1947	7(Rca Victor 2047)
15	Tomorrow		0	1947	25	1947	(Victor 2287)
16	Now Is The Hour (Maori Farewell Song)		0	1948	14	1948	(RCA Victor 2704)
17	Inner Sanctum		0	1948	23	1948	(Rca Victor 2864)
18	Mona Lisa		0	1950	16	1950	(london 619)

Charlotte   Female Vocalist from the UK

1	Queen Of Hearts	(Big Life Blrd 106)	54	1994	0	1994	

ISSUE	TITLE	UK LBL	UK POS	UK YEAR	US POS	US YEAR	US LBL
Charme	Mixed Vocal Group from the USA						
1	Georgy Porgy	(RCA 464)	68	1984	0	1984	
Charms	Names Richard Parker, Otis Williams, Donald Peak, Joe Penn & Rolland Bradley						
* 1	Hearts Of Stone		0	1954	15	1954	(Deluxe 6062)
+ 2	Two Hearts		0	1955	6	1955	(Deluxe 6065)
3	Ling, Ting, Tong		0	1955	26	1955	(Deluxe 6076)
4	Ivory Tower		0	1956	11	1956	(Deluxe 6093)
5	United		0	1957	5 +	1957	(Deluxe 6138)
	HIT 1 WAS NUMBER 1 IN THE USA R&B CHARTS HIT 4 IS CREDITED TO OTIS WILLIAMS AND HIS CHARMS • SEE ALSO 'OTIS WILLIAMS'						
Charo & The Salsoul Orchestra	Female Vocalist With Orchestra from the USA						
1	Dance A Little Bit Closer	(Salsoul Ssol 101)	44	1978	0	1978	
Chartbusters	Rock Quartet from Washington D.C						
1	She's The One		0	1964	33	1964	(Mutual 502)
Chas & Dave	Male Vocal/Instrumental Duo from the UK						
1	Strummin'	(EMI 2874)	52	1978	0	1978	
2	Gertcha	(EMI2947)	20	1979	0	1979	
3	The Sideboard Song	(EMI 2986)	55	1979	0	1979	
4	Rabbit	(Rockney 9)	8	1980	0	1980	
5	Stars Over 45	(Rockney Kor 12)	21	1981	0	1981	
6	Ain't No Pleasing You	(Rockney Kor 14)	2	1982	0	1982	
7	Margate	(Rockney Kor 15)	46	1982	0	1982	
8	London Girls	(Rockney Kor 17)	63	1983	0	1983	
9	My Melancholy Baby	(Rockney Kor 21)	51	1983	0	1983	
10	Snooker Loopy	(Rockney Pot 147)	6	1996	0	1996	
	HIT 1 IS CREDITED TO CHAS & DAVE WITH ROCKNEY • HIT 10 IS CREDITED TO MATCHROOM MOB WITH CHAS & DAVE SEE ALSO TOTTENHAM HOTSPUR F.C.						
Chas McDevitt Skiffle Group	Mixed Vocal/Instrumental Skiffle Group from the UK						
* 1	Freight Train	(Oriole Cb 1352)	5	1957	40	1957	(Chic 1008)
2	Greenback Dollar	(Oriole Cb 1371)	28	1957	0	1957	
3	Greenback Dollar (Re-Entry)	(Oriole Cb 1371)	30	1957	0	1957	
4	Freight Train (Re-Entry)	(Oriole Cb 1352)	27	1957	0	1957	
Chase	Jazz-Rock Band With Trumpeter Bill Chase from the USA						
1	Get It On		0	1971	24	1971	(Epic 10738)
	OBITUARY: BILL D: 9 AUG 1974 PLANE CRASH. THREE OTHER MEMBERS OF THE GROUP WERE KILLED IN THE SAME CRASH						
Cheap Trick	Male Vocal/Instrumental Group from the USA						
* 1	I Want You To Want Me	(Epic Epc 7258)	29	1979	7	1979	(Epic 50680)
2	Ain't That A Shame		0	1979	35	1979	(Epic 50743)
3	Dream Police		0	1979	26	1979	(Epic 50774)
4	Voices		0	1980	32	1980	(Epic 50814)
5	Way Of The World	(Epic Epc 8114)	73	1980	0	1980	
6	If You Want My Love	(Epic Epc A 2406)	57	1982	0	1982	
7	The Flame		0	1988	1	1988	(Epic 07745)
8	Don't Be Cruel		0	1988	4	1988	(Epic 07965)
9	Ghost Town		0	1988	33	1988	(Epic 08097)
10	Can't Stop Fallin' Into Love		0	1990	12	1990	(Epic 73444)
	NAMES: RICK NIELSEN, BRAD CARLSON, ROBIN ZANDER & TOM PETERSSON. JON BRANT REPLACED TOM IN 1980						
Checkmates	Sonny Charles, Bobby Stevens, Harvey Trees, Bill Van Buskirk & Marvin Smith						
1	Love Is All I Have To Give		0	1969	65	1969	(A&M 1039)
	See Also Sonny Charles, Emile Ford						
Cheech & Chong	Names Richard 'Cheech' Martin B: 13 Jul 1946 & Thomas Chong B: 24 May 1938						
1	Basketball Jones Featuring Tyrone Shoelaces		0	1973	15	1973	(Ode 66038)
2	Sister Mary Elephant (Shudd-Up!)		0	1973	24	1973	(Ode 66041)
3	Earache My Eyes (Featuring Alice Bowie)		0	1974	9	1974	(Ode 66102)
Cheers	Mixed Vocal Trio From Los Angeles Names: Gill Garfield, Sue Allen & Bert Convy						
1	(Bazoom) I Need Your Lovin'		0	1954	11	1954	(Capitol 2921)
2	Black Denim Trousers		0	1955	6	1955	(Capitol 3219)
	Obituary : Bert D: 15 Jul 1991 Brain Tumour.						
Cheetahs	Male Vocal/Instrumental Group from the UK						
1	Mecca	(Philips Bf 1362)	36	1964	0	1964	
2	Soldier Boy	(Philips Bf 1383)	39	1965	0	1965	
Chelsea F.C.	Male Vocal Soccer Team from the UK						
1	Blue Is The Colour	(Penny Farthing Pen 782)	5	1972	0	1972	

ISSUE	TITLE	UK LBL	UK POS	UK YEAR	US POS	US YEAR	US LBL
2	No One Can Stop Us Now	(Rca 74321210452)	23	1994	0	1994	
3	Blue Day	(Wea Wea 112cd)	24	1997	0	1997	
	HIT 3 IS CREDITED TO SUGGS & CO FEATURING CHELSEA TEAM						

Chemical Brothers Male Instrumental/Production Duo from the UK

1	Leave Home	(Junior Boy's Own Chemsd 1)	17	1995	0	1995	
2	Life Is Sweet	(Junior Boy's Own Chemsd 2)	25	1995	0	1995	
3	Loops Of Fury (EP)	(Junior Boy's Own Chemsd 3)	13	1996	0	1996	
4	Setting Sun	(Junior Boy's Own Chemsd 4)	1	1996	80	1997	(Caroline 6187)
5	Blockin' Rockin Beats	(Virgin Chemsd 5)	1	1997	0	1997	
6	Blockin' Rockin Beats (re-entry)	(Virgin Chemsd 5)	69	1997	0	1997	

Chequers Male Vocal/Instrumental Group from the UK

1	Rock On Brother	(Creole Cr 111)	21	1975	0	1975	
2	Hey Miss Payne	(Creole Cr 116)	32	1976	0	1976	

Cher Female Vocalist Real Name Cherilyn Lapierre Sakisian B: 20 May 1946 El Centro, California

1	All I Really Want To Do	(Liberty Lib 66114)	9	1965	15	1965	(Imperial 66114)
2	Where Do You Go		0	1965	25	1965	(Imperial 66136)
3	Bang Bang	(Liberty Lib 66160)	3	1966	2	1966	(Imperial 66160)
4	I Feel Something In The Air	(Liberty Lib 12034)	43	1966	0	1966	
5	Alfie		0	1966	32	1966	(Imperial 66192)
6	Sunny	(Liberty Lib 12083)	32	1966	0	1966	
7	You Better Sit Down Kids		0	1967	9	1967	(Imperial 66261)
* 8	Gypsies Tramps And Thieves	(MCA Mu 1142)	4	1971	1	1971	(Kapp 2146)
9	The Way Of Love		0	1972	7	1972	(Kapp 2158)
10	Living In A House Divided		0	1972	22	1972	(Kapp 2171)
* 11	Half-Bread		0	1973	1	1973	(MCA 40102)
* 12	Dark Lady	(MCA 101)	36	1974	1	1974	(MCA 40161)
13	Dark Lady (Re-Entry)	(MCA 101)	45	1974	0	1974	
14	Train Of Thought		0	1974	27	1974	(MCA 40245)
15	Take Me Home		0	1979	8	1979	(Casablanca 965)
16	I Found Someone	(Greffen Gef 31)	5	1987	10	1988	(Geffen 28191)
17	We All Sleep Alone	(Greffen Gef 35)	47	1988	14	1988	(Geffen 27986)
* 18	After All		0	1989	6	1989	(Geffen 27529)
* 19	If I Could Turn Back Time	(Greffen Gef 59)	6	1989	3	1989	(Geffen 22886)
20	Just Like Jesse James	(Greffen Gef 69)	11	1990	8	1989	(Geffen 22844)
21	Heart Of Stone	(Greffen Gef 75)	43	1990	20	1990	(Geffen 19953)
22	You Wouldn't Know Love	(Greffen Gef 77)	55	1990	0	1990	
23	It's In His Kiss (The Shoop Shoop Song)	(Epic 6566737)	1	1991	33	1991	(Geffen 19659)
24	Love And Understanding	(Greffen Gfs 5)	10	1991	17	1991	(Geffen 19023)
25	Save Up All Your Tears	(Greffen Gfs 11)	37	1991	37	1991	(Geffen 19105)
26	Love Hurts	(Greffen Gfs 16)	43	1991	0	1991	
27	Could've Been You	(Greffen Gfs 19)	31	1992	0	1992	
28	Oh No Not My Baby	(Greffen Gfs 29)	33	1992	0	1992	
29	Many Rivers To Cross	(Greffen Gfstd 31)	37	1993	0	1993	
30	Whenever You're Near	(Greffen Gfstd 32)	72	1993	0	1993	
31	I Got You Babe	(Greffen Gfstd 64)	35	1994	0	1994	
32	Love Can Build A Bridge	(London Cocd 1)	1	1995	0	1995	
33	Walking In Memphis	(Wea Wea 021cd1)	11	1995	0	1995	
34	One By One	(Wea Wea 032cd)	7	1996	52	1996	(Reprise 17695)
35	Not Enough Love In The World	(Wea Wea 052cd)	31	1996	0	1996	
36	The Sun Ain't Gonna Shine Anymore	(Wea Wea 071cd)	26	1996	0	1996	

Cherelle Female Vocalist B: Cheryl Norton, Los Angeles

1	Saturday Love	(Tabu A 6829)	6	1985	26	1985	(Tabu 05767)
2	Will You Satisfy	(Tabu A 6927)	57	1986	0	1986	
3	Never Knew Love Like This	(Tabu 6513827)	26	1988	28	1988	(Tabu 07646)
4	Affair	(Tabu 654673 7)	67	1989	0	1989	
5	Saturday Love (Re-Mix)	(Tabu 6558007)	55	1990	0	1990	
6	Baby Come To Me	(One World Ent. Owecd 1)	56	1997	0	1997	
	HIT 3, 6 IS CREDITED TO ALEXANDER O'NEAL FEATURING CHERELLE • HITS 1, 5 ARE CREDITED TO CHERELLE WITH ALEXANDER O'NEAL						

Cheri Female Vocal Duo, Names Rosalind Hunt & Lyn Cullerier from Canada

1	Murphy's Law	(Polydor Posp 459)	13	1982	39	1982	(Venture 149)

Cherokees Male Vocal/Instrumental Group from the UK

1	Seven Daffodils	(Columbia Db 7341)	33	1964	0	1964	

Cheryl Ladd Female Vocalist, Real Name Cheryl Stoppelmoor B: 2 Jul 1951 South Dakota   Played Kris Monroe In *Charlie's Angels*

1	Think It Over		0	1978	34	1978	(Capitol 4599)

ISSUE	TITLE	UK LBL	UK POS	UK YEAR	US POS	US YEAR	US LBL
Cheryl Lynn Female Vocalist, B: 11 Mar 1957 Los Angeles							
1	Got To Be Real		0	1979	12	1979	(Columbia 10808)
2	Encore	(Streetwave Khan 23)	68	1984	0	1984	
Cheryl Pepsii Riley Female R&B Vocalist From Brooklyn							
1	Thanks For My Child	(CBS 653153 7)	75	1989	32	1988	(Columbia 07996)
Chesney Hawkes Male Vocalist From The Uk							
1	The One And Only	(Chrysalis Chs 3627)	1	1991	11	1991	(Chrysalis 23730)
2	I'm A Man Not A Boy	(Chrysalis Chs 3708)	27	1991	0	1991	
3	Secrets Of The Heart	(Chrysalis Chs 3681)	57	1991	0	1991	
4	What's Wrong With This Picture	(Chrysalis Cdchs 3969)	63	1993	0	1993	
Chet Atkins Male Guitarist/Instrumentalist B: Chester Burton Atkins 20 June 1924 Tennessee							
! 1	Mister Sandman		0	1955	13	1955	(RCA 5956)
! 2	Silver Bell		0	1955	15	1955	(RCA 5995)
3	Teensville	(RCA 1174)	46	1960	0	1960	
4	Teensville (Re-Entry)	(RCA 1174)	49	1960	0	1960	
	HIT 1 IS CREDITED TO CHET ATKINS & HIS GALLOPIN' GUITAR						
Chi Coltrane Female Vocalist/Pianist, B: 16 Nov 1948 Wisconsin							
1	Thunder And Lightning		0	1972	17	1972	(Columbia 45640)
Chi-Lites Male Vocal Group from the USA							
+ 1	Give It Away		0	1969	10	1969	(Brunswick 55398)
+ 2	Are You My Woman (Tell Me So)		0	1970	8	1970	(Brunswick 55442)
3	(For Gods Sake) Give More Power To People	(MCA Mu 1138)	32	1971	26	1971	(Brunswick 55450)
* 4	Have You Seen Her	(MCA Mu 1146)	3	1972	3	1971	(Brunswick 55462)
* 5	Oh Girl	(MCA MU 1156)	14	1972	1	1972	(Brunswick 55471)
6	A Letter To Myself		0	1973	33	1973	(Brunswick 55491)
7	Stoned Out Of My Mind		0	1973	30	1973	(Brunswick 55500)
8	Homely Girl	(Brunswick BR 9)	5	1974	0	1974	
9	I Found Sunshine	(Brunswick BR 12)	35	1974	0	1974	
10	Too Good To Be Forgotten	(Brunswick BR 13)	10	1974	0	1974	
11	Have You Seen Her / Oh Girl (Re-Issue)	(Brunswick BR 20)	5	1975	0	1975	
12	It's Time For Love	(Brunswick BR 25)	5	1975	0	1975	
13	You Don't Have To Go	(Brunswick BR 34)	3	1976	0	1976	
14	Changing For You	(R&B RBS 215)	61	1983	0	1983	
	NAMES EUGENE RECORD, ROBERT LESTER, MARSHALL THOMPSON & CREADEL JONES. • GROUP FIRST RECORDED AS THE HI-LITES IN 1963						
Chic Mixed Vocal/Instrumental Group from the USA							
* 1	Dance Dance Dance (Yowsah Yowsah)	(Atlantic K 11038)	6	1977	6	1978	(Atlantic 3435)
2	Everybody Dance	(Atlantic K 11097)	9	1978	38	1978	(Atlantic 3469)
3	Le Freak	(Atlantic K 11029	7	1978	1	1978	(Atlantic 3519)
* 4	I Want You Love – Le Freak	(Atlantic Lv 16)	4	1979	7	1979	(Atlantic 3557)
* 5	Good Times	(Atlantic K 11385)	5	1979	1	1979	(Atlantic 3584)
6	My Forbidden Lover	(Atlantic K 11385)	15	1979	0	1979	
7	My Feet Keep Dancing	(Atlantic K 11415)	21	1979	0	1979	
8	Hangin'	(Atlantic A 9898)	64	1983	0	1983	
* 9	Jack Le Freak	(Atlantic A 9198)	19	1987	0	1985	
10	Megachic –Chic Medley	(East West A 7949)	58	1990	0	1990	
11	Chic Mystique	(Warner Bros W 0083)	48	1992	0	1992	
	NAMES: BERNARD EDWARDS, NILE RODGERS, NORMA JEAN WRIGHT & LUCI MARTIN • ALFA ANDERSON LATER REPLACED NORMA JEAN WRIGHT						
Chicago Male Vocal/Instrumental Group from the USA							
1	I'm A Man	(CBS 4715)	8	1970	0	1970	
2	Make Me Smile		0	1970	9	1970	(Columbia 45127)
3	25 Or 6 To 4	(CBS 5076)	7	1970	4	1970	(Columbia 45194)
4	Does Anybody Really Know What Time It Is		0	1970	7	1970	(Columbia 45264)
5	Free		0	1971	20	1971	(Columbia 45331)
6	Lowdown		0	1971	35	1971	(Columbia 45370)
7	Beginnings		0	1971	7	1971	(Columbia 45417)
8	Colour My World		0	1971	7	1971	(Columbia 45417)
9	Questions 67 And 68 (Re-Issue)		0	1971	24	1971	(Columbia 45467)
* 10	Saturday In The Park		0	1972	3	1972	(Columbia 45657)
11	Dialogue (Part 1-2)		0	1972	24	1972	(Columbia 45717)
12	Feelin' Stronger Every Day		0	1973	10	1973	(Columbia 45880)
* 13	Just You 'N' Me		0	1973	4	1973	(Columbia 45933)
14	(I've Been) Searchin' So Long		0	1974	9	1974	(Columbia 46020)
15	Call On Me		0	1974	6	1974	(Columbia 46062)

ISSUE	TITLE	UK LBL	UK POS	UK YEAR	US POS	US YEAR	US LBL
16	Wishing You Were Here		0	1974	11	1974	(Columbia 10049)
17	Harry Truman		0	1975	13	1975	(Columbia 10092)
18	Old Days		0	1975	5	1975	(Columbia 10131)
19	Another Rainy Day In New York City		0	1976	32	1976	(Columbia 10360)
* 20	If You Leave Me Now	(CBS 4603)	1	1976	1	1976	(Columbia 10390)
21	Baby What A Big Surprise	(CBS 5672)	41	1977	4	1977	(Columbia 10620)
22	Alive Again		0	1978	14	1978	(Columbia 10845)
23	No Tell Lover		0	1979	14	1979	(Columbia 10879)
* 24	Hard To Say I'm Sorry	(Full Moon K 79301)	4	1982	1	1982	(Full Moon 29979)
25	Love Me Tomorrow		0	1982	22	1982	(Full Moon 29911)
26	Stay The Night		0	1984	16	1984	(Full Moon 29306)
27	Hard Habit To Break	(Full Moon W 9214)	8	1984	3	1984	(Full Moon 29214)
28	You're The Inspiration	(Warner Bros W 9126)	14	1985	3	1985	(Full Moon 29126)
29	Along Comes A Woman		0	1985	14	1985	(Full Moon 29082)
30	Will You Still Love Me		0	1987	3	1987	(Full Moon 28512)
31	If She Would Have Been Faithful		0	1987	17	1987	(Warner Bros 28424)
32	I Don't Wanna Live Without Your Love		0	1988	3	1988	(Reprise 27855)
33	Look Away		0	1988	1	1988	(Reprise 27766)
34	You're Not Alone		0	1989	10	1989	(Reprise 27757)
35	What Kind Of Man Would I Be		0	1990	5	1990	(Reprise 22741)
36	Chasin' The Wind		0	1991	39	1991	(Reprise 19466)

HIT 9 WAS ISSUED IN 1969 AND REACHED NUMBER 71 IN THE USA. • ORIGINALLY CALLED THE BIG THING THEN CHICAGO TRANSIT AUTHORITY
NAMES: ROBERT LAMM, JAMES PANKOW, LEE LOUGHNANE, TERRY KATH, WALT PARAZAIDER, PETER CETERA & DANNY SERAPHINE
THERE HAVE BEEN MANY CHANGES IN PERSONNEL SINCE 1979. • OBITUARY: TERRY D: 23 JAN 1978 PLAYING RUSSIAN ROULETTE.

Chicago Loop   Lead Guitarist Is Stefan Grossman from Chicago

1	(When She Needs Good Lovin') She Comes To Me			0	1966	37	1966	(Dyno Voice 226)

Chicane   Male Instrumental Duo from the UK

1	Offshore	(Extravaganza 0091005)	14	1996	0	1996	
2	Sunstroke	(Xtravaganza 009125)	21	1997	0	1997	
3	Offshore '97	(Xtravaganza 0091255)	17	1997	0	1997	

Chicken Shack   Mixed Vocal/Instrumental Group from the UK

1	I'd Rather Go Blind	(Blue Horizon 57-3153)	14	1969	0	1969	
2	Tears In The Wind	(Blue Horizon 57-3160)	29	1969	0	1969	

Chico Debarge

1	Talk To Me		0	1986	21	1986	(Motown 1858)

Chicory Tip   Mixed Vocal/Instrumental Group from the UK

* 1	Son Of My Father	(CBS 7737)	1	1972	0	1972	
2	What's Your Name	(CBS 8021)	13	1972	0	1972	
3	Good Grief Christina	(CBS 1258)	17	1973	0	1973	

HIT 1 WAS CALLED 'NACHTS SCHEINT DIE SONNE' IN GERMANY • NAMES: PETER HEWSON, RICK FOSTER, BARRY MAYGER & BRIAN SHEARER

Chieftans   Male Vocalist With Instrumental Group From Ireland

1	Have I Told You Lately (That I Love You)	(RCA 74321271720)	71	1995	0	1995	

HIT IS CREDITED TO VAN MORRISON AND THE CHIEFTANS

Chiffons   Female Vocal Quartet From The Bronx

* 1	He's So Fine	(Stateside Ss 172)	16	1963	1	1963	(Laurie 3152)
2	One Fine Day	(Stateside Ss 202)	29	1963	5	1963	(Laurie 3179)
3	A Love So Fine		0	1963	40	1963	(Laurie 3195)
4	I Have A Boyfriend		0	1964	36	1964	(Laurie 3212)
5	Sweet Talkin' Guy	(Stateside Ss 512)	31	1966	10	1966	(Laurie 3340)
6	Sweet Talkin' Guy (Re-Issue)	(London Hl 10271)	4	1972	0	1972	

NAMES ARE BARBARA LEE, PATRICIA BENNETT, SYLVIA PETERSON & JUDY CRAIG. • ALSO RECORDED AS THE FOUR PENNIES

Child   Male Vocal/Instrumental Group from the UK

1	When You Walk In The Room	(Ariola Hansa Aha 511)	38	1978	0	1978	
2	It's Only Make Belleve	(Ariola Hansa Aha 522)	10	1978	0	1978	
3	Only You (And You Alone)	(Ariola Hansa Aha 536)	33	1979	0	1979	

Childliners   Mixed Vocal Group from the UK/Australia

1	The Gift Of Christmas	(London Loncd 376)	9	1995	0	1995	

Children For Rwanda   Mixed Choir from the UK

1	Love Can Build A Bridge	(East West Yz 849cd)	57	1994	0	1994	

Children Of Tansley School   Children's Choir from the UK

1	My Mum Is One In A Million	(EMI 5151)	27	1981	0	1981	

ISSUE	TITLE	UK LBL	UK POS	UK YEAR	US POS	US YEAR	US LBL
Children Of The Night Male Producer/Vocalist from the UK							
1	It's A Trip (Tune In, Turn On, Drop Out)	(Jive Jive 189)	52	1988	0	1988	
Chill Fac-Torr Male Vocal/Instrumental Group from the USA							
1	Twist (Round 'N' Round)	(Phillyworld Pws 109)	37	1983	0	1983	
Chilliwack Rock Group from Canada Led By Bill Henderson							
1	My Girl (Gone, Gone, Gone)		0	1981	22	1981	(Millennium 11813)
2	I Believe		0	1982	33	1982	(Millennium 13102)
Chimes (1) Male/Female Vocal And Instrumental Group from the UK							
1	1-2-3	(CBS 655166 7)	60	1989	0	1989	
2	Heaven	(CBS655432 7)	66	1989	0	1989	
3	Heaven (Re-Entry)	(CBS 655432 7)	69	1990	0	1990	
4	Still Haven't Found What I'm Looking For	(CBS Chim 1)	6	1990	0	1990	
5	True Love	(CBS Chim 2)	48	1990	0	1990	
6	Heaven (Re-Issue)	(CBS Chim 3)	24	1990	0	1990	
7	Love Comes To Mind	(CBS Chim 4)	49	1990	0	1990	
Chimes (2) Led By Leonard Cocco, A Brooklyn Based Quintet							
1	Once In A While		0	1961	11	1961	(Tag 444)
2	I'm In The Mood For Love		0	1961	38	1961	(Tag 445)
China Black Male Vocal/Instrumental Duo from the UK							
1	Searching	(Wild Card Cardd 7)	4	1994	0	1994	
2	Stars	(Wild Card Cardd 9)	17	1994	0	1994	
3	Searching (Re-Entry)	(Wild Card Cardd 7)	54	1994	0	1994	
4	Almost See You (Somewhere)	(Wild Card Cardd 15)	31	1995	0	1995	
5	Swing Low Sweet Chariot	(Polygram TV Swlow 2)	15	1995	0	1995	with Ladysmith Black Mambazo
China Crisis Male Vocal/Instrumental Group from the UK							
1	African And White	(Inevitable Inev 011)	45	1982	0	1982	
2	Christian	(Virgin Vs 562)	12	1983	0	1983	
3	Tragedy And Mystery	(Virgin Vs 587)	46	1983	0	1983	
4	Working With Fire And Steel	(Virgin Vs 620)	48	1983	0	1983	
5	Wishful Thinking	(Virgin Vs 647)	9	1984	0	1984	
6	Hanna Hanna	(Virgin Vs 665)	43	1984	0	1984	
7	Black Man Ray	(Virgin Vs 752)	14	1985	0	1985	
8	King In A Catholic Style (Wake Up)	(Virgin Vs 765)	19	1986	0	1986	
9	You Did Cut Me	(Virgin Vs 799)	54	1985	0	1985	
10	Arizona Sky	(Virgin Vs 898)	47	1986	0	1986	
11	Best Kept Secret	(Virgin Vs 926)	36	1987	0	1987	
China Drum Male Vocal/Instrumental Group from The UK							
1	Can't Stop These Things	(Mantra Mnt 8cd)	65	1996	0	1996	
2	Last Chance	(Mantra Mnt 10cd)	60	1996	0	1996	
3	Fiction Of Life	(Mantra Mnt 21cd)	65	1997	0	1997	
Chipmunks Male Vocalist David Seville from the USA See Also David Seville							
1	Achy Breaky Heart	(Epic 6588837)	53	1992	0	1992	
2	Macarena	(Sony Wonder 6639981)	65	1996	0	1996	
	HIT 1 IS CREDITED TO ALVIN & THE CHIPMUNKS FEATURING BILLY RAY CYRUS • HIT 2 IS CREDITED TO LOS DEL CHIPMUNKS						
Chippendales Male Vocal Group from the USA/UK							
1	Give Me Your Body	(XS Rhythm Xsr 3)	28	1992	0	1992	
Chiyo Okumura Female Singer from Japan. Hit Was Written By The Ventures							
* 1	Hokkaido Skies		0	1966	0	1966	
Chops-EMC + Extensive Male Instrumental/Rapper Group from the USA							
1	Me' Israelites	Faze 2 Faze 6)	60	1992	0	1992	
Chordettes Female Vocal Group from the USA							
* 1	Mr.Sandman	(Columbia Db 3553)	11	1954	1	1954	(Cadence 1247)
2	Eddie My Love		0	1956	14	1956	(Cadence 1284)
3	Born To Be With You	(London Hla 8302)	8	1956	5	1956	(Cadence 1291)
4	Lay Down Your Arms		0	1956	16	1956	(Cadence 1299)
5	Just Between You And Me		0	1957	8	1957	(Cadence 1330)
* 6	Lollipop	(London Hld 8584)	6	1958	2	1958	(Cadence 1345)
7	Zorro		0	1958	17	1958	(Cadence 1349)
8	No Other Arms, No Other Lips		0	1959	27	1959	(Cadence 1361)
9	Never On A Sunday		0	1961	13	1961	(Cadence 1402)
	NAMES: JANE ERTEL, CAROL BUSCHMAN, LYNN EVANS & JINNY LOCKARD						
	DOROTHY SCHWARTZ REPLACED LYNN EVANS, MARGIE NEEDHAM REPLACED JINNY LOCKARD						

ISSUE	TITLE	UK LBL	UK POS	UK YEAR	US POS	US YEAR	US LBL
Chords (1) Male R&B Quintet From New York, USA							
1	Sh-Boom		0	1954	9	1954	(Cat 104)
Chords (2) Male Vocal/Instrumental Group from the UK							
1	Now It's Gone	(Polydor 2059 141)	63	1979	0	1979	
2	Maybe Tomorrow	(Polydor Posp 101)	40	1980	0	1980	
3	Something's Missing	(Polydor Posp 146)	55	1980	0	1980	
4	The British Way Of Life	(Polydor 2059 258)	54	1980	0	1980	
5	In My Street	Polydor Posp 185)	50	1980	0	1980	
Chris & James Male Production Duo from the UK							
1	Calm Down (Bass Keeps Pumpin')	(Stress 12str 38)	74	1994	0	1994	
2	Fox Force Five	(Stress Cdstr 61)	71	1995	0	1995	
Chris Andrews Real Name Christopher Frederick Andrews B: 15 Oct 1942, Romford, Essex							
* 1	Yesterday Man	(Decca F 12236)	3	1965	0	1965	
2	To Whom It Concerns	(Decca F 22285)	13	1965	0	1965	
3	Something On My Mind	(Decca F 22365)	45	1966	0	1966	
4	Something On My Mind (Re-Entry)	Decca F 22365)	41	1966	0	1966	
5	Whatcha Gonna Do Now	(Decca F 22404)	40	1966	0	1966	
6	Stop That Girl	(Decca F 22472)	36	1966	0	1966	
Chris Barber's Jazz Band Male Jazz Bandleader/Trombonist, B: 17 Apr 1930 Welwyn Garden City, Hertfordshire, England)							
* 1	Petite Fleur (Little Flower)	(Pye Nixa 2026)	3	1959	5	1959	(Laurie 3022)
2	Petite Fleur (Little Flower) (Re-Entry)	(Pye Nixa 2026)	22	1959	0	1959	
3	Lonesome	(Columbia Db 4333)	27	1959	0	1959	
4	Revival	(Columbia Scd 2166)	50	1962	0	1962	
5	Revival (Re-Entry)	(Columbia Scd 2166)	43	1962	0	1962	
	LONNIE DONEGAN WAS A FORMER MEMBER OF THE BAND. HIT 3 IS CREDITED TO CHRIS BARBER FEATURING MONTY SUNSHINE						
Chris Bartley Soul Singer/Guitarist, B: 17 Apr 1949 New York City							
1	The Sweetest Thing This Side Of Heaven		0	1967	32	1967	(Vando 101)
	ALSO SANG WITH SOULFUL INSPIRATION						
Chris Christian Guitarist/Songwriter from the USA Also With The Trio Cotton, Lloyd & Christian							
1	I Want You, I Need Yo		0	1981	37	1981	(Boardwalk 126)
Chris Connor Female Vocalist, B: 8 Nov 1927 Kansas City, Missouri. She Was With Stan Kenton 1952-53							
1	I Miss You So		0	1957	34	1957	(Atlantic 1105)
Chris De Burgh Male Vocalist, Real Name Christopher John Davidson B: 15 Oct 1947 In Argentina							
1	Don't Pay The Ferryman	(A&M Ams 8256)	48	1982	34	1982	(A&M 2511)
2	High On Emotion	(A&M Am 190)	44	1984	0	1984	
3	The Lady In Red	(A&M Am 331)	1	1986	3	1987	(A&M 2848)
4	Fatal Hesitation	(A&M Am 348)	44	1986	0	1986	
5	A Spaceman Came Travelling	(A&M Am 365)	40	1986	0	1986	
6	The Lady In Red (Re-Entry)	(A&M Am 331)	74	1987	0	1987	
7	The Simple Truth (A Child Is Born)	(A&M Am 427)	69	1988	0	1988	
8	The Simple Truth (A Child Is Born) (Re-Entry)	(A&M Am 427)	55	1988	0	1988	
9	Missing You	(A&M Am 474)	3	1988	0	1988	
10	Tender Hands	(A&M Am 486)	43	1989	0	1989	
11	This Waiting Heart	(A&M Am 528)	59	1989	0	1989	
12	The Simple Truth (A Child Is Born) (Re-Issue)	(A&M Relf 1)	36	1991	0	1991	
13	Separate Tables	(A&M Am 863)	30	1992	0	1992	
14	Blonde Hair Blue Jeans	(A&M 5805932)	51	1994	0	1994	
15	The Snows Of New York	(A&M 5813132)	60	1995	0	1995	
Chris Farlowe Male Vocalist from the UK							
1	Think	(Immediate Im 023)	49	1966	0	1966	
2	Think (Re-Entry)	(Immediate Im 023)	37	1966	0	1966	
3	Out Of Time	(Immediate Im 035)	1	1966	0	1966	
4	Ride On Baby	(Immediate Im 038)	31	1966	0	1966	
5	My Way Of Giving In	(Immediate Im 041)	48	1967	0	1967	
6	Moanin'	(Immediate Im 056)	46	1967	0	1967	
7	Handbags And Gladrags	(Immediate Im 065)	33	1967	0	1967	
8	Out Of Time (Re-Issue)	(Immediate Ims 101)	44	1975	0	1975	
Chris Hill Male Producer/Vocalist from the UK							
1	Renta Santa	(Philips 6006 491)	10	1975	0	1975	
2	Bionic Santa	(Philips 6006 551)	10	1976	0	1976	

ISSUE	TITLE	UK LBL	UK POS	UK YEAR	US POS	US YEAR	US LBL
Chris Isaak Male Vocalist, B: 26 Jun 1956 Stockton, California							
* 1	Wicked Game	(London Lon 279)	10	1990	6	1991	(Reprise 19704)
2	Blue Hotel	(Reprise W 0005)	17	1991	0	1991	
3	Can't Do A Thing (To Stop Me)	(Reprise W 0161cd)	36	1993	0	1993	
4	San Francisco Days	(Reprise W 0182cd)	62	1993	0	1993	
Chris Kenner Singer/Songwriter, B: 25 Dec 1929 In Louisiana							
* 1	I Like It Like That (Part 1)		0	1961	2	1961	(Instant 3229)
2	Land Of A 1000 Dances		0	1963	77	1963	(Instant 3252)
	CHRIS FIRST RECORDED IN 1956. • OBITUARY: D: 28 JAN 1976 HEART ATTACK						
Chris Martin							
1	Six Buzzard Feathers And A Mocking Bird's Tail		0	1953	28	1953	(Smart 355)
Chris Montez Male Vocalist, Real Name Christopher Montanez B: 17 Jan 1943 In Los Angeles							
* 1	Let's Dance	(London Hlu 9596)	2	1962	4	1962	(Monogram 505)
* 2	Some Kinda Fun	(London Hlu 9650)	10	1963	0	1963	
3	Call Me		0	1966	22	1966	(A&M 780)
4	The More I See You	(Pye International 7n 25369)	3	1966	16	1966	(A&M 796)
5	There Will Never Be Another You	(Pye International 7n 5381)	37	1966	33	1966	(A&M 810)
6	Time After Time		0	1966	36	1966	(A&M 822)
7	Let's Dance (Re-Issue)	(London Hl 10205)	9	1972	0	1972	
8	Let's Dance (2nd Re-Issue)	(Lightning Lig 9011)	47	1979	0	1979	
Chris Paul Male Guitarist from the UK							
1	Expansions '86 (Expand Your Mind) (Fourth & Broadway Brw 48)		58	1986	0	1986	Featuring David Joseph
2	Back In My Arms	(Syncopate Sy 5)	74	1987	0	1987	
3	Turn The Music Up	(Syncopate Sy 13)	73	1988	0	1988	
Chris Rea Male Vocalist, B: 4 Mar 1951 Middlesborough, England							
1	Fool (If You Think It's Over)	(Magent Mag 111)	30	1978	12	1978	(United Artists 1198)
2	Diamonds	(Magnet Mag 144)	44	1979	0	1979	
3	Loving You	(Magnet Mag 215)	65	1982	0	1982	
4	I Can Hear Your Heartbeat	(Magnet Mag 244)	74	1983	0	1983	
5	I Don't Know What It Is But I Love It	(Magnet Mag 255)	65	1984	0	1984	
6	Stainsby Girls	(Magnet Mag 276)	26	1985	0	1985	
7	Josephine	(Magnet Mag 280)	67	1985	0	1985	
8	It's All Gone	(Magnet Mag 283)	69	1986	0	1986	
9	On The Beach	(Magnet Mag 294)	57	1986	0	1986	
10	On The Beach (Re-Entry)	(Magnet Mag 294)	75	1986	0	1986	
11	On The Beach (2nd Re-Entry)	(Magnet Mag 294)	66	1986	0	1986	
12	Let's Dance	(Magnet Mag 299)	12	1987	0	1987	
13	Loving You Again	(Magnet Mag 300)	47	1987	0	1987	
14	Joys Of Christmas	(Magnet Mag 314)	67	1987	0	1987	
15	Que Sera	(Magnet Mag 318)	73	1988	0	1988	
16	On The Beach Summer '88 (Re-Recording)	(Wea Yz 195)	12	1988	0	1988	
17	I Can Hear Your Heartbeat (Re-Recording)	(Wea Yz 320)	74	1988	0	1988	
18	Driving Home For Christmas	(Wea Yz 325)	53	1988	0	1988	
19	Working On It	(Wea Yz 50)	53	1989	0	1989	
20	The Road To Hell (Part 2)	(Wea Yz 431)	10	1989	0	1989	
21	Tell Me There's A Heaven	(Wea Yz 455)	24	1990	0	1990	
22	Texas	(Wea Yz 468)	69	1990	0	1990	
23	Auberge	(Wea Yz 555)	16	1991	0	1991	
24	Heaven	(East West Yz 566cd)	57	1991	0	1991	
25	Looking For The Summer	(East West Yz 584)	49	1991	0	1991	
26	Winter Song	(East West Yz 629)	27	1991	0	1991	
27	Nothing To Fear	(East West Yz 699)	16	1992	0	1992	
28	God's Great Banana Skin	(East West Yz 706)	31	1992	0	1992	
29	Soft Top Hard Shoulder	(East West Yz 710cd)	53	1993	0	1993	
30	Julia	(East West Yz 722cd)	18	1993	0	1993	
31	You Can Go Your Own Way	(East West Yz 835cd)	28	1994	0	1994	
32	Tell Me There's A Heaven (Re-Issue)	(East West Yz 885cd)	70	1994	0	1994	
33	'Disc O' La Passione	(East West Ew 072cd)	41	1996	0	1996	
34	Let's Dance (Re-Recording)	(Magnet Ew 112cd)	44	1997	0	1997	
	HIT 33 IS CREDITED TO CHRIS REA AND SHIRLEY BASSEY. • HIT 34 IS CREDITED TO 'MIDDLESBOROUGH F.C. FEATURING 'BOB MORTIMER' & 'CHRIS REA'						
Chris Sandford Male Vocalist from the UK							
1	Not Too Little Not Too Much	(Decca F 11778)	17	1963	0	1963	
Chris Spedding Male Vocal/Guitarist From The UK							
1	Motor Biking	(Rak 210)	14	1975	0	1975	

ISSUE	TITLE	UK LBL	UK POS	UK YEAR	US POS	US YEAR	US LBL
Chris Thompson Male Vocalist from the UK							
1	If You Remember Me	(Planet K 12389)	42	1979	17	1979	(Planet 45904)
	HIT IS CREDITED TO CHRIS THOMPSON & NIGHT						
Chris Walker Male Soul Singer/Jaxx Bassist from Houston							
1	Take Time		0	1992	29	1992	(Pendulum 64813)
Chris White Male Vocalist from the UK							
1	Spanish Wine	(Columbia CB 272)	37	1976	0	1976	
Chrissie Hynde							
1	I Got You Babe	(Dep International Dep 20)	1	1985	28	1985	(A&M 2600)
2	Breakfast In Bed	(Dep International Dep 29)	6	1988	0	1988	
3	Spiritual High (State Of Independance)	(Arista 114528)	66	1991	0	1991	
4	Spiritual High (Re-Issue)	(Arista 74321127712)	47	1993	0	1993	
5	Love Can Build A Bridge	(London Locd 1)	1	1995	0	1995	
1	Right And Exact	(Ore Ag7cd)	62	1995	0	1995	
2	Right And Exact (Re-Issue)	(XI Recordings Ag 21cd)	59	1997	0	199	
	HITS 1-2 ARE CREDITED TO UB40 FEATURING CHRISSIE HYNDE. • HITS 3-4 ARE CREDITED TO MOODSWINGS FEATURING CHRISSIE HYNDE							
	HIT 5 IS CREDITED TO CHER, CHRISSIE HYNDE & NENAH CHERRY.							
Christians Male Vocal/Instrumental Group from the UK							
1	Forgotten Town	(Island Is 291)	22	1987	0	1987	
2	Hooverville (They Promised Us The World)	(Island Is 326)	21	1987	0	1987	
3	When The Fingers Point	(Island Is 335)	34	1987	0	1987	
4	Ideal World	(Island Is 347)	14	1987	0	1987	
5	Born Again	(Island Is 365)	25	1988	0	1988	
6	Harvest For The World	(Island Is 395)	8	1988	0	1988	
7	Ferry 'Cross The Mersey	(Pwl Pwl 41)	1	1989	0	1989	
8	Words	(Island Is 450)	18	1989	0	1989	
9	I Found Out	(Island Is 453)	56	1990	0	1990	
10	Greenbank Drive	(Island Is 466)	63	1990	0	1990	
11	What's In A Word	(Island Is 536)	33	1992	0	1992	
12	Father	(Island Is 543)	55	1992	0	1992	
13	The Bottle	(Island Cid 549)	39	1993	0	1993	
	HIT 7 IS CREDITED TO CHRISTIANS, HOLLY JOHNSON, PAUL MCCARTNEY, GERRY MARSDEN & STOCK AITKEN WATERMAN							
Christie Male Vocal Trio from the UK Names: Jeff Christie, Vic Elmes & Michael Blakley							
* 1	Yellow River	(CBS 4911)	1	1970	23	1970	(Epic 10626)
2	San Bernardino	(Cbs 5169)	49	1970	0	1970	
3	San Bernardino (Re-Entry)	(CBS 5169)	7	1970	0	1970	
4	Iron Horse	(CBS 7747)	8	1988	0	1988	
Christine McVie Backup Singer With Fleetwood Mac Real Name Christine Perfect. B: 12 Jul 1943 Birmingham, England							
1	Got A Hold On Me		0	1984	10	1984	(Warner Bros 29372)
2	Love Will Show Us How		0	1984	30	1984	(Warner Bros 29313)
Christion							
1	Full of Smoke		0	1997	63	1997	(Mercury 573786)
Christopher Cross Male Vocalist, Real Name Christopher Geppert. B: 3 May 1951 San Antonio, Texas							
1	Ride Like The Wind	(Warner Bros K 17582)	69	1980	2	1980	(Warner Bros 49184)
2	Sailing	(Warner Bros K 17695)	48	1981	1	1980	(Warner Bros 49507)
3	Never Be The Same		0	1980	15	1980	(Warner Bros 49580)
4	Say You'll Be Mine		0	1981	20	1981	(Warner Bros 49705)
* 5	Arthur's Theme (Best That You Can Do)	(Warner Bros K 17847)	56	1981	1	1981	(Warner Bros 49787)
6	Arthur's Theme (Re-Entry)	(Warner Bros K 17847)	7	1982	0	1982	
7	All Right	(Warner Bros W 9843)	51	1983	12	1983	(Warner Bros 49843)
8	No Time To Talk		0	1983	33	1983	(Warner Bros 29662)
9	Think Of Laura		0	1984	9	1984	(Warner Bros 29658)
Chubb Rock Male Rapper from the USA							
1	Treat 'Em Right	(Champion Champ 272)	67	1991	0	1991	
Chubby Checker Male Vocalist, Real Name Ernest Evans. B: 3 Oct 1941 In Philadelphia							
1	The Class		0	1959	38	1959	(Parkway 804)
* 2	The Twist	(Columbia Db 4503)	49	1960	1	1960	(Parkway 811)
3	The Twist (Re-Entry)	(Columbia Db 4503)	44	1960	0	1960	
4	The Hucklebuck		0	1960	14	1960	(Parkway 813)
* 5	Pony Time	(Columbia Db 4591)	27	1961	1	1961	(Parkway 818)
6	Dance The Mess Around		0	1961	24	1961	(Parkway 822)
* 7	Let's Twist Again	(Columbia Db 4691)	37	1961	8	1961	(Parkway 824)

ISSUE	TITLE	UK LBL	UK POS	UK YEAR	US POS	US YEAR	US LBL
8	The Fly		0	1961	7	1961	(Parkway 830)
9	The Twist (2nd Re-Entry)	(Columbia Db 4691)	14	1962	1	1961	(Parkway 811)
10	Jingle Bell Rock	(Cameo-Parkway C 205)	40	1962	21	1961	(Cameo 205)
* 11	Slow Twistin'	(Columbia Db 4808)	23	1962	3	1962	(Parkway 835)
12	Let's Twist Again (2nd Re-Entry)	(Columbia Db 4691)	2	1961	22	1961	(Parkway 824)
13	Teach Me To Twist	(Columbia Db 4802)	45	1962	0	1962	
14	Dancin' Party	(Columbia Db 4876)	19	1962	12	1962	(Parkway 842)
15	Let's Twist Again (2nd Re-Entry)	(Columbia Db 4691)	46	1962	0	1962	
* 16	Limbo Rock	(Cameo-Parkway P 849)	32	1962	2	1962	(Parkway 849)
17	Popeye (The Hitchhiker)		0	1962	10	1962	(Parkway 849)
18	Let's Twist Again (3rd Re-Entry)	(Columbia Db 4691)	49	1962	0	1962	
19	Let's Limbo Some More		0	1963	15	1963	(Parkway 862)
20	Twenty Miles		0	1963	15	1963	(Parkway 862)
21	Birdland		0	1963	12	1963	(Parkway 873)
22	Twist It Up		0	1963	25	1963	(Parkway 879)
23	What Do You Say	(Cameo-Parkway P 806)	37	1963	0	1963	
24	Loddy Lo		0	1963	12	1963	(Parkway 890)
25	Hook Tooka		0	1964	17	1964	(Parkway 890)
26	Hey, Bobba Needle		0	1964	23	1964	(Parkway 907)
27	Lazy Elsie Molly		0	1964	40	1964	(Parkway 920)
28	Let's Do The Freddie		0	1965	40	1965	(Parkway 949)
29	Let's Twist Again - The Twist (Re-Issue)	(London Hl 10512)	5	1975	0	1975	
30	The Twist (Yo Twist)	(Urban Urb 20)	2	1968	16	1988	(Tin Pan 887571)

HIT 30 IS CREDITED TO FAT BOYS AND CHUBBY CHECKER • A CERTAIN MOBILE DJ CALLED HIM THE FAT DETECTIVE

Chubby Chunks Volume Ii Male Instrumental Duo from the UK

1	Testament 4	(Cleveland City Clecd 13017)	52	1994	0	1994	

Chuck Berry Male Vocal/Guitarist, Real Name Charles Edward Anderson Berry. B: 18 Oct 1926 California

* 1	Maybellene		0	1955	5	1955	(Chess 1604)
+ 2	Thirty Days		0	1955	8	1955	(Chess 1610)
+ 3	No Money Down		0	1956	11	1956	(Chess 1615)
4	Roll Over Beethoven		0	1956	29	1956	(Chess 1626)
+ 5	Too Much Monkey Business −Brown Eyed Handsome Man		0	1956	7	1956	(Chess 1635)
* 6	School Day	(Columbia Db 3951)	24	1957	3	1957	(Chess 1653)
7	School Day (Re-Entry)	(Columbia Db 3951)	24	1957	0	1957	
8	Oh Baby Doll		0	1957	47	1957	(Chess 1664)
9	Rock And Roll Music		0	1957	8	1957	(Chess 1671)
* 10	Sweet Little Sixteen	(London Hlm 8585)	16	1958	2	1958	(Chess 1683)
11	Johnny B Goode		0	1958	8	1958	(Chess 1691)
12	Carol		0	1958	18	1958	(Chess 1700)
13	Sweet Little Rock And Roll		0	1958	47	1958	(Chess 1709)
14	Anthony Boy		0	1959	60	1959	(Chess 1716)
15	Almost Grown		0	1959	32	1959	(Chess 1722)
16	Back In The Usa		0	1959	37	1959	(Chess 1729)
17	Too Pooped To Pop		0	1960	42	1960	(Chess 1883)
18	Go Go Go	(Pye International 7n 25209)	38	1963	0	1963	
19	Let It Rock - Memphis Tennessee	(Pye International 7n 25218)	6	1963	0	1963	
20	Run Rudolph Run	(Pye International 7n 25228)	36	1963	0	1963	
21	Nadine (Is It You)	(Pye International 7n 25236)	27	1964	23	1964	(Chess 1883)
22	Nadine (Is It You) (Re-Entry)	(Pye International 7n 25236)	43	1964	0	1964	
23	No Particular Place To Go	(Pye International 7n 25242)	3	1964	10	1964	(Chess 1898)
24	You Never Can Tell	(Pye International 7n 25257)	23	1964	14	1964	(Chess 1906)
25	Little Marie		0	1964	54	1964	(Chess 1912)
26	Promised Land	(Pye International 7n 25285)	26	1965	41	1964	(Chess 1916)
* 27	My Ding-A-Ling	(Chess 6145 019)	1	1972	1	1972	(Chess 2131)
28	Reelin' And Rockin'	(Chess 6145 020)	18	1973	27	1972	(Chess 2136)

'MY DING-A-LING' ORIGINALLY RECORDED UNDER THE TITLE OF 'MY TAMBOURINE' 1958. • IN 1959 HE WAS JAILED FOR TWO YEARS FOR SEXUAL OFFENCES

Chuck Brown & The Soul Searchers Nine-Member Group from Washington D.C.

1	Bustin' Loose (Part 1)		0	1979	34	1979	(Source 40967)
2	No	(Mercury Mercd 476)	55	1996	0	1996	

Chuck D Male Rapper from the USA

1	Bring The Noise	(Island Is 490)	14	1991	0	1991	

Hit 1 Is Credited To Anthrax Featuring Chuck D

Chuck Jackson Male Vocalist, B: 22 Jul 1937 South Carolina — Chuck Was With The Dell-Vikings In The Late 50s

1	I Don't Want To Cry		0	1961	36	1961	(Wand 106)

ISSUE	TITLE	UK LBL	UK POS	UK YEAR	US POS	US YEAR	US LBL
2	Any Day Now (My Wild Beautiful Bird)		0	1962	23	1962	(Wand 122)
3	I Keep Forgettin'		0	1962	55	1962	(Wand 126)
+ 4	(You Can't Let The Boy Overpower) The Man In You		0	1969	27	1969	(Motown 1118)

Chuck Mangione B: 29 Nov 1940 Rochester, New York

1	Feels So Good		0	1978	4	1978	(A&M 2001)
2	Gave It All You Got		0	1980	18	1980	(A&M 2211)

HE HAS ALSO RECORDED WITH THE JAZZ BROTHERS

Chuck Miller Pianist from California

1	The House Of Blue Lights		0	1955	9	1955	(Mercury 70627)

Chuck Willis Singer/Songwriter, B: 31 Jan 1928 Atlanta

1	C C Rider						
2	Betty And Dupree		0	1958	33	1958	(Atlantic 1168)
* 3	What Am I Living For		0	1958	9	1958	(Atlantic 1179)
4	Hang Up My Rock And Roll Shoes (FOR)			1958	24	1958	(Atlantic 1179)

CHUCK WORE A TURBAN AND CALLED HIMSELF THE 'KING OF THE STROLL'. OBITUARY: D: 10 APR 1958 PERITONITIS

Chucks Mixed Vocal Group from the UK

1	Loo-Be-Loo	(Decca F 11569)	22	1963	0	1963	

Chumbawamba Mixed Vocal/Instrumental Group from the UK

1	Enough Is Enough	(One Little Indian 79 Tp7cd)	56	1993	0	1993	
2	Timebomb	(One Little Indian 89 Tp7cd)	59	1993	0	1993	
3	Tubthumping	(EMI Cdem 486)	2	1997	0	1997	

HIT 1 IS CREDITED TO CHUMBAWAMBA & CREDIT TO THE NATION. • SEE ALSO CREDIT TO THE NATION

Chupito Male Vocalist from Spain

1	American Pie	(Eternal Wea 018cd)	54	1995	0	1995	

Chuy Reyes & His Hollywood Mocambo Orchestra Latin-American Rhumba Band from the USA

1	Rhumba Boogie		0	1948	27	1948	(Capitol 15067)

Chynna Phillips Female Vocalist from the USA

1	Naked And Sacred	(EMI Cdem 409)	62	1996	0	199	

Cicero Male Vocalist from the UK

1	Love Is Everywhere	(Spaghetti Ciao 3)	19	1992	0	1992	
2	That Loving Feeling	(Spaghetti Ciao 4)	46	1992	0	1992	
3	Heaven Must Have Sent You Back	(Spaghetti Ciao 5)	70	1992	0	1992	

Cilla Black Female Vocalist/Tv Host, Real Name Priscilla Maria Veronica White. B: 27 May 1943 from Liverpool, England

1	Love Of The Loved	(Parlophone R 5065)	35	1963	0	1963	
* 2	Anyone Who Had A Heart	(Parlophone R 5101)	1	1964	0	1964	
* 3	You're My World	(Parlophone R 5133)	1	1964	26	1964	(Capitol 5196)
4	It's For You	(Parlophone R 5162)	7	1964	0	1964	
5	You've Lost That Lovin' Feeling	(Parlophone R 5225)	2	1965	0	1965	
6	I've Been Wrong Before	(Parlophone R 5269)	17	1965	0	1965	
7	Loves Just A Broken Heart	(Parlophone R 5395)	5	1966	0	1966	
8	Alfie	(Parlophone R 5427)	9	1966	0	1966	
9	Don't Answer Me	(Parlophone R 5463)	6	1966	0	1966	
10	A Fool Am I	(Parlophone R 5515)	13	1966	0	1966	
11	What Good Am I	(Parlophone R 5608)	24	1967	0	1967	
12	I Only Live To Love You	(Parlophone R 5652)	26	1967	0	1967	
13	Step Inside Love	(Parlophone R 5674)	8	1968	0	1968	
14	Where Is Tomorrow	(Parlophone R 5706)	40	1968	0	1968	
15	Surround Youself With Sorrow	(Parlophone R 5759)	3	1969	0	1969	
16	Conversations	(Parlophone R 5785)	7	1969	0	1969	
17	If I Thought You'd Ever Change Your Mind	(Parlophone R 5820)	20	1969	0	1969	
18	Something Tells Me	(Parlophone R 5924)	3	1971	0	1971	
19	Baby We Can't Go Wrong	(EMI 2107)	36	1974	0	1974	
20	Through The Years	(Columbia 6596982)	54	1993	0	1993	
21	Heart And Soul	(Columbia 6598562)	75	1993	0	1993	

HIT 21 IS CREDITED TO CILLA BLACK AND DUSTY SPRINGFIELD

Cinderella Male Vocal/Instrumental Group from the USA   Names: Tom Keifer, Jeff Labar, Eric Brittingham & Fred Coury

1	Nobody's Fool		0	1987	13	1987	(Mercury 884851)
2	Gypsy Road	(Vertigo Ver 40)	54	1988	0	1988	
3	Don't Know What You've Got (Till It's Gone)	(Vertigo Ver 43)	54	1989	12	1988	(Mercury 870644)
4	The Last Mile		0	1989	36	1989	(Mercury 872148)
5	Coming Home		0	1989	20	1989	(Mercury 872982)
6	Shelter Me	(Vertigo Ver 51)	55	1990	36	1990	(Mercury 878700)
7	Heartbreak Station	(Vertigo Ver 63)	63	1991	0	1991	

ISSUE	TITLE	UK LBL	UK POS	UK YEAR	US POS	US YEAR	US LBL
Cindy & The Saffrons Female Vocal Group from the UK							
1	Past Present And Future	(Stilletto Stl 9)	56	1983	0	1983	
Circuit Mixed Vocal/Instrumental Group from the UK							
1	Shelter Me	(Cooltempo Cool 237)	44	1991	0	1991	
2	Shelter Me (Re-Issue)	(Pukka Cdpuka 2)	50	1995	0	1995	
Cirrus Male Vocal Group from the UK							
1	Rollin' On	(Jet 123)	62	1978	0	1978	
Cisco Houston Folk Singer/Songwriter from the USA							
1	Rose, Rose, I Love You		0	1951	21	1951	(Decca 27594)
	Obituary: D: 29 Apr 1961, (Aged 42).						
City Boy Male Vocal/Instrumental Rock Sextet from the UK, Led By Lol Mason							
1	5-7-0-5	(Vertigo 6059 207)	8	1978	27	1978	(Mercury 73999)
2	What A Night	(Vertigo 6059 211)	39	1978	0	1978	
3	The Day The Earth Caught Fire	(Vertigo 6059 238)	67	1979	0	1979	
Claire & Friends Female Vocalist And Mixed Young Friends from the UK							
1	It's Orrible Being In Love (When Your 8 ½)	(Bbc Resl 189)	13	1986	0	1986	
Clannad Mixed Vocal Group From Ireland							
1	Theme From Harry's Game	(RCA 292)	5	1982	0	1982	
2	New Grange	(RCA 340)	65	1983	0	1983	
3	Robin (The Hooded Man)	(RCAHood 1)	42	1984	0	1984	
4	In A Lifetime	(RCA Pb 40535)	20	1986	0	1986	
5	In A Lifetime (Re-Issue)	(RCA Pb 42873)	17	1989	0	1979	
6	Both Sides Now	(MCA Mcs 1546)	74	1991	0	1991	
	HITS 4-5 ARE CREDITED TO CLANNAD FEATURING BONO. HIT 6 IS CREDITED TO CLANNAD AND PAUL YOUNG						
Clarence 'Frogman' Henry Male Vocalist, B: 19 Mar 1937 Algiers, Louisiana							
1	Ain't Got No Home		0	1957	20	1957	(Argo 5259)
2	(I Don't Know Why I Love You) But I D	(Pye International 7n 25078)	3	1961	4	1961	(Argo 5378)
3	You Always Hurt The One You Love	(Pye International 7n 25089)	6	1961	12	1961	(Argo 5388)
4	Lonely Street / Why Can't You	(Pye International 7n 25108)	42	1961	57	1961	(Argo 5395)
5	(I Don't Know Why I Love You)... (Re-Issue)	(MCA Mcstd 1979)	65	1993	0	1993	
	GOT THE NICKNAME OF FROGMAN FROM THE HIT 'AIN'T GOT NO HOME'						
Clarence Carter Male Vocalist B: 1936 Montgomery, Alabama							
* 1	Slip Away		0	1968	6	1968	(Atlantic 2508)
* 2	Too Week To Fight		0	1968	13	1968	(Atlantic 2569)
3	Snatching It Back		0	1969	31	1969	(Atlantic 2605)
4	Doin' Our Thing		0	1969	46	1969	(Atlantic 2660)
+ 5	The Feeling Is Right		0	1969	9	1969	(Atlantic 2642)
* 6	Patches	(Atlantic 2091 030)	2	1970	4	1970	(Atlantic 2748)Married For
Clarence Reid Singer/Composer, B: 14 Feb 1945 Cochran, Georgia In The 60s He Was With The Delmiros. He Also Recorded As Blowfly							
1	Nobody But You Babe		0	1969	40	1969	(Alston 4574)
≠ 2	Funky Party		0	1974	17	1970	4(Alston 4621)
Clark Dennis							
1	Peg O' My Heart (From *Ziegfeld Follies* Of 1913)		0	1947	8	1947	(Capitol 346)
2	Galway Bay		0	1949	23	1949	(Capitol 15403)
3	Grenada		0	1954	24	1954	(Tiffany 1302)
Clash Male Vocal/Instrumental Group from the UK Names: Joe Strummer, Mick Jones, Paul Simonon & Topper Heado.							
1	White Riot	(CBS 5058)	38	1977	0	1977	
2	Complete Control	(CBS 5664)	28	1977	0	1977	
3	Clash City Rockers	(CBS 5834)	35	1978	0	1978	
4	(White Man) In Hammersmith Palais	(CBS 6383)	22	1978	0	1978	
5	Tommy Gun	(CBS 6788)	19	1978	0	1978	
6	English Civil War (Johnny Comes Marching Home)	(CBS 7082)	25	1979	0	1979	
7	The Cost Of Living (EP)	(CBS 7324)	22	1979	0	1979	
8	London Calling	(CBS 8087)	11	1979	0	1979	
9	Train In Vain (Stand By Me)		0	1980	23	1980	(Epic 50851)
10	Bankrobber	(CBS 8323)	12	1980	0	1980	
11	The Call Up	(CBS 9339)	40	1980	0	1980	
12	Hitsville Uk	(CBS 8480)	56	1981	0	1981	
13	The Magnificent Seven	(CBS 1133)	34	1981	0	1981	
14	This Is Radio Clash	(CBS 1797)	47	1981	0	1981	
15	Know Your Rights	(CBS A 2309)	43	1982	0	1982	
16	Rock The Casbah	(CBS A 2429)	30	1982	8	1982	(Epic 03245)

ISSUE	TITLE	UK LBL	UK POS	UK YEAR	US POS	US YEAR	US LBL
17	Should I Stay Or Should I Go / Straight To Hell	(CBS A 2646)	17	1982	0	1982	
18	This Is England	(CBS A 6122)	24	1985	0	1985	
19	I Fought The Law	(CBS Clash 1)	22	1979	0	1979	
20	London Calling (Re-Issue)	(CBS Clash 2)	46	1988	0	1988	
21	Return To Brixton	(CBS 656072 7)	57	1990	0	1990	
22	Should I Stay Or Should I Go (Re-Issue)	(CBS 6566677)	1	1991	0	1991	
23	Rock The Casbah (Re-Issue)	(CBS 6568147)	15	1991	0	1991	
24	London Calling (2nd Re-Issue)	(CBS 6569467)	64	1991	0	1991	
	PETER HOWARD REPLACED HEADON IN 1983, JONES LEFT IN 1984 • THE GROUP DISBANDED IN 1986						

Class Action Female Vocal Group from the USA

1	Weekend	(Jive Jive 35)	49	1983	0	1983	

Classics Names Emil Stucchio, Johnny Gambale, Tony Victor & Jamie Troy

1	Till Then		0	1963	20	1963	(Musicnote 1116)

Classics IV Male Vocal/Instrumental Group from the USA   Names: Dennis Yost, J.R. Cobb, Wally Eaton, Joe Wilson & Kim Venable

*	1	Spooky	(Liberty Lbs 15051)	46	1968	3	1968	(Imperial 66259)
*	2	Stormy		0	1968	5	1968	(Imperial 66328)
*	3	Traces		0	1969	2	1969	(Imperial 66352)
	4	Everyday With You Girl		0	1969	19	1969	(Imperial 66378)
	5	What Am I Crying For?		0	1972	39	1972	(Mgm South 7002)

HIT 4 IS CREDITED TO DENNIS YOST FEATURING CLASSICS IV • DEAN DAUGHTRY REPLACED WILSON. COBB, DAUGHTRY & BUDDY BUIE JOINED THE ATLANTA RHYTHM SECTION IN 1974

Classix Nouveaux Male Vocal/Instrumental Group from the UK

1	Guilty	(Liberty Bp 388)	43	1981	0	1981	
2	Tokyo	(Liberty Bp 397)	67	1981	0	1981	
3	Inside Outside	(Liberty Bp 403)	46	1981	0	1981	
4	Never Again (The Days Time Erased)	(Liberty Bp 406)	44	1981	0	1981	
5	Is It A Dream	(Liberty Bp 409)	11	1982	0	1982	
6	Because You're Young	(Liberty Bp 411)	43	1982	0	1982	
7	The End... Or The Beginning	(Liberty Bp 414)	60	1982	0	1982	

Claude Francois Male Vocalist from France

1	Tears On The Telephone	(Bradley's Brad 7528)	35	1976	0	1976	

Claude King Male Singer/Songwriter, B: 5 Feb 1933, Shreveport, Louisiana

*	1	Wolverton Mountain		0	1962	6	1962	(Columbia 42352)

Claude Thornhill & His Orchestra Male Arranger/Bandleader/Instrumentalist (Piano) from The USA

10	A Sunday Kind Of Love		0	1947	16	1947	(Columbia 37219)
11	You're Not So Easy To Forget		0	1947	25	1947	(Columbia 37558)
12	Warsaw Concerto		0	1948	26	1948	(Columbia 37940)
13	Love For Love		0	1947	28	1947	(Columbia 37940)
14	Early Autumn		0	1947	22	1947	(Columbia 37593)
15	Johnson Rag		0	1950	24	1950	(RCA Victor 78-3604)
16	Summer Is Gone		0	1953	29	1953	(Trend 60)

Claudia Brucken Female Vocalist from Germany

1	Absolut(E)	(Island Is 471)	71	1990	0	1990	
2	Kiss Like Ether	(Island Is 479)	63	1991	0	1991	

Claudine Clark Female Vocalist, B: 26 Apr 1941 Macon, Georgia   Also Recorded Under The Name Of Joy Dawn

1	Party Lights		0	1962	5	1962	(Chancellor 1113)

Clawfinger Male Vocal/Instrumental Group from Norway/Sweden

1	Warfair	(East West Yz 804cd1)	54	1994	0	1994	

Claytown Troupe Male Vocal/Instrumental Group from the UK

1	Ways Of Love	(Island Is 464)	57	1990	0	1990	
2	Wanted It All	(EMI USA Mt 102)	74	1992	0	1992	

Cledus Maggard & The Citizen's Band Real Name Jay Huguely. B: Quick Sand, Kentucky

1	The White Knight		0	1976	19	1976	(Mercury 73751)

Cleftones Names Herbie Cox, Charlie James, Berman Patterson, William Mcclain & Warren Corbin

+	1	Little Girl Of Mine		0	1956	8	1956	(Gee 1011)
	2	Heart And Soul		0	1961	18	1961	(Gee 1064)
	THE GROUP WAS ORIGINALLY THE SILVERTONES							

Cleo Laine Female Vocalist from the UK

1	Let's Slip Away	(Fontana H 269)	42	1960	0	1960	
2	You'll Answer To Me	(Fontana H 326)	5	1961	0	1961	

Cleveland Eaton Male Instrumentalist (Keyboards) from the USA

1	Bama Boogie Woogie	(Gull Guls 63)	35	1978	0	1978	

ISSUE	TITLE	UK LBL	UK POS	UK YEAR	US POS	US YEAR	US LBL
Click Male Rap Group from The USA							
1	Scandalous	(Jive Jivecd 393)	54	1996	0	1996	
Cliff Adams Orchestra Leader from the UK							
1	Lonley Man Theme	(Pye International 7n 25056)	39	1960	0	1960	
Cliff Bennett & The Rebel Rousers Male Vocal/Instrumental Group from the UK							
1	One Way Love	(Parlophone R 5173)	9	1964	0	1964	
2	I'll Take You Home	(Parlophone R 5229)	42	1965	0	1965	
3	Got To Get You Into My Life	(Parlophone R 5489)	6	1966	0	1966	
Cliff Deyoung Male Vocalist, B: 12 Feb 1946, Los Angeles							
1	My Sweet Lady		0	1974	17	1974	(MCA 40156)
Cliff Nobles & Co Singer/Bandleader, B: 1944, Mobile, Alabama							
* 1	The Horse		0	1968	2	1968	(Phil L.A. Soul 313)
Cliff Richard Real Name Harry Rodger Webb. B: 14 Oct 1940 Lucknow, India							
1	Move It	(Columbia Db 4178)	2	1958	0	1958	
2	High Class Baby	(Columbia Db 4203)	7	1958	0	1958	
3	Livin' Lovin' Doll	(Columbia Db 4249)	20	1959	0	1959	
4	Mean Streak	(Columbia Db 4290)	10	1959	0	1959	
5	Never Mind	(Columbia Db 4290)	21	1959	0	1959	
* 6	Living Doll	(Columbia Db 4306)	1	1959	30	1959	(Abc-Paramount 10042)
7	Travellin' Light	Columbia Db 4351)	16	1959	0	1959	
8	Dynamite	(Columbia Db 4351)	16	1959	0	1959	
9	Dynamite (Re-Entry)	(Columbia Db 4351)	21	1959	0	1959	
10	Living Doll (Re-Entry)	(Columbia Db 4306)	26	1959	0	1959	
11	Living Doll (2nd Re-Entry)	(Columbia Db 4306)	28	1960	0	1960	
12	Expresso Bongo (EP)	(Columbia Seg 7971)	14	1960	0	1960	
13	Voice In The Wilderness	(Columbia Db 4398)	2	1960	0	1960	
14	Fall In Love With You	(Columbia Db 4431)	2	1960	0	1960	
15	Voice In The Wilderness (Re-Entry)	(Columbia Db 4398)	36	1960	0	1960	
16	Please Don't Tease	(Columbia Db 4479)	1	1960	0	1960	
17	Nine Times Out Of Ten	(Columbia Db 4506)	3	1960	0	1960	
18	I Love You	(Columbia Db 4547)	1	1960	0	1960	
19	Theme For A Dream	(Columbia Db 4593)	3	1961	0	1961	
20	Gee Whiz It's You	(Columbia Dc 756)	4	1961	0	1961	
21	A Girl Like You	(Columbia Db 4667)	3	1961	0	1961	
22	When The Girl In Your Arms	(Columbia Db 4716)	3	1961	0	1961	
* 23	The Young Ones	(Columbia Db 4761)	1	1962	0	1962	
24	I'm Looking Out The Window	(Columbia Db 4828)	2	1962	0	1962	
25	It'll Be Me	(Columbia Db 4886)	2	1962	0	1962	
* 26	The Next Time – Bachelor Boy	(Columbia Db 4950)	1	1962	0	1962	
27	Summer Holiday	(Columbia Db 4977)	1	1963	0	1963	
* 28	Lucky Lips	(Columbia Db 7034)	4	1963	0	1963	
29	It's All In The Game	(Columbia Db 7089)	2	1963	25	1964	(Epic 9633)
30	Don't Talk To Him	(Columbia Db 7150)	2	1963	0	1963	
31	I'm The Lonely One	(Columbia Db 7203)	8	1964	0	1964	
32	Don't Talk To Him (Re-Entry)	(Columbia Db 7150)	50	1964	0	1964	
33	Constantly	(Columbia Db 7272)	4	1964	0	1964	
34	On The Beach	(Columbia Db 7305)	7	1964	0	1964	
35	The Twelfth Of Never	(Columbia Db 7372)	8	1964	0	1964	
36	I Could Easily Fall	(Columbia Db 7420)	9	1964	0	1964	
37	The Minute You're Gone	(Columbia Db 7496)	1	1965	0	1965	
38	On My Word	(Columbia Db 7596)	12	1965	0	1965	
39	The Time In Between	(Columbia Db 7660)	22	1965	0	1965	
40	Wind Me Up (Let Me Go)	(Columbia Db 7745)	2	1965	0	1965	
41	Blue Turns To Grey	(Columbia Db 7866)	15	1966	0	1966	
42	Visions	(Columbia Db 7968)	7	1966	0	1966	
43	Time Drags By	(Columbia Db 8017)	10	1966	0	1966	
44	In The Country	(Columbia Db 8094)	6	1966	0	1966	
45	It's All Over	(Columbia Db 8150)	9	1967	0	1967	
46	I'll Come Running	(Columbia Db 8210)	26	1967	0	1967	
47	The Day I Met Marie	(Columbia Db 8245)	10	1967	0	1967	
48	All My Love	(Columbia Db 8293)	6	1967	0	1967	
* 49	Congratulations	(Columbia Db 8376)	1	1968	0	1968	
50	I'll Love You Forever Today	(Columbia Db 8437)	27	1968	0	1968	
51	Marianne	(Columbia Db 8476)	22	1968	0	1968	

ISSUE	TITLE	UK LBL	UK POS	UK YEAR	US POS	US YEAR	US LBL
52	Don't Forget To Catch Me	(Columbia Db 8503)	21	1968	0	1968	
53	Goodtimes (Better Times)	(Columbia Db 8548)	12	1969	0	1969	
54	Big Ship	(Columbia Db 8581)	8	1969	0	1969	
55	Throw Down A Line	(Columbia Db 8615)	7	1969	0	1969	
56	With The Eyes Of A Child	(Columbia Db 8641)	20	1969	0	1969	
57	Joy Of Living (EP)	(Columbia Db 8657)	25	1970	0	1970	
58	Goodbye Sam Hello Samantha	(Columbia Db 8685)	6	1970	0	1970	
59	I Aint Got Time Anymore	(Columbia Db 8708)	21	1970	0	1970	
60	Sunny Honey Girl	(Columbia Db 8747)	19	1971	0	1971	
61	Silvery Rain	(Columbia Db 8774)	27	1971	0	1971	
62	Flying Machine	(Columbia Db 8797)	37	1971	0	1971	
63	Sing A Song Of Freedom	(Columbia Db 8836)	13	1971	0	1971	
64	Jesus	(Columbia Db 8864)	35	1972	0	1972	
65	Living In Harmony	(Columbia Db 8917)	12	1972	0	1972	
66	Power To All Our Friends	(EMI 2012)	4	1973	0	1973	
67	Help It Along - Tomorrow Rising	(EMI 2022)	29	1973	0	1973	
68	Take Me High	(EMI 2088)	27	1973	0	1973	
69	(You Keep Me) Hangin' On	(EMI 2150)	13	1974	0	1974	
70	Miss You Nights	(EMI 2376)	15	1976	0	1976	
* 71	Devil Woman	(EMI 2458)	9	1976	6	1976	(Rocket 40574)
72	I Can't Ask For Anymore Than You	(EMI 2499)	17	1976	0	1976	
73	Hey Mr.Dream Maker	(EMI 2559)	31	1976	0	1976	
74	My Kinda Life	(EMI 2584)	15	1977	0	1977	
75	When Two Worlds Drift Apart	(EMI 2633)	46	1977	0	1977	
76	Green Light	(EMI 2920)	46	1979	0	1979	
77	We Don't Talk Anymore	(EMI 2975)	1	1979	7	1979	(EMI America 8025)
78	Hot Shot	(EMI 5003)	46	1979	0	1979	
79	Carrie	(EMI 5006)	4	1980	34	1980	(EMI America 8035)
80	Dreamin'	(EMI 5095)	8	1980	10	1980	(EMI America 8057)
81	Suddenly	(Jet 7002)	15	1980	20	1980	(Mca 51007)
82	A Little In Love	(EMI 5123)	15	1981	17	1981	(EMI America 8068)
83	Wired For Sound	(EMI 5221)	4	1981	0	1981	
84	Daddy's Home	(EMI 5251)	2	1981	23	1981	(EMI America 8103)
85	The Only Way Out	(EMI 5318)	10	1982	0	1982	
86	Where Do We Go From Here	(EMI 5341)	60	1982	0	1982	
87	Little Town	(EMI 5348)	11	1982	0	1982	
88	She Means Nothing To Me	(Capitol Cl 276)	9	1983	0	1983	
89	True Love Ways	(EMI 5385)	8	1983	0	1983	
90	Drifting	(Djm Sheil 1)	64	1983	0	1983	
91	Never Say Die (Give A Little Bit More)	(EMI 5415)	15	1983	0	1983	
92	Please Don't Fall In Love	(EMI 5347)	7	1983	0	1983	
93	Baby You're Dynamite - Ocean Deep	(EMI 5457)	27	1984	0	1984	
94	Ocean Deep - Baby You're Dynamite (Re-Entry)	(EMI 5457)	72	1984	0	1984	
95	Shooting From The Heart	(EMI Rich 1)	51	1984	0	1984	
96	Heart User	(EMI Rich 2)	46	1985	0	1985	
97	She's So Beautiful	(EMI 5531)	17	1985	0	1985	
98	It's In Everyone Of Us	(EMI 5537)	45	1985	0	1985	
99	Living Doll	(Wea Yz 65)	1	1986	0	1986	
100	All I Ask Of You	(Polydor Posp 802)	3	1986	0	1986	
101	Slow Rivers	(Rocket Ejs 13)	44	1986	0	1986	
102	My Pretty One	(EMI Em 4)	6	1987	0	1987	
103	Some People	(EMI Em 18)	3	1987	0	1987	
104	Remember Me	(EMI Em 31)	35	1987	0	1987	
105	Two Hearts	(EMI Em 42)	34	1988	0	1988	
106	Mistletoe And Wine	(EMI Em 78)	1	1988	0	1988	
107	The Best Of Me	(EMI Em 78)	2	1989	0	1989	
108	I Just Don't Have The Heart	(EMI Em 101)	3	1989	0	1989	
109	Lean On You	(EMlem 105)	17	1989	0	1989	
110	Whenever God Shines His Light	(Polydor Vans 2)	20	1989	0	1989	
111	Stronger Than That	(EMI Em 129)	14	1990	0	1990	
112	Silhouettes	(EMI Em 152)	10	1990	0	1990	
113	From A Distance	(EMI Em 155)	11	1990	0	1990	
114	Saviour's Day	(EMI Exmas 90)	1	1990	0	1990	
115	More To Life	(EMI Em 205)	23	1991	0	1991	
116	We Should Be Together	(EMI Exmas 91)	10	1991	0	1991	

ISSUE	TITLE	UK LBL	UK POS	UK YEAR	US POS	US YEAR	US LBL
117	This New Year	(EMI Ems 216)	30	1990	0	1990	
118	I Still Believe In You	(EMI Em 255)	7	1992	0	1992	
119	Peace In Our Time	(EMI Cdems 265)	8	1993	0	1993	
120	Human Work Of Art	(EMI Cdems 267)	24	1993	0	1993	
121	Never Let Go	(EMI Cdems 281)	32	1993	0	1993	
122	Healing Love	(EMI Cdems 294)	19	1993	0	1993	
123	All I Have To Do Is Dream /Miss You Nights (Re-Issue)	(EMI Cdems 359) 14	1994	0	1994		
124	All I Have To Do Is Dream /... (Re-Issue)(Re-Entry)	(EMI Cdems 359)	58	1995	0	1995	
125	Misunderstood Man	(EMI cdem 394)	19	1995	0	1995	
127	The Wedding	(EMI Cdem 422)	40	1996	0	1996	
126	had to be	(EMIcdem 410)	22	1995	0	1995	
127	The Wedding	(EMI Cdem 422)	40	1996	0	1996	
128	Be With Me Always	(EMI Cdem 453)	52	1997	0	1997	

TO DATE CLIFF HAS HAD 11 CHART TOPPERS IN THE UK AS A SOLO ARTIST

Cliff Steward & The San Francisco Boys Male Bandleader from the USA

	ISSUE	TITLE	UK LBL	UK POS	UK YEAR	US POS	US YEAR	US LBL
	1	The Old Piano Roll Blues		0	1950	18	1950	(Coral 60177)
	2	The Aba Daba Honeymoon		0	1951	19	1951	(Coral 60374)

Cliffie Stone & His Orchestra Real Name Clifford Snyder B: 1 Mar 1917 Burbank, California

	ISSUE	TITLE	UK LBL	UK POS	UK YEAR	US POS	US YEAR	US LBL
	1	Silver Stars, Purple Sage, Eyees of Blue		0	1947	18	1947	(Capitol 354)
	2	Peepin' Thru The Keyhole (watching Jole Blon)		0	1948	4	1948	(Capitol America 40083)
	3	When My Blue Mooon Turns To Gols Again		0	1948	11	1948	(Capitol 15108)
	4	The Popcorn Song		0	1955	14	1955	(Capitol 3131)
	5	Littl Pink Mack		0	1966	30	1966	(Tower 269)

HIT 2 IS CREDITED TO 'CLIFFIE STONE & HIS BARN DANCE BAND' • HIT 5 IS CREDITED TO 'KAY ADAMS' WITH THE 'CLIFFIE STONE GROUP'

Clifford T. Ward Male Vocalist from the UK

	ISSUE	TITLE	UK LBL	UK POS	UK YEAR	US POS	US YEAR	US LBL
	1	Gaye	(Charisma Cb 205)	8	1973	0	1973	
	2	Scullery	(Charisma Cb 221)	37	1974	0	1974	

Climax Quintet Based In Los Angeles With Lead Singer Sonny Geraci

	ISSUE	TITLE	UK LBL	UK POS	UK YEAR	US POS	US YEAR	US LBL
*	1	Precious And Few		0	1971	3	1971	(Rocky Road 30055)

SONNY GERACI WAS WITH THE OUTSIDERS. THE GROUP WAS ORIGINALLY CALLED TOM KING & THE STARFIRES

Climax Blues Band Mental Group from the UK

	ISSUE	TITLE	UK LBL	UK POS	UK YEAR	US POS	US YEAR	US LBL
	1	Couldn't Get It Right	(Btm Sbt 105	10	1976	3	1977	(Sire 736)
	2	I Love You		0	1981	12	1981	(Warner Bros 49669)

NAMES: COLIN COOPER, PETER HAYCOCK, DEREK HOLT & JOHN CUFFLEY. • RICHARD JONES, GEORGE NEWSOME & ARTHUR WOOD WERE FORMER MEMBERS

Climie Fisher Male Vocal/Instrumental Duo Simon Climie & Rob Fisher From the UK

	ISSUE	TITLE	UK LBL	UK POS	UK YEAR	US POS	US YEAR	US LBL
	1	Love Changes (Everything)	(EMI Em 15)	67	1987	23	1988	(Capitol 44137)
	2	Rise To The Occasion	(EMI Em 33)	10	1987	0	1987	
	3	Love Changes Everything (Re-Mix)	(EMI Em 47)	2	1988	0	1988	
	4	This Is Me	(EMI Em 58)	22	1988	0	1988	
	5	I Won't Bleed For You	(EMI Em 66)	35	1988	0	1988	
	6	Love Like A River	(EMI Em 81)	57	1988	0	1988	
	7	Facts Of Love	(EMI Em 103)	50	1989	0	1989	

ROB WAS A MEMBER OF NAKED EYES WITH PETE BYRNE

Clint Black Male Vocalist B: Clint Patrick Black' 4 Feb 1962, Long Ranch, New Jersey

	ISSUE	TITLE	UK LBL	UK POS	UK YEAR	US POS	US YEAR	US LBL
!	1	Better Man		0	1989	1	1989	(RCA 8781)
!	2	Killin' Time		0	1989	1	1989	(RCA 8945)
!	3	Nobody's Home		0	1989	1	1989	(RCA 9078)
!	4	Walkin' Away		0	1990	1	1990	(RCA 2520)
!	5	Nothing's News		0	1990	3	1990	(RCA 2596)
!	6	Put Youself In My Shoes		0	1990	4	1990	(RCA 2678) !
!	7	Loving Blind		0	1991	1	1991	(RCA 2749)
!	8	One More Payment		0	1991	7	1991	(RCA 2819)
!	9	Where Are You Now		0	1991	1	1991	(RCA 62016)
!	10	Hold On Partner		0	1991	42	1991	(RCA 62061)
!	11	This Nightlife		0	1992	61	1992	(RCA Lp Cut)
!	12	We Tell Ourselves		0	1992	2	1992	(RCA 62194)
!	13	Burn One Down		0	1992	4	1992	(RCA 62337)
!	14	When My Ship Comes In		0	1993	1	1993	(RCA 62429)
	15	A Bad Goodbye		0	1993	43	1993	(RCA 62503)
!	16	No Time To Kill		0	1993	3	1993	(RCA 62609)
!	17	Desperado		0	1993	54	1993	(Giant LP Cut)
!	18	State Of Mind		0	1993	3	1993	(RCA 62700)

HIT 10 IS CREDITED TO 'ROY ROGERS' AND 'CLINT BLACK' • HIT 15 IS CREDITED TO 'CLINT BLACK WITH 'WYNONNA'

ISSUE	TITLE	UK LBL	UK POS	UK YEAR	US POS	US YEAR	US LBL

Clint Eastwood   Male Vocalist from the USA

1	I Talk To The Trees	(Paramount Para 3004)	18	1970	0	1970	

IN THE UK 'I TALK TO THE TREES' WAS BACKED WITH THE LEE MARVIN'S HIT FOR TWO WEEK. • SEE ALSO GENERAL SAINT

Clint Holmes   Male Vocalist, B: 9 May 1946 Bournemouth, England

* 1	Playground In My Mind		0	1972	2	1972	(Epic 10891)

THE CHILD'S VOICE IS BY PHILLIP VANCE

Clinton Ford   Male Vocalist from the UK

1	Old Shep	(Oriole Cb 1500)	27	1959	0	1959	
2	Too Many Beautiful Girls	(Oriole Cb 1632)	48	1961	0	1961	
3	Fanlight Fanny	(Oriole Cb 1706)	22	1962	0	1962	
4	Run To The Door	(Piccadilly 7n 35361)	25	1967	0	1967	

Clique   Pop-Rock Quintet from Texas

1	Sugar On Sunday		0	1969	22	1969	(White Whale 323)

Clive Dunn   Male Actor/Vocalist from the UK

1	Grandad	(Columbia Db 8726)	1	1970	0	1970	
2	Grandad (Re-Entry)	(Columbia Db 8726)	50	1971	0	1971	

Clive Griffin   Male Vocalist from the UK

1	Head Above Water	(Mercury Step 4)	60	1989	0	1989	
2	I'll Be Waiting	(Mercury Step 6)	56	1991	0	1991	

Clock   Mixed Vocal/Instrumental Group from the UK

1	Holding On	(Media Mrlcd 007)	66	1993	0	1993	
2	The Rhythm	(Media Mcstd 1971)	28	1994	0	1994	
3	Keep The Fires Burning	(Media Mcstd 1988)	36	1994	0	1994	
4	Axel F / Keep Pushin'	(MCA Mcstd 2041)	7	1995	0	1995	
5	Whoomph (There It Is)	(MCA Mcstd 2059)	4	1995	0	1995	
6	Everybody	(MCA Mcstd 2077)	6	1995	0	1995	
7	In The House	(MCA Mcstd 40005)	23	1995	0	1995	
8	Holding On 4 U (Re-Mix)	(Media/MCA Mcstd 40019)	27	1996	0	1996	
9	Oh What A Night	(Power Station/MCA Mcstd40057)	13	1996	0	1996	
10	It's Over	(Media Mcstd 40100)	10	1997	0	1997	

Clodagh Rodgers   Female Vocalist from Ireland

1	Come Back And Shake Me	(RCA 1792)	3	1969	0	1969	
2	Goodnight Midnight	(RCA 1852)	4	1969	0	1969	
3	Goodnight Midnight (Re-Entry)	(RCA 1852)	48	1969	0	1969	
4	Biljo	(RCA 1891)	22	1969	0	1969	
5	Everybody Go Home The Party's Over	(RCA 1930)	47	1970	0	1970	
6	Jack In The Box	(RCA 2066)	4	1971	0	1971	
7	Lady Love Bug	(RCA 2117)	28	1971	0	1971	

Cloud   Male Instrumental Group from the UK

1	All Night Long	(UK Champagne Funk 1)	72	1981	0	1981	

Clout   Female Vocal/Instrumental Group from South Africa

1	Substitute	(Carrere EMI 2788)	2	1978	0	1978	

Clovers   R&B Vocal Groupfrom Washington D.C

6	Love, Love, Love		0	1956	30	1956	(Atlantic 1094)
7	Love Potion No 9		0	1959	23	1959	(United Artists 180)

NAMES JOHN BAILEY, MATTHEW MCQUATER, HAROLD LUCAS, HAROLD WINELY, BILL HARRIS & BILLY MITCHELL
THEY NEVER MADE IT IN THE UK ALTHOUGH THEY WERE VERY SUCCESSFUL IN THE USA • OBITUARY: HARRIS D: 10 DEC 1988 CANCER.

Club 69   Mixed Vocal/Instrumental Duo from the USA/Austria

1	Let Me Be Your Underwear	(Ffrr F 204)	33	1992	0	1992	

Club Nouveau   Mixed Vocal/Instrumental Group from the USA

1	Lean On Me	(King Jay W 8430)	3	1987	1	1987	(Warner Bros 28430)
2	Why You Treat Me So Bad		0	1987	39	1987	(Warner Bros 28360)

Clubhouse   Male Vocal/Instrumental Group From Italy

1	Do It Again - Billie Jean (Medley)	(Island Is 132)	11	1983	0	1983	
2	Superstition - Good Times (Medley)	(Island Is 147)	59	1983	0	1983	
3	I'm A Man - Ye Ke Ye Ke (Medley)	(Music Man Mmps 7003)	69	1989	0	1989	
4	Deep In My Heart	(Ffrr F 157)	59	1991	0	1991	
5	Deep In My Heart (Re-Entry)	(Ffrr F 157)	55	1991	0	1991	
6	Light My Fire	(Pwl Continental Pwcd 272)	59	1993	0	1993	
7	Light My Fire (Re-Entry)	(Pwl Continental Pwcd 272)	45	1993	0	1993	
8	Light My Fire (2nd Re-Entry)	(Pwl Continental Pwcd 272)	53	1993	0	1993	

ISSUE	TITLE	UK LBL	UK POS	UK YEAR	US POS	US YEAR	US LBL
9	Light My Fire (Re-Mix)	(Pwl Continental Pwcd 288)	7	1994	0	1994	
10	Living In The Sunshine	(Pwl Continental Pwcd 309)	21	1994	0	1994	
11	Nowhere Land	(Pwl Continental Pwcd 318)	56	1995	0	1995	

Clubzone Male Vocal/Instrumental Group from the UK/Germany

1	Hands Up	(Logic 74321236982)	50	1994	0	1994	

Clueless

1	Don't Speak	(Zyx Zyx 660738)	61	1997	0	1997	

Clyde McPhatter Male Vocalist, Real Name Clyde Lensley Mcphatter B: 15 Nov 1932 In Durham, North Carolina

	ISSUE	TITLE	UK LBL	UK POS	UK YEAR	US POS	US YEAR	US LBL
+	1	Money Honey		0	1953	1	1953	(Atlantic 1006)
+	2	Honey Love		0	1954	1	1954	(Atlantic 1029)
*	3	Treasure Of Love	(London Hle 8293)	27	1956	16	1956	(Atlantic 1092)
*	4	Without Love (There Is Nothing)		0	1957	19	1957	(Atlantic 1117)
	5	Just To Hold My Hand		0	1957	26	1957	(Atlantic 1133)
*	6	A Lover's Question		0	1958	6	1958	(Atlantic 1199)
	7	Since You've Been Gone		0	1959	38	1959	(Atlantic 2028)
	8	Ta Ta		0	1960	23	1960	(Mercury 71660)
	9	Lover Please		0	1962	7	1962	(Mercury 71941)
	10	Little Bitty Pretty One		0	1962	25	1962	(Mercury 71987)

HE WAS WITH THE DOMINOES IN 1950 AND IN 1953 HE FORMED THE DRIFTERS • OBITUARY: D: 13 JUN 1972 HEART ATTACK.

Clyde Valley Stompers Male Instrumental Group from the UK

1	Peter And The Wolf	(Parlophone R 4928)	25	1962	0	1962	

Coast To Coast Male Vocal/Instrumental Group from the UK

1	(Do) The Hucklebuck	(Polydor Posp 214)	5	1981	0	1981	
2	Let's Jump The Broomstick	(Polydor Posp 249)	28	1981	0	1981	

Coasters Male Vocal Group from the USA   They Formed In Los Angeles In 1955 Singing Rhythm And Blues

	ISSUE	TITLE	UK LBL	UK POS	UK YEAR	US POS	US YEAR	US LBL
	1	One Kiss Led To Another		0	1956	73	1956	(Atco 6073)
*	2	Searchin'	(London Hle 8450)	30	1957	3	1957	(Atco 6087)
	3	Young Blood		0	1957	8	1957	(Atco 6087)
	4	Idol With The Golden Head		0	1957	64	1957	(Atco 6098)
*	5	Yakety Yak	(London Hle 8665)	12	1958	1	1958	(Atco 6116)
*	6	Charlie Brown	(London Hle 8819)	6	1959	2	1959	(Atco 6132)
	7	Along Came Jones		0	1959	9	1959	(Atco 6141)
*	8	Poison Ivy	(London Hle 8938)	15	1959	7	1959	(Atco 6146)
	9	I'm A Hog For You		0	1959	38	1959	(Atco 6146)
	10	Run Red Run		0	1959	36	1959	(Atco 6153)
	11	What About Us		0	1959	47	1959	(Atco 6153)
	12	Wait A Minute		0	1961	37	1961	(Atco 6186)
	13	Little Egypt (Ying-Yang)		0	1961	23	1961	(Atco 6192)
	14	Girls, Girls, Girls		0	1961	96	1961	(Atco 6204)
+	15	Love Potion No 9		0	1971	23	1971	(King 6385)
	16	Sorry But I'm Gonna Have To Pass	(Rhino A 4519cd)	41	1994	0	1994	

Cock Robin Pop/Vocal/Instrumental Quartet from Los Angeles

1	When Your Heart is Weak		0	1985	35	1985	(Coklumbia 04875)
2	The Promise You Made	(CBS A 6764)	28	1986	0	1986	

Cockerel Chorus Male Vocal Group from the UK

1	Nice One Cyril	(Youngblood Yb 1017)	14	1973	0	1973	

Cockney Rejects Male Vocal/Instrumental Group from the UK

1	I'm Not A Fool	(EMI5008	65	1979	0	1979	
2	Badman	(EMI5035)	65	1980	0	1980	
3	The Greatest Cockney Ripoff	(EMIZ 2)	21	1980	0	1980	
4	I'm Forever Blowing Bubbles	(EMIZ 4)	35	1980	0	1980	
5	We Can Do Anything	(EMIZ 6)	65	1980	0	1980	
6	We Are The Firm	(EMIZ 10)	54	1980	0	1980	

Co-Co Mixed Vocal/Instrumental Group from the UK

1	Bad Old Days	(Ariola Aha 513)	13	1978	0	1978	

Coconuts Female Vocal Group from the USA See Also Kid Creole & The Coconuts

1	Did You Have To Love Me Like You Did	(EMIAmerica Ea 156)	60	1983	0	1983	

Cocteau Twins Mixed Vocal/Instrumental Group from the UK

1	Pearly-Dewdrops' Drops	(4ad 405)	29	1984	0	1984	
2	Aikea-Guinea	(4ad Ad 501)	41	1985	0	1985	
3	Tiny Dynamine (Ep)	(4ad Bad 510)	52	1985	0	1985	
4	Echoes In A Shallow Bay (Ep	(4ad Bad 511)	65	1985	0	1985	

ISSUE	TITLE	UK LBL	UK POS	UK YEAR	US POS	US YEAR	US LBL
5	Love's Easy Tears	(4ad Ad 610)	53	1986	0	1986	
6	Iceblink Luck	(4ad Ad 0011)	38	1990	0	1990	
7	Evangeline	(Fontana Ctcd 1)	34	1993	0	1993	
8	Winter Wonderland / Frosty The Snowman	(Fontana Coccd 1)	58	1993	0	1993	
9	Bluebeard	(Fontana Ctcd 2)	31	1994	0	1994	
10	Twinlights (Ep)	(Fontana Ctcd 3)	59	1995	0	1995	
11	Otherness (Ep)	(Fontana Ctcd 4)	59	1995	0	1995	
12	Tishbite	(Fontana Ctdd 5)	34	1996	0	1996	
13	Violaine	(Fontana Ctdd 6)	56	1996	0	1996	
Code Red Male Vocal Group, Names Lee, Roger, Phil & Neal from the UK							
1	I Gave You Everything	(Polydor 5763992)	50	1996	0	1996	
2	This Is Our Song	(Polydor 5756332)	59	1996	0	1996	
3	Can We Talk	(Polydor 5710992)	29	1997	0	1997	
4	Is There Someone Out There?	(Polydor 5714652)	34	1997	0	1997	
Coffee Female Vocal Group from the USA							
1	Cassanova	(De-Lite Mer 38)	13	1980	0	1980	
2	Slip And Dip / I Wanna Be With You	(De-Lite De 1)	57	1980	0	1980	
Cola Boy Mixed Instrumental Duo from the UK							
1	7 Ways To Love	(Arista 114526)	8	1991	0	1991	
Coldcut Male Production Duo from the UK							
1	Doctorin' The House	(Ahead Of Our Time Ccut 27)	6	1988	0	1988	
2	Stop This Crazy Thing	(Ahead Of Our Time)	21	1988	0	1988	
3	People Hold On	(Ahead Of Our Time Ccut 5)	11	1989	0	1989	
4	My Telephone	(Ahead Of Our Time)	52	1989	0	1989	
5	Coldcut's Christmas Break	(Ahead Of Our Time)	67	1989	0	1989	
6	Find A Way	(Ahead Of Our Time Ccut 8)	52	1990	0	1990	
7	Dreamer	(Arista 74321156642)	54	1993	0	1993	
8	Autumn Leaves	(Arista 74321171052)	50	1994	0	1994	
9	More Beats & Pieces	(Ninja Tune Zencds 58)	37	1997	0	1997	
Cold Jam Mixed Vocal/Instrumental Group from the USA							
1	Last Night A Dj Saved My Life	(Big Wave Bwr 39)	64	1990	0	1990	
	HIT IS CREDITED TO COLD JAM FEATURING GRACE						
Coleman Hawkins Orchestra Male Saxophonist, B: 24 Nov 1904 St. Joseph, Missouri							
* 1	Body And Soul		0	1940	13	1940	(Bluebird 10523)
	OBITUARY: D: 19 MAY 1969 IN NEW YORK, (AGED 64)						
Colin Blunstone Male Vocalist, B: 24 Jun 1945 Hatfield, Hertfordshire, England							
1	Say You Don't Mind	(Epic Epc 7765)	15	1972	0	1972	
2	I Don't Believe In Miracles	(Epic Epc 8434)	31	1972	0	1972	
3	How Could We Dare To Be Wrong	(Epic Epc 1197)	45	1973	0	1973	
4	What Becomes Of The Broken Hearted	(Stiff Broken 1)	13	1981	0	1981	
5	Tracks Of My Tears	(Prt 7p 236)	60	1982	0	1982	
	HIT 4 IS CREDITED TO DAVE STEWART WITH SPECIAL VOCALS BY COLIN BLUNSTONE • SEE ALSO NEIL MACARTHUR, ZOMBIES AND DAVE STEWART						
Collage Male Vocal/Instrumental Group from the USA/Canada							
1	Romeo Where's Juliet?	(MCA MCA 1006)	46	1985	0	1985	
Collapsed Lung Male Vocal/Instrumental Group from the UK							
1	London Tonight / Eat My Goal	(Deceptive Bluff 029cd)	31	1996	0	1996	
Collective Soul Male Rock Quintet from Georgia, USA							
* 1	Shine		0	1994	11	1994	(Atlantic 87237)
2	December		0	1995	20	1995	(Atlantic 87157)
3	The World I Know		0	1995	19	1995	(Atlantic 87088)
4	Precious Declaration		0	1997	65	1997	(Atlantic 83003)
Colonel Abrams Male Vocalist from the USA							
1	Trapped	(MCA MCA 997)	3	1985	0	1985	
2	The Truth	(MCA Mca 1022)	53	1985	0	1985	
3	I'm Not Gonna Let You (Get The Best Of Me)	(MCA MCA 1031)	24	1986	0	1986	
4	How Soon We Forget	(MCA MCA 1179)	75	1987	0	1987	
Color Me Badd Male Vocal Group from the USA	Names Bryan Abrams, Sam Walters, Mark Calderon & Kevin Thornton						
* 1	I Wanna Sex You Up	(Giant W 0036)	1	1991	2	1991	(Giant 19382)
* 2	All 4 Love	(Giant W 0053)	5	1991	1	1991	(Giant 19236)
* 3	I Adore Mi Amor	(Giant W 0067)	44	1991	1	1991	(Giant 19204)
4	I Adore Mi Amor (Re-Issue)	(Giant W 0076)	59	1991	0	1991	
5	Heartbreaker	(Giant W 0078)	58	1992	0	1992	

ISSUE	TITLE	UK LBL	UK POS	UK YEAR	US POS	US YEAR	US LBL
6	Thinkin' Back		0	1992	16	1992	(Giant 19074)
7	Slow Motion		0	1992	18	1992	(Giant 18908)
8	Forever Love		0	1992	15	1992	(Giant 18727)
9	Time And Chance	(Giant 74321168992	62	1993	23	1993	(Giant 18339)
10	Choose	(Giant 74321199432)	65	1994	23	1994	(Giant 18270)
11	The Earth, The Sun, The Rain		0	1996	21	1996	(Giant 17654)

Colorado   Female Vocal Group from the UK

ISSUE	TITLE	UK LBL	UK POS	UK YEAR	US POS	US YEAR	US LBL
1	California Dreaming	(Pinnacle Pin 67)	45	1978	0	978	

Colour Field   Male Vocal/Instrumental Group from the UK

ISSUE	TITLE	UK LBL	UK POS	UK YEAR	US POS	US YEAR	US LBL
1	The Colour Field	(Chrysalis Colf 1)	43	1984	0	1984	
2	Take	(Chrysalis Colf 2)	70	1984	0	1984	
3	Thinking Of You	(Chrysalis Colf 3)	12	1985	0	1985	
4	Castles In The Air	(Chrysalis Colf 4)	51	1985	0	1985	

Coming Out Crew   Mixed Vocal Duo from the USA

ISSUE	TITLE	UK LBL	UK POS	UK YEAR	US POS	US YEAR	US LBL
1	Free, Gay And Happy	(Out On Vinyl Cdoov 002)	50	1995	0	1995	

Commander Cody & The Lost Planet Airmen   Is George Frayne , Group Formed In California In 1967

ISSUE	TITLE	UK LBL	UK POS	UK YEAR	US POS	US YEAR	US LBL
1	Hot Rod Lincoln		0	1972	9	1972	(Paramount 0146)
2	Smoke! Smoke Smoke		0	1973	94	1973	(Paramount 0216)

Commanders

ISSUE	TITLE	UK LBL	UK POS	UK YEAR	US POS	US YEAR	US LBL
1	Swanee River Boogie		0	1953	25	953	(Decca 28659)
	SEE ALSO DOLORES GRAY						

Commentators   Real Name Rory Bremner. Male Vocal/Impressionist from the UK

ISSUE	TITLE	UK LBL	UK POS	UK YEAR	US POS	US YEAR	US LBL
1	N-N-Nineteen Not Out	(Oval 100)	13	1985	0	1985	

Commitments   Mixed Vocal/Instrumental Group From Ireland

ISSUE	TITLE	UK LBL	UK POS	UK YEAR	US POS	US YEAR	US LBL
1	Mustang Sally	(Mca Mcs 1598)	63	1991	0	1991	

Commodores   Male Vocal/Instrumental Group from the USA

ISSUE	TITLE	UK LBL	UK POS	UK YEAR	US POS	US YEAR	US LBL
1	Machine Gun	(Tamla Motown Tmg 902)	20	1974	22	1974	(Motown 1307)
2	The Zoo (The Human Zoo)	(Tamla Motown Tmg 924)	44	1974	0	1974	
3	Slippery When Wet		0	1975	19	1975	(Motown 1338)
4	Sweet Love	(Tamla Motown Tmg 1086)	32	1977	5	1976	(Motown 1381)
5	Just To Be Close To You	(Motown Tmg 1127	62	1978	7	1976	(Motown 1402)
6	Fancy Dancer		0	1977	39	1977	(Motown 1408)
7	Easy	(Tamla Motown Tmg 1073)	9	1977	4	1977	(Motown 1418)
8	Brick House	(Tamla Motown Tmg 1086)	32	1977	5	1977	(Motown 1425)
9	Too Hot Ta Trot / Zoom	(Tamla Motown Tmg 1096)	38	1978	24	1978	(Motown 1432)
10	Flying High	(Motown Tmg 1111)	37	1978	38	1978	(Motown 1452)
11	Three Times A Lady	(Motown Tmg 1113)	1	1978	1	1978	(Motown 1443)
12	Sail On	(Motown Tmg 1155)	8	1979	4	1979	(Motown 1452)
13	Still	(Motown Tmg 1166)	4	1979	1	1979	(Motown 1474)
14	Wonderland	(Motown Tmg 1172)	40	1980	25	1980	(Motown 1479)
15	Old-Fashion Love		0	1980	20	1980	(Motown 1489)
16	Lady (You Bring Me Up)	(Motown Tmg 1238)	56	1981	8	1981	(Motown 1514)
17	Oh No	(Motown Tmg 1245)	44	1981	4	1981	(Motown 1527)
18	Nightshift	(Motown Tmg 1371)	3	1985	3	1985	(Motown 1773)
19	Animal Instinct	(Motown Zb 40097)	74	1985	0	1985	
20	Goin' To The Bank	(Polydor Pospa 826)	43	1986	0	1986	
21	Easy (Re-Issue)	(Motown Zb 41793)	15	1988	0	1988	

NAMES: LIONEL RICHIE, WILLIAM KING, THOMAS MCCLARY, MILAN WILLIAMS, RONALD LA-PREAD & WALTER ORANGE
HIT 18 IS A TRIBUTE TO MARVIN GAYE AND JACKIE WILSON. HIT 17 WAS THE LAST SONG WHERE RICHIE WAS LEAD SINGER LIONEL LEFT IN 1982

Communards   Male Vocal/Instrumental Duo from the UK

ISSUE	TITLE	UK LBL	UK POS	UK YEAR	US POS	US YEAR	US LBL
1	You Are My World	(London Lon 77)	21	1985	0	1985	
2	Disenchanted	(London Lon 89)	29	1986	0	1986	
3	Don't Leave Me This Way	(London Lon 103)	1	1986	40	1986	(MCA 52928)
4	So Cold The Night	(London Lon 110)	8	1986	0	1986	
5	You Are My World '87 (Re-Mix)	(London Lon 123)	21	1987	0	1987	
6	Tomorrow	(London Lon 143)	23	1987	0	1987	
7	Never Can Say Goodbye	(London Lon 158)	4	1987	0	1987	
8	For A Friend	(London Lon 166)	28	1988	0	1988	
9	There's More To Love	(London Lon 173)	20	1988	0	1988	

HIT 3 IS CREDITED TO COMMUNARDS WITH SARAH JANE MORRIS • NAMES: JIMMY SOMERVILLE AND RICHARD COLES

Compagnons De La Chanson   Female Vocal Group from France

ISSUE	TITLE	UK LBL	UK POS	UK YEAR	US POS	US YEAR	US LBL
1	The Three Bells	(Columbia Db 4358)	27	1959	0	1959	
2	The Three Bells (Re-Entry)	(Columbia Db 4358)	21	1959	0	1959	

ISSUE	TITLE	UK LBL	UK POS	UK YEAR	US POS	US YEAR	US LBL
Company B Names: Lori Leziee, Susan & Livrano Johnson							
1	Fascinated		0	1987	21	1987	(Atlantic 89294)
Comsat Angels Male Vocal/Instrumental Group from the UK							
1	Independence Day	(Jive Jive 54)	75	1984	0	1984	
2	Independance Day (Re-Entry)	(Jive Jive 54)	71	1984	0	1984	
Con Funk Shun Male Vocal/Instrumental Group from the USA Originally Known As Project Soul. Changed Their Name In 1972							
1	Ffun		0	1978	23	1978	(Mercury 73959)
2	Too Tight		0	1981	40	1981	(Mercury 76089)
3	Burnin' Love	(Club Jab 32)	68	1986	0	1986	
Concept Male Vocal/Instrumentalist Group from the UK							
1	Mr. Dj	(Fourth & Broadway Brw 40)	27	1985	0	1985	
Concrete Blonde Originally Known A Dream 6							
1	Joey		0	1990	19	1990	(I.R.S. 73014)
Congregation Mixed Choir from the UK							
1	Softly Whispering I Love You	(Columbia Db 8830)	4	1971	29	1972	(Atco 6865)
Congress Mixed Vocal/Instrumental Group from the UK							
1	40 Miles	(Inner Rhythm 7heart 01)	26	1991	0	1991	
Connee Boswell Female Vocalist From New Orleans							
23	Let It Snow! Let It Snow! Let It Snow!		0	1946	9	1946	(Decca 18741)
24	Who Told You That Lie?		0	1946	22	1946	(Decca 18881)
25	Ole Buttermilk Sky (From *Canyon Passage*)		0	1946	14	1946	(Decca 18913)
26	You Were Meant For Me		0	1948	19	1948	(Decca 25313)
27	My Little Nest Of Heavenly Blue (From *Rich, Young And Pretty*)		0	1952	25	1952	(Decca 283779
28	Singin' The Blues		0	1953	27	1953	(Decca 28498)
29	Main Street On Saturday Night		0	1953	29	1953	(Decca 28626)
30	I'm Gonna Sit Right Down And Write Myself A Letter		0	1953	29	1953	(Decca 28832)
31	The Philadelphia Waltz		0	1954	30	1954	(Decca 29051)
32	If I Give My Heart To You		0	1954	10	1954	(Decca 29148)
	OBITUARY : D: 12 OCT 1976, AGED 64.							
Connells Male Vocal/Instrumental Group From The USA							
1	74-75	(Tnt/London Loncd 369)	14	1995	0	1995	
2	74-75 (Re-Issue)	(Tnt/London Loncd 413)	21	1996	0	1996	
Connie Francis Female Vocalist, Real Name Concetta Rosa Maria Franconero. B: 12 Dec 1938 New Jersey							
* 1	Majesty Of Love		0	1957	1	1957	(MGM)
* 2	Who's Sorry Now	(MGM 975)	1	1958	4	1958	(MGM 12588)
3	I'm Sorry I Made You Cry	(MGM 982)	11	1958	36	1958	(MGM 12647)
4	Carolina Moon	(MGM 985)	1	1958	0	1958	
5	Stupid Cupid	(MGM 985)	1	1958	14	1958	(MGM 12683)
6	I'll Get By	(MGM 993)	19	1958	0	1958	
7	Fallin'	(MGM 993)	19	1958	30	1958	(MGM 12713)
* 8	My Happiness	(MGM 1001)	4	1959	2	1958	(MGM 12738)
9	You Always Hurt The One You Love	(MGM 998)	13	1958	0	1958	
10	If I Didn't Care		0	1959	22	1959	(MGM 12769)
11	My Happiness (Re-Entry)	(MGM 1001)	30	1959	0	1959	
* 12	Lipstick On Your Collar	(MGM 1018)	3	1959	5	1959	(MGM 12793)
13	Frankie		0	1959	9	1959	(MGM 12793)
14	Plenty Good Lovin'	(MGM 1036)	18	1959	0	1959	
15	You're Gonna Miss Me		0	1959	34	1959	(MGM 12824)
* 16	Among My Souvenirs	(MGM 1046)	11	1959	7	1959	(MGM 12841)
17	God Bless America		0	1959	36	1959	(MGM 12841)
* 18	Mamma	(MGM 1076)	2	1960	8	1960	(MGM 12878)
19	Teddy		0	1960	17	1960	(MGM 12878)
20	Robot Man	(MGM 1076)	2	1960	0	1960	
21	Valentino	(MGM 1060)	27	1960	0	1960	
* 22	Everybody's Somebody's Fool	(MGM 1086)	5	1960	1	1960	(MGM 12899)
23	Jealous Of You (Tango Della Gelosia)		0	1960	19	1960	(MGM 12899)
* 24	My Heart Has A Mind Of It's Own	(MGM 1100)	3	1960	1	1960	(MGM 12923)
* 25	Many Tears Ago	(MGM 1111)	12	1961	7	1960	(MGM 12964)
* 26	Where The Boys Are	(MGM 1121)	5	1961	4	1961	(MGM 12971)
27	No One		0	1961	34	1961	(MGM 12971)
28	Breakin' In A Brand New Broken Heart	(MGM 1136)	12	1961	7	1961	(MGM 12995)
29	Together	(MGM 1138)	6	1961	6	1961	(MGM 13019)

ISSUE	TITLE	UK LBL	UK POS	UK YEAR	US POS	US YEAR	US LBL
30	(He's My) Dreamboat		0	1961	14	1961	(MGM 13039)
31	When The Boy In Your Arms (Is The Boy In Your Heart)		0	1961	10	1961	(MGM 13051)
32	Baby's First Christmas	(MGM 1145)	30	1961	26	1962	(MGM 13051)
* 33	Don't Break The Heart That Loves You	(MGM 1157)	39	1962	1	1962	(MGM 13059)
34	Second Hand Love		0	1962	7	1962	(MGM 13074)
35	Vacation	(MGM 1165)	10	1962	9	1962	(MGM 13087)
36	I Was Such A Fool (To Fall In Love With You)		0	1962	24	1962	(MGM 13096)
37	I'm Gonna Be Warm This Winter	(MGM 1185)	48	1962	18	1963	(MGM 13116)
38	Follow The Boys		0	1963	17	1963	(MGM 13127)
39	If My Pillow Could Talk		0	1963	23	1963	(MGM 13143)
40	Drownin' My Sorrows		0	1963	36	1963	(MGM 13160)
41	Your Other Love		0	1963	28	1963	(MGM 13176)
42	Blue Winter		0	1964	24	1964	(MGM 13214)
43	Be Anything (But Be Mine)		0	1964	25	1964	(MGM 13237)
44	My Child	(MGM 1271)	26	1965	0	1965	
45	Jealous Heart	(MGM 1293)	44	1966	0	1966	
! 46	The Wedding Cake		0	1969	10	1969	(MGM 14034)
! 47	There's Still A Few Good Love Songs Left In Me		0	1983	84	1983	(Polydor 810087)

'BABY ROO' WAS LISTED WITH HIT 26 FOR EIGHT WEEKS HIT 46 REACHED NUMBER 91 IN THE US NATIONAL CHARTS
STOPPED PERFORMING AFTER BEING RAPED 8 NOV 1974, THEN MADE A COMEBACK IN 1978

Connie Haines   Female Vocalist, Real Name Marie Jamais from the USA

1	At The Darktown Strutter's Ball		0	1948	29	1948	(Signature 15197)
2	How It Lies, How It Lies, How It Lies!		0	1949	19	1949	(Coral 60044)
3	Maybe It's Because (From Along Fifth Avenue)		0	1949	20	1949	(Coral 60070)
4	Make A Joyful Noise Unto The Lord – Do Lord		0	1954	27	1954	(Coral 61113)

Connie Stevens   Female Vocalist, Real Name Concetta Ingolia B: 8 Apr 1938 Brooklyn

* 1	Kookie Kookie (Lend Me Your Comb)	(Warner Bros Wb 5)	27	1960	4	1959	(Warner Bros 5047)
* 2	Sixteen Reasons	(Warner Bros Wb 3)	9	1960	3	1960	(Warner Bros 5137)
3	Sixteen Reasons (Re-Entry)	(Warner Bros Wb 3)	45	1960	0	1960	

HIT 1 IS CREDITED TO EDWARD BYRNES AND CONNIE STEVENS

Connie Russell   Female Vocalist from the USA

1	You've Changed		0	1954	30	1954	(Capitol 2666)

Conny Froboess   Female Vocalist, B: 28 Oct 1943, Berlin

* 1	Zwei Kleiner Italiener (Two Little Italians)		0	1962	0	1962	

THE HIT SOLD OVER A MILLION IN EUROPE

Conner Reeves   Male Vocalist from the UK

1	My Father's Son	(Wildstar Cdwild 1)	12	1997	0	1997	

Conquering Lion   Male Vocal Group from the UK

1	Code Red	(Mango Cidm 821)	53	1994	0	1994	

Consortium   Male Vocal Group from the Uk

1	All The Love In The World	(Pye 7n 17635)	22	1969	0	1969	

Contours   Male R&B Vocal Group from Detroit

* 1	Do You Love Me		0	1962	3	1962	(Gordy 7005)
2	Shake Sherry		0	1963	43	1963	(Gordy 7012)
3	Can You Do It		0	1964	41	1964	(Gordy 7029)
4	Can You Jerk Like Me		0	1964	47	1964	(Gordy 7037)
+ 5	First Look At The Purse	(Tamla Motown Tmg 723)	31	1970	12	1965	(Gordy 7044)
+ 6	Just A Little Misunderstanding	(Tamla Motown Tmg 723)	31	1970	18	1966	(Gordy 7052)
7	Do You Love Me (Re-Issue)		0	1988	11	1988	(Motown Yest. 448)

NAMES: BILLY GORDON, BILLY HOGGS, JOE BILLINGSLEA, SYLVESTER POTTS, HUEY DAVIS & HUBERT JOHNSON
DENIS EDWARDS JOINED IN 1967 BUT WENT TO THE TEMPTATIONS IN 1968 • OBITUARY: HUBERT D: 11 JUL 1981.

Contraband   Mixed Vocal/Instrumental Group from The Usa/Germany

1	All The Way From Memphis	(Impact American Em 195)	65	1991	0	1991	

Control   Mixed Vocal/Instrumental Group from The Uk

1	Dance With Me	(All Around The World Globe 105)	17	1991	0	1991	

Convert   Male Production/Instrumental Duo from Belgium

1	Nightbird	(A&M Am 845)	39	1992	0	1992	
2	Rockin' To The Rhythm	(A&M 5802532)	42	1993	0	1993	

Conway Brothers   Male Vocal Group from The USA

1	Turn It Up	(10 Ten 57)	11	1985	0	1985	

Conway Twitty   Male Vocalist, Real Name Harold Lloyd Jenkis. B: 1 Sep 1933 Friars Point, Mississippi.

* 1	It's Only Make Believe	(MGM 992)	1	1958	1	1958	(MGM 12677)

ISSUE	TITLE	UK LBL	UK POS	UK YEAR	US POS	US YEAR	US LBL
2	Danny Boy		0	1959	10	1959	(MGM 12826)
3	Mona Lisa	(MGM 1029)	5	1959	29	1959	(MGM 12804)
4	Danny Boy		0	1959	10	1959	(MGM 12826)
* 5	Lonely Blue Boy		0	1960	6	1960	(MGM 12857)

THE REST ARE C/W HITS. • OBITUARY: D: 5 JUN 1993 ABDOMINAL ANEURISM.

Cookie Brown See Al Brown('s) Tunetoppers

Cookie Crew Female Vocal Group from the UK

1	Rok Da House	(Rhythm King Left 11)	5	1988	0	1988	
2	Born This Way (Let's Dance)	(Ffrr Ffr 19)	23	1989	0	1989	
3	Got To Keep On	(Ffrr Ffr 25)	17	1989	0	1989	
4	Come And Get Some	(Ffrr Ffr 110)	42	1989	0	1989	
5	Secrets Of Success	(Ffrr F 159)	53	1991	0	1991	

Cookies Female Vocal Group from the USA

1	Chains	(London Hlu 9634)	50	1963	17	1962	(Dimension 1002)
2	Don't Say Nothin' Bad (About My Baby)		0	1963	7	1963	(Dimension 1008)
3	Girls Grow Up Faster Than Boys		0	1964	33	1964	(Dimension 1020)

THE 1950S MEMBERS BECAME RAY CHARLES'S BACKING GROUP THE RAELETTS
THERE HAVE BEEN MANY CHANGES TO THE LINE-UP. THEY HAVE SANG BACKUP FOR NEIL SEDAKA, LITTLE EVA & CAROLE KING

Cool Down Zone Mixed Vocal/Instrumental Group from the UK

1	Heaven Knows	(10 Ten 309)	52	1990	0	1990	

Cool Jack Male Instrumental/Production Duo from Italy

1	Jus' Come	(Am-Pm 5819892)	44	1996	0	1996	

Coolio Male Rapper From The USA

* 1	Fantastic Voyage	(Tommy Boy Tb 0617cd)	41	1994	3	1994	(Tommy Boy 7617)
2	I Remember	(Tommy Boy Tbxcd 635)	73	1994	0	1994	
* 3	Gangsta's Paradise	(Tommy Boy Mcstd 2104)	1	1996	1	1995	(Mca 55104)
4	Too Hot	(Tommy Boy Tbcd 718)	9	1996	24	1995	(Tommy Boy 7718)
5	1, 2, 3, 4, (Sumpin' New)	(Tommy Boy Tbcd 7721)	13	1996	5	1996	
6	It's All The Way Live (Now) (From Eddie)	(Tommy Boy Tbcd 7731)	34	1996	29	1996	(Island 7731)
7	Hit 'em High (The Monstars' Anthem)	(Atlantic A 5449cd)	8	1997	0	1997	
8	The Winner	(Atlantic A 5433cd)	53	1997	0	1997	
9	C U When U Get There	(Tommy Boy Tbcd 785)	2	1997	0	1997	

Coolnotes Mixed Vocal/Instrumental Group from the UK

1	You're Never Too Young	(Abstract Dance Ad 1)	42	1984	0	1984	
2	I Forgot	(Abstract Dance Ad 2)	63	1984	0	1984	
3	Spend The Night	(Abstract Dance Ad 3)	11	1985	0	1985	
4	In Your Car	(Abstract Dance Ad 4)	13	1985	0	1985	
5	Have A Good Forever	(Abstract Dance Ad 5)	73	1985	0	1985	
6	Into The Motion	(Abstract Dance Ad 8)	66	1986	0	1986	

Corey Hart Singer/Songwriter, B: Montreal, Canada

1	Sunglasses At Night		0	1984	7	1984	(EMI America 8203)
2	It Ain't Enough		0	1984	17	1984	(EMI America 8236)
3	Never Surrender		0	1985	3	1985	(EMI America 8268)
4	Boy In The Box		0	1985	26	1985	(EMI America 8287)
5	Everything In My Heart		0	1985	30	1985	(EMI America 8300)
6	I Am By Your Side		0	1986	18	1986	(EMI America 8348)
7	Can't Help Falling In Love		0	1987	24	1987	(EMI America 8368)
8	In Your Soul		0	1988	38	1988	(EMI Manhattan 50134)
9	A Little Love		0	1990	37	1990	(EMI 50239)

Corina Female Dancer/Singer, B: Manhattan And Raised In The Bronx

1	Temptation		0	1991	6	1991	(Atco 98775)

SHE WON SECOND PLACE IN A MISS PUERTO RICO CONTEST 1983

Cornelius Brothers & Sister Rose A Family Of 15 Childrenfrom Florida   Names Eddie, Carter & Rose Cornelius. Billie Jo Arrived In 1973

* 1	Treat Her Like A Lady		0	1971	3	1971	(United Artist 50721)
* 2	Too Late To Turn Back Now		0	1972	2	1972	(United Artist 50910)
3	Don't Ever Be Lonely (A Poor Little Fool Like Me)		0	1972	23	1972	(United Artist 50954)
4	I'm Never Gonna Be Alone Anymore		0	1973	37	1973	(United Artist 50996)

Cornershop

1	Brimful Of Asha	(Wiiija Wij 75cd)	60	1997	0	1997	

Coro Mixed Production/Vocal Duo from Germany

1	Because The Night	(Zyx Zyx 68227)	61	1992	0	1992	with Talisa

ISSUE	TITLE	UK LBL	UK POS	UK YEAR	US POS	US YEAR	US LBL
Corona	Italian Producers Checco & Soul Train						
1	The Rhythm Of The Night	(Wea Yz 837cd1)	2	1994	11	1994	(East West 98192)
2	The Rhythm Of The Night (Re-Entry)	(Wea Yz 837cd1)	55	1994	0	1994	
3	Baby Baby	(Eternal Yx 919cd)	5	1995	0	1995	
4	Try Me Out	(East West Yz 955cd)	6	1995	0	1995	
5	I Don't Wanna Be A Star	(Eternal Wea 029cd)	22	1995	0	1995	
6	Megamix	(Eternal Wea 092cd)	36	1997	0	1997	
Coronets	Mixed Vocal Group from the UK						
	That's How A Love Song Was Born	(Columbia Db 3640)	14	1955	0	1955	
2	Twenty Tiny Fingers	(Columbia Db 3671)	20	1955	0	1955	
	HIT 1 IS CREDITED TO RAY BURNS WITH THE CORONETS						
Corrs	Mixed Vocal/Instrumental Group from Ireland Names: Jay, James & Moses Uzzell with George Wooten						
1	Runaway	(Atlantic A 5727cd)	49	1996	0	1996	
2	Runaway (Re-Entry)	(Atlantic A 5727cd)	60	1996	0	1996	
3	Love To Love You / Runaway	(Atlantic A 5621cd)	62	1997	0	1997	
Cosmic Baby	Male Producer from Germany						
1	Loops Of Infinity	(Logic 74321191432)	70	1994	0	1994	
Cougars	Male Instrumental Group From The UK						
1	Saturday Nite At The Duck Pond	(Parlophone R 4989)	33	1963	0	1963	
Council Collective	Mixed Vocal/Instrumental Group from the USA/UK						
1	Soul Deep (Part 1)	(Polydor Mine 1)	24	1984	0	1984	
Count Basie	Male Organ/Pianist/Bandleader, Real Name William Basie B: 21 Aug 1904 Red Bank, New Jersey						
16	Jivin' Joe Jackson		0	1946	12	1946	(Columbia 36889)
17	Patience And Fortitude		0	1946	14	1946	(Columbia 36946)
18	The Mad Boogie		0	1946	10	1946	(Columbia 36946)
19	Blue Skies (From Blues Skies)		0	1946	8	1946	(Columbia 37070)
20	Open The Door Richard!		0	1947	1	1947	(Victor 2127)
21	Free Eats		0	1947	7	1947	(Victor 2148)
22	One O'Clock Jump (Re-Issue)		0	1947	12	1947	(Decca 25056)
23	One O'clock Boogie		0	1947	8	1947	(Victor 2262)
24	I Ain't Mad At You (You Ain't Mad At Me)		0	1947	7	1947	(Victor 2314)
25	Blue And Sentimental		0	1948	21	1948	(Victor 2602)
26	Robbin's Nest		0	1948	22	1948	(Victor 2677)
27	Softly With Feeling		0	1954	29	1954	(Clef 89112)
28	16 Men Swinging		0	1954	29	1954	(Clef 89147)
29	April In Paris		0	1956	28	1956	(Clef 89162)
	OBITUARY : D: 26 APR 1984.						
Count Five	Rock Quintet from San José						
1	Psychotic Reaction		0	1966	5	1966	(Double Shot 104)
Count Indigo	Male Vocalist from the UK						
1	My Unknown Love	(Cowboy Rodeo 952cd)	59	1996	0	1996	
Counting Crows	Male Vocal/Instrumental Group from the USA						
1	Mr. Jones	(Geffen Gfstd 69)	28	1994	0	1994	
2	Round Here	(Geffen Gfstd 74)	70	1994	0	1994	
3	Rain King	(Geffen Gfstd 82)	49	1994	0	1994	
4	Angels Of The Silences	(Geffen Gfstd 22182)	41	1996	0	1996	
5	A Long December	(Geffen Gfstd 22190)	62	1996	0	1996	
6	Daylight Fading	(Geffen Gfstd 22247)	54	1997	0	1997	
Countrymen	Male Vocal Group from the UK						
1	I Know Where I'm Going	(Piccadilly 7n 35029)	45	1962	0	1962	
Courtney Pine	Male Saxophonist from the UK						
1	Like Dreamers Do	(Fourth & Broadway Brw 108)	26	1988	0	1988	
2	I'm Still Waiting	(Mango Mng 749)	66	1990	0	1990	
	HIT 2 IS CREDITED TO COURTNEY PINE FEATURING CAROLL THOMPSON. • HIT 1 IS CREDITED TO MICA PARIS FEATURING COURTNEY PINE SEE ALSO MOVEMENT 98						
Cours							
1	Ready Or Not	(The Brothers Cdbruv 2)	5	1997	0	1997	
Cousins	Names Adrien, Gus, Andre & Jacky Instrumental Quartet from Belgium						
* 1	Kili Watch		0	1961	0	1961	
Coven	Lead singer of the quintet is Jinx Dawson from the USA						
1	One Tin Soldier, the Legend of Billy Jack		0	1971	26	1971	(Warner Bros 7509)

ISSUE	TITLE	UK LBL	UK POS	UK YEAR	US POS	US YEAR	US LBL
Coventry City F.C. Male Vocal Soccer Team from the UK							
1	Go For It	(Sky Blue Skb 1)	61	1987	0	1987	
Cover Girls Female Vocal/Dance Trio From New York City							
1	Because Of You		0	1988	27	1988	(Fever 1914)
2	Promise Me		0	1988	40	1988	(Fever 1917)
3	My Heart Skips A Beat		0	1989	38	1989	(Capitol 44436)
4	We Can't Go Wrong		0	1990	8	1990	(Capitol 44498)
5	Wishing On A Star	(Epic 6581437)	38	1992	9	1992	(Epic74343)
Coverdale Page Male Vocal/Instrumental Duo from the UK							
1	Take Me For A Little While	(Emi Cdem 270)	29	1993	0	1993	
2	Take A Look At Yourself	(Emi Cdem 279)	43	1993	0	1993	
Cowboy Church Sunday School Lead Vocalist Is Carol Sue from the USA							
1	Open Up Your Heart (And Let The Sunshine In)		0	1955	8	1955	(Decca 29367)
Cowboy Copas Male Vocal/Guitarist, Real Name Lloyd T. Copas. B: 15 Jul 1913 In Muskogee, Oklahoma							
1	Filipino Baby		0	1946	4 !	1946	(King 505)
!* 2	Signed, Sealed And Delivered		0	1948	2	1948	(King 658
!* 3	Tennessee Waltz		0	1948	3	1948	(King 696)
4	Tennessee Waltz		0	1948	7	1948	(King 714)
5	Breeeze		0	1948	12	1948	(King 618)
6	I'm Waltzing With Tears In My Eyes		0	1948	12	1948	(King 775)
7	Candy Kisaes		0	1949	5	1949	(King 777)
8	Hangman's Boogie		0	1949	14	1949	(King 811)
9	The Strange Little Girl		0	1949	5	1949	(King 951)
10	Don't Leave My Poor Heart Breaking		0	1951	15	1951	(King 15137)
11	'Tis Sweet To Be Remembered		0	1952	8	1953	(King 1000)
12	Alabam		0	1960	1	1960	(Starday 501)
13	Flat Top		0	1961	9	1961	(Starday 542)
14	Sunny Tennessee		0	1961	12	1961	(Starday 552)
15	Signed, Sealed And Delivered (Re-Issue)		0	1961	10	1961	(Starday 559)
16	Goodbye Kisses		0	1963	12	1963	(Starday 621)
	OBITUARY : OB: D: 5 MAR 1963 PLANE CRASH						
Cowsills Names: Bill, Bob, Paul, Barry & John Are Five Brothers From Rhode Island, Together With Sister Susan And Mother Barbara Cowsilll							
* 1	The Rain, The Park And Other Things		0	1967	2	1967	(Mgm 13810)
2	We Can Fly		0	1968	21	1968	(Mgm 13886)
3	Indian Lake		0	1968	10	1968	(Mgm 13944)
* 4	Hair		0	1969	2	1969	(Mgm 14026)
	BOB, PAUL, JOHN & SUSAN GOT TOGETHER WHEN THEY TOURED IN 1990 • OBITUARY :- BARBARA D: 31 JAN 1985.						
Cozy Cole Male Instrumentalist, Real Name William Randolph Cole B: 17 Oct 1909 In East Orange, New Jersey							
1	Topsy (Part 2)		0	1958	3	1958	(Love 5004)
2	Topsy (Part 1)		0	1958	27	1958	(Love 5004)
3	Topsy (Part 1-2)	(London Hl 8750)	29	1958	0	1958	
4	Turvy (Part 2)		0	1958	36	1958	(Love 5014)
	OBITUARY: D: 29 JAN 1981 CANCER.						
Cozy Powell Male Instrumentalist (Drums) from the UK							
1	Dance With The Devil	(Rak 164)	3	1973	0	1973	
2	The Man In Black	(Rak 173)	18	1974	0	1974	
3	Na-Na-Na	(Rak 180)	10	1974	0	1974	
4	Theme One	(Ariola Aro 189)	62	1979	0	1979	
5	Resurrection	(Parlophone Cdrs 6351)	23	1993	0	1993	and Brian May
Crabby Appleton Rock Quintet, Led By "Michael Fennelly From The West Coast, USA							
1	Go Back		0	1970	26	1970	(Elektra 45687)
Cracker Male Vocal/Instrumental Group from the USA							
1	Low	(Virgin America Vusdg 80)	43	1994	0	1994	
2	Get Off This	(Virgin America Vusdg 83)	41	1994	0	1994	
3	Low (Re-Entry)	(Virgin America Vusdg 80)	54	1994	0	1994	
Craig Douglas Male Vocalist from the UK							
1	A Teenager In Love	(Top Rank Jar 133)	13	1959	0	1959	
2	Only Sixteen	(Top Rank Jar 159)	1	1959	0	1959	
3	Pretty Blue Eyes	(Top Rank Jar 268)	4	1960	0	1960	
4	The Heart Of A Teenage Girl	(Top Rank Jar 340)	10	1960	0	1960	
5	Oh! What A Day	(Top Rank Jar 406)	43	1960	0	1960	
6	A Hundred Pounds Of Clay	(Top Rank Jar 555)	9	1961	0	1961	

ISSUE	TITLE	UK LBL	UK POS	UK YEAR	US POS	US YEAR	US LBL
7	Time	(Top Rank Jar 569)	9	1961	0	1961	
8	When My Little Girl Is Smiling	(Top Rank Jar 610)	9	1962	0	1962	
9	Our Favourite Melodies	(Columbia Db 4854)	9	1962	0	1962	
10	Oh Lonesome Me	(Decca F 11523)	15	1962	0	1962	
11	Town Crier	(Decca F 11575)	36	1963	0	1963	

Craig Mack Male Rapper from the USA

1	Flava In Ya Ear	(Bad Boy 74321242582)	57	1994	9	1994	(Bad Boy 79001)
2	Get Down	(Puff Daddy 74321263402)	54	1995	38	1995	(Bad Boy 79012)
3	No One But You (From Baps)		0	1997	85	1997	(Island 34101)
4	Spirit	(A&M 5822312)	35	1997	0	1997	

HIT 3 IS CREDITED TO 'VERONICA' FEATURING 'CRAIG MACK' • HIT 4 IS CREDITED TO SOUNDS OF BLACKNESS FEATURING CRAIG MACK

Craig McLachlan Male Vocalist from Australia

1	Mona	(Epic 655784)	2	1990	0	1990	
2	Amanda	(Epic 656170)	19	1990	0	1990	
3	I Almost Felt Like Crying	(Epic 656310)	50	1990	0	1990	
4	One Reason Why	(Epic 6580677)	29	1992	0	1992	
5	On My Own	(Epic 6584677)	59	1992	0	1992	
6	You're The One That I Want	(Epic 6595222)	13	1993	0	1993	
7	Grease	(Epic 6600242)	44	1993	0	1993	
8	Everyday	(Mdmc Devcs 6)	65	1995	0	1995	

HITS 1-3 ARE CREDITED TO CRAIG MCLACHLAN AND CHECK • HIT 6 IS CREDITED TO CRAIG MCLACHLAN AND DEBBIE GIBSON • HIT 8 CRAIG MCLACHLAN & THE CULPRITS

Cramps Mixed Vocal/Instrumental Group from New York

1	Can Your Pussy Do The Dog?	(Big Beat Ns 110)	68	1985	0	1985	
2	Bikini Girl's With Machine Guns	(Enigma Env 17)	35	1990	0	1990	

Cranberries Mixed Vocal/Instrumental Group from Ireland

* 1	Linger	(Island Cid 556)	74	1993	8	1993	(Island 862800)
2	Linger (re-issue)	(Island cid 559)	14	1994	0	1994	
3	Dreams	(Island Cidx 594)	27	1994	0	1994	
4	Zombie	(Island Cid 600)	14	1994	0	1994	
5	Ode To My Family	(Island Cidx 601)	38	1994	0	1994	
6	I Can't Be With You	(Island Cid 605)	23	1995	0	1995	
7	Ridiculous Thoughts	(Island Cid 616)	20	1995	0	1995	
8	Salvation	(Island Cid 633)	13	1996	0	1996	
9	Free To Decide / When You're Gone	(Island Cid 637)	33	1996	22	1996	(Island 854802)

Cranes Mixed Vocal/Instrumental Group from the UK

1	Jewel	(RCA 74321201512)	29	1993	0	1993	
2	Shinning Road	(RCA 74321219622)	57	1994	0	1994	

Crash Test Dummies Mixed Vocal/Instrumental Group From Winniped, Canada, With Lead Vocals from Brad Roberts

* 1	Mmm Mmm Mmm Mmm	(RCA 74321201512)	2	1994	4	1994	(Arista 12654)
2	Afternoons And Coffeespoons	(RCA 74321219622)	23	1994	0	1994	
3	The Ballad Of Peter Pumkinhead	(RCA 74321276772)	30	1995	0	1995	

Crazy Elephant Male Vocal Group from the USA Touring Group Was Created After The Studio Manufactured Hit

1	Gimme Gimme Good Lovin'	(Major Minor Mm 609)	12	1969	12	1969	(Bell 763)

Crazy Otto Real Name Fritz Schulz-Reichel. B: 4 Jul 1912 Germany

1	Glad Rag Doll		0	1955	19	1955	(Decca 29403)
2	Smiles		0	1955	21	1955	(Decca 29403)

Crazy World Of Arthur Brown Male Vocal/Instrumental Group from the UK

* 1	Fire	(Track 604 022)	1	1968	2	1968	(Atlantic 2556)

Real Name Arthur Wilto. B: 24 Jun 1944 Whitby, Yorkshire, England Also Included Carl Palmer of Emerson, Lake & Palmer

Crazyhead Male Vocal/Instrumental Group from the UK

1	Time Has Taken It's Toll On You	(Food Food 12)	65	1988	0	1988	
2	Have Love, Will Travel (Ep)	(Food Sge 2025)	68	1989	0	1989	

Cream Male Vocal/Instrumental Group, Eric Clapton (Guitar) Ginger Baker (Drums) Jack Bruce (Bass) from the UK

1	Wrapping Paper	(Reaction 591 007)	34	1966	0	1966	
2	I Feel Free	(Reaction 591 011)	11	1966	0	1966	
3	Strange Brew	(Reaction 591 015)	17	1967	0	1967	
* 4	Sunshine Of Your Love	(Polydor 56 286)	25	1968	5	1968	(Atco 6544)
5	Anyone For Tennis (The Savage Seven Theme)	(Polydor 56 258)	40	1968	0	1968	
* 6	White Room	(Polydor 56 300)	28	1969	6	1968	(Atco 6617)
7	Crossroads		0	1969	28	1969	(Atco 6646)
8	Badge	(Polydor 56 315)	18	1969	0	1969	
9	Badge (Re-Issue)	(Polydor 2058 285)	42	1972	0	1972	

ERIC WAS INVOLVED WITH DEREK & THE DOMINOES, YARDBIRDS, DELANEY & BONNIE, BLIND FAITH, ROOSTERS AND BLUESBREAKERS
GINGER BAKER FORMED GINGER BAKER'S AIRFORCE

ISSUE	TITLE	UK LBL	UK POS	UK YEAR	US POS	US YEAR	US LBL
Creation	Male Vocal/Instrumental Group from the UK						
1	Marking Time	(Planet Plf 116)	49	1966	0	1966	
2	Painter Man	(Planet Plf 119)	36	1966	0	1966	
Creatures	Mixed Vocal/Instrumental Group from the UK						
1	Mad Eyed Screamer	(Polydor Pospd 354)	24	1981	0	1981	
2	Miss The Girl	(Wonderland She 1)	21	1983	0	1983	
3	Right Now	(Wonderland She 2)	14	1983	0	1983	
4	Standing There	(Wonderland She 17)	53	1989	0	1989	
Credit To The Nation	Male Rap Group from the UK						
1	Call It What You Want	(One Little Indian 94 Tp7cd)	57	1993	0	1993	
2	Enough Is Enough	(One Little Indian 79 Tp7cd)	56	1993	0	1993	
3	Timebomb	(One Little Indian 89 Tp7cd)	59	1993	0	1993	
4	Teenage Sensation	(One Little Indian 124 Tp7cd)	24	1994	0	1994	
5	Sowing The Seeds Of Hatred	(One Little Indian 134 Tp7cd)	72	1994	0	1994	
6	Liar Liar	(One Little Indian 144 Tp7cd)	60	1995	0	1995	
	HIT 2 IS CREDITED TO CHUMBAWAMBA AND CREDIT TO THE NATION						
Creedence Clearwater Revival	Male Vocal/Instrumental Group from the USA Names: John & Tom Fogerty, Stu Cook & Doug Clifford disbanded in 1972						
1	Suzie Q (Part 1)		0	1968	11	1968	(Fantasy 616)
2	I Put A Spell On You		0	1968	58	1968	(Fantasy 617)
* 3	Proud Mary	(Liberty Lbf 15223)	8	1969	2	1969	(Fantasy 619)
* 4	Bad Moon Rising	(Liberty Lbf 15230)	1	1969	2	1969	(Fantasy 622)
* 5	Green River	(Liberty Lbf 15250)	19	1969	2	1969	(Fantasy 625)
6	Commotion		0	1969	30	1969	(Fantasy 625)
* 7	Down On The Corner	(Liberty Lbf 15283)	31	1970	3	1969	(Fantasy 634)
8	Fortunate Son		0	1969	14	1969	(Fantasy 634)
* 9	Travellin' Band	(Liberty Lbf 15310)	8	1970	2	1970	(Fantasy 637)
10	Who'll Stop The Rain		0	1970	9	1970	(Fantasy 637)
11	Up Around The Bend	(Liberty Lbf 15354)	3	1970	4	1970	(Fantasy 641)
12	Travellin' Band (Re-Entry)	(Liberty Lbf 15310)	46	1970	0	1970	
* 13	Lookin' Out My Back Door		0	1970	2	1970	(Fantasy 645)
* 14	Have You Ever Seen The Rain	(Liberty Lbf 15440)	36	1971	8	1971	(Fantasy 655)
15	Sweet Hitch-Hiker	(United Artists Up 35261)	36	1971	6	1971	(Fantasy 665)
16	Someday Never Comes		0	1972	25	1972	(Fantasy 676)
17	Cotton Fields		0	1980	50!	1980	(Fantasy 920)
18	Bad Moon Rising (Re-Issue)	(Epic 6580047)	71	1992	0	1992	
	FIRST RECORDED AS THE BLUE VELVETS THEN THE GOLLIWOGS • OBITUARY : TOM D: 6 SEP 1990 RESPIRATORY FAILURE						
Crescendo	Mixed Vocal/Instrumental Duo from the UK/USA						
1	Are You Out There	(Frr Fcd 270)	20	1995	0	1995	
Crescendos	Originally Formed As The Spades In High School						
* 1	Oh Julie		0	1958	5	1958	(Nasco 6005)
	THIS WAS THE ONLY NATIONAL HIT FOR THE GROUP AND A MILLION SELLER						
Crests	Names Johnny Mastro, Jay Carter, Harold Torres & Tommy Gough						
* 1	16 Candles		0	1958	2	1959	(Coed 506)
2	Six Nights A Week		0	1959	28	1959	(Coed 509)
3	The Angels Listened In		0	1959	22	1959	(Coed 515)
4	Step By Step		0	1960	14	1960	(Coed 525)
5	Trouble In Paradise		0	1960	20	1960	(Coed 531)
Crew Cuts	Male Vocal Group from Toronto, Canada						
1	Crazy 'Bout You Baby		0	1954	8	1954	(Mercury 70341)
* 2	Sh-Boom	(Mercury Mb 3140)	12	1954	1	1954	(Mercury 70404)
3	I Spoke Too Soon		0	1954	24	1954	(Mercury 70404)
4	Oop-Shoop		0	1954	13	1954	(Mercury 70443)
5	Earth Angel	(Mercury Mb 3202)	4	1955	3	1955	(Mercury 70529)
6	Ko Ko Mo (I Love You So)		0	1955	6	1955	(Mercury 70529)
7	Don't Be Angry		0	1955	14	1955	(Mercury 70597)
8	A Story Untold		0	1955	16	1955	(Mercury 70634)
9	Gum Drop		0	1955	10	1955	(Mercury 70668)
10	Angels In The Sky		0	1955	11	1954	(Mercury 70741)
11	Mostly Martha		0	1956	31	1956	(Mercury 70741)
12	Seven Days		0	1956	18	1956	(Mercury 70782)
13	Young Love		0	1957	17	1957	(Mercury 71022)
	NAMES: JOHN & RAY PERKINS, PAT BARRETT & RUDI MAUGERI • ORIGINALLY CALLED THE CANADAIRES BUT CHANGED THEIR NAME IN 1954						
	FORMED IN 1952, THEY DISBANDED IN 1963						

ISSUE	TITLE	UK LBL	UK POS	UK YEAR	US POS	US YEAR	US LBL
Crickets	Names Buddy Holly (Vocals), Niki Sullivan (Drums) & Joe Maulin (Bass)						
* 1	That'll Be The Day	(Vogue Coral Q 72279)	1	1957	3	1957	(Brunswick 55009)
2	Oh Boy	(Coral Q 72298)	3	1957	10	1957	(Brunswick 55035)
3	That'll Be The Day (Re-Entry)	(Vogue Coral Q 72279)	29	1958	0	1958	
4	Maybe Baby	(Coral Q 72307)	4	1958	17	1958	(Brunswick 55053)
5	Think It Over	(Coral Q 72329)	11	1958	27	1958	(Brunswick 55072)
6	Love's Made A Fool Of You	(Coral Q 72365)	26	1959	0	1959	
7	Love's Made A Fool Of You (Re-Entry)	(Coral Q 72365)	30	1959	0	1959	
8	When You Ask About Love	(Coral Q 72382)	27	1960	0	1960	
9	More Than I Can Say	(Coral Q 72395)	42	1960	0	1960	
10	Baby My Heart	(Coral Q 72395)	33	1960	0	1960	
11	Don't Ever Change	(Liberty Lib 55441)	5	1962	0	1962	
12	My Little Girl	(Liberty Lib 10067)	17	1963	0	1963	
13	Don't Try To Change Me	(Liberty Lib 10092)	37	1963	0	1963	
14	You've Got Love	(Coral Q 72472)	40	1964	0	1964	
15	(They Call Her) La Bamba	(Liberty Lib 55696)	21	1964	0	1964	

HIT 14 IS CREDITED TO BUDDY HOLLY & THE CRICKETS
DIFFERENT VERSION OF HIT 1 WAS RELEASED ON DECCA 30434 AND CREDITED TO 'BUDDY HOLLY & THE THREE TUNES'

ISSUE	TITLE	UK LBL	UK POS	UK YEAR	US POS	US YEAR	US LBL
Criminal Element Orchestra	See Wally Jump Jr.						
Crispian St Peters							
1	You Were On My Mind	(Decca F 12287)	2	1966	36	1966	(Jamie 1310)
2	The Pied Piper	(Decca F 12359)	5	1966	4	1966	(Jamie 1320)
3	Changes	(Decca F 12480)	49	1966	0	1966	
Crispy & Company	Male Vocal/Instrumental Group from the USA						
1	Brazil	(Creole Cr 109)	26	1975	0	1975	
2	Get It Together	(Creole Cr 114)	21	1975	0	1975	
Critters	Male Vocal/Instrumental Quintet From New Jersey, USA Lead Singer Don Ciccone Who Later Left To Join The Four Seasons						
1	Younger Girl	(London HI 10047)	38	1966	0	1966	
2	Mr. Dieingly Sad		0	1966	17	1966	(Kapp 769)
3	Don't Let The Rain Fall Down On Me		0	1967	39	1967	(Kapp 838)
Crosby, Stills & Nash	Names David Crosby, Stephen Stills B: 3 Jan 1945 & Graham Nash B: 1942						
1	Marrakesh Express	(Atlantic 584 283)	17	1969	28	1969	(Atlantic 2652)
2	Suite Judy Blue Eyes		0	1969	21	1969	(Atlantic 2676)
3	Woodstock		0	1970	11	1970	(Atlantic 2723)
4	Teach Your Children		0	1970	16	1970	(Atlantic 2735)
5	Ohio		0	1970	14	1970	(Atlantic 2740)
6	Our House		0	1970	30	1970	(Atlantic 2760)
7	Just A Song Before I Go		0	1977	7	1977	(Atlantic 3401)
8	Wasted On The Way		0	1982	9	1982	(Atlantic 4058)
9	Southern Cross		0	1982	18	1982	(Atlantic 89969)
10	American Dream	(Atlantic A 9003)	55	1989	0	1989	

HITS 2-3 ARE CREDITED TO CROSBY, STILLS NASH & YOUNG • SEE ALSO STEPHEN STILLS, NEIL YOUNG • SEE ALSO DAVID CROSBY

ISSUE	TITLE	UK LBL	UK POS	UK YEAR	US POS	US YEAR	US LBL
Cross	Male Vocal/Instrumental Group from the USA/Uk						
1	Cowboys And Indians	(Virgin Vs 1007)	74	1987	0	1987	
Cross Country	Names: Jay Siegel, Phil & Mitch Margo Former Members With The Tokens						
1	In The Midnight Hour		0	1973	30	1973	(Atco 6934)
Crow	Lead Singer With Rock-Blues Quintet Is Dave Wagner From Minneapolis						
1	Evil Woman Don't Play Your Games With Me		0	1969	19	1969	(Amaret 112)
Crowd	Multi-National/Mixed Vocal/Instrumental Charity Assembly						
1	You'll Never Walk Alone	(Spartan Brad 1)	1	1985	0	1985	
Crowded House	Male Vocal/Instrumental Group from the USA/Australia/New Zealand						
1	Don't Dream It's Over	(Capitol Cl 438)	27	1987	2	1987	(Capitol 5614)
2	Something So Strong		0	1987	7	1987	(Capitol 5695)
3	Chocolate Cake	(Capitol Cl 618)	69	1991	0	1991	
4	Fall At Your Feet	(Capitol Cl 626)	17	1991	0	1991	
5	Weather With You	(Capitol Cl 643)	7	1992	0	1992	
6	Four Seasons In One Day	(Capitol Cl 655)	26	1992	0	1992	
7	It's Only Natural	(Capitol Cl 661)	24	1992	0	1992	
8	Distant Sun	(Capitol Cdcls 697)	19	1993	0	1993	
9	Nails In My Feet	(Capitol Cdcls 701)	22	1993	0	1993	
10	Locked Out	(Capitol Cdcls 707)	12	1994	0	1994	
11	Fingers Of Love	(Capitol Cdcls 715)	25	1994	0	1994	

ISSUE	TITLE	UK LBL	UK POS	UK YEAR	US POS	US YEAR	US LBL
12	Pineapple Head	(Capitol Cdcls 723)	27	1994	0	1994	
13	Instinct	(Capitol Cdcls 774)	12	1996	0	1996	
14	Not The Girl You Think You Are	(Capitol Cdcls 776)	20	1996	0	1996	
15	Don't Dream It's Over (Re-Issue)	(Capitol Cdcls 780)	25	1996	0	1996	
	NAMES: NEIL FINN, PAUL HESTER & NICK SEYMOUR. • THEY WERE LATER JOINED BY TIM FINN (OF SPLIT ENZ) IN 1991						

Crown Heights Affair Male Vocal/Instrumental Group from the USA

1	Galaxy Of Love	(Mercury 6168 801)	24	1978	0	1978	
2	I'm Gonna Love You Forever	(Mercury 6168 803)	47	1978	0	1978	
3	Dance Lady Dance	(Mercury 6168 804)	44	1979	0	1979	
4	You Gave Me Love	(De-Lite Mer 9)	10	1980	0	1980	
5	You've Been Gone	(De-Lite Mer 28)	44	1980	0	1980	

Crows Male R&B quartet from New York, USA

1	Gee		0	1954	14	1954	(RAMA 5)

Crusaders Male Vocal/Instrumental group from the USA

1	Street Life	(MCA 513)	5	1979	0	1979	
2	I'm So Glad I'm Standing Here Today	(MCA 741)	61	1981	0	1981	
3	Night Ladies	(MCA MCA 853)	55	1984	0	1984	
	VOCALS ON HIT 1 ARE BY RANDY CRAWFORD. • HIT 2 IS CREDITED TO THE CRUSADERS FEATURING JOE COCKER						

Crush Female Vocal Duo from the UK

1	Jellyhead	(Telstar CDsras 2833)	50	1996	72	1996	(Robbins 72002)
2	Luv'd Up	(Telstar Cdstas 2833)	45	1996	0	1996	

Cry Before Dawn Male Vocal/Instrumental Group from Ireland

1	Witness For The World	(Epic Gone 3)	67	1989	0	1989	

Cry Of Love Mixed Vocal/Instrumental Group from the USA

1	Bad Thing	(Columbia 6600462)	60	1994	0	1994	

Cry Sisco! Real Name Barry Blue Male Producer/Vocalist from the UK

1	Afro Dizzi Act	(Escape awol 1)	42	1989	0	1989	
2	Afro Dizzi Act (re-entry)	(Escape awol 1)	70	1990	0	1990	

Cryin' Shames male vocal/instrumental group from the UK

1	Please Stay	(Decca f 12340)	26	1966	0	1966	

Crystal Gayle Female vocalist, real name brenda gail webb b: 9 sep 1951 Paintsville, Kentucky

9	I'll Get Over You		0	1976	71	1976	(United Artist 781)
* 13	Don't It Make My Brown Eyes Blue	(United Artists up 36307)	5	1977	2	1977	(United Artist 1016)
15	Ready For The Times To Get Better		0	1978	52	1978	(United Artist 1136)
16	Talking in Your Sleep	(United Artists up 36422)	11	1978	18	1978	(columbia 1214)
20	Half the Way		0	1979	15	1979	(columbia 11087)
22	It's Like We Never Said Goodbye		0	1980	63	1980	(Columbia 11198)
27	Take It Easy		0	1981	17	1981	(Columbia 11436)
32	You andl		0	1982	7	1982	(elektra 69936)
33	'til I Gain Control Again		0	1982	1	1982	(Elektra 69893)
	OTHER HITS ARE C/W						

Crystal Palace F.C. Male Vocal Soccer Team from the UK)

1	Glad All Over / Where Eagles Fly	(Parkfield Pms 5019)	50	1990	0	1990	

Crystal Waters Female R&B-Dance Singer from South New Jersey

* 1	Gypsy Woman (La Da Dee)	(A&M Am 772)	2	1991	8	1991	(Mercury 868208)
2	Makin' Happy	(A&M Am 790)	18	1991	0	1991	
3	Megamix	(A&M Am 843)	39	1992	0	1992	
4	Gypsy Woman (La Da Dee) (Re-Mix)	(Epic 6584377)	35	1992	0	1992	
* 5	100% Pure Love	(A&M 8586692)	15	1994	11	1994	(Mercury 858485)
6	Ghetto Day	(A&M 8589592)	40	1994	0	1994	
7	Relax	(Manifesto Fescd 4)	37	1995	0	1995	
8	In De Ghetto	(Manifesto Fescd 12)	35	1996	0	1996	
9	Say... If You Feel Alright	(Mercury 5742912)	45	1997	40	1997	(Mercury 578943)
	THEB SIDE OF HIT 4 WAS HIT 4 BY SABRINA JOHNSON. • HIT 8 IS CREDITED TO 'DAVID MORALES & THE BAD YARD CLUB' FEATURING 'CRYSTAL WATERS' & 'DELTA'						

Crystals Female Vocal Group from the USA

1	There's No Other (Like My Baby)		0	1961	20	1961	(Philles 100)
2	Uptown		0	1962	13	1962	(Philles 102)
* 3	He's A Rebel	(London Hlu 9611)	19	1962	1	1962	(Philles 106)
4	He's Sure The Boy I Love		0	1962	11	1962	(Philles 109)
* 5	Da Doo Ron Ron	(London Hlu 9732)	5	1963	3	1963	(Philles 112)
* 6	Then He Kissed Me	(London Hlu 9773)	2	1963	6	1963	(Philles 115)
7	Little Boy		0	1964	92	1964	(Philles 119)

ISSUE	TITLE	UK LBL	UK POS	UK YEAR	US POS	US YEAR	US LBL
8	All Grown Up		0	1964	98	1964	(Philles 122)
9	I Wonder	(London Hlu 9852)	36	1964	0	1964	
10	Do Doo Ron Ron (Re-Issue)	(Warner Spector K 19010)	15	1974	0	1974	

HIT 3 WAS WRITTEN BY GENE PITNEY • NAMES: BARBARA ALSTON, LALA BROOKS, DEE DEE KENNIBREW, MARY THOMAS & PATRICA WRIGHT

Csilla   Female Vocalist from Hungary

1	Man In The Moon	(Worx Worxcd 001	69	1996	0	1996	

Cuba Gooding   Male Vocalist from the USA

1	Happiness Is Just Around The Bend	(London Lon 41)	72	1983	0	1983	

Cubic 22   Male Production/Instrumental Duo from Belgium

1	Night In Motion	(Xl Xls 20)	15	1991	0	1991	

Cud   Male Vocal/Instrumental Group from the UK

1	Oh No Won't Do (Ep)	(A&M Amb 829)	49	1991	0	1991	
2	Through The Roof	(A&M Am 857)	44	1992	0	1992	
	Rich And Strange	(A&M Am 871)	24	1992	0	1992	
4	Purple Love Balloon	(A&M Am 0024)	27	1992	0	1992	
5	Once Again	(A&M Am 0081)	45	1992	0	1992	
6	Neurotica	(A&M 5805172)	37	1994	0	1994	
7	Sticks And Stones	(A&M 5805472)	68	1994	0	1994	
8	One Giant Love	(A&M 5807292)	52	1994	0	1994	

Cuff Links   Male Vocal Group from the USA   Studio Created Group From The Voices Of Ron Dante

* 1	Tracy	(MCA Mu 1101)	4	1969	9	1969	(Decca 32533)
2	When Julie Comes Around	(MCA Mu 1112)	10	1970	0	1970	

Cult   Male Vocal/Instrumental Group from the UK

1	Ressurection Joe	(Beggars Banquet Beg 122)	74	1984	0	1984	
2	She Sells Sanctuary	(Beggars Banquet Beg 135)	15	1985	0	1985	
3	She Sells Sanctuary (Re-Entry)	(Beggars Banquet Beg 135)	61	1985	0	1985	
4	Rain	(Beggars Banquet Beg 147)	17	1985	0	1985	
5	Revolution	(Beggars Banquet Beg 152)	30	1985	0	1985	
6	Love Removal Machine	(Beggars Banquet Beg 182)	18	1987	0	1987	
7	Lil' Devil	(Beggars Banquet Beg 188)	11	1987	0	1987	
8	Wild Flower (Double Single)	(Beggars Banquet Beg 195)	30	1987	0	1987	
9	Fire Woman	(Beggars Banquet Beg 228)	15	1989	0	1989	
10	Edie (Ciao Baby)	(Beggars Banquet Beg 230)	32	1989	0	1989	
11	Sun King - Edie (Ciao Baby) (Re-Issue)	(Beggars Banquet Beg 235)	39	1989	0	1989	
12	Sweet Soul Sister	(Beggars Banquet Beg 241)	42	1990	0	1990	
13	Wild Hearted Son	(Beggars Banquet Beg 255)	40	1991	0	1991	
14	Heart And Soul	(Beggars Banquet Beg 260)	51	1992	0	1992	
15	She Sells Sanctuary (Re-Mix)	(Beggars Banquet Beg 253cd)	15	1993	0	1993	
16	Coming Down	(Beggars Banquet Bbq 40cd)	50	1994	0	1994	
17	Star	(Beggars Banquet Bbq 45cd)	65	1995	0	1995	

Culture Beat   Mixed Vocal/Instrumental Group from the USA/UK/Germany

1	Cherry Lips (Der Erdbeermund)	(Epic 65563 7)	55	1990	0	1990	
* 2	Mr. Vain	(Epic 6594682)	1	1993	17	1993	(550 Music 77259)
3	Got To Get It	(Epic 6597212)	4	1993	0	1993	
4	Anything	(Epic 6600252)	5	1994	0	1994	
5	World In Your Hands	(Epic 6602292)	20	1994	0	1994	
6	Inside Out	(Epic 6626562)	32	1996	0	1996	
7	Crying In The Rain	(Epic 6633582)	29	1996	0	1996	
8	Take Me Away	(Epic 6637552)	52	1996	0	1996	

Culture Club   Male Vocal/Instrumental Group from the UK   Names Boy George, Roy Hay, Michael Craig & Jon Moss.   See Also Boy George & Jesus Loves You

1	Do You Really Want To Hurt Me	(Virgin Vs 518)	1	1982	2	1983	(Virgin 03368)
2	Time (Clock Of The Heart)	(Virgin Vs 558)	3	1982	2	1983	(Virgin 03796)
3	Church Of The Poison Mind	(Virgin Vs 571)	2	1983	10	1983	(Epic 04144)
4	I'll Tumble 4 Ya		0	1983	9	1983	(Virgin 03912)
* 5	Karma Chameleon	(Virgin Vs 612)	1	1983	1	1984	(Virgin 04221)
6	Victims	(Virgin Vs 641)	3	1983	0	1983	
7	Miss Me Blind		0	1984	5	1984	(Virgin 04388)
8	It's A Miracle	(Virgin Vs 662)	4	1984	13	1984	(Virgin 04457)
9	The War Song	(Virgin Vs 694)	2	1984	17	1984	(Virgin 04638)
10	The Medal Song	(Virgin Vs 730)	32	1984	0	1984	
11	Mistake No.3		0	1985	33	1985	(Virgin 04727)
12	The Medal Song (Re-Entry)	(Virgin Vs 730)	74	1985	0	1985	
13	Move Away	(Virgin Vs 845)	7	1986	12	1986	(Virgin 05847)
14	God Thank You Woman	(Virgin Vs 861)	31	1986	0	1986	

ISSUE	TITLE	UK LBL	UK POS	UK YEAR	US POS	US YEAR	US LBL
Cupid's Inspiration Male Vocal/Instrumental Group from the UK							
1	Yesterday Has Gone	(Nems 56 3500)	4	1968	0	1968	
2	My World	(Nems 56 3702)	33	1968	0	1968	
Cure Male Vocal/Instrumental Group from the UK							
1	A Forest	(Fiction Fics 10)	31	1980	0	1980	
2	Primary	(Fiction Fics 12)	43	1981	0	1981	
3	Charlotte Sometimes	(Fiction Fics 14)	44	1981	0	1981	
4	Hanging Garden	(Fiction Fics 15)	34	1982	0	1982	
5	Let's Go To Bed	(Fiction Fics 17)	44	1982	0	1982	
6	Let's Go To Bed (Re-Entry)	(Fiction Fics 17)	75	1983	0	1983	
7	The Walk	(Fiction Fics 18)	12	1983	0	1983	
8	The Love Cats	(Fiction Fics 19)	7	1983	0	1983	
9	The Caterpillar	(Fiction Fics 20)	14	1984	0	1984	
10	In Between Days	(Fiction Fics 22)	15	1985	0	1985	
11	Close To Me	(Fiction Fics 23)	24	1985	0	1985	
12	Boys Don't Cry	(Fiction Fics 24)	22	1986	0	1986	
13	Why Can't I Be You	(Fiction Fics 25)	21	1987	0	1987	
14	Catch	(Fiction Fics 26)	27	1987	0	1987	
15	Just Like Heaven	(Fiction Fics 27)	29	1987	40	1987	(Elektra 69443)
16	Hot Hot Hot!!!	(Fiction Ficsx 28)	45	1988	0	1988	
17	Lullaby	(Fiction Fics 29)	5	1989	0	1989	
18	Love Song	(Fiction Fics 30)	18	1989	2	1989	(Elektra 69280)
19	Pictures Of You	(Fiction Fics 34)	24	1990	0	1990	
20	Never Enough	(Fiction Fics 35)	13	1990	0	1990	
21	Close To Me (Re-Mix)	(Fiction Fics 36)	13	1990	0	1990	
22	High	(Fiction Fics 39)	8	1992	0	1992	
23	High (Re-Mix)	(Fiction Ficxs 41)	44	1992	0	1992	
24	Friday I'm In Love	(Fiction Fics 42)	6	1992	18	1992	(Fiction 64742)
25	A Letter To Elise	(Fiction Fics 46)	28	1992	0	1992	
26	The 13th	(Fiction St 64692)	15	1996	44	1996	
27	Mint Car	(Fiction Ficcd 52)	31	1996	0	1996	
28	Gone	(Fiction Ficdd 53)	60	1996	0	1996	
Curiosity Male Vocal/Instrumental Group from the UK for hits 1-4 also Curiosity Killed the Cat							
1	Down To Earth	(Mercury Cat 2)	3	1986	0	1986	
2	Ordinary Day	(Mercury Cat 3)	11	1987	0	1987	
3	Misfit	(Mercury Cat 4)	7	1987	0	1987	
4	Free	(Mercury Cat 5)	56	1987	0	1987	
5	Name And Number	(Mercury Cat 6)	14	1989	0	1989	
6	Hang On In There Baby	(RCA Pb 45377)	3	1992	0	1992	
7	I Need Your Lovin'	(RCA 74321111377)	47	1992	0	1992	
8	Gimme The Sunshine	(RCA 74321168602)	73	1993	0	1993	
Curtis Hairston Male Vocalist from the USA							
1	I Want You (All Tonight)	(RCA 368)	44	1983	0	1983	
2	I Want Your Lovin'	(London Lon 66)	13	1985	0	1985	
3	Chillin' Out	(Atlantic A 9335)	57	1986	0	1986	
Curtis Lee							
1	Pretty Little Angel Eyes	(London Hlx 9397)	47	1961	7	1961	(Dunes 2007)
2	Pretty Little Angel Eyes (Re-Entry)	(London Hlx 9397)	48	1961	0	1961	
3	Under The Moon Of Love		0	1961	46	1961	(Dunes 2008)
Curtis Mayfield Male Vocalist, B: 3 Jun 1942 Chicago							
1	(Don't Worry) If There's A Hell Below, We're All Going To Go		0	1970	29	1970	(Curtom 1955)
* 2	Move On Up	(Buddah 2011 080)	12	1971	0	1971	
3	Freddie's Dead (Theme From Superfly)		0	1972	4	1972	(Curtom 1975)
* 4	Superfly (From Superfly)		0	1972	8	1972	(Curtom 1978)
5	Future Shock		0	1973	39	1973	(Curtom 1987)
6	Kung Fu		0	1974	40	1974	(Curtom 1999)
7	No Goodbyes	(Atlantic LV 1)	65	1978	0	1978	
8	(Celebrate) The Day After You	(RCA Monk 6)	52	1987	0	1987	
9	Superfly 1990	(Capitol Cl 586)	48	1990	0	1990	

HIT 8 IS CREDITED TO BLOW MONKEYS WITH CURTIS MAYFIELD. • HIT 9 IS CREDITED TO CURTIS MAYFIELD AND ICE-T
PREVIOUS GROUPS WERE THE IMPRESSIONS & NORTHERN JUBILEE SINGERS

ISSUE	TITLE	UK LBL	UK POS	UK YEAR	US POS	US YEAR	US LBL
Curtis Stigers Male Vocalist/Saxophonist from Boise, Idaho							
1	I Wonder Why	(Arista 114716)	5	1992	9	1991	(Arista 12331)
2	You're All That Matters To Me	(Arista 115273)	6	1992	0	1992	

ISSUE	TITLE	UK LBL	UK POS	UK YEAR	US POS	US YEAR	US LBL
3	Sleeping With The Lights On	(Arista 74321102307)	53	1992	0	1992	
4	Never Saw A Miracle	(Arista 74321117257)	34	1992	0	1992	
5	This Time	(Arista 74321286962)	28	1995	0	1995	
6	Keep Me From The Cold	(Arista 74321319162)	57	1995	0	1995	

Curve   Mixed Vocal Duo from the UK

ISSUE	TITLE	UK LBL	UK POS	UK YEAR	US POS	US YEAR	US LBL
1	The Blindfold (EP)	(Anxious Anx 27)	68	1991	0	1991	
2	Coast Is Clear	(Anxious Anx 30)	34	1991	0	1991	
3	Clipped	(Anxious Anx 35)	36	1991	0	1991	
4	Fait Accompli (EP)	(Anxious Anxt 36)	22	1992	0	1992	
5	Horror Head (EP)	(Anxious Anxt 38)	31	1992	0	1992	
6	Blackerthreetracker (EP)	(Anxious Anxcd 42)	39	1993	0	1993	

Curved Air   Mixed Vocal/Instrumental Group from the UK

ISSUE	TITLE	UK LBL	UK POS	UK YEAR	US POS	US YEAR	US LBL
1	Back Street Luv	(Warner Bros K 16092)	4	1971	0	1971	

Cut 'N' Move   Mixed Vocal/Instrumental Group from Denmark

ISSUE	TITLE	UK LBL	UK POS	UK YEAR	US POS	US YEAR	US LBL
1	Give It Up	(Emi Cdem 273)	61	1993	0	1993	
2	I'm Alive	(Emi Cdem 375)	49	1995	0	1995	

Cutting Crew   Male Vocal/Instrumental Group from the UK/Canada

ISSUE	TITLE	UK LBL	UK POS	UK YEAR	US POS	US YEAR	US LBL
1	(I Just) Died In Your Arms	(Siren Siren 21)	4	1986	1	1987	(Virgin 99481)
2	I've Been In Love Before	(Siren Siren 29)	31	1986	9	1987	(Virgin 99425)
3	I've Been In Love Before (Re-Entry)	(Siren Siren 29)	70	1987	0	1987	
4	One For The Mockingbird	(Siren Siren 40)	52	1987	38	1987	(Virgin 99464)
5	I've Been In Love Before (Re-Mix)	(Siren Siren 29)	24	1987	0	1987	
6	(Between A) Rock And A Hard Place	(Siren Srn 108)	66	1989	0	1989	

NAMES "NICK VAN EEDE, KEVIN SCOTT MACMICHAEL, COLIN FARLEY & MARTIN BEEDLE

Cybersonik   Male Sampling Group from the USA

ISSUE	TITLE	UK LBL	UK POS	UK YEAR	US POS	US YEAR	US LBL
1	Technarchy	(Champion Champ 264)	73	1990	0	1990	

Cyndi Lauper   Female Vocalist, B: 20 Jun 1953 Queens, New York

	ISSUE	TITLE	UK LBL	UK POS	UK YEAR	US POS	US YEAR	US LBL
*	1	Girls Just Want To Have Fun	(Portrait A 3943)	2	1984	2	1984	(Portrait 04120)
*	2	Time After Time	(Portrait A 4290)	54	1984	1	1984	(Portrait 04432)
	3	Time After Time (Re-Entry)	(Portrait A 4290)	3	1984	0	1984	
*	4	She Bop	(Portrait A 4620)	46	1984	3	1984	(Portrait 04516)
	5	All Through The Night	(Portrait A 4849)	64	1984	5	1984	(Portrait 04639)
	6	Money Changes Everything		0	1985	27	1985	(Portrait 04737)
	7	The Goonies 'R' Good Enough (From The Goonies)		0	1985	10	1985	(Portrait 04918)
	8	True Colours	(Portrait 650026 7)	12	1986	1	1986	(Portrait 06247)
	9	Change Of Heart	(Portrait Cyndi 1)	74	1986	3	1987	(Portrait 06431)
	10	Change Of Heart (Re-Entry)	(Portrait Cyndi 1)	67	1987	0	1987	
	11	What's Going On	(Portrait Cyn 1)	57	1987	12	1987	(Portrait 06970)
	12	I Drove All Night	(Portrait Cyn 4)	7	1989	6	1989	(Epic 68759)
	13	My First Night Without You	(Portrait Cyn 5)	53	1989	0	1989	
	14	Heading West	(Portrait Cyn 6)	68	1989	0	1989	
	15	The World Is Stone	(Epic 6579707)	15	1992	0	1992	
	16	That's What I Think	(Epic 6598782)	31	1993	0	1993	
	17	Who Let In The Rain	(Epic 6590392)	32	1994	0	1994	
	18	Hey Now (Girls Just Want To Have Fun)	(Epic 6608072)	4	1994	0	1994	
	19	I'm Gonna Be Strong	(Epic 6611962)	37	1995	0	1995	
	20	Come On Home	(Epic 6614255)	39	1995	0	1995	
	21	You Don't Know	(Epic 6641845)	27	1997	0	1997	

HIT 18 WAS A RE-RECORDING OF HIT 1. SHE ALSO RECORDED WITH A GROUP CALLED THE BLUE ANGELS IN 1980

Cypress Hill   Male Rap Trio Group from Los Angeles

	ISSUE	TITLE	UK LBL	UK POS	UK YEAR	US POS	US YEAR	US LBL
*	1	Insane In The Brain	(Ruff House 6595332)	32	1993	19	1993	(Ruffhouse 77135)
	2	When The Sh.. Goes Down	(Ruff House 6596702)	19	1993	0	1993	
	3	I Ain't Goin' Out Like That	(Ruff House 6596902)	15	1993	0	1993	
*	4	Blue Star (The Medic Theme)	(Decca F 10559)	2	1955	0	1955	
	5	The Italian Theme	(Decca F 10703)	18	1956	25	1956	(London 1672)
	6	The Happy Whistler	(Decca F 10735)	22	1956	0	1956	
	7	Forgotten Dreams	(Decca F 10912)	27	1957	0	1957	
	8	The Children's Marching Song (Nick Nack Paddy Wack)		0	1959	13	1959	(London 1851)

HIT 4 IS CREDITED TO CYRIL STAPLETON & HIS ORCHESTRA FEATURING JULIE DAWN.
HIT 6 IS TO CYRIL STAPLETON & HIS ORCHESTRA FEATURING DESMOND LANE, PENNY WHISTLE
HIT 8 IS WITH THE CHILDREN FROM THE FILM *THE INN OF THE SIXTH HAPPINESS*. • OBITUARY : D: 25 FEB 1974

Cyrkle   Originally The Rondells

	ISSUE	TITLE	UK LBL	UK POS	UK YEAR	US POS	US YEAR	US LBL
*	1	Red Rubber Ball		0	1966	2	1966	(Columbia 43589)
	2	Turn-Down Day		0	1966	16	1966	(Columbia 43729)

D

ISSUE	TITLE	UK LBL	UK POS	UK YEAR	US POS	US YEAR	US LBL
D Train Male Vocal/Instrumental Duo from the USA							
1	You're The One For Me	(Epic EPC A 2016)	30	1982	0	1982	
2	Walk On By	(Epic EPC A 2298)	44	1982	0	1982	
3	Music Part I	(Prelude A 3332)	23	1983	0	1983	
4	Keep Giving Me Love	(Prelude A 3479)	65	1983	0	1983	
5	You're The One For Me (Re-Mix)	(Prelude ZB 40302)	15	1985	0	1985	
6	Music	(Prelude ZB 40431)	62	1985	0	1985	
D'Angelo Male Singer/Songwriter from Richmond, Virginia, Full Name Michael D'Angelo Archer							
1	Brown Sugar	(Cooltempo CDCool 307)	24	1995	27	1995	(EMI 58360)
2	Cruisin'	(Cooltempo CDCool 316)	31	1996	0	1996	
3	Cold World	(Geffen GFSTD 22114)	40	1996	0	1996	
4	Lady	(Cooltempo CDCool 323)	21	1996	10	1996	
5	Me And Those Dreamin' Eyes Of Mine		0	1996	74	1996	(EMI 58570)
	HIT 3 IS CREDITED TO GENIUS/GZA FEATURING D'ANGELO						
D'Bora Female Vocalist from the USA							
1	Dream About You	(Polydor PO 161)	75	1991	0	1991	
2	Going Round	(MCA MCSTD 2055)	40	1995	0	1995	
3	Good Love, Real Love	(Music Plant MCSTD 40023)	58	1996	0	1996	
D'Lux Mixed Vocal/Instrumental Group from the UK							
1	Love Resurrection	(LOGIC 74321371012)	58	1996	0	1996	
D, B, M & T Male Vocal/Instrumental Group from the UK See Also Dave Dee, Dozy, Beaky, Mick & Tich							
1	Mr. President	(Fontana 6007022)	33	1970	0	1970	
D-Influence Mixed Vocal/Instrumental Group from the UK							
1	Good Lover	(East West A 8573)	46	1992	0	1992	
2	Good Lover (Re-Mix)	(East West A 8439CD)	61	1993	0	1993	
3	Midnight	(East West A 4418CD)	58	1995	0	1995	
4	Hypnotize	(Echo ECSCD 41)	33	1997	0	1997	
D-Mob Male Producer/Mixer Danny D from the UK Lead Singer Was Cathy Dennis Who Left In 1991							
1	We Call It Acieed	(FFRR FFR 13)	3	1988	0	1988	
2	It Is Time To Get Funky	(FFRR F 107)	9	1989	0	1989	
3	C'mon And Get My Love	(FFRR F 117)	15	1989	10	1990	(FFRR 996798)
4	Put Your Hands Together	(FFRR F 124)	7	1990	0	1990	
5	That's The Way Of The World	(FFRR F 132)	48	1990	0	1990	
6	Why	(FFRR FCD 227)	23	1994	0	1994	
7	One Day	(FFRR FCDP 239)	41	1994	0	1994	
D-Shake Male Production Duo from Holland							
1	Yaaah / Techno Trance	(Cooltempo Cool 213)	20	1990	0	1990	
2	My Heart The Beat	(Cooltempo Cool 228)	42	1991	0	1991	
D-Tek Male Production/Instrumental Group from the UK							
1	Drop The Rock (EP)	(Positiva 12TIV 5)	70	1993	0	1993	
D.B.M. Mixed Vocal/Instrumental Group from Germany							
1	Disco Beatlemania	(Atlantic K 11027)	45	1977	0	1977	
D.O.P. Male Instrumental/Production Duo from the UK							
1	Stop Starting To Start Stopping (EP)	(HI-LIFE 5779472)	58	1996	0	1996	
2	Groovy Beat	(Hi-Life 5750652)	54	1996	0	1996	
D.R.S. Male Vocal Quintet from the USA D.R.S. stands for Dirty Rotten Scoundrels							
* 1	Gangsta Lean		0	1993	4	1993	(Capitol 44958)
D.S.M. Male Rap Group from the USA							
1	Warrior Groove	(10 DAZZ 45-7)	68	1985	0	1985	

ISSUE	TITLE	UK LBL	UK POS	UK YEAR	US POS	US YEAR	US LBL
D.T.I. Male Vocal/Instrumental Group from the USA							
1	Keep This Frequency Clear/Keep It Clear	(Premiere UK ERE 501)	73	1988	0	1988	
D:Ream Male Vocal/Instrumental Duo from the UK							
1	U R The Best Thing	(FXU FXU 3)	72	1992	0	1992	
2	Things Can Only Get Better	(Magnet Mag 1010CD)	24	1993	0	1993	
3	U R The Best Thing (Re-Mix)	(Magnet Mag 1011CD)	19	1993	0	1993	
4	Unforgiven	(Magnet Mag1016CD)	29	1993	0	1993	
5	Star / I Like It	(Magnet Mag1019CD)	26	1993	0	1993	
6	Things Can Only Get Better (Re-Mix)	(Magnet Mag 1020CD)	1	1994	0	1994	
7	U R The Best Thing (2nd Re-Mix)	(Magnet Mag1021CD)	4	1994	0	1994	
8	Take Me Away	(Magnet Mag 025CD)	18	1994	0	1994	
9	Blame It On Me	(Magnet Mag1027CD)	24	1994	0	1994	
10	Shoot Me With Your Love	(Magnet Mag 1034CD)	7	1995	0	1995	
11	Party Up The World	(Magnet Mag 1037CD)	20	1995	0	1995	
12	The Power (Of All The Love In The World)	(Magnet Mag 1039CD)	40	1995	0	1995	
13	Things Can Only Get Better	(Magnet Mag 1050CD)	19	1997	0	1997	
Da Brat Female Rapper from the USA, Real Name Shawntae Harris							
* 1	Funkdafied	(Columbia 6609212)	65	1994	6	1994	(SO SO DEF 77532)
2	Fa All Y'all		0	1994	37	1994	(SO SO DEF 77594)
* 3	Give It 2 You		0	1995	26	1995	(SO SO DEF 77836)
4	Sittin' On Top Of The World		0	1996	30	1996	(SO SO DEF 78426)
5	Ghetto Love		0	1997	16	1997	(SO SO DEF 78527)
Da Lench Mob Male Rap Group from the USA							
1	Freedom Got An A.K.	(East West America 8431CD)A	51	1993	0	1993	
Dada Male Vocal/Instrumental Group from the USA							
1	Dog	(IRS CDEIRSS 185)	71	1993	0	1993	
Daddy Dewdrop Richard Monda is Daddy Dewdrop							
1	Chick-A-Boom (Don't Ya Jes' Love It)		0	1971	9	1971	(Sunflower 105)
Daddy-O's Male Producer, Billy Mure from the USA							
1	Got A Match		0	1958	39	1958	(Cabut 122)
Daffy Duck Male Production/Instrumental Group from Germany							
1	Party Zone	(East West YZ 592)	58	1991	0	1991	
	HIT IS CREDITED TO DAFFY DUCK FEATURING THE GROOVE GANG						
Dagmar Female Vocalist from the USA, Real Name Jennie Lewis Hit Is also Credited To Frank Sinatra							
1	Mama Will Bark		0	1951	21	1951	(Columbia 39425)
Daisy Chainsaw Mixed Vocal/Instrumental Group from the UK							
1	Love Your Money	(DEVA DEVA	26	1992	0	1992	
2	Pink Flower / Room Eleven	(DEVA 82 TP7)	65	1992	0	1992	
Dakotas Male Instrumental Group from the UK See Also Billy J. Kramer & The Dakotas							
1	The Cruel Sea	(Parlophone R 5044)	18	1963	0	1963	
Dale & Grace Mixed Vocal Duo from Louisiana, USA. Dale Houston & Grace Broussard							
* 1	I'm Leaving It Up To You	(London HL 9807)	42	1964	1	1963	(Montel 921)
2	Stop And Think It Over		0	1964	8	1964	(Montel 922)
Dale Hawkins Real Name Delmar Allen Hawkins B: 22 Aug 1938 Louisiana							
1	Susie-Q		0	1957	27	1957	(Checker 863)
2	La-Do-Dada		0	1958	32	1958	(Checker 900)
3	A House, A Car And A Wedding Ring		0	1958	88	1958	(Checker 906)
4	Class Cutter (Yeh Yeh)		0	1959	52	1959	(Checker 916)
Dale Sisters Female Vocal Group from the USA							
1	My Sunday Baby	(Ember S 140)	36	1961	0	1961	
Dale Wright & The Rock-Its Real Name Harian Dale Riffe B: 4 Feb 1938 Middletown, Ohio							
1	She's Neat		0	1958	38	1958	(Fraternity 792)
Dali's Car Male Vocal/Instrumental Duo from the UK							
1	The Judgement Is The Mirror	(Paradox DOX 1)	66	1984	0	1984	
Damage Male Vocal Group from the USA							
1	Anything	(Big Life BLRD 129)	68	1996	0	1996	
2	Love Ii Love	(Big Life BLRD 131)	12	1996	0	1996	
3	Forever	(Big Life BLRDB 132)	6	1996	0	1996	
4	Love Guaranteed	(Big Life BLRDA 133)	7	1997	0	1997	
5	Wonderful Tonight	(Big Life BLRDA 134)	3	1997	0	1997	

ISSUE	TITLE	UK LBL	UK POS	UK YEAR	US POS	US YEAR	US LBL
6	Love Guaranteed (Re-Entry)	Big Life BLRDA 133)	73	1997	0	1997	
7	Love Lady	(Big Life BLRDB 137)	33	1997	0	1997	
Damian	Male Vocalist from the UK						
1	The Time Warp 2	(Jive Jive 160)	51	1987	0	1987	
2	The Time Warp 2 (Re-Issue)	(Jive Jive 182)	64	1988	0	1988	
3	The Time Warp 2 (Re-Mix)	(Jive Jive 209)	7	1989	0	1989	
4	Wig Wam Bam	(Jive Jive 236)	49	1989	0	1989	
Damita Joe	Female Vocalist, B: Damita Jo DuBlanc In Austin, Texas						
1	I Don't Care		0	1953	29	1953	(RCA Victor 5022)
2	I'll Save The Last Dance For You		0	1960	22	1960	(Mercury 71690)
3	I'll Be There		0	1961	12	1961	(Mercury 71840)
Damn Yankees	Names Ted Nugent, Jack Blades, Tommy Shaw & Michael Cartellone						
* 1	High Enough		0	1990	3	1990	(Warner Bros. 19595)
2	Where You Goin' Now		0	1992	20	1992	(Warner Bros. 18728)
Damned	Male Vocal/Instrumental Group from the UK						
1	Love Song	(Chiswick CHIS 112)	20	1979	0	1979	
2	Smash It Up	(Chiswick CHIS 116)	35	1979	0	1979	
3	I Just Can't Be Happy Today	(Chiswick CHIS 120)	46	1979	0	1979	
4	History Of The World (Part 1)	(Chiswick CHIS 135)	51	1980	0	1980	
5	Friday 13th (EP)	(Stale One Try 1)	50	1981	0	1981	
6	Lovely Money	(Bronze BRO 149)	42	1982	0	1982	
7	Thanks For The Night	(Damned Damned 1)	42	1984	0	1984	
8	Grimly Fiendish	(MCA GRIM 1)	21	1985	0	1985	
9	The Shadow Of Love	(MCA GRIM 2)	25	1985	0	1985	
10	Is It A Dream	(MCA GRIM 3)	34	1985	0	1985	
11	Eloise	(MCA GRIM 4)	3	1986	0	1986	
12	Eloise (Re-Entry)	(MCA GRIM 4)	72	1986	0	1986	
13	Anything	(MCA GRIM 5)	32	1986	0	1986	
14	Gigolo	(MCA GRIM 6)	29	1987	0	1987	
15	Alone Again Or	(MCA GRIM 7)	27	1987	0	1987	
16	In Dulce Decorum	(MCA GRIM 8)	72	1987	0	1987	
Dan Baird	Male Vocalist, B: 12 Dec 1953 San Diego, Now Hails from Atlanta, USA						
1	I Love You Period		0	1993	26	1993	(DEF America18724)
Dan Fogelberg	Male Vocalist, B: 13 Aug 1951 Illinois						
1	Part Of The Plan		0	1975	31	1975	(Epic 50055)
2	The Power Of Gold		0	1978	24	1978	(Full Moon50606)
3	Longer	(Epic EPC 8230)	59	1980	2	1980	(Full Moon50824)
4	Heart Hotels		0	1980	21	1980	(Full Moon50862)
5	Same Old Lang Syne		0	1980	9	1980	(Full Moon 50961)
6	Hard To Say		0	1981	7	1981	(Full Moon 02488)
7	Leader Of The Band		0	1982	9	1982	(Full Moon 02647)
8	Run For The Roses		0	1982	18	1982	(Full Moon 02821)
9	Missing You		0	1982	23	1982	(Full Moon 03289)
10	Make Love Stay		0	1983	29	1983	(Full Moon 03525)
11	The Language Of Love		0	1984	13	1984	(Full Moon 04314)
12	Go Down Easy		0	1985	85	1985	(Full Moon 04835)
Dan Hartman	Male Vocalist from Harrisburg, Pennsylvania						
* 1	Instant Replay	(SKY 6706)	8	1978	29	1978	(Blue Sky 2772)
2	This Is It	(Blue Sky SKY 6999)	17	1979	0	1979	
3	I Can Dream About You	(MCA MCA 988)	12	1985	6	1984	(MCA 52378)
4	We Are The Young		0	1984	25	1984	(MCA 52471)
5	Second Nature	(MCA MCA 957)	66	1985	39	1985	(MCA 52519)
6	Keep The Fire Burnin'	(Columbia 6613022)	49	1995	0	1995	
Dan Hill	Male Vocalist, B: 3 Jun 1954 Toronto						
* 1	Sometimes When We Touch	(20th Century BTC 2355)	46	1978	3	1978	(20th Century 2355)
2	Sometimes When We Touch (Re-Entry)	(20th Century BTC 2355)	13	1978	0	1978	
3	Can't We Try		0	1987	6	1987	(Columbia 07050)
Dan McCafferty	Male Vocalist from the UK						
1	Out Of Time	(Mountain Top 1)	41	1975	0	1975	
Dan Reed Network	Male Vocal/Instrumental Group from the USA						
1	Ritual		0	1988	38	1988	(Mercury 870183)
2	Come Back Baby	(Mercury DRN 2)	51	1990	0	1990	
3	Rainbow Child	(Mercury DRN 3)	60	1990	0	1990	
4	Stardate 1990/Rainbow Child (Re-Issue)	(Mercury DRN 4)	39	1990	0	1990	

ISSUE	TITLE	UK LBL	UK POS	UK YEAR	US POS	US YEAR	US LBL
5	Mix It Up	(Mercury MER 345)	49	1991	0	1991	
5	Lover/Money	(Mercury DRN5)	45	1990	0	1990	
6	Baby Now I	(Mercury MER 352)	65	1991	0	1991	
Dan-I Male Vocalist from the UK							
1	Monkey Chop	(Island WIP 6520)	30	1979	0	1979	
Dana Female Vocalist, Real Name Rosemary Brown B: 20 Aug 1951 In London, England							
* 1	All Kinds Of Everything	(REX R 11054)	1	1970	0	1970	
2	All Kinds Of Everything (Re-Entry)	(REX R 11054)	47	1970	0	1970	
3	Who Put The Lights Out	(REX R 11062)	14	1971	0	1971	
4	Please Tell Him I Said Hello	(GTO GT 6)	8	1975	0	1975	
5	It's Gonna Be A Cold Cold Christmas	(GTO GT 45)	4	1975	0	1975	
6	Never Gonna Fall In Love Again	(GTO GT 55)	31	1976	0	1976	
7	Fairytale	(GTO GT 66)	13	1976	0	1976	
8	Something's Cookin' In The Kitchen	(GTO GT 243)	44	1979	0	1979	
9	I Feel Love Comin' On	(Creole CR 32)	66	1982	0	1982	
Dana Dawson Female Vocalist from the USA							
1	3 Is Family	(EMI CDEM 378)	9	1995	0	1995	
2	Got To Give Me Love	(EMI CDEM 392)	27	1995	0	1995	
3	Show Me	(EMI CDEMD 423)	28	1996	0	1996	
4	How I Wanna Be Loved	(EMI CDEMS 432)	42	1996	0	1996	
Dance 2 Trance Male Production/Instrumental Duo From Germany							
1	P.Ower Of A.Merican N.Atives	(Logic 74321139582)	25	1993	0	1993	
2	Take A Free Fall	(Logic 74321153602)	36	1993	0	1993	
3	Warrior	(Logic 74321257722)	56	1995	0	1995	
Dance Conspiracy Male Production/Instrumental Duo from the UK							
1	Dub War	(XL XLT 34)	72	1992	0	1992	
Dance Floor Virus Male Vocal/Instrumental Group from Italy							
1	Message In A Bottle	(Epic 6623742)	49	1995	0	1995	
Dandy Livingstone Male Vocalist from Jamaica							
1	Suzanne Beware Of The Devil	(Horse HOSS 16)	14	1972	0	1972	
2	Big City / Think About That	(Horse HOSS 25)	26	1973	0	1973	
Danger Danger Male Vocal/Instrumental Group from the USA							
1	(Too Much) Monkey Business	(Epic 6577517)	42	1992	0	1992	
2	Still Think About You	(Epic 6581337)	46	1992	0	1992	
3	Comin' Home	(Epic 6578387)	75	1992	0	1992	
Daniel Boone Male Vocalist, Real Name Peter Green Birmingham, England							
1	Daddy Don't You Walk So Fast	(Penny Farthing Pen 764)	17	1971	0	1971	
* 2	Beautiful Sunday	(Penny Farthing Pen 781)	48	1972	15	1972	(Mercury 73281)
3	Beautiful Sunday (Re-Entry)	(Penny Farthing Pen 781)	21	1972	0	1972	
Daniel O'Donnell Male Vocalist from Ireland							
1	I Just Want To Dance With You	(RITZ RITZ 250P)	20	1992	0	1992	
2	The Three Bells	(Ritz RitzCD 239)	71	1993	0	1993	
3	The Love In Your Eyes	(Ritz RitzCD 257)	47	1993	0	1993	
4	What Ever Happened To Old Fashioned Love	(Ritz RitzCD 262)	21	1993	0	1993	
5	Singing The Blues	(Ritz RitzCD 270)	23	1994	0	1994	
6	The Gift	(Ritz RitzCD 275)	46	1994	0	1994	
7	Secret Love	(Ritz RitzCD 285)	28	1995	0	1995	
8	Timeless	(Ritz RitzCD 293)	32	1996	0	1996	
9	Footsteps	(Ritz RitzCD 300)	25	1996	0	1996	
10	The Love Songs (EP)	(Ritz RitzCD 306)	27	1997	0	1997	
	HITS 7-8 ARE CREDITED TO DANIEL OÍDONNELL & MARY DUFF						
Danielle Brisebois Female Vocalist from the USA							
1	Gimme Little Sign	(Epic 6610782)	75	1995	0	1995	
Danleers Quintet from Brooklyn With Lead Singer Jimmy Weston							
1	One Summer Night		0	1958	7	1958	(Mercury 71322)
Danni'elle Gaha Female Vocalist from Australia							
1	Stuck In The Middle	(Epic 6581247)	68	1992	0	1992	
2	Do It For You	(Epic 6584612)	52	1993	0	1993	
3	Secret Love	(Epic 6592212)	41	1993	0	1993	
Dannii Minogue Female Vocalist from Australia, Sister Of Kylie							
1	Love And Kisses	(MCA MCS 1529)	8	1991	0	1991	

ISSUE	TITLE	UK LBL	UK POS	UK YEAR	US POS	US YEAR	US LBL
2	Success	(MCA MCS 1538)	11	1991	0	1991	
3	Jump To The Beat	(MCA MCS 1556)	8	1991	0	1991	
4	Baby Love	(MCA MCS 1580)	14	1991	0	1991	
5	I Don't Wanna Take This Pain	(MCA MCS 1600)	40	1991	0	1991	
6	Show You The Way To Go	(MCA MCS 1671)	30	1992	0	1992	
7	Love's On Every Corner	(MCA MCSR 1723)	44	1992	0	1992	
8	This Is It	(MCA MCSTD 1790)	10	1993	0	1993	
9	This Is The Way	(MCA MCSTD 1935)	27	1993	0	1993	
10	Get Into You	(MUSHROOM D 11751)	36	1994	0	1994	
11	All I Wanna Do	(WEA WEA 119CD)	4	1997	0	1997	

Danny & The Juniors Male Vocal Group from the USA, Danny Rapp, David White, Frank Maffel & Joe Terranove

* 1	At The Hop	(HMV POP 436)	3	1958	1	1957	(ABC-PARAMOUNT 9871)
2	Rock And Roll Is Here To Stay		0	1958	19	1958	(ABC-PARAMOUNT 9888)
3	Dottie		0	1958	39	1958	(ABC-PARAMOUNT 9926)
4	Twistin' USA		0	1960	27	1960	(SWAN 4060)
5	At The Hop (Re-Issue)	(ABC 4123)	39	1976	0	1976	

FORMED IN 1955 AS THE JUVENAIRS IN PHILADELPHIA • OBITUARY: DANNY D: 8 APR 1983 COMMITTED SUICIDE.

Danny Kaye Male Comedian/Vocalist Real Name David Kuminsky from the USA

1	Bloop Bleep		0	1947	21	1947	(Decca 23950)
2	Civilization (Bongo, Bongo, Bongo) (From *Angel In The Wings*)		0	1947	3	1947	(Decca 23940)
3	The Woody Woodpecker		0	1948	18	1948	(Decca 24462)
4	I've Got A Lovely Bunch Of Cocoanuts		0	1950	26	1950	(Decca 24784)
5	C'est Si Bon		0	1950	21	1950	(Decca 24932)
6	Blackstrap Molasses		0	1951	29	1951	(Decca 27748)
7	Thumbelina (From *Hans Christian Andersen*)		0	1952	28	1952	(Decca 28380)
8	Wonderful Copenhagen	(Brunswick 05023)	5	1953	0	1953	

Danny La Rue Male Vocalist/Female Impersonator from the UK

1	On Mother Kelly's Doorstep	(Page One POF 108)	33	1968	0	1968	

Danny Madden Male Vocalist from the USA

1	The Facts Of Life	(Eternal YZ 473)	72	1990	0	1990	

Danny Mirror Male Vocalist from Holland

1	I Remember Elvis Presley (The King Is Dead)	(SONET SON 2121)	4	1977	0	1977	

Danny O'Keefe Singer/Songwriter, B: Spokane, Washington

1	Good Time Charley's Got The Blues		0	1972	9	1972	(Sign Post 7006)
	Hit Reached Number 63 In The US C/W Charts						

Danny O'Neil Male Vocalist from the USA

1	Ole Buttermilk Sky		0	1948	12	1948	(Majestic 7199)

Danny Peppermint & The Jumping Jacks Male Vocal/Instrumental Group from the USA

1	Peppermint Twist	(London HLL 9478)	26	1962	0	1962	

Danny Rivers Male Vocalist from the UK

1	Can't You Hear My Heart	(Decca F 11294)	36	1961	0	1961	

Danny Storm Male Vocalist from the UK

1	Honest I Do	(Piccadilly 7N 35025)	42	1962	0	1962	

Danny Williams Male Vocalist, B: 17 Jan 1942 Port Elizabeth, South Africa

1	We Will Never Be As Young As This Again	(HMV POP 839)	44	1961	0	1961	
2	The Miracle Of You	(HMV POP 885)	41	1961	0	1961	
3	Moon River	(HMV POP 932)	1	1961	0	1961	
4	Jeannie	(HMV POP 968)	14	1962	0	1962	
5	Wonderful World Of The Young	(HMV POP 1002)	8	1962	0	1962	
6	Tears	(HMV POP 1035)	22	1962	0	1962	
7	My Own True Love	(HMV POP 1112)	45	1963	0	1963	
8	White On White		0	1964	9	1964	(United Artists 685)
9	Dancin' Easy	(Ensign ENY 3)	30	1977	0	1977	

Danny Wilson Male Vocal/Instrumental Group from the UK Names: Gary & Kit Clark With Ged Grimes, Disbanded In 1990

1	Mary's Prayer	(Virgin VS 934)	42	1987	23	1987	(Virgin 99465)
2	Mary's Prayer (Re-Entry)	(Virgin VS 934)	3	1988	0	1988	
3	The Second Summer Of Love	(Virgin VS 1186)	23	1989	0	1989	
4	Never Gonna Be The Same	(Virgin VS 1203)	69	1989	0	1989	

Danny Winchell Male Vocalist from the USA

1	Carolina In The Morning		0	1952	30	1952	(MGM 11335)

Danse Society Male Vocal/Instrumental Group from the UK

1	Wake Up	(Society SOC 5)	62	1983	0	1983	

ISSUE	TITLE	UK LBL	UK POS	UK YEAR	US POS	US YEAR	US LBL
2	Heaven Is Waiting	(Society SOC 6)	60	1983	0	1983	

Dante & The Evergreens Real Name Donald Drowty B: 8 Sep 1941also Bill Young, Tony Moon & Frank Rosenthal

1	Alley-Oop		0	1960	15	1960	(Madison 130)

Danyel Gerard Male Vocalist, B: 1941 France

* 1	Butterfly	(CBS 7454)	11	1971	0	1971	
	Hit Is A German Drinking Song						

Danzig Male Vocal/Instrumental Group from the USA

1	Mother	(American MOMDD 1)	62	1994	0	1994	

Daphne Female Vocalist from the USA

1	Change	(Stress CDSTR 54)	71	1995	0	1995	

Dardanelle Trio Dardanelle Is A Vocalist/Instrumentalist (Piano/Vibraphone) from the USA

1	September Song (From *Knickerbocker Holiday*)		0	1946	11	1946	(RCA Victor 1993)

Dare Male Vocal/Instrumental Group from the UK

1	The Raindance	(A&M AM 483)	62	1989	0	1989	
2	Abandon	(A&M AM 519)	71	1989	0	1989	
3	We Don't Need A Reason	(A&M AM 755)	52	1991	0	1991	
4	Real Love	(A&M AM 824)	67	1991	0	1991	

Darkman Male Rapper from the UK

1	Yabba Dabba Doo	(Wild Card Cardd 6)	49	1994	0	1994	
2	Who's The Darkman	(Wild Card Cardd 8)	46	1994	0	1994	
3	Yabba Dabba Doo (Re-Issue)	(Wild Card Cardd 11)	37	1994	0	1994	
4	Brand New Day	(Wild Card 5771892)	74	1995	0	1995	

Darlene Davis Female Vocalist from the USA

1	I Found Love	(Serious 7OUS 1)	55	1987	0	1987	

Darlene Lewis Female Vocalist from the USA

1	Let The Music (Lift You Up)	(KMS/Eastern Bloc KMSCD 10)	16	1994	0	1994	
	HIT IS CREDITED TO LOVELAND FEATURING RACHEL MCFARLANE VS DARLENE LEWIS						

Darlene Love Female Vocalist from the USA Has Also Sung Lead With The Blossoms And The Crystals

1	(Today I Met) The Boy I'm Gonna Marry		0	1963	39	1963	(PHILLES 111)
2	Wait 'Till My Bobby Gets Home		0	1963	26	1963	(PHILLES 114)
4	All Alone At Christmas	(Arista 7432112476)	31	1992	0	1992	
5	All Alone At Christmas (Re-Entry)	(Arista 7432112476)	72	1994	0	1994	

Darling Buds Mixed Vocal/Instrumental Group from the UK

1	Burst	(Epic Blond 1)	50	1988	0	1988	
2	Hit The Ground	(Epic Blond 2)	27	1989	0	1989	
3	Let's Go Round There	(Epic Blond 3)	49	1989	0	1989	
4	You've Got To Choose	(Epic Blond 4)	45	1989	0	1989	
5	Tiny Machine	(Epic Blond 5)	60	1990	0	1990	
6	Sure Thing	(Epic 6582157)	71	1992	0	1992	

Darrell Banks Male Vocalist, Real Name Darrell Eubanks B: 1938 Buffalo

1	Open The Door To Your Heart		0	1966	27	1966	(Revilot 201)
	OBITUARY: D: MARCH 1970 GUNSHOT WOUND.						

Darrell Glenn Male Country Vocalist from the USA

1	Crying In The Chapel		0	1953	6	1953	(Valley 105)

Darren Day Male Vocalist from the USA

1	Young Girl	(Bell 74321231082)	42	1994	0	1994	
2	Summer Holiday (Medley)	(RCA 74321384472)	17	1996	0	1996	

Dartells Rock Band from Oxnard, California

1	Hot Pastrami		0	1962	11	1962	(DOT 16453)
	NAMES: DOUG PHILLIPS, DICK BURNS, CORKY WILKIE, RICHARD PEIL, RANDY RAY & GARY PEELER						

Darts Mixed Vocal/Instrumental Group from the UK

1	Daddy Cool / The Girl Can't Help It	(Magnet Mag100)	6	1977	0	1977	
2	Come Back My Love	(Magnet Mag110)	2	1978	0	1978	
3	The Boy From New York City	(Magnet Mag116)	2	1978	0	1978	
4	It's Raining	(Magnet Mag126)	2	1978	0	1978	
5	Don't Let It Fade Away	(Magnet Mag134)	18	1978	0	1978	
6	Get It	(Magnet Mag140)	10	1979	0	1979	
7	Duke Of Earl	(Magnet Mag147)	6	1979	0	1979	
8	Can't Get Enough Of Your Love	(Magnet Mag156)	43	1979	0	1979	
9	Reet Petite	(Magnet Mag160)	51	1979	0	1979	

ISSUE	TITLE	UK LBL	UK POS	UK YEAR	US POS	US YEAR	US LBL
10	Let's Hang On	(Magnet Mag174)	11	1980	0	1980	
11	Peaches	(Magnet Mag179)	66	1980	0	1980	
12	White Christmas / Sh-Boom (Life Could Be A Dream)	(Magnet Mag184)	48	1980	0	1980	

Daryl Hall Male Vocalist, Real Name Daryl Franklin Hohl B: 11 Oct 1948 In Philadelphia

ISSUE	TITLE	UK LBL	UK POS	UK YEAR	US POS	US YEAR	US LBL
1	Dreamtime	(RCA HALL 1)	28	1986	5	1986	(RCA 14397)
2	Foolish Pride		0	1986	33	1986	(RCA 5038)
3	I'm In A Philly Mood	(Epic 6595555)	59	1993	0	1993	
4	Stop Loving Me, Stop Loving You	(Epic 6599982)	30	1994	0	1994	
5	I'm In A Philly Mood (Re-Entry)	(Epic 6599982)	52	1994	0	1994	
6	Help Me Find A Way To Your Heart	(Epic 6604102)	70	1994	0	1994	
7	Gloryland	(Mercury MERCD 404)	36	1994	0	1994	
8	Wherever Would I Be	(Columbia6620592)	44	1995	0	1995	

HIT 7 IS CREDITED TO DARYL HALL & THE SOUNDS OF BLACKNESS • SEE ALSO SOUNDS OF BLACKNESS • HIT 8 TO DUSTY SPRINGFIELD AND DARYL HALL

Daryl Hall & John Oates Male Vocal/Instrumental Duo from the USA

ISSUE	TITLE	UK LBL	UK POS	UK YEAR	US POS	US YEAR	US LBL
1	She's Gone		0	1974	60	1974	(Atlantic 3332)
* 2	Sara Smile		0	1976	4	1976	(RCA 10530)
3	She's Gone (USA Re-Entry)	(Atlantic K 10828)	42	1976	7	1976	(Atlantic 3332)
4	Do What You Want, Be What You Are		0	1976	39	1976	(RCA 10808)
* 5	Rich Girl		0	1977	1	1977	(RCA 10860)
6	Back Together Again		0	1977	28	1977	(RCA 10970)
7	It's A Laugh		0	1978	20	1978	(RCA 11371)
8	Wait For Me		0	1979	18	1979	(RCA 11747)
9	How Does It Feel To Be Back		0	1980	30	1980	(RCA 12048)
10	Running From Paradise	(RCA RUN 1)	41	1980	0	1980	
11	You've Lost That Lovin' Feelin'	(RCA 1)	55	1980	12	1980	(RCA 12103)
* 12	Kiss On My List	(RCA 15)	33	1980	1	1981	(RCA 12142)
13	You Make My Dreams		0	1981	5	1981	(RCA 12217)
* 14	Private Eyes	(RCA 134)	32	1982	1	1981	(RCA 12296)
* 15	I Can't Go For That (No Can Do)	(RCA 172)	8	1982	1	1981	(RCA 12357)
16	Did It In A Minute		0	1982	9	1982	(RCA 13065)
17	Your Imagination		0	1982	33	1982	(RCA 13252)
* 18	Maneater	(RCA 290)	6	1982	1	1982	(RCA 13354)
19	One On One	(RCA 305)	63	1983	7	1983	(RCA 13421)
20	Family Man	(RCA 323)	15	1983	6	1983	(RCA 13507)
21	Say It Isn't So	(RCA 375)	69	1983	2	1983	(RCA 13654)
22	Adult Education	(RCA 396)	63	1984	8	1984	(RCA 13714)
23	Out Of Touch	(RCA 449)	48	1984	1	1984	(RCA 13916)
24	Method Of Modern Love	(RCA RCA 472)	21	1985	5	1985	(RCA 13970)
25	Some Things Are Better Left Unsaid		0	1985	18	1985	(RCA 14035)
26	Possession Obsession		0	1985	30	1985	(RCA 14098)
27	Out Of Touch (Re-Mix)	(RCA PB 4 9967)	62	1985	0	1985	
28	A Night At The Apollo Live!	(RCA PB 49935)	58	1985	20	1985	(RCA 14178)
29	Everything Your Heart Desires		0	1988	3	1988	(Arista 9684)
30	Missed Opportunity		0	1988	29	1988	(Arista 9727)
31	Downtown Life		0	1988	31	1988	(Arista 9753)
32	So Close	(Arista 113600)	69	1990	11	1990	(Arista 2085)
33	Everywhere I Look	(Arista 113980)	74	1991	0	1991	

DARYL FRANKLIN HOHL, B: 11 OCT 1948 PHILADELPHIA • JOHN, B: 7 APR 1949 NEW YORK CITY

Das EFX Rap Duo Andre Weston, B: 9 Sep 1970 & Willie Hines B: 27 Nov 1970 From Virginia

ISSUE	TITLE	UK LBL	UK POS	UK YEAR	US POS	US YEAR	US LBL
* 1	They Want EFX		0	1992	25	1992	(East West 98600)
* 2	Check Yo Self		0	1993	20	1993	(Priority 53830)

HIT 2 IS CREDITED TO ICE CUBE FEATURING DAS EFX

Dave & Ansil Collins Male Vocal/Instrumental Duo From Jamaica

ISSUE	TITLE	UK LBL	UK POS	UK YEAR	US POS	US YEAR	US LBL
1	Double Barrell	(Technique TE 901)	1	1971	22	1971	(Big Tree 115)
2	Monkey Spanner	(Technique TE 914)	7	1971	0	1971	

BY 1983 THEY WERE KNOWN AS CLINT EASTWOOD & GENERAL SAINT

Dave 'Baby' Cortez Real Name David Cortez Clowney B: 13 Aug 1938 Detroit

ISSUE	TITLE	UK LBL	UK POS	UK YEAR	US POS	US YEAR	US LBL
* 1	The Happy Organ		0	1959	1	1959	(Clock 1009)
2	Rinky Dink		0	1962	9	1962	(Chess 1829)

HE WAS A MEMBER OF THE GROUP THE PEARLS 1955-57 AND THE VALENTINES

Dave Barbour Male Guitarist/Song Writer from the USA

ISSUE	TITLE	UK LBL	UK POS	UK YEAR	US POS	US YEAR	US LBL
1	The Mambo (Que Rico El Mambo)		0	1950	27	1950	(Capitol 973)

MARRIED TO PEGGY LEE, WORKED WITH ARTIE SHAW, BENNY GOODMAN AND OTHERS • OBITUARY: D: 11 DEC 1965, (AGED 53).

ISSUE	TITLE	UK LBL	UK POS	UK YEAR	US POS	US YEAR	US LBL
Dave Berry Male Vocalist from the UK							
1	Memphis Tennessee	(Decca F 11734)	19	1963	0	1963	
2	My Baby Left Me	(Decca F 11803)	41	1964	0	1964	
3	My Baby Left Me (Re-Entry)	(Decca F 11803)	37	1964	0	1964	
4	Baby It's You	(Decca F 11876)	24	1964	0	1964	
5	The Crying Game	(Decca F 11937)	5	1964	0	1964	
6	One Heart Between Two	(Decca F 12020)	41	1964	0	1964	
7	Little Things	(Decca F 12103)	5	1965	0	1965	
8	This Strange Effect	(Decca F 12188)	37	1965	0	1965	
9	Mama	(Decca F 12435)	5	1966	0	1966	
Dave Brubeck Quartet Male Instrumental Group from the USA							
* 1	Take Five	(Fontana H 339)	6	1961	25	1961	(Columbia 41479)
2	It's A Raggy Waltz	(Fontana H 352)	36	1962	0	1962	
3	Unsquare Dance	(CBS AAG 102)	14	1962	0	1962	
REAL NAME DAVID WARREN B: 6 DEC 1920 CONCORD, CALIFORNIA. • MEMBERS: ARE PAUL DESMOND, JOE MORELLO & EUGENE WRIGHT							
Dave Clark Five Male Vocal/Instrumental Group from the UK Other Members Are Mike Smith, Lenny Davidson, Dennis Payton & Rick Huxley							
* 1	Do You Love Me	(Columbia DB 7112)	30	1963	11	1964	(Epic 9678)
* 2	Glad All Over	(Columbia DB 7154)	1	1963	6	1964	(Epic 9656)
* 3	Bits And Pieces	(Columbia DB 7210)	2	1964	4	1964	(Epic 9671)
* 4	Can't You See That She's Mine	(Columbia DB 7291)	10	1964	4	1964	(Epic 9692)
* 5	Because		0	1964	3	1964	(Epic 9704)
6	Thinking Of You Baby	(Columbia DB 7335)	26	1964	0	1964	
7	Everybody Knows	(Columbia DB 7453)	37	1965	15	1964	(Epic 9722)
* 8	Anyway You Want It	(Columbia DB 7377)	25	1964	14	1964	(Epic 9739)
9	Come Home	(Columbia DB 7580)	16	1965	14	1965	(Epic 9763)
10	Reelin' And Rockin'	(Columbia DB 7503)	24	1965	23	1965	(Epic 9786)
* 11	I Like It Like That		0	1965	7	1965	(Epic 9811)
* 12	Catch Us If You Can	(Columbia DB 7625)	5	1965	4	1965	(Epic 9833)
* 13	Over And Over	(Columbia DB 7744)	45	1965	1	1965	(Epic 9863)
14	At The Scene		0	1966	18	1966	(Epic 9882)
15	Try Too Hard		0	1966	12	1966	(Epic 10004)
16	Look Before You Leap	(Columbia DB 7909)	50	1966	0	1966	
17	You Got What It Takes	(Columbia DB 8152)	28	1967	7	1967	(Epic 10144)
18	You Must Have Been A Beautiful Baby		0	1967	35	1967	(Epic 10179)
19	Everybody Knows	(Columbia DB 8286)	2	1967	0	1967	
20	No One Can Break A Heart Like You	(Columbia DB 8342)	28	1968	0	1968	
21	Red Balloon	(Columbia DB 8465)	7	1968	0	1968	
22	Live In The Sky	(Columbia DB 8505)	39	1968	0	1968	
23	Put A Little Love In Your Heart	(Columbia DB 8624)	31	1969	0	1969	
24	Good Old Rock 'N Roll	(Columbia DB 8638)	7	1969	0	1969	
25	Everybody Get Together	(Columbia DB 8660)	8	1970	0	1970	
26	Here Comes Summer	(Columbia DB 8689)	44	1970	0	1970	
27	More Good Old Rock 'N' Roll	(Columbia DB 8724)	34	1970	0	1970	
28	Glad All Over (Re-Issue)	(EMI CDEMCT 8)	37	1993	0	1993	
HITS 7 & 19 ARE TWO DIFFERENT RECORDINGS • DAVE B: 15 DEC 1942, TOTTENHAM, LONDON, ENGLAND							
Dave Clarke Male Producer from the UK							
1	Red Three: Thunder/Storm	(Deconstruction 74321306992)	45	1995	0	1995	
2	Southside	(Deconstruction 74321335382)	34	1996	0	1996	
3	No One's Driving	(Deconstruction 74321380162)	37	1996	0	1996	
Dave Davies Male Vocalist from the UK							
1	Death Of A Clown	(PYE 7N 17356)	3	1967	0	1967	
2	Suzanah's Still Alive	(PYE 7N 17429)	20	1967	0	1967	
Dave Dee Male Vocalist, Real Name David Harman B: 17 Dec 1943 Salisbury, Wiltshire, England							
1	My Woman's Man	(Fontana TF 1074)	42	1970	0	1970	
SEE ALSO DAVE DEE, DOZY, BEAKY, MICK & TICH							
Dave Dee, Dozy, Beaky, Mick & Tich Male Vocal/Instrumental Group from the UK							
1	You Make It Move	(Fontana TF 630)	26	1965	0	1965	
2	Hold Tight	(Fontana TF 671)	4	1966	0	1966	
3	Hideaway	(Fontana TF 711)	10	1966	0	1966	
* 4	Bend It	(Fontana TF 746)	2	1966	0	1966	
5	Save Me	(Fontana TF 775)	4	1966	0	1966	
6	Touch Me Touch Me	(Fontana TF 798)	13	1967	0	1967	
7	Okay!	(Fontana TF 830)	4	1967	0	1967	
8	Zabadak	(Fontana TF 873)	3	1967	0	1967	

ISSUE	TITLE	UK LBL	UK POS	UK YEAR	US POS	US YEAR	US LBL
* 9	Legend Of Xanadu	(Fontana TF 903)	1	1968	52	1968	
10	Last Night In Soho	(Fontana TF 953)	8	1968	0	1968	
11	Wreck Of The Antoinette	(Fontana TF 971)	14	1968	0	1968	
12	Don Juan	(Fontana TF1000)	23	1969	0	1969	
13	Snake In The Grass	(Fontana TF 1020)	23	1969	0	1969	

OFTEN REFERED TO AS DAVE DEE, DOZY, GREASY FISH & CHIPS • ORIGINALLY CALLED DAVE DEE & THE BOSTONS • SEE ALSO D, B, M & T

Dave Dudley   Male Vocalist, Real Name David Pedruska B: 3 May 1928 Stevens Point, Wisconsin

* 3	Six Days On The Road		0	1963	32	1963	(Golden Wing 3020)

ALL OTHERS ARE C/W HITS • HE WAS A PROFESSIONAL BASEBALL PLAYER UNTIL AN ARM INJURY FORCED HIM TO GIVE UP HIS CAREER

Dave Edmunds   Male Vocal/Multi-Instrumentalist, B: 15 Apr 1944 Cardiff, Wales

* 1	I Hear You Knocking	(MAM 1)	1	1970	1	1971	(MAM 3601)
2	Baby I Love You	(Rockfield ROC 1)	8	1973	0	1973	
3	Born To Be With You	(Rockfield ROC 2)	5	1973	0	1973	
4	I Knew The Bride	(Swansong SSK 19411)	26	1977	0	1977	
5	Girls Talk	(Swansong SSK 19418)	4	1979	0	1979	
6	Queen Of Hearts	(Swansong SSK 19419)	11	1979	0	1979	
7	Crawling From The Wreckage	(Swansong SSK 19420)	59	1979	0	1979	
8	Singing The Blues	(Swansong SSK 19422)	28	1980	0	1980	
9	Almost Saturday Night	(Swansong SSK 19424)	58	1981	0	1981	
10	The Race Is On	(Swansong SSK 19425)	34	1981	0	1981	
11	Slipping Away	(Arista Arist 522)	60	1983	39	1983	(Columbia 03877)
12	King Of Love	(Capitol CL 568)	68	1990	0	1990	

HIT 10 IS CREDITED TO DAVE EDMUNDS & THE STRAY CATS • DAVE FORMED THE GROUP LOVE SCULPTURE IN 1967

Dave Gardner   Male Vocalist, B: 11 Jun 1926 Jackson, Tennessee

1	White Silver Sands		0	1957	22	1957	(OJ 1002)

Dave King   Male Vocalist from Canada

1	Memories Are Made Of This	(Decca F 10684)	5	1956	0	1956	
2	You Can't Be True To Two	(Decca F 10720)	11	1956	0	1956	
3	Christmas And You	(Decca F 10791)	23	1956	0	1956	
4	The Story Of My Life	(Decca F 10973)	20	1958	0	1958	

HITS 1-2 ARE CREDITED TO DAVE KING FEATURING THE KEYNOTES • SEE ALSO ALL STAR HIT PARADE, VARIOUS ARTISTS (EP, LP, 78S)

Dave Loggins   Male Singer/Songwriter, B: 10 Nov 1947 Mountain City, Tennessee

1	Please Come To Boston		0	1974	5	1974	(Epic 11115)

Dave Mason   Male Vocal/Guitarist, B: 10 May 1946 Worcester, England. An Original Member Of Traffic

1	We Just Disagree		0	1977	12	1977	(Columbia 10575)
2	Will You Still Love Me Tomorrow		0	1978	39	1978	(Columbia 10749)

Dave Newman   Male Vocalist from the UK

1	The Lion Sleeps Tonight	(PYE 7N 45134)	48	1972	0	1972	
2	The Lion Sleeps Tonight (Re-Entry)	(PYE 7N 45134)	34	1972	0	1972	

Dave Sampson   Male Vocalist from the UK

1	Sweet Dreams	(Columbia DB 4449)	48	1960	0	1960	
2	Sweet Dreams (Re-Entry)	(Columbia DB 4449)	29	1960	0	1960	

Dave Stewart (1)   Male Instrumentalist (Keyboards) from the UK

1	What Becomes Of The Broken Hearted	(Stiff BROKEN 1)	12	1981	0	1981	
2	It's My Party	(Broken Broken 2)	1	1981	0	1981	
3	Busy Doing Nothing	(Broken Broken 5)	49	1983	0	1983	
4	The Locomotion	(Broken Broken 8)	70	1986	0	1986	

GUEST VOCALS ON HIT 1 ARE BY COLIN BLUNSTONE • HITS 2-4 ARE CREDITED TO DAVE STEWART WITH BARBARA GASKIN

Dave Stewart (2)   Male Multi-Instrumentalist, B: 9 Sep 1952 Sunderland, England.

1	Lily Was Here	(RCA ZB 43045)	6	1990	11	1991	(Arista 2187)
2	Jack Talking	(RCA PB 43907)	69	1990	0	1990	
3	Heart Of Stone	(East West YZ 845CD)	36	1994	0	1994	

HIT 1 IS CREDITED TO DAVID A. STEWART FEATURING CANDY DULFER • HIT 2 IS CREDITED TO DAVE STEWART & THE SPIRITUAL COWBOYS
DAVID IS MARRIED TO SIOBHAN FAHEY (BANANARAMA) AND HE WAS ALSO THE OTHER MEMBER OF THE DUO EURYTHMICS

David & David   Names David Baerwald & David Ricketts

1	Welcome To The Boomtown		0	1986	37	1986	(A&M 2857)

David & Jonathan   Male Vocal Duo from the UK, Roger Greenaway & Roger Cook

1	Michelle	(Columbia DB 7800)	11	1966	18	1966	(Capitol 5563)
2	Lovers Of The World Unite	(Columbia DB 7950)	7	1966	0	1966	

David Austin   Male Vocalist from the UK

1	Turn To Gold	(Parlophone R 6068)	68	1984	0	1984	

ISSUE	TITLE	UK LBL	UK POS	UK YEAR	US POS	US YEAR	US LBL
David Ball Male Country Singer, B: 9 Jul 1953 South Carolina							
1	Thinkin' Problem		0	1994	40	1994	(Warner Bros. 18250)
David Bendeth Male Vocalist and Multi-Instrumentalist from the UK							
1	Feel The Real	(Sidewalk SID 113)	44	1979	0	1979	
David Bowie Male Vocalist, Real Name David Robert Jones B: 8 Jan 1947 In Brixon, London, England							
1	Space Oddity	(Philips BF 1801)	48	1969	15	1973	(RCA 0876)
2	Space Oddity (Re-Entry)	(Philips BF 1801)	5	1969	0	1969	
3	Starman	(RCA 2199)	10	1972	0	1972	
4	John I'm Only Dancing	(RCA 2263)	12	1972	0	1972	
5	The Jean Genie	(RCA 2302)	2	1972	0	1972	
6	Drive-In Saturday	(RCA 2352)	3	1973	0	1973	
7	Life On Mars	(RCA 2316)	3	1973	0	1973	
8	The Laughing Gnome	(Deram DM 123)	6	1973	0	1973	
9	Sorrow	(RCA 2424)	3	1973	0	1973	
10	Rebel Rebel	(RCA LPBO 5009)	5	1974	0	1974	
11	Rock And Roll Suicide	(RCA LPBO 5021)	22	1974	0	1974	
12	Diamond Dogs	(RCA APBO 0293)	21	1974	0	1974	
13	Knock On Wood	(RCA 2466)	10	1974	0	1974	
14	Young Americans	(RCA 2523)	8	1975	28	1975	(RCA 10152)
* 15	Fame	(RCA 2579)	17	1975	1	1975	(RCA 10320)
16	Space Oddity (Re-Issue)	(RCA 2593)	1	1975	0	1975	
17	Golden Years	(RCA 2640)	8	1975	10	1976	(RCA 10441)
18	TVC 15	(RCA 2682)	33	1976	0	1976	
19	Sound And Vision	(RCA PB 0905)	3	1977	0	1977	
20	Heroes	(RCA PB 1121)	24	1977	0	1977	
21	Beauty And The Beast	(RCA PB 1190)	39	1978	0	1978	
22	Breaking Glass (EP)	(RCA BOW 1)	54	1978	0	1978	
23	Boys Keep Swinging	(RCA BOW 2)	7	1979	0	1979	
24	D.J.	(RCA BOW 3)	29	1979	0	1979	
25	John I'm Only Dancing (Again) (1975) / John I'm Only Dancing (1972)	(RCA BOW 4)	12	1979	0	1979	
26	Alabama Song	(RCA BOW 5)	23	1980	0	1980	
27	Ashes To Ashes	(RCA BOW 6)	1	1980	0	1980	
28	Fashion	(RCA BOW 7)	5	1980	0	1980	
29	Scary Monsters (And Super Creeps)	(RCA BOW 8)	20	1981	0	1981	
30	Up The Hill Backwards	(RCA BOW 9)	32	1981	0	1981	
31	Under Pressure	(EMI 5250)	1	1981	29	1981	(ELEKTRA 47235)
32	Wild Is The Wind	(RCA BOW 10)	24	1981	0	1981	
33	Baal's Hymn	(RCA BOW 11)	29	1982	0	1982	
34	Cat People (Putting Out Fire)	(MCA 770)	26	1982	0	1982	
35	Peace On Earth / Little Drummer Boy	(RCA BOW 12)	3	1982	0	1982	
36	Let's Dance	(EMI America EA 152)	1	1983	1	1983	(EMI America 8158)
37	China Cirl	(EMI America EA 157)	2	1983	10	1983	(EMI America 8165)
38	Modern Love	(EMI America EA 158)	2	1983	14	1983	(EMI America 8177)
39	White Light, White Heat	(RCA 372)	46	1983	0	1983	
40	Blue Jean	(EMI America EA 181)	6	1984	8	1984	(EMI America 8231)
41	Tonight	(EMI America EA 187)	53	1984	0	1984	
42	This Is Not America	(EMI America EA 190)	14	1985	32	1985	(EMI America 8251)
43	Loving The Alien	(EMI America EA 195)	19	1985	0	1986	
44	Loving The Alien (Re-Entry)	(EMI America EA 195)	67	1985	0	1985	
45	Dancing In The Street	(EMI America EA 204)	1	1985	7	1985	(EMI America 8288)
46	Absolute Beginners	(Virgin VS 838)	2	1986	0	1986	
47	Underground	(EMI America EA 216)	21	1986	0	1986	
48	When The Wind Blows	(Virgin VS 906)	44	1986	0	1986	
49	Day-In Day-Out	(EMI America EA 230)	17	1987	21	1987	(EMI America 8380)
50	Never Let Me Down	(EMI America EA 239)	34	1987	27	1987	(EMI America 73031)
51	Time Will Crawl	(EMI America EA 237)	33	1987	0	1987	
52	Fame (Re-Mix)	(EMI-USA FAME 90)	28	1990	0	1990	
53	Real Cool World	(Warner Bros. W 0127)	53	1992	0	1992	
54	Jump They Say	(Arista 74321139422)	9	1993	0	1993	
55	Black Tie White Noise	(Arista 74321148682)	36	1993	0	1993	
56	Miracle Goodnight	(Arista 74321162262)	40	1993	0	1993	
57	Buddha Of Surburbia	(Arista 74321177052)	35	1993	0	1993	
58	The Heart's Filthy Lesson	(RCA 74321307032)	35	1995	0	1995	
59	Strangers When We Meet / The Man Who Sold The World	(RCA 74321329402)	39	1995	0	1995	

ISSUE	TITLE	UK LBL	UK POS	UK YEAR	US POS	US YEAR	US LBL
60	Hallo Spaceboy	(RCA 74321353842)	12	1996	0	1996	
61	Little Wonder	(RCA 74321452072)	14	1997	0	1997	
62	Dead Man Walking	(RCA 74321475852)	32	1997	0	1997	
63	Seven Years In Tibet	(RCA 74321512542)	61	1997	0	1997	

HIT 31 IS CREDITED TO QUEEN AND DAVID BOWIE • IN 1988 HE FORMED THE GROUP THE TIN MACHINE. SEE SEPARATE ENTRY
FIRST RECORDED AS DAVID JONES & THE KING BEES, LOWER THIRD, MANISH BOYS

David Carroll   Real Name Nook Schrier B: 15 Oct 1913 Chicago

ISSUE	TITLE	UK LBL	UK POS	UK YEAR	US POS	US YEAR	US LBL
1	In A Little Spanish Town		0	1954	29	1954	(Mercury 70444)
2	Melody Of Love		0	1955	8	1955	(Mercury 70516)
3	It's Almost Tomorrow		0	1955	20	1955	(Mercury 70717)

HIT 1 IS CREDITED TO DAVID CARROLL & HIS ORCHESTRA

David Cassidy   Male Vocalist B: 12 Apr 1950 New York City

ISSUE	TITLE	UK LBL	UK POS	UK YEAR	US POS	US YEAR	US LBL
* 1	Cherish	(Bell 1224)	2	1971	9	1971	(Bell 45150)
2	Could It Be Forever	(Bell 1224)	2	1972	37	1972	(Bell 45187)
3	How Can I Be Sure	(Bell 1258)	1	1972	25	1972	(Bell 45220)
4	Rock Me Baby	(Bell 1268)	11	1972	38	1972	(Bell 45260)
5	I'm A Clown - Some Kind Of Summer	(Bell MABell 4)	3	1973	0	1973	
* 6	Daydreamer / Puppy Song	(Bell 1334)	1	1973	0	1973	
7	If I Didn't Care	(Bell 1350)	9	1974	0	1974	
8	Please Please Me	(Bell 1371)	16	1974	0	1974	
9	I Write The Songs - Get It Up For Love	(RCA 2571)	11	1975	0	1975	
10	Darlin'	(RCA 2622)	16	1975	0	1975	
11	The Last Kiss	(Arista ARIST 589)	6	1985	0	1985	
12	Romance (Let Your Heart Go)	(Arista Arist 620)	54	1985	0	1985	
13	Lyin' To Myself		0	1990	27	1990	(Enigma 75084)

SEE ALSO PARTRIDGE FAMILY

David Christie   Male Vocalist from France

ISSUE	TITLE	UK LBL	UK POS	UK YEAR	US POS	US YEAR	US LBL
1	Saddle Up	(KR KR 9)	9	1982	0	1982	

David Crosby   Real Name David Van Cortland B: 14 Aug 1941 Los Angeles

ISSUE	TITLE	UK LBL	UK POS	UK YEAR	US POS	US YEAR	US LBL
1	Immigration Man		0	1972	36	1972	(Atlantic 2873)
2	Hero	(Atlantic A 7360)	56	1993	0	1993	

HE WAS A FORMER MEMBER OF THE BYRDS AND CROSBY, STILLS & NASH

David Dundas   Male Vocalist, B: Oxford, England

ISSUE	TITLE	UK LBL	UK POS	UK YEAR	US POS	US YEAR	US LBL
1	Jeans On	(Air CHS 2094)	3	1976	17	1976	(Chrysalis 2094)
2	Another Funny Honeymoon	(Air CHS 2136)	29	1977	0	1977	

HIT 1 WAS USED AS A JINGLE FOR A TV ADVERT

David Essex   Male Actor/Vocalist, Real Name David Cook B: 23 Jun 1947 In Plaistow, London, England

ISSUE	TITLE	UK LBL	UK POS	UK YEAR	US POS	US YEAR	US LBL
* 1	Rock On	(CBS 1693)	3	1973	5	1974	(Columbia 45940)
2	Lamplight	(CBS 1902)	7	1973	0	1973	
3	America	(CBS 2176)	32	1974	0	1974	
4	Gonna Make You A Star	(CBS 2492)	1	1974	0	1974	
5	Stardust	(CBS 2828)	7	1974	0	1974	
6	Rollin' Stone	(CBS 3425)	5	1975	0	1975	
7	Hold Me Close	(CBS 3572)	1	1975	0	1975	
8	If I Could	(CBS 3776)	13	1975	0	1975	
9	City Lights	(CBS 4050)	24	1976	0	1976	
10	Coming Home	(CBS 4486)	24	1976	0	1976	
11	Cool Out Tonight	(CBS 5495)	23	1977	0	1977	
12	Stay With Me Baby	(CBS 6063)	45	1978	0	1978	
13	Oh What A Circus	(Mercury 6007 185)	3	1978	0	1978	
14	Brave New World	(CBS 6705)	55	1978	0	1978	
15	Imperial Wizard	(Mercury 6007 202)	32	1979	0	1979	
16	Silver Dream Machine (Part 1)	(Mercury BIKE 1)	4	1980	0	1980	
17	Hot Love	(Mercury HOT 11)	57	1980	0	1980	
18	Me And My Girl (Night Clubbing)	(Mercury MER 107)	13	1982	0	1982	
19	A Winter Tale	(Mercury MER 127)	2	1982	0	1982	
20	The Smile	(Mercury Essex 1)	52	1983	0	1983	
21	Tahiti	(Mercury BOUNT 1)	8	1983	0	1983	
22	You're In My Heart	(Mercury Essex 2)	67	1983	0	1983	
23	You're In My Heart (Re-Entry)	(Mercury Essex 2)	59	1983	0	1983	
24	Falling Angels Riding	(Mercury Essex 5)	29	1985	0	1985	
25	Myfanwy	(Arista RIS 11)	41	1987	0	1987	
26	True Love Ways	(Polygram TV TLWCD 2)	38	1994	0	1994	

HIT 26 IS CREDITED TO DAVID ESSEX & CATHERINE ZETA JONES

ISSUE	TITLE	UK LBL	UK POS	UK YEAR	US POS	US YEAR	US LBL
David Foster Composer from Victoria, British Columbia, Was Also A Member Of Skylark							
1	Love Theme From *St Elmo's Fire*		0	1985	15	1985	(Atlantic 89528)
David Garrick Male Vocalist from the UK							
1	Lady Jane	(Piccadilly 7N 35317)	28	1966	0	1966	
2	Dear Mrs. Applebee	(Piccadilly 7N 35335)	22	1966	0	1966	
David Gates Male Vocalist, B: 11 Dec 1940 Tulsa, Oklahoma							
1	Never Let Her Go		0	1975	29	1975	(Elektra 45450)
2	Goodbye Girl		0	1978	15	1978	(Elektra 45223)
3	Took The Last Train	(Elektra K 12307)	50	1978	30	1978	(Elektra 45500)
	HE WAS LEAD SINGER WITH, AND SEE ALSO BREAD						
David Geddes Male Vocal/Instrumentalist from the USA							
1	Run Joey Run		0	1975	4	1975	(Big Tree 16044)
2	The Last Game Of The Season (A Blind Man In The Bleachers)		0	1975	18	1975	(Big Tree 16052)
David Glasper See Breathe							
David Grant Male Vocalist from the UK							
1	Stop And Go	(Chrysalis GRAN 1)	19	1983	0	1983	
2	Watching You Watching Me	(Chrysalis GRAN 2)	10	1983	0	1983	
3	Love Will Find A Way	(Chrysalis GRAN 3)	24	1983	0	1983	
4	Rock The Midnight	(Chrysalis GRAN 4)	46	1983	0	1983	
5	Could It Be I'm Falling In Love	(Chrysalis GRAN 6)	5	1985	0	1985	
6	Mated	(EMI JAKI 6)	20	1985	0	1985	
7	Change	(Polydor POSP 871)	55	1987	0	1987	
8	Keep It Together	(Fourth & Broadway BRW 169)	56	1990	0	1990	
	HITS 5-6 ARE CREDITED TO DAVID GRANT AND JAKI GRAHAM • SEE ALSO JAKI GRAHAM						
David Hasselhoff Male Actor/Vocalist from the USA							
1	If I Could Only Say Goodbye	(Arista 74321172262)	35	1993	0	1993	
David Holmes Male Producer from the UK							
1	Gone	(Go!Disc GODCD 140)	75	1996	0	1996	
2	Gritty Shaker	(Go!Beat GOBCD 2)	53	1997	0	1997	
David Houston Male Guitarist/Singer/Songwriter, B: 9 Dec 1938 Bossier City, Louisiana							
9	Almost Persuaded		0	1966	24	1966	(Epic 10025)
	HIS 60 OTHER HITS WERE C/W • OBITUARY: D: 30 NOV 1993 RUPTURED BRAIN ANEURISM						
David Hughes Male Vocalist from the UK							
1	By The Fountain Of Rome	(Philips PB 606)	27	1956	0	1956	
David Joseph Male Vocalist from the UK							
1	You Can't Hide (Your Love From Me)	(Island IS 101)	13	1983	0	1983	
2	Let's Live It Up (Nite People)	(Island IS 116)	26	1983	0	1983	
3	Joys Of Life	(Island IS 153)	61	1984	0	1984	
4	Expansions '86 (Expand Your Mind)	(Fourth & Broadway BRW 48)	58	1986	0	1986	
	HIT 4 IS CREDITED TO CHRIS PAUL FEATURING DAVID JOSEPH						
David Lasley Male Vocalist, B: 20 Aug 1947 Michigan							
1	If I Had My Wish Tonight		0	1982	36	1982	(EMI America 8111)
	ALSO WORKED AS A BACK-UP SINGER FOR JAMES TAYLOR AND OTHERS						
David Lee Roth Male Vocalist, B: 10 Oct 1955 Bloomington, Indiana							
1	California Girls	(Warner Bros. W 9102)	68	1985	3	1985	(Warner Bros. 29102)
2	Just A Gigolo / I Ain't Got Nobody		0	1985	12	1985	(Warner Bros. 29040)
3	Yankee Rose		0	1986	16	1986	(Warner Bros. 28656)
4	Just Like Paradise	(Warner Bros. W 8119)	27	1988	6	1988	(Warner Bros.28119)
5	Damn Good / Stand Up	(Warner Bros. W 7753)	72	1988	0	1988	
6	A Lil' Ain't Enough	(Warner Bros. W 0002)	32	1991	0	1991	
7	She's My Machine	(Reprise W 0229CD)	64	1994	0	1994	
8	Night Life	(Reprise W 0249CD)	72	1994	0	1994	
	HE WAS LEAD SINGER WITH VAN HALEN						
David MacBeth Male Vocalist from the UK							
1	Mr. Blue	(PYE 7N 15231)	18	1959	0	1959	
David McAlmont Male Vocalist from the UK							
1	Yes	(Hut HUTCD 53)	8	1995	0	1995	
2	You Do	(Hut HUTDG 57)	17	1995	0	1995	
3	Hymn	(Blanco Y Negro NEG 87CD)	65	1996	0	1996	

ISSUE	TITLE	UK LBL	UK POS	UK YEAR	US POS	US YEAR	US LBL
4	Look At Yourself	(Hut HUTCD 87)	40	1997	0	1997	

HITS 1-2 ARE CREDITED TO MCALMONT AND BUTLER • HIT 3 IS CREDITED TO ULTRAMARINE FEATURING DAVID MCALMONT

David McCallum Male Vocalist from the UK

1	Communication	(Capitol CL 15439)	32	1966	0	1966	

David Morales & The Bad Yard Male Producer from the USA

1	Gimme Luv (Eenie Meenie Miny Mo)	(Mercury MERCD 390)	37	1993	0	1993	
2	The Program	(Mercury MERCD 396)	66	1993	0	1993	
3	In De Ghetto	(Manifesto FESCD 12)	35	1996	0	1996	

HIT 3 IS CREDITED TO DAVID MORALES & THE BAD YARD CLUB FEATURING CRYSTAL WATERS & DELTA • SEE ALSO BOSS, PULSE

David Naughton Male Vocalist from the USA

1	Makin' It (From *Meatballs*)	(RSO 32)	44	1979	5	1979	(RSO 916)

David Parton Male Vocalist from the UK

1	Isn't She Lovely	(PYE 7N 45663)	4	1977	0	1977	

David Rose & His Orchestra Male Orchestra Leader, B: 15 Jun 1910 London, England

*	1	Holiday For Strings		0	1943	2	1943	(Victor 27853)
	2	Poinciana (Song Of The Tree)		0	1944	11	1944	(Victor 1554)
*	3	The Stripper		0	1962	11	1962	(MGM 13064)

PREVIOUSLY MARRIED TO MARTHA RAYE 1938-41, AND JUDY GARLAND 1941-1943 • OBITUARY: D: 23 AUG 1990 HEART DISEASE.

David Ruffin Male Vocalist, Real Name Davis Eli Ruffin B: 18 Jan 1941 Meridian, Mississippi

+	1	I'm So Glad I Fell For You		0	1969	18	1969	(Motown 1158)
	2	My Whole World Ended (The Moment You Left Me)		0	1969	9	1969	(Motown 1140)
+	3	I've Lost Everything I've Ever Loved		0	1969	11	1969	(Motown 1149)
+	4	Stand By Me		0	1970	24	1970	(Soul 35076)
*	5	Walk Away From Love	(Tamla Motown TMG 1017)	10	1976	9	1975	(Motown 1376)
	6	A Night At The Apollo Live! The Way You Do The Things	(RCA PB 49935)	58	1985	20	1985	(RCA 14178)
		You Do/My Girl						

HIT 4 IS CREDITED TO DAVID AND JIMMY RUFFIN • HIT 6 IS CREDITED TO DARYL HALL, JOHN OATS WITH DAVID RUFFIN & EDDIE KENDRICK

OBITUARY : D: 1 JUN 1991 DRUG OVERDOSE. • SEE ALSO THE TEMPTATIONS

David Seville Male Vocalist, Real Name Ross Bagdasarian B: 27 Jan 1919 California.

*	1	Witch Doctor	(London HLU 8619)	11	1958	1	1958	(Liberty 55140)
	2	The Bird On My Head		0	1958	34	1958	(Liberty 55132)
*	3	The Chipmunk Song (Christmas Don't Be Late)		0	1958	1	1958	(Liberty 55168)
*	4	Alvin's Harmonica		0	1959	3	1959	(Liberty 55179)
	5	Ragtime Cowboy Joe	(London HLU 8916)	11	1959	16	1959	(Liberty 55200)
	6	Alvin's Orchestra		0	1960	33	1960	(Liberty 55233)
	7	Rudolph The Red Nosed Reindeer		0	1960	21	1960	(Liberty 55289)
	8	The Chipmunk Song (Re-Issue)		0	1962	39	1962	(Liberty 55250)
	9	The Alvin Twist		0	1962	40	1962	(Liberty 55424)
	10	The Chipmunks Song (2nd Re-Issue)		0	1962	40	1962	(Liberty 55250)

HITS 1-2 ARE CREDITED TO DAVID SEVILLE • HIT 3 IS CREDITED TO THE CHIPMUNKS WITH DAVID SEVILLE

HITS 4-10 ARE CREDITED TO DAVID SEVILLE & THE CHIPMUNKS • SEE ALSO CHIPMUNKS • OBITUARY : D: 16 JAN 1972.

David Soul Male Vocalist, Real Name David Solberg B: 28 Aug 1943 Chicago

*	1	Don't Give Up On Us	(Private Stock PVT 84)	1	1976	1	1977	(Private Stock 45129)
	2	Going In With My Eyes Wide Open	(Private Stock PVT 99)	7	1977	0	1977	
	3	Silver Lady	(Private Stock PVT 115)	1	1977	0	1977	
	4	Let's Have A Quiet Night In	(Private Stock PVT 130)	8	1977	0	1977	
	5	It Sure Bring Out The Love In Your Eyes	(Private Stock PVT 137)	12	1978	0	1978	

David Sylvian Male Vocalist from the UK

1	Bamboo Houses	(Virgin VS 510)	16	1983	0	1983	
2	Forbidden Colours	(Virgin VS 601)	16	1983	0	1983	
3	Red Guitar	(Virgin VS 633)	17	1984	0	1984	
4	The Ink In The Well	(Virgin VS 700)	36	1984	0	1984	
5	Pulling Punches	(Virgin VS 835)	56	1984	0	1984	
6	Words With The Shaman	(Virgin VS 835)	72	1985	0	1985	
7	Taking The Veil	(Virgin VS 815)	53	1986	0	1986	
8	Buoy	(Virgin VS 910)	63	1987	0	1987	
9	Let The Happiness In	(Virgin VS 1001)	66	1987	0	1987	
10	Heartbeat (Tainai Kaiki Ii) Returning To The Womb	(Virgin America VUS 57)	58	1992	0	1992	
11	Jean The Birdman	(Virgin VSCDG 1462)	68	1993	0	1993	

HIT 1 IS CREDITED TO SYLVIAN SAKAMOTO • HIT 2 IS CREDITED TO DAVID SYLVIAN AND RIUICHI SAKAMOTO

HIT 8 IS CREDITED TO MICK KARN FEATURING DAVID SYLVIAN

ISSUE	TITLE	UK LBL	UK POS	UK YEAR	US POS	US YEAR	US LBL
David Thorne Male Vocalist from the USA							
1	Alley Cat Song	(Stateside SS 141)	21	1963	0	1963	
David Van Day Male Vocalist from the UK							
1	Young Americans Talking	(WEA DAY 1)	43	1983	0	1983	
David Whitfield Male Vocalist, B: 2 Feb 1926 Hull, Yorkshire, England							
1	Bridge Of Sighs	(Decca F 10129)	9	1953	0	1953	
2	Answer Me	(Decca F 10192)	1	1953	0	1953	
3	Rags To Riches	(Decca F 10207)	12	1953	0	1953	
4	Rags To Riches (Re-Entry)	(Decca F 10207)	3	1954	0	1954	
5	Answer Me (Re-Entry)	(Decca F 10192)	12	1954	0	1954	
6	The Book	(Decca F 10242)	5	1954	0	1954	
7	The Book (Re-Entry)	(Decca F 10242)	10	1954	0	1954	
* 8	Cara Mia		0	1954	10	1954	(London 1486)
9	Smile		0	1954	25	1954	(London 1494)
10	Santo Natale	(Decca F 10399)	2	1954	19	1954	(London 1508)
11	Beyond The Stars	(Decca F 10458)	8	1955	0	1955	
12	Mama	(Decca F 10515)	20	1955	0	1955	
13	Mama (Re-Entry)	(Decca F 10515)	19	1955	0	1955	
14	Ev'rewhere	(Decca F 10515)	3	1955	0	1955	
15	Mama (2nd Re-Entry)	(Decca F 10515)	12	1955	0	1955	
16	When You Lose The One You Love	(Decca F 10627)	7	1955	0	1955	
17	My September Love	(Decca F 10690)	19	1956	0	1956	
18	My September Love (Re-Entry)	(Decca F 10690)	18	1956	0	1956	
19	My September Love (2nd Re-Entry)	(Decca F 10690)	3	1956	0	1956	
20	My Son John	(Decca F 10769)	22	1956	0	1956	
21	My Unfinished Symphony	(Decca F 10769)	29	1956	0	1956	
22	My September Love (3rd Re-Entry)	(Decca F 10690)	25	1956	0	1956	
23	Adoration Waltz	(Decca F 10833)	9	1957	0	1957	
24	I'll Find You	(Decca F 10864)	28	1957	0	1957	
25	I'll Find You (Re-Entry)	(Decca F 10864)	27	1957	0	1957	
26	Cry My Heart	(Decca F 10978)	22	1958	0	1958	
27	On The Street Where You Live	(Decca F 11018)	16	1958	0	1958	
28	The Right To Love	(Decca F 11039)	30	1958	0	1958	
29	I Believe	(Decca F 11289)	49	1960	0	1960	
	HITS 8, 11, 16 ARE CREDITED TO DAVID WHITFIELD WITH CHORUS AND MANTOVANI & HIS ORCHESTRA • SEE ALSO ALL STAR HIT PARADE, VARIOUS ARTISTS (EP, LP, 78S)						
Davie Allan & The Arrows Male Guitarist from the USA							
1	Apache '65		0	1965	64	1965	(Tower 116)
2	Blue's Theme		0	1967	37	1967	(Tower 295)
	SEE ALSO MAX FROST & THE TROOPERS						
Davis Sisters Female Vocal Duo, Full Names: Mary Frances Penick And Betty Davis from the USA							
1	I Forgot More Than You'll Ever Know		0	1953	18	1953	(RCA Victor 5345)
	OBITUARY: BETTY D: 1953, CAR ACCIDENT.						
Dawn Mixed Vocal Group from the USA Names: Tony Orlando, Joyce Vincent & Telma Hopkins							
* 1	Candida	(Bell 1118)	9	1971	3	1970	(Bell 903)
* 2	Knock Three Times	(Bell 1146)	1	1971	1	1970	(Bell 938)
3	I Play And Sing		0	1971	25	1971	(Bell 970)
4	Summer Sand		0	1971	33	1971	(Bell 45107)
5	What Are You Doing Sunday	(Bell 1169)	3	1971	39	1971	(Bell 45141)
* 6	Tie A Yellow Ribbon Round The Old Oak Tree	(Bell 1287)	1	1973	1	1973	(Bell 45318)
* 7	Say, Has Anybody Seen My Sweet Gypsy Rose	(Bell 1322)	12	1973	3	1973	(Bell 45374)
8	Who's In The Strawberry Patch With Sally	(Bell 1343)	37	1974	27	1974	(Bell 45424)
9	Tie A Yellow Ribbon Round The Old Oak Tree (Re-Entry)	(Bell 1287)	41	1974	0	1974	
10	Steppin' Out (Gonna Boogie Tonight)		0	1974	7	1974	(Bell 45601)
11	Look Into My Eyes Pretty Woman		0	1975	11	1975	(Bell 45620)
* 12	He Don't Love You (Like I Love You)		0	1975	1	1975	(Elektra 45240)
13	Mornin' Beautiful		0	1975	14	1975	(Elektra 45260)
14	You're All I Need To Get By		0	1975	34	1975	(Elektra 45275)
15	Cupid		0	1976	22	1976	(Elektra 45302)
	HIT 2 HAD GLOBAL SALES OF OVER SIX MILLION • DAWN CHANGED THEIR NAME BECAUSE THERE WERE 14 OTHER DAWNS AROUND THE WORLD AT THE TIME						
Dawn Penn Female Vocalist from Jamaica							
1	You Don't Love Me (No, No, No)	(BIG BEAT A 8295CD)	3	1994	0	1994	
Dayton Male Vocalist from the USA							
1	The Sound Of Music	(Capitol CL 318)	75	1983	0	1983	

ISSUE	TITLE	UK LBL	UK POS	UK YEAR	US POS	US YEAR	US LBL
Dazz Band	Male Vocal/Instrumental Group from the USA						
1	Let It Whip		0	1982	5	1982	(Motown 1609)
2	Let It All Blow	(Motown TMG 1361)	12	1984	0	1984	
De Castro Sisters	Female Vocal Group from the USA						
1	Teach Me Tonight	(London HL 8104)	20	1955	10	1954	(Abbott 3001)
2	Boom Boom Boomerang		0	1955	17	1955	(Abbott 3003)
	MALE VOICE ON HIT 2 ARE BY THURL RAVENSCROFT • NAMES: BABETTE, CHERIE & PEGGY FROM CUBA						
De Etta Little & Nelson Pigford	Mixed Vocal Duo from the USA						
1	You Take My Heart Away	(United Artists UP 36257)	35	1977	0	1977	
De John Sisters	Female Vocalist, Real Names Julie & Dux Degiovanni from the USA						
1	No More		0	1954	26	1954	(Epic 9085)
De La Soul	Male Rap Trio From Long Island, New York						
* 1	Me Myself And I	(Big Life BLR 7)	22	1989	34	1989	(Tommy Boy 7926)
2	Say No Go	(Big Life BLR 10)	18	1989	0	1989	
3	Eye Know	(Big Life BLR 13)	14	1989	0	1989	
4	The Magic Number	(Big Life BLR 14)	7	1989	0	1989	
5	Buddy	(Big Life BLR 14)	13	1989	0	1989	
6	Mama Gave Birth To The Soul Children	(GEE Street GEE 26)	14	1990	0	1990	
7	Ring Ring Ring (Ha Ha Hey)	(Big Life BLR 42)	10	1991	0	1991	
8	A Roller Skating Jam Named 'Saturdays'	(Big Life BLR 55)	22	1991	0	1991	
9	Keepin' The Faith	(Big Life BLR 62)	50	1991	0	1991	
10	Breakadawn	(Big Life BLRD 103)	39	1993	0	1993	
11	Fallin'	(Epic 6602522)	59	1994	0	1994	
12	Stakes Is High	(Tommy Boy TBCD 7730)	55	1996	0	1996	
13	4 More	(Tommy Boy TBCD 7779A)	52	1997	0	1997	
	HIT 13 IS CREDITED TO DE LA SOUL FEATURING ZHANE • HIT 6 IS CREDITED TO QUEEN LATIFAH + DE LA SOUL HIT 11 IS CREDITED TO TEENAGE FANCLUB AND DE LA SOUL						
De'lacy	Mixed Vocal/Instrumental Group from the USA						
1	Hideaway	(Slip 'n' Slide 74321310472)	9	1995	0	1995	
2	That Look	(Slip 'n' Slide 74321398322)	19	1996	0	1996	
De-Code (Featuring) Beverli Skeete	Mixed Vocal/Instrumental Group from the UK						
1	Wonderwall / Some Might Say	(Neotronic NRCD 2)	69	1996	0	1996	
Deacon Blue	Mixed Vocal/Instrumental Group from the UK						
1	Dignity	(CBS DEAC 4)	31	1988	0	1988	
2	When Will You Make My Telephone Ring	(CBS DEAC 5)	34	1988	0	1988	
3	Chocolate Girl	(CBS DEAC 6)	43	1988	0	1988	
4	Real Gone Kid	(CBS DEAC 7)	8	1988	0	1988	
5	Wages Day	(CBS DEAC 8)	18	1989	0	1989	
6	Fergus Sings The Blues	(CBS DEAC 9)	14	1989	0	1989	
7	Love And Regret	(CBS DEAC 10)	28	1989	0	1989	
8	Queen Of The New Year	(CBS DEAC 11)	21	1990	0	1990	
9	Four Bacharach And David Songs (EP)	(CBS DEAC 12)	2	1990	0	1990	
10	Your Swaying Arms	(Columbia 6568937)	23	1991	0	1991	
11	Twist And Shout	(Columbia 6573027)	10	1991	0	1991	
12	Closing Time	(Columbia 6575027)	42	1991	0	1991	
13	Cover From The Sky	(Columbia 6576737)	31	1991	5	1991	
14	Your Town	(Columbia 6587867)	14	1992	0	1992	
15	Will We Be Lovers	(Columbia 6589732)	31	1993	0	1993	
16	Only Tender Love	(Columbia 6591842)	22	1993	0	1993	
17	Hang Your Head (EP)	(Columbia 6594602)	21	1993	0	1993	
18	I Was Right And You Were Wrong	(Columbia 6602222)	32	1994	0	1994	
19	Dignity	(Columbia 6604485)	20	1994	0	1994	
	HIT 19 WAS THE ORIGINAL VERSION OF SONG 1, BUT NOT A HIT						
Dead Dred	Male Production/Instrumental Duo from the UK						
1	Dread Bass	(MOVING SHADOW SHADOW 50CD)	60	1994	0	1994	
Dead End Kids	Male Vocal/Instrumental Group from the UK						
1	Have I The Right	(CBS 4972)	6	1977	0	1977	
Dead Kennedys	Male Vocal/Instrumental Group from the USA						
1	Kill The Poor	(Cherry Red Cherry 16)	49	1980	0	1980	
2	Too Drunk To F—K	(Cherry Red Cherry 24)	36	1981	0	1981	
Dead Or Alive	Male Vocal/Instrumental Group from the UK						
1	That's The Way (I Like It)	(Epic A 4271)	22	1984	0	1984	
2	You Spin Me Round (Like A Record)	(Epic A 4861)	1	1984	11	1985	(Epic 04894)
3	Lover Come Back To Me	(Epic A 6086)	11	1985	0	1985	

ISSUE	TITLE	UK LBL	UK POS	UK YEAR	US POS	US YEAR	US LBL
4	In Too Deep	(Epic A 6360)	14	1985	0	1985	
5	My Heart Goes Bang (Get Me To The Doctor)	(Epic A 6571)	31	1985	0	1985	
6	Brand New Lover	(Epic A 650075	31	1986	15	1987	(Epic 06374)
7	Something In My House	(Epic Burns 1)	12	1987	0	1987	
8	Hooked On Love	(Epic Burns 2)	69	1987	0	1987	
9	Turn Around And Count 2 Ten	(Epic Burns 4)	70	1988	0	1988	
10	Come Home With Me Baby	(Epic Burns 5)	62	1989	0	1989	
	LEAD SINGER PETE BURNS B: 5 AUG 1959						

Deadeye Dick   Male Vocal/Instrumental Trio from New Orleans

* 1	New Age Girl		0	1994	27	1994	(ICHIBAN 232)

Deadly Sins   Male Vocal/Instrumental Duo from UK/Italy

1	We Are Going On Down	(FFRRREEDOM TABCD 220)	45	1994	0	1994	

Dean & Jean   Names Are Welton Young & Brenda Lee Jones

1	Tra La La La Suzy		0	1963	35	1963	(Rust 5067)
2	Hey Jean, Hey Dean		0	1964	32	1964	(Rust 5075)

Dean Friedman   Male Vocalist from the USA

* 1	Ariel		0	1977	26	1977	(Lifesong 45022)
2	Woman Of Mine	(Lifesong LS 401)	52	1978	0	1978	
3	Lucky Stars	(Lifesong LS 402)	3	1978	0	1978	
4	Lydia	(Lifesong LS 403)	31	1978	0	1978	

Dean Martin   Male Vocalist/Actor/TV Show Host(1965-74) Real Name Dino Crocetti. B: 7 Jun 1917 In Steubenville, Ohio

1	That Certain Party		0	1948	22	1948	(Capitol 15249)
2	Powder Your Face With Sunshine (Smile, Smile, Smile)		0	1949	10	1949	(Capitol 15351)
3	I'll Always Love You (From My Friend Irma Goes West)		0	1950	11	1950	(Capitol 1028)
4	If		0	1951	14	1951	(Capitol 1342)
5	You Belong To Me		0	1952	12	1952	(Capitol 2165)
6	Love Me, Love Me		0	1953	25	1953	(Capitol 2485)
7	Kiss	(Capitol CL 13893)	9	1953	0	1953	
8	Kiss (Re-Entry)	(Capitol CL 03893)	5	1953	0	1953	
* 9	That's Amore (From The Caddy)	(Capitol CL 14008)	2	1954	2	1953	(Capitol 2589)
10	I Cry Like A Baby		0	1954	21	1954	(Capitol 2749)
11	Sway	(Capitol CL 14138)	6	1954	8	1954	(Capitol 3818)
12	Money Burns A Hole In My Pocket (From Living It Up)		0	1954	23	1954	(Capitol 2818)
13	How Do You Speak To An Angel	(Capitol CL 14150)	15	1954	0	1954	
14	How Do You Speak To An Angel (Re-Entry)	(Capitol CL 14150)	17	1954	0	1954	
15	Naughty Lady Of Shady Lane	(Capitol CL 14226)	5	1955	0	1955	
16	Mambo Italiano	(Capitol CL 14227)	14	1955	0	1955	
17	Let Me Go Lover	(Capitol CL 14226)	3	1955	0	1955	
18	Under The Bridges Of Paris	(Capitol CL 14225)	6	1955	0	1955	
* 19	Memories Are Made Of This	(Capitol CL 14523)	1	1956	1	1955	(Capitol 3295)
20	Young And Foolish	(Capitol CL14519)	20	1956	0	1956	
21	Innamorata	(Capitol CL 14507)	21	1956	27	1956	(Capitol 3352)
22	Standing On The Corner		0	1956	22	1956	(Capitol 3414)
23	The Man Who Plays The Mandolino	(Capitol CL 14690)	21	1957	0	1957	
24	Return To Me	(Capitol CL14844)	2	1958	4	1958	(Capitol 3894)
25	Angel Baby		0	1958	30	1958	(Capitol 3988)
26	Volare	(Capitol CL 14910)	2	1958	12	1958	(Capitol 4028)
* 27	Everybody Loves Somebody	(Reprise R 20281)	11	1964	1	1964	(Reprise 0281)
28	The Door Is Still Open To My Heart	(Reprise R 20307)	42	1964	6	1964	(Reprise 0307)
29	You're Nobody Till Somebody Loves You		0	1965	25	1965	(Reprise 0333)
30	Send Me The Pillow You Dream On		0	1965	22	1965	(Reprise 0344)
31	(Remember Me) I'm The One Who Loves You		0	1965	32	1965	(Reprise 0369)
32	Houston		0	1965	21	1965	(Reprise 0393)
33	I Will		0	1965	10	1965	(Reprise 0415)
34	Somewhere There's A Someone		0	1966	32	1966	(Reprise 0443)
35	Come Running Back		0	1966	35	1966	(Reprise 0466)
36	In The Chapel In The Moonlight		0	1967	25	1967	(Reprise 0601)
37	Little Ole Wine Drinker, Me		0	1967	38	1967	(Reprise 0608)
38	Gentle On My Mind	(Reprise RS 23343)	2	1969	0	1969	
39	Gentle On My Mind (Re-Entry)	(Reprise RS 23343)	49	1969	0	1969	
! 40	My First Country Song		0	1983	35	1983	(Warner Bros. 29584)
41	That's Amore (Re-Issue)	(EMI PREMIER PRESCD 3)	43	1996	0	1996	

DEAN'S PREVIOUS JOBS INCLUDE STEEL WORKER & A PRIZE FIGHTER • OBITUARY : D: 25 DEC 1995 LIVER/KIDNEY FAILURE.

ISSUE	TITLE	UK LBL	UK POS	UK YEAR	US POS	US YEAR	US LBL
Dean Parrish Male Vocalist from the USA							
1	I'm On My Way	(UK USA 2)	38	1975	0	1975	
Deane Hawley Real Name William Dean Hawley from California							
1	Look For A Star (From The Film *Circus Of Horrors*)		0	1960	29	1960	(DORE 554)
Dear Jon Mixed Vocal/Instrumental Group from the UK							
1	One Gift Of Love	(MDMC DEVCS	68	1995	0	1995	
Debbie Gibson Female Vocalist, B: 31 Aug 1970 Long Island							
* 1	Only In My Dreams	(Atlantic A 9322)	54	1987	4	1987	(Atlantic 89322)
2	Shake Your Love	(Atlantic A 9187)	7	1988	4	1987	(Atlantic 89187)
3	Out Of The Blue	(Atlantic A 9091)	19	1988	3	1988	(Atlantic 89129)
4	Only In My Dreams (Re-Entry)	(Atlantic A 9322)	11	1988	0	1988	
5	Foolish Beat	(Atlantic A 9059)	9	1988	1	1988	(Atlantic 89109)
6	Staying Together	(Atlantic A 9020)	53	1988	22	1988	(Atlantic 89034)
7	Lost In Your Eyes	(Atlantic A 8970)	34	1989	1	1989	(Atlantic 88970)
8	Electric Youth	(Atlantic A 8919)	14	1989	11	1989	(Atlantic 88919)
9	No More Rhyme		0	1989	17	1989	(Atlantic 88885)
10	We Could Be Together	(Atlantic A 8896)	22	1989	0	1989	
11	Anything Is Possible	(Atlantic A 7735)	51	1991	26	1990	(Atlantic 87793)
12	Shock Your Mama	(Atlantic A 7386CD)	74	1993	0	1993	
13	You're The One That I Want	(Epic 6595222)	13	1993	0	1993	
	HIT 13 IS CREDITED TO GRAIG MCLACHLAN AND DEBBIE GIBSON						
Debbie Harry Female Vocalist, Former Lead Singer With Blondie from the USA							
1	Backfired	(Chrysalis CHS 2526)	32	1981	0	1981	
2	French Kissin' In The USA	(Chrysalis CHS 3066)	8	1986	0	1986	
3	Free To Fall	(Chrysalis CHS 3093)	46	1987	0	1987	
4	In Love With Love	(Chrysalis CHS 3128)	45	1987	0	1987	
5	I Want That Man	(Chrysalis CHS 3369)	13	1989	0	1989	
6	Brite Side	(Chrysalis CHS 3452)	59	1989	0	1989	
7	Sweet And Low	(Chrysalis CHS 3491)	57	1990	0	1990	
8	Well Did You Evah!	(Chrysalis CHS 3646)	42	1991	0	1991	
9	I Can See Clearly Now	(Chrysalis CDCHSS 4900)	23	1993	0	1993	
10	Strike Me Pink	(Chrysalis CDCHSS 5000)	46	1993	0	1993	
	HITS 1, 3, 4 ARE CREDITED TO DEBORAH HARRY • HIT 8 IS CREDITED TO DEBORAH HARRY AND IGGY POP						
Debbie Reynolds Female Vocalist, Real Name Mary Frances Reynolds B: 1 Apr 1932 El Paso, Texas.							
* 1	Ada Daba Honeymoon		0	1951	3	1951	(MGM 30282)
* 2	Tammy	(VOGUE Coral Q 72274)	2	1957	1	1957	(Coral 61851)
3	A Very Special Love		0	1958	20	1958	(Coral 61897)
4	Am I That Easy To Forget		0	1960	25	1960	(DOT 15985)
	HIT 1 IS CREDITED TO DEBBIE REYNOLDS AND CARLETON CARPENTER						
Debby Boone Female Vocalist, B: 22 Sep 1956 New Jersey, Daughter Of Pat Boone							
1	You Light Up My Life	(Warner Bros. K 17043)	48	1977	1	1977	(Warner Bros. 8455)
! 2	Baby I'm Yours		0	1978	33	1978	(Warner Bros. 8554)
3	God Knows		0	1978	74	1978	(Warner Bros. 8554)
	OTHER HITS WERE C/W						
Deborah Allen Female Country Singer/Songwriter, Real Name Deborah Lynn Thurmond. B: 30 Sep 1953 In Memphis							
8	Baby I Lied		0	1983	26	1983	(RCA 13600)
Deborah Cox Female Singer/Songwriter, B: 13 Jul 1974 Toronto, Canada							
1	Sentimental	(Arista 74321324962)	34	1995	27	1995	(Arista 12852)
2	Who Do U Love	(Arista 74321337942)	31	1996	17	1996	
3	Where Do We Go From Here		0	1996	48	1996	(Arista 1-3223)
4	The Sound Of My Tears		0	1997	97	1997	(Arista 13277)
Dee C. Lee Female Vocalist from the UK							
1	See The Day	(CBS A 6570)	3	1985	0	1985	
2	Come Hell Or Waters High	(CBS A 6869)	46	1986	0	1986	
3	No Time To Play	(Cooltempo CDCool 282)	25	1993	0	1993	
	HIT 3 IS CREDITED TO GURU FEATURING DEE C. LEE						
Dee Clark Male Vocalist, Real Name Delecta Clark B: 7 Nov 1938 Blythsville, Arkansas							
1	Nobody But You		0	1959	21	1959	(Abner 1019)
2	Just Keep It Up	(London HL 8915)	26	1959	18	1959	(Abner 1026)
3	Hey Little Girl		0	1959	20	1959	(Abner 1029)
4	How About That		0	1960	33	1960	(Abner 1032)
5	Your Friends		0	1961	34	1961	(VEE-JAY 372)
* 6	Raindrops		0	1961	2	1961	(VEE-JAY 383)

	ISSUE	TITLE	UK LBL	UK POS	UK YEAR	US POS	US YEAR	US LBL
	7	Ride A Wild Horse	(Chelsea 2005 037)	16	1975	0	1975	

HE WAS PREVIOUSLY A MEMBER OF THE GOLDENTONES, KOOL GENTS, DELEGATES & THE HAMBONE KIDS • OBITUARY: D: 7 DEC 1990 HEART ATTACK.

Dee D. Jackson Female Vocalist from the UK

	ISSUE	TITLE	UK LBL	UK POS	UK YEAR	US POS	US YEAR	US LBL
	1	Automatic Lover	(Mercury 6007 171)	4	1978	0	1978	
	2	Meteor Man	(Mercury 6007 182)	48	1978	0	1978	

Dee Dee Ford See Don Gardner

Dee Dee Sharp Female Vocalist, Real Name Dione Larue, B: 9 Sep 1945 Philadelphia

	ISSUE	TITLE	UK LBL	UK POS	UK YEAR	US POS	US YEAR	US LBL
	1	Slow Twistin'		0	1962	0	1962	(Parkway 835)
*	2	Mashed Potato Time		0	1962	2	1962	(Cameo 212)
	3	Do The Bird	(Cameo Parkway C 244)	46	1963	10	1963	(Cameo 244)
	4	Gravy (For My Mashed Potatoes)		0	1962	9	1962	(Cameo 219)
*	5	Ride!		0	1962	5	1962	(Cameo 230)
	6	Wild!		0	1963	33	1963	(Cameo 274)

SHE HAS ALSO RECORDED AS DEE DEE SHARP GAMBLE • HIT 1 IS CREDITED TO CHUBBY CHECKER WITH DEE DEE SHARP

Dee Fredrix Female Vocalist from the UK

	ISSUE	TITLE	UK LBL	UK POS	UK YEAR	US POS	US YEAR	US LBL
	1	And So I Will Wait For You	(East West YZ 725CD)	56	1993	0	1993	
	2	Dirty Money	(East West YZ 750CD)	74	1993	0	1993	

Dee Lewis Female Vocalist from the UK

	ISSUE	TITLE	UK LBL	UK POS	UK YEAR	US POS	US YEAR	US LBL
	1	The Best Of My Love	(Mercury DEE 3)	47	1988	0	1988	

Deee-Lite Dance/Vocal/Instrumental Trio Based In New York

	ISSUE	TITLE	UK LBL	UK POS	UK YEAR	US POS	US YEAR	US LBL
*	1	Groove Is In The Heart / What Is Love	(Elektra EKR 114)	2	1990	4	1990	(Elektra 64934)
	2	Power Of Love / Deee-Lite Theme	(Elektra EKR 117)	25	1990	0	1990	
	3	How Do You Say ...LOVE / Groove Is In The Heart (Re-Mix)	(Elektra EKR 118)	52	1991	0	1991	
	4	Good Beat / Riding On Through	(Elektra EKR 122)	53	1991	0	1991	
	5	Runaway	(Elektra EKR 148)	45	1992	0	1992	
	6	Picnic In The Summertime	(Elektra EKR 186CD1)	43	1994	0	1994	

Deele Funk Sextet Led By Darnell 'Dee' Bristol & Includes Mark Rooney & Keith Edmonds (Producers/Songwriter) from the USA

	ISSUE	TITLE	UK LBL	UK POS	UK YEAR	US POS	US YEAR	US LBL
	1	Two Occasions		0	1988	10	1988	(SOLAR 70015)

Deep Blue Real Name Sean O'Keefe Male Producer from the UK

	ISSUE	TITLE	UK LBL	UK POS	UK YEAR	US POS	US YEAR	US LBL
	1	Helicopter Tune	(Moving Shadow Shadow 41CD)	68	1994	0	1994	
	2	Josey	(Interscope IND 95518)	27	1996	0	1996	

Deep Blue Something Male Vocal/Instrumental Group Grom The USA

	ISSUE	TITLE	UK LBL	UK POS	UK YEAR	US POS	US YEAR	US LBL
	1	Breakfast At Tiffany's	(Interscope IND 80032)	55	1996	5	1995	(Rainmaker 98138)
	2	Breakfast At Tiffany's (Re-Entry)	(Interscope IND 80032)	1	1996	0	1996	
	3	Josey	(Interscope IND 95518)	27	1996	0	1996	

Deep C Mixed Vocal/Instrumental Group from the UK

	ISSUE	TITLE	UK LBL	UK POS	UK YEAR	US POS	US YEAR	US LBL
	1	African Reign	(M&G MAGS 4)	75	1991	0	1991	
	2	Chill To The Panic	(M&G MAGS 10)	73	1991	0	1991	

Deep Creed '94 Real Name Armand Van Helden Male Producer from the USA

	ISSUE	TITLE	UK LBL	UK POS	UK YEAR	US POS	US YEAR	US LBL
	1	Can You Feel It	(Eastern Bloc BlocCD 005)	59	1994	0	1994	

Deep Feeling Male Vocal/Instrumental Group from the UK

	ISSUE	TITLE	UK LBL	UK POS	UK YEAR	US POS	US YEAR	US LBL
	1	Do You Love Me	(Page One POF 165)	45	1970	0	1970	
	2	Do You Love Me (Re-Entry)	(Page One POF 165)	34	1970	0	1970	

Deep Fish Male Instrumental/Production Duo from the USA

	ISSUE	TITLE	UK LBL	UK POS	UK YEAR	US POS	US YEAR	US LBL
	1	Stay Gold	(Deconstruction 74321418222)	41	1996	0	1996	

Deep Forest Male Instrumental Duo from France

	ISSUE	TITLE	UK LBL	UK POS	UK YEAR	US POS	US YEAR	US LBL
	1	Sweet Lullaby	(Columbia 6599242)	10	1994	0	1994	
	2	Deep Forest	(Columbia 6604115)	20	1994	0	1994	
	3	Savanna Dance	(Columbia 6606355)	28	1994	0	1994	
	4	Marta's Song	(Columbia 6621402)	26	1995	0	1995	

Deep Purple Male Vocal/Instrumental Group from the UK

	ISSUE	TITLE	UK LBL	UK POS	UK YEAR	US POS	US YEAR	US LBL
*	1	Hush	(Harvest HAR 5020)	62	1968	4	1968	(Tetragramm 1503)
	2	Kentucky Woman		0	1968	38	1968	(Tetragramm 1508)
	3	Black Night		2	1970	0	1970	
	4	Strange Kind Of Woman	(Harvest HAR 5033)	8	1971	0	1971	
	5	Fireball	(Harvest HAR 5045)	15	1971	0	1971	
	6	Never Before	(Purple Pur 102)	35	1972	0	1972	
*	7	Smoke On The Water	(Purple Pur 132)	21	1977	4	1973	(Warner Bros.7710)
	8	New Live And Rare (EP)	(Purple Pur 135)	31	1977	0	1977	
	9	New Live And Rare (Vol 2)	(Purple Pur 137)	45	1978	0	1978	

ISSUE	TITLE	UK LBL	UK POS	UK YEAR	US POS	US YEAR	US LBL
10	Black Night (Re-Issue)	(Harvest HAR 5210)	43	1980	0	1980	
11	New Live And Rare (Vol 3)	(Harvest SHEP 101)	48	1980	0	1980	
12	Perfect Strangers	(Polydor POSP 719)	48	1985	0	1985	
13	Knocking At Your Back Door / Perfect Strangers	(Polydor Posp 749)	68	1985	0	1985	(Polydor POSP 749)
14	King Of Dreams	(RCA PB 49247)	70	1990	0	1990	
15	Love Conquers All	(RCA PB 49225)	57	1991	0	1991	
16	Black Night (Re-Mix)	(EMI CDEM 382)	66	1995	0	1995	

NAMES: RITCHIE BLACKMORE, ROD EVANS, JON LORD, IAN PAICE & NICKY SIMPER • THERE HAVE BEEN MANY CHANGES OVER THE YEARS

Deep River Boys   Male R&B Vocal Group from the USA

1	Recess In Heaven		0	1948	18	1948	(RCA Victor 3203)
2	That's Right	(HMV POP 263)	29	1956	0	1956	

THEY ALSO RECORDED WITH COUNT BASIE

Def Leppard   Male Vocal/Instrumental Group from Sheffield, England

1	Wasted	(Vertigo 6059 247)	61	1979	0	1979	
2	Hello America	(Vertigo LEPP1)	45	1980	0	1980	
3	Photograph	(Vertigo VER	66	1983	12	1983	(Mercury 811215)
4	Rock Of Ages	(Vertigo VER	41	1983	16	1983	(Mercury 812604)
5	Foolin'		0	1983	28	1983	(Mercury 814178)
6	Animal	(Bludgeon Riffola LEP 1)	6	1987	19	1987	(Mercury 888832)
7	Pour Some Sugar On Me	(Bludgeon Riffola LEP 2)	18	1987	2	1988	(Mercury 870298)
8	Hysteria	(Bludgeon Riffola LEP 3)	26	1987	0	1987	
9	Hysteria (Re-Entry)	(Bludgeon Riffola LEP 3)	74	1988	10	1988	(Mercury 870004)
10	Armageddon It	(Bludgeon Riffola LEP 4)	20	1988	3	1988	(Mercury 870692)
11	Love Bites	(Bludgeon Riffola LEP 5)	11	1988	1	1988	(Mercury 870402)
12	Rocket	(Bludgeon Riffola LEP 6)	15	1989	12	1989	(Mercury 872614)
13	Let's Get Rocked	(Bludgeon Riffola DEF 7)	2	1992	15	1992	(Mercury 866568)
14	Make Love Like A Man	(Bludgeon Riffola LEP 7)	12	1992	36	1992	(Mercury 864038)
15	Have You Ever Needed Someone So Bad	(Bludgeon Riffola LEP 8)	16	1992	12	1992	(Mercury 864136)
16	Stand Up (Kick Love Into Motion)		0	1993	34	1993	(Mercury 964604)
17	Heaven Is	(Bludgeon Riffola LEPCD 9)	13	1993	0	1993	
18	Tonight	(Bludgeon Riffola LEPCD 10)	34	1993	0	1993	
19	Two Steps Behind	(Bludgeon Riffola LEPCD 12)	32	1993	12	1993	(Columbia 77116)
20	Action	(Bludgeon Riffola LEPCD 13)	14	1994	0	1994	
21	Miss You In A Heartbeat		0	1994	39	1994	(Mercury 858080)
22	When Love And Hate Collide	(Bludgeon Riffola LEPDD 14)	2	1995	0	1995	
23	Slang	(Bludgeon Riffola LEPDD 15)	17	1996	0	1996	
24	Work It Out	(Bludgeon Riffola LEPCD 16)	22	1996	0	1996	
25	All I Want Is Everything	(Bludgeon Riffola LEPCD 17)	38	1996	0	1996	
26	Breathe A Sigh	(Bludgeon Riffola LEPCD 18)	43	1996	0	1996	

NAMES: JOE ELLIOT, PETE WILLIS, STEVE CLARK, RICK SAVAGE & RICK ALLEN (DRUMMER), WHO LOST HIS LEFT ARM IN A CAR ACCIDENT ON 31 DEC 1984.
OBITUARY: STEVE CLARK D: 8 JAN 1991 RESPIRATORY FAILURE.

Definition Of Sound   Male Rap Duo from the UK

1	Wear Your Love Like Heaven	(Circa YR 61)	17	1991	0	1991	
2	Now Is Tomorrow	(Circa YR 66)	48	1991	0	1991	
3	Moira Jane's Cafe	(Circa YR 80)	34	1992	0	1992	
4	What Are You Under	(Circa YR 95)	68	1992	0	1992	
5	Can I Get Over	(Circa YR 97)	61	1992	0	1992	
6	Boom Boom	(Fontana DOSCD 1)	59	1995	0	1995	
7	Pass The Vibes	(Fontana DOSCD 2)	23	1995	0	1995	
8	Child	(Fontana DOSCD 3)	48	1996	0	1996	

Defranco Family   Names Benny, Nino, Marisa, Tony & Merlina from Ontario

1	Heartbeat - It's A Lovebeat		0	1973	3	1973	(20th Century 2030)
2	Abra-Ca-Dabra		0	1974	32	1974	(20th Century 2070)
3	Save The Last Dance For Me		0	1974	18	1974	(20th Century 2088)

Degrees Of Motion   Female Vocal Group from the USA

1	Do You Want It Right Now	(FFRR F 184)	31	1992	0	1992	
2	Shine On	(FFRR F 192)	43	1992	0	1992	
3	Soul Freedom / Free Your Soul	(FFRR FX 201)	64	1992	0	1992	
4	Shine On (Re-Mix)	(FFRR FCD 229)	8	1994	0	1994	
5	Do You Want It Right Now (Re-Mix)	(FFRR FCD 246)	26	1994	0	1994	

HIT 2 IS CREDITED TO KIT WEST • ALL HITS ARE CREDITED TO DEGREES OF MOTION FEATURING BITI

Deja   Mixed Vocal Group from the USA

1	Serious	(10 TEN 132)	75	1987	0	1987	

ISSUE	TITLE	UK LBL	UK POS	UK YEAR	US POS	US YEAR	US LBL
Deja Vu Male Vocal/Instrumental Duo from the UK							
1	Why Why Why	(Cowboy Rodeo 941CD)	57	1994	0	1994	
Dejohn Sisters Names Julie B: 18 Mar 1931 & Dux B: 21 Jan 1933 Pennsylvania							
1	(My Baby Don't Love Me) No More		0	1955	6	1955	(Epic 9085)
Del Amitri Male Vocal/Instrumental/Rock Quartet from Scotland							
1	Kiss This Thing Goodbye	(A&M AM 515)	59	1989	35	1989	(A&M 1485)
2	Nothing Ever Happens	(A&M AM 536)	11	1990	0	1990	
3	Kiss This Thing Goodbye (Re-Issue)	(A&M AM 551)	43	1990	0	1990	
4	Move Away Jimmy Blue	(A&M AM 555)	36	1990	0	1990	
5	Spit In The Rain	(A&M AM 589)	21	1990	0	1990	
6	Always The Last To Know	(A&M AM 870)	12	1992	30	1992	(A&M 1604)
7	Be My Downfall	(A&M AM 884)	30	1992	0	1992	
8	Just Like A Man	(A&M AM 0057)	25	1992	0	1992	
9	When You Were Young	(A&M AMCD 0132)	20	1993	0	1993	
10	Driving With The Brakes On	(A&M 5810047)	18	1995	0	1995	
11	Roll To Me	(A&M 5822312)	22	1995	10	1995	(A&M 1114)
12	Tell Her This	(A&M 5812172)	32	1995	0	1995	
13	Here And Now	(A&M 5809592)	21	1995	0	1995	
14	Now Where It's At	(A&M 5822532)	21	1997	0	1997	
Del Shannon Male Vocalist, Charles Westover B: 30 Dec 1939 Coopersville, Michigan							
* 1	Runaway	(London HLX 9317)	1	1961	1	1961	(Big Top 3067)
* 2	Hats Off To Larry	(London HLX 9402)	6	1961	5	1961	(Big Top 3075)
3	So Long Baby	(London HLX 9462)	10	1961	28	1961	(Big Top 3083)
4	Hey! Little Girl	(London HLX 9515)	2	1962	38	1962	(Big Top 3091)
5	Cry Myself To Sleep	(London HLX 9587)	29	1962	0	1962	
6	Swiss Maid	(London HLX 9609)	2	1962	0	1962	
7	Little Town Flirt	(London HLX 9653)	4	1963	12	1963	(Big Top 3131)
8	Two Kinds Of Teardrops	(London HLX 9710)	5	1963	0	1963	
9	Two Silhouettes	(London HLX 9761)	23	1963	0	1963	
10	Sue's Gotta Be Mine	(London HLU 9800)	21	1963	0	1963	
11	Mary Jane	(Stateside SS 269)	35	1964	0	1964	
12	Handy Man	(Stateside SS 317)	36	1964	22	1964	(AMY 905)
* 13	Keep Searchin' (We'll Follow The Sun)	(Stateside SS 368)	3	1965	9	1965	(AMY 915)
14	Stranger In Town	(Stateside SS 395)	40	1965	30	1965	(AMY 919)
15	Sea Of Love		0	1982	33	1982	(NETWORK 47951)
! 16	In My Arms Again		0	1985	56	1986	(Warner Bros. 29098)
	OBITUARY D: 8 FEB 1990 SUICIDE (SHOT HIMSELF).						
Del Wood Female Vocal/Instrumentalist, B: Adelaide Hendricks, 22 Feb 1920 Nashville, Tennessee							
* 1	Down Yonder		0	1951	4	1951	(Tennessee 775)
2	Elmer's Tune		0	1953	24	1953	(Republic 7043)
	HIT 1 REACHED NUMBER 5 IN THE US C/W CHARTS • SHE WAS KNOWN AS THE DOWN YONDER GIRL BECAME A MEMBER OF THE 'GRAND OLE OPRY' IN 1951 • OBITUARY: D: 30 OCT 1989.						
Delage Female Vocal Group from the UK							
1	Rock The Boat	(PWL/Polydor PO 113)	63	1990	0	1990	
Delaney & Bonnie Names: Dalaney Bramlett & His Wife Bonnie Lynn Bramlett							
1	Never Ending Song Of Love		0	1971	13	1971	(ATCO 6804)
2	Only You Know And I Know		0	1971	20	1971	(ATCO 6838)
3	Comin' Home	(Atlantic 584 308)	16	1969	0	1969	
	SEE ALSO ERIC CLAPTON						
Delbert McClinton B: 4 Nov 1940 Lubbock, Texas							
1	Giving It Up For Your Love		0	1980	8	1980	(Capitol 4948)
	HE WAS THE HARMONICA PLAYER ON BRUCE CHANNEL'S 1962 SMASH HIT HEY BABY. ALSO LEADER OF THE RON-DELS						
Delegates Has Snippets of Hits from 1972, Featuring DJ Bob Decarlo							
1	Convention '72		0	1972	8	1972	(Mainstream 5525)
Delegation Male Vocal/Instrumental Group from the UK							
1	Where Is The Love (We Used To Know)	(State STAT 40)	22	1977	0	1977	
2	You've Being Doing Me Wrong	(State STAT 55)	49	1977	0	1977	
Delfonics Male Vocal Group from the USA							
1	La-La Means I Love You	(Bell 1165)	19	1971	4	1968	(Philly Groove 150)
2	I'm Sorry		0	1968	42	1968	(Philly Groove 151)
3	Break Your Promise		0	1968	35	1968	(Philly Groove 152)
4	Ready Or Not Here I Come (Can't Hide From Love)	(Bell 1175)	41	1971	35	1968	(Philly Groove 154)

ISSUE	TITLE	UK LBL	UK POS	UK YEAR	US POS	US YEAR	US LBL
5	You Got Your's And I'll Get Mine		0	1969	40	1969	(Philly Groove 157)
6	Didn't I (Blow Your Mind This Time)	(Bell 1099)	43	1971	10	1970	(Philly Groove 161)
7	Trying To Make A Fool Of Me		0	1970	40	1970	(Philly Groove 162)
+ 8	When You Get Right Down To It		0	1970	12	1970	(Philly Groove 163)
9	Didn't I (Blow Your Mind This Time) (Re-Entry)	(Bell 1099)	22	1971	0	1971	

NAMES: WILLIAM & WILBERT HART, RITCHIE DANIELS & RANDY CAIN • FORMED ORIGINALLY AS THE FOUR GENTS IN 1965

Delinquent Habits Vocal Group from the USA

1	Tres Delinquentes		0	1996	35	1996	(RCA 84526)

Deliverance Soundtrack See Eric Weissberg & Steve Mandell

Della Reese Real Name Delloreese Patricia Early B: 6 Jul 1931 Detroit

1	And That Reminds Me		0	1957	12	1957	(Jubilee 5292)
2	And That Reminds Me (Re-Entry)		0	1957	33	1957	(Jubilee 5292)
* 3	Don't You Know		0	1959	2	1959	(RCA 7591)
4	Not One Minute More		0	1959	16	1959	(RCA 7644)

Dells Male Vocal Group from the USA

+ 1	Oh, What A Night		0	1956	4	1956	(VEE-JAY 204)
+ 2	Stay In My Corner		0	1965	23	1965	(VEE-JAY 674)
3	There Is		0	1968	20	1968	(CADET 5590)
4	Stay In My Corner (Re-Recording)		0	1968	10	1968	(CADET 5612)
5	Always Together		0	1968	18	1968	(CADET 5621)
6	Does Anybody Know I'm Here		0	1969	38	1969	(CADET 5631)
7	I Can Sing A Rainbow / Love Is Blue	(Chess CRS 8099)	15	1969	22	1969	(CADET 5641)
* 8	Oh, What A Night (Re-Recording)		0	1969	10	1969	(CADET 5649)
9	Open Up My Heart		0	1970	51	1970	(CADET 5667)
10	The Love We Had (Stays On My Mind)		0	1971	30	1971	(CADET 5683)
* 11	Give Your Baby A Standing Ovation		0	1973	34	1973	(CADET 5696)

NAMES JOHNNY FUNCHES, MARVIN JUNIOR, VERNE ALLISON, MICKEY MCGILL & CHUCK BARKSDALE • THEY HAD 47 R & B HITS IN THE USA • SEE ALSO BARBARA LEWIS

Delta Rhythm Boys Male Vocal Group from the USA

1	Just A-Sittin' And A-Rockin'		0	1946	17	1946	(Decca 18739)

Deluxe Female Vocalist from the USA

1	Just A Little More	(UNYQUE UNQ 5)	74	1989	0	1989	

Demensions Names Phil Delgiudice, Lenny Dell, Howard Margolin & Marisa Martelli

1	Over The Rainbow		0	1960	16	1960	(Mohawk 116)

Demis Roussos Male Vocalist from Greece

1	Happy To Be On An Island In The Sun	(Philips 6042 033)	5	1975	0	1975	
2	Can't Say How Much I Love You	(PhilipsA 114)6042	35	1976	0	1976	
3	The Roussos Phenomenon (EP)	(Philips DEMIS 001)	1	1976	0	1976	
4	When Forever Has Gone	(Philips 6042 186)	2	1976	0	1976	
5	Because	(Philips 6042 245)	39	1977	0	1977	
6	Kyrila (EP)	(Philips DEMIS 002)	33	1977	0	1977	

Den Hegarty Male Vocalist from the UK

1	Voodoo Voodoo	(Magnet Mag143)	73	1979	0	1979	

Deniece Williams Female Vocalist, Real Name Deniece Chandler B: 3 Jun 1951 Gary, Indiana.

1	Free	(CBS 4978)	1	1977	25	1977	(Columbia 10429)
2	That's What Friends Are For	(CBS 5432)	8	1977	0	1977	
3	Baby Baby My Love's All For You	(CBS 5779)	32	1977	0	1977	
* 4	Too Much, Too Little, Too Late	(CBS 6164)	3	1978	1	1978	(Columbia 10693)
5	You're All I Need To Get By	(CBS 6483)	45	1978	0	1978	
6	It's Gonna Take A Miracle		0	1982	10	1982	(ABC 02812)
* 7	Let's Hear It For The Boy	(CBS A 4319)	2	1984	1	1984	(Columbia 04417)
8	Let's Hear It For The Boy (Re-Entry)	(CBS A 4319)	75	1984	0	1984	

HITS 4-5 ARE CREDITED TO JOHNNY MATHIS AND DENIECE WILLIAMS. • SHE WAS A MEMBER OF THE BACKING GROUP WONDERLOVE

Denis Leary Male Vocalist from the USA

1	Asshole	(A&M 5813352)	58	1996	0	1996	

Denise Johnson Female Vocalist from the UK

1	Don't Fight It Feel It	(Creation CRE 110)	41	1991	0	1991	
2	Rays Of The Rising Sun	(Magnet Mag1022CD)	45	1994	0	1994	

HIT 1 IS CREDITED TO PRIMAL SCREAM FEATURING DENISE JOHNSON

Denise Lasalle Female Vocalist, B: Denise Craig 16 Jul 1939 Mississippi

1	My Toot Toot	(Epic A 6334)	6	1985	0	1985	
* 2	Trapped By A Thing Called Love		0	1971	13	1971	(Westbound 182)

ISSUE	TITLE	UK LBL	UK POS	UK YEAR	US POS	US YEAR	US LBL
Denise Lopez Female Vocalist, B: Queens, New York							
1	Sayin' Sorry (Don't Make It Right)		0	1988	31	1988	(Vendetta 7200)
	RECORDED UNDER THE NAME OF NEECY DEE IN 1984						
Denise Lor Female Vocalist from the USA							
1	If I Give My Heart To You		0	1954	8	1954	(MAJOR 27)
Denise Welch Female Vocalist from the UK							
1	You Don't Have To Say You Love Me / Cry Me A River	(Virgin VSCDT 1569)	23	1995	0	1995	
Dennis Brown Male Vocalist from Jamaica							
1	Money In My Pocket	(Lightning LV 5)	14	1979	0	1979	
2	Love Has Found Its Way	(A&M AMS 8226)	47	1982	0	1982	
3	Halfway Up Halfway Down	(A&M AMS 8250)	56	1982	0	1982	
Dennis Coffey & The Detroit Guitar Band Male Guitarist, B: 1940							
* 1	Scorpio		0	1971	6	1971	(Sussex 226)
2	Taurus		0	1972	18	1972	(Sussex 233)
Dennis Day Male Vocalist (Tenor), Real Name Eugene McNulty From New York, USA							
1	Mam'selle (From *The Razor's Edge*)		0	1947	8	1947	(RCA Victor 2211)
2	Clancy Lowered The Boom		0	1949	23	1949	(RCA Victor 2810)
3	Dear Hearts And Gentle People		0	1950	14	1950	(RCA Victor 3102)
4	Goodnight Irene		0	1950	17	1950	(RCA Victor 3870)
5	Mona Lisa (From *Captain Carey, U.S.A.*)		0	1950	29	1950	(RCA Victor 3753)
6	All My Love		0	1950	22	1950	(RCA Victor 3870)
7	Mister And Mississippi		0	1951	13	1951	(RCA Victor 4140)
	HIT 3 WAS WITH THE RHYTHMAIRES						
Dennis Deyoung Former Singer/Instrumentalist (Keyboards) With Styx							
1	Desert Moon		0	1984	10	1984	(A&M 2666)
Dennis Edwards (Featuring) Siedah Garrett Mixed Vocal Duo from the USA							
1	Don't Look Any Further	(GORDY TMG 1334)	45	1984	0	1984	
2	Don't Look Any Further (Re-Entry)	(GORDY TMG 1334)	55	1987	0	1987	
	SEE ALSO MICHAEL JACKSON						
Dennis Waterman Male Actor/Vocalist from the UK							
1	I Could Be So Good For You	(EMI 5009)	3	1980	0	1980	
2	What Are We Gonna Get 'Er Indoors	(EMI MIN 101)	21	1983	0	1983	
	HIT 1 IS CREDITED TO THE DENNIS WATERMAN BAND • HIT 2 IS CREDITED TO DENNIS WATERMAN AND GEORGE COLE						
Dennis Yost See Classics IV							
Dennisons Male Vocal/Instrumental Group from the UK							
1	Be My Girl	(Decca F 11691)	46	1963	0	1963	
2	Walkin' The Dog	(Decca F 11880)	36	1964	0	1964	
Denny Martin Male Composer/Pianist, B: 10 Apr 1911 New York City							
1	Quite Village		0	1959	4	1959	(Liberty 55162)
2	The Enchanted Sea		0	1959	28	1959	(Liberty 55212)
	HITS CREDITED TO THE EXOTIC SOUNDS OF DENNY MARTIN						
Denny Seyton & The Sabres Male Vocal/Instrumental Group from the UK824)							
1	The Way You Look Tonight	(Mercury MF	48	1964	0	1964	
Deodato Real Name Eumir Deodato Almeida B: 21 Jun 1942 Brazil							
1	Also Sprach Zarathustra	(Creed Taylor CTI 4000)	7	1973	2	1973	(CTI 12)
	THEME FROM FILM *2001: A SPACE ODYSSEY*: WRITTEN BY RICHARD STRAUSS IN 1896						
Deon Estus Male Vocalist/Instrumentalist, B: Detroit And Formerly With Wham							
1	My Guy - My Girl (Medley)	(Sedition Edit 3310)	63	1986	0	1986	
2	Heaven Help Me	(MIKA MIKA 2)	41	1989	5	1989	(MIKA 871538)
	HIT 1 IS CREDITED TO AMII STEWART & DEON ESTUS • HIT 2 IS CREDITED TO DEON ESTUS WITH GEORGE MICHAEL						
Deon Jackson Male Vocal/Instrumentalist (Clarinet/Drums), B: 26 Jan 1946 Michigan							
1	Love Makes The World Go Round		0	1966	11	1966	(CARLA 2526)
Department S Male Vocal/Instrumental Group from the UK							
1	Is Vic There	(Demon D 1003)	22	1981	0	1981	
2	Going Left Right	(Stiff Buy 118)	55	1981	0	1981	
Depeche Mode Male Vocal/Instrumental Group from the UK							
1	Dreaming Of Me	(Mute Mute 013)	57	1981	0	1981	
2	New Life	(Mute Mute 014)	11	1981	0	1981	
3	Just Can't Get Enough	(Mute Mute 016)	8	1981	0	1981	

ISSUE	TITLE	UK LBL	UK POS	UK YEAR	US POS	US YEAR	US LBL
4	See You	(Mute Mute 018)	6	1982	0	1982	
5	The Meaning Of Love	(Mute Mute 022)	12	1982	0	1982	
6	Leave In Silence	(Mute Bong 1)	18	1982	0	1982	
7	Get The Balance Right	(Mute 7Bong 2)	13	1983	0	1983	
8	Everything Counts (Live)	(Mute 7Bong 3)	6	1983	0	1983	
9	Love In Itself 2	(Mute 7 Bong 4)	21	1983	0	1983	
10	People Are People	(Mute 7 Bong 5)	4	1984	13	1985	(SIRE 29221)
11	Master And Servant	(Mute 7Bong 6)	9	1984	0	1984	
12	Somebody / Blasphemous Rumours	(Mute 7Bong 7)	16	1984	0	1984	
13	Shake The Disease	(Mute Bong 8)	18	1985	0	1985	
14	It's Called A Heart	(Mute Bong 9)	18	1985	0	1985	
15	Stripped	(Mute Bong 10)	15	1986	0	1986	
16	A Question Of Lust	(Mute Bong 11)	28	1986	0	1986	
17 ·	A Question Of Time	(Mute Bong 12)	17	1986	0	1986	
18	Strangelove	(Mute Bong 13)	16	1987	0	1987	
19	Never Let Me Down Again	(Mute Bong 14)	22	1987	0	1987	
20	Behind The Wheel	(Mute Bong 15)	21	1988	0	1988	
21	Little 15 (Import)	(Mute Little15)	60	1988	0	1988	
22	Everything Counts	(Mute Bong 16)	22	1989	0	1989	
* 23	Personal Jesus	(Mute Bong 17)	13	1989	28	1990	(SIRE 19941)
* 24	Enjoy The Silence	(Mute Bong 18)	6	1990	8	1990	(SIRE 19885)
25	Policy Of Truth	(Mute Bong 19)	16	1990	15	1990	(SIRE 19842)
26	World In My Eyes	(Mute Bong 20)	17	1990	0	1990	
27	I Feel You	(Mute CDBong 21)	8	1993	37	1993	(SIRE 19600)
28	Walking In My Shoes	(Mute CDBong 22)	14	1993	0	1993	
29	Condemnation (EP)	(Mute CDBong 23)	9	1993	0	1993	
30	In Your Room	(Mute CDBong 24)	8	1994	0	1994	
31	Barrel Of A Gun	(Mute CDBong 25)	4	1997	47	1997	(Mute 17409)
32	It's No Good	(Mute CDBong 26)	5	1997	40	1997	(Mute 17390)
33	Home	(Mute CDBong 27)	23	1997	0	1997	

NAMES: DAVID GAHAN, MARTIN GORE, VINCE CLARKE & ANDY FLETCHER • CLARK LEFT IN 1982 TO FORM YAZZ AND THEN ERASURE

Depth Charge   Male Producer Jonathan Kane from the UK

1	Legend Of The Golden Snake (EP)	(DC Recordings DC01DC)	75	1995	0	1995	

Derek   Derek Is (And See Also) Johnny Cymbal

1	Cinnamon		0	1968	11	1968	(BANG 558)

Derek & The Dominos   See Eric Clapton

Derek B   Male Rapper from the UK

1	Good Groove	(Music Of Life 7NOTE 12)	16	1988	0	1988	
2	Bad Young Brother	(Tuff Audio DRKB 1)	16	1988	0	1988	
3	We've Got The Juice	(Tuff Audio DRKB 2)	56	1988	0	1988	

Dermot O'Brien   Male Vocalist from Ireland

1	The Merry Ploughboy	(Envoy ENV 016)	46	1966	0	1966	
2	The Merry Ploughboy (Re-Entry)	(Envoy ENV 016)	50	1966	0	1966	

Derrick Morgan   Male Vocalist From Jamaica

1	Moon Hop	(CRAB 32)	49	1970	0	1970	

Des O'Connor   Male Comedian/Talk-Show Host/Vocalist from the UK

1	Careless Hands	(Columbia DB 8275)	6	1967	0	1967	
2	I Pretend	(Columbia DB 8397)	1	1968	0	1968	
3	1-2-3 O'Leary	(Columbia DB 8492)	4	1968	0	1968	
4	Dick-A-Dum-Dum (King's Road)	(Columbia DB 8566)	14	1969	0	1969	
5	Loneliness	(Columbia DB 8632)	18	1969	0	1969	
6	I'll Go On Hoping	(Columbia DB 8661)	30	1970	0	1970	
7	The Tips Of My Fingers	(Columbia DB 8713)	15	1970	0	1970	
8	The Sky Boat Song	(TEMBO TML 119)	10	1976	0	1976	

HIT 8 IS CREDITED TO ROGER WHITTAKER AND DES O'CONNOR

Des'ree   Female Vocalist from London, Real Name Des'ree Weeks

1	Feel So High	(Dusted Sound 6573667)	51	1991	0	1991	
2	Feel So High (Re-Issue)	(Dusted Sound 6576897)	13	1992	0	1992	
3	Mind Adventures	(Dusted Sound 6578637)	43	1992	0	1992	
4	Why Should I Love You	(Dusted Sound 6580917)	44	1992	0	1992	
5	Delicate	(Columbia 6593312)	14	1993	0	1993	
6	You Gotta Be	(Dusted Sound 6601342)	20	1994	5	1994	(550 MUSIC 77551)

ISSUE	TITLE	UK LBL	UK POS	UK YEAR	US POS	US YEAR	US LBL
7	I Ain't Movin'	(Dusted Sound 6604672)	44	1994	0	1994	
8	Little Child	(Dusted Sound 6604515)	69	1994	0	1994	
9	You Gotta Be (Re-Mix)	(Dusted Sound 6613215)	14	1995	0	1995	

HIT 5 IS CREDITED TO TERENCE TRENT D'ARBY FEATURING DES'REE

Desireless Female Vocalist from France

1	Voyage Voyage	(CBS DESI 1)	53	1987	0	1987	
2	Voyage Voyage (Re-Mix)	(CBS DESI 2)	5	1988	0	1988	

Desiya Mixed Vocal/Instrumental Duo from the UK

1	Comin' On Strong	(Blackmarket 12MKT 2)	74	1992	0	1992	

HIT IS CREDITED TO DESIYA FEATURING MELISSA YIANNAKOU

Deskee Male Instrumentalist from the UK

1	Let There Be House	(Big One VBIG 19)	52	1990	0	1990	
2	Dance Dance	(Big One VBIG 22)	74	1990	0	1990	

Desmond Child Male Singer/Songwriter, Real Name John Charles Barrett Jr., B: 28 Oct 1953 from the USA

1	Love On A Rooftop		0	1991	40	1991	(Elektra)

Desmond Dekker & The Aces Male Vocal/Instrumental Group Real Name Desmond Dacris B: 16 Jul 1941, Kingston, Jamaica

1	007	(Pyramid PYR 6004)	14	1967	0	1967	
* 2	Israelites	(Pyramid PYR 6058)	1	1969	9	1969	(UNI 55129)
* 3	It Miek	(Pyramid PYR 6068)	7	1969	0	1969	
4	Israelites (Re-Entry)	(Pyramid PYR 6058)	45	1969	0	1969	
5	Pickney Gal	(Pyramid PYR 6078)	42	1970	0	1970	
6	You Can Get It If You Really Want	(Trojan TR 7777)	2	1970	0	1970	
7	Israelites (Re-Issue)	(Cactus CT 57)	10	1975	0	1975	
8	Sing A Little Song	(Cactus CT 73)	16	1975	0	1975	

HIT 6 IS CREDITED TO DESMOND DEKKER • THE TITLE 'IT MIEK' IS OF WEST INDIAN ORIGIN AND MEANS THAT'S WHY

Detergents Names: Ron Dante, Tommy Wynn & Danny Jordan For New York

1	Leader Of The Laundromat		0	1964	19	1964	(Roulette 4590)

Detroit Emeralds Male Vocal Group from the USA Formed By The Tilmon Brothers Abrim & Ivory

1	You Want It You Got It	(Westbound 6146 103)	12	1973	36	1972	(Westbound 192)
2	Baby Let Me Take You (In My Arms)		0	1972	24	1972	(Westbound 203)
3	Feel The Need In Me	(Janus 6146	4	1973	0	1973	
4	I Think Of You	(Westbound 6146 104)	27	1973	0	1973	
5	Feel The Need In Me (Re-Recording)	(Atlantic K 10945)	12	1977	0	1977	

Detroit Spinners Male R&B Group from Detroit Originally Known As The Domingoes

1	That's What Girls Are Made For		0	1961	27	1961	(TRI-PHI 1001)
2	I'll Always Love You		0	1965	35	1965	(Motown 1078)
+ 3	Truly Yours		0	1966	16	1966	(Motown 1093)
4	It's A Shame	(TAMLAMotown TMG 755)	20	1970	14	1970	(V.I.P. 25057)
+ 5	We'll Have It Made		0	1971	20	1971	(V.I.P. 25060)
* 6	I'll Be Around		0	1972	3	1972	(Atlantic 2904)
* 7	Could It Be I'm Falling In Love	(Atlantic K 10283)	11	1973	4	1972	(Atlantic 2927)
* 8	One Of A Kind (Love Affiar)		0	1973	11	1973	(Atlantic 2962)
9	Ghetto Child	(Atlantic K 10359)	7	1973	29	1973	(Atlantic 2973)
10	Mighty Love (Part 1)		0	1974	20	1974	(Atlantic 3006)
11	I'm Coming Home		0	1974	18	1974	(Atlantic 3027)
* 12	Then Came You	(Atlantic K 10495)	29	1974	1	1974	(Atlantic 3029)
13	Love Don't Love Nobody (Part 1)		0	1974	15	1974	(Atlantic 3206)
14	Living A Little, Laughing A Little		0	1975	37	1975	(Atlantic 3252)
+ 15	Sadie		0	1975	7	1975	(Atlantic 3268)
* 16	They Just Can't Stop It (Games People Play)		0	1975	5	1975	(Atlantic 3284)
17	Love Don't Love Nobody (Part 1) (Re-Issue)		0	1975	37	1975	(Atlantic 3206)
18	Love Or Leave		0	1976	36	1976	(Atlantic 3309)
* 19	The Rubberband Man	(Atlantic K 10807)	16	1976	2	1976	(Atlantic 3355)
20	Wake Up Susan	(Atlantic K 10799)	29	1977	0	1977	
21	Could It Be I'm Falling In Love (EP)	(Atlantic K 10935)	32	1977	0	1977	
* 22	Working My Way Back To You / Forgive Me Girl	(Atlantic K 11432)	1	1980	2	1980	(Atlantic 3637)
23	Body Language	(Atlantic K 11392)	40	1980	0	1980	
24	Cupid (I've Loved You For A Long Time) (Medley)	(Atlantic K 11498)	4	1980	4	1980	(Atlantic 3664)
25	I'll Be Around	(COOLTEMPOCDCOOL 306)	30	1995	39	1995	(RAG TOP 58331)

HIT 1 IS CREDITED TO THE MOTOWN SPINNERS • HIT 12 IS CREDITED TO DIONNE WARWICK & THE DETROIT SPINNERS

THEIR NAME HAS CHANGED OVER THE YEARS, SPINNERS, MOTOWN SPINNERS & DETROIT SPINNERS • HIT 25 IS CREDITED TO RAPPIN'4-TAY FEATURING THE SPINNERS

Deuce Mixed Vocal Group from the UK

1	Call It Love	(London LONCD 355)	11	1995	0	1995	

ISSUE	TITLE	UK LBL	UK POS	UK YEAR	US POS	US YEAR	US LBL
2	I Need You	(London LONCD 365)	10	1995	0	1995	
3	On The Bible	(London LONCD 368)	13	1995	0	1995	
4	No Surrender	(LOVE THIS LUVTHISCD 10)	29	1996	0	1996	

Deus   Male Vocal/Instrumental Group from Belgium

ISSUE	TITLE	UK LBL	UK POS	UK YEAR	US POS	US YEAR	US LBL
1	Hotel Lounge (Be The Death Of Me)	(Island CID 603)	55	1995	0	1995	
2	Theme From Turnpike (EP)	(Island CID 630)	68	1996	0	1996	
3	Little Arithmetics	(Island CID 643)	44	1996	0	1996	
4	Roses	(Island CID 645)	56	1997	0	1997	

Device   Male Vocal/Instrumental Pop-Rock Trio from Los Angeles

ISSUE	TITLE	UK LBL	UK POS	UK YEAR	US POS	US YEAR	US LBL
1	Hanging On A Heart Attack		0	1986	35	1986	(Chrysalis 42996)

NAMES: PAUL ENGERMANN, HOLLY KNIGHT & GENE BLACK • PAUL LEFT TO JOIN ANIMOTION IN 1988

Devo   Male Vocal/Instrumental Group from the USA   Names: Bob & Marc Mothersbaugh, Jerry And Bob Casale & Alan Myers

ISSUE	TITLE	UK LBL	UK POS	UK YEAR	US POS	US YEAR	US LBL
1	(I Can't Get Me No) Satisfaction	(Stiff Boy 1)	41	1978	0	1978	
2	Jocko Homo	(Stiff DEV 1)	62	1962	0	1962	
3	Be Stiff	(Stiff Boy 2)	71	1978	0	1978	
4	Come Back Jonee	(Virgin VS 223)	60	1978	0	1978	
5	Whip It	(Virgin VS 383)	51	1980	14	1980	(Warner Bros. 49550)

Devotions   Names: Ray Sanchez, Bob Weisbrod, Bob Hovorka And Frank & Joe Pardo

ISSUE	TITLE	UK LBL	UK POS	UK YEAR	US POS	US YEAR	US LBL
1	Rip Van Winkle		0	1964	36	1964	(Roulette 4541)

THE GROUP DISBANDED BEFORE THEIR HIT WAS RELEASED

Dexter Wansell   Male Instrumentalist (Keyboards) from the USA

ISSUE	TITLE	UK LBL	UK POS	UK YEAR	US POS	US YEAR	US LBL
1	All Night Long	(Philadelphia International PIR 6255)	59	1978	0	1978	

Dexy's Midnight Runners   Male Vocal/Instrumental Group from the UK

ISSUE	TITLE	UK LBL	UK POS	UK YEAR	US POS	US YEAR	US LBL
1	Dance Stance	(Oddball Productions R 6028)	40	1980	0	1980	
2	Geno	(Late Night Feelings R 6033)	1	1980	0	1980	
3	There There My Dear	(Late Night Feelings R 6038)	7	1980	0	1980	
4	Plan B	(Parlophone R 6046)	58	1981	0	1981	
5	Show Me	(Mercury DEXYS 6)	16	1981	0	1981	
6	The Celtic Soul Brothers	(Mercury DEXYS 8)	45	1982	0	1982	
7	Come On Eileen	(Mercury DEXYS 9)	1	1982	1	1983	(Mercury 76189)
8	Jackie Wilson Said	(Mercury DEXYS 10)	5	1982	0	1982	
9	Let's Get This Straight (From The Start)	(Mercury DEXYS 11)	17	1982	0	1982	
10	The Celtic Soul Brothers	(Mercury DEXYS 12)	20	1983	0	1983	
11	Because Of You	(Mercury BRUSH 1)	13	1986	0	1986	

HITS 6 & 10 ARE DIFFERENT RECORDINGS • HITS 6, 9 ARE CREDITED TO DEXY'S MIDNIGHT RUNNERS WITH EMERALD EXPRESS
HITS 8, 9, 10 CREDITED TO KEVIN ROWLAND & DEXY'S MIDNIGHT RUNNERS • EIGHT MEMBERS IN THE BAND LED BY KEVIN ROWLAND B: 17 AUG 1953

Dhar Braxton   Female Vocalist from the USA

ISSUE	TITLE	UK LBL	UK POS	UK YEAR	US POS	US YEAR	US LBL
1	Jump Back (Set Me Free)	(Fourth & Broadway BRW 47)	32	1986	0	1986	

Diamond Head   Male Vocal/Instrumental Group from the UK

ISSUE	TITLE	UK LBL	UK POS	UK YEAR	US POS	US YEAR	US LBL
1	In The Heat Of The Night	(MCA DHM 102)	67	1982	0	1982	

Diamonds   Male Vocal Group from Canada

	ISSUE	TITLE	UK LBL	UK POS	UK YEAR	US POS	US YEAR	US LBL
	1	Why Do Fools Fall In Love		0	1956	12	1956	(Mercury 70709)
	2	The Church Bells May Ring		0	1956	14	1956	(Mercury 70835)
	3	Love, Love, Love		0	1956	30	1956	(Mercury 70889)
	4	Soft Summer Breeze		0	1956	34	1956	(Mercury 70934)
	5	Ka-Ding-Dong		0	1956	35	1956	(Mercury 70934)
*	6	Little Darlin'	(Mercury MT 148)	3	1957	2	1957	(Mercury 71060)
	7	Words Of Love		0	1957	13	1957	(Mercury 71128)
	8	Zip Zip		0	1957	16	1957	(Mercury 71165)
	9	Silhouettes		0	1957	10	1957	(Mercury 71197)
*	10	The Stroll		0	1958	4	1958	(Mercury 71242)
	11	High Sign		0	1958	37	1958	(Mercury 71291)
	12	Kath-O		0	1958	16	1958	(Mercury 71330)
	13	Walking Along		0	1958	29	1958	(Mercury 71366)
	14	She Say (Oom Dooby Doom)		0	1959	18	1959	(Mercury 71404)
	15	One Summer Night		0	1961	22	1961	(Mercury 71831)
!	16	Just A Little Bit		0	1987	63	1987	(Churchill 94101)
!	17	Two Kinds Of Woman		0	1987	83	1987	(Churchill 94102)

NAMES: DAVE SOMERVILLE, TED KOWALSKI, PHIL LEAVITT & BILL REED • DIFFERENT LINE-UP FOR HITS 16-17 FRONTED BY LONG SERVING MEMBER BOB DUNCAN

Diana Brown & Barrie K. Sharpe   Mixed Vocal Duo from the UK

ISSUE	TITLE	UK LBL	UK POS	UK YEAR	US POS	US YEAR	US LBL
1	The Masterplan	(FFRR F 133)	39	1990	0	1990	
2	Sun Worshippers (Positive Thinking)	(FFRR F 144)	61	1990	0	1990	
3	Love Or Nothing	(FFRR F 152)	71	1991	0	1991	

ISSUE	TITLE	UK LBL	UK POS	UK YEAR	US POS	US YEAR	US LBL
4	Eating Me Alive	(FFRR F 190)	53	1992	0	1992	

Diana Decker Female Vocalist from the USA

ISSUE	TITLE	UK LBL	UK POS	UK YEAR	US POS	US YEAR	US LBL
1	Poppa Piccolino	(Columbia DB 3325)	2	1953	0	1953	
2	Poppa Piccolino (Re-Entry)	(Columbia DB 3325)	5	1954	0	1954	

Diana King Female Reggae Singer from Spain

ISSUE	TITLE	UK LBL	UK POS	UK YEAR	US POS	US YEAR	US LBL
* 1	Shy Guy	(Columbia 6621682)	2	1995	13	1995	(WORK 77678)
2	Ain't Nobody	(Columbia 6625495)	13	1995	0	1995	

Diana Ross Female Vocalist, Real Name Diana Earle B: 26 Mar 1944 Detroit

ISSUE	TITLE	UK LBL	UK POS	UK YEAR	US POS	US YEAR	US LBL
1	Reach Out And Touch (Somebody's Hand)	(Tamla Motown TMG 743)	0	1970	20	1970	(Motown 1165)
* 2	Ain't No Mountain High Enough	(TAMLAMotown TMG 751)	6	1970	1	1970	(Motown 1169)
3	Remember Me	(Tamla Motown TMG 768)	7	1971	16	1971	(Motown 1176)
4	Reach Out I'll Be There		0	1971	29	1971	(Motown 1184)
5	I'm Still Waiting	(Tamla Motown TMG 781)	1	1971	0	1971	
6	Surrender	(Tamla Motown TMG 792)	10	1971	38	1971	(Motown 1188)
7	Doobedood'ndoobe Doobedood'ndoobe	(Tamla Motown TMG 812)	12	1972	0	1972	
8	Good Morning Heartache		0	1973	34	1973	(Motown 1211)
* 9	Touch Me In The Morning	(Tamla Motown TMG 861)	9	1973	1	1973	(Motown 1239)
10	Touch Me In The Morning (Re-Entry)	(Tamla Motown TMG 861)	50	1973	0	1973	
11	You're A Special Part Of Me		0	1973	12	1973	(Motown 1280)
12	Last Time I Saw Him	(Tamla Motown TMG 893)	35	1974	14	1974	(Motown 1278)
13	All Of My Life	(Tamla Motown TMG 880)	9	1974	0	1974	
14	My Mistake (Was To Love You)		0	1974	19	1974	(Motown 1269)
15	You Are Everything	(Tamla Motown 890)	5	1974	0	1974	
16	Stop, Look, Listen (To Your Heart)	(Tamla Motown TMG 906)	25	1974	0	1974	
17	Love Me	(Tamla Motown TMG 917)	38	1974	0	1974	
18	Sorry Doesn't Always Make It Right	(Tamla Motown TMG 941)	23	1975	0	1975	
* 19	Theme From *Mahogany* (Do You Know Where You're Going To)	(Tamla Motown TMG 1010)	5	1976	1	1975	(Motown 1377)
20	Love Hangover	(Tamla Motown TMG 1024)	10	1976	1	1976	(Motown 1392)
21	I Thought It Took A Little Time	(Tamla Motown TMG 1032)	32	1976	0	1976	
22	One Love In My Lifetime		0	1976	25	1976	(Motown 1398)
23	I'm Still Waiting (Re-Issue)	(Tamla Motown TMG 1041)	41	1976	0	1976	
24	Gettin' Ready For Love	(Tamla Motown TMG 1090)	23	1977	27	1977	(Motown 1427)
25	Lovin' Livin' And Givin'	(Tamla Motown TMG 1112)	54	1978	0	1978	
26	Ease On Down The Road	(MCA 396)	45	1978	0	1978	
27	Pops We Love You	(Motown TMG 1136)	66	1979	0	1979	
28	The Boss	(Motown TMG 1150)	40	1979	19	1979	(Motown 1462)
29	No One Gets The Prize	(Motown TMG 1160)	59	1979	0	1979	
30	It's My House	(Motown TMG 1169)	32	1979	0	1979	
* 31	Upside Down	(Motown TMG 1195)	2	1980	1	1980	(Motown 1494)
32	My Old Piano	(Motown TMG 1202)	5	1980	0	1980	
33	I'm Coming Out	(Motown TMG 1210)	13	1980	5	1980	(Motown 1491)
34	It's My Turn	(Motown TMG 1217)	16	1981	9	1980	(Motown 1496)
35	One More Chance	(Motown TMG 1227)	49	1981	0	1981	
36	Cryin' My Heart Out For You	(Motown TMG 1233)	58	1981	0	1981	
* 37	Endless Love	(Motown TMG 1240)	7	1981	1	1981	(Motown 1519)
38	Why Do Fools Fall In Love	(Capitol CL 226)	4	1981	7	1981	(RCA 12349)
39	Tenderness	(Motown TMG 1248)	73	1982	0	1982	
40	Mirror Mirror	(Capitol CL 234)	36	1982	8	1982	(RCA 13021)
41	Tenderness (Re-Entry)	(Motown TMG 1248)	75	1982	0	1982	
42	Work That Body	(Capitol CL 241)	7	1982	0	1982	
43	It's Never Too Late	(Capitol CL256)	41	1982	0	1982	
44	Muscles	(Capitol CL 268)	15	1982	10	1982	(RCA 13348)
45	So Close	(Capitol CL 277)	43	1983	40	1983	(RCA 13424)
46	Pieces Of Ice	(Capitol CL 298)	46	1983	31	1983	(RCA 13549)
47	All Of You	(CBS A 4522)	43	1984	19	1984	(Columbia 04507)
48	Touch By Touch	(Capitol CL 337)	47	1984	0	1984	
49	Swept Away		0	1984	19	1984	(RCA 13864)
50	Missing You		0	1985	10	1985	(RCA 13966)
51	Eaten Alive	(Capitol CL 372)	71	1985	0	1985	
52	Chain Reaction	(Capitol CL 386)	1	1986	0	1986	
53	Experience	(Capitol CL 400)	47	1986	0	1986	
54	Dirty Looks	(EMI EM 2)	49	1987	0	1987	
55	Mr. Lee	(EMI EM 73)	58	1988	0	1988	

ISSUE	TITLE	UK LBL	UK POS	UK YEAR	US POS	US YEAR	US LBL
56	Love Hangover (Re-Mix)	(Motown ZB 42307)	75	1988	0	1988	
57	Workin' Overtime	(EMI EM 91)	32	1989	0	1989	
58	Paradise	(EMI EM 94)	61	1989	0	1989	
59	I'm Still Waiting (Re-Mix)	(Motown ZB 43781)	21	1990	0	1990	
60	When You Tell Me That You Love Me	(EMI EM 217)	2	1991	0	1991	
61	The Force Behind The Power	(EMI EM 221)	27	1992	0	1992	
62	One Shining Moment	(EMI EM 239)	10	1992	0	1992	
63	If We Hold On Together	(EMI EM 257)	11	1992	0	1992	
64	Heart (Don't Change My Mind)	(EMI CDEM 261)	31	1993	0	1993	
65	Chain Reaction (Re-Issue)	(EMI CDEM 290)	30	1993	0	1993	
66	Your Love	(EMI CDEM 299)	14	1993	0	1993	
67	The Best Years Of My Life	(EMI CDEM 305)	28	1994	0	1994	
68	Why Do Fools Fall In Love (Re-Mix) / I'm Coming Out	(EMI CDEM 332)	36	1994	0	1994	
69	Take Me Higher	(EMI CDEM 338)	32	1995	0	1995	
70	I'm Gone	(EMI CDEM 402)	36	1995	0	1995	
71	I Will Survive	(EMI CDEM 415)	14	1996	0	1996	
72	In The Ones You Love	(EMI CDEM 457)	34	1996	0	1996	

ORIGINALLY WITH THE PRIMETTES WHICH BECAME THE SUPREMES • SEE ALSO SUPREMES

Diana Williams Female Vocalist from the USA

1	Teddy Bear's Last Ride	(Capitol CL 207)	54	1981	0	1981	

Diane Ray Female Vocalist, B: 1 Sep 1942 Gastonia, North Carolina

1	Please Don't Talk To The Lifeguard		0	1963	31	1963	(Mercury 72117)

Diane Renay Female Vocalist, Full Name Is Diane Renee Kushner from Philadelphia

1	Navy Blue		0	1964	6	1964	(20th Century 456)
2	Kiss Me Sailor		0	1964	29	1964	(20th Century 477)

Dick & Deedee Mixed Vocal Duo from the USA   Dick St. John Gosting & Deedee Sperling

* 1	The Mountain's High	(London HLG 9408)	37	1961	2	1961	(Liberty 55350)
2	Tell Me		0	1962	22	1962	(Liberty 55412)
3	Young And In Love		0	1963	17	1963	(Warner Bros. 5342)
4	Turn Around		0	1963	27	1963	(Warner Bros. 5396)
5	Thou Shalt Not Steal		0	1965	13	1965	(Warner Bros. 5482)

Dick Charlesworth & His City Gents Male Jazz Band With Dick On Clarinet from the UK

1	Billy Boy	(Top Rank Jar 558)	43	1961	0	1961	

Dick Contino Male Accordionist from the USA

1	Yours		0	1954	23	1954	(Mercury 70455)

Dick Emery Male Comedian/Vocalist (Deceased) from the UK

1	If You Love Her	(PYE 7N 17644)	32	1969	0	1969	
2	You Are Awful	(PYE 7N 45202)	43	1973	0	1973	

Dick Farney Male Vocalist from the USA

1	I Wish I Didn't Love You So (From The Perils Of Pauline)		0	1947	13	1947	(Majestic 7225)

Dick Flood Male Singer/Songwriter, B: 13 Nov 1932 Philadelphia

1	Three Bells (The Jimmy Brown Story)		0	1959	23	1959	(Monument 408)

Dick Haymes Male Actor/Vocalist, B: 13 Sep 1916 Buenos Aires, Argentina

19	It's A Grand Night For Singing (From *State Fair*)		0	1946	21	1946	(Decca 18740)
20	Slowly (From *Fallen Angels*)		0	1946	12	1946	(Decca 18747)
21	You Make Me Feel So Young (From *Three Little Girls In Blue*)		0	1946	21	1946	(Decca 18914)
22	On The Boardwalk (In Atlantic City) (From *Three Little Girls In Blue*)		0	1946	21	1946	(Decca 18914)
23	For You, For Me, Forevermore (From *The Shocking Miss Pilgrim*)		0	1947	19	1947	(Decca 23687)
24	How Are Things In Glocca Mora? (From *Finian's Rainbow*)		0	1947	9	1947	(Decca 23830)
25	Mam'selle (From *The Razor's Edge*)		0	1947	3	1947	(Decca 23861)
26	There's No Business Like Show Business (From *Annie Get Your Gun*)		0	1947	25	1947	(Decca 40039)
27	Ivy (Movie Title Song)		0	1947	19	1947	(Decca 23877)
28	Naughty Angeline		0	1947	21	1947	(Decca 23977)
29	I Wish I Didn't Love You So (From *The Perils Of Pauline*)		0	1947	9	1947	(Decca 23977)
30	And Mimi		0	1947	15	1947	(Decca 24172)
31	Teresa		0	1948	21	1948	(Decca 24320)
* 32	Little White Lies		0	1948	3	1948	(Decca 24280)
33	You Can't Be True, Dear		0	1948	9	1948	(Decca 24439)
34	Nature Boy		0	1948	11	1948	(Decca 24439)
35	It's Magic (From *Romance On The High Seas*)		0	1948	9	1948	(Decca 23826)
36	Ev'ry Day I Love You (From *Two Guys From Texas*)		0	1948	24	1948	(Decca 24457)

ISSUE	TITLE	UK LBL	UK POS	UK YEAR	US POS	US YEAR	US LBL
37	Bouquet Of Roses		0	1949	22	1949	(Decca 24506)
38	Room Full Of Roses		0	1949	6	1949	(Decca 24632)
39	Maybe It's Because		0	1949	5	1949	(Decca 24650)
40	The Old Master Painter		0	1949	4	1949	(Decca 24801)
41	Roses		0	1950	29	1950	(Decca 27008)
42	Count Every Star		0	1950	10	1950	(Decca 27042)
43	Can Anyone Explain? (No! No! No!)		0	1950	23	1950	(Decca 27161)
44	You're Just In Love (From *Call Me Madam*)		0	1951	30	1951	(Decca 27317)
45	And So To Sleep Again		0	1951	28	1951	(Decca 27731)

HE WAS MARRIED FOR A TIME TO RITA HAYWORTH • SEE ALSO HELEN FORREST

Dick Hyman Trio Male/Instrumentalist (Keyboards), B: 8 Mar 1927 New York City

1	Unforgettable		0	1954	29	1954	(MGM 11743)
2	Theme From The *Threepenny Opera* (Moritat) (MGM 890)		9	1956	8	1956	(MGM 12149)
3	The Minotaur		0	1969	38	1969	(Command 4126)

HIT 3 IS CREDITED TO DICK HYMAN & HIS ELECTRIC ECLECTICS

Dick Jacobs & His Chorus And Orchestra Male Orchestra Leader, B: 29 Mar 1918 New York City

* 1	Main Title Theme From *The Man With The Golden Arm* - Molly-O		0	1956	22	1956	(Coral 61606)
2	Petticoats Of Portugal		0	1956	16	1956	(Coral 61724)
3	Fascination		0	1957	17	1957	(Coral 61864)

OBITUARY: D: 1988 CANCER.

Dick James Male Vocalist from the UK

1	Robin Hood	(Parlophone R 4117)	14	1956	0	1956	
2	Robin Hood / The Ballad Of Davy Crockett (Re-Entry)	(Parlophone R 4117)	29	1956	0	1956	
3	Garden Of Eden	(Parlophone R 4255)	18	1957	0	1957	

HIT 1 ARE CREDITED TO DICK JAMES WITH STEPHEN JAMES & HIS CHUMS

Dick Jordan Male Vocalist from the UK

1	Hallelujah I Love Her So	(Oriole CB 1534)	47	1960	0	1960	
2	Little Christine	(Oriole CB 1548)	39	1960	0	1960	

Dick Thomas Male Violinist/Accordionist, B: Richard Thomas Goldhahn, 4 Sep 1915 In Philadelphia

1	Sioux City Sue		0	1945	16	1945	(National 5007)

HIT 1 REACHED NUMBER 1 IN THE US C/W CHARTS

Dickey Lee Male Singer/Songwriter, Real Name Dickey Lipscomb B: 21 Sep 1941 In Memphis

* 1	Patches		0	1962	6	1962	(Smash 1758)
2	I Saw Linda Yesterday		0	1963	14	1963	(Smash 1791)
3	Laurie (Strange Things Happen)		0	1965	14	1965	(TCF HALL 102)
18	9,999,999 Texas		0	1976	52	1976	(RCA 10764)

OTHERS WERE C/W HITS

Dickie Goodman Male Comedy Writer, B: 19 Apr 1934 Hewlett, New York

1	Energy Crisis '74		0	1974	33	1974	(Rainy Wed. 206)
* 2	Mr. Jaws		0	1975	4	1975	(CASH 451)

SEE ALSO BUCHANAN & GOODMAN • OBITUARY: D: 6 NOV 1989 SUICIDE (SHOT HIMSELF).

Dickie Pride Male Vocalist from the UK

1	Primrose Lane	(Columbia DB 4340)	28	1959	0	1959	

Dickie Valentine Male Vocalist from the UK

1	Broken Wings	(Decca F 9954)	12	1953	0	1953	
2	All The Time And Everywhere	(Decca F 10038)	9	1953	0	1953	
3	In A Golden Coach	(Decca F 10098)	7	1953	0	1953	
4	Endless	(Decca F 10346)	19	1954	0	1954	
5	Mr. Sandman	(Decca F 10415)	5	1954	0	1954	
6	Finger Of Suspicion	(Decca F 10394)	1	1954	0	1954	
7	A Blossom Fell	(Decca F 10430)	9	1955	0	1955	
8	A Blossom Fell (Re-Entry)	(Decca F 10430)	18	1955	0	1955	
9	I Wonder	(Decca F 10493)	4	1955	0	1955	
10	Christmas Alphabet	(Decca F 10628)	1	1955	0	1955	
11	Old Pianna Rag	(Decca F 10645)	15	1955	0	1955	
12	Christmas Island	(Decca F 10798)	8	1956	0	1956	
13	Snowbound For Christmas	(Decca F 10950)	28	1957	0	1957	
14	Venus	(PYE NIXA 7N 15192)	28	1959	0	1959	
15	Venus (Re-Entry)	(PYE NIXA 7N 15192)	25	1959	0	1959	
16	Venus (2nd Re-Entry)	(PYE NIXA 7N 15192)	20	1959	0	1959	
17	Venus (3rd Re-Entry)	(PYE NIXA 7N15192)	25	1959	0	1959	
18	Venus (4th Re-Entry)	(PYE NIXA 7N 15192)	28	1959	0	1959	
19	One More Sunrise (Morgen)	(PYE 7N 15221)	14	1959	0	1959	

ISSUE	TITLE	UK LBL	UK POS	UK YEAR	US POS	US YEAR	US LBL

HIT 6 IS CREDITED TO DICKIE VALENTINE WITH THE STARGAZERS • SEE ALSO ALL STAR HIT PARADE, VARIOUS ARTISTS (EP, LP, 78S)

Dickies Male Vocal/Instrumental Group from the USA

ISSUE	TITLE	UK LBL	UK POS	UK YEAR	US POS	US YEAR	US LBL
1	Silent Night	(A&M AMS 7403)	47	1978	0	1978	
2	Banana Splits (Tra La La Song)	(A&M AMS 7431)	7	1979	0	1979	
3	Paranoid	(A&M AMS 7368)	45	1979	0	1979	
4	Nights In White Satin	(A&M AMS 7469)	39	1979	0	1979	
5	Fan Mail	(A&M AMS 7504)	57	1980	0	1980	
6	Gigantor	(A&M AMS 7544)	72	1980	0	1980	

Dicky Doo & The Don'ts Male Vocal Group from Brooklyn

ISSUE	TITLE	UK LBL	UK POS	UK YEAR	US POS	US YEAR	US LBL
1	Click-Clack		0	1958	28	1958	(SWAN 4001)
2	Nee Nee Na Na Na Nu Nu		0	1958	40	1958	(SWAN 4006)
3	Tear Drops Will Fall		0	1959	61	1959	

GERRY GRANTHAN, HARVEY DAVIS, RAY GANGI, AL WAYS & DAVE ALLDRED

Dictators Male Vocal/Instrumental Group from the USA

ISSUE	TITLE	UK LBL	UK POS	UK YEAR	US POS	US YEAR	US LBL
1	Search And Destroy	(Asylum K 13091)	49	1977	0	1977	
2	Search And Destroy (Re-Entry)	(Asylum K 13091)	50	1977	0	1977	

Diddy Male Producer from the USA

ISSUE	TITLE	UK LBL	UK POS	UK YEAR	US POS	US YEAR	US LBL
1	Give Me Love	(Positiva CDTIV 8)	52	1994	0	1994	
2	Give Me Love (Re-Recording)	(Feverpitch CDFVR 19)	23	1997	0	1997	

Diesel Rock Quintet With Lead Singer/Guitarist Rob Vunderink from Holland

ISSUE	TITLE	UK LBL	UK POS	UK YEAR	US POS	US YEAR	US LBL
1	Sausalito Summernight		0	1981	25	1981	(Regency 7339)

Diesel Park West Male Vocal/Instrumental Group from the UK

ISSUE	TITLE	UK LBL	UK POS	UK YEAR	US POS	US YEAR	US LBL
1	All The Myths On Sunday	(Food Food 17)	66	1989	0	1989	
2	Like Princes Do	(Food Food 19)	58	1989	0	1989	
3	When The Hoodoo Comes	(Food Food 20)	62	1989	0	1989	
4	Fall To Love	(Food Food 35)	48	1992	0	1992	
5	Boy On Top Of The News	(Food Food 36)	58	1992	0	1992	
6	God Only Knows	(Food Food 39)	57	1992	0	1992	

SEE ALSO THE FOOD CHRISTMAS (EP), VARIOUS ARTISTS (EP, LP, 78S)

Difford & Tilbrook Male Vocal/Instrumental Duo from the UK

ISSUE	TITLE	UK LBL	UK POS	UK YEAR	US POS	US YEAR	US LBL
1	Loves Crashing Waves	(A&M AM 193)	57	1984	0	1984	

Digable Planets Mixed Vocal/Instrumental Group from the USA

ISSUE	TITLE	UK LBL	UK POS	UK YEAR	US POS	US YEAR	US LBL
* 1	Rebirth Of Slick (Cool Like Dat)	(Pendulum 64674)	67	1993	15	1993	(Pendulum EKR 159CD)

Digital Dream Baby Real Name Peter Auty, Male Vocalist from the UK

ISSUE	TITLE	UK LBL	UK POS	UK YEAR	US POS	US YEAR	US LBL
1	Walking In The Air	(Columbia 6576067)	49	1991	0	1991	

Digital Orgasm Mixed Vocal/Instrumental Group from Belgium

ISSUE	TITLE	UK LBL	UK POS	UK YEAR	US POS	US YEAR	US LBL
1	Running Out Of Time	(Dead Dead Good Good 009)	16	1991	0	1991	
2	Startouchers	(DDG International GOOD 13)	31	1992	0	1992	
3	Moog Eruption	(DDG International GOOD 17)	62	1992	0	1992	

Digital Underground Male Vocal Group from the USA

ISSUE	TITLE	UK LBL	UK POS	UK YEAR	US POS	US YEAR	US LBL
1	The Humpty Dance		0	1990	11	1990	(Tommy Boy 7944)
2	Same Song	(Big Life BLR	52	1991	0	1991	

Dilemma Male Instrumental/Production Group from Italy

ISSUE	TITLE	UK LBL	UK POS	UK YEAR	US POS	US YEAR	US LBL
1	In Spirit	(FFRR FCD 274)	42	1996	0	1996	

Dimitri Tiomkin & His Orchestra Male Composer/Bandleader from Russia

ISSUE	TITLE	UK LBL	UK POS	UK YEAR	US POS	US YEAR	US LBL
1	The High And The Mighty		0	1954	29	1954	(Coral 61211)

Dimples D Female Rapper from the USA

ISSUE	TITLE	UK LBL	UK POS	UK YEAR	US POS	US YEAR	US LBL
1	Sucker DJ	(FBI FBI 11)	17	1990	0	1990	

Dina Carroll Female Vocalist from the UK

ISSUE	TITLE	UK LBL	UK POS	UK YEAR	US POS	US YEAR	US LBL
1	It's Too Late	(Mercury ITM 3)	8	1991	0	1991	
2	Naked Love (Just Say You Want Me)	(Mercury ITM 4)	39	1991	0	1991	
3	Ain't No Man	(A&M AM 0001)	16	1991	0	1991	
4	Special Kind Of Love	(A&M AM 0088)	16	1992	0	1992	
5	So Close	(A&M AM 0101)	20	1992	0	1992	
6	This Time	(A&M AMCD 0184)	23	1993	0	1993	
7	Express	(A&M 5802632)	12	1993	0	1993	
8	Don't Be A Stranger	(A&M 5803892)	3	1993	0	1993	
9	The Perfect Year	(A&M 5804812)	5	1993	0	1993	
10	Escaping	(Mercury DCCD 1)	3	1996	0	1996	
11	Only Human	(Mercury DCCD 2)	33	1996	0	1996	

HIT 1 IS CREDITED TO QUARTZ INTRODUCING DINA CARROLL • HIT 2 IS CREDITED TO QUARTZ AND DINA CARROLL

ISSUE	TITLE	UK LBL	UK POS	UK YEAR	US POS	US YEAR	US LBL

Dina Taylor See BBG

Dinah Shore Female Vocalist, Real Name Frances Rose Shore B: 1 Mar 1917 Winchester, Tennessee.

31	Personality		0	1946	10	1946	(Victor 1781)
32	Shoo-Fly Pie And Apple Pan Dowdy		0	1946	6	1946	(Columbia 36943)
33	Laughing On The Outside (Crying On The Inside)		0	1946	3	1946	(Columbia 36964)
34	The Gypsy		0	1946	1	1946	(Columbia 36964)
35	All That Glitters Is Not Gold		0	1946	9	1946	(Columbia 36971)
36	Doin' What Comes Natur'lly		0	1946	3	1946	(Columbia 36976)
37	You Keep Coming Back Like A Song		0	1946	5	1946	(Columbia 37072)
38	(I Love You) For Sentimental Reasons		0	1947	2	1947	(Columbia 37188)
39	Anniversary Song		0	1947	1	1947	(Columbia 37234)
40	The Egg And I		0	1947	16	1947	(Columbia 37278)
41	When Am I Gonna Kiss You Good Morning?		0	1947	23	1947	(Columbia 37291)
42	Tallahassee		0	1947	15	1947	(Columbia 37387)
43	I Wish I Didn't Love You So		0	1947	2	1947	(Columbia 37506)
44	You Do		0	1947	4	1947	(Columbia 37587)
45	It Takes A Long, Long Train With A Red Caboose (To Carry My Blues Away)		0	1947	23	1947	(Columbia 37840)
46	Golden Earrings		0	1947	25	1947	(Columbia 37932)
47	How Soon (Will I Be Seeing You)		0	1947	8	1947	(Columbia 37952)
48	At The Candlelight Cafe		0	1947	24	1947	(Columbia 37984)
49	The Best Things In Life Are Free		0	1948	18	1948	(Columbia 37984)
50	Little White Lies		0	1948	11	1948	(Columbia 38114)
* 51	Buttons And Bows		0	1948	1	1948	(Columbia 38284)
52	Lavender Blue (Dilly Dilly)		0	1948	9	1948	(Columbia 38299)
53	Far Away Places		0	1949	14	1949	(Columbia 38356)
54	So In Love		0	1949	20	1949	(Columbia 38399)
55	Forever, And Ever		0	1949	12	1949	(Columbia 38410)
56	Baby, It's Cold Outside		0	1949	4	1949	(Columbia 38463)
57	A Wonderful Guy		0	1949	22	1949	(Columbia 38460)
58	Dear Hearts And Gentle People		0	1949	2	1949	(Columbia 38605)
59	Bibbidi-Bobbidi-Boo		0	1950	25	1950	(Columbia 38659)
60	It's So Nice To Have A Man Around The House		0	1950	20	1950	(Columbia 38689)
61	Can Anyone Explain (No! No! No!)		0	1950	29	1950	(Columbia 38927)
62	My Heart Cries For You		0	1950	3	1950	(RCA Victor 3978)
63	Nobody's Chasing Me		0	1950	18	1950	(RCA Victor 3978)
64	A Penny A Kiss		0	1951	8	1951	(RCA Victor 4019)
65	In Your Arms		0	1951	24	1951	(RCA Victor 4019)
66	Sweet Violets		0	1951	3	1951	(RCA Victor 4174)
67	The Musicians		0	1951	24	1951	(RCA Victor 4225)
68	Delicado		0	1952	28	1952	(RCA Victor 4729)
69	Blues In Advance		0	1952	20	1952	(RCA Victor 4926)
70	Salomee (With Her Seven Veils)		0	1953	22	1953	(RCA Victor 5176)
71	Sweet Thing		0	1953	27	1953	(RCA Victor 5247)
72	Blue Canary		0	1953	11	1953	(RCA Victor 5390)
73	Changing Partners		0	1954	12	1954	(RCA Victor 5515)
74	Pass The Jam, Sam		0	1954	28	1954	(RCA Victor 5622)
75	If I Give My Heart To You		0	1954	28	1954	(RCA Victor 5838)
76	Whatever Lola Wants (Lola Gets)		0	1955	12	1955	(RCA 6077)
77	Love And Marriage		0	1955	20	1955	(RCA 6266)
78	Chantez-Chantez (Shan-Tay, Sing)		0	1957	19	1957	(RCA 6792)
79	Fascination		0	1957	15	1957	(RCA 6980)
80	I'll Never Say Never Again Again		0	1957	24	1957	(RCA 7056)
	OBITUARY: D: 24 FEB 1994 CANCER.						

Dinah Washington Female Vocalist, Real Name Ruth Lee Jones B: 29 Aug 1924 Tuscaloosa, Alabama.

1	I Wanna Be Loved		0	1950	22	1950	(Mercury 8181)
2	Teach Me Tonight		0	1954	23	1954	(Mercury 70497)
3	What A Diff'rence A Day Makes		0	1959	8	1959	(Mercury 71435)
4	Unforgettable		0	1959	17	1959	(Mercury 71508)
* 5	Baby (You Got What It Takes)		0	1960	5	1960	(Mercury 71565)
6	A Rockin' Good Way (To Mess Around And Fall In Love)		0	1960	7	1960	(Mercury 71629)
7	This Bitter Earth		0	1960	24	1960	(Mercury 71635)
8	Love Walked In		0	1960	30	1960	(Mercury 71696)
9	September In The Rain	(Mercury AMT 1162)	35	1961	23	1961	(Mercury 71876)
10	September In The Rain (Re-Entry)	(Mercury AMT 1162)	49	1962	0	1962	

ISSUE	TITLE	UK LBL	UK POS	UK YEAR	US POS	US YEAR	US LBL
11	Where Are You		0	1962	36	1962	(Roulette 4424)
12	Mad About The Boy	(Mercury Dinah 1)	41	1992	0	1992	

IN HER SHORT LIFE SHE'D BEEN MARRIED SEVEN TIMES • OBITUARY : D: 14 DEC 1963 DRUGS AND ALCOHOL.

Dino Male Singer/Songwriter, Real Name Dino Esposito B: 30 Jul 1963 California

1	I Like It		0	1989	7	1989	(4TH & Broadway 7483)
2	Sunshine		0	1989	23	1989	(4TH & Broadway 7489)
3	Romeo		0	1990	6	1990	(Island 878012)
4	Gentle		0	1990	31	1990	(Island 878472)
5	Ooh Child		0	1993	27	1993	(East West 98398)

Dino, Desi & Billy Names Dean Martin Jr, Desiderio Amaz IV & William Hinsche

1	I'm A Fool		0	1965	17	1965	(Reprise 0367)
2	Not The Lovin' Kind		0	1965	25	1965	(Reprise 0401)

Dinosaur Jr. Male Vocal/Instrumental Group from the USA

1	The Wagon	(Blanco Y Negro NEG 48)	49	1991	0	1991	
2	Get Me	(Blanco Y Negro NEG 60)	44	1992	0	1992	
3	Start Choppin'	(Blanco Y Negro NEG 61CD)	20	1993	0	1993	
4	Out There	(Blanco Y Negro NEG 63CD)	44	1993	0	1993	
5	Feel The Pain	(Blanco Y Negro NEG 74CD)	25	1994	0	1994	
6	I Don't Think So	(Blanco Y Negro NEG 77CD)	67	1995	0	1995	
7	Take A Run At The Sun	(Blanco Y Negro NEG 103CD)	53	1997	0	1997	

Dio Male Vocal/Instrumental Group from the USA/UK

1	Holy Diver	(Vertigo DIO 1)	72	1983	0	1983	
2	Rainbow In The Dark	(Vertigo DIO 2)	46	1983	0	1983	
3	We Rock	(Vertigo DIO 3)	42	1984	0	1984	
4	Mystery	(Vertigo DIO 4)	34	1984	0	1984	
5	Rock 'N' Roll Children	(Vertigo DIO 5)	26	1985	0	1985	
6	Hungry For Heaven	(Vertigo DIO 6)	72	1985	0	1985	
7	Hungry For Heaven (Re-Issue)	(Vertigo DIO 7)	56	1986	0	1986	
8	I Could Have Been A Dreamer	(Vertigo DIO 8)	69	1987	0	1987	

Dion & The Belmonts Male Vocalist, Real Name Dion Dimucci B: 18 Jul 1939 From USA

1	I Wonder Why		0	1958	22	1958	(Laurie 3013)
2	No One Knows		0	1958	19	1958	(Laurie 3015)
3	Don't Pity Me		0	1958	40	1958	(Laurie 3021)
* 4	A Teenager In Love	(London HLU 8874)	28	1959	5	1959	(Laurie 3027)
5	Where Or When		0	1960	3	1960	(Laurie 3044)
6	When You Wish Upon A Star		0	1960	30	1960	(Laurie 3052)
7	In The Still Of The Night		0	1960	38	1960	(Laurie 3059)
8	Lonely Teenager	(Top Rank Jar 521)	47	1961	12	1960	(Laurie 3070)
9	Havin' Fun		0	1961	42	1961	(Laurie 3081)
* 10	Runaround Sue	(Top Rank Jar 586)	11	1961	1	1961	(Laurie 3110)
* 11	The Wanderer	(HMV POP 971)	10	1962	2	1962	(Laurie 3115)
12	The Majestic		0	1961	36	1961	(Laurie 3115)
13	Lovers Who Wander		0	1962	3	1962	(Laurie 3123)
14	Little Diane		0	1962	8	1962	(Laurie 3134)
15	Love Came To Me		0	1962	10	1962	(Laurie 3145)
16	Ruby Baby		0	1963	2	1963	(Columbia 42662)
17	Sandy		0	1963	21	1963	(Laurie 3153)
18	This Little Girl		0	1963	21	1963	(Columbia 42776)
19	Be Careful Of The Stones You Throw		0	1963	31	1963	(Columbia 42810)
20	Donna The Prima Donna		0	1963	6	1963	(Columbia 42852)
21	Drip Drop		0	1963	6	1963	(Columbia 42917)
* 22	Abraham, Martin And John		0	1968	4	1968	(Laurie 3464)
23	The Wanderer (Re-Issue)	(Philips 6146 700)	16	1976	0	1976	
24	King Of The New York Street	(Arista 112556)	74	1989	0	1989	

HIT 22 REFERS TO LINCOLN, LUTHER KING AND J.F. KENNEDY • FIRST RECORDED AS DION & THE TIMBERLANES IN 1957

Dionne Female Vocalist from Canada

1	Come Get My Lovin'	(Citybeat CBC 745)	69	1989	0	1989	

Dionne Farris Female Vocalist from Bordentown, New Jersey

1	I Know	(Columbia 6613542)	47	1995	4	1995	(Columbia 77750)
2	I Know (Re-Entry)	(Columbia 6613542)	41	1995	0	1995	
3	Hopeless	(Columbia 6645165)	42	1997	0	1997	

Dionne Warwick Female Vocalist, Full Name Marie Dionne Warwick B: 12 Dec 1940 East Orange, New Jersey.

1	Don't Make Me Over		0	1963	21	1963	(Scepter 1239)

ISSUE	TITLE	UK LBL	UK POS	UK YEAR	US POS	US YEAR	US LBL
* 2	Anyone Who Had A Heart	(PYE International 7N 25234)	42	1964	8	1964	(Scepter 1262)
* 3	Walk On By	(PYE International 7N 25241)	9	1964	6	1964	(Scepter 1274)
4	You'll Never Get To Heaven (If You Break My Heart)	(PYE International 7N 25256)	20	1964	34	1964	(Scepter 1282)
5	Reach Out For Me	(PYE International 7N 25265)	23	1964	20	1964	(Scepter 1285)
6	You Can Have Him	(PYE International 7N 25290)	37	1965	0	1965	
7	Are You There (With Another Girl)		0	1966	39	1966	(Scepter 12122)
8	Message To Michael		0	1966	8	1966	(Scepter 12133)
9	Trains And Boats And Planes		0	1966	22	1966	(Scepter 12153)
10	I Just Don't Know What To Do With Myself		0	1966	26	1966	(Scepter 12167)
11	Alfie		0	1967	15	1967	(Scepter 12187)
12	The Windows Of The World		0	1967	32	1967	(Scepter 12196)
* 13	I Say A Little Prayer For You		0	1967	4	1967	(Scepter 12203)
14	(Theme From) Valley Of The Dolls	(PYE International 7N 25445)	28	1968	2	1968	(Scepter 12196)
15	Do You Know The Way To San Jose'	(PYE International 7N 25457)	8	1968	10	1968	(Scepter 12216)
16	Who Is Gonna Love Me?		0	1968	33	1968	(Scepter 12226)
17	Promises, Promises		0	1968	19	1968	(Scepter 12231)
18	This Girl's In Love With You		0	1969	7	1969	(Scepter 12241)
19	The April Fools (Movie Title Song)		0	1969	37	1969	(Scepter 12249)
20	You've Lost That Lovin' Feeling		0	1969	16	1969	(Scepter 12262)
21	I'll Never Fall In Love Again		0	1970	6	1970	(Scepter 12273)
22	Let Me Go To Him		0	1970	32	1970	(Scepter 12276)
23	Make It Easy On Yourself		0	1970	37	1970	(Scepter 12294)
* 24	Then Came You	(Atlantic K 10495)	29	1974	1	1974	(Atlantic 3029)
+ 25	Once You Hit The Road		0	1975	5	1975	(Warner Bros. 8154)
* 26	I'll Never Love This Way Again	(Arista ARIST 530)	62	1983	5	1979	(Arista 0419)
27	Deja Vu		0	1979	15	1979	(Arista 0459)
28	No Night So Long		0	1980	23	1980	(Arista 0527)
29	Friends In Love		0	1982	38	1982	(Arista 0673)
30	Heartbreaker	(Arista Arist 496)	2	1982	10	1982	(Arista 1015)
31	All The Love In The World	(Arista Arist 507)	10	1982	0	1982	
32	Yours	(Arista Arist 518)	66	1983	0	1983	
33	How Many Times Can We Say Goodbye		0	1983	27	1983	(Arista 9073)
* 34	That's What Friends Are For	(Arista Arist 638)	16	1985	1	1985	(Arista 9422)
35	Love Power	(Arista RIS 27)	63	1987	12	1987	(Arista 9567)

WITH HER SISTER DEE DEE WARWICK AND COUSIN CISSY HOUSTON FORMED THE GOSPELAIRES

Dire Straits Male Vocal/Instrumental Group from the UK

ISSUE	TITLE	UK LBL	UK POS	UK YEAR	US POS	US YEAR	US LBL
1	Sultans Of Swing	(Vertigo 6059 206)	8	1979	4	1979	(Warner Bros.8736)
2	Lady Writer	(Vertigo 6059 230)	51	1979	0	1979	
3	Romeo And Juliet	(Vertigo MOVIE 1)	8	1981	0	1981	
4	Skateaway	(Vertigo MOVIE 2)	37	1981	0	1981	
5	Tunnel Of Love	(Vertigo MOVIE 3)	54	1981	0	1981	
6	Private Investigations	(Vertigo DSTR 1)	2	1982	0	1982	
7	Twisting By The Pool	(Vertigo DSTR 2)	14	1983	0	1983	
8	Love Over Gold (Live) / Solid Rock (Live)	(Vertigo DSTR 6)	50	1984	0	1984	
9	So Far Away	(Vertigo DSTR 9)	20	1985	19	1986	(Warner Bros. 28789)
10	Money For Nothing	(Vertigo DSTR 10)	4	1985	1	1985	(Warner Bros.28950)
11	Brothers In Arms	(Vertigo DSTR 11)	16	1985	0	1985	
12	Walk Of Life	(Vertigo DSTR 12)	2	1986	7	1985	(Warner Bros.28878)
13	Your Latest Trick	(Vertigo DSTR 13)	26	1986	0	1986	
14	Sultans Of Swing (Re-Issue)	(Vertigo DSTR 15)	62	1988	0	1988	
15	Calling Elvis	(Vertigo DSTR16)	21	1991	0	1991	
16	Heavy Fuel	(Vertigo DSTR 17)	55	1991	0	1991	
17	On Every Street	(Vertigo DSTR 18)	42	1992	0	1992	
18	The Bug	(Vertigo DSTR 19)	67	1992	0	1992	
19	Encores (EP)	(Vertigo DSCD 20)	31	1993	0	1993	

NAMES: MARK & DAVID KNOPFLER, JOHN ILLSLEY & RICK WITHERS • VARIOUS PERSONNEL HAVE COME AND GONE SINCE 1979

Direckt Male Production/Instrumental Duo from the UK

ISSUE	TITLE	UK LBL	UK POS	UK YEAR	US POS	US YEAR	US LBL
1	Two Fat Guitars (Revisited)	(UFG UFG 7CD)	36	1994	0	1994	

Direct Drive Mixed Vocal/Instrumental Group from the UK

ISSUE	TITLE	UK LBL	UK POS	UK YEAR	US POS	US YEAR	US LBL
1	Anything?	(Polydor POSP 728)	67	1985	0	1985	
2	A.B.C (Falling In Love's Not Easy)	(Boiling Point POSP 742)	75	1985	0	1985	

Discharge Male Vocal/Instrumental Group from the UK

ISSUE	TITLE	UK LBL	UK POS	UK YEAR	US POS	US YEAR	US LBL
1	Never Again	(CLAY CLAY 6)	64	1981	0	1981	

ISSUE	TITLE	UK LBL	UK POS	UK YEAR	US POS	US YEAR	US LBL
Disco Anthem	Real Name Lex Van Coeverden Male Producer from Holland						
1	Screem	(SWEAT MCSTD 1977)	47	1994	0	1994	
Disco Citizens	Male Instrumental/Production Duo from the UK						
1	Right Here Right Now	(Deconstruction N 74321293872)	40	1995	0	1995	
2	Footprint	(Xtravaganza 0091115)	34	1997	0	1997	
Disco Evangelists	Male Production/Instrumental Group from the UK						
1	De Nero	(Positiva CDTIV 2)	59	1993	0	1993	
Disco Tex & The Sex-O-Lettes	Mixed Vocal Group from the USA						
1	Get Dancin'	(Chelsea 2005 013)	8	1974	10	1975	(Chelsea 3004)
2	I Wanna Dance Wit Choo	(Chelsea 2005 024)	6	1975	23	1975	(Chelsea 3015)
	HIT 2 FEATURES SIR MONTI ROCK III						
Disposable Heroes Of Hiphoprisy	Male Vocal/Instrumental Duo from the USA						
1	Television The Drug Of The Nation	(Fourth & Broadway BRW 241)	57	1992	0	1992	
2	Language Of Violence)	(Fourth & Broadway 12 BRW 248)	68	1992	0	1992	
3	Television The Drug Of The Nation (Re-Entry)	(Fourth & Broadway BRW 241)	44	1992	0	1992	
Diva	Female Vocal Duo from Norway						
1	The Sun Always Shines On TV	(East West YZ 947CD)	53	1995	0	1995	
2	Everybody (Move Your Body)	(East West EW 035CD)	44	1996	0	1996	
Diversions	Mixed Vocal/Instrumental Group from the UK						
1	Fattie Bum Bum	(GULL GULS 18)	34	1975	0	1975	
Divine	Male Vocalist from the USA						
1	Love Reaction	(Design Communications DES 4)	65	1983	0	1983	
2	You Think You're A Man	(Proto Ene 118)	16	1984	0	1984	
3	I'm So Beautiful	(Proto Ene 121)	52	1984	0	1984	
4	Walk Like A Man	(Proto Ene 125)	23	1985	0	1985	
5	Twistin' The Night Away	(Proto Ene 127)	47	1985	0	1985	
Divine Comedy	Male Vocal/Multi-Instrumentalist Neil Hannon from the UK						
1	Something For The Weekend	(Setanta SETCD 26)	14	1996	0	1996	
2	Becoming More Like Alfie	(Setanta SETCD 27)	27	1996	0	1996	
3	The Frog Princess	(Setanta SETCD 32)	15	1996	0	1996	
Divinyls	Mixed Vocal/Instrumental Duo From Australia, Formed In 1981						
1	I Touch Myself	(Virgin AmericaN VUS 36)	10	1991	4	1991	(Virgin 98873)
Dixie Cups	Female Vocal Group from the USA						
* 1	Chapel Of Love	(PYE International 7N 25245)	22	1964	1	1964	(Red Bird 10-001)
2	People Say		0	1964	12	1964	(Red Bird 10-006)
3	You Should Have Seen The Way He Looked At Me		0	1964	39	1964	(Red Bird 10-012)
4	Iko Iko	(Red Bird RB 10024)	23	1965	20	1965	(Red Bird 10-024)
	NAMES: BARBARA ANN & ROSA LEE HAWKINS & COUSIN JOAN MARIE JOHNSON						
Dixiebelles	Female Vocal Group from Memphis						
1	(Down At) Papa Joe's		0	1963	9	1963	(Sound Stage 7 2507)
2	Southtown, U.S.A.		0	1964	15	1964	(Sound Stage 7 2517)
	NAMES: SHIRLEY THOMAS, MARY HUNT & MILDRED PRATCHER						
Dizzy Gillespie	Male Jazz Instrumentalist (Trumpet) from the USA						
1	Salt Peanuts		0	1945	22	1945	(Guild 1003)
Dizzy Heights	Male Vocal/Instrumental Group from the UK						
1	Christmas Rapping	(Polydor WRAP 1)	49	1982	0	1982	
DJ Fast Eddie	Male Producer from the USA						
1	Can U Dance	(Champion Champ 41)	71	1987	0	1987	
2	Can U Dance (Re-Entry)	(Champion Champ 41)	67	1987	0	1987	
3	Hip House / I Can Dance	(DJ International DJIN 5)	47	1989	0	1989	
4	Yo-Yo Get Funky	(DJ International DJIN 7)	54	1989	0	1989	
5	Git On Up	(DJ International 655366)	49	1989	0	1989	
	HITS 1-2 ARE CREDITED TO KENNY 'JAMMING' JASON AND 'FAST' EDDIE SMITH • HIT 5 IS CREDITED TO DJ FAST EDDIE FEATURING SUNDANCE						
DJ Bobo	Male Vocalist, Real Name Rene Baumann from Switzerland						
1	Everybody	(PWL Continental PWCD 312)	47	1994	0	1994	
2	Love Is All Around	(AVEX UK AXEXCD 7)	49	1995	0	1995	
DJ Carl Cox	Male Producer from the UK						
1	I Want You (Forever)	(Perfecto PB 44885)	23	1991	0	1991	
2	Does It Feel Good To You	(Perfecto PB 74321102877)	35	1992	0	1992	
3	The Planet Of Love	(Perfecto PB 74321161772)	44	1993	0	1993	
4	Two Paintings And A Drum (EP)	(EDEL 0090715 COX)	24	1996	0	1996	

ISSUE	TITLE	UK LBL	UK POS	UK YEAR	US POS	US YEAR	US LBL
5	Sensual Sophis-Ti-Cat/The Player	(Ultimatum 0090875 COX)	25	1996	0	1996	
	THE '93 AND '96 HITS WERE RECORDED BY CARL COX						
DJ Dado Male Producer from Italy							
1	X-Files	(ZYX ZYX 8065R8)	8	1996	0	1996	
DJ Disciple Male Vocalist from the USA							
1	On The Dancefloor	(Mother MUMCD 55)	67	1994	0	1994	
DJ Doc Scott Male Producer from the UK							
1	NHS (EP)	(Absolute 2 ABS 001DJ)	64	1992	0	1992	
	THE HIT CONSISTED OF SURGERY AND NIGHT NURSE						
DJ Duke Male Producer from the USA							
1	Blow Your Whistle	(FFRR FCD 228)	15	1994	0	1994	
2	Turn It Up (Say Yeah)	(FFRR FCD 235)	31	1994	0	1994	
DJ Hype Male Producer from the UK							
1	Shot In The Dark	(Surburban Base SUBBASE 20CD)	63	1993	0	1993	
DJ Krush Male Producer from Japan							
1	Meiso	(MO WAX MW 042CD)	52	1996	0	1996	
2	Only The Strong Survive	(MO WAX MW 060CD	71	1996	0	1996	
DJ Miko Male Producer from Italy							
1	What's Up	(Systematic SYSCD 2)	6	1994	0	1994	
DJ Misjah & DJ Tim Male Instrumental/Production Duo From Holland							
1	Access	(FFRREEDOM TABCD 240)	16	1996	0	1996	
DJ Power Real Name Steve Gambaroli, Male Producer from Italy							
1	Everybody Pump	(COOLTEMPO COOL 252)	46	1992	0	1992	
DJ Professor Male Producer from Italy							
1	We Gotta Do It	(Fourth & Broadway BRW 225)	57	1991	0	1991	
2	Rock Me Steady	(Fourth & Broadway BRW 219)	49	1992	0	1992	
3	Rockin' Me	(Citra Citra 1CD)	56	1994	0	1994	
	HIT 1 IS CREDITED TO DJ PROFESSOR FEATURING FRANCESCO ZAPPALA • HIT 3 IS CREDITED TO PROFESSOR						
DJ Quik See Tony! Toni! Tone!							
DJ Scott (Featuring) Lorna B Mixed Vocal/Instrumental Duo from the UK							
1	Do You Wanna Party	(Love This SponCD 2)	36	1995	0	1995	
2	Sweet Dreams	(Steppin' Out SponCD 3)	37	1995	0	1995	
DJ Seduction Real Name John Kallum, Male Producer from the UK							
1	Hardcore Heaven / You And Me	(FFRREEDOM TAB 103)	26	1992	0	1992	
2	Come On	(FFRREEDOM TAB 111)	37	1992	0	1992	
DJ Shadow Male Producer from the UK							
1	What Does Your Soul Look Like	(NO WAX MW 027CD)	59	1995	0	1995	
2	Midnight In A Perfect World	(MO WAX MW 057CD)	54	1996	0	1996	
3	Stem	(MO WAX MW058CD)	74	1996	0	1996	
DJ Supreme Male Producer Nick Desri from the UK							
1	Tha Wild Style	(Distinctive DISNCD 19)	39	1996	0	1996	
2	Tha Wild Style (Re-Issue)	(Distinctive DISNCD 29)	24	1997	0	1997	
DJ's Rule Male Instrumental/Production Duo from Canada							
1	Get Into The Music	(Distinctive DISNCD 9)	72	1996	0	1996	
2	Get Into The Music (Re-Mix)	(Distinctive DISNCD 27)	65	1997	0	1997	
	HIT 2 IS CREDITED TO DJ'S RULE FEATURING KAREN BROWN						
Djaimin Male Producer from Switzerland							
1	Give You	(Cooltempo Cool 262)	45	1992	0	1992	
DJH Male Production/Instrumental Group From Italy							
1	Think About It	(RCA PB 44385)	22	1991	0	1991	
2	I Like It	(RCA PB 44741)	16	1991	0	1991	
3	Move Your Love	(RCA PB 44965)	73	1991	0	1991	
	HITS ARE CREDITED TO DJH FEATURING STEFY						
DJPC Male Producer from Belgium							
1	Inssomniak	(HYPE 7PUM 005)	62	1991	0	1991	
2	Inssomniak (Re-Issue)	(HYPE PUMR 005)	64	1992	0	1992	
DNA Two Production DJs from Bristol, England							
* 1	Tom's Diner	(A&M AM 592)	2	1990	5	1990	(A&M 1529)
2	La Serenissima	(Raw Bass RBASS 006)	34	1990	0	1990	

ISSUE	TITLE	UK LBL	UK POS	UK YEAR	US POS	US YEAR	US LBL
3	Rebel Woman	(DNA 7DNA 001)	42	1991	0	1991	
4	Can You Handle It	(EMI EM 219)	17	1992	0	1992	
5	Blue Love (Call My Name)	(EMI EM 226)	66	1992	0	1992	

Dobie Gray Male Vocalist, Real Name Leonard Victor Ainsworth B: 26 Jul 1942 Brookshire, Texas

ISSUE	TITLE	UK LBL	UK POS	UK YEAR	US POS	US YEAR	US LBL
1	The In Crowd	(London HL9953)	25	1965	13	1965	(Charger 105)
* 2	Drift Away		0	1973	5	1973	(Decca 33057)
3	Out On The Floor	(Black Magic BM 107)	42	1975	0	1975	
4	You Can Do It		0	1979	37	1979	(Infinity 50003)

OTHERS WERE C/W HITS • IN 1971 HE WAS LEAD SINGER WITH POLLUTION

Doc Holliday See Ivor Biggun

Doctor & The Medics Mixed Vocal/Instrumental Group from the UK

ISSUE	TITLE	UK LBL	UK POS	UK YEAR	US POS	US YEAR	US LBL
1	Spirit In The Sky	(IRS IRM 113)	1	1986	0	1986	
2	Burn	(IRS IRM 119)	29	1986	0	1986	
3	Waterloo	(IRS IRM 125)	45	1986	0	1986	

HIT 3 IS CREDITED TO DOCTOR & THE MEDICS FEATURING ROY WOOD

Doctor Spin Male Production/Instrumental Duo from the UK

ISSUE	TITLE	UK LBL	UK POS	UK YEAR	US POS	US YEAR	US LBL
1	Tetris	(Carpet CRPT 4)	6	1992	0	1992	

Dodgy Male Vocal/Instrumental Group from the UK

ISSUE	TITLE	UK LBL	UK POS	UK YEAR	US POS	US YEAR	US LBL
1	Lovebirds	(A&M AMCD 0177)	65	1993	0	1993	
2	I Need Another (EP)	(A&M 5803172)	67	1993	0	1993	
3	The Melod-EP	(Bostin 5806772)	53	1994	0	1994	
4	Staying Out For The Summer	(BOSTIN 5807972)	38	1994	0	1994	
5	So Let Me Go Far	(A&M 5809032)	30	1995	0	1995	
6	Making The Most Of	(A&M 5809892)	22	1995	0	1995	
7	Staying Out For The Summer (Re-Mix)	(A&M 5810952)	19	1995	0	1995	
8	In A Room	(A&M 5816252)	12	1996	0	1996	
9	Good Enough	(A&M 5818152)	4	1996	0	1996	
10	If You're Thinking Of Me	(A&M 5819992)	11	1996	0	1996	
11	Found You	(A&M 5821332)	19	1997	0	1997	

HIT 6 IS CREDITED TO DODGY WITH THE KICK HORNS

Dodie Stevens Real Name Geraldine Ann Pasquale B: 17 Feb 1947 Temple City, California

ISSUE	TITLE	UK LBL	UK POS	UK YEAR	US POS	US YEAR	US LBL
* 1	Pink Shoe Laces		0	1959	3	1959	(Crystalette 724)

Dodie West Female Vocalist from the UK

ISSUE	TITLE	UK LBL	UK POS	UK YEAR	US POS	US YEAR	US LBL
1	Goin' Out Of My Head	(Decca F 12046)	39	1965	0	1965	

Dog Eat Dog Male Vocal/Instrumental Group from the USA

ISSUE	TITLE	UK LBL	UK POS	UK YEAR	US POS	US YEAR	US LBL
1	No Fronts	(Roadrunner RR 23312)	64	1995	0	1995	
2	No Fronts (Re-Entry)	(Roadrunner RR 23313)	9	1996	0	1996	
3	Isms	(Roadrunner RR 23083)	43	1996	0	1996	

Dogs D'amour Male Vocal/Instrumental Group from the UK

ISSUE	TITLE	UK LBL	UK POS	UK YEAR	US POS	US YEAR	US LBL
1	How Come It Never Rains	(China China 13)	44	1989	0	1989	
2	Satellite Kid	(China China 17)	26	1989	0	1989	
3	Trail Of Tears	(China China 20)	47	1989	0	1989	
4	Victims Of Success	(China China 24)	36	1990	0	1990	
5	Empty World	(China China 27)	61	1990	0	1990	
6	All Or Nothing	(China WOKCD 2033)	53	1993	0	1993	

Doll Mixed Vocal/Instrumental Group from the UK

ISSUE	TITLE	UK LBL	UK POS	UK YEAR	US POS	US YEAR	US LBL
1	Desire Me	(Beggars Banquet BEG 11)	28	1979	0	1979	

Dollar Mixed Vocal Duo from the UK

ISSUE	TITLE	UK LBL	UK POS	UK YEAR	US POS	US YEAR	US LBL
1	Shooting Star	(Carrere 2871)	14	1978	0	1978	
2	Who Were You With In The Moonlight	(Carrere CAR 110)	14	1979	0	1979	
3	Love's Gotta Hold On Me	(Carrere CAR 122)	4	1979	0	1979	
4	I Wanna Hold Your Hand	(Carrere CAR 131)	9	1979	0	1979	
5	Takin' A Chance On You	(WEA K 18353)	62	1980	0	1980	
6	Hand Held In Black And White	(WEA Buck 1)	19	1981	0	1981	
7	Mirror Mirror (Mon Amour)	(WEA Buck 2)	4	1981	0	1981	
8	Ring Ring	(Carrere CAR 225)	61	1982	0	1982	
9	Give Me Back My Heart	(WEA Buck 3)	4	1982	0	1982	
10	Videotheque	(WEA Buck 4)	17	1982	0	1982	
11	Give Me Some Kinda Magic	(WEA Buck 5)	34	1982	0	1982	
12	We Walked In Love	(Arista DIME 1)	61	1986	0	1986	
13	O L'amour	(London LON 146)	7	1987	0	1987	
14	It's Nature's Way (No Problem)	(London LON 179)	58	1988	0	1988	

D

182

ISSUE	TITLE	UK LBL	UK POS	UK YEAR	US POS	US YEAR	US LBL
Dolly Dawn Female Singer, Real Name Theresa Maria Stabile from the USA							
Dolly Parton Female Vocalist, B: 19 Jan 1946 Sevier County, Tennessee							
18	Jolene	(RCA 2675)	7	1976	60	1973	(RCA 0145)
22	The Seeker		0	1975	2!	1975	(RCA 10310)
28	Two Doors Down		0	1978	19	1978	(RCA 11240)
29	Heartbreaker		0	1978	37	1978	(RCA 11296)
! 30	I Really Got The Feeling		0	1978	1	1978	(RCA 11420)
31	Baby I'm Burnin'		0	1979	25	1979	(RCA 11420)
32	You're The Only One		0	1979	59	1979	(RCA 11577)
35	Starting Over Again		0	1980	36	1980	(RCA 11926)
* 37	9 To 5	(RCA 25)	47	1981	1	1981	(RCA 12133)
38	But You Know I Love You		0	1981	41	1981	(RCA 12200)
43	I Will Always Love You (Re-Recording)		0	1982	53	1982	(RCA 13234)
* 48	Island In The Stream	(RCA 378)	7	1983	1	1983	(RCA 13615)
49	Save The Last Dance For Me		0	1983	45	1983	(RCA 13703)
* 51	Here You Come Again	(RCA 395)	75	1984	3	1977	(RCA 11123)
76	Romeo		0	1993	50	1993	(Columbia 74876)
79	The Day I Fall In Love	(Columbia 6600282)	64	1994	0	1994	
	OTHERS ARE US C/W HITS						
Dolores Gray Female Actress/Vocalist from the USA							
1	Shrimp Boats		0	1951	16	1951	(Decca 27832)
2	Kaw-Liga		0	1953	23	1953	(Decca 28582)
3	Big Mamou		0	1953	21	1953	(Decca 28676)
4	Lost In Loveliness (The Girl In Pink Tights)		0	1954	29	1954	(Decca 29109)
	HIT 2 WAS WITH THE COMMANDERS						
Domenico Modugno Male Vocalist, B: 9 Jan 1928 Polignano A Mare, Italy							
* 1	Volare (Nel Blu Dipinto Di Blu)	(OrioleICB 5000)	10	1958	1	1958	(Decca 30677)
2	Ciao Ciao Bambino	(Oriole CB 1489)	29	1959	0	1959	
Domino Male Rapper, Real Name Shawn Ivy from St. Louis							
1	Getto Jam	(Chaos 77298)	33	1994	7	1993	(Outburst 77298)
2	Sweet Potatoe Pie	(Chaos 77350)	42	1994	27	1994	(Outburst 77350)
Dominoes Male R&B Vocal Group With Clyde McPhatter & Billy Ward							
*+ 1	Do Something For Me		0	1951	6	1951	(Federal 12001)
* 2	Sixty Minute Man		0	1951	17	1951	(Federal 12022)
*+ 3	I Am With You		0	1951	8	1951	(Federal 12039)
See Also Billy Ward & His Dominoes							
Don & Juan Male Vocal Duo, Names Roland Trone & Claude Johnson from New York City							
1	What's Your Name		0	1962	7	1962	(BIG TOP 3079)
Don Azpiazu & His Havana Casino Orchestra Male Bandleader from Cuba							
* 1	The Peanut Vendor		0	1931	1	1931	(Victor 22483)
Don Campbell See General Saint							
Don Charles Male Vocalist from the UK							
1	Walk With Me My Angel	(Decca F 11424)	39	1962	0	1962	
Don Cherry Male Vocalist B: 11 Jan 1924 Wichita Falls, Texas							
1	Thinking Of You		0	1950	4	1950	(Decca 27128)
2	Vanity		0	1951	11	1951	(Decca 27618)
3	Belle, Belle, My Liberty Belle		0	1951	25	1951	(Decca 27717)
* 4	Band Of Gold	(Philips PB 549)	6	1956	4	1955	(Columbia 40597)
5	Wild Cherry		0	1956	29	1956	(Columbia 40665)
6	Ghost Town		0	1956	22	1956	(Columbia 40705)
Don Cornell Male Vocal/Guitarist from the USA							
1	I Need You So		0	1950	28	1950	(RCA Victor 3884)
2	I'll Walk Alone		0	1952	5	1952	(Coral 60659)
* 3	I'm Yours		0	1952	3	1952	(Coral 60690)
4	This Is The Beginning Of The End		0	1952	20	1952	(Coral 60748)
5	You'll Never Get Away		0	1952	17	1952	(Coral 60829)
6	I		0	1952	7	1952	(Coral 60860)
7	S'posin		0	1953	28	1953	(Coral 60903)
8	She Loves Me		0	1953	23	1953	(Coral 61011)

ISSUE	TITLE	UK LBL	UK POS	UK YEAR	US POS	US YEAR	US LBL
9	Please Play Our Song (Mister Record Man)		0	1953	18	1953	(Coral 61030)
10	Heart Of My Heart		0	1953	10	1953	(Coral 61076)
11	You're On Trial		0	1953	24	1953	(Coral 61068)
12	Size 12		0	1954	23	1954	(Coral 61125)
13	Believe In Me		0	1954	22	1954	(Coral 61171)
* 14	Hold My Hand	(VOGUE Q 2013)	1	1954	5	1954	(Coral 61206)
15	Stranger In Paradise	(VOGUE Q 72073)	19	1955	0	1955	
16	Most Of All		0	1955	14	1955	(Coral 61393)
17	The Bible Tells Me So		0	1955	7	1955	(Coral 61467)
18	Love Is A Many Splendoured Thing		0	1955	26	1955	(Coral 61467)
19	Young Abe Lincoln		0	1955	25	1955	(Coral 61521)

Don Costa Male Arranger/Orchestra from the USA, B: 10 Jun 1925 In Boston

ISSUE	TITLE	UK LBL	UK POS	UK YEAR	US POS	US YEAR	US LBL
1	Theme From *The Unforgiven* (The Need For Love)		0	1960	27	1960	(United Artists 221)
2	Never On Sunday	(London HLT 9195)	27	1960	19	1960	(United Artists 234)
3	Never On Sunday (Re-Entry)	(London HLT 9195)	0	1961	37	1961	(United Artists 234)
	OBITUARY: D: 19 JAN 1983.						

Don Covay Male Vocalist, β: 1938 Orangeburg, South Carolina

ISSUE	TITLE	UK LBL	UK POS	UK YEAR	US POS	US YEAR	US LBL
1	Mercy Mercy		0	1964	35	1964	(ROSEMART 801)
+ 2	Please Do Something		0	1965	21	1965	(Atlantic 2286)
3	Seesaw		0	1965	44	1965	(Atlantic 2301)
4	I Was Checkin' Out She Was Checkin' In		0	1973	29	1973	(Mercury 73385)
5	It's Better To Have (And Don't Need)	(Mercury 6052 634)	29	1974	0	1974	
	HITS 1-3 ARE CREDITED TO DON COVAY & THE GOODTIMERS						

Don Downing Male Vocalist from the USA

ISSUE	TITLE	UK LBL	UK POS	UK YEAR	US POS	US YEAR	US LBL
1	Lonely Days Lonely Nights	(People PEO 102)	32	1973	0	1973	

Don Fardon Male Vocalist, Real Name Don Maughn Coventry, England

ISSUE	TITLE	UK LBL	UK POS	UK YEAR	US POS	US YEAR	US LBL
* 1	Indian Reservation	(Young Blood YB 1015)	3	1970	20	1968	(GNP CRESC. 405)
2	Belfast Boy	(Young Blood YB 1010)	32	1970	0	1970	
	FORMER LEAD SINGER OF THE SORROWS						

Don Gardner & Dee Dee Ford Singing Duo from Philadelphia

ISSUE	TITLE	UK LBL	UK POS	UK YEAR	US POS	US YEAR	US LBL
1	I Need Your Loving		0	1962	20	1962	(FIRE 508)

Don Gibson Male Vocalist Donald Eugene Gibson B: 3 Apr 1928 Shelby, North Carolina

ISSUE	TITLE	UK LBL	UK POS	UK YEAR	US POS	US YEAR	US LBL
! 1	Sweet Dreams		0	1956	9	1956	(MGM 12194)
2	Oh Lonesome Me		0	1958	7	1958	(RCA 7133)
3	I Can't Stop Lovin' You		0	1958	81	1958	(RCA 7133)
4	Blue Blue Day		0	1958	20	1958	(RCA 7010)
5	Give Myself A Party		0	1958	46	1958	(RCA 7330)
6	Look Who's Blue		0	1958	58	1958	(RCA 7330)
7	Who Cares		0	1959	43	1959	(RCA 7437)
9	Lonesome Old House		0	1959	71	1959	(RCA 7505)
10	Don't Tell Me Your Troubles		0	1959	85	1959	(RCA 7566)
! 11	I'm Movin' On		0	1959	14	1959	(RCA 7629)
! 12	Big Hearted Me		0	1960	29	1960	(RCA 7629)
13	Just One Time		0	1960	29	1960	(RCA 7690)
14	Far, Far Away		0	1960	72	1960	(RCA 7762)
! 15	Sweet Dreams (Re-Recording)		0	1960	6	1960	(RCA 7805)
! 16	What About Me		0	1961	22	1961	(RCA 7841)
17	Sea Of Heartbreak	(RCA 1243)	14	1961	21	1961	(RCA 7890)
18	Lonesome Number One	(RCA 1272)	47	1962	59	1962	(RCA 7959)
	REST OF THE HITS ARE C/W						

Don Henley Male Vocalist, B: 22 Jul 1947 Gilmer, Texas

ISSUE	TITLE	UK LBL	UK POS	UK YEAR	US POS	US YEAR	US LBL
1	Leather And Lace		0	1981	6	1981	(Modern 7341)
* 2	Dirty Laundry	(Asylum E 9894)	59	1983	3	1982	(Asylum 69894)
3	The Boys Of Summer	(Geffen A 4945)	12	1985	5	1985	(Geffen 19141)
4	All She Wants To Do Is Dance		0	1985	9	1985	(Geffen 29065)
5	Not Enough Love In The World		0	1985	34	1985	(Geffen 29012)
6	Sunset Grill		0	1985	22	1985	(Geffen 28906)
7	The End Of The Innocence	(Geffen GEF 57)	48	1989	8	1989	(Geffen 22925)
8	The Last Worthless Evening		0	1989	21	1989	(Geffen 22771)
9	The Heart Of The Matter		0	1990	21	1990	(Geffen 19898)
* 10	Sometimes Love Just Ain't Enough	(MCA MCS 1692)	22	1992	2	1992	(MCA 54403)
	HIT 1 IS CREDITED TO STEVIE NICKS WITH DON HENLEY • HIT 10 IS CREDITED TO PATTY SMYTH WITH DON HENLEY • HE WAS A FORMER MEMBER OF THE EAGLES						

ISSUE	TITLE	UK LBL	UK POS	UK YEAR	US POS	US YEAR	US LBL
Don Howard Real Name Donald Howard Koplow B: 11 May 1935 Cleveland, Ohio							
* 1	Oh Happy Day		0	1952	4	1952	(Essex 311)
Don Johnson Male Vocalist, B: 15 Dec 1949 Flatt Creek, Missouri							
1	Heartbeat	(Epic 650064 7)	46	1986	5	1986	(Epic 06285)
2	Till I Loved You (Love Theme From *Goya*)	(CBS BARB 2)	16	1988	25	1988	(Columbia 08062)
	HIT 2 IS CREDITED TO BARBRA STREISAND AND DON JOHNSON							
Don Lang Male Vocalist from the UK							
1	Cloudburst	(HMV POP 115)	16	1955	0	1955	
2	Cloudburst (Re-Entry)	(HMV POP 115)	18	1955	0	1955	
3	Cloudburst (2nd E-Entry)	(HMV POP 115)	20	1956	0	1956	
4	School Day	(HMV POP 350)	26	1957	0	1957	
5	Witch Doctor	(HMV POP 488)	5	1958	0	1958	
6	Sink The Bismarck	(HMV POP 714)	43	1960	0	1960	
	HITS 4-5 ARE CREDITED TO DON LANG & HIS FANTASTIC FIVE							
Don McLean Male Singer/Songwiter, B: 2 Oct 1945 New Rochelle, New York							
* 1	American Pie	(United Artists UP 35325)	2	1972	1	1971	(United Artists 50856)
2	Vincent	(United Artists UP35359)	1	1972	12	1972	(United Artists 50887)
3	Castles in the Air	(EMI 5258)	47	1982	12	1972	(United Artists 50887)
4	Dreidel		0	1973	21	1973	(United Artists 51100)
5	Everyday	(United Artists UP 35519)	38	1973	0	1973	
6	Crying		1	1980	5	1981	(Millennium 11799)
7	Since I Don't Have You		0	1981	23	1981	(Millennium 11804)
8	Castles in the Air		0	1981	36	1981	(Millennium 11819)
9	American Pie (re-issue)	(Liberty EMCT 3)	12	1991	0	1991	
Don Pablo's Animals Male Instrumental Group from Italy							
1	Venus	(Rumour RUMA 18)	4	1990	0	1990	
Don Partridge Male Vocalist from the UK							
1	Rosie	(Columbia DB 8330)	4	1968	0	1968	
2	Blue Eyes	(Columbia DB 8416)	3	1968	0	1968	
3	Breakfast On Pluto	(Columbia DB 8538)	26	1969	0	1969	
Don Reid Male Vocalist from the USA							
1	Hurry! Hurry! Hurry!		0	1949	24	1949	(Peak 800)
2	Don't Be Afraid To Dream		0	1949	23	1949	(Peak 800)
Don Robertson Male Pianist/Whistler, B: 5 Dec 1922 Peking, China							
1	The Happy Whistler	(Capitol CL 14575)	8	1956	6	1956	(Capitol 3391)
	MOVED TO CHICAGO AT THE AGE OF FOUR							
Don Rondo Don sang on many advertising jingles and comes from New York City							
* 1	Two Different Worlds		0	1956	11	1956	(Jubilee 5256)
2	White Silver Sands		0	1957	7	1957	(Jubilee 5288)
Don Shirley Trio Male Organ/Pianist, B: 27 Jan 1927 Kingston, Jamaica							
1	Water Boy		0	1961	40	1961	(Cadence1392)
Don Spencer Male Vocalist from the UK							
1	Fireball	(HMV POP 1087)	32	1963	0	1963	
2	Fireball (Re-Entry)	(HMV POP 1087)	49	1963	0	1963	
Don Williams Male Vocalist, B: 27 May 1939 Floydada, Texas							
13	I Recall A Gypsy Woman	(ABC 4098)	13	1976	0	1976	
25	I Believe In You		0	1980	24	1980	(MCA 41304)
	REST ARE US C/W HITS • HIT 28 IS CREDITED TO EMMYLOU HARRIS AND DON WILLIAMS							
Don-E Male Vocalist from the UK							
1	Love Makes The World Go Round	(Fourth & Broadway BRW 242)	18	1992	0	1992	
2	Peace In The World	(Fourth & Broadway BRW 256)	41	1992	0	1992	
Donald Byrd Male Vocal/Instrumentalist from the USA							
1	Loving You / Love Has Come Around	(Elektra K 12559)	41	1981	0	1981	
Donald Fagen Male Vocalist, B: 10 Jan 1948 New Jersey							
1	I.G.Y (What A Beautiful World)		0	1982	26	1982	(Warner Bros. 29900)
2	Tomorrow's Girls	(Reprise W 0180CDX)	46	1993	0	1993	
	THE INITIALS I.G.Y. INTERNATIONAL GEOPHYSICAL YEAR (JUL '57 - DEC '58)							
Donald O'Connor Male Actor/Vocalist from the USA							
1	No Two People		0	1952	25	1952	(Columbia 39863)
	HIT WAS CREDITED TO DORIS DAY AND DONALD O'CONNOR							

ISSUE	TITLE	UK LBL	UK POS	UK YEAR	US POS	US YEAR	US LBL
Donald Peers	Male Vocalist from the UK						
1	Please Don't Go	(Columbia DB 8502)	3	1968	0	1968	
2	Please Don't Go (Re-Entry)	(Columbia DB 8502)	38	1969	0	1969	
3	Give Me One More Chance	(Decca F 13302)	36	1972	0	1972	
Donell Jones							
1	Knocks Me Off My Feet	(LAFACE 74321458502)	58	1997)			
Donell Rush	Male Vocalist from the USA						
1	Symphony	(ID 6587977)	66	1992	0	1992	
Donna Allen	Female Vocalist from the USA						
1	Serious	(Portrait PRT 650744 7)	8	1987	21	1987	(21 Records 99497)
2	Joy And Pain	(BCM BCM 257)	10	1989	0	1989	
3	Real	(Epic 6610992)	34	1995	0	1995	
Donna De Lory	Female Vocalist from the USA						
1	Just A Dream	(MCA MCSTD 1750)	71	1993	0	1993	
Donna Fargo	Female Vocalist, Real Name Yvonne Vaughan B: 10 Nov 1949 Mount Airy, North Carolina						
* 1	The Happiest Girl In The Whole Of The U.S.A.		0	1972	11	1972	(DOT 17409)
* 2	Funny Face		0	1972	5	1972	(DOT 17429)
3	Superman		0	1973	41	1973	(DOT 17444)
! 4	You Were Always There		0	1973	1	1973	(DOT 17460)
5	Little Girl Gone		0	1973	57	1973	(DOT 17476)
! 6	I'll Try A Little Bit Harder		0	1974	6	1974	(DOT 17491)
7	You Can't Be A Beacon (If Your Light Don't Shine)		0	1974	57	1974	(DOT 17506)
	THE REST ARE C/W HITS • IN 1979 SHE WAS STRICKEN WITH MULTIPLE SCLEROSIS						
Donna Giles	Male Vocalist from the USA						
1	And I'm Telling You I'm Not Going	(ORE AG 4CD)	43	1994	0	1994	
2	And I'm Telling You I'm Not Going (Re-Mix)	(EQUATORAXISCD 011)	27	1996	0	1996	
Donna Lewis	Female Vocalist from the UK						
1	I Love You Always Forever	(Atlantic A 5495CD)	5	1996	2	1996	(Atlantic 87072)
2	Without Love	(Atlantic A 5468CD)	39	1997	41	1996	(Atlantic 87028)
3	I Love You Always Forever (Re-Entry)	(Atlantic A 5495CD)	74	1996	0	1996	
Donna Summer	Female Vocalist, Real Name Adrian Donna Gaines B: 31 Dec 1948 Boston						
* 1	Love To Love You Baby	(GTO GT 17)	4	1976	2	1975	(OASIS 401)
2	Could It Be Magic	(GTO GT 60)	40	1976	0	1976	
3	Winter Melody	(GTO GT 76)	27	1976	0	1976	
* 4	I Feel Love	(GTO GT 100)	1	1977	6	1977	(Casablanca 884)
5	Down Deep Inside (Theme From *The Deep*)	(Casablanca CAN 111)	5	1977	0	1977	
6	I Remember Yesterday	(GTO GT 107)	14	1977	0	1977	
7	Love's Unkind	(GTO GT 113)	3	1977	0	1977	
8	I Love You	(Casablanca CAN 114)	10	1977	37	1978	(Casablanca 907)
9	Rumour Has It	(Casablanca CAN 122)	19	1978	0	1978	
10	Back In Love Again	(GTO GT 117)	29	1978	0	1978	
* 11	Last Dance	(Casablanca TGIF 2)	70	1978	3	1978	(Casablanca 926)
12	Last Dance (Re-Entry)	(Casablanca TGIF 2)	51	1978	0	1978	
* 13	Macarthur Park	(Casablanca CAN 131)	5	1978	1	1978	(Casablanca 939)
* 14	Heaven Knows	(Casablanca CAN 141)	34	1979	4	1979	(Casablanca 959)
* 15	Hot Stuff	(Casablanca CAN 151)	11	1979	1	1979	(Casablanca 978)
* 16	Bad Girls	(Casablanca CAN 155)	14	1979	1	1979	(Casablanca 988)
* 17	Dim All The Lights	(Casablanca CAN 162)	29	1979	2	1979	(Casablanca 2201)
* 18	No More Tears (Enough Is Enough)	(Casablanca CAN 174/CBS 8000)	3	1979	1	1979	Columbia 11125)
* 19	On The Radio	(Casablanca NB 2236)	32	1980	5	1980	(Casablanca 2236)
20	Sunset People	(Casablanca CAN 198)	46	1980	0	1980	
* 21	The Wanderer	(Warner Bros/Geffen K 79810)	48	1980	3	1980	(Geffen 49563)
22	Walk Away		0	1980	36	1980	(Casablanca 2300)
23	Cold Love	(Geffen K 79183)	44	1981	33	1981	(Geffen 49634)
24	Who Do You Think You're Foolin'		0	1981	40	1981	(Geffen 49664)
25	Love Is In Control (Finger On The Trigger)	(Warner Bros. K 79302)	18	1982	10	1982	(Geffen 29982)
26	State Of Independence	(Warner Bros. K 79344)	14	1982	0	1982	
27	I Feel Love (Re-Mix)	(Casablanca FEEL 7)	21	1982	0	1982	
28	The Woman In Me	(Warner Bros. U 9983)	62	1983	33	1983	(Geffen 29805)
29	She Works Hard For The Money	(Mercury Donna 1)	25	1983	3	1983	(Mercury 812370)
30	Unconditional Love	(Mercury Donna 2)	14	1983	0	1983	
31	Stop Look And Listen	(Mercury Donna 3)	57	1984	0	1984	
32	There Goes My Baby		0	1984	21	1984	(Geffen 29291)

ISSUE	TITLE	UK LBL	UK POS	UK YEAR	US POS	US YEAR	US LBL
33	Dinner With Gershwin	(Warner Bros. U 8237)	13	1987	0	1987	
34	All Systems Go	(WEA U 8122)	54	1988	0	1988	
* 35	This Time I Know It's For Real	(Warner Bros. U 7780)	3	1989	7	1989	(Atlantic 88899)
36	I Don't Wanna Get Hurt	(Warner Bros. U 7567)	7	1989	0	1989	
37	Love's About To Change My Heart	(Warner Bros. U 7494)	20	1989	0	1989	
38	When Love Takes Over You	(WEA U 7361)	72	1989	0	1989	
39	State Of Independance (Re-Issue)	(Warner Bros. U 2857)	45	1990	0	1990	
40	Breakaway	(Warner Bros. U 3308)	49	1991	0	1991	
41	Work That Magic	(Warner Bros. U 5937)	74	1991	0	1991	
42	Melody Of Love (Wanna Be Loved)	(Mercury MERCD 418)	21	1994	0	1994	
43	I Feel Love	(Manifesto FESCD 1)	8	1995	0	1995	
44	State Of Independence (Re-Mix)	(Manifesto FESCD 7)	13	1996	0	1996	

HIT 14 IS CREDITED TO DONNA SUMMER WITH BROOKLYN DREAMS • HIT 18 IS CREDITED TO DONNA SUMMER AND BARBRA STREISAND
HIT 30 HAS VOCALS BY MUSICAL YOUTH • HIT 44 IS CREDITED TO DONNA SUMMER FEATURING THE ALL STAR CHOIR • SHE WAS ALSO WITH THE GROUP CROW

Donnie & The Dreamers   Donnie Is Louis Burgio from New York City

ISSUE	TITLE	UK LBL	UK POS	UK YEAR	US POS	US YEAR	US LBL
1	Count Every Star		0	1961	35	1961	(Whale 500)

Donnie Brooks   Real Name John Faircloth Dallas, Texas

ISSUE	TITLE	UK LBL	UK POS	UK YEAR	US POS	US YEAR	US LBL
1	Mission Bell		0	1960	7	1960	(ERE 3018)
2	Doll House		0	1960	31	1960	(ERE 3028)

EARLY RECORDING NAMES: JOHHNY FAIRE, DICK BUSH & JOHNNY JORDON

Donnie Elbert   Male Vocalist/Multi-Instrumentalist, B: 25 May 1936 New Orleans

ISSUE	TITLE	UK LBL	UK POS	UK YEAR	US POS	US YEAR	US LBL
1	Where Did Our Love Go?	(London HL 10352)	8	1972	15	1971	(All Platinum 2330)
2	I Can't Help Myself	(AVCO 6105 009)	11	1972	22	1972	(AVCO 4587)
3	A Little Piece Of Leather	(London HL 10370)	27	1972	0	1972	

OBITUARY: D: 26 JAN 1989.

Donnie Iris   Real Name Dominic Ierace Pennsylvania, Formerly With Jaggerz

ISSUE	TITLE	UK LBL	UK POS	UK YEAR	US POS	US YEAR	US LBL
1	Ah! Leah!		0	1981	29	1981	(MCS 51025)
2	Love Is Like A Rock		0	1982	37	1982	(MCA 51223)
3	My Girl		0	1982	25	1982	(MCA 52031)

Donnie Owens   Male Pop-Country Singer, B: 30 Oct 1938 from the USA

ISSUE	TITLE	UK LBL	UK POS	UK YEAR	US POS	US YEAR	US LBL
1	Need You		0	1958	25	1958	(Guyden 2001)

Donny Hathaway & Roberta Flack   Donny B: 1 Oct 1945 Chicago

ISSUE	TITLE	UK LBL	UK POS	UK YEAR	US POS	US YEAR	US LBL
1	You've Got A Friend		0	1971	29	1971	(Atlantic 2808)
2	Where Is The Love	(Atlantic K 10202)	29	1972	5	1972	(Atlantic 2879)
3	The Closer I Get To You	(Atlantic K 11099)	42	1978	2	1978	(Atlantic 3463)
4	Back Together Again	(Atlantic K 11481)	3	1980	0	1980	

SEE ALSO ROBERTA FLACK

Donny Osmond   Male Vocalist, B: 9 Dec 1957 Ogden, Utah

ISSUE	TITLE	UK LBL	UK POS	UK YEAR	US POS	US YEAR	US LBL
* 1	Sweet And Innocent		0	1971	7	1971	(MGM 14227)
* 2	Go Away Little Girl		0	1971	1	1971	(MGM 14285)
* 3	Hey Girl / I Knew You When		0	1971	9	1971	(MGM 14322)
* 4	Puppy Love	(MGM 2006 104)	1	1972	3	1972	(MGM 14367)
5	Too Young	(MGM 2006 113)	5	1973	7	1972	(MGM 14407)
6	Why	(MGM 2006 119)	3	1972	13	1972	(MGM 14424)
7	Lonely Boy		0	1972	13	1972	(MGM 14424)
8	Puppy Love (Re-Entry)	(MGM 2006 104)	45	1972	0	1972	
9	Puppy Love (2nd Re-Entry)	(MGM 2006 104)	46	1972	0	1972	
10	Too Young (Re-Entry)	(MGM 2006 113)	47	1972	0	1972	
11	Puppy Love (3rd Re-Entry)	(MGM 2006 104)	48	1973	0	1973	
* 12	The Twelfth Of Never	(MGM 2006 199)	1	1973	8	1973	(MGM 14503)
13	A Million To One		0	1973	23	1973	(MGM 14583)
14	Young Love	(MGM 2006 300)	1	1972	25	1972	(MGM 14583)
15	When I Fall In Love	(MGM 2006 365)	4	1973	0	1974	
16	Are You Lonesome Tonight		0	1973	14	1973	(MGM 14677)
17	Where Did All The Good Times Go	(MGM 2006 468)	18	1974	0	1974	
18	C'mon Marianne		0	1976	38	1976	(Polydor 14320)
19	I'm In It For Love	(Virgin VS 994)	70	1987	0	1987	
20	Soldier Of Love	(Virgin VS 1094)	29	1988	2	1989	(Capitol 44369)
21	If It's Love That You Want	(Virgin VS 1140)	70	1988	0	1988	
22	My Love Is A Fire	(Capitol CL 600)	64	1991	21	1991	(Capitol 44379)
23	Sacred Emotion		0	1989	13	1989	(Capitol 44634)

SEE ALSO OSMONDS, DONNIE OSMOND & MARIE OSMOND

ISSUE	TITLE	UK LBL	UK POS	UK YEAR	US POS	US YEAR	US LBL

Donny Osmond & Marie Osmond Brother And Sister Vocal Duo from the USA

* 1	I'm Leaving It (All) Up To You	(MGM 2006 446)	2	1974	4	1974	(MGM 14735)
2	Morning Side Of The Mountain	(MGM 2006 274)	5	1974	8	1974	(MGM 14765)
3	Make The World Go Away	(MGM 2006 523)	18	1975	44	1975	(MGM 14807)
4	Deep Purple	(MGM 2006 561)	25	1976	14	1976	(MGM 14840)
5	Ain't Nothing Like The Real Thing		0	1976	21	1976	(Polydor 14363)
6	(Your My) Soul And Inspiration		0	1978	38	1978	(Polydor 14439)
7	On The Shelf		0	1978	38	1978	(Polydor 14510)

ALL HITS ARE CREDITED TO DONNY & MARIE OSMOND • SEE ALSO THE OSMONDS & SEPARATE ENTRIES

Donovan Male Vocalist, Full Name Donovan Phillip Leitch B: 10 Feb 1946, Glasgow, Scotland

1	Catch The Wind	(PYE 7N 15801)	4	1965	23	1965	(Hickory 1309)
2	Colours	(PYE 7N 15866)	4	1965	0	1965	
3	Turquoise	(PYE 7N 15984)	30	1965	0	1965	
* 4	Sunshine Superman	(PYE 7N 17241)	3	1966	1	1966	(Epic 10045)
* 5	Mellow Yellow	(PYE 7N 17267)	8	1967	2	1966	(Epic 10098)
6	Epistle To Dippy		0	1967	19	1967	(Epic 10127)
7	There Is A Mountain	(PYE 7N 17403)	8	1967	11	1967	(Epic 10212)
8	Wear Your Love Like Heaven		0	1967	23	1967	(Epic 10253)
9	Jennifer Juniper	(PYE 7N 17457)	5	1968	26	1968	(Epic 10300)
10	Hurdy Gurdy Man	(PYE 7N 17537)	4	1968	5	1968	(Epic 10345)
11	Lalena		0	1968	33	1968	(Epic 10393)
12	Atlantis	(PYE 7N 17660)	23	1968	7	1969	(Epic 10434)
13	To Susan On The West Coast Waiting		0	1969	35	1969	(Epic 10434)
14	Goo Goo Barabajagal (Love Is Hot)	(PYE 7N 17778)	12	1969	36	1969	(Epic 10510)
15	Jennifer Juniper	(Fontana SYP 1)	68	1990	0	1990	

HIT 5 HAS VOCALS FROM PAUL MCCARTNEY • HIT 14 IS CREDITED TO DONOVAN WITH THE JEFF BECK GROUP • HIT 15 IS CREDITED TO SINGING CORNER MEETS DONOVAN

Doobie Brothers Male Vocal/Instrumental Quartet from the USA

1	Listen To The Music	(Warner Bros K 16208).	29	1974	11	1972	(Warner Bros. 7619)
2	Jesus Is Just Alright		0	1973	35	1973	(Warner Bros. 7661)
3	Long Train Runnin'	(Warner Bros. W 0217CD)	7	1993	8	1973	(Warner Bros.7698)
4	China Grove		0	1973	15	1973	(Warner Bros. 7728)
5	Another Park, Another Sunday		0	1974	32	1974	(Warner Bros. 7795)
* 6	Black Water		0	1975	1	1975	(Warner Bros. 8062)
7	Take Me In Your Arms (Rock Me)	(Warner Bros. K 16559)	29	1975	11	1975	(Warner Bros. 8092)
8	Takin' It To The Streets		0	1976	13	1976	(Warner Bros. 8196)
8	Sweet Maxine		0	1975	40	1975	(Warner Bros. 8126)
9	It Keeps You Runnin'		0	1977	37	1977	(Warner Bros. 8282)
10	What A Fool Believes	(Warner Bros. K 17314)	31	1979	1	1979	(Warner Bros.8725)
11	What A Fool Believes (Re-Entry)	(Warner Bros. K 17314)	72	1979	0	1979	
12	Minute By Minute	(Warner Bros.k17411)	47	1979	14	1979	(Warner Bros.8828)
13	Dependin' On You		0	1979	25	1979	(Warner Bros. 49029)
14	Real Love		0	1980	5	1980	(Warner Bros. 49503)
15	One Step Closer		0	1980	24	1980	(Warner Bros. 49622)
16	What A Fool Believes (Re-Issue)	(Warner Bros. W 8451)	57	1987	0	1987	
17	The Doctor	(Capitol CL 536)	73	1989	9	1989	(Capitol 44376)
18	Listen To The Music (Re-Mix)	(Warner Bros. W 0228CD)	37	1994	0	1994	

HIT 6 WAS ORIGINALLY THE FLIP SIDE OF HIT 5 IN THE USA • NAMES: PAT SIMMONS, TOM JOHNSON, JOHN HARTMAN & DAVE SHOGREN

Dooley Silverspoon Male Vocalist from the USA

1	Let Me Be The Number One	(Seville SEV 1020)	44	1976	0	1976	

Dooley Wilson Male Vocalist from the USA

1	As Time Goes By	(United Artists UP 36331)	15	1977	0	1977	

HIT HAS VOICES OF HUMPHREY BOGART AND INGRID BERGMAN

Dooleys Mixed Vocal/Instrumental Group from the UK

1	Think I'm Gonna Fall In Love With You	(GTO GT 95)	13	1977	0	1977	
2	Love Of My Life	(GTO GT 110)	9	1977	0	1977	
3	Don't Take It Lyin' Down	(GTO GT 220)	60	1978	0	1978	
4	A Rose Has To Die	(GTO GT 229)	11	1978	0	1978	
5	Honey I'm Lost	(GTO GT 242)	24	1979	0	1979	
6	Wanted	(GTO GT 249)	3	1979	0	1979	
7	The Chosen Few	(GTO GT 258)	7	1979	0	1979	
8	Love Patrol	(GTO GT 260)	29	1980	0	1980	
9	Body Language	(GTO GT 276)	46	1980	0	1980	
10	And I Wish	(GTO GT 300)	52	1981	0	1981	

ISSUE	TITLE	UK LBL	UK POS	UK YEAR	US POS	US YEAR	US LBL
Doop	Male Instrumental Duo From Holland						
1	Doop	(Citybeat CBE 774CD)	1	1994	0	1994	
Doors	Male Vocal/Instrumental Quartet from Los Angeles						
* 1	Light My Fire	(Elektra EKSN 45014)	7	1967	1	1967	(Elektra 45615)
2	People Are Strange		0	1967	12	1967	(Elektra 45621)
3	Love Me Two Times		0	1967	25	1967	(Elektra 45624)
4	The Unknown Soldier		0	1968	39	1968	(Elektra 45628)
* 5	Hello I Love You	(Elektra EKSN 45037)	15	1968	1	1968	(Elektra 45635)
* 6	Touch Me		0	1969	3	1969	(Elektra 45646)
7	Wishful Sinful		0	1969	44	1969	(Elektra 45656)
8	Tell All The People		0	1969	57	1969	(Elektra 45663)
9	Runnin' Blue		0	1969	64	1969	(Elektra 45675)
10	You Make Me Real		0	1970	50	1970	(Elektra 45685)
11	Love Her Madly		0	1971	11	1971	(Elektra 45726)
12	Riders On The Storm	(Elektra K 12021)	50	1971	14	1971	(Elektra 45738)
13	Riders On The Storm (Re-Entry)	(Elektra K 12021)	22	1971	0	1971	
14	Riders On The Storm (Re-Issue)	(Elektra K 12203)	33	1976	0	1976	
15	Hello I Love You (Re-Issue)	(Elektra K 12215)	71	1979	0	1979	
16	Break On Through	(Elektra EKR 121)	64	1991	0	1991	
17	Light My Fire (Re-Issue)	(Elektra EKR 125)	7	1991	0	1991	
18	Riders On The Storm (2nd Re-Issue)	(Elektra EKR 131)	68	1991	0	1991	

NAMES: JIM MORRISON, RAY MANZAREK, ROBBY KRIEGER & JOHN DENSMORE • OBITUARY: MORRISON D: 3 JUL 1971 IN PARIS, FRANCE.

ISSUE	TITLE	UK LBL	UK POS	UK YEAR	US POS	US YEAR	US LBL
Dora Bryan	Female Actor/Vocalist from the UK						
1	All I Want For Christmas Is A Beatle	(Fontana TF 427)	20	1963	0	1963	
Dorian Gray	Male Vocalist from the UK						
1	I've Got You On My Mind	(Parlophone R 5667)	36	1968	0	1968	
Doris Day	Female Vocalist, Real Name Doris Kappelhoff B: 3 Apr 1922 Cincinnati, Ohio						
1	Papa, Won't You Dance With Me?		0	1947	21	1947	(Columbia 37931)
2	Thoughtless		0	1948	24	1948	(Columbia 38079)
* 3	Love Somebody		0	1948	1	1948	(Columbia 38174)
4	Confess		0	1948	16	1948	(Columbia 38174)
5	Put 'Em In A Box, Tie It With A Ribbon And Throw 'Em In The Deep Blue Sea		0	1948	27	1948	(Columbia 38188)
* 6	It's Magic (From *Romance On The High Seas*)		0	1948	2	1948	(Columbia 38188)
7	My Darling, My Darling (From *Where's Charley*)		0	1948	7	1948	(Columbia 38353)
8	Powder Your Face With Sunshine (Smile! Smile! Smile!)		0	1949	16	1949	(Columbia 38394)
9	Again (From *Roadhouse*)		0	1949	2	1949	(Columbia 38467)
10	Everywhere You Go		0	1949	22	1949	(Columbia 38467)
11	Let's Take An Old-Fashioned Walk (From *Miss Liberty*)		0	1949	17	1949	(Columbia 38513)
12	Now That I Need You (From Red, Hot, And Blue)		0	1949	20	1949	(Columbia 38507)
13	Canadian Capers (Cuttin' Capers) (From *My Dream Is Yours*)		0	1949	15	1949	(Columbia 38595)
14	Bluebird On Your Windowsill		0	1949	19	1949	(Columbia 38611)
15	Quicksilver		0	1950	20	1920	(Columbia 38638)
16	I Said My Pajamas (And Put On My Prayers)		0	1950	21	1950	(Columbia 38709)
17	Enjoy Yourself (It's Later Than You Think)		0	1950	24	1950	(Columbia 38709)
18	Hoop-Dee-Doo		0	1950	17	1950	(Columbia 38771)
19	Bewitched (From *Pal Joey*)		0	1950	9	1950	(Columbia 38698)
20	I Didn't Slip-I Wasn't Pushed-I Fell		0	1950	19	1950	(Columbia 38818)
21	A Bushel And A Peck (From *Guys And Dolls*)		0	1950	16	1950	(Columbia 39008)
22	It's A Lovely Day Today (From *Call Me Madam*)		0	1951	30	1951	(Columbia 39055)
23	Would I Love You (Love You, Love You)		0	1951	10	1951	(Columbia 39159)
24	Shanghai		0	1951	17	1951	(Columbia 39423)
25	Domino		0	1951	21	1951	(Columbia 39596)
* 26	A Guy Is A Guy		0	1952	1	1952	(Columbia 39673)
* 27	Sugarbush	(Columbia DB 3123)	8	1952	7	1952	(Columbia 39693)
28	When I Fall In Love (From *One Minute To Zero*)		0	1952	20	1952	(Columbia 39786)
29	No Two People (From *Hans Christian Andersen*)		0	1952	25	1952	(Columbia 39863)
30	My Love And Devotion	(Columbia DB 3157)	10	1952	0	1952	
31	Sugarbush (Re-Entry)	(Columbia DB 3123)	8	1952	0	1952	
32	A Full Time Job	(Columbia DB 3242)	11	1952	20	1952	(Columbia 39898)
33	Ma Says, Pa Says	(Columbia DB 3242)	12	1953	23	1952	(Columbia 39898
34	Mister Tap Toe		0	1953	10	1953	(Columbia 39906)
35	When The Red Red Robin Comes Bob-Bob-Bobbin' along		0	1953	29	1953	(Columbia 39970)
36	Candy Lips		0	1953	17	1953	(Columbia 40001)
37	Let's Walk Thata-Way	(Philips PB 157)	4	1953	0	1953	

ISSUE	TITLE	UK LBL	UK POS	UK YEAR	US POS	US YEAR	US LBL
38	Kiss Me Again, Stranger		0	1953	30	1953	(Columbia 40020)
39	A Purple Cow		0	1953	25	1953	(Columbia 40020)
40	Choo Choo Train (Ch-Ch-Foo)		0	1953	20	1953	(Columbia 40063)
* 41	Secret Love (From Calamity Jane)	(Philips PB 230)	1	1954	1	1954	(Columbia 40108)
42	I Speak To The Stars (From Lucky Me)		0	1954	16	1954	(Columbia 40210)
43	If I Give My Heart To You	(Philips PB 325)	4	1954	3	1954	(Columbia 40300)
44	Black Hills Of Dakota	(Philips PB 287)	7	1954	0	1954	
45	Anyone Can Fall In Love		0	1954	27	1954	(Columbia 40300)
46	Ready Willing And Able	(Philips PB 402)	7	1955	0	1955	
47	I'll Never Stop Loving You	(Philips PB 497)	17	1955	13	1955	(Columbia 40505)
48	Love Me Or Leave Me	(Philips PB 479)	20	1955	0	1955	
49	I'll Never Stop Loving You (Re-Entry)	(Philips PB 479)	19	1955	0	1955	
50	What Ever Will Be, Will Be (Que Sera, Sera)	(Philips PB 586)	1	1956	2	1956	(Columbia 40704)
51	A Very Precious Love	(Philips PB 799)	16	1958	0	1958	
52	Everybody Loves A Lover	(Philips PB 843)	25	1958	6	1958	(Columbia 41195)
53	Everybody Loves A Lover (Re-Entry)	(Philips PB 843)	27	1958	0	1958	
54	Move Over Darling	(CBS AAG 183)	8	1964	0	1964	
55	Move Over Darling (Re-Issue)	(CBS LEGS 1)	45	1987	0	1987	
	SEE ALSO LES BROWN ORCHESTRA						

Doris Drew   Female Vocalist from the USA

1	Sweet Violets		0	1951	22	1951	(Mercury 5673)

Doris Troy   Female Vocalist, Real Name Doris Payne B: 6 Jan 1937 New York City

1	Just One Look		0	1963	10	1963	(Atlantic 2188)
2	What'cha Gonna Do About It	(Atlantic AT 4011)	37	1964	0	1964	
3	What'cha Gonna Do About It (Re-Entry)	(Atlantic AT 4011)	38	1965	0	1965	

Dorothy   Male Instrumental Duo from the UK

1	What's That Tune (Doo Doo Doo Doo DOO-DOO-DOO-DOO-DOO-DOO)	(RCA 74321330912)	31	1995	0	1995	

Dorothy Collins   Real Name Marjorie Chandler B: 18 Nov 1926 Windsor, Ontario

1	My Boy-Flat Top		0	1955	16	1955	(Coral 61510)
2	Seven Days		0	1956	17	1956	(Coral 61562)

Dorothy Combs Morrison   See Edwin Hawkins Singers

Dorothy Moore   Female Vocalist, B: 1946 Jackson, Mississippi

1	Misty Blue	(Cooltempo CS 2087)	5	1976	3	1976	(Malaco 1029)
2	Funny How Time Slips Away	(CooltempoCS 2092)	38	1976	0	1976	
3	I Believe In You	(Epic EPC 5573)	20	1977	27	1977	(Malaco 1042)
	FORMER LEAD SINGER WITH THE POPPIES						

Dorothy Provine   Female Vocalist from the USA

1	Don't Bring Lulu	(Warner Bros. WB 53)	17	1961	0	1961	
2	Crazy Worlds Crazy Tune	(Warner Bros. WB 70)	45	1962	0	1962	

Dorothy Shay   Female Vocalist/Comedienne, B: Dorothy Sims In Jacksonville, Known As The Park Avenue Hillbilly from the USA

1	Feudin' And Fightin' (From Laffing Room Only)		0	1947	4	1947	(Columbia 37189)

Dorothy Squires   Female Vocalist from the UK

1	I'm Walking Behind You	(Polygon P 1068)	12	1953	0	1953	
2	Say It With Flowers	(Columbia DB 4665)	23	1961	0	1961	
3	For Once In My Life	(President PT 267)	24	1969	0	1969	
4	For Once In My Life (Re-Entry)	(President PT 267)	48	1969	0	1969	
5	Till	(President PT 281)	25	1970	0	1970	
6	Till (Re-Entry)	(President PT 281)	48	1970	0	1970	
7	My Way	(President PT 305)	25	1970	0	1970	
8	My Way (Re-Entry)	(President PT 305)	34	1970	0	1970	
9	My Way (2nd Re-Entry)	(President PT 305)	25	1970	0	1970	
	HIT 2 IS CREDITED TO DOROTHY SQUIRES AND RUSS CONWAY • SEE ALSO RUSS CONWAY						

Dorsey Burnette   Male Vocalist, B: 28 Dec 1932 Memphis

1	(There Was A) Tall Oak Tree		0	1960	23	1960	(ERA 3012)
	OTHERS WERE C/W HITS • OBITUARY: D: 19 AUG 1979 HEART ATTACK.						

Dose   See Mark E. Smith

Dottie O'Brien   Female Vocalist from the USA

1	I Wanna Be Loved		0	1950	23	1950	(Capitol 1044)

ISSUE	TITLE	UK LBL	UK POS	UK YEAR	US POS	US YEAR	US LBL
Dottie West	Female Country Singer, Real Name Dorothy Marie Marsh B: 11 Oct 1932 McMinnville, Tennessee						
31	Country Sunshine		0	1973	49	1973	(RCA 0072)
52	What Are We Doin' In Love		0	1981	14	1981	(Liberty 1404)
	OTHER HITS ARE C/W • HIT 52, 60 IS CREDITED TO KENNY ROGERS AND DOTTIE WEST • SEE ALSO KENNY ROGERS • OBITUARY: D: 4 SEP 1991 CAR ACCIDENT.						
Double	Male Vocal/Instrumental Duo from Switzerland Names: Kurt Maloo & Felix Haug And Also Played In Ping Pong						
1	The Captain Of Her Heart	(Polydor POSP 779)	8	1986	9	1986	(A&M 2838)
2	Devils Ball	(Polydor POSP 888)	71	1987	0	1987	
Double Dee	Male Vocal/Instrumental Group from the USA						
1	Found Love	(Epic 6563766)	63	1990	0	1990	
2	Found Love (Re-Mix)	(Sony S3 DANUCD 1)	33	1995	0	1995	
Double Trouble	Male Production/Instrumental Duo from the UK						
1	Just Keep Rockin'	(Desire Want 9)	11	1989	0	1989	
2	Street Tuff	(Desire Want 18)	3	1989	0	1989	
3	Talk Back	(Desire Want 27)	71	1990	0	1990	
4	Love Don't Live Here Anymore	(DESIRE WANT 32)	21	1990	0	1990	
5	Rub-A-Dub	(Desire Want 41)	66	1991	0	1991	
	HITS 1, 2 ARE CREDITED TO DOUBLE TROUBLE & THE REBEL MC • HIT 3 TO DOUBLE TROUBLE FEATURING JANETTE SEWELL						
	HIT 4 TO DOUBLE TROUBLE FEATURING JANETTE SEWELL & CARL BROWN						
• Double You?	Real Name Willie Morales Male Vocalist From Italy						
1	Please Don't Go	(ZYX ZYX 67487)	41	1992	0	1992	
Doug E. Fresh & The Get Fresh Crew	Male Vocal/Rap/Scratch Group from the USA						
1	The Show	(Cooltempo Cool 116)	7	1985	0	1985	
Doug Lazy	Male Vocalist from the USA						
1	Let It Roll	(Atlantic A 8866)	27	1989	0	1989	
2	Let The Rhythm Pump	(Atlantic A 8784)	45	1989	0	1989	
3	Let The Rhythm Pump (Re-Mix)	(East West A 7919)	63	1990	0	1990	
	HIT 1 IS CREDITED TO RAZE PRESENTS DOUG LAZY						
Doug Sheldon	Male Vocalist from the UK						
1	Runaround Sue	(Decca F 11398)	36	1961	0	1961	
2	Your Ma Said You Cried In Your Sleep Last Night	(Decca F 11416)	29	1962	0	1962	
3	I Saw Linda Yesterday	(Decca F 11564)	36	1963	0	1963	
Dovells	The Group Was Originally Called The Brooktones And Consisted Of Len Barry, Arnie Silver, Jerry Gross,						
	Mike Freda & Jim Meeley						
* 1	Bristol Stomp		0	1961	2	1961	(Parkway 827)
2	(Do The New) Continental		0	1962	37	1962	(Parkway 833)
3	Bristol Twistin' Annie		0	1962	27	1962	(Parkway 838)
4	Hully Gully Baby		0	1962	25	1962	(Parkway 845)
5	You Can't Sit Down		0	1963	6	1963	(Parkway 867)
	IN 1968 THE GROUP RECORDED UNDER THE NAME OF MAGISTRATES						
Dowlands	Male Vocal Duo from the UK						
1	All My Loving	(Oriole CB 1897)	33	1964	0	1964	
Dr. Alban	Male Producer from Nigeria						
1	It's My Life	(Logic 7432115330)	2	1992	0	1992	
2	One Love	(Logic 74321108727)	45	1992	0	1992	
3	Sing Hallelujah	(Logic 74321136202)	16	1993	0	1993	
4	Look Who's Talking	(Logic 74321195342)	55	1994	0	1994	
5	Away From Home	(Logic 74321222682)	42	1994	0	1994	
6	Sweet Dreams	(Logic 74321251552)	59	1995	0	1995	
	HIT 6 IS CREDITED TO SWING FEATURING DR. ALBAN						
Dr. Buzzard's Original 'Savannah'	Lead Singer With The '30s-Style Disco Band Is Cort-Day Band						
1	Whispering / Cherchez La Femme / Se Si Bon		0	1976	27	1976	(RCA 10827)
	THE BAND WAS FORMED BY THE BROTHERS STONY & AUGUST BROWDER, AUGUST LEFT TO FORM KID CREOLE & THE COCONUTS IN 1980						
Dr. Dre	Male Rapper, Real Name Andre Young from the USA						
1	Nuthin' But A G Thang	(Death Row A 8328CD)	31	1994	2	1993	(Death Row 53819)
* 2	Dre Day	(Death Row A 8292CD)	59	1994	8	1993	(Death Row 53827)
3	Let Me Ride		0	1993	34	1993	(Death Row 53839)
4	Natural Born Killaz	(Atlantic A 8197CD)	45	1995	0	1995	
* 5	Keep Their Heads Ringin'	(Priority/Virgin PTYCD 103)	25	1995	10	1995	(Priority 53188)
6	No Diggity	(Interscope IND 95003)	9	1996	1	1996	(Interscope)
7	California Love	(Death Row/Island DRWCD 3)	6	1996	6	1996	
	HIT 3 IS CREDITED TO ICECUBE FEATURING DR DRE • HIT 5 IS CREDITED TO BACKSTREET FEATURING DR DRE • HIT 6 IS CREDITED TO 2PAC FEATURING DR DRE						

ISSUE	TITLE	UK LBL	UK POS	UK YEAR	US POS	US YEAR	US LBL
Dr. Feelgood Male Vocal/Instrumental Group from the UK							
1	Sneakin' Suspicion	(United Artists UP 36255)	47	1977	0	1977	
2	She's A Wind Up	(United Artists UP 36304)	34	1977	0	1977	
3	Down At The Doctors	(United Artists UP 36444)	48	1977	0	1977	
4	Milk And Alcohol	(United Artists UP 36468)	9	1979	0	1979	
5	As Long As The Price Is Right	(United Artists YUP 36506)	40	1979	0	1979	
6	Put Him Out Of Your Mind	(United Artists BP 306)	73	1979	0	1979	
	NAMES ARE LEE BRILLEAUX, WILKO JOHNSON, JOHN SPARKS & JOHN MARTIN						
Dr. Hook Male Vocal/Instrumental Duo from the UK							
* 1	Sylvia's Mother	(CBS 7929)	2	1972	5	1972	(Columbia 45562)
* 2	The Cover Of 'Rolling Stone'		0	1972	6	1972	(Columbia 45732)
3	A Little Bit More	(Capitol CL15871)	2	1976	11	1976	(Capitol 4280)
! 4	A Couple More Years		0	1976	51	1976	(Capitol 4280)
5	Only Sixteen		0	1976	6	1976	(Capitol 4171)
! 6	If Not You	(Capitol CL15885)	5	1976	55	1976	(Capitol 4364)
7	Walk Right In		0	1977	46	1977	(Capitol 4423)
8	More Like The Movies	(Capitol CL 15967)	14	1978	0	1978	
* 9	Sharing The Night Together	(Capitol CL 16171)	43	1980	6	1978	(Capitol 4621)
! 10	All The Time In The World		0	1979	54	1979	(Capitol 4677)
* 11	When You're In Love With A Beautiful Woman	(Capitol CL 16039)	1	1979	6	1979	(Capitol 4705)
12	Better Love Next Time	(Capitol CL16112)	8	1980	12	1979	(Capitol 4785)
13	Sexy Eyes	(Capitol CL 16127)	4	1980	5	1980	(Capitol 4831)
14	Years From Now	(Capitol CL 16154)	47	1980	0	1980	
15	Girls Can Get It	(Mercury MER 51)	40	1980	34	1980	(Casablanca 2314)
16	Baby Makes Her Blue Jeans Talk		0	1982	25	1982	(Casablanca 2347)
17	When You're In Love With A Beautiful Woman (Re-Issue)	(Capitol EMCT4)	44	1992	0	1992	
18	A Little Bit More (Re-Issue)	(EMI EMCT 6)	47	1992	0	1992	
	REAL NAMES RAY SAYWER (DR HOOK) & DENNIS LOCORRIERE						
Dr. John Male Songwriter/Instrumentalist, Real Name Malcolm 'Mac' Rebennack B: 21 Nov 1940 In Philadelphia							
1	Right Place Wrong Time		0	1973	9	1973	(ATCO 6914)
Dr. Octagon Male Producer Keith Thornton from the USA							
1	Blue Flowers	(MO WAX MWO 55CD)	66	1996	0	1996	
Drafi Deutscher B: 9 May 1946, Berlin, He Was Once In The Group The Rainbows							
* 1	Marmor, Stein Und Eisen Bricht (Marble, Stone And Iron		0	1965	0	1965	
	HIT WAS NUMBER 1 IN GERMANY						
Dramatics Five Artists from Detroit, began singing together in the 60s							
* 1	Whatcha See Is Whatcha Get		0	1971	9	1971	(VOLT 4058)
* 2	In The Rain		0	1972	5	1972	(VOLT 4075)
	FIRST STARTED LIFE AS THE DYNAMICS IN 1966 • THEY HAD A FURTHER 33 R&B CHART HITS IN THE USA						
Dramatis Male Vocal/Instrumental Group from the UK							
1	Love Needs No Disguise	(Beggars Banquet BEG 68)	33	1981	0	1981	
2	I Can See Her Now	(Rocket XPRES 83)	57	1982	0	1982	
	HIT 1 IS CREDITED TO GARY NUMAN AND DRAMATIS • SEE ALSO GARY NUMAN						
Dread Flimstone & The New Tone Age Family Male Vocal/Instrumental Group from the USA							
1	From The Ghetto	(Urban URB)	66	1991	0	1991	
Dread Zeppelin Male Vocal/Instrumental Group from the USA							
1	Your Time Is Gonna Come	(IRS DREAD 1)	59	1990	0	1990	
2	Stairway To Heaven	(IRS DREAD 2)	62	1991	0	1991	
Dream Academy Mixed Vocal/Instrumental Trio from the UK							
1	Life In A Northern Town	(Blanco Y Negro NEG 10)	15	1985	7	1986	(Warner Bros.28841)
2	The Love Parade	(Blanco Y Negro NEG 16)	68	1985	36	1985	(Reprise 28750)
	NAMES: NICK LAIRD-CLOWES, GILBERT GABRIEL & KATE ST. JOHN						
Dream Frequency Real Name Ian Bland, Male Producer from the UK							
1	Love Peace And Harmony	(Citybeat CBE 756)	71	1991	0	1991	
2	Feel So Real	(Citybeat CBE 763)	23	1992	0	1992	
3	Take Me	(Citybeat CBE 768)	39	1992	0	1992	
4	Good Times / The Dream	(Citybeat CBE 773CD)	67	1994	0	1994	
5	You Make Me Feel Mighty Real	(Citybeat CBE 775CD)	64	1994	0	1994	
	HIT 2 IS CREDITED TO DREAM FREQUENCY FEATURING DEBBIE SHARP						
Dream Warriors Male Rap Group From Canada							
1	Wash Your Face In My Sink	(Fourth & Broadway BRW 183)	16	1990	0	1990	
2	My Definition Of A Boombastic Jazz Style	(Fourth & Broadway BRW 197)	13	1990	0	1990	
3	Ludi	(Fourth & Broadway BRW 206)	39	1992	0	1992	

ISSUE	TITLE	UK LBL	UK POS	UK YEAR	US POS	US YEAR	US LBL
Dreamhouse	Male Vocal/Instrumental Group from the UK						
1	Stay	(Chase CDPALACE 1)	62	1995	0	1995	
Dreamlovers	Black Quintet, Was The Backing Group On Most Of Chubby Checker's Hits						
1	When We Get Married		0	1961	10	1961	(Heritage 102)
Dreamweavers	Mixed Vocal Trio from Miami, Lead Singer Is Wade Buff						
* 1	It's Almost Tomorrow	(Brunswick 05515)	1	1956	7	1955	(Decca 29683)
2	A Little Love Can Go A Long Long Way		0	1956	33	1956	(Decca 29905)
Drifters	Male Vocal Group from the USA						
*+ 1	Money Honey		0	1953	1	1953	(Atlantic 1006)
9	Fools Fall In Love		0	1957	69	1957	(Atlantic 1123)
10	Drip Drop		0	1958	58	1958	(Atlantic 1187)
* 11	There Goes My Baby		0	1959	2	1959	(Atlantic 2025)
12	Dance With Me	(London HLE 8988)	17	1960	15	1959	(Atlantic 2040)
13	(If You Cry) True Love, True Love		0	1959	33	1959	(Atlantic 2040)
14	Dance With Me (Re-Entry)	(London HLE 8988)	35	1960	0	1960	
15	This Magic Moment		0	1960	16	1960	(Atlantic 2050)
* 16	Save The Last Dance For Me	(London HLK 9201)	2	1960	1	1960	(Atlantic 2071)
17	I Count The Tears	(London HLK 9287)	28	1961	17	1960	(Atlantic 2087)
18	Some Kind Of Wonderful		0	1961	32	1961	(Atlantic 2096)
19	Please Stay		0	1961	14	1961	(Atlantic 2105)
20	Sweets For My Sweet		0	1961	16	1961	(Atlantic 117)
21	When My Little Girl Is Smiling	(London HLK 9522)	31	1962	28	1962	(Atlantic 2134)
22	Up On The Roof		0	1963	5	1962	(Atlantic 2162)
23	On Broadway		0	1963	9	1963	(Atlantic 2182)
24	Rat Race		0	1963	71	1963	(Atlantic 2191)
25	I'll Take You Home	(London HLK 9785)	37	1963	25	1963	(Atlantic 2201)
26	Under The Broadwalk	(Atlantic AT 4001)	45	1964	4	1964	(Atlantic 2237)
27	I've Got Sand In My Shoes		0	1964	33	1964	(Atlantic 2253)
28	Saturday Night At The Movies		0	1964	18	1964	(Atlantic 2260)
29	At The Club	(Atlantic AT 4019)	35	1965	43	1965	(Atlantic 2268)
30	Come On Over To My Place	(Atlantic AT 4023)	40	1965	0	1965	
31	Baby What I Mean	(Atlantic 584 065)	49	1967	62	1967	(Atlantic 2366)
32	At The Club (Re-Issue)	(Atlantic K 10148)	39	1972	0	1972	
33	At The Club (Re-Issue)(Re-Entry)	(Atlantic K 10148)	3	1972	0	1972	
34	Come On Over To My Place (Re-Issue)	(Atlantic K 10216)	9	1972	0	1972	
35	Like Sister And Brother	(Bell 1313)	7	1973	0	1973	
+ 36	Kissin' In The Back Row Of The Movies	(Bell 1358)	2	1974	83	1974	(Bell 600)
37	Down On The Beach Tonight	(Bell 1381)	7	1974	0	1974	
38	Loves Games	(Bell 1396)	33	1975	0	1975	
39	There Goes My First Love	(Bell 1433)	3	1975	0	1975	
40	Can I Take You Home Little Girl	(Bell 1462)	10	1975	0	1975	
41	Hello Happiness	(Bell 1469)	12	1976	0	1976	
42	Every Nite's A Saturday Night With You	(Bell 1491)	29	1976	0	1976	
43	You're More Than A Number In My Little Red Book	(Arista 78)	5	1976	0	1976	
44	Save The Last Dance For Me (Re-Issue)	(Lightning LIG 9014)	69	1979	0	1979	

2-4 WERE R&B HITS • MOST OF THEIR HITS WERE SUNG BY DIFFERENT LEAD SINGERS • NAMES OF THE '53 SET-UP WERE CLYDE MCPHATTER, GERHART & ANDREW THRASHER & BILL PINKNEY • IN 1958 THE GROUP DISBANDED. THE GROUP FIVE CROWNS WAS LATER TO BE RENAMED THE DRIFTERS CHANGES IN PERSONNEL INCLUDE BEN E. KING, RUDY LEWIS & JOHNNY MOORE

ISSUE	TITLE	UK LBL	UK POS	UK YEAR	US POS	US YEAR	US LBL
Driver 67	Real Name Paul Phillips Male Vocalist from the UK						
1	Car 67	(LOGO GO 336)	7	1978	0	1978	
Drizabone	Male Production/Instrumental Duo from the UK						
1	Real Love	(Fourth & Broadway BRM 223)	16	1991	0	1991	
2	Catch The Fire	(Fourth & Broadway BRM 232)	54	1991	0	1991	
3	Pressure	(Fourth & Broadway BRCD 264)	33	1994	0	1994	
4	Real Love (Re-Recording)	(Fourth & Broadway BRCD 311)	24	1995	0	1995	
5	Brightest Star	(Fourth & Broadway BRCD 293)	45	1996	0	1996	
Drugstore	Mixed Vocal/Instrumental Group from the UK/USA/Brazil						
1	Fader	(HoneyHONCD 7)	72	1995	0	1995	
Drum Club	Male Production/Instrumental Duo from the UK						
1	Sound System	(Butterfly BFLD 10)	62	1993	0	1993	
Drum Theatre	Male Vocal/Instrumental Group from the UK						
1	Living In The Past	(Epic A 6798)	67	1986	0	1986	
2	Eldorado	(Epic EMU 1)	44	1987	0	1987	

ISSUE	TITLE	UK LBL	UK POS	UK YEAR	US POS	US YEAR	US LBL
Drupi	Male Vocalist From Italy						
1	Vado Via	(A&M AMS 7083)	17	1973	0	1973	
DSK	Male Production/Instrumental Duo from the UK						
1	What Would We Do / Read My Lips	(Boys Own BOI 6)	46	1991	0	1991	
Dtox	Mixed Vocal/Instrumental Group from the UK						
1	Shattered Glass	(Vitality VITAL 1)	75	1992	0	1992	
Duals	Names Henry Bellinger & Johnny Lageman						
1	Stick Shift		0	1961	25	1961	(Sue 745)
Duane Eddy & The Rebels	Male Guitarist, B: 26 Apr 1938 Corning, New York						
1	Movin 'N' Groovin		0	1958	72	1958	(Jamie 1101)
* 2	Rebel-Rouser	(London HL8669)	19	1958	6	1958	(Jamie 1104)
3	Ramrod		0	1958	27	1958	(Jamie 1109)
4	Cannonball	(London HL8764)	22	1959	15	1958	(Jamie1111)
5	The Lonely One		0	1959	23	1959	(Jamie 1117)
6	Yep		17	1959	30	1959	(JAMIE 1122)
7	Forty Miles Of Bad Road	(London HLW 8929)	11	1959	9	1959	(Jamie 1126)
8	Peter Gunn Theme	(London HLW 8879)	6	1959	27	1960	(Jamie 1168)
9	Peter Gunn Theme (Re-Entry)	(London HLW 8879)	27	1959	0	1959	
10	Some Kinda Earthquake	(London HLW 9007)	12	1959	37	1959	(Jamie 1130)
11	Bonnie Came Back	(London HLW 9050)	9	1960	26	1960	(Jamie 1144)
12	Shazam	(London HLW 9104)	4	1960	0	1960	
* 13	Because They're Young	(London HLW9162)	2	1960	4	1960	(Jamie 1156)
14	Kommotion	(London HLW 9225)	13	1960	0	1960	
15	Pepe	(London HLW 9257)	2	1961	18	1961	(Jamie 1175)
16	Theme From Dixie	(London HLW 9324)	7	1961	39	1961	(Jamie 1183)
17	Ring Of Fire	(London HLW 9370)	17	1961	0	1961	
18	Drivin' Home	(London HLW 9406)	30	1961	0	1961	
19	Caravan	(Parlophone R 4826)	42	1961	0	1961	
20	Deep In The Heart Of Texas	(RCA 1288)	19	1962	0	1962	
21	Ballad Of Paladin	(RCA 1300)	10	1962	33	1962	(RCA 8047)
* 22	Dance With The Guitar Man	(RCA 1316)	4	1962	12	1962	(RCA 8087)
23	Boss Guitar	(RCA 1329)	27	1963	28	1963	(RCA 8131)
24	Lonely Boy Lonely Guitar	(RCA 1344)	35	1963	0	1963	
25	Your Baby's Gone Surfin'	(RCA 1357)	49	1963	0	1963	
26	Play Me Like You Play Your Guitar	(GTO GT 11)	9	1975	0	1975	
! 27	You Are My Sunshine		0	1977	69	1977	(Elektra 45359)
28	Peter Gunn	(CHINA WOK 6)	8	1986	0	1986	

HITS 19-21 ARE CREDITED TO DUANE EDDY • HITS 22-26 ARE CREDITED TO DUANE EDDY & THE REBELETTES

HIT 27 IS WAS WITH WAYLON JENNINGS, WILLIE NELSON, DEED (DUANE'S WIFE) AND KIM VASSY • HIT 28 IS CREDITED TO ART OF NOISE FEATURING DUANE EDDY

ISSUE	TITLE	UK LBL	UK POS	UK YEAR	US POS	US YEAR	US LBL
Dub War	Male Vocal/Instrumental Group from the UK						
1	Strike It	(Earache Mosh 138CD)	70	1995	0	1995	
2	Enemy Maker	(Earache Mosh 147CD)	41	1996	0	1996	
3	Cry Dignity	(EEarache Mosh 163CDD)	59	1996	0	1996	
4	Million Dollar Love	(Earache Mosh 170CD1)	73	1997	0	1997	
Dubliners	Male Vocal/Instrumental Group from Ireland						
1	Seven Drunken Nights	(Major Minor MM 506)	7	1967	0	1967	
2	Black Velvet Band	(Major Minor MM 530)	15	1967	0	1967	
3	(Maids When You're Young) Never Wed An Old Man	(Major Minor MM 551)	43	1967	0	1967	
4	The Irish Rover	(Stiff Buy 258)	8	1987	0	1987	
5	Jack's Heroes /Whiskey In The Jar	(Pogue Mahone YZ 500)	63	1990	0	1990	

HITS 4-5 ARE CREDITED TO POGUES & THE DUBLINERS

ISSUE	TITLE	UK LBL	UK POS	UK YEAR	US POS	US YEAR	US LBL
Dubs	Lead Singer Of The R&B Quintet Is Richard Blandon from the USA						
1	Could This Be Magic		0	1957	23	1957	(GONE 5011)
Dubstar	Mixed Vocal/Instrumental Group from Newcastle With Lead Singer Sarah Blackwood						
1	Stars	(Food CDFOOD 61)	40	1995	0	1995	
2	Anywhere	(Food CDFOOD67)	37	1995	0	1995	
3	Not So Manic Now	(Food CDFOODS 71)	18	1996	0	1996	
4	Stars (Re-Issue)	(Food CDFOODS 75)	15	1996	0	1996	
5	Elevator Song	(Food CDFOOD 80)	25	1996	0	1996	
6	No More Talk	(Food CDFOOD 96)	20	1997	0	1997	
Duffo	Male Vocalist from Australia						
1	Give Me Back Me Brain	(Beggars Banquet BEG 15)	60	1979	0	1979	

ISSUE	TITLE	UK LBL	UK POS	UK YEAR	US POS	US YEAR	US LBL
Duice Male Rap Duo from Los Angeles/Barbados							
* 1	Dazzey Duks		0	1993	12	1993	(TMR/Bell 72501)
Duke Male Vocalist from the UK							
1	So In Love With You	(Encore CDCOR 009)	66	1996	0	1996	
2	So In Love With You (Re-Issue)	(Pukka CDPUKKA 11)	22	1996	0	1996	
Duke Baysee Male Vocalist from the UK							
1	Sugar Sugar	(Bell 74321228702)	30	1994	0	1994	
2	Do You Love Me	(Double Dekker CDDEK 1)	46	1995	0	1995	
Duke Ellington Orchestra Male Pianist/Jazz Composer/Orchestra Leader from Washington D.C.							
67	I'm Beginning To See The Light		0	1945	6	1945	(Victor 1618)
68	Come To Baby, Do		0	1946	13	1946	(Victor 1748)
69	Satin Doll		0	1953	27	1953	(Capitol 2458)
70	Boo-Dah		0	1953	30	1953	(Capitol 2598)
71	Skin Deep	(Philips PB 243)	7	1954	0	1954	
	VOCALS ON HITS 67,68 ARE BY JOYA SHERRILL • OBITUARY: D: 24 MAY 1974, (AGED 75).						
Dukes Male Vocal Duo from the UK							
1	Mystery Girl	(WEA K 18867)	47	1981	0	1981	
2	Thank You For The Party	(WEA K 19136)	53	1982	0	1982	
Dunblane Male Vocal/Instrumental Assembly With Children from Dunblane							
1	Knockin' On Heaven's Door / Throw These Guns Away	(BMG 74321442182)	1	1996	0	1996	
Duncan Browne Male Vocalist from the UK							
1	Journey	(RAK 135)	23	1972	0	1972	
2	Theme From *The Travelling Man*	(TOWERBell TOW 64)	68	1984	0	1984	
Duprees Names: Joseph Canzano, Mike Amone, Tom Bialablow, John Salvato & Joe Santollo							
1	You Belong To Me		0	1962	7	1962	(COED 569)
2	My Own True Love		0	1962	13	1962	(COED 571)
3	Why Don't You Believe Me		0	1963	37	1963	(COED 584)
4	Have You Heard		0	1963	18	1963	(COED 585)
Duran Duran Male Vocal/Instrumental Group from the UK							
1	Planet Earth	(EMI 6137)	12	1981	0	1981	
2	Carless Memories	(EMI 5168)	37	1981	0	1981	
3	Girls On Film	(EMI 5206)	5	1981	0	1981	
4	My Own Way	(EMI 5254)	14	1981	0	1981	
* 5	Hungry Like The Wolf	(EMI 5295)	5	1982	3	1983	(Harvest 5195)
6	Save A Prayer	(EMI 5327)	2	1982	16	1985	(Capitol 5438)
7	Rio	(EMI 5346)	9	1982	14	1983	(Capitol 5215)
8	Is There Something I Should Know	(EMI 5371)	1	1983	4	1983	(Capitol 5233)
9	Union Of The Snake	(EMI 5429)	3	1983	3	1983	(Capitol 5290)
10	Union Of The Snake (Re-Entry)	(EMI 5429)	66	1983	0	1966	
11	New Moon On Monday	(EMI Duran 1)	9	1984	10	1984	(Capitol 5309)
* 12	The Reflex	(EMI Duran 2)	1	1984	1	1984	(Capitol 5345)
* 13	Wild Boys	(EMI Duran 3)	2	1984	2	1984	(Capitol 5417)
14	A View To A Kill	(Parlophone Duran 007)	2	1985	1	1985	(Capitol 5475)
15	Notorious	(EMI DDN 45)	7	1986	2	1986	(Capitol 5648)
16	Notorious (Re-Entry)	(EMI DDN 45)	73	1987	0	1987	
17	Skin Trade	(EMI TRADE 1)	22	1987	39	1987	(Capitol 5670)
18	Meet El Presidente	(EMI TOUR 1)	24	1987	0	1987	
19	I Don't Want Your Love	(EMI YOUR 1)	14	1988	4	1988	(Capitol 44237)
20	All She Wants Is	(EMI DD 11)	9	1989	22	1989	(Capitol 44287)
21	Do You Believe In Shame	(EMI DD 12)	30	1989	0	1989	
22	Burning The Ground	(EMI DD 13)	31	1989	0	1989	
23	Violence Of Summer (Love's Taking Over)	(Parlophone DD 14)	20	1990	0	1990	
24	Serious	(Parlophone DD 15)	48	1990	0	1990	
* 25	Ordinary World	(Parlophone CDDDS 16)	6	1993	3	1993	(Capitol 44928)
26	Come Undone	(Parlophone CDDDS 17)	13	1993	7	1993	(Capitol 44918)
27	Too Much Information	(Parlophone CDDDS 18)	35	1993	0	1993	
28	Perfect Day	(Parlophone CDDDS 20)	28	1995	0	1995	
29	White Lines Don't Do It	(Parlophone CDDDS 19)	17	1995	0	1995	
30	Out Of My Mind	(Virgin VSCDT 1639)	21	1997	0	1997	
	NAMES SIMON LEBON, ANDY TAYLOR, NICK RHODES, JOHN TAYLOR & ROGER TAYLOR, THE SIZE OF THE GROUP HAS VARIED SINCE 1984						
Dusty Fletcher Male Comedian/Vocalist from the USA							
* 1	Open The Door Richard		0	1947	3	1947	(NATIONAL 4012)

ISSUE	TITLE	UK LBL	UK POS	UK YEAR	US POS	US YEAR	US LBL
Dusty Springfield Female Vocalist, Real Name Mary O'Brien B: 16 Apr 1939 Hampstead, London, England							
* 1	I Only Want To Be With You	(Philips BF 1292)	4	1963	12	1964	(Philips 40162)
2	Stay Awhile	(Philips BF 1313)	13	1964	38	1964	(Philips 40180)
3	I Just Don't Know What To Do With Myself	(Philips BF 1348)	3	1964	0	1964	
4	Wishin' And Hopin'		0	1964	6	1964	(Philips 40207)
5	Losing You	(Philips BF 1369)	9	1964	0	1964	
6	Your Hurtin' Kinda Love	(Philips BF 1396)	37	1965	0	1965	
7	In The Middle Of Nowhere	(Philips BF 1418)	8	1965	0	1965	
8	Some Of Your Lovin'	(Philips BF 1430)	8	1965	0	1965	
9	Little By Little	(Philips BF 1466)	17	1966	0	1966	
* 10	You Don't Have To Say You Love Me	(Philips BF 1482)	1	1966	4	1966	(Philips 40371)
11	Going Back	(Philips BF 1502)	10	1966	0	1966	
12	All I See Is You	(Philips BF 1510)	9	1966	20	1966	(Philips 40396)
13	I'll Try Anything	(Philips BF 153)	13	1967	40	1967	(Philips 40439)
14	Give Me Time	(Philips BF 1577)	24	1967	0	1967	
15	The Look Of Love		0	1967	22	1967	(Philips 40465)
16	I Close My Eyes And Count To Ten	(Philips BF 1682)	4	1968	0	1968	
17	Son Of A Preacher Man	(Philips BF 1730)	9	1968	10	1968	(Atlantic 2580)
18	The Windmills Of Your Mind		0	1969	31	1969	(Atlantic 2623)
19	Am I The Same Girl	(Philips BF 1811)	43	1969	0	1969	
20	Am I The Same Girl (Re-Entry)	(Philips BF 1811)	46	1969	0	1969	
21	A Brand New Me		0	1969	24	1969	(Atlantic 2685)
22	How Can I Be Sure	(Philips 6006 045)	36	1970	0	1970	
23	Baby Blue	(Mercury DUSTY 4)	61	1979	0	1979	
24	What Have I Done To Deserve This	(Parlophone R 6163)	2	1987	2	1988	(EMI-MAN. 50107)
25	Nothing Has Been Proved	(Parlophone R 6207)	16	1989	0	1989	
26	In Private	(Parlophone R 6234)	14	1989	0	1989	
27	Reputation	(Parlophone R 6253)	38	1990	0	1990	
28	Arrested By You	(Parlophone R 6266)	70	1990	0	1990	
29	Heart And Soul	(Columbia 6598562)	75	1993	0	1993	
30	Wherever Would I Be	(Columbia 6620592)	44	1995	0	1995	
31	Roll Away	(Columbia 6623682)	68	1995	0	1995	

HIT 24 IC CREDITED TO PET SHOP BOYS AND DUSTY SPRINGFIELD • HIT 29 IS CREDITED TO CILLA BLACK WITH DUSTY SPRINGFIELD
HIT 30 IS CREDITED TO DUSTY SPRINGFIELD AND DARYL HALL • SEE ALSO THE SPRINGFIELDS, CILLA BLACK & PET SHOP BOYS

ISSUE	TITLE	UK LBL	UK POS	UK YEAR	US POS	US YEAR	US LBL
Dweeb Mixed Trio from Lewisham/Watford, England							
1	Scoby Doo	(Blanco Y Negro 100CD)	63	1997	0	1997	
2	Oh Yeah, Baby	(Blanco Y Negro 102CD1)	70	1997	0	1997	
Dwight Twilley Singer/Songwriter/Pianist, B: 6 Jun 1951 Tulsa, Oklahoma							
1	I'm On Fire		0	1975	16	1975	(SHELTER
2	Girls		0	1984	16	1984	(EMI America 8196)

HIT 1 IS CREDITED TO THE DWIGHT TWILLEY BAND

ISSUE	TITLE	UK LBL	UK POS	UK YEAR	US POS	US YEAR	US LBL
Dyke & The Blazers Dyke's Real Name Is Arlester Christian B: 1943 Brooklyn							
1	We Got More Soul		0	1969	35	1969	(Original Sound 86)
2	Let A Woman Be A Woman - Let A Man Be A Man		0	1969	36	1969	(Original Sound 89)

OBITUARY: D: 1971 MURDERED (SHOT).

ISSUE	TITLE	UK LBL	UK POS	UK YEAR	US POS	US YEAR	US LBL
Dynamix II Male Vocal/Instrumental Group from the USA							
1	Just Give The DJ A Break	(Cooltempo COOL 151)	50	1987	0	1987	

HIT IS CREDITED TO DYNAMIX II FEATURING TOO TOUGH TEE

ISSUE	TITLE	UK LBL	UK POS	UK YEAR	US POS	US YEAR	US LBL
Dynasty Male Vocal/Instrumental Group from the USA							
1	I Don't Want To Be A Freak	(Solar FB 1694)	20	1979	0	1979	
2	I Just Begun To Love You	(Solar SO 10)	51	1980	0	1980	
3	Does That Ring A Bell	(Solar E 9911)	53	1983	0	1983	

Dynasty Of Two (Featuring) Rowetta See Further Adventures Of North (EP), Various Artists (EP, LP, 78s)

E

ISSUE	TITLE	UK LBL	UK POS	UK YEAR	US POS	US YEAR	US LBL
E'voke	Female Vocal Duo from the UK						
1	Runaway	(FFRREEDOM TABCD 238)	30	1995	0	1995	
2	Arms Of Loren	(Manifesto FESCD 10)	25	1996	0	1996	
E-Lustrious	Male Production/Instrumental Duo from the UK						
1	Dance No More	(MOS MOS 001T)	58	1992	0	1992	
2	In Your Dance	(UFG UFG 6CD)	69	1994	0	1994	
	HIT 1 IS CREDITED TO E-LUSTRIOUS FEATURING DEBORAH FRENCH						
E-Motion	Male Vocal/Instrumental Duo from the UK						
1	The Naughty North And The Sexy South	(Soundproof/MCA MCSTD 40017)	20	1996	0	1996	
2	I Stand Alone	(Soundproof/MCA MCSTD 40061)	60	1996	0	1996	
3	The Naughty North And The Sexy South (Re-Mix)	(Soundproof/MCA MCSTD 40076)	17	1996	0	1996	
E-Rotic	Mixed Vocal/Instrumental Group from the USA/Germany						
1	Max, Don't Have Sex With Your Ex	(STIP CDSTIP 2)	45	1995	0	1995	
E-Type	Male Vocalist from Sweden						
1	This Is The Way	(FFRREEDOM TABCD 237)	53	1995	0	1995	
E-Zee Possee	Mixed Vocal/Instrumental Group from the UK						
1	Everything Starts With An E	(More Protein PROT 1)	39	1989	0	1989	
2	Love On Love	(More Protein PROT 3)	59	1990	0	1990	
3	Everything Starts With An E (Re-Entry)	(More Protein PROT 1)	15	1990	0	1990	
4	The Sun Machine	(More Protein PROT 4)	62	1990	0	1990	
5	Breathing Is E-Zee	(More Protein PROT 12)	72	1991	0	1991	
	HIT 5 IS CREDITED TO E-ZEE POSSEE FEATURING TARA NEWLEY						
E.U.	E.U. (Experience Unlimited) Is A Ten-Man Band from Washington						
1	Da Butt		0	1988	35	1988	(EMI-MAN 50115)
2	Shake Your Thang (It's Your Thing)	(FFRR FFR 11)	22	1988	0	1988	
	HIT 1 REACHED NUMBER 87 IN THE UK CHARTS • HIT 2 IS CREDITED TO SALT-N-PEPA FEATURING E.U.						
E.V.E.	Female Vocal Group from the USA/UK						
1	Groove Of Love	(Gasoline ALLEYMCSTD 2007)	30	1994	0	1994	
2	Good Life	(Gasoline ALLEYMCSTD 2038)	39	1995	0	1995	
E.Y.C.	Male Vocal Group from the USA						
1	Feelin' Alright	(MCA MCSTD 1952)	16	1993	0	1993	
2	The Way You Work It	(MCA MCSTD 1963)	14	1994	0	1994	
3	Number One	(MCA MCSTD 1976)	27	1994	0	1994	
4	Black Book	(MCA MCSTD 1987)	13	1994	0	1994	
5	One More Chance	(MCA MCSTD 2025)	25	1994	0	1994	
6	Ohh-Ah-Aa (I Feel It)	(Gasoline ALLEY MCSTD 2096)	33	1995	0	1995	
7	In The Beginning	(Gasoline ALLEY MCSTD 2107)	41	1995	0	1995	
Eagles	Male Vocal/Instrumental Group from the USA Names: Glenn Frey, Randy Meisner, Don Henley & Bernie Leadon						
1	Take It Easy		0	1972	12	1972	(Asylum 11005)
2	Witchy Woman		0	1972	9	1972	(Asylum 11008)
3	Peaceful Easy Feeling		0	1973	22	1973	(Asylum 11013)
4	Already Gone		0	1974	32	1974	(Asylum 11036)
5	Best Of My Love		0	1975	1	1975	(Asylum 45218)
6	One Of These Nights	(Asylum AYM 543)	23	1975	1	1975	(Asylum 45257)
7	Lyin' Eyes	(Asylum AYM 548)	23	1975	2	1975	(Asylum 45279)
8	Take It To The Limit	(Asylum K 13029)	12	1976	4	1976	(Asylum 45293)
9	New Kid In Town	(Asylum K 13069)	20	1977	1	1977	(Asylum 45373)
10	Hotel California	(Asylum K 13079)	8	1977	1	1977	(Asylum 45386)
11	Life In The Fast Lane		0	1977	11	1977	(Asylum 45403)

ISSUE	TITLE	UK LBL	UK POS	UK YEAR	US POS	US YEAR	US LBL
12	Please Come Home For Christmas	(Asylum K 13145)	30	1978	18	1978	(Asylum 45555)
13	Heartache Tonight	(Asylum K 12394)	40	1979	1	1979	(Asylum 46545)
14	The Long Run	(Elektra K 12404)	66	1979	8	1979	(Asylum 46569)
15	I Can't Tell You Why		0	1980	8	1980	(Asylum 46608)
16	Seven Bridges Road		0	1981	21	1981	(Asylum 47100)
17	Get Over It		0	1994	31	1994	(Geffen 19376)
18	Love Will Keep Us Alive	(Geffen GFSTD 21980)	52	1996	0	1996	

Eamonn Andrews Male Vocalist/Chat Show Host, B: 1922 Dublin, Ireland

1	Shifting Whispering Sands (Part 1-2)	(Parlophone R 4106)	18	1956	0	1956	

OBITUARY: D: 5 NOV 1987 HEART ATTACK.

Earl Bostic Orchestra Male Writer/Saxophonist, B: 25 Apr 1913 In Tulsa, Oklahoma

*+ 3	Flamingo		0	1951	1	1951	(King 45-4475)

OBITUARY: D: 28 NOV 1965 IN NEW YORK.

Earl Gran Male Organ/Pianist/Vocalist, B: 1931 Oklahoma City

1	The End		0	1958	7	1958	(DECCA 30719)

Obituary: D: 10 Jun 1970 Car Crash.

Earl King (1) Male Vocalist B: Earl Connelly 19 Nov 1929 In Philadelphia

+ 1	Don't Take It So Hard		0	1955	13	1955	(King 4780)

Earl King (2) Male R&B Vocalist, B: Earl Silas Johnson, 7 Feb 1934 in New Orleans   Also Recorded As Handsome Earl

+ 1	Those Lonely, Lonely Nights		0	1955	7	1955	(ACE 509)
+ 2	Always A First Time		0	1962	17	1962	(Imperial 5811)

Earl-Jean Female Vocalist, Real Name Earl-Jean McCrae

1	I'm Into Something Good		0	1964	38	1964	(Colpix 729)

Earls Names Larry Figueiredo, Bob Del Din, Eddie Harder & Jack Wray

1	Remember Then		0	1963	24	1963	(Old Town 1130)

Early Music Consort Mixed Instrumental Group from the UK

1	Music From *The Six Wives Of Henry VIII* (EP)	(BBC RESL 1)	49	1971	0	1971	

Earth, Wind & Fire Male Vocal/Instrumental Group Formed By Maurice White In 1969 from the USA

1	Mighty Mighty		0	1974	29	1974	(Columbia 46007)
2	Devotion		0	1940	33	1974	(Columbia 10026)
* 3	Shining Star		0	1975	1	1975	(Columbia 10090)
4	That's The Way Of The World		0	1975	12	1975	(Columbia 10172)
* 5	Sing A Song		0	1975	5	1976	(Columbia 10251)
6	Can't Hide Love		0	1976	39	1976	(Columbia 10309)
7	Getaway		0	1976	12	1976	(Columbia 10373)
7	Saturday Nite	(CBS 4835)	17	1977	21	1976	(Columbia 10439)
8	Serpentine Fire		0	1977	13	1977	(Columbia 10625)
9	Fantasy	(CBS 6056)	14	1978	32	1978	(Columbia 10688)
10	Jupiter	(CBS 6267)	41	1978	0	1978	
11	Magic Mind	(CBS 6490)	75	1978	0	1978	
12	Magic Mind (Re-Entry)	(CBS 6490)	54	1978	0	1978	
13	Got To Get You Into My Life	(CBS 6553)	33	1978	9	1978	(Columbia 10796)
14	September	(CBS 6922)	3	1978	8	1979	(ARC 10854)
15	Boogie Wonderland	(CBS 7292)	4	1979	6	1979	(ARC 10956)
16	After The Love Has Gone	(CBS 7721)	4	1979	2	1989	(ARC 11033)
17	Star	(CBS 7092)	16	1979	0	1979	
18	Can't Let Go	(CBS 8077)	46	1979	0	1979	
19	In The Stone	(CBS 8252)	53	1980	0	1980	
20	Let Me Talk	(CBS 8982)	29	1980	0	1980	
21	Back On The Road	(CBS 9377)	63	1980	0	1980	
22	Let's Groove	(CBS A 1679)	3	1981	3	1981	(ARC 02536)
23	I've Had Enough	(CBS A 1959)	29	1982	0	1982	
24	Fall In Love With Me	(CBS A 2927)	47	1983	17	1983	(Columbia 03375)
25	System Of Survival	(CBS EWF 1)	54	1987	0	1987	

HIT 15 IS CREDITED TO EARTH, WIND & FIRE WITH THE EMOTIONS

Eartha Kitt Female Actress/Vocalist from the USA

1	Uska Dara - A Turkish Tale		0	1953	23	1953	(RCA Victor 5284)
2	C'est Si Bon		0	1953	8	1953	(RCA Victor 5358)
3	I Want To Be Evil		0	1953	22	1953	(RCA Victor 5442)
4	Santa Baby		0	1954	4	1954	(RCA Victor 5502)
5	Somebody Bad Stole De Wedding Bell (who's Got De Ding Dong)		0	1954	3	1954	(RCA Victor 5610)

ISSUE	TITLE	UK LBL	UK POS	UK YEAR	US POS	US YEAR	US LBL
6	Lovin' Spree		0	1954	20	1954	(RCA Victor 5610)
7	Under The Bridges Of Paris	(HMV B 10647)	7	1955	0	1955	
8	Under The Bridges Of Paris (Re-Entry)	(HMV B 10647)	20	1955	0	1955	
9	Where Is My Man	(Record Shack Soho 11)	36	1983	0	1983	
10	I Love Men	(Record Shack Soho 21)	50	1984	0	1984	
11	This Is My Life	(Record Shack Soho 61)	73	1986	0	1986	
12	Cha Cha Heels	(Arista 112331)	32	1989	0	1989	
13	If I Love Ya, Then I Need Ya...	(RCA 74321190342)	43	1994	0	1994	

HIT 12 IS CREDITED TO EARTHA KITT AND BRONSKI BEAT

Earthling Male Vocal/Instrumental Duo from the UK

1	Echo On My Mind (Part 1)	(Cooltempo CDCOOL 312)	61	1995	0	1995	
2	Blood Music (EP)	(Cooltempo CDCOOL 319)	69	1996	0	1996	

East 17 Male Vocal/Instrumental Group from the UK   Names: Tony Mortimer, Terry Coldwell, John Hendy & Brian Harvey

1	House Of Love	(London Lon 325)	10	1992	0	1992	
2	Gold	(London Lon331)	28	1992	0	1992	
3	Gold (Re-Entry)	(London Lon 331)	64	1992	0	1992	
4	Deep	(London LOCDP334)	5	1993	0	1993	
5	Slow It Down	(London LOCDP 339)	13	1993	0	1993	
6	West End Girls	(London LOCDP 344)	11	1993	0	1993	
7	It's Alright	(London LOCDP 345)	3	1993	0	1993	
8	Around The World	(London LOCDP 349)	3	1994	0	1994	
9	Steam	(London LOCDP 353)	7	1994	0	1994	
10	Stay Another Day	(London LOCDP 354)	1	1994	0	1994	
11	Let It Rain	(London LonCD 363)	10	1995	0	1995	
12	Stay Another Day (Re-Entry)	(London LonCD 354)	64	1995	0	1995	
13	Hold My Body Tight	(London LonCD 367)	12	1995	0	1995	
14	Thunder	(London LonCD 373)	4	1995	0	1995	
15	Do U Still?	(London LOCCD 379)	7	1996	0	1996	
16	Someone To Love	(London LonCD 385)	16	1996	0	1996	
17	If You Ever	(London LonCD 388)	2	1996	0	1996	
18	Hey Child	(London LonCD 390)	3	1997	0	1997	

BRIAN HARVEY WAS FIRED FROM THE GROUP WHEN HE PUBLICALLY PRAISED THE DRUG ECSTASY

East Of Eden Male Instrumental Group from the UK

1	Jig A Jig	(Deram DM 297)	7	1971	0	1971	

East Side Beat Male Vocal/Instrumental Duo from Italy

1	Ride Like The Wind	(FFRR F 176)	3	1991	0	1991	
2	Alive And Kicking	(FFRR F 206)	26	1992	0	1992	
3	You're My Everthing	(FFRR FCD 207)	65	1993	0	1993	

Eastside Connection Disco Aggregation from the USA

1	You're So Right For Me	(CREOLE CR 149)	44	1978	0	1978	

Easybeats Male Vocal/Instrumental Group formed in Australia 1964   Names: Steve Wright, Gordon Fleet, Dick Diamonde, Harry Vanda & George Young

* 1	Friday On My Mind	(United Artists 50106)	6	1966	16	1967	(United Artists UP 1157)
2	Hello How Are You	(United Artists UP 2209)	20	1968	0	1968	

HARRY VANDA WAS A MEMBER OF FLASH & THE PAN

Eat Mixed Vocal/Instrumental Group from the USA/UK

1	Bleed Me White	(FICTION FICCD 48)	73	1993	0	1993	

EAV Male Vocal/Instrumental Group from Austria   EAV Stands For Erste Allgemeine Verunsicherung

1	Ba-Ba-Bankrobbery (English Version)	(Columbia DB 9139)	63	1986	0	1986	

Eazy-E Male Rapper from the USA

1	Just Tah Let U Know	(Ruthless 6628162)	30	1996	0	1996	

Echo & The Bunnymen Male Vocal/Instrumental Group from the UK

1	Rescue	(Korova Kow 1)	62	1980	0	1980	
2	Crocodiles	(Korova ECHO 1)	37	1981	0	1981	
3	A Promise	(Korova Kow 15)	49	1981	0	1981	
4	The Back Of Love	(Korova Kow 24)	19	1982	0	1982	
5	The Cutter	(Korova Kow 26)	8	1983	0	1983	
6	Never Stop	(Korova Kow 28)	15	1983	0	1983	
7	The Killing Moon	(Korova Kow 32)	9	1984	0	1984	
8	Silver	(Korova Kow 34)	30	1984	0	1984	
9	Seven Seas	(Korova Kow 35)	16	1984	0	1984	
10	Bring On The Dancing Horses	(Korova Kow 43)	21	1985	0	1985	

ISSUE	TITLE	UK LBL	UK POS	UK YEAR	US POS	US YEAR	US LBL
11	The Game	(WEA YZ 134)	28	1987	0	1987	
12	Lips Like Sugar	(WEA YZ 144)	36	1987	0	1987	
13	People Are Strange	(WEA YZ 175)	29	1988	0	1988	
14	People Are Strange (Re-Issue)	(East West YZ 567)	34	1991	0	1991	
15	Nothing Lasts Forever	(London LOCDP 396)	8	1997	0	1997	
16	I Want To Be There When You Come	(London LonCD 399)	30	1997	0	1997	

Echobelly Mixed Vocal/Instrumental Group from the UK/Sweden

1	Insomniac	(Fauve Fauv 1CD)	47	1994	0	1994	
2	I Can't Imagine The World Without Me	(Fauve Fauv 2CD)	39	1994	0	1994	
3	Close...But	(Fauve Fauv4CD)	59	1994	0	1994	
4	Great Things	(Fauve Fauv 5CD)	13	1995	0	1995	
5	King Of The Kerb	(Fauve Fauv 7CD)	25	1995	0	1995	
6	Dark Therapy	(Fauve Fauv 8C)	20	1996	0	1996	
7	The World Is Flat	(EPIC 6648152)	31	1997	0	1997	

Echoes Names Tommy Duffy, Harry Doyle & Tom Morrissey

1	Baby Blue		0	1961	4	1961	(SEG-WEY 103)

Ed Ames See Also Ames Brothers

1	My Cup Runneth Over		0	1967	8	1967	(RCA 9002)
2	Who Will Answer?		0	1967	19	1967	(RCA 9400)

Ed Townsend Male Singer/Songwriter, B: 16 Apr 1929 Fayetteville, Tennessee

1	For Your Love		0	1958	13	1958	(CAPITOL 3926)

Eddi Reader Female Vocalist from the UK

1	Patience Of Angels	(Blanco Y Negro NEG 68CD)	33	1994	0	1994	
2	Joke (I'm Laughing)	(Blanco Y Negro NEG 72CD)	42	1994	0	1994	
3	Dear John	(Blanco Y Negro NEG 75CD1)	48	1994	0	1994	
4	Town Without Pity	(Blanco Y Negro NEG 90CD)	26	1996	0	1996	

Eddie 'Piano' Miller Male Honky-Tonk Pianist from the USA

1	She Wore A Yellow Ribbon		0	1949	14	1949	(Rainbow 80033)

Eddie & The Hotrods Male Vocal/Instrumental Group from the UK

1	Live At The Marquee (EP)	(Island IEP 2)	43	1976	0	1976	
2	Teenage Depression	(Island WIP 6354)	35	1976	0	1976	
3	I Might Be Lying	(Island WIP 6388)	44	1977	0	1977	
4	Do Anything You Wanna Do	(Island WIP 6401)	9	1977	0	1977	
5	Quit This Town	(Island WIP 6411)	36	1978	0	1978	

HIT 4 IS CREDITED TO RODS

Eddie Barclay Head Of A French Recording Company, B: 26 Jan 1921 Paris, France

1	The Bandit (O'Cangaceiro)		0	1955	18	1955	(TICO 249)

Eddie Calvert Male Instrumentalist, B: 15 Mar 1922 In Preston Lancashire, England

* 1	Oh Mein Papa (From The Swiss Movie Fireworks)	(Columbia DB 3337)	1	1953	6	1953	(Essex 336)
2	Cherry Pink And Apple Blossom White	(Columbia DB 3581)	1	1955	0	1955	
3	Stranger In Paradise	(Columbia DB 3594)	14	1955	0	1955	
4	John And Julia	(Columbia DB 3624)	6	1955	0	1955	
5	Zambesi	(Columbia DB 3747)	18	1956	0	1956	
6	Zambesi (Re-Entry)	(Columbia DB 3747)	13	1956	0	1956	
7	Mandy	(Columbia DB 3956)	9	1958	0	1958	
8	Little Serenade	(Columbia DB 4105)	28	1958	0	1958	

AT THE AGE OF 11 HE PLAYED PRINCIPAL CORNET WITH PRESTON TOWN SILVER BAND • OBITUARY: D: 7 AUG 1978.

Eddie Cantor Male Comedian, Real Name Eddie Israel Iskowitz from New York, USA

24	The Old Piano Roll Blues		0	1950	27	1950	(RCA Victor 3751)

Obituary : D: 10 Oct 1964.

Eddie Cochran Male Vocalist, Real Name Edward Ray Cochrane B: 3 Oct 1938 Oklahoma City, Oklahoma

1	Sittin' In The Balcony		0	1957	18	1957	(Liberty 55056)
2	Summertime Blues	(London HLU 8702)	18	1958	8	1958	(Liberty 55144)
3	C'mon Everybody	(London HLU 8792)	6	1959	35	1959	(Liberty 55166)
4	Somethin' Else	(London HLU 8944)	22	1959	0	1959	
5	Hallelujah I Love Her So	(London HLW 9022)	28	1960	0	1960	
6	Hallelujah I Love Her So (Re-Entry)	(London HLW 9022)	22	1960	0	1960	
7	Three Steps To Heaven	(London HLG 9115)	1	1960	0	1960	
8	Sweetie Pie	(London HLG 9196)	38	1960	0	1960	
9	Lonely	(London HLG 9196)	41	1960	0	1960	

ISSUE	TITLE	UK LBL	UK POS	UK YEAR	US POS	US YEAR	US LBL
10	Weekend	(London HLG 9362)	15	1961	0	1961	
11	Jeannie, Jeannie, Jeannie	(London HLG 9460)	31	1961	0	1961	
12	My Way	(Liberty LIB 10088)	23	1963	0	1963	
13	Summertime Blues (Re-Issue)	(Liberty LBF 15071)	34	1968	0	1968	
14	C'mon Everybody (Re-Issue)	(Liberty Eddie 501)	14	1988	0	1988	

OBITUARY: D: 17 APR 1960 CAR CRASH. • EDDIE & GENE VINCENT WERE BOTH INVOLVED IN THE ACCIDENT AT CHIPPENHAM, WILTSHIRE, ENGLAND

Eddie Cooley & The Dimples   Male Songwriter from New York With Female Duo

1	Priscilla		0	1956	20	1956	(Royal Roost 621)

Eddie Drennon & B.B.S. Unlimited   Male Vocal/Instrumental Group from the USA

1	Let's Do The Latin Hustle	(PYE International 7N 25702)	20	1976	0	1976	

Eddie Fisher   Male Vocalist, Real Name Edwin Jack Fisher B: 10 Aug 1928 In Philadelphia

ISSUE	TITLE	UK LBL	UK POS	UK YEAR	US POS	US YEAR	US LBL
1	Thinking Of You (From *Three Little Words*)		0	1950	5	1950	(RCA Victor 3901)
2	Bring Back The Thrill		0	1951	14	1951	(RCA Victor 4016)
3	Unless		0	1951	17	1951	(RCA Victor 4120)
4	I'll Hold You In My Heart		0	1951	18	1951	(RCA Victor 4191)
5	Turn Back The Hands Of Time		0	1951	8	1951	(RCA Victor 4257)
* 6	Any Time		0	1951	2	1951	(RCA Victor 4359)
* 7	Tell Me Why		0	1952	4	1952	(RCA Victor 4444)
8	Trust In Me		0	1952	25	1952	(RCA Victor 4444)
9	Forgive Me		0	1952	7	1952	(RCA Victor 4574)
10	That's The Chance You Take		0	1952	10	1952	(RCA Victor 4574)
11	I'm Yours		0	1952	3	1952	(RCA Victor 4680)
12	Just A Little Lovin'		0	1952	20	1952	(RCA Victor 4680)
13	Maybe		0	1952	3	1952	(RCA Victor 4744)
14	Watermelon Weather		0	1952	19	1952	(RCA Victor 4744)
15	I Remember When		0	1952	29	1952	(RCA Victor 4618)
* 16	Wish You Were Here (Musical Title Sing)	(HMV B 10564)	8	1953	3	1952	(RCA Victor 4618)
17	The Hand Of Fate		0	1952	24	1952	(RCA Victor 4830)
* 18	Lady Of Spain		0	1952	6	1952	(RCA Victor 4953)
19	Outside Of Heaven	(HMV B 10362)	1	1953	8	1952	(RCA Victor 4953)
20	Everything I Have Is Yours	(HMV B 10398)	12	1953	23	1952	(RCA Victor 4841)
21	Christmas Day		0	1952	22	1952	(RCA Victor 5038)
22	You're All I Want For Christmas		0	1953	22	1953	(RCA Victor 5065)
23	Even Now		0	1953	7	1953	(RCA Victor 5106)
24	Everything I Have Is Yours (Re-Entry)	(HMV B 10398)	8	1953	0	1953	
25	Downhearted	(HMV B 10450)	3	1953	5	1953	(RCA Victor 5137)
26	How Do You Speak To An Angel? (From *Hazel Flagg*)		0	1953	14	1953	(RCA Victor 5137)
* 27	I'm Walking Behind You	(HMV B 10489)	1	1953	1	1953	(RCA Victor 5293)
28	Just Another Polka		0	1953	24	1953	(RCA Victor 5293)
29	Outside Of Heaven (Re-Entry)	(HMV B 10362)	12	1953	0	1953	
30	With These Hands		0	1953	7	1953	(RCA Victor 5365)
31	Many Times		0	1953	4	1953	(RCA Victor 5453)
32	Just To Be With You		0	1953	18	1953	(RCA Victor 5453)
* 33	Oh My Papa	(HMV B 10614)	9	1954	1	1953	(RCA Victor 5552)
34	Oh My Papa (Re-Entry)	(HMV B 10614)	11	1954	0	1954	
35	Oh My Papa (2nd Re-Entry)	(HMV B 10614)	11	1954	0	1954	
36	Oh My Papa (3rd Re-Entry)	(HMV B 10614)	11	1954	0	1954	
37	A Girl, A Girl (Zoom-Ba Di Alli Nella)		0	1954	6	1954	(RCA Victor 5675)
38	Anema E Core (With All My Heart And Soul)		0	1954	14	1954	(RCA Victor 5675)
39	Green Years		0	1954	8	1954	(RCA Victor 5748)
40	My Friend		0	1954	15	1954	(RCA Victor 5748)
41	Heaven Was Never Like This		0	1954	21	1954	(RCA Victor 5830)
* 42	I Need You Now	(HMV B 10755)	16	1954	1	1954	(RCA Victor 5830)
43	Count Your Blessings (From *White Christmas*)		0	1954	5	1954	(RCA Victor 5871)
44	I Need You Now (Re-Entry)	(HMV B 10755)	13	1954	0	1954	
45	Fanny		0	1954	29	1954	(RCA Victor 5871)
46	I Need You Now (2nd Re-Entry)	(HMV B 10755)	19	1955	0	1955	
47	A Man Chases A Girl (Until She Catches Him)		0	1955	16	1955	(RCA 6015)
48	(I'm Always Hearing) Wedding Bells	(HMV B 10839)	5	1955	20	1955	(RCA 6015)
49	Heart (From *Damn Yankees*)		0	1955	6	1955	(RCA 6097)
50	Song Of The Dreamer		0	1955	11	1955	(RCA 6196)
* 51	Dungaree Doll		0	1956	7	1956	(RCA 6337)
52	Everybody's Got A Home But Me		0	1955	20	1950	(RCA 6337)

ISSUE	TITLE	UK LBL	UK POS	UK YEAR	US POS	US YEAR	US LBL
53	On The Street Where You Live		0	1956	18	1956	(RCA 6529)
54	Cindy Oh Cindy	(HMV POP 273)	5	1956	10	1956	(RCA 6677)

HIT 14 IS CREDITED TO PERRY COMO AND EDDIE FISHER • HIT 26 IS CREDITED TO EDDIE FISHER AND SALLY SWEETLAND

Eddie Floyd Male Vocalist, B: 25 Jun 1935 Alabama

	ISSUE	TITLE	UK LBL	UK POS	UK YEAR	US POS	US YEAR	US LBL
	1	Knock On Wood	(Atlantic 584 041)	50	1967	28	1966	(Stax 194)
	2	Knock On Wood (Re-Entry)	(Atlantic 584 041)	19	1967	0	1967	
+	3	Raise Your Hand	(Stax 601 001)	42	1967	16	1967	(Stax 208)
	4	Things Get Better	(Stax 601 016)	31	1967	0	1967	
	5	I've Never Found A Girl		0	1968	40	1968	(Stax 0002)
	6	Bring It On Home To Me		0	1968	17	1968	(Stax 0012)

Eddie Harris Vocal/Saxophonist, B: 20 Oct 1936 Chicago

	TITLE		UK POS	UK YEAR	US POS	US YEAR	US LBL
1	Exodus		0	1961	36	1961	(VEE-JAY 378)

Eddie Henderson Male Instrumentalist (Trumpet) from the USA

	TITLE	UK LBL	UK POS	UK YEAR	US POS	US YEAR	US LBL
1	Prance On	(CAPITOL CL 16015)	44	1978	0	1978	

Eddie Heywood Male Composer/Pianist, B: 4 Dec 1915 Atlanta

		TITLE		UK POS	UK YEAR	US POS	US YEAR	US LBL
*	1	Begin The Beguine		0	1945	16	1945	(DECCA 23398)
	2	Soft Summer Breeze		0	1956	11	1956	(MERCURY 70863)
	3	Canadian Sunset		0	1956	2	1956	(RCA 6537)

HIT 1 IS CREDITED TO THE EDDIE HEYWOOD ORCHESTRA • HIT 3 IS CREDITED TO HUGO WINTERHALTER AND EDDIE HEYWOOD • OBITUARY : D: 2 JAN 1989.

Eddie Hodges Male Vocalist, B: 5 Mar 1947 Mississippi

	TITLE	UK LBL	UK POS	UK YEAR	US POS	US YEAR	US LBL
1	I'm Gonna Knock On Your Door	(London HLA 9369)	37	1961	12	1961	(Cadence 1397)
2	Made To Love (Girls Girls Girls)	(London HLA 9576)	37	1962	14	1962	(Cadence 1421)

Eddie Holland

	TITLE		UK POS	UK YEAR	US POS	US YEAR	US LBL
1	Jamie		0	1962	30	1962	(Motown 1021)
2	Just Ain't Enough Love		0	1964	54	1964	(Motown 1058)
3	Candy To Me		0	1964	58	1964	(Motown 1063)

B: 30 OCT 1939 IN DETROIT, EDDIE WAS A VERY SUCCESSFUL MEMBER OF MOTOWN'S WRITING TEAM, HOLLAND-DOZIER-HOLLAND. (BRIAN HOLLAND AND LAMONT DOZIER)

Eddie Holman Male Vocalist, B: 3 Jun 1946 Norfolk, Virginia

		TITLE	UK LBL	UK POS	UK YEAR	US POS	US YEAR	US LBL
*	1	Hey There, Lonely Girl	(ABC 4012)	4	1974	2	1969	(ABC 11240)
+	2	My Mind Keeps Telling Me		0	1972	20	1972	(GSF 6873)

Eddie Kendricks Male Vocalist, B: 17 Dec 1939 Union Springs, Alabama

		TITLE	UK LBL	UK POS	UK YEAR	US POS	US YEAR	US LBL
*	1	Keep On Truckin (Part 1)	(Tamla Motown TMG 873)	18	1973	1	1973	(Tamla 54238)
*	2	Boogie Down	(Tamla Motown TMG 888)	39	1974	2	1973	(Tamla 54243)
	3	Son Of Sagittarius		0	1974	28	1974	(Tamla 54247)
	4	Shoeshine Boy		0	1975	18	1975	(Tamla 54257)
	5	He's A Friend		0	1976	36	1976	(Tamla 54266)
	6	A Night At The Apollo Live!	(RCA PB 49935)	58	1985	20	1985	(RCA 14178)

HIT 6 IS CREDITED TO DARYL HALL & JOHN OATES FEATURING DAVID RUFFIN & EDDIE KENDRICK • SEE ALSO THE TEMPTATIONS

Eddie Lawrence Comedian/Author/Actor/Playwright, B: 2 Mar 1919 New York City

	TITLE		UK POS	UK YEAR	US POS	US YEAR	US LBL
1	The Old Philosopher		0	1956	34	1956	(CORAL 61671)

Eddie Money Real Name Edward Mahoney B: 2 Mar 1949 Brooklyn, New York

	TITLE		UK POS	UK YEAR	US POS	US YEAR	US LBL
1	Baby Hold On		0	1978	11	1978	(Columbia 10663)
2	Two Tickets To Paradise		0	1978	22	1978	(Columbia 10765)
3	Maybe I'm A Fool		0	1979	22	1979	(Columbia 10900)
4	Think I'm In Love		0	1982	16	1982	(Columbia 02964)
5	Take Me Home Tonight		0	1986	4	1986	(Columbia 06231)
6	I Wanna Go Back		0	1987	14	1987	(Columbia 06569)
7	Endless Nights		0	1987	21	1987	(Columbia 07035)
8	Walk On Water		0	1988	9	1988	(Columbia 08060)
9	The Love In Your Eyes		0	1989	24	1989	(Columbia 68532)
10	Peace In Our Time		0	1989	11	1989	(Columbia 74109)
11	I'll Get By		0	1992	21	1992	(Columbia 74109)

Eddie Murphy Male Vocalist, B: 3 Apr 1961 Hampstead, New York

		TITLE	UK LBL	UK POS	UK YEAR	US POS	US YEAR	US LBL
*	1	Party All The Time		0	1985	2	1985	(Columbia 05609)
	2	Put Your Mouth On Me		0	1989	27	1989	(Columbia 68897)
	3	I Was A King	(Motown TMGCD 1414)	64	1993	0	1993	

Eddie Platt Male Bandleader/Saxophonist, from Cleveland, Ohio

	TITLE		UK POS	UK YEAR	US POS	US YEAR	US LBL
1	Tequila		0	1958	20	1958	(ABC-PARAMOUNT 9899)

Eddie Rabbitt Male Vocalist, Full Name Edward Thomas Rabbitt B: 27 Nov 1944 Brooklyn

		TITLE	UK LBL	UK POS	UK YEAR	US POS	US YEAR	US LBL
*	17	Drivin' My Life Away		0	1980	5	1980	(Elektra 46656)
*	18	I Love A Rainy Night	(Elektra K 12498)	53	1981	1	1981	(Elektra 47066)

ISSUE	TITLE	UK LBL	UK POS	UK YEAR	US POS	US YEAR	US LBL
19	Step By Step		0	1981	5	1981	(Elektra 47174)
20	Someone Could Lose A Heart Tonight		0	1982	15	1982	(Elektra 47239)
21	I Don't Know Where To Start		0	1982	35	1982	(Elektra 47435)
22	You And I		0	1982	7	1982	(Elektra 69936)

OTHER HITS ARE C/W • HIT 22 IS CREDITED TO EDDIE RABBIT WITH CRYSTAL GAYLE

Eddie Rambeau   Real Name Edward Flurie B: 30 Jun 1943 Hazleton, Pennsylvania

ISSUE	TITLE	UK LBL	UK POS	UK YEAR	US POS	US YEAR	US LBL
1	Concrete And Clay		0	1965	35	1965	(Dyno Voice 204)

Eddie Schwartz   Singer/Songwriter From Canada

ISSUE	TITLE	UK LBL	UK POS	UK YEAR	US POS	US YEAR	US LBL
1	All Our Tomorrows		0	1982	28	1982	(ATCO 7342)

Eddie Wilcox & His Orchestra   Male Bandleader/Pianist from the USA

ISSUE	TITLE	UK LBL	UK POS	UK YEAR	US POS	US YEAR	US LBL
1	Wheel Of Fortune		0	1952	13	1952	(Derby 787)

Vocals On Hit Are By Sunny Gale   Obituary: D: 29 Sep 1968.

Eddy   Female Vocalist from the UK

ISSUE	TITLE	UK LBL	UK POS	UK YEAR	US POS	US YEAR	US LBL
1	Someday	(Positiva CDTIV 14)	49	1994	0	1994	

Eddy & The Soul Band   Male Vocal/Instrumental Group from the USA

ISSUE	TITLE	UK LBL	UK POS	UK YEAR	US POS	US YEAR	US LBL
1	Theme From Shaft	(Club JAB 11)	13	1985	0	1985	

Eddy Arnold   Male Vocalist, Real Name Richard Edward Arnold B: 15 May 1918 Tennessee

ISSUE	TITLE	UK LBL	UK POS	UK YEAR	US POS	US YEAR	US LBL
* 8	I'll Hold You In My Heart (Till I Can Hold You In My Arms)		0	1947	22	1947	(RCA Victor 2332)
* 9	Anytime		0	1948	17	1948	(RCA Victor 2700)
10	What A Fool I Was		0	1948	29	1948	(RCA Victor 2700)
* 11	Bouquet Of Roses		0	1948	13	1948	(RCA Victor 2806)
12	Texarkana Baby		0	1948	18	1948	(RCA Victor 2806)
* 13	Just A Little Lovin' Will Go A Long Long Way		0	1948	13	1948	(RCA Victor 3013)
15	A Heart Full Of Love (From A Handful Of Kisses)		0	1948	23	1948	(RCA Victor 3174)
16	Then I Turned And Walked Slowly Away		0	1949	30	1949	(RCA Victor 3174)
19	Don't Rob Another Man's Castle		0	1949	23	1949	(RCA Victor 21-0002)
20	One Kiss Too Many		0	1949	23	1949	(RCA Victor 21-0051)
22	I'm Throwing Rice (At The Girl I Love)		0	1949	18	1949	(RCA Victor 21-0083)
!* 35	There's Been A Change In Me		0	1951	1	1951	(RCA Victor 0412)
!* 37	Kentucky Waltz		0	1951	1	1951	(RCA Victor 0444)
!* 38	I Wanna Play House With You		0	1951	1	1951	(RCA Victor 0476)
* 61	The Cattle Call		0	1955	42	1955	(RCA Victor 6139)
65	The Richest Man In The World		0	1955	99	1955	(RCA Victor 6290)
86	What's He Doing In My World		0	1965	60	1965	(RCA Victor 8516)
88	Make The World Go Away	(RCA 1496)	8	1966	6	1965	(RCA Victor 8679)
89	I Want To Go With You	(RCA 1519)	49	1966	36	1966	(RCA Victor 8749)
90	The Last Word In Lonesome		0	1966	40	1966	(RCA Victor 8818)
91	I Want To Go With You (Re-Entry)	(RCA 1519)	46	1966	0	1966	
92	The Tip Of My Fingers		0	1966	43	1966	(RCA Victor 8869)
93	If You Were Mine Mary	(RCA 1529)	49	1966	0	1966	
94	Somebody Like Me		0	1966	53	1966	(RCA Victor 8965)
96	Lonely Again		0	1967	87	1967	(RCA Victor 9080)
97	Misty Blue		0	1967	57	1967	(RCA Victor 9182)
98	Turn The World Around		0	1967	66	1967	(RCA Victor 9265)
100	Here Comes The Rain, Baby		0	1968	74	1968	(RCA Victor 9437)
101	It's Over		0	1968	74	1968	(RCA Victor 9525)
102	Then You Can Tell Me Goodbye		0	1968	84	1968	(RCA Victor 9606)
103	They Don't Make Love Songs Like They used To		0	1968	99	1968	(RCA Victor 9667)

THE REST ARE C/W HITS • HITS 55-67 ARE CREDITED TO EDDY ARNOLD & HIS GUITAR • EDDY'S NICKNAME IS THE TENNESSEE PLOWBOY

Eddy Grant   Male Vocal/Instrumentalist, Real Name Edmond Montague Grant B: 5 Mar 1948 Plaisance, Guyana

ISSUE	TITLE	UK LBL	UK POS	UK YEAR	US POS	US YEAR	US LBL
1	Living On The Front Line	(Ensign Eny 26)	11	1979	0	1979	
2	Do You Feel My Love	(Ensign Eny 45)	8	1980	0	1980	
3	Can't Get Enough Of You	(Ensign Eny 207)	13	1981	0	1981	
4	I Love You, Yes I Love You	(Ensign Eny 216)	37	1981	0	1981	
5	I Don't Wanna Dance	(Ice Ice 56)	1	1982	0	1982	
* 6	Electric Avenue	(Ice Ice 57)	2	1982	2	1983	(Portrait 03793)
7	Living On The Front Line / Do You Feel My Love (Re-Issue)	(Mercury MER 135)	47	1983	0	1983	
8	War Party	(Ice Ice 58)	42	1983	0	1983	
9	Till I Can't Take Love No More	(Ice Ice 60)	42	1983	0	1983	
10	Romancing The Stone	(Ice Ice 61)	52	1984	26	1984	(Portrait 04433)
11	Gimme Hope Jo'anna	(Ice Ice 78701)	7	1988	0	1988	

ISSUE	TITLE	UK LBL	UK POS	UK YEAR	US POS	US YEAR	US LBL
12	Walking On Sunshine	(Blue Wave R 6217)	63	1989	0	1989	
	IN 1967 HE FORMED THE EQUALS						

Eddy Howard Orchestra Male Vocalist/Orchestra Leader, B: 12 Sep 1914 California

ISSUE	TITLE	UK LBL	UK POS	UK YEAR	US POS	US YEAR	US LBL
* 3	To Each His Own		0	1946	1	1946	(Majestic 7188)
4	The Rickety Rickshaw Man		0	1946	6	1946	(Majestic 7192)
5	(I Love You) For Sentimental Reasons		0	1946	2	1946	(Majestic 7204)
6	My Best To You		0	1946	17	1946	(Majestic 1074)
7	The Girl That I Marry (From *Annie Get Your Gun*)		0	1947	23	1947	(Majestic 1083)
8	My Adobe Hacienda		0	1947	2	1947	(Majestic 1117)
9	Heartaches		0	1947	11	1947	(Majestic 1111)
10	I Wonder, I Wonder, I Wonder		0	1947	2	1947	(Majestic 1124)
11	Ragtime Cowboy Joe		0	1947	16	1947	(Majestic 1155)
12	On The Old Spanish Trail		0	1947	23	1947	(Majestic 1155)
13	Kate (Have I Come Too Early Too Late)		0	1947	7	1947	(Majestic 1160)
14	An Apple Blossom Wedding		0	1947	9	1947	(Majestic 1156)
15	A Tune For Humming		0	1947	21	1947	(Majestic 1177)
16	White Christmas		0	1947	21	1947	(Majestic 1175)
17	Now Is The Hour		0	1948	8	1948	(Majestic 1191)
18	Put 'Em In A Box (From *Romance On The High Seas*)		0	1948	23	1948	(Majestic 1252)
19	Just Because		0	1948	20	1948	(Majestic 1231)
20	On A Slow Boat To China		0	1948	6	1948	(Mercury 5210)
21	Dainty Brenda Lee		0	1948	27	1948	(Mercury 5208)
22	Candy Kisses		0	1949	20	1949	(Mercury 5272)
23	Love Me, Love Me, Love Me		0	1949	24	1949	(Mercury 5238)
24	Red Head		0	1949	29	1949	(Mercury 5274)
25	Room Full Of Roses		0	1949	4	1949	(Mercury 5296)
26	There's Yes! Yes! In Your Eyes		0	1949	21	1949	(Mercury 5296)
27	Maybe It's Because (From *Along Fifth Avenue*)		0	1949	9	1949	(Mercury 5314)
28	Tell Me Why		0	1949	25	1949	(Mercury 5314)
29	Half A Heart Is All You Left Me		0	1950	28	1950	(Mercury 5349)
30	Rag Mop		0	1950	24	1950	(Mercury 5371)
31	American Beauty Rose		0	1950	21	1950	(Mercury 5433)
32	To Think You've Chosen Me		0	1950	9	1950	(Mercury 5517)
33	A Penny A Kiss		0	1951	14	1951	(Mercury 5567)
34	What Will I Tell My Heart		0	1951	27	1951	(Mercury 5630)
35	A Strange Little Girl		0	1951	28	1951	(Mercury 5630)
36	Deadly Weapon		0	1951	22	1951	(Mercury 5663)
* 37	Sin (It's No Sin)		0	1951	1	1951	(Mercury 5711)
38	Stolen Love		0	1952	11	1952	(Mercury 5771)
39	Wishin'		0	1952	17	1952	(Mercury 5784)
40	Be Anything (But Be Mine)		0	1952	7	1952	(Mercury 5815)
41	Auf Weidersehn Sweetheart		0	1952	4	1952	(Mercury 5871)
42	I Don't Want To Take That Chance		0	1952	26	1952	(Mercury 5871)
43	Mademoiselle		0	1952	14	1952	(Mercury 5898)
44	It's Worth Any Price You Pay		0	1952	11	1952	(Mercury 70015)
45	Gomen-Nasai (Forgive Me)		0	1953	17	1953	(Mercury 70107)
46	Love Every Moment You Live		0	1953	24	1953	(Mercury 70176)
47	Skirts		0	1953	21	1953	(Mercury 70225)
48	Till We Two Are One		0	1954	22	1954	(Mercury 70293)
49	Melancholy Me		0	1954	16	1954	(Mercury 70304)
	OBITUARY : D: 23 MAY 1963.						

Edelweiss Mixed Vocal/Instrumental Group from Austria

ISSUE	TITLE	UK LBL	UK POS	UK YEAR	US POS	US YEAR	US LBL
1	Bring Me Edelweiss	(WEA YZ 353)	5	1989	0	1989	

Eden Mixed Vocal/Instrumental Group from the UK/Australia

ISSUE	TITLE	UK LBL	UK POS	UK YEAR	US POS	US YEAR	US LBL
1	Do U Feel 4 Me	(LOGIC 74321135422)	51	1993	0	1993	

Eden Kane Male Vocalist from the UK

ISSUE	TITLE	UK LBL	UK POS	UK YEAR	US POS	US YEAR	US LBL
1	Well I Ask You	(Decca F 11353)	1	1961	0	1961	
2	Get Lost	(Decca F 11381)	10	1961	0	1961	
3	Forget Me Not	(Decca F 11418)	3	1962	0	1962	
4	I Don't Know Why	(Decca F 11460)	7	1962	0	1962	
5	Boys Cry	(Fontana TF 438)	8	1964	0	1964	

ISSUE	TITLE	UK LBL	UK POS	UK YEAR	US POS	US YEAR	US LBL
Edgar Broughton Band	Male Vocal/Instrumental Group from the UK						
1	Out Demons Out	(Harvest HAR 5015)	39	1970	0	1970	
2	Apache Drop Out	(Harvest HAR 5032)	49	1971	0	1971	
3	Apache Dropout (Re-Entry)	(Harvest HAR 5032)	35	1971	0	1971	
4	Apache Dropout (2nd Re-Entry)	(Harvest HAR 5032)	35	1971	0	1971	
5	Apache Dropout (3rd Re-Entry)	(Harvest HAR 5032)	33	1971	0	1971	
Edgar Winter Group	Male Instrumentalist, B: 28 Dec 1946 Beaumont, Texas						
* 1	Frankenstein	(Epic EPC 1440)	18	1973	1	1973	(Epic 10967)
2	Free Ride		0	1973	14	1973	(Epic 11024)
3	River's Risin'		0	1974	33	1974	(Epic 11143)
	HIT 3 IS CREDITED TO EDGAR WINTER						
Edie Brickell & The New	Female Vocalist, Pronounced Bree-Kell , B: Oak Cliff, Texas, With The Band from Dallas						
1	What I Am	(Geffen GEF 49)	31	1989	7	1989	(Geffen 27696)
2	Circle	(Geffen GEF 51)	74	1989	0	1989	
3	Good Times	(Geffen GFSTD 78)	40	1994	0	1994	
Edison Lighthouse	Male Vocal/Instrumental Group from the UK						
* 1	Love Grows (Where My Rosemary Goes)	(Bell 1091)	1	1970	5	1970	(Bell 858)
2	It's Up To You Petula	(Bell 1136)	49	1971	0	1971	
	LEAD SINGER IS TONY BURROWS WHO WAS ALSO INVOLVED WITH WHITE PLAINS, BROTHERHOOD OF MAN & FIRST CLASS THE GROUP WAS ORIGINALLY CALLED GREENFIELD HAMMER						
Edith Piaf	Female Vocalist, Real Name Edith Giovanna Gassion B: 19 Dec 1915 France						
* 1	La Vie En Rose		0	1950	23	1950	(Columbia 38948)
2	Milord	(Columbia DC 754)	41	1960	0	1960	
3	Milord (Re-Entry)	(Columbia DC 754)	24	1960	0	1960	
	EDITH WENT BLIND AT THE AGE OF TWO, REGAINED HER SIGHT WHEN SHE WAS SEVEN • OBITUARY : D: 11 OCT 1963.						
Edmund Hockridge	Male Vocalist from Canada						
1	Young And Foolish	(NIXA N 15039)	10	1956	0	1956	
2	Young And Foolish (Re-Entry)	(NIXA N 15039)	28	1956	0	1956	
3	Young And Foolish (2nd Re-Entry)	(NIXA N 15039)	26	1956	0	1956	
4	No Other Love	(NIXA N 15048)	24	1956	0	1956	
5	No Other Love (Re-Entry)	(NIXA N 15048)	29	1956	0	1956	
6	No Other Love (2nd Re-Entry)	(NIXA N 15048)	30	1956	0	1956	
7	By The Fountains Of Rome	(PYE NIXA N 15063)	17	1956	0	1956	
Edmundo Ros & His Rumba Band	Male Bandleader/Drummer, B: 7 Dec 1910 Venezuela						
* 1	Wedding Samba		0	1949	16	1949	(London 499)
Edna Savage	Female Vocalist from the UK						
1	Arrivederci Darling	(Parlophone R 4097)	19	1956	0	1956	
Edsels	Lead Singer George Jones Jr. from Ohio						
1	Rama Lama Ding Dong		0	1961	21	1961	(TWIN 700)
Edward Ball	Male Vocalist from the UK						
1	The Mill Hill Self Hate Club	(Creation CRESCD 233)	57	1996	0	1996	
2	Love Is Blue	(Creation CRESCD 244)	59	1997	0	1997	
Edward Bear	Lead Singer Of The Trio Is Larry Evoy from Toronto						
* 1	Last Song		0	1973	3	1973	(Capitol 3452)
2	Close Your Eyes		0	1973	37	1973	(Capitol 3581)
Edward Byrnes & Connie	Edward's Real Name Is Edward Breitenberger B: 30 Jul 1933 New York						
* 1	Kookie Kookie (Lend Me Your Comb)		27	1960	4	1959	(Warner Bros. 5047)
	SOME OF HIS PREVIOUS JOBS INCLUDES AMBULANCE AND DELIVERY DRIVER • EDD WAS FAMOUS AS KOOKIE IN THE TV SERIES 77 *SUNSET STRIP*						
Edward R. Murrow	Edward R. Murrow B: 1904 In Greenboro, North Carolina, Was A Radio News Correspondent For K.B.E						
* 1	I Can Hear It Now		0	1948	0	1948	(Columbia)
	THE HIT INCLUDED SOME OF HIS PRE-WAR BROADCASTS • OBITUARY : D: 27 APR 1965.						
Edward Woodward	Male Actor/Vocalist from the UK						
1	The Way You Look Tonight	(DJM DJS 232)	50	1971	0	1971	
2	The Way You Look Tonight (Re-Entry)	(DJM DJS 232)	42	1971	0	1971	
Edwin Adderley	See Cannonball Adderley						
Edwin Hawkins Singers	Edwin Hawkins, B: Aug 1943, With Gospel Group from the USA Originally Called The Northern California State Youth Choir						
* 1	Oh Happy Day	(BUDDAH 201 048)	2	1969	4	1969	(PAVILION 20001)
2	Oh Happy Day (Re-Entry)	(Buddah 201 048)	43	1969	0	1969	
3	Lay Down (Candles In The Rain)		0	1970	6	1970	(Buddah 167)
	HITS 1-2 ARE CREDITED TO EDWIN HAWKINS SINGERS FEATURING DOROTHY COMBS MORRISON • HIT 3 IS CREDITED TO MELANIE WITH THE EDWIN HAWKINS SINGERS						

ISSUE	TITLE	UK LBL	UK POS	UK YEAR	US POS	US YEAR	US LBL
Edwin Starr	Male Vocalist, Real Name Charles Hatcher B: 21 Jan 1942 Nashville, Tennessee.						
1	Agent Double-O-Soul		0	1965	21	1965	(RIC-TIC 103)
2	Stop Her On Sight (Sos)	(Polydor BM 56 702)	35	1966	0	1966	
3	Headline News	(Polydor 56 717)	39	1966	0	1966	
4	Stop Her On Sight (Sos)/Headline News (Re-Issue)	(Polydor 56 753)	11	1968	0	1968	
5	Twenty Five Miles	(Tamla Motown TMG 672)	36	1969	6	1969	(Gordy 7083)
+ 6	I'm Still A Strugglin' Man		0	1969	27	1969	(Gordy 7087)
* 7	War	(Tamla Motown TMG 754)	39	1970	1	1970	(Gordy 7101)
8	Stop The War Now	(Tamla Motown TMG 764)	33	1971	26	1970	(Gordy 7104)
+ 9	Funky Music Sho Nuff Turns Me On		0	1971	6	1971	(Gordy 7107)
10	Contact	(20th Century BTC 2396)	6	1979	0	1979	
11	H.A.P.P.Y. Radio	(RCA TC 2408)	9	1979	0	1979	
12	It Ain't Fair	(Hippodrome HIP101)	56	1985	0	1985	
13	War (Re-Recording) / Wild Thing	(Weekend CDWEEK 103)	69	1993	0	1993	
	ALSO RECORDED WITH BLINKY, REAL NAME SANDRA WILLIAMS • EDWIN WAS ONCE IN THE GROUP THE FUTURETONES						
Edwyn Collins	Male Singer/Songwriter from Scotland, Was With Orange Juice						
1	Pale Blue Eyes	(Swamplands SWP 1)	72	1984	0	1984	
2	A Girl Like You	(Setanta ZOP 001CD1)	42	1994	32	1995	(Bar None 1234)
3	A Girl Like You (Re-Issue)	(Setanta ZOP 003CD)	4	1995	0	1995	
4	Keep On Burning	(Setanta ZOP 004CD1)	45	1996	0	1996	
5	The Magic Piper (Of Love)	(Setanta SETCDA 041)	32	1997	0	1997	
	HIT 1 IS CREDITED TO PAUL QUINN AND EDWYN COLLINS • HIT 2 WAS LISTED AS EXPRESSLY EP						
EFUA	Female Vocalist from the UK						
1	Somewhere	(Virgin VSCDT 1463)	42	1993	0	1993	
Eggs On Legs	Male Vocalist from the UK						
1	Cock A Doodle Do It	(AVEX AVEXCD	42	1995	0	1995	
Egyptian Empire	Real Name Tim Taylor Male Producer from the UK						
1	The Horn Track	(FFRREEDOM TAB 115)	61	1992	0	1992	
18 Wheeler							
1	Stay	(Creation Crescd 249)	59	1997	0	1997	
808 State	Male Instrumental Group from the UK						
1	Pacific State	(Ztt Zang 1)	10	1989	0	1989	
2	The Extended Pleasure Of Dance (EP)	(Ztt 2t)	56	1990	0	1990	
3	The Only Rhyme That Bites	(Ztt Zang 3)	10	1990	0	1990	
4	Tunes Splits The Atom	(Ztt Zang 6)	18	1990	0	1990	
5	Cubik / Olympic	(Ztt Zang 5)	10	1990	0	1990	
6	In Yer Face	(Ztt Zang 14)	9	1991	0	1991	
7	Ooops	(Ztt Zang 19)	42	1991	0	1991	
8	Lift / Open Your Mind	(Ztt Zang 20)	38	1991	0	1991	
9	Time Bomb / Nimbus	(Ztt Zang 33)	59	1992	0	1992	
10	One In Ten	(Ztt Zang 39)	17	1992	0	1992	
11	Plan 9	(Ztt Zang 38cd)	50	1993	0	1993	
12	10 X 10	(Ztt Zang 42cd)	67	1993	0	1993	
13	Bombadin	(Ztt Zang 54cd)	67	1994	0	1994	
14	Bond	(Ztt Zang 80cd)	57	1996	0	1996	
15	Lopez	(Ztt Zang 87cd)	20	1997	0	1997	
	HITS 3-4 ARE CREDITED TO MC TUNES VERSUS 808 STATE • HIT 7 IS CREDITED TO 808 STATE FEATURING BJORK • HIT 12 IS CREDITED TO 808 STATE VS UB40						
88.3							
1	Wishing On A Star	(Urban Gorilla Ugr 3cd)	61	1995	0	1995	
	HIT IS CREDITED TO 88.3 FEATURING LISA MAY						
8th Day	Eight Member Session Musicians from Detroit						
* 1	She's Not Just Another Woman		0	1971	11	1971	(Invictus 9087)
2	You've Got To Crawl	(Before You Walk)	0	1971	28	1971	(Invictus 9098)
Eighth Wonder	Mixed Vocal/Instrumental Group from the UK						
1	Stay With Me	(CBS A 6594)	65	1985	0	1985	
2	I'm Not Scared	(CBS Scare 1)	7	1988	0	1988	
3	Cross My Heart	(CBS 651552 7)	13	1988	0	1988	
4	Baby Baby	(CBS Babe 1)	65	1988	0	1988	
Eileen Barton	Female Vocalist, B: Brooklyn, New York						
* 1	If I Knew You Were Coming I'd Have Baked A Cake		0	1950	1	1950	(National 9103)

ISSUE	TITLE	UK LBL	UK POS	UK YEAR	US POS	US YEAR	US LBL
2	May I Take Two Giant Steps		0	1950	25	1950	(National 9112)
3	Cry		0	1951	10	1951	(Coral 60592)
4	Wishin'		0	1952	30	1952	(Coral 60651)
5	Pretend		0	1953	17	1953	(Coral 60927)
6	Don't Let The Stars Get In Your Eyes		0	1953	24	1953	(Coral 60882)
7	Toys		0	1953	21	1953	(Coral 61019)
8	Don't Ask Me Why		0	1954	25	1954	(Coral 61109)
9	Pine Tree, Pine Over Me		0	1954	26	1954	(Coral 61126)
10	Sway (Quien Sera)		0	1954	21	1954	(Coral 61185)

HIT 1 IS WITH THE NEW YORKERS • HIT 9 IS CREDITED TO JOHNNY DESMOND, EILEEN BARTON AND THE MCGUIRE SISTERS

Eileen Rodgers   Female Vocalist, B: 1933 Pittsburgh, Sang With Charlie Spivak's Band In The 50s

ISSUE	TITLE	UK LBL	UK POS	UK YEAR	US POS	US YEAR	US LBL
1	Miracle Of Love		0	1956	18	1956	(Columbia 40708)
2	Treasure Of Your Love		0	1958	26	1958	(Columbia 41214)

Eileen Wilson   Female Vocalist from the USA

1	Cold, Cold Heart		0	1951	19	1951	(Decca 27761)

Eimear Quinn   Female Vocalist from Ireland

1	The Voice	(Polydor 5768842)	40	1996	0	1996	

Einstein   Male Rapper from the UK

1	Another Monsterjam	(FFRR F 116)	65	1989	0	1989	
2	Turn It Up	(Swanyard SYD 9)	42	1990	0	1990	
3	The Power	(Arista 74321398672)	42	1996	0	1996	

HIT 1 IS CREDITED TO SIMON HARRIS FEATURING EINSTEIN • HIT 2 TO TECHNOTRONIC FEATURING MELISSA & EINSTEIN • HIT 3 TO SNAP FEATURING EINSTEIN

El Chicano   Lead Singer Jerry Salas, Formed In 1965 As The VIPs

1	Viva Triado (Part 1)		0	1970	28	1970	(KAPP 2085)
2	Tell Her She's Lovely		0	1973	40	1973	(MCA 40104)

El Coco   Male Vocal/Instrumental Group from the USA

1	Cocomotion	(PYE International 7N 25761)	31	1978	0	1978	

El Debarge   Mixed Family Group from Grand Rapids, Michigan, USA   Real Name Eldra Debarge B: 4 Jun 1961 Michigan

1	I Like It		0	1983	31	1983	(GORDY 1645)
2	All This Love		0	1983	17	1983	(Gordy 1660)
3	Time Will Reveal		0	1983	18	1983	(Gordy 1705)
4	Rhythm Of The Night	(Gordy TMG 1376)	4	1985	3	1985	(Gordy 1770)
5	Who's Holding Donna Now		0	1985	6	1985	(Gordy 1793)
6	You Wear It Well	(Gordy ZB 40345)	54	1985	0	1985	
7	Who's Johnny (Short Circuit Theme)	(Gordy ELD 1)	60	1986	3	1986	(Gordy 1842)
* 8	Secret Garden (Sweet Seduction Suite)	(QWEST Q 9992)	67	1990	31	1990	(QWEST 19992)

HITS 1-4 ARE CREDITED TO DEBARGE • HIT 8 TO QUINCY JONES FEATURING AL B. SURE!, JAMES INGRAM, EL DEBARGE & BARRY WHITE

El Dorados   Male R&B Quintet from Chicago

1	At My Front Door		0	1955	17	1955	(VEE-JAY 147)

El Mariachi   Male Producer Roger Sanchez from the USA

1	Cuba	(FFRR FCD 286)	38	1996	0	1996	

Elaine Paige   Female Vocalist from the UK

1	Don't Walk Away Till I Touch You	(EMI 2862)	46	1978	0	1978	
2	Memory	(Polydor POSP 279)	6	1981	0	1981	
3	Memory (Re-Entry)	(Polydor POSP 279)	67	1982	0	1982	
4	Sometimes (Theme From The Champions)	(Island IS 174)	72	1984	0	1984	
5	I Know Him So Well	(RCA CHESS 3)	1	1985	0	1985	
6	The Second Time (Theme From The Bilitis)	(WEA YZ 163)	69	1987	0	1987	
7	Hymne A L'amour (If You Love Me)	(WEA YZ 899CD)	68	1995	0	1995	

HIT 5 IS CREDITED TO ELAINE PAIGE AND BARBARA DICKSON • SEE ALSO BARBARA DICKSON

Elastica   Mixed Vocal/Instrumental Group from the UK/Germany

1	Line Up	(Deceptive Bluff 004CD)	20	1994	0	1994	
2	Connection	(Deceptive Bluff 010CD)	17	1994	0	1994	
3	Waking Up	(Deceptive Bluff 011CD)	13	1995	0	1995	

Elbow Bones & The Racketeers   Male Group Leader With A Female Backing Group from the USA

1	A Night In New York	(EMI America EA165)	33	1984	0	1984	

Electra   Male Vocal/Instrumental Group from the UK

1	Jibaro	(FFRR FFR 9)	54	1988	0	1988	
2	It's Your Destiny / Autumn Love	(London F 121)	51	1989	0	1989	

Electrafixion   Male Vocal/Instrumental Group from the UK

1	Zephyr	(WEA YZ 865CD)	47	1994	0	1994	

ISSUE	TITLE	UK LBL	UK POS	UK YEAR	US POS	US YEAR	US LBL
2	Lowdown	(East West YZ 977CD)	54	1995	0	1995	
3	Never	(Spacejunk WEA 022CD)	58	1995	0	1995	
4	Sister Pain (Live)	(Spacejunk WEA WEA 037CD1)	27	1996	0	1996	

Electribe 101 Mixed Vocal/Instrumental Group from the UK/Germany

1	Tell Me When The Fever Ended	(Mercury MER 310)	32	1989	0	1989	
2	Talking With Myself	(Mercury MER 316)	23	1990	0	1990	
3	You're Walking	(Mercury MER 328)	50	1990	0	1990	

Electric Indian Instrumental Group From Philadelphia

1	Keem-O-Sabe		0	1969	16	1969	(United Artists 50563)

Electric Light Orchestra Male Vocal/Instrumental Group from the UK Formed In 1971 Names Roy Wood, Bev Bevans & Jeff Lynne

1	10538 Overture	(Harvest HAR 5053)	9	1972	0	1972	
2	Roll Over Beethoven	(Harvest HAR 5063)	6	1973	0	1973	
3	Showdown	(Harvest HAR 5077)	12	1973	0	1973	
4	Ma-Ma-Ma-Belle	(Warner Bros. K 16349)	22	1974	0	1974	
5	Can't Get It Out Of My Head		0	1978	9	1975	(United Artists 573)
6	Evil Woman	(Jet 764)	10	1976	10	1976	(United Artists 729)
7	Strange Magic	(Jet 779)	38	1976	14	1976	(United Artists 770)
8	Livin' Thing	(Jet UP 36184)	4	1976	13	1977	(United Artists 888)
9	Rockaria!	(Jet UP 36209)	9	1977	0	1977	
10	Do Ya (Re-Recording)		0	1977	24	1977	(United Artists 939)
11	Telephone Line	(Jet UP 36254)	8	1977	7	1977	(United Artists 1000)
12	Turn To Stone	(Jet UP 36313)	18	1977	13	1978	(Jet 1099)
13	Mr. Blue Sky	(Jet UP 36342)	6	1978	35	1978	(Jet 5050)
14	Sweet Talkin' Woman	(Jet 121)	6	1978	17	1978	(Jet 1145)
15	Wild West Hero	(Jet Jet 109)	6	1978	0	1978	
16	ELO (EP)	(Jet ELO 1)	34	1978	0	1978	
17	Shine A Little Love	(Jet 144)	6	1979	8	1979	(Jet 5057)
18	The Diary Of Horace Wimp	(Jet 150)	8	1979	0	1979	
19	Don't Bring Me Down	(Jet 153)	3	1979	4	1979	(Jet 5060)
20	Confusion	(Jet 166)	8	1979	37	1979	(Jet 5064)
21	Last Train To London	(Jet 166)	8	1979	39	1979	(Jet 5067)
22	I'm Alive	(Jet 179)	20	1980	16	1980	(MCA 41246)
23	Xanadu	(Jet 185)	1	1980	8	1980	(MCA 41285)
24	All Over The World	(Jet 195)	11	1980	13	1980	(MCA 41289)
25	Don't Walk Away	(Jet 7004)	21	1980	0	1980	
26	Hold On Tight	(Jet 7011)	4	1981	10	1981	(Jet 02408)
27	Twilight	(Jet 7015)	30	1981	38	1981	(Jet 02559)
28	Ticket To The Moon / Here Is The News	(Jet 7018)	24	1982	0	1982	
29	Rock And Roll Is King	(Jet A 3500)	13	1983	19	1983	(Jet 03964)
30	Secret Messages	(Jet A 3720)	48	1983	0	1983	
31	Calling America	(Epic A 6844)	28	1986	18	1986	(CBS ASSOC. 05766)
32	Honest Men	(TELSTAR ELO 100)	60	1991	0	1991	

HIT 23 IS CREDITED TO OLIVIA NEWTON-JOHN & ELECTRIC LIGHT ORCHESTRA • HIT 32 TO ELECTRIC LIGHT ORCHESTRA PART 2

Electric Prunes Male Vocal/Instrumental Rock Quintet From Seattle

1	I Had Too Much To Dream Last Night	(Reprise RS 20532)	49	1967	11	1967	(Reprise 0532)
2	Get Me To The World On Time	(Reprise RS 20564)	42	1967	27	1967	(Reprise 0564)

Electronic Male Vocal/Instrumental Group from the UK   Names: Bernard Sumner, Johnny Marr, Neil Tennant, Anne Dudley & David Palmer

1	Getting Away With It	(Factory FAC 2577)	12	1989	38	1989	
2	Get The Message	(Factory FAC 2877)	8	1991	0	1991	
3	Feel Every Beat	(Factory FAC 287)	39	1991	0	1991	
4	Disappointed	(Parlophone R 6311)	6	1992	0	1992	
5	Forbidden City	(Parlophone CDR 6436)	14	1996	0	1996	
6	For You	(Parlophone CDR 6445)	16	1996	0	1996	
7	Second Nature	(Parlophone CDR 6455)	35	1997	0	1997	

SEE ALSO NEW ORDER, SMITHS, PET SHOP BOYS & ART OF NOISE

Electronicas Male Instrumental Group from Holland

1	Original Bird Dance	(Polydor POSP 360)	22	1981	0	1981	

Electroset Male Production/Instrumental Group from the UK

1	How Does It Feel	(FFRR F 203)	27	1992	0	1992	
2	Sensation	(FFRR TABCD 231)	69	1995	0	1995	

Elegants Male Vocal Group from New York, Formed In 1957

* 1	Little Star	(HMV POP 520)	25	1958	1	1958	(APT 25005)

THE HIT IS A MODERN VERSION OF 'TWINKLE, TWINKLE LITTLE STAR'

ISSUE	TITLE	UK LBL	UK POS	UK YEAR	US POS	US YEAR	US LBL
Elevation	Male Production/Instrumental Duo from the UK						
1	Can You Feel It	(NOVA MUTE 12NOMU 3)	62	1992	0	1992	
Elevatorman	Male Instrumental/Production Group from the UK						
1	Funk And Drive	(Wired Wired 211)	37	1995	0	1995	
2	Fired Up	(Wired Wired 216)	44	1995	0	1995	
Elgins	Mixed Vocal Group from the USA						
+ 1	Darling Baby		0	1966	4	1966	(V.I.P. 25029)
2	Heaven Must Have Sent You	(Tamla Motown TMG 771)	3	1971	50	1966	(V.I.P. 25037)
3	Put Yourself In My Place	(Tamla Motown TMG 771)	3	1971	0	1971	
4	Put Yourself In My Place (Re-Issue)	(Tamla Motown TMG 787)	28	1971	0	1971	
	SEE ALSO THE TEMPTATIONS						
Elias & His Zigzag Jive Flutes	Male Instrumental Group From South Africa						
1	Tom Hark	(Columbia DB 4109)	2	1958	0	1958	
Elisa Fiorillo	Female Vocalist from the UK						
1	Who Found Who	(Chrysalis CHS JEL 1)	10	1987	16	1987	(Chrysalis 43120)
2	How Can I Forget You	(Chrysalis Elisa 1)	50	1988	0	1988	
3	On The Way Up		0	1987	16	1987	(Chrysalis 23497)
	HIT 1 IS CREDITED TO JELLYBEAN FEATURING ELISA FIORILLO • SEE ALSO JELLYBEAN						
Elizabeth Frazer	See Ian McCulloch						
Elkie Brooks	Female Vocalist, B: 1945 In Lancashire, England						
1	Pearl's A Singer	(A&M AMS 7275)	8	1977	0	1977	
2	Sunshine After The Rain	(A&M AMS 7306)	10	1977	0	1977	
3	Lilac Wine	(A&M AMS 7333)	16	1978	0	1978	
4	Only Love Can Break Your Heart	(A&M AMS 7353)	43	1978	0	1978	
5	Don't Cry Out Loud	(A&M AMS 7395)	12	1978	0	1978	
6	The Runaway	(A&M AMS 7428)	50	1979	0	1979	
7	Fool If You Think It's Over	(A&M AMS 8187)	17	1982	0	1982	
8	Our Love	(A&M AMS 8214)	43	1982	0	1982	
9	Nights In White Satin	(A&M AMS 8235)	33	1982	0	1982	
10	Gasoline Alley	(A&M AMS 8305)	52	1983	0	1983	
11	No More The Fool	(LEGEND LM 4)	5	1986	0	1986	
12	Break The Chain	(LEGEND LM 8)	55	1987	0	1987	
13	We've Got Tonight	(LEGEND LM 9)	69	1987	0	1987	
	IN 1968 SHE FORMED A 12-PIECE JAZZ-ROCK BAND CALLED DADA ALTHOUGH IT LASTED ONLY TWO YEARS THE NUCLEUS LEAVING IN 1972 TO FORM VINEGAR JOE						
Ella Fitzgerald	Female Jazz Vocalist, B: 25 Apr 1918 Newport News, Virginia						
* 9	A-Tisket, A-Tasket		0	1938	0	1938	(Decca 1840)
* 31	I'm Making Believe (From *Sweet And Low-Down*)		0	1944	1	1900	(Decca 23356)
* 32	Into Each Life Some Rain Must Fall		0	1944	1	1944	(Decca 23356)
36	You Won't Be Satisfied (Until You Break My Heart)		0	1946	10	1946	(Decca 23496)
37	Stone Cold Dead In The Market (He Had It Coming)		0	1946	7	1946	(Decca 23546)
38	(I Love You) For Sentimental Reasons		0	1946	8	1946	(Decca 23670)
39	Guilty		0	1947	11	1947	(Decca 23844)
40	My Happiness		0	1948	6	1948	(Decca 24446)
41	Tea Leaves		0	1948	24	1948	(Decca 24446)
42	Baby It's Cold Outside (From *Neptune's Daughter*)		0	1949	9	1949	(Decca 24644)
43	Can Anyone Explain? (No! No! No!)		0	1950	30	1950	(Decca 27209)
44	Smooth Sailing		0	1951	23	1951	(Decca 27693)
45	Trying		0	1952	21	1952	(Decca 28375)
46	Walking By The River		0	1952	29	1952	(Decca 28433)
47	Crying In The Chapel		0	1953	15	1953	(Decca 28762)
48	Melancholy Me		0	1954	25	1954	(Decca 29008)
49	I Need		0	1954	30	1954	(Decca 29108)
50	Swingin' Shepherd Blues	(HMV POP 486)	15	1958	0	1958	
51	But Not For Me	(HMV POP 657)	25	1959	0	1959	
52	But Not For Me (Re-Entry)	(HMV POP 657)	29	1959	0	1959	
53	Mack The Knife	(HMV POP 736)	19	1960	27	1960	(Verve 10209)
54	How High The Moon	(HMV POP 782)	46	1960	0	1960	
55	Desafinado	(Verve VS 502)	38	1962	0	1962	
56	Desafinado (Re-Entry)	(Verve VS 502)	41	1962	0	1962	
57	Can't Buy Me Love	(Verve VS 519)	34	1964	0	1964	

ISSUE	TITLE	UK LBL	UK POS	UK YEAR	US POS	US YEAR	US LBL

Hits 28,31, 32,3 4 Are With The Ink Spots   Hits 35 & 38 Are With The Delta Rhythm Boys   Hits 36, 43 Are With Louis Armstrong
Hits 37,42 To Ella Fitzgerald And Louis Jordan   Hit 40 Is With The Song Spinners   Hit 47 Is With The Ray Charles Singers And Bill Goggett Orchestra
OBITUARY : D: 1996.

Ella Mae Morse Female Vocalist, B: Dallas, Texas

* 1	Cow-Cow Boogie		0	1942	9	1942	(Capitol 102)
8	Buzz Me		0	1946	15	1946	(Capitol 226)
* 9	The Blacksmith Blues		0	1952	3	1952	(Capitol 1922)
10	Oakie Boogie		0	1952	23	1952	(Capitol 2072)
11	40 Cups Of Coffee		0	1953	26	1953	(Capitol 2539)

Ellen Sutton Female Vocalist from the USA   With Sir H. Pimm

1	I Wanna Say Hello		0	1952	21	1952	(KEM 2710)

Elliot Lawrence & His Orchestra Male Orchestra Leader/Pianist, Real Name Elliot Lawrence Broza from the USA

1	Who Do You Hope I Love		0	1946	9	1946	(Columbia 37047)
2	You Broke The Only Heart That Ever Loved You		0	1946	16	1946	(Columbia 37084)
3	Near You		0	1947	4	1947	(Columbia 37838)
4	At The Flying W		0	1948	21	1948	(Columbia 38215)

Ellis, Beggs & Howard Male Vocal/Instrumental Group from the UK

1	Big Bubbles No Troubles	(RCA PB 42089)	59	1988	0	1988	
2	Big Bubbles No Troubles (Re-Entry)	(RCA PB 42089)	41	1989	0	1941	

Elmer Bernstein Male Composer/Conductor, B: 4 Apr 1922 New York City

1	Main Title Theme From *The Man With The Golden Arm*		0	1956	16	1956	(Decca 29869)
2	Staccato's Theme	(Capitol CL 15101)	4	1959	0	1959	
3	Staccato's Theme (Re-Entry)	(Capitol CL 15101)	40	1960	0	1960	

Elmo Tanner See Ted Weems & His Orchestra

Elton Britt Male Vocalist/Yodeler, B: 27 Jun 1913 Marshall, Arkansas

* 1	There's A Star Spangled Banner Waving Somewhere		0	1942	7	1942	(Bluebird 9000)
! 2	I'm A Convict With Old Glory In My Heart		0	1945	7	1945	(Bluebird 33-0517)
! 3	Someday		0	1946	2	1946	(Bluebird 33-0521)
4	Wave To Me, My Lady		0	1946	19	1946	(Victor 20-1789)

OTHER HITS ARE C/W • OBITUARY : D: 23 JUN 1972, AGED 59

Elton John Male Vocal/Pianist, Real Name Reginald Kenneth Dwight B: 25 Mar 1947 Pinner, Middlesex, England

1	Border Song		0	1970	92	1970	(UNI 55246)
2	Your Song	(DJM DJS 233)	7	1971	8	1971	(UNI 55265)
3	Friends		0	1971	34	1971	(UNI 55277)
4	Levon		0	1971	24	1971	(UNI 55314)
5	Tiny Dancer		0	1972	41	1972	(UNI 55318)
* 6	Rocket Man	(DJM DJX 501)	2	1972	6	1972	(UNI 55328)
* 7	Honky Cat	(DJM DJS)	31	1972	7	1972	(UNI 55343)
* 8	Crocodile Rock	(DJM DJS 271)	5	1972	1	1973	(MCA 40000)
* 9	Daniel	(DJM DJS 275)	4	1973	2	1973	(MCA 40046)
* 10	Saturday Night Alright For Fighting	(DJM DJX 502)	7	1973	4	1973	(MCA 40105)
* 11	Goodbye Yellow Brick Road	(DJM DJS 285)	6	1973	2	1973	(MCA 40148)
12	Step Into Christmas	(DJM DJS 290)	24	1973	0	1973	
13	Candle In The Wind	(DJM DJS 297)	11	1974	0	1974	
* 14	Bennie And The Jets	(DJM DJS 10705)	37	1976	1	1974	(MCA 40198)
* 15	Don't Let The Sun Go Down On Me	(DJM DJS 302)	1	1991	2	1974	(MCA 40259)
16	The Bitch Is Back	(DJM DJS 322)	15	1974	4	1974	(MCA 40297)
* 17	Lucy In The Sky With Diamonds	(DJM DJS 340)	10	1974	1	1974	(MCA 40344)
* 18	Philadelphia Freedom	(DJM DJS 354)	12	1975	1	1975	(MCA 40364)
* 19	Someone Saved My Life Tonight	(DJM DJS 385)	22	1975	1	1975	(MCA 40421)
* 20	Island Girl	(DJM DJS 610)	14	1975	1	1975	(MCA 40461)
21	Grow Some Funk Of Your Own		0	1976	14	1976	(MCA 40505)
* 22	Don't Go Breaking My Heart	(Rocket ROKN 512)	1	1976	1	1976	(Rocket 40585)
23	Pinball Wizzard	(DJM DJS 652)	7	1976	0	1976	
* 24	Sorry Seems To Be The Hardest Word	(Rocket ROKN 517)	11	1976	6	1976	(MCA/Rocket 40645)
25	Crazy Water	(Rocket ROKN 521)	27	1977	0	1977	
26	Bite Your Lip (Get Up And Dance)	(Rocket ROKN 526)	28	1977	28	1977	(MCA/Rocket 40677)
27	Ego	(Rocket ROKN 538)	34	1978	34	1978	(MCA 40892)
28	Part-Time Love	(Rocket XPRES 1)	15	1978	22	1978	(MCA 40973)

ISSUE	TITLE	UK LBL	UK POS	UK YEAR	US POS	US YEAR	US LBL
29	Song For Guy	(Rocket XPRES 5)	4	1978	0	1978	
30	Are You Ready For Love	(Rocket XPRES 13)	42	1979	0	1979	
31	Mama Can't Buy You Love		0	1979	9	1979	(MCA 41042)
32	Victim Of Love		0	1979	31	1979	(MCA 41126)
* 33	Little Jeannie	(Rocket XPRES 32)	33	1980	3	1980	(MCA 41236)
34	Sartorial Eloquence	(Rocket XPRES 41)	44	1980	39	1980	(MCA 41293)
35	I Saw Her Standing There	(DJM DJS 10965)	40	1981	0	1981	
36	Nobody Wins	(Rocket XPRES 54)	42	1981	21	1981	(Geffen 49722)
37	Chloe		0	1981	34	1981	(Geffen 49788)
38	Blue Eyes	(Rocket XPRES 71)	8	1982	12	1982	(Geffen 29954)
39	Empty Garden (Hey Hey Johnny)	(Rocket XPRES 77)	51	1982	13	1992	(Geffen 50049)
40	I Guess That's Why They Call It The Blues	(Rocket XPRES 91)	5	1983	4	1983	(Geffen 29460)
41	I'm Still Standing	(Rocket EJS 1)	4	1983	12	1983	(Geffen 29639)
42	Kiss The Bride	(Rocket EJS 2)	20	1983	25	1983	(Geffen 29568)
43	Cold As Christmas	(Rocket EJS 3)	33	1983	0	1983	
44	Sad Songs (Say So Much)	(Rocket PH 7)	7	1984	5	1984	(Geffen 29292)
45	Passengers	(Rocket EJS 5)	5	1984	0	1984	
46	Who Wears These Shoes?	(Rocket EJS 6)	50	1984	16	1984	(Geffen 29189)
47	In Neon		0	1985	38	1985	(Geffen 29111)
48	Breaking Hearts (Ain't What It used To Be)	(Rocket EJS 7)	59	1985	0	1985	
49	Act Of War	(Rocket EJS 8)	32	1985	0	1985	
50	Nikita	(Rocket EJS 9)	3	1985	7	1986	(Geffen 28800)
51	Wrap Her Up	(Rocket EJS 10)	12	1985	20	1985	(Geffen 28873)
* 52	That's What Friends Are For	(Arista ARIST 638)	16	1985	1	1985	(Arista 9422)
53	Cry To Heaven	(Rocket EJS 11)	47	1986	0	1986	
54	Heartache All Over The World	(Rocket EJS 12)	45	1986	0	1986	
55	Slow Rivers	(Rocket EJS 13)	44	1986	0	1986	
56	Candle In The Wind (Live)	(Rocket EJS 15)	5	1988	6	1987	(MCA 53196)
57	Flames Of Paradise	(CBS 6508657)	59	1987	36	1987	(Epic 07119)
58	I Don't Wanna Go On With You Like That	(Rocket EJS 16)	30	1988	2	1988	(MCA 43345)
59	Town Of Plenty	(Rocket EJS 17)	74	1988	0	1988	
60	A Word In Spanish		0	1988	19	1988	(MCA 53408)
61	Through The Storm	(Arista 112185)	41	1989	16	1989	(Arista 9809)
62	Healing Hands	(Rocket EJS 19)	45	1989	13	1989	(MCA 53692)
63	Sacrifice	(Rocket EJS 20)	55	1989	18	1989	(MCA 43750)
64	Sacrifice / Healing Hands (Re-Issue)	(Rocket EJS 22)	1	1990	0	1990	
65	Club At The End Of The Street / Whispers	(Rocket EJS 23)	47	1990	28	1990	(MCA 79026)
66	You Gotta Love Someone	(Rocket EJS 24)	33	1990	0	1990	
67	Easier To Walk Away	(Rocket EJS 25)	67	1990	0	1990	
68	Easier To Walk Away (Re-Entry)	(Rocket EJS 25)	63	1990	0	1990	
* 69	Don't Let The Sun Go Down On Me	(Epic 6576467)	1	1991	1	1992	(Columbia 74086)
70	The One	(Rocket EJS 28)	10	1992	9	1992	(MCA 54423)
71	Runaway Train	(Rocket EJS 29)	31	1992	0	1992	
72	The Last Song	(Rocket EJS 30)	21	1992	23	1992	(MCA 54510)
73	Simple Life	(Rocket EJSCD 31)	44	1993	0	1993	
74	True Love	(Rocket EJSCX 32)	2	1993	0	1993	
75	Don't Go Breaking My Heart	(Rocket EJCD	7	1994	0	1994	
76	Ain't Nothing Like The Real Thing	(London LonCD 350)	24	1994	0	1994	
* 77	Can You Feel The Love Tonight	(Mercury EJCD 34)	14	1994	4	1994	(Hollywood 64543)
78	Circle Of Life	(Rocket EJSCD 35)	11	1994	18	1994	(Hollywood 64516)
79	Believe	(Rocket EJSCD 36)	15	1995	34	1995	(Rocket 856014)
80	Made In England	(Rocket EJSDD 37)	18	1995	0	1995	
81	Blessed		0	1996	34	1996	(Rocket 852394)
82	Please	(Rocket EJSCD 40)	33	1996	0	1996	
83	You Can Make History (Young Again)		0	1996	70	1996	(MCA 55222)
84	Live Like Horses	(Rocket LLHCD 1)	9	1996	0	1996	
* 85	Something About The Way.../ Candle In The Wind 1997	(Rocket PTCD 1)	1	1997	0	1997	

HITS 21,72 ARE WITH KIKI DEE • HIT 16 WAS BY THE ELTON JOHN BAND • HIT 33 WAS WITH JOHN LENNON AND THE MUSIC SCOALS HORNS
HIT 47 IS WITH MILLIE JACKSON
HIT 50 IS CREDITED TO DIONNE AND FRIENDS • HIT 50 IS WITH DIONNE WARWICK, GLADY'S NIGHT & STEVIE WONDER • HIT 55 IS WITH CLIFF RICHARD
HIT 57 IS WITH JENNIFER RUSH • HIT 59 IS WITH ARETHA FRANKLIN • HIT 67 IS WITH GEORGE MICHAEL • HIT 69 IS WITH ERIC CLAPTON • HIT 73 IS WITH RUPAUL
HIT 74 IS WITH MARCELLA DETROIT • HIT 84 IS CREDITED TO ELTON JOHN AND LUCIANO PAVAROTTI • HIS FIRST GROUP WAS CALLED THE BLUESOLOGY IN 1966
HIT 85 IS THE LARGEST SELLING RECORD OF ALL TIME, A RE-WRITTEN VERSION OF HIT 13 IN MEMORY OF DIANA, PRINCESS OF WALES D: 31 AUG 1997.

ISSUE	TITLE	UK LBL	UK POS	UK YEAR	US POS	US YEAR	US LBL
Elvin Bishop	Male Guitarist, B: 21 Oct 1942 Tulsa, Oklahoma Vocals On The Hit Are By Mickey Thomas						
1	Fooled Around And Fell In Love	(Capricorn 2089 024)	34	1976	3	1976	(Capricorn 0252)
Elvis Costello	Male Vocalist, Real Name Declan McManus B: 25 Aug 1954 Liverpool, England						
1	Watching The Detectives	(Stiff Buy 20)	15	1977	0	1977	
2	I Don't Want To Go To Chelsea	(Radar Ada 3)	16	1978	0	1978	
3	Pump It Up	(Radar Ada 10)	24	1978	0	1978	
4	Radio Radio	(Radar Ada 24)	29	1978	0	1978	
5	Oliver's Army	(Radar Ada 31)	2	1979	0	1979	
6	Accidents Will Happen	(Radar Ada 35)	28	1979	0	1979	
7	I Can't Stand Up For Falling Down	(F. BEAT XX 1)	4	1980	0	1980	
8	High Fidelity	(F. BEAT XX 3)	30	1980	0	1980	
9	New Amsterdam	(F. BEAT XX 5)	36	1980	0	1980	
10	Clubland	(F. BEAT XX 12)	60	1980	0	1980	
11	A Good Year For The Roses	(F. BEAT XX 17)	6	1981	0	1981	
12	Sweet Dreams	(F. BEAT XX 19)	42	1981	0	1981	
13	I'm Your Toy	(F. BEAT XX 21)	51	1982	0	1982	
14	You Little Fool	(F. BEAT XX 26)	52	1982	0	1982	
15	Man Out Of Time	(F. BEAT XX 28)	58	1982	0	1982	
16	From Head To Toe	(F. BEAT XX 30)	43	1982	0	1982	
17	Party Party	(A&M AMS 8267)	48	1982	0	1982	
18	Pills And Soap	(IMP IMP 001)	16	1983	0	1983	
19	Everyday I Write The Book	(F. BEAT XX 32)	28	1983	36	1983	(Columbia 04045)
20	Let Them All Talk	(F. BEAT XX 33)	59	1983	0	1983	
21	Peace In Our Time	(Imposter Truce 1)	48	1984	0	1984	
22	I Wanna Be Loved / Turning The Town Red	(F. BEAT XX 35)	25	1984	0	1984	
23	The Only Flame In Town	(F. BEAT XX 37)	71	1984	0	1984	
24	Green Shirt	(F. BEAT ZB 40085)	71	1985	0	1985	
25	Green Shirt (Re-Entry)	(F. BEAT ZB 40085)	68	1985	0	1985	
26	Don't Let Me Be Misunderstood	(F. BEAT ZB 40555)	33	1986	0	1986	
27	Tokyo Storm Warning	(IMP IMP 007)	73	1986	0	1986	
28	Veronica	(Warner Bros. W 7558)	31	1989	19	1989	(Warner Bros. 22981)
29	Baby Plays Around (EP)	(Warner Bros. W 2949)	65	1989	0	1989	
30	The Other Side Of Summer	(Warner Bros. W 0025)	43	1991	0	1991	
31	Sulky Girl	(Warner Bros. W 0234CD)	22	1994	0	1994	
32	13 Steps Lead Down	(Warner Bros. W 0245CD)	59	1994	0	1994	
33	London's Brilliant Parade	(Warner Bros. W 0270CD)	48	1994	0	1994	
34	It's Time	(Warner Bros. W 0348CD)	58	1996	0	1996	

HITS 2-6, 10, 31 ARE CREDITED TO ELVIS COSTELLO & THE ATTRACTIONS • HIT 13 IS CREDITED TO ELVIS COSTELLO & THE ATTRACTIONS WITH THE ROYAL PHILHARMONIC ORCHESTRA • HITS 18,21 ARE CREDITED TO IMPOSTER • HIT 26 IS CREDITED TO COSTELLO SHOW FEATURING THE CONFEDERATES

ISSUE	TITLE	UK LBL	UK POS	UK YEAR	US POS	US YEAR	US LBL
Elvis Presley	Male Vocalist, Elvis Aaron Presley B: 8 Jan 1935 Tupelo, Mississippi						
! 1	Baby Let's Play House / I'm Left, You're Right, She's Gone		0	1955	5	1955	(SUN 217)
! 2	Mystery Train / I Forgot To Remember To Forget	(HMV POP 295)	25	1957	1	1955	(SUN 223)
* 3	Heartbreak Hotel / I Was The One	(HMV POP 182)	2	1956	1	1956	(RCA 47-6420)
4	Blue Suede Shoes	(HMV POP 213)	9	1956	20	1956	(RCA EPA-747)
* 5	I Want You, I Need You, I Love You	(IIMV POP 235)	25	1956	1	1956	(RCA 47-6540)
* 6	Hound Dog - Don't Be Cruel	(HMV POP 249)	2	1956	1	1956	(RCA 47-6604)
7	I Want You,I Need You, I Love You (Re-Entry)	(HMV POP 235)	14	1956	0	1956	
8	Blue Suede Shoes (Re-Entry)	(HMV POP 213)	26	1956	0	1956	
* 9	Love Me Tender	(HMV POP 253)	11	1956	1	1956	(RCA 47-6643)
10	Heartbreak Hotel / I Was The One (Re-Entry)	(HMV POP 182)	23	1956	0	1956	
11	Blue Moon	(HMV POP 272)	9	1956	0	1956	
12	I Don't Care If The Sun Don't Shine	(HMV POP 272)	29	1956	0	1956	
13	Love Me / When My Blue Moon Turns To Gold Again		0	1956	2	1956	(AGAIN RCA EPA-992)
14	I Don't Care If The Sun Don't Shine (Re-Entry)	(HMV POP 272)	23	1956	0	1956	
15	Poor Boy		0	1956	24	1956	(RCA EPA-4006)
16	Old Shep		0	1956	47	1956	(RCA EPA 993)
17	(There'll Be) Peace In The Valley		0	1957	25	1957	(RCA EPA-4054)
* 18	Too Much / Playing For Keeps	(HMV POP 330)	6	1957	1	1957	(RCA 47-6800)
19	Rip It Up	(HMV POP 305)	27	1957	0	1957	
* 20	All Shook Up	(HMV POP 359)	24	1957	1	1957	(RCA 47-6870)
21	All Shook Up (Re-Entry)	(HMV POP 359)	1	1957	0	1957	
* 22	Teddy Bear	(RCA 1013)	3	1957	1	1957	(RCA 47-7000)
23	Too Much / Playing For Keeps (Re-Entry)	(HMV POP 330)	26	1957	0	1957	

	ISSUE	TITLE	UK LBL	UK POS	UK YEAR	US POS	US YEAR	US LBL
	24	Loving You	(RCA 1013)	24	1957	20	1957	(RCA 47-7000)
	25	Paralyzed	(HMV POP 378)	8	1957	0	1957	
	26	Party	(RCA 1020)	2	1957	0	1957	
	27	Got A Lot O' Livin' To Do	(RCA 1020)	17	1957	0	1957	
	28	Treat Me Nice		0	1957	18	1957	(RCA 47-7035)
	29	Trying To Get To You	(HMV POP 408)	16	1957	0	1957	
	30	Lawdy Miss Clawdy	(HMV POP 408)	15	1957	0	1957	
	31	Santa Bring My Baby Back To Me	(RCA 1025)	7	1957	0	1957	
!	32	I'm Left You're Right She's Gone	(HMV POP 428)	21	1958	10	1958	(SUN 217)
*	33	Jailhouse Rock	(RCA 1028)	1	1958	1	1957	(RCA 47-7035)
*	34	Don't	(RCA 1043)	2	1958	1	1958	(RCA 47-7150)
	35	Jailhouse Rock (EP)	(RCA RCX 106)	18	1958	0	1958	
	36	I'm Left You're Right She's Gone (Re-Entry)	(HMV POP 428)	29	1958	0	1958	
*	37	Wear My Ring Around Your Neck	(RCA 1058)	3	1958	2	1958	(RCA 47-7240)
*	38	Hard Headed Woman	(RCA 1070)	2	1958	1	1958	(RCA 47-7280)
	39	King Creole	(RCA 1081)	2	1958	0	1958	
*	40	I Got Stung / One Night	(RCA 1100)	1	1959	4	1958	(RCA 47-7410)
*	41	A Fool Such As I / I Need Your Love Tonight	(RCA 1113)	1	1959	2	1959	(RCA 47-7506)
*	42	A Big Hunk O'love	(RCA 1136)	4	1959	1	1959	(RCA 47-7600)
	43	Strictly Elvis (EP)	(RCA RCX 175)	26	1960	0	1960	
*	44	Stuck On You / Fame And Fortune	(RCA 1187)	3	1960	1	1960	(RCA 47-7740)
*	45	It's Now Or Never	(RCA 1207)	1	1960	1	1960	(RCA 47-7777)
	46	A Mess Of Blues	(RCA 1194)	2	1960	32	1960	(RCA 47-7777)
*	47	Are You Lonesome Tonight / I Gotta Know	(RCA 1216)	1	1961	1	1960	(RCA 47-7810)
*	48	Surrender	(RCA 1227)	1	1961	1	1961	(RCA 47-7850)
*	49	Wooden Heart	(RCA 1226)	1	1961	0	1960	
	50	Lonely Man		0	1961	32	1961	(RCA 47-7850)
	51	Flaming Star		0	1961	14	1961	(RCA LPC-128)
	52	I Feel So Bad	(RCA 1244)	0	1961	5	1961	(RCA 47-7880)
	53	Wild In The Country	(RCA 1244)	4	1961	26	1961	(RCA 47-7880)
	54	His Latest Flame / Little Sister	(RCA 1258)	1	1961	4	1961	(RCA 47-7908)
*	55	Can't Help Falling In Love / Rock-A-Hula Baby	(RCA 1270)	1	1962	2	1961	(RCA 47-7968)
*	56	Good Luck Charm	(RCA 1280)	1	1962	1	1962	(RCA 47-7992)
	57	King Of The Whole Wide World		0	1962	30	1962	(RCA EPA-4371)
	58	Follow That Dream (EP)	(RCA RCX 211)	34	1962	15	1962	(RCA EPA-4368)
	59	She's Not You	(RCA 1303)	1	1962	5	1962	(RCA 47-8041)
*	60	Return To Sender	(RCA 1320)	1	1962	2	1962	(RCA 47-8100)
*	61	One Broken Heart For Sale	(RCA 1337)	12	1963	11	1963	(RCA 47-8134)
*	62	Devil In Disguise	(RCA 1355)	1	1963	3	1963	(RCA 47-8188)
*	63	Bossa Nova Baby	(RCA 1374)	13	1963	8	1963	(RCA 47-8243)
	64	Kiss Me Quick	(RCA 1375)	14	1963	34	1964	(RCA 447-063)
*	65	Kissin' Cousins / It Hurts Me	(RCA 1404)	10	1964	12	1964	(RCA 47-8307)
*	66	Viva Las Vegas	(RCA 1390)	17	1964	21	1964	(RCA 47-8360)
	67	Such A Night	(RCA 1411)	13	1964	16	1964	(RCA 47-8400)
	68	Ask Me		0	1964	12	1964	(RCA 47-8440)
*	69	Ain't That Lovin' You Baby	(RCA 1422)	15	1964	13	1964	(RCA 47-8440)
	70	Blue Christmas	(RCA 1430)	11	1964	0	1964	
	71	Do The Clam	(RCA 1443)	19	1965	21	1965	(RCA 47-8500)
*	72	Crying In The Chapel	(RCA 1455)	1	1965	3	1965	(RCA 447-064)
	73	(Such An) Easy Question		0	1965	11	1965	(RCA 47-8585)
*	74	I'm Yours / It's A Long Lonely Highway		0	1965	11	1965	(RCA 47-8657)
	75	Puppet On A String		0	1965	14	1965	(RCA 447-0650)
	76	Puppet On A String		0	1965	14	1965	(RCA 447-0650)
*	77	Tell Me Why	(RCA 1489)	15	1965	33	1966	(RCA 47-8740)
	78	Blue River	(RCA 1504)	22	1966	0	1966	
*	79	Frankie And Johnny	(RCA 1509)	21	1966	25	1966	(RCA 47-8780)
*	80	Love Letters	(RCA 1526)	6	1966	19	1966	(RCA 47-8870)
	81	Spinout		0	1966	40	1966	(RCA 47-8941)
*	82	If Every Day Was Like Christmas	(RCA 1557)	13	1966	0	1966	
*	83	Indescribably Blue	(RCA 1565)	21	1967	33	1967	(RCA 47-9056)
	84	You Gotta Stop / Love Machine	(RCA 1593)	38	1967	0	1967	
	85	Long Legged Girl	(RCA RCA 1616)	49	1967	0	1967	
	86	Big Boss Man		0	1967	38	1967	(RCA 47-9341)
	87	Guitar Man	(RCA 1663)	19	1968	43	1968	(RCA 47-9425)

ISSUE	TITLE	UK LBL	UK POS	UK YEAR	US POS	US YEAR	US LBL
88	U.S. Male	(RCA 1688)	15	1968	28	1968	(RCA 47-9465)
89	Your Time Hasn't Come Yet Baby	(RCA 1714)	22	1968	0	1968	
90	You'll Never Walk Alone	(RCA 1747)	44	1968	0	1968	
* 91	If I Can Dream	(RCA 1795)	11	1969	12	1968	(RCA 47-9670)
92	Memories		0	1969	35	1969	(RCA 47-9731)
* 93	In The Ghetto	(RCA 1831)	2	1969	3	1969	(RCA 47-9741)
94	Clean Up Your Own Back Yard	(RCA 1869)	21	1969	35	1969	(RCA 47-9747)
* 95	Suspicious Minds	(RCA 1900)	2	1969	1	1969	(RCA 47-9764)
96	In The Ghetto (Re-Entry)	(RCA 1831)	50	1969	0	1969	
* 97	Don't Cry Daddy	(RCA 1916)	8	1970	6	1969	(RCA 47-9768)
* 98	Kentucky Rain	(RCA 1949)	21	1970	16	1970	(RCA 47-9791)
* 99	The Wonder Of You	(RCA 1974)	1	1970	9	1970	(RCA 47-9835)
100	Kentucky Rain (Re-Entry)	(RCA 1949)	46	1970	0	1970	
101	I've Lost You	(RCA 1999)	9	1970	32	1970	(RCA 47-9873)
* 102	You Don't Have To Say You Love Me	(RCA 2046)	9	1971	11	1970	(RCA 47-9916)
103	I Really Don't Want To Know		0	1970	21	1970	(RCA 47-9960)
104	There Goes My Everything	(RCA 2060)	6	1971	21	1971	(RCA 47-9960)
105	The Wonder Of You (Re-Entry)	(RCA 1974)	47	1971	0	1971	
106	You Don't Have To Say You Love Me (Re-Entry)	(RCA 2046)	35	1971	0	1971	
107	Rags To Riches - Where Did They Go, Lord	(RCA 2084)	9	1971	33	1971	(RCA 47-9980)
108	Heartbreak Hotel / Hound Dog (Re-Issue)	(RCA Maximillion 2104)	10	1971	0	1971	
109	I'm Leavin'	(RCA 2125)	23	1971	36	1971	(RCA 47-9998)
110	I Just Can't Help Believing	(RCA 2158)	6	1971	0	1971	
111	Jailhouse Rock (Re-Issue)	(RCA Maximillion 2153)	42	1971	0	1971	
112	Until It's Time For You To Go	(RCA 2188)	5	1972	40	1972	(RCA 74-0619)
113	American Trilogy	(RCA 2229)	8	1972	0	1972	
* 114	Burning Love	(RCA 2267)	7	1972	2	1972	(RCA 74-0789)
115	Always On My Mind	(RCA 2304)	9	1972	0	1972	
116	Separate Ways		0	1972	20	1972	(RCA 74-0815)
117	Steamroller Blues	(RCA 2393)	15	1973	17	1973	(RCA 74-0910)
118	Polk Salad Annie	(RCA 2359)	23	1973	0	1973	
119	Fool	(RCA 2393)	15	1973	0	1973	
120	Raised On Rock	(RCA 2435)	36	1973	41	1973	(RCA 0088)
121	I've Got A Thing About You Baby	(RCA APBO 0196)	33	1974	39	1974	(RCA APBO-0196)
122	If You Talk In Your Sleep	(RCA APBO 0280)	40	1974	17	1974	(RCA APBO-0280)
123	Promised Land	(RCA PB 10074)	9	1975	14	1974	(RCA PB-10074)
124	My Boy	(RCA 2458)	5	1974	20	1975	(RCA PB-10191)
125	T-R-O-U-B-L-E	(RCA 2562)	31	1975	35	1975	(RCA PB-10278)
126	Green Green Grass Of Home	(RCA 2635)	29	1975	0	1975	
127	Hurt	(RCA 2674)	37	1976	0	1976	(RCA PB-10601)
128	Girl Of My Best Friend	(RCA 2729)	9	1976	0	1976	
129	Suspicion	(RCA 2768)	9	1976	0	1976	
130	Moody Blue	(RCA PB 0857)	6	1977	0	1977	(RCA PB-10857)
131	Way Down	(RCA PB 0998)	1	1977	18	1977	(RCA PB-10998)
132	All Shook Up (Re-Issue)	(RCA PB 2694)	41	1977	0	1977	
133	Are You Lonesome Tonight (Re-Issue)	(RCA PB 2699)	46	1977	0	1977	
134	Crying In The Chapel (Re-Issue)	(RCA PB 2708)	43	1977	0	1977	
135	It's Now Or Never (Re-Issue)	(RCA PB 2698)	39	1977	0	1977	
136	Jailhouse Rock (2nd Re-Issue)	(RCA PB 2695)	44	1977	0	1977	
137	Return To Sender (Re-Issue)	(RCA PB 2706)	42	1977	0	1977	
138	The Wonder Of You (Re-Issue)	(RCA PB 2709)	48	1977	0	1977	
139	Wooden Heart (Re-Issue)	(RCA PB 2700)	49	1977	0	1977	
140	My Way	(RCA PB 1165)	9	1977	0	1977	(RCA PB-11165)
! 141	Unchained Melody		0	1978	6	1978	(RCA PB-11212)
! 142	Softly, As I Leave You		0	1978	6	1978	(RCA PB-11212)
143	Don't Be Cruel	(RCA PB 9265)	24	1978	0	1978	
! 144	Are You Sincere		0	1979	10	1979	(RCA PB-11533)
! 145	Solitaire		0	1979	10	1979	(RCA PB-11533)
! 146	There's A Honky Tonk Angel (Who Will Take Me Back In)		0	1979	6	1979	(RCA PB-11679)
! 147	I Got A Feelin' In My Body		0	1979	6	1979	(RCA PB-11679)
148	It Won't Seem Like Christmas (Without You)	(RCA PB 9464)	13	1979	0	1979	
149	It's Only Love / Beyond The Reef	(RCA 4)	3	1980	0	1980	
150	Santa Claus Is Back In Town	(RCA 16)	41	1980	0	1980	
151	Guitar Man (Re-Mix)	(RCA 43)	43	1981	28	1981	(RCA PB-12158)
! 152	Loving Arms	(RCA 48)	47	1981	8	1981	(RCA PB-12205)

ISSUE	TITLE	UK LBL	UK POS	UK YEAR	US POS	US YEAR	US LBL
! 153	You Asked Me To		0	1981	8	1981	(RCA PB-12205)
! 154	You'll Never Walk Alone (Re-Issue)		0	1982	73	1982	(RCA PB-13058)
! 155	There Goes My Everything (Re-Issue)		0	1982	73	1982	(RCA PB-13058)
156	Are You Lonesome Tonight (Re-Issue)	(RCA 196)	25	1982	0	1982	
157	The Sound Of Your Cry	(RCA 232)	59	1982	0	1982	
158	The Elvis Medley	(RCA 476)	51	1985	71	1982	(RCA PB-13351)
159	Jailhouse Rock (Re-Entry)	(RCA 1028)	27	1983	0	1983	
! 160	I Was The One (Re-Issue)		0	1983	92	1983	(RCA PB-13500)
! 161	Wear My Ring Around Your Neck (Re-Issue)		0	1983	92	1983	(RCA PB-13500)
162	Baby I Don't Care	(RCA 332)	61	1983	0	1983	
163	I Can Help	(RCA 369)	30	1983	0	1983	
164	The Last Farewell	(RCA 459)	48	1984	0	1984	
165	Always On My Mind	(RCA PB 49944)	59	1985	0	1985	
166	Ain't That Lovin' You Baby / Bossa Nova Baby	(RCA ARON 1)	47	1987	0	1987	
167	Love Me Tender / If I Can Dream (Re-Issue)	(RCA ARON 2)	56	1987	0	1987	
168	Stuck On You (Re-Issue)	(RCA PB 49595)	58	1988	0	1988	
169	Are You Lonesome Tonight (Live) (Re-Issue)	(RCA PB 49177)	68	1991	0	1991	
170	Don't Be Cruel (Re-Issue)	(RCA 74321110777)	42	1992	0	1992	
171	Heartbreak Hotel / I Was The One (Re-Issue)	(RCA 74321336862)	45	1996	0	1996	
172	The Twelfth Of Never	(RCA 74321320122)	21	1995	0	1995	
173	Always On My Mind (Re-Issue)	(RCA 74321485412)	13	1997	0	1997	
	OBITUARY: D: 16 AUG 1977 IN MEMPHIS FROM HEART FAILURE, HIS TWIN BROTHER JESSE GARON D: 8 JAN 1935 AT BIRTH						

Emerson, Lake & Palmer Male Instrumental Group from the UK

	TITLE	UK LBL	UK POS	UK YEAR	US POS	US YEAR	US LBL
1	From The Beginning		0	1972	39	1972	(COTILLION 44158)
2	Fanfare For The Common Man	(Atlantic K 10946)	2	1977	0	1977	
	NAMES KEITH EMERSON, GREG LAKE & CARL PALMER, DISBANDED IN 1979 SEE ALSO GREG LAKE						

EMF Male Vocal/Instrumental Group from the UK   The Group's Initials Stand For Epson Mad Funkers

	TITLE	UK LBL	UK POS	UK YEAR	US POS	US YEAR	US LBL
* 1	Unbelievable	(Parlophone R 6273)	3	1990	1	1991	(EMI 50350)
2	I Believe	(Parlophone R 6279)	6	1991	0	1991	
3	Children	(Parlophone R 6288)	19	1991	0	1991	
4	Lies	(Parlophone R 6295)	28	1991	18	1991	(EMI 50363)
5	Unexplained (EP)	(Parlophone SGE 2026)	18	1992	0	1992	
6	They're Here	(Parlophone R 6321)	29	1992	0	1992	
7	It's You	(Parlophone R6327)	23	1992	0	1992	
8	Perfect Day	(EMI CDR 6401)	27	1995	0	1995	
9	I'm A Believer	(EMI CDR 6412)	3	1995	0	1995	
10	Afro King	(Parlophone CDR 6416)	51	1995	0	1995	
	NAMES: JAMES ATKIN, IAN DENCH, MARK DECLOEDT & DERRY BROWNSON • HIT 9 IS CREDITED TO EMF AND REEVES & MORTIMER						

Emile Cote Serenaders Vocal Group from the USA

	TITLE	UK LBL	UK POS	UK YEAR	US POS	US YEAR	US LBL
1	Tea Leaves		0	1948	22	1948	(Columbia 38230)

Emile Ford & The Checkmates Male Vocalist, B: 16 Oct 1937 Nassau, Bahamas

	TITLE	UK LBL	UK POS	UK YEAR	US POS	US YEAR	US LBL
* 1	What Do You Want To Make Those Eyes At Me For	(PYE 7N 15225)	1	1959	0	1959	
2	On A Slow Boat To China	(PYE 7N 15245)	3	1960	0	1960	
3	You'll Never Know What Your Missing	(PYE 7N 15268)	12	1960	0	1960	
4	Them There Eyes	(PYE 7N 15282)	18	1960	0	1960	
5	Counting Tear Drops	(PYE 7N 15314)	4	1960	0	1960	
6	What Am I Gonna' Do	(PYE 7N 15331)	33	1961	0	1961	
7	Half Of My Heart	(PICCADILLY 7N 35003)	50	1961	0	1961	
8	Half Of My Heart (Re-Entry)	(PICCADILLY 7N 35003)	42	1961	0	1961	
9	I Wonder Who's Kissing Her Now	(PICCADILLY 7N 35033)	43	1962	0	1962	
	HITS 4, 7, 8 ARE CREDITED TO EMILE FORD • THE CHECKMATES ARE A MALE VOCAL/INSTRUMENTAL GROUP FROM THE UK						

Emilio Pericoli Male Vocalist, B: 1928 Cesenatico, Italy

	TITLE	UK LBL	UK POS	UK YEAR	US POS	US YEAR	US LBL
* 1	Al Di La'	(Warner Bros. WB 69)	30	1962	6	1961	(Warner Bros. 5259)

Emma Female Vocalist from the UK

	TITLE	UK LBL	UK POS	UK YEAR	US POS	US YEAR	US LBL
1	Give A Little Love Back To The World	(BIG WAVE BWR 33)	33	1990	0	1990	

Emmylou Harris Female Vocalist, B: 2 Apr 1947 Birmingham, Alabama

	TITLE	UK LBL	UK POS	UK YEAR	US POS	US YEAR	US LBL
! 1	Too Far Gone		0	1975	73	1975	(Reprise 1326)
2	If I Could Only Win Your Love		0	1975	58	1975	(Reprise 1332)
! 3	Light Of The Stable		0	1975	99	1975	(Reprise 1341)
! 4	The Sweetest Gift		0	1976	12	1976	(Asylum 45294)
5	Here There And Everywhere	(RCA 74321110777)	30	1976	65	1976	(Reprise 1346)
! 6	Together Again		0	1976	1	1976	(Reprise 1346)
! 7	One Of These Days		0	1976	3	1976	(Reprise 1353)

ISSUE	TITLE	UK LBL	UK POS	UK YEAR	US POS	US YEAR	US LBL
! 8	Sweet Dreams		0	1976	1	1976	(Reprise 1371)
! 9	(You Never Can Tell) C'est La Vie		0	1977	6	1977	(Warner Bros. 8329)
! 10	Making Believe		0	1977	8	1977	(Warner Bros. 8388)
! 11	To Daddy		0	1977	3	1977	(Warner Bros. 8495)
! 12	Two More Bottles Of Wine		0	1978	1	1978	(Warner Bros. 8553)
! 13	Easy From Now On		0	1978	12	1978	(Warner Bros. 8623)
! 14	Too Far Gone (Re-Recording)		0	1979	13	1979	(Warner Bros. 8732)
! 15	Play Together Again Again		0	1979	11	1979	(Warner Bros. 8830)
! 16	Save The Last Dance For Me		0	1979	4	1979	(Warner Bros. 8815)
! 17	Love Don't Care		0	1979	91	1979	(Little Darlin' 7922)
! 18	Blue Kentucky Girl		0	1979	6	1979	(Warner Bros. 49056)
! 19	Beneath Still Waters		0	1980	1	1980	(Warner Bros. 49164)
! 20	Wayfaring Stranger		0	1980	7	1980	(Warner Bros. 49239)
21	That Lovin' You Feelin' Again		0	1980	55	1980	(Warner Bros. 49262)
! 22	The Boxer		0	1980	13	1980	(Warner Bros. 49551)
23	Mister Sandman		0	1981	37	1981	(Warner Bros. 49684)

ALL THE REST ARE C/W HITS HIT 2 REACHED NUMBER 4 IN THE USA C/W CHARTS • HIT 3 WITH DOLLY PARTON, LINDA RONSTADT WITH BACKING VOCALS FROM NEIL YOUNG • HIT 4 IS CREDITED TO LINDA RONSTADT AND EMMYLOU HARRIS • HIT 11 REACHED NUMBER 102 IN THE USA NATIONAL CHARTS
HIT 15 IS CREDITED TO BUCK OWENS AND EMMYLOU HARRIS • HIT 17 IS CREDITED TO CHARLIE LOUVIN AND EMMYLOU HARRIS

Emotions Female Vocal Trio from Chicago   Names Wanda, Sheila And Jeanette Hutchinson

1	So I Can Love You		0	1969	39	1969	(VOLT 4010)
2	Best Of My Love	(CBS 5555)	4	1977	1	1977	(Columbia 10544)
3	I Don't Wanna Lose Your Love	(CBS 5819)	40	1977	0	1977	
4	Boogie Wonderland	(CBS 7292)	4	1979	6	1979	(ARC 10956)

HIT 4 IS CREDITED TO EARTH, WIND & FIRE WITH THE EMOTIONS

Empirion Male Instrumental/Production Group from the UK

1	Narcotic Influence	(XL RECORDINGSXLS 72CD)	64	1996	0	1996	
2	Beta	(XL RECORDINGSXLS 77CD)	75	1997	0	1997	

En Vogue Female Vocal Quartet, Names Dawn Robinson, Terry Ellis, Cindy Herron & Maxine Jones

* 1	Hold On	(East West America 7908)	5	1990	2	1990	(Atlantic 87984)
2	Lies	(East West America 7893)	44	1990	38	1990	(Atlantic 87893)
* 3	My Lovin' (You're Never Gonna Get It)	(East West America A 8578)	69	1992	2	1992	(East West 98586)
4	My Lovin' (Re-Entry)	(East West America A 8578)	4	1992	0	1992	
5	Give Him Something He Can Feel / Free Your Mind	(East West America A 8524)	44	1992	6	1992	(East West 98560)
6	Give Him Something He Can Feel / Free Your Mind (Re-Issue)	(E/W AM A 8524)	16	1992	0	1992	
7	Give It Up, Turn It Loose	(East West America A 8445CD)	22	1993	15	1992	(EASTWEST 98455)
8	Love Don't Love You	(East West America 8424CD)	64	1993	36	1993	(EASTWEST 98432)
9	Runaway Love	(East West America A 8359CD)	36	1993	0	1993	
* 10	Whatta Man	(FFRR FCD 222)	7	1994	3	1994	(NEXT PLAT. 857390)
11	Don't Let Go (Love) (From Set It Off)	(East West A 3976CD)	5	1997	2	1996	(EASTWEST 64231)
12	Whatever	(East West E 3642CD)	14	1997	0	1997	
13	Too Gone, Too Long	(East West E 3908CD)	20	1997	0	1997	

HIT 10 IS CREDITED TO SALT-N-PEPA WITH EN VOGUE • HIT 'FREE YOUR MIND' WAS RELEASED SEPERATELY IN THE USA AND REACHED NO.8 IN 1992 ON EASTWEST 98487.

Enchantment Quintet Formed In 1966 from Detroit

1	Gloria		0	1977	25	1977	(United Artists912)
2	It's You That I Need		0	1978	33	1978	(Roadshow 1124)

Energise Male Vocal/Instrumental Group from the UK

1	Report To The Dance Floor	(NETWORK NWKT16)	69	1991	0	1991	

Energy Orchard Male Vocal/Instrumental Group from Ireland

1	Belfast	(MCA MCA 1392)	52	1990	0	1990	
2	Sailortown	(MCA MCA 1402)	73	1990	0	1990	

Engelbert Humperdinck Male Vocalist, Real Name Arnold George Dorsey B: 2 May 1936 In Madras, India Name Is Taken From A Famous German Opera Composer

* 1	Release Me	(Decca F 12541)	1	1967	4	1967	(Parrot40011)
* 2	There Goes My Everything	(Decca F 12610)	2	1967	20	1967	(Parrot40015)
* 3	The Last Waltz	(Decca F 12655)	1	1967	25	1967	(Parrot40019)
4	Am I That Easy To Forget	(Decca F 12722)	3	1968	18	1968	(Parrot40023)
5	A Man Without Love	(Decca F 12770)	2	1968	19	1968	(Parrot40027)
6	Les Bicyclettes De Belsize	(Decca F 12834)	5	1968	31	1968	(Parrot40032)
7	The Way It used To Be	(Decca F 12879)	3	1969	0	1969	
8	I'm A Better Man	(Decca F 12957)	15	1969	38	1969	(Parrot40040)
9	Winter World Of Love	(Decca F 12980)	7	1969	16	1970	(Parrot40044)

ISSUE	TITLE	UK LBL	UK POS	UK YEAR	US POS	US YEAR	US LBL
10	My Marie	(Decca F 13032)	31	1970	0	1970	
11	Sweetheart	(Decca F 13068)	22	1970	0	1970	
12	Sweetheart (Re-Entry)	(Decca F 13068)	50	1970	0	1970	
13	Another Time Another Place	(Decca F 13212)	13	1971	0	1971	
14	Too Beautiful To Last	(Decca F 13281)	14	1972	0	1972	
15	Love Is All	(Decca F 13443)	44	1973	0	1973	
16	Love Is All (Re-Entry)	(Decca F 13443)	45	1973	0	1973	
* 17	After The Lovin'		0	1976	8	1976	(Epic 50270)
18	Goodbye My Friend		0	1977	97	1977	(Epic 50365)
19	This Moment In Time		0	1979	58	1979	(Epic 50632)
20	Til You And Your Lover Are Lovers Again		0	1983	77	1983	(Epic 03817)

England Dan & John Ford Coley Male Vocal Duo from the USA Names Dan Seals B: 8 Feb 1948, John Ford Coley B: 12 Oct 1948

* 1	I'd Really Love To See You Tonight	(Atlantic K 10810)	26	1976	2	1976	(Big Tree 16069)
2	Nights Are Forever Without You		0	1976	10	1976	(Big Tree 16079)
3	It's Sad To Belong		0	1977	21	1977	(Big Tree 16088)
4	Gone Too Far		0	1977	23	1977	(Big Tree 16102)
5	We'll Never Have To Say Goodbye Again		0	1978	9	1978	(Big Tree 16110)
6	Love Is The Answer	(Big Tree K 11296)	45	1979	10	1979	(Big Tree 16131)

England Sisters Female Vocal Group from the UK

1	Heartbeat	(HMV POP 710)	33	1960	0	1960	

England World Cup Squad Male Vocal Soccer Team from the UK

1	Back Home	(PYE 7N 17920)	1	1970	0	1970	
2	Back Home (Re-Entry)	(PYE 7N 17920)	46	1970	0	1970	
3	This Time (We'll Get It Right)	(ENGLAND ER 1)	2	1982	0	1982	
4	We've Got The Whole World At Our Feet	(Columbia DB 9128)	66	1986	0	1986	
5	All The Way	(MCA GOAL 1)	64	1988	0	1988	
6	World In Motion	(Factory/MCA FAC 2937)	1	1990	0	1990	

HIT 5 IS CREDITED TO ENGLAND FOOTBALL TEAM & THE 'SOUND' OF STOCK, AITKEN & WATERMAN • HIT 6 IS CREDITED TO ENGLANDNEWORDER

Englandneworder See New Order

Enigma (1) Michael Cretu Is Enigma, B: 18 May 1957 Bucharest

* 1	Sadness (Part 1)	(Virgin INTER DINS 101)	1	1990	5	1991	(Charisma 98864)
2	Mea Culpa Part II	(Virgin INTER DINS 104)	55	1991	0	1991	
3	Principles Of Lust	(Virgin INTER DINS 110)	59	1991	0	1991	
4	The Rivers Of Belief	(Virgin INTER DINS 112)	68	1992	0	1992	
* 5	Return To Innocence	(Virgin INTER DINSD 123)	3	1994	4	1994	(Charisma 38423)
6	The Eyes Of Truth	(Virgin INTER DINSD 126)	21	1994	0	1994	
7	Age Of Loneliness	(Virgin INTER DINSD 135)	21	1994	0	1994	
8	Beyond The Invisible	(Virgin DINSD 155)	26	1997	81	1996	(Virgin 38572)
9	Tnt For The Brain	(Virgin DINSD 161)	60	1997	0	1997	

Enigma (2) Male Vocal/Instrumental Group from the UK

1	Ain't No Stoppin'	(Creole CR 9)	11	1981	0	1981	
2	I Love Music	(Creole CR 14)	25	1981	0	1981	

Ennio Morricone Orchestra from Italy

1	Chi Mai (Theme From The Life And Times Of David Lloyd George)	(BBC 92)	2	1981	0	1981	

Enrico Caruso Male Opera Singer, B: 25 Feb 1873 Naples

* 1	Pagliacci - Vesti La Ciubba (On With The Play)		0	1904	2	1904	(Victor 81032)

OBITUARY: D: 2 AUG 1921 IN NAPLES.

Enya Female Vocalist, Real Name Eithne Ni Bhraonain B: Donegal, Ireland   Former Member Of Clannad

1	Orinoco Flow (Sail Away)	(WEA YZ 312)	1	1988	24	1988	(Geffen 27633)
2	Evening Falls	(WEA YZ 356)	20	1988	0	1988	
3	Storms In Africa (Part 11)	(WEA YZ 368)	41	1989	0	1989	
4	Caribbean Blue	(WEA YZ 604)	13	1991	0	1991	
5	How Can I Keep From Singing	(WEA YZ 365)	32	1991	0	1991	
6	Book Of Days	(WEA YZ 640)	10	1992	0	1992	
7	The Celts	(WEA YZ 705)	29	1992	0	1992	
8	Anywhere Is	(WEA WEA 023CD)	7	1995	0	1995	
9	On My Way Home	(WEA WEA 047CD)	26	1996	0	1996	

Eon Real Name Ian Bela Male Producer from the UK

1	Fear: The Mindkiller	(Vinyl Solution Storm 33)	63	1991	0	1991	

ISSUE · TITLE	UK LBL	UK POS	UK YEAR	US POS	US YEAR	US LBL
Equals Male Vocal/Instrumental Group from the UK/Guyana		Lead Singer Eddy Grant				
1 I Get So Excited	(President PT 180)	44	1968	0	1968	
* 2 Baby Come Back	(President PT 135)	50	1968	32	1968	(RCA 9583)
3 Baby Come Back (Re-Entry)	(President PT 135)	1	1968	0	1968	
4 Laurel And Hardy	(President PT 200)	35	1968	0	1968	
5 Softly Softly	(President PT 222)	48	1968	0	1968	
6 Michael And The Slipper Tree	(President PT 240)	24	1969	0	1969	
7 Viva Bobby Joe	(President PT 260)	6	1969	0	1969	
8 Rub A Dub Dub	(President PT 275)	34	1969	0	1969	
9 Black Skin Blue Eyed Boy	(President PT 325)	9	1970	0	1970	
Erasure Male Vocal/Instrumental Duo, Vince Clark And Andy Bell from the UK						
1 Who Needs Love (Like That)	(Mute Mute 40)	55	1985	0	1985	
2 Sometimes	(Mute Mute 51)	2	1986	0	1986	
3 It Doesn't Have To Be	(Mute Mute 56)	12	1987	0	1987	
4 Victim Of Love	(Mute Mute 61)	7	1987	0	1987	
5 The Circus	(Mute Mute 66)	6	1987	0	1987	
6 Ship Of Fools	(Mute Mute 74)	6	1988	0	1988	
7 Chains Of Love	(Mute Mute 83)	11	1988	12	1988	(SIRE 278449
8 A Little Respect	(Mute Mute 85)	4	1988	14	1988	(SIRE 27738)
9 Crackers International (EP)	(Mute Mute 93)	3	1988	0	1988	
10 Drama!	(Mute Mute 89)	4	1989	0	1989	
11 You Surround Me	(Mute Mute 99)	15	1989	0	1989	
12 Blue Savannah	(Mute Mute 109)	3	1990	0	1990	
13 Star	(Mute Mute 111)	11	1990	0	1990	
14 Chorus	(Mute Mute 125)	3	1991	0	1991	
15 Love To Hate You	(Mute Mute 131)	4	1991	0	1991	
16 Am I Right (EP)	(Mute Mute 134)	15	1991	0	1991	
17 Am I Right (EP) (Re-Mix)	(Mute L12Mute 134)	22	1992	0	1992	
18 Breath Of Life	(Mute Mute 142)	8	1992	0	1992	
19 Abba-Esque (EP)	(Mute Mute 144)	1	1992	0	1992	
20 Who Needs Love (Like That) (Re-Mix)	(Mute Mute 150)	10	1992	0	1992	
21 Always	(Mute CDMute 152)	4	1994	0	1994	
22 Run To The Sun	(Mute CDMute 153)	6	1994	0	1994	
23 I Love Saturday	(Mute CDMute 166)	20	1994	0	1994	
24 Stay With Me	(Mute CDMute 174)	15	1995	0	1995	
25 Fingers And Thumbs (Cold Summer's Day)	(Mute CDMute 178)	20	1995	0	1995	
26 In My Arms	(Mute CDMute 190)	13	1997	55	1997	(Warner Bros. 17371)
27 Don't Say Your Love Is Killing Me	(Mute CDMute 195)	23	1997	0	1997	
Eric & The Good Good Feeling Mixed Vocal/Instrumental Group from the UK						
1 Good Good Feeling	(Equinox EQN 1)	73	1989	0	1989	
Eric B & Rakim Make Vocal/Instrumental Duo from the USA						
1 Paid In Full	(Fourth & BroadwayBRW 78)	15	1987	0	1987	
2 Move The Crowd	(Fourth & BroadwayBRW 88)	53	1988	0	1988	
3 I Know You Got Soul	(Cooltempo COOL 146)	13	1988	0	1988	
4 Fullow The Leader	(MCA 1256)	21	1988	0	1988	
5 The Microphone Fiend	(MCA 1300)	74	1988	0	1988	
6 Friends	(MCA 1352)	21	1989	9	1989	
Hit 6 Is Credited To Jody Watley With Eric B & Rakim						
Eric Carmen Male Vocalist B: 11 Aug 1949 Cleveland, Ohio		Lead Singer Of The Raspberries 1970-1974				
* 1 All By Myself	(Arista 42)	12	1976	2	1975	(Arista 0165)
2 Never Gonna Fall In Love Again		0	1976	11	1976	(Arista 0184)
3 Sunrise		0	1976	34	1976	(Arista 0200)
4 She Did It		0	1977	23	1977	(Arista 0266)
6 I Wanna Hear It From Your Lips		0	1985	35	1985	(Geffen 29118)
7 Hungry Eyes (From Dirty Dancing)		0	1988	4	1988	(RCA 5315)
8 Make Me Lose Control		0	1988	3	1988	(Arista 9686)
Eric Clapton Male Vocal/Instrumentalist B: 30 Mar 1945 Ripley, Surrey, England						
1 Comin' Home	(Atlantic 584 308)	16	1969	0	1969	
2 After Midnight		0	1970	18	1970	(ATCO 6784)
3 Layla		0	1971	51	1971	(ATCO 6809)
4 Layla (USA Re-Issue)	(Polydor 2058 130)	7	1972	10	1972	(ATCO 6809)
* 5 I Shot The Sheriff	(RSO 2090 132)	9	1974	1	1974	(RSO 409)

ISSUE	TITLE	UK LBL	UK POS	UK YEAR	US POS	US YEAR	US LBL
6	Willie And The Hand Jive		0	1974	26	1974	(RSO 503)
7	Swing Low Sweet Chariot	(RSO 2090 158)	19	1975	0	1975	
8	Knockin' On Heavens Door	(RSO 2090 166)	38	1975	0	1975	
9	Hello Old Friend		0	1976	24	1976	(RSO 861)
10	Lay Down Sally	(RSO 2090 264)	39	1977	3	1978	(RSO 886)
11	Wonderful Tonight		0	1978	16	1978	(RSO 895)
12	Promises	(RSO 21)	37	1978	9	1978	(RSO 910)
13	Watch Out For Lucy		0	1979	40	1979	(RSO 910)
14	Tulsa Time		0	1980	30	1980	(RSO 1039)
15	Cocaine		0	1980	30	1980	(RSO 1039)
16	I Can't Stand It		0	1981	10	1981	(RSO 1060)
17	Layla (Re-Issue)	(RSO 87)	4	1982	0	1982	
18	I Shot The Sheriff (Re-Issue)	(RSO 88)	64	1982	0	1982	
19	I've Got A Rock N' Roll Heart		0	1983	18	1983	(Duck29780)
20	The Shape You're In	(DuckW 9701)	75	1983	0	1983	
21	Forever Man	(Warner Bros. W 9069)	51	1985	26	1985	(Duck29081)
22	Edge Of Darkness	(BBC RESL 178)	65	1986	0	1986	
23	Behind The Mask	(DuckW 8461)	15	1987	0	1987	
24	Tearing Us Apart	(DuckW 8299)	56	1987	0	1987	
25	Bad Love	(DuckW 2644)	25	1990	0	1990	
26	No Alibis	(DuckW 9981)	53	1990	0	1990	
27	Wonderful Tonight (Live)	(DuckW 0069)	30	1991	0	1991	
* 28	Tears In Heaven	(Reprise W 0081)	50	1992	2	1992	(Reprise 19038)
29	Tears In Heaven (Re-Entry)	(Reprise W 0081)	5	1992	0	1992	
30	Runaway Train	(Rocket EJS 29)	31	1992	0	1992	
31	It's Probably Me	(A&M AM 883)	30	1992	0	1992	
32	Layla (Acoustic)	(DuckW 0134)	45	1992	12	1992	(Duck18787)
33	Motherless Child	(DuckW 0271CD)	63	1994	0	1994	
34	Love Can Build A Bridge	(London COCD 1)	1	1995	0	1995	
35	Change The World (From *Phenomenon*)	(Reprise W 0358CD)	18	1996	5	1996	(Reprise 17621)

SEE ALSO YARDBIRDS, CREAM

Eric Gable Male Vocalist from the USA

1	Process Of Elimination	(Epic 6602282)	63	1994	0	1994	

Eric Idle (Featuring) Richard Wilson Male Actor/Vocal Duo from the UK

1	One Foot In The Grave	(VICTA CDVICTA 1)	50	1994	0	1994	

Eric Weissberg & Steve Mandell Male Instrumental Duo from the USA

* 1	Dueling Banjos	(Warner Bros. K 16223)	17	1973	2	1973	(Warner Bros. 7659)
! 2	Yakety Yak		0	1975	91	1975	(Epic 50072)

HIT 2 CREDITED TO ERIC WEISSBERG & DELIVERANCE • ERIC PLAYED THE BANJO WITH STEVE ON GUITAR
HIT 1 ORIGINALLY WRITTEN IN 1955 BY ARTHUR SMITH & DON RENO AS FEUDIN' BANJOS

Erick 'More' Morillo Presents Raw Mixed Vocal/Instrumental Duo from the USA

1	Higher (Feel It)	(A&M 5809412)	74	1995	0	1995	

Erik Female Vocalist from the UK

1	Looks Like I'm In Love Again	(PWL Sanctury PWCD 252)	46	1993	0	1993	
2	Got To Be Real	(PWL International)	43	1994	0	1994	
3	We've Got The Love	(PWL International PWCD 305)	55	1994	0	1994	

HIT 1 IS CREDITED TO KEY WEST FEATURING ERIK

Erma Franklin Female Vocalist from the USA

1	(Take A Little) Piece Of My Heart	(Epic 6583847)	9	1992	0	1992	

Ernest Tubb Male C/W Vocalist, B: 9 Feb 1914 Near Crisp, Texas

* 1	Walkin' The Floor Over You		0	1941	23	1941	(Decca 5958)
17	Forever Is Ending Today		0	1948	30	1948	(Decca 46134
23	I'm Bitin' My Fingernails And Thinking Of You		0	1949	30	1949	(Decca 24592)
26	Slippin' Around		0	1949	17	1949	(Decca 46173)
30	Blue Christmas		0	1949	21	1949	(Decca 46186)
* 40	Goodnight Irene		0	1950	10	1950	(Decca 46255)
54	I'll Miss You When You Go		0	1953	22	1953	(Decca 28550)
55	Counterfeit Kisses		0	1953	25	1953	(Decca 28869)

OTHERS WERE C/W HITS HIT 23 IS CREDITED TO ANDREW SISTERS AND ERNEST TUBB WITH THE TEXAS TROUBADORS
HIT 40 CREDITED TO ERNEST TUBB AND RED FOLE • OBITUARY: D: 6 SEP 1984, EMPHYSEMA (AGED 70).

Ernest Van (Pop) Stoneman Male Vocalist, B: 25 May 1893 Iron Ridge, Carroll County, Virginia

* 1	The Sinking Of The *Titanic*		0	1924	0	1924	

OBITUARY: D: 14 JUN 1968.

ISSUE	TITLE	UK LBL	UK POS	UK YEAR	US POS	US YEAR	US LBL

Ernie See Jim Henson

Ernie Fields Orchestra Male Trombonist/Pianist/Orchestra Leader, B: 26 Aug 1905 Texas

	1	In The Mood	(London HL 8985)	13	1959	4	1959	(Rendezvous 110)

Ernie Freeman Male Producer/Pianist, B: 16 Aug 1922 Cleveland

	1	Raunchy		0	1957	4	1957	(Imperial 5474)

Obituary : D: 16 May 1981 Heart Attack.

Ernie K-Doe Male Vocalist, Real Name Ernest Kador Jr. B: 22 Feb 1936 In New Orleans   With The Group The Blue Diamonds In The Mid-50s

	1	Mother-In-Law	(London HLU 9330)	29	1961	1	1961	(MINIT 623)
	2	Te, Ta, Te, Ta, Ta		0	1961	53	1961	(MINIT 627)

Ernie Maresca Male Singer/Songwriter, B: 21 Apr 1939 Bronx

	1	Shout Shout (Knock Yourself Out)		0	1962	6	1962	(Seville 117)

Erotic Drum Band Mixed Vocal/Instrumental Group From The Canada

	1	Love Disco Style	(SCOPE SC 1)	47	1979	0	1979	

Errol Brown Male Vocalist from the UK

	1	Personel Touch	(WEA YZ 130)	25	1987	0	1987	
	2	Body Rockin'	(WEA YZ 162)	51	1987	0	1987	

Erroll Dunkley Male Vocalist From Jamaica

	1	O.K. Fred	(SCOPE SC 6)	11	1979	0	1979	
	2	Sit Down And Cry	(SCOPE SC 11)	52	1980	0	1980	

Erroll Garner Trio Male Jazz Instrumentalist (Piano) from the USA

	1	Misty		0	1954	30	1954	(Mercury 70442)

Erskine Hawkins Orchestra Male Bandleader/Composer/Instrumentalist (trumpet) from the USA

	16	Gabriel's Heater		0	1948	28	1948	(RCA Victor 2836)

Eruption Mixed Vocal/Instrumental Group from the USA

	1	I Can't Stand The Rain	(Atlantic K 11068)	5	1978	18	1978	(ARIOLA 7686)
	2	One Way Ticket	(Atlantic/HANSA K 11266)	9	1979	0	1979	

HIT 1 IS CREDITED TO ERUPTION FEATURING PRECIOUS WILSON

Escape Club Names Trevor Steel, John Holliday, Johnnie Christo & Milan Zekavica

*	1	Wild, Wild West		0	1988	1	1988	(Atlantic 89048)
	2	Shake For The Sheik		0	1989	28	1989	(Atlantic 88983)
*	3	I'll Be There		0	1991	8	1991	(Atlantic 87683)

Escorts Male Vocal/Instrumental Group from the UK

	1	The One To Cry	(Fontana TF 474)	49	1964	0	1964	

Escrima Male Producer Paul Newman from the UK

	1	Train Of Thought	(FFRREEDOM TABCD 225)	36	1995	0	1995	
	2	Deeper	(HOOJ CHOONS TABCD 236)	27	1995	0	1995	

Eskimos & Egypt Male Vocal/Instrumental Group from the UK

	1	Fall From Grace	(One Little Indian EEF 96CD)	51	1993	0	1993	
	2	UK-USA	(One Little Indian99 TP7CD)	52	1993	0	1993	

Espiritu Mixed Vocal/Instrumental Duo from the UK/Trance

	1	Conquistador	(Heavenly HVN 28CD)	47	1993	0	1993	
	2	Los Americanos	(Heavenly HVN 33CD)	45	1993	0	1993	
	3	Bonita Manana	(Columbia 6606925)	50	1994	0	1994	
	4	Always Something There To Remind Me	(East West YZ 911CD)	14	1995	0	1995	

HIT 4 IS CREDITED TO TIN TIN OUT FEATURING ESPIRITU

Esquires Soul Quintet Formed In 1957

	1	Get On Up		0	1967	11	1967	(Bunky 7750)
	2	And Get Away		0	1967	22	1967	(Bunky 7752)

Essex Mixed Vocal Group from the USA   Names Anita Humes, Walter Vickers, Rodney Taylor, Billie Hill, & Rudolph Johnson

*	1	Easier Said Than Done	(Columbia DB 7077)	41	1963	1	1963	(Roulette 4494)
	2	A Walkin' Miracle		0	1963	12	1963	(Roulette 4515)

Esther & Abi Ofarim Husband And Wife Vocal Duo from Israel   B: Esther Zaled B: 13 Jun 1943, Abraham Reichstadt B: 5 Oct 1939

*	1	Cinderella Rockefella	(Philips BF 1640)	1	1968	68	1968	(Philips)
	2	One More Dance	(Philips BF 1678)	13	1968	0	1968	

Esther Phillips Female Vocalist, Real Name Esther Mae Jones B: 23 Dec 1935 Galveston, Texas

*	1	Release Me		0	1962	8	1962	(Lenox 5555)

ISSUE	TITLE	UK LBL	UK POS	UK YEAR	US POS	US YEAR	US LBL
2	Release Me (Re-Entry)		0	1967	93	1967	(Lenox 5555)
3	What A Difference A Day Makes	(Kudu 925)	6	1975	20	1975	(Kudu 925)

ALSO RECORDED AND TOURED AS LITTLE ESTHER • OBITUARY : D: 8 JUL 1984 LIVER FAILURE.

Esther Williams & Ricardo Montalban Esther B: 8 Aug 1923 Los Angeles, Ricardo B: 25 Nov 1923 Mexico

* 1	Baby, It's Cold Outside		0	1949	0	1949	

Esy Morales & His Latin-American Band Male Bandleader/Instrumentalist (Flute) & Rumba Band from the USA

1	Jungle Fantasy		0	1948	27	1948	(Rainbow 10050)

Eternal Female Vocal Quartet from the UK

1	Stay	(EMI CDEM 283)	4	1993	19	1994	(EMI 58113)
2	Save Our Love	(EMI CDEM 296)	8	1994	0	1994	
3	Just A Step From Heaven	(EMI CDEM 311)	8	1994	0	1994	
4	So Good	(EMI CDEMS 339)	13	1994	0	1994	
5	Oh Baby I	(EMI CDEM 353)	4	1994	0	1994	
6	Crazy	(EMI CDEMX 364)	15	1994	0	1994	
7	Power Of A Woman	(EMI CDEM 396)	5	1995	0	1995	
8	I Am Blessed	(EMI CDEMS 408)	34	1995	0	1995	
9	Good Thing	(EMI CDEM 419)	8	1996	0	1996	
10	Someday	(EMI CDEMS 439)	4	1996	0	1996	
11	Someday (Re-Entry)	(EMI CDEMS 439)	64	1996	0	1996	
12	Secrets	(EMI CDEM 459)	9	1996	0	1996	
13	Don't You Love Me	(EMI CDEMS 465)	3	1997	0	1997	
14	I Wanna Be The Only One	(EMI CDEM 472)	1	1997	0	1997	

HIT 14 IS CREDITED TO ETERNAL FEATURING BEBE WINANS

Ethel Merman Female Actress/Vocalist, Real Name Ethel Zimmerman from the USA

1	How Deep Is The Ocean?		0	1932	14	1932	(Victor 24146)
2	Eadie Was A Lady		0	1933	8	1933	(Brunswick 5456)
3	An Earful Of Music		0	1934	11	1934	(Brunswick 6995)
4	You're The Top		0	1934	4	1934	(Brunswick 7342)
5	I Get A Kick Out Of You		0	1935	12	1935	(Brunswick 7342)
6	Move It Over		0	1943	14	1943	(Victor 1521)
7	They Say It's Wonderful		0	1946	20	1946	(Decca 23586)
8	Dearie		0	1950	12	1950	(Decca 24873)
9	I Said My Pajamas (And Put On My Prayers)		0	1950	20	1950	(Decca 24873)
10	If I Knew You Were Coming' I'd've Baked A Cake		0	1950	15	1950	(Decca 24944)
11	You're Just In Love		0	1951	30	1951	(Decca 27317)
12	Once Upon A Nickel		0	1951	29	1951	(Decca 27506)

HIT 7 IS CREDITED TO ETHEL MERMAN AND RAY MIDDLETON • HIT 11 IS CREDITED TO ETHEL MERMAN AND DICK HAYMES
HIT 12 IS CREDITED TO ETHEL MERMAN AND RAY BOLGER • OBITUARY : D: 15 FEB 1984 (AGED 75).

Ethics Male Producer Patrick Prinz from Holland

1	La Luna (To The Beat Of The Drum)	(Virgin VCRD 5)	13	1995	0	1995	

Ethiopians Male Vocal/Instrumental Group from Jamaica

1	Train To Skaville	(RIO RIO 130)	21	1977	0	1977	

Ethna Campbell Female Vocalist from the UK

1	The Old Rugged Cross	(Philips 6006 475)	33	1975	0	1975	

Etta James Real Name Jamesetta Hawkins B: 25 Jan 1938 Los Angeles

1	All I Could Do Is Cry		0	1960	33	1960	(ARGO 5359)
2	My Dearest Darling		0	1960	34	1960	(ARGO 5368)
3	Trust In Me		0	1961	30	1961	(ARGO 5385)
4	Don't Cry, Baby		0	1961	39	1961	(ARGO 5393)
5	Something's Got A Hold On Me	(ARGO 5409)	0	1962	37	1962	(ARGO 5409)
6	Stop The Wedding		0	1962	34	1962	(ARGO 5418)
7	Pushover		0	1963	25	1963	(ARGO 5437)
8	Tell Mama		0	1967	23	1967	(CADET 5578)
9	Security		0	1968	35	1968	(CADET 5594)
10	I Just Want To Make Love To You	(MCA MCSTD 48003)	5	1996	0	1996	

Etta Jones Jazz Singer, B: 25 Nov 1928 In South Carolina

1	Don't Go To Strangers		0	1960	36	1960	(Prestige180)

Eugene Church & The Fellows Eugene Was B: 23 Jan 1938 Los Angeles A Former Member Of The Cliques

1	Pretty Girls Everywhere		0	1959	36	1959	(Class 235)

BACKING VOCALS ON HIT BY BOBBY DAY • OBITUARY : D: 16 APR 1993 FROM AIDS.

ISSUE	TITLE	UK LBL	UK POS	UK YEAR	US POS	US YEAR	US LBL
Eugene Wilde Male Vocalist from the UK							
1	Gotta Get You Home Tonight	(Fourth & BroadwayBRW 15)	18	1984	0	1984	
2	Personality	(Fourth & BroadwayBRW 18)	34	1985	0	1985	
Eugenie Baird Fomerly A Vocalist With The Tony Pastor Orchestra, from the USA							
1	Fall In Love Too Easily (From *Anchors Aweigh*)		0	1945	20	1945	(Decca 18707)
2	Say Si Si		0	1953	26	1953	(VINROB 3)
	HIT 1 IS CREDITED TO EUGENIE BAIRD WITH MEL TORME'S MEL-TONES						
Eurogroove Mixed Vocal Group from the UK							
1	Move Your Body	(AVEX AVEXCD 4)	29	1995	0	1995	
2	Dive To Paradise	(AVEX AVEXCD 10)	31	1995	0	1995	
3	It's On You (Scan Me)	(AVEX AVEXCD 17)	25	1995	0	1995	
4	Move Your Body (Re-Mix)	(AVEX AVEXCD 22)	44	1996	0	1996	
Europe Male Vocal/Instrumental Group from Sweden Names: Joey Tempest, Kee Marcello, John Leven, Mic Michaeli & Ian Haugland							
1	The Final Countdown	(Epic A 7127)	1	1986	8	1987	(Epic 06416)
2	Rock The Night	(Epic EUR 1)	12	1987	30	1987	(Epic 07091)
3	Carrie	(Epic EUR 2)	22	1987	3	1987	(Epic 07292)
4	Superstitious	(Epic EUR 3)	34	1988	31	1988	(Epic 07979)
5	I'll Cry For You	(Epic 6576977)	28	1992	0	1992	
6	Halfway To Heaven	(Epic 6578517)	42	1992	0	1992	
Eurythmics Vocal/Instrumental Duo, Names: Annie Lennox & David Stewart from the UK							
1	Never Gonna Cry Again	(RCA 68)	63	1981	0	1981	
2	Love Is A Stranger	(RCA DA 1)	54	1982	0	1982	
* 3	Sweet Dreams (Are Made Of This)	(RCA DA 2)	2	1983	1	1983	(RCA 13533)
4	Love Is A Stranger (Re-Entry)	(RCA DA 1)	6	1983	23	1983	(RCA 13618)
5	Who's That Girl?	(RCA DA 3)	3	1983	21	1983	(RCA 13800)
6	Right By Your Side	(RCA DA 4)	10	1983	29	1984	(RCA 13695)
7	Here Comes The Rain Again	(RCA DA 5)	8	1984	4	1984	(RCA 13725)
8	Sexcrime (Nineteen Eighty Four)	(Virgin VS 728)	4	1984	0	1984	
9	Julia	(Virgin VS 734)	44	1985	0	1985	
10	Would I Lie To You?	(RCA PB 40101)	17	1985	5	1985	(RCA 14078)
11	There Must Be An Angel (Playing With My Heart)	(RCA PB 40247)	1	1985	22	1985	(RCA 14160)
12	Sisters Are Doin' It For Themselves	(RCA PB 40339)	9	1985	18	1985	(RCA 14214)
13	It's Alright (Baby's Coming Back)	(RCA PB 40375)	12	1986	0	1986	
14	When Tomorrow Comes	(RCA DA 7)	30	1986	0	1986	
15	Missionary Man	(RCA DA 10)	31	1987	14	1986	(RCA 14414)
16	Thorn In My Side	(RCA DA 8)	5	1986	0	1986	
17	The Miracle Of Love	(RCA DA 9)	23	1986	0	1986	
18	Beethoven (I Love To Listen To)	(RCA DA 11)	25	1987	0	1987	
19	Shame	(RCA DA 14)	41	1987	0	1987	
20	I Need A Man	(RCA DA 15)	26	1988	0	1988	
21	You Have Placed A Chill In My Heart	(RCA DA 16)	16	1988	0	1988	
22	Revival	(RCA DA 17)	26	1989	0	1989	
23	Don't Ask Me Why	(RCA DA 19)	25	1989	40	1989	(Arista 9880)
24	The King And Queen Of America	(RCA DA 20)	29	1990	0	1990	
25	Angel	(RCA DA 21)	23	1990	0	1990	
26	Love Is A Stranger (Re-Issue)	(RCA PB 44265)	46	1991	0	1991	
27	Sweet Dreams Are Made Of This (Re-Mix)	(RCA PB 45031)	48	1991	0	1991	
	HIT 9 IS CREDITED TO EURYTHMICS AND ARETHA FRANKLIN						
Eusebe Mixed Vocal Group from the UK							
1	Summertime Healing	(Mama's Yard CDMAMA 4)	32	1995	0	1995	
Evasions Mixed Vocal/Instrumental Group from the UK							
1	Wikka Wrap	(GROOVE GP 107)	20	1981	0	1981	
Eve Boswell Female Vocalist from Hungary							
1	Pickin' A Chicken	(Parlophone R 4082)	9	1955	0	1955	
2	Pickin' A Chicken (Re-Entry)	(Parlophone R 4082)	16	1956	0	1956	
3	Pickin' A Chicken (2nd Re-Entry)	(Parlophone R 4082)	20	1956	0	1956	
Eve Gallagher Female Vocalist from the ÜK							
1	Love Come Down	(More Protein PROT 6)	61	1990	0	1990	
2	Love Come Down (Re-Entry)	(More Protein PROT 6)	68	1990	0	1990	
3	You Can Have It All	(Cleveland City Imports CLECD13023)	43	1995	0	1995	
4	Love Come Down (Re-Issue)	(Cleveland City Imports CLECDCITY13028)	57	1995	0	1995	

ISSUE	TITLE	UK LBL	UK POS	UK YEAR	US POS	US YEAR	US LBL
5	Heartbreak	(REACT CDREACT 78)	44	1996	0	1996	

HIT 5 IS CREDITED TO MRS. WOOD FEATURING EVE GALLAGHER

Eve Young Female Vocalist from the USA

1	Cuanto La Gusta		0	1948	29	1948	(RCA Victor 3077)
2	My Darling, My Darling		0	1949	26	1929	(RCA Victor 3187)

HIT 1 IS CREDITED TO EVE YOUNG & THE DRUGSTORE COWBOYS • HIT 2 IS CREDITED TO EVE YOUNG AND JACK LATHROP • SEE ALSO KAREN CHANLER

Evelyn 'Champagne' King Female Vocalist, B: 29 Jun 1960 Bronx

* 1	Shame	(RCA PC 1122)	39	1978	9	1978	(RCA 11122)
* 2	I Don't Know If It's Right	(RCA PB 1386)	67	1979	23	1979	(RCA 11386)
3	I'm In Love	(RCA 95)	27	1981	40	1981	(RCA 12243)
4	If You Want My Lovin'	(RCA 131)	43	1981	0	1981	
5	Love Come Down	(RCA 249)	7	1982	17	1982	(RCA 13273)
6	Back To Love	(RCA 287)	40	1982	0	1982	
7	Get Loose	(RCA 315)	45	1983	0	1983	
8	Your Personal Touch	(RCA PB 49915)	37	1985	0	1985	
9	High Horse	(RCA PB 49891)	55	1986	0	1986	
10	Hold On To What You've Got	(Manhattan MT 49)	47	1988	0	1988	
11	Shame (Re-Mix)	(Network NWKTEN 56)	74	1992	0	1992	

HITS 3-7 ARE CREDITED TO EVELYN KING • HIT 11 IS CREDITED TO ALTERN 8 VS EVELYN KING • PREVIOUSLY A CLEANING LADY FOR SIGMA STUDIOS

Evelyn Knight Female Vocalist from Washington D.C.

1	Dance With A Dolly (With A Hole In Her Stocking)		0	1944	6	1944	(Decca 18614)
2	Chickery Chick		0	1945	10	1945	(Decca 18725)
3	Brush Those Tears From Your Eyes		0	1948	9	1948	(Decca 24514)
* 4	A Little Bird Told Me		0	1948	1	1948	(Decca 24514)
5	Buttons And Bows (From *Paleface*)		0	1947	14	1948	(Decca 24489)
6	Powder Your Face With Sunshine		0	1948	1	1948	(Decca 24530)
7	It's Too Late Now		0	1949	22	1949	(Decca 24636)
8	You're So Understanding		0	1949	21	1949	(Decca 24636)
9	Candy And Cake		0	1950	9	1950	(Decca 24943)
10	All Dressed Up To Smile		0	1950	25	1950	(Decca 27103)
11	My Heart Cries For You		0	1951	28	1951	(Decca 27378)

HIT 2 WAS WITH THE THREE JESTERS • HITS 3-6 ARE WITH THE STARDUSTERS • HITS 7, 8 ARE WITH FOUR HITS & A MISS
HIT 10 IS WITH THE RAY CHARLES SINGERS • HIT 11 IS CREDITED TO RED FOLEY AND EVELYN KNIGHT

Evelyn Thomas Female Vocalist from the USA

1	Weak Spot	(20th Century BTC 1014)	26	1976	0	1976	
2	Doomsday	(20th Century BTC 1017)	41	1976	0	1976	
3	Doomsday (Re-Entry)	(20th Century BTC 1017)	45	1976	0	1976	
4	High Energy	(Record Shack Soho 18)	5	1984	0	1984	
5	Masquerade	(Record Shack Soho 25)	60	1984	0	1984	

Everclear Male Vocal/Instrumental Group from the USA

1	Heartspark Dollarsign	(Capitol CDCLS 773)	48	1996	0	1996	
2	Santa Monica (Watch The World Die)	(Capitol CDCL 775)	40	1996	0	1996	

Everly Brothers Male Vocal Duo from the USA

* 1	Bye Bye Love	(London HLA 8440)	6	1957	2	1957	(Cadence 1315)
* 2	Wake Up Little Susie	(London HLA 8498)	2	1957	1	1957	(Cadence 1337)
3	This Little Girl Of Mine		0	1958	26	1958	(Cadence 1342)
* 4	All I Have To Do Is Dream	(London HLA 8618)	1	1958	1	1958	(Cadence 1348)
5	Claudette	(London HLA 8618)	1	1958	30	1958	(Cadence 1348)
* 6	Bird Dog	(London HLA 8685)	2	1958	1	1958	(Cadence 1350)
7	Devoted To You	(London HLA 8685)	2	1958	10	1958	(Cadence 1350)
* 8	Problems	(London HLA 8781)	6	1959	2	1958	(Cadence 1355)
9	Love Of My Life		0	1958	40	1958	(Cadence 1355)
10	Take A Message To Mary	(London HLA 8863)	29	1959	16	1959	(Cadence 1364)
11	Poor Jenny	(London HLA 8863)	14	1959	22	1959	(Cadence 1364)
12	Take A Message To Mary (Re-Entry)	(London HLA 8863)	27	1959	0	1959	
13	Take A Message To Mary (2nd Re-Entry)	(London HLA 8863)	20	1959	0	1959	
14	('Til) I Kissed You	(London HLA 8934)	2	1959	4	1959	(Cadence 1369)
15	Let It Be Me	(London HLA9039)	13	1960	7	1960	(Cadence 1376)
16	Let It Be Me (Re-Entry)	(London HLA 9039)	26	1960	0	1960	
17	Cathy's Clown	(Warner Bros. WB 1)	1	1960	1	1960	(Warner Bros. 5151)
18	When Will I Be Loved	(London HLA 9157)	4	1960	8	1960	(Cadence 1380)
19	Lucille	(Warner Bros. WB 19)	4	1960	21	1960	(Warner Bros. 5163)
20	So Sad (To Watch Good Love Go Bad)	(Warner Bros. WB 19)	4	1960	7	1960	(Warner Bros. 5163)
21	Like Strangers	(London HLA 9250)	11	1960	22	1960	(Cadence 1388)

ISSUE	TITLE	UK LBL	UK POS	UK YEAR	US POS	US YEAR	US LBL
22	Walk Right Back	(Warner Bros. WB 33)	1	1961	7	1961	(Warner Bros. 5199)
23	Ebony Eyes	(Warner Bros. WB 33)	1	1961	8	1961	(Warner Bros. 5199)
24	Temptation	(Warner Bros. WB 42)	1	1961	27	1961	(Warner Bros. 5220)
25	Muskrat / Don't Blame Me	(Warner Bros. WB 50)	20	1961	20	1961	(Warner Bros. 5501/2)
26	Cryin' In The Rain	(Warner Bros. WB 56)	6	1962	6	1962	(Warner Bros. 5250)
27	How Can I Meet Her	(Warner Bros. WB 67)	12	1962	0	1962	
28	Thats Old Fashioned (That's The Way Love Should Be)		0	1962	9	1962	(Warner Bros. 5273)
29	Don't Ask Me To Be Friends		0	1962	48	1962	(Warner Bros. 5297)
30	No One Can Make My Sunshine Smile	(Warner Bros. WB 79)	11	1962	0	1962	
31	So It Always Will Be	(Warner Bros. WB 94)	23	1963	0	1963	
32	It's Been Nice	(Warner Bros. WB 99)	26	1963	0	1963	
33	The Girl Sang The Blues	(Warner Bros. WB 109)	25	1963	0	1963	
34	Gone Gone Gone	(Warner Bros. WB 146)	36	1964	31	1964	(Warner Bros. 5478)
35	Ferris Wheel	(Warner Bros. WB 135)	22	1964	0	1964	
36	That'll Be The Day	(Warner Bros. WB 158)	30	1965	0	1965	
37	The Price Of Love	(Warner Bros. WB 161)	2	1965	0	1965	
38	I'll Never Get Over You	(Warner Bros. WB 5639)	35	1965	0	1965	
39	Love Is Strange	(Warner Bros. WB 5649)	11	1965	0	1965	
40	Bowling Green		0	1967	40	1967	(Warner Bros. 7020)
41	It's My Time	(Warner Bros. WB 7192)	39	1968	0	1968	
42	On The Wings Of A Nightingale	(Mercury MER 880213)	41	1984	50	1984	(Mercury 170)

LSATS HITS WERE C/W • DONALD ISAAC, B: 1 FEB 1937, & PHILIP, B: 19 JAN 1939 • HIT 47 IS CREDITED TO JOHNNY CASH WITH ROSANNE CASH AND THE EVERLY BROTHERS THEIR PARENTS ARE IKE AND MARGARET EVERLY AND ARE WELL-KNOWN COUNTRY SINGERS, THE BOYS WORKED WITH THEM ON LOCAL RADIO SHOWS

Everton F.C. Male Vocal Soccer Team from the UK

1	Here We Go	(Columbia DB 9106)	14	1985	0	1985	
2	All Together Now	(MDMC DEVCS 3)	24	1995	0	1995	

Every Mother's Son Rock Quintet from Greenwich Village, Lead By Dennis & Lary Larden

1	Come On Down To My Boat		0	1967	6	1967	(MGM 13733)

Everything But The Girl Mixed Vocal/Instrumental Duo from the UK

1	Each And Everyone	(Blanco Y Negro NEG 1)	28	1984	0	1984	
2	Mine	(Blanco Y Negro NEG 3)	58	1984	0	1984	
3	Native Land	(Blanco Y Negro NEG 6)	73	1984	0	1984	
4	Come On Home	(Blanco Y Negro NEG 21)	44	1986	0	1986	
5	Don't Leave Me Behind	(Blanco Y Negro NEG 23)	72	1986	0	1986	
6	These Early Days	(Blanco Y Negro NEG 30)	75	1988	0	1988	
7	I Don't To Talk About It	(Blanco Y Negro NEG 34)	3	1988	0	1988	
8	Driving	(Blanco Y Negro NEG 40)	54	1990	0	1990	
9	Covers (EP)	(Blanco Y Negro NEG 54)	13	1992	0	1992	
10	The Only Living Boy In New York (EP)	(Blanco Y Negro NEG 62CD)	42	1993	0	1993	
11	I Didn't Know I Was Looking For Love (EP)	(Blanco Y Negro NEG 64CD)	72	1993	0	1993	
12	Rollercoaster (EP)	(Blanco Y Negro NEG 69CD)	65	1994	0	1994	
13	Missing	(Blanco Y Negro NEG 71CD1)	69	1994	2	1995	(Atlantic 87124)
14	Missing (Re-Mix)	(Blanco Y Negro NEG 84CD)	3	1996	0	1996	
15	Walking Wounded	(Virgin VSCDT 1577)	6	1996	0	1996	
16	Wrong	(Virgin VSCDT 1589)	8	1996	0	1996	
17	Single	(Virgin VSCDT 1600)	20	1996	0	1996	
18	Driving (Re-Mix)	(Blanco Y Negro NEG 99CD1)	36	1996	0	1996	
19	Before Today	(Virgin VSCDT 1624)	25	1997	0	1997	

Evolution Mixed Vocal/Instrumental Group from the UK

1	Love Thing	(Deconstruction 74321134272)	32	1993	0	1993	
2	Everybody Dance	(Deconstruction 74321152012)	19	1993	0	1993	
3	Evolutiondance Part 1 (EP)	(Deconstruction 74321171912)	52	1994	0	1994	
4	Look Up To The Light	(Deconstruction 74321318042)	55	1995	0	1995	
5	Your Love Is Calling	(Deconstruction 74321422872)	60	1996	0	1996	

Ex Pistols Male Vocal/Instrumental Group from the UK

1	Land Of Hope And Glory	(Virginia Pistol 76)	69	1985	0	1985	

Exciters Mixed Vocal Quartet from the USA   Names: Herb Rooney, Brenda Reid, Carol Johnson & Lillian Walker

1	Tell Him	(United Artists UP 1011)	46	1963	4	1962	(United Artists 544)
2	Reaching For The Best	(20th Century BTC 1005)	31	1975	0	1975	

Exeter Bramdean Boy's Choir Male Choir from the UK

1	Remembering Christmas	(Golden Sounds DSCC 1)	46	1993	0	1993	

Exile Male Vocal/Instrumental Group from the USA

1	Kiss You All Over	(RAK 279)	6	1978	1	1978	(Warner Bros. 8589)

ISSUE	TITLE	UK LBL	UK POS	UK YEAR	US POS	US YEAR	US LBL
2	You Thrill Me		0	1979	40	1979	(Warner Bros. 8711)
3	How Could This Go Wrong	(RAK 293)	67	1979	0	1979	
4	Heart And Soul	(RAK 333)	54	1981	0	1981	

HITS 5 UP TO 25 ARE ALL C/W • FORMED IN LEXINGTON, KENTUCKY IN 1963 AS THE EXILES • HIT 10 IS A RE-ISSUE OF A RECORDING FROM 1978

Exoterix   Real Name Duncan Millar Male Producer from the UK

1	Void	(Positiva CDTIV 1)	58	1993	0	1993	
2	Satisfy My Love	(Union UCRCD 26)	62	1994	0	1994	

Exotica (Featuring) Itsy Foster   Mixed Vocal/Instrumental Group from the UK/Italy

1	The Summer Is Magic '95	(Polydor 5798392)	68	1995	0	1995	

Exploited   Male Vocal/Instrumental Group from the UK

1	Dogs Of War	(Secret SHH 110)	63	1981	0	1981	
2	Dead Cities	(Secret SHH 120)	31	1981	0	1981	
3	Don't Let 'Em Grind You Down	(Superville EXP1003)	70	1981	0	1981	
4	Attack	(SEecret SHH 130)	50	1982	0	1982	

HIT 3 IS CREDITED TO EXPLOITED AND ANTI-PASTI

Expose   Female Vocal Trio, Names: Ann Curless, Jeanette Jurado & Gioia Bruno from the USA

1	Come Go With Me		0	1987	5	1987	(Arista 9555)
2	Point Of No Return (Re-Recording)		0	1987	5	1987	(Arista 9579)
3	Let Me Be The One		0	1987	7	1987	(Arista 9617)
4	Seasons Change		0	1988	1	1988	(Arista 9640)
* 5	What You Don't Know		0	1989	8	1989	(Arista 9836)
6	When I Looked At Him		0	1989	10	1989	(Arista 9868)
7	Tell Me Why		0	1990	9	1990	(Arista 9916)
8	You're Baby Never Looked Good In Blue		0	1990	17	1990	(Arista 9916)
9	I Wish The Phone Would Ring		0	1992	9	1992	(Arista 12466)
* 10	I'll Never Get Over You (Getting Over Me)	(Arista 74321158962)	75	1993	8	1993	(Arista 12518)

Express Of Sound   Male Instrumental/Production Group from Italy

1	Real Vibration (Want Love)	(Positiva CDTIV 66)	45	1996	0	1996	

Expressos   Mixed Vocal/Instrumental Group from the UK

1	Hey Girl	(WEA K 18246)	60	1980	0	1980	
2	Tango In Mono	(WEA K 18431)	70	1981	0	1981	

Extreme   Male Vocal/Instrumental Quartet from the USA   Names: Gary Cherone, Nuno Bettencourt, Pat Badger & Paul Geary

1	Get The Funk Out	(A&M AM 737)	19	1991	0	1991	
2	More Than Words	(A&M AM 792)	2	1991	1	1991	(A&M 1552)
3	Decadence Dance	(A&M AM 773)	36	1991	0	1991	
4	Hole Hearted	(A&M AM 839)	12	1991	4	1991	(A&M 1564)
5	Song For Love	(A&M AM 698)	12	1992	0	1992	
6	Rest In Peace	(A&M AM 0055)	13	1992	0	1992	
7	Stop The World	(A&M AM 0096)	22	1992	0	1992	
8	Tragic Comic	(A&M AMCD 0156)	15	1993	0	1993	
9	Hip Today	(A&M 5809932)	44	1995	0	1995	

Eydie Gorme   Female Vocalist, B: 16 Aug 1931 Bronx, New York City

1	Fini		0	1954	19	1954	(Coral 61093)
2	Too Close For Comfort (From Mr. Wonderful)		0	1956	39	1956	(ABC-Paramount 9684)
3	Mama Teach Me To Dance		0	1956	34	1956	(ABC-Paramount 9722)
4	Love Me Forever	(HMV POP 432)	21	1958	24	1957	(ABC-Paramount 9863)
5	You Need Hands		0	1958	11	1958	(ABC-Paramount 9925)
6	Yes My Darling Daughter	(CBS AAG 105)	10	1962	0	1962	
* 7	Blame It On The Bossa Nova	(CBS AAG 131)	32	1963	7	1963	(Columbia 42661)
8	I Want To Stay Here	(CBS AAG 163)	3	1963	28	1963	(Columbia 42815)
9	I Can't Stop Talking About You		0	1964	35	1964	(Columbia 42932)
! 10	Take One Step		0	1973	94	1973	(MGM 14563)

HIT 8 IS CREDITED TO STEVE & EYDIE • RECORDED WITH STEVE LAWRENCE AS PARKER & PENNY 1979

Eye To Eye   Names: Deborah Berg & Julian Marshall

1	Nice Girls		0	1982	37	1982	(Warner Bros. 50050)

Ezio Pinza   Male Vocalist from Italy

* 1	Some Enchanted Evening		0	1949	7	1949	(Columbia 4559)

OBITUARY: D: 9 MAY 1957 (AGED 64).

Ezz Reco & The Launchers With   Male Vocal/Instrumental Group from Jamaica

1	King Of Kings	(Columbia DB 7217)	68	1984	0	1984	

F

ISSUE	TITLE	UK LBL	UK POS	UK YEAR	US POS	US YEAR	US LBL
F L B	See Fat Larry's Band						
F.K.W.	Male Vocal/Instrumental Group from the UK						
1	Never Gonna	(PWL International Pwcd 273)	48	1993	0	1993	
2	Seize The Day	(PWL International Pwcd 279)	45	1993	0	1993	
3	Jingo	(PWL International Pwcd 283)	30	1994	0	1994	
4	This Is The Way	(PWL International Pwcd 307)	63	1994	0	1994	
F.R. David	Male Vocalist From France						
1	Words	(Carrere Car 248)	2	1983	0	1983	
2	Music	(Carrere Car 282)	71	1983	0	1983	
Fab	Male Producers from the UK						
1	Thunderbirds Are Go	(Brothers Organisation Fab 1)	5	1990	0	1990	
2	The Prisoner	(Brothers Organisation Fab 6)	56	1990	0	1990	
	HIT 1 IS CREDITED TO FAB FEATURING MC PARKER HIT 2 IS CREDITED TO FAB FEATURING MC NUMBER 6 • HIT 3 IS CREDITED TO FAB FEATURING AQUA MARINA						
Fabian	Male Vocalist, Real Name Fabiano Forte Bonaparte B: 6 Feb 1943 Phildelphia						
1	I'm A Man		0	1959	31	1959	(Chancellor 1029)
2	Turn Me Loose		0	1959	9	1959	(Chancellor 1033)
* 3	Tiger	Rothers Organisation Fab 2)	0	1959	3	1959	(Chancellor 1037)
* 3	Tiger		0	1959	3	1959	(Chancellor 1037)
4	Come On And Get Me		0	1959	29	1959	(Chancellor 1041)
5	Hound Dog Man	(HMV Pop 695)	46	1960	9	1959	(Chancellor 1044)
6	This Friendly World		0	1959	12	1959	(Chancellor 1044)
7	About This Thing Called Love		0	1960	31	1960	(Chancellor 10479)
8	String Along		0	1960	39	1960	(Chancellor 1047)
Fabulous Thunderbirds	Male R&B Band from Texas 1990 Line-Up Are Kim Wilson, Jimmie & Stevie Vaughan, Preston Hubbard & Fran Christina						
1	Tuff Enuff		0	1986	10	1986	(CBS Assoc. 05838)
Face To Face	Rock Quintet Hails From Boston						
1	10-9-8		0	1984	38	1984	(Epic 04430)
Faces	Male Vocal/Instrumental Group from the UK Former Lead Singers Are Steve Marriott & Rod Stewart, Disbanded 1975						
1	(I Know) I'm Losing You		0	1971	24	1971	(Mercury 73244)
2	Stay With Me	(Warner Bros K 16136)	6	1971	17	1972	(Warner Bros 7545)
3	Cindy Incidentally	(Warner Bros K 16247)	2	1973	0	1973	
4	Pool Hall Richard / I Wish It Would Rain	(Warner Bros K 16341)	8	1973	0	1973	
5	You Can Make Me Dance Sing Or Anything	(Warner Bros K 16494)	12	1974	0	1974	
6	Faces (Ep)	(Riva 8)	41	1977	0	1977	
	HITS 1, 5 ARE CREDITED TO ROD STEWART & THE FACES. • SEE ALSO SMALL FACES						
Factory Of Unlimited Rhythm	Mixed Vocal/Instrumental Group From Jamaica						
1	The Sweetest Surrender	(Kuff Kuffd 6)	59	1996	0	1996	
Facts Of Life	Formed By Millie Jackson And Originally Known As The Gospel Truth						
1	Sometimes		0	1977	31	1977	(Kayvette 5128)
Fair Weather	Male Vocal/Instrumental Group from the UK						
1	Natural Sinner	(RCA 1977)	6	1970	0	1970	
	SEE ALSO ANDY FAIRWEATHER-LOW						
Fairground Attraction	Mixed Vocal/Instrumental Group from the UK						
1	Perfect	(RCA Pb 41845)	1	1988	80	1988	(RCA 8789)
2	Find My Love	(RCA Pb 42079)	7	1988	0	1988	
3	A Smile In A Whisper	(RCA Pb 42249)	75	1988	0	1988	
4	Clare	A Pb 42607)	49	1989	0	1989	
Fairport Convention	Mixed Vocal/Instrumental Group from the UK						
1	Si Tu Dois Partir	(Island Wip 6064	21	1969	0	1969	
2	Si Tu Dois Partir (Re-Entry)	(Island Wip 6064)	49	1969	0	1969	

ISSUE	TITLE	UK LBL	UK POS	UK YEAR	US POS	US YEAR	US LBL
Faith Female R&B Vocalist, Real Name Faith Evans from the USA							
1	You Used To Love Me		0	1995	24	1995	(Bad Boy 79025)
* 2	Soon As I Get Home		0	1995	2	1995	(Bad Boy 79040)
	HIT 2 IS CREDITED TO FAITH EVANS						
Faith Brothers Male Vocal/Instrumental Group from the UK							
1	The Country Of The Blind	(Siren Siren 4)	63	1985	0	1985	
2	A Stranger On Home Ground	(Siren Siren 2)	69	1985	0	1985	
Faith Evans Female Vocalist from the USA							
1	You Used To Love Me	(Arista 74321299812)	42	1995	0	1995	
2	Soon As I Get Home		0	1996	24	1996	
3	Stressed Out	(Jive Jivecd 404)	33	1996	0	1996	
* 4	I'll Be Missing You	(Arista 74321499102)	1	1997	0	1997	
	HIT 4 IS CREDITED TO PUFF DADDY & FAITH EVANS • HIT 3 IS CREDTIED TO A TRIBE CALLED QUEST FEATURING FAITH EVANS & RAPHAEL SAADIQ						
Faith No More Male Vocal/Instrumental Group from the USA							
1	We Care A Lot	(Slash Lash 17)	53	1988	0	1988	
2	Epic	(Slash Lash 21)	37	1990	9	1990	(Slash 19813)
3	From Out Of Nowhere	(Slash Lash 24)	23	1990	0	1990	
4	Falling To Pieces	(Slash Lash 25)	41	1990	0	1990	
5	Epic (Re-Issue)	(Slash Lash 26)	25	1990	0	1990	
6	Midlife Crisis	(Slash Lash 37)	10	1992	0	1992	
7	A Small Victory	(Slash Lash 39)	29	1992	0	1992	
8	A Small Victory (Re-Mix)	(Slash Lash 40)	55	1992	0	1992	
9	Everything's Ruined	Slash Lash 43)	28	1992	0	1992	
10	I'm Easy - Be Aggressive	(Slash Lacdp 44)	3	1993	0	1993	
11	I'm Easy - Be Aggressive (Re-Entry)	(Slash Lacdp 44)	75	1993	0	1993	
12	Another Boy Murdered	(Epic 6597942)	36	1993	0	1993	
13	Digging The Grave	(Slash Lascd 51)	16	1995	0	1995	
14	Ricochet	(Slash Lascd 53)	27	1995	0	1995	
15	Evidence	(Slash Lascd 54)	32	1995	0	1995	
16	Ashes To Ashes	(Slash Lascd 61)	15	1997	0	1997	
17	Last Cup Of Sorrow	(Slash Lascd 62)	51	1997	0	1997	
	HIT 12 IS CREDITED TO FAITH NO MORE AND BOO-YAA T.R.I.B.E. • NAMES: MICHAEL PATTON, JIM MARTIN, RODDY BOTTUM, BILLY GOULD & MIKE BORDIN						
Faith, Hope & Charity (1) Female Vocal Group from the UK							
1	Battle Of The Sexes	(WEA YZ 480)	53	1990	0	1990	
Faith, Hope & Charity (2) Female Vocal Group from the USA							
1	Just One Look	(RCA 2632)	38	1976	0	1976	
Faithless Mixed Vocal/Instrumental Group from the UK							
1	Salva Mea (Save Me)	(Cheeky Chekcd 008)	30	1995	0	1995	
2	Insomnia	(Cheeky Chekcd 010)	27	1995	0	1995	
3	Don't Leave	(Cheeky Chekcd 012)	34	1996	0	1996	
4	Insomnia (Re-Mix)	(Cheeky Chekcd 017)	3	1996	62	1997	(Arista 13332)
5	Salva Mea (Re-Issue)	(Cheeky Chekcd 018)	9	1996	0	1996	
6	Reverence	(Cheeky Chekcd 019)	10	1997	0	1997	
Falco Male Vocalist, Real Name Johann Holzel B: 19 Feb 1957 In Vienna, Austria							
1	Rock Me Amadeus	(A&M Am 278)	1	1986	1	1986	(A&M 2821)
2	Vienna Calling	(A&M Am 318)	10	1986	18	1986	(A&M 2832)
3	Jeanny	(A&M Am 333)	68	1986	0	1986	
4	The Sound Of Musik	(Wea U 8591)	61	1986	0	1986	
Falcons Male R&B Group from the USA							
1	You're So Fine		0	1959	17	1959	(Unart 2013)
2	I Found A Love		0	1962	6 +	1962	(Lupine 1003)
	NAMES EDDIE FLOYD, BONNY RICE, JOE STUBBS, WILLIE SCHOFIELD & LANCE FINNIE • FLOYD WAS REPLACED BY WILSON PICKETT IN 1961						
Fall Real Name Mark E. Smith, Male Vocal/Multi-Instrumentalist from the UK							
1	Mr. Pharmacist	(Beggars Banquet Beg 168)	75	1986	0	1986	
2	Hey! Luciani	(Beggars Banquet Beg 176)	59	1986	0	1986	
3	There's A Ghost In My House	(Beggars Banquet Beg 187)	30	1987	0	1987	
4	Hit The North	(Beggars Banquet Beg 200)	57	1987	0	1987	
5	Victoria	(Beggars Banquet Beg 206)	35	1988	0	1988	
6	Big New Prinz / Jerusalem (Double Single)	(Beggars Banquet Fall 213)	59	1988	0	1988	
7	Telephone Thing	(Cog Sinister Sin 4)	58	1990	0	1990	
8	White Lightning	(Cog Sinister Sin 6)	56	1990	0	1990	
9	Free Range	(Cog Sinister Sins 8)	40	1992	0	1992	
10	Why Are People Grudgeful	(Permanent Cdsperm 9)	43	1993	0	1993	

ISSUE	TITLE	UK LBL	UK POS	UK YEAR	US POS	US YEAR	US LBL
11	Behind The Counter	(Permanent Cdsperm 13)	75	1993	0	1993	
12	15 Ways	(Permanent Cdsperm 14)	65	1994	0	1994	
13	The Chiselers	(Jet Jetscd 500)	60	1996	0	1996	
Family Male Vocal/Instrumental Group from the UK							
1	No Mule's Fool	(Reprise Rs 27001)	29	1969	0	1969	
2	Strange Band	(Reprise Rs 27009)	11	1970	0	1970	
3	In My Own Time	(Reprise K 14090)	4	1971	0	1971	
4	Burlesque	(Reprise K 14196)	13	1972	0	1972	
Family Cat Male Vocal/Instrumental Group from the UK							
1	Airplane Gardens / Atmospheric Road	(Dedicated Fcuk 003cd)	69	1993	0	1993	
2	Wonderful Excuse	(Dedicated 74321208432)	48	1994	0	1994	
3	Golden Book	(Dedicated 74321220072)	42	1994	0	1994	
Family Dogg Mixed Vocal Group from the UK							
1	A Way Of Life	(Bell 1055)	6	1969	0	1969	
Family Foundation Mixed Vocal/Instrumental Group from the UK							
1	Xpress Yourself	(380 Pew 1)	42	1992	0	1992	
Family Stand Mixed Vocal/Instrumental Group from the USA							
1	Ghetto Heaven	(East West A 7997)	10	1990	0	1990	
Fancy Lead Singer Of The Quartet Is Helen Court							
1	Wild Thing		0	1974	14	1974	(Big Tree 15004)
2	Touch Me		0	1974	19	1974	(Big Tree 16026)
Fanny Names Jean & June Millington, Nickey Barclay & Alice Debuhr							
1	Charity Ball		0	1971	40	1971	(Reprise 1033)
2	Butter Boy		0	1975	29	1975	(Casablanca 814)
Fantastic Four Male Vocal Group from the USA							
1	B.Y.O.F. (Bring Your Own Funk)	(Atlantic LV 14)	62	1979	0	1979	
Fantastic Johnny C Real Name Johnny Corley B: 28 Apr 1943, South Carolina							
1	Boogaloo Down Broadway		0	1967	7	1967	(Phil-L.A. 305)
2	Hitch It To The Horse		0	1967	7	1967	(Phil-L.A. 315)
Fantastics Male Vocal Group from the USA							
1	Something Old, Something New	(Bell 1141)	9	1971	0	1971	
Fantasy UFO Male Instrumental Group from the USA							
1	Fantasy	(Xl Xlt 15)	56	1990	0	1990	
2	Mind Body Soul	(Strictly Underground Yz 591)	0	1991	0	1991	
HIT 2 IS CREDITED TO FANTASY UFO FEATURING JAY GROOVE							
Far Corporation Male Vocal/Instrumental Group from the USA/UK/Germany/Switzerland							
1	Stairway To Heaven	(Arista Arist 639)	8	1985	0	1985	
Fargetta Mixed Vocal/Instrumental Duo from The USA/Italy							
1	Music	(Synthetic Cdr 6334)	34	1993	0	1993	
2	The Music Is Moving	(Arista 74321381572)	74	1996	0	1996	
HIT 1 IS CREDITED TO FARGETTA AND ANN-MARIE SMITH							
Farley 'Jackmaster' Funk Male Producer from the USA							
1	Love Can't Turn Around	(D.J. International Lon 105	10	1986	0	1986	
2	As Always	(Champion Champ 90)	49	1989	0	1989	
3	Love Can't Turn Around (Re-Mix)	(4 Liberty Libtcd 27)	40	1996	0	1996	
HIT 2 IS CREDITED TO FARLEY JACKMASTER' FUNK FEATURING RICKY DILLARD • HIT 3 IS CREDITED TO FARLEY JACKMASTER FUNK FEATURING DARRYL PANDY							
Farm Male Vocal/Instrumental Group from the UK							
1	Stepping Stone / Family Of Man	(Produce Milk 101)	58	1990	0	1990	
2	Groovy Train	(Produce Milk 102)	6	1990	0	1990	
3	All Together Now	(Produce Milk 103)	4	1990	0	1990	
4	Sinful!	(Siren Srn 138)	28	1991	0	1991	
5	Don't Let Me Down	(Produce Milk 104)	36	1991	0	1991	
6	Mind	(Produce Milk 105)	31	1991	0	1991	
7	Love See No Colour	(Produce Milk 106)	58	1991	0	1991	
8	Rising Sun	(End Product 6581737)	48	1992	0	1992	
9	Don't You Want Me	(End Product 6584687)	18	1992	0	1992	
10	Love See No Colour (Re-Issue)	(End Product 6588682)	35	1993	0	1993	
HIT 4 IS CREDITED TO PETE WYLIE WITH THE FARM							
Farmers Boys Male Vocal/Instrumental Group From The Uk							
1	Muck It Out	(Emi 5380)	48	1983	0	1983	

ISSUE	TITLE	UK LBL	UK POS	UK YEAR	US POS	US YEAR	US LBL
2	For You	(Emi 5401)	66	1983	0	1983	
3	In The Country	(Emi Fab 2)	44	1984	0	1984	
4	Phew Wow (Phew Row)	(Emi Fab 3)	59	1984	0	1984	
Faron Young Male Vocalist, B: 25 Feb 1932 Shreveport, Louisiana							
1	Goin' Steady		0	1953	2	1953	(Capitol 2299)
2	I Can't Wait (For The Sun To Go Down)		0	1953	5	1953	(Capitol 2461)
	0	1960	5	1960 (Capitol 4351)			
* 36	Hello Walls		0	1961	12	1961	(Capitol 4533)
*! 59	She Went A Little Bit Farther		0	1968	14	1968	(Merc 72774)
	HIS NICKNAME IS THE YOUNG SHERIFF • HIT 36 REACHED NUMBER 1 IN THE C/W CHARTS						
	REST OF THE HITS ARE C/W • OBITUARY: D: 10 DEC 1996, COMMITED SUICIDE (SHOT HIMSELF), AGED 64.						
Fascinations Female Vocal Group from the USA							
+ 1	Girls Are Out To Get You	(Mojo 2092 004)	32	1971	13	1967	(Mayfield 7714)
Fashion Male Vocal/Instrumental Group from the UK							
1	Streetplayer (Mechanik)	(Arista Arist 456)	46	1982	0	1982	
2	Love Shadow	(Arista Arist 483)	51	1982	0	1982	
3	Eye Talk	(De Stijl A 4106	69	1984	0	1984	
Faster Pussycat Hard-Rock Quinter from Los Angeles							
1	House Of Pain		0	1990	28	1990	(Elektra 64995)
Fastway Male Vocal/Instrumental Group from the UK							
1	Easy Livin'	(Cbs A 3196)	74	1983	0	1983	
Fatboy Slim							
1	Going Out Of My Head	(Skint Skint 19cd)	57	1997	0	1997	
Fat Boys Male Vocal Rap Trio from the USA Names Darren Robinson, Mark Morales & Damon Wimley							
1	Jail House Rap	(Sultra U 9123)	63	1985	0	1985	
2	Wipeout	(Urban Urb 5)	2	1987	12	1987	(Tin Pan 885960)
3	The Twist (Yo Twist)	(Urban Urb 20)	2	1988	16	1988	(Tin Pan 887571)
4	Louie Louie	(Urban Urb 26)	46	1988	0	1988	
	HIT 2 IS CREDITED TO FAT BOYS & THE BEACH BOYS • HIT 3 IS CREDITED TO FAT BOYS & CHUBBY CHECKER						
Fat Lady Sings Male Vocal/Instrumental Group from Ireland							
1	Drunkard Logic	(East West Yz 756cd)	56	1993	0	1993	
Fat Larry's Band Male Vocal/Instrumental Group from the USA							
1	Center City	(Atlantic K 10951)	31	1977	0	1977	
2	Boogie Town	(Fantasy Ftc 168)	46	1979	0	1979	
3	Lookin' For Love Tonight	(Fantasy Ftc 179)	46	1979	0	1979	
4	Zoom	(Virgin Vs 546)	2	1982	0	1982	
Fatback Band Male Vocal/Instrumental Group from the USA							
1	Yum Yum (Gimme Some)	(Polydor 2066 590)	40	1975	0	1975	
2	(Are You Ready) Do The Bus Stop	(Polydor 2066 637)	18	1975	0	1975	
3	(Do The) Spanish Hustle	(Polydor 2066 656)	10	1976	0	1976	
4	Party Time	(Polydor 2066 682)	41	1976	0	1976	
5	Night Fever	(Polydor 2066 706)	38	1976	0	1976	
6	Double Dutch	(Polydor 2066 777)	31	1977	0	1977	
7	Backstrokin'	(Spring Posp 149)	41	1980	0	1980	
8	I Found Lovin'	(Master Mix Che 8401)	49	1984	0	1984	
9	Girls On My Mind	(Atlantic/Cotillion Fback 1)	69	1985	0	1985	
10	I Found Lovin' Re-Mix)	(Important Tan 10)	55	1986	0	1986	
11	I Found Lovin' (Re-Entry)	(Master Mix Che 8401)	7	1987	0	1987	
Father Abraham & The Smurfs Male Vocalist from Holland							
1	The Smurfs Song	(Decca F 13759)	2	1978	0	1978	
2	Dippety Day	(Decca F 13798)	13	1978	0	1978	
3	Christmas In Smurfland	(Decca F 13819)	19	1978	0	1978	
Father M.C. Male Reggae Singer, Real Name Timothy Brown From Brooklyn, He Dropped The MC From His Name In 1993							
* 1	I'll Do 4 U		0	1991	20	1991	(Uptown 53914)
2	Everything's Gonna Be Alright		0	1993	37	1993	(Uptown 54523)
Fatima Mansions Male Vocal/Instrumental Group From Ireland. See Also Manic Street Preachers							
1	Evil Man	(Radioactive Skx 56)	59	1992	0	1992	
2	1000%	(Radioactive Skx 59)	61	1992	0	1992	
3	(Everything I Do) I Do For You	(Columbia 6583827)	7	1992	0	1992	
4	The Loyaliser	(Kitchenware Skcd 67)	58	1994	0	1994	

ISSUE	TITLE	UK LBL	UK POS	UK YEAR	US POS	US YEAR	US LBL
Fats Domino	Male Vocal/Pianist, Real Name Antoine Domino B: 26 Feb 1928 In New Orleans						
+ * 1	The Fat Man / Detroit City Blues		0	1950	6	1950	(Imperial 5058)
+* 2	Every Night About This Time		0	1950	5	1950	(Imperial 5099)
+* 3	Rockin' Chair		0	1951	9	1951	(Imperial 5145)
4	Goin' Home		0	1952	30	1952	(Imperial 5180)
* 5	Goin' To The River		0	1953	24	1953	(Imperial 5231)
+ 6	How Long		0	1952	9	1952	(Imperial 5209)
+* 7	Please Don't Leave Me		0	1953	5	1953	(Imperial 5240)
+ 8	Rose Mary		0	1953	10	1953	(Imperial 5251)
+ 9	Something's Wrong		0	1953	6	1953	(Imperial 5262)
+ 10	You Done Me Wrong		0	1954	10	1954	(Imperial 5272)
+ 11	Don't You Know		0	1955	12	1955	(Imperial 5340)
* 12	Ain't That A Shame	(London Hlu 8173)	23	1957	10	1955	(Imperial 5348)
+* 13	All By Myself		0	1955	3	1955	(Imperial 5357)
+* 14	Poor Me		0	1955	3	1955	(Imperial 5369)
* 15	Bo Weevil		0	1956	35	1956	(Imperial 4375)
* 16	I'm In Love Again	(London Hlu 8280)	28	1956	3	1956	(Imperial 5386)
17	My Blue Heaven		0	1956	19	1956	(Imperial 5386)
18	When My Dreamboat Comes Home		0	1956	14	1956	(Imperial 5396)
19	I'm In Love Again (Re-Entry)	(London Hlu 8280)	12	1956	0	1956	
* 20	Blueberry Hill	(London Hlu 8330)	26	1956	2	1956	(Imperial 5407)
21	Blueberry Hill (Re-Entry)	(London Hlu 8330)	6	1956	0	1956	
* 22	Blue Monday	(London Hlp 8377)	23	1957	5	1956	(Imperial 5417)
* 23	I'm Walkin'	(London Hlp 8407)	19	1957	4	1957	(Imperial 5428)
24	Honey Chile	(London Hlu 8356)	29	1957	0	1957	
25	I Want You To Know		0	1957	32	1957	(Imperial 5477)
26	It's You I Love		0	1957	6	1957	(Imperial 5442)
27	Blue Monday (Re-Entry)	(London Hlp 8377)	30	1957	0	1957	
28	Valley Of Tears	(London Hlp 8449)	25	1957	8	1957	(Imperial 5442)
29	Wait And See		0	1957	23	1957	(Imperial 5467)
30	When I See You		0	1957	29	1957	(Imperial 5467)
31	Sick And Tired	(London Hlp 8628)	26	1958	22	1958	(Imperial 5515)
32	Little Mary		0	1958	49	1958	(Imperial 5526)
33	The Big Beat	(London Hlp 8575)	20	1958	26	1957	(Imperial 5477)
* 34	Whole Lotta Loving		0	1958	6	1958	(Imperial 5553)
35	Margie	(London Hlp 8865)	18	1959	0	1959	
36	Telling Lies		0	1959	50	1959	(Imperial 5569)
37	I'm Ready		0	1959	16	1959	(Imperial 5585)
38	I Want To Walk You Home	(London Hlp 8942)	14	1959	8	1959	(Imperial 5606)
39	I'm Gonna Be A Wheel Some Day		0	1959	17	1959	(Imperial 5606)
40	Be My Guest	(London Hlp 9005)	11	1959	8	1959	(Imperial 5629)
41	I've Been Around		0	1959	33	1959	(Imperial 5629)
42	Country Boy	(London Hlp 9073)	19	1960	25	1960	(Imperial 5645)
43	Be My Guest (Re-Entry)	(London Hlp 9005)	19	1960	0	1960	
44	Don't Come Knockin'		0	1960	21	1960	(Imperial 5675)
45	Walkin' To New Orleans	(London Hlp 9163)	19	1960	6	1960	(Imperial 5675)
46	Three Nights A Week	(London Hlp 9198)	45	1960	15	1960	(Imperial 5687)
47	My Girl Josephine	(London Hlp 9244)	32	1961	14	1960	(Imperial 5704)
48	Natural Born Lover		0	1960	38	1960	(Imperial 5704)
49	What A Price		0	1961	22	1961	(Imperial 5723)
50	Ain't That Just Like A Woman		0	1961	33	1961	(Imperial 5723)
51	Fell In Love On Monday		0	1961	32	1961	(Imperial 5734)
52	Shu Rah		0	1961	32	1961	(Imperial 5734)
53	It Keeps Rainin'	(London Hlp 9374)	49	1961	23	1961	(Imperial 5753)
54	Let The Four Winds Blow		0	1961	15	1961	(Imperial 5764)
55	What A Party	(London Hlp 9456)	43	1961	22	1961	(Imperial 5779)
56	Jambalaya (On The Bayou)	(London Hlp 9520)	41	1962	30	1961	(Imperial 5796)
57	You Win Again		0	1962	22	1962	(Imperial 5816)
58	Red Sails In The Sunset	(HMV Pop 1219)	34	1963	35	1963	(ABC-Paramount 10484)
59	Blueberry Hill (Re-Issue)	(United Artists Up 35797)	41	1976	0	1976	
! 60	Whiskey Heaven (From Any Which Way You Can)		0	1980	51	1951	(Warner Bros 49610)
Fausto Leali	Hit Is The Italian Version Of 'Hurt' By Timi Yuro						
* 1	A Chi		0	1967	0	1967	

ISSUE	TITLE	UK LBL	UK POS	UK YEAR	US POS	US YEAR	US LBL
Faye Adams Female R&B Vocalist, Real Name Faye Scruggs from the USA							
* 1	Shake A Hand		0	1953	22	1953	(Herald 416)
+ 2	I'll Be True		0	1954	1	1954	
+ 3	Hurts Me To My Heart		0	1954	1	1954	
Feargal Sharkey Male Vocalist from the UK							
1	Listen To Your Father	(Zarjazz Jazz 1)	23	1984	0	1984	
2	Loving You	(Virgin Vs 770)	26	1985	0	1985	
3	A Good Heart	(Virgin Vs 808)	1	1985	0	1985	
4	You Little Thief	(Virgin Vs 840)	5	1986	0	1986	
5	Someone To Somebody	(Virgin Vs 828)	64	1986	0	1986	
6	More Love	(Virgin Vs 992)	44	1988	0	1988	
7	I've Got News For You	(Virgin Vs 1294)	12	1991	0	1991	
Feeder							
1	Tangerine	(Echo Ecscd 32)	60	1997	0	1997	
2	Cement	Echo Ecscx 36)	53	1997	0	1997	
3	Crash	(Echo Ecscd 42)	48	1997	0	1997	
Felice Taylor from the USA							
1	I Feel Love Coming On	(President Pt 155)	11	1967	0	1967	
Felicia Sanders Female Vocalist, B: New York City							
1	Blue Star (The Medic Theme)		0	1955	29	1955	(Columbia 40508)
	Sang Vocals On Percy Faith's 'Song From Moulin Rouge			Obituary: 1975.			
Felix Male Producer from the UK							
1	Don't You Want Me	(Deconstruction 74321110507)	6	1992	0	1992	
2	It Will Make You Crazy	(Deconstruction 74321118137)	11	1992	0	1992	
3	Stars	(Deconstruction 74321147102)	29	1993	0	1993	
4	Don't You Want Me (Re-Mix)	(Deconstruction 74321293972)	10	1996	0	1996	
5	Don't You Want Me (2nd Re-Mix)	(Deconstruction 74321418142)	17	1996	0	1996	
Felix Cavaliere							
1	Only A Lonely Heart Sees		0	1980	36	1980	(Epic 50829)
Femme Fatale Mixed Vocal/Instrumental Group from the USA							
1	Falling In And Out Of Love	(MCA MCA 1309)	69	1989	0	1989	
Fendermen Male Vocal/Instrumental Duo, Phill Humphrey & Jim Sundquist from the USA							
1	Mule Skinner Blues	(Top Rank Jar 395)	50	1960	5	1960	(Soma 1137)
2	Mule Skinner Blues (Re-Entry)	(Top Rank Jar 395)	37	1960	0	1960	
3	Mule Skinner Blues (2nd Re-Entry)	(Top Rank Jar 395)	32	1960	0	1960	
Fentones Group from the UK							
1	The Mexican	(Parlophone R 4899)	41	1962	0	1962	
2	The Breeze And I	(Parlophone R 4937)	48	1962	0	1962	
	See Also Shane Fenton & The Fentones, Alvin Stardust						
Ferko String Band Male Vocal/Instrumental Group from the USA							
1	Heartbreaker		0	1948	21	1948	(Palda 109)
2	Alabama Jubilee	(London Hl 8140)	20	1955	14	1955	(Media 1010)
Ferlin Husky Male Country Singer/Songwriter/Guitarist B: 3 Dec 1927 In Flat River, Missouri							
1	Dear John Letter		0	1953	4	1953	(Capitol 2502)
2	Forgive Me, John		0	1953	24	1953	(Capitol 2586)
7	Gone		0	1957	4	1957	(Capitol 3628)
8	A Fallen Star		0	1957	47	1957	(Capitol 3742)
! 14	Black Sheep		0	1959	21	1959	(Capitol 4278)
15	Wings Of A Dove		0	1961	12	1961	(Capitol 4406)
21	Timber I'm Falling		0	1964	13	1964	(Capitol 5111)
22	True, True Lovin'		0	1965	46	1965	(Capitol 5355)
23	Money Greases The Wheels		0	1965	48	1965	(Capitol 5522)
24	I Could Sing All Night		0	1966	27	1966	(Capitol 5615)
25	I Hear Little Rock Calling		0	1966	17	1966	(Capitol 5679)
26	Once		0	1966	4	1966	(Capitol 5775)
27	What Am I Gonna Do Now		0	1967	37	1967	(Capitol 5852)
28	You Pushed Me Too Far		0	1967	14	1967	(Capitol 5938)
29	Just For You		0	1967	4	1967	(Capitol 2048)
30	I Promised You The World		0	1968	26	1968	(Capitol 2154)
31	White Fences And Evergreen Trees		0	1968	25	1968	(Capitol 2288)
32	Flat River, Mo.		0	1969	33	1969	(Capitol 2411)

ISSUE	TITLE	UK LBL	UK POS	UK YEAR	US POS	US YEAR	US LBL
33	That's Why I Love You So Much		0	1969	16	1969	(Capitol 2512)
34	Every Step Of The Way		0	1969	21	1969	(Capitol 2666)
35	Heavenly Sunshine		0	1970	11	1970	(Capitol 2793)
36	Your Sweet Love Lifted Me		0	1970	45	1970	(Capitol 2882)
37	Sweet Misery		0	1970	14	1970	(Capitol 2999)
38	One More Time		0	1971	28	1971	(Capitol 3069)
39	Open Up The Book (And Take A Look)		0	1971	45	1971	(Capitol 3165)
40	Just Plain Lonely		0	1972	39	1972	(Capitol 3308)
41	How Could You Be Anything But Love		0	1972	53	1972	(Capitol 3415)
42	True, True Lovin' (Re-Recording)		0	1973	35	1973	(ABC 11345)
43	Between Me And Blue		0	1973	46	1973	(ABC 11360)
44	Baby's Blue		0	1973	75	1973	(ABC 11381)
45	Rosie Cries A Lot		0	1973	17	1973	(ABC 11395)
46	Freckles And Polliwog Days		0	1974	26	1974	(ABC 11432)
47	A Room For A Boy...Never Used		0	1974	60	1974	(ABC 12021)
48	Champagne Ladies And Blue Ribbon Babies		0	1974	34	1974	(ABC 12048)
49	Burning		0	1975	37	1975	(ABC 12085)
50	An Old Memory (Got In My Eye)		0	1975	90	1975	(ABC/Dot 17574)
51	She's Not Your Anymore		0	1975	74	1975	(ABC/Dot 17574)

UNLISTED HITS ARE C/W • 33 IS CREDITED TO FERLIN HUSKY & HIS HUSH PUPPIES HITS 7, 15 REACHED NUMBER 1 IN THE US C/W CHARTS
HIT 15 WAS ORIGINALLY RECORDED BY HUSKY IN 1952 • ALSO RECORDED UNDER THE NAME OF TERRY PRESTON

Fern Kinney   Female Vocalist from the USA

| | 1 | Together We Are Beautiful | (WEA K 79111) | 1 | 1980 | 0 | 1980 | |

Ferrante & Teicher   Names Arthur Ferrante B: 7 Sep 1921 New York & Louis Teicher B: 24 Aug 1924 In Wilks-Barre, Pennsylvans

*	1	Theme From The Apartment	(London Hlt 916 4)	44	1960	10	1960	(United Artists 231)
*	2	Theme From Exodus	(London Hlt 9298/HMV Pop 881)	6	1961	2	1960	(United Artists 274)
	3	Love Theme From One Eyed Jacks		0	1961	37	1961	(United Artists 300)
*	4	Tonight		0	1961	8	1961	(United Artists 373)
*	5	Midnight Cowboy		0	1969	10	1969	(United Artists 50554)

Ferry Aid   Mixed International Charity Assembly

| | 1 | Let It Be | (The Sun Aid 1) | 1 | 1987 | 0 | 1987 | |

Fess Parker   Male Actor/Vocalist, B: 16 Aug 1927 Fort Worth

| | 1 | Ballad Of Davy Crockett | | 0 | 1955 | 5 | 1955 | (Columbia 40449) |
| | 2 | Wringle Wrangle | | 0 | 1957 | 12 | 1957 | (Disneyland 43) |

Fever & Tippairie

| | 1 | Staying Alive '95 | (Xs Rhythm Cdstas 2776) | 48 | 1995 | 0 | 1995 | |

Fiat Lux   Male Vocal/Instrumental Group from the UK

| | 1 | Secrets | (Polydor Fiat 2) | 65 | 1984 | 0 | 1984 | |
| | 2 | Blue Emotion | (Polydor Fiat 3) | 59 | 1984 | 0 | 1984 | |

Fiction Factory   Male Vocal/Instrumental Group from the UK

| | 1 | (Feels Like) Heaven | (CBS A 3996) | 6 | 1984 | 0 | 1984 | |
| | 2 | Ghost Of Love | (CBS A 3819) | 64 | 1984 | 0 | 1984 | |

Fiddler's Dram   Mixed Vocal/Instrumental Group from the UK

| | 1 | Day Trip To Bangor | (Dingles Sid 211) | 3 | 1979 | 0 | 1979 | |

Fiddlin' John Carson   Male Hillbilly Fiddle Player, B: 13 Mar 1868 Fannin County, Virginia

	1	The Little Old Log Cabin In The Lane		0	1923	9	1923	(Okeh 4890)
*	2	You Will Never Miss Your Mother Until She Is Gone		0	1923	2	1923	(Okeh 4994)
*	3	Fare You Well, Old Joe Clark		0	1924	2	1924	(Okeh 40038)

OBITUARY : D: 11 DEC 1949, (AGED 81).

Fidelfatti   Mixed Production/Vocalist Duo from Italy

| | 1 | Just Wanna Touch Me | (Urban Urb 46) | 65 | 1990 | 0 | 1990 | |

HIT IS CREDITED TO FIDELFATTI FEATURING RONNETTE

Fields Of The Nephilim   Male Vocal/Instrumental Group from the UK

	1	Blue Water	(Situation Two Sit 48)	75	1987	0	1987	
	2	Moonchild	(Situation Two Sit 52)	28	1988	0	1988	
	3	Psychonaut	(Situation Two St 57)	35	1989	0	1989	
	4	For Her Light	(Beggars Banquet Beg 244t)	54	1990	0	1990	
	5	Sumerland (Dreamed)	(Beggars Banquet Beg 250)	37	1990	0	1990	

Fiestas   Names Eddie Morris, Tommy Bullock, Sam Ingalls & Preston Lane

| | 1 | So Fine | | 0 | 1959 | 11 | 1959 | (Old Town 1062) |

ISSUE	TITLE	UK LBL	UK POS	UK YEAR	US POS	US YEAR	US LBL
5th Dimension Mixed Vocal Group from the USA) Formed In 1965 As The Versatiles And Consisted Of Two Girls And Three Men							
1	Go Where You Wanna Go		0	1967	16	1967	(Soul City 753)
* 2	Up-Up And Away		0	1967	7	1967	(Soul City 756)
3	Paper Cup		0	1967	7	1967	(Soul City 760)
4	Carpet Man		0	1968	29	1968	(Soul City 762)
* 5	Stoned Soul Picnic		0	1968	3	1968	(Soul City 766)
6	Sweet Blindness		0	1968	13	1968	(Soul City 768)
7	California Soul		0	1969	25	1969	(Soul City 770)
* 8	Aquarius - Let The Sunshine In (Medley)	(Liberty Lbf 15193)	11	1969	1	1969	(Soul City 772)
9	Workin' On A Groovy Thing		0	1969	20	1969	(Soul City 776)
* 10	Wedding Bell Blues	(Liberty Lbf 15288)	16	1970	1	1969	(Soul City 779)
11	Blowing Away		0	1970	21	1970	(Soul City 780)
12	Puppet Man		0	1970	24	1970	(Bell 880)
13	Save The Country		0	1970	27	1970	(Bell 895)
* 14	One Less Bell To Answer		0	1970	2	1970	(Bell 940)
15	Love's Lines, Angels And Rhymes		0	1971	19	1971	(Bell 965)
16	Never My Love		0	1971	12	1971	(Bell 45134)
17	Together Let's Find Love		0	1972	37	1972	(Bell 45170)
* 18	(Last Night) I Didn't Get To Sleep At All		0	1972	8	1972	(Bell 45195)
19	If I Could Reach You		0	1972	10	1972	(Bell 45261)
20	Living Together, Growing Together		0	1973	32	1973	(Bell 45310)
Fifth Estate							
1	Ding Dong! The Witch Is Dead		0	1967	11	1967	(Jubilee 5573)
52nd Street Mixed Vocal/Instrumental Group from the UK							
1	Tell Me (How It Feels)	(10 Ten 74)	54	1985	0	1985	
2	You're My Last Chance	(10 Ten 89)	49	1986	0	1986	
3	I Can't Let You Go	(10 Ten 114)	57	1986	0	1986	
Fine Young Cannibals Male Vocal/Instrumental Trio from the UK Names Roland Gift, David Steele & Andy Cox							
1	Johnny Come Home	(London Lon 68)	8	1985	0	1985	
2	Blue	(London Lon 79)	41	1985	0	1985	
3	Suspicious Minds	(London Lon 82)	8	1986	0	1986	
4	Funny How Love Is	(London Lon 88)	58	1986	0	1986	
5	Ever Fallen In Love	(London Lon 121)	9	1987	0	1987	
6	She Drives Me Crazy	(London Lon 199)	5	1989	1	1989	(I.R.S. 53483)
7	Good Thing	(London Lon 218)	7	1989	1	1989	(I.R.S. 53639)
8	Don't Look Back	(London Lon 220)	34	1989	11	1989	(I.R.S. 53695)
9	I'm Not The Man I Used To Be	(London Lon 244)	20	1989	0	1989	
10	I'm Not Satisfied	(London Lon 252)	46	1990	0	1990	
11	The Flame	(Ffrr Loncd 389)	17	1996	0	1996	
12	She Drives Me Crazy (Re-Issue)	(Ffrr Loncd 391)	36	1997	0	1997	
Finitribe Male Production/Instrumental Duo from the UK							
1	Forevergreen	(One Little Indian 74 Tp12f)	51	1992	0	1992	
2	Brand New	(Ffrr Fcd 247)	69	1994	0	1994	
Fink Brothers Male Vocal/Instrumental Duo from the UK							
1	Mutants In Mega City One	(Zarjazz Jazz 2)	50	1985	0	1985	
Finley Quaye							
1	Sunday Shining	(Epic 6644552)	16	1997	0	1997	
2	Even After All	(Epic 6649712)	10	1997	0	1997	
Finn Male Vocal/Instrumental Duo from New Zealand							
1	Suffer Never	(Parlophone Cdrs 6417)	29	1995	0	1995	
2	Angel's Heap	(Parlophone Cdrs 6421)	41	1995	0	1995	
Fire Island Male Production/Instrumental Group from the UK							
1	In Your Bones / Fire Island	(Boys Own Boix 11)	66	1992	0	1992	
2	There But For The Grace Of God	(Junior Boy's Own Jbo 18cd)	32	1994	0	1994	
3	If You Should Need A Friend	(Junior Boy's Own Jbo 26cd)	51	1995	0	1995	
HIT 2 IS CREDITED TO FIRE ISLAND FEATURING LOVE NELSON • HIT 3 IS CREDITED TO FIRE ISLAND FEATURING MARK ANTHONI							
Fireballs Male Instrumental Group from the USA							
1	Torquay		0	1959	39	1959	(Top Rank 2008)
2	Bulldog		0	1960	24	1960	(Top Rank 2026)
3	Quite A Party	(Pye International 7n 25092)	29	1961	27	1961	(Warwick 644)
* 4	Sugar Shack	(London Hld 9789)	45	1963	1	1963	(Dot 16487)
5	Sugar Shack (Re-Entry)	(London Hld 9789	46	1963	0	1963	

ISSUE	TITLE	UK LBL	UK POS	UK YEAR	US POS	US YEAR	US LBL
6	Daisy Petal Pickin'		0	1964	15	1964	(Dot 16539)
7	Bottle Of Wine		0	1968	9	1968	(Atco 6491)

HITS 3-5 ARE CREDITED TO JIMMY GILMER & THE FIREBALLS • NAMES: GEORGE TOMSCO, DAN TRAMMELL, ERIC BUDD, STAN LARK & CHUCK THARP

Firefall Names Rick Roberts, Larry Burnett, Jack Bartley, Mark Andes, Mike Clarke & David Muse

ISSUE	TITLE	UK LBL	UK POS	UK YEAR	US POS	US YEAR	US LBL
1	You Are The Woman		0	1976	9	1976	(Atlantic 3335)
2	Cinderella		0	1977	34	1977	(Atlantic 3392)
3	Just Remember I Love You		0	1977	11	1977	(Atlantic 3420)
4	Strange Way		0	1978	11	1978	(Atlantic 3518)
5	Headed For A Fall		0	1980	35	1980	(Atlantic 3657)
6	Staying With It		0	1981	37	1981	(Atlantic 3791)

Fireflies   Lead Singer Of The Quartet Is Ritchie Adams

| 1 | You Were Mine | | 0 | 1959 | 21 | 1959 | (Ribbon 6901) |

Firehouse Male Vocal/Instrumental Group from the USA   Names: Richardson, Foster, Perry & Snare make up the quartet

ISSUE	TITLE	UK LBL	UK POS	UK YEAR	US POS	US YEAR	US LBL
1	Don't Treat Me Bad	(Epic 6567807)	71	1991	19	1991	(Epic 73676)
* 2	Love Of A Lifetime		0	1991	5	1991	(Epic 73771)
3	When I Look Into Your Eyes	(Epic 6588347)	65	1992	8	1992	(Epic 74440)
4	I Live My Life For You		0	1995	26	1995	(Epic 77812)

Firm Male Vocal/Instrumental Quartet from the UK   Names Jimmy Page, Paul Rodgers, Chris Slade & Tony Franklin

ISSUE	TITLE	UK LBL	UK POS	UK YEAR	US POS	US YEAR	US LBL
1	Arthur Daley ('Es Alright)	(Bark Hid 1)	14	1982	0	1982	
2	Radioactive		0	1985	28	1985	(Atlantic 89586)
3	Star Trekkin'	(Bark Trek 1)	1	1987	0	1987	

First Choice Female Vocal Group from the USA , Rochelle Fleming & Annette Guest

ISSUE	TITLE	UK LBL	UK POS	UK YEAR	US POS	US YEAR	US LBL
1	Armed And Extremely Dangerous	(Bell 1297)	16	1973	28	1973	(Philly Groove 175)
2	Smarty Pants	(Bell 1324)	9	1973	0	1973	
+ 3	The Player (Part 1)		0	1974	7	1974	(Philly Groove 200)
+ 4	Guilty		0	1975	19	1975	(Philly Groove 202)

First Class Male Vocal Quartet from the UK   Names: Tony Burrows, John Carter, Del John & Chas Mills

| 1 | Beach Baby | (UK 66) | 13 | 1974 | 4 | 1974 | (UK 49022) |

First Light Male Vocal/Instrumental Duo from the UK

| 1 | Explain The Reasons | (London Lon 26) | 65 | 1983 | 0 | 1983 | |
| 2 | Wish You Were Here | (London Lon 43) | 71 | 1984 | 0 | 1984 | |

Fischer-Z Male Vocal/Instrumental Group from the UK

| 1 | The Worker | (United Artists UP 36509) | 53 | 1979 | 0 | 1979 | |
| 2 | So Long | (United Artists BP 342) | 72 | 1980 | 0 | 1980 | |

Fish Male Vocalist from the UK

ISSUE	TITLE	UK LBL	UK POS	UK YEAR	US POS	US YEAR	US LBL
1	Short Cut To Somewhere	(Charisma Cb 426)	75	1986	0	1986	
2	State Of Mind	(Emi Em 109)	32	1989	0	1989	
3	Big Wedge	(Emi Em 125)	25	1990	0	1990	
4	A Gentleman's Excuse Me	(Emi Em 135)	0	1990	0	1990	
5	Internal Exile	(Polydor Fishy 1)	37	1991	0	1991	
6	Credo	(Polydor Fishy 2)	38	1992	0	1992	
7	Something In The Air	(Polydor Fishy 3)	51	1992	0	1992	
8	Lady Let It Lie	(Dick Bros Ddick 3cd1)	46	1994	0	1994	
9	Fortunes Of War	(Dick Bros Ddick 008cd1)	67	1994	0	1994	
10	Just Good Friends	(Dick Bros Ddick 014cd1)	63	1995	0	1995	

HIT 1 IS CREDITED TO FISH AND TONY BANKS • HIT 10 IS CREDITED TO FISH AND SAM BROWN

Fishbone Vocal/Instrumental Group from the USA

| 1 | Everyday Sunshine / Fight The Youth | (Columbia 6581937) | 60 | 1992 | 0 | 1992 | |
| 2 | Swim | (Columbia 6596252) | 54 | 1993 | 0 | 1993 | |

Fits Of Gloom Male Vocal Duo from the UK/Italy

| 1 | Heaven | (Media Mcstd 1981) | 47 | 1994 | 0 | 1994 | |
| 2 | The Power Of Love | (Media Mcstd 2016) | 49 | 1994 | 0 | 1994 | Featuring Lizzy Mack |

Five Americans Lead Singer Of The Quintet Is Michael Rabon

ISSUE	TITLE	UK LBL	UK POS	UK YEAR	US POS	US YEAR	US LBL
1	See The Light		0	1966	26	1966	(Hbr 454)
2	Western Union		0	1967	5	1967	(Abnak 118)
3	Sound Of Love		0	1967	36	1967	(Abnak 120)
4	Zip Code		0	1967	36	1967	(Abnak 123)

Five Blobs The hit was dreated in a studio with vocals by Bernie Nee

| 1 | The Blob | | 0 | 1958 | 33 | 1958 | (Columbia 41250) |

Five Flights Up Five Man Group from the USA

| 1 | Do What You Wanna Do | | 0 | 1970 | 37 | 1970 | (T-A 202) |

ISSUE	TITLE	UK LBL	UK POS	UK YEAR	US POS	US YEAR	US LBL
Five Keys Originally Called The Sentimental Four in the 1940s without Pierce			Names Rudy & Bernie West, Ripley & Raphael Ingram And Maryland Pierce				
+* 1	Glory Of Love		0	1951	1	1951	(Capitol 0000)
2	Ling, Tong, TOng		0	1954	28	1954	(Captiol 2945)
+ 3	Close Your Eyes		0	1955	6	1955	(Capitol 3032)
4	Out Of Sight, Out Of Mind		0	1956	23	1956	(Capitol 3502)
+ 5	Gee Whittakers!		0	1956	14	1956	(capitol 0000)
6	Wisdom of a Fool		0	1957	35	1957	(capitol 3597)
Five-Man Electrical Band Les Emmerson Is The Lead Singer Of This Canadian Rock Group							
* 1	Signs		0	1971	3	1971	(Lionel 3213)
2	Absolutely Right		0	1971	26	1971	(Lionel 3220)
5 Royals Male R&B Vocal Group from the USA							
* +1	Baby Don't Do It		0	1953	1	1953	(Apollo 443)
+ 2	Help Me Somebody - Crazy, Crazy, Crazy		0	1953	1	1953	(Apollo 446)
+ 3	Too Much Lovin'		0	1953	4	1953	(Apollo 448)
Five Satins Names Fred Parris, Jim Freeman, Eddie Martin, Al Denby & Jessie Murphy							
* 1	In The Still Of The Nite		0	1956	24	1956	(Ember 1005)
2	To The Aisle		0	1957	25	1957	(Ember 1019)
	LEAD SINGER ON HIT 1 IS BILL BAKER, AS PARRIS WAS IN THE ARMY						
Five Smith Brothers Male Vocal Group from the UK							
1	I'm In Favour Of Friendship	(Decca F 10527)	20	1955	0	1955	
Five Stairsteps Chicago-Based Soul Group							
1	World Of Fantasy		0	1966	49	1966	(Windy C 602) with Cubie
* 2	Ooh-Ooh-Child		0	1970	8	1970	(Buddah 165)
Five Star Mixed Family Group Of Deniece, Doris, Stedman, Lorraine & Delroy Pearson from the UK							
1	All Fall Down	(Tent Pb 40039)	15	1985	0	1985	
2	Let Me Be The One	(Tent Pb 40193)	18	1985	0	1985	
3	Love Take Over	(Tent Pb 40353)	25	1985	0	1985	
4	R.S.V.P.	(Tent Pb 40445)	45	1985	0	1985	
5	System Addict	(Tent Pb 40515)	3	1986	0	1986	
6	Can't Wait Another Minute	(Tent Pb 40697)	7	1986	0	1986	
7	Find The Time	(Tent Pb 40799)	7	1986	0	1986	
8	Rain Or Shine	(Tent Pb 40901)	2	1986	0	1986	
9	If I Say Yes	(Tent Pb 40981)	15	1986	0	1986	
10	Stay Out Of My Life	(Tent Pb 41131)	9	1987	0	1987	
11	The Slightest Touch	(Tent Pb 41265)	4	1987	0	1987	
12	Whenever You're Ready	(Tent Pb 41477)	11	1987	0	1987	
13	Strong As Steel	(Tent Pb 41565)	16	1987	0	1987	
14	Somewhere Somebody	(Tent Pb 41661)	23	1987	0	1987	
15	Another Weekend	(Tent Pb 42081)	18	1988	0	1988	
16	Rock My World	(Tent Pb 42145)	28	1988	0	1988	
17	There's A Brand New World	(Tent Pb 42235)	61	1988	0	1988	
18	Let Me Be Yours	(Tent Pb 42343)	51	1988	0	1988	
19	With Every Heartbeat	(Tent Pb 42693)	49	1989	0	1989	
20	Treat Me Like A Lady	(Tent Five 1)	54	1990	0	1990	
21	Hot Love	(Tent Five 2)	68	1990	0	1990	
Five Thirty Male Vocal/Instrumental Group from the UK							
1	Abstain	(East West Yz 530)	75	1990	0	1990	
2	13th Disciple	(East West Yz 577)	67	1991	0	1991	
3	Supernova	(East West Yz 594)	75	1991	0	1991	
4	You (EP)	(East West Yz 624)	72	1991	0	1991	
5000 Volts Mixed Vocal/Instrumental Group from the UK							
1	I'm On Fire	(Philips 6006 464)	4	1975	26	1975	(Philips 40801)
2	Dr. Kiss Kiss	(Philips 6006 533)	8	1976	0	1976	
Fixx Male Vocal/Instrumental Group from the UK			Names: Cy Curnin, Jamie West-Oram, Adam Woods, Dan Brown & Rupert Greenall				
1	Stand Or Fall	(Mca Fixx 2)	54	1982	0	1982	
2	Red Skies	(Mca Fixx 3)	57	1982	0	1982	
3	Saved By Zero		0	1983	20	1983	(MCA 52213)
4	One Thing Leads To Another		0	1983	4	1983	(MCA 52264)
5	The Sign Of Fire		0	1983	32	1983	(MCA 52316)
6	Are We Ourselves?		0	1984	15	1984	(MCA 52444)
7	Secret Separation		0	1986	19	1986	(MCA 52832)
8	How Much Is Enough		0	1991	35	1991	(Impact 54028)

ISSUE	TITLE	UK LBL	UK POS	UK YEAR	US POS	US YEAR	US LBL
Flaming Ember Soul-Rock Band from Detroit Names Bill Ellis, Jim Bugnel, Jerry Plunk & Joe Sladich							
1	Mind, Body And Soul		0	1969	26	1969	(Hot Wax 6902)
2	Westbound Number 9		0	1970	24	1970	(Hot Wax 7003)
3	I'm Not My Brother's Keeper		0	1970	34	1970	(Hot Wax 7006)
	THEIR NAME WAS ORIGINALLY THE FLAMING EMBERS						
Flaming Lips Male Vocal/Instrumental Group from the USA							
1	This Here Giraffe / Life On Mars	(Warner Bros W 0335cd)	72	1996	0	1996	
Flamingos Male Vocal Group from the USA							
+ 1	I'll Be Home		0	1956	5	1956	(Checker 830)
+ 2	Lovers Never Say Goodbye		0	1959	25	1959	(End 1035)
3	I Only Have Eyes For You		0	1959	11	1959	(End 1046)
4	Nobody Loves Me Like You		0	1960	30	1960	(End 1068)
5	Boogaloo Party	(Philips Bf 1786)	26	1969	0	1969	
	NAMES: JAKE & ZEKE CAREY, PAUL WILSON, JOHNNY CARTER & SOLLIE MCELROY. • THERE HAS BEEN MANY CHANGES IN THE LINE-UP SINCE 1952						
Flares Lead Singer Of The Quintet Is Aaron Collins A Former Member Of The Cadets							
1	Foot Stomping (Part 1)		0	1961	25	1961	(Felsted 8624)
Flash Lead Singer Of The Quartet Is Colin Carter)							
1	Small Beginnings		0	1972	29	1972	(Capitol 3345)
Flash & The Pan Male Vocal/Instrumental Group from Australia							
1	And The Band Played On (Down Among The Dead Men)	(Ensign Eny 15)	54	1978	0	1978	
2	Waiting For A Train	(Easybeat Easy 1)	7	1983	0	1983	
Flash Cadillac & The Continental Kids Lead Singer Is Samuel McFadden							
1	Did You Boogie (With Your Baby)		0	1976	29	1976	(Private Stock 45079)
Flee-Rekkers Male Instrumental Group from the UK							
1	Green Jeans	(Triumph Rmg 1008)	23	1960	0	1960	
Fleetwood Mac Mixed Vocal/Instrumental Group from the USA/UK							
1	Black Magic Woman	(Blue Horizon 57 3138)	37	1968	0	1968	
2	Need Your Love So Bad	(Blue Horizon 57 3139)			31	1968	0	1968
* 3	Albatross	(Blue Horizon 57 3145)	1	1968	0	1968	
4	Man Of The World	(Immediate Im 080)	2	1969	0	1969	
5	Need Your Love So Bad (Re-Issue)	(Blue Horizon 57 3157)	32	1969	0	1969	
6	Need Your Love So Bad (Re-Issue) (Re-Entry)	(Blue Horizon 57 3157)	42	1969	0	1969	
* 7	Oh Well	(Reprise Rs 27000)	2	1969	0	1969	
8	The Green Manalishi (With The Two-Prong Crown)	(Reprise Rs 27007)	10	1970	0	1970	
9	Albatross (Re-Issue)	(Cbs 8306)	2	1973	0	1973	
10	Over My Head		0	1975	20	1975	(Reprise 1339)
11	Rhiannon (Will You Ever Win)	(Reprise K 14430)	46	1979	11	1976	(Reprise 1345)
12	Say You Love Me	(Reprise K 14447)	40	1976	11	1976	(Reprise 1356)
13	Go Your Own Way	(Warner Bros K 16872)	38	1977	10	1977	(Warner Bros 8304)
14	Don't Stop	(Warner Bros K 16930)	32	1977	3	1977	(Warner Bros 8413)
* 15	Dreams	(Warner Bros K 16969)	24	1977	1	1977	(Warner Bros 8371)
16	You Make Loving Fun	(Warner Bros K 17013)	45	1977	9	1977	(Warner Bros 8483)
17	Tusk (Live)		0	1979	8	1979	(Warner Bros 49077)
18	Sara	(Warner Bros K 17533)	37	1979	7	1980	(Warner Bros 49150)
19	Think About Me		0	1980	20	1980	(Warner Bros 49196)
20	Hold Me		0	1982	4	1982	(Warner Bros 29966)
21	Gypsy	(Warner Bros K 17997)	46	1982	12	1982	(Warner Bros 19928)
22	Love In Store		0	1982	22	1982	(Warner Bros 29848)
23	Oh Diane	(Warner Bros Fleet 1)	9	1982	0	1982	
24	Big Love	(Warner Bros W 8398)	9	1987	5	1987	(Warner Bros 28398)
25	Seven Wonders	(Warner Bros W 8317)	56	1987	19	1987	(Warner Bros 28317)
26	Little Lies	Warner Bros W 8291	5	1987	4	1987	(Warner Bros 28291)
27	Family Man	(Warner Bros W 8114)	54	1987	0	1987	
28	Everywhere	(Warner Bros W 8143)	4	1988	14	1988	(Warner Bros 18143)
29	Isn't It Midnight	(Warner Bros W 7860)	60	1988	0	1988	
30	As Long As You Follow	(Warner Bros W 7644)	66	1988	0	1988	
31	Save Me	(Warner Bros W 9866)	53	1990	33	1990	(Warner Bros 19866)
32	In The Back Of My Mind	(Warner Bros W 9739)	58	1990	0	1990	
	NAMES PETER GREEN, MICK FLEETWOOD, JOHN MCVIE & JEREMY SPENCER						
	MICK FLEETWOOD B: 24 JUN 1947. FIRST STARTED LIFE AS THE CHEYNES WHICH WENT ON TO BE SHOTGUN EXPRESS WITH VOCALIST ROD STEWART						
	THE GROUP WAS MALE ONLY UP TO AND INCLUDING 1973. • MANY CHANGES SINCE THE ORIGINAL LINE-UP IN 1967						

	ISSUE	TITLE	UK LBL	UK POS	UK YEAR	US POS	US YEAR	US LBL
		Fleetwoods Mixed Vocal Group from the USA	Names: Barbara Ellis, Gretchen Christopher, Gary Troxel, Formed In 1958					
*	1	Come Softly To Me	(London Hlu 8841)	6	1959	1	1959	(Dolphin 1)
	2	Graduation's Here		0	1959	39	1959	(Dolton 3)
*	3	Mr. Blue		0	1959	1	1959	(Dolton 5)
	4	Outside My Window		0	1960	28	1960	(Dolton 15)
	5	Runaround		0	1960	23	1960	(Dolton 22)
	6	Tragedy		0	1961	10	1961	(Dolton 40)
	7	(He's) The Great Imposter		0	1961	30	1961	(Dolton 45)
	8	Lovers By Night, Strangers By Day		0	1962	36	1962	(Dolton 62)
	9	Goodnight My Love		0	1963	32	1963	(Dolton 75)
		Flintlock Male Vocal/Instrumental Group from the UK						
	1	Dawn	(Pinnacle P 8419)	30	1976	0	1976	
		Flirtations Names: Viola Billups And Sisters Eamestine & Shirley Pearce	The Sisters Were Members Of The Gypsies					
	1	Nothing But A Heartache		0	1969	34	1969	(Deram 85038)
		Floaters Male Vocal/Instrumental Quartet from the USA Names Paul And Ralph Mitchell, Larry Cunningham & Charles Clarke						
*	1	Float On	(ABC 4187)	1	1977	2	1977	(ABC 12284)
		Flock Of Seagulls Male Vocal/Instrumental Group from the UK. Lead Singer Mike Score						
	1	I Ran (So Far Away)	(Jive Jive 14)	43	1982	9	1982	(Jive 102)
	2	Space Age Love Song	(Jive Jive 17)	34	1982	30	1982	(Jive 2003)
	3	Wishing (I Had A Photograph Of You)	(Jive Jive 25)	10	1982	26	1982	(Jive 2006)
	4	Nightmares	(Jive Jive 33)	53	1983	0	1983	
	5	Transfer Affection	(Jive Jive 41)	38	1983	0	1983	
	6	The More You Live The More You Love	(Jive Jive 62)	26	1984	0	1984	
	7	Who's That Girl (She's Got It)	(Jive Jive 106)	66	1985	0	1985	
		Floorplay Male Instrumental/Production Duo from the UK						
	1	Automatic	(Perfecto Perf 115cd)	50	1996	0	1996	
		Florian Zabach He Became A Concert Violinist At The Age Of Twelve						
*	1	The Hot Canary		0	1951	13	1951	(Decca 27509)
	2	Red Canary		0	1953	22	1953	(Decca 28646)
		Flowered Up Male Vocal/Instrumental Group from the UK						
	1	It's On	(Heavenly HNV 3)	54	1990	0	1990	
	2	Phobia	(Heavenly HNV 7)	75	1990	0	1990	
	3	Take It	(London FUP 1)	34	1991	0	1991	
	4	It's On / Egg Rush	(London FUP 2)	38	1991	0	1991	
	5	Weekender	(Heavenly HNV 16)	20	1992	0	1992	
		Flowerpot Men Male Vocal Group from the UK						
	1	Let's Go To San Francisco	(Deram Dm 142)	4	1967	0	1967	
		Floyd Cramer Male Pianist, B: 27 Oct 1933 Shreveport, Louisiana						
	1	Fancy Pants		0	1954	28	1954	(Fabor 146)
*	2	Last Date		0	1960	2	1960	(RCA Victor 7775)
*	3	On The Rebound	(RCA 1231)	1	1961	4	1961	(RCA Victor 7840)
	5	Chattanooga Choo Choo		0	1962	36	1962	(RCA 7978)
	6	Hot Pepper	(RCA 1301)	46	1962	0	1962	
!	7	Stood Up		0	1967	53	1967	(RCA 9065)
!	8	Rhythm Of The Rain		0	1977	67	1977	(RCA 10908)
!	9	Dallas		0	1980	32	1980	(RCA 11916)
		HIT 8 IS CREDITED TO FLOYD CRAMER & THE KEYBOARD KICK BAND • HIT 9 REACHED NUMER 104 IN THE US NATIONAL CHARTS						
		Floyd Dixon						
*	1	Too Much Jelly Roll		0	1951	0	1951	
		Floyd Robinson Male Vocalist, B: 1937 Nashville						
	1	Makin' Love	(RCA 1146)	9	1959	20	1959	(RCA 7529)
		Fluffy Female Vocal/Instrumental Group from the UK						
	1	Husband	(Parkway Park 006cd)	58	1996	0	1996	
	2	Nothing	(Virgin Vscdt 1614)	52	1996	0	1996	
		Fluke Male Production/Instrumental Group from the UK						
	1	Slid	(Circa Yrcd 103)	59	1993	0	1993	
	2	Electric Guitar	(Circa Yrcd 104)	58	1993	0	1993	
	3	Groove Feeling	(Circa Yrcd 106)	45	1993	0	1993	
	4	Bubble	(Circa Yrcd 110)	37	1994	0	1994	
	5	Bullet	(Circa Yrcd 121)	23	1995	0	1995	
	6	Tosh	(Circa Yrcd 122)	32	1995	0	1995	

ISSUE	TITLE	UK LBL	UK POS	UK YEAR	US POS	US YEAR	US LBL
7	Atom Bomb	(Circa Yrcd 125)	20	1996	0	1996	
8	Absurd	(Virgin Yrcd 126)	25	1997	0	1997	
Flying Lizards	Mixed Vocal/Instrumental Group from the UK						
1	Money	(Virgin Vs 276)	5	1979	0	1979	
2	T.V.	(Virgin Vs 325)	43	1980	0	1980	
Flying Machine	Male Songwriters/Prodecers Geoff Stephens & Tony Macauley from the UK						
* 1	Smile A Little Smile For Me		0	1969	5	1969	(Congress 6000)
Flying Pickets	Male Vocal Group from the UK						
1	Only You	(10 Ten 14)	1	1983	0	1983	
2	When You're Young And In Love	(10 Ten 20)	7	1984	0	1984	
3	Who's That Girl	(10 Girl 1)	71	1984	0	1984	
FM	Male Vocal/Instrumental Group from the UK						
1	Frozen Heart	(Portrait Didge 1)	64	1987	0	1987	
2	Let Love Be The Leader	(Portrait Merv 1)	71	1987	0	1987	
3	Bad Luck	(Epic 655031 7)	54	1989	0	1989	
4	Someday (You'll Come Running)	(CBS Dink 2)	64	1989	0	1989	
5	Everytime I Think Of You	(Epic Dink 2)	73	1990	0	1990	
Focus	Dutch Instrumental Quartet Led By Jan Akkerman						
1	Hocus Pocus	(Polydor 2001 211)	20	1973	9	1973	(Sire 704)
2	Sylvia	(Polydor 2001 422)	4	1973	0	1973	
Fog	Mixed Vocal/Instrumental Group from the USA						
1	Been A Long Time	(Columbia 6601212)	44	1994	0	1994	
Foghat	Names Rod Price, Dave Peverett, Tony Stevens & Roger Earl						
1	Slow Ride		0	1976	20	1976	(Bearsville 0306)
2	Drivin' Wheel		0	1976	34	1976	(Bearsville 0313)
3	I Just Want To Make Love To You (Live Version)		0	1977	33	1977	(Bearsville 0319)
4	Stone Blue		0	1978	36	1978	(Bearsville 0325)
5	Third Time Lucky (First Time I Was A Fool)		0	1979	23	1979	(Bearsville 49125)
Fogwell Flax & The Anklebiters	Male Vocalist And School Choir from the UK						
1	One Nine For Santa	(EMI 5255)	68	1981	0	1981	
Folk Crusaders							
* 1	Kaette Kita Yopparai (I Only Live Twice)		0	1967	0	1967	
	HIT WAS NUMBER 1 IN JAPAN						
Folk Implosion	Male Vocal/Instrumental Group from the USA						
1	Natural One	(London Locdp 382)	45	1996	35	1996	
Fonda Rae	Female Vocalist from the USA						
1	Touch Me	(Streetwave Khan 28)	49	1984	0	1984	
Fontane Sisters	Names: Geri, Marge & Bea Rosse From New Jersey						
1	Tennessee Waltz		0	1951	20	1951	(RCA Victor 3979)
2	Let Me In		0	1951	24	1951	(RCA Victor 4077)
3	Castle Rock		0	1951	27	1951	(RCA Victor 4213)
4	Cold, Cold Heart		0	1951	16	1951	(RCA Victor 4274)
5	Kissing Bridge		0	1954	22	1954	(RCA Victor 5524)
6	Happy Days And Lonely Nights		0	1954	18	1954	(Dot 15171)
* 7	Hearts Of Stone		0	1954	1	1954	(Dot 15236)
8	Rock Love		0	1955	13	1955	(Dot 15333)
9	Rollin' Stone		0	1955	13	1955	(Dot 15370)
10	Seventeen		0	1955	3	1955	(Dot 15396)
11	Daddy-O		0	1955	11	1955	(Dot 15428)
12	Nuttin' For Christmas		0	1955	36	1955	(Dot 15434)
13	Eddie My Love		0	1956	11	1956	(Dot 15450)
14	I'm In Love Again		0	1956	38	1956	(Dot 15462)
15	Banana Boat Song		0	1957	13	1957	(Dot 15527)
16	Chanson D'amour (Song Of Love)		0	1958	12	1958	(Dot 15736)
	THE SISTERS ALSO TEAMED UP WITH THEIR BROTHER FRANK • HIT 2 IS WITH TEXAS JIM ROBERTSON • OBITUARY: FRANK D: IN W.W.2.						
Fontella Bass	Female Vocalist, B: 24 Aug 1942 In St. Louis, Missouri (B: 24 Aug 1942, St Louis, Missouri)						
1	Don't Mess Up A Good Thing		0	1965	33	1965	(Checker 1097)
* 2	Rescue Me	(Chess Crs 8023)	11	1965	4	1965	(Checker 1120)
3	Recovery	(Chess Crs 8027)	32	1966	37	1966	(Checker 1131)
Foo Fighters	Male Vocal/Instrumental Group from the USA						
1	This Is A Call	(Roswell Cdcl 753)	5	1995	0	1995	

ISSUE	TITLE	UK LBL	UK POS	UK YEAR	US POS	US YEAR	US LBL
2	I'll Stick Around	(Roswell Cdcl 757)	18	1995	0	1995	
3	For All The Cows	(Roswell Cdcl 762)	26	1995	0	1995	
4	Big Me	(Roswell Cdcl 768)	19	1996	0	1996	
5	Monkey Wrench	(Roswell Cdcls 788)	12	1997	0	1997	
6	Everlong	(Roswell Cdcl 792)	18	1997	0	1997	

Fool's Garden Male Vocal/Instrumental Group from Germany

ISSUE	TITLE	UK LBL	UK POS	UK YEAR	US POS	US YEAR	US LBL
1	Lemon Tree	(Encore Cdcore 014)	61	1996	0	1996	
2	Lemon Tree (Re-Issue)	(Encore Cdcore 018)	26	1996	0	1996	

For Real

ISSUE	TITLE	UK LBL	UK POS	UK YEAR	US POS	US YEAR	US LBL
1	You Don't Know Nothin'	(A&M 5811232)	54	1995	0	1995	
2	Like I Do	(Rowdy 74321486582)	45	1997	72	1996	(Arista 35079)

Force MDs US Quintet Originally Called Dr. Rock & The M.C.S

ISSUE	TITLE	UK LBL	UK POS	UK YEAR	US POS	US YEAR	US LBL
1	Tender Love	(Tommy Boy Is 269)	23	1986	10	1986	(Warner Bros 28818)

Foreigner Mixed Vocal/Instrumental Group from the USA/UK   Names Lou Gramm, Ian Mcdonald, Mick Jones, Ed Gagllardi, Al Greenwood & Dennis Elliot

ISSUE	TITLE	UK LBL	UK POS	UK YEAR	US POS	US YEAR	US LBL
1	Feels Like The First Time	(Atlantic K 11086)	39	1978	4	1977	(Atlantic 3394)
2	Cold As Ice	(Atlantic K 10986)	24	1978	6	1977	(Atlantic 3410)
3	Long, Long Way From Home		0	1978	20	1978	(Atlantic 3439)
* 4	Hot Blooded	(Atlantic K 11167)	42	1978	3	1978	(Atlantic 3488)
* 5	Double Vision		0	1978	2	1978	(Atlantic 3514)
6	Blue Morning, Blue Day	(Atlantic K 11236)	45	1979	15	1979	(Atlantic 3543)
7	Dirty White Boy		0	1979	12	1979	(Atlantic 3618)
8	Head Games		0	1979	14	1979	(Atlantic 3633)
9	Urgent	(Atlantic K 11665)	54	1981	4	1981	(Atlantic 3831)
10	Juke Box Hero	(Atlantic K 11678)	48	1981	26	1982	(Atlantic 4017)
* 11	Waiting For A Girl Like You	(Atlantic K 11696)	8	1981	2	1981	(Atlantic 3868)
12	Urgent (Re-Issue)	(Atlantic K 11728)	45	1982	0	1982	
13	Break It Up		0	1982	26	1982	(Atlantic 4044)
* 14	I Want To Know What Love Is	(Atlantic A 9596)	1	1984	1	1985	(Atlantic 89596)
15	That Was Yesterday	(Atlantic A 9571)	28	1985	12	1985	(Atlantic 89571)
16	Cold As Ice (Re-Mix)	(Atlantic A 9539)	64	1985	0	1985	
17	Say You Will	Atlantic A 9169	71	1987	6	1988	(Atlantic 89169)
18	I Don't Want To Live Without You		0	1988	5	1988	(Atlantic 89101)
19	White Lie	(Arista 74321232862)	58	1994	0	1994	

Formations Male Vocal Group from the USA

ISSUE	TITLE	UK LBL	UK POS	UK YEAR	US POS	US YEAR	US LBL
1	At The Top Of The Stairs	(Mojo 2027 001)	50	1971	0	1971	
2	At The Top Of The Stairs (Re-Entry)	(Mojo 2027 001)	28	1971	0	1971	

Forrest Male Vocalist from the USA

ISSUE	TITLE	UK LBL	UK POS	UK YEAR	US POS	US YEAR	US LBL
1	Rock The Boat	(CBS A 3121)	4	1983	0	1983	
2	Feel The Need In Me	(CBS A 3411)	17	1983	0	1983	
3	One Lover (Don't Stop The Show)	(CBS A 3734)	67	1983	0	1983	

45 King Real Name Mark King Male Producer from the USA

ISSUE	TITLE	UK LBL	UK POS	UK YEAR	US POS	US YEAR	US LBL
1	The King Is Here /The 900 Number	(Dance Trax Drx 9)	60	1989	0	1989	
2	The King Is Here / The 900 Number (Re-Entry)	(Dance Trax Drx 9)	73	1990	0	1990	

Fortunes Male Vocal/Instrumental Group from the UK   Quintet Led By Glen Dale Who Was Replaced By Shel Macrae In 1966

ISSUE	TITLE	UK LBL	UK POS	UK YEAR	US POS	US YEAR	US LBL
1	You've Got Your Troubles	(Decca F 12173)	2	1965	7	1965	(Press 9773)
2	Here It Comes Again	(Decca F 12243)	4	1965	27	1965	(Press 9798)
3	This Golden Ring	(Decca F 12321)	15	1966	0	1966	
4	Here Comes That Rainy Day Feeling Again		0	1971	15	1971	(Columbia 3086)
5	Freedom Come Freedom Go	(Capitol Cl 15693)	6	1971	0	1971	
6	Storm In A Teacup	(Capitol Cl 15707)	7	1972	0	1972	

Foster & Allen Male Vocal Duo from Ireland

ISSUE	TITLE	UK LBL	UK POS	UK YEAR	US POS	US YEAR	US LBL
1	A Bunch Of Thyme	(Ritz Ritz 5)	18	1982	0	1982	
2	Old Flames	(Ritz Ritz 028)	51	1982	0	1982	
3	Maggie	(Ritz Ritz 025)	27	1983	0	1983	
4	I Will Love You All Of My Life	(Ritz Ritz 056)	49	1983	0	1983	
5	Just For Old Times Sake	(Ritz Ritz 066)	47	1984	0	1984	
6	After All These Years	(Ritz Ritz 106)	43	1986	0	1986	

Foster Sylvers Male Vocalist, B: 25 Feb 1962 Memphis

ISSUE	TITLE	UK LBL	UK POS	UK YEAR	US POS	US YEAR	US LBL
1	Misdemeanor		0	1973	22	1973	(Mgm 14580)

Foundations Male Vocal/Instrumental Group from the UK

ISSUE	TITLE	UK LBL	UK POS	UK YEAR	US POS	US YEAR	US LBL
* 1	Baby Now That I've Found You	(Pye 7n 17366)	1	1967	11	1968	(Uni 55038)

ISSUE	TITLE	UK LBL	UK POS	UK YEAR	US POS	US YEAR	US LBL
2	Back On My Feet Again	(Pye 7n 17477)	18	1968	0	1968	
3	Any Old Time	(Pye 7n 17503)	48	1968	0	1968	
4	Any Old Time (Re-Entry)	(Pye 7n 17503)	50	1968	0	1968	
* 5	Build Me Up Buttercup	(Pye 7n 17636)	2	1968	3	1968	(Uni 55101)
6	In The Bad Bad Old Days	(Pye 7n 17702)	8	1969	0	1969	
7	Born To Live And Born To Die	(Pye 7n 17809)	46	1969	0	1969	

NAMES PETER MACBETH, TIM HARRIS, TONY GOMEZ, MIKE ELLIOT, PAT BURKE & ERIC ALLANDALE
LEAD SINGER CLEM CURTIS REPLACED BY COLIN YOUNG. • THE GROUP DISBANDED IN 1970

Fountains Of Wayne

1	Radiation Vibe	(Atlantic 7567956262)	32	1997	0	1997	
2	Sink To The Bottom	(Atlantic A 5612cd)	42	1997	0	1997	
3	Survival Car	(Atlantic At 0004cd)	3	1997	0	1997	

Four Aces   Male Vocal Group From Chester, Pennsylvania

* 1	Sin (It's No Sin)		0	1951	4	1951	(Victoria 101)
* 2	Tell Me Why		0	1952	2	1952	(Decca 27860)
3	Garden In The Rain		0	1952	14	1952	(Decca 27860)
4	Perfidia		0	1952	7	1952	(Decca 27987)
5	Two Little Kisses		0	1952	29	1952	(Flash 103)
6	I'm Yours		0	1952	21	1952	(Decca 28162)
7	Should I		0	1952	9	1952	(Decca 28323)
8	Heart And Soul		0	1952	11	1952	(Decca 28390)
9	Just Squeeze Me		0	1952	20	1952	(Decca 28390)
10	La Rosita		0	1953	24	1953	(Decca 28393)
11	I'll Never Smile Again		0	1953	21	1953	(Decca 28391)
12	You Fooled Me		0	1953	22	1953	(Decca 28560)
13	Organ Grinder's Swing		0	1953	17	1953	(Decca 28691)
14	Honey In The Horn		0	1953	24	1953	(Decca 28691)
15	False Love		0	1930	24	1953	(Decca 28744)
16	Laughing On The Outside (Crying On The Inside)		0	1953	22	1953	(Decca 28843)
* 17	Stranger In Paradise (From Kismet)	(Brunswick 05418)	6	1955	3	1953	(Decca 28927)
18	The Gang That Sang 'Heart Of My Heart')		0	1953	7	1953	(Decca 28927)
19	Amor		0	1954	21	1954	(Decca 29036)
20	So Long		0	1954	26	1954	(Decca 29036)
* 21	Three Coins In The Fountain	(Brunswick 05308)	5	1954	2	1954	(Decca 29036)
22	Wedding Bells (Are Breaking Up That Old Gang Of Mine)		0	1954	22	1954	(Decca 29123)
23	Dream		0	1954	17	1954	(Decca 29217)
24	Three Coins In The Fountain (Re-Entry)	(Brunswick 05308)	17	1954	0	1954	
25	It's A Woman's World (From Woman's World)		0	1954	11	1954	(Decca 29269)
26	Mr.Sandman	(Brunswick 05355)	9	1955	5	1954	(Decca 29344)
27	Melody Of Love		0	1955	3	1955	(Decca 29395)
28	Heart		0	1955	13	1955	(Decca 29476)
* 29	Love Is A Many Splendoured Thing	(Brunswick 05480)	2	1955	1	1955	(Decca 29625)
30	Woman In Love	(Brunswick 05589)	19	1956	14	1956	(Decca 29725)
31	I Only Know I Love You		0	1956	22	1956	(Decca 29989)
32	You Can't Run Away From It		0	1956	20	1956	(Decca 30041)
33	Friendly Persuasion	(Brunswick 05623)	29	1957	0	1957	
34	The World Outside	(Brunswick 05773)	18	1959	0	1959	

HITS 27-34 ARE CREDITED TO THE FOUR ACES FEATURING AL ROBERTS • LEAD SINGER AL ALBERTS, DAVE MAHONY, SOL VACCARO & LOU SILVESTRI

Four Bucketeers   Mixed Vocal Group from the UK

1	The Bucket Of Water Song	(CBS 8393)	26	1980	0	1980	

Four Coins   Male Vocal Group from Pennsylvania, USA   Names: George Gregorakis, George Mantalis, George & Michael Mahramas

1	We'll Be Married In The Church In The Wildwood		0	1954	30	1954	(Epic 9074)
2	I Love You Madly		0	1955	28	1955	(Epic 9082)
3	Memories Of You		0	1955	22	1955	(Epic 9129)
4	Shangri-La		0	1957	11	1957	(Epic 9213)
5	My One Sin		0	1957	28	1957	(Epic 9229)
6	The World Outside		0	1958	21	1958	(Epic 9295)

Four Esquires   Male Vocal Quartet from the USA.   Names Wally Gold, Bob Golden, Bill Courtney And Frank Mahoney

1	Love Me Forever	(London Hlo 8533)	23	1958	25	1958	(Paris 509)
2	Hideaway		0	1958	21	1958	(Paris 520)

Four Freshmen   Names Bob Flanigan, Ken Errair, Arthur Jordan And Don Barbour

1	It's A Blue World		0	1952	30	1952	(Capitol 2152)
2	It Happened Once Before		0	1953	29	1953	(Capitol 2564)
3	Mood Indigo		0	1954	24	1954	(Capitol 2961)

ISSUE	TITLE	UK LBL	UK POS	UK YEAR	US POS	US YEAR	US LBL
4	Graduation Day		0	1956	17	1956	(Capitol 3410)

400 Blows Male Vocal/Instrumental Duo from the UK

ISSUE	TITLE	UK LBL	UK POS	UK YEAR	US POS	US YEAR	US LBL
1	Movin'	(Illuminated Ill 61)	54	1985	0	1985	

Four Jacks & A Jill

ISSUE	TITLE	UK LBL	UK POS	UK YEAR	US POS	US YEAR	US LBL
1	Master Jack		0	1968	18	1968	(RCA 9473)

JILL IS LEAD SINGER GLENYS LYNNE OF THE SOUTH AFRICAN QUINTET

Four Knights Male Vocal Group from North Carolina, USA

ISSUE	TITLE	UK LBL	UK POS	UK YEAR	US POS	US YEAR	US LBL
1	I Love The Sunshine Of Your Smile		0	1951	23	1951	(Capitol 1587)
2	(It's No) Sin		0	1951	14	1951	(Capitol 1806)
3	Cry		0	1951	21	1951	(Capitol 1875)
4	Oh, Happy Day		0	1953	8	1953	(Capitol 2315)
* 5	I Get So Lonely (When I Dream About You)	(Capitol CI 14076)	5	1954	2	1954	(Capitol 2654)
6	Period		0	1954	22	1954	(Capitol 2847)
7	I Get So Lonely (When I Dream About You) (Re-Entry)	(Capitol CI 14076)	10	1954	0	1954	
8	In The Chapel In The Moonlight		0	1954	30	1954	(Capitol 2840)
9	If I May		0	1955	8	1955	(Capitol 3095)
10	That's All There Is To That		0	1956	16	1956	(Capitol 3456)
11	My Personal Possession		0	1957	21	1957	(Capitol 3737)

HIT 5 IS ALSO KNOWN AS 'OH BABY MINE' • HITS 9-11 IS CREDITED TO NAT 'KING COLE & THE FOUR KNIGHTS

Four Lads Male Vocal Group from Canada   Names: Jimmie Arnold, Bernie Toorish, Frankie Busseri & Connie Codarin

ISSUE	TITLE	UK LBL	UK POS	UK YEAR	US POS	US YEAR	US LBL
1	The Mocking Bird		0	1952	23	1952	(Okeh 6885)
2	Faith Can Move Mountains	(Columbia DB 3154)	7	1952	0	1952	
3	Somebody Loves Me		0	1952	22	1952	(Columbia 39865)
4	He Who Has Love		0	1953	16	1953	(Columbia 39958)
5	Faith Can Move Mountains (Re-Entry)	(Columbia DB 3154)	9	1953	0	1953	
6	Down By The Riverside		0	1953	17	1953	(Columbia 40005)
7	I Should Have Told You Long Ago		0	1953	26	1953	(Columbia 40082)
8	Instanbul (Not Constantinople)		0	1953	10	1953	(Columbia 40082)
9	Oh, That'll Be Joyful		0	1954	30	1954	(Columbia 40220)
10	Gilly, Gilly, Ossenfeffer, Katzenellen Bogen By The Sea		0	1954	18	1954	(Columbia 40236)
11	Skokiaan		0	1954	7	1954	(Columbia 40306)
12	Rain Rain Rain	(Philips Pb 311)	8	1954	21	1954	(Columbia 40295)
* 13	Moments To Remember		0	1955	2	1955	(Columbia 40539)
14	The Mocking Bird (Re-Entry)		0	1956	67	1956	(Okeh 6885)
* 15	No, Not Much		0	1956	2	1956	(Columbia 40629)
16	Standing On The Corner (From Most Happy Fella)	(Philips Pb 1000)	34	1960	3	1956	(Columbia 40674)
17	My Little Angel		0	1956	22	1956	(Columbia 40674)
18	A House With Love In It		0	1956	16	1956	(Columbia 40736)
19	The Bus Stop Song (A Paper Of Pins) (From *Bus Stop*)		0	1956	17	1956	(Columbia 40736)
20	Who Needs You		0	1957	9	1957	(Columbia 40811)
21	I Just Don't Know		0	1957	17	1957	(Columbia 40914)
22	Put A Light In The Window		0	1957	8	1957	(Columbia 41058)
23	There's Only One Of You		0	1958	10	1958	(Columbia 41136)
24	Enchanted Island		0	1958	12	1958	(Columbia 41194)
25	The Mocking Bird (New Version)		0	1958	32	1958	(Columbia 41266)

HITS 2, 5 ARE CREDITED TO JOHNNIE RAY AND THE FOUR LADS. • HIT 12 IS CREDITED TO FRANKIE LAINE AND THE FOUR LADS

4 Hero Male Instrumental Group from the UK

ISSUE	TITLE	UK LBL	UK POS	UK YEAR	US POS	US YEAR	US LBL
1	Mr. Kirk's Nightmare	(Reinforced Rivet 1203)	73	1990	0	1990	
2	Cookin' Up Yah Brain	(Reinforced Rivet 1216)	59	1992	0	1992	

4mandu Male Vocal Group from the UK

ISSUE	TITLE	UK LBL	UK POS	UK YEAR	US POS	US YEAR	US LBL
1	This Is It	(Arista 74321292122)	45	1995	0	1995	
2	Do It For Love	(Arista 74321343902)	45	1996	0	1996	
3	Baby Don't Go	(Arista 74321375914)	47	1996	0	1996	

4 Non Blondes Mixed Vocal/Instrumental Group from the USA

ISSUE	TITLE	UK LBL	UK POS	UK YEAR	US POS	US YEAR	US LBL
* 1	What's Up	(Interscope A 8412cd)	2	1993	14	1993	(Interscope 98430)
2	Spaceman	(Interscope A 8349cd)	53	1993	0	1993	

4 Of Us Male Vocal/Instrumental Group from Ireland

ISSUE	TITLE	UK LBL	UK POS	UK YEAR	US POS	US YEAR	US LBL
1	She Hits Me	(Columbia 6589192)	35	1993	0	1993	
2	I Miss You	(Columbia 6591722)	62	1993	0	1993	

Four Pennies Male Vocal/Instrumental Group from the UK

ISSUE	TITLE	UK LBL	UK POS	UK YEAR	US POS	US YEAR	US LBL
1	Do You Want Me To	(Philips Bf 1296)	47	1964	0	1964	
2	Do You Want Me To (Re-Entry)	(Philips Bf 1296)	49	1964	0	1964	
3	Juliet	(Philips Bf 1322)	1	1964	0	1964	

ISSUE	TITLE	UK LBL	UK POS	UK YEAR	US POS	US YEAR	US LBL
4	I Found Out The Hard Way	(Philips Bf 1349)	14	1964	0	1964	
5	Black Girl	(Philips Bf 1366)	20	1964	0	1964	
6	Until It's Time For You To Go	(Philips Bf 1435)	19	1965	0	1965	
7	Trouble Is My Middle Name	(Philips BF 1469)	32	1966	0	1966	

4 P.M. (For Positive Music) Male Vocal Quartet from Baltimore, USA

ISSUE	TITLE	UK LBL	UK POS	UK YEAR	US POS	US YEAR	US LBL
* 1	Sukiyaki		0	1994	8	1994	(Next Plat. 857736)

Four Preps Male Vocal Quintet from the USA   Names Glen Larson, Bruce Belland, Ed Cobb And Marvin Ingraham

ISSUE	TITLE	UK LBL	UK POS	UK YEAR	US POS	US YEAR	US LBL
* 1	26 Miles (Santa Catalina)		0	1958	2	1958	(Capitol 3845)
* 2	Big Man	(Capitol Cl 14873)	2	1958	3	1958	(Capitol 3960)
3	Lazy Summer Night		0	1958	21	1958	(Capitol 4023)
4	Big Man (Re-Entry)	(Capitol Cl 14873)	22	1958	0	1958	
5	Down By The Station		0	1960	13	1960	(Capitol 4312)
6	Got A Girl	(Capitol Cl 15128)	28	1960	24	1960	(Capitol 4362)
7	Got A Girl (Re-Entry)	(Capitol Cl 15128)	47	1960	0	1960	
8	More Money For You And Me	(Capitol Cl 15217)	39	1961	17	1961	(Capitol 4599)

Four Seasons Male Vocal Group from the USA

ISSUE	TITLE	UK LBL	UK POS	UK YEAR	US POS	US YEAR	US LBL
* 1	Sherry	(Stateside Ss 122)	8	1962	1	1962	(Vee-Jay 456)
* 2	Big Girls Don't Cry	(Stateside Ss 145)	13	1963	1	1962	(Vee-Jay 465)
3	Santa Claus Is Coming To Town		0	1962	23	1962	(Vee-Jay 478)
* 4	Walk Like A Man	(Stateside Ss 169)	12	1963	1	1963	(Vee-Jay 485)
5	Ain't That A Shame	(Stateside Ss 194)	38	1963	22	1963	(Vee-Jay 512)
6	Candy Girl		0	1963	3	1963	(Vee-Jay 539)
7	Marlena		0	1963	36	1963	(Vee-Jay 539)
8	New Mexican Rose		0	1963	36	1963	(Vee-Jay 562)
9	Dawn (Go Away)		0	1964	3	1964	(Philips 40166)
10	Stay		0	1964	16	1964	(Vee-Jay 582)
11	Ronnie		0	1964	6	1964	(Philips 40185)
* 12	Rag Doll	(Philips Bf 1347)	2	1964	1	1964	(Philips 40211)
13	Alone		0	1964	28	1964	(Vee-Jay 597)
14	Save It For Me		0	1964	10	1964	(Philips 40225)
15	Big Man In Town		0	1964	20	1964	(Philips 40238)
16	Bye, Bye, Baby (Baby Goodbye)		0	1965	12	1965	(Philips 40260)
17	Girl Come Running		0	1965	30	1965	(Philips 40305)
* 18	Let's Hang On	(Philips BF 1439)	4	1965	3	1965	(Philips 40317)
19	Don't Think Twice		0	1965	12	1965	(Philips 40324)
20	Working My Way Back To You	(Philips BF1474)	50	1966	9	1966	(Philips 40350)
21	Opus 17 (Don't You Worry 'Bout Me)	(Philips Bf 1493)	20	1966	13	1966	(Philips 40370)
22	I've Got You Under My Skin	(Philips BF 1511)	12	1966	9	1966	(Philips 40393)
23	Tell It To The Rain	(Philips BF 1538)	37	1967	10	1966	(Philips 40412)
24	Beggin'		0	1967	16	1967	(Philips 40433)
25	C'mon Marianne		0	1967	9	1967	(Philips 40460)
26	Watch The Flowers Grow		0	1967	30	1967	(Philips 40490)
27	Will You Love Me Tomorrow		0	1968	24	1968	(Philips 40523)
28	And That Reminds Me		0	1969	45	1969	(Crewe 333)
29	Night	(Mowest Mw 3024)	7	1975	0	1975	
30	Who Loves You	(Warner Bros K 16602)	6	1975	3	1975	(Warner Bros 8122)
* 31	December '63 (Oh What A Night)	(Warner Bros K 16688)	1	1976	1	1975	(Warner Bros 8168)
32	Silver Star	(Warner Bros K 16742)	3	1976	38	1976	(Warner Bros 8203)
33	We Can Work It Out	(Warner Bros K 16845)	34	1976	0	1976	
34	Rhapsody	(Warner Bros K 6932)	37	1977	0	1977	
35	Down The Hall	(Warner Bros K 16982)	34	1977	0	1977	
36	December '63 (Oh What A Night) (Re-Mix)	(Philips Br 45277)	49	1988	0	1988	
37	December '63 (Oh, What A Night) (Re-Issue)		1994	14	1994		(Curb 76917)

HITS 12, 18 CREDITED TO FOUR SEASONS WITH THE SOUND OF FRANKIE VALLI • HIT 19 TO WONDER WHO • HITS 29,36 ARE FRANKIE VALLI & THE FOUR SEASONS
HITS 22-23 ARE CREDITED TO FOUR SEASONS WITH FRANKIE VALLI • ORIGINALLY FORMED AS THE VARIATONES. • LATER CHANGED NAME TO THE FOUR LOVERS.

Four Tops Male Vocal Group from the USA.   Names Abdul Fakir, Levi Stubbs, Renaldo Benson & Lawrence Payton

ISSUE	TITLE	UK LBL	UK POS	UK YEAR	US POS	US YEAR	US LBL
* 1	Baby I Need Your Loving		0	1964	11	1964	(Motown 1062)
2	Without The One You Love		0	1964	43	1964	(Motown 1069)
3	Ask The Lonely		0	1965	24	1965	(Motown 1073)
* 4	I Can't Help Myself	(Tamla Motown Tmg 515)	23	1965	1	1965	(Motown 1076)
5	It's The Same Old Song	(Tamla Motown Tmg 528)	34	1965	5	1965	(Motown 1081)
6	Something About You		0	1965	19	1965	(Motown 1084)
7	Shake Me, Wake Me (When It's Over)		0	1966	18	1966	(Motown 1090)
8	Loving You Is Sweeter Than Ever	(Tamla Motown Tmg 568)	21	1966	45	1966	(Motown 1096)

ISSUE	TITLE	UK LBL	UK POS	UK YEAR	US POS	US YEAR	US LBL
* 9	Reach Out I'll Be There	(Tamla Motown Tmg 579)	1	1966	1	1966	(Motown 1098)
* 10	Standing In The Shadows Of Love	(Tamla Motown Tmg 589)	6	1967	6	1966	(Motown 1102)
11	Bernadette	(Tamla Motown Tmg 601)	8	1967	4	1967	(Motown 1104)
12	7 Rooms Of Gloom	(Tamla Motown Tmg 612)	0	1967	14	1967	(Motown 1110)
13	You Keep Running Away	(Tamla Motown Tmg 623)	26	1967	19	1967	(Motown 1113)
14	Walk Away Renee	(Tamla Motown Tmg 634)	3	1967	14	1968	(Motown 1119)
15	If I Were A Carpenter	(Tamla Motown Tmg 647)	7	1968	20	1968	(Motown 1124)
16	Yesterday's Dreams	(Tamla Motown Tmg 665)	23	1968	0	1968	
+ 17	I'm In A Different World	(Tamla Motown Tmg 675)	27	1968	23	1968	(Motown 1132)
18	What Is A Man	(Tamla Motown Tmg 698)	16	1969	0	1969	
19	Don't Let Him Take Your Love Away From Me		0	1969	45	1969	(Motown 1159)
20	Do What You Gotta Do	(Tamla Motown Tmg 710)	11	1969	0	1969	
21	I Can't Help Myself (Re-Issue)	(Tamla Motown Tmg 732)	10	1970	0	1970	
22	It's All In The Game	(Tamla Motown Tmg 736)	5	1970	24	1970	(Motown 1164)
23	It's All In The Game (Re-Entry)	(Tamla Motown Tmg 736)	48	1970	0	1970	
24	Still Water (Love)	(Tamla Motown Tmg 752)	10	1970	11	1970	(Motown 1170)
25	River Deep Mountain High	(Tamla Motown Tmg 777)	11	19711	4	1970	(Motown 1173)
26	Still Water (Love) (Re-Entry)	(Tamla Motown Tmg 752)	44	1970	0	1970	
+ 27	In These Changing Times		0	1971	28	1971	(Motown 1185)
28	Just Seven Numbers	(Tamla Motown Tmg 770)	36	1971	40	1971	(Motown 1175)
29	Simple Game	(Tamla Motown Tmg 785)	3	1971	0	1971	
30	Macarthur Park (Part 2)		0	1971	38	1971	(Motown 1189)
31	You Gotta Have Love In Your Heart	(Tamla Motown Tmg 793)	25	1971	0	1971	
32	Bernadette (Re-Issue)	(Tamla Motown Tmg 803)	23	1972	0	1972	
33	Walk With Me Talk With Me Darling	(Tamla Motown Tmg 823)	32	1972	0	1972	
* 34	Keeper Of The Castle	(Probe Pro 575)	18	1972	10	1972	(Dunhill 4330)
* 35	Ain't No Woman (Like The One I've Got)		0	1973	4	1973	(Dunhill 4339)
36	Are You Man Enough		0	1973	15	1973	(Dunhill 4354)
37	Sweet Understanding Love	(Probe Pro 604)	29	1973	33	1973	(Dunhill 4366)
38	When She Was My Girl	(Casablanca Can 1005)	3	1981	11	1981	(Casablanca 2338)
39	Don't Walk Away	(Casablanca Can 1006)	16	1981	0	1981	
40	Tonight I'm Gonna Love You All Over	(Casablanca Can 1008)	43	1982	0	1982	
41	Back To School Again	(RSO 89)	62	1982	0	1982	
42	Reach Out I'll Be There (Re-Mix)	(Motown Zb 41943)	11	1988	0	1988	
43	Indestructible	(Arista 111717)	55	1988	35	1988	(Arista 9706)
44	Loco In Acapulco	(Arista 111850)	7	1988	0	1988	
45	Indestructible	(Arista 112074)	30	1989	0	1989	

Four Tunes   Male R&B Vocal Group from the USA   Names: are, James Nabbie, Danny Owens, William Best And James Gordon

1	Marie		0	1954	13	1954	(Jubilee 5128)
* 2	I Understand (Just How You Feel)		0	1954	6	1954	(Jubilee 5132)
3	Sugar Lump		0	1954	25	1954	(Jubilee 5132)

Four Voices   Names: Allan Chase, Frank Fosta, Sal Mayo & Bill McBride

1	Lovely One		0	1956	20	1956	(Columbia 40643)

Fourmost   Male Vocal/Instrumental Group from the UK

1	Hello Little Girl	(Parlophone R 5056)	9	1963	0	1963	
2	I'm In Love	(Parlophone R 5078)	17	1963	0	1963	
3	A Little Lovin'	(Parlophone R 5128)	6	1964	0	1964	
4	How Can I Tell Her	(Parlophone R 5157)	33	1964	0	1964	
5	Baby I Need Your Lovin'	(Parlophone R 5194)	24	1964	0	1964	
6	Girls Girls Girls	(Parlophone R 5379)	33	1964	0	1964	

14-18   Real Name Peter Waterman Male Vocalist from the UK

1	Goodbye-Ee	(Magnet Mag 48)	33	1975	0	1975	

Fox   Mixed Vocal/Instrumental Group from the USA/UK

1	Only You Can	(Gto Gt 8)	3	1975	0	1975	
2	Imagine Me Imagine You	(Gto Gt 21)	15	1975	0	1975	
3	S-S-S-Single Bed	(Gto Gt 57)	4	1976	0	1976	

Foxy   Lead Singer Of The Dance Band Is "Ish Ledesma

1	Get Off		0	1978	9	1978	(Dash 5046)
2	Hot Number		0	1979	21	1979	(Dash 5050)

Foxy Brown

1	Ain't No Nigga / Dead Presidents		0	1996	50	1996	
2	Touch Me, Tease Me (From *The Nutty Professor*)	(Def Jam Defcd 18)	26	1996	14	1996	(Mercury 854620)
3	I'll Be		0	1997	7	1997	(Mercury 574029)

ISSUE	TITLE	UK LBL	UK POS	UK YEAR	US POS	US YEAR	US LBL
4	Get Me Home	(Def Jam Defcd 32)	11	1997	0	1997	
5	Ain't No Playa	(Northwestside 74321474842)	31	1997	0	1997	
6	I'll Be	(Def Jam 5710432)	9	1997	0	1997	
FPI Project Male Production/Instrumental Group from Italy							
1	Going Back To My Roots / Rich In Paradise	(Rumour Rumat 99)	9	1989	0	1989	
2	Everybody (All Over The World)	(Rumour Ruma 29)	65	1991	0	1991	
3	Come On (And Do It)	(Synthetic Synth 006cd)	59	1993	0	1993	
Fraggles Puppets from the USA/Uk							
1	Fraggle Rock Theme	(RCA 389)	33	1984	0	1984	
Fran Allison Female TV Host/Vocalist from the USA							
1	Peter Cottontail		0	1950	26	1950	(RCA Victor 3727)
2	Too Young		0	1951	20	1951	(RCA Victor 4105)
Fran Warren Female Vocalist from the USA							
1	A Wonderful Guy		0	1949	17	1949	(RCA Victor 3403)
2	Envy		0	1941	2	1949	(RCA Victor 78-3613)
3	I Said My Pajamas (And Put On My Prayers)		0	1950	3	1950	(RCA Victor 78-3613)
4	Dearie		0	1950	22	1950	(RCA Victor 78-3696)
5	I Love That Guy		0	1950	22	1950	(RCA Victor 3848)
6	It's Anybody's Heart		0	1953	26	1953	(MGM 11616)
France Joli French Canadian Vocalist, B: 1963 Montreal							
1	Come To Me		0	1979	15	1979	(Prelude 8001)
Frances Nero Female Vocalist from the USA							
1	Footsteps Following Me	(Debut Debt 3109)	17	1991	0	1991	
Frances Ruffelle Female Vocalist from the UK							
1	Lonely Symphony	(Virgin Vscdt 1499)	25	1994	0	1994	
Francesco Zappala Male Producer From Italy							
1	We Gotta Do It	(Fourth & Broadway Brw 225)	57	1991	0	1991	
2	No Way Out	(Pwl Continental Pwl 230)	69	1992	0	1992	
Francis Craig Orchestra Male Pianist/Orchestra Leader, B: 10 Sep 1900 Dickson, Tennessee							
* 1	Near You		0	1947	1	1947	(Bullet 1001)
2	Beg Your Pardon		0	1948	3	1948	(Bullet 1012)
	VOCALS ON THE HITS 1-2 ARE BY BOB LAMM • VOCALS ON HIT 2 ARE BY-BOB LAMM • OBITUARY :- D: 19 NOV 1966 IN SEWANEE, TENNESSEE.						
Francis Lai Orchestra							
* 1	Lee Passager De La Pluie (Passenger In The Rain)		0	1970	0	1970	(Paramount)
2	Theme From Love Story		0	1971	31	1971	(Paramount 0064)
Francis Rossi Male Vocalist from the UK							
1	Modern Romance (I Want To Fall In Love Again)	(Vertigo Fros 1)	54	1985	0	1985	
2	Give Myself To Love	(Virgin Vscdt 1594)	42	1996	0	1996	
	HIT 1 IS CREDITED TO FRANCIS ROSSI AND BERNARD FROST • HIT 2 IS CREDITED TO FRANCIS ROSSI AND STATUS QUO						
Franck Pourcel's French Fiddles Male Orchestra Leader/Violinist/Composer/Arranger, B: 1 Jan 1915 Marseilles, France)							
1	Only You		0	1959	9	1959	(Capitol 4165)
Françoise Hardy Female Vocalist, B: 17 Jan 1944, Paris							
* 1	Tous Les Garçons Et Les Filles (All The Boys And Girls)	(Pye 7n 15740)	36	1964	0	1964	
2	All Over The World	(Pye 7n 15802)	16	1964	0	1964	
Frank & Walters Male Vocal/Instrumental Group From Ireland							
1	Happy Busman	(Setanta Hoo 2)	49	1992	0	1992	
2	This Is Not A Song	(Setanta Hoo 3)	46	1992	0	1992	
3	After All	(Setanta Hocd 4)	11	1993	0	1993	
4	Fashion Crisis Hits New York	(Setanta Hoocd 5)	42	1993	0	1993	
Frank Black Male Vocalist from the USA							
1	Headache	(4ad Radd 4007cd)	53	1994	0	1994	
2	Men In Black	(Dragnet 6627862)	37	1996	0	1996	
3	I Don't Want To Hurt You (Every Single Time)	(Dragnet 6634635)	63	1996	0	1996	
Frank Bruno Male Boxer/Voalist from the UK							
1	Eye Of The Tiger	(RCA 74321336282)	28	1995	0	1995	
Frank Chacksfield & His Orchestra Male Orchestra Leader, B: 9 May 1914 In Battle, Sussex, England							
1	Limelight (Terry's Theme)	(Decca F 10106)	2	1953	5	1953	(London 1342)
2	Little Red Monkey	(Parlophone R 3658)	10	1953	0	1953	
* 3	Ebb Tide	(Decca F 10122)	9	1954	2	1954	(London 1358)
4	In Old Lisbon	(Decca F 10689)	15	1956	0	1956	

ISSUE	TITLE	UK LBL	UK POS	UK YEAR	US POS	US YEAR	US LBL
5	Port Au Prince	(Decca F 10727)	18	1956	0	1956	
6	Donkey Cart	(Decca F 10743)	26	1956	0	1956	

HIT 2 IS CREDITED TO FRANK CHACKSFIELD TUNESMITHS • HIT 5 IS CREDITED TO WINIFRED ATWELL & FRANK CHACKSFIELD ORCHESTRA

Frank Cordell Male Orchestra Leader from the UK

ISSUE	TITLE	UK LBL	UK POS	UK YEAR	US POS	US YEAR	US LBL
1	Sadie's Shawl	(HMV Pop 229)	29	1956	0	1956	
2	The Black Bear	(HMV Pop 824)	44	1961	0	1961	

Frank D'Rone Male Vocalist from the USA

ISSUE	TITLE	UK LBL	UK POS	UK YEAR	US POS	US YEAR	US LBL
1	Strawberrry Blonde	(Mercury Amt 1123)	24	1960	0	1960	

Frank Devol Orchestra Male Saxophonist/Orchestra Leader from the USA

ISSUE	TITLE	UK LBL	UK POS	UK YEAR	US POS	US YEAR	US LBL
1	Dream Awhile		0	1950	28	1950	(Capitol 1143)

Frank Gallagher Male Vocalist from the USA

ISSUE	TITLE	UK LBL	UK POS	UK YEAR	US POS	US YEAR	US LBL
1	You're All I Want For Christmas		0	1948	25	1948	(Dana 2026)

Frank Gallop Male Comedian/Tv Announcer from the USA

ISSUE	TITLE	UK LBL	UK POS	UK YEAR	US POS	US YEAR	US LBL
1	The Ballad Of Irving		0	1966	34	1966	(Kapp 745)

Frank Gari Male Actor/Vocalist, B: 1 Apr 1942 New York City

ISSUE	TITLE	UK LBL	UK POS	UK YEAR	US POS	US YEAR	US LBL
1	Utopia		0	1961	27	1961	(Crusade 1020)
2	Lullaby Of Love		0	1961	23	1961	(Crusade 1021)
3	Princess		0	1961	30	1961	(Crusade 1022)

Frank Hooker & Positive People Male Vocal/Instrumental Group from the USA

ISSUE	TITLE	UK LBL	UK POS	UK YEAR	US POS	US YEAR	US LBL
1	This Feelin'	(Djm Djs 10947)	48	1980	0	1980	

Frank Ifield Male Vocalist, B: 30 Nov 1937 Coventry, England

ISSUE	TITLE	UK LBL	UK POS	UK YEAR	US POS	US YEAR	US LBL
1	Lucky Devil	(Columbia Db 4399)	22	1960	0	1960	
2	Lucky Devil (Re-Entry)	(Columbia Db 4399)	33	1960	0	1960	
3	Gotta Get A Date	(Columbia Db 4496)	49	1960	0	1960	
* 4	I Remember You	(Columbia Db 4856)	1	1962	5	1962	(Vee-Jay 457)
* 5	Love Sick Blues	(Columbia Db 4913)	1	1962	44	1962	(Vee-Jay)
6	Wayward Wind	(Columbia Db 4960)	1	1963	0	1963	
7	Nobody's Darlin' But Mine	(Columbia Db 7007)	4	1963	0	1963	
8	Confessin'	(Columbia Db 7062)	1	1963	0	1963	
9	Mule Train	(Columbia Db 7131)	22	1963	0	1963	
10	Don't Blame Me	(Columbia Db 7184)	8	1964	0	1964	
11	Angry At The Big Oak Tree	(Columbia Db 7263)	25	1964	0	1964	
12	I Should Care	(Columbia Db 7319)	33	1964	0	1964	
13	Summer Is Over	(Columbia Db 7355)	25	1964	0	1964	
14	Paradise	(Columbia Db 7655)	26	1965	0	1965	

BEGAN HIS CAREER IN AUSTRALIA • HIT 4 SOLD OVER 100,000 COPIES IN ONE DAY • HIT 19 IS CREDITED TO FRANK IFIELD FEATURING THE BACKROOM BOYS

Frank K (Featuring) Wiston Office Male Vocal/Instrumental Duo from the USA/Italy

ISSUE	TITLE	UK LBL	UK POS	UK YEAR	US POS	US YEAR	US LBL
1	Everybody Let's Somebody Love	(Urban Urb 66)	61	1991	0	1991	

Frank Kelly Male Vocalist from Ireland

ISSUE	TITLE	UK LBL	UK POS	UK YEAR	US POS	US YEAR	US LBL
1	Christmas Countdown	(Ritz Ritz 062)	26	1983	0	1983	
2	Christmas Countdown (Re-Entry)	(Ritz Ritz 062)	54	1984	0	1984	

Frank Mills Male Pianist/Composer/Arranger, B: 1943 Toronto

ISSUE	TITLE	UK LBL	UK POS	UK YEAR	US POS	US YEAR	US LBL
1	Music Box Dancer		0	1979	3	1979	(Polydor 14517)

Frank Petty Trio

ISSUE	TITLE	UK LBL	UK POS	UK YEAR	US POS	US YEAR	US LBL
1	Rain		0	1950	17	1950	(Mgm 10669)
2	Down Yonder		0	1951	26	1951	(Mgm 11057)

Frank Sinatra Male Vocalist, Real Name Francis Albert Sinatra. B: 12 Dec 1915 Hoboken, New Jersey

ISSUE	TITLE	UK LBL	UK POS	UK YEAR	US POS	US YEAR	US LBL
1	Night And Day		0	1942	16	1942	(Bluebird 11463)
* 2	All Or Nothing At All (Re-Issue)		0	1943	2	1943	(Columbia 35587)
3	You'll Never Know (From *Hello, Frisco, Hello*)		0	1943	2	1943	(Columbia 36678)
4	Close To You		0	1943	10	1943	(Columbia 36678)
5	Sunday, Monday, Or Always		0	1943	9	1943	(Columbia 36679)
6	People Will Say We're In Love (From "Oklahoma!)		0	1943	3	1943	(Columbia 36682)
7	Oh, What A Beautiful Mornin' (From "Oklahoma!)		0	1943	12	1943	(Columbia 36682)
8	I Couldn't Sleep A Wink Last Night (From *Higher And Higher*)		0	1944	4	1944	(Columbia 36687)
9	A Lovely Way To Spend A Evening (From *Higher And Higher*)		0	1944	11	1944	(Columbia 36687)
10	On A Little Street In Singapore		0	1944	27	1944	(Columbia 36700)
11	Every Day Of My Life		0	1944	17	1944	(Columbia 36700)
12	Night And Day (Re-Issue)		0	1944	15	1944	(Victor 1589)
13	It's Funny To Everyone But Me		0	1944	21	1944	(Columbia 36738)

ISSUE	TITLE	UK LBL	UK POS	UK YEAR	US POS	US YEAR	US LBL
* 14	White Christmas (From *Holiday Inn*)		0	1944	7	1944	(Columbia 36756)
15	Saturday Night (Is The Loneliest Night Of The Week)		0	1945	2	1945	(Columbia 36756)
16	I Dream Of You		0	1945	7	1945	(Columbia 36762)
17	If You Are But A Dream		0	1945	19	1945	(Columbia 36786)
18	What Make The Sun Set (From Anchors Aweigh)		0	1945	13	1945	(Columbia 36774)
19	Dream		0	1945	5	1945	(Columbia 36797)
20	I Should Care (From *Thrill Of A Romance*)		0	1945	8	1945	(Columbia 36791)
21	If I Loved You (From Carousel)		0	1945	7	1945	(Columbia 36825)
22	You'll Never Walk Alone (From *Carousel*)		0	1945	9	1945	(Columbia 36825)
23	Homesick - That's All		0	1945	23	1945	(Columbia 36820)
24	Don't Forget Tonight Tomorrow		0	1945	9	1945	(Columbia 36854)
25	Nancy (With The Laughing Face)		0	1945	10	1945	(Columbia 36868)
26	White Christmas (Re-Issue)		0	1945	5	1945	(Columbia 36860)
27	The House I Live In		0	1946	22	1946	(Columbia 36886)
28	Oh! What It Seemed To Be		0	1946	1	1946	(Columbia 36905)
29	Day By Day		0	1946	5	1946	(Columbia 36905)
30	Full Moon		0	1946	17	1946	(Columbia 36947)
31	They Say It's Wonderful (From Annie Get Your Gun)		0	1946	2	1946	(Columbia 36975)
32	The Girl That I Marry (From Annie Get Your Gun)		0	1946	11	1946	(Columbia 36975)
33	All Through The Day (From *Centennial Summer*)		0	1946	7	1946	(Columbia 36962)
34	From This Day Forward		0	1946	18	1946	(Columbia 36898)
35	Five Minutes More (From *Sweetheart Of Sigm Chi*)		0	1946	1	1946	(Columbia 37048)
36	The Coffee Song		0	1946	6	1946	(Columbia 37089)
37	Something Old, Something New		0	1946	21	1946	(Columbia 36987)
38	Begin The Beguine (From *Jubilee*)		0	1946	23	1946	(Columbia 37064)
39	The Things We Did Last Summer		0	1946	8	1946	(Columbia 37089)
40	September Song (From *Knickerbocker Holiday*)		0	1946	8	1946	(Columbia 37161)
41	White Christmas (2nd Re-Issue)		0	1946	6	1946	(Columbia 37132)
42	This Is The Night		0	1947	11	1947	(Columbia 37193)
43	That's How Much I Love You		0	1947	10	1947	(Columbia 37231)
44	I Believe (From *It Happened In Brooklyn*)		0	1947	5	1947	(Columbia 37300)
45	Time After Time (From *It Happened In Brooklyn*)		0	1947	16	1947	(Columbia 37300)
46	Mam'selle (From *The Razor's Edge*)		0	1947	1	1947	(Columbia 37343)
47	Almost Like Being In Love (From *Brigadoon*)		0	1947	20	1947	(Columbia 37382)
48	Stella By Starlight		0	1947	21	1947	(Columbia 37343)
49	I Have But One Heart		0	1947	13	1947	(Columbia 37554)
50	Ain'tcha Ever Comin' Back		0	1947	21	1947	(Columbia 37554)
51	So Far (From *Allegro*)		0	1947	8	1947	(Columbia 37883)
52	A Fellow Needs A Girl (From *Allegro*)		0	1947	24	1947	(Columbia 37883)
53	The Dum-Dot Song		0	1947	21	1947	(Columbia 37966)
54	Christmas Dreaming		0	1947	26	1947	(Columbia 37809)
55	You're My Girl (From *High Button Shoes*)		0	1948	23	1948	(Columbia 37966)
56	What'll I Do? (From *Music Box Revue* Of 1923)		0	1948	23	1948	(Columbia 38045)
57	My Cousin Louella		0	1948	24	1948	(Columbia 38045)
58	I've Got A Crush On You (From *Treasure Girl*)		0	1948	21	1948	(Columbia 38151)
60	All Of Me		0	1948	21	1948	(Columbia 38163)
61	Nature Boy		0	1948	7	1948	(Columbia 38210)
62	Just For Now		0	1948	25	1948	(Columbia 38225)
63	Everybody Loves Somebody		0	1948	25	1948	(Columbia 38225)
64	It Only Happens When I Dance With You (From *Easter Parade*)		0	1948	19	1948	(Columbia 38192)
65	Autumn In New York		0	1949	27	1949	(Columbia 38316)
66	Sunflower		0	1949	14	1949	(Columbia 38391)
67	Some Enchanted Evening (From *South Pacific*)		0	1949	6	1949	(Columbia 38446)
68	Bali Ha'i (From *South Pacific*)		0	1949	18	1949	(Columbia 38446)
69	The Hucklebuck		0	1949	10	1949	(Columbia 38486)
70	Let's Take An Old-Fashioned Walk (From *Miss Liberty*)		0	1949	17	1949	(Columbia 38513)
71	Don't Cry, Joe (Let Her Go, Let Her Go, Let Her Go)		0	1949	9	1949	(Columbia 38555)
72	That Licky Old Sun		0	1949	16	1949	(Columbia 38608)
73	The Old Master Painter		0	1949	13	1949	(Columbia 38650)
74	Sorry		0	1950	28	1950	(Columbia 38662)
75	Chattanoogie Shoe Shine Boy		0	1950	10	1950	(Columbia 38708)
76	God's Country		0	1950	25	1950	(Columbia 38708)

ISSUE	TITLE	UK LBL	UK POS	UK YEAR	US POS	US YEAR	US LBL
77	American Beauty Rose		0	1950	26	1950	(Columbia 38809)
78	Goodnight Irene		0	1950	5	1950	(Columbia 38892)
79	One Finger Melody		0	1950	9	1950	(Columbia 39014)
80	Nevertheless (From *Three Little Words*)		0	1950	14	1950	(Columbia 39044)
81	You're The One		0	1951	17	1951	(Columbia 39213)
82	We Kiss In The Shadow (From *The King An I*)		0	1951	22	1951	(Columbia 39294)
83	I'm A Fool To Want You		0	1951	14	1951	(Columbia 39425)
84	Mama Will Bark		0	1951	21	1951	(Columbia 39425)
85	Castle Rock		0	1951	8	1951	(Columbia 39527)
86	I Hear A Rhapsody		0	1952	25	1952	(Columbia 39652)
87	Bim Bam Baby		0	1952	20	1952	(Columbia 39819)
88	Azure-Te (Paris Blues)		0	1952	30	1952	(Columbia 39819)
89	The Birth Of The Blues (From *George White's Scandals* Of 1926)		0	1952	19	1952	(Columbia 39882)
90	I'm Walking Behind You		0	1953	7	1953	(Capitol 2450)
91	Lean Baby		0	1953	25	1953	(Capitol 2450)
92	I've Got The World On A String		0	1953	14	1953	(Capitol 2505)
93	My One And Only Love		0	1953	28	1953	(Capitol 2505)
94	From Here To Eternity		0	1953	15	1953	(Capitol 2560)
95	South Of The Border		0	1953	18	1953	(Capitol 2638)
* 96	Young-At-Heart (Movie Title Song)	(Capitol Cl 14064)	12	1954	2	1954	(Capitol 2703)
97	Don't Wory 'Bout Me		0	1954	17	1954	(Capitol 2787)
98	I Could Have Told You		0	1954	21	1954	(Capitol 2787)
99	Three Coins In A Fountain (Movie Title Song)	(Capitol Cl 14120)	1	1954	4	1954	(Capitol 2816)
100	The Gal That Got Away (From *A Star Is Born*)		0	1954	21	1954	(Capitol 2864)
101	Half As Lovely (Twice As True)		0	1954	4	1954	(Capitol 2864)
102	It Worries Me		0	1954	30	1954	(Capitol 2922)
103	Melody Of Love		0	1955	19	1955	(Capitol 3018)
* 104	Learnin' The Blues	(Capitol Cl 14296)	2	1955	1	1955	(Capitol 3102)
105	You My Love	(Capitol Cl 14240)	13	1955	0	1955	
106	You My Love (Re-Entry)	(Capitol Cl 14240)	17	1955	0	1955	
107	You My Love (2nd Re-Entry)	(Capitol Cl 14240)	17	1955	0	1955	
108	Not As A Stranger	(Capitol Cl 14326)	18	1955	0	1955	
109	Same Old Saturday Night		0	1955	13	1955	(Capitol 3218)
* 110	Love And Marriage	(Capitol Cl 14503)	18	1956	5	1955	(Capitol 3260)
111	(Love Is) The Tender Trap	(Capitol Cl 14511)	2	1956	7	1955	(Capitol 3290)
112	Flowers Mean Forgiveness		0	1956	21	1956	(Capitol 3350)
113	(How Little It Matters) How Little We Know		0	1956	13	1956	(Capitol 3423)
114	Songs For Swinging Lovers	(Capitol Lct 6106)	12	1956	0	1956	
115	Hey! Jealous Lover		0	1956	3	1956	(Capitol 3552)
116	Can I Steal A Little Love		0	1957	15	1957	(Capitol 3608)
117	You're Cheatin' Yourself (If You're Cheatin' On Me)		0	1957	25	1957	(Capitol 3744)
118	All The Way	(Capitol Cl 14800)	29	1957	2	1957	(Capitol 3793)
119	Chicago	(Capitol Cl 14800)	25	1957	12	1957	(Capitol 3793)
120	All The Way / Chicago (Re-Entry)	(Capitol Cl 14800)	21	1957	0	1957	
121	All The Way (2nd Re-Entry)	(Capitol Cl 14800)	3	1957	0	1957	
122	Witchcraft	(Capitol Cl 14819)	12	1958	6	1958	(Capitol 3859)
123	How Are Ya' Fixed For Love?		0	1958	22	1958	(Capitol 3952)
124	Mr. Success	(Capitol Cl 14956)	29	1958	0	1958	
125	Mr. Success (Re-Entry)	(Capitol Cl 14956)	25	1958	0	1958	
126	Mr. Success (2nd Re-Entry)	(Capitol Cl 14956)	26	1959	0	1959	
127	French Foreign Legion	(Capitol Cl 14997)	18	1959	0	1959	
128	Come Dance With Me (Ep)	(Capitol Lct 6179)	30	1959	0	1959	
129	High Hopes (From A Hole In The Head)	(Capitol Cl 15052)	28	1959	30	1959	(Capitol 4214)
130	High Hopes (Re-Entry)	(Capitol Cl 15052)	6	1959	0	1959	
131	Talk To Me		0	1959	38	1959	(Capitol 4284)
132	High Hopes (2nd Re-Entry)	(Capitol Cl 15052)	42	1960	0	1960	
133	It's Nice To Go Trav'ling	(Capitol Cl 15116)	48	1960	0	1960	
134	River Stay 'Way From My Door	(Capitol Cl 15135)	18	1960	0	1960	
135	Nice 'N' Easy	(Capitol Cl 15150)	15	1960	0	1960	
136	Ol' Mac Donald	(Capitol Cl 15168)	11	1960	25	1960	(Capitol 4466)
137	My Blue Heaven	(Capitol Cl 15193)	33	1961	0	1961	
138	Granada	(Reprise R 20010)	15	1961	0	1961	
139	The Coffee Song	(Reprise R 20035)	39	1961	0	1961	
140	Pocketful Of Miracles		0	1962	34	1962	(Reprise 20040)
141	Everybody's Twisting	(Reprise R 20063)	22	1962	0	1962	

ISSUE	TITLE	UK LBL	UK POS	UK YEAR	US POS	US YEAR	US LBL
142	Me And My Shadow	(Reprise R 20128)	20	1962	0	1962	
143	Me And My Shadow (Re-Entry)	(Reprise R 20128)	47	1963	0	1963	
144	My Kind Of Girl	(Reprise R 20148)	35	1963	0	1963	
145	Hello Dolly	(Reprise R 20351)	47	1964	0	1964	
146	Softly, As I Leave You		0	1964	27	1964	(Reprise 0301)
147	Somewhere In Your Heart		0	1965	32	1965	(Reprise 0332)
148	It Was A Very Good Year		0	1966	28	1966	(Reprise 0429)
* 149	Strangers In The Night	(Reprise R 23052)	1	1966	1	1966	(Reprise 0470)
150	Summer Wind	(Reprise Rs 20509)	36	1966	25	1966	(Reprise 0509)
151	That's Life	(Reprise Rs 20531)	46	1966	4	1966	(Reprise 0531)
* 152	Somethin' Stupid	(Reprise Rs 23166)	1	1967	1	1967	(Reprise 0561)
153	The World We Knew (Over And Over)	(Reprise Rs 20610)	33	1967	30	1967	(Reprise 0610)
154	Cycles		0	1968	23	1968	(Reprise 0764)
* 155	My Way	(Reprise Rs 20817)	5	1969	27	1969	(Reprise 0817)
156	Loves Been Good To Me	(Reprise Rs 20852)	8	1969	0	1969	
157	My Way (Re-Entry)	(Reprise Rs 20817)	49	1970	0	1970	
158	My Way (2nd Re-Entry)	(Reprise Rs 20817)	30	1970	0	1970	
159	My Way (3rd Re-Entry)	(Reprise Rs 20817)	33	1970	0	1970	
160	My Way (4th Re-Entry)	(Reprise Rs 20817)	28	1970	0	1970	
161	My Way (5th Re-Entry)	(Reprise Rs 20817)	18	1970	0	1970	
162	I Will Drink The Wine	(Reprise Rs 23487)	16	1971	0	1971	
163	My Way (6th Re-Entry)	(Reprise Rs 20817)	22	1971	0	1971	
164	My Way (7th Re-Entry)	(Reprise Rs 20817)	39	1971	0	1971	
165	My Way (8th Re-Entry)	(Reprise Rs 20817)	50	1972	0	1972	
166	I Believe I'm Gonna Love You	(Reprise K 14400)	34	1975	0	1975	
167	Theme From New York, New York	(Reprise K 14502)	59	1980	32	1980	(Reprise 49233)
168	Theme From New York, New York (Re-Entry	)(Reprise K 14502)	4	1986	0	1986	
169	I've Got You Under My Skin	(Island Cid 578)	4	1993	0	1993	
170	My Way (Re-Issue)	(Reprise W 0163cd)	45	1994	0	1994	

HITS 2, 10-11, 13, 85 ARE CREDITED TO FRANK SINATRA WITH HARRY JAMES & HIS ORCHESTRA
HITS 3-9 ARE WITH THE BOBBY TUCKER SINGERS • HITS 22-23 ARE WITH THE KEN LANE SINGERS • HIT 55 WAS WITH THE PIED PIPERS
HIT 66 WAS WITH THE HILLBILLY BAND • HIT 70 IS CREDITED TO FRANK SINATRA AND DORIS DAY • HITS 72, 76 ARE WITH THE JEFF ALEXANDER CHOIR
HITS 73-74 ARE WITH PAULA KELLY & THE MODERNAIRES • HIT 78 IS WITH THE MITCH MILLER & TRIO
HIT 84 IS CREDITED TO FRANK SINATRA AND DAGMAR • HITS 92-94, 96-102 ARE WITH NELSON RIDDLE'S ORCHESTRA)
HIT 123 IS CREDITED TO FRANK SINATRA AND KEELY SMITH • HIT 129 IS CREDITED TO FRANK SINATRA & A BUNCH OF KIDS
HITS 142-143 ARE CREDITED TO FRANK SINATRA AND SAMMY DAVIS JR. • HITS 144-145 ARE CREDITED TO FRANK SINATRA WITH COUNT BASIE
HIT 152 IS CREDITED TO NANCY SINATRA AND FRANK SINATRA • HIT 169 IS CREDITED TO FRANK SINATRA AND BONO • SEE ALSO BONO AND U2

Frank Stallone   Male Vocalist, Brother Of The Actor Sylvester Stallone from the USA

1	Far From Over	(RSO 95)	68	1983	10	1983	(RSO 815023)

Frank Weir & His Orchestra   Male Soprano Saxophonist/Bandleader from the UK

1	The Happy Wanderer		0	1954	4	1954	(London 1448)
2	My Son My Son	(Decca F9985)	1	1954	0	1954	
3	Caribbean Honeymoon	(Oriole Cb 1559)	42	1960	0	1960	

HIT 2 IS CREDITED TO VERA LYNN WITH FRANK WEIR, HIS SAXOPHONE, HIS ORCHESTRA AND CHORUS. • ALSO VERA LYNN

Frank Yankovic & His Yanks   A Self-Taught Accordionist From Davis, West Virginia

1	Just Because		0	1948	9	1948	(Columbia 12359)
* 2	Blue Skirt Waltz		0	1949	12	1949	(Columbia 12394)

Frank Zappa   Full Name Francis Vincent Zappa B: 21 Dec 1940 Baltimore, Maryland

1	Valley Girl		0	1982	32	1982	(Brking P. 02972)

HIT FEATURED FRANK'S DAUGHTER MOON UNIT ZAPPA. • IN 1965 HE FORMED THE GROUP MOTHERS OF INVENTION

Frank'O Moiraghi (Featuring) Amnesia   Mixed Vocal/Instrumental Duo From Italy

1	Feel My Body	(Multiply Cdmulty 10)	39	1996	0	1996	
2	Feel My Body (Re-Mix)	(Multiply Cdmulty 15)	40	1996	0	1996	

Franke   Real Name Franke Pharoah Male Vocalist from the UK

1	Understand This Groove	(China Wok 2028)	60	1992	0	1992	
2	Love Come Home	(Triangle Bluescd 001)	73	1994	0	1994	

HIT 2 IS CREDITED TO OUR TRIBE WITH FRANKE PHAROAH AND KRISTINE W

Franke & The Knockouts   Lead Singer Of The Quintet Is Frenke Previte

1	Sweetheart		0	1981	10	1981	(Millennium 11801)
2	You're My Girl		0	1981	27	1981	(Millennium 11808)
3	Without You (Not Another Lonely Night)		0	1982	24	1982	(Millennium 13105)

Frankie Avalon   Male Vocalist from the USA.

1	Dede Dinah		0	1958	7	1958	(Chancellor 1011)

ISSUE	TITLE	UK LBL	UK POS	UK YEAR	US POS	US YEAR	US LBL
2	Ginger Bread	(HMV Pop 517	30	1958	9	1958	(Chancellor 1021)
3	I'll Wait For You		0	1958	15	1958	(Chancellor 1026)
* 4	Venus	(HMV Pop 603)	16	1959	1	1959	(Chancellor 1031)
5	A Boy Without A Girl		0	1959	10	1959	(Chancellor 1036)
6	Bobby Sox To Stockings		0	1959	8	1959	(Chancellor 1036)
7	Just Ask Your Heart		0	1959	7	1959	(Chancellor 1040)
8	Swingin' On A Rainbow		0	1960	39	1960	(Chancellor 1045)
* 9	Why	(HMV Pop 688)	20	1960	1	1959	(Chancellor 1045)
10	Don't Throw Away All Those Teardrops	(HMV Pop 727)	37	1960	22	1960	(Chancellor 1048)
11	Where Are You		0	1960	32	1960	(Chancellor 1052)
12	Togetherness		0	1960	26	1960	(Chancellor 1056)
13	You Are Mine		0	1962	26	1962	(Chancellor 1107)

NAME FRANCIS AVALLONE B: 19 SEP 1939 PHILADELPHIA. • HIT 9 WAS SUBJECTED TO LEGAL PROCEEDINGS BECAUSE OF COPYRIGHT

Frankie Carle Orchestra Male Orchestra Leader/Composer/Pianist from the USA

6	Oh! What It Seemed To Be		0	1946	1	1946	(Columbia 36892)
7	One More Tomorrow		0	1946	10	1946	(Columbia 36978)
8	I'd Be Lost Without You		0	1946	14	1946	(Columbia 36994)
9	Without You		0	1946	24	1946	(Columbia 37069)
10	Rumors Are Flying		0	1946	1	1946	(Columbia 37069)
11	It's All Over Now		0	1946	6	1946	(Columbia 37146)
12	Roses In The Rain		0	1947	9	1947	(Columbia 37252)
13	And Mimi		0	1947	24	1947	(Columbia 37819)
14	Peggy O'Neil		0	1947	21	1947	(Columbia 37930)
15	(I'm A-Comin', I'm A-Courtin') Corabelle		0	1948	22	1948	(Columbia 37972)
16	Beg Your Pardon		0	1948	5	1948	(Columbia 38036)
17	Dreamy Lullaby		0	1948	25	1948	(Columbia 38090)
18	Twelfth Street Rag		0	1948	10	1948	(Columbia 35572)
19	Cruising Down The River (On A Sunday Afternoon)		0	1949	8	1949	(Columbia 38411)

Frankie Cutlass

| 1 | The Cypher; Part 3 | (Epic 6641445) | 59 | 1997 | 0 | 1997 | |

Frankie Ford Real Name Frank Guzzo B: 4 Aug 1939 Gretna, Louisiana

| * 1 | Sea Cruise | | 0 | 1959 | 14 | 1959 | (Ace 554) |
| 2 | Time After Time | | 0 | 1960 | 75 | 1960 | (Ace 580) |

Frankie Goes To Hollywood Male Vocal/Instrumental Group from the UK

1	Relax	(ZTT ZTAS1)	1	1983	67	1984	(Island 99805)
2	Two Tribes	(ZTT ZTAS3)	1	1984	0	1984	
3	Two Tribes (Re-Entry)	(ZTT ZTAS3)	73	1984	0	1984	
4	The Power Of Love	(ZTT ZTAS5)	1	1984	0	1984	
5	Relax (Re-Entry)	(ZTT ZTAS1)	58	1985	10	1985	(Island 99805)
6	The Power Of Love (Re-Entry)	(ZTT ZTAS5)	64	1985	0	1985	
7	Welcome To The Pleasure Dome	(ZTT ZTAS7)	2	1985	0	1985	
8	Rage Hard	(ZTT ZTAS22)	4	1986	0	1986	
9	Warriors (Of The Wasteland)	(ZTT ZTAS25)	19	1986	0	1986	
10	Watching The Wild Life	(ZTT ZTAS26)	28	1987	0	1987	
11	Relax (Re-Issue)	(Ztt Fgth 1cd)	5	1993	0	1993	
12	Welcome To The Pleasure Dome (Re-Mix)	(ZTT Fgth 2cd)	18	1993	0	1993	
13	The Power Of Love (Re-Issue)	(ZTTFgth 3cd)	10	1993	0	1993	
14	Two Tribes (Re-Mix)	(ZTT Fgth 4cd)	16	1994	0	1994	

Frankie Kelly Male Vocal/Instrumentalist from the USA

| 1 | Ain't That The Truth | (10 Ten 87) | 65 | 1985 | 0 | 1985 | |

Frankie Knuckles Male Producer from the UK

1	Tears	(Ffrr F 108)	50	1989	0	1989	
2	Your Love	(Trax Traxt 3)	59	1989	0	1989	
3	The Whistle Song	(Virgin America Vus 47)	17	1991	0	1991	
4	It's Hard Sometimes	(Virgin America Vus 52)	67	1991	0	1991	
5	Rain Falls	(Virgin America Vus 60)	48	1992	0	1992	
6	Too Many Fish	(Virgin America Vuscd 89)	34	1995	0	1995	
7	Whadda U Want (From Me)	(Virgin America Vuscd 98)	36	1995	0	1995	

HIT 1 IS CREDITED TO FRANKIE KNUCKLES PRESENTS SATOSHI TOMIIE • HIT 5 IS CREDITED TO FRANKIE KNUCKLES FEATURING LISA MICHAELIS
HIT 6 IS CREDITED TO FRANKIE KNUCKLES FEATURING ADEVA

Frankie Laine Male Vocalist, Real Name Frank Paul Lovecchio. B: 30 Mar 1913 in Chicago

| * 1 | That's My Desire | | 0 | 1947 | 4 | 1947 | (Mercury 5007) |
| 2 | Mam'selle (From Razor's Edge) | | 0 | 1947 | 14 | 1947 | (Mercury 5048) |

ISSUE	TITLE	UK LBL	UK POS	UK YEAR	US POS	US YEAR	US LBL
3	Two Loves Have I		0	1947	21	1947	(Mercury 5064)
4	Black And Blue		0	1947	27	1947	(Mercury 1026)
5	Shine		0	1948	9	1948	(Mercury 5091)
6	Monday Again		0	1948	24	1948	(Mercury 5105)
7	Baby, That Ain't Right		0	1948	20	1948	(Mercury 5114)
8	Ah, But It Happens		0	1948	21	1948	(Mercury 5158)
9	You're All I Want For Christmas		0	1948	11	1948	(Mercury 5177)
* 10	That Lucky Old Sun		0	1949	1	1949	(Mercury 5316)
11	Now That I Need You (From Red, Hot, And Blue)		0	1949	20	1949	(Mercury 5311)
* 12	Mule Train		0	1949	1	1949	(Mercury 5345)
13	You're All I Want For Christmas (Re-Entry)		0	1950	29	1950	(Mercury 5117)
* 14	Cry Of The Wild Goose		0	1950	1	1950	(Mercury 5363)
15	Satan Wears A Satin Gown		0	1950	28	1950	(Mercury 5358)
16	Swamp Girl		0	1950	12	1950	(Mercury 5390)
17	The Stars And Stripes Forever		0	1950	20	1950	(Mercury 5421)
18	Music Maestro Please		0	1950	13	1950	(Mercury 5488)
19	Dream A Little Dream Of Me		0	1950	18	1950	(Mercury 5488)
20	Nevertheless (I'm In Love With You)		0	1950	11	1950	(Mercury 5495)
21	If I Were A Bell (From Guys And Dolls)		0	1950	30	1950	(Mercury 5500)
22	Metro Polka		0	1951	19	1951	(Mercury 5581)
* 23	Jezebel		0	1951	2	1951	(Columbia 39367)
24	Rose Rose I Love You		0	1951	3	1951	(Columbia 39367)
25	Pretty Eyed Baby		0	1951	13	1951	(Columbia 39388)
26	In The Cool, Cool, Cool Of The Evening		0	1951	17	1951	(Columbia 39466)
27	The Girl In The Wood		0	1951	23	1951	(Columbia 39489)
28	Wonderful, Wasn't It		0	1951	17	1951	(Columbia 39489)
29	Hey, Good Lookin'		0	1951	9	1951	(Columbia 39570)
30	Gambella (The Gamblin' Lady)		0	1951	19	1951	(Columbia 39570)
* 31	Jealousy (Jalousie)		0	1951	3	1951	(Columbia 39585)
32	Hambone		0	1952	6	1952	(Columbia 39672)
33	The Grandy Dancer's Ball		0	1952	21	1952	(Columbia 39685)
34	When You're In Love		0	1952	30	1952	(Columbia 39685)
* 35	Sugarbush	(Columbia Db 3123)	8	1952	7	1952	(Columbia 39693)
* 36	High Noon (Do Not Forsake Me)	(Columbia Db 3113)	7	1952	5	1952	(Columbia 39770)
37	The Rock Of Gibraltar		0	1952	20	1952	(Columbia 39770)
38	Tonight We're Setting The Woods On Fire		0	1952	21	1952	(Columbia 38967)
39	Sugarbush (Re-Entry)	(Columbia Db 3123)	8	1952	0	1952	
40	I'm Just A Poor Bachelor		0	1953	14	1953	(Columbia 39903)
41	Tonight You Belong To Me		0	1953	26	1953	(Columbia 39903)
* 42	I Believe	(Philips Pb 117)	1	1953	2	1953	(Columbia 39938)
43	Your Cheatin' Heart		0	1953	18	1953	(Columbia 39938)
* 44	Tell Me A Story	(Philips Pb 126)	5	1953	4	1953	
45	The Little Boy And The Old Man		0	1953	24	1953	(Columbia 39570)
46	Girl In The Wood	(Columbia Db 2907)	11	1953	0	1953	
47	I Let Her Go		0	1953	27	1953	(Columbia 39979)
48	Hey Joe!	(Philips Pb 172)	1	1953	6	1953	(Columbia 40036)
49	Where The Winds Blow	(Philips Pb 167)	2	1953	0	1953	
50	Tell Me A Story (Re-Entry)	(Philips Pb 126)	12	1953	0	1953	
51	Answer Me (Lord Above)	(Philips Pb 196)	1	1953	24	1953	(Columbia 40079)
52	Blowing Wind (The Ballad Of Black Gold)	(Philips Pb 207)	2	1954	21	1953	(Columbia 40036)
53	Way Down Yonder In New Orleans		0	1953	26	1953	(Columbia 40116)
54	Grenada (Granada)	(Philips Pb 242)	10	1954	17	1954	(Columbia 40136)
55	The Kid's Last Fight	(Philips Pb 258)	3	1954	20	1954	(Columbia 40170)
56	Grenada (Granada) (Re-Entry)	(Philips Pb 242)	9	1954	0	1954	
57	Some Day		0	1954	14	1954	(Columbia 40235)
58	My Friend	(Philips Pb 316)	3	1954	0	1954	
59	Rain, Rain, Rain	(Philips Pb 311)	8	1954	21	1954	(Columbia 40295)
60	There Must Be A Reason	(Philips Pb 306)	9	1954	0	1954	
61	Your Heart, My Heart		0	1954	28	1954	(Columbia 40295)
62	In The Beginning	(Philips Pb 404)	20	1955	0	1955	
63	Cool Water	(Philips Pb 465)	2	1955	0	1955	
64	Strange Lady In Town	(Philips Pb 478)	6	1955	0	1955	
65	Humming Bird	(Philips Pb 498)	16	1955	17	1955	(Columbia 40526)
66	Hawkeye	(Philips Pb 519)	7	1955	0	1955	
67	A Woman In Love	(Philips Pb 617)	1	1956	19	1956(	Columbia 40583)
68	Sixteen Tons	(Philips Pb 539)	10	1956	0	1956	

ISSUE	TITLE	UK LBL	UK POS	UK YEAR	US POS	US YEAR	US LBL
69	Hell Hath No Fury	(Philips Pb 585)	28	1956	0	1956	
* 70	Moonlight Gambler	(Philips Pb 638)	13	1956	3	1956	(Columbia 40780)
71	Moonlight Gambler (Re-Entry)	(Philips Pb 638)	28	1957	0	1957	
72	Love Is A Golden Ring	(Philips Pb 676)	19	1957	10	1957	(Columbia 40856)
73	Good Evening Friends / Up Above My Head	(Philips Pb 708)	25	1957	0	1957	
74	Rawhide	(Philips Pb 965)	6	1959	0	1959	
75	Rawhide (Re-Entry)	(Philips Pb 965)	41	1960	0	1960	
76	Gunslinger	(Philips Pb 1135)	50	1961	0	1961	
77	I'll Take Care Of Your Cares		0	1967	39	1967	(ABC 10891)
78	Making Memories		0	1967	35	1967	(ABC 10924)
79	You Gave Me A Mountain		0	1969	24	1969	(ABC11174)

HIT 12 WAS WITH THE MULESKINNERS • HITS 26, 30, 53 TO FRANKIE LAINE AND JO STAFFORD • HITS 35, 39 TO DORIS DAY AND FRANKIE LAINE
HITS 44, 45,5 0 ARE CREDITED TO FRANKIE LAINE AND JIMMY BOYD • HIT 59 IS CREDITED TO FRANKIE LAINE & THE FOUR LADS AND BUDDY COLE QUARTET
HIT 72 IS CREDITED TO FRANKIE LAINE WITH THE EASY RIDERS • HIT 76 IS CREDITED TO FRANKIE LAINE AND JOHNNIE RAY • HE WAS WITH THE THREE BLAZERS FOR A TIME

Frankie Lymon & The Teenagers   R&B Male Vocal Group from the USA   Names: Herman Santiago, Joe Negroni & Sherman Games

ISSUE	TITLE	UK LBL	UK POS	UK YEAR	US POS	US YEAR	US LBL
* 1	Why Do Fools Fall In Love	(Columbia Db 3772)	1	1956	6	1956	(Gee 1002)
2	I Want You To Be My Girl		0	1956	13	1956	(Gee 1012)
+ 3	I Promise To Remember		0	1956	10	1956	(Gee 1018)
+ 4	The ABCs Of Love		0	1956	14	1956	(Gee 1022)
5	I'm Not A Juvenile Delinquent	(Columbia Db 3878)	12	1957	0	1957	
6	Baby Baby	(Columbia Db 3878)	4	1957	0	1957	
7	Goody Goody	(Columbia Db 3983)	24	1957	20	1957	(Gee 1039)

OBITUARY : FRANKIE D: 28 FEB 1968 DRUG OVERDOSE. • JOE D : 5 SEP 1978. • SHERMAN D: 26 FEB 1977. FRANKIE B: 30 SEP 1942 IN NEW YORK.
THEY FORMED AS THE PREMIERS IN 1955 WITH JIMMY MERCHANT, HERMAN SANTIAGO, JOE NEGRONI & SHERMAN GAMES •
HIT 1 IS CREDITED TO TEENAGERS FEATURING FRANKIE LYMON

Frankie Mcbride   Male Vocalist from Ireland

ISSUE	TITLE	UK LBL	UK POS	UK YEAR	US POS	US YEAR	US LBL
1	Five Little Fingers	(Emerald Md 1081)	19	1967	0	1967	

Frankie Miller   Male Vocalist from the UK

ISSUE	TITLE	UK LBL	UK POS	UK YEAR	US POS	US YEAR	US LBL
1	Be Good To Yourself	(Chrysalis Chs 2147)	27	1977	0	1977	
2	Darlin'	(Chrysalis Chs 2255)	6	1978	0	1978	
3	When I'm Away From You	(Chrysalis Chs 2276)	42	1979	0	1979	
4	Caledonia	(MCA MCA 2001)	45	1992	0	1992	

Frankie Oliver

ISSUE	TITLE	UK LBL	UK POS	UK YEAR	US POS	US YEAR	US LBL
1	Give Her What She Wants	(Island Jamaica Ijcd 2011)	58	1997	0	1997	

Frankie Smith   Frankie Is A Writer/Producer From Philadelphia

ISSUE	TITLE	UK LBL	UK POS	UK YEAR	US POS	US YEAR	US LBL
* 1	Double Dutch Bus		0	1981	30	1981	(Wmot 5356)

Frankie Valli   Male Vocalist, Real Name Francis Castellicio. B: 3 May 1937 Newark, New Jersey

ISSUE	TITLE	UK LBL	UK POS	UK YEAR	US POS	US YEAR	US LBL
1	(Your Gonna) Hurt Yourself		0	1966	39	1966	(Smash 2015)
* 2	Can't Take My Eyes Off You		0	1967	2	1967	(Philips 40446)
3	I Make A Fool Of Myself		0	1967	18	1967	(Philips 40484)
4	To Give (The Reason I Live)		0	1967	29	1967	(Philips 40510)
5	You're Ready Now	(Philips 320226)	11	1970	0	1970	
* 6	My Eyes Adored You	(Private Stock Pvt 1)	5	1975	1	1974	(Private Stock 45003)
7	Swearin' To God	(Private Stock Pvt 21)	31	1975	6	1975	(Private Stock 45021)
8	Our Day Will Come		0	1975	11	1975	(Private Stock 45043)
9	Fallen Angel	(Private Stock Pvt 51)	11	1976	36	1976	(Private Stock 45074)
* 10	Grease	(RSO 897)	3	1976	1	1978	(Rso 897)
11	Grease - The Dream Mix	(PO 136)	47	1991	0	1991	

HIT 11 IS CREDITED TO FRANKIE VALLI, JOHN TRAVOLTA AND OLIVIA NEWTON-JOHN • SEE ALSO FOUR SEASONS. • PREVIOUSLY RECORDED UNDER THE NAME OF
FRANK VALLEY IN 1953 • IN 1955 HE FORMED THE GROUP THE VARIATONES WHICH BECAME FOUR LOVERS AND IN 1961 FINALLY BECAME THE FOUR SEASONS

Frankie Vaughan   Male Vocalist, Real Name Frank Abeison. B: 3 Feb 1928 Liverpool, England

ISSUE	TITLE	UK LBL	UK POS	UK YEAR	US POS	US YEAR	US LBL
1	Istanbul	(HMV B 10599)	11	1954	0	1954	
2	Happy Days And Lonely Nights	(HMV B 10783)	12	1955	0	1955	
3	Tweedle Dee	(Philips Pb 423)	17	1955	0	1955	
4	Seventeen	(Philips Pb 511)	18	1955	0	1955	
5	My Boy Flat Top	(Philips Pb 544)	20	1956	0	1956	
6	Green Door	(Philips Pb 640)	2	1956	0	1956	
7	Garden Of Eden	(Philips Pb 660)	1	1957	0	1957	
8	Man On Fire / Wanderin' Eyes	(Philips Pb 729)	6	1957	0	1957	
9	Gotta Have Something In The Bank Frank	(Philips Pb 751)	8	1957	0	1957	
10	Kisses Sweeter Than Wine	(Philips Pb 775)	8	1957	0	1957	
11	Can't Get Along Without You / We Are Not Alone	(Philips Pb 793)	11	1958	0	1958	
12	Kewpie Doll	(Philips Pb 825)	10	1958	0	1958	

ISSUE	TITLE	UK LBL	UK POS	UK YEAR	US POS	US YEAR	US LBL
13	Wonderful Things	(Philips Pb 834)	22	1958	0	1958	
14	Judy		0	1958	22	1958	(Epic 9273)
15	Wonderful Things (Re-Entry)	(Philips Pb 834)	27	1958	0	1958	
16	Am I Wasting My Time On You	(Philips Pb 865)	25	1958	0	1958	
17	Am I Wasting My Time On You (Re-Entry)	(Philips Pb 865)	27	1959	0	1959	
18	That's My Doll	(Philips Pb 895)	28	1959	0	1959	
19	Come Softly To Me	(Philips Pb 913)	9	1959	0	1959	
20	The Heart Of A Man	(Philips Pb 930)	5	1959	0	1959	
21	Walkin' Tall	(Philips Pb 931)	28	1959	0	1959	
22	Walkin' Tall (Re-Entry)	(Philips Pb 931)	29	1959	0	1959	
23	What More Do You Want	(Philips Pb 985)	25	1960	0	1960	
24	Kookie Little Paradise	(Philips Pb 1054)	31	1960	0	1960	
25	Milord	(Philips Pb 1066)	34	1960	0	1960	
26	Tower Of Strength	(Philips Pb 1195)	1	1961	0	1961	
27	Don't Stop Twist	(Philips 1219)	22	1962	0	1962	
28	Herecules	(Philips 326542 Bf)	42	1962	0	1962	
29	Hello Dolly	(Philips Bf 1339)	18	1964	0	1964	
30	Loop-De-Loop	(Philips 326566 Bf)	5	1963	0	1963	
31	Hey Mama	(Philips Bf 1254)	21	1963	0	1963	
32	Someone Must Have Hurt You A Lot	(Philips BF 1394)	46	1965	0	1965	
33	There Must Be A Way	Columbia Db 8248)	7	1967	0	1967	
34	So Tired	(Columbia Db 8298)	21	1967	0	1967	
35	Nevertheless	(Columbia Db 8354)	29	1968	0	1968	

HITS 9, 19 ARE CREDITED TO FRANKIE VAUGHAN & THE KAYE SISTERS

Frankie Yankovic & His Yanks Male Bandleader/Instrumentalist (Accordion),

1	Just Because		0	1948	9	1948	(Columbia 12359)
! 2	The Iron Range		0	1949	13	1949	(Columbia 12381)
* 3	Blue Skirt Waltz		0	1949	12	1949	(Columbia 12394)

FRANKIE IS A MEMBER OF THE INTERNATIONAL POLKA HALL OF FAME
B: 28 JUL 1915 IN DAVIS, WEST VIRGINIA & RAISED IN CLEVELAND • HIT 3 IS CREDITED TO FRANKIE YANKOVIC & HIS YANKS WITH THE MARLIN SISTERS

Frantique Female Vocal Group from the USA

1	Strut Your Funky Stuf	(Philadelphia Int Pir 7728)	10	1979	0	1979	

Frash Male Vocal/Instrumental Group from the UK

1	Here I Go Again	(PWL International Flipcd 1)	69	1995	0	1995	

Frazier Chorus Mixed Vocal/Instrumental Group from the UK

1	Dream Kitchen	(Virgin Vs 1145)	57	1989	0	1989	
2	Typical!	(Virgin Vs 1174)	53	1989	0	1989	
3	Sloppy Heart	(Virgin Vs 1192)	73	1989	0	1989	
4	Cloud 8	(Virgin Vs 1252)	52	1990	0	1990	
5	Nothing	(Virgin Vs 1284)	51	1990	0	1990	
6	Walking On Air	(Virgin Vs 1330)	30	1991	0	1991	

Freak Nasty

1	Da' Dip		0	1997	15	1997	(Hard Hood/Power 0112)

Freak Power Male Vocal/Instrumental Group from the USA/UK

1	Turn On, Tune In, Cop Out	(Fourth & Broadway Brcd 284)	29	1993	0	1993	
2	Rush	(Fourth & Broadway Brcd 291)	62	1994	0	1994	
3	Turn On, Tune In, Cop Out (Re-Issue)	(Fourth & Broadway Brcd 317)	3	1995	0	1995	
4	New Direction	(Fourth & Broadway Brcd 331)	60	1996	0	1996	

Freaky Realistic Mixed Vocal/Instrumental Group From Uk/Japan

1	Koochie Ryder	(Frealism Frecd 2)	52	1993	0	1993	
2	Leonard Nimoy	(Frealism Frecd 3)	71	1993	0	1993	

Fred Astaire Male Actor/Song And Dance, Real Name Frederick Austerlitz B: 10 May 1899 Omaha, Nedraska.

* 36	How Could You Believe Me When I Said I Loved You		0	1951	30	1951	(MGM 30316)

WHEN YOU KNOW I'VE BEEN A LIAR ALL MY LIFE
HIT 36 IS CREDITED TO FRED ASTAIRE AND JANE POWELL • JANE POWELL'S REAL NAME IS SUZANNE BRUCE. B: OREGON ON APRIL FOOLS DAY

Fred Bertelmann & The Hansen Quartet

* 1	Der Lachend Vagabund		0	1958	1	1958	

Fred Hughes Fred Hails From Arkansas And Formed The Band The Creators

1	Oo Wee Baby, I Love You		0	1965	23	1965	(Vee-Jay 684)

Fred Knoblock Male Vocalist, B: Jackson, Mississippi

1	Why Not Me		0	1980	18	1980	(Scotti Brothers 518)
3	Killin Time		0	1980	28	1980	(Scotti Brothers 609)

ISSUE	TITLE	UK LBL	UK POS	UK YEAR	US POS	US YEAR	US LBL
Fred Wedlock Male Vocalist from the UK							
1	Oldest Swinger In Town	(Rocket Xpres 46)	6	1981	0	1981	
Fred Wesley & The JB's							
* 1	Doin' It To Death		0	1973	22	1973	(People 621)
Freda Payne Female Vocalist, B: 19 Sep 1945 Detroit Sister Of Supremes' Cherrie Payne							
* 1	Band Of Gold	(Invictus Inv 502)	1	1970	3	1970	(Invictus 9075)
2	Deeper And Deeper	(Invictus Inv 505)	33	1970	24	1970	(Invictus 9080)
3	Cherish What Is Dear To You	(Invictus Inv 509)	46	1971	0	1971	
* 4	Bring The Boys Home		0	1971	12	1971	(Invictus 9092)
Freddie & The Dreamers Male Vocal/Instrumental Group from the UK Real Name Freddie Garrity B: 14 Nov 1940, Manchester, England							
1	If You Gotta Make A Fool Of Somebody	(Columbia Db 7032)	3	1963	0	1963	
* 2	I'm Telling You Now	(Columbia Db 7086)	2	1963	1	1965	(Tower 125)
* 3	You Were Made For Me	(Columbia Db 7147)	3	1963	21	1964	(Tower 127)
4	Over You	(Columbia Db 7214)	13	1964	0	1964	
5	I Love You Baby	(Columbia Db 7286)	16	1964	0	1964	
6	Just For You	(Columbia Db 7322)	41	1964	0	1964	
* 7	I Understand (Just How You Feel)	(Columbia Db 7381)	5	1964	36	1965	(Mercury 72377)
8	A Little You	(Columbia Db 7526)	26	1965	0	1965	
9	Do The Freddie		0	1965	18	1965	(Mercury 72428)
10	Thou Shalt Not Steal	(Columbia Db 7720)	44	1965	0	1965	
Freddie Bell & The Bell Boys Male Vocal/Instrumental Group from the USA							
1	Giddy Up A Ding Dong	(Mercury Mt 122)	4	1956	0	1956	
Freddie Hart Real Name Fred Segrest B: 21 Dec 1926 Lochapoka, Alabama							
* 16	Easy Loving		0	1971	17	1971	(Capitol 3115)
	OTHER HITS WERE C/W						
Freddie Jackson Male Vocalist, B: 2 Oct 1956 And Raised In Harlem He Worked For Many Years As A Backup Singer							
1	Rock Me Tonight (For Old Times Sake)	(Capitol Cl 358)	18	1986	18	1985	(Capitol 5459)
2	You Are My Lady	(Capitol Cl 379)	49	1985	12	1985	(Capitol 5495)
3	He'll Never Love You (Like I Do)		0	1986	25	1986	(Capitol 5535)
4	Tasty Love	(Capitol Cl 428	73	1986	0	1986	
5	Have You Ever Loved Somebody	(Capitol Cl 437)	33	1987	0	1987	
6	Jam Tonight		0	1987	32	1987	(Capitol 44037)
7	Nice 'N' Slow	(Capitol Cl 502)	56	1988	0	1988	
8	Crazy (For Me)	(Capitol Cl 510)	41	1988	0	1988	
9	Me And Mrs. Jones	(Capitol Cl 668)	32	1992	0	1992	
10	Make Love Easy	(RCA 74321179162)	70	1994	0	1994	
Freddie James Male Vocalist from Canada							
1	Get Up And Boogie	(Warner Bros K 17478)	54	1979	0	1979	
Freddie King							
1	Hide Away		0	1961	29	1961	(Federal 12401)
Freddie McGregor Male Vocalist from Jamaica							
1	Just Don't Want To Be Lonely	(Germain Dg 24)	9	1987	0	1987	
2	That Girl (Groovy Situation)	(Polydor Posp 884)	46	1987	0	1987	
Freddie Mercury Male Vocalist, Real Name Fred Bulsara. B: 5 Sep 1946 from Zanzibar							
1	Love Kills	(CBS A 4735)	10	1984	0	1984	
2	I Was Born To Love You	(CBS A 6019)	11	1985	0	1985	
3	Made In Heaven	CBS A 6413)	57	1985	0	1985	
4	Living On My Own	(CBS A 6555)	50	1985	0	1985	
5	Time	(EMI EMI 5559)	32	1986	0	1986	
6	The Great Pretender	(Parlophone R 6151)	4	1987	0	1987	
7	Barcelona	(Polydor Posp 887)	8	1987	0	1987	
8	Barcelona (Re-Issue)	(Polydor Po 221)	2	1992	0	1992	
9	In My Defence	(Parlophone R 6331)	8	1992	0	1992	
10	The Great Pretender (Re-Issue)	(Parlophone Cdr 6336)	29	1993	0	1993	
11	Living On My Own (Re-Mix)	(Parlophone CDR 6355)	1	1993	0	1993	
	HITS 7-8 ARE CREDITED TO FREDDIE MERCURY & MONTSERRAT CABALLE • SEE ALSO QUEEN • OBITUARY : D: 24 NOV 1991 OF AIDS.						
Freddie North Freddie Hails From Nashville And Is A DJ For WLAC							
1	She's All I Got		0	1971	39	1971	(Mankind 12004)
Freddie Notes & The Rudies Male Vocal/Instrumental Group From Jamaica							
1	Montego Bay	(Trojan Tr 7791)	45	1970	0	1970	

ISSUE	TITLE	UK LBL	UK POS	UK YEAR	US POS	US YEAR	US LBL
Freddie Scott	Male Songwriter/Vocalist, B: 24 Apr 1933 Providence, Rhode Island						
1	Hey Girl		0	1963	10	1963	(Colpix 692)
2	Are You Lonely For Me		0	1967	39	1967	(Shout 207)
Freddie Starr	Male Comedian/Vocalist from the UK						
1	It's You	(Tiffany 6121 501)	9	1974	0	1974	
2	White Christmas	(Thunderbird The 102)	41	1975	0	1975	
Freddy Breck	Male Vocalist from Germany						
1	So In Love With You	(Decca F 13481)	44	1974	0	1974	
Freddy Cannon	Male Vocalist, Real Name Frederick Picariell. B: 4 Dec 1939 Lynn, Massachusetts						
* 1	Tallahassee Lassie	(Top Rank Jar 135)	17	1959	6	1959	(Swan 4031)
* 2	Way Down Yonder In New Orleans	(Top Rank Jar 247)	3	1960	3	1959	(Swan 4043)
3	Chattanooga Shoe-Shine Boy		0	1960	34	1960	(Swan 4050)
4	California Here I Come	(Top Rank Jar 309)	33	1960	0	1960	
5	Indiana	(Top Rank Jar 309)	42	1960	0	1960	
6	California Here I Come (Re-Entry)	(Top Rank Jar 309)	46	1960	0	1960	
7	The Urge	(Top Rank Jar 369)	18	1960	0	1960	
8	Jump Over		0	1960	28	1960	(Swan 4053)
9	Muskrat Ramble	(Top Rank Jar 548)	32	1961	0	1961	
10	Transistor Sister		0	1961	35	1961	(Swan 4078)
* 11	Palasades Park	(Stateside Ss 101)	20	1962	3	1962	(Swan 4106)
12	Abigail Beecher		0	1964	16	1964	(Warner Bros 5409)
* 13	Action		0	1965	13	1965	(Warner Bros 4645)
Freddy Fender	Male Vocalist, Real Name Baldemar Huerta B: 4 Jun 1937 San Benito, Texas						
* 1	Before The Next Teardrop Falls		0	1975	1	1975	(ABC/Dot 17540)
* 2	Wasted Days And Wasted Nights		0	1975	3	1975	(ABC/Dot 17558)
3	Since I Met You Baby		0	1975	45	1975	(Grt 031)
4	Secret Love		0	1975	20	1975	(ABC/Dot 17585)
! 5	Wild Side Of Life		0	1976	13	1976	(Grt 039)
6	You'll Lose A Good Thing		0	1976	32	1976	(ABC/Dot 17607)
7	Vaya Con Dios		0	1976	59	1976	(ABC/Dot 17627)
8	Living It Down		0	1976	72	1976	(ABC/Dot 17652)
	HIT 2 WAS ORIGINALLY RECORDED IN 1959 ON THE DUNCAN LABEL						
Freddy King	Real Name Freddie Christian B: 30 Sep 1934 Gilmer, Texas						
1	Hide Away		0	1961	29	1961	(Federal 12401)
	OBITUARY : D: 28 DEC 1976 HEART ATTACK.						
Freddy Martin & His Orchestra	Male Bandleader/Saxophonist, B: 9 Dec In Springfield, Ohio, The Year Of His Birth Is Unclear)						
* 35	Piano Concerto In B Flat		0	1941	1	1941	(Bluebird 11211)
61	One-Zy, Two-Zy (I Love You-Zy)		0	1946	4	1946	(RCA Victor 1826)
62	Bumble Boogie		0	1946	7	1946	(RCA Victor 1829)
63	Doin' What Comes Natur'lly		0	1946	2	1946	(RCA Victor 1878)
64	To Each His Own		0	1946	1	1946	(RCA Victor 1921)
65	Managua Nicaragua		0	1947	1	1947	(RCA Victor 2026)
66	Santa Catalina (Island Of Romance)		0	1947	20	1947	(RCA Victor 2136)
67	Moon-Faced, Starry-Eyed		0	1947	14	1947	(RCA Victor 2176)
68	The Lady From 29 Palms		0	1947	5	1947	(RCA Victor 2347)
69	Come To The Mardi Gras		0	1947	16	1947	(RCA Victor 2288)
70	Don't You Love Me Anymore?		0	1947	23	1947	(RCA Victor 2473)
71	Treasure Of The Sierra Madre		0	1948	23	1948	(RCA Victor 2590)
72	Don't Call It Love		0	1948	23	1948	(RCA Victor 2590)
73	Sabre Dance Boogie		0	1948	6	1948	(RCA Victor 2721)
74	The New Look		0	1948	21	1948	(RCA Victor 2769)
75	The Dickey-Bird Song		0	1948	5	1948	(RCA Victor 2617)
76	On A Slow Boat To China		0	1948	4	1948	(RCA Victor 3123)
* 77	I've Got A Lovely Bunch Of Coconuts		0	1949	8	1949	(RCA Victor 78-3554)
78	Music! Music! Music!		0	1950	5	1950	(RCA Victor 78-3693)
79	The Third Man Theme		0	1950	17	1950	(RCA Victor 3797)
80	The Aba Daba Honeymoon		0	1951	12	1951	(RCA Victor 4065)
81	Never Been Kissed		0	1951	19	1951	(RCA Victor 4099)
82	My Truly, Truly Fair		0	1951	18	1951	(RCA Victor 4159)
83	Down Yonder		0	1951	15	1951	(RCA Victor 4267)
84	April In Portugal (The Whisp'ring Serenade)		0	1953	15	1953	(RCA Victor 5052)
85	Lonesome Polecat		0	1954	27	1954	(RCA Victor 5833)

ISSUE	TITLE	UK LBL	UK POS	UK YEAR	US POS	US YEAR	US LBL
Freddy Quinn	Male Actor/Vocalist, Real Name Manfred Petz from Vienna						
* 1	Heimweh (Memories Are Made Of This)		0	1956	1	1956	
* 2	Heimatlos (Homeless)		0	1958	0	1958	
* 3	Unter Freemden Sternen (Under Foreign Stars)		0	1960	0	1960	
* 4	La Paloma		0	1961	0	1961	
* 5	Junge Komm Bald Wieder (Son, Come Home Soon)		0	1962	0	1962	
* 6	Vergangen, Vergessen, Vorueber (Gone, Forgotten,All Over)		0	1964	0	1964	
	HE IS THE EUROPEAN POP CHAMPION FOR MILLION SELLERS, UP TO 1969 HAD SOLD OVER 20 MILLION UNITS						
Frederick Knight	Male Vocalist, B: 15 Aug 1944 Alabama						
1	I've Been Lonely For So Long	(Stax 2025 098)	22	19722	7	1972	(Stax 0117)
Free	Male Vocal/Instrumental Group from the UK						
1	All Right Now	(Island Wip 6082)	2	1970	4	1970	(A&M 1206)
2	My Brother Jake	(Island Wip 6100)	4	1971	0	1971	
3	A Little Bit Of Love	(Island Wip 6129)	13	1972	0	1972	
4	Wishing Well	(Island Wip 6146)	7	1973	0	1973	
5	All Right Now (Re-Entry)	(Island Wip 6082)	15	1973	0	1973	
6	Free (EP)	(Island Iep 6)	11	1978	0	1978	
7	Free (EP) (Re-Entry)	(Island Iep 6)	57	1982	0	1982	
8	All Right Now (Re-Mix)	(Island Is 486	8	1991	0	1991	
	ORIGINAL MEMBERS WERE PAUL RODGERS, PAUL KOSSOFF, SIMON KIRKE & ANDY FRASER • OBITUARY: KOSSOFF D: 19 MAR 1976 HEART ATTACK						
Free Movement	Vocal Sextet From Los Angeles						
1	I've Found Someone On My Own		0	1971	5	1971	(Decca 32818)
Free Spirit	Mixed Vocal Duo from the UK						
1	No More Rainy Days	(Columbia 6612822)	68	1995	0	1995	
Freedom Williams	Male Rapper from the USA						
1	Gonna Make You Sweat (Everybody Dance Now)	(CBS 6564540)	3	1990	0	1990	
2	Here We Go	(Columbia 6567537)	20	1991	0	1991	
3	Things That Make You Go Hmmm	(Columbia 6566907)	4	1991	0	1991	
4	Voice Of Freedom	(Columbia 6593342)	62	1993	0	1993	
Freeez	Male Vocal/Instrumental Group from the UK						
1	Keep In Touch	(Calibre Cab 103)	49	1980	0	1980	
2	Southern Freeez	(Beggars Banquet Beg 51)	8	1981	0	1981	
3	Flying High	(Beggars Banquet Beg 55)	35	1981	0	1981	
4	I.O.U.	(Beggars Banquet Beg 96)	2	1983	0	1983	
5	Pop Goes My Love	(Beggars Banquet Beg 98)	26	1983	0	1983	
6	I.O.U. (Re-Mix)	(Citybeat CBE 709)	23	1987	0	1987	
7	Southern Freeez (Re-Mix)	(Total Control Toco 14)	63	1987	0	1987	
Freefall	Male Production/Instrumental Group from The USA/UK						
1	Feel Surreal	(FFRR FX 160)	63	1991	0	1991	
Freiheit	Male Vocal/Instrumental Group from Germany						
1	Keeping The Dream Alive	(CBS 652989 7)	15	1988	0	1988	
Fresh 4 featuring Lizz E	Male Scratch Group With Female Vocal Group from the UK						
1	Wishing On A Star	(10 Ten 287)	10	1989	0	1989	
Freshies	Male Vocal/Instrumental Group From The Uk						
1	I'm In Love With The Girl On A Certain	(MCA 670)	54	1981	0	1981	
	MANCHESTER MEGASTORE CHECKOUT DESK						
Freur	Male Vocal/Instrumental Group from the UK						
1	Doot Doot	(CBS A 3141)	59	1983	0	1983	
Frida	Female Vocalist, Real Name Anni-Frid Lyngstad B: 15 Nov 1945 In Narvik, Norway						
1	I Know There's Something Going On	(Epic Epc A2603)	43	1982	13	1983	(Atlantic 89984)
2	Time	(Epic A 3983)	45	1983	0	1983	
	(B: 15 NOV 1945 NARVIK, NORWAY) • HIT 2 IS CREDITED TO FRIDA AND B.A. ROBERTSON • SEE ALSO ABBA						
Friend & Lover	Real Names James & Cathy Post						
1	Reach Out Of The Darkness		0	1968	10	1968	(Verve F. 5069)
Friends Again	Male Vocal/Instrumental Group From the UK						
1	The Friends Again (EP)	(Mercury Fa 1)	59	1984	0	1984	
Friends Of Distinction	Names Are Harry Elston, Floyd Butler, Jessica Cleaves & Barbara Jean Love						
* 1	Crazin' In The Grass		0	1969	3	1969	(RCA 0107)
* 2	Going In Circles		0	1969	15	1969	(RCA 0204)
3	Love Or Let Me Be Lonely		0	1970	6	1970	(RCA 0319)

ISSUE	TITLE	UK LBL	UK POS	UK YEAR	US POS	US YEAR	US LBL
Frijid Pink	Male Vocal/Instrumental Quartet from Detroit, Kelly Green, Gary Thompson, Thomas Harris & Rich Stevens						
* 1	The House Of The Rising Sun	(Deram Dm 288)	4	1970	7 *	1970	(Parrot 341)
Frogmen							
1	Underwater		0	1961	44	1961	(Candix 314)
Front 242	Male Vocal/Instrumental Group from the USA/Belgium						
1	Religion	(Rre Rre 106cd)	46	1993	0	1993	
Fugees							
1	Fu-Gee-La	(Columbia 6630662)	21	1996	29	1996	
2	Killing Me Softly	(Columbia 6633435)	1	1996	0	1996	
3	Ready Or Not	(Columbia 6637215)	1	1996	0	1996	
4	No Woman, No Cry	(Columbia 6639925)	2	1996	0	1996	
5	Killing Me Softly (Re-Entry)	(Columbia 6633435)	61	1996	0	1996	
6	Rumble In The Jungle	(Mercury 5740692)	3	1997	0	1997	
7	Hip-Hopera		0	1997	81	1997	(TVT 1464)
Fuifui (Fifi) Ouyang							
* 1	Ame No Midoosuji		0	1971	0	1971	
Full Circle	Male Vocal Group From the USA						
1	Workin' Up A Sweat	(EMI America Ea 229)	41	1987	0	1987	
Full Force	Male Vocal/Instrumental Group From the USA						
1	I Wonder If I Take You Home	(CBS A 6057)	53	1985	0	1985	
2	I Wonder If I Take You Home (Re-Entry)	(CBS A 6057)	12	1985	0	1985	
3	Alice I Want You Just For Me	(CBS A 6640)	9	1985	0	1985	
4	Naughty Girls (Need Love Too)	(Jive Foxy 9)	31	1988	5	1988	
5	I'm Real	(Scotti Brothers Jsb 1)	31	1988	0	1988	
Full Intention	Male Instrumental/Production Duo from the UK						
1	America (I Love America)	(Stress Cdstr 56)	32	1996	0	1996	
2	Uptown Downtown	(Stress Cdstr 67)	61	1996	0	1996	
3	Shake Your Body (Down To The Ground)	(Stress Cdstr 82)	34	1997	0	1997	
Full Monty Allstars (Featuring) T.J. Davis	Male Vocal/Instrumental Group from the UK						
1	Brilliant Feeling	(Arista 74321380902)	72	1996	0	1996	
Fun Boy Three	Male Vocal/Instrumental Group From the UK						
1	The Lunatics (Have Taken Over The Asylum)	(Chrysalis Chs 2563)	20	1981	0	1981	
2	It Ain't What You Do It's The Way That You Do It	(Chrysalis Chs 2570)	4	1982	0	1982	
3	Really Saying Something	(Deram Nana 1)	5	1982	0	1982	
4	The Telephone Always Rings	(Chrysalis Chs 2609)	17	1982	0	1982	
5	Summertime	(Chrysalis Chs 2629)	18	1982	0	1982	
6	The More I See (The Less I Believe)	(Chrysalis Chs 2554)	68	1983	0	1983	
7	Tunnel Of Love	(Chrysalis Chs 2678)	10	1983	0	1983	
8	Our Lips Are Sealed	(Chrysalis Funb 1)	7	1983	0	1983	
	HIT 3 IS CREDITED TO BANANARAMA WITH THE FUN BOY THREE • HIT 2 IS CREDITED TO FUN BOY THREE &BANANARAMA • SEE ALSO BANANARAMA						
Fun Lovin' Criminals	Male Vocal/Instrumental Group from the USA						
1	The Grave And The Constant	(Chrysalis Cdchs 5031)	72	1996	0	1996	
2	Scooby Snacks	(Chrysalis Cdchs 5034)	22	1996	0	1996	
3	The Fun Lovin' Criminal	(Chrysalis Cdchs 5040)	26	1996	0	1996	
4	King Of New York	(Chrysalis Cdchs 5049)	28	1997	0	1997	
5	I'm Not In Love / Scooby Snacks	(Chrysalis Cdchs 5060)	12	1997	0	1997	
Funk Masters	Mixed Vocal/Instrumental Group From the UK						
1	It's Over	(Master Funk Records 7mp 004)	8	1983	0	1983	
Funkadelic	Male Vocal/Instrumental Group From the USA						
* 1	One Nation Under A Groove (Part 1)	(Warner Bros K 17246)	9	1978	28	1978	(Warner Bros 8618)
Funkapolitan	Male Vocal/Instrumental Group From the UK						
1	As The Time Goes By	(London Lon 001)	41	1981	0	1981	
Funkdoobiest	Male Rap Group from the USA						
1	Wopbabalubop	(Immortal 6597112)	37	1993	0	1993	
2	Bow Wow Wow	(Immortal 6594052)	34	1994	0	1994	
Funky Green Dogs							
1	Fired Up!	(Twisted UK Twcd 10016)	17	1997	80	1997	(MCA 55221)
2	The Way	(Twisted Uk Twcd 10026)	43	1997	0	1997	
Funky Poets	Male Vocal Group from the USA						
1	Born In The Ghetto	(Epic 6603522)	72	1994	0	1994	

ISSUE	TITLE	UK LBL	UK POS	UK YEAR	US POS	US YEAR	US LBL
Funky Worm Mixed Vocal/Instrumental Group from the UK							
1	Hustle! (To The Music...)	(Fon Fon 15)	13	1988	0	1988	
2	The Spell!	(Fon Fon 16)	61	1988	0	1988	
3	U + Me = Love	(Fon Fon 19)	46	1989	0	1989	
Fureys Male Vocal Group from Ireland							
1	When You Were Sweet Sixteen	(Ritz Ritz 003)	14	1981	0	1981	
2	I Will Love You (Ev'ry Time When We Are Gone)	(Ritz Ritz 012)	54	1982	0	1982	
Furniture Mixed Vocal/Instrumental Group from the UK							
1	Brilliant Mind	(Stiff Buy 251)	21	1986	0	1986	
Fu-Schnickens With Shaquille O'Neal (Shag-Fu) Rap Trio from Brooklyn							
* 1	What's Up Doc? (Can We Rock?)		0	1993	39	1993	(Jive 42164)
Future Breeze							
1	Why Don't You Dance With Me	(Am:Pm 5823312)	50	1997	0	1997	
Future Force Mixed Vocal/Instrumental Duo from the UK/USA							
1	What You Want	(Am:Pm 5816592)	47	1996	0	1996	
Future Sound Of London Male Production/Instrumental Duo From the UK							
1	Papua New Guinea	(Jumpin' & Pumpin' Tot 17)	22	1992	0	1992	
2	Cascade	(Virgin Vscdt 1478)	27	1993	0	1993	
3	Expander	(Jumpin' & Pumpin' Cdstot 37)	72	1994	0	1994	
4	Lifeforms	(Virgin Vscd 1484)	14	1994	0	1994	
5	Far-Out Son Of Lung (And The Ramblings Of A Madman)	(Virgin Vscdt 1540)	22	1995	0	1995	
6	My Kingdom	(Virgin Vscdt 1605)	13	1996	0	1996	
7	We Have Explosive	(Virgin Vscdx 1616)	12	1997	0	1997	
Fuzz Names Barbara Gilliam, Sheila Young & Val Williams The Washington Trio Was Originally Called The Passionettes							
1	I Love You For All Seasons		0	1971	21	1971	(Calla 174)

G

ISSUE	TITLE	UK LBL	UK POS	UK YEAR	US POS	US YEAR	US LBL
G-Clefs	Male Vocal Group from the USA						
1	Ka-Ding Dong		0	1956	24	1956	(Pilgrim 715)
2	I Understand (Just How You Feel)	(London Hlu 9433)	17	1961	9	1961	(Terrace 7500)
	NAMES RAY GIBSON WITH BROTHERS CHRIS, TIMMY, TEDDY & ARNOLD SCOTT						
G Nation							
1	Feel The Need	(Cooltempo Cdcool 327)	58	1997	0	1997	
	HIT IS CREDITED TO G NATION FEATURING ROSIE						
G.O.S.H.	Mixed Charity Assembly from the UK						
1	The Wishing Well	(MBS Gosh 1)	22	1987	0	1987	
G.T.O.	Mixed Vocal/Instrumental/Production Duo from the UK						
1	Pure	(Cooltempo Cool 218)	57	1990	0	1990	
2	Listen To The Rhythm Flow / Bullfrog	(React React 7001)	72	1991	0	1991	
3	Elevation	(React React 4)	59	1992	0	1992	
	SEE ALSO TECHNOHEAD & TRICKY DISCO						
Gabrielle	Female Vocalist, Louise Gabrielle Bobb B: 19 Jun 1969 Hackney, East London, England.						
1	Dreams	(Go.Beat Godcd 99)	1	1993	26	1993	(Go!/London 857298)
2	Going Nowhere	(Go.Beat Godcd 106)	9	1993	0	1993	
3	I Wish	(Go.Beat Godcd 108)	26	1993	0	1993	
4	Because Of You	(Go.Beat Godcd 109)	24	1994	0	1994	
5	Give Me A Little More Time	(Go.Beat Godcd 139)	5	1996	0	1996	
6	Forget About The World	(Go.Beat Golcd 146)	23	1996	0	1996	
7	If You Really Cared	(Go.Beat Godcd 153)	15	1996	0	1996	
8	If You Ever	(London Loncd 388)	2	1996	0	1996	
9	Walk On By	(Go.Beat Godcd 159)	7	1997	0	1997	
	HIT 8 IS CREDITED TO EAST 17 FEATURING GABRIELLE						
Gadabouts	Male Quartet from Illinois Jonnie Barr, Eddie Hayes, Larry Craig & 'Wild Bill' Putnam						
1	Stranded In The Jungle		0	1956	39	1956	(Mercury 70898)
Gala							
1	Freed From Desire	(Big Life Blrd 135)	2	1997	0	1997	
Gale Garnett	Female Actress/Vocalist, B: 17 Jul 1942, Auckland, New Zealand		She Has Had Acting Roles In 77 Sunset Strip, Bonanza And Others				
* 1	We'll Sing In The Sunshine		0	1964	4	1964	(Rca 8388)
Gale Storm	Real Name Josephine Cottle B: 5 Apr 1922 Bloomington, Texas						
* 1	I Hear You Knocking		0	1955	2	1955	(Dot 15412)
2	Teenage Prayer		0	1956	6	1956	(Dot 15436)
3	Memories Are Made Of This		0	1955	5	1955	(Dot 15436)
4	Why Do Fools Fall In Love		0	1956	9	1956	(Dot 15448)
5	Ivory Tower		0	1956	6	1956	(Dot 15458)
6	Dark Moon		0	1957	4	1957	(Dot 15558)
Gallagher & Lyle	Male Vocal/Instrumental Group from the UK						
1	I Wanna Stay With You	(A&M Ams 7211)	6	1976	0	1976	
2	Heart On My Sleeve	(A&M Ams 7227)	6	1976	0	1976	
3	Breakaway	(A&M Ams 7245)	35	1976	0	1976	
4	Every Little Teardrop	(A&M Ams 7274)	32	1977	0	1977	
Gallagher & Shean	Male Comedy Duo, Real Names Ed Gallagher And Al Shean						
* 1	Mr Gallagher And Mr. Shean		0	1922	1	1922	(Victor 18941)
Gallery	Lead Singer Jim Gold from Detroit						
* 1	Nice To Be With You		0	1972	4	1972	(Sussex 232)
2	I Believe In Music		0	1972	22	1972	(Sussex 239)
3	Big City Miss Ruth Ann		0	1973	23	1973	(Sussex 248)

ISSUE	TITLE	UK LBL	UK POS	UK YEAR	US POS	US YEAR	US LBL
Galliano	Male Vocal/Instrumental Group from the UK						
1	Skunk Funk	(Talkin Loud Tlk 23)	41	1992	0	1992	
2	Prince Of Peace	(Talkin Loud Tlk 24)	47	1992	0	1992	
3	Jus' Reach (Recycled)	(Talkin Loud Tlk 29)	66	1992	0	1992	
4	Long Time Gone	(Talkin Loud Tlkcd 48	15	1994	0	1994	
5	Twyford Down	(Talkin Loud Tlkdd 49)	37	1994	0	1994	
6	Ease Your Mind	(Talkin Loud Tldd 10)	45	1996	0	1996	
Gang Of Four	Male Vocal/Instrumental Group From the UK						
1	At Home He's A Tourist	(EMI 2956)	58	1979	0	1979	
2	I Love A Man In A Uniform	(EMI 5299)	65	1982	0	1982	
Gang Starr	Male Rap Group From the USA						
1	Jazz Thing	(CBS 356377 7)	66	1990	0	1990	
2	Take A Rest	(Cooltempo Cool 230)	63	1991	0	1991	
3	Lovesick	(Cooltempo Cool 234)	50	1991	0	1991	
4	2 Deep	(Cooltempo Cool 256)	67	1992	0	1992	
Gap Band	Male Vocal/Instrumental Trio From Tulsa, USA Names Of The Brothers Are Ronnie, Charles And Robert Wilson						
1	Oops Up Side Your Head	(Mercury Mer 22)	6	1980	0	1980	
2	Party Lights	(Mercury Mer 37)	30	1980	0	1980	
3	Burn Rubber On Me (Why You Wanna Hurt Me)	(Mercury Mer 52)	22	1980	0	1980	
4	Humpin'	(Mercury Mer 63)	36	1981	0	1981	
5	Yearning For Your Love	(Mercury Mer 73)	4	1981	0	1981	
6	Early In The Morning	(Mercury Mer 97)	55	1982	24	1982	(Total Exp. 8201)
7	You Dropped A Bomb On Me		0	1982	31	1982	(Total Exp. 8203)
8	Outstanding	(Total Experience Te 001)	68	1983	0	1983	
9	Someday	(Total Experience Te 5)	17	1984	0	1984	
10	Jammin' In America	(Total Experience Te 6)	64	1984	0	1984	
11	Big Fun	(Total Experience Fb 49779)	4	1986	0	1986	
12	How Music Came About (Bop B Da B Da Da)	(Total Experience Fb 49755)	61	1987	0	1987	
13	Oops Upside Your Head (Re-Mix)	(Club Jab 54)	20	1987	0	1987	
14	I'm Gonna Git You Sucka	(Arista 112016)	63	1989	0	1989	
Garbage							
1	Subhuman	(Mushroom D 1138)	50	1995	0	1995	
2	Only Happy When It Rains	(Mushroom D 1199)	29	1995	0	1995	
3	Queer	(Mushroom D 1237)	13	1995	0	1995	
4	Stupid Girl	(Mushroom D 1271)	4	1996	24	1996	(Geffen 89004)
5	Milk	(Mushroom D 1494)	10	1996	0	1996	
6	Milk (Re-Entry)	(Mushroom D 1494)	74	1997	0	1997	
Garland Green	Real Name Garfield Green Jr. B: 24 Jun 1942 Leland, Mississippi						
* 1	Jealous Kind Of Fella		0	1969	20	1969	(Uni 55143)
Garland Jeffreys	From the USA						
1	Hail Hail Rock 'N' Roll	(RCA Pb 49171)	72	1992	0	1992	
Garnet Mimms & Truckin' Co	Male Vocal/Instrumental Group From the UK						
* 1	Cry Baby		0	1963	4	1963	(United Artists 629)
2	For Your Precious Love		0	1963	26	1963	(United Artists 658)
3	Baby Don't You Weep		0	1963	30	1963	(United Artists 628)
4	I'll Take Good Care Of You		0	1966	30	1966	(United Artists 995)
5	What It Is	(Arista 109)	44	1977	0	1977	
	REAL NAME GARRETT MIMMS B: 16 NOV 1933 ASHLAND, WEST VIRGINIA • HITS 1-3 ARE CREDITED TO GARNET MIMMS & THE ENCHANTERS						
Garry Lee & Showdown	Male Vocal/Instrumental Group from Canada						
1	The Rodeo Song	(Party Dish Vcd 101)	44	1993	0	1993	
Garry Miles	Real Name James Cason B: 27 Nov 1939 Nashville						
1	Look For A Star (From Circus Of Horrors)		0	1960	16	1960	(Liberty 55261)
	HE ALSO RECORDED AS BUZZ CASON. THE HIT SHOULD NOT BE CONFUSED WITH THE OTHER VERSION OF THE SAME SONG BY GARRY MILLS						
Garry Mills	Male Vocalist From the UK						
1	Look For A Star (Part 1) (From Circus Of Horrors)	(Top Rank Jar 336)	7	1960	26	1960	(Liberty 5674)
2	Top Teen Baby	(Top Rank Jar 500)	24	1960	0	1960	
3	I'll Step Down	(Decca F 11358)	39	1961	0	1961	
Garth Brooks	Male Vocalist Troyal Garth Brooks B: 7 Feb 1962 Luba, Oklahoma						
26	The Red Strokes / Ain't Goin' Down	(Liberty Cdcls 704)	13	1994	0	1994	
27	Standing Outside The Fire	(Liberty Cdcl 712)	28	1994	0	1994	
28	The Dance / Friends In Low Places	(Capitol Cdcl 735)	36	1995	0	1995	
29	She's Every Woman	(Capitol Cdcl 767)	55	1996	0	1996	
	OTHER HITS ARE C/W						

ISSUE	TITLE	UK LBL	UK POS	UK YEAR	US POS	US YEAR	US LBL
Gary Barlow Male Vocalist from the UK							
1	Forever Love	(RCA 74321397922)	1	1996	0	1996	
2	Forever Love (Re-Entry)	(RCA 74321397922)	56	1996	0	1996	
3	Love Won't Wait	(RCA 74321470842)	1	1997	0	1997	
4	So Help Me Girl	(RCA 74321501202)	11	1997	0	1997	
5	Love Won't Wait (Re-Entry)	(RCA 74321470842)	64	1997	0	1997	
6	Love Won't Wait (2nd Re-Entry)	(RCA 74321470842)	67	1997	0	1997	
Gary Benson Male Vocalist From the UK							
1	Don't Throw It All Away	(State Stat 10)	20	1975	0	1975	
Gary Byrd & The GB Experience Male Vocalist/Mixed Instrumental Group from the USA							
1	The Crown	(Motown Tmgt 1312)	6	1983	0	1983	
Gary Clark Male Vocalist from the UK							
1	We Sail On The Stormy Waters	(Circa Yrcdx 93)	34	1993	0	1993	
2	Free Floating	(Circa Yrcdx 94)	50	1993	0	1993	
3	Make A Family	(Circa Yrcdx 105)	70	1993	0	1993	
Gary Crosby Son Of Bing Crosby from the USA							
* 1	Play A Simple Melody (From *Watch Your Step*)		0	1950	2	1950	(Decca 27112)
2	Sam's Song		0	1950	3	1950	(Decca 27112)
3	When You And I Were Young, Maggie, Blues		0	1951	8	1951	(Decca 27577)
4	Moonlight Bay		0	1951	14	1951	(Decca 27577)
5	Down By The Riverside		0	1954	28	1954	(Decca 28955)
	HIT 5 IS CREDITED TO BING CROSBY AND GARY CROSBY						
Gary Glail On-U Sound System Male Producer From the UK							
1	Beef	(RCA Pb 49265)	64	1990	0	1990	
2	Human Nature	(Perfecto Pb 44401)	10	1991	0	1991	
3	Escape	(Perfecto Pb 44563)	44	1991	0	1991	
4	Who Pays The Piper	(Perfecto 74321117017)	1	1992	0	1992	
5	These Things Are Worth Fighting For	(Perfecto 74321147222)	45	1993	0	1993	
	HIT 1 IS CREDITED TO GARY GLAIL • SEE ALSO GIMME SHELTER (EP), VARIOUS ARTISTS (EP, LP, 78S)						
Gary Glitter Male Vocalist, Real Name Paul Gadd. B: 8 May 1944 In Banbury, Oxfordshire, England							
* 1	Rock And Roll (Part 1-2)	(Bell 1216)	2	1972	7	1972	(Bell 45237)
2	I Didn't Know I Loved You (Till I Saw You Rock 'N' Roll)	(Bell 1259)	4	1972	35	1972	(Bell 45276)
3	Do You Wanna Touch Me? (Oh Yeah)	(Bell 1280)	2	1973	0	1973	
4	Hello Hello I'm Back Again	(Bell 1299)	2	1973	0	1973	
* 5	I'm The Leader Of The Gang (I Am)	(Bell 1321)	1	1973	0	1973	
* 6	I Love You Love Me Love	(Bell 1337)	1	1973	0	1973	
7	Remember Me This Way	(Bell 1349)	3	1974	0	1974	
8	Always Yours	(Bell 1359)	1	1974	0	1974	
9	Oh Yes! You're Beautiful	(Bell 1391)	2	1974	0	1974	
10	Love Like You And Me	(Bell 1423)	10	1975	0	1975	
11	Doing Alright With The Boys	(Bell 1429)	6	1975	0	1975	
12	Papa Ooh Mow Mow	(Rell 1451)	38	1975	0	1975	
13	You Belong To Me	(Bell 1473)	40	1976	0	1976	
14	It Takes All Night Long	(Arista 85)	25	1977	0	1977	
15	A Little Boogie Woogie In The Back Of My Mind	(Arista 112)	31	1977	0	1977	
16	Gary Glitter (Ep)	(Gto Gt 282)	57	1980	0	1980	
17	And Then She Kissed Me	(Bell Bell 1497)	39	1981	0	1981	
18	All That Glitters	(Bell Bell 1498)	48	1981	0	1981	
19	Dance Me Up	(Arista Arist 570)	25	1984	0	1984	
20	Another Rock And Roll Christmas	(Arista Arist 592)	7	1984	0	1984	
21	And The Leader Rocks On	(EMI Em 252)	58	1992	0	1992	
22	Through The Years	(EMI Fm 256)	49	1992	0	1992	
23	Hello, Hello, I'm Back Again (Again!)	(Carlton Sounds 3036000192)	50	1995	0	1995	
	PREVIOUS RECORDING NAMES INCLUDE PAUL RAVEN & PAUL MONDAY • FIRST RECORD WAS ALONE IN THE NIGHT FOR DECCA IN 1960						
Gary Lewis & The Playboys Male Vocal/Instrumental Group from the USA Gary, Male Vocalist, B: 31 Jul 1946 The Son Of Jerry Lewis							
* 1	This Diamond Ring		0	1965	1	1965	(Liberty 55756)
2	Count On Me		0	1965	2	1965	(Liberty 55778)
3	Save Your Heart For Me		0	1965	2	1965	(Liberty 55809)
4	Everybody Loves A Clown		0	1965	4	1965	(Liberty 55818)
5	She's Just My Style		0	1966	3	1966	(Liberty 55846)
6	Sure Gonna Miss Her		0	1966	9	1966	(Liberty 55865)
7	Green Grass		0	1966	8	1966	(Liberty 55880)

ISSUE	TITLE	UK LBL	UK POS	UK YEAR	US POS	US YEAR	US LBL
8	My Hearts Symphony	(United Artists Up 35780)	36	1975	13	1966	(Liberty 55898)
9	(You Don't Have To) Paint Me A Picture		0	1966	15	1966	(Liberty 55914)
10	Where Will The Words Come From		0	1967	21	1967	(Liberty 55933)
11	Girls In Love		0	1967	39	1967	(Liberty 55971)
12	Sealed With A Kiss		0	1968	19	1968	(Liberty 56037)

Gary Low   Male Vocalist from Italy

ISSUE	TITLE	UK LBL	UK POS	UK YEAR	US POS	US YEAR	US LBL
1	I Want You	(Savoir Faire Fais 004)	52	1983	0	1983	

Gary Miller   Male Vocalist from the UK

ISSUE	TITLE	UK LBL	UK POS	UK YEAR	US POS	US YEAR	US LBL
1	Yellow Rose Of Texas	(Nixa N 15004)	13	1955	0	1955	
2	Robin Hood	(Nixa N 15020)	10	1956	0	1956	
3	Garden Of Eden	(Pye Nixa N 15070)	14	1957	0	1957	
4	Garden Of Eden (Re-Entry)	(Pye Nixa N 15070)	27	1957	0	1957	
5	Wonderful Wonderful	(Pye Nixa N 15094)	29	1957	0	1957	
6	Story Of My Life	(Pye Nixa N 15120)	14	1958	0	1958	
7	There Goes That Song Again - The Night Is Young	(Pye 7n 15404)	29	1961	0	1961	
8	There Goes That Song Again (Re-Entry)	(Pye 7n 15404)	48	1962	0	1962	

Gary Moore   Male Vocal/Guitarist from the UK

ISSUE	TITLE	UK LBL	UK POS	UK YEAR	US POS	US YEAR	US LBL
1	Parisienne Walkways	(Mca 419)	8	1979	0	1979	
2	Hold On To Love	(10 Ten 13)	65	1984	0	1984	
3	Empty Rooms	(10 Ten 25)	51	1984	0	1984	
4	Out In The Field	(10 Ten 49)	5	1985	0	1985	
5	Empty Rooms (Re-Issue)	(10 Ten 58)	23	1985	0	1985	
6	Over The Hills And Far Away	(10 Ten 134)	20	1986	0	1986	
7	Wild Frontier	(10 Ten 159)	35	1987	0	1987	
8	Friday On My Mind	(10 Ten 164)	26	1987	0	1987	
9	The Loner	(10 Ten 178)	53	1987	0	1987	
10	Takes A Little Time (Double Single)	(10 Ten 190)	75	1987	0	1987	
11	After The War	(Virgin Gms 1)	37	1989	0	1989	
12	Ready For Love	(Virgin Gms 2)	56	1989	0	1989	
13	Oh Pretty Woman	(Virgin Vs 1233)	48	1990	0	1990	
14	Still Got The Blues (For You)	(Virgin Vs 1267)	31	1990	0	1990	
15	Walking By Myself	(Virgin Vs 1281)	48	1990	-	1990	
16	Too Tired	(Virgin Vs 1306)	71	1990	0	1990	
17	Cold Day In Hell	(Virgin Vs1393)	24	1992	0	1992	
18	Story Of The Blues	(Virgin Vs 1412)	40	1992	0	1992	
19	Since I Met You Baby	(Virgin Vs 1423)	59	1992	0	1992	
20	Separate Ways	(Virgin Vs 1437)	59	1992	0	1992	
21	Parisienne Walkways (Re-Mix)	(Virgin Vscdx 1456)	32	1993	0	1993	
22	Need Your Love So Bad	(Virgin Vscdg 146)	8	1995	0	1995	

HIT 4 IS CREDITED TO GARY MOORE AND PHIL LYNOTT • HIT 13 IS CREDITED TO GARY MOORE FEATURING ALBERT KING
HIT 19 IS CREDITED TO GARY MOORE AND B.B. KING • SEE ALSO PHILIP LYNOT

Gary Numan   Male Vocalist, Real Name Gary Webb B: 8 Mar 1958 Hammersmith, West London, England

ISSUE	TITLE	UK LBL	UK POS	UK YEAR	US POS	US YEAR	US LBL
1	Are 'Friends' Electric?	(Beggars Banquet Beg 18)	1	1979	0	1979	
2	Cars	(Beggars Banquet Beg 23)	1	1979	9	1980	(Atco 7211)
3	Complex	(Beggars Banquet Beg 29)	6	1979	0	1979	
4	We Are Glass	(Beggars Banquet Beg 35)	5	1980	0	1980	
5	I Die: You Die	(Beggars Banquet Beg 46)	6	1980	0	1980	
6	This Wreckage	(Beggars Banquet Beg 50)	20	1980	0	1980	
7	She's Got Claws	(Beggars Banquet Beg 62)	6	1981	0	1981	
8	Love Needs No Disguise	(Beggars Banquet Beg 68)	33	1981	0	1981	
9	Music For Chameleons	(Beggars Banquet Beg 70)	19	1982	0	1982	
10	We Take Mystery (To Bed)	(Beggars Banquet Beg 77)	9	1982	0	1982	
11	White Boys And Heroes	(Beggars Banquet Beg 81)	20	1982	0	1982	
12	Warriors	(Beggars Banquet Beg 95)	20	1983	0	1983	
13	Sister Surprise	(Beggars Banquet Beg 101)	32	1983	0	1983	
14	Berserker	(Numa Nu 4)	32	1984	0	1984	
15	My Dying Machine	(Numa Nu 6)	66	1984	0	1984	
16	Change Your Mind	(Polydor Posp 722)	17	1985	0	1985	
17	The Live (EP)	(Numa Nu 7)	27	1985	0	1985	
18	Your Fascination	(Numa Nu 9)	46	1985	0	1985	
19	Call Out The Dogs	(Numa Nu 11)	49	1985	0	1985	
20	Miracles	(Numa Nu 13)	49	1985	0	1985	
21	This Is Love	(Numa Nu 16)	28	1986	0	1986	

ISSUE	TITLE	UK LBL	UK POS	UK YEAR	US POS	US YEAR	US LBL
22	I Can't Stop	(Numa Nu 17)	27	1986	0	1986	
23	New Things From London Town	(Numa Nu 19)	52	1986	0	1986	
24	I Still Remember	(Numa Nu 21)	74	1986	0	1986	
25	Radio Heart	(Gfm Gfm 109)	35	1987	0	1987	
26	London Times	(Gfm Gfm 112)	48	1987	0	1987	
27	Cars (E Reg Model)/Are Friends Electric? (Re-Mix)	(Beggars B. Beg 199)	16	1987	0	1987	
28	No More Lies	(Polydor Posp 894)	34	1988	0	1988	
29	New Anger	(Illegal Ils 1003)	46	1988	0	1988	
30	America	(Illegal Ils 1004)	49	1988	0	1988	
32	I'm On Automatic	(Polydor Po 43)	44	1989	0	1989	
33	Heart	(Irs Numan 1)	43	1991	0	1991	
34	The Skin Game	(Numa Nu 23)	68	1992	0	1992	
35	Machine + Soul	(Numa Nu 124)	72	1992	0	1992	
36	Cars (2nd Re-Mix)	(Beggars Banquet Beg 264cd)	53	1993	0	1993	
37	Cars (Premier Mix)	(Polygram Tv Prmcd 1)	17	1996	0	1996	

Gary Portnoy Male Vocalist From the USA

1	Theme From Cheers	(Starblend Cheer 1)	58	1984	0	1984	

Gary Puckett & The Union Gap Male Vocalist, B: 7 Oct 1942 Hibbing, Minnesota, With Instrumental Group

* 1	Woman Woman	(CBS 3110)	48	1968	4	1967	(Columbia 44297)
* 2	Young Girl	(CBS 3365)	1	1968	2	1968	(Columbia 44450)
3	Lady Willpower	(Cbs 3551)	5	1968	2	1968	(Columbia 44547)
* 4	Over You		0	1968	7	1968	(Columbia 44644)
5	Don't Give Into Him		0	1969	15	1969	(Columbia 44788)
6	This Girl Is A Woman Now		0	1969	9	1969	(Columbia 44967)
7	Young Girl (Re-Issue)	(CBS 8202)	6	1974	0	1974	

Gary Shearston Male Vocalist from Australia

1	I Get A Kick Out Of You	(Charisma Cb 234)	7	1974	0	1974	

Gary Stites Male Singer/Songwriter/Guitarist, B: 23 Jul 1940 Denver

1	Lonely For You		0	1959	24	1959	(Carlton 508)

Gary U.S. Bonds Writer. Real Name Gary Anderson B: 6 Jun 1939 Jacksonville, Florida)

1	New Orleans	(Top Rank Jar 527)	16	1961	6	1960	(Legrand 1003)
* 2	Quarter To Three	(Top Rank Jar 575)	7	1961	1	1961	(Legrand 1008)
3	School It Out		0	1961	5	1961	(Legrand 1009)
4	School Is In		0	1961	28	1961	(Legrand 1012)
* 5	Dear Lady Twist		0	1962	9	1962	(Legrand 1015)
6	Twist Twist Senora		0	1962	9	1962	(Legrand 1018)
7	Seven Day Weekend		0	1962	27	1962	(Legrand 1019)
8	This Little Girl	(EMI America EA 122)	43	1981	11	1981	(Emi America 8079)
9	Jole Blon	(EMI America EA 127)	51	1981	0	1981	
10	It's Only Love	(EMI America EA 128)	43	1981	0	1981	
11	Out Of Work		0	1982	21	1982	(Emi America 8117)
12	Soul Deep	(EMI America EA 140)	59	1982	0	1982	

Gary Walker Male Vocalist From the USA

1	You Don't Love Me	(Cb 202036)	26	1966	0	1966	
2	Twinkle Lee	(Cbs 202081)	26	1966	0	1966	

Gary Wright Male Singer/Songwriter, B: 26 Apr 1943 Creskill, New Jersey

1	Dream Weaver		0	1976	2	1976	(Warner Bros 8167)
2	Love Is Alive		0	1976	6	1976	(Warner Bros 8143)
3	Really Wanna Know You		0	1981	9	1981	(Warner Bros 49769)

Gary's Gang Male Vocal/Instrumental Group from the USA

1	Keep On Dancin'	(Cbs 7109)	8	1979	0	1979	
2	Let's Love Dance Tonight	(CBS 7328)	49	1979	0	1979	
3	Knock Me Out	(Arista Arist 499)	45	1982	0	1982	

Gat Decor Male Instrumental Group From the UK

1	Passion	(Effective Effs 1)	29	1992	0	1992	
2	Passion (Re-Issue)	(Way Of Life Wayda 1)	6	1996	0	1996	

Gavin Christopher

1	One Step Closer To You		0	1986	22	1986	(Manhattan 50028)

Gay Gordon & The Mince Pies Mixed Vocal/Instrumental Group from the UK

1	The Essential Wally Party Medley	(Lifestyle Xy 2)	60	1986	0	1986	

ISSUE	TITLE	UK LBL	UK POS	UK YEAR	US POS	US YEAR	US LBL
Gaye Bykers On Acid	Male Vocal/Instrumental Group from the UK						
1	Git Down (Shake Your Thang)	(Purple Fluid Vs 1008)	54	1987	0	1987	
Gayla Peevey	Eleven-Year-Old Gayla & Orchestra Directed By Norman Leyden						
1	I Want A Hippopotamus For Christmas		0	1953	24	1953	(Columbia 40106)
Gayle & Gillian	Female Vocal Duo from Australia						
1	Mad If Ya Don't	(Mushroom Cdmush 1)	75	1993	0	1993	
2	Wanna Be Your Lover	(Mushroom D 11598)	62	1994	0	1994	
Gayle Adams	Female Singer from the USA						
1	Stretchin' Out	(Epic Epc 8791)	64	1980	0	1980	
Gaylords	Ronnie Gaylord Was A Solo Artist, Then A Trio, Then A Duo With Burt Bonaldi from Detroit						
* 1	Tell Me You're Mine		0	1953	2	1953	(Mercury 70030)
2	Spinning A Web		0	1953	16	1953	(Mercury 70112)
3	Ramona		0	1953	12	1953	(Mercury 70112)
4	The Strings Of My Heart		0	1953	21	1953	(Mercury 70258)
5	Rom The Vine Came The Grape		0	1954	7	1954	(Mercury 70296)
6	Isle Of Capri		0	1954	14	1954	(Mercury 70350)
7	Love I You (You I Love)		0	1954	2	1954	(Mercury 70350)
8	The Little Shoemaker		0	1954	2	1954	(Mercury 70403)
9	Mecque, Mecque		0	1954	28	1954	(Mercury 70403)
10	Veni-Vidi-Vici (I Came, I Saw, I Conquered)		0	1954	30	1954	(Mercury 70427)
	HIT 8 IS WITH HUGO PERELLI • SEE ALSO RONNIE GAYLORD						
Gaz	Male Vocal/Instrumental Group from the USA						
1	Sing Sing	(Salsoul Ssol 116)	60	1979	0	1979	
Gazza	Male Vocalist/Soccer Player, Real Name Paul Gascoigne from the UK						
1	Fog On The Tyne (Revisited)	(Best Zb 44083)	2	1990	0	1990	
2	Geordie Boys (Gazza Rap)	(Best Zb 44229)	31	1990	0	1990	
GBH	Male Vocal/Instrumental Group from the UK						
1	0 Survivors	(Clay Clay 8)	63	1982	0	1982	
2	Give Me Fire	(Clay Clay 16)	69	1982	0	1982	
Gemini	Male Vocal Duo from the UK						
1	Even Though You Broke My Heart	(EMI Cdems 391)	40	1995	0	1995	
2	Steal Your Love Away	(EMI Cdems 407)	37	1996	0	1996	
3	Could It Be Forever	(EMI Cdems 426)	38	1996	0	1996	
Gems For Jem	Male Instrumental/Production Duo from the UK						
1	Lifting Me Higher	(Box 21 Cdsboxs 3)	28	1995	0	1995	
Gene	Male Vocal/Instrumental Group from the UK						
1	Be My Light Be My Guide	(Costermonger Cost 002cd)	54	1994	0	1994	
2	Sleep Well Tonight	(Costermonger Cost 003cd)	36	1994	0	1994	
3	Haunted By You	(Costermonger Cost 004cd)	32	1995	0	1995	
4	Olympian	(Costermonger Cost 005cd)	18	1995	0	1995	
5	For The Dead	(Costermonger Cost 006cd)	14	1996	0	1996	
6	Fighting Fit	(Polydor Cost 9cd)	22	1996	0	1996	
7	We Could Be Kings	(Polydor Coscd 10)	17	1997	0	1997	
8	Where Are They Now?	(Polydor Cdcsd 11)	22	1997	0	1997	
Gene & Debbe	Names Gene Thomas & Debbe Nevills						
* 1	Playboy		0	1967	17	1967	(Trx 5006)
Gene & Jim Are Into Shakes	Mixed Vocal/Instrumental Duo From the UK						
1	Shake (How About A Sampling Gene)	(Rough Trade Rt 216)	68	1988	0	1988	
Gene Allison	R&B Vocalist, B: 29 Aug 1934 Nashville						
1	You Can Make It If You Try		0	1958	36	1958	(Vee-Jay 256)
Gene Austin	Real Name Eugene Lucas B: 24 Jun 1900 Gainsville, Texas						
* 24	My Blue Heaven		0	1927	1	1927	(Victor 20964)
* 29	Ramona		0	1928	1	1928(	Victor 21334)
	OBITUARY :- D: 24 JAN 1972, (AGED 71).						
Gene Autry	Male Country Singer, Orvon Gene Autry B: 29 Sep 1907 Near Tioga, Texas						
* 4	That Silver Haired Daddy Of Mine		0	1935	7	1935	(Vocalion 2991)
11	Here Comes Santa Claus (Down Santa Claus Lane)		0	1947	9	1947	(Columbia 37942)
12	Buttons And Bows (From *Paleface*)		0	1948	17	1948	(Columbia 20469)
* 13	Here Comes Santa Claus (Down Santa Claus Lane) (Re-Issue)		0	1947	1	1947	(Columbia 20377)
* 14	Rudolph The Red-Nosed Reindeer		0	1949	1	1949	(Columbia 38610)

ISSUE	TITLE	UK LBL	UK POS	UK YEAR	US POS	US YEAR	US LBL
15	Here Comes Santa Claud (Re-Issue) (Re-Entry)		0	1950	24	1950	(Columbia 20377)
* 16	Peter Cottontail		0	1950	5	1950	(Columbia 38750)
17	Rudolph The Red-Nosed Reindeer (Re-Entry)		0	1950	3	1950	(Columbia 38610)
* 18	Frosty The Snowman		0	1950	7	1950	(Columbia 38907)
19	Peter Cottontail (Re-Entry)		0	1951	19	1951	(Columbia 28750)
20	Rudolph The Red-Nosed Reindeer (2nd Re-Entry)		0	1951	16	1951	(Columbia 38610)
21	The Night Before Christmas Song		0	1952	9	1952	(Columbia 39876)
22	Frosty The Snowman (Re-Entry)		0	1952	23	1952	(Columbia 38907)
23	Rudolph The Red-Nosed Reindeer (3rd Re-Entry)		0	1952	12	1952	(Columbia 38610)
24	Rudolph The Red-Nosed Reindeer (4th Re-Entry)		0	1953	26	1953	(Columbia 38610)

Gene Chandler Male Vocalist, Real Name Eugene Dixon B: 6 Jul 1937 Chicago

ISSUE	TITLE	UK LBL	UK POS	UK YEAR	US POS	US YEAR	US LBL
* 1	Duke Of Earl		0	1962	1	1962	(Vee-Jay 416)
2	Rainbow		0	1963	47	1963	(Vee-Jay 468)
3	Man's Temptation		0	1963	71	1963	(Vee-Jay 536)
4	Just Be True		0	1964	19	1964	(Constellation 130)
5	Bless Our Love		0	1964	39	1964	(Constellation 136)
6	What Now		0	1965	40	1965	(Constellation 141)
7	Nothing Can Stop Me	(Soul City Sc 102)	41	1968	18	1965	(Constellation 149)
8	Rainbow '65		0	1965	69	1965	(Constellation 158)
9	I Fooled You This Time		0	1966	45	1966	(Checker 1155)
+ 10	To Be A Lover		0	1967	9	1967	(Checker 1165)
* 11	Groovy Situation		0	1970	12	1970	(Mercury 73083)
12	Get Down	(20th Century Btc 1040)	11	1979	0	1979	
13	When You're Number One	(20th Century Tc 2411)	43	1979	0	1979	
14	Does She Have A Friend	(20th Century Tc 2451)	28	1980	0	1980	

Gene Cotton Male Vocalist, B: Columbus, Ohio

ISSUE	TITLE	UK LBL	UK POS	UK YEAR	US POS	US YEAR	US LBL
1	You've Got Me Runnin'		0	1977	33	1977	(ABC 1227)
2	Before My Heart Finds Out		0	1978	23	1978	(Ariola Am. 7675)
3	You're A Part Of Me		0	1978	36	1978	(Ariola Am. 7704)
4	Like A Sunday In Salem (The Amos And Andy Song)		0	1978	40	1978	(Ariola Am. 7723)
5	If I Could Get You (Into My Life)		0	1982	76	1982	(Knoll 5002)

Gene Farrow & G.F. Band Male Vocal/Instrumental Group from the UK

ISSUE	TITLE	UK LBL	UK POS	UK YEAR	US POS	US YEAR	US LBL
1	Move Your Body	(Magnet Mag 109)	33	1978	0	1978	
2	Move Your Body (Re-Entry)	(Magnet Mag 109)	67	1978	0	1978	
3	Don't Stop Now	(Magnet Mag 125)	71	1978	0	1978	
4	Don't Stop Now (Re-Entry)	(Magnet Mag 125)	74	1978	0	1978	

Gene Krupa Orchestra Male Bandleader/Drummer from the USA

ISSUE	TITLE	UK LBL	UK POS	UK YEAR	US POS	US YEAR	US LBL
25	Boogie Blues		0	1946	9	1946	(Columbia 36986)
26	Old Devil Moon (From *Finian's Rainbow*)		0	1947	21	1947	(Columbia 37270)
27	Bonaparte's Retreat		0	1950	9	1950	(RCA Victor 3766)

Gene Loves Jezebel Male Vocal/Instrumental Group from the UK

ISSUE	TITLE	UK LBL	UK POS	UK YEAR	US POS	US YEAR	US LBL
1	Sweetest Thing	(Beggars Banquet Beg 156)	75	1986	0	1986	
2	Heartache	(Beggars Banquet Beg 161)	71	1986	0	1986	
3	The Motion Of Love	(Beggars Banquet Beg 192)	56	1987	0	1987	
4	Gorgeous	(Beggars Banquet Beg 202)	68	1987	0	1987	

Gene McDaniels Male Vocalist, Full Name Eugene B. McDaniels B: 12 Feb 1935 Kansas City

ISSUE	TITLE	UK LBL	UK POS	UK YEAR	US POS	US YEAR	US LBL
* 1	A Hundred Pounds Of Clay		0	1961	3	1961	(Liberty 55308)
2	A Tear		0	1961	31	1961	(Liberty 55344)
3	Tower Of Strength	(London Hlg 9448)	49	1961	5	1961	(Liberty 55371)
4	Tower Of Strength (Re-Entry)	(London Hlg 9448)	49	1961	0	1961	
5	Chip Chip		0	1962	10	1962	(Liberty 55405)
6	Point Of No Return		0	1962	21	1962	(Liberty 55480)
7	Spanish Lace		0	1962	31	1962	(Liberty 55510)

Gene Pitney Male Vocalist, B: 17 Feb 1941 Hartford, Connecticut

ISSUE	TITLE	UK LBL	UK POS	UK YEAR	US POS	US YEAR	US LBL
1	I Wanna Love My Life Away	(London Hl 9270)	26	1961	39	1961	(Musicor 1002)
* 2	Town Without Pity	(Hmv Pop 952)	32	1962	13	1961	(Musicor 1009)
3	Every Breath I Take		0	1961	42	1961	(Musicor 1011)
* 4	(The Man Who Shot) Liberty Valance		0	1962	4	1962	(Musicor 1020)
* 5	Only Love Can Break A Heart		0	1962	2	1962	(Musicor 1022)
6	Half Heaven-Half Heartache		0	1963	12	1963	(Musicor 1026)
7	Mecca		0	1963	12	1963	(Musicor 1028)
8	True Love Never Runs Smooth		0	1963	21	1963	(Musicor 1032)
* 9	Twenty Four Hours From Tulsa	(United Artists Up 1035)	5	1963	17	1963	(Musicor 1034)
10	That Girl Belongs To Yesterday	(United Artists Up 1045)	7	1964	0	1964	

ISSUE	TITLE	UK LBL	UK POS	UK YEAR	US POS	US YEAR	US LBL
11	It Hurts To Be In Love	(United Artists Up 1063)	36	1964	7	1964	(Musicor 1040)
12	I'm Gonna Be Strong	(Stateside Ss 358)	2	1964	9	1964	(Musicor 1045)
13	I Must Be Seeing Things	(Stateside Ss 390)	6	1965	31	1965	(Musicor 1070)
! 14	I've Got Five Dollars And It's Saturday Night		0	1965	16	1965	(Musicor 1066)
15	Last Chance To Turn Around		0	1965	13	1965	(Musicor 1093)
! 16	Louisiana Man		0	1965	25	1965	(Musicor 1097)
* 17	Looking Through The Eyes Of Love	(Stateside Ss 420)	3	1965	28	1965	(Musicor 1103)
! 18	Big Job		0	1965	50	1965	(Musicor 1115)
19	Princess In Rags	(Stateside Ss 471)	9	1965	37	1965	(Musicor 1130)
! 20	Baby Ain't That Fine		0	1966	15	1966	(Musicor 1135)
21	Backstage	(Stateside Ss 490)	4	1966	25	1966	(Musicor 1171)
! 22	That's All It Took		0	1966	47	1966	(Musicor 1165)
23	Nobody Needs Your Love	(Stateside Ss 518)	2	1966	0	1966	
24	Just One Smile	(Stateside Ss 558)	8	1966	0	1966	
25	Cold Light Of Day	(Stateside Ss 597)	38	1967	0	1967	
26	Something's Gotten Hold Of My Heart	(Stateside Ss 2060)	5	1967	0	1967	
27	Somewhere In The Country	(Stateside Ss 2103)	19	1968	0	1968	
28	She's A Heartbreaker		0	1968	16	1968	(Musicor 1306)
29	Your's Until Tomorrow	(Stateside Ss 2131)	34	1968	0	1968	
30	Maria Elena	(Stateside Ss 2142)	25	1969	0	1969	
31	A Street Called Hope	(Stateside Ss 2164)	37	1970	0	1970	
32	Shady Lady	(Stateside Ss 2177)	29	1970	0	1970	
33	24 Sycamore	(Pye International 7n 25606)	34	1973	0	1973	
34	Blue Angel	(Bronze Bro 11)	39	1974	0	1974	
35	Blue Angel (Re-Entry)	(Bronze Bro 11)	39	1974	0	1974	
36	Something's Gotten Hold Of My Heart	(Parlophone R 6201)	1	1989	0	1989	

ALSO RECORDED AS BILLY BRYAN • HIT 14 REACHED NUMBER 99 IN THE US NATIONAL CHARTS • HIT 20 IS CREDITED TO GENE PITNEY AND MELBA MONTGOMERY
HIT 22 IS CREDITED TO GEORGE & GENE (GEORGE JONES) • HIT 36 IS CREDITED TO MARC ALMOND FEATURING SPECIAL GUEST STAR GENE PITNEY

Gene Redding   Male Vocalist, B: 1945 Anderson, Indiana

1	This Heart		0	1974	24	1974	(Haven 7000)

Gene Simmons   Male Rockabilly Singer, B: 1933 In Tupelo, Mississippi

1	Haunted House		0	1964	11	1964	(Hi 2076)
! 2	Why Didn't I Think Of That		0	1977	88	1977	(Deltune 1201)
3	Radioactive	(Casablanca Can 134)	41	1979	0	1979	

HIS NICKNAME IS JUMPIN' GENE

Gene Vincent & His Blue Caps   Male Vocal/Guitarist, Real Name Vincent Eugene Craddock B: 11 Feb 1935 Norfolk, Virginia.

* 1	Be-Bop-A-Lula	(Capitol Cl 14599)	30	1956	7	1956	(Capitol 3450)
2	Be-Bop-A-Lula (Re-Entry)	(Capitol Cl 14599)	16	1956	0	1956	
3	Be-Bop-A-Lula (2nd Re-Entry)	(Capitol Cl 14599)	23	1956	0	1956	
4	Race With The Devil	(Capitol Cl 14628)	28	1956	96	1956	(Capitol 3530)
5	Blue Jean Bop	(Capitol Cl 14637)	16	1956	0	1956	
6	Lotta Lovin'		0	1957	13	1957	(Capitol 3763)
7	Wear My Ring		0	1957	13	1957	(Capitol 3763)
8	Dance To The Bop		0	1958	23	1958	(Capitol 3839)
9	Wild Cat	(Capitol Cl 15099)	21	1960	0	1960	
10	My Heart	(Capitol Cl 15115)	16	1960	0	1960	
11	Wild Cat (Re-Entry)	(Capitol Cl 15099)	39	1960	0	1960	
12	My Heart (Re-Entry)	(Capitol Cl 15115)	47	1960	0	1960	
13	My Heart (2nd Re-Entry)	(Capitol Cl 15115)	36	1960	0	1960	
14	Pistol Packin' Mama	(Capitol Cl 15136)	15	1960	0	1960	
15	She She Little Sheila	(Capitol Cl 15202)	22	1961	0	1961	
16	She She Little Sheila (Re-Entry)	(Capitol Cl 15202)	44	1961	0	1961	
17	I'm Going Home	(Capitol Cl 15215)	36	1961	0	1961	

HE WAS INVOLVED IN A THE CAR CRASH THAT KILLED EDDIE COCHRAN • HE WAS INJURED IN A MOTORCYCLE ACCIDENT IN 1953 WHICH
RESULTED IN HIM HAVING TO WEAR A STEEL LEG BRACE. • HIT 1 REACHED NUMBER 5 IN THE US C/W CHARTS • OBITUARY: D: 12 OCT 1971 ULCER HAEMORRHAGE.

General Levy   Male Vocalist from the UK

1	Monkey Man	(Ffrr Fcd 214)	75	1993	0	1993	
2	Incredible	(Renk Renkt 42cd)	39	1994	0	1994	
3	Incredible (Re-Mix)	(Renk Cdrenk 44)	8	1994	0	1994	

General Public   Male Vocal/Instrumental Group from the UK

1	General Public	(Virgin Vs 659)	60	1984	0	1984	
2	Tenderness		0	1985	27	1985	(I.R.S. 9934)
3	I'll Take You There	(Epic 6605532)	73	1994	0	1994	

ISSUE	TITLE	UK LBL	UK POS	UK YEAR	US POS	US YEAR	US LBL
General Saint	Male Vocalist from the UK						
1	Last Plane (One Way Ticket)	(MCA MCA 910)	51	1984	0	1984	
2	Oh Carol!	(Copasetic Copcd 0009)	54	1994	0	1994	
3	Save the Last Dance for Me	(Copasetic Copcd 12)	75	1994	0	1994	

HIT 1 IS CREDITED TO CLINT EASTWOOD & GENERAL SAINT • HITS 2-3 ARE CREDITED TO GENERAL SAINT FEATURING DON CAMPBELL • SEE ALSO DAVE AND ANSIL COLLINS

ISSUE	TITLE	UK LBL	UK POS	UK YEAR	US POS	US YEAR	US LBL
Generation X	Male Vocal/Instrumental Group from the UK						
1	Your Generation	(Chrysalis Chs 2165)	36	1977	0	1977	
2	Ready Steady Go	(Chrysalis Chs 2207)	47	1978	0	1978	
3	King Rocker	(Chrysalis Chs 2261)	11	1979	0	1979	
4	Valley Of The Dolls	(Chrysalis Chs 2310)	23	1979	0	1979	
5	Friday's Angels	(Chrysalis Chs 2330)	62	1979	0	1979	
6	Dancing With Myself	(Chrysalis Chs 2444)	62	1980	0	1980	
7	Dancing With Myself (EP)	(Chrysalis Chs 2488)	60	1981	0	1981	

ISSUE	TITLE	UK LBL	UK POS	UK YEAR	US POS	US YEAR	US LBL
Genesis	Male Vocal/Instrumental Group from the UK						
1	I Know What I Like (In Your Wardrobe)	(Charisma Cb 224)	21	1974	0	1974	
2	Your Own Special Way	(Charisma Cb 300)	43	1977	0	1977	
3	Spot The Pigeon (EP)	(Charisma Gen 001)	14	1977	0	1977	
4	Follow You Follow Me	(Charisma Cb 309)	7	1978	23	1978	(Atlantic 3474)
5	Many Too Many	(Charisma Cb 315)	43	1978	0	1978	
6	Turn It On Again	(Charisma Cb 356)	8	1980	0	1980	
7	Duchess	(Charisma Cb 363)	46	1980	0	1980	
8	Misunderstanding	(Charisma Cb 369)	42	1980	14	1980	(Atlantic 3662)
9	Abacab	(Charisma Cb 388)	9	1981	26	1982	(Atlantic 3891)
10	Keep It Dark	(Charisma Cb 391)	33	1981	0	1981	
11	No Reply At All		0	1981	29	1981	(Atlantic 3858)
12	Man On The Corner	(Charisma Cb 393)	41	1982	40	1982	(Atlantic 4025)
13	3 X 3 (EP)	(Charisma Gen 1)	10	1982	0	1982	
14	Paperlate		0	1982	32	1982	(Atlantic 4053)
15	Mama	(Virgin/Charisma Mama 1)	4	1983	0	1983	
16	Thats All!	(Charisma/Virgin Tata 1)	16	1983	6	1984	(Atlantic 89724)
17	Illegal Alien	(Virgin/Charisma Al1)	46	1984	0	1984	
18	Illegal Alien (Re-Entry)	(Virgin/Charisma Al1)	70	1984	0	1984	
19	Invisible Touch	(Virgin Gens 1)	15	1986	1	1986	(Atlantic 89407)
20	In Too Deep	(Virgin Gens 2)	19	1986	3	1987	(Atlantic 89316)
21	Throwing It All Away	(Virgin Gens 5)	22	1987	4	1986	(Atlantic 89372)
22	Land Of Confusion	(Virgin Gens 3)	14	1986	4	1986	(Atlantic 89336)
23	Tonight Tonight Tonight	(Virgin Gens 4)	18	1987	3	1987	(Atlantic 89290)
24	No Son Of Mine	(Virgin Gens 6)	6	1991	12	1991	(Atlantic 87571)
25	No Son Of Mine (Re-Entry)	(Virgin Gens 6)	70	1992	0	1992	
26	I Can't Dance	(Virgin Gens 7)	7	1992	7	1992	(Atlantic 87532)
27	Hold On My Heart	(Virgin Gens 8)	16	1992	12	1992	(Atlantic 87481)
28	Jesus He Knows Me	(Virgin Gens 9)	20	1992	23	1992	(Atlantic 87454)
29	Invisible Touch (Live)	(Virgin Gens 10)	7	1992	0	1992	
30	Never A Time		0	1992	2	1992	(Atlantic 87411)
31	Tell My Why	(Virgin Gendg 11)	40	1993	0	1993	

NAMES PETER GABRIEL, ANTHONY PHILLIPS, TONY BANKS, MICHAEL RUTHERFORD & JOHN MAYHEW • MANY CHANGES OVER THE YEARS INCLUDING PHIL COLLINS

ISSUE	TITLE	UK LBL	UK POS	UK YEAR	US POS	US YEAR	US LBL
Geneva	Male Vocal/Instrumental Group from the UK						
1	No One Speaks	(Nude Nud 22cd)	32	1996	0	1996	
2	Into The Blue	(Nude Nud 25cd)	26	1997	0	1997	
3	Tranquillizer	(Nude Nud 28cd)	24	1997	0	1997	
4	Best Regrets	(Nude Nud 31cd1)	38	1997	0	1997	
Genevieve	Female Vocalist from France						
1	Once	(CBS 202061)	43	1966	0	1966	
Genius							
1	Cold World	(Geffen Gfstd 22114)	40	1996	0	1996	
Geno Washington & The Ram Jam Band	Male Vocalist With Male Instrumental Backing Group from the UK						
1	Water	(Piccadilly 7n 35312)	39	1966	0	1966	
2	Hi Hi Hazel	(Piccadilly 7n 35329)	45	1966	0	1966	
3	Hi Hi Hazel (Re-Entry)	(Piccadilly 7n 35329)	48	1966	0	1966	
4	Que Sera Sera	(Piccadilly 7n 35346)	43	1966	0	1966	
5	Michael	(Piccadilly 7n 35359)	39	1967	0	1967	
Gentrys	Lead Singer Of The Rock Band Is Larry Raspberry						
* 1	Keep On Dancing		0	1965	4	1965	(Mgm 13379)

ISSUE	TITLE	UK LBL	UK POS	UK YEAR	US POS	US YEAR	US LBL
Geoffrey Burgon Orchestra from the UK							
1	Brideshead Theme	(Chrysalis Chs 2562)	48	1981	0	1981	
Geoffrey Williams Male Vocalist from the UK							
1	It's Not A Love Thing	(EMI EM 228)	63	1992	0	1992	
2	Summer Breeze	(EMI EM 245)	56	1992	0	1992	
3	Drive	(Hands On Cdhor 11)	52	1997	0	1997	
4	Sex Life	(Hands On Cdhor 12)	71	1997	0	1997	
Geordie Male Vocal/Instrumental Group from the UK							
1	Don't Do That	(Regal Zonophone Rz 3067)	32	1972	0	1972	
2	All Because Of You	(EMI2008)	6	1973	0	1973	
3	Can You Do It	(EMI2031)	13	1973	0	1973	
4	Electric Lady	(EMI 2048)	32	1973	0	1973	
George Baker Selection Mixed Vocal/Instrumental Group from Holland Baker's Real Name Johannes Bouwens B: 9 Dec 1944.							
* 1	Little Green Bag		0	1970	21	1970	(Colossus 112)
* 2	Una Paloma Blanca	(Warner Bros K 16541)	10	1975	26	1975	(Warner Bros 8115)
George Benson Male Vocal/Instrumentalist, B: 22 Mar 1943 From Pittsburgh							
1	Supership	(Cti Ctsp 002)	30	1975	0	1975	
2	This Masquerade		0	1976	10	1976	(Warner Bros 8209)
3	The Greatest Love Of All	(Arista 133)	27	1977	24	1977	(Arista 0251)
4	Nature Boy	(Warner Bros K 16921)	26	1977	0	1977	
5	On Broadway		0	1978	7	1978	(Warner Bros 8542)
6	Love Ballad	(Warner Bros K 17333)	29	1979	18	1979	(Warner Bros 8759)
7	Give Me The Night	(Warner Bros K 17673)	7	1980	4	1980	(Warner Bros 49505)
8	Love X Love	(Warner Bros K 17699)	10	1980	0	1980	
9	What's On Your Mind	(Warner Bros K 17748)	45	1981	0	1981	
10	Love All The Hurt Away	(Arista Arist 428)	49	1981	0	1981	
11	Turn Your Love Around	(Warner Bros K 17877)	29	1981	5	1981	(Warner Bros 49846)
12	Never Give Up On A Good Thing	(Warner Bros K 17902)	14	1982	0	1982	
13	Lady Love Me (One More Time)	(Warner Bros W 9614)	11	19833	0	1983	(Warner Bros 29563)
14	Feel Like Makin' Love	(Warner Bros W 9551)	28	1983	0	1983	
15	In Your Eyes	(Warner Bros W 9487)	7	1983	0	1983	
16	Inside Love (So Personal)	(Wea Int W 9427)	57	1983	0	1983	
17	20/20	(Warner Bros W 9120)	29	1985	0	1985	
18	Beyond The Sea (La Mer)	(Warner Bros W 9014)	60	1985	0	1985	
19	Kisses In The Moonlight	(Warner Bros W 9640)	60	1986	0	1986	
20	Shiver	(Warner Bros W 8523)	19	1986	0	1986	
21	Teaser	(Warner Bros W 8437)	45	1987	0	1987	
22	Let's Do It Again	(Warner Bros W 7780)	56	1988	0	1988	
23	I'll Keep Your Dreams Alive	(Ammi Ammi 101)	68	1992	0	1992	
George Chakiris Male Vocalist from the USA							
1	Heart Of A Teenage Girl	(Triumph Rgm 1010)	49	1960	0	1960	
George Clinton Male Vocalist from the USA							
1	Loopzilla	(Capitol Cl 271)	57	1982	0	1982	
2	Do Fries Go With That Shake	(Capitol Cl 402)	57	1986	0	1986	
3	Bop Gun (One Nation)	(Fourth & Broadway Brcd 308)	22	1994	0	1994	
George Duke Male Vocal/Instrumentalist, B: 12 Jan 1946 California							
1	Brazilian Love Affair	(Epic Epc 8751)	36	1980	0	1980	
2	Sweet Baby		0	1981	19	1981	(Epic 01052)
George Fenton & Jonas Gwangwa Male Production/Instrumental Duo from the UK/South Africa							
1	Cry Freedom	(MCA MCA 1228)	75	1988	0	1988	
	See Also Thuli Dumakude						
George Formby Male Actor/Instrumentalist (Ukelele) from the UK							
1	Happy Go Lucky Me / Banjo Boy	(Pye 7n 15269)	40	1960	0	1960	
George Hamilton IV Male Vocalist, B: 19 Jul 1937 In Winston-Salem, North Carolina							
* 1	A Rose And A Baby Ruth		0	1956	6	1956	(ABC-Paramount 9765)
2	Only One Love		0	1957	33	1957	(Abc-Paramount 9782)
3	Why Don't They Understand	(HMV Pop 429)	22	1958	10	1957	(ABC-Paramount 9862)
4	Now And For Always		0	1958	25	1958	(Abc-Paramount 9898)
5	I Know Where I'm Going	(HMV Pop 505)	29	1958	0	1958	
6	I Know Where I'm Going (Re-Entry)	(HMV Pop 505)	23	1958	0	1958	
7	The Teen Commandments		0	1958	29	1958	(ABC-Paramount 9974)
14	Abilene		0	1963	15	1963	(RCA 8181)

ISSUE	TITLE	UK LBL	UK POS	UK YEAR	US POS	US YEAR	US LBL

HIT 7 IS CREDITED TO PAUL ANKA, GEORGE HAMILTON IV & JOHNNY NASH • HIT 14 REACHED NUMBER 1 IS THE US C/W CHARTS
OTHER HITS ARE C/W

George Harrison Male Vocalist, B: 25 Feb 1943 Liverpool, England

ISSUE	TITLE	UK LBL	UK POS	UK YEAR	US POS	US YEAR	US LBL
* 1	My Sweet Lord	(Apple R 5884)	1	1971	1	1970	(Apple 2995)
2	Isn't It A Pity		0	1970	1	1970	(Apple 2995)
3	What Is Life		0	1971	10	1971	(Apple 1828)
4	Bangla Desh	(Apple R 5912	10	1971	23	1971	(Apple 1836)
* 5	Give Me Love (Give Me Peace On Earth)	Apple R 5988)	8	1973	1	1973	(Apple 1862)
6	Dark Horse		0	1974	15	1974	(Apple 1877)
7	Ding Dong; Ding Dong	(Apple R 6002)	38	1974	36	1974	(Apple 1879)
8	You	(Apple R 6007)	38	1975	20	1975	(Apple 1884)
9	This Song		0	1976	25	1976	(Dark Horse 8294)
10	Crackerbox Palace		0	19771	9	1977	(Dark Horse 8313)
11	Blow Away	(Dark Horse K 17327)	51	1979	16	1979	(Dark Horse 8763)
12	All Those Years Ago	(Dark Horse 3k 17807)	13	1981	2	1981	(Dark Horse 49725)
13	Got My Mind Set On You	(Dark Horse W 8178)	2	1987	1	1987	(Dark Horse 28178)
14	When We Was Fab	(Dark Horse W 8131)	25	1988	23	1988	(Dark Horse 28131)
15	This Is Love	(Dark Horse W 7913)	55	1988	0	1988	

GEORGE & JOHN LENNON RECORDED AS THE BEAT BROTHERS FOR POLYDOR WHILST IN HAMBURG, WEST GERMANY
FORMED THE GROUP THE REBEL IN 1956, JOINED THE QUARRYMEN IN 1958) • SEE ALSO THE BEATLES AND TRAVELING WILBURYS

George Lamond Real Name George Garcia B: 25 Feb 1967 Washington, D.C.

ISSUE	TITLE	UK LBL	UK POS	UK YEAR	US POS	US YEAR	US LBL
1	Bad Of The Heart		0	1990	25	1990	(Columbia 73339)

George Maharis Male Actor/Vocalist, B: 1 Sep 1928 New York City

ISSUE	TITLE	UK LBL	UK POS	UK YEAR	US POS	US YEAR	US LBL
1	Teach Me Tonight		0	1962	25	1962	(Epic 9504)

George McCrae Male Vocalist, B: 19 Oct 1944 Florida

ISSUE	TITLE	UK LBL	UK POS	UK YEAR	US POS	US YEAR	US LBL
* 1	Rock Your Baby	(Jayboy Boy 85)	1	1974	1	1974	(Tk 1004)
2	I Can't Leave You Alone	(Jayboy Boy 90)	9	1974	50	1974	(Tk 1007)
3	You Can Have It All	(Jayboy Boy 92)	23	1974	0	1974	
4	I Get Lifted		0	1975	37	1975	(Tk 1007)
5	Sing A Happy Song	(Jayboy Boy 95)	38	1975	0	1975	
6	It's Been So Long	(Jayboy Boy 100)	4	1975	0	1975	
7	I Ain't Lyin'	(Jayboy Boy 105)	12	1975	0	1975	
8	Honey I	(Jayboy Boy 107)	33	1976	0	1976	
9	One Step Closer (To Love)	(President Pt 522)	57	1984	0	1984	

George Melachrino & His Orchestra Male Orchestra Leader from the UK

ISSUE	TITLE	UK LBL	UK POS	UK YEAR	US POS	US YEAR	US LBL
1	Autumn Concerto	(HMV B 10958)	18	1956	0	1956	

George Michael Male Vocalist, Real Name Georgios Kyriacos Panayiotou B: 26 Jun 1963 Bushey, Hertfordshire, England.

ISSUE	TITLE	UK LBL	UK POS	UK YEAR	US POS	US YEAR	US LBL
* 1	Careless Whisper	(Epic A 4603)	1	1984	1	1985	(Columbia 04691)
2	A Different Corner	(Epic A 7033)	1	1986	7	1986	(Columbia 05888)
3	I Knew You Were Waiting (For Me)	(Epic Duet 2)	1	1987	1	1987	(Arista 9559)
4	I Want Your Sex (From "Beverly Hills Cop II")	(Epic Lust 1)	3	1987	2	1987	(Columbia 07164)
* 5	Faith	(Epic Emu 3)	2	1987	1	1987	(Columbia 07623)
6	Father Figure	(Epic Emu 4)	11	1988	1	1988	(Columbia 07682)
* 7	One More Try	(Epic Emu 5)	8	1988	1	1988	(Columbia 07773)
8	Monkey	(Epic Emu 6)	13	1988	1	1988	(Columbia 07941)
9	Kissing A Fool	(Epic Emu 7)	18	1988	5	1988	(Columbia 08050)
10	Heaven Help Me		0	1989	5	1989	(Miki 871538)
11	Praying For Time	(Epic Geo 1)	6	1990	1	1990	(Columbia 73512)
12	Waiting For That Day	(Epic Geo 2)	23	1990	27	1990	(Columbia 73663)
* 13	Freedom '90	(Epic Geo 3)	28	1990	8	1990	(Columbia 73559)
14	Heal The Pain	(Epic 6566477)	31	1991	0	1991	
15	Cowboys And Angels	(Epic 6567747)	45	1991	0	1991	
* 16	Don't Let The Sun Go Down On Me	(Epic 6576467)	1	1991	11	1992	(Columbia 74086)
* 17	Too Funky	(Epic 6580587)	4	1992	10	1992	(Columbia 74353)
18	Five Live (Ep)	(Parlophone R Cdrs 6340)	1	1993	0	1993	
19	Somebody To Love		0	1993	30	1993	(Hollywood 64647)
20	Five Live (EP) (Re-Entry)	(Parlophone R Cdrs 6340)	74	1993	0	1993	
21	Fastlove	(Virgin Vscdg 1579)	1	1996	8	1996	(Geffen 59001)
22	Jesus To A Child	(Virgin Vscdg 1571)	1	1996	7	1996	(Abcdef 00000)
23	Jesus To A Child (Re-Entry)	(Virgin Vscdg 1571)	66	1996	0	1996	
24	Jesus To A Child (2nd Re-Entry)	(Virgin Vscdg 1571)	68	1996	0	1996	
25	Jesus To A Child (3rd Re-Entry)	(Virgin Vscdg 1571)	65	1996	0	1996	
26	Spinning The Wheel	(Virgin Vscdg 1595)	2	1996	0	1996	
27	Older / I Can't Make You Love Me	(Virgin Vscdg 1626)	3	1997	0	1997	

ISSUE	TITLE	UK LBL	UK POS	UK YEAR	US POS	US YEAR	US LBL
28	Older / I Can't Make You Love Me (Re-Entry)	(Virgin Vscdg 1626)	70	1997	0	1997	
29	Star People '97	(Virgin Vscdg 1641)	2	1997	0	1997	
30	Waltz Away Dreaming	(Aegean Aecd 01)	10	1997	0	1997	
31	Star People '97 (Re-Entry)	(Virgin Vscdg 1641)	59	1997	0	1997	

HIT 3 IS CREDITED TO AREATHA FRANKLIN AND GEORGE MICHAEL • HIT 16 IS CREDITED TO GEORGE MICHAEL AND ELTON JOHN
HIT 13 IS A DIFFERENT TUNE TO THE '85 WHAM HIT • HITS 18-19 ARE CREDITED TO GEORGE MICHAEL AND QUEEN WITH LISA STANSFIELD
HIT 30 IS CREDITED TO TOBY BOURKEWITH GEORGE MICHAEL

George Morel (Featuring) Heather Wildman   Mixed Vocal/Instrumental Duo from the USA

ISSUE	TITLE	UK LBL	UK POS	UK YEAR	US POS	US YEAR	US LBL
1	Let's Groove	(Positiva Cdtiv 62)	42	1996	0	1996	

George Shearing   Male Pianist, B: 13 Aug 1920 Battersea, London

ISSUE	TITLE	UK LBL	UK POS	UK YEAR	US POS	US YEAR	US LBL
* 1	September In The Rain		0	1949	25	1949	(MGM 30250)
2	Let There Be Love	(Capitol Cl 15257)	11	1992	0	1992	
3	Baubles Bangles And Beads	(Capitol Cl 15269)	49	1962	0	1962	

FORMED A QUINTET IN 1949 WITH DENZIL BEST, JOHN LEVY & CHUCK WAYNE HIT 1 IS CREDITED TO GEORGE SHEARING QUINTET

George Van Dusen   Male Vocalist from the UK

ISSUE	TITLE	UK LBL	UK POS	UK YEAR	US POS	US YEAR	US LBL
1	It's Party Time Again	(Bri-Tone 7bt 001)	43	1988	0	1988	

Georghe Zamfir   Male Instrumentalist From Romania

ISSUE	TITLE	UK LBL	UK POS	UK YEAR	US POS	US YEAR	US LBL
1	(Light Of Experience) Doina De Jale	(Epic Epc 4310)	4	1976	0	1976	

Georgia Gibbs   Female Vocalist, Real Name Fredda Gibbons B: 17 Aug 1920 Worcester, Massachusetts.

ISSUE	TITLE	UK LBL	UK POS	UK YEAR	US POS	US YEAR	US LBL
1	If I Knew You Were Comin' I'd've Baked A Cake		0	1950	5	1950	(Coral 60169)
2	Play A Simple Melody (From Watch Your Step)		0	1950	25	1950	(Coral 60227)
3	I Still Feel The Same About You		0	1951	18	1951	(Coral 60353)
4	Tom's Tune		0	1951	21	1951	(Mercury 5644)
5	Good Morning Mr.Echo		0	1951	21	1951	(Mercury 5662)
6	While You Danced, Danced, Danced (I Walked In With A Smile)		0	1951	6	1951	(Mercury 5681)
7	Cry		0	1951	24	1951	(Mercury 5749)
* 8	Kiss Of Fire		0	1952	1	1952	(Mercury 5823)
9	So Madly In Love		0	1952	21	1952	(Mercury 5874)
10	My Favorite Song		0	1952	22	1952	(Mercury 5912)
11	Seven Lonely Days		0	1953	5	1953	(Mercury 70095)
12	For Me, For Me		0	1953	23	1953	(Mercury 70172)
13	The Bridge Of Sighs		0	1953	30	1953	(Mercury 70238)
14	A Home Lovin' Man		0	1953	30	1953	(Mercury 70238)
15	Somebady Bad Stole De Wedding Bell		0	1954	18	1954	(Mercury 70298)
16	My Sin		0	1954	21	1954	(Mercury 70339)
17	Wait For Me, Darling		0	1954	24	1954	(Mercury 70386)
* 18	Tweedle Dee	(Mercury Mb 3196)	20	1955	2	1955	(Mercury 70517)
* 19	Dance With Me Henry (Wallflower)		0	1955	1	1955	(Mercury 70572)
20	Sweet And Gentle		0	1955	12	1955	(Mercury 70647)
21	I Want You To Be My Baby		0	1955	14	1955	(Mercury 70685)
22	Rock Right		0	1956	36	1956	(Mercury 70811)
23	Kiss Me Another	(Mercury Mt 110)	24	1956	30	1956	(Mercury 70850)
24	Happiness Street		0	1956	20	1956	(Mercury 70920)
25	Tra La La		0	1956	24	1956	(Mercury 70998)
26	The Hula Hoop Song		0	1958	32	1958	(Roulette 4106)

HIT 1 WAS WITH MAX KAMINSKY'S DIXIELANDERS HIT 2WITH THE BOB CROSBY ORCHESTRA • HIT 3WITH THE OWEN BRADLEY SEXTET
HIT 11 WAS WITH THE YALE BROTHERS

Georgia Jones (Featuring) Plux

ISSUE	TITLE	UK LBL	UK POS	UK YEAR	US POS	US YEAR	US LBL
1	Over & Over	(Ffrr Fcd 277)	33	1996	0	1996	

Georgia Satellites   Male Vocal/Instrumental Quartet from the USA

ISSUE	TITLE	UK LBL	UK POS	UK YEAR	US POS	US YEAR	US LBL
1	Keep Your Hands To Yourself	(Elektra Ekr 50)	69	1987	2	1987	(Elektra 69502)
2	Battleship Chains	(Elektra Ekr 58)	44	1987	0	1987	
3	Hippy Hippy Shake	(Elektra Ekr 86)	63	1989	0	1989	

NAMES DAN BAIRD, RICK RICHARDS, RICH PRICE & MAURO MAGELLAN

Georgie Fame   Male Vocal/Pianist, Real Name Clive Powell B: 26 Jun 1943 In Leigh, Manchester, England

ISSUE	TITLE	UK LBL	UK POS	UK YEAR	US POS	US YEAR	US LBL
* 1	Yeh Yeh	(Columbia Db 7428)	1	1964	21	1965	(Imperial 66086)
2	In The Meantime	(Columbia Db 7494)	22	1965	0	1965	
3	Like We Used To Be	(Columbia Db 7633)	33	1965	0	1965	
4	Something	(Columbia Db 7727)	23	1965	0	1965	
5	Get Away	(Columbia Db 7946)	1	1966	0	1966	
6	Sunny	(Columbia Db 8015)	13	1966	0	1966	
7	Sitting In The Park	(Columbia Db 8096)	12	1966	0	1966	
8	Because I Love You	(CBS 202587)	15	1967	0	1967	
9	Try My World	(CBS 2945)	37	1967	0	1967	

ISSUE	TITLE	UK LBL	UK POS	UK YEAR	US POS	US YEAR	US LBL
* 10	Ballad Of Bonnie And Clyde	(CBS 3124)	1	1967	7	1968	(Epic 10283)
11	Peaceful	(CBS 4295)	16	1969	0	1969	
12	Seventh Son	(CBS 4659)	25	1969	0	1969	
13	Rosetta	(CBS 7108)	11	1971	0	1971	

(B: 26 JUN 1943, LEIGH, MANCHESTER, ENGLAND) • HIT 13 IS CREDITED TO FAME AND PRICE TOGETHER
HITS 1-5,7 ARE CREDITED TO GEORGIE FAME & THE BLUE FLAMES

Georgie Porgie   Male Producer from the USA

1	Everybody Must Party	(MCA Mcstd 2068)	61	1995	0	1995	
2	Take Me Higher	(Music Plant Mcstd 40031)	61	1996	0	1996	

Georgie Shaw

1	Til We Two Are One		0	1954	7	1954	(Decca 28937)
2	Someone Else's Love Song		0	1954	29	1954	(Decca 29160)
3	No Arms Can Ever Hold You (Like These Arms Of Mine)		0	1955	23	1955	(Decca 29679)
4	Go On With The Wedding		0	1956	39	1956	(Decca 29776)

Georgio   Male Vocalist from the USA

1	Lover's Lane	(Motown Zb 41611)	54	1988	0	1988	

Gerald Alston   Male Vocalist from the USA

1	Activated	(RCA Zb 42681)	73	1989	0	1989	

Geraldine Hunt   Female Vocalist from Canada

1	Can't Fake The Feeling	(Champagne Fizz 501)	44	1980	0	1980	

Gerard Kenny   Male Vocalist from the USA

1	New York, New York	(RCA Pb 5117)	43	1978	0	1978	
2	Fantasy	(RCA Pb 5256)	65	1980	0	1980	
3	Fantasy (Re-Entry)	(RCA Pb 5256)	34	1980	0	1980	
4	The Other Woman, The Other Man	(Impression Ims 3)	69	1984	0	1984	
5	No Mans Land (Widows Theme)	(Wea Yz 38)	56	1985	0	1985	

Gerald Levert   Male Vocalist from the USA

1	Baby Hold On To Me		0	1992	37	1992	(Eastwest 98639)
2	I'd Give Anything		0	1994	28	1994	(Eastwest 98244)

Gerardo   Male Rapper/Actor, Real Name Gerardo Mejia 111 B: 16 Apr 1965 Ecuador

* 1	Rico Suave		0	1991	7	1991	(Interscope 98871)
2	We Thank The Funk		0	1991	16	1991	(Interscope 98815)

Gerhard Wendland   B: 1932, Berlin

* 1	Tanze Mit Mir In Den Morgen (Dance With Me In The Morning)		0	1962	0	1962	

Gerideau   See Project

Gerri Granger   Female Vocalist from the USA

1	I Go To Pieces (Everytime)	(Casino Classics Cc3)	50	1978	0	1978	

Gerry & The Pacemakers   Male Vocal/Instrumental Group from the UK   Other Members Are Leslie Maguire, Les Chadwick And Gerry's Brother Freddie Marsden

1	How Do You Do It	(Columbia Db 4987)	1	1963	9	1964	(Laurie 3261)
2	I Like It	(Columbia Db 7041)	1	1963	17	1964	(Laurie 3271)
3	You'll Never Walk Alone	(Columbia Db 7126)	1	1963	0	1963	
4	I'm The One	(Columbia Db 7189)	2	1964	0	1964	
* 5	Don't Let The Sun Catch You Crying	(Columbia Db 7268)	6	1964	4	1964	(Laurie 3251)
6	It's Gonna Be All Right	(Columbia Db 7353)	24	1964	23	1964	(Laurie 3293)
7	Ferry 'Cross The Mersey	(Columbia Db 7437)	8	1964	6	1965	(Laurie 3284)
8	I'll Be There	(Columbia Db 7504)	15	1965	14	1964	(Laurie 3279)
9	Walk Hand In Hand	(Columbia Db 7738)	29	1965	0	1965	
10	Girl on a Swing		19662	1966	8	1966	(laurie 3354)

GERRY'S REAL NAME GERRY MARSDEN B: 24 SEP 1942, LIVERPOOL, ENGLAND • ANOTHER GROUP GERRY WAS INVOLVED IN PRIOR TO THIS WAS THE MARS-BARS

Gerry Granahan   B: 17 Jun 1939 Pittston, Pennsylvania

1	No Chemise Please		0	1958	23	1958	(Sunbeam 102)

Gerry Marsden   Male Vocalist From Liverpool, England, See Also Gerry & The Pacemakers

1	Ferry 'Cross The Mersey	Pwl Pwl 41)	1	1989	0	1989	

Gerry Monroe   Male Vocalist from the UK

1	Sally	(Chapter One Ch 122)	4	1970	0	1970	
2	Cry	(Chapter One Ch 128)	38	1970	0	1970	
3	My Prayer	(Chapter One Ch 132)	9	1970	0	1970	
4	It's A Sin To Tell A Lie	(Chapter One Ch 144)	13	1971	0	1971	
5	Little Drops Of Silver	(Chapter One Ch 152)	37	1971	0	1971	
6	Girl Of My Dreams	(Chapter One Ch 159)	43	1972	0	1972	

ISSUE	TITLE	UK LBL	UK POS	UK YEAR	US POS	US YEAR	US LBL
Gerry Rafferty	Male Vocalist, B: 16 Apr 1947 Paisley, Scotland, Ex Member Of Stealers Wheel						
* 1	Baker Street	(United Artists Up 36346)	3	1979	2	1978	(United Artists 1192)
2	Right Down The Line		0	1978	12	1978	(United Artists 1233)
3	Home And Dry		0	1979	28	1979	(United Artists 1266)
4	Night Owl	(United Artists Up 36512)	5	1979	0	1979	
5	Days Gone Down (Still Got The Light In Your Eyes)		0	1979	17	1979	(United Artists 1298)
6	Get It Right Next Time	(United Artists Bp 301)	30	1979	21	1979	(United Artists 1316)
7	Bring It All Home	(United Artists Bp 3400)	54	1980	0	1980	
8	Royal Mile	(United Artists Bp 345)	67	1980	0	1980	
9	Baker Street (Re-Mix)	(EMI EM 132)	53	1990	0	1990	
Gertrude Niesen	Female Vocalist from the USA						
1	Tony's Wife		0	1933	19	1933	(Columbia 2759)
2	Hold Your Man		0	1933	14	1933	(Columbia 2787)
3	Where Are You?		0	1937	14	1937	(Brunswick 7837)
4	I Wanna Get Married		0	1945	10	1945	(Decca 23382)
Get Ready	Male Vocal Group from the UK						
1	Wild Wild West	(Mega Gacxcd 2698)	65	1995	0	1995	
Get Wet	Lead Singer Sherri Beachfront, Although Cannot Confirm The Name						
1	Just So Lonely		0	1981	39	1981	(Boardwalk 02018)
Geto Boys	Male Rap Outfit From Houston, Texas						
* 1	Mind Playing Tricks On Me		0	1991	23	1991	(Rap-A-Lot 7241)
2	Six Feet Deep		0	1993	40	1994	(Rap-A-Lot 53823)
3	The World Is A Ghetto	(Vision Vuscdx 104)	49	1996	0	1996	
Ghost Dance	Male Vocal/Instrumental Group from the UK						
1	Down To The Wire	(Chrysalis Chs 3376)	66	1989	0	1989	
Ghost Town DJs							
1	My Boo		0	1996	31	1996	(Columbia 78358)
Ghostface Killah							
1	All That I Got Is You	(Epic 6646842)	11	1997	0	1997	
Gianni Morandi							
* 1	In Ginocchio Da Te (On My Knees To You)		0	1964	0	1964	
* 2	Non Son Degna Di Te (Not Good Enough For You)		0	1964	0	1964	
* 3	Scende La Poggia (It's Raining)		0	1969	0	1969	
Giant	Brothers Dann & David Huff form half of this rock quartet						
1	I'll See You In My Dreams		0	1990	20	1990	(A&M 1495)
Giant Steps	ames: McFarlane & Campsie Ex Members Of Grand Hotel						
1	Another Lover		0	1988	13	1988	(A&M 1226)
Gibson Brothers	Male Vocal/Instrumental Group From Martinique						
1	Cuba	(Island Wip 6483)	41	1979	0	1979	
2	Ooh! What A Life	(Island Wip 6503)	10	1979	0	1979	
3	Que Sera Mi Vida (If You Should Go)	(Island Wip 6525)	5	1979	0	1979	
4	Cuba / Better Do It Salsa (Re-Issue)	(Island Wip 6561)	12	1980	0	1980	
5	Mariana	(Island Wip 6617)	11	1980	0	1980	
6	My Heart's Beating Wild (Tic Tac Tic Tac)	(Stiff Buy 184)	56	1983	0	1983	
Gid Tanner & His Skillet Lickers	Male Instrumentalist, Real Name James Gideon Tanner B: 1886 Thomas Bridge, Near Monroe, Georgia.						
* 3	Down Yonder		0	1934	10	1934	(Bluebird 5562)
Gidea Park	Real Name Adrian Baker Male Vocal/Instrumentalist from the UK						
1	Beachboy Gold	(Stone Son 2162)	11	1981	0	1981	
2	Seasons Of Gold	(Polo Polo 14)	28	1981	0	1981	
Gifted							
1	Do I	(Perfecto Perf 140cd)	60	1997	0	1997	
Gigliola Cinquetti	Female Vocalist B: 20 Dec 1947, Verona, Italy						
* 1	Non Ho L'eta Per Amarti	(Decca F 21882)		17	1964	0	1964
	(I'm Not Old Enoughto Love You)						
2	Go (Before You Break My Heart)	(CBS 2294)	8	1974	0	1974	
	HIT 1 WON THE SAN REMO FESTIVAL AND THE EUROVISON SONG CONTEST AND WAS NUMBER 1 IN FIVE OTHER EUROPEAN COUNTRIES						
Gigolo Aunts	Male Vocal/Instrumental Group from the USA						
1	Mrs. Washington	(Fire Blaze 68cd)	74	1994	0	1994	
2	Where I Find My Heaven	(Fire Blaze 87cd)	29	1995	0	1995	
Gilbert Becaud	Male Vocalist from France						
1	A Little Love And Understanding	(Decca F 13537)	10	1975	0	1975	

ISSUE	TITLE	UK LBL	UK POS	UK YEAR	US POS	US YEAR	US LBL
Gilbert O'Sullivan	Male Vocal/Pianist, Real Name Raymond O'Sullivan B: 1 Dec 1946 In Waterford, Southern Ireland				(B: 1 Dec 1946 Waterford, Southern Ireland)		
1	Nothing Rhymed	(Mam 3)	8	1970	0	1970	
2	Underneath The Blanket Go	(Mam 13)	40	1971	0	1971	
3	Underneath The Blanket Go (Re-Entry)	(Mam 13)	42	1971	0	1971	
4	We Will	(Mam 30)	16	1971	0	1971	
5	No Matter How I Try	(Mam 53)	5	1971	0	1971	
* 6	Alone Again (Naturally)	(Mam 66)	3	1972	1	1972	(Mam 3619)
7	Ohh-Wakka-Doo-Wakka-Day	(Mam 78)	8	1972	0	1972	
* 8	Clair	(Mam 84)	1	1972	2	1972	(Mam 3626)
* 9	Get Down	(Mam 96)	1	1973	7	1973	(Mam 3629)
10	Out Of The Question		0	1973	17	1973	(Mam 3628)
11	Ooh Baby	(Mam 107)	18	1973	25	1973	(Mam 3633)
12	Why Oh Why Oh Why	(Mam 111)	6	1973	0	1973	
13	Happiness Is Me And You	(Mam 114)	19	1974	0	1974	
14	A Woman's Place	(Mam 122)	42	1974	0	1974	
15	Christmas Song	(Mam 124)	12	1974	0	1974	
16	I Don't Love You But I Think I Like You	(Mam 130)	14	1975	0	1975	
17	What's In A Kiss	(CBS 8929)	19	1980	0	1980	
18	So What	(Dover Roj 3)	70	1990	0	1990	
Gillan	Male Vocal/Instrumental Group from the UK						
1	Sleeping On The Job	(Virgin Vs 355)	55	1980	0	1980	
2	Trouble	(Virgin Vs 377)	14	1980	0	1980	
3	Mutually Assured Destruction	(Virgin Vs 103)	32	1981	0	1981	
4	New Orleans	(Virgin Vs 406)	17	1981	0	1981	
5	No Laughing In Heaven	(Virgin Vs 425)	31	1981	0	1981	
6	Nightmare	(Virgin Vs 441)	36	1981	0	1981	
7	Restless	(Virgin Vs 465)	25	1982	0	1982	
8	Living For The City	(Virgin Vs 519)	50	1982	0	1982	
Gin Blossoms	Male Vocal/Instrumental Group from the USA						
1	Hey Jealousy	(Fontana Gincd 3)	24	1994	25	1993	(A&M 0242)
2	Found Out About You	(Fontana Gincd 4)	40	1994	25	1994	(A&M 0418)
3	Til I Hear It From You	(A&M 5812272)	39	1996	9	1996	(A&M 581380)
4	Follow You Down	A&M 5815512	30	1996	0	1996	
5	As Long As It Matters		0	1996	75	1996	(A&M 581672)
Gina G	Female Vocalist From Australia						
1	Ooh Aah...Just A Little Bit	(Eternal/Wea 041cd)	1	1996	0	1996	
2	Ooh Aah...Just A Little Bit (Re-Entry)	(Eternal/Wea 041cd)	62	1996	0	1996	
3	Ooh Aah...Just A Little Bit (2nd Re-Entry)	(Eternal/Wea 041cd)	64	1996	12	1996	(Warner Bros 17455)
4	I Belong To You	(Eternal/Wea 081cd)	6	1996	0	1996	
5	Fresh!	(Eternal/Wea 095cd)	6	1997	0	1997	
6	Ti Amo	(Eternal/WEA 107cd1)	11	1997	0	1997	
7	Gimme Some Love	(Eternal/WEA 101cd1)	25	1997	0	1997	
Gina Thompson	Female Vocalist from the USA						
1	The Things That You Do		0	1996	41	1996	(Mercury 578158)
Ginny Gibson	Female Vocalist from the USA						
1	You Blew Me A Kiss		0	1953	25	1953	(Mgm 11383)
Ginny Simms	Female Actress/Vocalist from the USA						
1	Walkin' By The River		0	1941	16	1941	(Okeh 6025)
2	Irresistable You		0	1944	27	1944	(Columbia 36693)
Gino & Gina	Real Names Aristedes & Irene Giosasi – Brother & Sister						
1	(It's Been A Long Time) Pretty Baby		0	1958	20	1958	(Mercury 71283)
Gino Latino	Male Producer From Italy						
1	Welcome	(Ffrr F 126)	17	1990	0	1990	
Gino Soccio	Male Instrumentalist (Keyboards) From Canada						
1	Dancer	(Warner Bros K 17357)	46	1979	0	1979	
Gino Vannelli	B: 16 Jun 1952 Montreal, Canada						
1	People Gotta Move		0	1974	22	1974	(A&M 1614)
2	I Just Wanna Stop		0	1978	4	1978	(A&M 2072)
3	Living Inside Myself		0	1981	6	1981	(A&M 0588)
Ginuwine	Male R&B Singer, Real Name Elgin Lumpkin From Washington D.C.						
* 1	Pony	(Epic 6641282)	16	1997	6	1996	(Music 78373)
3	When Doves Cry	(Epic 6649245)	10	1997	0	1997	
3	When Doves Cry	(Epic 6649245)	10	1997	0	1997	

ISSUE	TITLE	UK LBL	UK POS	UK YEAR	US POS	US YEAR	US LBL
Giorgio Moroder	Male Instrumentalist (Synthesizer) B: 26 Apr 1940 Italy						
1	From Here To Eternity		16	1977	0	1977	
2	Chase		48	1979	33	1979	(Casablanca 956)
3	Together In Electric Dreams		3	1984	0	1984	
4	Goodbye Bad Times		44	1985	0	1985	
Gipsy Kings	Male Vocal/Instrumental Group from France						
1	Hits Medley	(Columbia 6606022)	53	1994	0	1994	
Girl	Male Vocal/Instrumental Group from the UK						
1	Hollywood Tease	(Jet 176)	50	1980	0	1980	
Girlfriend	Female Vocal Group from Australia						
1	Take It From Me	(Arista 74321114252)	47	1993	0	1993	
2	Girl's Life	(Arista 74321138452)	68	1993	0	1993	
Girlschool	Female Vocal/Instrumental Group from the UK						
1	Race With The Devil	(Bronze Bro 100)	49	1980	0	1980	
2	St.Valentine's Day Massacre (EP)	(Bronze Bro 116)	5	1981	0	1981	
3	Hit And Run	(Bronze Bro 118)	32	1981	0	1981	
4	C'mon Let's Go	(Bronze Bro 126)	42	1981	0	1981	
5	Wildlife (EP)	(Bronze Bro 144)	58	1982	0	1982	
	MOTORHEAD AND GIRLSCHOOL ARE ALSO KNOWN AS HEADGIRL. • HIT 2 IS CREDITED TO MOTORHEAD AND GIRLSCHOOL						
Gisele Jackson							
1	Love Commandments	(Manifesto Fescd 28)	54	1997	0	1997	
Gisele Mackenzie	Female Vocalist, Real Name Giseie Lefieche B: 10 Jan 1927 Winnipeg, Canada						
1	La Fiacre		0	1952	20	1952	(Capitol 1907)
2	Adios		0	1952	14	1952	(Capitol 2156)
3	Water Can't Quench The Fire Of Love		0	1952	21	1952	(Capitol 2266)
4	Don't Let The Stars Get In Your Eyes		0	1952	11	1952	(Capitol 2256)
5	Lipstick-A-Powder-N' Paint		0	1953	25	1953	(Capitol 2404)
6	Seven Lonely Days	(Capitol Cl 13920)	12	1953	0	1953	
7	Seven Lonely Days (Re-Entry)	(Capitol Cl 13920)	11	1953	0	1953	
8	Seven Lonely Days (2nd Re-Entry)	(Capitol Cl 13920	6	1953	0	1953	
9	Hard To Get		0	1955	4	1955	(X 0137)
Gitte	Her Real Name Is Gitte Haenning B: 29 Jul 1946, Copenhagen, Denmark						
* 1	Ich Will Einen Cowboy Als Mann (I Want To Marry A Cowboy)		0	1963	0	1963	
Giuffria	Rock Quintet Based In California Led By Gregg Gluffria						
1	Call To The Heart		0	1985	15	1985	(Mca 52497)
Gladiators	Mixed Vocal Group from the UK						
1	The Boys Are Back In Town	(RCA 74321417002)	70	1996	0	1996	
Gladiolas							
1	Little Darlin'		0	1957	41	1957	(Excello 2101)
Gladys Knight & The Pips	Female Vocalist/Male Backing Group from the USA						
1	Every Beat Of My Heart		0	1991	6	1991	(Vee-Jay 386)
2	Letter Full Of Tears		0	1962	19	1962	(Fury 1054)
3	Giving Up		0	1964	38	1964	(Maxx 326)
4	Take Me In Your Arms And Love Me	(Tamla Motown Tmg 604)	13	1967	0	1967	
5	Everybody Needs Love		0	1967	3	1967	(Soul 35034)
* 6	I Heard It Through The Grapevine	(Tamla Motown Tmg 629)	47	1967	2	1967	(Soul 35039)
7	The End Of Our Road		0	1968	15	1968	(Soul 35042)
8	It Should Have Been Me		0	1968	40	1968	(Soul 35045)
9	I Wish It Would Rain		0	1968	41	1968	(Soul 35047)
+ 10	Didn't You Know		0	1969	11	1969	(Soul 35057)
11	The Nitty Gritty		0	1969	19	1969	(Soul 35063)
12	Friendship Train		0	1969	17	1969	(Soul 35068)
13	You Need Love Like I Do (Don't You)		0	1970	25	1970	(Soul 35071)
14	If I Were Your Woman		0	1970	9	1970	(Soul 35078)
15	I Don't Want To Do Wrong		0	1971	17	1971	(Soul 35083)
16	Make Me The Woman That You Go Home To		0	1971	27	1971	(Soul 35091)
17	Help Me Make It Through The Night	(Tamla Motown Tmg 830)	11	1972	33	1972	(Soul 35039)
18	Just Walk In My Shoes	(Tamla Motown Tmg 813)	35	1972	0	1972	
* 19	Neither One Of Us	(TMG 855)	31	1973	2	1973	(Soul 35098)
	(Wants To Be The First To Say Goodbye)						
20	Look Of Love	(Tamla Motown Tmg 844)	21	1973	0	1973	
21	Daddy Could Swear, I Declare		0	1973	19	1973	(Soul 35105)

ISSUE	TITLE	UK LBL	UK POS	UK YEAR	US POS	US YEAR	US LBL
22	Where Peaceful Waters Flow		0	1973	28	1973	(Buddah 363)
* 23	Midnight Train To Georgia	(Buddah Bds 444)	10	1976	1	1973	(Buddah 383)
* 24	I've Got To Use My Imagination		0	1973	4	1973	(Buddah 393)
* 25	Best Thing That Ever Happened To Me	(Buddah Bds 432)	7	1975	3	1974	(Buddah 403)
* 26	On And On		0	1974	5	1974	(Buddah 423)
27	I Feel A Song (In My Heart)		0	1974	21	1974	(Buddah 433)
28	The Way We Were - Try To Remember (Medley)	(Buddah Bds 428)	4	1975	11	1975	(Buddah 463)
29	Part Time Love	(Buddah Bds 438)	30	1975	22	1975	(Buddah 513)
30	Make Yours A Happy Home	(Buddah Bds 447)	35	1976	0	1976	
31	So Sad The Song	(Buddah Bds 448)	20	1976	0	1976	
32	Nobody But You	(Buddah Bds 541)	34	1977	0	1977	
33	Baby Don't Change Your Mind	(Buddah Bds 458)	4	1977	0	1977	
34	Home Is Where The Heart Is	(Buddah Bds 460)	35	1977	0	1977	
35	The One And Only	(Buddah Bds 470)	32	1978	0	1978	
36	The One And Only (Re-Entry)	(Buddah Bds 470)	66	1978	0	1978	
37	Come Back And Finish What You Started	(Buddah Bds 473)	15	1978	0	1978	
38	It's Better Than Good Time	(Buddah Bds 478)	59	1978	0	1978	
39	Taste Of Bitter Love	(CBS 8890)	35	1980	0	1980	
40	Bourgie Bourgie	(CBS 9081)	32	1980	0	1980	
41	When A Child Is Born	(CBS S 1758)	74	1981	0	1981	
* 42	That's What Friends Are For	(Arista Arist 638)	16	1985	1	1985	(Arista 9422)
43	Love Overboard	(MCA MCA 1223)	42	1988	13	1988	(MCA 53210)
44	Licence To Kill	(MCA MCA 1339)	6	1989	0	1989	

FIRST SINGLE WAS 'CHING CHONG' IN 1957 WHEN SHE WAS ONLY 13 • LEGAL PROBLEMS PREVENTED GLADYS RECORDING WITH THE PIPS FROM 1977-80

Glam Male Production/Instrumental Group from Italy

1	Hell's Party	(Six6 Sixcd 001)	42	1993	0	1993	

Glam Metal Detectives Mixed Vocal Group from the UK

1	Everybody Up	(Ztt Zang 62cd)	29	1995	0	1995	

Glass Bottle Lead Singer Gary Criss

1	I Ain't Got Time Anymore		0	1971	36	1971	(Avco Emb. 4575)

Glass Tiger Male Vocal/Instrumental Group from Canada   Names: Sam Reid, Alan Frew, Al Connelly, Michael Hanson & Wayne Parker

1	Don't Forget Me (When I'm Gone)	(Manhattan Mt 13)	29	1986	2	1986	(Manhattan 50037)
2	Someday	(Manhattan Mt 17)	66	1987	7	1987	(Manhattan 50048)
3	I Will Be There		0	1987	34	1987	(Manhattan 50066)
4	I'm Still Searching		0	1988	31	1988	(Emi-Manhattan 50116)
5	My Town	(Emi Em 212)	33	1991	0	1991	

HIT 5 HAS UNCREDITED VOCALS BY ROD STEWART

Glen Campbell Male Vocalist/Guitarist/Composer, B: The Seventh Son Of A Seventh Son Born on 22 Apr 1936 Arkansas

	ISSUE	TITLE	UK LBL	UK POS	UK YEAR	US POS	US YEAR	US LBL
!	1	Kentucky Means Paradise		0	1962	20	1962	(Capitol 4867)
!	2	Burning Bridges		0	1966	18	1966	(Capitol 5773)
!	3	I Gotta Have My Baby Back		0	1967	73	1967	(Capitol 5854)
	4	Gentle On My Mind		0	1967	39	1967	(Capitol 5939)
	5	By The Time I Get To Phoenix		0	1967	26	1967	(Capitol 2015)
!	6	Hey Little One		0	1968	13	1968	(Capitol 2076)
	7	I Wanna Live		0	1968	36	1968	(Capitol 2146)
	8	Dreams Of The Everyday Housewife		0	1968	32	1968	(Capitol 2224)
	9	Gentle On My Mind (Re-entry)		0	1968	32	1968	(Capitol 5839)
*	10	Wichita Lineman	(Ember Embs 261)	7	1969	3	1968	(Capitol 2302)
	11!	Less Of Me		0	1968	44	1968	(Capitol 2314)
	12	Mornin' Glory		0	1967	74	1968	(Capitol 2314)
	13	Let It Be Me		0	1969	36	1969	(Capitol 2387)
*	14	Galveston	(Ember Embs 263)	14	1969	4	1969	(Capitol 2428)
	15	Where's The Playground Susie		0	1969	26	1969	(Capitol 2494)
	16	True Grit		0	1969	35	1969	(Capitol 2574)
	17	Try A Little Kindness	(Capitol Cl 15622)	45	1970	23	1970	(Capitol 2659)
	18	Honey Come Back	(Capitol Cl 15638)	4	1970	19	1970	(Capitol 2718)
	19	All I Have To Do Is Dream	(Capitol Cl 15619)	3	1969	27	1969	(Capitol 2745)
	20	Oh Happy Day		0	1970	40	1970	(Capitol 2787)
	21	It's Only Make Believe	(Capitol Cl 15663)	4	1970	10	1970	(Capitol 2905)
	22	Everything A Man Could Ever Need	(Capitol Cl 15653)	32	1970	0	1970	
	23	Dream Baby (How Long Must I Dream)	(Capitol Cl 15674)	39	1971	31	1971	(Capitol 3062)
*	23	Rhinestone Cowboy	(Capitol Cl 15824)	4	1975	1	1975	(Capitol 4095)
	24	The Last Time I Saw Her		0	1971	61	1971	(Capitol 3062)
	25	I Say A Little Prayer / By The Time I Get To Phoenix		0	1971	81	1971	(Capitol 3200)

ISSUE	TITLE	UK LBL	UK POS	UK YEAR	US POS	US YEAR	US LBL
! 26	Oklahoma Sunday Morning		0	1972	15	1972	(Capitol 3254)
! 27	Manhattan Kansa		0	1972	6	1972	(Capitol 3305)
28	I Will Never Pass This Way Again		0	1972	6	1972	(Capitol 3411)
29	One Last Time		0	1972	78	1972	(Capitol 3483)
30	I Knew Jesus (Before He Was A Star)		0	1973	45	1973	(Capitol 3548)
! 33	Bring Back My Yesterday		0	1973	49	1973	(Capitol 3669)
! 32	Wherefore And Wh		0	1973	20	1973	(Capitol 3735)
33	Houston (I'm Comin' To See You)		0	1974	68	1974	(Capitol 3808)
! 34	Bonaparte's Retreat		0	1974	3	1974	(Capitol 3926)
! 35	It's A Sin When You Love Somebody		0	1974	16	1974	(Capitol 3988)
36	Rhoinestone Cowboy	(Capitol CL15824)	4	1975	1	1975	(Capitol 4095)
37	Country Boy (You've Got Your Feet In L.A.)		0	1976	11	1976	(Capitol 4155)
38	Don't Pull Your Love / Then You Can Tell Me Goodbye)		0	1976	27	1976	(Capitol 4245)
! 39	See You On Sunday		0	1976	18	1976	(Capitol 4288)
* 40	Southern Nights	(Capitol CI 15824)	28	1977	1	1977	(Capitol 4376)
41	Sunflower		0	1977	39	1977	(Capitol 4445)
! 42	God Must Have Blessed America		0	1977	39	1977	(Capitol 4515)
! 43	Another Fine Mess (From The End)		0	1978	21	1978	(Capitol 4584)
44	Can You Fool		0	1978	38	1978	(Capitol 4584)
! 45	I'm Gonna Love You		0	1979	13	1979	(Capitol 4682)
! 46	California		0	1979	45	1979	(Capitol 4715)
! 47	Hound Dog Man		0	1979	25	1979	(Capitol 4769)
48!	My Prayer		0	1979	66	1979	(Capitol 4799)
49	Somethin''Bout You Baby I Like		0	1980	42	1980	(Capitol 4865)
! 50	Hollywood Smiles		0	1980	80'	1980	(Capitol 4909)
! 51	Dream Lover		0	1980	59	1980	(MCA 41323)
! 52	Any Which Way You Can (Movie Title Song)		0	1980	10	1980	(Warner Bros 49609)
53	I Don't Want To Know Your Name		0	1981	65	1981	(Capitol 4959)
! 54	Why Don't We Just Sleep On It Tonight		0	1981	85	1981	(Capitol 4986)
55	I Love My Truck		0	1981	94	1981	(Mirage 3845)
56	Old Home Town		0	1982	44!	1982	(Altn. Am. 99967)
! 57	I Love How You Love Me		0	1983	17	1983	(Altn. Am. 99930)
! 58	On The Wings Of My Victory		0	1983	85	1983	(Altn. Am. 99893)
! 59	Faithless Love		0	1984	10	1984	(Altn. Am. 99768)
! 60	Slow Nights		0	1984	47	1984	(Mca 52474)
! 61	A Lady Like You		0	1984	4	1984	(Altn. Am. 99691)
62!	(Love Ways) Letter To Home		0	1985	14	1985	(Altn. Am. 99647)
! 63	It's Just A Matter Of Time		0	1985	7	1985	(Altn. Am. 99600)
! 64	Cowpoke		0	1986	38	1986	(Altn. Am. 99559)
65	Call Home		0	1986	52	1986	(Altn. Am. 99525)
66	The Hand That Rocks The Cradle		0	1987	6	1987	(MCA 53108)
67	Still Within The Sound Of My Voice		0	1987	5	1987	(MCA 53172)
68	I Remember You		0	1988	32	1988	(MCA 53245)
69	I Have You		0	1988	7	1988	(MCA 53218)
70	Light Years		0	1988	35	1988	(MCA 53426)
71	More Than Enough		0	1989	47	1989	(MCA 53493)
72	She's Gone, Gone, Gone		0	1989	6	1989	(Universal 66024)
73	Walkin' In The Sun		0	1990	61	1990	(Capitol Lp Cut)
74	Unconditional Love		0	1991	27	1991	(Capitol Lp Cut)
75	Livin' In A House Full Of Love		0	1991	70	1991	(Capitol Lp Cut)
76	Somebody Like That		0	1993	66	1993	(Liberty Lp Cut)

Glen Goldsmith Male Vocalist from the USA

1	I Won't Cry	(Reproduction Pb 41493)	34	1987	0	1987	
2	Dreaming	(Reproduction Pb 41711)	12	1988	0	1988	
3	What You See Is What You Get	(Reproduction Pb 42075)	33	1988	0	1988	
4	Save A Little Bit	(Reproduction Pb 42147	73	1988	0	1988	

Glen Mason Male Vocalist from the UK

1	Glendora	(Parlophone R 4203)	28	1956	0	1956	
2	Green Door	(Parlophone R 4244)	24	1956	0	1956	

Glencoves Names Brian Bolger, Bull Byme & Don Connors

1	Hootenanny		0	1963	38	1963	(Select 724)

Glenn & Chris Male Vocal Duo from the UK

1	Diamond Lights	(Record Shack Kick 1)	12	1987	0	1987	

Glenn Frey   Male Vocalist, B: 6 Nov 1948 Detroit   He Was One Of The Original Members of The Eagles

ISSUE	TITLE	UK LBL	UK POS	UK YEAR	US POS	US YEAR	US LBL
1	I Found Somebody		0	1982	31	1982	(Asylum 47466)
2	The One You Love		0	1982	15	1982	(Asylum 69974)
3	Sexy Girl		0	1984	20	1984	(MCA 52413)
4	The Heat Is On	(MCA MCA 941)	12	1985	2	1985	(MCA 52512)
5	Smuggler's Blues	(BBCResl 170)	22	1985	12	1985	(MCA 52546)
6	You Belong To The City		0	1985	2	1985	(MCA 52651)
7	True Love		0	1988	13	1988	(MCA 53363)

Glenn Medeiros   Male Vocalist, B: 24 Jun 1970 Hawaii

ISSUE	TITLE	UK LBL	UK POS	UK YEAR	US POS	US YEAR	US LBL
1	Nothing's Gonna Change My Love For You	(London Lon 184)	1	1988	12	1987	(Amherst 311)
2	Long And Lasting Love (One In A Lifetime)	(London Lon 202)	42	1988	0	1988	
* 3	She Ain't Worth It	(London Lon 265)	12	1990	1	1990	(MCA 79047)
4	All I'm Missing Is You		0	1990	32	1990	(MCA 53886)

Glenn Miller & His Orchestra   Male Orchestra Leader, Real Name Alton Glenn Miller B: 1 Mar 1904 Clarinda, Iowa.

ISSUE	TITLE	UK LBL	UK POS	UK YEAR	US POS	US YEAR	US LBL
* 4	Moonlight Serenade		0	1939	3	1939	(Bluebird 10214)
* 22	In The Mood		0	1939	1	1939	(Bluebird 10416)
* 37	Tuxedo Junction		0	1940	1	1940	(Bluebird 10612)
* 54	Pennsyvania 6-5000		0	1940	5	1940	(Bluebird 10754)
* 89	Chattanooga Choo Choo (From It Happened In Sun Valley)		0	1941	1	1941	(Bluebird 11230)
* 98	A String Of Pearls		0	1942	1	1942	(Bluebird 11382)
* 104	Moonlight Cocktail		0	1942	1	1942	(Bluebird 11401)
* 112	I've Got A Gal In) Kalamazoo		0	1942	1	1942	(Victor 27934)
129	Adios (Re-Issue)		0	1948	25	1948	(Victor 2942)
130	Moonlight Serenade	(HMV Bd 5942)	12	1954	0	1954	
131	Moonlight Serenade / Little Brown Jug etc (Re-Issue) (RCA 2644)		13	1976	0	1976	
	OBITUARY : D: 15 DEC 1944 DISAPPEARED OVER THE ENGLISH CHANNEL.						

Glenn Yarbrough   B: 12 Jan 1930 Milwaukee, Former Lead Singer With The Limeliters

ISSUE	TITLE	UK LBL	UK POS	UK YEAR	US POS	US YEAR	US LBL
1	Baby, The Rain Must Fall		0	1965	12	1965	(RCA 8498)

Glitter Band   Male Vocal/Instrumental Group from the USA/UK

ISSUE	TITLE	UK LBL	UK POS	UK YEAR	US POS	US YEAR	US LBL
1	Angel Face	(Bell 1348)	4	1974	0	1974	
2	Just For You	(Bell 1368)	10	1974	0	1974	
3	Let's Get Together Again	(Bell 1383)	8	1974	0	1974	
4	Goodbye My Love	(Bell 1395)	2	1975	0	1975	
5	The Tears I Cried	(Bell 1416)	8	1975	0	1975	
6	Love In The Sun	(Bell 1437)	15	1975	0	1975	
7	People Like You And People Like Me	(Bell 1471	5	1976	0	1976	
	SEE ALSO GARY GLITTER						

Global

ISSUE	TITLE	UK LBL	UK POS	UK YEAR	US POS	US YEAR	US LBL
1	The Way –The Deep	(Dedicated Globa 002cd)	51	1997	0	1997	

Gloria D. Brown   Female Vocalist from the USA

ISSUE	TITLE	UK LBL	UK POS	UK YEAR	US POS	US YEAR	US LBL
1	The More They Knock, The More I Love You	(10 Ten 52)	57	1985	0	1985	

Gloria Dehaven   Female Actress/Vocalist from the USA

ISSUE	TITLE	UK LBL	UK POS	UK YEAR	US POS	US YEAR	US LBL
1	Because Of You		0	1951	11	1951	(Decca 27666)

Gloria Estefan   Female Vocalist, Real Name Gloria Fajardo B: 1 Dec 1957 Cuba

ISSUE	TITLE	UK LBL	UK POS	UK YEAR	US POS	US YEAR	US LBL
1	Dr. Beat	(Epic A 4614)	6	1984	0	1984	
2	Conga		0	1986	10	1986	(Epic 05457)
3	Bad Boy	(Epic A 6537)	16	1986	8	1986	(Epic 05805)
4	Words Get In The Way		0	1986	5	1986	(Epic 06120)
5	Falling In Love (Uh-Oh)		0	1986	25	1986	(Epic 06352)
6	Rhythm Is Gonna Get You	(Epic 654514 7)	16	1988	5	1987	(Epic 07059)
7	Betcha Say That		0	1987	36	1987	(Epic 07371)
8	Can't Stay Away From You	(Epic 651444 7)	7	1989	6	1988	(Epic 07641)
9	Anything For You	(Epic 651673 7)	10	1988	1	1988	(Epic 07759)
10	1-2-3	(Epic 652958 7)	9	1988	3	1988	(Epic 07921)
11	1-2-3 (Re-Entry)	(Epic 652958 7)	72	1988	0	1988	
12	Don't Wanna Lose You	(Epic 655054 0)	6	1989	1	1989	(Epic 68959)
13	Get On Your Feet	(Epic 655450 7)	23	1989	11	1989	(Epic 69064)
14	Oye Mi Canto (Hear My Voice)	(Epic 655287 7)	16	1989	0	1989	
15	Here We Are	(Epic 655473 9)	23	1990	6	1990	(Epic 73084)
16	Cuts Both Ways	(Epic 655982 7)	49	1990	0	1990	
17	Coming Out Of The Dark	(Epic 6565747)	25	1991	1	1991	(Epic 73666)
18	Seal Our Fate	(Epic 6567737)	24	1991	0	1991	
19	Remember Me With Love	(Epic 6569687)	22	1991	0	1991	

ISSUE	TITLE	UK LBL	UK POS	UK YEAR	US POS	US YEAR	US LBL
20	Live For Loving You	(Epic 6573827)	33	1991	22	1991	(Epic 73962)
21	Always Tomorrow	(Epic 6583977)	24	1992	0	1992	
22	Miami Hit Mix - Christmas Through Your Eyes	(Epic 6588377)	8	1992	0	1992	
23	I See Your Smile	(Epic 6589612)	48	1993	0	1993	
24	Go Away	(Epic 6590952)	13	1993	0	1993	
25	Mi Tierra	(Epic 6593512)	36	1993	0	1993	
26	If We Were Lovers	(Epic 6595702)	40	1993	0	1993	
27	Montuno	(Epic 6599972)	55	1993	0	1993	
* 28	Turn The Beat Around	(Epic 6606822)	21	1994	13	1994	(Cresent M. 77630)
29	Hold Me, Thrill Me, Kiss Me	(Epic 6610802)	11	1994	0	1994	
30	Everlasting Love	(Epic 6611595)	19	19952	7	1995	(Epic 77756)
31	Hold Me, Thrill Me, Kiss Me (Re-Entry)	(Epic 6610802)	68	1995	0	1995	
32	Reach	(Epic 6632642)	15	1996	42	1996	(Epic 78285)
33	Reach (Re-Entry)	(Epic 6632642)	68	1996	0	1996	
34	Reach (2nd Re-Entry)	(Epic 6632642)	55	1996	0	1996	
35	You'll Be Mine (Party Time)	(Epic 6636505)	18	1996	70	1996	(Epic 78378)
36	I'm Not Giving You Up	(Epic 6640222)	28	1996	40	1996	(Epic 78464)

Gloria Gaynor Female Vocalist, B: 7 Sep 1949 Newark, New Jersey Former Singer With The Soul Satisfiers

1	Never Can Say Goodbye	(MGM 2006 463)	2	1974	9	1974	(MGM 14748)
2	Reach Out I'll Be There	(MGM 2006 499)	14	1975	0	1975	
3	All I Need Is Your Sweet Lovin'	(MGM 2006 531)	44	1975	0	1975	
4	How High The Moon	(MGM 2006 558)	33	1976	0	1976	
* 5	I Will Survive	(Polydor 2095 017)	1	1979	1	1979	(Polydor 14508)
6	Let Me Know (I Have A Right)	(Polydor Step 5)	32	1979	0	1979	
7	I Am What I Am	(Chrysalis Chs 2765)	13	1983	0	1983	
8	I Will Survive (Re-Mix)	(Polydor Pzcd 270)	5	1993	0	1993	

Gloria Hart Female Vocalist from the USA

1	Oh How I Love You		0	1951	28	1951	(Sharp 36)
2	I Would Rather Look At You		0	1952	18	1952	(Mercury 5881)

Gloria Loring Female Actress/Vocalist, B: 10 Dec 1946 from the USA

1	Friends And Lovers		0	1986	2	1986	(Usa Carrere 06122)

She Played Liz Curtis In The Tv Soap 'Days Of Our Lives'   Hit Is Credited To Gloria Loring And Carl Anderson

Gloria Lynne Female Vocalis, B: 23 Nov 1931 New York City

1	I Wish You Love		0	1964	28	1964	(Everest 2036)

Gloria Mann Mother Of Will To Power Lead Singer Bob Rosenberg

1	Earth Angel		0	1955	18	1955	(Sound 109)
2	Teen Age Prayer		0	1955	19	1955	(Sound 126)

Glove Male Vocal/Instrumental Group from the UK

1	Like An Animal	(Wonderland She 3)	52	1983	0	1983	

Gloworm Male Vocal/Instrumental Group from the USA/UK

1	I Lift My Cup	(Pulse 8 Cdlose 37)	20	1993	0	1993	
2	Carry Me Home	(Go.Beat Godcd 112)	9	1994	0	1994	
3	I Lift My Cup (Re-Issue)	(Pulse 8 Cdlose 67)	46	1994	0	1994	

Glyn Poole Male Vocalist from the UK

1	Milly Molly Mandy	(York Syk 565)	35	1973	0	1973	

Go Go Lorenzo & The Davis Pinckney Project Male Vocal/Instrumental Group from the USA

1	You Can Dance (If You Want To)	(Boiling Point Posp 836)	46	1986	0	1986	

Go West Male Vocal/Instrumental Duo from the UK   Names: Richard Drummie & Peter Cox

1	We Close Our Eyes	(Chrysalis Chs 2850)	5	1985	0	1985	
2	Call Me	(Chrysalis Gow 1)	12	1985	0	1985	
3	Goodbye Girl	(Chrysalis Gow 2)	25	1985	0	1985	
4	Don't Look Down (The Sequel)	(Chrysalis Gow 3)	13	1987	39	1987	(Chrysalis 43141)
5	True Colours	(Chrysalis Gow 4)	48	1986	0	1986	
6	I Want To Hear It From You	(Chrysalis Gow 5)	43	1987	0	1987	
7	The King Is Dead	(Chrysalis Gow 6)	67	1987	0	1987	
8	The King Of Wishful Thinking	(Chrysalis Gow 8)	18	1990	8	1990	(Emi 50307)
9	Faithful	(Chrysalis Gow 9)	13	1992	14	1992	(Emi 50411)
10	What You Won't Do For Love	(Chrysalis Cdgows 10)	15	1993	0	1993	
11	Still In Love	(Chrysalis Cdgows 11)	43	1993	0	1993	
12	Tracks Of My Tears	(Chrysalis Cdgows 12)	16	1993	0	1993	
13	We Close Our Eyes (Re-Mix)	(Chrysalis Cdgows 13)	40	1993	0	1993	

ISSUE	TITLE	UK LBL	UK POS	UK YEAR	US POS	US YEAR	US LBL
Go-Go's Female Vocal/Instrumental Group from the USA		Names: Belinda Carlisle, Jane Wiedlin, Charlotte Caffey, Kathy Valentine & Gina Schock					
1	Our Lips Are Sealed	(Irs Gdn 102)	47	1982	20	1981	(Irs 9901)
2	We Got The Beat		0	1982	2	1982	(Irs 9903)
3	Vacation		0	1982	8	1982	(Irs 9907)
4	Head Over Heels		0	1984	11	1984	(Irs 99026)
5	Turn To You		0	1984	32	1984	(Irs 9928)
6	Cool Jerk	(Irs Am 712)	60	1991	0	1991	
7	The Whole World's Lost Its Head	(Irs Am 190)	29	1995	0	1995	
Goats Male Rap Group from the USA							
1	Aaah D Yaaa / Typical American	(Ruff House 6593032)	53	1993	0	1993	
God Machine Male Vocal/Instrumental Group from the USA							
1	Home	(Fiction Ficcd 47)	65	1993	0	1993	
Godiego Male Vocal/Instrumental Group from the USA/Japan							
1	The Water Margin	(Bbc Resl 50)	37	1977	0	1977	
2	Gandhara	(Bbc Resl 66)	56	1980	0	1980	
Godley & Creme Male Vocal /Instrumental Duo from the UK		Kevin Godley B: 7 Oct 1945 & Lol Creme B: 19 Sep 1947. Both former members Of 10cc and Hotlegs					
1	Under Your Thumb	(Polydor Posp 322)	3	1981	0	1981	
2	Wedding Bells	(Polydor Posp 369)	7	1981	0	1981	
3	Cry	(Polydor Posp 732)	19	1985	16	1985	(Polydor 881786)
4	Cry (Re-Entry)	(Polydor Posp 732)	66	1986	0	1986	
Godspell Lead Vocals Are By Robin Lamont							
1	Day By Day		0	1972	13	1972	(Bell 45210)
Gogi Grant Female Vocalist, Real Name Audrey Brown B: 20 Sep 1924 in Philadelphia							
* 1	Suddenly There's A Valley		0	1955	9	1955	(Era 1003)
* 2	The Wayward Wind	(London Hlb 8282)	9	1956	1	1956	(Era 1013)
Gold Blade							
1	Strictly Hardcore	(Ultimate Topp 056cd)	64	1997	0	1997	
Goldbug Mixed Vocal/Instrumental Group from the UK							
1	Whole Lotta Love	(Acid Jazzid 125cd)	3	1996	0	1996	
Golden Earring Male Vocal/Instrumental Group from Holland							
1	Radar Love	(Track 2094 116)	7	1973	13	1974	(Track 40202)
2	Radar Love	(Polydor 2121 335)	4	1977	0	1977	
3	Twilight Zone		0	1983	10	1983	(21 Records 103)
HITS 1-2 ARE TWO DIFFERENT RECORDINGS OF THE SAME SONG • THE '75 LINE-UP WERE BARRY HAY, GEORGE KOOYMANS, CESAR ZUIDERWILK & RINUS GERRITSEN							
Goldie (1) Male Vocal/Instrumental Group from the UK							
1	Making Up Again	(Bronze Bro 50)	7	1978	0	1978	
Goldie (2) Male Producer from the UK							
1	Inner City Life	(Ffrr Fcd 251)	49	1994	0	1994	
2	Angel	(Ffrr Fcd 266)	41	1995	0	1995	
3	Inner City Life (Re-Mix)	(Ffrr Fcd 267)	39	1995	0	1995	
Goldie & The Gingerbreads Female Vocal/Instrumental Group from the USA							
1	Can't You Hear My Heartbeat	(Decca F 12070)	25	1965	0	1965	
Gompie Male Vocal/Instrumental Group From Holland							
1	Alice (Who The Fuck Is Alice) (Living Next Door To Alice)	(Habana Habscd 5)	34	1995	0	1995	
2	Alice (Who The Fuck Is Alice) (Living Next Door To Alice) (Re-Entry)	(Habana Habscd 5)	17	1995	0	1995	
Gone All Stars Male Arranger/Producer George Goldner							
1	"7-11"		0	1958	30	1958	(Gone 5016)
Gonzalez American/British Soul Disco Band							
1	Haven't Stopped Dancing Yet	(Sidewalk Sid 102)	15	1979	26	1979	(Capitol 4674)
Goo Goo Dolls Rock Trio From Buffalo, New York							
1	Name		0	1995	5	1995	(Warner Bros 17758)
Goodfellaz							
1	Sugar Honey Ice Tea	(Wild Card 5736132)	25	1997	0	1997	
Goodie Mob Rap Quartet From Atlanta							
1	Cell Therapy		0	1995	39	1995	(La Face 24113)
Goodbye Mr. Mackenzie Mixed Vocal/Instrumental Group from the UK							
1	Goodbye Mr. Mackenzie	(Capitol Cl 501)	62	1988	0	1988	

ISSUE	TITLE	UK LBL	UK POS	UK YEAR	US POS	US YEAR	US LBL
2	The Rattler	(Capitol Cl 522)	7	1989	0	1989	
3	Goodwill City / I'm Sick Of You	(Capitol Cl 538)	49	1989	0	1989	
4	Love Child	(Parlophone R 6247)	52	1990	0	1990	
5	Blacker Than Black	(Parlophone R 6257)	61	1990	0	1990	

Goodies Male Actor/Vocalist Trio from the UK

ISSUE	TITLE	UK LBL	UK POS	UK YEAR	US POS	US YEAR	US LBL
1	The Inbetweenies	(Bradley's Brad 7421)	7	1974	0	1974	
2	The Funky Gibbon / Sick Man Blues	(Bradley's Brad 7504)	4	1975	0	1975	
3	Black Pudding Bertha	(Bradley's Brad 7517)	19	1975	0	1975	
4	Nappy Love / Wild Thing	(Bradley's Brad 7524)	21	1975	0	1975	
5	Make A Daft Noise For Christmas	(Bradley's Brad 7533)	20	1975	0	1975	

Goodmen Male Production/Instrumental Duo from Holland

ISSUE	TITLE	UK LBL	UK POS	UK YEAR	US POS	US YEAR	US LBL
1	Give It Up	(Fresh Fruit Tabcd 118)	23	1993	0	1993	
2	Give It Up (Re-Entry)	(Fresh Fruit Tabcd 118)	5	1993	0	1993	

Goody Goody Female Vocal Duo from the USA

ISSUE	TITLE	UK LBL	UK POS	UK YEAR	US POS	US YEAR	US LBL
1	Number One Dee Jay	(Atlantic Lv 3)	55	1978	0	1978	

Goombay Dance Band Mixed Vocal/Instrumental Group from Germany/Montserrat

ISSUE	TITLE	UK LBL	UK POS	UK YEAR	US POS	US YEAR	US LBL
1	Seven Tears	(Epic Epc A 1242)	1	1982	0	1982	
2	Sun Of Jamaica	(Epic Epc A 2345)	50	1982	0	1982	

Goons Names: Harry Secombe, Spike Milligan, Michael Bentine & Peter Sellers

ISSUE	TITLE	UK LBL	UK POS	UK YEAR	US POS	US YEAR	US LBL
1	I'm Walking Backwards For Christmas	(Decca F 10756)	4	1956	0	1956	
2	Bloodnok's Rock'n'roll Call / Ying Tong Song	(Decca F 10780)	3	1956	0	1956	
3	Ying Tong Song (Re-Issue)	(Decca F 13414)	9	1973	0	1973	

HIT 1 'B' SIDE, BLUEBOTTLE BLUES PEAKED AT NUMBER 5 • OBITUARY PETER SELLERS • 1980. • MICHAEL BENTINE D: 20 NOV 1996 CANCER.

Gordon Giltrap Male Guitarist from the UK

ISSUE	TITLE	UK LBL	UK POS	UK YEAR	US POS	US YEAR	US LBL
1	Heartsong	(Electric Wot 19)	21	1978	0	1978	
2	Fear Of The Dark	(Electric Wot 29)	58	1979	0	1979	

Gordon Jenkins Orchestra Male Orchestra Leader, B: 12 May 1910 Webster Groves, Missouri

ISSUE	TITLE	UK LBL	UK POS	UK YEAR	US POS	US YEAR	US LBL
* 3	Maybe You'll Be There		0	1948	3	1948	(Decca 24403)
4	I Don't See Me In Your Eyes Anymore		0	1949	5	1949	(Decca 24576)
5	Again (From Roadhouse)		0	1949	2	1949	(Decca 24602)
6	Don't Cry Joe (Let Her Go, Let Her Go, Let Her Go)		0	1949	3	1949	(Decca 24720)
7	A Dreamer's Holiday		0	1949	26	1949	(Decca 24738)
8	My Foolish Heart (Movie Title Song)		0	1950	3	1950	(Decca 24830)
9	Bewitched (From Pal Joey)		0	1950	4	1950	(Decca 24983)
* 10	Tzena, Tzena, Tzena		0	1950	2	1950	(Decca 27077)
11	Goodnight Irene		0	1950	1	1950	(Decca 27077)
12	I'm Forever Blowing Bubbles (From *The Passing Show* Of 1918)		0	1950	10	1950	(Decca 27186)
13	So Long (It's Been Good To Know Ya)		0	1951	4	1951	(Decca 27376)
14	Rose, Rose I Love You		0	1951	21	1951	(Decca 27594)
15	Unless		0	1951	30	1951	(Decca 27594)
16	Whispering		0	1951	27	1951	(Decca 27585)
17	Charmaine (From What Price Glory)		0	1951	18	1951	(Decca 27859)
18	Wimoweh		0	1952	14	1952	(Decca 27928)
19	Around The Corner (Beneath The Berry Tree)		0	1952	19	1952	(Decca 28054)
20	Fury		0	1953	26	1953	(Decca 28806)
21	Blueberry Hill		0	1956	29	1956	(Decca 30091)

HIT 21 IS CREDITED TO LOUIS ARMSTRONG AND GORDON JENKINS • VOCALS ON HITS 1, 17 ARE BY BOB CARROLL • VOCALS ON HIT 3 ARE BY CHARLES LAVERE
OBITUARY : D: 2 MAY 1984. (AGED 73).

Gordon Lightfoot Male Vocalist, B: 17 Nov 1938 Orillia, Canada He Formed The Two Tones In The 60s With Jim Whalen

ISSUE	TITLE	UK LBL	UK POS	UK YEAR	US POS	US YEAR	US LBL
* 1	If You Could Read My Mind	(Reprise Rs 20974)	30	1971	5	1971	(Reprise 0974)
* 2	Sundown	(Reprise K 14327)	33	1974	1	1974	(Reprise 1194)
3	Carefree Highway		0	1974	10	1974	(Reprise 1309)
4	Rainy Day People		0	1975	26	1975	(Reprise 1328)
5	The Wreck Of Edmund Fitzgerald	(Reprise K 14451)	40	1977	2	1976	(Reprise 1369)
6	The Circle Is Small (I Can See It In Your Eyes)		0	1978	33	1978	(Warner Bros 8518)
! 7	Dreamland		0	1978	99	1978	(Warner Bros 8644)
8	Daylight Katy	(Warner Bros K 17214)	41	1978	0	1978	

Gordon MacRae Male Vocalist, B: 12 Mar 1921 East Orange, New Jersey

ISSUE	TITLE	UK LBL	UK POS	UK YEAR	US POS	US YEAR	US LBL
1	I Still Get Jealous		0	1947	25	1947	(Capitol 15002)
2	At The Candlelight Cafe (From *Tisa*)		0	1947	20	1947	(Capitol 15014)
3	Thoughtless		0	1948	28	1948	(Capitol 15027)
4	You Were Meant For Me		0	1948	22	1948	(Capitol 15027)
5	That Feathery Feelin'		0	1948	27	1948	(Capitol 15041)

ISSUE	TITLE	UK LBL	UK POS	UK YEAR	US POS	US YEAR	US LBL
6	It's Magic (From *Romance On The High Seas*)		0	1948	9	1948	(Capitol 15072)
7	Hankerin'		0	1948	23	1948	(Capitol 15128)
8	Hair Of Gold, Eyes Of Blue (From *Silver Spurs*)		0	1948	7	1948	(Capitol 15178)
9	Rambling Rose		0	1948	27	1948	(Capitol 15178)
10	So In Love (From *Kiss Me Kate*)		0	1949	20	1949	(Capitol 15357)
11	Younger Than Springtime (From *South Pacific*)		0	1949	30	1949	(Capitol 598)
12	Mule Train		0	1949	14	1949	(Capitol 777)
13	Dear Hearts And Gentle People		0	1949	19	1949	(Capitol 777)
14	How Do You Speak To An Angel? (From *Haxel Flagg*)		0	1953	30	1953	(Capitol 2352)
15	Congratulations To Someone		0	1953	28	1953	(Capitol 2352)
16	C'est Magnifique (From *Can-Can*)		0	1953	29	1953	(Capitol 2465)
17	Stranger In Paradise (From *Kismet*)		0	1953	29	1953	(Capitol 2652)
18	Face To Face		0	1954	30	1954	(Capitol 2760)
19	The Secret		0	1958	18	1958	(Capitol 4033)

HITS 8-9 ARE WITH THE STARLIGHTERS • SEE ALSO JO STAFFORD • OBITUARY : D: 24 JAN 1986.

Gordon Sinclair   Male Author/Broadcaster, B: 3 Jun 1900 Toronto, Canada

1	The Americans (A Canadian's Opinion)		0	1974	24	1974	(Avco 4628)

OBITUARY: D: 17 MAY 1984.

Gorky's Zygotic Mynci   Mixed Vocal/Instrumental Group from the UK

1	Patio Song	(Fontana Gzmcd 1)	41	1996	0	1996	
2	Diamond Dew	(Fontana Gzmcd 2)	42	1997	0	1997	
3	Young Girl & Happy Endings / Dark Night	(Fontana Gzmcd 3)	49	1997	0	1997	

GQ   Male Vocal/Instrumental Group from the USA

* 1	Disco Nights (Rock-Freak)	(Arista Arist 245)	42	1979	12	1979	(Arista 0388)
2	I Do Love You		0	1979	20	1979	(Arista 0426)

NAMES EMMANUEL RAHIEM LEBLANC, KEITH CRIER, HERB LANE & PAUL SERVICE PAUL LEFT THE GROUP IN 1980

Grace   Female Vocalist from the UK

1	Not Over Yet	(Perfecto Perf 104cd)	6	1995	0	1995	
2	I Want To Live	(Perfecto Perf 109cd)	30	1995	0	1995	
3	Skin On Skin	(Perfecto Perf 116cd)	21	1996	0	1996	
4	Down To Eart	(Perfecto Perf 120cd)	20	1996	0	1996	
5	If I Could Fly	(Perfecto Perf 127cd)	29	1996	0	1996	
6	Hand In Hand	(Perfecto Perf 129cd)	38	1997	0	1997	
7	Down To Earth	(Perfecto Perf 142cd1)	29	1997	0	1997	

Grace Brothers   Male Instrumental Duo from the UK

1	Are You Being Served?	(Emi Premier Prescd 1)	51	1996	0	1996	

Grace Jones   Female Vocalist from the USA

1	Private Life	(Island Wip 6629)	17	1980	0	1980	
2	Pull Up To The Bumper	(Island Wip 6696)	53	1981	0	1981	
3	The Apple Stretching / Nipple To The Bottle	(Island Wip 6779)	50	1982	0	1982	
4	My Jamaican Guy	(Island Is 103)	56	1983	0	1983	
5	Slave to the Rhythm	(ZTTis 206)	12	1985	0	1985	
6	Pull Up To The Bumper / La Vie En Rose (Re-Issue)	(Island Is 240)	12	1986	0	1986	
7	Love Is The Drug	(Island Is 266)	35	1986	0	1986	
8	I'm Not Perfect (But I'm Perfect For You)	(Manhattan Mt 15)	56	1986	0	1986	
9	Slave To The Rhythm (Re-Mix)	(Zance Zang 50cd1)	28	1994	0	1994	

Grace Kelly   Female Vocalist from the USA

* 1	True Love	(Capitol Cl 14645)	4	1956	3	1956	(Capitol 3507)

HIT IS CREDITED TO BING CROSBY AND GRACE KELLY • D: 14 SEP 1982 CAR ACCIDENT.

Grace Slick   Female Vocalist from the USA

1	Dreams	(RCA Pb 9534)	50	1980	0	1980	

Gracie Fields   Female Actress/Vocalist from the UK

1	Now Is The Hour		0	1948	3	1948	(London 110)
2	Forever And Ever		0	1949	23	1949	(London 362)
3	Around The World	(Columbia Db 3953)	8	1957	0	1957	
4	Around The World (Re-Entry)	(Columbia Db 3953)	24	1957	0	1957	
5	Little Donkey	(Columbia Db 4360)	30	1959	0	1959	
6	Little Donkey (Re-Entry)	(Columbia Db 4360)	20	1959	0	1959	

Graham Bonnet   Male Vocalist from the UK

1	Night Games	(Vertigo Ver 1)	6	1981	0	1981	
2	Liar	(Vertigo Ver 2)	51	1981	0	1981	

ISSUE	TITLE	UK LBL	UK POS	UK YEAR	US POS	US YEAR	US LBL
Graham Bonney Male Vocalist, B: 2 Jun 1945, Stratford, East London, England							
* 1	Supergirl	(Columbia Db 7843)	19	1966	0	1966	
Graham Gouldman Male Vocalist from the UK							
1	Sunburn	(Mercury Sunny 1)	52	1979	0	1979	
Graham Kendrick Male Vocalist from the UK							
1	Let The Flame Burn Brighter	(Power P 30)	55	1989	0	1989	
Graham Nash B: 2 Feb 1942 Blackpool, Lancashire, England							
1	Chicago		0	1971	35	1971	(Atlantic 2804)
2	Immigration Man		0	1972	36	1972	(Atlantic 2873)
	HIT 2 IS CREDITED TO GRAHAM NASH AND DAVID CROSBY • FORMED CROSBY, STILLS & NASH IN 1970, ALSO CO-FOUNDER OF THE HOLLIES						
Graham Parker & The Rumour Male Vocalist, B: 1950 East London, England							
1	The Pink Parker (EP)	(Vertigo Park 001)	24	1977	0	1977	
2	Hey Lord Don't Ask Me Questions	(Vertigo Park 002)	32	1978	0	1978	
3	Temporary Beauty	(Vertigo Park 100)	50	1982	0	1982	
4	Wake Up (Next To You)		0	1985	39	1985	(Elektra 69654)
	HIT 3 IS CREDITED TO GRAHAM PARKER • HIT 4 IS CREDITED TO GRAHAM PARKER & THE SHOT • GRAIG MCLACHLAN • SEE DEBBIE GIBSON						
Grand Funk Railroad Male Vocal/Instrumental Group from the USA							
1	Closer To Home		0	1970	22	1970	(Capitol 2877)
2	Inside Looking Out	(Capitol Cl 15668)	40	1971	0	1971	
3	Footstompin' Music		0	1972	29	1972	(Capitol 3255)
4	Rock 'N Roll Soul		0	1972	29	1972	(Capitol 3363)
* 5	We're An American Band		0	1973	1	1973	(Capitol 3660)
6	Walk Like A Man		0	1973	19	1973	(Capitol 3760)
* 7	The Loco-Motion		0	1974	1	1974	(Capitol 3840)
8	Shinin' On		0	1974	11	1974	(Capitol 3917)
9	Some Kind Of Wonderful		0	1975	3	1975	(Capitol 4002)
11	Bad Time		0	1975	4	1975	(Capitol 4046)
	HIT 4 IS CREDITED TO GRAND FUNK • ORIGINAL LINE-UP WERE MEL SCHACHER, MARK FAMER & DON BREWER						
Grand Plaz Production Group from the UK							
1	Wow Wow - Na Na	(Urban Urb 6 0)	41	1990	0	1990	
Grand Prix Male Vocal/Instrumental Group from the UK							
1	Keep On Believing	(RCA 162)	75	1982	0	1982	
Grand Puba Male Rapper from the USA							
1	Why You Treat Me So Bad	(Virgin Vscdt 1566)	11	1996	0	1996	
2	Will You Be My Baby?	(GHQ 74321339092)	53	1996	0	1996	
	HIT 1 IS CREDITED TO SHAGGY FEATURING GRAND PUBA • HIT 2 IS CREDITED TO INFINITI FEATURING GRAND PUBA						
Grandmaster Flash, Melle Mel & The Furious Five Male Vocal Duo With Male Vocal Group from the USA							
1	The Message	(Sugarhill Shl 117)	8	1982	0	1982	
2	Message Ii (Survival)	(Sugarhill Sh 119)	74	1983	0	1983	
3	White Lines (Don't Don't Do It)	(Sugarhill Sh 130)	60	1983	0	1983	
4	White Lines (Don't Don't Do It) (Re-Entry)	(Sugarhill Sh 130)	7	1984	0	1984	
5	Beat Street Breakdown	(Atlantic A 9659)	42	1984	0	1984	
6	We Don't Work For Free	(Sugarhill Sh 136)	45	1984	0	1984	
7	White Lines (2nd Re-Entry)	(Sugarhill Sh 130)	75	1984	0	1984	
8	Step Off (Part 1)	(Sugarhill Sh 139)	8	1984	0	1984	
9	White Lines (3rd Re-Entry)	(Sugarhill Sh 130)	73	1985	0	1985	
10	Sign Of The Times	(Elektra E 9677)	72	1985	0	1985	
11	Pump Me Up	(Sugarhill Sh 141)	45	1985	0	1985	
12	White Lines (Don't Do It) (Re-Mix)	(Wgaf Wgafcd 103)	59	1994	0	1994	
Grandmixer Male Scratch DJ from the USA							
1	Crazy Cuts	(Island Is 146)	73	1983	0	1983	
2	Crazy Cuts (Re-Entry)	(Island Is 146)	71	1984	0	1984	
Grange Hill Cast Mixed Vocal Charity Assembly from the UK							
1	Just Say No	(BBC Resl 183)	5	1986	0	1986	
Grapefruit Male Vocal/Instrumental Group from the UK							
1	Dear Delilah	(RCA 1656)	21	1968	0	1968	
2	C'mon Marianne	(RCA 1716)	31	1968	0	1968	
Grass Roots Originally Called The Bedouins, Lead Singer Bill Fulton							
1	Where Were You When I Needed You		0	1966	28	1966	(Dunhill 4029)
* 2	Let's Live For Today		0	1967	8	1967	(Dunhill 4084)
3	Things I Should Have Said		0	1967	23	1967	(Dunhill 4094)

ISSUE	TITLE	UK LBL	UK POS	UK YEAR	US POS	US YEAR	US LBL
* 4	Midnight Confessions		0	1968	5	1968	(Dunhill 4144)
5	Bella Linda		0	1969	28	1969	(Dunhill 4162)
6	The River Is Wide		0	1969	31	1969	(Dunhill 4187)
7	I'd Wait A Million Years		0	1969	15	1969	(Dunhill 4198)
8	Heaven Knows		0	1969	24	1969	(Dunhill 4217)
9	Baby Hold On		0	1970	35	1970	(Dunhill 4237)
10	Temptation Eyes		0	1971	15	1971	(Dunhill 4263)
11	Sooner Or Later		0	1971	9	1971	(Dunhill 4279)
12	Two Divided By Love		0	1971	16	1971	(Dunhill 4289)
13	Glory Bound		0	1972	34	1972	(Dunhill 4302)
14	The Runway		0	1972	39	1972	(Dunhill 4316)

Grateful Dead   Original Line-Up Included Jerry Garcia, Bob Weir, Ron Mckeman, Phil Lesh, Bill Kreutzmann & Mickey Hart

1	Touch Of Grey		0	1987	9	1987	(Arista 9606)

VARIOUS MEMBERS HAVE COME AND GONE SINCE THEY FORMED IN 1966 • OBITUARY : GODCHAUX D: 23 JUL 1980 MOTORCYCLE ACCIDENT.
MCKEMAN D: 8 MAR 1973 LIVER AILMENT. • MYDLAND D: 26 JUL 1990 DRUG OVERDOSE.

Gravediggaz   Male Rap Group from the USA

1	Six Feet Deep (EP)	(Gee Street Gescd 62)	64	1995	0	1995	
2	The Hell (Ep)	(Fourth & Broadway Brcd 326)	12	1995	0	1995	

HIT 2 IS CREDITED TO TRICKY VS THE GRAVEDIGGAZ

Great White   Male Vocal/Instrumental Quartet from the USA Names: Jack Russell, Mark Kendall, Michael Lardie, Tony Montana & Audie Desbrow

* 1	Once Bitten Twice Shy		0	1989	5	1989	(Capitol 44366)
2	The Angel Song		0	1989	30	1989	(Capitol 44449)
3	House Of Broken Love	(Capitol Cl 562)	44	1990	0	1990	
4	Congo Square	(Capitol Cl 605)	62	1991	0	1991	
5	Call It Rock 'N' Roll	(Capitol Cl 625)	67	1991	0	1991	

Greed & Ricardo Da Force

1	Pump Up The Volume	(Cdstr 49)	51	1995	0	1995	

Greedies   Male Vocal/Instrumental Group from the USA/Uk/Ireland

1	A Merry Jingle	Vertigo Greed 1)	28	1979	0	1979	

Green Day   Male Vocal/Instrumental Group from the USA

1	Basket Case	(Reprise W 0257cd)	55	1994	0	1994	
2	Welcome To Paradise	(Reprise W 0269cdx)	20	1994	0	1994	
3	Basket Case (Re-Issue)	(Reprise W 0279cd)	7	1995	0	1995	
4	Longview	(Reprise W 0287cd)	30	1995	0	1995	
5	When I Come Around	(Reprise W 0294cd)	27	1995	0	1995	
6	Geek Stink Breath	(Reprise W 0320cd)	16	1995	0	1995	
7	Stuck With Me	(Reprise W 0327c)	24	1996	0	1996	
8	Brain Stew / Jaded	(Reprise W 0339cd)	28	1996	0	1996	

Green Jelly   Male Vocal/Instrumental Group From Kenmore, New York

1	Three Little Pigs	(Zoo 74321151422)	5	1993	17	1993	(Zoo 14088)
2	Anarchy In The U.K.	(Zoo 74321159052)	27	1993	0	1993	
3	I'm The Leader Of The Gang	(Arista 74321174892)	25	1993	0	1993	

HIT 3 IS CREDITED TO HULK HOGAN WITH GREEN JELLY

Greg Guidry   Singer/Songwriter/Pianist, B. 1950 St. Louis

1	Goin' Down		0	1982	17	1982	(Columbia 02691)

Greg Kihn Band   Male Vocal/Instrumental Group from the USA, formed by Greg Kihn in 1975

1	The Breakup Song (They Don't Write 'Em)		0	1981	15	1981	(Beserkley 47149)
2	Jeopardy	(Beserkley E 9847)	63	1983	2	1983	(Beserkley 69847)
3	Lucky		0	1985	30	1985	(Emi America 8255)

Greg Lake   Male Vocalist from the UK   See Also Emerson, Lake & Palmer

1	I Believe In Father Christmas	(Manticore K 13511)	2	1975	0	1975	
2	I Believe In Father Christmas (Re-Entry)	(Manticore K 13511)	72	1982	0	1982	
3	I Believe In Father Christmas (2nd Re-Entry)	(Manticore K 13511)	65	1983	0	1983	

Gregg Allman   Male Vocal/Instrumentalist (Keyboards), B: 8 Dec 1947 Nashville   In '65 Formed Allman Joy Which Became Allman Brothers

1	Midnight Rider		0	1974	19	1974	(Capricorn 0035)

Gregg Diamond Bionic Boogie   Mixed Vocal Group from the USA

1	Cream (Always Rises To The Top)	(Polydor Posp 18)	61	1979	0	1979	

Gregory Abbott   Singer/Songwriter From New York

1	Shake You Down	(CBS A 7326)	6	1986	1	1986	(Columbia 06191)

Greyhound   Male Vocal/Instrumental Group From Jamaica

1	Black And White	(Trojan Tr 7820)	6	1971	0	1971	

ISSUE	TITLE	UK LBL	UK POS	UK YEAR	US POS	US YEAR	US LBL
2	Moon River	(Trojan Tr 7848)	12	1972	0	1972	
3	I Am What I Am	(Trojan Tr 7853)	20	1972	0	1972	

Grid Male Production/Instrumental Duo from the UK

1	Floatation	(East West Yz 475)	60	1990	0	1990	
2	A Beat Called Love	(East West Yz 498)	64	1990	0	1990	
3	Figure Of 8	(Virgin Vstg 1421)	50	1992	0	1992	
4	Heartbeat	(Virgin Vst 1427)	72	1992	0	1992	
5	Crystal Clear	(Virgin Vscdt 1442)	27	1993	0	1993	
6	Texas Cowboys	(Deconstruction 74321167762)	21	1993	0	1993	
7	Swamp Thing	(Deconstruction 74321205842)	3	1994	0	1994	
8	Rollercoaster	(Deconstruction 74321230772)	19	1994	0	1994	
9	Texas Cowboys (Re-Issue)	(Deconstruction 74321244032)	17	1994	0	1994	
10	Diablo	(Deconstruction 74321308402)	32	1995	0	1995	

Groove Corporation Mixed Vocal/Instrumental Group from the UK/Italy

1	Rain	(6six Sixcd 109)	71	1994	0	1994	

Groove Theory Mixed R&B Duo, Bryce Wilson & Amel Larrieux from the USA

* 1	Tell Me	(Epic 6623882)	31	1995	5	1996	(Epic 77961)
2	Baby Luv		0	1996	65	1996	(Epic 78359)

Ground Level Male Production/Instrumental Group from Australia

1	Dreams Of Heaven	(Faze 2 Cdfaze 14)	54	1993	0	1993	

Group Therapy Male Rap Group from the USA

1	East Coast/West Coast Killas	(Interscope Ind 95516)	51	1996	0	1996	

Grover Washington Jr. Male Saxophonist, B: 12 Dec 1943 Buffalo

1	Just The Two Of Us	(Elektra K 12514)	34	1981	2	1981	(Elektra 47103)

THE HIT WAS WITH BILL WITHERS ALTHOUGH UNCREDITED

GSP Male Production/Instrumental Duo from the UK

1	The Banana Song	(Yoyo Yoyo 1)	37	1992	0	1992	

GTR British Quintet Which Includes Max Bacon, Steve Hackett & Steve Howe

1	When The Heart Rules The Mind		0	1986	14	1986	(Arista 9470)

Guess Who Male Vocal/Instrumental Rock Group from Canada   Names Allan 'Chad Allan' Kobel, Randy Bachman, Garry Peterson, Bob Ashley & Jim Kale

1	Shakin' All Over		0	1965	22	1965	(Septer 1295)
2	His Girl	(King Kg 1044)	45	1967	0	1967	
* 3	These Eyes		0	1969	6	1969	(RCA 0102)
4 *	Laughing		0	1969	10	1969	(RCA 0195)
5	Undun		0	1969	22	1969	(RCA 0195)
* 8	No Time		0	1969	5	1969	(RCA 0300)
* 7	American Woman	(RCA 1943)	45	1970	1	1970	(RCA 0325)
8	No Sugar Tonight		0	1970	1	1970	(RCA 0325)
9	American Woman (Re-Entry)	(RCA 1943)	19	1970	0	1970	
10	Hand Me Down World		0	1970	17	1970	(RCA 0367)
* 11	Share The Land		0	1970	10	1970	(RCA 0388)
12	Albert Flasher		0	1971	29	1971	(RCA 0458)
13	Rain Dance		0	1971	19	1971	(RCA 0522)
14	Star Baby		0	1974	39	1974	(RCA 0217)
15	Clap For The Woolfman		0	1974	6	1974	(RCA 0324)
17	Dancin' Fool		0	1974	28	1974	(RCA 10075)

HIT 1 WAS ACTUALLY CHAD ALLAN & THE EXPRESSIONS ALSO RECORDED AS THE REFLECTIONS.
THERE HAVE BEEN MANY CHANGES IN LINE-UP SINCE THEY FORMED IN 1963

Guitar Slim Male Guitarist, Real Name Eddie Jones B: 9 Dec 1926

* 1	The Things That I Used To Do		0	1954	23	1954	(Specialty 482)

THE HIT WAS NUMBER 1 IN THE US R&B CHARTS • OBITUARY :- D: 7 FEB 1959.

Gun (1) Male Vocal/Instrumental Group from the UK

1	Race With The Devil	(CBS 3724)	8	1968	0	1968	

Gun (2) Male Vocal/Instrumental Group from the UK

1	Better Days	(A&M Am 505)	33	1989	0	1989	
2	Money (Everybody Loves Her)	(A&M Am 520)	73	1989	0	1989	
3	Inside Out	(A&M Am 531)	57	1989	0	1989	
4	Taking On The World	(A&M Am 541)	50	1990	0	1990	
5	Shame On You	(A&M Am 573)	33	1990	0	1990	
6	Steal Your Fire	(A&M Am 851)	24	1992	0	1992	
7	Higher Ground	(A&M Am 869)	48	1992	0	1992	
8	Welcome To The Real World	(A&M Am 885)	43	1992	0	1992	
9	Word Up	(A&M 5806672)	8	1994	0	1994	

ISSUE	TITLE	UK LBL	UK POS	UK YEAR	US POS	US YEAR	US LBL
10	Don't Say It's Over	(A&M 5807572)	19	1994	0	1994	
11	The Only One	(A&M 5809532)	29	1995	0	1995	
12	Something Worthwhile	(A&M 5810452)	39	1995	0	1995	
13	Crazy You	(A&M 5821932)	21	1997	0	1997	
14	My Sweet Jane	(A&M 5822792)	51	1997	0	1997	

Gunhill Road Names Steve Goldrich, Glen Leopolo & Gil Roman

1	Back When My Hair Was Short		0	1973	40	1973	(Kama Sutra 569)

Guns N' Roses Male Vocal/Instrumental Group from the USA   Lead Singer Of This Rock Quintet Is William Bailey

	ISSUE	TITLE	UK LBL	UK POS	UK YEAR	US POS	US YEAR	US LBL
	1	Welcome To The Jungle	(Geffen Gef 30)	67	1987	7	1988	(Geffen 27759)
*	2	Sweet Child O'mine	(Geffen Gef 43)	24	1988	1	1988	(Geffen 27963)
	3	Welcome To The Jungle / Nightrain (Re-Issue)	(Geffen Gef 47)	24	1988	0	1988	
	4	Paradise City	(Geffen Gef 50)	6	1989	5	1989	(Geffen 27570)
*	5	Patience	(Geffen Gef 56)	10	1989	4	1989	(Geffen 22996)
	6	Sweet Child O'Mine (Re-Mix)	(Geffen Gef 55)	6	1989	0	1989	
	7	Nightrain (Re-Issue)	(Geffen Gef 60)	17	1989	0	1989	
*	8	You Could Be Mine	(Geffen Gfs 6)	3	1991	29	1991	(Geffen 19039)
*	9	Don't Cry	(Geffen Gfs 9)	8	1991	10	1992	(Geffen 19027)
	10	Live And Let Die	(Geffen Gfs 17)	5	1991	33	1992	(Geffen 19114)
*	11	November Rain	(Geffen Gfs 18)	4	1992	3	1992	(Geffen 19067)
	12	Knockin' On Heaven's Doo	(Geffen Gfs 21)	2	1992	0	1992	
	13	Yesterday's/ November's Rain (Re-Issue)	(Geffen Gfs 27)	8	1992	0	1992	
	14	The Civil War (EP)	(Geffen Gefstd 43)	11	1993	0	1993	
	15	Ain't It Fun	(Geffen Gfstd 62)	9	1993	0	1993	
	17	Since I Don't Have You	(Geffen Gfstd 70)	10	1994	0	1994	
	18	Sympathy For The Devil	(Geffen Gfstd 86)	9	1995	0	1995	

Gunter Kallman Choir Mixed Vocal Group from Germany

1	Elisabeth Serenade	(Polydor Nh 24678	45	1964	0	1964	

Guru Male Instrumentalist from the USA   See also DC Lee

1	Trust Me	(Cooltempo Cdcool 278)	34	1993	0	1993	
2	No Time To Play	(Cooltempo Cdcool 282)	25	1993	0	1993	
3	Watch What You Say	(Cooltempo Cdcool 308)	28	1995	0	1995	
4	Feel The Music	(Cooltempo Cdcool 313)	34	1995	0	1995	
5	Livin' In This World / Lifesaver	(Cooltempo Cdcool 320)	61	1996	0	1996	

HIT 1 IS CREDITED TO GURU FEATURING N'DEA DAVENPORT • HIT 2 IS CREDITED TO GURU FEATURING D.C. LEE • HIT 3 IS CREDITED TO GURU FEATURING CHAKA KHAN

Guru Josh Male Vocal/Instrumental Group from the UK

1	Infinity	(Deconstruction Pb 43475)	5	1990	0	1990	
2	Whose Law (Is It Anyway)	(Deconstruction Pb 43647)	26	1990	0	1990	

Gusto Male Producer Edward Green from the USA

1	Disco's Revenge	(Manifesto Fescd 6)	9	1996	0	1996	
2	Let's All Chant	(Manifesto Fescd 13)	21	1996	0	1996	

Guy Male Vocal Group from the USA

1	Her	(MCA MCS 1575)	58	1991	0	1991	

Guy Darrell Male Vocalist from the UK

1	I've Been Hurt	(Santa Ponsa Pns 4)	12	1973	0	1973	

Guy Little & Shawn Monifah See Various Artists

1	New York Undercover	(Uptown Mcstd 48002)	39	1996	0	1996	

Guy Lombardo & His Royal Canadians Male Bandleader, B: 19 Jun 1902 London, Ontario

	ISSUE	TITLE	UK LBL	UK POS	UK YEAR	US POS	US YEAR	US LBL
	171	Symphony		0	1946	10	1946	(Decca 18737)
	172	Seems Like Old Times		0	1946	7	1946	(Decca 18737)
	173	Shoo-Fly Pie And Apple Pan Dowdy		0	1946	6	1946	(Decca 18809)
	174	Give Me The Moon Over Brooklyn		0	1946	12	1946	(Decca 18809)
	175	Love On A Greyhound Bus (From No Leave, No Love)		0	1946	23	1946	(Decca 18873)
	176	I'd Be Lost Without You		0	1946	14	1946	(Decca 18901)
	177	Managua, Nicaragua		0	1947	1	1947	(Decca 23782)
	178	Anniversary Song		0	1947	2	1947	(Decca 23799)
*	179	Easter Parade (Re-Recording)		0	1947	21	1947	(Decca 23817)
	180	April Showers (The Jolson Story)		0	1947	9	1947	(Decca 23845)
	181	I Wonder, I Wonder, I Wonder		0	1947	3	1947	(Decca 23865)
	182	The Echo Said "No		0	1947	16	1947	(Decca 24115)
	183	Thoughtless		0	1948	22	1848	(Decca 24318)
	184	I'm My Own Grandpaw		0	1948	10	1948	(Decca 24288)
	185	Red Roses For A Blue Lady		0	1949	8	1949	(Decca 24549)
	186	Everywhere You Go		0	1949	19	1949	(Decca 24549)

ISSUE	TITLE	UK LBL	UK POS	UK YEAR	US POS	US YEAR	US LBL
187	Down By The Station		0	1949	20	1949	(Decca 24555)
188	Merry-Go-Round Waltz		0	1949	18	1949	(Decca 24624)
189	Need You		0	1949	30	1949	(Decca 24614)
190	The Four Winds And The Seven Seas		0	1949	19	1949	(Decca 24648)
191	Hop-Scotch Polka (Scotch Hot)		0	1949	16	1949	(Decca 24704)
192	The Blue Skirt Waltz		0	1949	30	1949	(Decca 24714)
193	Enjoy Yourself (It's Later Than You Think)		0	1950	10	1950	(Decca 24825)
* 194	The Third Man Theme (Movie Title Song)		0	1950	1	1950	(Decca 24839)
195	The Wedding Samba		0	1950	28	1950	(Decca 24838)
196	Dearie (From The Copacabana Show Of 1950)		0	1950	5	1950	(Decca 24899)
197	Tiddley Winkey Woo		0	1950	24	1950	(Decca 27005)
198	Our Little Ranch House		0	1950	19	1950	(Decca 27092)
199	Nola		0	1950	25	1950	(Decca 27178)
200	All My Love		0	1950	10	1950	(Decca 27118)
201	The Petite Waltz (La Petite Valse)		0	1950	22	1950	(Decca 27208)
202	Harbour Lights		0	1950	2	1950	(Decca 27208)
203	Tennessee Waltz		0	1950	6	1950	(Decca 27336)
204	Frosty The Snowman		0	1951	28	1951	(Decca 27257)
205	Get Out Those Old Records		0	1951	29	1951	(Decca 27336)
206	Velvet Lips		0	1951	21	1951	(Decca 27393)
207	The Chicken Song (I Ain't Gonna Take It Settin' Down)		0	1951	22	1951	(Decca 27393)
208	If		0	1951	20	1951	(Decca 27449)
209	Because Of You		0	1951	11	1951	(Decca 27666)
210	Undecided		0	1951	28	1951	(Decca 27835)
211	Crazy Heart		0	1952	20	1952	(Decca 27888)
212	Blue Tango		0	1952	9	1952	(Decca 28031)
213	Kiss Of Fire		0	1952	30	1952	(Decca 28179)
214	Auf Wiedersehen Sweetheart		0	1952	13	1952	(Decca 28271)
215	Half As Much		0	1952	20	1952	(Decca 28271)
216	Wish You Were Here (Musical Title Song)		0	1952	20	1952	(Decca 28271)
217	John, John, John (Every Tom, Dick And Harry's Called John)		0	1953	26	1953	(Decca 28546)
218	Hernando's Hideaway (From Pajama Game)		0	1954	14	1954	(Decca 29173)

OBITUARY: CARMEN D: 17 APR 1971 (AGED 67). • OBITUARY : GUY D: 5 NOV 1977 IN HOUSTON, TEXAS.

Guy Marks Male Vocalist from Australia

1	Loving You Has Made Me Bananas	(ABC 4211)	25	1978	0	1978	

Guy Mitchell Male Vocalist, Real Name Al Cernik B: 21 Feb 1927 Detroit

1	My Heart Cries For You		0	1950	2	1950	(Columbia 78-39067)
2	The Roving Kind		0	1950	4	1950	(Columbia 78-39067)
3	You're Just In Love (From Call Me Madam)		0	1951	24	1951	(Columbia 29052)
4	Sparrow In The Tree Top		0	1951	8	1951	(Columbia 39190)
5	Christopher Columbus		0	1951	27	1951	(Columbia 39331)
6	Unless		0	1951	17	1951	(Columbia 39331)
* 7	My Truly, Truly Fair		0	1951	2	1951	(Columbia 39415)
8	Belle, Belle, My Liberty Belle		0	1951	9	1951	(Columbia 39512)
9	Sweetheart Of Yesterday		0	1951	23	1951	(Columbia 39512)
10	There's Always Room At Our House		0	1951	20	1951	(Columbia 39595)
11	I Can't Help It		0	1951	28	1951	(Columbia 39595)
* 12	Pittsburgh, Pennsylvania (There's A Pawnshop Round The Corner In)		0	1952	4	1952	(Columbia 39753)
13	Day Of Jubilo		0	1952	26	1952	(Columbia 39753)
14	Feet Up (Pat Him On The Po-Po)	(Columbia Db 3151)	2	1952	14	1952	(Columbia 39822)
15	'Cause I Love You, That's Why		0	1952	24	1952	(Columbia 39879)
16	She Wears Red Feathers	(Columbia Db 3238)	1	1953	19	1953	(Columbia 39909)
17	Pretty Little Black Eyed Susie	(Columbia Db 3255)	2	1953	0	1953	
18	She Wears Red Feathers (Re-Entry)	(Columbia Db 3238)	12	1953	0	1953	
19	Tell Us Where The Good Times Are		0	1953	23	1953	(Columbia 39992)
0	Look At That Girl	(Philips Pb 162)	1	1953	0	1953	
21	Chicka Boom	(Philips Pb 178)	5	1953	0	1953	
22	Cloud Lucky Seven	(Philips Pb 210)	2	1953	0	1953	
23	Chicka Boom (Re-Entry)	(Philips Pb 178)	4	1954	0	1954	
24	Cuff Of My Shirt	(Philips Pb 225)	9	1954	0	1954	
25	Sippin' Soda	(Philips Pb 210)	11	1954	0	1954	
26	Cuff Of My Shirt (Re-Entry)	(Philips Pb 225)	12	1954	0	1954	
27	Cuff Of My Shirt (2nd Re-Entry)	(Philips Pb 225)	11	1954	0	1954	
28	Dime And A Dollar	(Philips Pb 248)	8	1954	0	1954	
29	Dime And A Dollar (Re-Entry)	(Philips Pb 248)	8	1954	0	1954	

ISSUE	TITLE	UK LBL	UK POS	UK YEAR	US POS	US YEAR	US LBL
30	Ninety Nine Years (Dead Or Alove)		0	1956	23	1956	(Columbia 40631)
* 31	Singing The Blues	(Philips Pb 650)	1	1956	1	1956	(Columbia 40769)
32	Knee Deep In The Blues	(Philips Pb 669)	3	1957	16	1957	(Columbia 40820)
33	Rock-A-Billy	(Philips Pb 685)	1	1957	10	1957	(Columbia 40877)
34	In The Middle Of A Dark Dark Night / Sweet Stuff	(Philips Pb 712)	27	1957	0	1957	
35	In The Middle Of A Dark Dark Night / Sweet Stuff (Re-Entry)	(Pb 712)	25	1957	0	1957	
36	Call Rosie On The Phone	(Philips Pb 743)	17	1957	0	1957	
* 37	Heartaches By The Number	(Philips Pb 964)	26	1959	1	1959	(Columbia 41476)
38	Heartaches By The Numbers (Re-Entry)	(Philips Pb 964)	5	1959	0	1959	

HE WORKED AS A CHILD SINGER AT WARNER BROTHERS MOVIE STUDIO

Guys & Dolls Mixed Vocal Group from the UK

1	There's A Whole Lot Of Loving	(Magnet Mag 20)	2	1975	0	1975	
2	Here I Go Again	(Magnet Mag 30)	33	1975	0	1975	
3	You Don't Have To Say You Love Me	(Magnet Mag 50)	5	1976	0	1976	
4	Stoney Ground	(Magnet Mag 76)	38	1976	0	1976	
5	Only Lovin' Does It	(Magnet Mag 115)	42	1978	0	1978	

Gwen Dickey Female Vocalist from the USA

1	Car Wash	(Swanyard Syr 7)	72	1990	0	1990	
2	Ain't Nobody (Loves Me Better)	(X-Clusive Xclu 010cd)	21	1994	0	1994	with KWS

Gwen Guthrie Female Vocalist from the USA

1	Ain't Nothin' Goin' On But The Rent	(Boiling Point Posp 807)	5	1986	0	1986	
2	(They Long To Be) Close To You	(Boiling Point Posp 822)	25	1986	0	1986	
3	Good To Go Lover / Outside In The Rain	(Boiling Point Posp 841)	37	1987	0	1987	
4	Ain't Nothing Goin' On But The Rent (Re-Mix)	(Boiling Point Pzcd 276)	42	1993	0	1993	

Gwen McCrae Female Vocalist, B: 21 Dec 1943 Florida

+ 1	For Your Love		0	1973	17	1973	(Cat 1989)
2	Rockin' Chair		0	1975	9	1975	(Cat 1996)
3	All This Love That I'm Giving	(Flame Melt 7)	63	1988	0	1988	
4	All This Love I'm Giving	(Ktda Cdktda 2)	36	1993	0	1993	

Gyres Male Vocal/Instrumental Group from the UK

1	Pop Cop	(Sugar Suga 9cd)	71	1996	0	1996	
2	Are You Ready?	(Sugar Suga 11cd)	71	1996	0	1996	

H

ISSUE	TITLE	UK LBL	UK POS	UK YEAR	US POS	US YEAR	US LBL
H-Town	Male Vocal Trio, Shazam & John Conner And Darryl Jackson from Houston						
* 1	Knockin' Da Boots		0	1993	3	1993	(Luke 161)
2	A Thin Line Between Love And Hate		0	1996	37	1996	
H.B. Barnum	Male Vocalist, B: 15 Jul 1936 Houston, Texas	Former Member Of The Dyna-Sores					
1	Lost Love		0	1961	35	1961	(Eldo 111)
HHC							
1	We're Not Alone	(Perfecto Perf 138cd)	44	1997	0	1997	
H2o	Male Vocal/Instrumental Group from the UK						
1	Dream To Sleep	(RCA330)	17	1983	0	1983	
2	Just Outside Of Heaven	(RCA349)	38	1983	0	1983	
3	Satisfied (Take Me Higher)	(Am:Pm 5823252)	66	1997	0	1997	
4	Time After Time	(M&G Magcd 34)	71	1993	0	1993	
H2o (Featuring) Billie	Mixed Vocal/Instrumental Group from the USA/Switzerland						
1	Nobody's Business	(Am:Pm 5818832)	19	1996	0	1996	
Habit	Male Vocal/Instrumental Group from the UK						
1	Lucy	(Virgin Vs 1063)	56	1988	0	1988	
Haddaway	Male Dancer/Vocalist, Real Name Nestor Alexander Haddaway from Trinidad And Tobago						
* 1	What Is Love	(Logic 74321148502)	2	1993	11	1993	(Arista 12575)
2	Life	(Logic 74321164212)	6	1993	0	1993	
3	I Miss You	(Logic 74321181522)	9	1993	0	1993	
4	Rock My Heart	(Logic 74321194122)	9	1994	0	1994	
5	Fly Away	(Logic 74321286942)	20	1995	0	1995	
6	Catch A Fire	(Logic 74321306652)	39	1995	0	1995	
Haircut 100	Male Vocal/Instrumental Group from the UK	Nick Heyward Formed The Sextet Although They Disbanded In 1983					
1	Favourite Shirts	(Arista Clip 1)	4	1981	0	1981	
2	Love Plus One	(Arista Clip 2)	3	1982	37	1982	(Arista 0672)
3	Fantastic Day	(Arista Clip 3)	9	1982	0	1982	
4	Nobody's Fool	(Arista Clip 4)	9	1982	0	1982	
5	Prime Time	(Polydor Hc 1)	46	1983	0	1983	
Hal (Featuring) Gillian Anderson							
1	Extremis	(Virgin Vscdt 1636)	23	1997	0	1997	
Hal Derwin	Male Vocalist (Baritone) from the USA						
1	The Old Lamplighter		0	1946	5	1946	(Capitol 288)
2	My, How The Time Goes By		0	1947	25	1947	(Capitol
3	Worry, Worry, Worry		0	1948	23	1948	(Capitol 498)
Hal McIntyre & His Orchestra	Male Bandleader/Saxophonist from the USA						
7	The Gypsy		0	1946	8	1946	(Cosmo 475)
8	Cement Mixer (Put-Ti, Put-Ti)		0	1946	18	1946	(Cosmo 475)
9	There's No One Else But You		0	1946	17	1946	(Cosmo 479)
	OBITUARY: D: 5 MAY 1959 (AGED 44).						
Hal Page & The Whalers	Male Vocal/Instrumental Group from the USA						
1	Going Back To My Home Town	(Melodisc Mel 1553)	50	1960	0	1960	
Hale And Pace & The Stonkers	Male Comedy Duo And Backing Group from the UK						
1	The Stonk	(London Lon 296)	1	1991	0	1991	
Halo James	Male Vocal/Instrumental Group from the UK						
1	Wanted	(Epic Halo 1)	45	1989	0	1989	
2	Could Have Told You So	(Epic Halo 2)	6	1989	0	1989	
3	Baby	(Epic Halo 3)	43	1990	0	1990	

ISSUE	TITLE	UK LBL	UK POS	UK YEAR	US POS	US YEAR	US LBL
	~~Magic Hour~~	(Epic Halo 1)	59	1996		1996	

Halos   Based In New York City This R&B Group Also Backed Curtis Lee On His '61 Hit Pretty Little Angel Eyes

ISSUE	TITLE	UK LBL	UK POS	UK YEAR	US POS	US YEAR	US LBL
1	Nag		0	1961	25	1961	(7 Arts 709)

Hamilton Bohannon   Male Vocal/Instrumentalist from the USA

1	South African Man	(Brunswick Br 16)	22	1975	0	1975	
2	Disco Stomp	(Brunswick Br 19)	6	1975	0	1975	
3	Foot Stompin' Music	(Brunswick Br 21)	23	1975	0	1975	
4	Happly Feeling	(Brunswick Br 24)	49	1975	0	1975	
5	Let's Start The Dance	(Mercury 6167 700)	56	1978	0	1978	
6	Let's Start The Dance Again	(London Hl 10582)	49	1982	0	1982	

Hamilton, Joe Frank & Reynolds   Male Vocal Group from the USA, Names Dan Hamilton, Joe Frank Carollo & Tommy Reynolds

* 1	Don't Pull Your Love		0	1971	4	1971	(Dunhill 4276)
* 2	Fallin' In Love	(Pye International 7n 25690)	33	1975	1	1975	(Playboy 6024)
3	Winners And Losers		0	1974	21	1974	(Playboy 6054)

FORMER MEMBERS OF THE T-BONES, ALAN DENNISON REPLACED REYNOLDS IN 1972, THEY DID NOT CHANGE THE GROUPS NAME UNTIL 1976

Hamish Menzies   Male Singer/Songwriter from Scotland

1	Less Than Tomorrow		0	1953	22	1953	(Decca 28601)
2	Dare I?		0	1953	25	1953	(Decca 28811)

Hammer   Male Rapper, Real Name Stanley Kirk Burrell B: 30 Mar 1963 Oakland

1	U Can't Touch This	(Capitol Cl 578)	3	1990	8	1990	(Capitol 15571)
* 2	Have You Seen Her	(Capitol Cl 590)	8	1990	4	1990	(Capitol 44573#)
* 3	Pray	(Capitol Cl 599)	8	1990	2	1990	(Capitol 44609#)
4	Here Comes The Hammer	(Capitol Cl 610)	15	1991	0	1991	
5	Yo!! Sweetness	(Capitol Cl 616)	16	1991	0	1991	
6	(Hammer Hammer) They Put Me In The Mix	(Capitol Cl 607)	20	1991	0	1991	
7	2 Legit 2 Quit	(Capitol Cl 6369)	60	1991	5	1991	(Capitol 44785)
8	Addams Groove	(Capitol Cl 642)	4	1991	7	1991	(Capitol 44794)
9	Do Not Pass Me By	(Capitol Cl 650)	14	1992	0	1992	
10	It's All Good	(RCA 74321188612)	52	1994	0	1994	
11	Don't Stop	(RCA 74321220012)	72	1994	0	1994	
* 12	Pumps And A Bump		0	1994	26	1994	(Giant 18218)
13	Straight To My Feet	(Priority Ptycd 102)	57	1995	0	1995	

HITS 1-6 ARE CREDITED TO MC HAMMER • HIT 13 IS CREDITED TO HAMMER FEATURING DEION SANDERS • IN 1991 HE DROPPED THE MC PREFIX FROM HIS NAME

Handbaggers   Mixed Vocal/Instrumental Group from the UK

1	U Found Out	(Tidy Trax Tidy 104cd)	55	1996	0	1996	

Handley Family   Mixed Vocal Group From The Uk

1	Wam Bam	(Gl 100)	30	1973	0	1973	

Hank Ballard & The Midnighters   Hank, B: 18 Nov 1936 Detroit, The Group Was Originally Called The Royals

+ 1	Get It		0	1953	6	953	(Federal 12133)
* 2	Work With Me Annie		0	1954	22	1954	(Federal 12169)
*+ 3	Sexy Ways		0	1954	2	1954	(Federal 12185)
* 4	Annie Had A Baby		0	1954	23	1954	(Federal 12195)
+ 5	Annie's Aunt Fanny		0	1954	10	1954	(Federal 12200)
+ 6	Henry's Got Flat Feet (Can't Dance No More)		0	1955	14	1955	(Federal 12224)
+ 7	It's Love Baby (24 Hours A Day)		0	1955	10	1955	(Federal 12227)
+ 8	Teardrops On Your Letter		0	1959	4	1959	(King 5171)
+ 9	The Twist		0	1959	16	1959	(King 5171)
10	Kansas City		0	1959	72	1959	(King 5195)
+ 11	The Coffee Grind		0	1960	21	1960	(King 5312)
12	Finger Poppin' Time		0	1960	7	1960	(King 5341)
13	The Twist (Re-Entry)		0	1960	28	1960	(King 5171)
14	Let's Go, Let's Go, Let's Go		0	1960	6	1960	(King 5400)
15	The Hoochi Coochi Coo		0	1961	23	1961	(King 5430)
16	Let's Go Again (Where We Went Last Night)		0	1961	39	1961	(King 5459)
17	The Continental Walk		0	1961	33	1961	(King 5491)
18	The Switch-A-Roo		0	1961	26	1961	(King 5510)
+ 19	The Float		0	1961	10	1961	(King 5510)
20	Nothing But Good		0	1961	49	1961	(King 5535)

THE MIDNIGHTERS CONSIST OF HENRY BOOTH, CHARLES SUTTON, LAWSON SMITH & SONNY WOODS. • HIT 1 IS CREDITED TO THE ROYALS

Hank C. Burnette   Male Multi-Instrumentalist From Sweden

1	Spinning Rock Boogie	(Sonet Son 2094)	21	1976	0	1976	

Hank Levine   Orchestra Leader from the USA

1	Image	(Hmv Pop 947)	45	1961	0	1961	

ISSUE	TITLE	UK LBL	UK POS	UK YEAR	US POS	US YEAR	US LBL
Hank Locklin Male Vocalist, Real Name Lawrence Hankins Locklin B: 15 Feb 1918 In McLellean, Florida							
4	Geisha Girl		0	1957	66	1957	(RCA 6984)
* 9	Please Help Me I'm Falling	(RCA 1188)	9	1960	8	1960	(RCA 7692)
22	I Feel A Cry Coming On	(RCA 1510)	28	1966	0	1966	
	HIT 4 REACHED NUMBER 4 IN THE US C/W CHARTS • HIT 9 REACHED NUMBER 1 IN THE US C/W CHARTS							
Hank Marvin Male Vocal/Guitarist, B: 28 Oct 1941 Newcastle, England							
1	Throw Down A Line	(Columbia Db 8615)	7	1969	0	1969	
2	Joy Of Living (EP)	(Columbia Db 8657)	25	1990	0	1990	
3	Don't Talk	(Polydor Posp 420)	49	1982	0	1982	
4	Living Doll	(WEA Yz 65)	1	1986	0	1986	
5	London Kid	(Polydor Po 32	52	1989	0	1989	
6	We Are The Champions	(Polygram Tv Tv Po 229)	66	1992	0	1992	
Hank Mizell Male Vocalist from the USA							
1	Jungle Rock	(Charly CS 1005)	3	1976	0	1976	
Hank Snow Male vocalist. B Clarence Eugene Snow 9 May 1914 in Liverpool, Nova Scotia							
* 2	I'm Moving On		0	1950	27	1950	(RCA Victor 0328)
* 19	I Don't Hurt Anymore		0	1954	22	1954	(RCA 5698)
	THOSE UNLISTED ARE C/W HITS • HIT 2 REACHED NUMBER 1 IN THE US C/W CHARTS							
	HIT 19 REACHED NUMBER 1 IN THE US C/W CHARTS • HIT 23 IS CREDITED TO HANK SNOW AND CHET ATKINS							
Hank Thompson & His Brazos Valley Boys Male Vocalist, Real Name Henry William Thompson B: 3 Sep 1925 Waco, Texas							
8	Soft Lips		0	1949	10	1949	(Capitol 40211)
9	The Grass Looks Greener Over Yonder		0	1949	15	1949	(Capitol 40211)
* 10	The Wild Side Of Life		0	1952	27	1952	(Capitol 1942)
11	Waiting In The Lobby Of Your Heart		0	1952	3	1952	(Capitol 2063)
12	The New Wears Off Too Fast		0	1952	10	1952	(Capitol 2269)
13	You're Walking On My Heart		0	1953	21	1953	(Capitol 2269)
28	Don't Take It Out On Me		0	1955	5	1955	(Capitol 3275)
47	I Wasn't Even In The Running		0	1963	23	1963	(Capitol 4968)
48	Too In Love		0	1963	22	1963	(Capitol 5008)
49	Twice As Much		0	1964	45	1964	(Capitol 5071)
50	Then I'll Start Believing In You		0	1965	42	1965	(Capitol 5422)
52	He's Got A Way With Women		0	1967	16	1967	(Warner Bros 5886)
53	On Tap, In The Can, Or In The Bottle		0	1968	7	1968	(Dot 17108)
75	I'm Just Gettin' By		0	1978	92	1978	(ABC12409)
76	Dance With Me Molly		0	1979	88	1979	(Abc 12447)
80	Once In A Blue Moon		0	1983	82	1983	(Churchill 94026)
	THOSE UNLISTED ARE C/W HITS							
Hank Williams & His Drifting Cowboys Male Vocalist, B: Hiram King Williams, 17 Sep 1923 In Mount Olive, Alabama							
* 4	Lovesick Blues		0	1949	24	1949	(MGM 10352)
7	Never Again (Re-Recording)		0	1949	6	1949	(MGM 10352)
* 21	Cold, Cold Heart		0	1951	27	1951	(MGM 10904)
22	Howlin' at the Moon		0	1951	2	1951	(MGM 10961)
* 25	Hey, Good Looking		0	1951	29	1951	(MGM 11000)
* 31	Jambalaya (On The Bayou)		0	1952	20	1952	(MGM 11283)
* 35	Kaw-Liga		0	1953	23	1953	(MGM 11416)
* 36	Your Cheatin' Heart		0	1953	25	1953	(MGM 11416)
	HANK FORMED THE DRIFTING COWBOYS IN 1935 AND CONSISTED OF DON HELMS, JETTY RIVERS, HILLOUS BUTTRAM & BOB MCNETT							
	OBITUARY : D: 1 JAN 1953 CAR ACCIDENT WHILST TRAVELLING TO A CONCERT IN CANTON, OHIO. • THOSE UNLISTED SONGS ARE C/W HITS							
Hannah Jones Female Vocalist from the USA							
1	Bridge Over Troubled Water	(Dance Pool 6565467)	21	1991	0	1991	
2	Keep It On	(Tmrc Cdtmrc 7)	67	1993	0	1993	
Hanoi Rocks Male Vocal/Instrumental Group from Finland							
1	Up Around The Bend	(CBS A 4513)	61	1984	0	1984	
Hanson Male Teenage Trio Of Brothers from the UK							
* 1	Mmmbop	(Mercury 5745012)	1	1997	1	1997	(Mercury 574261)
2	Where's The Love	(Mercury 5749032)	4	1997	0	1997	
Happenings Names Dave Libert, Tom Giuliano, Bob Miranda & Ralph Divito							
* 1	See You In September		0	1966	3	1966	(B.T. Puppy 520)
* 2	Go Away Little Girl		0	1966	12	1966	(B.T. Puppy 522)
* 3	I Got Rhythm	(Stateside Ss 2013)	28	1967	3	1967	(B.T. Puppy 527)
* 4	My Mammy	(Pye Int 7n 25501)	34	1967	13	1967	(B.T. Puppy 530)

ISSUE	TITLE	UK LBL	UK POS	UK YEAR	US POS	US YEAR	US LBL
Happy Clappers Mixed Vocal/Instrumental Group from the UK							
1	I Believe	(Shindig Shin 4cd)	7	1995	0	1995	
2	Hold On	(Shindig Shin 7cd)	27	1995	0	1995	
3	I Believe (Re-Issue)	(Shindig Shin 9cd)	7	1995	0	1995	
4	Can't Help It	(Coliseum Toga 004cd)	18	1996	0	1996	
5	Never Again	(Coliseum Toga 012cd)	49	1996	0	1996	
Happy Mondays Male Vocal/Instrumental Group from The Uk							
1	Wfl	(Factory Fac 2327)	68	1989	0	1989	
2	Madchester Rave On (Ep)	(Factory Fac 2427)	19	1989	0	1989	
3	Step On	(Factory Fac 2727)	5	1990	0	1990	
4	Lazyitis - One Armed Boxer	(Factory Fac 2227)	46	1990	0	1990	
5	Kinky Afro	Factory Fac 3027)	5	1990	0	1990	
6	Loose Fit	(Factory Fac 3127)	17	1991	0	1991	
7	Judge Fudge	(Factory Fac 3327)	24	1991	0	1991	
8	Stinkin' Thinkin'	(Factory Fac 3627)	31	1992	0	1992	
9	Sunshine And Love	(Factory Fac 3727)	62	1992	0	1992	
Hardcore Rhythm Team Vocal/Production Group from the UK							
1	Hardcore - The Final Conflict	(Furious Frut 001)	69	1992	0	1992	
Hardfloor Male Production/Instrumental Group from Germany							
1	Hardtrance Acperience	(Hardhouse Uk Hartuk 1)	65	1992	0	1992	
2	Trancescript	(Hardhouse Uk Hartuk 5cd)	72	1993	0	1993	
Harlequin 4's & Bunker Kru US Male Vocal/Instrumental Group With Production Duo from the UK							
1	Set It Off	(Champion Champ 64)	55	1988	0	1988	
Harley Quinne Male Vocal Group from the UK							
1	New Orleans	(Bell 1255)	19	1972	0	1972	
Harlow Wilcox & The Oakies Top Session Musician from Norman, Oklahoma							
1	Groovy Grubworm		0	1969	30	1969	(Plantation 28)
Harmonicats Male Harmonica Players, Jerry Murad, Al Fiore & Bob Nes							
* 1	Peg O' My Heart (From Ziegfeld Follies Of 1913)		0	1947	1	1947	(Vitacoustic 1)
2	Peggy O'Neil		0	1947	21	1947	(Vitacoustic 7)
3	Hair Of Gold (Eyes Of Blue) (From Singin' Spurs)		0	1948	15	1948	(Universal 121)
4	Bewitched (From Pal Joey)		0	1950	8	1950	(Mercury 5399)
5	Charmaine		0	1951	21	1951	(Mercury 5747)
6	Till I Waltz Again With You		0	1953	26	1953	(Mercury 70069)
Harmonix Male Producer Hamish Brown from the UK							
1	Landslide	(Deconstruction 74321330762)	28	1996	0	1996	
Harmony Grass Male Vocal/Instrumental Group from the UK							
1	Move In A Little Closer Baby	(RCA 1772)	24	1969	0	1969	
Harold Dorman Male Vocalist, B: 23 Dec 1926 In Drew, Mississippi							
1	Mountain Of Love		0	1960	21	1960	(Rita 1003)
Harold Faltermeyer Songwriter/Producer/Instrumentalist (Keyboards) from Germany							
1	Axel F (From *Beverly Hills Cop*)	(MCA Mca 949)	62	1985	3	1985	(MCA 52536)
2	Axel F (From *Beverly Hills Cop*) (Re-Entry)	(MCA MCA 949)	2	1985	0	1985	
3	Fletch Theme	(MCA MCA 991)	74	1985	0	1985	
Harold Melvin & The Bluenotes Male Vocal Group from the USA							
1	I Miss You		0	1972	58	1972	(Phil/Inter 3516)
* 2	If You Don't Know Me By Now	(CBS 8496)	9	1973	3	1973	(Phil/Inter 3520)
	Yesterday I Had The Blues		0	1973	63	1973	(Phil/Inter 3525)
* 4	The Love I Lost (Part 1)	(Philadelphia Int. Pir 1879)	21	1974	7	1973	(Phil/Inter 3533)
5	Yesterday I Had The Blues (Re-Issue)		0	1973	7	1973	(Phil/Inter 3533)
+ 6	Satisfaction Guaranteed	(Philadelphia Int. Pir 2187)	32	1974	6	1974	(Phil/Inter 3543)
+ 7	Where Are All My Friends		0	1974	8	1974	(Phil/Inter 3552)
8	Bad Luck (Part 1)		0	1975	15	1975	(Phil/Inter 8-3562)
9	Get Out (And Let Me Cry)	(Route Rt 06)	35	1975	0	1975	
10	Hope That We Can Be Together Soon		0	1975	42	1975	(Phil/Inter 8-3569)
11	Wake Up Everybody (Part 1)	(Philadelphia Int. Pir 3866)	23	1976	12	1976	(Phil/Inter 3579)
12	Don't Leave Me This Way	(Philadelphia Int. Pir 4909)	5	1977	0	1977	
13	Reaching For The World	(Abc 4161)	48	1977	0	1977	
14	Don't Give Me Up	(London Lon 47)	59	1984	0	1984	
15	Today's Your Luck Day	(London Lon 52)	66	1984	0	1984	

NAMES HAROLD MELVIN, THEODORE PENDERGRASS, LAWRENCE BROWN, BERNARD WILSON & LLOYD PARKS • HIT 10 WAS WITH SHARON PAIGE

ISSUE	TITLE	UK LBL	UK POS	UK YEAR	US POS	US YEAR	US LBL
Harpers Bizarre USA, Male Quintet Led By Ted Templeman							
1	59th Street Bridge Song (Feeling Groovy)	(Warner Bros Wb 5890)	34	1967	13	1967	(Warner Bros 5890)
2	Come To The Sunshine		0	1967	37	1967	(Warner Bros 7028)
3	Anything Goes	(Warner Bros Wb 7063)	33	1967	0	1967	
Harpo Male Vocalist From Sweden							
1	Movie Star	(Djm Djs 400)	24	1976	0	1976	
Harptones R&B Group Lead By Willie Winfield from the USA							
1	Why Should I Love You?		0	1954	25	1954	(Bruce 109)
	THE HIT WAS WITH THE SHYTANS						
Harriet Real Name Harriet Roberts Sheffield, Yorkshire, England							
1	Temple Of Love		0	1991	39	1991	(East West 98863)
Harry Belafonte Male Vocalist, Real Name Harold George Belafonte B: 1 Mar 1927 Harlem, New York							
1	Scarlet Ribbons	(Hmv Pop 360)	18	1957	30	1952	(RCA Victor 5051)
2	Gomen Nasai (Forgive Me)		0	1953	19	1953	(RCA Victor 5210)
3	Hold 'Em Joe (From John Murray Anderson's Almanac)		0	1954	20	1954	(RCA Victor 5617)
4	Jamaica Farewell		0	1957	14	1957	(RCA 6663)
* 5	Mary's Boy Child	(RCA 1022)	1	1957	12	1957	(RCA 6735)
* 6	Banana Boat Song (Day-O)	(Hmv Pop 308)	2	1957	5	1957	(RCA 6771)
7	Mama Looka Bubu		0	1957	11	1957	(RCA 6830)
8	Cocoanut Woman		0	1957	25	1957	(RCA 6885)
9	Island In The Sun	(RCA 1007)	3	1957	30	1957	(RCA 6885)
10	Little Bernadette	(RCA 1072)	16	1958	0	1958	
11	Mary's Boy Child (Re-Entry)	(RCA 1022)	10	1958	0	1958	
12	Son Of Mary	(RCA 1084)	18	1958	0	1958	
13	Mary's Boy Child (2nd Re-Entry)	(RCA 1022)	30	1959	0	1959	
14	Hole In The Bucket	(RCA 1247)	32	1961	0	1961	
15	Hole In The Bucket (Re-Entry)	(RCA 1247)	34	1961	0	1961	
	HITS 14-15 ARE CREDITED TO HARRY BELAFONTE AND ODETTA						
Harry Chapin Male Vocalist, B: 7 Dec 1942 New York City							
1	Taxi		0	1972	24	1972	(Elektra 45770)
2	W.O.L.D.	(Elektra K 12133)	34	1974	36	1974	(Elektra 45874)
* 3	Cat's In The Cradle		0	1974	1	1974	(Elektra 45203)
4	Sequel		0	1980	23	1980	(Boardwalk 5700)
	THE HIT SEQUEL WAS A SEQUEL TO TAXI. • OBITUARY : D: 16 JUL 1981 CAR ACCIDENT						
Harry Connick Jr. Male Vocalist from the USA							
1	Recipe For Love / It Had To Be You	(Columbia 6568907)	32	1991	0	1991	
2	We Are In Love	(Columbia 6572847)	62	1991	0	1991	
3	Blue Light Red Light (Someone's There)	(Columbia 6575367)	54	1991	0	1991	
Harry Cool Male Vocalist from the USA With Mindy Carson							
1	Rumors Are Flying		0	1946	12	1946	(Signature 15043)
Harry Enfield Male Comedian/Vocalist from the UK							
1	Loadsmoney (Doin' Up The House)	(Mercury Dosh 1)	4	1988	0	1988	
Harry Grove Trio							
1	Meet Mr.Callaghan		0	1952	11		1952 (London 1248)
Harry J. All Stars Male Instrumental Group from Jamaica							
1	Liquidator	(Trojan Tr 675)	9	1969	0	1969	
2	Liquidator (Re-Issue)	(Trojan Tro 9063)	42	1980	0	1980	
Harry James Orchestra Real Name Harry Haag James B: 15 Mar 1916 Albany, Georgia							
* 1	One O'Clock Jump		0	1938	7	1938	(Brunswick 8055)
* 4	Ciribiribin		0	1940	10	1940	(Columbia 35316)
* 9	You Made Me Love You		0	1941	5	1941	(Columbia 36296)
* 14	Easter Parade (From As Thousands Cheer)		0	1942	11	1942	(Columbia 36545)
* 24	I Had The Craziest Dream (From Springtime In The Rockies)		0	1942	1	1942	(Columbia 36659)
* 27	I've Heard That Song Before (From Youth On Parade)		0	1943	1	1943	(Columbia 36688)
* 31	All Or Nothing At All (Re-Issue		0	1943	1	1943	(Columbia 35587)
57	I'm Always Chasing Rainbows (From Oh, Look!)		0	1946	9	1946	(Columbia 36899)
58	Easter Parade (Re-Entry)		0	1946	23	1946	(Columbia 36545)
59	Who's Sorry Now		0	1946	18	1946	(Columbia 36973)
60	Do You Love Me (Movie Title Song)		0	1946	15	1946	(Columbia 36965)
61	And Then It's Heaven (From Sweetheart Of Sigma Chi)		0	1946	13	1946	(Columbia 37060)
62	This Is Always (From Three Little Girls In Blue)		0	1946	10	1946	(Columbia 38052)

ISSUE	TITLE	UK LBL	UK POS	UK YEAR	US POS	US YEAR	US LBL
63	Oh! But I Do (From *The Time, The Place, And The Girl*)		0	1947	12	1947	(Columbia 35156)
64	Heartaches		0	1947	4	1947	(Columbia 37305)
65	Jalousie (Jealousy)		0	1947	17	1947	(Columbia 37218)
66	I Tipped My Hat (And Slowly Rode Away)		0	1947	21	1947	(Columbia 37305)
67	Stella By Starlight (From *The Uninvited*)		0	1947	21	1947	(Columbia 37323)
68	I Still Get Jealous (From *High Button Shoes*)		0	1947	23	1947	(Columbia 37929)
69	Mona Lisa (From *Captain Carey, U.S.A.*)		0	1950	14	1950	(Columbia 38768)
70	Would I Love You (Love You, Love You)		0	1951	10	1951	(Columbia 39159)
71	Castle Rock		0	1951	8	1951	(Columbia 39527)
72	You'll Never Know (From *Hello Frisco, Hello*)		0	1953	18	1953	(Columbia 39905)
73	Ruby (From *Ruby Gentry*)		0	1953	20	1953	(Columbia 39994)

Harry Kari & His Six Saki Sippers   Real Name Yorgi Yorgesson from the USA

1	Yokohama Mama		0	1953	22	1953	(Capitol 2392)

Harry Secombe   Male Vocalist from the UK   See Also The Goons

1	On With The Motley	(Philips Pb 523)	16	1955	0	1955	
2	If I Ruled The World	(Philips Pb 1261)	44	1963	0	1963	
3	If I Ruled The World (Re-Entry)	(Philips Pb 1261)	18	1963	0	1963	
4	This Is My Song	(Philips Pb 1539)	2	1967	0	1967	

Harry Simeone Chorale   Male Arranger/Conductor, B: 9 May 1911 Newark, New Jersey

* 1	Little Drummer Boy	Top Rank Jar 101)	13	1959	13	1958	(20th Century Fox 121)
2	Little Drummer Boy (Re-Entry)		0	1959	15	1959	(20th Century Fox 121)
3	Little Drummer Boy (2nd Re-Entry)		0	1960	24	1960	(20th Century Fox 121)
4	Onwards Christian Soldiers	(Ember Embs 118)	35	1960	0	1960	
5	Onwards Christian Soldiers (Re-Entry)	(Ember Embs 118)	38	1961	0	1961	
6	Little Drummer Boy (3rd Re-Entry)		0	1961	22	1961	(20th Century Fox 121)
7	Onwards Christian Soldiers (2nd Re-Entry)	(Ember Embs 118)	36	1961	0	1961	
8	Little Drummer Boy (4th Re-Entry)		0	1962	28	1962	(20th Century Fox 121)
9	Onwards Christian Soldiers (Re-Issue)	(Ember Embs 118)	38	1962	0	1962	

Harry Thumann   Male Instrumentalist (Keyboards) from Germany

1	Underwater	(Decca F 13901)	41	1981	0	1981	

Harry's Tavern Band   The Band Backed Billy Murray In The Early 40s

1	Bartender Polka		0	1940	26	1940	(Bluebird 10806)

Havana   Male Production/Instrumental Group from The UK

1	Ethnic Prayer	(Limbo Limbo 007cd)	71	1993	0	1993	

Hawkwind   Male Vocal/Instrumental Group With Female Dancers from the UK

1	Silver Machine	(United Artists Up 35381)	3	1972	0	1972	
2	Urban Guerrilla	(United Artists Up 5566)	39	1973	0	1973	
3	Silver Machine (Re-Entry)	(United Artists Up 35381)	34	1978	0	1978	
4	Shot Down In The Night	(Bronze Bro 98)	59	1980	0	1980	
5	Silver Machine (2nd Re-Entry)	(United Artists Up 35381)	67	1983	0	1983	
	SEE ALSO GIMME SHELTER (EP), VARIOUS ARTISTS (EP, LP, 78S)						

Hawkshaw Hawkins   Male Country Singer Harold Franklin Hawkins B: 22 Dec 1921 Huntington, West Virginia

6	Slow-Poke		0	1952	26	1952	(King 998)
	HIT 6 REACHED NUMBER 7 IN THE US C/W CHARTS • OBITUARY : D: 5 MAR 1963 PLANE CRASH IN TENNESSEE						

Hayley Mills   Female Actress/Vocalist, B: 18 Apr 1946 London, England

1	Let's Get Together	(Decca F 21396)	17	1961	8	1961	(Vista 385)
2	Johnny Jingo		0	1962	21	1962	(Vista 395)

Haysi Fantayzee   Mixed Vocal Duo from the UK

1	John Wayne Is Big Leggy	(Regard Rg 100)	11	1982	0	1982	
2	Holy Joe	(Regard Rg 104)	51	1982	0	1982	
3	Shiny Shiny	(Regard Rg 106)	16	1983	0	1983	
4	Sister Friction	(Regard Rg 108)	62	1983	0	1983	

Haywoode   Female Vocalist from the UK

1	A Time Like This	(CBS A 3651)	48	1983	0	1983	
2	I Can't Let You Go	(CBS A 4664)	63	1984	0	1984	
3	Roses	Cbs A 6069)	65	1985	0	1985	
4	Getting Closer	(CBS A 6582)	67	1985	0	1985	
5	Roses (Re-Issue)	(CBS A 7224)	11	1986	0	1986	
6	I Can't Let You Go (Re-Issue)	(CBS 650076 7)	50	1986	0	1986	

Hazel O'Connor   Female Vocalist from the UK

1	Eighth Day	(A&M Ams 7553)	5	1980	0	1980	
2	Give Me An Inch	(A&M Ams 7569)	41	1980	0	1980	

ISSUE	TITLE	UK LBL	UK POS	UK YEAR	US POS	US YEAR	US LBL
3	D-Days	(Albion Ion 1009)	10	1981	0	1981	
4	Will You	(A&M Ams 8131)	8	1981	0	1981	
5	(Cover Plus) Were All Grown Up	(Albion Ion 1018)	41	1981	0	1981	
6	Hanging Around	(Albion Ion 1022)	45	1981	0	1981	
7	Calls The Tune	(A&M Ams 8203)	60	1982	0	1982	

Hazell Dean   Female Vocalist from the UK

1	Evergreen / Jealous Love	(Proto Ena 114)	63	1984	0	1984	
2	Searchin' (I Gotta Find A Man)	(Proto Ena 109)	6	1984	0	1984	
3	Whatever I Do (Wherever I Go)	(Proto Ena 119)	4	1984	0	1984	
4	Back In My Arms (Once Again)	(Proto Ena 122)	41	1984	0	1984	
5	No Fool (For Love)	(Proto Ena 123)	41	1985	0	1985	
6	They Say It's Gonna Rain	(Parlophone R 6107)	58	1985	0	1985	
7	Who's Leaving Who	(EMI Em 45)	4	1988	0	1988	
8	Maybe (We Should Call It A Day)	(EMI Em 62)	15	1988	0	1988	
9	Turn It Into Love	(EMI Em 71)	21	1988	0	1988	
10	Love Pains	(Lisson Dole 12)	48	1989	0	1989	
11	Better Off Without You	(Lisson Dole 19)	2	1991	0	1991	

Headbangers   Male Vocal/Instrumental Group from the UK

1	Status Rock	(Magnet Mag 206)	60	1981	0	1981	

Headboys   Male Vocal/Instrumental Group from the UK

1	The Shape Of Things To Come	(RSO 40)	45	1979	0	1979	

Heads   Male Instrumental Group Talking Heads Without Lead Singer David Byrne from the UK

1	Aztec Lightning (Theme From *World Cup Grandstand*)	(BBC Resl 184)	45	1986	0	1986	
2	Don't Take My Kindness For Weakness	(Radioactive Mcstd 48024)	60	1996	0	1996	

Headswim   Male Vocal/Instrumental Group from the UK

1	Crawl	(Crush 6612252)	64	1995	0	1995	

Hear 'N Aid   Mixed International Vocal/Instrumental Assembly

1	Stars	(Vertigo Hear 1)	26	1986	0	1986	

Heart   Mixed Vocal/Instrumental Group from Seattle

1	Crazy On You		0	1976	35	1976	(Mushroom 7021)
2	Magic Man		0	1976	9	1976	(Mushroom 7011)
3	Barracuda		0	1977	11	1977	(Portrait 70004)
4	Heartless		0	1978	24	1978	(Mushroom 7031)
5	Straight On		0	1978	15	1978	(Portrait 70020)
6	Dog And Butterfly		0	1979	34	1979	(Portrait 70025)
7	Even It Up		0	1980	33	1980	(Epic 50847)
8	Tell It Like It Is		0	1980	8	1980	(Epic 50950)
9	This Man Is Mine		0	1982	33	1982	(Epic 02925)
10	What About Love?	(Capitol Cl 487)	41	9881	0	1985	(Capitol 5481)
11	Never		0	1985	4	1985	(Capitol 5512)
12	These Dreams	(Capitol Cl 394)	8	1986	1	1986	(Capitol 5541)
13	Nothin' At All	(Capitol Cl 507)	38	1988	10	1986	(Capitol 5572)
14	Alone	(Capitol Cl 448)	3	1987	1	1987	(Capitol 44002)
15	Who Will You Run To	(Capitol Cl 457)	30	1987	7	1987	(Capitol 44040)
16	There's The Girl	(Capitol Cl 473)	34	1987	12	1988	(Capitol 44089)
17	Never / These Dreams (Re-Issue)	(Capitol Cl 482)	8	1988	0	1988	
* 18	All I Wanna Do Is Make Love To You	(Capitol Cl 569)	8	1990	2	1990	(Capitol 44507)
19	I Didn't Want To Need You	(Capitol Cl 580)	47	1990	23	1990	(Capitol 44553)
20	Stranded	(Capitol Cl 595)	60	1990	13	1990	(Capitol 44621)
21	You're The Voice	(Capitol Cls 624)	56	1991	0	1991	
22	Will You Be There (In The Morning)	(Capitol Cdcls 700)	19	1993	39	1994	(Capitol 58040)

ORIGINALLY KNOWN AS THEARMY WHICH BECAME WHITE HEART THEN FINALLY IN 1974 BECAME HEART

Heartbeat   Mixed Vocal/Instrumental Group from the UK

1	Tears From Heaven	(Priority P 17)	32	1987	0	1987	
2	The Winner	(Priority P 19)	70	1988	0	1988	

Heartbeat Country   Actor/Vocalist, Real Name Bill Maynard from the UK

1	Heartbeat	(Mmm Mmm 01cd)	75	1994	0	1994	

Hearts   R&B Vocal Group from the USA

1	Lonely Nights		0	1955	8 +	1955	(Baton 208)

Heather Nova   Female Vocalist from Bermuda

1	Walk This World	(Butterfly Bfld 19)	69	1995	0	1995	

ISSUE	TITLE	UK LBL	UK POS	UK YEAR	US POS	US YEAR	US LBL

Heatwave Mixed Vocal/Instrumental Group from the USA/UK   Group Formed By Brothers Keith And Johnnie Wilder

* 1	Boogie Nights	(GTO GT 77)	2	1977	2	1977	(Epic 50370)
2	Too Hot To Handle / Slip Your Disc To This	(GTO GT 91)	15	1977	0	1977	
* 3	The Groove Line	(GTO GT 115)	12	1978	7	1978	(Epic 50524)
* 4	Always And Forever		0	1978	18	978	(Epic 50490)
5	Mind Blowing Decisions	(GTO GT 226)	12	1978	0	1978	
6	Always And Forever / Mind Blowing Decisions (Re-Mix)	(GTO GT 236)	9	1978	0	1978	
7	Razzle Dazzle	(GTO GT 248)	23	1979	0	1979	
8	Gangsters Of The Groove	(GTO GT 285)	19	1981	0	1981	
9	Jitter Buggin'	(GTO GT 290)	34	1981	0	1981	
10	Mind Blowing Decisions (Re-Issue	(Brothers Organisation HW 1)	65	1990	0	1990	

HIT 6 IS THE EXTENDED RE-MIX VERSION   JOHNNIE WAS INVOLVED IN A SERIOUS CAR ACCIDENT IN 1979 AND IS NOW SADLY A PARAPLEGIC

Heaven 17 Male Vocal/Instrumental Group from the UK

1	(We Don't Need This) Fascist Groove Thang	(Virgin VS 400)	45	1981	0	1981	
2	Play To Win	(Virgin VS 433)	46	1981	0	1981	
3	Penthouse And Pavement	(Virgin VS 455)	57	1981	0	1981	
4	Let Me Go	(Virgin VS 532)	41	1982	0	1982	
5	Temptation	(Virgin VS 570)	2	1983	0	1983	
6	Come Live With Me	(Virgin VS 607)	5	1983	0	1983	
7	Crushed By The Wheels Of Industry	(Virgin VS 628)	17	1983	0	1983	
8	Sunset Now	(Virgin VS 708)	24	1984	0	1984	
9	This Is Mine	(Virgin VS 722)	23	1984	0	1984	
10	...(And That's No Lie)	(Virgin VS 740)	52	1985	0	1985	
11	Trouble	(Virgin VS 920)	51	1987	0	1987	
12	Temptation (Re-Mix)	(Virgin VS 1446)	4	1992	0	1992	
13	(We Don't Need This) Facist Groove Thang	(Virgin Vscdt 1451)	40	1993	0	1993	
14	Penthouse And Pavement (Re-Mix)	(Virgin Vscdt 1457)	54	1993	0	1993	

HIT 13 IS A RE-RECORDING • SEE ALSO GIMME SHELTER (EP), VARIOUS ARTISTS (EP, LP, 78S)

Heavy D. & The Boyz Male Vocal/Instrumental Group from the USA/Jamaica

1	Mr. Big Stuff	(MCA MCA 1106)	65	1986	0	1986	
2	We Got Our Own Thang	(MCA MCA 23942)	69	1989	0	1989	
* 3	Now That We Found Love	(MCA MCS 1550)	2	1991	11	1991	(Uptown/MCA 54090)
4	Is It Good For You	(MCA MCS 1564)	46	1991	32	1991	(Uptown/MCA 54200)
5	Got Me Waiting		0	1994	20	1994	(Uptown/Mca 54815)
6	Nuttin' But Love		0	1994	40	1994	(Uptown/MVCA 54865)
7	This Is Your Right	(MCA Mcstd 2010)	30	1994	0	1994	
8	Big Daddy		0	1997	18	1997	(Universal 56039)

HIT 8 IS CREDITED TO HEAVY D. • NAMES: DWIGHT MEYERS, GLEN PARRISH, TROY DIXSON & EDWARD FERRELL • OBITUARY : TROY D: 15 JUL 1990 ACCIDENTAL FALL

Heavy Pettin' Male Vocal/Instrumental Group from the UK

1	Love Times Love	(Polydor Hep 3)	69	1984	0	1984	

Heavy Stereo Male Vocal/Instrumental Group from the UK

1	Sleep Freak	(Creation Crescd 203)	46	1995	0	1995	
2	Smiler	(Creation Crescd 213)	46	1995	0	1995	
3	Chinese Burn	(Creation Crescd 218)	45	1996	0	1996	
4	Mouse In A Hole	(Creation Crescd 230)	53	1996	0	1996	

Heavy Weather Male Vocalist Peter Lee from the USA

1	Love Can't Turn Around	(Pukka Cdpukka 6)	56	1996	0	1996	

Hed Boys Male Production/Instrumental Duo from the UK

1	Girls + Boys	(Deconstruction 74321223322)	21	1994	0	1994	
2	Girls + Boys (Re-Mix)	(Deconstruction 74321322032)	36	1995	0	1995	

Hedgehoppers Anonymous Male Vocal/Instrumental Group from the UK

1	It's Good News Week	(Decca F 12241)	5	1965	0	1965	

Hedva & David

* 1	I Dream Of Naomi		0	1971	0	1971	

Heidi Bruhl Actress/Vocalist, B: 30 Jan 1942 from Germany

* 1	Wir Wollen Neimals Auseinandergeh'n (We Will Never Part)		0	1960	0		1960

Heights Cast Members Of The TV Show Heights from the USA

* 1	How Do You Talk To An Angel		0	1992	1	1992	(Capitol 44890)

Heintje Boy Vocalist B: 12 Aug 1956 Bleijerheide, South Holland

* 1	Du Sollst Nicht Weinen (You Shouldn't Cry)		0	1967	0	1967	
* 2	Mama		0	1967	0	1967	

ISSUE	TITLE	UK LBL	UK POS	UK YEAR	US POS	US YEAR	US LBL
* 3	Heidschi Bumbeidschi		0	1968	0	1968	
	BOTH 1967 AND 1968 HITS WERE NUMBER 1 IN GERMANY						
Heinz	Male Vocalist from the UK						
1	Just Like Eddie	(Decca F 11693)	5	1963	0	1963	
2	Country Boy	(Decca F 11768)	26	1963	0	1963	
3	You Were There	(Decca F 11831)	26	1964	0	1964	
4	Questions I Can't Answer	(Columbia Db 7374)	39	1964	0	1964	
5	Digging My Potatoes	(Columbia Db 7482)	49	1965	0	1965	
Helen Carroll	Female Vocalist from the USA						
1	Ole Buttermilk Sky (From *Canyon Passage*)		0	1946	7	1946	(RCA Victor 1982)
2	Cruising Down The River		0	1949	29	1949	(Mercury 5249)
Helen Forrest	Female Vocalist from the USA						
5	I'll Buy That Dream		0	1945	2	1945	(Decca 23434)
6	Some Sunday Morning		0	1945	9	1945	(Decca 23434)
7	I'm Always Chasing Rainbows (From Oh Look!)		0	1946	7	1946	(Decca 23472)
8	Oh! What It Seemed To Be		0	1946	4	1946	(Decca 23481)
9	Come Rain Or Come Shine (From St.Louis Women)		0	1946	23	1946	(Decca 23548)
10	In Love In Vain (From Centennial Summer)		0	1946	12	1946	(Decca 23528)
11	Why Does It Get So Late So Early		0	1946	22	1946	(Decca 23611)
	SHE ALSO WORKED WITH HARRY JAMES AND BENNY GOODMAN • SEE ALSO DICK HAYMES • HIT 6 IS WITH THE GORDON JENKINS ORCHESTRA						
	HITS 1, 3-11 ARE CREDITED TO HELEN FORREST AND DICK HAYMES • HITS 1, 3, 4 ARE WITH THE VICTOR YOUNG ORCHESTRA						
Helen Grayco	Female Vocalist, Wife Of Spike Jones from the USA						
1	Oop Shoop		0	1954	24	1954	(X 0051)
2	Teach Me Tonight		0	1954	29	1954	(X 0051)
Helen O'Connell	Female Vocalist from the USA						
1	Would I Love You (Love You, Love You)		0	1951	16	1951	(Capitol 1368)
2	Slow Poke		0	1951	8	1951	(Capitol 1837)
3	Be Anything (But Be Mine)		0	1952	27	1952	(Capitol 2011)
4	Water Can't Quench The Fire Of Love		0	1952	21	1952	(Capitol 2266)
5	Lipstick-A-Powder-'N Paint		0	1953	25	1953	(Capitol 2404)
Helen Reddy	Female Vocalist, B: 25 Oct 1942 Melbourne, Australia						
1	I Don't Know How To Love Him		0	1971	6	1971	(Capitol 3027)
* 2	I Am Woman		0	1972	1	1972	(Capitol 3350)
3	Peaceful		0	1973	4	1973	(Capitol 3527)
* 4	Delta Dawn		0	1973	1	1973	(Capitol 3645)
* 5	Leave Me Alone (Ruby Red Dress)		0	1973	12	1973	(Capitol 3768)
6	Keep On Singing		0	1974	9	1974	(Capitol 3845)
7	You And Me Against The World		0	1974	8	1974	(Capitol 3897)
* 8	Angie Baby	(Capitol Cl 15799)	5	1975	1	1974	(Capitol 3972)
9	Emotion		0	1975	22	1975	(Capitol 4021)
10	Bluebird		0	1975	35	1975	(Capitol 4108)
11	Ain't No Way To Treat A Lady		0	1975	9	1975	(Capitol 4128)
12	Somewhere In The Night		0	1975	19	1975	(Capitol 4192)
13	I Can't Hear You No More		0	1976	29	1976	(Capitol 4312)
14	Music Is My Life		0	1976	29	1976	(Capitol 4312)
15	You're My World		0	1977	18	1977	(Capitol 4418)
16	I Can't Say Goodbye To You	(MCA 744)	43	1981	0	1981	
Helen Shapiro	Female Vocalist, B: 28 Sep 1946 East End, London, England						
1	Don't Treat Me Like A Child	(Columbia Db 4589)	3	1961	0	1961	
* 2	You Don't Know	(Columbia Db 4670)	1	1961	0	1961	
* 3	Walkin' Back To Happiness	(Columbia Db 4715)	1	1961	0	1961	
4	Tell Me What He Said	(Columbia Db 4782)	2	1962	0	1962	
5	Let's Talk About Love	(Columbia Db 4824)	23	1962	0	1962	
6	Little Miss Lonely	(Columbia Db 4869)	8	1962	0	1962	
7	Keep Away From Other Girls	(Columbia Db 4908)	40	1962	0	1962	
8	Queen For Tonight	(Columbia Db 4966)	33	1963	0	1963	
9	Woe Is Me	(Columbia Db 7026)	35	1963	0	1963	
10	Look Who It Is	(Columbia Db 7130)	47	1963	0	1963	
11	Fever	(Columbia Db 7190)	38	1964	0	1964	
Helen Terry	Female Vocalist from the UK						
1	Love Lies Lost	(Virgin Vs 678)	34	1984	0	1984	
Helen Ward	Female Vocalist from the USA						
1	You Brought A New Kind Of Love To Me		0	1953	30	1953	(Columbia 49709)

ISSUE	TITLE	UK LBL	UK POS	UK YEAR	US POS	US YEAR	US LBL
Helene Dixon							
1	The Breeze (That's Bringin' My Honey Back To Me)		0	1953	21	1953	(Okeh 6964)
2	Don't Call My Name		0	1953	27	1953	(Okeh 6964)
Helicopter Male Production/Instrumental Duo from the UK							
1	On Ya Way	(Helicopter Tig 007cd)	32	1994	0	1994	
2	On Ya Way (Re-Mix)	(Systematic Syscd 27)	37	1996	0	1996	
Heliocentric World Mixed Vocal/Instrumental Group from the UK							
1	Where's Your Love Been	(Talkin' Loud Tlkcd 51)	71	1995	0	1995	
Heller & Farley Project Male Instrumental/Production Duo from the UK							
1	Ultra Flava	(Am:Pm 5814372)	22	1996	0	1996	
2	Ultra Flava (Re-Mix)	(Am:Pm 5820552)	32	1996	0	1996	
Hello Male Vocal/Instrumental Group from the UK							
1	Tell Him	(Bell 1377)	9	1974	0	1974	
2	New York Groove	(Bell 1438)	9	1975	0	1975	
Helloween Male Vocal/Instrumental Group from the USA							
1	Dr. Stein	(Noise International 7hello 1)	57	1988	0	1988	
2	I Want Out	(Noise International 7hello 2)	69	1988	0	1988	
3	Kids Of The Century	(EMI EM 178)	56	1991	0	1991	
Helmut Zacharias & His Magic Violins Male Violinist And Orchestra from Germany							
1	When The White Lilacs Bloom Again		0	1956	12	1956	(Decca 30039)
2	Tokyo Melody	(Polydor Ynh 52341)	9	1964	0	1964	
Heltah Skeltah & Originoo Gunn Clappaz As The Fabulous Five Male Vocal/Instrumental Duo from the USA							
1	Blah	(Priority Ptycd 117)	60	1996	0	1996	
Henri Rene & His Orchestra Male Bandleader/Arranger/Conductor, Raised In Germany							
3	Toolie Oolie Doolie (The Yodel Polka)		0	1948	30	1948	(RCA Victor 1114)
4	The Song From *Moulin Rouge* (Where Is Your Heart)		0	1953	24	1953	(RCA Victor 5264)
Henry Gross Male Vocalist From Brooklyn, Was Originally Lead Guitar With Sha-Na-Na							
1	Shannon	(Lifesong Els 45002)	32	1976	6	1976	(Lifesong 45002)
2	Springtime Mama		0	1976	37	1976	(Lifesong 45008)
Henry Jerome Orchestra Male Composer/Bandleader From New York							
1	Here's To The Ladies		0	1953	22	1953	(MGM 11526)
2	Tipica Serenade		0	1953	21	1953	(MGM 11594)
Henry King Orchestra Male Pianist/Bandleader from the USA							
14	Baby Face		0	1948	14	1948	(Decca 25356)
	VOCALS ON HIT 14 ARE BY SIGGY LANE						
Henry Lee Summer Rock Singer From Indiana							
1	I Wish I Had A Girl		0	1988	20	1988	(CBS Assoc. 07720)
2	Hey Baby		0	1989	18	1989	(CBSAssoc. 68891)
Henry Mancini & His Orchestra Male Orchestra Leader, B: 16 Apr 1924 Cleveland							
1	Mr. Lucky		0	1960	21	1960	(RCA 7705)
2	Moon River (From Breakfast At Tiffany's)	(RCA 1256)	46	1961	11	1961	(RCA 7916)
3	Moon River (Re-Entry)	(RCA 1256)	44	1961	32	1962	(RCA 7916)
4	Days Of Wine And Roses		0	1963	33	1963	(RCA 8120)
5	Charade		0	1964	36	1964	(RCA 8256)
6	The 'Pink Panther' Theme		0	1964	31	1964	(RCA 8286)
7	How Soon	(RCA 1414)	10	1964	0	1964	
* 8	Love Theme From *Romeo And Juliet*		0	1969	1	1969	(RCA 0131)
9	Theme From Love Story		0	1971	13	1971	(RCA 9927)
10	Theme From Cade's Country	(RCA 2182)	42	1972	0	1972	
11	Theme From The Thornbirds	(Warner Bros 9677)	23	1984	0	1984	
	THE HIT 'ROMEO AND JULIET' SOLD OVER 200,000 COPIES IN ONE WEEK						
Henson Cargill Male Country Singer, B: 5 Feb 1941 Oklahoma City							
1	Skip A Rope		0	1968	25	1968	(Monument 1041)
	REST OF THE HITS ARE C/W						
Herb Alpert Male Trumpeter/Bandleader, B: 31 Mar 1935 Los Angeles							
* 1	The Lonely Bull	(Stateside Ss 138)	22	1963	6	1962	(A&M 703)
2	Taste Of Honey		0	1965	7	1965	(A&M 775)
3	Zorba The Greek		0	1966	11	1966	(A&M 787)
* 4	Spanish Flea	(Pye International 7 N 25335)	3	1965	27	1966	(A&M 792)
5	Tijuana Taxi	(Pye International 7 N 25352)	37	1963	38	1966	(A&M 787)

ISSUE	TITLE	UK LBL	UK POS	UK YEAR	US POS	US YEAR	US LBL
6	What Now My Love		0	1966	24	1966	(A&M 792)
7	The Work Song		0	1966	18	1966	(A&M 805)
8	Flamingo		0	1966	28	1966	(A&M 813)
9	Mame		0	1966	19	1966	(A&M 823)
10	Wade In The Water		0	1967	37	1967	(A&M 840)
11	The Happening		0	1967	32	1967	(A&M 860)
12	Keep Your Eye On Me	(Breakout USA 602	19	1987	0	1987	
13	Casino Royale	(A&M Ams 700)	27	1967	27	1967	(A&M 850)
14	A Banda		0	1967	35	1967	(A&M 870)
* 15	This Guy's In Love With You	(A&M Ams 727)	3	1968	1	1968	(A&M 929)
16	This Guy's In Love With You (Re-Entry)	(A&M Ams 727)	47	1969	0	1969	
17	This Guy's In Love With You (2nd Re-Entry)	(A&M Ams 727)	49	1969	0	1969	
18	This Guy's In Love With You (3rd Re-Entry)	(A&M Ams 727)	50	1969	0	1969	
19	Without Her	(A&M Ams 755)	36	1969	0	1969	
20	Jerusalem	(A&M Ams 810)	47	1970	0	1970	
21	Jerusalem (Re-Entry)	(A&M Ams 810)	42	1971	0	1971	
22	Rise	(A&M Ams 7465)	13	1979	1	1979	(A&M 2151)
23	Rotation	(A&M Ams 7500	46	1980	30	1979	(A&M 2202)
24	Route 101		0	1982	37	1982	(A&M 2422)
25	Diamonds	(Breakout US 605)	27	1987	5	1987	(A&M 2929)
26	Making Love In The Rain		0	1987	35	1987	(A&M 2949)

HITS 2-11, 14 ARE CREDITED TO HERB ALPERT & THE TIJUANA BRASS • VOCALS ON HIT 26 ARE FROM LISA KEITH
HIT 1 IS CREDITED TO TIJUANA BRASS FEATURING HERB ALPERT

Herb Jeffries Male Vocalist (Baritone) from the USA

ISSUE	TITLE	UK LBL	UK POS	UK YEAR	US POS	US YEAR	US LBL
1	When I Write My Song		0	1947	21	1947	(Exclusive 16)
2	The Four Winds And The Seven Seas		0	1949	18	1949	(Columbia 38511)

Herbie Fields Orchestra Male Orchestra Leader/Saxophonist from the USA

ISSUE	TITLE	UK LBL	UK POS	UK YEAR	US POS	US YEAR	US LBL
1	A-Huggun' And A-Kissin'		0	1947	14	1947	(RCA Victor 2036)
2	Connecticut		0	1947	26	1947	(RCA Victor 2104)
3	Harlem Nocturne		0	1953	24	1953	(Parrot 775)

OBITUARY : D: 17 SEP 1958 COMMITED SUICIDE. (AGED 39).

Herbie Hancock Male Vocal/Instrumentalist (Keyboards) from the UK

ISSUE	TITLE	UK LBL	UK POS	UK YEAR	US POS	US YEAR	US LBL
1	I Thought It Was You	(CBS 6530)	15	1978	0	1978	
2	You Bet Your Love	(CBS 7010)	18	1979	0	1979	
3	Rockit	(CBS A 3577)	8	1983	0	1983	
4	Auto Drive	(CBS A 3802)	33	1983	0	1983	
5	Future Shock	(CBS A 4075)	54	1974	0	1974	
6	Hardrock	(CBS A 4616)	65	1984	0	1984	

Herbie Mann Real Name Herbert Jay Solomon B: 16 Apr 1930 Brooklyn

ISSUE	TITLE	UK LBL	UK POS	UK YEAR	US POS	US YEAR	US LBL
1	Hijack		0	1975	14	1975	(Atlantic 3246)
2	Superman		0	1979	26	1979	(Atlantic 3547)

Herd Male Vocal/Instrumental Group from the UK

ISSUE	TITLE	UK LBL	UK POS	UK YEAR	US POS	US YEAR	US LBL
1	From The Underworld	(Fontana Tf 856)	6	1967	0	1967	
2	Paradise Lost	(Fontana Tf 887)	15	1967	0	1967	
3	I Don't Want Our Loving To Die	(Fontana Tf 925)	5	1968	0	1968	

Herman Brood Rock Band Leader, B: 5 Nov 1946 Zwolle, Holland

ISSUE	TITLE	UK LBL	UK POS	UK YEAR	US POS	US YEAR	US LBL
1	Saturday Night		0	1979	35	1979	(Ariola 7754)

Herman's Hermits Male Vocal/Instrumental Group from the UK

ISSUE	TITLE	UK LBL	UK POS	UK YEAR	US POS	US YEAR	US LBL
1	I'm In To Something Good	(Columbia Db 7338	1	1964	13	1964	(MGM 13280)
2	Show Me Girl	(Columbia Db 7408)	19	1964	0	1964	
* 3	Silhouettes	(Columbia Db 7475)	3	1965	5	1965	(MGM 13332)
* 4	Can't You Hear My Heartbeat		0	1965	2	1965	(MGM 13310)
* 5	Wonderful World	(Columbia Db 7546)	7	1965	4	1965	(MGM 13354)
* 6	Mrs. Brown You've Got A Lovely Daughter		0	1965	1	1965	(MGM 13341)
*7	I'm Henry Viii I Am		0	1965	1	1965	(MGM 13367)
* 8	Just A Little Bit Better	(Columbia Db 7670)	15	1965	7	1965	(MGM 13398)
9	A Must To Avoid (From Hold On)	(Columbia Db 7791)	6	1965	8	1965	(MGM 13437)
* 10	Listen People (From When The Boys Meet The Girls)		0	1966	3	1966	(MGM 13462)
11	You Won't Be Leaving	(Columbia Db 7861)	20	1966	0	1966	
12	Leaning On A Lamp Post (From Hold On)		0	1966	9	1966	(MGM 13500)
13	This Door Swings Both Ways	(Columbia Db 7947)	18	1966	12	1966	(MGM 13548)
14	No Milk Today	(Columbia Db 8012)	7	1966	35	1966	(MGM 13681)
15	Dandy		0	1966	5	1966	(MGM 13603)
16	East West	(Columbia Db 8076)	37	1966	27	1966	(MGM 13639)

ISSUE	TITLE	UK LBL	UK POS	UK YEAR	US POS	US YEAR	US LBL
* 17	There's A Kind Of Hush	(Columbia Db 8123)	7	1967	4	1967	(MGM 13681)
18	Don't Go Out In The Rain (You're Going To Melt)		0	1967	18	1967	(MGM 13761)
19	Museum		0	1967	39	1967	(MGM 13787)
20	I Can Take Or Leave Your Loving	(Columbia Db 8327)	11	1968	22	1968	(MGM 13885)
21	Sleepy Joe	(Columbia Db 8404)	12	1968	0	1968	
22	Sunshine Girl	(Columbia Db 8446)	8	1968	0	1968	
23	Something's Happening	(Columbia Db 8504)	6	1968	0	1968	
24	My Sentimental Friend	(Columbia Db 8563)	2	1969	0	1969	
25	Here Comes The Star	(Columbia Db 8626)	33	1969	0	1969	
26	Years May Come, Years May Go	(Columbia Db 8656)	7	1970	0	1970	
27	Years May Come, Years May Go (Re-Entry)	(Columbia Db 8656)	45	1970	0	1970	
28	Bet Yer Life I Do	(Rak 102)	22	1970	0	1970	
29	Lady Barbar	(Rak 101)	13	1970	0	1970	

Hernandez Male Vocalist from the UK

1	All My Love	(Epic Her 1)	58	1989	0	1989	

Herreys Male Vocal Group from Sweden

1	Diggi Loo-Diggi Ley	(Panther Pan 5	46	1984	0	1984	

Hesitations Soul Group From Cleveland With Lead Singer George 'King' Scott

1	Born Free		0	1968	38	1968	(Kapp 878)

OBITUARY : SCOTT D: FEB 1968 ACCIDENTALLY SHOT BY FRED DEAL.

Hi Gloss Male Disco Group from the USA

1	You'll Never Know	(Epic Epc A 1387)	12	1981	0	1981	

Hi Power Male Rap Group from Germany

1	Cult Of Snap / Simba Groove	(Rumour Rumat 24)	73	1990	0	1990	

Hi Tension Male Vocal/Instrumental Group from the UK

1	Hi Tension	(Island Wip 6422)	13	1978	0	1978	
2	British Hustle	(Island Wip 6446)	8	1978	0	1978	

Hi-Five Male Vocal Quartet from the USA

* 1	I Like The Way (The Kissing Game)	(Jive Jive 271)	43	1991	1	991	(Jive 1424)
2	I Can't Wait Another Minute		0	1991	8	1991	(Jive 1445)
3	She's Playing Hard To Get	(Jive Jive 316)	55	1992	5	1992	(Jive 42067)
4	Quality Time		0	1993	38	1993	(Jive 42109)
5	Never Should've Let You Go		0	1993	30	1993	(Jive 42178)Names Tony

THOMPSON, RODERICK CLARK, RUSSELL NEAL, MARCUS SANDERS & TORIANO EASLEY WHO HAS SINCE LEFT

Hi-Los Male Vocal Quartet, Don Shelton, Clark Burroughs, Gene Puerling & Bob Mors from the USA

1	My Baby Just Cares For Me		0	1954	29	1954	(Trend 74)

Hi-Lux Male Instrumental/Production Duo from the UK

1	Feel It	(Cheeky Chekk 006)	41	1995	0	1995	
2	Never Felt This Way	(Champion Champcd 319)	58	1995	0	1995	

Hi-Tek 3 Mixed Vocal/Instrumental Group from Belgium

1	Spin That Wheel	(Brothers Organisation Borg 1)	69	1990	0	1990	
2	Spin That Wheel (Turtles Get Real) (Re-Issue)	(Brothers Organisation Borg 16)	15	1990	0	1990	

HITS 1-2 ARE CREDITED TO HI-TEK 3 FEATURING YA KID • SEE ALSO TECHNOTRONIC

High Male Vocal Group from the UK

1	Up And Down	(London Lon 272)	53	1990	0	1990	
2	Take Your Time	(London Lon 280)	56	1990	0	1990	
3	Box Set Go	(London Long 286)	28	1991	0	1991	
4	More...	(London Lon 297)	67	1991	0	1991	

High Inergy Female Group fom Passadena, California   Names Barbara And Vernessa Mitchell, Linda Howard & Michelle Rumph

1	You Can't Turn Me Off (In The Middle Of Turning Me On)		0	1977	12	1977	(Gordy 7155)

High Numbers Male Vocal/Instrumental Group from the UK

1	I'm The Face	(Back Door Door 4)	49	1980	0	1980	

NAMES ROGER DALTREY, PETE TOWNSHEND, JOHN ENTWISTLE, KEITH MOON • SEE ALSO THEWHO

High Society Male Vocal/Instrumental Group from the UK

1	I Never Go Out In The Rain	(Eagle Ers 002)	53	1980	0	1980	

Highlights Names Frank Pizani, Frank & Tony Calzaretta, Jerry Oleski & Bill Melshimer

1	City Of Angels		0	1956	19	1956	(Bally 1016)

Highly Likely Male Vocal/Instrumental Group from the UK

1	Whatever Happened To You (*Likely Lads Theme*)	(BBC Resl 10)	35	1973	0	1973	

Highwaymen Male Vocal Group, Bob Burnett, Steve Trott, Dave Fisher, Steve Butts & Chan Daniels

* 1	Michael	(HMV Pop 910)	1	1961	1	1961	(United Artists 258)

ISSUE	TITLE	UK LBL	UK POS	UK YEAR	US POS	US YEAR	US LBL
2	Gypsy Rover	(HMV Pop 948)	41	1961	0	1961	
3	Cotton Fields		0	1961	13	1961	(United Artists 370)
4	Gypsy Rover (Re-Entry)	(HMV Pop 948)	43	1962	0	1962	

OBITUARY : CHAN D: 2 AUG 1975

Hijack Male Producer from the UK

1	The Badman Is Robbin'	(Rhyme Syndicate 655517 7)	56	1990	0	1990	

Hildegarde Real Name, Hildegarde Loretta Sell, Vocalist from the USA

1	Pennies From Heaven (Movie Title Song)		0	1936	16	1936	(Columbia 1598)
2	Darling, Je Vous Aime Beaucoup		0	1943	21	1943	(Decca 23218)
3	Leave Us Face It (We're In Love)		0	1944	29	1944	(Decca 23297)
4	Suddenly It's Spring (From Lady In The Dark)		0	1944	15	1944	(Decca 23297)
5	June Is Bustin' Out All Over (From Carousel)		0	1945	11	1945	(Decca 23428)
6	One-Zy, Two-Zy (I Love You-Zy)		0	1946	15	1946	(Decca 23511)
7	The Gypsy		0	1946	7	1946	(Decca 23511)

HITS 5-7 ARE WITH GUY LOMBARDO & HIS ROYAL CANADIANS

Hillside Singers The Group Consisted Of Nine Members

* 1	I'd Like To Teach The World To Sing (In Perfect Harmony)		0	1971	13	1971	(Metromedia 231)

THE HIT WAS RELEASED BEFORE THE NEW SEEKERS' VERSION

Hilltoppers Male Vocal Group from the USA , Jimmy Sacca, Don McGuire, Seymour Spiegelman, Billy Vaughn Formed In Western Centre College In Kentucky In 1952

1	Trying		0	1952	7	1952	(Dot 15018)
2	I Keep Telling Myself		0	1953	26	1953	(Dot 15034)
3	Must I Cry Again		0	1953	15	1953	(Dot 15034)
4	If I Were King		0	1953	22	1953	(Dot 15055)
5	I'd Rather Die Young		0	1953	8	1953	(Dot 15085)
* 6	P.S. I Love You		0	1953	4	1953	(Dot 15085)
7	To Be Alone		0	1953	8	1953	(Dot 15105)
8	Love Walked In (From The Goldwyn Follies)		0	1953	8	1953	(Dot 15105)
9	Time Will Tell		0	1954	27	1954	(Dot 15127)
10	From The Wine Came The Grape		0	1954	2	1954	(Dot 15127)
11	Till Then		0	1954	10	1954	(Dot 15132)
12	Poor Butterfly (From The Big Show)		0	1954	12	1954	(Dot 15156)
13	Sweetheart (Will You Remember)		0	1954	24	1954	(Dot 15201)
14	If I Didn't Care		0	1954	17	1954	(Dot 15220)
15	Time Waits For No One (From Shine On, Harvest Moon)		0	1954	25	1954	(Dot 15249)
16	Kentuckian Song		0	1955	20	1955	(Dot 15375)
17	Only You	(London Hld 8221)	3	1956	8	1955	(Dot 15423)
18	My Treasure		0	1956	31	1956	(Dot 15437)
19	Ka-Ding-Dong		0	1956	38	1956	(Dot 15489)
20	Only You (Re-Entry)	(London Hld 8221)	24	1956	0	1956	
21	Tryin'	(London Hld 8298)	24	1956	0	1956	
22	Marianne	(London Hld 8381)	20	1957	3	1957	(Dot 15537)
23	Marianne (Re-Entry)	(London Hld 8381)	23	1957	0	1957	
24	The Joker (That's What They Call Me)		0	1957	22	1957	(Dot 15662)

BILLY LEFT TO BECOME A MUSICAL DIRECTOR IN 1955 • HIT 16 IS CREDITED TO HILLTOPPERS FEATURING JIMMY SACCA
THEY FORMED IN WESTERN CENTRE COLLEGE IN KENTUCKY IN 1952)

Hipsway Male Vocal/Instrumental Group from the UK

1	The Broken Years	(Mercury Mer 193)	72	1985	0	1985	
2	Ask The Lord	(Mercury Mer 195)	72	1985	0	1985	
3	The Honeythief	(Mercury Mer 212)	17	1986	19	1987	(Columbia 06579)
4	Ask The Lord (Re-Recording)	(Mercury Lord 1)	50	1986	0	1986	
5	Long White Car	(Mercury Mer 230)	55	1986	0	1986	
6	Your Love	(Mercury Mer 279)	66	1989	0	1989	

LEAD SINGER OF THE QUARTET IS GRAHAME SKINNER

History Mixed Rap Group from the USA

1	Afrika	(Sbk Sbk 7008)	42	1990	0	1990	

HIT IS CREDITED TO HISTORY FEATURING Q-TEE

Hithouse Male Producer, Real Name Peter Slaghuis From Holland

1	Jack To The Sound Of The Underground	(Supreme Supe 137)	14	1988	0	1988	
2	Move Your Feet To The Rhythm Of The Beat	(Supreme Supe 149)	69	1989	0	1989	

Hoagy Carmichael Male Actor/Composer/Vocalist, B: 22 Nov 1899 Bloomington, Indiana

4	Hong Kong Blues (From To Have And Have Not)		0	1945	6	1945	(Ara 123)
5	Doctor, Lawyer, Indian Chief (From Stork Club)		0	1946	18	1946	(Ara 126)
6	Ole Buttermilk Sky (From Canyon Passage)		0	1946	2	1946	(Ara 155)

ISSUE	TITLE	UK LBL	UK POS	UK YEAR	US POS	US YEAR	US LBL
7	Huggin' And Chalkin'		0	1946	1	1946	(Decca 23675)
8	The Old Piano Roll Blues		0	1950	11	1950	(Decca 24977)
9	The Aba Daba Honeymoon (From *Two Weeks With Love*)		0	1951	23	1951	(Decca 27474)

VOCALS ON HIT 2 ARE BY LOUIS ARMSTRONG AND HOAGY CARMICHAEL • VOCALS ON HIT 3 ARE BY HOAGY CARMICHAEL AND ELLA LOGAN
OBITUARY : D: 27 DEC 1981, (AGED 82)

Hole   Mixed Vocal/Instrumental Group from the USA

ISSUE	TITLE	UK LBL	UK POS	UK YEAR	US POS	US YEAR	US LBL
1	Beautiful Son	(City Slang Efa 0491603)	54	1993	0	1993	
2	Miss World	(City Slang Efa 049362)	64	1994	0	1994	
3	Doll Parts	(Geffen Gfstd 91)	16	1995	0	1995	
4	Violet	(Geffen Grstd 94)	17	1995	0	1995	

OBITUARY : CHAN D: 2 AUG 1975

Hole In One

ISSUE	TITLE	UK LBL	UK POS	UK YEAR	US POS	US YEAR	US LBL
1	Life's Too Short	(Manifesto Fescd 21)	36	1997	0	1997	

Holland-Dozier (Featuring) Lamont Dozier   Male Songwriter/Vocal Duo from the USA

ISSUE	TITLE	UK LBL	UK POS	UK YEAR	US POS	US YEAR	US LBL
1	Why Can't We Be Lovers	(Invictus Inv 525)	29	1972	0	1972	

Hollies   Male Vocal/Instrumental Group from the UK

ISSUE	TITLE	UK LBL	UK POS	UK YEAR	US POS	US YEAR	US LBL
1	Just Like Me	(Parlophone 5030)	25	1963	0	1963	
2	Searchin'	(Parlophone R 5052)	12	1963	0	1966	
3	Stay	(Parlophone R 5077)	8	1963	0	1966	
4	Just One Look	(Parlophone R 5104)	2	1964	0	1964	
5	Here I Go Again	(Parlophone R 5137)	4	1964	0	1964	
6	We're Through	(Parlophone R 5178)	8	1964	0	1964	
7	Yes I Will	(Parlophone R 5232)	7	1965	0	1965	
8	I'm Alive	(Parlophone R 5287	1	1965	0	1966	
9	Look Through Any Window	(Parlophone R 5322)	4	19653	2	1965	(Imperial 66134)
10	If I Needed Someone	(Parlophone R 392)	20	1965	0	1965	
* 11	I Can't Let Go	(Parlophone R 5409)	2	1966	0	1966	
12	Bus Stop	(Parlophone R 5469)	5	1966	5	1966	(Imperial 66186)
* 13	Stop Stop Stop	(Parlophone R 5508)	2	1966	7	1966	(Imperial 66214)
* 14	On A Carousel	(Parlophone R 5562)	4	1967	11	1967	(Imperial 66231)
* 15	Carrie-Anne	(Parlophone R 5602)	3	1967	9	1967	(Epic 10180)
16	Pay You Back With Interest		0	1967	28	1967	(Imperial 66240)
17	King Midas In Reverse	(Parlophone R 5637)	18	1967	0	1967	
18	Jennifer Eccles	(Parlophone R 5680)	7	19684	0	1968	(Epic 10298)
19	Listen To Me	(Parlophone R 5733)	11	1968	0	1968	
20	Sorry Suzanne	(Parlophone R 5765)	3	1969	0	1969	
*21	He Ain't Heavy, He's My Brother	(Parlophone R 5806)	3	1969	7	1970	(Epic 10532)
22	I Can't Tell The Botton From The Top	(Parlophone R 5837)	7	1970	0	1970	
23	Gasoline Alley Bred	(Parlophone R 5862)	14	1970	0	1970	
24	Hey Willy	(Parlophone R 5905)	22	1971	0	1971	
25	The Baby	(Polydor 2058 199)	26	1972	0	1972	
* 26	Long Cool Woman In A Black Dress	(Parlophone R 5939)	32	1972	2	1972	(Epic 10871)
27	The Day That Curly Billy Shot Crazy Sam McGee	(Polydor 2058 403)	24	1973	0	1973	
28	Long Dark Road		0	1972	26	1972	(Epic 10920)
* 29	The Air That I Breathe	(Polydor 2058 435)	2	1974	6	1974	(Epic 11100)
30	Soldiers Song	(Polydor 2059 246)	58	1980	0	1980	
31	Holliedaze (Medley)	(EMI 5229)	28	1981	0	1981	
32	Stop In The Name Of Love		0	1983	29	1983	(Atlantic 89819)
33	He Ain't Heavy, He's My Brother (Re-Issue)	(EMI Em 74)	1	1988	0	1988	
34	The Air That I Breathe (Re-Issue)	(EMI Em 80)	60	1988	0	1988	
35	The Woman I Love	(EMI Cdem 264)	42	1993	0	1993	

NAMES ALLAN CLARK, GRAHAM NASH, TONY HICKS, ERIC HAYDOCK & DON RATHBONE
WERE THE FOURTONES, THEN THE DELTAS, WHICH BECAME THE HOLLIES IN 1962

Holly & The Ivys   Male Vocal/Instrumental Group from the UK

ISSUE	TITLE	UK LBL	UK POS	UK YEAR	US POS	US YEAR	US LBL
1	Christmas On 45	(Decca Santa 1)	40	1981	0	1981	

Holly Johnson   Male Vocalist from the UK

ISSUE	TITLE	UK LBL	UK POS	UK YEAR	US POS	US YEAR	US LBL
1	Love Train	(MCA MCA 1306)	4	1989	0	1989	
2	Americanos	(MCA MCA 1323)	4	1989	0	1989	
3	Ferry 'Cross The Mersey	(Pwl Pwl 41)	1	1989	0	1989	
4	Atomic City	(MCA MCA 1342)	18	989	0	1989	
5	Heaven's Here	(MCA MCA 1365)	62	1989	0	1989	
6	Where Has Love Gone	(MCA MCA 1460)	73	1990	0	1990	

Holly Sherwood   Female Vocalist from the USA

ISSUE	TITLE	UK LBL	UK POS	UK YEAR	US POS	US YEAR	US LBL
1	Day By Day	(Bell 1182)	29	1972	0	1972	

ISSUE	TITLE	UK LBL	UK POS	UK YEAR	US POS	US YEAR	US LBL
Hollywood Argyles	Male Vocal Group from the USA						
* 1	Alley-Oop	(London Hlu 9146)	24	1960	1	1960	(Lute 5905)
	Lead Singer Gary Paxton Is Also 'Flip' In Skip & Flip • The Hit Was Recorded By Gary Before He Formed The Group						
Hollywood Beyond	Male Vocalist from the UK						
1	What's The Colour Of Money?	(Wea Yz 76)	7	1986	0	1986	
	No More Tears	(Wea Yz 81)	47	1986	0	1986	
Hollywood Flames	Formed In 1950 By And See Also Bobby Day Group Was Also Known As The Flames, Four Flames, Satellites And The Hollywood Four Flames						
1	Buzz Buzz Buzz		0	1958	11	1958	(EBB 119)
Hombres	Male Vocal Quartet from Memphis						
1	Let It Out (Let It All Hang Out)		0	1967	12	1967	(Verve 5058)
	NAMES B.B. CUNNINGHAM, GARY MCEWEN, JOHNNY HUNTER, & JERRY MASTERS • OBITUARY :- HUNTER D: 1976.						
Homer & Jethro	Male Country/Vocal Comedy Duo From Knoxville, Tennessee						
2	Baby, It's Cold Outside (From Neptune's Daughter)		0	1949	22	1949	(RCA Victor 0078)
4	That Hound Dog In The Window		0	1953	17	1953	(RCA Victor 5280)
6	The Battle Of Kookamonga		0	1959	14	1959	(RCA 7585)
	NAMES HENRY 'HOMER' HAYNES B: 29 JUL 1917 & KENNETH 'JETHRO' BURNES B: 10 MAR 1917 • OBITUARY : HENRY D: 7 AUG 1971.						
Hondells	Lead Singer Of The Quartet Is Ritchie Burns						
1	Little Honda		0	1964	9	1964	(Mercury 72324)
Hondy							
1	Hondy (No Access)	(Manifesto Fescd 20)	26	1997	0	1997	
Honey Bane	Female Vocalist from the UK						
1	Turn Me On Turn Me Off	(Zonophone Z 15)	37	1981	0	1981	
2	Baby Love	(Zonophone Z 19)	58	1981	0	1981	
Honey Cone	Names Shelly Clark, Carolyn Willis & Edna Wright						
* 1	Want Ads		0	1971	1	1971	(Hot Wax 7011)
* 2	Stick-Up		0	1971	11	1971	(Hot Wax 7106)
3	One Monkey Don't Stop No Show (Part 1)		0	1972	15	1972	(Hot Wax 7110)
4	The Day I Found Myself		0	1972	23	1972	(Hot Wax 7113)
Honeybus	Male Vocal/Instrumental Group from the UK						
1	I Can't Let Maggie Go	(Deram Dm 182)	8	1968	0	1968	
Honeycombs	Male Vocal/Instrumental Group from the UK						
* 1	Have I The Right	(Pye 7n 15664)	1	1964	5	1964	(Interphon 7707)
2	Is It Because	(Pye 7n 15705)	38	1964	0	1964	
3	Something Better Beginning	(Pye 7n 15827)	39	1965	0	1965	
4	That's The Way	(Pye 7n 15890)	12	1965	0	1965	
	LEAD SINGER OF THE QUINTET IS DENNIS DALZIEL						
Honeycrack	Male Vocal/Instrumental Group from the UK						
1	Sitting At Home	(Epic 6625382	42	1995	0	1995	
2	Go Away	(Epic 6628642)	41	1996	0	1996	
3	King Of Misery	(Epic 6631472)	32	1996	0	1996	
4	Sitting At Home (Re-Issue)	(Epic 6635032)	32	1996	0	1996	
5	Anyway	(Eg Ego 52a)	67	1996	0	1996	
Honeydrippers	Male Vocal/Instrumental Group from the USA/UK Names Robert Plant, Jimmy Page, Jeff Beck & Nile Rodgers						
1	Sea Of Love	(Es Paranza Yz 33)	56	1985	3	1984	(Es Paranza 99701)
2	Rockin' At Midnight		0	1985	25	1985	(Es Paranza 99686)
Honeymoon Suite	Names: Dave Betts, Gary Lalonde, Johnnie Dee, Derry Grehan & Rob Preuss						
1	Feel It Again		0	1986	34	1986	(Warner Bros 28779)
Honky (1)	Male Vocal/Instrumental Group from the UK						
1	Join The Party	(Creole Cr 137)	28	1977	0	1977	
Honky (2)	Male Vocal/Instrumental Group from the UK						
1	The Honky Doodle Day (EP)	(Ztt Zang 45cd)	61	1993	0	1993	
2	The Whistler	(Ztt Zang 48cd)	41	1994	0	1994	
3	Hip Hop Don't Ya Drop	(Higher Ground Highs 1cd)	70	1996	0	1996	
4	What's Goin' Down	(Higher Ground Highs 2cd)	49	1996	0	1996	
Hooters	Male Vocal/Instrumental Rock Quintet from Philadelphia						
1	And We Danced		0	1985	21	1985	(Columbia 05568)
2	Day By Day		0	1986	18	1986	(Columbia 05730)
3	Where Do The Children Go		0	1986	38	1986	(Columbia 05854)
4	Satellite	(CBS 651168 7)	22	1987	0	1987	

ISSUE	TITLE	UK LBL	UK POS	UK YEAR	US POS	US YEAR	US LBL
Hootie & The Blowfish Male Vocal/Instrumental Group, Lead Vocals Darius Rucker from South Carolina							
1	Hold My Hand	(Atlantic A 7230cd)	50	1995	10	1995	(Atlantic 87230)
2	Let Her Cry	(Atlantic A 7188cd)	75	1995	9	1995	(Atlantic 87231)
3	Only Wanna Be With You		0	1996	6	1995	(Atlantic 87132)
4	Time		0	1995	14	1995	(Atlantic 87095)
5	Tucker's Town		0	1996	38	1996	(Atlantic 87051)
6	Old Man And Me (When I Get To Heaven)	(Atlantic A 5513cd)	57	1996	13	1996	(Atlantic 87074)
Hope A.D. Male Producer, Real Name David Hope from the UK			See Also Mind Of Kane				
1	Tree Frog	(Sun-Up Sun 003cd)	73	1994	0	1994	
Horace Brown Male Vocalist from the USA							
1	Taste Your Love	(Uptown Mcstd 2026)	58	1995	0	1995	
2	One For The Money	(Motown 8605232)	12	1996	0	1996	
3	Things We Do For Love	(Motown 8605712)	27	1996	0	1996	
Horace Faith Male Vocalist from Jamaica							
1	Black Pearl	(Trojan Tr 7790)	13	1970	0	1970	
Horse Mixed Vocal/Instrumental Group from the UK							
1	Careful	(Capitol Cl 587)	52	1990	0	1990	
2	Shake This Mountain	(Oxygen Gaspd 7)	52	1993	0	1993	
3	God's Home Movie	(Oxygen Gasxd 10)	56	1993	0	1993	
4	Celebrate	(Oxygen Gaspd 11)	49	1994	0	1994	
5	Careful (Re-Issue)	(Stress Cdstrx 79)	44	1997	0	1997	
Horst Jankowski Male Pianist, B: 30 Jan 1936, Berlin, Germany							
* 1	A Walk In The Black Forest	(Mercury Mf 861)	3	1965	12	1965	(Mercury 72425)
	THE HIT SOLD OVER 250,000 IN THE UK ALONE						
Hot The Trio Was First Known As Sugar & Spice							
* 1	Angel In Your Arms		0	1977	6	1977	(Big Tree 16085)
	NAMES CATHY CARSON, GWEN OWENS & JUANITA CURIEL						
Hot Blood Male Instrumental Group From France							
1	Soul Dracula	(Creole Cr 132)	32	1976	0	1976	
Hot Butter Male Instrumentalist (Moog Synthesizer) from the USA							
1	Popcorn	(Pye International 7n 25583)	5	1972	9	1972	(Musicor 1458)
2	Popcorn (Re-Entry)	(Pye International 7n 25583)	50	1972	0	1972	
	HOT BUTTER IS STAN FREE						
Hot Chocolate Male Vocal/Instrumental Group from the UK							
1	Love Is Life	(RAK 103)	6	1970	0	1970	
2	You Could've Been A Lady	(RAK 110)	22	1971	0	1971	
3	I Believe In Love	(RAK 118)	8	1971	0	1971	
4	You'll Always Be A Friend	(RAK 139)	23	1972	0	1972	
5	Brother Louie	(RAK 149)	7	1973	0	1973	
6	Rumours	(RAK 157)	44	1973	0	1973	
7	Emma	(RAK 168)	3	1974	8	1975	(Big Tree 16031)
8	Cheri Babe	(RAK 188)	31	1974	0	1974	
9	Disco Queen	(RAK 202)	11	1975	28	1975	(Big Tree 16038)
10	A Child's Prayer	(RAK 212)	7	1975	0	1975	
* 11	You Sexy Thing	(RAK 221)	2	1975	3	1975	(Big Tree 16047)
12	Don't Stop It Now	(RAK 230)	11	1976	0	1976	
13	Man To Man	(RAK 238)	14	1976	0	1976	
14	Heaven Is The Back Seat Of My Cadillac	(RAK 240)	25	1976	0	1976	
15	So You Win Again	(RAK 259)	1	1977	31	1977	(Big Tree 16096)
16	Put Your Love In Me	(RAK 266)	10	1977	0	1977	
* 17	Every 1's A Winner	(RAK 270)	12	1978	6	1979	(Infinity 50002)
18	I'll Put You Together Again	(RAK 286)	13	1978	0	1978	
19	Mindless Boogie	(RAK 292)	46	1979	0	1979	
20	Going Through The Motions	(RAK 296)	53	1979	0	1979	
21	No Doubt About It	(RAK 310)	2	1980	0	1980	
22	Are You Getting Enough Of What Makes You Happy	(RAK 318)	17	1980	0	1980	
23	Love Me To Sleep	(RAK 324)	50	1980	0	1980	
24	You'll Never Be So Wrong	(RAK 331)	52	1981	0	1981	
25	Girl Crazy	(RAK 341)	7	1982	0	1982	
26	It Started With A Kiss	(RAK 344)	5	1982	0	1982	
27	Chances	(RAK 350)	32	1982	0	1982	

ISSUE	TITLE	UK LBL	UK POS	UK YEAR	US POS	US YEAR	US LBL
28	What Kinda Boy You Looking For (Girl)	(RAK 357)	10	1983	0	1983	
29	Tears On The Telephone	(RAK 363)	37	1983	0	1983	
30	I Gave You My Heart (Didn't I)	(RAK 369)	13	1984	0	1984	
31	You Sexy Thing (Re-Mix)	(EMI 5592)	69	1987	0	1987	
32	Every 1's A Winner (Re-Mix)	(EMI 5607)	69	1987	0	1987	
33	It Started With A Kiss (Re-Issue)	(EMI Cdemcts 7)	31	1993	0	1993	

NAMES ERROL BROWN, HARVEY HINSLEY, LARRY FERGUSON, TONY WILSON, PATRICK OLIVE & TONY CONNOR • TONY WILSON MOVED ON IN 1975

Hot House   Mixed Vocal/Instrumental Group from the UK

ISSUE	TITLE	UK LBL	UK POS	UK YEAR	US POS	US YEAR	US LBL
1	Don't Come To Stay	(Deconstruction Chez 1)	74	1987	0	1987	
2	Don't Come To Stay (Re-Issue)	(Deconstruction Pb 42233)	70	1988	0	1988	

Hot Streak   Male Vocal/Instrumental Group from the USA

ISSUE	TITLE	UK LBL	UK POS	UK YEAR	US POS	US YEAR	US LBL
1	Bodywork	(Polydor Posp 642)	19	1983	0	1983	

Hothouse Flowers   Male Vocal/Instrumental Group from Ireland

ISSUE	TITLE	UK LBL	UK POS	UK YEAR	US POS	US YEAR	US LBL
1	Don't Go	(London Lon 174)	11	1988	0	1988	
2	I'm Sorry	(London Lon 187)	53	1988	0	1988	
3	Give It Up	(London Lon 258)	30	1990	0	1990	
4	I Can See Clearly Now	(London Lon 269)	23	1990	0	1990	
5	Movies	(London Lon 276)	68	1990	0	1990	
6	Emotional Time	(London Lon 335)	38	1993	0	1993	
7	One Tongue	(London Locdp 340)	45	1993	0	1993	
8	Isn't It Amazing	(London Locdp 343)	46	1993	0	1993	
9	This Is It (Your Soul)	(London Loncd 346)	67	1993	0	1993	

Hotlegs   Male Vocal/Instrumental Group from the UK

ISSUE	TITLE	UK LBL	UK POS	UK YEAR	US POS	US YEAR	US LBL
* 1	Neanderthal Man	(Fontana 6007 019)	2	1970	22	1970	(Capitol 2886)

NAMES: ERIC STEWART, KEVIN GODLEY & LOL CREME • GRAHAM GOULDMAN JOINED THE TRIO LATER WHICH BECAME 10CC

Hotshots   Male Vocal Group from the UK

ISSUE	TITLE	UK LBL	UK POS	UK YEAR	US POS	US YEAR	US LBL
* 1	Snoopy V.S. The Red Baron	(Mooncrest Moon 5)	4	1973	0	1973	

House Engineers   Male Vocal/Instrumental Duo from the UK

ISSUE	TITLE	UK LBL	UK POS	UK YEAR	US POS	US YEAR	US LBL
1	Ghost House	(Syncopate Sy 8)	69	1987	0	1987	

House Of Love   Male Vocal/Instrumental Group from the UK

ISSUE	TITLE	UK LBL	UK POS	UK YEAR	US POS	US YEAR	US LBL
1	Never	(Fontana Hol 1)	4	1989	0	1989	
2	I Don't Know Why I Love You	(Fontana Hol 2)	41	1989	0	1989	
3	Shine On	(Fontana Hol 3)	20	1990	0	1990	
4	Beatles And The Stones	(Fontana Hol 4)	36	1990	0	1990	
5	The Girl With The Loneliest Eyes	(Fontana Hol 5)	58	1991	0	1991	
6	Free	(Fontana Hol 6)	45	1992	0	1992	
7	You Don't Understand	(Fontana Hol 7)	46	1992	0	1992	
8	Crush Me	(Fontana Hol 810)	67	1992	0	1992	

House Of Pain   Male Rap Group from the USA

ISSUE	TITLE	UK LBL	UK POS	UK YEAR	US POS	US YEAR	US LBL
1	Jump Around	(Ruffness Xls 32)	32	1992	3	1992	(Tommy Boy 7526)
2	Jump Around Re-Issue / Top O' The Morning To Ya	(Ruffness Xls 443cd)	8	1993	0	1993	
3	Shamrocks And Shenanigans / Who's The Man	(Ruffness Xls 46cd)	23	1993	0	1993	
4	On Point	(Ruffness Xls 52cd)	19	1994	0	1994	
5	It Ain't A Crime	(Ruffness Xls 55cd1)	37	1994	0	1994	
6	Over There (I Don't Care)	(Ruffness Xls 61cd1)	20	1995	0	1995	
7	Fed Up	(Tommy Boy Tbcd 7744)	68	1996	0	1996	

House Of Virginism   Male Vocal/Instrumental Group from Sweden

ISSUE	TITLE	UK LBL	UK POS	UK YEAR	US POS	US YEAR	US LBL
1	I'll Be There For You (Doya Dododo Doya)	(Ffrr Fcd 221)	29	1993	0	1993	
2	Reachin'	(Ffrr Fcd 238)	35	1994	0	1994	
3	Exclusive	(Arista 74321342102)	67	1996	0	1996	

Housemartins   Male Vocal/Instrumental Group from the UK

ISSUE	TITLE	UK LBL	UK POS	UK YEAR	US POS	US YEAR	US LBL
1	Sheep	(Go! Discs God 9)	54	1986	0	1986	
2	Sheep (Re-Entry)	(Go! Discs God 9)	71	1986	0	1986	
3	Happy Hour	(Go! Discs God 11)	3	1986	0	1986	
4	Think For A Minute	(Go! Discs God 13)	18	1986	0	1986	
5	Caravan Of Love	(Go! Discs God 16)	1	1986	0	1986	
6	Five Get Over Excited	(Go! Discs God 18)	11	1987	0	1987	
7	Me And The Farmer	(Go! Discs God 19)	15	1987	0	1987	
8	Build	(Go! Discs God 21)	15	1987	0	1987	
9	There Is Always Something There To Remind Me	(Go! Discs God 22)	35	1988	0	1988	

ISSUE	TITLE	UK LBL	UK POS	UK YEAR	US POS	US YEAR	US LBL
Housemaster & The Rude Boy Of House	Male Vocal/Instrumental Group from the USA						
1	House Nation	(Magnetic Dance Magd 1)	48	1987	0	1987	
2	House Nation (Re-Entry)	(Magnetic Dance Magd 1)	8	1987	0	1987	
Houston Wells	Male Vocalist from the UK						
1	Only The Heartaches	(Parlophone R 5031)	22	1963	0	1963	
Howard Johnson	Male Vocalist from the USA						
1	So Fine	(A&M Usa 1221)	45	1982	0	1982	
2	Keeping Love New	(A&M USA 1221)	64	1982	0	1982	
Howard Jones	Male Vocalist, B: 23 Feb 1955 Southampton, England						
1	New Song	(Wea How 1)	3	1983	27	1984	(Elektra 69766)
2	What Is Love?	(Wea How 2)	2	1983	33	1984	(Elektra 39737)
3	New Song (Re-Entry)	(Wea How 1)	60	1984	0	1984	
4	Hide And Seek	(Wea How 3)	12	1984	0	1984	
5	Pearl In The Shell	(Wea How 4)	7	1984	0	1984	
6	Like To Get To Know You Well	(Wea How 5)	4	1984	0	1984	
7	Things Can Only Get Better	(Wea How 6)	6	1985	5	1985	(Elektra 69651)
8	Look Mama	(Wea How 7)	10	1985	0	1985	
9	Life In One Day	(Wea How 8)	14	1985	19	1985	(Elektra 69631)
10	No One Is To Blame	(Wea How 9)	16	1986	4	1986	(Elektra 69549)
11	All I Want	(Wea How 10)	35	1986	0	1986	
12	You Know I Love You... Don't You?	(Wea How 11)	43	1986	17	1986	(Elektra 69512)
13	A Little Bit Of Snow	(Wea How 12)	70	1987	0	1987	
14	Everlasting Love	(Wea How 13)	62	1989	12	1989	(Elektra 69308)
15	The Prisoner		0	1989	30	1989	(Elektra 69288)
16	Lift Me Up	(East West How 15)	52	1992	32	1992	(Elektra 64779)
Howie B	Male vocal/musician/DJ from Glasgow, Scotland						
1	Angels Go Bald:Two	(Polydor 5711672)	36	1997	0	1997	
Howlin' Wolf	Name Chester Burnett B: 1910 In West Point, Mississippi						
1	Smokestack Lightnin'	(Pye International 7n 25244)	42	1964	0	1964	
Hoyt Axton	Male Vocalist B: 25 Mar 1938 from Duncan, Oklahoma						
! 1	When The Morning Comes		0	1974	54	1974	(A&M 1497)
! 2	Boney Fingers		0	1974	8	1974	(A&M 1607)
! 3	Nashville		0	1975	61	1975	(A&M 1657)
! 4	Lion In The Water		0	1975	57	1975	(A&M 1683)
! 5	Flash Of Fire		0	1976	18	1976	(A&M 1811)
! 6	You're The Hangnail In My Life		0	1977	57	1977	(MCA 40711)
! 7	Little White Moon		0	1977	65	1977	(MCA 40731)
8	Della And The Dealer	(Young Blood Yb 82)	48	1980	17	1979	(Jeremiah 1000)
! 9	A Rusty Old Halo		0	1979	14	1979	(Jeremiah 1001)
! 10	Wild Bull Rider		0	1980	21	1980	(Jeremiah 1003)
! 1	Evangelina		0	1980	37	1980	(Jeremiah 1005)
! 12	Where Did The Money Go		0	1980	80	1980	(Jeremiah 1008)
! 13	Flo's Yellow Rose		0	1981	78	1981	(Elektra 47133)
! 14	The Devil		0	1981	86	1981	(Jeremiah 1011)

FEMALE VOCALS ON HIT 2 ARE BY RENEE ARMAND • GUEST VOCALS ON HITS 1,4 ARE BY LINDA RONSTADT

Hudson Brothers	Names Are Bill, Brett & Mark From Portland						
1	So You Are A Star		0	1974	21	1971	(Casablanca 0108)
2	Rendezvous		0	1975	26	1975	(Rocket 40417)
Hudson-Ford	Male Vocal/Instrumental Duo from the UK	See also Monks					
1	Pick Up The Pieces	(A&M Ams 7078)	8	1973	0	1973	
2	Burn Baby Burn	(A&M Ams 7096)	15	1974	0	1974	
3	Floating In The Wind	(A&M Ams 7116)	35	1974	0	1974	
Hue & Cry	Male Vocal/Instrumental Duo from the UK						
1	Labour Of Love	(Circa Yr 4)	6	1987	0	1987	
2	Strength To Strength	(Circa Yr 6)	46	1987	0	1987	
3	I Refuse	(Circa Yr 8)	47	1988	0	1988	
4	Ordinary Angel	(Circa Yr 18)	42	1988	0	1988	
5	Looking For Linda	(Circa Yr 24)	15	1989	0	1989	
6	Violently (EP)	(Circa Yr 29)	21	1989	0	1989	
7	Sweet Invisibility	(Circa Yr 37)	55	1989	0	1989	
8	My Salt Heart	(Circa Yr 64)	47	1991	0	1991	
9	Long Term Lovers Of Pain (EP)	(Circa Yr 71)	48	1991	0	1991	

ISSUE	TITLE	UK LBL	UK POS	UK YEAR	US POS	US YEAR	US LBL
10	Profoundly Yours	(Fidelity Fidel 1)	74	1992	0	1992	
11	Labour Of Love (Re-Mixes)	(Circa Huescd 1)	25	1993	0	1993	

Hues Corporation   Mixed Vocal Group from Los Angeles

ISSUE	TITLE	UK LBL	UK POS	UK YEAR	US POS	US YEAR	US LBL
* 1	Rock The Boat	(RCA Apbo 0232)	6	1974	1	1974	(RCA 0232)
2	Rockin' Soul	(RCA Pb 10066)	24	1974	18	1974	(RCA 10066)

NAMES: BERNARD HENDERSON, FLEMING WILLIAMS & ANN KELLEY • WILLIAMS REPLACED TOMMY BROWN, WHO WAS REPLACED BY KARL RUSSELL IN 1975

Huey 'Piano' Smith & The Clowns   Male Rock & Roll Pianist, B: 26 Jan 1934 New Orleans

ISSUE	TITLE	UK LBL	UK POS	UK YEAR	US POS	US YEAR	US LBL
* 1	Rocking Pneumonia And The Boogie Woogie Flu		0	1957	52	1957	(Ace 530)
* 2	Don't You Just Know It		0	1958	9	1958	(Ace 545)
3	Don't You Know Yockomo		0	1958	56	1958	(Ace 553)
* 4	Sea Cruise		0	1959	14	1959	(Ace 554)
5	Pop-Eye		0	1962	46	1962	(Ace 649)

Huey Lewis & The News   Male Vocal/Instrumental Group from the USA

ISSUE	TITLE	UK LBL	UK POS	UK YEAR	US POS	US YEAR	US LBL
1	Do You Believe In Love	(Chrysalis Chs 2829)	9	1986	7	1982	(Chrysalis 2589)
2	Hope You Love Me Like You Say You Do		0	1982	3	1982	(Chrysalis 2604)
3	Heart And Soul (EP)	(Chrysalis Huey 2)	61	1985	8	1983	(Chrysalis 42726)
* 4	I Want A New Drug		0	1984	6	1984	(Chrysalis 42766)
5	The Heart Of Rock And Roll	(Chrysalis Huey 4)	49	1986	6	1984	(Chrysalis 42782)
6	If This Is It	(Chrysalis Chs 2829)	7	1984	6	1984	(Chrysalis 42803)
7	Walking On A Thin Line		0	1984	18	1984	(Chrysalis 42825)
* 8	The Power Of Love (From *Back To The Future*)	(Chrysalis Huey 1)	11	1985	1	1985	(Chrysalis 42876)
9	The Power Of Love (Re-Issue)/ Do You Believe In Love	(Chrysalis Huey 3)	9	1986	0	1986	
10	Stuck With You	(Chrysalis Huey 5)	12	1986	1	1986	(Chrysalis 43019)
11	Hip To Be Square	(Chrysalis Huey 6)	41	1986	3	1988	(Chrysalis 43065)
12	Jacob's Ladder		0	1987	1	1987	(Chrysalis 43097)
13	Simple As That	(Chrysalis Huey 7)	47	1987	0	1987	
14	I Know What I Like		0	1987	9	1987	(Chrysalis 43108)
15	Doing It All For My Baby		0	1987	6	1987	(Chrysalis 43143)
16	Perfect World	(Chrysalis Huey 10)	48	1988	3	1988	(Chrysalis 43265)
17	Small World		0	1988	25	1988	(Chrysalis 43306)
18	Couple Days Off		0	1991	11	1991	(EMI 50346)
19	It Hit Me Like A Hammer		0	1991	21	1991	(EMI 50364)

REAL NAME HUGH CREGG III B: 5 JUL 1950 NEW YORK CITY • HIT 4 WAS WITH FRANKIE FORD

Huff & Puff   Male Instrumental/Production Duo from the UK

ISSUE	TITLE	UK LBL	UK POS	UK YEAR	US POS	US YEAR	US LBL
1	Help Me Make It	(Skyway Skywcd 4)	31	1996	0	1996	
2	Help Me Make It (Re-Recording)	(Skyway Skywcd 8)	37	1997	0	1997	

Hugh Cornwell   Male Vocal/Guitarist from the UK

ISSUE	TITLE	UK LBL	UK POS	UK YEAR	US POS	US YEAR	US LBL
1	Facts + Figures	(Virgin Vs 922)	61	1987	0	1987	
2	Another Kind Of Love	(Virgin Vs 945)	71	1988	0	1988	

Hugh Masekela   Real Name Hugh Ramapolo Masekela B: 4 Apr 1939 Witbank, Johannesburg

ISSUE	TITLE	UK LBL	UK POS	UK YEAR	US POS	US YEAR	US LBL
* 1	Grazing In The Grass		0	1968	1	1968	(Uni 55066)

Hugo & Luigi   Male Producer/Songwriters Duo from the USA

ISSUE	TITLE	UK LBL	UK POS	UK YEAR	US POS	US YEAR	US LBL
1	La Plume De Ma Tante	(RCA 1127)	29	1959	0	1959	
2	Just Come Home		0	1960	35	1960	(RCA 7639)

NAMES HUGO PERETTI & LUIGI CREATORE. • OBITUARY : HUGO D: 1 MAY 1986.

Hugo Montenegro   Orchestra Leader, B: 1925 And Raised In New York City

ISSUE	TITLE	UK LBL	UK POS	UK YEAR	US POS	US YEAR	US LBL
1	The Good The Bad And The Ugly	(RCA 1727)	1	1968	2	1968	(RCA 9432)
2	Hang 'Em High	(RCA 1771)	50	1969	0	1969	
3	The Good The Bad And The Ugly (Re-Entry)	(RCA 1727)	48	1969	0	1969	

OBITUARY D: 6 FEB 1981.

Hugo Winterhalter & His Orchestra   Male Orchestra Leader, B: 15 Aug 1909 Wilkes-Barre, Pennsylvania

ISSUE	TITLE	UK LBL	UK POS	UK YEAR	US POS	US YEAR	US LBL
1	Jealous Heart		0	1949	10	1949	(Columbia 38593)
2	Blue Christmas		0	1949	9	1949	(Columbia 38635)
3	Music! Music! Music		0	1950	17	1950	(Columbia 38704)
4	Count Every Star		0	1950	10	1950	(RCA Victor 78-3697)
5	The Third Man Theme		0	1950	21	1950	(Columbia 38706)
6	My Foolish Heart		0	1950	29	1950	(Columbia 38697)
7	I Wanna Be Loved		0	1950	11	1950	(RCA Victor 3772)
8	I Need You So		0	1950	25	1950	(RCA Victor 3884)
9	Mr. Touchdown, U.S.A.		0	1950	9	1950	(RCA Victor 3913)
10	Blue Christmas (Re-Entry)		0	1950	20	1950	(Columbia 38635)

ISSUE	TITLE	UK LBL	UK POS	UK YEAR	US POS	US YEAR	US LBL
11	Across The Wide Missouri		0	1951	21	1951	(RCA Victor 4017)
12	Belle, Belle, My Liberty Belle		0	1951	25	1951	(RCA Victor 4217)
13	Beyond The Blue Horizon		0	1951	23	1951	(RCA Victor 4288)
14	Blue December		0	1952	18	1952	(RCA Victor 4412)
15	A Kiss To Build A Dream On		0	1952	10	1952	(RCA Victor 4455)
16	Blue Tango		0	1952	6	1952	(RCA Victor 4518)
17	Vanessa		0	1952	9	1952	(RCA Victor 4691)
18	Blue Violins		0	1952	19	1952	(RCA Victor 4997)
19	Fandango		0	1952	30	1952	(RCA Victor 4997)
20	The Magic Tough		0	1953	24	1953	(RCA Victor 5209)
21	The Velvet Glove		0	1953	8	1953	(RCA Victor 5405)
22	Latin Lady		0	1954	22	1954	(RCA Victor 5655)
23	The Little Shoemaker		0	1954	9	1954	(RCA Victor 5769)
24	The Magic Tango		0	1954	22	1954	(RCA Victor 5769)
25	Land Of Dreams		0	1954	28	1954	(RCA Victor 5888)
26	Song Of The Barefoot Contessa		0	1954	25	1954	(RCA Victor 5888)
27	Canadian Sunset		0	1956	2	1956	(RCA 6537)

HIT 27 IS CREDTITED TO HUGO WINTERHALTER AND EDDIE HEYWOOD • OBITUARY : D: 17 SEP 1973 (AGED 64) CANCER.

Human Beinz   Rock Band From Youngstown, Ohio

1	Nobody But Me	0		1968	8	1968	(Capitol 5990)

Human League   Mixed Vocal/Instrumental Group from Sheffield, UK

ISSUE	TITLE	UK LBL	UK POS	UK YEAR	US POS	US YEAR	US LBL
1	Holiday 80 (Double Single)	(Virgin Vs 105)	56	1980	0	1980	
2	Empire State Human	(Virgin Vs 351)	62	1980	0	1980	
3	Boys And Girls	(Virgin Vs 395)	48	1981	0	1981	
4	The Sound Of The Crowd	(Virgin Vs 416)	12	1981	0	1981	
5	Love Action (I Believe In Love)	(Virgin Vs 435)	3	1981	0	1981	
6	Open Your Heart	(Virgin Vs 453)	6	1981	0	1981	
* 7	Don't You Want Me	(Virgin Vs 466)	1	1981	1	1982	(A&M 2397)
8	Being Boiled	(EMI Fast 4)	6	1982	0	1982	
9	Holiday 80 (Double Single) (Re-Entry)	(Virgin Vs 105)	46	1982	0	1982	
10	Mirror Man	(Virgin Vs 522)	2	1982	30	1983	(A&M 2587)
11	(Keep Feeling) Fascination	(Virgin Vs 569)	2	1983	8	1983	(A&M 2547)
12	The Lebanon	(Virgin Vs 672)	11	1984	0	1984	
13	The Lebanon (Re-Entry)	(Virgin Vs 672)	5	1984	0	1984	
14	Life On Your Own	(Virgin Vs 688)	16	1984	0	1984	
15	Louise	(Virgin Vs 723)	13	1984	0	1984	
16	Human	(Virgin Vs 880)	8	1986	1	1986	(A&M 2861)
17	I Need Your Loving	(Virgin Vs 900)	72	1986	0	1986	
18	Love Is All That Matters	(Virgin Vs 1025)	41	1988	0	1988	
19	Heart Like A Wheel	(Virgin Vs 1262)	29	1990	32	1990	(Virgin/A&M 1520)
20	Tell Me When	(East West Yz 882cd1)	6	1995	31	1995	(Eastwest 64443)
21	One Man In My Heart	(East West Yz 904cd1)	13	1995	0	1995	
22	Filling Up With Heaven	(East West Yz 944cd1)	36	1995	0	1995	
23	Don't You Want Me (Re-Mix)	(Virgin Vscdt 1557)	16	1995	0	1995	
24	Stay With Me Tonight	(East West Ew 20cd)	40	1996	0	1996	

NAMES MARTYN WARE, IAN MARSH, PHILLIP OAKEY. JOANNE CATHERALL, SUSAN SULLEY. • IAN AND MARTIN LEFT TO FORM HEAVEN 17

Human Nature   Male quartet from Australia

1	Wishes	(Epic 6644485)	44	1997	0	1997	
2	Whisper Your Name	(Epic 6649465)	53	1997	0	1997	

Human Resource   Male Production/Instrumental Group from Holland

1	Dominator	(R&S Rsuk 4)	36	1991	0	1991	
2	The Complete Dominator (Re-Mix)	(R&S Rsuk 4x)	18	1991	0	1991	

Humanoid   Male Producer from the UK

1	Stakker Humanoid	(Westside Wsr 12)	17	1988	0	1988	
2	Slam	(Westside Wsr 14)	54	1989	0	1989	
3	Stakker Humanoid (Re-Issue)	(Jumpin' + Pumpin' Tot 27)	40	1992	0	1992	

Humble Pie   Male Vocal/Instrumental Group from the UK

1	Natural Born Bugie	(Immediate Im 082)	4	1969	0	1969	
	See Also Small Faces						

Humphrey Lyttelton Band   Male Bandleader/Instrumentalist (Trumpet) With The Male Jazz Band from the UK

1	Bad Penny Blues	(Parlophone R 4184)	19	1956	0	1956	

100 Proof Aged In Soul   Names: Joe Stubbs, Eddie Anderson & Steve Mancha

* 1	Somebody's Been Sleeping		0	1970	8	1970	(Hot Wax 7004)

ISSUE	TITLE	UK LBL	UK POS	UK YEAR	US POS	US YEAR	US LBL
Hunter							
1	Shakaboom	(Telstar Huntcd 1)	64	1995	0	1995	
	Hit Was With Ruby Turner						
Hurricane #1							
1	Step Into My World	(Creation Crescd 253)	29	1997	0	1997	
2	Just Another Illusion	(Creation Crescd 264)	35	1997	0	1997	
3	Chain Reaction	(Creation Crescd 271)	30	1997	0	1997	
Hurricane Smith Male Vocalist, Real Name Norman Smit B: 1923 England							
1	Don't Let Is Die	(Columbia Db 8785)	2	1971	0	1971	
2	Oh Babe What Would You Say	(Columbia Db 8878)	4	1972	3	1973	(Capitol 3383)
3	Who Was It	(Columbia Db 8916)	23	1972	0	1972	
Hustlers Convention Male Instrumental/Production Duo from the UK							
1	The Dance To The Music (EP)	(Stress Cdstr 53)	71	1995	0	1995	
HWA (Featuring) Sonic The Hedgehog Male Producer, Real Name Jeremy Healey from the UK							
1	Supersonic	(Internal Affairs)	33	1992	0	1992	
Hylda Baker & Arthur Mullard Mixed Actors/Vocal Duo from the UK							
1	You're The One That I Want	(Pye 7n 46121)	22	1978	0	1978	
	THE HIT WAS A COMEDY VERSION OF THE NUMBER 1 HIT BY JOHN TRAVOLTA & OLIVIA NEWTON-JOHN						
Hyper Go-Go Male Production/Instrumental Duo from the UK							
1	High	(Deconstruction 74321110497)	30	1992	0	1992	
2	Never Let Go	(Positiva Cdtiv 3)	45	1993	0	1993	
3	Raise	(Positiva Cdtiv 9)	36	1994	0	1994	
4	It's Alright	(Positiva Cdtiv 20)	49	1994	0	1994	
5	Do Watcha Do	(Avex Uk Avexcd 24)	54	1996	0	1996	
6	High (Re-Mix)	(Distinctive Disncd 24)	32	1996	0	1996	
7	Do Watcha Do (Re-Mix)	(Distinctive Disncd 28)	60	1997	0	1997	
Hyperlogic Male Instrumental/Production Duo from the UK							
1	Only Me	(Systematic Syscd 15)	35	1995	0	1995	
Hypnotist Male Producer, Real Name Caspar Pound from the UK							
1	The House Is Mine	(Rising High Rsn 4)	65	1991	0	1991	
2	The Hardcore (EP)	(Rising High Rsn 13)	68	1991	0	1991	
Hysteric Ego Male Producer Rob White from the UK							
1	Want Love	(Wea Wea 070cd)	28	1996	0	1996	
2	Ministry Of Love	(Wea Wea 094cd)	39	1997	0	1997	
Hysterics Male Vocal/Instrumental Group from the UK							
1	Jingle Bells Laughing All The Way	(Record Delivery Ka 5)	44	1981	0	1981	
Hysterix Mixed Vocal/Instrumental Group from the UK							
1	Must Be The Music	(Deconstruction 74321207362)	40	1994	0	1994	
2	Everything	(Deconstruction 74321236882)	65	1995	0	1995	

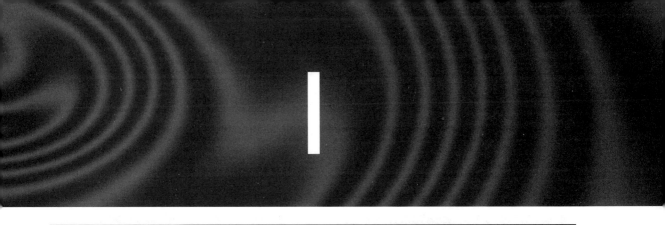

ISSUE	TITLE	UK LBL	UK POS	UK YEAR	US POS	US YEAR	US LBL
I-Level Male Vocal/Instrumental Group from the UK							
1	Minefield	(Virgin Vs 563)	52	1983	0	1983	
2	Teacher	(Virgin Vs 595)	56	1983	0	1983	
Iain Gregory Male Vocalist from the UK							
1	Can't You Hear The Beat Of A Broken Heart	(Pye 7n 15397)	39	1962	0	1962	
Ian Campbell Folk Group Male Vocal/Instrumental Group from the UK							
1	The Times They Are A-Changin'	(Transatlantic Sp 5)	42	1965	0	1965	
2	The Times They Are A-Changin' (Re-Entry)	(Transatlantic Sp 5)	47	1965	0	1965	
3	The Times They Are A-Changin' (2nd Re-Entry)	(Transatlantic Sp 5)	46	1965	0	1965	
Ian Dury & The Blockheads Male Vocal/Instrumental Group from the UK							
1	What A Waste	(Stiff Buy 27)	9	1978	0	1978	
2	Hit Me With Your Rhythm Stick	(Stiff Buy 38)	1	1978	0	1978	
3	Reasons To Be Cheerful Part 3	(Stiff Buy 50)	3	1979	0	1979	
4	I Want To Be Straight	(Stiff Buy 90)	22	1980	0	1980	
5	Superman's Big Sister	(Stiff Buy 100)	51	1980	0	1980	
6	Hit Me With Your Rhythm Stick (Re-Mix)	(Stiff Buy 214)	55	1985	0	1985	
7	Profoundly In Love With Pandora	(EMI Emi 5534)	45	1985	0	1985	
8	Hit Me With Your Rhythm Stick (2nd Re-Mix)	(Flying Flyr 1)	73	1991	0	1991	
Ian Gomm Male Vocalist, B: 17 Mar 1947 Ealing, West London, England							
1	Hold On		0	1979	18	1979	(Stiff/Epic 50747)
Ian Hunter Male Vocalist from the UK							
1	Once Bitten Twice Shy	(CBS3194)	14	1975	0	1975	
Ian Matthews Male Vocalist, Real Name Ian Matthews Macdonald B: Jun 1946 Lincolnshire, England							
1	Shake It		0	1978	13	1978	(Mushroom 7039)
Ian McCulloch Male Vocalist from the UK							
1	September Song	(Korova Kow 40)	51	1984	0	1984	
2	Proud To Fall	(WEA Yz 417)	51	1989	0	1989	
3	Candleland (The Second Coming)	(East West Yz 452)	75	1990	0	1990	
4	Lover Lover Lover	(East West Yz 643)	47	1992	0	1992	
	HIT 3 IS CREDITED TO IAN MCCULLOCH FEATURING ELIZABETH FRASER						
Ian McNabb Male Vocalist from the UK							
1	If Love Was Like Guitars	(This Way Up Way 233)	67	1993	0	1993	
2	You Must Be Prepared To Dream	(This Way Up Way 3199)	54	1994	0	1994	
3	Get Into The Light	(This Way Up Way 3699)	66	1994	0	1994	
4	Don't Put Your Spell On Me	(This Way Up Way 5033)	72	1996	0	1996	
5	Merseybeast	(This Way Up Way 5266)	74	1996	0	1996	
Ian Thomas Singer/Songwriter from Canada							
1	Painted Ladies	0		1973	34	1973	
Ian Whitcomb & Bluesville Male Singer/Songwriter, B: 10 Jul 1941 Woking, Surrey, England							
1	You Turn Me On	0		1965	8	1965	(Tower 134)
Ian Wright Male Vocalist from the UK							
1	Do The Right Thing	(M&G Magcd 45)	43	1993	0	1993	
Ice Cube Male Rapper from the USA							
* 1	It Was A Good Day	(Fourth & Broadway Brcd 270)	27	1993	15	1993	(Priority 53817)
* 2	Check Yo Self	(Fourth & Broadway Brcd 283)	36	1993	20	1993	(Priority 53830)
3	Wicked	(Fourth & Broadway Brcd 282)	62	1993	0	1993	
4	Really Doe	(Fourth & Broadway Brcd 302)	66	1993	0	1993	
5	You Know How We Do It	(Fourth & Broadway Brcd 303)	41	1994	30	1994	(Priority 53847)

ISSUE	TITLE	UK LBL	UK POS	UK YEAR	US POS	US YEAR	US LBL
* 6	Bop Gun (One Nation)	(Fourth & Broadway Brcd 308)	22	1994	23	1994	(Priority 53155)
7	You Know How We Do It (Re-Entry)	(Fourth & Broadway Brcd 303)	46	1994	0	1994	
8	Hand Of The Dead Body	(Virgin America Vuscd 88)	41	1995	0	1995	
9	Natural Born Killaz	(Death Row A 8197cd)	45	1995	0	1995	
10	World Is Mine	(Jive Jivecd 419)	60	1997	0	1997	

Ice Mc Male Rapper from Italy

ISSUE	TITLE	UK LBL	UK POS	UK YEAR	US POS	US YEAR	US LBL
1	Think About The Way (Bom Digi Digi Bom)	(WEA Yz 829cd)	42	1994	0	1994	
2	It's A Rainy Day	(Eternal Yz 902cd)	73	1995	0	1995	
3	Bom Digi Bom (Think About The Way) (Re-Issue)	(Eternal Wea 073cd)	38	1996	0	1996	

Ice-T Male Rapper from the USA

ISSUE	TITLE	UK LBL	UK POS	UK YEAR	US POS	US YEAR	US LBL
1	High Rollers	(Sire W 7574)	63	1989	0	1989	
2	You Played Yourself	(Sire W 9994)	64	1990	0	1990	
3	Superfly 1990	(Capitol Cl 586)	48	1990	0	1990	
4	I Ain't New Ta This	(Rhythm Syndicate Syndd 1)	62	1993	0	1993	
5	That's How I'm Livin'	(Rhythm Syndicate Syndd 2)	21	1993	0	1993	
6	Gotta Lotta Love	(Rhythm Syndicate Syndd 3)	24	1994	0	1994	
7	Born To Raise Hell	(Fox 74321230152)	47	1994	0	1994	
8	I Must Stand	(Rhythm Syndicate Syndd 5)	23	1996	0	1996	
9	The Lane	(Rhythm Syndicate Syndd 6)	18	1996	0	1996	

Icehouse Vocal/Instrumental Rock Quartet from Australia led by Iva Davies Originally Known As The Flowers

ISSUE	TITLE	UK LBL	UK POS	UK YEAR	US POS	US YEAR	US LBL
1	Hey Little Girl	(Chrysalis Chs 2670)	17	1983	0	1983	
2	Street Cafe	(Chrysalis Cool 1)	62	1983	0	1983	
3	No Promises	(Chrysalis Chs 2978)	72	1986	0	1986	
4	Crazy	(Chrysalis Chs 3156)	74	1987	14	1987	(Chrysalis 43156)
5	Crazy (Re-Entry)	(Chrysalis Chs 3156)	38	1988	0	1988	
6	Electric Blue	(Chrysalis Chs 3239)	53	1988	7	1988	(Chrysalis 43201)

Icicle Works Male Vocal/Instrumental Group from the UK
Names Robert Ian Mcnabb, Chris Layhe & Chris Sharrock

ISSUE	TITLE	UK LBL	UK POS	UK YEAR	US POS	US YEAR	US LBL
1	Love Is A Wonderful Colour	(Beggars Banquet Beg 99)	15	1983	0	1983	
2	Birds Fly (Whispers To A Scream)	(Beggars Banquet Beg 108)	53	1984	37	1984	(Arista 9155)
3	Understanding Jane	(Beggars Banquet Beg 160)	52	1986	0	1986	
4	Who Do You Want For Your Love	(Beggars Banquet Beg 172)	54	1986	0	1986	
5	Evangeline	(Beggars Banquet Beg 181)	53	1987	0	1987	
6	Little Girl Lost	(Beggars Banquet Beg 215)	59	1988	0	1988	
7	Motorcycle Rider	(Epic Works 100)	73	1990	0	1990	

Icon Mixed Vocal/Instumental Duo from the UK

ISSUE	TITLE	UK LBL	UK POS	UK YEAR	US POS	US YEAR	US LBL
1	Tainted Love	(Eternal/WEA 057cd)	51	1996	0	1996	

Ideal Life Male Producer, Real Name Jon Da Silva from the UK

ISSUE	TITLE	UK LBL	UK POS	UK YEAR	US POS	US YEAR	US LBL
1	Hot	(Cleveland City Clecd 13019)	49	1994	0	1994	

Ides Of March Male Vocal/Instrumental Group from the USA

ISSUE	TITLE	UK LBL	UK POS	UK YEAR	US POS	US YEAR	US LBL
* 1	Vehicle	(Warner Bros Wb 7378)	31	1970	2	1970	(Warner Bros 7378)

Idris Muhammad Male Vocalist from the USA

ISSUE	TITLE	UK LBL	UK POS	UK YEAR	US POS	US YEAR	US LBL
1	Could Heaven Ever Be Like This	(Kudu 935)	42	1977	0	1977	

Iggy Pop Male Vocalist, Real Name James Jewel Osterberg B: 21 Apr 1947 From Muskegan, Michigan

ISSUE	TITLE	UK LBL	UK POS	UK YEAR	US POS	US YEAR	US LBL
1	Real Wild Child (Wild One)	(A&M Am 368)	10	1986	0	1986	
2	Livin' On The Edge Of The Night	(Virgin America Vus 18)	51	1990	0	1990	
3	Candy	(Virgin America Vus 29)	67	1990	28	1991	(Virgin 98900)
4	Well Did You Evah!	(Chrysalis Chs 3646)	42	1991	0	1991	
5	The Wild America (EP)	(Virgin America Vuscd 740)	63	1993	0	1993	
6	Beside You	(Virgin America Vuscd 77)	47	1994	0	1994	
7	Lust For Life	(Virgin America Vuscd 116)	26	1996	0	1996	

Ignorants Male Vocal Duo from the UK

ISSUE	TITLE	UK LBL	UK POS	UK YEAR	US POS	US YEAR	US LBL
1	Phat Girls	(Spaghetti Ciocd 8)	59	1993	0	1993	

Ike & Tina Turner Mixed Vocal/Instrumental Duo from the USA

ISSUE	TITLE	UK LBL	UK POS	UK YEAR	US POS	US YEAR	US LBL
1	A Fool In Love		0	1960	27	1960	(Sue 730)
2	It's Gonna Work Out Fine		0	1961	14	1961	(Sue 749)
3	Poor Fool		0	1962	38	1962	(Sue 753)
4	River Deep Mountain High	(London Hl 10046)	3	1966	88	1966	(Philles 131)
5	Tell Her I'm Not Home	(Warner Bros Eb 5753)	48	1966	0	1966	
6	A Love Like Yours	(London Hl 10083)	16	1966	0	1966	

ISSUE	TITLE	UK LBL	UK POS	UK YEAR	US POS	US YEAR	US LBL
7	River Deep Mountain High (Re-Issue)	(London Hlu 10242)	33	1969	0	1969	
8	I Want To Take You Higher		0	1970	34	1970	(Liberty 56177)
* 9	Proud Mary		0	1971	4	1971	(Liberty 56216)
* 10	Nutbush City Limits	(United Artists Up 35582)	4	1973	22	1973	(United Artists 298)

IKE WAS B: 5 NOV 1931 CLARKSDALE, MISSISSIPPI • HE ALSO WORKED WITH SONNY BOY WILLIAMS AND THE NIGHTHAWKS
EARLY IN HIS CAREER HE FORMED HIS OWN BAND THE KINGS OF RHYTHM • HIT 8 IS CREDITED TO IKE & TINA TURNER & THE IKETTES • IKE & TINA TURNER

Ikettes   Names Are Delores Johnson, Eloise Hester & Jo 'Joshie' Armstead

			UK POS	UK YEAR	US POS	US YEAR	US LBL
1	I'm Blue (The Gong-Gong Song)		0	1962	19	1962	(Atco 6212)
2	Peaches 'n' Cream		0	1965	36	1965	(Modern 1005)

Ilene Woods   Female Vocalist from the USA

			UK POS	UK YEAR	US POS	US YEAR	US LBL
1	Bibbidi-Bobbidi-Boo (From Cinderella)		0	1950	22	1950	(Bluebird 0019)

SHE IS THE VOICE OF CINDERELLA IN THE WALT DISNEY CLASSIC ANIMATION

Illegal Motion (Featuring) Simone Chapman   Mixed Vocal/Instrumental Duo from the UK

			UK POS	UK YEAR	US POS	US YEAR	US LBL
1	Saturday Love	(Arista 74321163032)	67	1993	0	1993	

Illusion   The Rock Quintet Is Led By John Vinci

			UK POS	UK YEAR	US POS	US YEAR	US LBL
1	Did You See Her Eyes		0	1969	32	1969	(Steed 718)

Imagination   Male Vocal/Instrumental Group from the UK

			UK POS	UK YEAR	US POS	US YEAR	US LBL
1	Body Talk	(R&B Rbs 201)	4	1981	0	1981	
2	In And Out Of Love	(R&B Rbs 202)	16	1981	0	1981	
3	Flashback	(R&B Rbs 206)	16	1981	0	1981	
4	Just An Illusion	(R&B Rbs 208)	2	1982	0	1982	
5	Music And Lights	(R&B Rbs 210)	5	1982	0	1982	
6	In The Heat Of The Night	(R&B Rbs 211)	22	1982	0	1982	
7	Changes	(R&B Rbs 213)	31	1982	0	1982	
8	Looking At Midnight	(R&B Rbs 214)	29	1983	0	1983	
9	New Dimension	(R&B Rbs 216)	56	1983	0	1983	
10	State Of Love	(R&B Rbs 218)	67	1984	0	1984	
11	Thank You My Love	(R&B Rbs 219)	22	1984	0	1984	
12	Instinctual	(RCA Pb 41697)	62	1988	0	1988	

Immaculate Fools   Male Vocal/Instrumental Group from the UK

			UK POS	UK YEAR	US POS	US YEAR	US LBL
1	Immaculate Fools	(A&M Am 227)	51	1985	0	1985	

Immature   Male R&B Trio From Los Angeles

			UK POS	UK YEAR	US POS	US YEAR	US LBL
* 1	Never Lie		0	1994	5	1994	(MCA 54850)
* 2	Constantly		0	1994	16	1994	(MCA 54948)
3	Please Don't Go		0	1996	36	1996	
4	We Got It	(MCA Mcstd 48009)	26	1996	37	1996	
5	Watch Me Do My Thing (From All That)		0	1997	32	1997	(RCA 64737)

Impalas   Male Vocal Group from Brooklyn, USA Names Joe Frazier, Richard Wagner, Lenny Renda & Tony Cartucci

			UK POS	UK YEAR	US POS	US YEAR	US LBL
* 1	Sorry (I Ran All The Way Home)	(MGM 1015)	28	1959	2	1959	(Club 9022)

Impedance   Male Producer, Real Name Daniel Haydon from the UK

			UK POS	UK YEAR	US POS	US YEAR	US LBL
1	Tainted Love	(Jumpin' & Pumpin' Tot 4)	54	1989	0	1989	

Imperial Drag   Male Vocal/Instrumental Group from the UK

			UK POS	UK YEAR	US POS	US YEAR	US LBL
1	Boy Or A Girl	(Columbia 6632992)	54	1996	0	1996	

Imperial Teen   Mixed Vocal/Instrumental Group from the USA

			UK POS	UK YEAR	US POS	US YEAR	US LBL
1	You're One	(Slash Lascd 57)	69	1996	0	1996	

Impressions   Male Vocal Group from the USA

			UK POS	UK YEAR	US POS	US YEAR	US LBL
1	For Your Precious Love		0	1958	11	1958	(Abner 1013)
2	Gypsy Woman		0	1961	20	1961	(ABC-Paramount 10241)
3	It's All Right		0	1963	4	1963	(ABC-Paramount 10487)
4	Talking About My Baby		0	1964	12	1964	(ABC-Paramount 10511)
5	I'm So Proud		0	1964	14	1964	(ABC-Paramount 10544)
6	Keep On Pushing		0	1964	10	1964	(ABC-Paramount 10554)
7	You Must Believe Me		0	1964	15	1964	(ABC-Paramount 10581)
8	Amen		0	1965	7	1965	(ABC-Paramount 10602)
9	People Get Ready		0	1965	14	1965	(ABC-Paramount 10622)
10	Woman's Got Soul		0	1965	29	1965	(ABC-Paramount 10647)
11	You've Been Cheatin'		0	1965	33	1965	(ABC-Paramount 10750)
12	We're A Winner		0	1968	14	1968	(ABC-Paramount 11022)
13	I Loved And I Lost		0	1968	61	1968	(Abc-Paramount 11103)
14	Fool For You		0	1968	22	1968	(Curtom 1932)
15	This Is My Country		0	1968	25	1968	(Curtom 1934)

ISSUE	TITLE	UK LBL	UK POS	UK YEAR	US POS	US YEAR	US LBL
16	Choice Of Colours		0	1969	21	1969	(Curtom 1943)
17	Say You Love Me		0	1969	58	1969	(Curtom 1946)
18	Check Out Your Mind		0	1970	28	1970	(Curtom 1951)
19	(Baby) Turn On To Me		0	1970	56	1970	(Curtom 1954)
20	Finally Got Myself Together (I'm A Changed Man)		0	1974	17	1974	(Curtom 1997)
21	First Impression	(Curtom K 16638)	16	1975	0	1975	

Inaura Male Vocal/Instrumental Group from the UK

1	Coma Aroma	(EMI Cdem 421)	57	1996	0	1996	

Incantation Male Vocal/Instrumental Group from the UK

1	Cacharpaya (Andes Pumpsa Daesi)	(Beggars Banquet Beg 84)	12	1982	0	1982	

In Crowd Male Vocal/Instrumental Group from the UK

1	That's How Strong My Love Is	(Parlophone R 5276)	48	1965	0	1965	

Incognito Mixed Vocal/Instrumental Group From France

1	Parisienne Girl	(Ensign Eny 44)	73	1980	0	1980	
2	Always There	(Talkin Loud Tlk 10)	6	1991	0	1991	
3	Crazy For You	(Talkin Loud Tlk 14)	59	1991	0	1991	
4	Don't You Worry 'bout A Thing	(Talkin Loud Tlk 21)	19	1992	0	1992	
5	Change	(Talkin Loud Tlk 26)	52	1992	0	1992	
6	Still A Friend Of Mine	(Talkin Loud Tlkcd 42)	47	1993	0	1993	
7	Givin' It Up	(Talkin Loud Tlkcd 44)	43	1993	0	1993	
8	Pieces Of A Dream	(Talkin Loud Tlkcd 46)	35	1994	0	1994	
9	Everyday	(Talkin Loud Tlkcd 55)	23	1995	0	1995	
10	I Hear Your Name	(Talkin Loud Tlcd 56)	42	1995	0	1995	
11	Jump To My Love / Always There	(Talkin Loud Tlcd 7)	29	1996	0	1996	
12	Out Of The Storm	(Talkin Loud Tlcd 14)	57	1996	0	1996	

Indecent Obsession Names:David Dixon, Michael Szumowski, Andrew Coyne & Darryl Simms

1	Tell Me Something		0	1990	31	1990	(MCA 79029)

Indeep Mixed Vocal Duo from the USA

1	Last Night A DJ Saved My Life	(Sound Of New York SNY 1)	13	1983	0	1983	
2	When Boys Talk	(Sound Of New York SNY 3)	67	1983	0	1983	

Independents Names: Chuck Jackson, Maurice Jackson, Eric Thomas, Marvin Yancy Jr. & Helen Curry

* 1	Leaving Me		0	1973	21	1973	(Wand 11252)

India Female Vocalist from the USA

1	Love And Happiness (Yemaya Y Ochun)	(Cooltempo Cdcool 287)	50	1994	0	1994	
2	I Can't Get No Sleep	(A&M 5811412)	44	1995	0	1995	
3	Oye Como Va	(Media Mcstd 40013)	36	1996	0	1996	

Indian Vibes Male Vocal/Instrumental Group from the UK

1	Mathar	(Virgin International Dinsd 136)	68	1994	0	1994	

Inez Foxx Female Vocalist, B: 9 Sep 1942, Greensboro, North Carolina

* 1	Mockingbird	(Sue Wi 323)	34	1969	7	1963	(Symbol 919)
2	Hurt By Love	(United Artists Up 2269)	40	1964	0	1964	
3	Mockingbird (Re-Entry)	(Sue Wi 323)	34	1969	0	1969	

Infiniti

1	Will You Be My Baby?	(GHQ 74321339092)	53	1996	0	1996	

Information Society Names Paul Robb, Kurt Valaquen, Amanda Kramer & James Cassidy

* 1	What's On Your Mind (Pure Energy)		0	1988	3	1988	(Tommy Boy 27826)
2	Walking Away		0	1989	9	1989	(Tommy Boy 27736)
3	Think		0	1990	28	1990	(Tommy Boy 19591)
	ANANDA KRAMER LEFT THE GROUP IN 1990						

Ingram Male Vocal/Instrumental Group from the USA

1	Smoothin' Groovin'	(Streetwave Wave 3)	56	1983	0	1983	

Ini Kamoze Male Reggae Singer/Author From Kingston, Jamaica

* 1	Here Comes The Hot Stepper	(Columbia 6610472)	4	1995	1	1994	(Columbia 77614)

Ink Spots Male Vocal Group from the USA

* 32	I'm Making Believe (From Sweet And Low-Down)		0	1944	1	1944	(Decca 23356)
* 35	The Gypsy		0	1946	1	1946	(Decca 18817)
36	Prisoner Of Love		0	1946	9	1946	(Decca 18864)
* 37	To Each His Own		0	1946	1	1946	(Decca 23615)
38	You Can't See The Sun When You're Crying		0	1947	19	1947	(Decca 23809)
39	Ask Anyone Who Knows		0	1947	17	1947	(Decca 23900)

ISSUE	TITLE	UK LBL	UK POS	UK YEAR	US POS	US YEAR	US LBL
40	Say Something Sweet To Your Sweetheart		0	1948	22	1948	(Decca 24507)
41	You Were Only Fooling (While I Was Falling In Love)		0	1948	8	1948	(Decca 24507)
42	You're Breaking My Heart		0	1949	9	1949	(Decca 24693)
43	Who Do You Know In Heaven (That Made You The Angel You Are?)		0	1949	21	1949	(Decca 24693)
44	Echoes		0	1950	24	1950	(Decca 24741)
45	Sometime		0	1950	26	1950	(Decca 27102)
46	If		0	1951	23	1951	(Decca 27391)
47	Melody Of Love	(Parlophone R 3977)	10	1955	0	1955	

NAMES ORVILLE JONES, BILLY KENNY, CHARLIE FUQUA, IVORY WATSON • HITS 28, 34 ARE CREDITED TO ELLA FITZGERALD & THE INK SPOTS   OBITUARY: JONES D: NOV 1944.

Inmates Male Vocal/Instrumental Group from the UK

1	The Walk	(Radar Ada 47)	36	1979	0	1979	

Inner Circle Male Vocal/Instrumental Group From Jamaica

1	Everything Is Great	(Island Wip 6472)	37	1979	0	1979	
2	Stop Breaking My Heart	(Island Wip 6488)	50	1979	0	1979	
3	Sweat (A La La La La Long)	(Magnet 9031776802)	43	1992	16	1993	(Big Beat 98429)
4	Sweat (A La La La La Long) (Re-Entry)	(Magnet 9031776802)	3	1993	10	1993	
* 5	Bad Boys	(Magnet Mag 1017cd)	52	1993	8	1993	(Big Beat 98426)
6	Games People Play	(Magnet Mag 1026cd)	67	1994	0	1994	

Inner City Mixed Vocal/Instrumental Duo from the USA

1	Big Fun	(10 Ten 240)	8	1988	0	1988	
2	Good Life	(10 Ten 249)	4	1988	0	1988	
3	Ain't Nobody Better	(10 Ten 252)	10	1989	0	1989	
4	Do You Love What You Feel	(10 Ten 237)	16	1989	0	1989	
5	Watcha Gonna Do With My Lovin'	(10 Ten 290)	12	1989	0	1989	
6	That Man (He's All Mine)	(10 Ten 334)	42	1990	0	1990	
7	Till We Meet Again	(10 Ten 337)	47	1991	0	1991	
8	Let It Reign	(Ten Ten 392)	51	1991	0	1991	
9	Hallelujah '92	(Ten Ten 398)	22	1992	0	1992	
10	Pennies From Heaven	(Ten Ten 405)	24	1992	0	1992	
11	Praise	(Ten Tenx 408)	59	1992	0	1992	
12	Till We Meet Again (Re-Mix)	(Ten Tencd 414)	55	1993	0	1993	
13	Do Ya	(Six6 Sixcd 107)	44	1994	0	1994	
14	Share My Life	(Six6 Sixcd 114)	62	1994	0	1994	
15	Your Love	(Six6 Sixcd 127)	28	1996	0	1996	
16	Do Me Right	(Six6 Sixxcd 2)	47	1996	0	1996	

Innerzone Orchestra Male Producer Carl Craig from the USA

1	Bug In The Bassbin	(Mo Wax Mw 049cd)	68	1996	0	1996	

Innocence (1) Mixed Vocal/Instrumental Group from the UK

1	Natural Thing	(Cooltempo Cool 201)	16	1990	0	1990	
2	Silent Voice	(Cooltempo Cool 212)	37	1990	0	1990	
3	Let's Push It	(Cooltempo Cool 220)	25	1990	0	1990	
4	A Matter Of Fact	(Cooltempo Cool 223)	37	1990	0	1990	
5	Remember The Day	(Cooltempo Cool 226)	56	1991	0	1991	
6	I'll Be There	(Cooltempo Cool 255)	26	1992	0	1992	
7	One Love In My Lifetime	(Cooltempo Cool 263)	40	1992	0	1992	
8	Build	(Cooltempo Cool 267)	72	1992	0	1992	

Innocence (2) Singer/Songwriting Duo Pete Anders & Vinnie Poncia

1	There's Got To Be A Word		0	1967	34	1967	(Kama Sutra 214)
	The Duo Have Also Recorded As The Trade Winds						

Innocents Names James West, Al Candelaria & Darron Stankey With Backup Vocals From Kath Young

1	Honest I Do		0	1960	28	1960	(Indigo 105)
2	Gee Whiz		0	1960	28	1960	(Indigo 111)

Inspiral Carpets Male Vocal/Instrumental Group from the UK

1	Move	(Cow Dung 6)	49	1989	0	1989	
2	This Is How It Feels	(Cow Dung 7)	14	1990	0	1990	
3	She Comes In The Fall	(Cow Dung 10)	27	1990	0	1990	
4	Island Head (EP)	(Cow Dung 11)	21	1990	0	1990	
5	Caravan	(Cow Dung 13)	30	1991	0	1991	
6	Please Be Cruel	(Cow Dung 15)	50	1991	0	1991	
7	Dragging Me Down	(Cow Dung 16)	12	1992	0	1992	
8	Two Worlds Collide	(Cow Dung 17)	32	1992	0	1992	
9	Generations	(Cow Dung 18t)	28	1992	0	1992	
10	Bitches Brew	(Cow Dung 20t)	36	1992	0	1992	

	ISSUE	TITLE	UK LBL	UK POS	UK YEAR	US POS	US YEAR	US LBL
	11	How It Should Be	(Cow Dung 22cd)	49	1993	0	1993	
	12	Saturn 5	(Cow Dung 23cd)	20	1994	0	1994	
	13	I Want You	(Cow Dung 24cd)	18	1994	0	1994	
	14	Uniform	(Cow Dung 26cd)	51	1994	0	1994	
	15	Joe	(Cow Dung 27cd)	37	1995	0	1995	

Inspirational Choir Mixed Vocal Choir from the USA

	ISSUE	TITLE	UK LBL	UK POS	UK YEAR	US POS	US YEAR	US LBL
	1	Abide With Me	(Epic A 4997)	44	1984	0	1984	
	2	Abide With Me (Re-Issue)	(Portrait A 4997)	36	1985	0	1985	

Instant Funk Male Vocal/Instrumental Group from the USA   Formed in 1977 and led by James Carmichael

	ISSUE	TITLE	UK LBL	UK POS	UK YEAR	US POS	US YEAR	US LBL
	1	Got My Mind Made Up (You Can Get It Girl)	(Salsoul Ssol 114)	46	1979	20	1979	(Salsoul 2078)

Intastella Mixed Vocal/Instrumental Group from the UK

	ISSUE	TITLE	UK LBL	UK POS	UK YEAR	US POS	US YEAR	US LBL
	1	Dream Some Paradise	(Mca Mcs 1520)	69	1991	0	1991	
	2	People	(MCA MCS 1559)	74	1991	0	1991	
	3	Century	(MCA MCS 1585)	70	1991	0	1991	
	4	The Night	(Planet 3 Gxy 2005cd)	60	1995	0	1995	

Intelligent Hoodlum Male Rap Group from the USA

	ISSUE	TITLE	UK LBL	UK POS	UK YEAR	US POS	US YEAR	US LBL
	1	Back To Reality	(A&M Am 598)	55	1990	0	1990	

Interactive Male Instrumental/Production Group From Germany

	ISSUE	TITLE	UK LBL	UK POS	UK YEAR	US POS	US YEAR	US LBL
	1	Forever Young	(Ffreedom Tabcd 235)	28	1996	0	1996	

Intrigues Soul Trio Hails From Philadelphia

	ISSUE	TITLE	UK LBL	UK POS	UK YEAR	US POS	US YEAR	US LBL
	1	In A Moment		0	1969	31	1969	(Yew 1001)

Intro Male Vocal Trio From New York

	ISSUE	TITLE	UK LBL	UK POS	UK YEAR	US POS	US YEAR	US LBL
	1	Come Inside		0	1993	33	1993	(Atlantic 87317)

Intruders Male Vocal Group from the USA   Names: Sam Brown, Eugene Daughtry, Phill Terry & Robert Edwards

	ISSUE	TITLE	UK LBL	UK POS	UK YEAR	US POS	US YEAR	US LBL
	1	Together		0	1967	48	1967	(Gamble 205)
*	2	Cowboys To Girls		0	1968	6	1968	(Gamble 214)
	3	(Love Is Like A) Baseball Game		0	1968	26	1968	(Gamble 217)
+	4	Slow Drag		0	1968	12	1968	(Gamble 221)
	5	Sad Girl		0	1969	47	1969	(Gamble 235)
	6	When We Get Married		0	1970	45	1970	(Gamble 4004)
+	7	I'm Girl Scouting		0	1971	16	1971	(Gamble 4009)
	8	I Bet He Don't Love You (Like I Love You)		0	1971	20	1971	(Gamble 4016)
+	9	(Win Place Or Show) She's A Winner	(Philadelphia Int. Pir 2212)	14	1974	12	1972	(Gamble 672)
	10	I'll Always Love My Mama (Part 1)	(Philadelphia Int. Pir 2149)	32	1974	36	1973	(Gamble 2506)
	11	I Wanna Know Your Name		0	1973	60	1973	(Gamble 2508)
	12	Who Do You Love	(Streetwave Khan 34)	65	1984	0	1984	

In Tua Nua Mixed Vocal/Instrumental Group From Ireland

	ISSUE	TITLE	UK LBL	UK POS	UK YEAR	US POS	US YEAR	US LBL
	1	All I Wanted	(Virgin Vs 1072)	69	1988	0	1988	

INXS Male Vocal/Instrumental Group from Australia

	ISSUE	TITLE	UK LBL	UK POS	UK YEAR	US POS	US YEAR	US LBL
	1	The One Thing		0	1983	30	1983	(Atco 99905)
	2	What You Need	(Mercury Inxs 5)	51	1986	5	1986	(Atlantic 89460)
	3	Listen Like Thieves	(Mercury Inxs 6)	46	1986	0	1986	
	4	Kiss The Dirt (Falling Down The Mountain)	(Mercury Inxs 7)	54	1986	0	1986	
	5	Need You Tonight	(Mercury Inxs 8)	58	1987	1	1987	(Atlantic 89188)
	6	New Sensation	(Mercury Inxs 9)	25	1988	3	1988	(Atlantic 89144)
	7	Devil Inside	(Mercury Inxs 10)	47	1988	2	1988	(Atlantic 89080)
	8	Never Tear Us Apart	(Mercury Inxs 11)	24	1988	7	1988	(Atlantic 89038)
	9	Need You Tonight (Re-Issue)	(Mercury Inxs 12)	2	1988	0	1988	
	10	Mystify	(Mercury Inxs 13)	14	1989	0	1989	
*	11	Suicide Blonde	(Mercury Inxs 14)	11	1990	9	1990	(Atlantic 87860)
	12	Disappear	(Mercury Inxs 15)	21	1990	8	1991	(Atlantic 87784)
	13	Good Times	(Atlantic A 7751)	18	1991	0	1991	
	14	By My Side	(Mercury Inxs 16)	42	1991	0	1991	
	15	Bitter Tears	(Mercury Inxs 17)	30	1991	0	1991	
	16	Shining Star (EP)	(Mercury Inxs 18)	27	1991	0	1991	
	17	Heaven Sent	(Mercury Inxs 19)	31	1992	0	1992	
	18	Baby Don't Cry	(Mercury Inxs 20)	20	1992	0	1992	
	19	Not Enough Time		0	1992	28	1992	(Atlantic 87437)
	20	Taste It	(Mercury Inxs 23)	21	1992	0	1992	
	21	Beautiful Girl	(Mercury Inxcd 24)	23	1993	0	1993	
	22	The Gift	(Mercury Inxcd 25)	11	1993	0	1993	
	23	Please (You Got That...)	(Mercury Inxcd 26)	50	1993	0	1993	
	24	The Strangest Party (These Are The Times)	(Mercury Inxcd 27)	15	1994	0	1994	

ISSUE	TITLE	UK LBL	UK POS	UK YEAR	US POS	US YEAR	US LBL
25	Elegantly Wasted	(Mercury Inxcd 28)	20	1997	0	1997	
26	Everything	(Mercury Inxdd 29)	71	1997	0	1997	

Irene Cara Female Vocalist/Pianist, B: 18 Mar 1959 New York City

ISSUE	TITLE	UK LBL	UK POS	UK YEAR	US POS	US YEAR	US LBL
1	Fame	(RSO 90)	1	1982	4	1980	(RSO 1034)
2	Out Here On My Own	(RSO 66)	58	1982	19	1982	(RSO 1048)
* 3	Flashdance - What A Feeling	(Casablanca Can 1016)	2	1983	1	1983	(Casablanca 811440)
4	Why Me?		0	1983	13	1983	(Geffen 29464)
5	The Dream (Hold On To Your Dream)		0	1984	37	1984	(Geffen 29396)
6	Breakdance		0	1984	8	1984	(Geffen 29328)

Iris Williams Female Vocalist from the UK

ISSUE	TITLE	UK LBL	UK POS	UK YEAR	US POS	US YEAR	US LBL
1	He Was Beautiful (Cavantina)	(Columbia Db 9070)	18	1979	0	1979	

Irish Rovers Names Will & George Millar, Joe Millar, Jimmy Ferguson & Wilcil McDowell

ISSUE	TITLE	UK LBL	UK POS	UK YEAR	US POS	US YEAR	US LBL
1	The Unicorn		0	1968	7	1968	(Decca 32254)
2	Wasn't That A Party		0	1981	37	1981	(Epic 51007)

Irma Thomas Real Name Irma Lee B: 18 Feb 1941 Ponchatoula, Louisiana

ISSUE	TITLE	UK LBL	UK POS	UK YEAR	US POS	US YEAR	US LBL
1	Wish Someone Would Care		0	1964	17	1964	

Iron Butterfly Names Doug Ingle, Erik Braunn, Lee Dorman & Ron Bushy

ISSUE	TITLE	UK LBL	UK POS	UK YEAR	US POS	US YEAR	US LBL
1	In-A-Gadda-Da-Vida		0	1968	30	1968	(Atco 6606)

Iron Maiden Male Vocal/Instrumental Group from the UK

ISSUE	TITLE	UK LBL	UK POS	UK YEAR	US POS	US YEAR	US LBL
1	Running Free	(EMI 5032)	34	1980	0	1980	
2	Sanctuary	(EMI 5065)	29	1980	0	1980	
3	Women In Uniform	(EMI 5105)	35	1980	0	1980	
4	Twilight Zone / Wrath Child	(EMI 5145)	31	1981	0	1981	
5	Purgatory	(EMI 5184)	52	1981	0	1981	
6	Maiden Japan	(EMI 5219)	43	1981	0	1981	
7	Run To The Hills	(EMI 5263)	7	1982	0	1982	
8	The Number Of The Beast	(EMI 5287)	18	1982	0	1982	
9	Flight Of Icarus	(EMI 5378)	11	1983	0	1983	
10	The Trooper	(EMI 5397)	12	1983	0	1983	
11	2 Minutes To Midnight	(EMI 5849)	11	1984	0	1984	
12	Aces High	(EMI 5502)	20	1984	0	1984	
13	Running Free (Live)	(EMI Emi 5532)	19	1985	0	1985	
14	Run To The Hills (Live)	(EMI Emi 5542)	26	1985	0	1985	
15	Wasted Years	(EMI Emi 5583)	18	1986	0	1986	
16	Stranger In A Strange Land	(EMI Emi 5589)	22	1986	0	1986	
17	Stranger In A Strange Land (Re-Entry)	(EMI Emi 5589)	71	1986	0	1986	
18	Can I Play With Madness	(EMI Em 49)	3	1988	0	1988	
19	The Evil That Men Do	(EMI Em 64)	5	1988	0	1988	
20	The Clairvoyant	(EMI Em 79)	6	1988	0	1988	
21	Infinite Dreams	(EMI Em 117)	6	1989	0	1989	
22	Infinite Dreams (Re-Entry)	(EMI Em 117)	74	1989	0	1989	
23	Holy Smoke	(EMI Em 153)	3	1990	0	1990	
24	Bring Your Daughter To The Slaughter	(EMI Empd 171)	1	1991	0	1991	
25	Be Quick Or Be Dead	(EMI Em 229)	2	1992	0	1992	
26	From Here To Eternity	(EMI Ems 240)	21	1992	0	1992	
27	Fear Of The Dark (Live)	(EMI Cdems 263)	8	1993	0	1993	
28	Hallowed Be Thy Name (Live)	(EMI Cdem 288)	9	1993	0	1993	
29	Man On The Edge	(EMI Cdem 398)	10	1995	0	1995	
30	Virus	(EMI Cdem 443)	16	1996	0	1996	

Ironhorse Rock Band Formed By Randy Bachman Of Bachman-Turner Overdrive Fame

ISSUE	TITLE	UK LBL	UK POS	UK YEAR	US POS	US YEAR	US LBL
1	Sweet Lui-Louise	(Scotti Brothers K 11271)	60	1979	36	1979	(Scotti Brothers 406)

Irving Fields Male Pianist/Combo Leader from the USA

ISSUE	TITLE	UK LBL	UK POS	UK YEAR	US POS	US YEAR	US LBL
1	The Wedding Song		0	1948	24	1948	(RCA Victor 9035)

Isaac Hayes Male Vocalist/Instrumentalist, B: 20 Aug 1942 Covington, Tennessee

ISSUE	TITLE	UK LBL	UK POS	UK YEAR	US POS	US YEAR	US LBL
1	By The Time I Get To Phoenix		0	1969	37	1969	(Enterprise 9003)
2	Walk On By		0	1969	30	1969	(Enterprise 9003)
3	Never Can Say Goodbye		0	1971	22	1971	(Enterprise 9031)
* 4	Theme From *Shaft*	(Stax 2025 069)	4	1971	1	1971	(Enterprise 9038)
5	Do Your Thing		0	1972	30	1972	(Enterprise 9042)
6	Theme From Men		0	1972	38	1972	(Enterprise 9058)
7	Joy (Part 1)		0	1974	30	1974	(Enterprise 9085)
8	Don't Let Go		0	1979	18	1979	(Polydor 2011)
9	Disco Connection	(ABC 4100)	10	1976	0	1976	

ISSUE	TITLE	UK LBL	UK POS	UK YEAR	US POS	US YEAR	US LBL
Isha-D	Mixed Vocal/Instrumental Duo from the UK						
1	Stay (Tonight)	(Cleveland City Blues Ccbcd 15005)	18	1995	0	1995	
2	Stay	(Satellite/3 Beat 74321498212)	58	1997	0	1997	
Isham Jones Orchestra	Male Orchestra Leader, B: 31 Jan 1894 Coalton, Ohio						
* 7	Wabash Blues		0	1921	1	1921	(Brunswick 5065)
Islanders	Names Randy Starr & Frank Metis Of Guitar And Accordian						
1	The Enchanted Sea		0	1959	15	1959	(Mayflower 16)
Isley Brothers	Male Vocal/Instrumental Group from the USA						
1	Shout (Part 1-2)		0	1959	47	1959	(RCA Victor)
* 2	Twist And Shout	(Stateside Ss 112)	42	1963	17	1962	(Wand 124)
3	This Old Heart Of Mine	(Tamla Motown Tmg 555)	47	1966	12	1966	(Tamla 54128)
4	I Guess I'll Always Love You	(Tamla Motown Tmg 572)	45	1966	0	1966	
+ 5	Take Me In Your Arms (And Rock Me A Little While)		0	1968	22	1968	(Tamla 54164)
6	This Old Heart Of Mine (Re-Entry)	(Tamla Motown Tmg 555)	3	1968	0	1968	
7	I Guess I'll Always Love You (Re-Issue)	(Tamla Motown Tmg 683)	11	1969	0	1969	
* 8	It's Your Thing	(Major Minor Mm 621)	30	1969	2	1969	(T-Neck 901)
9	Behind A Painted Smile	(Tamla Motown Tmg 693)	5	1969	0	1969	
10	I Turned You On		0	1969	23	1969	(T-Neck 902)
11	Put Yourself In My Place	(Tamla Motown Tmg 708)	13	1969	0	1969	
12	Love The One You're With		0	1971	18	1971	(T-Neck 930)
13	Pop That Thang		0	1972	24	1972	(T-Neck 935)
* 14	That Lady (Part 1)	(Epic Epc 1704)	14	1973	6	1973	(T-Neck 2251)
15	Highway Of My Life	(Epic Epc 1980)	25	1974	0	1974	
16	Summer Breeze	(Epic Epc 2244)	16	1974	0	1974	
* 17	Fight The Power (Part 1)		0	1975	4	1975	(T-Neck 2256)
18	For The Love Of You (Part 1-2)		0	1975	22	1975	(T-Neck 2259)
19	Harvest For The World	(Epic Epc 4369)	10	1976	0	1976	
20	Livin' In The Life		0	1977	40	1977	(T-Neck 2264)
21	Take Me To The Next Phase	(Epic Epc 6292)	50	1978	0	1978	
22	It's A Disco Night	(Epic Epc 7911)	14	1979	0	1979	
23	Don't Say Goodnight (It's Time For Love) (Part 1-2)		0	1980	39	1980	(T-Neck 2290)
24	Between The Sheets	(Epic A 3513)	52	1983	0	1983	
25	Floatin' On Your Love		0	1996	47	1996	(Island 854738)
26	Tears		0	1997	55	1997	(Island 854862)
Isley Jasper Isley	Male Vocal/Instrumental Group from the USA						
1	Caravan Of Love	(Epic A 6612)	52	1985	0	1985	
Isotonik	Male Producer, Real Name Chris Paul from the UK						
1	Different Strokes	(Ffrreedom Tab 101)	12	1992	0	1992	
2	Everywhere I Go / Let's Get Down	(Ffrreedom Tab 108)	25	1992	0	1992	
It Bites	Male Vocal/Instrumental Group from the UK						
1	Calling All The Heroes	(Virgin Vs 872)	6	1986	0	1986	
2	Whole New World	(Virgin Vs 896)	54	1986	0	1986	
3	The Old Man And The Angel	(Virgin Vs 941)	72	1987	0	1987	
4	Still Too Young To Remember	(Virgin Vs 1184)	60	1989	0	1989	
5	Still Too Young To Remember (Re-Issue)	(Virgin Vs 1238)	60	1990	0	1990	
It's Immaterial	Male Vocal/Instrumental Group from the UK						
1	Driving Away From Home (Jim's Tune)	(Siren Siren 15)	18	1986	0	1986	
2	Ed's Funky Diner (Friday Night, Saturday Morning)	(Siren Siren 24)	65	1986	0	1986	
Itty Bitty Boozy Woozy	Male Instrumental/Production Duo from Holland Duo Also Known As Klubbheads						
1	Tempo Fiesta (Party Time)	(Systematic Syscd 23)	34	1995	0	1995	
Ivan Matias	Male Vocalist from the USA						
1	So Good (To Come Home To) /I've Had Enough	(Arista 74321345072)	69	1996	0	1996	
Ivan Neville	Male Bassist From New Orleans, The Son Of Aaron Neville						
1	Not Just Another Girl		0	1988	26	1988	(Polydor 887814)
Ivor Biggun	Male Vocalist Doc Holliday from the UK						
1	The Winkers Song (Misprint)	(Beggars Banquet Bop 1)	22	1978	0	1978	
2	Bras On 45 (Family Version)	(Beggars Banquet Bop 6)	50	1981	0	1981	
Ivo Robic	Male Vocalist, B: 1927 Zagreb, Yugoslavia						
1	Morgen	(Polydor 23923)	23	1959	13	1959	(Laurie 3033)
	His Name Is Pronounced 'Eevo Robish'						

ISSUE	TITLE	UK LBL	UK POS	UK YEAR	US POS	US YEAR	US LBL
Ivory Joe Hunter	Male Pianist/Composer/R&B Vocalist, B: 10 Oct 1914 Kirbyville, Texas						
*+ 1	I Almost Lost My Mind		0	1950	1	1950	
* 2	Since I Met You Baby		0	1956	12	1956	
* 3	Empty Arms		0	1957	43	1957	
Ivy League	Male Vocal Group from the UK						
1	Funny How Love Can Be	(Piccadilly 7n 35222)	8	1965	0	1965	
2	That's Why I'm Crying	(Piccadilly 7n 35228)	22	1965	0	1965	
3	Tossing And Turning	(Piccadilly 7n 35251)	3	1965	0	1965	
4	Willow Tree	(Piccadilly 7n 35326)	50	1966	0	1966	
Ivy Three	Names Charles Koppelman, Art Berkowitz & Don Rubin						
1	Yogi		0	1960	8	1960	(Shell 720)
Izhar Cohen & Alphabeta	Mixed Vocal Group From Israel						
1	A-Ba-Ni-Bi	(Polydor 2001 781)	20	1978	0	1978	
Izit	Mixed Vocal/Instrumental Group from the UK						
1	Stories	(Ffrr F 122)	52	1989	0	1989	
Izzy Stradlin'	Male Vocal/Guitarist from the USA						
1	Pressure Drop	(Geffen GFS 25)	45	1992	0	1992	

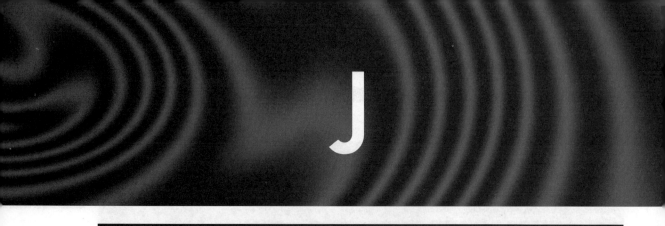

J

ISSUE	TITLE	UK LBL	UK POS	UK YEAR	US POS	US YEAR	US LBL
J Pac Male Vocal/Instrumental Duo from the UK							
1	Rock N' Roll (Dole)	(East West YZ 953CD)	51	1995	0	1995	
J. Blackfoot Male Vocalist from the USA							
1	Taxi	(Allegiance ALES 2)	48	1984	0	1984	
J. Frank Wilson & The Cavaliers Male Vocalist, B: 11 Dec 1941, Lufkin, Texas							
* 1	Last Kiss		0	1964	2	1964	(Josie 923)
J. Geils Band Male Vocal/Instrumental Group from the USA							
1	Looking For A Love		0	1972	39	1972	(Atlantic 2844)
2	Give It To Me		0	1973	30	1973	(Atlantic 2953)
3	Must Of Got Lost		0	1974	12	1974	(Atlantic 3214)
4	One Last Kiss	(EMI America AM 507)	74	1979	35	1979	(EMI America 8007)
5	Come Back		0	1980	32	1980	(EMI AMERICA 8032)
6	Love Stinks		0	1980	38	1980	(EMI AMERICA 8039)
* 7	Centerfold	(EMI America EA135)	3	1982	1	1981	(EMI America 8102)
* 8	Freeze-Frame	(EMI America EA 134)	27	1982	4	1982	(EMI America 8108)
9	Angel In Blue	(EMI America EA 138)	55	1982	40	1982	(EMI America 8100)
10	I Do		0	1982	24	1982	(EMI AMERICA 8148)
	NAMES JEROME GELLS, PETER BLANKFIELD, DICK SALWITZ, SETH JUSTMAN, DANNY KLEIN AND STEPHEN JO BLADD						
J.A.L.N. Band Male Vocal/Instrumental Group from the UK/Jamaica							
1	Disco Music / I Like It	(Magnet MAG 73)	21	1976	0	1976	
2	I Got To Sing	(Magnet MAG 97)	40	1977	0	1977	
3	Get Up	(Magnet MAG 118)	53	1978	0	1978	
J.C. 001 Male Rapper from the UK							
1	Never Again	(Anxious ANX 1012CD)	67	1993	0	1993	
2	Cupid	(Anxious ANX 1014CD)	56	1993	0	1993	
J.D. Souther Real Name John David Souther B: Detroit & Raised In Amarillo, Texas							
1	You're Only Lonely		0	1979	7	1979	(Columbia 11079)
2	Her Town Too		0	1981	11	1981	(Columbia 60514)
J.J. Barrie Male Vocalist from Canada							
1	No Charge	(Power Exchange PX 209)	1	1976	0	1976	
J.J. Cale Male Vocalist, Real Name John J Cale B: 5 Dec 1938 Oklahoma City							
1	Crazy Mama		0	1972	22	1972	(Shelter 7314)
J.J. Fad Female Rap Trio from Los Angeles							
* 1	Supersonic		0	1988	30	1988	(Ruthless 99328)
	Names Juana Burns, Diana Birks & Michelle Franklin						
J.J. Jackson Real Name Jerome Louis Jackson B: 8 Apr 1941 Brooklyn							
1	But It's Alright		0	1966	22	1966	(Calla 119)
J.M. Silk Male Vocal/Instrumental Duo from the USA							
1	I Can't Turn Around	(RCA PB 49793)	62	1986	0	1986	
2	Let The Music Take Control	(RCA PB 49767)	47	1987	0	1987	
J.T. Taylor Male Vocalist from the USA							
1	Long Hot Summer Night	(MCA MCS 1567)	63	1991	0	1991	
2	Feel The Need	(MCA MCS 1592)	57	1991	0	1991	
3	Follow Me	(MCA MCS 161)	59	1992	0	1992	
J.X. Male Producer, Real Name Jake Williams from the UK							
1	Son Of A Gun	(Internal Dance IDC 5)	13	1994	0	1994	
2	You Belong To Me		17	1995	0	1995	
3	There's Nothing I Won't Do	(FFRREEDOM TABCD 241)	4	1996	0	1996	

ISSUE	TITLE	UK LBL	UK POS	UK YEAR	US POS	US YEAR	US LBL
Jack 'N' Chill	Male Instrumental Group from the UK						
1	The Jack That House Built	(OVAL TEN 174)	48	1987	0	1987	
2	The Jack That House Built (Re-entry)	(OVAL TEN 174)	6	1988	0	1988	
3	Beatin' The Heat	(10 TEN 234)	42	1988	0	1988	
Jack Blanchard & Misty Morgan	Husband And Wife Country Singers from the USA						
! 1	Big Black Bird (Spirit Of Our Love)		0	1969	59	1969	(Wayside 1028)
2	Tennessee Bird Walk		0	1970	23	1970	(Wayside010)
3	Humphrey The Camel		0	1970	78	1970	(Wayside 013)
Jack E. Makossa	Male Producer From Kenya						
1	The Opera House	(CHAMPION CHAMP 50)	48	1987	0	1987	
Jack Jones	Male Vocalist, B: 14 Jan 1938 Los Angeles						
1	Wives And Lovers		0	1964	14	1964	(KAPP 551)
2	Dear Heart		0	1964	30	1964	(KAPP 635)
3	The Race Is On		0	1965	15	1965	(KAPP 651)
4	The Impossible Dream (The Quest)		0	1966	35	1966	(KAPP 755)
5	Lady		0	1967	39	1967	(KAPP 800)
Jack Kilty	Male Vocalist, Previously Sang With Leo Reisman from the USA						
1	Sunflower		0	1949	28	1949	(MGM 10339)
Jack Lathrop & The Drugstore Cowboys	Male Singer/Guitarist from the USA						
1	You Call Everybody Darling		0	1948	27	1948	(RCA Victor 3109)
2	Hair Of Gold, Eyes Of Blue		0	1948	19	1948	(RCA Victor 3109)
3	My Darling, My Darling		0	1949	26	1949	(RCA Victor 3187)
Jack Nitzsche	Real Name Bernard Nitzsche B: 22 Apr 1937 Chicago						
1	The Lonely Surfer		0	1963	39	1963	(REPRISE 20202)
Jack Owens	Male Vocalist from the USA						
1	How Soon (Will I Be Seeing You)		0	1947	2	1947	(TOWER 1258)
2	Jealous Heart		0	1949	11	1949	(Decca 24711)
3	You're The Only One I Care For		0	1950	22	1950	(Decca 27412)
4	You're A Sweetheart		0	1950	29	1950	(Decca 24935)
5	Dream A Little Dream Of Me		0	1950	14	1950	(Decca 27096)
Jack Richards & The Marksmen	Orchestra Directed By Dick Jacobs from the USA						
1	Hers And His		0	1954	27	1954	(Coral 61164)
Jack Ross	Male Instrumentalist (Trumpet), B: 1916						
1	Cinderella		0	1962	16	1962	(DOT 16333)
	OBITUARY : D: 16 DEC 1982 (AGED 66).						
Jack Scott	Male Vocalist, Real Name Jack Scafone Jr B: 28 Jan 1936 Windsor, Ontario, Canada.						
* 1	My True Love	(London HLU 8626)	9	1958	3	1958	(Carlton 462)
2	Leroy	(London HLU 8626)	9	1958	11	1958	(Carlton 462)
3	With Your Love		0	1958	28	1958	(Carlton 483)
4	Goodbye Baby		0	1959	8	1959	(Carlton 493)
5	The Way I Walk	(London HLU 8912)	30	1959	35	1959	(Carlton 514)
* 6	What In The World's Come Over You	(Top Rank JAR 280)	11	1960	5	1960	(Top Rank 2028)
7	Burning Bridges	(Top Rank JAR 375)	32	1960	3	1960	(Top Rank 2041)
8	Oh, Little One	(Top Rank JAR 375)	32	1960	34	1960	(Top Rank 2041)
9	It Only Happened Yesterday		0	1960	38	1960	(Top Rank 2055)
! 10	You're Just Gettin' Better		0	1974	92	1974	(DOT 17504)
	JACK WROTE LEROY AFTER HIS FRIEND LEROY JOHNSON WAS JAILED FOR FIGHTING						
Jack Smith	Male Actor/Vocalist from the USA						
1	Jack! Jack! Jack!		0	1947	18	1947	(Capitol 403)
2	Civilization (Bongo, Bongo, Bongo)		0	1947	9	1947	(Capitol 465)
3	Big Brass Band From Brazil		0	1948	26	1948	(Capitol 15029)
4	Shaunty O'shea		0	1948	26	1948	(Capitol 484)
5	Baby Face		0	1948	13	1948	(Capitol 15078)
6	Takin' Miss Mary To The Ball		0	1948	26	1948	(Capitol 15073)
7	Tea Leaves		0	1948	17	1948	(Capitol 15102)
* 8	You Call Everybody Darling		0	1948	13	1948	(Capitol 15156)
9	Cuanto Le Gusta (La Parranda)		0	1948	14	1948	(Capitol 15280)
10	Lavender Blue (Dilly Dilly)		0	1949	17	1949	(Capitol 15225)
11	Cruising Down The River		0	1949	3	1949	(Capitol 15372)
12	Sunflower		0	1949	13	1949	(Capitol 15394)
	HIT 8 IS CREDITED TO JACK SMITH AND THE CLARK SISTERS • HIT 12 IS WITH THE CREW CHIEFS						

ISSUE	TITLE	UK LBL	UK POS	UK YEAR	US POS	US YEAR	US LBL
Jack Teagarden & His Orchestra	Male Bandleader/Singer/Instrumentalist (Trombone) from the USA						
1	Someone Stole Gabriel's Horn		0	1933	7	1933	(Columbia 2802)
2	I've Got It		0	1934	16	1934	(Columbia 2913)
3	The Sheik Of Araby		0	1939	14	1939	(Brunswick 8370)
4	Cinderella, Stay In My Arms		0	1939	19	1939	(Brunswick 8378)
5	The Waiter And The Porter And The Upstairs Maid		0	1941	23	1941	(Decca 3970)
	HIT 5 IS CREDITED TO BING CROSBY, MARY MARTIN & JACK TEAGARDEN WITH HIS ORCHESTRA • OBITUARY : D: 15 JAN 1964 (AGED 58).						
Jack Teter Trio	Male Trio, Guitar, Piano And Organ						
1	Johnson Rag		0	1949	6	1949	(LONDON 501)
Jack Wagner	Male Actor/Vocalist, B: Washington, Missouri						
1	All I Need		0	1984	2	1984	(QWEST 29238)
	PLAYS FRISCO JONES IN THE TV SOAP *GENERAL HOSPITAL*						
Jack Wild	Male Vocalist from the UK						
1	Some Beautiful	(Capitol CL 15635)	46	1970	0	1970	
Jackie Brenston	Male Vocal/Saxophonist, B: 15 Aug 1930 In Clarksdale, Mississippi						
*+ 1	Rocket 88		0	1951	1	1951	(Chess 1458)
	THE HIT WAS ACTUALLY RECORDED BY THE TURNER'S BAND WITH JACKIE SINGING LEAD AND PLAYING SAXOPHONE OBITUARY : D: 15 DEC 1979 HEART ATTACK						
Jackie De Shannon	Female Vocalist, Real Name Sharon Myers B: 21 Aug 1944 Hazel, Kentucky						
1	What The World Needs Now Is Love		0	1965	7	1965	(Imperial 66110)
* 2	Put A Little Love In Your Heart		0	1969	4	1969	(Imperial 66385)
3	Love Will Find A Way		0	1989	40	1989	(Imperial 66419)
Jackie Dennis	Male Vocalist from the UK						
1	La Dee Dah	(Decca F 10992)	4	1958	0	1958	
2	The Purple People Eater	(Decca F 11033)	29	1958	0	1958	
Jackie Gleason Orchestra	Male Comedian/Orchestra Leader, B: 26 Feb 1916 Brooklyn, New York						
* 1	Melancholy Serenade (From *The Honeymooners*)		0	1953	22	1953	(Capitol 2361)
2	Terry's Theme (From *Limelight*)		0	1953	30	1953	(Capitol 2507)
Jackie Lee (1)	Female Vocalist from the UK						
1	White Horses	(Philips BF 1674)	10	1968	0	1968	
2	Rupert	(PYE 7N 45003)	14	1971	0	1971	
Jackie Lee (2)	Real Name Is Earl Nelson B: 8 Sep 1928 Louisiana						
1	The Duck		0	1966	14	1966	(MIRWOOD 5502)
	EARL WAS THE OTHER HALF OF BOB & EARL. SEE SEPARATE ENTRY HIS STAGE NAME WAS A COMBINATION OF HIS & HIS WIFE'S MIDDLE NAMES						
Jackie Lee & His Orchestra	Male Pianist/Bandeader from the USA						
1	Isle Of Capri		0	1954	17	1954	(CORAL 61149)
Jackie McLean	Male Saxophonist from the USA						
1	Dr. Jackyll And Mr. Funk	(RCA PB 1575)	53	1979	0	1979	
Jackie Moore	Female Vocalist From Jacksonville, Florida						
* 1	Precious Precious		0	1971	30	1971	(Atlantic 2681)
2	Sweet Charlie Babe		0	1973	42	1973	(Atlantic 2956)
3	This Time Baby	(CBS 7722)	49	1979	0	1979	
Jackie Ross	Female Vocalist, B: 30 Jan 1946 In St. Louis, Raised In Chicago						
1	Selfish One		0	1964	11	1964	(CHESS 1903)
Jackie Trent	Female Vocalist from the UK						
1	Where Are You Now (My Love)	(PYE 7N 15776)	1	1965	0	1965	
2	When The Summer Is Over	(PYE 7N 15865)	39	1965	0	1965	
3	I'll Be There	(PYE 7N 17693)	38	1969	0	1969	
Jackie Wilson	Male Vocalist, B: 9 Jun 1934 Detroit						
1	Reet Petite	(Coral Q 72290)	6	1957	62	1957	(Brunswick 55024)
2	To Be Loved	(Coral Q 72306)	27	1958	22	1958	(Brunswick 55052)
3	To Be Loved (Re-entry)	(Coral Q 72306)	23	1958	0	1958	
4	To Be Loved (2nd Re-entry)	(Coral Q 72306)	23	1958	0	1958	
* 5	Lonely Teardrops		0	1959	7	1959	(Brunswick 55105)
6	That's Why (I Love You So)		0	1959	13	1959	(Brunswick 55121)
7	I'll Be Satisfied		0	1959	20	1959	(Brunswick 55136)
8	You Better Know It		0	1959	37	1959	(Brunswick 55149)
9	Talk That Talk		0	1959	34	1959	(Brunswick 55165)
* 10	Night		0	1960	4	1960	(Brunswick 55166)
11	Doggin' Around		0	1960	15	1960	(Brunswick 55166)
12	(You Were Made For) All My Love	(Coral Q 72407)	33	1960	12	1960	(Brunswick 55167)
13	A Woman, A Lover, A Friend		0	1960	15	1960	(Brunswick 55167)

ISSUE	TITLE	UK LBL	UK POS	UK YEAR	US POS	US YEAR	US LBL
14	(You Were Made For) All My Love (Re-entry)	(Coral Q 72407)	47	1960	0	1960	
15	Alone At Last	(Coral Q 72412)	50	1960	8	1960	(Brunswick 55170)
16	Am I The Man		0	1960	32	1960	(Brunswick 55170)
17	My Empty Arms / The Tear Of The Year		0	1961	9	1961	(Brunswick55201)
18	Please Tell Me Why		0	1961	20	1961	(Brunswick55208)
19	Your One And Only Love		0	1961	40	1961	(Brunswick 55208)
20	I'm Coming On Back To You		0	1961	19	1961	(Brunswick 55216)
21	Years From Now / You Don't Know What It Means		0	1961	37	1961	(Brunswick 55219)
22	The Greatest Hurt		0	1962	34	1962	(Brunswick 55221)
+ 23	I Just Can't Help It		0	1962	17	1962	(Brunswick 55229)
24	Baby Workout		0	1987	5	1963	(Brunswick 55239)
25	Shake! Shake! Shake!		0	1963	33	1963	(Brunswick 55246)
+ 26	Danny Boy		0	1965	25	1965	(Brunswick 55277)
+ 27	No Pity (In The Naked City)		0	1965	25	1965	(Brunswick 55280)
28	Whispers (Getting Louder)		0	1966	11	1966	(Brunswick 55300)
+ 29	I Don't Want To Lose You		0	1967	11	1967	(Brunswick 55309)
30	(Your Love Keeps Lifting Me) Higher And Higher	(MCA BAG 2)	11	1969	6	1967	(Brunswick 55336)
31	Since You Showed Me How To Be Happy		0	1967	32	1967	(Brunswick 55354)
32	I Get The Sweetest Feeling	(MCA MU 1160)	9	1972	34	1968	(Brunswick 55381)
+ 33	Helpless		0	1969	21	1969	(Brunswick 55418)
34	This Love Is Real		0	1970	56	1970	(Brunswick 55443)
+ 35	Love Is Funny That Way		0	1971	18	1971	(Brunswick 55461)
36	I Get The Sweetest Feeling / Higher And Higher (Re-Issue)	(Brunswick BR 18)	25	1975	0	1975	
37	Reet Petite (Re-Issue)	(SMP SKM 3)	1	1986	0	1986	
38	I Get The Sweetest Feeling (2nd Re-Issue)	(SMP SKM 1)	3	1987	0	1987	
39	(Your Love Keeps Lifting Me) (2nd re entry)	(SMP SKM10)	15	1987	0	1987	

OBITUARY : JACKIE SUFFERED A STROKE ON STAGEIN NEW JERSEY ON THE 25 SEP 1975 AND NEVER REALLY RECOVERED • D: 21 JAN 1984.

Jacks Male R&B Group from the USA

+ 1	Why Don't You Write Me		0	1955	4	1955	(RPM 428)

Jackson Browne Male Vocalist, B: 9 Oct 1948 Heidelberg, Germany

1	Doctor My Eyes		0	1972	8	1972	(Asylum 11004)
2	Here Comes Those Tears Again		0	1977	23	1977	(Asylum 45379)
3	Runnin' On Empty		0	1978	11	1978	(Asylum 45460)
4	Stay	(Asylum K 13128)	12	1978	20	1978	(Asylum 45485)
5	The Load-Out		0	1978	7	1978	(Asylum 45485)
6	Boulevard		0	1980	19	1980	(Asylum 47003)
7	That Girl Could Sing		0	1980	22	1980	(Asylum 47036)
8	Somebody's Baby		0	1982	7	1982	(Asylum 69982)
9	Lawyers In Love		0	1983	13	1983	(Asylum 69826)
10	Tender Is The Night		0	1983	25	1983	(Asylum 69791)
11	You're A Friend Of Mine		0	1985	18	1985	(Columbia
12	For America		0	1986	30	1986	(Asylum 69566)
13	In The Shape Of A Heart	(Elektra EKR 42)	66	1986	0	1986	
14	Everywhere I Go	(Elektra EKR 184CD1)	67	1994	0	1994	

OBITUARY: JACKSON D: 25 MAR 1976 COMMITTED SUICIDE.

Jackson Sisters Female Vocal Group from the USA

1	I Believe In Miracles	(URBAN URB 4)	72	1987	0	1987	

Jacksons/Jackson Five Male Vocal Group/Female Backing Vocals from the USA

* 1	I Want You Back	(Tamla Motown TMG 724)	2	1970	1	1969	(Motown 1157)
* 2	ABC	(Tamla Motown TMG 738)	8	1970	1	1970	(Motown 1163)
* 3	The Love You Save	(Tamla Motown TMG 746)	7	1970	1	1970	(Motown 1166)
* 4	I'll Be There	(Tamla Motown TMG 758)	4	1970	1	1970	(Motown 1171)
* 5	Mama's Pearl	(Tamla Motown TMG 769)	25	1971	2	1971	(Motown 1177)
* 6	Never Can Say Goodbye	(Tamla Motown TMG 778)	33	1971	2	1971	(Motown 1179)
7	Maybe Tomorrow		0	1971	20	1971	(Motown 1186)
8	Sugar Daddy		0	1971	10	1971	(Motown 1194)
9	Little Bitty Pretty One		0	1972	13	1972	(Motown 1199)
10	Lookin' Through The Windows	(TAMLA TMG 833)	9	1972	16	1972	(Motown 1205)
11	Corner Of The Sky (From *Pippin*)		0	1972	18	1972	(Motown 1214)
12	Santa Claus Is Comin' To Town	(Tamla Motown TMG 837)	43	1972	0	1972	
13	Doctor My Eyes	(Tamla Motown TMG 842)	9	1973	0	1973	
14	Hallelujah Day	(Tamla Motown TMG 856)	20	1973	28	1973	(Motown 1224)

ISSUE	TITLE	UK LBL	UK POS	UK YEAR	US POS	US YEAR	US LBL
15	Skywriter	(Tamla Motown TMG 865)	25	1973	0	1973	
16	Get It Together		0	1973	28	1973	(Motown 1277)
* 17	Dancing Machine		0	1974	2	1974	(Motown 1286)
18	Whatever You Got, I Want		0	1974	38	1974	(Motown 1308)
19	I Am Love (Part 1-2)		0	1975	15	1975	(Motown 1310)
* 20	Enjoy Yourself	(Epic EPC 5063)	42	1977	6	1977	(Epic 50289)
21	Show You The Way To Go	(Epic EPC 5266)	1	1977	28	1977	(Epic 50350)
22	Dreamer	(Epic EPC 5458)	22	1977	0	1977	
23	Goin' Places	(Epic EPC 5732)	26	1977	0	1977	
24	Even Though You've Gone	(Epic EPC 5919)	31	1978	0	1978	
25	Blame It On The Boogie	(Epic EPC 6683)	8	1978	0	1978	
26	Destiny	(Epic EPC 6983)	39	1979	0	1979	
* 27	Shake Your Body (Down To The Ground)	(Epic EPC 7181)	4	1979	7	1979	(Epic 50656)
28	Lovely One	(Epic EPC 9302)	29	1980	12	1980	(Epic 50938)
29	Heartbreak Hotel	(Epic EPC 9391)	44	1980	22	1981	(Epic 50959)
30	Can You Feel It	(Epic EPC 9554)	6	1981	0	1981	
31	Walk Right Now	(Epic EPC A 1294)	7	1981	0	1981	
32	State Of Shock	(Epic A 4431)	14	1984	3	1984	(Epic 04503)
33	Torture	(Epic A 4675)	26	1984	17	1984	(Epic 04575)
34	I Want You Back (Re-Mix)	(Motown ZB 41913)	8	1988	0	1988	
35	Nothin' (That Compares 2 U)	(Epic 654808 7)	33	1989	0	1989	

NAMES SIGMUND 'JACKIE', TITO, JERMAINE, MARION, MICHAEL & RANDY • REBBIE, LA TOYA & JANET BACKED THE GROUP

Jacky Noguez Bandleader Hails from Paris, France

1	Ciao, Ciao Bambina		0	1959	24	1959	(JAMIE 1127)

Jacqueline Boyer Female Vocalist from France

1	Tom Pillibi	(Columbia DB 4452)	33	1960	0	1960	

Jade Female Vocal Trio from Los Angeles

1	I Wanna Love You	(Giant 74321151662)	13	1993	16	1992	(Giant 18950)
* 2	Don't Walk Away	(Giant W 0160CD)	7	1993	4	1993	(Giant 18686)
3	One Woman	(Giant 74321165122)	22	1993	22	1993	(Giant 18606)
4	All Thru The Nite	(Giant 74321187552)	32	1994	0	1994	
5	Everyday Of The Week	(Giant 74321260242)	19	1995	20	1994	(Giant 17988)

Jagged Edge Male Vocal/Instrumental Group from the UK

1	You Don't Love Me	(Decca F 13067)	66	1990	0	1990	

Jaggerz Lead Singer Of The Rock Group Is Donnie Iris

* 1	The Rapper		0	1969	2	1969	(KAMA SUTRA 502)

Jags Male Vocal/Instrumental Group from the UK

1	Back Of My Hand	(Island WIP 6501)	17	1979	0	1979	
2	Woman's World	(Island WIP 6531)	75	1980	0	1980	

Jah Wobble's Invaders Of The Male Vocal/Multi-Instrumentalist from the UK

1	Vision Of You	(OVAL OVAL 103)	35	1992	0	1992	
2	Becoming More Like A God	(Island CID 571)	36	1994	0	1994	
3	The Sun Does Rise	(Island CID 587)	41	1994	0	1994	

HIT 1 HAS UNCREDITED VOCALS FROM SINEAD O'CONNOR

Jaki Graham Female Vocalist from the UK

1	Could It Be I'm Falling In Love	(Chrysalis GRAN 6)	5	1985	0	1985	
2	Round And Round	(EMI JAKI 4)	9	1985	0	1985	
3	Heaven Knows	(EMI JAKI 5)	59	1985	0	1985	
4	Mated	(EMI JAKI 6)	20	1985	0	1985	
5	Set Me Free	(EMI JAKI 7)	7	1986	0	1986	
6	Breaking Away	(EMI JAKI 8)	16	1986	0	1986	
7	Step Right Up	(EMI JAKI 9)	15	1986	0	1986	
8	No More Tears	(EMI JAKI 12)	60	1988	0	1988	
9	From Now On	(EMI JAKI 15)	73	1989	0	1989	
10	Ain't Nobody	(PULSE 8 CDLOSE 64)	44	1994	0	1994	
11	You Can Count On Me	(AVEX AVEXCD 1)	62	1995	0	1995	
12	Absolute E-Sensual	(AVEX AVEXCD 5)	69	1995	0	1995	

HITS 1 AND 4 ARE CREDITED TO DAVID GRANT AND JAKI GRAHAM • SEE ALSO DAVID GRANT

Jakie Quartz Female Vocalist from France

1	A La Vie, A L'amour	(PWL PWL 30)	55	1989	0	1989	

Jam Male Vocal/Instrumental Group from the UK

1	In The City	(Polydor 2058 866)	40	1977	0	1977	

ISSUE	TITLE	UK LBL	UK POS	UK YEAR	US POS	US YEAR	US LBL
2	All Around The World	(Polydor 2058 903)	13	1977	0	1977	
3	The Modern World	(Polydor 2058 945)	36	1977	0	1977	
4	News Of The World	(Polydor 2058 995)	27	1978	0	1978	
5	David Watts / 'A' Bomb In Wardour Street	(Polydor 2059 054)	25	1978	0	1978	
6	Down The Tube Station At Midnight	(Polydor POSP 8)	15	1978	0	1978	
7	Strange Town	(Polydor POSP 34)	15	1979	0	1979	
8	When You're Young	(Polydor POSP 69)	17	1979	0	1979	
9	The Eton Rifles	(Polydor POSP 83)	3	1979	0	1979	
10	Going Underground / Dreams Of Children	(Polydor POSP 113)	1	1980	0	1980	
11	All Around The World (Re-entry)	(Polydor 2058 903)	43	1980	0	1980	
12	David Watts / (Re-entry)	(Polydor 2059 054)	54	1980	0	1980	
13	In The City (Re-entry)	(Polydor 2058 866)	40	1980	0	1980	
14	News Of The World (Re-entry)	(Polydor 2058 995)	53	1980	0	1980	
15	Strange Town (Re-entry)	(Polydor POSP 34)	44	1980	0	1980	
16	The Modern World (Re-entry)	(Polydor 2058 945)	52	1980	0	1980	
17	Start	(Polydor 2059 266)	1	1980	0	1980	
18	That's Entertainment (Import)	(Metronome 0030 364)	21	1981	0	1981	
19	Funeral Pyre	(Polydor POSP 257)	4	1981	0	1981	
20	Absolute Beginners	(Polydor POSP 350)	4	1981	0	1981	
21	Town Callled Malice / Precious	(Polydor POSP 400)	1	1982	0	1982	
22	Just Who Is The Five O'clock Hero	(Polydor 2059 504)	8	1982	0	1982	
23	The Bitterest Pill (I Ever Had To Swallow)	(Polydor POSP 505)	2	1982	0	1982	
24	Beat Surrender	(Polydor POSP 540)	1	1982	0	1982	
25	All Around The World (2nd Re-entry)	(Polydor 2058 903)	38	1983	0	1983	
26	David Watts / '(2nd Re-entry)	(Polydor 2058 054)	50	1983	0	1983	
27	Down The Tube Station At Midnight (Re-entry)	(Polydor POSP 8)	30	1983	0	1983	
28	Going Underground / (Re-entry)	(Polydor POSP 113)	21	1983	0	1983	
29	In The City (2nd Re-entry)	(Polydor 2058 866)	47	1983	0	1983	
30	News Of The World (2nd Re-entry)	(Polydor 2058 995)	39	1983	0	1983	
31	Strange Town (2nd Re-entry)	(Polydor POSP 34)	42	1983	0	1983	
32	The Modern World (2nd Re-entry)	(Polydor 2058 945)	51	1983	0	1983	
33	When You're Young (Re-entry)	(Polydor POSP 69)	53	1983	0	1983	
34	That's Entertainment (Re-Issue)	(Polydor POSP 482)	60	1983	0	1983	
35	Start (Re-entry)	(Polydor 2059 266)	62	1983	0	1983	
36	The Eton Rifles (Re-entry)	(Polydor POSP 83)	54	1983	0	1983	
37	Town Called Malice / Precious (Re-entry)	(Polydor POSP 400)	73	1983	0	1983	
38	That's Entertainment (2nd Re-Issue)	(Polydor PO 155)	57	1991	0	1991	

Jam & Spoon (Featuring) Plavka Male Production/Instrumental Duo from Germany

1	Tales From A Danceographic Ocean (EP)	(R&S RSUK 14)	49	1992	0	1992	
2	The Complete Stella (Re-Mix)	(R&S RSUK 14X)	66	1992	0	1992	
3	Right In The Night (Fall In Love With Music)	(Epic 6600822)	31	1994	0	1994	
4	Find Me (Odyssey To Anyoona)	(Epic 6608082)	22	1995	0	1995	
5	Right In The Night (Re-Issue)	(Epic 6620182)	10	1995	0	1995	
6	Find Me (Odyssey To Anyoona (Re-Issue)	(Epic 6623242)	22	1995	0	1995	
7	Angel (Ladadi O-Hey O)	(Epic 6626392)	26	1995	0	1995	
8	Kaleidoscope Skies	(Epic 6646714)	48	1997	0	1997	

Jam Machine Male Vocal/Instrumental Group from the USA/Italy

1	Everyday	(Deconstruction PB 43299)	68	1989	0	1989	

Jam On The Mutha Male Vocal/Instrumental Group from the UK

1	Hotel California	(M&G MAGS 3)	62	1990	0	1990	

Jam Tronik Mixed Vocal/Instrumental Group from Germany

1	Another Day In Paradise	(Debut DEBT 3093)	19	1990	0	1990	

James Male Vocal/Instrumental Group from the UK

1	How Was It For You	(Fontana JIM 5)	32	1990	0	1990	
2	Come Home	(Fontana JIM 6)	32	1990	0	1990	
3	Lose Control	(Fontana JIM 7)	38	1990	0	1990	
4	Sit Down	(Fontana JIM 8)	2	1991	0	1991	
5	Sound	(Fontana JIM 9)	9	1991	0	1991	
6	Born Of Frustration	(Fontana JIM 10)	13	1992	0	1992	
7	Ring Of Bells	(Fontana JIM 11)	37	1992	0	1992	
8	Seven (EP)	(Fontana JIM 12)	46	1992	0	1992	
9	Sometimes	(Fontana JIM 13)	18	1993	0	1993	
10	Laid	(Fontana JIMCD 14)	25	1993	0	1993	
11	Jam J / Say Something	(Fontana JIMCD152)	24	1994	0	1994	

ISSUE	TITLE	UK LBL	UK POS	UK YEAR	US POS	US YEAR	US LBL
12	She's A Star	(Fontana JIMCD 16)	9	1997	0	1997	
13	Tomorrow	(Fontana JIMCD 17)	12	1997	0	1997	
14	Waltzing Along	(Fontana JIMCD 18)	23	1997	0	1997	

James & Bobby Purify Male Vocal Duo, James B: 12 May 1944, Robert Lee Dickey B: 2 Sep 1939)

* 1	I'm Your Puppet	(Mercury 6167 324)	12	1976	6	1966	(Bell 648)
2	Wish You Didn't Have To Go		0	1967	38	1967	(Bell 660)
3	Shake A Tail Feather		0	1967	25	1967	(Bell 669)
4	Let Love Come Between Us		0	1967	23	1967	(Bell 685)
5	Morning Glory	(Mercury 6167 380)	27	1976	0	1976	

ROBERT DICKEY LEFT IN LATE '60 WHEN BEN MOORE JOINED AS BOBBY PURIFY

James Boys Male Vocal Duo from the UK

1	Over And Over	(Penny Farthing PEN 806)	39	1973	0	1973	

James Brown Male Vocalist from the USA

+ 1	Please, Please, Please		0	1956	6	1956	(Federal 12258)
* 2	Try Me (I Need You)		0	1958	48	1958	(Federal 12337)
+ 3	I Want You So Bad		0	1959	20	1959	(Federal 12348)
+ 4	I'll Go Crazy		0	1960	15	1960	(Federal 12369)
5	Think / You've Got The Power		0	1960	33	1960	(Federal 12370)
+ 6	This Old Heart		0	1960	20	1960	(Federal 12378)
7	Bewildered		0	1961	40	1961	(King 5442)
8	I Don't Mind		0	1961	47	1961	(King 5466)
9	Baby You're Right		0	1961	49	1961	(King 5524)
+ 10	Just You And Me Darling		0	1961	17	1961	(King 5547)
11	Lost Someone		0	1961	48	1961	(King 5573)
12	Night Train		0	1962	35	1962	(King 5614)
+ 13	Shout And Shimmy		0	1962	16	1962	(King 5657)
+ 14	Three Hearts In A Tangle		0	1962	18	1962	(King 5701)
15	Prisoner Of Love		0	1963	18	1963	(King 5739)
16	Oh Baby Don't You Weep (Part 1)		0	1964	23	1964	(King 5842)
17	Out Of Sight		0	1964	24	1964	(SMASH 1919)
* 18	Papa's Got A Brand New Bag	(London HL 9990)	25	1965	8	1965	(King 5999)
* 19	I Got You (I Feel Good)	(PYE International7N 25350)	29	1966	3	1965	(King 6015)
20	Ain't That A Groove		0	1966	42	1966	(King 6025)
21	It's A Man's Man's Man's World	(PYE International7N 25371)	13	1966	8	1966	(King 6035)
+ 22	Money Won't Change You		0	1966	11	1966	(King 6048)
23	Don't Be A Drop-Out		0	1966	50	1966	(King 6056)
24	Bring It Up		0	1967	29	1967	(King 6071)
+ 25	Kansas City		0	1967	21	1967	(King 6086)
26	Let Yourself Go		0	1967	46	1967	(King 6100)
* 27	Cold Sweat (Part 1)		0	1967	7	1967	(King 6110)
28	Get It Together		0	1967	40	1967	(King 6122)
29	I Can't Stand Myself (When You Touch Me) /There Was A Time		0	1968	28	1968	(King 6144)
30	I Got The Feelin'		0	1968	6	1968	(King 6155)
31	Licking Stick-Licking Stick (Part 1)		0	1968	14	1968	(King 6166)
+ 32	America Is My Home		0	1968	13	1968	(King 6112)
+ 33	I Guess I'll Have To Cry, Cry, Cry		0	1968	15	1968	(King 6141)
34	Say It Loud - I'm Black And I'm Proud Of It (Part 1)		0	1968	10	1968	(King 6187)
35	Goodbye My Love		0	1968	31	1968	(King 6198)
36	Give It Up Or Turnit A Loose		0	1969	15	1969	(King 6213)
37	I Don't Want Nobody To Give Me Nothing		0	1969	20	1969	(King 6224)
38	The Popcorn		0	1969	30	1969	(King 6240)
39	Mother Popcorn (You Got To Have A Mother For Me (Part 1)		0	1969	11	1969	(King 6245)
40	Lowdown Popcorn		0	1969	41	1969	(King 6250)
41	World (Part 1)		0	1969	37	1969	(King 6258)
42	Let A Man Come In And Do The Popcorn (Part 1)		0	1969	21	1969	(King 6255)
43	Ain't It Funky Now (Part 1)		0	1969	24	1969	(King 6280)
44	Let A Man Come In And Do The Popcorn (Part 2)		0	1969	40	1969	(King 6275)
45	It's A New Day (Part 1-2)		0	1970	32	1970	(King 6292)
+ 46	Funky Drummer (Part 1)		0	1970	20	1970	(King 6290)
47	Brother Rapp (Part 1-2)		0	1970	32	1970	(King 6310)
48	Get Up I Feel Like A Being A Sex Machine	(Polydor 2001071)	32	1970	15	1970	(King 6318)
49	Super Bad (Part 1-2)		0	1970	13	1970	(King 6329)
50	Get Up, Get Into It, Get Involved (Part 1)		0	1971	34	1971	(King 6347)
51	Soul Power (Part 1)		0	1971	29	1971	(King 6368)
52	I Cried		0	1971	50	1971	(King 6363)

ISSUE	TITLE	UK LBL	UK POS	UK YEAR	US POS	US YEAR	US LBL
53	Escape-Ism (Part 1)		0	1971	35	1971	(PEOPLE 2500)
* 54	Hot Pants (She Got To Use What She Got To Get What She Wants)		0	1971	15	1971	(PEOPLE 2501)
55	Make It Funky (Part 1)		0	1971	22	1971	(Polydor 14088)
56	I'm A Greedy Man (Part 1)		0	1971	35	1971	(Polydor 14100)
57	Talking Loud And Saying Nothing (Part 1)		0	1972	27	1972	(Polydor 14109)
58	King Heroin		0	1972	40	1972	(Polydor 14116)
59	There It Is		0	1972	43	1972	(Polydor 14125)
60	Honky Tonk		0	1972	44	1972	(Polydor 14129)
* 61	Get On The Good Foot (Part 1)		0	1972	18	1972	(Polydor 14139)
62	I Got A Bag Of My Own		0	1972	44	1972	(Polydor 14153)
63	What My Baby Needs Now Is A Little More Lovin'		0	1972	56	1972	(Polydor 14157)
64	I Got Ants In My Pants (Part 1) (And I Want To Dance)		0	1973	27	1973	(Polydor 14162)
65	Down And Out In N.Y. City		0	1973	50	1973	(Polydor 14168)
66	Think		0	1973	77	1973	(Polydor 14177)
67	Sexy, Sexy, Sexy		0	1973	50	1973	(Polydor 14194)
68	Stoned To The Bone		0	1973	58	1973	(Polydor 14210)
* 69	The Payback (Part 1)		0	1974	26	1974	(Polydor 14223)
70	My Thang		0	1974	29	1974	(Polydor 14244)
71	Papa Don't Take No Mess (Part 1)		0	1974	31	1974	(Polydor 14255)
72	Funky President (People It's Bad) / Coldblooded		0	1974	44	1974	(Polydor 14258)
+ 73	Reality		0	1975	19	1975	(Polydor 14268)
+ 74	Sex Machine		0	1975	16	1975	(Polydor 14270)
+ 75	Hustle!!! (Dread On It)		0	1975	11	1975	(Polydor 14281)
76	Get Up Offa That Thing	(Polydor 2066 687)	22	1976	0	1976	
77	Body Heat	(Polydor 2066 763)	36	1977	0	1977	
78	Rapp Payback (Where Iz Moses?)	(RCA 28)	39	1981	0	1981	
79	Bring It On...Bring It On	(SONET SON 2258)	45	1966	0	1966	
80	Unity (Part 1 - The Third Coming)	(TOMMY BOY AFR 2)	49	1984	0	1984	
81	Froggy Mix	(Boiling Point FROG 1)	50	1985	0	1985	
82	Get Up I Feel Like Being A Sex Machine (Re-Issue)	(Boiling Point POSP 751)	47	1985	0	1985	
83	Living In America	(Scotti Brothers 05682)	5	1986	4	1986	(Scotti 6701)
84	Get Up I Feel Like Being(Re-Issue) (Re-entry)	(Boiling Point POSP 751)	46	1986	0	1986	
85	Gravity	(Scotti Brothers650059 7)	65	1986	0	1986	
86	She's The One	(URBAN URB 13)	45	1988	0	1988	
87	The Playback Mix	(URBAN URB 17)	12	1988	0	1988	
88	I'm Real	(Scotti BrothersJSB 1)	31	1988	0	1988	
89	I Got You (I Feel Good) (Re-Issue)	(A&M AM 444)	52	1988	0	1988	
90	Get Up (I Feel Like Being A (2nd Re-Issue)	Polydor PO 185	69	1991	0	1991	
91	I Got You (I Feel Good) (Re-Mix)	(FBI FBI 9)	72	1992	0	1992	
92	Can't Get Any Harder	(Polydor PZCD 262)	59	1993	0	1993	

SERVED 2 YEARS OF A 6-YEAR JAIL SENTENCE FOR A INTERSTATE POLICE CAR CHASE ON THE 15 DEC 1988

James Carr Male R&B Vocalist from the USA

+ 1	You've Got My Mind Messed Up		0	1965	7	1965	(Goldwax 302)
+ 2	The Dark End Of The Street		0	1967	10	1967	(Goldwax 317)
+ 3	A Man Needs A Woman		0	1968	16	1968	(Goldwax 332)

James Darren Male Vocalist, Real Name James William Ercolani B: 30 Oct 1936 Philadelphia

1	Because They're Young	(PYE International7N 25059)	29	1960	0	1960	
2	Goodbye Cruel World	(PYE International 7N 25116)	28	1961	3	1961	(COLPIX 609)
3	Her Royal Majesty	(PYE International 7N 25125)	36	1962	6	1962	(COLPIX 622)
4	Conscience	(PYE International7N 25138)	30	1962	11	1962	(COLPIX 630)
5	Mary's Little Lamb		0	1962	39	1962	(COLPIX 644)
6	All (From Run For Your Wife)		0	1967	35	1967	(Warner Bros. 5874)
! 7	Let Me Take You In My Arms Again		0	1978	53	1978	(RCA 11316)

James Galway Male Flautist from the UK

1	Annie's Song	(RCA RED SEAL RB 5085)	3	1978	0	1978	

James Gilreath Male Vocalist, B: 14 Nov 1939 Mississippi

1	Little Band Of Gold	(PYE International7N 25190)	29	1963	21	1963	(JOY 274)

James Ingram Male Vocalist From Akron, Ohio

1	Just Once		0	1981	17	1981	(A&M 2357)
2	One Hundred Ways		0	1982	14	1982	(A&M 2387)
* 3	Baby Come To Me	(QWEST K 15005)	11	1983	1	1982	(QWEST 50036)
4	Yah Mo B There	(QWEST W 9394)	44	1984	19	1984	(QWEST 29394)
5	Yah Mo B There (Re-enter)	(QWEST W 9394)	69	1984	0	1984	

ISSUE	TITLE	UK LBL	UK POS	UK YEAR	US POS	US YEAR	US LBL
6	What About Me?		0	1984	15	1984	(RCA 13899)
7	Yah Mo B There (Re-Mix)	(QWEST W 9394)	12	1985	0	1985	
8	Somewhere Out There	(MCA MCA 1132)	8	1987	2	1987	(MCA 52973)
9	Secret Garden (Sweet Seduction Suite)	(QWEST W 9992)	67	1990	31	1990	(QWEST 19992)
10	I Don't Have The Heart		0	1990	1	1990	(Warner Bros. 19911)
11	The Day I Fall In Love	(Columbia 6600282)	64	1994	0	1994	

James Last Band Orchestra Leader, B: 17 Apr 1929 Bremen, Germany

1	The Seduction (Love Theme)	(Polydor PD 2071)	48	1980	28	1980	(Polydor 2071)

James Ray Male R&B Vocalist, B: 1941 Washington D.C.

1	If You Gotta Make A Fool Of Somebody		0	1961	22	1961	(CAPRICE 110)

James Taylor Male Vocalist, B: 12 Mar 1948 Boston, Massachusetts

1	Fire And Rain	(Warner Bros. 7423)	42	1970	3	1970	(Warner Bros. WB 6104)
2	Country Road		0	1971	37	1971	(Warner Bros. 7460)
* 3	You've Got A Friend	(Warner Bros. WB 16085)	4	1971	1	1971	(Warner Bros. 7498)
4	Long Ago And Far Away		0	1971	31	1971	(Warner Bros. 7521)
5	Don't Let Me Be Lonely Tonight		0	1973	14	1973	(Warner Bros. 7655)
* 6	Mockingbird	(ELEKTRA K 12134)	34	1974	5	1974	(ELEKTRA 45880)
7	How Sweet It Is (To Be Loved By You)		0	1975	5	1975	(Warner Bros. 8109)
8	Shower The People		0	1976	22	1976	(Warner Bros. 8222)
9	Handy Man		0	1977	4	1977	(Columbia 10557)
! 10	Bartender's Blues		0	1977	88	1977	(Columbia 10557)
11	Your Smiling Face		0	1977	20	1977	(Columbia 10602)
12	(What A) Wonderful World		0	1978	17	1978	(Columbia 10676)
13	Devoted To You		0	1978	36	1978	(ELEKTRA 45506)
14	Up On The Roof		0	1979	28	1979	(Columbia 11005)
15	Her Town Too		0	1981	11	1981	(Columbia 60514)

Jamie J. Morgan Male Vocalist from the USA

1	Walk On The Wild Side	(TABU 655596 7)	27	1990	0	1990	

Jamie Walters Male Actor/Vocalist from the USA

1	Hold On		0	1995	16	1995	(Atlantic 87240)

Jamies Tom Jamison & His Sister Serena Lead The Massachusetts Based Quartet

1	Summertime, Summertime		0	1958	26	1958	(Epic 9281)

Jamiroquai Male Vocal/Instrumental Group from the UK

1	When You Gonna Learn	(ACID JAZZ JAZID 46T)	52	1992	0	1992	
2	When You Gonna Learn (Re-entry)	(ACID JAZZ JAZID 46T)	69	1993	0	1993	
3	Too Young To Die	(SONY S2 6590112)	12	1993	0	1993	
4	Blow Your Mind	(SONY S2 6592972)	10	1993	0	1993	
5	Emergency On Planet Earth	(SONY S2 6595782)	32	1993	0	1993	
6	When You Gonna Learn (Re-Issue)	(SONY S2 6596952)	28	1993	0	1993	
7	Space Cowboy	(SONY S2 6608512)	17	1994	0	1994	
8	Half The Man	(SONY S2 6610032)	15	1994	0	1994	
9	Stillness In Time	(SONY S2 6620255)	9	1995	0	1995	
10	Do U Know Where You're Coming From	(RENK CDRENK 63)	12	1996	0	1996	with M-People
11	Virtual Insanity	(SONY S2 6636132)	3	1996	0	1996	
12	Cosmic Girl	(SONY S2 6638292)	6	1996	0	1996	
13	Alright	(SONY S2 66423525)	6	1997	0	1997	

Jammers Male Vocal/Instrumental Group from the USA

1	Be Mine Tonight	(SALSOUL SAL101)	59	1983	0	1983	

Jamo Thomas Male Vocalist from the USA

1	I Spy (For The FBI)	(Polydor 56755)	48	1969	0	1969	
2	I Spy (For The FBI) (Re-entry)	(Polydor 56755)	44	1969	0	1969	

Jan & Dean Male Vocal Duo, Real Names Jan Berry B: 4 Mar 1941, Dean Torrence B: 40 Mar 1940

1	Jennie Lee		0	1958	6	1958	(ARWIN 108)
2	Baby Talk		0	1959	10	1959	(DORE 522)
3	Heart And Soul	(London HLH 9395)	24	1961	25	1961	(CHALLENGE 9111)
4	Linda		0	1963	28	1963	(Liberty 55531)
* 5	Surf City	(Liberty LIB 55580)	6	1963	1	1963	(Liberty 55580)
6	Honolulu Lulu		0	1963	11	1963	(Liberty 55613)
7	Drag City		0	1964	10	1964	(Liberty 55641)
8	Dead Man's Curve		0	1964	8	1964	(Liberty 55672)
9	The New Girl In School		0	1964	37	1964	(Liberty 55672)
10	Little Old Lady From Pasadena		0	1964	3	1964	(Liberty 55704)
11	Ride The Wild Surf		0	1964	16	1964	(Liberty 55724)

ISSUE	TITLE	UK LBL	UK POS	UK YEAR	US POS	US YEAR	US LBL
12	Sidewalk-Surfin'		0	1964	25	1964	(Liberty 55727)
13	You Really Know How To Hurt A Guy		0	1965	27	1965	(Liberty 55792)
14	I Found A Girl		0	1965	30	1965	(Liberty 55833)
15	Popsicle		0	1966	21	1966	(Liberty 55886)
	HIT 1 IS CREDITED TO JAN & ARNIE • IN APRIL 1966 JAN WAS SERIOUSLY INJURED IN A CAR ACCIDENT F						

Jan & Kjeld   The Male Vocal Duo Are from Copenhagen, Denmark

* 1	Banjo Boy	(EMBER S 101)	36	1965	58	1960	(ARIOLA)

Jan August   Female Vocalist/Pianist, Real Name Jan Augustoff from the USA

1	Misirou		0	1946	7	1946	(DIAMOND 2009)
2	Bewitched		0	1950	8	1950	(Mercury 5399)
3	Theme From The Threepenny Opera (Moritat)	(MGM 890)	9	1956	8	1956	(MGM 12149)
	HIT 2 IS CREDITED TO JAN AUGUST AND JERRY MURAD'S HARMONICATS • HIT 3 IS CREDITED TO DICK HYMAN TRIO AND JAN AUGUST						

Jan Bradley   Real Name Addie Bradley B: 6 Jul 1943 Mississippi

1	Mama Didn't Lie		0	1963	14	1963	(CHESS 1845)

Jan Garber Orchestra   Male Orchestra Leader from the USA

58	The Gypsy		0	1946	14	1946	(BLACK & WHITE 774)
59	Bedelia		0	1948	22	1948	(Columbia 38205)
60	Bella Bella Marie		0	1949	28	1949	(Capitol 15181)
61	You're Breaking My Heart		0	1949	19	1949	(Capitol 719)
62	Jealous Heart		0	1949	22	1949	(Capitol 759)
63	The Old Piano Roll Blues		0	1950	30	1950	(Capitol 970)
64	I Wanna Be Loved		0	1950	28	1950	(Capitol 1044)
65	If		0	1951	26	1951	(Capitol 1351)
66	The Morning Side Of The Mountain		0	1951	29	1951	(Capitol 1594)

Jan Hammer   Male Instrumentalist (Keyboards), B: 1950 Prague, Czechoslovakia

1	Miami Vice Theme	(MCA MCA 1000)	5	1985	1	1985	(MCA 52666)
2	Crockett's Theme	(MCA MCA 1193)	2	1987	0	1987	
3	Crockett's Theme (Re-Issue)	(MCA MCS 1541)	47	1991	0	1991	

Jan Peerce   Male Vocalist (Tenor) from the USA

1	Bluebird Of Happiness		0	1948	23	1948	(RCA Victor 9007)
2	What Is A Boy?		0	1951	22	1951	(RCA Victor 3425)
3	Because Of You		0	1951	12	1951	(RCA Victor 3425)
	Obituary : D: 15 Dec 1984 (Aged 80).						

Jane Birkin & Serge Gainsbourg   Mixed Vocal Duo, Jane B: 1947, London, Serg B: 1929 France

1	Je T'aime... Moi Non Plus	(Fontana TF 1042)	2	1969	0	1969	
2	Je T'aime... Moi Non Plus (Re-Issue)	(Fontana TF 1042)	1	1969	0	1969	
3	Je T'aime...Moi Non Plus (2nd Re-Issue)	(Fontana TF 1042)	31	1974	0	1974	

Jane Child   Female Vocalist From Canada

* 1	Don't Wanna Fall In Love	(Warner Bros. 9817)	22	1990	2	1990	(Warner Bros. 19933)

Jane Froman   Female Vocalist from the USA

1	I Only Have Eyes For You (From *Dames*)		0	1934	20	1934	(Decca 181)
2	I'll Walk Alone (From *Follow The Boys*)		0	1952	14	1952	(Capitol 2044)
3	Wish You Were Here (Musical Title Song)		0	1952	25	1952	(Capitol 2154)
4	I Believe		0	1953	11	1953	(Capitol 2332)
5	Robe Of Calvary		0	1953	28	1953	(Capitol 2639)
6	I Wonder	(Capitol CL 14254)	14	1955	0	1955	

Jane Kennaway & Strange Behaviour   Female Vocalist/Male Instrumental Group from the UK

1	I.O.U.	(DERAM DM 436)	65	1981	0	1981	

Jane Morgan   Female Vocalist, Real Name Jane Currier B: Boston, Massachusetts

1	Fascination		0	1957	7	1957	(KAPP 191)
2	The Day The Rains Came	(London HLR 8751)	1	1958	21	1958	(KAPP 235)
3	If Only I Could Live My Life Again	(London HLR 8810)	27	1959	0	1959	
4	With Open Arms		0	1959	39	1959	(KAPP 284)
5	Romantica	(London HLR 9120)	39	1960	0	1960	
! 6	A Girl Named Johnny Cash		0	1970	61	1970	(RCA 9839)
! 7	The First Day		0	1970	70	1970	(RCA 9901)
	HIT 1 HAS INSTRUMENTAL INTRO BY THE TROUBADOURS						

Jane Powell   Real Name Suzanne Burce B: 1 Apr 1929 Portland, Oregon

1	True Love		0	1956	15	1956	(VERVE 2018)

Jane Russell   Female Actress/Vocalist from the USA

1	Make A Joyful Noise Unto The Lord - Do Lord		0	1954	27	1954	(Coral 61113)

ISSUE	TITLE	UK LBL	UK POS	UK YEAR	US POS	US YEAR	US LBL
Jane Turzy Female Vocalist From Chicago							
1	God Morning, Mister Echo		0	1951	12	1951	(Decca 27622)
2	Sweet Violets		0	1951	11	1951	(Decca 27668)
3	I Like It		0	1951	20	1951	(Decca 27851)
Jane Wiedlin Female Vocalist, B: 20 May 1958 Oconomowoc, Wisconsin							
1	Rush Hour	(Manhattan MT 36)	12	1988	9	1988	(EMI-Manhattan 50118)
2	Inside A Dream	(Manhattan MT 55)	64	1988	0	1988	
Jane Wyman Female Actress/Vocalist from the USA							
1	In The Cool, Cool, Cool Of The Evening		0	1951	11	1951	(Decca 27678)
2	Blackstrap Molasses		0	1951	29	1951	(Decca 27748)
3	Zing A Little Zong		0	1952	18	1952	(Decca 28255)
	SHE WAS MARRIED TO ACTOR/EX PRESIDENT RONALD REAGAN						
Jane's Addiction Male Vocal/Instrumental Group from the USA							
1	Been Caught Stealing	(Warner Bros. W 0011)	34	1991	0	1991	
2	Classic Girl	(Warner Bros. W 0031)	60	1991	0	1991	
Janet Brace Female Vocalist from the USA							
1	Teach Me Tonight		0	1954	23	1954	(Decca 28990)
Janet Jackson Female Vocalist, B: 16 May 1966 Indiana							
* 1	What Have You Done For Me Lately	(A&M AM 308)	3	1986	4	1986	(A&M 2812)
* 2	Nasty	(A&M AM 316)	19	1986	3	1986	(A&M 2830)
* 3	When I Think Of You	(A&M AM 337)	10	1986	1	1986	(A&M 2855)
* 4	Control	(A&M AM 359)	42	1986	5	1986	(A&M 2877)
5	Let's Wait A While	(Breakout USA 601)	3	1987	2	1987	(A&M 2906)
6	Pleasure Principle	(Breakout USA 604)	24	1987	14	1987	(A&M 2927)
7	Funny How Time Flies	(Breakout USA 613)	59	1987	0	1987	
* 8	Miss You Much	(Breakout USA 663)	22	1989	1	1989	(A&M 1145)
* 9	Rhythm Nation	(Breakout USA 673)	23	1989	2	1989	(A&M 1455)
* 10	Escapade	(Breakout USA 684)	17	1990	1	1990	(A&M 1490)
11	Come Back To Me	(Breakout USA 681)	20	1990	2	1990	(A&M 1475)
* 12	Alright	(A&M USA 693)	20	1990	4	1990	(A&M 1479)
* 13	Black Cat	(A&M EM 587)	15	1990	1	1990	(A&M 1477)
* 14	Love Will Never Do (Without You)	(A&M EM 700)	34	1990	1	1990	(A&M 1538)
15	The Best Things In Life Are Free	(PERSS 7400)	2	1992	10	1992	(Perspective 0010)
* 16	That's The Way Love Goes	(Virgin VSCDG 1460)	2	1993	1	1993	(Virgin 12650)
* 17	If	(Virgin VSCDT 1474)	14	1993	4	1993	(Virgin 12676)
* 18	Again	(Virgin VSCDG 1481)	6	1993	1	1993	(Virgin 38404)
19	Because Of Love	(Virgin VSCDG 1488)	19	1994	10	1994	(Virgin 38422)
* 20	Any Time Any Place / And On And On	(Virgin VSCDT 1501)	13	1994	2	1994	(Virgin 38435)
21	You Want This / 70's Love Groove	(Virgin VSCDT 1519)	14	1994	8	1994	(Virgin 38455)
22	Whoops Now / What'll I Do	(Virgin VSCDT 1533)	9	1995	0	1995	
23	Scream	(Epic 6620222)	3	1995	5	1995	(Epic 78000)
24	Scream (Re-Mix)	(Epic 6621277)	43	1995	0	1995	
* 25	Runaway	(A&M 5811972)	6	1995	3	1996	(A&M 1194)
26	Scream (Re-entry)	(Epic 6620222)	72	1995	0	1995	
27	The Best Things In Life Are Free (Re-Issue)	(A&M 5813092)	7	1995	0	1995	
28	Twenty Foreplay	(A&M 5815112)	22	1996	0	1996	
	HITS 15, 25 ARE CREDITED TO LUTHER VANDROSS AND JANET JACKSON WITH SPECIAL GUESTS BELL BIV DEVOE & RALPH TRESVANT						
	HITS 23-24, 26 ARE CREDITED TO MICHAEL JACKSON AND JANET JACKSON						
Janet Kay Female Vocalist from the UK							
1	Silly Games	(Scope SC 2)	2	1979	0	1979	
2	Silly Games	(Arista 113452)	22	1990	0	1990	
3	Silly Games (Re-Mix)	(MUsic Factory Dance MFD 006)	62	1990	0	1990	
	HIT 2 IS CREDITED TO LINDY LAYTON FEATURING JANET KAY						
Janie Grant Real Name Rose Marie Cosili from Paterson, New Jersey							
1	Triangle		0	1961	29	1961	(CAPRICE 104)
Janie Jones Female Vocalist from the UK							
1	Witches Brew	(HMV POP 1495)	46	1966	0	1966	
Janis Ian Female Vocalist, Real Name Janis Eddy Fink B: 7 Apr 1951 New York City							
1	Society's Child (Baby I've Been Thinking)		0	1967	14	1967	(VERVE 5027)
2	At Seventeen		0	1975	3	1975	(Columbia
3	Fly Too High	(CBS 7936)	44	1979	0	1979	
4	The Other Side Of The Sun	(CBS 8611)	44	1980	0	1980	

ISSUE	TITLE	UK LBL	UK POS	UK YEAR	US POS	US YEAR	US LBL
Janis Joplin Female Vocalist, B: 19 Jan 1943 Port Arthur, Texas							
* 1	Me And Bobby McGee		0	1971	1	1971	(Columbia 45314)
	HER NICKNAME WAS PEARL • OBITUARY : D: 4 OCT 1970 HEROIN OVERDOSE.						
Jann Arden Female Vocalist From Canada							
1	Insensitive (From Bed Of Roses)	(A&M 581 2652)	40	1996	12	1996	(A&M 581274)
Japan Male Vocal/Instrumental Group from the UK							
1	Gentlemen Take Polaroids	(Virgin VS 379)	60	1980	0	1980	
2	The Art Of Parties	(Virgin VS 409)	48	1981	0	1981	
3	Quiet Life	(Hansa Hansa 6)	19	1981	0	1981	
4	Visions Of China	(Virgin VS 436)	32	1981	0	1981	
5	European Son	(Hansa Hansa 10)	31	1982	0	1982	
6	Ghosts	(Virgin VS 472)	5	1982	0	1982	
7	Cantonese Boy	(Virgin VS 502)	24	1982	0	1982	
8	I Second That Emotion	(Hansa Hansa 12)	9	1982	0	1982	
9	Like In Tokyo	(Hansa Hansa17)	28	1982	0	1982	
10	Night Porter	(Virgin VS 554)	29	1982	0	1982	
11	All Tomorrow's Parties	(Hansa Hansa 18)	38	1983	0	1983	
12	Canton (Live)	(Virgin VS 581)	42	1983	0	1983	
	RECORDED UNDER THE NAME OF, AND SEE ALSO RAIN TREE CROW						
Jarmels Names Nathaniel Ruff, Ray Smith, Paul Burnett, Earl Christian & Tom Eldridge							
1	A Little Bit Of Soap		0	1961	12	1961	(LAURIE 3098)
Jasmine Guy Female Actress/Singer, B: 10 Mar 1964 From Boston, USA							
1	Just Want To Hold You		0	1991	34	1991	(Warner Bros. 19330)
Jason Donovan Male Actor/Vocalist from Australia							
1	Nothing Can Devide Us	(PWL PWL 17)	5	1988	0	1988	
2	Especially For You	(PWL PWL 24)	1	1988	0	1988	
3	Too Many Broken Hearts	(PWL PWL 32)	1	1989	0	1989	
4	Sealed With A Kiss	(PWL PWL 39)	1	1989	0	1989	
5	Every Day (I Love You More)	(PWL PWL 43)	2	1989	0	1989	
6	When You Come Back To Me	(PWL PWL 46)	2	1989	0	1989	
7	Hang On To Your Love	(PWL PWL 51)	8	1990	0	1990	
8	Another Night	(PWL PWL 58)	18	1990	0	1990	
9	Rhythm Of The Rain	(PWL PWL 60)	9	1990	0	1990	
10	I'm Doing Fine	(PWL PWL 69)	22	1990	0	1990	
11	RSVP	(PWL PWL 80)	17	1991	0	1991	
12	Any Dream Will Do	(Really Useful RUR 7)	1	1991	0	1991	
13	Happy Together	(PWL PWL 203)	10	1991	0	1991	
14	Joseph Mega (Re-Mix)	(Really Useful RUR 9)	13	1991	0	1991	
15	Mission Of Love	(Polydor PO 222)	26	1992	0	1992	
16	As Time Goes By	(Polydor PO 245)	26	1992	0	1992	
17	All Around The World	(Polydor PZCD 278)	41	1993	0	1993	
	HIT 2 IS CREDITED TO KYLIE MINOQUE AND JASON DONOVAN • HIT 14 ITO JASON DONOVAN & ORIGINAL LONDON CAST FEATURING LINZI HATELY, DAVID EASTER & JOHNNY AMOBI						
Jasper Carrott Male Comedian/Vocalist from the UK							
1	Magic Roundabout / Funky Moped	(DJM DJS 388)	5	1975	0	1975	
Javells Mixed Vocal/Instrumental Group from the UK							
1	Goodbye Nothing To Say	(PYE disco demand DDS 2003)	26	1974	0	1974	
	THE HIT WAS CREDITED TO JAVELLS FEATURING NOSMO KING						
Jay & The Americans Group Formed In The Late 50s As Harbor-Lites							
1	She Cried		0	1962	5	1962	(United Artists 415)
2	Only In America		0	1963	25	1963	(United Artists 626)
3	Come A Little Bit Closer		0	1964	3	1964	(United Artists 759)
4	Let's Lock The Door (And Throw Away The Key)		0	1965	11	1965	(United Artists 805)
5	Cara Mia		0	1965	4	1965	(United Artists 881)
6	Some Enchanted Evening		0	1965	13	1965	(United Artists 919)
7	Sunday And Me		0	1965	18	1965	(United Artists 948)
8	Crying		0	1966	25	1966	(United Artists 50016)
* 9	This Magic Moment		0	1969	6	1969	(United Artists 50475)
10	Walkin' In The Rain		0	1970	19	1970	(United Artists 50605)
Jay & The Techniques Names Jay Proctor, Karl Landis, Ronnie Goosly, John Walsh, George Lloyd, Chuck Crowl, & Dante							
* 1	Apples Peaches Pumkin Pie		0	1967	6	1967	(Smash 2086)
* 2	Keep The Ball Rollin'		0	1967	14	1967	(Smash 2124)
3	Strawberry Shortcake		0	1968	39	1968	(Smash 2142)

ISSUE	TITLE	UK LBL	UK POS	UK YEAR	US POS	US YEAR	US LBL
Jay 'Bird' Uzzell See Corsairs							
Jay Ferguson B: 10 May 1943 California. Former Member Of spirit And Jo Jo Gunne							
1	Thunder Island		0	1978	9	1978	(Asylum 45444)
2	Shakedown Cruise		0	1979	31	1979	(Asylum 46041)
Jay McShann & His Orchestra Male Pianist/Bandleader from the USA							
1	Confessin' The Blues		0	1941	24	1941	(Decca 8559)
2	Get Me On Your Mind		0	1943	18	1943	(Decca 4418)
+ 3	Hands Off		0	1955	1	1955	(Decca 0000)
Jay Mondi & The Living Bass Mixed Vocal/Instrumental Group from the USA							
1	All Night Long	(10 TEN 304)	63	1990	0	1990	
Jaye P. Morgan Female Vocalist, Real Name Mary Margaret Morgan B: 3 Dec 1931 Colorado							
1	Just A Gigolo		0	1953	22	1953	(Derby 828)
2	Life Is Just A Bowl Of Cherries		0	1953	26	1953	(Derby 837)
3	That's All I Want From You		0	1954	3	1954	(RCA 5896)
4	Danger! Heartbreak Ahead		0	1955	12	1955	(RCA 6016)
5	Softly, Softly		0	1955	12	1955	(RCA 6016)
6	Chee Chee-Oo-Chee (Sang The Little Bird)		0	1955	12	1955	(RCA 6137)
7	Two Lost Souls		0	1955	18	1955	(RCA 6137)
8	The Longest Walk		0	1955	6	1955	(RCA 6182)
9	Swanee		0	1955	6	1955	(RCA 6182)
10	Pepper-Hot Baby		0	1955	14	1955	(RCA 6282)
11	If You Don't Want My Love		0	1955	12	1955	(RCA 6282)
	HITS 6-7 ARE CREDITED TO PERRY COMO AND JAYE P. MORGAN						
Jayhawks (1) Names James Johnson, Dave Govan, Carlton Fisher & Carver Bunkum							
1	Stranded In The Jungle		0	1956	18	1956	(Flash 109)
	THE NAME OF THE GROUP WAS CHANGED IN 1960 TO THE VIBRATIONS						
Jayhawks (2) Mixed Vocal/Instrumental Group from the USA							
1	Bad Times	(American 74321291632)	70	1995	0	1995	
Jayn Hanna Female Vocalist from the UK							
1	Lovelight (Ride On A Love Train)	(VC Recordings VCRD 10)	42	1996	0	1996	
2	Lost Without You	(VC Recordings VCRD 16)	44	1997	0	1997	
Jaynetts Female R&B Group From The Bronx							
1	Sally Go Round The Roses		0	1963	2	1963	(TUFF 369)
Jazz & The Brothers Grimm Male Vocal/Instrumental Group from the UK							
1	Let's All Go Back (Disco Nights)	(ENSIGN ENY 616)	57	1988	0	1988	
Jazzi P Female Vocalist from the USA							
1	Get Loose	(Breakout USA 659)	25	1989	0	1989	
2	Feel The Rhythm	(A&M AMUSA 691)	51	1990	0	1990	
3	Rebel Woman	(DNA 7DNS 001)	42	1991	0	1991	
	HIT 1 IS CREDITED TO L.A. MIX PERFORMED BY JAZZI P • HIT 3 IS CREDITED TO DNA PERFORMED BY JAZZI P						
Jazzy Dee Male Vocalist from the USA							
1	Get On Up	(Laurie LRS 101)	53	1983	0	1983	
Jazzy Jeff & The Fresh Prince Male Vocal/Instrumental Rap Duo From Philadelphia							
1	Girls Ain't Nothing But Trouble	(Champion Champ18)	21	1986	0	1986	
2	Parents Just Don't Understand		0	1988	12	1988	(Jive 1099)
3	A Nightmare On My Street		0	1988	15	1988	(Jive 1124)
* 4	Summertime	(Jive Jive 279)	8	1991	4	1991	(Jive 1465)
* 5	Ring My Bell	(Jive Jive 288)	53	1991	20	1991	(Jive 42024)
* 6	Boom! Shake The Room	(Jive JiveCD 335)	1	1993	13	1993	(Jive 42108)
7	I'm Looking For The One (To Be With Me)	(Jive JiveCD 345)	24	1993	0	1993	
8	Can't Wait To Be With You	(Jive JiveCD 348)	29	1994	0	1994	
9	Twinkle Twinkle (I'm Not A Star)	(Jive JiveCD 354)	62	1994	0	1994	
10	Summertime (Re-entry)	(Jive JiveCD 279)	29	1994	0	1994	
11	Boom! Shake The Room (Re-Mix)	(Jive JiveCD 387)	40	1995	0	1995	
	HITS 1,4,5 ARE CREDITED TO DJ JAZZY JEFF & THE FRESH PRINCE NAMES JEFF TOWNES & WILL SMIT						
JB's All Stars Mixed Vocal/Instrumental Group from the UK							
1	Backfield In Motion	(RCA Victor RCA 384)	48	1984	0	1984	
	JAMES BROWN'S BACKUP BAND LED BY FRED WESLEY SEE ALSO FRED WESLEY & THE JBS						
Jean Knight Female Vocalist, B: 26 Jan 1943 New Orleans							
* 1	Mr. Big Stuff		0	1971	2	1971	(STAX 0088)

ISSUE	TITLE	UK LBL	UK POS	UK YEAR	US POS	US YEAR	US LBL
Jean Shepard Female Vocalist, B: Ollie Imogene Shepard, 21 Nov 1933 In Pauls Valley, Oklahoma							
1	A Dear John Letter		0	1953	4	1953	(Capitol 2502)
2	Forgive Me, John		0	1953	24	1953	(Capitol 2586)
	HITS 1-2 ARE CREDITED TO JEAN SHEPARD AND FERLIN HUSKY • HIT 1 REACHED NUMBER 1 IN THE USA C/W CHARTS						
	REST ARE C/W HITS • OBITUARY : D: 5 MAR 1963 PLANE CRASH.						
Jean-Michel Jarre Male Producer/Instrumentalist from France							
1	Oxygene Part Iv	(Polydor 2001721)	4	1977	0	1977	
2	Equinoxe Part 5	(Polydor POSP 20)	45	1979	0	1979	
3	Fourth Rendez-Vous	(Polydor POSP 788)	65	1986	0	1986	
4	Revolutions	(Polydor PO 25)	52	1988	0	1988	
5	London Kid	(Polydor PO 32)	52	1989	0	1989	with Hank Marvin
6	Oxygene Part Iv (Re-Mix)	(Polydor PO 55)	65	1989	0	1989	
7	Chronologie Part 4	(Polydor POCS 274)	55	1993	0	1993	
8	Chronologie Part 4 (Re-Mix)	(Polydor POCS 274)	56	1993	0	1993	
9	Oxygene 8	(Epic 6643232)	17	1997	0	1997	
Jeanette MacDonald Female Actress/Vocalist, B: 18 Jun 1907, Philadelphia							
1	Beyond The Blue Horizon		0	1930	9	1930	(Victor 22514)
* 2	Indian Love Call		0	1936	8	1936	(Victor 4323)
Jeanie Tracy Female Vocalist from the USA							
1	If This Is Love	(PULSE 8 CDLOSE 63)	73	1994	0	1994	
2	Do You Believe In The Wonder	(PULSE 8 CDLOSE 74)	57	1994	0	1994	
3	It's A Man's Man's Man's World	(PULSE 8 CDLOSE 89)	73	1995	0	1995	
	3 IS CREDITED TO JEANIE TRACY AND BOBBY WOMACK						
Jeanne Black Female Vocalist, Real Name Gloria Jeanne Black B: 25 Oct 1937 California							
* 1	He'll Have To Stay	(Capitol CL 151319)	41	1960	4	1960	(Capitol 4368)
Jeanne Pruett Real Name Norma Jean Bowman B: 30 Jan 1937 Pell City, Alabama							
1	Satin Sheets		0	1973	28	1973	(MCA 40015)
Jeannie C. Riley Female Vocalist, Real Name Jeanne Carolyn Stephenson B: 19 Oct 1945 Anson, Texas.							
* 1	Harper Valley P.T.A.	(Polydor 65748)	12	1968	1	1968	(Plantation 3)
Jeff Beck Male Vocal/Instrumentalist, B: 24 Jun 1944 In Surrey, England							
1	Hi Ho Silver Lining	(Columbia DB 8151)	14	1967	0	1967	
2	Tallyman	(Columbia DB 8227)	30	1967	0	1967	
3	Love Is Blue	(Columbia DB 8359)	23	1968	0	1968	
4	Goo Goo Barabajagal (Love Is Hot)	(PYE 7N 17778)	12	1969	36	1969	(Epic 10510)
5	Hi Ho Silver Lining (Re-Issue)	(RAK RR 3)	17	1972	0	1972	
6	I've Been Drinking	(RAK RR 4)	27	1973	0	1973	
7	Hi Ho Silver Lining (Re-Issue) (Re-entry)	(RAK RR 3)	62	1982	0	1982	
8	People Get Ready	(Epic 6577567)	49	1992	0	1992	
	HITS 6,8 ARE CREDITED TO JEFF BECK AND ROD STEWART • HIT 4 IS CREDITED TO JEFF BECK GROUP AND DONOVAN • JEFF WAS ALSO WITH THE YARDBIRDS AND VANILLA FUDGE						
Jeff Buckley Male Vocalist from the USA							
1	Last Goodbye	(Columbia 6620422)	54	1995	0	1995	
Jeff Chandler Male Actor/Vocalist from the USA							
1	I Should Care		0	1954	21	1954	(Decca 29004)
Jeff Collins Male Vocalist from the UK							
1	Only You	(Polydor 2058 287)	40	1972	0	1972	
Jeff Healey Band Other Members Of The Trio Are Tom Stephen & Joe Rockman							
1	Angel Eyes		0	1989	5	1989	(Arista 9808)
Jeff Lorber Featuring Karyn White Male Jazz Instrumentalist (Keyboards) from the USA							
1	Facts Of Love		0	1987	27	1987	(Warner Bros. 28588)
Jeff Lynne Male Vocalist from the UK							
1	Every Little Thing	(REPRISE W 9799)	59	1990	0	1990	
Jeff Wayne Orchestra from the USA							
1	Matador	(CBS A 2493)	57	1982	0	1982	
	SEE ALSO JEFF WAYNE'S WAR OF THE WORLDS						
Jeff Wayne's War Of The Worlds Mixed Vocal/Instrumental Cast from the UK/USA.							
1	The Eve Of The War	(CBS 6496)	36	1978	0	1978	
2	The Eve Of The War (Re-Mix)	(CBS 6551267)	3	1989	0	1989	
	SEE ALSO JEFF WAYNE						
Jefferson Male Vocalist from the UK							
1	Colour Of My Love	(PYE 7N 17706)	22	1969	0	1969	
2	Baby Take Me In Your Arms		0	1970	23	1970	(JANUS 106)

ISSUE	TITLE	UK LBL	UK POS	UK YEAR	US POS	US YEAR	US LBL
Jefferson Airplane/Starship	Mixed Vocal/Instrumental Group from the USA						
1	Somebody To Love		0	1967	5	1967	(RCA Victor 9140)
2	White Rabbit		0	1967	8	1967	(RCA Victor 9248)
3	Ballad Of You And Me And Pooneil		0	1967	42	1967	(RCA Victor 9297)
4	Watch Her Ride		0	1967	61	1967	(RCA Victor 9389)
5	Greasy Heart		0	1968	98	1968	(RCA Victor 9496)
6	Crown Of Creation		0	1968	64	1968	(RCA Victor 9644)
7	Volunteers		0	1969	65	1969	(RCA 0245)
8	Pretty As You Feel		0	1971	60	1971	(Grunt 0500)
9	Ride The Tiger		0	1974	84	1974	(Grunt 10080)
10	Miracles		0	1975	3	1975	(Grunt 10367)
11	Play On Love		0	1975	49	1975	(Grunt 10456)
12	With Your Love		0	1976	12	1976	(Grunt 10746)
13	Count On Me		0	1978	8	1978	(Grunt 11196)
14	Runaway		0	1978	12	1978	(Grunt 11274)
15	Jane	(Grunt FB 1750)	21	1980	14	1979	(Grunt 11750)
16	Find Your Way Back		0	1981	29	1981	(Grunt 12211)
17	Be My Lady		0	1982	28	1982	(Grunt 13350)
18	Winds Of Change		0	1983	38	1983	(Grunt 13439)
19	No Way Out		0	1984	23	1984	(Grunt 13811)
* 20	We Built This City	(RCA PB 49929)	12	1985	1	1985	(Grunt 14170)
21	Sara	(RCA PB 49893)	66	1986	1	1986	(Grunt 14253)
22	Tomorrow Doesn't Matter Tonight		0	1986	26	1986	(Grunt 14332)
* 23	Nothing's Gonna Stop Us Now (From *Mannequin*)	(Grunt FB 49757)	1	1987	1	1987	(Grunt 5109)
24	It's Not Over ('Til It's Over)		0	1987	9	1987	(RCA/Grunt 5225)
25	It's Not Enough		0	1989	12	1989	(RCA 9032)
	FORMED AS JEFFERSON AIRPLANE IN SAN FRANCISCO IN 1965 • DUE TO LEGAL PROBLEMS THEIR NAME WAS SHORTENED TO STARSHIP THE GROUP DISBANDED IN 1990						
Jeffrey Osborne	Male Vocalist, B: 9 Apr 1948 Providence, Rhode Island Former Lead Singer with Ltd until 1980						
1	I Really Don't Need No Light		0	1982	39	1982	(A&M 2410)
2	On The Wing Of Love	(A&M AM 198)	11	1984	29	1982	(A&M 2434)
3	Don't You Get So Mad	(A&M AM 140)	54	1983	25	1983	(A&M 2561)
4	Stay With Me Tonight	(A&M AM 188)	18	1984	30	1983	(A&M 2591)
5	The Last Time I Made Love		0	1984	40	1984	(A&M 2656)
6	Don't Stop	(A&M AM 222)	61	1984	0	1984	
7	The Borderlines		0	1985	38	1985	(A&M 2695)
8	You Should Be Mine (The Woo Woo Song)		0	1986	13	1986	(A&M 2814)
9	Soweto	(A&M AM 334)	44	1986	0	1986	
10	Soweto (Re-entry)	(A&M AM 334)	75	1986	0	1986	
11	Love Power	(Arista RIS 27)	63	1987	12	1987	(Arista 9567)
	HIT 11 IS CREDITED TO DIONNE WARWICK AND JEFFREY OSBORNE • HIT 5 IS CREDITED TO JOYCE KENNEDY AND JEFFREY OSBORNE						
Jelly Beans	Names: Elyse And Maxine Herbert, Alma Brewer, Diane Taylor & Charles Thomas						
1	I Wanna Love Him So Bad		0	1964	9	1964	(Red Bird 10-003)
Jellybean	Male Producer, Real Name John Benitez B: Bronx						
1	Sidewalk Talk	(EMI America EA 210)	47	1986	18	1985	(EMI America 8297)
2	Who Found Who	(Chrysalis CHS JEL 1)	10	1987	16	1987	(Chrysalis 43120)
3	The Real Thing	(Chrysalis CHS 3167)	13	1987	0	1987	
4	Jingo	(Chrysalis JEL 2)	12	1987	0	1987	
5	Just A Mirage	(Chrysalis JEL 3)	13	1988	0	1988	
6	Coming Back For More	(Chrysalis JEL 4)	41	1988	0	1988	
Jellyfish	Male Vocal/Instrumental Group from the USA						
1	The King Is Half Undressed	(Charisma CUSS 1)	39	1991	0	1991	
2	Baby's Coming Back	(Charisma CUSS 2)	51	1991	0	1991	
3	The Scary-Go-Round (EP)	(Charisma CUSS 3)	49	1991	0	1991	
4	I Wanna Stay Home	(Charisma CUSS 4)	59	1991	0	1991	
5	The Ghost At Number One	(Charisma CUDG 10)	43	1993	0	1993	
6	New Mistake	(Charisma CUSDG 11)	55	1993	0	1993	
Jennifer Holliday	Female Vocalist, B: 19 Oct 1960 Riverside, Texas						
1	And I'm Telling You I'm Not Going	(Geffen GEF 2644)A	32	1982	22	1982	(Geffen 29983)
Jennifer Rush	Female Vocalist from Queens, New York						
1	The Power Of Love	(CBS A 5003)	1	1985	0	1985	
2	Ring Of Ice	(CBS A 4745)	14	1985	0	1985	
3	The Power Of Love (Re-entry)	(CBS A 5003)	55	1986	0	1986	
4	Flames Of Paradise	(CBS 650865 7)	59	1987	36	1987	(Epic 07119)

ISSUE	TITLE	UK LBL	UK POS	UK YEAR	US POS	US YEAR	US LBL
5	Till I Loved You	(CBS 654843 7)	24	1989	0	1989	

HIT 4 IS CREDITED TO JENNIFER RUSH AND ELTON JOHN • HIT 5 IS CREDITED TO PLACIDO DOMINGO AND JENNIFER RUSH

Jennifer Warnes Female Vocalist, B: Seattle And Raised In Orange County, California

	ISSUE	TITLE	UK LBL	UK POS	UK YEAR	US POS	US YEAR	US LBL
	1	Right Time Of The Night		0	1977	6	1977	(Arista 0223)
	2	I Know A Heartache When I See One		0	1979	19	1979	(Arista 0430)
!	3	Don't Make Me Over		0	1980	84	1980	(Arista 0455)
!	4	Lost The Good Thing		0	1980	76	1986	(REGENCY 45002)
	5	Could It Be Love		0	1982	47	1982	(Arista 0611)
*	6	Up Where We Belong	(Island WIP 6830)	7	1983	1	1982	(Island 99996)
!	7	Ain't No Cure For Love		0	1987	86	1987	(CYPRESS 661111)
	8	First We Take Manhattan	(CYPRESS PB 49709)	74	1987	0	1987	
*	9	(I've Had) The Time Of My Life	(RCA PB 49625)	6	1987	1	1987	(RCA 5224)
	10	(I've Had) The Time Of My Life (Re-entry)	(RCA PB 49625)	8	1990	0	1990	

Jenny Barrett Female Vocalist from the USA

	ISSUE	TITLE	UK LBL	UK POS	UK YEAR	US POS	US YEAR	US LBL
	1	He Loves Me		0	1953	21	1953	(VOGUE 1024)

Jenny Burton Female Vocalist from the USA

	ISSUE	TITLE	UK LBL	UK POS	UK YEAR	US POS	US YEAR	US LBL
	1	Bad Habits	(Atlantic A 9583)	68	1985	0	1985	

Jeremy Faith

	ISSUE	TITLE	UK LBL	UK POS	UK YEAR	US POS	US YEAR	US LBL
*	1	Jesus	Not Known	0	1971	0	1971	Not Known

THE HIT WAS A RELIGIOUS SONG AND WAS SUNG ACROSS EUROPE BY MANY ARTISTS

Jeremy Jordan Male Vocalist, Real Name Don Henson B: 19 Sep 1973 Indiana

	ISSUE	TITLE	UK LBL	UK POS	UK YEAR	US POS	US YEAR	US LBL
	1	The Right Kind Of Love		0	1993	14	1993	(GIANT 18718)
	2	Wannagirl		0	1993	28	1993	(GIANT 18548)

Jeri Southern Female Vocalist/Instrumentalist (Piano) from Nebraska

	ISSUE	TITLE	UK LBL	UK POS	UK YEAR	US POS	US YEAR	US LBL
	1	You Better Go Now		0	1951	30	1951	(Decca 27840)
	2	Joey		0	1954	25	1954	(Decca 29184)
	3	Fire Down Below	(Brunswick 05665)	22	1957	0	1957	

Jermaine Jackson Male Vocalist, B: 11 Dec 1954 Indiana, USA

	ISSUE	TITLE	UK LBL	UK POS	UK YEAR	US POS	US YEAR	US LBL
*	1	Daddy's Home		0	1972	9	1972	(Motown 1216)
	2	Let's Get Serious	(Motown TMG 1183)	8	1980	9	1980	(Motown 1469)
	3	Burnin' Hot	(Motown TMG 1194)	32	1980	0	1980	
	4	You're Supposed To Keep Your Love For Me		0	1980	34	1980	(Motown 1490)
	5	You Like Me Don't You	(Motown TMG 1222)	41	1981	0	1981	
	6	Let Me Tickle Your Fancy		0	1982	18	1982	(Motown 1628)
	7	Sweetest Sweetest	(Arista JJK 1)	52	1984	0	1984	
	8	Dynamite		0	1984	15	1984	(Arista 9190)
	9	When The Rain Begins To Fall	(Arista ARIST 584)	68	1984	0	1984	
	10	Do What You Do	(Arista ARIST 609)	6	1985	13	1985	(Arista 9279)
	11	I Think It's Love		0	1986	16	1986	(Arista 9444)
	12	Don't Take It Personal	(Arista 112634)	69	1989	0	1989	

BACKING VOCALS ON HIT 6 ARE BY DEVO • HIT 9 IS CREDITED TO JERMAINE JACKSON AND PIA ZADORA

Jermaine Stewart Male Singer/Dancer From Chicago

	ISSUE	TITLE	UK LBL	UK POS	UK YEAR	US POS	US YEAR	US LBL
	1	We Don't Have To Take Our Clothes Off	(10 TEN 96)	2	1986	5	1986	(Arista 9424)
	2	Jody	(10 TEN 143)	50	1986	0	1986	
	3	Say It Again	(10 TEN 188)	7	1988	27	1988	(Arista 9636)
	4	Get Lucky	(SIREN SRN 82)	13	1988	0	1988	
	5	Don't Talk Dirty To Me	(SIREN SRN 86)	61	1988	0	1988	

Jerry Burns Female Vocalist from the UK

	ISSUE	TITLE	UK LBL	UK POS	UK YEAR	US POS	US YEAR	US LBL
	1	Pale Red	(Columbia6579467)	64	1992	0	1992	

Jerry Butler Male Vocalist, B: 8 Dec 1939, Sunflower, Missouri

	ISSUE	TITLE	UK LBL	UK POS	UK YEAR	US POS	US YEAR	US LBL
	1	For Your Precious Love		0	1958	11	1958	(ABNER 1013)
	2	He Will Break Your Heart		0	1960	7	1960	(VEE-JAY 354)
	3	Find Another Girl		0	1961	27	1961	(VEE-JAY 375)
	4	I'm A Telling You		0	1961	25	1961	(VEE-JAY 390)
*	5	Moon River		0	1961	11	1961	(VEE-JAY 405)
	6	Make It Easy On Yourself		0	1962	20	1962	(VEE-JAY 451)
	7	Need To Belong		0	1963	31	1963	(VEE-JAY 567)
	8	Giving Up On Love		0	1964	56	1964	(VEE-JAY 588)
	9	I Stand Accused		0	1964	61	1964	(VEE-JAY 598)
	10	Let It Be Me		0	1964	5	1964	(VEE-JAY 613)
	11	Mr. Dream Merchant		0	1967	38	1967	(Mercury 72721)
	12	Never Give You Up		0	1968	20	1968	(Mercury 72789)

ISSUE	TITLE	UK LBL	UK POS	UK YEAR	US POS	US YEAR	US LBL
13	Hey, Western Union Man		0	1968	16	1968	(Mercury 72850)
14	Are You Happy		0	1968	39	1968	(Mercury 72876)
* 15	Only The Strong Survive		0	1969	4	1969	(Mercury 72898)
16	Moody Woman		0	1969	24	1969	(Mercury 72929)
17	What's The Use Of Breaking Up		0	1969	20	1969	(Mercury 72960)
18	Don't Let Love Hang You Up		0	1969	44	1969	(Mercury 72991)
19	I Could Write A Book		0	1970	46	1970	(Mercury 73045)
* 20	Ain't Understanding Mellow		0	1972	21	1972	(Mercury 73255)

Jerry Byrd   Male Country Steel Guitarist from the USA

1	Harbour Lights		0	1950	19	1950	(Mercury 5461)

Jerry Jaye   Full Name Jerald Jaye Hatley B: 19 Oct 1937 In Manila, Arkansas

1	My Girl Josephine		0	1967	29	1967	(HI 2120)
! 2	It's All In The Game		0	1975	53	1975	(Columbia 10170)
! 3	Honky Tonk Women Love Red Neck Men		0	1976	32	1976	(HI 2310)
! 4	Hot And Still Heatin'		0	1976	78	1976	(HI 2318)

Jerry Keller   Male Vocalist, B: 20 Jun 1937 Ford Smith, Arkansas   Also Involved In The Quartet The Lads Of Note

1	Here Comes Summer	(London HLR 8890)	1	1959	14	1959	(KAPP 277)

Jerry Lee Lewis   Male Vocal/Pianist, B: 29 Sep 1935 Ferriday, Louisiana

* 1	Whole Lotta Shakin' Goin' On	(London HLS 8457)	8	1957	3	1957	(SUN 267)
* 2	Great Balls Of Fire	(London HLS 8529)	1	1957	2	1957	(SUN 281)
3	You Win Again		0	1957	95	1957	(SUN 281)
4	Whole Lotta Shakin' Goin' On (Re-entry)	(London HLS 8457)	26	1957	0	1957	
5	Breathless	(London HLS 8592)	8	1958	7	1958	(SUN 288)
6	High School Confidential	(London HLS 8780)	12	1959	21	1958	(SUN 296)
7	I'll Make It All Up To You		0	1958	85	1958	(SUN 303)
8	Break Up		0	1958	52	1958	(SUN 303)
9	I'll Sail My Ship Alone		0	1959	93	1959	(SUN 312)
10	Lovin' Up A Storm	(London HLS 8840)	28	1959	0	1959	
11	Baby Baby Bye Bye	(London HLS 9131)	47	1960	0	1960	
12	What'd I Say	(London HLS 9335)	10	1961	30	1961	(SUN 256)
13	What'd I Say (Re-entry)	(London HLS 9335)	49	1961	0	1961	
! 14	Cold Cold Heart		0	1961	22	1961	(SUN 364)
15	Sweet Little Sixteen	(London HLS 9584)	38	1962	0	1962	
16	Good Golly Miss Molly	(London HLS 9688)	31	1963	0	1963	
! 17	Pen And Paper		0	1964	36	1964	(SMASH 1857)
18	Another Place Another Time		0	1968	97	1968	(SMASH 2146)
19	What Made Milwaukee Famous (Made A Loser Out Of Me)		0	1968	94	1968	(SMASH 2164)
37	Me And Bobby Mcgee		0	1971	40	1971	(Mercury 73248)
38	Chantilly Lace	(Mercury 6052 141)	33	1972	43	1972	(Mercury 73273)
41	Turn On Your Love Light		0	1972	95	1972	(Mercury 73296)
44	Drinking Wine Spo-Dee-O-Dee		0	1973	41	1973	(Mercury 73374)

UNLISTED HITS ARE C/W • NICKNAMED THE KILLER, HIS POPULARITY DECLINED AFTER MARRYING HIS 13YR OLD COUSIN IN 1958.

Jerry Lester   Male Vocalist/Comedian from the USA

1	Orange Coloured Sky		0	1950	30	1950	(Coral 60325)

Jerry Lewis   Male Vocalist, Real Name Joseph Levitch B: 16 Mar 1925 New Jersey

1	That Certain Party		0	1948	22	1948	(Capitol 1529)
* 2	Rock-A-Bye Your Baby (With A Dixie Melody)	(Brunswick 05636)	12	1957	10	1956	(Decca 30124)
3	Rock-A-Bye Your Baby (With A Dixie Melody) (Re-entry)	(Brunswick 05636)	22	1957	0	1957 with Dean Martin	

Jerry Lordan   Male Vocalist from the UK

1	I'll Stay Single	(Parlophone R 4588)	26	1960	0	1960	
2	Who Could Be Bluer	(Parlophone R 4627)	17	1960	0	1960	
3	I'll Stay Single (Re-entry)	(Parlophone R 4588)	41	1960	0	1960	
4	Who Could Be Bluer (Re-entry)	(Parlophone R 4627)	45	1960	0	1960	
5	Sing Like An Angel	(Parlophone R 4653)	36	1960	0	1960	

Jerry Reed   Male Singer/Guitarist Real Name Jerry Reed Hubbard B: 20 Mar 1937 Atlanta

* 10	Amos Moses		0	1970	8	1970	(RCA 9904)
11	The Preacher And The Bear		0	1970	8	1970	(RCA 9904)
* 12	When You're Hot, You're Hot		0	1971	9	1971	(RCA 9976)

Jerry Vale   Male Vocalist, Real Name Genero Vitaliano B: 8 Jul 1932 Bronx

1	You Can Never Give Me Back My Heart		0	1953	29	1953	(Columbia 39929)
2	Two Purple Shadows		0	1954	20	1954	(Columbia 40131)
3	I Live Each Day		0	1954	29	1954	(Columbia 40201)
4	Innamorata (Sweetheart)		0	1956	30	1956	(Columbia 40634)

ISSUE	TITLE	UK LBL	UK POS	UK YEAR	US POS	US YEAR	US LBL
5	You Don't Know Me		0	1956	14	1956	(Columbia 40710)
6	Have You Looked Into Your Heart		0	1965	24	1965	(Columbia 43181)

Jerry Wallace Male Vocalist, B: 15 Dec 1928 Guilford, Missouri

1	Little Miss One		0	1954	30	1954	(ALLIED 5015)
2	How The Time Flies		0	1958	11	1958	(Challenge 59013)
* 3	Primrose Lane		0	1959	8	1959	(Challenge 59047)
4	Little Coco Palm		0	1960	36	1960	(Challenge 59060)
5	You're Singing Our Love Song To Somebody Else	(London HLH 9110)	46	1960	0	1960	
6	There She Goes		0	1961	26	1961	(Challenge 59098)
7	Shutters And Boards		0	1962	24	1962	(Challenge 9171)
8	In The Misty Moonlight		0	1964	19	1964	(Challenge 59246)
22	To Get To You		0	1972	48	1972	(Decca 32914)
23	If You Leave Me Tonight I'll Cry		0	1972	38	1972	(Decca 32989)

Jerry Wayne Male Actor/Vocalist from the USA

1	You Call Everybody Darling		0	1948	14	1948	(Columbia 38286)
2	A Little Bird Told Me		0	1949	15	1949	(Columbia 28386)
3	Room Full Of Roses		0	1949	6	1949	(Columbia 38525)

HIT 2 IS CREDITED TO JERRY WAYNE WITH JANETTE DAVIS • SEE ALSO KEN GRIFFIN

Jeru The Damaja Male Rapper from the USA

1	Ya Playin' Yaself	(FFRR FCD 289)	67	1996	0	1996	

Jess Conrad Male Vocalist from the UK

1	Cherry Pie	(Decca F 11236)	39	1960	0	1960	
2	Mystery Girl	(Decca F 11315)	44	1961	0	1961	
3	Mystery Girl (Re-entry)	(Decca F 11315)	18	1961	0	1961	
4	Pretty Jenny	(Decca F 11511)	50	1962	0	1962	

Jesse Belvin Real Name Jessie Lorenzo Belvin B: 15 Dec 1932 San Antoinio, Texas

1	Guess Who		0	1959	31	1959	(RCA 7469)

Jesse Green Male Vocalist from the USA

1	Nice And Slow	(EMI 2492)	17	1976	0	1976	
2	Flip	(EMI 2564)	26	1976	0	1976	
3	Come With Me	(EMI 2615)	29	1977	0	1977	

Jesse Lee Turner Texas-Born Rockabilly Singer

1	The Little Space Girl		0	1959	20	1959	(Carlton 496)

Jesse Rae Male Vocalist from the UK

1	Over The Sea	(Scotland-Video YZ 36)	65	1985	0	1985	

Jesse Winchester Male Singer/Songwriter/Guitarist, B: 17 May 1944 Shreveport, Louisiana

1	Say What		0	1981	32	1981	(Bearsville 49711)

Jessi Colter Female Vocalist, Real Name Miriam Johnson B: 25 May 1947 Phoenix

1	I'm Not Lisa		0	1975	4	1975	(Capitol 4009)
2	What's Happened To Blue Eyes		0	1975	57	1975	(Capitol 4087)

Her Marriages Include Duane Eddy 1962-68 And Waylon Jennings 1969 • Hits 9-13 Are Credited To Waylon & Jessi

Jessie Hill Male Singer/Drummer/Pianist, B: 9 Dec 1932 New Orleans

1	Ooh Poo Pah Doo (Part 2)		0	1960	28	1960	(MINIT 607)

Jesus & Mary Chain Male Vocal/Instrumental Group from the UK

1	Never Understand	(Blanco Y Negro NEG 8)	47	1985	0	1985	
2	You Trip Me Up	(Blanco Y Negro NEG 13)	55	1985	0	1985	
3	Just Like Honey	(Blanco Y Negro NEG 17)	45	1985	0	1985	
4	Some Candy Talking	(Blanco Y Negro NEG 19)	13	1986	0	1986	
5	April Skies	(Blanco Y Negro NEG 24)	8	1987	0	1987	
6	Happy When It Rains	(Blanco Y Negro NEG 25)	25	1987	0	1987	
7	Darklands	(Blanco Y Negro NEG 29)	33	1987	0	1987	
8	Sidewalking	(Blanco Y Negro NEG 32)	30	1988	0	1988	
9	Blues From A Gun	(Blanco Y Negro NEG 41)	32	1989	0	1989	
10	Head On	(Blanco Y Negro NEG 42)	57	1989	0	1989	
11	Rollercoaster (EP)	(Blanco Y Negro NEG 45)	46	1990	0	1990	
12	Reverence	(Blanco Y Negro NEG 55)	10	1992	0	1992	
13	Far Gone And Out	(Blanco Y Negro NEG 56)	23	1992	0	1992	
14	Almost Gold	(Blanco Y Negro NEG 57)	41	1992	0	1992	
15	Sound Of Speed (EP)	(Blanco Y Negro NEG 66CD)	30	1993	0	1993	
16	Sometimes Always	(Blanco Y Negro NEG 70CD)	22	1994	0	1994	
17	Come On	(Blanco Y Negro NEG 73CD1)	52	1994	0	1994	
18	I Hate Rock N' Roll	(Blanco Y Negro NEG 81CD)	61	1995	0	1995	

ISSUE	TITLE	UK LBL	UK POS	UK YEAR	US POS	US YEAR	US LBL
Jesus Jones Male Vocal/Instrumental Group from the UK							
1	Info-Freako	(Food Food 18)	42	1989	0	1989	
2	Never Enough	(Food Food 21)	42	1989	0	1989	
3	Bring It On Down	(Food Food 22)	46	1989	0	1989	
4	Real Real Real	(Food Food 24)	19	1990	4	1991	(SBK 07364)
5	Right Here Right Now	(Food Food 25)	31	1990	2	1991	(SBK 07345)
6	International Bright Young Thing	(Food Food 27)	7	1991	0	1991	
7	Who Where Why	(Food Food 28)	21	1991	0	1991	
8	Right Here Right Now (Re-Issue)	(Food Food 30)	31	1991	2	1991	
9	The Devil You Know	(FOOD CDPERV 1)	10	1993	0	1993	
10	The Right Decision	(FOOD CDPERV 2)	36	1993	0	1993	
11	Zeroes And Ones	(FOOD CDFOODS 44)	30	1993	0	1993	
12	The Next Big Thing	(FOOD CDFOOD 95)	49	1997	0	1997	
13	Chemical #1	(FOOD CDFOOD 102)	71	1997	0	1997	

LEAD SINGER MIKE EDWARDS OF THIS QUINTET FROM LONDON, ENGLAND • SEE ALSO THE FOOD CHRISTMAS (EP), VARIOUS ARTISTS (EP, LP, 78S)

ISSUE	TITLE	UK LBL	UK POS	UK YEAR	US POS	US YEAR	US LBL
Jesus Lizard Male Vocal/Instrumental Group from the USA							
1	Puss	(Touch and Go TG 83CD)	12	1993	0	1993	

ON THE FLIP SIDE OF THE HIT WAS HIT 5 BY NIRVANA

ISSUE	TITLE	UK LBL	UK POS	UK YEAR	US POS	US YEAR	US LBL
Jesus Loves You Male Vocalist, Real Name George O'dowd from the UK							
1	After The Love	(More Protein PROT 2)	68	1989	0	1989	
2	Bow Down Mister	(More Protein PROT 8)	27	1991	0	1991	
3	Generations Of Love	(More Protein PROT 10)	35	1991	0	1991	
4	Sweet Toxic Music	(Virgin VS 1449)	65	1992	0	1992	

SEE ALSO BOY GEORGE AND CULTURE CLUB

ISSUE	TITLE	UK LBL	UK POS	UK YEAR	US POS	US YEAR	US LBL
Jet Bronx & The The Forbidden Male Vocal/Instrumental Group from the UK							
1	Ain't Doin' Nothin'	(LIGHTNING LIG 50)	49	1977	0	1977	
Jet Harris Male Bass Guitarist, B: 7 Jul 1939 Kingsbury, London, England							
1	Besame Mucho	(Decca F 11466)	22	1962	0	1962	
2	Main Title Theme From						
	The Man With The Golden Arm	(Decca F 11488)	12	1962	0	1962	
Jet Harris & Tony Meehan Male Instrumental Duo from the UK							
1	Diamonds	(Decca F 11563)	1	1963	0	1963	
2	Scarlett O'hara	(Decca F 11644)	2	1963	0	1963	
3	Applejack	(Decca F 11710)	4	1963	0	1963	

TONY IS A DRUMMER, B: 2 MAR 1942 LONDON, ENGLAND • SEE ALSO JET HARRIS

ISSUE	TITLE	UK LBL	UK POS	UK YEAR	US POS	US YEAR	US LBL
Jethro Tull Male Vocal/Instrumental Group from the UK							
1	Love Story	(Island WIP 6048)	29	1969	0	1969	
2	Living In The Past	(Island WIP 6056)	3	1969	11	1972	(Chrysalis 2006)
3	Sweet Dream	(Island WIP 6070)	9	1969	0	1969	
4	Teacher / The Witch's Promise	(Island WIP 6077)	4	1970	0	1970	
5	Life Is A Long Song / Up The Fool	(Island WIP 6106)	11	1971	0	1971	
6	Bungle In The Jungle		0	1975	12	1975	(Chrysalis 2101)
7	Ring Out Solstice Bells	(Chrysalis CXP 2)	28	1976	0	1976	
8	Lap Of Luxury	(Chrysalis TULL 1)	70	1984	0	1984	
9	Said She Was A Dancer	(Chrysalis TULL 4)	55	1987	0	1987	
10	Rocks On The Road	(Chrysalis TULLX 7)	47	1992	0	1992	
11	Living In The (Slightly More Recent Past)	(Chrysalis CSCHSS 3970)	32	1993	0	1993	

'68 LINE-UP, IAN ANDERSON, MICK ABRAHAMS, GLENN COMICK & CLIVE BUNKER

ISSUE	TITLE	UK LBL	UK POS	UK YEAR	US POS	US YEAR	US LBL
Jets (1) Male Vocal/Instrumental Group from the UK							
1	Sugar Doll	(EMI 5211)	55	1981	0	1981	
2	Yes Tonight Josephine	(EMI 5247)	25	1981	0	1981	
3	Love Makes The World Go Round	(EMI 5262)	21	1982	0	1982	
4	The Honeydripper	(EMI 5289)	58	1982	0	1982	
5	Somebody To Love	(EMI 5342)	56	1982	0	1982	
6	Blue Skies	(EMI 5405)	53	1983	0	1983	
7	Rockin' Around The Christmas Tree	(PRT 7P 297)	62	1983	0	1983	
8	Party Doll	(PRT JETS 2)	72	1984	0	1984	
Jets (2) Mixed Vocal/Instrumental Group from the USA							
1	Crush On You	(MCA MCA 1048)	5	1987	3	1986	(MCA 52774)
2	You Got It All		0	1987	3	1987	(MCA 52968)
3	Curiosity	(MCA MCA 1119)	41	1987	0	1987	
4	Cross My Broken Heart (From *Beverly Hills Cop II*)		0	1987	7	1987	(MCA 53123)
5	I Do You		0	1987	20	1987	(MCA 53193)

ISSUE	TITLE	UK LBL	UK POS	UK YEAR	US POS	US YEAR	US LBL
6	Rocket 2 U	(MCA MCA 1226)	69	1988	6	1988	(MCA 53254)
7	Make It Real		0	1988	4	1988	(MCA 53311)

EIGHT BROTHERS & SISTERS, LEROY, EDDIE, EUGENE, HAINI, RUDY, KATHY, ELIZABETH & MOANA WOLFGRAMM • EUGENE LEFT TO FORM THE BOYS CLUB IN 1988

Jewel Akens Male Vocalist, B: 1940 Houston, Texas

* 1	The Birds And The Bees	(London HLN 9954)	29	1965	3	1965	(ERA 3141)

HIS UNUSUAL CHRISTIAN NAME IS SAID TO HAVE COME ABOUT, BECAUSE HIS MOTHER WANTED A DAUGHTER. HE IS ONE OF TEN

Jhelisa Female Vocalist from the USA

1	Friendly Pressure	(DORADO DOR040CD)	75	1995	0	1995	

Jigsaw Male Vocal/Instrumental Quartet from the UK

1	Sky High	(SPLASH CPI 1)	9	1975	3	1975	(CHELSEA 3022)
2	Love Fire		0	1976	30	1976	(CHELSEA 3037)
3	If I Have To Go Away	(SPLASH CP 11)	36	1977	0	1977	

NAMES: DES DEYER, CLIVE SCOTT, TONY CAMPBELL & BARRIE BERNARD

Jill Corey Female Vocalist, Real Name Norma Jean Speranza B: 30 Sep 1935

1	Robe Of Calvary		0	1954	22	1954	(Columbia 40123)
2	I Love My Baby (My Baby Loves Me)		0	1957	21	1957	(Columbia 40794)
3	Love Me To Pieces		0	1957	11	1957	(Columbia 40955)

Jill Francis Female Vocalist from the UK

1	Make Love To Me	(GLADY WAX GW 003CD)	70	1993	0	1993	

Jilted John Male Vocalist from the UK

1	Jilted John	(EMI International INT 567)	4	1978	0	1978	

Jim Bakus & Friend Male Actor/Vocalist, Real Name Jim Backus B: 25 Feb 1913 Cleveland

1	Delicious		0	1958	40	1958	(Jubilee 5330)

FAMOUS AS THE VOICE OF MR. MAGOO • OBITUARY : D: 3 JUL 1989 PNEUMONIA.

Jim Boles Male Vocalist from the USA

1	For You		0	1930	9	1930	

Jim Capaldi Male Vocalist B: 24 Jun 1944 Evesham, England

1	It's All Up To You	(Island WIP 6198)	27	1974	0	1974	
2	Love Hurts	(Island WIP 6246)	4	1975	0	1975	
3	That's Love		0	1983	28	1983	(Atlantic 89849)

Jim Carrey Male Vocalist from the USA

1	Cuban Pete	(Columbia 6606622)	31	1995	0	1995	

Jim Croce Male Vocalist, B: 10 Jan 1943 Philadelphia

1	You Don't Mess Around With Jim		0	1972	8	1972	(ABC 11328)
2	Operator (That's Not The Way It Feels)		0	1972	17	1972	(ABC 11335)
3	One Less Set Of Footsteps		0	1973	37	1973	(ABC 11346)
* 4	Bad, Bad Leroy Brown		0	1973	1	1973	(ABC 11359)
5	I Got A Name		0	1973	10	1973	(ABC 11389)
* 6	Time In A Bottle		0	1973	1	1973	(ABC 11405)
7	I'll Have To Say I Love You In A Song		0	1974	9	1974	(ABC 11424)
8	Workin' At The Car Wash Blues		0	1974	32	1974	(ABC 11447)

OBITUARY : D: 20 SEP 1972 PLANE CRASH.

Jim Dale Male Vocalist from the UK

1	Be My Girl	(Parlophone R 4343)	2	1957	0	1957	
2	Just Born	(Parlophone R 4376)	27	1958	0	1958	
3	Crazy Dream	(Parlophone R 4376)	24	1958	0	1958	
4	Sugartime	(Parlophone R 4402)	25	1958	0	1958	

Jim Davidson Male Comedian/Vocalist from the UK

1	White Christmas / Too Risky	(SCRATCH SCR 001)	52	1980	0	1980	

Jim Diamond Male Vocalist from Isleworth, West London, England

1	I Should Have Known Better	(A&M AM 220)	1	1984	0	1984	
2	I Sleep Alone At Night	(A&M AM 229)	72	1985	0	1985	
3	Remember I Love You	(A&M AM 247)	42	1985	0	1985	
4	Hi Ho Silver	(A&M AM 296)	5	1986	0	1986	

Jim Gilstrap Male Vocalist from the USA

1	Swing Your Daddy	(CHELSEA 2005 021)	4	1975	0	1975	

Jim Henson Creator Of The Muppets, B: 24 Sep 1936 Greenville, Mississippi

1	Rubber Duckie		0	1970	16	1970	(Columbia
2	Rainbow Connection		0	1979	25	1979	(Atlantic 3610)

HIT 1 IS CREDITED TO ERNIE • HIT 2 IS CREDITED TO KERMIT • SEE ALSO THE MUPPETS • OBITUARY : D: 16 MAY 1990 SUDDEN VIRUS.

ISSUE	TITLE	UK LBL	UK POS	UK YEAR	US POS	US YEAR	US LBL
Jim Lowe Male Dj/Vocalist, B: 7 May 1927 Springfield, Missouri							
1	Gambler's Guitar		0	1953	26	1953	(Mercury 70163)
* 2	The Green Door	(London HLD8317)	8	1956	1	1956	(DOT 15486)
3	Four Walls		0	1957	15	1957	(DOT 15569)
4	Talkin' To The Blues		0	1957	20	1957	(DOT 15569)
	HIT 2 IS CREDITED TO JIM LOWE & THE HIGH FIVES • HIT 4 REACHED NUMBER 8 IN THE USA C/W CHARTS						
Jim Photoglo Male Vocalist From Los Angeles							
1	We Were Meant To Be Lovers		0	1980	31	1980	(20TH CENTURY 2446)
2	Fool In Love With You		0	1981	25	1981	(20TH CENTURY 2487)
	THE 1980 HIT WAS CREDITED TO PHOTOGLO						
Jim Reeves Male Vocalist, Real Name James Travis Reeves B: 20 Aug 1924 Panola County, Texas.							
* 1	Mexican Joe		0	1953	23	1953	(ABBOTT 116)
2	Bimbo		0	1953	26	1953	(ABBOTT 148)
* 26	He'll Have To Go	(RCA 1168)	36	1960	2	1959	(RCA 7643)
27	He'll Have To Go (Re-entry)	(RCA 1168)	12	1960	0	1960	
28	I'm Gettin' Better		0	1960	37	1960	(RCA 7756)
31	Am I Losing You (Re-Issue)		0	1960	31	1960	(RCA 7800)
33	Whispering Hope	(RCA 1223)	50	1961	0	1961	
!* 48	I Love You Because	(RCA 1385)	5	1964	54	1976	(RCA 10557)
52	There's A Heartache Following Me	(RCA 1423)	6	1964	0	1964	
53	I Won't Forget You (Re-entry)	(RCA 1400)	47	1965	0	1965	
54	It Hurts So Much	(RCA 1437)	8	1965	0	1965	
56	Not Until The Next Time	(RCA 1446)	13	1965	0	1965	
57	How Long Has It Been	(RCA 1445)	45	1965	0	1965	
58	This World Is Not My Home	(RCA 1412)	22	1965	0	1965	
65	Trying To Forget	(RCA 1611)	33	1967	0	1967	
	(In Your Pretty Brown Eyes)	(RCA 1672)	33	1968	9	1968	(RCA 9455)
70	But You Love Me Daddy	(RCA 1899)	15	1969	0	1969	
74	Angels Don't Lie (Re-entry)	(RCA 1997)	32	1970	0	1970	
76	I Love You Because/He'll Have To Go/ Moonlight & Roses (Re-Issue)	(RCA Maximillion 2092)	34	1971	0	1971	
77	You're Free To Go	(RCA 2174)	48	1972	0	1972	
	UNLISTED HITS ARE C/W • HE WAS A PROFESSIONAL BASEBALL PITCHER WITH THE HOUSTON BUFFALOES • OBITUARY : D: 31 JUL 1964 PLANE CRASH.						
Jim Stafford Male Vocalist, B: 16 Jan 1944 In Eloise, Florida							
1	Swamp Witch		0	1973	39	1973	(MGM 14496)
* 2	Spiders And Snakes	(MGM 2006 374)	14	1974	3	1973	(MGM 14648)
3	My Girl Bill	(MGM 2006 423)	20	1974	12	1974	(MGM 14718)
4	Wildwood Weed		0	1974	7	1974	(MGM 14737)
5	Your Bulldog Drinks Champagne		0	1975	24	1975	(MGM 14775)
6	I Got Stoned And I Missed It		0	1975	37	1975	(MGM 14819)
Jim Steinman Male Vocalist, B: New York City, Vocals On The 1981 Hit Are By Rory Dodd							
1	Rock And Roll Dream Come Through	(Epic EPC A 1236)	52	1981	32	1981	(Epic 02111)
2	Tonight Is What It Means To Be Young	(MCA MCA 889)	67	1984	0	1984	
Jim Weatherly Male Songwriter/Vocalist, B: 17 Mar 1943 Pontotoc, Mississippi							
1	The Need To Be		0	1974	11	1974	(BUDDAH 420)
Jimi Hendrix Male Vocalist/Instrumentalist, B: 27 Nov 1942 Seattle							
1	Hey Joe	(Polydor 56 139)	6	1967	0	1967	
2	Purple Haze	(TRACK 604 001)	3	1967	0	1967	
3	The Wind Cries Mary	(TRACK 604 004)	6	1967	0	1967	
4	The Burning Of The Midnight Lamp	(TRACK 604 007)	18	1967	0	1967	
5	All Along The Watchtower	(TRACK 604 025)	5	1968	20	1968	(REPRISE 0767)
6	Crosstown Traffic	(TRACK 604 029)	37	1969	0	1969	
7	Voodoo Chile	(TRACK 2095 001)	1	1970	0	1970	
8	Gypsy Eyes / Remember	(TRACK 2094 010)	35	1971	0	1971	
9	Johnny B Goode	(Polydor 2001 277)	35	1972	0	1972	
10	Crosstown Traffic (Re-Issue)	(Polydor PO 71)	61	1990	0	1990	
11	All Along The Watchtower (EP)	(Polydor PO 100)	52	1990	0	1990	
	JIMI FORMED JIMMY JAMES & THE BLUE FLAMES IN 1965 & THE BAND OF GYPSYS IN 1969 • HITS 3-8 ARE CREDITED TO JIMI HENDRIX EXPERIENCE JIMI HENDRIX EXPERIENCE FORMED IN 1966 • OBITUARY :-D: 18 SEP 1970 DRUG OVERDOSE.						
Jimi Polo Male Producer from the USA							
1	Never Goin' Down	(MCA MCS 1578)	51	1991	0	1991	with Adamski
2	Express Yourself	(PERFECTO 74321101827)	59	1992	0	1992	
3	Express Yourself (Re-Recording)	(PERFECTO PERF 146CD1)	62	1997	0	1997	

ISSUE	TITLE	UK LBL	UK POS	UK YEAR	US POS	US YEAR	US LBL

Jimmie Rodgers 1) Male Vocalist, B: James Charles Rodgers, 8 Sep 1897 Meridian, Mississippi. The Father Of Country Music

*	1	The Soldiers Sweetheart		0	1927	9	1927	(Victor 20864)
*	2	Blue Yodel		0	1928	2	1928	(Victor 21142)
*	4	The Brakemen's Blues		0	1928	7	1928	(Victor 21291)
		OBITUARY : D: 26 MAY 1933 TUBERCULOSIS.						

Jimmie Rodgers (2) Male Vocalist/Guitarist, Real Name James Frederick Rodgers B: 18 Sep 1933 Camas, Washington.

*	1	Honeycomb	(Columbia DB 3986)	30	1957	1	1957	(ROULETTE 4015)
*	2	Kisses Sweeter Than Wine	(Columbia DB 4052)	7	1957	3	1957	(ROULETTE 4031)
	3	Oh-Oh, I'm Falling In Love Again	(Columbia DB 4078)	18	1958	7	1957	(ROULETTE 4045)
*	4	Secretly		0	1958	3	1958	(ROULETTE 4070)
	5	Make Me A Miracle		0	1956	16	1956	(ROULETTE 4070)
	6	Are You Really Mine		0	1958	10	1958	(ROULETTE 4090)
	7	Bimbombey		0	1958	11	1958	(ROULETTE 4116)
	8	Woman From Liberia	(Columbia DB 4206)	18	1958	0	1958	
	9	I'm Never Gonna Tell		0	1959	36	1959	(ROULETTE 4129)
	10	Ring-A-Ling-Laro		0	1959	32	1959	(ROULETTE 4158)
	11	Wonderful You		0	1959	40	1959	(ROULETTE 4158)
	12	Tucumcari		0	1959	32	1959	(ROULETTE 4191)
	13	T.L.C. (Tender Loving Care)		0	1960	24	1960	(ROULETTE 4218)
	14	English Country Garden	(Columbia DB 4847)	5	1962	0	1962	
	15	It's Over		0	1966	37	1966	(DOT 16861)
	16	Child Of Clay		0	1967	31	1967	(A&M 871)

Jimmy 'Bo' Horne Miami Based Soul Singer, B: 28 Sep 1949 In West Palm Beach, Florida

| | 1 | Dance Across The Floor | | 0 | 1978 | 38 | 1978 | (SUNSHINE S. 1003) |

Jimmy Bowen & The Rhythm Orchids Male Vocalist/Producer, B: 30 Nov 1937 New Mexico

| | 1 | I'm Stickin' With You | | 0 | 1957 | 14 | 1957 | (ROULETTE 4001) |

Jimmy Boyd Male Vocalist, B: 9 Jan 1940 Mccomb, Missouri

*	1	I Saw Mommy Kissing Santa Claus	(Columbia DB 3365)	3	1953	1	1952	(Columbia 39871)
*	2	Tell Me A Story	(Philips PB 126)	5	1953	4	1953	(Columbia 39945)
	3	The Little Boy And The Old Man		0	1953	24	1943	(Columbia 39945)
	4	Dennis The Menace		0	1953	25	1953	(Columbia 39988)
	5	Tell Me A Story (Re-entry)	(Philips PB 126)	12	1953	0	1953	
		HITS 1-3 ARE CREDITED TO FRANKIE LAINE AND JIMMY BOYD • HIT 4 IS CREDITED TO ROSEMARY CLOONEY AND JIMMY BOYD • HE RECORDED HIT 1 AT THE AGE OF 12						

Jimmy Buffett Male Vocalist, B: 25 Dec 1946 Alabama

!	1	The Great Filling Station Holdup		0	1973	58	1973	(DUNHILL 4348)
	2	Come Monday		0	1974	30	1974	(DUNHILL 4385)
!	3	Door Number Three		0	1975	88	1975	(ABC 12113)
	4	Margaritaville		0	1977	8	1977	(ABC 12254)
	5	Changes In Latitudes, Changes In Attitudes		0	1977	37	1977	(ABC 12305)
	6	Cheeseburger In Paradise		0	1978	32	1978	(ABC 12358)
	7	Livingston Saturday Night		0	1978	52	1978	(ABC 12391)
	8	Fins		0	1979	35	1979	(MCA 41109)
		REST ARE C/W HITS • HE NOW HAILS FROM KEY WEST SELLING HIS OWN LINE IN TROPICAL CLOTHING						

Jimmy Castor Male Composer/Singer/Saxophonist/Arranger, B: 2 Jun 1943 New York

	1	Hey, Leroy, Your Mama's Callin' You		0	1967	31	1967	(SMASH 2069)
*	2	Troglodyte (Cave Man)		0	1972	2	1972	(RCA 1029)
	3	The Bertha Butt Boogie (Part 1)		0	1975	16	1975	(Atlantic 3232)
		HITS 2-3 ARE CREDITED TO THE JIMMY CASTOR BUNCH • JIMMY FORMED THE BUNCH IN 1972						

Jimmy Charles Male R&B Singer, B: 1942 New Jersey

| | 1 | A Million To One | | 0 | 1960 | 5 | 1960 | (PROMO 1002) |

Jimmy Clanton Male Vocalist B: 2 Sep 1940 Baton Rouge, Louisiana

*	1	Just A Dream		0	1958	4	1958	(ACE 546)
*	2	A Letter To An Angel		0	1958	25	1958	(ACE 546)
	3	A Part Of Me		0	1958	38	1958	(ACE 546)
	4	My Own True Love		0	1959	33	1959	(ACE 567)
	5	Go, Jimmy, Go		0	1960	5	1960	(ACE 575)
	6	Another Sleepless Night	(Top Rank JAR 382)	50	1960	22	1960	(ACE 585)
*	7	Venus In Blue Jeans		0	1962	7	1962	(ACE 8001)

Jimmy Cliff Male Vocalist, Real Name James Chambers B: 1948 Jamaica

	1	Wonderful World Beautiful People	(TROJAN TR 690)	6	1969	25	1969	(A&M 1146)
	2	Vietnam	(TROJAN TR	47	1970	0	1970	
	3	Vietnam (Re-entry)	(TROJAN TR	46	1970	0	1970	

	ISSUE	TITLE	UK LBL	UK POS	UK YEAR	US POS	US YEAR	US LBL
	4	Wild World	(Island WIP 6087)	8	1970	0	1970	
	5	I Can See Clearly Now	(Columbia 6601982)	23	1994	0	1994	

Jimmy Crawford Male Vocalist from the UK

	ISSUE	TITLE	UK LBL	UK POS	UK YEAR	US POS	US YEAR	US LBL
	1	Love Or Money	(Columbia DB 4633)	49	1961	0	1961	
	2	I Love How You Love Me	(Columbia DB 4717)	18	1961	0	1961	

Jimmy Dean Male Vocalist, B: 10 Aug 1928 Near Plainview, Texas

	ISSUE	TITLE	UK LBL	UK POS	UK YEAR	US POS	US YEAR	US LBL
!	1	Bumming Around		0	1953	5	1953	(4 STAR 1613)
	2	Little Sandy Sleighfoot		0	1958	32	1958	(Columbia 41025)
*	3	Big Bad John	(Philips PB 1187)	2	1961	1	1961	(Columbia 42175)
	4	Dear Ivan		0	1962	24	1962	(Columbia 42259)
	5	The Cajun Queen		0	1962	22	1962	(Columbia 42282)
	6	To A Sleeping Beauty		0	1962	26	1962	(Columbia 42282)
	7	P.T. 109		0	1962	8	1962	(Columbia 42338)
	8	Little Black Book	(CBS AAG 122)	33	1962	29	1962	(Columbia 42529)
	24	I.O.U.		0	1976	35	1976	(CASINO 052)

Jimmy Dorsey Orchestra Male Orchestra Leader, B: 9 Feb 1904 Pennsylvania

	ISSUE	TITLE	UK LBL	UK POS	UK YEAR	US POS	US YEAR	US LBL	
*	37	Amapola (From *First Love*)		0	1941	1	1941	(Decca 3629)	
*	42	Green Eyes		0	1941	1	1941	(Decca 3698)	
*	43	Maria Elena		0	1941	1	1941	(Decca 3698)	
*	83	Besame Mucho (Kiss Me)		0	1943	1	1943	(Decca 18574)	58
	94	Doin' What Comes Natur'lly (From Annie Get Your Gun)		0	1946	8	1946	(Decca 18872)	
	95	The Whole World Is Singing My Song		0	1946	12	1946	(Decca 18917)	
	96	Heartaches		0	1947	11	1947	(MGM 10001)	
	97	Ballerina		0	1948	10	1948	(MGM 10035)	
	98	On Green Dolphin Street (From Green Dolphin Street)		0	1948	25	1948	(MGM 10098)	
	99	Johnson Rag		0	1950	13	1950	(Columbia 38649)	
	100	Rag Mop		0	1950	15	1950	(Columbia 38710)	
*	101	So Rare		0	1957	2	1957	(FRATERNITY 755)	
	102	June Night		0	1957	21	1957	(FRATERNITY 777)	

OBITUARY : D: 12 JUN 1957 CANCER.

Jimmy Durante (1) Male Comedian/Vocalist/Actor, Nicknamed Schnozzola from the USA

	ISSUE	TITLE	UK LBL	UK POS	UK YEAR	US POS	US YEAR	US LBL
	3	Blackstrap Molasses		0	1951	29	1951	(Decca 27748)

HIT 3 IS CREDITED TO DANNY KAYE, JIMMY DURANTE, GROUCHO MARX & JANE WYMAN • OBITUARY :D: 29 JAN 1980, AGED 86.

Jimmy Durante (2) Male Vocalist from the USA

	ISSUE	TITLE	UK LBL	UK POS	UK YEAR	US POS	US YEAR	US LBL
	1	Make Someone Happy	(Warner Bros. W 0385CD)	69	1996	0	1996	

Jimmy Elledge Male Vocalist, B: 8 Jan 1943, Nashville, Tennessee

	ISSUE	TITLE	UK LBL	UK POS	UK YEAR	US POS	US YEAR	US LBL
*	1	Funny (How Time Slips Away)		0	1961	22	1961	(RCA 7946)

Jimmy Hall Hails From Alabama And Is Leader Of Wet Willie

	ISSUE	TITLE	UK LBL	UK POS	UK YEAR	US POS	US YEAR	US LBL
	1	I'm Happy That Love Has Found You		0	1980	27	1980	(Epic 50931)

Jimmy Helms Male Vocalist from the UK

	ISSUE	TITLE	UK LBL	UK POS	UK YEAR	US POS	US YEAR	US LBL
	1	Gonna Make You An Offer You Can't Refuse	(CUBE BUG 27)	8	1973	0	1973	

Jimmy Hughes Jimmy Hails From Alabama And Is Cousin To Percy Sledge

	ISSUE	TITLE	UK LBL	UK POS	UK YEAR	US POS	US YEAR	US LBL
	1	Steal Away		0	1964	17	1964	(FAME 6401)

Jimmy James & The Vagabonds Male Vocal/Instrumental Group from the UK

	ISSUE	TITLE	UK LBL	UK POS	UK YEAR	US POS	US YEAR	US LBL
	1	Red Red Wine	(PYE 7N 17579)	36	1968	0	1968	
	2	I'll Go Where Your Music Takes Me	(PYE 7N 45585)	23	1976	0	1976	
	3	Now Is The Time	(PYE 7N 45606)	5	1976	0	1976	

Jimmy Jones Male Vocalist, B: 2 Jun 1937 Birmingham, Alabama

	ISSUE	TITLE	UK LBL	UK POS	UK YEAR	US POS	US YEAR	US LBL
*	1	Handy Man	(MGM 1051)	3	1960	2	1960	(CUB 9049)
*	2	Good Timin'	(MGM 1078)	1	1960	3	1960	(CUB 9067)
	3	Handy Man (Re-entry)	(MGM 1051)	32	1960	0	1960	
	4	I Just Go For You	(MGM 1091)	35	1960	0	1960	
	5	Ready For Love	(MGM 1103)	46	1960	0	1960	
	6	I Told You So	(MGM 1123)	33	1961	0	1961	

JIMMY'S PREVIOUS GROUPS INCLUDE SPARKS OF RHYTHM, SAVOYS & THE PRETENDERS

Jimmy Justice Male Vocalist from the UK

	ISSUE	TITLE	UK LBL	UK POS	UK YEAR	US POS	US YEAR	US LBL
	1	When My Little Girl Is Smiling	(PYE 7N 15421)	9	1962	0	1962	
	2	Ain't That Funny	(PYE 7N 15443)	8	1962	0	1962	
	3	Spanish Harlem	(PYE 7N 15457)	20	1962	0	1962	

Jimmy McCracklin B: 13 Aug 1921 St. Louis

	ISSUE	TITLE	UK LBL	UK POS	UK YEAR	US POS	US YEAR	US LBL
	1	The Walk		0	1958	7	1958	(CHECKER 885)

JIMMY FIRST RECORDED WITH THE BAND BLUES BLASTERS IN 1949

ISSUE	TITLE	UK LBL	UK POS	UK YEAR	US POS	US YEAR	US LBL
Jimmy McGriff Male R&B/Jazz Multi-Instrumentalist, B: 3 Apr 1936 Philadelphia							
1	I've Got A Woman (Part 1)		0	1962	20	1962	(SUE 770)
Jimmy Nail Male Actor/Vocalist from the UK							
1	Love Don't Live Here Anymore	(Virgin VS 764)	3	1985	0	1985	
2	Ain't No Doubt	(East West YZ 686)	1	1992	0	1992	
3	Laura	(East West YZ 702)	58	1992	0	1992	
4	Crocodile Shoes	(East West YZ 867CD)	4	1994	0	1994	
5	Cowboy Dreams	(East West YZ 878CD)	13	1995	0	1995	
6	Crocodile Shoes (Re-entry)	(East West YZ 867CD)	68	1995	0	1995	
7	Crocodile Shoes (2nd Re-entry)	(East West 867CD)YZ	56	1995	0	1995	
8	Calling Out Your Name	(East West YZ935CD)	65	1995	0	1995	
9	Big River	(East West EW 008CD)	18	1995	0	1995	
10	Love	(East West EW 018CD)	33	1995	0	1995	
11	Big River (Re-Mix)	(East West EW 024CD)	72	1996	0	1996	
12	Country Boy	(East West EW 070CD)	25	1996	0	1996	
Jimmy Newman Male Vocal/Guitarist, B: Jimmy Yeve Newman 27 Aug 1927 Big Mamou, Louisiana							
7	A Fallen Star		0	1957	23	1957	(DOT 15574)
Jimmy Osmond Male Vocalist, B: 16 Apr 1963 Canoga Park, California All Hits Credited To Little Jimmy Osmond							
1	Long Haired Lover From Liverpool	(MGM 2006 109)	1	1972	38	1972	(MGM 14376)
2	Tweedlee Dee	(MGM 2006 175)	4	1973	0	1973	
3	Long Haired Lover From Liverpool (Re-entry)	(MGM 2006 109)	41	1973	0	1973	
4	I'm Gonna Knock On Your Door	(MGM 2006 389)	11	1974	0	1974	
Jimmy Parkinson Male Vocalist From Australia							
1	The Great Pretender	(Columbia DB 3729)	9	1956	0	1956	
2	Walk Hand In Hand	(Columbia DB 3775)	30	1956	0	1956	
3	Walk Hand In Hand (Re-entry)	(Columbia DB 3775)	26	1956	0	1956	
4	In The Middle Of The House	(Columbia DB 3833)	26	1956	0	1956	
5	In The Middle Of The House (Re-entry)	(Columbia DB 3833)	20	1956	0	1956	
Jimmy Radcliffe Male Vocalist from the USA							
1	Long After Tonight Is All Over	(STATESIDE SS 374)	40	1965	0	1965	
Jimmy Reed Male Vocalist, Real Name Mathis James Reed B: 6 Sep 1925 Dunleith, Mississippi.							
1	Shame Shame Shame	(STATESIDE SS 330)	45	1964	0	1964	
2	Honest I Do		0	1957	32	1957	(VEE-JAY 253)
3	Baby What You Want Me To Do		0	1960	37	1960	(VEE-JAY 333)
	OBITUARY: D: 29 AUG 1976 EPILEPTIC SEIZURE.						
Jimmy Roselli Male Vocalist from the USA							
1	When Your Old Wedding Ring Was New	(A1 282)	51	1983	0	1983	
2	When Your Old Wedding Ring Was New (Re-Issue)	(FIRST NIGHT SCORE 9)	52	1987	0	1987	
Jimmy Ruffin Male Vocalist, B: 7 May 1939 Collinsville, Mississippi							
1	What Becomes Of The Broken Hearted	(Tamla Motown TMG 577)	10	1966	7	1966	(SOUL 35022)
2	I've Passed This Way Before	(Tamla Motown TMG 593)29		1967	17	1966	(SOUL 35027)
3	Gonna Give Her All The Love I've Got	(Tamla Motown TMG 603)	26	1967	29	1967	(SOUL 35032)
+ 4	Don't You Miss Me A Little Bit Baby		0	1967	27	1967	(SOUL 35035)
5	I've Passed This Way Before (Re-Issue)	(Tamla Motown TMG 703)	33	1969	0	1969	
6	Farewell Is A Lonely Sound	(Tamla Motown TMG 726)	8	1970	0	1970	
7	I'll Say Forever My Love	(Tamla Motown TMG 740)	7	1970	0	1970	
8	It's Wonderful	(Tamla Motown TMG 753)	6	1970	0	1970	
+ 9	Stand By Me		0	1970	24	1970	(SOUL 35076)
10	What Becomes Of The Brokenhearted (Re-Issue)	(Tamla Motown TMG 911)	4	1974	0	1974	
11	Farewell Is A Lonely Sound (Re-Issue)	(Tamla Motown TMG 922)	30	1974	0	1974	
12	Tell Me What You Want	(Polydor 2058 433)	39	1974	0	1974	
13	Hold On To My Love	(RSO 57)	7	1980	10	1980	(RSO 1021)
14	There Will Never Be Another You	(EMI 5541)	68	1985	0	1985	
	JIMMY BECAME A REGULAR ON THE BRITISH CLUB CIRCUIT INCLUDING THE ALL NIGHT TWISTED WHEEL IN MANCHESTER ALTHOUGH IT NO LONGER EXISTS. HIT 9 IS CREDITED TO DAVID AND JIMMY RUFFIN • SEE ALSO DAVID RUFFIN						
Jimmy Sacca See Hilltoppers							
Jimmy Shand Male Dance Band from the UK							
1	Bluebell Polka	(Parlophone F 3436)	20	1955	0	1955	
Jimmy Smith Male Instrumentalist (Organ) B: 8 Dec 1925 Norristown, Pennsylvania							
1	Walk On The Wild Side (Part 1)		0	1962	21	1962	(VERVE 10255)
2	Got My Mojo Working	(VERVE VS 536)	48	1966	0	1966	

ISSUE	TITLE	UK LBL	UK POS	UK YEAR	US POS	US YEAR	US LBL
3	Got My Mojo Working (Re-entry)	(VERVE VS 536)	48	1966	0	1966	

HIT 1 IS CREDITED TO JIMMY SMITH & THE BIG BAND • JIMMY HAD HIS OWN TRIO CALLED THE BLUE NOTES IN THE EARLY 50S

Jimmy Somerville   Male Vocalist from the UK

1	Comment Te Dire Adieu	(London LON 241)	14	1989	0	1989	
2	You Make Me Feel (Mighty Real)	(London LON 249)	5	1990	0	1990	
3	Read My Lips (Enough Is Enough)	(London LON 254)	26	1990	0	1990	
4	Smalltown Boy (Re-Mix)	(London LON 287)	32	1991	0	1991	
5	To Love Somebody	(London LON 281)	8	1990	0	1990	
6	Run From Love	(London LON 301)	52	1991	0	1991	
7	Heartbeat	(London LONCD 358)	24	1995	0	1995	
8	Hurt So Good	(London LONCD 364)	15	1995	0	1995	
9	By Your Side	(London LONCD 372)	41	1995	0	1995	
10	Dark Sky	(GUT CXGUT 11)	66	1997	0	1997	

HIT 1 IS CREDITED TO JIMMY SOMERVILLE FEATURING JUNE MILES-KINGSTON • HIT 4 IS CREDITED TO JIMMY SOMERVILLE WITH BRONSKI BEAT

Jimmy Soul   Male Vocalist, Real Name Jimmy Mccleese B: 1942, Harlem

1	Twistin' Matilda		0	1962	22	1962	(S.P.Q.R. 300)
* 2	If You Wanna Be Happy	(STATESIDE SS 178)	39	1963	1	1963	(S.P.Q.R. 3305)
3	If You Wanna Be Happy (Re-Issue)	(Epic 6569647)	68	1991	0	1991	

JIMMY WAS A PREACHER AT THE AGE OF SEVEN • HE TOURED WITH THE FAMED GOSPEL GROUP THE NIGHTINGALES

Jimmy Tarbuck   Male Comedian/Vocalist from the UK

1	Again	(SAFARI SAFE 68)	74	1985	0	1985	
2	Again (Re-entry)	(SAFARI SAFE 68)	68	1985	0	1985	

Jimmy The Hoover   Mixed Vocal/Instrumental Group from the UK

1	Tantalise (Wo Wo Ee Yeh Yeh)	(INNERVISION A 3406)	18	1983	0	1983	

Jimmy Wakely   Male Actor/Guitarist/Pianist/Vocalist, B: 16 Feb 1914 Near Mineola, Arkansas & Raised In Oklahoma

4	One Has My Name (The Other Has My Heart)		0	1948	10	1948	(Capitol 15162)
5	I Love You So Much It's Hurts		0	1948	21	1948	(Capitol 15243)
* 12	Slippin' Around		0	1949	1	1949	(Capitol 40224)
13	Wedding Bell Will Soon Be Ringing		0	1949	30	1949	(Capitol 40224)
14	I'll Never Slip Around Again		0	1949	8	1949	(Capitol 40246)
15	Broken Down Merry-Go-Round		0	1950	12	1950	(Capitol 800)
16	The Gods Were Angry With Me		0	1950	17	1950	(Capitol 800)
17	Let's Go To Church (Next Sunday Morning)		0	1950	13	1950	(Capitol 960)
18	Peter Cottontail		0	1950	26	1950	(Capitol 929)
20	A Bushel And A Peck		0	1950	6	1950	(Capitol 1234)
21	My Heart Cries For You		0	1951	12	1951	(Capitol 1328)
22	Beautiful Brown Eyes		0	1951	12	1951	(Capitol 1393)
23	When You And I Were Young, Maggie		0	1951	20	1951	(Capitol 1500)

OTHER HITS ARE C/W HITS • OBITUARY : D: 25 SEP 1982 (AGED 68).

Jimmy Witherspoon   Male Vocalist from the USA

* 1	Real Ugly Woman		0	1950	0	1950	

Jimmy Young   Male Dj/Vocalist from the UK

1	Faith Can Move Mountains	(Decca F 9986)	11	1953	0	1953	
2	Eternally	(Decca F 10130)	8	1953	0	1953	
3	Unchained Melody	(Decca F 10502)	1	1955	0	1955	
4	The Man From Laramie	(Decca F 10597)	1	1955	0	1955	
5	Someone On Your Mind	(Decca F 10640)	13	1955	0	1955	
6	Chain Gang	(Decca F 10694)	9	1956	0	1956	
7	Wayward Wind	(Decca F 10736)	27	1956	0	1956	
8	Rich Man Poor Man	(Decca F 10736)	25	1956	0	1956	
9	More	(Decca F 10774)	4	1956	0	1956	
10	Round And Round	(Decca F 10875)	30	1957	0	1957	
11	Miss You	(Columbia DB 7119)	15	1963	0	1963	
12	Unchained Melody	(Columbia DB 7234)	43	1964	0	1964	

HIT 10 WAS WITH THE MICHAEL SAMMES SINGERS • HITS 3 & 12 ARE DIFFERENT RECORDINGS • SEE ALSO ALL STAR HIT PARADE, VARIOUS ARTISTS (EP, LP, 78S)

Jingle Belles   Female Vocal Group from the USA/UK

1	Christmas Spectre	(PASSION PASH 14)	37	1983	0	1983	

Jinny   Female Vocalist From Italy

1	Keep Warm	(Virgin VS 1356)	11	1991	0	1991	
2	Feel The Rhythm	(LOGIC 401633001022)	74	1993	0	1993	
3	Keep Warm (Re-Mix)	(MULTIPLY CDMULTY 5)	11	1995	0	1995	
4	Wanna Be With You	(MULTIPLY CDMULTY 8)	30	1995	0	1995	

ISSUE	TITLE	UK LBL	UK POS	UK YEAR	US POS	US YEAR	US LBL
Jive Bombers Names Earl Johnson, Al Tinney, Clarence Palmer & William Tinney							
1	Bad Boy		0	1957	36	1957	(SAVOY 1508)
Jive Bunny & The Mastermixers Male Production/Mixing Group from the UK							
* 1	Swing The Mood	(Music Factory MFD 001)	1	1989	11	1990	(Music Factory 99140)
2	That's What I Like	(Music Factory MFD 002)	1	1989	0	1989	
3	Let's Party	(Music Factory MFD 003)	1	1989	0	1989	
4	That Sounds Good To Me	(Music Factory MFD 004)	4	1990	0	1990	
5	Can Can You Party	(Music Factory MFD 007)	8	1990	0	1990	
6	Let's Swing Again	(Music Factory MFD 009)	19	1990	0	1990	
7	The Crazy Party Mixes	(Music Factory MFD 010)	13	1990	0	1990	
8	Over To You John (Here We Go Again)	(Music Factory MFD 012)	28	1991	0	1991	
9	Hot Summer Salsa	(Music Factory MFD 013)	43	1991	0	1991	
10	Rock 'N' Roll Party	(Music Factory MFD 015)	48	1991	0	1991	
	NAMES: LES HEMSTOCK, IAN MORGAN, JOHN & ANDY PICKLES • SEE ALSO LIZ KERSHAW & BRUNO BROOKES						
Jive Five Formed In 1959 With Lead Singer Eugene Pitt							
1	My True Story		0	1961	3	1961	(BELTONE 1006)
2	I'm A Happy Man		0	1965	36	1965	(United Artists 853)
JJ Mixed Vocal/Instrumental Duo from the UK							
1	If This Is Love	(Columbia 6566097)	55	1991	0	1991	
JKD Band Male Vocal/Instrumental Group from the UK							
1	Dragon Power	(SATRIL SAT 132)	58	1978	0	1978	
Jo Ann Campbell Female Vocalist, B: 20 Jul 1938 Jacksonville, Florida							
1	Motorcycle Michael	(HMV POP 873)	41	1961	0	1961	
2	(I'm The Girl On) Wolverton Mountain		0	1962	38	1962	(CAMEO 223)
Jo Ann Tolley Female Vocalist from the USA							
1	I'd Never Forgive Myself		0	1953	29	1953	(MGM 11471)
1Jo Boxers Male Vocal/Instrumental Group from the UK Lead Singer Of The Quintet Is Dig Wayne							
1	Boxer Beat	(RCA BOXX 1)	3	1983	0	1983	
2	Just Got Lucky	(RCA BOXX 2)	7	1983	36	1983	(RCA 13601)
3	Johnny Friendly	(RCA BOXX 3)	31	1983	0	1983	
4	Jealous Love	(RCA BOXX 4)	72	1983	0	1983	
Jo Jo Gunne Rock Quartet Formed By Mark Andes & Jay Ferguson From Los Angeles							
1	Run Run Run	(Asylum AYM 501)	6	1972	27	1972	(Asylum 11003)
Jo Stafford Female Vocalist, B: 12 Nov 1920 Coalinga, California.							
13	Day By Day		0	1946	8	1946	(Capitol 227)
14	This Is Always (From *Three Little Girls In Blue*)		0	1946	11	1946	(Capitol 277)
15	You Keep Coming Back Like A Song (From *Blue Skies*)		0	1946	11	1946	(Capitol 297)
16	The Things We Did Last Summer		0	1946	10	1946	(Capitol 2970
17	White Christmas (From *Holiday Inn*)		0	1946	9	1946	(Capitol 319)
18	Sonata		0	1947	10	1947	(Capitol 337)
19	Ivy (Movie Title Song)		0	1947	13	1947	(Capitol 388)
20	A Sunday Kind Of Love		0	1947	15	1947	(Capitol 388)
* 21	Temptation (Tim-Tayshun)		0	1947	1	1947	(Capitol 412)
22	I'm So Right Tonight		0	1947	15	1947	(Capitol 423)
23	Feudin' And Fightin' (From *Laffing Room Only*)		0	1947	7	1947	(Capitol 443)
24	The Stanley Steemer (From *Summer Holiday*)		0	1947	11	1947	(Capitol 454)
25	Love And The Weather		0	1947	25	1947	(Capitol 443)
26	The Gentleman Is A Dope (From *Allegro*)		0	1947	20	1947	(Capitol 15007)
27	Serenade Of The Bells		0	1947	6	1947	(Capitol 15007)
28	The Best Things In Life Are Free (From *Good News*)		0	1948	21	1948	(Capitol 15017)
29	I Never Loved Anyone		0	1948	23	1948	(Capitol 15017)
30	I'm My Own Grandmaw		0	1948	21	1948	(Capitol 15023)
31	Haunted Heart (From *Inside U.S.A.*)		0	1948	23	1948	(Capitol 15023)
32	Suspicion		0	1948	23	1948	(Capitol 15068)
33	Better Luck Next Time		0	1948	26	1948	(Capitol 15084)
34	Ev'ry Day I Love (Just A Little Bit More) (From *Two Guys From Texas*)		0	1948	25	1948	(Capitol 15139)
35	Say Something Sweet To Your Sweetheart		0	1948	10	1948	(Capitol 15207)
36	Bluebird Of Happiness		0	1948	16	1948	(Capitol 15207)
37	My Darling, My Darling (From *Where's Charley*)		0	1948	1	1948	(Capitol 15270)
38	Congratulations		0	1949	13	1949	(CAPIOL 15319)
39	Here I'll Stay		0	1949	28	1949	(Capitol 15319)
40	The Pussy Cat Song		0	1949	26	1949	(Capitol 15342)
41	A You're Adorable (The Alphabet Song)		0	1949	4	1949	(Capitol 15393)

ISSUE	TITLE	UK LBL	UK POS	UK YEAR	US POS	US YEAR	US LBL
42	Need You		0	1949	7	1949	(Capitol 15393)
43	Once And For Always		0	1949	16	1949	(Capitol 15424)
44	Some Enchanted Evening (From *South Pacific*)		0	1949	4	1949	(Capitol 544)
45	Homework		0	1949	11	1949	(Capitol 665)
46	Just One Way To Say I Love You		0	1949	12	1949	(Capitol 665)
* 47	Whispering Hope		0	1949	4	1949	(Capitol 690)
48	Ragtime Cowboy Joe		0	1949	10	1949	(Capitol 710)
49	The Last Mile Home		0	1949	16	1949	(Capitol 710)
50	If I Ever Loved Again		0	1949	20	1949	(Capitol 742)
51	Bibbidi-Bobbidi-Boo (From *Cinderella*)		0	1949	13	1949	(Capitol 782)
52	Echoes		0	1949	18	1949	(Capitol 782)
53	Scarlet Ribbons (For Her Hair)		0	1950	14	1950	(Capitol 785)
54	Diamonds Are A Girl's Best Friend (From *Gentlemen Prefer Blondes*)		0	1950	30	1950	(Capitol 824)
55	Dearie (From *The Copacabana Show* Of 1950)		0	1950	10	1950	(Capitol 858)
56	Play A Simple Melody (From Watch Your Step)		0	1950	18	1950	(Capitol 1039)
57	No Other Love		0	1950	8	1950	(Capitol 1053)
58	Sometime		0	1950	27	1950	(Capitol 1053)
59	Goodnight Irene		0	1950	9	1950	(Capitol 1142)
60	Tennessee Waltz		0	1950	7	1950	(Columbia 78-39065)
61	If You've Got The Money, I've Got The Time		0	1950	14	1950	(Columbia 78-39065)
62	If		0	1951	8	1951	(Columbia 78-39082)
63	It Is No Secret		0	1951	15	1951	(Columbia 78-39082)
64	Pretty Eyed Baby		0	1951	13	1951	(Columbia 39388)
65	Somebody		0	1951	12	1951	(Columbia 39389)
66	In The Cool, Cool, Cool Of The Evening (From *Here Comes The Groom*)		0	1951	17	1951	(Columbia 39466)
67	Kissing Bug Boogie		0	1951	20	1951	(Columbia 39529)
68	Hey, Good Lookin'		0	1951	9	1951	(Columbia 39570)
69	Gambella (The Gamblin' Lady)		0	1951	19	1951	(Columbia 39570)
* 70	Shrimp Boats		0	1951	2	1951	(Columbia 39581)
71	Hambone		0	1952	6	1952	(Columbia 39672)
72	A-Round The Corner		0	1952	9	1952	(Columbia 39653)
* 73	You Belong To Me	(Columbia DB 3152)	1	1952	1	1952	(Columbia 39811)
* 74	Jambalaya	(Columbia DB 3169)	11	1952	3	1952	(Columbia 39838)
75	Tonight We're Setting The Woods On Fire		0	1952	21	1952	(Columbia 39867)
76	Early Autumn		0	1952	23	1952	(Columbia 39838)
77	Keep It A Secret		0	1952	4	1952	(Columbia 39891)
78	Chow Willy		0	1953	25	1953	(Columbia 39893)
79	(Now And Then There's) A Fool Such As I		0	1953	16	1953	(Columbia 39930)
80	Without My Lover		0	1953	27	1953	(Columbia 39951)
81	Just Another Polka		0	1953	22	1953	(Columbia 40000)
82	Way Down Yonder In New Orleans		0	1953	26	1953	(Columbia 40116)
* 83	Make Love To Me!	(Philips PB 233)	8	1954	1	1954	(Columbia 40143)
84	Indiscretion (From *Indiscretion Of An American Wife*)		0	1954	30	1954	(Columbia 40170)
85	Thank You For Calling		0	1954	12	1954	(Columbia 40250)
86	Teach Me Tonight		0	1954	15	1954	(Columbia 40351)
87	Suddenly There's A Valley	(Philips PB 509)	12	1955	13	1955	(Columbia 40559)
88	It's Almost Tomorrow		0	1955	14	1955	(Columbia 40595)
89	Suddenly There's A Valley (Re-entry)	(Philips PB 509)	19	1956	0	1956	
90	On London Bridge		0	1956	38	1956	(Columbia 40782)

SHE FORMED A TRIO WITH HER SISTERS IN 1935 TO SING ON A RADIO SERIES.

Joan Armatrading   Female Vocalist from the UK

1	Love And Affection	(A&M AMS 7249)	10	1976	0	1976	
2	Rosie	(A&M AMS 7506)	49	1980	0	1980	
3	Me Myself I	(A&M AMS 7527)	21	1980	0	1980	
4	All The Way From America	(A&M AMS 7552)	54	1980	0	1980	
5	I'm Lucky	(A&M AMS 8163)	46	1981	0	1981	
6	No Love	(A&M AMS 8179)	50	1982	0	1982	
7	Drop The Pilot	(A&M AMS 8306)	11	1983	0	1983	
8	Temptation	(A&M AM 238)	65	1985	0	1985	
9	More Than One Kind Of Love	(A&M 561)	75	1990	0	1990	
10	Wrapped Around Her	(A&M AM 877)	56	1992	0	1992	

Joan Baez   Female Vocalist B: 9 Jan 1941 Staten Island, New York City

1	We Shall Overcome	(Fontana TF 564)	26	1965	0	1965	
2	There But For Fortune	(Fontana TF 587)	8	1965	50	1965	(VANGUARD 35031)
3	It's All Over Now Baby Blue	(Fontana TF 604)	22	1965	0	1965	

ISSUE	TITLE	UK LBL	UK POS	UK YEAR	US POS	US YEAR	US LBL
4	Farewell Angelina	(Fontana TF 639)	35	1965	0	1965	
5	Farewell Angelina (Re-entry)	(Fontana TF 639)	49	1966	0	1966	
6	Pack Up Your Sorrows	(Fontana TF 727)	50	1966	0	1966	
* 7	The Night They Drove Old Dixie Down	(VANGUARD 35138)	6	1971	3	1970	(VANGUARD 35138)
8	Diamonds And Rust		0	1975	35	1975	(A&M 1737)

Joan Collins Fan Club Male Comedian /Vocalist, Real Name Julian Clary from the UK

1	Leader Of The Pack	(10 TEN 227)	60	1988	0	1988	

Joan Jett & The Blackhearts Female Vocalist, B: 22 Sep 1960 Philadelphia She Played In The Band Runaways, Before Forming Blackhearts In 1980

* 1	I Love Rock 'N' Roll	(Epic EPC A 2087)	4	1982	1	1982	(BOARDWALK
2	Crimson And Clover	(Epic EPC A 2485)	60	1982	7	1982	(BOARDWALK
3	Do You Wanna Touch Me (Oh Yeah)		0	1982	20	1982	(BOARDWALK
4	Fake Friends		0	1983	35	1983	(BLACKHEART 52240)
5	Everyday People		0	1983	37	1983	(BLACKHEART 52272)
6	Light Of Day		0	1987	33	1987	(BLACKHEART 06692)
7	I Hate Myself For Loving You	(London LON 195)	48	1988	8	1988	(BLACKHEART 07919)
8	Little Liar		0	1988	19	1988	(BLACKHEART 08095)
9	Dirty Deeds	(Chrysalis CHS 3518)	69	1990	36	1990	(BLACKHEART 73267)
10	I Love Rock 'N' Roll (Re-Issue)	(REPRISE W 0232CD)	75	1994	0	1994	

HIT 4 WAS ALSO RELEASED ON BLACKHEART 52256 IN 1983 • HIT 6 IS CREDITED TO BARBUSTERS IN A FILM OF SAME NAME

Joan Osborne Female Singer/Songwriter/Guitarist, B: 8 Jul 1962 From Kentucky

* 1	One Of Us	(BLUE GORILLAJOACD 1)	6	1996	4	1995	(BLUE GOR./MER852368)
2	St. Teresa	(BLUE GORILLA JOACD 3)	33	1996	0	1996	

Joan Regan Female Vocalist from the UK

1	Till They've All Gone Home		0	1953	23	1953	(London 1353)
2	Ricochet	(Decca F 10193)	8	1953	0	1953	
3	Ricochet (Re-entry)	(Decca F 10193)	9	1954	0	1954	
4	Someone Else's Roses	(Decca F 10257)	5	1954	0	1954	
5	If I Give My Heart To You	(Decca F 10373)	20	1954	0	1954	
6	If I Give My Heart To You (Re-entry)	(Decca F 10373)	3	1954	0	1954	
7	Wait For Me Darling	(Decca F 10362)	18	1954	0	1954	
8	Prize Of Gold	(Decca F 10432)	6	1955	0	1955	
9	Open Up Your Heart	(Decca F 10474)	19	1955	0	1955	
10	May You Always	(HMV POP 593)	9	1959	0	1959	
11	Happy Anniversary	(PYE 7N 15238)	29	1960	0	1960	
12	Happy Anniversary (Re-entry)	(PYE 7N 15238)	29	1960	0	1960	
13	Papa Loves Mama	(PYE 7N 15278)	29	1960	0	1960	
14	One Of The Lucky Ones	(PYE 7N 15310)	47	1960	0	1960	
15	It Must Be Santa	(PYE 7N 15303)	42	1961	0	1961	

SEE ALSO ALL STAR HIT PARADE, VARIOUS ARTISTS (EP, LP, 78S) • HITS 1-2 ARE CREDITED TO JOAN REGAN WITH THE SQUADRONAIRES
HIT 6 IS CREDITED TO JOAN REGAN & THE JOHNSTON BROTHERS

Joan Weber Female Vocalist, B: 1936 Paulsboro, New Jersey

* 1	Let Me Go Lover	(Philips PB 389)	16	1955	1	1954	(Columbia 40366)

THE HIT WAS ORIGINALLY TITLED 'LET ME GO DEVIL'. THE EMPHASIS WAS ON ALCOHOL, THE DEMON DRINK BEING RUM. • OBITUARY: D: 13 MAY 1981.

Joanie Sommers Female Vocalist, B: 24 Feb 1941 Buffalo

1	Johnny Get Angry		0	1962	7	1962	(Warner Bros. 5275)

Joanna Law Female Vocalist from the UK

1	First Time Ever	(Citybeat CBE 752)	67	1990	0	1990	
2	The Gift	(Deconstruction 74321401912)	15	1996	0	1996	

Joanne Farrell Female Vocalist from the USA

1	All I Wanna Do	(Atlantic A 8194CD)	40	1995	0	1995	

Jocelyn Brown Female Vocalist from the USA

1	Somebody Else's Guy	(Fourth & Broadway BRW5)	13	1984	0	1984	
2	I Wish You Would	(Fourth & Broadway BRW14)	51	1984	0	1984	
3	Love's Gonna Get You	(Warner Bros. W 8889)	70	1986	0	1986	
4	Always There	(Talkin Loud TLK 10)	6	1991	0	1991	
5	She Got Soul	(A&M AM 819)	57	1991	0	1991	
6	Don't Talk Just Kiss	(TUG SNOG 2)	3	1991	0	1991	
7	Take Me Up	(A&M AMCD 210)	61	1993	0	1993	
8	No More Tears (Enough Is Enough)	(DING DONG 74321209032)	13	1994	0	1994	
9	Gimme All Your Lovin'	(DING DONG 74321231322)	22	1994	0	1994	
10	Keep On Jumpin'	(MANIFESTO FESCD 11)	8	1996	0	1996	
11	It's Alright, I Feel It!	(TALKIN' LOUD TLCD 22)	26	1997	0	1997	

ISSUE	TITLE	UK LBL	UK POS	UK YEAR	US POS	US YEAR	US LBL
Jocelyn Enriquez Female Vocalist from the USA							
1	Do You Miss Me		0	1996	49	1996	(TOMMY BOY 7186)
2	A Little Bit Of Ecstasy		0	1997	61	1997	(TOMMY BOY 0190)
Jocko Male Vocalist from the USA							
1	Rhythm Talk	(PHILADELPHIA INT. PIR 8222)	56	1980	0	1980	
Jodeci Male Vocal Group From Tiny Grove, North Carolina							
1	Forever My Lady		0	1991	25	1991	(UPTOWN/MCA 54197)
* 2	Come And Talk To Me		0	1992	11	1992	(UPTOWN/MCA 54175)
* 3	Lately		0	1993	4	1993	(UPTOWN/MCA 54652)
4	.Cherish	(MCA MCSTD 1726)	56	1993	0	1993	
* 5	Cry For You	(MCA MCSTD 1951)	56	1993	15	1993	(UPTOWN/MCA 54723)
6	Feenin'	(MCA MCSTD 1984)	18	1994	25	1994	(UPTOWN/MCA 54798)
7	Cry For You (Re-Issue)	(MCA MCSTD 2039)	20	1995	0	1995	
* 8	Freek N' You	(MCA MCSTD 2072)	17	1995	14	1995	(UPTOWN/MCA 55023)
9	Love U 4 Life	(MCA MCSTD 2105)	23	1995	31	1995	(UPTOWN/MCA 55133)
10	Get On Up	(MCA MCSTD 48010)	20	1996	22	1996	(MCA 55123)
Jodie Female Vocalist From Australia							
1	Anything You Want	(Mercury MERCD 423)	47	1995	0	1995	
Jodie Sands Female Vocalist From Philadelphia							
1	With All My Heart		0	1957	15	1957	CHANCELLOR 1003)
2	Someday	(HMV POP 533)	14	1958	0	1958	
Jody Miller Female Vocalist, B: Myrna Joy Miller 29 Nov 1941 In Phoenix							
1	Queen Of The House		0	1965	12	1965	(Capitol 5402)
2	Home Of The Brave	(Capitol CL 15415)	0	1965	25	1965	(Capitol 5483)
6	He's So Fine		0	1971	53	1971	(Epic 10734)
Jody Reynolds Male Vocalist, B: 3 Dec 1938 Denver							
1	Endless Sleep	(Lightning LIG 9015)	66	1979	5	1958	DEMON 1507)
Jody Watley Female Vocalist, B: 30 Jan 1959 Chicago, Was With Shalamar 1977-84							
1	Looking For A New Love	(MCA MCA 1107)	13	1987	2	1987	(MCA 52956)
2	Don't You Want Me	(MCA MCA 1198)	55	1987	6	1987	(MCA 53162)
3	Some Kind Of Lover		0	1988	10	1988	(MCA 53235)
* 4	Real Love	(MCA MCA 1324)	31	1989	2	1989	(MCA 53484)
5	Friends	(MCA MCA 1352)	21	1989	9	1989	(MCA 53660)
6	Everything	(MCA MCA 1395)	74	1990	4	1989	(MCA 53714)
7	I'm The One You Need	(MCA MCS 1608)	50	1992	19	1992	(MCA 54276)
8	When A Man Loves A Woman	(MCA MCSTD 1964)	33	1994	0	1994	
	HIT 5 IS CREDITED TO JODY WATLEY WITH ERIC B. AND RAKIM						
Joe Male Vocalist from the USA							
1	I'm In Luv	(Mercury JOECD 1)	22	1994	0	1994	
2	The One For Me	(Mercury JOECD 2)	34	1994	0	1994	
3	All Or Nothing	(Mercury JOECD 3)	56	1994	0	1994	
4	All The Things (Your Man Won't Do)	(Island CID 634)	34	1996	11	1996	
5	Don't Wanna Be A Player (From Booty Call)	(Jive JiveCD 410)	16	1997	21	1997	(Jive 42450)
Joe 'Fingers' Carr Male Instrumentalist (Piano) from the USA							
1	Sam's Song		0	1950	7	1950	(Capitol 962)
2	Down Yonder		0	1951	14	1951	(Capitol 1777)
3	Until Sunrise		0	1954	24	1954	(Capitol 2730)
4	Portuguese Washerwoman	(Capitol CL 14587)	20	1956	19	1956	(Capitol 3418)
Joe 'Mr. Piano' Henderson Male Pianist from the UK							
1	Sing It With Joe	(Polygon P	14	1955	0	1955	
2	Sing It Again With Joe	(Polygon P	18	1955	0	1955	
3	Trudie	(PYE NIXA N 15147)	14	1958	0	1958	
4	Trudie (Re-entry)	(PYE NIXA N 15147)	23	1958	0	1958	
5	Treble Chance	(PYE 7N 15224)	28	1959	0	1959	
6	Ooh La La	(PYE 7N 15257)	46	1960	0	1960	
Joe Barry Male Vocalist, Real Name Joe Barious B: Cut Off, Louisiana							
* 1	I'm A Fool To Care	(Mercury AMT 1149)	49	1961	24	1961	(Smash 1702)
Joe Bennett & The Sparkletones Names Joe Bennett, Howard Childress, Wayne Arthur And Irving Denton							
1	Black Slacks		0	1957	17	1957	(ABC-Paramount 9837)
Joe Brown Male Vocalist from the UK							
1	The Darktown Strutter's Ball	(Decca F 11207)	34	1960	0	1960	

ISSUE	TITLE	UK LBL	UK POS	UK YEAR	US POS	US YEAR	US LBL
2	Shine	(PYN 7N 15322)	33	1961	0	1961	
3	What A Crazy World We're Living In	(Piccadilly 7N 35024)	37	1962	0	1962	
4	A Picture Of You	(Piccadilly 7N 35047)	2	1962	0	1962	
5	Your Tender Look	(Piccadilly 7N 35058)	31	1962	0	1962	
6	It Only Took A Minute	(Piccadilly 7N 35082)	6	1962	0	1962	
7	That's What Love Will Do	(Piccadilly 7N 35106)	3	1963	0	1963	
8	It Only Took A Minute (Re-entry)	(Piccadilly 7N 35082)	50	1963	0	1963	
9	Nature's Time For Love	(Piccadilly 7N 35129)	26	1963	0	1963	
10	Sally Ann	(Piccadilly 7N 35138)	28	1963	0	1963	
11	With A Little Help From My Friends	(PYE 7N 17339)	32	1967	0	1967	
12	Hey Mama	(AMMO AMO 101)	33	1973	0	1973	

HE PLAYED GUITAR FOR CLAY NICHOLLS & THE BLUE FLAMES IN A HOLIDAY CAMP • HITS 2, 11, 12 ARE CREDITED TO JOE BROWN & HIS BRUVVERS

Joe Cocker Male Vocalist, Real Name John Robert Cocker B: 20 May 1944 In Sheffield, England

1	Marjorine	(Regal-Zonophone RZ 3006)	48	1968	0	1968	
2	With A Little Help From My Friends	(Regal-Zonophone RZ 013)	1	1968	0	1968	
3	Feeling Alright		0	1969	69	1969	(A&M 1063)
4	Delta Lady	(Regal-Zonophone RZ 3024)	10	1969	0	1969	
5	She Came In Through The Bathroom Window		0	1970	30	1970	(A&M 1147)
6	The Letter	(Regal-Zonophone RZ 3027)	39	1970	7	1970	(A&M 1174)
* 7	Cry Me A River		0	1970	11	1970	(A&M 1200)
8	High Time We Went		0	1971	22	1971	(A&M 1258)
9	Feeling Alright (Re-Issue)		0	1972	33	1972	(A&M 1063)
10	Midnight Rider		0	1972	27	1972	(A&M 1370)
11	You Are So Beautiful		0	1975	5	1975	(A&M 1641)
12	I'm So Glad I'm Standing Here Today	(MCA 741)	61	1981	0	1981	
* 13	Up Where We Belong	(Island WIP 6830)	7	1983	1	1982	(Island 99996)
14	Unchain My Heart	(Capitol CL 465)	46	1987	0	1987	
15	When The Night Comes	(Capitol CL 535)	65	1990	11	1990	(Capitol 44437)
16	(All I Know) Feels Like Forever	(Capitol CL 645)	25	1992	0	1992	
17	Now That The Magic Has Gone	(Capitol CL 657)	28	1992	0	1992	
18	Unchain My Heart (Re-Issue)	(Capitol CL 664)	17	1992	0	1992	
19	When The Night Comes (Re-Issue)	(Capitol CL 674)	61	1992	0	1992	
20	The Simple Things	(Capitol CDCLS 722)	17	1994	0	1994	
21	Take Me Home	(Capitol CDCLS729)	45	1994	0	1994	
22	Let The Healing Begin	(Capitol CDCLS 727)	32	1994	0	1994	
23	Have A Little Faith In Me	(Capitol CDCLS 744)	67	1995	0	1995	
24	Don't Let Me Be Misunderstood	(Parlophone CDCLS 779)	53	1996	0	1996	

BEFORE HIS CAREER TOOK OFF JOE WAS A PLUMBER IN HIS HOME TOWN • IN THE LATE 1950S PLAYED WITH THE SKIFFLE BAND THE CAVALIERS

Joe Dolan Male Vocalist from Ireland)

1	Make Me An Island	(PYE 7N 17738)	3	1969	0	1969	
2	Teresa	(PYE 7N 17833)	20	1969	0	1969	
3	Make Me An Island (Re-entry)	(PYE 7N 17738)	48	1969	0	1969	
4	You're Such A Good Looking Woman	(PYE 7N 17891)	17	1970	0	1970	
5	I Need You	(PYE 7N 45702)	43	1977	0	1977	

Joe Dolce Male Vocalist from the USA

1	Shaddap Your Face	(Epic EPC 9518)	1	1981	0	1981	

Joe Dowell Male Vocalist, B: 1943 In Bloomington, Indiana

* 1	Wooden Heart		0	1961	1	1961	(SMASH 1708)
2	Little Red Rented Rowboat		0	1962	23	1962	(SMASH 1759)

Joe Fagin Male Vocalist from the UK

1	That's Livin' Alright	(TowerBell TOW 46)	3	1984	0	1984	
2	Back With The Boys Again	(TowerBell TOW 84)	53	1986	0	1986	

Joe Farrell Male Saxophonist from the USA

1	Night Dancing	(Warner Bros. LV 2)	57	1978	0	1978	

Joe Foley Male Vocalist from the USA

1	All Or Nothing At All		0	1954	28	1954	(JUBILEE 5146)

Joe Harnell Male Conductor/Arranger, B: 2 Aug 1924 Bronx

1	Fly Me To The Moon / Bossa Nova		0	1963	14	1963	(KAPP 497)

Joe Hayman Male Comedian/Vocalist from the USA

* 1	Cohen On The Telephone		0	1914	1	1914	(Columbia 1516)
2	Cohen Telephones From Brighton		0	1916	5	1916	(Columbia 1885)
3	Cohen Telephones About His Auto		0	1923	15	1923	(Columbia 3772)

ISSUE	TITLE	UK LBL	UK POS	UK YEAR	US POS	US YEAR	US LBL
Joe Henderson (2) Male R&B Singer, B: 1938 Como, Mississippi							
1	Snap Your Fingers		0	1962	8	1962	(TODD 1072)
	OBITUARY : D: 7 NOV 1964.							
Joe Hinton Male Vocalist, B: 1929 from the USA							
* 1	Funny (How Time Slips Away)		0	1964	13	1964	(BACK BEAT 541)
	OBITUARY : D: 13 AUG 1968 IN BOSTON.							
Joe Jackson Male Singer/Songwriter/Pianist, B: 11 Aug 1955 Burton-on-Trent, Nottinghamshire, England							
1	Is She Really Going Out With Him?	(A&M AMS 7459)	13	1979	21	1979	(A&M 2132)
2	It's Different For Girls	(A&M AMS 7493)	5	1980	0	1980	
3	Jumpin' Jive	(A&M AMS 8145)	43	1981	0	1981	
4	Steppin' Out	(A&M AMS 8262)	6	1983	6	1982	(A&M 2428)
5	Breaking Us In Two	(A&M AM 101)	59	1983	18	1983	(A&M 2510)
6	Happy Ending	(A&M AM 186)	58	1984	0	1984	
7	You Can't Get What You Want (Till You Know What You Want)		0	1984	15	1984	(A&M 2628)
8	Be My Number Two	(A&M AM 200)	70	1984	0	1984	
9	Left Of Centre	(A&M AM 320)	32	1986	0	1986	
	HIT 3 IS CREDITED TO JOE JACKSON'S JUMPIN' JIVE • HIT 9 IS CREDITED TO SUZANNE VEGA FEATURING JOE JACKSON • SEE ALSO SUZANNE VEGA							
Joe Jeffrey Group Male R&B Vocal/Guitarist from the USA							
1	My Pledge Of Love		0	1969	14	1969	(WAND 11200)
Joe Jones Male Producer/Pianist, B: 12 Aug 1926 New Orleans							
1	California Sun		0	1961	89	1961	(ROULETTE 4344)
2	You Talk Too Much		0	1960	3	1960	(RIC 972)
Joe Liggins Male R&B Vocalist, B: 9 Jul 1916 Guthrie, Oklahoma							
* 1	Honeydripper		0	1945	13	1945	(Exclusive 207)
2	Got A Right To Cry		0	1946	12	1946	(Exclusive210)
* 3	Pink Champagne		0	1950	30	1950	(Specialty 355)
Joe Longthorne Male Vocalist from the UK							
1	Young Girl	(EMI CDEM 310)	61	1994	0	1994	
2	Passing Strangers	(EMI CDEM 362)	32	1994	0	1994	
	HIT 2 IS CREDITED TO JOE LONGTHORNE AND LIZ DAWN							
Joe Loss & His Orchestra Male Orchestra Leader from the UK							
1	A Tree In The Meadow		0	1948	17	1948	(RCA Victor 2965)
2	Wheels Cha Cha	(HMV POP 880)	21	1961	0	1961	
3	Sucu-Sucu	(HMV POP 937)	48	1961	0	1961	
4	The Maigret Theme	(HMV POP 995)	20	1962	0	1962	
5	Must Be Madison	(HMV POP 1075)	20	1962	0	1962	
6	March Of The Mods	(HMV POP 1351)	35	1964	0	1964	
7	March Of The Mods (Re-entry)	(HMV POP 1351)	31	1964	0	1964	
Joe Publi Male R&B Group From Buffalo, New York							
1	Live And Learn	(Columbia 6575267)	43	1992	4	1992	(Columbia 74012)
2	I've Been Watchin'	(Columbia 6587657)	75	1992	0	1992	
Joe Reichman & His Orchestra Male Bandleader/Pianist from the USA							
1	Afraid To Say Hello (Since You Said Goodbye)		0	1941	24	1941	(Victor 27357)
	OBITUARY : D: 14 APR 1970 (AGED 72).							
Joe Roberts Male Vocalist from the UK							
1	Back In My Life	(FFRR FCD 215)	59	1993	0	1993	
2	Lover	(FFRR FCD 220)	22	1994	0	1994	
3	Back In My Life (Re-Issue)	(FFRR FCD 230)	39	1994	0	1994	
4	Adore	(FFRR FCD 240)	45	1994	0	1994	
5	You Are Everything	(Columbia 611755)	28	1995	0	1995	
6	Happy Days	(GRASS GREEN GRASS 10CD)	63	1996	0	1996	
	HIT 5 IS CREDITED TO MELANIE WILLIAMS AND JOE ROBERTS • HIT 6 IS CREDITED TO SWEET MERCY FEATURING JOE ROBERTS							
Joe Satriani Male Vocal/Guitarist from the USA							
1	The Satch (EP)	(Relativity 6589532)	53	1993	0	1993	
Joe Simon Male Vocalist, B: 2 Sep 1943 Simmesport, Louisiana							
5	(You Keep Me) Hangin' On		0	1968	25	1968	(Sound Stage 7 2608)
* 6	The Chokin' Kind		0	1969	13	1969	(Sound Stage7 2628)
+ 7	Baby, Don't Be Looking In My Mind		0	1969	16	1969	Sound Stage 7 2634
8	Your Time To Cry		0	1971	40	1971	(Spring 108)
* 9	Drowning In The Sea Of Love		0	1971	11	1971	(Spring 120)
10	Pool Of Bad Luck		0	1972	42	1972	(Spring 124)
* 11	Power Of Love		0	1972	11	1972	(Spring 128)

ISSUE	TITLE	UK LBL	UK POS	UK YEAR	US POS	US YEAR	US LBL
12	Step By Step	(MOJO 2093 030)	14	1973	37	1973	(Spring 133)
13	Theme From Cleopatra Jones		0	1973	18	1973	(Spring 138)
14	Get Down, Get Down (Get On The Floor)		0	1975	8	1975	(Spring 156)

FIRST 4 WERE R&B HITS • HIT 11 IS CREDITED TO JOE SIMON FEATURING THE MAINSTREETERS • JOE WAS WITH THE GOLDEN TONES IN 1960

Joe Smooth Male Vocalist from the USA

1	Promised Land	(DJ International DJIN 6)	56	1989	0	1989	

Joe South Male Vocalist, Real Name Joe Souter B: 28 Feb 1940 Atlanta

! 1	You're The Reason		0	1961	16	1961	(FAIRLANE 21006)
2	Games People Play	(Capitol CL 15579)	6	1969	12	1969	(Capitol 2248)
! 3	Don't It Make You Want To Go Home		0	1969	27	1969	(Capitol 2592)
4	Walk A Mile In My Shoes		0	1970	12	1970	(Capitol 2704)

HITS 3-4 ARE CREDITED TO JOE SOUTH & THE BELIEVERS • HIT 4 REACHED NUMBER 56 IN THE USA C/W CHARTS

Joe Stampley B: 6 Jun 1943 Springhill, Louisiana

4	Soul Song		0	1973	37	1973	(DOT 17442)

HIT 4 REACHED NUMBER 1 IN THE USA C/W CHARTS • OTHER HITS WERE C/W • JOE IS THE LEADER OF THE GROUP THE UNIQUES

Joe Strummer Male Vocalist from the UK

1	Love Kills	(CBA A 7244)	69	1986	0	1986	
2	Just The One	(CHINA WOKCD 2076)	12	1995	0	1995	
3	England's Irie	(RADIOACTIVE RAXTD 25)	6	1996	0	1996	

HIT 2 IS CREDITED TO LEVELLERS SPECIAL GUEST JOE STRUMMER • HIT 3 IS CREDITED TO BLACK GRAPE FEATURING JOE STRUMMER & KEITH ALLEN

Joe T. Vannelli Project Male Producer from Italy

1	Sweetest Day Of May	(Positiva CDTIV 36)	45	1995	0	1995	

Joe Tex Male Vocalist, Real Name Joseph Arrington Jr B: 8 Aug 1933 Rogers, Texas.

* 1	Hold What You've Got		0	1964	5	1964	(Dial 4001)
2	You Got What It Takes / You Better Get It		0	1965	46	1965	(Dial 4003)
+ 3	A Woman Can Change A Man		0	1965	12	1965	(Dial 4006)
+ 4	One Monkey Don't Stop No Show		0	1965	20	1965	(Dial 4011)
5	I Want To (Do Everything For You)		0	1965	23	1965	(Dial 4016)
6	A Sweet Woman Like You		0	1965	29	1965	(Dial 4022)
+ 7	The Love You Save		0	1965	2	1965	(Dial 4026)
8	S.Y.S.L.J.F.M. (The Letter Song)		0	1966	39	1966	(Dial 4028)
+ 9	I Believe I'm Gonna Make It		0	1966	8	1966	(Dial 4033)
+ 10	I've Got To Do A Little Bit Better		0	1966	20	1966	(Dial 4045)
11	Papa Was Too		0	1966	44	1966	(Dial 4051)
12	Show Me		0	1967	35	1967	(Dial 4055)
* 13	Skinny Legs And All		0	1967	10	1967	(Dial 4063)
14	Men Are Gettin' Scarse		0	1968	33	1968	(Dial 4069)
+ 15	Keep The One You Got		0	1968	13	1968	(Dial 4083)
16	Buying A Book		0	1969	47	1969	(Dial 4090)
* 17	I Gotcha		0	1972	2	1972	(Dial 1010)
* 18	Ain't Gonna Bump No More (With No Big Fat Woman)	(Epic EPC 5035)	2	1977	12	1977	(Epic 50313)

JOE BECAME KNOWN AS JOSEPH X • BECAUSE OF HIS FAITH HE CHANGED HIS NAME TO JOSEPH HAZZIEZ IN 1972 • OBITUARY : D: 13 AUG 1982 HEART ATTACK.

Joe Turner Male R&B Vocalist, B: 18 May 1911 Kansas City

* 1	Chains Of Love		0	1951	30	1951	(Atlantic 939)
* 2	Honey Hush		0	1953	23	1953	(Atlantic 1001)
3	Shake, Rattle, And Roll		0	1954	22	1954	(Atlantic 1026)

OBITUARY : D: 24 NOV 1985 (AGED 74).

Joe Valino Male Vocalist from Philadelphia

1	Garden Of Eden	(HMV POP 293)	23	1957	12	1956	(VIK 0226)

Joe Walsh Male Vocalist, B: 20 Nov 1947 Wichita, Kansas Former Member Of The James Gang And The Eagles 1975-82

1	Rocky Mountain Way (EP)	(ABC ABE 12002)	39	1977	23	1973	(Dunhill 4361)
2	Life's Been Good	(Asylum K 13129)	14	1978	12	1978	(Asylum 45493)
3	All Night Long		0	1980	19	1980	(Full Moon 46639)
4	A Life Of Illusion		0	1981	34	1981	(Asylum 47144)

Joe Ward Joe Hails From Cincinnati And Was Eight Years Old At The Time Of The Hit

1	Nuttin' For Xmas		0	1955	20	1955	(King 4854)

Joey B. Ellis Male Vocalist from the USA

1	Go For It (Heart And Fire)	(Capitol CL 601)	20	1991	0	1991	
2	Thought You Were The One For Me	(Capitol CL 614)	58	1991	0	1991	

Joey Dee & The Starliters Male Vocal/Instrumental Group from the USA

* 1	Peppermint Twist (Part 1)	(Columbia DB 4758)	33	1962	1	1961	(Roulette 4401)

ISSUE	TITLE	UK LBL	UK POS	UK YEAR	US POS	US YEAR	US LBL
2	Hey, Let's Twist		0	1962	20	1962	(Roulette 4408)
* 3	Shout (Part 1)		0	1962	6	1962	(Roulette 4416)
4	What Kind Of Love Is This		0	1962	18	1962	(Roulette 4438)
5	Hot Pastrami With Mashed Potato's (Part 1)		0	1963	36	1963	(Roulette 4488)

REAL NAME JOSEPH DINICOLA B: 11 JUN 1941 PASSAIC, NEW JERSEY • OTHER MEMBERS ARE CARLTON LATIMOR, WILLIE DAVIS, LARRY VERNIERI & DAVID BRIGATI

Joey Heatherton Female Actress/Vocalist, B: 14 Sep 1944 Rockville Centre, New York

1	Gone		0	1972	24	1972	(MGM 14387)

Joey Lawrence Male Actor/Vocalist, B: 20 Apr 1976 from Philadelphia

1	Nothin' My Love Can't Fix	(EMI CDEM 271)	13	1993	19	1993	(IMPACT 54562)
2	I Can't Help Myself	(EMI CDEM 277)	27	1993	0	1993	
3	Stay Forever	(EMI CDEM 289)	41	1993	0	1993	

Joey Negro Male Producer from the UK, Real Name Dave Lee

1	Reachin'	(REPUBLIC LIC 006)	70	1989	0	1989	
2	Do What You Feel	(TEN TEN 391)	36	1991	0	1991	
3	Reachin' (Re-Mix)	(REPUBLIC LIC160)	70	1991	0	1991	
4	Enter Your Fantasy (EP)	(TEN TEN 397)	35	1992	0	1992	
5	What Happened To The Music	(Virgin VSCD 1466)	51	1993	0	1993	

HIT 1 IS CREDITED TO PHASE II • HIT 3 IS CREDITED TO JOEY NEGRO PRESENTS PHASE II

Joey Powers Male Vocalist, B: 1939 Canonsburg, Pennsylvania

1	Midnight Mary		0	1963	10	1963	(AMY 892)

Joey Scarbury Male Vocalist, B: 7 Jun 1955 Ontario, California

* 1	Believe It Or Not (Theme From Greatest American Hero')		0	1981	2	1981	(Elektra 47147)

Johann Male Producer Johann Bley from Germany

1	New Kicks (Mixes)	(PERFECTO PERF 118CD)	54	1996	0	1996	

John & Ernest Full Names: John Free & Ernest Smith

1	Super Fly Meets Shaft		0	1973	31	1973	(RAINY WED. 201)

John Alford Male Vocalist from the UK

1	Smoke Gets In Your Eyes	(LoveThis Luvthis CD7)	13	1996	0	1996	
2	Blue Moon / Only You	(Love This Luvthis CDX9)	9	1996	0	1996	
3	If / Keep On Running	(Love This Luvthis CD15)	24	1996	0	1996	

John Anderson Big Band Big Band from the UK

1	Glenn Miller Medley	(Modern GLEN 1)	63	1985	0	1985	
2	Glenn Miller Medley (Re-entry)	(Modern GLEN 1)	61	1986	0	1986	

John Asher Male Vocalist from the UK

1	Let's Twist Again	(CreoleCR 112)	14	1975	0	1975	

John Barry Male Instrumentalist/Bandleader from the USA

1	Hit And Miss	(Columbia DB 4414)	10	1960	0	1960	
2	Beat For Beatniks	(Columbia DB 4446)	40	1960	0	1960	
3	Hit And Miss (Re-entry)	(Columbia DB 4414)	45	1960	0	1960	
4	Never Let Go	(Columbia DB4480)	49	1960	0	1960	
5	Blueberry Hill	(Columbia DB 4480)	34	1960	0	1960	
6	Walk Don't Run	(Columbia DB 4505)	49	1960	0	1960	
7	Walk Don't Run (Re-entry)	(Columbia DB 4505)	11	1960	0	1960	
8	Black Stockings	(Columbia DB 4554)	27	1960	0	1960	
9	The Magnificent Seven	(Columbia DB 4598)	48	1961	0	1961	
10	The Magnificent Seven (Re-entry)	(Columbia DB 4598)	45	1961	0	1961	
11	The Magnificent Seven (2nd Re-entry)	(Columbia DB 4598)	50	1961	0	1961	
12	The Magnificent Seven (3rd Re-entry)	(Columbia DB 4598)	47	1961	0	1961	
13	Cutty Sark	(Columbia DB 4806)	35	1962	0	1962	
14	James Bond Theme	(Columbia DB 4898)	13	1962	0	1962	
15	From Russia With Love	(EMBER S 181)	39	1963	0	1963	
16	From Russia With Love (Re-entry)	(EMBER S 181)	39	1963	0	1963	
17	The Persuaders (Theme)	(CBS 7469)	13	1971	0	1971	

HITS 1, 2, 3, AND 6-13 INCLUSIVE ARE CREDITED TO JOHN BARRY SEVEN • ALL OTHER HITS ARE CREDITED TO JOHN BARRY ORCHESTRA

John Cafferty & The Beaver Brown Band Rock Sextet From Rhode Island Led By John Cafferty

1	On The Dark Side		0	1983	64	1983	(SCOTTI BR 04594)
2	On The Dark Side (Re-entry)		0	1984	7	1984	(SCOTTI BR 04594)
3	Tender Years		0	1984	78	1984	(SCOTTI BR 04682)
4	Tender Years (Re-entry)		0	1984	31	1984	(SCOTTI BR 04682)
5	Tough All Over		0	1985	22	1985	(SCOTTI BR 04891)
6	C-I-T-Y		0	1985	18	1985	(SCOTTI BR 05452)

OTHER MEMBERS BOB COTOIA, KENNY JO SILVA, GARY GRAMOLINI, PAT LUPO & MICHAEL ANTUNES

ISSUE	TITLE	UK LBL	UK POS	UK YEAR	US POS	US YEAR	US LBL
John Christie Male Vocalist from Australia							
1	Here's To Love (Auld Lang Syne)	(EMI 2554)	24	1976	0	1976	
John Cooper Clarke Male Vocalist from the UK							
1	Gimmix! Play Loud	(Epic EPC 7009)	39	1979	0	1979	
John Cougar Mellencamp Male Vocalist, B: 7 Oct 1951 Seymour, Indiana							
1	I Need A Lover		0	1979	28	1979	(RIVA 202)
2	This Time		0	1980	27	1980	(RIVA 205)
3	Ain't Even Done With The Night		0	1981	17	1981	(RIVA 207)
* 4	Hurt So Good		0	1982	2	1982	(RIVA 209)
* 5	Jack And Diane	(RIVA RIVA 37)	25	1982	1	1982	(RIVA 210)
6	Hand To Hold On To		0	1982	19	1982	(RIVA 211)
7	Crumblin' Down		0	1983	9	1983	(RIVA 214)
8	Pink Houses		0	1983	8	1983	(RIVA 215)
9	Authority Song		0	1984	15	1984	(RIVA 216)
10	Lonely Ol' Night		0	1985	6	1985	(RIVA 880984)
11	Small Town	(RIVA JCM 5)	53	1986	6	1985	(RIVA 884202)
12	R.O.C.K. In The USA	(RIVA JCM 6)	67	1986	2	1986	(RIVA 884455)
13	Rain On The Scarecrow		0	1986	21	1986	(RIVA 884635)
14	Rumbleseat		0	1986	28	1986	(RIVA 884856)
15	Paper In Fire		0	1987	9	1987	(Mercury 888763)
16	Cherry Bomb		0	1987	8	1987	(Mercury 888934)
17	Check It Out		0	1988	14	1988	(Mercury 870126)
18	Pop Singer		0	1989	15	1989	(Mercury 874012)
19	Get A Leg Up		0	1991	14	1991	(Mercury 867890)
20	Again Tonight		0	1992	36	1992	(Mercury 866414)
21	Wild Night	(Mercury MERCD 409)	34	1994	0	1994	
22	Key West Intermezzo (I Saw You First)		0	1996	14	1996	(Mercury 578398)
23	Just Another Day		0	1997	46	1997	(Mercury 578816)

HITS 1-5 ARE CREDITED TO JOHN COUGAR • HIT 21 IS CREDITED TO JOHN COUGAR MELLENCAMP FEATURING ME'SHELL NDEGEOCELLO

HITS 19-20, 23 ARE CREDITED TO JOHN MELLENCAMP

ISSUE	TITLE	UK LBL	UK POS	UK YEAR	US POS	US YEAR	US LBL
John D. Loudermilk Male Vocalist/Songwriter, B: 31 Mar 1934 Durham, North Carolina							
1	Sittin' In The Balcony		0	1957	38	1957	(COLONIAL 430)
2	Language Of Love	(RCA 1269)	13	1962	32	1962	(RCA 7938)

HIT 1 IS CREDITED TO JOHNNY DEE • HIT 4 REACHED NUMBER 132 IN THE USA NATIONAL CHARTS • RECORDED UNDER NAMES OF JOHNNY DEE AND EBE SNEEZER IN THE 50S

ISSUE	TITLE	UK LBL	UK POS	UK YEAR	US POS	US YEAR	US LBL
John Davis & The Monster Orchestra Male Vocal/Instrumental Group from the USA							
1	Ain't That Enough For You	(MIRACLE M 2)	70	1979	0	1979	
John Denver Male Vocalist, Real Name John Henry Deutschendorf B: 31 De 1943 New Mexico							
* 1	Take Me Home, Country Roads		0	1971	2	1971	(RCA 0445)
2	Please, Daddy		0	1973	69	1973	(RCA 0445)
* 3	Rocky Mountain High		0	1972	9	1972	(RCA 0829)
* 4	Sunshine On My Shoulders		0	1974	1	1974	(RCA 0213)
* 5	Annie's Song	(RCA APBO 0295)	1	1974	1	1974	(RCA 0295)
* 6	Back Home Again		0	1974	5	1974	(RCA 10065)
7	Sweet Surrender		0	1975	13	1975	(RCA 10148)
* 8	Thank God I'm A Country Boy		0	1975	1	1975	(RCA 10239)
* 9	I'm Sorry		0	1975	1	1975	(RCA 10353)
10	Calypso		0	1975	2	1975	(RCA 10353)
11	Fly Away		0	1976	13	1976	(RCA 10517)
12	Looking For Space		0	1976	29	1976	(RCA 10586)
13	It Makes Me Giggle		0	1976	60	1976	(RCA 10687)
14	Like A Sad Song		0	1976	36	1976	(RCA 10774)
15	Baby, You Look Good To Me Tonight		0	1976	65	1976	(RCA 10854)
16	My Sweet Lady		0	1977	32	1977	(RCA 10911)
17	How Can I Leave You Again		0	1977	44	1977	(RCA 11036)
18	It Amazes Me		0	1978	59	1978	(RCA 11214)
! 19	Downhill Stuff		0	1979	64	1979	(RCA 11479)
! 20	What's On Your Mind		0	1979	47	1979	(RCA 11535)
! 21	Sweet Melinda		0	1979	47	1979	(RCA 11535)
22	Autograph		0	1980	52	1980	(RCA 11915)
23	Some Days Are Diamonds Some Days Are Stones		0	1981	36	1981	(RCA 12246)
24	The Cowboy And The Lady		0	1981	66	1981	(RCA 12345)
25	Perhaps Love	(CBS A 1905)	46	1981	0	1981	
26	Shanghai Breezes		0	1982	31	1982	(RCA 13071)

ISSUE	TITLE	UK LBL	UK POS	UK YEAR	US POS	US YEAR	US LBL

HIT 16 WAS ALSO B-SIDE OF HIT 9 • HIT 19 REACHED NUMBER 106 IN THE USA NATIONAL CHARTS • HIT 20 REACHED NUMBER 107 IN THE USA NATIONAL CHARTS
HIT 25 IS CREDITED TO PLACIDO DOMINGO WITH JOHN DENVER • OBITUARY: D: 14 OCT 1997 PLANE CRASH.

John Du Cann Male Vocalist from the UK

| | 1 | Don't Be A Dummy | (VERTIGO 6059 241) | 33 | 1979 | 0 | 1979 | |

John Dummer & Helen April Mixed Vocal Duo from the UK

| | 1 | Blue Skies | (SPEED SPEED 8) | 54 | 1982 | 0 | 1982 | |

John Farnham Male Vocalist from Australia

| | 1 | You're The Voice | (WHEATLEY PB 41093) | 6 | 1987 | 0 | 1987 | |

John Fogerty Male Vocalist/Songwriter B: 28 May 1945 California

| | 1 | Hearts Of Stone | | 0 | 1973 | 37 | 1973 | (FANTASY 700) |

MEMBER OF THE BLUE VELVETS WHO BECAME THE GOLLIWOGS IN 1964, LATER RENAMED AS CREEDENCE CLEARWATER REVIVAL • SEE ALSO BLUE RIDGE RANGERS

John Foxx Male Vocalist from the UK

	1	Underpass	(Virgin VS 318)	31	1980	0	1980	
	2	No-One Driving (Double Single)	(Virgin VS 338)	32	1980	0	1980	
	3	Burning Car	(Virgin VS 360)	35	1980	0	1980	
	4	Miles Away	(Virgin VS 382)	51	1980	0	1980	
	5	Europe (After The Rain)	(Virgin VS 393)	40	1981	0	1981	
	6	Endlessly	(Virgin VS 543)	66	1983	0	1983	
	7	Your Dress	(Virgin VS 615)	61	1983	0	1983	

John Fred & The Playboy Band Male Vocal/Instrumental Group from the USA

| * | 1 | Judy In Disguise | (PYE International 7N 25442) | 3 | 1968 | 1 | 1967 | (PAULA 282) |

Real Name John Fred Gourrier B: 8 May 1941 Louisiana

John Holt Male Vocalist From Jamaica

| | 1 | Help Me Make It Through The Night | (TROJAN TR 7909) | 6 | 1974 | 0 | 1974 | |

John Hunter Male Singer/Instrumentalist (Keyboards) From Chicago

| | 1 | Tragedy | | 0 | 1985 | 39 | 1985 | (PRIVATE I 04643) |

John Inman Male Actor/Vocalist from the UK

| | 1 | Are You Being Served Sir? | (DJM DJS 602) | 39 | 1975 | 0 | 1975 | |

John Kongos Male Vocal/Multi-Instrumentalist From South Africa

| | 1 | He's Gonna Step On You Again | (FLY BUG 8) | 4 | 1971 | 0 | 1971 | |
| | 2 | Tokoloshe Man | (FLY BUG 14) | 4 | 1971 | 0 | 1971 | |

John Laurenz Male Vocalist (Baritone) from the USA.

	1	My Happiness		0	1948	26	1948	(Mercury 5144)
	2	A Tree In The Meadow		0	1948	18	1948	(Mercury 5148)
	3	Hair Of Gold, Eyes Of Blue (From Silver Spurs)		0	1948	22	1948	(Mercury 5172)
	4	The Mountaineer And The Jabberwock		0	1948	29	1948	(Mercury 5202)
	5	Red Roses For A Blue Lady		0	1949	21	1949	(Mercury 5201)
	6	Some Enchanted Evening (From South Pacific)		0	1949	28	1949	(Mercury 5276)

John Lee Hooker Male Vocalist/Guitarist, B: 22 Aug 1917 Clarksdale, Mississippi

*	1	I'm In The Mood		0	1951	30	1951	(Modern 835)
*	2	Dimples	(Stateside SS 297)	23	1964	0	1964	
	3	Boom Boom	(Pointblank POB 3)	16	1992	0	1992	
	4	Boogie At Russian Hill	(Pointblank POB DX 4)	53	1993	0	1993	
	5	Gloria	(EXILE VANCD 11)	31	1993	0	1993	
	6	Chill Out (Things Gonna Change)	(Pointblank POBD 10)	45	1995	0	1995	
	7	Baby Lee	(Silvertone ORECD 81)	65	1996	0	1996	

HIT 5 IS CREDITED TO VAN MORRISON AND JOHN LEE HOOKER

John Lennon Male Singer/Songwriter/Instrumentalist (Guitar), Real Name John Winston Lennon, B: 9 Oct 1940 Liverpool,

*	1	Give Peace A Chance	(Apple 13)	2	1969	14	1969	(Apple 1809)
	2	Cold Turkey	(Apple 1001)	14	1969	30	1969	(Apple 1813)
*	3	Instant Karma (We All Shine On)	(Apple 1003)	5	1970	3	1970	(Apple 1818)
*	4	Power To The People	(Apple R 5892)	7	1971	11	1971	(Apple 1830)
	5	Imagine	(Apple R 6009)	6	1975	3	1971	(Apple 1840)
*	6	Happy Xmas (War Is Over)	(Apple R 5970)	4	1972	0	1972	
	7	Mind Games	(Apple R 5994)	26	1973	18	1973	(Apple 1868)
	8	What Ever Gets You Thru The Night	(Apple R 5998)	36	1974	1	1974	(Apple 1874)
	9	Happy Xmas (War Is Over) (Re-entry)	(Apple R 5970)	48	1975	0	1975	
	10	Number 9 Dream	(Apple R 6003)	23	1975	9	1975	(Apple 1878)
	11	Stand By Me	(Apple R 6005)	30	1975	20	1975	(Apple 1881)
*	12	(Just Like) Starting Over	(Geffen K 79186)	1	1980	1	1980	(Geffen 49604)
	13	Happy Xmas (War Is Over) (2nd Re-entry)	(Apple R 5970)	2	1980	0	1980	
	14	Imagine (Re-entry)	(Apple R 6009)	1	1980	0	1980	

ISSUE	TITLE	UK LBL	UK POS	UK YEAR	US POS	US YEAR	US LBL
* 15	Woman	(Geffen K 79195)	1	1981	2	1981	(Geffen 49644)
16	Give Peace A Chance (Re-entry)	(Apple 13)	33	1981	0	1981	
17	I Saw Her Standing There	(DJM DJS 10965)	40	1981	0	1981	
18	Watching The Wheels	(Geffen K 79207)	30	1981	10	1981	(Geffen 49695)
19	Happy Xmas (War Is Over) (3rd Re-entry)	(Apple R 5970)	28	1981	0	1981	
20	Love	(PARLOPHONR R 6059)	41	1982	0	1982	
21	Happy Xmas (War Is Over) (4th Re-entry)	(Apple R 5970)	56	1982	0	1982	
22	Nobody Told Me	(ONO MUSIC/POLYDOR 817254)	6	1984	5	1984	(Polydor POSP 700)
23	Borrowed Time	(Polydor POSP 701)	32	1984	0	1984	
24	Jealous Guy	(Parlophone R 6117)	65	1985	0	1985	
25	Imagine/Jealous Guy/Happy Xmas (War Is Over) (Re-Issue)	(Parlophone R 6199)	45	1988	0	1988	

OBITUARY : D: 8 DEC 1980 MURDERED (SHOT) IN NEW YORK CITY.

John Leyton Male Vocalist from the UK

	TITLE	UK LBL	UK POS	UK YEAR	US POS	US YEAR	US LBL
1	Johnny Remember Me	(Top Rank JAR 577)	1	1961	0	1961	
2	Wild Wind	(Top Rank JAR 585)	2	1961	0	1961	
3	Son This Is She	(HMV POP 956)	15	1961	0	1961	
4	Lone Rider	(HMV POP 992)	40	1962	0	1962	
5	Lonely City	(HMV POP 1014)	14	1962	0	1962	
6	Down The River Nile	(HMV POP 1054)	42	1962	0	1962	
7	Cupboard Love	(HMV POP 1122)	22	1963	0	1963	
8	I'll Cut Your Tail Off	(HMV POP 1175)	50	1963	0	1963	
9	I'll Cut Your Tail Off (Re-entry)	(HMV POP 1175)	36	1963	0	1963	
10	Make Love To Me	(HMV POP 1264)	49	1964	0	1964	

John Lydon Male Vocalist from the UK

	TITLE	UK LBL	UK POS	UK YEAR	US POS	US YEAR	US LBL
1	Sun	(Virgin VUSCD 122)	42	1997	0	1997	

John McEnroe & Pat Cash With The Full Metal Rackets USA/Australia Male Vocal/Instrumental Duo With Backing Group from the UK

	TITLE	UK LBL	UK POS	UK YEAR	US POS	US YEAR	US LBL
1	Rock 'N' Roll	(Music For Nations KUT 141)	66	1991	0	1991	

John Miles Male Vocal/Multi-Instrumentalist, B: 23 Apr 1949 Jarrow, England

	TITLE	UK LBL	UK POS	UK YEAR	US POS	US YEAR	US LBL
1	High Fly	(Decca F 13595)	17	1975	0	1975	
2	Music	(Decca F 13627)	3	1976	0	1976	
3	Remember Yesterday	(Decca F 13667)	32	1976	0	1976	
4	Slow Down	(Decca F 13709)	10	1977	34	1977	(London 20092)

John O'Banion Male Vocalist From From Kokomo, Indiana

	TITLE	UK LBL	UK POS	UK YEAR	US POS	US YEAR	US LBL
1	Love You Like I Never Loved Before		0	1981	24	1981	(Elektra 47125)

John O'Kane Male Vocalist from the UK

	TITLE	UK LBL	UK POS	UK YEAR	US POS	US YEAR	US LBL
1	Stay With Me	(Circa YR 88)	41	1992	0	1992	

John Otway & Wild Willy Barrett Male Vocal/Instrumental Duo from the UK

	TITLE	UK LBL	UK POS	UK YEAR	US POS	US YEAR	US LBL
1	Really Free	(Polydor 2058 951)	27	1977	0	1977	
2	Dk 50-80	(Polydor 2059 250)	45	1980	0	1980	

HIT 2 IS CREDITED TO OTWAY AND BARRETT

John Parr Male Vocalist, B: Nottingham, England

	TITLE	UK LBL	UK POS	UK YEAR	US POS	US YEAR	US LBL
1	Naughty Naughty	(London LON 80)	58	1986	23	1986	(Atlantic 89612)
2	St. Elmo's Fire (Man In Motion)	(London LON 73)	6	1985	1	1985	(Atlantic 89541)
3	Rock N' Roll Mercenaries	(Arista ARIST 666)	31	1986	0	1986	

HIT 3 IS CREDITED TO MEAT LOAF FEATURING JOHN PARR • SEE ALSO MEAT LOAF

John Paul Joans Male Vocalist from the UK

	TITLE	UK LBL	UK POS	UK YEAR	US POS	US YEAR	US LBL
1	Man From Nazareth	(RAK 107)	41	1970	0	1970	
2	Man From Nazareth (Re-entry)	(RAK 107)	25	1971	0	1971	

John Paul Young Male Singer/Songwriter B: 1953 Glasgow, Scotland

	TITLE	UK LBL	UK POS	UK YEAR	US POS	US YEAR	US LBL
1	Love Is In The Air	(Ariola ARO 117)	5	1978	7	1978	(Scotti Brothers402)
2	Love Is In The Air (Re-Mix)	(Columbia 6587697)	49	1992	0	1992	

John Phillips Male Vocalist, B: 30 Aug 1935 Paris Island, South Carolina

	TITLE	UK LBL	UK POS	UK YEAR	US POS	US YEAR	US LBL
1	Mississippi		0	1970	32	1970	(Dunhill4236)

John Rowles Male Vocalist From New Zealand

	TITLE	UK LBL	UK POS	UK YEAR	US POS	US YEAR	US LBL
1	If I Only Had Time	(MCA MU 1000)	3	1968	0	1968	
2	Hush Not A Word To Mary	(MCA MU 1023)	12	1968	0	1968	

John Schneider Male Actor/Country Singer, B: 8 Apr 1954 Mount Kisco, New York

	TITLE	UK LBL	UK POS	UK YEAR	US POS	US YEAR	US LBL
1	It's Now Or Never		0	1981	14	1981	(Scotti Brothers 02105)
! 2	Them Good Ol' Boys Are Bad		0	1981	13	1981	(Scotti Brothers 02489)
3	Still		0	1981	69	1981	(Scotti Brothers02489)

ISSUE	TITLE	UK LBL	UK POS	UK YEAR	US POS	US YEAR	US LBL
John Sebastian Male Writer/Vocalist, B: 17 Mar 1944 New York City							
* 1	Welcome Back		0	1976	1	1976	(REPRISE 1349)
	HE PLAYED WITH THE EVEN DOZEN JUG BAND AS JOHN BENSON • FORMED THE LOVIN' SPOONFUL IN 1965						
John Steele & Sandra Steele Mixed Vocal Duo from the USA							
* 1	My Happiness		0	1948	2	1948	(DAMON 11133)
John Stewart Male Vocalist, B: 5 Sep 1939 San Diego							
1	Gold	(RSO 35)	43	1979	5	1979	(RSO 931)
2	Midnight Wind		0	1979	28	1979	(RSO 1000)
3	Lost Her In The Sun		0	1980	34	1980	(RSO 1016)
	BACKING VOCALS ON HIT 1 ARE BY STEVIE NICKS & LINDSEY BUCKINGHAM • HE WAS A MEMBER OF THE KINGSTON TRIO						
John Taylor Male Vocalist, B: 20 Jun 1960 Birmingham, England Like Andy Taylor, John Was With Duran Duran And Power Station							
1	I Do What I Do (Theme From *9 1/2 Weeks*)	(Parlophone R 6125)	42	1986	23	1986	(Capitol 5551)
John Travolta Male Actor/Vocalist, B: 18 Feb 1954 Englewood, New Jersey							
1	Let Her In		0	1976	10	1976	(MIDLAND I. 10623)
2	Whenever I'm Away From You		0	1976	38	1976	(MIDLAND I. 10780)
3	All Strung Out On You		0	1977	34	1977	(MIDLAND I. 10907)
* 4	You're The One That I Want	(RSO 006)	1	1978	1	1978	(RSO 891)
* 5	Summer Nights	(RSO 18)	1	1978	5	1978	(RSO 906)
6	Sandy	(Polydor POSP 6)	2	1978	0	1978	
7	Greased Lightnin'	(Polydor POSP 14)	11	1978	0	1978	
8	Grease Megamix	(Polydor PO 114)	3	1990	0	1990	
9	Grease - The Dream Mix	(PWL/Polydor PO 1236)	47	1991	0	1991	
	HITS 4-5, 8 ARE CREDITED TO JOHN TRAVOLTA AND OLIVIA NEWTON-JOHN • HIT 9 IS CREDITED TO FRANKIE VALLI, JOHN TRAVOLTA AND OLIVIA NEWTON-JOHN						
John Valenti Soul Singer from Chicago							
1	Anything You Want		0	1976	37	1976	(EMI AM. 7625)
John Waite Male Vocalist, B: 4 Jul 1955 England He Was Lead Singer With Babys And Bad English							
1	Missing You	(EMI AMERICA EA 182)	9	1984	1	1984	(EMI AMERICA 8212)
2	Tears		0	1984	37	1984	(EMI AMERICA 8238)
3	Every Step Of The Way		0	1985	25	1985	(EMI AMERICA 8282)
4	Missing You (Re-Issue)	(Chrysalis CDCHS 3938)	56	1993	0	1993	
John Walker Male Vocalist from the USA See Also The Walker Brothers							
1	Annabella	(Philips BF 1593)	58	1967	0	1967	
2	Annabella (Re-entry)	(Philips BF 1593)	24	1967	0	1967	
John Williams (1) Male Instrumentalist (Guitar) from the UK							
1	Cavatina	(CUBE BUG 80)	13	1979	0	1979	
John Williams (2) Male Orchestra Leader, B: 8 Feb 1932 New York City							
1	Main Title Theme From *Jaws*		0	1975	32	1975	(MCA 40439)
2	Theme From (*Star Wars*)		0	1977	10	1977	(20TH Century 2345)
3	Theme From (*Close Encounters Of The Third Kind*)		0	1978	13	1978	(Arista 0300)
4	Theme From *E.T.* (The Extra Terrestrial)	(MCA 800)	17	1982	0	1982	
5	Theme From *Jurassic Park*	(MCA MCSTD)	45	1993	0	1993	
John Zacherle (The Cool Ghoul) B: 26 Sep 1918 Philadelphia, WCAU-TV Host For Horror Movies							
1	Dinner With Drac (Part 1)		0	1958	6	1958	(CAMEO 130)
Johnna Female Vocalist from the USA							
1	Do What You Feel	(PWL International PWL 232CD)	43	1996	0	1996	
2	In My Dreams	(PWL International PWL 325CD)	66	1996	0	1996	
Johnnie & Joe R&B Duo, Real Names Joe Rivers & Johnnie Louise Richardson From The Bronx							
1	Over The Mountain; Across The Sea		0	1957	8	1957	(CHESS 1654)
	OBITUARY : RICHARDSON D: 25 OCT 1988 FROM A STROKE.						
Johnnie Lee Wills & His Boys Male Instrumentalist (Fiddle/Banjo), B: 2 Sep 1912 In Jewett, Texas							
1	Rag Mop		0	1950	9	1950	(BULLET 696)
Johnnie Ray Male Vocalist, B: 10 Jan 1927 Dallas,							
* 1	Cry		0	1951	1	1951	(Okeh 6840)
* 2	The Little White Cloud That Cried		0	1951	2	1951	(Okeh 6840
* 3	Please Mr. Sun		0	1952	6	1952	(Columbia 39636)
4	Here I Am-Broken Hearted		0	1952	8	1952	(Columbia 39636)
5	What's The Use		0	1952	13	1952	(Columbia 39698)
6	Walking My Baby Back Home	(Columbia DB3060)	12	1952	4	1952	(Columbia 39750)
7	All Of Me		0	1952	12	1952	(Columbia 39788)
8	A Sinner Am I		0	1952	20	1952	(Columbia 39788)
9	Love Me (Baby Can't You Love Me)		0	1952	25	1952	(Columbia 39837)

ISSUE	TITLE	UK LBL	UK POS	UK YEAR	US POS	US YEAR	US LBL
10	A Full-Time Job	(Columbia DB 3242)	11	1953	20	1952	(Columbia 39898)
11	Faith Can Move Mountains	(Columbia DB 3154)	7	1952	0	1952	
12	Ma Says Pa Says	(Columbia DB 3242)	12	1953	23	1952	(Columbia 39898)
13	I'm Gonna Walk And Talk With My Lord		0	1953	24	1953	(Columbia 39908)
14	Faith Can Move Mountains (Re-entry)	(Columbia DB 3154)	9	1953	0	1953	
15	Somebody Stole My Gal	(Philips PB 123)	6	1953	8	1953	(Columbia 39961)
16	Somebody Stole My Gal (Re-entry)	(Philips PB 123)	6	1953	0	1953	
17	Somebody Stole My Gal (2nd Re-entry)	(Philips PB 123)	12	1953	0	1953	
18	Candy Lips		0	1953	17	1953	(Columbia 40001)
19	Let's Walk That-A-Way	(Philips PB 157)	4	1953	0	1953	
20	Somebody Stole My Gal (3rd Re-entry)	(Philips PB 123)	11	1953	0	1953	
21	With These Hands		0	1953	29	1953	(Columbia 40026)
22	All I Do Is Dream Of You		0	1953	27	1953	(Columbia 40046)
23	Please Don't Talk About Me When I'm Gone		0	1953	29	1953	(Columbia 40090)
24	You'd Be Surprised		0	1954	25	1954	(Columbia 40154)
25	Such A Night	(Philips PB 244)	1	1954	19	1954	(Columbia 40200)
26	Hey There	(Philips PB 495)	5	1955	27	1954	(Columbia 40224)
27	Hernando's Hideaway	(Philips PB 495)	11	1955	14	1954	(Columbia 40224)
28	To Ev'ry Girl-To Ev'ry Boy (The Meaning Of Love)		0	1954	26	1954	(Columbia 40252)
29	If You Believe	(Philips PB 379)	15	1955	0	1955	
30	If You Believe (Re-entry)	(Philips PB 379)	7	1955	0	1955	
31	Paths Of Paradise	(Philips PB 441)	20	1955	0	1955	
32	Song Of The Dreamer	(Philips PB 516)	10	1955	0	1955	
33	Who's Sorry Now	(Philips PB 546)	17	1956	0	1956	
34	Ain't Misbehavin'	(Philips PB 580)	17	1956	0	1956	
35	Ain't Misbehavin' (Re-entry)	(Philips PB 580)	24	1956	0	1956	
* 36	Just Walkin' In The Rain	(Philips PB 624)	1	1956	2	1956	(Columbia 40729)
37	You Don't Owe Me A Thing	(Philips PB 655)	12	1957	10	1957	(Columbia 40803)
38	Look Homeward Angel	(Philips PB 655)	7	1957	36	1957	(Columbia 40803)
39	Yes Tonight Josephine	(Philips PB 686)	1	1957	12	1957	(Columbia 40893)
40	Build Your Love	(Philips PB 721)	17	1957	0	1957	
41	Good Evening Friends / Up Above My Head	(Philips PB 708)	25	1957	0	1957	
42	I'll Never Fall In Love Again	(Philips PB 952)	26	1959	0	1959	
43	I'll Never Fall In Love Again (Re-entry)	(Philips PB 952)	26	1960	0	1960	
44	I'll Never Fall In Love Again (2nd Re-entry)	(Philips PB 952)	28	1960	0	1960	

HE WAS PARTIALLY DEAF AND WAS FAMOUS FOR HIS TEARS ON STAGE. • HITS 1-5, 8, 11, 14, 21 ARE CREDITED TO JOHNNIE RAY WITH THE FOUR LADS

HIT 41 IS CREDITED TO FRANKIE LAINE AND JOHNNIE RAY) • HITS 10,12,18 ARE CREDITED TO DORIS DAY AND JOHNNIE RAY) • OBITUARY : D: 25 FEB 1990 LIVER FAILURE.

Johnnie Spence   Orchestra from the UK

	1	Theme From *Dr Kildare*	(Parlophone R 4872)	15	1962	0	1962	

Johnnie Taylor   Male Vocalist, B: 5 May 1938, Crawfordville, Arkansas

	ISSUE	TITLE	UK LBL	UK POS	UK YEAR	US POS	US YEAR	US LBL
+	1	I Had A Dream		0	1966	19	1966	(STAX 186)
+	2	I've Got To Love Somebody Baby		0	1966	15	1966	(STAX 193)
*	3	Who's Making Love		0	1968	5	1968	(STAX 0009)
	4	Take Care Of Your Homework		0	1969	20	1969	(STAX 0023)
	5	Testify (I Wonna)		0	1969	36	1969	(STAX 0033)
	6	I Could Never Be President		0	1969	48	1969	(STAX 0046)
	7	Love Bones		0	1969	43	1969	(STAX 0055)
	8	Steal Away		0	1970	37	1970	(STAX 0068)
	9	I Am Somebody (Part II)		0	1970	39	1970	(STAX 0078)
	10	Jody's Got Your Girl And Gone		0	1971	28	1971	(STAX 0085)
+	11	Hijackin' Love		0	1971	10	1971	(STAX 0096)
*	12	I Believe In You (You Believe In Me)		0	1973	11	1973	(STAX 0161)
	13	Cheaper To Keep Her		0	8197	15	1973	(STAX 0176)
	14	We're Getting Careless With Our Love		0	1974	34	1974	(STAX 0193)
*	15	Disco Lady	(CBS 4044)	25	1976	1	1976	(Columbia 10281)
	16	Somebody's Gettin' It		0	1976	33	1976	(Columbia 10334)

HE WAS WITH THE GROUP THE FIVE ECHOES IN 1954, AND PRIOR TO GOING SOLO HE WAS WITH THE SOUL STIRRERS

Johnny & Charley   Male Vocal Duo From Spain

	1	La Yenka	(PYE Internationall7N 25326)	49	1965	0	1965	

Johnny & The Hurricanes   Male Instrumental Group from the USA   Originally Formed As The Orbits In 1958

	1	Crossfire		0	1959	23	1959	(WARWICK 502)
	2	Red River Rock	(London HL 8948)	3	1959	5	1959	(Warwick 509)
	3	Reveille Rock	(London HL 9017)	14	1959	25	1959	(Warwick 513)
	4	Beatnik Fly	(London HLI 9072)	8	1960	15	1960	(Warwick 520)

ISSUE	TITLE	UK LBL	UK POS	UK YEAR	US POS	US YEAR	US LBL
5	Down Yonder	(London HLX 9134)	8	1960	0	1960	
6	Rocking Goose	(London HLX 9190)	3	1960	0	1960	
7	Ja-Da	(London HLX 9289)	14	1961	0	1961	
8	Old Smokie / High Voltage	(London HLX 9378)	24	1961	0	1961	

NAMES JOHN POCISK 'PARIS', DAVE YORKO, PAUL TESLUK, LIONEL MATTICE & TONY KAYE • TONY WAS REPLACED BY BO SAVISH IN LATE 1959

Johnny 'Guitar' Watson   Male Vocal/Guitarist from the USA

1	I Need It	(DJM DJS 10694)	35	1976	0	1976	
2	A Real Mother For Ya	(DJM DJT 10762)	44	1977	0	1977	

Johnny Ace   Real Name John Marshall Alexande Jr. B: 9 Jun 1929 Memphis

+ 1	My Song		0	1952	1	1952	
+ 2	The Clock		0	1953	1	1953	
3	Pledging My Love		0	1955	17	1955	(DUKE 136)

OBITUARY : D: PLAYING RUSSIAN ROULETTE IN HOUSTON, TEXAS, ON CHRISTMAS EVE 1954.

Johnny Adams   Real Name Latham John Adams B: 5 Jan 1932 New Orleans

1	Reconsider Me		0	1969	28	1969	(SSS INT'L 770)

HIS NICKNAME WAS THE TAN CANARY

Johnny Bond   Real Name Cyrus Whitfield Bond B: 1 Jun 1915 Enville, Oklahoma

1	Hot Rod Lincoln		0	1960	26	1960	(REPUBLIC 2005)

OBITUARY : D: 12 JUN 1978 HEART ATTACK.

Johnny Brandon   Male Vocalist from the UK

1	Tomorrow	(Polygon P 1131)	8	1955	0	1955	
2	Tomorrow (Re-entry)	(Polygon P 1131)	16	1955	0	1955	
3	Don't Worry	(Polygon P 1163)	18	1955	0	1955	

HIT 1-2 ARE CREDITED TO JOHNNY BRANDON & THE PHANTOMS

Johnny Bristol   Soul Singer From North Carolina, Worked As A Producer For Motown

1	Hang On In There Baby	(MGM 2006 443)	3	1974	8	1974	(MGM 14715)
2	My Guy-My Girl (Medley)	(Atlantic/Hansa K 11550)	39	1980	0	1980	

HIT 2 IS CREDITED TO AMII STEWART AND JOHNNY BRISTOL

Johnny Burnette   Male Vocalist, B: 25 Mar 1934 Memphis

* 1	Dreamin' / Cincinnati Fireball	(London HLG 9172)	5	1960	11	1960	(Liberty 55258)
* 2	You're Sixteen	(London HLG 9254)	3	1961	8	1960	(Liberty 55285)
3	Little Boy Sad	(London HLG 9315)	12	1961	17	1961	(Liberty 55298)
4	Girls	(London HLG 9388)	37	1961	0	1961	
5	God, Country And My Baby		0	1961	18	1961	(Liberty 55379)
6	Clown Shoes	(Liberty LIB 55416)	35	1962	0	1962	

SOME OF HIS EARLY JOBS WERE A DECKHAND AND A BOXER • HE FORMED A TRIO WITH HIS BROTHER DORSEY & PAUL BURLISON IN 1952
OBITUARY: D: 1 AUG 1964 BOATING ACCIDENT AT CLEAR LAKE, CALIFORNIA.

Johnny Cash   Male Country Singer/Guitarist, B:26 Feb 1932 in Knigsland, Arkansas

* 4	I Walk The Line		0	1956	17	1956	(SUN 241)
11	Ballad Of A Teenage Queen		0	1958	14	1958	(SUN 283)
12	Big River		0	1958	14	1958	(SUN 283)
13	Guess Things Happen That Way / Come In Stranger		0	1958	11	1958	(SUN 295)
14	Come In Stranger		0	1958	66	1958	(SUN 295)
15	The Ways Of A Woman In Love		0	1958	24	1958	(SUN 302)
16	You're The Nearest Thing To Heaven		0	1958	24	1958	(SUN 302)
17	All Over Again		0	1958	38	1958	(Columbia 41251)
18	What Do I Care		0	1958	52	1958	(Columbia 41251)
19	Don't Take Your Guns To Town		0	1959	32	1959	(Columbia 41313)
20	It's Just About Time		0	1959	47	1959	(SUN 309)
23	Frankie's Man, Johnny		0	1959	57	1959	(Columbia 41371)
25	Katy Too		0	1959	66	1959	(SUN 321)
26	I Got Stripes		0	1959	43	1959	(Columbia 41427)
27	Five Feet High And Rising		0	1959	76	1959	(Columbia 41427)
29	The Little Drummer Boy		0	1960	63	1960	(Columbia 41481)
30	Straight A's In Love		0	1960	84	1960	(SUN 334)
34	Second Honeymoon		0	1960	79	1960	(Columbia 41707)
36	Oh Lonesome Me		0	1961	93	1961	(SUN 355)
38	Tennessee Flat-Top Box		0	1961	84	1961	(Columbia 42147)
42	Ring Of Fire		0	1963	17	1963	(Columbia 42788)
43	The Matador		0	1963	44	1963	(Columbia 42880)
44	Understand Your Man		0	1964	35	1964	(Columbia 42964)
49	It Ain't Me Babe	(CBS 201760)	28	1965	0	1965	
53	The One On The Right Is On The Left		0	1966	46	1966	(Columbia 43496)

ISSUE	TITLE	UK LBL	UK POS	UK YEAR	US POS	US YEAR	US LBL
54	Everybody Loves A Nut		0	1966	96	1966	(Columbia 43673)
58	Rosanna's Going Wild		0	1967	91	1967	(Columbia 44373)
59	Folsom Prison Blues (Live)		0	1956	32	1956	(Columbia 44513)
60	Daddy Sang Bass		0	1968	42	1968	(Columbia 44689)
* 61	A Boy Named Sue	(CBS 4460)	4	1969	2	1969	(Columbia 44944)
62	Get Rhythm (Re-Issue)		0	1969	60	1969	(SUN 1103)
63	Blistered		0	1969	50	1969	(Columbia 45020)
66	If I Were A Carpenter		0	1970	36	1970	(Columbia 45064)
67	What Is Truth	(CBS 4934)	21	1970	19	1970	(Columbia 45134)
68	Sunday Morning Coming Down		0	1970	46	1970	(Columbia 45211)
70	Flesh And Blood		0	1970	54	1970	(Columbia 45269)
71	Man In Black		0	1971	58	1971	(Columbia 45339)
75	A Thing Called Love (Re-entry)	(CBS 7797)	48	1972	0	1972	
90	One Piece At A Time	(CBS 4287)	32	1976	29	1976	(Columbia 10321)
	UNLISTED HITS ARE C/W						

Johnny Cash & June Carter Husband And Wife Country Vocal/Instrumental Duo from the USA

1	It Ain't Me, Babe		0	1964	58	1964	(Columbia 43145)
! 2	Jackson		0	1967	2	1967	(Columbia 44011)
! 3	Long-Legged Guitar Pickin' Man		0	1976	6	1967	(Columbia 44158)
4	If I Were A Carpenter		0	1970	36	1970	(Columbia 45064)

/Instrumental Group from the UK/South Africa

1	Scatterlings Of Africa	(EMI EMI 5605)	75	1987	0	1987	

Johnny Crawford Male Actor/Vocalist, B: 26 Mar 1946 Los Angeles

1	Cindy's Birthday		0	1962	8	1962	(DEL-FI 4178)
2	Your Nose Is Gonna Grow		0	1962	14	1962	(DEL-FI 4181)
3	Rumors		0	1962	12	1962	(DEL-FI 4188)
4	Proud		0	1963	29	1963	(DEL-FI 413)
	PLAYED MARK MCCAIN IN THE TV SERIES *THE RIFLEMAN* 1958-63						

Johnny Cymbal Male Vocalist, B: 3 Feb 1945 Ochitree, Scotland

1	Mr. Bass Man	(London HLR 9682)	24	1963	16	1963	(KAPP 503)

Johnny Dankworth Male Saxophonist/Orchestra/Group Leader from the UK

1	Experiments With Mice	(Parlophone R 4185)	7	1956	0	1956	
2	African Waltz	(Columbia DB 4590)	9	1961	0	1961	

Johnny Desmond Male Vocalist, Real Name Giovanni Desimons B: 14 Nov 1920 Detroit

1	Don't You Remember Me?		0	1946	21	1946	(Victor 1796)
2	Guilty		0	1947	12	1947	(RCA Victor 2109)
3	Don't Cry Joe (Let Her Go, Let Her Go)		0	1949	22	1949	(MGM 10613)
4	C'est Si Bon (It's So Good)		0	1950	25	1950	(MGM 10613)
5	The Picnic Song		0	1950	20	1950	(MGM 10703)
6	Just Say I Love Her		0	1950	24	1950	(MGM 10758)
7	A Bushel And A Peck (From Guys And Dolls)		0	1950	29	1950	(MGM 10800)
8	Because Of You		0	1951	17	1951	(MGM 10947)
9	I Want To Be Near You		0	1951	30	1951	(MGM 11027)
10	Nina Never Knew		0	1952	19	1952	(Coral 60848)
11	Stay Where You Are		0	1952	26	1952	(Coral 60848)
12	Trying		0	1953	23	1953	(Coral 60823)
13	Woman		0	1953	9	1953	(Coral 61069)
14	Heart Of My Heart		0	1953	10	1953	(Coral 61076)
15	Pine Tree, Pine Over Me		0	1954	26	1954	(Coral 61126)
16	East Side, West Side		0	1954	28	1954	(Coral 61176)
17	The High And The Mighty (From the movie of same name)		0	1954	17	1954	(Coral 61204)
18	My Own True Love (*Tara's Theme*)		0	1954	23	1954	(Coral 61301)
19	Play Me Hearts And Flowers (I Wanna Cry)		0	1955	6	1955	(Coral 61379)
20	The Yellow Rose Of Texas		0	1955	3	1955	(Coral 61476)
21	Sixteen Tons		0	1955	17	1955	(Coral 61529)
	HIT 14 IS CREDITED TO DON CORNELL, JOHNNY DESMOND & ALAN DALE • HIT 15 IS CREDITED TO JOHNNY DESMOND, EILEEN BARTON AND MCGUIRE SISTERS HIT 16 IS CREDITED TO JOHNNY DESMOND, ALAN DALE & BUDDY GRECO • OBITUARY : D: 6 SEP 1985.						

Johnny Duncan & The Blue Grass Boys Male Vocal/Instrumental Group from the USA

1	Last Train To San Fernando	(Columbia DB 3959)	2	1957	0	1957	
2	Blue Blue Heartache	(Columbia DB 3996)	27	1957	0	1957	
3	Footprints In The Snow	(Columbia DB 4029)	27	1957	0	1957	
4	Footprints In The Snow (Re-entry)	(Columbia DB 4029)	28	1958	0	1958	

Johnny Ferguson Male Dj/Vocalist, B: 22 Mar 1937 Nashville

1	Angela Jones		0	1960	27	1960	(MGM 12855)

ISSUE	TITLE	UK LBL	UK POS	UK YEAR	US POS	US YEAR	US LBL
Johnny Gill Male Vocalist from Washington D.C. Ex Member Of New Edition							
1	Rub You The Right Way		0	1990	3	1990	(Motown 1982)
2	My, My, My		0	1990	10	1990	(Motown 919)
3	Fairweather Friend		0	1990	28	1990	(Motown 2049)
4	Wrap My Body Tight	(Motown ZB 44271)	57	1991	0	1991	
5	Silent Prayer		0	1992	31	1992	(Motown 2165)
* 6	Slow And Sexy	(Epic 6587727)	17	1992	33	1993	(Epic 74741)
7	The Floor	(Motown TMGCD 1416)	53	1993	0	1993	
8	A Cute, Sweet Love Addiction	(Motown TMGCD 1420)	46	1994	0	1994	
9	Let's Get The Mood Right		0	1996	53	1996	(Motown 860510)
10	It's Your Body		0	1996	43	1996	(Motown 860462)
	HIT 5 IS CREDITED TO SHANICE FEATURING JOHNNY GILL • HIT 6 IS CREDITED TO SHABBA RANKS FEATURING JOHNNY GILL							
	HIT 9 IS CREDITED TO JOHNNY GILL FEATURING ROGER TROUTMAN							
Johnny Hallyday Real Name Jean Philippe Smet. B: 1943 Paris, France							
* 1	Let's Twist Again		0	1961	0	1961	
	JOHNNY HAD A FRENCH MOTHER AND A BELGIAN FATHER							
Johnny Hates Jazz Male Vocal/Instrumental Group from the UK							
1	Shattered Dreams	(Virgin VS 948)	5	1987	2	1988	(Virgin 99383)
2	I Don't Want To Be A Hero	(Virgin VS 1000)	11	1987	31	1987	(Virgin 99304)
3	Turn Back The Clock	(Virgin VS 1017)	12	1987	0	1987	
4	Heart Of Gold	(Virgin VS 1045)	23	1988	0	1988	
5	Don't Say It's Love	(Virgin VS 1081)	48	1988	0	1988	
	NAMES: MIKE NOCITO, CLAVIN HAYES AND CLARK DATCHLER • CLARK WAS REPLACED BY PHIL THORNALLEY IN 1988							
Johnny Hodges Orchestra Male Orchestra Leader/Saxophonist from the USA							
1	A Sailboat In The Moonlight		0	1937	17	1937	(VARIETY 586)
2	Prelude To A Kiss		0	1938	13	1938	(VOCALION 4386)
3	Castle Rock		0	1951	28	1951	(Mercury 8944)
	VOCALS ON HIT 1 ARE BY BUDDY CLARK • VOCALS ON HIT 2 ARE BY MARY MCHUGH • HE WAS WITH DUKE ELLINGTON FOR MANY YEARS							
	OBITUARY : D: 11 MAY 1970, (AGED 63).							
Johnny Horton Male Vocalist, B: 30 Apr 1925 Los Angeles							
! 1	Honky-Tonk Man		0	1956	9	1956	(Columbia 21504)
! 2	I'm A One-Woman Man		0	1956	7	1956	(Columbia 21538)
! 3	I'm Coming Home		0	1957	11	1957	(Columbia 40813)
! 4	The Woman I Need		0	1957	9	1957	(Columbia 40919)
! 5	All Grown Up		0	1958	8	1958	(Columbia 41210)
! 6	When It's Springtime In Alaska (It's Forty Below)		0	1959	1	1959	(Columbia 41308)
* 7	The Battle Of New Orleans	(Philips PB 932)	16	1959	1	1959	(Columbia 41339)
8	Johnny Reb		0	1959	54	1959	(Columbia 41437)
9	Sal's Got A Sugar Lip		0	1959	81	1959	(Columbia 41437)
10	Sink The Bismarck		0	1960	3	1960	(Columbia 41568)
11	North To Alaska	(Philips PB 1062)	23	1961	4	1960	(Columbia 41782)
12	Sleepy-Eyed John		0	1961	54	1961	(Columbia 41963)
! 13	Honky-Tonk Man (Re-Issue)		0	1962	11	1962	(Columbia 42302)
! 14	All Grown Up (Re-Issue)		0	1963	26	1963	(Columbia 42653)
	HIT 7 WAS ORIGINALLY WRITTEN IN CELEBRATION OF THE FINAL BATTLE IN 1812 • HIT 11 REACHED NUMBER 1 IN THE USA C/W CHARTS							
	HIT 13 REACHED NUMBER 96 IN THE USA NATIONAL CHARTS • OBITUARY : D: 5 NOV 1960 CAR ACCIDENT.							
Johnny Johnson & The Bandwagon Male Vocal Group from the USA							
1	Breaking Down The Walls Of Heartache	(DIRECTION 58-3670)	4	1968	0	1968	
2	You	(DIRECTION 583923)	34	1969	0	1969	
3	Let's Hang On	(DIRECTION 584180)	36	1969	0	1969	
4	Sweet Inspiration	(Bell 1111)	10	1970	0	1970	
5	Sweet Inspiration (Re-entry)	(Bell 1111)	46	1970	0	1970	
6	Blame It On The Pony Express	(Bell 1128)	7	1970	0	1970	
	HITS 1-3 ARE CREDITED TO BANDWAGON							
Johnny Keating Orchestra from the UK							
1	Theme From Z Cars	(Piccadilly 7N 35032)	8	1962	0	1962	
Johnny Kemp Male Vocalist, B: Nassau, Bahamas							
* 1	Just Got Paid	(CBS 651470 7)	68	1988	10	1988	(Columbia 07744)
2	Birthday Suit		0	1989	36	1989	(Columbia 68569)
Johnny Kidd & The Pirates Male Vocal/Instrumental Group from the UK							
1	Please Don't Touch	(HMV POP 615)	26	1959	0	1959	
2	Please Don't Touch (Re-entry)	(HMV POP 615)	25	1959	0	1959	
3	You Got What It Takes	(HMV POP 698)	25	1960	0	1960	

ISSUE	TITLE	UK LBL	UK POS	UK YEAR	US POS	US YEAR	US LBL
4	Skakin' All Over	(HMV POP 753)	1	1960	0	1960	
5	Restless	(HMV POP 790)	22	1960	0	1960	
6	Linda Lu	(HMV POP 853)	47	1961	0	1961	
7	Shot Of Rhythm And Blues	(HMV POP 1088)	48	1963	0	1963	
8	I'll Never Get Over You	(HMV POP 1173)	4	1963	0	1963	
9	Hungry For Love	(HMV POP 1228)	20	1963	0	1963	
10	Always And Ever	(HMV POP 1269)	46	1964	0	1964	

HITS 1-2 ARE CREDITED TO JOHNNY KIDD • OBITUARY : D: 1966 CAR ACCIDENT

Johnny L   Male Vocalist from the UK

1	Ooh I Like It	(XL ALS 44CD)	73	1993	0	1993	

Johnny Lee   Real Name John Lee Ham B: 3 Jul 1946 Texas

* 7	Lookin' For Love		0	1980	5	1980	(Full Moon 47004)
12	Bet Your Heart On Me		0	1981	54	1981	(Full Moon 47215)

OTHER HITS ARE C/W

Johnny Logan   Male Vocalist from Ireland

1	What's Another Year	(Epic EPC 8572)	1	1980	0	1980	
2	Hold Me Now	(Epic LOG 1)	2	1987	0	1987	
3	I'm Not In Love	(Epic LOG 2)	51	1987	0	1987	

HE WAS TWICE THE EUROVISION SONG CONTEST WINNER IN 1980 & 1987, ALSO WROTE THE 1992 WINNER FOR LINDA MARTIN

Johnny Long & His Orchestra   Male Orchestra Leader, B: 1916 Newall, North Carolina

11	In A Shanty In Old Shanty Town (From *The Crooner*)		0	1946	13	1946	(Decca 23622)
12	Sweet Sue, Just You		0	1949	19	1949	(SIGNATURE 15243)
13	We'll Build A Bungalow		0	1950	22	1950	(King 15018)

OBITUARY : D: 31 OCT 1972 IN PARKERSBURG, VIRGINIA.

Johnny Maddox & The Rhythmasters   Male Honky-Tonk Pianist/Bandleader, B: 1929 Gallatin, Tennessee

1	The Little Green Shack		0	1952	26	1952	(DOT 15020)
2	In The Mood		0	1953	16	1953	(DOT 15045)
3	Twilight Time		0	1953	21	1953	(DOT 15062)
4	Eight Beat Boogie		0	1953	21	1953	(DOT 15090)
5	Dipsy Doodle		0	1953	15	1953	(DOT 15182)
* 6	Crazy Otto Medley (Part 1-2)		0	1955	2	1955	(DOT 15325)

Johnny Maestro   Real Name Johnny Mastrangelo B: 7 May 1939 New York City

1	Model Girl		0	1961	20	1961	(COED 545)
2	What A Surprise		0	1961	33	1961	(COED 549)

Johnny Mann Singers   Mixed Vocal Group from the USA

1	Up, Up And Away	(Liberty LIB 55972)	6	1967	0	1967	

Johnny Mathis   Male Vocalist, B: 30 Sep 1935 San Francisco

* 1	Wonderful, Wonderful		0	1957	14	1957	(Columbia 40784)
* 2	It's Not For Me To Say		0	1957	5	1957	(Columbia 40851)
* 3	Chances Are		0	1957	1	1957	(Columbia 40993)
4	The Twelfth Of Never		0	1957	9	1957	(Columbia 40993)
5	Wild Is The Wind		0	1957	21	1957	(Columbia 41060)
6	No Love (But Your Love)		0	1958	21	1958	(Columbia 41060)
7	Come Io Me		0	1958	22	1958	(Columbia 41082)
8	All The Time		0	1958	21	1958	(Columbia 41152)
9	Teacher, Teacher	(Fontana H 130)	27	1958	21	1958	(Columbia 41152)
10	A Certain Smile	(Fontana H 142)	4	1958	14	1958	(Columbia 41193)
11	Call Me		0	1958	21	1958	(Columbia 41253)
12	Winter Wonderland	(Fontana H 165)	17	1958	0	1958	
13	Someone	(Fontana H 199)	6	1959	35	1959	(Columbia 41355)
14	Small World (From Gypsy)	(Fontana H 219)	0	1959	20	1959	(Columbia 41410)
15	Misty	(Fontana H 219)	12	1960	12	1959	(Columbia 41483)
16	The Best Of Everythng		30	1959	0	1959	
17	You Are Beautiful	(Fontana H 234)	38	1960	0	1960	
18	Starbright	(Fontana H 254)	47	1960	25	1960	(Columbia 41583)
19	Misty (Re-entry)	(Fontana H 219)	46	1960	0	1960	
20	You Are Beautiful (Re-entry)	(Fontana H 234)	46	1960	0	1960	
21	My Love For You	(Fontana H 267)	9	1960	0	1960	
22	Gina		0	1962	6	1962	(Columbia 42582)
23	What Will My Mary Say	(CBS AAG 135)	49	1963	9	1963	(Columbia 42666)
24	Every Step Of The Way		0	1963	30	1963	(Columbia 42799)
25	I'm Stone In Love With You	(CBS 2653)	10	1975	0	1975	
26	When A Child Is Born (Soleado)	(CBS 4599)	1	1976	0	1976	

ISSUE	TITLE	UK LBL	UK POS	UK YEAR	US POS	US YEAR	US LBL
* 27	Too Much Too Little Too Late	(CBS 6164)	3	1978	1	1978	(Columbia 10693)
28	You're All I Need To Get By	(CBS 6483)	45	1978	0	1978	
29	Gone Gone Gone/Begin The Beguine	(CBS 7730)	15	1979	0	1979	
30	When A Child Is Born	(CBS S 1758)	74	1981	0	1981	
31	Friends In Love		0	1982	38	1982	(Arista 0673)

HITS 27-28 ARE CREDITED TO JOHNNY MATHIS AND DENIECE WILLIAMS • HIT 30 IS CREDITED TO JOHNNY MATHIS AND GLADY'S KNIGHT
HIT 31 IS CREDITED TO DIONNE WARWICK AND JOHNNY MATHIS

Johnny Mercer Male Songwriter/Vocalist B: 18 Nov 1809 In Savannah.

	TITLE	UK LBL	UK POS	UK YEAR	US POS	US YEAR	US LBL
1	Mr. Gallagher And Mr. Shean		0	1938	7	1938	(Decca 1960)
2	Small Fry		0	1938	3	1938	(Decca 1960)
3	Mister Meadowlark		0	1940	18	1940	(Decca 2182)
4	Strip Polka		0	1942	7	1942	(Capitol 103)
5	I Lost My Sugar In Salt Lake City		0	1943	18	1943	(Capitol 122)
6	G.I. Jive		0	1944	11	1944	(Capitol 141)
7	San Fernando Valley		0	1944	21	1944	(Capitol 150)
8	Sam's Got Him		0	1944	24	1944	(Capitol 164)
9	Ac-Cent-Tchu-Ate The Positive		0	1945	1	1945	(Capitol 180)
10	Candy		0	1945	1	1945	(Capitol 183)
11	I'm Gonna See My Baby		0	1945	12	1945	(Capitol 183)
12	On The Acheson, Topeka And The Santa Fe		0	1945	1	1945	(Capitol 195)
13	Surprise Party		0	1945	16	1945	(Capitol 217)
14	Personality		0	1946	1	1946	(Capitol 230)
15	My Sugar Is So Refined		0	1946	11	1946	(Capitol 268)
16	Ugly Chile (You're Some Pretty Doll)		0	1946	22	1946	(Capitol 268)
17	Zi-A-Dee-Doo-Dah		0	1946	8	1946	(Capitol 323)
18	A Gal In Calico		0	1946	5	1946	(Capitol 316)
19	Winter Wonderland		0	1947	4	1947	(Capitol 316)
20	Huggin' And A-Chalkin'		0	1947	8	1947	(Capitol 334)
21	I Do Do Do Like You		0	1947	13	1947	(Capitol 367)
22	Moon Faced, Starry-Eyed		0	1947	21	1947	(Capitol 1376)
23	Sugar Blues		0	1947	4	1947	(Capitol 448)
24	Save The Bones For Henry Jones (Cause Henry Don't Eat Meat)		0	1947	12	1947	(Capitol 15000)
25	Harmony		0	1947	12	1947	(Capitol 15000)
26	The Thousand Island Song		0	1948	28	1948	(Capitol 15028)
27	Hooray For Love		0	1948	25	1948	(Capitol 15028)
28	Baby, It's Cold Outside		0	1949	3	1949	(Capitol 567)
29	The Glow-Worm (Re-Issue)		0	1952	30	1952	(Capitol 2248)

HITS 1-3 ARE CREDITED TO BING CROSBY AND JOHNNY MERCER • HIT 10 IS CREDITED TO JOHNNY MERCER, JO STAFFORD & PIED PIPERS
HIT 28 IS CREDITED TO MARGARET WHITING AND JOHNNY MERCE • HIT 29 WAS ORIGINALLY RELEASED ON CAPITOL 15412 IN 1949
OBITUARY : D: 25 JUN 1976 (AGED 66).

Johnny Nash Male Vocalist, B: 19 Aug 1940 Houston, Texas

	TITLE	UK LBL	UK POS	UK YEAR	US POS	US YEAR	US LBL
1	A Very Special Love		0	1958	23	1958	(ABC-Paramount 9874)
2	The Teen Commandments		0	1958	29	1958	(ABC-Paramount 9974)
3	Hold Me Tight	(Regal Zonophone RZ 3010)	5	1968	5	1968	(JAD 207)
4	You Got Soul	(Major Minor MM 586)	6	1969	0	1969	
5	Cupid	(Major Minor MM 603)	6	1969	39	1970	(JAD 220)
6	Cupid (Re-entry)	(Major Minor MM 603)	50	1969	0	1969	
7	Stir It Up	(CBS 7800)	13	1972	12	1973	(Epic 10949)
* 8	I Can See Clearly Now	(CBS 8133)	5	1972	1	1972	(Epic 10902)
9	There Are More Questions Than Answers	(CBS 8351)	9	1972	0	1972	
10	Tears On My Pillow	(CBS 3220)	1	1975	0	1975	
11	Let's Be Friends	(CBS 3597)	42	1975	0	1975	
12	(What A) Wonderful World	(Epic EPC 4294)	25	1976	0	1976	
13	Rock Me Baby	(2000 A.D. FED 19)	47	1985	0	1985	
14	I Can See Clearly Now (Re-Mix)	(Epic JN 1)	54	1989	0	1972	

Hit 2 Is Credited To Paul Anka, George Hamilton IV, Johnny Nash • In The USA Hit 5 Was Originally The B Side Of Hit 3

Johnny Otis Show Real Name John Veliotes B: 8 Dec 1921 California

	TITLE	UK LBL	UK POS	UK YEAR	US POS	US YEAR	US LBL
1	Ma He's Makin' Eyes At Me	(Capitol CL 14794)	2	1957	0	1957	
2	Bye Bye Baby	(Capitol CL 14817)	20	1958	0	1958	
3	Willie And The Hand Jive		0	1958	9	1958	(Capitol 3966)

Had Number 1 R&B Hits With Double Crossing Blues & Mistrustin' Blues In 1950 With Orchestra And Chorus from the USA

Johnny Panic & The Bible Of Dreams Mixed Vocal/Instrumental Group from the UK

	TITLE	UK LBL	UK POS	UK YEAR	US POS	US YEAR	US LBL
1	Johnny Panic And The Bible Of Dreams	(Fontana PANIC 1)	70	1991	0	1991	

ISSUE	TITLE	UK LBL	UK POS	UK YEAR	US POS	US YEAR	US LBL

Johnny Pearson Orchestra Pianist/Orchestra Leader, B: 18 Jun 1925, Plaistow, London, England

| | 1 | Sleepy Shores | (Penny Farthing PEN 778) | 8 | 1971 | 0 | 1971 | |

IN 1934 HE WON A SCHOLARSHIP TO THE LONDON ACADEMY OF MUSIC

Johnny Preston Male Vocalist, Real Name John Preston Courville B: 18 Aug 1939 Port Arthur, Texas.

*	1	Running Bear	(Mercury AMT 1079)	1	1960	1	1960	(Mercury 71474)
	2	Cradle Of Love	(Mercury AMT 1092)	2	1960	7	1960	(Mercury 71598)
	3	Running Bear (Re-entry)	(Mercury AMT 1079)	41	1960	0	1960	
	4	I'm Starting To Go Steady	(Mercury AMT 1104)	49	1960	0	1960	
	5	Feel So Fine	(Mercury AMT	18	1960	14	1960	(Mercury 71651)1104)
	6	Charming Billy	(Mercury AMT 1114)	34	1960	0	1960	
	7	Charming Billy (Re-entry)	(Mercury AMT 1114)	42	1960	0	1960	

JOHNNY FORMED A COMBO CALLED THE SHADES • INDIAN SOUNDS ON HIT 1 ARE BY THE BIG BOPPER & GEORGE JONES

Johnny Rivers Male Vocalist, Real Name John Ramistella B: 7 Nov 1942, New York

*	1	Memphis		0	1964	2	1964	(Imperial 66032)
	2	Maybelline		0	1964	12	1964	(Imperial 66056)
	3	Mountain Of Love		0	1964	9	1964	(Imperial 66075)
	4	Midnight Special		0	1965	20	1965	(Imperial 66087)
	5	Seventh Son		0	1965	7	1965	(Imperial 66112)
	6	Where Have All The Flowers Gone		0	1965	26	1965	(Imperial 66133)
	7	Under Your Spell Again		0	1966	35	1966	(Imperial 66144)
*	8	Secret Agent Man		0	1966	3	1966	(Imperial 66159)
	9	(I Washed My Hands In) Muddy Water		0	1966	19	1966	(Imperial 66175)
*	10	Poor Side Of Town		0	1966	1	1966	(Imperial 66205)
	11	Baby I Need Your Lovin'		0	1967	3	1967	(Imperial 66227)
	12	The Tracks Of My Tears		0	1967	10	1967	(Imperial 66244)
	13	Summer Rain		0	1968	14	1968	(Imperial 66267)
*	14	Rockin' Pneumonia And The Boogie Woogie Flu		0	1972	6	1972	(United Artists 50960)
	15	Blue Suede Shoes		0	1973	38	1973	(United Artists 198)
!	16	Six Day's On The Road		0	1974	58	1974	(Atlantic 3028)
	17	Help Me Rhonda		0	1975	22	1975	(Epic/SOUL CITY 50121)
*	18	Swayin' To The Music (Slow Dancin')		0	1977	10	1977	(BIG TREE 16094)

Johnny Sea Vocalist, B: 15 Jul 1940 Gulfport, Mississippi

| | 5 | Day For Decision | | 0 | 1966 | 35 | 1966 | (Warner Bros. 5820) |

HIT 5 REACHED NUMBER 14 IN THE US C/W CHARTS

Johnny Thunder Real Name Gil Hamilton B: 15 Aug 1941 Leesburg, Florida

| | 1 | Loop De Loop | | 0 | 1963 | 4 | 1963 | (DIAMOND 129) |

Johnny Tillotson Male Vocalist, B: 20 Apr 1939 Jacksonville, Florida

	1	Dreamy Eyes		0	1958	63	1958	(CADENCE 1409)
*	2	Poetry In Motion	(London HLA 9231)	1	1960	2	1960	(CADENCE 1384)
	3	Jimmy's Girl	(London HLA 9275)	50	1961	25	1961	(CADENCE 1391)
	4	Jimmy's Girl (Re-entry)	(London HLA 9275)	43	1961	0	1961	
	5	Without You		0	1961	7	1961	(CADENCE 1404)
	6	Dreamy Eyes (Re-entry)		0	1962	35	1962	(CADENCE 1409)
	7	It Keeps Right On A Hurtin'	(London HLA 9550)	31	1962	3	1962	(CADENCE 1418)
	8	Send Me The Pillow You Dream On	(London HLA 9598)	21	1962	17	1962	(CADENCE 1424)
	9	I Can't Help It (If I'm Still In Love With You)	(London HLA 9642)	42	1962	24	1962	(CADENCE 1432)
	10	I Can't Help It (If I'm Still In Love With You) (Re-entry)	(London HLA 9642)	47	1963	0	1963	
	11	I Can't Help It (If I'm Still In Love With You) (2nd Re-entry)	(London HLA 9642)	41	1963	0	1963	
	12	Out Of My Mind	(London HLA 9695)	34	1963	24	1963	(CADENCE 1434)
	13	You Can Never Stop Me Loving You		0	1963	18	1963	(CADENCE 1437)
	14	Talk Back Trembling Lips		0	1963	7	1963	(MGM 13181)
	15	Worried Guy		0	1964	37	1964	(MGM 13193)
	16	I Rise, I Fall		0	1964	36	1964	(MGM 13232)
	17	She Understands Me		0	1964	31	1964	(MGM 13284)
	18	Heartaches By The Numbers		0	1965	35	1965	(MGM 13376)
!	19	You're The Reason		0	1967	48	1967	(MGM 13829)
!	21	I Can Spot A Cheater		0	1968	63	1968	(MGM 13888)
!	22	Toy Hearts		0	1977	99	1977	(United Artists 986)
	23	Poetry In Motion (Re-Issue)	(LIGHTNING LIG 9016)	67	1979	0	1979	
!	24	Lay Back (In The Arms Of Someone)		0	1984	91	1984	(REWARD 04346)

HIT 7 REACHED NUMBER 4 IN THE USA C/W CHARTS • HIT 8 REACHED NUMBER 11 IN THE USA C/W CHARTS

ISSUE	TITLE	UK LBL	UK POS	UK YEAR	US POS	US YEAR	US LBL
Johnny Wakelin Male Vocalist from the UK							
1	Black Superman (Muhammad Ali)	(PYE 7N 45420)	7	1975	21	1975	(PYE 71012)
2	In Zaire	(PYE 7N 45595)	4	1976	0	1976	
	HIT 1 IS CREDITED TO JOHNNY WAKELIN & THE KINSHASA BAND						
JJohnston Brothers (1) Male Baritone Quartet from the USA							
1	Crystal Ball		0	1954	28	1954	(London 1423)
2	The Bandit		0	1954	26	1954	(London 1470)
Johnston Brothers (2) Male Vocal Group from the UK							
1	Oh Happy Day	(Decca F 10071)	4	1953	0	1953	
2	Wait For Me Darling	(Decca F 10362)	18	1954	0	1954	
3	Happy Days And Lonely Nights	(Decca F 10389)	14	1955	0	1955	
4	Hernando's Hideaway	(Decca F 10608)	1	1955	0	1955	
5	Join In And Sing Again	(Decca F 10636)	9	1955	0	1955	
6	No Other Love	(Decca F 10731)	22	1956	0	1956	
7	In The Middle Of The House	(Decca F 10781)	27	1956	0	1956	
8	Join In And Sing (No.3)	(Decca F 10814)	30	1956	0	1956	
9	Join In And Sing (No.3) (Re-entry)	(Decca F 10814)	24	1956	0	1956	
10	Give Her My Love	(Decca F 10828)	27	1957	0	1957	
11	Heart	(Decca F 10860)	23	1957	0	1957	
	HIT 2 IS CREDITED TO JOAN REGAN & THE JOHNSTON BROTHERS • HIT 3 IS CREDITED TO SUZI MILLER & THE JOHNSTON BROTHERS						
Jolly Brothers Male Vocal/Instrumental Group From Jamaica							
1	Conscious Man	(United Artists UP 36515)	46	1979	0	1979	
Jolly Roger Male Vocalist from the UK							
1	Acid Man	(10 TEN 236)	23	1988	0	1988	
Jomanda Female R&B Vocal Trio From New Jersey							
1	Make My Body Rock	(RCA PB 42749)	44	1989	0	1989	
2	Got A Love For You	(GIANT W 0040)	43	1991	40	1991	(BIG BEAT 5031)
3	I Like It	(BIG BEAT A 8377CD)	67	1993	0	1993	
4	Never	(BIG BEAT A 8347CD)	40	1993	0	1993	
Jon & Robin And The In Crowd Names John Abnor & Robin Wright							
1	Do It Agin A Little Bit Slower		0	1967	18	1967	(ABNAK 119)
Jon & Sandra Steele Mixed Vocal Duo from the USA							
1	My Happiness		0	1948	2	1948	(DAMON 11133)
Jon & Vangelis Male Vocal/Multi-Instrumentalist From Greece							
1	I Hear You Now	(Polydor POSP 96)	8	1980	0	1980	
2	I'll Find My Way Home	(Polydor JV 1)	6	1981	0	1981	
3	He Is Sailing	(Polydor JV 4)	61	1983	0	1983	
4	State Of Independence	(Polydor JV 5)	67	1984	0	1984	
Jon B. Male Vocalist, Real Name Jon Buck From Rhode Island							
* 1	Someone To Love		0	1995	10	1995	(YAB YUM 77895)
2	Pretty Girl		0	1995	25	1995	(YAB YUM 77813)
Jon Bon Jovi Male Vocalist from the USA							
1	Blaze Of Glory	(VERTIGO JBJ 1)	13	1990	1	1990	(Mercury 875896)
2	Miracle	(VERTIGO JBVJ 2)	29	1990	12	1990	(Mercury 878392)
3	Midnight In Chelsea	(Mercury MERCD 488)	4	1997	0	1997	
4	Queen Of New Orleans	(Mercury MERCD 493)	10	1997	0	1997	
Jon Of The Pleased Wimmin Male Dj from the UK							
1	Passion	(EASTWEST YZ 884C)	27	1995	0	1995	
2	Give Me Strength	(PERFECTO PERF 119CD)	30	1996	0	1996	
Jon Pertwee Male Actor/Vocalist from the UK							
1	Worzel's Song	(Decca F 13885)	33	1980	0	1980	
Jon Secada Male Singer/Songwriter From Cuba							
* 1	Just Another Day	(SBK SBK 35)	5	1992	5	1992	(SBK 07383)
2	Do You Believe In Us	(SBK SBK 37)	30	1992	13	1992	(SBK 50408)
3	Angel	(SBK CDSBK 39)	23	1993	18	1993	(SBK 50406)
4	Do You Really Want Me	(SBK CDSBK 41)	30	1993	0	1993	
5	I'm Free	(SBK CDSBK 44)	50	1993	27	1993	(SBK 50434)
6	If You Go	(SBK CDSBK 51)	39	1994	10	1994	(SBK 58156)
7	If You Go (Re-entry)	(SBK CDSBK 51)	71	1994	0	1994	
8	Mental Picture	(CDSBK 54)	44	1995	29	1995	(SBK 58272)
9	If I Never Knew You						

ISSUE	TITLE	UK LBL	UK POS	UK YEAR	US POS	US YEAR	US LBL
	(Love Theme From *Pocahontas*)	(WALT DISNEY WD 7023C)	51	1995	0	1995	
10	Too Late, Too Soon	(SBK CDSBK 57)	43	1997	41	1997	(EMI 58628)
	HIT 9 IS CREDITED TO JON SECADA AND SHANICE						

Jona Lewie Male Vocalist, Real Name Terry Dactyl from the UK

1	You'll Always Find Me In The Kitchen At Parties	(STIFF BUY 73)	16	1980	0	1980	
2	Stop The Cavalry	(STIFF BUY 104)	3	1980	0	1980	
	SEE ALSO TERRY DACTYL						

Jonathan Butler Male Vocal/Guitarist, B: Capetown, South Africa

1	If You're Ready (Come Go With Me)	(Jive Jive 109)	34	1974	0	1974	
2	Lies	(Jive Jive 141)	18	1987	27	1987	(Jive 1038)
	HIT 1 IS CREDITED TO RUBY TURNER FEATURING JONATHAN BUTLER						

Jonathan Edwards Male Vocalist, B: 28 Jul 1946 Minnesota   Formed The Group Sugar Creek In 1965

* 1	Sunshine		0	1971	4	1971	(CAPRICORN 8021)

Jonathan King Male Vocalist, Real Name Kenneth King B: 6 Dec 1944 London, England

* 1	Everyone's Gone To The Moon	(Decca F 12187)	4	1965	17	1965	(PARROT 9774)
2	Let It All Hang Out	(Decca F 12988)	26	1970	0	1970	
3	It's The Same Old Song	(B&C CD 139)	19	1971	0	1971	
4	Sugar Sugar	(RCA 2064)	12	1971	0	1971	
5	Lazy Bones	(Decca F 13177)	23	1971	0	1971	
6	Hooked On A Feelin	(Decca F 13241)	23	1971	0	1971	
7	Flirt	(Decca F 13276)	22	1972	0	1972	
8	Loop Di Love	(UK 7)	4	1972	0	1972	
9	I Can't Get No Satisfaction	(UK 53)	29	1974	0	1974	
10	Una Paloma Blanca	(UK 105)	5	1975	0	1975	
11	Chick A Boom (Don't Ya Jes Love It)	(UK 2012 002)	36	1975	0	1975	
12	In The Mood	(UK 121)	46	1976	0	1976	
13	It Only Takes A Minute	(UK 135)	9	1976	0	1976	
14	One For You One For Me	(GTO GT 237)	29	1978	0	1978	
15	Lick A Smurf For Christmas (All Fall Down)	(PETROL GAS1/MAGNET MAG 139)	58	1978	0	1978	
16	You're The Greatest Lover	(UK International INT 586)	67	1979	0	1979	
17	Gloria	(ARIOLA ARO 198)	65	1979	0	1979	

Jonathan Richman & The Modern Lovers Male Vocal/Instrumental Group from the UK

1	Roadrunner	(BESERKLEY BZZ 1)	11	1977	0	1977	
2	Egyptian Reggae	(BESERKLEY BZZ 2)	5	1977	0	1977	
3	Morning Of Our Lives	(BESERKLEY BZZ 7)	28	1978	0	1978	
	HIT 3 IS CREDITED TO MODERN LOVERS						

Jones Girls Names Shirley, Brenda & Valorie Jones from Detroit   Sang Backup Vocals For Diana Ross, Aretha Franklin And Others

* 1	You Gonna Make Me Love Somebody Else		0	1979	38	1979	(Philadelphia INT. 3680)

Joni James Female Vocalist, Real Name Joan Carmello Babbo B: 22 Sep 1930 In Chicago

* 1	Why Don't You Believe Me	(MGM 582)	11	1953	1	1952	(MGM 11333)
2	Purple Shades		0	1952	26	1952	(MGM 11333)
* 3	Have You Heard		0	1953	4	1953	(MGM 11390)
4	Wishing Ring		0	1953	17	1953	(MGM 11390)
* 5	Your Cheatin' Heart		0	1953	2	1953	(MGM 11426)
6	Almost Always		0	1953	9	1953	(MGM 11470)
7	Is It Any Wonder		0	1953	16	1953	(MGM 11470)
8	My Love, My Love		0	1953	8	1953	(MGM 11543)
9	You're Fooling Someone		0	1953	11	1953	(MGM 11543)
10	I'd Never Stand In Your Way		0	1953	23	1953	(MGM 11606)
11	Nina-Mon		0	1953	27	1953	(MGM 11637)
12	Maybe Next Time		0	1954	22	1954	(MGM 11696)
13	Am I In Love		0	1954	22	1954	(MGM 11696)
14	In A Garden Of Roses		0	1954	22	1954	(MGM 11753)
15	Mama, Don't Cry At My Wedding		0	1954	23	1954	(MGM 11802)
16	When We Come Of Age		0	1954	28	1954	(MGM 11865)
* 17	How Important Can It Be		0	1955	2	1955	(MGM 11919)
18	You Are My Love		0	1955	6	1955	(MGM 12066)
19	Give Us This Day		0	1956	30	1956	(MGM 12288)
20	There Goes My Heart		0	1958	19	1958	(MGM 12706)
21	There Must Be A Way	(MGM 1002)	24	1959	33	1959	(MGM 12746)
22	Little Things Mean A Lot		0	1960	35	1960	(MGM 12849)
23	My Last Date (With You)		0	1961	38	1961	(MGM 12933)
	HIT 8 IS WITH THE JACK HALLORAN CHOIR						

ISSUE	TITLE	UK LBL	UK POS	UK YEAR	US POS	US YEAR	US LBL
Joni Mitchell	Female Vocalist, Real Name Roberta Joan Anderson B: 7 Nov 1943 In Fort Mcleod, Alberta						
1	Big Yellow Taxi	(REPRISE RS 20906)	11	1970	67	1970	
2	You Turn Me On, I'm A Radio		0	1972	25	1972	(Asylum 11010)
3	Help Me		0	1974	7	1974	(Columbia 11034)
4	Free Man In Paris		0	1974	22	1974	(Columbia 11041)
5	Big Yellow Taxi (Live)		0	1974	24	1974	(Columbia 45221)
Jonny Chingas	Male Vocalist from the USA						
1	Phone Home	(CBS A 3121)	43	1983	0	1983	
Jonny L	Male Vocalist from the UK						
1	Ooh I Like It	(AL XLS 44CD)	73	1993	0	1993	
Jorgen Ingmann & His Guitar	Real Name Jorgen Ingmann-Pedersen B: 26 Apr 1925 Copenhagen, Denmark						
1	Apache		0	1961	2	1961	(ATCO 5184)
Jose Carreras	Male Vocalist (Tennor) From Italy						
1	Amigos Para Siempre (Friends For Life)	(REALLY USEFUL RUR 10)	11	1992	0	1992	
2	Libiamo / La Donna E Mobile	(TELDEC YZ 843CD)	21	1994	0	1994	
	HIT 1 IS CREDITED TO JOSE CARRERAS AND SARAH BRIGHTMAN • HIT 2 IS CREDITED TO JOSE CARRERAS, PLACIDO DOMINGO AND LUCIANO PAVAROTTI • SEE ALSO SARAH BRIGHTMAN						
Jose Iturbi	Male Actor/Pianist, B: 28 Nov 1895 Valencia						
* 1	Chopin's Polonaise In A Flat (From A Song To Remember)		0	1945	20	1945	(Victor 8848)
2	Clair De Lune		0	1946	21	1946	(Victor 8851)
	OBITUARY : D: 28 JUN 1980, AGED 84.						
Jose Jimenez	Real Name Bill Dana, B: William Szarthmary 5 Oct 1924 Massachusetts						
1	The Astronaut (Part 1-2)		0	1961	19	1961	(KAPP 409)
Jose' Feliciano	Male Vocal/Guitarist, Real Name Jose Monserrate Feliciano B: 8 Sep 1945 Puerto Rico						
* 1	Light My Fire	(RCA 1715)	6	1968	3	1968	(RCA 9550)
2	Hi-Heel Sneakers		0	1968	25	1968	(RCA 9641)
3	And The Sun Will Shine	(RCA 1871)	25	1969	0	1969	
! 4	Let's Find Each Other Tonight		0	1983	64	1983	(Motown 1674)
Jose' Ferrer	Male Vocalist from the USA						
1	The Heat's On (From *Miss Sadie Thompson*)		0	1954	30	1954	(MGM 25181)
2	Woman (Uh-Huh)	(Philips PB 220)	7	1954	2	1954	(Columbia 40144)
	HE WAS MARRIED TO, AND SEE ALSO ROSEMARY CLOONEY • HIT 1 IS CREDITED TO RITA HAYWORTH AND JOSE FERRER						
Josh Wink	Male Producer from the USA						
1	Don't Laugh	(XL RECORDINGS XLS 62CD)	38	1995	0	1995	
2	Higher State Of Consciousness	(MANIFESTO FESCD 3)	8	1995	0	1995	
3	Higher State Of Conciousness (Re-entry)	(MANIFESTO FESCD 3)	60	1995	0	1995	
4	Hypnotizin'	(XL RECORDINGS XLS 71CD)	35	1996	0	1996	
5	Higher State Of Consciousness (Re-Mix)	(MANIFESTO FESCD 9)	7	1996	0	1996	
	HITS 1, 4, 5 ARE CREDITED TO WINK • SEE ALSO SIZE 9						
Joshua Kadison	Male Singer/Songwriter/Pianist, B: 8 Feb 1965 Los Angeles						
1	Jessie	(SBK CDSBK 43)	69	1994	26	1993	(SBK 50429)
2	Jessie (Re-entry)	(SBK CDSBK 43)	48	1994	0	1994	
3	Beautiful In My Eyes	(SBK CDSBK 50)	37	1994	19	1994	(SBK 58099)
4	Jessie (Re-Issue)	(SBK CDSBK 43)	15	1995	0	1995	
5	Beautiful In My Eyes (Re-Issue)	(SBK CDSBK 55)	37	1995	0	1995	
Journey	Male Vocal/Instrumental Group from the USA						
1	Lovin', Touchin', Squeezin'		0	1979	16	1979	(Columbia
2	Any Way You Want It		0	1980	23	1980	(Columbia
3	Walks Like A Lady		0	1980	32	1980	(Columbia
4	The Party's Over (Hopelessly In Love)		0	1981	34	1981	(Columbia
5	Who's Crying Now	(CBS A 2725)	46	1982	4	1981	(Columbia
6	Don't Stop Believing	(CBS A 1728)	62	1982	9	1981	(Columbia
7	Open Arms		0	1982	2	1982	(Columbia
8	Still They Ride		0	1982	19	1982	(Columbia
9	Separate Ways (Worlds Apart)		0	1983	8	1983	(Columbia
10	Faithfully		0	1983	12	1983	(Columbia
11	After The Fall		0	1983	23	1983	(Columbia
12	Send Her My Love		0	1983	23	1983	(Columbia
13	Only The Young (From Vision Quest)		0	1985	9	1985	(Geffen 29090)
14	Be Good To Yourself		0	1986	9	1986	(Columbia
15	Suzanne		0	1986	17	1986	(Columbia
16	Girl Can't Help It		0	1986	17	1986	(Columbia
17	I'll Be Alright Without You		0	1987	14	1987	(Columbia

ISSUE	TITLE	UK LBL	UK POS	UK YEAR	US POS	US YEAR	US LBL
18	When You Love A Woman		0	1996	12	1996	(Columbia

NAMES: GEORGE TICKNER, NEAL SCHON, GREGG ROLIE, ROSS VALORY & AYNSLEY DUNBAR • MOST OF THE MEMBERS HAVE MOVED ON TO OTHER GROUPS

Joy Division   Male Vocal/Instrumental Group from the UK

1	Love Will Tear Us Apart	(FACTORY FAC	13	1980	0	1980	
2	Love Will Tear Us Apart (Re-entry)	(FACTORY FAC	19	1983	0	1983	
3	Atmosphere	(FACTORY FAC2137)	34	1988	0	1988	
4	Love Will Tear Us Apart (Re-Mix)	London YOJCD	19	1995	0	1995	

Joy Layne   Female Vocalist, B: Chicago In The 30's

1	Your Wild Heart		0	1957	20	1957	(Mercury 71038)

Joy Marshall   Female Vocalist from the UK

1	The More I See You	(Decca F 12422)	34	1966	0	1966	

Joy Nichols & Benny Lee   Mixed Vocal Duo from the USA

1	The Pussy Cat Song		0	1949	21	1949	(London 365)

Joy Sarney   Female Vocalist from the UK

1	Naughty Naughty Naughty	(ALASKA ALA	26	1977	0	1977	

Joy Strings   Mixed Vocal/Instrumental Group from the UK

1	It's A Open Secret	(REGALZONOPHONE RZ 501)	32	1964	0	1964	
2	A Starry Night	(REGAL ZONOPHONE RZ 504)	35	1964	0	1964	

Joyce Kennedy   See Jeffrey Osborne

Joyce Sims   Female Vocalist from the USA

1	All And All	(London LON 94)	16	1986	0	1986	
2	Lifetime Love	(London LON 137)	34	1987	0	1987	
3	Come Into My Life	(London LON 161)	7	1987	0	1987	
4	Walk Away	(London LON 176)	24	1988	0	1988	
5	Looking For A Love	(FFRR F 109)	39	1989	0	1989	
6	Come Into My Life (Re-Mix)	(CLUB TOOLS 60435 CLU)	72	1995	0	1995	

Joyrider   Male Vocal/Instrumental Group from the UK

1	Rush Hour	(PARADOX PDOXDX 012)	22	1996	0	1996	
2	All Gone Away	(A&M 5819552)	54	1996	0	1996	

JR WALKER AND THE ALL STARS • SEE JUNIOR WALKER & THE ALL STARS

JT & The Big Family   Mixed Vocal/Instrumental Group From Italy

1	Moments In Soul	(CHAMPION CHAMP 237)	7	1990	0	1990	

JTQ   Male Instrumental Group With Male Vocalist from the UK

1	Love The Life	(BIG LIFE BLRD	34	1993	0	1993	
2	See A Brighter Day	(BIG LIFE BLRD	49	1993	0	1993	
3	Love Will Keep Us Together	(ACID JAZZ JAZID 112CD)	63	1995	0	1995	

HITS 1-2 ARE CREDITED TO J.T.Q. WITH NOEL MCKOY • HIT 3 IS CREDITED TO J.T.Q. FEATURING ALISON LIMERICK

Juan Martin   Male Guitarist from Spain

1	Theme From *The Thorn Birds*	(WEA X 9518)	10	1984	0	1984	

Juanita Hall   Female Actress/Vocalist from the USA

1	Don't Cry, Joe (Let Her Go, Let Her Go, Let Her Go)		0	1949	22	1949	(RCA Victor 3557)

Jubilaires   Harmony Vocal Group from the USA

1	I Know		0	1946	14	1946	(Decca 18782)
2	The Old Piano Roll Blues		0	1950	25	1950	(Capitol 845)

Jud Strunk   Real Name Justin Strunk Jr B: 11 Jun 1936 Jamestown, New York

	1	Daisy A Day		0	1973	14	1973	(MGM 14463)
!	2	Next Door Neighbour's Kid		0	1973	86	1973	(MGM 14572)
	3	The Biggest Parakeets In Town		0	1975	50	1975	(MELODYLAND 6015)
!	4	Pamela Brown		0	1976	88	1976	(MELODYLAND 6027)

HIT 1 REACHED NUMBER 33 IN THE USA C/W CHARTS • HIT 3 REACHED NUMBER 51 IN THE USA C/W CHARTS • OBITUARY : D: 15 OCT 1981 PLANE CRASH.

Judas Priest   Male Vocal/Instrumental Group from the UK

1	Take On The World	(CBS 6915)	14	1979	0	1979	
2	Evening Star	(CBS 7312)	53	1979	0	1979	
3	Living After Midnight	(CBS 8379)	12	1980	0	1980	
4	Breaking The Law	(CBS 8644)	12	1980	0	1980	
5	United	(CBS 8897)	26	1980	0	1980	
6	Don't Go	(CBS 9520)	51	1981	0	1981	
7	Hot Rockin'	(CBS 1153)	60	1981	0	1981	
8	You've Got Another Thing Comin'	(CBS A 2611)	66	1982	0	1982	

ISSUE	TITLE	UK LBL	UK POS	UK YEAR	US POS	US YEAR	US LBL
9	Freewheel Burnin'	(CBS A 4054)	42	1984	0	1984	
10	Johnny B. Goode	(Atlantic 9114)	64	1988	0	1988	
11	Painkiller	(CBS 656273 7)	74	1990	0	1990	
12	A Touch Of Evil	(Columbia 6565897)	58	1991	0	1991	
13	Night Crawler	(Columbia 6590972)	63	1993	0	1993	

Jude Cole   Male Guitartist/Vocalist, Hails From East Moline, Illinois

ISSUE	TITLE	UK LBL	UK POS	UK YEAR	US POS	US YEAR	US LBL
1	Baby, It's Tonight		0	1990	16	1990	(REPRISE 19869)
2	Time For Letting Go		0	1990	32	1990	(REPRISE 19743)

Judge Dread   Male Vocalist from the UK

ISSUE	TITLE	UK LBL	UK POS	UK YEAR	US POS	US YEAR	US LBL
1	Big Six	(BIG SHOT BI 608)	11	1972	0	1972	
2	Big Seven	(BIG SHOT BI 613)	8	1972	0	1972	
3	Big Eight	(BIG SHOT BI 619)	14	1973	0	1973	
4	Je T'aime...Moi Non Plus	(CACTUS CT 65)	9	1975	0	1975	
5	Big Ten	(CACTUS CT 77)	14	1975	0	1975	
6	Christmas In Dreadland / Come Outside	(CACTUS CT 80)	14	1975	0	1975	
7	The Winkle Man	(CACTUS CT 90)	35	1976	0	1976	
8	Y Viva Suspenders	(CACTUS CT 99)	27	1976	0	1976	
9	5th Anniversary (EP)	(CACTUS CT 98)	31	1977	0	1977	
10	Up With The Cock / Big Punk	(CACTUS CT 110)	49	1978	0	1978	
11	Hokey Cokey / Jingle Bells	(EMI 2881)	59	1979	0	1979	

Judie Tzuke   Female Vocalist from the UK

ISSUE	TITLE	UK LBL	UK POS	UK YEAR	US POS	US YEAR	US LBL
1	Stay With Me Till Dawn	(ROCKET XPRES 17)	16	1979	0	1979	

Judith Durham   Female Vocalist, B: 3 Jul 1943 Australia

ISSUE	TITLE	UK LBL	UK POS	UK YEAR	US POS	US YEAR	US LBL
1	The Olive Tree	(Columbia DB 8207)	33	1967	0	1967	

SHE WAS ALSO LEAD SINGER WITH AND SEE ALSO THE SEEKERS

Judson Spence   Singer/Songwriter from Mississippi

ISSUE	TITLE	UK LBL	UK POS	UK YEAR	US POS	US YEAR	US LBL
1	Yeah, Yeah, Yeah		0	1988	32	1988	(Atlantic 88999)

Judy Boucher   Female Vocalist from the UK

ISSUE	TITLE	UK LBL	UK POS	UK YEAR	US POS	US YEAR	US LBL
1	Can't Be With You Tonight	(Orbitone OR 721)	2	1987	0	1987	
2	You Caught My Eye	(Orbitone OR 722)	18	1987	0	1987	

Judy Cheeks   Female Vocalist from the USA

ISSUE	TITLE	UK LBL	UK POS	UK YEAR	US POS	US YEAR	US LBL
1	So In Love (The Real Deal)	(Positiva CDTIV 6)	27	1993	0	1993	
2	Reach	(Positiva CDTIV 12)	17	1994	0	1994	
3	This Time / Respect	(Positiva CDTIV 28)	23	1995	0	1995	
4	You're The Story Of My Life / As Long As You're Good To	(Positiva CDTIV 34)	30	1995	0	1995	
5	Reach (Re-Mix)	(Positiva CDTIV 42)	22	1996	0	1996	

Judy Clay   Female Vocalist, Real Name Judy Gulon from New York

ISSUE	TITLE	UK LBL	UK POS	UK YEAR	US POS	US YEAR	US LBL
+ 1	Private Number	(Stax 101)	8	1968	17	1968	(STAX 0005)
2	Country Girl-City Man		0	1968	36	1968	(Atlantic 2480)
3	Tryin' To Love Two		0	1977	10	1977	(Mercury 73839)

HITS 1,3 ARE CREDITED TO WILLIAM BELL AND JUDY CLAY • HIT 2 IS CREDITED TO BILLY VERA AND JUDY CLAY

Judy Collins   Female Vocalist, B: 1 May 1939 Seattle

ISSUE	TITLE	UK LBL	UK POS	UK YEAR	US POS	US YEAR	US LBL
1	Both Sides Now	(Elektra EKSN 45043)	14	1970	8	1968	(Elektra 45639)
2	Amazing Grace	(Elektra 2101 020)	5	1970	0	1971	
* 3	Amazing Grace (Re-entry)	(Elektra 2101020)	48	1971	15	1971	(Elektra 45709)
4	Amazing Grace (2nd Re-entry)	(Elektra 2101 020)	40	1971	0	1971	
5	Amazing Grace (3rd Re-entry)	(Elektra 2101020)	50	1971	0	1971	
6	Amazing Grace (4th Re-entry)	(Elektra 2101 020)	48	1971	0	1971	
7	Amazing Grace (5th Re-entry)	(Elektra 2101 020)	20	1972	16	1972	
8	Amazing Grace (6th Re-entry)	(Elektra 2101 020)	46	1972	32	1972	
9	Amazing Grace (7th Re-entry)	(Elektra 2101 020)	49	1972	0	1972	
10	Cook With Honey		0	1973	32	1973	(Elektra 45831)
11	Send In The Clowns	(Elektra 2101020)	6	1975	36	1975	(Elektra 45253)
12	Send In The Clowns (Re-entry)		0	1977	19	1977	(Elektra 45253)

Judy Garland   Female Actress/Vocalist, Real Name Francis Gumm B: 10 Jun 1922 From Grand Rapids, Minnesota

ISSUE	TITLE	UK LBL	UK POS	UK YEAR	US POS	US YEAR	US LBL
* 1	Over The Rainbow (From *The Wizard Of Oz*)		0	1939	5	1939	(Decca 2672)
13	Wait And See (From *The Harvey Girls*)		0	1946	24	1946	(Decca 23459)
14	You'll Never Walk Alone (From *Carousel*)		0	1946	21	1946	(Decca 23539)
15	For You, For Me, Forevermore (From *The Shocking Miss Pilgrim*)		0	1947	19	1947	(Decca 23687)
16	Without A Memory		0	1953	29	1953	(Columbia 40010)
* 17	The Man That Got Away	(Philips PB 366)	18	1955	22	1954	(Columbia 40270)

ISSUE	TITLE	UK LBL	UK POS	UK YEAR	US POS	US YEAR	US LBL
7	I'll Never Be Free		0	1950	3	1950	(Capitol 1124)
8	Ain't Nobody's Business But My Own		0	1950	22	1950	(Capitol 1124)
9	Oh, Babe!		0	1950	7	1950	(Capitol 1278)
10	Oceans Of Tears		0	1950	15	1950	(Capitol 1567)
11	You're My Sugar		0	1951	22	1951	(Capitol 1567)
12	Come On-A My House (From *The Son*)		0	1951	8	1951	(Capitol 1710)
13	Angry		0	1951	26	1951	(Capitol 1796)
* 14	Wheel Of Fortune		0	1952	1	1952	(Capitol 1964)
15	I Waited A Little Too Long		0	1952	20	1952	(Capitol 2062)
16	Kay's Lament		0	1952	18	1952	(Capitol 2151)
17	Fool, Fool, Fool		0	1952	13	1952	(Capitol 2151)
* 18	Comes A-Long A-Love	(Capitol CI 13808)	1	1952	9	1952	(Capitol 2213)
19	Three Letters		0	1952	22	1952	(Capitol 2213)
20	Side By Side	(Capitol CI 1871)	7	1953	3	1953	(Capitol 2334)
21	Half A Photograph		0	1953	7	1953	(Capitol 2464)
22	Allez-Vous-En (From *Can-Can*)		0	1953	11	1953	(Capitol 2464)
23	When My Dreamboat Comes Home		0	1953	18	1953	(Capitol 2595)
24	Swamp Fire		0	1953	30	1953	(Capitol 2595)
25	Changing Partners	(Capitol CI 14050)	4	1954	7	1953	(Capitol 2657)
26	The Man Upstairs		0	1954	7	1954	(Capitol 2769)
27	If You Love Me (Really Love Me)		0	1954	4	1954	(Capitol 2769)
28	Am I A Toy Or A Treasure?	(Capitol CI 14151)	17	1954	22	1954	(Capitol 2887)
29	Fortune Of Dreams		0	1954	17	1954	(Capitol 2887)
30	Am I A Toy Or A Treasure? (Re-Entry)	(Capitol CI 14151)	20	1954	0	1954	
31	Good And Lonesome		0	1955	17	1955	(RCA 6146)
* 32	Rock And Roll Walt	(Hmv Pop 168)	1	1956	1	1956	(RCA 6359)
33	Second Fiddle		0	1956	40	1956	(RCA 6541)
34	My Heart Reminds Me		0	1957	9	1957	(RCA 6981)
	SHE WAS BORN ON AN INDIAN RESERVATION AND SANG ON LOCAL RADIO AT THIRTEEN						

Kay Thompson Female Authoress/Actress, B: 9 Nov 1913 St. Louis

ISSUE	TITLE	UK LBL	UK POS	UK YEAR	US POS	US YEAR	US LBL
1	Eloise		0	1956	39	1956	(Cadence 1286)

Kaye Sisters Female Vocal Trio from the UK

ISSUE	TITLE	UK LBL	UK POS	UK YEAR	US POS	US YEAR	US LBL
1	Ivory Tower	(Hmv Pop 209)	20	1956	0	1956	
2	Gotta Have Something In The Bank Frank	(Philips Pb 751)	8	1957	0	1957	
3	Shake Me I Rattle / Alone	(Philips Pb 752)	27	1958	0	1958	
4	Come Softly To Me	(Philips Pb 913)	9	1959	0	1959	
5	Paper Roses	(Philips Pb 1024)	7	1960	0	1960	

KC & The Sunshine Band Male Vocal/Instrumental Group from the USA

ISSUE	TITLE	UK LBL	UK POS	UK YEAR	US POS	US YEAR	US LBL
+ 1	Blow Your Whistle		0	1973	27	1973	(T.K. 1001)
2	Queen Of Club	(Joyboy Boy 88)	7	1974	0	197	
+ 3	Sound Your Funky Horn	(Joyboy Boy 83)	17	1974	21	1974	(Tk 1003)
* 4	Get Down Tonight	(Joyboy Boy 93)	21	1975	1	1975	(Tk 1009)
* 5	That's The Way I Like It	(Joyboy Boy 99)	4	1975	1	1975	(Tk 1015)
6	I'm So Crazy ('Bout You)	(Joyboy Boy 101)	34	1975	0	1975	
7	(Shake Shake Shake) Shake Your Booty	(Joyboy Boy 110)	22	1976	1	1976	(T.K. 1019)
8	Keep It Comin' Love	(Joyboy Boy 112)	31	1976	2	1977	(T.K. 1023)
9	I Like To Do It		0	1977	37	1977	(T.K. 1020)
10	I'm Your Boogie Man	(TI Xb 2167)	41	1977	1	1977	(T.K. 1022)
11	Boogie Shoes	(Tk Tkr 6025)	34	1978	35	1978	(T.K. 1025)
12	It's The Same Old Song	(Tk Tkr 6037)	49	1978	35	1978	(T.K. 1028)
13	Please Don't Go	(Tk Tkr 7558)	3	1979	1	1979	(T.K. 1035)
* 14	Yes, I'm Ready		0	1982	2	1980	(Casablanca 2227)
15	Give It Up	(Epic Epc A 3017)	1	1983	18	1983	(Meca 1001)
16	(You Said) You'd Gimme Some More	(Epic A 2760)	41	1983	0	1983	
17	That's The Way I Like It (Re-Mix)	(Music Factory Dance M7fac 2)	59	1991	0	1991	
	LEAD SINGER HARRY KC' CASEY B: 31 JAN 1951 FLORIDA • HIT 15 IS CREDITED TO KC • HIT 14 IS CREDITED TO TERI DESARIO WITH KC						

Ke Male Vocalist from the USA

ISSUE	TITLE	UK LBL	UK POS	UK YEAR	US POS	US YEAR	US LBL
1	Strange World	(RCA 74321349412)	73	1996	0	1996	

Keedy Female Vocalist, Real Name Kelly Keedy B: 26 Jul 1965 Abilene, Texas

ISSUE	TITLE	UK LBL	UK POS	UK YEAR	US POS	US YEAR	US LBL
1	Save Some Love		0	1991	15	1991	(Arista 2153)

Keely Smith Female Vocalist from the USA

ISSUE	TITLE	UK LBL	UK POS	UK YEAR	US POS	US YEAR	US LBL
1	How Are Ya' Fixed For Love?		0	1958	22	1958	(Capitol 3952)
2	That Old Black Magic		0	1958	18	1958	(Capitol 4063)

ISSUE	TITLE	UK LBL	UK POS	UK YEAR	US POS	US YEAR	US LBL
3	You're Breaking My Heart	(Reprise R 20346)	14	1965	0	1965	
	HIT 1 IS CREDITED TO FRANK SINATRA AND KEELY SMITH • HIT 2 IS CREDITED TO LOUIS PRIMA & HIS ORCHESTRA AND KEELY SMITH						
Keith Male vocalist, real name James Barry Keefer. B. & May 1949 Philadelphia							
1	Ain't Gonna Lie		0	1966	39	1966	(Mercury 72596)
* 2	98.6	(Mercury Mf 955)	24	1967	7	1967	(Mercury 72639)
3	Tell Me To My Face	(Mercury Mf 968)	50	1967	37	1967	(Mercury 72652)
	KEITH FIRST RECORDED AS KEITH AND THE ADMIRATIONS IN 1965						
Keith Barbour Male Singer/Songwriter from the USA He Was With The New Christy Minstrels							
1	Echo Park		0	1969	40	1969	(Epic 10486)
Keith Carradine Male Actor/Vocalist, B: 8 Aug 1949 California							
1	I'm Easy (From The Movie Nashville)		0	1976	17	1976	(Abc 12117)
Keith Emerson Male Pianist from the UK							
1	Honk Tonk Train Blues	(Manticore K 13513)	21	1976	0	1976	
	SEE ALSO EMERSON, LAKE & PALMER						
Keith Harris & Orville Male Ventriloquist/Vocalist With Orville (Duck) from the UK							
1	Orville's Song	(BBC Resl 124)	4	1982	0	1982	
2	Come To My Party	(BBC Resl 138)	44	1983	0	1983	
3	White Christmas	(Columbia Db 9121)	0	1985	0	1985	
Keith Kelly Male Vocalist from the UK							
1	Tease Me	(Parlophone R 4640)	46	1960	0	1960	
2	Tease Me (Re-Entry)	(Parlophone R 4640)	27	1960	0	1960	
3	Listen Little Girl	(Parlophone R 4676)	47	1960	0	1960	
Keith Mac Project Mixed Vocal/Instrumental Group from the UK							
1	De Dah Dah (Spice Of Life)	(Public Demand Ppdcd 3)	66	1994	0	1994	
Keith Marshall Male Vocalist from the UK							
1	Only Crying	(Arrival Pik 2)	12	1981	0	1981	
Keith Michell Male Vocalist from Australia							
1	I'll Give You The Earth	(Spark Sel 1046)	43	1971	0	1971	
2	I'll Give You The Earth(Re-Entry)	(Spark Sel 1046)	30	1971	0	1971	
3	Captain Beaky / Wilfred The Weasel	(Polydor Posp 106)	5	1980	0	1980	
4	The Trial Of Hissing Sid	(Polydor Hiss 1)	53	1980	0	1980	
	Hit 4 Is Credited To Keith Michell, Captain Beaky & His Band						
Keith Murray Male rapper from the USA							
1	The Rhyme	(Jive Jivecd 407)	59	1996	0	1996	
Keith Relf Male Vocalist from the UK							
1	Mr. Zero	(Columbia Db 7920)	50	1966	0	1966	
Keith Sweat Male Singer/Songwriter from Harlem							
* 1	I Want Her	(Vintertainment Ekr 68)	26	1988	5	1988	(Vintertainment 69431)
2	Something Just Ain't Right	(Vintertainment Ekr 72)	55	1988	0	1988	
* 3	Make You Sweat		0	1990	14	1990	(Vintertainment 64961)
4	I'll Give All My Love To You		0	1990	7	1990	(Vintertainment 64915)
5	Keep It Coming		0	1992	17	1992	(Elektra 64812)
6	How Do You Like It	(Elektra Ekr 185cd)	71	1994	0	1994	
* 7	Nobody	(Elektra Ekr 233cd)	30	1997	3	1996	(Elektra 64245)
8	Just A Touch	(Elektra Ekr 227cd	35	1996	0	1996	
* 9	Twisted	(Elektra Ekr 223cd)	39	1996	2	1996	(Elektra 64282)
Keith Washington Male Vocalist from Detroit							
1	Kissing You		0	1991	40	1991	(Qwest 19414)
Keith West Male Vocalist from the UK							
1	Excerpt From A Teenage Opera	(Parlophone R 5623)	2	1967	0	1967	
2	Sam	(Parlophone R 5651)	38	1967	0	1967	
Kellee Patterson Female Vocalist from the USA							
1	If It Don't Fit Don't Force It	(EMI International Int 544)	44	1978	0	1978	
Kelli Rich See Nu Soul							
Kelly Family Male Vocalist from the USA							
1	An Angel	(Cdem 390)	69	1995	0	1995	
Kelly Llorenna See Also N-Trance							
1	Set You Free	All Around The World Cdglobe 124)39		1994	0	1994	
2	Set You Free (Re-Issue)	(All Around The World Cdglobe 124)2		1995	0	1995	
3	Brighter Day	(Pukka Cdpukka 5)	43	1996	0	1996	

ISSUE	TITLE	UK LBL	UK POS	UK YEAR	US POS	US YEAR	US LBL
Kelly Marie Female Vocalist from the UK							
1	Feels Like I'm In Love	(Calibre Plus 1)	1	1980	0	1980	
2	Loving Just For Fun	(Calibre Plus 4)	21	1980	0	1980	
3	Hot Love	(Calibre Plus 5)	22	1981	0	1981	
4	Love Trial	(Calibre Plus 7)	51	1981	0		1981
Ken Barrie Male Vocalist from the UK							
1	Postman Pat	(Post Music Pp 001)	44	1982	0	1982	
2	Postman Pat (Re-Entry)	(Post Music Pp 001)	54	1982	0	1982	
3	Postman Pat (2nd Re-Entry)	(Post Music Pp 001)	59	1983	0	1983	
Ken Boothe Male Vocalist from Jamaica							
1	Everything I Own	(Trojan Tr 7920)	1	1974	0	1974	
2	Crying Over You	(Trojan Tr 7944)	11	1974	0	1974	
Ken Carson Male Vocalist from the USA							
1	Wond'rous Word (Of The Lord)		0	1951	30	1951	(Silvertone 770)
Ken Copeland Male Vocal/Televangelist, B: 1937 Texas							
1	Pledge Of Love		0	1957	12	1957	(Imperial 5432)
Ken Dodd Male Comedian/Vocalist, Kenneth Arthur Dodd B: 8 Nov 1932 In Liverpool, England							
1	Love is Like A Violin	(DeLuxe 3093)	0	1948	11	1948	
2	Once In Every Lifetime	(Decca F 11355)	28	1961	0	1961	
3	Once In Every Lifetime (Re-Entry)	(Decca F 11355)	47	1961	0	1961	
4	Once In Every Lifetime (2nd Re-Entry)	(Decca F 11355)	31	1961	0	1961	
5	Pianassimo	(Decca F 11422)	21	1962	0	1962	
6	Still	(Columbia Db 7094)	35	1963	0	1963	
7	Eight By Ten	(Columbia Db 7191)	22	1964	0	1964	
8	Happiness	(Columbia Db 7325)	31	1964	0	1964	
9	So Deep Is The Night	(Columbia Db 7398)	31	1964	0	1964	
* 10	Tears	(Columbia Db 7659)	1	1965	0	1965	
11	The River (Le Colline Sono In Fioro)	(Columbia Db 7750)	3	1965	0	1965	
12	Promises	(Columbia Db 7914)	6	1966	0	1966	
13	More Than Love	(Columbia Db 7976)	14	1966	0	1966	
14	It's Love	(Columbia Db 8031)	36	1966	0	1966	
15	Let Me Cry On Your Shoulder	(Columbia Db 8101)	11	1967	0	1967	
16	Tears Won't Wash Away These Heartaches	(Columbia Db 8600)	22	1969	0	1969	
17	Broken Hearted	(Columbia Db 8725)	15	1970	0	1970	
18	Broken Hearted (Re-Entry)	(Columbia Db 8725)	38	1971	0	1971	
19	When Love Comes Around Again	(Columbia Db 8796)	19	1971	0	1971	
20	Just Out Of Reach (Of My Two Empty Arms)	(Columbia Db 8947)	29	1972	0	1972	
21	(Think Of Me) Wherever You Are	(EMI 2342)	21	1975	0	1975	
22	Hold My Hand	(Images Imgs 0002)	44	1981	0	1981	
	HIS FIRST JOB WAS SELLING POTS & PANS WITH HIS FATHER						
Ken Doh Male Producer, Michael Devlin, from the UK							
1	Nakasaki (I Need A Lover Tonight) (EP)	(FFRR Fcd 272)	7	1996	0	1996	
Ken Griffin Male Instrumentalist (Organ) from the USA							
* 1	You Can't Be True, Dear		0	1948	1	1948	(Rondo 228)
2	Cuckoo Waltz		0	1948	19	1948	(Rondo 128)
3	You Can't Be True, Dear (Instrumental)		0	1948	2	1948	(Rondo 128)
4	You, You, You Are The One		0	1949	29	1949	(Rondo 186)
5	Beautiful Wisconsin		0	1949	26	1949	(Rondo 192)
6	Harbour Lights		0	1950	11	1950	(Columbia 38889)
	VOCALS ON HIT 1 ARE BY ACTOR JERRY WAYNE • VOCALS ON HIT 2 ARE BY NIKOLA MEINKOFF • VOCALS ON HIT 5 ARE BY JOHNNY HILL						
Ken Mackintosh Male Orchestra Leader from the UK							
1	The Creep	(HMV Bd 1295)	12	1954	0	1954	
2	The Creep (Re-Entry)	(HMV Bd 1295)	10	1954	0	195	
3	Raunchy	(HMV Pop 426)	19	1958	0	1958	
4	No Hiding Place	(HMV Pop 713)	45	1960	0	1960	
Ken Remo							
1	Mexico		0	1953	29	1953	(MGM 11419)
Ken Thorne & His Orchestra Male Orchestra Leader, from the UK							
1	Theme From The Legion's Last Patrol	(HMV Pop 1176)	4	1963	0	1963	
Keneckie Mixed Vocal/Instrumental Group from the UK							
1	Punka	(EMI disc Cddisc 001)	43	1996	0	1996	
2	Millionaire Sweeper	(EMIdisc Cddisc 002)	60	1996	0	1996	

ISSUE	TITLE	UK LBL	UK POS	UK YEAR	US POS	US YEAR	US LBL
3	In Your Car	(EMIdisc Cddisc 005)	24	1997	0	1997	
4	Nightlife	(EMIdisc Cddisc 006)	27	1997	0	1997	
5	Punka	(EMIdisc Cddisc 007)	38	1997	0	1997	

HIT 5 IS CREDITED TO KENICKIE

Keni Burke   Male Vocalist from the USA
| 1 | Let Somebody Love You | (RCA 93) | 59 | 1981 | 0 | 1981 | |
| 2 | Risin' To The Top | (RCA Pb 49103) | 70 | 1992 | 0 | 1992 | |

Kenneth McKellar   Make Vocalist from Scotland
| 1 | A Man Without Lov | (Decca F 12341) | 30 | 1966 | 0 | 1966 | |

Kenny (1)   Male Vocalist From Ireland
| 1 | Heart Of Stone | (Rak 144) | 11 | 1973 | 0 | 1973 | |
| 2 | Give It To Me Now | (Rak 153) | 38 | 1973 | 0 | 1973 | |

Kenny (2)   Male Vocal/Instrumental Group from the UK
1	The Bump	(Rak 186)	3	1974	0	1974	
2	Fancy Pants	(Rak 196)	4	1975	0	1975	
3	Baby I Love You O.K.	(Rak 207)	12	1975	0	1975	
4	Julie Anne	(Rak 214)	10	1975	0	1975	

Kenny Baker   Male Actor/Vocalist from the USA
| 8 | The Old Lamplighter | | 0 | 1947 | 11 | 1947 | (Decca 23781) |
| 9 | My Adobe Hacienda | | 0 | 1947 | 16 | 1947 | (Decca 23846) |

Kenny Ball & His Jazzmen   Male Jazz Band Leader/Vocalist/Trumpeter
1	Samantha	(Pye Jazz Today 7nj 4040)	13	1961	0	1961	
2	I Still Love You All	(Pye Jazz 7nj 2402)	24	1961	0	1961	
3	Someday	(Pye Jazz 7nj 2047)	28	1961	0	1961	
* 4	Midnight In Moscow	(Pye Jazz 7nj 2049)	2	1961	2	1962	(Kapp 442)
5	March Of The Siamese Children	(Pye Jazz 7nj 2051)	4	1962	0	1962	
6	The Green Leaves Of Summer	(Pye Jazz 7nj 2054)	7	1962	0	1962	
7	So Do I	(Pye Jazz 7nj 2056)	14	1962	0	1962	
8	The Pay Off	(Pye Jazz 7nj 2061)	23	1962	0	1962	
9	Sukiyaki	(Pye Jazz 7nj 2062)	10	1963	0	1963	
10	Casablanca	(Pye Jazz 7nj 2064)	21	1963	0	1963	
11	Rondo	(Pye Jazz 7nj 2065)	24	1963	0	1963	
12	Acapulco 1922	(Pye Jazz 7nj 2067)	27	1963	0	1963	
13	Hello Dolly	(Pye Jazz 7nj 2071)	30	1964	0	1964	
14	When I'm 64	(Pye 7n 17348)	43	1967	0	1967	

Kenny Damon   Male Vocalist from the USA
| 1 | While I Live | (Mercury Mf 907) | 48 | 1966 | 0 | 1966 | |

Kenny Dino   Male Vocalist, B: 12 Sep 1939 Long Island, New York
| 1 | Your Ma Said You Cried In Your Sleep Last Night | | 0 | 1961 | 24 | 1961 | (Musicor 1013) |

Kenny Everett   Male DJ/Comedian/Vocalist from the UK
| 1 | Captain Kremmen (Retribution) | (Djm Djs 10810) | 32 | 1977 | 0 | 1977 | |
| 2 | Snot Rap | (RCA Ken 1) | 9 | 1983 | 0 | 1983 | |

HIT 1 IS CREDITED TO KENNY EVERETT AND MIKE VICKERS • OBITUARY: D: AIDS.

Kenny G   Male Saxophonist, Real Name Kenny Gorelick from the USA
1	Hi! How Ya Doin'	(Arista Arist 561)	70	1984	0	1984	
2	What Does It Take (To Win Your Love)	(Arista Arist 672)	64	1986	0	1986	
3	Songbird	(Arista Ris 18)	22	1987	4	1987	(Arista 9588)
4	Don't Make Me Wait For Love		0	1987	15	1987	(Arista 9625)
5	Silhouette		0	1988	13	1988	(Arista 9751)
6	Missing You Now	(Columbia 6579917)	28	1992	12	1992	(Columbia 74184)
7	Forever In Love	(Arista 74321145552)	47	1993	18	1993	(Arista 12482)
8	By The Time The Night Is Over	(Arista 74321157142)	56	1993	25	1993	(Arista 12565)
9	The Moment		0	1996	63	1996	(Arista 13260)
10	Havana		0	1997	66	1997	(Arista 13326)

HIT 6 IS CREDITED TO MICHAEL BOLTON FEATURING KENNY G • HIT 8 IS CREDITED TO KENNY G WITH PEABO BRYSON HE WAS WITH THE LOVE UNLIMITED ORCHESTRA

Kenny Lattimore   Male Vocalist from the USA
| 1 | For You | | 0 | 1997 | 33 | 1997 | (Columbia 78456) |

Kenny Loggins   Male Vocalist, B: 7 Jan 1947 Everett, Washington, Cousin Of Dave Loggins
1	Whenever I Call You 'Friend'		0	1978	5	1978	(Columbia 10794)
2	This Is It		0	1980	11	1980	(Columbia 11109)
3	Keep The Fire		0	1980	36	1980	(Columbia 11215)
4	I'm Alright (From Caddyshack)		0	1980	7	1980	(Columbia 11317)

ISSUE	TITLE	UK LBL	UK POS	UK YEAR	US POS	US YEAR	US LBL
5	Don't Fight It		0	1982	17	1982	(Columbia 03192)
6	Heart To Heart		0	1983	15	1983	(Columbia 03377)
7	Welcome To Heartlight		0	1983	24	1983	(Columbia 03555)
* 8	Footloose (From film Of same name)	(CBS A 4101)	6	1984	1	1984	(Columbia 04310)
9	I'm Free (Heaven Helps The Man) (From *Footloose*)		0	1984	22	1984	(Columbia 04452)
10	Vox Humana		0	1985	29	1985	(Columbia 04849)
11	Forever		0	1985	40	1985	(Columbia 04931)
12	Danger Zone (From *Top Gun*)	(CBS A 7188)	45	1986	2	1986	(Columbia 05893)
13	Meet Me Half Way (From *Over The Top*)		0	1987	11	1987	(Columbia 06690)
14	Nobody's Fool (From Caddyshack II)		0	1988	8	1988	(Columbia 07971)

Kenny Lynch   Male Vocalist from the UK

ISSUE	TITLE	UK LBL	UK POS	UK YEAR	US POS	US YEAR	US LBL
1	Mountain Of Love	(HMV Pop 751)	33	1960	0	1960	
2	Puff	(HMV Pop 1057)	33	1962	0	1962	
3	Puff (Re-Entry)	(HMV Pop 1057)	46	1962	0	1962	
4	Upon The Roof	(HMV Pop 1090)	10	1962	0	1962	
5	You Can Never Stop Me From Loving You	(HMV Pop 1165)	10	1963	0	1963	
6	Stand By Me	(HMV Pop 1280)	39	1964	0	1964	
7	What Am I To Do	(HMV Pop 1321)	37	1964	0	1964	
8	What Am I To Do (Re-Entry)	(HMV Pop 1321)	44	1964	0	1964	
9	I'll Stay By You	(HMV Pop 1430)	29	1965	0	1965	
10	Half The Days Gone And We Haven't Earnt A Penny	(Satril Sat 510)	50	1983	0	1983	

Kenny Nolan   Kenny was involved with the studio group Eleventh Hour

ISSUE	TITLE	UK LBL	UK POS	UK YEAR	US POS	US YEAR	US LBL
* 1	I Like Dreamin'		0	1977	3	1977	(20th Century 2287)
2	Love's Grown Deep		0	1977	20	1977	(20th Century 2331)

Kenny Rogers   Male Vocalist, Real Name Kenneth Donald Rogers B: 21 Aug 1938 Houston, Texas.

ISSUE	TITLE	UK LBL	UK POS	UK YEAR	US POS	US YEAR	US LBL
1	Just Dropped In (To See What Condition My Condition Was In)		0	1968	5	1968	(Reprise 0655)
2	But You Know I Love You		0	1969	19	1969	(Reprise 0799)
* 3	Ruby Don't Take Your Love To Town	(Reprise Rs 20829)	2	1969	6	1969	(Reprise 0829)
4	Ruben James (Reuben James)		0	1969	36	1969	(Reprise 0854)
5	Something's Burning	(Reprise Rs 20888)	8	1970	11	1970	(Reprise 0888)
6	Tell It All Brother		0	1970	17	1970	(Reprise 0923)
7	Heed The Call		0	1970	33	1970	(Reprise 0953)
* 12	Lucille	(United Artists Up 36242)	1	1977	5	1977	(United Artists 929)
13	Daytime Friends	(United Artists Up 36289)	39	1977	28	1977	(United Artists 1027)
15	Love Or Something Like It		0	1978	32	1978	(United Artists 1210)
16	The Gambler		0	1978	16	1978	(United Artists 1250)
* 18	She Believes In Me	(United Artists Up 614)	42	1979	5	1979	(United Artists 1273)
20	You Decorated My Life		0	1979	7	1979	(United Artists 1315)
* 21	Coward Of The County	(United Artists Up 614)	1	1980	3	1980	(United Artists 1327)
22	Don't Fall In Love With A Dreamer		0	1980	4	1980	(United Artists 1345)
23	Love The World Away		0	1980	14	1980	(United Artists 1359)
* 24	Lady	(United Artists Up 635)	12	1980	1	1980	(Liberty 1380)
25	What Are We Doin' In Love		0	1981	14	1981	(Liberty 1404)
26	I Don't Need You		0	1981	3	1981	(Liberty 1415)
27	Share Your Love With Me		0	1981	14	1981	(Liberty 1430)
29	Through The Years		0	1982	13	1982	(Liberty 1444)
30	Love Will Turn You Around		0	1982	13	1982	(Liberty 1471)
32	We've Got Tonight	(Liberty Up 658)	28	1983	6	1983	(Liberty 1492)
33	All My Life		0	1983	37	1983	(Liberty 1495)
* 35	Island In The Stream	(RCA 378)	7	1983	1	1983	(RCA 13615)
36	Eyes That See In The Dark	(RCA 358)	61	1983	0	1983	
39	This Woman		0	1984	23	1984	(RCA 13710)
44	What About Me?		0	1984	15	1984	(RCA 1899)
	OTHER HITS WERE C/W						

Kenny Thomas   Male Vocalist from the UK

ISSUE	TITLE	UK LBL	UK POS	UK YEAR	US POS	US YEAR	US LBL
1	Outstanding	(Cooltempo Cool 227	12	1991	0	1991	
2	Thinking About Your Love	(Cooltempo Cool 235)	4	1991	0	1991	
3	Best Of You	(Cooltempo Cool 243)	11	1991	0	1991	
4	Tender Love	(Cooltempo Cool 247)	26	1991	0	1991	
5	Stay	(Cooltempo Cdcool 271)	22	1993	0	1993	
6	Trippin' On Your Love	(Cooltempo Cdcool 277)	17	1993	0	1993	
7	Piece By Piece	(Cooltempo Cdcool 283)	36	1993	0	1993	
8	Destiny	(Cooltempo Cdcool 289)	59	1994	0	1994	
9	When I Think Of You	(Cooltempo Cdcool 309)	27	1995	0	1995	

ISSUE	TITLE	UK LBL	UK POS	UK YEAR	US POS	US YEAR	US LBL
Kenny Williams Male Vocalist from the USA							
1	(You're) Fabulous Babe	(Decca Fr 13731)	35	1977	0	1977	
Kerbdog Male Vocal/Instrumental Group From Ireland							
1	Dry Riser	(Vertigo Vercc 83)	60	1994	0	1994	
2	Dummy Crusher	(Vertigo Vercd 86)	37	1994	0	1994	
3	Sally	(Fontana Kercd 2)	69	1996	0	1996	
4	Mexican Wave	(Fontana Kercd 3)	49	1997	0	1997	
Kerri & Mick Mixed Vocal Duo from Australia							
1	Sons And Daughters Theme	(A1 A1 286)	68	1984	0	1984	
Ketty Lester Female Vocalist, Real Name Revoyda Frierson B: 16 Aug 1934, Hope, Arkansas							
* 1	Love Letters	(London Hln 9527)	4	1962	5	1962	(Era 3068)
2	But Not For Me	(London Hln 9574)	45	1962	0	1962	
Kevin Johnson Male Vocalist from Australia							
1	Rock 'N Roll (I Gave You The Best Years)	(UK Ukr 84)	23	1975	0	1975	
Kevin Keegan Male Soccer Player/Manager/Vocalist from the UK							
1	Head Over Heels In Love	(EMI 2965)	31	1979	0	1979	
Kevin Kitchen Male Vocalist from the UK							
1	Put My Arms Around You	(China Wok 1)	64	1985	0	1985	
Kevin Paige Male Vocalist From Memphis							
1	Don't Shut Me Out		0	1989	18	1989	(Chrysalis 23389)
2	Anything I Want		0	1990	29	1990	(Chrysalis 23444)
Kevin The Gerbil Male Vocalist from the UK							
1	Summer Holiday	(Magnet Rat 3)	50	1984	0	1984	
Kick Squad Male Vocal/Instrumental Group from the UK/Germany							
1	Sound Clash (Champion Sound)	(Kickin' Kick 2)	59	1990	0	1990	
Kicking Back With Taxman Mixed Vocal/Instrumental Duo With Male Rapper from the UK							
1	Devotion	(10 Ten 297)	47	1990	0	1990	
2	Everything	(10 Ten 307)	54	1990	0	1990	
Kicks Like A Mule Male Production/Instrumental Duo from the UK							
1	The Bouncer	(Tribal Bass Tribe 3s)	7	1992	0	1992	
Kid 'N' Play Male Vocal/Instrumental Duo from the USA							
1	Last Night	(Cooltempo Cool 148)	71	1987	0	1987	
2	Do This My Way	(Cooltempo Cool 164)	48	1987	0	1987	
3	Gittin' Funky	(Cooltempo Cool 168)	55	1988	0	1988	
Kid Creole & The Coconuts Male Vocalist And Female Vocal Group from the USA							
1	Me No Pop 1	(Ze Wip 6711)	32	1981	0	1981	
2	I'm A Wonderful Thing Baby	(Ze Wip 6756)	4	1982	0	1982	
3	Stool Pigeon	(Ze Wip 6793)	7	1982	0	1982	
4	Annie I'm Not Your Daddy	(Ze Wip 6801)	2	1982	0	1982	
5	Dear Addy	(Ze Wip 6840)	29	1982	0	1982	
6	There's Something Wrong In Paradise	(Island Is 130)	35	1983	0	1983	
7	The Lifeboat Part	(Island Is 142)	49	1983	0	1983	
8	The Sex Of It	(CBS 655698 7)	29	1990	0	1990	
9	I'm A Wonderful Thing Baby (Re-Mix)	(Island Cid 551)	60	1993	0	1993	
Kid Unknown Male Producer, Real Name Paul Fitzpatrick from the UK							
1	Nightmare	(Warp Wap 20cd)	64	1992	0	1992	
Kids From 'Fame' Mixed Vocal Group from the USA							
1	Hi-Fidelity	(RCA 254)	5	1982	0	1982	
2	Starmaker	(RCA 280)	3	1982	0	1982	
3	Mannequin	(RCA 299)	50	1982	0	1982	
4	Friday Night (Live)	(RCA 320)	13	1983	0	1983	
	HIT 1 IS CREDITED TO KIDS FROM 'FAME' FEATURING VALERIE LANDSBERG • HIT 2 TO KIDS FROM 'FAME' FEATURING GENE ANTHONY RAY						
Kiki Dee Female Vocalist, Real Name Pauline Matthews B: 6 Mar 1947 Yorkshire, England							
1	Amoureuse	(Rocket Pig 4)	13	1973	0	1973	
2	I've Got The Music In Me	(Rocket Pig 12)	19	1974	12	1974	(Rocket 40293)
3	(You Don't Know) How Glad Am I	(Rocket Pig 16)	33	1975	0	1975	
* 4	Don't Go Breaking My Heart	(Rocket Rokn 512)	1	1976	1	1976	(Rocket 40585)
5	Loving And Free - Amoureuse (Re-Issue)	(Rocket Rokn 515)	13	1976	0	1976	
6	First Thing In The Morning	(Rocket Rokn 520)	32	1977	0	1977	
7	Chicago	(Rocket Rokn 526)	28	1977	0	1977	
8	Star	(Ariola Aro 251)	3	1981	0	1981	
9	Perfect Timing	(Ariola Aro 257)	66	1981	0	1981	
10	True Love	(Rocket Elscx 32)	2	1993	0	1993	
	HITS 2-3 ARE CREDITED TO KIKI DEE BAND • HITS 4,10 ARE CREDITED TO ELTON JOHN AND KIKI DEE						

ISSUE	TITLE	UK LBL	UK POS	UK YEAR	US POS	US YEAR	US LBL
Killing Joke	Male Vocal/Instrumental Group from the UK						
1	Follow The Leaders	(Malicious Damage Egmds 101)	55	1981	0	1981	
2	Empire Song	(Malicious Damage Ego 4)	43	1982	0	1982	
3	Birds Of A Feather	(Eg Ego 10)	64	1982	0	1982	
4	Let's All Go (To The Fire Dances)	(Eg Ego 11)	51	1983	0	1983	
5	Me Or You?	(Eg Ego 14)	57	1983	0	1983	
6	Eighties	(Eg Ego 16)	60	1984	0	1984	
7	A New Day	(Eg Ego 17)	56	1984	0	1984	
8	Love Like Blood	(Eg Ego 20)	16	1985	0	1985	
9	Kings And Queens	(Eg Ego 21)	58	1985	0	1985	
10	Adorations	(Eg Ego 27)	42	1986	0	1986	
11	Sanity	(Eg Ego 30)	70	1986	0	1986	
12	Millennium	(Butterfly Bfld 12)	34	1994	0	1994	
13	The Pandemonium Single	(Butterfly Bflda 17)	28	1994	0	1994	
14	Jana	(Butterfly Bflda 21)	54	1995	0	1995	
15	Democracy	(Butterfly Bfldb 33)	39	1996	0	1996	
Kim Appleby	Female Vocalist from the UK						
1	Don't Worry	(Parlophone R 6272)	2	1990	0	1990	
2	G.L.A.D.	(Parlophone R 6281)	10	1991	0	1991	
3	Mama	(Parlophone R 6291)	19	1991	0	1991	
4	If You Cared	(Parlophone R 6297)	44	1991	0	1991	
5	Light Of The World	(Parlophone R 6352)	41	1993	0	1993	
6	Breakaway	(Parlophone Cdr 6362	56	1993	0	1993	
7	Free Spirit	(Parlophone Cdr 6397)	51	1994	0	1994	
Kim Carnegie	Female Vocalist from the UK						
1	Jazz Rap	(Best Zb 44085)	73	1991	0	1991	
Kim Carnes	Female Vocalist/Pianist/Composer B: 20 Jul 1945 Los Angeles						
1	You're A Part Of Me		0	1978	36	1978	(Ariola 7704)
2	Don't Fall In Love With A Dreamer		0	1980	4	1980	(United Artists 1345)
3	More Love		0	1980	10	1980	(EMI America 8045)
* 4	Bette Davis Eyes	(EMI America Ea 121)	10	1981	1	1981	(EMI America 8077)
5	Draw Of The Cards	(EMI America Ea 125)	49	1981	28	1981	(EMI America 8087)
6	Voyeur	(EMI America Ea 143)	68	1982	29	1982	(EMI America 8127)
7	Does It Make You Remember		0	1982	36	1982	(EMI America 8147)
8	Invisible Hands		0	1983	40	1983	(EMI America 8181)
9	What About Me?		0	1984	15	1984	(RCA 13899)
10	Crazy In The Night (Barking At Aeroplanes)		0	1985	15	1985	(EMI America 8267)
Kim English	Female Vocalist from the USA						
1	Nite Life	(Hi-Life Pzcd 323)	35	1994	0	1994	
2	Time For Love	(Hi-Life Hicd 8)	48	1995	0	1995	
3	I Know A Place	(Polydor 5798072)	52	1995	0	1995	
4	Nite Life (Re-Mix)	(Polydor 5755332)	35	1996	0	1996	
5	Supernatural	(Polydor 5736972)	50	1997	0	1997	
Kim Weston	Female Vocalist, Real Name Agatha Natalie Weston B: Detroit						
+ 1	Love Me All The Way		0	1963	24	1963	(Tamla 54076)
2	Take Me In Your Arms (And Rock Me A Little While)		0	1965	50	1965	(Gordy 7046)
+ 3	Helpless		0	1966	13	1966	(Gordy 7050)
4	It Takes Two	(Tamla Motown Tmg 590)	16	1967	14	1967	(Tamla 54141)
	HIT 4 IS CREDITED TO MARVIN GAYE AND KIM WESTON						
Kim Wilde	Female Vocalist, Real Name Kim Smith B: 18 Nov 1960 West London, England.						
1	Kids In America	(Rak 327)	2	1981	25	1982	(EMI Amercia 8110)
2	Chequered Love	(Rak 330)	4	1981	0	1981	
3	Water On Glass / Boys	(Rak 334)	11	1981	0	1981	
4	Cambodia	(Rak 336)	12	1981	0	1981	
5	View From A Bridge	(Rak 342)	16	1982	0	1982	
6	Child Come Away	(Rak 352)	43	1982	0	1982	
7	Love Blonde	(Rak 360)	23	1983	0	1983	
8	Dancing In The Dark	(Rak 365)	67	1983	0	1983	
9	The Second Time	(MCA Kim 1)	29	1984	0	1984	
10	The Touch	(MCA Kim 2)	56	1984	0	1984	
11	Rage To Lov	(MCA Kim 3)	19	1985	0	1985	
12	You Keep Me Hangin' O	(MCA Kim 4)	2	1986	1	1987	(MCA 53024)
13	Another Step (Closer To You)	(MCA Kim 5)	6	1987	0	1987	
14	Say You Really Want Me	(MCA Kim 6)	29	1987	0	1987	
16	Hey Mister Heartache	(MCA Kim 7)	31	1988	0	1988	
15	Rockin' Around The Christmas Tree	(10 Ten 2)	3	1987	0	1987	
17	You Came	(MCA Kim 8)	3	1988	0	1988	

ISSUE	TITLE	UK LBL	UK POS	UK YEAR	US POS	US YEAR	US LBL
18	Never Trust A Stranger	(MCA Kim 9)	7	1988	0	1988	
19	Four Letter Word	(MCA Kim 10)	14	1988	0	1988	
20	Love Is The Natural Way	(MCA Kim 11)	32	1989	0	1989	
21	It's Here	(MCA Kim 12)	42	1990	0	1990	
22	Time	(MCA Kim 13)	71	1990	0	1990	
23	I Can't Say Goodbye	(MCA Kim 14)	51	1990	0	1990	
24	Love Is Holy	(MCA Kim 15)	16	1992	0	1992	
25	Heart Over Mind	(MCA Kim 16)	34	1992	0	1992	
26	Who Do You Think You Are	(MCA Kim 17)	49	1992	0	1992	
27	If I Can't Have You	(MCA Kimtd 18)	12	1993	0	1993	
28	In My Life	(MCA Kimtd 19)	54	1993	0	1993	
29	Breakin' Away	(MCA Kimtd 21)	43	1995	0	1995	
30	This I Swear	(MCA Kimtd 22)	46	1996	0	1996	

HIT 13 IS CREDITED TO KIM WILDE AND JUNIOR, DAUGHTER OF MARTY WILDE • HIT 15 IS CREDITED TO MEL & KIM

King Male Vocal/Instrumental Group from the UK/Ireland

1	Love On Pride	(CBS A 4988)	2	1985	0	1985	
2	Won't You Hold My Hand	(CBS A 6094)	24	1985	0	1985	
3	Alone Without You	(CBS A 6308)	8	1985	0	1985	
4	The Taste Of Your Tears	(CBS A 6618)	11	1985	0	1985	
5	Torture	(CBS A 6761)	23	1986	0	1986	
6	I Know	(CBS Pking 1)	59	1987	0	1987	

HIT 6 IS CREDITED TO PAUL KING

King Bee Male Rapper from the UK

1	Must Bee The Music	(Columbia 6565827)	44	1991	0	1991	
2	Back By Dope Demand	(First Bass 7ruff 6x)	61	1991	0	1991	

King Brothers Male Vocal/Instrumental Group from the UK

1	A White Sport Coat	(Parlophone R 4310)	6	1957	0	1957	
2	In The Middle Of An Island	(Parlophone R 4338)	19	1957	0	1957	
3	Wake Up Little Susie	(Parlophone R 4367)	22	1957	0	1957	
4	Put A Light In The Window	(Parlophone R 4389)	29	1958	0	1958	
5	Put A Light In The Window (Re-Entry)	(Parlophone R 4389)	28	1958	0	1958	
6	Put A Light In The Window (2nd Re-Entry)	Parlophone R 4389)	25	1958	0	1958	
7	Standing On The Corner	(Parlophone R 4639)	4	1957	0	1957	
8	Mais Oui	(Parlophone R 4672)	16	1960	0	1960	
9	Doll House	(Parlophone R 4715)	21	1961	0	1961	
10	76 Trombones	(Parlophone R 4737)	19	1961	0	1961	

SEE ALSO STUTZ BEARCATS

King Curtis Real Name Curtis Ousley B: 7 Feb 1934 Fort Worth, Texas

1	Soul Twist		0	1962	17	1962	(Enjoy 1000)
2	Memphis Soul Stew		0	1967	33	1967	(Atco 6511)
3	Ode To Billie Jo		0	1967	28	1967	
4	Soul Serenade		0	1964	51	1964	(Capitol 5109)

OBITUARY : D: 13 AUG 1971 STABBED TO DEATH

King Floyd Male Singer/Songwriter, B: 13 Feb 1945 In New Orleans

* 1	Groove Me		0	1971	6	1971	(Chimneyville 435)
2	Baby Let Me Kiss You		0	1971	29	1971	(Chimneyville 437)

King Harvest Male Vocal/Instrumental Group from the USA

1	Dancing In The Moonlight		0	1973	13	1973	(Perception 515)

King Kurt Male Vocal/Instrumental Group from the UK

1	Destination Zululand	(Stiff Buy 189)	36	1983	0	1983	
2	Mack The Knife	(Stiff Buy 199)	55	1984	0	1984	
3	Banana Banana	(Stiff Buy 206)	54	1984	0	1984	
4	America	(Polydor Kurt 1)	73	1986	0	1986	
5	The Land Of Ring Dang Do	(Polydor Kurt 2)	67	1987	0	1987	

King Sun-D'moet Male Rap-Scratch Duo from the USA

1	Hey Love	(Flame Melt 5)	66	1987	0	1987	

King Trigger Mixed Vocal/Instrumental Group from the UK

1	The River	(Chrysalis Chs 2623)	57	1982	0	1982	

Kingdom Come Male Vocal/Instrumental Group from the USA

1	Get It On	(Polydor Kcs 1)	75	1988	0	1988	
2	Do You Like It	(Polydor Kcs 2)	73	1989	0	1989	

ISSUE	TITLE	UK LBL	UK POS	UK YEAR	US POS	US YEAR	US LBL
Kingmaker	Male Vocal/Instrumental Group from the UK						
1	Idiots At The Wheel (EP)	(Scorch Scorch 3)	30	1992	0	1992	
2	Eat Yourself Whole	(Scorch Scorchg 5)	15	1992	0	1992	
3	Armchair Anarchist	(Scorch Scorchg 6)	47	1992	0	1992	
4	10 Years Asleep	(Scorch Cdscorchs 8)	15	1993	0	1993	
5	Queen Jane	(Scorch Cdscors 9)	29	1993	0	1993	
6	Saturday's Not What It Used To Be	(Scorch Cdscorch 10)	63	1993	0	1993	
7	You And I Will Never See Things Eye To Eye	(Scorch Cdscorchs 11)	33	1995	0	1995	
8	In The Best Possible Taste (Part 2)	(Scorch Cdscorchs 12)	41	1995	0	1995	
Kings Of Swing Orchestra	Orchestra from Australia						
1	Switched On Swing	(Philips Swing 1)	48	1982	0	1982	
Kingsmen (1)	Male Vocal/Instrumental Group from the USA Names Jack Ely, Lynn Easton, Mike Mitchell, Bob Nordby & Don Gallucci						
* 1	Louie Louie	(Pue International 7n 25231)	26	1964	2	1963	(Wand 143)
2	Money		0	1964	16	1964	(Wand 150)
3	The Jolly Green Giant		0	1965	4	1965	(Wand 172)
Kingsmen (2)	The Group Is Bill Haley's Band, The Comets Without Haley						
1	Week End		0	1958	35	1958	(East West 115)
Kingston Trio	Male Vocal/Instrumental Group from the USA Names Bob Shane, Nick Reynolds & Dave Guard						
* 1	Tom Dooley	(Capitol CI 14951)	5	1958	1	1958	(Capitol 4049)
2	The Tijuana Jail		0	1959	12	1959	(Capitol 4167)
3	M.T.A. (Metropolitan Transit Authority) (Boston)		0	1959	15	1959	(Capitol 4221)
4	A Worried Man		0	1959	20	1959	(Capitol 4271)
5	San Muguel	(Capitol CI 15073)	29	1959	0	1959	
7	El Matador		0	1960	32	1960	(Capitol 4338)
8	Bad Man Blunder		0	1960	37	1960	(Capitol 4379)
9	Where Have All The Flowers Gone		0	1962	21	1962	(Capitol 4671)
10	Greenback Dollar		0	1963	21	1963	(Capitol 4898)
11	Reverend Mr. Black		0	1963	8	1963	(Capitol 4951)
12	Desert Pete		0	1963	33	1963	(Capitol 5005)
	JOHN STEWARD REPLACED DAVE GUARD IN 1961, TRIO DISBANDED IN 1968 • TOM DULA WHO WAS HANGED FOR MURDERING LAURA FOSTER						
Kinks	Male Vocal/Instrumental Group from the UK						
* 1	You Really Got Me	(Pye 7n 15673)	1	1964	7	1964	(Reprise 0306)
2	All Day And All Of The Night	(Pye 7n 15714)	2	1964	7	1964	(Reprise 0334)
* 3	Tired Of Waiting For You	(Pye 7n 15759)	1	1965	6	1965	(Reprise 0347)
4	Everybody's Gonna Be Happy	(Pye 7n 15813)	17	1965	0	1965	
5	Set Me Free	(Pye 7n 15854)	9	1965	23	1965	(Reprise 0379)
6	Who'll Be The Next In Line		0	1965	34	1965	(Reprise 0366)
7	See My Friend	(Pye 7n 15919)	9	1965	0	1965	
8	Till The End Of The Day	(Pye 7n 15981)	8	1965	50	1966	(Reprise 0454)
9	A Well Repected Man		0	1966	13	1966	(Reprise 0420)
10	Dedicated Follower Of Fashion	(Pye 7n 17064)	4	1966	36	1966	(Reprise 0471)
11	Sunny Afternoon	(Pye 7n 17125)	1	1966	14	1966	(Reprise 0497)
12	Dead End Street	(Pye 7n 17222)	5	1966	73	1967	(Reprise 0540)
13	Mr. Pleasant		0	1967	80	1967	(Reprise 0587)
14	Waterloo Sunset	(Pye 7n 17321)	2	1967	0	1967	
15	Autumn Almanac	(Pye 7n 17400)	3	1967	0	1967	
16	Wonder Boy	(Pye 7n 17468)	36	1968	0	1968	
17	Days	(Pye 7n 17573)	12	1968	0	1968	
18	Plastic Man	(Pye 7n 17724)	31	1969	0	1969	
19	Victoria	(Pye 7n 17865)	33	1970	62	1970	(Reprise 0863)
20	Lola	(Pye 7n 17961)	2	1970	9	1970	(Reprise 0930)
21	Apeman	(Pye 7n 45016)	5	1970	45	1971	(Reprise 0979)
22	Supersonic Rocket Ship	(RCA 2211)	16	1972	0	1972	
23	A Rock 'N' Roll Fantasy		0	1978	30	1978	(Arista 0342)
24	Better Things	(Arista Arist 415)	46	1981	0	1981	
25	Come Dancing	(Arista Arist 502)	12	1983	6	1983	(Arista 1054)
26	Don't Forget To Dance	(Arista Arist 524)	58	1983	29	1983	(Arista 9075)
27	You Really Got Me (Re-Issue)	(Prt Kd1)	47	1983	0	1983	
28	The Days (EP)	(When! Wenx 1016)	35	1997	0	1997	
	THE GROUP WAS FORMED BY LEAD SINGER RAY DAVIES IN 1963 IN 1980 A LIVE VERSION OF HIT 20 REACHED NUMBER 81 IN THE USA						
	HIT 20 WAS ORIGINALLY CALLED 'PEPSI COLA' AND WAS RE-RECORDED WHEN THE BBC REFUSED TO PLAY IT AS THEY CLAIMED IT WAS ADVERTISING						
Kinky	Female Rapper from the UK						
1	Everybody	(Feverpitch Cdfvrs 1009)	26	1996	0	1996	

ISSUE	TITLE	UK LBL	UK POS	UK YEAR	US POS	US YEAR	US LBL
Kinky Machine	Male Vocal/Instrumental Group from the UK						
1	Supernatural Giver	(Lemon Lemon 006cd)	70	1993	0	1993	
2	Shockaholic	(Oxygen Gaspd 5)	70	1993	0	1993	
3	Going Out With God	Oxygen Gaspd 9)	74	1993	0	1993	
4	10 Second Bionic Man	(Oxygen Gaspd 14)	66	1994	0	1994	
Kirby Stone Four	B: 27 Apr 1918 New York City						
1	Baubles, Bangles And Beads		0	1958	25	1958	(Columbia 41183)
	THE OTHER THREE MEMBERS ARE LARRY FOSTER, EDDIE HALL & MIKE GARDNER						
Kiri Te Kanawa	Female Vocalist from New Zealand						
1	World In Union	(Columbia 6574817)	4	1991	0	1991	
Kirsty MacColl	Female Vocalist from the UK						
1	There's A Guy Works Down The Chip Shop Swears He's Elvis	(Polydor Posp250)	14	1981	0	1981	
3	Greetings To The New Brunette	(Go! Discs God 12)	59	1986	0	1986	
2	A New England	(Stiff Buy 216)	7	1985	0	1985	
4	Fairytale Of New York	(Pogue Mahone Ny 7)	2	1987	0	1987	
5	Free World	(Virgin Kma 1)	43	1989	0	1989	
6	Days	(Virgin Kma 2)	12	1989	0	1989	
7	Walking Down Madison	(Virgin Vs 1348)	23	1991	0	1991	
8	My Affair	(Virgin Vs 1354)	56	1991	0	1991	
9	Fairytale Of New York	(Pm Yz 628)	36	1991	0	1991	
10	Caroline	(Virgin Vscdt 1517)	58	1995	0	1995	
11	Perfect Day	(Virgin Vscdt 1552)	75	1995	0	1995	
12	Days (Re-Issue)	(Virgin Vscdt 1558)	42	1995	0	1995	
	HIT 3 IS CREDITED TO BILLY BRAGG WITH JOHNNY MARR & KIRSTY MACCOLL • HIT 11 IS CREDITED TO KIRSTY MACCOLL AND ECAN DANDO						
	HITS 4, 9 ARE CREDITED TO THE POGUES FEATURING KIRSTY MACCOLL						
Kiss	Male Vocal/Instrumental Group from the USA						
1	Rock And Roll All Nite (Live)		0	1975	12	1975	(Casablanca 850)
2	Shout It Out Loud		0	1976	31	1976	(Casablanca 854)
* 3	Beth		0	1976	7	1976	(Casablanca 863)
4	Hard Luck Woman		0	1977	15	1977	(Casablanca 873)
5	Calling Dr. Love		0	1977	16	1977	(Casablanca 880)
6	Christine Sixteen		0	1977	25	1977	(Casablanca 889)
7	Rocket Ride		0	1978	39	1978	(Casablanca 915)
* 8	I Was Made For Lovin' You	(Casablanca Can 152)	50	1979	11	1979	(Casablanca 983)
9	A World Without Heros	(Casablanca Kiss 002)	55	1982	0	1982	
10	Creatures Of The Night	(Casablanca Kiss 4)	34	1983	0	1983	
11	Lick It Up	(Vertigo Kiss 5)	31	1983	0	1983	
12	Heaven's On Fire	(Vertigo Ver 12)	43	1984	0	1984	
13	Tears Are Falling	(Vertigo Kiss 6)	57	1985	0	1985	
14	Crazy Crazy Nights	(Vertigo Kiss 7)	4	1987	0	1987	
15	Reason To Live	(Vertigo Kiss 8)	33	1987	0	1987	
16	Turn On The Night	(Vertigo Kiss 9)	41	1988	0	1988	
17	Hide Your Heart	(Vertigo Kiss 10)	59	1989	0	1989	
18	Forever	(Vertigo Kiss 11)	65	1990	8	1990	(Mercury 876716)
19	God Gave Rock And Roll To You II	(Interscope A 8696)	4	1992	0	1992	
20	Unholy	(Mercury Kiss 12)	26	1992	0	1992	
Kiss AMC	Female Vocal Duo from the UK						
1	A Bit Of...	(Syncopate Sy 29)	58	1989	0	1989	
2	A Bit Of U2 (Re-Entry)	(Syncopate Sy 29)	58	1989	0	1989	
3	My Docks	(Syncopate Xamc 1)	66	1990	0	1990	
	COPYRIGHT PROBLEMS PREVENTED FULL TITLE OF HIT 1, BEFORE THE RE-ENTRY						
Kissing The Pink	Mixed Vocal/Instrumental Group from the UK						
1	Last Film	(Magnet KTP 3)	19	1983	0	1983	
Kit Carson	Orchestra Conductor, Real Name Liza Morrow						
1	Band Of Gold		0	1955	11	1955	(Capitol 3283)
Kitty Kallen	Female Vocalist, B: 25 May 1922 South Philadelphia						
* 1	Besame Mucho (Kiss Me)		0	1943	1	1943	(Decca 18574)
2	Kiss Me Sweet		0	1949	30	1949	(Mercury 5265)
3	Juke Box Annie		0	1950	17	1950	(Mercury 5417)
4	The Aba Daba Honeymoon		0	1950	10	1950	(Mercury 5466)
5	Are You Looking For A Sweetheart?		0	1953	27	1953	(Decca 28904)
* 6	Little Things Mean A Lot	(Brunswick 05287)	1	1954	1	1954	(Decca 29037)

ISSUE	TITLE	UK LBL	UK POS	UK YEAR	US POS	US YEAR	US LBL
* 7	In The Chapel In The Moonlight		0	1954	4	1954	(Decca 29130)
8	I Want You All To Myself (Just You)		0	1954	23	1954	(Decca 29268)
9	Go On With The Wedding		0	1956	39	1956	(Decca 29776)
10	If I Give My Heart To You		0	1959	34	1959	(Columbia 41473)
11	My Colouring Book		0	1963	18	1963	(RCA 8124)

Kitty Wells Female Vocalist, Real Name Muriel Ellen Deason B: 30 Aug 1919 Nashville, Tennessee

1	It Wasn't God Who Made Honky Tonk Angels		0	1952	27	1952	(Decca 28232)
2	The Things I Might Have Done		0	1953	22	1953	(Decca 28525)

OTHER HITS ARE C/W • KNOWN AS THE QUEEN OF COUNTRY MUSIC WITH A LIFE-TIME RECORDING CONTRACT WITH DECCA

Kix Names Ronnie Younkins, Brian Forsythe, Steve Whiteman, Donnie Pumell & Jimmy Chalfant

* 1	Don't Close Your Eyes		0	1989	11	1989	(Atlantic 88902)

Kiyohiko Ozaki Male Vocalist From Japan

* 1	Mata Au Hi Made (Lovers And Fools)		0	1972	0	1972	

Kiyoko Suizenji The Hit Was Number 1 In Japan

* 1	Daishobu		0	1970	0	1970	

Klark Kent Male Vocal/Multi-Instrumentalist from the USA

1	Don't Care	(A&M Ams 7376)	48	1978	0	1978	

Klaxons Male Vocal/Instrumental Group from Belgium

1	The Clap Clap Song	(PRT 7p 290)	45	1983	0	1983	

Kleeer Mixed Vocal/Instrumental Group from the USA

1	Keep Your Body Working	(Atlantic LV 21	51	1979	0	1979	
2	Get Tough	(Atlantic 11560)	49	1981	0	1981	

KLF Male Vocal/Instrumental Duo, Names Jimmy Cauty & Bill Drummond

1	What Time Is Love (Live At Trancentral)	(Klf Communications Klf 004)	2	1990	0	1990	
* 2	3 A.M. Eternal	(Klf Communications Klf 005)	1	1991	5	1991	(Arista 2230)
3	Last Train To Trancentral	(Klf Communications Klf 008)	2	1991	0	1991	
4	Justified And Ancient	(Klf Communications Klf 099)	2	1991	11	1992	(Arista 12401)
5	America: What Time Is Love	(Klf Communications Klfusa 004)	4	1992	0	1992	

INITIALS STAND FOR KOPYRIGHT LIBERATION FRONT • HIT 4 IS CREDITED TO KLF FEATURING TAMMY WYNETTE

Klubbheads Male Instrumental/Production Duo from Holland Duo Also Known As Itty Bitty Boozy Woozy

1	Klubbhopping	(Am:Pm 5815572)	10	1996	0	1996	
2	Discohoppin	(Am:Pm 5823032)	35	1997	0	1997	

Klymaxx Black Female Band from Los Angeles

1	I Miss You		0	1985	5	1985	(Constellation 52606)
2	Man Size Love		0	1986	15	1986	(MCA 52841)
3	I'd Still Say Yes		0	1987	18	1987	(Constellation 53028)

Knack Male Vocal/Instrumental Group from the USA Names Berton Averre, Doug Fieger, Bruce Gary & Prescott Niles

*1	My Sharona	(Capitol CI 16087)	6	1979	1	1979	(Capitol 4731)
2	Good Girls Don't	(Capitol CI 16097)	66	1979	11	1979	(Capitol 4771)
3	Baby Talks Dirty		0	1980	38	1980	(Capitol 822)

Knickerbockers Male Vocal/Instrumental Group from New Jersey Originally Known As The Castle Kings In 1964

1	Lies		0	1966	20	1966	(Challenge 59321)

Kobie Powell & Rahsaan See US3

Kokomo (1) Mixed Vocal/Instrumental Group from the UK

1	A Little Bit Further Away	(CBS A 2064)	45	1982	0	1982	

Kokomo (2) Male Pianist, Real Name Jimmy Wisner B: 8 Dec 1931 Philadelphia

1	Asia Minor	(London Hlu 9305)	35	1961	8	1961	(Felsted 8612)

Kon Kan Male Vocal/Instrumental Duo from Canada Names Kevin Wynne & Barry Harris, Kevin Left In 1989

1	I Beg Your Pardon	(Atlantic A 8969)	5	1989	15	1989	(Atlantic 88969)

Kool & The Gang Male Vocal/Instrumental Group from the USA

1	Funky Stuff		0	1973	29	1973	(De-Lite 557)
* 2	Jungle Boogie		0	1974	4	1974	(De-Lite 559)
* 3	Hollywood Swinging		0	1974	6	1974	(De-Lite 561)
4	Higher Plane		0	1974	37	1974	(De-Lite 1562)
5	Spirit Of The Boogie		0	1975	35	1975	(De-Lite 1567)
* 6	Ladies Night	(Mercury Kool 7)	9	1979	8	1979	(De-Lite 801)
* 7	Too Hot	(Mercury Kool 8)	23	1980	5	1980	(De-Lite 802)
8	Hangin' Out	(De-Lite Kool 9	52	1980	0	1980	
* 9	Celebration	(De-Lite Kool 10)	7	1980	1	1981	(De-Lite 807)
10	Jones Vs Jones	(De-Lite Kool 11)	17	1981	39	1981	(De-Lite 813)

ISSUE	TITLE	UK LBL	UK POS	UK YEAR	US POS	US YEAR	US LBL
11	Take It To The Top	(De-Lite De 2)	15	1981	0	1981	
12	Steppin' Out	(De-Lite De 4)	12	1981	0	1981	
13	Take My Heart (You Can Have It If You Want It)	(De-Lite De 6)	29	1982	17		1982 (De-Lite 815)
* 14	Get Down On It	(De-Lite De 5)	3	1981	10	1982	(De-Lite 818)
15	Big Fun	(De-Lite De 7)	14	1982	21	1982	(De-Lite 822)
16	Ooh La, La, La (Let's Go Dancin')	(De-Lite De 9)	6	1982	30	1982	(De-Lite 824)
17	Hi De Hi Ho De Ho	(De-Lite De 14)	29	1982	0	1982	
* 18	Joanna	(De-Lite De 16)	2	1984	2	1984	(De-Lite 829)
19	Straight Ahead	(De-Lite De 15)	15	1983	0	1983	
20	Tonight	(De-Lite De 16)	2	1984	13	1984	(De-Lite 830)
21	(When You Say You Love Somebody) In The Heart	(De-Lite De 17)	7	1984	0	1984	
22	Fresh	(De-Lite De 18)	11	1984	9	1985	(De-Lite 880623)
23	Misled	(De-Lite De 19)	28	1985	10	1985	(De-Lite 880431)
* 24	Cherish	(De-Lite De 20)	4	1985	2	1985	(De-Lite 880869)
25	Emergency	(De-Lite De 21)	50	1985	18	1985	(De-Lite 884199)
26	Victory	(Club Jab 44)	67	1986	10	1986	(De-Lite 888074)
27	Victory (Re-Entry)	(Club Jab 44)	30	1986	0	1986	
28	Stone Love	(Club Jab 47)	45	1987	10	1987	(Mercury 888292)
29	Celebration (Re-Mix)	(Club Jab 78)	56	1988	0	1988	
30	Get Down On It (Re-Mix)	(Mercury Mer 346)	69	1991	0	1991	

NAMES ROBERT 'KOOL' EARL, RONALD BELL, CLAUDE SMITH, ROBERT MICKENS, GEORGE BROWN & REEDMAN THOMAS

Korgis Male Vocal/Instrumental Duo, Andy Davis & James Warren from the UK

Names Andy Davis & James Warren

1	If I Had You	(Rialto Treb 103)	13	1979	0	1979	
2	Everybody's Got To Learn Sometime	(Rialto Treb 115)	5	1980	18	1980	(Asylum 47055)
3	If It's Alright With You Baby	(Rialto Treb 118)	56	1980	0	1980	

Korn Male Vocal/Instrumental Group from the USA

1	No Place To Hide	(Epic 6638452)	26	1996	0	1996	
2	A.D.I.D.A.S.	(Epic 6642042)	22	1997	0	1997	
3	Good God	(Epic 6646585)	25	1997	0	1997	

Kraftwerk Male Vocal/Instrumental Group from Germany, Formed In West Germany In 1970, The Name Means Power Station

1	Autobahn	(Vertigo 6147 012)	11	1975	25	1975	(Vertigo 203)
2	Neon Lights	(Capitol Cl 15998)	53	1978	0	1978	
3	Pocket Calculator	(EMI 5175)	39	1981	0	1981	
4	Computer Love / The Model	(EMI 5207)	36	1981	0	1981	
5	Computer Love / The Model (Re-Entr	(EMI 5207)	1	1981	0	1981	
7	Show Room Dummies	(EMI 5272)	25	1982	0	1982	
8	Tour De France	(EMI 5413)	22	1983	0	1983	
9	Tour De France (Re-Entry)	(EMI 5413)	24	1984	0	1984	
10	The Robots	(EMI Em 192)	20	1991	0	1991	
11	Radioactivity	(EMI Em 201)	43	1991	0	1991	

Krankies Husband And Wife Vocal Duo From Scotland

1	Fan'dabi'dozi	Monarch Mon 21)	71	1981	0	1981	
2	Fan'dabi'dozi (Re-Entry)	(Monarch Mon 21)	46	1981	0	1981	

Kraze Mixed Vocal/Instrumental Group from the USA

1	The Party	(MCA MCA 1288)	29	1988	0	1988	
2	Let's Play House	(MCA MCA 1337)	71	1989	0	1989	

Kreuz Male Vocal Group from the UK

1	Party All Night	w(Diesel Des 004c)	75	1995	0	1995	

Krew-Kats Male Instrumental Group from the UK

1	Trambone	(HMV Pop 840)	33	1961	0	1961	
2	Trambone (Re-Entry)	(HMV Pop 840)	49	1961	0	1961	

Kris Jensen Real Name Peter Jensen B: 4 Apr 1942 New Haven, Connecticut

1	Torture		0	1962	20	1962	(Hickory 1173)

Kris Kristofferson Male Actor/Vocalist, B: 22 Jun 1936 Brownsville, Texas

1	Loving Her Was Easier (Than Anything I'll Ever Do Again)		0	1971	26	1971	(Monument 8525)
2	Josie		0	1972	63	1972	(Monument 8536)
* 3	Why Me Lord?		0	1973	16	1973	(Monument 8571)
4	A Song I'd Like To Sing		0	1973	49	1973	(A&M 1475)
5	Loving Arms		0	1974	86	1974	(A&M 1498)

Kris Kross Male Rap Duo from the USA)

* 1	Jump	(Ruff House 6578547)	2	1992	1	1992	(Ruffhouse 74197)

ISSUE	TITLE	UK LBL	UK POS	UK YEAR	US POS	US YEAR	US LBL
* 2	Warm It Up	(Ruff House 6582187)	16	1992	13	1992	(Ruffhouse 74376)
3	I Missed The Bus	(Ruff House 6583927)	57	1992	0	1992	
4	It's A Shame	(Ruff House 6588587)	31	1992	0	1992	
* 5	Alright	(Ruff House 6595652)	47	1993	19	1993	(Ruddhouse 77103)
* 6	Tonite's Tha Night		0	1995	12	1995	(Ruffhouse 78092)

Kristin Hersh Female Vocalist from the USA

1	Your Ghost	(4ad Ban 4001cd)	49	1994	0	1994	
2	Strings	(4ad Ban 4006cd)	60	1994	0	1994	

Kristine W Female Vocalist from the USA

1	Love Come Home	(Triangle Bluescd 001)	73	1994	0		1994
2	Feel What You Want	(Champion Champcd 304)	33	1994	0	1994	
3	One More Try	(Champion Champcd 317)	41	1996	78	1996	(RCA 64533)
4	Land Of The Living	(Champion Champcd 324)	57	1996	0	1996	
5	Feel What You Want (Re-Recording)	(Champion Champcd 329)	40	1997	0	1997	

HIT 1 IS CREDITED TO OUR TRIBE WITH FRANKE PHAROAH AND KRISTINE W

Krokus Male Vocal/Instrumental Group from Argenti, Switzerland

1	Industrial Strength (EP)	(Ariola Aro 258)	62	1981	0	1981	

KRS One Male Rapper from the USA

1	Rappaz Rn Dainja	(Jive Jivecd 396)	47	1996	0	1996	
2	Word Perfect	(RCA 74321424732)	70	1997	0	1997	
3	Step Into A World (Rapture's Delight)	(Jive Jivecd 411)	24	1997	71	1997	(Jive 42442)

Krush Mixed Vocal/Instrumental Group from the UK

1	House Arrest	(Club Jab 63)	3	1987	0	1987	
2	Walking On Sunshine	(Network Nwk 55)	71	1992	0	1992	

Krush Perspective Female Vocal Group from the UK

1	Let's Get Together (So Goovy Now)	(Perspective Perd 7416)	61	1993	0	1993	

Kula Shaker Male Vocal/Instrumental Group from the UK

1	Grateful When You're Dead - Jerry Was There	(Columbia Kulacd 2)	35	1996	0	1996	
2	Tattva	(Columbia Kulacd 3)	4	1996	0	1996	
3	Hey Dude	(Columbia Kulacd 4)	2	1996	0	1996	
4	Govinda	(Columbia Kulacd 5)	7	1996	0	1996	
5	Hush	(Columbia Kulacd 6)	2	1997	0	1997	
6	Hush (Re-Entry)	(Columbia Kulacd 6)	70	1997	0	1997	

LEAD SINGER CRISPIAN MILLS, SON OF ACTRESS HAYLEY MILLS

Kursaal Flyers Male Vocal/Instrumental Group from the UK

1	Little Does She Know	(CBS 4689)	14	1976	0	1976	

Kurtis Blow Male Vocalist from the USA

1	Christmas Rappin'	(Mercury Blow 7)	30	1979	0	1979	
2	The Breaks	(Mercury Blow 8)	47	1980	0	1980	
3	Party Time	(Club Jab 12)	67	1985	0	1985	
4	Save Your Love (For Number 1)	(Club Jab 14)	66	1985	0	1985	
5	If I Ruled The World	(Club Jab 26)	24	1986	0	1986	
6	I'm Chillin'	(Club Jab 42)	64	1986	0	1986	

HIT 4 IS CREDITED TO RENE' AND ANGELA FEATURING KURTIS BLOW

Kut Klose Female Vocal Trio from the USA

1	I Like	(Elektra Ekr 200cd	72	1995	34	1995	(Keia/Elektra 64486)

KWS Male Vocal/Instrumental Trio from Nottingham. England

1	Please Don't Go / Game Boy	(Network Nwk 46)	1	1992	6	1992	(Next Plat. 339)
2	Rock Your Baby	(Network Nwk 54)	8	1992	0	1992	
3	Hold Back The Night	(Network Nwk 65)	30	1992	0	1992	
4	Can't Get Enough Of Your Love	(Network Nwkcd 72)	71	1993	0	1993	
5	It Seems To Hang On	(X-Clusive Xclu 006cd)	58	1994	0	1994	
6	Ain't Nobody (Loves Me Better)	(X-Clusive Xclu 010cd)	21	1994	0	1994	
7	The More I Get The More I Want	(X-Clusive Xclu 011cd)	35	1994	0	1994	

Kylie Minogue Female Actress/Vocalist, B: 28 May 1968 Melbourne, Australia

1	I Should Be So Lucky	(Pwl Pwl 8)	1	1988	28	1988	(Geffen 27922)
2	Got To Be Certain	(Pwl Pwl 12)	2	1988	0	1988	
3	The Loco-Motion	(Pwl Pwl 14)	2	1988	3	1988	(Geffen 27752)
4	Je Ne Sais Pas Pourquoi	(Pwl Pwl 21)	2	1988	0	1988	
5	Especially For You	(Pwl Pwl 24)	1	1988	0	1988	
6	It's No Secret		0	1989	37	1989	(Geffen 27651)
7	Hand On Your Heart	(Pwl Pwl 35)	1	1989	0	1989	

ISSUE	TITLE	UK LBL	UK POS	UK YEAR	US POS	US YEAR	US LBL
8	Wouldn't Change A Thing	(Pwl Pwl 42)	2	1989	0	1989	
9	Never Too Late	(Pwl Pwl 45)	4	1989	0	1989	
10	Tears On My Pillow	(Pwl Pwl 47)	1	1990	0	1990	
11	Better The Devil You Know	(Pwl Pwl 56)	2	1990	0	1990	
12	Step Back In Time	(Pwl Pwl 64)	4	1990	0	1990	
13	What Do I Have To Do	(Pwl Pwl 72)	6	1991	0	1991	
14	Shocked	(Pwl Pwl 81)	6	1991	0	1991	
15	Word Is Out	(Pwl Pwl 204)	16	1991	0	1991	
16	If You Were With Me Now	(Pwl Pwl 208)	4	1991	0	1991	
17	Keep On Pumping It	(Pwl Pwl 207)	49	1991	0	1991	
18	Give Me Just A Little More Time	(Pwl Pwl 212)	2	1992	0	1992	
19	Finer Feelings	(Pwl International Pwl 227)	11	1992	0	1992	
20	What Kind Of Fool (Heard It All Before)	(Pwl International Pwl 241)	14	1992	0	1992	
21	Celebration	(Pwl International Pwl 257)	0	1992	0	1992	
22	Confide In Me	(Deconstruction 74321227482)	73	1994	0	1994	
23	Put Yourself In My Place	(Deconstruction 74321246572)	11	1994	0	1994	
24	Where Is The Feeling	(Deconstruction 74321293612)	16	1995	0	1995	
25	Where The Wild Roses Grow	(Mute Cdmute 185)	11	1995	0	1995	

Kym Mazelle   Female Vocalist from the USA

ISSUE	TITLE	UK LBL	UK POS	UK YEAR	US POS	US YEAR	US LBL
1	Useless (I Don't Need You Now)	(Syncopate Sy 18)	53	1988	0	1988	
2	Wait	(RCA Pb 42595)	7	1989	0	1989	
3	Got To Get You Back	(Syncopate Sy 25)	29	1989	0	1989	
4	Love Strain	(Syncopate Sy 30)	52	1989	0	1989	
5	Was That All It Was	(Syncopate Sy 32)	33	1990	0	1990	
6	Useless (I Don't Need You Now) (Re-Mix)	(Syncopate Sy 36)	48	1990	0	1990	
7	Missing You	(Ten Ten 345)	22	1990	0	1990	
8	No One Can Love You More Than Me	(Parlophone R 6287)	62	1991	0	1991	
9	Love Me The Right Way	(Logic 74321128097)	22	1992	0	1992	
10	No More Tears (Enough Is Enough)	(Ding Dong 74321209032)	13	1994	0	1994	
11	Gimme All Your Lovin'	(Ding Dong 74321231322)	22	1994	0	1994	
12	Searching For The Golden Eye	(Eternal Wea 027cd)	40	1995	0	1995	
13	Love Me The Right Way (Re-Mix)	(Logic 74321404442)	55	1996	0	1996	
14	Young Hearts Run Free		20	1997	0	1997	

HIT 2 IS CREDITED TO ROBERT HOWARD AND KYM MAZELLE • HIT 7 IS CREDITED TO SOUL II SOUL FEATURING KYM MAZELLE
HITS 9, 13 ARE CREDITED TO RAPINATION AND KYM MAZELLE • HIT 12 IS CREDITED TO MOTIV 8 AND KYM MAZELLE

Kym Sims   Female Vocalist, B: 28 Dec 1966 from Chicago

ISSUE	TITLE	UK LBL	UK POS	UK YEAR	US POS	US YEAR	US LBL
1	Too Blind To See It	(Atco B 8667)	5	1991	38	1992	(Atco 98667)
2	Take My Advice	(Atco B 8591)	13	1992	0	1992	
3	A Little Bit More	(Atco B 8528)	30	1992	0	1992	
4	We Gotta Love	(Pulse 8 Cdlose 104)	58	1996	0	1996	

Kyper   B: Randall Kyper From Baton Rouge, Louisiana

ISSUE	TITLE	UK LBL	UK POS	UK YEAR	US POS	US YEAR	US LBL
1	Tic-Tac-Toe		0	1990	14	1990	(Atlantic 87910)

Kyu Sakamoto   Male Vocalist, B: 1942 Kawasaki, Japan

ISSUE	TITLE	UK LBL	UK POS	UK YEAR	US POS	US YEAR	US LBL
* 1	Sukiyaki	(HMV Pop 1171)	6	1963	1	1963	(Capitol 4945)

HIT RELEASED IN JAPAN AS UE O MUITE ARUKO (I LOOK UP WHEN I WALK)) • OBITUARY : D: 12 AUG 1985 PLANE CRASH

L

ISSUE	TITLE	UK LBL	UK POS	UK YEAR	US POS	US YEAR	US LBL
L.A. Guns Mixed Vocal/Instrumental Group from the USA							
1	The Ballad Of Jayne	(Mercury NER 358)	53	1991	33	1990	(Vertigo 87698)
2	Some Lie 4 Love	(Mercury NER 361)	61	1991	0	1991	
L.A. Mix Mixed Vocal/Instrumental Duo from the UK							
1	Don't Stop (Jammin')	(Breakout USA 615)	47	1987	0	1987	
2	Check This Out	(Breakout USA 629)	6	1988	0	1988	
3	Get Loose	(Breakout USA659)	25	1989	0	1989	
4	Love Together	(Breakout USA 662)	66	1989	0	1989	
5	Coming Back For More	(A&M AM 579)	50	1990	0	1990	
6	Mysteries Of Love	(A&M AM 707)	46	1991	0	1991	
7	We Shouldn't Hold Hands In The Dark	(A&M AM 755)	69	1991	0	1991	
L.J. Johnson Male Vocalist from the USA							
1	Your Magic Put A Spell On Me	(Philips 6006 492)	27	1976	0	1976	
L.J. Reynolds Male Vocalist from the USA							
1	Don't Let Nobody Hold You Down	(CLUB JAB 5)	53	1984	0	1984	
L.L. Cool J Male Rapper, Real Name James Todd Smith And Hails From New York, His Stage Name Means Ladies Love Cool James							
1	I'm Bad	(DEF JAM 6508567)	71	1987	0	1987	
2	I Need Love	(DEF JAM 6511017)	8	1987	14	1987	(DEF JAM 07350)
3	Go Cut Creator Go	(DEF JAM LLCD 1)	66	1987	0	1987	
* 4	Going Back To Cali (From *Less Than Zero*)	(DEF JAM LLCD 2)	37	1988	31	1988	(DEF JAM 07679)
* 5	I'm The Type Of Guy	(DEF JAM LLCJ 3)	43	1989	15	1989	(DEF JAM 68902)
* 6	Around The Way Girl	(DEF JAM 6564470)	41	1990	9	1990	(DEF JAM 73609)
7	Mama Said Knock You Out	(DEF JAM 6564470)	41	1990	17	1991	(DEF JAM 73706)
* 8	Around The Way Girl (Re-Issue)	(DEF JAM 6564470)	36	1991	9	1991	(DEF JAM 73609)
9	How I'm Comin'	(DEF JAM 6591692)	37	1993	0	1993	
* 10	Hey Lover	(DEF JAM DEFCD14)	17	1996	3	1995	(DEF JAM/RAL 577494)
11	Doin' It	(DEF JAM DEFCD 15)	15	1996	9	1996	(DEF JAM)
* 12	Loungin'	(DEF JAM DEFCD 30)	7	1996	3	1996	(Mercury 575)
13	Ain't Nobody (From *Beavis And Butt-Head Do America*)	(Geffen GFSTD 22195)	1	1997	46	1996	(Geffen 19410)
14	Hit 'Em High (The Monstars' Anthem)	(Atlantic A 5449CD)	8	1997	0	1997	
L.N.R. Male Vocal/Instrumental Duo from the USA							
1	Work It To The Bone	(Kool Kat Kool 501)	64	1989	0	1989	
L.T.D. Male Vocal/Instrumental Group from the USA, The Initials Stand For Love, Togetherness And Devotion							
1	Love Ballad		0	1976	20	1976	(A&M 1847)
* 2	(Every Time I Turn Around) Back In Love Again		0	1977	4	1977	(A&M 1974)
3	Holding On (When Love Is Gone)	(A&M AMS 7378)	70	1978	0	1978	
4	Shine On		0	1981	40	1981	(A&M 2283)
L.V. Male Vocalist/Rapper from Los Angeles							
* 1	Gangsta's Paradise	(Tommy Boy MCSTD 2104)	1	1995	1	1995	(MCA 55104) with Coolio
2	Throw Your Hands Up/Gangsta's Paradise	(Tommy Boy TBCD 699)	24	1995	0	1995	
3	I Am Lv	(Tommy Boy TBCD 7724)	64	1996	0	1996	
L.W.S. Male Instrumental Group from Italy							
1	Gosp	(Transworld Tranny 4CD)	65	1994	0	1994	
L7 Female Vocal/Instrumental Group from the USA							
1	Pretend We're Dead	(Slash Lash 34)	21	1992	0	1992	
2	Everglade	(Slash Lash 36)	27	1992	0	1992	
3	Monster	(Slash Lash 38)	33	1992	0	1992	
4	Pretend We're Dead (Re-Issue)	(Slash Lash)	50	1992	0	1992	
5	Andres	(Slash LASCD 48)	34	1994	0	1994	

ISSUE	TITLE	UK LBL	UK POS	UK YEAR	US POS	US YEAR	US LBL
La Belle Epoque	Female Vocal Duo from France						
1	Black Is Black	(Harvest HAR 5133)	48	1977	0	1977	
2	Black Is Black (Re-Entry)	(Harvest HAR 5133)	2	1977	0	1977	
La Bionda	Mixed Vocal Group from Italy						
1	One For You One For Me	(Philips 6198 227)	54	1978	0	1978	
La Bouche	Mixed Rap/Vocal Duo, Lane McCray and Melanie Thornton, from the USA						
1	Sweet Dreams	(Bell 7432122912)	63	1994	0	1994	
* 2	Be My Lover	(Arista 74321265402)	27	1995	6	1995	(RCA 64446)
3	Falling In Love	(Arista74321305102)	43	1995	0	1995	
4	Be My Lover (Re-Mix)	(Arista74321339822)	25	1996	6	1996	(RCA)
5	Sweet Dreams (Re-Issue)	(Arista 74321398542)	44	1996	13	1996	(RCA 64505)
La Fleur	Mixed Vocal/Instrumental Group from Holland						
1	Boogie Nights	(PROTO ENA 111)	51	1983	0	1983	
La Ganz	Male Vocal/Instrumental Group from the USA						
1	Like A Playa	(JIVE JIVECD 405)	75	1996	0	1996	
La's	Male Vocal/Instrumental Group from the UK						
1	There She Goes	(Go! Discs Golas 2)	59	1989	0	1989	
2	Timeless Melody	(Go! Discs Golas 4)	57	1990	0	1990	
3	There She Goes (Re-Issue)	(Go! Discs Golas 5)	13	1990	0	1990	
4	Feelin'	(Go! Discs Golas 6)	43	1991	0	1991	
Labelle	Female Vocal Group from the USA						
* 1	Lady Marmalade	(Epic EPC 2852)	17	1975	1	1975	(Epic 50048)
	Names: Patti Labelle, Nona Hendryx, Sarah Dash, Cindy Birdsong • See Also Patti Labelle						
Labi Siffre	Male Vocal Group from the UK						
1	It Must Be Love	(PYE International 7N 25572)	14	1971	0	1971	
2	Crying Laughing Loving Lying	(PYE International 7N 25576)	11	1972	0	1972	
3	Watch Me	(PYE International 7N 25586)	29	1972	0	1972	
4	(Something Inside) So Strong	(China Wok 12)	4	1987	0	1987	
5	Nothin's Gonna Change	(China Wok16)	52	1987	0	1987	
Ladies Choice	Male Vocalist from the UK						
1	Funky Sensation	(Sure Delight SD 01)	41	1986	0	1986	
Lady Flash	Barry Manilow's Backing Singers. Lead Singer Lorraine Mazzola						
1	Street Singin'		0	1976	27	1976	(RSO 852)
Lady Of Rage	Female Rapper from the USA						
1	Afro Puffs	(Interscope A 8288CD)	72	1994	0	1994	
Ladysmith Black Mambazo	Male Vocal Group from South Africa						
1	Swing Low Sweet Chariot	(Polygram TV SWLOW 2)	15	1995	0	1995	
2	World In The Union '95	(Polygram TV Rugby 2)	47	1995	0	1995	
Laid Back	Male Vocal/Instrumental Duo, John Guldberg & Tim Stahl From Denmark						
1	White Horse		0	1984	26	1984	(SIRE 29346)
2	Bakerman	(Arista 112356)	44	1990	0	1990	
Lalah Hathaway	Female Vocalist from the USA						
1	Heaven Knows	(Virgin American VUS 28)	66	1990	0	1990	
2	Baby Don't Cry	(Virgin American VUS 35)	54	1991	0	1991	
3	Family Affair	(TEN TEN 369)	37	1991	0	1991 with BEF	
Lalo Schifrin	Orchestra from the USA						
1	Jaws	(CTI CTSP 005)	14	1976	0	1976	
Lambrettas	Male Vocal/Instrumental Group from the UK						
1	Poison Ivy	(Rocket XPRESS 25)	7	1980	0	1980	
2	D-A-A-Ance	(Rocket XPRESS 33)	12	1980	0	1980	
3	Another Day (Another Girl)	(Rocket XPRESS 36)	49	1980	0	1980	
Lamont Dozier	Male Singer/Songwriter, B: 16 Jun 1941 Detroit						
1	Trying To Hold On To My Woman		0	1974	3	1974	(ABC 11407)
2	Fish Ain't Bitin'		0	1974	26	1974	(ABC 11438)
Lancastrians	Male Vocal/Instrumental Group from the UK						
1	We'll Sing In The Sunshine	(PYE 7N 15732)	47	1964	0	1964	
Lance Ellington	Male Vocalist from the UK						
1	Lonely (Have We Lost Our Love)	(RCA 74321158332)	57	1993	0	1993	

|---|---|---|---|---|---|---|---|
Lance Fortune	Male Vocalist from the UK						
1	Be Mine	(PYE 7N 15240)	4	1960	0	1960	
2	This Love I Have For You	(PYE 7N 15260)	26	1960	0	1960	
Lance Percival	Male Actor/Vocalist from the UK						
1	Shame And Scandal In The Family	(Parlophone R 5335)	37	1965	0	1965	
Lancers	Male Vocal Group, often sang backup vocals for other artists such as Kay Starr.						
1	Sweet Mama Tree Top Fall		0	1953	13	1953	(Trend 63)
2	Stop Chasin' Me, Baby		0	1954	26	1954	(Trend 70)
3	Mister Sandman		0	1954	28	1954	(Coral 61288)
Landscape	Male Vocal/Instrumental Group from the UK						
1	Einstein A Go-Go	(RCA 22)	5	1981	0	1981	
2	Norman Bates	(RCA 60)	40	1981	0	1981	
Larks	Names Don Julian, Charles Morrison & Ted Walters, Originally Called Don Julian & The Meadowlarks						
1	The Jerk		0	1964	7	1964	(Money 106)
Larry Cunningham	Male Vocalist from Ireland, With The Instrumental Group The Mighty Avons						
1	Tribute To Jim Reeves	(King KG 1016)	40	1964	0	1964	
2	Tribute To Jim Reeves (Re-Entry)	(King KG 1016)	46	1965	0	1965	
Larry Douglas	Male Vocalist from the USA						
1	Linda (From The Story Of G.I. Joe)		0	1947	14	1947	(Signature 15106)
Larry Elgart & His Manhattan	B: 20 Mar 1922 New London, Connecticut, Swing Orchestra						
1	Hooked On Swing		0	1982	31	1982	(RCA 13219)
Larry Finnegan	Fulll Name John Lawrence Finneran B: 10 Aug 1938 New York City						
* 1	Dear One		0	1962	11	1962	(Old Town 1113)
	Obituary: D: 22 Jul 1973 of a brain tumour.						
Larry Graham	Male Vocalist, B: 14 Aug 1946 Beaumont, Texas						
1	Your Love		0	1975	38	1975	(Warner Bros. 8105)
2	One In A Million		0	1980	9	1980	(Warner Bros. 49221)
3	Sooner Or Later	(Warner Bros. K 17925)	54	1982	0	1982	
	Hit 1 Is Credited To Graham Central Station						
Larry Green Orchestra	Male Pianist/Bandleader from the USA						
1	Near You		0	1947	3	1947	(RCA Victor 2421)
2	Gonna Get A Girl		0	1947	23	1947	(RCA Victor 2560)
3	Song Of New Orleans		0	1947	23	1947	(RCA Victor 2560)
4	Beg Your Pardon		0	1948	8	1948	(RCA Victor 2647)
5	Bella Bella Marie		0	1948	21	1948	(RCA Victor 3072)
6	Bewitched (From Pal Joey)		0	1950	13	1950	(RCA Victor 3726)
7	Can Anyone Explain? (No! No! No!)		0	1950	28	1950	(RCA Victor 3902)
Larry Groce	Male Pop-Folk Singer/Songwriter, B: 22 Apr 1948 Dallas						
1	Junk Food Junkie (Live)		0	1976	9	1976	(Warner Bros. 8165)
Larry Hall	Male Vocalist, B: 3 Jun 1941 Cincinnati						
1	Sandy (Re-Issue)		0	1959	15	1959	(STRAND 25007)
	THE HIT WAS FIRST RELEASED ON A DIFFERENT LABEL, HOT 1						
Larry Santos	Male Vocalist, B: 2 Jun 1941 Oneonto, New York						
1	We Can't Hide It Anymore		0	1976	36	1976	(Casablanca 844)
Larry Verne	Male Vocalist, B: 8 Feb 1936 Minneapolis						
* 1	Mr. Custer		0	1960	1	1960	(ERA 3024)
Larry Williams	Male Vocalist, B: 10 May 1935 New Orleans						
* 1	Short Fat Fannie	(London HLN 8472)	21	1957	5	1957	(Specialty 608)
2	High School Dance		0	1957	5	1957	(Specialty 608)
3	Bony Moronie	(London HLU 8532)	11	1958	14	1957	(Specialty 615)
	OBITUARY: D: 7 JAN 1980 SHOT IN THE HEAD, THE OFFICIAL VERDICT: SUICIDE.						
Larsen-Feiten Band	Session Musicians, Real Name Neil Larson & Buzz Feiten						
1	Who'll Be The Fool Tonight		0	1980	29	1980	(Warner Bros. 49282)
Last Rhythm	Male Instrumental/Production Group from Italy						
1	Last Rhythm	(Stress CDSTR 76)	62	1996	0	1996	
Late Show	Male Vocal/Instrumental Group from the UK						
1	Bristol Stomp	(Decca F 13822)	40	1979	0	1979	
Latimore	Real Name Benjamin Latimore B: 7 Sep 1939 Charleston, Tennessee						
1	Let's Straighten It Out		0	1974	31	1974	(Glades 1722)
2	Somethin''Bout 'Cha		0	1977	37	1977	(Glades 1739)

ISSUE	TITLE	UK LBL	UK POS	UK YEAR	US POS	US YEAR	US LBL
Latin Quarter	Mixed Vocal/Instrumental Group from the UK						
1	Radio Africa	(Rockin' Horse PH 102)	19	1986	0	1986	
2	Nomzamo (One People One Cause)	(Rockin' Horse PH 113)	73	1987	0	1987	
Latin Thing	Mixed Vocal/Instrumental Group from Canada/Spain						
1	Latin Thing	(Faze 2 CDDAZE 33)	41	1996	0	1996	
Latour	Male Producer/Vocalist, Real Name William Latour from Chicago						
1	People Are Still Having Sex	(Polydor PO 147)	15	1991	35	1991	(Smash 879666)
Laura Branigan	Female Vocalist, B: 3 Jul 1957 Brewster, New York						
1	Gloria	(Atlantic K 4048)	6	1982	1	1982	(Atlantic 11759)
2	Solitaire		0	1983	7	1983	(Atlantic 89868)
3	How Am I Supposed To Live Without You		0	1983	12	1983	(Atlantic 89805)
4	Self Control	(Atlantic A 9676)	5	1984	4	1984	(Atlantic 89676)
5	The Lucky One	(Atlantic A 9636)	56	1984	20	1984	(Atlantic 89636)
6	Spanish Eddie		0	1985	40	1985	(Atlantic 89531)
7	Power Of Love		0	1987	26	1987	(Atlantic 89191)
Laura Lee	Full Name Laura Lee Rundless, B: 1945 Chicago						
1	Women's Love Rights		0	1971	36	1971	(Hot Wax 7105)
Laurel & Hardy (1)	UK Male Actor/Vocal Duo with Male Vocal Group from the USA						
1	The Trail Of The Lonesome Pine	(United Artists UP 36026)	2	1975	0	1975	
Laurel & Hardy (2)	Male Vocal/Instrumental Duo from the UK						
1	Clunk Clink	(CBS A 3213)	65	1983	0	1983	
Laurel Aitken & The Unitone	Male Vocal/Instrumental Group from Jamaica/Cuba						
1	Rudi Got Married	(I-SPY SEE 6)	60	1980	0	1980	
Lauren Wood	Singer/Songwriter from Pittsburgh						
1	Please Don't Leave		0	1979	24	1979	(Warner Bros. 49043)
Laurie Anders	Male Comic/Vocalist from the USA						
1	I Like The Wide Open Spaces		0	1951	13	1951	(Columbia 39404) with Arthur Godfrey
Laurie Anderson	Female Vocal/Instrumentalist from the USA						
1	O Superman	(Warner Bros. K 17870)	2	1981	0	1981	
Laurie Johnson	Orchestra from the UK						
1	Sucu Sucu	(PYE 7N 15383)	9	1961	0	1961	
Laurie Lingo & The Dipsticks	Male DJ/Vocal Duo: Dave Lee Travis & Paul Burnett from the UK						
1	Convoy G.B.	(State STAT 23)	4	1976	0	1976	
Laurie London	Male Vocalist, B: 19 Jan 1944 London, Recorded Hit At The Age Of 13						
* 1	He's Got The Whole World In His Hands	(Parlophone R 4359)	12	1957	1	1958	(Capitol 3891)
Laurie Sisters	Female Vocal Group from the USA						
1	Dixie Danny		0	1955	30	1955	(Mercury 70548)
Lavern Baker	Female Vocalist, Real Name Delores Williams, B: 11 Nov 1928 Chicago						
* 1	Tweedle Dee		0	1955	14	1955	(Atlantic 1047)
2	I Can't Love You Enough		0	1956	22	1956	(Atlantic 1104)
3	Jim Dandy		0	1957	17	1957	(Atlantic 1116)
* 4	I Cried A Tear		0	1959	6	1959	(Atlantic 2007)
5	I Waited Too Long		0	1959	33	1959	(Atlantic 2021)
6	You're The Boss		0	1961	81	1961	(Atlantic 2090)
7	Saved		0	1961	37	1961	(Atlantic 2099)
8	See See Rider		0	1963	34	1963	(Atlantic 2167)
Lavine Hudson	Female Vocalist from the UK						
1	Intervention	(Virgin VS 1067)	57	1988	0	1988	
Lavinia Jones	Female Vocalist from South Africa						
1	Sing It To You (Dee-Doob-Dee-Doo)	(Virgin International DINDG 142)	45	1995	0	1995	
Lawrence Cook	Male Pianist from the USA, Nickname Piano Roll						
1	He Old Piano Roll Blues		0	1950	13	1950	(Abbey 15003)
2	Own Yonder		0	1951	22	1951	(Abbey 15053)
Lawrence Reynolds	Male Vocalist from Mobile, Alabama						
1	Jesus Is A Soul Man		0	1969	28	1969	(Warner Bros. 7322)
Lawrence Welk & His Orchestra	Male Orchestra Leader, B: 11 Mar 1903, Strasbourg, North Dakota						
20	Oh Happy Day		0	1953	5	1953	(Coral 60893)
21	Moritat (Theme From *The Threepenny Opera*)		0	1956	17	1956	(Coral 61574)

ISSUE	TITLE	UK LBL	UK POS	UK YEAR	US POS	US YEAR	US LBL
22	The Poor People Of Paris		0	1956	17	1956	(Coral 61592)
23	Weary Blues		0	1956	32	1956	(Coral 61670)
24	Tonight You Belong To Me		0	1956	15	1956	(Coral 61710)
25	Last Date		0	1960	21	1960	(DOT 16145)
* 26	Calcutta		0	1960	1	1960	(DOT 16161)

Le Roux Lead singer with the six-man rock band is Jeff Pollard
| 1 | Nobody Said It Was Easy (Lookin' For The Lights) | | 0 | 1982 | 18 | 1982 | (RCA 13059) |

Leann Rimes Female Vocalist from the USA, Name pronounced Le Ann
| 1 | Blue | | 0 | 1996 | 26 | 1996 | (CURB 76959) |

Leapy Lee Male Vocalist, Real Name Lee Graham B: 2 Jul 1942 In Eastbourne, Sussex, England
* 1	Little Arrows	(MCA MU 1028)	2	1968	16	1968	(Decca 32380)
! 2	Good Morning	(MCA MK 5021)	47	1969	55	1970	(Decca 32625)
3	Good Morning (Re-Entry)	(MCA MK 5021)	29	1970	0	1970	

Leblanc & Carr Names: Lenny Leblanc & Pete Carr from Alabama
| 1 | Falling | | 0 | 1978 | 13 | 1978 | (Big Tree 16100) |

Led Zeppelin First Known As The New Yardbirds, Names: Jimmy Page, John Paul Jones, John Bonham & Robert Plant
* 1	Whole Lotta Love	(Atlantic AT 0013CD)	21	1997	4	1969	(Atlantic 2690)
2	Immigrant Song		0	1970	16	1970	(Atlantic 2777)
3	Black Dog / Misty Mountain Hop		0	1972	15	1972	(Atlantic 2849)
4	D'yer Mak'er		0	1973	20	1973	(Atlantic 2986)
5	Trampled Under Foot		0	1975	38	1975	(Swan Song 70102)
6	Fool In The Rain		0	1980	21	1980	(Swan Song 71003)

IN 1984 PLANT & PAGE FORMED THE HONEYDRIPPERS • OBITUARY: BONHAM D: 25 SEP 1980 OF ASPHYXIATION.

Lee Andrews & The Hearts Real Name Arthur Lee Andrew Thompson from Goldsboro, North Carolina
1	Long Lonely Nights		0	1957	45	1957	(Chess 1665)
2	Tear Drops		0	1957	20	1957	(Chess 1675)
3	Try The Impossible		0	1958	33	1958	(United Artists 123)

Lee Dorsey Male Vocalist, Irving Lee Dorsey B: 24 Dec 1924 Portland, Oregon
* 1	Ya Ya		0	1961	7	1961	(Fury 1053)
2	Do-Re-Mi		0	1962	27	1962	(Fury 1056)
3	Ride Your Pony		0	1965	28	1965	(AMY 927)
4	Get Out Of My Life Woman	(Stateside SS 485)	22	1966	0	1966	
5	Confusion	(Stateside SS 506)	38	1966	0	1966	
6	Working In The Coalmine	(Stateside SS 528)	8	1966	9	1966	(AMY 958)
7	Holy Cow	(Stateside SS 552)	6	1966	23	1966	(AMY 965)

Lee Garrett Male Vocalist from the USA
| 1 | You're My Everything | (Chrysalis CHS 2087) | 15 | 1976 | 0 | 1976 | |

Lee Greenwood Male Vocalist, Melvin Lee Greenwood B: 27 Oct 1942 In Southgate, California
| 1 | The Wind Beneath My Wings | (MCA 877) | 49 | 1974 | 0 | 1974 | |
| 6 | I.O.U. | | 0 | 1983 | 53 | 1983 | (MCA 52199) |

OTHER HITS WERE C/W

Lee Lawrence Male Vocalist from the UK
1	Crying In The Chapel	(Decca F 10177)	11	1953	0	1953	
2	Crying In The Chapel (Re-Entry)	(Decca F 10177)	7	1953	0	1953	
3	Suddenly There's A Valley	(Columbia DB 3681)	19	1955	0	1955	
4	Suddenly There's A Valley (Re-Entry)	(Columbia DB 3681)	14	1955	0	1955	

Lee Marvin Male Actor/Vocalist, B: 19 Feb 1924 New York
* 1	Wand'rin' Star	(Paramount PARA 3004)	1	1970	0	1970	
2	Wand'rin Star (Re-Entry)	(Paramount PARA 3004)	42	1970	0	1970	
3	Wand'rin Star (2nd Re-Entry)	(Paramount PARA 3004)	47	1970	0	1970	

Lee Michaels Male Vocal/Organist, B: 24 Nov 1946 Los Angeles
| 1 | Do You Know What I Mean | | 0 | 1971 | 6 | 1971 | (A&M 1262) |
| 2 | Can I Get A Witness | | 0 | 1971 | 39 | 1971 | (A&M 1303) |

Lee Ritenour Male Guitarist/Composer/Arranger, B: 11 Jan 1952 Los Angeles, nickname is Captain Fingers
| 1 | Is It You | | 0 | 1981 | 15 | 1981 | (Elektra 47124) |
| 2 | Waiting In Vain | (GRP MCSC 1921) | 65 | 1993 | 0 | 1993 | with Maxi Priest |

Leeds United F.C. Male Vocal Soccer Team from the UK
1	Leeds United	(Chapter One SCH 168)	10	1972	0	1972	
2	Leeds Leeds Leeds	(Q Music LUFC 2)	61	1992	0	1992	
3	Leeds Leeds Leeds (Re-Entry)	(Q Music LUFC 2)	54	1992	0	1992	

Leena Conquest Female Vocal Group from the USA
| 1 | Boundaries | (Natural Response 74321208522) | 67 | 1994 | 0 | 1994 | |

ISSUE	TITLE	UK LBL	UK POS	UK YEAR	US POS	US YEAR	US LBL
Left Banke Lead Singer Of The Rock Quintet Is Steve Martin							
1	Walk Away Renee		0	1966	5	1966	(Smash 2041)
2	Pretty Ballerina		0	1967	15	1967	(Smash 2074)
Leftfield Male Production/Instrumental Duo from the UK							
1	Song Of Life	(Hard Hands Hand 002T)	59	1992	0	1992	
2	Open Up	(Hard Hands Hand 009CD)	13	1993	0	1993	
3	Original	(Hard Hands Hand 18CD)	18	1995	0	1995	
4	The Afro-Left (EP)	(Hard Hands Hand 23CD)	22	1995	0	1995	
5	Release The Pressure	(Hard Hands Hand 29CD)	13	1996	0	1996	
Lefty Frizzell Male Country Vocalist William Orville Frizzel B: 31 Mar 1929 In Corsicana, Texas							
5	I Want To Be With You Always		0	1951	29	1951	(Columbia 20799)
21	Saginaw, Michigan		0	1964	85	1964	(Columbia 42924)
	OTHERS ARE C/W HITS. • OBITUARY : D: 19 JUL 1975, (AGED 47).						
Leif Garrett Male Vocalist, B: 8 Nov 1961 Hollywood							
1	Surfin' USA		0	1977	20	1977	(Atlantic 3423)
2	Runaround Sue		0	1977	13	1977	(Atlantic 34409
3	I Was Made For Dancin'	(Scotti Brothers K 11202)	4	1979	10	1978	(Scotti Brothers 403)
4	Feel The Need	(Scotti Brothers K 11274)	38	1979	0	1979	
Leila K Female Vocalist from Sweden							
1	Got To Get	(Arista 112696)	8	1989	0	1989	
2	Rock The Nation	(Arista 112971)	41	1990	0	1990	
3	Open Sesame	(Polydor PQCD 1)	23	1993	0	1993	
4	Ca Plane Pour Moi	(Polydor PQCD 3)	69	1993	0	1993	
	HITS 1 & 2 ARE CREDITED TO ROB 'N' RAZ FEATURING LIELA K						
Lemon Pipers Male Vocal/Instrumental Group from the USA Lead Singer Is Ivan Browne							
* 1	Green Tamborine	(PYE International 7N 25444)	7	1968	1	1968	(Buddah 23)
2	Rice Is Nice	(PYE International 7N 25454)	41	1968	0	1968	
Lemon Trees Male Vocal/Instrumental Group from the UK							
1	Love Is In Your Eyes	(Oxygen GASP 1)	75	1992	0	1992	
2	The Way I Feel	(Oxygen GASP 2)	62	1992	0	1992	
3	Let It Loose	(Oxygen GASPD 3)	55	1993	0	1993	
4	Child Of Love	(Oxygen GASPD 4)	55	1993	0	1993	
5	I Can't Face The World	(Oxygen GASPD 6)	52	1993	0	1993	
Lemonheads Male Vocal/Instrumental Group from the USA/Australia							
1	It's A Shame About Ray	(Atlantic A 7423)	70	1992	0	1992	
2	Mrs Robinson / Bein' Around	(Atlantic A 7401)	19	1992	0	1992	
3	Confetti / My Drug Buddy	(Atlantic A 7430CD)	44	1993	0	1993	
4	It's A Shame About Ray (Re-Issue)	(Atlantic A 5764CD)	31	1993	0	1993	
5	Into Your Arms	(Atlantic A 7302CD)	14	1993	0	1993	
6	It's About Time	(Atlantic A 7396CD)	57	1993	0	1993	
7	Big Gay Heart	(Atlantic A 7259CD)	55	1994	0	1994	
8	If I Could Talk I'd Tell You	(Atlantic A 5495CD)	39	1996	0	1996	
9	It's All True	(Atlantic A 5635CD)	61	1996	0	1996	
Len Barry Male Vocalist, Real Name Leonard Borisoff B: 6 Dec 1942, West Philadelphia							
* 1	1-2-3	(Brunswick 05942)	3	1965	2	1965	(Decca 31827)
2	Like A Baby	(Brunswick 05949)	10	1966	27	1966	(Decca 31889)
3	Somewhere		0	1966	26	1966	(Decca 31923)
Lena Fiagbe Female Vocalist from the UK							
1	You Came From Earth	(Mother MUMCD 42)	69	1993	0	1993	
2	Gotta Get It Right	(Mother MUMCD 44)	20	1993	0	1993	
3	What's It Like To Be Beautiful	(Mother MUMCD 49)	52	1994	0	1994	
4	Visions	(Mother MUMCD 53)	48	1994	0	1994	
5	African Dream	(Mercury MERCD 453)	44	1996	0	1996 with Wasis Diop	
Lena Horne Female Actress/Vocalist, B: 30 Jun 1917 Brooklyn							
3	Deed I Do		0	1948	26	1948	(MGM 10165)
4	Love Me Or Leave Me		0	1955	19	1955	(RCA 6073)
Lena Martell Female Vocalist from the UK							
1	One Day At A Time	(PYE 7N 46021)	1	1979	0	1979	
Lena Zavaroni Female Vocalist from the UK							
1	Ma He's Making Eyes At Me	(Philips 6006 367)	10	1974	0	1974	
2	Personality	(Philips 6006 391)	33	1974	0	1974	

ISSUE	TITLE	UK LBL	UK POS	UK YEAR	US POS	US YEAR	US LBL
Lene Lovich Female Vocalist from the USA							
1	Lucky Number	(Stiff Buy 42)	3	1979	0	1979	
2	Say When	(Stiff Buy 46)	19	1979	0	1979	
3	Bird Song	(Stiff Buy 53)	39	1979	0	1979	
4	What Will I Do Without You	(Stiff Buy 69)	58	1980	0	1980	
5	New Toy	(Stiff Buy 97)	53	1981	0	1981	
6	It's You Only You (Mein Schmerz)	(Stiff Buy 164)	68	1982	0	1982	
Lenny Dee Male Organist, B: In The 1920s In Illinois							
1	Plantation Boogie		0	1955	19	1955	(Decca 29360)
Lenny Kravitz Male Vocalist from the USA							
1	Mr. Cabdriver	(Virgin America VUS 20)	58	1990	0	1990	
2	Let Love Rule	(Virgin America VUS 26)	39	1990	0	1990	
3	Always On The Run	(Virgin America VUS 34)	41	1991	0	1991	
4	It Ain't Over 'Til It's Over	(Virgin America VUS 43)	11	1991	2	1991	(Virgin 98795)
5	Stand By My Woman	(Virgin America VUS 45)	55	1991	0	1991	
6	Are You Gonna Go My Way	(Virgin America VUSDG 65)	4	1993	0	1993	
7	Believe	(Virgin America VUSCD 72)	30	1993	0	1993	
8	Heaven Help	(Virgin America VUSDG 73)	20	1993	0	1993	
9	Is There Any Love In Your Heart	(Virgin America VUSDG 76)	52	1993	0	1993	
10	Rock And Roll Is Dead	(Virgin VUSCD 93)	22	1995	0	1995	
11	Circus	(Virgin VUSCD 96)	54	1995	0	1995	
12	Can't Get You Off My Mind	(Virgin VUSCD 100)	54	1996	0	1996	
Lenny Welch Male Vocalist, B: 15 May 1938 Asbury Park, New Jersey							
1	Since I Fell For You		0	1963	4	1963	(Cadence 1439)
2	Ebb Tide		0	1964	25	1964	(Cadence 1422)
3	Breaking Up Is Hard To Do		0	1970	34	1970	(Common. U. 3004)
Lenny Williams Male Vocalist from the USA							
1	Shoo Doo Fu Fu Ooh	(ABC 4194)	38	1977	0	1977	
2	You Got Me Burning	(ABC 4228)	67	1978	0	1978	
Leo Diamond Male Harmonica Player, B: 29 Jun 1915 New York							
1	Off Shore		0	1953	14	1953	(Ambassador 1005)
2	Melody Of Love		0	1955	30	1955	(RCA 5973)
Leo Sayer Male Vocalist, Real Name Gerald Sayer B: 21 May 1948 Shoreham, Kent, England.							
1	The Show Must Go On	(Chrysalis CHS 2023)	2	1973	0	1973	
2	One Man Band	(Chrysalis CHS 2045)	6	1974	0	1974	
3	Long Tall Glasses (I Can Dance)	(Chrysalis CHS 2052)	4	1974	9	1975	(Warner Bros. 8043)
4	Moonlighting	(Chrysalis CHS 2076)	2	1975	0	1975	
* 5	You Make Me Feel Like Dancing	(Chrysalis CHS 2119)	2	1976	1	1976	(Warner Bros. 8283)
* 6	When I Need You	(Chrysalis CHS 2127)	1	1977	1	1977	(Warner Bros. 8332)
7	How Much Love	(Chrysalis CHS 2140)	10	1977	17	1977	(Warner Bros. 8319)
8	Thunder In My Heart	(Chrysalis CHS 2163)	22	1977	38	1977	(Warner Bros. 8465)
9	Easy To Love		0	1978	36	1978	(Warner Bros. 8502)
10	I Can't Stop Loving You		6	1978	0	1978	
11	Raining In My Heart	(Chrysalis CHS 2277)	21	1978	47	1978	(Warner Bros. 8682)
* 12	More Than I Can Say	(Chrysalis CHS 242)	2	1980	2	1980	(Warner Bros. 49565)
13	Living In A Fantasy		0	1981	23	1981	(Warner Bros.49657)
14	Have You Ever Been In Love	(Chrysalis CHS 2596)	10	1982	0	1982	
15	Heart (Stop Beating In Time)	(Chrysalis CHS 2616)	22	1982	0	1982	
16	Orchard Road	(Chrysalis CHS 2677)	16	1983	0	1983	
17	Till You Come Back To Me	(Chrysalis LEO 01)	51	1983	0	1983	
18	Unchained Melody	(Chrysalis LEO 3)	54	1986	0	1986	
19	When I Need You (Re-Issue)	(Chrysalis CDCHS 3926)	65	1993	0	1993	
Leon Berry Male Instrumentalist (Organ) from the USA							
1	Misirlou		0	1953	26	1953	(DOT 15063)
Leon Haywood Male Vocalist, B: 11 Feb 1942 Houston, Texas							
1	I Want a Do Something Freaky To You		0	1975	15	1975	(20th Century 2228)
2	Don't Push It Don't Force It	(20th Century FOX TC 2443)	12	1980	0	1980	
Leon Russell Male Vocalist/Songwriter, B: 2 Apr 1941 Lawton, Oklahoma							
1	Tight Rope		0	1972	11	1972	(Shelter 7325)
4	Lady Blue		0	1975	14	1975	(Shelter 40378)
	OTHERS WERE C/W HITS						

ISSUE	TITLE	UK LBL	UK POS	UK YEAR	US POS	US YEAR	US LBL
Leonard Bernstein Male Conductor, Orchestra And Chorus from the USA							
1	America - World Cup Theme 1994	(Deutsche Grammophon USACD 1)44		1994	0	1994	
Leopold Stokowski & The Philadelphia Symphony Orchestra B: 18 Apr 1882 In London, England							
* 1	Tales From The Vienna Woods - The Blue Danube		0	1939	0	1939	
Leroy Anderson Orchestra Male Orchestra Leader, B: 29 Jun 1908 Cambridge, Massachusetts							
* 1	The Syncopated Clock		0	1951	12	1951	(Decca 16005)
* 2	Blue Tango		0	1951	1	1951	(Decca 27875)
3	A Christmas Festival		0	1953	22	1953	(Decca 16041)
4	The Typewriter		0	1953	21	1953	(Decca 28881)
5	Forgotten Dreams	(Brunswick 05485)	28	1957	0	1957	
6	Forgotten Dreams (Re-Entry)	(Brunswick 05485)	30	1957	0	1957	
7	Forgotten Dreams (2nd Re-Entry)	(Brunswick 05485)	24	1957	0	1957	
Leroy Holmes Orchestra B: 22 Sep 1913 Pittsburgh, Studied Music At Northwest University							
* 1	The High And The Mighty (Movie Title Song)		0	1954	9	1954	(MGM 11761)
2	Tara's Theme (From *Gone With The Wind*)		0	1954	21	1954	(MGM 11854)
Leroy Van Dyke Male Vocalist, B: 4 Oct 1929 Spring Fork, Missouri							
1	Auctioneer		0	1956	19	1956	(DOT 15503)
* 2	Walk On By	(Mercury AMT 1166)	5	1962	5	1961	(Mercury 71834)
3	If A Woman Answers (Hang Up The Phone)		0	1962	35	1962	(Mercury 71926)
4	Big Man In A Big House	(Mercury AMT 1173)	34	1962	0	1962	
	OTHERS ARE C/W HITS • ONE OF HIS PREVIOUS JOBS WAS A LIVESTOCK AUCTIONEER						
Les Baxter Orchestra Leader, B: 14 Mar 1922 Mexia, Texas							
1	Because Of You		0	1951	4	1951	(Capitol 1760)
2	Blue Tango		0	1952	10	1952	(Capitol 1966)
3	Lovely Wine		0	1952	26	1952	Capitol 2106)
4	Auf Wiederseh'n Sweetheart		0	1952	20	1952	(Capitol 2143)
5	April In Portugal		0	1953	2	1953	(Capitol 2374)
6	Ruby		0	1953	7	1953	(Capitol 2457)
7	Gigi (From *Can Can*)		0	1953	23	1953	(Capitol 2479)
8	I Love Paris (From *Can Can*)		0	1953	13	1953	(Capitol 2479)
9	The High And The Mighty		0	1954	8	1954	(Capitol 2845)
* 10	Unchained Melody	(Capitol CL 14257)	10	1955	1	1955	(Capitol 3055)
11	Wake The Town And Tell The People		0	1955	5	1955	(Capitol 3120)
* 12	The Poor People Of Paris		0	1956	1	1956	(Capitol 3336)
Les Brown Orchestra Male Clarinetist/Bandleader, B: 14 Mar 1912 Reinertown, Pennsylvania							
14	You Won't Be Satisfied (Until You Break My Heart)		0	1946	4	1946	(Columbia 36884)
15	Doctor, Lawyer, Indian Chief (From *The Stork Club*)		0	1946	6	1946	(Columbia 36945)
16	Day By Day		0	1946	15	1946	(Columbia 36945)
17	I Got The Sun In The Morning (From *Annie Get Your Gun*)		0	1946	10	1946	(Columbia 36977)
18	I Guess I'll Get The Papers (And Go Home)		0	1946	11	1946	(Columbia 37066)
19	The Whole World Is Singing My Song		0	1946	6	1946	(Columbia 37066)
20	The Best Man		0	1946	15	1946	(Columbia 37086)
21	The Christmas Song		0	1947	12	1947	(Columbia 37174)
22	Sooner Or Later (From *The Song Of The South*)		0	1947	13	1947	(Columbia 37153)
* 23	I've Got My Love To Keep Me Warm (From *On The Avenue*)		0	1949	1	1949	(Columbia 38234)
24	It Isn't Fair		0	1950	22	1950	(Columbia 38735)
25	I'll Be Hangin' Around		0	1953	26	1953	(Coral 60946)
26	Ruby (From *Ruby Gentry*)		0	1953	29	1953	(Coral 60959)
	OTHERS WERE PRE-1946						
Les Compagnons De La Chanson Vocal Group from France, sometimes backed Edith Piaf							
1	The Three Bells (Jimmy Brown Song)		0	1952	14	1952	(Columbia 39657)
Les Cooper & The Soul Rockers Male Pianist/Vocalist, B: 15 Mar 1931 Norfolk, Virginia							
1	Wiggle Wobble		0	1962	22	1962	(Everlast 5019)
Les Crane Male Vocalist and a Talk Show Host from San Francisco							
* 1	Desiderata	(Warner Bros. K 16119)	7	1972	8	1971	(Warner Bros. 7520)
Les Gray Male Vocalist from the UK							
1	A Groovy Kind Of Love	(Warner Bros. K 16883)	32	1977	0	1977	(Warner Bros. K 16883)
Les Paul Played guitar for Fred Waring 1938-1940.							
1	Rumours Are Flying		0	1946	4	1946	(Decca 23656)
2	Lover		0	1948	21	1948	(Capitol 15037)
3	Brazil		0	1948	22	1948	(Capitol 15037)
4	What Is This Thing Called Love?		0	1948	11	1948	(Capitol 15070)
5	Nola		0	1950	9	1950	(Capitol 1014)

ISSUE	TITLE	UK LBL	UK POS	UK YEAR	US POS	US YEAR	US LBL
6	Goofus		0	1950	21	1950	(Capitol 1192)
7	Little Rock Getaway		0	1950	18	1950	(Capitol 1316)
8	Jazz Me Blues		0	1951	23	1951	(Capitol 1825)
9	Josephine		0	1951	12	1951	(Capitol 1592)
10	Whispering		0	1951	7	1951	(Capitol 1748)
11	Jingle Bells		0	1951	10	1951	(Capitol 1881)
12	Carioca		0	1952	14	1952	(Capitol 2080)
13	Meet Mister Callghan		0	1952	5	1952	(Capitol 2193)
14	Lady Of Spain		0	1952	8	1952	(Capitol 2265)
15	Sleep		0	1953	21	1953	(Capitol 2400)
16	The Kangaroo		0	1953	25	1953	(Capitol 2614)
17	Mandolino		0	1954	19	1954	(Capitol 2928)
	HIT 1 IS CREDITED TO THE ANDREW SISTERS AND LES PAUL						

Les Paul & Mary Ford Male Guitarist And Female Vocalist from the USA. Colleen Summer B: 7 Jul 1928 Pasadena, California

ISSUE	TITLE	UK LBL	UK POS	UK YEAR	US POS	US YEAR	US LBL
1	Tennessee Waltz		0	1950	6	1950	(Capitol 1316)
* 2	Mockin' Bird Hill		0	1951	2	1951	(Capitol 1373)
* 3	How High The Moon (From *Two For The Show*)		0	1951	1	1951	(Capitol 1451)
4	Whither Thou Goest		0	1954	10	1954	(Capitol 2928)
* 5	The World Is Waiting For The Sunrise		0	1951	2	1951	(Capitol 1748)
6	Just One More Chance		0	1951	5	1951	(Capitol 1825)
7	Tiger Rag		0	1952	2	1952	(Capitol 1920)
8	I'm Confessin' (That I Love You)		0	1952	13	1952	(Capitol 2080)
9	In The Good Old Summertime		0	1952	15	1952	(Capitol 2123)
10	Smoke Rings		0	1952	14	1952	(Capitol 2123)
11	Take Me In Your Arms And Hold Me		0	1952	15	1952	(Capitol 2193)
12	Me Baby's Coming Home		0	1952	7	1952	(Capitol 2316)
13	Bye Bye Blues		0	1953	5	1953	(Capitol 2316)
14	I'm Sitting On Top Of The World		0	1953	10	1953	(Capitol 2400)
* 15	Vaya Con Dios (May God Be With You)	(Capitol CL 13943)	7	1953	1	1953	(Capitol 2486)
16	Johnny (Is The Boy For Me)		0	1953	15	1953	(Capitol 2486)
17	Don'cha Hear Them Bells		0	1953	13	1953	(Capitol 2614)
18	I Really Don't Want To Know		0	1954	11	1954	(Capitol 2735)
19	I'm A Fool To Care		0	1954	3	1954	(Capitol 2839)
20	Whither Thou Goest		0	1954	10	1954	(Capitol 2928)
21	Hummingbird		0	1955	7	1955	(Capitol 3165)
22	Amukiriki (The Lord Willing)		0	1955	38	1955	(Capitol 3248)
23	Cinco Robles (Five Oaks)		0	1957	35	1957	(Capitol 3612)
24	Put A Ring On My Finger		0	1958	32	1958	(Columbia 41222)
25	Jura (I Swear I Love You)		0	1961	37	1961	(Columbia 41994)
	OBITUARY : MARY D: 1 OCT 1977.						

Lesley Garrett & Amanda   Female Vocal/Instrumental Duo from the UK

ISSUE	TITLE	UK LBL	UK POS	UK YEAR	US POS	US YEAR	US LBL
1	Ave Maria	(Internal Affairs KGBD 012)	16	1993	0	1993	

Lesley Gore   Female Vocalist, B: 25 May 1946 New York City

ISSUE	TITLE	UK LBL	UK POS	UK YEAR	US POS	US YEAR	US LBL
* 1	It's My Party	(Mercury AMT 1205)	9	1963	1	1963	(Mercury 72119)
2	Judy's Turn To Cry		0	1963	5	1963	(Mercury 72143)
3	She's A Fool		0	1963	5	1963	(Mercury 72180)
* 4	You Don't Own Me		0	1963	2	1963	(Mercury 72206)
5	That's The Way Boys Are		0	1964	12	1964	(Mercury 72259)
6	I Don't Wanna Be A Loser		0	1964	37	1964	(Mercury 72270)
7	Maybe I Know	(Mercury MF 829)	20	1964	14	1964	(Mercury 72309)
8	Look Of Love		0	1965	27	1965	(Mercury 72372)
9	Sunshine, Lollipops And Rainbows		0	1965	13	1965	(Mercury 72433)
10	My Town, My Guy And Me		0	1965	32	1965	(Mercury 72475)
11	California Nights		0	1967	16	1967	(Mercury 72649)

Leslie Caron & Mel Ferrer   Leslie B: 1 Jul 1931 Paris, France, Mel B: 25 Aug 1917 New Jersey

ISSUE	TITLE	UK LBL	UK POS	UK YEAR	US POS	US YEAR	US LBL
* 1	Hi-Lili, Hi-Lo (From *Lili*)		0	1953	30	1953	(MGM 30759)

Leslie Fyson   See Michael Medwin

Leslie Pearl   Hails from Pennsylvania, And The Singer/songwriter Is Also A Successful Jingle Writer

ISSUE	TITLE	UK LBL	UK POS	UK YEAR	US POS	US YEAR	US LBL
1	If The Love Fits Wear It		0	1982	28	1982	(RCA 13235)

Lester Flatt & Earl Scruggs   Male Bluegrass Duo, Lester Raymond Flatt

ISSUE	TITLE	UK LBL	UK POS	UK YEAR	US POS	US YEAR	US LBL
8	The Ballad Of Jed Clampett		0	1962	44	1962	(Columbia 42606)
18	Foggy Mountain Breakdown	(CBS 3038/Mercury MF 1007)	39	1967	55	1968	(Columbia 44380)

ISSUE	TITLE	UK LBL	UK POS	UK YEAR	US POS	US YEAR	US LBL

B: 19 Jun 1914 Tennessee & Earl Eugene Scruggs B: 6 Jan 1924 North Carolina   Others hits are C/W

Let Loose Male Vocal/Instrumental Group from the UK

1	Crazy For You	(Vertigo VERCD74)	44	1993	0	1993	
2	Seventeen	(Vertigo MERCD 400)	44	1994	0	1994	
3	Crazy For You (Re-Issue)	(Vertigo MERCD 402)	2	1994	0	1994	
4	Seventeen (Re-Issue)	(Vertigo MERCD406)	11	1994	0	1994	
5	Crazy For You (Re-Issue) (Re-Entry)	(Vertigo MERCD 402)	52	1994	0	1994	
6	Seventeen (Re-Issue) (Re-Entry)	(Vertigo MERCD 406)	47	1995	0	1995	
7	One Night Stand	(Mercury MERCD 419)	12	1995	0	1995	
8	Best In Me	(Mercury MERCD 428)	8	1995	0	1995	
9	Everybody Say Everybody Do	(Mercury MERCD 446)	29	1995	0	1995	
10	Everybody Say Everybody Do (Re-Entry)	(Mercury MERCD 446)	71	1996	0	1996	
11	Make It With You	(Mercury MERCD 464)	7	1996	0	1996	
12	Take It Easy	(Mercury MERCD 472)	25	1996	0	1996	
13	Darling Be Home Soon	(Mercury MERCD 475)	65	1996	0	1996	

Letitia Dean & Paul Medford Mixed Vocal Duo from the UK

1	Something Outa Nothing	(BBC RESL 203)	12	1986	0	1986	

Lettermen Male Vocal Group from the USA   Names: Jim Pike, Bob Engemann & Tony Butala.

1	The Way You Look Tonight	(Capitol CL 15222)	36	1961	13	1961	(Capitol 4586)
2	When I Fall In Love		0	1961	7	1961	(Capitol 4658)
3	Come Back Silly Girl		0	1962	17	1962	(Capitol 4699)
4	Theme From A Summer Place		0	1965	16	1965	(Capitol 5437)
5	Goin' Out Of My Head / Can't Take My Eyes Off You		0	1968	7	1968	(Capitol 2054)
6	Hurt So Bad		0	1969	12	1969	(Capitol 2482)

Level 42 Male Vocal/Instrumental Group from the UK

1	Love Meeting Love	(Polydor POSP 170)	61	1980	0	1980	
2	Love Games	(Polydor POSP 234)	38	1981	0	1981	
3	Turn It On	(Polydor POSP 286)	57	1981	0	1981	
4	Starchild	(Polydor POSP 343)	47	1981	0	1981	
5	Are You Hearing (What I Hear)?	(Polydor POSP 396)	49	1982	0	1982	
6	Weave Your Spell	(Polydor POSP 500)	43	1982	0	1982	
7	The Chinese Way	(Polydor POSP 538)	24	1983	0	1983	
8	Out Of Sight Out Of Mind	(Polydor POSP 570)	41	1983	0	1983	
9	The Sun Goes Down (Living It Up)	(Polydor POSP 622)	10	1983	0	1983	
10	Micro Kids	(Polydor POSP 643)	37	1983	0	1983	
11	Hot Water	(Polydor POSP 697)	18	1984	0	1984	
12	The Chant Has Begun	(Polydor POSP 710)	41	1984	0	1984	
13	Something About You	(Polydor POSP 759)	6	1985	7	1986	(Polydor 883362)
14	Leaving Me Now	(Polydor POSP 776)	15	1985	0	1985	
15	Lessons In Love	(Polydor POSP 790)	3	1986	12	1987	(Polydor 883956)
16	Running In The Family	(Polydor POSP 842)	6	1987	0	1987	
17	To Be With You Again	(Polydor POSP 855)	10	1987	0	1987	
18	It's Over	(Polydor POSP 900)	10	1987	0	1987	
19	Children Say	(Polydor POSP 911)	22	1987	0	1987	
20	Heaven In My Hands	(Polydor PO 14)	12	1988	0	1988	
21	Take A Look	(Polydor PO 24)	32	1988	0	1988	
22	Tracie	(Polydor PO 34)	25	1989	0	1989	
23	Take Care Of Yourself	(Polydor PO 58)	39	1989	0	1989	
24	Guaranteed	(RCA PB 44745)	17	1991	0	1991	
25	Overtime	(RCA PB 44997)	62	1991	0	1991	
26	My Father's Shoes	(RCA PB 45271)	55	1992	0	1992	
27	Forever Now	(RCA 74321190272)	19	1994	0	1994	
28	All Over You	(RCA 74321205662)	26	1994	0	1994	
29	Love In A Peaceful World	(RCA 74321220332)	31	1994	0	1994	

NAMES PHIL AND BOON GOULD, MIKE LINDUP AND MARK KING. • GARY HUSBAND AND ALAN MURPHY REPLACED PHIL AND BOON IN 1987

Levellers Male Vocal/Instrumental Group from the UK

1	One Way	(China Wok 2008)	51	1991	0	1991	
2	Far From Home	(China Wok 2010)	71	1991	0	1991	
3	15 Years (EP)	(China Wok X 2020)	11	1992	0	1992	
4	Belaruse	(China Wok CD 2034)	12	1993	0	1993	
5	This Garden	(China WokCD 2039)	12	1993	0	1993	
6	Julie (EP)	(China WokCD 2042)	17	1994	0	1994	

ISSUE	TITLE	UK LBL	UK POS	UK YEAR	US POS	US YEAR	US LBL
7	Hope St.	(China WokCD 2059)	12	1995	0	1995	
8	Fantasy	(China WokCD 2067)	16	1995	0	1995	
9	Just The One	(China WokCD 2076)	12	1995	0	1995	
10	Exodus - Live	(China WokCD 2082)	24	1996	0	1996	
11	What A Beautiful Day	(China WokCD 2088)	13	1997	0	1997	
	HIT 9 IS CREDITED TO LEVELLERS SPECIAL GUEST JOE STRUMMER						

Levert Male Vocal Trio from the UK

| 1 | Casanova | (Atlantic A9217) | 9 | 1987 | 5 | 1987 | (Atlantic 89217) |
| | NAMES SEAN AND GERALD LEVERT & MARC GORDON | | | | | | |

Leviticus Male Vocalist from the UK

| 1 | Burial | (FFRR FCD 255) | 66 | 1995 | 0 | 1995 | |

Lew Douglas Orchestra Male Orchestra Leader from the USA

| 1 | Turn Around Boy | | 0 | 1954 | 27 | 1954 | (MGM 11654) |

Leyton Buzzards Male Vocal/Instrumental Group from the UK

| 1 | Saturday Night (Beneath The Plastic Palm Trees) | (Chrysalis CHS 2288) | 53 | 1979 | 0 | 1979 | |

LFO Male Instrumental Group from the UK

1	LFO	(WARP WAP 5)	12	1990	0	1990	
2	We Are Back /Nurture	(WARP 7WAP 14)	47	1991	0	1991	
3	What Is House (EP)	(WARP WAP 17)	62	1992	0	1992	

Li Kwan Male Producer, Real Name Joey Negro from the UK

| 1 | I Need A Man | (Deconstruction 74321252192) | 51 | 1994 | 0 | 1994 | |

Liberace Male Vocal/Pianist, Full Name Wladziu Valentino Liberace from Milwaukee.

1	September Song (From *Knickerbocker Holiday*)		0	1952	27	1952	(Columbia 39709)
2	The Story Of Three Loves		0	1953	21	1953	(Columbia 40099)
3	Christmas Melody		0	1953	21	1953	(Columbia 48001)
4	Indiscretion with Jo Stafford		0	1954	30	1954	(Columbia 40170)
5	Easter Parade (From *As Thousands Cheer*)		0	1954	26	1954	(Columbia 48007)
6	Twelfth Street Rag		0	1954	23	1954	(Columbia 40217)
7	Unchained Melody	(Philips PB 430)	20	1955	0	1955	
8	I Don't Care	(Columbia DB 430)	28	1956	0	1956	

Liberation Male Production/Instrumental Duo from the UK

| 1 | Liberation | (XYZ XYZ 68657) | 28 | 1992 | 0 | 1992 | |

Libra Male Vocal/Instrumental Group from the UK

| 1 | Anomaly/Calling Your Name | | 71 | 1996 | 0 | 1996 | |

Lick The Tins Mixed Vocal/Instrumental Group from the UK

| 1 | Can't Help Falling In Love | (Sedition EDIT 3308) | 42 | 1986 | 0 | 1986 | |

Lidell Townsell & M.T.F. Male DJ/Mixer Townsell from Chicago, With M.T.F. (More Than Friends) Singer Martell & Rapper Silk E

| 1 | Nu Nu | | 0 | 1992 | 26 | 1992 | (Mercury 866780) |

Lieutenant Pigeon Mixed Instrumental Group from the UK

| 1 | Mouldy Old Dough | (Decca F 13278) | 1 | 1972 | 0 | 1972 | |
| 2 | Desperate Dan | (Decca F 13365) | 17 | 1972 | 0 | 1972 | |

Light Of The World Male Vocal/Instrumental Group from the UK

1	Swingin'	(Ensign Eny 22)	45	1979	0	1979	
2	Midnight Groovin'	(Ensign Eny 29)	72	1979	0	1979	
3	London Town	(Ensign Eny 43)	41	1980	0	1980	
4	I Shot The Sheriff	(Ensign Eny 46)	41	1981	0	1981	
5	I'm So Happy	(Ensign Eny 64)	35	1981	0	1981	
6	Ride The Love Train	(EMI 5242)	49	1981	0	1981	

Lighter Shade Of Brown Male Vocal Duo from the USA

| 1 | Hey DJ | (Mercury MERCD 401) | 33 | 1994 | 0 | 1994 | |

Lighthouse Lead Singer With The Rock Band Is Bob McBride

| 1 | One Fine Morning | | 0 | 1971 | 24 | 1971 | (Evolution 1048) |
| 2 | Sunny Days | | 0 | 1972 | 34 | 1972 | (Evolution 1069) |

Lighthouse Family Male Vocal/Instrumental Duo from the UK

1	Lifted	(Wild Card CARDD 17)	61	1995	0	1995	
2	Ocean Drive	(Wild Card 5797072)	34	1995	0	1995	
3	Lifted (Re-Issue)	(Wild Card 5779432)	4	1996	0	1996	
4	Ocean Drive (Re-Issue)	(Wild Card 5766192)	11	1996	0	1996	
5	Goodbye Heartbreak	(Wild Card 5753492)	14	1996	0	1996	
6	Loving Every Minute	(Wild Card 5731012)	20	1996	0	1996	

ISSUE	TITLE	UK LBL	UK POS	UK YEAR	US POS	US YEAR	US LBL
Lightning Seeds	There have been many changes in their line-up. Producer Is Ian Broudie						
1	Pure	(Ghetto GTG 4)	16	1989	31	1989	(MCA 53816)
2	He Life Of Riley	(Virgin VS 1402)	28	1992	0	1992	
3	Sense	(Virgin VS 1414)	31	1992	0	1992	
4	Lucky You	(Epic 6606282)	43	1994	0	1994	
5	Change	(Epic 6609865)	13	1995	0	1995	
6	Marvellous	(Epic 6614265)	24	1995	0	1995	
7	Perfect	(Epic 6621792)	18	1995	0	1995	
8	Lucky You (Re-Issue)	(Epic 6625182)	15	1995	0	1995	
9	Ready Or Not	(Epic 6629672)	20	1996	0	1996	
10	Three Lions	(Epic 6632732)	1	1996	0	1996	
11	What If...	(Epic 6638635)	14	1996	0	1996	
12	What If...(Re-Entry)	(Epic 6638635)	64	1997	0	1997	
13	Sugar Coated Iceberg	(Epic 6640435)	12	1997	0	1997	
14	You Showed Me	(Epic 6643282)	8	1997	0	1997	
	HIT 10 IS CREDITED TO BADDIEL & SKINNER AND THE LIGHTNING SEEDS AND WAS THE OFFICIAL SONG OF THE ENGLAND SOCCER TEAM						
Lil Mo' Yin Yang	Male Instrumental/Production Duo from the USA						
1	Reach (Mixes)	(Multiply CDMULTY 9)	28	1996	0	1996	
	SEE ALSO LIL' LOUIS						
Lil' Louis	Male Producer from the USA						
1	French Kiss	(FFRR FX 115)	2	1989	0	1989	
2	I Called U	(FFRR FX 123)	16	1990	0	1990	
3	Saved My Life	(FFRR FX 197)	74	1992	0	1992	
	HIT 3 IS CREDITED TO LIL' LOUIS & THE WORLD						
Lillian Briggs	Hails from Philadelphia And Worked In An All-girl Orchestra						
1	I Want You To Be My Baby		0	1955	18	1955	(Epic 9115)
Lillo Thomas	Male Vocalist from the USA						
1	Settle Down	(Capitol CL 356)	66	1985	0	1985	
2	Sexy Girl	(Capitol CL 445)	23	1987	0	1987	
3	I'm In Love	(Capitol CL 450)	54	1987	0	1987	
Lily Ann Carol	Female Vocalist from the USA, was with The Louis Prima Band						
1	More Luck Than Money		0	1953	25	1953	(RCA Victor 5184)
Limahl	Male Vocalist ex Kajagoogoo, Real Name Chris Hamill from the UK, Name Is An Anagram Of His Surname						
1	Only For Love	(EMI LML 1)	16	1983	0	1983	
2	Only For Love (Re-Entry)	(EMI LML 1)	75	1984	0	1984	
3	Too Much Trouble	(EMI LML 2)	64	1984	0	1984	
4	Never Ending Story	(EMI LML 3)	4	1984	17	1984	(EMI America 8230)
Limit	Male Vocal/Instrumental Duo from Holland						
1	Say Yeah	(Portrait A 4808)	17	1985	0	1985	
Limmie & The Family Cookin'	Mixed Vocal Group from the USA						
1	You Can Do Magic	(AVCO 6105 019)	3	1973	0	1973	
2	Dreamboat	(AVCO 6105 025)	31	1973	0	1973	
3	A Walkin' Miracle	(AVCO 6105 027)	6	1974	0	1974	
Lina Santiago	Female Vocalist from the USA						
1	Feels So Good (Show Me You..)		0	1996	35	1996	(Universal 00000)
2	Just Because I Love You		0	1996	78	1996	(Universal 56012)
Linda Carr	Female Vocalist from the USA						
1	Highwire	(Columbia DB 4275)	15	1975	0	1975	(Chelsea 2005 025)
2	Sold My Rock 'N' Roll (Gave It For Funky Soul)	(Columbia DB 4603)	36	1976	0	1976	(Spark SRL 1139)
Linda Clifford	Female Vocalist from the USA						
1	If My Friends Could See Me Now	(CURTOM K 17163)	50	1978	0	1978	
2	Bridge Over Troubled Water	(RSO 30)	28	1979	0	1979	
Linda Jones	Female Vocalist, B: 14 Jan 1944 Newark, New Jersey						
1	Hypnotized		0	1967	21	1967	(LOMA 2070)
	FIRST RECORDED AS LINDA LANE IN 1963						
	OBITUARY : D: 14 MAR 1972 DIABETES.						
Linda Lewis	Female Vocalist from the UK						
1	Rock A Doodle Doo	(RAFT RA 18502)	15	1973	0	1973	
2	It's In His Kiss	(Arista 17)	6	1975	0	1975	
3	Baby I'm Yours	(Arista 43)	33	1976	0	1976	
4	I'd Be Surprisingly Good For You	(ARIOLA ARO 166)	40	1979	0	1979	

ISSUE		TITLE	UK LBL	UK POS	UK YEAR	US POS	US YEAR	US LBL
Linda Martin Female Vocalist from Ireland								
1	1	Why Me	(Columbia 6581317)	59	1992	0	1992	
Linda Ronstadt Female Vocalist, B: 15 Jul 1946 Tucson, Arizona								
	1	Different Drum		0	1967	13	1967	(Capitol 2004)
	2	Long Long Time		0	1970	25	1970	(Capitol 2846)
	4	You're No Good		0	1974	1	1974	(Capitol 3990)
	6	When Will I Be Loved		0	1975	2	1975	(Capitol 4050)
	8	Heat Wave		0	1975	5	1975	(Asylum 45282)
	10	Tracks Of My Tears	(Asylum K 13034)	42	1976	25	1976	(Asylum 45295)
	12	That'll Be The Day		0	1976	11	1976	(Asylum 45340)
	14	Someone To Lay Down Beside Me		0	1976	42	1976	(Asylum 45361)
*	15	Blue Bayou	(Asylum K 13106)	35	1978	3	1977	(Asylum 45431)
	16	It's So Easy		0	1977	5	1977	(Asylum 45438)
	17	Poor Poor Pitiful Me		0	1978	31	1978	(Asylum 45462)
	18	Tumbling Dice		0	1978	32	1978	(Asylum 45479)
	20	Back In The U.S.A.		0	1978	16	1978	(Asylum 45519)
	21	Ooh Baby Baby		0	1978	7	1978	(Asylum 45546)
	22	Just One Look		0	1979	44	1978	(Asylum 46011)
	24	Alison	(Asylum K 13149)	66	1979	0	1979	
	25	How Do I Make You		0	1980	10	1980	(Asylum 46602)
	27	Hurt So Bad		0	1980	8	1980	(Asylum 46624)
	28	I Can't Let Go		0	1980	31	1980	(Asylum 46654)
	30	Get Closer		0	1982	29	1982	(Asylum 69948)
	31	I Knew You When		0	1983	37	1983	(Asylum 69853)
*	32	Somewhere Out There (From *An American Trail*)	(MCA MCA 1132)	8	1987	2	1987	(MCA 5273)
!*	37	Don't Know Much	(Elektra EKR 100)	2	1989	2	1989	(Elektra 64987)
	38	All My Life		0	1990	11	1990	(Elektra 64987)
		UNLISTED HITS ARE C/W • LINDA WAS INVOLVED WITH HER SISTER AND BROTHER AS THE THREE RONSTADTS, LATER ON WITH BOBBY KIMMEL SHE FORMED THE STONE							
Linda Scott Female Vocalist, Real Name Linda Joy Sampson, B: 1 Jun 1945 Queens, New York.								
*	1	I've Told Every Little Star	(Columbia DB 4638)	7	1961	3	1961	(Canadian AmericaN 123)
	2	Don't Bet Money Honey	(Columbia DB 4692)	50	1961	9	1961	(Canadian American 127)
	3	I Don't Know Why		0	1961	12	1961	(Canadian American 129)
Lindisfarne Male Vocal/Instrumental Group from the UK, Lead Singer With The Quintet is Alan Hull								
	1	Meet Me On The Corner	(Charisma CB 173)	5	1972	0	1972	
	2	Lady Eleanor/ og On The Tyne	(Charisma CB 153)	3	1972	0	1972	
	3	All Fall Down	(Charisma CB 191)	34	1972	0	1972	
	4	Run For Home	(Mercury 6007 177)	10	1978	33	1978	(ATCO 7093)
	5	Juke Box Gypsy	(Mercury 6007 187)	56	1978	0	1978	
	6	Fog On The Tyne (Revisited)	(BEST ZB 44083)	2	1990	0	1990 with Gazza	
Lindsey Buckingham Male Vocalist, B: 3 Oct 1947 California, Joined Fleetwood Mac In 1975								
	1	Trouble	(Mercury MER 85)	31	1982	9	1981	(Asylum 47223)
	2	Go Insane		0	1984	23	1984	(Elektra 69714)
Lindy Layton Female Vocalist from the UK								
	1	Dub Be Good To Me	(Gu.Beat Gud 39)	1	1990	0	1990	
	2	Silly Games	(Arista 113452)	22	1990	0	1990	
	3	Echo My Heart	(Arista 113845)	42	1991	0	1991	
	4	Without You (One And One)	(Arista 114636)	71	1991	0	1991	
	5	We Got The Love	(PWL International PWCD 250)	38	1993	0	1993	
	6	Show Me	(PWL International PWCD 275)	47	1993	0	1993	
Linear Trio Based In Miami With Vocals By Charlie Pennachio								
*	1	Sending All My Love		0	1990	5	1990	(Atlantic 87961)
	2	T.L.C		0	1992	30	1992	(Atlantic 87484)
Liner Male Vocal/Instrumental Group from the UK								
	1	Keep Reaching Out For Love	(Atlantic K 11235)	49	1979	0	1979	
	2	You And Me	(Atlantic K 11285)	44	1979	0	1979	
Link Wray & His Ray Men Wray B: 2 May 1935 Fort Brag, North Carolina								
*	1	Rumble		0	1958	16	1958	(Cadence 1347)
	2	Rawhide		0	1959	23	1959	(Epic 9300)
Linx Male Vocal/Instrumental Duo from the UK								
	1	You're Lying	(Chrysalis CHS 2461)	15	1980	0	1980	
	2	Intuition	(Chrysalis CHS 2500)	7	1981	0	1981	
	3	Throw Away The Key	(Chrysalis CHS 2519)	21	1981	0	1981	
	4	So This Is Romance	(Chrysalis CHS 2546)	15	1981	0	1981	

ISSUE	TITLE	UK LBL	UK POS	UK YEAR	US POS	US YEAR	US LBL
5	Can't Help Myself	(Chrysalis CHS 2565)	55	1981	0	1981	
6	Plaything	(Chrysalis CHS 2621)	48	1982	0	1982	

Lionel Bart Male Vocalist from the UK

ISSUE	TITLE	UK LBL	UK POS	UK YEAR	US POS	US YEAR	US LBL
1	Happy Endings (Give Yourself A Pinch)	(EMI EM 121)	68	1989	0	1989	
2	Happy Endings (Give Yourself A Pinch) (Re-Entry)	(EMI EM 121)	71	1989	0		1989

Lionel Hampton Orchestra Male Orchestra Leader/Instrumentalist from the USA

ISSUE	TITLE	UK LBL	UK POS	UK YEAR	US POS	US YEAR	US LBL
10	Hey! Ba-Ba-Re-Bop		0	1946	9	1946	(Decca 18754)
11	Blow Top Blues		0	1947	21	1947	(Decca 23792)
12	Rag Mop		0	1950	7	1950	(Decca 24855)

VOCALS ON HIT 11 ARE BY DINAH WASHINGTON   VOCALS ON HIT 12 ARE BY THE HAMPTONES

Lionel Richie Male Vocalist, B: 20 Jun 1949 Tuskegee, Alabama

	ISSUE	TITLE	UK LBL	UK POS	UK YEAR	US POS	US YEAR	US LBL
*	1	Endless Love	(Motown TMG 1240)	7	1981	1	1981	(Motown 1519)
*	2	Truly	(Motown TMG 1284)	6	1982	1	1982	(Motown 1644)
	3	You Are	(Motown TMG 1290)	43	1983	4	1983	(Motown 1657)
	4	My Love	(Motown TMG 1300)	70	1983	5	1983	(Motown 1677)
*	5	All Night Long (All Night)	(Motown TMG 1319)	2	1983	1	1983	(Motown 1698)
	6	Running With The Night	(Motown TMG 1324)	9	1983	7	1983	(Motown 1710)
*	7	Hello	(Motown TMG 1330)	1	1984	1	1984	(Motown 1722)
	8	Stuck On You	(Motown TMG 1341)	12	1984	3	1984	(Motown 1746)
	9	Penny Lover	(Motown TMG 1356)	18	1984	8	1984	(Motown 1762)
*	10	Say You, Say Me	(Motown ZB 40421)	8	1985	1	1985	(Motown 1819)
	11	Dancing On The Ceiling	(Motown L10 1)	7	1986	2	1986	(Motown 1843)
	12	Love Will Conquer All	(Motown L10 2)	45	1986	9	1986	(Motown 1866)
!	13	Deep River Woman		0	1986	10	1986	(Motown 1873)
	14	Ballerina Girl	(Motown L10 3)	17	1986	7	1987	(Motown 1873)
	15	Se La	(Motown L10 4)	43	1987	20	1987	(Motown 1883)
	16	Do It To Me	(Motown TMG 1407)	33	1992	21	1992	(Motown 2160)
	17	My Destiny	(Motown TMG 1408)	7	1992	0	1992	
	18	Love Oh Love	(Motown TMG 1413)	52	1992	0	1992	
	19	Love Oh Love (Re-Entry)	(Motown TMG 1413)	73	1992	0	1992	
	20	Don't Wanna Lose You	(Mercury MERDD 461)	17	1996	39	1996	
	21	Still In Love	(Mercury MERCD 477)	66	1996	0	1996	

HIT 1 IS CREDITED TO DIANA ROSS AND LIONEL RICHIE • HIT 13 IS CREDITED TO LIONEL RICHIE WITH ALABAMA AND REACHED NUMBER 71 IN THE US NATIONAL CHARTS

Lionrock Male Producer, Real Name Justin Robertson from the UK

ISSUE	TITLE	UK LBL	UK POS	UK YEAR	US POS	US YEAR	US LBL
1	Lionrock	(Deconstruction 74321124381)	63	1992	0	1992	
2	Packet Of Peace	(Deconstruction 74321144372)	32	1993	0	1993	
3	Carnival	(Deconstruction 74321164862)	34	1993	0	1993	
4	Tripwire	(Deconstruction 74321204702)	44	1994	0	1994	
5	Straight At Yer Head	(Deconstruction 74321342972)	33	1996	0	1996	
6	Fire Up The Shoesaw	(Deconstruction 74321382652)	43	1996	0	1996	

Lipps Inc. Mixed Vocal/Instrumental Group from the USA

	ISSUE	TITLE	UK LBL	UK POS	UK YEAR	US POS	US YEAR	US LBL
*	1	Funkytown	(Casablanca CAN 194)	2	1980	1	1980	(Casablanca 2233)

THE NAME IS PRONOUNCED LIP-SYNCH WITH VOCALS BY CYNTHIA JOHNSON

Lippy Lou Female Rapper from the UK

ISSUE	TITLE	UK LBL	UK POS	UK YEAR	US POS	US YEAR	US LBL
1	Liberation	(More Protein PROCD 105)	57	1995	0	1995	

Liquid Male Production/Instrumental Duo from the UK

ISSUE	TITLE	UK LBL	UK POS	UK YEAR	US POS	US YEAR	US LBL
1	Sweet Harmony	(XL XLS 28)	15	1992	0	1992	
2	The Future Music (EP)	(XL XLT 33)	59	1992	0	1992	
3	Time To Get Up	(XL XLS 40CD)	46	1993	0	1993	
4	Sweet Harmony (Re-Mix) One Love Family	(XL XLS 65CD)	14	1995	0	1995	
5	Closer	(XL XLS 66CD)	47	1995	0	1995	

Liquid Gold Mixed Vocal/Instrumental Group from the UK

ISSUE	TITLE	UK LBL	UK POS	UK YEAR	US POS	US YEAR	US LBL
1	Anyway You Do It	(CREOLE CR 159)	41	1978	0	1978	
2	Dance Yourself Dizzy	(Polo Polo 1)	2	1980	0	1980	
3	Substitute	(Polo Polo 4)	8	1980	0	1980	
4	The Night The Wine And The Roses	(Polo Polo 6)	32	1980	0	1980	
5	Don't Panic	(Polo Polo 8)	42	1981	0	1981	
6	Where Did We Go Wrong	(Polo Polo 23)	56	1982	0	1982	

Liquid Oxygen Male Producer from the USA

ISSUE	TITLE	UK LBL	UK POS	UK YEAR	US POS	US YEAR	US LBL
1	The Planet Dance	(Champion Champ 242)	56	1990	0	1990	

Lisa B Female Vocalist from the USA

ISSUE	TITLE	UK LBL	UK POS	UK YEAR	US POS	US YEAR	US LBL
1	Glam	(FFRR FCD 210)	49	1993	0	1993	
2	Fascinated	(FFRR FCD 218)	35	1993	0	1993	
3	You And Me	(FFRR FCD 226)	39	1994	0	1994	

ISSUE	TITLE	UK LBL	UK POS	UK YEAR	US POS	US YEAR	US LBL
Lisa Fischer	Female Vocalist, Hails from New York, Worked Mostly As A Session Singer						
1	How Can I Ease The Pain		0	1991	11		1991 (Elektra 64897)
	LISA HUNT SEE LOVESTATION						
Lisa Keith	Female Singer/Songwriter from Minneapolis, USA						
1	Better Than You		0	1993	36	1993	(Perspective 7430)
	SEE ALSO HERB ALPERT						
Lisa Kirk	Female Actress/Vocalist from the USA						
1	Dearie		0	1950	22	1950	(RCA Victor 78-3696)
2	The Old Piano Roll Blues		0	1950	27	1950	(RCA Victor 3751)
3	Boomerang		0	1952	25	1952	(RCA Victor 5016)
4	Ohio (From *Wonderful Town*)		0	1953	27	1953	(RCA Victor 5187)
Lisa Lisa & Cult Jam	Mixed Vocal/Instrumental Group from Harlem, Names: Lisa Velez, Mike Hughes & Alex Moseley						
* 1	I Wonder If I Take You Home	(CBS A 6057)	53	1985	34	1985	(Columbia 04886)
2	I Wonder If I Take You Home (Re-Entry)	(CBS A 6057)	12	1985	0	1985	
3	All Cried Out		0	1986	8	1986	(Columbia 05844)
4	Head To Toe		0	1987	1	1987	(Columbia 07008)
5	Lost In Emotion	(CBS 651036)	58	1987	1	1987	(Columbia 07267)
6	Little Jackie Wants To Be A Star		0	1989	29	1989	(Columbia 68674)
7	Let The Beat Hit Em'	(Columbia 6575867)	17	1991	0	1991	
* 8	Let The Beat Hit Em' Part 2	(Columbia 6573747)	49	1991	37	1991	(Columbia 73847)
9	Skip To My Lu	(Chrysalis CDCHS 5006)	34	1994	0	1994	
Lisa Loeb & Nine Stories	Mixed Vocal/Instrumental Group From New York						
* 1	Stay (I Missed You)	(RCA 74321212522)	6	1994	1	1994	(RCA 62870)
2	Do You Sleep?	(Geffen GFSTD 96)	45	1995	18	1995	(Geffen 19388)
Lisa Marie Experience	Male Instrumental/Production Duo from the UK						
1	Keep On Jumpin'	(FFRR FCD 271)	7	1996	0	1996	
2	Keep On Jumpin' (Re-Entry)	(FFRR FCD 271)	67	1996	0	1996	
3	Do That To Me	(Positiva CDTIV 57)	33	1996	0	1996	
	SEE ALSO MALCOLM MCLAREN						
Lisa May	Female Vocalist from the UK						
1	Wishing On A Star	(Urban Gorilla UG 3CD)	16	1995	0	1995	
2	The Curse Of Voodoo Ray	(Fontana VOOCD 1)	64	1996	0	1996	
Lisa Moorish	Female Vocalist from the UK						
1	Just The Way It Is	(Go! Beat GODCD 123)	42	1995	0	1995	
2	I'm Your Man	(Go! Beat GODCD 128)	24	1995	0	1995	
3	Mr. Friday Night	(Go! Beat GODCD 137)	24	1996	0	1996	
4	Love For Life	(Go! Beat GODCD 145)	37	1996	0	1996	
	HIT 2 HAS UNCREDITED VOCALS FROM GEORGE MICHAEL						
Lisa Stansfield	Female Vocalist, From Rochdale, Lancashire, England, Lead Singer With The Band Blue Zone						
1	People Hold On	(Ahead Of Our Time CCUT 5)	11	1989	0	1989	
2	This Is The Right Time	(Arista 112512)	13	1989	21	1990	(Arista 2049)
* 3	All Around The World	(Arista 112693)	1	1989	3	1990	(Arista 9928)
4	Live Together	(Arista 112914)	10	1990	0	1990	
5	What Did I Do To You (EP)	(Arista 113168)	25	1990	0	1990	
6	You Can't Deny It		0	1990	14	1990	(Arista 2024)
7	Change	(Arista 114820)	10	1991	27	1991	(Arista 12362)
8	All Woman	(Arista 115000)	20	1991	0	1991	
9	Time To Make You Mine	(Arista 115113)	14	1992	0	1992	
10	Set Your Loving Free	(Arista 74321100587)	28	1992	0	1992	
11	Someday (I'm Coming Back)	(Arista 74321123567)	10	1992	0	1992	
12	Five Live (EP)	(Parlophone CDRS 6340)	1	1993	0	1993	
13	In All The Right Places	(MCA MCSTD	8	1993	0	1993	
14	Five Live (EP) (Re-Entry)	(Parlophone CDRS 6340)	74	1993	0	1993	
15	So Natural	(Arista 74321169132)	15	1993	0	1993	
16	Little Bit Of Heaven	(Arista 74321178202)	32	1993	0	1993	
17	People Hold On (The Bootleg Mixes)	(Arista 74321452012)	4	1997	0	1997	
18	The Real Thing	(Arista74321453222)	9	1997	0	1997	
19	Never Never Gonna Give You Up	(Arista 74321490392)	25	1997	0	1997	
Lisette Melendez	Female Dancer/Singer from East Harlem, New York						
1	Together Forever		0	1991	35	1991	(Fever 73629)
Lita Ford	Female Vocalist from the USA						
1	Kiss Me Deadly	(RCA PB 49575)	75	1988	12	1988	(RCA 6866)

ISSUE	TITLE	UK LBL	UK POS	UK YEAR	US POS	US YEAR	US LBL
* 2	Close My Eyes Forever	(RCA PB 49409)	47	1989	8	1989	(RCA 8899)
3	Shot Of Poison	(RCA PB 49145)	63	1992	0	1992	

Lita Roza Female Vocalist from the UK

ISSUE	TITLE	UK LBL	UK POS	UK YEAR	US POS	US YEAR	US LBL
1	(How Much) Is That Doggie In The Window	(Decca F 10070)	1	1953	0	1953	
2	Hey There	(Decca F 10611)	17	1955	0	1955	
3	Jimmy Unknown	(Decca F 10679)	15	1956	0	1956	

Little Angels Male Vocal/Instrumental Group from the UK

ISSUE	TITLE	UK LBL	UK POS	UK YEAR	US POS	US YEAR	US LBL
1	Big Bad (EP)	(Polydor LTLEP 2)	74	1989	0	1989	
2	Kicking Up Dust	(Polydor LTL 5)	46	1990	0	1990	
3	Radical Your Lover	(Polydor LTL 6)	34	1990	0	1990	
4	She's A Little Angel	(Polydor LTL 7)	21	1990	0	1990	
5	Boneyard	(Polydor LTL 8)	33	1991	0	1991	
6	Product Of The Working Class	(Polydor LTL 9)	40	1991	0	1991	
7	Young Gods	(Polydor LTL 10)	34	1991	0	1991	
8	I Ain't Gonna Cry	(Polydor LTL 11)	26	1991	0	1991	
9	Too Much Too Young	(Polydor LTL 12)	22	1992	0	1992	
10	Womankind	(Polydor LTLCD 13)	12	1993	0	1993	
11	Soapbox	(Polydor LTLCD 14)	33	1993	0	1993	
12	Sail Away	(Polydor LTLCD15)	45	1993	0	1993	
13	Ten Miles High	(Polydor LTLCD 16)	18	1994	0	1994	

Little Anthony & The Imperials Male Vocal Group from the USA, Little Tony's Real Name Is Anthony Gourdine B: 8 Jan 1941

ISSUE	TITLE	UK LBL	UK POS	UK YEAR	US POS	US YEAR	US LBL
* 1	Tears On My Pillow		0	1958	4	1958	(END 1027)
2	Shimmy Shimmy Ko-Ko-Bop		0	1959	24	1959	(END 1060)
3	I'm On The Outside (Looking In)		0	1964	15	1964	(DCP 1104)
4	Goin' Out Of My Head		0	1964	6	1964	(DCP 1119)
5	Hurt So Bad		0	1965	10	1965	(DCP 1128)
6	Take Me Back		0	1965	16	1965	(DCP 1136)
7	I Miss You So		0	1965	34	1965	(DCP 1149)
8	Better Use Your Head	(United Artists UP 36141)	42	1976	0	1976	
9	Who's Gonna Love Me	(Power Exchange PX 266)	17	1977	0	1977	

Little Benny & The Masters Male Rapper/Trumpet With Male Instrumental Group from the USA

ISSUE	TITLE	UK LBL	UK POS	UK YEAR	US POS	US YEAR	US LBL
1	Who Comes To Boogie	(Bluebird 10 BR 13)	33	1985	0	1985	

Little Caesar Male Vocalist from the UK

ISSUE	TITLE	UK LBL	UK POS	UK YEAR	US POS	US YEAR	US LBL
1	The Whole Of The Moon	(A1 EAU 1)	68	1990	0	1990	

Little Caesar & The Romans R&B Quintet Led By David 'Little Caesar' Johnson B: 16 Jun 1934 In Chicago

ISSUE	TITLE	UK LBL	UK POS	UK YEAR	US POS	US YEAR	US LBL
1	Those Oldies But Goodies (Remind Me Of You)		0	1961	9	1961	(DEL FI 4158)

Little Dippers Names: Emily Gilmore, Delores Dinning, Hurshel Wigintin & Darrell McCall

ISSUE	TITLE	UK LBL	UK POS	UK YEAR	US POS	US YEAR	US LBL
1	Forever		0	1960	9	1960	(University 210)

Little Eva Female Vocalist, Real Name Eva Narcissus Boyd B: 29 Jun 1945 In Belhaven, Carolina

ISSUE	TITLE	UK LBL	UK POS	UK YEAR	US POS	US YEAR	US LBL
* 1	The Loco-motion	(London HL 9581)	2	1962	1	1962	(Dimension 1000)
2	Keep Your Hands Of My Baby	(London HLU9633)	30	1963	12	1962	(Dimension 1003)
3	Let's Turkey Trot	(London HLU 9687)	13	1963	20	1963	(Dimension 1006)
4	Swinging On A Star	(COPIX PX 11010)	7	1963	38	1963	(Dimension 1010)
5	The Loco-motion (Re-Entry)	(London HL 9581)	11	1972	0	1972	

Little Jack Little & His Orchestra Male Vocalist/Bandleader from London, England

ISSUE	TITLE	UK LBL	UK POS	UK YEAR	US POS	US YEAR	US LBL
* 1	I'm In The Mood For Love		0	1935	8	1935	(Columbia 3069)

Little Jimmy Dickens Male Country Singer, James Cecil Dickens B: 19 Dec 1920 In Bolt, West Virginia

ISSUE	TITLE	UK LBL	UK POS	UK YEAR	US POS	US YEAR	US LBL
11	May The Bird Of Paradise Fly Up Your Nose		0	1965	15	1965	(Columbia 43388)

Little Joe & The Thrillers Names Farris Hill, Joe Cook, Harry Pascie, Richard Frazier & Donald Burnett

ISSUE	TITLE	UK LBL	UK POS	UK YEAR	US POS	US YEAR	US LBL
1	Peanuts		0	1957	22	1957	(Okeh 7088)

Joe's Daughter Is Lead Singer With The Sherrys

Little Joey & The Flips Lead Singer With The Quintet Is Joey Hall

ISSUE	TITLE	UK LBL	UK POS	UK YEAR	US POS	US YEAR	US LBL
1	Bongo Stomp		0	1962	33	1962	(JOY 262)

Little Johnny Taylors Real Name Johnny Young B: 11 Feb 1943 Memphis

ISSUE	TITLE	UK LBL	UK POS	UK YEAR	US POS	US YEAR	US LBL
1	Part Time Love		0	1963	19	1963	(Galaxy 722)

Little Milton Male Blues Vocalist/Guitarist, Real Name Milton Campbell Jr. B: 7 Sep 1934 In Inverness, Mississippi

ISSUE	TITLE	UK LBL	UK POS	UK YEAR	US POS	US YEAR	US LBL
1	We're Gonna Make It		0	1965	25	1965	(Checker 1105)

Little Peggy March Female Vocalist, Margaret Battavio, B: 7 Mar 1948, Lansdale, Pennsylvania

ISSUE	TITLE	UK LBL	UK POS	UK YEAR	US POS	US YEAR	US LBL
* 1	I Will Follow Him (aka Chariot)		0	1963	1	1963	(RCA 8139)
2	I Wish I Were A Princess		0	1963	32	1963	(RCA 8189)
3	Hello Heartache Goodbye Love	(RCA 1362)	29	1963	26	1963	(RCA 8221)

ISSUE	TITLE	UK LBL	UK POS	UK YEAR	US POS	US YEAR	US LBL
Little Richard Male Vocal/Pianist, Real Name Richard Wayne Penniman B: 5 Dec 1932 In Macon, Georgia							
1	Tutti Frutti	(London HLO 8366)	29	1957	17	1956	(Specialty 561)
* 2	Long Tall Sally	(London HLO 8366)	3	1957	6	1956	(Specialty 572)
3	Slippin' And Slidin' (Peepin' And Hidin')		0	1956	33	1956	(Specialty 572)
4	Rip It Up	(London HLO 8336)	30	1956	17	1956	(Specialty 579)
+ 5	She's Got It	(London HLO 8382)	15	1957	15	1956	(Specialty 584)
6	The Girl Can't Help It	(London HLO 8382)	9	1957	49	1957	(Specialty 591)
7	Lucille	(London HLO 8446)	10	1957	21	1957	(Specialty 598)
8	She's Got It (Re-Entry)	(London HLO 8382)	28	1957	0	1957	
9	Jenny Jenny	(London HLO 8470)	11	1957	10	1957	(Specialty 606)
10	Keep A Knockin'	(London HLO 8509)	21	1957	8	1957	(Specialty 611)
11	Good Golly Miss Molly	(London HLO 8560)	8	1958	10	1958	(Specialty 624)
12	Ooh My Soul	(London HLO 8647)	30	1958	31	1958	(Specialty 633)
13	Ooh My Soul (Re-Entry)	(London HLO 8647)	22	1958	0	1958	
14	Baby Face	(London HLU 8770)	2	1959	41	1958	(Specialty 645)
15	By The Light Of The Silvery Moon	(London HLU 8831)	17	1959	0	1959	
16	Kansas City	(London HLU 8868)	26	1959	0	1959	
17	He Got What He Wanted	(Mercury AMT 1189)	38	1962	0	1962	
18	Bama Lama Bama Loo	(London HL 9896)	20	1964	82	1964	(Specialty 692)
+ 19	I Don't Know What You've Got But It's Got Me - Part 1		0	1965	92	1965	(VEE-JAY 698)
20	Freedom Blues		0	1970	47	1970	(Reprise 0907)
21	Good Golly Miss Milly/Rip It Up	(CREOLE CR 140)	37	1977	0	1977	
22	Great Gosh A'mighty (It's A Matter Of Time)	(MCA MCA 1049)	62	1986	0	1986	
23	Operator	(WEA YZ 89)	67	1986	0	1986	
	HIT 21 IS A RE-RECORDINGS OF HITS 4 & 11						
Little River Band Rock Band formed in Australia in 1975 with lead singer Glenn Shorrock							
1	It's A Long Way There		0	1976	28	1976	(Harvest 4318)
2	Help Is On Its Way		0	1977	14	1977	(Harvest 4428)
3	Happy Aniversary		0	1978	16	1978	(Harvest 4524)
4	Reminiscing		0	1978	3	1978	(Harvest 4605)
5	Lady		0	1979	10	1979	(Harvest 4667)
6	Lonesome Loser		0	1979	6	1979	(Capitol 4748)
7	Cool Change		0	1979	10	1979	(Capitol 4789)
8	The Night Owls		0	1981	6	1981	(Capitol 5033)
9	Take It Easy On Me		0	1982	10	1982	(Capitol 5057)
10	Man On Your Mind		0	1982	14	1982	(Capitol 5061)
11	The Other Guy		0	1983	11	1982	(Capitol 5185)
12	We Two		0	1983	22	1983	(Capitol 5231)
13	You're Driving Me Out Of My Mind		0	1983	35	1983	(Capitol 5256)
Little Sister Female Soul Trio, Mary Rand, Elva Melton & Vanetta Stewart from the USA							
1	You're The One (Part 1)		0	1970	22	1970	(Stone Flower 9000)
2	Somebody's Watching You		0	1971	32	1971	(Stone Flower 9001)
Little Steven Male Vocal/Guitarist from the USA							
1	Bitter Fruit	(Manhattan MT 21)	66	1987	0	1987	
Little Tony & His Brothers Male Vocalist, Real Name Antonio Ciacci B: 1940, San Marino, Italy							
1	Too Good	(Decca F 11190)	19	1960	0	1960	
* 2	Cuore Matto (Crazy Heart)	(PYE/Durium)	0	1967	0	1967	
	ALTHOUGH HIT 2 DIDN'T HIT THE CHARTS IN EITHER COUNTRY, THE COLLECTIVE SALES ARE OVER A MILLION						
Little Willie John Real Name William Edgar John B: 15 Nov 1937 In Cullendale, Arkansas, Convicted Of Manslaughter In 1966							
* 1	Fever		0	1956	24	1956	(King 4935)
2	Talk To Me, Talk To Me		0	1958	20	1958	(King 5108)
3	Heartbreak 'It's Hurtin' Me)		0	1960	38	1960	(King 5356)
4	Sleep		0	1960	13	1960	(King 5394)
	OBITUARY: D: 26 MAY 1968 HEART ATTACK, WHILST IN WASHINGTON STATE PENITENTIARY.						
Live Male Vocal/Instrumental Group from the USA							
1	I Alone	(Radioactive RAXTD 13)	48	1995	0	1995	
2	Selling The Drama	(Radioactive RAXTD 17)	30	1995	0	1995	
3	All Over You	(Radioactive RAXTD 20)	48	1995	0	1995	
4	Lightning Crashes	(Radioactive RAXTD 23)	33	1996	0	1996	
5	Lakini's Juice	(Radioactive RAD 49023)	29	1997	0	1997	
6	Freaks	(Radioactive RAXTD 29)	60	1997	0	1997	
Live Report Male Vocal/Instrumental Group from the UK							
1	Why Do I Always Get It Wrong	(BrouhahaCUE 7)	73	1989	0	1989	

ISSUE	TITLE	UK LBL	UK POS	UK YEAR	US POS	US YEAR	US LBL
Liverpool Express Male Vocal/Instrumental Group from the UK							
1	You Are My Love	(Warner Bros. K 16743)	11	1976	0	1976	
2	Hold Tight	(Warner Bros. K 16799)	46	1976	0	1976	
3	Every Man Must Have A Dream	(Warner Bros. K 16854)	17	1976	0	1976	
4	Dreamin'	(Warner Bros. K 16933)	40	1977	0	1977	
Liverpool F.C. Male Vocal Soccer Team from the UK							
1	We Can Do It (EP)	(State STAT 50)	15	1977	0	1977	
2	Liverpool (We're Never Gonna…) / Liverpool	(Anthem) (Meanmean 102)	54	1983	0	1983	
3	Sitting On Top Of The World	Columbia DB 9116)	50	1986	0	1986	
4	Anfield Rap (Red Machine In Full Effect)	(Virgin LFC 1)	3	1988	0	1988	
5	Pass And Move (It's The Liverpool Groove)	(TELSTAR LFCCD 96)	4	1996	0	1996	
	HIT 5 IS CREDITED TO LIVERPOOL F.C. & THE BOOT ROOM BOYZ						
Livin' Joy Mixed Vocal/Instrumental Group from the USA/Italy							
1	Dreamer	(Undiscovered MCSTD 1993)	18	1994	0	1994	
2	Dreamer (Re-Mix)	(Undiscovered MCSTD 2056)	1	1995	0	1995	
3	Don't Stop Movin'	(Undiscovered MCSTD 40041)	5	1996	67	1997	(MCA 55301)
4	Follow The Rules	(Undiscovered MCSTD 40081)	9	1996	0	1996	
5	Where Can I Find Love	(Undiscovered MCSTD 40108)	12	1997	0	1997	
6	Deep In You	(Universal MCSTD 40136)	17	1997	0	1997	
Living Colour Male Instrumental/Rock Quartet from New York With Vocalist Corey Glover							
1	Cult Of Personality	(Epic 6575357)	67	1991	13	1989	(Epic 68611)
2	Glamour Boys		0	1989	31	1989	(Epic 68548)
3	Type	(Epic LCL 7)	75	1990	0	1990	
4	Love Rears It's Ugly Head	(Epic 6565937)	12	1991	0	1991	
5	Solace Of You	(Epic 6569087)	33	1991	0	1991	
6	Leave It Alone	(Epic 6589762)	34	1993	0	1993	
7	Auslander	(Epic 6591732)	53	1993	0	1993	
Living In A Box Male Vocal/Instrumental Trio from the UK, Names Richard Darbyshire, Marcus Vere & Anthony Critchlow							
1	Living In A Box	(Chrysalis LIB 1)	5	1987	17	1987	(Chrysalis 43104)
2	Scales Of Justice	(Chrysalis LIB 2)	30	1987	0	1987	
3	So The Story Goes	(Chrysalis LIB 3)	34	1987	0	1987	
4	Love Is The Art	(Chrysalis LIB 4)	45	1988	0	1988	
5	Blow The House Down	(Chrysalis LIB 5)	10	1989	0	1989	
6	Gatecrashing	(Chrysalis LIB 6)	36	1989	0	1989	
7	Room In Your Heart	(Chrysalis LIB 7)	5	1989	0	1989	
8	Different Air	(Chrysalis LIB 8)	64	1989	0	1989	
9	Different Air (Re-Entry)	(Chrysalis LIB 8)	57	1990	0	1990	
Livingston Taylor Male Vocalist, B: 21 Nov 1950 Boston, Younger Brother Of James Taylor							
1	First Time Love		0	1980	38	1980	(Epic 50894)
2	I Will Be In Love With You		0	1978	30	1978	(Epic 50604)
Liz Damon('S) Orient Express Mixed Vocal/Instrumental Group from Hawaii							
1	Yesterday		0	1971	33	1971	(White Whale 368)
Liz Kershaw & Bruno Brookes Mixed Vocal Duo from the UK							
1	It Takes Two Baby	(Spartan CIN 101)	53	1989	0	1989	
2	Let's Dance	(Jiveruno 1)	54	1990	0	1990	
Liza Minnelli Female Actress/Vocalist from the USA							
1	Losing My Mind	(Epic ZEE 1)	6	1989	0	1989	
2	Don't Drop Bombs	(Epic ZEE 2)	46	1989	0	1989	
3	So Sorry I Said	(Epic ZEE 3)	62	1989	0	1989	
4	Love Pains	(Epic ZEE 4)	41	1990	0	1990	
Lizzy Mack Female Vocalist from the UK							
1	The Power Of Love	(MEDIA NCSTD 2016)	49	1994	0	1994	
2	Don't Go	(Power Station MCSTD 40004)	52	1995	0	1995	
Lloyd Cole Male Vocalist from the UK							
1	Perfect Skin	(Polydor Cole 1)	71	1984	0	1984	
2	Perfect Skin (Re-Entry)	(Polydor Cole 1)	26	1984	0	1984	
3	Forest Fire	(Polydor Cole 2)	41	1984	0	1984	
4	Rattlesnakes	(Polydor Cole 3)	65	1984	0	1984	
5	Brand New Friend	(Polydor Cole 4)	19	1985	0	1985	
6	Lost Weekend	(Polydor Cole 5)	17	1985	0	1985	
7	Cut Me Down	(Polydor Cole 6)	36	1986	0	1986	

ISSUE	TITLE	UK LBL	UK POS	UK YEAR	US POS	US YEAR	US LBL
8	My Bag	(Polydor Cole 7)	46	1987	0	1987	
9	Jennifer She Said	(Polydor Cole 8)	31	1988	0	1988	
10	From The Hip (EP)	(Polydor Cole 9)	59	1988	0	1988	
11	No Blue Skies	(Polydor Cole 11)	42	1990	0	1990	
12	Don't Look Back	(Polydor Cole 12)	59	1990	0	1990	
13	She's A Girl And I'm A Man	(Polydor Cole 14)	55	1991	0	1991	
14	So You'd Like To Save The World	(Fontana VIBE D1)	72	1993	0	1993	
15	Like Lovers Do	(Fontana LCCD 1)	24	1995	0	1995	
16	Sentimental Fool	(Fontana LCCD 2)	73	1995	0	1995	

Lloyd Price Male Vocalist, B: 9 Mar 1933 Kenner, Louisiana

	ISSUE	TITLE	UK LBL	UK POS	UK YEAR	US POS	US YEAR	US LBL
*+	1	Lawdy Miss Clawdy		0	1952	1	1952	(Specialty 428)
+	2	Oooh-Oooh-Oooh / Restless Heart		0	1952	5	1952	(Specialty 440)
+	3	Ain't It A Shame?/Tell Me Pretty Baby		0	1953	7	1953	(Specialty 452)
	4	Just Because		0	1957	29	1957	(ABC-Paramount 9792)
*	5	Stagger Lee	(HMV POP 580)	7	1959	1	1959	(ABC-Paramount 9972)
	6	Where Were You (On Our Wedding Day)?	(HMV POP 598)	15	1959	23	1959	(ABC-Paramount 9997)
*	7	Personality	(HMV POP 626)	9	1959	2	1959	(ABC-Paramount 10018)
	8	Personality (Re-Entry)	(HMV POP 626)	25	1959	0	1959	
*	9	I'm Gonna Get Married	(HMV POP 650)	23	1959	3	1959	(ABC-Paramount 10032)
	10	Come Into My Heart / Wont'cha Come Home		0	1959	20	1959	(ABC-Paramount 10062)
	11	Lady Luck	(HMV POP 712)	45	1960	14	1960	(ABC-Paramount 10075}
	12	No If's-No And's		0	1960	40	1960	(ABC-Paramount 10102)
	13	Question		0	1960	19	1960	(ABC-Paramount 10123)
	14	Misty		0	1963	21	1963	(Double-L 722)
		HIT 1 HAS FATS DOMINO ON PIANO						

LNR See L.N.R.

Lo-Key? Male Funk Fivesome from The US Midwest

| | 1 | I Got A Thang 4 Ya! | | 0 | 1992 | 27 | 1992 | (Perspective 0008) |

Lobo (1) Male Vocalist, Real Name Roland Kent Lavoie B: 31 Jul 1943 Tallahassee, Florida

*	1	Me And You And A Dog Named Boo	(Philips 6073 801)	4	1971	5	1971	(Big Tree 112)
*	2	I'd Love You To Want Me	(UK 68)	5	1974	2	1972	(Big Tree 147)
	3	Don't Expect Me To Be Your Friend		0	1973	8	1973	(Big Tree 158)
	4	It Sure Took A Long, Long Time		0	1973	27	1973	(Big Tree 16001)
	5	How Can I Tell Her		0	1973	22	1973	(Big Tree 16004)
	6	Standing At The End Of The Line		0	1974	37	1974	(Big Tree 15001)
	7	Don't Tell Me Goodnight		0	1975	27	1975	(Big Tree 16033)
	8	Where Were You When I Was Falling In Love		0	1979	23	1979	(MCA 41065)

Lobo (2) Male Vocalist from Holland

| | 1 | The Caribbean Disco Show | (Polydor POSP 302) | 8 | 1981 | 0 | 1981 | |

Locksmith Male Vocal/Instrumental Group from the USA

| | 1 | Unlock The Funk | (Arista ARIST 364) | 42 | 1980 | 0 | 1980 | |

Locomotive Male Vocal/Instrumental Group from the UK

| | 1 | Rudi's In Love | (Parlophone R 5718) | 25 | 1968 | 0 | 1968 | |

Loggins & Messina Real Names Kenneth Clark Loggins B: 7 Jan 1947 Fron Everett, Washington & James Messina B: 5 Dec 1947

*	1	Your Mama Don't Dance		0	1972	4	1972	(Columbia 45719)
	2	Thinking Of You		0	1973	18	1973	(Columbia 45815)
	3	My Music		0	1973	16	1973	(Columbia 45952)
!	4	Oh, Lonesome Me		0	1975	92	1975	(Columbia 10222)
	5	A Lovers Question		0	1975	89	1975	(Columbia 10222)

Lola Female Vocalist from the USA

| | 1 | Wax The Van | (SYNCOPATE SY 1) | 65 | 1987 | 0 | 1987 | |

Lola Ameche See Also All Trace

| | 1 | Hitsity Hotsity | | 0 | 1951 | 24 | 1951 | (Mercury 5675) |

Loleatta Holloway Female Vocalist from the USA

	1	Good Vibrations	(Interscope A 8764)	14	1991	9	1991	(Interscope 98764)
	2	Take Me Away	(Continental PWL 210)	25	1992	0	1992	
	3	Stand Up	(SIX6 SIXCD 111)	68	1994	0	1994	
	4	Keep The Fire Burnin'	(Columbia 6611552)	49	1995	0	1995	

Lolita Real Name Lolita Ditta St. Poelten, Austria

| * | 1 | Sailor (Your Home Is The Sea) | | 0 | 1960 | 5 | 1960 | (KAPP 349) |

London Boys Male Vocal Duo from the UK

| | 1 | Requiem | (WEA YZ 345) | 59 | 1988 | 0 | 1988 | |

ISSUE	TITLE	UK LBL	UK POS	UK YEAR	US POS	US YEAR	US LBL
2	Requiem (Re-Entry)	(WEA YZ 345)	4	1989	0	1989	
3	London Nights	(WEA YZ 393)	2	1989	0	1989	
4	Harlem Desire	(WEA YZ 415)	17	1989	0	1989	
5	My Love	(WEA YZ 433)	46	1989	0	1989	
6	Chapel Of Love	(East West YZ 458)	75	1990	0	1990	
7	Freedom	(East West YZ 554)	54	1991	0	1990	

London String Chorale Orchestra And Choir from the UK

1	Galloping Home	(Polydor 2058 280)	49	1973	0	1973	
2	Galloping Home (Re-Entry)	(Polydor 2058 280)	31	1974	0	1974	

London Symphony Orchestra UK Orchestra Conducted By John Williams

1	Theme From *Superman* (Main Title)	(Warner Bros. K 17292)	32	1979	0	1979	

Londonbeat Male Vocal Group from the USA/UK

1	9 Am (The Comfort Zone)	(Anxious ANX 008)	19	1988	0	1988	
2	Falling In Love Again	(Anxious ANX 007)	60	1989	0	1989	
* 3	I've Been Thinking About You	(Anxious ANX 14)	2	1990	1	1991	(Radioactive 54005)
4	A Better Love	(Anxious ANX 21)	52	1990	18	1990	(Radioactive 54101)
5	No Woman No Cry	(Anxious ANX 25)	64	1991	0	1991	
6	A Better Love (Re-Issue)	(Anxious ANX 32)	23	1991	0	1991	
7	You Bring On The Sun	(Anxious ANX 37)	32	1992	0	1992	
8	That's How I Feel About You	(Anxious ANX 40)	69	1992	0	1992	
9	I'm Just Your Puppet On A...(String)	(Anxious 74321270982)	55	1995	0	1995	
10	Come Back	(Anxious 74321226682)	69	1995	0	1990	

Lone Justice Mixed Vocal/Instrumental Group from the USA

1	I Found Love	(Geffen GEF 18)	45	1987	0	1987	

Long & The Short Male Vocal/Instrumental Group from the UK

1	The Letter	(Decca F 11964)	30	1964	0	1964	
2	Choc Ice	(Decca F 12043)	49	1964	0	1964	

Long John Baldry Male Vocalist from the UK

1	Let The Heartaches Begin	(PYE 7N 17385)	1	1967	0	1967	
2	When The Sun Comes Shinning Thru'	(PYE 7N 17593)	29	1968	0	1968	
3	Mexico	(PYE 7N 17563)	15	1968	0	1968	
4	It's Too Late Now	(PYE 7N 17664)	21	1969	0	1969	

Long Ryders Male Vocal/Instrumental Group from the USA

1	Looking For Lewis And Clark	(Island IS 237)	59	1985	0	1985	

Longpigs Male Vocal/Instrumental Group from the UK

1	She Said	(Mother MUMCD 66)	67	1995	0	1995	
2	Jesus Christ	(Mother MUMCD 68)	61	1995	0	1995	
3	Far	(Mother MUMCD 71)	37	1996	0	1996	
4	On And On	(Mother MUMCD 74)	16	1996	0	1996	
5	She Said (Re-Issue)	(Mother MUMXD 77)	16	1996	0	1996	
6	Lost Myself	(Mother MUMCD 82)	22	1996	0	1996	

Longsy D Male Vocalist from the UK

1	This Is Ska	(ONE BIG 13)	56	1989	0	1989	

Loni Clark Female Vocalist from the USA

1	Rushing	(A&M 5802862)	37	1993	0	1993	
2	U	(A&M 5804752)	28	1994	0	1994	
3	Love's Got Me On A Trip So High	(A&M 5808872)	59	1994	0	1994	

Lonnie Donegan Real Name Anthony Donegan B: 29 Apr 1931 Glasgow, Scotland

* 1	Rock Island Line	(Decca F 10647)	8	1956	8	1956	(London 1650)
2	Rock Island Line (Re-Entry)	(Decca F 10647)	16	1956	0	1956	
3	Stewball	(PYE NIXA N 15036)	27	1956	0	1956	
4	Lost John / Stewball	(PYE NIXA N 15036)	2	1956	0	1956	
5	Rock Island Line (2nd Re-Entry)	(Decca F 10647)	19	1956	0	1956	
6	Skiffle Session (EP)	(PYE NIXA NJE 1017)	20	1956	0	1956	
7	Bring A Little Water Sylvie / Dead Or Alive	(PYE NIXA N 15071)	7	1956	0	1956	
8	Lonnie Donegan Showcase (Lp)	(PYE NIXA NPT 19012)	26	1956	0	1956	
9	Bring A Little Water Sylvie / Dead Or Alive (Re-Entry)	(PYE NIXA N 15071)	30	1957	0	1957	
10	Don't You Rock Me Daddy-O	(PYE NIXA N 15080)	4	1957	0	1957	
11	Cumberland Gap	(PYE NIXA N 15087)	1	1957	0	1957	
12	Gamblin' Man / Putting On The Style	(PYE NIXA N 15093)	1	1957	0	1957	
13	My Dixie Darling	(PYE NIXA N 15108)	10	1957	0	1957	

ISSUE	TITLE	UK LBL	UK POS	UK YEAR	US POS	US YEAR	US LBL
14	Jack O' Diamonds	(PYE NIXA 7N 15116)	14	1957	0	1957	
15	Grand Coolie Dam	(PYE NIXA 7N 15129)	6	1958	0	1958	
16	Sally Don't You Greeve / Betty Betty Betty	(PYE NIXA 7N 15148)	11	1958	0	1958	
17	Lonesome Traveller	(PYE NIXA 7N 15158)	28	1958	0	1958	
18	Lonnie's Skiffle Party	(PYE NIXA 7N 15165)	23	1958	0	1958	
19	Tom Dooley	(PYE NIXA 7N 15172)	3	1958	0	1958	
* 20	Does Your Chewing Gum Lose It's Flavour On The Bedpost Overnight	(PYE NIXA 7N 15181)	3	1959	5	1961	(DOT 15911)
21	Fortworth Jail	(PYE NIXA 7N 15198)	14	1959	0	1959	
22	Battle Of New Orleans	(PYE 7N 15206)	2	1959	0	1959	
23	Sals Got A Sugar Lip	(PYE 7N 15223)	13	1959	0	1959	
24	San Miguel	(PYE 7N 15237)	19	1959	0	1959	
* 25	My Old Man's A Dustman / The Golden Venity	(PYE 7N 15256)	1	1960	1	1960	
26	I Wanna Go Home/Jimmy Brown The News Boy	(PYE 7N 15267)	5	1960	0	1960	
27	Lorelie/In All My Wildest Dreams	(PYE 7N 15275)	10	1960	0	1960	
28	Lively / Black Cat	(PYE 7N 15312)	13	1960	0	1960	
29	Virgin Mary/Beyond The Sunset	(PYE 7N 15315)	27	1960	0	1960	
30	Have A Drink On Me / Seven Daffodils	(PYE 7N 15354)	8	1961	0	1961	
31	Michael Row The Boat/Lumbered	(PYE 7N 15371)	6	1961	0	1961	
32	The Comancheros/Ramblin' Round	(PYE 7N 15410)	14	1962	0	1962	
33	The Party's Over/Over The Rainbow	(PYE 7N 15424)	9	1962	0	1962	
34	Pick A Bale Of Cotton/Steal Away	(PYE 7N 15455)	11	1962	0	1962	

Lonnie Gordon   Female Vocalist from the USA

1	(I've Got Your) Pleasure Control	(FFRR F 106)	60	1989	0	1989	
2	Happenin' All Over Again	(Supreme SUPE 159)	4	1990	0	1990	
3	Beyond Your Wildest Dreams	(Supreme SUPE 167)	48	1990	0	1990	
4	If I Have To Stand Alone	(Supreme SUPE 181)	68	1990	0	1990	
5	Gonna Catch You	(Supreme SUPE 185)	32	1991	0	1991	
6	Love Eviction	(X-PLODE BANG 2CD)	32	1995	0	1995	

Lonnie Hill   Male Vocalist from the USA

1	Galveston Bay	(10 TEN 111)	51	1986	0	1986	

Lonnie Johnson   Male Blues Guitarist, B: 8 Feb 1900 New Orleans

* 1	Tomorrow Night		0	1948	19	1948	(King 4201)

Lonnie Mack   Male Guitarist, Real Name Lonnie McIntosh B: 18 Jul 1941 In Harrison, Indiana

* 1	Memphis	(Lightning LIG 9011)	47	1979	5	1963	(Fraternity 906)
2	Wham!		0	1963	24	1963	(Fraternity 912)

Look   Male Vocal/Instrumental Group from the UK

1	I Am The Beat	(MCA 647)	6	1980	0	1980	
2	Feeding Time	(MCA 736)	50	1981	0	1981	

Looking Glass   Names Elliot Lurie, Pieter Sweval, Larry Gonsky And Jeff Grob

* 1	Brandy (You're A Fine Girl)		0	1972	1	1972	(Epic 10874)
2	Jimmy Loves Mary-Anne		0	1973	33	1973	(Epic 11001)

Loose Ends   Mixed Vocal/Instrumental Group from the UK

1	Tell Me What You Want	(Virgin VS 658)	74	1984	0	1984	
2	Emergency (Dial 999)	(Virgin VS 677)	41	1984	0	1984	
3	Choose Me (Rescue Me)	(Virgin VS 697)	59	1984	0	1984	
4	Hangin' On A String (Contemplating)	(Virgin VS 748)	13	1985	0	1985	
5	Magic Touch	(Virgin VS 761)	16	1985	0	1985	
6	Golden Years	(Virgin VS 795)	59	1985	0	1985	
7	Stay A Little While Child	(Virgin VS 819)	52	1986	0	1986	
8	Slow Down	(Virgin VS 884)	27	1986	0	1986	
9	Nights Of Pleasure	(Virgin VS 919)	42	1986	0	1986	
10	Mr. Bachelor	(Virgin VS 1080)	50	1988	0	1988	
11	Don't Be A Fool	(10 TEN 312)	13	1990	0	1990	
12	Love's Got Me	(10 TEN 330)	40	1990	0	1990	
13	Hangin' On A String (Re-Mix)	(TEN TEN 406)	25	1992	0	1992	
1 14	Magic Touch (Re-Mix)	(TEN TEN 409)	75	1992	0	1992	

Lord Rockingham's XI   Male Instrumental Group from the UK

1	Hoots Mon	(Decca F 11059)	1	1958	0	1958	
2	Wee Tom	(Decca F 11104)	16	1959	0	1959	
3	Hoots Mon (Re-Issue)	(Decca 8820982)	60	1993	0	1993	

Lord Tanamo   Male Vocalist From Trinidad And Tobago

ISSUE	TITLE	UK LBL	UK POS	UK YEAR	US POS	US YEAR	US LBL
1	I'm In The Mood For Love	(MOONCREST MMON 1009)	58	1990	0	1990	

Lori & The Chameleons Mixed Vocal/Instrumental Group from the UK

ISSUE	TITLE	UK LBL	UK POS	UK YEAR	US POS	US YEAR	US LBL
1	Touch	(SIRE SIR 4025)	70	1979	0	1979	

Lorne Greene Male Actor/Vocalist, B: 12 Feb 1914 Ottawa, Canada

ISSUE	TITLE	UK LBL	UK POS	UK YEAR	US POS	US YEAR	US LBL
* 1	Ringo	(RCA 1428)	22	1964	1	1964	(RCA 8444)

He Is Best Known For His Role As Pa Cartwright In *Bonanza*   Obituary : D: 11 Sep 1987 Heart Attack.

Lorraine Cato Female Vocalist from the UK

ISSUE	TITLE	UK LBL	UK POS	UK YEAR	US POS	US YEAR	US LBL
1	How Can You Tell Me It's Over	(Columbia 6587662)	46	1993	0	1993	
2	I Was Made To Love You	(MCA MCSTD 40055)	41	1996	0	1996	

Lorry Raine Female Vocalist from the USA

ISSUE	TITLE	UK LBL	UK POS	UK YEAR	US POS	US YEAR	US LBL
1	Strangers		0	1950	24	1950	(London 30178)
2	A-Wooin' We Will Go		0	1953	22	1953	(KEM 2723)
3	There's Nothin' Left To Do (But Cry)		0	1953	21	1953	(KEM 2723)
4	I'm In Love With A Guy		0	1953	24	1953	(KEM 2729)
5	What Would I Do		0	1954	22	1954	(DOT 15224)

Los Bravos Male Vocal/Instrumental Group from Spain/Germany, An Amalgamation Of Two Groups, Los Sonor and The Runaways

ISSUE	TITLE	UK LBL	UK POS	UK YEAR	US POS	US YEAR	US LBL
* 1	Black Is Black	(Decca F 22419)	2	1966	4	1966	(PRESS 60002)
2	I Don't Care	(Decca F 22484)	16	1966	0	1966	

Los Del Mar Male Vocal/Instrumental Group from Canada/Cuba

ISSUE	TITLE	UK LBL	UK POS	UK YEAR	US POS	US YEAR	US LBL
1	Macarena	(PULSE 8 CDLOSE 101)	66	1996	0	1996	
2	Macarena (Re-Entry)	(PULSE 8 CDLOSE 101)	43	1996	0	1996	

Los Del Rio Male Vocal/Instrumental Duo From Spain

ISSUE	TITLE	UK LBL	UK POS	UK YEAR	US POS	US YEAR	US LBL
1	Macarena	(RCA 74321345372)	64	1996	23	1996	(Ariola 39227)
* 2	Macarena (Re-Entry)	(RCA 74321345372)	2	1996	1	1996	(RCA 64407)
3	Macarena Christmas		0	1996	66	1996	(Ariola 44124)

Los Indios Tabajaras Brazilian Duo, Two Brothers, Musiperi And Herundy Lima, Brazil

ISSUE	TITLE	UK LBL	UK POS	UK YEAR	US POS	US YEAR	US LBL
* 1	Maria Elena	(RCA 1365)	5	1963	6	1963	(RCA 8216)

Los Lobos Male Vocal/Instrumental Quintet From East Los Angeles, Lead Vocals David Hidalgo

ISSUE	TITLE	UK LBL	UK POS	UK YEAR	US POS	US YEAR	US LBL
1	Don't Worry Baby / Will The Wolf Survive	(London LASH 4)	57	1985	0	1985	
2	La Bamba	(Slash Lash 13)	1	1987	1	1987	(Slash 28336)
3	Come On Let's Go	(Slash Lash 14)	18	1987	21	1987	(Slash 28186)

Lost Male Production/Instrumental Duo from the UK

ISSUE	TITLE	UK LBL	UK POS	UK YEAR	US POS	US YEAR	US LBL
1	Techno Funk	(Perfecto PT 44560)	75	1991	0	1991	

Lost Generation Names: Lowrell And Fred Simon, Larry Browniee & Jesse Dean, The Group Disbanded In 1974

ISSUE	TITLE	UK LBL	UK POS	UK YEAR	US POS	US YEAR	US LBL
1	The Sly, Slick, And Wicked		0	1970	30	1970	(Brunswick 55436)

Lotus Eaters Male Vocal/Instrumental Duo from the UK

ISSUE	TITLE	UK LBL	UK POS	UK YEAR	US POS	US YEAR	US LBL
1	First Picture Of You	(Sylvan SYL 1)	15	1983	0	1983	
2	You Don't Need Someone New	(Sylvan SYL 2)	53	1983	0	1983	

Lou Busch Male Orchestra Leader And Chorus from the USA

ISSUE	TITLE	UK LBL	UK POS	UK YEAR	US POS	US YEAR	US LBL
1	Zambezi	(Capitol CL 14504)	2	1956	0	1956	

Lou Christie Male Vocalist Real Name Lugee Sacco B: 19 Feb 1943 In Glen Willard, Pittsburgh

ISSUE	TITLE	UK LBL	UK POS	UK YEAR	US POS	US YEAR	US LBL
* 1	The Gypsy Cried		0	1962	24	1962	(Roulette 4457)
* 2	Two Faces Have I		0	1963	6	1963	(Roulette 4481)
* 3	Lightnin' Strikes	(MGM 1297)	11	1966	1	1965	(MGM 13412)
4	Rhapsody In The Rain	(MGM 1308)	37	1966	16	1966	(MGM 13473)
5	I'm Gonna Make You Mine	(Buddah 201 057)	2	1969	10	1969	(Buddah 116)
6	She Sold Me Magic	(Buddah 201 073)	25	1969	0	1969	
	RECORDED AS LUGEE & THE LIONS IN 1961						

Lou Gramm B: 2 May 1950 Rochester, New York. Former member of Foreigner

ISSUE	TITLE	UK LBL	UK POS	UK YEAR	US POS	US YEAR	US LBL
1	Midnight Blue		0	1987	5	1987	(Atlantic 89304)
2	Just Between You And Me		0	1990	6	1990	(Atlantic 88781)
3	True Blue Love		0	1990	40	1990	(Atlantic 88768)

Lou Johnson Male Vocalist from the USA

ISSUE	TITLE	UK LBL	UK POS	UK YEAR	US POS	US YEAR	US LBL
1	Message To Martha	(London HL 9929)	36	1964	0	1964	

Lou Monte Male Vocal/Guitarist, B: 2 Apr 1917, Oakland, New Jersey

ISSUE	TITLE	UK LBL	UK POS	UK YEAR	US POS	US YEAR	US LBL
1	At The Darktown Strutter's Ball		0	1954	7	1954	(RCA Victor 5611)
2	Somewhere There Is Someone		0	1951	21	1954	(RCA Victor 5691)
3	Italian Hucklebuck		0	1954	30	1954	(RCA Victor 5832)
4	Lazy Mary		0	1958	12	1958	(RCA 7160)
* 5	Pepino The Italian Mouse		0	1963	5	1963	(Reprise 20106)

ISSUE	TITLE	UK LBL	UK POS	UK YEAR	US POS	US YEAR	US LBL
Lou Rawls Male Vocalist, B: 1 Dec 1935 Chicago, Also Worked With The Pilgrim Travelers							
1	Love Is A Hurtin' Thing		0	1966	13	1966	(Capitol 5709)
2	Dead End Street		0	1967	29	1967	(Capitol 5869)
* 3	Your Good Thing (Is About To End)		0	1969	18	1969	(Capitol 2550)
4	A Natural Man		0	1971	17	1971	(MGM 14262)
* 5	You'll Never Find Another Love Like Mine	(Philadelphia International PIR 4372)	10	1976	2	1976	(Philadelphia INT. 3592)
6	Lady Love		0	1978	24	1978	(Philadelphia INT. 3634)
Lou Reed Male Vocalist, Real Name Louis Firbank B: 2 Mar 1942 Long Island, New York.							
1	Walk On The Wild Side	(RCA 203)	10	1973	16	1973	(RCA 0887)
2	Soul Man	(A&M AM 364)	30	1987	0	1987	with Sam Moore
Lou Stein Male Pianist, B: 22 Apr 1922 Philadelphia							
1	Almost Paradise		0	1957	31	1957	(RKO Unique 385)
Louchie Lou & Michie One Female Vocal Duo from the UK							
1	Shout	(FFRR FCD 211)	7	1993	0	1993	
2	Somebody Else's Guy	(FFRR FCD 216)	54	1993	0	1993	
3	Get Down On It	(China WOKCD 2054)	58	1995	0	1995	
4	Cecilia	(WEA WEA 042CD1)	4	1996	0	1996	
5	Good Sweet Lovin'	(INDOCHINA ID 050CD)	34	1996	0	1996	
6	Cecilia (Re-Entry)	(WEA WEA 042CD1)	65	1996	0	1996	
7	Cecilia (2nd Re-Entry)	(WEA WEA042CD1)	59	1996	0	1996	
1 8	No More Alcohol	(WEA WEA 065CD1)	24	1996	0	1996	
Loud Male V2ocal/Instrumental Group from the UK							
1	Easy	(China Wok 2016)	67	1992	0	1992	
Loudon Wainwright III Male Singer/Songwriter, B: 5 Sep 1946 Chapel Hill, North Carolina							
1	Dead Shunk		0	1973	16	1973	(Columbia 45726)
Louie Louie Male Vocalist, Real Name Louie Cordero From Southern California							
1	Sittin' In The Lap Of Luxury		0	1990	19	1990	(WTG 73266)
2	The Thought Of It	(Hardback YZ 724)	34	1992	0	1992	
Louie Vega & Marc Anthony Male Vocal/Instrumental Duo from the USA							
1	Ride On The Rhythm	(Atlantic A 7602)	71	1991	0	1991	
2	Ride On The Rhythm (Re-Issue)	(Atlantic A 7486)	70	1992	0	1992	
	ORIGINAL RECORDING WAS BY 'LITTLE LOUIE VEGA & MARK ANTHONY						
Louis Armstrong Male Vocalist/Jazz Bandleader/Instrumentalist, Full Name Daniel Louis Armstrong B: 4 Aug 1901 New							
58	You Won't Be Satisfied (Until You Break My Heart)		0	1946	10	1946	(Decca 23496)
59	That Lucky Old Sun		0	1949	19	1949	(Decca 24752)
60	La Vie En Rose		0	1950	28	1950	(Decca 27113)
61	Can Anyone Explain? (No! No! No!)		0	1950	30	1950	(Decca 27209)
62	Gone Fishin'		0	1951	19	1951	(Decca 27623)
63	(When We Are Dancing) I Get Ideas		0	1951	10	1951	(Decca 27720)
64	A Kiss To Build A Dream On (From *The Strip*)		0	1951	16	1951	(Decca 27720)
65	When It's Sleepy Time Down South		0	1952	19	1952	(Decca 27899)
66	Kiss Of Fire		0	1952	20	1952	(Decca 28177)
67	Takes Two To Tango	(Brunswick 04995)	6	1952	19	1952	(Decca 28394)
68	Chloe		0	1953	26	1953	(Decca 28524)
69	The Dummy Song		0	1953	30	1953	(Decca 28803)
70	Sittin' In The Sun (Countin' My Money)		0	1953	30	1953	(Decca 28803)
71	Skokiaan (South Africa Song)		0	1954	29	1954	(Decca 29256)
72	Muskrat Ramble (Re-Recording)		0	1954	28	1954	(Decca 29280)
73	Theme From The Threepenny Opera	(Philips PB 574)	8	1956	20	1956	(Columbia 40587)
74	Take It Satch (EP)	(Philips BBE 12035)	29	1956	0	1956	
75	The Faithfull Hussar	(Philips PB 604)	27	1956	0	1956	
76	Blueberry Hill		0	1956	29	1956	(Decca 30091)
77	Mack The Knife	(Philips PB 967)	24	1959	0	1959	
* 78	Hello Dolly	(London HLR 9878)	4	1964	1	1964	(KAPP 573)
* 79	What A Wonderful World - Caberet	(HMV POP 1615)	1	1968	32	1967	(A&M 3010)
80	Sunshine Of Love	(Stateside SS 2116)	41	1968	0	1968	
81	What A Wonderful World (Re-Issue)	(A&M AM 435)	53	1988	0	1988	
82	We Have All The Time In The World	(EMI CDEM 357)	3	1994	0	1994	
83	We Have All The Time In The World (Re-Entry)	(EMI CDEM 357)	66	1995	0	1995	
	OBITUARY : D: 6 JUL 1971.						

ISSUE	TITLE	UK LBL	UK POS	UK YEAR	US POS	US YEAR	US LBL

Louis Jordan & His Tympany Male Vocal/Saxophonist, B: 8 Jul 1908 Brinkley, Arkansas
Five

* 3	G.I. Jive		0	1944	1	1944	(Decca 8659)
* 6	Caldonia Boogie		0	1945	6	1945	(Decca 8670)
8	Buzz Me		0	1946	9	1946	(Decca 18734)
* 9	Beware (Brother, Beware)		0	1946	20	1946	(Decca 18818)
10	Stone Cold Dead In The Market (He Had It Coming)		0	1946	7	1946	(Decca 23546)
* 11	Choo Choo Ch'boogie		0	1946	7	1946	(Decca 23610)
12	Ain't It Just Like A Woman		0	1946	17	1946	(Decca 23669)
13	Ain't Nobody Here But Us Chickens		0	1947	6	1947	(Decca 23741)
14	Open The Door, Richard		0	1947	6	1947	(Decca 23841)
15	Texas And Pacific		0	1947	20	1947	(Decca 23810)
16	Jack, You're Dead		0	1947	21	1947	(Decca 23901)
17	Boogie Woogie Blue Plate		0	1947	21	1947	(Decca 24108)
18	Run, Joe		0	1948	23	1948	(Decca 24448)
19	Baby, It's Cold Outside (From *Neptune's Daughter*)		0	1949	9	1949	(Decca 24644)
* 20	Saturday Night Fish Fry		0	1949	21	1949	(Decca 24725)

Louis Prima & His Orchestra Male Vocalist/Orchestra Leader, B: 7 Dec 1911 New Orleans.

8	Civilization (Bongo, Bongo, Bongo)		0	1947	8	1947	(RCA Victor 2400)
9	Oh, Babe!		0	1950	12	1950	(ROBIN HOOD 101)
10	Buona Sera	(Capitol CL 14841)	25	1958	0	1958	
11	That Old Black Magic		0	1958	18	1958	(Capitol 4063)
12	Wonderland By Night		0	1961	1	1961	(DOT 16151)

Louise Female Vocalist from the UK

1	Light Of My Life	(EMI CDEMS 397)	8	1995	0	1995	
2	In Walked Love	(EMI CDEMS 413)	17	1996	0	1996	
3	Naked	(EMI CDEEM 431)	5	1996	0	1996	
4	Undivided Love	(EMI CDEM 441)	5	1996	0	1996	
5	One Kiss From Heaven	(EMI CDEM 454)	9	1996	0	1996	

Louise Cordet Female Vocalist From France

1	I'm Just A Baby	(Decca F 11476)	13	1962	0	1962	

Louise Tucker Female Vocalist From Holland

1	Midnight Blue	(ARIOLA ARO 289)	59	1983	0	1983	

Love Lead Singer/Guitarist Of This Rock Group Is Arthur Lee From Memphis

1	7 Is		0	1966	33	1966	(Elektra 45605)

Love & Kisses Studio Group, Don Daniels, Dianne Brooks, Jean Graham & Elaine Hill

1	Thank God It's Friday		0	1978	22	1978	(CASABLANCA 925)

Love & Money Male Vocal/Instrumental Group from the UK

1	Candybar Express	(Mercury Money 1)	56	1986	0	1986	
2	Love And Money	(Mercury Money 4)	68	1987	0	1987	
3	Hallelujah Man	(Fontana Money 5)	63	1988	0	1988	
4	Strange Kind Of Love	(Fontana Money 6)	45	1989	0	1989	
5	Jocelyn Square	(Fontana Money 7)	51	1989	0	1989	
6	Winter	(Fontana Money 9)	52	1991	0	1991	

Love & Rockets Lead Singer With This British Trio Is Daniel Ash, Who Left In 1991

1	So Alive		0	1989	3	1989	(RCA 8956)

Love Affair Male Vocal/Instrumental Group from the UK

1	Everlasting Love	(CBS 3125)	1	1968	0	1968	
2	Rainbow Valley	(CBS 3366)	5	1968	0	1968	
3	A Day Without Love	(CBS 3674)	6	1968	0	1968	
4	One Road	(CBS 3994)	19	1969	0	1969	
5	Bring On Back The Good Times	(CBS 4300)	9	1969	0	1969	

Love City Groove Mixed Vocal/Instrumental Group from the UK

1	Love City Groove	(Planet 3 GXY 2003CD)	7	1995	0	1995	

Love Decade Mixed Vocal/Instrumental Group from the UK

1	Dream On (Is This A Dream)	(Around the World Globe100)	52	1991	0	1991	
2	So Real	(Around the World Globe 106)	14	1991	0	1991	
3	I Feel You	(Around the World Globe 107)	34	1992	0	1992	
4	When The Morning Comes	(Around the World CDGLOBE 114)	69	1993	0	1993	
5	Is This A Dream	(Around the World CDGLOBE 132)	39	1996	0	1996	

ISSUE	TITLE	UK LBL	UK POS	UK YEAR	US POS	US YEAR	US LBL
Love Decree Male Vocal/Instrumental Group from the UK							
1	Something So Real (*Chinheads* Theme)	(Ariola 112642)	61	1989	0	1989	
Love Inc Male Vocal/Production Duo from the UK							
1	Love Is The Message	(Love Evol 1)	59	1991	0	1991	
Love Nelson See Fire Island							
Love Sculpture Instrumental Group from the UK							
1	Sabre Dance	(Parlophone R 5744)	5	1968	0	1968	
Love To Infinity Mixed Vocal/Instrumental Group from the UK							
1	Keep Love Together	(Mushroom D 00467)	38	1995	0	1995	
2	Someday	(Mushroom D 1143)	75	1995	0	1995	
3	Pray For Love	(Mushroom D 1213)	69	1996	0	1996	
Love Tribe Mixed Vocal/Instrumental Duo from the USA							
1	Stand Up	(AM:PM 5816272)	23	1996	89	1997	(A&M 127057)
Love Unlimited Female Vocal Group from the USA							
* 1	Walkin' In The Rain With The One I Love	(UNI UN 539)	14	1972	14	1972	(UNI 55319)
2	I Belong To You		0	1975	27	1975	(20th Century 2141)
3	It May Be Winter Outside (But In My Heart It's Spring)	(20th Century 2149)	11	1975	0	1975	
Love Unlimited Orchestra Studio Orchestra Conducted/Arranged By Barry White							
* 1	Love's Theme	(PYE International 7N 25635)	10	1974	1	1974	(20th Century2069)
2	Satin Soul		0	1975	22	1975	(20th Century 2162)
	SEE ALSO BARRY WHITE, LOVE UNLIMITED						
Love/Hate Male Vocal/Instrumental Group from the USA							
1	Evil Twin	(Columbia 6575967)	59	1991	0	1991	
2	Wasted In America	(Columbia 6578897)	38	1992	0	1992	
Lovebug Starski Male Vocalist from the USA							
1	Amityville The House On The Hill	(Epic A 7182)	12	1986	0	1986	
Lovehappy Mixed Vocal/Instrumental Group from the USA/UK							
1	Message Of Love	(MCA MCSTD 2040)	37	1995	0	1995	
2	Message Of Love (Re-Mix)	(MCA MCSTD 40052)	70	1996	0	1996	
Loveland (Featuring) Rachel Mixed Vocal/Instrumental Group from the UK							
McFarlane							
1	Let The Music (Lift You Up)	(KMS/Eastern Bloc KMSCD 10)	16	1994	0	1994	
2	(Keep On) Shining / Hope (Never Give Up)	(Eastern Bloc Bloc CD 016)	37	1994	0	1994	
3	I Need Somebody	(Eastern Bloc Bloc 23CD)	38	1995	0	1995	
4	Don't Make Me Wait	(Eastern Bloc Bloc 20CD)	22	1995	0	1995	
5	The Wonder Of Love	(Eastern Bloc BLOC 22CD)	53	1995	0	1995	
6	I Need Somebody (Re-Mix)	(Eastern Bloc Bloc 23CD)	38	1995	0	1995	
	HIT 1 IS CREDITED TO LOVELAND FEATURING RACHEL MCFARLANE VS DARLENE LEWIS						
Lover Speaks Male Vocal/Instrumental Duo from the UK							
1	No More 'I Love You's	(A&M AM 326)	58	1986	0	1986	
Loverboy Lead Singer Of This Rock Quintet from Canada Is Mike Reno							
1	Turn Me Loose		0	1981	35	1981	(Columbia 11421)
2	Working For The Weekend		0	1982	29	1982	(Columbia 02589)
3	When It's Over		0	1982	26	1982	(Columbia 02814)
4	Hot Girls In Love		0	1983	11	1983	(Columbia 03941)
5	Queen Of Broken Hearts		0	1983	34	1983	(Columbia 04096)
6	Lovin' Every Minute Of It		0	1985	9	1985	(Columbia 05569)
7	This Could Be The Night		0	1986	10	1986	(Columbia 05765)
8	Heaven In Your Eyes		0	1986	12	1986	(Columbia 06178)
9	Notorious		0	1987	38	1987	(Columbia 07324)
Lovestation Male Production Group from the UK							
1	Shine On Me	(RCA 743211337912)	71	1993	0	1993	
2	Best Of My Love	(Fresh FRSHD 1)	73	1993	0	1993	
3	Love Come Rescue Me	(Fresh FRSHD 22)	42	1995	0	1995	
Lovin' Spoonful Male Vocal/Instrumental Group from the USA/Canada							
1	Do You Believe In Magic		0	1965	9	1965	(Kama Sutra 201)
2	You Didn't Have To Be So Nice		0	1965	10	1965	(Kama Sutra 205)
* 3	Daydream	(PYE International 7N 25361)	2	1966	2	1966	(Kama Sutra 208)
4	Did You Ever Have To Make Up Your Mind		0	1966	2	1966	(Kama Sutra 209)

ISSUE	TITLE	UK LBL	UK POS	UK YEAR	US POS	US YEAR	US LBL
* 5	Summer In The City	(Kama Sutra 200)	8	1966	1	1966	(Kama Sutra 211)
6	Rain On The Roof		0	1966	10	1966	(Kama Sutra 216)
7	Nashville Cats	(Kama Sutra 204)	26	1967	8	1966	(Kama Sutra 219)
8	Darling Be Home Soon	(Kama Sutra 207)	44	1967	15	1967	(Kama Sutra 220)
9	Six O'Clock		0	1967	18	1967	(Kama Sutra 225)
10	She Is Still A Mystery		0	1967	27	1967	(Kama Sutra 239)

Lovindeer Male Vocalist from the UK

1	Man Shortage	(TSOJ TS 1)	69	1986	0	1986	

Lowrell Male Vocalist from the USA

1	Mellow Mellow Right On	(AVI AXIS 108)	37	1979	0	1979	
	SEE ALSO LOST GENERATION						

LTD See L.T.D.

Lu Ann Simms Female Vocalist from the USA

1	Moving Away		0	1953	30	1953	(Columbia 39928)

Lucas Male Rapper from Denmark

1	Lucas With The Lid Off	(WEA YZ 1482)	37	1994	29	1994	(Big Beat 98219)

Luciana Female Vocalist from the UK

1	Get It Up For Love	(Chrysalis CDCHS 5008)	55	1994	0	1994	
2	If You Want	(Chrysalis CDCHS 5009)	47	1994	0	1994	
3	What Goes Around / One More River	(Chrysalis CDCHS 5015)	67	1994	0	1994	

Luciano Pavarotti Male Vocalist (Tennor) from Italy

1	Nessun Dorma	(Decca PAV 03)	2	1990	0	1990	
2	Miserere	(London Lon 329)	15	1992	0	1992	
3	Libiamo /La Donna E Mobile	(TELDEC YZ 843CD)	21	1994	0	1994	
4	Live Like Horses	(Rocket LLHCD 1)	9	1996	0	1996	

Lucille Starr B: St. Boniface, Manitoba, She's Otherwise Known As Fern Regan

* 1	The French Song		0	1964	54	1964	(ALMO)

Lucky Monkeys Male Instrumental Group from the UK

1	Bjango	(HI-LIFE/Polydor 5757132)	50	1996	0	1996	

Luisa Fernandez Female Vocalist from Spain

1	Lay Love On You	(Warner Bros. K 17061)	31	1978	0	1978	

Luke See 2 Live Crew

Luke Goss & The Band Of Thieves Male Vocal/Instrumental Group from the UK

1	Sweeter Than Midnight Rain	(Sabre CDSAB 1)	52	1993	0	1993	
2	Give Me One More Chance	(Sabre CDSAB 2)	68	1993	0	1993	

Lukk (Featuring) Felicia Collins Mixed Vocal/Instrumental Group from the USA

1	One The One	(Important TAN 6)	72	1985	0	1985	

Lulu Female Vocalist, Real Name Marie McDonald McLaughlin Lawrie B: 3 Nov 1948 In Glasgow

1	Shout	(Decca F 11884)	7	1964	0	1964	
2	Here Comes The Night	(Decca F 12017)	50	1964	0	1964	
3	Leave A Little Love	(Decca F 12169)	8	1965	0	1965	
4	Try To Understand	(Decca F 12214)	25	1965	0	1965	
5	The Boat That I Row	(Columbia DB 8169)	6	1967	0	1967	
6	Let's Pretend	(Columbia DB 8221)	11	1967	0	1967	
* 7	To Sir With Love		0	1967	1	1967	(Epic 10187)
8	Love Loves To Love Love	(Columbia DB 8295)	32	1967	0	1967	
9	Me The Peaceful Heart	(Columbia DB 8358)	9	1968	0	1968	
10	Best Of Both Worlds		0	1968	32	1968	(Epic 10260)
11	Boy	(Columbia DB 8425)	15	1968	0	1968	
12	I'm A Tiger	(Columbia DB 8500)	9	1968	0	1968	
13	Boom Bang-A-Bang	(Columbia DB 8550)	2	1969	0	1969	
14	Oh Me Oh My (I'm A Fool For You Baby)	(ATCO 226008)	47	1969	22	1970	(ATCO 6722)
15	The Man Who Sold The World	(POLTDOR 2001 490)	3	1974	0	1974	
16	Take Your Mama For A Ride	(Chelsea 2005 022)	37	1965	0	1965	
17	I Could Never Miss You (More Than I Do)	(ALFA ALFA 1700)	62	1981	18	1981	(ALFA 7006)
18	I Could Never Miss You (More Than I Do) (Re-Entry)	(ALFA ALFA 1700)	63	1982	0	1982	
19	Shout	(JIVE LULU 1/Decca SHOUT 1)	8	1986	0	1986	

ISSUE	TITLE	UK LBL	UK POS	UK YEAR	US POS	US YEAR	US LBL
20	Independance	(DOME CDDOME 1001)	11	1993	0	1993	
21	I'm Back For More	(DOME CDDOME 1002)	27	1993	0	1993	
22	Let Me Wake Up In Your Arms	(DOME CDDOME 1005)	51	1993	0	1993	
23	Relight My Fire	(RCA 74321167722)	1	1993	0	1993	
24	How 'Bout Us	(DOME CDDOME 1007)	46	1993	0	1993	
25	Goodbye Baby And Amen	(DOME CDDOME 1011)	40	1994	0	1994	
26	Every Woman Knows	(DOME CDDOME 1013)	44	1994	0	1994	

Luniz Rap Duo From Oakland, USA

ISSUE	TITLE	UK LBL	UK POS	UK YEAR	US POS	US YEAR	US LBL
* 1	I Got 5 On It	(Virgin America VUSCD 101)	3	1996	8	1995	(NOO TRYBE 38474)
2	Playa Hata	(Virgin America VUSCD 103)	20	1996	0	1996	

Lurkers Male Vocal/Instrumental Group from the UK

ISSUE	TITLE	UK LBL	UK POS	UK YEAR	US POS	US YEAR	US LBL
1	Ain't Got A Clue	(Beggars Banquet BEG 6)	45	1978	0	1978	
2	I Don't Need To Tell Her	(Beggars Banquet BEG 9)	49	1978	0	1978	
3	Just Thirteen	(Beggars Banquet BEG 14)	66	1979	0	1979	
4	Out In The Dark / Cyanide	(Beggars Banquet BEG 19)	72	1979	0	1979	
5	New Guitar In Town	(Beggars Banquet BEG 28)	72	1979	0	1979	

Luscious Jackson Female Vocal/Instrumental Group from the USA

ISSUE	TITLE	UK LBL	UK POS	UK YEAR	US POS	US YEAR	US LBL
1	Deep Shag / Citysong	(EMI CDCL 739)	69	1995	0	1995	
2	Here	(Capitol CDCL 758)	59	1995	0	1995	
3	Naked Eye	(Capitol CDCL 786)	25	1997	36	1996	(Capitol 58619)

Lush Mixed Vocal/Instrumental Group from the UK

ISSUE	TITLE	UK LBL	UK POS	UK YEAR	US POS	US YEAR	US LBL
1	Mad Love (EP)	(4AD BAD 003)	55	1990	0	1990	
2	Sweetness And Light	(4AD BAD 0013)	47	1990	0	1990	
3	Nothing Natural	(4AD BAD 1016)	43	1991	0	1991	
4	For Love (EP)	(4AD BAD 2001)	35	1992	0	1992	
5	Hypocrite	(4AD BAD 4008CD)	52	1994	0	1994	
6	Desire Lines	(4AD BAD 4010CD)	60	1994	0	1994	
7	Single Girl	(4AD BAD 6001CD)	21	1996	0	1996	
8	Ladykillers	(4AD BAD 6002CD)	22	1996	0	1996	
9	500 (Shake Baby Shake)	(4AD BAD 6009CD)	21	1996	0	1996	

Luther Ingram Male Soul Singer/songwriter, B: 30 Nov 1944 Jackson, Tennessee

ISSUE	TITLE	UK LBL	UK POS	UK YEAR	US POS	US YEAR	US LBL
1	Ain't That Loving You (For More Reasons Than One)		0	1970	45	1970	(KOKO 2105)
* 2	(If Loving You Is Wrong) I Don't Want To Be Right		0	1972	3	1972	(KOKO 2111)
3	I'll Be Your Shelter (In Time Of Storm)		0	1973	40	1973	(KOKO 2113)

Luther Vandross Male Vocalist, B: 20 Apr 1951 New York City

ISSUE	TITLE	UK LBL	UK POS	UK YEAR	US POS	US YEAR	US LBL
1	Never Too Much	(Epic EPC A 3101)	44	1983	33	1981	(Epic 02409)
2	How Many Times Can We Say Goodbye		0	1983	27	1983	(Arista 9073)
3	'Til My Baby Comes Home		0	1985	29	1985	(Epic 04760)
4	Give Me The Reason	(Epic EPC A 7288)	60	1986	0	1986	
5	Stop To Love	(Epic LUTH 2)	24	1987	15	1986	(Epic 06523)
6	Give Me The Reason (Re-Issue)	(Epic 6502167)	71	1987	0	1987	
7	See Me	(Epic LUTH 1)	60	1987	0	1987	
8	I Really Didn't Mean It	(Epic LUTH 3)	16	1987	0	1987	
9	So Amazing	(Epic LUTII 4)	33	1987	0	1987	
10	Give Me The Reason (2nd Re-Issue)	(Epic LUTH 5)	26	1988	0	1988	
11	I Gave It Up (When I Fell In Love)	(Epic LUTH 6)	28	1988	0	1988	
12	There's Nothing Better Than Love	(Epic LUTH 7)	72	1988	0	1988	
13	Any Love	(Epic LUTH 8)	31	1988	0	1988	
14	She Won't Talk To Me	(Epic LUTH 9)	34	1989	30	1989	(Epic 08513)
15	Come Back	(Epic LUTH 10)	53	1989	0	1989	
16	Never Too Much (Re-Mix)	(Epic LUTH 12)	13	1989	0	1989	
* 17	Here And Now	(Epic LUTH 13)	43	1990	6	1990	(Epic 73029)
18	Power Of Love / Love Power	(Epic 6568227)	46	1991	4	1991	(Epic 73778)
19	Don't Want To Be A Fool		0	1991	9	1991	(Epic 73879)
20	The Rush	(Epic 6577237)	53	1992	0	1992	
21	The Best Things In Life Are Free	(Perspective PERSS 7400)	2	1992	10	1992	(Perspective 0010)
22	Little Miracles (Happen Every Day)	(Epic 6590442)	28	1993	0	1993	
23	Heaven Knows	(Epic 6596522)	34	1993	0	1993	
24	Love Is On The Way	(Epic 6599592)	38	1993	0	1993	
* 25	Endless Love	(Epic 6608062)	3	1994	2	1994	(Columbia 77629)
26	Love The One You're With	(Epic 6610612)	31	1994	0	1994	
27	Endless Love (Re-Entry)	(Epic 6608062)	70	1995	0	1995	
28	Always And Forever	(Epic 6611945)	20	1995	0	1995	
29	Endless Love (2nd Re-Entry)	(Epic 6608062)	55	1995	0	1995	

ISSUE	TITLE	UK LBL	UK POS	UK YEAR	US POS	US YEAR	US LBL
30	Ain't No Stopping Us Now	(Epic 6614242)	22	1995	0	1995	
31	Power Of Love-Love Power (Re-Mix)	(Epic 6625902)	31	1995	0	1995	
32	The Best Things In Life Are Free (Re-Mix)	(A&M 5813092)	7	1995	0	1995	
33	Every Year, Every Christmas	(Epic 6627762)	43	1995	0	1995	
34	Your Secret Love	(Epic 6638385)	14	1996	52	1996	(Epic 78400)
35	I Can Make It Better	(Epic 6640632)	44	1996	83	1996	(Epic 78466)

Lydia Murdock Female Vocalist from the USA

ISSUE	TITLE	UK LBL	UK POS	UK YEAR	US POS	US YEAR	US LBL
1	Superstar	(Korova Kow 30)	14	1983	0	1983	

Lyn Paul Female Vocalist from the UK

ISSUE	TITLE	UK LBL	UK POS	UK YEAR	US POS	US YEAR	US LBL
1	It Oughta Sell A Million	(Polydor 2058 602)	37	1975	0	1975	

Lynn Anderson Female Vocalist, B: 26 Sep 1947 Grand Forks, North Dakota

ISSUE	TITLE	UK LBL	UK POS	UK YEAR	US POS	US YEAR	US LBL
24	How Can I Unlove You		0	1971	63	1971	(Columbia 45429)
25	Cry		0	1972	71	1972	(Columbia 45529)
29	Top Of The World		0	1973	74	1973	(Columbia 45857)
33	What A Man, My Man Is		0	1974	93	1974	(Columbia 10041)
	OTHERS ARE C/W HITS						

Lynn Cornell Female Vocalist from the UK

ISSUE	TITLE	UK LBL	UK POS	UK YEAR	US POS	US YEAR	US LBL
1	Never On Sunday	(Decca F 11277)	30	1960	0	1960	

Lynne Hamilton Female Vocalist from Australia

ISSUE	TITLE	UK LBL	UK POS	UK YEAR	US POS	US YEAR	US LBL
1	On The Inside (Theme From *Prisoner Cell Block H*)	(A.1. A1 311)	3	1989	0	1989	

Lynsey De Paul Female Vocalist from the UK

ISSUE	TITLE	UK LBL	UK POS	UK YEAR	US POS	US YEAR	US LBL
1	Sugar Me	(MAM 81)	5	1972	0	1972	
2	Getting A Drag	(MAM 88)	18	1972	0	1972	
3	Won't Somebody Dance With Me	(MAM 109)	14	1973	0	1973	
4	Ooh I Do	(Warner Bros. K 16401)	25	1974	0	1974	
5	No Honestly	(Jet 747)	7	1974	0	1974	
6	My Man And Me	(Jet 750)	40	1975	0	1975	
7	Rock Bottom	(Polydor 2058 859)	19	1977	0	1977	And Mike Moran

Lynyrd Skynyrd Male Vocal/Instrumental Rock Band Formed In Florida In 1965

ISSUE	TITLE	UK LBL	UK POS	UK YEAR	US POS	US YEAR	US LBL
1	Sweet Home Alabama		0	1974	8	1974	(MCA 40258)
2	Free Bird	(MCA 251)	31	1976	19	1975	(MCA 40328)
3	Saturday Night Special		0	1975	27	1975	(MCA 40416)
4	Free Bird (Live)		0	1977	38	1977	(MCA 40665)
5	What's Your Name		0	1978	13	1978	(MCA 40819)
6	Free Bird (Re-Entry)	(MCA 251)	43	1979	0	1979	
7	Free Bird (2nd Re-Entry)	(MCA 251)	21	1982	0	1982	

OBITUARY : CASSIE GAINES, STEVE GAINES AND VAN ZANT • D: 20 OCT 1977 PLANE CRASH • COLLINS   D: 23 JAN 1990 PNEUMONIA.

M

ISSUE	TITLE	UK LBL	UK POS	UK YEAR	US POS	US YEAR	US LBL
M Male Vocal/Multi-Instrumentalist, Real Name Robin Scott from the UK							
* 1	Pop Muzic	(MCA 413)	2	1979	1	1979	(Sire 49033)
2	Moonlight And Muzak	(MCA 541)	33	1979	0	1979	
3	That's The Way The Money Goes	(MCA 570)	45	1980	0	1980	
4	Official Secrets	(MCA 650)	64	1980	0	1980	
5	Pop Muzik (Re-Mix)	(Freestyle FRS 1)	15	1989	0	1989	
M & O Band Male Vocal/Instrumental Group from the UK							
1	Let's Do The Latin Hustle	(Creole CR 120)	16	1976	0	1976	
M-Beat Male Producer from the UK							
1	Incredible	(Renk Renk 42CD)	39	1994	0	1994	
2	Incredible (Re-Mix)	(Renk CDRENK 44)	8	1994	0	1994	
3	Sweet Love	(Renk CDRENK 49)	18	1994	0	1994	
4	Do U Know Where You're Coming From	(Renk CDRENK 63)	12	1996	0	1996	
HITS 1-2 ARE CREDITED TO M-BEAT FEATURING GENERAL LEVY • HIT 3 M-BEAT FEATURING NAZLYN, HIT 4 IS M-BEAT FEATURING JAMIROQUAI							
M-D-Emm Male Producer, Real Name Mark Ryder from the UK							
1	Get Down	(Strictly Underground 7STUR 13)	55	1992	0	1992	
2	Move Your Feet	(Strictly Underground 7STUR 15)	67	1992	0	1992	
M-People Mixed Vocal/Instrumental Group from the UK							
1	How Can I Love You More	(Deconstruction PB 44855)	29	1991	0	1991	
2	Colour My Life	(Deconstruction PB 45241)	35	1992	0	1992	
3	Someday	(Deconstruction PB 45369)	38	1992	0	1992	
4	Excited	(Deconstruction 74321116337)	29	1992	0	1992	
5	How Can I Love You More (Re-Mix)	(Deconstruction 74321130232)	8	1993	0	1993	
6	One Night In Heaven	(Deconstruction 74321151852)	6	1993	0	1993	
7	Moving On Up	(Deconstruction 74321166162)	2	1993	34	1994	(EPIC 77392)
8	Don't Look Any Further	(Deconstruction 74321177112)	9	1993	0	1993	
9	Renaissance	(Deconstruction 74321194132)	5	1994	0	1994	
10	Elegantly American: One Night In Heaven	(Deconstruction 74321231882)	31	1994	0	1994	
11	Sight For Sore Eyes	(Deconstruction 74321245472)	6	1994	0	1994	
12	Open Your Heart	(Deconstruction 74321261532)	9	1995	0	1995	
13	Search For The Hero	(Deconstruction 74321287962)	9	1995	0	1995	
14	Love Rendezvous	(Deconstruction 74321319282)	32	1995	0	1995	
15	Itchycoo Park	(Deconstruction 74321330732)	11	1995	0	1995	
M.A.N.I.C. Male Production/Vocal Duo from the UK							
1	I'm Comin' Hardcore	(Union CityUCRT 2)	60	1992	0	1992	
M.K. Male Producer Mark Kinchen from the USA							
1	Always	(Activ CDTV 3)	69	1995	0	1995	
2	Burning	(Activ CDTVR6)	44	1995	0	1995	
M.N.O. Male Production/Instrumental Group from Belgium							
1	God Of Abraham	(A&M AM 820)	66	1991	0	1991	
M/A/R/R/S Male Instrumental/Scratch Group from the UK Names: Steve & Martyn Young With Rudi & Alex Kane							
* 1	Pump Up The Volume / Anitina (The First Time I See She)	(4AD AD 70)	1	1987	13	1988	(FOURTH & B. 7452)
Mable John Female Vocalist from the USA							
1	Your Good Thing (Is About To End)		0	1966	6	1966	(STAX 192)
Mac & Katie Kissoon Brother & Sister Vocal Duo from Trinidad							
1	Chirpy Chirpy Cheep Cheep	(Young Blood YB 1026)	41	1971	20	1971	(ABC 11306)
2	Sugar Candy Kisses	(Polydor 2058 531)	3	1975	0	1975	
3	Don't Do It Baby	(State STAT 4)	9	1975	0	1975	

ISSUE	TITLE	UK LBL	UK POS	UK YEAR	US POS	US YEAR	US LBL
4	Like A Butterfly	(State STAT 9)	18	1975	0	1975	
5	The Two Of Us	(State STAT 21)	46	1976	0	1976	

Mac Band (Featuring) The McCampbell Brothers   Male Vocal Group from the USA

1	Roses Are Red	(MCA MCA 1264)	8	1988	0	1988	
2	Stalemate	(MCA MCA 1271)	40	1988	0	1988	

Mac Davis   Male Writer/Guitarist/Vocalist, B: 21 Jan 1942 Lubock, Texas

1	Whoever Finds This, I Love You		0	1970	53	1970	(Columbia 45117)
! 2	I'll Paint You A Song		0	1970	68	1970	(Columbia 45192)
* 3	Baby Don't Get Hooked On Me	(CBS 8250)	29	1972	1	1972	(Columbia 45618)
4	Dream Me Home		0	1973	73	1973	(Columbia 45773)
5	Your Side Of The Bed		0	1973	88	1973	(Columbia 45839)
! 6	Kiss It And Make It Better		0	1973	29	1973	(Columbia 45911)
7	One Hell Of A Woman		0	1974	11	1974	(Columbia 46004)
8	Stop And Smell The Roses		0	1974	9	1974	(Columbia 10018)
9	Rock N' Roll (I Gave You The Best Years Of My Life)		0	1974	15	1974	(Columbia 10070)
10	(If You Add) All The Love In The World		0	1975	54	1975	(Columbia 10111)
11	Burnin' Thing		0	1975	53	1975	(Columbia 10148)
! 12	I Still Love You (You Still Love Me)		0	1975	81	1975	(Columbia 10187)
13	Forever Lovers		0	1976	76	1976	(Columbia 10304)
! 14	Every Now And Then		0	1976	34	1976	(Columbia 10418)
! 15	Picking Up The Pieces Of My Life		0	1977	42	1977	(Columbia 10535)
! 16	Music In My Life		0	1978	92	1978	(Columbia 10745)
17	It's Hard To Be Humble	(Casablanca CAN 210)	27	1980	43	1980	(Casablanca 2244)
! 18	Let's Keep It That Way		0	1980	10	1980	(Casablanca 2286)
19	Texas In My Rear View Mirror		0	1980	51	1980	(Casablanca 2305)
! 20	Hooked On Music		0	1981	2	1981	(Casablanca 2327)
21	Secrets		0	1981	76	1981	(Casablanca 2336)
! 22	You're My Bestest Friend		0	1981	5	1981	(Casablanca 2341)
! 23	Rodeo Clown		0	1982	37	1982	(Casablanca 2350)
! 24	The Beer Drinkin' Song		0	1982	58	1982	(Casablanca 2355)
! 25	Lying Here Lying		0	1982	62	1982	(Casablanca 2363)
! 26	Most Of All		0	1984	41	1984	(Casablanca 818168)
! 27	Caroline's Still In Georgia		0	1984	76	1984	(Casablanca 818929)
! 28	I Never Made Love (Till I Made Love With You)		0	1985	10	1985	(MCA 52573)
! 29	I Feel The Country Callin' Me		0	1985	34	1985	(MCA 52669)
! 30	Sexy Young Girl		0	1986	46	1986	(MCA 52765)
! 31	Somewhere In America		0	1986	65	1986	(MCA 52826)

Mac McAnally   Real Name Lyman McAnally Jr. B: 1957 Red Bay, Alabama

1	It's A Crazy World		0	1977	37	1977	(Ariola AM.7665)

Maccrarys   Male Vocal/Instrumental Group from the USA

1	Love On A Summer Night	(Capitol CL 251)	52	1982	0	1982	

Maceo & The Macs   Male Vocal/Instrumental Group from the USA

1	Cross The Track (We Better Go Back)	(Urban URBX 1)	54	1987	0	1987	

Machel   Male Vocalist from Trinidad

1	Come Dig It	(London LONCD 386)	56	1996	0	1996	

Machine Head   Male Vocal/Instrumental Group from the UK

1	Old	(Roadrunner RR 23403)	43	1995	0	1995	

Mack Vibe (Featuring) Jacqueline   Mixed Vocal/Instrumental Duo from the USA

1	I Can't Let You Go	(MCA MC 20020)STD	53	1995	0	1995	

Mad Cobra (Featuring) Ritchie Stephens   Male Vocal Duo From Jamaica/UK

* 1	Flex		0	1993	13	1992	(Columbia 74373)
2	Legacy	(Columbia 6592852)	64	1993	0	1993	

Mad Jocks (Featuring) Jockmaster B.A.   Male Vocal/Instrumental Group from the UK

1	Jock Mix 1	(Debut DEBT 3037)	46	1987	0	1987	
2	Party Four (EP)	(SMP CDSSKM 24)	57	1993	0	1993	

Madder Rose   Mixed Vocal/Instrumental Group from the USA

1	Panic On	(Atlantic A8301CD)	65	1994	0	1994	
2	Car Song	(SEED A 7256CD)	68	1994	0	1994	

Madeline Bell   Female Vocalist, Formed The Group Blue Mink In 1969

1	I'm Gonna Make You Love Me		0	1968	26	1968	(Philips 40517)

ISSUE	TITLE	UK LBL	UK POS	UK YEAR	US POS	US YEAR	US LBL
Madness Male Vocal/Instrumental Group from the UK							
1	The Prince	(2 TONE TT 3)	16	1979	0	1979	
2	One Step Beyond	(Stiff Buy 56)	7	1979	0	1979	
3	My Girl	(Stiff Buy 62)	3	1980	0	1980	
4	Work Rest And Play (EP)	(Stiff Buy 71)	6	1980	0	1980	
5	Baggy Trousers	(Stiff Buy 84)	3	1980	0	1980	
6	Embarrassment	(Stiff Buy 102)	4	1980	0	1980	
7	The Return Of The Los Palmas Seven	(Stiff Buy 108)	7	1981	0	1981	
8	Grey Day	(Stiff Buy 112)	4	1981	0	1981	
9	Shut Up	(Stiff Buy 126)	7	1981	0	1981	
10	It Must Be Love	(Stiff Buy 134)	4	1981	33	1983	(Geffen 29562)
11	Cardiac Arrest	(Stiff Buy 140)	14	1982	0	1982	
12	House Of Fun	(Stiff Buy 146)	1	1982	0	1982	
13	Driving In My Car	(Stiff Buy 153)	4	1982	0	1982	
14	Our House	(Stiff Buy 163)	5	1982	7	1983	(Geffen 29668)
15	Tomorrow's Just Another Day	(Stiff Buy 169)	8	1983	0	1983	
16	Wings Of A Dove	(Stiff Buy 181)	2	1983	0	1983	
17	The Sun And The Rain	(Stiff Buy 192)	5	1983	0	1983	
18	Michael Caine	(Stiff Buy 196)	11	1984	0	1984	
19	One Better Day	(Stiff Buy 201)	17	1984	0	1984	
20	Yesterdays Men	(ZARJAZZ JAZZ 5)	18	1985	0	1985	
21	Uncle Sam	(ZARJAZZ JAZZ 7)	21	1985	0	1985	
22	Sweetest Girl	(ZARJAZZ JAZZ 8)	35	1986	0	1986	
23	(Waiting For) The Ghost Train	(ZARJAZZ JAZZ 9)	18	1986	0	1986	
24	(Waiting For) The Ghost Train (Re-Entry)	(ZARJAZZ JAZZ 9)	74	1987	0	1987	
25	I Pronounce You	(Virgin VS 1054)	44	1988	0	1988	
26	It Must Be Love (Re-Issue)	(Virgin VS 1405)	6	1992	0	1992	
27	House Of Fun (Re-Issue)	(Virgin VS 1413)	40	1992	0	1992	
28	My Girl (Re-Issue)	(Virgin VS 1425)	27	1992	0	1992	
29	The Harder They Come	(GO! DISC GOD 93)	44	1992	0	1992	
30	Night Boat To Cairo	(Virgin VSCDT 1447)	56	1993	0	1993	
Madonna Female Vocalist, Full Name Madonna Louise Ciccone B: 16 Aug 1958 Bay City, Michigan							
1	Holiday	(Sire W 9405)	6	1984	16	1983	(Sire 29478)
2	Lucky Star	(Sire W 9522)	14	1984	4	1984	(Sire 29177)
3	Borderline	(Sire W 9260)	2	1984	10	1984	(Sire 29354)
* 4	Like A Virgin	(Sire W 9210)	3	1984	1	1984	(Sire 29210)
5	Material Girl	(Sire W 9083)	3	1985	2	1985	(Sire 29083)
* 6	Crazy For You	(Geffen A 6323)	2	1985	1	1985	(Geffen 29051)
* 7	Angel	(Sire W 8881)	5	1985	5	1985	(Sire 29088)
8	Into The Groove	(Sire W 8934)	1	1985	0	1985	
9	Holiday (Re-Entry)	(Sire W 9405)	2	1985	0	1985	
10	Dress You Up	(Sire W 8848)	5	1985	5	1985	(Sire 28919)
11	Gambler	(Geffen A 6585)	4	1985	0	1985	
12	Borderline (Re-Entry)	(Sire W 9260)	2	1986	0	1986	
13	Gambler (Re-Entry)	(Geffen A 6585)	61	1986	0	1986	
14	Live To Tell	(Sire W 8717)	2	1986	1	1986	(Sire 28717)
15	Papa Don't Preach	(Sire W 8636)	1	1986	1	1986	(Sire 28660)
16	True Blue	(Sire W 8550)	1	1986	3	1986	(Sire 28591)
17	Open Your Heart	(Sire W 8480)	4	1986	1	1987	(Sire 28508)
18	La Isla Bonita	(Sire W 8378)	1	1987	4	1987	(Sire 28425)
19	Who's That Girl	(Sire W 8341)	1	1987	1	1987	(Sire 28341)
20	Causing A Commotion	(Sire W 8224)	4	1987	2	1987	(Sire 28224)
21	The Look Of Love	(Sire W 8115)	9	1987	0	1987	
* 22	Like A Prayer	(Sire W 7539)	1	1989	1	1989	(Sire 27539)
* 23	Express Yourself	(Sire W 2948)	5	1989	2	1989	(Sire 27948)
24	Cherish	(Sire W 2883)	3	1989	2	1989	(Sire 22883)
25	Oh Father	(Sire W 2723)	16	1996	20	1989	(Sire 22723)
26	Dear Jessie	(Sire W 2668)	5	1989	0	1989	
27	Keep It Together		0	1990	8	1990	(Sire 19986)
* 28	Vogue	(Sire W 9851)	1	1990	1	1990	(Sire 19863)
* 29	Hanky Panky	(Sire W 9789)	2	1990	10	1990	(Sire 19789)
* 30	Justify My Love	(Sire W 9000)	2	1990	1	1990	(Sire 19485)
* 31	Rescue Me	(Sire W 0024)	3	1991	9	1991	(Sire 19490)
32	Crazy For You (Re-Mix)	(Sire W 0008)	2	1991	0	1991	

ISSUE	TITLE	UK LBL	UK POS	UK YEAR	US POS	US YEAR	US LBL
33	Holiday (Re-Issue)	(Sire W 0037)	5	1991	0	1991	
* 34	This Used To Be My Playground	(Sire W 0122)	3	1992	1	1992	(Sire 18822)
* 35	Erotica	(Maverick W 0138)	3	1992	2	1992	(Maverick 18782)
36	Deeper And Deeper	(Maverick W 0138)	6	1992	7	1992	(Maverick 18639)
37	Erotica (Re-Entry)	(Maverick W 0138)	65	1993	0	1993	
38	Bad Girl	(Maverick W 0145CD)	10	1993	36	1993	(Maverick 18650)
39	Fever	(Maverick W 0168CD)	6	1993	0	1993	
40	Rain	(Maverick W 0190CD)	7	1993	14	1993	(Maverick 18505)
* 41	I'll Remember	(Maverick W 0240CD)	7	1994	2	1994	(Maverick/Sire 18247)
* 42	Secret	(Maverick W 0268CD)	5	1994	3	1994	(Maverick/Sire 18035)
* 43	Take A Bow	(Maverick W0278CD)	16	1994	1	1994	(Maverick/Sire 18000)
44	Bedtime Story	(Maverick W 0285CD)	4	1995	0	1995	
45	Bedtime Story (Re-Entry)	(Maverick W 0285CD)	66	1995	0	1995	
46	Human Nature	(Maverick W 0300CD)	8	1995	0	1995	
47	You'll See	(Maverick W 0324CD)	5	1995	6	1996	(Maverick 17719)
48	Oh Father	(Maverick W 0326CD)	16	1996	0	1996	
49	One More Chance / You'll See	(Maverick W 0337CD)	11	1996	0	1996	
50	You Must Love Me (From *Evita*)	(Warner Bros. W 0378CD)	10	1996	18	1996	(Warner Bros. 17485)
51	Don't Cry For Me Argentina (From *Evita*)	(Warner Bros. W 0384CD)	3	1996	8	1997	(Warner Bros. 43809)
52	You Must Love Me (From *Evita*) (Re-Entry)	(Warner Bros. W 0378CD)	75	1997	0	1997	
53	You Must Love Me (From *Evita*) (2nd Re-Entry)	(Warner Bros. W 0378CD)	71	1997	0	1997	
54	Another Suitcase In Another Hall	(Warner Bros. W 0388CD)	7	1997	0	1997	

Magazine Male Vocal/Instrumental Group from the UK

1	Shot By Both Sides	(Virgin VS 200)	41	1978	0	1978	
2	Sweet Heart Contract	(Virgin VS 368)	54	1980	0	1980	

Maggie Bell Female Vocalist from the UK

1	Hazell	(Swansong SSK 19412)	37	1978	0	1978	
2	Hazell (Re-Entry)	(Swansong SSK 19412)	74	1978	0	1978	
3	Hold Me	(Swansong BAM 1)	11	1981	0	1981	with B.A. Robertson

Magic Affair Mixed Vocal/Instrumental Group from the USA/Germany

1	Omen III	(EMI CDEM 317)	17	1994	0	1994	
2	Give Me All Your Love	(EMI CDEM 340)	30	1994	0	1994	
3	In The Middle Of The Night	(EMI CDEM 349)	38	1994	0	1994	

Magic Lady Female Vocal Duo from the USA

1	Betcha Can't Lose (With My Love)	(Motown ZB 42003)	58	1988	0	1988	

Magic Lanterns Male Vocal/Instrumental Group from the UK

1	Excuse Me Baby	(CBS 202094)	46	1966	0	1966	
2	Excuse Me Baby (Re-Entry)	(CBS 202094)	44	1966	0	1966	
3	Excuse Me Baby (2nd Re-Entry)	(CBS 202094)	46	1966	0	1966	
4	Shame, Shame		0	1968	29	1968	(Atlantic 2560)

Magnum Male Vocal/Instrumental Group from the UK

1	Magnum	(JET 175)	47	1980	0	1980	
2	Lonely Nights	(Polydor POSP 798)	70	1986	0	1986	
3	Days Of No Trust	(Polydor POSP 910)	32	1988	0	1988	
4	Start Talking Love	(Polydor POSP 920)	22	1988	0	1988	
5	It Must Have Been Love	(Polydor POSP 930)	33	1988	0	1988	
6	Rockin' Chair	(Polydor PO 88)	27	1990	0	1990	
7	Heartbroke And Busted	(Polydor PO 94)	49	1990	0	1990	

Mahalia Jackson Female Gospel Singer, B: 26 Oct 1911 New Orleans, Louisiana

* 1	Move On Up A Little Higher		0	1948	21	1948	(Apollo 164)

Mai Tai Female Vocal Group from Holland

1	History	(Virgin VS 773)	8	1985	0	1985	
2	Body And Soul	(Virgin VS 801)	9	1985	0	1985	
3	Female Intuition	(Virgin VS 844)	54	1986	0	1986	

Main Ingredient Male Vocal Group from the USA   Original Names: Luther Simmons Jr, Tony Silvester & Cuba Gooding

* 1	Everybody Plays The Fool		0	1972	3	1972	(RCA 0731)
* 2	Just Don't Want To Be Lonely	(RCA APBO 0205)	27	1974	10	1974	(RCA 0205)
3	Happiness Is Just Around The Bend		0	1974	35	1974	(RCA 0305)

Maisonettes Mixed Vocal/Instrumental Group from the UK

1	Heartache Avenue	(Ready Steady Go! RSG 1)	7	1982	0	1982	

Major Harris Male Vocalist, B: 9 Feb 1947 Richmond, Virginia, Sang With The Jarrels, Teenagers, Impacts And Delfonics

* 1	Love Won't Let Me Wait	(Atlantic K 10585)	37	1975	5	1975	(Atlantic 3248)
2	All My Life	(London LON 37)	61	1983	0	1983	

ISSUE	TITLE	UK LBL	UK POS	UK YEAR	US POS	US YEAR	US LBL
Major Lance Male Vocalist, B: 4 Apr 1942 Chicago							
1	The Monkey Time		0	1963	8	1963	(Okeh 7175)
2	Hey Little Girl		0	1963	13	1963	(Okeh 7181)
3	Um Um Um Um Um Um	(Columbia DB 7205)	40	1964	5	1964	(Okeh 7187)
4	The Matador		0	1964	20	1964	(Okeh 7191)
5	Rhythm		0	1964	24	1964	(Okeh 7203)
6	Sometimes I Wonder		0	1965	64	1965	(Okeh 7209)
7	Come And See		0	1965	40	1965	(Okeh 7216)
Majors Names Frank Troutt, Eugene Glass, Ronald Gathers & Idella Morris							
1	A Wonderful Dream		0	1962	22	1962	(Imperial 5855)
Makadopoulos & His Greek Serenaders Male Vocal/Instrumental Group from Greece							
1	Never On Sunday	(Palette PG 9005)	36	1960	0	1960	
Malaika Female Vocalist from the UK							
1	Gotta Know (Your Name)	(A&M 5802732)	68	1993	0	1993	
Malandra Burrows Female Vocalist from the UK							
1	Just This Side Of Love	11	1990	0	1990		
Malcolm McLaren Male Vocalist from the UK							
1	Buffalo Gals	(Charisma MALC 1)	9	1982	0	1982	
2	Soweto	(Charisma MALC 2)	32	1983	0	1983	
3	Double Dutch	(Charisma MALC 3)	3	1983	0	1983	
4	Duck For The Oyster	(Charisma MALC 4)	54	1983	0	1983	
5	Madam Butterfly (Un Bel Di Vedremo)	(Charisma MALC 5)	13	1984	0	1984	
6	Waltz Darling	(Epic WALTZ 2)	31	1989	0	1989	
7	Something's Jumping In Your Shirt	(Epic WALTZ 3)	29	1989	0	1989	
8	House Of The Blue Danube	(Epic WALTZ 4)	73	1989	0	1989	
9	Magic's Back (Theme From *The Ghosts Of Oxford Street*)	(RCA PB 45223)	42	1991	0	1991	
Malcolm Roberts Male Vocalist from the UK							
1	Time Alone Will Tell	(RCA 1578)	45	1967	0	1967	
2	May I Have The Next Dream With You	(Major Minor MM 581)	8	1968	0	1968	
3	May I Have The Next Dream With You (Re-Entry)	(Major Minor MM 581)	45	1969	0	1969	
4	Love Is All	(Major Minor MM 637)	12	1969	0	1969	
Malcolm Vaughan Male Vocalist from the UK							
1	Every Day Of My Life	(HMV B 10874)	5	1955	0	1955	
2	With Your Love	(HMV POP 130)	20	1956	0	1956	
3	With Your Love (Re-Entry)	(HMV POP 130)	18	1956	0	1956	
4	With Your Love (2nd Re-Entry)	(HMV POP 130)	20	1956	0	1956	
5	St. Therese Of The Roses	(HMV POP 250)	27	1956	0	1956	
6	St. Therese Of The Roses (Re-Entry)	(HMV POP 250)	3	1956	0	1956	
7	The World Is Mine	(HMV POP 303)	30	1957	0	1957	
8	The World Is Mine (Re-Entry)	(HMV POP 303)	29	1957	0	1957	
9	Chapel Of The Roses	(HMV POP 325)	13	1957	0	1957	
10	The World Is Mine (2nd Re-Entry)	(HMV POP 303)	26	1957	0	1957	
11	My Special Angel	(HMV POP 419)	3	1957	0	1957	
12	To Be Loved	(HMV POP 459)	14	1958	0	1958	
13	More Than Ever (Come Prima)	(HMV POP 538)	5	1958	0	1958	
14	Wait For Me / Willingly	(HMV POP 590)	28	1959	0	1959	
15	Wait For Me / Willingly (Re-Entry)	(HMV POP 590)	13	1959	0	1959	
Malcolm X Male Orator from the USA							
1	No Sell Out	(Tommy Boy IS 165)	60	1984	0	1984	
Malo Latin-Rock Band Formed By Carlos Santana's Brother Jorge							
1	Suavecito		0	1972	18	1972	(Warner Bros. 7559)
Mama Cass Female Vocalist, Real Name Ellen Naomi Cohen B: 19 Sep 1941							
1	Dream A Little Dream Of Me	(RCA 1726)	11	1968	12	1968	(Dunhill 4145)
2	It's Getting Better	(StateSIDE SS 8021)	8	1969	30	1969	(Dunhill 4195)
3	Make Your Own Kind Of Music		0	1969	36	1969	(Dunhill 4214)
	HIT 3 IS CREDITED TO MAMA CASS ELLIOT • OBITUARY : D: 29 JUL 1974 HEART ATTACK.						
Mamas & The Papas Mixed Vocal Group from the USA Formed In 1963 – John Phillips, Holly Phillips, Dennis Doherty & Cass Elliot							
* 1	California Dreamin'	(RCA 1503)	23	1966	4	1966	(Dunhill 4020)
* 2	Monday Monday	(RCA 1516)	3	1966	1	1966	(Dunhill 4026)
3	I Saw Her Again	(RCA 1533)	11	1966	5	1966	(Dunhill 4031)

	ISSUE	TITLE	UK LBL	UK POS	UK YEAR	US POS	US YEAR	US LBL
	4	Look Through My Window		0	1966	24	1966	(Dunhill 4050)
	5	Words Of Love	(RCA 1564)	47	1967	5	1967	(Dunhill 4057)
*	6	Dedicated To The One I Love	(RCA 1576)	2	1967	2	1967	(Dunhill 4077)
	7	Creeque Alley	(RCA 1613)	9	1967	5	1967	(Dunhill 4083)
	8	Twelve Thirty (Young Girls Are Coming To The Canyon)		0	1967	20	1967	(Dunhill 4099)
	9	Glad To Be Unhappy		0	1967	26	1967	(Dunhill 4107)
	10	California Dreamin' (Re-Issue)	(MCA MCSTD 48058)	9	1997	0	1997	

Man Parrish Male Mixer from the UK

	ISSUE	TITLE	UK LBL	UK POS	UK YEAR	US POS	US YEAR	US LBL
	1	Hop Hop, Be Bop (Don't Stop)	(Polydor POSP 575)	41	1983	0	1983	
	2	Boogie Town (Bronx)	(Boiling Point POSP 731)	56	1985	0	1985	
	3	Male Stripper	(Bolts Bolts 4)	64	1986	0	1986	
	4	Male Stripper (Re-Entry)	(Bolts Bolts 4)	63	1987	0	1987	
	5	Male Stripper (2nd Re-Entry)	(Bolts Bolts4)	4	1987	0	1987	

Man To Man Male Vocal/Instrumental Duo from the USA

	ISSUE	TITLE	UK LBL	UK POS	UK YEAR	US POS	US YEAR	US LBL
	1	Male Stripper	(Bolts Bolts 4)	64	1986	0	1986	
	2	Male Stripper (Re-Entry)	(Bolts Bolts 4)	63	1987	0	1987	
	3	Male Stripper (2nd Re-Entry)	(Bolts Bolts 4)	4	1987	0	1987	
	4	I Need A Man / Energy Is Eurobeat	(Bolts Bolts 5)	43	1987	0	1987	

Man With No Name Male Producer Martin Freeland from the UK

	ISSUE	TITLE	UK LBL	UK POS	UK YEAR	US POS	US YEAR	US LBL
	1	Floor / Essence	(Perfecto PERF 108CD)	68	1995	0	1995	
	2	Paint A Picture	(Perfecto PERF 114CD)	42	1996	0	1996	
	3	Teleport / Sugar Rush	(Perfecto PERF 126CD)	55	1996	0	1996	

Manchester United F.C. Male Vocal Soccer Team from the UK

	ISSUE	TITLE	UK LBL	UK POS	UK YEAR	US POS	US YEAR	US LBL
	1	Manchester United	(Decca F 13633)	50	1976	0	1976	
	2	Glory Glory Man. United	(EMI 5390)	13	1983	0	1983	
	3	We All Follow Man. United	(Columbia DB 9107)	10	1985	0	1985	
	4	United (We Love You)	(Living Beat LBECD 026)	37	1993	0	1993	
	5	Come On You Reds	(Polygram TV MANU 2)	1	1994	0	1994	
	6	We're Gonna Do It Again	(Polygram TV MANU 952)	6	1995	0	1995	
	7	Move Move Move (The Red Tribe)	(Music Collection MANUCD 1)	6	1996	0	1996	
	8	Move Move Move (The Red Tribe) (Re-Entry)	(Music Collection MANUCD 1)	50	1996	0	1996	

Mandy Smith Female Vocalist from the UK

	ISSUE	TITLE	UK LBL	UK POS	UK YEAR	US POS	US YEAR	US LBL
	1	Don't You Want Me Baby	(PWL PWL 3)	59	1989	0	1989	

Manfred Mann Male Vocalist, Real Name Michael Lubowitz B: 21 Oct 1940 Johannesburg, South Africa

	ISSUE	TITLE	UK LBL	UK POS	UK YEAR	US POS	US YEAR	US LBL
	1	5-4-3-2-1	(HMV POP 1252)	5	1964	0	1964	
	2	Hubble Bubble Toil And Trouble	(HMV POP 1282)	11	1964	0	1964	
*	3	Doo Wah Diddy Diddy	(HMV POP 1320)	1	1964	1	1964	(ASCOT 2157)
*	4	Sha La La	(HMV POP 1346)	3	1964	12	1964	(Ascot 2165)
	5	Come Tomorrow	(HMV POP 1381)	4	1965	0	1965	
	6	Oh No Not My Baby	(HMV POP 1413)	11	1965	0	1965	
	7	If You Gotta Go, Go Now	(HMV POP 1466)	2	1965	0	1965	
	8	Pretty Flamingo	(HMV POP 1523)	1	1966	29	1966	(United Artists 50040)
	9	You Gave Me Somebody To Love	(HMV POP 1541)	36	1966	0	1966	
	10	Just Like A Woman	(Fontana TF 730)	10	1966	0	1966	
	11	Semi-Detached Surburban Mr. Jones	(Fontana TF 757)	2	1966	0	1966	
	12	Ha Ha Said The Clown	(Fontana TF 812)	4	1967	0	1967	
	13	Sweet Pea	(Fontana TF 828)	36	1967	0	1967	
*	14	Mighty Quinn	(Fontana TF 897)	1	1968	10	1968	(Mercury 72770)
	15	My Name Is Jack	(Fontana TF 943)	8	1968	0	1968	
	16	Fox On The Run	(Fontana TF 985)	5	1968	0	1968	
	17	Ragamuffin Man	(Fontana TF 1013)	8	1969	0	1969	
	18	Joybringer	(Vertigo 6059 083)	9	1973	0	1973	
	19	Spirit In The Night		0	1976	97	1976	(Warner Bros.)
*	20	Blinded By The Light	(Bronze BRO 29)	6	1976	1	1976	(Warner Bros. 8252)
	21	Spirit In The Night (Re-Mix)		0	1977	40	1977	(Warner Bros. 8355)
	22	Davy's On The Road Again	(Bronze BRO 52)	6	1978	0	1978	
	23	You Angel You	(Bronze BRO 68)	54	1979	0	1979	
	24	Don't Kill It Carol	(Bronze BRO 77)	45	1979	0	1979	
	25	Runner		0	1984	22	1984	(Arista 9143)

Manhattan Transfer Mixed Vocal Group from the USA

	ISSUE	TITLE	UK LBL	UK POS	UK YEAR	US POS	US YEAR	US LBL
	1	Operator		0	1975	22	1975	(Atlantic 3292)
	2	Tuxedo Junction	(Atlantic K 10670)	24	1976	0	1976	
	3	Chanson D'amour	(Atlantic K 10886)	1	1977	0	1977	

ISSUE	TITLE	UK LBL	UK POS	UK YEAR	US POS	US YEAR	US LBL
4	Don't Let Go	(Atlantic K 10930)	32	1977	0	1977	
5	Walk In Love	(Atlantic K 11075)	48	1978	0	1978	
6	Walk In Love (Re-Entry)	(Atlantic K 11075)	12	1978	0	1978	
7	On A Little Street In Singapore	(Atlantic K 11136)	20	1978	0	1978	
8	Where Did Our Love Go / Je Voulais Te Dire	(Atlantic K 11182)	40	1978	0	1978	
9	Who What When Where Why	(Atlantic K 11233)	49	1978	0	1978	
10	Twilight Zone - Twilight Tone (Medley)	(Atlantic K 11476)	25	1980	30	1980	(Atlantic 3649)
11	Boy From New York City		0	1981	7	1981	(Atlantic 3816)
12	Spice Of Life	(Atlantic A 9728)	19	1984	40	1983	(Atlantic 89786)

Manhattans Male Vocal Group from the USA

ISSUE	TITLE	UK LBL	UK POS	UK YEAR	US POS	US YEAR	US LBL
1	Don't Take Your Love From Me		0	1975	37	1975	(Columbia 3-10045)
* 2	Kiss And Say Goodbye	(CBS 4317)	4	1976	1	1976	(Columbia 3-10310)
+ 3	Hurt	(CBS 4562)	4	1976	10	1975	(Columbia 3-10140)
4	It's You	(CBS 5093)	43	1977	0	1977	
* 5	Shining Star	(CBS 8624)	45	1980	5	1980	(Columbia 11222)
6	Crazy	(CBS A 3578)	63	1983	0	1983	

LEAD SINGER WITH THE SOUL GROUP WAS GEORGE SMITH • OBITUARY: D: GEORGE D: 1970 SPINAL MENINGITIS.

Manic MCs (Featuring) Sara Male Production Duo With Female Vocalist from the UK

ISSUE	TITLE	UK LBL	UK POS	UK YEAR	US POS	US YEAR	US LBL
1	Mental	(RCA PB 43037)	30	1989	0	1989	

Manic Street Preachers Male Vocal/Instrumental Group from the UK

ISSUE	TITLE	UK LBL	UK POS	UK YEAR	US POS	US YEAR	US LBL
1	You Love Us	(Heavenly HVN 10)	62	1991	0	1991	
2	Stay Beautiful	(Columbia6573377)	40	1991	0	1991	
3	Love's Sweet Exile / Repeat	(Columbia 6575827)	26	1991	0	1991	
4	You Love Us (Re-Issue)	(Columbia 6577247)	16	1992	0	1992	
5	Slash 'N' Burn	(Columbia 6578737)	20	1992	0	1992	
6	Motorcycle Emptiness	(Columbia 6580837)	17	1992	0	1992	
7	Theme From M.A.S.H. (Suicide Is Painless)	(Columbia 6583827)	7	1992	0	1992	
8	Little Baby Nothing	(Columbia 6587967)	29	1992	0	1992	
9	From Despair To Where	(Columbia 6593372)	25	1993	0	1993	
10	La Tristesse Durera (Scream To A Sigh)	(Columbia 6594772)	22	1993	0	1993	
11	Roses In The Hospital	(Columbia 6597272)	15	1993	0	1993	
12	Life Becoming A Landslide	(Columbia 6600702)	36	1994	0	1994	
13	Faster / Pcp	(Columbia 6604472)	16	1994	0	1994	
14	Revol	(Epic 6606862)	22	1994	0	1994	
15	She Is Suffering	(Epic 6608952)	25	1994	0	1994	
16	A Design For Life	(Epic 6630705)	2	1996	0	1996	
17	A Design For Life (Re-Entry)	(Epic 6630705)	71	1996	0	1996	
18	Everything Must Go	(Epic 6634685)	5	1996	0	1996	
19	Kevin Carter	(Epic 6637752)	9	1996	0	1996	
20	Australia	(Epic 6640442)	7	1996	0	1996	
21	Motorcycle Emptiness	(Epic Manic 5CD)	41	1997	0	1997	
22	You Love Us	(Eplc Manic3CD)	49	1997	0	1997	
23	Little Baby Nothing	(Epic Manic 6CD)	50	1997	0	1997	
24	Stay Beautiful	(Epic Manic 1CD)	52	1997	0	1997	
25	Slash 'N' Burn	(Epic Manic 4CD)	54	1997	0	1997	
26	Love's Sweet Exile	(Epic Manic 2CD)	55	1997	0	1997	

Manix Mixed Vocal/Instrumental Group from the UK

ISSUE	TITLE	UK LBL	UK POS	UK YEAR	US POS	US YEAR	US LBL
1	Manic Minds	(Reinforced Rivet 1209)	63	1991	0	1991	
2	Oblivion (Head In The Clouds) (EP)	(Reinforced Rivet 1212)	43	1992	0	1992	
3	Rainbow People	(Reinforced Rivet 1221)	57	1992	0	1992	

Mankey Male Producer Andy Manston from the UK

ISSUE	TITLE	UK LBL	UK POS	UK YEAR	US POS	US YEAR	US LBL
1	Believe In Me	(Frisky Disky 3)	74	1996	0	1996	

Mankind Male Instrumental Group from the UK

ISSUE	TITLE	UK LBL	UK POS	UK YEAR	US POS	US YEAR	US LBL
1	Dr. Who	(Pinnacle Pin 71)	25	1978	0	1978	

Mansun Male Vocal/Instrumental Trio from the UK

ISSUE	TITLE	UK LBL	UK POS	UK YEAR	US POS	US YEAR	US LBL
1	One (EP)	(ParlophoneCDR 6430)	37	1996	0	1996	
2	Two (EP)	(Parlophone CDR 6437)	32	1996	0	1996	
3	Stripper Vicar	(Parlophone CDR 6447)	19	1996	0	1996	
4	Wide Open Space	(Parlophone CDR 6453)	15	1996	0	1996	
5	She Makes My Nose Bleed	(Parlophone CDR 6458)	9	1997	0	1997	
6	Taxloss	(Parlophone CDRS 6465)	15	1997	0	1997	

Mantell Jordan Male R&B Vocalist from Los Angeles

ISSUE	TITLE	UK LBL	UK POS	UK YEAR	US POS	US YEAR	US LBL
* 1	This Is How We Do It		0	1995	1	1995	(PMP/RAL 851468)

ISSUE	TITLE	UK LBL	UK POS	UK YEAR	US POS	US YEAR	US LBL
* 2	Somethin' 4 Da Honeyz		0	1995	21	1995	(PMP/RAL 856962)

Mantovani & His Orchestra Male Orchestra Leader, Real Name Annunzio Paolo Mantovani B: 15 Nov 1905

ISSUE	TITLE	UK LBL	UK POS	UK YEAR	US POS	US YEAR	US LBL
* 3	Charmaine		0	1951	10	1951	(London 1020)
4	Greensleeves		0	1952	25	1952	(London 1171)
5	Dancing With Tears In My Eyes		0	1952	26	1952	(London 1175)
6	White Christmas (From *Holiday Inn*)	(Decca F 10017)	6	1952	23	1952	(London 1280)
* 7	The Moulin Rouge Theme (Where Is Your Heart)	(Decca F 10094)	1	1953	8	1953	(London 1328)
* 8	Swedish Rhapsody	(Decca F 10168)	2	1953	0	1953	
* 9	Cara Mia	(Decca F 10327)	1	1954	10	1954	—(London 1486)
10	The Moulin Rouge Theme (Re-Entry)	(Decca F 10094)	10	1953	0	1953	
11	The Moulin Rouge Theme (2nd Re-Entry)	(Decca F 10094)	12	1953	0	1953	
12	Swedish Rhapsody (Re-Entry)	(Decca F 10168)	12	1954	0	1954	
* 13	Lonely Ballerina	(Decca F 10395)	16	1955	0	1955	
14	Lonely Ballerina (Re-Entry)	(Decca F 10395)	18	1955	0	1955	
15	Around The World	(Decca F 10888)	20	1957	12	1957	(London 1746)
16	Main Theme From *Exodus* (Ari's Theme)		0	1961	31	1961	(London 1953)

Mantronix Male Vocal/Instrumental Duo from the USA/Jamaica

ISSUE	TITLE	UK LBL	UK POS	UK YEAR	US POS	US YEAR	US LBL
1	Ladies	(10 TEN 116)	55	1986	0	1986	
2	Bassline	(10 TEN 118)	34	1986	0	1986	
3	Who Is It	(10 TEN 137)	40	1987	0	1987	
4	Scream (Primal Scream)	(10 TEN 169)	46	1987	0	1987	
5	Sing A Song (Break It Down)	(10 TEN 206)	61	1988	0	1988	
6	Simple Simon (You Gotta Regard)	(10 TEN 217)	72	1988	0	1988	
7	Got To Have Your Love	(Capitol CL 559)	4	1990	0	1990	
8	Take Your Time	(Capitol CL 573)	10	1990	0	1990	
9	Don't Go Messin' With My Heart	(Capitol CL 608)	22	1991	0	1991	
10	Step To Me (Do Me)	(Capitol CL 613)	59	1991	0	1991	

HITS 7-8 ARE CREDITED TO MANTRONIX FEATURING WONDRESS

Manu Dibango Male Saxophonist/Pianist, B: 1934 Cameroon, Africa

ISSUE	TITLE	UK LBL	UK POS	UK YEAR	US POS	US YEAR	US LBL
1	Soul Makossa		0	1973	35	1973	(Atlantic 2971)

Manuel & His Music Of The Mountains Male Orchestra Leader, Real Name Geoff Love from the UK

ISSUE	TITLE	UK LBL	UK POS	UK YEAR	US POS	US YEAR	US LBL
1	Theme From *Honeymoon*	(Columbia DB 4323)	29	1959	0	1959	
2	Theme From Honeymoon (Re-Entry)	(Columbia DB 4323)	22	1959	0	1959	
3	Theme From Honeymoon (2nd Re-Entry)	(Columbia DB 4323)	27	1959	0	1959	
4	Never On Sunday	(Columbia DB 4515)	29	1960	0	1960	
5	Somewhere My Love	(Columbia DB 7969)	42	1966	0	1966	
6	Rodrigo's Guitar Concerto De Aranjeuz	(EMI 2383)	3	1987	0	1987	

Mao Tse-Tung Red China's Chairman

ISSUE	TITLE	UK LBL	UK POS	UK YEAR	US POS	US YEAR	US LBL
* 1	Sing Along With Mao		0	1966	0	1966	

Mar-Keys Names Terry Johnson, Steve Cropper, Don 'Duck' Dunn, Charles Axton, Don Nix, Wayne Jackson & Jerry

ISSUE	TITLE	UK LBL	UK POS	UK YEAR	US POS	US YEAR	US LBL
* 1	Last Night		0	1961	3	1961	(SATELLITE 107)

Marathon Male Vocal/Instrumental Group from the UK/Germany

ISSUE	TITLE	UK LBL	UK POS	UK YEAR	US POS	US YEAR	US LBL
1	Movin'	(TEN TEN 395)	36	1992	0	1992	

Marauders Male Vocal/Instrumental Group from the UK

ISSUE	TITLE	UK LBL	UK POS	UK YEAR	US POS	US YEAR	US LBL
1	That's What I Want	(Decca F 11695)	48	1963	0	1963	
2	That's What I Want (Re-Entry)	(Decca F 11695)	43	1963	0	1963	

Marbles Male Vocal Duo from the UK

ISSUE	TITLE	UK LBL	UK POS	UK YEAR	US POS	US YEAR	US LBL
1	Only One Woman	(Polydor 56 272)	5	1968	0	1968	
2	The Walls Fell Down	(Polydor 56 310)	28	1969	0	1969	

Marc Almond Male Vocalist from the UK

ISSUE	TITLE	UK LBL	UK POS	UK YEAR	US POS	US YEAR	US LBL
1	Black Heart	(Some Bizarre BZS 19)	49	1983	0	1983	
2	The Boy Who Came Back	(Some Bizarre BZS 23)	52	1984	0	1984	
3	You Have	(Some Bizarre BZS 24)	57	1984	0	1984	
5	Stories Of Johnny	(Some Bizarre BONK 1)	23	1985	0	1985	
6	Love Letter	(Some Bizarre BONK 2)	68	1986	0	1986	
7	The House Is Haunted (By Your Last Goodbye)	(Some Bizarre GLOW 1)	55	1986	0	1986	
8	A Womans Story	(Some Bizarre GLOW 2)	41	1986	0	1986	
9	Ruby Red	(Some Bizarre GLOW 3)	47	1986	0	1986	
10	Melancholy Rose	(Some Bizarre GLOW 4)	71	1987	0	1987	
11	Tears Run Rings	(Parlophone R 6186)	26	1988	0	1988	
12	Bitter Sweet	(Some Bizarre R 6194)	40	1988	0	1988	
13	Something's Gotten Hold Of My Heart	(Parlophone R 6201)	1	1989	0	1989	

ISSUE	TITLE	UK LBL	UK POS	UK YEAR	US POS	US YEAR	US LBL
14	Only The Moment	(Parlophone R 6210)	45	1989	0	1989	
15	A Lover Spurned	(Some Bizarre R 6229)	29	1990	0	1990	
16	The Desperate Hours	(Some Bizarre R 6252)	45	1990	0	1990	
17	Say Hello Wave Goodbye '91	(Mercury SOFT 1)	38	1991	0	1991	
18	Tainted Love (Re-Issue)	(Mercury SOFT 2)	5	1991	0	1991	
19	Jacky	(Some Bizarre YZ 610)	17	1991	0	1991	
20	My Hand Over My Heart	(Some Bizarre YZ 633)	33	1992	0	1992	
21	The Days Of Pearly Spencer	(Some Bizarre YZ 638)	4	1992	0	1992	
22	What Makes A Man A Man (Live)	(Some Bizarre YZ 720CD)	60	1993	0	1993	
23	Adored And Explored	(Some Bizarre/Mercury MERCD 431)	25	1995	0	1995	
24	The Idol	(Some Bizarre/Mercury MERCD 437)	44	1995	0	1995	
25	Child Star	(Some Bizarre/Mercury MERCD 450)	41	1995	0	1995	
26	Yesterday Has Gone	(EMI Premier CDPRES 13)	58	1996	0	1996	
27	Yesterday Has Gone (Re-Entry)	(EMI PremierCDPRESX 13)	69	1997	0	1997	

Marc Cohn   Male Vocalist, B: Cleveland, Formed The Supreme Court

ISSUE	TITLE	UK LBL	UK POS	UK YEAR	US POS	US YEAR	US LBL
1	Walking In Memphis	(Atlantic A 7747)	66	1991	13	1991	(Atlantic 87747)
2	Silver Thunderbird	(Atlantic A 7657)	54	1991	0	1991	
3	Walking In Memphis (Re-Issue)	(Atlantic 7585)A	22	1991	0	1991	
4	Walk Through The World	(Atlantic A 7340CD)	37	1993	0	1993	

Marcella Detroit   Female Vocalist

ISSUE	TITLE	UK LBL	UK POS	UK YEAR	US POS	US YEAR	US LBL
1	I Believe	(London LONCD 347)	11	1994	0	1994	
2	Ain't Nothing Like The Real Thing	(London LONCD 350)	24	1994	0	1994 with Elton John	
3	I'm No Angel	(London LOCDP 351)	33	1994	0	1994	

Marcello Minerbi   Orchestra Leader from Italy

ISSUE	TITLE	UK LBL	UK POS	UK YEAR	US POS	US YEAR	US LBL
1	Zorba's Dance	(Durium DRS 54001)	6	1964	0	1964	

Marcels   Male R&B Vocal Group from the USA, Lead Singer Was Cornelius Harp

ISSUE	TITLE	UK LBL	UK POS	UK YEAR	US POS	US YEAR	US LBL
* 1	Blue Moon	(PYE International7N 25073)	1	1961	1	1961	(COLPIX 186)
2	Summertime	(PYE International 7N 25083)	46	1961	0	1961	
3	Heartaches		0	1961	7	1961	(COLPIX 612)

Marcie Blaine   Female Vocalist, B: 21 May 1944, In Brooklyn, New York

ISSUE	TITLE	UK LBL	UK POS	UK YEAR	US POS	US YEAR	US LBL
* 1	Bobby's Girl		0	1962	3	1962	(Seville 120)

Marco Polo   Male Instrumental/Production Duo from Italy

ISSUE	TITLE	UK LBL	UK POS	UK YEAR	US POS	US YEAR	US LBL
1	A Prayer To The Music	(Hi-Life HICD 7)	65	1995	0	1995	

Mardi Gras   Male Vocal/Instrumental Group from the UK

ISSUE	TITLE	UK LBL	UK POS	UK YEAR	US POS	US YEAR	US LBL
1	Too Busy Thinking 'Bout My Baby	(Bell 1226)	19	1972	0	1972	

Marek Weber & His Orchestra   Male Bandleader from Australia

ISSUE	TITLE	UK LBL	UK POS	UK YEAR	US POS	US YEAR	US LBL
1	Blue Danube Waltz		0	1941	25	1941	(Victor 25199)

Margaret Whiting   Female Vocalist, B: 22 Jul 1924 Mineola, Arkansas

ISSUE	TITLE	UK LBL	UK POS	UK YEAR	US POS	US YEAR	US LBL
1	All Through The Day		0	1946	11	1946	(Capitol 240)
2	In Love In Vain		0	1461	2	1946	(Capitol 240)
3	Come Rain Or Come Shine		0	1946	17	1946	(Capitol 247)
4	Along With Me		0	1946	13	1946	(Capitol 269)
5	Passe		0	1946	12	1946	(Capitol 294)
6	Guilty		0	1946	4	1946	(Capitol 324)
7	Oh, But I Do		0	1946	7	1946	(Capitol 324)
8	Beware My Heart		0	1947	21	1947	(Capitol 360)
9	Old Devil Moon		0	1947	11	1947	(Capitol 360)
10	Ask Anyone Who Knows		0	1947	21	1947	(Capitol 410)
11	Little Girl Blue		0	1947	25	1947	(Capitol 20116)
12	You Do		0	1947	5	1947	(Capitol 438)
13	Lazy Countryside		0	1947	21	1947	(Capitol 461)
14	Pass The Peace Pipe		0	1947	8	1947	(Capitol 15010)
15	Let's Be Sweethearts Again		0	1948	22	1948	(Capitol 15010)
16	But Beautiful		0	1948	21	1948	(Capitol 15024)
17	Now Is The Hour (Maori Farewell Song)		0	1948	2	1948	(Capitol 15024)
18	What's Good About Goodbye?		0	1948	29	1948	(Capitol 15038)
19	Please Don't Kiss Me		0	1948	23	1948	(Capitol 15058)
* 20	A Tree In The Meadow		0	1948	1	1948	(Capitol 15122)
21	Far Away Places		0	1948	2	1948	(Capitol 15278)
22	Forever And Ever		0	1949	5	1949	(Capitol 15386)

	ISSUE	TITLE	UK LBL	UK POS	UK YEAR	US POS	US YEAR	US LBL
	23	A Wonderful Guy		0	1949	12	1949	(Capitol 542)
	24	Baby, It's Cold Outside		0	1949	3	1949	(Capitol 567)
*	25	Slippin' Around		0	1949	1	1949	(Capitol 40224)
	26	Wedding Bells Will Soon Be Ringing		0	1949	30	1949	(Capitol 40224)
	27	Dime A Dozen		0	1949	19	1919	(Capitol 709)
	28	I'll Never Slip Around Again		0	1949	8	1949	(Capitol 40246)
	29	Broken Down Merry-Go-Round		0	1950	12	1950	(Capitol 800)
	30	The Gods Were Angry With Me		0	1950	17	1950	(Capitol 800)
	31	I Said My Pajamas (And Put On My Pray'rs)		0	1950	21	1950	(Capitol 841)
	32	Let's Got To Church (Next Sunday Morning)		0	1950	13	1950	(Capitol 960)
	33	My Foolish Heart		0	1950	17	1950	(Capitol 934)
	34	Blind Date		0	1950	16	1950	(Capitol 1042)
	35	A Bushel And A Peck		0	1950	6	1950	(Capitol 1234)
	36	When You And I Were Young, Maggie, Blues		0	1951	20	1951	(Capitol 1500)
	37	Good Morning, Mr. Echo		0	1951	14	1951	(Capitol 1702)
!	38	I Don't Want To Be Free		0	1951	5	1951	(Capitol 1816)
	39	I'll Walk Alone		0	1952	29	1952	(Capitol 2000)
	40	Outside Of Heaven		0	1952	22	1952	(Capitol 2217)
	41	Why Don't You Believe Me?		0	1953	29	1953	(Capitol 2292)
	42	Moonlight In Vermont		0	1954	29	1954	(Capitol 2681)
	43	The Money Tree		0	1956	20	1956	(Capitol 3586)
	44	The Wheel Of Hurt		0	1966	26	1966	(London 101)
Margie Rayburn Female Singer, B: In Madera, California, Also A Member Of The Sunnysiders							
	1	I'm Available		0	1957	9	1957	(Liberty 55102)
Mari Wilson Female Vocalist from the UK							
	1	Beat The Beat	(Compact Pink 2)	59	1982	0	1982	
	2	Baby It's True	(Compact Pink 3)	42	1982	0	1982	
	3	Just What I Always Wanted	(Compact Pink 4)	8	1982	0	1982	
	4	(Beware) Boyfriend	(Compact Pink 5)	51	1982	0	1982	
	5	Cry Me A River	(Compact Pink 6)	27	1983	0	1983	
	6	Wonderful	(Compact Pink7)	47	1983	0	1983	
Maria McKee Female Vocalist from the USA							
	1	Show Me Heaven	(Epic 656303 7)	1	1990	0	1990	
	2	Breathe	(Geffen GFS 1)	59	1991	0	1991	
	3	Sweetest Child	(Geffen GFS 23)	45	1992	0	1992	
	4	I'm Gonna Soothe You	(Geffen GFSTD 39)	35	1993	0	1993	
	5	I Can't Make It Alone	(Geffen GFSTD 53)	74	1993	0	1993	
Maria Muldaur Female Vocalist, Real Name Maria D'amato, B: 12 Sep 1943 New York City							
	1	Midnight At The Oasis	(Reprise K 14331)	21	1974	6	1974	(Reprise 1183)
	2	I'm A Woman		0	1975	12	1975	(Reprise 1319)
Maria Nayler Female Vocalist from the UK							
	1	Be As One	(Deconstruction 74321342962)	17	1996	0	1996	
	2	One And One	(Deconstruction 74321427692)	3	1996	0	1996	
Maria Rowe Female Vocalist from the UK							
	1	Sexual	(FFRR FCD 248)	67	1995	0	1995	
Maria Vidal Female Vocalist from the USA							
	1	Body Rock	(EMI America EA 189)	11	1985	0	1985	
Mariah Carey Female Vocalist B: 27 Mar 1970 from the USA							
*	1	Vision Of Love	(CBS 6559320)	9	1990	1	1990	(Columbia 73348)
*	2	Love Takes Time	(CBS 6563647)	37	1990	1	1990	(Columbia 73455)
*	3	Someday	(CBS 6565837)	38	1991	1	1991	(Columbia 73561)
	4	I Don't Wanna Cry		0	1991	1	1991	(Columbia 73743)
	5	There's Got To Be A Way	(Columbia 6569317)	54	1991	0	1991	
*	6	Emotions	(Columbia 6574037)	17	1991	1	1991	(Columbia 73977)
	7	Can't Let Go	(Columbia6576627)	20	1992	2	1991	(Columbia 74088)
	8	Make It Happen	(Columbia 6579417)	17	1992	5	1992	(Columbia 74239)
	9	I'll Be There	(Columbia 6581377)	2	1992	1	1992	(Columbia 74330)
*	10	Dreamlover	(Columbia 6594445)	9	1993	1	1993	(Columbia 77080)
*	11	Hero	(Columbia 6598122)	7	1993	1	1993	(Columbia 77224)
*	12	Without You	(Columbia 6599192)	1	1994	3	1994	(Columbia 77358)
	13	Never Forget You		0	1994	20	1994	(Columbia 77358)
	14	Anytime You Need A Friend	(Columbia 6603542)	8	1994	12	1994	(Columbia 77499)
*	15	Endless Love	(Epic 6608062)	3	1994	2	1994	(Columbia 77629)

ISSUE	TITLE	UK LBL	UK POS	UK YEAR	US POS	US YEAR	US LBL
16	All I Want For Christmas Is You	(Columbia 6610702)	2	1994	0	1994	
17	Endless Love (Re-Entry)	(Epic 6608062)	70	1995	0	1995	
18	Endless Love (2nd Re-Entry)	(Epic 6608062)	55	1996	0	1996	
19	All I Want For Christmas Is You (Re-Entry)	Columbia 6610702	59	1995	0	1995	
* 20	Fantasy	(Columbia 6624952)	4	1995	1	1995	(Columbia 78043)
* 21	One Sweet Day	(Columbia 6626035)	6	1996	1	1996	(Columbia 78074)
22	Open Arms	(Columbia 6629772)	4	1996	0	1996	
23	Always Be My Baby	(Columbia 6633345)	3	1996	0	1996	
24	Honey	(Columbia 6650192)	3	1997	0	1997	

HIT 9 ALTHOUGH UNCREDITED IS MARIAH CAREY AND TRAY LORENZ • HITS 15, 17 ,18 ARE CREDITED TO LUTHER VANDROSS AND MARIAH CAREY
HIT 21 IS CREDITED TO MARIAH CAREY AND BOYZ II MEN • SEE ALSO TREY LORENZ

Marian Caruso   Female Vocalist With Don Costa's Orchestra And The Overtones

1	My Favorite Song		0	1952	28	1952	(Devon 1001)

Marianne Faithfull   Female Vocalist, B: 29 Dec 1946 Hamstead, London, England

1	As Tears Go By	(Decca F 11923)	9	1964	22	1964	(London 9697)
2	Come And Stay With Me	(Decca F 12075)	4	1965	26	1965	(London 9731)
3	This Little Bird	(Decca F 12162)	6	1965	32	1965	(London 9759)
4	Summer Nights	(Decca F 12193)	10	1965	24	1965	(London 9780)
5	Yesterday	(Decca F 12268)	36	1965	0	1965	
6	Is This What I Get For Loving You	(Decca F 22524)	42	1967	0	1967	
7	The Ballad Of Lucy Jordan	(Island WIP 6491)	48	1979	0	1979	

Marie Myriam   Female Vocalist from France, Won Eurovision Song Contest

1	L'oiseau Et L'enfant	(Polydor 2056 634)	42	1977	0	1977	

Marie Osmond   Female Vocalist, B: Olive Marie Osmond, 13 Oct 1959 In Ogden, Utah

* 1	Paper Roses	(MGM 2006 315)	2	1973	5	1973	(MGM 14609)
! 2	In My Little Corner Of The World		0	1974	33	1974	(MGM 14694)
3	Who's Sorry Now		0	1975	40	1975	(MGM 14786)
! 4	A My Name Is Alice		0	1976	85	1976	(Polydor 14333)
5	That Is The Way That I Feel		0	1977	39	1977	(Polydor 14385)

OTHERS WERE C/W HITS

Marillion   Male Vocal/Instrumental Group from the UK

1	Market Square Heroes	(EMI 5351)	60	1982	0	1982	
2	He Knows You Know	(EMI 5362)	35	1983	0	1983	
3	Market Square Heroes (Re-Entry)	(EMI 5351)	53	1983	0	1983	
4	Garden Party	(EMI 5393)	16	1983	0	1983	
5	Punch And Judy	(EMI Maril 1)	29	1984	0	1984	
6	Assassing	(EMI Maril 2)	22	1984	0	1984	
7	Keyleigh	(EMI Maril 3)	2	1985	0	1985	
8	Lavender	(EMI Maril 4)	5	1985	0	1985	
9	Heart Of Lothian	(EMI Maril 5)	29	1985	0	1985	
10	Incommunicado	(EMI Maril 6)	6	1987	0	1987	
11	Sugar Mice	(EMI Maril 7)	22	1987	0	1987	
12	Warm Wet Circles	(EMI Maril 8)	22	1987	0	1987	
13	Freaks (Live)	(EMI Maril 9)	24	1988	0	1988	
14	Hooks In You	(EMI Maril 10)	30	1989	0	1989	
15	Univited Guest	(EMI Maril 11)	53	1989	0	1989	
16	Easter	(EMI Maril 12)	34	1990	0	1990	
17	Cover My Eyes (Pain And Heaven)	(EMI Maril 13)	34	1991	0	1991	
18	No One Can	(EMI Maril 14)	33	1991	0	1991	
19	Dry Land	(EMI Maril 15)	34	1991	0	1991	
20	Sympathy	(EMI Maril 16)	17	1992	0	1992	
21	No One Can (Re-Issue)	(EMI Maril 17)	26	1992	0	1992	
22	The Hollow Man	(EMI CDEMS 307)	30	1994	0	1994	
23	Alone Again In The Lap Of Luxury	(EMI CDEMS 318)	53	1994	0	1994	
24	Beautiful	(EMI CDMarilS 18)	29	1995	0	1995	

Marilyn   Male Vocalist from the UK

1	Calling Your Name	(Mercury MAZ 1)	4	1983	0	1983	
2	Cry And Be Free	(Mercury MAZ 2)	31	1984	0	1984	
3	You Don't Love Me	(Mercury MAZ 3)	40	1984	0	1984	

ISSUE	TITLE	UK LBL	UK POS	UK YEAR	US POS	US YEAR	US LBL
4	Baby U Left Me (In The Cold)	(Mercury MAZ 4)	70	1985	0	1985	

Marilyn Manson Mixed Vocal/Instrumental Rock Band from the USA

1	The Beautiful People	(Interscope IND 95541)	18	1997	0	1997	

Marilyn Martin Female Vocalist, Raised In Louisville

1	Separate Lives (From White Nights)	(Virgin VS 818)	4	1985	1	1986	(Atlantic 89498)
2	Night Movies		0	1986	28	1986	(Atlantic 89465)

HIT 1 IS CREDITED TO PHIL COLLINS AND MARILYN MARTIN • SANG BACKING VOCALS FOR STEVIE NICKS, KENNY LOGGINS AND MANY MORE

Marilyn McCoo & Billy Davis Jr. Mixed Vocal Duo from the USA

* 1	You Don't Have To Be A Star (To Be In My Show)	(ABC 4147)	7	1977	1	1976	(ABC 12208)
2	Your Love		0	1977	15	1977	(ABC 12262)

BILLY B: 26 JUN 1939, ST. LOUIS • MARILYN B: 30 SEP 1943, JERSEY CITY • BOTH FORMER MEMBERS OF THE 5TH DIMENSION

Marilyn Monroe Female Actress/Vocalist, Real Name Norma Jean Baker from the USA

1	River Of No Return		0	1954	30	1954	(RCA Victor 5754)

OBITUARY : D: 5 AUG 1962 (AGED 36).

Marilyn Sellars Female Country Singer from Northfield, Minnesota

1	One Day At A Time		0	1974	37	1974	(MEGA 1205)

SHE USED TO WORK AS AN AIRLINE STEWARDESS

Mariners Vocal Group from the USA

1	Sometime		0	1950	16	1950	(Columbia 38781)
2	They Call The Wind Maria (From Paint Your Wagon)		0	1951	30	1951	(Columbia 39568)
3	I See The Moon		0	1953	14	1953	(Columbia 40047)

Marino Marini & His Quartet Male Vocalist from Italy

1	Volare	(DURIUM DC 16632)	13	1958	0	1958	
2	Come Prima	(DURIUM DC 16632)	2	1958	0	1958	
3	Ciao, Ciao Bambina	(DURIUM DC 16636)	25	1959	0	1959	
4	Ciao, Ciao Bambina (Re-Entry)	(DURIUM DC 16636)	24	1959	0	1959	

Mario Lanza Male Vocalist, Real Name Alfredo Arnold Cocozza B: 31 Jan 1921

* 1	Be My Love		0	1950	1	1950	(RCA Victor 78-1561)
2	Vesti La Giubba (From I Pagliacci)		0	1951	21	1951	(RCA Victor 3228)
* 3	The Loveliest Night Of The Year		0	1951	3	1951	(RCA Victor 3300)
* 4	Because		0	1952	16	1952	(RCA Victor 3207)
* 5	Because Your Mine	(HMV DA 2017)	3	1952	7	1900	(RCA Victor 3914)
6	Song Of India (From Sadko)		0	1953	20	1953	(RCA Victor 4209)
7	Drinking Song (Drink, Drink, Drink) (From Student Prince)	(HMV DA 2065)	13	1955	21	1954	(RCA Victor 4220)
8	I'll Walk With God	(HMV DA 2062)	18	1955	0	1955	
9	Serenade	(HMV DA 2065)	19	1955	0	1955	
10	I'll Walk With God (Re-Entry)	(HMV DA 2062)	20	1955	0	1955	
11	Serenade (Re-Entry)	(HMV DA 2065)	15	1955	0	1955	
12	Serenade	(HMV DA 2085)	25	1956	0	1956	
13	Serenade (Re-Entry)	(HMV DA 2085)	29	1956	0	1956	

HITS 9, 11 ARE DIFFERENT RECORDING OF HITS 12-13 • HIS STAGE NAME IS SAID TO HAVE BEEN TAKEN FROM HIS MOTHER'S MARIA LANZA

Marion Male Vocal/Instrumental Group from the UK

1	Sleep	(London LONCD 360)	53	1995	0	1995	
2	Toys For Boys	(London LONCD 366)	57	1995	0	1995	
3	Let's All Go Together	(London LONCD 371)	37	1995	0	1995	
4	Time	(London LONCD 377)	29	1996	0	1996	
5	Sleep (Re-Mix)	(London LONCD 381)	17	1996	0	1996	

Marion Marlowe Ballad Singer, Was With Arthur Godfrey And His Friends In The 50s

1	Whither Thou Goest		0	1954	27	1954	(Columbia 40315)
2	The Man In The Raincoat		0	1955	14	1955	(Cadence 1266)

Marion Vocalist from the UK, Mother Of Paul And Barry Ryan

1	Love Me Forever	(PYN NIXA N 15121)	5	1958	0	1958	

Marjorie Hughes Female Vocalist from the USA

1	You Told A Lie		0	1949	18	1949	(Columbia 38500)

Mark 'Oh Male Producer Marko Albrecht from Germany

1	Tears Don't Lie	(Systematic SYSCD 9)	24	1995	0	1995	

Mark Dinning Male Vocalist, B: 17 Aug 1933 Grant County, Oklahoma

* 1	Teen Angel	(MGM 1053)	37	1960	1	1960	(MGM 12845)
2	Teen Angel (Re-Entry)	(MGM 1053)	42	1960	0	1960	

OBITUARY: D: 22 MAR 1986 HEART ATTACK.

ISSUE	TITLE	UK LBL	UK POS	UK YEAR	US POS	US YEAR	US LBL
Mark E. Smith Male Vocalist from the UK							
1	I Want You	(Cow Dung 24CD)	18	1994	0	1994	
2	Plug Myself In	(Colliseum Toga 001CD1)	50	1996	0	1996	
	HIT 1 IS CREDITED TO INSPIRAL CARPETS FEATURING MARK E. SMITH • HIT 2 IS CREDITED TO DOSE FEATURING MARK E. SMITH						
See Also Fall							
Mark Fisher Male Instrumentalist (Keyboards) And Female Vocalist from the UK							
1	Love Situation	(Total Control TOCO 3)	59	1985	0	1985	
	HIT IS CREDITED TO MARK FISHER FEATURING DOTTY GREEN						
Mark IV Pop-Rock Quartet from Chicago							
1	I Got A Wife		0	1959	24	1959	(Mercury 71403)
Mark Knopfler Male Vocal/Guitarist from the UK							
1	Going Home (Theme From Local Hero)	(Vertigo DSTR 4)	56	1983	0	1983	
2	Darling Pretty	(Vertigo VERCD 88)	33	1996	0	1996	
3	Cannibals	(Vertigo VERCD 89)	42	1996	0	1996	
Mark Lindsay Male Saxophonist/Vocalist, B: 9 Mar 1942 Cambridge, Idaho							
* 1	Arizona		0	1970	10	1970	(Columbia 45037)
2	Silver Bird		0	1970	25	1970	(Columbia 45180)
	PREVIOUS GROUPS WERE THE UNKNOWNS AND PAUL REVERE & THE RAIDERS						
Mark Morrison Male Vocalist from the UK							
1	Crazy	(WEA YZ 907CD)	19	1995	0	1995	
2	Let's Get Down	(WEA WEA 001CD)	39	1995	0	1995	
* 3	Return Of The Mack	(WEA WEA 040CD)	1	1996	3	1997	(Atlantic 84868)
4	Crazy (Re-Mix)	(WEA WEA 054CD1)	6	1996	0	1996	
5	Return Of The Mack (Re-Entry)	(WEA WEA 040CD)	60	1996	0	1996	
6	Crazy (Re-Mix) (Re-Entry)	(WEA WEA 054CD)	71	1996	0	1996	
7	Trippin'	(WEA WEA 079CD1)	8	1996	0	1996	
8	Horny	(WEA WEA 090CD1)	5	1996	0	1996	
9	Return Of The Mack (2nd Re-Entry)	(WEA WEA 040CD)	60	1996	0	1997	
10	Moan & Groan	(WEA WEA 096CD1)	7	1997	0	1997	
Mark Owen Male Vocalist from the UK							
1	Child	(RCA 74321424422)	3	1996	0	1996	
2	Clementine	(RCA 74321424422)	3	1997	0	1997	
3	Child (Re-Entry)	(RCA 74321424422)	45	1997	0	1997	
4	I Am What I Am	(RCA 74321501222)	29	1997	0	1997	
Mark Shaw Male Vocalist from the UK							
1	Love So Bright	(EMI EM 161)	54	1990	0	1990	
Mark Snow Male Instrumentalist (Keyboards) from the USA							
1	The X Files	(Warner Bros. W 0341CD)	2	1996	0	1996	
Mark Summers Male Producer from the UK							
1	Summer's Magic	(Fourth & Broadway BRW 205)	27	1991	0	1991	
Mark Valentino Real Name Anthony Busillo B: 12 Mar 1942 Philadelphia							
1	The Push And Kick		0	1962	27	1962	(Swan 4121)
Mark Warnow & His Orchestra Male Bandleader from the USA							
1	Who Put That Dream In Your Eye?		0	1948	26	1948	(Coast 8026)
	OBITUARY: D: OCT 1949 (AGED 47).						
Mark Wynter Male Vocalist from the UK							
1	Image Of A Girl	(Decca F 11263)	11	1960	0	1960	
2	Kicking Up The Leaves	(Decca F 11279)	24	1960	0	1960	
3	Dream Girl	(Decca F 11323)	27	1961	0	1961	
4	Exclusively Yours	(Decca F 11354)	32	1961	0	1961	
5	Venus In Blue Jeans	(PYE /N 15466)	4	1962	0	1962	
6	Go Away Little Girl	(PYE 7N 15492)	6	1962	0	1962	
7	Shy Girl	(PYR 7N 15525)	28	1963	0	1963	
8	It's Almost Tomorrow	(PYE 7N 15577)	12	1963	0	1963	
9	Only You	(PYE 7N 15626)	38	1964	0	1964	
Marketts Male Instrumental Group from Hollywood, California							
1	Surfer's Stomp		0	1962	31	1962	(Liberty 55401)
* 2	Out Of Limits		0	1964	3	1964	(Warner Bros. 5391)

ISSUE	TITLE	UK LBL	UK POS	UK YEAR	US POS	US YEAR	US LBL
3	Batman Theme		0	1966	17	1966	(Warner Bros. 5696)

Marky Mark & The Funky Bunch Mixed Vocal/Instrumental Group from the USA

ISSUE	TITLE	UK LBL	UK POS	UK YEAR	US POS	US YEAR	US LBL
* 1	Good Vibrations	(Interscope A 8764)	14	1991	1	1991	(Interscope 98764)
* 2	Wildside	(Interscope A 8674)	42	1991	10	1991	(Interscope 98673)
3	You Gotta Believe	(Interscope A 8480)	54	1992	0	1992	

Marlene Dietrich Female Actress/Vocalist, Real Name Maria Magdalene Dietrich Von Losch B: In Weimar, West Germany

ISSUE	TITLE	UK LBL	UK POS	UK YEAR	US POS	US YEAR	US LBL
1	Too Old To Cut The Mustard		0	1952	12	1952	(Columbia 39812)
	HIT IS CREDITED TO ROSEMARY CLOONEY AND MARLENE DIETRICH						

Marmalade Male Vocal/Instrumental Group from the UK

ISSUE	TITLE	UK LBL	UK POS	UK YEAR	US POS	US YEAR	US LBL
1	Lovin' Things	(CBS 3412)	6	1968	0	1968	
2	Wait For Me Marianne	(CBS 3708)	30	1968	0	1968	
* 3	Ob-La-Di Ob-La-Da	(CBS 3892)	1	1968	0	1968	
4	Baby Make It Soon	(CBS 4287)	9	1969	0	1969	
* 5	Reflections Of My Life	(Decca F 12982)	3	1969	10	1970	(London 20058)
6	Rainbow	(Decca F 13035)	3	1970	0	1970	
7	My Little One	(Decca F 13135)	15	1971	0	1971	
8	Cousin Norman	(Decca F 13214)	6	1971	0	1971	
9	Back On The Road	(Decca F 13251)	35	1971	0	1971	
10	Back On The Road (Re-Entry)	(Decca F 13251)	50	1972	0	1972	
11	Radancer	(Decca F 13297)	6	1972	0	1972	
12	Falling Apart At The Seams	(Target TGT 105)	9	1976	0	1976	

Marmion Male Instrumental/Production Duo from Holland/Spain

ISSUE	TITLE	UK LBL	UK POS	UK YEAR	US POS	US YEAR	US LBL
1	Schoneberg	(HOOJ CHOONS HOOJCD 43)	53	1996	0	1996	

Marradona Mixed Vocal/Instrumental Group from the UK

ISSUE	TITLE	UK LBL	UK POS	UK YEAR	US POS	US YEAR	US LBL
1	Out Of My Head	(Peach PWCD 282)	38	1994	0	1994	
2	Out Of My Head (Re-Mix)	(SOOPA SPCD 1)	39	1997	0	1997	

Marsha Hunt Female Vocalist from the USA

ISSUE	TITLE	UK LBL	UK POS	UK YEAR	US POS	US YEAR	US LBL
1	Walk On Gilded Splinters	(Track 604 030)	46	1969	0	1969	
2	Keep The Customer Satisfied	(Track 604 037)	41	1970	0	1970	

Marshall Crenshaw Male Singer/Songwriter from Detroit

ISSUE	TITLE	UK LBL	UK POS	UK YEAR	US POS	US YEAR	US LBL
1	Someday, Someway		0	1982	36	1982	(Warner Bros. 29974)

Marshall Hain Mixed Vocal/Instrumental Duo from the UK

ISSUE	TITLE	UK LBL	UK POS	UK YEAR	US POS	US YEAR	US LBL
1	Dancing In The City	(Harvest HAR 5157)	3	1978	0	1978	
2	Coming Home	(Harvest HAR 5168)	39	1978	0	1978	

Marshall Tucker Band Southern Rock Band from South Carolina With Lead Singer Doug Gray

ISSUE	TITLE	UK LBL	UK POS	UK YEAR	US POS	US YEAR	US LBL
1	Fire On The Mountain		0	1975	38	1975	(Capricorn 0244)
4	Heard It In A Love Song		0	1977	14	1977	(Capricorn 0270)
	OBITUARY : TOMMY D: 28 APR 1980 CAR ACCIDENT. TOY D: 25 FEB 1993 RESPIRATORY FAILURE.						

Martha & The Muffins Mixed Vocal/Instrumental Group From Canada

ISSUE	TITLE	UK LBL	UK POS	UK YEAR	US POS	US YEAR	US LBL
1	Echo Beach	(DINDISC DIN 9)	10	1980	0	1980	
2	Black Stations White Stations	(RCA 426)	46	1984	0	1984	
	HIT 2 IS CREDITED TO M+M						

Martha Reeves & The Vandellas Female Vocal Group from the USA, Martha B: 18 Jul 1941 Alabama, Left The Group In 1972.

ISSUE	TITLE	UK LBL	UK POS	UK YEAR	US POS	US YEAR	US LBL
1	Hitch Hike		0	1963	30	1963	(TAMLA 54075)
2	Pride And Joy		0	1963	10	1963	(TAMLA 54079)
3	Come And Get These Memories		0	1963	29	1963	(Gordy 7014)
* 4	Heatwave		0	1963	4	1963	(Gordy 7022)
5	Quicksand		0	1963	8	1963	(Gordy 7025)
6	Live Wire		0	1964	42	1964	(Gordy 7027)
7	In My Lonely Room		0	1964	44	1964	(Gordy 7031)
* 8	Dancing In The Street	(StateSIDE SS 345)	28	1964	2	1964	(Gordy 7033)
9	Wild One		0	1964	34	1964	(Gordy 7036)
10	Nowhere To Run	(Tamla Motown TMG 502)	26	1965	8	1965	(Gordy 7039)
11	You've Been In Love Too Long / Love (Makes Me Do Foolish Things)		0	1965	36	1965	(Gordy 7045)
12	My Baby Loves Me		0	1966	22	1966	(Gordy 7048)
13	I'm Ready For Love	(Tamla Motown TMG 582)	29	1966	9	1966	(Gordy 7056)
14	Jimmy Mack	(Tamla Motown TMG 599)	21	1967	10	1967	(Gordy 7058)
15	Love Bug Leave My Heart Alone		0	1967	25	1967	(Gordy 7062)
16	Honey Chile	(Tamla Motown TMG 636)	30	1968	11	1967	(Gordy 7067)
17	Dancing In The Street (Re-Issue)	(Tamla Motown TMG 684)	4	1969	0	1969	
18	Nowhere To Run (Re-Issue)	(Tamla Motown TMG 694)	42	1969	0	1969	

ISSUE	TITLE	UK LBL	UK POS	UK YEAR	US POS	US YEAR	US LBL
19	Jimmy Mack (Re-Entry)	(Tamla Motown TMG 699)	21	1970	0	1970	
20	Forget Me Not	(Tamla Motown TMG 762)	11	1971	0	1971	
+ 21	Bless You	(Tamla Motown TMG 794)	33	1972	29	1971	(Gordy 7110)
22	Nowhere To Run (2nd Re-Issue)	(A&M AM 444)	52	1988	0	1988	

OTHER MEMBERS ARE ANNETTE BEARD & ROSALIND ASHFORD

Martha Tilton Female Vocalist from the USA

	TITLE		UK POS	UK YEAR	US POS	US YEAR	US LBL
5	How Are Things In Glocca Mora?		0	1947	8	1947	(Capitol 345)
6	That's My Desire		0	1947	10	1947	(Capitol 395)
7	I Wonder, I Wonder, I Wonder		0	1947	9	1947	(Capitol 395)
8	That's Gratitude		0	1948	22	1948	(Capitol 15042)
9	I'll Always Love You		0	1950	23	1950	(CAORAL 60258)

Martha Wash Female Vocalist from the USA

	TITLE		UK POS	UK YEAR	US POS	US YEAR	
1	Carry On	(RCA 74321125457)	74	1992	0	1992	
2	Give It To You	(RCA 74321136562)	37	1993	0	1993	
3	Runaround / Carry On (Re-Mix)	(RCA 74321153702)	49	1993	0	1993	
4	Take A Toke	(Columbia 6612112)	26	1995	0	1995	
5	Keep On Jumpin'	(Manifesto FESCD 11)	8	1996	0	1996	

HIT 4 IS CREDITED TO C & C MUSIC FACTORY FEATURING MARTHA WASH • HIT 5 IS CREDITED TO TODD TERRY FEATURING MARTHA WASH AND JOCELYN BROWN

Marti Webb Female Vocalist from the UK

	TITLE		UK POS	UK YEAR	US POS	US YEAR	
1	Take That Look Of Your Face	(Polydor POSP 100)	3	1980	0	1980	
2	Tell Me On A Sunday	(Polydor POSP 111)	67	1980	0	1980	
3	Your Ears Should Be Burning Now	(Polydor POSP 166)	61	1980	0	1980	
4	Ben	(Starblend STAR 6)	5	1985	0	1985	
5	Always There	(BBC RESL 190)	13	1986	0	1986	
6	I Can't Let Go	(Rainbow RBR 12)	65	1987	0	1987	

Martika Female Vocalist, Real Name Martika Marrero From Los Angeles

	TITLE		UK POS	UK YEAR	US POS	US YEAR	
1	More Than You Know	(Columbia 655526 7)	15	1990	18	1989	(Columbia08103)
* 2	Toy Soldiers	(Columbia 655049 7)	5	1989	1	1989	(Columbia 68747)
3	I Feel The Earth Move	(Columbia 655294 7)	7	1989	25	1989	(Columbia 68996)
4	Water	(Columbia 6557317)	59	1990	0	1990	
5	Love...Thy Will Be Done	(Columbia6573137)	9	1991	10	1991	(Columbia 73853)
6	Martika's Kitchen	(Columbia 6575687)	17	1991	0	1991	
7	Coloured Kisses	(Columbia 6577097)	41	1992	0	1992	

Martin Briley Male Songwriter/Session Musician

	TITLE		UK POS	UK YEAR	US POS	US YEAR	
1	The Salt In My Tears		0	1983	36	1983	(Mercury 812165)

B: IN THE UK AND MOVED TO NEW YORK CITY IN 1977

Martin Denny Orchestra Male Composer/Pianist, B: 10 Apr 1911 And Comes From New York City

	TITLE		UK POS	UK YEAR	US POS	US YEAR	
* 1	Quite Village		0	1959	5	1959	(Liberty 55162)
2	The Enchanted Sea		0	1959	28	1959	(Liberty 55212)

Martin Page Male Singer/Songwriter, B: 23 Sep 1959 From Southampton, England

	TITLE		UK POS	UK YEAR	US POS	US YEAR	
1	In The House Of Stone And Light		0	1995	14	1995	(Mercury 858940)

Martin Stephenson & The Daintees Male Vocal/Instrumental Group from the UK

	TITLE		UK POS	UK YEAR	US POS	US YEAR	
1	Boat To Bolivia	(Kitchenware SL 27)	70	1986	0	1986	
2	Trouble Town	(Kitchenware SK 13)	58	1987	0	1987	
3	Big Sky New Light	(Kitchenware SK 57)	71	1992	0	1992	

HIT 2 IS CREDITED TO THE DAINTEES

Martine Girault Female Vocalist from the USA

	TITLE		UK POS	UK YEAR	US POS	US YEAR	
1	Revival	(FFRR FX 195)	53	1992	0	1992	
2	Revival (Re-Issue)	(FFRR FCD 205)	37	1993	0	1993	
3	Been Thinking About You	(RCA	63	1995	0	1995	
4	Revival (2nd Re-Issue)	(RCA	61	1997	0	1997	

Marty Balin B: 30 Jan 1943 Cincinnati, Co-Founder Of Jefferson Airplane/Starship

	TITLE		UK POS	UK YEAR	US POS	US YEAR	
1	Hearts		0	1981	8	1981	(EMI America 8084)
2	Atlanta Lady (Something About Your Love)		0	1981	27	1981	(EMI America 8093)

Marty Robbins Male Vocalist, Born Martin David Robinson B: 26 Sep 1925 Glendale, Arizona.

	TITLE		UK POS	UK YEAR	US POS	US YEAR	
8	Singing The Blues		0	1956	17	1956	(Columbia 21545)
* 12	A White Sport Coat (And A Pink Carnation)		0	1957	2	1957	(Columbia 40864)
15	The Story Of My Life		0	1957	15	1957	(Columbia 41013)
16	Just Married		0	1958	26	1958	(Columbia 41143)
	More)		0	1958	27	1958	(Columbia 41208)
20	The Hanging Tree		0	1959	38	1959	(Columbia 41325)
* 21	El Paso	(Fontana H 233)	19	1960	1	1959	(Columbia 41511)

ISSUE	TITLE	UK LBL	UK POS	UK YEAR	US POS	US YEAR	US LBL
22	Big Iron	(Fontana H 229)	48	1960	26	1960	(Columbia 41589)
23	El Paso (Re-Entry)	(Fontana H 233)	44	1960	0	1960	
24	Is There Any Chance		0	1960	31	1960	(Columbia 41686)
25	Ballad Of The Alamo		0	1960	34	1960	(Columbia 41809)
27	Don't Worry		0	1961	3	1961	(Columbia 41922)
32	Devil Woman	(CBS AAG 114)	5	1962	16	1962	(Columbia 42486)
33	Ruby Ann	(CBS AAG 128)	24	1962	18	1962	(Columbia 42614)

UNLISTED HITS ARE C/W • OBITUARY : D: 8 DEC 1982 HEART ATTACK.

Marty Wilde Male Vocalist, Father Of Kim Wilde from the UK

ISSUE	TITLE	UK LBL	UK POS	UK YEAR	US POS	US YEAR	US LBL
1	Endless Sleep	(Philips PB 835)	4	1958	0	1958	
2	Donna	(Philips PB 902)	3	1959	0	1959	
3	A Teenager In Love	(Philips PB 926)	2	1959	0	1959	
4	Donna (Re-Entry)	(Philips PB 902)	25	1959	0	1959	
5	Sea Of Love	(Philips PB 959)	3	1959	0	1959	
6	Bad Boy	(Philips PB 972)	7	1959	0	1959	
7	Johnny Rocco	(Philips PB 1002)	30	1960	0	1960	
8	The Fight	(Philips PB 1022)	47	1960	0	1960	
9	Little Girl	(Philips PB 1078)	16	1960	0	1960	
10	Rubber Ball	(Philips PB 1101)	9	1961	0	1961	
11	Hide And Seek	(Philips PB 1161)	47	1961	0	1961	
12	Tomorrow's Clown	(Philips PB 1191)	33	1961	0	1961	
13	Jezebel	(Philips PB 1240)	19	1962	0	1962	
14	Ever Since You Said Goodbye	(Philips 326546 BF)	31	1962	0	1962	

Martyn Ford Orchestra from the UK

ISSUE	TITLE	UK LBL	UK POS	UK YEAR	US POS	US YEAR	US LBL
1	Let Your Body Go Downtown	(Mountain Top 26)	38	1977	0	1977	

Martyn Joseph Male Vocalist from the UK

ISSUE	TITLE	UK LBL	UK POS	UK YEAR	US POS	US YEAR	US LBL
1	Dolphins Make Me Cry	(Epic 6581347)	34	1992	0	1992	
2	Working Mother	(Epic 6582937)	65	1992	0	1992	
3	Please Sir	(Epic 6588552)	45	1993	0	1993	
4	Talk About It In The Morning	(Epic 6613342)	45	1995	0	1995	

Marv Johnson Male Vocalist, B: 15 Oct 1938 Detroit

	ISSUE	TITLE	UK LBL	UK POS	UK YEAR	US POS	US YEAR	US LBL
	1	Come To Me		0	1959	30	1959	(United Artists 160)
	2	You Got What It Takes	(London HLT 9013)	5	1960	10	1960	(United Artists 185)
	3	I Love The Way You Love	(London HLT 9109)	35	1960	9	1960	(United Artists208)
	4	Ain't Gonna Be That Way	(London HLT 9165)	50	1960	0	1960	
*	5	(You've Got To) Move Two Mountains		0	1960	20	1960	(United Artists 241)
	6	I'll Pick A Rose For My Rose	(Tamla Motown TMG 680)	10	1969	0	1969	
	7	I Miss You Baby	(Tamla Motown TMG 713)	25	1969	0	1969	

Marvelettes Female Vocalist from the USA, Names: Gladys Horton, Georgeanna Gordon, Wanda Young, Katherine Anderson & Juanita Cowart

	ISSUE	TITLE	UK LBL	UK POS	UK YEAR	US POS	US YEAR	US LBL
*	1	Please Mr. Postman		0	1961	1	1961	(Tamla 54046)
	2	Twistin' Postman		0	1962	34	1962	(Tamla 54054)
	3	Playboy		0	1962	7	1962	(Tamla 54060)
	4	Beechwood 4-5789 / Someday Someway		0	1962	17	1962	(Tamla 54065)
	5	Strange I Know		0	1962	49	1962	(Tamla 54072)
	6	Locking Up My Heart / Forever		0	1963	44	1963	(Tamla 54077)
	7	As Long As I Know He's Mine		0	1963	47	1963	(Tamla 54088)
	8	He's A Good Guy		0	1964	55	1964	(Tamla 54091)
	9	You're My Remedy		0	1964	48	1964	(Tamla 54097)
	10	Too Many Fish In The Sea		0	1964	25	1964	(Tamla 54105)
	11	I'll Keep Holding On		0	1965	34	1965	(Tamla 54116)
+	12	Danger Heartbreak Dead Ahead		0	1965	11	1965	(Tamla 54120)
	13	Don't Mess With Bill		0	1966	7	1966	(Tamla 54126)
	14	You're The One		0	1966	48	1966	(Tamla 54131)
	15	The Hunter Gets Captured By The Game		0	1967	13	1967	(Tamla 54143)
	16	When Your Young And In Love	(Tamla Motown TMG 609)	13	1967	23	1967	(Tamla 54150)
	17	My Baby Must Be A Magician		0	1967	17	1967	(Tamla 54158)
	18	Here I Am Baby		0	1968	44	1968	(Tamla 54166)
+	19	Destination Anywhere		0	1968	28	1968	(Tamla 54171)

Marvelows R&B Group From Chicago Heights, Illinois

ISSUE	TITLE	UK LBL	UK POS	UK YEAR	US POS	US YEAR	US LBL
1	I Do		0	1965	37	1965	(ABC-Paramount 10629)

FIRST KNOWN AS THE MYSTICS WITH LEAD SINGER MELVIN MASON

Marvin Gaye Real Name Marvin Pentz Gay Jr. B: 2 Apr 1939 In Washington

ISSUE	TITLE	UK LBL	UK POS	UK YEAR	US POS	US YEAR	US LBL
1	Stubborn Kind Of Fellow		0	1962	46	1962	(Tamla 54068)
2	Hitch Hike		0	1963	30	1963	(Tamla 54075)

ISSUE	TITLE	UK LBL	UK POS	UK YEAR	US POS	US YEAR	US LBL
3	Pride And Joy		0	1963	10	1963	(Tamla 54079)
4	Can I Get A Witness		0	1963	22	1963	(Tamla 54087)
5	You're A Wonderful One		0	1964	15	1964	(Tamla 54093)
6	Once Upon A Time	(Stateside SS 316)	50	1964	17	1964	(Motown 1057)
7	What's The Matter With You Baby		0	1964	17	1964	(Motown 1057)
8	Try It Baby		0	1964	15	1964	(Tamla 54095)
9	Once Upon A Time	(Stateside SS 316)	50	1964	0	1964	
10	Baby Don't Do It		0	1964	27	1964	(Tamla 54101)
11	How Sweet It Is (To Be Loved By You)	(StateSIDE SS 360)	49	1964	6	1964	(Tamla 54107)
12	I'll Be Doggone		0	1965	8	1965	(Tamla 54112)
13	Pretty Little Baby		0	1965	25	1965	(Tamla 54117)
14	Ain't That Peculiar		0	1965	8	1965	(Tamla 54122)
15	One More Heartache		0	1966	29	1966	(Tamla 54129)
16	Take This Heart Of Mine		0	1966	44	1966	(Tamla 54132)
17	Little Darlin' (I Need You)	(Tamla Motown TMG 574)	50	1966	47	1966	(Tamla 54138)
18	It Takes Two	(Tamla Motown TMG 590)	16	1967	14	1967	(Tamla 54141)
19	Ain't No Mountain High Enough		0	1967	19	1967	(Tamla 54149)
20	Your Unchanging Love		0	1967	33	1967	(Tamla 54153)
21	Your Precious Love		0	1967	5	1967	(Tamla 54156)
22	If I Could Build My Whole World Around You	(Tamla Motown TMG 635)	41	1968	10	1968	(Tamla 54161)
23	You		0	1968	34	1968	(Tamla 54160)
* 24	Ain't Nothing Like The Real Thing	(Tamla Motown TMG 655)	34	1968	8	1968	(Tamla 54163)
25	You're All I Need To Get By	(Tamla Motown TMG 668)	19	1968	7	1968	(Tamla 54169)
26	Chained		0	1968	32	1968	(Tamla 54170)
27	Keep On Loving Me Honey		0	1968	24	1968	(Tamla 54173)
28	You Ain't Livin' Till You're Lovin'	(Tamla Motown TMG 681)	21	1969	0	1969	
* 29	I Heard It Through The Grapevine	(Tamla Motown TMG 686)	1	1969	1	1968	(Tamla 54176)
30	Too Busy Thinking About My Baby	(Tamla Motown TMG 705)	5	1969	4	1969	(Tamla 54181)
31	Good Lovin' Ain't Easy To Come By	(Tamla Motown TMG 697)	26	1969	30	1969	(Tamla 54179)
32	Good Lovin' Ain't Easy To Come By (Re-Entry)	(Tamla Motown TMG 697)	48	1969	0	1969	
33	That's The Way Love Is		0	1969	7	1969	(Tamla 54184)
34	What You Gave Me		0	1969	49	1969	(Tamla 54187)
35	Onion Song	(Tamla Motown TMG 715)	9	1969	50	1970	(Tamla 54192)
36	How Can I Forget		0	1970	41	1970	(Tamla 54190)
37	Abraham, Martin And John	(Tamla Motown TMG 734)	9	1970	0	1970	
38	The End Of Our Road		0	1970	40	1970	(Tamla 54195)
* 39	What's Goin' On		0	1971	2	1971	(Tamla 54201)
* 40	Mercy Mercy Me (The Ecology)		0	1971	4	1971	(Tamla 54207)
41	Inner City Blues (Makes Me Wanna Holler)		0	1971	9	1971	(Tamla 54209)
42	Save The Children	(Tamla Motown TMG 796)	41	1971	0	1971	
43	Trouble Man		0	1973	7	1973	(Motown 54228)
* 44	Let's Get It On	(Tamla Motown TMG 868)	31	1973	1	1973	(Motown 54234)
45	You're A Special Part Of Me		0	1973	12	1973	(Motown 1280)
46	Come Get To This		0	1973	21	1973	(Tamla 54241)
47	You Are Everything	(Tamla Motown TMG 890)	5	1974	0	1964	
48	My Mistake (Was To Love You)		0	1974	19	1974	(Motown 1269)
49	Stop, Look, Listen (To Your Heart)	(Tamla Motown TMG 906)	25	1974	0	1974	
50	Distant Lover		0	1974	28	1974	(Tamla 54253)
51	I Want You		0	1976	15	1976	(Tamla 54234)
52	Got To Give It Up (Part 1)	(Tamla Motown TMG 1069)	7	1977	1	1977	(Tamla 54280)
53	Pops We Love You	(Tamla Motown TMG 1136)	66	1979	0	1979	
* 54	Sexual Healing	(CBS A 2855)	4	1982	3	1982	(Columbia 03302)
55	My Love Is Waiting	(CBS A 3048)	34	1983	0	1983	
56	Sanctified Lady	(CBS A 4894)	51	1985	0	1985	
57	I Heard It Through The Grapevine (Re-Issue)	(Tamla Motown ZB 40701)	8	1986	0	1986	
58	Lucky Lucky Me	(Motown TMGCD 1426)	67	1994	0	1994	

OBITUARY: D: 4 JAN 1984 SHOT BY HIS FATHER. • MARVIN'S FATHER RECEIVED 5-YEAR PROBATION FOR SHOOTING HIM

Marvin Hamlisch Male Pianist, B: 2 Jun 1944 New York City

* 1	The Entertainer	(MCA 121)	25	1974	1	1974	(MCA 40174)

THE HIT WAS WRITTEN BY SCOTT JOPLIN IN 1902

Marvin Rainwater Male Vocalist, Real Name Marvin Karlton Percy B: 2 Jul 1925 Wichita, Kansas.

* 1	Gonna Find Me A Bluebird		0	1957	18	1957	(MGM 12412)
2	So You Think You've Got Troubles		0	1957	18	1957	(MGM 12412)
3	Whole Lotta Woman	(MGM 974)	1	1958	0	1958	

ISSUE	TITLE	UK LBL	UK POS	UK YEAR	US POS	US YEAR	US LBL
4	I Dig You Baby	(MGM 980)	19	1958	0	1958	

Marvin The Paranoid Android Robot from the UK

1	Marvin	(Polydor POSP 261)	53	1981	0	1981	

Marxman Rap/Instrumental Group from the UK/Ireland

1	All About Eve	(Talkin' LoudTLKCD 35)	28	1993	0	1993	
2	Ship Ahoy	(Talkin' Loud TLKCD 39)	64	1993	0	1993	

Vocals On Hit 2 Are By Sinead O'Connor

Mary Duff See Daniel O'Donnell

Mary Hopkin Female Vocalist, B: 3 May 1950, Pontardawe, Wales

* 1	Those Were The Days	(Apple 2)	1	1968	2	1968	(Apple 1801)
2	Goodbye	(Apple 10)	2	1969	13	1969	(Apple 1806)
3	Temma Harbour	(Apple 22)	6	1970	39	1970	(Apple 1816)
4	Knock Knock Who's There	(Apple 26)	2	1970	0	1970	
5	Think About Your Children	(Apple 30)	19	1970	0	1970	
6	Think About Your Children (Re-Entry)	(Apple 30)	46	1971	0	1971	
7	Let Me Name Be Sorrow	(Apple 34)	46	1971	0	1971	
8	If You Love Me	(Good Earth GD 2)	32	1976	0	1976	

SEE ALSO THE APPLE (EP), VARIOUS ARTISTS (EP, LP, 78S)

Mary J. Blige Female R&B Vocalist From Atlanta, USA

1	You Remind Me	(Uptown MCSTD1770)	48	1993	29	1992	(Uptown/MCA 54327)
2	Real Love	(Uptown MCS 1721)	68	1992	7	1992	(Uptown/MCA 54455)
3	Sweet Thing		0	1993	28	1993	(Uptown/MCA 54586)
4	Reminisce	(Uptown MCSTD 1731)	31	1993	0	1993	
5	Real Love (Re-Mix)	(Uptown MCSTD 1922)	26	1993	0	1993	
6	You Don't Have To Worry	(Uptown MCSTD1948)	36	1993	0	1993	
7	My Love	(Uptown MCSTD 1972)	29	1994	0	1994	
8	Be Happy	(Uptown MCSTD 2033)	30	1994	29	1994	(Uptown/MCA 54927)
9	I'm Goin' Down	(Uptown MCSTD 2053)	12	1995	22	1995	(Uptown/MCA 55008)
10	I'll Be There For You-You're All I Need To Get By	(DEF JAM DEFCD 11)	10	1995	3	1995	(DEF JAM/RAL 1878)
11	Mary Jane (All Night Long)	(MCA MCSTD 2088)	17	1995	0	1995	
12	(You Make Me Feel Like A) Natural Waman	(MCA MCSTD 2108)	23	1995	0	1995	
13	Not Gon' Cry / Chaka Khan	(Arista 74321358252)	39	1996	2	1996	
14	Can't Knock The Hustle	(Northwestside 74321447192)	30	1997	0	1997	
15	Love Is All We Need	(MCA MCSTD 48053)	15	1997	0	1997	
16	Everything	(MCA MCSTD 48059)	6	1997	0	1997	

HIT 10 IS CREDITED TO MARY J. BLIGE AND METHOD MAN • HIT 14 IS CREDITED TO JAY-Z FEATURING MARY J. BLIGE

Mary Jane Girls Female Vocal Group from the USA Names: Candice Ghant, Kim Wuletick, Joanne McDuffle & Yvette Marina

1	Candy Man	(Motown TMG 1301)	60	1983	0	1983	
2	All Night Long	(Gordy TMG 1309)	13	1983	0	1983	
3	Boys	(Gordy TMG 1315)	74	1983	0	1983	
4	In My House		0	1985	7	1985	(Gordy 1741)
5	All Night Long (Re-Mix)	(Motown TMGCD 1436)	51	1995	0	1995	

Mary Kiani Female Vocalist from the UK

1	When I Call Your Name	(Mercury MERCD 440)	18	1995	0	1995	
2	I Give It All To You / I Imagine	(Mercury MERCD 449)	35	1995	0	1995	
3	Let The Music Play	(Mercury MERCD 456)	19	1996	0	1996	
4	100%	(Mercury MERCD 469)	23	1997	0	1997	
5	With Or Without You	(Mercury MERCD 487)	46	1997	0	1997	

Mary MacGregor Female Vocalist, B: 6 May 1948 St Paul, Minnesota

* 1	Torn Between Two Lovers	(Ariola America AA 111)	4	1977	1	1976	(Ariola America 7638)
2	This Girl (Has Turned Into A Woman)		0	1977	46	1977	(Ariola America 7662)
3	For A While		0	1977	90	1977	(Ariola America 7667)
4	Good Friend		0	1979	39	1979	(RSO 938)

Mary Martin Female Actress/Vocalist from the USA

5	Almost Like Being In Love		0	1947	21	1947	(Decca 24156)
6	Go To Sleep, Go To Sleep, Go To Sleep		0	1952	8	1950	(Columbia 38744)

Mary Mason Female Vocalist from the UK

1	Angel Of The Morning - Any Way That You Want Me	(Epic EPC 5552)	27	1977	0	1977	

ISSUE	TITLE	UK LBL	UK POS	UK YEAR	US POS	US YEAR	US LBL
Mary May Female Vocalist from the UK							
1	Anyone Who Had A Heart	(Fontana TF 440)	49	1964	0	1964	
Mary Wells Female Vocalist, Real Name Mary Esther Wells B: 13 May 1943 Detroit							
1	I Don't Want To Take A Chance		0	1961	33	1961	(Motown 1011)
2	The One Who Really Loves You		0	1962	8	1962	(Motown 1024)
3	You Beat Me To The Punch		0	1962	9	1962	(Motown 1032)
* 4	Two Lovers		0	1963	7	1963	(Motown 1035)
5	Laughing Boy		0	1963	15	1963	(Motown 1039)
6	Your Old Stand By		0	1963	40	1963	(Motown 1042)
7	You Lost The Sweetest Boy		0	1963	22	1963	(Motown 1048)
8	What's Easy For Two Is So Hard For One		0	1963	22	1963	(Motown 1048)
* 9	My Guy	(StateSIDE SS 288)	5	1964	1	1964	(Motown 1056)
10	What's The Matter With You Baby		0	1964	17	1964	(Motown 1057)
11	Once Upon A Time	(StateSIDE SS 316)	50	1964	19	1964	(Motown 1057)
12	Use Your Head		0	1965	34	1965	(20th Century 555)
13	My Guy (Re-Issue)	(Tamla Motown TMG 820)	14	1972	0	1972	
	HITS 10-11 ARE CREDITED TO MARY WELLS AND MARVIN GAYE • OBITUARY: D: AUG 1990 THROAT CANCER.						
Mary-Chapin Carpenter Female Vocalist B: 21 Feb 1958 Princeton, New Jersey							
11	Passionate Kisses		0	1992	57	1992	(Columbia 74795)
14	He Thinks He'll Keep Her	(Columbia 6598632)	71	1993	0	1993	
15	One Cool Remove	(Columbia 6611342)	40	1995	0	1995	
16	Shut Up And Kiss Me	(Columbia 6613672)	35	1995	0	1995	
	OTHER HITS ARE C/W						
Mash Mixed Vocal Group from the USA/UK							
1	Theme From *Mash* (Suicide Is Painless)	(CBS 8536)	1	1980	0	1980	
Mash! Male Vocal/Instrumental Group from the USA							
1	U Don't Have To Say U Love Me	(REACT CDREACT 37)	37	1994	0	1994	
2	Let's Spend The Night Together	(PLAYA CDXPLAYA 2)	66	1995	0	1995	
Mashmakhan Lead Singer With The Quartet Is Puerre Senecal							
* 1	As The Years Go By		0	1970	31	1970	(Epic 10634)
	JERRY MERCER LEFT THE GROUP AND JOINED APRIL WINE						
Mason Williams Male Guitarist, B: 24 Aug 61938, Abilene, Texas							
* 1	Classical Gas	(Warner Bros. WB 7190)	9	1968	2	1968	(Warner Bros. 7190)
Masquerade Mixed Vocal Group from the UK							
1	One Nation	(Streetwave KHAN 59)	54	1986	0	1986	
2	(Solution To) The Problem	(Streetwave KHAN 67)	65	1986	0	1986	
3	(Solution To) The Problem (Re-Entry)	(Streetwave KHAN 67)	64	1986	0	1986	
Mass Order Male Vocal/Instrumental Duo from the USA							
1	Lift Every Voice (Take Me Away)	(Columbia 6577487)	35	1992	0	1992	
2	Let's Get Happy	(Columbia 6580737)	45	1992	0	1992	
Mass Production Male Vocal/Instrumental Group from the USA							
1	Welcome To Our World (Of Merry Music)	(Atlantic K 10898)	44	1977	0	1977	
2	Shante	(Atlantic K 11475)	59	1980	0	1980	
Massiel Female Vocalist from Spain							
1	La La La	(Philips BF 1667)	35	1968	0	1968	
Massive Attack Mixed Vocal/Instrumental Group from the UK							
1	Unfinished Sympathy	((Wild Bunch WBRS 2)	13	1991	0	1991	
2	Safe From Harm	(Wild Bunch WBRS 3)	25	1991	0	1991	
3	Massive Attack (EP)	((Wild Bunch WBRS 4)	27	1992	0	1992	
4	Sly	((Wild Bunch WBRDX 5)	24	1994	0	1994	
5	Protection	(W(Wild Bunch WBRX 6)	14	1995	0	1995	
6	Karmacoma (EP)	((Wild Bunch WBRX 7)	28	1995	0	1995	
7	Risingson	((Wild Bunch WBRX 8)	11	1997	0	1997	
Massivo (Featuring) Tracy Mixed Vocal/Instrumental Group from the UK							
1	Loving You	(Debut Debt 3097)	25	1990	0	1990	
Masta Ace Incorporated Male Rapper from Brownsville, USA							
1	Born To Roll		0	1994	23	1994	(Delicious V. 98315)
Master Singers Male Vocal Group from the UK							
1	Highway Code	(Parlophone R 5428)	25	1966	0	1966	
2	Weather Forcast	(Parlophone R 5523)	50	1966	0	1966	

ISSUE	TITLE	UK LBL	UK POS	UK YEAR	US POS	US YEAR	US LBL
Masters At Work	See India						
Match Male Vocal/Instrumental Group from the UK							
1	Boogie Man	(Flamingo FM 2)	48	1979	0	1979	
Matchbox Male Vocal/Instrumental Group from the UK							
1	Rockabilly Rebel	(Magnet MAG 155)	18	1979	0	1979	
2	Buzz Buzz A Diddle It	(Magnet MAG 157)	22	1980	0	1980	
3	Midnite Dynamos	(Magnet MAG 169)	14	1980	0	1980	
4	When You Ask About Love	(Magnet MAG 191)	4	1980	0	1980	
5	Over The Rainbow - You Belong To Me (Medley)	(Magnet MAG 192)	19	1980	0	1980	
6	Babe's In The Wood	(Magnet MAG 193)	46	1981	0	1981	
7	Love's Made A Fool Of You	(Magnet MAG 194)	63	1981	0	1981	
8	One More Saturday Night	(Magnet MAG 223)	63	1982	0	1982	
Matchroom Mob	See Chas & Dave						
Matt Bianco Mixed Vocal/Instrumental Group from The UK/Poland							
1	Get Out Of Your Lazy Bed	(WEA BIANCO 1)	15	1984	0	1984	
2	Sneaking Out The Back Door / Matt's Mood	(WEA YZ 3)	44	1984	0	1984	
3	Half A Minute	(WEA YZ 26)	23	1984	0	1984	
4	More Than I Can Bear	(WEA YZ 34)	50	1985	0	1985	
5	Yeh Yeh	(WEA YZ 46)	13	1985	0	1985	
6	Just Can't Stand It	(WEA YZ 62)	66	1986	0	1986	
7	Dancing In The Street	(WEA YZ 72)	64	1986	0	1986	
8	Don't Blame It On That Girl / Wap-Bam Boogie	(WEA YZ 188)	11	1988	0	1988	
9	Good Times	(WEA YZ 302)	55	1988	0	1988	
10	Nervous - Wap Bam Boogie (Re-Mix)	(WEA YZ 328)	59	1989	0	1989	
	AFTER THE FIRST FIVE HITS THE GROUP WERE ALL FROM THE UK						
Matt Fretton Male Vocalist from the UK							
1	It's So High	(Chrysalis MATT 1)	50	1983	0	1983	
Matt Goss Male Vocalist from the UK							
1	The Key	(Polydor 5811532)	40	1995	0	1995	
2	If You Were Here Tonight	(ATLAS 5762932)	23	1996	0	1996	
Matt Monro Male Vocalist, Real Name Terrence Parsons B: 1 Dec 1932 London, England							
1	Portrait Of My Love	(Parlophone R 4714)	3	1960	0	1960	
2	My Kind Of Girl	(Parlophone R 4755)	5	1961	18	1961	(Warwick 636)
3	Why Not Now / Can This Be Love	(Parlophone R 4775)	24	1961	0	1961	
4	Gonna Build A Mountain	(Parlophone R 4819)	44	1961	0	1961	
5	Softly As I Leave You	(Parlophone R 4868)	10	1962	0	1962	
6	When Love Comes Along	(Parlophone R 4911)	46	1962	0	1962	
7	My Love And Devotion	(Parlophone R 4954)	29	1962	0	1962	
8	From Russia With Love	(Parlophone R 5068)	20	1963	0	1963	
9	Walk Away	(Parlophone R 5171)	4	1964	23	1964	(Liberty 55745)
10	For Mama	(Parlophone R 5215)	36	1964	0	1964	
11	Without You	(Parlophone R 5251)	37	1965	0	1965	
12	Yesterday	(Parlophone R 5348)	8	1965	0	1965	
13	And You Smiled	(EMI 2091)	28	1973	0	1973	
	OBITUARY: D: 7 FEB 1985 LIVER CANCER.						
Matthew Wilder Male Singer/Songwriter, B: 24 Jan 1953 Manhattan							
1	Break My Stride	(Epic A 3908)	4	1984	5	1983	(Private I 04113)
2	The Kid's American		0	1984	33	1984	(Private I 04363)
Matthews Southern Comfort Male Vocal/Instrumental Group from the UK							
1	Woodstock	(UNI UNS 526)	1	1970	23	1971	(Decca 32774)
	SEE ALSO IAN MATTHEWS						
Matumbi Male Vocal/Instrumental Group from the UK							
1	Point Of View	(Matumbi RIC 101)	35	1979	0	1979	
Maureen Female Vocalist from the UK							
1	Say A Little Prayer	(Rhythm King DOOD 3)	10	1988	0	1988	with Bomb The Bass
2	Thinking Of You	(Urban URB 55)	11	1990	0	1990	
3	Where Has All The Love Gone	(Urban URB 65)	51	1991	0	1991	
Maureen Evans Female Vocalist from the UK							
1	The Big Hurt	(Oriole CB 1533)	26	1960	0	1960	

ISSUE	TITLE	UK LBL	UK POS	UK YEAR	US POS	US YEAR	US LBL
2	Love Kisses And Heartaches	(Oriole CB 1540)	44	1960	0	1960	
3	Paper Roses	(Oriole CB 1550)	40	1960	0	1960	
4	Like I Do	(Oriole CB 1760)	3	1962	0	1962	
5	I Love How You Love Me	(Oriole CB 1906)	34	1964	0	1964	
6	I Love How You Love Me (Re-Entry)	(Oriole CB 1906)	50	1964	0	1964	

Maureen McGovern Female Actress/Vocalist, B: 27 Jul 1949 Youngstown, Ohio

ISSUE	TITLE	UK LBL	UK POS	UK YEAR	US POS	US YEAR	US LBL
* 1	The Morning After (From The Poseidon Adventure)		0	1973	1	1973	(20th Century 2010)
2	The Continental	(20th Century BTC 2222)	16	1976	0	1976	
3	Can You Read My Mind		0	1979	52	1979	(Warner/Curb 8750)
4	Different Worlds		0	1979	18	1979	(Warner Bros. 8835)

Maurice Williams & The Zodiacs Male Vocal Group from the USA, Originally Recorded As The Gladiolas Also Known As The Charms, Royal Charms & Excellos

ISSUE	TITLE	UK LBL	UK POS	UK YEAR	US POS	US YEAR	US LBL
* 1	Stay	(Top Rank Jar 526)	14	1961	1	1960	(Herald 552)

Max Bygraves Male Vocalist from the UK

ISSUE	TITLE	UK LBL	UK POS	UK YEAR	US POS	US YEAR	US LBL
1	Cowpuncher's Cantata	(HMV B 10250)	11	1952	0	1952	
2	Cowpuncher's Cantata (Re-Entry)	(HMV B 10250)	8	1953	0	1953	
3	Cowpuncher's Cantata (2nd Re-Entry)	(HMV B 10250)	6	1953	0	1953	
4	Cowpuncher's Cantata (3rd Re-Entry)	(HMV B 10250)	10	1953	0	1953	
5	Heart Of My Heart	(HMV B 10654)	7	1954	0	1954	
6	Gilly Gilly Ossenfeffer	(HMV B 10734)	7	1954	0	1954	
7	Gilly Gilly Ossenfeffer (Re-Entry)	(HMV B 10734)	20	1954	0	1954	
8	Mr. Sandman	(HMV B 10801)	16	1955	0	1955	
9	Meet Me On The Corner	(HMV POP 116)	2	1955	0	1955	
10	Ballad Of Davy Crockett	(HMV POP 153)	20	1956	0	1956	
11	Out Of Town	(HMV POP 164)	18	1956	0	1956	
12	Heart	(Decca F 10862)	14	1957	0	1957	
13	You Need Hands / Tulips From Amsterdam	(Decca F 11004)	3	1958	0	1958	
14	Little Train / Gotta Have Rain	(Decca F 11046)	28	1958	0	1958	
15	My Ukelele	(Decca F 11077)	19	1959	0	1959	
16	Jingle Bell Rock	(Decca F 11176)	7	1959	0	1959	
17	Fing's Ain't What They Used T'be	(Decca F 11214)	5	1960	0	1960	
18	Consider Yourself	(Decca F 11251)	50	1960	0	1960	
19	Bells Of Avignon	(Decca F 11350)	36	1961	0	1961	
20	You're My Everything	(PYE 7N 17705)	50	1969	0	1969	
21	Your My Everything (Re-Entry)	(PYE 7N 17705)	34	1969	0	1969	
22	Deck Of Cards	(PYE 7N 45276)	13	1973	0	1973	
23	White Christmas	(PARKFIELD PMS 5012)	71	1989	0	1989	

Max Frost & The Troopers Max Frost Is Played By Christopher Jones In The Film Wild In The Streets

ISSUE	TITLE	UK LBL	UK POS	UK YEAR	US POS	US YEAR	US LBL
1	Shape Of Things To Come		0	1968	22	1968	(TOWER 419)

Max Harris Orchestra from the UK

ISSUE	TITLE	UK LBL	UK POS	UK YEAR	US POS	US YEAR	US LBL
1	Gurney Slade	(Fontana H 282)	11	1960	0	1960	

Max Q Male Vocal/Instrumental Duo From Australia

ISSUE	TITLE	UK LBL	UK POS	UK YEAR	US POS	US YEAR	US LBL
1	Sometimes	(Mercury MXQ 2)	53	1990	0	1990	

Max Romeo Male Vocalist from Jamaica

ISSUE	TITLE	UK LBL	UK POS	UK YEAR	US POS	US YEAR	US LBL
1	Wet Dream	(Unity UN 503)	10	1969	0	1969	
2	Wet Dream (Re-Entry)	(Unity UN 503)	50	1969	0	1969	

Max Webster Male Vocal/Instrumental Group from Canada

ISSUE	TITLE	UK LBL	UK POS	UK YEAR	US POS	US YEAR	US LBL
1	Paradise Skies	(Capitol CL 16079)	43	1979	0	1979	

Maxi Priest Male Vocalist, B: Max Elliot From London, England

ISSUE	TITLE	UK LBL	UK POS	UK YEAR	US POS	US YEAR	US LBL
1	Strollin' On	(10 TEN 84)	32	1986	0	1986	
2	In The Springtime	(10 TEN 127)	54	1986	0	1986	
3	Crazy Love	(10 TEN 135)	67	1986	0	1986	
4	Let Me Know	(10 TEN 156)	49	1987	0	1987	
5	Some Guys Have All The Luck	(10 TFN 198)	12	1987	0	1987	
6	How Can We Ease The Pain	(10 TEN 207)	41	1988	0	1988	
7	Wild World	(10 TEN 221)	5	1988	25	1988	(Virgin 99269)
8	Goodbye To Love Again	(10 TEN 238)	57	1988	0	1988	
* 9	Close To You	(10 TEN 294)	7	1990	1	1990	(Charisma 98951)
10	Peace Throughout The World	(10 TEN 317)	41	1990	0	1990	
11	Human Work Of Art	(10 TEN 328)	75	1990	0	1990	
12	Human Work Of Art (Re-Entry)	(10 TEN 328)	71	1990	0	1990	
13	Housecall (You're Body Can't Lie To Me)	(Epic 6573477)	31	1991	37	1991	(Epic 73928)
14	Set The Night To Music		0	1991	6	1991	(Atlantic 87607)
15	The Maxi Priest (EP)	(TEN TEN 343)	62	1991	0	1991	
16	Groovin' In The Midnight	(TEN TEN 412)	50	1992	0	1992	

ISSUE	TITLE	UK LBL	UK POS	UK YEAR	US POS	US YEAR	US LBL
17	Just Wanna Know / Fe' Real	(TEN TEN 416)	33	1992	0	1992	
18	One More Chance	(TEN TENCD 420)	40	1993	0	1993	
19	Housecall (Re-Mix)	(Epic 6592842)	8	1993	0	1993	
20	Waiting In Vain	(GRP MCSC 1921)	65	1993	0	1993	
21	That Girl	(Virgin VUSDX 106)	15	1996	20	1996	(Virgin 38550)
22	Watching The World Go By	(Virgin VUSD 108)	36	1996	0	1996	

Maxima Mixed Vocal/Instrumental Group from the UK/Spain

1	Ibiza	(YO! YO! CDLILY ??)	55	1993	0	1993	

Maxine Brown Female Vocalist, B: Kingstree, South Carolina

1	All In My Mind		0	1961	19	1961	(NOMAR 103)
2	Funny		0	1961	25	1961	(NOMAR 106)
3	Oh No Not My Baby		0	1964	24	1964	(WAND 162)

Maxine Nightingale Female Vocalist, B: 2 Nov 1952 Wembley, Middlesex, England

* 1	Right Back Where We Started From	(United Artists UP 36015)	8	1975	2	1976	(United Artists 752)
2	Love Hit Me	(United Artists UP 36215)	11	1977	0	1977	
* 3	Lead Me On		0	1979	5	1979	(Windsong 11530)

Maxine Singleton Female Vocalist from the USA

1	You Can't Run From Love	(Creole CR 50)	57	1983	0	1983	

Maxine Sullivan Female Vocalist, Real Name Marietta Williams from the USA

1	Nice Work If You Can Get It		0	1937	10	1937	(Vocalion 3848)
2	Loch Lomond		0	1937	9	1937	(Vocalion 3654)
3	My Ideal		0	1943	11	1943	(Decca 18555)

Maxwell Male Vocalist from the USA

1	...Til The Cops Come Knockin' The Opus	(Columbia 6631792)	63	1996	0	1996	
2	Ascension No One's Gona Love You, So Don't Ever Wander	(Columbia 6636265)	39	1996	36	1996	(Columbia78372)
3	Sumthin' Sumthin' The Mantra	(Columbia 6638642)	27	1997	0	1997	
4	Ascension Don't Ever Wander	(Columbia 6645952)	28	1997	0	1997	

Maxx Mixed Vocal/Instrumental Group from the UK/Germany/Sweden

1	Get-A-Way	(Pulse8 CDLOSE 59)	4	1994	0	1994	
2	No More (I Can't Stand It)	(Pulse8 CDLOSE 66)	8	1994	0	1994	
3	You Can Get It	(Pulse8 CDLOSE 75)	21	1994	0	1994	
4	I Can Make You Feel Like	(Pulse8 CDLOSE 88)	56	1995	0	1995	

Maynard Ferguson Male Jazz Instrumentalist (Trumpet), B: 4 May 1928 Quebec, Canada

1	Gonna Fly Now (Theme From *Rocky*)		0	1977	28	1977	(Columbia 10468)

Maytals Male Vocal/Instrumental Group from Jamaica

1	Monkey Man	(Trojan TR 7711)	50	1970	0	1970	
2	Monkey Man (Re-Entry)	(Trojan TR 7711)	47	1970	0	1970	

Mayte Female Vocalist from the USA

1	If Eye Love U 2 Night	(NPG 0061635)	67	1995	0	1995	

Maze Male Vocal/Instrumental Group from the USA

1	Joy And Pain	(Capitol CL 363)	57	1989	0	1989	
2	I Wanna Be With You	(Capitol CL 421)	55	1986	0	1986	
3	Too Many Games	(Capitol CL 531)	36	1985	0	1985	

Mazzy Star Mixed Vocal/Instrumental Duo from the USA

1	Fade Into You	(Capitol CDCL 720)	48	1994	0	1994	
2	Flowers In December	(Capitol CDCL 781)	40	1996	0	1996	

MC Brains Male Rapper, Real Name James De Shannon Davis From Cleveland, USA

* 1	Oochie Coochie		0	1992	21	1992	(Motown 2146)

MC Duke Male Rapper from the UK

1	I'm Riffin (English Rasta)	(Music Of Life 7NOTE 25)	75	1989	0	1989	

MC Lethal Male Producer from the UK

1	The Rave Digger	(Network NWKT 60)	66	1992	0	1992	

MC Lyte Female Rapper from the USA

* 1	Ruffneck	(Atlantic A8336CD)	67	1994	35	1993	(FIRST PRI. 98401)
2	Keep On, Keeping On	(East West A 4287CD)	39	1996	10	1996	(Flavour Unit)
3	Cold Rock A Party	(East West A 3975)	15	1997	11	1996	(East West 64212)
4	Keep On, Keeping On (Re-Mix)	(East West A 3950CD1)	27	1997	0	1997	
5	Come On		0	1997	51	1997	(East West 64239)

HITS 2,4 ARE CREDITED TO MC LYTE FEATURING XSCAPE • HIT 5 IS CREDITED TO BILLY LAWRENCE FEATURING MC LYTE

	ISSUE	TITLE	UK LBL	UK POS	UK YEAR	US POS	US YEAR	US LBL
		MC Miker 'G' & Deejay Sven Male Vocal/Instrumental Rap Duo from Holland						
	1	Holiday Rap	(Debut Debt 3008)	6	1986	0	1986	
		MC Skat Kat & The Stray Mob Male Vocal/Instrumental Group from the USA						
	1	Skat Strut	(Virgin AmericaVUS 51)	64	1991	0	1991	
		MC Spy-D+ Friends Mixed Vocal/Instrumental Group from the UK						
	1	The Amazing Spiderman	(Parlophone CDR 6404)	37	1995	0	1995	
		MC Tunes Male Rapper from the UK						
	1	The Only Rhyme That Bites	(ZTT ZANG 3)	10	1990	0	1990	
	2	Tunes Splits The Atom	(ZTT ZANG 6)	18	1990	0	1990	
	3	Primary Rhyming	(ZTT ZANG 10)	67	1990	0	1990	
		MC Wildski Male Rapper from the UK						
	1	Blame It On The Bassline	(GO.BEAT GOD	29	1989	0	1989	
	2	Warrior	(Arista 112956)	49	1990	0	1990	
		HIT 1 IS CREDITED TO NORMAN COOK FEATURING MC WILDSKI						
		McCoys Male Vocal/Instrumental Group from the USA						
*	1	Hang On Sloopy	(Immediate IM 001)	5	1965	1	1965	(BANG 506)
	2	Fever	(Immediate IM 021)	44	1965	7	1965	(BANG 511)
	3	Come On Let's Go		0	1966	22	1966	(BANG 522)
		NAMES RICK AND RANDY ZEHRINGER, RANDY HOBBS & RONNIE BRANDON						
		McFadden & Whitehead Gene Mcfadden & John Whitehead from the USA						
*	1	Ain't No Stoppin' Us Now	(Philadelphia INT. PIR 7365)	5	1979	13	1979	(PHIL INT. 3681)
		McGuinn, Clark & Hillman Gene Clark B: 17 Nov 1944, Roger McGuinn B: 13 Jul 1942 & Chris Hillman B: 4 Jun 1942						
	1	Don't You Write Her Off		0	1979	33	1979	(Capitol 4693)
		ALL WERE WITH THE GROUP THE BYRDS • OBITUARY : CLARK D: 24 MAY 1991.						
		McGuinness Flint Male Vocal/Instrumental Group from the UK						
	1	When I'm Dead And Gone	(Capitol CL 15662)	2	1970	0	1970	
	2	Malt And Barley Blues	(Capitol CL 15682)	5	1971	0	1971	
		McGuire Sisters Female Vocal Group from the USA						
	1	Pine Tree, Pine Over Me		0	1954	26	1954	(Coral 61126)
	2	Goodnight, Sweetheart, Goodnight		0	1954	7	1954	(Coral 61187)
	3	Muskrat Ramble		0	1954	10	1954	(Coral 61278)
	4	Christmas Alphabet		0	1954	25	1954	(Coral 61303)
*	5	Sincerely	(Vogue Coral Q 72050)	14	1955	1	1955	(Coral 61323)
	6	No More	(Vogue Coral Q 72050)	20	1955	17	1955	(Coral 61323)
	7	It May Sound Silly		0	1955	11	1955	(Coral 61369)
	8	Something's Gotta Give		0	1955	5	1955	(Coral 61423)
	9	He		0	1955	10	1955	(Coral 61501)
	10	Picnic		0	1956	13	1956	(Coral 61627)
	11	Deliliah Jones (From Man With The Golden Arm)	(Vogue Coral Q 72161)	24	1956	37	1956	(Coral 61627)
	12	Weary Blues		0	1956	32	1956	(Coral 61670)
	13	Ev'ry Day Of My Life		0	1956	37	1956	(Coral 61703)
	14	Goodnight My Love, Pleasant Dreams		0	1956	32	1956	(Coral 61748)
*	15	Sugartime	(Vogue Coral Q 72305)	14	1958	1	1958	(Coral 61924)
	16	Ding Dong		0	1958	25	1958	(Coral 61991)
	17	May You Always	(Vogue Coral Q 72356)	15	1959	11	1959	(Coral 62059)
	18	May You Always (Re-Entry)	(Vogue Coral Q 72356)	28	1959	0	1959	
	19	Just For Old Time's Sake		0	1961	20	1961	(Coral 62249)
		McKoy Mixed Vocal Group from the UK						
	1	Fight	(Ringtrackcdtum 1)	54	1993	0	1993	
		Me & You (Featuring) We The Mixed Vocal/Instrumental Group from the UK/Jamaica						
		People Band						
	1	You Never Know What You've Got	(LASER LAS 8)	31	1979	0	1979	
		Me Me Me Male Vocal/Instrumental Group from the UK						
	1	Hanging Around	(Indolent/RCA DUFF 005CD)	19	1996	0	1996	
		Me'shell Ndegeocello Female Vocal/Instrumentalist (Bass) from the USA						
	1	If That's Your Boyfriend (It Wasn't Last Night)	(Maverick W 0223CD1)	74	1994	0	1994	
	2	Wild Night	(Mercury MERCD 409)	34	1994	0	1994	

ISSUE	TITLE	UK LBL	UK POS	UK YEAR	US POS	US YEAR	US LBL
Meat Beat Manifesto Male Production/Instrumental Duo from the UK							
1	Mindstream	(PLAY IT AGAIN SAM BIAS 232CD) 55		1993	0	1993	
Meat Loaf Male Actor/Vocalist, Real Name Marvin Lee Aday B: 27 Sep 1947 In Dallas							
* 1	Two Out Of Three Ain't Bad	(Epic EPC 6281)	32	1978	11	1978	(Epic 50513)
2	You Took The Words Right Out Of My Mouth	(Epic EPC 5980)	33	1978	39	1979	(Epic 50634)
3	Paradise By The Dashboard Light		0	1978	39	1978	(Epic 50588)
4	Bat Out Of Hell	(Epic EPC 7018)	15	1979	0	1979	
5	I'm Gonna Love Her For Both Of Us	(Epic EPCA 1580)	62	1981	0	1981	
6	Dead Ringer For Love	(Epic EPCA 1697)	5	1981	0	1981	
7	If You Really Want To	(Epic A 3357)	59	1983	0	1983	
8	Midnight At The Lost And Found	(Epic A 3748)	17	1983	0	1983	
9	Razor's Edge	(Epic A 4080)	41	1984	0	1984	
10	Modern Girl	(Arista ARIST 585)	17	1984	0	1984	
11	Nowhere Fast	(Arista ARIST 600)	67	1984	0	1984	
12	Piece Of The Action	(Arista ARIST 603)	47	1985	0	1985	
13	Rock 'N' Roll Mercenaries	(Arista ARIST 666)	31	1986	0	1986	
14	Dead Ringer For Love (Re-Issue)	(Epic 6569827)	53	1991	0	1991	
15	Two Out Of Three Ain't Bad (Re-Issue)	(Epic 6574917)	69	1992	0	1992	
* 16	I'll Do Anything For Love (But I Won't Do That)	(Virgin VSCDT 1443)	1	1993	1	1993	(MCA 54626)
17	Bat Out Of Hell (Re-Issue)	(Epic 6600062)	8	1993	0	1993	
18	Rock And Roll Dreams Come Though	(Virgin VSCDT 1479)	11	1994	13	1994	(MCA 54757)
19	Objects In The Rear View Mirror May Appear Closer Than They Are	(Virgin VSCDT 1492)	26	1994	38	1994	(MCA 54848)
* 20	I'd Lie For You (And That's The Truth)	(Virgin VSCDT 1563)	2	1995	13	1995	(MCA 55134)
21	Not A Dry Eye In The House	(Virgin VSCDT 1567)	7	1996	0	1996	
22	Runnin' For The Red Light (I Gotta Life)	(Virgin VSCDX 1582)	21	1996	0	1996	
Meco Orchestra Leader, Real Name Meco Monardo B: 29 Nov 1939 Johnsonburg, Pennsylvania							
* 1	Star Wars Theme-Cantina Band	(RCA XB 1028)	7	1977	1	1977	(Millennium 604)
2	Theme From *Close Encounters*		0	1978	25	1978	(Millennium 608)
3	Theme's From Wizzard Of Oz		0	1978	35	1978	(Millennium 620)
4	Empire Strikes Back		0	1980	18	1980	(RSO 1038)
5	Pop Goes The Movies (Part 1)		0	1982	35	1982	(Arista 0660)
Medicine Head Male Vocal/Instrumental Duo from the UK							
1	(And The) Picture In The Sky	(Dandelion DAN 7003)	22	1971	0	1971	
2	One And One Is One	(Polydor 2001 432)	3	1973	0	1973	
3	Rising Sun	(Polydor 2058 389)	11	1973	0	1973	
4	Slide And Slide	(Polydor 2058 436)	22	1974	0	1974	
Meechie Female Vocalist from the USA							
1	You Bring Me Joy	(Vibe MCSTD 2069)	74	1995	0	1995	
Mega City Four Male Vocal/Instrumental Group from the UK							
1	Words That Say	(Big Life MEGA 2)	66	1991	0	1991	
2	Stop (EP)	(Big Life MEGA 3)	36	1992	0	1992	
3	Shivering Sand	(Big Life MEGA 4)	35	1992	0	1992	
4	Iron Sky	(Big Life MEGA 4)	48	1993	0	1993	
5	Wallflower	(Big Life MEGA 6)	69	1993	0	1993	
Megadeth Male Vocal/Instrumental Group from the USA							
1	Wake Up Dead	(Capitol CL 476)	65	1987	0	1987	
2	Anarchy In The U.K.	(Capitol CL 480)	45	1988	0	1988	
3	Mary Jane	(Capitol CL 489)	46	1988	0	1988	
4	No More Mr. Nice Guy	(SBK SBK 4)	13	1990	0	1990	
5	Holy Wars...The Punishment Due	(Capitol CPL 588)	24	1990	0	1990	
6	Hangar 18	(Capitol CLS 604)	26	1991	0	1991	
7	Symphony Of Destruction	(Capitol CLS 662)	15	1992	0	1992	
8	Skin O' My Teeth	(Capitol CLP 669)	13	1992	0	1992	
9	Sweating Bullets	(Capitol CDCL 682)	26	1993	0	1993	
10	Train Of Consequences	(Capitol CDCL 730)	22	1995	0	1995	
Mel & Kim Female Vocal Duo from the UK							
1	Showing Out (Get Fresh At The Weekend)	(SupremeSUPE 107)	3	1986	0	1986	
2	Respectable	(Supreme SUPE 111)	1	1987	0	1987	
3	F.L.M.	(Supreme SUPE 113)	7	1987	0	1987	
4	That's The Way It Is	(SupremeSUPE 117)	10	1988	0	1988	
Mel & Tim Real Names Mel Hardin & Tim McPherson From Mississippi							

ISSUE	TITLE	UK LBL	UK POS	UK YEAR	US POS	US YEAR	US LBL
* 1	Backfield In Motion		0	1969	10	1969	(Bamboo 107)
2	Starting All Over Again		0	1972	19	1972	(Stax 0127)

Mel Blanc Male Vocalist from the USA

1	Clink, Clink, Another Drink		0	1942	23	1942	(Bluebird 11466)
2	Woody Woodpecker		0	1948	2	1948	(Capitol 15145)
3	Toot, Toot, Tootsie (Good-Bye)		0	1949	26	1949	(Capitol 780)
4	I Taut I Taw A Puddy Cat		0	1951	9	1951	(Capitol 1360)

FAMOUS FOR THE VOICES OF BUGS BUNNY, DAFFY DUCK AND OTHERS

Mel Brooks Male Vocalist from the USA

1	To Be Or Not To Be (The Hitler Rap)	(Island IS 158)	12	1984	0	1984	

Mel Carter Male Actor/Vocalist, B: 22 Apr 1943, Cincinnati

* 1	Hold Me Thrill Me Kiss Me		0	1965	8	1965	(Imperial 66113)
2	(All Of A Sudden) My Heart Sings		0	1965	38	1965	(Imperial 66138)
3	Band Of Gold		0	1966	32	1966	(Imperial 66165)

Mel Smith Male Vocalist from the UK

1	Rockin' Around The Christmas Tree	(10 TEN 2)	3	1987	0	1987	
2	Another Blooming Christmas	(Epic 6576877)	59	1991	0	1991	

HIT 1 IS CREDITED TO MEL AND KIM   MEL SMITH IS PART OF THE DUO MEL AND KIM WITH KIM WILDE

Mel Torme Male Vocalist, Real Name Melvin Howard B: 13 Sep 1925 Chicago

1	I Fall In Love Too Easily		0	1945	20	1945	(Decca 18707)
2	Day By Day		0	1946	15	1946	(Decca 18746)
3	It's Dreamtime		0	1947	24	1947	(Musicraft 15102)
4	Careless Hands		0	1949	1	1949	(Capitol 15379)
5	Again		0	1949	3	1949	(Capitol 15428)
6	Blue Moon		0	1949	20	1949	(Capitol 15428)
7	The Four Winds And The Seven Seas		0	1949	10	1949	(Capitol 671)
8	The Old Master Painter		0	1950	9	1950	(Capitol 791)
9	Bewitched (From Pal Joey		0	1950	8	1950	(Capitol 1000)
10	Anywhere I Wonder		0	1952	30	1950	(Capitol 2263)
11	Mountain Greenery	(Vogue Coral Q 72150)	15	1956	0	1956	
12	Mountain Greeery (Re-Entry)	(Vogue Coral Q 72150)	4	1956	0	1956	
13	Comin' Home Baby	(London HLK 9643)	13	1963	36	1962	(Atlantic 2165)

HIT 1 IS CREDITED TO EUGENE BAIRD WITH MEL TORME'S MEL-TONES• HIT 2 IS CREDITED TO BING CROSBY WITH MEL TORME & HIS MEL-TONES

Melanie Female Vocalist, Real Name Melanie Safka B: 3 Feb 1947 New York City

1	Lay Down (Candles In The Rain)		0	1970	6	1970	(Buddah 167)
2	Peace Will Come (According To Plan)		0	1970	32	1970	(Buddah 186)
3	Ruby Tuesday	(Buddah 2011 038)	9	1970	0	1970	
4	Ruby Tuesday (Re-Entry)	(Buddah 2011 038)	43	1971	0	1971	
5	What Have They Done To My Song Ma	(Buddah 2011 038)	39	1971	0	1971	
* 6	Brand New Key	(Buddah 2011 105)	4	1972	1	1971	(Neighborhood 4201)
7	Ring The Living Bell		0	1972	31	1972	(Neighborhood 4202)
8	The Nickel Song		0	1972	35	1972	(Buddah 268)
9	Bitter Bad		0	1973	36	1973	(Neighborhood 4210)
10	Will You Love Me Tomorrow	(Neighborhood NBH 9)	37	1974	0	1974	
11	Every Breath Of The Way	(Neighborhood HOOD NB1)	70	1983	0	1983	

HIT 1 IS CREDITED TO MELANIE WITH THE EDWIN HAWKINS SINGERS

Melanie Williams Female Vocalist from the UK

1	Ain't No Love (Ain't No Use)	(Rob's CDROB 9)	3	1993	0	1993	
2	All Cried Out	(Columbia 6601872)	60	1994	0	1994	
3	Everyday Thang	(Columbia 6604712)	38	1994	0	1994	
4	Not Enough	(Columbia 6607752)	65	1994	0	1994	
5	You Are Everything	(Columbia6611755)	28	1995	0	1995	

HIT 1 CREDITED TO SUB SUB FEATURING MELANIE WILLIAMS
HIT 5 IS CREDITED TO MELANIE WILLIAMS AND JOE ROBERTS

Melba Montgomery Country Singer/Fiddler/Guitarist, B: 14 Oct 1938 Iron City, Tennessee

21	No Charge		0	1974	39	1974	(Elektra 45883)

OTHER HITS ARE C/W

Melba Moore Female Vocalist from the USA

1	This Is It	(Buddah BDS 443)	9	1976	0	1976	
2	Pick Me Up I'll Dance	(Epic EPC 7234)	48	1979	0	1979	
3	Love's Comin' At Ya	(EMI America EA 146)	15	1982	0	1982	
4	Mind Up Tonight	(Capitol CL 272)	22	1983	0	1983	

ISSUE	TITLE	UK LBL	UK POS	UK YEAR	US POS	US YEAR	US LBL
5	Underlove	(Capitol CL 281)	60	1983	0	1983	

Meli'sa Morgan Female Vocalist from the USA

1	Fool's Paradise	(Capitol CL 415)	41	1986	0	1986	
2	Good Love	(Capitol CL 483)	59	1988	0	1988	

Melissa Etheridge Female Singer/Guitarist, B: 29 May 1961 From Levenworth, Kansas

1	Come To My Window		0	1994	25	1994	(Island 858028)
2	I'm The Only One		0	1994	8	1994	(Island 854068)
3	If I Wanted To		0	1995	16	1995	(Island 854238)
4	I Want To Come Over		0	1996	22	1996	(Island 000000)
5	Nowhere To Go		0	1996	40	1996	(Island 854664)

Melissa Manchester Female Vocalist ,B: 15 Feb 1951 Bronx

1	Midnight Blue		0	1975	6	1975	(Arista 0116)
2	Just Too Many People		0	1975	30	1975	(Arista 0146)
3	Just You And I		0	1976	27	1976	(Arista 0168)
4	Don't Cry Out Loud		0	1979	10	1979	(Arista 0373)
5	Pretty Girls		0	1979	39	1979	(Arista 0456)
6	Fire In The Morning		0	1980	32	1980	(Arista 0485)
7	You Should Hear How She Talks About You		0	1982	5	1982	(Arista 0676)
8	The Music Of Goodbye (Love Theme From *Out Of Africa*)	(MCA MCA 1038)	75	1986	0	1986	

HIT 8 IS CREDITED TO MELISSA MANCHESTER AND AL JARREAU • SHE HAS BEEN BACKUP SINGER FOR BETTE MIDLER

Mellow Man Ace Male Rapper, Real Name Ulpiano Sergio Reyez B: 12 Apr 1967 Cuba

1	Mentirosa		0	1990	14	1990	(Capitol 44533)

Melodians Male Vocal/Instrumental Group from Jamaica

1	Sweet Sensation	(Trojan TR 695)	41	1970	0	1970	

Meltdown Male Instrumental/Production Duo from the USA/UK

1	My Life In Your Hands	(SONY S3 DANU 7CD)	44	1996	0	1996	

Members Male Vocal/Instrumental Group from the UK

1	The Sound Of The Suburbs	(Virgin VS 242)	12	1979	0	1979	
2	Off Shore Banking Business	(Virgin VS 248)	31	1979	0	1979	

Men At Large Male R&B Duo, David Tolliver & Jason Champio From Cleveland, USA

1	So Alone		0	1993	31	1993	(EASTWEST 98459)

Men At Work Male Vocal/Instrumental Group from Australia Names: Ron Strykert, Jerry Speiser, Greg Ham, Colin Hay & John Rees

1	Who Can It Be Now	(Epic EPC A2392)	45	1982	1	1982	(Columbia 02888)
* 2	Down Under	(Epic EPC A 1980)	1	1983	1	1982	(Columbia 03303)
3	Overkill	(Epic EPC A 3220)	21	1983	3	1983	(Columbia 03795)
4	It's A Mistake	(Epic EPC A 3475)	33	1983	6	1983	(Columbia 03959)
5	Dr. Heckyll And Mr. Jive	(Epic EPC A 3668)	31	1983	28	1983	(Columbia 04111)

Men They Couldn't Hang Male Vocal/Instrumental Group from the UK

1	The Colours	(Magnet SELL 6)	61	1988	0	1988	

Men Without Hats Male Vocal/Instrumental Group from Canada, Lead Singer Is Ivan Doroschuk

1	The Safety Dance	(STATIK TAK 1)	6	1983	3	1983	(Backstreet 52232)
2	Pop Goes The World		0	1987	20	1987	(Mercury 888859)

Menswear Male Vocal/Instrumental Group from the UK

1	I'll Manage Somehow	(Laurel Laucd 4)	49	1995	0	1995	
2	Daydreamer	(Laurel Laucd 5)	14	1995	0	1995	
3	Stardust	(Laurel Laucd 6)	16	1995	0	1995	
4	Sleeping In	(Laurel Laucd 7)	24	1995	0	1995	
5	Being Brave	(Laurel Laucd 8)	10	1996	0	1996	
6	We Love You	(Laurel Laucd 11)	22	1996	0	1996	

Mental As Anything Male Vocal/Instrumental Group from Australia

1	Live It Up	(Epic ANY 1)	3	1987	0	1987	

Mercy Lead Singer With The Group Is Jack Sigler Jr. From Florida

* 1	Love (Can Make You Happy)		0	1969	2	1969	(Sundi 6811)

Mercy Mercy Male Vocal/Instrumental Group from the UK

1	What Are We Gonna Do About It	(Ensign ENY 522)	59	1985	0	1985	

Meri Wilson Female Vocalist, B: Japan And Moved To Marietta, Georgia, USA.

* 1	Telephone Man	(PYE International 7N 25747)	6	1977	18	1977	(GRT 127)

Merle Haggard Male Country Vocalist, B: 6 Apr 1937 And Raised In Bakersfield, California

ISSUE	TITLE	UK LBL	UK POS	UK YEAR	US POS	US YEAR	US LBL
19	Okie From Muskogee		0	1969	41	1969	(Capitol 2626)
20	The Fightin' Side Of Me		0	1970	92	1970	(Capitol 2719)
25	Soldier's Last Letter		0	1971	90	1971	(Capitol 3024)
28	Carolyn		0	1971	58	1971	(Capitol 3222)
34	Everybody's Had The Blues		0	1973	62	1973	(Capitol 3641)
35	If We Make It Through December		0	1973	28	1973	(Capitol 3746)
50	From Graceland To The Promised Land		0	1977	58	1977	(MCA 40804)

OTHER HITS ARE C/W • HE WAS IN SAN QUENTIN PRISON FOR BURGLARY FROM 1957-60 UNTIL RONALD REAGAN GRANTED HIM A FULL PARDON

Merle Travis   Male Country Singer Songwriter/Guitarist, B: 29 Nov 1917 In Rosewood, Kentucky

3	Divorce Me C.O.D.		0	1946	25	1946	(Capitol 290)
5	So Round, So Firm, So Fully Packed		0	1947	21	1947	(Capitol 349)

OTHER HITS ARE C/W • OBITUARY: D: 20 OCT 1983 (AGED 65).

Merril Bainbridge   Female Vocalist from Australia

1	Mouth	(Gotham 74321431012)	51	1996	4	1996	(Universal 56018)
2	Under The Water		0	1997	91	1997	(Universal 56112)

Merrilee Rush & The Turnabouts   Female Vocalist, from Seattle, Washington

* 1	Angel Of The Morning		0	1968	7	1968	(Bell 705)

Merry Clayton   Female Vocalist from the USA

1	Yes	(RCA PB 49563)	70	1988	0	1988	

Merseybeats   Male Vocal/Instrumental Group from the UK

1	It's Love That Really Counts	(Fontana TF 412)	24	1963	0	1963	
2	I Think Of You	(Fontana TF 431)	5	1964	0	1964	
3	Don't Turn Around	(Fontana TF 459)	13	1964	0	1964	
4	Wishin' And Hopin'	(Fontana TF 482)	13	1964	0	1964	
5	Last Night	(Fontana TF 504)	40	1964	0	1964	
6	I Love You, Yes I Do	(Fontana TF 607)	22	1965	0	1965	
7	I Stand Accused	(Fontana TF 645)	38	1966	0	1966	

Merseys   Male Vocal Duo from the UK

1	Sorrow	(Fontana TE 694)	4	1966	0	1966	

Merton Parkas   Male Vocal/Instrumental Group from the UK

1	You Need Wheels	(Beggars Banquet BEG 22)	40	1979	0	1979	

Merv Griffin   Male Vocalist/Talk-Show Host from the USA

1	The Morning Side Of The Mountain		0	1951	27	1951	(RCA Victor 4181)
2	Twenty-Three Starlets (And Me)		0	1951	30	1951	(RCA Victor 4270)

Mervin Shiner   Male Country Singer, B: 20 Feb 1921 Bethlehem, Pennsylvania

* 2	Peter Cottontail		0	1950	8	1950	(Decca 46221)

HIT 2 REACHED NUMBER 6 IN THE USA C/W CHARTS

Messiah   Male Production/Instrumental Group from the UK

1	Temple Of Dreams	(Kickin Kick 125)	20	1992	0	1992	
2	I Feel Love	(Kickin Kick 225)	19	1992	0	1992	
3	Thunderdome	(WEA YZ 790CD1)	29	1993	0	1993	

Metal Gurus   Male Vocal/Instrumental Group from the UK

1	Merry Xmas Everybody	(Mercury GURU 1)	55	1990	0	1990	

Metallica   Male Vocal/Instrumental Quartet formed in Los Angeles in 1981

1	The $5.98 (EP) - Garage Days Revisited	(Vertigo METAL 112)	27	1987	0	1987	
2	Harvester Of Sorrow	(Vertigo Metal 212)	20	1988	0	1988	
* 3	One	(Vertigo Metal 5)	13	1989	35	1989	(Elektra 69329)
4	Enter Sandman	(Vertigo Metal 7)	5	1991	16	1991	(Elektra 64857)
5	The Unforgiven	(Vertigo Metal 8)	15	1991	35	1992	(Elektra 64814)
6	Nothing Else Matters	(Vertigo Metal 10)	6	1992	34	1992	(Elektra 64770)
7	Wherever I May Roam	(Vertigo Metal 9)	25	1992	0	1992	
8	Sad But True	(Vertigo Metal 11)	20	1993	0	1993	
9	Until It Sleeps	(Vertigo UKMETCD 12)	5	1996	10	1996	(Elektra 64276)
10	Hero Of The Day	(Vertigo METCD 13)	17	1996	60	1996	(Elektra 64248)
11	Mama Said	(Vertigo METCD 14)	19	1996	0	1996	
12	King Nothing		0	1997	90	1997	(Elektra 64197)

Meteors   Male Vocal/Instrumental Group from the UK

1	Johnny Remember Me	(ID EYE 1)	66	1983	0	1983	

Meters   R&B Instrumental Group formed in 1966 and disbanded in 1977

1	Sophisticated Cissy		0	1969	34	1969	(Josie 1001)
2	Cissy Strut		0	1969	23	1969	(Josie 1005)

ISSUE	TITLE	UK LBL	UK POS	UK YEAR	US POS	US YEAR	US LBL
Method Man Male Rapper, Real Name Clifford Smith from Staten Island, New York							
1	Release Yo'delf	(DEF JAM DEFCD 6)	46	1995	0	1995	
* 2	I'll Be There For You / You're All I Need To Get By	(DEF JAM DEFCD 11)	10	1995	3	1995	(DEF JAM/RAL 1878)
* 3	How High		0	1995	13	1995	(DEF JAM/RAL 9924)
4	Ice Cream		0	1995	37	1995	(LOUD/RCA 64426)
5	Hit 'Em High (The Monstars' Anthem)	(Atlantic A 5449CD)	8	1997	0	1997	
Mezzoforte Male Instrumental Group from Iceland							
1	Garden Party	(Steinar STE 705)	17	1983	0	1983	
2	Rockall	(Steinar STE 710)	75	1983	0	1983	
MFSB Orchestra from the USA, MFSB = Mother Father Sister Brother							
* 1	Tsop (The Sound Of Philadelphia)	(Philadelphia INT. PIR 2289)	22	1974	1	1974	(Phil/Inter 3540)
2	Sexy	(Philadelphia INT. PIR 3381)	37	1975	42	1975	(Phil/Inter 3567)
3	Mysteries Of The World	(Philadelphia INT. PIR 9501)	41	1981	0	1981	
	MIAMI SOUND MACHINE SEE GLORIA ESTEFAN							
Mica Paris Female Vocalist from the UK							
1	My One Temptation	(Fourth & Broadway BRW 85)	7	1988	0	1988	
2	Like Dreamers Do	(Fourth & Broadway BRW 108)	26	1988	0	1988	
3	Breathe Life Into Me	(Fourth & Broadway BRW 115)	26	1988	0	1988	
4	Where Is The Love	(Fourth & Broadway BRW 122)	19	1989	0	1989	
5	Contribution	(Fourth & Broadway BRW 188)	33	1990	0	1990	
6	South Of The River	(Fourth & Broadway BRW 199)	50	1990	0	1990	
7	If I Love U 2 Nite	(Fourth & Broadway BRW 207)	43	1991	0	1991	
8	Young Soul Rebels	(Big Life BLR 57)	61	1991	0	1991	
9	I Never Felt Like This Before	(Fourth & Broadway BRCD263)	15	1993	0	1993	
10	I Wanna Hold On To You	(Fourth & Broadway BRCD 275)	27	1993	0	1993	
11	Two In A Million	(Fourth & Broadway BRCD 285)	51	1993	0	1993	
12	Whisper A Prayer	(Fourth & Broadway BRCD 287)	65	1993	0	1993	
13	One	(Cooltempo Cdcool 304)	29	1995	0	1995	
	HIT 2 IS CREDITED TO MICA PARIS FEATURING COURTNEY PINE • HIT 4 IS CREDITED TO MICA PARIS AND WILL DOWNING							
Michael Ball Male Vocalist from the UK							
1	Love Changes Everything	(Really Useful RUR 3)	2	1989	0	1989	
2	The First Man To Remember	(Really Useful RUR 6)	68	1989	0	1989	And Diana Morrison
3	It's Still You	(Polydor PO160)	58	1991	0	1991	
4	One Step Out Of Time	(Polydor PO 206)	20	1992	0	1992	
5	If I Can Dream (EP)	(Polydor PO248)	51	1992	0	1992	
6	If I Can Dream (EP) (Re-Entry)	(Polydor PO 248)	68	1992	0	1992	
7	Sunset Boulevard	(Polydor PZCD 293)	72	1993	0	1993	
8	From Here To Eternity	(Columbia 6606905)	36	1994	0	1994	
9	The Lovers We Were	(Columbia 6607972)	63	1994	0	1994	
10	The Rose	(Columbia 6614535)	42	1995	0	1995	
11	(Something Inside) So Strong	(Columbia 6629005)	40	1996	0	1996	
Michael Barrymore Male Comedian/Vocalist from the UK							
1	Too Much For One Heart	(EMI CDEM 412)	25	1995	0	1995	
Michael Bolton Male Vocalist, Real Name Michael Bolotin B: 25 Feb 1954 New Haven							
1	That's What Love Is All About		0	1987	19	1987	(Columbia 7322)
2	(Sittin' On) The Dock Of The Bay		0	1988	11	1988	(Columbia 07680)
3	Soul Provider	(Columbia 6629812)	35	1996	17	1989	(Columbia 68909)
4	How Am I Supposed To Live Without You	(CBS 655397 7)	3	1990	1	1989	(Columbia 73017)
5	How Can We Be Lovers	(CBS 655918 7)	10	1990	3	1990	(Columbia 73318)
6	When I'm Back On My Feet Again	(CBS 656077 7)	44	1990	7	1990	(Columbia 73342)
7	Georgia On My Mind		0	1990	36	1990	(Columbia 73490)
8	Love Is A Wonderful Thing	(Columbia 6567717)	23	1991	4	1991	(Columbia73719)
9	Time, Love And Tenderness	(Columbia 6569897)	28	1991	7	1991	(Columbia 73889)
10	When A Man Loves A Woman	(Columbia 6574887)	6	1991	1	1991	(Columbia 74020)
11	Steel Bars	(Columbia 6577257)	17	1992	0	1992	
12	Missing You Now	(Columbia 6579917)	28	1992	12	1992	(Columbia 74184)
13	To Love Somebody	(Columbia 6584557)	16	1992	11	1992	(Columbia 74733)
14	Drift Away	(Columbia 6588657)	18	1992	0	1992	
15	Reach Out I'll Be There	(Columbia 6588972)	37	1993	0	1993	
* 16	Said I Love You ...But I Lied	(Columbia 598762)	15	1993	6	1993	(Columbia 77260)
17	Soul Of My Soul	(Columbia 6601772)	32	1994	0	1994	
18	Completely		0	1994	32	1994	(Columbia 77376)

ISSUE	TITLE	UK LBL	UK POS	UK YEAR	US POS	US YEAR	US LBL
19	Lean On Me	(Columbia 6604132)	14	1994	0	1994	
20	Can I Touch You...There	(Columbia6624385)	6	1995	27	1995	(Columbia 77991)
21	A Love So Beautiful	(Columbia6627092)	27	1995	0	1995	
22	Soul Provider	(Columbia6629812)	35	1996	0	1996	

HIT 12 IS CREDITED TO MICHAEL BOLTON FEATURING KENNY G • MICHAEL WAS WITH THE BLACKJACKS IN THE 1970S

Michael Cox Male Vocalist from the UK

1	Angela Jones	(Triumph RGM 1011)	7	1960	0	1960	
2	Along Came Caroline	(HMV POP 789)	41	1960	0	1960	

Michael Crawford Male Vocalist from the UK

1	The Music Of The Night	(Polydor POSP 803)	7	1987	0	1987	
2	The Music Of The Night	(Columbia 6597382)	54	1994	0	1994	

HIT 2 IS CREDITED TO BARBRA STREISAND DUET WITH MICHAEL CRAWFORD • HIT 2 WAS THE B SIDE OF HIT 8 BY SARAH BRIGHTMAN

Michael Damian Male Vocalist, Real Name Michael Weir B: 26 Apr 1962 In San Diego

1	Rock On		0	1989	1	1989	(Cypress 1420)
2	Cover Of Love		0	1989	31	1989	(Cypress 1430)
3	Was It Nothing At All		0	1989	24	1989	(Cypress 1451)

Michael Flanders Male Vocalist from the UK

1	Little Drummer Boy	(Parlophone R 4528)	20	1959	0	1959	
2	Little Drummer Boy (Re-Entry)	(Parlophone R 4528)	24	1959	0	1959	

Michael Holliday Male Vocalist from the UK

1	Nothin' To Do	(Columbia DB 3746)	20	1956	0	1956	
2	Nothin' To Do (Re-Entry)	(Columbia DB 3746)	23	1956	0	1956	
3	Gal With The Yaller Shoes	(Columbia DB 3783)	13	1956	0	1956	
4	Hot Diggity	(Columbia DB 3783)	14	1956	0	1956	
5	Hot Diggity / Gal With The Yaller Shoes (Re-Entry)	(Columbia DB 3783)	17	1956	0	1956	
6	Ten Thousand Miles / The Runaway Train	(Columbia DB 3813)	24	1956	0	1956	
7	The Story Of My Life / Keep Your Heart	(Columbia DB 4058)	1	1958	0	1958	
8	In Love / Money	(Columbia DB 4087)	26	1958	0	1958	
9	Stairway Of Love/May I?	(Columbia DB 4121)	3	1958	0	1958	
10	I'll Always Be In Love With You	(Columbia DB 4155)	27	1958	0	1958	
11	Starry Eyed/The Steady Game	(Columbia DB 4378)	1	1960	0	1960	
12	Skylark	(Columbia DB 4437)	39	1960	0	1960	
13	Little Boy Lost / The 1 Finger Symphony	(Columbia DB 4475)	50	1960	0	1960	

Michael Jackson Male Vocalist, B: 29 Aug 1958 Indiana

	1	Got To Be There	(Tamla Motown TMG 15147)	5	1972	4	1971	(Motown 1191)
*	2	Rockin' Robin	(Tamla Motown TMG 816)	3	1972	2	1972	(Motown 1197)
	3	I Wanna Be Where You Are		0	1972	16	1972	(Motown 1202)
	4	Ain't No Sunshine	(Tamla Motown TMG 826)	8	1972	0	1972	
*	5	Ben	(Tamla Motown TMG 834)	7	1972	1	1972	(Motown 1207)
	6	Just A Little Bit Of You		0	1975	23	1975	(Motown 1349)
	7	Ease On Down The Road	(MCA 396)	45	1978	0	1978	
*	8	Don't Stop Till You Get Enough	(Epic EPC 7763)	3	1979	1	1979	(Epic 50742)
*	9	Off The Wall	(Epic EPC 8045)	7	1979	10	1980	(Epic 50838)
*	10	Rock With You	(Epic EPC 8206)	7	1980	1	1979	(Epic 50797)
*	11	She's Out Of My Life	(Epic EPC 8384)	3	1980	10	1980	(Epic 50871)
	12	Girlfriend	(Epic EPC 8782)	41	1981	0	1981	
	13	One Day In Your Life	(Motown TMG976)	1	1981	0	1981	
	14	We're Almost There	(Motown TMG 977)	46	1981	0	1981	
*	15	The Girl Is Mine	(Epic EPC A 2729)	8	1982	2	1982	(Epic 03288)
	16	The Girl Is Mine (Re-Entry)	(Epic EPC A2729)	75	1983	0	1983	
*	17	Billie Jean	(Epic EPC A 3084)	1	1983	1	1983	(Epic 03509)
*	18	Beat It	(Epic EPC A 3258)	3	1983	1	1983	(Epic 03759)
	19	Wanna Be Startin' Somethin'	(Epic A 3427)	8	1983	5	1983	(Epic 03914)
	20	Happy (Love Theme From *Lady Sings The Blues*)	(Tamla Motown TMG 986)	52	1983	0	1983	
	21	Human Nature		0	1983	7	1983	(Epic 04026)
*	22	Say Say Say	(Parlophone R 6062)	2	1983	1	1983	(Columbia 04168)
	23	P.Y.T. (Pretty Young Thing)	(Epic A 4136)	11	1984	10	1984	(Epic 04165)
*	24	Thriller	(Epic A 3643)	10	1983	4	1984	(Epic 04364)
	25	Farewell My Summer Love (Re-Mix)	(Motown TMG 1342)	7	1984	38	1984	(Motown 1739)
	26	Girl You're So Together	(Motown TMG 1355)	33	1984	0	1984	
*	27	I Just Can't Stop Loving You	(Epic 650202 7)	1	1987	1	1987	(Epic 07253)
	28	Bad	(Epic 651155 7)	3	1987	1	1987	(Epic 07418)
	29	The Way You Make Me Feel	(Epic 651275 7)	3	1987	1	1987	(Epic 07645)

ISSUE	TITLE	UK LBL	UK POS	UK YEAR	US POS	US YEAR	US LBL
30	The Man In The Mirror	(Epic 651388 7)	21	1988	1	1988	(Epic 07668)
31	Dirty Diana	(Epic 651546 7)	4	1988	1	1988	(Epic 07739)
32	Get It	(Motown ZB 41883)	37	1988	0	1988	
33	Another Part Of Me	(Epic 652844 7)	15	1988	11	1988	(Epic 07962)
34	Smooth Criminal	(Epic 653026 7)	8	1988	7	1988	(Epic 08044)
35	Leave Me Alone	(Epic 654672 7)	2	1989	0	1989	
36	Liberian Girl	(Epic 654947 0)	13	1989	0	1989	
* 37	Black Or White	(Epic 6575987)	1	1991	1	1991	(Epic 74100)
38	Black Or White (Re-Mix)	(Epic 6577316)	14	1992	0	1992	
* 39	Remember The Time / Come Together	(Epic 6577747)	3	1992	3	1992	(Epic 74200)
* 40	In The Closet	(Epic 6580187)	8	1992	6	1992	(Epic 74266)
41	Who Is It	(Epic 6581797)	10	1992	14	1993	(Epic 74406)
42	Jam	(Epic 6583607)	13	1992	26	1992	(Epic 74333)
43	Heal The World	(Epic 6584887)	2	1992	27	1993	(Epic 74708)
44	Give In To Me	(Epic 6590692)	2	1993	0	1993	
45	Will You Be There	(Epic 6592222)	9	1993	7	1993	(MJJ/Epic 77060)
46	Gone Too Soon	(Epic 6599762)	33	1993	0	1993	
* 47	Scream	(Epic 6620222)	3	1995	5	1995	(Epic 78000)
48	Childhood		0	1995	5	1995	(Epic 78000)
* 49	You Are Not Alone	(MJJ MUSIC 6623102)	1	1995	1	1995	(Epic 78002)
50	Scream (Re-Mix)	(Epic 6621277)	43	1995	0	1995	
51	Scream (Re-Entry)	(Epic 6620222)	72	1995	0	1995	
52	Earth Song	(Epic 6626955)	16	1995	0	1995	
53	They Don't Care About Us	(Epic 6629502)	4	1996	30	1996	(Epic 78264)
54	Stranger In Moscow	(Epic 6637872)	4	1996	0	1996	
55	They Don't Care About Us (Re-Entry)	(Epic 6629502)	66	1996	0	1996	
56	They Don't Care About Us (2nd Re-Entry)	(Epic 6629502)	66	1996	0	1996	
57	Why	(Epic 6629502)	2	1996	0	1996	
58	Stranger In Moscow	(Epic 6637872)	4	1996	0	1996	
59	Stranger In Moscow (Re-Entry)	(Epic 6637872)	69	1997	0	1997	
60	Blood On The Dance Floor	(Epic 6644624/5)	1	1997	42	1997	(Epic 78007)
61	History / Ghosts	(Epic 6647962)	5	1997	0	1997	

HIT 7 IS CREDITED TO DIANA ROSS AND MICHAEL JACKSON • HITS 15-16 TO MICHAEL JACKSON AND PAUL McCARTNEY HIT 22 ALSO TO PAUL McCARTNEY
HIT 32 IS CREDITED TO STEVIE WONDER AND MICHAEL JACKSON • HITS 47, 50, 51 ATO MICHAEL AND JANET JACKSON
HIT 56 TO MICHAEL JACKSON FEATURING 3T

Michael Johnson Male Vocalist/Guitarist, B: 6 Jul 1944 Alamosa, Colorado

1	Bluer Than Blue		0	1978	12	1978	(EMI America 8001)
2	Almost Like Being In Love		0	1978	32	1978	(EMI America 8004)
3	This Night Won't Last Forever		0	1979	19	1979	(EMI America 8019)

Michael Lovesmith Male Vocalist from the USA

1	Ain't Nothin' Like It	(Motown ZB 40369)	75	1985	0	1985	

Michael McDonald Male Vocalist, B: 1952 St. Louis, Missouri

1	I Keep Forgettin' (Every Time You're Near)	(Warner Bros. K 17992)	43	1986	4	1982	(Warner Bros. 29933)
2	Yah Mo B There	(QWEST W 9394)	44	1984	19	1984	(QWEST 29394)
3	Yah Mo B There (Re-Enter)	(QWEST W 9394)	69	1984	0	1984	
4	No Lookin' Back		0	1985	34	1985	(Warner Bros. 28960)
5	Yah Mo B There	(QWEST W 9394)	12	1985	0	1985	
* 6	On My Own	(MCA MCA 1045)	2	1986	1	1986	(MCA 52770)
7	Sweet Freedom (From *Running Scared*)	(MCA MCA 1073)	12	1986	7	1986	(MCA 52857)
8	The Right Kind Of Lover	(MCA MCSTD 1995)	50	1994	0	1994	

HITS 2, 3, 5 ARE CREDITED TO JAMES INGRAM WITH MICHAEL McDONALD   HIT 5 IS A RE-MIX VERSION BUT THE SAME CATALOGUE NUMBER
HITS 6, 8 ARE CREDITED TO PATTI LABELLE WITH MICHAEL McDONALD   WAS ALSO WITH THE DOOBIE BROTHERS AND STEELY DAN

Michael Medwin Male Vocal Group from the UK

1	Signature Tune Of The Army Game	(HMV POP 490)	5	1958	0	1958	

HIT IS CREDITED TO MICHAEL MEDWIN, BERNARD BRESSLAW, ALFIE BASS AND LESLIE FYSON

Michael Morales Male Vocalist, B: 25 Apr 1963 And Hails From San Antonio, Texas

1	Who Do You Give Your Love To?		0	1989	15	1989	(Wing 887743)
2	What I Like About You		0	1989	28	1989	(Wing 889678)

Michael Murphey Male Vocalist, Full Name Michael Martin Murphey B: 5 May 1958 In Dallas

1	Geronimo's Cadillac		0	1972	37	1972	(A&M 1368)
* 2	Wildfire		0	1975	3	1975	(Epic 50084)
3	Carolina In The Pines		0	1975	21	1975	(Epic 50131)
4	Renegade		0	1976	39	1976	(Epic 50184)

ISSUE	TITLE	UK LBL	UK POS	UK YEAR	US POS	US YEAR	US LBL
11	What's Forever For		0	1982	19	1982	(Liberty 1466)
Michael Nesmith Male Vocalist, B: 30 Dec 1943 Houston							
1	Joanne		0	1970	21	1970	(RCA 0368)
2	Rio	(Island WIP6373)	28	1977	0	1977	
Michael Nyman Male Pianist from the UK							
1	The Heart Asks Pleasure First - The Promise	(Virgin VEND 3)	60	1994	0	1994	
Michael Parks Male Actor/Singer, B: 4 Apr 1938 Corona, California							
1	Long Lonesome Highway		0	1970	20	1970	(MGM 14104)
Michael Penn Male Singer/Songwriter, Older Brother Of Sean Penn, Lives In Los Angeles							
1	No Myth		0	1990	13	1990	(RCA 9111)
Michael Schenker Group Male Vocal/Instrumental Group from the UK/Germany							
1	Armed And Ready	(Chrysalis CHS 2455)	53	1980	0	1980	
2	Cry For The Nations	(Chrysalis CHS 2471)	56	1980	0	1980	
3	Dancer	(Chrysalis CHS 2636)	52	1982	0	1982	
Michael Sembello Male Vocalist, B: 17 Apr 1954 Philadelphia							
1	Maniac		43	1983	1	1983	(Casablanca 812516)
2	Automatic Man		0	1983	34	1983	(Warner Bros. 29485)
Michael Stanley Band Cleveland Rock Band, Michael Gismondi, Rick Bell & Gary Markashy							
1	He Can't Love You		0	1981	33	1981	(EMI America 8063)
2	My Town		0	1983	39	1983	(EMI America 8178)
Michael W. Smith Male Singer/Songwriter from West Virginia							
1	Place In This World		0	1991	6	1991	(Reunion 19019)
2	I Will Be Here For You		0	1992	27	1992	(Reunion 19139)
Michael Ward Male Vocalist from the UK							
1	Let There Be Peace On Earth	(Philips 6006 340)	15	1973	0	1973	
2	Let There Be Peace On Earth (Re-Entry)	(Philips 6006 340)	50	1973	0	1973	
Michael Watford Male Vocalist from the USA							
1	So Into You	(East West A 8309CD)	53	1994	0	1994	
Michael Wycoff Male Vocalist from the USA							
1	(Do You Really Love Me) Tell Me Love	(RCA 348)	60	1983	0	1983	
Michael Zager Band Mixed Vocal/Instrumental Group from the USA, Michael B: 1943 Jersey City, New Jersey.							
1	Let's All Chant	(Private Stock PVT 143)	8	1978	36	1978	(Private Stock 45184)
	MICHAEL WAS A MEMBER OF THE GROUP TEN WHEEL DRIVE						
Michaela Female Vocalist from the UK							
1	H-A-P-P-Y Radio	(London H 1)	62	1989	0	1989	
2	Take Good Care Of My Heart	(London WAC 90)	66	1990	0	1990	
Michel'le Black Vocalist, Pronounced Mee-Shell-Lay Toussant From Los Angeles							
* 1	No More Lies		0	1990	7	1990	(Ruthless 99149)
2	Nicety		0	1990	29	1990	(Ruthless 98980)
3	Something In My Heart		0	1991	31	1991	(Ruthless 98885)
	FORMER BACKING VOCALIST WITH WORLD CLASS WRECKIN' CRU						
Michelle Female Vocalist from Trinidad							
1	Standing Here All Alone	(Positiva CDTIV 54)	69	1996	0	1996	
Michelle Gayle Female Vocalist from the UK							
1	Looking Up	(RCA 74321154532)	11	1993	0	1993	
2	Sweetness	(RCA 74321230192)	4	1994	0	1994	
3	I'll Find You	(RCA 74321247762)	26	1994	0	1994	
4	Freedom	(RCA 74321284692)	16	1995	0	1995	
5	Happy Just To Be With You	(RCA 74321302692)	11	1995	0	1995	
6	Do You Know	(RCA 74321419282)	6	1997	0	1997	
7	Sensational	(RCA 74321419302)	14	1997	0	1997	
Michelle Shocked Female Vocalist from the USA							
1	Anchorage	(Cooking Vinyl Lon 193)	60	1988	0	1988	
2	If Love Was A Train	(Cooking Vinyl Lon 212)	63	1989	0	1989	
3	When I Grow Up	(Cooking Vinyl Lon 219)	67	1989	0	1989	
Michelle Sweeney Female Vocalist from the USA							
1	This Time	(Big Beat A 8229CD)	57	1994	0	1994	

ISSUE	TITLE	UK LBL	UK POS	UK YEAR	US POS	US YEAR	US LBL
Mick Jackson Male Vocalist from the UK							
1	Blame It On The Boogie	(Atlantic K 11102)	15	1978	0	1978	
2	Weekend	(Atlantic K 11224)	38	1979	0	1979	
Mick Jagger Male Vocalist, Real Name Michael Phillip Jagger B: 7 Jul 1943 In Dartford, Essex, England							
1	Memo From Turner	(Decca F 13067)	32	1970	0	1970	
2	State Of Shock	(Epic A 4431)	14	1984	3	1984	(Epic 04503)
3	Just Another Night	(CBS A 4722)	32	1985	12	1985	(Columbia 04743)
4	Lucky In Love		0	1985	38	1985	(Columbia 04893)
5	Dancing In The Street	(EMI America EA 204)	1	1985	7	1985	(EMI America8288)
6	Let's Work	(CBS 651028 7)	31	1987	39	1987	(Columbia 07306)
7	Sweet Thing	(Atlantic A 7410CD)	24	1993	0	1993	
	HIT 2 CREDITED TO JACKSONS, MICK JAGGER AND MICHAEL JACKSON • HIT 5 TO DAVID BOWIE AND MICK JAGGER • MICK WAS ALSO THE LEAD SINGER WITH BLUES INC						
Mick Karn Male Saxohphonist from the UK							
1	After A Fashion	(MUSICFEST FEST 1)	39	1983	0	1983	
2	Buoy	(Virgin VS 910)	63	1987	0	1987	
	HIT 1 IS CREDITED TO MIDGE URE AND MICK KARN • HIT 2 IS CREDITED TO MICK KARN FEATURING DAVID SYLVIAN						
Mick Ronson With Joe Elliott Mixed Instrumental Duo from the UK							
1	Don't Look Down	(Epic 6603582)	55	1994	0	1994	
Mickey & Sylvia Born McHouston 'Mickey' Baker 15 Oct 1925 & Sylvia Vanderpool B: 6 Mar 1936							
* 1	Love Is Strange		0	1957	11	1957	(Groove 0175)
	SYLVIA BEGAN HER RECORDING LIFE AS SYLVIA. (SEE SYLVIA (3))						
Mickey Gilley Male Country Vocalist/Pianist, B: 9 Mar 1936 In Natchez, Louisiana							
2	Room Full Of Roses		0	1974	50	1974	(Playboy 50056)
21	True Love Ways		0	1980	66	1980	(Epic 50876)
22	Stand By Me		0	1980	22	1980	(FULL MOON 46640)
25	You Don't Know Me		0	1981	55	1981	(Epic 02172)
	OTHERS ARE C/W HITS						
Mickey Katz Orchestra Male Bandleader, Formerly With Spike Jones from the USA							
1	Music! Music! Music!		0	1950	18	1950	(Capitol 862)
2	Come On-A My House (From The Son)		0	1951	22	1951	(Capitol 1788)
3	Herring Boats		0	1952	28	1952	(Capitol 1961)
Mickey Lee Lane B: 1945 Rochester, New York							
1	Shaggy Dog		0	1964	38	1964	(Swan 4183)
Mickey Mozart Quintet Pseudonym for Robert Maxwell, See Also Robert Maxwell							
1	Little Dipper		0	1959	30	1959	(Roulette 4148)
Mickey Newbury Male Vocalist, Real Name Milton S Newbury Jr. B: 19 May 1940 In Houston							
1	An American Trilogy	(Elektra K 12047)	42	1972	26	1972	(Elektra 45750)
Mickie Most Male Vocalist from the UK							
1	Mister Porter	(Decca F 11664)	45	1963	0	1963	
Microbe Originally The Voice Was Used As A Jingle For DJ David Simon's BBC Radio 1 Show							
1	Groovy Baby	(CBS 4158)	29	1969	0	1969	
Microdisney Male Vocal/Instrumental Group from Ireland							
1	Town To Town	(Virgin VS 927)	55	1987	0	1987	
Middle Of The Road Mixed Vocal/Instrumental Group from Glasgow, Scotland, Names Eric & Ian Campbell, Ken Andrew, Sally Carr							
* 1	Chirpy Chirpy Cheep Cheep	(RCA 2047)	1	1971	0	1971	
* 2	Tweele Dee Tweedle Dum	(RCA 2110)	2	1971	0	1971	
* 3	Soley Soley	(RCA 2151)	5	1971	0	1971	
4	Sacramento	(RCA 2184)	49	1972	0	1972	
5	Sacramento (Re-Entry)	(RCA 2184)	23	1972	0	1972	
6	Samson And Delilah	(RCA 2237)	26	1972	0	1972	
Middlesborough F.C. Male Soccer Team Vocalists from the UK							
1	Let's Dance	(Magnet EW 112CD)	44	1997	0	1997	
Midge Ure Male Vocalist from the UK							
1	No Regrets	(Chrysalis CHS 2618)	9	1982	0	1982	
2	After A Fashion	(MUSICFEST FEST 1)	39	1983	0	1983	And Mick Karn
3	If I Was	(Chrysalis URE 1)	1	1985	0	1985	
4	That Certain Smile	(Chrysalis URE 2)	46	1985	0	1985	
5	Wastelands	(Chrysalis URE 3)	46	1986	0	1986	
6	Call Of The Wild	(Chrysalis URE 4)	27	1986	0	1986	

ISSUE	TITLE	UK LBL	UK POS	UK YEAR	US POS	US YEAR	US LBL
7	Answers To Nothing	(Chrysalis URE 5)	49	1988	0	1988	
8	Dear God	(Chrysalis URE 6)	55	1988	0	1988	
9	Cold Cold Heart	(Arista 114555)	17	1991	0	1991	
10	Breathe	(Arista743211371172)	70	1996	0	1996	

Midi Xpress Male Vocal/Instrumental Duo from the UK

1	Chase	(Labello Dance Lad 26CD)	73	1996	0	1996	

Midnight Cowboy Soundtrack Orchestra from the USA

1	Midnight Cowboy	(United Artists UP 634)	47	1980	0	1980	

Midnight Oil Male Vocal/Instrumental Group From Australia, Lead Singer With The Quintet Is Peter Garrett

1	Beds Are Burning	(Sprint Oil 1)	48	1988	17	1988	(Columbia 07433)
2	The Dead Heart	(Sprint Oil 2)	68	1988	0	1988	
3	Beds Are Burning (Re-Issue)	(Sprint Oil 3)	6	1989	0	1989	
4	The Dead Heart (Re-Issue)	(Sprint Oil 4)	62	1989	0	1989	
5	Blue Sky Mine	(CBS OIL 5)	66	1990	0	1990	
6	Truganini	(Columbia 6590492)	29	1993	0	1993	
7	My Country	(Columbia 6593702)	66	1993	0	1993	
8	In The Valley	(Columbia 6598492)	60	1993	0	1993	

Midnight Star R&B Group formed in 1976 With Lead Singer Belinda Lipscomb

1	Operator	(Solar MCA 942)	66	1985	18	1985	(Solar 69684)
2	Headlines	(Solar MCA 1065)	16	1986	0	1986	
3	Midas Touch	(Solar MCA 1096)	8	1986	0	1986	
4	Engine No 9	(Solar MCA 1117)	64	1987	0	1987	
5	Wet My Whistle	(Solar MCA 1127)	60	1987	0	1987	

Mig29 Male Production/Instrumental Group from Italy

1	Mig29	(Champion Champ 292)	62	1992	0	1992	

Mighty Avengers Male Vocal/Instrumental Group from the UK

1	So Much In Love	(Decca F 11962)	46	1964	0	1964	

Mighty Dub Katz See Norman Cook

Mighty Lemon Drops Male Vocal/Instrumental Group from the UK

1	The Other Side Of You	(Blue Guitar Azur 1)	67	1986	0	1986	
2	Out Of Hand	(Blue Guitar Azur 4)	66	1987	0	1987	
3	Inside Out	(Blue Guitar Azur 6)	74	1988	0	1988	

Mighty Morph'n Power Rangers Mixed Vocal Group from the USA

1	Power Rangers	(RCA 74321253022)	3	1994	0	1994	
2	Power Rangers (Re-Entry)	(RCA 74321253022)	57	1995	0	1995	
3	Power Rangers (2nd Re-Entry)	(RCA 74321253022)	65	1995	0	1995	

Migil Five Male Vocal/Instrumental Group from the UK

1	Mockingbird Hill	(PYE 7N 15597)	10	1964	0	1964	
2	Near You	(PYE 7N 15645)	31	1964	0	1964	

Miguel Rios Male Vocalist, B: 1944 Granada, Spain

* 1	Song Of Joy (Himno A La Alegria)	(A&M AMS 790)	16	1970	14	1970	(A&M 1193)

Mike Male Producer, Real Name Mark Jolley from the UK

1	Twangling Three Fingers In A Box	(Pukka CDMIKE 100)	40	1994	0	1994	

Mike & The Mechanics Male Vocal/Instrumental Group from the UK Names: Mike Rutherford, Paul Carrack, Paul Young, Peter Van Hooke & Adrian Lee

1	Silent Running (On Dangerous Ground)	(WEA U 8908)	21	1986	6	1986	(Atlantic 89488)
2	All I Need Is A Miracle	(WEA U 8765)	53	1986	5	1986	(Atlantic 89450)
3	Taken In		0	1986	32	1986	(Atlantic 89404)
4	The Living Years	(WEA U 7717)	2	1989	1	1989	(Atlantic 88964)
5	Word Of Mouth	(Virgin VS 1345)	13	1991	0	1991	
6	A Time And Place	(Virgin VS 1351)	58	1991	0	1991	
7	Everybody Gets A Second Chance	(Virgin VS 1396)	56	1992	0	1992	
8	Over My Shoulder	(Virgin VSCDT 1526)	12	1995	0	1995	
9	A Beggar On A Beach Of Gold	(Virgin VSCDT 1535)	33	1995	0	1995	
10	Another Cup Of Coffee	(Virgin VSCDG 1554)	51	1995	0	1995	
11	All I Need Is A Miracle (Re-Mix)	(Virgin VSCDG 1576)	27	1996	0	1996	
12	Silent Running (Re-Issue)	(Virgin VSCDT 1585)	61	1996	0	1996	

Mike 'Hitman' Wilson Male Producer from the USA

1	Another Sleepless Night	(Arista 113506)	74	1990	0	1990	

ISSUE	TITLE	UK LBL	UK POS	UK YEAR	US POS	US YEAR	US LBL
Mike Batt Male Vocalist from the UK							
1	Summer Time City	(Epic EPC 3460)	4	1975	0	1975	
	THE HIT WAS CREDITED TO MIKE BATT - NEW EDITION • SEE ALSO THE WOMBLES						
Mike Berry Male Vocalist from the UK							
1	Tribute To Buddy Holly	(HMV POP 912)	24	1961	0	1961	
2	Don't You Think It's Time	(HMV POP 1105)	6	1963	0	1963	
3	My Little Baby	(HMV POP 1142)	34	1963	0	1963	
4	The Sunshine Of Your Smile	(Polydor 2059 161)	9	1980	0	1980	
5	If I Could Only Make You Care	(Polydor POSP 202)	37	1980	0	1980	
6	Memories	(Polydor POSP 287)	55	1981	0	1981	
Mike Clifford Male Vocalist, B: 6 Nov 1943 Los Angeles							
1	Close To Cathy		0	1962	12	1962	(United Artists 489)
Mike Cotton's Jazzmen Male Trumpet/Instrumental Band from the UK							
1	Swing That Hammer	(Columbia DB 7029)	36	1963	0	1963	
Mike Curb Congregation Male Music Mogul, B: 24 Dec 1944 Savannah, Georgia							
1	Burning Bridges		0	1971	34	1971	(MGM 14151)
	MIKE IS PRESIDENT OF MGM RECORDS, HIS OWN RECORD COMPANY IS CURB RECORDS						
Mike Douglas Male Vocalist, Real Name Michael Dowd Jr. B: 11 Aug 1925 Chicago							
1	The Men In My Little Girl's Life		0	1966	1	1966	(Epic 9876)
Mike Flowers Pops Mixed Vocal/Instrumental Group from the UK							
1	Wonderwall	(London LONCD 378)	2	1995	0	1995	
2	Wonderwall (Re-Entry)	(London LONCD 378)	52	1996	0	1996	
3	Light My Fire / Please Release Me	(London LONCD 384)	39	1996	0	1996	
4	Don't Cry For Me Argentina	(LOVE THIS LUVTHISCD 16)	30	1996	0	1996	
Mike Harding Male Comedian/Vocalist from the UK							
1	Rochdale Cowboy	(Rubber ADUB 3)	22	1975	0	1975	
Mike McGear Male Vocalist from the UK							
1	Leave It	(Warner Bros. K 16446)	36	1974	0	1974	
Mike Oldfield Male Vocal/Multi-Instrumentalist B: 15 May 1953 In Reading, Berkshire, England							
* 1	Mike Oldfield's Single	(Virgin VS 101)	31	1974	7	1974	(Virgin 55100)
2	In Dulci Jubilo / On Horseback	(Virgin VS 131)	4	1975	0	1975	
3	Portsmouth	(Virgin VS 163)	3	1976	0	1976	
4	Take 4 (EP)	(Virgin VS 238)	72	1978	0	1978	
5	Guilty	(Virgin VS 245)	22	1979	0	1979	
6	Blue Peter	(Virgin VS 317)	19	1979	0	1979	
7	Five Miles Out	(Virgin VS 464)	43	1982	0	1982	
8	Family Man	(Virgin VS 489)	45	1982	0	1982	
9	Moonlight Shadow	(Virgin VS 586)	4	1983	0	1983	
10	Crime Of Passion	(Virgin VS 648)	61	1984	0	1984	
11	To France	(Virgin VS 686)	48	1984	0	1984	
12	Pictures In The Dark	(Virgin VS 836)	50	1985	0	1985	
13	Sentinel	(WEA YZ 698)	10	1992	0	1992	
14	Tattoo	(WEA YZ 708)	33	1992	0	1992	
15	The Bell	(WEA YZ 737CD)	50	1993	0	1993	
16	Moonlight Shadow (Re-Issue)	(Virgin VSCDT 1477)	52	1993	0	1993	
17	Hibernaculum	(WEA YZ 871CD)	47	1994	0	1994	
18	Let There Be Light	(WEA YZ 880CD)	51	1995	0	1995	
Mike Post Orchestra Leader, B: 29 Sep 1944 Los Angeles							
1	The Rockford Files		0	1975	10	1975	(MGM 14772)
2	Afternoon Of The Rhino	(Warner Bros. K 16588)	48	1975	0	1975	
3	Afternoon Of The Rhino (Re-Entry)	(Warner Bros. K 16588)	47	1975	0	1975	
4	Theme From *Hill Street Blues*	(Elektron K 12576)	25	1982	10	1981	(Elektra 47186)
5	(Theme From) *Magnum P.I.*		0	1982	25	1982	(Elektra 47400)
6	The A Team	(RCA 443)	45	1984	0	1984	
Mike Preston Male Vocalist from the UK							
1	Mr. Blue	(Decca F 11167)	12	1959	0	1959	
2	I'd Do Anything	(Decca F 11255)	23	1960	0	1960	
3	Togetherness	(Decca F 11287)	41	1960	0	1960	

ISSUE	TITLE	UK LBL	UK POS	UK YEAR	US POS	US YEAR	US LBL
4	Marry Me	(Decca F 11335)	14	1961	0	1961	

Mike Reid Male Comedian/Actor/Vocalist from the UK

1	The Ugly Duckling	(PYE 7N 45434)	10	1975	0	1975	

Mike Reno & Ann Wilson Mixed Vocal Duo, Lead Singers With Loverboy & Heart Respectively

1	Almost Paradise...Love Theme From *Footloose*		0	1984	7	1984	(Columbia 04418)

Mike Sagar Male Vocalist from the UK

1	Deep Feeling	(HMV POP 819)	44	1960	0	1960	

Mike Sammes Singers Mixed Vocal Group from the UK

1	Somewhere My Love	(HMV POP 1546)	22	1966	0	1966	
2	Somewhere My Love (Re-Entry)	(HMV POP 1546)	14	1967	0	1967	

Mike Sarne Male Vocalist from the UK

1	Come Outside	(Parlophone R4902)	1	1962	0	1962	
2	Will I What	(Parlophone R 4932)	18	1962	0	1962	
3	Just For Kicks	(Parlophone R 4974)	22	1963	0	1963	
4	Code Of Love	(Parlophone R 5010)	29	1963	0	1963	
	HIT 1 IS CREDITED TO MIKE SARNE WITH WENDY RICHARDS HIT 2 TO MIKE SARNE WITH BILLIE DAVIS						

Mike Scott Male Vocal/Multi-Instrumentalist from the UK

1	Bring 'Em All In	(Chrysalis CDCHS 5025)	56	1995	0	1995	
2	Building The City Of Light	(Chrysalis CDCHS 5026)	60	1995	0	1995	

Miki & Griff Mixed Vocal Duo from the UK

1	Hold Back Tomorrow	(PYE 7N 15213)	26	1959	0	1959	
2	Rockin' Alone	(PYE 7N 15296)	44	1960	0	1960	
3	Little Bitty Tear	(PYE 7N 15412)	16	1962	0	1962	
4	I Wanna Stay Here	(PYE 7N 15555)	23	1963	0	1963	

Miki Anthony Male Vocalist from the UK

1	If It Wasn't For The Reason That I Love You	(Bell 1275)	27	1973	0	1973	

Miki Howard Female Vocalist from the USA

1	Until You Come Back To Me (That's What I'm Gonna Do)	(East West	67	1990	0	1990	

Mildred Bailey Female Jazz Vocalist from the USA

22	Almost Like Being In Love		0	1947	21	1947	(MAJESTIC 1140)

Milk & Honey Mixed Vocal/Instrumental Group from Israel

1	Hallelujah	(Polydor 2001 870)	5	1979	0	1979	
	HIT IS CREDITED TO MILK & HONEY FEATURING GALI ATARI • EUROVISION SONG CONTEST ENTRY						

Milla Female Vocalist from the USA

1	Gentleman Who Fell	(SBK CDSBK 49)	65	1994	0	1994	

Milli Vanilli Vocalist Are Brad Howe, John Davis & Charles Shaw

*	1	Girl You Know It's True	(Cooltempo Cool 170)	3	1988	2	1989	(Arista 9781)
*	2	Baby Don't Forget My Number	(Cooltempo Cool 178)	41	1988	1	1989	(Arista 9832)
	3	Blame It On The Rain	(Cooltempo Cool 180)	53	1989	0	1989	
*	4	Girl I'm Gonna Miss You	(Cooltempo Cool 191)	2	1989	1	1989	(Arista 9870)
*	5	Blame It On The Rain (Re-Entry)	(Cooltempo Cool 180)	52	1989	1	1989	(Arista 9904)
	6	All Or Nothing	(Cooltempo Cool 199)	74	1990	4	1990	(Arista 9923)

Millican & Nesbitt Male Vocal Duo from the UK

1	Vaya Con Dios	(PYE 7N 45310)	20	1973	0	1973	
2	For Old Times Sake	(PYE 7N 45357)	38	1974	0	1974	

Millie Female Vocalist, Real Name Millicent 'Dolly May' Smith B: 6 Oct 1946, Clarendon, Jamaica

*	1	My Boy Lollipop	(Fontana TF449)	2	1964	2	1964	(Smash 1893)
	2	Sweet William	(Fontana TF479)	30	1964	40	1964	(Smash 1920)
	3	Blood Shot Eyes	(Fontana TF617)	48	1965	0	1965	
	4	My Boy Lollipop (Re-Issue)	(Island WIP 6574)	46	1987	0	1987	
		HIT 1 SOLD OVER 600,000 IN THE UK ALONE						

Millie Jackson Female Vocalist, B: 15 Jul 1944 Thompson, Georgia

1	Ask Me What You Want		0	1972	27	1972	(Spring 123)
2	My Man's A Sweet Man	(MOJO 2093 022)	50	1972	0	1972	
3	Hurts So Good (From Cleopatra Jones)		0	1973	24	1973	(Spring 139)
4	I Feel Like Walkin' In The Rain	(Sire W 9348)	55	1984	0	1984	
5	Act Of War	(Rocket EJS 8)	32	1985	0	1985 with Elton John	

ISSUE	TITLE	UK LBL	UK POS	UK YEAR	US POS	US YEAR	US LBL
Millie Scott Female Vocalist from the USA							
1	Prisoner Of Love	(Fourth & Broadway BRW 45)	52	1986	0	1986	
2	Automatic	(Fourth & Broadway BRW51)	56	1986	0	1986	
3	Ev'ry Little Bit	(Fourth & Broadway BRW 58)	63	1987	0	1987	
Millionaire Hippies Male Producer, Real Name Danny Rampling from the UK							
1	I Am The Music, Hear Me!	(Deconstruction 74321175432)	52	1993	0	1993	
2	C'mon	(Deconstruction 74321229372)	59	1994	0	1994	
Mills Brothers Male Vocal Group from the UK							
* 1	Tiger Rag		0	1931	1	1931	(Brunswick 6197)
* 30	Paper Doll (Re-Entry)		0	1943	1	1943	(Decca 18318)
* 32	You Always Hurt The One You Love		0	1944	1	1944	(Decca 18599)
36	Don't Be A Baby, Baby		0	1946	12	1946	(Decca 18753)
37	I Don't Know Enough About You		0	1946	7	1946	(Decca 18834)
38	There's No One But You		0	1946	22	1946	(Decca 18834)
39	I Guess I'll Get The Papers (And Go Home)		0	1946	12	1946	(Decca 23638)
40	Across The Alley From The Alamo		0	1947	2	1947	(Decca 23863)
41	Oh! My Achin' Heart		0	1947	21	1947	(Decca 23979)
42	When You Where Sweet Sixteen		0	1947	15	1947	(Decca 23627)
43	Gloria		0	1948	17	1948	(Decca 24509)
44	I Love You So Much It Hurts		0	1949	8	1949	(Decca 24550)
45	I've Got My Love To Keep Me Warm (From *On The Avenue*)		0	1949	9	1949	(Decca 24550)
46	Someday (You'll Want Me To Want You)		0	1949	5	1949	(Decca 24694)
47	Who'll Be The Next One (To Cry Over You)		0	1949	24	1949	(Decca 24749)
48	Daddy's Little Girl		0	1950	5	1950	(Decca 24872)
49	Nevertheless (I'm In Love With You) (From *Three Little Words*)		0	1950	4	1950	(Decca 27253)
50	Be My Life's Companion		0	1952	7	1952	(Decca 27889)
* 51	The Glow-Worm	(Brunswick 05007)	10	1953	2	1952	(Decca 27384)
52	Lazy River		0	1952	22	1952	(Decca 28458)
53	Twice As Much		0	1953	14	1953	(Decca 28586)
54	Say Si Si		0	1953	12	1953	(Decca 28670)
55	Pretty Butterfly		0	1953	21	1953	(Decca 28736)
56	Who Put The Devil In Evelyn's Eyes		0	1953	23	1953	(Decca 28818)
57	The Jones Boy		0	1953	15	1953	(Decca 28945)
58	She Was Five And He Was Ten		0	1954	27	1954	(Decca 28945)
59	You Didn't Want Me When You Had Me		0	1954	22	1954	(Decca 29019)
60	A Carnival In Venice		0	1954	26	1954	(Decca 29115)
61	How Blue?		0	1954	25	1954	(Decca 29185)
62	Queen Of The Senior Prom		0	1957	39	1957	(Decca 30299)
63	Get A Job		0	1958	21	1958	(DOT 15695)
64	Cab Driver		0	1968	23	1968	(DOT 17041)
	OBITUARY : JOHN JNR D: 28 JUN 1982. JOHN SNR D: 8 DEC 1967.						
Milltown Brothers Male Vocal/Instrumental Group from the UK							
1	Which Way Should I Jump	(A&M AM 711)	38	1991	0	1991	
2	Here I Stand	(A&M AM 758)	41	1991	0	1991	
3	Apple Green	(A&M AM 787)	43	1991	0	1991	
4	Turn Off	(A&M 5802692)	55	1993	0	1993	
5	It's All Over Now Baby Blue	(A&M 5803332)	48	1993	0	1993	
Mind Of Kane Male Producer, Real Name David Hope from the UK							
1	Stabbed In The Back	(DEJA VU DJV 007)	64	1991	0	1991	
Minds Of Men Mixed Vocal/Instrumental Group from the UK							
1	Brand New Day	(Perfecto PERF 121CD)	41	1996	0	1996	
Mindy Carson Female Vocalist, B: 16 Jul 1927 New York City							
1	Rumors Are Flying		0	1946	12	1946	(SIGNATURE 15043)
2	Candy And Cake		0	1950	12	1950	(RCA Victor 3204)
3	My Foolish Heart		0	1950	6	1950	(RCA Victor 3204)
4	A Rainy Day Refrain		0	1950	24	1950	(RCA Victor 3921)
5	Lonely Little Robin		0	1951	25	1951	(RCA Victor 4151)
6	'Cause I Love You, That's A-Why		0	1952	24	1952	(Columbia 39879)
7	Tell Me You're Mine (Per Un Bacio D'amour)		0	1953	22	1953	(Columbia 39914)
8	Tell Us Where The Good Times Are		0	1953	23	1953	(Columbia 39992)
9	This Above All		0	1954	29	1954	(Columbia 40206)
10	Wake The Town And Tell The People		0	1955	13	1955	(Columbia 40537)

ISSUE	TITLE	UK LBL	UK POS	UK YEAR	US POS	US YEAR	US LBL
11	Since I Met You Baby		0	1957	34	1957	(Columbia 40789)
Mini Pops Mixed Vocal Group from the UK							
1	Songs For Christmas '87 (EP)	(Bright Bulb 9)	39	1987	0	1987	
Ministry Male Vocal/Instrumental Group from the UK							
1	Nwo	(Sire W 0125TE)	49	1992	0	1992	
2	The Fall	(Warner Bros. 0328CD)	53	1996	0	1996	
Mink De Ville Male Vocal/Instrumental Group from the USA							
1	Spanish Stroll	(Capitol CLX 103)	20	1977	0	1977	
Minnie Riperton Female Vocalist, B: 8 Nov 1947 Chicago, Also Recorded As Andrea Davis.							
* 1	Lovin' You	(Epic EPC 3121)	2	1975	1	1975	(Epic 50057)
Mint Condition Male Funk Sextet from Minneapolis							
* 1	Breakin' My Heart (Pretty Brown Eyes)		0	1992	6	1992	(Perspective 0004)
2	U Send Me Swingin'		0	1994	39	1994	(Perspective 7439)
3	What Kind Of Man Would I Be	(WILD CARD/Polydor 5710492)	38	1997	17	1996	(A&M 587558)
4	You Don't Have To Hurt No More		0	1997	32	1997	(Perspective 587564)
Mint Juleps Female Vocal Group from the UK							
1	Only Love Can Break Your Heart	(Stiff Buy 241)	62	1986	0	1986	
2	Every Kinda People	(Stiff Buy 257)	58	1987	0	1987	
Miquel Brown Female Vocalist from the USA							
1	He's A Saint He's A Sinner	(Record Shack Soho 15)	68	1984	0	1984	
2	Close To Perfection	(Record Shack Soho 48)	63	1985	0	1985	
Mirage Male Vocal/Instrumental Group from the UK							
1	Give Me The Night	(Passion Pash 15)	49	1984	0	1984	
2	Jack Mix II/Iii	(Debut Debt 3022)	4	1987	0	1987	
3	Serious Mix	(Debut Debt 3028)	42	1987	0	1987	
4	Jack Mix Iv	(Debut Debt 3035)	8	1987	0	1987	
5	Jack Mix Vii	(Debut Debt 3042)	50	1988	0	1988	
6	Push The Beat	(Debut Debt 3050)	67	1988	0	1988	
7	Latino House	(Debut Debt 3085)	70	1989	0	1989	
Mireille Mathieu Female Vocalist from France							
1	La Derniera Valse	(Columbia DB 8323)	26	1967	0	1967	
Miriam Makeba Female Vocalist, Real Name Zensi B: 4 Mar 1932 In Johannesburg, South Africa							
1	Pata Pata		0	1967	12	1967	(Reprise 0606)
Miss X Female Vocalist, Real Name Joice Blair from the UK							
1	Christine	(EMBER 5 175)	37	1963	0	1963	
Mission Male Vocal/Instrumental Group from the UK							
1	Serpents Kiss	(Chapter 22 CHAP 6)	70	1986	0	1986	
2	Garden Of Delight / Like A Hurricane	(Chapter 22 CHAP 7)	50	1986	0	1986	
3	Stay With Me	(Mercury MYTH 1)	30	1986	0	1986	
4	Wasteland	(Mercury MYTH 2)	11	1987	0	1987	
5	Severina	(Mercury MYTH 3)	25	1987	0	1987	
6	Tower Of Strength	(MercuryMYTH 4)	12	1988	0	1988	
7	Beyond The Pale	(Mercury MYTH 6)	32	1988	0	1988	
8	Butterfly On A Wheel	(Mercury MYTH 8)	12	1990	0	1990	
9	Deliverance	(MercuryMYTH 9)	27	1990	0	1990	
10	Into The Blue	(Mercury MYTH 10)	32	1990	0	1990	
11	Hands Across The Ocean	(Mercury MYTH 11)	28	1990	0	1990	
12	Never Again	(Mercury MYTH 12)	34	1992	0	1992	
13	Like A Child Again	(Mercury MYTH 13)	30	1992	0	1992	
14	Shades Of Green	(Mercury MYTH 14)	49	1992	0	1992	
15	Tower Of Strength (Re-Mix)	(Vertigo MYTCD 15)	53	1994	0	1994	
16	Afterglow	(Vertigo MYTCD 16)	53	1994	0	1994	
17	Swoon	(Neverland HOOKCD 002)	73	1995	0	1995	
Mista E Male Producer from the UK, Real Name Damon Rochort							
1	Don't Believe The Hype	(Urban URB 28)	41	1988	0	1988	
Mistura Male Instrumental Group With Lloyd Michels On Trumpet, from the UK							
1	The Flasher	(Route RT 30	23	1976	0	1976	
Misty Morgan See Jack Blanchard							

ISSUE	TITLE	UK LBL	UK POS	UK YEAR	US POS	US YEAR	US LBL
Misty Oldland	Female Vocalist from the UK						
1	Got Me A Feeling	(Columbia 6597872)	59	1993	0	1993	
2	A Fair Affair (Je T'aime)	(Columbia 6601612)	49	1994	0	1994	
3	I Wrote You A Song	(Columbia 6603732)	73	1994	0	1994	
Mitch Miller & His Orchestra	Male Orchestra Leader, B: 4 Jul 1916 Rochester, New York						
1	Tzena, Tzena, Tzena		0	1950	3	1950	(Columbia 38885)
2	Meet Mister Callaghan		0	1952	23	1952	(Columbia 39851)
3	Without My Lover		0	1953	25	1953	(Columbia 39901)
4	Under Paris Skies		0	1953	26	1953	(Columbia 40100)
5	Napoleon		0	1954	25	1954	(Columbia 40261)
* 6	The Yellow Rose Of Texas	(Philips PB 505)	2	1955	1	1955	(Columbia 40540)
7	Lisbon Antigua (In Old Lisbon)		0	1956	19	1956	(Columbia 40635)
8	Theme Song From *Song For A Summer Night*		0	1956	8	1956	(Columbia 40730)
* 9	March From The River Kwai And Colonel Bogey		0	1958	20	1958	(Columbia 41066)
10	The Children's Marching Song		0	1959	16	1959	(Columbia 41317)
Mitch Ryder & The Detroit Wheels	Male Vocalist With Male Instrumental Group from the USA						
* 1	Jenny Take A Ride! (Medley)	(StateSIDE SS 481)	44	1966	10	1966	(New Voice806)
2	Jenny Take A Ride! (Medley) (Re-Entry)	(Stateside SS 481)	33	1966	0	1966	
3	Little Latin Lupe Lu		0	1966	17	1966	(New Voice 808)
4	Devil With A Blue Dress On / Good Golly Miss Molly		0	1966	4	1966	(New Voice 817)
5	Sock It To Me-Baby!		0	1967	6	1967	(New Voice 820)
6	Too Many Fish In The Sea / Three Little Fishes		0	1967	24	1967	(New Voice 822)
7	What Now My Love		0	1967	30	1967	(DYNO VOICE 901)
	REAL NAME WILLIAM LEVISE B: 26 FEB 1945 DETROIT,						
Mitchell Torok	Male Vocalist, B: 28 Oct 1929 Houston, First Recorded In 1948						
1	Caribbean		0	1953	26	1953	(ABBOTT 140)
! 2	Hootchy Kootchy Henry (From *Hawaii*)		0	1954	9	1954	(Abbott 150)
3	When Mexico Gave Up The Rhumba	(Brunswick 05586)	6	1956	0	1956	
4	Red Light Green Light	(Brunswick 05626)	29	1957	0	1957	
5	When Mexico Gave Up The Rhumba (Re-Entry)	(Brunswick 05586)	30	1957	0	1957	
6	Pledge Of Love		0	1957	25	1957	(Decca 30230)
7	Caribbean (Re-Issue)		0	1959	27	1959	(GUYDEN 2018)
Mix Factory	Mixed Vocal/Instrumental Group from the UK						
1	Take Me Away (Paradise)	(All Around The World Cdglobe 120)	51	1993	0	1993	
Mixmaster	Male Producer, Real Name Daniele Daroli from Italy						
1	Grand Piano	(BCM BCM 344)	9	1989	0	1989	
Mixmasters	See U.K. Mixmasters						
Mixtures	Male Vocal/Instrumental Group From Australia						
1	The Push Bike Song	(Polydor 2058 083)	2	1971	0	1971	
MN8	Male Vocal Group from the UK/Trinidad						
1	I've Got A Little Something For You	(Columbia 6608802)	2	1995	0	1995	
2	If You Only Let Me In	(Columbia 6613252)	6	1995	0	1995	
3	Happy	(Columbia 6622192)	8	1995	0	1995	
4	Baby It's You	(Columbia 6624522)	22	1995	0	1995	
5	Baby It's You (Re-Entry)	(Columbia 6624522)	59	1996	0	1996	
6	Pathway To The Moon	(Columbia 6629212)	25	1996	0	1996	
7	Tuff Act To Follow	(Columbia 6635345)	15	1996	0	1996	
8	Dreaming	(Columbia 6638302)	21	1996	0	1996	
Mobiles	Mixed Vocal/Instrumental Group from the UK						
1	Drowning In Berlin	(RIALTO RIA 3)	9	1982	0	1982	
2	Amour Amour	(RIALTO RIA 5)	45	1982	0	1982	
Moby	Male Producer, Real Name Richard Hall from the USA						
1	Go	(Outer Rhythm Foot 15)	46	1991	0	1991	
2	Go (Re-Entry)	(Outer Rhythm Foot15)	10	1991	0	1991	
3	I Feel It	(EQUINOX AXISCD 001)	38	1993	0	1993	
4	Move	(Mute CDMute158)	21	1993	0	1993	
5	Hymn	(Mute CDMute161)	31	1994	0	1994	
6	Feeling So Real	(Mute CDMute173)	30	1994	0	1994	
7	Everytime You Touch Me	(Mute CDMute176)	28	1995	0	1995	
8	Into The Blue	(Mute CDMute179A)	34	1995	0	1995	

ISSUE	TITLE	UK LBL	UK POS	UK YEAR	US POS	US YEAR	US LBL
9	That's When I Reach For My Revolver	(Mute CDMute184)	50	1996	0	1996	

Mocedades Spanish Sextet from Bilbao with Sisters Izaskum & Amaya Amezaga

1	Eres Tu (Touch The Wind)		0	1974	9	1974	(TARA 100)

Mock Turtles Male Vocal/Instrumental Group from the UK

1	And Then She Smiles	(Siren SRN 139)	44	1991	0	1991	
2	Can You Dig It	(Siren SRN 136)	18	1991	0	1991	

Models Lead Vocals from Australian Quintet are by Sean Kelly & James Freud

1	Out Of Mind Out Of Sight		0	1986	37	1986	(Geffen 28762)

Modern Romance Male Vocal/Instrumental Group from the UK

1	Everybody Salsa	(WEA K 18815)	12	1981	0	1981	
2	Ay Ay Ay Ay Moosey	(WEA K 18883)	10	1981	0	1981	
3	Queen Of The Rapping Scene	(WEA K 18928)	37	1982	0	1982	
4	Cherry Pink And Apple Blossom White	(WEA K 19245)	15	1982	0	1982	
5	Best Years Of Our Lifes	(WEA ROM 1)	4	1982	0	1982	
6	High Life	(WEA ROM 2)	8	1983	0	1983	
7	Don't Stop That Crazy Rhythm	(WEA ROM 3)	14	1983	0	1983	
8	Walking In The Rain	(WEA X 9733)	7	1983	0	1983	
	HIT 4 IS CREDITED TO MODERN ROMANCE FEATURING JOHN DU PREZ						

Modern Talking Male Vocal/Instrumental Duo from Germany

1	You're My Heart, You're My Soul	(Magnet MAG 277)	69	1986	0	1986	
2	You're My Heart, You're My Soul (Re-Entry)	(Magnet MAG 277)	56	1985	0	1985	
3	You Can Win If You Want	(Magnet MAG 282)	70	1985	0	1985	
4	Brother Louie	(RCA PB 40875)	4	1986	0	1986	
5	Atlantis Is Calling	(RCA PB 40969)	55	1986	0	1986	

Modettes Female Vocal/Instrumental Group from the UK

1	Paint It Black	(Deram DET-R 1)	42	1980	0	1980	
2	Tonight	(Deram DET 3)	68	1981	0	1981	

Moe Koffman Quartett Male Flautist, B: 28 Dec 1928 Toronto, Canada

1	Swingin' Shepherd Blues	(London HLJ 8549)	23	1958	23	1958	(Jubilee 5311)

Mohawks Male Vocal/Instrumental Group from Jamaica

1	The Champ	(Pama PM 1)	58	1987	0	1987	

Moira Anderson Female Vocalist from the UK

1	Holy City	(Decca F 12989)	43	1969	0	1969	

Moist Male Vocal/Instrumental Group from Canada

1	Push	(Chrysalis CDCHS 5016)	20	1994	0	1994	
2	Silver	(Chrysalis CDCHS 5019)	50	1995	0	1995	
3	Freaky Be Beautiful	(Chrysalis CDCHS 5022)	47	1995	0	1995	
4	Push (Re-Issue)	(Chrysalis CDCHS 5024)	20	1995	0	1995	

Mojo Male Instrumental Group from the UK

1	Dance On	(Creole CR 17)	70	1981	0	1981	

Mojo Men Originally Known As Sly & The Mojo Men, Members Paul Curcio, Jimmy Alalmo, Don Metchick & Dennis De-Carr

1	Sit Down, I Think I Love You		0	1967	36	1967	(Reprise 0539)

Mojos Male Vocal/Instrumental Group from the UK

1	Everything's Al'right	(Decca F 11853)	9	1964	0	1964	
2	Why Not Tonight	(Decca F 11918)	25	1964	0	1964	
3	Seven Daffodils	(Decca F 11959)	30	1964	0	1964	

Mokenstef Female Vocal Trio from Los Angeles

*	1	He's Mine	(DEF JAM DEFCD 13)	70	1995	7	1995	(Outburst 851704)

Molly Bee Female Vocalist from the USA

1	I Saw Mommy Kissing Santa Claus		0	1953	19	1953	(Capitol 2285)

Molly Half Head Male Vocal/Instrumental Group from the UK

1	Shine	(Columbia 6620732)	73	1995	0	1995	

Moloko Mixed Vocal/Instrumental Duo from the UK/Ireland

1	Dominoid	(ECHO ECSCD 016)	65	1996	0	1996	
2	Fun For Me	(ECHO ECSCD 20)	36	1996	0	1996	

ISSUE	TITLE	UK LBL	UK POS	UK YEAR	US POS	US YEAR	US LBL
Moments	Male Vocal Group from the USA						
* 1	Love On A Two-Way Street		0	1970	3	1970	(STANG 5012)
2	Sexy Mama		0	1974	17	1974	(STANG 5052)
3	Girls	(All Platinum 6146 302)	3	1975	0	1975	
4	Dolly My Love	(All Platinum 6146 306)	10	1975	0	1975	
5	Look At Me (I'm In Love)	(All Platinum 6146 309)	42	1975	39	1975	(STANG 5060)
6	Jack In The Box	(All Platinum 6146 318)	7	1977	0	1977	
7	Special Lady		0	1980	5	1980	(Polydor 2033)
Moms Mabley	Female Actress/Comedienne, Real Name Loretta Mary Aiken B: 19 Mar 1894 North Carolina						
1	Abraham, Martin And John		0	1969	35	1969	(Mercury 72935)
	OBITUARY: D: 23 MAY 1975.						
Mondo Kane	Male Vocal/Instrumental Group from the UK						
1	New York Afternoon	(LISSON DOLE 2)	70	1986	0	1986	
Mone'	Female Vocalist from the USA						
1	We Can Make It	(A&M 5811592)	64	1995	0	1995	
2	Movin'	(AM:PM 5814392)	48	1996	0	1996	
Mongo Santamaria	Real Name Ramon Santamaria B: 7 Apr 1922 Havana, Cuba						
1	Watermelon Man		0	1963	10	1963	(Battle 45909)
2	Cloud Nine		0	1969	32	1969	(Columbia 44740)
Monica	Female Vocalist from Atlanta, Real Name Monica Arnold B: 24 Oct 1980						
* 1	Don't Take It Personal (Just One Of Dem Days)	(Arista 74321301452)	32	1995	2	1995	(ROWDY 35040)
* 2	Before You Walk Out Of My Life	(Arista 74321374042)	22	1996	7	1995	(Rowdy 35052)
3	Like This And Like That	(Arista 74321344222)	33	1996	7	1995	(Rowdy 25052)
4	Why I Love You So Much / Ain't Nobody		0	1996	9	1996	(Arista 3-5072)
5	For You I Will (From *Space Jam*)	(Atlantic 5437CD)A	27	1997	4	1997	(Atlantic 87003)
Monica Lewis	Female Vocalist/Actress from the USA						
1	Midnight Masquerade		0	1947	16	1947	(Signature 15078)
2	A Tree In The Meadow		0	1948	21	1948	(Decca 24411)
Monie Love	Female Rapper, Real Name Simone Wilson B: 1971						
1	I Can Do This	(Cooltempo Cool 117)	37	1989	0	1989	
2	Grandpa's Party	(Cooltempo Cool 184)	16	1989	0	1989	
3	Monie In The Middle	(Cooltempocool 210)	46	1990	0	1990	
4	It's A Shame (My Sister)	(Cooltempo Cool 219)	12	1990	26	1990	(Warner Bros. 19515)
5	Down To Earth	(Cooltempo Cool 222)	31	1990	0	1990	
6	Ring My Bell	(Cooltempo Cool 224)	20	1991	0	1991	
7	Full Term Love	(Cooltempo Cool 258)	34	1992	0	1992	
8	Born 2 B.R.E.E.D.	(Cooltempo Cdcool 269)	18	1993	0	1993	
9	In A Word Or 2 - The Power	(Cooltempo Cdcool 273)	33	1993	0	1993	
10	Never Give Up	(COOLTEMPOCDCOOL 276)	41	1993	0	1993	
Monkees	Male Vocal/Instrumental Group from the USA/UK Names: Mickey Dolenz, Peter Tork, Robert Nesmith & David Jones						
* 1	Last Train To Clarksville	(RCA 1547)	23	1967	1	1966	(Colgems 1001)
* 2	I'm A Believer	(RCA 1560)	1	1967	1	1966	(Colgems 1002)
3	I'm Not Your Stepping Stone		0	1966	20	1966	(Colgems 1002)
* 4	A Little Bit Me A Little Bit You	(RCA 1580)	3	1967	2	1967	(Colgems 1004)
5	The Girl I Knew Somewhere		0	1967	39	1967	(Colgems 1004)
6	Alternative Title	(RCA 1604)	2	1967	0	1967	
* 7	Pleasant Valley Sunday	(RCA 1620)	11	1967	3	1967	(Colgems 1007)
8	Words		0	1967	9	1967	(Colgems 1007)
* 9	Daydream Believer	(RCA 1645)	5	1967	1	1967	(Colgems 1012)
* 10	Valleri	(RCA 1673)	12	1967	3	1968	(Colgems 1019)
11	Tapioca Tundra		0	1968	34	1968	(Colgems 1019)
12	D.W. Washburn	(RCA 1706)	17	1968	19	1968	(Colgems 1023)
13	Teardrop City	(RCA 1802)	46	1969	0	1969	
14	Someday Man	(RCA 1824)	47	1969	0	1969	
15	The Monkees (EP)	(Arista ARIST 326)	33	1980	0	1980	
16	That Was Then, This Is Now	(Arista ARIST 673)	68	1986	20	1986	(Arista 9505)
17	The Monkeeys (EP)	(Arista 112157)	62	1989	0	1989	
	HIT 16 IS CREDITED TO MICKY DOLENZ & PETER TORK OF THE MONKEES • THE GROUP DISBANDED IN 1969 ONLY TO REFORM IN 1986 WITHOUT NESMITH						
Monks	This is Hudson-Ford under a different name						
1	Nice Legs Shame About Her Face	(Carrere CAR 104)	19	1979	0	1979	
Monotones	Lead Singer With The Group Is Charles Patrick						
1	Book Of Love		0	1958	5	1958	(ARGO 5290)

ISSUE	TITLE	UK LBL	UK POS	UK YEAR	US POS	US YEAR	US LBL
Monsoon	Mixed Vocal/Instrumental Group from the UK						
1	Ever So Lonely	(Mobile Soup Corp 2)	12	1982	0	1982	
2	Shakti	(Mobile Soup Corp 4)	41	1983	0	1983	
Monster Magnet	Male Vocal/Instrumental Group from the UK						
1	Twin Earth	(A&M 5802812)	67	1993	0	1993	
2	Negasonic Teenage Warhead	(A&M 5809812)	49	1995	0	1995	
3	Dopes To Infinity	(A&M 5810332)	58	1995	0	1995	
Montana Sextet	Mixed Vocal/Instrumental Group from the USA						
1	Heavy Vibes	(Virgin VS 560)	59	1983	0	1983	
Montell Jordan	Male Vocalist from the USA						
1	This Is How We Do It	(DEF JAM DEFCD 07)	11	1995	0	1995	
2	Somethin' 4 Da Honeyz	(DEF JAM DEFCD 10)	15	1995	0	1995	
3	I Like (From *The Nutty Professor*)	(DEF JAM DEFCD19)	24	1996	28	1996	(Mercury 575046)
4	Falling		0	1996	18	1996	(Mercury 575648)
5	What's On Tonight		0	1997	21	1997	(DEF JAM 574032)
	HIT 3 IS CREDITED TO MONTELL JORDAN FEATURING SLICK RICK						
Montrose	Male Vocal/Instrumental Group from the UK						
1	Space Station No 5 / Good Rockin' Tonight	(WB HM 9)	71	1980	0	1980	
Monty Kelly Orchestra	Male Arranger/Instrumentalist (Trumpet), B: 1919 And Hails From Oakland						
1	Tropicana		0	1953	19	1953	(Essex 325)
2	Three O'Clock In The Morning		0	1953	21	1953	(Essex 328)
3	Summer Set		0	1960	30	1960	(Carlton 527)
Monty Python	Male Comedy Group from the UK						
1	Always Look On The Bright Side Of Life	(Virgin PYTH 1)	3	1991	0	1991	
Monyaka	Male Vocal/Instrumental Group from the USA/Jamaica						
1	Go Deh Yaka (Go To The Top)	(Polydor POSP 641)	14	1983	0	1983	
Mood	Male Vocal/Instrumental Group from the UK						
1	Don't Stop	(RCA 171)	59	1982	0	1982	
2	Paris Is One Day Away	(RCA 211)	42	1982	0	1982	
3	Passion In Dark Rooms	(RCA 276)	74	1982	0	1982	
Moodswings (Featuring) Chrissie Hynde	Mixed Vocal/Instrumental Group from the USA/UK						
1	Spiritual High (State Of Independance)	(Arista 114528)	66	1991	0	1991	
2	Spiritual High (Re-Issue)	(Arista74321127712)	47	1993	0	1993	
Moody Blues	Male Vocal/Instrumental Group from the UK Names: Ray Thomas, Denny Laine, Mike Pinder, Clint Warwick & Graeme Edge						
* 1	Go Now	(Decca F 12022)	1	1964	10	1965	(London 9726)
2	I Don't Want To Go On Without You	(Decca F 12095)	33	1965	0	1965	
3	From The Bottom Of My Heart	(Decca F 12166)	22	1965	0	1965	
4	Everyday	(Decca F 12266)	44	1965	0	1965	
5	Nights In White Satin	(DERAM DM 161)	19	1967	0	1967	
6	Voices In The Sky	(DERAM DM 196)	27	1968	0	1968	
7	Tuesday Afternoon (Forever Afternoon)		0	1968	24	1968	(DERAM 85028)
8	Ride My See-Saw	(DERAM DM 213)	42	1968	0	1968	
9	Question	(Threshold TH 4)	2	1970	21	1970	(Threshold 67004)
10	The Story In Your Eyes		0	1971	23	1971	(Threshold 67006)
11	Isn't Life Strange	(Threshold TH	13	1972	29	1972	(Threshold 67009)
* 12	Nights In White Satin (Re-Entry)	(DERAM DM 161)	9	1972	2	1972	(DERAM 85023)
13	I'm Just A Singer (In A Rock And Roll Band)	(Threshold TH 13)	36	1973	12	1973	(Threshold 67012)
14	Steppin' In A Slide Zone		0	1978	39	1978	(London 270)
15	Nights In White Satin (2nd Re-Entry)	(DERAM DM 161)	14	1979	0	1979	
16	Gemini Dream		0	1981	7	1981	(Threshold 601)
17	The Voice		0	1981	15	1981	(Threshold 602)
18	Blue World	(Threshold TH 30)	35	1983	0	1983	
19	Sitting At The Wheel		0	1983	27	1983	(Threshold 604)
20	Your Wildest Dreams		0	1986	9	1986	(Polydor 883906)
21	I Know You're Out There Somewhere	(Polydor POSP 921)	52	1988	30	1988	(Polydor 887600)
Moon Martin	Real Name John Martin Oklahoma, Played Lead Guitarist for Southwind						
1	Rolene		0	1979	30	1979	(Capitol 4765)
Moon Mullican	Male Country Singer, Real Name Aubrey Mullican B: 29 Mar 1909 Polk County, Texas.						
1	New Pretty Blonde (Jole Blon)		0	1947	21	1947	(KING 578)
* 4	I'll Sail My Ship Alone		0	1950	17	1950	(KING 830)

HIT 1 IS CREDITED TO MOON MULLICAN & THE SHOWBOYS • OBITUARY : D: 1 JAN 1967, HEAR ATTACK (AGED 57).

ISSUE	TITLE	UK LBL	UK POS	UK YEAR	US POS	US YEAR	US LBL
Moonglows Names Harvey Fuque, Bobby Lester, Billy Johnson, Alex Graves & Prentiss Barnes							
1	Sincerely		0	1955	20	1955	(CHESS 1581)
+ 2	Most Of All		0	1955	11	1955	(CHESS 1589)
3	See Saw		0	1956	25	1956	(CHESS 1629)
4	Ten Commandments Of Love		0	1958	22	1958	(CHESS 1705)
	HIT 4 IS CREDITED TO HARVEY & THE MOONGLOWS • OBITUARY: BOBBY D: 15 OCT 1980 CANCER.						
Moontrekkers Male Instrumental Group from the UK							
1	Night Of The Vampire	(Parlophone R 4814)	50	1961	0	1961	
Moran & Mack Humorous Duologues On 10 Disks							
* 1	Two Black Crows		0	1926	0	1926	
Morcheeba Mixed Vocal/Instrumental Group from the UK							
1	Tape Loop	(INDOCHINA ID 045CD)	42	1996	0	1996	
2	Trigger Hippie	(INDOCHINA ID 052CD)	40	1996	0	1996	
3	The Music That We Hear (Moog Island)	(INDOCHINA ID 054CD)	47	1997	0	1997	
More Male Vocal/Instrumental Group from the UK							
1	We Are The Band	(Atlantic K 11561)	59	1981	0	1981	
Mormon Tabernacle Choir Hit was sung by a huge gathering directed by Richard Condie							
1	Battle Hymn Of The Republic		0	1959	13	1959	(Columbia 41459)
Morris Albert Male Vocalist from Brazil, Full Name Morris Albert Kaisermann							
* 1	Feelings	(Decca F 13591)	4	1975	6	1975	(RCA 1027)
Morris Day B: Springfield, Illinois, Leader Of Prince's Backing Group The Time							
1	Fishnet		0	1988	23	1988	(Warner Bros. 28201)
Morris Minor & The Majors Male Vocal Group from the UK							
1	Stutter Rap (No Sleep 'Til Bedtime)	(10 TEN 203)	4	1987	0	1987	
Morris Stoloff Male Orchestra Leader, B: 1 Aug 1898 Philadelphia							
* 1	Moonglow /Theme From *Picnic*	(Brunswick 05553)	7	1956	1	1956	(Decca 29888)
	OBITUARY: D: 16 APR 1980.						
Morrissey Male Vocalist from the UK							
1	Suedehead	(HMV POP 1618)	5	1988	0	1988	
2	Everyday Is Like Sunday	(HMV POP 1619)	9	1988	0	1988	
3	Last Of The Famous International Playboys	(HMV POP 1620)	6	1989	0	1989	
4	Interesting Drug	(HMV POP 1621)	9	1989	0	1989	
5	Ouija Board Ouija Board	(HMV POP 1622)	18	1989	0	1989	
6	November Spawned A Monster	(HMV POP 1623)	12	1990	0	1990	
7	Piccadilly Palare	(HMV POP 1624)	18	1990	0	1990	
8	Our Frank	(HMV POP 1625)	26	1991	0	1991	
9	Sing Your Life	(HMV POP 1626)	33	1991	0	1991	
10	Pregnant For The Last Time	(HMV POP 1627)	25	1991	0	1991	
11	My Love Life	(HMV POP 1628)	29	1991	0	1991	
12	We Hate It When Our Friends Become Successful	(HMV POP 1629)	17	1992	0	1992	
13	You're The One For Me, Fatty	(HMV POP 1630)	19	1992	0	1992	
14	Certain People I Know	(HMV POP 1631)	35	1992	0	1992	
15	The More You Ignore Me, The Closer I Get	(Parlophone CDR 6372)	8	1994	0	1994	
16	Hold On To Your Friends	(Parlophone CDR 6383)	47	1994	0	1994	
17	Interlude	(Parlophone CDR 6365)	25	1994	0	1994	
18	Boxers	(Parlophone CDR 6400)	23	1995	0	1995	
19	Dagenham Dave	(RCA Victor 74321299802)	26	1995	0	1995	
20	The Boy Racer	(RCA Victor 74321332952)	36	1995	0	1995	
21	Sunny	(Parlophone CDR 6243)	42	1995	0	1995	
22	Alma Matters	(Island CID 667)	16	1997	0	1997	
	HIT 17 IS CREDITED TO MORRISSEY AND SIOUXSIE						
Morten Harket Male Vocalist from Norway							
1	A Kind Of Christmas Card	(Warner Bros. W 0304C)	53	1995	0	1995	
Mory Kante Male Vocalist from Guinea							
1	Yeke Yeke	(London LON 171)	29	1988	0	1988	
2	Yeke Yeke (Re-Mix)	(FFRREEDOM TABCD 226)	25	1995	0	1995	
3	Yeke Yeke (2nd Re-Mix)	(FFRR FCD 288)	28	1996	0	1996	

Motels Mixed Vocal/Instrumental Group from the USA/UK

	TITLE	UK LBL	UK POS	UK YEAR	US POS	US YEAR	US LBL
1	Whose Problem	(Capitol CL 16162)	42	1980	0	1980	
2	Days Are O.K.	(Capitol CL 16149)	41	1981	0	1981	
3	Only The Lonely		0	1982	9	1982	(Capitol 5114)
4	Suddenly Last Summer		0	1983	9	1983	(Capitol 5271)
5	Remember The Nights		0	1984	36	1984	(Capitol 5246)
6	Shame		0	1985	21	1985	(Capitol 6497)

LEAD SINGER WITH THE QUINTET IS MARTHA DAVIS • THE GROUP DISBANDED FOR THE SECOND TIME IN 1987

Mother Male Production/Instrumental Duo from the UK

	TITLE	UK LBL	UK POS	UK YEAR	US POS	US YEAR	US LBL
1	All Funked Up	(BOSTING BYSNCD 101)	34	1993	0	1993	
2	Get Back	(SIX6 SIXT 119)	73	1994	0	1994	
3	All Funked Up (Re-Mix)	(SIX6 SIXX CD1)	66	1996	0	1996	

Motherlode Quartet from Canada Led By William Smith

	TITLE	UK LBL	UK POS	UK YEAR	US POS	US YEAR	US LBL
1	When I Die		0	1969	18	1969	(Buddah 131)

Motiv 8 Male Producer, Real Name Steve Rodway from the UK

	TITLE	UK LBL	UK POS	UK YEAR	US POS	US YEAR	US LBL
1	Rockin' For Myself	(NUFF RESPECT NUFF 002CD)	67	1993	0	1993	
2	Rockin' For Myself (Re-Mix)	(WWA YZ 814CD)	18	1994	0	1994	
3	Break The Chain	(WEA WEA 010CD)	31	1995	0	1995	
4	Searching For The Golden Eye	(WEA WEA 027CD)	40	1995	0	1995	

Motley Crue Hard-Rock Quartet from Los Angeles

	TITLE	UK LBL	UK POS	UK YEAR	US POS	US YEAR	US LBL
1	Smokin' In The Boys Room	(Elektra EKR 16)	71	1985	16	1985	(Elektra 69625)
2	Home Sweet Home / Smokin' In The Boys Room	(Elektra EKR 33)	51	1985	0	1985	
3	Girls, Girls, Girls	(Elektra EKR 59)	26	1987	12	1987	(Elektra 69465)
4	You're All I Need	(Elektra EKR 65)	23	1988	0	1988	
5	Wild Side	(Elektra EKR 65)	26	1988	0	1988	
* 6	Dr. Feelgood	(Elektra EKR 97)	50	1989	6	1989	(Elektra 69271)
7	Kickstart My Heart		0	1990	27	1990	(Elektra 69248)
8	Without You	(Elektra EKR 109)	39	1990	8	1990	(Elektra 64985)
9	Don't Go Away Mad (Just Go Away)		0	1990	19	1990	(Elektra 64962)
10	Primal Scream	(Elektra EKR 133)	32	1991	0	1991	
11	Home Sweet Home (Re-Mix)	(Elektra EKR 136)	37	1992	37	1992	(Elektra 64818)
12	Hooligan's Holiday	(Elektra EKR 180CDX)	36	1994	0	1994	
13	Afraid	(Elektra E3936 CD)	58	1997	0	1997	

Motorhead Male Vocal/Instrumental Group from the UK

	TITLE	UK LBL	UK POS	UK YEAR	US POS	US YEAR	US LBL
1	Louie Louie	(BRONZE BRO 60)	75	1978	0	1978	
2	Louie Louie (Re-Entry)	(BRONZE BRO 60)	68	1978	0	1978	
3	Overkill	(BRONZE BRO 67)	39	1979	0	1979	
4	Overkill (Re-Entry)	(BRONZE BRO67)	57	1979	0	1979	
5	No Class	(BRONZE BRO 78)	61	1979	0	1979	
6	Bomber	(BRONZE BRO 85)	34	1979	0	1979	
7	The Golden Years (EP)	(BRONZE BRO 92)	8	1980	0	1980	
8	Ace Of Spades	(BRONZE BRO 1106)	5	1980	0	1980	
9	Beer Drinkers And Hell Raisers	(BIG BEAT SWT 61)	43	1980	0	1980	
10	St. Valentine's Day Massacre (EP)	(BRONZE BRO 116)	5	1981	0	1981	
11	Motorhead (Live)	(BRONZE BRO 124)	6	1981	0	1981	
12	Iron Fist	(BRONZE BRO 146)	29	1982	0	1982	
13	I Got Mine	(BRONZE BRO 165)	46	1983	0	1983	
14	Shine	(BRONZE BRO 167)	59	1983	0	1983	
15	Killed By Death	(BRONZE BRO 185)	51	1984	0	1984	
16	Deaf Forever	(GWR GWR 2)	67	1986	0	1986	
17	The One To Sing The Blues	(Epic 6565787)	45	1991	0	1991	
18	'92 Tour (EP)	(Epic 6588096)	63	1992	0	1992	
19	Ace Of Spades (Re-Mix)	(WGAF CDWGAF 101)	23	1993	0	1993	
20	Born To Raise Hell	(FOX 74321230152)	47	1994	0	1994	

HIT 10 IS CREDITED TO MOTORHEAD AND GIRLSCHOOL • HIT 20 IS CREDITED TO MOTORHEAD/ICE-T/WHITFIELD CRANE

Motors Male Vocal/Instrumental Group from the UK

	TITLE	UK LBL	UK POS	UK YEAR	US POS	US YEAR	US LBL
1	Dancing The Night Away	(Virgin VS 186)	42	1977	0	1977	
2	Airport	(Virgin VS 219)	4	1978	0	1978	
3	Forget About You	(Virgin VS 222)	13	1978	0	1978	
4	Love And Loneliness	(Virgin VS 263)	58	1980	0	1980	

Mott The Hoople British Rock Group With Lead Singer Ian Hunter

	TITLE	UK LBL	UK POS	UK YEAR	US POS	US YEAR	US LBL
1	All The Young Dudes	(CBS 8271)	3	1972	37	1972	(Columbia 45673)
2	Honaloochie Boogie	(CBS 1530)	12	1973	0	1973	

ISSUE	TITLE	UK LBL	UK POS	UK YEAR	US POS	US YEAR	US LBL
3	All The Way From Memphis	(CBS 1764)	10	1973	0	1973	
4	Roll Away The Stone	(CBS 1895)	8	1973	0	1973	
5	The Golden Age Of Rock 'N' Roll	(CBS 2177)	16	1974	0	1974	
6	Foxy Foxy	(CBS 2439)	33	1974	0	1974	
7	Saturday Gigs	(CBS 2754)	41	1974	0	1974	

Mountain New York Based Rock Group With Leslie Weinstein & Felix Pappalardi

1	Mississippi Queen		0	1970	21	1970	(WINDFALL 532)

OBITUARY: FELIX D: 17 APR 1983 MURDERED (SHOT) IN NEW YORK.

Mouth & MacNeal Names Willem Duyn & Sjoukje Vant Spijker From Holland

* 1	How Do You Do		0	1972	8	1972	(Philips 40715)
2	I See A Star	(Decca F 13504)	8	1974	0	1974	

Move Male Vocal/Instrumental Group, Carl Wanyne, Roy Wood, Trevor Burton, Chris Kefford & Bev Bevan

1	Night Of Fear	(DERAM DM 109)	2	1967	0	1967	
2	I Can Hear The Grass Grow	(DERAM DM 117)	5	1967	0	1967	
3	Flowers In The Rain	(Regal Zonophone RZ3001)	2	1967	0	1967	
4	Fire Brigade	(Regal Zonophone RZ3005)	3	1968	0	1968	
5	Blackberry Way	(Regal Zonophone RZ3015)	1	1968	0	1968	
6	Curly	(Regal Zonophone RZ3021)	12	1969	0	1969	
7	Brontosaurus	(Regal Zonophone RZ3026)	7	1970	0	1970	
8	Tonight	(Harvest HAR 5038)	11	1971	0	1971	
9	Chinatown	(Harvest HAR 5043)	23	1971	0	1971	
10	California Man	(Harvest HAR 5050)	7	1972	0	1972	

Movement Male Vocal/Instrumental Group from the UK

1	Jump	(Arista 74321116677)	57	1992	0	1992	

Movement 98 Mixed Vocal/Instrumental Group from the UK

1	Joy And Heartbreak	(CIRCA YR 45)	27	1990	0	1990	
2	Sunrise	(CIRCA YR 51)	58	1990	0	1990	

Hits 1-2 Are Credited To Movement 98 Featuring Carroll Thompson

Movin' Melodies Male Producer Patrick Prinz From Holland

1	La Luna	(EFFECTIVE EFFS 017CD)	64	1994	0	1994	
2	Indica	(HOOJ CHOONS HOOJCD 44)	62	1996	0	1996	
3	Rollerblade	(MOVIN' MELODIES 5822352)	71	1997	0	1997	

HIT 1 IS CREDITED TO MOVIN' MELODIES PRODUCTION

Moving Pictures Lead Singer In This Australian Six-Man Group Is Alex Smith

1	What About Me		0	1982	29	1982	(Network 69952)
2	What About Me (Re-Entry)		0	1989	46	1989	(Network 69952)

Mozaic Female Vocal Group from the UK

1	Sing It (The Hallelujah Song)	(Perfecto PERF 106CD)	14	1995	0	1995	
2	Rays Of The Rising Sun	(Perfecto PERF 123CD)	32	1996	0	1996	
3	Moving Up Moving On	(Perfecto PERF 131CD)	62	1996	0	1996	

Mr. & Mrs. Smith Mixed Vocal/Instrumental Production Group from the UK

1	Gotta Get Loose	(HOOJ CHOONS HOOJCD 46)	70	1996	0	1996	

Mr. Bean & Smear Campaign Male Comedian, Rowan Atkinson/Vocal/Instrumental Group from the UK

1	(I Want To Be) Elected	(London LON 319)9		1992	0	1992	

HIT IS CREDITED TO MR. BEAN & SMEAR CAMPAIGN FEATURING BRUCE DICKINSON

Mr. Big **(1)** Male Vocal/Instrumental Group from the UK

1	Romeo	(EMI 2567)	4	1977	0	1977	
2	Feel Like Calling Home	(EMI 2610)	35	1977	0	1977	

Mr. Big **(2)** Male Vocal/Instrumental Quartet from the USA

* 1	To Be With You	(Atlantic A 7514)	3	1992	1	1992	(Atlantic 87580)
2	Just Take My Heart	(Atlantic A 7490)	26	1992	16	1992	(Atlantic 87509)
3	Green Tinted Sixties Mind	(Atlantic A 7468)	72	1992	0	1992	
4	Wild World	(Atlantic A 7310CD)	59	1993	27	1993	(Atlantic 87308)

Mr. Blobby Male Vocalist from the UK

1	Mr. Blobby	(DESTINY MUSIC CDDMUS 104)	1	1993	0	1993	
2	Christmas In Blobbyland	(DESTINY MUSIC DMUSCD 108)	36	1995	0	1995	

Mr. Bloe Male Instrumentalist (Harmonica) from the UK

1	Groovin With Mr. Bloe	(DJM DJS 216)	2	1970	0	1970	

Mr. Fingers Male Producer, Real Name Larry Heard from the USA

1	What About This Love	(FFRR F 131)	74	1990	0	1990	
2	Closer	(MCA MCS 1601)	50	1992	0	1992	

ISSUE	TITLE	UK LBL	UK POS	UK YEAR	US POS	US YEAR	US LBL
3	On My Way	(MCA MCS 1630)	71	1992	0	1992	
Mr. Food	Male Vocalist from the UK						
1	...And That's Before Me Tea!	(TANGIBLE TGB 005)	62	1990	0	1990	
Mr. Goon Bones & Mr. Ford	Male Instrumentalists (Bones & Organ) from the USA						
1	Ain't She Sweet		0	1949	14	1949	(CRYSTALETTE 1803)
Mr. Lee	Male Producer, Real Name Leroy Haggard from the USA						
1	Pump Up London	(BREAKOUT USA 639)	64	1988	0	1988	
2	Get Busy	(JIVE JIVE 231)	71	1989	0	1989	
3	Get Busy (Re-Entry)	(JIVE JIVE 231)	41	1990	0	1990	
Mr. Mister	Male Vocal/Instrumental Group from the USA						
1	Broken Wings	(RCA PB 49945)	4	1985	1	1985	(RCA 14136)
2	Kyrie	(RCA PB 49927)	11	1986	1	1986	(RCA 14258)
3	Is It Love		0	1986	8	1986	(RCA 14313)
4	Something Real (Inside Me / Inside You)		0	1987	29	1987	(RCA 5273)
	VOCALS WITH THIS POP-ROCK QUARTET ARE BY RICHARD PAGE						
Mr. Roy	Male Production/Instrumental Group from the UK						
1	Something About You	(Fresh FRSHT 11)	74	1994	0	1994	
2	Saved	(Fresh FRSHD 21)	24	1995	0	1995	
3	Something About U (Can't Be Beat) (Re-Mix)	(Fresh FRSHD 33)	49	1994	0	1994	
Mr. V	Male Producer, Real Name Rob Villiers from the UK						
1	Give Me Life	(Cheeky CHEKCD 005)	40	1994	0	1994	
Mrs. Mills	Female pianist from the UK						
1	Mrs. Mills Medley	(Parlophone R 4856)	18	1961	0	1961	
Mrs. Wood	Female artist from the UK						
1	Joanna	(React CDREACT 066)	40	1995	0	1995	
2	Heartbreak	(React CDREACT 78)	44	1996	0	1996	
Mtume	Mixed Vocal/Instrumental Group from the USA						
1	Juicy Fruit	(Epic A 3424)	34	1983	0	1983	
2	Prime Time	(Epic A 4720)	57	1984	0	1984	
Mud	Male Vocal/Instrumental Group from the UK, Names: Les Gray, Dave Mount, Rob Davis, Ray Stiles						
1	Crazy	(RAK 146)	12	1973	0	1973	
2	Hypnosis	(RAK 152)	16	1973	0	1973	
3	Dyna-Mite	(RAK 159)	4	1973	0	1973	
* 4	Tiger Feet	(RAK 166)	1	1974	0	1974	
5	The Cat Crept In	(RAK 170)	2	1974	0	1974	
6	Rocket	(RAK 178)	6	1974	0	1974	
7	Lonely This Christmas	(RAK 187)	1	1974	0	1974	
8	The Secrets That You Keep	(RAK 194)	3	1975	0	1975	
9	Oh Boy	(RAK 201)	1	1975	0	1975	
10	Moonshine Sally	(RAK 208)	10	1975	0	1975	
11	One Night	(RAK 213)	32	1975	0	1975	
12	L-L-Lucy	(Private Stock PVT 41)	10	1975	0	1975	
13	Show Me You're A Woman	(Private Stock PVT 45)	8	1975	0	1975	
14	Shake It Down	(Private Stock PVT 65)	12	1976	0	1976	
15	Lean On Me	(Private Stock PVT 85)	7	1976	0	1976	
16	Lonely This Christmas (Re-Entry)	(RAK 187)	61	1985	0	1985	
Muddy Waters	Male Vocal/Guitarist, Real Name McKinley Morganfield B: 1915 In Mississippi.						
1	Mannish Boy	(Epic MUD 1)	51	1988	0	1988	
	OBITUARY : D: 1983 IN CHICAGO.						
Mudhoney	Male Vocal/Instrumental Group from the USA						
1	Let It Slide	(SUBPOP SP 15154)	60	1991	0	1991	
2	Suck You Dry	(Reprise W 0137)	65	1992	0	1992	
Mudlarks	Mixed Vocal Group from the UK						
1	Lollipop	(Columbia DB 4099)	2	1958	0	1958	
2	Book Of Love	(Columbia DB 4133)	8	1958	0	1958	
3	The Love Game	(Columbia DB 4250)	30	1959	0	1959	
Mukkaa	Male Production/Instrumental Duo from the UK						
1	Buruchacca	(Limbo Limbo 008)	74	1993	0	1993	
Mulcays	Male Harmonica Group from the USA						
1	My Happiness		0	1953	26	1953	(CARDINAL 1011)
2	Alabamy Bound		0	1954	24	1954	(CARDINAL 1014)

ISSUE	TITLE	UK LBL	UK POS	UK YEAR	US POS	US YEAR	US LBL
Mundy Male Vocalist from Ireland							
1	To You I Bestow	(Epic MUNDY 1CD)	60	1996	0	1996	
2	Life's A Cinch	(Epic MUNDY 2CD)	75	1996	0	1996	
Mungo Jerry Male Vocal/Instrumental Group from the UK Names: Ray Dorset, Paul King, Colin Earl & Mike Cole							
* 1	In The Summertime	(Dawn DNX 2502)	1	1970	3	1970	(JANUS 125)
2	Baby Jump	(Dawn DNX 2505)	32	1971	0	1971	
3	Baby Jump (Re-Entry)	(Dawn DNX 2505)	1	1971	0	1971	
4	Lady Rose	(Dawn DNX 2510)	5	1971	0	1971	
5	You Don't Have To Be In The Army To Fight In A War	(Dawn DNX 2513)	13	1971	0	1971	
6	Open Up	(Dawn DNX 2514)	21	1972	0	1972	
7	Alright Alright Alright	(Dawn DNS 1037)	3	1973	0	1973	
8	Wild Love	(Dawn DNS 1051)	32	1973	0	1973	
9	Long Legged Woman Dressed In Black	(DAWN DNS 1061)	13	1974	0	1974	
Munich Machine Male Instrumental Duo from Germany							
1	Get On The Funk Train	(OASIS OASIS 2)	41	1977	0	1977	
2	A Whiter Shade Of Pale	(OASIS OASIS 5)	42	1978	0	1978	
Muppets Puppets from the USA, See Also Jim Henson							
1	Halfway Down The Stairs	(PYE 7N 45698)	7	1977	0	1977	
2	The Muppet Show Music Hall (EP)	(PYE 7NX 8004)	19	1977	0	1977	
Muriel Smith Female Vocalist from the UK							
1	Hold Me Thrill Me Kiss Me	(Philips PB 122)	3	1953	0	1953	
Murmaids Names Sally Gordon With Sisters Terry & Carol Fischer							
1	Popsicles And Icicles		0	1963	3	1963	(CHATTAHOOCHE E 628)
Murray Head British Male Vocalist							
1	Superstar (From *Jesus Christ Superstar*)	(MCA MMKS 5077)	47	1972	14	1971	(Decca 32603)
2	One Night In Bangkok (From *Chess*)	(RCA CHESS 1)	12	1984	3	1985	(RCA 13988)
3	One Night In Bangkok (Re-Entry)	(RCA CHESS 1)	74	1985	0	1985	
Music & Mystery The Hit Is Credited To Music And Mystery Featuring Gwen McCrae							
1	All This Love I'm Giving SEE ALSO GWEN MCCRAE	(KTDA CDKTDA 2)	36	1993	0	1993	
Music Explosion Lead Singer With The Quintet Is Jamie Lyons							
* 1	Little Bit O' Soul		0	1967	2	1967	(Laurie3380)
Music Machine Lead Singer With The Quintet Is Sean Bonniwell							
1	Talk Talk		0	1967	15	1967	(Original Sound 61)
Music Relief '94 Mixed Vocal/Instrumental Group from the UK							
1	What's Going On	(Jive RWANDACD 1)	70	1994	0	1994	
Musical Youth Names Dennis Seaton, Michael & Kelvin Grant With Patrick & Junior Waite							
1	Pass The Dutchie	(MCA YOU 1)	1	1982	10	1983	(MCA 52149)
2	Youth Of Today	(MCA YOU 2)	13	1982	0	1982	
3	Pass The Dutchie (Re-Entry)	(MCA YOU 1)	65	1983	0	1983	
4	Never Gonna Give You Up	(MCA YOU 3)	6	1983	0	1983	
5	Heartbreaker	(MCA YOU 4)	44	1983	0	1983	
6	Tell Me Why	(MCA YOU 5)	33	1983	0	1983	
7	007	(MCA YOU 6)	26	1983	0	1983	
8	Sixteen	(MCA YOU 7)	23	1984	0	1984	
	THE HIT 'PASS THE DUTCHIE' IS A CLEAN VERSION OF 'PASS THE KOUCHIE', WHICH MEANS PASS THE JOINT. A DUTCHIE IS A JAMAICAN COOKING POT						
Musique Female Vocalist from the USA							
1	In The Bush	(CBS 6791)	16	1978	0	1978	
MXM Mixed Vocal/Instrumental Group from Italy							
1	Nothing Compares 2 U	(London LON 267)	68	1990	0	1990	
My Bloody Valentine Mixed Vocal/Instrumental Group from the UK							
1	Soon	(CREATION CRE 073)	41	1990	0	1990	
2	To Here Knows When	(CREATION CRE 085)	29	1991	0	1991	
My Life Story Mixed Vocal/Instrumental Group from the UK							
1	12 Reasons Why I Love Her	(ParlophoneCDR 6442)	32	1996	0	1996	
2	Sparkle	(Parlophone CDR 6450)	34	1996	0	1996	
3	The King Of Kissingdom	(Parlophone CDRS 6457)	35	1997	0	1997	

ISSUE	TITLE	UK LBL	UK POS	UK YEAR	US POS	US YEAR	US LBL
4	Strumpet	(Parlophone CDR 6464)	27	1997	0	1997	
5	Duchess	(Parlophone CDR 6474)	39	1997	0	1997	
Mystic Merlin	Male Vocal/Instrumental/Magic Group from the USA						
1	Just Can't Give You Up	(Capitol CL 16133)	20	1980	0	1980	
Mystics	Names: Bob Ferrante, George Galfo, Phil Cracolici, Albee Cracolici & Allie Contrera						
1	Hushabye		0	1959	20	1959	(Laurie 3028)

N

ISSUE	TITLE	UK LBL	UK POS	UK YEAR	US POS	US YEAR	US LBL
N'Dea Davenport See Guru							
N-Joi Production/Instrumental Group from the UK							
1	Anthem	(Deconstruction Pb 44041)	45	1990	0	1990	
2	Adrenalin (EP)	(Deconstruction Pt 44344)	23	1991	0	1991	
3	Anthem (Re-Issue)	(Deconstruction Pb 44445)	8	1991	0	1991	
4	Live In Manchester (Part 1-2)	(Deconstruction Pt 45252)	12	1992	0	1992	
5	The Drumstick (EP)	(Deconstruction 74321154832)	33	1993	0	1993	
6	Papillon	(Deconstruction 74321252132)	70	1994	0	1994	
7	Bad Things	(Deconstruction 74321277292)	57	1995	0	1995	
N-Trance Mixed Vocal/Instrumental Group from the UK							
1	Set You Free	(All Around The World Cdglobe 124)	39	1994	0	1994	
2	Turn Up The Power	(All Around The World Cdglobe 125)	23	1994	0	1994	
3	Set You Free (Re-Mix)	(All Around The Worls Cdglobe 126)	2	1995	0	1995	
4	Stayin Alive	(All Around The World Cdglobe 131)	2	1995	0	1995	
5	Electronic Pleasure	(All Around The World Cdglobe 135)	11	1996	0	1996	
6	D.I.S.C.O.	(All Around The World Cdglobe 153)	11	1997	0	1997	
7	The Mind Of The Machine	(All Around The World Cdglobe 159)	15	1997	0	1997	
N-Tyce							
1	Hey Dj! (Play That Song)	(Telstar Cdstas 2885)	20	1997	0	1997	
2	We Come To Party	(Telstar Cdstas 2915)	12	1997	0	1997	
N.T. Gang Male Vocal/Instrumental Group from Germany							
1	Wam Bam	(Cooltempo Cool 163)	71	1988	0	1988	
N.W.A. Male Rap Group from the USA							
1	Express Yourself	(Fourth & Broadway Brw 144)	50	1989	0	1989	
2	Express Yourself (Re-Entry)	(Fourth & Broadway Brw 144)	26	1990	0	1990	
3	Gangsta, Gangsta	(Fourth & Broadway Brw 191)	70	1990	0	1990	
4	100 Miles And Runnin'	(Fourth & Broadway Brw 200)	38	1990	0	1990	
5	Alwayz Into Somethin'	(Fourth & Broadway Brw 238)	60	1991	0	1991	
N2deep Male Rap Group from California							
* 1	Back To The Hotel		0	1992	14	1992	(Profile 5367)
Naked Eyes Names Peter Byrn & Rob Fisher Who Disbanded In 1984							
1	Always Something There To Remind Me	(RCA 348)	59	1983	8	1983	(EMI America 8155)
2	Promises Promises		0	1983	11	1983	(EMI America 8170)
3	When The Lights Go Out		0	1983	37	1983	(EMI America 8183)
4	(What) In The Name Of Love		0	1984	39	1984	(EMI America 8219)
	SEE ALSO CLIMIE FISHER						
Nana Mouskouri Female Vocalist, B: 10 Oct 1936 Athens, Greece							
* 1	White Rose Of Athens (Weisse Rosen Aus Athen)	(Fontana/Philips)	0	1961	0	1961	
2	Only Love	(Philips Ph 38)	2	1986	0	1986	
Nancy Martinez Female Actress/Vocalist, B: Quebec, Canada							
1	For Tonight		0	1986	32	1986	(Atlantic 89371)
Nancy Nova Female Vocalist from the UK							
1	No No No	(EMI 5328)	63	1982	0	1982	
Nancy Sinatra Female Vocalist, B: 8 Jun 1940, Jersey City, New Jersey							
* 1	These Boots Are Made For Walkin'	(Reprise R 20432)	1	1966	1	1966	(Reprise 0432)
2	How Does That Grab You Darlin'?	(Reprise R 20461)	19	1966	7	1966	(Reprise 0461)
3	Friday's Child		0	1966	36	1966	(Reprise 0491)

ISSUE	TITLE	UK LBL	UK POS	UK YEAR	US POS	US YEAR	US LBL
* 4	Sugar Town	(Reprise Rs 20527)	8	1967	5	1966	(Reprise 0527)
* 5	Somethin' Stupid	(Reprise Rs 23166)	1	1967	1	1967	(Reprise 0561)
6	Love Eyes		0	1967	15	1967	(Reprise 0559)
7	You Only Live Twice	(Reprise Rs 20595)	11	1967	0	1967	
8	Jackson	(Reprise Rs 20595)	11	1967	14	1967	(Reprise 0595)
9	Lightning's Girl		0	1967	24	1967	(Reprise 0620)
10	Lady Bird	(Reprise Rs 20629)	47	1967	20	1967	(Reprise 0629)
11	Some Velvet Morning		0	1968	26	1968	(Reprise 0651)
12	Highway Song	(Reprise Rs 20869)	21	1969	0	1969	
13	Did You Ever	(Reprise Rs 14093)	2	1971	0	1971	

HIT 5 IS CREDITED TO NANCY SINATRA AND FRANK SINATRA • HITS 8,10-11 ARE CREDITED TO NANCY SINATRA AND LEE HAZLEWOOD
HIT 13 IS CREDITED TO NANCY AND LEE • NANCY WHISKEY SEE CHAS MCDEVITT SKIFFLE GROUP

Nancy Wilson   Female Vocalist, B: 20 Feb 1947 Chillicothe, Ohio

	TITLE	UK LBL	UK POS	UK YEAR	US POS	US YEAR	US LBL
1	(You Don't Know) How Glad I Am		0	1964	11	1964	(Capitol 5198)
2	Face It Girl, It's Over		0	1968	29	1968	(Capitol 2136)

SHE FIRST RECORDED IN 1956

Naomi Campbell   Female Model/Vocalist from the UK

	TITLE	UK LBL	UK POS	UK YEAR	US POS	US YEAR	US LBL
1	Love And Tears	(Epic 6608352)	40	1994	0	1994	

Naomi Chiaki

	TITLE	UK LBL	UK POS	UK YEAR	US POS	US YEAR	US LBL
* 1	Kassai (Applause)		0	1972	0	1972	

Napoleon XIV   Male Vocalist, Real Name Jerry Samuels From New York

	TITLE	UK LBL	UK POS	UK YEAR	US POS	US YEAR	US LBL
* 1	They're Coming To Take Me Away Ha-Haaa!	(Warner Bros Wb 5831)	4	1966	3	1966	(Warner Bros 5831)

Nappy Brown   Real Name Napoleon Brown Culp B: 12 Oct 1929 Charlotte, North Carolina

	TITLE	UK LBL	UK POS	UK YEAR	US POS	US YEAR	US LBL
1	Don't Be Angry		0	1955	25	1955	(Savoy 1155)

Narada Michael Walden   Male Vocalist/Producer from the USA

	TITLE	UK LBL	UK POS	UK YEAR	US POS	US YEAR	US LBL
1	Tonight I'm All Right	(Atlantic K 11437)	34	1980	0	1980	
2	I Shoulda Loved Ya	(Atlantic K 11413)	8	1980	0	1980	
3	Devine Emotions	(Atlantic W 7967)	8	1988	0	1988	

HIT 3 IS CREDITED TO NARADA

Nas   Male Rapper from the USA

	TITLE	UK LBL	UK POS	UK YEAR	US POS	US YEAR	US LBL
1	It Ain't Hard To Tell	(Columbia 6604702)	64	1994	0	1994	
2	If I Ruled The World	(Columbia 6634022)	12	1996	53	1996	(Columbia 78327)
3	Street Dreams	(Columbia 6641302)	12	1997	22	1996	(Columbia 78409)
4	Head Over Heals		0	1997	35	1997	(Track Masters 78522)

Nashville Teens   Male Vocal/Instrumental Group from the UK   Lead Singer With The Sextet Is Arthur Sharp

	TITLE	UK LBL	UK POS	UK YEAR	US POS	US YEAR	US LBL
1	Tobacco Road	(Decca F 11930)	6	1964	14	1964	(London 9689)
2	Google Eye	(Decca F 12000)	10	1964	0	1964	
3	Find My Way Back Home	(Decca F 12089)	34	1965	0	1965	
4	The Little Bird	(Decca F 12143)	38	1965	0	1965	
5	The Hard Way	(Decca F 12346)	45	1966	0	1966	
6	The Hard Way (Re-Entry)	(Decca F 12346)	48	1966	0	1966	

Nat 'King' Cole   Male Vocalist, Real Name Nathaniel Adams Coles B: 17 Mar 1917 Alabama

	TITLE	UK LBL	UK POS	UK YEAR	US POS	US YEAR	US LBL
1	All For You		0	1943	18	1943	(Capitol 139)
2	Straighten Up And Fly Right		0	1944	9	1944	(Capitol 154)
3	I Can't See For Lookin'		0	1944	28	1944	(Capitol 154)
4	Gee, Baby, Ain't I Good To You?		0	1944	15	1944	(Capitol 169)
5	The Frim Fram Sauce		0	1946	19	1946	(Capitol 224)
6	Get Your Kicks On Route 66		0	1946	11	1946	(Capitol 256)
7	You Call It Madness		0	1946	10	1946	(Capitol 274)
8	(I Love You) For Sentimental Reasons		0	1946	1	1946	(Capitol 304)
9	The Best Man		0	1946	14	1946	(Capitol 304)
* 10	The Christmas Song		0	1946	3	1946	(Capitol 311)
11	You Don't Learn That In School		0	1947	22	1947	(Capitol 393)
12	Save The Bones For Henry Jones		0	1947	12	1947	(Capitol 15000)
13	Harmony		0	1947	12	1947	(Capitol 15000)
14	Those Things Money Can't Buy		0	1947	22	1947	(Capitol 15011)
15	The Christmas Song (Re-Entry)		0	1947	23	1947	(Capitol 311)
16	What'll I Do (From Music Box Revue Of 1923)		0	1948	22	1948	(Capitol 15019)
* 17	Nature Boy		0	1948	1	1948	(Capitol 15054)
18	Lost April		0	1948	20	1948	(Capitol 15054)
19	A Boy From Texas		0	1948	24	1948	(Capitol 15085)
20	Put 'Em In A Box, Tie It With A Ribbon (From Romance On The High Seas)		0	1948	30	1948	(Capitol 15060)
21	Don't Blame Me		0	1948	21	1948	(Capitol 15110)

	ISSUE	TITLE	UK LBL	UK POS	UK YEAR	US POS	US YEAR	US LBL
*	22	Little Girl		0	1948	25	1948	(Capitol 15165)
	23	The Christmas Song (Re-Issue)		0	1949	24	1949	(Capitol 15201)
	24	I Almost Lost My Mind		0	1950	26	1950	(Capitol 889)
*	25	Mona Lisa		0	1950	1	1950	(Capitol 1010)
	26	Home		0	1950	22	1950	(Capitol 1133)
	27	Orange Colored Sky		0	1950	5	1950	(Capitol 1184)
	28	Frosty The Snowman		0	1951	9	1951	(Capitol 1203)
	29	Jet		0	1951	20	1951	(Capitol 1365)
	30	Always You		0	1951	28	1951	(Capitol 1401)
*	31	Too Young		0	1951	1	1951	(Capitol 1449)
	32	Red Sails In The Sunset (From Provincetown Follies)		0	1951	24	1951	(Capitol 1468)
	33	Because Of Rain		0	1951	17	1951	(Capitol 1501)
	34	Unforgettable		0	1951	12	1951	(Capitol 1808)
	35	Somewhere Along The Way	(Capitol CI 13774)	3	1952	8	1952	(Capitol 2069)
	36	Walking My Baby Back Home		0	1952	8	1952	(Capitol 2130)
	37	Funny (Not Much)		0	1952	26	1952	(Capitol 2130)
	38	Because You're Mine	(Capitol CI 13811)	6	1952	16	1952	(Capitol 2212)
	39	I'm Never Satisfied		0	1952	22	1952	(Capitol 2212)
	40	The Ruby And The Pearl (From Thunder In The East)		0	1952	23	1952	(Capitol 2230)
	41	Faith Can Move Mountains	(Capitol CI 13811)	11	1952	24	1952	(Capitol 2230)
	42	Faith Can Move Mountains (Re-Entry)	(Capitol CI 13811)	12	1953	0	1953	
	43	Because You're Mine (Re-Entry)	(Capitol CI 13811)	10	1953	0	1953	
	44	The Christmas Song (Re-Entry)		0	1953	30	1953	(Capitol 15201)
	45	Strange		0	1953	20	1953	(Capitol 2309)
	46	Faith Can Move Mountains (2nd Re-Entry)	(Capitol CI 13811)	10	1953	0	1953	
	47	Pretend	(Capitol CI 13878)	2	1953	2	1953	(Capitol 2346)
	48	Because You're Mine (2nd Re-Entry)	(Capitol CI 13811)	11	1953	0	1953	
	49	Don't Let Your Eyes Go Shopping (For Your Heart)		0	1953	3	1953	(Capitol 2346)
	50	Can't I?	(Capitol CI 13937)	9	1953	16	1953	(Capitol 2389)
	51	I Am In Love (From Can-Can)		0	1953	19	1953	(Capitol 2459)
	52	Return To Paradise		0	1953	15	1953	(Capitol 2498)
	53	A Fool Was I		0	1953	17	1953	(Capitol 2540)
	54	If Love Is Good To Me		0	1953	28	1953	(Capitol 2540)
	55	Can't I? (Re-Entry)	(Capitol CI 13937)	6	1953	0	1953	
	56	Mother Nature And Father Time	(Capitol CI 13912)	7	1953	0	1953	
	57	Can't I? (2nd Re-Entry)	(Capitol CI 13937)	10	1953	0	1953	
	58	Lover, Come Back To Me! (From New Moon)		0	1953	16	1953	(Capitol 2610)
*	59	Answer Me, My Love		0	1954	6	1954	(Capitol 2687)
	60	Tenderly	(Capitol CI 14061)	10	1954	0	1954	
	61	Why		0	1954	27	1954	(Capitol 2687)
	62	It Happens To Be Me		0	1954	16	1954	(Capitol 2754)
	63	Alone Too Long (From The Beautiful Sea)		0	1954	25	1954	(Capitol 2754)
	64	Make Her Mine	(Capitol CI 14149)	11	1954	19	1954	(Capitol 2803)
	65	Smile (From Modern Times)	(Capitol CI 14149)	2	1954	10	1954	(Capitol 2897)
	66	Unbelievable		0	1954	26	1954	(Capitol 2949)
	67	Haji Baba (Persian Lament) (From The Adventures Of Haji Baba)		0	1954	14	1954	(Capitol 2949)
	68	The Christmas Song (Re-Recording)		0	1954	29	1954	(Capitol 2955)
	69	Darling Je Vous Aime Beaucoup		0	1955	7	1955	(Capitol 3027)
	70	The Sand And The Sea		0	1955	23	1955	(Capitol 3027)
*	71	A Blossom Fell	(Capitol CI 14235)	3	1955	2	1955	(Capitol 3095)
	72	If I May		0	1955	8	1955	(Capitol 3095)
	73	My One Sin	(Capitol CI 14327)	18	1955	24	1955	(Capitol 3136)
	74	My One Sin (Re-Entry)	(Capitol CI 14327)	17	1955	0	1955	
	75	Forgive My Heart		0	1955	13	1955	(Capitol 3234)
	76	Someone To Love		0	1955	13	1955	(Capitol 3234)
	77	Dreams Can Tell A Lie	(Capitol CI 14513)	10	1956	0	1956	
	78	Ask Me		0	1956	18	1956	(Capitol 3328)
	79	Too Young To Go Steady	(Capitol CI 14573)	8	1956	21	1956	(Capitol 3390)
	80	That's All There Is To That		0	1956	16	1956	(Capitol 3456)
	81	Love Me As Though There Were No Tomorrow	(Capitol CI 14621)	24	1956	0	1956	
	82	Love Me As Though... (Re-Entry)	(Capitol CI 14621)	11	1956	0	1956	
	83	Night Lights		0	1956	11	1956	(Capitol 3551)
	84	To The Ends Of The Earth		0	1956	25	1956	(Capitol 3551)
	85	Ballerina		0	1957	18	1957	(Capitol 3619)
	86	When I Fall In Love	(Capitol CI 14709)	2	1957	0	1957	

ISSUE	TITLE	UK LBL	UK POS	UK YEAR	US POS	US YEAR	US LBL
87	Send For Me		0	1957	6	1957	(Capitol 3737)
88	My Personal Possession	(Capitol Cl 14765)	21	1957	6	1957	(Capitol 3737)
89	When Rock And Roll Came To Trinidad	(Capitol Cl 14733)	28	1957	0	1957	
90	With You On My Mind		0	1957	30	1957	(Capitol 3782)
91	Stardust	(Capitol Cl 14787)	24	1957	0	1957	
92	Angel Smile		0	1958	33	1958	(Capitol 3860)
93	Looking Back		0	1958	5	1958	(Capitol 3939)
94	Come Closer To Me		0	1958	38	1958	(Capitol 4004)
95	You Made Me Love You	(Capitol Cl 15017)	22	1959	0	1959	
96	Midnight Flyer	(Capitol Cl 15056)	27	1959	0	1959	
97	Midnight Flyer (Re-Entry)	(Capitol Cl 15056)	23	1959	0	1959	
98	Time And The River	(Capitol Cl 15111)	29	1960	30	1960	(Capitol 4325)
99	Time And The River (Re-Entry)	(Capitol Cl 15111)	23	1960	0	1960	
100	Time And The River (2nd Re-Entry)	(Capitol Cl 15111)	47	1960	0	1960	
101	That's You	(Capitol Cl 15129)	10	1960	0	1960	
102	Just As Much As Ever	(Capitol Cl 15163)	18	1960	0	1960	
103	Let True Love Begin	(Capitol Cl 15224)	29	1961	0	1961	
104	The World In My Arms	(Capitol Cl 15178)	36	1961	0	1961	
105	Brazilian Love Song	(Capitol Cl 15241)	34	1962	0	1962	
106	The Right Thing To Say	(Capitol Cl 15250)	0	1962	42	1962	(Capitol 0000)
107	Let There Be Love	(Capitol Cl 15257)	11	1992	0	1992	
* 108	Ramblin' Rose	(Capitol Cl 15270)	5	1962	2	1962	(Capitol 4804)
109	Dear Lonely Hearts	(Capitol Cl 15280)	37	1962	13	1962	(Capitol 4870)
110	Those Lazy Hazy Crazy Days Of Summer		0	1963	6	1963	(Capitol 4965)
111	That Sunday, That Summer		0	1963	12	1963	(Capitol 5027)
112	I Don't Want To Be Hurt Anymor		0	1964	22	1964	(Capitol 5155)
113	I Don't Want To See Tomorrow		0	1964	34	1964	(Capitol 5261)
114	When I Fall In Love (Re-Issue)	(Capitol Cl 15975)	4	1987	0	1987	
115	The Christmas Song	(Capitol Cl 641)	69	1991	0	1991	
116	Let's Face The Music And Dance	(EMI Cdem 312)	30	1994	0	1994	

Obituary :- D: 15 Feb 1965 Lung Cancer.

Natalie Casey Female Vocalist from the UK

1	Chick Chick Chicken	(Polydor Chick 1)	72	1984	0	1984	

Natalie Cole Female Vocalist, B: 6 Feb 1950 Los Angeles

1	This Will Be	Capitol Cl 15834	32	1975	6	1975	(Capitol 4109)
2	Inseparable		0	1976	32	1976	(Capitol 4193)
3	Sophisticated Lady (She's A Different Lady)		0	1976	25	1976	(Capitol 4259)
* 4	I've Got Love On My Mind		0	1977	5	1977	(Capitol 4360)
* 5	Our Love		0	1978	10	1978	(Capitol 4509)
6	Someone That I Used To Love		0	1980	21	1980	(Capitol 4869)
7	Jump Start	(Manhattan Mt 22)	44	1987	13	1987	(Manhattan 50073)
8	I Live For Your Love	(Manhattan Mt 57)	23	1988	13	1987	(Manhattan 50094)
9	Pink Cadillac	(Manhattan Mt 35)	5	1988	5	1988	(EMI-Manhattan 50117)
10	Everlasting	(Manhattan Mt 46)	28	1988	0	1988	
11	Jump Start (Re-Issue)	(Manhattan Mt 50)	33	1988	0	1988	
12	Miss You Like Crazy	(EMI-Usa Mt 63)	2	1989	7	1989	(EMI 50185)
13	Best Of The Night	(EMI-Usa Mt 69)	56	1989	0	1989	
14	Starting Over Again	(EMI-Usa Mt 77)	56	1986	0	1986	
15	Wild Women Do (From Pretty Woman)	(EMI-USA MT 81)	16	1990	34	1990	(EMI 50275)
* 16	Unforgettable	(Elektra Ekr 128)	19	1991	14	1991	(Elektra 64875)
17	The Very Thought Of You	(Elektra Ekr 147)	71	1992	0	1992	

HIT 16 HAVE VOCALS FROM HER FATHER'S 1951 HIT 35 • SHE IS THE DAUGHTER OF THE GREAT NAT 'KING' COLE

Natalie Merchant Female Vocalist, B: 26 Oct 1963 In Jamestown, New York. Former Lead Singer Of 10,000 Maniacs

1	Carnival		0	1995	10	1995	(Elektra 64413)
2	Jealousy		0	1996	23	1996	(Electra 6430)
3	Wonder		0	1996	20	1996	(Elektra 64376)

Natasha Female Vocalist from the UK

1	Iko-Iko	(Towerbell Tow 22)	10	1982	0	1982	
2	The Boom Boom Room	(Towerbell Tow 25)	44	1982	0	1982	

Nate Dogg

1	Regulate	(Death Row A 8290cd)	5	1994	0	1994	
2	Never Leave Me Alone		0	1996	33	1996	(Interscope 97012)

HIT 1 IS CREDITED TO WARREN G AND NATE DOG • HIT 2 IS CREDITED TO NATE DOGG FEATURING SNOOP DOGGY DOGG

ISSUE	TITLE	UK LBL	UK POS	UK YEAR	US POS	US YEAR	US LBL
Nathaniel Mayer & The Fabulous Twilights R&B Singer From Detroit							
1	Village Of Love		0	1962	22	1962	(Fortune 449)
Natural Born Grooves Male Instrumental/Production Duo From Holland							
1	Forerunner	(Xl Recordings Xls 76cd)	64	1996	0	1996	
2	Groovebird	(Positiva Cdtiv 75)	21	1997	0	1997	
Natural Four Soul Group from San Francisco Led By Chris James							
1	Can This Be Real		0	1974	31	1974	(Curtom 1990)
Natural Life Mixed Vocal/Instrumental Group from the UK							
1	Natural Life	(Tribe Nlife 3)	47	1992	0	1992	
Natural Selection Male Funk Duo, Elliot Erickson & Frederick Thomas From Minneapolis							
1	Do Anything	(East West A 8724)	69	1991	2	1991	(East West 98724)
2	Hearts Don't Think (They Feel)		0	1992	28	1992	(East West 98652)
Naturals Male Vocal/Instrumental Group from the UK							
1	I Should Have Known Better	(Parlophone R 5165)	24	1964	0	1964	
Naughty By Nature Male Rap Trio From East Orange, New Jersey							
* 1	O.P.P.	(Big Life Blr 62)	73	1991	6	1991	(Tommy Boy 988)
2	O.P.P. (Re-Issue)	(Big Life Blr 74)	35	1992	0	1992	
* 3	Hip Hop Hooray	(Big Life Blrd 89)	22	1993	8	1993	(Tommy Boy 554)
4	It's On	(Big Life Blrd 99)	48	1993	0	1993	
5	Hip Hop Hooray (Re-Mix)	(Big Life Blrd 104)	20	1993	0	1993	
* 6	Feel Me Flow	(Big Life Blrd 115)	23	1995	17	1995	(Tommy Boy 7682)
Nazareth Male Vocal/Instrumental Group from the UK Names: Dan McCafferty, Manny Charlton, Pete Agnew, & Darryl Sweet							
1	Broken Down Angel	(Mooncrest Moon 1)	9	1973	0	1973	
2	Bad Bad Boy	(Mooncrest Moon 9)	10	1973	0	1973	
3	This Flight Tonight	(Mooncrest Moon 14)	11	1973	0	1973	
4	Shanghai'd In Shangai	(Mooncrest Moon 22)	41	1974	0	1974	
5	My White Bicycle	(Mooncrest Moon 47)	14	1975	0	1975	
6	Holy Roller	(Mountain Top 3)	36	1975	0	1975	
* 7	Love Hurts		0	1977	8	1976	(A&M 1671)
8	Hot Tracks (EP)	(Mountain Naz 1)	15	1977	0	1977	
9	Gone Dead Train	(Mountain Naz 002)	49	1978	0	1978	
10	Place In Your Heart	(Mountain Top 37)	70	1978	0	1978	
11	Place In Your Heart (Re-Entry)	(Mountain Top 37)	74	1978	0	1978	
12	May The Sun Shine	(Mountain Naz 003)	22	1979	0	1979	
13	Star	(Mountain Top 45)	54	1979	0	1979	
DAN, PETE & DARRYL WAS THE SHADETTES BEFORE MANNY JOINED THEM, JOHN LOCKE & BILLY RANKIN JOINED THE GROUP IN 1981							
Neal Hefti Male Orchestra, B: 29 Oct 1922 Hastings, Nebraska							
1	Batman Theme	(RCA Pb 49571)	55	1988	35	1966	(RCA 8755)
Nearly God Mixed Vocal/Instrumental Group from the UK							
1	Poems	(Durban Poison Dpcd 3)	28	1996	0	1996	
Nebula II Male Production/Instrumental Group from the UK							
1	Seance / Atheama	(Reinforced Rivet 1211)	55	1992	0	1992	
2	Flatliners	(J4m 12nebula 2)	54	1992	0	1992	
Ned Miller Male Singer/Songwriter, B: Henry Ned Miller 12 Apr 1925, Rains, Utah, USA							
* 1	From A Jack To A King	(London Hl 9658)	2	1963	6	1963	(Fabor 114)
! 2	One Among The Many		0	1963	27	1963	(Fabor 116)
! 3	Another Fool Like Me		0	1963	28	1963	(Fabor 121)
! 4	Invisible Tears		0	1964	13	1964	(Fabor 128)
5	Do What You Do, Do Well	(London Hl 9937)	48	1965	52	1965	(Fabor 137)
! 6	Whistle Walkin'		0	1965	28	1965	(Capitol 5431)
! 7	Summer Roses		0	1966	39	1966	(Capitol 5661)
! 8	Teardrop Lane		0	1966	44	1966	(Capitol 5742)
! 9	Hobo		0	1967	53	1967	(Capitol 5868)
! 10	Only A Fool		0	1968	61	1968	(Capitol 2074)
! 11	The Lover's Song		0	1970	39	1970	(Republic 1411)
HIT 4 REACHED NUMBER 131 IN THE US NATIONAL CHARTS • HIT 5 REACHED NUMBER 7 IN THE US C/W CHARTS							
HIT 1 WAS ORIGINALLY RELEASED IN THE USA IN 1957 ON DOT 15601							
Ned's Atomic Dustbin Male Vocal/Instrumental Group from the UK							
1	Kill Your Television	(Chapter 22 Chap 48)	53	1990	0	1990	
2	Until You Find Out	(Chapter 22 Chap 52)	51	1990	0	1990	
3	Happy	(Columbia 6566807)	16	1991	0	1991	

ISSUE	TITLE	UK LBL	UK POS	UK YEAR	US POS	US YEAR	US LBL
4	Trust	(Furtive 6574627)	21	1991	0	1991	
5	Not Sleeping Around	(Furtive 6583866)	19	1992	0	1992	
6	Intact	(Furtive 6588166)	36	1992	0	1992	
7	All I Ask Of Myself Is That I Hold Together	(Furtive 6613565)	33	1995	0	1995	
8	Stuck	(Furtive 6620562)	64	1995	0	1995	

Neighborhood Vocal/Instrumental Group from the USA

1	Big Yellow Taxi		0	1970	29	1970	(Big Tree 102)

Neil Male Vocalist from the UK

1	Hole In My Shoe	(Wea Yz 10)	2	1984	0	1984	

Neil Arthur Male Vocalist from the UK

1	I Love, I Hate	(Chrysalis Cdchss 5005)	50	1994	0	1994	

Neil Christian Male Vocalist from the UK

1	That's Nice	(Strike Jh 301)	14	1966	0	1966	

Neil Diamond Male Vocalist, B: 24 Jan 1941, Coney Island, New York

1	Solitary Man		0	1966	55	1966	(Bang 578)
* 2	Cherry Cherry		0	1966	6	1966	(Bang 528)
3	I Got The Feelin' (Oh No No)		0	1966	16	1966	(Bang 536)
4	You Got To Me		0	1967	18	1967	(Bang 540)
5	Girl, You'll Be A Woman Soon		0	1967	10	1967	(Bang 542)
6	I Thank The Lord For The Night Time		0	1967	13	1967	(Bang 547)
7	Kentucky Woman		0	1967	22	1967	(Bang 551)
8	Brother Love's Travelling Salvation Show		0	1969	22	1969	(Uni 55109)
* 9	Sweet Carolin	(Uni Un 531)	8	1971	4	1969	(Uni 55136)
* 10	Holly Holy		0	1969	6	1969	(Uni 55175)
11	Shilo		0	1970	24	1970	(Bang 575)
12	Soolaimon (African Trilogy II)		0	1970	30	1970	(Uni 55224)
13	Solitary Man (Re-Entry)		0	1970	21	1970	(Bang 528)
* 14	Cracklin Rosie	(Uni Un 529)	3	1970	1	1970	(Uni 55250)
15	He Ain't Heavy... He's My Brother		0	1970	20	1970	(Uni 55264)
16	Do It		0	1970	36	1970	(Bang 580)
17	I Am...I Said	(Uni Un 532)	4	1971	4	1971	(Uni 55278)
18	Stones		0	1971	14	1971	(Uni 55310)
* 19	Song Sung Blue	(Uni Un 538)	14	1972	1	1972	(Uni 55326)
20	Play Me		0	1972	11	1972	(Uni 55346)
21	Walk On Water		0	1972	17	1972	(Uni 55352)
22	Cherry Cherry (Live Version)		0	1973	31	1973	(MCA 40017)
23	Be		0	1973	34	1973	(Columbia 45942)
24	Longfellow Serenade		0	1974	5	1974	(Columbia 10043)
25	I've Been This Way Before		0	1975	34	1975	(Columbia 10084)
26	If You Know That I Mean	(CBS 4398)	35	1976	11	1976	(Columbia 10366)
27	Beautiful Noise	(Cbs 4601)	13	1976	0	1976	
28	Desiree	(Cbs 5869)	39	1977	16	1978	(Columbia 10657)
* 29	You Don't Bring Me Flowers	(Cbs 6803)	5	1978	1	1978	(Columbia 10840)
30	Forever In Blue Jeans	(Cbs 7047)	16	1979	20	1979	(Columbia 10897)
31	September Morn'		0	1980	17	1980	(Columbia 11175)
32	Love On The Rocks	(Capitol Cl 16173)	17	1980	2	1980	(Capitol 4939)
33	Hello Again	(Capitol Cl 16176)	51	1981	6	1981	(Capitol 4960)
34	America		0	1981	8	1981	(Capitol 4994)
35	Yesterday's Songs		0	1981	11	1981	(Columbia 02604)
36	On The Way To The Sky		0	1982	27	1982	(Columbia 02712)
37	Be Mine Tonight		0	1982	35	1982	(Columbia 02928)
38	Heartlight	(Cbs A 2814)	47	1982	5	1982	(Columbia 03219)
39	I'm Alive		0	1983	35	1983	(Columbia 03503)
40	Morning Has Broken	(Columbia 6588267)	36	1992	0	1992	

Hit 29 Is Credited To Barbra & Neil

Neil MacArthur Male Vocalist, Colin Blunstone Under A False Name

1	She's Not Ther	(Deram Dm 225)	34	1969	0	1969	

Neil Reid Male Vocalist from the UK

* 1	Mother Of Mine	(Decca F 13264)	2	1971	0	1971	
2	That's What I Want To Be	(Decca F 13300)	49	1972	0	1972	
3	That's What I Want To Be (Re-Entry)	(Decca F 13300)	45	1972	0	1972	

ISSUE	TITLE	UK LBL	UK POS	UK YEAR	US POS	US YEAR	US LBL
Neil Sedaka Male Singer/Songwriter/Pianist, B: 13 Mar 1939 Brooklyn							
1	The Diary		0	1958	14	1958	(RCA 7408)
2	I Go Ape	(RCA 1115)	9	1959	42	1959	(RCA)
3	Oh Carol	(RCA 1152)	3	1959	9	1959	(RCA 7595)
4	Stairway To Heaven	(RCA 1178)	8	1960	9	1960	(RCA 7709)
5	You Mean Everything To Me	(RCA 1198)	45	1960	17	1960	(RCA 7781)
6	Run Samson Run		0	1960	28	1960	(RCA 7781)
7	Calendar Girl	(RCA 1220)	8	1961	4	1961	(RCA 7829)
8	Little Devil	(RCA 1236)	9	1961	11	1961	(RCA 7874)
9	Happy Birthday Sweet Sixteen	(RCA 1266)	3	1961	6	1961	(RCA 7957)
10	King Of Clowns	(RCA 1282)	23	1962	0	1962	
* 11	Breaking Up Is Hard To Do	(RCA 1298)	7	1962	1	1962	(RCA 8046)
12	Next Door To An Angel	(RCA 1319)	29	1962	5	1962	(RCA 8086)
13	Alice In Wonderland		0	1963	17	1963	(RCA 8137)
14	Let's Go Steady Again	(RCA 1343)	42	1963	26	1963	(RCA 8169)
15	Let's Go Steady Again (Re-Entry)	(RCA 1343)	43	1963	0	1963	
16	Bad Girl		0	1963	33	1963	(RCA 8254)
17	Oh Carol/Breaking Up Is Hard To Do (Re-Issue)	(RCA Maximillion 2259)	19	1972	0	1972	
18	Beautiful You	(RCA 2269)	43	1972	0	1972	
19	That's When The Music Takes Me	(RCA 2310)	18	1973	27	1975	(Rocket 40426)
20	Standing On The Inside	(Mgm 2006 267	26	1973	0	1973	
21	Our Last Song Together	(Mgm 2006 307)	31	1973	0	1973	
22	A Little Lovin'	(Polydor 2058 434)	34	1974	0	1974	
23	Laughter In The Rain	(Polydor 2058 494)	15	1974	1	1974	(Rocket 40313)
24	The Queen Of 1964	(Polydor 2058 546)	35	1975	0	1964	
25	The Immigrant		0	1975	22	1975	(Rocket 40370)
* 26	Bad Blood		0	1975	1	1975	(Rocket 40460)
27	Breaking Up Is Hard To Do (Slow Version)		0	1975	8	1975	(Rocket 40500)
28	Love In The Shadows		0	1976	16	1976	(Rocket 40543)
29	Steppin' Out		0	1976	36	1976	(Rocket 40582)
30	Should've Never Let You Go		0	1980	19	1980	(Elektra 46615)
	BACKING VOCALS ON HIT 26 ARE BY ELTON JOHN, SEE ALSO THE TOKENS N • HIT 30 IS CREDITED TO NEIL SEDAKA AND DARA SEDAKA (DAUGHTER)							
Neil Young Male Rock Singer/Songwriter/Guitarist, B: 12 Nov 1945 Toronto, Canada							
1	Only Love Can Break Your Heart		0	1970	33	1970	(Reprise 0958)
* 2	Heart Of Gold	(Reprise K 14140)	10	1972	1	1972	(Reprise 1065)
3	Old Man		0	1972	31	1972	(Reprise 1084)
4	Four Strong Winds	Reprise K 14493)	57	1979	0	1979	
! 5	Get Back To The Country		0	1985	33	1985	(Geffen 28883)
6	Harvest Moon	(Reprise W 0139cd)	36	1993	0	1993	
7	The Needle And The Damage Done	(Reprise W 0191cd)	75	1993	0	1993	
8	Long May You Run (Live)	(Reprise W 0207cd)	71	1993	0	1993	
9	Philadelphia	(Reprise W 0242cd)	62	1994	0	1994	
Nelson Male Vocal Duo from the USA							
* 1	(Can't Live Without Your) Love And Affection	(DGC Gef 82)	54	1990	1	1990	(DGC 19689)
2	After The Rain		0	1991	6	1991	(Dgc 19667)
3	More Than Ever		0	1991	14	1991	(Dgc 19002)
4	Only Time Will Tell		0	1991	28	1991	(Dgc 19014)
	MATTHEW & GUNNAR NELSON B: 20 SEP 1967 IDENTICAL TWINS SONS OF ERIC HILLIARD AKA RICKY NELSON							
Nelson Eddy Male Actor/Vocalist, B: 29 Jun 1901 Providence, Rhode Island Obituary: D: 6 Mar 1967, (Aged 65)							
* 4	Indian Love Call (From Rose Marie)		0	1936	8	1936	(Victor 4323)
Nelson Keene Male Vocalist from the UK							
1	Image Of A Girl	(HMV Pop 771)	37	1960	0	1960	
2	Image Of A Girl (Re-Entry)	(HMV Pop 771)	45	1960	0	1960	
Nelson Riddle & His Orchestra Male Orchestra Leader, B: 1 Jun 1921 Oradell, New Jersey							
1	Brother John		0	1954	23	1954	(Capitol 2744)
* 2	Lisbon Antigua		0	1956	1	1956	(Capitol 3287)
3	Port Au Prince		0	1956	20	1956	(Capitol 3374)
4	Theme From The Proud Ones		0	1956	39	1956	(Capitol 3472)
5	Route 66 Theme		0	1962	30	1962	(Capitol 4741)
	OBITUARY : D: 6 OCT 1985 (AGED 64).							
Nena Female Vocalist, Real Name Gabriele Nena Kerner, B: 26 Mar 1960 Germany							
* 1	99 Red Baloons (99 Luftballons)	(Epic A 4074)	1	1984	2	1984	(Epic 04108)
2	Just A Dream	(Epic H 3249)	70	1984	0	1984	

ISSUE	TITLE	UK LBL	UK POS	UK YEAR	US POS	US YEAR	US LBL

Neneh Cherry   Female Vocalist B: 10 Aug 1964 Stockholm

* 1	Buffalo Stance	(Circa Yr 21)	7	1988	3	1989	(Virgin 99231)
2	Manchild	(Circa Yr 30)	5	1989	0	1989	
3	Kisses On The Wind	(Circa Yr 33)	20	1989	8	1989	(Virgin 99183)
4	Inna City Mamma	(Circa Yr 42)	31	1989	0	1989	
5	I've Got You Under My Skin	(Circa Yr 53)	25	1990	0	1990	
6	Money Love	(Circa Yr 83)	23	1992	0	1992	
7	Buddy X	(Circa Yrcd 98)	35	1993	0	1993	
8	7 Seconds	(Columbia 6605082)	3	1994	0	1994	
9	7 Seconds (Re-Entry)	(Columbia 6605082)	54	1994	0	1994	
10	Love Can Build A Bridge	(London Cocd1	1	1995	0	1995	
11	Woman	(Hut Hutd 70)	9	1996	0	1996	
12	Kootchi	(Hut Hutcd 75)	38	1996	0	1996	
13	Feel It	(Hut Hutcd 79)	68	1997	0	1997	

HITS 8-9 ARE CREDITED TO YOUSSOU N'DOUR FEATURING NENEH CHERRY
HIT 10 IS CREDITED TO CHER, CHRISSY HYNDE, NENEH CHERRY & ERIC CLAPTON

Neon Philharmonic   Chamber-Sized Orchestra Of The Nashville Symphony Orchestra

1	Morning Girl		0	1969	17	1969	(Warner Bros 7261)

MUSICIANS HEADED BY TUPPER SAUSSY   VOCALS ARE BY DON GRANT B: 1943
OBITUARY : DON D: 6 MAR 1987

Nero & The Gladiators   Male Instrumental Group from the UK

1	Entry Of The Gladiators	(Decca F 11329)	50	1961	0	1961	
2	Entry Of The Gladiators (Re-Entry)	(Decca F 11329)	37	1961	0	1961	
3	In The Hall Of The Mountain King	(Decca F 11367)	48	1961	0	1961	

Nervous Norvus   Male Vocalist, Real Name Jimmy Drake B: 1912 California

1	Transfusion		0	1956	8	1956	(Dot 15470)
2	Ape Call		0	1956	24	1956	(Dot 15485)

THE APE CALLS ON THE HIT 2 ARE BY RED BLANCHARD • OBITUARY : D: 1968.

Network   Male Vocal/Instrumental Group from the UK

1	Broken Wings	(Chrysalis Chs 3923)	46	1992	0	1992	

Nevada   Mixed Vocal/Instrumental Group from the UK

1	In The Bleak Mid Winter	(Polydor Posp 203)	71	1983	0	1983	

Neville Brothers   Male Vocal/Instrumental Group from the USA

1	With God On Our Side	(A&M Am 545)	47	1989	0	1989	
2	Bird On A Wire	(A&M Am 568)	72	1990	0	1990	

Neville Dickie   Male Pianist from the UK

1	Robin's Return	(Major Minor Mm 644)	33	1969	0	1969	
2	Robin's Return (Re-Entry)	(Major Minor Mm 644)	43	1969	0	1969	

New Atlantic   Male Production/Instrumental Duo from the UK

1	I Know	(3 Beat 3bt 1)	12	1992	0	1992	
2	Into The Future	(3 Beat 3bt 2)	70	1992	0	1992	
3	Take Off Some Time	(3 Beat 3btcd 14)	64	1993	0	1993	
4	The Sunshine After The Rain	(3 Beat Tabcd 223)	4	1994	0	1994	

HIT 4 IS CREDITED TO NEW ATLANTIC/U4EA FEATURING BERRI

New Birth

1	I Can Understand It		0	1973	35	1973	(RCA 0912)
2	Dream Merchant		0	1975	36	1975	(Buddah 470)

New Christy Minstrels   Lead Singer Barry McGuire

* 1	Green Green		0	1963	14	1963	(Columbia 42805)
2	Saturday Night		0	1963	29	1963	(Columbia 42887)
3	Today		0	1964	17	1964	(Columbia 43000)

New Colony Six   Based In Chicago Which Include Ronnie Rice, Gerry Van Kollenburg, Patrick McBride, Les Kummel, Chuck Jobes & William Herman

1	I Will Always Think About You		0	1968	22	1968	(Mercury 72775)
2	Things I'd Like To Say		0	1969	16	1969	(Mercury 72858)

New Edition   R&B Quintet Includes Ralph Tresvant, Ronald Devoe, Michael Bivins, Ricky Bell & Bobby Brown

1	Candy Girl	(London Lon 21)	1	1983	0	1983	
2	Popcorn Love	(London Lon 31)	43	1983	0	1983	
* 3	Cool It Now		0	1984	4	1984	(MCA 52455)
4	Mr. Telephone Man	(MCA Mca 938)	19	1985	12	1985	(MCA 52484)
5	Lost In Love		0	1985	35	1985	(MCA 52553)
6	A Little Bit Of Love (Is All It Takes)		0	1986	38	1986	(MCA 52768)
7	Earth Angel		0	1986	21	1986	(MCA 52905)

ISSUE	TITLE	UK LBL	UK POS	UK YEAR	US POS	US YEAR	US LBL
8	If It Isn't Love		0	1988	7	1988	(MCA 53264)
9	Crucial	(MCA MCA 23934)	70	1989	0	1989	
10	Hit Me Off	(MCA Mcstd 48014)	20	1996	3	1996	(MCA 55210)
11	I'm Still In Love With You		0	1996	7	1996	(MCA 55264)
12	Something About You	(MCA Mcstd 48032)	16	1997	0	1997	

New England Names Jimmy Waldo, Gary Shea, John Fannon & Hirsh Gardner

ISSUE	TITLE	UK LBL	UK POS	UK YEAR	US POS	US YEAR	US LBL
1	Don't Ever Wanna Lose Ya		0	1979	40	1979	(Infinity 50013)

New Generation Male Vocal/Instrumental Group from the UK

ISSUE	TITLE	UK LBL	UK POS	UK YEAR	US POS	US YEAR	US LBL
1	Smokey Blues Away	(Spark Srl 1007)	38	1968	0	1968	

New Kids On The Block Male Vocal Group from Boston Originally Called Nynuk

ISSUE	TITLE	UK LBL	UK POS	UK YEAR	US POS	US YEAR	US LBL
1	Please Don't Go Girl		0	1988	10	1988	(Columbia 07700)
* 2	You Got It (The Right Stuff)	(Cbs Block 2)	1	1989	3	1989	(Columbia 08092)
* 3	I'll Be Loving You (Forever)	(Cbs Block 4)	5	1990	1	1989	(Columbia 68671)
*4	Hangin' Tough	(Cbs Block 1)	52	1989	1	1989	(Columbia 68960)
* 5	Cover Girl	(Cbs Block 5)	4	1990	2	1989	(Columbia 69088)
6	Didn't I Blow Your Mind	(Cbs Block 8)	8	1990	8	1989	(Columbia 68960)
* 7	This One's For The Children	(Cbs Block 9)	9	1990	7	1989	(Columbia 73064)
8	Hangin' Tough (Re-Issue)	(Cbs Block 3)	1	1990	0	1990	
* 9	Step By Step	(Cbs Block 6)	2	1990	1	1990	(Columbia 73343)
10	Tonight	(Cbs Block 7)	3	1990	7	1990	(Columbia 73461)
11	Let's Try Again	(Cbs Block 8)	8	1990	0	1990	
12	Games	(Cbs 6566267)	14	1991	0	1991	
13	Call It What You Want	(Cbs 6567857)	12	1991	0	1991	
14	If You Go Away	(Cbs 6576667)	9	1991	16	1992	(Columbia 74255)
15	Dirty Dawg	(Cbs 6600362)	27	1994	0	1994	
16	Never Let You Go	(Cbs 6602072)	42	1994	0	1994	

NAMES DONNY WAHLBERG, JORDON AND JON KNIGHT, JOE MCINTYRE & DANNY WOOD   HITS 15-16 ARE CREDITED TO NKOTB

New Model Army Male Vocal/Instrumental Group from the UK

ISSUE	TITLE	UK LBL	UK POS	UK YEAR	US POS	US YEAR	US LBL
1	No Rest	(EMI Nma 1)	28	1985	0	1985	
2	Better Than Them / No Sense	(EMI Nma 2)	49	1985	0	1985	
3	Brave New World	(EMI Nma 3)	57	1985	0	1985	
4	Fifty-First State	(EMI Nma 4)	71	1986	0	1986	
5	Poison Street	(EMI Nma 5)	64	1987	0	1987	
6	White Coats (EP)	(EMI Nma 6)	50	1987	0	1987	
7	Stupid Question	(EMI Nma 7)	1	1989	0	1989	
8	Vagabonds	(EMI Nma 8)	37	1989	0	1989	
9	Green And Grey	(EMI Nma 9)	37	1989	0	1989	
10	Get Me Out	(EMI Nma 10)	34	1990	0	1990	
11	Purity	(EMI Nma 11)	61	1990	0	1990	
12	Space	(EMI Nma 12)	39	1991	0	1991	
13	Here Comes The War	(Epic 6589352)	25	1993	0	1993	
14	Living In The Rose (The Ballads) (EP)	(Epic 6592492)	51	1993	0	1993	

See Also Gimme Shelter (Ep), Various Artists (EP, LP, 78s)

New Musik Male Vocal/Instrumental Group from the UK

ISSUE	TITLE	UK LBL	UK POS	UK YEAR	US POS	US YEAR	US LBL
1	Straight Lines	(Gto Gt 255)	53	1979	0	1979	
2	Living By Numbers	(Gto Gt 261)	13	1980	0	1980	
3	This World Of Water	(Gto Gt 268)	31	1980	0	1980	
4	Sanctuary	(Gto Gt 275)	31	1980	0	1980	

New Order Mixed Vocal/Instrumental Group from the UK

ISSUE	TITLE	UK LBL	UK POS	UK YEAR	US POS	US YEAR	US LBL
1	Ceremony	(Factory Fac 33)	34	1981	0	1981	
2	Procession / Everything's Gone Green	(Factory Fac 53)	38	1981	0	1981	
3	Temptation	(Factory Fac 63)	29	1982	0	1982	
4	Blue Monday	(Factory Fac 73)	12	1983	0	1983	
5	Blue Monday (Re-Entry)	(Factory Fac 73)	9	1983	0	1983	
6	Confusion	(Factory Fac 93)	12	1983	0	1983	
7	Blue Monday (2nd Re-Entry)	(Factory Fac 73)	52	1984	0	1984	
8	Thieves Like Us	(Factory Fac 103)	18	1984	0	1984	
9	The Perfect Kiss	(Factory Fac 123)	46	1985	0	1985	
10	Sub-Culture	(Factory Fac 133)	63	1985	0	1985	
11	Shellshock	(Factory Fac 143)	28	1986	0	1986	
12	State Of The Nation	(Factory Fac 153)	30	1986	0	1986	
13	The Peel Sessions (1st June 1992)	(Strange Fruit Sfps 001)	54	1986	0	1986	
14	Bizarre Love Triangle	(Factory Fac 163)	56	1986	0	1986	
15	True Faith	(Factory Fac 183/7)	4	1987	32	1987	(Qwest 28271)
16	Touched By The Hand Of God	(Factory Fac 1937)	20	1987	0	1987	

ISSUE	TITLE	UK LBL	UK POS	UK YEAR	US POS	US YEAR	US LBL
17	Blue Monday (Re-Mix)	(Factory Fac 737)	3	1988	0	1988	
18	Fine Time	(Factory Fac 2237)	11	1988	0	1988	
19	Round And Round	(Factory Fac 2637)	21	1989	0	1989	
20	Run 2	(Factory Fac 273)	49	1989	0	1989	
21	World In Motion	(Factory/Mva Fac 2937)	1	1990	0	1990	
22	Regret	(Centredate Co. Nuocd 1)	4	1993	28	1993	(Qwest 18586)
23	Ruined In A Day	(Centredate Co. Nuocd 2)	22	1993	0	1993	
24	World (The Price Of Love)	(Centredate Co. Nuocd 3)	13	1993	0	1993	
25	Spooky	(Centredate Co. Nuocd 4)	22	1993	0	1993	
26	True Faith (Re-Mix)	(Centredate Co. Nuocd 5)	9	1994	0	1994	
27	Nineteen 63	(London Nucdp 6)	21	1995	0	1995	
28	Blue Monday (2nd Re-Mix)	(London Nuocd 7)	17	1995	0	1995	

NAMES STEPHEN MORRIS, PETER HOOK, BERNARD SUMNER & GILLIAN GILBERT

HIT 21 IS CREDITED TO ENGLANDNEWORDER • THE GROUP WAS ORIGINALLY KNOWN AS JOY DIVISION

New Power Generation   Mixed Vocal/Instrumental Group from the USA

1	Get Wild	(Npg 0061045)	19	1995	0	1995	
2	The Good Life	(Npg 0061515)	29	1995	0	1995	
3	The Good Life (Re-Entry)	(Npg 0061515)	15	1997	0	1997	

SEE ALSO PRINCE

New Seekers   Mixed Vocal/Instrumental Group from the UK

1	Look What They've Done To My Song Ma	(Philips 6006 027)	48	1970	14	1970	(Elektra 45699)
2	Look What They've Done... (Re-Entry)	(Philips 6006 027)	44	1970	0	1970	
3	Never Ending Song Of Love	(Philips 6006 125)	2	1971	0	1971	
* 4	I'd Like To Teach The World To Sing	(Polydor 2058 184)	1	1971	7	1972	(Elektra 45762)
5	Beg Steal Or Borrow	(Polydor 2058 201)	2	1972	0	1972	
6	Circles	(Polydor 2058 242)	4	1972	0	1972	
7	Come Softly To Me	(Polydor 2058 315)	20	1972	0	1972	
8	Pinball Wizard - See Me Feel Me	(Polydor 2058 338)	16	1973	29	1973	(Verve 10709)
9	Nevertheless	(Polydor 2068 340)	34	1973	0	1973	
10	Goodbye Is Just Another Word	(Polydor 2058 368)	36	1973	0	1973	
11	You Won't Find Another Fool Like Me	(Polydor 2058 421)	1	1973	0	1973	
12	I Get A Little Sentimental Over You	(Polydor 2058 439)	5	1974	0	1974	
13	It's So Nice (To Have You Home)	(Cbs 4391)	44	1976	0	1976	
14	I Wanna Go Back	(Cbs 4786)	25	1977	0	1977	
15	Anthem (One Day In Every Week)	(Cbs 6413)	21	1978	0	1978	

THE GROUP WAS FORMED BY EX SEEKERS KEITH POTGER CONSISTING OF EVE GRAHAM. LYN PAUL, PETER DOYLE, PAUL LAYTON & MARTY KRISTIAN

New Vaudeville Band   Male Vocal/Instrumental Group from the UK

* 1	Winchester Cathedral	(Fontana Tf 741)	4	1966	1	1966	(Fontana 1562)
2	Peek-A-Boo	(Fontana Tf 784)	7	1967	0	1967	
3	Finchley Central	(Fontana Tf 824)	11	1967	0	1967	
4	Green Street Green	(Fontana Tf 853)	37	1967	0	1967	

New World   Male Vocal/Instrumental Group From Australia

1	Rose Garden	(RAK 111)	15	1971	0	1971	
2	Tom Tom Turnaround	(RAK 117)	6	1971	0	1971	
3	Kara Kara	(RAK 123)	17	1971	0	1971	
4	Sister Jane	(RAK 130)	9	1972	0	1972	
5	Roof Top Singing	(RAK 148)	50	1973	0	1973	

New York City   Male Vocal Group from the USA

1	I'm Doing Fine Now	(RCA 2351)	20	1973	17	1973	(Chelsea 0113)

Names John Brown, Ed Shell, Tim McQueen & Claude Johnson

The Group Began Life As The Triboro Exchange

New York Skyy   Mixed Vocal/Instrumental Group from the USA

1	Let's Celebrate	(Epic Epc A 1898)	71	1982	0	1982	
2	Let's Celebrate (Re-Entry)	(Epic Epc A 1898)	67	1982	0	1982	

Newbeats   Male Vocal Trio from the USA

* 1	Bread And Butter	(Hickory 1269)	15	1964	2	1964	(Hickory 1269)
2	Everything's Alright		0	1964	16	1964	(Hickory 1282)
3	Break Away (From That Boy)		0	1965	40	1965	(Hickory 1290)
4	Run Baby Run (Back Into My Arms)	(London Hl 10341)	10	1971	12	1965	(Hickory 1332)

DEAN MATHIS B: 17 MAR 1939, MARK MATHIS B: 9 FEB 1942 & LARRY HENLEY B: 30 JUN 1941

Newcleus   Male Vocal/Instrumental Group from the USA

1	Jam In Revenge (The Wikki Wikki Song)	(Beckett Bks 8)	44	1983	0	1983	

ISSUE	TITLE	UK LBL	UK POS	UK YEAR	US POS	US YEAR	US LBL
News	Male Vocal/Instrumental Group from the UK						
1	Audio Video	(George George 1)	52	1981	0	1981	
Newton	Male Vocalist from the UK						
1	Sky High	(Bags Of Fun Bagscd 6)	56	1995	0	1995	
2	Sometimes When We Touch	(Dominion Cddmin 202)	32	1997	0	1997	
3	Don't Worry	(Dominion Cddmin 206)	61	1997	0	1997	
Nia Peeples	Female Actress/Vocalist, B: 10 Dec 1961 from the USA						
1	Trouble		0	1988	35	1988	(Mercury 87015)
2	Street Of Dreams		0	1991	12	1991	(Charisma 98690)
Niamh Kavanagh	Female Actress/Vocalist, B: 10 Dec 1961 From Ireland						
1	In Your Eyes	(Arista 74321154152)	24	1993	0	1993	
Nic Haverson	Male Vocalist from the UK						
1	Head Over Heels	(Telstar Cdhoh 1)	48	1993	0	1993	
Nice	Male Instrumental Group from the UK						
1	America	(Immediate Im 068)	21	1968	0	1968	
Nick Berry	Male Actor/Vocalist from the UK						
1	Every Loser Wins	(Bbc Resl 204)	1	1986	0	1986	
2	Every Loser Wins (Re-Entry)	(Bbc Resl 204)	72	1986	0	1986	
3	Hearbeat	(Columbia 6581517)	2	1992	0	1992	
4	Long Live Love	(Columbia 6587597)	47	1992	0	1992	
Nick Cave & The Bad Seeds	Male Vocal/Instrumental Group From Australia/Germany						
1	Straight To You / Jack The Ripper	(Mute Mute 140)	68	1992	0	1992	
2	What A Wonderful World	(Mute Mute 151)	72	1992	0	1992	
3	Do You Love Me?	(Mute Cdmute 160)	68	1994	0	1994	
4	Where The Wild Roses Grow	(Mute Cdmute 185)	11	1995	0	1995	
5	Henry Lee (EP)	(Mute Cdmute 189)	36	1996	0	1996	
6	Into My Arms	(Mute Cdmute 192)	53	1997	0	1997	
7	(Are You) The One That I've Been	(Mute Cdmute 206)	67	1997	0	1997	

HIT 3 IS CREDITED TO NICK CAVE AND SHANE MCGOWAN • HIT 4 IS CREDITED TO NICK CAVE & THE BAD SEEDS WITH LYLIE MINOGUE
HIT 5 IS CREDITED TO NICK CAVE & THE BAD SEEDS AND P.J. HARVEY

ISSUE	TITLE	UK LBL	UK POS	UK YEAR	US POS	US YEAR	US LBL
Nick Gilder	Male Vocalist, B: 7 Nov 1951 London, England						
* 1	Hot Child In The City		0	1978	1	1978	(Chrysalis 2226)
	FOUNDING MEMBER OF THE GROUP SWEENEY TODD						
Nick Heyward	Male Vocalist from the UK						
1	Whistle Down The Wind	(Arista Hey 1)	13	1983	0	1983	
2	Take That Situation	(Arista Hey 2)	20	1983	0	1983	
3	Blue Hat For A Blue Day	(Arista Hey 3)	14	1983	0	1983	
4	On A Sunday	(Arista Hey 4)	52	1983	0	1983	
5	Love All Day	(Arista Hey 5)	31	1984	0	1984	
6	Warning Sign	(Arista Hey 6)	25	1984	0	1984	
7	Warning Sign (Re-Entry)	(Arista Hey 6)	72	1985	0	1985	
8	Laura	(Arista Hey 8)	45	1985	0	1985	
9	Over The Weekend	(Arista Hey 9)	43	1986	0	1986	
10	You're My World	(Warner Bros W 7758)	67	1988	0	1988	
11	Kite	(Epic 6594882)	44	1993	0	1993	
12	He Doesn't Love You Like I Do	(Epic 6597282)	58	1993	0	1993	
13	The World	(Epic 6623845)	47	1995	0	1995	
14	Rollerblade	(Epic 6627912)	37	1996	0	1996	
Nick Howard	Male Vocalist From Australia						
1	Everybody Needs Somebody	(Bell 74321220942)	64	1995	0	1995	
Nick Kamen	Male Vocalist from the UK						
1	Each Time You Break My Heart	(Wea Yz 90)	5	1986	0	1986	
2	Loving You Is Sweeter Than Ever	(Wea Yz 106)	16	1987	0	1987	
3	Nobody Else	(Wea Yz 122)	47	1987	0	1987	
4	Tell Me	(Wea Yz 184)	40	1988	0	1988	
5	I Promised Myself	(Wea Yz 454)	50	1990	0	1990	
Nick Lowe	Male Vocalist, B: 25 Mar 1949 Woodbridge, Suffolk, England						
1	I Love The Sound Of Breaking Glass	(Radar Ada)	7	1978	0	1978	
2	Crackin' Up	(Radar Ada 34)	34	1979	0	1979	
3	Cruel To Be Kind	(Radar Ada 43)	12	1979	12	1979	(Columbia 11018)

N

473

ISSUE	TITLE	UK LBL	UK POS	UK YEAR	US POS	US YEAR	US LBL
4	Half A Boy Half A Man	(F. Beat Xx 34)	53	1984	0	1984	

Nick Noble   Real Name Nicholas Valkan B: 21 Jun 1936 Chicago

1	The Bible Tells Me So		0	1955	22	1955	(Wing 90003)
2	To You, My Love		0	1955	27	1955	(Mercury 70821)
3	A Fallen Star		0	1957	20	1957	(Mercury 71124)
4	Moonlight Swim		0	1957	37	1957	(Mercury 71169)

Nick Straker Band   Male Vocal/Instrumental Group from the UK

1	A Walk In The Park	(Cbs 8525)	20	1980	0	1980	
2	Leaving On The Midnight Train	(Cbs 9088)	61	1980	0	1980	

Nick Todd   Real Name Nicholas Boone B: 1 Jun 1935 Jacksonville, Florida   Younger Brother Of Pat Boone

1	At The Hop		0	1958	21	1958	(Dot 15675)

Nicki French   Female Vocalist From Carlisle, England

* 1	Total Eclipse Of The Heart	(Bags Of Fun Bagscd 1)	54	1994	2	1995	(Critique 15539)
2	Total Eclipse Of The Heart (Re-Entry)	(Bags Of Fun Bagscd 1)	5	1995	0	1995	
3	For All We Know	(Bags Of Fun Bagscd 4)	42	1995	0	1995	
4	Did You Ever Really Love Me	(Love This Luvthiscd 2)	55	1995	0	1995	

Nicko McBrain   Male Vocalist/Drummer from the UK

1	Rhythm Of The Beast	(EMI Nick 01)	72	1991	0	1991	

Nicky Thomas   Male Vocalist From Jamaica

1	Love Of The Common People	(Trojan Tr 7750)	9	1970	0	1970	

Nicole (1)   Female Vocalist From Germany

1	A Little Peace	(Cbs A 2365)	1	1982	0	1982	
2	Give Me More Time	(Cbs A 2467)	75	1982	0	1982	

Nicole (2)   Female Vocalist from the USA

1	New York Eyes	(Portrait A 6805)	41	1985	0	1985	
2	Rock The House	(React 12react 12)	63	1992	0	1992	
3	Runnin' Away	(Xl Recordings Ag 18cd)	69	1996	0	1996	

HIT 1 IS CREDITED TO NICOLE WITH TIMMY THOMAS • HIT 2 IS CREDITED TO SOURCE FEATURING NICOLE

Nicolette   Female Vocalist from the UK

1	No Government	(Talkin Loud Tlcd 1)	67	1995	0	1995	

Nicolette Larson   Female Vocalist, B: 17 Jul 1952 Helena, Montana

1	Lotta Love		0	1979	8	1979	(Warner Bros 8664)
2	Let Me Go, Love		0	1980	35	1980	(Warner Bros 49130)

Nielsen/Pearson   Lead Singers With The Quartet Is Reed Nielsen & Mark Pearson

1	If You Should Sail		0	1980	38	1980	(Capitol 4910)

Nigel Olsson   He Was The Drummer In Elton John's Band From 1971-76

1	Dancin' Shoes		0	1979	18	1979	(Bang 740)
2	Little Bit Of Soap		0	1979	34	1979	(Bang 4800)

Night   Lead Singer With The Sextet Is Stevie Lange

1	Hot Summer Nights		0	1979	18	1979	(Planet 45903)
2	If You Remember Me	(Planet K 12389)	42	1979	17	1979	(Planet 45904)

Night Ranger   Lead Singers With The Rock Group Are Jack Blades & Kelly Keagy

1	Don't Tell Me You Love Me		0	1983	40	1983	(Boardwalk 171)
2	Sister Christian		0	1984	5	1984	(MCA/Camel 52350)
3	When You Close Your Eyes		0	1984	14	1984	(MCA/Camel 52420)
4	Sentimental Street		0	1985	8	1985	(MCA/Camel 52591)
5	Four In The Morning (I Can't Take Anymore)		0	1985	19	1985	(MCA/Camel 52661)
6	Goodbye		0	1985	17	1985	(MCA/Camel 52729)

Nightcrawlers (Featuring) John Reid   Male Production/Instrumental Duo from the UK

1	Push The Feeling On	(Ffrr Fcd 245)	22	1994	0	1994	
2	Push The Feeling On (Re-Mix)	(Ffrr Fcd 257)	3	1995	0	1995	
3	Surrender Your Love	(Final Vinyl 74321283982)	7	1995	0	1995	
4	Don't Let The Feeling Go	(Final Vinyl 74321293882)	13	1995	0	1995	
5	Let's Push It	(Final Vinyl 74321328152)	23	1996	0	1996	
6	Should I Ever (Fall In Love)	(Arista 74321358072)	34	1996	0	1996	
7	Keep On Pushing Our Love	(Arista 74321390422)	30	1996	0	1996	

HIT 7 IS CREDITED TO NIGHTCRAWLERS FEATURING JOHN REID AND ALYSHA WARREN

Nightmares On Wax   Male Instrumental Group from the UK

1	Aftermath / I'm For Real	(Warp Wap 6)	38	1990	0	1990	

ISSUE	TITLE	UK LBL	UK POS	UK YEAR	US POS	US YEAR	US LBL
Nightwriters	Male Vocal/Instrumental Duo from the USA						
1	Let The Music Use You	(Ffrreedom Tabx 112)	51	1992	0	1992	
Niiu	Male R&B Quartet From New Jersey						
1	I Miss You		0	1995	22	1995	(Arista 12768)
Nik Kershaw	Male Vocalist from the UK						
1	I Won't Let The Sun Go Down On Me	(MCA Mca 816)	47	1983	0	1983	
2	Wouldn't It Be Good	(MCA Nik 2)	4	1984	0	1984	
3	Dancing Girls	(MCA Nik 3)	13	1984	0	1984	
4	I Won't Let The Sun Go Down On Me (Re-Issue)	(MCA Nik 4)	2	1984	0	1984	
5	Human Racing	(MCA Nik 5)	19	1984	0	1984	
6	The Riddle	(MCA Nik 6)	3	1984	0	1984	
7	Wide Boy	(MCA Nik 7)	9	1985	0	1985	
8	Don Quixote	(MCA Nik 8)	10	1985	0	1985	
9	When A Heart Beats	(MCA Nik 9)	27	1985	0	1985	
10	Nobody Knows	(MCA Nik 10)	44	1986	0	1986	
11	Radio Musicola	(MCA Nik 11)	43	1986	0	1986	
12	One Step Ahead	(MCA Nik 12)	55	1989	0	1989	
Nikita Warren	Female Vocalist from Italy						
1	I Need You	(VC Recordings Vcrd 12)	48	1996	0	1996	
Nikke? Nicole!	Female Rapper from the USA						
1	Nikke Does It Better	(Love Evol 5)	73	1991	0	1991	
Nikki	Male Singer/Multi-Instrumentalist, B: Okinawa, Japan. He Was Once A Backing Singer With Sun						
1	Notice Me		0	1990	21	1990	(Geffen 19946)
Nikki D	Female Rapper from the USA						
1	My Love Is So Raw	(Def Jam 6548987)	34	1989	0	1989	
2	Daddy's Little Girl	(Def Jam 6567347)	75	1991	0	1991	
	HIT 1 IS CREDITED TO ALYSON WILLIAMS FEATURING NIKKI D						
Nils Lofgren	Male Vocal/Guitarist from the USA						
1	Secrets In The Street	(Towerbell Tow 68)	53	1985	0	1985	
Nilsson	Male Vocalist, Real Name Harry Edward Nelson 111 B: 16 Jun 1941 In Brooklyn						
1	Everybody's Talkin' (From Midnight Cowboy)	(RCA 1876)	50	1969	6	1969	(RCA 0161)
2	Everybody's Talkin' (Re-Entry)	(RCA 1876)	73	1969	0	1969	
3	I Guess The Lord Must Be In New York City		0	1969	34	1969	(RCA 0261)
4	Everybody's Talkin' (2nd Re-Entry)	(RCA 1876)	39	1970	0	1970	
5	Me And My Arrow		0	1971	34	1971	(RCA 0443)
* 6	Without You	(RCA 2165)	1	1972	1	1971	(RCA 0604)
7	Jump Into The Fire		0	1972	27	1972	(RCA 0673)
8	Coconut	(RCA 2214)	42	1972	8	1972	(RCA 0718)
9	Spaceman		0	1972	23	1972	(RCA 0788)
10	Daybreak		0	1974	39	1974	(RCA 0246)
11	Without You (Re-Issue)	(RCA 2733)	22	1976	0	1976	
12	All I Think About Is You	(RCA Pb 9104)	43	1977	0	1977	
13	Without You (Re-Issue)	(RCA 74321193092)	47	1994	0	1994	
Nina & Frederick	Mixed Vocal Duo From Denmark						
1	Mary's Boy Child	(Columbia Db 4375)	26	1959	0	1959	
2	Listen To The Ocean	(Columbia Db 4332)	47	1960	0	1960	
3	Listen To The Ocean (Re-Entry)	(Columbia Db 4332)	46	1960	0	1960	
4	Little Donkey	(Columbia Db 4536)	3	1960	0	1960	
5	Longtime Boy	(Columbia Db 4703)	43	1961	0	1961	
6	Sucu Sucu	(Columbia Db 4632)	23	1961	0	1961	
Nina Simone	Female Vocalist, Real Name Eunice Waymon B: 21 Feb 1933 Tryon, South Carolina						
1	I Loves You, Porgy		0	1959	18	1959	(Bethlehem 11021)
2	I Put A Spell On You	(Philips BF 1415)	49	1965	0	1965	
3	Ain't Go No-I Got Life	(RCA 1743)	2	1968	0	1968	
4	Do What You Gotta Do	(RCA 1743)	7	1968	0	1968	
5	To Love Somebody	(RCA 1779)	5	1969	0	1969	
6	I Put A Spell On You (Re-Issue)	(Philips Bf 1736)	28	1969	0	1969	
7	My Baby Just Cares For Me	(Charly Cyz 7112)	5	1987	0	1987	
8	Feeling Good	(Mercury Mercd 403)	40	1994	0	1994	
Nine Inch Nails	Male Vocalist, Trent Reznor & Backing Musicians from the USA						
1	Head Like A Hole	(Tvt Is 484)	45	1991	0	1991	
2	Sin	(Tvt Is 508)	35	1991	0	1991	

ISSUE	TITLE	UK LBL	UK POS	UK YEAR	US POS	US YEAR	US LBL
3	March Of The Pigs	(Tvt Cid 592)	45	1994	0	1994	
4	Closer	(TVT Cid 596)	25	1994	0	1994	
5	The Perfect Drug (From Lost Highway)	(Interscope Ind 95542)	43	1997	48	1997	(Interscope 95007)

999 Male Vocal/Instrumental Group from the UK

1	Homicide	(United Artists Up 36467)	40	1978	0	1978	
2	Found Out Too Late	(Radar Ada 46)	69	1979	0	1979	
3	Obsessed	(Albion Ion 1011)	71	1981	0	1981	
4	Lil' Red Riding Hood	(Albion Ion 1017)	59	1981	0	1981	
5	Indian Reservation	(Albion Ion 1023)	51	1981	0	1981	

9ers Real Name Gianfranco Bortolotti Male Producer From Italy

1	Touch Me	(Fourth & Broadway Brw 157)	3	1989	0	1989	
2	Don't You Love Me	(Fourth & Broadway Brw 167)	12	1990	0	1990	
3	Girl To Girl	(Fourth & Broadway Brw 174)	31	1990	0	1990	
4	Got To Be Free	(Fourth & Broadway Brw 255)	46	199	20	1992	
5	The Message	(Fourth & Broadway Brw 257)	68	1992	0	1992	
6	Rockin' My Body	(Media Mcstd 2021)	31	1995	0	1995	

HIT 6 IS CREDITED TO THE 49ERS FEATURING ANN MARIE SMITH

1910 Fruitgum Company Male Vocal/Instrumental Group from the USA

*	1	Simon Says	(Pye International 7n 25447)	2	1968	4	1968	(Buddah 24)
*	2	1, 2, 3, Red Light		0	1968	5	1968	(Buddah 54)
	3	Goody Goody Gumdrops		0	1968	37	1968	(Buddah 71)
*	4	Indian Giver		0	1969	5	1969	(Buddah 91)
	5	Special Delivery		0	1969	38	1969	(Buddah 114)

FLOYD MARCUS, PAT KARWAN, MARK GUTKOWSKI, STEVE MORTKOWITZ & FRANK JECKELL A QUINTET ALL FROM LYNDEN, NEW JERSEY

1927 Male Vocal/Instrumental Group from Australia

1	That's When I Think Of You	(Wea Yz 351)	46	1989	0	1989	

9.9 Mixed Vocal Group from the USA

1	All Of Me For All Of You	(RCA Pb 49951)	53	1985	0	1985	

95 South Male Vocal Group (Named After The Interstate Highway) From Miami

*	1	Whoot, There It Is		0	1993	11	1993	(Wrap 162)

911 Male Vocal Group from the UK

1	Night To Remember	(Ginga Cdginga 1)	38	1996	0	1996	
2	Love Sensation	(Ginga Cdginga 2)	21	1996	0	1996	
3	Don't Make Me Wait	(Ginga Vscdt 1618)	10	1996	0	1996	
4	Don't Make Me Wait (Re-Entry)	(Ginga Vscdt 1618)	63	1997	0	1997	
5	The Day We Find Love	(Ginga Vscdg 1619)	4	1997	0	1997	
6	Bodyshakin'	(Jive Jivecd 415)	3	1997	0	1997	
7	The Journey	(Virgin Vscdt 1645)	3	1997	0	1997	

99th Floor Elevators

1	Hooked	(Labello Dance/Pwl Lad 18cd)	28	1995	0	995	
2	I'll Be There	(Labello Dance/Pwl Lad 25cd2)	37	1996	0	1996	

HIT 2 IS CREDITED TO 99TH FLOOR ELEVATORS WITH TONY DE VIT

Nini Rosso Male Instrumentalist (Trumpet) B: 19 Sep 1926, Turin, Italy

*	1	Il Silenzio	(Durium Drs 54000)	8	1985	0	1965	

Nino De Angelo Male Vocalist from Germany

1	Guardian Angel	(Carrere Car 335)	57	1984	0	1984	

Nino Tempo & April Stevens Mixed Vocal Duo, Real Names Antonio Lo B: 6 Jan 1935 And Carol Lo Tempio B: 29 Apr 1936 from the USA

*	1	Deep Purple	(London Hlk 9782)	17	1963	1	1963	(Atco 6273)
	2	Whispering	(London Hlk 9829)	20	1964	11	1964	(Atco 6281)
	3	Stardust		0	1964	32	1964	(Atco 6286)
	4	All Strung Out		0	1966	26	1966	(White Whale 236)

Nirvana (1) Male Vocal/Instrumental Duo from the UK/Ireland

1	Rainbow Chaser	(Island Wip 6029)	34	1968	0	1968	

Nirvana (2) Male Vocal/Instrumental Group from the USA

*	1	Smells Like Team Spirit	(Dgc Dgcs 5)	7	1991	6	1991	(Dgc 19050)
	2	Come As You Are	(Dgc Dgcs 7)	9	1992	32	1992	(Dgc 19120)
	3	Lithium	(Dgc Dgcs 9)	11	1992	0	1992	
	4	In Bloom	(Geffen Gfs 34)	28	1992	0	1992	
	5	Oh The Guilt	(Touch And Go Tg 83cd)	12	1993	0	1993	
	6	Heart-Shaped Box	(Geffen Gfstd 54)	5	1993	0	1993	

	ISSUE	TITLE	UK LBL	UK POS	UK YEAR	US POS	US YEAR	US LBL
	7	All Apologies / Rape Me	(Geffen Gfstd 66)	32	1993	0	1993	

Nite-Liters Formed In 1963 And Later Renamed As The New Birth
| | 1 | K-Jee | | 0 | 1971 | 39 | 1971 | (RCA 0461) |

Niteflyte Disco Group Led By Howard Johnson & Sandy Torano
| | 1 | If You Want Me | | 0 | 1979 | 37 | 1979 | (Ariola Am. 7747) |

Nitro Deluxe Male Multi-Instrumentalist, Real Name Lee Junior from the USA
	1	This Brutal House	(Cooltempo Cool 142)	47	1987	0	1987	
	2	This Brutal House (Re-Entry)	(Cooltempo Cool 142)	62	1987	0	1987	
	3	Let's Get Brutal (remix of hit 1)	(Cooltempo Cool 142)	4	1988	0	1988	

Nitty Gritty Dirt Band Country-Folk-Rock Group Led By Jeff Hanna, Changed Their Name To Dirt Band In 1976, Changed The Name Back Again In 1982
	1	Mr. Bojangles		0	1971	9	1971	(Liberty 56197)
!	2	I Saw The Light		0	1971	56	1971	(United Artist 50849)
!	3	Grand Ole Opry Song		0	1973	97	1973	(United Artist 247)
	4	(All I Have To Do Is) Dream		0	1975	66	1975	(United Artist 655)
	5	An American Dream		0	1980	13	1980	(United Artists 1330)
	6	Make A Little Magic		0	1980	25	1980	(United Artists 1356)
	7	Fire In The Sky		0	1981	76	1981	(Liberty 1429)
		OTHER HITS ARE C/W						

Nitzer Ebb Male Vocal/Instrumental Group from the UK
	1	Godhead	(Mute 1mute 135t)	56	1992	0	1992	
	2	Ascend	(Mute 110mute 145t)	52	1992	0	1992	
	3	Kick It	(Mute Lcdmute 155)	75	1995	0	1995	

No Dice Male Vocal/Instrumental Group from the UK
| | 1 | Come Dancing | (EMI 2927) | 65 | 1979 | 0 | 1979 | |

No Doubt Mixed Vocal/Instrumental Group from the USA
	1	Just A Girl	(Interscope Ind 80034)	38	1996	23	1996	
	2	Don't Speak	(Interscope Ind 95515)	1	1997	0	1997	
	3	Just A Girl	(Interscope Ind 95539)	3	1997	0	1997	

No Mercy
	1	Where Do You Go	(Arista 74321401502	2	1997	7	1996	(Arista 13225)
	2	Please Don't Go	(Arista 74321481372)	4	1997	21	1997	(Arista 13304)
	3	Kiss You All Over	(Arista 74321514452)	16	1997	0	1997	

No Sweat Male Vocal/Instrumental Group From Ireland
| | 1 | Heart And Soul | (London Lon 274) | 64 | 1990 | 0 | 1990 | |
| | 2 | Tear Down The Walls | (London Lon 288) | 61 | 1991 | 0 | 1991 | |

No Way Jose' Male Instrumental Group from the USA
| | 1 | No Way Jose' | (Fourth & Broadway Brw 28) | 47 | 1985 | 0 | 1985 | |

No Way Sis Male Vocal/Instrumental Group from the USA
| | 1 | I'd Like To Teach The World To Sing | (EMI Cdem 461) | 27 | 1996 | 0 | 1996 | |

Noel Harrison Male Vocalist from the UK
| | 1 | The Windmills Of Your Mind | (Reprise Rs 20758) | 8 | 1969 | 0 | 1969 | |

Noel Murphy Male Vocalist From Ireland
| | 1 | Murphy And The Bricks | (Murphy's Stack 1) | 57 | 1987 | 0 | 1987 | |

Nolans Female Vocal Group From Ireland
	1	Spirit Body And Soul	(Epic Epc 7796)	34	1979	0	1979	
	2	I'm In The Mood For Dancing	(Epic Epc 8068)	3	1979	0	1979	
	3	Don't Make Waves	(Epic Epc 8349)	12	1980	0	1980	
	4	Gotta Pull Myself Together	(Epic Epc 8878)	9	1980	0	1980	
	5	Who's Gonna Rock You	(Epic Epc 9325)	12	1980	0	1980	
	6	Attention To Me	(Epic Epc 9571)	9	1981	0	1981	
	7	Chemistry	(Epic Epc A 1485)	15	1981	0	1981	
	8	Don't Love Me Too Hard	(Epic Epc A 1927)	14	1982	0	1982	
	9	I'm In The Mood For Dancing (Re-Mix)	(Living Beat Lbecd 31)	51	1995	0	1995	

Nomad Mixed Vocal/Instrumental Duo from the UK
	1	I Wanna Give You (Devotion)	(Rumour Ruma 25)	2	1991	0	1991	
	2	Just A Groove	(Rumour Ruma 33)	16	1991	0	1991	
	3	Something Special	(Rumour Ruma 35)	73	1991	0	1991	
	4	Your Love Is Lifting Me	(Rumour Ruma 48)	60	1992	0	1992	
	5	24 Hours A Day	(Rumour Ruma 60)	61	1992	0	1992	
	6	I Wanna Give You (Devotion) (Re-Mix)	(Rumour Rumacd 75)	42	1995	0	1995	

ISSUE	TITLE	UK LBL	UK POS	UK YEAR	US POS	US YEAR	US LBL
Non Blondes Rock Band Formed In San Francisco In 1989							
1	What's Up		0	1993	14	1993	(Interscope 98430)
Nona Hendryx Female Vocalist from the USA							
1	Why Should I Cry	(EMI America EA 234)	60	1987	0	1987	
Nonchalant Female Vocalist from the USA							
1	5 O'Clock	(MCA Mcstd 48011)	44	1996	24	1996	(MCA)
Noosha Fox Female Vocalist from the UK							
1	Georgina Bailey	(GTO GT 106)	31	1977	0	1977	
Nootropic Male Instrumental/Production Duo from the UK							
1	I See Only You	(Hi-Life/Polydor 5779832)	42	1996	0	1996	
Norma Tanega Female Vocalist, B: 30 Jan 1939 Vallejo, California							
1	Walkin' My Cat Named Dog	(Stateside Ss 496)	22	1966	22	1966	(New Voice 807)
Norman Brooks Male Vocalist, Real Name Norman Joseph Arie From Canada							
1	Hello Sunshine		0	1953	20	1953	(Zodiac 101)
2	You Shouldn't Have Kissed Me The First Time		0	1953	22	1953	(Zodiac 102)
3	Somebody Wonderful		0	1953	22	1953	(Zodiac 102)
4	A Sky Blue Shirt And A Rainbow Tie	(London L 1228)	17	1954	0	1954	
Norman Connors Male Drummer, B: 1 Mar 1948 Phiadelphia							
1	You Are My Starship		0	1976	27	1976	(Buddah 542)
Norman Cook Male Producer/Multi-Instrumental from the UK							
1	Won't Talk About It	(Go.Beat God 33)	29	1989	0	1989	
2	Blame It On The Bassline	(Go.Beat God 33)	29	1989	0	1989	
3	For Spacious Lies	(Go.Beat God 37)	48	1989	0	1989	
4	Just Another Groove	(Ffrr Fcd 287)	43	1996	0	1996	
Norman Greenbaum Male Vocalist, B: 20 Nov 1942 Malden, Massachusetts In 1965 Formed Dr West's Medicine Show And Junk Band							
* 1	Spirit In The Sky	(Reprise Rs 20885)	1	1970	3	1970	(Reprise 0885)
Norman Petty Trio							
1	Mood Indigo		0	1954	14	1954	(X 0040)
2	On The Alamo		0	1954	29	1954	(X 0071)
Norman Vaughan Male Comedian/Vocalist from the UK							
1	Swinging In The Rain	(Pye 7n 15438)	34	1962	0	1962	
Norman Wisdom Male Comedian/Vocalist from the UK							
1	Don't Laugh At Me	(Columbia Db 3133)	3	1954	0	1954	
2	The Wisdom Of A Fool	(Columbia Db 3903)	13	1957	0	1957	
Norrie Paramor Orchestra Leader from the UK							
1	Theme From A Summer Place	(Columbia Db 4419)	36	1960	0	1960	
2	Theme From Z Cars	(Columbia Db 4789)	33	1962	0	1962	
North & South							
1	I'm A Man Not A Boy	(RCA 74321461142)	7	1997	0	1997	
2	Tarantino's New Star	(RCA 74321501242)	18	1997	0	1997	
Northern Uproar Male Vocal/Instrumental Group from the UK							
1	Rollercoaster / Rough Boys	(Heavenly Hvn 047cd)	41	1995	0	1995	
2	From A Window / This Morning	(Heavenly Hvn 051cd)	17	1996	0	1996	
3	Livin' It Up	(Heavenly Hvn 52cd)	24	1996	0	1996	
4	Town	(Heavenly Hvn 54cd)	48	1996	0	1996	
5	Any Way You Look	(Heavenly Hvn 70cd)	36	1997	0	1997	
6	A Girl I Once Knew	(Heavenly Hvn 73cd)	63	1997	0	1997	
Northside Male Vocal/Instrumental Group from the UK							
1	Shall We Take A Trip / Moody Places	(Factory Fac 268)	50	1990	0	1990	
2	My Rising Star	(Factory Fac 2987)	32	1990	0	1990	
3	Take 5	(Factory Fac 3087)	40	1991	0	1991	
Notorious B.I.G. Male Rapper from the USA							
* 1	Juicy	(Bad Boy 74321240102)	72	1994	27	1994	(Bad Boy 79004)
2	Unbelievable		0	1994	27	1994	(Bad Boy 79004)
* 3	Big Poppa	(Arista 74321263412)	63	1995	6	1995	(Bad Boy 79015)
4	Warning		0	1995	6	1995	(Bad Boy 79015)
* 5	Can't You See	(Tommy Boy Tbcd 700)	43	1995	13	1995	(Tommy Boy 7676)
* 6	One More Chance / Stay With Me	(Puff Daddy 74321300782)	34	1995	2	1995	(Bad Boy 79031)
7	The What		0	1995	2	1995	(Bad Boy 79031)
8	Only You		0	1996	13	1996	(Arista 79060)

ISSUE	TITLE	UK LBL	UK POS	UK YEAR	US POS	US YEAR	US LBL
9	Runnin'		0	1997	84	1997	(Solar 70134)
10	Runnin' (Re-Entry)		0	1997	81	1997	(Solar 70134)
11	Hypnotize	(Arista 74321466412)	10	1997	1	1997	(Arista 79092)
12	Stop The Gunfight		0	1997	77	1997	(Intersound 9269)
13	Mo Money Mo Problems	(Arista 74321492492)	6	1997		1997	
NRG							
1	Never Lost His Hardcore	(Top Banana Topcd 04)	71	1997	0	1997	
NT Gang Male Vocal/Instrumental Group From Germany							
1	Wam Bam	(Cooltempo Cool 163)	71	1988	0	1988	
Nu-Birth							
1	Anytime	(Xl Recordings Xls 85cd)	48	1997	0	1997	
Nu Colours Mixed Vocal/Instrumental Group from the UK							
1	Tears	(Wild Card Card 1)	55	1992	0	1992	
2	Power	(Wild Card Card 3)	64	1992	0	1992	
3	What In The World	(Wild Card Cardd 4)	57	1993	0	1993	
4	Power (Re-Issue)	(Wild Card Cardd 5)	40	1993	0	1993	
5	Desire	(Wild Card 5763652)	31	1996	0	1996	
6	Special Kind Of Lover	(Wild Card 5752012)	38	1996	0	1996	
Nu Flavor (featuring Roger)							
1	Sweet Sexy Thing		0	1997	67	1997	(Reprise 17402)
Nu Matic Male Production/Instrumental Duo from the UK							
1	Spring In My Step	(Xl Xls 31)	58	1992	0	1992	
Nu Shooz Mixed Vocal/Instrumental Group from Portland, Oregon Lead Singers Are John Smith And His Wife Valerie Day							
1	I Can't Wait	(Atlantic A 9446)	2	1986	3	1986	(Atlantic 89446)
2	Point Of No Return	(Atlantic A 9392)	48	1986	28	1986	(Atlantic 89392)
Nu Soul (featuring Kelly Rich) Mixed Vocal/Instrumental Duo from the USA							
1	Hide-A-Way	(Ffrr Fcd 269)	27	1996	0	1996	
Nu Tornados Names: Eddie Dono, Louie Mann, Tom Dell, Phil Dale & Mike Perna							
1	Philadelphia Usa		0	1958	26	1958	(Carlton 492)
Nuance (Featuring) Vikki Love Mixed Vocal/Instrumental Group from the USA							
1	Loveride	(Fourth & Broadway Brw 20)	59	1985	0	1985	
Number One Cup Male Vocal/Instrumental Group From The US							
1	Divebomb	(Blue Rose/Flydaddy Brrc 10032)	61	1996	0	1996	
Nush Male Production/Instrumental Duo from the UK							
1	U Girls	(Blunted Vinyl Blncdx 006)	58	1994	0	1994	
2	Move That Body	(Blunted Vinyl Blncd 12)	46	1995	0	1995	
3	U Girls (Look So Sexy) (Re-Mix)	(Blunted Vinyl Blncd 13)	15	1995	0	1995	
Nut Female Vocalist from the UK							
1	Brains	(Epic Nutcd 2)	64	1996	0	1996	
2	Crazy	(Epic Nutcd 5)	56	1996	0	1996	
3	Scream	(Epic Nutcd 6)	43	1997	0	1997	
Nutmegs R&B Vocal Group from the USA							
* 1	Story Untold		0	1955	2	1955	(Herald 452)
Nuttin' Nyce Female Vocal Group from the USA							
1	Down 4 Whateva	(Jive Jivecd 365)	62	1995	0	1995	
2	Froggy Sryle	(Jive Jivecd 381)	68	1995	0	1995	
Nutty Squirrels Voices From Sascha Burland & Don Elliot							
1	Uh! Oh! (Part 2)		0	1959	14	1959	(Hanover 4540)
Nuyorican Soul							
1	Runaway	(Talkin' Loud Tlcd 20)	24	1997	0	1997	with India
2	It's Alright, I Feel It!	(Talkin' Loud Tlcd 22)	26	1997	0	1997	with Jocelyn Brown

ISSUE	TITLE	UK LBL	UK POS	UK YEAR	US POS	US YEAR	US LBL
Nylon Moon Male Instrumental Duo from Italy							
1	Sky Plus	(Positiva Cdtiv 50)	43	1996	0	1996	
Nylons Male Vocal Quartet from Canada							
1	Kiss Him Goodbye		0	1987	12	1987	(Open Air 0022)
'N Sync							
1	Tearin' Up My Heart	(Arista 74321505152)	40	1997	0	1997	

O

ISSUE	TITLE	UK LBL	UK POS	UK YEAR	US POS	US YEAR	US LBL
O'Jays Names: Eddie Levert, Walter Williams & Bill Powell							
+ 1	One Night Affair		0	1969	15	1969	(Neptune 12)
+ 2	Deeper (In Love With You)		0	1970	21	1970	(Neptune 22)
+ 3	Looky Looky (Look At Me Girl)		0	1970	17	1970	(Neptune 31)
* 4	Back Stabbers	(CBS 8270)	14	1972	3	1972	(Phil/Inter 3517)
5	992 Arguments		0	1972	57	1972	(Phil/Inter 3522)
* 6	Love Train	(Philadelphia Int. Pir 3879)	9	1973	1	1973	(Phil/Inter 3524)
7	Time To Get Down		0	1973	33	1973	(Phil/Inter 3531)
8	Put Your Hands Together		0	1974	10	1974	(Phil/Inter 3535)
* 9	For The Love Of Money		0	1974	9	1974	(Phil/Inter 3544)
10	Sunshine (Part 2)		0	1974	48	1974	(Phil/Inter 3558)
+ 11	Let Me Make Love To You		0	1975	10	1975	(Phil/Inter 8-3558)
12	Give The People What They Want		0	19754	5	1975	(Hi 2282)
13	I Love Music (Part 1)	(Philadelphia Int. Pir 3879)	13	1976	5	1975	(Phil/Inter 3577)
* 14	Livin' For The Weekend		0	1976	20	1976	(Phil/Inter 3587)
15	Darlin' Darlin' Baby	(Philadelphia Int. Pir 4834)	24	1977	0	1977	
16	I Love Music (Part 1) (Re-Entry)	(Philadelphia Int. Pir 6093)	36	1978	0	1978	
* 17	Use Ta Be My Girl	(Philadelphia Int. Pir 6332)	12	1978	4	1978	(Phil/Inter 3642)
18	Brandy	(Philadelphia Int. Pir 6658)	21	1978	0	1978	
19	Sing A Happy Song	(Philadelphia Int. Pir 7825)	38	1979	0	1979	
20	Forever Mine		0	1980	28	1980	(Phil/Inter 3727)
21	Put Our Heads Together	(Philadelphia Int. A 3642)	45	1983	0	1983	
	THE GROUP WAS ORIGINALLY KNOWN AS THE TRIUMPHS WITH BOBBY MASSEY & BILL ISLES IN 1958 • TOOK THEIR NAME FROM THEIR MANAGER EDDIE O'JAY ALSO RECORDED AS THE MASCOTS IN 1961						
O'Kaysions Names: Donny Weaver, Ron Turner, Wayne Pittman, Jim Spidel, Jimmy Hennant & Bruce Joyner Originally Called The Kays							
* 1	Girl Watcher		0	1968	5	1968	(ABC 11094)
O.C. Smith Male Vocalist, Real Name Ocie Lee Smith B: 21 Jun 1936 Mansfield, Louisiana							
1	The Son Of Hickory Holler's Tramp	(CBS 3343)	2	1968	40	1968	(Columbia 44425)
2	Together	(Caribou Crb 4910)	25	1977	0	1977	
* 3	Little Green Apples		0	1968	2	1968	(Columbia 44616)
4	Daddy's Little Man		0	1969	34	1969	(Columbia 44948)
O.V. Wright Male R&B vocalist from the USA							
+ 1	You're Gonna Make Me Cry		0	1965	6	1965	(Backbeat 548)
+ 2	Eight Men Four Women		0	1967	4	1967	(Backbeat 580)
3	Ace Of Spade		0	1970	54	1970	(Backbeat 615)
Oak Ridge Boys Formed In 1940 As A Gospel Quartet In Tennessee, Now Switched To A Country-Pop Style							
* 15	Elvira		0	1981	5	1981	(MCA 51084)
17	Bobbie Sue		0	1982	12	1982	(MCA 51231)
Oasis Male Vocal/Instrumental Group Lead By Noel & Liam Gallagher from the UK							
1	Supersonic	(Creation Crescd 176)	31	1994	0	1994	
2	Shakermaker	(Creation Crescd 182)	11	1994	0	1994	
3	Live Forever	(Creation Crescd 185)	10	1994	0	1994	
4	Cigarettes And Alcohol	(Creation Crescd 190)	7	1994	0	1994	
5	Whatever	(Creation Crescd 195)	3	1994	0	1994	
6	Cigarettes And Alcohol (Re-Entry)	(Creation Crescd 190)	69	1994	0	1994	
7	Some Might Say	(Creation Crescd 204)	1	1995	0	1995	
8	Some Might Say (Re-Entry)	(Creation Cre 201t)	71	1995	0	1995	
9	Supersonic (Re-Entry)	(Creation Crescd 176)	44	1995	0	1995	
10	Whatever (Re-Entry)	(Creation Crescd 195)	48	1995	0	1995	
11	Live Forever (Re-Entry)	(Creation Crescd 185)	50	1995	0	1995	
12	Shakermaker (Re-Entry)	(Creation Crescd 182)	52	1995	0	1995	

ISSUE	TITLE	UK LBL	UK POS	UK YEAR	US POS	US YEAR	US LBL
13	Cigarettes And Alcohol (2nd Re-Entry)	(Creation Crescd 190)	53	1995	0	1995	
14	Roll With It	(Creation Crescd 212)	2	1995	0	1995	
15	Some Might Say (Re-Entry)	(Creation Crescd 204)	73	1995	0	1995	
16	Wonderwall	(Creation Crescd 215)	2	1996	8	1996	(Epic 00000)
17	Sibbling Rivalry	(Fierce Panda Ning 12cd)	52	1995	0	1995	
	(Interviews With Noel & Liam Gallagher)						
18	Whatever (2nd Re-Entry)	(Creation Crescd 195)	75	1995	0	1995	
19	Cigarettes And Alcohol (3rd Re-Entry)	(Creation Crescd 190)	58	1996	0	1996	
20	Whatever (3rd Re-Entry)	(Creation Crescd 195)	55	1995	0	1995	
21	Supersonic (2nd Re-Entry)	(Creation Crescd 176)	54	1996	0	1996	
22	Shakermaker (2nd Re-Entry)	(Creation Crescd 182)	61	1996	0	1996	
23	Live Forever (2nd Re-Entry)	(Creation Crescd 185)	64	1996	0	1996	
24	Some Might Say (2nd Re-Entry)	(Creation Crescd 204)	59	1996	0	1996	
25	Roll With It (Re-Entry)	(Creation Crescd 212)	65	1996	0	1996	
26	Live Foever (3rd Re-Entry)	(Creation Crescd 185)	71	1996	0	1996	
27	Whatever (4th Re-Entry)	(Creation Crescd 195)	61	1996	0	1996	
28	Whatever (5th Re-Entry)	(Creation Crescd 195)	55	1996	0	1996	
29	Don't Look Back In Anger	(Creation Crescd 221)	1	1996	55	1996	(Epic 78356)
30	Cigarettes And Alcohol (4th Re-Entry)	(Creation Crescd 190)	62	1996	0	1996	
31	Supersonic (3rd Re-Entry)	(Creation Crescd 176)	71	1997	0	1997	
32	Shakermaker (3rd Re-Entry)	(Creation Crescd 182)	74	1996	0	1996	
33	Live Forever (4th Re-Entry)	(Creation Crescd 185)	74	1996	0	1996	
34	Some Might Say (3rd Re-Entry)	(Creation Crescd 204)	75	1996	0	1996	
35	Cigarettes And Alcohol (5th Re-Entry)	(Creation Crescd 190)	72	1996	0	1996	
36	Cigarettes And Alcohol (6th Re-Entry)	(Creation Crescd 190)	72	1996	0	1996	
37	Whatever (6th Re-Entry)	(Creation Crescd 195)	62	1996	0	1996	
38	Wonderwall (Re-Entry)	(Creation Crescd 215)	60	1996	0	1996	
39	Some Might Say (4th Re-Entry)	(Creation Crescd 204)	70	1996	0	1996	
40	Cigarettes And Alcohol (7th Re-Entry)	(Creation Crescd 190)	72	1996	0	1996	
41	Whatever (7th Re-Entry)	(Creation Crescd 195)	66	1996	0	1996	
42	Whatever (8th Re-Entry)	(Creation Crescd 195)	34	1996	0	1996	
43	Wonderwall (2nd Re-Entry)	(Creation Crescd 215)	36	1996	0	1996	
44	Cigarettes And Alcohol (8th Re-Entry)	(Creation Crescd 190)	38	1996	0	1996	
45	Some Might Say (5th Re-Entry)	(Creation Crescd 204)	40	1996	0	1996	
46	Live Forever (5th Re-Entry)	(Creation Crescd 185)	42	1996	0	1996	
47	Supersonic (4th Re-Entry)	(Creation Crescd 176)	47	1996	0	1996	
48	Shakermaker (4th Re-Entry)	(Creation Crescd 182)	48	1996	0	1996	
49	Don't Look Back In Anger (Re-Entry)	(Creation Crescd 221)	53	1996	0	1996	
50	Roll With It (2nd Re-Entry)	(Creation Crescd 212)	55	1996	0	1996	
51	Don't Look Back In Anger (2nd Re-Entry)	(Creation Crescd 221)	67	1996	0	1996	
52	Cigarettes And Alcohol (9th Re-Entry)	(Creation Crescd 190)	71	1996	0	1996	
53	Some Might Say (6th Re-Entry)	(Creation Crescd 204)	73	1996	0	1996	
54	Live Forever (6th Re-Entry)	(Creation Crescd 185)	75	1996	0	1996	
55	D'you Know What I Mean?	(Creation Crescd 256)	1	1996	0	1997	
	HIT 17 IS CREDITED TO OAS*S • HIT 8 WAS IN A 12 FORMAT						

Obernkirchen Children's Choir Children's Choir from Germany

1	The Happy Wanderer	(Parlophone R 3799)	2	1954	0	1954	
2	The Happy Wanderer (Re-Entry)	(Parlophone R 3799)	8	1954	0	1954	
	The Hit And All The Children's Song Translations Were Written By Mr.S Antonia Ridge						

Ocean Names: Janice Morgan, David Tamblyn, Greg Brown, Jeff Jones & Charles Slater

* 1	Put Your Hand In The Hand		0	1971	2	1971	(Kama Sutra 519)

Ocean Colour Scene Male Vocal/Instrumental Group from the UK

1	Yesterday Today	(!Phfft Fit 2)	49	1991	0	1991	
2	The Riverboat Song	(MCA Mcstd 40021)	15	1996	0	1996	
3	You've Got It Bad	(MCA Mcstd 40036)	7	1996	0	1996	
4	The Day We Caught The Train	(MCA Mcstd 40046)	4	1996	0	1996	
5	The Circle	(MCA Mcstd 40077)	6	1996	0	1996	
6	Hundred Mile High City	(MCA Mcstd 40133)	4	1997	0	1997	
7	Travellers Tune	(MCA Mcstd 40144)	5	1997	0	1997	

Oceanic Mixed Vocal/Instrumental Group from the UK

1	Insanity	(Dead Dead Good Good 4)	3	1991	0	1991	
2	Wicked Love	(Dead Dead Good Good 5)	25	1991	0	1991	
3	Wicked Love (Re-Entry)	(Dead Dead Good Good 5)	65	1991	0	1991	
4	Controlling Me	(Dead Dead Good Good 14)	14	1992	0	1992	

ISSUE	TITLE	UK LBL	UK POS	UK YEAR	US POS	US YEAR	US LBL
5	Ignorance	(Dead Dead Good Good 22)	72	1992	0	1992	

HIT 5 IS CREDITED TO OCEANIC OCTOPUS FEATURING SIOBHAN MAHER

Octopus   Mixed Vocal/Instrumental Group from the UK/France

ISSUE	TITLE	UK LBL	UK POS	UK YEAR	US POS	US YEAR	US LBL
1	Your Smile	(Food Cdfood 78)	42	1996	0	1996	
2	Saved	(Food Cdfoods 84)	40	1996	0	1996	
3	Jealousy	(Food Cdfoods 87)	59	1996	0	1996	

Odyssey   Mixed Vocal Trio from the USA   Names are Tony Reynolds, Louise & Lillian Lopez

ISSUE	TITLE	UK LBL	UK POS	UK YEAR	US POS	US YEAR	US LBL
1	Native New Yorker	(RCA PC 1129)	5	1977	21	1977	(RCA 11129)
2	Use It Up And Wear It Out	(RCA PB 1962)	1	1980	0	1980	
3	If You're Lookin' For A Way Out	(RCA 5)	6	1980	0	1980	
4	Hang Together	(RCA 23)	36	1981	0	1981	
5	Going Back To My Roots	(RCA 85)	4	1981	0	1981	
6	It Will Be Alright	(RCA 128)	43	1981	0	1981	
7	Inside Out	(RCA 226)	3	1982	0	1982	
8	Magic Touch	(RCA 275)	41	1982	0	1982	
9	(Joy) I Know It	(Mirror Butch 12)	51	1985	0	1985	

Off-Shore   Male Production/Instrumental Duo from Germany

ISSUE	TITLE	UK LBL	UK POS	UK YEAR	US POS	US YEAR	US LBL
1	I Can't Take The Power	(CBS 6565707)	7	1990	0	1990	
2	I Got A Little Song	(Dance Pool 6568257)	64	1991	0	1991	

Offspring   Male Vocal/Instrumental Group from the USA

ISSUE	TITLE	UK LBL	UK POS	UK YEAR	US POS	US YEAR	US LBL
1	Self Esteem	(Golf Cdshole 001)	37	1995	0	1995	
2	Gotta Get Away	(Out Of Step Woos 2cds)	43	1995	0	1995	
3	All I Want	(Epitaph 64912)	31	1997	0	1997	
4	Gone Away	(3 Beat 3 Btcd1)	42	1997	0	1997	

Ofra Haza   Female Vocalist from Israel

ISSUE	TITLE	UK LBL	UK POS	UK YEAR	US POS	US YEAR	US LBL
1	Im Nin' Alu	(WEA Yz 190)	15	1988	0	1988	

Oh Well   Male Producer, Real Name Ackim Faulker from Germany

ISSUE	TITLE	UK LBL	UK POS	UK YEAR	US POS	US YEAR	US LBL
1	Oh Well	(Parlophone R 6236)	28	1989	0	1989	
2	Radar Love	(Parlophone R 6244)	65	1990	0	1990	

Ohio Express   Male Vocal/Instrumental Group from Mansfield, Ohio

ISSUE	TITLE	UK LBL	UK POS	UK YEAR	US POS	US YEAR	US LBL
1	Beg, Borrow And Steal		0	1967	29	1967	(Cameo 483)
* 2	Yummy Yummy Yummy	(Pye International 7n 25459)	5	1968	4	1968	(Buddah 38)
3	Down A Lulu's		0	1968	33	1968	(Buddah 56)
* 4	Chewy Chewy		0	1968	15	1968	(Buddah 70)
5	Mercy		0	19693	0	1969	(Buddah 102)

NAMES: DOUGLAS GRASSEL, DALE POWERS, JIM PFAHLER, TIM CORWIN & DEAN KASTRAN

Ohio Players   Male Vocal/Instrumental Group from the USA   Originally Known As The Ohio Untouchables

ISSUE	TITLE	UK LBL	UK POS	UK YEAR	US POS	US YEAR	US LBL
* 1	Funky Worm		0	1973	15	1973	(Westbound 214)
2	Ecstasy		0	1973	31	1973	(Westbound 216)
* 3	Skin Tight		0	1974	13	1974	(Mercury 73609)
* 4	Fire		0	1974	1	1974	(Mercury 73643)
5	Sweet Sticky Thing		0	1975	33	1975	(Mercury 73713)
* 6	Love Rollercoaster		0	1975	1	1975	(Mercury 73734)
7	Fopp		0	1976	30	1976	(Mercury 73775)
8	Who'd She Coo	(Mercury Play 001)	43	1976	18	1976	(Mercury 73814)

Oleta Adams   Female Singer from Yakima, Washington

ISSUE	TITLE	UK LBL	UK POS	UK YEAR	US POS	US YEAR	US LBL
1	Rhythm Of Life	(Fontana Oleta 1)	52	1990	0	1990	
2	Rhythm Of Life (Re-Entry)	(Fontana Oleta 1)	56	1990	0	1990	
3	Get Here	(Fontana Oleta 3)	4	1991	5	1991	(Fontana 878476)
4	You've Got To Give Me Room (Re-Issue)	(Fontana Oleta 4)	49	1991	0	1991	
5	Circle Of One	(Fontana Oleta 5)	73	1991	0	1991	
6	Don't Let The Sun Go Down On Me	(Fontana Tribo 1)	33	1991	0	1991	
7	Woman In Chains (Re-Issue)	(Fontana Idea 16)	57	1989	0	1989	
8	I Just Had To Hear Your Voice	(Fontana Olecd 6)	42	1993	0	1993	
9	Never Knew Love	(Fontana Olecd 9)	22	1995	0	1995	
10	Rhythm Of Life (Re-Mix)	(Fontana Olecd 10)	38	1995	0	1995	
11	We Will Meet Again	(Fontana Olecd 11)	51	1996	0	1996	

HIT 4 WAS BACKED WITH THE RHYTHM OF LIFE • HIT 7 IS CREDTIED TO TEARS FOR FEARS FEATURING OLETA ADAMS
SHE SANG BACKING VOCALS ON TOUR WITH TEARS FOR FEARS

Olga   Female Vocalist from Italy

ISSUE	TITLE	UK LBL	UK POS	UK YEAR	US POS	US YEAR	US LBL
1	I'm A Bitch	(Umm Umm 144ukcd)	68	1994	0	1994	

ISSUE	TITLE	UK LBL	UK POS	UK YEAR	US POS	US YEAR	US LBL
Olive	Mixed Vocal/Instrumental Group from the UK						
1	You're Not Alone	(RCA 74321406272)	42	1996	0	1996	
2	Miracle	(RCA 74321461242)	41	1997	0	1997	
3	You're Not Alone (Re-Issue)	(RCA 74321473232)	1	1997	0	1997	
4	Outlaw	(RCA 74321508372)	14	1997	0	1997	
Oliver	Male Vocalist, Real Name William Oliver Swofford. B: 22 Feb 1945 In North Carolina						
1	Good Morning Starshine	(CBS 4435)	6	1969	3	1969	(Jubilee 5659)
* 2	Jean		0	1969	2	1969	(Crewe 334)
3	Sunday Mornin		0	1969	35	1969	(Crewe 337)
4	Good Morning Starshine (Re-Entry)	(CBS 4435)	39	1969	0	1969	
Oliver Cheatham	Male Vocalist from the USA						
1	Get Down Saturday Night	(MCA 828)	38	1983	0	1983	
Olivia Newton-John	Female Vocalist B: 26 Sep 1948 In Cambridge, England, Moved To Australia In 1953						
1	If Not For You	(Pye International 7n 25543)	7	1971	25	1971	(Uni 55281)
2	Banks Of The Ohio	(Pye International 7n 25568)	6	1971	0	1971	
3	What Is Life	(Pye International 7n 25575)	16	1972	0	1972	
4	Take Me Home Country Road	(Pye International 7n 25599)	15	1973	0	1973	
* 5	Let Me Be There		0	1974	6	1974	(MCA 40101)
6	Long Live Love	(Pye International 7n 25638)	11	1974	0	1974	
* 7	If You Love Me (Let Me Know)		0	1974	5	1974	(MCA 40209)
* 8	I Honestly Love You	(EMI 2216)	22	1974	1	1974	(MCA 40280)
* 9	Have You Never Been Mellow		0	1975	1	1975	(MCA 40349)
* 10	Please Mr. Please		0	1975	3	1975	(MCA 40418)
11	Something Better To Do		0	1975	13	1975	(MCA 40459)
12	Let It Shine		0	1976	30	1976	(MCA 40495)
13	Come On Over		0	1976	23	1976	(MCA 40525)
14	Don't Stop Believin'		0	1976	33	1976	(MCA 40600)
15	Every Face Tells A Story		0	1976	55	1976	(MCA 40642)
16	Sam	(EMI 2616)	6	1977	20	1977	(MCA 40670)
* 17	You're The One That I Want	(RSO 006)	1	1978	1	1978	(Rso 891)
18	Hopelessly Devoted To You (From Grease)	(RSO 17)	2	1978	3	1978	(Rso 903)
* 19	Summer Nights	(RSO 18)	1	1978	5	1978	(RSO 906)
* 20	A Little More Love	(EMI 2879)	4	1978	3	1979	(MCA 40975)
21	Deeper Than The Night	(EMI 2954)	64	1979	11	1979	(MCA 41009)
22	Dancin''Round And 'Round		0	1979	82	1979	(MCA 41074)
23	Totally Hot		0	1979	52	1979	(MCA 41074)
24	I Can't Help It		0	1980	12	1980	(Rso 1026)
* 25	Magic	(Jet 196)	32	1980	1	1980	(MCA 41247)
26	Xanadu	(Jet 185)	1	1980	8	1980	(MCA 41285)
27	Suddenly	(Jet 702)	15	1980	20	1980	(MCA 51007)
* 28	Physical	(EMI 5234)	7	1981	1	1981	(MCA 51182)
29	Landslide	(EMI 5257)	18	1982	0	1982	
30	Make A Move On Me	(EMI 5291)	43	1982	5	1982	(MCA 52000)
31	Heart Attack	(EMI 5347)	46	1982	3	1982	(MCA 52100)
32	I Honestly Love You (Re-Issue)	(EMI 5360)	52	1983	0	1983	
33	Tied Up		0	1983	38	1983	(MCA 52115)
34	Twist Of Fate	(EMI 5438)	5	7198	35	1983	(MCA 52284)
35	Livin' In Desperate Times		0	1984	31	1984	(MCA 52341)
36	Soul Kiss		0	1985	20	1985	(MCA 52686)
37	The Grease Megamix	(Polydor Po 114)	3	1990	0	1990	
38	Grease - The Dream Mix	(PWL/Polydor Po 136)	47	1991	0	1991	
39	I Need Love	(Mercury Mer 370)	75	1992	0	1992	
40	Had To Be	(EMI Cdems 410)	22	1995	0	1995	

HIT 26 IS CREDITED TO OLIVIA NEWTON-JOHN & ELECTRIC LIGHT ORCHESTRA • HIT 27 IS CREDITED TO OLIVIA NEWTON-JOHN & CLIFF RICHARD
HIT 38 IS CREDITED TO FRANKIE VALLI, JOHN TRAVOLTA & OLIVIA NEWTON-JOHN • HIT 40 IS CREDITED TO CLIFF RICHARD & OLIVIA NEWTON-JOHN

ISSUE	TITLE	UK LBL	UK POS	UK YEAR	US POS	US YEAR	US LBL
Ollie & Jerry	Male Vocal Duo from the USA						
1	Breakin'....There's No Stopping Us	(Polydor Posp 690)	5	1984	9	1984	(Polydor 821708)
2	Electric Boogaloo	(Polydor Posp 730)	57	1985	0	1985	
Olympic Orchestra	Orchestra from the UK						
1	Reilly	(Red Bus Rbus 82)	26	1983	0	1983	
Olympic Runners	Male Vocal/Instrumental Group from the UK						
1	Whatever It Takes	(RCA Pc 5078)	61	1978	0	1978	
2	Get It While You Can	(Polydor Run 7)	35	1978	0	1978	

ISSUE	TITLE	UK LBL	UK POS	UK YEAR	US POS	US YEAR	US LBL
3	Sir Dancealot	(Polydor Posp 17)	35	1979	0	1979	
4	The Bitch	(Polydor Posp 63)	37	1979	0	1979	

Olympics Male Vocal Trio from the USA They Were Originally Called The Challengers In 1954

ISSUE	TITLE	UK LBL	UK POS	UK YEAR	US POS	US YEAR	US LBL
1	Western Moves	(Hmv Pop 528)	12	1958	8	1958	(Demon 1508)
2	Big Boy Pete		0	1960	50	1960	(Arvee 595)
3	I Wish I Could Shimmy Like My Sister Kate	(Vogue V 9174)	45	1961	0	1961	
4	The Bounce		0	1963	40	1963	(Tri Disc 106)

Omar Male Vocalist from the UK

ISSUE	TITLE	UK LBL	UK POS	UK YEAR	US POS	US YEAR	US LBL
1	There's Nothing Like This	(Talkin Loud Tlk 9	14	1991	0	1991	
2	Your Loss My Gain	(Talkin Loud Tlk 22)	47	1992	0	1992	
3	Music	(Talkin Loud Tlk 28)	53	1992	0	1992	
4	Outside / Saturday	(RCA 74321213982)	43	1994	0	1994	
5	Keep Steppin'	(RCA 74321233682)	57	1994	0	1994	
6	Say Nothin'	(RCA 74321502872)	29	1997	0	1997	

OMC Male Vocalist from New Zealand

ISSUE	TITLE	UK LBL	UK POS	UK YEAR	US POS	US YEAR	US LBL
1	How Bizarre	(Polydor 5776202)	5	1996	0	1996	
2	On The Run	(Polydor 5732452)	56	1997	0	1997	

One 2 Many Mixed Vocal/Instrumental Trio from Norway Names Sag Kolsrud, Jan Gisle & Camilla Griehsel

ISSUE	TITLE	UK LBL	UK POS	UK YEAR	US POS	US YEAR	US LBL
1	Downtown	(A&M Am 476)	65	1988	0	1988	
2	Downtown (Re-Issue)	(A&M Am 476)	43	1989	37	1989	(A&M 1272)

One Dove Mixed Vocal/Instrumental Group from the UK

ISSUE	TITLE	UK LBL	UK POS	UK YEAR	US POS	US YEAR	US LBL
1	White Love	(Boy's Own Boicd 14)	43	1993	0	1993	
2	Breakdown	(Boy's Own Boicd 15)	24	1993	0	1993	
3	Why Don't You Take Me	(Boy's Own Boicd 16)	30	1994	0	1994	

112

ISSUE	TITLE	UK LBL	UK POS	UK YEAR	US POS	US YEAR	US LBL
1	Only You		0	1996	13	1996	(Arista 79060)
2	Come See Me		0	1996	33	1996	(Arista 79073)
3	Cupid		0	1997	13	1997	(Bad Boy 78087)

1300 Drums (Featuring) Unjustified Ancients Of Mu Male Instrumental/Production Group from the UK

ISSUE	TITLE	UK LBL	UK POS	UK YEAR	US POS	US YEAR	US LBL
1	Ooh! Aah! Cantona	(Dynamo Dynd 5)	11	1996	0	1996	

One The Juggler Male Vocal/Instrumental Group from the UK

ISSUE	TITLE	UK LBL	UK POS	UK YEAR	US POS	US YEAR	US LBL
1	Passion Killer	(Regard Rg 107)	71	1983	0	1983	

Only Ones Male Vocal/Instrumental Group from the UK

ISSUE	TITLE	UK LBL	UK POS	UK YEAR	US POS	US YEAR	US LBL
1	Another Girl - Another Planet	(Columbia 6577507)	57	1992	0	1992	

Onslaught Male Vocal/Instrumental Group from the UK

ISSUE	TITLE	UK LBL	UK POS	UK YEAR	US POS	US YEAR	US LBL
1	Let There Be Rock	(London Lon 224)	50	1989	0	1989	

Onyx Male Rap Group from New York

ISSUE	TITLE	UK LBL	UK POS	UK YEAR	US POS	US YEAR	US LBL
* 1	Slam	(Columbia 6596302)	31	1993	4	1993	(Jmj/Ral 77053)
2	Throw Ya Gunz	(Columbia 6598312)	34	1993	0	1993	

Oo La La Male Vocal/Instrumental Group from the UK

ISSUE	TITLE	UK LBL	UK POS	UK YEAR	US POS	US YEAR	US LBL
1	Oo...Ah...Cantona	(North Speed Ooah 1)	64	1992	0	1992	

Open Arms (Featuring) Rowetta Mixed Vocal/Instrumental Group from the UK

ISSUE	TITLE	UK LBL	UK POS	UK YEAR	US POS	US YEAR	US LBL
1	Hey Mr. DJ	(All Around The World Cdglobe 136)	62	1996	0	1996	

Optimystic Mixed Vocal Group from the UK

ISSUE	TITLE	UK LBL	UK POS	UK YEAR	US POS	US YEAR	US LBL
1	Cought Up In My Heart	(WEA Yz 841cd)	49	1994	0	1994	
2	Nothing But Love	(WEA Yz 864cd1)	37	1994	0	1994	
3	Best Thing In The World	(WEA Yz 920cd	70	1995	0	1995	

Opus Male Vocal/Instrumental Group from Austria Lead Singer With The Quintet Is Herwig Rudisser

ISSUE	TITLE	UK LBL	UK POS	UK YEAR	US POS	US YEAR	US LBL
1	Live Is Life	(Polydor Posp 743)	6	1985	32	1986	(Polydor 883730)

Opus III Mixed Vocal/Instrumental Group from the UK

ISSUE	TITLE	UK LBL	UK POS	UK YEAR	US POS	US YEAR	US LBL
1	It's A Fine Day	(PWL International Pwl 215)	5	1992	0	1992	
2	I Talk To The Wind	(PWL International Pwl 235)	52	1992	0	1992	
3	When You Made The Mountain	(PWL International Pwcd 302)	71	1994	0	1994	

Oran 'Juice' Jones Male Vocalist, B: 1959 Houston

ISSUE	TITLE	UK LBL	UK POS	UK YEAR	US POS	US YEAR	US LBL
1	The Rain	(Def Jam A 7303)	4	1986	9	1986	(Def Jam 06209)

Orange Male Vocal/Instrumental Group from the UK

ISSUE	TITLE	UK LBL	UK POS	UK YEAR	US POS	US YEAR	US LBL
1	Judy Over The Rainbow	(Chrysalis Cdchs 5012)	73	1994	0	1994	

Orange Juice Male Vocal/Instrumental Group from the UK

ISSUE	TITLE	UK LBL	UK POS	UK YEAR	US POS	US YEAR	US LBL
1	L.O.V.E...Love	(Polydor Posp 357)	65	1981	0	1981	

ISSUE	TITLE	UK LBL	UK POS	UK YEAR	US POS	US YEAR	US LBL
2	Felicity	(Polydor Posp 386)	63	1982	0	1982	
3	Two Hearts Together	(Polydor Posp 470)	60	1982	0	1982	
4	I Can't Help Myself	(Polydor Posp 522)	42	1982	0	1982	
5	Rip It Up	(Polydor Posp 547)	8	1983	0	1983	
6	Flesh Of My Flesh	(Polydor Oj 4)	41	1983	0	1983	
7	Bridge	(Polydor Oj 5)	67	1984	0	1984	
8	What Presence?	(Polydor Oj 6)	47	1984	0	1984	
9	Lean Period	(Polydor Oj 7)	74	1984	0	1984	

Orb Male Production/Instrumental Duo from the UK

ISSUE	TITLE	UK LBL	UK POS	UK YEAR	US POS	US YEAR	US LBL
1	Perpetual Dawn	(Big Life Blr 46	61	1991	0	1991	
2	Blue Room	(Big Life Blrt 75)	8	1992	0	1992	
3	Assassin	(Big Life Blrt 81)	12	1992	0	1992	
4	Little Fluffy Clouds	(Big Life Blrd 98)	10	1993	0	1993	
5	Perpetual Dawn (Re-Entry)	(Big Life Blrd 46)	18	1994	0	1994	
6	Oxbow Lakes	(Island Cid 609)	38	1995	0	1995	
7	Toxygene	(Island Cid 652)	4	1997	0	1997	
8	Asylum	(Island Cid 657)	20	1997	0	1997	

Orbital Male Instrumental Duo from the UK

ISSUE	TITLE	UK LBL	UK POS	UK YEAR	US POS	US YEAR	US LBL
1	Chime	(Ffrr F B5)	17	1990	0	1990	
2	Omen	(Ffrr F 145)	46	1990	0	1990	
3	Satan	(Ffrr Fx 149)	31	1991	0	1991	
4	Mutations (EP)	(Ffrr Fx 181)	24	1992	0	1992	
5	Radiccio (EP)	(Internal Liarx 1)	37	1992	0	1992	
6	Lush	(Internal Liecd 7)	43	1993	0	1993	
7	Are We Here	(Internal Liecd 15)	33	1994	0	1994	
8	Belfast	(Internal Vol Cd1)	53	1995	0	1995	
9	The Box	(Internal Liecd 30)	11	1996	0	1996	
10	Satan	(Internal Liecd 37)	3	1997	0	1997	
11	The Saint	(Ffrr Fcd 296)	3	1997	0	1997	

HIT 8 IS CREDITED TO ORBITAL AND THERAPY

Orchestra On The Half Shell Male Vocal/Instrumental Group from the USA

ISSUE	TITLE	UK LBL	UK POS	UK YEAR	US POS	US YEAR	US LBL
1	Turtle Rhapsody	(SBK SBK 17)	36	1990	0	1990	

Orchestral Manoeuvres In The Dark Male Vocal/Instrumental Group from the UK

ISSUE	TITLE	UK LBL	UK POS	UK YEAR	US POS	US YEAR	US LBL
1	Red Flame White Light	(Dindisc Din 6)	67	1980	0	1980	
2	Messages	(Dindisc Din 15)	13	1980	0	1980	
3	Enola Gay	(Dindisc Din 22)	8	1980	0	1980	
4	Souvenir	(Dindisc Din 24)	3	1981	0	1981	
5	Joan Of Arc	(Dindisc Din 36)	5	1981	0	1981	
6	Maid Of Orleans (The Waltz Joan Of Arc)	(Dindisc Din 40)	4	1982	0	1982	
7	Genetic Engineering	(Virgin Vs 527)	20	1983	0	1983	
8	Telegraph	(Virgin Vs 580)	42	1983	0	1983	
9	Locomotion	(Virgin Vs 660)	5	1984	0	1984	
10	Talking Loud And Clear	(Virgin Vs 685)	11	1984	0	1984	
11	Telsa Girls	(Virgin Vs 705)	21	1984	0	1984	
12	Never Turn Away	(Virgin Vs 727)	70	1984	0	1984	
13	So In Love	(Virgin Vs 766)	27	1985	26	1985	(A&M 2746)
14	Secret	(Virgin Vs 796)	34	1985	0	1985	
15	La Femme Accident	(Virgin Vs 811)	42	1985	0	1985	
16	If You Leave (From Pretty In Pink)	(Virgin Vs 843)	48	1986	4	1986	(A&M 2811)
17	(Forever) Live And Die	(Virgin Vs 888)	11	1986	19	1986	(A&M 2872)
18	We Love You	(Virgin Vs 911)	54	1986	0	1986	
19	Shame	(Virgin Vs 938)	52	1987	0	1987	
20	Dreaming	(Virgin Vs 987)	50	1988	16	1988	(A&M 3002)
21	Dreaming (Re-Entry)	(Virgin Vs 987)	60	1988	0	1988	
22	Sailing On The Seven Sea	(Virgin Vs 1310)	3	1991	0	1991	
23	Pandora's Box	(Virgin Vs 1331)	7	1991	0	1991	
24	Then You Turn Away	(Virgin Vs 1368)	50	1991	0	1991	
25	Call My Name	(Virgin Vs 1380)	50	1991	0	1991	
26	Stand Above Me	(Virgin Vscdg 1444)	21	1993	0	1993	
27	Dream Of Me (Based On Love's Theme)	(Virgin Vscdt 1461)	24	1993	0	1993	
28	Everyday	(Virgin Vscdt 1471)	59	1993	0	1993	
29	Walking On The Milky Way	(Virgin Vscdt 1599)	17	1996	0	1996	
30	Universal	(Virgin Vscdt 1606)	55	1996	0	1996	

NAMES: PAUL HUMPHREYS, ANDREW MCCLUSKEY, MALCOLM HOLMES & MARTIN COOPER. PAUL LATER LEFT THE BAND • GROUP OFTEN CALLED OMD

ISSUE	TITLE	UK LBL	UK POS	UK YEAR	US POS	US YEAR	US LBL
Orchestre De Chambre Jean-Francois Paillard Male Conductor And Orchestra from France							
1	Theme From Vietnam (Canon In D)	(Debut Debt 3053)	61	1988	0	1988	
Origin Unknown Male Instrumental/Production Duo from the UK							
1	Valley Of The Shadows	(Ram Ramm 16cd)	60	1996	0	1996	
Original Male Vocal/Instrumental Duo from the USA							
	I Luv U Baby	(Ore Agr8cd)	31	1995	0	1995	
2	I Luv U Baby (Re-Mix)	(Ore Agr8cd)	2	1995	66	1996	(Next Plateau 1436)
3	B 2 Gether	(Ore Age12cd)	29	1995	0	1995	
Original Caste Lead Singer With The Quintet Is Dixie Lee Innes							
1	One Tin Soldier		0	1970	34	1970	(T-A 186)
Originals Names: Walter Gaines, Crathman Spencer, Henry Dixon & Freddie Gorman							
1	Baby, I'm For Real		0	1969	14	1969	(Soul 35066)
* 2	The Bells		0	1970	12	1970	(Soul 35069)
+ 3	We Can Make It Baby		0	1970	20	1970	(Soul 35074)
+ 4	God Bless Whoever Sent You		0	1971	14	1971	(Soul 35079)
	SPENCER WAS REPLACED IN 1971 BY TY HUNTER						
Orioles R&B Group from Knoxville, Tennessee, Originally from Baltimore, Usa							
1	It's Too Soon To Know		0	1948	13	1948	(Natural 5000)
* 2	Crying In The Chapel		0	1953	11	1953	(Jubilee 5122)
	HIT 2 IS CREDITED TO ORIOLES FEATURING SONNY TIL						
Orleans Rock Group Formed By John Hall In New York							
1	Dance With Me		0	1975	6	1975	(Asylum 45261)
2	Still The One		0	1976	5	1976	(Asylum 45336)
3	Love Takes Time		0	1979	11	1979	(Asylum 50006)
Orlons Mixed Vocal Group from the USA Names: Rosetta Hightower, Steve Caldwell, Marlena Davis & Shirley Brickley							
* 1	The Wah Watusi		0	1962	2	1962	(Cameo 218)
* 2	Don't Hang Up	(Cameo Parkway C 231)	50	1962	4	1962	(Cameo 231)
3	Don't Hang Up (Re-Entry)	(Cameo Parkway C 231)	39	1963	0	1963	
* 4	South Street		0	1963	3	1963	(Cameo 243)
5	Not Me		0	1963	12	1963	(Cameo 257)
6	Cross Fire		0	1963	19	1963	(Cameo 273)
	SHIRLEY BRICKLEY B: 23 JUN 1944. THEY DISBANDED IN 1968 • OBITUARY: SHIRLEY D: 13 OCT 1977 MURDERED (SHOT).						
Orn							
1	Snow	(Deconstruction 74321447612)	61	1997	0	1997	
Orrin Tucker & His Orchestra Male Dance Band Leader, B: 17 Feb 1911 St Louis, Missouri, See Also Wee Bonnie Baker							
* 2	Oh, Johnny, Oh Johnny, Oh!		0	1939	2	1939	(Columbia 35228)
Oscar Toney Jr Male R&B Vocalist, B: 26 May 1939 Selma, Alabama							
1	For Your Precious Love		0	1967	23	1967	(Bell 672)
Osibisa Male Vocal/Instrumental Group from Ghana/Nigeria							
1	Sunshine Day	(Bronze Bro 20)	17	1976	0	1976	
2	Dance The Body Music	(Bronze Bro 26)	31	1976	0	1976	
Osmond Boys Male Vocal Group from the USA							
1	Boys Will Be Boys	(Curb 6573847)	65	1991	0	1991	
2	Show Me The Way	(Curb 6577227)	60	1992	0	1992	
Osmonds Male Vocal/Instrumental Group, Alan B: 22 Jun 1949, Wayne B: 28 Aug 1951, Merrill B: 30 Apr 1953 & Jay B: 2 Mar 1955							
* 1	One Bad Apple		0	1971	1	1971	(Mgm 14193)
2	Double Lovin'		0	1971	14	1971	(Mgm 14259)
* 3	Yo-Yo		0	1971	3	1971	(Mgm 14295)
* 4	Down By The Lazy River	(Mgm 2006 096)	40	1972	4	1972	(Mgm 14324)
5	Hold Her Tight		0	1972	14	1972	(Mgm 14405)
6	Crazy Horses	(Mgm 2006 142)	2	1972	14	1972	(Mgm 14450)
7	Goin' Home	(Mgm 2006 288)	4	1972	36	1972	(Mgm 14562)
8	Let Me In	(Mgm 2006 321)	2	1973	36	1973	(Mgm 14617)
9	I Can't Stop	(MCA 129)	12	1974	0	1974	
10	Love Me For A Reason	(Mgm 2006 458)	1	1974	10	1974	(Mgm 14746)
11	Having A Party	(Mgm 2006 492)	28	1975	0	1975	
12	The Proud One	(Mgm 2006 520)	5	1975	22	1975	(Mgm 14791)
13	I'm Still Gonna Need You	(Mgm 2006 551)	32	1975	0	1975	
14	I Can't Live A Dream	(Polydor 2066 726)	37	1976	0	1976	
26	Crazy Horses (Re-Mix)	(Polydor 5793212)	50	1995	0	1995	
	UNLISTED HITS ARE C/W • THE OSMONDS NAMES ARE ALAN, WAYNE, MERRILL, JAY, JIMMY, MARIE, DONNY, VIRL & TOM STARTED SINGING RELIGIOUS AND BARBERSHOP-QUARTET SONGS						

ISSUE	TITLE	UK LBL	UK POS	UK YEAR	US POS	US YEAR	US LBL
Other Ones	Lead Singers With This Australian Sextet Is Alf & Johnny Klimek						
1	Holiday		0	1987	29	1987	(Virgin 99428)
Other Two	Mixed Vocal/Instrumental Duo from the UK						
1	Tasty Fish	(Factory Fac 3297)	41	1991	0	1991	
2	Selfish	(London Twocd 1)	46	1993	0	1993	
Otis Redding	Male Vocalist From Dawson, Georgia, B: 9 Sep 1941						
1	These Arms Of Mine		0	1963	85	1963	(Volt 103)
+ 2	That's What My Heart Needs		0	1963	27	1963	(Volt 109)
3	Pain In My Heart		0	1963	61	1963	(Volt 112)
4	Come To Me		0	1964	69	1964	(Volt 116)
5	Security		0	1954	97	1964	(Volt 117)
6	Chained And Bound		0	1964	70	1964	(Volt 121)
7	Mr. Pitiful / That's How Strong My Love Is		0	1965	41	1965	(Volt 124)
8	I've Been Loving You Too Long		0	1965	21	1965	(Volt 126)
9	Respect		0	1965	35	1965	(Volt 128)
10	My Girl	(Atlantic At 4050)	11	1965	0	1965	
+ 11	I Can't Turn You Loose	(Atlantic 584 030)	29	1966	11	1965	(Volt 130)
12	Satisfaction	(Atlantic At 4080)	33	1966	31	1966	(Volt 132)
+ 13	My Lover's Prayer	(Atlantic 584 019)	37	1966	10	1966	(Volt 136)
14	Fa-Fa-Fa-Fa Fa Sad Song	(Atlantic 584 049)	23	1966	29	1966	(Volt 138)
15	Try A Little Tenderness	(Atlantic 584 070)	46	1967	25	1966	(Volt 141)
16	Tramp	(Stax 601 012)	18	1967	26	1967	(Stax 216)
17	Day Tripper	(Stax 601 005)	43	1967	0	1967	
+ 18	I Love You More Than Words Can Say		0	1967	30	1967	(Volt 146)
19	Let Me Come On Home	(Stax 601 007)	48	1967	0	1967	
20	Shake	(Stax 601 011)	28	1967	47	1967	(Volt 149)
+ 21	Glory Of Love		0	1967	19	1967	(Volt 152)
22	Knock On Wood	(Stax 601 021)	35	1967	30	1967	(Stax 228)
* 23	(Sittin' On) The Dock Of The Bay	(Stax 601 031)	3	1968	1	1968	(Volt 157)
24	My Girl (Re-Issue)	(Atlantic 584 092)	36	1968	0	1968	
25	The Happy Song (Dum Dum)	(Stax 601 040)	24	1968	25	1968	(Volt 163)
+ 26	Hard To Handle	(Atlantic 584 199)	15	1968	11	1968	
27	Amen		0	1968	36	1968	(Atco 6592)
28	I've Got Dreams To Remember		0	1968	41	1968	(Atco 6612)
29	Papa's Got A Brand New Bag		0	1968	21	1968	(Atco 6636)
30	A Lovers Question		0	1969	48	1969	(Atco 6654)

THE HIT '(SITTIN' ON) THE DOCK OF THE BAY' WAS RECORDED 3 DAYS BEFORE HIS DEATH • HITS 16,22 ARE CREDITED TO OTIS REDDING AND CARLA THOMAS
OBITUARY: D: 10 DEC 1967 PLANE CRASH.

ISSUE	TITLE	UK LBL	UK POS	UK YEAR	US POS	US YEAR	US LBL
OTT							
1	Let Me In	(Epic 6642052)	12	1997	0	1997	
2	Forever Girl	(Epic 6645082)	24	1997	0	1997	
3	All Out Of Love	(Epic 6649152)	11	1997	0	1997	
Ottawan	Mixed Vocal Duo from France						
1	D.I.S.C.O.	(Carrere Car 161)	2	1980	0	1980	
2	You're O.K.	(Carrere Car 168	56	1980	0	1980	
3	Hands Up (Give Me Your Heart)	(Carrere Car 183)	3	1981	0	1981	
4	Help, Get Me Some Help!	(Carrere Car 215)	49	1981	0	1981	
Oui 3	Mixed Vocal/Instrumental Group from the USA/UK/Switzerland						
1	For What It's Worth	(MCA Mcstd 1736)	28	1993	0	1993	
2	Arms Of Solitude	(MCA Mcstd 1759)	54	1993	0	1993	
3	Break From The Old Routine	(MCA Mcstd 1793)	17	1993	0	1993	
4	For What It's Worth (Re-Mix)	(MCA Mcstd 1941)	26	1993	0	1993	
5	Facts Of Life	(MCA Mcstd 1939)	38	1994	0	1994	
6	Joy Of Living	(MCA Mcstd 2057)	55	1995	0	1995	
Our Daughter's Wedding	Male Vocal/Instrumental Group from the USA						
1	Lawnchairs	(EMI America Ea 124)	49	1981	0	1981	
Our House	Male Vocal/Instrumental Group from the USA						
1	Floor Space	(Perfecto Perf 125cd)	52	1996	0	1996	
Our Kid	Male Vocal Group from the UK						
1	You Just Might See Me Cry	(Polydor 2058 729)	2	1976	0	1976	

ISSUE	TITLE	UK LBL	UK POS	UK YEAR	US POS	US YEAR	US LBL
Our Tribe/One Tribe Mixed Vocal/Instrumental Group from the USA/Uk							
1	What Have You Done (Is This All)	(Inner Rhythm Heart 03)	52	1992	0	1992	
2	I Believe In You	(Ffrreedom Tabcd 117)	42	1993	0	1993	
3	Hold That Sicker Down	(Cheeky Chekcd 004)	24	1994	0	1994	
4	Love Comes Home	(Triangle Bluescd 001)	73	1994	0	1994	
5	High As A Kite	(Ffrr Fcd 259)	55	1995	0	1995	
6	Hold That Sucker Down (Re-Mix)	(Cheeky Chekcd 004)	26	1995	0	1995	
Outfield Names: Tony Lewis, John Spinks & Alan Jackman. When Alan Left Tony & John Continued As A Duo							
1	Your Love		0	1986	6	1986	(Columbia 05796)
2	All The Love In The World		0	1986	19	1986	(Columbia 05894)
3	Since You've Been Gone		0	1987	31	1987	(Columbia 07170)
4	Voices Of Babylon		0	1989	25	1989	(Columbia 68601)
5	For You		0	1990	21	1990	(MCA 53935)
Outhere Brothers Male Vocal/Instrumental Duo from the USA							
1	Don't Stop (Wiggle Wiggle)	(Eternal Yz 917cd)	1	1995	0	1995	
2	Boom Boom Boom	(Eternal Yz 938cd)	1	1995	0	1995	
3	La La La Hey Hey	(Eternal Yz 974cd)	7	1995	0	1995	
4	If You Wanna Party	(Eternal Wea 030cd)	9	1995	0	1995	
5	Let Me Hear You Say 'Ole Ole'	(Wea Wea 089cd)	18	1997	0	1997	
	HIT 4 IS CREDITED TO MOLELLA FEATURING OUTHERE BROTHERS						
Outkast Male Rap Duo from Atlanta, USA							
* 1	Player's Ball		0	1994	37	1994	(MCA 53935)
2	Elevators (Me & You)		0	1996	12	1996	(Arista 24177)
3	Atliens		0	1996	35	1996	(Arista 24196)
4	Jazzy Belle		0	1997	52	1997	(Arista 24224)
Outlander Male Producer, Real Name Marcos Salon from Belgium							
1	Vamp	(R&S Rsuk 1)	51	1991	0	1991	
Outlaws (1) Male Instrumental Group from the UK							
1	Swingin' Low	(Hmv Pop 844)	46	1961	0	1961	
2	Ambush	(Hmv Pop 877)	43	1961	0	1961	
	See Also Mike Berry						
Outlaws (2) Southern Rock Band from Tampa, USA							
1	There Goes Another Love Song		0	1975	34	1975	(Arista 0150)
2	Ghost Riders In The Sky		0	1981	31	1981	(Arista 0582)
Outrage Male Vocalist from the USA							
1	Tall 'N' Handsome	(Effective Ecfl 001cd)	57	1995	0	1995	
2	Tall 'N' Handsome (Re-Mix)	(Positiva Cdtiv 64)	51	1996	0	1996	
Outsiders Names: Sonny Geraci, Tom King, Mert Madsen, Bill Bruno & Rick Baker. Sonny Went On To Lead The Group Climax							
1	Time Won't Let Me		0	1966	15	1966	(Capitol 5573)
2	Girl In Love		0	1966	21	1966	(Capitol 5646)
3	Respectable		0	1966	15	1966	(Capitol 5701)
4	Help Me Girl		0	1966	37	1966	(Capitol 5759)
Overlanders Male Vocal/Instrumental Group from the UK							
1	Michelle	(Pye 7n 17034)	1	1966	0	1966	
Owen Bradley Quintet Male Producer/Organist, B: 21 Oct 1915 Westmoreland, Tennessee							
1	Blues Stay Away From Me		0	1949	11	1949	(Coral 60107)
2	The Third Man Theme		0	1950	23	1950	(Coral 60159)
3	White Silver Sands		0	1957	18	1957	(Decca 30363)
	VOCAL DUET ON HIT 1 BY JACK SHOOK AND DOTTIE DILLARD • VOCALS ON HIT 3 ARE BY THE ANITA KERR QUARTET						
Owen Paul Male Vocalist from the UK							
1	My Favourite Waste Of Time	(Epic A 7125)	3	1986	0	1986	
Oxo Lead Singer With The Quartet Is Ish Ledesma							
1	Whirly Girl		0	1983	28	1983	(Geffen 29765)
Ozark Mountain Daredevils Country-Rock Group from Missouri, USA							
1	If You Wanna Get To Heaven		0	1974	25	1974	(A&M 1515)
2	Jackie Blue		0	1975	3	1975	(A&M 1654)
Ozzy Osbourne Male Vocalist, Real Name John Osbourne B: 3 Dec 1948, Birmingham, England							
1	Crazy Train	(Jet 197)	49	1980	0	1980	
2	Mr. Crowley	(Jet 7003)	46	1980	0	1980	
3	Bark At The Moon	(Epic A 3915)	21	1983	0	1983	

ISSUE	TITLE	UK LBL	UK POS	UK YEAR	US POS	US YEAR	US LBL
4	So Tired	(Epic A 4452)	20	1984	0	1984	
5	Shot In The Dark	(Epic A 6859)	20	1986	0	1986	
6	The Ultimate Sin / Lightning Strikes	(Epic A 7311)	72	1986	0	1986	
* 7	Close My Eyes Forever	(Dreamland Pb 49409)	47	1989	8	1989	(RCA 8899)
8	No More Tears	(Epic 6574407)	32	1991	0	1991	
9	Mama I'm Coming Home	(Epic 6576177)	46	1991	28	1992	(Epic/Assoc. 74093)
10	Perry Mason	(Epic 6626395)	23	1995	0	1995	
11	I Just Want You	(Epic 6635702)	43	1996	0	1996	

HITS 1-2 ARE CREDITED TO OZZY OSBOURNE'S BLIZZARD OF OZZ • HIT 7 IS CREDITED TO LITA FORD DUET WITH OZZY OSBOURNE

P

ISSUE	TITLE	UK LBL	UK POS	UK YEAR	US POS	US YEAR	US LBL
P.F. Sloan Male Vocalist from the USA							
1	Sins Of The Family	(RCA 1482)	38	1965	0	1965	
P.J. & Duncan Male Vocal Duo from the UK							
1	Tonight I'm Free	(Telstar CDSTAS 2706)	62	1993	0	1993	
2	Why Me	(Telstar CDSTAS 2719)	27	1994	0	1994	
3	Let's Get Ready To Rhumble	(XS Rhythm CDDEC 1)	9	1994	0	1994	
4	If I Give You My Number	(XS Rhythm CDDEC 29)	15	1994	0	1994	
5	Eternal Love	(XS Rhythm CDDEC 3)	12	1994	0	1994	
6	Our Radio Rocks	(XS Rhythm CDDEC 4)	15	1995	0	1995	
7	Stuck On U	(XS Rhythm CDDEC 5)	12	1995	0	1995	
8	U Krazy Katz	(XS Rhythm CDANT 6)	15	1995	0	1995	
9	Perfect	(XS Rhythm CDANT 7)	16	1995	0	1995	
10	Stepping Stone	(Telstar CDANT 8)	11	1996	0	1996	
11	Better Watch Out	(Telstar CDANT 9)	10	1996	0	1996	
12	When I Fall In Love	(Telstar CDANT 10)	12	1996	0	1996	
13	Shout	(Telstar CDDEC 11)	10	1997	0	1997	
14	Falling	(Telstar CDDEC I2)	14	1997	0	1997	
	HITS 11-14 ARE CREDITED TO ANT & DEC						
P.J. Harvey Female Vocalist Poly Jean Harvey from the UK							
1	Sheela-Na-Gig	(too pure pure 008)	69	1992	0	1992	
2	50ft Queenie	(Island CID 538)	27	1993	0	1993	
3	Man-Size	(Island CID 569)	42	1993	0	1993	
4	Down By The Water	(Island IS 607)	38	1995	0	1995	
5	C'mon Billy	(Island CIDX 614)	29	1995	0	1995	
6	Send His Love To Me	(Island CID 610)	34	1995	0	1995	
7	Henry Lee (EP)	(Mute CDMUTE 189)	36	1996	0	1996	
8	That Was My Veil	(Island CID 648)	75	1996	0	1996	
P.J. Proby Male Vocalist, Real Name James Marcus Smith B: 6 Nov 1938 Houston							
1	Hold Me	(Decca F 11904)	3	1964	0	1964	
2	Together	(Decca F 11967)	8	1964	0	1964	
3	Somewhere	(Liberty LIB 10182)	6	1964	0	1964	
4	I Apologise	(Liberty LIB 10188)	11	1965	0	1965	
5	Let The Water Run Down	(Liberty LIB 10206)	19	1965	0	1965	
6	That Means A Lot	(Liberty LIB 10215)	30	1965	0	1965	
7	Maria	(Liberty LIB 10218)	8	1965	0	1965	
8	You've Come Back	(Liberty LIB 10223)	25	1966	0	1966	
9	To Make A Big Man Cry	(Liberty LIB 10236)	34	1966	0	1966	
10	I Can't Make It Alone	(Liberty LIB 10250)	37	1966	0	1966	
11	Niki Hoeky		0	1967	23	1967	(Liberty 55936)
12	It's Your Day Today	(Liberty LBF 15046)	32	1968	0	1968	
13	Yesterday Has Gone	(EMI Premier CDPRESX 13)	58	1996	0	1996	
14	Yesterday Has Gone (Re-Entry)	(EMI Premier CDPRESX 13)	69	1997	0	1997	
	WAS ALSO FAMOUS FOR SPLITTING HIS TROUSERS ON STAGE • HIS 13-14 ARE CREDITED TO P.J. PROBY AND MARC ALMOND						
P.P. Arnold Female Vocalist from the USA							
1	The First Cut Is The Deepest	(Immediate IM 047)	18	1967	0	1967	
2	The Time Has Come	(Immediate IM 055)	47	1967	0	1967	
3	(If You Think) You're Groovy	(Immediate IM 061)	41	1968	0	1968	
4	Angel Of The Morning	(Immediate IM 067)	29	1968	0	1968	
5	Burn It Up	(Rhythm King LEFT 27)	14	1988	0	1988	
	HITS 5-8 ARE CREDITED TO BEATMASTERS WITH P.P. ARNOLD						
Pablo Cruise Pop-Rock Quartet formed in San Francisco in 1973							
1	Whatcha Gonna Do?		0	1977	6	1977	(A&M 1920)

ISSUE	TITLE	UK LBL	UK POS	UK YEAR	US POS	US YEAR	US LBL
2	Love Will Find A Way		0	1978	6	1978	(A&M 2048)
3	Don't Want To Live Without It		0	1978	21	1978	(A&M 2076)
4	I Want You Tonight		0	1979	19	1979	(A&M 2195)
5	Cool Love		0	1981	13	1981	(A&M 2349)

Pacific Gas & Electric Lead Singer With The Quintet Is Charles Allen

1	Are You Ready?		0	1970	14	1970	(Columbia 45158)

Pack Male Vocal/Instrumental Group from the UK

1	Stand And Fight	(IQ ZB 44237)	61	1990	0	1990	Featuring Nigel Benn

Packabeats Male Instrumental Group from the UK

1	Gypsy Beat	(Parlophone R 4729)	49	1961	0	1961	

Pagliaro Male Vocalist from Canada

1	Lovin' You Ain't Easy	(PYE 7N 45111)	31	1972	0	1972	

Pale Male Vocal/Instrumental Group from Ireland

1	Dogs With No Tails	(A&M AM 866)	51	1992	0	1992	

Pale Fountains Male Vocal/Instrumental Group from the UK

1	Thank You	(Virgin VS 557)	48	1982	0	1982	

Pale Saints Mixed Vocal/Instrumental Group from Australia

1	Kinky Love	(4AD AD 1009)	72	1991	0	1991	

Pam Hall Female Vocalist From Jamaica

1	Dear Boopsie	(Bluemountain BM 027)	54	1986	0	1986	

Pamela Fernandez Female Vocalist from the USA

1	Kickin' In The Beat	(ORE AG 5CD)	43	1994	0	1994	
2	Let's Start Over / Kickin' The Beat (Re-Mix)	(ORE AG 9CD)	59	1995	0	1995	

Pan Position Male Production/Instrumental Group from Italy/Venezuela

1	Elephant Paw (Get Down To The Funk)	(POSITIVA CDTIV 13)	55	1994	0	1994	

Pandora's Box Mixed Vocal/Instrumental Group from the USA

1	It's All Coming Back To Me Now	(Virgin VS 1216)	51	1989	0	1989	

Pantera Male Vocal/Instrumental Group from the USA

1	Mouth For War	(ATCO A 5845T)	73	1992	0	1992	
2	Walk	(ATCO B 6076CD)	35	1993	0	1993	
3	I'm Broken	(ATCO B ???)	19	1994	0	1994	
4	Planet Caravan	(East WestA 5836CD1)	26	1994	0	1994	

Paper Dolls Female Vocal Group from the UK

1	Something Here In My Heart (Keeps A-Tellin'me No)	(PYE 7N 17456)	11	1968	0	1968	

Paper Lace Male Vocal/Instrumental Group from the UK   Names Michael Vaughn, Cliff Fish, Philip Wright, Chris Morris & Carlos Santana, Formed In 1969

	1	Billy Don't Be A Hero	(Bus Stop Bus 1014)	1	1974	0	1974	
*	2	The Night Chicago Died	(Bus Stop Bus 1016)	3	1974	1	1974	(Mercury 73492)
	3	The Black Eyed Boys	(Bus Stop Bus 1019)	11	1974	0	1974	
	4	We've Got The Whole World In Our Hands	(Warner Bros. K 17110)	24	1978	0	1978	

Paperboy Male Rapper from Los Angeles

*	1	Ditty		0	1993	10	1993	(Next Pl AT 357012)

Parade Names Jerry Riopelle, Murray MacLeod & Smokey Roberds

1	Sunshine Girl		0	1967	20	1967	(A&M 841)

Paradise Male Vocal/Instrumental Group from the UK

1	One Minds Two Hearts	(Priority P 1)	42	1983	0	1983	

Paradise Lost Male Vocal/Instrumental Group from the UK

1	The Last Time	(Music For Nations CDKUT 165)	60	1995	0	1995	
2	Forever Failure	(Music For NationsCDKUT 169)	66	1995	0	1995	
3	Say Just Words	(Music For Nations CDKUT 174)	53	1997	0	1997	

Paradise Organisation Male Production/Instrumental Group from the UK

1	Prayer Tower	(Cowboy Rodeo 13)	70	1993	0	1993	

Paradons R&B Group From California Includes West Tyler, Chuck Weldon, Billy Myers & William Powers

1	Diamonds And Pearls		0	1960	18	1960	(Milestone 2003)

Paradox Male Instrumental Duo from the UK

1	Jailbreak	(RONIN 7R2)	66	1990	0	1990	

Paramounts Male Vocal/Instrumental Group from the UK

1	Poison Ivy	(Parlophone R 5093)	35	1964	0	1964	

Parchment Mixed Vocal/Instrumental Group from the UK

1	Light Up The Fire	(PYE 7N 45178)	31	1972	0	1972	

ISSUE	TITLE	UK LBL	UK POS	UK YEAR	US POS	US YEAR	US LBL
Paris (1)	Mixed Vocal Group from the UK						
1	No Getting Over You	(RCA 222)	49	1982	0	1982	
Paris (2)	Male Vocalist from the USA						
1	Guerrilla Funk	(Priority/Virgin PTYCD 100)	38	1995	0	1995	
Paris Angels	Male Vocal/Instrumental Group from Ireland						
1	Scope	(Sheer Joy Sheer 0047)	75	1990	0	1990	
2	Perfume	(Virgin VS 1360)	55	1991	0	1991	
3	Fade	(Virgin VS 1365)	70	1991	0	1991	
Paris Red	Mixed Vocal/Instrumental Duo from the USA/Germany						
1	Good Friend	(Columbia 6569417)	61	1992	0	1992	
2	Promises	(Columbia 6592342)	59	1993	0	1993	
Paris Sisters	Names Priscilla, Albeth & Sherrell Paris						
1	Be My Boy		0	1961	56	1961	(Gregmark 2)
2	I Love How You Love Me		0	1961	5	1961	(Gregmark 6)
3	He Knows I Love Him Too Much		0	1962	34	1962	(Gregmark 10)
Parliament	The Group Is Led By George Clinton						
* 1	Tear The Roof Of The Sucker (Give Up The Funk)		0	1976	15	1976	(Casablanca 856)
* 2	Flash Light		0	1978	16	1978	(Casablanca 909)
	THE GROUP HAVE HAD MANY OTHER NAMES, THE PARLIAMENTS BEING ONE						
Parliaments	Other Names Include Parlet And Funk All Stars, See Also Previous Entry						
1	(I Wanna) Testify		0	1967	20	1967	(Revilot 207)
Partland Brothers	Male Vocal Duo From Canada						
1	Soul City		0	1987	27	1987	(Manhattan 50065)
Partners In Kryme	Male Vocal/Instrumental Duo from the USA Names Richard Usher & James Alpem From New York						
* 1	Turtle Power		1	1990	13	1990	(SBK 07325)
Partridge Family	Mixed Vocal Group from the USA						
* 1	I ThInk I Love You	(Bell 1130)	18	1971	1	1970	(Bell 910)
* 2	Doesn't Somebody Want To Be Wanted		0	1971	6	1971	(Bell 963)
3	I'll Meet You Halfway		0	1971	9	1971	(Bell 996)
4	I Woke Up In Love This Morning		0	1971	13	1971	(Bell 45130)
5	It's One Of Those Nights (Yes Love)	(Bell 1203)	11	1972	20	1972	(Bell 45160)
6	Breaking Up Is Hard Io Do	(Bell MABEL I)	3	1972	28	1972	(Bell 45235)
7	Looking Through The Eyes Of Love	(Bell 1278)	9	1973	39	1973	(Bell 45301)
8	Walking In The Rain	(Bell 1293)	10	1973	0	1973	
Party	Dance Quintet from Florida						
1	In My Dreams		0	1992	34	1992	(HOLLYWOOD 64832)
Party Animals	Male Instrumental/Production Duo from Holland						
1	Have You Ever Been Mellow?	(Mokum/Roadrunner DB 17553)	56	1996	0	1996	
2	Have You Ever Been Mellow? (EP)	(Mokum/Roadrunner DB 17413)	43	1996	0	1996	
Party Faithful	Mixed Vocal/Instrumental Group from the UK						
1	Brass / Let There Be House	(ORE AG 10CD)	54	1995	0	1995	
Pasadenas	Male Vocal Group from the UK						
1	Tribute (Right On)	(CBS PASA 1)	5	1988	0	1988	
2	Riding On A Train	(CBS PASA 2)	13	1988	0	1988	
3	Enchanted Lady	(CBS PASA 3)	31	1988	0	1988	
4	Love Thing	(CBS PASA 4)	22	1990	0	1990	
5	Reeling	(CBS PASA 5)	75	1990	0	1990	
6	I'm Doing Fine Now	(Columbia 6577187)	4	1992	0	1992	
7	Make It With You	(Columbia 6579257)	20	1992	0	1992	
8	I Believe In Miracles	(Columbia 6580567)	34	1992	0	1992	
9	Moving In The Right Direction	(Columbia 6583417)	49	1992	0	1992	
10	Let's Stay Together	(Columbia 6587747)	22	1992	0	1992	
Passengers	Male Vocal/Instrumental Group from the UK/Ireland/Italy						
1	Miss Sarajevo	(Island CID 625)	6	1995	0	1995	
Passions	Mixed Vocal/Instrumental Group from the UK						
1	I'm In Love With A German Film Star	(Polydor POSP 222)	25	1981	0	1981	
Pastel Six	Septet from California						
1	The Cinnamon Cinder (It's A Very Nice Dance)		0	1963	25	1963	(ZEN 102)
Pastels	Lead Singer With The Quartet Is Defosca Ervin, See Also Big Dee Irwin						
1	Been So Long		0	1958	24	1958	(ARGO 5287)

ISSUE	TITLE	UK LBL	UK POS	UK YEAR	US POS	US YEAR	US LBL
Pat & Mick Male Vocal Duo from the UK							
1	Let's All Chant	(PWL PWL 10)	11	1988	0	1988	
2	On The Night	(PWL PWL 10)	70	1988	0	1988	
3	I Haven't Stopped Dancing Yet	(PWL PWL 33)	9	1989	0	1989	
4	Use It Up And Wear It Out	(PWL PWL 55)	22	1990	0	1990	
5	Gimme Some	(PWL PWL 75)	53	1991	0	1991	
6	Hot Hot Hot	(PWL International PARKCD 1)	47	1993	0	1993	
Pat Benatar Female Vocalist, Real Name Patricia Andrzejewski B: 1952 Long Island, New York							
1	Heartbreaker		0	1980	23	1980	(Chrysalis 2395)
2	We Live For Love		0	1980	27	1980	(Chrysalis 2419)
3	Hit Me With Your Best Shot		0	1980	9	1980	(Chrysalis 2464)
4	Treat Me Right		0	1981	18	1981	(Chrysalis 2487)
5	Fire And Ice		0	1981	17	1981	(Chrysalis 2529)
6	Promises In The Dark		0	1981	38	1981	(Chrysalis 2555)
7	Shadows Of The Night	(Chrysalis PAT 2)	50	1985	13	1982	(Chrysalis 2647)
8	Little Too Late		0	1983	20	1983	(Chrysalis 03536)
9	Looking For A Stranger		0	1983	39	1983	(Chrysalis 42688)
10	Love Is A Battlefield	(Chrysalis CHS 2747)	49	1984	5	1983	(Chrysalis 42732)
11	We Belong	(Chrysalis CHS 2821)	22	1985	5	1984	(Chrysalis 42826)
12	Ooh Ooh Song		0	1985	36	1985	(Chrysalis 42843)
13	Love Is A Battlefield (Re-Issue)	(Chrysalis PAT 1)	17	1985	0	1985	
14	Invincible	(Chrysalis PAT 3)	53	1985	10	1985	(Chrysalis 42877)
15	Sex As A Weapon	(Chrysalis PAT 4)	67	1986	28	1986	(Chrysalis 42927)
16	All Fired Up	(Chrysalis PAT 5)	19	1988	19	1988	(Chrysalis 43268)
17	Don't Walk Away	(Chrysalis PAT 6)	42	1988	0	1988	
18	One Love	(Chrysalis PAT 7)	59	1989	0	1989	
19	Somebody's Baby	(Chrysalis CDCHS 5001)	48	1993	0	1993	
Pat Boone Male Vocalist, Real Name Charles Eugene Boone B: 1 Jun 1934 Jacksonville, Florida							
1	Two Hearts		0	1955	16	1955	(DOT 15338)
* 2	Ain't That A Shame	(London HLD 8173)	7	1955	1	1955	(DOT 15377)
3	At My Front Door (Crazy Little Mamma)		0	1955	7	1955	(DOT 15422)
4	No Other Arms (No Arms Can Ever Hold You)		0	1955	26	1955	(DOT 15422)
5	Gee Whittakers!		0	1955	19	1955	(DOT 15435)
* 6	I'll Be Home	(London HLD 8253)	1	1956	4	1956	(DOT 15443)
7	Tutti' Frutti'		0	1956	12	1956	(DOT 15443)
8	Long Tall Sally	(London HLD 8291)	18	1956	8	1956	(DOT 15457)
* 9	I Almost Lost My Mind	(London HLD 8303)	14	1956	1	1956	(DOT 15472)
10	Long Tall Sally (Re-Entry)	(London HLD 8291)	22	1957	0	1957	
* 11	Friendly Persuasion	(London HLD 8346)	3	1956	5	1956	(DOT 15490)
12	Chains Of Love		0	1956	10	1956	(DOT 15490)
* 13	Don't Forbid Me	(London HLD 8370)	2	1957	1	1957	(DOT 15521)
14	Ain't That A Shame (Re-Entry)	(London HLD 8173)	22	1957	0	1957	
15	I'll Be Home (Re-Entry)	(London HLD 8253)	18	1957	0	1957	
16	Anastasia		0	1957	37	1957	(DOT 15521)
* 17	Why Baby Why	(London IILD 8404)	17	1957	5	1957	(DOT 15545)
18	I'm Waiting Just For You		0	1957	27	1957	(DOT 15545)
* 19	Love Letters In The Sand	(London HLD 8445)	2	1957	1	1957	(DOT 15570)
20	Bernardine		0	1957	14	1957	(DOT 15570)
* 21	Remember Your Mine /	(London HLD 8479)	5	1957	6	1957	(DOT 15602)
* 22	April Love	(London HLD 8512)	7	1957	1	1957	(DOT 15660)
23	White Christmas/Jingle Bells	(London HLD 8520)	29	1957	0	1957	
* 24	A Wonderful Time Up There	(London HLD 8574)	2	1958	4	1958	(DOT 15690)
* 25	It's Too Soon To Know	(London HLD 8574)	0	1958	4	1958	(DOT 15690)
26	Sugar Moon / Cherie I Love You	(London HLD 8640)	6	1958	5	1958	(DOT 15750)
27	If Dreams Came True	(London HLD 8675)	16	1958	7	1958	(DOT 15785)
28	Gee But It's Lonely / For My Good Fortune	(London HLD 8739)	30	1958	21	1958	(DOT 15825)
29	I'll Remember Tonight	(London HLD 8775)	28	1959	34	1958	(DOT 15840)
30	With The Wind And Rain In Your Hair	(London HLD 8824)	21	1959	21	1959	(DOT 15888)
31	I'll Remember Tonight (Re-Entry)	(London HLD 8775)	21	1959	0	1959	
32	I'll Remember Tonight (2nd Re-Entry)	(London HLD 8775)	18	1959	0	1959	
33	For A Penny / Wang Dang Toffy Apple Tango	(London HLD 8855)	28	1959	23	1959	(DOT 15914)
34	For A Penny	(London HLD 8855)	19	1959	0	1959	
35	Twixt Twelve And Twenty / Rock Bow Weevil	(London HLD 8910)	18	1959	17	1959	(DOT 15955)
36	Fools Hall Of Fame		0	1959	29	1959	(DOT 15982)
37	Twixt Twelve And Twenty	(London 8910)	26	1959	0	1959	

ISSUE	TITLE	UK LBL	UK POS	UK YEAR	US POS	US YEAR	US LBL
38	(Welcome) New Lovers		0	1960	18	1960	(DOT 16048)
39	Walkin' The Floor Over You/Spring Rain	(London HLD 9138)	40	1960	0	1960	
40	Walkin' The Floor Over You / Spring Rain (Re-Entry)	(London HLD 9138)	46	1960	0	1960	
41	Walkin' The Floor Over You/Spring Rain (2nd Re-Entry)	(London HLD 9138)	39	1960	0	1960	
* 42	Moody River/A Thousand Years	(London HLD 9350)	18	1961	1	1961	(DOT 16209)
43	Big Cold Wind		0	1961	19	1961	(DOT 16244)
44	Johnny Will / Just Let Me Dream	(London HLD 9461)	4	1961	35	1961	(DOT 16284)
45	I'll See You In My Dreams / Pictures In The Fire	(London HLD 9504)	27	1962	32	1962	(DOT 16312)
46	Quando Quando Quando / Willing And Eager	(London HLD 49543)	1	1962	0	1962	
* 47	Speedy Gonzales	(London HLD 9573)	2	1962	6	1962	(DOT 16368)
! 48	The Main Attraction / Amore Baciami	(London HLD 9620)	12	1962	0	1962	
49	Indiana Girl		0	1975	72	1972	(MELODYLAND 6005)
! 50	I'd Do It WIth You		0	1975	84	1975	(Melodyland 6018)
! 51	Texas Woman		0	1976	34	1976	(LONDON 6037)
! 52	Oklahoma Sunshine		0	1976	86	1976	(LONDON 6042)
! 53	Colorado Country Morning		0	1980	60	1980	(Warner/CURB 49596)

Pat Campbell   Male Vocalist from Ireland

1	The Deal	(Major Minor MM 648)	31	1969	0	1969	

Pat Suzuki   Female Vocalist from the USA

1	I Enjoy Being A Girl	(RCA 1171)	49	1960	0	1960	

Pat Terry   Male Vocalist from the USA

1	Love Me Again		0	1953	23	1953	(Jubilee 6044)

Patience & Prudence   Mixed Vocal Duo from the USA   Real Names Patience McIntyre B: 1945, Prudence McIntyre B: 1942

* 1	Tonight You Belong To Me	(London HLU 8321)	28	1956	4	1956	(Liberty 55022)
2	Gonna Get Along Without Ya Now	(London HLU 8369)	22	1957	11	1956	(Liberty 55040)
3	Gonna Get Along Without Ya Now (Re-Entry)	(London HLU 8369)	24	1957	0	1957	

Pato Banton   Male Vocalist from the UK

1	Baby Come Back	(Virgin VSCDT 1522)	1	1994	0	1994	
2	Bubling Hot	(Virgin VSCDT 1530)	15	1995	0	1995	
3	Spirits In The Material World	(MCA MCSDT	36	1996	0	1996	
4	Groovin'	(IRIS CDEIRS 195)	14	1996	0	1996	

Patra   Female Vocalist from Jamaica

1	Family Affair	(Polydor PZCD 304)	18	1993	0	1993	
2	Pull Up To The Bumper	(Epic 6623942)	50	1995	0	1995	
3	Work Mi Body	(Heavenly HUN 53CD)	75	1996	0	1996	
4	15 Steps (EP)	(Heavenly HVN 67CD)	67	1997	0	1997	

Patric   Male Vocalist from the UK

1	Love Me	(Bell 7432125352)	54	1994	0	1994	

Patrice Munsel   Female Actress/Vocalist from the USA

1	Bela Bimba		0	1951	27	1951	(RCA Victor 455)

Patrice Rushen   Male Vocalist, B: 30 Sep 1954 Los Angeles

1	Haven't You Heard	(Elektra K 12414)	62	1980	0	1980	
2	Never Gonna Give You Up (Won't Let You Be)	(Elektra K 12494)	66	1981	0	1981	
3	Forget Me Nots	(Elektra K 13173)	8	1982	23	1982	(Elektra 47427)
4	I Was Tired Of Being Alone	(Elektra K 13184)	39	1982	0	1982	
5	Feels So Real (Won't Let Go)	(Elektra E 9742)	51	1984	0	1984	

Patrick Hernandez   Male Vocalist, B: 1949 Paris, France

* 1	Born To Be Alive	(GEM GEM 4)	10	1979	16	1979	(Columbia 10986)

Patrick Juvet   Male Vocalist from France

1	Got A Feeling	(Casablanca CAN 127)	34	1978	0	1978	
2	I Love America	(Casablanca CAN 132)	12	1978	0	1978	

Patrick MacNee & Honor Blackman   Male And Female Actor/Actress/Vocal Duo from the UK

1	Kinky Boots	(Deram Kinky 1)	5	1990	0	1990	

Patrick Simmons   Male Vocal/Guitarist, B: 23 Jan 1950 Aberdeen, Washington

1	So Wrong		0	1983	30	1983	(Elektra 69839)
	Patrick Was A Founding Member Of The Doobie Brothers						

Patrick Swayze (Featuring) Wendy Frase   Patrick B: 18 Aug 1952 Houston   Mixed Vocal Duo from the USA

1	She's Like The Wind	(RCA PB 49565)	17	1988	3	1988	(RCA 5363)

ISSUE	TITLE	UK LBL	UK POS	UK YEAR	US POS	US YEAR	US LBL

P

495

Patsy Cline Female Vocalist, Real Name Virginia Patterson Hensley B: 8 Sep 1932 In Winchester, Virginia

ISSUE	TITLE	UK LBL	UK POS	UK YEAR	US POS	US YEAR	US LBL
1	Walking After Midnight		0	1957	12	1957	(Decca 30221)
! 2	A Poor Man's Roses (Or A Rich Man's Gold)		0	1957	14	1957	(Decca 30221)
3	I Fall To Pieces		0	1961	12	1961	(Decca 31205)
4	Crazy	(MCA MCA 1465)	14	1990	9	1961	(Decca 31317)
5	She's Got You	(Brunswick 05866)	43	1962	14	1962	(Decca 31354)
6	When I Get Thru With You (You'll Love Me Too)		0	1962	53	1962	(Decca 31354)
9	Heartaches	(Brunswick 05878)	31	1962	0	1962	
11	Sweet Dreams (Of You)		0	1964	44	1964	(Decca 31483)

UNKISTED HITS ARE C/W OBITUARY : D: 5 MAR 1963 IN PLANE CRASH WITH COWBOY COPAS AND HAWKSHAW HAWKINS.

Patsy Gallant Female Vocalist From Canada

ISSUE	TITLE	UK LBL	UK POS	UK YEAR	US POS	US YEAR	US LBL
1	From New York To L.A.	(EMI 2620)	6	1977	0	1977	

Patsy Montana Female Country Singer, Real Name Rubye Blevins B: 30 Oct 1914 In Hot Springs, Montana

ISSUE	TITLE	UK LBL	UK POS	UK YEAR	US POS	US YEAR	US LBL
* 1	I Want To Be A Cowboy's Sweetheart - Ridin' Old Paint		0	1936	10	1936	(Vocalion 3010)

Patti Austin Female Vocalist B: 10 Aug 1948 New York

ISSUE	TITLE	UK LBL	UK POS	UK YEAR	US POS	US YEAR	US LBL
1	Razzamatazz	(A&M AMS 8140)	11	1981	0	1981	
* 2	Baby Come To Me	(QWEST K 15005)	11	1983	1	1983	(QWEST 50036)
3	I Don't Have The Heart		0	1990	10	1990	(Warner Bros. 19911)
4	I'll Keep Your Dreams Alive	(AMMI AMM 101)	68	1992	0	1992	

Patti Day Female Vocalist from the USA

ISSUE	TITLE	UK LBL	UK POS	UK YEAR	US POS	US YEAR	US LBL
1	Right Before My Eyes	(Debut DEBT 3080)	69	1989	0	1989	

Patti Labelle Female Vocalist, Real Name Patricia Holt B: 24 May In Philadelphia

ISSUE	TITLE	UK LBL	UK POS	UK YEAR	US POS	US YEAR	US LBL
1	Down The Aisle (Wedding Song)		0	1963	37	1963	(Newtown 5777)
2	You'll Never Walk Alone		0	1964	34	1964	(Parkway 896)
3	New Attitude		0	1985	17	1985	(MCA 52517)
* 4	On My Own	(MCA MCA 1045)	2	1986	1	1986	(MCA 52770)
5	Oh, People	(MCA MCA 1075)	26	1986	29	1986	(MCA 52877)
6	The Right Kind Of Lover	(MCA MCSTD	50	1994	0	1994	

Patti Lynn Female Vocalist from the UK

ISSUE	TITLE	UK LBL	UK POS	UK YEAR	US POS	US YEAR	US LBL
1	Johnny Angel	(Fontana H 391)	37	1962	0	1962	

Patti Page Female Vocalist, Real Name Clara Ann Fowler B: 8 Nov 1927 Muskogee, Oklahoma.

ISSUE	TITLE	UK LBL	UK POS	UK YEAR	US POS	US YEAR	US LBL
1	Confess		0	1948	12	1948	(Mercury 5129)
2	Say Something Sweet To Your Sweetheart		0	1948	23	1948	(Mercury 5192)
3	So In Love (From Kiss Me, Kate)		0	1949	13	1949	(Mercury 5230)
4	Money, Marbles And Chalk		0	1949	27	1949	(Mercury 5251)
5	I'll Keep The Lovelight Burning		0	1949	26	1949	(Mercury 5310)
* 6	With My Eyes Wide Open I'm Dreaming (From *Shoot The Works*)		0	1950	11	1950	(Mercury 5344)
7	I Don't Care If The Sun Don't Shine		0	1950	8	1950	(Mercury 5396)
* 8	All My Love		0	1950	1	1950	(Mercury 5455)
9	Back In Your Own Back Yard		0	1950	23	1950	(Mercury 5463)
* 10	The Tennessee Waltz		0	1951	1	1951	(Mercury 5534)
* 11	Would I Love You (Love You, Love You)		0	1951	4	1951	(Mercury 5571)
* 12	Mockin' Bird Hill		0	1951	2	1951	(Mercury 5595)
13	Down The Trail Of Achin' Hearts		0	1951	17	1951	(Mercury 5579)
14	Ever True Ever More		0	1951	24	1951	(Mercury 5579)
* 15	Mister And Mississippi		0	1951	8	1951	(Mercury 5645)
16	These Things I Offer You		0	1951	26	1951	(Mercury 5645)
* 17	Detour		0	1951	5	1951	(Mercury 5682)
18	And So To Sleep Again		0	1951	4	1951	(Mercury 5706)
19	Retreat (Cries My Heart)		0	1952	22	1952	(Mercury 5772)
20	Come What May		0	1952	9	1952	(Mercury 5772)
21	Whispering Winds		0	1952	16	1952	(Mercury 5816)
22	Once In A While		0	1952	9	1952	(Mercury 5867)
* 23	I Went To Your Wedding		0	1952	1	1952	(Mercury 5899)
24	You Belong To Me		0	1954	4	1952	(Mercury 5899)
25	Why Don't You Believe Me		0	1952	4	1952	(Mercury 70025)
26	Conquest		0	1952	18	1952	(Mercury 70025)
* 27	(How Much Is) That Doggie In The Window	(ORIOLE CB 1156)	9	1953	1	1953	(Mercury 70070)
28	My Jealous Eyes		0	1953	17	1953	(Mercury 70070)
29	Now That I'm In Love		0	1953	18	1953	(Mercury 70127)
30	Oo! What You Do To Me		0	1953	16	1953	(Mercury 70127)
31	Butterflies		0	1953	10	1953	(Mercury 70183)

ISSUE	TITLE	UK LBL	UK POS	UK YEAR	US POS	US YEAR	US LBL
32	This Is My Song		0	1953	20	1953	(Mercury 70183)
33	Father, Father		0	1953	21	1953	(Mercury 70222)
34	Milwaukee Polka		0	1953	23	1953	(Mercury 70230)
* 35	Changing Partners		0	1953	3	1953	(Mercury 70260)
* 36	Cross Over The Bridge		0	1954	2	1954	(Mercury 70302)
37	My Restless Lover		0	1954	21	1954	(Mercury 70302)
38	Steam Heat (From *The Pajama Game*)		0	1954	8	1954	(Mercury 70380)
39	I Cried		0	1954	13	1954	(Mercury 70416)
40	What A Dream		0	1954	10	1954	(Mercury 70416)
41	I Can't Tell A Waltz From A Tango		0	1954	30	1954	(Mercury 70458)
42	The Mama Doll Song		0	1954	24	1954	(Mercury 70458)
43	Let Me Go Lover		0	1954	8	1954	(Mercury 70511)
44	Croce Di Oro (Cross Of Gold)		0	1955	16	1955	(Mercury 70713)
45	Go On With The Wedding		0	1956	11	1956	(Mercury 70766)
* 46	Allegheny Moon		0	1956	2	1956	(Mercury 70878)
47	Mama From The Train		0	1956	11	1956	(Mercury 70971)
48	A Poor Man's Roses (Or A Rich Man's Gold)		0	1957	14	1957	(Mercury 71059)
* 49	Old Cape Cod		0	1956	3	1956	(Mercury 71101)
50	Wondering		0	1957	12	1957	(Mercury 71101)
51	I'll Remember Today		0	1957	23	1957	(Mercury 71189)
52	Belonging To Someone		0	1958	13	1958	(Mercury 71247)
53	Another Time, Another Place		0	1958	20	1958	(Mercury 71294)
54	Left Right Out Of Your Heart (Hi Lee Hi Lo Hi Lup Up Up)		0	1958	9	1958	(Mercury 71331)
55	Fibbin'		0	1958	39	1958	(Mercury 71355)
56	One Of Us (Will Weep Tonight)		0	1960	31	1960	(Mercury 71639)
57	Mom And Dad's Waltz		0	1961	58	1961	(Mercury 71823)
58	Go On Home		0	1962	42	1962	(Mercury 71906)
59	Most People Get Married		0	1962	27	1962	(Mercury 71950)
60	Hush Hush, Sweet Charlotte (Movie Title Song)		0	1965	8	1965	(Columbia 43251)

HIT 2 IS CREDITED TO VIC DAMONE AND PATTI PAGE • HIT 6 IS CREDITED TO PATTI PAGE QUARTET

Patti Smith Group Female Vocalist, B: 31 Dec 1946 In Chicago

	TITLE	UK LBL	UK POS	UK YEAR	US POS	US YEAR	US LBL
1	Because The Night	(Arista 181)	5	1978	13	1978	(Arista 0318)
2	Privilege (Set Me Free)	(Arista 197)	72	1978	0	1978	
3	Frederick	(Arista 264)	63	1979	0	1979	

Patty & The Emblems Lead Singer With The Group Is Pat Russell

	TITLE	UK LBL	UK POS	UK YEAR	US POS	US YEAR	US LBL
1	Mixed-Up Shook-Up Girl		0	1964	37	1964	(Herald 590)

Patty Andrews Female Vocalist, Lead Singer With Her Sisters The Andrew Sisters

	TITLE	UK LBL	UK POS	UK YEAR	US POS	US YEAR	US LBL
1	The Pussy Cat Song (Nyow! Nyot! Nyow!)		0	1949	12	1949	(Decca 24533) with Bing Crosby
2	Too Young		0	1951	19	1951	(Decca 27569)

Patty Duke Real Name Anna Marie Duke B: 14 Dec 1928 New York

	TITLE	UK LBL	UK POS	UK YEAR	US POS	US YEAR	US LBL
1	Don't Just Stand There		0	1965	8	1965	(United Artists 875)
2	Say Something Funny		0	1965	22	1965	(United Artists 915)

Paul & Barry Ryan Male Vocal Duo, Real Names Paul And Barry Stevens B: 24 Oct 1948

	TITLE	UK LBL	UK POS	UK YEAR	US POS	US YEAR	US LBL
1	Don't Bring Me Your Heartaches	(Decca F 12260)	13	1965	0	1965	
2	Have Pity On The Boy	(Decca F 12319)	18	1966	0	1966	
3	I Love Her	(Decca F 12391)	17	1966	0	1966	
4	I Love How You Love Me	(Decca F 12445)	21	1966	0	1966	
5	Have You Ever Loved Somebody	(Decca F 12494)	49	1966	0	1966	
6	Missy Missy	(Decca F 12520)	43	1966	0	1966	
7	Keep It Out Of Sight	(Decca F 12567)	30	1967	0	1967	
8	Claire	(Decca F 12633)	47	1967	0	1967	

SEE ALSO BARRY RYAN

Paul & Paula Mixed Vocal Duo from the USA Real Names Ray Hildebrand B: 21 Dec 1940 and Jill Jackson B: 20 May 1942

	TITLE	UK LBL	UK POS	UK YEAR	US POS	US YEAR	US LBL
* 1	Hey Paula	(Philips 304012 BF)	8	1963	1	1963	(Philips 40084)
2	Young Lovers	(Philips 304016 BF)	9	1963	6	1963	(Philips 40096)
3	Hey Paula (Re-Entry)	(Philips 304012 BF)	37	1963	0	1963	
4	First Quarrel		0	1963	27	1963	(Philips 40114)

Paul Anka Male Vocalist, B: 30 Jul 1941 Ottawa, Canada

	TITLE	UK LBL	UK POS	UK YEAR	US POS	US YEAR	US LBL
* 1	Diana	(Columbia DB 3980)	1	1957	1	1957	(ABC-Paramount 9831)
2	I Love You Baby	(Columbia DB 4022)	3	1957	0	1957	
3	Tell Me That You Love Me	(Columbia DB 4022)	25	1957	0	1957	
4	You Are My Destiny	(Columbia DB 4063)	6	1958	7	1958	(ABC-Paramount 9880)
5	Crazy Love	(Columbia DB 4110)	26	1958	15	1958	(ABC-Paramount 9907)

ISSUE	TITLE	UK LBL	UK POS	UK YEAR	US POS	US YEAR	US LBL
6	Let The Bells Keep Ringing		0	1958	16	1958	(ABC-Paramount 9907)
7	Midnight	(Columbia DB 4172)	26	1958	0	1958	
8	The Teen Commandments		0	1958	29	1958	(ABC-Paramount 9974)
9	(All Of A Sudden) My Heart Sings	(Columbia DB 4241)	10	1959	15	1959	(ABC-Paramount 9987)
10	I Miss You So		0	1959	33	1959	(ABC-Paramount 10011)
* 11	Lonely Boy	(Columbia DB 4324)	3	1959	1	1959	(ABC-Paramount 10022)
12	Put Your Head On My Shoulder	(Columbia DB 4355)	7	1959	2	1959	(ABC-Paramount 10040)
13	It's Time To Cry	(Columbia DB 4390)	28	1960	4	1959	(ABC-Paramount 10064)
* 14	Puppy Love	(Columbia DB 4434)	33	1960	2	1960	(ABC-Paramount 10082)
15	It's Time To Cry (Re-Entry)	(Columbia DB 4390)	37	1960	0	1960	
16	Puppy Love (Re-Entry)	(Columbia DB 4434)	37	1960	0	1960	
17	My Home Town		0	1960	8	1960	(ABC-Paramount 10106)
18	Hello Young Lovers	(Columbia DB 4504)	44	1960	23	1960	(ABC-Paramount 10132)
19	I Love You In The Same Old Way		0	1960	40	1960	(ABC-Paramount 10132)
20	Summer's Gone		0	1960	11	1960	(ABC-Paramount 10147)
21	The Story Of My Love		0	1961	16	1961	(ABC-Paramount 10168)
22	Tonight My Love, Tonight		0	1961	13	1961	(ABC-Paramount 10194)
23	Dance On Little Girl		0	1961	10	1961	(ABC-Paramount 10220)
24	Kissin' On The Phone		0	1961	35	1961	(ABC-Paramount 10239)
25	Love Me Warm And Tender	(RCA 1276)	19	1962	12	1962	(RCA 7977)
26	A Steel Guitar And A Glass Of Wine	(RCA 1292)	41	1962	13	1962	(RCA 8030)
27	Eso Beso (That Kiss)		0	1962	19	1962	(RCA 8097)
28	Love Makes The World Go Round		0	1963	26	1963	(RCA 8115)
29	Remember Diana		0	1963	39	1963	(RCA 8170)
* 30	Every Time	(RCA)	0	1964	0	1964	
31	Goodnight My Love		0	1969	27	1969	(RCA 9648)
* 32	You're Having My Baby	(United Artists UP 35713)	6	1974	1	1974	(United Artists 454)
33	One Man Woman - One Woman Man		0	1975	7	1975	(United Artists 569)
34	I Don't Like To Sleep Alone		0	1975	8	1975	(United Artists 615)
35	I Believe There's Something Stronger Than Our Love		0	1975	15	1975	(United Artists 685)
36	Times Of Your Life		0	1975	7	1975	(United Artists 737)
37	Anytime I'll Be There		0	1976	33	1976	(United Artists 789)
38	This Is Love		0	1978	35	1978	(RCA 11395)
39	Hold Me 'Til The Morning Comes		0	1983	40	1983	(Columbia 03897)

Paul Brady   Male Vocalist from the UK

1	The World Is What You Make It	(Mercury PBCD 5)	67	1996	0	1996	

Paul Carrack   Male Vocalist B: 22 Apr 1951 Sheffield, England, Lead Singer With Ace, Squeeze, Mike + Mechanics

1	I Need You		0	1982	37	1982	(Epic 03146)
2	When You Walk In The Room	(Chrysalis CHS 3109)	48	1987	0	1987	
3	Don't Shed A Tear	(Chrysalis CHS 3164)	60	1989	9	1988	(Chrysalis 43164)
4	One Good Reason		0	1988	28	1988	(Chrysalis 43204)
5	I Live By The Groove		0	1989	31	1989	(Chrysalis 23427)
6	How Long?	(IRS CDEIRS 193)	32	1996	0	1996	
7	Eyes Of Blue (Re-Mix)	(IRS CDEIRS 194)	45	1996	0	1996	

Paul Da Vinci   Male Vocalist from the UK

1	Your Baby Ain't Your Baby Anymore	(Penny Farthing PEN 843)	20	1974	0	1974	

Paul Davidson   Male Vocalist from Jamaica

1	Midnight Rider	(Tropical ALO 56)	10	1975	0	1975	

Paul Davis   Male Singer/Songwriter/Producer, B: 21 Apr 1948 Mississippi

1	Ride 'Em Cowboy		0	1974	23	1974	(BANG 712)
2	Superstar		0	1976	35	1976	(BANG 726)
3	I Go Crazy		0	1978	7	1978	(BANG 733)
4	Sweet Life		0	1978	17	1978	(BANG 738)
5	Do Right		0	1980	23	1980	(BANG 4808)
6	Cool Night		0	1982	11	1982	(Arista 0645)
7	'65 Love Affair		0	1982	6	1982	(Arista 0661)
8	Love Or Let Me Be Lonely		0	1982	40	1982	(Arista 0697)
	HIT 2 IS A TRIBUTE TO JONI MITCHELL, STEVIE WONDER, ELTON JOHN & LINDA RONSTADT						

Paul Dino   Real Name Paul Dino Bertuccini Jr B: 2 Mar 1935 Philadelphia

1	Ginnie Bell		0	1961	38	1961	(PROMO 2180)

Paul Evans   Male Vocalist, B: 5 Mar 1938 New York City

* 1	Seven Little Girls Sitting In The Back Seat	(London HLL8968)	25	1959	9	1959	(Guaranteed 200)
2	Midnight Special	(London HLL 9045)	41	1960	16	1960	(Guaranteed 205)

ISSUE	TITLE	UK LBL	UK POS	UK YEAR	US POS	US YEAR	US LBL
3	Happy-Go-Lucky-Me		0	1960	10	1960	(Guaranteed 208)

HIT 1 IS CREDITED TO PAUL EVANS & THE CURLS — SUE SINGLETON & SUE TERRY

Paul Gardiner Male Bassist from the UK

ISSUE	TITLE	UK LBL	UK POS	UK YEAR	US POS	US YEAR	US LBL
1	Stormtrooper In Drag	(Beggars Banquet BEG 61)	49	1981	0	1981	

UNCREDITED VOCALS ON HIT ARE BY GARY NUMAN

Paul Gayten Male Jazz Pianist from the USA

ISSUE	TITLE	UK LBL	UK POS	UK YEAR	US POS	US YEAR	US LBL
1	Since I Fell For You		0	1947	20	1947	(Deluxe 1082)
2	True		0	1947	5	1947	(Deluxe 1063)
3	Cuttin Out		0	1949	6	1949	(REGAL 3235)
*+ 4	I'll Never Be Free		0	1950	8	1950	(Regal 3258)
5	Goodnight Irene		0	1950	6	1950	(Regal 3281)
6	The Hunch		0	1959	68	1959	(ANNA 1106)

VOCALS ON HIT 1 ARE BY ANNIE LAURIE • HIT 4 IS CREDITED TO PAUL GAYTEN AND ANNIE LAURIE

Paul Haig Male Vocalist from the UK

ISSUE	TITLE	UK LBL	UK POS	UK YEAR	US POS	US YEAR	US LBL
1	Heaven Sent	(Island IS 111)	74	1983	0	1983	

Paul Hardcastle Male Producer, B: 10 Dec 1957 London, England

ISSUE	TITLE	UK LBL	UK POS	UK YEAR	US POS	US YEAR	US LBL
1	You're The One For Me - Daybreak - A.M.	(Total Control TOCO 1)	41	1984	0	1984	
2	Guilty	(Total Control TOCO 2)	55	1984	0	1984	
3	Rain Forest	(Bluebird BR 8)	41	1984	0	1984	
4	Eat Your Heart Out	(Cooltempo COOL 102)	59	1984	0	1984	
5	Nineteen	(Chrysalis CHS 2860)	1	1985	15	1985	(Chrysalis 42860)
6	Rain Forest (Re-Issue)	(Bluebird10 BR 15)	53	1985	0	1985	
7	Just For Money	(Chrysalis CASH 1)	19	1985	0	1985	
8	Don't Waste My Time	(Chrysalis PAUL 1)	8	1986	0	1986	
9	Foolin' Yourself	(Chrysalis PAUL 2)	51	1986	0	1986	
10	The Wizard	(Chrysalis PAUL 3)	15	1986	0	1986	
11	Walk In The Night	(Chrysalis PAUL 4)	54	1988	0	1988	
12	40 Years	(Chrysalis PAUL 5)	53	1988	0	1988	

HIT 5 REFERS TO THE AVERAGE AGE OF U.S. SOLDIERS IN VIETNAM • HIT 8 CREDITED TO PAUL HARDCASTLE FEATURING CAROL KENYON. HE FORMED TOTAL CONTROL RECORDS

Paul Henry & The Mayson Glen Orchestra Male Vocalist And Orchestra from the UK

ISSUE	TITLE	UK LBL	UK POS	UK YEAR	US POS	US YEAR	US LBL
1	Benny's Theme	(PYE 7N 46027)	39	1978	0	1978	

Paul Humphrey & His Cool Aid Chemists Male Session Drummer, B: 12 Oct 1935 Detroit

ISSUE	TITLE	UK LBL	UK POS	UK YEAR	US POS	US YEAR	US LBL
1	Cool Aid		0	1971	29	1971	(Lizard 21006)

Paul Johnson Male Vocalist from the UK

ISSUE	TITLE	UK LBL	UK POS	UK YEAR	US POS	US YEAR	US LBL
1	When Love Comes Calling	(CBS PJOHN 1)	52	1987	0	1987	
2	No More Tomorrows	(CBS PJOHN 7)	67	1989	0	1989	

Paul Jones Male Vocalist from the UK

ISSUE	TITLE	UK LBL	UK POS	UK YEAR	US POS	US YEAR	US LBL
1	High Time	(HMV POP 1554)	4	1966	0	1966	
2	I've Been A Bad Bad Boy	(HMV POP 1576)	5	1967	0	1967	
3	Thinkin' Ain't For Me	(HMV POP 1602)	47	1967	0	1967	
4	Thinkin' Ain't For Me (Re-Entry)	(HMV POP 1602)	32	1967	0	1967	
5	Aquarius	(Columbia DB 8514)	45	1969	0	1969	

Paul Lekakis Male Vocalist from the USA

ISSUE	TITLE	UK LBL	UK POS	UK YEAR	US POS	US YEAR	US LBL
1	Boom Boom (Let's Go Back To My Room)	(Champion Champ 43)	60	1987	0	1987	

Paul Mauriat Male Conductor/Arranger/Orchestra Leader, B: 1925 France

ISSUE	TITLE	UK LBL	UK POS	UK YEAR	US POS	US YEAR	US LBL
* 1	Love Is Blue	(Philips BF 1637)	12	1968	1	1968	(Philips 40495)

Paul McCartney Male Vocal/Songwriter/Instrumentalist, James Paul McCartney, B: 19 Jun 1942 Liverpool, England

ISSUE	TITLE	UK LBL	UK POS	UK YEAR	US POS	US YEAR	US LBL
* 1	Another Day	(Apple R 5889)	2	1971	5	1971	(Apple 1829)
2	Back Seat Of My Car / Heart Of The Country	(Apple R 5914)	39	1971	0	1971	
* 3	Uncle Albert-Admiral Halsey		0	1971	1	1971	(Apple 1837)
4	Give Ireland Back To The Irish	(Apple R 5936)	16	1972	21	1972	(Apple 1847)
5	Mary Had A Little Lamb	(Apple R 5949)	9	1972	28	1972	(Apple 1851)
6	Hi Hi Hi / C Moon	(Apple R 5973)	5	1972	10	1973	(Apple 1857)
* 7	My Love	(Apple R 5985)	9	1973	1	1973	(Apple 1861)
* 8	Live And Let Die (Movie Title Song)	(Apple R 5987)	9	1973	2	1973	(Apple 1863)
9	Live And Let Die (Re-Entry)	(Apple R 5987)	49	1973	0	1973	
10	Helen Wheels	(Apple R 5993)	12	1973	10	1973	(Apple 1869)
11	Jet	(Apple R 5996)	7	1974	7	1974	(Apple 1871)
* 12	Band On The Run	(Apple R 5997)	3	1974	1	1974	(Apple 1873)
13	Juniors Farm	(Apple R 5999)	16	1974	3	1974	(Apple 1875)
14	Sally G	(Apple R 5999)	16	1974	17	1974	(Apple 1875)
* 15	Listen To What The Man Said	(Capitol R 6006)	6	1975	1	1975	(Capitol 4091)
16	Letting Go	(Capitol R 6008)	41	1975	39	1975	(Capitol 4145)

ISSUE	TITLE	UK LBL	UK POS	UK YEAR	US POS	US YEAR	US LBL
17	Venus And Mars Rock Show		0	1975	12	1975	(Capitol 4175)
* 18	Silly Love Songs	(Parlophone R 6014)	2	1976	1	1976	(Capitol 4256)
* 19	Let 'Em In	(Parlophone R 6015)	2	1976	3	1976	(Capitol 4293)
20	Maybe I'm Amazed	(Parlophone R 6017)	28	1977	10	1977	(Capitol 4385)
21	Mull Of Kintyre / Girls School	(Capitol R 6018)	1	1977	33	1977	(Capitol 4504)
22	With A Little Luck	(Parlophone R 6019)	5	1978	1	1978	(Capitol 4559)
23	I've Had Enough	(Parlophone R 6020)	42	1978	25	1978	(Capitol 4594)
24	London Town	(Parlophone R 6021)	60	1978	39	1978	(Capitol 4625)
* 25	Goodnight Tonight	(Parlophone R 6023)	5	1979	5	1979	(Columbia 10939)
26	Old Siam Sir	(MPL R 6026)	35	1979	0	1979	
27	Getting Closer	(Parlophone R 6027)	60	1979	20	1979	(Columbia 11020)
28	Arrow Through Me		0	1979	29	1979	(Columbia 11070)
29	Wonderful Christmas Time	(Parlophone R 6029)	6	1979	0	1979	
* 30	Coming Up (Live At Glasgow)	(Parlophone R 6035)	2	1980	1	1980	(Columbia 11263)
31	Waterfalls	(Parlophone R 6037)	9	1980	0	1980	
* 32	Ebony And Ivory	(Parlophone R 6054)	1	1982	1	1982	(Columbia 02860)
33	Take It Away	(Parlophone R 6056)	15	1982	10	1982	(Columbia 03018)
34	Tug Of War	(Parlophone R 6057)	53	1982	0	1982	
* 35	The Girl Is Mine	(Epic EPC A 2729)	8	1992	2	1982	(Epic 03288)
36	The Girl Is Mine (Re-Entry)	(Epic EPC A 2729)	75	1983	0	1983	
* 37	Say Say Say	(Parlophone R 6062)	2	1983	1	1983	(Columbia 04168)
38	Pipes Of Peace	(Parlophone R 6064)	1	1983	0	1983	
39	So Bad		0	1984	23	1984	(Columbia 04296)
40	No More Lonely Nights (Ballad)	(Parlophone R 6080)	2	1984	6	1984	(Columbia 04581)
41	We All Stand Together	(Parlophone R 6086)	3	1984	0	1984	
42	Spies Like Us	(Parlophone R 6118)	13	1985	7	1986	(Capitol 5537)
43	We All Stand Together (Re-Entry)	(Parlophone R 6086)	32	1985	0	1985	
44	Press	(Parlophone R 6133)	25	1986	21	1986	(Capitol 5597)
45	Only Love Remains	(Parlophone R 6148)	34	1986	0	1986	
46	Once Upon A Long Ago	(Parlophone R 6170)	10	1987	0	1987	
47	Ferry 'Cross The Mersey	(PWL PWL 41)	1	1989	0	1989	
48	My Brave Face	(Parlophone R 6213)	18	1989	25	1989	(Capitol 44367)
49	This One	(Parlophone R 6223)	18	1989	0	1989	
50	Figure Of Eight	(Parlophone R 6235)	42	1989	0	1989	
51	Put It There	(Parlophone R 6246)	32	1990	0	1990	
52	Birthday	(Parlophone R 6271)	29	1990	0	1990	
53	All My Trials	(Parlophone R 6278)	35	1990	0	1990	
54	Hope Of Deliverance	(Parlophone CDR 6330)	18	1993	0	1993	
55	C'mon People	(Parlophone CDRS 6338)	41	1993	0	1993	
56	Young Boy	(Parlophone CDRS 6462)	19	1997	0	1997	
57	The World Tonight (From *Fathers' Day*)	(Parlophone CDR 6472)	23	1997	64	1997	(Capitol 58650)

WINGS FORMED IN 1971, WITH DENNY LAINE, DENNY SEIWELL & LINDA MCCARTNEY

Paul Nicholas Male Vocalist, Real Name Paul Beuselinck B: 3 Dec 1945 In Peterborough, England

1	Reggae Like It Used To Be	(RSO 2090 185)	17	1976	0	1976	
2	Dancing With The Captain	(RSO 2090 206)	8	1976	0	1976	
3	Grandma's Party	(RSO 2090 216)	9	1976	0	1976	
* 4	Heaven On The 7th Floor	(RSO 2090 249)	40	1977	6	1977	(RSO 878)

Paul Petersen Male Vocalist/Actor/Author, B: 23 Sep 1945 Glendale, California

1	She Can't Find Her Keys		0	1962	19	1962	(COLPIX 620)
2	My Dad		0	1962	6	1962	(COLPIX 663)

Paul Phoenix Male Vocalist from the UK

1	Nunc Dimittis	(Different Have 20)	56	1979	0	1979	

Paul Revere & The Raiders B: 7 Jan 1942 Boise, Idaho

1	Like, Long Hair		0	1961	38	1961	(Gardena 116)
2	Just Like Me		0	1965	11	1965	(Columbia 43461)
3	Kicks		0	1966	4	1966	(Columbia 43556)
4	Hungry		0	1966	6	1966	(Columbia 43678)
5	The Great Airplane Strike		0	1966	20	1966	(Columbia 43810)
6	Good Thing		0	1967	4	1967	(Columbia 43907)
7	Ups And Downs		0	1967	22	1967	(Columbia 44018)
8	Him Or Me-What's It Gonna Be		0	1967	5	1967	(Columbia 44094)
9	I Had A Dream		0	1967	17	1967	(Columbia 44227)
10	Too Much Talk		0	1968	19	1968	(Columbia 44444)
11	Don' Take It So Hard		0	1968	27	1968	(Columbia 44553)

ISSUE	TITLE	UK LBL	UK POS	UK YEAR	US POS	US YEAR	US LBL
12	Mr. Sun, Mr. Moon		0	1969	18	1969	(Columbia 44744)
13	Let Me		0	1969	20	1969	(Columbia 44854)
* 14	Indian Reservation (Lament Of The Cherokee Reservation Indian)		0	1971	1	1971	(Columbia 45332)
15	Birds Of A Feather		0	1971	23	1971	(Columbia 45453)
	LEAD SINGER WITH THE GROUP IS MARK LINDSEY • HITS 14-15 ARE CREDITED TO THE RAIDERS						

Paul Rodgers Male Vocalist from the UK

ISSUE	TITLE	UK LBL	UK POS	UK YEAR	US POS	US YEAR	US LBL
1	Muddy Water Blues	(Creation CRESCD 178)	45	1994	0	1994	

Paul Rutherford Male Vocalist from the UK

ISSUE	TITLE	UK LBL	UK POS	UK YEAR	US POS	US YEAR	US LBL
1	Get Real	(Fourth & BroadwayBRW 113)	47	1988	0	1988	
2	Oh World	(Fourth & BroadwayBRW 136)	61	1989	0	1989	

Paul Shane & The Yellowcoats Male Actor/Vocalist With Mixed Vocal Group from the UK

ISSUE	TITLE	UK LBL	UK POS	UK YEAR	US POS	US YEAR	US LBL
1	Hi-De-Hi (Holiday Rock)	(EMI 5180)	36	1981	0	1981	

Paul Simon Male Vocalist, B: 5 Nov 1941 Newark, New Jersey

ISSUE	TITLE	UK LBL	UK POS	UK YEAR	US POS	US YEAR	US LBL
1	Mother And Child Reunion	(CBS 7793)	5	1972	4	1972	(Columbia 45547)
2	Me And Julio Down By The School Yard	(CBS 7964)	15	1972	22	1972	(Columbia 45585)
3	Kodachrome		0	1973	2	1973	(Columbia 45859)
4	Take Me To The Mardi Gras	(CBS 1578)	7	1973	0	1973	
* 5	Love Me Like A Rock	(CBS 1700)	39	1973	2	1973	(Columbia 45907)
6	American Tune		0	1974	35	1974	(Columbia 45900)
7	Gone At Last		0	1975	23	1975	(Columbia 10197)
* 8	50 Ways To Leave Your Lover	(CBS 3887)	23	1976	1	1976	(Columbia 10270)
9	Still Crazy After All These Years		0	1976	40	1976	(Columbia 10332)
10	Slip Sliding Away	(CBS 5770)	27	1977	5	1977	(Columbia 10630)
11	(What A) Wonderful World		0	1978	17	1978	(Columbia 10676)
12	Late In The Evening	(Warner Bros. K 17666)	58	1980	6	1980	(Warner Bros. 49511)
13	One-Trick Pony		0	1980	40	1980	(Warner Bros.49601)
14	You Can Call Me Al	(Warner Bros. W 8667)	4	1986	23	1987	(Warner Bros. 28667)
15	The Boy In The Bubble	(Warner Bros. W 8509)	26	1986	0	1986	
16	Musical Freedom (Moving On Up)	(Cooltempo COOL 182)	22	1989	0	1989	
17	The Obvious Child	(Warner Bros. W 9549)	15	1990	0	1990	
18	Something So Right	(RCA	44	1995	0	1995	

Paul Stookey Male Vocalist, B: 30 Nov 1937 Baltimore

ISSUE	TITLE	UK LBL	UK POS	UK YEAR	US POS	US YEAR	US LBL
1	Wedding Song (There Is Love)		0	1971	24	1971	(Warner Bros. 7511)

Paul Weller Male Vocalist from the UK

ISSUE	TITLE	UK LBL	UK POS	UK YEAR	US POS	US YEAR	US LBL
1	Into Tomorrow	(Freedom HIGH FHP 1)	36	1991	0	1991	
2	Above The Clouds	(Go! Discs God 91)	47	1992	0	1992	
3	Sunflower	(Go! Discs God 102)	16	1993	0	1993	
4	Uh Huh Oh Yeh	(Go! Discs God 86)	18	1992	0	1992	
5	Wild Wood	(Go! Discs God 104)	14	1993	0	1993	
6	The Weaver (EP)	(Go! Discs God 107)	18	1993	0	1993	
7	Hung Up	(Go! Discs GodCD 111)	11	1994	0	1994	
8	Out Of The Sinking	(Go! Discs GodCD 121)	20	1994	0	1994	
9	The Changingman	(Go! Discs GodCD 127)	7	1995	0	1995	
10	You Do Something To Me	(Go! Discs GodCD 130)	9	1995	0	1995	
11	Broken Stones	(GO! DISCS GPDCD 132)	20	1995	0	1995	
12	Out Of The Sinking (Re-Recording)	(Go! Discs GodCD 143)	16	1996	0	1996	
13	Peacock Suit	(Go! Discs GodCD 149)	5	1996	0	1996	
14	Brushed	(Island CID 666)	14	1997	0	1997	
	HIT 1 IS CREDITED TO THE PAUL WELLER MOVEMENT						

Paul Weston & His Orchestra Male Conductor/Arranger/Bandleader, Paul Wetstein from the USA See Also Pied Pipers

ISSUE	TITLE	UK LBL	UK POS	UK YEAR	US POS	US YEAR	US LBL
1	It Might As Well Be Spring		0	1945	6	1945	(Capitol 214)
2	Ole Buttermilk Sky		0	1946	6	1946	(Capitol 285)
3	Just Squeeze Me (But Don't Tease Me)		0	1946	21	1946	(Capitol 285)
4	Linda		0	1947	8	1947	(Capitol 362)
5	Clair De Lune		0	1948	15	1948	(Capitol 15153)
6	Deep Purple		0	1949	20	1949	(Capitol 15294)
7	The Hot Canary		0	1949	12	1949	(Capitol 15373)
8	Bali Ha'i		0	1949	10	1949	(Capitol 629)
9	Some Enchanted Evening		0	1949	9	1949	(Capitol 629)
10	Reckon I'm In Love		0	1949	23	1949	(Capitol 697)
11	Lingering Down The Lane		0	1949	16	1949	(Capitol 57725)
12	I Know, I Know, I Know		0	1949	25	1949	(Capitol 57725)
13	Fairy Tales		0	1950	30	1950	(Capitol 826)

ISSUE	TITLE	UK LBL	UK POS	UK YEAR	US POS	US YEAR	US LBL
14	La Vie En Rose		0	1950	12	1950	(Capitol 826)
15	Nevertheless (I'm In Love With You)		0	1950	2	1950	(Columbia 38982)
16	Across The Wide Missouri		0	1951	19	1951	(Columbia 39160)
17	So Long (It's Been Good To Know Yuh)		0	1951	21	1951	(Columbia 39160)
18	The Morningside Of The Mountain		0	1951	16	1951	(Columbia 38424)
19	And So To Sleep Again		0	1951	30	1951	(Columbia 39569)
20	Charmaine		0	1951	8	1951	(Columbia 39616)
21	Shane (The Call Of The Far-Away Hills)		0	1953	29	1953	(Columbia 40014)
22	I Went Out Of My Way		0	1954	30	1954	(Columbia 40237)

Paul Whiteman & His Orchestra Male Orchestra Leader, B: 28 Mar 1890 Denver, Colorado

	ISSUE	TITLE	UK LBL	UK POS	UK YEAR	US POS	US YEAR	US LBL
*	1	Whispering		0	1920	1	1920	(Victor 18690)
*	3	Wang Wang Blues		0	1920	1	1920	(Victor 18694)
*	35	Three O'Clock In The Morning		0	1922	1	1922	(Victor 18940)
*	55	Linger Awhile		0	1924	1	1924	(Victor 19211)

Paul Young Male Vocal/Guitarist, B: 17 Jan 1956 In Bedfordshire, England

	ISSUE	TITLE	UK LBL	UK POS	UK YEAR	US POS	US YEAR	US LBL
	1	Wherever I Lay My Hat (That's My Home)	(CBS A 3371)	1	1983	0	1983	
	2	Come Back And Stay	(CBS A 3636)	4	1983	22	1984	(Columbia 04313)
	3	Love Of The Common People	(CBS A 3585)	2	1983	0	1983	
	4	I'm Gonna Tear Your Playhouse Down	(CBS A 4786)	9	1984	13	1985	(Columbia 0557)
	5	Everything Must Change	(CBS A 4972)	9	1984	0	1984	
*	6	Every Time You Go Away	(CBS A 6300)	4	1985	1	1985	(Columbia 04867)
	7	Tomb Of Memories	(CBS A 6321)	16	1985	0	1985	
	8	Tomb Of Memories (Re-Entry)	(CBS A 6321)	74	1985	0	1985	
	9	Wonderland	(CBS YOUNG 1)	24	1986	0	1986	
	10	Some People	(CBS YOUNG 2)	56	1986	0	1986	
	11	Why Does A Man Have To Be Strong	(CBS Young 3)	63	1987	0	1987	
	12	Softly Whispering I Love You	(CBS Young 5)	21	1990	0	1990	
	13	Oh Girl	(CBS Young 6)	25	1990	8	1990	(Columbia 73377)
	14	Heaven Can Wait	(CBS Young 6)	71	1990	0	1990	
	15	Calling You	(CBS Young 7)	57	1991	0	1991	
	16	Senza Una Donna (Without A Woman)	(London LON 294)	4	1991	0	1991	
	17	Both Sides Now	(MCA MCS 1546)	74	1991	0	1991	
	18	Don't Dream It's Over	(Columbia 6574117)	20	1991	0	1991	
	19	What Becomes Of The Brokenhearted		0	1992	22	1992	(MCA 54331)
	20	Now I Know What Made Otis Blue	(Columbia 6596412)	14	1993	0	1993	
	21	Hope In A Hopeless World	(Columbia 6598652)	42	1993	0	1993	
	22	I'll Be With You	(Columbia 6602812)	34	1994	0	1994	
	23	I Wish You Love	(East West EW 100CD1)	33	1997	0	1997	

HIT 16 IS CREDITED TO ZUCCHERO AND PAUL YOUNG • HIT 17 IS CREDITED TO CLANNAD AND PAUL YOUNG

Paula Abdul Female Vocalist, B: 19 Jun 1962 Los Angeles

ISSUE	TITLE	UK LBL	UK POS	UK YEAR	US POS	US YEAR	US LBL
1	Straight Up	(Siren SRN 111)	3	1989	1	1988	(Virgin 99256)
2	It's Just The Way That You Love Me	(Siren SRN 101)	74	1988	88	1988	(Virgin 99282)
3	Forever Your Girl	(Siren SRN 112)	24	1989	1	1989	(Virgin 99230)
4	Knocked Out	(Siren SRN 92)	45	1989	0	1989	
5	It's Just The Way That You Love Me(Re Entry)	(Siren SRN 101)	74	1989	3	1989	(Virgin 99282)
6	Opposites Attract	(Siren SRN 124)	2	1990	1	1990	(Virgin 99158)
7	Knocked Out (Re-Mix)	(Virgin America VUS 23)	21	1990	0	1990	
8	Cold Hearted	(Virgin America VUS 27)	46	1990	1	1989	(Virgin 99196)
9	Rush Rush	(Virgin America VUS 38)	6	1991	1	1991	(Virgin 98828)
10	The Promise Of A New Day	(Virgin America VUS 44)	52	1991	1	1991	(Virgin 98752)
11	Blowing Kisses In The Wind		0	1991	6	1991	(Virgin 98683)
12	Vibeology	(Virgin America VUS 53)	19	1992	16	1992	(Virgin 98737)
13	Will You Marry Me	(Virgin America VUS 58)	73	1992	19	1992	(Virgin 98584)
14	My Love Is For Real	(Virgin America VUSCD 91)	28	1995	28	1995	(CAPTIVE/Virgin 38493)

HIT 6 IS CREDITED TO PAULA ABDUL WITH THE WILD PAIR • THE RAP ON THE HIT IS BY DERRICK DELITE (SOUL PURPOSE)

Paula Cole Female Vocalist from the USA

ISSUE	TITLE	UK LBL	UK POS	UK YEAR	US POS	US YEAR	US LBL
1	Where Have All The Cowboys Gone?	(Warner Bros. W 0406CD)	15	1997	9	1997	(Warner Bros.17373)

Paula Watson Female R&B Vocalist from the USA

ISSUE	TITLE	UK LBL	UK POS	UK YEAR	US POS	US YEAR	US LBL
1	A Little Bird Told Me		0	1948	6	1948	(Supreme 1507)

Pauline Henry Female Vocalist from the UK

ISSUE	TITLE	UK LBL	UK POS	UK YEAR	US POS	US YEAR	US LBL
1	Too Many People	(Sony S2 6595942)	38	1993	0	1993	
2	Feel Like Making Love	(Sony S2 6597972)	12	1993	0	1993	
3	Can't Take Your Love	(Sony S2 6599902)	30	1994	0	1994	
4	Watch The Miracle Start	(Sony S2 6602772)	54	1994	0	1994	

ISSUE	TITLE	UK LBL	UK POS	UK YEAR	US POS	US YEAR	US LBL
5	Sugar Free	(Sony S2 6624362)	57	1995	0	1995	
6	Love Hangover	(Sony S2 6626132)	37	1995	0	1995	
7	Never Knew Love Like This	(Sony S2 6629382)	40	1996	0	1996	
8	Happy	(Sony S2 6630692)	46	1996	0	1996	
Pauline Murray & The Invisible Girls Female Vocalist With Male Vocal/Instrumental Group from the UK							
1	Dream Sequence (One)	(Illusive IVE 1)	67	1980	0	1980	
Pauline Taylor Female Vocalist from the UK							
1	Let This Be A Prayer	(Cheeky Chek CD013)	26	1996	0	1996	
2	Constantly Waiting	(Cheeky Chek CD015)	51	1996	0	1996	
	HIT 1 IS CREDITED TO ROLLO GOES SPIRITUAL FEATURING PAULINE TAYLOR							
Pavement Male Vocal/Instrumental Group from the UK							
1	Watery Domestic (EP)	(Big Cat ABB 38T)	58	1992	0	1992	
2	Cut Your Hair	(Big Cat ABB 55SCD)	52	1994	0	1994	
3	Stereo	(Domino RUG 51CD)	48	1997	0	1997	
4	Shady Lane	(Domino RUG 53CD)	40	1997	0	1997	
Peabo Bryson Male Vocalist, Real Name Robert Peabo Bryson B: 13 Apr 1951 Greenville, South Carolina							
1	Tonight I Celebrate My Love	(Capitol CL 302)	2	1983	16	1983	(Capitol 5242)
2	If Ever You're In My Arms Again		0	1984	10	1984	(Elektra 69728)
3	Beauty And The Beast	(Epic 6576607)	9	1992	3	1992	(Epic 74090)
* 4	A Whole New World (Aladdin's Cave)	(Columbia 6599002)	12	1993	1	1993	(Columbia 74751)
5	By The Time The Night Is Over	(Arista 74321157142)	56	1993	25	1993	(Arista 12565)
Peace By Piece Male Vocal Group from the UK							
1	Sweet Sister	(Blanco Y Negro NEG 94CD)	46	1996	0	1996	
Peaches & Herb Mixed Vocal Duo from the USA							
1	Let's Fall In Love		0	1967	21	1967	(Date 1523)
2	Close Your Eyes		0	1967	8	1967	(Date 1549)
3	For Your Love		0	1967	20	1967	(Date 1563)
4	Love Is Strange		0	1967	11	1967	(Date 1574)
5	Two Little Kids		0	1968	31	1968	(Date 1586)
* 6	Shake Your Groove Thing	(Polydor 2066 992)	26	1979	5	1979	(Polydor 14514)
* 7	Reunited	(Polydor POSP 43)	4	1979	1	1979	(Polydor 14547)
8	I Pledge My Love		0	1980	19	1980	(Polydor 2053)
	ORIGINAL NAMES HERBERT FEEMSTER AND FRANCINE BAKER (NEE HURD) • MARLENE MACK REPLACED BAKER FROM 1968-69 UNTIL HER RETURN. A DUET REFORMED IN 1977 WITH LINDA GREEN							
Pearl Bailey Female Actress/Vocalist from the USA							
1	Takes Two To Tango		0	1952	7	1952	(Coral 60817)
Pearl Carr & Teddy Johnson Mixed Vocal Duo from the UK							
1	Sing Little Birdie	(Columbia DB 4275)	12	1959	0	1959	
2	How Wonderful To Know	(Columbia DB 4603)	23	1961	0	1961	
Pearl Jam Male Vocal/Instrumental Group from the UK							
1	Alive	(Epic 6575727)	16	1992	0	1992	
2	Even Flow	(Epic 6578577)	27	1992	0	1992	
3	Jeremy	(Epic 6582587)	15	1992	0	1992	
4	Daughter	(Epic 6600202)	18	1994	0	1994	
5	Dissident	(Epic 6604415)	14	1994	0	1994	
6	Spin The Black Circle	(Epic 6610362)	10	1994	0	1994	
7	Tremor Christ		0	1994	18	1994	(Epic 77771)
8	Not For You	(Epic 6612037)	34	1995	0	1995	
9	Merkinball	(Epic 6627162)	25	1995	0	1995	
10	I Got Id	(Epic 6635392)	18	1996	7	1995	(Epic 78199)
11	Who Are You	(Epic 6635392)	18	1996	31	1996	(Epic 78389)
Pearls Female Vocal Duo from the UK							
1	Third Finger Left Hand	(Bell 1217)	31	1972	0	1972	
2	You Came You Saw You Conquered	(Bell 1254)	32	1972	0	1972	
3	You Are Everything	(Bell 1284)	41	1973	0	1973	
4	Guilty	(Bell 1352)	10	1974	0	1974	
Pebbles Female Vocalist, Real Name Perri Alette McKissack from Oakland							
1	Girlfriend	(MCA MCA 1233)	8	1988	5	1988	(MCA 53185)
2	Mercedes Boy	(MCA MCA 1248)	42	1988	2	1988	(MCA 53279)
3	Giving You The Benefit	(MCA MCA 1448)	73	1990	4	1990	(MCA 53891)
4	Love Makes Things Happen		0	1991	13	1991	(MCA 53973)

ISSUE	TITLE	UK LBL	UK POS	UK YEAR	US POS	US YEAR	US LBL
Peddlers Male Vocal/Instrumental Group from the UK							
1	Let The Sunshine In	(PHILLIPS BF 1375)	50	1965	0	1965	
2	Birth	(CBS 4449)	17	1969	0	1969	
3	Girlie	(CBS 4720)	34	1970	0	1970	
Pee Bee Squad Male Vocalist, Real Name Paul Burnett from the UK							
1	Rugged And Mean, Butch And On Screen	(PROJECT PRO 3)	52	1985	0	1985	
Pee Wee Hunt Orchestra Male Singer/Trombonist, B: 1907 Mount Healthy, Ohio							
* 1	Twelfth Street Rag		0	1948	1	1948	(Capitol 15105)
* 2	Oh		0	1953	3	1953	(Capitol 2442)
3	San		0	1953	24	1953	(Capitol 2442)
Pee Wee King & His Golden West Cowboys Male Instrumentalist (Harmonica/Accordion), Real Name Julius Frank Kuczynski B: 18 Feb 1914 In Abrams, Wisconsin							
1	Tennessee Waltz		0	1948	30	1948	(RCA Victor 2680)
* 6	Slow-Poke		0	1951	1	1951	(RCA Victor 0489)
7	Silver And Gold		0	1952	18	1952	(RCA Victor 4458)
8	Busybody		0	1952	27	1952	(RCA Victor 4655)
Peech Boys Male Vocal/Instrumental Group from the UK							
1	Don't Make Me Wait	(TMT QTMT 7001)	49	1982	0	1982	
Peggy King Female Actress/Vocalist from the USA							
1	Make Yourself Comfortable		0	1955	30	1955	(Columbia 40363)
Peggy Lee Female Vocalist, Real Name Norma Jean Egstrom B: 26 May 1920 Jamestown, North Dakota.							
1	Waitin' For The Rain To Come In		0	1945	4	1945	(Capitol 218)
2	I'm Glad I Waited For You (From *Tars And Spars*)		0	1946	24	1946	(Capitol 218)
3	I Don't Know Enough About You		0	1946	7	1946	(Capitol 236)
4	Linger In My Arms A Little Longer Baby		0	1946	16	1946	(Capitol 263)
5	It's All Over Now		0	1946	10	1946	(Capitol 292)
6	It's A Good Day		0	1947	16	1947	(Capitol 322)
7	Everything's Movin' Too Fast		0	1947	21	1947	(Capitol 343)
8	Chi-Baba, Chi-Baba (My Bambino Go To Sleep)		0	1947	10	1947	(Capitol 419)
9	Golden Earrings (Movie Title Song)		0	1947	2	1947	(Capitol 15009)
10	I'll Dance At Your Wedding		0	1947	11	1947	(Capitol 15009)
* 11	Manana (Is Soon Enough For Me)		0	1948	1	1948	(Capitol 15022)
12	All Dressed Up With A Broken Heart		0	1948	21	1948	(Capitol 15022)
13	For Every Man There's A Woman (From *Casbah*)		0	1948	25	1948	(Capitol 15030)
14	Laroo, Laroo, Lili Bolero		0	1948	13	1948	(Capitol 15048)
15	Talking To Myself About You		0	1948	23	1948	(Capitol 15048)
16	Don't Smoke In Bed		0	1948	22	1948	(Capitol 10120)
17	Caramba It's The Samba		0	1948	13	1948	(Capitol 15090)
18	Baby Don't Be Mad At Me		0	1948	21	1948	(Capitol 15090)
19	Bubble Loo, Bubble Loo		0	1948	23	1948	(Capitol 15118)
20	Blum Blum, I Wonder Who I Am		0	1949	27	1949	(Capitol 15371)
21	Similau (See-Me-Lo)		0	1949	17	1949	(Capitol 15416)
22	Bali Ha'i (From *South Pacific*)		0	1949	13	1949	(Capitol 543)
23	Riders In The Sky (A Cowboy Legend)		0	1949	2	1949	(Capitol 608)
24	The Old Master Painter		0	1950	9	1950	(Capitol 791)
25	Show Me The Way To Get Out Of This World		0	1950	28	1950	(Capitol 1105)
26	I Get Ideas		0	1951	14	1951	(Capitol 1573)
27	Be Anything (But Be Mine)		0	1952	21	1952	(Decca 28142)
* 28	Lover (From *Love Me Tonight*)		0	1952	3	1952	(Decca 28215)
29	Watermelon Weather		0	1952	28	1952	(Decca 28238)
30	Just One Of Those Thing (From *Jubilee*)		0	1952	14	1952	(Decca 28313)
31	River, River		0	1952	23	1952	(Decca 28395)
32	Who's Gonna Pay The Check		0	1953	22	1953	(Decca 28631)
33	Baubles, Bangles, And Beads (From *Kismet*)		0	1953	30	1953	(Decca 28890)
34	Where Can I Go Without You?		0	1954	28	1954	(Decca 29003)
35	Let Me Go Lover		0	1954	26	1954	(Decca 29373)
36	Mr. Wonderful	(Brunswick 05671)	5	1957	14	1956	(Decca 29834)
37	Fever	(Capitol CL 14902)	5	1958	8	1958	(Capitol 3998)
38	Till There Was You	(Capitol CL 15184)	40	1961	0	1961	
39	Till There Was You (Re-Entry)	(Capitol CL 15184)	30	1961	0	1961	
40	Is That All There Is		0	1969	11	1969	(Capitol 2602)
41	Fever (Re-Issue)	(Capitol PEG 1)	75	1992	0	1992	
Peggy Scott & Jo Jo Benson Mixed Studio Vocal Duo, Benson Was With Chuck Willis & The Blue Notes							
1	Lover's Holiday		0	1968	31	1968	(SSS INT'L 736)

ISSUE	TITLE	UK LBL	UK POS	UK YEAR	US POS	US YEAR	US LBL
2	Pickin' Wild Mountain Berries		0	1968	27	1968	(SSS INT'L 748)
3	Soulshake		0	1969	37	1969	(SSS INT'L 761)
Pele Mixed Vocal/Instrumental Group from the UK							
1	Megalowmania	(M&G MAGS 20)	73	1992	0	1992	
2	Fair Blows The Wind For France	(M&G MAGS 24)	62	1992	0	1992	
3	Fat Black Heart	(M&G MAGCD 43)	75	1993	0	1993	
Penguins Names: Cleveland Duncan, Bruce Tate, Curtis Williams & Dexter Tisby							
* 1	Earth Angel		0	1955	8	1955	(DOOTONE 348)
Penny Ford Female Vocalist from the USA, Former Backing Vocalist With The Gap Band							
1	Dangerous	(total experience FB 49975)	43	1985	0	1985	
2	Daydreaming	(Columbia 6590592)	43	1993	0	1993	
Pentangle Mixed Vocal/Instrumental Group from the UK							
1	Once I Had A Sweetheart	(BIG T BIG 124)	46	1969	0	1969	
2	Light Flight	(BIG T BIG 128)	43	1970	0	1970	
3	Light Flight (Re-Entry)	(BIG T BIG 128)	45	1970	0	1970	
Penthouse 4 Male Vocal/Instrumental Duo from the UK							
1	Bust This House Down	(Syncopate SY 10)	56	1988	0	1988	
People Lead Singer With The Sextet Is Jeff Levin							
1	I Love You		0	1968	14	1968	(Capitol 2078)
People's Choice Male Vocal/Instrumental Group from the USA Names: Frankie Brunson, David Thompson, Roger Andrews & Darnell Jordon							
1	I Likes To Do It		0	1971	38	1971	(Philadelphia L.A. 349)
* 2	Do It Anyway You Wanna	(Philadelphia International PIR 3500)	36	1975	11	1975	(TSOP 8-4769)
3	Jam Jam Jam	(Philadelphia International PIR 5891)	40	1978	0	1978	
Peppermint Harris Male R&B Vocalist/Guitarist, B: Harrison D. Nelson 17 July 1925 in Texarkana, Texas							
1	Raining in My Heart		0	1950	4	1950	(Sittin' In With 45-453)
*+ 2	I Got Loaded		0	1951	1	1951	(ALADIN 45-3097)
Peppermint Rainbow Vocal/Instrumental Group from the USA							
* 1	Will You Be Staying After Sunday		0	1968	32	1968	(Decca 32410)
	THE HIT WAS WRITTEN BY A. KASHA & J. HIRSCHHORN						
Peppers Male Instrumental Group From France							
1	Pepper Box	(Spark SRL 1100)	6	1974	0	1974	
Pepsi & Shirlie Female Vocal Duo from the UK							
1	Heartache	(Polydor POSP 837)	2	1987	0	1987	
2	Goodbye Stranger	(Polydor POSP 865)	9	1987	0	1987	
3	Can't Give Me Love	(Polydor POSP 885)	58	1987	0	1987	
4	All Right Now	(Polydor POSP 896)	50	1987	0	1987	
Perception Male Vocal Group from the UK							
1	Feed The Feeling	(Talkin Loud TLK 17)	58	1992	0	1992	
Percy Faith Male Orchestra Leader B: 7 Apr 1908 Toronto, Canada							
1	Cross My Fingers		0	1950	20	1950	(Columbia 38786)
2	All My Love		0	1950	7	1950	(Columbia 38918)
3	Christmas In Killarney		0	1950	28	1950	(Columbia 39048)
4	On Top Of Old Smoky		0	1951	10	1951	(Columbia 39328)
5	When The Saints Go Marching In		0	1951	29	1951	(Columbia 39528)
6	I Want To Be Near You		0	1951	30	1951	(Columbia 39528)
* 7	Delicado		0	1952	1	1952	(Columbia 39708)
8	Swedish Rhapsody (Midsummer Vigil)		0	1953	21	1953	(Columbia 39944)
* 9	Song From Moulin Rouge (Where Is Your Heart)		0	1953	1	1953	(Columbia 39944)
10	Return To Paradise (Movie Title Song)		0	1953	19	1953	(Columbia 39998)
11	Many Times		0	1953	30	1953	(Columbia 40076)
12	Dream, Dream, Dream		0	1954	25	1954	(Columbia 40185)
13	The Bandit (From *Cangaceiro*)		0	1954	25	1954	(Columbia 40323)
* 14	Theme From A Summer Place	(Philips PB 989)	2	1960	1	1960	(Columbia 41490)
15	Theme From *Young Lovers*		0	1960	35	1960	(Columbia 41655)
Percy Mayfield Male R&B Vocalist, B: 12 Aug 1920 Shreveport, Louisiana							
* 1	Please Send Me Someone To Love		0	1950	1	1950	(Specialty 375)
Percy Sledge Male Vocalist, B: 1941, Muscle Shoals, Alabama							
* 1	When A Man Loves A Woman	(Atlantic 584 001)	4	1966	1	1966	(Atlantic 2326)
2	Warm And Tender Love	(Atlantic 584 034)	34	1966	17	1966	(Atlantic 2342)
3	It Tears Me Up		0	1966	20	1966	(Atlantic 2358)
4	Love Me Tender		0	1967	40	1967	(Atlantic 2414)

ISSUE	TITLE	UK LBL	UK POS	UK YEAR	US POS	US YEAR	US LBL
5	Take Time To Know Her		0	1968	11	1968	(Atlantic 2490)
6	When A Man Loves A Woman (Re-Issue)	(Atlantic 584 001)	2	1987	0	1987	

Perez Prado   Orchestra Leader, Full Name Damaso Perez Prado B: 11 Dec 1916 Mamtanzas, Cuba

ISSUE	TITLE	UK LBL	UK POS	UK YEAR	US POS	US YEAR	US LBL
1	Anna (Movie Title Theme)		0	1953	29	1953	(RCA Victor 5367)
2	Skokiaan		0	1954	26	1954	(RCA Victor 5839)
* 3	Cherry Pink And Apple Blossom White	(HMV B 10833)	1	1955	1	1955	(RCA 5965)
* 4	Patricia	(RCA 1067)	8	1958	1	1958	(RCA 7245)
5	Guaglione	(RCA 74321250192)	41	1994	0	1994	
6	Guaglione (Re-Entry)	(RCA 74321250192)	58	1995	0	1995	
7	Guaglione (2nd Re-Entry)	(RCA 74321250192)	2	1995	0	1995	
	OBITUARY: D: 14 SEP 1989 FROM A STROKE.						

Perfect Day   Male Vocal/Instrumental Group from the UK

ISSUE	TITLE	UK LBL	UK POS	UK YEAR	US POS	US YEAR	US LBL
1	Liberty Town	(London LON 214)	58	1989	0	1989	
2	Jane	(London LON 188)	68	1989	0	1989	

Perfect Gentlemen   Names Maurice Starr Jr., Corey Blakely & Tyrone Sutton

ISSUE	TITLE	UK LBL	UK POS	UK YEAR	US POS	US YEAR	US LBL
1	Ooh La La (I Can't Get Over You)		0	1990	10	1990	(Columbia 73379)

Perfectly Ordinary People   Male Vocal/Instrumental Group from the UK

ISSUE	TITLE	UK LBL	UK POS	UK YEAR	US POS	US YEAR	US LBL
1	Theme From *P.O.P.*	(Urban URB 25)	61	1988	0	1988	

Perfecto Allstarz   Male Instrumental/Production Duo from the UK

ISSUE	TITLE	UK LBL	UK POS	UK YEAR	US POS	US YEAR	US LBL
1	Reach Up (Papa's Got A Brand New Pig Bag)	(Perfecto YZ 892CD)	6	1995	0	1995	

Perfume   Male Vocal/Instrumental Group from the UK

ISSUE	TITLE	UK LBL	UK POS	UK YEAR	US POS	US YEAR	US LBL
1	Haven't Seen You	(Aromasound Aroma 005CDS)	71	1996	0	1996	

Perry Como   Male Vocalist, Real Name Pierino Como B: 18 May 1912 Pennsylvania

ISSUE	TITLE	UK LBL	UK POS	UK YEAR	US POS	US YEAR	US LBL
* 11	I'm Gonna Love That Gal		0	1945	4	1945	(Victor 1676)
* 12	If I Loved You		0	1945	3	1945	(Victor 1676)
* 17	I'm Always Chasing Rainbows		0	1946	5	1946	(Victor 1788)
18	You Won't Be Satisfied (Until You Break My Heart)		0	1946	5	1946	(Victor 1788)
* 19	Prisoner Of Love		0	1946	1	1946	(RCA Victor 1814)
20	All Through The Day (From *Centennial Summer*)		0	1946	8	1946	(RCA Victor 1814)
21	They Say It's Wonderful		0	1960	4	1946	(RCA Victor 1857)
22	If You Were The Only Girl In The World		0	1946	14	1946	(RCA Victor 1857)
23	Surrender		0	1946	1	1946	(RCA Victor 1877)
24	More Than You Know (From *Great Day!*)		0	1946	19	1946	(RCA Victor 1877)
25	Temptation		0	1946	21	1946	(RCA Victor 1658)
26	A Garden In The Rain		0	1946	22	1946	(RCA Victor 1916)
27	If I'm Lucky		0	1946	19	1946	(RCA Victor 1945)
28	Sonata		0	1946	9	1946	(RCA Victor 2033)
29	That's The Beginning Of The End		0	1947	19	1947	(RCA Victor 2033)
30	Winter Wonderland		0	1946	10	1946	(RCA Victor 1968)
31	I Want To Thank Your Folks		0	1947	21	1947	(RCA Victor 2117)
32	That's Where I Came In		0	1947	21	1947	(RCA Victor 2117)
* 33	Chi-Baba, Chi-Baba (My Bambino Go To Sleep		0	1947	1	1947	(Victor 2259)
34	When You Were Sweet Sixteen		0	1947	2	1947	(RCA Victor 2259)
35	I Wonder Who's Kissing Her Now (From *The Prince Of Tonight*)		0	1947	2	1947	(Decca 25078)
36	So Far		0	1947	11	1947	(RCA Victor 2402)
37	A Fellow Needs A Girl (From *Allegro*)		0	1947	25	1947	(RCA Victor 2402)
38	Two Loves Have I		0	1947	21	1947	(RCA Victor 2545)
39	White Christmas		0	1947	23	1947	(RCA Victor 1970)
40	Pianissimo		0	1948	21	1948	(RCA Victor 2593)
* 41	Because		0	1948	4	1948	(RCA Victor 2653)
42	Haunted Heart (From *Inside U.S.A.*)		0	1948	20	1948	(RCA Victor 2713)
43	Laroo, Laroo, Lilli Bolero		0	1948	20	1948	(RCA Victor 2734)
44	Rambling Rose		0	1948	18	1948	(RCA Victor 2947)
45	Far Away Places		0	1949	4	1949	(RCA Victor 3316)
46	N'yot N'yow (The Pussycat Song)		0	1949	20	1949	(RCA Victor 3288)
47	Blue Room (From *The Girl Friend*)		0	1949	18	1949	(RCA Victor 3329)
48	Forever And Ever		0	1949	2	1949	(RCA Victor 78-3347)
49	I Don't See Me In Your Arms Anymore		0	1949	11	1900	(RCA Victor 78-3347)
50	A Your Adorable		0	1949	1	1949	(RCA Victor 78-3381)
* 51	Some Enchanted Evening (From *South Pacific*)		0	1949	1	1949	(RCA Victor 78-3402)
52	Bali Ha'i (From *South Pacific*)		0	1949	5	1949	(RCA Victor 78-3402)
53	Just One Way To Say I Love You		0	1949	23	1949	(RCA Victor 78-3469)
54	Let's Take An Old-Fashioned Walk		0	1949	15	1949	(RCA Victor78-3469)

ISSUE	TITLE	UK LBL	UK POS	UK YEAR	US POS	US YEAR	US LBL
55	Give Me Your Hand		0	1949	23	1949	(RCA Victor 78-3521)
56	A Dreamer's Holiday		0	1949	3	1949	(RCA Victor 78-3543)
57	I Wanna Go Home		0	1949	18	1949	(RCA Victor 78-3586)
58	The Lord's Prayer		0	1949	28	1949	(RCA Victor78-0436)
59	Ave Maria		0	1949	22	1949	(RCA Victor 78-0436)
60	Bibbidi-Bobbodi-Boo (From *Cinderella*)		0	1950	14	1950	(RCA Victor 78-3113)
61	Hoop-Dee-Doo		0	1950	1	1950	(RCA Victor 3747)
62	On The Outgoing Tide		0	1950	16	1950	(RCA Victor 3747)
63	I Cross My Fingers		0	1950	25	1950	(RCA Victor 3846)
64	Patricia		0	1950	7	1950	(RCA Victor 3905)
65	A Bushel And A Peck (From *Guys And Dolls*)		0	1950	3	1950	(RCA Victor 3930)
66	You're Just In Love (From *Call Me Madam*)		0	1950	5	1950	(RCA Victor 3945)
* 67	If		0	1951	1	1951	(RCA Victor 3997)
68	Zing Zing-Zoom Zoom		0	1951	12	1951	(RCA Victor 3997)
69	Hello, Young Lovers (From *The King And I*)		0	1951	27	1951	(RCA Victor 4112)
70	There's No Boat Like A Rowboat		0	1951	20	1951	(RCA Victor 4158)
71	There's A Big Blue Cloud (Next To Heaven)		0	1951	25	1951	(RCA Victor 4158)
72	Rollin' Stone		0	1951	24	1951	(RCA Victor 4269)
73	With All My Heart And Soul		0	1951	28	1950	(RCA Victor 4269)
74	It's Beginning To Look Like Christmas		0	1951	19	1951	(RCA Victor 4314)
75	Tulips And Heather		0	1952	16	1952	(RCA Victor 4453)
76	Please Mr.Sun		0	1952	12	1952	(RCA Victor 4453)
77	Noodlin' Rag		0	1952	23	1952	(RCA Victor 4542)
78	One Little Candle		0	1952	18	1952	(RCA Victor 4631)
79	Maybe		0	1952	3	1952	(RCA Victor 4744)
80	Watermelon Weather		0	1952	19	1952	(RCA Victor 4744)
81	My Love And Devotion		0	1952	22	1952	(RCA Victor 4877)
82	To Know You (Is To Love You)		0	1952	19	1952	(RCA Victor 4959)
* 83	Don't Let The Stars Get In Your Eyes	(HMV B 10400)	1	1953	1	1952	(RCA Victor 5064)
84	Lies		0	1952	30	1952	(RCA Victor 5064)
85	Winter Wonderland (Re-Entry)		0	1952	27	1952	(RCA Victor 1968)
86	Wild Horses		0	1953	6	1953	(RCA Victor 5152)
87	I Confess		0	1953	17	1953	(RCA Victor 5152)
88	Say You're Mine Again		0	1953	3	1953	(RCA Victor 5277)
89	My One And Only Heart		0	1953	11	1953	(RCA Victor 5277)
90	No Other Love		0	1953	1	1953	(RCA Victor 5317)
91	Keep It Gay		0	1953	30	1953	(RCA Victor 5317)
92	Pa-Paya Mama		0	1953	11	1953	(RCA Victor 5447)
93	You Alone		0	1953	9	1953	(RCA Victor 5447)
* 94	Wanted	(HMV B 10667)	4	1954	1	1954	(RCA Victor 5647)
95	Look Out The Window (And See How I'm Standing In The Rain)		0	1954	24	1954	(RCA Victor 5647)
96	Idle Gossip	(HMV B 10710)	3	1954	0	1900	
97	Hit And Run Affair		0	1954	15	1954	(RCA Victor 5749)
98	There Never Was A Night So Beautiful		0	1954	21	1954	(RCA Victor 5749)
99	Wanted (Re-Entry)	(HMV B 10667)	18	1954	0	1954	
* 100	Papa Loves Mambo	(HMV B 10776)	16	1954	4	1954	(RCA Victor 5857)
101	The Things I Didn't Do		0	1954	22	1954	(RCA Victor 5857)
102	Home For The Holidays		0	1954	8	1954	(RCA Victor 5950)
103	Ko Ko Mo (I Love You So)		0	1955	2	1955	(RCA 5994)
104	Chee Chee-Oo-Chee (Sang The Little Bird)		0	1955	12	1955	(RCA 6137)
105	Two Lost Souls		0	1955	18	1955	(RCA 6137)
106	Tina Marie	(HMV POP 103)	24	1955	5	1955	(RCA 6192)
107	Fooled		0	1955	20	1955	(RCA 6192)
108	All At Once You Love Her		0	1955	11	1955	(RCA 6294)
* 109	Hot Diggity	(HMV POP 221)	4	1956	1	1956	(RCA 6427)
110	Juke Box Baby	(HMV POP 191)	22	1956	10	1956	(RCA 6427)
* 111	More	(HMV POP 240)	10	1956	4	1956	(RCA 6554)
112	Glendora	(HMV POP 240)	18	1956	8	1956	(RCA 6554)
113	Somebody Up There Likes Me		0	1956	18	1956	(RCA 6590)
114	More (Re-Entry)	(HMV POP 240)	29	1956	0	1956	
* 115	Round And Round		0	1957	1	1957	(RCA 6815)
116	The Girl With The Golden Braids		0	1957	13	1957	(RCA 6815)
117	Dancin'		0	1957	76	1957	(RCA Victor 6991)
118	Just Born (To Be Your Baby)		0	1957	12	1957	(RCA 7050)
119	Ivy Rose		0	1957	18	1957	(RCA 7050)
* 120	Catch A Falling Star	(RCA 1036)	1	1958	1	1958	(RCA 7128)

ISSUE	TITLE	UK LBL	UK POS	UK YEAR	US POS	US YEAR	US LBL
* 121	Magic Moments	(RCA 1036)	1	1958	4	1958	(RCA 7128)
122	Kewpie Doll	(RCA 1055)	9	1958	6	1958	(RCA 7202)
123	Dance Only With Me		0	1958	19	1958	(RCA 7202)
124	I May Never Pass This Way Again	(RCA 1062)	15	1958	0	1958	
125	Moon Talk	(RCA 1071)	17	1958	28	1958	(RCA 7274)
126	Love Makes The World Go Round	(RCA 1086)	6	1958	33	1958	(RCA 7353)
127	Mandolins In The Moonlight	(RCA 1086)	13	1958	0	1958	
128	Tomboy	(RCA 1111)	10	1959	29	1959	(RCA 7464)
129	I Know	(RCA 1126)	13	1959	0	1959	
130	Delaware	(RCA 1170)	3	1960	22	1960	(RCA 7670)
131	Caterina	(RCA 1283)	37	1962	23	1962	(RCA 7004)
132	Caterina (Re-Entry)	(RCA 1283)	45	1962	0	1962	
133	(I Love You) Don't You Forget It		0	1963	39	1963	(RCA 8186)
134	Dream On Little Dreamer		0	1965	25	1965	(RCA 8533)
135	Seattle		0	1969	38	1969	(RCA 9722)
* 136	It's Impossible	(RCA 2043)	4	1971	10	1970	(RCA 0387)
137	I Think Of You	(RCA 2075)	14	1971	0	1971	
138	And I Love You So	(RCA 2346)	3	1973	29	1973	(RCA 0906)
139	For The Good Times	(RCA 2402)	7	1973	0	1973	
140	Walk Right Back	(RCA 2432)	33	1973	0	1973	
141	And I Love You So (Re-Entry)	(RCA 2346)	40	1974	0	1974	
142	I Want To Give	(RCA LPBO 7518)	31	1974	0	1974	
! 143	Just Out Of Reach		0	1976	99	1976	(RCA 10402)

PERRY OWNED A BARBER'S SHOP IN CANONSBURG WHERE THEY HAVE RENAMED ONE OF THE STREETS PERRY COMO AVENUE

Persuaders Names Douglas Scott, Willie Holland, James Barnes & Charles Stodghill

* 1	Thin Line Between Love And Hate		0	1971	15	1971	(ATCO 6822)
2	Some Guys Have All The Luck		0	1973	39	1973	(ATCO 6943)

Pet Shop Boys Male Vocal/Instrumental Duo from the UK, Names Neil Tennant And Chris Lowe

1	West End Girls	(Parlophone R 6115)	1	1985	1	1986	(EMI America 8307)
2	Love Comes Quickly	(Parlophone R 6116)	19	1986	0	1986	
3	Opportunities (Let's Make Lots Of Money)	(Parlophone R 6129)	11	1986	10	1986	(EMI America 8330)
4	Surburbia	(Parlophone R6140)	8	1986	0	1986	
5	It's A Sin	(Parlophone R 6158)	1	1987	9	1987	(EMI America 43027)
6	What Have I Done To Deserve This	(Parlophone R 6163)	2	1987	2	1988	(EMI-MAN 50107)
7	Rent	(Parlophone R 6168)	8	1987	0	1987	
8	Always On My Mind	(Parlophone R 6171)	1	1987	4	1988	(EMI-MAN 50123)
9	Heart	(Parlophone R 6177)	1	1988	0	1988	
10	Domino Dancing	(Parlophone R 6190)	7	1988	18	1988	(EMI-MAN 50161)
11	Left To My Own Devices	(Parlophone R 6198)	4	1988	0	1988	
12	It's Alright	(Parlophone R 6220)	5	1989	0	1989	
13	So Hard	(Parlophone R 6269)	4	1990	0	1990	
14	Being Boring	(Parlophone R 6275)	20	1990	0	1990	
15	Where The Streets Have No Name (EP)	(Parlophone R 6285)	4	1991	0	1991	
16	Jealousy	(Parlophone R 6283)	12	1991	0	1991	
17	DJ Culture	(Parlophone R 6301)	13	1991	0	1991	
18	DJ Culture (Re-Mix)	(Parlophone 12RX 6301)	40	1991	0	1991	
19	Was It Worth It	(Parlophone R 6306)	24	1991	0	1991	
20	Can You Forgive Her	(Parlophone CDR 6348)	7	1993	0	1993	
21	Go West	(Parlophone CDR 6356)	2	1993	0	1993	
22	I Wouldn't Normally Do This Kind Of Thing	(Parlophone CDR 6370)	13	1993	0	1993	
23	Liberation	(Parlophone CDRS 6377)	14	1994	0	1994	
24	Absolutely Fabulous	(Spaghetti CDR 6382)	6	1994	0	1994	
25	Yesterday When I Was Mad	(Parlophone CDRS 6386)	13	1994	0	1994	
26	Paninaro '95	(Parlophone CDRS 6414)	15	1995	0	1995	
27	Before	(Parlophone CDRS 6431)	7	1996	0	1996	
28	Se A Vida E (That's The Way Life Is)	(Parlophone CDRS 6443)	8	1996	0	1996	
29	Single	(Parlophone CDRS 6452)	14	1996	0	1996	
30	A Red Letter Day	(Parlophone CDR 6460)	9	1997	0	1997	
31	Somewhere	(Parlophone CDR 6470)	9	1997	0	1997	

HIT 6 IS CREDITED TO PET SHOP BOYS AND DUSTY SPRINGFIELD • HIT 24 IS CREDITED TO ABSOLUTELY FABULOUS

Pete Drake B: 8 Oct 1932 Atlanta, Georgia

* 1	Forever		0	1964	25	1964	(SMASH 1867)

HIT WAS CREDITED TO PETE DRAKE & HIS TALKING STEEL GUITAR • PETER WAS NICKNAMED THE TALKING STEEL GUITAR MAN • OBITUARY : D: 29 JUL 1988.

ISSUE	TITLE	UK LBL	UK POS	UK YEAR	US POS	US YEAR	US LBL
Pete Hanley Male Vocalist from the USA							
1	Big Mamou		0	1953	19	1953	(Okeh 6956)
2	Help Me Mend A Broken Heart		0	1953	28	1953	(Okeh 6980)
Pete Mac Jr. Male Vocalist from the USA							
1	The Water Margin	(BBC RESL50)	37	1977	0	1977	
Pete Mac Jr For The Japanese Version See Godiego							
Pete Shelley Male Vocalist from the UK							
1	Telephone Operator	(Genetic XX1)	66	1983	0	1983	
Pete Townshend Male Vocalist, B: 19 May 1945 London, England, Lead Guitarist With The Who							
1	Rough Boys	(ATCO K 11460)	39	1980	0	1980	
2	Let My Love Open The Door	(ATCO K 11486)	46	1980	9	1980	(ATCO 7217)
3	Uniforms (Corps D'esprit)	(ATCO K 11751)	48	1982	0	1982	
4	Face The Face		0	1985	26	1985	(ATCO 99590)
Pete Wingfield Male Vocalist/Instrumentalist (Keyboard), B: 17 May 1948 England							
1	Eighteen With A Bullet	(Island WIP 6231)	7	1975	15	1975	(Island 026)
Pete Wylie Male Vocalist from the UK							
1	Sinful	(Eternal MDM 7)	13	1986	0	1986	
2	Diamond Girl	(Eternal MDM 12)	57	1986	0	1986	
3	Sinful!	(Siren SRN 138)	28	1991	0	1991	
Peter & Gordon Male Vocal Duo from the UK							
* 1	A World Without Love	(Columbia DB 7225)	1	1964	1	1964	(Capitol 5175)
* 2	Nobody I Know	(Columbia DB 7292)	10	1964	12	1964	(Capitol 5211)
3	I Don't Want To See You Again		0	1964	16	1964	(Capitol 5272)
4	I Go To Pieces		0	1965	9	1965	(Capitol 5335)
* 5	True Love Ways	(Capitol DB 7524)	2	1965	14	1965	(Capitol 5406)
6	To Know You Is To Love You	(Capitol DB 7617)	5	1965	24	1965	(Capitol 5461)
7	Baby I'm Yours	(Capitol DB 7729)	19	1965	0	1965	
8	Woman	(Capitol DB 8003)	28	1966	14	1966	(Capitol 5579)
* 8	Lady Godiva	(Capitol DB 7834)	16	1966	6	1966	(Capitol 5740)
9	Knight In Rusty Armour		0	1967	15	1967	(Capitol 5808)
10	Sunday For Tea		0	1967	31	1967	(Capitol 5864)
	REAL NAMES PETER ASHER B. 22 JUN 1944, GORDON WALLER B: 4 JUN 1945						
Peter Andre Male Vocalist from the UK							
1	Turn It Up	(Mushroom D 1000)	64	1995	0	1995	
2	Mysterious Girl	(Mushroom D 11921)	53	1995	0	1995	
3	Only One	(Mushroom D 1307)	16	1996	0	1996	
4	Only One (Re-Entry)	(Mushroom D 1307)	69	1996	0	1996	
5	Mysterious Girl (Re-Issue)	(Mushroom D 2000)	2	1996	0	1996	
6	Flava	(Mushroom DX 2003)	1	1996	0	1996	
7	I Feel You	(Mushroom D 1521)	1	1996	0	1996	
8	Only One (Re-Entry)	(Mushroom D 1307)	69	1996	0	1996	
9	I Feel You (Re-Entry)	(Mushroom D 1521)	65	1997	0	1997	
10	Natural	(Mushroom DX 1577)	6	1997	0	1997	
11	I Feel You (2nd Re-Entry)	(Mushroom D 1521)	74	1997	0	1997	
12	Natural (Re-Entry)	(Mushroom DX1577)	58	1997	0	1997	
13	Natural (2nd Re-Entry)	(Mushroom DX 1577)	68	1997	0	1997	
14	All About Us	(Mushroom MUSH 5CD)	3	1997	0	1997	
	HIT 5 IS CREDITED TO PETER ANDRE FEATURING BUBBLER RANX						
Peter Blake Male Vocalist from the UK							
1	Lipsmakin' Rock 'N' Rollin'	(Pepper UP 36295)	40	1977	0	1977	
Peter Brown Male Vocalist/Instrumentalist, B: 11 Jul 1953 Blue Island, Illinois							
1	Do Ya Wanna Get Funky With Me	(TK TKR 6027)	43	1978	18	1978	(Drive 6258)
2	Dance With Me	57	1978	8	1978	(DRIVE 6269)	
Peter Cetera Male Vocalist B: 13 Sep 1944 Chicago. See Also Chicago							
1	Glory Of Love (From The Karate Kid Part 11)	(Full Moon W 8662)	3	1986	1	1989	(Full Moon 28662)
2	The Next Time I Fall		0	1986	1	1986	(Full Moon 28597)
3	One Good Woman		0	1986	4	1986	(Full Moon 27824)
4	After All (From *Chances Are*)		0	1989	6	1989	(Geffen 27529)
5	Restless Heart		0	1992	35	1992	(Warner Bros. 18897)
6	Hard To Say I'm Sorry		0	1997	8	1997	(Arista 24223)

ISSUE	TITLE	UK LBL	UK POS	UK YEAR	US POS	US YEAR	US LBL
Peter Cook	Male Comedian/Vocalist from the UK						
1	Goodbyee	(Decca F 12158)	18	1965	0	1965	
2	The Ballad Of Spotty Muldoon	(Decca F 12182)	34	1965	0	1965	
	HIT 1 IS CREDITED TO PETER COOK AND DUDLEY MOOREN OBITUARY : D: DRINK-RELATED DEATH.						
Peter Cox	Male Vocalist from the UK						
1	Ain't Gonna Cry Again	(Chrysalis CDCHS 5056)	37	1997	0	1997	
Peter E. Bennett & The Co-operation Choir	Male Vocalist from the UK						
1	The Seagul's Name Was Nelson	(RCA 1991)	45	1970	0	1970	
Peter Fenton	Male Vocalist from the UK						
1	Marble Breaks Iron Bends	(Fontana TF 748)	46	1966	0	1966	
Peter Frampton	Male Vocalist, B: 22 Apr 1950 Beckenham, Kent, England						
1	Show Me The Way	(A&M AMS 7218)	10	1976	6	1976	(A&M 1795)
2	Baby I Love Your Way	(A&M AMS 7246)	43	1976	12	1976	(A&M 1832)
3	Do You Feel Like We Do	(A&M AMS 7260)	39	1976	10	1976	(A&M 1867)
4	I'm In You	(A&M AMS 7298)	41	1977	2	1977	(A&M 1941)
5	Signed, Sealed, Delivered (I'm Yours)		0	1977	18	1977	(A&M 1972)
6	I Can't Stand It No More		0	1979	14	1979	(A&M 2148)
Peter Gabriel	Male Vocalist, B: 13 Feb 1950 London, England, He Was Lead Singer With Genesis 1966-1975						
1	Solsbury Hill	(Charisma CB 301)	13	1977	0	1977	
2	Games Without Frontiers	(Charisma CB 354)	4	1980	0	1980	
3	No Self Control	(Charisma CB 360)	33	1980	0	1980	
4	Biko	(Charisma CB 370)	38	1980	0	1980	
5	Shock The Monkey	(Charisma SHOCK 1)	58	1982	29	1982	(Geffen 29883)
6	I Don't Remember	(Charisma GAB 1)	62	1983	0	1983	
7	Walk Through The Fire	(Virgin VS 689)	69	1984	0	1984	
8	Sledgehammer	(Virgin PGS 1)	4	1986	1	1986	(Geffen 28718)
9	In Your Eyes		0	1986	26	1986	(Geffen 28622)
10	Don't Give Up	(Virgin PGS 2)	9	1986	0	1986	
11	Big Time	(Virgin PGS 3)	13	1987	8	1987	(Geffen 28503)
12	Red Rain	(Virgin PGS 4)	46	1987	0	1987	
13	Biko (Live)	(Virgin PGS 6)	49	1987	0	1987	
14	Shaking The Tree	(Virgin VS 1167)	61	1989	0	1989	
15	Solsbury Hill / Shaking The Tree (Re-Issue)	(Virgin VS 1322)	57	1990	0	1990	
16	Digging The Dirt	(Realworld PGS 7)	24	1992	0	1992	
17	Steam	(Realworld PGSDG 8)	10	1993	32	1993	(Geffen 19145)
18	Blood Of Eden	(Realworld PGSDG 9)	43	1993	0	1993	
19	Kiss That Frog	(Realworld PGSDG 10)	46	1993	0	1993	
20	Lovetown	(Epic 6604802)	49	1994	0	1994	
21	SW Live (EP)	(Realworld PGSCD 11)	39	1994	0	1994	
Peter Jay & The Jaywalkers	Peter Jay (Drums) With The Male Instrumental Group from the UK						
1	Can Can 62	(Decca F 11531)	31	1962	0	1962	
Peter McCann	Peter Hails from Connecticut And Is A Writer With A Music Company						
* 1	Do You Wanna Make Love		0	1977	5	1977	(20th Century 2335)
Peter Nero	Male Pianist, B: 22 May 1934 Brooklyn						
1	Theme From Summer Of '42		0	1971	21	1971	(Columbia 45399)
Peter Noone	Male Vocalist, B: 5 Nov 1947, Manchester, England						
1	Lady Barbara	(RAK 101)	13	1970	0	1970	
2	Oh You Pretty Things	(RAK 114)	12	1971	0	1971	
	HIT 1 IS CREDITED TO PETER NOONE & HERMAN'S HERMITS • SEE ALSO HERMAN'S HERMITS						
Peter Polycarpou	Male Vocalist from the UK						
1	Love Hurts	(Soundtrack Music CDEM 259)	26	1993	0	1993	
Peter Sarstedt	Male Vocalist from the UK						
1	Where Do You Go To My Lovely	(United Artists UP 2262)	1	1969	0	1969	
2	Frozen Orange Juice	(United ArtistsUP 35021)	10	1969	0	1969	
Peter Schilling	Male Vocalist, B: 21 Jan 1956 Stuttgart, Germany						
1	Major Tom (Coming Home)	(PSP/WEA X 9438)	42	1984	14	1983	(Elektra 69811)
2	Major Tom (Coming Home) (Re-Entry)	(PSP/WEA X 9438)	73	1984	0	1984	
Peter Sellers	Male Actor/Vocalist from the UK						
1	Any Old Iron	(Parlophone R 4337)	21	1957	0	1957	
2	Any Old Iron (Re-Entry)	(Parlophone R 4337)	17	1957	0	1957	
3	Goodness Gracious Me	(Parlophone R 4702)	4	1960	0	1960	

ISSUE	TITLE	UK LBL	UK POS	UK YEAR	US POS	US YEAR	US LBL
4	Bangers And Mash	(Parlophone R 4724)	22	1961	0	1961	
5	A Hard Day's Night	(Parlophone R 5393)	14	1965	0	1965	
6	A Hard Day's Night (Re-Issue)	(EMI CDEMS 293)	52	1993	0	1993	

HITS 3-4 ARE CREDITED TO PETER SELLERS AND SOPHIA LOREN • SEE ALSO THE GOONS

Peter Shelley   Male Vocalist from the UK

1	Gee Baby	(Magnet MAG 12)	4	1974	0	1974	
2	Love Me Love My Dog	(Magnet MAG 22)	3	1975	0	1975	

Peter Skellern   Male Vocalist from the UK

1	You're A Lady	(Decca F 13333)	3	1972	0	1972	
2	Hold On To Love	(Decca F 13568)	14	1975	0	1975	
3	Love Is The Sweetest Thing	(Mercury 6008 603)	60	1978	0	1978	

Peter Straker & The Hands Of Dr. Teleny   Male Vocalist/Male Vocal/Instrumental Group from the UK

1	The Spirit Is Willing	(RCA 2163)	40	1972	0	1972	

Peter Tosh   Male Vocalist from Jamaica

1	(You Gotta Walk) Don't Look Back	(Rolling Stones 2859)	43	1978	0	1978	
2	Johnny B. Goode	(EMI RIC 115)	48	1983	0	1983	

Peter Wolf   Real Name Peter Blankfield B: 7 Mar 1946 Bronx

1	Lights Out		0	1984	12	1984	(EMI America 8208)
2	I Need You Tonight		0	1984	36	1984	(EMI America 8241)
3	Come As You Are		0	1987	15	1987	(EMI America 8350)

Peter, Paul & Mary   Mixed Vocal/Instrumental Trio from the USA

	1	Lemon Tree		0	1962	35	1962	(Warner Bros. 5274)
	2	If I Had A Hammer		0	1962	10	1962	(Warner Bros. 5296)
*	3	Puff (The Magic Dragon)		0	1963	2	1963	(Warner Bros. 5348)
*	4	Blowin' In The Wind	(Warner Bros. WB 104)	13	1963	2	1963	(Warner Bros. 5368)
	5	Don't Think Twice It's All Right		0	1963	9	1963	(Warner Bros. 5385)
	6	Stewball		0	1963	35	1963	(Warner Bros. 5399)
	7	Tell It To The Mountain	(Warner Bros. WB 127)	33	1964	33	1964	(Warner Bros. 5418)
	8	The Times They Are A Changin'	(Warner Bros. WB 142)	44	1964	0	1964	
	9	For Lovin' Me		0	1965	30	1965	(Warner Bros. 5496)
	10	Too Much Of Nothing		0	1967	35	1967	(Warner Bros. 092)
	11	I Dig Rock And Roll Music		0	1967	9	1967	(Warner Bros. 7067)
	12	Day Is Done		0	1969	21	1969	(Warner Bros. 7279)
*	13	Leavin' On A Jet Plane	(Warner Bros. WB 7340)	2	1970	1	1969	(Warner Bros. 7340)

Peters & Lee   Mixed Vocal Duo, Lennie Peters And Dianne Lee from the UK

!	1	Welcome Home	(Philips 6006 307)	1	1973	79	1974	(Philips 40729)
	2	By Your Side	(Philips 6006 339)	39	1973	0	1973	
	3	Don't Stay Away Too Long	(Philips 6006 388)	3	1974	0	1974	
	4	Rainbow	(Philips 6006 4060)	17	1974	0	1974	
	5	Hey Mr. Music Man	(Philips 6006 502)	16	1976	0	1976	

THEY GOT THEIR FIRST BREAK AFTER WINNING A TV TALENT SHOW • OBITUARY: LENNIE D: 10 OCT 1992 (AGED 59) FROM CANCER

Pets   Male Vocal/Instrumental Group from the USA

1	Cha-Hua-Hua		0	1958	34	1958	(ARWIN 109)

Petula Clark   Female Actress/Vocalist Petula Sally Olwen Clark B: 15 Nov 1932 In West Ewell, Surrey, England

	1	The Little Shoemaker	(PolygonP 1117)	12	1954	0	1954	
	2	The Little Shoemaker (Re-Entry)	(PolygonP 1117)	7	1954	0	1954	
	3	Majorca	(PolygonP 1146)	12	1955	0	1955	
	4	Majorca (Re-Entry)	(PolygonP 1146)	18	1955	0	1955	
	5	Suddenly There's A Valley	(PYE NIXA N 15013)	7	1955	0	1955	
	6	With All My Heart	(PYE NIXA N 15096)	4	1957	0	1957	
	7	Alone	(PYE NIXA N 15112)	8	1957	0	1957	
	8	Baby Lover	(PYE NIXA N 15126)	12	1958	0	1958	
	9	Sailor	(PYE 7N 15324)	7	1961	0	1961	
	10	Something Missing	(PYE 7N 15337)	44	1961	0	1961	
*	11	Romeo	(PYE 7N 15361)	3	1961	0	1961	
	12	My Friend The Sea	(PYE 7N 15389)	7	1961	0	1961	
*	13	Monsieur	(Vogue Germany)	0	1962	0	1962	
	14	I'm Counting On You	(PYE 7N 15407)	41	1962	0	1962	
	15	Ya Ya Twist	(PYE 7N 15448)	14	1962	0	1962	
	16	Ya Ya Twist (Re-Entry)	(PYE 7N 15448)	45	1962	0	1962	
*	17	Casanova / Chariot	(PYE 7N 15522)	39	1963	0	1963	
*	18	Downtown	(PYE 7N 15722)	2	1964	1	1965	(Warner Bros. 5494)

ISSUE	TITLE	UK LBL	UK POS	UK YEAR	US POS	US YEAR	US LBL
19	I Know A Place	(PYE 7N 15772)	17	1965	3	1965	(Warner Bros. 5612)
20	You Better Come Home	(PYE 7N 15864)	44	1965	22	1965	(Warner Bros. 5643)
21	Round Every Corner	(PYE 7N 15945)	43	1965	21	1965	(Warner Bros. 5661)
22	You're The One	(PYE 7N 15991)	23	1965	0	1965	
* 23	My Love	(PYE 7N 17038)	4	1966	1	1965	(Warner Bros. 5684)
24	A Sign Of The Times	(PYE 7N 17071)	49	1966	11	1966	(Warner Bros. 5802)
25	I Couldn't Live Without Your Love	(PYE 7N 17133)	6	1966	9	1966	(Warner Bros. 5835)
26	Who Am I		0	1966	21	1966	(Warner Bros. 5863)
27	Colour My World		0	1966	16	1966	(Warner Bros. 5882)
* 28	This Is My Song	(PYE 7N 17258)	1	1967	3	1967	(Warner Bros. 7002)
29	Don't Sleep In The Subway	(PYE 7N 17325)	12	1967	5	1967	(Warner Bros. 7049)
30	The Cat In The Window (The Bird In The Sky)		0	1967	26	1967	(Warner Bros. 7073)
31	The Other Man's Grass	(PYE 7N 17416)	20	1967	31	1967	(Warner Bros. 7097)
32	Kiss Me Goodbye	(PYE 7N 17466)	50	1968	15	1968	(Warner Bros.7170)
33	Don't Give Up		0	1968	37	1968	(Warner Bros. 7216)
34	The Song Of My Life	(PYE 7N 45026)	41	1971	0	1971	
35	The Song Of My Life (Re-Entry)	(PYE 7N 45026)	32	1971	0	1971	
36	I Don't Know How To Love Him	(PYE 7N 45112)	47	1972	0	1972	
37	I Don't Know How To Love Him (Re-Entry)	(PYE 7N 45112)	49	1972	0	1972	
38	Natural Love		0	1982	66	1982	(Scotti Brothers 02676)
39	Downtown (Re-Mix)	(PRT PYS 19)	10	1988	0	1988	

HIT 11 WAS ORIGINALLY RELEASED IN GERMANY CALLED 'SALOME' • HIT 17 (CHARIOT) IS ALSO KNOWN AS 'I WILL FOLLOW HIM'

Pharao Mixed Vocal/Instrumental Group From Germany

1	There Is A Star	(Epic 6611832)	43	1995	0	1995	

Pharcyde Male Rap Group from the USA

1	Passin' Me By	(Atlantic A 8360CD)	55	1993	0	1993	
2	Runnin'	(Go.Beat Godcd 142)	36	1996	0	1996	
3	She Said	(Go.Beat Godcd 144)	51	1996	0	1996	

PHD Male Vocal/Instrumental Duo from the UK

1	I Won't Let You Down	(WEA K 79209)	3	1982	0	1982	

Phil Collins Male Vocalist, B: 31 Jan 1951 London, England

1	In The Air Tonight	(Virgin VSK 102)	2	1981	19	1981	(Atlantic 3790)
2	I Missed Again	(Virgin VS 402)	14	1981	19	1981	(Atlantic 3790)
3	If Leaving Me Is Easy	(Virgin VS 423)	17	1981	0	1981	
4	Thru' These Walls	(Virgin VS 524)	56	1982	0	1982	
5	You Can't Hurry Love	(Virgin VS 531)	1	1982	10	1982	(Atlantic 89933)
6	I Don't Care Anymore		0	1983	39	1983	(Atlantic 89877)
7	Don't Let Him Steal Your Heart Away	(Virgin VS 572)	45	1983	0	1983	
* 8	Against All Odds (Take A Look At Me Now)	(Virgin VS 674)	2	1984	1	1984	(Atlantic 89700)
* 9	Easy Lover	(CBS A 4915)	1	1985	2	1984	(Columbia 04679)
* 10	Sussudio	(Virgin VS 736)	12	1985	1	1985	(Atlantic 89560)
* 11	One More Night	(Virgin VS 755)	4	1985	1	1985	(Atlantic 89588)
12	Take Me Home	(Virgin VS 777)	19	1985	7	1986	(Atlantic 89472)
13	Don't Lose My Number		0	1985	4	1985	(Atlantic 89536)
14	Separate Lives (From White Nights)	(Virgin VS 818)	4	1985	1	1985	(Atlantic 89498)
16	In The Air Tonight (Re-Mix)	(Virgin VS 102)	4	1988	0	1988	
* 17	A Groovy Kind Of Love (From *Buster*)	(Virgin VS 1117)	1	1988	1	1988	(Atlantic 89017)
18	Two Hearts (From Buster)	(Virgin VS 1141)	6	1988	1	1988	(Atlantic 88980)
* 19	Another Day In Paradise	(Virgin VS 1234)	2	1989	1	1989	(Atlantic 88774)
20	I Wish It Would Rain Down	(Virgin VS 1240)	7	1990	3	1990	(Atlantic 88738)
21	Something Happened On The Way To Heaven	(Virgin VS 1251)	15	1990	4	1990	(Atlantic 87885)
22	Do You Remember (Live)	(Virgin VS 1305)	57	1990	4	1990	(Atlantic 87955)
23	That's Just The Way It Is	(Virgin VS 1277)	26	1990	0	1990	
24	Hang In Long Enough	(Virgin VS 1300)	34	1990	23	1990	(Atlantic 87800)
25	Hero	(Atlantic A 7360)	56	1993	0	1993	
26	Both Sides Of The Story	(Virgin VSCDT 1500)	7	1993	25	1993	(Atlantic 87299)
27	Both Sides Of The Story (Re-Entry)	(Virgin VSCDT 1500)	61	1994	0	1994	
28	Everyday	(Virgin VSCDT 1505)	15	1994	24	1994	(Atlantic 87300)
29	We Wait And We Wonder	(Virgin VSCD 1510)	45	1994	0	1994	
30	Dance Into The Light	(Face Value EW 066CD)	9	1996	45	1996	(Atlantic 87043)
31	It's In Your Eyes	(Face Value EW 076CD1)	30	1996	77	1997	(Atlantic 87016)
32	Wear My Hat	(Face Value EW 113CD)	43	1997	0	1997	

ISSUE	TITLE	UK LBL	UK POS	UK YEAR	US POS	US YEAR	US LBL
Phil Everly	Male Vocalist from the USA						
4	Louise	(Capitol CL 266)	47	1982	0	1982	
5	She Means Nothing To Me	(Capitol CL 276)	9	1983	0	1983	
6	All I Have To Do Is Dream	(EMI CDEMS 359)	14	1994	0	1994	
7	All I Have To Do Is Dream (Re-Entry)	(EMI CDEMS 359)	58	1995	0	1995	

HIT 5 IS CREDITED TO PHIL EVERLY AND CLIFF RICHARD • HITS 6-7 ARE CREDITED TO CLIFF RICHARD AND PHIL EVERLY

ISSUE	TITLE	UK LBL	UK POS	UK YEAR	US POS	US YEAR	US LBL
Phil Fearon	Male Vocalist from the UK						
1	Dancing Tonight	(Ensign ENY 501)	4	1983	0	1983	
2	Wait Until Tonight (My Love)	(Ensign ENY 503)	20	1983	0	1983	
3	Fantasy Real	(Ensign ENY507)	41	1983	0	1983	
4	What Do I Do	(Ensign ENY 510)	5	1984	0	1984	
5	Everybody's Laughing	(Ensign ENY 514)	10	1984	0	1984	
6	You Don't Need A Reason	(Ensign ENY 517)	42	1985	0	1985	
7	This Kind Of Love	(Ensign ENY 521)	70	1985	0	1985	
8	I Can Prove It	(Ensign PF 1)	8	1986	0	1986	
9	Ain't Nothing But A House Party	(Ensign PF 2)	60	1986	0	1986	

HITS 1-2 ARE CREDITED TO GALAXY FEATURING PHIL FEARON • HITS 3-6 ARE CREDITED TO PHIL FEARON AND GALAXY
HIT 7 IS CREDITED TO PHIL FEARON & GALAXY FEATURING DEE GALDES

ISSUE	TITLE	UK LBL	UK POS	UK YEAR	US POS	US YEAR	US LBL
Phil Harris	Male Bandleader/Drummer from Linton, Indiana						
4	One-Zy, Two-Zy (I Love You-Zy)		0	1946	2	1946	(ARA 136)
5	The Darktown Poker Club (From *Ziegfeld Follies* Of 1914)		0	1946	10	1946	(ARA 116)
6	That's What I Like About The South		0	1947	21	1947	(RCA Victor 2089)
7	The Preacher And The Bear		0	1947	22	1947	(RCA Victor 2143)
8	Smoke! Smoke! Smoke (That Cigarette)		0	1947	8	1947	(RCA Victor 2370)
9	The Dark Town Poker Club (Re-Recording)		0	1947	27	1947	(RCA Victor 2471)
10	Deck Of Cards		0	1948	20	1948	(RCA Victor 2821)
11	The Old Master Painter		0	1949	10	1949	(RCA Victor 78-3608)
12	Chattanoogie Shoe-Shine Boy		0	1950	8	1950	(RCA Victor 78-3692)
13	Play A Simply Melody (From *Watch Your Step*)		0	1950	30	1950	(RCA Victor 3781)
* 14	The Thing		0	1950	1	1950	(RCA Victor 3968)
15	The Musicians		0	1951	24	1951	(RCA Victor 4225)
16	Hambone		0	1952	19	1952	(RCA Victor 4584)

ISSUE	TITLE	UK LBL	UK POS	UK YEAR	US POS	US YEAR	US LBL
Phil Hurtt	Male Vocalist from the USA						
1	Giving It Back	(Fantasy FTC 161)	36	1978	0	1978	

ISSUE	TITLE	UK LBL	UK POS	UK YEAR	US POS	US YEAR	US LBL
Phil McLean	Male Vocalist/DJ from Detroit						
1	Small Sad Sam	(Top Rank Jar 597)	34	1962	21	1961	(Versatile 107)

HIT WAS A PARODY TO BIG BAD JOHN

ISSUE	TITLE	UK LBL	UK POS	UK YEAR	US POS	US YEAR	US LBL
Phil Phillips With The Twilights	Real Name John Phillip Baptists B: 14 Mar 1931 Louisiana						
1	Sea Of Love		0	1959	2	1959	(Mercury 4236)

ISSUE	TITLE	UK LBL	UK POS	UK YEAR	US POS	US YEAR	US LBL
Phil Seymour	Male Bassist/Drummer/Vocalist, B: 15 May 1952 In Tulsa, Oklahoma						
1	Precious To Me		0	1981	22	1981	(Broadwalk 5703)

ISSUE	TITLE	UK LBL	UK POS	UK YEAR	US POS	US YEAR	US LBL
Phil Spitalny & His Orchestra	Male Bandleader/Instrumentalist (Clarinet) & An All-girl Orchestra						
5	Our Lady Of Fatima		0	1950	23	1950	(RCA Victor 3920)

ISSUE	TITLE	UK LBL	UK POS	UK YEAR	US POS	US YEAR	US LBL
Phil Upchurch Combo	Male Instrumentalist (Bass Guitar), B: 19 Jul 1941 Chicago						
* 1	You Can't Sit Down (Part 1-2)	(SUE WI 4005)	39	1961	29	1961	(Boyd 3398)

ISSUE	TITLE	UK LBL	UK POS	UK YEAR	US POS	US YEAR	US LBL
Philadelphia International All-Stars	Collection Of Various Acts from the USA						
1	Let's Clean Up The Ghetto	(Philadelphia International PIR 5451)	34	1977	0	1977	

ISSUE	TITLE	UK LBL	UK POS	UK YEAR	US POS	US YEAR	US LBL
Philharmonia Orchestra	Orchestra from the UK Conducted By Male Producer Lorin Maazel from the USA						
1	Thus Spake Zarathustra	(Columbia DB 8607)	33	1969	0	1969	

ISSUE	TITLE	UK LBL	UK POS	UK YEAR	US POS	US YEAR	US LBL
Philip Bailey	Male Vocalist B: 8 May 1951 Denver						
1	Easy Lover with Phil Collins	(CBS A 4915)	1	1985	2	1985	(Columbia 04679)
2	Walking On The Chinese Wall	(CBS A 6206)	34	1985	0	1985	

ISSUE	TITLE	UK LBL	UK POS	UK YEAR	US POS	US YEAR	US LBL
Philip Jap	Male Vocalist from the UK						
1	Save Us	(A&M AMS 8217)	53	1982	0	1982	
2	Total Erasure	(A&M JAP 1)	41	1982	0	1982	

ISSUE	TITLE	UK LBL	UK POS	UK YEAR	US POS	US YEAR	US LBL
Philip Lynott	Male Vocalist From Ireland						
1	Dear Miss Lonely Hearts	(Vertigo SOLO 1)	32	1980	0	1980	
2	Kings Call	(Vertigo SOLO 2)	35	1980	0	1980	
3	Yellow Pearl	(Vertigo SOLO 3)	56	1981	0	1981	
4	Yellow Pearl (Re-Entry)	(Vertigo SOLO 3)	14	1981	0	1981	
5	Out In The Fields	(10 TEN 49)	5	1985	0	1985	

ISSUE	TITLE	UK LBL	UK POS	UK YEAR	US POS	US YEAR	US LBL
6	Kings Call (Re-Mix)	(Vertigo LYN 1)	68	1987	0	1987	
	HIT 5 IS CREDITED TO GARY MOORE AND PHILIP LYNOTT						

Phillip Leo Male Vocalist from the UK

1	Second Chance	(EMI CDEM 327)	57	1994	0	1994	
2	Thinking About Your Love	(EMI CDEM 358)	64	1995	0	1995	

Phillip Scofield Male Vocalist from the UK

1	Close Every Door	(Really Useful RUR 11)	27	1992	0	1992	

Phoebe Snow Female Vocalist, Real Name Phoebe Laub B: 17 Jul 1952 New York City

1	Poetry Man		0	1975	5	1975	(Shelter 40353)
2	Gone At Last		0	1975	23	1975	(Columbia 10197)
3	Everynight	(CBS 6842)	37	1979	0	1979	

Photos Mixed Vocal/Instrumental Group from the UK

1	Irene	(Epic EPC 8517)	56	1980	0	1980	

Phuture Assassins Male Production/Instrumental Group from the UK

1	Future Sounds (EP)	(Suburban Base Subbase 010)	64	1992	0	1992	

Phyllis Hyman Female Vocalist from the USA

1	You Know How To Love Me	(Arista ARIST 323)	47	1980	0	1980	
2	You Sure Look Good To Me	(Arista ARIST 424)	56	1981	0	1981	

Phyllis Nelson Female Vocalist from the USA

1	Move Closer	(Carrerre CAR 337)	1	1985	0	1985	
2	Move Closer (Re-Issue)	(EMI CDEMCT 9)	34	1994	0	1994	

Pia Zadora Female Actress/Vocalist, Real Name Pia Schipani B: 1955 In New York City

5	The Clapping Song		0	1983	36	1983	(Elektra/Curb 69889)
6	When The Rain Begins To Fall	(Arista ARIST 574)	68	1984	0	1984	
7	Dance Out Of My Head	(Epic 652886)	65	1988	0	1988	
	HIT 6 IS CREDITED TO JERMAINE JACKSON AND PIA ZADORA • HIT 7 IS CREDITED TO PIA						

Pianoman Male Producer James Salmon from the USA

1	Blurred	(FFRREEDOM TABCD 243)	6	1996	0	1996	
2	Party People (Live Your Life Be Free)	(3 BEAT 3 BTCD1)	43	1997	0	1997	

Picketty Witch Mixed Vocal/Instrumental Group from the UK

1	That Same Old Feeling	(PYE 7N 17887)	5	1970	0	1970	
2	(It's Like A) Sad Old Kinda Movie	(PYE 7N 17951)	16	1970	0	1970	
3	Baby I Won't Let You Down	(PYE 7N 45002)	27	1970	0	1970	

Pied Pipers Names John Huddlestone, Chuck Lowry, Clark Yokum & Jo Stafford

* 3	Dream		0	1945	1	1945	(Capitol 185)
6	In The Middle Of May		0	1946	14	1946	(Capitol 225)
7	In The Moon Mist		0	1946	8	1946	(Capitol 243)
8	Open The Door, Richard		0	1947	8	1947	(Capitol 369)
9	Mam'selle		0	1947	3	1947	(Capitol 396)
10	Penny		0	1947	28	1947	(Capitol 478)
11	Ok'l Baby Dok'l		0	1948	25	1948	(Capitol 495)
* 12	My Happiness / Highway To Love		0	1948	3	1948	(Capitol 15094)

Piero Umiliani Orchestra And Chorus From Italy

1	Mah Na Mah Na	(EMI InternationalINT 530)	8	1977	0	1977	

Pigbag Male Instrumental Group from the UK

1	Sunny Day	(Y Records Y 12)	53	1981	0	1981	
2	Getting Up	(Y Records Y 16)	61	1982	0	1982	
3	Papa's Got A Brand New Pigbag	(Y Records Y 10)	3	1982	0	1982	
4	The Big Bean	(Y Records Y 24)	40	1982	0	1982	

Piglets Female Vocal Group from the UK

1	Johnny Reggae	(Bell 1180)	3	1971	0	1971	

Pigmeat Markham Male Comedian/Vocalist, Real Name Dewey Markham B: 1906 In Durham, North Carolina

1	Here Comes The Judge	(Chess CRS	19	1968	19	1968	(Chess 2049)
0	bituary: D: 13 Dec 1981.						

Pilot Male Vocal/Instrumental Trio from the UK, Names: David Paton, Stuart Tosh & Bill Lyall

* 1	Magic	(EMI 2217)	11	1974	5	1975	(EMI 3992)
2	January	(EMI 2255)	1	1975	0	1975	
3	Call Me Around	(EMI 2287)	34	1975	0	1975	
4	Just A Smile	(EMI 2338)	31	1975	0	1975	

ISSUE	TITLE	UK LBL	UK POS	UK YEAR	US POS	US YEAR	US LBL
Piltdown Men Male Instrumental Group from the USA							
1	McDonald's Cave	(Capitol CL 15149)	14	1960	0	1960	
2	Piltdown Rides Again	(Capitol CL 15175)	14	1961	0	1961	
3	Goodnight Mrs Flintstone	(Capitol CL 15186)	18	1961	0	1961	
Pinetoppers Group Formed By Brothers Roy & Vaughn Horton From Pennsylvania							
1	Mockin' Bird Hill		0	1951	10	1951	(CORAL 64061)
2	Lonely Little Robin		0	1951	14	1951	(CORAL 60508)
Ping Ping & Al Verlaine Male Vocal Duo from Belgium							
1	Sucu Sucu	(ORIOLE CB 1589)	41	1961	0	1961	
Pink Floyd Male Vocal/Instrumental Group from the UK Names: David Gilmour, Nick Mason, Roger Waters & Richard Wright							
1	Arnold Layne	(Columbia DB 8156)	20	1967	0	1967	
2	See Emily Play	(Columbia DB 8214)	6	1967	0	1967	
3	Money		0	1973	13	1973	(Harvest 3609)
* 4	Another Brick In The Wall	(Harvest HAR 5194)	1	1979	1	1980	(Columbia 11187)
5	When The Tigers Broke Free	(Harvest HAR 5222)	39	1982	0	1982	
6	Not Now John	(Harvest HAR 5224)	30	1983	0	1983	
7	On The Turning Away	(EMI EM 34)	55	1987	0	1987	
8	One Slip	(EMI EM 52)	50	1988	0	1988	
9	Take It Back	(EMI CDEMS 309)	23	1994	0	1994	
10	High Hopes / Keep Talking	(EMI CDEMS 342	26	1994	0	1994	
	GILMOUR REPLACED SYD BARRETT IN 1968						
Pink Lady Female Disco Duo, Real Names Mei & Kei from Japan							
1	Kiss In The Dark		0	1979	37	1979	(Elektra 46040)
Pinkees Male Vocal/Instrumental Group from the UK							
1	Danger Games	(Creole CR 39)	8	1982	0	1982	
Pinkerton's Assorted Colours Male Vocal/Instrumental Group from the UK							
1	Mirror Mirror	(Decca F 12307)	9	1966	0	1966	
2	Don't Stop Loving Me Baby	(Decca F 12377)	50	1966	0	1966	
Pinky & Perky TV/Puppet Duo from the UK							
1	Reet Petite	(Telstar CDPIGGY 1)	47	1993	0	1993	
Pioneers Male Vocal/Instrumental Group from Jamaica							
1	Long Shot Kick De Bucket	(Trojan TR 672)	21	1969	0	1969	
2	Long Shot Kick De Bucket (Re-Entry)	(Trojan TR 672)	40	1970	0	1970	
3	Let Your Yeh Be Yeh	(Trojan TR 7825)	5	1971	0	1971	
4	Give And Take	(Trojan TR 7846)	35	1972	0	1972	
5	Long Shot Kick De Bucket (Re-Issue)	(Trojan TRO 9063)	42	1980	0	1980	
Pipkins Male Vocal Duo from the UK Real Names Roger Greenaway & Tony Burrows							
1	Gimme Dat Ding	(Columbia DB 8662)	6	1970	9	1970	(Capitol 2819)
Piranhas Male Vocal/Instrumental Group from the UK							
1	Tom Hark	(Sire SIR 4044)	6	1980	0	1980	
2	Zambezi	(Dakota DAK 6)	17	1982	0	1982	
Pixies Mixed Vocal/Instrumental Group from the USA							
1	Monkey Gone To Heaven	(4AD AD 904)	60	1989	0	1989	
2	Here Comes Your Man	(4AD AD 909)	54	1989	0	1989	
3	Velouria	(4AD AD 0009)	28	1990	0	1990	
4	Dig For Fire	(4AD AD 0014)	62	1990	0	1990	
5	Planet Of Sound	(4AD AD 1008)	27	1991	0	1991	
Pixies Three Female Vocal Trio from Hanover, Pennsylvania							
1	Birthday Party		0	1963	40	1963	(Mercury 72130)
Pizzaman Male Production/Instrumental Group from the UK							
1	Trippin On Sunshine	(LoadedCDLOAD 16)	33	1994	0	1994	
2	Sex On The Streets	(LoadedCDLOAD 24)	23	1995	0	1995	
3	Happiness	(LoadedCDLOAD 29)	19	1995	0	1995	
4	Sex On The Streets (Re-Entry)	(LoadedCDLOAD 24)	23	1996	0	1996	
5	Trippin On Sunshine (Re-Issue)	(LoadedCDLOAD 32)	18	1996	0	1996	
6	Hello Honky Tonks (Rock Your Body)	(LoadedCDLOAD 39)	41	1996	0	1996	
PKA Male Producer, Real Name Phil Kelsey from the UK							
1	Temperature Rising	(STRESS SS 4)	68	1991	0	1991	
2	Powergen (Only Your Love)	(STRESS PKA 1)	70	1992	0	1992	

ISSUE	TITLE	UK LBL	UK POS	UK YEAR	US POS	US YEAR	US LBL
Placebo	Male Instrumental/Production Group from Sweden/USA						
1	Teenage Angst	(Elevator Music FloorCD 3)	30	1996	0	1996	
2	Nancy Boy	(Elevator Music FloorCD 4)	4	1997	0	1997	
3	Bruise Pristine	(Elevator Music FloorCD 5)	14	1997	0	1997	
Placido Domingo	Male Vocalist (Tenor) from Spain						
1	Perhaps Love	(CBS A 1905)	46	1981	0	1981	
2	Till I Loved You	(CBS 654843)	24	1989	0	1989	
3	Nessun Dorma (From *Turandot*)	(Epic 656005)	59	1990	0	1990	
4	Libiamo / La Donna E Mobile	(TELDEC YZ 843CD)	21	1994	0	1994	
Planet Patrol	Male Vocal/Instrumental Group from the USA						
1	Cheap Thrills	(Polydor POSP 639)	64	1983	0	1983	
Planet Soul	Male Producer George Costa And Vocalist Nadine Renne from Miami Brenda Lee Replaced Nadine In 1966						
1	Set U Free		0	1995	26	1995	(Strictly R. 12362)
Planets	Male Vocal/Instrumental Group from the UK						
1	Lines	(Rialto TREB 104)	66	1979	0	1979	
2	Don't Look Now	(Rialto TREB 116)	66	1980	0	1980	
Plasmatics	Mixed Vocal/Instrumental Group from the USA						
1	Butcher Baby	(Stiff Buy 76)	55	1980	0	1980	
Plastic Bertrand	Male Vocalist from Belgium						
1	Ca Plane Pour Moi	(SIRE 6078 616)	8	1978	0	1978	
2	Sha La La La Lee	(VERTIGO 6059 209)	39	1978	0	1978	
Plastic Penny	Male Vocal/Instrumental Group from the UK						
1	Everything I Am	(PAGE ONE POF 051)	6	1968	0	1968	
Platinum Hook	Male Vocal/Instrumental Group from the USA						
1	Standing On The Verge (Of Getting It On)	(MOTOWN TMG 1115)	72	1978	0	1978	
Platters	Mixed Vocal R&B Vocal Group from the USA	Names Tony Williams, David Lynch, Paul Robi, Herb Reed & Zola Taylor					
* 1	The Great Pretender - Side Of Diamonds		0	1955	1	1955	(Mercury 70753)
* 2	Only You	(Mercury MT 70633)	5	1956	5	1955	(Mercury 117)
* 3	The Great Pretender	(Mercury MT 70753)	5	1956	1	1956	(Mercury 117)
4	(You've Got) The Magic Touch		0	1956	4	1956	(Mercury 70819)
* 5	My Prayer	(Mercury MT 70893)	4	1956	1	1956	(Mercury 120)
6	Heaven On Earth		0	1956	39	1956	(Mercury 70893)
7	You'll Never Never Know	(Mercury MT 70948)	23	1957	11	1956	(Mercury 130)
8	It Isn't Right	(Mercury MT 70948)	23	1957	13	1956	(Mercury 130)
9	The Great Pretender / Only You (Re-Entry)	(Mercury MT 117)	21	1956	0	1956	
10	On My Word Of Honor		0	1957	20	1957	(Mercury 71011)
11	You'll Never Never Know / It Isn't Right	(Mercury MT 30)	23	1957	0	1957	
12	One In A Million		0	1957	20	1957	(Mercury 71011)
13	My Prayer (Re-Entry)	(Mercury MT 120)	28	1957	0	1957	
14	You'll Never Never Know / It Isn't Right (Re-Entry)	(Mercury MT 130)	29	1957	0	1957	
15	I'm Sorry	(Mercury MT 71032)	18	1957	11	1957	(Mercury 145)
16	My Prayer (2nd Re-Entry)	(Mercury MT 120)	22	1957	0	1957	
17	He's Mine		0	1957	16	1957	(Mercury 71032)
18	Only You (2nd Re-Entry)	(Mercury MT 117)	18	1957	0	1957	
19	You'll Never Never Know / It Isn't Right (2nd Re-Entry)	(Mercury MT 130)	29	1957	0	1957	
20	My Dream		0	1957	24	1957	(Mercury 71093)
21	I Wanna		0	1957	24	1957	(Mercury 71093)
22	I'm Sorry (Re-Entry)	(Mercury MT 145)	23	1957	0	1957	
23	I'm Sorry (2nd Re-Entry)	(Mercury MT 145)	22	1957	0	1957	
* 24	Twilight Time	(Mercury MT 214)	3	1958	1	1958	(Mercury 71289)
* 25	Smoke Gets In Your Eyes	(Mercury AMT 1016)	1	1958	1	1958	(Mercury 71383)
26	Enchanted		0	1959	12	1959	(Mercury 71427)
27	Remember When	(Mercury AMT 1053)	25	1959	0	1959	
28	Harbour Lights	(Mercury AMT 1081)	11	1960	8	1960	(Mercury 71563)
29	Red Sails In The Sunset		0	1960	36	1960	(Mercury 71656)
30	To Each His Own		0	1960	21	1960	(Mercury 71697)
31	If I Didn't Care		0	1961	30	1961	(Mercury 71749)
32	I'll Never Smile Again		0	1961	25	1961	(Mercury 71847)
33	I Love You 1000 Times		0	1966	31	1966	(Musicor 1166)
34	With This Ring		0	1967	14	1967	(Musicor 1229)

ISSUE	TITLE	UK LBL	UK POS	UK YEAR	US POS	US YEAR	US LBL
Player	Male Vocal/Instrumental Group from the USA/UK Names: Peter Beckett, John Crowley, John Friesen, Ronn Moss & Wayne Cooke						
* 1	Baby Come Back	(RSO 2090 254)	32	1978	1	1977	(RSO 879)
2	This Time I'm In It For Love		0	1978	10	1978	(RSO 890)
3	Prisoner Of Your Love		0	1978	27	1978	(RSO 908)
Players Association	Mixed Vocal/Instrumental Group from the USA						
1	Turn The Music Up	(Vanguard VS 5011)	8	1979	0	1979	
2	Ride The Groove	(Vanguard VS 5012)	42	1979	0	1979	
3	We Got The Groove	(Vanguard VS 5016)	61	1980	0	1980	
Playmates	Chic Hetti B: 26 Feb 1930, Morey Carr B: 31 Jul 1932 & Donny Conn B: 29 Mar 1930. From Waterbury, Connecticut						
1	Jo-Ann		0	1958	19	1958	(Roulette 4037)
2	Don't Go Home		0	1958	22	1958	(Roulette 4072)
* 3	Beep Beep		0	1958	4	1958	(Roulette 4115)
4	What Is Love?		0	1959	15	1959	(Roulette 4160)
5	Wait For Me		0	1960	37	1960	(Roulette 4276)
Plus One (Featuring) Sirron	Mixed Vocal/Instrumental Group from the UK						
1	It's Happenin'	(MCA MCA 1405)	40	1990	0	1990	
Pluto Shervington	Male Vocalist From Jamaica						
1	Dat	(OPAL PAL 5)	6	1976	0	1976	
2	Ram Goat Liver	(Trojan TR 7978)	43	1976	0	1976	
3	Your Honour	(KR KR 4)	19	1982	0	1982	
PM Dawn	Male Vocal/Instrumental Rap Duo Atrell & Jarrett Cordes From New Jersey						
1	A Watcher's Point Of View	(Gee Street Gee 32)	36	1991	0	1991	
* 2	Set Adrift On Memory Bliss	(Gee Street Gee33)	3	1991	1	1991	(Gee Street 866094)
3	Paper Doll	(Gee Street Gee35)	49	1991	28	1991	(Gee Street 866374)
4	Reality Used To Be A Friend Of Mine	(Gee Street Gee37)	29	1992	0	1992	
* 5	I'd Die Without You	(Gee Street Gee39)	30	1992	3	1992	(Gee Street/LAF.24034)
6	Looking Through Patient Eyes	(Gee Street GESCD 47)	11	1993	6	1993	(Gee Street 862024)
7	More Than Likely	(Gee Street GESCD 49)	40	1993	0	1993	
8	Downtown Venus	(Gee Street GESCD 63)	58	1995	0	1995	
9	Sometimes I Miss You So Much	(Gee Street GESCD 65)	58	1996	0	1996	
	HIT 7 IS CEDITED TO PM DAWN FEATURING BOY GEORGE						
Poco	Country-Rock Band from Los Angeles, Formed By Rusty Young, Richie Furay & Jim Messina						
1	Crazy Love		0	1979	17	1979	(ABC 12439)
2	Heart Of The Night		0	1979	20	1979	(MCA 41023)
3	Call It Love		0	1989	18	1989	(RCA 9038)
4	Nothin' To Hide		0	1990	39	1990	(RCA 9131)
Poets	Male Vocal/Instrumental Group from the UK						
1	Now We're Thru	(Decca F 11995)	31	1964	0	1964	
Pogues	Mixed Vocal/Instrumental Group from the UK/Ireland						
1	A Pair Of Brown Eyes	(Stiff Buy 220)	72	1985	0	1985	
2	Sally MacLennane	(Stiff Buy 224)	51	1985	0	1985	
3	Dirty Old Town	(Stiff Buy 229)	62	1985	0	1985	
4	Poguetry In Motion	(Stiff Buy 243)	29	1986	0	1986	
5	Haunted	(MCA MCA 1084)	42	1986	0	1986	
6	The Irish Rover	(Stiff Buy 258)	8	1987	0	1987	
7	Fairytale Of New York	(Pogue Mahone NY 7)	2	1987	0	1987	
8	If I Should Fall From Grace With God	(Pogue Mahone PG 1)	58	1988	0	1988	
9	Fiesta	(Pogue Mahone PG 2)	24	1988	0	1988	
10	Yeah Yeah Yeah Yeah Yeah	(Pogue Mahone YZ 355)	43	1988	0	1988	
11	Misty Morning, Albert Bridge	(Pogue Mahone YZ 407)	41	1989	0	1989	
12	Jack's Hero's / Whiskey In The Jar	(PM YZ 500)	63	1990	0	1990	
13	Summer In Siam	(PM YZ 519)	64	1990	0	1990	
14	A Rainy Night In Soho	(PM YZ 603)	67	1991	0	1991	
15	Fairytale Of New York (Re-Issue)	(PM YZ 628)	36	1991	0	1991	
16	Honky Tonk Women	(PM YZ 673)	56	1992	0	1992	
17	Tuesday Morning	(PM YZ 758CD)	18	1993	0	1993	
18	Once Upon A Time	(PM YZ 771CD)	66	1994	0	1994	
Point Blank	Lead Singer With The Six-Man Band from Texas Is Bubba Keith, Who Replaced John O'Daniel						
1	Nicole		0	1981	39	1981	(MCA 51132)
Pointer Sisters	Female Soul Group, With Sisters Bonnie, June, Anita, & Ruth Pointer from Oakland						
1	Yes We Can Can		0	1973	11	1973	(Blue Thumb 229)
2	Fairytale		0	1974	13	1974	(ABC/Blue Thumb 254)

ISSUE	TITLE	UK LBL	UK POS	UK YEAR	US POS	US YEAR	US LBL
3	How Long (Betcha' Got A Chick On The Side)		0	1975	20	1975	(ABC/Blue Thumb 265)
* 4	Fire	(Planet K 12339)	34	1979	2	1978	(Planet 45901)
5	Everybody Is A Star	(Planet K 12324)	61	1979	0	1979	
6	Happiness		0	1979	30	1979	(Planet 45902)
* 7	He's So Shy		0	1980	3	1980	(Planet 47916)
* 8	Slow Hand	(Planet K 12530)	10	1981	2	1981	(Planet 47929)
9	Should I Do It	(REPRISE K 12578)	50	1981	13	1982	(Planet 47960)
10	American Music		0	1982	16	1982	(Planet 13254)
11	I'm So Excited		0	1982	30	1982	(Planet 13327)
12	Autmatic	(Planet RPS 105)	2	1984	5	1984	(Planet 13730)
13	Jump (For My Love)	(Planet RPS 106)	6	1984	3	1984	(Planet 13780)
14	I Need You	(Planet RPS 107)	25	1984	0	1984	
15	I'm So Excited (Re-Mix)	(Planet RPS 108)	11	1984	9	1984	(Planet 13857)
16	Neutron Dance	(Planet RPS 109)	31	1985	6	1985	(Planet 13951)
17	Dare Me	(Planet PB 49957)	17	1985	11	1985	(RCA 14126)
18	Goldmine		0	1986	33	1986	(RCA 5062)

HIT 2 REACHED NUMBER 37 IN THE US C/W CHARTS

Poison Vocals In This Quartet from Pennsylvania Are from Bret Michaels

1	Talk Dirty To Me	(Music For Nations KUT 125)	67	1987	9	1987	(Capitol 5686)
2	I Won't Forget You		0	1987	13	1987	(Enigma 44038)
3	Nothin' But A Good Time	(Capitol CL 486)	35	1988	6	1988	(Enigma 44145)
4	Fallen Angel	(Capitol CL 500)	59	1988	12	1988	(Enigma 44191)
* 5	Every Rose Has It's Thorn	(Capitol CL 520)	13	1989	1	1988	(Enigma 44203)
6	Your Mamma Don't Dance	(Capitol CL 523)	13	1989	10	1989	(Enigma 44293)
7	Nothin' But A Good Time (Re-Entry)	(Capitol CL 539)	48	1989	0	1989	
* 8	Unskinny Bop	(Capitol CL 582)	15	1990	3	1990	(Enigma 44584)
9	Something To Believe In	(Capitol CL 594)	35	1990	4	1990	(Enigma 44617)
10	Ride The Wind		0	1991	38	1991	(Enigma 44616)
11	Life Goes On		0	1991	35	1991	(Enigma 44705)
12	So Tell Me Why	(Capitol CL 640)	25	1991	0	1991	
13	Stand	(Capitol CL 679)	25	1993	0	1993	
14	Until You Suffer Some (Fire And Ice)	(Capitol CDCL 685)	32	1993	0	1993	

Polecats Male Vocal/Instrumental Group from the UK

1	John I'm Only Dancing / Big Green Car	(Mercury Pole 1)	35	1981	0	1981	
2	Rockabilly Guy	(Mercury Pole 2)	35	1981	0	1981	
3	Jeepster / Marie Celeste	(Mercury Pole 3)	53	1981	0	1981	

Police Male Vocal/Instrumental Group from the USA/UK

1	Can't Stand Losing You	(A&M AMS 7381)	42	1978	0	1978	
2	Roxanne	(A&M AMS 7348)	12	1979	32	1979	(A&M 2096)
3	Can't Stand Losing You (Re-Entry)	(A&M AMS 7381)	2	1979	0	1979	
4	Message In A Bottle	(A&M AMS 7474)	1	1979	0	1979	
5	Fall Out	(Illegal IL 001)	47	1979	0	1979	
6	Walking On The Moon	(A&M AMS 7494)	1	1979	0	1979	
7	So Lonely	(A&M AMS 7402)	6	1980	0	1980	
8	Slx Pack	(A&M AMPP 6001)	17	1980	0	1980	
9	Don't Stand So Close To Me	(A&M AMS 7564)	1	1980	10	1981	(A&M 2301)
10	De Do Do Do De Da Da Da	(A&M AMS 7578)	5	1980	10	1980	(A&M 2275)
11	Invisible Sun	(A&M AMS 8164)	2	1981	0	1981	
12	Every Little Thing She Does Is Magic	(A&M AMS 8174)	1	1981	3	1981	(A&M 2371)
13	Spirits Of The Material World	(A&M AMS 8194)	12	1981	11	1982	(A&M 2390)
* 14	Every Breath You Take	(A&M AM 117)	1	1983	1	1983	(A&M 2542)
15	Wrapped Around Your Finger	(A&M AM 127)	7	1983	8	1984	(A&M 2614)
16	Synchronicity Ii	(A&M AM 153)	17	1983	16	1983	(A&M 2571)
17	King Of Pain	(A&M AM 176)	17	1984	3	1983	(A&M 2569)
18	Don't Stand So Close To Me '86 (Re-Mix)	(A&M AM 354)	24	1986	0	1986	
19	Can't Stand Losing You (Live)	(A&M 5810372)	27	1995	0	1995	

NAMES GORDON SUMNER, ANDY SUMMERS & STEWART COPELAND • HENRI PADOVANI WAS REPLACED BY SUMMERS IN 1977

Polly Brown Female Vocalist from the UK

1	Up In A Puff Of Smoke	(GTO GT 2)	43	1974	16	1974	(GTO 1002)

ALSO LEAD SINGER WITH PICKETTYWITCH AND SWEET DREAMS

Poltergeist Male Producer Simon Berry from the UK

1	Vicious Circles	(Manifesto FESCD 8)	32	1996	0	1996	

Polygon Window Male Producer, Real Name Richard James from the UK

1	Quoth	(WARP WAP 33CD)	49	1993	0	1993	

ISSUE	TITLE	UK LBL	UK POS	UK YEAR	US POS	US YEAR	US LBL
Poni-Tails Female Vocal Trio from the USA Names Toni Cistone, Laverne Novak & Patti McCabe							
1	Born Too Late	(HMV POP 516)	26	1958	7	1958	ABC-Paramount 9934)
2	Early To Bed	(HMV POP 5960	26	1959	0	1959	
Pop Will Eat Itself Male Vocal/Instrumental Group from the UK							
1	There Is No Love Between Us Anymore	(Chapter 22 CHAP 20)	66	1988	0	1988	
2	Def. Con One	(Chapter 22 PWE 001)	63	1988	0	1988	
3	Can U Dig It	(RCA PB 42621)	38	1989	0	1989	
4	Wise Up! Sucker	(RCA PB 42761)	41	1989	0	1989	
5	Very Metal Noise Pollution (EP)	(RCA PB 42883)	45	1989	0	1989	
6	Touched By The Hand Of Cicciolina	(RCA PB 43735)	28	1990	0	1990	
7	Dance Of The Mad	(RCA PB 44023)	32	1990	0	1990	
8	X Y And Zee	(RCA PB 44243)	15	1991	0	1991	
9	92 Degrees	(RCA PB 44555)	23	1991	0	1991	
10	Karmadrome / Eat Me Drink Me Love Me	(RCA PB 45467)	17	1992	0	1992	
11	Bulletproof	(RCA 74321110137)	24	1992	0	1992	
12	Get The Girl! Kill The Baddies	(RCA 74321128802)	9	1993	0	1993	
13	R.S.V.P. / Familius Horribilus	(Infectious INFECT 1CD)	27	1993	0	1993	
14	Ich Bin Ein Auslander	(Infectious INFECT 4CD)	28	1994	0	1994	
15	Everything's Cool	(Infectious INFECT 9CD)	23	1994	0	1994	
Poppy Family Mixed Vocal/Instrumental Group from Canada Names: Terry & Susan Jacks, Craig MacCaw & Satwan Singh							
* 1	Which Way You Goin' Billy?	(Decca F 22976)	7	1970	2	1970	(London 129)
2	That's Where I Went Wrong		0	1970	29	1970	(London 139)
Porn Kings Male Instrumental/Production Group from the UK							
1	Up To No Good	(All Around The World Cdglobe 145)28		1996	0	1996	
2	Amour (C'mon)	(All Around The World Cdglobe 152)17		1997	0	1997	
Porno For Pyros Male Vocal/Instrumental Group from the USA							
1	Pets	(Warner Bros. 0777CDX)	53	1993	0	1993	
Portishead Mixed Vocal/Instrumental Duo from the UK							
1	Sour Times	(Go.Beat Godcd 116)	57	1994	0	1994	
2	Glory Box	(Go.Beat Godcd 120)	13	1995	0	1995	
3	Sour Times (Re-Entry)	(Go.Beat Godcd 116)	13	1995	0	1995	
Portrait Male Vocal Quartet From Rhode Island, USA							
1	Here We Go Again!	(Capitol CDCL 683)	37	1993	11	1992	(Capitol 44865)
2	I Can Call You	(Capitol CDCL 740)	61	1995	0	1995	
3	How Deep Is Your Love	(Capitol CDCL 751)	41	1995	0	1995	
Portsmouth Sinfonia Orchestra from the UK							
1	Classical Muddley	(Island WIP 6736)	38	1981	0	1981	
Posies Male Vocal/Instrumental Group from the USA							
1	Definite Door	(Geffen GFSTD 68)	67	1994	0	1994	
Positive Force Female Vocal Duo from the USA							
1	We Got The Funk	(Sugarhill SHL 102)	18	1979	0	1979	
Positive Gang Mixed Vocal/Instrumental Group from the UK							
1	Sweet Freedom	(PWL Continental PWCD 261)	34	1993	0	1993	
2	Sweet Freedom (Part 2)	(PWL Continental PWCD 264)	67	1993	0	1993	
Positive K Male Rapper, Real Name Darryl Gibson From The Bronx							
* 1	I Got A Man	(Fourth & BroadwayBRCD 280)	43	1993	14	1993	(Island 864305)
Potters Male Vocal Group from the UK							
1	We'll Be With You	(PYE JT 100)	34	1972	0	1972	
Powder Mixed Vocal/Instrumental Group from the UK							
1	Afrodisiac	(Parkway Park 002CD)	72	1995	0	1995	
Power Of Dreams Male Vocal/Instrumental Group From Ireland							
1	American Dream	(Polydor PO 117)	74	1991	0	1991	
2	There I Go Again	(Polydor PO 200)	65	1992	0	1992	
Power Station Male Vocal/Instrumental Quartet from the USA/UK Names: Robert Palmer, Tony Thompson, John Taylor & Andy Taylor							
1	Some Like It Hot	(Parlophone R 6091)	14	1985	6	1985	(Capitol 5444)
2	Get It On	(Parlophone R 6096)	22	1985	9	1985	(Capitol 5479)
3	Communication	(Parlophone R 6114)	75	1985	34	1985	(Capitol 5511)
4	She Can Rock It	(Chrysalis CDCHS 5039)	63	1996	0	1996	
Powercut (Featuring) Nubian Prinz Male Vocal/Instrumental Group from the USA							
1	Girls	(Eternal YZ 570)	50	1991	0	1991	

ISSUE	TITLE	UK LBL	UK POS	UK YEAR	US POS	US YEAR	US LBL
Powerpill Male Production/Instrumental Group from the UK							
1	Pac-Man	(FFRREEDOM TABX 110)	43	1992	0	1992	
Pozo-Seco Singers Names: Susan Taylor, Lofton Kline & Don Williams From Texas							
1	I Can Make It With You		0	1966	32	1966	(Columbia 43784)
2	Look What You've Done		0	1967	32	1967	(Columbia 43927)
Praga Khan Male Producer from Belgium							
1	Free Your Body / Injected With A Poison	(Profile Proft 347)	16	1992	0	1992	
2	Rave Alert	(Profile Proft369)	39	1992	0	1992	
Praise Mixed Vocal/Instrumental Group from the UK							
1	Only You	(Epic 6566117)	4	1991	0	1991	
Pratt & McClain With Brotherlove Male Vocal Duo,							
1	Happy Days	(Reprise K 14435)	31	1977	5	1976	(Reprise 1351)
Praxis Mixed Vocal/Instrumental Group from the UK							
1	Turn Me Out	(Stress CDSTR 40)	44	1995	0	1995	
Praying Mantis Male Vocal/Instrumental Group from the UK							
1	Cheated	(Arista ARIST 378)	69	1981	0	1981	
Prefab Sprout Mixed Vocal/Instrumental Group from the UK							
1	Don't Sing	(Kitchenware SK 9)	64	1984	0	1984	
2	Faron Young	(Kitchenware SK 22)	74	1985	0	1985	
3	When Love Breaks Down	(Kitchenware SK 21)	25	1985	0	1985	
4	Johnny Johnny	(Kitchenware SK 24)	64	1986	0	1986	
5	Cars And Girls	(Kitchenware SK 35)	44	1988	0	1988	
6	The King Of Rock N' Roll	(Kitchenware SK 37)	7	1988	0	1988	
7	Hey Manhattan	(Kitchenware SK 38)	72	1988	0	1988	
8	Looking For Atlantis	(Kitchenware SK 47)	51	1990	0	1990	
9	We Let The Stars Go	(Kitchenware SK 48)	50	1990	0	1990	
10	Jordan: The (EP)	(Kitchenware SK 49)	35	1991	0	1991	
11	The Sound Of Crying	(Kitchenware SK 58)	23	1992	0	1992	
12	If You Don't Love Me	(Kitchenware SK 60)	33	1992	0	1992	
13	All The World Loves Lovers	(Kitchenware SK 62)	61	1992	0	1992	
14	Life Of Surprises	(Kitchenware SKCD 63)	24	1993	0	1993	
15	A Prisoner Of The Past	(Columbia SKZD 70)	30	1997	0	1997	
16	Electric Guitars	(Columbia SKZD 71)	53	1997	0	1997	
Prelude Mixed Vocal/Instrumental Group from the UK Names Brian & Irene Hume With Ian Vardy							
1	After The Goldrush	(Dawn DNS 1052)	21	1974	22	1974	(Island 002)
2	Platinum Blonde	(EMI 5046)	45	1980	0	1980	
3	After The Goldrush (Re-Recording)	(AAfter Hours AFT 02)	28	1982	0	1982	
4	Only The Lonely	(After Hours AFT 06)	55	1982	0	1982	
Premiers Latin-Rock Band from California							
1	Farmer John		0	1964	19	1964	(Warner Bros. 5443)
Presidents Male Soul Group, Bill Shorter, Tony Boyd & Archie Powell from the USA							
1	5-10-15-20 (20-30 Years Of Love)		0	1970	11	1970	(Sussex 207)
Presidents Of The United States Of America Male Vocal/Instrumental Group from the USA							
1	Lump	(Columbia 6624962)	15	1996	0	1996	
2	Peaches	(Columbia 6631072)	8	1996	29	1996	(Columbia)
3	Dune Buggy	(Columbia 6634892)	15	1996	0	1996	
4	Mach 5	(Columbia 6638812)	29	1996	0	1996	
Preston Epps Male Bongo Player, B: 1931 Oakland							
1	Bongo Rock		0	1959	14	1959	(Original Sound 4)
Pretenders Mixed Vocal/Instrumental Group from the USA/UK							
1	Stop Your Sobbing	(Real Are 6)	34	1979	0	1979	
2	Kid	(Real Are 9)	33	1979	0	1979	
3	Brass In Pocket (I'm Special)	(Real Are 11)	1	1979	14	1980	(Sire 49181)
4	Talk Of The Town	(Real Are 12)	8	1980	0	1980	
5	Message Of Love	(Real Are 15)	11	1981	0	1981	
6	Day After Day	(Real Are 17)	45	1981	0	1981	
7	I Go To Sleep	(Real Are18)	7	1981	0	1981	
8	Back On The Chain Gang	(Real Are 19)	17	1982	5	1983	(Sire 29840)
9	2000 Miles	(Real Are 20)	15	1983	0	1983	
10	Middle Of The Road		0	1984	19	1984	(Sire 29444)
11	Show Me		0	1984	28	1984	(Sire 29317)

ISSUE	TITLE	UK LBL	UK POS	UK YEAR	US POS	US YEAR	US LBL
12	Thin Line Between Love And Hate	(Real Are 22)	49	1984	0	1984	
13	Don't Get Me Wrong	(REAL YZ 85)	10	1986	10	1986	(Sire 28630)
14	Hymn To Her	(REAL YZ 93)	8	1986	0	1986	
15	If There Was A Man	(REAL YZ 149)	49	1987	0	1987	
16	I'll Stand By You	(WEA YZ 815CD)	10	1994	16	1994	(Sire/Warner Bros. 18160)
17	Night In My Veins	(WEA YZ 825CD)	25	1994	0	1994	
18	977	(WEA YZ	66	1994	0	1994	
19	Kid	(WEA 014CD)	73	1995	0	1995	
20	Fever Pitch The EP	(Blanco Y Negro NEG 104CD)	65	1997	0	1997	

LEAD SINGER WITH THE QUARTET IS CHRISSIE HYNDE • HIT 15 IS CREDITED TO PRETENDERS FOR 007

Pretty Boy Floyd Male Vocal/Instrumental Group from the USA

1	Rock And Roll (Is Gonna Set The Night On Fire)	(MCA MCA 1393)	75	1990	0	1990	

Pretty Poison Lead Singer With The Dance Band from Philadelphia Is Jade Starling

* 1	Catch Me (I'm Falling)		0	1987	8	1987	(Virgin 99416)
+ 2	Nightime		0	1984	82	1984	(Svengali 8403(T))
3	Nightime (Re-Mix)		0	1988	36	1988	(Virgin 99350)

Pretty Things Male Vocal/Instrumental Group from the UK

1	Rosalyn	(Fontana TF 469)	41	1964	0	1964	
2	Don't Bring Me Down	(Fontana TF 503)	10	1964	0	1964	
3	Honey I Need	(Fontana TF 537)	13	1965	0	1965	
4	Cry To Me	(Fontana TF 585)	28	1965	0	1965	
5	Midnight To Six Man	(Fontana TF 674)	46	1966	0	1966	
6	Come See Me	(Fontana TF 688)	43	1966	0	1966	
7	A House In The Country	(Fontana TF 722)	50	1966	0	1966	
8	A House In The Country (Re-Entry)	(Fontana TF 722)	50	1966	0	1966	

Prima Donna Mixed Vocal Group from the UK

1	Love Enough For Two	(Ariola ARO 221)	48	1980	0	1980	

Primal Scream Male Vocal/Instrumental Group from the UK

1	Loaded	(Creation CRE 070)	16	1990	0	1990	
2	Come Together	(Creation CRE 0778)	26	1990	0	1990	
3	Higher Than The Sun	(Creation CRE 096)	40	1991	0	1991	
4	Don't Fight It Feel It	(Creation CRE 110)	41	1991	0	1991	
5	Disco-Narco (FP)	(Creation CRE 117)	11	1992	0	1992	
6	Rocks / Funky Jam	(Creation CRESCD 129)	7	1994	0	1994	
7	Jailbird	(Creation CRESCD 145)	29	1994	0	1994	
8	(I'm Gonna) Cry Myself Blind	(Creation CRESCD 183)	49	1994	0	1994	
9	The Big Man And The Scream Team Meet The Barmy Army Uptown	(Creation CRESCD 194)	17	1996	0	1996	
10	Kowalski	(Creation CRESCD 245)	8	1997	0	1997	
11	Star	(Creation CRESCD 263)	16	1997	0	1997	

HIT 4 IS CREDITED TO PRIMAL SCREAM FEATURING DENISE JOHNSON • HIT 9 IS CREDITED TO PRIMAL SCREAM, IRVINE WELSH & ON-U SOUND

Prime Movers Male Vocal/Instrumental Group from the USA

1	On The Trail	(Island IS 263)	74	1986	0	1986	

Primitive Radio Gods Male Vocalist Chris O'Connor from the USA

1	Standing Outside A Broken Phone Booth With No Money In My Hand	(Columbia 6626952)	74	1996	0	1996	

Primitives Mixed Vocal/Instrumental Group from the UK

1	Crash	(Lazy PB 41761)	5	1988	0	1988	
2	Out Of Reach	(Lazy PB 42011)	25	1988	0	1988	
3	Way Behind Me	(Lazy PB 42209)	36	1988	0	1988	
4	Sick Of It	(Lazy PB 42947)	24	1989	0	1989	
5	Secrets	(Lazy PB 43173)	49	1989	0	1989	
6	You Are The Way	(Lazy PB 44481)	58	1991	0	1991	

Primo Scala & Banjo & Accordion Orchestra With The Keynotes Male Bandleader And Vocalist from the UK

1	Underneath The Arches		0	1948	6	1948	(London 238)
2	Jingle Bells		0	1949	24	1949	(London 302)
3	The Mistletoe Kiss		0	1949	27	1949	(London 302)
4	Cruising Down The River		0	1949	27	1949	(London 356)

Prince Male Vocalist, Real Name Prince Roger Nelson, B: 7 Jun 1958 Minneapolis.

* 1	I Wanna Be Your Lover	(Warner Bros. K 17537)	41	1980	11	1979	(Warner Bros. 49050)
2	1999	(Warner Bros. W 9896)	25	1983	12	1983	(Warner Bros. 29896)
3	Little Red Corvette	(Warner Bros. W 9688)	54	1983	6	1983	(Warner Bros. 29746)

ISSUE	TITLE	UK LBL	UK POS	UK YEAR	US POS	US YEAR	US LBL
4	Delirious		0	1983	8	1983	(Warner Bros. 29503)
5	Little Red Corvette (Re-Issue)	(Warner Bros. W 9436)	66	1983	0	1983	
* 6	When Doves Cry	(Warner Bros. W 9286)	4	1984	1	1984	(Warner Bros. 29286)
* 7	Let's Go Crazy	(Warner Bros. W 2000)	7	1985	1	1984	(Warner Bros. 29216)
* 8	Purple Rain	(Warner Bros. W 9174)	8	1984	2	1984	(Warner Bros. 29174)
9	I Would Die 4 U	(Warner Bros. W 9121)	58	1984	8	1984	(Warner Bros. 29121)
10	Little Red Corvette - 1999 (Re-Issue)	(Warner Bros. W 1999)	2	1985	0	1985	
11	Rasberry Beret	(WEA W 8929)	25	1985	2	1985	(Paisley Park 28972)
12	Take Me With U		0	1985	25	1985	(Warner Bros. 29079)
13	Paisley Park	(WEA W 9052)	18	1985	0	1985	
14	Pop Life	(Paisley Park W 8858)	60	1985	7	1985	(Paisley Park 28998)
* 15	Kiss	(Paisley Park W 8751)	6	1986	1	1986	(Paisley Park 28751)
16	Mountains	(Paisley Park W 8711)	45	1986	23	1986	(Paisley Park 28711)
17	Girls And Boys	(Paisley Park W 8586)	11	1986	0	1986	
18	Anotherloverholenyohead	(Paisley Park W 8521)	36	1986	0	1986	
19	Sign 'O' The Times	(Paisley Park W 8399)	10	1987	3	1987	(Paisley Park 28399)
20	If I Was Your Girlfriend	(Paisley Park W 8334)	20	1987	0	1987	
21	U Got The Look	(Paisley Park W 8289)	11	1987	2	1987	(Paisley Park 28289)
22	I Could Never Take The Place Of Your Man	(Paisley Park W 8288)	29	1987	10	1988	(Paisley Park 28288)
23	Alphabet Street	(Paisley Park W7900)	9	1988	8	1988	(Paisley Park 27900)
24	Gram Slam	(Paisley Park W 7806)	29	1988	0	1988	
25	I Wish U Heaven	(Paisley Park W 7745)	24	1988	0	1988	
* 26	Batdance	(Warner Bros. W 2924)	2	1989	1	1989	(Warner Bros. 22924)
* 27	Partyman	(Warner Bros. W 2814)	14	1989	18	1989	
28	The Arms Of Orion	(Warner Bros. W 2757)	27	1989	36	1989	(Warner Bros. 22757)
* 29	Thieves In The Temple	(Paisley Park W9751)	7	1990	6	1990	(Paisley Park 19751)
30	New Power Generation	(Paisley Park W 9525)	26	1990	0	1990	
* 31	Gett Off	(Paisley Park W 0056)	4	1991	21	1991	(Paisley Park 19225)
* 32	Cream	(Paisley Park W 0061)	15	1991	1	1991	(Paisley Park 19175)
33	Diamonds And Pearls	(Paisley Park W19083)	25	1991	3	1991	(Paisley Park 0075)
34	Money Don't Matter 2 Night	(Paisley Park W 0091)	19	1992	23	1992	(Paisley Park 19020)
35	Thunder	(Paisley Park W 01132P)	28	1992	0	1992	
36	Sexy MF - Strollin'	(Paisley Park W 0123)	4	1992	0	1992	
37	My Name Is Prince	(Paisley Park W 0132)	7	1992	36	1992	(Paisley Park 18707)
38	My Name Is Prince (Re-Mix)	(Paisley Park W 0142T)	27	1992	0	1992	
* 39	7	(Paisley Park W 0147)	27	1992	7	1992	Paisley Park 18824)
40	The Morning Papers	(Paisley Park W 0162CD)	52	1993	0	1993	
41	Peach	(Paisley Park W 0210CD)	14	1993	0	1993	
42	Controversy	(Paisley Park W 0215CD1)	5	1993	0	1993	
* 43	The Most Beautiful Girl In The World	(NPG NPG 60155)	1	1994	3	1994	(NPG/Bell 72514)
44	A Most Beautiful Experience (Re-Mix)	(NPG NPG 60212)	18	1994	0	1994	
45	Letitgo	(Warner Bros. W 0260CD)	30	1994	31	1994	(Warner Bros. 18074)
46	Purple Medley	(Paisley Park W 0289CD)	33	1995	0	1995	
47	I Hate You		0	1995	12	1995	(NPG/Warner Bros. 17811)
48	Gold	(Warner Bros. W 0325CD)	36	1996	0	1996	
49	Dinner With Delores	(Warner Bros. 9632437422)	36	1996	0	1996	
51	The Holy River	(EMI CDEM 467)	19	1997	0	1997	

Prince Buster Male Vocalist, B: Buster Campbell 24 May 1938 in Kingston, Jamaica

1	Ten Commandments		0	1967	17	1967	(Phillips 40427)
2	Al Capone	(Blue Beat)	18	1967	0	1967	

Prince Charles & The City BeatBand Male Vocalist And Male Vocal/Instrumental Group from the USA

1	We Can Make It Happen	(PRT 7P 348)	56	1986	0	1986	

Princess Female Vocalist from the UK

+ 1	Say I'm Your No.1	(Supreme SUPE 101)	7	1985	20	1985	(Next lat. 50035)
2	After The Love Has Gone	(Supreme SUPE 103)	28	1985	41	1985	(Next Plat. 50037)
3	I'll Keep On Loving You	(Supreme SUPE 105)	16	1986	0	1986	
4	Tell Me Tomorrow	(Supreme SUPE 106)	34	1986	0	1986	
5	In The Heat Of A Passionate Moment	(Supreme SUPE 109)	74	1986	0	1986	

Princess Ivori Female Rapper from the USA

1	Wanted	(Supreme SUPE 163)	69	1990	0	1990	

Priscilla Wright Female Vocalist from the USA

1	The Man In The Raincoat		0	1955	16	1955	(Unique 303)

Prism Lead Singer With The Canadian Rock Group Is Ron Tabak

1	Don't Let Him Know		0	1982	39	1982	(Capitol 5082)

ISSUE	TITLE	UK LBL	UK POS	UK YEAR	US POS	US YEAR	US LBL
Private Lives Male Vocal/Instrumental Duo from the UK							
1	Living In A World (Turned Upside Down)	(EMI PRIV 2)	53	1984	0	1984	
Prizna (Featuring) Demolition Man Male Vocal/Instrumental Group from the USA							
1	Fire	(Labello Blanco NLBCDX 18)	33	1995	0	1995	
Proclaimers Male Vocal/Instrumental Duo from the UK							
1	Letter From America	(Chrysalis CHS 3178)	3	1987	0	1987	
2	Make My Heart Fly	(Chrysalis Claim 1)	63	1988	0	1988	
3	I'm Gonna Be (500 Miles)	(Chrysalis Claim 2)	11	1988	3	1993	(Chrysalis 24846)
4	Sunshine On Leith	(Chrysalis Claim 3)	41	1988	0	1988	
5	I'm On My Way	(Chrysalis Claim 4)	43	1989	0	1989	
6	King Of The Road (EP)	(Chrysalis Claim 5)	9	1990	0	1990	
7	Let's Get Married	(Chrysalis CDClaimS 6)	21	1994	0	1994	
8	What Makes You Cry	(Chrysalis CDClaim 7)	38	1994	0	1994	
9	These Arms Of Mine	(Chrysalis CDClaim 8)	51	1994	0	1994	
Procol Harum Male Vocal/Instrumental Group from the UK, Led By Gary Brooker							
* 1	A Whiter Shade Of Pale	(DERAM DM 126)	1	1967	5	1967	(DERAM 7507)
2	Homburg	(Regal Zonophone RZ 3003)	6	1967	34	1967	(A&M 885)
3	Quite Rightly So	(Regal Zonophone RZ3007)	50	1968	0	1968	
4	Salty Dog	(Regal Zonophone RZ 3019)	44	1969	0	1969	
5	Salty Dog (Re-Entry)	(Regal Zonophone RZ 3019)	44	1969	0	1969	
6	Salty Dog (2nd Re-Entry)	(Regal Zonophone RZ3019)	44	1969	0	1969	
7	A Whiter Shade Of Pale (Re-Issue)	(Magnifly Echo 10)	13	1972	0	1972	
8	Conquistador	(Chrysalis CHS 2003)	22	1972	16	1972	(A&M 1347)
9	Pandora's Box	(Chrysalis CHS 2073)	16	1975	0	1975	
	HIT 1 IS BASED ON BACH CANTATA 'SLEEPERS AWAKE' AND REACHED NUMBER 22 IN THE USA R&B CHARTS						
Prodigy Male Producer, Real Name Liam Howlett And Dancers from the UK							
1	Charly	(XL Recordings XLS 21)	3	1991	0	1991	
2	Everybody In The Place (FP)	(XL Recordings XLS 26)	2	1992	0	1992	
3	Fire / Jericho	(XL Recordings XLS 30)	11	1992	0	1992	
4	Out Of Space / Ruff In The Jungle Bizness	(XL Recordings XLS 35)	5	1992	0	1992	
5	Wind It Up (Rewound)	(XL Recordings XLS 39CD)	11	1993	0	1993	
6	One Love	(XL Recordings XLS 47CD)	8	1993	0	1993	
7	No Good (Srart The Dance)	(XL Recordings XLS 51CD)	4	1994	0	1994	
8	Voodoo People	(XL Recordings XLS 54CD)	13	1994	0	1994	
9	Poison	(XL Recordings XLS 58CD)	15	1995	0	1995	
10	Firestarter	(XL Recordings XLS 70CD)	1	1996	0	1996	
11	Out Of Space / Ruff In The Jungle Bizness (Re-Entry)	(XL XLS 35CD)	52	1996	0	1996	
12	No Good (Start The Dance) (Re-Entry)	(XL Recordings XLS 51CD)	57	1996	0	1996	
13	Poison (Re-Entry)	(XL Recordings XLS 58CD)	62	1996	0	1996	
14	Fire /Jerico (Re-Entry)	(XL Recordings XLS 30CD)	63	1996	0	1996	
15	Charly (Re-Entry)	(XL Recordings XLS 21)	66	1996	0	1996	
16	Wind It Up (Rewound) (Re-Entry)	(XL Recordings XL 39CD)	71	1996	0	1996	
17	Voodoo People (Re-Entry)	(XL Recordings XL 54CD)	75	1996	0	1996	
18	Everybody In The Place (EP) (Re-Entry)	(XL Recordings XLS 26)	69	1996	0	1996	
19	Breathe	(XL Recordings XLS 80CD)	1	1996	0	1996	
20	Firestarter (2nd Re-Entry)	(XL Recordings XLS 70CD)	62	1996	30	1997	(Warner Bros. 43843)
21	No Good (Start The Dance) (Re-Entry)	(XL Recordings XLS 51CD)	57	1996	0	1996	
22	Out Of Space (Re-Issue)	(XL Recordings XLS 35CD)	52	1996	0	1996	
23	Firestarter (3rd Re-Entry)	(XL Recordings XLS 70CD)	53	1997	0	1997	
24	Breathe (Re-Entry)	(XL Recordings XLS 80CD)	71	1997	0	1997	
Professionals Male Vocal/Instrumental Group from the UK							
1	1-2-3	(Virgin VS 376)	43	1980	0	1980	
Project (Featuring) Gerideau Male Vocal/Instrumental Duo from the USA							
1	Bring It Back 2 Luv	(FRUITTREE FTREE 10CD)	65	1994	0	1994	
Project 1 Male Producer, Real Name Mark Williams from the UK							
1	Roughneck (EP)	(Rising High RSN 22)	49	1992	0	1992	
2	Don Cargon Comin'	(Rising High RSN 35)	64	1992	0	1992	
Pron Male Vocal/Instrumental Group from the USA							
1	Whose Fist Is This Anyway (EP)	(Epic 6580026)	58	1992	0	1992	
Propaganda Mixed Vocal/Instrumental Group from Germany							
1	Dr Mabuse	(ZTT ZTAS 2)	27	1984	0	1984	

ISSUE	TITLE	UK LBL	UK POS	UK YEAR	US POS	US YEAR	US LBL
2	Duel	(ZTT ZTAS 8)	21	1985	0	1985	
3	P Machinery	(ZTT ZTAS 12)	50	1985	0	1985	
4	Heaven Give Me Words	(Virgin VS 1245)	36	1990	0	1990	
5	Only One Word	(Virgin VS 1271)	71	1990	0	1990	
Propellerheads	**Male Instrumental/Production Duo from the UK**						
1	Take California	(Wall Of Sound WALLD 024)	69	1996	0	1996	
2	Spybreak!	(Wall Of Sound WALLD 029)	40	1997	0	1997	
Pseudo Echo	**Male Vocal/Instrumental Group from Australia Lead Singer Is Brian Canham**						
1	Funky Town	(RCA PB 49705)	8	1987	6	1987	RCA 5217)
Psychedelic Furs	**Male Vocal/Instrumental Group from the UK Names: Tim And Richard Butler, John Aston, Vince Ely**						
1	Dumb Waiters	(CBS 1166)	59	1981	0	1981	
2	Pretty In Pink	(CBS 1327)	43	1981	0	1981	
3	Love My Way	(CBS A 2549)	42	1982	0	1982	
4	Heaven	(CBS A 4300)	29	1984	0	1984	
5	Ghost In You	(CBS A 4470)	68	1984	0	1984	
6	Pretty In Pink (Re-Recording)	(CBS A 7242)	18	1986	0	1986	
7	Heartbreak Beat		0	1987	26	1987	(Columbia 06420)
8	All That Money Wants	(CBS FURS 4)	75	1988	0	1988	
Psychic TV	**Mixed Vocal/Instrumental Group from the UK**						
1	Godstar	(Temple Topy 009)	67	1986	0	1986	
2	Good Vibrations / Roman P	(Temple TOPY 23)	65	1986	0	1986	
Public Enemy	**Male Rap Group from the USA, led by Charlton Ridenhauer (Chuck D)**						
1	Rebel Without A Pause	(DEF JAM 651245 7)	37	1987	0	1987	
2	Rebel Without A Pause (Re-Entry)	(DEF JAM 651245 7)	71	1988	0	1988	
10	Can't Do Nuttin' For Ya Man	(DEF JAM 656385 7)	53	1990	0	1990	
11	Can't Truss It	(DEF JAM 6575307)	22	1991	50	1991	(DEF JAM 73870)
13	Nighttrain	(DEF JAM 6578647)	55	1992	0	1992	
14	Give It Up	(DEF JAM DEFCD1)	18	1994	33	1994	(DEF JAM 853316)
15	So Whatcha Gonna Do Now	(DEF JAM DEFCD5)	50	1995	0	1995	
	UNLISTED HITS WERE R&B						
Public Image Ltd	**Male Vocal/Instrumental Group from the UK**						
1	Public Image	(Virgin VS 228)	9	1978	0	1978	
2	Death Disco (Part 1-2)	(Virgin VS 274)	20	1979	0	1979	
3	Memories	(Virgin VS 299)	60	1979	0	1979	
4	Flowers Of Romance	(Virgin VS 397)	24	1981	0	1981	
5	This Is Not A Love Song	(Virgin VS 529)	5	1983	0	1983	
6	Bad Life	(Virgin VS 675)	71	1984	0	1984	
7	Rise	(Virgin VS 841)	11	1986	0	1986	
8	Home	(Virgin VS 855)	75	1986	0	1986	
9	Seattle	(Virgin VS 988)	47	1987	0	1987	
10	Disappointed	(Virgin VS 1181)	38	1989	0	1989	
11	Don't Ask Me	(Virgin VS 1231)	22	1990	0	1990	
12	Cruel	(Virgin VS 1390)	49	1992	0	1992	
Pulp	**Mixed Vocal/Instrumental Group from the UK**						
1	Lip Gloss	(Island CID 567)	50	1993	0	1993	
2	Do You Remember The First Time	(Island CID 574)	33	1994	0	1994	
3	The Sisters (EP)	(Island CID 595)	19	1994	0	1994	
4	Common People	(Island CID 613)	2	1995	0	1995	
5	Mis-Shapes / Sorted For Es And Whizz	(Island CID 620)	2	1995	0	1995	
6	Disco 2000	(Island CID 623)	7	1996	0	1996	
7	Mis-Shapes/Sorted For Es And Wizz (Re-Entry)	(Island CID 620)	62	1995	0	1995	
8	Something Changed	(Island CID 632)	10	1996	0	1996	
9	Something Changed (Re-Entry)	(Island CID 632)	62	1996	0	1996	
10	Something Changed (2nd Re-Entry)	(Island CID 632)	61	1996	0	1996	
11	Do You Remember The First Time (Re-Entry)	(Island CID 574)	73	1996	0	1996	
Pulse (Featuring) Antoinette Roberson	**Mixed Vocal/Instrumental Duo from the USA**						
1	The Lover That You Are	(FFRR FCD 278)	22	1996	0	1996	
Puppies	**Brother & Sister Rap Duo, Calvin & Tamara Mills From Miami**						
1	Funky Y-2-C		0	1994	40	1994	(Chaos/COL. 77461)
Pure Prairie League	**Male Country Rock Group from Cincinnati, US**						
1	Amie		0	1975	27	1975	(RCA 10184)
2	Love Me Love You Tonight		0	1980	10	1980	(Casablanca 2266)
3	I'm Almost Ready		0	1980	34	1980	(Casablanca 2294)

ISSUE	TITLE	UK LBL	UK POS	UK YEAR	US POS	US YEAR	US LBL
4	Still Right Here In My Heart		0	1981	28	1981	(Casablanca 2332)
Purple Hearts Male Vocal/Instrumental Group from the UK							
1	Millions Like Us	(Fiction FICS 003)	57	1979	0	1979	
2	Jimmy	(Fiction FICS 9)	60	1980	0	1980	
Purple Kings Male Vocal/Instrumental Duo from the UK							
1	That's The Way You Do It	(Positiva CDTIV 21)	26	1994	0	1994	
Pussycat Mixed Vocal/Instrumental Group From Holland							
1	Mississippi	(Sonet SON 20770	1	1976	0	1976	
2	Smile	(SON 2096)	24	1976	0	1976	
Pyramids Male Vocal/Instrumental Group from Jamaica							
1	Penetration		0	1964	18	1964	(BEST 13002)
2	Train Tour To Rainbow City	(President PT 161)	35	1967	0	1967	
Python Lee Jackson Male Vocal/Instrumental Group from Australia							
1	In A Broken Dream	(YoungBlood YB 1002)	3	1972	0	1972	

LEAD VOCALS ON THE HIT ARE BY, AND SEE ALSO, ROD STEWART

ISSUE	TITLE	UK LBL	UK POS	UK YEAR	US POS	US YEAR	US LBL
Q (1)	Quartet from Beaver Falls, Pennnnsylvania, USA						
	Dancin' Man		0	1977	23	1977	Epic 50335)
Q (2)	Male Production/Instrumental Duo from the UK						
1	Get There	(Arista 74321145972)	37	1993	0	1993	
2	(Everything I Do) I Do It For You	(Bell 74321193062)	47	1994	0	1994	
Q-Bass	Male Production/Instrumental Group from the UK						
1	Hardcore Will Never Die	(Surburban Base Subbase 007)	64	1992	0	1992	
Q-Club	Mixed Vocal/Instrumental Group from Italy						
1	Tell It To My Heart	(Manifesto Fescd 5)	28	1996	0	1996	
Q-Tee	Female Rap Group from the UK						
1	Afrika	(Sbk Sbk 7008)	42	1990	0	1990	
2	Gimme That Body	(Deconstruction Hvn 48cd)	40	1996	0	1996	
3	My Baby Mama		0	1997	94	1997	(Arista 35093)
Q-Tex	Mixed Vocal/Instrumental Group from the UK						
1	The Power Of Love	(Stoatin' Stoat 002cd)	65	1994	0	1994	
2	Believe	(23rd Precinct Third 2cd)	41	1994	0	1994	
3	Let The Love	(23rd Precinct Third 4t)	30	1996	0	1996	
4	Do You Want Me	(23rd Precinct Third 5cd)	48	1996	0	1996	
5	Power Of Love (Re-Mix)	(23rd Precinct Third 7cd)	49	1997	0	1997	
QFX	Male Producer Kirk Turnbull from the UK						
1	Freedom (Ep)	(Epidemic Epicd 4)	41	1995	0	1995	
2	Everytime You Touch Me	(Epidemic Epicd 006)	22	1996	0	1996	
3	You Got The Power	(Epidemic Epicd 007)	33	1996	0	1996	
4	Freedom 2	(Epidemic Epicd 008)	21	1997	0	1997	
Quad City Dj's							
* 1	C'mon N'ride It (The Train)		0	1996	3	1996	(Atlantic 98083)
2	Space Jam (From *Space Jam*)		0	1996	37	1996	(Atlantic 87018)
Quadrophonia	Male Production/Instrumental Group From Belgium						
1	Quadrophonia	(Ars 6567687)	14	1991	0	1991	
2	The Way Of The Future	(Ars 6569937)	40	1991	0	1991	
3	Find The Time (Part One)	(Ars 6576260)	41	1991	0	1991	
Quads	Male Vocal/Instrumental Group from the UK						
1	There Must Be Thousands	(Big Bear Bb23)	66	1979	0	1979	
Quaker City Boys	Lead Singer With This String Band Is Tommy Reilly						
1	Teasin'		0	1959	39	1959	(Swan 4023)
Quantum Jump	Male Vocal/Instrumental Group from the UK						
1	The Lone Ranger	(Electric Wot 33)	5	1979	0	1979	
Quarterflash	Mixed Vocal/Instrumental Group from the USA, Originally Known A Seafood Mama						
1	Harden My Heart	(Geffen Gef A 1838)	49	1982	3	1981	(Geffen 49824)
2	Find Another Fool		0	1982	16	1982	(Geffen 50006)
3	Take Me To Heart		0	1983	14	1983	(Geffen 29603)
Quartz	Male Instrumental Group with Female Vocalist from the UK						
1	We're Comin' At Ya	(Mercury Itmr 2)	65	1990	0	1990	
2	It's Too Late	(Mercury Itm 3)	8	1991	0	1991	
3	Naked Love (Just Say You Want Me)	(Mercury Itm 4)	39	1991	0	1991	
Quartz Lock							
1	Love Eviction	(Warner Bros Bang 2cd)	32	1995	0	1995	

ISSUE	TITLE	UK LBL	UK POS	UK YEAR	US POS	US YEAR	US LBL
Qattara							
1	Come With Me	(Postiva Cdtiv 71)	31	1997	0	1997	
Queen Male Vocal/Instrumental Rock Rand Names: Freddie Mercury, Brian May, John Deacon & Roger Taylor							
1	Seven Seas Of Rhye	(EMI 2121	10	1974	0	1974	
2	Killer Queen	(EMI 2229)	2	1974	12	1975	(Elektra 45226)
3	Now I'm Here	(EMI 2256)	11	1975	0	1975	
* 4	Bohemian Rhapsody	(EMI 2375)	1	1975	9	1976	(Elektra 45297)
5	You're My Best Friend	(EMI 2494)	7	1976	16	1976	(Elektra 45318)
6	Somebody To Love	(EMI 2565)	2	1976	13	1977	(Elektra 45362)
7	Tie Your Mother Down	(EMI 2593)	31	1977	0	1977	
8	Queen's First EP	(EMI 2623)	17	1977	0	1977	
* 9	We Are The Champions	(EMI 2708)	2	1977	4	1978	(Elektra 45441)
10	Spread Your Wings	(EMI 2757)	34	1978	0	1978	
11	Bicycle Race	(EMI 2870)	11	1978	24	1978	(Elektra 45541)
12	Fat Bottomed Girls	(EMI 2870)	11	1978	24	1978	(Elektra 45541)
13	Don't Stop Me Now	(EMI 2910)	9	1979	0	1979	
14	Love Of My Life	(EMI 2959)	63	1979	0	1979	
* 15	Crazy Little Thing Called Love	(EMI 5001)	2	1979	1	1980	(Elektra 46579)
16	Save Me	(EMI 5022)	11	1980	0	1980	
17	Play The Game	(EMI 5076)	14	1980	0	1980	
* 18	Another One Bites The Dust	(EMI 5102)	7	1980	1	1980	(Elektra 47031)
19	Flash	(EMI 5126)	10	1980	0	1980	
20	Under Pressure	(EMI 5250)	1	1981	29	1981	(Elektra 47235)
21	Body Language	(EMI 5293)	25	1982	11	1982	(Elektra 47452)
22	Las Palabras De Amour	(EMI 5316)	17	1982	0	1982	
23	Back Chat	(EMI 5325)	40	1982	0	1982	
24	Radio Ga Ga	(EMI Queen 1)	2	1984	16	1984	(Capitol 5317)
25	I Want To Break Free	(EMI Queen 2)	3	1984	0	1984	
26	It's A Hard Life	(EMI Queen 3)	6	1984	0	1984	
27	Hammer To Fall	(EMI Queen 4)	13	1984	0	1984	
28	Thank God It's Christmas	(EMI Queen 5)	21	1984	0	1984	
29	One Vision	(EMI Queen 6)	7	1985	0	1985	
30	A Kind Of Magic	(EMI Queen 7)	3	1986	0	1986	
31	Friends Will Be Friends	(EMI Queen 8)	14	1986	0	1986	
32	Who Wants To Live For Ever	(EMI Queen 9)	24	1986	0	1986	
33	I Want It All	(EMI Queen 10)	3	1989	0	1989	
34	Breakthru'	(EMI Queen 11)	7	1989	0	1989	
35	The Invisible Man	(EMI Queen 12)	12	1989	0	1989	
36	Scandal	(EMI Queen 14)	25	1989	0	1989	
37	The Miracle	(EMI Queen 15)	21	1989	0	1989	
38	Innuendo	(EMI Queen 16)	1	1991	0	1991	
39	I'm Going Slightly Mad	(Parlophone Queen 17)	22	1991	0	1991	
40	Headlong	(Parlophone Queen 18)	14	1991	0	1991	
41	The Show Must Go On	(Parlophone Queen 19)	16	1991	0	1991	
42	The Show Must Go On (Re-Entry)	(Parlophone Queen 19)	27	1991	0	1991	
43	Bohemian Rhapsody (Re-Issue)	(Parlophone Queen 20)	1	1991	2	1992	(Hollywood 64794)
44	Live Live (EP)	(Parlophone Cdrs 6340)	1	1993	0	1993	
45	Somebody To Love (Re-Issue)		0	1993	30	1993	(Hollywood 64647)
46	Live Live (Ep) (Re-Entry)	(Parlophone Cdrs 6340)	74	1993	0	1993	
47	Heaven For Everyone	(Parlophone Cdqueen 21)	2	1995	0	1995	
48	A Winter Tale	(Parlophone Cdqueen 22)	6	1995	0	1995	
49	Too Much Love Will Kill You	(Parlophone Cdqueen 23)	15	1996	0	1996	
50	Let Me Live	(Parlophone Cdqueen 24)	9	1996	0	1996	
51	You Don't Fool Me	(Parlophone Cdqueen 25)	17	1996	0	1996	
Queen Latifah Female Rapper from the USA							
1	Mama Gave Birth To The Soul Children	(Gee Street Gee 26)	14	1990	0	1990	
2	Find A Way	(Ahead Of Our Time Ccut 8)	52	1990	0	1990	
3	Fly Girl	(Gee Street Gee 34)	67	1991	0	1991	
4	What'cha Gonna Go	(Epic 6593072)	21	1993	0	1993	
5	U.N.I.T.Y.	(Motown Tmgcd 1422)	74	1994	23	1993	(Motown 2225)
6	Mr. Big Stuff	(Motown 5736572)	31	1997	0	1997	
Queensryche Male Vocal/Instrumental Group from the USA Names: Chris Degarmo, Michael Wilton, Geoff Tate, Eddie Jackson & Scott Rockenfield							
1	Eyes Of A Stranger	(EMI USA Mt 65)	59	1989	0	1989	
2	Empire	(EMI USA Mt 90)	61	1990	0	1990	
3	Silent Lucidity	(EMI USA Mt 94)	34	1991	9	1991	(EMI 50345)

ISSUE	TITLE	UK LBL	UK POS	UK YEAR	US POS	US YEAR	US LBL
4	Best I Can	(EMI USA Mt 97)	36	1991	0	1991	
5	Jet City Woman	(EMI USA Mt 98)	39	1991	0	1991	
6	Silent Lucidity (Re-Issue)	(EMI USA Mt 104)	18	1992	0	1992	
7	I Am I	(EMI Cdmts 109)	40	1995	0	1995	
8	Bridge	(EMI Manhattan Cdmts 111)	40	1995	0	1995	
Quench Male Instrumental/Production Duo from Australia							
1	Dreams	(Infectious Infect 3cdr)	75	1996	0	1996	
Quentin & Ash Female Vocal Duo from the UK							
1	Tell Him	(East West Ew 049cd)	25	1996	0	1996	
Questions Male Vocal/Instrumental Group from the UK							
1	Price You Pay	(Respond Kob 702)	56	1983	0	1983	
2	Tear Soup	(Respond Kob 705)	66	1983	0	1983	
3	Tuesday Sunshine	(Respond Kob 707)	46	1984	0	1984	
Quick Male Vocal/Instrumental Group from the UK							
1	Rhythm Of The Jungle Rock	(Epic Epc A 2013)	41	1982	0	1982	
Quiet Five Male Vocal/Instrumental Group from the UK							
1	When The Morning Sun Dries The Dew	(Parlophone R 5273)	45	1965	0	1965	
2	Homeward Bound	(Parlophone R 5421)	44	1966	0	1966	
Quiet Riot Male Vocal/Instrumental Group from the USA Lead Singer with the quartet is Kevin Dubrow							
* 1	Cum On Feel The Noize	(Epic A 3968)	45	1983	5	1983	(Pasha 04005)
2	Bang Your Head (Mental Health)	(Epic A 3968)	45	1984	31	1984	(Pasha 04267)
Quincy Jones Male Producer/Instrumentalist – Quincy Delight Jones Jr B: 14 Mar 1933 Chicago							
1	Stuff Like That	(A&M Ams 7367)	34	1978	21	1978	(A&M 2043)
2	Ai No Corrida (I-No-Ko-Ree-Da)	(A&M Ams 8109)	14	1981	28	1981	(A&M 2309)
3	Razzamatazz	(A&M Ams 8140)	11	1981	0	1981	
4	Just Once		0	1981	17	1981	(A&M 2357)
5	Betcha' Wouldn't Hurt Me	(A&M Ams 8157)	52	1981	0	1981	
6	One Hundred Ways		0	1982	14	1982	(A&M 2387)
7	I'll Be Good To You	(Qwest W 2697)	21	1990	18	1989	(Qwest 22697)
* 8	Secret Garden (Sweet Seduction Suite)	(Qweat W 9992)	67	1990	31	1990	(Qwest 19992)
9	Stomp	(Qwest W 0372cd)	28	1996	0	1996	
Quin-Tones Names: Carolyn Holmes, Kenny Sexton, Roberta Haymon, Jeannie Crist & Ronnie Scott							
1	Down The Aisle Of Love		0	1958	18	1958	(Hunt 321)
Quireboys Male Vocal/Instrumental Group from the UK							
1	7 o'Clock	(Parlophone R 6230)	36	1989	0	1989	
2	Hey You	(Parlophone R 6241)	14	1990	0	1990	
3	I Don't Love You Anymore	(Parlophone R 6248)	24	1990	0	1990	
4	There She Goes Again / Misled	(Parlophone R 6267)	37	1990	0	1990	
5	Tramps And Thieves	(Parlophone R 6323)	41	1992	0	1992	
6	Brother Louie	(Parlophone Cdr 6335)	31	1993	0	1993	
Quivver Male Production/Instrumental Duo from the UK							
1	Saxy Lady	(A&M 5805152)	58	1994	0	1994	
2	Believe In Me	(Perfecto Perf 111cd)	56	1995	0	1995	
Qwilo & Felix Da Housecat							
1	Dirty Motha	(Manifesto Fescd 29)	66	1997	0	1997	

R

ISSUE	TITLE	UK LBL	UK POS	UK YEAR	US POS	US YEAR	US LBL
R & J Stone Mixed Vocal Duo from the USA/UK							
1	We Do It	(RCA 2616)	5	1976	0	1976	
R. Dean Taylor Male Vocalist, B: 1939 In Toronto							
1	Gotta See Jane	(Tamla Motown Tmg 656)	17	1968	0	1968	
2	Indiana Wants Me	(Tamla Motown Tmg 763)	2	1971	5	1970	(Rare Earth 5013)
3	There's A Ghost In My House	(Tamla Motown Tmg 896)	3	1974	0	1974	
4	Window Shopping	(Polydor 2058502)	36	1974	0	1974	
5	Gotta See Jane (Re-Issue)	(Tamla Motown Tmg 918)	41	1974	0	1974	
R. Kelly Male Vocalist/Multi-Instrumentalist from Chicago							
1	She's Got That Vibe	(Jive Jive 292)	57	1992	0	1992	
2	Honey Love		0	1992	39	1992	(Jive 42031)
3	Dedicated		0	1993	31	1993	(Jive 42115)
* 4	Sex Me	(Jive Jivecd 346)	75	1993	20	1993	(Jive 42161)
* 5	Your Body's Callin'	(Jive Jivecd 353)	19	1994	13	1994	(Jive 42220)
6	Summer Bunnies	(Jive Jivecd 358)	23	1994	0	1994	
7	She's Got That Vibe (Re-Issue)	(Jive Jivecd 364)	3	1994	0	1994	
* 8	Bump N' Grind	(Jive Jivecd 368)	8	1995	1	1994	(Jive 42207)
9	The 4 Play (EP)	(Jive Jivecd 376)	23	1995	0	1995	
* 10	You Remind Me Of Something	(Jive Jivecd 388)	24	1995	4	1995	(Jive 42344)
11	Down Low (Nobody Has To Know)	(Jive Jivercd392)	23	1996	4	1996	
12	Thank God It's Friday	(Jive Jivercd395)	14	1996	0	1996	
* 13	I Can't Sleep Baby (If I)		0	1996	5	1996	(Jive 42377)
14	I Believe I Can Fly (From Space Jam)	(Jive Jivecd 415)	1	1997	2	1996	(Atlantic 42422)
15	Gotham City	(Jive Jivecd 428)	9	1997	0	1997	
R.B. Greaves Real Name Ronald Bertram Aloysius Greaves B: 28 Nov 1944							
* 1	Take A Letter Maria		0	1969	2	1969	(Atco 6714)
2	Always Something There To Remind Me		0	1970	27	1970	(Atco 6726)
R.E.M. Male Vocal/Instrumental Group from the USA Names: Peter Buck, Mike Mills, Bill Berry & Michael Stipe							
1	The One I Love	(Irs Irm 46)	51	1987	9	1987	(Irs 53171)
2	Finest Worksong	(Irs Irm 161)	50	1988	0	1988	
3	Stand	(Warner Bros W 7577)	51	1989	6	1989	(Warner Bros 27688)
4	Orange Crush	(Warner Bros W 2960)	28	1989	0	1989	
5	Stand (Re-Issue)	(Warner Bros W 2833)	48	1989	0	1989	
* 6	Losing My Religion	(Warner Bros W 0015)	19	1991	4	1991	(Warner Bros 19392)
7	Shiny Happy People	(Warner Brosw 0027)	6	1991	10	1991	(Warner Bros 19242)
8	Near Wild Heaven	(Warner Brosw 0055)	27	1991	0	1991	
9	The One I Love (Re-Issue)	(Irs Irm 178)	16	1991	0	1991	
10	Radio Song	(Warner Brosw 0072)	28	1991	0	1991	
11	It's The End Of The World As We Know It	(Irs Irm 180)	39	1991	0	1991	
12	Drive	(Warner Bros W 0136)	11	1992	28	1992	(Warner Bros 18729)
13	Man On The Moon	(Warner Bros W 0143)	18	1992	30	1993	(Warner Bros 18642)
14	The Sidewinder Sleeps Tonight	(Warner Bros W 0152cd1)	17	1993	0	1993	
15	Everybody Hurts	(Warner Bros W 0169cd1)	7	1993	29	1993	(Warner Bros 18638)
16	Nightswimming	(Warner Bros W 0184cd)	27	1993	0	1993	
17	Find The River	(Warner Bros W 0211cd)	54	1993	0	1993	
18	What's The Frequency, Kenneth?	(Warner Bros W 0265cd)	9	1994	21	1994	(Warner Bros 18050)
19	Bang And Blame	(Warner Brosw 0275cd)	15	1994	19	1995	(Warner Bros 17994)
20	Crush With Eyeliner	(Warner 1952 (Warner Bros W 0281cd)	23	1995	0	1995	
21	Strange Currencies	(Warner Bros	9	1995	0	1995	
22	Tongue	(Warner Bros W 0308cd)	13	1995	0	1995	

ISSUE	TITLE	UK LBL	UK POS	UK YEAR	US POS	US YEAR	US LBL
23	Bittersweet Me	(Warner Bros W 0377cd)	19	1996	46	1996	(Warner Bros 17490)
24	E-Bow The Letter	(Warner Bros W 0369cd)	4	1996	49	1996	(Warner Bros 17529)
25	Electrolite	(Warner Brosw 0383cd)	29	1996	96	1997	(Warner Bros 17446)
Racey Male Vocal/Instrumental Group from the UK							
1	Lay Your Love On Me	(Rak 284)	3	1978	0	1978	
2	Some Girls	(Rak 291)	2	1979	0	1979	
3	Boy Oh Boy	(Rak 297)	22	1979	0	1979	
4	Runaround Sue	(Rak 325)	13	1980	0	1980	
Rachel Sweet Female Vocalist, B: 1963 Akron, Ohio							
! 1	We Live In Two Different Worlds		0	1976	96	1976	(Derrick 1000)
2	B-A-B-Y	(Stiff Buy 39)	35	1978	0	1978	
3	Everlasting Love	(CBS A 1405)	35	1981	0	1981	
Racing Cars Male Vocal/Instrumental Group from the UK							
1	They Shoot Horses Don't They	(Chrysalis Chs2129)	14	1977	0	1977	
Radha Krishna Temple Mixed Vocal/Instrumental Group From Oxford Street, London, England							
1	Hare Krishna Mantra	(Apple 15)	12	1969	0	1969	
2	Govinda	(Apple 25)	23	1970	0	1970	
Radiants R&B Vocal Group from the USA							
1	Voice Your Choice		0	1965	51	1965	(Chess 1904)
Radical Rob Male Producer, Real Name Rob McLuan from the UK							
1	Monkey Wah	(R&S Rsuk 8)	67	1992	0	1992	
Radio Stars Male Vocal/Instrumental Group from the UK							
1	Nervous Wreck	(Chiswick Ns 23)	39	1978	0	1978	
Radiohead Male Vocal/Instrumental Group from the UK							
1	Anyone Can Play Guitar	(Parlophonecdr 6333)	32	1993	0	1993	
2	Pop Is Dead	(Parlophonecdr 6345)	42	1993	0	1993	
3	Creep	(Parlophone Cdr 6359)	7	1993	34	1993	(Capitol 44932)
4	My Iron Lung	(Parlophonecdr 6394)	24	1994	0	1994	
5	High And Dry / Planet Telex	(Parlophonecdr 6405)	17	1995	0	1995	
6	Fake Plastic Trees	(Parlophonecdrs 6411)	20	1995	0	1995	
7	Just	(Parlophonecdrs 6415)	19	1995	0	1995	
8	Street Spirit (Fade Out)	(Parlophonecdrs 6419)	5	1996	0	1996	
9	Paranoid Android	(Parlophonecdodata 01)	3	1997	0	1997	
10	Karma Police	(Parlophonecdodatas 03)	8	1997	0	1997	
Raekwon Male Vocalist, Real Name Shallah Raekwon Aka Chef Raekwon & Lou Diamonds							
1	Ice Cream		0	1995	37	1995	(Loud/RCA 64426)
Raf Mixed Vocal/Instrumental Group From Italy							
1	We've Got To Live Together	(PWLcontinental PWL 218)	34	1992	0	1992	
2	Take Me Higher	(Media Mrlcd0012)	71	1994	0	1994	
3	Take Me Higher (Re-Mix)	(Media Mcstd40026)	59	1996	0	1996	
4	Angel's Symphony	(Media Mcstd40051)	73	1996	0	1996	
Raffaella Carra Female Vocalist from Italy							
1	Do It Do It Again	(Epic Epc 6094)	9	1978	0	1978	
Rage Male Vocal/Instrumental Group from the UK							
1	Run To You	(Pulse 8 Lose 33)	3	1992	0	1992	
2	Why Don't You	(Pulse 8 Cdlose39)	44	1993	0	1993	
3	House Of The Rising Sun	(Pulse 8 Cdlose43)	41	1993	0	1993	
Rage Against The Machine Male Vocal/Instrumental Group from the USA							
1	Killing In The Name	(Epic 6584922)	25	1993	0	1993	
2	Bullet In The Head	(Epic 6592582)	16	1993	0	1993	
3	Bombtrack	(Epic 6594712)	37	1993	0	1993	
4	Bulls On Parade	(Epic 6631522)	8	1996	0	1996	
5	People Of The Sun	9epic 6636282)	26	1996	0	1996	
Ragga Twins Male Vocal Group from the UK							
1	Illegal Gunshot / Spliffhead	(Shut Up Anddance Suad 7)	51	1990	0	1990	
2	Wipe The Needle / Juggling	(Shut Up Anddance Suad 125)	71	1991	0	1991	
3	Hooligan 69	(Shut Up And Dance Suad 165)	56	1991	0	1991	
4	Mixed Truth / Bring Up The Mic Some	(Shut Up Anddance Suad 275)	65	1992	0	1992	
5	Shine Eye	(Shut Up Anddance Suad 325)	63	1992	0	1992	

ISSUE	TITLE	UK LBL	UK POS	UK YEAR	US POS	US YEAR	US LBL
Ragtimers	Male Vocal/Instrumental Group from the UK						
1	The Sting	(Pye 7n 45323)	46	1974	0	1974	
2	The Sting (Re-Entry)	(Pye 7n 45323)	31	1974	0	1974	
Rah Band	Mixed Vocal/Instrumental Group from the UK						
1	The Crunch	(Good Earth Gd7)	6	1977	0	1977	
2	Falcon	(Djm Djs 10954)	35	1980	0	1980	
3	Slide	(Djm Djs 10964)	50	1981	0	1981	
4	Perfumed Garden	(Kr Kr 5)	45	1982	0	1982	
5	Messages From The Stars	(Tmt Tmt 5)	42	1983	0	1983	
6	Are You Satisfied? (Funka Nova)	(RCA RCA 470)	70	1985	0	1985	
7	Clouds Across The Moon	(RCA Pb 40025)	6	1985	0	1985	
Rahni Harris & F.L.O.	Male Instrumental Group from the USA						
1	Six Million Steps	(Mercury 6007198)	43	1978	0	1978	
Railway Children	Male Vocal/Instrumental Group from the UK						
1	Every Beat Of My Heart	(Virgin Vs 1237)	68	1990	0	1990	
2	Music Stop	(Virgin Vs 1255)	66	1990	0	1990	
3	So Right	(Virgin Vs 1289)	68	1990	0	1990	
4	Every Beat Of My Heart (Re-Entry)	(Virgin Vs 1237)	24	1991	0	1991	
5	Something So Good	(Virgin Vs 1318)	57	1991	0	1991	
Rain Tree Crow	Male Vocal/Instrumental Group from the UK						
1	Blackwater	(Virgin Vs 1340)	62	1991	0	1991	
Rainbow	Hard Rock Band Led By Ritchie Blackmore And Roger Glover from the UK						
1	Kill The King	(Polydor 2066845)	44	1977	0	1977	
2	Long Live Rock 'n' Roll	(Polydor 2066913)	33	1978	0	1978	
3	L.A. Connection	(Polydor 2066968)	40	1978	0	1978	
4	Since You've Been Gone	(Polydor Posp70)	6	1979	0	1979	
5	All Night Long	(Polydor Posp104)	5	1980	0	1980	
6	I Surrender	(Polydor Posp221)	3	1981	0	1981	
7	Can't Happen Here	(Polydor Posp251)	20	1981	0	1981	
8	Kill The King (Re-Issue)	(Polydor Posp274)	41	1981	0	1981	
9	Stone Cold	(Polydor Posp421)	34	1982	40	1982	(Mercury 76146)
10	Street Of Dreams	(Polydor Posp631)	52	1983	0	1983	
11	Can't Let You Go	(Polydor Posp654)	43	1983	0	1983	
Rainbow Cottage	Male Vocal/Instrumental Group from the UK						
1	Seagull	(Pennyfarthing Pen 906)	33	1976	0	1976	
Raindrops	Husband And Wife Team Of Jeff Barry & Ellie Greenwich						
1	The Kind Of Boy You Can't Forget		0	1963	17	1963	(Jubilee 5455)
Rainmakers	Male Vocal/Instrumental Group from the UK						
1	Let My People Go-Go	(Mercury Mer238)	18	1987	0	1987	
Raja Nee	Female Vocalist from the USA						
1	Turn It Up	(Perspective5874872)	42	1995	0	1995	
Ral Donner	Male Vocalist, B: 10 Feb 1943 Chicago						
1	Girl Of My Best Friend		0	1961	19	1961	(Gone 5102)
2	You Don't Know What You've Got (Until You Lose It)	(Parlophone R4820)	25	1961	4	1961	(Gone 5108)
3	Please Don't Go		0	1961	39	1961	(Gone 5114)
4	She's Everything (I Wanted You To Be)		0	1962	18	1962	(Gone 5121)
Ralf Bendix	A Former Director With TWA Airlines In Germany						
* 1	Baby Sittin' Boogie	Not Known	0	1961	0	1961	Not Known
Ralph Flanagan Orchestra	Male Pianist/Orchestra Leader from the USA						
1	You're Breaking My Heart		0	1949	14	1949	(Bluebird 0001)
2	Don't Cry, Joe (Let Her Go, Let Her Go, Le Ther Go)		0	1949	9	1949	(Bluebird 0007)
3	My Hero (From The Chocolate Soldiers)		0	1949	27	1949	(Bluebird 0006)
4	Dear Hearts And Gentle People		0	1950	24	1950	(Bluebird 0016)
5	Rag Mop		0	1950	3	1950	(RCA Victor 78-3688)
6	Joshua		0	1950	17	1950	(RCA Victor 3724)
7	The Stars And Stripes Forever		0	1950	28	1950	(RCA Victor 3762)
8	Tzena Tzena Tzena		0	1950	16	1950	(RCA Victor 3847)
9	Mona Lisa (From Captain Carey, U.S.A.)		0	1950	16	1950	(RCA Victor 3888)
10	The Red We Want Is The Red We've Got (In The Old Red, White, & Blue)		0	1950	13	1950	(RCA Victor 3904)

ISSUE	TITLE	UK LBL	UK POS	UK YEAR	US POS	US YEAR	US LBL
11	Nevertheless (I'm In Love With You)		0	1950	10	1950	(RCA Victor 3904)
12	La Vie En Rose		0	1950	27	1950	(RCA Victor 3889)
13	Harbour Lights		0	1950	5	1950	(RCA Victor 3911)
14	Oh, Babe!		0	1950	27	1950	(RCA Victor 3954)
15	Blues (From An American In Paris)		0	1951	15	1951	(RCA Victor 4247)
16	Slow-Poke		0	1951	6	1951	(RCA Victor 4373)
17	Delicado		0	1952	26	1952	(RCA Victor 4706)
18	I Should Care		0	1952	4	1952	(RCA Victor 4885)
19	Hot Toddy		0	1953	7	1953	(RCA Victor 5095)
20	A-L-B-U-Q-U-E-R-Q-U-E		0	1953	18	1953	(RCA Victor 5237)
21	Rub-A-Dub-Dub		0	1953	18	1953	(RCA Victor 5361)
22	Angela Mia		0	1954	27	1954	(RCA Victor 5676)

Ralph Marterie & His Orchestra Male Orchestra Leader, B: 24 Dec 1914 Naples, Italy

ISSUE	TITLE	UK LBL	UK POS	UK YEAR	US POS	US YEAR	US LBL
1	So Long (It's Been Good To Know You)		0	1951	26	1951	(Mercury 5570)
2	Pretend		0	1953	6	1953	(Mercury 70045)
* 3	Caravan		0	1953	6	1953	(Mercury 70097)
4	Crazy, Man, Crazy		0	1953	13	1953	(Mercury 70153)
5	Warsaw Concerto (From Suicide Squadron)		0	1953	27	1953	(Mercury 70221)
6	The Creep (From O Cangaceiro)		0	1954	25	1954	(Mercury 70281)
7	Skokiaan		0	1954	3	1954	(Mercury 70432)
8	Tricky		0	1957	25	1957	(Mercury 71050)
9	Shish-Kebab		0	1957	10	1957	(Mercury 71092)

RALPH BEGAN HIS CAREER WITH THE DANNY ORIOLE ORCHESTRA AS A TRUMPETER • OBITUARY: D: 8 OCT 1978.

Ralph McTell Male Vocalist from the UK

ISSUE	TITLE	UK LBL	UK POS	UK YEAR	US POS	US YEAR	US LBL
1	Streets Of London	(Reprise K 14380)	2	1974	0	1974	
2	Dreams Of You	(Warner Brosk 16648)	36	1975	0	1975	

Ralph Tresvant Male Vocalist, B: 16 May 1968 And Raised In Massachusetts

ISSUE	TITLE	UK LBL	UK POS	UK YEAR	US POS	US YEAR	US LBL
* 1	Sensitivity	(MCA Mcs 1462)	18	1991	4	1990	(MCA 53932)
2	Stone Cold Gentleman		0	1991	34	1991	(MCA 54043)
3	The Best Things In Life Are Free	(Perss 7400)	2	1992	10	1992	(Perspective 0010)
4	The Best Things In Life Are Free (Re-Issue)	(A&M 5813112)	7	1995	0	1995	

HITS 3,4 ARE CREDITED TO LUTHER VANDROSS AND JANET JACKSON WITH SPECIAL GUESTS BBD AND RALPH TRESVANT
HE WAS ALSO WITH THE R&B QUINTET NEW EDITION

Ram Jam Male Vocal/Instrumental Rock Quartet from the USA, Led By Bill Bartlett

ISSUE	TITLE	UK LBL	UK POS	UK YEAR	US POS	US YEAR	US LBL
1	Black Betty	(Epic Epc 5492)	7	1977	18	1977	(Epic 50357)
2	Black Betty (Re-Mix)	(Epic 655430 7)	13	1990	0	1990	

Ramblers (From The Abbey Hey Junior School) Children's Choir from the UK

ISSUE	TITLE	UK LBL	UK POS	UK YEAR	US POS	US YEAR	US LBL
1	The Sparrow	(Decca F 13860)	11	1979	0	1979	

Ramones Male Vocal/Instrumental Group from the USA

ISSUE	TITLE	UK LBL	UK POS	UK YEAR	US POS	US YEAR	US LBL
1	Sheena Is A Punk Rocker	(Sire Ram 001)	22	1977	0	1977	
2	Swallow My Pride	(Sire 6078 607)	36	1977	0	1977	
3	Don't Come Close	(Sire Sre 1031)	39	1978	0	1978	
4	Rock 'n' Roll High School	(Sire Sir 4021)	67	1979	0	1979	
5	Baby I Love You	(Sire Sir 4031)	80	1980	0	1980	
6	Do You Remember Rock 'n' Roll Radio	(Sire Sir 4037)	54	1980	0	1980	
7	Somebody Put Something In My Drink	(Beggarsbanquet Beg 157)	69	1986	0	1986	
8	Something To Believe In	(Beggars Banquet Beg 157)	69	1986	0	1986	
9	Poison Heart	(Chrysalis Chs3917)	69	1992	0	1992	

Ramp Male Instrumental/Production Duo from the UK

ISSUE	TITLE	UK LBL	UK POS	UK YEAR	US POS	US YEAR	US LBL
1	Rock The Discotek '96	(Loaded Loadcd 30)	49	1996	0	1996	

Rampage Male Vocal/Instrumental/Production Duo from the UK

ISSUE	TITLE	UK LBL	UK POS	UK YEAR	US POS	US YEAR	US LBL
1	The Monkees	(Almo Soundscdalmos 017)	51	1995	0	1995	

Ramrods Mixed Instrumental Group from the USA Names: Eugene Morrow, Richard Lane, Vincent Bell Lee & his sister Claire

ISSUE	TITLE	UK LBL	UK POS	UK YEAR	US POS	US YEAR	US LBL
1	(Ghost) Riders In The Sky	(London Hlu9282)	8	1961	30	1961	(Amy 813)

Ramsey Lewis Male Pianist, B: 27 May 1935, Chicago

ISSUE	TITLE	UK LBL	UK POS	UK YEAR	US POS	US YEAR	US LBL
* 1	The In Crowd		0	1965	5	1965	(Argo 5506)
* 2	Hang On Sloopy		0	1965	11	1965	(Chess 5522)
3	A Hard Day's Night		0	1966	29	1966	(Chess 5525)
* 4	Wade In The Water	(Chess 6145 004)	31	1972	19	1966	(Chess 5541)

Ran-Dells Real Names Steve & Robert Rappaport With John Spirit

ISSUE	TITLE	UK LBL	UK POS	UK YEAR	US POS	US YEAR	US LBL
1	Martian Hop		0	1963	16	1963	(Chairman 4403)

ISSUE	TITLE	UK LBL	UK POS	UK YEAR	US POS	US YEAR	US LBL
Rancid Male Vocal/Instrumental Group from the USA							
1	Time Bomb	(Out Of Stepwoos 8cds)	56	1995	0	1995	
Randy & The Rainbows Originally Called Jr & The Counts, Lead Singer With The Group Is Dominick Safuto							
1	Denise		0	1963	10	1963	(Rust 5059)
Randy Crawford Female Vocalist from the USA							
1	Last Night At Dance Land	(Warner Brosk 17631)	61	1980	0	1980	
2	One Day I'll Fly Away	(Warner Brosk 17680)	2	1980	0	1980	
3	You Might Need Somebody	(Warner Bros k 17803)	11	1981	0	1981	
4	Rainy Night In Georgia	(Warner Bros k 17840)	18	1981	0	1981	
5	Secret Conbination	(Warner Bros k 17872)	48	1981	0	1981	
6	Imagine	(Warner Brosk 17906)	60	1982	0	1982	
7	Imagine (Re-Entry)	(Warner Bros k 17906)	75	1982	0	1982	
8	One Hello	(Warner Bros k 17948)	48	1982	0	1982	
9	He Reminds Me	(Warner Brosk 17970)	65	1983	0	1983	
10	Night Line	(Warner Bros w 9530)	51	1983	0	1983	
11	Almaz	(Warner Bros w 8583)	4	1986	0	1986	
12	Diamante	(London Lon313)	44	1992	0	1992	
Randy Edelman Male Vocalist from the USA							
1	Concrete And Clay	(20th Century Btc 2261)	11	1976	0	1976	
2	Uptown Uptempo Woman	(20th Century Btc 2225)	25	1976	0	1976	
3	You	(20th Century Btc 2253)	49	1977	0	1977	
4	Nobody Made Me	(Rocketxpress 81)	60	1982	0	1982	
Randy Meisner Male Vocalist, B: 8 Mar 1946 Nebraska, With The Eagles From 1971-77							
1	Deep Inside My Heart		0	1980	22	1980	(Epic 50939)
2	Hearts On Fire		0	1981	19	1981	(Epic 50964)
3	Never Been In Love		0	1982	28	1982	(Epic 03032)
Randy Newman Male Singer/Pianist, B: 28 Nov 1943 New Orleans							
* 1	Short People		0	1977	2	1977	(Warner Bros 8492)
Randy Starr Real Name Warren Nadel B: 2 Jul 1930 New York City							
1	After School		0	1957	32	1957	(Dale 100)
Randy Vanwarmer Male Singer/Songwriter/Guitarist, Real Name Randall Van Wormer B: 30 Mar 1955 Indian Hills, Colorado.							
* 1	Just When I Needed You Most	(Bearsville Wip6516)	8	1979	4	1979	(Bearsville 0334)
Raphael Saadiq Male Vocalist, Former Member Of Tony! Toni! Tone!							
1	Ask Of You		0	1995	19	1995	(550 Music 77862)
Rapination Male Prodction/Instrumental Duo From Italy							
1	Love Is The Right Way	(Logic74321128097)	22	1992	0	1992	
2	Here's My A	(Logic74321153092)	69	1993	0	1993	
3	Love Me The Right Way (Re-Mix)	(Logic74321404442)	55	1996	0	1996	
Rappin' 4-Tay Male Rapper, Real Name Anthony Forte From San Francisco							
1	Playaz Club	(Cooltempodcool 310	63	1995	36	1994	(Chrysalis 58267)
2	I'll Be Around	(Cooltempodcool 306)	30	1995	39	1995	(Rag Top 58331)
Rare Mixe Vocal/Instrumental Group from the UK							
1	Something Wild	(Equatoraxiscd 011)	57	1996	0	1996	
Rare Bird Male Vocal/Instrumental Group from the UK, Stephen Gould, Mark Ashton, Dave Kaffinetti & Graham Field							
* 1	Sympathy	(Charisma Cd120)	27	1970	0	1970	
Rare Earth Names Gil Bridges, John Parrish, Rod Richards, Kenny James & Pete Rivers							
* 1	Get Ready		0	1970	4	1970	(Rare Earth 5012)
2	(I Know) I'm Losing You		0	1970	7	1970	(Rare Earth 5017)
3	Born To Wander		0	1971	17	1971	(Rare Earth 5021)
4	I Just Want To Celebrate		0	1971	7	1971	(Rare Earth 5031)
5	Hey Big Brother		0	1971	19	1971	(Rare Earth 5038)
6	Warm Ride		0	1978	39	1978	(Prodigal 0640)
Group Used The Name Sunliners In The 60s							
Rascals Male Vocal/Instrumental Group from the USA							
1	I Ain't Gonna Eat Out My Heart Anymore		0	1965	52	1965	(Atlantic 2312)
* 2	Good Lovin'		0	1966	1	1966	(Atlantic 2321)
3	You Better Run		0	1966	20	1966	(Atlantic 2338)
4	Come On Up		0	1966	43	1966	(Atlantic 2353)
5	I've Been Lonely Too Long		0	1967	16	1967	(Atlantic 2377)
* 6	Groovin'	(Atlantic 584111)	8	1967	1	1967	(Atlantic 2401)
7	A Girl Like You	(Atlantic 584128)	31	1967	10	1967	(Atlantic 2424)

ISSUE	TITLE	UK LBL	UK POS	UK YEAR	US POS	US YEAR	US LBL
8	How Can I Be Sure		0	1967	4	1967	(Atlantic 2438)
9	It's Wonderful		0	1967	20	1967	(Atlantic 2463)
* 10	A Beautiful Morning		0	1968	3	1968	(Atlantic 2493)
* 11	People Got To Be Free		0	1968	1	1968	(Atlantic 2537)
12	A Ray Of Hope		0	1968	24	1968	(Atlantic 2584)
13	Heaven		0	1969	39	1969	(Atlantic 2599)
14	See		0	1969	27	1969	(Atlantic 2634)
15	Carry Me Back		0	1969	26	1969	(Atlantic 2664)

NAMES DINO DANELLI, FELIX CAVALIERE, EDDIE BRIGATI & GENE COMISH • HIT 1-7 ARE CREDITED TO THE YOUNG RASCALS

Raspberries Names Eric Carmen, Wally Bryson, David Smalley & Jim Bonifanti

ISSUE	TITLE	UK LBL	UK POS	UK YEAR	US POS	US YEAR	US LBL
* 1	Go All The Way		0	1972	5	1972	(Capitol 3348)
2	I Wanna Be With You		0	1972	6	1972	(Capitol 3473)
3	Let's Pretend		0	1973	35	1973	(Captiol 3546)
4	Overnight Sensation (Hit Record)		0	1974	18	1974	(Captol 3946)

Ratpack Male Production/Instrumental Duo from the UK

ISSUE	TITLE	UK LBL	UK POS	UK YEAR	US POS	US YEAR	US LBL
1	Searchin' For My Rizla	(Big Giant Bigt02)	58	1992	0	1992	

Ratt Lead Singer With The Quintet Is Stephen Pearcy

ISSUE	TITLE	UK LBL	UK POS	UK YEAR	US POS	US YEAR	US LBL
1	Round And Round		0	1984	12	1984	(Atlantic 89693)
2	Lay It Down		0	1985	40	1985	(Atlantic 89546)

Rattles Male Vocal/Instrumental Group From Germany

ISSUE	TITLE	UK LBL	UK POS	UK YEAR	US POS	US YEAR	US LBL
* 1	The Witch	(Decca F 23058)	8	1970	0	1970	

Raul Orellana Male Producer From France

ISSUE	TITLE	UK LBL	UK POS	UK YEAR	US POS	US YEAR	US LBL
1	The Real Wild House	(RCA Bcm 322)	29	1989	0	1989	

Raven Maize Male Vocalist from the USA

ISSUE	TITLE	UK LBL	UK POS	UK YEAR	US POS	US YEAR	US LBL
1	Forever Together	(Republic Lic014)	67	1989	0	1989	

Ravesignal Iii Male Producer, Real Name Raymond Bolland From Belgium

ISSUE	TITLE	UK LBL	UK POS	UK YEAR	US POS	US YEAR	US LBL
1	Horsepower	(R&S Rsuk 6)	61	1991	0	1991	

Raw Silk Female Vocal Group from the USA

ISSUE	TITLE	UK LBL	UK POS	UK YEAR	US POS	US YEAR	US LBL
1	Do It To The Music	(Kr Kr 14)	18	1982	0	1982	
2	Just In Time	(West End Wend2)	49	1983	0	1983	

Raw Stylus Mixed Vocal/Instrumental Duo from the UK

ISSUE	TITLE	UK LBL	UK POS	UK YEAR	US POS	US YEAR	US LBL
1	Believe In Me	(Wired Wired234)	66	1996	0	1996	

Ray Anthony Real Name Raymond Antonini B: 20 Jan 1922 Bentleyville, Pennsylvania

ISSUE	TITLE	UK LBL	UK POS	UK YEAR	US POS	US YEAR	US LBL
1	A Dreamer's Holiday		0	1949	11	1949	(Capitol 761)
2	Sitting By The Window		0	1950	21	1950	(Capitol 794)
3	Sentimental Me		0	1950	7	1950	(Capitol 923)
4	Count Every Star		0	1950	4	1950	(Capitol 979)
5	Roses		0	1950	19	1950	(Capitol 1001)
6	Can Anyone Explain		0	1950	5	1950	(Capitol 1131)
7	Harbour Lights		0	1950	4	1950	(Capitol 1190)
8	Nevertheless (I'm In Love With You)		0	1950	9	1950	(Capitol 1190)
9	The Night Is Young And You're So Beautiful		0	1951	26	1951	(Capitol 1310)
10	Be My Love		0	1951	13	1951	(Capitol 1352)
11	These Things I Offer You (For A Lifetime)		0	1951	17	1951	(Capitol 1522)
12	My Truly, Truly Fair		0	1951	28	1951	(Capitol 1583)
13	Undecided		0	1951	10	1951	(Capitol 1824)
14	At Last		0	1952	2	1952	(Capitol 1912)
15	Bermuda		0	1952	24	1952	(Capitol 1956)
16	As Time Goes By		0	1952	10	1952	(Capitol 2104)
17	Slaughter On 10th Avenue		0	1952	21	1952	(Capitol 2085)
18	Marilyn		0	1952	20	1952	(Capitol 2207)
19	Bunny Hop		0	1952	13	1952	(Capitol 2251)
20	On The Trail		0	1953	26	1953	(Capitol 2327)
21	Wild Horses		0	1953	28	1953	(Capitol 2349)
22	Thunderbird		0	1953	26	1953	(Capitol 2451)
23	Dragnet	(Capitol Cl13983)	7	1953	2	1953	(Capitol 2562)
24	O Mein Papa (Oh! My Papa)		0	1953	15	1953	(Capitol 2678)
25	Dragnet (Re-Entry)	(Capitol Cl13983)	11	1954	0	1954	
26	Secret Love		0	1954	29	1954	(Capitol 2678)
27	Skokiaan		0	1954	18	1954	(Capitol 2896)
28	Melody Of Love		0	1955	19	1955	(Capitol 3018)
29	Peter Gunn		0	1959	8	1959	(Capitol 4041)

R

533

ISSUE	TITLE	UK LBL	UK POS	UK YEAR	US POS	US YEAR	US LBL
Ray Barber	Male Vocalist (Baritone) from the USA						
1	Because Of You		0	1951	23	1951	(Mercury 5643)
Ray Barretto	Male Percussionist, B: April 1939 In Brooklyn						
1	El Watusi		0	1963	17	1963	(Tico 419)
Ray Bloch Orchestra	Male Orchestra Leader from the USA						
1	Kate (Have I Come Too Early Too Late)		0	1947	11	1947	(Signature 15114)
2	Anna		0	1953	22	1953	(Coral 60963)
	VOCALS ON HIT 1 ARE BY ALAN DALE • OBITUARY : D: 31 MAR 1982, (AGED 79).						
Ray Bolger	Male Comedian/Dancer/Actor/Vocalist from the USA						
1	Once In Love With Amy (From Where's Charley)		0	1949	16	1949	(Decca 40065)
2	Dearie (From *Copacabana Show* Of 1950)		0	1950	12	1950	(Decca 24873)
3	I Said My Pajamas (And Put On My Prayers)		0	1950	20	1950	(Decca 24873)
4	If I Knew You Were Coming I'd've Baked A Cake		0	1950	15	1950	(Decca 24944)
5	Once Upon A Nickel		0	1951	29	1951	(Decca 27506)
	HIT 1, 2, 3 AND 4 ARE CREDITED TO ETHEL MERMAN AND RAY BOLGER • HE PLAYED THE SCARECROW IN THE FILM *WIZARD OF OZ*						
Ray Bryant Combo	Real Name Raphael Bryant B: 24 Dec 1931 Philadelphia						
1	The Madison Time (Part 1)		0	1960	30	1960	(Columbia 41628)
Ray Burns	Male Vocalist from the UK						
1	Mobile	(Columbia Db3563)	4	1955	0	1955	
2	That's How A Love Song Was Born	(Columbia Db3640)	14	1955	0	1955	
	HIT 2 IS CREDITED TO RAY BURNS WITH THE CORONETS						
Ray Charles	Male Vocal/Pianist, Real Name Ray Charles Robinson B: 23 Sep 1930 In Georgia						
*+ 1	Baby Let Me Hold Your Hand		0	1951	7	1951	(Swing Time 250)
12	Swanee River Rock (Talkin''bout That River)		0	1957	34	1957	(Atlantic 1154)
* 16	What'd I Say (Part 1-2)		0	1959	6	1959	(Atlantic 2031)
17	I'm Movin' On		0	1959	40	1959	(Atlantic 2043)
20	Sticks And Stones		0	1960	40	1960	(ABC-Paramount 10118)
* 22	Georgia On My Mind	(HMV Pop 792)	47	1960	1	1960	(ABC-Paramount 10135)
23	Ruby		0	1960	28	1960	(ABC-Paramount 10164)
24	Georgia On My Mind (Re-Entry)	(HMV Pop 792)	24	1960	0	1960	
26	One Mint Julep		0	1961	8	1961	(Impulse 200)
* 28	Hit The Road Jack	(HMV Pop 935)	6	1961	1	1961	(ABC-Paramount 10244)
29	Unchain My Heart		0	1961	9	1961	(ABC-Paramount 10266)
30	Hide Nor Hair / At The Club		0	1962	20	1962	(ABC-Paramount 10314)
* 31	I Can't Stop Loving You	(HMV Pop 1034)	1	1962	1	1962	(ABC-Paramount 10330)
32	You Don't Know Me	(HMV Pop 1064)	9	1962	2	1962	(ABC-Paramount 10345)
33	You Are My Sunshine		0	1962	7	1962	(ABC-Paramount 10375)
34	Your Cheating Heart	(HMV Pop 1099)	13	1962	29	1962	(ABC-Paramount 10375)
35	Don't Set Me Free	(HMV Pop 1133)	37	1963	20	1963	(ABC-Paramount 10405)
36	Take These Chains From My Heart	(HMV Pop 1161)	5	1963	8	1963	(ABC-Paramount 10435)
37	No One	(HMV Pop 1202)	35	1963	21	1963	(ABC-Paramount 10453)
38	Without Love (There Is Nothing)		0	1963	29	1963	(ABC-Paramount 10453)
39	Busted	(HMV Pop 1221)	21	1963	4	1963	(ABC-Paramount 10481)
40	That Lucky Old Sun		0	1963	20	1963	(ABC-Paramount 10509)
41	My Heart Cries For You		0	1964	38	1964	(ABC-Paramount 10530)
42	Baby, Don't You Cry		0	1964	39	1964	(ABC-Paramount 10530)
44	No One To Cry To	(HMV Pop 1333)	3	1964	0	1964	
45	Makin' Whoopee	(HMV Pop 1383)	42	1965	14	1965	(ABC-Paramount 10609)
46	Cryin' Time	(HMV Pop 1502)	50	1966	6	1966	(ABC-Paramount 10739)
47	Together Again	(HMV Pop 1519)	48	1966	19	1966	(ABC-Paramount 10785)
48	Let's Go Get Stoned		0	1966	31	1966	(ABC 10808)
49	I Chose To Sing The Blues		0	1966	32	1966	(ABC 10840)
50	Here We Go Again	(HMV Pop 1595)	38	1967	15	1967	(ABC 10938)
51	Here We Go Again (Re-Entry)	(HMV Pop 1595)	45	1967	0	1967	
52	In The Heat Of The Night		0	1967	33	1967	(ABC 10970)
53	Yesterday	(Stateside Ss2071)	44	1967	25	1967	(ABC 11009)
+ 54	That's A Lie		0	1968	11	1968	(ABC 11045)
55	Eleanor Rigby / Understanding	(Stateside Ss2120)	36	1968	35	1968	(ABC 11090)
58	Don't Change On Me		0	1971	36	1971	(ABC 11291)
60	Booty Butt		0	1971	36	1971	(Tangerine 1015)
74	I'll Be Good To You	(Qwest W 2697)	21	1990	18	1989	(Qwest 22697)
	OTHERS ARE R&B OR C/W HITS						

ISSUE	TITLE	UK LBL	UK POS	UK YEAR	US POS	US YEAR	US LBL
Ray Charles Singers Real Name Charles Raymond Offenberg B: 13 Sep 1918 Chicago							
1	Love Me With All Your Heart (Cuando Calienta El Sol)		0	1964	3	1964	(Command 4046)
2	Al-Di-La		0	1964	29	1964	(Command 4049)
3	One More Time		0	1964	32	1964	(Command 4057)
Ray Conniff Male Bandleader/Trombonist, B: 6 Nov 1916, Attleboro, Massachusetts							
* 1	Somewhere My Love		0	1966	9	1966	(Columbia 43626)
	THE HIT WAS CREDITED TO RAY CONNIFF & THE SINGERS						
Ray Dorey Male Vocalist, Previously Sang With Larry Green's Orchestra From Usa							
1	Mam'selle (From The Razor's Edge)		0	1947	7	1947	(Majestic 7217)
Ray Ellington Male Orchestra Leader from the UK							
1	The Madison	(Ember S 102)	41	1962	0	1962	
2	The Madison (Re-Entry)	(Ember S 102)	36	1962	0	1962	
Ray Martin Orchestra Leader from the UK							
1	Blue Tango	(Columbia Db3051)	8	1952	0	1952	
2	Blue Tango (Re-Entry)	(Columbia Db3051)	10	1952	0	1952	
3	Swedish Rhapsody	(Columbia Db3346)	10	1953	0	1953	
4	Swedish Rhapsody (Re-Entry)	(Columbia Db3346)	4	1953	0	1953	
5	Carousel Waltz	(Columbia Db3771)	28	1956	0	1956	
6	Carousel Waltz (Re-Entry)	(Columbia Db3771)	24	1956	0	1956	
Ray McKinley & His Orchestra Male Bandleader/Drummer from the USA							
1	Big Boy		0	1943	14	1943	(Capitol 131)
2	Hoodle-Addle		0	1947	15	1947	(Majestic 7207)
3	Red Silk Stockings And Green Perfume		0	1947	10	1947	(Majestic 7216)
4	Civilization (Bongo, Bongo, Bongo)		0	1947	8	1947	(Majestic 7274)
5	Your Red Wagon		0	1947	22	1947	(Majestic 7275)
6	Airizay		0	1948	21	1948	(RCA Victor 2736)
7	A Man Could Be A Wonderful Thing		0	1948	24	1948	(RCA Victor 2768)
8	You Came A Long Way (From St. Louis)		0	1948	13	1948	(RCA Victor 2913)
9	Sunflower		0	1949	19	1949	(RCA Victor 3334)
Ray Moore Male Vocalist from the UK							
1	O' My Father Had A Rabbit	(Play Play 213)	24	1986	0	1986	
2	Bog-Eyed Jog	(Play Play 224)	61	1987	0	1987	
Ray Morgan Male Vocalist from the UK							
1	The Long And Winding Road	(B&C Cb 128)	32	1970	0	1970	
Ray Noble & His Orchestra Male Composer/Bandleader, B: 17 Dec 1903 Brighton, Sussex, England							
51	Full Moon And Empyt Arms		0	1946	18	1946	(Columbia 36893)
52	Linda		0	1947	1	1947	(Columbia 37215)
53	I Wonder Who's Kissing Her Now		0	1947	11	1947	(Columbia 37544)
54	I'll Dance At Your Wedding		0	1947	3	1947	(Columbia 37967)
55	Suspicion		0	1948	25	1948	(Columbia 38146)
56	It's A Most Unusual Day		0	1948	21	1948	(Columbia 38206)
57	Lady Of Spain (Re-Recording)		0	1949	19	1949	(RCA Victor 3302)
	OBITUARY :- D: 2 APR 1978 LONDON, ENGLAND (AGED 75).						
Ray Parker Jr./Raydio Male Vocalist, B: 1 May 1954 Detroit & Mixed Vocal/Instrumental Group from the USA							
* 1	Jack And Jill	(Arista 161)	11	1978	8	1978	(Arista 0283)
2	Is This A Love Thing	(Arista 193)	27	1978	0	1978	
3	You Can't Change That		0	1979	9	1979	(Arista 0399)
4	Two Places At The Same Time		0	1980	30	1980	(Arista 0494)
5	A Woman Needs Love (Just Like You Do)		0	1981	4	1981	(Arista 0592)
6	The Old Song		0	1981	21	1981	(Arista 0616)
7	The Other Woman		0	1982	4	1982	(Arista 0669)
8	Let Me Go		0	1982	38	1982	(Arista 0695)
9	Bad Boy		0	1983	35	1983	(Arista 1030)
10	I Still Can't Get Over Loving You		0	1984	12	1984	(Arista 9116)
* 11	Ghostbusters	(Arista Arist580)	2	1984	1	1984	(Arista 9212)
12	Jamie		0	1985	14	1985	(Arista 9293)
13	Girls Are More Fun	(Arista Arist641)	46	1986	34	1986	(Arista 9352)
14	I Don't Think Man Should Sleep Alone	(Geffen Gef 27)	13	1987	0	1987	
15	Over You	(Geffen Gef 33)	65	1988	0	1988	
16	All I'm Missing Is You		0	1990	32	1990	(MCA 53886)

ISSUE	TITLE	UK LBL	UK POS	UK YEAR	US POS	US YEAR	US LBL
Ray Peterson Male Vocalist, B: 23 Apr 1939 Denton, Texas							
1	The Wonder Of You	(RCA 1131)	23	1959	25	1959	(RCA 7513)
2	Answer Me	(RCA 11750	47	1960	0	1960	
3	Tell Laura I Love Her		0	1960	7	1960	(RCA 7745)
4	Corinna, Corinna	(London Hlx9246)	48	1961	9	1960	(Dunes 2002)
5	Corinna, Corinna (Re-Entry)	(London Hlx9246)	41	1961	0	1961	
6	Missing You		0	1961	29	1961	(Dunes 2006)
7	I Could Have Loved You So Well		0	1961	57	1961	(Dunes 2009)
Ray Price Male Country Singer, B: 12 Jan 1926 Perryville, Texas							
56	For The Good Times		0	1970	11	1970	(Columbia 45178)
57	Grazin' In Greener Pasture		0	1970	11	1970	(Columbia 45178)
58	I Won't Mention It Again		0	1971	42	1970	(Columbia 45329)
	REST ARE C/W HITS • HE'S KNOWN AS THE CHEROKEE COWBOY						
Ray Smith Male Vocal/Instrumentalist, B: 31 Oct 1934 Melber, Kentucky							
* 1	Rockin' Little Angel		0	1960	22	1960	(Judd 1016)
	OBITUARY : D: 29 NOV 1979 COMMITTED SUICIDE.						
Ray Stevens Male Vocalist, Real Name Ray Ragsdale B: 24 Jan 1939 Clarkdale, Georgia							
1	Jeremiah Peabody's Poly Unstaturated Quick Dissolving Fast-Acting Pleasant Tasting Green And Purple Pills *		0	1961	35	1961	(Mercury 71843)
2	Ahab The Arab		0	1962	5	1962	(Mercury 71966)
3	Harry The Hairy Ape		0	1963	17	1963	(Mercury 72125)
4	Mr. Businessman		0	1968	28	1968	(Monument 1083)
! 5	Sunday Mornin' Coming Down		0	1969	55	1969	(Monument 1163)
* 6	Gitarzan		0	1969	8	1969	(Monument 1131)
7	Along Came Jones		0	1969	27	1969	(Monument 1150)
! 8	Have A Little Talk With Myself		0	1969	63	1969	(Monument 1171)
* 9	Everything Is Beautiful	(CBS 4953)	6	1970	1	1970	(Barnaby 2011)
10	Bridget The Midget (The Queen Of The Blues)	(CBS 7070)	2	1971	0	1971	
11	Turn Your Radio On	(CBS 7634)	33	1972	63	1972	(Barnaby 2048)
! 12	Nashville		0	1973	37	1973	(Barnaby 5020)
* 13	The Streak	(Janus 6146 201)	1	1974	1	1974	(Barnaby 600)
! 14	Everybody Needs A Rainbow		0	1974	37	1974	(Barnaby 610)
15	Misty	(Janus 6146 204)	2	1975	14	1975	(Barnaby 614)
16	Indian Love Call	(Janus 6146 205)	34	1975	68	1975	(Barnaby 616)
20	In The Mood	(Warner Brosk 16875)	31	1977	40	1977	(Warner Bros 8301)
24	I Need Your Help Barry Manilow		0	1979	49	1979	(Warner Bros 8785)
Raymond Lefevre Orchestra Leader From France							
1	The Day The Rains Came		0	1958	30	1958	(Kapp 231)
2	Ame Caline (Soul Coaxing)	(Major Minormm 559)	46	1968	37	1968	(Four Corners147)
Rays Names: Harold Miller, Harry James, David Jones & Walter Ford							
* 1	Silhouettes		0	1957	3	1957	(Cameo 117)
Raze Mixed Vocal/Instrumental Group from the USA							
1	Jack The Groove	(Championchamp 23)	57	1986	0	1986	
2	Jack The Groove (Re-Entry)	(Championchamp 23)	20	1987	0	1987	
3	Let The Music Move U	(Championchamp 27)	57	1987	0	1987	
4	Break 4 Love	(Championchamp 67)	28	1988	0	1988	
5	Let It Roll	(Atlantic A 8866)	27	1989	0	1989	
6	Break 4 Love (Re-Entry)	(Championchamp 67)	59	1989	0	1989	
7	All 4 Love (Break 4 Love 1990)	(Championchamp 228)	30	1990	0	1990	
8	Can You Feel It / Can You Feel It	(Championchamp 227)	62	1990	0	1990	
9	Break 4 Love (2nd Re-Mix)	(Championchampcd 314)	44	1994	0	1994	
Re-Flex Male Vocal/Instrumental Group from the UK							
1	The Politics Of Dancing	(EMI Flex 2)	28	1984	24	1984	(Capitol 5301)
Ready For The World Male Vocal/Instrumental Group from the USA							
1	Oh Sheila	(MCA MCA 1005)	50	1985	1	1985	(MCA 52636)
2	Digital Display		0	1986	21	1986	(MCA 52734)
3	Love You Down	(MCA MCA 1110)	60	1987	9	1987	(MCA 52947)
	LEAD SINGER WITH THE SEXTET IS MELVIN RILEY JR						
Real Emotion Mixed Vocal/Instrumental Group from the UK							
1	Back For Good	Living Beatlbecd Tcls D 015)	67	1995	0	1995	

ISSUE	TITLE	UK LBL	UK POS	UK YEAR	US POS	US YEAR	US LBL
Real Life	Lead Singer With The Australian Quartet Is David Sterry						
1	Send Me An Angel		0	1984	29	1984	(Curb 52287)
2	Catch Me I'm Falling		0	1984	40	1984	(Curb 52362)
3	Send Me An Angel '89		0	1989	26	1989	(Curb 10531)
Real McCoy	Mixed Vocal/Instrumental Trio Olaf Jelitza, Patricia Petersen & Vanessa Mason from Berlin, Germany.						
* 1	Another Night	(Logic74321173732)	61	1993	3	1994	(Arista 12724)
2	Another Night (Re-Issue)	(Logic74321236992)	2	1994	0	1994	
* 3	Run Away	(Logic74321258822)	6	1995	3	1995	(Arista 12808)
4	Love And Devotion	(Arista 74321272702)	11	1995	0	1995	
5	Come And Get Your Love	(Arista74321301272)	19	1995	19	1995	(Arista 12834)
6	Automatic Lover (Call For Love)	(Arista74321325042)	58	1995	0	1995	
7	One More Time		0	1997	27	1997	(Arista 13328)
	HITS 2-3 ARE CREDITED TO (MCSAR &) THE REAL MCCOY						
Real People	Male Vocal/Instrumental Group from the UK						
1	Open Up Your Mind (Let Me In)	(CBS 6566127)	70	1991	0	1991	
2	The Truth	(CBS 6567877)	73	1991	0	1991	
3	Window Pane (Ep)	(CBS 6569327)	60	1991	0	1991	
4	The Truth (Re-Issue)	(CBS 6576987)	41	1992	0	1992	
5	Believer	(CBS 6580067)	38	1992	0	1992	
Real Roxanne	Female Vocalist from the USA						
1	Bang Zoom Let's Go Go	(Cooltempocool 124)	11	1986	0	1986	
2	Respect	(Cooltempocool 176)	60	1987	0	1987	
	HIT 1 IS CREDITED TO REAL ROXANNE WITH HITMAN HOWIE TEE						
Real Thing	Male Vocal/Instrumental Group from the UK						
1	You To Me Are Everything	(Pyeinternational 7n 25709)	1	1976	0	1976	
2	Can't Get By Without You	(Pye 7n 45618)	2	1976	0	1976	
3	You'll Never Now What Your Missing	(Pye 7n 45662)	16	1977	0	1977	
4	Love's Such A Wonderful Thing	(Pye 7n 45701)	33	1977	0	1977	
5	Whenever You Want My Love	(Pye 7n 46045)	18	1978	0	1978	
6	Let's Go Disco	(Pye 7n 46078)	39	1978	0	1978	
7	Rainin' Through My Sunshine	(Pye 7n 46113)	40	1978	0	1978	
8	Can You Feel The Force	(Pye 7n 46147)	5	1979	0	1979	
9	Boogie Down (Get Funky Now)	(Pye 7p 109)	33	1979	0	1979	
10	She's A Groovy Freak	(Calibre Cab105)	52	1980	0	1980	
11	You To Me Are Everything	(Prt 7p 349)	5	1986	0	1986	
12	Can't Get By Without You	(Prt 7p 352)	6	1986	0	1986	
13	You To Me Are Everything	(Prt 7p 349)	72	1986	0	1986	
14	Can You Feel The Force ('86 Re-Mix)	(Prt 7p 358)	24	1986	0	1986	
15	Straight To The Heart	(Jive Jive 129)	71	1986	0	1986	
Real To Reel	Male Vocal/Instrumental Group from the USA						
1	Love Me Like This	(Arista Arist565)	68	1984	0	1984	
Rebbie Jackson	Real Name Maureen Jackson B: 29 May 1950 Indiana						
1	Centipede		0	1984	24	1984	(Columbia 04547)
Rebecca De Ruvo	Female Vocalist From Sweden						
1	I Caught You Out	(Arista74321230782)	72	1994	0	1994	
Rebecca Storm	Female Vocalist from the UK						
1	The Show (Theme From *Connie*)	(Towerbell Tvp3)	22	1985	0	1985	
Rebekah Ryan	Female Vocalist from the UK						
1	You Lift Me Up	(MCA Mcstd40022)	26	1996	0	1996	
2	Just A Little Bit Of Love	(MCA Mcstd40063)	51	1996	0	1996	
3	Woman In Love	(MCA Mcstd40109)	64	1997	0	1997	
Rebel MC	Male Vocalist from the UK						
1	Just Keep Rockin'	(Desire Want 9)	11	1989	0	1989	
2	Street Tuff	(Desire Want 18)	3	1989	0	1989	
3	Better World	(Desire Want 25)	20	1990	0	1990	
4	Rebel Music	(Desire Want 31)	53	1990	0	1990	
5	Wickedest Sound	(Desire Want 40)	43	1991	0	1991	
6	Tribal Base	(Desire Want 41)	20	1991	0	1991	
7	Black Meaning Good	(Desire Want 47)	73	1991	0	1991	
8	Rich Ah Getting Richer	(Big Life Blr 70)	48	1992	0	1992	
9	Humanity	(Big Life Blr 78)	62	1992	0	1992	

ISSUE	TITLE	UK LBL	UK POS	UK YEAR	US POS	US YEAR	US LBL
Rebels	Mickey & Jim Kipler, Tom Gorman & Paul Balon From Buffalo						
1	Wild Weekend		0	1963	8	1963	(Swan 4125)
	HIT FIRST RELEASED IN 1960, THE GROUP WERE ALSO KNOWN AS ROCKIN' REBELS						
Recoil	Male Vocal/Instrumental Group from the UK						
1	Faith Healer	(Mute Mute 110)	62	1992	0	1992	
Red Box	Male Vocal/Instrumental Duo from the UK						
1	Lean On Me (Ah-Li-Ayo)	(Sire W 8926)	3	1985	0	1985	
2	For America	(Sire Yz 84)	10	1986	0	1986	
3	Heart Of The Sun	(Sire Yz 100)	71	1987	0	1987	
Red Buttons	Male Actor/Vocalist from the USA						
1	The Ho Ho Song		0	1953	9	1953	(Columbia 39981)
2	Strange Things Are Happening (Ho Ho, Hee Hee, Ha Ha)		0	1953	15	1953	(Columbia 39981)
Red Car & The Blue Car	Male Vocal/Instrumental Group from the UK						
1	Home For Christmas Day	(Virgin Vs 1394)	44	1991	0	1991	
Red Dragon With Brian & Tony Gold	Male Vocal Group From Jamaica						
1	Compliments On Your Kiss	(Mango Cidm820)	2	1994	0	1994	
2	Compliments On Your Kiss (Re-Entry)	(Mango Cidm820)	49	1994	0	1994	
Red Eye	Male Production/Instrumental Duo from the UK						
1	Kut It	(Champion Champcd 315)	62	1994	0	1994	
Red Foley	Male Vocalist, Real Name Clyde Julian Foley B: 17 Jun 1910 In Blue Lick, Kentucky						
1	Smoke On The Water		0	1944	7	1944	(Decca 6102)
5	Shame On You		0	1945	13	1945	(Decca 18698)
* 25	Chatanoogie Shoe-Shine Boy		0	1950	1	1950	(Decca 46205)
26	Sugarfoot Rag		0	1950	24	1950	(Decca 46205)
* 28	Birmingham Bounce		0	1950	14	1950	(Decca 46234)
30	M-I-S-S-I-S-S-I-P-P-I		0	1950	22	1950	(Decca 46241)
* 32	Goodnight Irene		0	1950	10	1950	(Decca 46255)
34	Cincinatti Dancing Pig		0	1950	7	1950	(Decca 46261)
35	Our Lady Of Fatima		0	1950	16	1950	(Decca 14526)
36	My Heart Cries For You		0	1951	28	1951	(Decca 27378)
!* 40	(There'll Be) Peace In The Valley (For Me)		0	1951	5	1951	(Decca 46319)
41	Alabama Jubilee		0	1951	28	1951	(Decca 27810)
46	Don't Let The Stars Get In Your Eyes		0	1952	25	1952	(Decca 28460)
51	Put Christ Back Into Christmas		0	1953	23	1953	(Decca 28940)
! 52	As Far As I'm Concerned		0	1954	8	1954	(Decca 29000)
	UNLISTED HITS ARE C/W • OBITUARY : D: 19 SEP 1968 FORT WAYNE, INDIANA.						
Red Hill Children	Mixed Vocal Group from the UK						
1	When Children Rule The World	(Really Useful5797262)	40	1996	0	1996	
Red Hot Chili Peppers	Male Vocal/Instrumental Group from the UK						
1	Higher Ground	(EMI-Usa Mt 75)	55	1990	0	1990	
2	Taste The Pain	(EMI-Usa Mt 85)	29	1990	0	1990	
3	Higher Ground (Re-Issue)	(EMI-Usa Mt 88)	54	1990	0	1990	
* 4	Under The Bridge	(Warner Bros W 0084)	26	1992	2	1992	(Warner Bros 18978)
5	Breaking The Girl	(Warner Brosw 0126)	41	1992	0	1992	
6	Soul To Squeeze		0	1993	22	1993	(Warner Bros 18401)
7	Give It Away	(Warner Brosw 0225cd1)	9	1994	0	1994	
8	Under The Bridge (Re-Issue)	(Warner Brosw 0237cdx)	13	1994	0	1994	
9	Warped	(Warner Brosw 0316cd)	31	1995	0	1995	
10	My Friends	(Warner Brosw 0317cd)	29	1995	0	1995	
11	Aeroplane	(Warner Brosw 0331cd)	11	1996	0	1996	
12	Love Rollercoaster	(Geffen Gfstd22188)	7	1997	0	1997	
Red Ingle & The Natural Seven	Real Name Ernest Jansen Ingle B: 1906 Toledo, Ohio						
* 1	Temptation (Tim-Tayshun) (From Going Hollywood)		0	1947	1	1947	(Capitol 412)
2	Them Durn Fool Things		0	1947	26	1947	(Capitol 451)
3	Nowhere		0	1947	24	1947	(Capitol 476)
* 4	Cigareets, Whusky And Wild, Wild Women		0	1948	15	1948	(Capitol 15045)
5	Serutan Yob (A Song For Backward Boys And Girls Under 40)		0	1948	12	1948	(Capitol 15210)
	VOCALS ON HIT 1 ARE BY JO STAFFORD						
	HIT 4 WAS CREDITED TO THE MAIN ST. CHORAL SOCIETY						
	VOCALS ON HIT 8 ARE BY KAREN TEDDER & HAWTHORNE						
	SEE ALSO JO STAFFORD						

Red Nichols & His Five Pennies Male Bandleader/Instrumentalist (Cornet), Real Name Ernest Loring Nichols B: 8 May 1905 Ogden, Utah

* 3	Ida, Sweet As Apple Cider		0	1927	1	1927	(Brunswick 3626)

OBITUARY : RED D: 28 JUN 1965 (AGED 60).

Red Saunders & His Orchestra Male Bandleader/Instrumentalist (Vibraphone, Drums), Real Name Theodore Saunders From Chicago.

1	Hambone		0	1952	20	1952	(Okeh 6862)

Red Sovine Male Vocalist, Real Name Woodrow Wilson Sovine B: 17 Jul 1918 Charleston, West Virginia.

* 23	Teddy Bear	(Starday Sd 12)	4	1981	40	1976	(Starday 142)

OBITUARY : D: 14 APR 1980 HEART ATTACK.

Redbone Male Vocal/Instrumental Group from the USANames Lolly And Pat Vegas With Anthony Bellamy & Peter De Poe

1	Witch Queen Of New Orleans	(Epic Epc 7351)	2	1971	21	1971	(Epic 10749)
* 2	Come And Get Your Love		0	1974	5	1974	(Epic 11035)

Redd Kross Male Vocal/Instrumental Group from the USA

1	Visionary	(This Way Upway 2733)	75	1994	0	1994	
2	Yesterday Once More	(A&M 5807932)	45	1994	0	1994	
3	Get Out Of Myself	(This Way Upway 5466)	63	1997	0	1997	

FLIP SIDE OF HIT 2 WAS HIT 5 BY SONIC YOUTH

Redeye Rock Quartet Led By Dave Hodgkins & Douglas Mark

1	Games		0	1970	27	1970	(Pentagram ???

Redhead Kingpin & The Fbi Male Vocalist from the USA

1	Do The Right Thing	(10 Ten 271)	13	1989	0	1989	
2	Superbad Superslick	(10 Ten 26)	68	1989	0	1989	

Redman Male Rapper From Newark, New Jersey

1	How High		0	1995	13	1995	(Def Jam/Ral 9924)
2	Whateva Man		0	1997	42	1997	(Def Jam 574026)

HIT IS CREDITED TO REDMAN AND METHOD MAN

Rednex Mixed Vocal/Instrumental Group From Sweden

1	Cotton Eye Joe	(Internal Affairs Kgbcd 016)	1	1994	25	1995	(Battery 46501)
2	Old Pop In An Oak	(Internalaffairs Kgbd 019)	12	1995	0	1995	
3	Wild 'n' Free	(Internalaffairs Kgbd 024)	55	1995	0	1995	

Redskins Male Vocal/Instrumental Duo from the UK

1	Keep On Keepin' On	(Decca F 1)	43	1984	0	1984	
2	Bring It Down (This Insane Thing)	(Decca F 2)	33	1985	0	1985	
3	The Power Is Yours	(Decca F 3)	59	1986	0	1986	

Reef Male Vocal/Instrumental Group from the UK

1	Good Feeling	(Sony Soho26613602)	24	1995	0	1995	
2	Naked	(Sony Soho26620622)	11	1995	0	1995	
3	Weird	(Sony Soho26622772)	19	1995	0	1995	
4	Place Your Hands	(Sony S2 6635712)	6	1996	0	1996	
5	Place Your Hands (Re-Entry)	(Sony S2 6635712)	72	1996	0	1996	
6	Come Back Brighter	(Sony S2 6640972)	8	1997	0	1997	
7	Consideration	(Sony S2 6643125)	13	1997	0	1997	
8	Yer Old	(Sony S2 6647032)	21	1997	0	1997	

Reel 2 Real Male Vocal/Instrumental Group from the USA

1	I Like To Move It	(Positiva Cdtiv10)	5	1994	0	1994	
2	Go On Move	(Positiva Cdtiv15)	7	1994	0	1994	
3	Can You Feel It	(Positiva Cdtiv22)	13	1994	0	1994	
4	Raise Your Hands	(Positiva Cdtiv27)	14	1994	0	1994	
5	Conway	(Positiva Cdtic30)	27	1995	0	1995	
6	Jazz It Up	(Positiva Cdtiv59)	7	1996	0	1996	
7	Are You Ready For Some More?	(Positiva Cdtiv56)	24	1996	0	1996	

HITS 1-5 ARE CREDITED TO REEL 2 REAL FEATURING MAD STUNTMAN
SEE ALSO REAL TO REEL

Reese Project Male Producer, Real Name Kevin Saunderson from the USA

1	The Colour Of Love	(Network Nwk51)	52	1992	0	1992	
2	I Believe	(Network Nwk63)	74	1992	0	1992	
3	So Deep	(Networknwkcd 68)	54	1993	0	1993	
4	The Colour Of Love (Re-Mix)	(Networknwkcd 81)	55	1994	0	1994	
5	Direct Me	(Networknwkcd 87)	44	1995	0	1995	

Reflections Lead Singer With The Quartet Is Tony Micale

1	(Just Like) Romeo And Juliet		0	1964	6	1964	(Golden World 9)

ISSUE	TITLE	UK LBL	UK POS	UK YEAR	US POS	US YEAR	US LBL
Reg Owen	British Orchestra Leader B: 1928						
1	Manhattan Spiritual	(Pye International 7n 25009)	20	1959	10	1958	(Palette 5005)
2	Obsession	(Palette Pg9004)	43	1960	0	1960	
Regents (1)	Vocal Group From The Bronx Originally Known As The Desires In 1958						
1	Barbara-Ann		0	1961	13	1961	(Gee 1065)
2	Runaround		0	1961	28	1961	(Gee 1071)
	NAMES GUY VILLARI, SAL CULOMO, CHARLES FASSERT, DON JACOBUCCI & TONY GRAVAGNA						
Regents (2)	Mixed Vocal/Instrumental Group from the UK						
1	7 Teen	(Rialto Treb 111)	11	1979	0	1979	
2	See You Later	(Arista Arist350)	55	1980	0	1980	
Reggae Philharmonic Orchestra	Mixed Vocal/Instrumental Group from the UK						
1	Minnie The Moocher	(Mango Is 378)	35	1988	0	1988	
2	Lovely Thing	(Mango Mng 742)	71	1990	0	1990	
Reggie Goff	Male Vocalist (Baritone) from the UK						
1	I Love You So Much It Hurts		0	1949	13	1949	(London 312)
	SEE ALSO PAUL FENNELLY ORCHESTRA						
Regina	Female Vocalist Regina Richards Comes From New York						
1	Baby Love	(Funkin'marvellous Marv 01)	50	1986	10	1986	
Regina Belle	Female Vocalist from the USA						
1	Good Lovin'	(CBS 655230)	73	1989	0	1989	
2	A Whole New World	(Columbia6599002)	12	1993	0	1993	
	HIT 2 IS CREDITED TO PEABO BRYSON AND REGINA BELLE						
Reid	Male Vocal Group from the UK						
1	One Way Out	(Syncopate Sy16)	66	1988	0	1988	
2	Real Emotion	(Syncopate Sy24)	65	1989	0	1989	
3	Good Times	(Syncopate Sy27)	55	1989	0	1989	
4	Lovin' On The Side	(Syncopayereid 1)	71	1989	0	1989	
Rembrandts	Male Vocal Duo, Were Also Members Of Great Buildings	Real Names Danny Wilde & Phil Solem					
1	Just The Way It Is Baby		0	1991	14	1991	(Atco 98874)
2	I'll Be There For You (Theme From *Friends*)	(East West 4390cd) A	3	1995	17	1995	(Eastwest 64384)
3	This House Is Not A Home	(Atlantic A4366cd)	58	1996	17	1995	(Eastwest 64384)
4	I'll Be There For You	(East West4390cd) A	5	1997	0	1997	
	(THEME FROM *FRIENDS*) (RE-ENTRY)						
Renaissance	Mixed Vocal/Instrumental Group from the UK						
1	Northern Lights	(Warner Brosk 17117)	10	1978	0	1978	
Renato Carosone & His Sextet	Male Vocalist/Instrumental Backing Group From Italy						
1	Terero - Cha Cha Cha	(Parlophone R4433)	25	1958	18	1958	(Capitol 71080)
Rene & Angela	Mixed Vocal Duo from the USA						
1	Save Your Love (For Number 1)	(Club Jab 14)	66	1985	0	1985	
2	I'll Be Good	(Club Jab 18)	22	1985	0	1985	
3	Secret Rendezvous	(Championchamp 5)	54	1985	0	1985	
Rene & Rene	Real Names Rene Omelas & Rene Herrera						
1	Lo Mucho Que Te Quiero (The More I Love You)		0	1968	14	1968	(White Whale 287)
Rene & Yvette	Mixed Actor/Actress Vocal Duo from the UK						
1	Je T'aime (Allo Allo) / Rene D.M.C. (Devastating Macho Charisma)	(Sedition Edit3319)	57	1986	0	1986	
Renee & Renato	Mixed Vocal Duo From Uk/Italy						
1	Save Your Love	(Hollywoodhwd 003)	1	1982	0	1982	
2	Just One More Kiss	(Hollywoodhwd 006)	48	1983	0	1983	
Renegade Soundwave	Male Vocal/Instrumental Group from the UK						
1	Probably A Robbery	(Mute Mute 102)	38	1990	0	1990	
2	Renegade Soundwave	(Mute Cdmute146)	64	1994	0	1994	
Reo Speedwagon	Male Vocal/Instrumental Group from the USA						
* 1	Keep On Loving You	(Epic Epc 9544)	7	1981	1	1981	(Epic 50953)
* 2	Take It On The Run	(Epic Epc A 1207)	19	1981	5	1981	(Epic 01054)
3	Don't Let Him Go		0	1981	24	1981	(Epic 02127)
4	In Your Letter		0	1981	20	1981	(Epic 02457)
5	Keep The Fire Burnin'		0	1982	7	1982	(Epic 02967)
6	Sweet Time		0	1982	26	1982	(Epic 03175)
7	I Do'wanna Know		0	1984	29	1984	(Epic 04659)
* 8	Can't Fight This Feeling	(Epic A 4880)	16	1985	1	1985	(Epic 04713)

ISSUE	TITLE	UK LBL	UK POS	UK YEAR	US POS	US YEAR	US LBL
9	One Lonely Night		0	1985	19	1985	(Epic 04848)
10	Live Every Moment		0	1985	34	1985	(Epic 05412)
11	That Ain't Love		0	1987	16	1987	(Epic 06656)
12	In My Dreams		0	1987	19	1987	Epic 07255)
13	Here With Me		0	1988	20	1988	(Epic 07901)

LEAD VOCALS WITH THE QUINTET IS KEVIN CRONIN • THE GROUP TOOK THEIR NAME FROM AN AMERICAN 1911 FIRE APPLIANCE

Reparata & The Delrons Female Vocal Group from the USA

1	Captain Of Your Ship	(Bell 1002)	13	1968	0	1968	
2	Shoes	(Dart 2066 562)	43	1975	0	1975	

HIT 2 IS CREDITED TO REPARATA

Republica Mixed Vocal/Instrumental Group from the UK

1	Ready To Go	(Deconstruction 7421326132)	43	1996	56	1996	(RCA 64540)
2	Drop Dead Gorgeous	(Deconstruction 74321408442)	7	1997	93	1997	(RCA 64767)
3	Ready To Go (Re-Issue)	(Deconstruction 74321421332)	13	1997	0	1997	

Restless Heart Male Country-Rock Quintet, Names David Innis, Greg Jennings, Larry Stewart, Paul Gregg & John Ditrich

6	I'll Still Be Loving You		0	1987	33	1987	(RCA 5065)
19	When She Cries		0	1992	11	1992	(RCA 62412)

OTHER HITS ARE C/W

Retta Young Female Vocalist from the USA

1	Sending Out An S.O.S.	(All Platinum6146 305)	28	1975	0	1975	

Reunion Lead Singer With The Studio Group Is Joey Levine from the USA

1	Life Is A Rock (But The Radio Rolled Me)	(RCA Pb 10056)	33	1974	8	1974	(RCA 10056)

SEE ALSO OHIO EXPRESS

Reva Rice & Greg Ellis Mixed Vocal Duo from the UK

1	Next Time You Fall In Love	(Really Usefulrurcd 12)	59	1993	0	1993	

Revels Group Formed By John Kelly In Philadelphia

1	Midnight Stroll		0	1959	35	1959	(Norgolde 103)

HIT WAS ORIGINALLY RELEASED AS DEAD MAN'S STROLL

Revolting Cocks Male Vocal/Instrumental Group from the USA

1	Do Ya Think I'm Sexy	(Devotioncddvn 111)	61	1993	0	1993	

Rex Allen Male Actor/Vocalist/Guitarist, B: 31 Dec 1922 Wilcox, Arizona

2	The Roving Kind		0	1951	20	1951	(Mercury
3	Sparrow In The Tree Top		0	1951	28	1951	(Mercury
* 4	Crying In The Chapel		0	1953	8	1953	(Decca 28758)
6	Don't Go Near The Indians		0	1962	17	1962	(Mercury 71997)

REX MADE HIS DEBUT ON A RADIO STATION IN PHOENIX AT THE AGE OF THIRTEEN • HIT 1 IS CREDITED TO REX ALLEN & THE ARIZONA WRANGLERS WITH JERRY BYRD

Rex Smith Male Actor/Vocalist, B: 19 Sep 1956 Jacksonville, Florida

* 1	You Take My Breath Away		0	1979	10	1979	(Columbia 10908)
2	Everlasting Love	(CBS A 1405)	35	1981	32	1981	(Columbia 02169)

HIT 2 IS CREDITED TO REX SMITH AND RACHEL SWEET

Reynolds Girls Female Vocal Duo from the UK

				•			
1	I'd Rather Jack	(PWL PWL 25)	8	1989	0	1989	

Rezillos Mixed Vocal/Instrumental Group from the UK

1	Top Of The Pops	(Sire Sir 4001)	17	1978	0	1978	
2	Destination Venus	(Sire Sir 4008)	24	1978	0	1978	
3	I Wanna Be Your Man / I Can't Stand My Baby	(Sensible Sab 1)	71	1979	0	1979	
4	I Wanna Be Your Man / I Can't Stand My Baby	(Sensible Sab 1)	75	1979	0	1979	
5	Motorbike Beat	(Dindisc Din 5)	45	1980	0	1980	

HIT 5 IS CREDITED TO THE REVILLOS

Rhc Mixed Vocal/Instrumental Duo From Balgium

1	Fever Called Love	(R&S Rsuk 9)	65	1992	0	1992	

Rhet Stoller Male Instrumentalist (Guitar) from the UK

1	Chariot	(Decca F 11302)	26	1961	0	1961	

Rhythm Eternity Mixed Vocal/Instrumental Group from the UK

1	Pink Champagne	(Dead Deadgood Good 15t)	72	1992	0	1992	

Rhythm Factor Mixed Vocal/Instrumental Group from the USA

1	You Bring Me Joy	(Multiplycdmulty 4)	53	1995	0	1995	

Rhythm Heritage Vocals With The Studio Group Are By Luther & Oren Waters

* 1	Theme From S.W.A.T.		0	1975	1	1975	(ABC 12135)
2	Barretta's Theme (Keep Your Eyes On The Sparrow)		0	1976	20	1976	(ABC 12177)

ISSUE	TITLE	UK LBL	UK POS	UK YEAR	US POS	US YEAR	US LBL
Rhythm Is Rhythm Male Instrumental Duo from the USA							
1	Strings Of Life '89	(Kool Kat Kool509)	74	1989	0	1989	
Rhythm On The Loose Male Producer Geoff Hibbert from the UK							
1	Break Of Dawn	(Six6 Sixcd 126)	36	1995	0	1995	
Rhythm Quest Male Producer, Real Name Mark Hadfield Fr6m The Uk							
1	Closer To All Your Dreams	(Network Nwk40)	45	1992	0	1992	
Rhythm Section Male Vocal/Instrumental Group from the UK							
1	Midsummer Madness (Ep)	(Rhythm Section Rsec 006)	66	1992	0	1992	
Rhythm Source Mixed Vocal/Instrumental Group from the UK							
1	Love Shine	(A&M 5810672)	74	1995	0	**1995**	
Rhythm-N-Bass Male Rap Group from the UK							
1	Roses	(Epic 6582907)	56	1992	0	1992	
2	Can't Stop The Feeling	(Epic 6592002)	59	1993	0	1993	
Rhythmatic Male Instrumental Group from the UK							
1	Take Me Back	(Network Nwk8)	74	1990	0	1990	
2	Take Me Back (Re-Entry)	(Network Nwk8)	71	1990	0	1990	
3	Frequency	(Network Nwk13)	62	1990	0	1990	
Ric Ocasek Real Name Richard Otcasek From Baltimore							
1	Emotion In Motion		0	1986	15	1986	(Geffen 28617)
Ricardo Da Force Male Rapper from the UK							
1	Pump Up The Volume	(Stress Cdstr49)	51	1995	0	1995	
2	Stayin' Alive	(Around Theworld Cdglobe 131)	2	1995	0	1995	
3	Why?	(Ffrr Fcd 280)	58	1996	0	1996	
Rich Kids Male Vocal/Instrumental Group from the UK							
1	Rich Kids	(EMI 2738)	24	1978	0	1978	
Richard 'dimples' Fields Male Vocalist from the USA							
1	I've Got To Learn To Say No	(Epic Epc A 1918)	56	1982	0	1982	
Richard Ace Male Vocalist From Jamaica							
1	Stayin' Alive	(Blue Inc. Inc 2)	66	1978	0	1978	
Richard Allan Male Vocalist from the UK							
1	As Time Goes By	(Parlophone R4634)	44	1960	0	1960	
Richard Anthony Real Name Richard Anthony Btesh B: 13 Jan 1938 Egypt							
* 1	500 Miles Away From Home (J'entends Sifflerle Train)		0	1962	0	1962	(Columbia)
2	Walking Alone	(Columbia Db7235)	37	1963	0	1963	
3	If I Loved You	(Columbia Db7133)	48	1964	0	1964	
4	If I Loved You (Re-Entry)	(Columbia Db7133)	18	1964	0	1964	
Richard Barnes Male Vocalist from the UK							
1	Take To The Mountains	(Philips Bf 1840)	35	1970	0	1970	
2	Go North	(Philips 6006 039)	49	1970	0	1970	
3	Go North (Re-Entry)	(Philips 6006 039)	38	1970	0	1970	
Richard Bowers Male Vocalist from the USA							
1	Gomen Nasai (Forgive Me)		0	1953	15	1953	(Columbia 39954)
2	Baby Let Me Kindle Your Flame		0	1953	21	1953	(Columbia 40016)
Richard Chamberlain Male Vocalist B: 31 Mar 1935 Los Angeles							
1	Theme From *Dr Kildare* (Three Stars Will Shine Tonight)	(Mgm 1160)	12	1962	10	1962	(Mgm 13075)
2	Love Me Tender	(Mgm 1173)	15	1962	21	1962	(Mgm 13097)
3	Hi-Lili Hi-Lo	(Mgm 1189)	20	1963	0	1963	
4	All I Have To Do Is Dream		0	1963	14	1963	(Mgm 13121)
5	True Love	(Mgm 1205)	30	1963	0	1963	
Richard Darbyshire Male Vocalist from the USA							
1	Coming Back For More	(Chrysalis Jel ??)	41	1988	0	1988	
2	This I Swear	(Dome Cddome1003)	50	1993	0	1993	
3	When Only Love Will Do	(Dome Cddome1008)	54	1994	0	1994	
	HIT 1 IS CREDITED TO JELLYBEAN FEATURING RICHARD DARBYSHIRE						
Richard Denton & Martin Cook Male Orchestral Leaders/Instrumental Duo from the UK							
1	Theme From The Hong Kong Beat	(Bbc Resl 52)	25	1978	0	1978	
Richard Harris Male Vocalist, B: 1 Oct 1930, Limerick, Ireland							
* 1	Macarthur Park	(RCA 1699)	4	1968	2	1968	(Dunhill 4134)
2	Macarthur Park (Re-Issue)	(Probe Gff 101)	38	1972	0	1972	

ISSUE	TITLE	UK LBL	UK POS	UK YEAR	US POS	US YEAR	US LBL
Richard Hartley & Michael Reed Male Instrumentalist (Synthesizer) And Orchestra from the UK							
Orchestra							
1	Music Of Torvill And Dean (Ep)	(Safari Skate 1)	9	1984	0	1984	
Richard Hayes Male Vocalist from the USA							
1	The Old Master Painter		0	1949	2	1949	(Mercury ???)
2	My Foolish Heart		0	1950	21	1950	(Mercury ???)
3	Our Lady Of Fatima		0	1950	10	1950	(Mercury ???)
4	The Aba Daba Honeymoon		0	1951	9	1951	(Mercury ???)
5	Too Young		0	1951	24	1951	(Mercury ???)
6	Come On-A My House (From The Son)		0	1951	14	1951	(Mercury ???)
7	Go! Go! Go! Go!		0	1951	23	1951	(Mercury ???)
8	Out In The Cold Again		0	1951	9	1951	(Mercury ???)
9	Junco Partner		0	1952	15	1952	(Mercury ???)
10	I'll Walk Alone (From Follow The Boys)		0	1952	24	1952	(Mercury ???)
11	The Mask Is Off		0	1952	23	1952	(Mercury ???)
12	Forgetting You		0	1952	15	1952	(Mercury ???)
13	Midnight In Paris		0	1953	24	1953	(Mercury 70169)
	VOCALS ON HIT 4 ARE BY RICHARD HAYES AND KITTY KALLEN						
Richard Hayman Male Conductor/Harmonica/Arranger, B: 27 Mar 1920 Massachusetts							
1	Ruby (From Ruby Gentry)		0	1953	3	1953	(Mercury 70115)
2	April In Portugal		0	1953	12	1953	(Mercury 70114)
3	Limelight (Terry's Theme)		0	1953	13	1953	(Mercury 70168)
4	Eyes Of Blue (From Shane)		0	1953	23	1953	(Mercury 70168)
5	The Story Of Three Loves		0	1953	14	1953	(Mercury 70202)
6	Off Shore		0	1954	16	1954	(Mercury 70232)
7	Sadie Thompson's Song (From *Miss Sadie Thompson*)		0	1954	20	1954	(Mercury 70237)
8	Theme From *The Threepenny Opera* (Moritat)		0	1956	11	1956	(Mercury 70781)
	OBITUARY : JAN D: 17 JAN 1976.						
Richard Jon Smith Male Vocalist From South Africa							
1	She's The Master Of The Game	(Jive Jive 38)	63	1983	0	1983	
Richard Maltby & His Orchestra Male Trumpeter/Bandleader, B: 26 Jun 1914 Chicago							
1	St. Louis Blues Mambo		0	1954	21	1954	(X 0042)
2	Stardust Mambo		0	1954	27	1954	(X 0075)
3	Main Title Theme From The Man With The Golden Arm		0	1956	14	1956	(Vik 0196)
	OBITUARY : D: 19 AUG 1991.						
Richard Marx Male Vocalist, B: 16 Sep 1963 In Chicago							
1	Don't Mean Nothing		0	1987	3	1987	(Manhattan 50079)
2	Should've Known Better	(Manhattan Mt32)	50	1988	3	1987	(Manhattan 50083)
3	Endless Summer Nights	(Manhattan Mt39)	50	1988	2	1988	(EMI-Manhattan50113)
4	Hold On To The Nights		0	1988	1	1988	(EMI-Manhattan50106)
5	Satisfied	(EMI-Usa Mt 64)	52	1989	1	1989	(EMI 50189)
* 6	Right Here Waiting	(EMI-Usa Mt 72)	2	1989	1	1989	(EMI 50219)
7	Angelina	(EMI-Usa Mt 74)	45	1989	4	1989	(EMI 50218)
8	Too Late To Say Goodbye	(EMI Usa Mt 80)	38	1990	12	1990	(EMI 50234)
9	Children Of The Night	(EMI-Usa Mt 84)	54	1990	13	1990	(EMI 50288)
10	Endless Summer Nights (Re-Issue)	(EMI-Usa Mt 89)	60	1990	0	1990	
11	Keep Coming Back	(Capitol Cl 634)	55	1991	12	1991	(Capitol 44753)
12	Hazard	(Capitol Cl 654)	3	1992	9	1992	(Capitol 44796)
13	Take This Heart	(Capitol Cl 667)	13	1992	20	1992	(Capitol 44782)
14	Chains Around My Heart	(Capitol Cl 676)	29	1992	0	1992	
15	Now And Forever	(Capitol Cdcls703)	13	1994	7	1994	(Capitol 58005)
16	Silent Scream	(Capitol Cdcls714)	32	1994	0	1994	
17	The Way She Loves Me	(Capitol Cdcl721)	38	1994	20	1994	(Capitol 58167)
18	Until I Find You Again		0	1997	42	1997	(Capitol 58633)
	FIRST WORKED AS A JINGLE SINGER						
Richard Myhill Male Vocalist from the UK							
1	It's Take Two To Tango	(Mercury 6007167)	17	1978	0	1978	
Richie Furay B: 9 May 1944 Yello Springs, Ohio							
1	Still Have Dreams		0	1979	39	1979	(Asylum 46534)
Richie Havens Male Folk Singer/Guitarist, B: 21 Jan 1941 Brooklyn							
1	Here Comes The Sun		0	1971	16	1971	(Stormy Forest 656)

ISSUE	TITLE	UK LBL	UK POS	UK YEAR	US POS	US YEAR	US LBL
Richie Rich	Male Vocalist from the UK						
1	Turn It Up	(Club Jab 68)	48	1988	0	1988	
2	I'll House You	(Gee Streetgee 003)	22	1988	0	1988	
3	My Dj (Pump It Up Some)	(Gee Streetgee 7)	74	1988	0	1988	
4	Salsa House	(Ffrr F 113)	50	1989	0	1989	
5	You Used To Salsa	(Ffrr F 156)	52	1991	0	1991	
6	Let's Ride		0	1996	67	1996	(Mercury 575774)
7	Do G's Get To Go To Heaven?		0	1997	57	1997	(Def Jam 574030)
8	Stay With Me	(Castle Communicationcatx 1001)58		1997	0	1997	
Richie Sambora	Male Vocal/Instrumentalist (Bass) from the USA						
1	Ballad Of Youth	(Mercury Mer350)	59	1991	0	1991	
Rick Astley	Male Vocalist, B: 6 Feb 1966 Warrington, Manchester, England						
1	Never Gonna Give You Up	(RCA Pb 41447)	1	1987	1	1988	(RCA 5347)
2	Whenever You Need Somebody	(RCA Pb 41567)	3	1987	0	1987	
3	When I Fall In Love	(RCA Pb 41683)	2	1987	0	1987	
4	Together Forever	(RCA Pb 41817)	2	1988	1	1988	(RCA 8319)
5	She Wants To Dance With Me	(RCA Pb 42189)	6	1988	6	1989	(RCA 8838)
6	It Would Take A Strong Man		0	1988	10	1988	(RCA 8663)
7	Take Me To Your Heart	(RCA Pb 42573)	8	1988	0	1988	
8	Hold Me In Your Arms	(RCA Pb 42615)	10	1989	0	1989	
9	Giving Up On Love		0	1989	38	1989	(RCA 8872)
10	Cry For Help	(RCA Pb 44247)	7	1991	7	1991	(RCA 2774)
11	Move Right Out	(RCA Pb 44407)	58	1991	0	1991	
12	Never Knew Love	(RCA Pb 44737)	70	1991	0	1991	
13	The Ones You Love	(RCA ???)	48	1993	0	1993	
14	Hopelessly	(RCA ???)	33	1993	28	1993	(RCA 62597)
Rick Clarke	Male Vocalist from the UK						
1	I'll See You Along The Way	(Wa Wa 1)	63	1988	0	1988	
Rick Dees & His Cast Of Idiots	Male Vocalist/Mixed Vocal/Instrumental Group from the USA						
* 1	Disco Duck (Part 1)	(Rso 2090 204)	6	1976	1	1976	(Rso 857)
	REAL NAME RIGDON OSMOND DEES 111 FROM MEMPHIS						
Rick Derringer	Real Name Richard Zehringer B: 5 Aug 1947 Ohio						
1	Rock And Roll, Hoochie Koo		0	1974	23	1974	(Blue Sky 2751)
Rick James	Male Vocalist, Real Name James Johnson B: 1 Feb 1952 Buffalo						
1	You And I	(Motown Tmg1110)	46	1978	13	1978	(Gordy 7156)
2	I'm A Sucker For Your Love	(Motown Tmg1146)	43	1979	0	1979	
3	Big Time	(Motown Tmg1198)	41	1980	0	1980	
4	Give It To Me Baby	(Motown Tmg1229)	47	1981	40	1981	(Gordy 7197)
5	Super Freak (Part 1)		0	1981	16	1981	(Gordy 7205)
6	Standing On The Top (Part 1)	(Motown Tmg1263)	53	1982	0	1982	
7	Dance Wit' Me	(Motown Tmg1266)	53	1982	0	1982	
8	Cold Blooded		0	1983	40	1983	(Gordy 1687)
9	17		0	1984	36	1984	(Gordy 1730)
Rick Springfield	Male Vocalist, B: 23 Aug 1949 Sidney, Australia						
1	Speak To The Sky		0	1972	14	1972	(Capitol 3340)
* 2	Jessie's Girl	(RCA Rick 2)	43	1984	1	1981	(RCA 12201)
3	I've Done Everything For You		0	1981	8	1981	(RCA 12166)
4	Love Is Alright Tonight		0	1981	20	1981	(RCA 13008)
5	Don't Talk To Strangers		0	1982	2	1982	(RCA 13070)
6	What Kind Of Fool Am I		0	1982	21	1982	(RCA 13245)
7	I Get Excited		0	1982	32	1982	(RCA 13303)
8	Affair Of The Heart		0	1983	9	1983	(RCA 13497)
9	Human Touch	(RCA Rick 1)	23	1984	18	1983	(RCA 13576)
10	Souls	(RCA Rick 1)	24	1984	23	1983	(RCA 13650)
11	Love Somebody		0	1984	5	1984	(RCA 13738)
12	Don't Walk Away		0	1984	26	1984	(RCA 13813)
13	Bop 'til You Drop		0	1984	20	1984	(RCA 13861)
14	Bruce		0	1984	27	1984	(Mercury 880405)
15	Celebrate Youth		0	1985	26	1985	(RCA 14047)
16	State Of The Heart		0	1985	22	1985	(RCA 14120)
17	Rock Of Life		0	1988	22	1988	(RCA 6853)

ISSUE	TITLE	UK LBL	UK POS	UK YEAR	US POS	US YEAR	US LBL

Rickie Lee Jones Female Vocalist, B: 8 Nov 1954 Chicago

1	Chuck E's In Love	(Warner Brosk 17390)	18	1979	4	1979	(Warner Bros 8825)
2	Young Blood		0	1979	40	1979	(Warner Bros 49018)

Ricky Nelson Male Vocalist, Real Name Eric Hilliard Nelson B: 8 May 1940 In Teaneck, New Jersey

	ISSUE	TITLE	UK LBL	UK POS	UK YEAR	US POS	US YEAR	US LBL
	1	I'm Walking		0	1957	4	1957	(Verve 10047)
*	2	A Teenager's Romance		0	1957	4	1957	(Verve 10047)
	3	You're My One And Only One		0	1957	14	1957	(Verve 10070)
*	4	Be-Bop Baby		0	1957	3	1957	(Imperial 5463)
	5	Have I Told You Lately That I Love You?		0	1957	29	1957	(Imperial 5463)
*	6	Stood Up	(London Hlp 8542)	27	1958	2	1957	(Imperial 5483)
	7	Waitin' In School		0	1957	18	1957	(Imperial 5483)
	8	Stood Up (Re-Entry)	(London Hlp8542)	29	1958	0	1958	
*	9	Believe What You Say		0	1958	4	1958	(Imperial 5503)
	10	My Bucket's Got A Hole In It		0	1958	12	1958	(Imperial 5503)
*	11	Poor Little Fool	(London Hlp8670)	4	1958	1	1958	(Imperial 5528)
	12	Lonesome Town	(London Hlp8732)	0	1958	7	1958	(Imperial 5545)
	13	I Got A Feeling	(London Hlp8732)	27	1958	10	1958	(Imperial 5545)
	14	Someday	(London Hlp8732)	9	1958	0	1957	
	15	Poor Little Fool (Re-Entry)	(London Hlp8670)	28	1958	0	1958	
	16	Never Be Anyone Else But You	(London Hlp8817)	19	1959	6	1959	(Imperial 5565)
*	17	It's Late	(London Hlp8817)	3	1959	9	1959	(Imperial 5565)
	18	Never Be Anyone Else By You (Re-Entry)	(London Hlp8817)	14	1959	0	1959	
	19	Just A Little Too Much	(London Hlp8927)	11	1959	9	1959	(Imperial 5595)
	20	Sweeter Than You	(London Hlp8927)	19	1959	9	1959	(Imperial 5595)
	21	I Wanna Be Loved	(London Hlp9021)	30	1960	20	1959	(Imperial 5614)
	22	Mighty Good		0	1959	38	1959	(Imperial 5614)
	23	Young Emotions	(London Hlp9121)	48	1960	12	1960	(Imperial 5663)
	24	I'm Not Afraid		0	1960	27	1960	(Imperial 5685)
	25	Yes Sir, That's My Baby		0	1960	34	1960	(Imperial 5685)
	26	You Are The Only One		0	1961	25	1961	(Imperial 5707)
*	27	Travellin' Man	(London Hlp9347)	2	1961	1	1961	(Imperial 5741)
	28	Hello Mary Lou	(London Hlp9347)	2	1961	9	1961	(Imperial 5741)
	29	A Wonder Like You		0	1961	11	1961	(Imperial 5770)
	30	Everlovin'	(London Hlp9440)	23	1961	16	1961	(Imperial 5770)
	31	Young World	(London Hlp9524)	19	1962	5	1962	(Imperial 5805)
	32	Teenage Idol	(London Hlp9583)	39	1962	5	1962	(Imperial 5864)
	33	It's Up To You	(London Hlp9648)	22	1963	6	1962	(Imperial 5901)
	34	String Along		0	1963	25	1963	(Decca 31495)
	35	Fools Rush In	(Brunswick05895)	12	1963	12	1963	(Decca 31533)
	36	For You	(Brunswick05900)	14	1964	6	1964	(Decca 31574)
	37	The Very Thought Of You		0	1964	26	1964	(Decca 31612)
!	38	Take A City Bride		0	1967	58	1967	(Decca 32120)
	39	She Belongs To Me		0	1970	33	1970	(Decca 32550)
*	40	Garden Party	(MCA Mu 1165)	41	1972	6	1972	(Decca 32980)
!	41	One Night Stand		0	1974	89	1974	(Epic 50674)
!	42	Dream Lover		0	1979	59	1979	(Epic 50674)
!	43	Dream Lover (Re-Issue)		0	1986	88	1986	(Epic 06066)
	44	Hello Mary Lou (Goodbye Heart) (Re-Issue)	(Liberty Emct 2)	45	1991	0	1991	
		OBITUARY : D: 31 DEC 1985 PLANE CRASH.						

Ricky Ross Male Vocalist from the UK

1	Radio On	(Epic 6631352)	35	1996	0	1996	
2	Good Evening Philadelphia	(Epic 6635335)	58	1996	0	1996	

Ricky Stevens Male Vocalist from the UK

1	I Cried For You	(Columbia Db4739)	34	1961	0	1961	

Ricky Valance Male Vocalist, Real Name David Spence from the UK

1	Tell Laura I Love Her	(Columbia Db4493)	1	1960	0	1960	
	THE HIT WAS THE FIRST RECORD TO BE BANNED BY THE BBC AND REACH NUMBER 1						

Ricky Zahnd & The Blue Jeaners Male Vocalist, B: 22 Jul 1946 New York City

1	(I'm Gettin') Nuttin' For Christmas		0	1955	21	1955	(Columbia 40576)

Ride Male Vocal/Instrumental Group from the UK

1	Ride (Ep)	(Creation Cre07t2)	71	1990	0	1990	
2	Play (Ep)	(Creation Cre075t)	32	1990	0	1990	

ISSUE	TITLE	UK LBL	UK POS	UK YEAR	US POS	US YEAR	US LBL
3	Fall (Ep)	(Creation Cre087t)	34	1990	0	1990	
4	Today Forever	(Creation Cre100t)	14	1991	0	1991	
5	Leave Them All Behind	(Creation Cre123t)	9	1992	0	1992	
6	Twisterella	(Creation Cre150t)	36	1992	0	1992	
7	Birdman	(Creation Crescd 155)	38	1994	0	1994	
8	How Does It Feel To Feel	(Creation Crescd 184)	58	1994	0	1994	
9	I Don't Know Where It Comes From	(Creation Crescd 189r)	46	1994	0	1994	
10	Black Nite Crash	(Creation Crescd 199)	67	1996	0	1996	

Riff Names: Steven Capers Jr, Michael Best, Kenny Kelly, Dwayne Jones & Anthony Fuller

1	My Heart Is Failing Me		0	1991	25	1991	(Sbk 07342)

Righeira Male Vocal Duo From Spain

1	Vamos A La Playa	(A&M Am 137)	53	1983	0	1983	

Right Said Fred Vocal/Instrumental Group, Fred & Richard Fairbrass With Rob Manzoli from the UK

* 1	I'm Too Sexy	(Tug Snog 1)	2	1991	1	1992	(Charisma ???
2	Don't Talk Just Kiss	(Tug Snog 2)	3	1991	0	1991	
3	Deeply Dippy	(Tug Snog 3)	1	1992	0	1992	
4	Those Simple Things / Daydream	(Tug Snog 4)	29	1992	0	1992	
5	Stick It Out	(Tug Cdcomic 1)	4	1993	0	1993	
6	Bumped	(Tug Cdsnog 7)	32	1993	0	1993	
7	Hands Up (4 Lovers)	(Tug Cdsnog 8)	60	1993	0	1993	
8	Wonderman	(Tug Cdsnog 9)	55	1994	0	1994	

Righteous Brothers Male Vocal Duo from the USA   Real Names Bill Medley B: 19 Sep 1940, Bobby Hatfield B: 10 Aug 1940

* 1	You've Lost That Lovin' Feelin'	(London Hlu 943)	1	1965	1	1964	(Philles 124)
2	Just Once In My Life		0	1965	9	1965	(Philles 127)
3	Unchained Melody	(London Hl 9975)	14	1965	4	1965	(Philles 129)
4	Ebb Tide	(London Hl10011)	3	1966	5	1965	(Philles 130)
* 5	(Your My) Soul And Inspiration	(Verve Vs 535)	15	1966	1	1966	(Verve 10383)
6	He		0	1966	18	1966	(Verve 10406)
7	Go Ahead And Cry		0	1966	30	1966	(Verve 10430)
8	White Cliffs Of Dover	(London Hl10086)	21	1966	0	1966	
9	Island In The Sun	(Verve Vs 547)	36	1966	0	1966	
10	You've Lost That Lovin' Feelin' (Re-Issue)	(London Hl10241)	10	1969	0	1969	
11	Rock And Roll Heaven		0	1974	3	1974	(Haven 7002)
12	Give It To The People		0	1974	20	1974	(Haven 7004)
13	Dream On		0	1974	32	1974	(Haven 7006)
14	You've Lost That Lovin' Feelin' (2nd Re-Issue)	(Phil Spector International) 2010 022	42	1977	0	1977	
15	Unchained Melody (Re-Issue)	(Verve/Polydorpo 101)	1	1990	13	1990	(Verve F. 871882)
16	Unchained Melody (Re-Recording)		0	1990	19	1990	(Curb 76842)
17	You've Lost That Lovin' Feelin' (3rd Re-Issue)	(Verve/Polydorpo 116)	3	1990	0	1990	

Rimshots Male Vocal/Instrumental Group from the USA

1	7-6-5-4-3-2-1 (Blow Your Whistle)	(All Platinum6146 304)	26	1975	0	1975	

Ringo Starr Male Drummer/Vocalist, Real Name Richard Starkey B: 7 Jul 1940 Liverpool, England.

* 1	It Don't Come Easy	(Apple R 5898)	4	1971	4	1971	(Apple 1831)
2	Back Off Boogaloo	(Apple R 5944)	2	1972	9	1972	(Apple 1849)
* 3	Photograph	(Apple R 5992)	8	1973	1	1973	(Apple 1865)
* 4	You're Sixteen	(Apple R 5995)	4	1974	1	1974	(Apple 1870)
5	Oh My My		0	1974	5	1974	(Apple 1872)
6	Only You	(Apple R 6000)	28	1974	6	1974	(Apple 1876)
7	No No Song		0	1975	3	1975	(Apple 1880)
9	Snookeroo		0	1975	3	1975	(Apple 1880)
10	It's All Down To Goodnight Vienna		0	1975	31	1975	(Apple 1882)
11	Oo-Wee		0	1975	31	1975	(Apple 1882)
12	A Dose Of Rock 'n' Roll		0	1976	26	1976	(Atlantic 3361)
13	Wrack My Brain		0	1981	38	1981	(Broadwalk 130)
14	Weight Of The World	(Private Music115392)	74	1992	0	1992	

Rio & Mars Mixed Vocal/Instrumental Duo from the UK/France

1	Boy I Gotta Have You	(Dome Cddome1014)	43	1995	0	1995	
2	Boy I Gotta Have You (Re-Issue)	(Feverpitchcdfvr 1007)	46	1996	0	1996	

Rip Chords Terry Melcher & Bruce Johnson Featured With The Californian Quartet

1	Hey Little Cobra		0	1964	4	1964	(Columbia 42921)
2	Three Window Coupe		0	1964	28	1964	(Columbia 43035)

ISSUE	TITLE	UK LBL	UK POS	UK YEAR	US POS	US YEAR	US LBL
Rita Coolidge Female Vocalist, B: 1 May 1944 In Nashville							
1	A Song I'd Like To Sing		0	1973	49	1973	(A&M 1475)
2	Loving Arms		0	1974	86	1974	(A&M 1498)
! 3	Mama Lou		0	1974	94	1974	(A&M 1545)
! 4	Rain		0	1974	87	1974	(Monument 8630)
* 5	(Your Love Has Lifted Me) Higher And Higher	(A&M Ams 7315)	49	1977	2	1977	(A&M 1922)
* 6	We're All Alone	(A&M Ams 7295)	6	1977	7	1977	(A&M 1965)
7	(Your Love Has Lifted Me) Higher And Higher (Re-Enry) (A&M Ams 7315)		48	1977	0	1977	
8	Words	(A&M Ams 7330)	25	1978	0	1978	
9	The Way You Do The Things You Do		0	1978	20	1978	(A&M 2004)
10	You		0	1978	25	1978	(A&M 2058)
! 11	The Jealous Kind		0	1978	63	1978	(A&M 2090)
12	Love Me Again		0	1978	68	1978	(A&M 2090)
13	I'd Rather Leave While I'm In Love		0	1980	38	1980	(A&M 2199)
14	Something 'bout You Baby I Like		0	1980	42	1980	(Capitol 4865)
15	All Time High	(A&M Am 007)	75	1983	36	1983	(A&M 2551)
16	Fool That I Am		0	1981	46	1981	(A&M 2281)
Rita Hayworth (And Jose Ferrer) Female Actress/Vocalist from the USA							
1	The Heat's On (From *Miss Sadie Thompson*)		0	1954	30	1954	(Mgm 70259)
Rita Macneil Female Vocalist From Canada							
1	Working Man	(Polydor Po 98)	11	1990	0	1990	
Rita Pavone Female Vocalist, B: 23 Aug 1945 Turin, Italy							
1	Remember Me		0	1964	26	1964	(RCA 8365)
2	Heart	(RCA 1553)	27	1966	0	1966	
3	You Only You	(RCA 1561)	21	1967	0	1967	
	KNOWN AS LITTLE QUEEN OF ITALIAN SONG • SHE IS ONLY FIVE FEET TALL, AND HER RECORDS HAVE SOLD MILLIONS IN EUROPE						
Ritchie Family Group Made Up Of Studio Session Musicians And Singers from the USA							
1	Brazil	(Polydor 2058 625)	41	1975	11	1975	(20th Century 2218)
2	The Best Disco In Town	(Polydor 2058 777)	10	1976	17	1976	(Marlin 3306)
3	American Generation	(Mercury 6007199)	49	1979	0	1979	
Ritchie Valens Male Vocalist, Real Name Richard Valenzuela B: 13 May 1941							
* 1	Donna	(London Hl	29	1959	1	1959	(Del-Fi 4110)
2	La Bamba	(RCA Pb 41435)	49	1987	22	1987	(Del-Fi 4110)
	OBITUARY : D: 3 FEB 1959 PLANE CRASH. RITCHIE, THE BIG BOPPER & BUDDY HOLLY WERE ALL ON THE SAME AEROPLANE.						
River City People Mixed Vocal/Instrumental Group from the UK							
1	(What's Wrong With) Dreaming	(EMI Em 95)	70	1989	0	1989	
2	Walking On Ice	(EMI Em 130)	62	1990	0	1990	
3	Carry The Blame / California Dreamin'	(EMI Em 145)	13	1990	0	1990	
4	(What's Wrong With) Dreaming (Re-Issue)	(EMI Em 156)	40	1990	0	1990	
5	When I Was Young	(EMI Em 176)	62	1991	0	1991	
6	Special Way	(EMI Em 207)	44	1991	0	1991	
7	Standing In The Need Of Love	(EMI Em 216)	36	1992	0	1992	
River Detectives Male Vocal/Instrumental Duo from the UK							
1	Chains	(Wea Yz 383)	51	1989	0	1989	
River Ocean (Featuring) India Mixed Vocal/Instrumental Duo from the USA							
1	Love And Happiness (Yemaya Y Ochun)	(Cooltempocdcool 287)	50	1994	0	1994	
Rivieras Lead Singer On The Hit Was Marty Fortson Who Was Replaced By Bill Dobslaw							
1	California Sun		0	1964	5	1964	(Epic 1401)
Roach Motel Male Production/Instrumental Group from the UK							
1	Afro Sleeze / Transatlantic	(Junior Boy's Own Jbo 1412)	73	1993	0	1993	
2	Happy Bizzness / Wild Luv	(Junior Boy's Own Jbo 24)	75	1994	0	1994	
Roachford Vocal/Instrumental Group from the UK Ames Andrew Roachford, Chris Taylor, Derrick Taylor & Hawl Gondwe							
1	Cuddly Toy (Feel For Me)	(CBS Roa 2)	61	1988	0	1989	
2	Cuddly Toy (Feel For Me) (Re-Issue)	(CBS Roa 4)	4	1989	25	1989	(Epic 68549)
3	Family Man	(CBS Roa 5)	25	1989	0	1989	
4	Kathleen	(CBS Roa 6)	43	1989	0	1989	
5	Get Ready	(Columbia 6567057)	22	1991	0	1991	
6	Only To Be With You	(Columbia 6601562)	21	1994	0	1994	
7	Lay Your Love On Me	(Columbia 6603722)	36	1994	0	1994	
8	This Generation	(Columbia 6607452)	38	1994	0	1994	

ISSUE	TITLE	UK LBL	UK POS	UK YEAR	US POS	US YEAR	US LBL
9	Cry For Me	(Columbia 6610742)	46	1994	0	1994	
10	I Know You Don't Love Me	(Columbia 6612525)	42	1995	0	1995	
Road Apples Vocal/Instrumental Group from the USA							
1	Let's Live Together		0	1975	35	1975	(Polydor 14285)
Rob Base & Dj E-Z Rock Male Vocal Duo from the USA							
* 1	It Takes Two	(Citybeat Cbe724)	24	1988	36	1988	(Profile 5186)
2	Get On The Dance Floor	(Supreme Supe139)	14	1989	0	1989	
3	It Takes Two (Re-Entry)	(Citybeat Cbe724)	49	1989	0	1989	
4	Joy And Pain	(Supreme Supe143)	47	1989	0	1989	
	NAMES RODNEY BRYCE & ROBERT GINYARD						
Robbie Dupree Real Name Robert Dupulis B: 1947 Brooklyn							
1	Steal Away		0	1980	6	1980	(Elektra 46621)
2	Hot Rod Hearts		0	1980	15	1980	(Elektra 47005)
Robbie Nevil Singer/Songwriter From Los Angeles							
1	C'est La Vie	(Manhattan Mt14)	3	1986	2	1986	(Manhattan 50047)
2	Dominoes	(Manhattan Mt19)	26	1987	14	1987	(Manhattan 50053)
3	Wot's It To Ya	(Manhattan Mt24)	43	1987	10	1987	(Manhattan 50075)
4	Back On Holiday		0	1989	34	1989	(EMI 50152)
5	Just Like You		0	1991	25	1991	(EMI 50356)
Robbie Patton Male Singer/Songwriter from the USA							
1	Don't Give It Up		0	1981	26	1981	(Liberty 1420)
Robbie Robertson Male Vocalist From Canada							
1	Somewhere Down The Crazy River	(Geffen Gef 40)	15	1988	0	1988	
Robbie Williams Male Vocalist from the UK							
1	Freedom	(Chrysaliscdfree 1)	2	1996	0	1996	
2	Freedom (Re-Entry)	(Chrysaliscdfree 1)	59	1996	0	1996	
3	Freedom (2nd Re-Entry)	(Chrysaliscdfree 1)	61	1996	0	1996	
4	Freedom (3rd Re-Entry)	(Chrysaliscdfree 1)	56	1996	0	1996	
5	Old Before I Die	(Chrysaliscdchs 5055)	2	1997	0	1997	
6	Old Before I Die (Re-Entry)	(Chrysaliscdchs 5055)	72	1997	0	1997	
7	Old Before I Die (2nd Re-Renty)	(Chrysaliscdchs 5055)	69	1997	0	1997	
8	Lazy Days	(Chrysaliscdchs 5063)	8	1997	0	1997	
Robert & Johnny Names Robert Carr & Johnny Mitchell							
1	We Belong Together		0	1958	32	1958	(Old Town 1047)
Robert Cray Band Male Vocal/Instrumental Group from the USA							
1	Smoking Gun		0	1987	22	1987	(Mercury 888343)
2	Right Next Door (Because Of Me)	(Mercurycray 3)	50	1987	0	1987	
3	Baby Lee	(Silvertoneorecd 81)	65	1996	0	1996	
	HIT 3 IS CREDITED TO JOHN LEE HOOKER WITH ROBERT CRAY						
Robert Downey Jr. Male Vocalist from the USA							
1	Smile	(Epic 6589052)	68	1993	0	1993	
Robert Earl Male Vocalist from the UK							
1	I May Never Pass This Way Again	(Philips Pb 805)	14	1958	0	1958	
2	More Than Ever (Come Prima)	(Philips Pb 867)	26	1958	0	1958	
3	More Than Ever (Come Prima) (Re-Entry)	(Philips Pb 867)	28	1958	0	1958	
4	The Wonderful Secret Of Love	(Philips Pb 891)	17	1959	0	1959	
Robert Ellis Orrall With Carlene Carter Male Singer/Songwriter/Pianist From Boston							
1	I Couldn't Say No		0	1983	32	1983	(RCA 13431)
	CARLENE WAS B: 26 SEP 1955 AND DAUGHTER OF JUNE CARTER CASH AND CARL SMITH						
Robert Goulet Male Actor/Vocalist, B: 26 Nov 1933 Lawrence, Massachusetts							
1	My Love, Forgive Me (Amore, Scusami)		0	1964	16	1964	(Columbia 43131)
Robert John Male Vocalist, Real Name Robert John Pedrick Jr. B: 1946 Brooklyn							
1	If You Don't Want My Love	(CBS 3436)	42	1968	0	1968	
* 2	The Lion Sleeps Tonight		0	1972	3	1972	(Atlantic 2846)
* 3	Sad Eyes	(EMI America Ea101)	31	1979	1	1979	(EMI America8015)
4	Hey There Lonely Girl		0	1980	31	1980	(EMI America 8049)
	HIT 2 IS ADAPTED FROM SOUTH AFRICA CALLED WIMOWEH						
	HE WAS LEAD SINGER WITH BOBBY & THE CONSOLES						
Robert Knight Male Vocalist, B: 21 Apr 1945 Tennessee							
1	Everlasting Love	(Monumentmon 1008)	40	1968	13	1967	(Rising Sons 705)
2	Love On A Mountain Top	(Monumentmnt 1875)	10	1973	0	1973	

ISSUE	TITLE	UK LBL	UK POS	UK YEAR	US POS	US YEAR	US LBL
3	Everlasting Love (Re-Issue)	(Monumentmnt 2106)	19	1974	0	1974	

Robert Maxwell   Male Jazz Harpist/Composer, B: 19 Apr 1921 New York City

1	Shangri-La		0	1964	15	1964	(Decca 25622)
	SEE ALSO MICKEY MOZART QUINTET						

Robert Merrill   Male Opera Singer

1	The Wiffenpoof Song		0	1947	14	1947	(RCA Victor 1313)

Robert Miles   Male Instrumentalist (Keyboards) From Italy

1	Children	(Deconstruction 74321348322)	2	1996	21	1996	(Arista 13006)
2	Fable	(Deconstruction 74321382622)	7	1996	0	1996	
3	Fable (Re-Entry)	(Deconstruction 74321382622)	71	1996	0	1996	
4	Fable (2nd Re-Entry)	(Deconstruction 74321382622)	69	1996	0	1996	
5	One And One	(Deconstruction 74321427692)	3	1996	54	1996	(Arista 13247)
	HIT 5 IS CREDITED TO ROBERT MILES FEATURING MARIA NAYLER						

Robert Owens   Male Vocalist from the UK

1	I'll Be Your Friend	(Perfecto Pb45161)	75	1991	0	1991	
2	I'll Be Your Friend (Re-Mix)	(Perfectoperf 137cd1)	25	1997	0	1997	
	SEE ALSO GIMME SHELTER (EP), VARIOUS ARTISTS (EP, LP, 78S)						

Robert Palmer   Male Vocalist, Real Name Alan Palmer B: 19 Jan 1949 In Batley, Yorkshire, England

1	Every Kinda People	(Island Wip 6425)	53	1978	16	1978	(Island 100)
2	Bad Case Of Lovin' You (Doctor, Doctor)	(Island Wip 6481)	61	1979	14	1979	(Island 49016)
3	Johnny And Mary	(Island Wip 6638)	44	1980	0	1980	
4	Looking For Clues	(Island Wip 6651)	33	1980	0	1980	
5	Some Guys Have All The Luck	(Island Wip 6754)	16	1982	0	1982	
6	You Are In My System	(Island Is 104)	53	1983	0	1983	
7	You Can Have It (Tame My Heart)	(Island Is 121)	66	1983	0	1983	
* 8	Addicted To Love	(Island Is 270)	5	1986	1	1986	(Island 99570)
9	Hyperactive		0	1986	33	1986	(Island 99545)
10	I Didn't Mean To Turn You On	(Island Is 283)	9	1986	2	1986	(Island 99537)
11	Discipline Of Love	(Island Is 242)	68	1986	0	1986	
12	Sweet Lies	(Island Is 352)	58	1988	0	1988	
13	Simply Irresistible	(EMI Em 61)	44	1988	2	1988	(EMI-Manhattan 50133)
14	She Makes My Day	(EMI Em 65)	6	1988	0	1988	
15	Early In The Morning		0	1988	19	1988	(EMI-Manhattan 50157)
16	Change His Ways	(EMI Em 85)	28	1989	0	1989	
17	It Could Happen To You	(EMI Em 99)	71	1989	0	1989	
18	I'll Be Your Baby Tonight	(EMI Em 167)	6	1990	0	1990	
19	You're Amazing		0	1990	28	1990	(EMI 50338)
20	Mercy Mercy Me (The Ecology) / I Want You	(EMI Em 173)	9	1991	16	1991	(EMI 50344)
21	Dreams To Remember	(EMI Em 193)	68	1991	0	1991	
22	Every Kinda People (Re-Issue)	(Island Is 498)	43	1992	0	1992	
23	Witchcraft	(EMI Em 251)	50	1992	0	1992	
24	Girl U Want	(EMI Cdems 331)	57	1994	0	1994	
25	Know By Now	(EMI Cdems 343)	25	1994	0	1994	
26	You Blow Me Away	(EMI Cdems 350)	38	1994	0	1994	
27	Respect Yourself	(EMI Cdem 399)	45	1995	0	1995	
	HIT 18 IS CREDITED TO ROBERT PALMER AND UB40 • PREVIOUS INVOLVEMENTS WITH MANDRAKE PADDLE STEAMER & POWER STATION						

Robert Parker   Male Vocalist, B: 14 Oct 1930 Crescent City, Louisiana

* 1	Barefootin'	(Island Wi 286)	24	1966	7	1966	(Nola 721)

Robert Plant   Male Vocalist, B: 20 Aug 1948 West Bromwich, England

1	Burning Down One Side	(Swansong Ssk19429)	73	1982	0	1982		
2	Big Log	(Wea B 9848)	11	1983	20	1983	(Es Paranza	99844)
3	In The Mood		0	1983	39	1983	(Es Paranza	99820)
4	Little By Little		0	1985	36	1985	(Es Paranza	99644)
5	Heaven Knows	(Es Paranza A9373)	33	1988	0	1988		
6	Tall Cool One		0	1988	25	1988	(Es Paranza	99348)
7	Hurting Kind (I've Got My Eyes On You)	(Es Paranza A8985)	45	1990	0	1990		
8	29 Palms	(Fontana Fatex1)	21	1993	0	1993		
9	I Believe	(Fontana Fatex2)	64	1993	0	1993		
10	If I Were A Carpenter	(Fontana Fatex4)	63	1993	0	1993		
11	Gallows Pole	(Fontana Ppcd2)	35	1994	0	1994		
	HIT 11 IS CREDITED TO JIMMY PAGE AND ROBERT PLANT							
	ALSO LEAD SINGER WITH LED ZEPPELIN AND HONEYDIPPERS							

ISSUE	TITLE	UK LBL	UK POS	UK YEAR	US POS	US YEAR	US LBL
Robert Q. Lewis Male Vocalist/Dj/Tv Host from the USA							
1	Where's A Your House		0	1951	22	1951	(Mgm 11056)
Robert Tepper Robert Is From New Jersey							
1	No Easy Way Out		0	1986	22	1986	(Scotti Brothers 05750)
Robert Wyatt Male Vocalist from the UK							
1	I'm A Believer	(Virgin Vs 114)	29	1974	0	1974	
2	Shipbuilding	(Rough Tradert 115)	35	1983	0	1983	
Roberta Flack Female Vocalist, B: 10 Feb 1939 Asheville, North Carolina							
1	You've Got A Friend		0	1971	29	1971	(Atlantic 2808)
* 2	The First Time Ever I Saw Your Face	(Atlantic K10161)	14	1972	1	1972	(Atlantic 2864)
* 3	Where Is The Love	(Atlantic K10202)	29	1972	5	1972	(Atlantic 2879)
* 4	Killing Me Softly With His Song	(Atlantic K10282)	6	1973	1	1973	(Atlantic 2940)
5	Jesse		0	1973	30	1973	(Atlantic 2982)
* 6	Feel Like Makin' Love	(Atlantic K10467)	34	1974	1	1974	(Atlantic 3025)
7	The Closer I Get To You	(Atlantic K11099)	42	1978	2	1978	(Atlantic 3463)
8	If I Ever See You Again		0	1978	24	1978	(Atlantic 3483)
9	Back Together Again	(Atlantic K11481)	3	1980	0	1980	
10	Don't Make Me Wait Too Long	(Atlantic K11555)	44	1980	0	1980	
11	Making Love (Movie Title Song)		0	1982	13	1982	(Atlantic 4005)
12	Tonight I Celebrate My Love	(Capitol Cl 302)	2	1983	16	1983	(Capitol 5242)
13	Uh-Uh Ooh Ooh Look Out (Here It Comes)	(Atlantic A 8941)	72	1989	0	1989	
14	Set The Night To Music		0	1991	6	1991	(Atlantic 87607)
Roberta Kelly Female Vocalist from the USA							
1	Zodiacs	(Oasis/Hansa 3)	48	1978	0	1978	
2	Zodiacs (Re-Entry)	(Oasis/Hansa 3)	44	1978	0	1978	
Roberta Lee Female R&B Vocalist from the USA							
1	Slow Poke		0	1951	13	1951	(Decca 27792)
Roberta Quinlan Female Tv Personality/Vocalist from the USA							
1	Buffalo Billy		0	1950	22	1950	(Mercury ???)
2	Molasses Molasses		0	1950	30	1950	(Mercury ???)
Robin Beck Female Vocalist from the USA							
1	First Time	(Mercury Mer270)	1	1988	0	1988	
Robin George Male Vocal/Guitarist from the UK							
1	Heartline	(Bronze Bro191)	68	1985	0	1985	
Robin Gibb Male Vocalist, B: 22 Sep 1949							
* 1	Saved By The Bell	(Polydor 56-337)	2	1969	0	1969	
2	Saved By The Bell (Re-Entry)	(Polydor 56-337)	49	1969	0	1969	
3	August October	(Polydor 56-371)	45	1970	0	1970	
4	Oh! Darling		0	1978	15	1978	(Rso 907)
5	Another Lonely Night In New York	(Polydor Posp668)	71	1984	0	1984	
6	Boys Do Fall In Love		0	1984	37	1984	(Mirage 99743)
Robin Luke Male Vocalist, B: 19 Mar 1942 Los Angeles							
* 1	Susie Darlin'	(London Hld8676)	24	1958	5	1958	(Dot 15781)
2	Susie Darlin' (Re-Entry)	(London Hld8676)	23	1958	0	1958	
3	Susie Darlin' (2nd Re-Entry)	(London Hld8676)	23	1958	0	1958	
	THE HIT WAS MADE WITH REFERENCE TO HIS SISTER SUSIE						
Robin McnNamara He Was Involved With The Original Cast Of *Hair*							
1	Lay A Little Lovin' On Me		0	1970	11	1970	(Steed 724)
Robin S Female Vocalist, Real Name Robin Stone from Jamaica, New York							
* 1	Show Me Love	(Championchampcd 300)	59	1993	5	1993	(Big Beat 10118)
2	Show Me Love (Re-Entry)	(Championchampcd 300)	6	1993		1993	
3	Luv 4 Luv	(Championchampcd 301)	11	1993	0	1993	
4	What I Do Best	(Championchampcd 307)	43	1993	0	1993	
5	I Want To Thank You	(Championchampcd 310)	48	1994	0	1994	
6	Back It Up	(Championchampcd 312)	43	1994	0	1994	
7	Show Me Love	(Championchampcd 326)	9	1997	0	1997	
8	It Must Be Love	(Atlantic A	37	1997	96	1997	(Atlantic 98023)
Robin Sarstedt Male Vocalist from the UK							
1	My Resistance Is Low	(Decca F 13624)	3	1976	0	1976	

ISSUE	TITLE	UK LBL	UK POS	UK YEAR	US POS	US YEAR	US LBL
Robin Ward Real Name Jackie Ward From Nebraska							
1	Wonderful Summer		0	1963	14	1963	(Dot 16530)
Robson & Jerome Male Actor/Vocalists, Real Names Robson Green & Jerome Flynn from the UK							
1	Unchained Melody / (There'll Be Bluebirds Over) (RCA 74321284362) The White Cliffs Of Dover		1	1995	0	1995	
2	Unchained Melody / (There'll Be Bluebirds Over) (RCA 74321284362) The White		63	1995	0	1995	
3	I Believe / Up On The Roof	(RCA 74321326882)	1	1995	0	1995	
4	What Becomes Of The Broken Hearted/ Saturday Night Atthe Movies	(RCA 74321424732)	1	1996	0	1996	
Robyn Female Vocalist From Sweden							
1	You've Got That Something	(RCA 74321393462)	54	1996	0	1996	
2	Do You Know (What It Takes)	(RCA 74321509932)	26	1997	36	1997	(RCA 64865)
Rocco Granata & The International Quintet Singer/Songwriter/Accordionist, B: 1938 Waterschei, Belgium							
* 1	Marina		0	1960	31	1960	(Laurie 3041)
	THE HIT WAS A SMASH IN EUROPE AND SOLD OVER A MILLION IN GERMANY ALONE						
Rochell & The Candles R&B Group From Los Angeles With Johnny Wyatt, Rochell Henderson, Melvin Sasso & T.C. Henderson							
1	Once Upon A Time		0	1961	26	1961	(Swingin' 623)
Obituary: Wyatt D: 1983.							
Rochelle Female Vocalist from the UK							
1	My Magic Man	(Warner Brosw 8838)	27	1986	0	1986	
Rock Aid Armenia Male Vocal/Instrumental Charity Assembly from the UK							
1	Smoke On The Water	(Life Aid Armenia Armen39001)		1989	0	1989	
Rock Candy Male Vocal/Instrumental Group from the UK							
1	Remember	(MCA Mk 5069)	32	1971	0	1971	
Rock Goddess Female Vocal/Instrumental Group from the UK							
1	My Angel	(A&M Ams 8311)	64	1983	0	1983	
2	I Didn't Know I Loved You	(A&M Ams 185)	57	1984	0	1984	
Rock-A-Teens Rock And Roll Sextet Led By Vic Mizelle from the USA							
1	Woo-Hoo		0	1959	16	1959	(Roulette 4192)
Rocker's Revenge Mixed Vocal/Instrumental Group from the USA							
1	Walking On Sunshine	(London Lon 11)	4	1982	0	1982	
2	The Harder They Come	(London Lon 18)	30	1983	0	1983	
	HIT 1 IS CREDITED TO ROCKER'S REVENGE FEATURING DONNIE CALVIN						
Rocket From The Crypt Male Vocal/Instrumental Group from the USA							
1	Born In '69	(Elemental Elm32cd)	68	1996	0	1996	
2	Young Livers	(Elemental Elm33cds)	67	1996	0	1996	
3	On A Rope	(Elemental Elh38cds1)	12	1996	0	1996	
Rockets Detroit Band Led By David Gilbert							
1	Oh Well		0	1979	30	1979	(Rso 935)
Rockford Files Male Instrumental/Production Duo from the UK							
1	You Sexy Dancer	(Escapade/Rumour Cdjape 7)	34	1995	0	1995	
2	You Sexy Dancer (Re-Issue)	(Escapade/Rumour Cdjape 14)	59	1996	0	1996	
Rockin' Berries Male Vocal/Instrumental Group from the UK							
1	I Didn't Mean To Hurt You	(Piccadilly 7n35197)	43	1964	0	1964	
2	He's In Town	(Piccadilly 7n35203)	3	1964	0	1964	
3	What In The World's Come Over You	(Piccadilly 7n35217)	23	1965	0	1965	
4	Poor Mans Son	(Piccadilly 7n35236)	5	1965	0	1965	
5	You're My Girl	(Piccadilly 7n35254)	40	1965	0	1965	
6	The Water Is Over My Head	(Piccadilly 7n35270)	43	1966	0	1966	
7	The Water Is Over My Head (Re-Entry)	(Piccadilly 7n35270)	50	1966	0	1966	
Rocksteady Crew Mixed Vocal Group from the USA							
1	(Hey You) The Rocksteady Crew	(Charisma/Virgin Rsc 1)	6	1983	0	1983	
2	Uprock	(Charisma/Virgin Rsc 2)	64	1984	0	1984	
Rockwell Male Vocalist, Real Name Kennedy Gordy B: 15 Mar 1964 Detroit							
* 1	Somebody's Watching Me	(Motown Tmg1331)	6	1984	2	1984	(Motown 1702)
2	Obscene Phone Caller		0	1984	35	1984	(Motown 1731)
3	I Fell In Love		0	1996	61	1996	(Robbins 72007)
	BACKING VOCALS ON HIT 1 ARE BY MICHAEL JACKSON						

ISSUE	TITLE	UK LBL	UK POS	UK YEAR	US POS	US YEAR	US LBL
Rocky Burnette Male Vocalist, B: 12 Jun 1953 Memphis, Son Of Johnny Burnette, Nephew Of Dorsey Burnette							
1	Tired Of Toein' The Line		58	1979	8	1980	(EMI America 8043)
Rocky Fellers Family Group Of Eddie, Tony, Albert & Junior Feller							
1	Killer Joe		0	1963	16	1963	(Scepter 1246)
Rocky Sharpe & The Replays Mixed Vocal Group from the UK							
1	Rama Lama Ding Dong	(Chiswick Chis104)	17	1978	0	1978	
2	Imagination	(Chiswick Chis110)	39	1979	0	1979	
3	Love Will Make You Fail In School	(Chiswick Chis114)	60	1979	0	1979	
4	Martian Hop	(Chiswick Chis121)	55	1980	0	1980	
5	Shout Shout (Knock Yourself Out)	(Chiswick Dice	19	1982	0	1982	
6	Clap Your Hands	(Rak 345)	54	1982	0	1982	
7	If You Wanna Be Happy	(Polydor Posp560)	46	1983	0	1983	
	HITS 3-4 ARE CREDITED TO ROCKY SHARPE & THE REPLAYS FEATURING THE TOP LINERS						
Rococo Mixed Vocal/Instrumental Group from the UK/Italy							
1	Italo House Mix	(Mercury Mer314)	54	1989	0	1989	
Rod Bernard Male R&B Vocal/Guitarist, B: 12 Aug 1940 Louisiana							
1	This Should Go On Forever		0	1959	20	1959	(Argo 5327)
Rod Lauren Male Vocalist, B: 26 Mar 1940							
1	If I Had A Girl		0	1960	31	1960	(RCA 7645)
Rod Stewart Male Vocalist, Real Name Roderick Stewart B: 10 Jan 1945 London, England.							
* 1	Maggie May	(Mercury 6052097)	1	1971	1	1971	(Mercury 73224)
2	Reason To Believe	(Mercury 6052097)	19	1971	0	1971	
3	(I Know) I'm Losing You		0	1971	24	1971	(Mercury 73244)
4	You Wear It Well	(Mercury 6052171)	1	1972	13	1972	(Mercury 73330)
5	Angel	(Mercury 6052 198)	4	1972	40	1972	(Mercury 73344)
6	What Made Milwaukee Famous (Has Made A Loser Out Of Me)	(Mercury 6052198)	4	1972	0	1972	
7	I've Been Drinking	(Rak Rr 4)	27	1973	0	1973	
8	Oh No Not My Baby	(Mercury 6052371)	6	1973	0	1973	
9	Farewell - Bring It On Home To Me / You Send Me	(Mercury 667033)	7	1974	0	1974	
10	Sailing	(Warner Brosk 16600)	1	1975	0	1975	
11	This Old Heart Of Mine	(Riva 1)	4	1975	0	1976	
* 12	Tonight's The Night (Gonna Be Alright)	(Riva 3)	5	1976	1	1976	(Warner Bros 8262)
13	The Killing Of Georgie	(Riva 4)	2	1976	30	1976	(Warner Bros 8396)
14	Sailing (Re-Entry)	(Wrner Bros K16600)	3	1976	0	1976	
15	Get Back	(Riva 6)	11	1976	0	1976	
16	Maggie May (Re-Entry)	(Mercury 6160006)	31	1976	0	1976	
17	I Don't Want To Talk About It	(Riva 7)	1	1977	0	1977	
18	The First Cut Is The Deepest	(Riva 7)	1	1977	21	1977	(Warner Bros 8321)
* 19	You're In My Heart (The Final Acclaim)	(Riva 11)	3	1977	4	1977	(Warner Bros 8475)
20	Hotlegs	(Riva 10)	5	1978	28	1978	(Warner Bros 8535)
21	I Was Only Joking	(Rica 10)	5	1978	22	1978	(Warner Bros 8568)
22	Ole Ola (Mulher Brasileira)	(Riva 15)	4	1978	0	1978	
* 23	Da Ya Think I'm Sexy	(Riva 17)	1	1978	1	1979	(Warner Bros 8724)
24	Ain't Love A Bitch	(Riva 18)	11	1979	22	1979	(Warner Bros 8810)
25	Blondes (Have More Fun)	(Riva 19)	63	1979	0	1979	
26	If Loving You Is Wrong (I Don't Want To Be Right)	(Riva 23)	23	1980	0	1980	
27	Passion	(Riva 26)	17	1980	5	1980	(Warner Bros 49617)
28	My Girl	(Riva 28)	32	1980	0	1980	
29	Tonight I'm Yours (Don't Hurt Me)	(Riva 33)	8	1981	20	1982	(Warner Bros 49886)
30	Young Turks	(Riva 34)	11	1981	5	1981	(Warner Bros 49843)
31	How Long	(Riva 35)	41	1982	0	1982	
32	Baby Jane	(Warner Brosw 9608)	1	1983	14	1983	(Warner Bros 29608)
33	What Am I Gonna Do (I'm So In Love With You)	(Warner Bros W 9564)	3	1983	35	1983	(Warner Bros 29564)
34	Sweet Surrender	(Warner Brosw 9440)	23	1983	0	1983	
35	Infatuation	(Warner Brosw 9256)	27	1984	6	1984	(Warner Bros 29256)
36	Some Guys Have All The Luck	(Warner Brosw 9204)	15	1984	10	1984	(Warner Bros 29215)
37	Love Touch	(Warner Bros W 8668)	27	1986	6	1986	(Warner Bros 28668)
38	Love Touch (Re-Entry)	(Warner Brosw 8668)	69	1986	0	1986	
39	Every Beat Of My Heart	(Warner Brosw 8625)	2	1986	0	1986	

ISSUE	TITLE	UK LBL	UK POS	UK YEAR	US POS	US YEAR	US LBL
40	Another Heartache	(Warner Brosw 8631)	54	1986	0	1986	
41	Sailing (2nd Re-Entry)	(Warner Brosk 16600)	41	1987	0	1987	
42	Lost In You	(Warner Brs W7927)	21	1988	12	1988	(Warner Bros 27927)
43	Forever Young	(Warner Brosw 7796)	57	1988	12	1988	(Warner Bros 27796)
44	My Heart Can't Tell You No	(Warner Brosw 7729)	49	1989	4	1989	(Warner Bros 27729)
45	Crazy About Her		0	1989	11	1989	(Warner Bros 27657)
46	This Old Heart Of Mine	(Warner Brosw 2686)	51	1989	10	1990	(Warner Bros 19983)
47	Downtown Train	(Warner B W2647) Ros	10	1990	3	1989	(Warner Bros 22685)
48	It Takes Two	(Warner Brosrod 1)	5	1990	0	1990	
49	Rhythm Of My Heart	(Warner Brosw 0017)	3	1991	5	1991	(Warner Bros 19366)
50	The Motown Song	(Warner Brosw 0030)	10	1991	10	1991	(Warner Bros 19322)
51	My Town	(EMI Em 212)	33	1991	0	1991	
52	Broken Arrow	(Warner Brosw 0059)	41	1991	20	1991	(Warner Bros 19274)
53	People Get Ready	(Epic 6577567)	49	1992	0	1992	
54	Your Song / Broken Arrow (Re-Issue)	(Warner Brosw 0104)	41	1992	0	1992	
55	Tom Traubert's Blues (Waltzing Matilda)	(Warner Brosw 0144)	6	1992	0	1992	
56	Ruby Tuesday	(Warner Brosw 0158cd)	11	1993	0	1993	
57	Shotgun Wedding	(Warner Brosw 0171cd)	21	1993	0	1993	
* 58	Have I Told You Lately	(Warner Brosw 0185cd)	5	1993	5	1993	(Warner Bros 18511)
* 59	Reason To Believe (Re-Recording)	(Warner Brosw 0198cd1)	51	1993	19	1993	(Warner Bros 18427)
60	People Get Ready (Re-Recording)	(Warner Bros W 0226cd1)	45	1993	0	1993	
* 61	All For Love	(A&M 5804772)	2	1994	1	1993	(A&M 0476)
62	Having A Party		0	1994	36	1994	(Warner Bros 18424)
63	You're The Star	(Warner Brosw 0296cd)	19	1995	0	1995	
64	Lady Luck	(Warner Brosw 0310cd1)	56	1995	0	1995	
65	Purple Heather	(Warner Brosw 0345cd)	16	1996	0	1996	
66	If We Fall In Love Tonight	(Warner Brosw 0380cd)	58	1996	54	1996	(Warner Bros 17459)

Rodeo Jones Mixed Vocal/Instrumental Group from the UK/Grenada

1	Natural World	(A&M Amcd 0165)	75	1993	0	1993	
2	Shades Of Summer	(A&M Amcd 212)	59	1993	0	1993	

Rodger Collins Male Vocalist from the USA

1	You Sexy Sugar Plum (But I Like It)	(Fantasy Ftc132)	22	1976	0	1976	

Rodney Crowell Male Country Singer/Songwriter/Guitarist, B: 7 Aug 1950 Houston

3	Ashes By Now		0	1980	37	1980	(Warner Bros 4922)

Rodney Franklin Male Pianist from the USA

1	The Groove	(CBS 8529)	7	1980	0	1980	

Rofo Male Production/Instrumental Duo from the UK

1	Rofo's Theme	(PWLcontinentalpwlt 236)	44	1992	0	1992	

Roger Male Vocalist, Real Name Roger Troutman Hamilton, Ohio

1	I Want To Be Your Man	(Reprise 8229)	61	1987	3	1988	(Reprise 28229)
2	Boom! There She Was	(Virgin Vs 1143)	55	1988	0	1988	

HIT 2 IS CREDITED TO SCRITTI POLITTI FEATURING ROGER • ROGER WAS THE LEADER OF ZAPP, SEE ALSO SCRITTI POLITTI

Roger Christian Male Vocalist from the UK

1	Take It From Me	(Island Is 427)	89	1994	0	1994	

Roger Coleman Male Vocalist from the USA

1	You Say It With Your Eyes		0	1953	29	1953	(Decca 28529)

Roger Daltrey Male Vocalist, B: 1 Mar 1944 London, England

1	Giving It All Away	(Track 2094 110)	5	1973	0	1973	
2	I'm Free	(Ode Ods 66302)	13	1973	0	1973	
3	Written On The Wind	(Polydor 2121319)	46	1977	0	1977	
4	Free Me	(Polydor 2001980)	39	1980	0	1980	
5	Without Your Love	(Polydor Posp181)	55	1980	20	1980	(Polydor 2121)
6	Walking In My Sleep	(Wea U 9686)	56	1984	0	1984	
7	After The Fire	(10 Ten 69)	50	1985	0	1985	
8	Under The Raging Moon	(10 Ten 81)	43	1986	0	1986	

SEE ALSO THE WHO

Roger Miller Male Vocalist, Real Name Roger Dean Miller B: 2 Jan 1936 In Fort Worth, Texas

* 4	Dang Me		0	1964	7	1964	(Smash 1881)
* 5	Chug-A-Lug		0	1964	9	1964	(Smash 1926)
6	Do-Wacka-Do		0	1965	31	1965	(Smash 1947)
* 7	King Of The Road	(Philips Bf 1397)	1	1965	4	1965	(Smash 1965)
8	Engine Engine Number 9	(Philips Bf 1416)	33	1965	7	1965	(Smash 1983)

ISSUE	TITLE	UK LBL	UK POS	UK YEAR	US POS	US YEAR	US LBL
9	One Dyin' And A Buryin'		0	1965	34	1965	(Smash 1994)
10	Kansas City Star	(Philips Bf 1437)	48	1965	31	1965	(Smash 1998)
11	England Swings	(Philips Bf 1456)	45	1965	8	1965	(Smash 2010)
12	England Swings (Re-Entry)	(Philips Bf 1456)	13	1966	0	1966	
13	Husbands And Wives		0	1966	26	1966	(Smash 2024)
! 14	I've Been A Long Time Leavin' (But I'll Be A Long Time Gone)		0	1966	13	1966	(Smash 2024)
15	You Can't Roller Skate In A Buffalo Herd		0	1966	40	1966	(Smash 2043)
16	My Uncle Used To Love Me But She Died		0	1966	58	1966	(Smash 2055)
17	Heartbreak Hotel		0	1966	84	1966	(Smash 2066)
18	Walkin' In The Sunshine		0	1967	37	1967	(Smash 2081)
19	Little Green Apples	(Mercury Mf1021)	19	1968	39	1968	(Smash 2148)
20	Vance		0	1968	80	1968	(Smash 2197)
21	Little Green Apples (Re-Entry)	(Mercury Mf1021)	48	1969	0	1969	
22	Little Green Apples (2nd Re-Entry)	(Mercury Mf1021)	39	1969	0	196	

OTHER HITS ARE C/W • HITS 43-44 ARE CREDITED TO ROGER MILLER AND WILLIE NELSON (WITH RAY PRICE)

Roger Taylor Male Vocalist from the UK

	1	Future Management	(EMI 5157)	49	1981	0	1981	
	2	Man On Fire	(EMI 5478)	66	1984	0	1984	
	3	Radio	(Epic 6584367)	37	1992	0	1992	
	4	Nazis	(Parlophonecdr 6379)	22	1994	0	1994	
	5	Foreign Sand	(Parlophonecdr 6389)	26	1994	0	1994	
	6	Happiness	(Parlophonecdr 6399)	32	1994	0	1994	

HIT 3 IS CREDITED TO SHAKY FEATURING ROGER TAYLOR • HIT 5 IS CREDITED TO ROGER TAYLOR AND YOSHIKI

Roger Voudouris Male Singer/Songwriter, B: 29 Dec 1954 Sacramento, California

	1	Get Used To It		0	1979	21	1979	(Warner Bros 8762)

Roger Waters Male Vocal/Instrumentalist from the UK

	1	Radio Waves	(Harvest Em 6)	74	1987	0	1987	
	2	The Tide Is Turning (After Live Aid)	(Harvest Em 37)	84	1987	0	1987	
	3	What God Wants (Part 1)	(Columbia 6581390)	35	1992	0	1992	

Roger Whittaker Male Vocalist, B: 22 Mar 1936 Nairobi, Kenya

	1	Durham Town	(Columbia Db8613)	12	1969	0	1969	
	2	I Don't Believe In If Anymore	(Columbia Db8664)	8	1970	0	1970	
	3	New World In The Morning	(Columbia Db8718)	17	1970	0	1970	
	4	Why	(Columbia Db8752)	47	1971	0	1971	
	5	Mammy Blue	(Columbia Db8822)	31	1971	0	1971	
	6	The Last Farewell	(EMI 2294)	2	1975	19	1975	(RCA 50030)
	7	The Skye Boat Song	(Tembo Tml 119)	10	1976	0	1976	

HIT 7 IS CREDITED TO ROGER WHITTAKER AND DES O' CONNOR

Roger Williams Real Name Louis Weertz B: 1925 Omaha

*	1	Autumn Leaves		0	1955	1	1955	(Kapp 116)
	2	Wanting You		0	1956	38	1956	(Kapp 127)
	3	La Mer (Beyond The Sea)		0	1956	37	1956	(Kapp 138)
	4	Almost Paradise		0	1957	15	1957	(Kapp 175)
	5	Till		0	1957	22	1957	(Kapp 197)
	6	Near You		0	1958	10	1958	(Kapp 233)
	7	Born Free		0	1966	7	1966	(Kapp 767)

Rokes Male Vocal/Instrumental Group from the UK

*	1	Piangi Con Me (Cry With Me)		0	1967	0	1967	

NAMES SHEL, JOHNY, BOBBY & MIKE

Rokotto Male Vocal/Instrumental Group from the UK

	1	Boogie On Up	(State Stat 62)	40	1977	0	1977	
	2	Funk Theory	(State Stat 80)	49	1978	0	1978	

Roland Rat Male Rat/Vocalist from the UK

	1	Rat Rapping	(Rodent Rat 1)	14	1983	0	1983	
	2	Love Me Tender	(Rodent Rat 2)	32	1984	0	1984	
	3	No. 1 Rat Fan	(Rodent Rat 4)	72	1985	0	1985	

Roland Stone The Hit Was Written By Mac Rebennack

*	1	Something Special		0	1960	0	1960	(Ace)

Rolf Harris Male Vocalist, B: 30 Mar 1930 Perth, Australia

*	1	Tie Me Kangaroo Down Sport	(Columbia Db4483)	9	1960	3	1963	(Epic 9596)
	2	Sun Arise	(Columbia Db4888)	3	1962	0	1962	
	3	Johnny Day	(Columbia Db4979)	44	1963	0	1963	
	4	Bluer Than Blue	(Columbia Db8553)	30	1969	0	1969	

ISSUE	TITLE	UK LBL	UK POS	UK YEAR	US POS	US YEAR	US LBL
* 5	Two Little Boys	(Columbia Db8630)	1	1969	0	1969	
6	Two Little Boys (Re-Entry)	(Columbia Db8630)	50	1970	0	1970	
7	Stairway To Heaven	(Vertigo Vercd73)	7	1993	0	1993	
8	Bohemian Rhapsody	(Living Beatlbecd 41)	50	1996	0	1996	

HE RECEIVED THE M.B.E IN 1968 AND THE O.B.E. IN 1977 • THE SON OF WELSH PARENTS FROM CARDIFF WHO EMIGRATED TO AUSTRALIA IN 1958

Rolling Stones   Male Vocal/Instrumental Group from the UK

ISSUE	TITLE	UK LBL	UK POS	UK YEAR	US POS	US YEAR	US LBL
1	Come On	(Decca F 11675)	21	1963	0	1963	
2	I Wanna Be Your Man	(Decca F 11764)	12	1963	0	1963	
3	Not Fade Away	(Decca F 11845)	3	1964	48	1964	(London 9657)
* 4	It's All Over Now	(Decca F 11934)	1	1964	26	1964	(London 9687)
5	Tell Me (You're Coming Back)		0	1964	24	1964	(London 9682)
* 6	Time Is On My Side	(Rollingstones Rsr 111)	62	1982	6	1964	(London 9708)
7	Little Red Rooster	(Decca F 12014)	1	1964	0	1964	
8	Heart Of Stone		0	1965	19	1965	(London 9725)
* 9	The Last Time	(Decca F 12104)	1	1965	9	1965	(London 9741)
* 10	(I Can't Get No) Satisfaction	(Decca F 12220)	1	1965	1	1965	(London 9766)
* 11	Get Off Of My Cloud	(Decca F 12263)	1	1965	1	1965	(London 9792)
* 12	As Tears Go By		0	1966	6	1966	(London 9808)
* 13	19th Nervous Breakdown	(Decca 12331)	2	1966	2	1966	(London 9823)
* 14	Paint It Black	(Decca F 12395)	1	1966	1	1966	(London 901)
* 15	Mother's Little Helper		0	1966	8	1966	(London 902)
16	Lady Jane			1966	24	1966	(London 902)
* 17	Have You Seen Your Mother Baby Standing In The Shadow	(Decca F 12497)	5	1966	9	1966	(London 903)
18	Let's Spend The Night Together	(Decca F 12546)	3	1967	0	1967	
* 19	Ruby Tuesday	(Decca F 12546)	3	1967	1	1967	(London 904)
20	We Love You	(Decca F 12654)	8	1967 *	21	Dandelion	(Decca F 12654) 8 1967 14 1967 (London 905)
22	She's A Rainbow		0	1967	25	1967	(London 906)
* 23	Jumping Jack Flash	(Decca F 12782)	1	1968	3	1968	(London 908)
* 24	Honky Tonk Woman	(Decca F 12952)	1	1969	1	1969	(London 910)
* 25	Brown Sugar	(Rollingstones Rs 19100)	2	1971	1	1971	(Rolling Stones 19100)
26	Wild Horses		0	1971	28	1971	(Rolling Stones 19101)
27	Street Fighting Man	(Decca F 13195)	21	1971	48	1968	(London 909)
28	Tumbling Dice	(Rollingstones Rs 19103)	5	1972	7	1972	(Rolling Stones 19103)
29	Happy		0	1972	22	1972	(Rolling Stones 19104)
30	You Can't Always Get What You Want		0	1973	42	1973	(London 910)
* 31	Angie	(Rollingstones Rs 19105)	5	1973	1	1973	(Rolling Stones 19105)
32	Doo Doo Doo Doo Doo (Heartbreaker)		0	1974	15	1974	(Rolling Stones 19109)
33	It's Only Rock And Roll (But I Like It)	(Rollingstones Rs 19114)	20	1974	16	1974	(Rolling Stones 19301)
34	Ain't Too Proud To Beg		0	1974	17	1974	(Rolling Stones 19302)
35	Out Of Time	(Decca F 13597)	45	1975	81	1975	(Abkco 4702)
36	I Don't Know Why		0	1975	42	1975	(Abkco 4701)
37	Fool To Cry	(RollingStones Rs 19121)	6	1976	10	1976	(Rolling Stones 19304)
* 38	Miss You	(Rollingstones Emi 2802)	3	1978	1	1978	(Rolling Stones 19307)
39	Far Away Eyes	(RollIngstones EmI 2802)	10	1978	0	1978	
40	Beast Of Burden		0	1978	8	1978	(Rolling Stones 19309)
41	Respectable	(Rollingstones Emi 2861)	23	1978	0	1978	
42	Shattered		0	1979	31	1979	(Rolling Stones 19310)
43	Emotional Rescue	(Rollingstones Rsr 105)	9	1980	3	1980	(Rolling Stones 20001)
44	She's So Cold	(Rolling Stones Rsr 106)	33	1980	26	1980	(Rolling Stones 21001)
45	Start Me Up	(Rolling Stones Rsr 108)	7	1981	2	1981	(Rolling Stones 21003)
46	Waiting On A Friend	(Rolling Stones Rsr 109)	50	1982	13	1982	(Rolling Stones 21004)
47	Hang Fire		0	1982	20	1982	(Rolling Stones 21300)
48	Going To A Go-Go (Live)	(Rolling Stones Rsr 110)	26	1982	25	1982	(Rolling Stones 21301)
49	Time Is On My Side	(Rolling Stones Rsr 111)	62	1982	0	1982	
50	Undercover Of The Night	(Rollingstones 99813)	11	1983	9	1983	(Rolling Stones Rsr 113)
51	She Was Hot	(Rollingstones Rsr 114)	42	1984	0	1984	
52	Brown Sugar (Re-Issue)	(Rollingstones Sugar 1)	58	1984	0	1984	
53	Harlem Shuffle	(Rollingstones A 6864)	13	1986	5	1986	(Rolling Stones 05802)
54	One Hit (To The Body)		0	1986	28	1986	(Rolling Stones 05906)
55	Mixed Emotions	(Rolling Stones 655193 7)	36	1989	5	1989	(Rolling Stones 69008)
56	Rock And A Hard Place	(Rollingstones 655422 7)	63	1989	23	1989	(Rolling Stones 73057)
57	Paint It Black (Re-Issue)	(London Lon264)	61	1990	0	1990	
58	Almost Hear You Sigh	(Rollingstones 656065 7)	31	1990	0	1990	

R
556

ISSUE	TITLE	UK LBL	UK POS	UK YEAR	US POS	US YEAR	US LBL
59	Highwire	(Rolling Stones 6567567)	29	1991	0	1991	
60	Ruby Tuesday (Live)	(Rollingstones 6568927)	59	1991	0	1991	
61	Love Is Strong	(Virgin Vscdt1503)	14	1994	0	1994	
62	You Got Me Rocking	(Virgin Vscdg1518)	23	1994	0	1994	
63	Out Of Tears	(Virgin Vscdt1524)	36	1994	0	1994	
64	I Go Wild	(Virgin Vscdx1539)	29	1995	0	1995	
65	Like A Rolling Stone	(Virgin Vscdt1562)	12	1995	0	1995	

NAMES: MICK JAGGER, KEITH RICHARDS, BRIAN JONES, BILL WYMAN & CHARLIE WATTS. JONES WAS REPLACED BY MICK TAYLOR. • OBITUARY: JONES D: 3 JUL 1969 DROWNED.

Rollins Band   Male Vocal/Instrumental Group from the USA

1	Tearing	(Imago72787250187)	54	1992	0	1992	
2	Liar / Disconnected	(Imago74321213052)	27	1994	0	1994	

Rollo   Male Producer, Full Name Rollo Armstring from the UK

1	Get Off Your High Horse	(Cheeky Chekcd003)	43	1994	0	1994	
2	Get Off Your High Horse (Re-Entry)	(Cheeky Chekce003)	47	1994	0	1994	
3	Love, Love, Love, Here I Come	(Cheeky Chekcd007)	32	1995	0	1995	
4	Let This Be A Prayer	(Cheeky Chekcd013)	26	1996	0	1996	

HITS 1-2 ARE CREDITED TO ROLLO GOES CAMPING • HIT 3 IS CREDITED TO ROLLO GOES MYSTIC
HIT 4 IS CREDITED TO ROLLO GOES SPIRITUAL FEATURING PAULINE TAYLOR

Roman Holiday   Male Vocal/Instrumental Group from the UK

1	Stand By	(Jive Jive 31)	61	1983	0	1983	
2	Don't Try To Stop It	(Jive Jive 39)	14	1983	0	1983	
3	Motormania	(Jive Jive 49)	40	1983	0	1983	

Romantics   Lead Singer With The Rock Quartet Is Wally Palmer

1	Talking In Your Sleep		0	1983	3	1983	(Nemperor 04135)
2	On In A Million		0	1984	37	1984	(Nemperor 04373)

Romeo Void   Lead Singer With The Quintet Is Debora Lyall

1	A Girl In Trouble (Is A Temporary Thing)		0	1984	35	1984	(Columbia 04534)

Ron Goodwin Orchestra   Orchestra from the UK

1	Theme From 'limelight'	(Parlophone R3686)	3	1953	0	1953	
2	Blue Star (The Medic Theme)	(Parlophone R4074)	20	1955	0	1955	
3	Shifting Whispering Sands (Part 1-2)	(Parlophone R4106)	18	1956	0	1956	

HIT 3 IS CREDITED TO EAMONN ANDREWS & RON GOODWIN ORCHESTRA & CHORUS

Ron Grainer & His Orchestra   Male Orchestra Leader from the UK

1	A Touch Of Velvet A Sting Of Brass	(Casinoclassics Cc 5)	60	1978	0	1978	

Ron Holden   Male R&B Vocalist, B: 7 Aug 1939 Seattle And Former Singer With The Playboys

1	Love You So		0	1960	7	1960	(Donna 1315)

THE BACKING GROUP ON THE HIT ARE THE THUNDERBIRDS

Ronald & Ruby   Names Ronald Gumby & Beverly Ross

1	Lollipop		0	1958	20	1958	(RCA 7174)

Rondo Veneziana   Orchestra From Italy

1	La Serenissima (Theme From *Venice In Peril*)	(Ferroway 7ron 1)	58	1983	0	1983	

Ronettes   Female Vocal Group from the USA   Originally Formed As The Darling Sisters In 1958

* 1	Be My Baby	(London Hlu9793)	4	1963	2	1963	(Philles 116)
2	Baby, I Love You	(London Hlu9826)	11	1964	24	1963	(Philles 118)
3	(The Best Part Of) Breaking Up	(London Hlu9905)	43	1964	39	1964	(Philles 120)
4	Do I Love You?	(London Hlu9922)	35	1964	34	1964	(Philles 121)
5	Walking In The Rain		0	1964	23	1964	(Philles 123)
6	Born To Be Together		0	1965	52	1965	(Philles 126)
7	Is This What I Get For Loving You		0	1965	75	1965	(Philles 128)

DISBANDED IN 1966.

Roni Hill   Female Vocalist from the USA

1	You Keep Me Hangin' On - Stop In The Name Of Love	(Creole Cr 138)	36	1977	0	1977	

Ronni Simon   Male Vocalist from the UK

1	B Good 2 Me	(Networknwkcd 80)	73	1994	0	1994	
2	Take You There	(Networknwkcd 85)	58	1995	0	1995	

Ronnie & The Hi-Lites   Lead Singer With The Rock Quintet Is Ronnie Goodson

1	I Wish That We Were Married		0	1962	16	1962	(Joy 260)

OBITUARY: GOODSON D: 4 NOV 1980 BRAIN TUMOUR.

Ronnie Bond   Male Vocalist from the UK

1	It's Written On Your Body	(Mercury Mer13)	52	1980	0	1980	

ISSUE	TITLE	UK LBL	UK POS	UK YEAR	US POS	US YEAR	US LBL
Ronnie Carroll	Male Vocalist from the UK						
1	Walk Hand In Hand	(Philips Pb 605)	13	1956	0	1956	
2	The Wisdom Of A Fool	(Philips Pb 667)	20	1957	0	1957	
3	Footsteps	(Philips Pb 1004)	36	1960	0	1960	
4	Ring-A-Ding Girl	(Philips Pb 1222)	46	1962	0	1962	
5	Roses Are Red	(Philips 326532bf)	3	1962	0	1962	
6	If Only Tomorrow	(Philips 326550bf)	33	1962	0	1962	
7	Say Wonderful Things	(Philips 326574bf)	6	1963	0	1963	
Ronnie Dove	Male Vocalist, B: 7 Sep 1940 Virginia						
1	Say You		0	1964	40	1964	(Diamond 167)
2	Right Or Wrong		0	1964	14	1964	(Diamond 173)
3	One Kiss For Old Time's Sake		0	1965	5	1965	(Diamond 179)
4	A Little Bit Of Heaven		0	1965	16	1965	(Diamond 184)
5	I'll Make All Your Dreams Come True		0	1965	21	1965	(Diamond 188)
6	Kiss Way		0	1965	25	1965	(Diamond 191)
7	When Liking Turns To Loving		0	1966	18	1966	(Diamond 195)
8	Let's Start All Over Again		0	1966	20	1966	(Diamond 198)
9	Happy Summer Days		0	1966	27	1966	(Diamond 205)
10	I Really Don't Want To Know		0	1966	22	1966	(Diamond 208)
11	Cry		0	1966	18	1966	(Diamond 214)
Ronnie Dyson	Male Vocalist, B: 5 Jun 1950 Washington						
1	(If You Let Me Make Love To You Then) Why Can't I Touch		0	1970	8	1970	(Columbia 45110)
2	When You Get Right Down To It	(CBS 7449)	34	1971	0	1971	
3	One Man Band (Plays All Alone)		0	1973	28	1973	(Columbia 45776)
	OBITUARY : D: 10 NOV 1990 HEART FAILURE.						
Ronnie Gaylord	Male Vocalist And Lead Singer With, And See Also The Gaylords						
1	Cuddle Me		0	1954	13	1954	(Mercury 70285)
Ronnie Griffith	Female Vocalist from the USA						
1	The Best Part Of Breaking Up	(Making Wavessurf 101)	63	1984	0	1984	
Ronnie Harris	Male Vocalist from the UK						
1	Story Of Tina	(Columbia Db3499)	12	1954	0	1954	
Ronnie Hawkins	Male Vocalist, B: 10 Jan 1935 Huntsville, Arkansas						
1	Forty Days		0	1959	45	1959	(Roulette 4154)
2	Mary Lou		0	1959	26	1959	(Roulette 4177)
Ronnie Hilton	Male Vocalist from the UK						
1	I Still Believe	(HMV B 10785)	3	1954	0	1954	
2	Veni Vidi Vici	(HMV B 10785)	12	1954	0	1954	
3	A Blossom Fell	(HMV B 10808)	10	1955	0	1955	
4	Stars Shine In Your Eyes	(HMV B 10901)	13	1955	0	1955	
5	Yellow Rose Of Texas	(HMV B 10924)	15	1955	0	1955	
6	Young And Foolish	(HMV Pop 154)	17	1956	0	1956	
7	Young And Foolish (Re-Entry)	(HMV Pop 154)	20	1956	0	1956	
8	Young And Foolish (2nd Re-Entry)	(HMV Pop 154)	19	1956	0	1956	
9	No Other Love	(HMV Pop 198)	1	1956	0	1956	
10	Who Are We	(HMV Pop 221)	6	1956	0	1956	
11	Woman In Love	(HMV Pop 248)	30	1956	0	1956	
12	Two Different Worlds	(HMV Pop 274)	13	1956	0	1956	
13	Around The World	(HMV Pop 338)	4	1957	0	1957	
14	Wonderful Wonderful	(HMV Pop 364)	27	1957	0	1957	
15	Magic Moments	(HMV Pop 446)	22	1958	0	1958	
16	I May Never Pass This Way Again	(HMV Pop 468)	30	1958	0	1958	
17	I May Never Pass This Way Again (Re-Entry)	(HMV Pop 468)	30	1958	0	1958	
18	I May Never Pass This Way Again (2nd Re-Entry)	(HMV Pop 468)	27	1958	0	1958	
19	The World Outside	(HMV Pop 559)	18	1959	0	1959	
20	The Wonder Of You	(HMV Pop 638)	22	1959	0	1959	
21	Don't Let The Rain Come Down	(HMV Pop 1291)	11	1964	0	1964	
22	A Windmill In Old Amsterdam	(HMV Pop 1378)	21	1965	0	1965	
Ronnie Lane & Slim Chance	Male Vocalist With Male Instrumental Group from the UK						
1	How Come	(Gm Gms 011)	11	1974	0	1974	
2	The Poacher	(Gm Gms 024)	36	1974	0	1974	
Ronnie McDowell	Male Country Singer, B: 26 Mar 1950 From Fountain Head, Tennessee						
* 1	The King Is Gone		0	1977	13	1977	(Scorpion 135)

ISSUE	TITLE	UK LBL	UK POS	UK YEAR	US POS	US YEAR	US LBL
	HIT IS A TRIBUTE TO ELVIS PRESLEY • REST ARE C/W HITS						
Ronnie Milsap Blind Male Country Singer/Multi-Instrumentalist B: 16 Jan 1946 From Robbinsville, North Carolina							
32	(There's No) Gettin' Over Me		0	1981	5	1981	(RCA 12264)
33	I Wouldn't Have Missed It For The World		0	1981	20	1981	(RCA 12342)
34	Any Day Now		0	1982	14	1982	(RCA 13216)
35	He Got You		0	1982	59	1982	(RCA 13286)
43	She Loves My Car		0	1984	84	1984	(RCA 13847)
Ronny & The Daytonas Real Name John Wilkin B: 26 Apr 1946, Tulsa, Oklahoma, The Daytonas Were Session Musicians							
* 1	G.T.O.		0	1964	4	1964	(Mala 481)
2	Sandy		0	1966	27	1966	(Mala 513)
Ronny Jordan Male Guitarist from the UK							
1	So What!	(Antilles Ann 14)	32	1992	0	1992	
2	Under Your Spell	(Island Cid 565)	72	1993	0	1993	
3	Tinsel Town	(Island Cid 566)	64	1994	0	1994	
4	Come With Me	(Island Cid 584)	63	1994	0	1994	
Rooftop Singers Mixed Vocal Trio From New York, Erik Darling, Lynee Taylor & Bill Svanoe. They Disbanded In 1967.							
* 1	Walk Right In	(Fontana Tf271700)	10	1963	1	1963	(Vanguard 35017)
2	Tom Cat		0	1963	20	1963	(Vanguard 35019)
	OBITUARY: D: LYNNE 1982.						
Rosanne Cash Female Vocalist B: 24 May 1955 Memphis, Daughter Of Johnny Cash							
4	Seven Year Ache		0	1981	22	1981	(Columbia 11426)
Rose Brennan Female Vocalist from Ireland							
1	Tall Dark Stranger	(Philips Pb 1193)	31	1961	0	1961	
Rose Garden Lead Singer With The Quintet Is Diana Di Rose							
1	Next Plane To London		0	1967	17	1967	(Atco 6510)
Rose Marie Female Vocalist from the UK							
1	When I Leave The World Behind	(A1 284)	75	1983	0	1983	
2	When I Leave The World Behind (Re-Entry)	(A1 284)	63	1983	0	1983	
3	When I Leave The World Behind (2nd Re-Entry)	(A1 284)	66	1983	0	1983	
Rose Of Romance Orchestra Orchestra from the UK							
1	Tara's Theme From (Gone With The Wind)	(Bbs Resl 108)	71	1982	0	1982	
Rose Royce Mixed Vocal/Instrumental Group from the USA, Formerly A Backing Group							
* 1	Car Wash	(MCA 267)	9	1976	1	1976	(MCA 40615)
2	Put Your Money Where Your Mouth Is	(MCA 259)	44	1977	0	1977	
3	I Wanna Get Next To You	(MCA 278)	14	1977	10	1977	(MCA 40662)
4	Do Your Dance (Part 1)	(Whitfield K17006)	30	1977	39	1977	(Whitfield 8440)
5	Wishing On A Star	(Warner Bros k 17060)	3	1978	0	1978	
6	It Makes You Feel Like Dancin'	(Warner Brosk 17060)	16	1978	0	1978	
7	Love Don't Live Here Anymore	(Whitfield F17236)	2	1978	32	1979	(Whitfield 8712)
8	I'm In Love And I Love The Feeling	(Whitfield K17291)	51	1979	0	1979	
9	Is It Love Your After	(Whitfield K17456)	13	1979	0	1979	
10	Ooh Boy	(Whitfield K17575)	46	1980	0	1980	
11	Rose Royce Express	(Warner Brosk 17875)	52	1981	0	1981	
12	Magic Touch	(Streetwavekhan 21)	43	1984	0	1984	
13	Love Me Right Now	(Streetwavekhan 39)	60	1985	0	1985	
14	Car Wash / Is It Love You're After (Re-Issue)	(MCA MCA 1253)	20	1988	0	1988	
Rose Tattoo Male Vocal/Instrumental Group from Australia							
1	Rock 'n' Roll Outlaw	(Carrere Car 200)	60	1981	0	1981	
Rosemary Clooney Female Vocalist B: 23 May 1928 Maysville, Kentucky							
1	You're Just In Love		0	1951	24	1951	(Columbia 39052)
* 2	Beautiful Brown Eyes		0	1951	11	1951	(Columbia 39212)
* 3	Come-On-A My House (From *The Son*)		0	1951	1	1951	(Columbia 39467)
4	Mixed Emotions		0	1951	22	1951	(Columbia 39333)
5	I'm Waiting Just For You		0	1951	21	1951	(Columbia 39535)
6	If Teardrops Were Pennies		0	1951	24	1951	(Columbia 39535)
7	I Wish I Wuz (From Slaughter Trail)		0	1951	27	1951	(Columbia 39536)
8	Be My Life's Companion		0	1952	18	1952	(Columbia 39631)
* 9	Tenderly		0	1952	30	1952	(Columbia 39631)
* 10	Half As Much	(Columbia Db3129)	3	1952	2	1952	(Columbia 39710)
* 11	Botch-A-Me (Ba-Ba-Baciami Piccina)		0	1952	26	1952	(Columbia 39767)
12	Too Old To Cut The Mustard		0	1952	12	1952	(Columbia 39812)
13	Blues In The Night		0	1952	17	1952	(Columbia 398713)
14	Who Kissed Me Last Night?		0	1953	23	1953	(Columbia 39816)
15	The Night Before Christmas Song		0	1952	9	1952	(Columbia 39876)

ISSUE	TITLE	UK LBL	UK POS	UK YEAR	US POS	US YEAR	US LBL
16	You'll Never Know (From *Hello, Frisco, Hello*)		0	1953	18	1953	(Columbia 39905)
17	If I Had A Penny		0	1953	26	1953	(Columbia 39910)
18	Dennis The Menace		0	1953	25	1953	(Columbia 39988)
19	Man	(Philips Pb 220)	7	1954	0	1954	
20	Happy Christmas, Little Friend		0	1954	30	1954	(Columbia 40102)
* 21	Hey There	(Philips Pb 494)	4	1955	1	1954	(Columbia 40266)
* 22	This Ole House	(Philips Pb 336)	1	1954	1	1954	(Columbia 40266)
23	Sisters		0	1954	30	1954	(Columbia 40305)
* 24	Mambo Italiano	(Philips Pb 382)	1	1954	10	1954	(Columbia 40361)
25	Count Your Blessing (Instead Of Sheep)		0	1954	27	1954	(Columbia 40370)
26	Where Will The Baby's Dimple Be	(Philips Pb 428)	6	1955	0	1955	
27	Memories Of You		0	1956	20	1956	(Columbia 40616)
28	Mangos	(Philips Pb 671)	25	1957	10	1957	(Columbia 40835)
29	Mangos (Re-Entry)	(Philips Pb 671)	17	1957	0	1957	

Rosemary June   Female Vocalist from the USA

1	In Apple Blossom Time	(Pye Internation 7n 25005)	14	1959	0	1959	

Rosetta Howard   Female Blues Vocalist From Chicago

1	Ebony Rhapsody		0	1948	21	1948	(Columbia 37573)
	OBITUARY: D: 1974.						

Rosie & The Originals   Lead Singer With The Group Is Rosalle Hamlin

1	Angel Baby		0	1960	5	1960	(Highland 1011)

Rosie Gaines   Female Vocalist from the USA

1	I Want U	(Motown8604852)	70	1995	0	1995	
2	Closer Than Close	(Big Bangcd Bbang 1)	4	1997	0	1997	

Rosie Vela   Female Vocalist from the USA

1	Magic Smile	(A&M Am 369)	27	1987	0	1987	

Rotterdam Termination Source   Male Production/Instrumental Duo from Holland

1	Poing	(Sep Edge 74)	27	1992	0	1992	
2	Merry X-Mess	(Reactcdreact 33)	73	1993	0	1993	

Routers   Rock And Roll Quintet from the USA, led by Mike Gordon

1	Let's Go	(Warner Bros WB 77)	32	1962	19	1962	(Warner Bros 5283)

Rover Boys   Lead Singer With The Quartet Is Billy Albert

1	Graduation Day		0	1956	16	1956	(ABC-Paramount 9700)

Roxanne Shante   Female Rapper from the USA

1	Have A Nice Day	(Breakout USA 612)	58	1987	0	1987	
2	Go On Girl	(Breakout USA 633)	55	1988	0	1988	
3	Sharp As A Knife	(Club Jab 73)	45	1988	0	1988	with Brandon Cooke
4	Go On Girl (Re-Mix)	(Breakout USA 689)	74	1990	0	1990	

Roxette   Mixed Vocal/Instrumental Duo, Per Gessele & Marie Fredriksson From Sweden)

* 1	The Look	(EMI Em 87)	7	1989	1	1989	(EMI 50190)
2	Dressed For Success	(EMI Em 96)	48	1989	14	1989	(EMI 50204)
3	Listen To Your Heart	(EMI Em 108)	62	1989	1	1989	(EMI 50223)
4	Dangerous		0	1990	2	1990	(EMI 50233)
* 5	It Must Have Been Love	(EMI Em 141)	3	1990	1	1990	(EMI 50283)
6	Listen To Your Heart (Re-Issue)	(EMI Em 149)	6	1990	0	1990	
7	Dressed For Success (Re-Issue)	(EMI Em 162)	18	1990	0	1990	
8	Joyride	(EMI Em 177)	4	1990	1	1991	(EMI 50342)
9	Fading Like A Flower (Every Time You Leave)	(EMI Em 190)	12	1991	2	1991	(EMI 50355)
10	The Big L	(EMI Em 204)	21	1991	0	1991	
11	Spending My Time	(EMI Em 215)	22	1991	32	1991	(EMI 50366)
12	Church Of Your Heart	(EMI Em 227)	21	1992	36	1992	(EMI 50380)
13	How Do You Do	(EMI Em 241)	13	1992	0	1992	
14	Queen Of Rain	(EMI Em 253)	28	1992	0	1992	
15	Almost Unreal	(EMI Em 268)	7	1993	0	1993	
16	It Must Have Been Love (Re-Issue)	(EMI Cdem 285)	10	1993	0	1993	
17	Sleeping In My Car	(EMI Cdem 314)	14	1994	0	1994	
18	Crash! Boom! Bang!	(EMI Cdems 324)	26	1994	0	1994	
19	Fireworks	(EMI Cdems 345)	30	1994	0	1994	
20	Run To You	(EMI Cdem 360)	27	1994	0	1994	
21	Vulnerable	(EMI Cdem 369)	44	1995	0	1995	
22	The Look (Re-Mix)	(EMI Cdem 406)	28	1995	0	1995	
23	You Don't Understand Me	(EMI Cdem 418)	42	1996	0	1996	

ISSUE	TITLE	UK LBL	UK POS	UK YEAR	US POS	US YEAR	US LBL
24	June Afternoon	(EMI Cdem 437)	52	1996	0	1996	

Roxy Music   Male Vocal/Instrumental Group from the UK

1	Virginia Plain	(Island Wip 6144)	4	1972	0	1972	
2	Pyjamarama	(Island Wip 6159)	10	1973	0	1973	
3	Street Life	(Island Wip 6173)	9	1973	0	1973	
4	All I Want Is You	(Island Wip 6208)	12	1974	0	1974	
5	Love Is The Drug	(Island Wip 6248)	2	1975	30	1976	(Atco 7042)
6	Both Ends Burning	(Island Wip 6262)	25	1975	0	1975	
7	Virginia Plain (Re-Issue)	(Polydor 2001739)	11	1977	0	1977	
8	Trash	(Polydor Posp32)	40	1979	0	1979	
9	Dance Away	(Polydor Posp44)	2	1979	0	1979	
10	Angel Eyes	(Polydor Posp67)	4	1979	0	1979	
11	Over You	(Polydor Posp93)	5	1980	0	1980	
12	Oh Yeah (On The Radio)	(Polydor 2001972)	5	1980	0	1980	
13	The Same Old Scene	(Polydor Roxy1)	12	1980	0	1980	
14	Jealous Guy	(EG ROXY 2)	1	1981	0	1981	
15	More Than This	(EG ROXY 3)	6	1982	0	1982	
16	Avalon	(EG ROXY 4)	13	1982	0	1982	
17	Take A Chance With Me	(EG ROXY 5)	26	1982	0	1982	
18	Love Is The Drug (Re-Mix)	(EG VSCDT 1580)	33	1996	0	1996	

Roy 'Chubby' Brown   Male Vocalist With Male Vocal/Instrumental Group From The UK

1	Living Next Door To Alice (Who The Fuck Is Alice)	(North Of Watford Cdwag 245)	64	1995	0	1995	
2	Living Next Door To Alice (Who The Fuck Is Alice) (Re-Entry) (North Of Watford Cdwag 245)		3	1995	0	1995	
3	Rockin' Good Christmas	(Polystar 5732612)	51	1996	0	1996	

HIT 1 IS CREDITED TO SMOKIE FEATURING ROY 'CHUBBY' BROWN

Roy Acuff   Male C/W Vocalist, B: Roy Claxton Acuff 15 Sep 1903 Maynardsville, Tennessee

1	Great Speckle Bird		0	1938	13	1938	(Vocalion 4252)
* 2	Wabash Cannon Ball		0	1938	12	1938	(Vocalion 4466)
3	The Prodigal Son		0	1944	19	1944	(Okeh 6716)
4	I'll Forgive You, But I Can't Forget		0	1944	26	1944	(Okeh 6723)

HIT 1 IS CREDITED TO ROY ACUFF & THE CRAZY TENNESSEEANS • OTHER HITS ARE C/W • OBITUARY: D: 23 NOV 1992 HEART FAILURE.

Roy Ayers   Male Vocal/Instrumentalist from the USA

1	Get On Up, Get On Down	(Polydor Ayers7)	41	1978	0	1978	
2	Eat Of The Beat	(Polydor Pops16)	43	1979	0	1979	
3	Don't Stop The Feeling	(Polydor Step6)	56	1980	0	1980	

Roy Brown   Male Vocal/Pianist/Writer, B: 10 Sep 1925 New Orleans

*+ 1	Cadillac Baby / Long About Sundown		0	1950	6	1950	(Deluxe 0000)
*+ 2	Hard Luck Blues		0	1950	1	1950	(Deluxe 3304)
*+ 3	Love Don't Love Nobody		0	1950	2	1950	(Deluxe 3306)
*+ 4	Big Town		0	1951	8	1951	(Deluxe 3318)
5	Let The Four Winds Blow		0	1957	29	1957	(Imperial 5439)

OBITUARY : D: 25 MAY 1981 HEART ATTACK IN LOS ANGELES.

Roy Buchanan   Male Guitarist from the USA

1	Sweet Dreams	(Polydor 2066307)	40	1973	0	1973	

Roy C   Male Vocalist from the USA

1	Shotgun Wedding	(Island Wi 273)	6	1966	0	1966	
2	Shotgun Wedding (Re-Issue)	(Uk 19)	8	1972	0	1972	

Roy Castle   Male Vocal/Multi-Instrumentalist from the UK

1	Little White Berry	(Philips Pb 1087)	40	1960	0	1960	

OBITUARY: D: 1995 CANCER.

Roy Clark   Male Guitarist/Banjo And Fiddle Player, B: 15 Apr 1933 Virginia

1	Tips Of My Fingers		0	1963	45	1963	(Capitol 4956)
6	Yesterday, When I Was Young		0	1969	19	1969	(Dot 17246)

OTHERS WERE C/W HITS

Roy Drusky   Male Country Singer, B: 22 Jun 1930 Atlanta

5	Three Hearts In A Tangle		0	1961	35	1961	(Decca 31193)

Roy Hamilton   Male Vocalist, B: 16 Apr 1929 Leesburg, Georgia

1	You'll Never Walk Alone (From *Carousel*)		0	1954	21	1954	(Epic 9015)
2	If I Loved You (From *Carousel*)		0	1954	26	1954	(Epic 9047)
3	Ebb Tide		0	1954	30	1954	(Epic 9068)
4	Unchained Melody		0	1955	6	1955	(Epic 9102)

ISSUE	TITLE	UK LBL	UK POS	UK YEAR	US POS	US YEAR	US LBL
5	Don't Let Go		0	1958	13	1958	(Epic 9257)
6	You Can Have Her		0	1961	12	1961	(Epic 9434)
	OBITUARY : D: 20 JUL 1969 FROM A STROKE.						

Roy Head & The Traits Male Vocalist, B: 9 Jan 1943 Three Rivers, Texas

1	Treat Her Right	(Vocalion V-P9248)	30	1965	2	1965	(Back Beat 546)
2	Just A Little Bit		0	1965	39	1965	(Scepter 12116)
3	Apple Of My Eye		0	1965	32	1965	(Back Beat 555)

Roy Milton Male Singer/Drummer, B: 1915 Tulsa, Oklahoma

* 1	R.M. Blues		0	1946	20	1946	(Juke Box 504)

Roy Orbison Male Vocalist, Real Name Roy Kelton Orbison B: 23 Apr 1936 In Vernon, Texas

1	Ooby Dooby		0	1956	59	1956	(Sun 242)
2	Uptown		0	1960	72	1960	(Monument 412)
* 3	Only The Lonely (Know How I Feel)	(London Hlu9149)	36	1960	2	1960	(Monument 421)
4	Only The Lonely (Know How I Feel) (Re-Entry)	(London Hlu9149)	1	1960	0	1960	
* 5	Blue Angel	(London Hlu9207)	11	1960	9	1960	(Monument 425)
6	I'm Hurtin'		0	1960	27	1960	(Monument 433)
* 7	Running Scared	(London Hlu9342)	9	1961	1	1961	(Monument 438)
* 8	Cryin'	(London Hlu9405)	25	1961	2	1961	(Monument 447)
9	Candy Man		0	1961	25	1961	(Monument 447)
* 10	Dream Baby	(London Hlu9511)	2	1962	4	1962	(Monument 456)
11	The Crowd	(London Hlu9561)	40	1962	26	1962	(Monument 461)
12	Leah		0	1962	25	1962	(Monument 467)
* 13	Workin' For The Man	(London Hlu9607)	50	1962	33	1962	(Monument 467)
* 14	In Dreams	(London Hlu9676)	6	1963	7	1963	(Monument 806)
* 15	Falling	(London Hlu9727)	9	1963	22	1963	(Monument 815)
16	Mean Woman Blues	(London Hlu9777)	3	1963	5	1963	(Monument 824)
* 17	Blue Bayou	(London Hlu9777)	3	1963	29	1963	(Monument 824)
18	Pretty Paper	(London Hlu9930)	6	1964	15	1963	(Monument 830)
19	Borne On The Wind	(London Hlu9845)	15	1964	0	1964	
* 20	It's Over	(London Hlu9882)	1	1964	9	1964	(Monument 837)
* 21	Oh Pretty Woman	(London Hlu9919)	1	1964	1	1964	(Monument 851)
22	Goodnight	(London Hlu9951)	14	1965	21	1965	(Monument 873)
23	(Say) Your My Girl	(London Hlu9978)	23	1965	39	1965	(Monument 891)
24	Ride Away	(London Hlu9986)	34	1965	25	1965	(Mgm 13386)
25	Crawlin' Back	(London Hlu10000)	19	1965	46	1965	(Mgm 13410)
26	Breakin' Up Is Breakin' My Heart	(London Hl10015)	22	1966	31	1966	(Mgm 13446)
27	Twinkle Toes	(London Hlu10034)	29	1966	39	1966	(Mgm 13498)
28	Lana	(London Hl10051)	15	1966	0	1966	
29	Too Soon To Know	(London Hlu10067)	3	1966	0	1966	
30	There Won't Be Many Coming Home	(London Hl10096)	18	1966	0	1966	
31	So Good	(London Hl10113)	32	1967	0	1967	
32	Walk On	(London Hlu10206)	39	1968	0	1968	
33	Heartache	(London Hlu10222)	44	1968	0	1968	
34	My Friend	(London Hl10261)	35	1969	0	1969	
35	Penny Arcade	(London Hl10285)	40	1969	0	1969	
36	Penny Arcade (Re-Entry)	(London Hl10285)	27	1969	0	1969	
37	That Lovin' You Feelin' Again		0	1980	55	1980	(Warner Bros 49262)
40	You Got It	(Virgin Vs 1166)	3	1989	9	1989	(Virgin 99245)
41	She's A Mystery To Me	(Virgin Vs 1173)	27	1989	0	1989	
44	I Drove All Night	(MCA Mcs 1652)	7	1992	0	1992	
45	Heartbreak Radio	(Virgin Americavus 68)	36	1992	0	1992	
46	I Drove All Night (Re-Issue)	(Virgin Americavuscd 79)	47	1993	0	1993	
	UNLISTED HITS WERE C/W • HIT 43 WAS RECORDED WITH BACKING VOCALS FROM BRUCE SPRINGSTEEN AND OTHERS						
	OBITUARY : CLAUDETTE (WIFE) D: 7 JUN 1966 MOTOR CYCLE ACCIDENT • TWO SONS D: 1969 IN A HOUSE FIRE. ROY D: 6 DEC 1988 HEART ATTACK.						

Roy Ross & His Orchestra Male Bandleader/Instrumentalist (Accordion, Piano) from the USA

1	Bewitched (From *Pal Joey*)		0	1950	28	1950	(Coral 60182)

Roy Wood Male Vocal/Multi-Instrumentalist from the UK

1	Dear Elaine	(Harvest Har5074)	18	1973	0	1973	
2	Forever	(Harvest Har5078)	13	1973	0	1973	
3	Going Down The Road	(Harvest Har5083)	13	1974	0	1974	
4	Oh! What A Shame	(Jet 754)	18	1975	0	1975	
5	Waterloo	(IRS Irm 125)	45	1986	0	1986	
6	I Wish It Could Be Christmas Every Day	(Woody Woody001cd)	59	1995	0	1995	
	HIT 5 IS CREDITED TO DOCTOR & THE MEDICS FEATURING ROY WOOD • HIT 6 IS CREDITED TO ROY WOOD BIG BAND						

ISSUE	TITLE	UK LBL	UK POS	UK YEAR	US POS	US YEAR	US LBL
Royal Guardsmen	Male Vocal/Instrumental Group from the USA Names John Burdett, Bill Balogh, Barry Winslow, Tom Richards, Billy Taylor & Chris Nunley.						
* 1	Snoopy Vs. The Red Barron	(Stateside Ss574)	8	1967	2	1966	(Laurie 3366)
2	Return Of The Red Barron	(Stateside Ss2010)	37	1967	15	1967	(Laurie 3379)
3	Baby Let's Wait		0	1969	35	1969	(Laurie 3461)
Royal House	Mixed Vocal/Instrumental Group from the USA						
1	Can You Party	(Championchamp 79)	14	1988	0	1988	
2	Yeah! Buddy	(Championchamp 9)	35	1989	0	1989	
Royal Philharmonic Orchestra	Orchestra Conducted By Louis Clark From Birmingham, UK						
1	Hooked On Classics	(RCA 109)	2	1981	10	1981	(RCA 12304)
2	Hooked On A Can-Can	(RCA 151)	47	1981	0	1981	
3	BBC World Cup Grandstand	(Bbc Resl 116)	61	1982	0	1982	
4	If You Knew Sousa (And Friends)	(RCA 256)	71	1982	0	1982	
Royal Scots Dragoon Guards	The Pipes And Drums & Military Band Of The Royal Scots Dragoon Guards from the UK.						
* 1	Amazing Grace	(RCA 2191)	1	1972	11	1972	(RCA 0709)
2	Heyken's Serenade	(RCA 2251)	30	1972	0	1972	
3	Little Drummer Boy	(RCA 2301)	13	1972	0	1972	
4	Amazing Grace (Re-Entry)	(RCA 2191)	42	1972	0	1972	
Royal Teens	Pop Quartet From New Jersey						
1	Short Shorts		0	1958	3	1958	(ABC-Paramount 9882)
2	Believe Me		0	1959	26	1959	(Capitol 4261)
	HIT 1 WAS FIRST RELEASED IN 1957						
Royalle Delite	Female Vocalist from the USA						
1	(I'll Be A) Freek For You	(Streetwavekhan 51)	45	1985	0	1985	
Royaltones	The Group Originally Formed As The Paragons In 1957						
1	Poor Boy		0	1958	17	1958	(Jubilee 5338)
Rozalla	Female Vocalist, Real Name Rozalla Miller B: 18 Mar 1964 From Ndola, Zambia						
1	Faith (In The Power Of Love)	(Pulse 8 Lose 7)	65	1991	0	1991	
2	Everybody's Free (To Feel Good)	(Pulse 8 Lose 13)	6	1991	37	1992	(Epic 74388)
3	Faith (In The Power Of Love) (Re-Issue)	(Pulse 8 Lose 15)	11	1991	0	1991	
4	Are You Ready To Fly	(Pulse 8 Lose 21)	14	1992	0	1992	
5	Love Breakdown	(Pulse 8 Lose 25)	65	1992	0	1992	
6	In 4 Choons Later	(Pulse 8 Lose 29)	50	1992	0	1992	
7	Don't Play With Me	(Pulse 8 Lose 52)	50	1993	0	1993	
8	I Love Music	(Epic 6598932)	18	1994	0	1994	
9	This Time I Found Love	(Epic 6603742)	33	1994	0	1994	
10	You Never Love The Same Way Twice	(Epic 6609052)	16	1994	0	1994	
11	Baby	(Epic 6611955)	26	1995	0	1995	
12	Everybody's Free (Re-Mix)	(Pulse 8 Cdlose110)	30	1996	0	1996	
Rtz	Rock Quintet From Boston						
1	Until Your Love Comes Back Around		0	1992	26	1992	(Giant 19051)
Rubettes	Male Vocal/Instrumental Group from the UK Names: Alan Williams, Tony Thorpe, Mick Clarke, Bill Hurd & John Richardson.						
* 1	Sugar Baby Love	(Polydor 2058442)	1	1974	37	1974	(Polydor 15089)
2	Tonight	(Polydor 2058529)	12	1974	0	1974	
3	Juke Box Jive	(Polydor 2058529)	3	1974	0	1974	
4	I Can Do It	(State Stat 1)	7	1975	0	1975	
5	Foe-Dee-O-Dee	(State Stat 7)	15	1975	0	1975	
6	Little Darling	(State Stat 13)	30	1975	0	1975	
7	You're The Reason Why	(State Stat 20)	28	1976	0	1976	
8	Under The Roof	(State Stat 27)	40	1976	0	1976	
9	Baby I Know	(State Stat 37)	10	1977	0	1977	
Rubicon	A Septet Led By Jerry Martini from the USA						
1	I'm Gonna Take Care Of Everything		0	1978	28	1978	(20th Century 2362)
Ruby & The Romantics	Mixed Vocal/Instrumental Group from the USA, Ed Roberts, George Lee, Ronald Mosley & Leroy Fann						
* 1	Our Day Will Come	(London Hlr9679)	38	1963	1	1963	(Kapp 501)
2	My Summer Love		0	1963	16	1963	(Kapp 525)
3	Hey There, Lonely Boy		0	1963	27	1963	(Kapp 544)
	LEAD IS RUBY NASH CURTIS B: 12 NOV 1939 • OBITUARY : ED D: 10 AUG 1993 AGED 57 CANCER. LEROY D: 1973.						
Ruby Murray	Female Vocalist from the UK						
1	Heartbeat	(Columbia Db3542)	3	1954	0	1954	
2	Softly Softly	(Columbia Db3558)	1	1955	0	1955	

ISSUE	TITLE	UK LBL	UK POS	UK YEAR	US POS	US YEAR	US LBL
3	Happy Days And Lonely Nights	(Columbia Db3577)	6	1955	0	1955	
4	Let Me Go Lover	(Columbia Db3577)	5	1955	0	1955	
5	If Anyone Finds This I Love You	(Columbia Db3580)	4	1955	0	1955	
6	Evermore	(Columbia Db3617)	3	1955	0	1955	
7	Softly Softly (Re-Entry)	(Columbia Db3558)	20	1955	0	1955	
8	I'll Come When You Call	(Columbia Db3643)	6	1955	0	1955	
9	You Are My First Love	(Columbia Db3770)	16	1956	0	1956	
10	You Are My First Love (Re-Entry)	(Columbia Db3770)	21	1956	0	1956	
11	Real Love	(Columbia Db4192)	18	1958	0	1958	
12	Goodbye Jimmy Goodbye	(Columbia Db4305)	10	1959	0	1959	
13	Goodbye Jimmy Goodbye (Re-Entry)	(Columbia Db4305)	26	1959	0	1959	

Ruby Turner   Female Vocalist from the UK

ISSUE	TITLE	UK LBL	UK POS	UK YEAR	US POS	US YEAR	US LBL
1	If You're Ready (Come Go With Me)	(Jive Jive 109)	30	1986	0	1986	
2	I'm In Love	(Jive Jive 118)	61	1986	0	1986	
3	Bye Baby	(Jive Jive 126)	52	1986	0	1986	
4	I'd Rather Go Blind	(Jive Rts 1)	24	1987	0	1987	
5	I'm In Love	(Jive Rts 2)	57	1987	0	1987	
6	It's Gonna Be Alright	(Jive Rts 7)	57	1990	0	1990	
7	Stay With Me Baby	(M&G Magcd 53)	39	1994	0	1994	
8	Shakaboom!	(Telstar Huntcd 1)	64	1995	0	1995	

Ruby Winters   Female Vocalist from the USA

ISSUE	TITLE	UK LBL	UK POS	UK YEAR	US POS	US YEAR	US LBL
1	I Will	(Creole Cr 141)	4	1977	0	1977	
2	Come To Me	(Creole Cr 153)	11	1978	0	1978	
3	I Won't Mention It Again	(Creole Cr 160)	45	1978	0	1978	
4	Baby Lay Down	(Creole Cr 171)	43	1979	0	1979	

Ruby Wright   Female Vocalist from the UK

ISSUE	TITLE	UK LBL	UK POS	UK YEAR	US POS	US YEAR	US LBL
1	Bimbo	(Parlophone R3816)	7	1954	0	1954	
2	Bimbo (Re-Entry)	(Parlophone R3816)	12	1954	0	1954	
3	Three Stars	(Parlophone R4556)	19	1959	0	1959	

Rude Boys   Vocal Quintet Led By Larry Marcus

ISSUE	TITLE	UK LBL	UK POS	UK YEAR	US POS	US YEAR	US LBL
1	Written All Over Your Face		0	1991	16	1991	(Atlantic 87805)

Rudy Grant   Male Vocalist From Guyana

ISSUE	TITLE	UK LBL	UK POS	UK YEAR	US POS	US YEAR	US LBL
1	Lately	(Ensign Eny 202)	58	1981	0	1981	

Rudy Vallee & His Connecticut Yankees   Male Bandleader/Vocalist, Real Name Herbert Pryor Vallee B: 28 Jul 1901 Island Point, Usa

ISSUE	TITLE	UK LBL	UK POS	UK YEAR	US POS	US YEAR	US LBL
73	The Whiffenpoof Song		0	1946	20	1946	(Enterprise 181)

Ruffneck (Featuring) Yavahn   Mixed Vocal/Instrumental Group from the USA

ISSUE	TITLE	UK LBL	UK POS	UK YEAR	US POS	US YEAR	US LBL
1	Everybody Be Somebody	(Positiva Cdtiv46)	13	1995	0	1995	
2	Move Your Body	(Positiva Cdtiv61)	60	1996	0	1996	

Rufus Thomas   Male Vocalist, B: 26 Mar 1917 Cayce, Mississippi, He Was Formerly A Dj In Memphis

ISSUE	TITLE	UK LBL	UK POS	UK YEAR	US POS	US YEAR	US LBL
1	Walking The Dog		0	1963	10	1963	(Stax 140)
+ 2	The Dog		0	1963	22	1963	(Stax 130)
3	Do The Funky Chicken	(Stax 144)	18	1970	28	1970	(Stax 0059)
4	(Do The) Push And Pull (Part 1)		0	1970	25	1970	(Stax 0079)
5	The Breakdown (Part 1)		0	1971	31	1971	(Stax 0098)

Rugbys   Names: Ed Vernon, Steve McNichol, Mike Momel & Glenn Howerton

ISSUE	TITLE	UK LBL	UK POS	UK YEAR	US POS	US YEAR	US LBL
1	You, I		0	1969	24	1969	(Amazon 1)

Rumple-Stilts-Skin   Mixed Vocal/Instrumental Group from the USA

ISSUE	TITLE	UK LBL	UK POS	UK YEAR	US POS	US YEAR	US LBL
1	I Think I Want To Dance With You	(Polydor Posp649)	51	1983	0	1983	

Run D.M.C.   Male Rap Trio, Joseph Simmons, Darryl McDaniels & Jason Mizell from the USA.

ISSUE	TITLE	UK LBL	UK POS	UK YEAR	US POS	US YEAR	US LBL
1	My Adidas / Peter Piper	(London Lon101)	62	1986	0	1986	
2	Walk This Way	(London Lon104)	8	1986	4	1986	(Profile 5112)
3	You Be Illin'	(Profile Lon118)	42	1987	29	1986	(Profile 5119)
4	It's Tricky	(Profile Lon130)	16	1987	0	1987	
5	Christmas In Hollis	(Profile Lon163)	56	1987	0	1987	
6	Run's House	(Profile Lon177)	37	1988	0	1988	
7	Ghostbusters	(MCA Profilemca 1360)	65	1989	0	1989	
8	What's It All About	(Profile Prof315)	48	1990	0	1990	
* 9	Down With The King	(Profileprofcd 39)	69	1993	21	1993	(Profile 5391)

Run Tings   Male Production/Instrumental Duo from the UK

ISSUE	TITLE	UK LBL	UK POS	UK YEAR	US POS	US YEAR	US LBL
1	Fires Burning	(Surburbanbase Subbase 009)	58	1992	0	1992	

SEE ALSO SUBPLATES VOLUME 1 (EP), VARIOUS ARTISTS (EP, LP, 78S)

ISSUE	TITLE	UK LBL	UK POS	UK YEAR	US POS	US YEAR	US LBL
Runrig	Male Vocal/Instrumental Group from the UK						
1	Capture The Heart (EP)	(Chrysalis Chs3594)	49	1990	0	1990	
2	Hearthammer (EP)	(Chrysalis Chs3754)	25	1991	0	1991	
3	Flower Of The West	(Chrysalis Chs3805)	43	1991	0	1991	
4	Wonderful	(Chrysaliscdchs 3952)	29	1993	0	1993	
5	The Greatest Flame	(Chrysaliscdchs 3975)	36	1993	0	1993	
6	This Time Of Year	(Chrysaliscdchs 5018)	38	1995	0	1995	
7	An Ubhalas Airde (Highest Apple)	(Chrysaliscdchs 5021)	18	1995	0	1995	
8	Things That Are	(Chrysaliscdchs 5029)	40	1995	0	1995	
9	Rhythm Of My Heart	(Chrysaliscdchs 5035)	24	1996	0	1996	
10	The Greatest Flame	(Chrysaliscdchs 5045)	30	1997	0	1997	
Rupaul	Male Vocalist from the USA						
1	Supermodel (You Better Work)	(Union Cityucrd 21)	61	1994	0	1994	
2	House Of Love / Back To My Roots	(Union Cityucrd 23)	40	1993	0	1993	
3	Supermodel (Re-Mix) / Little Drummer Boy	(Union Cityucrd 25)	61	1994	0	1994	
4	Don't Go Breaking My Heart	(Rocket Ejcd	7	1994	0	1994	
5	House Of Love (Re-Mix)	(Union Cityucrdg 29)	68	1994	0	1994	
6	Snapshot		0	1996	95	1996	(Rhino 74454)
Rupert Holmes	Male Vocalist, B: 24 Feb 1947 Cheshire, England						
* 1	Escape (The Pina Colada Song)	(Infinity Inf 120)	23	1980	1	1979	(Infinity 50035)
2	Him	(MCA 565)	31	1980	6	1980	(MCA 41173)
3	Answering Machine		0	1980	32	1980	(MCA 41235)
Rupie Edwards	Male Vocalist from Jamaica						
1	Ire Feeling (Skanga)	(Cactus Ct 38)	9	1974	0	1974	
2	Lego Shanga	(Cactus Ct 51)	32	1975	0	1975	
Rush	Names Geddy Lee, Alex Lifeson & Neil Peart						
1	Closer To The Heart	(Mercury Rush 7)	7	1978	0	1978	
2	Spirit Of Radio	(Mercury Radio 7)	13	1980	0	1980	
3	Vital Signs / A Passage To Bangkok	(Mercury Vital7)	41	1981	0	1981	
4	Tom Sawyer	(Exit Exit 7)	25	1981	0	1981	
5	New World Man	(Mercuryrush 8)	42	1982	21	1982	(Mercury 76179)
6	Subdivisions	(Mercuryrush 9)	53	1982	0	1982	
7	Countdown / New World Man	(Mercuryrush 10)	36	1983	0	1983	
8	The Body Electric	(Vertigo Rush11)	56	1984	0	1984	
9	The Big Money	(Vertigo Rush12)	46	1985	0	1985	
10	Time Stand Still	(Vertigo Rush13)	42	1987	0	1987	
11	Prime Mover	(Vertigo Rush14)	43	1988	0	1988	
12	Roll The Bones	(Atlantic A 7524)	49	1992	0	1992	
Russ Abbot	Male Vocalist/Comedian Uk						
1	A Day In The Life Of Vince Prince	(EMI 5249)	61	1982	0	1982	
2	A Day In The Life Of Vince Prince (Re-Entry)	(EMI 5249)	75	1982	0	1982	
3	Atmosphere	(Spirit Fire 6)	7	1984	0	1984	
4	All Night Holiday	(Spirit Fire 4)	20	1985	0	1985	
Russ Case Orchestra	Male Orchestra Leader/Instrumentalist (Trumpet) from the USA						
1	You're Breaking My Heart		0	1949	26	1949	(MGM 10478)
Russ Conway	Male Pianist, Real Name Tevor H. Stanford B: 2 Sep 1927 Bristol, England						
1	Party Pops	(Columbia Db4031)	24	1957	0	1957	
2	Got A Match	(Columbia Db4166)	30	1958	0	1958	
3	More Party Pops	(Columbia Db4204)	10	1958	0	1958	
4	The World Outside	(Columbia Db4234)	24	1959	0	1959	
* 5	Side Saddle	(Columbia Db4256)	1	1959	0	1959	
6	The World Outside (Re-Entry)	(Columbia Db4256)	24	1959	0	1959	
7	Roulette	(Columbia Db4298)	1	1959	0	1959	
8	China Tea	(Columbia Db4337)	5	1959	0	1959	
9	Snow Coach	(Columbia Db4368)	7	1959	0	1959	
10	More And More Party Pops	(Columbia Db4373)	5	1959	0	1959	
11	Royal Event	(Columbia Db4418)	15	1960	0	1960	
12	Fings Ain't Wot They Used To Be	(Columbia Db4422)	47	1960	0	1960	
13	Lucky Five	(Columbia Db4457)	14	1960	0	1960	
14	Passing Breeze	(Columbia Db4508)	16	1960	0	1960	
15	Even More Party Pops	(Columbia Db4535)	27	1960	0	1960	
16	Pepe	(Columbia Db5464)	19	1961	0	1961	

ISSUE	TITLE	UK LBL	UK POS	UK YEAR	US POS	US YEAR	US LBL
17	Pablo	(Columbia Db4649)	45	1961	0	1961	
18	Say It With Flowers	(Columbia Db4665)	23	1961	0	1961	
19	Toy Balloons	(Columbia Db4738)	7	1961	0	1961	
20	Lesson One	(Columbia Db4784)	21	1962	0	1962	
21	Always You And Me	(Columbia Db4934)	33	1962	0	1962	
22	Always You And Me (Re-Entry)	(Columbia Db4934)	35	1963	0	1963	

HE LOST THE TOP OF HIS THIRD FINGER COURTESY OF A BREAD SLICER WHEN HE WAS A GALLEY BOY IN THE NAVY

Russ Hamilton Male Vocalist, Real Name Ronald Hulme B: 1934 Liverpool England

1	We Will Make Love	(Oriole Cb 1359)	2	1957	0	1957	
2	Rainbow		0	1957	4	1957	(Kapp 184)
3	Wedding Ring	(Oriole Cb 1388)	20	1957	0	1957	

Russ Irwin Male Singer/Songwriter, B: 1968 In Huntington, Long Island

1	My Heart Belongs To You		0	1991	28	1991	(Sbk 07363)

Russ Morgan & His Orchestra Male Bandleader/Instrumentalist (Trombone, Piano, Violinist) From Scranton, Pennsylvania.

36	(Did You Ever Get) The Feeling In The Moonlight		0	1946	17	1946	(Decca 18724)
37	You're Nobody 'til Somebody Loves You		0	1946	14	1946	(Decca 18724)
38	I'm Looking Over A Four-Leaf Clover		0	1948	6	1948	(Decca 24319)
39	Bye Bye Blackbird		0	1948	20	1948	(Decca 24319)
40	So Tired		0	1948	3	1948	(Decca 24521)
* 41	Cruising Down The River		0	1949	1	1949	(Decca 24568)
42	Sunflower		0	1949	5	1949	(Decca 24568)
43	Forever And Ever		0	1949	1	1949	(Decca 24569)
44	You, You, You Are The One		0	1949	17	1949	(Decca 24569)
45	Barroom Polka		0	1949	20	1949	(Decca 24608)
46	That's My Weekness Now		0	1949	17	1949	(Decca 24692)
47	Blue Christmas		0	1949	13	1949	(Decca 24766)
48	Johnson Rag		0	1949	7	1949	(Decca 24819)
49	Careless Kisses		0	1950	24	1950	(Decca 24814)
50	Sentimental Me		0	1950	7	1950	(Decca 24904)
51	Hoop-De-Doo		0	1950	15	1950	(Decca 24986)
52	You Dreamer You		0	1950	28	1950	(Decca 27006)
53	Beloved, Be Faithful		0	1950	28	1950	(Decca 27006)
54	Mockin' Bird Hill		0	1951	16	1951	(Decca 27444)
55	Dance Me Loose		0	1952	30	1952	(Decca 27906)
56	Till I Waltz Again With You		0	1953	23	1953	(Decca 28539)
57	I'll Be Hangin' Around		0	1953	21	1953	(Decca 28590)
58	Dogface Soldier		0	1955	30	1955	(Decca 29703)
59	The Poor People Of Paris		0	1956	19	1956	(Decca 29835)

OBITUARY : D: 8 AUG 1969 IN LAS VEGAS.

Rusty Bryant Male Saxophonist/Bandleader from the USA

1	All Night Long		0	1954	25	1954	(Dot 15134)

THE HIT IS CREDITED TO RUSTY BRYANT & THE CAROLYN CLUB BAND

Male Vocalist, Real Name Farrell H. Draper From Kirksville, Missouri

1	No Help Wanted		0	1953	10	1953	(Mercury 70077)
* 2	Gambler's Guitar		0	1953	6	1953	(Mercury 70167)
3	Lighthouse		0	1953	23	1953	(Mercury 70188)
4	Native Dancer		0	1953	23	1953	(Mercury 70258)

S

ISSUE	TITLE	UK LBL	UK POS	UK YEAR	US POS	US YEAR	US LBL
S*M*A*S*H* Male Vocal/Instrumental Group from the UK							
1	(I Want To) Kill Someone	(Hi-Rise FlatsCD5)	26	1994	0	1994	
1S-Express Mixed Vocal/Instrumental Group from the UK							
1	Theme From *S-Express*	(Rhythm KingLEFT 21)	1	1988	0	1988	
2	Superfly Guy	(Rhythm King LEFT 28)	5	1988	0	1988	
3	Hey Music Lover	(Rhythm King LEFT 30)	6	1989	0	1989	
4	Mantra For A State Of Mind	(Rhythm King LEFT 35)	21	1989	0	1989	
5	Nothing To Lose	(Rhythm King SEXY 01)	32	1990	0	1990	
6	Find Em', Fool Em', Forget Em'	(Rhythm King 6580137)	43	1992	0	1992	
7	Theme From *S-Express* (Re-Mix)	(Rhythm King Sexy 9CD)	14	1996	0	1996	
S.F.X. Male Production/Instrumental Duo from the UK							
1	Lemmings	(Parlophone CDR 6343)	51	1993	0	1993	
S.O.S. Band Mixed Vocal/Instrumental Group from the UK The S.O.S. Stands For Sounds Of Success							
* 1	Take Your Time (Do It Right) (Part 1)	(Tabu TBU 8564)	51	1980	3	1980	(Tabu 5522)
2	Groovin' (That's What We're Doin')	(Tabu TBU A	72	1983	0	1983	
3	Just Be Good To Me	(Tabu TBU A	13	1984	0	1984	
4	Just The Way You Like It	(Tabu A 4621)	32	1984	0	1984	
5	Weekend Girl	(Tabu A 4785)	51	1984	0	1984	
6	The Finest	(Tabu A 6997)	17	1986	0	1986	
7	Borrowed Love	(Tabu A 7241)	50	1986	0	1986	
8	No Lies	(Tabu 650444 7)	64	1987	0	1987	
S.O.U.L. S.Y.S.T.E.M. Mixed Vocal/Instrumental Group from the USA (Introducing) Michelle Visage							
1	It's Gonna Be A Lovely Day	(Arista 74321125692)	17	1993	34	1993	(Arista 12486)
S.W.V. Female Vocal Group from the USA, S.W.V. Stands For Sisters With Voices							
* 1	I'm So Into You	(RCA 74321144972)	17	1993	6	1993	(RCA 62451)
* 2	Week	(RCA 74321153352)	33	1993	1	1993	(RCA 62521)
* 3	Right Here (Human Nature)	(RCA 74321160482)	3	1993	2	1993	(RCA 62614)
4	Downtown	(RCA 74321189012)	19	1994	2	1994	(RCA 62614)
5	Anything	(RCA 74321212212)	24	1994	18	1994	(RCA 62834)
6	You're The One	(RCA 74321383312)	13	1996	5	1996	(RCA 64516)
7	Use Your Heart		0	1996	22	1996	(RCA 64607)
8	It's All About U	(RCA 74321442152)	36	1996	61	1997	(RCA 64735)
9	Can We	(JIVE JIVECD 423)	18	1997	0	1997	
10	Someone	(RCA 74321513942)	34	1997	0	1997	
Sa-Fire Latin American Dance/Singer Real Name Wilma Cosme from New York City.							
1	Thinking Of You		0	1989	12	1989	(Cutting 872502)
Sabre (Featuring) President Brown Male Vocal Duo from Jamaica							
1	Wrong Or Right	(Greensleeves GRECD 485)	71	1995	0	1995	
Sabres Of Paradise Male Instrumental Group from the UK							
1	Smokebelch II	(Sabres Of Paradise PT009CD)	55	1993	0	1993	
2	Theme	(Sabres Of Paradise PT 014CD)	56	1994	0	1994	
3	Wilmot	(Warp WAP 50CD)	36	1994	0	1994	
Sabrina Female Vocalist from Italy							
1	Boys (Summertime Love)	(Ibiza IBIZ 1)	60	1988	0	1988	
2	Boys (Summertime Love) (Re-Entry)	(Ibiza IBIZ 1)	3	1988	0	1988	
3	All Of Me	(PWL PWL 19)	25	1988	0	1988	
4	Like A Yo-Yo	(Videogram DCUP 1)	72	1989	0	1989	
Sabrina Johnston Female Vocalist from the USA							
1	Peace	(East West YZ 616)	8	1991	0	1991	
2	Friendship	(East West YZ 637)	58	1991	0	1991	

ISSUE	TITLE	UK LBL	UK POS	UK YEAR	US POS	US YEAR	US LBL
3	I Wanna Sing	(East West YZ 661)	46	1992	0	1992	
4	Peace (Re-Mix)	(Epic 6584377)	35	1992	0	1992	
5	Satisfy My Love	(Champion CHAMPCD 311)	62	1994	0	1994	
	THE FLIP SIDE OF HIT 4 WAS HIT 4 BY CRYSTAL WATERS						
Sacha Distel Male Vocalist from France							
1	Raindrops Keep Fallin' On My Head	(Warner Bros. WB 7345)	50	1970	0	1970	
2	Raindrops Keep Fallin' On My Head (Re-Entry)	(Warner Bros. WB 7345)	10	1970	0	1970	
3	Raindrops Keep Fallin' On My Head (2nd Re-Entry)	(Warner Bros. WB 7345)	43	1970	0	1970	
4	Raindrops Keep Fallin' On My Head (3rd Re-Entry)	(Warner Bros. WB 7345)	47	1970	0	1970	
5	Raindrops Keep Fallin' On My Head (4th Re-Entry)	(Warner Bros. WB 7345)	44	1970	0	1970	
Sacred Spirit Unknown European Producer With Chants from Native America							
1	Yeha-Noha	(Virgin CSCDT 1514)	71	1995	0	1995	
2	Wishes Of Happiness And Prosperity	(Virgin VSCDT 1514)	37	1995	0	1995	
3	Winter Ceremony	(Virgin VSCDT 1574)	45	1996	0	1996	
Sad Cafe Male Vocal/Instrumental Group from the UK							
1	Every Day Hurts	(RCA PB 5180)	3	1979	0	1979	
2	Strange Little Girl	(RCA PB 5202)	32	1980	0	1980	
3	My Oh My	(RCA SAD 3)	14	1980	0	1980	
4	Nothing Left Toulouse	(RCA SAD 4)	62	1980	0	1980	
5	La-Di-Da	(RCA SAD 5)	41	1980	0	1980	
6	I'm In Love Again	(RCA SAD 6)	40	1980	0	1980	
Sade Female Vocalist, Real Name Helen Folasade Adu B: 16 Jan 1959 Ibandan, Nigeria, Raised In Clacton, Essex, England							
1	Your Love Is King	(Epic A 4137)	6	1984	0	1984	
2	Your Love Is King (Re-Entry)	(Epic A 4137)	75	1984	0	1984	
3	When Am I Gonna Make A Living	(Epic A 4437)	36	1984	0	1984	
4	Smooth Operator	(Epic A 4655)	19	1984	5	1985	(Portrait 04807)
5	Sweetest Taboo	(Epic A 6609)	31	1985	5	1986	(Portrait 05713)
6	Is It A Crime	(Epic A 6742)	49	1986	0	1986	
7	Love Is Stronger Than Pride	(Epic SADE 1)	44	1988	0	1988	
8	Never As Good As The First Time		0	1986	20	1986	(Portrait 05846)
9	Paradise	(Epic SADE 2)	29	1988	16	1988	(Epic 07904)
10	No Ordinary Love	(Epic 6583567)	26	1992	28	1993	(Epic 74734)
11	Feel No Pain	(Epic 6588297)	56	1992	0	1992	
12	Kiss Of Life	(Epic 6591162)	44	1993	0	1993	
13	No Ordinary Love (Re-Entry)	(Epic 6583562)	14	1993	0	1993	
14	Cherrish The Day	(Epic 6594812)	53	1993	0	1993	
Safaris Lead Singer With The Quartet Is Jim Stephens							
1	Image Of A Girl		0	1960	6	1960	(Eldo101)
Saffron Female Vocalist from the UK							
1	Circles	(WEA SAFF 9CD)	60	1993	0	1993	
Saga Names: Michael Sadler, Jim And Ian Crichton, Jim Gilmour & Steve Negus							
1	On The Loose		0	1983	26	1983	(PORTRAIT 03359)
Sagat Male Rapper from the USA							
1	Funk Dat	(FFRR FCD 224)	25	1993	0	1993	
2	Luvstuff	(FFRR FCD 250)	71	1994	0	1994	
Saigon Kick Male Rock Quartet From Miami, Lead Vocals Are By Matt Krammer							
* 1	Love Is On The Way		0	1992	12	1992	(Third Stone 98530)
Sailcat Male Country-Rock Duo, John Wyker & Court Pickett							
1	Motorcycle Mama		0	1972	12	1972	(Elektra 45782)
Sailor Male Vocal/Instrumental Group from the UK							
1	Glass Of Champagne	(Epic EPC 3770)	2	1975	0	1975	
2	Girls Girls Girls	(Epic EPC 3858)	7	1976	0	1976	
3	One Drink Too Many	(Epic EPC 4804)	35	1977	0	1977	
Saint Etienne Mixed Vocal/Instrumental Group from the UK							
1	Nothing Can Stop Us / Speedwell	(Heavenly HVN 009)	54	1991	0	1991	
2	Only Love Can Break Your Heart / Filthy	(Heavenly HVN 12)	39	1991	0	1991	
3	Join Our Club / People Get Real	(HeavenlyHVN 15)	21	1992	0	1992	
4	Avenue	(Heavenly HVN 2312)	40	1992	0	1992	
5	You're In A Bad Way	(Heavenly HVN 25CD)	12	1993	0	1993	
6	Hobart Paving / Who Do You Think You Are	(Heavenly HVN 29CD)	23	1993	0	1993	

ISSUE	TITLE	UK LBL	UK POS	UK YEAR	US POS	US YEAR	US LBL
7	I Was Born On Christmas Day	(Heavenly HVN 36CD)	37	1993	0	1993	
8	Pale Movie	(Heavenly HVN 37CD)	28	1994	0	1994	
9	Like A Motorway	(Heavenly HVN 40CD)	47	1994	0	1994	
10	Hug My Soul	(Heavenly HVN 42CD)	32	1994	0	1994	
11	He's On The Phone	(Heavenly HNV 50CD)	11	1995	0	1995	

Saints Male Vocal/Instrumental Group from Australia

1	This Perfect Day	(Harvest HAR 5130)	34	1977	0	1977	

Sal Mineo Male Vocalist, B: 10 Jan 1939 New York

1	Start Movin' (In My Direction)	(Philips PB 707)	16	1957	9	1957	(Epic 9216)
2	Lasting Love		0	1957	27	1957	(Epic 9227)

Obituary : D: 12 Feb 1976 Murdered.

Sal Solo Male Vocalist from the UK

1	San Damiano (Heart And Soul)	(MCA MCA 930)	15	1984	0	1984	
2	Music And You	(MCA MCA 946)	52	1985	0	1985	

Salad Mixed Vocal/Instrumental Group from the UK/Holland

1	Drink The Elixir	(Island Red CIRD 104)	66	1995	0	1995	
2	Motorbike To Heaven	(Island Red CIRD 106)	42	1995	0	1995	
3	Granite Statue	(Island Red CIRD 108)	50	1995	0	1995	
4	I Want You	(Island CID 646)	60	1996	0	1996	
5	Cardboy King	(Island CID 654)	65	1997	0	1997	

Salena Female Vocalist, Real Name Selena Quintanilla Perez B: 16 Apr 1971 from Corpus Christi, Texas

1	Dreaming Of You		0	1995	22	1995	(EMI Latin 58490)

OBITUARY: D: 31 MAR 1995 SHOT BY YOLANDA SALDIVAR (FOUNDER OF SALENA'S FAN CLUB)

Salford Jets Male Vocal/Instrumental Group from the UK

1	Who You Looking At	(RCA PB 5239)	72	1980	0	1980	

Sally Oldfield Female Vocalist from the UK

1	Mirrors	(Bronze BRO 66)	19	1978	0	1978	

Salsoul Orchestra Disco Orchestra Conducted By Vincent Montana Jr.

1	Tangerine		0	1976	18	1976	(Salsoul 2004)
2	Nice 'N' Naasty		0	1976	30	1976	(Salsoul 2011)

Salt Tank Male Instrumental Group from the UK

1	Eugina	(Internal LIECD 29)	40	1996	0	1996	

Salt-N-Pepa Female Rap Trio from the USA Names Cheryl James, Sandy Denton & Dee Dee Roper

*	1	Push It / I Am Down	(FFRR FFR 2)	41	1988	19	1988	(Next Plat. 315)
	2	Push It - Tramp	(CHAMP 51 & FFRR FFR 2)	2	1988	0	1988	
	3	Shake Your Thang (It's Your Thing)	(FFRR FFR 11)	22	1988	0	1988	
	4	Twist And Shout	(FFRR FFR 16)	4	1988	0	1988	
*	5	Expression	(FFRR F 127)	40	1990	26	1990	(Next Plat. 329)
*	6	Do You Want Me	(FFRR F 151)	5	1991	21	1991	(Next Plat. 331)
*	7	Let's Talk About Sex	(FFRR F 162)	2	1991	13	1991	(Next Plat. 333)
	8	You Showed Me	(FFRR F 174)	15	1991	0	1991	
	9	Expression (Re-Issue)	(FFRR F 182)	23	1992	0	1992	
	10	Start Me Up	(FFRR F 196)	39	1992	0	1992	
*	11	Shoop	(FFRR FCD 219)	29	1993	4	1993	(Next Plat. 857314)
*	12	Whatta Man	(FFRR FCD 222)	7	1994	3	1994	(Next Plat. 857390)
	13	Shoop (Re-Mix)	(FFRR FCD 234)	13	1994	0	1994	
	14	None Of Your Business	(FFRR FCD 244)	19	1994	32	1994	(Next Plat. 857776)
	15	None Of Your Business (Re-Entry)	(FFRR FCD 244)	64	1995	0	1995	
	16	Ain't Nuthin' But A She Thing		0	1995	38	1995	(London 850346)
	17	Champagne	(MCA MCSTD 48025)	23	1996	0	1996	

Sam & Dave Male Vocal Duo, Samual Moore B: 12 Oct 1935 & David Prater B: 9 May 1937 from the USA.

+	1	You Don't Know Like I Know		0	1966	7	1966	(Stax 180)
*	2	Hold On! I'm Coming		0	1966	21	1966	(Stax 189)
+	3	Said I Wasn't Gonna Tell Nobody		0	1966	8	1966	(Stax 198)
+	4	You Got Me Hummin'		0	1966	7	1966	(Stax 204)
	5	When Something Is Wrong With My Baby		0	1967	42	1967	(Stax 210)
	6	Soothe Me	(Stax 601 004)	48	1967	56	1967	(Stax 218)
	7	Soothe Me (Re-Entry)	(Stax 601 004)	35	1967	0	1967	
*	8	Soul Man	(Stax 601 023)	24	1967	2	1967	(Stax 231)
*	9	I Thank You	(Stax 601 030)	34	1968	9	1968	(Stax 242)
	10	You Don't Know What You Mean To Me		0	1968	48	1968	(Atlantic 2517)
	11	Can't You Find Another Way		0	1968	54	1968	(Atlantic 2540)

ISSUE	TITLE	UK LBL	UK POS	UK YEAR	US POS	US YEAR	US LBL
12	Soul Sister Brown Sugar	(Atlantic 584 237)	15	1969	0	1969	

SEE ALSO LOU REED • OBITUARY: DAVE D: 9 APR 1988, CAR ACCIDENT.

Sam Brown Female Vocalist from the UK

ISSUE	TITLE	UK LBL	UK POS	UK YEAR	US POS	US YEAR	US LBL
1	Stop	(A&M AM 440)	52	1988	0	1988	
2	Stop (Re-Entry)	(A&M AM 440)	4	1989	0	1989	
3	Can I Get A Witness	(A&M AM 509)	15	1989	0	1989	
4	With A Little Love	(A&M AM 539)	44	1990	0	1990	
5	Kissing Gate	(A&M AM 549)	23	1990	0	1990	
6	Just Good Friends	(Dick Bros DDICK 014CD1)	63	1995	0	1995	with Fish

Sam Browne Male Vocalist from the USA, Was With The Ambrose Orchestra For A Time

ISSUE	TITLE	UK LBL	UK POS	UK YEAR	US POS	US YEAR	US LBL
1	A Tree In The Meadow		0	1948	22	1948	(London 123)

Sam Cooke Male Vocalist, B: 2 Jan 1931 Mississippi

	ISSUE	TITLE	UK LBL	UK POS	UK YEAR	US POS	US YEAR	US LBL
*	1	You Send Me	(London HLU 8506)	29	1958	1	1957	(Keen 34013)
	2	I'll Come Running Back To You		0	1957	18	1957	(Specialty 619)
	3	(I Love You) For Sentimental Reasons / Desire Me		0	1958	17	1958	(Keen 34002)
	4	Lonely Island		0	1958	26	1958	(Keen 4009)
	5	You Were Made For Me		0	1958	27	1958	(Keen 4009)
	6	Win Your Love For Me		0	1958	33	1958	(Keen 2006)
	7	Love You Most Of All		0	1958	26	1958	(Keen 2008)
	8	Everybody Likes To Cha Cha		0	1959	31	1959	(Keen 2018)
	9	Only Sixteen	(HMV POP 642)	23	1959	28	1959	(Keen 2022)
+	10	There I've Said It Again		0	1959	25	1959	(Keen 2105)
	11	Teenage Sonata		0	1960	50	1960	(RCA Victor 47-7701)
*	12	Wonderful World	(HMV POP 754)	27	1960	12	1960	(Keen 2112)
*	13	Chain Gang	(RCA 1202)	9	1960	2	1960	(RCA Victor 47-7783)
	14	Sad Mood		0	1960	29	1960	(RCA Victor 47-7816)
	15	That's It, I Quit, I'm Movin' On		0	1961	31	1961	(RCA Victor 47-7853)
	16	Cupid	(RCA 1242)	7	1961	17	1961	(RCA Victor 47-7883)
*	17	Twistin' The Night Away	(RCA 1277)	6	1962	9	1962	(RCA Victor 47-7983)
	18	Having A Party		0	1962	17	1962	(RCA 47-8036)
	19	Bring It On Home To Me		0	1962	13	1962	(RCA Victor 47-8036)
	20	Nothing Can Change This Love / Somebody Have Mercy		0	1962	12	1962	(RCA Victor 47-8088)
	21	Send Me Some Lovin'		0	1963	13	1963	(RCA Victor 47-8129)
	22	Another Saturday Night	(RCA 1341)	23	1963	10	1963	(RCA Victor 47-8164)
	23	Frankie And Johnny	(RCA 1361)	30	1963	14	1963	(RCA Victor 47-8215)
	24	Little Red Rooster		0	1963	11	1963	(RCA Victor 47-8247)
	25	Good News		0	1964	11	1964	(RCA Victor 47-8299)
	26	Good Times		0	1964	11	1964	(RCA Victor 47-8368)
	27	Tennessee Waltz		0	1964	35	1964	(RCA 47-8368)
	28	Cousin Of Mine / That's Where It's At		0	1964	31	1964	(RCA Victor 47-8426)
	29	Shake		0	1965	7	1965	(RCA Victor 47-8486)
	30	A Change Is Gonna Come		0	1965	31	1965	(RCA 8486)
	31	It's Got The Whole World Shakin'		0	1965	41	1965	(RCA Victor 47-8539)
	32	Sugar Dumpling		0	1965	32	1965	(RCA Victor 47-8631)
	33	Wonderful Land (Re-Issue)	(RCA PB 49871)	2	1986	0	1986	
	34	Another Saturday Night (Re-Issue)	(RCA PB 49849)	75	1986	0	1986	

SAM HAS ALSO RECORDED UNDER THE NAME OF DALE COOK • OBITUARY: D: FROM GUNSHOT WOUNDS ON 11 DEC 1964

Sam Donahue Orchestra Male Saxophonist/Orchestra Leader from the USA

ISSUE	TITLE	UK LBL	UK POS	UK YEAR	US POS	US YEAR	US LBL
1	Do You Care?		0	1941	17	1941	(Bluebird 11198)
2	Dinah		0	1946	9	1946	(Capitol 260)
3	Just The Other Day		0	1946	8	1946	(Capitol 275)
4	Put That Kiss Back Where You Found It		0	1946	8	1946	(Capitol 293)
5	A Rainy Night In Rio		0	1946	7	1946	(Capitol 325)
6	My Melancholy Baby		0	1947	5	1947	(Capitol 357)
7	I Never Knew		0	1947	2	1947	(Capitol 405)
8	Red Wind		0	1947	9	1947	(Capitol 472)
9	The Whistler		0	1947	6	1947	(Capitol 472)
10	Racos, Enchiladas And Beans		0	1948	21	1948	(Capitol 493)
11	Robbins Nest		0	1948	23	1948	(Capitol 493)
12	Saxa-Boogie		0	1948	24	1948	(Capitol 1508)
13	I'll Get Along Somehow		0	1948	26	1948	(Capitol 15081)
14	September In The Rain (From *Melody For Two*)		0	1948	26	1948	(Capitol 15172)

ISSUE	TITLE	UK LBL	UK POS	UK YEAR	US POS	US YEAR	US LBL
Sam Harris	Male Vocalist from the UK						
1	Sugar Don't Bite		0	1984	36	1984	(Motown 1743)
2	Hearts On Fire / Over The Rainbow	(Motown TMG 1370)	67	1985	0	1985	
Sam Moore	Male Vocalist, Half Of The Duo Sam & Dave						
1	Soul Man	(A&M AM 364)	30	1987	0	1987	And Lou Reed
Sam Neely	Male Vocalist, B: 22 Aug 1948 Cuero, Texas						
1	Loving You Just Crossed My Mind		0	1972	29	1972	(Capitol 3381)
2	You Can Have Her		0	1974	34	1974	(A&M 1612)
3	I Fought The Law		0	1975	54	1975	(A&M 1651)
4	Sail Away		0	1977	84	1977	(Elektra 45419)
Sam The Sham & The Pharoahs	Male Vocal/Instrumental Group from the USA, Lead Singer Is Domingo 'Sam' Samudio						
* 1	Wooly Bully	(MGM 1269)	11	1965	2	1965	(MGM 13322)
2	Ju Ju Hand		0	1965	26	1965	(MGM 13364)
3	Ring Dang Doo		0	1965	33	1965	(MGM 13397)
* 4	Lil' Red Riding Hood	(MGM 1315)	48	1966	2	1966	(MGM 13506)
5	Lil' Red Riding Hood (Re-Issue)	(MGM 1315)	46	1966	0	1966	
6	The Hair On My Chinny Chin Chin		0	1966	22	1966	(MGM 13581)
7	How Do You Catch A Girl		0	1967	27	1967	(MGM 13649)
Samantha Fox	Female, Former Topless Model/Vocalist, B: 15 Apr 1966 England						
1	Touch Me (I Want Your Body)	(Jive Foxy 1)	3	1986	4	1987	(JIVE 1006)
2	Do Ya Do Ya (Wanna Please Me)	(Jive Foxy 2)	10	1986	0	1986	
3	Hold On Tight	(Jive Foxy 3)	26	1986	0	1986	
4	I'm All You Need	(Jive Foxy 4)	41	1986	0	1986	
5	Nothing's Gonna Stop Me Now	(Jive Foxy 5)	8	1987	0	1987	
6	I Surrender (To The Spirit Of The Night)	(Jive Foxy 6)	25	1987	0	1987	
7	I Promise You (Get Ready)	(Jive Foxy 7)	58	1987	0	1987	
8	True Devotion	(Jive Foxy 8)	62	1987	0	1987	
9	Naughty Girls (Need Love Too)	(Jive Foxy 9)	31	1988	5	1988	(JIVE 1089)
10	Love House	(Jive Foxy 10)	32	1988	0	1988	
* 11	I Wanna Have Some Fun	(Jive Foxy 12)	63	1989	8	1988	(JIVE 1154)
12	I Only Wanna Be With You	(Jive Foxy 11)	16	1989	31	1989	(JIVE 1192)
	HIT 9 IS CREDITED TO SAMANTHA FOX FEATURING FULL FORCE						
Samantha Janus	Female Vocalist from the UK						
1	A Message To Your Heart	(Hollywood HWD 104)	30	1991	0	1991	
Samantha Sang	Female Vocalist, Real Name Cheryl Gray B: 5 Aug 1953 Melbourne, Australia						
* 1	Emotions	(Private Stock PVT 128)	11	1978	3	1978	(Private Stock 45178)
Sami Jo Cole	Female Vocalist from Batesville, Arkansas						
1	Tell Me A Lie		0	1974	21	1974	(MGM South 7029)
2	It Could Have Been Me		0	1974	46	1974	(MGM South 7034)
Sammi Smith	Female Country Singer, B: 5 Aug 1943 Orange, California. She Is One Of America's Top C/W Singers						
* 5	Help Me Make It Through The Night		0	1971	8	1971	(Mega 0015)
	HIT 5 REACHED NUMBER 1 IN THE US C/W CHARTS • UNLISTED SONGS WERE C/W HITS						
Sammy Davis Jr.	Male Actor/Dancer/Vocalist, B: 8 Dec 1925, New York						
1	Hey There (From *The Pajama Game*)		0	1954	16	1954	(Decca 29199)
2	The Red Caps		0	1954	28	1954	(Decca 29310)
3	Love Me Or Leave Me	(Brunswick 05428)	8	1955	12	1955	(Decca 29484)
4	Something's Gotta Give	(Brunswick 05428)	19	1955	9	1955	(Decca 29484)
5	That Old Black Magic	(Brunswick 05450)	16	1955	13	1955	(Decca 29541)
6	Something's Gotta Give (Re-Entry)	(Brunswick 05428)	11	1955	0	1955	
7	Hey There		0	1954	9	1954	(Decca 29119)
8	Love Me Or Leave Me (Re-Entry)	(Brunswick 05428)	18	1955	0	1955	
9	In A Persian Market	(Brunswick 05518)	28	1956	0	1956	
10	All Of You	(Brunswick 05629)	28	1956	0	1956	
* 11	Happy To Make Your Acquaintance	(Brunswick 05830)	46	1960	0	1960	
12	What Kind Of Fool Am I	(Reprise R 20048)	26	1962	17	1962	(Reprise 20048)
13	Me And My Shadow	(Reprise R 20128)	20	1962	0	1962	
14	Me And My Shadow (Re-Entry)	(Reprise R 20128)	47	1963	0	1963	
15	The Shelter Of Your Arms		0	1964	17	1964	(Reprise 20216)
16	Don't Blame The Children		0	1967	37	1967	(Reprise 0566)
17	I've Gotta Be Me		0	1969	11	1969	(Reprise 0779)
* 18	The Candy Man		0	1972	1	1972	(MGM 14320)
	HIT 11 IS CREDITED TO SAMMY DAVIS JR. AND CARMEN MCRAE • HITS 13,14 ARE CREDITED TO FRANK SINATRA AND SAMMY DAVIS JR. OBITUARY : D: 16 MAY 1990 THROAT CANCER.						

S

571

ISSUE	TITLE	UK LBL	UK POS	UK YEAR	US POS	US YEAR	US LBL
Sammy Hagar Male Vocal/Guitarist, B: 13 Oct 1947 Monterey, California								
1	This Planets On Fire / Space Station No 5	(Capitol CL 16114)	52	1979	0	1979	
2	I've Done Everything For You	(Capitol CL 16120)	36	1980	0	1980	
3	Heartbeat / Love Or Money	(Capitol RED 1)	67	1980	0	1980	
4	Piece Of My Heart	(Geffen GEFA 1884)	67	1982	0	1982	
5	Piece Of My Heart (Re-Entry)	(Geffen GEFA1884)	67	1982	0	1982	
6	Your Love Is Driving Me Crazy		0	1983	13	1983	(Geffen 29816)
7	Two Sides Of Love		0	1984	38	1984	(Geffen 29246)
8	I Can't Drive 55		0	1984	26	1984	(Geffen 29173)
9	Give To Live		0	1987	23	1987	(Geffen 28314)
Sammy Johns Male Vocalist, B: 7 Feb 1946 Charlotte, North Carolina, He Had His Own Band The Devilles From 1963-73								
1	Early Morning Love		0	1974	68	1974	(GRC 2021)
* 2	Chevy Van		0	1975	5	1975	(GRC 2046)
Sammy Kaye Orchestra Male Orchestra Leader, B: 13 Mar 1910 Rocky River, Ohio								
65	Atlanta G.A.		0	1946	6	1946	(Victor 1795)
66	I'm A Big Girl Now		0	1946	1	1946	(Victor 1812)
67	The Gypsy		0	1946	3	1946	(RCA Victor 1844)
68	Laughing On The Outside, Crying On The Inside		0	1946	3	1946	(RCA Victor 1856)
69	The Old Lamp-Lighter		0	1946	1	1946	(RCA Victor 1963)
70	Sooner Or Later (You're Gonna Be Comin' Around)		0	1946	8	1946	(RCA Victor 1976)
71	Zip-A-Dee-Doo-Dah (From *Song Of The South*)		0	1946	11	1946	(RCA Victor 1976)
72	The Egg And I (Movie Title Song)		0	1947	16	1947	(RCA Victor 2209)
73	After Graduation Day		0	1947	22	1947	(RCA Victor 2209)
74	That's My Desire		0	1947	2	1947	(RCA Victor 2251)
75	The Red Silk Stockings And Green Perfume		0	1947	8	1947	(RCA Victor 2251)
76	The Echo Says No		0	1947	17	1947	(RCA Victor 2330)
77	An Apple Blossom Wedding		0	1947	5	1947	(RCA Victor 2330)
78	The Little Old Mill (Went Round And Round)		0	1947	24	1947	(RCA Victor 2434)
79	Serenade Of The Bells		0	1947	3	1947	(RCA Victor 2372)
80	Hand In Hand		0	1947	21	1947	(RCA Victor 2482)
81	Dream Again		0	1947	21	1947	(RCA Victor 2524)
82	I Hate Myself In The Morning		0	1947	20	1947	(RCA Victor 2524)
83	I Love You, Yes I Do		0	1948	10	1948	(RCA Victor 2674)
84	Tell Me A Story		0	1948	8	1948	(RCA Victor 2761)
85	Baby Face		0	1948	11	1948	(RCA Victor 2879)
86	Down Among The Sheltering Palms		0	1948	14	1948	(RCA Victor 3100)
87	Lavender Blue (Dilly Dilly) (From *So Dear To My Heart*)		0	1948	4	1948	(RCA Victor 3100)
88	Careless Hands		0	1949	3	1949	(RCA Victor 78-3321)
89	Powder Your Face With Sunshine		0	1949	13	1949	(RCA Victor 78-3321)
90	Kiss Me Sweet		0	1949	29	1949	(RCA Victor 3420)
91	Room Full Of Roses		0	1949	2	1949	(RCA Victor 78-3441)
92	The Four Winds And The Seven Seas		0	1949	3	1949	(RCA Victor 78-3459)
93	Baby It's Cold Outside (From *Neptune's Daughter*)		0	1949	12	1949	(RCA Victor 78-3532)
94	Dime A Dozen		0	1949	24	1949	(RCA Victor 78 3532)
95	It Isn't Fair		0	1950	2	1950	(RCA Victor 78-3609)
96	Wanderin'		0	1950	11	1950	(RCA Victor 78-3680)
97	Roses		0	1950	5	1950	(RCA Victor 3754)
98	Harbour Lights		0	1950	1	1950	(Columbia 78-38963)
99	Longing For You		0	1951	16	1951	(Columbia 39499)
100	Sin		0	1951	25	1951	(Columbia 39567)
101	You		0	1952	28	1952	(Columbia 39724)
102	Walkin' To Missouri		0	1952	11	1952	(Columbia 29769)
103	In The Mission Of St.Augustine		0	1953	15	1953	(Columbia 40061)
104	Charade (Movie Title Theme)		0	1964	36	1964	(Decca 31589)
	OBITUARY: D: 2 JUN 1987, CANCER.							
Sammy Masters Male Vocalist from the USA								
1	Rockin' Red Wing	(Warner Bros. WB 10)	36	1960	0	1960	
Sammy Salvo Pop Singer from Birmingham, Alabama								
1	Oh Julie		0	1958	23	1958	(RCA 7097)
Sammy Turner Real Name Samuel Black B: 2 Jun 1932 Paterson, New Jersey								
1	Lavender-Blue		0	1959	3	1959	(Big Top3016)
2	Always	(London HLX 8963)	26	1959	19	1959	(Big Top 3029)

ISSUE	TITLE	UK LBL	UK POS	UK YEAR	US POS	US YEAR	US LBL
Samson Male Vocal/Instrumental Group from the UK							
1	Riding With The Angels	(RCA 67)	55	1981	0	1981	
2	Losing My Grip	(Polydor POSP 471)	63	1982	0	1982	
3	Red Skies	(Polydor POSP 554)	65	1983	0	1983	
San Jose' (Featuring) Rodriguez Argentina Male Instrumental Group from the UK, Rodriguez Argentina Is Rod Argent							
1	Argentine Melody (Cancion De Argentina)	(MCA 369)	14	1978	0	1978	
San Remo Strings Orchestra from the USA							
1	Hungry For Love		0	1965	27	1965	(RIC-TIC 104)
2	Festival Time	(TAMLA MotownTMG 795)	39	1971	0	1971	
Sandie Shaw Female Vocalist, Real Name Sandra Goodrich B: 26 Feb 1947 Dagenham, Essex, England.							
1	(There's) Always Something There To Remind Me	(PYE 7N 15704)	1	1964	0	1964	
2	Girl Don't Come	(PYE 7N 15743)	3	1964	0	1964	
3	I'll Stop At Nothing	(PYE 7N 15783)	4	1965	0	1965	
4	Long Live Love	(PYE 7N 15841)	1	1965	0	1965	
5	Message Understood	(PYE 7N 15940)	6	1965	0	1965	
6	How Can You Tell	(PYE 7N 15987)	21	1965	0	1965	
7	Tomorrow	(PYE 7N 17036)	9	1966	0	1966	
8	Nothing Comes Easy	(PYE 7N 17086)	14	1966	0	1966	
9	Run	(PYE 7N 17163)	32	1966	0	1966	
10	Think Sometimes About Me	(PYE 7N 17212)	32	1966	0	1966	
11	I Don't Need Anything	(PYE 7N 172390)	50	1967	0	1967	
* 12	Puppet On A String	(PYE 7N 17272)	1	1967	0	1967	
13	Tonight In Tokyo	(PYE 7N 17346)	21	1967	0	1967	
14	You've Not Changed	(PYE 7N 17378)	18	1967	0	1967	
15	Today	(PYE 7N 17441)	27	1968	0	1968	
16	Monsieur Dupont	(PYE 7N 17675)	6	1969	0	1969	
17	Think It All Over	(PYE 7N 17726)	42	1969	0	1969	
18	Hand In Glove	(ROUGH TRADE RT 130)	27	1984	0	1984	
19	Are You Ready To Be Heartbroken	(Polydor POSP 793)	68	1986	0	1986	
20	Nothing Less Than Brilliant	(Virgin VSCDT1521)	66	1994	0	1994	
Sandpebbles Names: Calvin White, Lonzine Wright & Andrea Bolden							
1	Love Power		0	1968	22	1968	(Calla 141)
Sandpipers Male Vocal Trio, Michael Piano, Jim Brady & Richard Shoff							
1	Quantanamera	(PYE International 7N 25380)	7	1966	9	1966	(A&M 806)
· 2	Louie, Louie		0	1966	30	1966	(A&M 819)
3	Quando M' Innamoro (A Man Without Love)	(A&M AMS 723)	33	1968	0	1968	
4	Kumbaya	(A&M AMS 744)	39	1969	0	1969	
5	Kumbaya (Re-Entry)	(A&M AMS 744)	49	1969	0	1969	
6	Come Saturday Morning		0	1970	17	1970	(A&M 1134)
7	Hang On Sloopy	(Satril SAT 114)	32	1976	0	1976	
Sandra Female Vocalist from Germany							
1	Everlasting Love	(Siren SRN 85)	54	1988	0	1988	
Sandy B Female Vocalist from the USA							
1	Feel Like Singin'	(Nervous SANCD 1)	60	1993	0	1993	
2	Make The World Go Round	(Champion Champ CD 322)	73	1996	0	1996	
3	Make The World Go Round (Re-Recording)	(Champion Champ CD 327)	35	1997	0	1997	
Sandy Nelson Male Instrumentalist (Drums), Real Name Sander Nelson B: 1 Dec 1938 In Santa Monica, California							
* 1	Teen Beat	(Top Rank Jar 197)	9	1959	4	1959	(Original Sound 5)
2	Teen Beet (Re-Entry)	(Top Rank Jar 197)	25	1960	0	1960	
3	Let There Be Drums	(London HLP 9466)	3	1961	7	1961	(Imperial 5775)
4	Drums Are My Beat	(London HLP 9521)	30	1962	29	1962	(Imperial 5809)
5	Drummin' Up A Storm	(London HLP 9558)	39	1962	0	1962	
	LOST PART OF RIGHT LEG IN A MOTORCYCLE ACCIDENT IN 1963						
Sandy Posey Female Vocalist, B: 18 Jun 1944, Jasper, Alabama & Raised In West Memphis							
* 1	Born A Woman	(MGM 1321)	24	1966	12	1966	(MGM 13501)
* 2	Single Girl	(MGM 1330)	15	1967	12	1966	(MGM 13612)
3	What A Woman In Love Won't Do	(MGM 1335)	48	1967	31	1967	(MGM 13702)
4	I Take It Back		0	1967	12	1967	(MGM 13744)
9	Single Girl (Re-Issue)	(MGM 2006 533)	35	1975	0	1975	
	OTHER HITS ARE C/W • SHE WORKED AS A SESSION SINGER IN MEMPHIS & NASHVILLE IN THE 60S						
Sandy Stewart (1) Female Vocalist, Real Name Sandra Galitz B: 10 Jul 1937 Philadelphia							
1	Since You Went Away From Me		0	1953	27	1953	(Okeh 6941)

ISSUE	TITLE	UK LBL	UK POS	UK YEAR	US POS	US YEAR	US LBL
2	My Colouring Book		0	1963	20	1963	(COLPIX 669)

Sanford Clark Male Vocalist B: 1935 Tulsa, Now Hails From Phoenix

ISSUE	TITLE	UK LBL	UK POS	UK YEAR	US POS	US YEAR	US LBL
1	The Fool		0	1956	7	1956	(DOT 15481)

Sanford/Townsend Band Rock Band from Los Angeles Led By Ed Sanford & John Townsend

ISSUE	TITLE	UK LBL	UK POS	UK YEAR	US POS	US YEAR	US LBL
1	Smoke From A Distant Fire		0	1977	9	1977	(Warner Bros. 8370)

Santa Claus & The Christmas Male Vocal/Instrumental Group from the UK

ISSUE	TITLE	UK LBL	UK POS	UK YEAR	US POS	US YEAR	US LBL
1	Singalong-A-Santa	(Polydor IVY 1)	19	1982	0	1982	
2	Singalong-A-Santa Again	(Polydor IVY 2)	39	1983	0	1983	

Santa Esmeralda & Leroy Gomez Mixed Vocal/Instrumental Producers Nicolas Skorsky & Jean-Manuel De Scarano from the USA/France.

ISSUE	TITLE	UK LBL	UK POS	UK YEAR	US POS	US YEAR	US LBL
1	Don't Let Me Be Misunderstood	(Philips 6042 325)	41	1977	15	1977	(Casablanca 902)

Santana Male Vocal/Instrumental Group from the USA

ISSUE	TITLE	UK LBL	UK POS	UK YEAR	US POS	US YEAR	US LBL
1	Evil Ways		0	1970	9	1970	(Columbia 45069)
2	Black Magic Woman		0	1970	4	1970	(Columbia 45270)
3	Oye Como Va		0	1971	13	1971	(Columbia 45330)
4	Everybody's Everything		0	1971	12	1971	(Columbia 45472)
5	No One To Depend On		0	1972	36	1972	(Columbia 45552)
6	Samba Pa Ti	(CBS 2561)	27	1974	0	1974	
7	She's Not There	(CBS 5671)	11	1977	27	1977	(Columbia 10616)
8	Well All Right	(CBS 6755)	53	1978	0	1978	
9	Stormy		0	1979	32	1979	(Columbia 10873)
10	You Know That I Love You		0	1980	35	1980	(Columbia 11144)
11	All I Ever Wanted	(CBS 8160)	57	1980	0	1980	
12	Winning		0	1981	17	1981	(Columbia 01050)
13	Hold On		0	1982	15	1982	(Columbia 03160)

NAMES: CARLOS SANTANA, GREGG ROLIE, AUTLAN DE NAVARRO & DAVID BROWN

Santo & Johnny Male Guitarist Brothers, Santo Farina B: 24 Oct 1937 & Johnny B: 30 Apr 1941 from Brooklyn, USA.

ISSUE	TITLE	UK LBL	UK POS	UK YEAR	US POS	US YEAR	US LBL
1	Sleep Walk	(PYE International 7N 25037)	22	1959	1	1959	(Canada/American 103)
2	Teardrops	(Parlophone R 4619)	50	1960	23	1959	(Canada/American 107)

Sapphires Names Carol Jackson, Joe Livingston & George Gainer

ISSUE	TITLE	UK LBL	UK POS	UK YEAR	US POS	US YEAR	US LBL
1	Who Do You Love		0	1964	25	1964	(SWAN 4162)

Sarah Brightman Female Vocalist from the UK

ISSUE	TITLE	UK LBL	UK POS	UK YEAR	US POS	US YEAR	US LBL
1	I Lost My Heart To A Starship Trooper	(Ariola/Hansa AHA 527)	6	1978	0	1978	
2	The Adventures Of The Love Crusader	(Ariola/Hansa AHA 538)	53	1979	0	1979	
3	Him	(Polydor POSP 625)	55	1983	0	1983	
4	Pie Jesu	(HMV WEBBER 1)	3	1985	0	1985	
5	The Phantom Of The Opera	(Polydor POSP 800)	7	1986	0	1986	
6	All I Ask Of You	(Polydor POSP 802)	3	1986	0	1986	
7	Wishing You Were Somehow Here Again	Polydor POSP 803)	7	1987	0	1987	
8	Amigos Para Siepre (Friends For Life)	(REally Useful RUR 10)	11	1992	0	1992	
* 9	Time To Say Goodbye (Con Te Partiro)	(Coalition COLA003CD)	2	1997	0	1997	
10	Who Wants To Live Forever	(Coalition COLA014CD)	45	1997	0	1997	

Sarah Cracknell Female Vocalist from the UK

ISSUE	TITLE	UK LBL	UK POS	UK YEAR	US POS	US YEAR	US LBL
1	Anymore	(Gut CDGUT 3)	39	1996	0	1996	

Sarah Vaughan Female Jazz Vocalist, B: 27 Mar 1924 Newark, New Jersey.

ISSUE	TITLE	UK LBL	UK POS	UK YEAR	US POS	US YEAR	US LBL
1	Tenderly		0	1947	27	1947	(Musicraft 504)
2	Nature Boy		0	1948	9	1948	(Musicraft 567)
3	It's Magic (From *Romance On The High Seas*)		0	1948	11	1948	(Musicraft 557)
4	Black Coffee		0	1949	13	1949	(Columbia 38462)
5	That Lucky Old Sun (Just Rolls Around Heaven All Day)		0	1949	14	1949	(Columbia 38559)
6	Make Believe (You Are Glad When You're Sorry)		0	1949	20	1949	(Columbia 38559)
7	I'm Crazy To Love You		0	1950	26	1950	(Columbia 38701)
8	Our Very Own (Movie Title Song)		0	1950	15	1950	(Columbia 38860)
9	I Love The Guy		0	1950	10	1950	(Columbia 38925)
10	Thinking Of You		0	1950	16	1950	(Columbia 38925)
11	These Things I Offer You (For A Lifetime)		0	1951	11	1951	(Columbia 39370)
12	Vanity		0	1951	19	1951	(Columbia 39446)
13	I Ran All The Way Home		0	1951	18	1951	(Columbia 39576)
14	Sinner Or Saint		0	1952	22	1952	(Columbia 39873)
15	My Tormented Heart		0	1952	27	1952	(Columbia 39839)
16	A Lover's Quarrel		0	1953	28	1953	(Columbia 39932)
17	Time		0	1953	30	1953	(Columbia 40041)
18	Make Yourself Comfortable		0	1954	6	1954	(Mercury 70469)

ISSUE	TITLE	UK LBL	UK POS	UK YEAR	US POS	US YEAR	US LBL
19	How Important Can It Be		0	1955	12	1955	(Mercury 70534)
20	Whatever Lola Wants		0	1955	6	1955	(Mercury 70595)
21	Experience Unnecessary		0	1955	14	1955	(Mercury 70646)
22	C'est La Vie		0	1955	11	1955	(Mercury 70727)
23	Mr. Wonderful		0	1956	13	1956	(Mercury 70777)
24	Fabulous Character		0	1956	19	1956	(Mercury 70885)
25	Banana Boat Song		0	1957	19	1957	(Mercury 71020)
26	Passing Strangers	(Mercury MT 164)	22	1957	0	1957	
* 27	Broken-Hearted Melody	(Mercury AMT1057)	7	1959	7	1959	(Mercury 71477)
28	Let's / Serenata	(Columbia DB 4542)	37	1960	0	1960	
29	Let's / Serenata (Re-Entry)	(Columbia DB 4542)	47	1961	0	1961	
30	Passing Strangers (Re-Issue)	(Mercury MF 1082)	20	1969	0	1969	
	OBITUARY: D: 3 APR 1990 FROM LUNG CANCER.						

Sarah Washington Female Vocalist from the UK

1	I Will Always Love You	(Almighty CDALMY 33)	12	1993	0	1993	
2	Careless Whisper	(Almighty CDALMY 43)	45	1993	0	1993	
3	Heaven	(AM:PM 5815352)	28	1996	0	1996	
4	Everything	(AM:PM 5818872)	30	1996	0	1996	

Sarr Band Mixed Vocal/Instrumental Group from the UK/France/Italy

1	Magic Mandrake	(CalendarDay 111)	68	1978	0	1978	

Sartorello Mixed Vocal/Instrumental Duo From Italy

1	Move Baby Move	(Multiply CDMULTY 12)	56	1996	0	1996	

Sasha Male Producer from the UK

1	Together	(FFRR FCD 212)	57	1993	0	1993	
2	Higher Ground	(Deconstruction 74321189002)	19	1994	0	1994	
3	Magic	(Deconstruction 74321221862)	32	1994	0	1994	
4	Be As One	(Deconstruction 74321342962)	17	1996	0	1996	

Saturday Night Band Male Vocal/Instrumental Group from the USA

1	Come On Dance Dance	(CBS 6367)	16	1978	0	1978	

Sauter-Finegan Orchestra Male Arrangers, Eddie Sauter And Bill Finegan

1	Doodletown Fifers		0	1952	12	1952	(RCA Victor 4866)
2	Nina Never Knew		0	1952	13	1952	(RCA Victor 5065)
3	Midnight Sleighride		0	1953	29	1953	(RCA Victor 4995)
4	The Moon Is Blue		0	1953	20	1953	(RCA Victor 5359)

Savanna Male Vocal/Guitarist from the USA

1	I Can't Turn Away	(R&B RBS 203)	61	1981	0	1981	

Savannah Churchill Jazz/R&B Vocalist from the USA

1	I Want To Be Loved		0	1947	21	1947	(Manor 1046)
2	Time Out For Tears		0	1948	20	1948	(Manor1116)
3	(It's No) Sin		0	1951	5	1951	(RCA Victor 4280)
4	Shake A Hand		0	1953	22	1953	(Decca 28836)
	OBITUARY: D: 19 APR 1974, (AGED 54).						

Saw Doctors Male Vocal/Instrumental Group From Ireland

1	Small Bit Of Love	(Shamtown SAW001CD)	24	1994	0	1994	
2	World Of Good	(Shamtown SAW002CD)	15	1996	0	1996	
3	To Win Just Once	(Shamtown SAW004CD)	14	1996	0	1996	

Saxon Male Vocal/Instrumental Group from the UK

1	Wheels Of Steel	(Carrere CAR 143)	20	1980	0	1980	
2	747 (Strangers In The Night)	(Carrere CAR 151)	13	1980	0	1980	
3	Backs To The Wall	(Carrere HM 6)	64	1980	0	1980	
4	Big Teaser / Rainbow Theme	(Carrere HM 5)	66	1980	0	1980	
5	Strong Arm Of The Law	(Carrere CAR 170)	63	1980	0	1980	
6	And The Bands Played On	(Carrere CAR 180)	12	1981	0	1981	
7	Never Surrender	(Carrere CAR 204)	18	1981	0	1981	
8	Princess Of The Night	(Carrere CAR 208)	57	1981	0	1981	
9	Power And The Glory	(Carrere SAXON 1)	32	1983	0	1983	
10	Nightmare	(Carrere CAR 284)	50	1983	0	1983	
11	Back On The Streets	(Parlophone R 6103)	75	1985	0	1985	
12	Rock N' Roll Gypsy	(Parlophone R 6112)	71	1986	0	1986	
13	Waiting For The Night	(EMI EM 43)	66	1986	0	1986	
14	Ride Like The Wind	(EMI EM 43)	52	1988	0	1988	
15	I Can't Wait Anymore	(EMI EM 54)	71	1988	0	1988	

ISSUE . TITLE	UK LBL	UK POS	UK YEAR	US POS	US.YEAR	US LBL
Scaffold Male Vocal Group from the UK						
1 Thank U Very Much	(Parlophone R 5643)	4	1967	0	1967	
2 Do You Remember	(Parlophone R 5679)	34	1968	0	1968	
* 3 Lily The Pink	(Parlophone R 5734)	1	1968	0	1968	
4 Gin Gan Goolie	(Parlophone R 5812)	38	1969	0	1969	
5 Gin Gan Goolie (Re-Entry)	(Parlophone R 5812)	50	1970	0	1970	
6 Liverpool Lou	(Warner Bros. K 16400)	7	1974	0	1974	
GROUP FORMED IN 1962, THE FRENCH VERSION 'LE SIROP TYPHON', SOLD 800,000						
Scandal (Featuring) Patty Smyth Rock Band Led By Patty Smyth & Zack Smith from New York						
1 The Warrior		0	1984	7	1984	(Columbia 04424)
Scarface Male Vocalist, Real Name Brad Jordan B: 9 Nov 1969 from Houston						
1 Hand Of The Dead Body	(Virgin VUSCD 88)	41	1995	0	1995	
2 I Never Seen A Man Cry (Aka I Seen A Man Die)	(Virgin VUDCD 94)	55	1995	37	1994	(RAP-ALOT 38461)
3 Game Over	(Virgin VUSCD 121)	34	1997	0	1997	
Scarlet Fantastic Mixed Vocal/Instrumental Group from the UK						
1 No Memory	(Arista RIS 36)	24	1987	0	1987	
2 Plug Me In (To The Central Love Line)	(Arista 109693)	67	1988	0	1988	
Scarlet Party Male Vocal/Instrumental Group from the UK						
1 101 Dam-Nations	(Parlophone R 6058)	44	1982	0	1982	
Scarlett & Black Names Robin Hild And Sue West						
1 You Don't Know		0	1988	20	1988	(Virgin 99405)
Scatman Male Vocalist from the USA						
1 Scatman (Ski-Ba-Bop-Ba Do Bop)	(Arista 74321281712)	3	1995	0	1995	
2 Scatman's World	(Arista 74321289952)	10	1995	0	1995	
Scientist Male Instrumentalist from the UK						
1 The Exorcist	(Kickin Kick 1)	62	1990	0	1990	
2 The Exorcist (Re-Mix)	(Kickin Kick 1TR)	46	1990	0	1990	
3 The Bee	(Kickin Kick 35)	52	1990	0	1990	
4 The Bee (Re-Entry)	(Kickin Kick 35)	47	1991	0	1991	
5 Spiral Symphony	(Kickin Kick 5)	74	1991	0	1991	
Scooter Male Vocal/Instrumental Group from the UK/Germany						
1 The Move Your Ass (EP)	(Club Tools 0061675 CLU)	23	1995	0	1995	
2 Back In The UK	(Club Tools 0061955 CLU)	18	1996	0	1996	
3 Rebel Yell	(Club Tools 0062575 CLU)	30	1996	0	1996	
4 I'm Raving	(Club Tools 0063015 CLU)	33	1996	0	1996	
5 Fire	(Club Tools 0060005 CLU)	45	1997	0	1997	
Scorpions Male Vocal/Instrumental Quintet from Germany Lead Singer WKlaus Meine						
1 Is There Anybody There / Another Piece Of Meat	(Harvest Har 5185)	39	1979	0	1979	
2 Lovedrive	(Harvest Har 5188)	69	1979	0	1979	
3 Make It Real	(Harvest Har5206)	72	1980	0	1980	
4 The Zoo	(Harvest Har 5212)	75	1980	0	1980	
5 No One Like You	(Harvest Har 5219)	65	1982	0	1982	
6 No Onc Like You (Re-Entry)	(Harvest Har 5219)	64	1982	0	1982	
7 Can't Live Without You	(Harvest Har 5221)	63	1982	0	1982	
8 Rock You Like A Hurricane		0	1984	25	1984	(Mercury 818440)
9 Rhythm Of Love	(Harvest Har 5240)	59	1988	0	1988	
10 Passion Rules The Game	(Harvest Har5242)	74	1989	0	1989	
* 11 Wind Of Change	(Vertigo VER 54)	53	1991	4	1991	(Mercury 868180)
12 Wind Of Change (Re-Issue)	(Vertigo VER 58)	2	1991	0	1991	
13 Send Me An Angel	(Vertigo VER 60)	27	1991	0	1991	
14 Send Me An Angel (Re-Entry)	(Vertigo VER 60)	68	1991	0	1991	
Scot Project Male Producer Frank De Zenk from Germany						
1 U (I Got A Feeling)	(Positiva CDTIV 55)	66	1996	0	1996	
Scotland Rugby Team National Male Rugby Team Vocalist						
1 Flower Of Scotland	(Greentrax STRAX 1001)	73	1990	0	1990	
Scotland World Cup Squad National Male Soccer Team Vocalists						
1 Easy Easy	(Polydor 2058 452)	20	1974	0	1974	
2 Ole Ola (Mulher Brasileira)	(RIVA 15)	4	1978	0	1978 with Rod Stewart	
3 We Have A Dream	(WEA K 19145)	5	1982	0	1982	
4 Say It With Pride	(RCA PB 43791)	45	1990	0	1990	

ISSUE	TITLE	UK LBL	UK POS	UK YEAR	US POS	US YEAR	US LBL
Scott Bradley Male Vocalist from the UK							
1	Zoom	(Hidden Agenda HIDDCD 1)	61	1994	0	1994	
Scott English Male Vocalist from the USA							
1	Brandy	(Horse HOSS 7)	12	1971	0	1971	
Scott Fitzgerald Male Vocalist from the UK							
1	If I Had Words	(Pepper UP 36333)	3	1978	0	1978	
2	Go	(PRT PYS 10)	52	1988	0	1988	
Scott McKenzie Male Vocalist, Real Name Phillip Blondheim B: 10 Jan 1939 In Jacksonville, Florida							
* 1	San Francisco (Be Sure To Wear Some Flowers...)	(CBS 2816)	1	1967	4	1967	(ODE 103)
2	Like An Old Time Movie	(CBS 3009)	50	1967	24	1967	(ODE 105)
	HIT 2 IS CREDITED TO THE VOICE OF SCOTT MCKENZIE • SCOTT FAILED AN AUDITION WITH THE MONKEES						
Scott Walker Male Vocalist from the USA							
1	Jackie	(Philips BF 1628)	22	1967	0	1967	
2	Joanna	(Philips BF 1662)	7	1968	0	1968	
3	Lights Of Cincinnati	(Philips BF 1793)	13	1969	0	1969	
Scottish Euro '96 Squad National Soccer Team Vocalist							
1	Purple Heather	(Warner Bros. W 0345CD)	16	1996	0	1996	
Screamin' Jay Hawkins Male Vocalist from the USA							
1	Heart Attack And Vine	(Columbia 6591092)	42	1993	0	1993	
Screaming Blue Messiahs Male Vocal/Instrumental Group from the UK							
1	I Wanna Be A Flintstone	(WEA YZ 166)	28	1988	0	1988	
Screaming Trees Male Vocal/Instrumental Group from the USA							
1	Nearly Lost You	(Epic 6582372)	50	1993	0	1993	
2	Dollar Bill	(Epic 6591792)	52	1993	0	1993	
Scritti Politti Male Vocal/Instrumental Group from the UK Names: Green Gartside, David Gamson & Fred Maher							
1	The Sweetest Girl	(Rough Trade RT 091)	64	1981	0	1981	
2	Faithless	(Rough Trade RT 101)	56	1982	0	1982	
3	Asylums In Jerusalem / Jacques Derrida	(Rough Trade RT 111)	43	1982	0	1982	
4	Wood Beez (Pray Like Aretha Franklin)	(Virgin VS 657)	10	1984	0	1984	
5	Absolute	(Virgin VS 680)	17	1984	0	1984	
6	Hypnotise	(Virgin VS 725)	68	1984	0	1984	
7	The Word Girl	(Virgin VS 747)	6	1985	0	1985	
8	Perfect Way	(Virgin VS 780)	48	1985	11	1985	(Warner Bros. 28949)
9	Oh Patti (Don't Feel Sorry For Loverboy)	(Virgin VS 1006)	13	1988	0	1988	
10	First Boy In This Town	(Virgin VS 1082)	63	1988	0	1988	
11	Boom! There She Was	(Virgin VS 1143)	55	1988	0	1988	
12	She's A Woman	(Virgin VS 1333)	55	1991	0	1991	
13	Take Me In Your Arms And Love Me	(Virgin VS 1346)	47	1991	0	1991	
Sea Level Instrumental Group from the USA							
1	Fifty-Four	(Capricorn POSP 28)	63	1979	0	1979	
Seal Male Vocalist, Real Name Sealhenry Samuel B: Paddington, London, England							
1	Crazy	(ZTT ZANG 8)	2	1990	7	1991	(SIRE 19298)
2	Future Love (EP)	(ZTT ZANG 11)	12	1991	0	1991	
3	The Beginning	(ZTT ZANG 21)	24	1991	0	1991	
4	Killer (EP)	(ZTT ZANG 23)	8	1991	0	1991	
5	Violet	(ZTT ZANG 27)	39	1992	0	1992	
6	Prayer For The Dying / Don't Cry	(ZTT ZANG 51CD)	14	1994	21	1994	(ZTT/SIRE 18138)
* 7	Kiss From A Rose	(ZTT ZANG 52CD1)	4	1994	1	1995	(ZTT/SIRE 17896)
8	Newborn Friend	(ZTT ZANG 58CD)	45	1994	0	1994	
9	Don't Cry / Prayer For The Dying (Re-Issue)	(ZTT ZANG 75CD)	51	1995	0	1995	
10	Fly Like An Eagle (From *Space Jam*)	(ZTT ZEAL 1CD)	13	1997	10	1996	(Atlantic 87046)
Seals & Crofts Real Names Jim Seals B: 17 Oct 1941, Dash Crofts B: 14 Aug 1940 from the USA.							
1	Summer Breeze		0	1972	6	1972	(Warner Bros. 7606)
2	Hummingbird		0	1973	20	1973	(Warner Bros. 7671)
3	Diamond Girl		0	1973	6	1973	(Warner Bros. 7708)
4	We May Never Pass This Way (Again)		0	1973	21	1973	(Warner Bros. 7740)
5	I'll Play For You		0	1975	18	1975	(Warner Bros. 8075)
6	Get Closer		0	1976	6	1976	(Warner Bros. 8190)
7	My Fair Share		0	1977	28	1977	(Warner Bros. 8405)
8	You're The Love		0	1978	18	1978	(Warner Bros. 8551)

ISSUE	TITLE	UK LBL	UK POS	UK YEAR	US POS	US YEAR	US LBL
Sean Maguire Male Vocalist from the UK							
1	Someone To Love	(Parlophone CDRS 6390)	14	1994	0	1994	
2	Take This Time	(Parlophone CDR 6395)	27	1994	0	1994	
3	Take This Time (Re-Entry)	(ParlophoneCDR 6395)	74	1994	0	1994	
4	Suddenly	(Parlophone CDR 6403)	18	1995	0	1995	
5	Now I've Found You	(ParlophoneCDLEEPYS 1)	22	1995	0	1995	
6	You To Me Are Everything	(Parlophone CDRS 6420)	16	1995	0	1995	
7	Good Day	(Parlophone CDRS 6432)	12	1996	0	1996	
8	Don't Pull Your Love	(Parlophone CDRS 6440)	14	1996	0	1996	
9	Today's The Day	(Parlophone CDR 6459)	27	1997	0	1997	
Searchers Male Vocal/Instrumental Group from the UK Names: John McNally, Mike Pender, Tony Jackson & Chris Curtis							
1	Sweets For My Sweet	(PYE 7N 15533)	1	1963	0	1963	
2	Sweet Nothin's	(Philips BF 1274)	48	1963	0	1963	
3	Sugar And Spice	(PYE 7N 15566)	2	1963	44	1964	(Liberty 55689)
* 4	Needles And Pins	(PYE 7N 15594)	1	1964	13	1964	(KAPP 577)
5	Don't Throw Your Love Away	(PYE 7N 15630)	1	1964	16	1964	(KAPP 593)
6	Someday We're Gonna Love Again	(PYE 7N 15670)	11	1964	34	1964	(KAPP 609)
7	When You Walk In The Room	(PYE 7N 15694)	3	1964	34	1964	(KAPP 618)
8	What Have They Done To The Rain	(PYE 7N 15739)	13	1964	29	1965	(KAPP 644)
9	Love Potion Number 9		0	1964	3	1964	(KAPP 27)
10	Goodbye My Love	(PYE 7N 15794)	4	1965	0	1965	
11	Bumble Bee		0	1965	21	1965	(KAPP 49)
12	He's Got No Love	(PYE 7N 15878)	12	1965	0	1965	
13	When I Get Home	(PYE 7N 15950)	35	1965	0	1965	
14	Take Me For What I'm Worth	(PYE 7N 15992)	20	1965	0	1965	
15	Take It Or Leave It	(PYE 7N 17094)	31	1966	0	1966	
16	Have You Ever Loved Somebody	(PYE 7N 17170)	48	1966	0	1966	
Seashells Female Vocal Group from the UK							
1	Maybe I Know	(CBS 8218)	32	1972	0	1972	
Seb Male Instrumentalist (Keyboards) from the UK							
1	Sugar Shack	(React CDREACT 50)	61	1995	0	1995	
Sebadoh Male Vocal/Instrumental Group from the USA							
1	Beauty Of The Ride	(DominoRUG 47CD)	74	1996	0	1996	
Secchi (Featuring) Orlando Male Vocal/Instrumental Duo from the USA/Italy							
1	I Say Yeah	(Epic 6568467)	46	1991	0	1991	
Second City Sound Male Instrumental Group from the UK							
1	Tchaikovsky One	(Decca F 12310)	22	1966	0	1966	
2	The Dream Of Olwen	(Major Minor MM 600)	43	1969	0	1969	
Second Image Male Vocal/Instrumental Group from the UK							
1	Star	(Polydor POSP 457)	60	1982	0	1982	
2	Better Take Time	(Polydor POSP 565)	67	1983	0	1983	
3	Don't You	(MCA 848)	68	1983	0	1983	
4	Sing And Shout	(MA MCA 882)	53	1984	0	1984	
5	Starting Again	(MCA 936)	65	1985	0	1985	
Second Phase Male Producer, Real Name Joey Beltram from the USA							
1	Mentasm	(R&S RSUK 2)	48	1991	0	1991	
Secret Affair Male Vocal/Instrumental Group from the UK							
1	Time For Action	(I-SPY SEE 1)	13	1979	0	1979	
2	Let Your Heart Dance	(I-SPY SEE 3)	32	1979	0	1979	
3	My World	(I-SPY SEE 5)	16	1980	0	1980	
4	Sound Of Confusion	(I-SPY SEE 8)	45	1980	0	1980	
5	Do You Know	(I-SPY SEE 10)	57	1981	0	1981	
Secret Knowledge Mixed Vocal/Instrumental Duo from the UK/USA							
1	Love Me Now	(Deconstruction 74321342432)	66	1996	0	1996	
2	Sugar Daddy	(Deconstruction 74321400242)	75	1996	0	1996	
Secret Life Male Vocal Group from the UK							
1	As Always	(Cowboy 7 Rodeo 9)	45	1992	0	1992	
2	Love So Strong	(Cowboy Rodeo18CD)	38	1993	0	1993	
3	She Holds The Key	(Pulse 8 CDLOSE58)	63	1994	0	1994	
4	I Want You	(Pulse 8 CDLOSE71)	70	1994	0	1994	
5	Love So Strong (Re-Mix)	(Pulse 8 CDLOSE79)	37	1995	0	1995	

ISSUE	TITLE	UK LBL	UK POS	UK YEAR	US POS	US YEAR	US LBL
Secrets Names: Josie Allen, Carole Raymont, Pat Miller & Kragen Gray							
1	The Boy Next Door		0	1963	18	1963	(Philips 40146)
Seduction Female Vocal Trio, April Harris, Idalis Leon & Michelle Visage from New York							
1	You're My One And Only (True Love)		0	1989	23	1989	(Vendetta 1433)
* 2	Two To Make It Right		0	1990	2	1990	(Vendetta 1464)
3	Heartbeat	(Breakout USA 685)	75	1990	13	1990	(Vendetta 1473)
4	Could This Be Love		0	1990	11	1990	(Vendetta 1509)
	VOCALS ON HIT 2 ARE BY MARTHA WASH • SINOA LOREN REPLACED MICHELLE IN 1990						
Seeds Lead Singer With The Quartet Is Richard Marsh							
1	Pushin' Too Hard		0	1967	36	1967	(GNP Crescendo 372)
Seekers Mixed Vocal Group from Australia/Sri Lanka Names: Judith Durham, Keith Potger, Bruce Woodley & Athol Guy							
* 1	I'll Never Find Another You	(Columbia DB 7431)	1	1965	4	1965	(Capitol 5383)
* 2	A World Of Our Own	(Columbia DB 7532)	3	1965	19	1965	(Capitol 5430)
* 3	The Carnival Is Over	(Columbia DB 7711)	1	1965	0	1965	
4	Someday One Day	(Columbia DB 7867)	11	1966	0	1966	
5	Walk With Me	(Columbia DB 8000)	10	1966	0	1966	
6	Morningtown Ride	(Columbia DB 8060)	2	1966	0	1966	
* 7	Georgy Girl	(Columbia DB 8134)	3	1967	2	1966	(Capitol 5756)
8	When Will The Good Apples Fall	(Columbia DB 8273)	11	1967	0	1967	
9	Emerald City	(Columbia DB8313)	50	1967	0	1967	
Seiko & Donnie Wahlberg Mixed Vocal Duo from the USA/Japan							
1	The Right Combination	(Epic 656203 7)	44	1990	0	1990	
Selecter Mixed Vocal/Instrumental Group from the UK							
1	On My Radio	(2 Tone CHS TT	8	1979	0	1979	
2	Three Minute Hero	(2 Tone CHS TT	16	1980	0	1980	
3	Missing Words	(2 Tone CHS TT 10)	23	1980	0	1980	
4	The Whisper	(Chrysalis CHSS 1)	36	1980	0	1980	
Semprini Male Orchestra Leader from the UK							
1	Theme From *Exodus*	(HMV POP 842)	25	1961	0	1961	
Senator Bobby Real Name Bill Minkin							
1	Wild Thing		0	1967	20	1967	(Parkway 127)
Senator Everett Mckinley Dirksen Male US Senator (1950-69), B: 1896 Pekin, Illinois							
1	Gallant Men		0	1967	29	1967	(Capitol 5805)
Sensational Alex Harvey Band Male Vocal/Instrumental Group from the UK							
1	Delilah	(Vertigo Alex 001)	7	1975	0	1975	
2	Gamblin' Bar Room Blues	(Vertigo Alex 002)	38	1975	0	1975	
3	Boston Tea Party	(Mountain Top 12)	13	1976	0	1976	
Sensations Lead Singer With The Quartet Is Yvonne Mills Baker							
1	Let Me In		0	1962	4	1962	(ARGO 5405)
Senseless Things Male Vocal/Instrumental Group from the UK							
1	Everybody's Gone	(Epic 6569807)	73	1991	0	1991	
2	Got It At The Delmar	(Epic 6574497)	50	1991	0	1991	
3	Easy To Smile	(Epic 6576957)	18	1992	0	1992	
4	Hold It Down	(Epic 6579267)	19	1992	0	1992	
5	Homophobic Asshole	(Epic 6588337)	52	1992	0	1992	
6	Primary Instinct	(Epic 6589402)	41	1993	0	1993	
7	Too Much Kissing	(Epic 6592502)	69	1993	0	1993	
8	Christine Keeler	(Epic 6609572)	56	1994	0	1994	
9	Something To Miss	(Epic 6611162)	57	1995	0	1995	
Senser Mixed Vocal/Instrumental Group from the UK							
1	The Key	(Ultimate TOPP019CD)	47	1993	0	1993	
2	Switch	(Ultimate TOPP 022CD)	39	1994	0	1994	
3	Age Of Panic	(UltimateTOPP 027CD)	52	1994	0	1994	
4	Charming Demons	(Ultimate TOPP 045CD)	42	1996	0	1996	
Sepultura Male Vocal/Instrumental Group from Brazil							
1	Territory	(Roadrunner RR 23823)	66	1993	0	1994	
2	Refuse-Resist	(Roadrunner RR 23773)	51	1994	0	1994	
3	Slave New World	(Roadrunner RR 23745)	46	1994	0	1994	
4	Roots Bloody Roots	(Roadrunner RR 23205)	19	1996	0	1994	
5	Ratamahatta	(Roadrunner RR 23145)	23	1996	0	1996	
6	Attitude	(Roadrunner RR 22995)	46	1996	0	1996	

ISSUE	TITLE	UK LBL	UK POS	UK YEAR	US POS	US YEAR	US LBL
Serendipity Singers	A Large Pop-Folk Group from Colorado, USA						
1	Don't Let The Rain Come Down (Crooked Little Man)		0	1964	6	1964	(Philips 40175)
2	Beans In My Ears		0	1964	30	1964	(Philips 40198)
Sergio Mendes	Male Conductor, B: 11 Feb 1941 Niterol, Brazil						
1	The Look Of Love		0	1968	4	1968	(A&M 924)
2	The Fool On The Hill		0	1968	6	1968	(A&M 961)
3	Scarborough Fair		0	1968	16	1968	(A&M 986)
4	Never Gonna Let You Go	(A&M AM 118)	45	1983	4	1983	(A&M 2540)
5	Alibis		0	1984	29	1984	(A&M 2639)
	HITS 1-3 ARE CREDITED TO SERGIO MENDES & BRASIL '66						
Serious Intention	Male Vocal/Instrumental Group from the USA						
1	You Don't Know (Oh-Oh-Oh)	(Important TAN8)	75	1985	0	1985	
2	Serious	(Pow Wow LON 93)	51	1986	0	1986	
Serious Rope	Mixed Vocal/Instrumental Group from the UK						
1	Happiness	(Rumour RUMACD 64)	54	1993	0	1993	
2	Happiness - You Make Me Happy (Re-Mix)	(Mercury MERCD 407)	70	1994	0	1994	
	Hit 1 Is Credited To Serious Rope Presents Sharon Dee Clarke						
Set The Tone	Male Vocal/Instrumental Group from the UK						
1	Dance Sucker	(Island WIP 6836)	62	1983	0	1983	
2	Rap Your Love	(Island IS 110)	67	1983	0	1983	
Settlers	Mixed Vocal/Instrumental Group from the UK						
1	The Lightning Tree	(York SYK 505)	36	1971	0	1971	
Seven Grand Housing Authority	Male Producer, Real Name Terence Parker from the UK						
1	The Question	(Olympic ELYCD 010)	70	1993	0	1993	
702	Female Vocal Group from the USA						
1	Steelo	(Motown 8606072)	41	1996	32	1996	(Motown 860530)
2	Get It Together		0	1997	10	1997	(Motown 860612)
740 Boyz	Male Vocal/Instrumental Duo from the USA						
1	Shimmy Shake	(MCA Mcstd 40002)	54	1995	0	1995	
7669	Female Rap Group from the USA						
1	Joy	(Motown Tmgcd 1429)	60	1994	0	1994	
7th Heaven	Male Vocal Group from the UK						
1	Hot Fun	(Mercury Mer 199)	47	1985	0	1985	
Severine	Female Vocalist from France						
1	Un Banc, Un Arbre, Une Rue	(Philips 6009 135)	9	1971	0	1971	
Sex Club (Featuring) Brown Sugar	Mixed Vocal/Instrumental Duo from the USA						
1	Big Dick Man	(Club Tools CLU 60775)	67	1995	0	1995	
Sex Pistols	Male Vocal/Instrumental Group from the UK						
1	Anarchy In The U.K.	(EMI 2566)	38	1976	0	1976	
2	God Save The Queen	(Virgin VS 181)	2	1977	0	1977	
3	Pretty Vacant	(Virgin VS 84)	6	1977	0	1977	
4	Holidays In The Sun	(Virgin VS 191)	8	1977	0	1977	
5	No One Is Innocent / My Way	(Virgin VS 220)	7	1978	0	1978	
6	Something Else / Friggin' In The Riggin'	(Virgin VS 240)	3	1979	0	1979	
7	Silly Things / Who Killed Bambi	(Virgin CS 256)	6	1979	0	1979	
8	C'mon Everybody	(Virgin VS 272)	3	1979	0	1979	
9	The Great Rock 'N' Roll Swindle / Rock Around The Clock	(Virgin VS 290)	21	1979	0	1979	
10	(I'm Not Your) Stepping Stone	(Virgin VS 339)	21	1980	0	1980	
11	Anarchy In The U.K. (Re-Issue)	(Virgin VS 1431)	33	1992	0	1992	
12	Pretty Vacant (Re-Issue)	(Virgin VS 1448)	56	1992	0	1992	
13	Pretty Vacant (Live)	(Virgin VUSCD 113)	18	1996	0	1996	
	HIT 5 IS CREDITED TO SEX PISTOLS, PUNK PRAYER BY RONALD BIGGS • HITS 'ROCK AROUND THE CLOCK' & 'WHO KILLED BAMBI' ARE CREDITED TO TEN POLE TUDOR • OBITUARY: SID VICIOUS D: 2 FEB 1979 DRUG OVERDOSE.						
Shabba Ranks	Male Vocalist From Jamaica						
1	She's A Woman	(Virgin VS 1333)	20	1991	0	1991	
2	Trailer Load Of Girls	(Epic 6568747)	63	1991	0	1991	
3	Housecall	(Epic 6573477)	31	1991	37	1991	(Epic 73928)
4	Mr. Loverman	(Epic 6582517)	23	1992	40	1992	(Epic 74257)
* 5	Slow And Sexy	(Epic 6587727)	17	1992	33	1993	(Epic 74741)
6	Mr.Loverman (Re-Issue)	(Epic 6590782)	3	1993	0	1993	
7	Housecall (Re-Mix)	(Epic 6592842)	8	1993	0	1993	

ISSUE	TITLE	UK LBL	UK POS	UK YEAR	US POS	US YEAR	US LBL
8	What'cha Gonna Do	(Epic 6593072)	21	1993	0	1993	
9	Family Affair	(Polydor PZCD 304)	18	1993	0	1993	
10	Let's Get It On	(Epic 6614122)	22	1995	0	1995	
11	Shine Eye Gal	(Epic 6622332)	46	1995	0	1995	

Shades Of Blue Mixed Vocal/Instrumental Froup from the USA

1	Oh How Happy		0	1966	12	1966	(Impact 1007)

Shades Of Love Male Instrumental/Production Duo from the USA

1	Keep In Touch	(Visious Muzic MUZCD 102)	64	1995	0	1995	

Shades Of Rhythm Male Production/Instrumental Group from the UK

1	Homicide / Exorcist	(ZTT ZANG 13)	53	1991	0	1991	
2	Sweet Sensation	(ZTT ZANG 18)	54	1991	0	1991	
3	The Sound Of Eden	(ZTT ZANG 22)	35	1991	0	1991	
4	Extacy	(ZTT ZANG 24)	16	1991	0	1991	
5	Sweet Revival (Keep It Comin')	(ZTT ZANG 40CD)	61	1993	0	1993	
6	Sound Of Eden (Re-Issue)	(ZTT ZANG 44CD)	37	1993	0	1993	
7	The Wandering Dragon	(Public Demand PPDCD 5)	55	1994	0	1994	
8	Psycho Base	(Coalition Drum 002CD)	57	1997	0	1997	

Shadows Male Vocal/Instrumental Group from the UK

	ISSUE	TITLE	UK LBL	UK POS	UK YEAR	US POS	US YEAR	US LBL
*	1	Apache	(Columbia DB 4484)	1	1960	0	1960	
	2	Man Of Mystery / The Stranger	(Columbia DB 4530)	5	1960	0	1960	
	3	F.B.I.	(Columbia DB 4580)	6	1961	0	1961	
	4	Frightened City	(Columbia DB 4637)	3	1961	0	1961	
	5	Kon-Tiki	(Columbia DB 4698)	1	1961	0	1961	
	6	The Savage	(Columbia DB 4726)	10	1961	0	1961	
	7	Kon-Tiki (Re-Entry)	(Columbia DB 4698)	37	1961	0	1961	
*	8	Wonderful Land	(Columbia DB4790)	1	1962	0	1962	
	9	Guitar Tango	(Columbia DB 4870)	4	1962	0	1962	
	10	Dance On!	(Columbia DB4948)	1	1962	0	1962	
	11	Foot Tapper	(Columbia DB 4984)	1	1963	0	1963	
	12	Atlantis	(Columbia DB 7047)	2	1963	0	1963	
	13	Shindig	(Columbia DB 7106)	6	1963	0	1963	
	14	Geronimo	(Columbia DB 7163)	11	1963	0	1963	
	15	Theme For Young Lovers	(Columbia DB 7231)	12	1964	0	1964	
	16	The Rise And Fall Of Flingle Bunt	(Columbia DB 7261)	5	1964	0	1964	
	17	Rhythm And Greens	(Columbia DB 7342)	22	1964	0	1964	
	18	Genie With The Light Brown Lamp	(Columbia DB 7416)	17	1964	0	1964	
	19	Mary Anne	(Columbia DB 7476)	17	1965	0	1965	
	20	Stingray	(Columbia DB7588)	19	1965	0	1965	
	21	Don't Make My Baby Blue	(Columbia DB 7650)	10	1965	0	1965	
	22	War Lord	(Columbia DB 7769)	18	1965	0	1965	
	23	I Met A Girl	(Columbia DB 7853)	22	1966	0	1966	
	24	A Place In The Sun	(Columbia DB 7952)	24	1966	0	1966	
	25	The Dreams I Dream	(Columbia DB 8034)	42	1966	0	1966	
	26	Maroc 7	(Columbia DB 8170)	24	1967	0	1967	
	27	Let Me Be The One	(EMI 2269)	12	1975	0	1975	
	28	Don't Cry For Me Argentina	(EMI 2890)	5	1978	0	1978	
	29	Theme From The Deer Hunter (Cavatina)	(EMI 2939)	9	1979	0	1979	
	30	Riders In The Sky	(EMI 5027)	12	1980	0	1980	
	31	Equinox (Part V)	(Polydor POSP 148)	50	1980	0	1980	
	32	The Third Man	(Polydor POSP 255)	44	1981	0	1981	

NAMES: HANK MARVIN, BRUCE WELCH, TERENCE 'JET' HARRIS & TONY MEEHAN BRUCE WELCH B: 2 NOV 1941 BOGNOR REGIS, SUSSEX, ENGLAND

Shadows Of Knight Lead Singer With The Chicago-Based Band Is Jim Sohns

*	1	Gloria		0	1966	10	1966	(Dunwich 116)
	2	Oh Yeah		0	1966	39	1966	(Dunwich 122)

Shaft Male Production/Instrumental Duo from the UK

1	Roobarb And Custard	(FFRREEDOM TAB 100)	7	1991	0	1991	
2	Monkey	(FFRREEDOM TAB 114)	61	1992	0	1992	

Shaggy Male Vocalist from Jamaica

	1	Oh Carolina	(Greensleeves GRECD 361)	1	1993	0	1993	
	2	Soon Be Done	(Greensleeves GRECD 380)	46	1993	0	1993	
*	3	Boombastic	(Virgin VSCDT 1536)	1	1995	3	1995	(Virgin 38482)
	4	In The Summertime	(Virgin VCSDT 1542)	5	1995	3	1995	(Virgin 38482)
	5	Why You Treat Me So Bad	(Virgin VSCDT 1566)	11	1996	0	1996	

ISSUE	TITLE	UK LBL	UK POS	UK YEAR	US POS	US YEAR	US LBL
6	That Girl	(Virgin VUSDX 106)	15	1996	20	1996	(Virgin 38550)
7	Something Different / The Train Is Coming	(Virgin VSCDX 1581)	21	1996	0	1996	
8	Piece Of My Heart	(Virgin VSCDT 1647)	7	1997	0	1997	
	HIT 5 IS CREDITED TO SHAGGY AND GRAND PUBAM • HIT 6 TO MAXI PRIEST FEATURING SHAGGY • HIT 8 TO SHAGGY FEATURING MARSHA						

Shai Male Vocal Quartet from Washington D.C.

* 1	If I Ever Fall In Love	(MCA MCS 1727)	36	1992	2	1992	(Gasoline A. 54518)
* 2	Comforter		0	1993	10	1993	(Gasoline A. 54596)
3	Baby I'm Yours		0	1993	10	1993	(Gasoline A. 54574)
4	The Place Where You Belong		0	1994	34	1994	(MCA 54807)

Shakatak Mixed Vocal/Instrumental Group from the UK

1	Feels Like The Right Time	(Polydor POSP 188)	41	1980	0	1980	
2	Living In The U.K.	(Polydor POSP 230)	52	1981	0	1981	
3	Brazilian Dawn	(Polydor POSP 282)	48	1981	0	1981	
4	Easier Said Than Done	(Polydor POSP 375)	12	191	0	1981	
5	Night Birds	(Polydor POSP 407)	9	1982	0	1982	
6	Street Walkin'	(Polydor POSP 452)	38	1982	0	1982	
7	Invitations	(Polydor POSP 502)	24	1982	0	1982	
8	Stranger	(Polydor POSP 530)	43	1982	0	1982	
9	Dark Is The Night	(Polydor POSP 595)	15	1983	0	1983	
10	If You Could See Me Now	(Polydor POSP 635)	49	1983	0	1983	
11	Down On The Street	(Polydor POSP 688)	9	1984	0	1984	
12	Don't Blame It On Love	(Polydor POSP 699)	55	1984	0	1984	
13	Day By Day	(Polydor POSP 770)	53	1985	0	1985	
14	Mr. Manic And Sister Cool	(Polydor MANIC1)	56	1987	0	1987	
	HIT 13 IS CREDITED TO SHAKATAK WITH AL JARREAU						

Shakespears Sister Female Vocal/Instrumental Group from the USA/UK

1	You're History	(FFRR F 112)	7	1989	0	1989	
2	Run Silent	(FFRR F 119	54	1989	0	1989	
3	Dirty Mind	(FFRR F 128)	71	1990	0	1990	
4	Goodbye Cruel World	(London LON 309)	59	1991	0	1991	
* 5	Stay	(London LON 314)	1	1992	4	1992	(London 869730)
6	I Don't Care	(London LON 318)	7	1992	0	1992	
7	Goodbye Cruel World (Re-Issue)	(London LON 322)	32	1992	0	1992	
8	Hello (Turn Your Radio On)	(London LON 330)	14	1992	0	1992	
9	My 16th Apology (EP)	(London LONCD 337)	61	1993	0	1993	
10	I Can Drive	(London LONCD 383)	30	1996	0	1996	

Shakin' Stevens Male Vocalist, Real Name Michael Barrett, B: 1948 Cardiff, Wales

1	Hot Dog	(Epic EPC 8090)	24	1980	0	1980	
2	Marie Marie	(Epic EPC 8725)	19	1980	0	1980	
3	This Ole House	(Epic EPC 9555)	1	1981	0	1981	
4	You Drive Me Crazy	(Epic A 1165)	2	1981	0	1981	
5	Green Door	(Epic A 1354)	1	1981	0	1981	
6	It's Raining	(Epic A 1643)	10	1981	0	1981	
7	Oh Julie	(Epic EPC A 1742)	1	1982	0	1982	
8	Shirley	(Epic EPC A 2087)	6	1982	0	1982	
9	Give Me Your Heart Tonight	(Epic EPC A 2656)	11	1982	0	1982	
10	I'll Be Satisfied	(Epic EPC A 2846)	10	1982	0	1982	
11	The Shakin' Stevens (EP)	(Epic SHAKY 1)	2	1982	0	1982	
12	It's Late	(Epic A 3565)	11	1983	0	1983	
13	Cry Just A Little Bit	(Epic A 3774)	3	1983	0	1983	
14	A Rockin' Good Way	(Epic A 4071)	5	1984	0	1984	
15	A Love Worth Waiting For	(Epic A 4291)	2	1984	0	1984	
16	A Letter To You	(Epic A 4677)	10	1984	0	1984	
17	Teardrops	(Epic A 4882)	5	1984	0	1984	
18	Breaking Up My Heart	(Epic A 6072)	14	1985	0	1985	
19	Lipstick Powder And Paint	(Epic A 6610)	11	1985	0	1985	
20	Merry Christmas Everyone	(Epic A 6769)	1	1985	0	1985	
21	Turning Away	(Epic A 6819)	15	1986	0	1986	
22	Because I Love You	(Epic Shaky 2)	14	1986	0	1986	
23	Merry Christmas Everyone (Re-Entry)	(Epic A 6769)	58	1986	0	1986	
24	A Little Boogie Woogie (In The Back Of My Mind)	(Epic Shaky 3)	12	1987	0	1987	
25	Come See About Me	(Epic Shaky 4)	24	1987	0	1987	
26	What Do You Want To Make Those Eyes	(Epic Shaky 5)	5	1987	0	1987	
27	Feel The Need In Me	(Epic Shaky 6)	26	1988	0	1988	

ISSUE	TITLE	UK LBL	UK POS	UK YEAR	US POS	US YEAR	US LBL
28	How Many Tears Can You Hide	(Epic Shaky 7)	47	1988	0	1988	
29	True Love	(Epic Shaky 8)	23	1988	0	1988	
30	Jezzebel	(Epic Shaky 9)	58	1989	0	1989	
31	Love Attack	(Epic Shaky 10)	28	1989	0	1989	
32	I Might	(Epic Shaky 11)	18	1990	0	1990	
33	Yes I Do	(Epic Shaky 12)	60	1990	0	1990	
34	Pink Champagne	(Epic Shaky 13)	59	1990	0	1990	
35	My Cutie Cutie	(Epic Shaky 14)	75	1990	0	1990	
36	The Best Christmas Of Them All	(Epic Shaky 15)	19	1990	0	1990	
37	I'll Be Home This Christmas	(Epic 6576507)	34	1991	0	1991	
38	Radio	(Epic 6584367)	37	1992	0	1992	

HIT 14 IS CREDITED TO SHAKY AND BONNIE • HIT 38 TO SHAKY FEATURING ROGER TAYLOR
HITS 24-26 ARE CREDITED TO SHAKIN' STEVENS & THE SUNSETS

Shalamar Mixed Vocal Group from the USA

1	Uptown Festival	(Soul Train FB 0885)	30	1977	25	1977	(Soul Train 10885)
2	Take That To The Bank	(RCA FB 1379)	20	1978	0	1978	
* 3	The Second Time Around	(Solar FB 1709)	45	1979	8	1980	(Solar 11709)
4	Right In The Socket	(Solar SO2)	44	1980	0	1980	
5	I Owe You One	(Solar SO 11)	13	1980	0	1980	
6	Make That Move	(Solar SO 17)	30	1981	0	1981	
7	I Can Make You Feel Good	(Solar K 12599)	7	1982	0	1982	
8	A Night To Remember	(Solar K 13162)	5	1982	0	1982	
9	There It Is	(Solar K 13194)	5	1982	0	1982	
10	Friends	(Solar CHUM 1)	12	1982	0	1982	
11	Dead Giveaway	(Solar E 9819)	8	1983	22	1983	(Solar 69819)
12	Disappearing Act	(Solar E 9807)	18	1983	0	1983	
13	Over And Over	(Solar E 9792)	23	1983	0	1983	
14	Dancing In The Sheets	(CBS A 4171)	41	1984	17	1984	(Columbia 04372)
15	Deadline U.S.A.	(MCA MCA 866)	52	1984	0	1984	
16	Amnesia	(Solar/MCA SHAL 1)	61	1984	0	1984	
17	My Girl Loves Me	(MCA SHAL 2)	45	1985	0	1985	
18	A Night To Remember (Re-Mix)	(MCA SHAL 3)	52	1986	0	1986	

NAMES: JODY WATLEY, JEFFREY DANIELS & GERALD BROWN • BROWN WAS REPLACED BY HOWARD HEWETT IN 1979

Sham 69 Male Vocal/Instrumental Group from the UK

1	Angels With Dirty Faces	(Polydor 2059 023)	19	1978	0	1978	
2	If The Kids Are United	(Polydor 2059 050)	9	1978	0	1978	
3	Hurry Up Harry	(Polydor POSP 7)	10	1978	0	1978	
4	Questions And Answers	(Polydor POSP 27)	18	1979	0	1979	
5	Hersham Boys	(Polydor POSP 64)	6	1979	0	1979	
6	You're A Better Man Than I	(Polydor POSP 82)	49	1979	0	1979	
7	Tell The Children	(Polydor POSP 136)	45	1980	0	1980	

Shamen Mixed Vocal/Instrumental Group from the UK

1	Pro-Gen	(One Little Indian 36 TP7)	55	1990	0	1990	
2	Make It Mine	(One Little Indian 46 TP7)	42	1990	0	1990	
3	Hyperreal	(One Little Indian 48 TP7)	29	1991	0	1991	
4	Move Any Mountain (Progen 91) (Re-Mix)	(One Little Indian 52 TP7)	4	1991	38	1992	(Epic 74044)
5	LSI	(One Little Indian 68 TP7)	6	1992	0	1992	
6	Ebeneezer Goode	(One Little Indian 78 TP7)	1	1992	0	1992	
7	Boss Drum	(One Little Indian 8 TP7)	4	1992	0	1992	
8	Boss Drum (Re-Mix)	(One Little Indian 88 TP12)	58	1992	0	1992	
9	Phorever People	(One Little Indian 98 TP7)	5	1992	0	1992	
10	Re: Evolution	(One Little Indian TP7CD)118	18	1993	0	1993	
11	The S.O.S. (EP)	(One Little Indian 108 TP7CD)	14	1993	0	1993	
12	Destination Eschaton	(One Little Indian 128 TP7CDL)	15	1995	0	1995	
13	Transamazonia	(One Little Indian 138 TP7CD)	28	1995	0	1995	
14	Heal (The Separation)	(One Little Indian 158 TP7CDL)	31	1996	0	1996	
15	Move Any Mountain (2nd Re-Mix)	(One Little Indian 169 TP7CD)	35	1996	0	1996	

HIT 10 IS CREDITED TO SHAMEN WITH TERENCE MCKENNA

Shampoo Female Vocal Duo from the UK

1	Trouble	(FOOD CDFOOD 51)	11	1994	0	1994	
2	Viva La Megababes	(FOOD CDFOOD 54)	27	1994	0	1994	
3	Delicious	(FOOD CDFOOD 58)	21	1995	0	1995	
4	Trouble (Re-Issue)	(FOOD CDFOOD 66)	36	1995	0	1995	
5	Girl Power	(FOOD CDFOOD 76)	25	1996	0	1996	
6	I Know What Boys Like	(FOOD CDFOOD 83)	42	1996	0	1996	

ISSUE	TITLE	UK LBL	UK POS	UK YEAR	US POS	US YEAR	US LBL
Shana Real Name Shana Petrone B: 8 May 1972 Parkridge, Illinios							
1	I Want You		0	1990	40	1990	(Vision 4511)
Shane Fenton & The Fentones Male Vocal/Instrumental Group from the UK							
1	I'm A Moody Guy	(Parlophone R 4827)	22	1961	0	1961	
2	Walk Away	(Parlophone R 4866)	38	1962	0	1962	
3	It's All Over Now	(Parlophone R 4883)	29	1962	0	1962	
4	Cindy's Birthday	(Parlophone R 4921)	19	1962	0	1962	
Shane Mcgowan Male Vocalist from the UK							
1	What A Wonderful World	(MUTE MUTE 151)	72	1992	0	1992	
2	The Church Of The Holy Spook	(ZTT ZANG 57CD)	74	1994	0	1994	
3	That Woman's Got Me Drinking	(ZTT ZANG 57CD)	34	1994	0	1994	
4	Haunted	(ZTT ZANG 65CD)	30	1995	0	1995	
5	My Way	(ZTT ZANG 79CD)	29	1996	0	1996	
	HIT 1 IS CREDITED TO NICK CAVE AND SHANE MCGOWAN • HITS 2, 3 ARE CREDITED TO SHANE MCGWAN & THE POPES HIT 4 IS CREDITED TO SHANE MCGOWAN AND SINEAD O'CONNOR						
Shangri-Las Female Vocal Group from Queens, New York							
* 1	Remember (Walkin In The Sand)	(Red Bird RB 10008)	14	1964	5	1964	(Red Bird10-008)
* 2	Leader Of The Pack	(Red Bird RB 10014)	11	1965	1	1964	(Red Bird10-014)
3	Give Him A Great Big Kiss		0	1964	18	1964	(Red Bird10-018)
4	Give Us Your Blessings		0	1965	29	1965	(Red Bird10-030)
5	I Can Never Go Home Anymore		0	1965	6	1965	(Red Bird10-043)
6	Long Live Our Love		0	1966	33	1966	(Red Bird048)
7	Leader Of The Pack (Re-Issue)	(KAMA SUTRA 2013 024)	3	1972	0	1972	
8	Leader Of The Pack (2nd Re-Issue)	(CHARLY CS	7	1976	0	1976	
9	Leader Of The Pack (3rd Re-Issue)	(CONTEMPO CS 903232)	7	1976	0	1976	
	TWINS, MARY ANN & MARGE GANSER WITH SISTERS BETTY & MARY WEISS • OBITUARY : MARGE • D: DRUG OVERDOSE. MARY ANN D: ENCEPHALITIS.						
Shania Twain Female Vocalist, B: 28 Aug 1965 From Windsor, Ontario							
1	Any Man Of Mine		0	1995	31	1995	(Mercury 856448)
Shanice Female Vocalist, Shanice Wilson B: 14 May 1973 Pittsburgh, USA							
1	I Love Your Smile	(Motown ZB 44907)	55	1991	2	1992	(Motown 2093)
2	I Love Your Smile (Re-Mix)	(Motown TMG 1401)	2	1992	0	1992	
3	Silent Prayer		0	1992	31	1992	(Motown 2165)
4	Lovin' You	(Motown TMG 1409)	54	1992	0	1992	
5	Saving Forever For You	(GIANT W 0148CD)	42	1993	4	1992	(GIANT 18719)
6	I Like	(Motown TMG 1427)	49	1994	0	1994	
7	If I Never Knew (Love Theme from *Pocahontas*	(Walt Disney WD7023CD)	51	1995	0	1995	
	HIT 3 IS CREDITED TO SHANICE FEATURING JOHNNY GILL • HIT 7 IS CREDITED TO JON SECADA AND SHANICE						
Shannon Female Vocalist, Real Name Brenda Shannon Greene From Washington D.C.							
* 1	Let The Music Play	(CLUB LET 1)	51	1983	8	1984	(MIRAGE 99810)
2	Let The Music Play (Re-Entry)	(CLUB LET 1)	14	1984	0	1984	
3	Give Me Tonight	(Club Jab 1)	24	1984	0	1984	
4	Sweet Somebody	(Club Jab 3)	25	1984	0	1984	
5	Stronger Together	(Club Jab 15)	46	1985	0	1985	
Shaquille O'Neal Male Rapper B: 6 Mar 1972 From Newark, New Jersey							
* 1	What's Up Doc? (Can We Rock?)		0	1993	39	1993	(JIVE 42164)
2	I'm Outstanding	(JIVE JIVECD 349)	70	1994	0	1994	
* 3	(I Know I Got) Skillz		0	1993	35	1993	(JIVE 42177)
4	You Can't Stop The Reign	(Interscope IND95522)	40	1997	0	1997	
	HIT 1 IS CREDITED TO FU-SCHNICKENS WITH SHAQUILLE O'NEAL (SHAG-FU)						
Shara Nelson Female Vocalist from the UK							
1	Down That Road	(Cooltempo CDCOOL 275)	19	1993	0	1993	
2	One Goodbye In Ten	(Cooltempo CDCOOL 279)	21	1993	0	1993	
3	Uptight	(Cooltempo CDCOOL 286)	19	1994	0	1994	
4	Nobody	(Cooltempo CDCOOL 290)	49	1994	0	1994	
5	Inside Out / Down That Road (Re-Mix)	(Cooltempo CDCOOLX 295)	34	1994	0	1994	
6	Rough With The Smooth	(Cooltempo CDCOOL 311)	30	1995	0	1995	
Sharada House Gang Mixed Vocal/Instrumental Group From Italy							
1	Keep It Up	(MCA MCSTD 2071)	36	1995	0	1995	
2	Let The Rhythm Move You	(MCA MCSTD 40035)	50	1996	0	1996	
Sharon Brown Female Vocalist from the USA							
1	I Specialize In Love	(Virgin VS 494)	38	1982	0	1982	
2	I Specialize In Love (Re-Entry)	(Virgin VS 494)	62	1994	0	1994	

ISSUE	TITLE	UK LBL	UK POS	UK YEAR	US POS	US YEAR	US LBL
Sharon Bryant Lead Singer With Atlantic Starr From 1976-84							
1	Let Go		0	1989	34	1989	(WING 871722)
Sharon Forrester Female Vocalist From Jamaica							
1	Love In Side	(FFRR FCD 253)	50	1995	0	1995	
Sharon Redd Female Vocalist from the USA							
1	Can You Handle It	(Epic EPC 9572)	31	1981	0	1981	
2	Never Give You Up	(Prelude PRL A 2755)	20	1982	0	1982	
3	In The Name Of Love	(Prelude PRL A 2905)	31	1983	0	1983	
4	Love How You Feel	(Prelude A 3868)	39	1983	0	1983	
5	Can You Handle It	(Epic EPC 9572)	17	1992	0	1992	
	HIT 5 IS CREDITED TO DNA FEATURING SHARON REDD						
Sharonettes Female Vocal Group from the UK							
1	Papa O-Oh Mow Mow	(Black Magic BM 102)	26	1975	0	1975	
2	Going To A Go Go	(Black Magic BM 104)	46	1975	0	1975	
Shaun Cassidy Male Vocalist, B: 27 Sep 1959 Los Angeles, He Is Half Brother To David Cassidy							
* 1	Da Doo Ron Ron		0	1977	1	1977	(Warner Bros. 8365)
* 2	That's Rock 'N' Roll		0	1977	3	1977	(Warner Bros. 8423)
* 3	Hey Deanie		0	1977	3	1977	(Warner Bros. 8488)
4	Do You Believe In Magic		0	1978	31	1978	(Warner Bros. 8533)
Shawn Christopher Female Vocalist from the USA							
1	Another Sleepless Night	(Arista 114186)	50	1991	0	1991	
2	Don't Lose The Magic	(Arista 115097)	30	1992	0	1992	
3	Make My Love	(BTB BTBCD 502)	57	1994	0	1994	
Shawn Colvin Female Vocalist from the USA							
1	I Don't Know Why	(Columbia 6598272)	52	1993	0	1993	
2	Round Of Blues	(Columbia 6594282)	73	1994	0	1994	
3	Every Little Thing She Does Is Magic	(Columbia 6607742)	65	1994	0	1994	
4	One Cool Remove	(Columbia 6611342)	40	1995	0	1995	
5	I Don't Know Why (Re-Issue)	(Columbia 6622725)	52	1995	0	1995	
6	Get Out Of This House	(Columbia 6638522)	70	1997	0	1997	
	HIT 4 IS CREDITED TO SHAWN COLVIN WITH MARY CHAPIN CARPENTER						
Shaye Cogan Female Vocalist from the USA							
1	Mean To Me	(MGM 1063)	43	1960	0	1960	
She Rockers Female Vocal Duo from the UK							
1	Jam It Jam	(JIVE JIVE 233)	58	1990	0	1990	
Sheb Wooley Male Singer/Songwriter/Actor, Real Name Shelby F. Wooley B: 10 Apr 1921 Erick, Oklahoma							
* 1	The Purple People Eater	(MGM 981)	12	1958	1	1958	(MGM 12651)
Shed Seven Male Vocal/Instrumental Group from the UK							
1	Dolphin	(Polydor YORCD 2)	28	1994	0	1994	
2	Speakeasy	(PolydorYORCD 3)	24	1994	0	1994	
3	Ocean Pie	(Polydor YORCD 4)	33	1994	0	1994	
4	Where Have You Been Tonight	(Polydor YORCD 5)	23	1995	0	1995	
5	Getting Better	(Polydor 5778912)	14	1996	0	1996	
6	Going For Gold	(Polydor 5762152)	8	1996	0	1996	
7	Bully Boy	(Polydor 5765972)	22	1996	0	1996	
8	On Standby	(Polydor 5762732)	12	1996	0	1996	
9	Chasing Rainbows	(Polydor 5759292)	17	1996	0	1996	
Sheena Easton Female Vocalist, Real Name Sheena Orr B: 27 Apr 1959 In Glasgow, Scotland							
1	Modern Girl	(EMI 5042)	56	1980	18	1981	(EMI America 8080)
* 2	9 To 5 (Morning Train)	(EMI 5066)	3	1980	1	1981	(EMI America 8071)
3	Modern Girl (Re-Entry)	(EMI 5042)	8	1980	0	1980	
4	One Man Woman	(EMI 5114)	14	1980	0	1980	
5	Take My Time	(EMI 5135)	44	1981	0	1981	
6	For Your Eyes Only	(EMI 5195)	33	1981	4	1981	(Liberty 1418)
7	Just Another Broken Heart	(EMI 5232)	33	1981	0	1981	
8	When He Shines	(EMI 5166)	12	1981	30	1981	(EMI America 8113)
9	You Could Have Been With Me	(EMI 5252)	54	1981	15	1981	(EMI America 8101)
10	Machinery	(EMI 5326)	38	1982	0	1982	
11	We've Got Tonight	(Liberty UP 658)	28	1983	6	1983	(Liberty 1492)
12	Telefone (Long Distance Love Affair)		0	1983	9	1983	(EMI America 8172)
13	Almost Over You		0	1984	25	1984	(EMI America 8186)
14	Strut		0	1984	7	1984	(EMI America 8227)

ISSUE	TITLE	UK LBL	UK POS	UK YEAR	US POS	US YEAR	US LBL
15	Sugar Walls		0	1985	9	1985	(EMI America 8253)
16	Do It For Love		0	1985	29	1985	(EMI America 8295)
17	The Lover In Me	(MCA MCA 1289)	15	1989	2	1988	(MCA 53416)
18	Days Like This	(MCA MCA 1325)	43	1989	0	1989	
19	101	(MCA MCA 1348)	54	1989	0	1989	
20	The Arms Of Orion	(Warner Bros. W 2757)	27	1989	36	1989	(Warner Bros. 22757)
21	What Comes Naturally		0	1991	19	1991	(MCA 53742)

HIT 11 IS CREDITED TO KENNY ROGERS & SHEENA EASTON • HIT 20 IS CREDITED TO PRINCE WITH SHEENA EASTON

Sheep On Drugs   Male Vocal/Instrumental Duo from the UK

1	15 Minutes Of Fame	(Transglobal CID 564)	44	1993	0	1993	
2	From A To H And Back Again	(Transglobal CID 575)	40	1993	0	1993	
3	Let The Good Times Roll	(Transglobal CID 576)	56	1994	0	1994	

Sheer Bronze (Featuring) Lisa   Mixed Vocal/Instrumental Duo from the UK

1	Walkin' On	(GO.BEAT GODCD115)	63	1994	0	1994	

Sheer Elegance   Male Vocal Group from the UK

1	Milky Way	(PYE International 7N 25697)	18	1975	0	1975	
2	Life Is Too Short Girl	(PYE International 7N 25703)	9	1976	0	1976	
3	It's Temptation	(PYE International 7N 25715)	41	1976	0	1976	

Sheila B. Devotion   Female Vocalist from France

1	Singin' In The Rain (Part 1)	(Carrere EMI 2751)	11	1978	0	1978	
2	You Light My Fire	(Carrere EMI 2828)	44	1978	0	1978	
3	Spacer	(Carrere CAR 128)	18	1979	0	1979	

HIT 3 IS CREDITED TO SHEILA AND B. DEVOTION

Sheila E   Female Vocalist, Real Name Sheila Escovedo B: 12 Dec 1959 In San Francisco, Former Drummer With Prince's Revolution

1	The Glamorous Life		0	1984	7	1984	(Warner Bros. 29285)
2	The Belle Of St.Mark	(Warner Bros. W 9180)	18	1985	34	1985	(Warner Bros. 29180)
3	A Love Bizarre		0	1985	11	1985	(Paisley Park 28890)

Sheila Ferguson   Female Vocalist from the USA

1	When Will I See You Again	(XSRHYTHM CDSTAS 2711)	60	1994	0	1994	

Sheila Hylton   Female Vocalist from Jamaica

1	Breakfast In Bed	(United Artists BP 304)	57	1979	0	1979	
2	The Bed's Too Big Without You	(Island WIP 6671)	35	1981	0	1981	

Shelby Flint   Singer/Songwriter And Hails From California

1	Angel On My Shoulder		0	1961	22	1961	(Valiant 6001)

Shelby Lynne   Female Vocalist, B: 22 Oct 1968 In Quanico, Virginia, Raised In AlabamaFabares B: 19 Jan 1944 In Santa Monica, California

*	1	Johnny Angel	(PYE International 7N 25132)	41	1962	1	1962	(Colpix 621)
	2	Johnny Loves Me		0	1962	21	1962	(Colpix 636)

Shells   B: 19 Jan 1944 In Santa Monica, CaliforniaNames Nathaniel Bouknight, Bobby Nurse, Gus Geter, Randy Alston & Danny Small

1	Baby Oh Baby		0	1960	21	1960	(Johnson 104)

Shep & The Limelites   Names: James Sheppard, Clarence Bassett & Charles Baskerville

	1	Daddy's Home		0	1961	2	1961	(HULL 740)
+	2	Our Anniversary		0	1962	7	1962	(HULL 748)

Shepherd Sisters   Female Vocal Group, Names Mary Lou, Martha, Gayle & Judy

1	Alone (Why Must I Be Alone)	(HMV POP 441)	14	1957	18	1957	(Lance 125)
2	Alone (Why Must I Be Alone) (Re-Entry)	(HMV POP 441)	22	1958	0	1958	

Sherbet   Male Vocal/Instrumental Group from Australia

1	Howzat	(Epic EPC 4574)	4	1976	0	1976	

Sheriff   Lead Singer With The Quintet Was Freddy Curci

	1	When I'm With You		0	1983	61	1983	(Capitol)
*	2	When I'm With You (Re-Issue)		0	1988	1	1988	(Capitol 44302)

THE GROUP DISBANDED IN 1983

Sherrick   Male Vocalist from the USA

1	Just Call	(Warner Bros. W 8380)	23	1987	0	1987	
2	Let's Be Lovers Tonight	(Warner Bros. W 8146)	63	1987	0	1987	

Sherrys   Female Group Formed By Joe Cook Of Little Joe & The Thrillers

1	Pop Pop Pop-Pie		0	1962	35	1962	(Guyden 2068)

LEAD SINGER WITH THE QUINTET IS DINELL COOK

Sheryl Crow   Female Vocalist, B: 11 Feb 1963 Kennett, Missouri

	1	Leaving Las Vegas	(A&M 6806472)	66	1994	0	1994	
*	2	All I Wanna Do	(A&M 5808452)	4	1994	2	1994	(A&M 0702)

	ISSUE	TITLE	UK LBL	UK POS	UK YEAR	US POS	US YEAR	US LBL
	3	Strong Enough	(A&M 5809192)	33	1995	5	1995	(A&M 0798)
	4	Can't Cry Anymore	(A&M 5810552)	33	1995	36	1995	(A&M 0638)
	5	Run Baby, Run	(A&M 5811492)	24	1995	0	1995	
	6	What I Can Do For You	(A&M 5812292)	43	1995	0	1995	
	7	If It Makes You Happy	(A&M 5819032)	9	1996	10	1996	(A&M 581874)
	8	Everyday Is A Winding Road	(A&M 5820232)	12	1996	11	1997	(A&M 582032)
	9	Hard To Make A Stand	(A&M 5821492)	22	1997	0	1997	
	10	A Change Would Do You Good	(A&M 5822092)	8	1997	0	1997	

Sheryl Lee Ralp Female Vocalist from the USA

	ISSUE	TITLE	UK LBL	UK POS	UK YEAR	US POS	US YEAR	US LBL
	1	In The Evening	(Arista ARIST 595)	64	1985	0	1985	

Shields Lead Singer With The Group Specially Assembled For The Hit Is Frankie Ervin

	ISSUE	TITLE	UK LBL	UK POS	UK YEAR	US POS	US YEAR	US LBL
	1	You Cheated		0	1958	12	1958	(Tender 513)

Shinehead Male Vocalist from Jamaica

	ISSUE	TITLE	UK LBL	UK POS	UK YEAR	US POS	US YEAR	US LBL
	1	Jamaican In New York	(Elektra EKR 161CD)	30	1993	0	1993	
	2	Let 'Em In	(Elektra EKR 168CD)	70	1993	0	1993	

Ship's Company & The Royal Marine Band Of H.M.S. Ark Royal Male Choir And Marine Band from the UK

	ISSUE	TITLE	UK LBL	UK POS	UK YEAR	US POS	US YEAR	US LBL
	1	Last Farewell	(BBC RESL 61)	46	1978	0	1978	

Shirelles Female Vocal Group from the USA

	ISSUE	TITLE	UK LBL	UK POS	UK YEAR	US POS	US YEAR	US LBL
	1	I Met Him On A Sunday		0	1958	50	1958	(Decca 30588)
	2	Dedicated To The One I Love		0	1959	83	1959	(Scepter 1203)
*	3	Tonight's The Night		0	1960	39	1960	(Scepter 1208)
*	4	Will You Love Me Tomorrow	(Top Rank Jar 540)	4	1961	1	1961	(Scepter 1211)
*	5	Dedicated To The One I Love (Re-Issue)		0	1961	3	1961	(Scepter 1203)
	6	Mama Said		0	1961	4	1961	(Scepter 1217)
	7	Big John		0	1961	21	1961	(Scepter 1223)
	8	Baby It's You		0	1962	8	1962	(Scepter 1227)
*	9	Soldier Boy	(HMV POP 1019)	23	1962	1	1962	(Scepter 1228)
	10	Wecome Home Baby		0	1962	22	1962	(Scepter 1234)
	11	Stop The Music		0	1962	36	1962	(Scepter 1237)
	12	Everybody Loves A Lover		0	1962	19	1962	(Scepter 1243)
	13	Foolish Little Girl	(STATESIDE SS 181)	38	1963	4	1963	(Scepter 1248)
	14	Don't Say Goodnight And Mean Goodbye		0	1963	26	1963	(Scepter 1255)
		NAMES SHIRLEY OWENS ALSTON, BEVERLY LEE, DORIS KENNER & ADDIE HARRIS						

Shirley & Company Female Vocalist With Male Vocal/Instrumental Group from the USA

	ISSUE	TITLE	UK LBL	UK POS	UK YEAR	US POS	US YEAR	US LBL
	1	Shame Shame Shame	(All Platinum 6146 301)	6	1975	12	1975	(Vibration 532)
		REAL NAME SHIRLEY GOODMAN. SEE ALSO SHIRLEY & LEE						

Shirley & Lee Real Names Shirley Goodman B: 19 Jun 1936, Leonard Lee B: 29 Jun 1936

	ISSUE	TITLE	UK LBL	UK POS	UK YEAR	US POS	US YEAR	US LBL
+	1	I'm Gone		0	1952	2	1952	(Aladdin 3153)
	2	Let The Good Times Roll		0	1956	20	1956	(Aladdin 3325)
	3	I Feel Good		0	1957	38	1957	(Aladdin 3289)

Shirley Bassey Female Vocalist, Shirley Veronica Bassey B: 8 Jan 1937, Tiger Bay, Cardiff

	ISSUE	TITLE	UK LBL	UK POS	UK YEAR	US POS	US YEAR	US LBL
	1	Banana Boat Song	(Philips PB 668)	8	1957	0	1957	
	2	Fire Down Below	(Philips PB 723)	30	1957	0	1957	
	3	You You Romeo	(Philips PB 723)	29	1957	0	1957	
	4	As I Love You	(Philips PB 845)	27	1958	0	1958	
	5	Kiss Me Honey Honey Kiss Me	(Philips PB 860)	3	1958	0	1958	
	6	As I Love You (Re-Entry)	(Philips PB 845)	1	1959	0	1959	
	7	With These Hands	(Columbia DB 4421)	31	1960	0	1960	
	8	With These Hands (Re-Entry)	(Columbia DB 4421)	31	1960	0	1960	
	9	With These Hands (2nd Re-Entry)	(Columbia DB 4421)	41	1960	0	1960	
	10	As Long As He Needs Me	(Columbia DB 4490)	2	1960	0	1960	
	11	You'll Never Now	(Columbia DB 4643)	6	1961	0	1961	
	12	Reach For The Stars - Climb Every Mountain	(Columbia DB 4685)	1	1961	0	1961	
	13	I'll Get By	(Columbia DB 4737)	10	1961	0	1961	
	14	Reach For The Stars (Re-Entry)	(Columbia DB 4685)	40	1961	0	1961	
	15	Tonight	(Columbia DB 4777)	21	1962	0	1962	
	16	Ave Maria	(Columbia DB 4816)	34	1962	0	1962	
	17	Far Away	(Columbia DB 4836)	24	1962	0	1962	
	18	What Now My Love	(Columbia DB 4882)	5	1962	0	1962	
	19	What Kind Of Fool Am I	(Columbia DB 4974)	47	1963	0	1963	
	20	I (Who Have Nothing)	(Columbia DB 7113)	6	1963	0	1963	
	21	My Special Dream	(Columbia DB 7185)	32	1964	0	1964	
	22	Gone	(Columbia DB 7248)	36	1964	0	1964	

ISSUE	TITLE	UK LBL	UK POS	UK YEAR	US POS	US YEAR	US LBL
* 23	Goldfinger	(Columbia DB7360)	21	1964	8	1965	(United Artists 790)
24	No Regrets	(Columbia DB 7535)	39	1965	0	1965	
25	Big Spender	(United ArtistsUP 1192)	21	1967	0	1967	
26	Something	(United ArtistsUP 35125)	4	1970	0	1970	
27	The Fool On The Hill	(United ArtistsUP 35156)	48	1971	0	1971	
28	Something (Re-Entry)	(United ArtistsUP 35125)	50	1971	0	1971	
29	(Where Do I Begin) Love Story	(United ArtistsUP 35194)	34	1971	0	1971	
30	For All We Know	(United ArtistsUP 35267)	46	1971	0	1971	
31	For All We Know (Re-Entry)	(United ArtistsUP 35267)	6	1971	0	1971	
32	Diamonds Are Forever	(United ArtistsUP 35293)	38	1972	0	1972	
33	Never Never Never	(United ArtistsUP 35490)	8	1973	0	1973	
34	Never Never Never (Re-Entry)	(United ArtistsUP 35490)	48	1973	0	1973	
35	The Rhythm Devine	(Mercury MER253)	54	1987	0	1987	
36	'Disco' La Passione	(East West EW 072CD)	41	1996	0	1996	
	SHIRLEY FIRST STARTED WORK IN AN ENAMEL FACTORY						

Shirley Brown Female Soul Vocalist, B: 6 Jan 1947 Memphis, Arkansas

* 1	Woman To Woman		0	1974	22	1974	(Truth 3206)

Shirley Ellis Female Vocalist, B: 1941 Bronx, USA,   She Was Also In The Group The Metronomes

1	The Nitty Gritty		0	1963	8	1963	(Congress 202)
2	The Name Game		0	1965	3	1965	(Congress 230)
* 3	The Clapping Song	(London HLR 9961)	6	1965	8	1965	(Congress 234)
4	The Clapping Song (EP)	(MCA MCEP 1)	59	1978	0	1978	

Shirley Murdock Female Vocalist from the USA, Also Sang Backup Vocals For Zapp

1	Truth Or Dare	(Elektra EKR 36)	60	1986	0	1986	
2	As We Lay		0	1987	23	1987	(Elektra 69518)

Shiva Mixed Vocal/Instrumental Group from the UK

1	Work It Out	(FFRR FCD 261)	36	1995	0	1995	
2	Freedom	(FFRR FCD 263)	18	1995	0	1995	

Sho Nuff Male Vocal/Instrumental Group from the USA

1	It's Alright	(Ensign ENY 37)	53	1980	0	1980	

Shocking Blue Mixed Vocal/Instrumental Group from Holland, Lead Singer With The Quartet was Mariska Veres

* 1	Venus	(Penny Farthing Pen 702)	8	1970	1	1969	(Colossus 108)
* 2	Mighty Joe	(Penny Farthing Pen 703)	43	1970	0	1970	

Shooting Party Male Vocal Duo from the UK

1	Let's Hang On	(Lisson DOLE 15)	66	1990	0	1990	

Shorty Long Male Vocalist, Real Name Frederick Earl Long B: 20 May 1940 Birmingham, Alabama.

1	Here Comes The Judge	(Tamla MotownTMG 663)	30	1968	8	1968	(SOUL 35044)
	OBITUARY: 29 JUN 1969 DROWNED.						

Showaddywaddy Male Vocal/Instrumental Group from the UK

1	Hey Rock And Roll	(Bell 1357)	2	1974	0	1974	
2	Rock 'N' Roll Lady	(Bell 1374)	15	1974	0	1974	
3	Hey Mr. Christmas	(Bell 1387)	13	1974	0	1974	
4	Sweet Music	(Bell 1403)	14	1975	0	1975	
5	Three Steps To Heaven	(Bell 1426)	2	1975	0	1975	
6	Heartbeat	(Bell 1450)	7	1975	0	1975	
7	Heavenly	(Bell 1460)	34	1975	0	1975	
8	Trocadero	(Bell 1476)	32	1976	0	1976	
9	Under The Moon Of Love	(Bell 1495)	1	1976	0	1976	
10	When	(Arista 91)	3	1977	0	1977	
11	You Got What It Takes	(Arista 1260	2	1977	0	1977	
12	Dancin' Party	(Arista 149)	4	1977	0	1977	
13	I Wonder Why	(Arista 174)	2	1978	0	1978	
14	A Little Bit Of Soap	(Arista 191)	5	1978	0	1978	
15	Pretty Little Angel Eyes	(Arista ARIST 222)	5	1978	0	1978	
16	Remember Then	(Arista 247)	17	1979	0	1979	
17	Sweet Little Rock 'N' Roller	(Arista 278)	15	1979	0	1979	
18	A Night At Daddy Gee's	(Arista 314)	39	1979	0	1979	
19	Why Do Lovers Break Each Other's Heart	(Arista ARIST 359)	22	1980	0	1980	
20	Blue Moon	(Arista ARIST 416)	32	1980	0	1980	
21	Multiplication	(Arista ARIST 416)	39	1981	0	1981	
22	Footsteps	(Bell Bell 1499)	31	1981	0	1981	
23	Who Put The Bomp (In The Bomp-A-Bomp-A-Bomp)	(RCA 236)	37	1982	0	1982	

ISSUE	TITLE	UK LBL	UK POS	UK YEAR	US POS	US YEAR	US LBL
Showdown Male Vocal/Instrumental Group from the USA							
1	Keep Doin' It	(STATE STAT 63)	41	1977	0	1977	
Showstoppers Male Vocal Group from the UK							
1	Ain't Nothing But A House Party	(Beacon 3-100)	11	1968	0	1968	
2	Eeny Meeny	(MGM 1436)	33	1968	0	1968	
3	Ain't Nothing But A House Party (Re-Issue)	(Beacon BEA 100)	43	1971	0	1971	
4	Ain't Nothing But A House Party (Re-Issue) (Re-Entry)	(Beacon BEA 100)	33	1971	0	1971	
5	Ain't Nothing But A House Party (Re-Issue) (2nd Re-Entry)	(Beacon BEA 100)	36	1971	0	1971	
Shriekback Male Vocal/Instrumental Group from the UK							
1	Hand On My Heart	(Arista SHRK 1)	52	1984	0	1984	
Shut Up & Dance Male Production/Vocal Group from the UK							
1	£20 To Get It	(Shut Up And Dance Suad 3)	56	1990	0	1990	
2	Lamborghini	(Shut Up And Dance Suad 4)	55	1990	0	1990	
3	Autobiography Of A Crackhead - The Green Man	(Shut Up And Dance Suad 21)	43	1992	0	1992	
4	Raving I'm Raving	(Shut Up And Dance Suad 305)	2	1992	0	1992	
5	The Art Of Moving Butts	(Shut Up And Dance Suad 345)	69	1992	0	1992	
6	Save It 'Til The Morning After	(Pulse 8 PULS 84CD)	25	1995	0	1995	
7	I Love U	(Pulse 8 PULS 90CD)	68	1995	0	1995	
Shy Male Vocal/Instrumental Group from the UK							
1	Girl (It's All I Have)	(Gallery GA 1)	60	1980	0	1980	
Shyheim Male Rapper from the USA							
1	This Iz Real	(NOO TRYBE/Virgin VUSCD 105)	61	1996	0	1996	
Sid Owen & Patsy Palmer Mixed Vocal Duo from the UK							
1	Better Believe It (Children In Need)	(Trinity Direct Marketing TDM001MC)	60	1995	0	1995	
Sidney Bechet & The Claud Luter Orchestra Claud B: 23 Jul 1923 Paris, France							
* 1	Les Oignons		0	1949	0	1949	
Sidney Devine Male Vocalist from Scotland							
1	Scotland Forever	(Philips SCOT 1)	48	1978	0	1978	
Sigue Sigue Sputnik Male Vocal/Instrumental Group from the UK							
1	Love Missile F1-11	(Parlophone SSS 1)	3	1986	0	1986	
2	Twenty-First Century Boy	(Parlophone SSS 2)	20	1986	0	1986	
3	Success	(Parlophone SSS 3)	31	1988	0	1988	
4	Dancerama	(Parlophone SSS 5)	50	1989	0	1989	
5	Albinoni Vs Star Wars	(Parlophone SSS 4)	75	1989	0	1989	
Sil Austin Real Name Sylvester Austin B: 1929 Donellon, Florida							
1	Slow Walk		0	1956	17	1956	(Mercury 70963)
Silencers Male Vocal/Instrumental Group from the UK							
1	Painted Moon	(RCA HUSH 1)	57	1988	0	1988	
2	Scottish Rain	(RCA PB 42701)	71	1989	0	1989	
3	I Can Feel It	(RCA	62	1993	0	1993	
Silent Underdog Male Instrumentalist, Real Name Paul Hardcastle from the UK							
1	Papa's Got A Brand New Pig Bag	(KAZ KAZ 50)	73	1985	0	1985	
Silhouettes Names William Horton, Earl Beal, Richard Lewis & Raymond Edwards							
* 1	Get A Job		0	1957	1	1957	(EMBER 1029)
	The Group Was Originally Called The Tornadoes						
Silje Female Vocalist from Norway							
1	Tell Me Where You're Going	(EMI EM 159)	55	1990	0	1990	
Silk Male Vocal R&B Quintet from Atlanta, USA							
* 1	Freak Me	(Elektra EKR 165CD)	46	1993	1	1993	(KEIA/Elektra 64654)
2	Girl U For Me	(Elektra EKR 167CD)	67	1993	26	1993	(KEIA/Elektra 64643)
3	Lose Control		0	1993	26	1993	(KEIA/Elektra 64643)
4	Baby It's You	(Elektra EKR 173CD)	44	1993	0	1993	
5	Freak Me (Re-Entry)	(Elektra EKR 165CD)	72	1994	0	1994	
Silkie Mixed Vocal/Instrumental Group Formed At Hull University In 1963.							
1	You've Got To Hide Your Love Away	(Fontana TF 603)	28	1965	10	1965	(Fontana 1525)
	Lead Singer With The Quartet Is Silvia Tatler						
Silsoe Male Instrumentalist (Keyboards) from the UK							
1	Aztec Gold	(CBA A 7231)	48	1986	0	1986	

ISSUE	TITLE	UK LBL	UK POS	UK YEAR	US POS	US YEAR	US LBL
Silvana Mangano Female Actress/Vocalist from Italy							
1	Anna (Movie Title Song)		0	1953	5	1953	(MGM 11457)
Silver Country-Rock Quintet Led By John Batdorf							
1	Wham Bam		0	1976	16	1976	(Arista 0189)
	HIT SHOWS TITLE AS WHAM BAM SHANG-A-LANG						
Silver Bullet Male Vocal/Instrumental Duo from the UK							
1	Bring Forth The Guillotine	(TAM TAM TTT 013)	70	1989	0	1989	
2	20 Seconds To Comply	(TAM TAM TTT 019)	11	1989	0	1989	
3	Bring Forth The Guillotine (Re-Entry)	(TAM TAM TTT 013)	45	1990	0	1990	
4	Undercover Anarchist	(Parlophone R 6284)	33	1991	0	1991	
Silver City Mixed Vocal/Instrumental Duo from the UK							
1	Love Infinity	(Silver City GFJMCD 1)	62	1993	0	1993	
Silver Condor Rock Quintet Led By Joe Cerisano							
1	You Could Take My Heart Away		0	1981	32	1981	(Columbia 02268)
Silver Convention Female Vocal Trio from the USA/Germany							
1	Save Me	(MAGNET MAG 26)	30	1975	0	1975	
* 2	Fly Robin Fly	(Magnet MAG 43)	28	1975	1	1975	(Midland I. 10339)
* 3	Get Up And Boogie (That's Right)	(Magnet MAG 55)	7	1976	2	1976	(Midland I. 10571)
4	Tiger Bay / No No Joe	(Magnet MAG 69)	41	1976	0	1976	
5	Everybody's Talkin''Bout Love	(Magnet MAG 81)	25	1977	0	1977	
	NAMES: RAMONA WULF, LINDA THOMPSON & PENNY MCLEAN						
Silver Sun Male Vocal/Instrumental Group from the UK							
1	Lava	(Polydor 5756872)	54	1996	0	1996	
2	Last Day	(Polydor 5732432)	48	1997	0	1997	
3	Golden Skin	(Polydor 5738272)	32	1997	0	1997	
4	Julia	(Polydor 5711752)	51	1997	0	1997	
Silverchair Male Vocal/Instrumental Group from Australia							
1	Pure Massacre	(Columbia 6622642)	71	1995	0	1995	
2	Tomorrow	(Columbia 6623952)	59	1995	0	1995	
3	Freak	(Columbia 6640765)	34	1997	0	1997	
4	Abuse Me	(Columbia 6647905)	40	1997	0	1997	
Silvetti Real Name Bebu Silvetti from Argentina							
1	Spring Rain		0	1977	39	1977	(SALSOUL 2014)
Simon & Garfunkel Male Vocal Duo First Recorded As Tom And Jerry							
* 1	The Sound Of Silence		0	1965	1	1965	(Columbia 43396)
2	Homeward Bound	(CBS 202045)	9	1966	5	1966	(Columbia 43617)
3	I Am A Rock	(CBS 202303)	17	1966	3	1966	(Columbia 43617)
4	The Dangling Conversation		0	1966	25	1966	(Columbia 43728)
5	A Hazy Shade Of Winter		0	1966	13	1966	(Columbia 43873)
6	At The Zoo		0	1967	16	1967	(Columbia 44046)
7	Fakin' It		0	1967	23	1967	(Columbia 44232)
8	Scarborough Fair / Canticle		0	1968	11	1968	(Columbia 44465)
* 9	Mrs. Robinson	(CBS 3443)	4	1968	1	1968	(Columbia 44511)
10	Mrs. Robinson (EP)	(CBS EP 6400)	9	1969	0	1969	
11	The Boxer	(CBS 4162)	6	1969	7	1969	(Columbia 44785)
* 12	Bridge Over Troubled Water	(CBS 4790)	1	1970	1	1970	(Columbia 45079)
* 13	Cecilia		0	1970	4	1970	(Columbia 45133)
14	Bridge Over Troubled Water (Re-Entry)	(CBS 4790)	45	1970	0	1970	
15	El Condor Pasa		0	1970	18	1970	(Columbia 45237)
16	America	(CBS 8336)	25	1972	0	1972	
17	My Little Town		0	1975	9	1975	(Columbia 10230)
18	(What A) Wonderful World		0	1978	17	1978	(Columbia 10676)
19	Wake Up Little Susie		0	1982	27	1982	(Warner Bros. 50053)
20	A Hazy Shade Of Winter / Silent Night / Seven O'clock News	(Columbia 6576537)	30	1991	0	1991	
21	The Boxer (Re-Issue)	(Columbia 6578067)	75	1992	0	1992	
	'SCARBOROUGH FAIR' WAS ALSO KNOWN AS PARSLEY, SAGE, ROSEMARY AND THYME • HIT 18 IS CREDITED TO ART GARFUNKEL WITH JAMES TAYLOR & PAUL SIMON						
Simon Climie Male Vocalist from the UK							
1	Soul Inspiration	(Epic 6582837)	60	1992	0	1992	
Simon Dupree & The Big Sound Male Vocal/Instrumental Group from the UK							
1	Kites	(Parlophone R 5646)	9	1967	0	1967	
2	For Whom The Bell Tolls	(Parlophone R 5670)	43	1968	0	1968	

ISSUE	TITLE	UK LBL	UK POS	UK YEAR	US POS	US YEAR	US LBL
Simon Harris	Male Producer from the UK						
1	Bass (How Low Can You Go)	(FFRR FFR 4)	12	1988	0	1988	
2	Here Comes That Sound	(FFRR FFR 12)	38	1988	0	1988	
3	(I've Got Your) Pleasure Control	(FFRR F 106)	60	1989	0	1989	
4	Another Monsterjam	(FFRR F 116)	65	1989	0	1989	
5	Ragga House (All Night Long)	(LIVING BEAT 75SMASH 9)	56	1990	0	1990	

HIT 3 IS CREDITED TO SIMON HARRIS FEATURING LONNIE GORDON • HIT 4TO SIMON HARRIS FEATURING EINSTEIN
HIT 5 IS CREDITED TO SIMON HARRIS FEATURING DADDY FREDDY

ISSUE	TITLE	UK LBL	UK POS	UK YEAR	US POS	US YEAR	US LBL
Simon May	Male Vocalist from the UK						
1	Summer Of My Life	(PYE 7N 45627)	7	1976	0	1976	
2	We'll Gather Lilacs / All My Loving (Medley)	(PYE 7N 45688)	49	1977	0	1977	
3	We'll Gather Lilacs / All My Loving (Medley)	(RE-ENTRY) (PYE 7N 45688)	50	1977	0	1977	
4	Theme From *Howard's Way*	(BBC RESL 174)	21	1985	0	1985	
5	Anyone Can Fall In Love	(BBC RESL 191)	4	1986	0	1986	

HIT 4 IS CREDITED TO THE SIMON MAY ORCHESTRA • HIT 5 IS CREDITED TO ANITA DOBSON FEATURING SIMON MAY ORCHESTRA

ISSUE	TITLE	UK LBL	UK POS	UK YEAR	US POS	US YEAR	US LBL
Simon Park	Orchestra Leader, B: 1946 Market Harborough, England						
1	Eye Level	(Columbia DB 8946)	41	1972	0	1972	
* 2	Eye Level (Re-Entry)	(Columbia DB 8946)	1	1972	0	1973	
Simon Scott	Male Vocalist from the UK						
1	Move It Baby	(Parlophone R 5164)	37	1964	0	1964	
Simone	Female Vocalist from the USA						
1	My Family Depends On Me	(Strictly Rhythm A 8678)	75	1991	0	1991	
Simone Angel	Female Vocalist From The Holland						
1	Let This Feeling	(A&M 5803652)	60	1993	0	1993	
Simple Minds	Male Vocal/Instrumental Group from Scotland, Lead Singer With The Group Was Jim Kerr						
1	Life In A Day	(ZOOM ZUM 10)	62	1979	0	1979	
2	The American	(Virgin VS 410)	59	1981	0	1981	
3	Love Song	(Virgin VS 434)	47	1981	0	1981	
4	Sweat In Bullet	(Virgin VS 451)	52	1981	0	1981	
5	Promised You A Miracle	(Virgin VS 488)	13	1982	0	1982	
6	Glittering Prize	(Virgin VS 511)	16	1982	0	1982	
7	Someone Somewhere (In The Summertime)	(Virgin VS 538)	36	1982	0	1982	
8	Waterfront	(Virgin VS 636)	13	1983	0	1983	
9	Speed Your Love To Me	(Virgin VS 649)	20	1984	0	1984	
10	Up On The Catwalk	(Virgin VS 661)	27	1984	0	1984	
11	Don't You (Forget About Me)	(Virgin VS 749)	7	1985	1	1985	(A&M 2703)
12	Don't You (Forget About Me) (Re-Entry)	(Virgin VS 749)	61	1985	0	1985	
13	Alive And Kicking	(Virgin VS 817)	7	1986	3	1985	(A&M 2783)
14	Don't You (Forget About Me) (2nd Re-Entry)	(Virgin VS 749)	74	1985	0	1985	
15	Alive And Kicking (Re-Entry)	(Virgin VS 817)	60	1986	0	1986	
16	Sanctify Yourself	(Virgin SM 1)	10	1986	14	1986	(A&M 2810)
17	Don't You (Forget About Me) (3rd Re-Entry)	(Virgin VS 779)	62	1986	0	1986	
18	Don't You (Forget About Me) (4th Re-Entry)	(Virgin VS 779)	68	1986	0	1986	
19	All The Things She Said	(Virgin VS 860)	9	1986	28	1986	(A&M 2828)
20	All The Things She Said (Re-Entry)	(Virgin VS 860)	73	1986	0	1986	
21	Ghostdancing	(Virgin VS 907)	13	1986	0	1986	
22	Ghostdancing (Re-Entry)	(Virgin VS 907)	68	1987	0	1987	
23	Promised You A Miracle (Live)	(Virgin SM 2)	19	1987	0	1987	
24	Belfast Child	(Virgin SMX 3)	1	1989	0	1989	
25	This Is Your Land	(Virgin SMX 4)	13	1989	0	1989	
26	Kick It In	(Virgin SM 5)	15	1989	0	1989	
27	The Amsterdam (EP)	(Virgin SMX 6)	18	1989	0	1989	
28	Let There Be Love	(Virgin VS 1332)	6	1991	0	1991	
29	See The Lights	(Virgin VS 1343)	20	1991	40	1991	(A&M 1553)
30	Stand By Love	(Virgin VS 1358)	13	1991	0	1991	
31	Real Life	(Virgin VS 1382)	34	1991	0	1991	
32	Love Song - Alive And Kicking (Re-Issue)	(Virgin VS 1440)	6	1992	0	1992	
33	She's A River	(Virgin VSCDX 1509)	9	1995	0	1995	
34	Hypnotised	(Virgin VSCDX 1534)	18	1995	0	1995	
Simplicious	Male Vocal Group from the USA						
1	Let Her Feel It	(Fourth & Broadway BRW 13)	65	1984	0	1984	
2	Let Her Feel It (Re-Issue)	(Fourth & Broadway BRW18)	34	1985	0	1985	

ISSUE	TITLE	UK LBL	UK POS	UK YEAR	US POS	US YEAR	US LBL
Simply Red Male Vocal/Instrumental Group from the UK							
1	Money's Too Tight (To Mention)	(Elektra EKR 9)	13	1985	28	1985	(Elektra 69528)
2	Come To My Aid	(Elektra EKR	66	1985	0	1985	
3	Holding Back The Years	(Elektra EKR	51	1985	1	1986	(Elektra 69564)
4	Jericho	(WEA YZ 63)	53	1986	0	1986	
5	Holding Back The Years (Re-Issue)	(WEA YZ 70)	2	1986	0	1986	
6	Open Up The Red Box	(WEA YZ 75)	61	1986	0	1986	
7	The Right Thing	(WEA YZ 103)	11	1987	27	1987	(Elektra 69487)
8	Infidelity	(Elektra YZ 114)	31	1987	0	1987	
9	Ev'ry Time We Say Goodbye	(Elektra YZ 161)	11	1987	0	1987	
10	I Won't Feel Bad	(Elektra YZ 172)	68	1988	0	1988	
11	It's Only Love	(Elektra YZ 349)	13	1989	0	1989	
* 12	If You Don't Know Me By Now	(Elektra YZ 377)	2	1989	1	1989	(Elektra 69297)
13	A New Flame	(WEA YZ 404)	17	1989	0	1989	
14	You've Got It	(Elektra YZ 424)	46	1989	0	1989	
15	Something Got Me Started	(East West YZ 614)	11	1991	23	1991	(East West 98711)
16	Stars	(East West YZ 626)	8	1991	0	1991	
17	For Your Babies	(East West YZ 642)	9	1992	0	1992	
18	Thrill Me	(East West YZ 671)	33	1992	0	1992	
19	Your Mirror	(East West YZ 689)	17	1992	0	1992	
20	Montreux (EP)	(East West YZ 716)	11	1992	0	1992	
21	Fairground	(East West EW 001CD1)	1	1995	0	1995	
22	Remembering The First Time	(East West EW 015CD1)	22	1995	0	1995	
23	Never Never Love	(East West EW 029CD1)	18	1996	0	1996	
24	We're In This Together	(East West EW 046CD1)	11	1996	0	1996	
25	Angel	(East West EW 074CD1)	4	1996	0	1996	
	LEAD SINGER MICK HUCKNALL B: 8 JUN 1960						
Simply Red & White Male Vocal Group from the UK							
1	Daydream Believer (Cheer Up Peter Reid)	(Ropery SHAYISGOD 1D)	41	1996	0	1996	
2	Daydream Believer (Cheer Up Peter Reid) (Re-Entry)	(Ropery SHAYISGOD 1D)	74	1996	0	1996	
Simpsons Mixed Vocal Cartoon Group from the USA							
1	Do The Batman	(Geffen GEF 87)	1	1991	0	1991	
2	Deep Deep Trouble	(Geffen GEF 88)	7	1991	0	1991	
Sin With Sebastian Male Vocalist Sebastian Roth from Germany							
1	Shut Up (And Sleep With Me)	(SING SING 74321253592)	44	1995	0	1995	
2	Shut Up (And Sleep With Me) (Re-Mix)	(SING SING 74321337972)	46	1996	0	1996	
Sinclair Male Vocalist from the UK							
1	Ain't No Casanova	(DOME CDDOME 1004)	28	1993	0	1993	
2	(I Wanna Know) Why	(DOME CDDOME 1009)	58	1994	0	1994	
3	Don't Lie	(DOME CDDOME 1010)	70	1994	0	1994	
Sindy Female Vocalist from the UK							
1	Saturday Night	(Love This LUVTHISCD 13)	70	1996	0	1996	
Sine Disco Assembly from the USA							
1	Just Let Me Do My Thing	(CBS 6351)	33	1978	0	1978	
Sinead O'Conno Female Vocalist, Pronounced Shin-Nayd B: 1967 & Raised In Dublin, Southern Ireland							
1	Mandinka	(Ensign ENY 611)	17	1988	0	1988	
* 2	Nothing Compares 2 U	(Ensign ENY 630)	1	1990	1	1990	(Ensign 23488)
3	The Emperor's New Clothes	(Ensign ENY 633)	31	1990	0	1990	
4	Three Babies	(Ensign ENY 635)	42	1990	0	1990	
5	My Special Child	(Ensign ENY 646)	42	1991	0	1991	
6	Silent Night	(Ensign ENY 652)	60	1991	0	1991	
7	Success Has Made A Failure Of Our Home	(Ensign ENY 656)	18	1992	0	1992	
8	Don't Cry For Me Argentina	(Ensign ENY 657)	53	1992	0	1992	
9	You Made Me The Thief Of Your Heart	(Island CID 588)	42	1994	0	1994	
10	Thank You For Hearing Me	(Ensign CDENYS662)	13	1994	0	1994	
11	Haunted	(ZZT ZAND 65CD)	30	1995	0	1995	
12	Famine	(Ensign CDENY 663)	51	1995-	0	1995	
13	Gospel Oak (EP)	(Chrysalis CDCHS 5051)	28	1997	0	1997	
	HIT 11 IS CREDITED TO SHANE MCGOWAN & SINEAD O'CONNOR						
Singing Dogs Don Charles And Four Dogs Barking							
1	The Singing Dogs (Medley)	(NIXA N 15009)	13	1955	22	1955	(RCA 6344)

ISSUE	TITLE	UK LBL	UK POS	UK YEAR	US POS	US YEAR	US LBL
Singing Sheep Computerised Sheep Noises from the UK							
1	Baa-Baa Black Sheep	(Sheep BAA 1)	42	1982	0	1982	
Sinitta Female Vocalist from the USA							
1	So Macho / Cruising	(Fanfare Fan 7)	47	1986	0	1986	
2	So Macho / Cruising (Re-Entry)	(Fanfare Fan 7)	2	1986	0	1986	
3	Feels Like The First Time	(Fanfare Fan 8)	45	1986	0	1986	
4	Toy Boy	(Fanfare Fan 12)	4	1987	0	1987	
5	G.T.O.	(Fanfare Fan 14)	15	1987	0	1987	
6	Cross My Broken Heart	(Fanfare Fan 15)	6	1988	0	1988	
7	I Don't Believe In Miracles	(Fanfare Fan 16)	22	1988	0	1988	
8	Right Back Where We Started From	(Fanfare Fan 18)	4	1989	0	1989	
9	Love On A Mountain Top	(Fanfare Fan 21)	20	1989	0	1989	
10	Hitchin' A Ride	(Fanfare Fan 24)	24	1990	0	1990	
11	Love And Affection	(Fanfare Fan 31)	62	1990	0	1990	
12	Shame Shame Shame	(Arista 74321100327)	28	1992	0	1992	
13	The Supreme (EP)	(Arista 74321139592)	49	1993	0	1993	
Sinnamon Male Vocal/Instrumental Group from the USA							
1	I Need You Now	(WORX WORXCD 003)	70	1996	0	1996	
Siouxsie & The Banshees Mixed Vocal/Instrumental Group from the UK							
1	Hong Kong Garden	(Polydor 2059 052)	7	1978	0	1978	
2	The Staircase (Mystery)	(Polydor POSP 9)	24	1979	0	1979	
3	Playground Twist	(Polydor POSP 59)	28	1979	0	1979	
4	Mittageisen (Metal Postcard)	(Polydor 2059 151)	47	1979	0	1979	
5	Happy House	(Polydor POSP 117)	17	1980	0	1980	
6	Christine	(Polydor 2059 249)	24	1980	0	1980	
7	Israel	(Polydor POSP 205)	41	1980	0	1980	
8	Spellbound	(Polydor POSP 273)	22	1981	0	1981	
9	Arabian Knights	(Polydor POSP 309)	32	1981	0	1981	
10	Fire Works	(Polydor POSPG 450)	22	1982	0	1982	
11	Slowdive	(Polydor POSP 510)	41	1982	0	1982	
12	Melt / Il Est Ne Le Divin Enfant	(Polydor POSP 539)	49	1982	0	1982	
13	Dear Prudence	(Wonderland SHE 4)	3	1983	0	1983	
14	Swimming Horses	(Wonderland SHE 6)	28	1984	0	1984	
15	Dazzle	(Wonderland SHE 7)	33	1984	0	1984	
16	The Thorn (EP)	(Wonderland SHEEP 8)	47	1984	0	1984	
17	Cities In Dust	(Wonderland SHE 9)	21	1985	0	1985	
18	Candyman	(Wonderland SHE 10)	34	1986	0	1986	
19	This Wheel's On Fire	(Wonderland SHE 11)	14	1987	0	1987	
20	The Passenger	(Wonderland SHE 12)	41	1987	0	1987	
21	Song From The Edge Of The World	(Wonderland SHE 13)	59	1987	0	1987	
22	Peek-A-Boo	(Wonderland SHE 14)	16	1988	0	1988	
23	The Killing Jar	(Wonderland SHE 15)	41	1988	0	1988	
24	The Last Beat Of My Heart	(Wonderland SHE 16)	44	1988	0	1988	
25	Kiss Them For Me	(Wonderland SHE 19)	32	1991	23	1991	(Geffen 19031)
26	Shadowtime	(Wonderland SHE 20)	57	1991	0	1991	
27	Face To Face	(Wonderland SHE 21)	21	1992	0	1992	
28	Interlude	(Parlophone CDR 6365)	25	1994	0	1994	
30	O Baby	(Wonderland SHECD 22)	34	1995	0	1995	
31	Stargazer	(Wonderland SHECD 23)	64	1995	0	1995	
	HIT 28 IS CREDITED TO MORRISSEY AND SIOUXSIE						
Sir Douglas Quintet Male Vocal/Instrumental Group from the USA, Led By Doug Sahm B: 6 Nov 1941 San Francisco							
1	She's About A Mover	(London HLU 9964)	15	1965	13	1965	(Tribe 8308)
2	The Rains Came		0	1966	31	1966	(Tribe 8314)
* 3	Mendocino		0	1968	27	1968	(Smash 2191)
Sir Mix-A-Lot Male Rapper, Anthony Ray from Seattle, USA							
* 1	Baby Got Back	(DEF American DEFA 20)	56	1992	1	1992	(DEF American 18947)
2	Jump To It		0	1996	97	1996	(Reprise 17626)
Sister Bliss With Colette Female Vocal Duo from the USA/UK							
1	Cantgetaman Cantgetajob (Life's A Bitch)	(GO.BEAT GODCD124)	31	1994	0	1994	
2	Oh! What A World	(GO.DISCS GODCD 126)	40	1995	0	1995	
3	Badman	(JUNK DOG JDOGCD 1)	51	1996	0	1996	
Sister Janet Mead Female Vocalist, B: 1938, Member Of The Mercy Convent In Adelaide							
* 1	The Lords Prayer		0	1974	4	1974	(A&M 1491)

Sister Sledge   Female Vocal Group from Philadelphia, Joan, Kim, Debra & Kathie

ISSUE	TITLE	UK LBL	UK POS	UK YEAR	US POS	US YEAR	US LBL
1	Mama Never Told Me	(Atlantic K 10619)	20	1975	0	1975	
2	He's The Greatest Dancer	(Atlantic/Cotillion K 11257)	6	1979	9	1979	(Cotillion 44245)
* 3	We Are Family	(Atlantic/Cotillion K 11293)	8	1979	2	1979	(Cotillion 44251)
4	Lost In Music	(Atlantic/Cotillion K 11337)	17	1979	0	1979	
5	Got To Love Somebody	(Atlantic/Cotillion K 11404)	34	1980	64	1980	(Cotillion 45007)
6	All American Girls	(Atlantic K 11656)	41	1981	79	1981	
7	My Guy		0	1982	23	1982	(Cotillion 47000)
8	Thinking Of You	(Cotillion/Atlantic B 9744)	11	1984	0	1984	
9	Lost In Music (Re-Mix)	(Cotillion/Atlantic B 9718)	4	1984	0	1984	
10	We Are Family (Re-Mix)	(Cotillion/Atlantic B 9692)	33	1984	0	1984	
11	Frankie	(Atlantic A 9547)	1	1985	0	1985	
12	Dancing On A Jagged Edge	(Atlantic A 9520)	50	1985	71	1985	(Atlantic 89520)
13	We Are Family (2nd Re-Mix)	(Atlantic A 4508CD)	5	1993	0	1993	
14	Lost In Music (2nd Re-Mix)	(Atlantic A 4509CD)	14	1993	0	1993	
15	Thinking Of You (Re-Mix)	(Atlantic A 4515CD)	17	1993	0	1993	

Sisters Of Mercy   Male Vocalist, Real Name Andrew Eldritch & Backing Musicians from the UK

ISSUE	TITLE	UK LBL	UK POS	UK YEAR	US POS	US YEAR	US LBL
1	Body And Soul / Train	(Merciful Release MR 029)	46	1984	0	1984	
2	Walk Away	(Merciful Release MR 033)	45	1984	0	1984	
3	No Time To Cry	(Merciful Release MR 035)	63	1985	0	1985	
4	This Corrosion	(Merciful Release MR 39)	7	1987	0	1987	
5	Dominion	(Merciful Release MR 43)	13	1987	0	1987	
6	Lucretia My Reflection	(Merciful Release MR 45)	20	1988	0	1988	
7	More	(Merciful Release MR 47)	14	1990	0	1990	
8	Doctor Jeep	(Merciful Release MR 51)	37	1990	0	1990	
9	Temple Of Love	(Merciful Release MR 53)	3	1992	0	1992	
10	Under The Gun	(Merciful Release MR 59CDX)	19	1993	0	1993	

Siv Malmquist   Female Vocalist, B: 31 Dec 1936 Landskrona, Sweden, Her First Record Was Tweedle Dee

ISSUE	TITLE	UK LBL	UK POS	UK YEAR	US POS	US YEAR	US LBL
* 1	Liebeskummer Lonhnt Sich Nicht (Love Problems Aren't Worthwhile)		0	1964	0	1964	

HIT WAS A MILLION SELLER IN GERMANY AFTER WINNING THE POP MUSIC FESTIVAL

Sivuca   Male Vocalist from Brazil

ISSUE	TITLE	UK LBL	UK POS	UK YEAR	US POS	US YEAR	US LBL
1	Ain't No Sunshine	(London LON 51)	56	1984	0	1984	

Six Hits & A Miss   Vocal Group from the USA, They Have Sung Backing Vocals For Many Famous Artists

ISSUE	TITLE	UK LBL	UK POS	UK YEAR	US POS	US YEAR	US LBL
1	You'd Be So Nice To Come Home To		0	1943	11	1943	(Capitol 127)

6 By Six   Male Instrumental/Production Duo from the UK

ISSUE	TITLE	UK LBL	UK POS	UK YEAR	US POS	US YEAR	US LBL
1	Into Your Heart	(Six6 Sixcd 130)	51	1996	0	1996	

60ft Dolls   Male Vocal/Instrumental Group from the UK

ISSUE	TITLE	UK LBL	UK POS	UK YEAR	US POS	US YEAR	US LBL
1	Stay	(Indolent Dolls 002)	48	1996	0	1996	
2	Talk To Me	(Indolent Dolls 003cd)	37	1996	0	1996	
3	Happy Shopper	(Indolent Dolls 005cd)	38	1996	0	1996	

69 Boyz   Hip-Hop Quartet from Hacksonville, Florida

ISSUE	TITLE	UK LBL	UK POS	UK YEAR	US POS	US YEAR	US LBL
1	Toosee Roll		0	1994	8 *	1994	(Rip-It 6911)

Six Teens   Lead From Trudy Williams & Ed Wells Of The Los Angeles Based Sextet

ISSUE	TITLE	UK LBL	UK POS	UK YEAR	US POS	US YEAR	US LBL
1	A Casual Look		0	1956	25	1956	(FLIP 315)

Size 9   Male Producer Josh Wink from the USA

ISSUE	TITLE	UK LBL	UK POS	UK YEAR	US POS	US YEAR	US LBL
1	I'm Ready	(Virgin VUSCD 92)	52	1995	0	1995	
2	I'm Ready (Re-Issue)	(VC VCRD 2)	30	1995	0	1995	

HIT 2 IS CREDITED TO JOSH WINK'S SIZE 9

Skatalites   Male Instrumental Group from Jamaica

ISSUE	TITLE	UK LBL	UK POS	UK YEAR	US POS	US YEAR	US LBL
1	Guns Of Navarone	(Island WI 168)	36	1967	0	1967	

Skee-Lo   Male Rapper from Riverside, California

ISSUE	TITLE	UK LBL	UK POS	UK YEAR	US POS	US YEAR	US LBL
* 1	I Wish	(Wild Card 5755652)	15	1995	13	1995	(SUNSHINE 78032)
2	Top Of The Stairs	(Wild Card 5763352)	38	1996	0	1996	

Skeeter Davis   Female Vocalist, Real Name Mary Penick B: 30 Dec 1931 In Sparta, Kentucky

ISSUE	TITLE	UK LBL	UK POS	UK YEAR	US POS	US YEAR	US LBL
5	(I Can't Help You) I'm Falling Too		0	1960	39	1960	(RCA 7767)
6	My Last Date (With You)		0	1961	26	1961	(RCA 7825)
* 12	The End Of The World	(RCA 1328)	18	1963	2	1963	(RCA 8098)
13	I'm Saving My Love		0	1963	41	1963	(RCA 8176)
14	I Can't Stay Mad At You		0	1963	7	1963	(RCA 8219)
15	He Says The Same Things To Me		0	1964	47	1964	(RCA 8288)
16	Gonna Get Along Without You Now		0	1964	48	1964	(RCA 8347)

OBITUARY: D: 2 AUG 1953 CAR ACCIDENT. • OTHER HITS ARE C/W

ISSUE	TITLE	UK LBL	UK POS	UK YEAR	US POS	US YEAR	US LBL
Skid Row	Vocals With The New York Based Quintet Are From Sebastian Bierk						
* 1	18 And Life	(Atlantic A 8883)	12	1989	4	1989	(Atlantic 88883)
2	I Remember You	(East West A 8836)	36	1989	6	1989	(Atlantic 88886)
3	Youth Gone Wild	(Atlantic A 8935)	42	1989	0	1989	
4	Monkey Business	(Atlantic A 7673)	19	1991	0	1991	
5	Slave To The Grind	(Atlantic A 7603)	43	1991	0	1991	
6	Wasted Time	(Atlantic A 7570)	20	1991	0	1991	
7	Youth Gone Wild (Re-Issue)	(Atlantic A 7444)	22	1992	0	1992	
8	Breakin' Down	(Atlantic A 7135CD1)	48	1995	0	1995	
Skids	Male Vocal/Instrumental Group from the UK						
1	Sweet Suburbia	(Virgin VS 227)	70	1978	0	1978	
2	Sweet Suburbia (Re-Entry)	(Virgin VS 227)	71	1978	0	1978	
3	The Saints Are Coming	(Virgin VS 232)	48	1978	0	1978	
4	Into The Valley	(Virgin VS 241)	10	1979	0	1979	
5	Masquerade	(Virgin VS 262)	14	1979	0	1979	
6	Charade	(Virgin VS 288)	31	1979	0	1979	
7	Working For The Yankee Dollar	(Virgin VS 306)	20	1979	0	1979	
8	Animation	(Virgin VS 323)	56	1980	0	1980	
9	Circus Games	(Virgin VS 359)	32	1980	0	1980	
10	Goodbye Civilian	(Virgin VS 373)	52	1980	0	1980	
11	Woman In Winter	(Virgin VSK 101)	49	1980	0	1980	
Skin	Male Vocal/Instrumental Group from the UK/germany						
1	The Skin Up (EP)	(Parlophone CDR 6363)	67	1993	0	1993	
2	House Of Love	(Parlophone CDR 6374)	45	1994	0	1994	
3	Money / Unbelieveable	(Parlophone CDR 6381)	18	1994	0	1994	
4	Tower Of Strength	(Parlophone CDR 6387)	19	1994	0	1994	
5	Look But Don't Touch	(Parlophone CDR 6391)	33	1994	0	1994	
6	Take Me Down To The River	(Parlophone CDR 6409)	26	1995	0	1995	
7	How Lucky You Are	(Parlophone CDR 6426)	32	1996	0	1996	
8	Perfect Day	(Parlophone CDR 6433)	33	1996	0	1996	
Skin Up	Male Producer from the UK						
1	Ivory	(Love EVOL 4)	48	1991	0	1991	
2	A Juicy Red Apple	(Love EVOL 11)	32	1992	0	1992	
3	Accelerate	(Love EVOL 17)	45	1992	0	1992	
Skip & Flip	Real Names Gary Paxton & Clyde Battin						
1	It Was I		0	1959	11	1959	(Brent 7002)
2	Cherry Pie		0	1960	11	1960	(Brent 7010)
Skipworth & Turner	Male Vocal Duo from the USA						
1	Thinking About Your Love	(Fourth & Broadway BRW 23)	24	1985	0	1985	
2	Make It Last	(Fourth & Broadway BRW 118)	60	1989	0	1989	
Skitch Henderson Orchestra	Male Pianist/Bandleader from the USA						
1	Five Minutes More (From *Sweetheart Of Sigma Chi*)		0	1946	9	1946	(Capitol 257)
2	Papa Won't You Dance With Me? (From *High Button Shoes*)		0	1947	27	1947	(Capitol 471)
Skunk Anansie	Mixed Vocal/Instrumental Group from the UK						
1	Selling Jesus	(One Little Indian 101 TP7CD)	46	1995	0	1995	
2	I Can Dream	(One Little Indian 121 TP7CD)	41	1995	0	1995	
3	Charity	(One Little Indian 131 TP7CD)	40	1995	0	1995	
4	Weak	(One Little Indian 141 TP7CD)	20	1996	0	1996	
5	Charity (Re-Issue)	(One Little Indian 151 TP7CD)	20	1996	0	1996	
6	All I Want	(One Little Indian 161 TP7CD)	14	1996	0	1996	
7	Twisted (Everyday Hurts)	(One Little Indian 171 TP7CD)	26	1996	0	1996	
8	Hedonism (Just Because You Feel Good)	(One Little Indian 181 TP7CD)	13	1997	0	1997	
9	Brazen 'Weep	(One Little Indian 191TP7CD1)	11	1997	0	1997	
Sky	Male Instrumental Group from the UK/Australia						
1	Toccata	(Ariola ARO 300)	5	1980	0	1980	
Skyhooks	Male Vocal/Instrumental Group from Australia						
1	Women In Uniform	(United ArtistsUP 36508)	73	1979	0	1979	
Skylark	Lead Singers With The Group Are Bonnie Jean Cook & Donny Gerrard						
1	Wildflower		0	1973	9	1973	(Capitol 3511)
Skylarks	Vocal Group from the USA						
1	I Had The Craziest Dream		0	1953	28	1953	(RCA Victor 5257)

ISSUE	TITLE	UK LBL	UK POS	UK YEAR	US POS	US YEAR	US LBL
Skyliners Mixed Vocal Quintet from Pittsburgh, Jimmy Beaumont, Wally Lester, Joe Ver-Scharen, Jackie Taylor & Janet Vogel							
1	Since I Don't Have You		0	1959	12	1959	(Calico 103)
2	This I Swear		0	1959	26	1959	(Calico 106)
3	Pennies From Heaven		0	1960	24	1960	(Calico 117)
	OBITUARY: JANET D: 21 FEB 1980 COMMITTED SUICIDE.						
Skyy Vocals from sisters Delores, Denise & Bonnie Dunning							
1	Call Me		0	1982	26	1982	(Salsoul 2152)
SL2 Male Production/Instrumental Duo from the UK							
1	DJs Take Control / Way In My Brain	(XL XLS 24)	11	1991	0	1991	
2	DJs Take Control (Re-Entry)	(XL XLS 24)	71	1992	0	1992	
3	On A Ragga Tip	(XL XLS 29)	2	1992	0	1992	
4	Way In My Brain (Re-Issue)	(XL XLS 36)	26	1992	0	1992	
5	On A Ragga Tip '97	(XL RecordingsXLSR 29CD)	31	1997	0	1997	
Slade Male Vocal/Instrumental Group from the UK							
1	Get Down And Get With It	(Polydor 2058 112)	16	1971	0	1971	
2	Coz I Love You	(Polydor 2058 155)	1	1971	0	1971	
3	Look Wot You Dun	(Polydor 2058 195)	4	1972	0	1972	
4	Take Me Bak 'Ome	(Polydor 2058 231)	1	1972	0	1972	
5	Mama Weer All Crazee Now	(Polydor 2058 274)	1	1972	0	1972	
6	Gud Buy T' Jane	(Polydor 2058 312)	2	1972	0	1972	
7	Cum On Feel The Noize	(Polydor 2058 339)	1	1973	0	1973	
8	Skweeze Me Pleeze Me	(Polydor 2058 377)	1	1973	0	1973	
9	My Friend Stan	(Polydor 2058 407)	2	1973	0	1973	
* 10	Merry Xmas Everybody	(Polydor 2058 422)	1	1973	0	1973	
11	Everyday	(Polydor 2058 453)	3	1974	0	1974	
12	Bangin' Man	(Polydor 2058 492)	3	1974	0	1974	
13	Far Far Away	(Polydor 2058 522)	2	1974	0	1974	
14	How Does It Feel	(Polydor 2058 547)	15	1975	0	1975	
15	Thanks For The Memory	(Polydor 2058 585)	7	1975	0	1975	
	(Wham Bam Thank You Mam)						
16	In For A Penny	(Polydor 2058 663)	11	1975	0	1975	
17	Let's Call It Quits	(Polydor 2058 690)	11	1976	0	1976	
18	Gypsy Road Hog	(BARN 2014 105)	48	1977	0	1977	
19	My Baby Left Me / That's All Right (Medley)	(BARN 2014 114)	32	1977	0	1977	
20	Slade Alive At Reading '80 (EP)	(Cheapskate Cheap 5)	44	1980	0	1980	
21	Merry Xmas Everybody	(Cheapskate Cheap 11)	70	1980	0	1980	
22	We'll Bring The House Down	(Cheapskate Cheap 16)	10	1981	0	1981	
23	Wheels Ain't Coming Down	(Cheapskate Cheap 21)	60	1981	0	1981	
24	Lock Up Your Daughters	(RCA 124)	29	1981	0	1981	
25	Merry Xmas Everybody (Re-Entry)	(Polydor 2058 422)	32	1981	0	1981	
25	Ruby Red	(Polydor 2058 422)	51	1982	0	1982	
26	(And Now-The Waltz) C'est La Vie	(RCA 291)	50	1982	0	1982	
27	Merry Xmas Everybody (2nd Re-Entry)	(Polydor 2058 422)	67	1982	0	1982	
28	My Oh My	(RCA 373)	2	1983	37	1984	(CBS Association 04528)
29	Merry Xmas Everybody (3rd Re-Entry)	(Polydor 2058 422)	20	1983	0	1983	
30	Run Run Away	(RCA 385)	7	1984	20	1984	(CBS Association 04398)
31	All Join Hands	(RCA 385)	15	1984	0	1984	
32	Merry Xmas Everybody (4th Re-Entry)	(Polydor 2058 422)	47	1984	0	1984	
33	7 Year Bitch	(RCA 475)	60	1985	0	1985	
34	Myzsterious Mizter Jones	(RCA PB 40027)	50	1985	0	1985	
35	Do You Believe In Miracles	(RCA PB 40449)	54	1985	0	1985	
36	Merry Xmas Everybody (Re-Issue)	(Polydor POSP 780)	48	1985	0	1985	
37	Merry Xmas Everybody (Re-Issue) (Re-Entry)	(Polydor POSP 780)	71	1986	0	1986	
38	Still The Same	(RCA PB 41137)	73	1987	0	1987	
39	Radio Wall Of Sound	(Polydor PO 180)	21	1991	0	1991	
	HIT 21 IS CREDITED TO SLADE & THE READING CHOIR • LEAD SINGER NODDY HOLDER B: 15 JUN 1950 WALSALL, BIRMINGHAM, ENGLAND						
	OTHER MEMBERS ARE JIM LEA, DAVE HILL & DON POWELL • GROUP WAS FIRST KNOWN AS THE 'N'BETWEENS IN THE LATE 60S						
Slamm Male Vocal/Instrumental Group from the UK							
1	Energize	(PWL International PWCD 266)	57	1993	0	1993	
2	Virginia Plain	(PWL International PWCD 274)	60	1993	0	1993	
3	That's Where My Mind Goes	(PWL International PWCD 310)	68	1994	0	1994	
4	Can't Get By	(PWL International PWCD 316)	47	1995	0	1995	

ISSUE	TITLE	UK LBL	UK POS	UK YEAR	US POS	US YEAR	US LBL
Slaughter Hard-Rock Quartet from Las Vegas Led By Mark Slaughter							
1	Up All Night	(Chrysalis CHS 3556)	62	1990	27	1990	(Chrysalis 23486)
2	Fly To The Angels	(Chrysalis CHS 3634)	55	1991	19	1990	(Chrysalis 23527)
3	Spend My Life		0	1991	39	1991	(Chrysalis 23605)
Slave Hard-Rock Vocal/Instrumental Band From Ohio							
1	Slide		0	1977	32	1977	(Cotillion 44218)
2	Just A Touch Of Love	(Atlantic/Cotillion K 11442)	64	1980	0	1980	
Slayer Male Vocal/Instrumental Group from the USA							
1	Criminally Insane	(DEF JAM LON	64	1987	0	1987	
2	Seasons Of The Abyss	(DEF American DEFA 9)	51	1991	0	1991	
3	Serenity In Murder	(American 74321262347)	50	1995	0	1995	
Sleazesisters With Vikki Shepard Mixed Vocal/Instrumental Group from the UK/USA							
1	Sex	(PULSE 8 CDLOSE92)	53	1995	0	1995	
2	Let's Whip It Up (You Go Girl)	(PULSE 8 CDLOSE102)	46	1996	0	1996	
Sleeper Mixed Vocal/Instrumental Group from the UK							
1	Delicious	(Indolent Sleep003CD)	75	1994	0	1994	
2	Inbetweener	(Indolent Sleep006CD)	16	1995	0	1995	
3	Vegas	(Indolent Sleep008CD)	33	1995	0	1995	
4	What Do I Do Now	(Indolent Sleep09CD1)	14	1995	0	1995	
5	Sale Of The Century	(Indolent Sleep011CD)	10	1996	0	1996	
6	Nice Guy Eddie	(Indolent Sleep013CD)	10	1996	0	1996	
7	Statuesque	(Indolent Sleep014CD1)	17	1996	0	1996	
Slick Mixed Vocal/Instrumental Group from the USA							
1	Space Bass	(Fantasy FTC 176)	16	1979	0	1979	
2	Sexy Cream	(Fantasy FTC 182)	47	1979	0	1979	
Slik Male Vocal/Instrumental Group from the UK							
1	Forever And Ever	(Bell 1464)	1	1976	0	1976	
2	Requiem	(Bell 1478)	24	1976	0	1976	
Slim Dusty Male Vocalist from Australia							
1	A Pub With No Beer	(Columbia DB 4212)	3	1959	0	1959	
Slim Gaillard Trio Male Pianist And Half Of The Duo Slim & Slam from the USA							
1	Cement Mixer (Put-Ti, Put-Ti)		0	1946	21	1946	(Cadet 201)
Slim Harpo Male Harmonica/Vocalist, Real Name James Moore B: 11 Jan 1924 In Lobdell, Louisiana							
1	Rainin' In My Heart		0	1961	34	1961	(Excello 2194)
2	Baby Scratch My Back		0	1966	16	1966	(Excello 2273)
Also Known As Harmonica Slim	Obituary : D: 31 Jan 1970 Heart Attack.							
Slim Whitman Male Yodeller/Vocalist, B: Otis Dewey Whitman, 20 Jan 1924 In Tampa, Florida							
* 2	Indian Love Call	(London L 1149)	7	1955	9	1952	(Imperial 8156)
!* 6	Secret Love		0	1954	2	1954	(Imperial 8223)
* 7	Rose Marie	(London HL 8061)	1	1955	22	1954	(Imperial 8236)
10	China Doll	(London L 1149)	15	1955	0	1955	
11	Tumbling Tumbleweeds	(London HLU 8230)	19	1956	0	1956	
12	I'm A Fool	(London HLU 8252)	16	1956	0	1956	
13	I'm A Fool (Re-Entry)	(London HLU 8252)	29	1956	0	1956	
14	Serenade	(London HLU 8287)	24	1956	0	1956	
15	Serenade (Re-Entry)	(London HLU 8287)	8	1956	0	1956	
16	I'll Take You Home Again Kathleen	(London HLP 8403)	7	1957	0	1957	
	UNLISTED HITS ARE C/W							
Slipstreem Male Vocal Group from the UK							
1	We Are Raving - The Anthem	(Boogie FOOD 7BF 1)	18	1992	0	1992	
Slits Female Vocal/Instrumental Group from the UK							
1	Typical Girls / I Heard It Throught The Grapevine	(Island WIP 6505)	60	1979	0	1979	
Slo-Moshun Male Production/Instrumental Duo from the UK							
1	Bells Of N.Y.	(SIX6 SIXCD 108)	29	1994	0	1994	
2	Help My Friend	(SIX6 SIXCD 117)	52	1994	0	1994	
Slowdive Mixed Vocal/Instrumental Group from the UK							
1	Catch The Breeze / Shine	(Creation CRE 112)	52	1991	0	1991	
2	Outside Your Room (EP)	(Creation CRESCD 119)	69	1993	0	1993	

	ISSUE	TITLE	UK LBL	UK POS	UK YEAR	US POS	US YEAR	US LBL
Sly & Robbie Male Vocal/Instrumental Duo From Jamaica								
	1	Boops (Here To Go)	(Fourth & Broadway BRW 61)	12	1987	0	1987	
	2	Fire	(Fourth & Broadway BRW 71)	60	1987	0	1987	
Sly & The Family Stone Mixed Soul Band From San Francisco Formed By Sylvester Stewart								
	1	Dance To The Music	(Direction 58 3568)	7	1968	8	1968	(Epic 10256)
	2	M'lady	(Direction 58 3707)	32	1968	93	1968	(Epic 10353)
*	3	Everyday People	(Direction 58 3938)	36	1969	1	1969	(Epic 10407)
	4	Everyday People (Re-Entry)	(Direction 58 3938)	37	1969	0	1969	
	5	Stand		0	1969	60	1969	(Epic 10450)
	6	Stand (Re-Entry)		0	1969	22	1969	(Epic 10450)
	7	Hot Fun In The Summertime		0	1969	2	1969	(Epic 10497)
*	8	Thank You Falettinme Be Mice Elf Agin'		0	1970	1	1970	(Epic 10555)
	9	Everybody Is A Star		0	1970	1	1970	(Epic 10555)
	10	I Want To Take You Higher (Re-Entry)		0	1970	38	1970	(Epic 10450)
*	11	Family Affair	(Epic EPC 7632)	15	1972	1	1971	(Epic 10805)
	12	Runnin' Away	(Epic EPC 7810)	17	1972	23	1972	(Epic 10829)
	13	Smilin'		0	1972	42	1972	(Epic 10850)
*	14	If You Want Me To Stay		0	1973	12	1973	(Epic 11017)
	15	Frisky		0	1973	79	1973	(Epic 11060)
	16	Time For Livin'		0	1974	32	1974	(Epic 11140)
	17	Loose Booty		0	1974	84	1974	(Epic 50033)
	18	I Get High On You		0	1975	52	1975	(Epic 8-50135)
		NAMES ARE SLY STONE, ROSE STONE (SISTER), JERRY MARTINI, CYNTHIA ROBINSON, FREDDIE STONE, GREGG ERRICO & LARRY GRAYHAM.						
Sly Fox Male Vocal/Instrumental Duo from the USA								
	1	Let's Go All The Way	(Capitol CL 403)	3	1986	7	1986	(Capitol 5552)
		REAL NAMES GARY 'MUDBONE' COOPER & MICHAEL CAMACHO						
Small Ads Male Vocal/Instrumental Group from the UK								
	1	Small Ads	(Bronze BRO 115)	63	1981	0	1981	
Small Faces Male Vocal/Instrumental Group from the UK								
	1	Watcha Gonna Do About It	(Decca F 12208)	14	1965	0	1965	
	2	Sha-La-La-La-Lee	(Decca F 12317)	3	1966	0	1966	
	3	Hey Girl	(Decca F 12393)	10	1966	0	1966	
	4	All Or Nothing	(Decca F 12470)	1	1966	0	1966	
	5	My Minds Eye	(Decca F 12500)	4	1966	0	1966	
	6	I Can't Make It	(Decca F 12565)	26	1967	0	1967	
	7	Here Comes The Nice	(Immediate IM 050)	12	1967	0	1967	
*	8	Itchycoo Park	(Immediate IM 057)	3	1967	16	1968	(Immediate 501)
	9	Tin Soldier	(Immediate IM 062)	9	1967	0	1967	
	10	Lazy Sunday	(Immediate IM 064)	2	1968	0	1968	
	11	Universal	(Immediate IM 069)	16	1968	0	1968	
	12	Afterglow Of Your Love	(Immediate IM 077)	36	1969	0	1969	
	13	Itchycoo Park (Re-Issue)	(Immediate IMS 102)	9	1975	0	1975	
	14	Lazy Sunday (Re-Issue)	(Immediate IMS 106)	39	1976	0	1976	
		NAMES STEVE MARRIOTT, RONNIE LANE, KENNEY JONES & IAN MCLAGEN • STEVE WENT ON TO FORM HUMBLE PIE OBITUARY : MARRIOTT D: 20 APR 1991 IN A FIRE.						
Smaller Male Vocal/Instrumental Group from the UK								
	1	Wasted	(Better BETSCD006)	72	1996	0	1996	
	2	Is	(Better BETSCD008)	55	1997	0	1997	
Smart E's Male Production/Instrumental Group from the UK								
	1	Sesame's Treet	(Suburban Base Subbase	2	1992	0	1992	
Smashing Pumpkins Mixed Vocal/Instrumental Quartet from Chicago								
	1	I Am One	(HUT HUTT 18)	73	1992	0	1992	
	2	Cherub Rock	(Hut HutCD 31)	31	1993	0	1993	
	3	Today	(Hut HutCD 37)	44	1993	0	1993	
	4	Disarm	(Hut HutCD 43)	11	1994	0	1994	
*	5	Bullet With Butterfly Wings	(Hut HutCD 63)	20	1995	22	1995	(Virgin 38522)
	6	1979	(Hut HutCD 67)	16	1996	12	1996	(Virgin)
	7	Tonight, Tonight	(Hut HUTDX 69)	7	1996	36	1996	(Virgin 38547)
	8	Thirty-Three	(Hut HutCD 78)	21	1996	39	1996	(Virgin 38574)
	9	The End Is The Beginning Is The End	(Warner Bros. W 0404CD)	10	1997	0	1997	
	10	The End Is The Beginning Is The End (Re-Recording)	(Warner Bros. W 0410CD)	72	1997	0	1997	

ISSUE	TITLE	UK LBL	UK POS	UK YEAR	US POS	US YEAR	US LBL
Smells Like Heaven Male Producer, Real Name Fabi Paras From Italy							
1	Londres Strutt	(Deconstruction 74321154312)	57	1993	0	1993	
Smiley Culture Male Vocalist from the UK							
1	Police Officer	(Fashion Fad 7012)	12	1984	0	1984	
2	Cockney Translation	(Fashion Fad 7028)	71	1985	0	1985	
3	School Time Chronicle	(Polydor POSP 815)	59	1986	0	1986	
Smith Quintet From Los Angeles, Consisting Of One Women & Four Men							
* 1	Baby It's You		0	1969	5	1969	(Dunhill 4206)
Smith Brothers Male Vocal Group from the USA							
1	Melancholy Me		0	1954	21	1954	(X 0003)
2	(These Are) The Things I Love		0	1954	23	1954	(X 0009)
Smithereens Pop Quartet, Vocals Are By Pat Dinizio							
1	A Girl Like You		0	1990	38	1990	(Enigma 44480)
2	Too Much Passion		0	1992	37	1992	(Capitol 44784)
Smiths Male Vocal/Instrumental Group from the UK							
1	This Charming Man	(Rough Trade RT 136)	25	1983	0	1983	
2	What Difference Does It Make	(Rough Trade RT 146)	12	1984	0	1984	
3	Heaven Knows I'm Miserable Now	(Rough Trade RT 156)	10	1984	0	1984	
4	William It Was Really Nothing	(Rough Trade RT 166)	17	1984	0	1984	
5	How Soon Is Now	(Rough Trade RT 176)	16	1985	0	1985	
6	Shakespeare's Sister	(Rough Trade	26	1985	0	1985	
7	That Joke Isn't Funny Anymore	(Rough Trade RT 186)	49	1985	0	1985	
8	The Boy With The Thorn In His Side	(Rought Trade RT 191)	23	1985	0	1985	
9	Big Mouth Strikes Again	(Rough Trade RT 192)	26	1986	0	1986	
10	Panic	(Rought Trade RT 193)	11	1986	0	1986	
11	Ask	(Rough Trade RT 194)	14	1986	0	1986	
12	Shoplifters Of The World Unite	(Rough Trade RT 195)	12	1987	0	1987	
13	Sheila Take A Bow	(Rough Trade RT 196)	10	1987	0	1987	
14	Girl Friend In A Coma	(Rough Trade RT 197)	13	1987	0	1987	
15	I Started Something I Couldn't Finish	(Rough Trade RT 198)	23	1987	0	1987	
16	Last Night I Dreamt Somebody Loved Me	(Rough Trade RT 200)	30	1987	0	1987	
17	This Charming Man (Re-Issue)	(WEA YZ 0001)	8	1992	0	1992	
18	How Soon Is Now (Re-Issue)	(WEA YZ 002)	16	1992	0	1992	
19	There Is A Light That Never Goes Out	(WEA YZ 223)	25	1992	0	1992	
20	Ask (Re-Issue)	(WEA YZ 0004CDX)	62	1995	0	1995	
Smoke Male Vocal/Instrumental Group from the UK							
1	My Friend Jack	(Columbia DB 8115)	45	1967	0	1967	
Smokey Robinson & The Miracles Names: William Robinson, Emerson & Bobby Rogers, Ronnie White & Warren Moore							
* 1	Shop Around		0	1961	2	1961	(Tamla 54034)
2	What's So Good About Good-By		0	1962	35	1962	(Tamla 54053)
3	I'll Try Something New		0	1962	39	1962	(Tamla 54059)
* 4	You've Really Got A Hold On Me		0	1963	8	1963	(Tamla 54073)
5	A Love She Can Count On		0	1963	31	1963	(Tamla 54078)
6	Mickey's Monkey		0	1963	8	1963	(Tamla 54083)
7	I Gotta Dance To Keep From Crying		0	1963	35	1963	(Tamla 54089)
8	(You Can't Let The Boy Overpower) The Man In You		0	1964	59	1964	(Tamla 54092)
9	I Like It Like That		0	1964	27	1964	(Tamla 54098)
10	That's What Love Is Made Of		0	1964	35	1964	(Tamla 54102)
11	Come On Do The Jerk		0	1964	50	1964	(Tamla 54109)
12	Ooo Baby Baby		0	1965	16	1965	(Tamla 54113)
13	The Tracks Of My Tears		0	1965	16	1965	(Tamla 54118)
14	My Girl Has Gone		0	1965	14	1965	(Tamla 54123)
* 15	Going To A Go-Go	(Tamla MotownTMG 547)	44	1966	11	1966	(Tamla 54127)
16	(Come Round Here) I'm The One You Need	(Tamla MotownTMG 584)	45	1966	17	1966	(Tamla 54140)
17	Whole Lot Of Shakin' In My Heart		0	1966	46	1966	(Tamla 54134)
18	The Love I Saw In You Was Just A Mirage		0	1967	20	1967	(Tamla 54145)
19	More Love		0	1967	23	1967	(Tamla 54152)
* 20	I Second That Emotion	(Tamla MotownTMG 631)	27	1967	4	1967	(Tamla 54159)
21	If You Can Want	(Tamla MotownTMG 648)	50	1968	11	1968	(Tamla 54162)
22	Yester Love		0	1968	31	1968	(Tamla 54167)
23	Special Occasion		0	1968	26	1968	(Tamla 54172)
24	Baby, Baby Don't Cry		0	1969	8	1969	(Tamla 54178)

ISSUE	TITLE	UK LBL	UK POS	UK YEAR	US POS	US YEAR	US LBL
* 25	Tracks Of My Tears	(Tamla MotownTMG 696)	9	1969	16	1965	(Tamla 54118)
26	Abraham, Martin And John		0	1969	33	1969	(Tamla 54184)
27	Doggone Right		0	1969	32	1969	(Tamla 54183)
28	Here I Go Again		0	1969	37	1969	(Tamla 54183)
29	Point It Out		0	1969	37	1969	(Tamla 54189)
30	Who's Gonna Take The Blame		0	1970	46	1970	(Tamla 54194)
* 31	The Tears Of A Clown	(Tamla MotownTMG 745)	1	1970	1	1970	(Tamla 54199)
33	I Don't Blame You At All	(Tamla MotownTMG 774)	11	1971	18	1971	(Tamla 54205)
34	(Come 'Round Here) I'm The One You Need (Re-Issue)	(Tamla Motown TMG 761)	13	1971	0	1971	
+ 35	Crazy About The La La La		0	1971	20	1971	(Tamla 54206)
36	Satisfaction		0	1971	49	1971	(Tamla 54211)
* 37	Baby Come Close		0	1974	27	1974	(Tamla 54239)
38	Just My Soul Responding	(Tamla Motown TMG 883)	35	1974	0	1974	
* 39	Do It Baby		0	1974	13	1974	(Tamla 54248)
40	Baby That's Backatcha		0	1975	26	1975	(Tamla 54258)
41	The Agony And The Ecstasy		0	1975	36	1975	(Tamla 54261)
* 42	Love Machine (Part 1)	(Tamla MotownTMG 1015)	3	1976	1	1975	(Tamla 54262)
43	The Tears Of A Clown (Re-Issue)	(Tamla MotownTMG 1048)	34	1976	0	1976	
44	Pops We Love You	(Motown TMG 1136)	66	1979	0	1979	
45	Cruisin'		0	1979	4	1979	(Tamla 54306)
46	Let Me Be The Clock		0	1980	31	1980	(Tamla 54311)
* 47	Being With You	(Motown TMG 1223)	1	1981	2	1981	(Tamla 54321)
48	Tell Me Tomorrow (Part 1)	(Motown TMG 1255)	51	1982	33	1982	(Tamla 1601)
49	Just To See Her	(Motown ZB 41147)	52	1987	8	1987	(Motown 1877)
50	One Heartbeat		0	1987	10	1987	(Motown 1897)
51	Indestructible	(Arista 112074)	30	1989	35	1989	(Arista 9706)

HITS 1-16, 42 ARE CREDITED TO THE MIRACLES • SMOKEY, REAL NAME WILLIAM ROBINSON B: 19 FEB 1940 DETROIT

Smokie   Male Vocal/Instrumental Group from the UK,   Names: Chris Norman, Terry Utley, Pete Spencer & Alan Silson

1	If You Think You Know How To Love Me	(RAK 206)	3	1975	0	1975	
2	Don't Play That Rock 'N' Roll To Me	(RAK 217)	8	1975	0	1975	
3	Somethings Been Making Me Blue	(RAK 227)	17	1976	0	1976	
4	I'll Meet You At Midnight	(RAK 241)	11	1976	0	1976	
5	Living Next Door To Alice	(RAK 244)	5	1976	25	1977	(RSO 860)
6	Lay Back In The Arms Of Someone	(RAK 251)	12	1977	0	1977	
7	It's Your Life	(RAK 260)	5	1977	0	1977	
8	Needles And Pins	(RAK 263)	10	1977	0	1977	
9	For A Few Dollars More	(RAK 267)	17	1978	0	1978	
10	Oh Carol	(RAK 276)	5	1978	0	1978	
11	Mexican Girl	(RAK 283)	19	1978	0	1978	
12	Take Good Care Of My Baby	(RAK 309)	34	1980	0	1980	
13	Living Next Door To Alice (Who The Fuck Is Alice) (North Of Watford CDWAG 245)		64	1995	0	1995	
14	Living Next Door To Alice (Who The Fuck Is Alice) (Re-Entry) (North Of Watford CDWAG 245)		3	1995	0	1995	

Smokin' Mojo Filters   Mixed Vocal/Instrumental Group from the UK/USA

1	Come Together	(GO! DISC GODCD136)	19	1995	0	1995	

Smooth   Female Vocalist from the USA

1	Mind Blowin'	(JIVE JIVECD 379)	36	1995	0	1995	
2	It's Summertime (Let It Get Into You)	(JIVE JIVECD 383)	46	1995	0	1995	
3	We Got It	(MCA MCSTD 48009)	26	1996	0	1996	
4	Love Groove (Groove With You)	(JIVE JIVECD 390)	46	1996	0	1996	
5	Undercover Lover	(JIVE JIVECD 397)	41	1996	0	1996	

HIT 3 IS CREDITED TO IMMATURE FEATURING SMOOTH

Smooth Touch   Male Production/Instrumental Duo from the USA

1	House Of Love (In My House)	(SIXG SIXCD 112)	58	1994	0	1994	

Smoothies   Vocal Group from the USA

1	Down By The O-Hi-O		0	1940	29	1940	(Bluebird 10710)

Smurfs   Vocal Puppets from Holland

1	The Smurf Song	(Decca F 13759)	2	1978	0	1978	
2	Dippety Day	(Decca F 13798)	13	1978	0	1978	
3	Christmas In Smurfland	(Decca F 13819)	19	1978	0	1978	
4	I've Got A Little Puppy	(EMI TV CDSMURF 100)	4	1996	0	1996	
5	Your Christmas Wish	(EMI CDSMURF 102)	8	1996	0	1996	

HITS 1-3 ARE CREDITED TO FATHER ABRAHAM & THE SMURFS

ISSUE	TITLE	UK LBL	UK POS	UK YEAR	US POS	US YEAR	US LBL
Snap	Mixed Dance Band Duo From Pittsburgh. Turbo B A London-based Rapper With His Cousin Jackie Harris, Replaced In 1991 By Penny Ford.						
* 1	The Power	(Arista 113133)	1	1990	2	1990	(Arista 2013)
* 2	Ooops Up	(Arista 113296)	5	1990	35	1990	(Arista 2060)
3	Cult Of Snap	(Arista 113596)	8	1990	0	1990	
4	Mary Had A Little Boy	(Arista 113831)	8	1990	0	1990	
5	Snap Megamix	(Arista 114169)	10	1991	0	1991	
6	The Colour Of Love	(Arista 114678)	54	1991	0	1991	
* 7	Rhythm Is A Dancer	(Arista 115309)	1	1992	5	1992	(Arista 12437)
8	Exterminate	(Arista 74321106962)	2	1993	0	1993	
9	Do You See The Light (Looking For)	(Arista 74321147622)	10	1993	0	1993	
10	Welcome To Tomorrow	(Arista 74321223852)	6	1994	0	1994	
11	Welcome To Tomorrow (Re-Entry)	(Arista 74321223852)	75	1995	0	1995	
12	The First, The Last, The Eternity (Til The End)	(Arista 74321254672)	15	1995	0	1995	
13	The World In My Hands	(Arista 74321314792)	44	1995	0	1995	
14	Rame	(Arista 74321368902)	50	1996	0	1996	
15	The Power '96	(Arista 74321398672)	42	1996	0	1996	
Sneaker	Sextet Based In Los Angeles						
1	More Than Just The Two Of Us		0	1981	34	1981	(Handshake 02557)
Sneaker Pimps	Mixed Vocal/Instrumental Group from the UK						
1	6 Underground	(Clean Up Cup 023CDD)	15	1996	79	1997	(Virgin 38582)
2	Spin Spin Sugar	(Clean Up Cup 033CDS)	21	1997	0	1997	
3	Six Underground	(Clean Up Cup 036CDS)	9	1997	0	1997	
4	Post Modern Sleaze	(Clean Up Cup 038CDM)	22	1997	0	1997	
Sniff 'N' The Tears	Male Vocal/Instrumental Group from the UK, Vocals With This Rock Band are by Paul Roberts						
1	Driver's Seat	(Chiswick CHIS 105)	42	1979	15	1979	(Atlantic 3604)
Snooky Lanson	Male Vocalist, Real Name Roy Landman B: 27 Apr 1914 Memphis						
1	On A Slow Boat To China		0	1948	24	1948	(Mercury
2	The Old Master Painter		0	1949	12	1949	(London 555)
3	It's Almost Tomorrow		0	1955	20	1955	(DOT 15424)
	OBITUARY: D: 2 JUL 1990.						
Snoop Doggy Dogg	Male Rapper, Real Name Calvin Broadus B: 1971 from Long Beach, California						
* 1	What's My Name?	(Death Row A 8337CD)	20	1993	8	1993	(Death Row 98340)
* 2	Gin And Juice	(Death Row A 8316CD)	39	1994	8	1994	(Death Row 98318)
3	Doggy Dogg World	(Death Row A 8289CD)	32	1994	0	1994	
4	Never Leave Me Alone		0	1996	39	1996	(Death Row 97012)
5	Snoops's Upside Ya Head	(Interscope IND95520)	12	1996	0	1996	
6	Vapors	(Interscope IND95530)	18	1997	0	1997	
	HIT 4 IS CREDITED TO NATE DOGG FEATURING SNOOP DOGGY DOGG • HIT 5 TO SNOOP DOGGY DOGG FE6TURING CHARLIE WILSON						
Snow	Male Reggae Vocalist, Darren O'brien B: 30 Oct 1969 From Toronto						
* 1	Informer	(East West America A 98471)	2	1993	1	1993	(East West 8436CD)
2	Girl I've Been Hurt	(East West America A 98438)	48	1993	19	1993	(East West 8417CD)
3	Uhh In You	(Atlantic A 8378CD)	67	1993	0	1993	
Snowmen	Male Vocal/Instrumental Group from the UK						
1	Hokey Cokey	(STIFF ODB 1)	18	1971	0	1971	
2	Xmas Party	(Solid Stop 006)	44	1982	0	1982	
Snowy White	Male Vocal/Guitarist from the UK						
1	Bird Of Paradise	(TowerBell TOW 42)	6	1983	0	1983	
2	For You	(R4 FOR 3)	65	1985	0	1985	
3	For You (Re-Entry)	(R4 FOR 3)	72	1986	0	1986	
So	Male Vocal/Instrumental Group from the UK						
1	Are You Sure	(Parlophone R 6173)	62	1988	0	1988	
Soapy	Male Instrumental/Production Duo from the UK						
1	Horny As Funk	(WEA WEA 074CD)	35	1996	0	1996	
Soft Cell	Male Vocal/Instrumental Duo, Real Names Marc Almond & David Bell						
1	Tainted Love	(Some Bizarre BZS 2)	1	1981	8	1982	(SIRE 49855)
2	Bed Sitter	(Some Bizarre BZS 6)	4	1981	0	1981	
3	Tainted Love (Re-Entry)	(Some Bizarre BZS 2)	43	1982	0	1982	
4	Say Hello Wave Goodbye	(Some Bizarre BZS 7)	3	1982	0	1982	
5	Torch	(Some Bizarre BZS 9)	2	1982	0	1982	
6	Tainted Love (2nd Re-Entry)	(Some Bizarre BZS 2)	50	1982	0	1982	
7	What	(Some Bizarre BZS 11)	3	1982	0	1982	

ISSUE	TITLE	UK LBL	UK POS	UK YEAR	US POS	US YEAR	US LBL
8	Where The Heart Is	(Some Bizarre BZS 16)	21	1982	0	1982	
9	Numbers / Barriers	(Some Bizarre BZS 17)	25	1983	0	1983	
10	Soul Inside	(Some Bizarre BZS 20)	16	1983	0	1983	
11	Down In The Subway	(Some Bizarre BZS 22)	24	1984	0	1984	
12	Tainted Love (3rd Re-Entry)	(Some Bizarre BZS 2)	43	1985	0	1985	
13	Say Hello Wave Goodbye '91	(Mercury SOFT 1)	38	1991	0	1991	
14	Tainted Love (Re-Issue)	(Mercury SOFT 2)	5	1991	0	1991	

Hit 12-13 Are Credited To Soft Cell/Marc Almond

Soho   Mixed Vocal/Instrumental Trio from the USA

	ISSUE	TITLE	UK LBL	UK POS	UK YEAR	US POS	US YEAR	US LBL
*	1	Hippy Chick	(Savage 7SAV 106)	67	1990	14	1990	(Savage/ATCO 98908)
	2	Hippy Chick (Re-Entry)	(Savage 7SAV 106)	8	1991	0	1991	
	3	Born To Be Alive	(MCA MCS 1578)	51	1991	0	1991	

HIT 3 IS CREDITED TO ADAMSKI FEATURING SOHO • NAMES JACQUELINE & PAULINE CUFF WITH TIM BRINKHURST

Solo   **(1)**   Male Producer, Real Name Stuart Crichton from the UK

ISSUE	TITLE	UK LBL	UK POS	UK YEAR	US POS	US YEAR	US LBL
1	Rainbow (Sample Free)	(REVERB RVBT 003)	59	1991	0	1991	
2	Come On	(REVERB RVBT 008)	75	1992	0	1992	
3	Come On (Re-Mix)	(STOATIN' STOAT003CD)	63	1993	0	1993	

Solo   **(2)**   Male Vocal Group from the USA

ISSUE	TITLE	UK LBL	UK POS	UK YEAR	US POS	US YEAR	US LBL
1	Heaven	(Perspective 5875212)	35	1996	0	1996	
2	Where Do You Want Me To Put It	(Perspective 5875312)	45	1996	50	1996	(SOLO Perspective)

Solomon Burke   Male Soul Singer, B: 1936 Philadelphia, First Recorded In 1954

	ISSUE	TITLE	UK LBL	UK POS	UK YEAR	US POS	US YEAR	US LBL
	1	Just Out Of Reach (Of My Two Open Arms)		0	1961	24	1961	(Atlantic 2114)
	2	Cry To Me		0	1962	44	1962	(Atlantic 2131)
+	3	I'm Hanging Up My Heart For You / Down In The Valley		0	1962	15	1962	(Atlantic 2147)
	4	If You Need Me		0	1963	37	1963	(Atlantic 2185)
	5	You're Good For Me		0	1963	49	1963	(Atlantic 2205)
	6	He'll Have To Go		0	1964	51	1964	(Atlantic 2218)
	7	Goodbye Baby (Baby Goodbye)		0	1964	33	1964	(Atlantic 2226)
	8	Everybody Needs Somebody To Love		0	1964	58	1964	(Atlantic 2241)
	9	The Price		0	1964	57	1964	(Atlantic 2259)
	10	Got To Get You Off My Mind		0	1965	22	1965	(Atlantic 2276)
	11	Tonight's The Night		0	1965	28	1965	(Atlantic 2288)
+	12	Someone Is Watching		0	1965	24	1965	(Atlantic 2299)
+	13	Keep A Light In The Window Till I Come Home		0	1967	15	1967	(Atlantic 2378)
	14	Take Me (Just As I Am)		0	1967	49	1967	(Atlantic 2416)
	15	Proud Mary		0	1969	45	1969	(Bell 783)

Solomon King   Male Vocalist from the USA

ISSUE	TITLE	UK LBL	UK POS	UK YEAR	US POS	US YEAR	US LBL
1	She Wears My Ring	(Columbia DB 8325)	3	1968	0	1968	
2	When We Were Young	(Columbia DB8402)	21	1968	0	1968	

Somethin' Smith & The Redheads   Male Trio From ULCA

ISSUE	TITLE	UK LBL	UK POS	UK YEAR	US POS	US YEAR	US LBL
1	It's A Sin To Tell A Lie		0	1955	7	1955	(Epic 9093)
2	In A Shanty In Old Shanty Town		0	1956	27	1956	(Epic 9168)

Son'z Of A Loop Da Loop Era   Male Producer, Real Name Danny Breaks from the UK

ISSUE	TITLE	UK LBL	UK POS	UK YEAR	US POS	US YEAR	US LBL
1	Far Out	(Suburban Base Subbase 008)	36	1992	0	1992	
2	Peace+ Loveism	(Suburban Base Subbase 14)	60	1992	0	1992	

Song Spinners   Vocal Group from the USA

ISSUE	TITLE	UK LBL	UK POS	UK YEAR	US POS	US YEAR	US LBL
1	Comin' In On A Wing And A Prayer		0	1943	1	1943	(Decca 18553)
2	Johnny Zero		0	1943	4	1943	(Decca 18553)

Sonia   Female Vocalist from the UK

ISSUE	TITLE	UK LBL	UK POS	UK YEAR	US POS	US YEAR	US LBL
1	You'll Never Stop Me Loving You	(Chrysalis CHS 3385)	1	1989	0	1989	
2	Can't Forget You	(Chrysalis CHS 3419)	17	1989	0	1989	
3	Listen To Your Heart	(Chrysalis CHS 3465)	10	1989	0	1989	
4	Counting Every Minute	(Chrysalis CHS 3492)	16	1990	0	1990	
5	You've Got A Friend	(JIVE CHILD 90)	14	1990	0	1990	
6	End Of The World	(Chrysalis CHS 3557)	18	1990	0	1990	
7	Only Fools (Never Fall In Love)	(IQ ZB 44613)	10	1991	0	1991	
8	Be Young Be Foolish Be Happy	(IQ ZB 44935)	22	1991	0	1991	
9	You To Me Are Everything	(IQ ZB 45121)	13	1991	0	1991	
10	Boogie Nights	(Arista 74321113467)	30	1992	0	1992	
11	Better The Devil You Know	(Arista 74321146872)	15	1993	0	1993	
12	Hopelessly Devoted To You	(Cockney COCCD 2)	61	1994	0	1994	

HIT 5 IS CREDITED TO BIG FUN AND SONIA

ISSUE	TITLE	UK LBL	UK POS	UK YEAR	US POS	US YEAR	US LBL
Sonic Solution	Male Producer, Real Name Steve Cop from the UK						
1	Beatstime	(R&S RSUK 11)	59	1992	0	1992	
Sonic Surfers	Male Producer/Instrumental Duo from Holland						
1	Take Me Up	(A&M AMCD 210)	61	1993	0	1993	
2	Don't Give Up	(BrilliantCDBRIL 6)	54	1994	0	1994	
	HIT 1 IS CREDITED TO SONIC SURFERS FEATURING JOCELYN BROWN						
Sonic Youth	Mixed Vocal/Instrumental Group from the USA						
1	100%	(DGC DGCS 11)	28	1992	0	1992	
2	Youth Against Fascism	(Geffen GFS 26)	52	1992	0	1992	
3	Sugar Kane	(Geffen GFS 37)	26	1993	0	1993	
4	Bull In The Heather	(Geffen GFSTD 72)	24	1994	0	1994	
5	Superstar	(A&M 5807932)	45	1994	0	1994	
	FLIP SIDE OF HIT 5 IS HIT 2 BY REDD KROSS						
Sonny & Cher	Husband And Wife Vocal Duo from the USA						
* 1	I Got You Babe	(Atlantic AT 4035)	1	1965	1	1965	(ATCO 6359)
2	Laugh At Me	(Atlantic AT 4038)	9	1965	10	1965	(ATCO 6369)
3	Baby Don't Go	(Reprise R	11	1965	8	1965	(Reprise 0309)
4	Just You		0	1965	20	1965	(ATCO 6345)
5	But Your Mine	(Atlantic AT 4047)	17	1965	15	1965	(ATCO 6381)
6	What Now My Love	(Atlantic AT 4069)	13	1966	14	1966	(ATCO 6395)
7	Have I Stayed Too Long	(Atlantic 584 018)	42	1966	0	1966	
8	Little Man	(Atlantic 584 040)	4	1966	21	1966	(ATCO 6440)
9	Living For You	(Atlantic 584 057)	44	1966	0	1966	
* 10	The Beat Goes On	(Atlantic 584 078)	29	1967	6	1967	(ATCO 6461)
* 11	All I Ever Need Is You	(MCA MU 1145)	8	1971	7	1971	(KAPP 2151)
12	A Cowboys Work Is Never Done		0	1972	8	1972	(KAPP 2163)
13	When You Say Love		0	1972	32	1972	(KAPP 2176)
14	I Got You Babe (Re-Issue)	(Epic 6592402)	66	1993	0	1993	
SONNY, REAL NAME SALVATORE BONO B: 16 FEB 1935, DETROIT							
Sonny Charles	Male Vocal/Instrumental Group from the USA						
1	Put It In A Magazine		0	1963	40	1963	(HIGHRISE 2001)
2	Black Pearl		0	1969	13	1969	(A&M 1053)
3	Proud Mary	(A&M AMS 769)	30	1969	69	1969	(A&M 1127)
	HITS 2-3 ARE CREDITED TO SONNY CHARLES & THE CHECKMATES LTD • FORMER LEAD SINGER WITH THE CHECKMATES LTD AND HAILS FROM INDIANA						
Sonny Curtis	Male Vocal And Former Guitarist With Buddy Holly from the USA						
1	The Best Way To Hold A Girl		0	1953	28	1953	(CORAL 61023)
Sonny James	Male Vocalist, Real Name James Hugh Loden B: 1 May 1929 In Hackleburg, Alabama						
* 6	Young Love	(Capitol CL 14683)	11	1957	1	1957	(Capitol 3602)
8	First Date, First Kiss, First Love		0	1957	25	1957	(Capitol 3674)
	REST ARE C/W HITS						
Sonny Knight	Real Name Joseph C. Smith B: 1934 Illinois						
1	Confidential		0	1956	17	1956	(DOT 15507)
Sonny Thompson & His Three Sharps and Flats	Male R&B Pianist, B: 22 Aug 1923 Chicago						
* 1	Long Gone		0	1948	29	1948	(MIRACLE 126)
Sons Of The Pioneers	Country & Western Group Founded By Roy Rogers from the USA						
1	Tumbling Tumbleweeds		0	1934	13	1934	(Decca 5047)
2	Cool Water		0	1941	25	1941	(Decca 5939)
Sophia George	Female Vocalist from Jamaica						
1	Girlie Girlie	(Winner WIN 01)	7	1985	0	1985	
Sophie B. Hawkins	Female Vocalist from the USA						
1	Damn I Wish I Was Your Lover	(Columbia 6581077)	14	1992	5	1992	(Columbia 74164)
2	California Here I Come	(Columbia 6583177)	53	1992	0	1992	
3	I Want You	(Columbia 6587772)	49	1993	0	1993	
4	Right Beside You	(Columbia 6606915)	13	1994	0	1994	
5	Don't Don't Tell Me No	(Columbia 6610152)	36	1994	0	1994	
6	As I Lay Me Down	(Columbia 6612125)	24	1995	6	1996	(Columbia 77801)
7	Only Love (Ballad Of Sleeping)		0	1996	49	1996	(Columbia)
Sophie Lawrence	Female Vocalist from the UK						
1	Love's Unkind	(IQ ZB 44821)	21	1991	0	1991	

ISSUE	TITLE	UK LBL	UK POS	UK YEAR	US POS	US YEAR	US LBL
Sopwith Camel	Lead Singer With The Quintet Is Peter Kraemer						
1	Hello Hello		0	1967	26	1967	(Kama Sutra 217)
Sorrows	Male Vocal/Instrumental Group from the UK						
1	Take A Heart	(Piccadilly 7N 35260)	21	1965	0	1965	
Soul Asylum	Male Vocal/Instrumental Rock Group From Minneapolis, USA.						
* 1	Runaway Train	(Columbia 74966)	37	1993	5	1993	(Columbia 6593902)
2	Somebody To Shove	(Columbia 6596492)	34	1993	0	1993	
3	Runaway Train (Re-Entry)	(Columbia 6593902)	7	1993	0	1993	
4	Black Gold	(Columbia 6598442)	26	1994	0	1994	
5	Somebody To Shove (Re-Issue)	(Columbia 6602245)	32	1994	0	1994	
6	Misery	(Columbia 6621092)	30	1995	20	1995	(Columbia 77959)
7	Just Like Anyone	(Columbia 6624785)	52	1995	0	1995	
Soul Brothers	Male Vocal/Instrumental Group from the UK						
1	I Keep Ringing My Baby	(Decca F 12116)	42	1965	0	1965	
Soul Children	Names Shelbra Bennett, Anita Louis, Norman West & John Colbert						
1	I'll Be The Other Woman		0	1974	36	1974	(Stax 0182)
2	The Sweeter He Is		0	1969	52	1969	(Stax 0050)
Soul City Orchestra	Production/Instrumental Duo from the UK/Holland						
1	It's Jurassic	(London JURCD 1)	70	1993	0	1993	
Soul Family Sensation	Mixed Vocal/Instrumental Group from the UK						
1	I Don't Even Know If I Should Call You Baby	(One Little Indian 47 TP7)	49	1991	0	1991	
Soul For Real	Vocal Quartet from Long Island						
* 1	Candy Rain	(UPTOWN MCSTD 2052)	23	1995	2	1995	(UPTOWN 54906)
* 2	Every Little Thing I Do	(Uptown MCSTD48005)	31	1996	17	1995	(Uptown 55032)
Soul II Soul	Soul Group Led By Beresford Romeo & Neilee Hooper, Features Female Vocals By Caron Wheeler,						
Do'reen & Rose Windross							
1	Fairplay	(10 TEN 228)	63	1988	0	1988	
2	Feel Free	(10 TEN 236)	64	1988	0	1988	
* 3	Keep On Moving	(10 TEN 263)	5	1989	11	1989	(Virgin 99205)
* 4	Back To Life (However Do You Want Me)	(10 TEN 265)	1	1989	4	1989	(Virgin 99171)
5	Get A Life	(10 TEN 284)	3	1989	0	1989	
6	A Dream's A Dream	(10 TEN 300)	6	1990	0	1990	
7	Missing You	(10 TEN 345)	22	1990	0	1990	
8	Joy	(TEN TEN 350)	4	1992	0	1992	
9	Move Me No Mountain	(TEN TEN 400)	31	1992	0	1992	
10	Just Right	(TEN TEN 410)	38	1992	0	1992	
11	Wish	(Virgin VSCDG 1480)	24	1993	0	1993	
12	Love Enuff	(Virgin VSCDG 1527)	12	1995	0	1995	
13	I Care	(Virgin VSCDT 1560)	17	1995	0	1995	
14	Keep On Movin' (Re-Mix)	(Virgin VSCDT 1612)	31	1996	0	1996	
15	Represent	(Island CID 668)	39	1997	0	1997	
Soul Survivors	Soul Band from New York City/Philadelphia						
* 1	Expressway To Your Heart		0	1967	4	1967	(Crimson 1010)
2	Explosion (In Your Soul)		0	1968	33	1968	(Crimson 1012)
Souled Out	Mixed Vocal/Instrumental Group from the USA/UK/Italy						
1	In My Life	(Columbia 6578367)	75	1992	0	1992	
Sound Factory	Male Vocal/Instrumental Duo from Sweden						
1	2 The Sound Of One	Mixed Vocal/Instrumental Duo from the USA					
1	As I Am	(Cooltempo CDCOOL 280)	65	1993	0	1993	
Soundgarden	Male Vocal/Instrumental Group from the USA						
1	Jesus Christ Pose	(A&M AM 862)	30	1992	0	1992	
2	Rusty Cage	(A&M AM 874)	41	1992	0	1992	
3	Outshined	(A&M AM 0102)	52	1992	0	1992	
4	Spoonman	(A&M 5805392)	20	1994	0	1994	
5	The Day I Tried To Live	(A&M 5805952)	42	1994	0	1994	
6	Black Hole Sun	(A&M 5807532)	12	1994	0	1994	
7	Fell On Black Days	(A&M 5809472)	24	1995	0	1995	
8	Pretty Noose	(A&M 5816202)	14	1996	0	1996	
9	Burden In My Hand	(A&M 5818552)	33	1996	0	1996	
10	Blow Up The Outside World	(A&M 5819862)	40	1996	0	1996	

ISSUE TITLE	UK LBL	UK POS	UK YEAR	US POS	US YEAR	US LBL
Soundman & D. Lloydie With Mixed Vocal/Instrumental Group from the UK						
Elizabeth Troy						
1 Greater Love	(Sound Of Underground SOURCD 016)	49	1995	0	1995	
Sounds Incorporated Male Instrumental Group from the UK						
1 The Spartans	(Columbia DB 7239)	30	1964	0	1964	
2 Spanish Harlem	(Columbia DB 7321)	35	1964	0	1964	
Sounds Nice Male Instrumental Group With Tim Mycroft On Organ from the UK						
1 Love At First Sight (Je T'aime...Moi Non Plus)	(Parlophone R 5797)	18	1969	0	1969	
Sounds Of Blackness Mixed Gospel Choir from the USA						
1 Optimistic	(IPerspectivePERSS 786)	45	1991	0	1991	
2 The Pressure (Part 1)	(IPerspectivePERSS 816)	71	1991	0	1991	
3 Optimistic (Re-Issue)	(IPerspectivePERSS 849)	28	1992	0	1992	
4 Pressure (Part 1) (Re-Issue)	(IPerspectivePERSS 867)	49	1992	0	1992	
5 I'm Going All The Way	(IPerspective5874252)	27	1993	0	1993	
6 I Believe	(A&M 5874512)	17	1994	0	1994	
7 Gloryland	(Mercury MERCD 404)	36	1994	0	1994	
8 Everything Is Gonna Be Alright	(A&M 5874672)	29	1994	0	1994	
9 I'm Going All The Way (Re-Issue)	(A&M 5874832)	14	1995	0	1995	
10 Spirit	(A&M 5822312)	35	1997	0	1997	
Sounds Of Sunshine Names Walt, George & Warner Wilder from Los Angeles, Also Recorded As Wilder Brothers						
1 Love Means (You Never Have To Say You're Sorry)		0	1971	39	1971	(Ranwood 896)
Sounds Orchestral Producer John Schroeder & Orchestra from the UK						
1 Cast Your Fate To The Wind	(Piccadilly 7N 35206)	5	1964	10	1965	(Parkway 942)
2 Moonglow	(Piccadilly 7N 35248)	43	1965	0	1965	
Soundsource Male Production/Instrumental Group from the UK/sweden						
1 Take Me Up	(FFRR FX 177)	62	1992	0	1992	
Soundstation Male Producer from the UK						
1 Peace And Joy	(FFRREEDOM TABCD 224)	48	1995	0	1995	
Soup Dragons Male Vocal/Instrumental Group from Glasgow, Scotland.						
1 Can't Take No More	(RAW TV RTV 3)	65	1987	0	1987	
2 Soft As Your Face	(RAW TV RTV 4)	66	1987	0	1987	
3 I'm Free	(RAW TV RTV 9)	5	1990	0	1990	
4 Mother Universe	(Big Life BLR 30)	26	1990	0	1990	
5 Devine Thing	(Big Life BLR 68)	53	1992	35	1992	(BIG LIFE 865764)
HIT 3 IS CREDITED TO SOUP DRAGONS FEATURING JUNIOR REID • NAMES ARE SEAN DICKINSON, JIM MCCULLOCK, SUSHIL DADE & PAUL QUINN.						
Source Male Producer, Real Name John Truelove from the UK						
1 You Got The Love	(Truelove TLOVE 7001)	4	1991	0	1991	
2 Rock The House	(React 12REACT12)	63	1992	0	1992	
3 You Got The Love (Re-Issue)	(React CDREACT 89)	3	1997	0	1997	
4 Clouds	(XL RECORDINGSXLS 83CD)	38	1997	0	1997	
HITS 1, 3 ARE CREDITED TO SOURCE FEATURING CANDI STATON • HIT 2 IS CREDITED TO SOURCE FEATURING NICOLE						
Souther, Hillman, Furay Band Sextet With J.D. Souther, Chris Hillman & Richie Furay						
1 Fallin' In Love		0	1974	27	1974	(Asylum 45201)
Southlanders Male Vocal Group from the UK						
1 Alone	(Decca F 10946)	17	1957	0	1957	
Sovereign Collection Orchestra from the UK						
1 Mozart 40	(Capitol CL 15676)	27	1971	0	1971	
Sox Female Vocal Group from the UK						
1 Go For The Heart	(Living Beat LBECD 33)	47	1995	0	1995	
Space (1) Male Instrumental Group from France						
1 Magic Fly	(PYE International 7N 25746)	2	1977	0	1977	
Space (2) Male Vocal/Instrumental Group from the UK						
1 Neighbourhood	(GUT CDGUT 1)	56	1996	0	1996	
2 Female Of The Species	(GUT CDGUT 2)	14	1996	0	1996	
3 Me And You Versus The World	(GUT CXGUT 4)	9	1996	0	1996	
4 Neighbourhood (Re-Issue)	(GUT CXGUT 5)	11	1996	0	1996	
5 Dark Clouds	(GUT CDGUT 6)	14	1997	0	1997	
Space 2000 Male Vocal/Instrumental Duo from the UK						
1 Do U Wanna Funk	(WIRED WIRED 218)	50	1995	0	1995	

ISSUE	TITLE	UK LBL	UK POS	UK YEAR	US POS	US YEAR	US LBL
Space Kittens Male Instrumental/Production Group from the UK							
1	Storm	(HOOJ CHOONSHOOJCD 41)	58	1996	0	1996	
Space Monkeys Male Producer, Real Name Paul Goodchild from the UK							
1	Can't Stop Running	(Innervision A 3742)	53	1983	0	1983	
Spacebaby Male Producer Matt Darey from the UK							
1	Free Your Mind	(HOOJ CHOONS HOOJ 34CD)	55	1995	0	1995	
Spacehog Male Vocal/Instrumental Group from the UK							
1	In The Meantime	(SIRE 7559643162)	70	1996	32	1996	(SPACEHOG)
2	In The Meantime (Re-Entry)	(SIRE 7559643162)	27	1996	0	1996	
Spaghetti Surfers Male Instrumental/Production Duo from the UK							
1	Misirlou (Theme From *Pulp Fiction*)	(TEMPO TUNES CDTOON 4)	55	1995	0	1995	
Spagna Female Vocalist from Italy							
1	Call Me	(CBS 650279 7)	2	1987	0	1987	
2	Easy Lady	(CBS 651169 7)	62	1987	0	1987	
3	Every Girl And Boy	(CBS SPAG 1)	23	1988	0	1988	
Spandau Ballet Male Vocal/Instrumental Group from the UK							
1	To Cut A Long Story Short	(Reformation CHS 2473)	5	1980	0	1980	
2	The Freeze	(Reformation CHS 2486)	17	1981	0	1981	
3	Musclebound	(Reformation CHS 2509)	10	1981	0	1981	
4	Chant No.1 (I Don't Need This Pressure On)	(Reformation CHS 2528)	3	1981	0	1981	
5	Paint Me Down	(Chrysalis CHS 2560)	30	1981	0	1981	
6	She Loved Like Diamond	(Chrysalis CHS 2585)	49	1982	0	1982	
7	Instinction	(Chrysalis CHS 2602)	10	1982	0	1982	
8	Lifeline	(Chrysalis CHS 2642)	7	1982	0	1982	
9	Communication	(Reformation CHS 2662)	12	1983	0	1983	
10	True	(Reformation SPAN 1)	1	1983	4	1983	(Chrysalis 42720)
11	Gold	(Reformation SPAN 2)	2	1983	29	1983	(Chrysalis 42743)
12	Only When You Leave	(Reformation SPAN 3)	3	1984	34	1984	(Chrysalis 42792)
13	Only When You Leave (Re-Entry)	(Reformation SPAN 3)	74	1984	0	1984	
14	I'll Fly For You	(Reformation SPAN 4)	9	1984	0	1984	
15	Highly Strung	(Reformation SPAN 5)	15	1984	0	1984	
16	Round And Round	(Reformation SPAN 6)	18	1984	0	1984	
17	Fight For Ourselves	(Reformation A7264)	15	1986	0	1986	
18	Through The Barricades	(Reformation SPANS 1)	6	1986	0	1986	
19	How Many Lies	(Reformation SPANS 2)	34	1987	0	1987	
20	Raw	(CBS SPANS 3)	47	1988	0	1988	
21	Be Free With Your Love	(CBS SPANS 4)	42	1989	0	1989	
	LEAD SINGER WITH THE QUINTET IS TONY HADLEY, WITH JOHN KEEBLE, STEVE NORMAN, GARY & MARTIN KEMP						
Spaniels Male Vocal Doo-Wop Quintet Led By Pookie Hudson, from the USA							
+ 1	Baby It's You		0	1953	10	1953	(Chance141)
2	Goodnite Sweetheart Goodnite		0	1954	24	1954	(VEE-JAY 107)
Spanky & Our Gang Mixed Vocal/Instrumental Group From Chicago, Lead Vocals Elaine 'Spanky' McFarlane B: 19 Jun 1942 In Peoria, Illinois							
* 1	Sunday Will Never Be The Same		0	1967	9	1967	(Mercury 72679)
2	Making Every Minute Count		0	1967	31	1967	(Mercury 72714)
3	Lazy Day		0	1967	14	1967	(Mercury 72732)
4	Sunday Mornin'		0	1968	30	1968	(Mercury 72765)
5	Like To Get To Know You		0	1968	17	1968	(Mercury 72795)
Sparklehorse Male Vocal/Instrumental Group from the USA							
1	Rainmaker	(Capitol CDCL 777)	61	1996	0	1996	
Sparks Male Vocal/Instrumental Sibling Duo from Los Angeles, USA							
1	This Town Ain't Big Enough For The Both Of Us	(Island WIP 6193)	2	1974	0	1974	
2	Amateur Hour	(Island WIP 6203)	7	1974	0	1974	
3	Never Turn Your Back On Mother Earth	(Island WIP 6211)	13	1974	0	1974	
4	Something For The Girl With Everything	(Island WIP 6221)	17	1975	0	1975	
5	Get In The Swing	(Island WIP 6236)	27	1975	0	1975	
6	Looks Looks Looks	(Island WIP 6249)	26	1975	0	1975	
7	The Number One Song In Heaven	(Virgin VS 244)	14	1979	0	1979	
8	Beat The Clock	(Virgin VS 270)	10	1979	0	1979	
9	Tryouts For The Human Race	(Virgin VS 289)	45	1979	0	1979	
10	When Do I Get To Sing 'My Way'	(LOGIC 74321234472)	38	1994	0	1994	
11	When I Kiss You (I Hear Charlie Parker)	(Arista 74321264272)	36	1995	0	1995	

ISSUE	TITLE	UK LBL	UK POS	UK YEAR	US POS	US YEAR	US LBL
12	When Do I Get To Sing 'My Way' (Re-Issue)	(Arista 74321274002)	32	1995	0	1995	
13	Now That I Own The BBC	(Arista 74321348672)	60	1996	0	1996	
	FOR THE FIRST SIX HITS THEY WERE MALE VOCAL/INSTRUMENTAL GROUP FROM THE UK/USA. STARTED OUT AS HALF NELSON						
Spear Of Destiny Male Vocal/Instrumental Group from the UK							
1	The Wheel	(Epic A 3372)	59	1983	0	1983	
2	Prisoner Of Love	(Epic A 4068)	59	1984	0	1984	
3	Liberator	(Epic A 4310)	67	1984	0	1984	
4	All My Love (Ask Nothing)	(Epic A 6333)	61	1985	0	1985	
5	Come Back	(Epic 6445)	55	1985	0	1985	
6	Strangers In Our Town	(10 TEN 148)	49	1987	0	1987	
7	Never Take Me Alive	(10 TEN 162)	14	1987	0	1987	
8	Was That You	(10 TEN 173)	55	1987	0	1987	
9	The Traveller	(10 TEN 189)	44	1987	0	1987	
10	So In Love With You	(Virgin VS 1123)	36	1988	0	1988	
Spearhead Male Vocal/Instrumental Group from the USA							
1	Of Course You Can	(Capitol CDCL 733)	74	1994	0	1994	
2	Hole In The Bucket	(Capitol CDCL 742)	55	1995	0	1995	
3	People In Tha Middle	(Capitol CDCL752)	49	1995	0	1995	
4	Why Oh Why	(Capitol CDCL 785)	45	1997	0	1997	
Specials Male Vocal/Instrumental Group from the UK							
1	Gangsters	(2 TONE CHS TT 1)	6	1979	0	1979	
2	A Message To You Rudy / Nite Club	(2 TONE CHS TT 5)	10	1979	0	1979	
3	The Special A.K.A Live (EP)	(2 TONE CHS TT 7)	1	1980	0	1980	
4	Rat Race / Rude Boys Outa Jail	(2 TONE CHS TT 11)	5	1980	0	1980	
5	Sterotype / International Jet Set	(2 TONE CHSTT13)	6	1980	0	1980	
6	Do Nothing / Maggie's Farm	(2 TONE CHS TT16)	4	1980	0	1980	
7	Ghost Town	(2 TONE CHS TT17)	1	1981	0	1981	
8	The Boiler	(2 TONE CHS TT 18)	35	1982	0	1982	
9	Racist Friend	(2 TONE CHS TT 25)	60	1983	0	1983	
10	Nelson Mandela	(2 TONE CHS TT 26)	9	1984	0	1984	
11	What I Like Most About You Is Your Girlfriend	(2 TONE CHS TT 27)	51	1984	0	1984	
12	Hypocrite	(KUFF KUFFD 3)	66	1996	0	1996	
Spectrum Male Production/Instrumental Group from the UK							
1	True Love Will Find You In The End	(Slvertone ORE44)	70	1992	0	1992	
Speech Male Vocalist from the USA							
1	Like Marvin Gaye Said (What's Goin' On)	(Cooltempo CDCOOL 314)	35	1996	0	1996	
Speedy Male Vocal/Instrumental Group from the UK							
1	Boy Wonder	(Boiler House Boil 2CD)	56	1996	0	1996	
Spencer Davis Group Male Vocal/Instrumental Group from the UK							
1	I Can't Stand It	(Fontana TF 499)	47	1964	0	1964	
2	Every Little Bit Hurts	(Fontana TF 530)	43	1965	0	1965	
3	Every Little Bit Hurts (Re-Entry)	(Fontana TF 530)	41	1965	0	1965	
4	Strong Love	(Fontana TF 571)	50	1965	0	1965	
5	Strong Love (Re-Entry)	(Fontana TF 571)	44	1965	0	1965	
6	Keep On Running	(Fontana TF 632)	1	1965	0	1965	
7	Somebody Help Me	(Fontana TF 679)	1	1966	0	1966	
8	When I Come Home	(Fontana TF 739)	12	1966	0	1966	
* 9	Gimme Some Lovin'	(Fontana TF 762)	2	1966	7	1967	(United Artists50108)
* 10	I'm A Man	(Fontana TF 785)	9	1967	10	1967	(United Artists50144)
11	Time Seller	(Fontana TF 854)	30	1967	0	1967	
12	Mr. Second Class	(United ArtistsUP 1203)	35	1968	0	1968	
	SINGER/GUITARIST, DAVIS, B: 14 JUL 1941, FORMED THE GROUP IN 1963						
Spencer Ross Male Conductor/Arranger, Real Name Robert Mersey from the USA							
1	Tracy's Theme		0	1960	13	1960	(Columbia 41532)
Sphinx Male Vocal/Instrumental Group from the UK/USA							
1	What Hope Have I	(Champion ChampCD 318)	43	1995	0	1995	
Spice Girls Female Vocal Quintet, Geri Halliwell, Emme Bunton, Melanie Brown, Melanie Chisholm & Victoria Adams from the UK							
* 1	Wannabe	(Virgin VSCDX 1588)	1	1996	1	1997	(Virgin 38579)
2	Wannabe (Re-Entry)	(Virgin CSCDX 1588)	30	1996	0	1996	
3	Say You'll Be There	(Virgin VSCDT 1601)	1	1996	5	1997	(Virgin 38592)
4	2 Become 1	(Virgin VSCDT 1607)	1	1996	0	1996	
* 5	Mama /Who Do You Think You Are	(Virgin VSCDT1623)	1	1997	0	1997	

ISSUE	TITLE	UK LBL	UK POS	UK YEAR	US POS	US YEAR	US LBL
6	2 Become 1 (Re-Entry)	(Virgin VSCDT	54	1997	0	1997	
7	Say You'll Be There		0	1997	3	1997	(Virgin 38592)

Spider (1) Male Vocal/Instrumental Group from the UK

ISSUE	TITLE	UK LBL	UK POS	UK YEAR	US POS	US YEAR	US LBL
1	Why D'ya Lie To Me	(RCA 313)	65	1983	0	1983	
2	Here We Go Rock N' Roll	(A&M AM 180)	57	1984	0	1984	

Spider (2) New York Based Rock Quintet

ISSUE	TITLE	UK LBL	UK POS	UK YEAR	US POS	US YEAR	US LBL
1	New Romance (It's A Mystery)		0	1980	39	1980	(Dreamland 100)

Spike Jones & His City Slickers Male Drummer/Vocalist, Real Name Lindley Armstrong Jones B: 14 Dec 1911 Long Beach, California.

ISSUE	TITLE	UK LBL	UK POS	UK YEAR	US POS	US YEAR	US LBL
* 2	Der Fuehrer's Face		0	1942	3	1942	(Bluebird 11586)
* 5	Cocktails For Two (From Murder At The Vanities)		0	1945	4	1945	(Victor 1628)
9	Hawaiian War Chant (Ta-Hu-Wa-Hu-Wai)		0	1946	8	1900	(RCA Victor 1893)
10	William Tell Overture		0	1948	6	1948	(RCA Victor 2861)
* 11	All I Want For Christmas (Is My Two Front Teeth)		0	1948	1	1948	(RCA Victor 3177)
12	Ya Wanna Buy A Bunny?		0	1949	24	1949	(RCA Victor 3359)
13	Dance Of The Hours (Rca Victor 45-2992)		0	1949	13	1949	(RCA Victor 78-3516)
14	All I Want For Christmas (Is My Two Front Teeth) (Re-Entry)		0	1950	18	1950	(RCA Victor 78-3177)
15	Chinese Mule Train (From *Singing Guns*)		0	1950	16	1950	(RCA Victor 2741)
16	Rudolph, The Red-Nosed Reindeer		0	1950	7	1950	(RCA Victor 3934)
17	Tennessee Waltz		0	1951	13	1951	(RCA Victor 4011)
18	I Saw Mommy Kissing Santa Claus		0	1952	4	1952	(RCA Victor 5067)
19	Winter		0	1953	23	1953	(RCA Victor 5067)
20	I Went To Your Wedding		0	1953	20	1953	(RCA Victor 5107)

THE CITY SLICKERS ARE A NOVELTY BAND   OBITUARY: D: 1 MAY 1965, AGED 52.

Spin Doctors Male Vocal/Instrumental Quartet from New York

ISSUE	TITLE	UK LBL	UK POS	UK YEAR	US POS	US YEAR	US LBL
1	Little Miss Can't Be Wrong	(Epic 6584892)	23	1993	17	1992	(Epic/Association 74473)
2	Two Princes	(Epic 6591452)	3	1993	7	1993	(Epic/Association 74804)
3	Jimmy Olsen's Blues	(Epic 6597582)	40	1993	0	1993	
4	What Time Is It	(Epic 6599552)	56	1993	0	1993	
5	Cleopatra's Cat	(Epic 6604192)	29	1994	0	1994	
6	You Let Your Heart Go Too Fast	(Epic 6606612)	66	1994	0	1994	
7	Mary Jane	(Epic 6609772)	55	1994	0	1994	
8	She Used To Be Mine	(Epic 6632682)	55	1996	0	1996	

Spinal Tap Male Vocal/Instrumental Group from the USA/UK

ISSUE	TITLE	UK LBL	UK POS	UK YEAR	US POS	US YEAR	US LBL
1	Bitch School	(MCA MCS 1624)	35	1992	0	1992	
2	The Majesty Of Rock	(MCA MCS 1629)	61	1992	0	1992	

Spiral Starecase Names Pat Upton, Dick Lopes, Bobby Raymond, Havey Kaplan & Vinny Parello

ISSUE	TITLE	UK LBL	UK POS	UK YEAR	US POS	US YEAR	US LBL
* 1	More Today Than Yesterday		0	1969	12	1969	(Columbia 44741)

Spiral Tribe Mixed Vocal/Instrumental Group from the UK

ISSUE	TITLE	UK LBL	UK POS	UK YEAR	US POS	US YEAR	US LBL
1	Breach The Peace (EP)	(Butterfly BLRT 79)	66	1992	0	1992	
2	Forward The Revolution	(Butterfly BLRT 85)	70	1992	0	1992	

Spirit Lead Singer With The Rock Group Is Jay Ferguson

ISSUE	TITLE	UK LBL	UK POS	UK YEAR	US POS	US YEAR	US LBL
1	I Got A Line On You		0	1969	25	1969	(ODE 115)

Spirits Mixed Vocal Duo from the UK

ISSUE	TITLE	UK LBL	UK POS	UK YEAR	US POS	US YEAR	US LBL
1	Don't Bring Me Down	(MCA MCSTD 2018)	31	1994	0	1994	
2	Spirit Inside	(MCA MCSTD 2045)	39	1995	0	1995	

Spiritualized Male Vocal/Instrumental Group from the UK

ISSUE	TITLE	UK LBL	UK POS	UK YEAR	US POS	US YEAR	US LBL
1	Anyway You Want Me / Step Into The Breeze	(DedicatedZB 43783)	75	1990	0	1990	
2	Run	(Dedicated Spirit 002)	59	1991	0	1991	
3	Medication	(Dedicated Spirit 005T)	55	1992	0	1992	
4	Electric Mainline	(Dedicated Spirit 007CD)	49	1993	0	1993	
5	Let It Flow	(Dedicated Spirit 009CD1)	30	1995	0	1995	
6	Electricity	(Dedicated Spirit 012CD1)	32	1997	0	1997	

HIT 5 IS CREDITED TO SPIRITUALIZED ELECTRIC MAINLINE

Spiro & Wix Male Instrumental Duo from the UK

ISSUE	TITLE	UK LBL	UK POS	UK YEAR	US POS	US YEAR	US LBL
1	Tara's Theme	(EMI PREMIER PRESCD 4)	29	1996	0	1996	

Spitting Image Mixed Vocal Puppets from the UK

ISSUE	TITLE	UK LBL	UK POS	UK YEAR	US POS	US YEAR	US LBL
1	The Chicken Song	(Virgin SPIT 1)	1	1986	0	1986	
2	The Chicken Song (Re-Entry)	(Virgin SPIT 1)	67	1986	0	1986	
3	Santa Claus Is On The Dole/First Atheist Tabernacle Choir	(Virgin VS 921)	22	1986	0	1986	

Splinter Male Vocal/Instrumental Duo from the UK

ISSUE	TITLE	UK LBL	UK POS	UK YEAR	US POS	US YEAR	US LBL
1	Costafine Town	(Dark Horse AMS 7135)	17	1974	0	1974	

ISSUE	TITLE	UK LBL	UK POS	UK YEAR	US POS	US YEAR	US LBL
Split Enz Male Vocal/Instrumental Group from the UK/New Zealand							
1	I Got You	(A&M AMS 7546)	12	1980	0	1980	
2	History Never Repeats	(A&M AMS 8128)	63	1981	0	1981	
Splodgenessabounds Male Vocal/Instrumental Group from the UK							
1	Two Pints Of Lager And A Packet Of Crisps	(DERAM BUM 1)	7	1980	0	1980	
2	Two Little Boys / Horse	(DERAM ROLF 1)	26	1980	0	1980	
3	Cowpunk Medlum	(DERAM BUM 3)	69	1981	0	1981	
Spokesmen Names Dave White, Roy Gilmore & Johnny Madara							
1	The Dawn Of Correction		0	1965	36	1965	(Decca 31844)
Sponge Male Vocal/Instrumental Group from the USA							
1	Plowed	(Columbia 6623162)	74	1995	0	1995	
Spooky Male Vocal/Instrumental Duo from the UK							
1	Schmoo	(Guerilla GRRR45CD)	72	1993	0	1993	
Sportsmen Vocal Group from the USA							
1	What Do You Do In The Infantry?		0	1943	22	1943	(Decca 18562)
2	Tutti Tutti Pizzicato		0	1948	24	1948	(Capitol 496)
3	You Can't Be True, Dear		0	1948	6	1948	(Capitol 15077)
4	Toolie Oolie Doolie		0	1948	11	1948	(Capitol 15077)
5	Woody Woodpecker		0	1948	2	1948	(Capitol 15145)
	HIT 5 IS CREDITED TO SPORTSMEN AND MEL BLANC						
SPOTNICKS MALE INSTRUMENTAL GROUP FROM SWEDEN							
1	Orange Blossom Special	(Oriole CB 1724)	29	1962	0	1962	
2	The Rocket Man	(riole CB 1755)	38	1962	0	1962	
3	Hava Nagila	(Oriole CB 1790)	13	1963	0	1963	
4	Just Listen To My Heart	(Oriole CB 1818)	36	1963	0	1963	
Springfields Mixed Vocal/Instrumental Group from the UK							
1	Breakaway	(Philips BF 1168)	31	1961	0	1961	
2	Bambino	(Philips BF 1178)	16	1961	0	1961	
* 3	Silver Threads And Golden Needles		0	1962	20	1962	(Philips 40038)
4	Island Of Dreams	(Philips 326557 BF)	5	1962	0	1962	
5	Say I Won't Be There	(Philips 326577 BF)	5	1963	0	1963	
6	Come On Home	(Philips BF 1263)	31	1963	0	1963	
	NAMES MARY O'BRIEN & HER BROTHER TOM WITH TIM FEILD TIM WAS REPLACED BY MIKE LONGHURST-PICKWORTH						
Springwater Male Instrumentalist, Real Name Phil Cordell from the UK							
1	I Will Return	(Polydor 2058 141)	5	1971	0	1971	
Spyder Turner Real Name Dwight D. Turner B: 1947 Beckley, West Virginia							
1	Stand By Me		0	1967	12	1967	(MGM 13617)
Spyro Gyra Jazz-Pop Band Formed In Buffalo 1975							
1	Morning Dance	(Infinity INF 111)	17	1979	24	1979	(Infinity 50011)
Squeeze Male Vocal/Instrumental Band from the UK, Led By Chris Difford							
1	Take Me I'm Yours	(A&M AMS 7335)	19	1978	0	1978	
2	Bang Bang	(A&M AMS 7360)	49	1978	0	1978	
3	Goodbye Girl	(A&M AMS 7398)	63	1978	0	1978	
4	Cool For Cats	(A&M AMS 7426)	2	1979	0	1979	
5	Up The Junction	(A&M AMS 7444)	2	1979	0	1979	
6	Slap And Tickle	(A&M AMS 7466)	24	1979	0	1979	
7	Another Nail In My Heart	(A&M AMS 7507)	17	1980	0	1980	
8	Pulling Mussels (From The Shell)	(A&M AMS 753)	44	1980	0	1980	
9	Is That Love	(A&M AMS 8129)	35	1981	0	1981	
10	Tempted	(A&M AMS 8147)	41	1981	0	1981	
11	Labelled With Love	(A&M AMS 8166)	4	1981	0	1981	
12	Black Coffee In Bed	(A&M AMS 8219)	51	1982	0	1982	
13	Annie Get Your Gun	(A&M AMS 8259)	43	1982	0	1982	
14	Last Time Forever	(A&M AM 255)	45	1985	0	1985	
15	Hourglass	(A&M AM 400)	16	1987	15	1987	(A&M 2967)
16	Trust Me To Open My Mouth	(A&M AM 412)	72	1987	0	1987	
17	853-5937		0	1988	32	1988	(A&M 2994)
18	Cool For Cats (Re-Issue)	(A&M AM 860)	62	1992	0	1992	
19	Third Rail	(A&M 5803372)	39	1993	0	1993	
20	Some Fantastic Place	(A&M 5803792)	73	1993	0	1993	
21	This Summer	(A&M 5811892)	36	1995	0	1995	
22	Electric Trains	(A&M 5812692)	44	1995	0	1995	

ISSUE	TITLE	UK LBL	UK POS	UK YEAR	US POS	US YEAR	US LBL
23	Heaven Knows	(A&M 5816052)	27	1996	0	1996	
24	This Summer (Re-Mix)	(A&M 5818372)	32	1996	0	1996	

THE WERE ORIGINALLY KNOWN AS THE UK SQUEEZE TO AVOID CONFUSION WITH THE BAND TIGHT SQUEEZE.

Ssgt Barry Sadler   Male Vocalist, B: 1 Nov 1940 Carlsbad, New Mexico

* 1	Ballad Of The Green Berets	(RCA 1506)	24	1966	1	1966	(RCA 8739)
2	The A Team		0	1966	28	1966	(RCA 8804)

OBITUARY : D: 5 NOV 1989 SUFFERED HEART FAILURE AFTER BEING SHOT BY AN INTRUDER AT HIS HOME.

St. Andrews Chorale   Church Choir from the UK

1	Cloud 99 (Soleado)	(Decca F 13617)	31	1976	0	1976	

St. Cecilia   Male Vocal/Instrumental Group from the UK

1	Leap Up And Down	(Polydor 2058 104)	12	1971	0	1971	

St. Germain   Male Producer from France

1	Alabama Blues (Revisited)	(F Communications F 050CD)	50	1996	0	1996	

St. Johns College School Choir   School Choir And Military Band from the UK

1	The Queen's Birthday Song	(Columbia Q1)	40	1986	0	1986	

St. Louis Union   Male Vocal/Instrumental Group from the UK

1	Girl	(Decca F 12318)	11	1966	0	1966	

St. Philips Choir   Choir from the UK

1	Sing For Ever	(BBC RESL 222)	49	1987	0	1987	

St. Winifred's School Choir   School Choir from the UK

1	There's No One Quite Like Grandma	(MFP FP 900)	1	1980	0	1980	

Stabbs   Male Production/Instrumental Group from the USA/Finland/Cameroon

1	Joy And Happiness	(HI-LIFE HICD 3)	65	1994	0	1994	

Staccato   Mixed Vocal/Instrumental Duo from the UK/holland

1	I Wanna Know	(Multiplu CDMULTY 11)	65	1996	0	1996	

Stacey Q   Real Name Stacey Swain from Los Angeles

1	Two Of Hearts		0	1986	3	1986	(Atlantic 89381)
2	We Connect		0	1987	35	1987	(Atlantic 89331)

Stacy Earl   Female Vocalist, B; 28 Dec 1962 Boston, USA

1	Love Me All Up		0	1991	26	1991	(RCA 62116)
2	Romeo & Juliet		0	1992	27	1992	(RCA 62192)

HIT 2 IS CREDITED TO STACY EARL FEATURING THE WILD PAIR

Stacy Lattisaw   Female Vocalist, B: 12 Nov 1966 Washington D.C.

1	Let Me Be Your Angel		0	1980	21	1980	(Cotillion 46001)
2	Jump To The Beat	(Atlantic/Cotillion K 11496)	3	1980	0	1980	
3	Dynamite	(Atlantic K 11554)	51	1980	0	1980	
4	Love On A Two Way Street		0	1981	26	1981	(Cotillion 46015)
5	Miracles		0	1983	40	1983	(Cotillion 99855)

Staiffi & His Mustafas   Male Vocal/Instrumental Group From France

1	Mustafa	(PYE International 7N 25057)	43	1960	0	1960	

Stakka Bo   Male Producer from Sweden

1	Here We Go	(Polydor PZCD 280)	13	1993	0	1993	
2	Down The Drain	(Polydor PZCD 301)	64	1993	0	1993	

Stallion   Lead Singer With The Quintet Is Buddy Stephens

1	Old Fashioned Boy (You're The One)		0	1977	37	1977	(Casablanca 877)

Stamford Bridge   Male Vocal Group from the UK

1	Chelsea	(Penny Farthing Pen 715)	47	1970	0	1970	

Stampeders   Names Rick Dodson, Ronnie King & Kim Berly, Originally A Sextet In 1963

1	Sweet City Woman		0	1971	8	1971	(Bell 45120)
2	Hit The Road Jack		0	1976	40	1976	(Quality 501)

Stan   Male Vocal/Instrumental Duo from the UK

1	Suntan	(HUG CDBUM 1)	40	1993	0	1993	

Stan Campbell   Male Vocalist from the UK

1	Years Go By	(WEA YZ 127)	65	1987	0	1987	

Stan Freberg   Male Vocalist, B: 7 Aug 1926 Pasadena, California

1	John And Marsha		0	1951	21	1951	(Capitol 1356)
2	I've Got You Under My Skin (From Born To Dance)		0	1951	11	1951	(Capitol 1711)
3	That's My Boy		0	1951	30	1951	(Capitol 1711)
4	Try		0	1952	15	1952	(Capitol 2029)

ISSUE	TITLE	UK LBL	UK POS	UK YEAR	US POS	US YEAR	US LBL
5	The World Is Waiting For The Sunrise		0	1952	24	1952	(Capitol 2279)
* 6	St George And The Dragonet		0	1953	1	1953	(Capitol 2596)
7	Little Blue Riding Hood		0	1953	9	1953	(Capitol 2596)
8	C'est Si Bon		0	1953	13	1953	(Capitol 2677)
9	Christmas Dragnet		0	1953	13	1953	(Capitol 2671)
10	Dear John And Marsha Letter		0	1954	23	1954	(Capitol 2677)
11	Point Of Order		0	1954	15	1954	(Capitol 2838)
12	Sh-Boom	(Capitol CL14187)	15	1954	14	1954	(Capitol 2929)
13	The Yellow Rose Of Texas		0	1955	16	1955	(Capitol 3249)
14	Rock Island Line / Heartbreak Hotel	(Capitol CL 14608)	24	1956	0	1956	
15	Rock Island Line / Hearbreak Hotel (Re-Entry)	(Capitol CL 14608)	29	1956	0	1956	
16	Banana Boat (Day-O)		0	1957	25	1957	(Capitol 3687)
17	Wun'erful, Wun'erful! (Sides Uh-One & Uh-Two)		0	1957	32	1957	(Capitol 3815)
18	The Old Payola Roll Blues	(Capitol CL 15122)	40	1960	0	1960	

Stan Getz Male Saxophonist, Real Name Stan Gayetzsky B: 2 Feb 1927 In Philadelphia

ISSUE	TITLE	UK LBL	UK POS	UK YEAR	US POS	US YEAR	US LBL
* 1	Desafinado	(HMV POP 1061)	11	1962	15	1962	(Verve 10323)
* 2	The Girl From Ipanema (Garota De Ipanema)	(Verve VS 520)	29	1964	5	1964	(Verve 10323)
3	The Girl From Ipanema (Re-Issue)	(Verve IPA 1)	55	1984	0	1984	

OBITUARY: STAN D: 6 JUN 1991 LIVER CANCER.

Stan Kenton Orchestra Male Orchestra Leader, B: 19 Feb 1912 From Wichita, Kansas

ISSUE	TITLE	UK LBL	UK POS	UK YEAR	US POS	US YEAR	US LBL
7	Artistry Jumps		0	1946	13	1946	(Capitol 229)
8	Just A-Sittin' And A-Rockin'		0	1946	16	1946	(Capitol 229)
* 9	Shoo-Fly Pie And Apple Pan Dowdy		0	1946	8	1946	(Capitol 235)
10	His Feet Too Big For De Bed		0	1947	12	1947	(Capitol 361)
11	Across The Alley From The Alamo		0	1947	11	1947	(Capitol 387)
12	Curiosity		0	1947	23	1947	(Capitol 15005)
13	I Told Ya I Love Ya, Now Get Out		0	1948	26	1948	(Capitol 15018)
14	Lonely Woman		0	1948	23	1948	(Capitol 10125)
15	How High The Moon		0	1948	20	1948	(Capitol 15117)
16	Orange Coloured Sky		0	1950	5	1950	(Capitol 1184)
17	September Song		0	1951	17	1951	(Capitol 1480)
18	Laura		0	1951	12	1951	(Capitol 1704)
19	Delicado		0	1952	25	1952	(Capitol 2040)
20	And The Bull Walked Around, Olay		0	1953	30	1953	(Capitol 2388)
21	Hush-A-Bye		0	1953	27	1953	(Capitol 2373)
22	The Creep		0	1954	28	1954	(Capitol 2685)
23	Mama Sang A Song		0	1962	32	1962	(Capitol 4847)

Stan Ridgway Male Vocalist from the USA

ISSUE	TITLE	UK LBL	UK POS	UK YEAR	US POS	US YEAR	US LBL
1	Camouflage	(IRS IRM 114)	4	1986	0	1986	

Standells Lead Singer With The Quartet Is Dick Dodd

ISSUE	TITLE	UK LBL	UK POS	UK YEAR	US POS	US YEAR	US LBL
1	Dirty Water		0	1966	11	1966	(TOWER 185)

Stanley Clarke Male R&B Jazz Bassist/Violinist/Cellist, B: 30 Jun 1951 Philadelphia

ISSUE	TITLE	UK LBL	UK POS	UK YEAR	US POS	US YEAR	US LBL
1	Sweet Baby		0	1981	19	1981	(Epic 01052)

Staple Singers Mixed Vocal Group from the USA

ISSUE	TITLE	UK LBL	UK POS	UK YEAR	US POS	US YEAR	US LBL
* 1	Heavy Makes You Happy (Sha-Na-Boom Boom)		0	1971	27	1971	(Stax 0083)
* 2	Respect Yourself		0	1971	12	1971	(Stax 0104)
* 3	I'll Take You There	(STAK 2025 110)	30	1972	1	1972	(STAK 0125)
4	This World		0	1972	38	1972	(STAK 0137)
5	Oh La De Da		0	1973	33	1973	(Stax 0156)
* 6	If You're Ready (Come Go With Me)	(Stax 2025 224)	34	1974	9	1973	(Stax 0179)
7	Touch A Hand, Make A Friend		0	1974	23	1974	(Stax 0196)
* 8	Let's Do It Again		0	1975	1	1975	(CURTOM 0109)

REAL NAME ROEBUCK 'POP' STAPLES, B: 28 DEC 1914, AND DAUGHTERS MAVIS, CLEO, & YVONNE.

Starbuck Lead Singer With The Septet Is Bruce Blackman

ISSUE	TITLE	UK LBL	UK POS	UK YEAR	US POS	US YEAR	US LBL
1	Moonlight Feels Right		0	1976	3	1976	(Private Stock 45039)
2	Everybody Be Dancin'		0	1977	38	1977	(Private Stock 45144)

32Stardust Mixed Vocal/Instrumental Group from Sweden

ISSUE	TITLE	UK LBL	UK POS	UK YEAR	US POS	US YEAR	US LBL
1	Ariana	(Satril SAT 120)	42	1977	0	1977	

Stargard Female Vocal Trio from the USA, Names Janice Williams, Debra Anderson & Rochelle Runnells

ISSUE	TITLE	UK LBL	UK POS	UK YEAR	US POS	US YEAR	US LBL
1	Theme From Which Way Is Up	(MCA 346)	19	1978	21	1978	(MCA 40825)
2	Love Is So Easy	(MCA 354)	45	1978	0	1978	
3	What You Waiting For	(MCA 382)	39	1978	0	1978	

ISSUE	TITLE	UK LBL	UK POS	UK YEAR	US POS	US YEAR	US LBL
Stargazers	**(1)** Male Vocal/Instrumental Group from the UK						
1	Broken Wings	(Decca F 10047)	11	1953	0	1953	
2	Broken Wings (Re-Entry)	(Decca F 10047)	1	1953	0	1953	
3	I See The Moon	(Decca F 10213)	1	1954	0	1954	
4	The Happy Wanderer	(Decca F 10259)	12	1954	0	1954	
5	Somebody	(Decca F 10437)	20	1955	0	1955	
6	Crazy Otto Rag	(Decca F 10523)	18	1955	0	1955	
7	Close The Door	(Decca F 10594)	6	1955	0	1955	
8	Twenty Tiny Fingers	(Decca F 10626)	4	1955	0	1955	
9	Hot Diggity	(Decca F 10731)	28	1956	0	1956	
Stargazers	**(2)** Male Vocal/Instrumental Group from the UK						
1	Groove Baby Groove	(Epic EPC A 1924)	56	1982	0	1982	
Starjets	Male Vocal/Instrumental Group from the UK						
1	War Stories	(Epic EPC 7770)	51	1979	0	1979	
Starland Vocal Band	Mixed Vocal Group from the USA						
* 1	Afternoon Delight	(RCA 2716)	18	1976	1	1976	(Windsong 10588)
Starlets	Names: Dynetta Boone, Jane Hall, Maxine Edwards, Mickey Mckinney, Jeanette Miles & Bernice Williams						
1	Better Tell Him No		0	1961	38	1961	(PAM 1003)
2	I Sold My Heart To The Junkman		0	1962	15	1962	(Newtown 5000)
Starlight	Male Production/Instrumental Group from Italy						
1	Numero Uno	(Citybeat CBE 742)	9	1989	0	1989	
Starlighters	Vocal Group, Sang Backing Vocals With Jo Stafford						
1	Maria From Bahia		0	1948	23	1948	(Capitol 15114)
2	I've Got My Love To Keep Me Warm		0	1949	26	1949	(Capitol 15330)
3	Room Full Of Roses		0	1949	21	1949	(Capitol 617)
4	Rag Mop		0	1950	12	1950	(Capitol 844)
Starpoint	Ernesto, George, Orlando & Gregory Phillips With Renee Diggs & Kayode Adeyemo						
1	Object Of My Desire		0	1985	25	1985	(Elektra 69621)
Starsound	Male Producer, Real Name Jaap Eggermont With Mixed Session Singers from Holland.						
* 1	Stars On 45 (Vol 1)	(CBS A 1102)	2	1981	1	1981	(Rsdio3810)
2	Stars On 45 (Vol 2)	(CBS A 1407)	7	1981	0	1981	
3	Stars On 45 (Vol 3)	(CBS A 1521)	17	1981	0	1981	
4	Stars On Stevie (Stevie Wonder)	(CBS A 2041)	14	1982	28	1982	(RADIO 4019)
Startrax	Mixed Session Group from the UK						
1	Startrax Club Disco	(PICKSY KSY 1001)	18	1981	0	1981	
Starturn On 45 (Pints)	Male Vocal Group from the UK						
1	Starturn On 45 (Pints)	(V TONE V TONE 003)	45	1981	0	1981	
2	Pump Up The Bitter	(Pacific Drink 1)	12	1988	0	1988	
Starvation	Multi-National Mixed Vocal/Instrumental Assembly						
1	Starvation / Tam-Tam Pour L'ethiope	(ZARJAZZ JAZZ 3)	33	1985	0	1985	
Starving Souls	Male Vocal/Instrumental Group from the UK						
1	I Be The Prophet (EP)	(Durban PoisonDPCE 001)	66	1995	0	1995	
Starz	Lead Singer With The Quartet Is Michael Lee Smith						
1	Cherry Baby		0	1977	33	1977	(Capitol 4399)
Statler Brothers	Male Quartet from Staunton, Virginia, Originally Formed As The Kingsmen In 1955						
1	Flowers On The Wall	(CBS 201976)	38	1966	4	1965	(Columbia 43315)
	REST ARE C/W HITS • OBITUARY : DEWITT D: 15 AUG 1990 FROM CROHN'S DISEASE.						
Status IV	Male Vocal Group from the USA						
1	You Ain't Really Down	(TMT TMT 4)	56	1983	0	1983	
Status Quo	Male Vocal/Instrumental Group from the UK, Names: Francis Michael Rossi, Rick Parfitt, Roy Lynes, John Coghlan & Alan Lancaster						
* 1	Pictures Of Matchstick Men	(PYE 7N 17449)	7	1968	12	1968	(Cadet 7001)
2	Ice In The Sun	(PYE 7N 17581)	8	1968	0	1968	
3	Are You Growing Tired Of My Love	(PYE 7N 17728)	46	1969	0	1969	
4	Are You Growing Tired Of My Love (Re-Entry)	(PYE 7N 17728)	50	1969	0	1969	
5	Down The Dustpipe	(PYE 7N 17907)	12	1970	0	1970	
6	In My Chair	(PYE 7N 17998)	21	1970	0	1970	
7	Paper Plane	(Vertigo 6059 071)	8	1973	0	1973	
8	Mean Girl	(PYE 7N 45229)	20	1973	0	1973	
9	Caroline	(Vertigo 6059 085)	5	1973	0	1973	
10	Break The Rules	(Vertigo 6059 101)	8	1974	0	1974	

ISSUE	TITLE	UK LBL	UK POS	UK YEAR	US POS	US YEAR	US LBL
11	Down Down	(Vertigo 6059 114)	1	1974	0	1974	
12	Roll Over Lay Down	(Vertigo QUO	9	1975	0	1975	
13	Rain	(Vertigo 6059 133)	7	1976	0	1976	
14	Mystery Song	(Vertigo 6059 146)	11	1976	0	1976	
15	Wild Side Of Life	(Vertigo 6059 153)	9	1976	0	1976	
16	Rockin' All Over The World	(Vertigo 6059 184)	3	1977	0	1977	
17	Again And Again	(Vertigo QUO 1)	13	1978	0	1978	
18	Accident Prone	(Vertigo QUO 2)	36	1978	0	1978	
19	Whatever You Want	(Vertigo 6059 242)	4	1979	0	1979	
20	Living On An Island	(Vertigo 6059 248)	16	1979	0	1979	
21	What Your Proposing	(Vertigo QUO 3)	2	1980	0	1980	
22	Lies / Don't Drive My Car	(Vertigo QUO 4)	11	1980	0	1980	
23	Something 'Bout You Baby I Like	(Vertigo QUO 5)	9	1981	0	1981	
24	Rock 'N' Roll	(Vertigo QUO 6)	8	1981	0	1981	
25	Dear John	(Vertigo QUO 7)	10	1982	0	1982	
26	She Don't Fool Me	(Vertigo QUO 8)	36	1982	0	1982	
27	Caroline (Live At The N.E.C.)	(Vertigo QUO 10)	13	1982	0	1982	
28	Ol' Rag Blues	(Vertigo QUO 11)	9	1983	0	1983	
29	A Mess Of The Blues	(Vertigo QUO 12)	15	1983	0	1983	
30	Marguerita Time	(Vertigo QUO 14)	3	1983	0	1983	
31	Going Down Town Tonight	(Vertigo QUO 15)	11	1974	0	1974	
32	The Wanderer	(Vertigo QUO 16)	7	1984	0	1984	
33	Rollin' Home	(Vertigo QUO 18)	9	1986	0	1986	
34	Red Sky	(Vertigo QUO 19)	19	1986	0	1986	
35	In The Army Now	(Vertigo QUO 20)	2	1986	0	1986	
36	Dreamin'	(Vertigo QUO 21)	15	1986	0	1986	
37	Ain't Complaining	(Vertigo QUO 22)	19	1988	0	1988	
38	Who Gets The Love	(Vertigo QUO 23)	34	1988	0	1988	
39	Running All Over The World	(Vertigo QUAID 1)	17	1988	0	1988	
40	Burning Bridges (On And Off And On Again)	(Vertigo QUO 25)	5	1988	0	1988	
41	Not At All	(Vertigo QUO 26)	50	1989	0	1989	
42	The Anniversary Waltz (Part 1)	(Vertigo QUO 28)	2	1990	0	1990	
43	The Anniversary Waltz (Part 2)	(Vertigo QUO 29)	16	1990	0	1990	
44	Can't Give You More	(Vertigo QUO 30)	37	1991	0	1991	
45	Rock 'Til You Drop	(Vertigo QUO 32)	38	1992	0	1992	
46	Roadhouse Medley (Annivarsary Waltz Part 25)	(Polydor QUO 33)	21	1992	0	1992	
47	I Didn't Mean It	(Polydor QUOCD 34)	21	1994	0	1994	
48	Sherri Don't Fail Me Now	(Polydor QUOCD 35)	38	1994	0	1994	
49	Restless	(Polydor QUOCD 36)	39	1994	0	1994	
50	When You Walk In The Room	(POLYGRAM TV 5775122)	34	1995	0	1995	
51	Fun Fun Fun	(POLYGRAM TV 5762632)	24	1996	0	1996	
52	Don't Stop	(POLYGRAM TV 5766352)	35	1996	0	1996	
53	All Around My Hat	(POLYGRAM TV 5759452)	47	1996	0	1996	

HIT 51 IS CREDITED TO STATUS QUO WITH THE BEACH BOYS • HIT 53 IS CREDITED TO STATUS QUO AND MADDY PRIOR

Staxx   Mixed Vocal/Instrumental Group from the UK

1	Joy	(Champion ChampCD 303)	25	1993	0	1993	
2	You	(Champion ChampCD 316)	50	1995	0	1995	
3	Joy (Re-Recording)	(Champion ChampCD 328)	14	1997	0	1997	

HITS 2-3 ARE CREDITED TO STAXX FEATURING CAROL LEEMING

Stealers Wheel   Male Vocal/Instrumental Group from the UK

* 1	Stuck In The Middle With You	(A&M AMS 7036)	8	1973	6	1973	(A&M 1416)
2	Everything'l Turn Out Fine	(A&M AMS 7079)	33	1973	0	1973	
3	Star	(A&M AMS 7094)	25	1974	29	1974	(A&M 1483)

NAMES: JOE EGAN, GERRY RAFFERTY, LUTHER GROSVENOR, DELISLE HARPER, ROD COOMBES & PAIL PILNICK

Steam   Male Vocal/Instrumental Group Of Six Men from the USA

* 1	Na Na Hey Hey Kiss Him Goodbye	(Fontana TF 1058)	9	1970	1	1969	(Fontana 1667)

Steel Breeze   Lead Vocals Of This Six-Man Group Is Ric Jacobs From California

1	You Don't Want Me Anymore		0	1982	16	1982	(RCA 13283)
2	Dreamin' Is Easy		0	1983	30	1983	(RCA 13427)

Steel Pulse   Male Vocal/Instrumental Group from the UK

1	Ku Klux Klan	(Island WIP 6428)	41	1978	0	1978	
2	Prodigal Son	(Island WIP 6449)	35	1978	0	1978	
3	Sound System	(Island WIP 6490)	71	1979	0	1979	

ISSUE	TITLE	UK LBL	UK POS	UK YEAR	US POS	US YEAR	US LBL
Steeleye Span Mixed Vocal/Instrumental Group from the UK								
1	Gaudete	(Chrysalis CHS 2007)	14	1973	0	1973	
2	All Around My Hat	(Chrysalis CHS 2078)	5	1975	0	1975	
Steelheart Vocals In The Quintet Are From Michael Matijevic								
1	I'll Never Let You Go (Angel Eyes)		0	1991	23	1991	(MCA 53801)
Steely Dan Male Vocal/Instrumental Group From New Jersey								
1	Do It Again	(ABC 4075)	39	1975	6	1972	(ABC 11338)
2	Reelin The Years		0	1973	11	1973	(ABC 11352)
3	Rikki Don't Lose That Number	(ABC 4241)	58	1979	4	1974	(ABC 11439)
4	Black Friday		0	1975	37	1975	(ABC 12101)
5	Haitian Divorce	(ABC 4152)	17	1976	0	1976	
6	Peg		0	1978	11	1978	(ABC 12320)
7	Deacon Blues		0	1978	19	1978	(ABC 12355)
8	F.M. (No Static At All)	(MCA 374)	49	1978	22	1978	(MCA 40894)
9	F.M. (No Static At All) (Re-Entry)	(MCA 374)	75	1978	0	1978	
10	Josie		0	1978	26	1978	(ABC 12404)
11	Hey Nineteen		0	1981	10	1981	(MCA 51036)
12	Time Out Of Mind		0	1981	22	1981	(MCA 51082)
	DONALD FAGEN & WALTER BECKER FORMED THE GROUP • OBITUARY : JIMMY HOLDER (DRUMMER) D: 5 JUN 1990 DROWNED.								
Stefan Dennis Male Vocalist from Australia								
1	Don't It Make You Feel Good	(Sublime Lime 105)	16	1989	0	1989	
2	This Love Affair	(Sublime Lime 113)	67	1989	0	1989	
Steinski & Mass Media Male Producer And Rapper from the USA								
1	We'll Be Right Back	(Fourth & Broadway BRW 59)	63	1987	0	1987	
Stella Parton Female Vocalist from the USA								
1	The Danger Of A Stranger	(Elektra K 12272)	35	1977	0	1977	
Stephanie De Sykes Female Vocalist from the UK								
1	Born With A Smile On My Face	(Bradley's BRAD7409)	2	1974	0	1974	
2	We'll Find Our Day	(BRADLEY'S BRAD7509)	17	1975	0	1975	
	HIT 1 IS CREDITED TO STEPHANIE DE SYKES WITH RAIN								
Stephanie Mills Female Vocalist, B: 1957 Brooklyn								
1	What Cha Gonna Do With My Lovin'		0	1979	22	1979	(20th Century 2403)
* 2	Never New Love Like This Before	(20th Century TC 2460)	4	1980	6	1980	(20th Century 2460)
3	Two Hearts	(20th Century TC 2492)	49	1981	40	1981	(20th Century 2492)
4	The Medicine Song	(Club Jab 8)	29	1984	0	1984	
5	(You're Puttin') A Rush On Me	(MCA MCA 1187)	62	1987	0	1987	
6	Never Do You Wrong	(MCA MCSTD	57	1993	0	1993	
7	All Day, All Night	(MCA MCSTD	68	1993	0	1993	
	HIT 3 IS CREDITED TO STEPHANIE MILLS FEATURING TEDDY PENDERGRASS								
Stephen 'Tin Tin' Duffy Male Vocalist from the UK								
1	Hold It	(CURVE X 9763)	55	1983	0	1983	
2	Kiss Me	(10 TIN 2)	4	1985	0	1985	
3	Icing On The Cake	(10 TIN 3)	14	1985	0	1985	
Stephen Bishop Male Singer/Songwriter, B: 14 Dec 1951 In San Diego								
1	Save It For A Rainy Day		0	1977	22	1977	(ABC 12232)
2	On And On		0	1977	11	1977	(ABC 12260)
3	Everybody Needs Love		0	1978	32	1978	(ABC 12406)
4	It Might Be You (Theme From Toosie)		0	1983	25	1993	(Warner Bros. 29791)
Stephen Stills Male Vocalist, B: 3 Jan 1945 Dallas								
1	Love The One Your With	(Atlantic 2091 046)	37	1971	14	1971	(Atlantic 2778)
2	Sit Yourself Down		0	1971	37	1971	(Atlantic 2790)
	SEE ALSO CROSBY STILLS AND NASH & BUFFALO SPRINGFIELD								
Steppenwolf Male Vocal/Instrumental Group From Canada								
* 1	Born To Be Wild	(STATESIDE SS 8017)	30	1969	2	1968	(Dunhill 4138)
* 2	Magic Carpet Ride		0	1968	3	1968	(Dunhill 4161)
* 3	Rock Me		0	1969	10	1969	(Dunhill 4182)
4	Move Over		0	1969	31	1969	(Dunhill 4205)
5	Born To Be Wild (Re-Entry)	(STATESIDE SS 8017)	50	1969	0	1969	
6	Monster		0	1970	39	1970	(Dunhill 4221)
7	Hey Lawdy Mama		0	1970	35	1970	(Dunhill4234)
8	Straight Shootin' Woman		0	1974	29	1974	(MUMS 6031)
	NAMES: JOACHIM KRAULEDAT (JOHN KAY), MICHAEL MONARCH, GOLDY MCJOHN, NICK ST. NICHOLAS, DENNIS EDMONTON (MARS BONFIRE) & JERRY EDMONTON.								

ISSUE	TITLE	UK LBL	UK POS	UK YEAR	US POS	US YEAR	US LBL
Stereo MCs Male Studio Mixers, Rob Birch,Nick Hallam & Owen Rossitet							
1	Elevate My Mind	(Fourth & Broadway BRW186)	74	1990	39	1991	(Fourth & Broadway 447519)
2	Lost In Music	(Fourth & Broadway BRW198)	46	1991	0	1991	
3	Connected	(Fourth & Broadway BRW 864744)	18	1992	20	1993	(GEE STREET 262)
4	Step It Up	(Fourth & Broadway BRW 266)	12	1992	0	1992	
5	Ground Level	(Fourth & Broadway BRCD268)	19	1993	0	1993	
6	Creation	(Fourth & Broadway BRCD 276)	19	1993	0	1993	
Stereo Nation Male Vocal Duo from the UK							
1	I've Been Waiting	(EMI PremierPRESCD 5)	53	1996	0	1996	
Stereolab Mixed Vocal/Instrumental Group from the UK/France							
1	Jenny Ondioline /French Disko	(Duophonic UHFDUHFD 01)	75	1994	0	1994	
2	Ping Pong	(Duophonic UHFDUHFCD 04)	70	1994	0	1994	
3	Wow And Flutter	(Duophonic UHFDUHFCD 07)	70	1994	0	1994	
4	Cybell's Reverie / Brigette	(Duophonic UHFDUHFCD 10)	62	1996	0	1996	
5	Miss Modular	(Duophonic UHFDUHFCD 16)	60	1997	0	1997	
Stereos Names Nathaniel Hicks, George Otis, Sam Profit, Bruce Robinson & Ronnie Collins							
1	I Really Love You		0	1961	29	1961	(CUB 9095)
	ORIGINALLY CALLED THE BUCKEYES						
Sterling Void Male Vocalist from the UK							
1	Runaway Girl / It's Alright	(FFRR FFR 21)	53	1989	0	1989	
Stetasonic Male Rap Group from the USA							
1	Talkin' All That Jazz	(BREAKOUT USA 640)	73	1988	0	1988	
Steve 'Silk' Hurley Male Vocalist from the USA							
1	Jack Your Body	(DJ International LON 117)	1	1987	0	1987	
Steve Allan Male Vocalist from the UK							
1	Together We Are Beautiful	(CREOLE CR 164)	67	1979	0	1979	
2	Together We Are Beautiful (Re-Entry)	(Creole CR 164)	70	1979	0	1979	
Steve Allen Comedian/Actor/Composer, B: 26 Dec 1921 New York City, See George Cates Orchestra							
Steve Arrington Male Vocalist from the USA							
1	Feel So Real	(Atlantic A 9576)	5	1985	0	1985	
2	Dancin' In The Key Of Life	(Atlantic A 9534)	21	1985	0	1985	
3	Dancin' In The Key Of Life (Re-Entry)	(Atlantic A 9534)	75	1985	0	1985	
Steve Earle Male Vocal/Guitarist from the USA							
1	Copperhead Road	(MCA MCA 1280)	45	1988	0	1988	
2	Johnny Come Lately	(MCA MCA 1301)	75	1988	0	1988	
Steve Forbert B: 1955 Meridian, Mississippi							
1	Romeo's Tune		0	1980	11	1980	(MEMPEROR 7525)
Steve Gibbons Band Male Vocal/Instrumental Group from the UK							
1	Tulane	(Polydor 2058 889)	13	1987	0	1987	
2	Eddy Vortex	(Polydor 2059 017)	56	1978	0	1978	
Steve Hackett Male Vocal/Instrumentalist from the UK							
1	Cell 151	(CHARISMA CELL 1)	66	1983	0	1983	
Steve Harley & Cockney Rebel Male Vocalist, Real Name Steven Nice from the UK							
1	Judy Teen	(EMI 2128)	5	1974	0	1974	
2	Mr. Soft	(EMI 2191)	8	1974	0	1974	
* 3	Make Me Smile (Come Up And See Me)	(EMI 2263)	1	1975	0	1975	
4	Mr. Raffles (Man It Was Mean)	(EMI 2299)	13	1975	0	1975	
5	Here Comes The Sun	(EMI 2505)	10	1976	0	1976	
6	I Believe Love's A Prima Donna	(EMI 2539)	41	1976	0	1976	
7	Freedom's Prisoner	(EMI 2994)	58	1979	0	1979	
8	Ballerina (Prima Donna)	(STILLETTO STL 14)	51	1983	0	1983	
9	The Phantom Of The Opera	(Polydor POSP 800)	7	1986	0	1986	
10	Make Me Smile (Come Up And See Me)	(EMI EMCT 5)	46	1992	0	1992	
11	Make Me Smile (Come Up And See Me)	(EMI CDHARLEY 1)	33	1995	0	1995	
Other Members, Milton Reame-James, Jean Crocker, Paul Jeffreys & Stuart Elliot							
Steve Harvey Male Vocalist from the UK							
1	Something Special	(London LON 25)	46	1983	0	1983	
2	Tonight	(London LON 36)	63	1983	0	1983	

ISSUE	TITLE	UK LBL	UK POS	UK YEAR	US POS	US YEAR	US LBL
Steve Lawrence Male Vocalist, Real Name Sidney Leibowitz B: 8 Jul 1935 Brooklyn							
1	Poinciana		0	1952	21	1952	(KING 15185)
2	How Many Stars Have To Shine		0	1953	26	1953	(KING 15208)
3	Banana Boat Song		0	1957	18	1957	(CORAL 61761)
4	Party Doll		0	1957	5	1957	(CORAL 61792)
5	Pretty Blue Eyes		0	1959	9	1959	(EMI-Parammount 10058)
6	Footsteps	(HMV POP 726)	4	1960	7	1960	(Columbia 10085)
7	Girls Girls Girls	(London HLT 9166)	49	1960	0	1960	
8	Portrait Of My Love		0	1961	9	1961	(United Artists291)
9	My Clair De Lune		0	1961	68	1961	(United Artists335)
* 10	Go Away Little Girl		0	1962	1	1962	(Columbia 42601)
11	Don't Be Afraid, Little Darlin'		0	1963	26	1963	(Columbia 42699)
12	Poor Little Rich Girl		0	1963	27	1963	(Columbia 42795)
13	I Want To Stay Here	(CBS AAG 163)	3	1963	28	1953	(Columbia 42815)
14	Walking Proud		0	1963	26	1963	(Columbia 42865)
15	I Can't Stop Talking About You		0	1964	35	1964	(Columbia 42932)
	HIT 11 IS CREDITED TO STEVE & EYDIE						
	STEVE AND EYDIE GORME WERE MARRIED IN DEC 1957 AND RECORDED AS PARKER AND PENNY IN 1979. SEE ALSO EYDIE GORME						
Steve Martin & The Toot Uncommons Male TV/Movie Comedian/Writer, B: 8 Jun 1945 Waco, Texas							
* 1	King Tut		0	1978	17	1978	(Warner Bros. 8577)
Steve Miller Band Male Vocal/Instrumental Group from Dallas. Steve B: 5 Oct 1943 In Milwaukee							
* 1	The Joker	(Capitol CL 583)	1	1990	1	1973	(Capitol 3732)
2	Take The Money And Run		0	1976	11	1976	(Capitol 4260)
3	Rock 'N' Me	(Mercury 6078804)	11	1976	1	1976	(Capitol 4323)
* 4	Fly Like An Eagle		0	1977	2	1977	(Capitol 4372)
5	Jet Airliner		0	1977	8	1977	(Capitol 4424)
6	Jungle Love		0	1977	23	1977	(Capitol 4466)
7	Swingtown		0	1977	17	1977	(Capitol 4496)
8	Heart Like A Wheel		0	1981	24	1981	(Capitol 5068)
* 9	Abracadabra	(Mercury STEVE 3)	2	1982	1	1982	(Capitol 5126)
10	Keeps Me Wondering Why	(Mercury Steve 4)	52	1982	0	1982	
	HITS 2-4 ARE CREDITED TO STEVE MILLER						
	STEVE WAS INVOLVED WITH THE ARDELLS WHICH BECAME THE FABULOUS NIGHT TRAINS, IN HIGH SCHOOL HE FORMED THE						
	MARKSMEN WHICH INCLUDED BOZ SCAGGS						
Steve Perry (1) Male Vocalist from the UK							
1 1	Step By Step	(HMV POP 745)	41	1960	0	1960	
Steve Perry (2) Male Vocalist, B: 22 Jan 1949 Hanford, California, See Also Journey							
1	Don't Fight It		0	1982	17	1982	(Columbia 03192)
2	Oh Sherrie		0	1964	3	1984	(Columbia 04391)
3	She's Mine		0	1984	21	1984	(Columbia 04496)
4	Strung Out		0	1984	40	1984	(Columbia 04598)
5	Foolish Heart		0	1984	18	1984	(Columbia 04693)
6	You Better Wait		0	1994	29	1994	(Columbia 77580)
	HIT 1 IS CREDITED TO KENNY LOGGINS WITH STEVE PERRY						
Steve Race Male Pianist from the UK							
1	The Pied Piper (The Beeje)	(Parlophone R 4981)	29	1963	0	1963	
Steve Walsh Male Vocalist from the UK							
1	I Found Lovin'	(A1 A1 299)	74	1987	0	1987	
2	I Found Lovin' (Re-Entry)	(A1 A1 299)	9	1987	0	1987	
3	Let's Get Together Tonite	(A1 A1 303)	74	1987	0	1987	
4	Ain't No Stoppin' Us Now (Party For The World)	(A1 A1 304)	44	1988	0	1988	
Steve Winwood Male Vocalist, B: 12 May 1948 Birmingham, England							
1	While You See A Chance	(Island WIP 6655)	45	1981	7	1981	(Island 19656)
2	Valerle	(Island WIP 6818)	51	1982	0	1982	
3	Higher Love	(Island IS 288)	13	1986	1	1986	(Island 28710)
4	Freedom Overspill	(Island IS 294)	69	1986	20	1986	(Island 28595)
5	Back In The High Life Again	(Island IS 303)	53	1987	13	1987	(Island 28472)
6	The Finer Things		0	1987	8	1987	(Island 28498)
7	Valerie (Re-Recording)	(Island IS 336)	19	1987	9	1987	(Island 28231)
8	Roll With It	(Island VS 1085)	53	1988	1	1988	(Virgin 99326)
9	Don't You Know What The Night Can Do		0	1988	6	1988	(Virgin 99290)
10	Holding On		0	1989	11	1989	(Virgin 99261)

ISSUE	TITLE	UK LBL	UK POS	UK YEAR	US POS	US YEAR	US LBL
11	One And Only Man		0	1990	18	1990	(Virgin 98892)
	ALSO LEAD SINGER WITH BLIND FAITH, TRAFFIC AND SPENCER DAVIS GROUP						

Steve Wright   Male DJ/Vocalist from the UK

1	I'm Alright	(RCA 296)	40	1982	0	1982	
2	Get Some Therapy	(RCA RCA 362)	75	1983	0	1983	
3	The Gay Cavalieros (The Story So Far)	(MCA 925)	61	1984	0	1984	
	HIT 1 IS CREDITED TO YOUNG STEVE & THE AFTERNOON BOYS • HIT 2 IS CREDITED TO STEVE WRIGHT & THE SISTERS OF SOUL						

Steven Dante   Male Vocalist from the UK

1	The Real Thing	(Chrysalis CHS 3167)	13	1987	0	1987	
2	I'm Too Scared	(Cooltempo DANTE 1)	34	1988	0	1988	
	HIT 1 IS CREDITED TO JELLYBEAN FEATURING STEVEN DANTE						

Stevenson's Rocket   Male Vocal/Instrumental Group from the UK

1	Alright Baby	(Magnet MAG 47)	37	1975	0	1975	
2	Alright Baby (Re-Entry)	(Magnet MAG 47)	45	1975	0	1975	

Stevie B   Male Vocalist, Real Name Steven B. Hill, B: Miami

1	I Wanna Be The One		0	1989	32	1989	(LMR 74003)
2	In My Eyes		0	1989	37	1989	(LMR 74004)
3	Love Me For Life		0	1990	29	1990	(LMR 84006)
4	Love And Emotion		0	1990	15	1990	(LMR 2645)
* 5	Because I Love You (The Postman Song)	(Polydor PO 126)	6	1991	1	1990	(LMR 2724)
6	I'll Be By Your Side		0	1991	12	1991	(LMR 2758)
7	Dream About You		0	1995	29	1995	(Emporia/THUM P 2205)
8	Funky Melody		0	1995	29	1995	(EMPORIA/THUM P 2205)

Stevie Marsh   Female Vocalist from the UK

1	The Only Boy In The World	(Decca F 11181)	29	1959	0	1959	
2	The Only Boy In The World (Re-Entry)	(Decca F 11181)	24	1959	0	1959	

Stevie Nicks   Female Vocalist, Real Name Stephanie Nicks B: 26 May 1948 In Phoenix, Joined Fleetwood Mac In

1	Stop Draggin' My Heart Around	(WEA K 79231)	50	1981	3	1981	(Modern 7336)
2	Leather And Lace		0	1981	6	1981	(Modern 7341)
3	Edge Of Seventeen (Just Like The White Winged Dove)		0	1982	11	1982	(Modern 7401)
4	After The Glitter Fades		0	1982	32	1982	(Modern 7405)
5	Stand Back		0	1983	5	1983	(Modern 99863)
6	If Anyone Falls		0	1983	14	1983	(Modern 99832)
7	Nightbird		0	1984	33	1984	(Modern 99799)
8	Talk To Me	(Parlophone R 6124)	68	1986	4	1985	(Modern 99582)
9	I Can't Wait	(Parlophone R 6110)	54	1986	16	1986	(Modern 99565)
10	Needles And Pins		0	1986	37	1986	(MCA 52772)
11	Rooms On Fire	(EMI EM 90)	16	1989	16	1989	(Modern 99216)
12	Long Way To Go	(EMI EM 97)	60	1989	0	1989	
13	Whole Lotta Trouble	(EMI EM 114)	62	1989	0	1989	
14	Sometimes It's A Bitch	(EMI EM 203)	40	1991	0	1991	
15	I Can't Wait (Re-Issue)	(EMI EM 214)	47	1991	0	1991	
16	Maybe Love	(EMI CDEMS 328)	42	1994	0	1994	
	WAS ORIGINALLY A SINGER WITH FRITZ						

Stevie Wonder   Real Name Steveland Morris B: 13 May 1950, Saginaw, Michigan

* 1	Fingertips (Part 1-2)		0	1963	1	1963	(Tamla 54080)
+ 2	Workout Stevie, Workout / Money Talk		0	1963	33	1963	(Tamla 54086)
3	Hey Harmonica Man		0	1964	29	1964	(Tamla 54096)
+ 4	High Heel Sneakers		0	1965	30	1965	(Tamla 54119)
* 5	Uptight	(Tamla MotownTMG 545)	14	1966	3	1966	(Tamla 54124)
6	Nothing's Too Good For My Baby / With A Child's Heart		0	1966	20	1966	(Tamla 54130)
7	Blowin' In The Wind	(Tamla MotownTMG 570)	36	1966	9	1966	(Tamla 54136)
8	A Place In The Sun	(Tamla MotownTMG 588)	20	1967	9	1966	(Tamla 54139)
9	Travlin' Man		0	1967	32	1967	(Tamla 54147)
* 10	I Was Made To Love Her	(Tamla MotownTMG 613)	5	1967	2	1967	(Tamla 54151)
11	I'm Wondering	(Tamla MotownTMG 626)	22	1967	12	1967	(Tamla 54157)
12	Shoo-Be-Doo-Be-Doo-Da-Day	(TamlaTMG 653) Motown	46	1968	9	1968	(Tamla 54165)
13	You Met Your Match		0	1968	35	1968	(Tamla 54168)
* 14	For Once In My Life	(Tamla MotownTMG 679)	3	1968	2	1968	(Tamla 54174)
15	I Don't Know Why	(Tamla MotownTMG 690)	14	1969	0	1969	
* 16	My Cherie Amour	(Tamla MotownTMG 690)	4	1969	4	1969	(Tamla 54180)
17	I Don't Know Why (Re-Entry)	(Tamla MotownTMG 690)	43	1969	0	1969	
* 18	Yester-Me Yester-You Yesterday	(Tamla MotownTMG 717)	2	1969	7	1969	(Tamla 54188)

ISSUE	TITLE	UK LBL	UK POS	UK YEAR	US POS	US YEAR	US LBL
19	Never Had A Dream Come True	(Tamla MotownTMG 731)	6	1970	26	1970	(Tamla 54191)
* 20	Signed, Sealed, Delivered I'm Yours	(Tamla MotownTMG 744)	15	1970	3	1970	(Tamla 54196)
21	Signed, Sealed, Delivered I'm Yours (Re-Entry)	(Tamla MotownTMG 744)	49	1970	0	1970	
22	Heaven Help Us All	(Tamla MotownTMG 757)	29	1970	9	1970	(Tamla 54200)
23	We Can Work It Out	(Tamla MotownTMG 772)	27	1971	13	1971	(Tamla 54202)
24	If You Really Love Me	(Tamla MotownTMG 798)	20	1972	8	1971	(Tamla 54208)
25	Superwoman (Where Were You When I Needed You)		0	1972	33	1972	(Tamla 54216)
* 26	Superstition	(Tamla MotownTMG 841)	11	1973	1	1973	(Tamla 54226)
* 27	You Are The Sunshine Of My Life	(Tamla MotownTMG 852)	7	1973	1	1973	(Tamla 54232)
28	Higher Ground	(Tamla Motown TMG 959)	29	1973	0	1973	
29	Living For The City	(Tamla MotownTMG 881)	15	1974	8	1973	(Tamla 54252)
30	He's Misstra Know It All	(Tamla MotownTMG 892)	10	1974	0	1974	
31	Don't You Worry 'Bout A Thing		0	1974	16	1974	(Tamla 54245)
* 32	You Haven't Done Nothin'	(Tamla Motown TMG 921)	30	1974	1	1974	(Tamla 54252)
* 33	Boogie On Reggae Woman	(Tamla Motown TMG 928)	12	1975	3	1974	(Tamla 54254)
34	I Wish	(Tamla MotownTMG 1054)	5	1976	1	1976	(Tamla 54274)
35	Sir Duke	(Motown TMG 1068)	2	1977	1	1977	(Tamla 54281)
36	Another Star	(Motown TMG 1083)	29	1977	32	1977	(Tamla 54286)
37	As		0	1977	36	1977	(Tamla 54291)
38	Pops We Love You	(Motown TMG 1136)	66	1979	0	1979	
39	Send One Your Love	(Motown TMG 1149)	52	1979	4	1979	(Tamla 54303)
40	Black Orchid	(Motown TMG 1173)	63	1980	0	1980	
41	Outside My Window	(Motown TMG 1179)	52	1980	0	1980	
42	Masterblaster (Jammin')	(Motown TMG 1204)	2	1980	5	1980	(Tamla 54317)
43	I Ain't Gonna Stand For It	(Motown TMG 1215)	10	1980	11	1981	(Tamla 54320)
44	Lately	(MOTOWM TMG 1226)	3	1981	0	1981	
45	Happy Birthday	(Motown TMG 1235)	2	1981	0	1981	
46	That Girl	(Motown TMG 1254)	39	1982	4	1982	(Tamla 1602)
* 47	Ebony And Ivory	(Parlophone R 6054)	1	1982	1	1982	(Columbia 02860)
48	Do I Do	(Motown TMG 1269)	10	1982	13	1982	(Tamla 1612)
49	Ribbon In The Sky	(Motown TMG 1280)	45	1982	0	1982	
* 50	I Just Called To Say I Love You	(Motown TMG 1349)	1	1984	1	1984	(Motown 1745)
51	Love Light In Flight	(Motown TMG 1364)	44	1984	17	1984	(Motown 1769)
52	Don't Drive Drunk	(Motown TMG 1372)	71	1984	0	1984	
53	Don't Drive Drunk (Re-Entry)	(Motown TMG 1372)	62	1985	0	1985	
54	Part Time Lover	(Motown ZB 40351)	3	1985	1	1985	(Tamla 1808)
* 55	That's What Friends Are For	(Arista ARIST 638)	16	1985	1	1985	(Arista 9422)
56	Go Home	(Motown ZB 40501)	67	1985	10	1985	(Tamla 1817)
57	I Just Called To Say I Love You (Re-Entry)	(Motown TMG 1349)	64	1985	0	1985	
58	Overjoyed	(Motown ZB 40567)	17	1986	24	1986	(Tamla 1832)
59	Stranger On The Shore Of Love	(Motown WOND 2)	55	1987	0	1987	
60	Skeletons	(Motown ZB 41439)	59	1987	19	1987	(Motown 1907)
61	Get It	(Motown ZB 41883)	37	1988	0	1988	
62	My Love	(CBS JULIO 2)	5	1988	0	1988	
63	Free	(Motown ZB 42855)	49	1989	0	1989	
64	Fun Day	(Motown ZB 44957)	63	1991	0	1991	
65	For Your Love	(Motown TMGCD 1437)	23	1995	0	1995	
66	Tomorrow Robins Will Sing	(Motown 8603732)	71	1995	0	1995	

Stevie Woods   Male R&B Vocalist, B: Columbus, Ohio, Now Based In Los Angeles

1	Steal The Night		0	1981	25	1981	(Cotillion 46016)
2	Just Can't Win 'Em All		0	1982	38	1982	(Cotillion 46030)

Stex   Male Vocal Group from the UK

1	Still Feel The Rain	(Some Bizarre SBZ 7002)	63	1991	0	1991	

Stiff Little Fingers   Male Vocal/Instrumental Group from the UK

1	Straw Dogs	(Chrysalis CHS 2368)	44	1979	0	1979	
2	At The Edge	(Chrysalis CHS 2406)	15	1980	0	1980	
3	Nobody's Hero / Tin Soldiers	(Chrysalis CHS 2424)	36	1980	0	1980	
4	Back To Front	(Chrysalis CHS 2447)	49	1980	0	1980	
5	Just Fade Away	(Chrysalis CHS 2510)	47	1981	0	1981	
6	Silver Lining	(Chrysalis CHS 2517)	68	1981	0	1981	
7	Listen (EP)	(Chrysalis CHS 2580)	33	1982	0	1982	
8	Bits Of Kids	(Chrysalis CHS 2637)	73	1982	0	1982	

Stiltskin   Male Vocal/Instrumental Group from the UK

1	Inside	(WHITE WATER LEV 1CD)	1	1994	0	1994	
2	Footsteps	(WHITE WATER WWRD 2)	34	1994	0	1994	

ISSUE	TITLE	UK LBL	UK POS	UK YEAR	US POS	US YEAR	US LBL
Sting	Male Vocalist, Real Name Gordon Sumner B: 2 Oct 1951 England						
1	Spread A Little Happiness	(A&M AMS 8217)	16	1982	0	1982	
2	If You Love Somebody Set Them Free	(A&M AM 258)	26	1985	3	1985	(A&M 2738)
3	Love Is The Seventh Wave	(A&M AM 272)	41	1985	17	1985	(A&M 2787)
4	Fortress Around Your Heart	(A&M AM 286)	49	1985	8	1985	(A&M 2767)
5	Russians	(A&M AM 292)	12	1985	16	1985	(A&M 2799)
6	Moon Over Bourbon Street	(A&M AM 305)	44	1986	0	1986	
8	We'll Be Together	(A&M AM 410)	41	1987	7	1987	(A&M 2983)
9	Be Still My Beating Heart		0	1988	15	1988	(A&M 2992)
10	English Man In New York	(A&M AM 431)	51	1988	0	1988	
11	Fragile	(A&M AM 439)	70	1988	0	1988	
12	Englishman In New York (Re-Mix)	(A&M AM 580)	15	1990	0	1990	
13	All This Time	(A&M AM 713)	22	1991	5	1991	(A&M 1541)
14	Mad About You	(A&M AM 721)	56	1991	0	1991	
15	The Soul Cages	(A&M AM 759)	57	1991	0	1991	
16	It's Probably Me	(A&M AM 883)	30	1992	0	1992	
17	If I Ever Lose My Faith In You	(A&M AMCD 0172)	14	1993	17	1993	(A&M 0111)
18	Seven Days	(A&M 5802232)	25	1993	0	1993	
19	Fields Of Gold	(A&M 5803012)	16	1993	23	1993	(A&M 0258)
20	Shape Of My Heart	(A&M 5803532)	57	1993	0	1993	
21	Demolition Man	(A&M 5804512)	21	1993	0	1993	
* 22	All For Love	(A&M 5804772)	2	1994	1	1993	(A&M 1476)
23	Nothing 'Bout Me	(A&M 5805292)	32	1994	0	1994	
24	When We Dance	(A&M 5808612)	9	1994	38	1994	(A&M 0846)
25	This Cowboy Song	(A&M 5809652)	15	1995	0	1995	
26	Spirits In The Material World	(MCA MCSTD 2113)	36	1996	0	1996	
27	Let Your Soul Be Your Pilot	(A&M 5813312)	15	1996	0	1996	
28	You Still Touch Me	(A&M 5815472)	27	1996	0	1996	
29	Live At Tfi Friday	(A&M 5817652)	53	1996	0	1996	
30	I Was Brought To My Senses (Steve Lipson Re-Mix)	(A&M 5818912)	31	1996	0	1996	
31	I'm So Happy I Can't Stop Crying	(A&M 5820312)	54	1996	94	1996	(A&M 581982)
	SEE ALSO POLICE. • HE GOT HIS NICKNAME FROM A JERSEY HE USED TO WEAR						
Stix 'N' Stoned	Male Instrumental/Production Duo from the UK						
1	Outrageous	(Positiva CDTIV 52)	39	1996	0	1996	
Stock Aitken Waterman	Male Producers from the UK						
1	Roadblock	(BREAKOUT USA 611)	13	1987	0	1987	
2	Mr. Sleaze	(London NANA 14)	3	1987	0	1987	
3	Packjammed (With The Party Posse)	(BREAKOUT USA620)	41	1987	0	1987	
4	All The Way	(MCA GOAL 1)	64	1988	0	1988	
5	Ss Paparazzi	(PWL PWL 22)	68	1988	0	1988	
6	Ferry 'Cross The Mersey	(PWL PWL 41)	1	1989	0	1989	
Stone Roses	Male Vocal/Instrumental Group from the UK						
1	She Bangs The Drums	(SILVERTONE ORE 6)	36	1989	0	1989	
2	What The World Is Waiting For - Fool's Gold	(SILVERTONE ORE 13)	8	1989	0	1989	
3	Sally Cinnamon	(REVOLVER REV 36)	75	1990	0	1990	
4	Sally Cinnamon (Re-Entry)	(REVOLVER REV 36)	46	1990	0	1990	
5	Elephant Stone	(SILVERTONE ORE 1)	8	1990	0	1990	
6	Made Of Stone	(SILVERTONE ORE 2)	20	1990	0	1990	
7	She Bangs The Drums (Re-Entry)	(SILVERTONE ORE 6)	4	1990	0	1990	
8	One Love	(SILVERTONE ORE 17)	4	1990	0	1990	
9	What The World Is Waiting For (Re-Entry)	(SILVERTONE ORE 13)	22	1990	0	1990	
10	I Wanna Be Adored	(SILVERTONE ORE 31)	20	1991	0	1991	
11	Waterfall	(SILVERTONE ORE 35)	27	1992	0	1992	
12	I Am The Resurrection	(SILVERTONE ORE 40)	33	1992	0	1992	
13	Fool's Gold (Re-Mix)	(SILVERTONE ORET 13)	73	1992	0	1992	
14	Love Spreads	(Geffen GFSTD 84)	2	1994	0	1994	
15	Ten Storey Love Song	(Geffen GFSTD 87)	11	1995	0	1995	
16	Fools Gold (2nd Re-Mix)	(SILVERTONE ORECD 71)	25	1995	0	1995	
17	Begging You	(Geffen GFSTD 22060)	16	1995	0	1995	
Stone Temple Pilots	Male Vocal/Instrumental Group from the USA						
1	Sex Type Thing	(Atlantic A 5769CD)	60	1993	0	1993	
2	Plush	(Atlantic A 7349CD)	23	1993	0	1993	
3	Sex Type Thing (Re-Issue)	(Atlantic A 7239CD)	55	1993	0	1993	

ISSUE	TITLE	UK LBL	UK POS	UK YEAR	US POS	US YEAR	US LBL
4	Vasoline	(Atlantic A 5650CD)	48	1994	0	1994	
5	Interstate Love Song	(Atlantic A 7192CD)	53	1994	0	1994	

Stonebolt Lead Singer With The Quintet Is David Wills

1	I Will Still Love You		0	1978	29	1978	(PARACHUTE 512)

Stonebridge Mcguinness Male Vocal/Instrumental Duo from the UK

1	Oo-Eeh Baby	(RCA PB 5163)	54	1979	0	1979	

Stonefree Male Vocalist from the UK

1	Can't Say Bye	(EMSIGN ENY 607)	73	1987	0	1987	

Stonewall Jackson Male Vocalist, B: 6 Nov 1932 In Emerson, North Carolina

* 2	Waterloo	(Philips PB 941)	24	1959	4		
5	Mary Don't You Weep		0	1960	41	1960	(Columbia 41533)
	OTHERS WERE C/W HITS						

Stop The Violence Mixed Rap Charity Assembly from the USA

1	Self Destruction	(JIVE BDPST 1)	75	1989	0	1989	

Stories Lead Singer With The Quartet Is Ian Lloyd

* 1	Brother Louie		0	1973	1	1973	(KAMA SUTRA 577)

Storm (1) Mixed Vocal/Instrumental Group from the UK

1	It's My House	(SCOPE SC 10)	36	1979	0	1979	

Storm (2) Male Vocal/Instrumental Group With Vocal From Gregg Rolie & Kevin Chalfant

1	I've Got A Lot To Learn About Love		0	1992	26	1992	(INTERSCOPE 98726)

Strangelove Male Vocal/Instrumental Group from the UK

1	Living With The Human Machines	(FOOD/Parlophone CDFOOD 70)	53	1996	0	1996	
2	Beautiful Alone	(FOOD/Parlophone CDFOOD 81)	35	1996	0	1996	
3	Sway	(FOOD/Parlophone CDFOOD 82)	47	1996	0	1996	
4	The Greatest Show On Earth	(FOOD/Parlophone CDFOOD 97)	36	1997	0	1997	

Strangeloves Male Producers/Writers, Jerry Goldstein, Richard Gottehrer & Robert Feldman from the USA

1	I Want Candy		0	1955	11	1955	(BANG 501)
2	Cara-Lin		0	1965	39	1965	(BANG 508)
3	Night Time		0	1966	30	1966	(BANG 514)

Stranglers Male Vocal/Instrumental Group from the UK

1	(Get A) Grip (On Yourself)	(United Artists UP 36211)	44	1977	0	1977	
2	Peaches / Go Buddy Go	(United Artists UP 36248)	8	1977	0	1977	
3	Something Better Change / Straighten Out	(United Artists UP 36277)	9	1977	0	1977	
4	No More Heroes	(United Artists UP 36300)	8	1977	0	1977	
5	Five Minutes	(United Artists UP 36350)	11	1978	0	1978	
6	Nice 'N Sleazy	(United Artists UP 36379)	18	1978	0	1978	
7	Walk On By	(United Artists UP 36429)	21	1978	0	1978	
8	Duchess	(United Artists BP 308)	14	1979	0	1979	
9	Nuclear Device / The Wizzard Of Aus	(United Artists BP 308)	36	1979	0	1979	
10	Don't Bring Harry (EP)	(United Artists STR 1)	41	1979	0	1979	
11	Bear Cage	(United ArtistsBP 344)	36	1980	0	1980	
12	Who Wants The World	(United ArtistsBPX 355)	39	1980	0	1980	
13	Thrown Away	(United Artists BP 383)	42	1981	0	1981	
14	Let Me Introduce You To The Family	(United Artists BP 405)	42	1981	0	1981	
15	Golden Brown	(United Artists BP 407)	2	1982	0	1982	
16	La Folie	(United Artists BP 410)	47	1982	0	1982	
17	Strange Little Girl	(Liberty BP 412)	7	1982	0	1982	
18	European Female	(Epic EPC A 2893)	9	1983	0	1983	
19	Midnight Summer Dream	(Epic EPC A 3167)	35	1983	0	1983	
20	Paradise	(Epic A 3387)	48	1983	0	1983	
21	Skin Deep	(Epic A 4738)	15	1984	0	1984	
22	No Mercy	(Epic A 4921)	37	1984	0	1984	
23	Let Me Down Easy	(Epic A 6045)	48	1985	0	1985	
24	Nice In Nice	(Epic 650057)	30	1986	0	1986	
25	Always The Sun	(Epic Solar 1)	30	1986	0	1986	
26	Big In America	(Epic HUGE 1)	48	1986	0	1986	
27	Shakin' Like A Leaf	(Epic SHEIK 1)	58	1987	0	1987	
28	All Day And All Of The Night	(Epic VICE 1)	7	1988	0	1988	
29	Grip '89 (Get A) Grip (On Yourself) (Re-Mix)	(EMI EM 84)	33	1989	0	1989	
30	96 Tears	(Epic TEARS 1)	17	1990	0	1990	
31	Sweet Smell Of Sucess	(Epic TEARS 2)	65	1990	0	1990	
32	Always The Sun (Re-Mix)	(Epic 6564307)	29	1991	0	1991	
33	Golden Brown (Re-Mix)	(Epic 6567617)	68	1991	0	1991	
34	Heaven Or Hell	(PSYCHO WOK 2025)	46	1992	0	1992	

ISSUE	TITLE	UK LBL	UK POS	UK YEAR	US POS	US YEAR	US LBL
Strawberry Alarm Clock	Lead Guitar In This Sextet Is Ed King						
* 1	Incense And Peppermints		0	1967	1	1967	(UNI 55018)
2	Tomorrow		0	1968	23	1968	(UNI 55046)
Strawberry Switchblade	Female Vocal Duo from the UK						
1	Since Yesterday	(KOROVA KOW 38)	5	1984	0	1984	
2	Let Her Go	(KOROVA KOW 39)	59	1985	0	1985	
3	Jolene	(KOROVA KOW 42)	53	1983	0	1983	
Strawbs	Male Vocal/Instrumental Group from the UK						
1	Laydown	(A&M AMS 7035)	12	1972	0	1975	
2	Part Of The Union	(A&M AMS 7047)	2	1973	0	1973	
3	Shine On Silver Sun	(A&M AMS 7082)	34	1973	0	1973	
Stray Cats	Male Rockabilly Trio From Long Island, New York						
1	Runaway Boys	(Arista SCAT 1)	9	1980	0	1980	
2	Rock This Town	(Arista SCAT 2)	9	1981	9	1982	(EMI America 8132)
3	Stray Cat Strut	(Arista SCAT 3)	11	1981	3	1983	(EMI America 8122)
4	The Race Is On	(SWANSONG SSK19425)	34	1981	0	1981	
5	You Don't Believe Me	(Arista SCAT 4)	57	1981	0	1981	
6	(She's) Sexy And 17	(Arista SCAT 6)	29	1983	5	1983	(EMI America 8168)
7	I Won't Stand In Your Way		0	1983	35	1983	(EMI America 8185)
8	Bring It Back Again	(EMI USA MT 62)	64	1989	0	1989	
	NAMES ARE BRIAN SETZER, JIM PHANTOM & LEE ROCKER (B: LEON DRUCHER) • THE GROUP DISBANDED IN 1984						
Street People	Mixed Studio Quartet from the USA						
1	Jennifer Tomkins		0	1970	36	1970	(MUSICOR 1365)
Streetband	Male Vocal/Instrumental Group from the UK						
1	Toast / Hold On	(LOGO GO 325)	18	1978	0	1978	
Stress	Male Vocal/Instrumental Group from the UK						
1	Beautiful People	(ETERNAL YZ 95)	74	1990	0	1990	
Stretch	Male Vocal/Instrumental Group from the UK, Used The Name Fleetwood Mac When A Member Of The Original Group Left To Form Stretch						
1	Why Did You Do It	(ANCHOR ANC 1021)	16	1975	0	1975	
Stretch & Vern	Male Instrumental/Production Duo from the UK						
1	I'm Alive	(FFRR FCD 284)	6	1996	0	1996	
2	Get Up! Go Insane!	(FFRR FCD 304)	17	1997	0	1997	
	HIT 1 IS CREDITED TO STRETCH & VERN FEATURING MADDOG • HIT 2 IS CREDITED TO STRETCH 'N' VERN PRESENTS MADDOG						
Strike	Mixed Vocal/Instrumental Group From Australia						
1	U Sure Do	(FRESH FRSHD 19)	31	1994	0	1994	
2	U Sure Do (Re-Entry)	(FRESH FRSHT 19)	4	1995	0	1995	
3	The Morning After (Free At Last)	(FRESH FSSHT 37)	38	1995	0	1995	
4	Inspiration	(FRESH FRSHD 45)	27	1996	0	1996	
5	My Love Is For Real	(FRESH FRSHD 46)	35	1996	0	1996	
6	I Have Peace	(FRESH FRSHD 58)	17	1997	0	1997	
Strikers	Male Vocal/Instrumental Group from the UK						
1	Body Music	(Epic EPC A 1290)	45	1981	0	1981	
String-A-Longs	Male Instrumental Guitar Group from the USA, Keith McCormack, Aubrey Lee De-Gordova, Jimmy Torres, Richard Stephens & Don Allen.						
* 1	Wheels	(London HLU 9278)	8	1961	3	1961	(WARWICK 603)
2	Brass Buttons		0	1961	35	1961	(WARWICK 625)
Strings Of Love	Mixed Vocal/Instrumental Group from Italy						
1	Nothing Has Been Proved	(BREAKOUT USA 688)	59	1990	0	1990	
Stryper	Vocals With This Heavy Metal Band From California Are By Michael Sweet						
1	Honestly		0	1987	23	1987	(ENIGMA 75009)
Stuart Gillies	Male Vocalist from the UK						
1	Amanda	(Philips 6006 293)	13	1973	0	1973	
Stuart Hamblen	Male Country/Gospel/Songwriter/Singer from the USA						
1	This Ole House		0	1954	26	1954	(RCA Victor 5739)
Stump	Male Vocal/Instrumental Group from the UK						
1	Charlton Heston	(Ensign ENY 614)	72	1988	0	1988	
Stutz Bearcats & The Denis King Orchestra	Mixed Vocal Group With Orchestra from the UK						
1	The Song That I Sing (Theme From We'll Meet Again)		36	1982	0	1982	(MULTI-MEDIA TAPES MMT 6)
	SEE ALSO KING BROTHERS						

Style Council   Male Vocal/Instrumental Trio from the UK, Names: Paul Weller & Mick Talbot & Dee C. Lee (Joined In 1988)

ISSUE	TITLE	UK LBL	UK POS	UK YEAR	US POS	US YEAR	US LBL
1	Speak Like A Child	(Polydor TSC 1)	4	1983	0	1983	
2	Money Go Round (Part 1)	(Polydor TSC 2)	11	1983	0	1983	
3	Long Hot Summer / Paris Match	(Polydor TSC 3)	3	1983	0	1983	
4	Money Go Round (Part 1) (Re-Entry)	(Polydor TSC 2)	74	1983	0	1983	
5	Solid Bond In Your Heart	(Polydor TSC 4)	11	1983	0	1983	
6	My Ever Changing Moods	(Polydor TSC 5)	5	1984	29	1984	(Geffen 29359)
7	Groovin' (You're The Best Thing) / Big Boss Groove	(Polydor TSC 6)	5	1984	0	198	
8	Shout To The Top	(Polydor TSC 7)	7	1984	0	1984	
9	Walls Come Tumbling Down	(Polydor TSC 8)	6	1985	0	1985	
10	Come To Milton Keynes	(Polydor TSC 9)	23	1985	0	1985	
11	The Lodgers	(Polydor TSC 10)	13	1985	0	1985	
12	Have You Ever Had It Blue	(Polydor CINE	14	1986	0	1986	
13	It Didn't Matter	(Polydor TSC 12)	9	1987	0	1987	
14	Waiting	(Polydor TSC 13)	52	1987	0	1987	
15	Wanted	(Polydor TSC 14)	20	1987	0	1987	
16	Life At A Top Peoples Health Farm	(Polydor TSC 15)	28	1988	0	1988	
17	How She Threw It All Away (EP)	(Polydor TSC 16)	4	1988	0	1988	
18	Promised Land	(Polydor TSC 17)	27	1989	0	1989	
19	Long Hot Summer '89 (Re-Mix)	(Polydor LHS 1)	48	1989	0	1989	

Stylistics   Male Vocal Group from the USA Names Russell Thompkins Jr, James Smith, Airron Love, James Dunn & Herbie Murrell.

ISSUE	TITLE	UK LBL	UK POS	UK YEAR	US POS	US YEAR	US LBL
*+ 1	You're A Big Girl Now		0	1971	7	1971	(Avco Embassy 4555)
2	Stop, Look, Listen (To Your Heart)		0	1971	39	1971	(Avco Embassy 4572)
* 3	You Are Everything		0	1971	9	1971	(Avco 4581)
* 4	Betcha By Golly Wow	(Avco 6105 011)	13	1972	3	1972	(Avco 4591)
5	People Make The World Go Round		0	1972	25	1972	(Avco 4595)
* 6	I'm Stone In Love With You	(Avco 610 015)	9	1972	10	1972	(Avco 4603)
* 7	Break Up To Make Up	(Avco 6105 020)	34	1973	5	1973	(Avco 4611)
8	You'll Never Get To Heaven (If You Break My Heart)		0	1973	23	1973	(Avco 4618)
9	Peek-A-Boo	(Avco 6105 023)	35	1973	0	1973	
10	Rockin' Roll Baby	(Avco 6105 026)	6	1974	14	1973	(Avco 4625)
* 11	You Make Me Feel Brand New	(Avco 6105 028)	2	1974	2	1974	(Avco 4634)
12	Let's Put It All Together	(Avco 6105 032)	9	1974	18	1974	(Avco 4640)
13	Star On A Tv Show	(Avco 6105 035)	12	1975	0	1975	
14	Sing Baby Sing	(Avco 6105 036)	3	1975	0	1975	
15	Can't Give You Anything (But My Love)	(Avco 6105 039)	1	1975	0	1975	
16	Na Na Is The Saddest Word	(Avco 6105 041)	5	1975	0	1975	
17	Funky Weekend	(Avco 6105 044)	10	1976	0	1976	
18	Can't Help Falling In Love	(Avco 6105 050)	4	1976	0	1976	
19	16 Bars	(H&L 6105 059)	7	1976	0	1976	
20	You'll Never Get To Heaven (EP)	(H&L STYL 001)	24	1976	0	1976	
21	7000 Dollars And You	(H&L 6105 073)	24	1977	0	1977	

HIT 4 IS CREDITED TO STYLISTICS FEATURING RUSSELL THOMPKINS JR.

Styx   Male Vocal/Instrumental Group from the UK

ISSUE	TITLE	UK LBL	UK POS	UK YEAR	US POS	US YEAR	US LBL
1	Lady		0	1975	6	1975	(Wooden N. 10102)
2	Lorelie		0	1976	27	1976	(A&M 1786)
3	Mademoiselle		0	1976	36	1976	(A&M 1877)
4	Come Sail Away		0	1977	8	1977	(A&M 1977)
5	Fooling Yourself (The Angry Young Man)		0	1978	29	1978	(A&M 2007)
6	Blue Collar Man (Long Nights)		0	1978	21	1978	(A&M 2087)
7	Renegade		0	1979	16	1979	(A&M 2110)
* 8	Babe	(A&M AMS 7489)	6	1980	1	1979	(A&M 2188)
9	Why Me		0	1980	26	1980	(A&M 2206)
10	The Best Of Times	(A&M AMS 8102)	42	1981	3	1981	(A&M 2300)
11	Too Much Time On My Hands		0	1981	9	1981	(A&M 2323)
* 12	Mr. Roboto		0	1983	3	1983	(A&M 2525)
13	Don't Let It End	(A&M AM 120)	56	1983	6	1983	(A&M 2543)
14	Music Time		0	1984	40	1984	(A&M 2625)
15	Show Me The Way		0	1991	3	1991	(A&M 1536)
16	Love At First Sight		0	1991	25	1991	(A&M 1548)

VOCALS WITH THE QUINTET ARE BY DENNIS DEYOUNG

Su Pollard   Female Actress/Vocalist from the UK

ISSUE	TITLE	UK LBL	UK POS	UK YEAR	US POS	US YEAR	US LBL
1	Come To Me (I Am Woman)	(Rainbow RBR 1)	71	1985	0	1985	
2	Starting Together	(Rainbow RBR 4)	2	1986	0	1986	

ISSUE	TITLE	UK LBL	UK POS	UK YEAR	US POS	US YEAR	US LBL
Suave Male Vocalist, B: 22 Feb 1966 from Los Angeles							
1	My Girl		0	1988	20	1988	(Capitol 44124)
Sub Sub Male Production/Instrumental Duo from the UK							
1	Ain't No Love (Ain't No Use)	(ROB'S CDROB 9)	3	1993	0	1993	
2	Respect	(ROB'S CDROB 19)	49	1994	0	1994	
	HIT 1 IS CREDITED TO SUB SUB FEATURING MELANIE WILLIAMS						
Subliminal Cuts Male Producer Patrick Prinz from Holland							
1	Le Voie Le Soleil	(XL XLS 53CD)	69	1994	0	1994	
2	Le Voie Le Soleil (Re-Mix)	(XL XLSR 53CD)	23	1996	0	1996	
Subsonic 2 Male Rap Duo from the UK							
1	The Unsung Heroes Of Hip Hop	(UNITY 6577947)	63	1991	0	1991	
Subterrania(Featuring Ann Consuelo) Mixed Vocal/Instrumental Duo from Sweden							
1	Do It For Love	(Champion ChampCD 297)	68	1993	0	1993	
Subway Vocal Quartet from Chicago							
* 1	This Lil' Game We Play		0	1995	15	1995	(SUGAR HILL 542)
Sue Chaloner Female Vocalist from the UK							
1	Move On Up	(PULSE 8 CDLOSE41)	64	1993	0	1993	
Sue Jones-Davies See Julie Covington							
Sue Nicholls Female Vocalist from the UK							
1	Where Will You Be	(PYE 7N 17565)	17	1968	0	1968	
Sue Thompson Female Vocalist, Real Name Eva Sue McCkee B: 19 Jul 1926 Nevada, Missouri							
* 1	Sad Movies (Make Me Cry)	(Polydor NH 66967)	46	1961	5	1961	(HICKORY 1153)
* 2	Sad Movies (Make Me Cry) (Re-Entry)	(Polydor NH 66967)	48	1961	0	1961*	
3	Norman		0	1962	3	1962	(HICKORY 1159)
4	Have A Good Time		0	1962	31	1962	(HICKORY 1174)
5	James (Hold The Ladder Steady)		0	1962	17	1962	(HICKORY 1183)
6	Paper Tiger	(HICKORY 1284)	50	1965	23	1965	(HICKORY 1284)
7	Paper Tiger (Re-Entry)	(HICKORY 1284)	30	1965	0	1965	
Sue Wilkinson Female Vocalist from the UK							
1	You Gotta Be A Hustler If You Want To Get On	(Cheapskate Cheap 2)	25	1980	0	1980	
Suede Male Vocal/Instrumental Group from the UK							
1	The Drowners - To The Birds	(NUDE NUD 1S)	49	1992	0	1992	
2	Metal Mickey	(NUDE NUD 3S)	17	1992	0	1992	
3	Animal Nitrate	(NUDE NUD 4CD)	7	1993	0	1993	
4	So Young	(NUDE NUD 5CD)	22	1993	0	1993	
5	Stay Together	(NUDE NUD 9CD)	3	1994	0	1994	
6	We Are The Pigs	(NUDE NUD 10CD)	18	1994	0	1994	
7	The Wild Ones	(NUDE NUD 11CD1)	18	1994	0	1994	
8	New Generation	(NUDE NUD 12CD1)	21	1995	0	1995	
9	New Generation (Re-Entry)	(NUDE NUD 12CD1)	75	1995	0	1995	
10	Trash	(NUDE NUD 21CD1)	3	1996	0	1996	
11	Beautiful Ones	(NUDE NUD 23CD1)	8	1996	0	1996	
12	Saturday Night	(NUDE NUD 24CD1)	6	1997	0	1997	
13	Lazy	(NUDE NUD 27CD1)	9	1997	0	1997	
14	Filmstar	(NUDE NUD 30CD1)	9	1997	0	1997	
Sueno Latino (Featuring) Carolina Damas Male Production Duo With Female Vocalist From Italy							
1	Sueno Latino	(BCM BCM 323)	47	1989	0	1989	
Sugar Male Vocal/Instrumental Group from the USA							
1	A Good Idea	(Creation CRE 143)	65	1992	0	1992	
2	If I Can't Change Your Mind	(Creation CRESCD 149)	30	1993	0	1993	
3	Tilted	(Creation CRECD 156)	48	1993	0	1993	
4	Your Favorite Thing	(Creation CRESCD 186)	40	1994	0	1994	
5	Believe What You're Saying	(Creation CRESCD 193)	73	1994	0	1994	
Sugar Cane Mixed Vocal Group from the USA							
1	Montego Bay	(ARIOLA HANSA AHA 524)	54	1978	0	1978	
Sugar Minott Male Vocalist from the UK							
1	Good Thing Going (We've Got A Good Thing Going)	(RCA 58)	4	1981	0	1981	
2	Never My Love	(RCA 138)	52	1981	0	1981	

ISSUE	TITLE	UK LBL	UK POS	UK YEAR	US POS	US YEAR	US LBL
Sugarcubes	Mixed Vocal/Instrumental Group From Iceland						
1	Birthday	(One Little Indian TP 7)	65	1987	0	1987	
2	Cold Sweat	(One Little Indian 7TP 9)	56	1988	0	1988	
3	Deus	(One Little Indian 7TP 10)	51	1988	0	1988	
4	Birthday (Re-Recording)	(One Little Indian 7TP 11)	65	1989	0	1989	
5	Regina	(One Little Indian 26TP7)	55	1989	0	1989	
6	Hit	(One Little Indian 62 TP7)	17	1992	0	1992	
7	Birthday (Re-Mix)	(One Little Indian 104 TP12)	64	1992	0	1992	
Sugarhill Gang	Male Rap Trio from the USA, Names: Michael Wright, Guy O'Brien & Henry Jackson						
1	Rapper's Delight	(SUGARHILL SHL 101)	3	1979	36	1980	(SUGAR HILL 542)
2	The Lover In You	(SUGARHILL SH 116)	54	1982	0	1982	
3	Rapper's Delight (Re-Mix)	(SUGARHILL SHRD 0007)	58	1989	0	1989	
Sugarloaf	Lead Singer With The Quartet Is Jerry Corbetta						
1	Green-Eyed Lady		0	1970	3	1970	(Liberty 56183)
2	Don't Call Us We'll Call You		0	1975	9	1975	(CLARIDGE 402)
	HIT 2 IS CREDITED TO SUGARLOAF/JERRY CORBETTA						
Suggs	Male Vocalist from the UK						
1	I'm Only Sleeping / Off On Holiday	(WEA YZ 975CD)	7	1995	0	1995	
2	Camden Town	(WEA WEA 019CD)	14	1995	0	1995	
3	The Tune	(WEA WEA 031CD)	33	1995	0	1995	
4	Cecilia	(WEA WEA042CD1)	4	1996	0	1996	
5	Cecilia (Re-Entry)	(WEA WEA 042CD1)	65	1996	0	1996	
6	Cecilia (2nd Re-Entry)	(WEA WEA 042CD1)	59	1996	0	1996	
7	No More Alcohol	(WEA WEA 065CD1)	24	1996	0	1996	
8	Blue Day	(WEA WEA 112CD)	26	1997	0	1997	
	HITS 4-7 ARE CREDITED TO SUGGS FEATURING LOUCHIE LOU & MICHIE ONE • HIT 8 IS CREDITED TO SUGGS & CO FEATURING CHELSEA TEAM						
Sultana	Male Production/Instrumental Group From Italy						
1	Te Amo	(UNION CITY UCRD 28)	57	1994	0	1994	
Sultans Of Ping	Male Vocal/Instrumental Group From Ireland						
1	Where's Me Jumper	(DIVINE ATHY 01)	67	1992	0	1992	
2	Stupid Kid	(DIVINE ATHY 02)	67	1992	0	1992	
3	Veronica	(DIVINE ATHY 03)	69	1992	0	1992	
4	You Talk Too Much	(Rhythm King6588872)	26	1993	0	1993	
5	Teenage Punks	(Epic 6595792)	49	1993	0	1993	
6	Michiko	(Epic 6598222)	43	1993	0	1993	
7	Wake Up And Scratch Me	(Epic 6601122)	50	1994	0	1994	
	HITS 1-4 ARE CREDITED TO SULTANS OF PING FC						
Summer Daze	Male Instrumental/Production Duo from the UK						
1	Samba Magic	(VC VCRD 14)	61	1996	0	1996	
Sundays	Mixed Vocal/Instrumental Group from the UK						
1	Can't Be Sure	(Rought Trade RT 218)	46	1989	0	1989	
2	Goodbye	(Parlophone R 6319)	27	1992	0	1992	
Sundragon	Male Vocal/Instrumental Group from the UK						
1	Green Tamborine	(MGM 1380)	50	1968	0	1968	
Sunfire	Male Vocal/Instrumental Group from the USA						
1	Young Free And Single	(Warner Bros. W 9897)	20	1983	0	1983	
Sunny	Female Vocalist from the UK						
1	Doctor's Orders	(CBS 2068)	7	1974	0	1974	
Sunny & The Sunglows	Formed In San Antonio, Texas In 1959						
1	Talk To Me		0	1963	11	1963	(TEAR DROP 3014)
Sunny Gale	Sunny Hails From Clayton, New Jersey						
1	Wheel Of Fortune		0	1952	13	1952	(Decca 787)
2	I Laughed At Love		0	1952	14	1952	(RCA Victor 4789)
3	Teardrops On My Pillow		0	1953	12	1953	(RCA Victor 5103)
4	A Stolen Waltz		0	1953	18	1953	(RCA Victor 5103)
5	Love Me Again		0	1953	22	1953	(RCA Victor 5424)
6	Before It's Too Late		0	1953	27	1953	(RCA Victor 5424)
7	Goodnight, Sweetheart, Goodnight		0	1954	26	1954	(RCA Victor 5746)
8	Smile (From Modern Times)		0	1954	19	1954	(RCA Victor 5836)
9	Let Me Go Lover!		0	1955	17	1955	(RCA 5952)
	HIT 1 IS CREDITED TO EDDIE WILCOX ORCHESTRA WITH SUNNY GALE						

ISSUE	TITLE	UK LBL	UK POS	UK YEAR	US POS	US YEAR	US LBL
Sunnysiders Vocal/Instrumental Group from the UK, Names Jad Paul, Margie Raybum & Freddy Morgan							
1	Hey, Mr. Banjo		0	1955	12	1955	(KAPP 113)
FREDDY WAS A MEMBER OF SPIKE JONES & HIS CITY SLICKERS FROM 1947 UNTIL EARLY 1958 • OBITUARY :MORGAN D: 1970.							
Sunscreem Mixed Vocal/Instrumental Group from the UK							
1	Pressure	(SONY S2 6578017)	60	1992	0	1992	
2	Love U More	(SONY S2 6581727)	23	1992	36	1993	(Columbia 74769)
3	Perfect Motion	(SONY S2 6584057)	18	1992	0	1992	
4	Broken English	(SONY S2 6589032)	13	1993	0	1993	
5	Pressure Us (Re-Mix)	(SONY S2 6591102)	19	1993	0	1993	
6	When	(SONY S2 6623222)	47	1995	0	1995	
7	Exodus	(SONY S2 6625342)	40	1995	0	1995	
8	White Skies	(SONY S2 6627425)	25	1996	0	1996	
9	Secrets	(SONY S2 6629342)	36	1996	0	1996	
10	Catch	(PULSE-8 CDLOSE117)	55	1997	0	1997	
Sunshine Company Lead Singer With The Quintet Is Mary Nance							
1 1	Back On The Streets Again		0	1967	36	1967	(IMPERIAL 66260)
Super Furry Animals Male Vocal/Instrumental Group from the UK							
1	Hometown Unicorn	(Creation CRESCD 222)	47	1996	0	1996	
2	God! Show Me Magic	(Creation CRESCD 231)	33	1996	0	1996	
3	Something 4 The Weekend	(Creation CRESCD 235)	18	1996	0	1996	
4	If You Don't Want Me To Destroy You	(Creation CRESCD 243)	18	1996	0	1996	
5	The Man Don't Give A Fuck	(Creation CRESCD 247)	22	1996	0	1996	
6	Hermann Loves Pauline	(Creation CRESCD 252)	26	1997	0	1997	
7	The International Language Of Screaming	(Creation CRESCD 269)	24	1997	0	1997	
Supercat Mixed Vocal Duo from Jamaica							
1	It Fe Done	(Columbia 6582737)	66	1992	0	1992	
2	My Girl Josephine	(Columbia 6614702)	22	1995	0	1995	
HIT 2 IS CREDITED TO SUPERCAT FEATURING JACK RADICS							
Supergrass Male Vocal/Instrumental Group from the UK							
1	Caught By The Fuzz	(Parlophone CDR 6396)	43	1994	0	1994	
2	Mansize Rooster	(Parlophone CDR 6402)	20	1995	0	1995	
3	Lose It	(SUB POP SP 281)	75	1995	0	1995	
4	Lenny	(ParlophoneCDR 6410)	10	1995	0	1995	
5	Alright / Time	(ParlophoneCDR 6413)	2	1995	0	1995	
6	Going Out	(Parlophone CDR 6428)	5	1996	0	1996	
7	Richard Iii	(Parlophone CDR 6461)	2	1997	0	1997	
8	Sun Hits The Sky	(Parlophone CDR 6469)	10	1997	0	1997	
Supernaturals Male Vocal/Instrumental Group from the UK							
1	Lazy Lover	(FOOD/Parlophone CDFOOD 85)	34	1996	0	1996	
2	The Day Before Yesterday's Man	(FOOD/Parlophone CDFOOD 88)	25	1997	0	1997	
3	Smile	(FOOD/Parlophone CDFOOD 92)	23	1997	0	1997	
4	Love Has Passed Away	(Food/Parlophone CDFOOD 99)	38	1997	0	1997	
Supernova Mixed Vocal/Instrumental Duo from the UK							
1	Some Might Say	(Sing Sing 74321369442)	55	1996	0	1996	
Supertramp Male Vocal/Instrumental Group from the USA/UK, Roger Hodgson, John Helliwell, Dougie Thompson, Rick Davies & Bob Siebenberg							
1	Dreamer	(A&M AMS 7132)	13	1975	10	1980	(A&M 2193)
2	Bloody Well Right		0	1975	35	1975	(A&M 1660)
3	Give A Little Bit	(A&M AMS 7293)	29	1977	15	1977	(A&M 1938)
4	The Logical Song	(A&M AMS 7427)	7	1979	6	1979	(A&M 2128)
5	Breakfast In America	(A&M AMS 7451)	9	1979	0	1979	
6	Goodbye Stranger	(A&M AMS 7481)	57	1979	15	1979	(A&M 2162)
7	Take The Long Way Home		0	1979	10	1979	(A&M 2193)
8	Dreamer (Live)		0	1980	15	1980	(A&M 2269)
9	It's Raining Again	(A&M AMS 8255)	26	1982	11	1982	(A&M 2502)
10	My Kind Of Lady		0	1983	31	1983	(A&M 2517)
11	Cannonball		0	1985	28	1985	(A&M 2731)
HIT 9 IS CREDITED TO SUPERTRAMP FEATURING ROGER HODGSON							
Supremes Female Vocal Group from Detroit, Diana Ross, Mary Wilson, Barbara Martin & Florence Ballard							
+ 1	Let Me Go The Right Way		0	1962	26	1962	(Motown 1034)
2	Can I Get A Witness		0	1963	22	1963	(Tamla 54087)
3	When The Lovelight Start Shining Through His Eyes		0	1963	23	1963	(Motown 1051)
* 4	Where Did Our Love Go	(STATESIDE SS 327)	3	1964	1	1964	(Motown 1060)

ISSUE	TITLE	UK LBL	UK POS	UK YEAR	US POS	US YEAR	US LBL
* 5	Baby Love	(STATESIDE SS 350)	1	1964	1	1964	(Motown 1066)
* 6	Come See About Me	(STATESIDE SS 376)	27	1965	1	1964	(Motown 1068)
* 7	Stop In The Name Of Love	(Tamla MotownTMG 501)	7	1965	1	1965	(Motown 1074)
* 8	Back In My Arms Again	(Tamla MotownTMG 516)	40	1965	1	1965	(Motown 1075)
* 9	Nothing But Heartaches		0	1965	11	1965	(Motown 1080)
* 10	I Hear A Symphony	(Tamla MotownTMG 543)	50	1965	1	1965	(Motown 1083)
11	I Hear A Symphony (Re-Entry)	(Tamla MotownTMG 543)	39	1965	0	1965	
* 12	My World Is Empty Without You		0	1966	5	1966	(Motown 1089)
13	Love Is Like An Itching In My Heart		0	1966	9	1966	(Motown 1094)
* 14	You Can't Hurry Love	(Tamla MotownTMG 575)	3	1966	1	1966	(Motown 1097)
* 15	You Keep Me Hangin' On	(Tamla MotownTMG 585)	8	1966	1	1966	(Motown 1101)
* 16	Love Is Here And Now You're Gone	(Tamla MotownTMG 597)	17	1967	1	1967	(Motown 1103)
* 17	The Happening	(Tamla MotownTMG 607)	6	1967	1	1967	(Motown 1107)
18	Reflections	(Tamla MotownTMG 616)	5	1967	2	1967	(Motown 1111)
19	In And Out Of Love	(Tamla MotownTMG 632)	13	1967	9	1967	(Motown 1116)
20	Forever Came Today	(Tamla MotownTMG 650)	28	1968	28	1968	(Motown 1122)
21	Somethings You Never Get Used To	(Tamla MotownTMG 662)	34	1968	30	1968	(Motown 1126)
22	Love Child	(Tamla MotownTMG 677)	15	1968	1	1968	(Motown 1135)
23	I'm Gonna Make You Love Me	(Tamla MotownTMG 685)	3	1969	2	1968	(Motown 1137)
24	I'm Livin' In Shame	(Tamla MotownTMG 695)	14	1969	10	1969	(Motown 1139)
25	I'll Try Something New		0	1969	25	1969	(Motown 1142)
26	The Composer		0	1969	27	1969	(Motown 1146)
27	I'm Gonna Make You Love Me (Re-Entry)	(Tamla MotownTMG 685)	49	1969	0	1969	
28	No Matter What Sign You Are	(Tamla Motown TMG 704)	37	1969	31	1969	(Motown 1148)
29	I'm Livin' In Shame (Re-Entry)	(Tamla Motown TMG 695)	50	1969	0	1969	
30	I Second That Emotion	(Tamla Motown TMG 709)	18	1969	0	1969	
31	Someday We'll Be Together	(Tamla Motown TMG 721)	13	1969	1	1969	(Motown 1156)
* 32	Up The Ladder To The Roof	(Tamla Motown TMG 735)	6	1970	10	1970	(Motown 1162)
33	Why Must We Fall In Love	(Tamla Motown TMG 730)	31	1970	0	1970	
34	Everybody's Got The Right To Love		0	1970	21	1970	(Motown 1167)
* 35	Stoned Love	(Tamla MotownTMG 760)	3	1971	7	1970	(Motown 1172)
36	River Deep Mountain High	(Tamla Motown TMG 777)	11	1971	14	1971	(Motown 1173)
* 37	Nathan Jones	(Tamla Motown TMG 782)	5	1971	16	1971	(Motown 1182)
38	You Gotta Have Love In Your Heart	(Tamla MotownTMG 793)	25	1971	0	1971	
* 39	Floy Joy	(Tamla Motown TMG 804)	9	1972	16	1972	(Motown 1195)
40	Automatically Sunshine	(Tamla MotownTMG 821)	10	1972	37	1972	(Motown 1200)
41	Bad Weather	(Tamla Motown TMG 847)	37	1973	0	1973	
42	Baby Love (Re-Issue)	(Tamla MotownTMG 915)	12	1974	0	1974	
43	I'm Gonna Let My Heart Do The Walking		0	1976	40	1976	(Motown 1391)
44	Stop In The Name Of Love (Re-Issue)	(Tamla ZB 41963)	62	1989	0	1989	

STARTED WITH MOTOWN AS THE PRIMETTES, THE TEMPTATIONS WERE THE PRIMES • OBITUARY : FLORENCE D: 22 FEB 1976 DRINK-RELATED HEART ATTACK.

Surface   Male Vocal/Instrumental Trio from the USA,   Names: Bernard Jackson, David Townend & Dave Conley

ISSUE	TITLE	UK LBL	UK POS	UK YEAR	US POS	US YEAR	US LBL
1	Falling In Love	(SALSOUL SAL104)	67	1983	0	1983	
2	When Your 'Ex' Wants You Back	(SALSOUL SAL 106)	52	1984	0	1984	
3	Happy	(CBS 650393 7)	56	1987	20	1987	(Columbia 06611)
* 4	Shower Me With Your Love		0	1989	5	1989	(Columbia 68746)
* 5	The First Time	(Columbia 6564767)	60	1991	1	1990	(Columbia 73502)
6	Never Gonna Let You Down		0	1991	17	1991	(Columbia 73643)

Surface Noise   Male Instrumental Group from the UK

ISSUE	TITLE	UK LBL	UK POS	UK YEAR	US POS	US YEAR	US LBL
1	The Scratch	(WEA K 18291)	26	1980	0	1980	
2	Dancin' On A Wire	(Groove GP 102)	59	1980	0	1980	

Surfaris   Male Instrumental Group from the USA

ISSUE	TITLE	UK LBL	UK POS	UK YEAR	US POS	US YEAR	US LBL
* 1	Wipe Out	(London HLD 9751)	5	1963	2	1963	(DOT 16479)
2	Wipe Out (Re-Issue)		0	1966	16	1966	(DOT 144)

NAMES RON WILSON, JIM FULLER, BOB BERRYHILL, PAT CONNOLLY & JIM PASH

Surprise Sisters   Female Vocal Group from the UK

ISSUE	TITLE	UK LBL	UK POS	UK YEAR	US POS	US YEAR	US LBL
1	La Booga Rooga	(Good Earth GD 1)	38	1976	0	1976	

Survivor   Male Vocal/Instrumental Group from the USA

ISSUE	TITLE	UK LBL	UK POS	UK YEAR	US POS	US YEAR	US LBL
1	Poor Man's Son		0	1981	33	1981	(Scotti Brothers 02560)
* 2	Eye Of The Tiger	(Scotti Brothers SCT 02912)	1	1982	1	1982	(Scotti Brothers A 2411)
3	American Heartbeat		0	1982	17	1982	(Scotti Brothers 03213)
4	I Can't Hold Back		0	1984	13	1984	(Scotti Brothers 04603)
5	High On You		0	1985	8	1985	(Scotti Brothers 04685)
6	The Search Is Over		0	1985	4	1985	(Scotti Brothers 04871)
7	Burning Heart	(Scotti Brothers A05663)	5	1986	2	1985	(Scotti Brothers 6708)

ISSUE	TITLE	UK LBL	UK POS	UK YEAR	US POS	US YEAR	US LBL
8	Is This Love		0	1986	9	1986	(Scotti Brothers 06381)
	LEAD SINGER WITH THE GROUP IS DAVE BICKLER						

Susan Cadogan   Female Vocalist from the UK

| 1 | Hurt So Good | (Magnet MAG 23) | 4 | 1975 | 0 | 1975 | |
| 2 | Love Me Baby | (Magnet MAG 36) | 22 | 1975 | 0 | 1975 | |

Susan Fassbender   Female Vocalist from the UK

| 1 | Twilight Cafe | (CBS 9468) | 21 | 1981 | 0 | 1981 | |

Susan Maughan   Female Vocalist from the UK

1	Bobby's Girl	(Philips 326544 BF)	3	1962	0	1962	
2	Hand A Hankerchief To Helen	(Philips 326562 BF)	41	1963	0	1963	
3	She's New To You	(Philips 326586 BF)	45	1963	0	1963	

Susanna Hoffs   Female Vocalist, B: 17 Jan 1957 from the USA., Former Lead Singer With The Bangles

1	My Side Of The Bed	(Columbia 6565547)	44	1991	30	1991	(Columbia 73529)
2	Unconditional Love	(Columbia 6567827)	65	1991	0	1991	
3	All I Want	(London LONCD 387)	32	1996	77	1996	(Island 850686)

Sutherland Brothers & Quiver   Male Vocal/Instrumental Group from the UK

1	Arms Of Mary	(CBS 4001)	5	1976	0	1976	
2	Secrets	(CBS 4668)	35	1976	0	1976	
3	Easy Come Easy Go	(CBS 7121)	50	1979	0	1979	

Suzanne Vega   Female Singer/Songwriter, B: 12 Aug 1959 From New York

	1	Small Blue Thing	(A&M AM 294)	65	1986	0	1986	
	2	Marlene On The Wall	(A&M AM 309)	21	1986	0	1986	
	3	Left Of Centre	(A&M AM 320)	32	1986	0	1986	
	4	Luka	(A&M VEGA 1)	23	1987	3	1987	(A&M 2937)
	5	Tom's Diner	(A&M VEGA 2)	58	1987	0	1987	
	6	Book Of Dreams	(A&M AM 559)	66	1990	0	1990	
*	7	Ton's Diner	(A&M AM 592)	2	1990	5	1990	(A&M 1529)
	8	In Liverpool	(A&M AM 0029)	52	1992	0	1992	
	9	99.9f	(A&M AM 0085)	46	1992	0	1992	
	10	Blood Makes Noise	(A&M AM 0112)	60	1992	0	1992	
	11	When Hero's Go Down	(A&M AMCD 0158)	58	1993	0	1993	
	12	No Cheap Thrill	(A&M 5818692)	40	1997	0	1997	

HIT 3 IS CREDITED TO SUZANNE VEGA FEATURING JOE JACKSON • HIT 7 IS CREDITED TO DNA FEATURING SUZANNE VEGA

Suzette Charles   Female Vocalist from the USA

| 1 | Free To Love Again | (RCA 74321158372) | 58 | 1993 | 0 | 1993 | |

Suzi Carr   Female Vocalist from the USA

| 1 | All Over Me | (Cowboy Rodeo 947CD) | 45 | 1994 | 0 | 1994 | |

Suzi Quatro   Female Vocal/Instrumentalist (Bass Guitar), B: 3 Jun 1950 Detroit, Michigan

*	1	Can The Can	(RAK 150)	1	1973	0	1973	
*	2	48 Crash	(RAK 158)	3	1973	0	1973	
	3	Daytona Demond	(RAK 161)	14	1973	0	1973	
*	4	Devil Gate Drive	(RAK 167)	1	1974	0	1974	
	5	Too Big	(RAK 175)	14	1974	0	1974	
	6	The Wild One	(RAK 185)	7	1974	0	1974	
	7	You're Mamma Won't Like Me	(RAK 191)	31	1975	0	1975	
	8	Tear Me Apart	(RAK 248)	27	1977	0	1977	
	9	If You Can't Give Me Love	(RAK 271)	4	1978	0	1978	
	10	The Race Is On	(RAK 278)	43	1978	0	1978	
	11	Stumblin' In	(RAK 285)	41	1978	4	1979	(RSO 917)
	12	She's In Love With You	(RAK 299)	11	1979	0	1979	
	13	Mama's Boy	(RAK 303)	34	1980	0	1980	
	14	I've Never Be In Love	(RAK 307)	56	1980	0	1980	
	15	Rock Hard	(Dreamland DLSP 6)	68	1980	0	1980	
	16	Heart Of Stone	(Polydor POSP 477)	60	1982	0	1982	

HIT 11 IS CREDITED TO SUZI QUATRO AND CHRIS NORMAN

Sven Vath   Male Producer from Germany

1	L'esperance	(EYE Q YZ 757)	63	1993	0	1993	
2	An Accident In Paradise	(EYE Q YZ 778CD)	57	1993	0	1993	
3	Harlequin - The Beauty And The Beast	(EYE Q YZ 857)	72	1994	0	1994	

Swan Lake   Male Vocal/Multi-Instrumentalist from the USA

| 1 | In The Name Of Love | (Champion Champ 86) | 53 | 1988 | 0 | 1988 | |

ISSUE	TITLE	UK LBL	UK POS	UK YEAR	US POS	US YEAR	US LBL

Swans Way Mixed Vocal/Instrumental Group from the UK

| | 1 | Soul Train | (EXIT EXT 3) | 20 | 1984 | 0 | 1984 | |
| | 2 | Illuminations | (Balgier PH 5) | 57 | 1984 | 0 | 1984 | |

Sweathog Rock Quartet Includes Lenny Lee Goldsmith

| | 1 | Hallelujah | | 0 | 1971 | 33 | 1971 | (Columbia 45492) |

Sweet Male Vocal/Instrumental Group from the UK   Names: Brian Connolly, Andy Scott, Steve Priest & Mick Tucker

*	1	Funny Funny	(RCA 2051)	13	1971	0	1971	
*	2	Co-Co	(RCA 2087)	2	1971	0	1971	
	3	Alexander Graham Bell	(RCA 2121)	33	1971	0	1971	
*	4	Popa Joe	(RCA 2164)	11	1972	0	1972	
*	5	Little Willy	(RCA 2225)	4	1972	3	1973	(Bell 45251)
*	6	Wig-Wam Bam	(RCA 2260)	4	1972	0	1972	
*	7	Blockbuster	(RCA 2305)	1	1973	0	1993	
*	8	Hell Raiser	(RCA 2357)	2	1973	0	1973	
*	9	Ballroom Blitz	(RCA 2403)	2	1973	5	1975	(Capitol 4055)
*	10	Teenage Rampage	(RCA LPBO 5004)	2	1974	0	1974	
	11	The Six Teens	(RCA LPBO 5037)	9	1974	0	1974	
	12	Turn It Down	(RCA 2480)	41	1974	0	1974	
*	13	Fox On The Run	(RCA 2524)	2	1975	5	1975	(Capitol 4157)
*	14	Action	(RCA 2578)	15	1975	20	1976	(Capitol 4220)
	15	Lies In Your Eyes	(RCA 2641)	35	1976	0	1976	
	16	Love Is Like Oxygen	(Polydor POSP 1)	9	1978	8	1978	(Capitol 4549)
	17	It's It's The Sweet Mix	(Anagram ANA 28)	45	1985	0	1985	

OBITUARY : BRIAN D: 10 FEB 1997, LIVER FAILURE.

Sweet Dreams (1) Mixed Vocal Duo from the UK

| | 1 | Honey Honey | (Bradley's Brad 7408) | 10 | 1974 | 0 | 1974 | |

Sweet Dreams (2) Mixed Vocal Group from the UK

| | 1 | I'm Ever Giving Up | (Ariola ARO 333) | 21 | 1983 | 0 | 1983 | |

Sweet Inspirations R&B Quartet, Names Estelle Brown, Sylvia Shemwell, Cissy Houston & Myrna Smith

| | 1 | Sweet Inspirations | | 0 | 1968 | 18 | 1968 | (Atlantic 2476) |

Sweet People Male Vocal/Instrumental Group from France

| | 1 | Et Les Oiseaux Chantaient (And The Birds Were Singing) | (Polydor POSP 179) | 4 | 1980 | 0 | 1980 | |
| | 2 | Et Les Oiseaux Chantaient (And The Birds Were Singing) | (Polydor POSP 179) | 73 | 1987 | 0 | 1987 | |

Sweet Sensation (1) Eight Member Soul Group from Manchester, England

| | 1 | Sad Sweet Dreamer | (PYE 7N 45385) | 1 | 1974 | 14 | 1975 | (PYE 71002) |
| | 2 | Purely By Coincidence | (PYE 7N 45421) | 11 | 1975 | 0 | 1975 | |

Sweet Sensation (2) Female Trio Of Betty Lebron, Margie & Mari Fernandez from New York

	1	Hooked On You		0	1987	64	1987	(Atco 00000)
	2	Sincerely Yours		0	1989	14	1989	(Atco 99246)
	3	Hooked On You (Re-Mix)		0	1989	23	1989	(Atco 99210)
	4	Love Child		0	1990	13	1990	(Atco 98983)
	5	If Wishes Came True		0	1990	1	1990	(Atco 98953)

Sweet Tee Female Rapper from the USA

| | 1 | It's Like That Y'all / I Got Da Feelin' | (Cooltempo COOL 160) | 31 | 1988 | 0 | 1988 | |
| | 2 | The Feeling | (Deep Distraxion OILYCD 029) | 32 | 1994 | 0 | 1994 | |

HIT 2 IS CREDITED TO TIN TIN OUT FEATURING SWEET TEE

Swervedriver Male Vocal/Instrumental Group from the UK

	1	Sandblasted (EP)	(Creation CRE 102)	67	1991	0	1991	
	2	Never Lose That Feeling	(Creation CRE 120)	62	1992	0	1992	
	3	Duel	(Creation CRESCD 136)	60	1993	0	1993	

Swimming With Sharks Female Vocal Group from Germany

| | 1 | Careless Love | (WFA YZ 173) | 63 | 1988 | 0 | 1988 | |

Swing 52 Male Vocal/Instrumental Group from the USA

| | 1 | Color Of My Skin | (FFRR FCD 256) | 60 | 1995 | 0 | 1995 | |

Swing Out Sister Mixed Vocal/Instrumental Group from the UK   Names: Corinne Drewery, Andy Connell & Martin Jackson (Left In 1989)

	1	Breakout	(Mercury Swing 2)	4	1986	6	1987	(Mercury 888016)
	2	Surrender	(Mercury Swing 3)	7	1987	0	1987	
	3	Twilight World	(Mercury Swing 4)	32	1987	31	1988	(Mercury 888484)
	4	Fooled By A Smile	(Mercury Swing 5)	43	1987	0	1987	
	5	You On My Mind	(Fontana Swing 6)	28	1989	0	1989	
	6	Where In The World	(Fontana Swing7)	47	1989	0	1989	

S

627

ISSUE	TITLE	UK LBL	UK POS	UK YEAR	US POS	US YEAR	US LBL
7	Am I The Same Girl	(Fontana Swing 9)	21	1992	0	1992	
8	Notgonnachange	(Fontana Swing 10)	49	1992	0	1992	
9	La La (Means I Love You)	(Fontana SWIDD11)	37	1994	0	1994	

Swingin' Medallions Eight-Man Rock Band Led By John McElrath

ISSUE	TITLE	UK LBL	UK POS	UK YEAR	US POS	US YEAR	US LBL
1	Double Shot (Of My Baby's Love)		0	1965	17	1965	(Smash 2033)

Swinging Blue Jeans Male Vocal/Instrumental Group from the UK, Names: Ralph Ellis, Ray Ennis, Norman Kuhike & Les Braid

ISSUE	TITLE	UK LBL	UK POS	UK YEAR	US POS	US YEAR	US LBL
1	It's Too Late Now	(HMV POP 1170)	30	1963	0	1963	
2	It's Too Late Now (Re-Entry)	(HMV POP 1170)	46	1963	0	1963	
3	Hippy Hippy Shake	(HV POP 1242)	2	1963	24	1964	(Imperial 66021)
4	Good Golly Miss Molly	(HMV POP 1273)	11	1964	0	1964	
5	You're No Good	(HMV POP 1304)	3	1964	0	1964	
6	Don't Make Me Over	(HMV POP 1501)	31	1966	0	1966	

Switch Male Vocal/Instrumental Group from Mansfield, Ohio, Lead Vocals With The Sextet Is Phillip Ingram

ISSUE	TITLE	UK LBL	UK POS	UK YEAR	US POS	US YEAR	US LBL
1	There'll Never Be		0	1978	36	1978	(Gordy 7159)
2	Keeping Secrets	(Total Experience XE 502)	41	1984	0	1984	

Sybil Female Vocalist, Real Name Sybil Lynch from Paterson, New Jersey

ISSUE	TITLE	UK LBL	UK POS	UK YEAR	US POS	US YEAR	US LBL
1	Falling In Love	(Champion Champ 22)	68	1986	0	1986	
2	Let Yourself Go	(Champion Champ 42)	32	1987	0	1987	
3	My Love Is Guaranteed	(Champion Champ 55)	42	1987	0	1987	
* 4	Don't Make Me Over	(Champion Champ 213)	59	1989	20	1989	(Next Plat. 325)
5	Don't Make Me Over (Re-Entry)	(Champion Champ 213)	19	1989	0	1989	
6	Walk On By	(PWL PWL 48)	6	1990	0	1990	
7	Crazy For You	(PWL PWL 53)	71	1990	0	1990	
8	The Love I Lost	(PWL Sanctuary PWCD 253)	3	1993	0	1993	
9	When I'm Good And Ready	(PWL International PWCD 260)	5	1993	0	1993	
10	Beyond Your Wildest Dreams	(PWL International PWCD 265)	41	1993	0	1993	
11	Stronger Together	(PWL International PWCD 269)	41	1993	0	1993	
12	My Love Is Guaranteed (Re-Mix)	(PWL International PWCD 227)	48	1993	0	1993	
13	So Tired Of Being Alone	(PWL International PWL 324CD)	53	1996	0	1996	
14	When I'm Good And Ready	(Next PlatEAU NP 14183)	66	1997	0	1997	
15	Still A Thrill	(Coalition COLA07CD)	55	1997	0	1997	

HIT 8 IS CREDITED TO WEST END FEATURING SYBIL

Sydney Youngblood Male Vocalist from the USA

ISSUE	TITLE	UK LBL	UK POS	UK YEAR	US POS	US YEAR	US LBL
1	If Only I Could	(Circa YR 34)	3	1989	0	1989	
2	Sit And Wait	(Circa YR 40)	16	1989	0	1989	
3	I'd Rather Go Blind	(Circa YR 43)	44	1990	0	1990	
4	Hooked On You	(Circa YR 65)	72	1991	0	1991	
5	Anything	(RCA 74321138672)	48	1993	0	1993	

Sylvana Mangano Female Italian movie star, before her hit she worked as a model until 1949

ISSUE	TITLE	UK LBL	UK POS	UK YEAR	US POS	US YEAR	US LBL
* 1	Anna (Movie Title Song)		0	1953	5	1953	(MGM 11457)

Sylvers Names Of The Family Are Leon, Charmaine, James, Edmund, Ricky, Olympia-Ann, Foster, Jonathon,

ISSUE	TITLE	UK LBL	UK POS	UK YEAR	US POS	US YEAR	US LBL
* 1	Boogie Fever		0	1976	1	1976	(Capitol 4179)
* 2	Hot Line		0	1976	5	1976	(Capitol 4336)
3	High School Dance		0	1977	17	1977	(Capitol 4405)

Sylvester Male Vocalist, Full Name Sylvester James B: Los Angeles

ISSUE	TITLE	UK LBL	UK POS	UK YEAR	US POS	US YEAR	US LBL
1	You Make Me Feel (Mighty Real)	(Fantasy FTC 160)	8	1978	36	1979	(Fantasy 846)
2	Dance (Disco Heat)	(Fantasy FTC 163)	29	1978	19	1978	(Fantasy 827)
3	I (Who Have Nothing)	(Fantasy FTC 171)	46	1979	40	1979	(Fantasy 855)
4	Stars	(Fantasy FTC 177)	47	1979	0	1979	
5	Do Ya Wanna Funk	(London LON 13)	32	1982	0	1982	
6	Band Of Gold	(London LON 33)	67	1983	0	1983	

HIT 5 IS CREDITED TO SYLVESTER WITH PATRICK COWLEY

Sylvia **(1)** Female Vocalist from Sweden, Real Name Sylvia Vrethammar

ISSUE	TITLE	UK LBL	UK POS	UK YEAR	US POS	US YEAR	US LBL
* 1	Y Viva Espana	(Sonet Son 2037)	4	1974	0	1974	
2	Y Viva Espana (Re-Entry)	(Sonet Son 2037)	38	1975	0	1975	
3	Hasta La Vista	(Sonet Son 2055)	38	1975	0	1975	

Sylvia **(2)** Female Vocalist, Real Name Sylvia Kirby Allen B: 9 Dec 1956 Kokomo, Indiana.

ISSUE	TITLE	UK LBL	UK POS	UK YEAR	US POS	US YEAR	US LBL
* 8	Nobody		0	1982	15	1982	(RCA 13223)

OTHERS WERE C/W HITS

ISSUE	TITLE	UK LBL	UK POS	UK YEAR	US POS	US YEAR	US LBL
Sylvia	**(3)** Female Vocalist, Real Name Sylvia Vanderpool B: 6 May 1936 New York						
* 1	Pillow Talk	(London HL 10415)	14	1973	3	1973	(Vibration 521)
Sylvia Syms	Female Vocalist, B: 2 Dec 1917 In Brooklyn						
1	I Could Have Danced All Night		0	1956	20	1956	(Decca 29903)
2	English Muffins And Irish Stew		0	1956	21	1956	(Decca 29969)
	OBITUARY: D: 10 MAY 1992, COLLAPSED ON STAGE IN MANHATTAN WITH A HEART ATTACK.						
Symarip	Male Vocal/Instrumental Group from the UK						
1	Skinhead Moonstomp	(Trojan TRO 9062)	54	1980	0	1980	
Symbols	Male Vocal/Instrumental Group from the UK						
1	Bye Bye Baby	(President PT 144)	44	1967	0	1967	
2	The Best Part Of Breaking Up	(President PT 173)	25	1968	0	1968	
Synch	Pop-Rock Group from Wilkes-Barre, Pennsylvania						
1	Where Are You Now? (Re-Issue)		0	1989	10	1989	(WTG 68625)
Syndicate Of Sound	Lead Singer With The Quintet Is Don Baskin						
1	LIttle Girl		0	1966	8	1966	(Bell 640)
Syreeta	Female Vocalist, Syreeta Wright from the USA						
1	Spinnin' And Spinnin'	(Tamla MotownTMG 912)	49	1974	0	1974	
2	Your Kiss Is Sweet	(Tamla MotownTMG 933)	12	1975	0	1975	
3	Harmour Love	(Tamla MotownTMG 954)	32	1975	0	1975	
4	With You I'm Born Again	(Motown TMG 1159)	2	1979	4	1980	(Motown 1477)
5	It Will Come In Time	(Tamla MotownTMG 1175)	47	1980	0	1980	
	HIT 4-5 ARE CREDITED TO BILLY PRESTON AND SYREETA						
System	Male Vocal/Instrumental Duo, David Frank & Mic Murphy from the USA						
1	I Wanna Make You Feel Good	(Polydor POSP 685)	73	1984	0	1984	
2	Don't Disturb The Groove		0	1987	4	1987	(Atlantic 89320)
System 7	Mixed Vocal/Instrumental Duo from the UK/France						
1	7:7 Xpansion	(Butterfly BFLD 2)	39	1993	0	1993	
2	Sinbad Quest	(Butterfly BFLD 8)	74	1993	0	1993	

T

ISSUE	TITLE	UK LBL	UK POS	UK YEAR	US POS	US YEAR	US LBL
T Rex	Male Vocal/Instrumental Group from the UK, Lead Singer, Marc Bolan, Real Name Marc Feld B: 30 Jul 1947, Hackney, London, England.						
1	Debora	(Regalzonophone RZ 3008)	7	1968	0	1968	
2	One Inch Rock	(Regalzonophone RZ 3011)	28	1968	0	1968	
3	King Of The Rumbling Spires	(Regalzonophone RZ 3022)	44	1969	0	1969	
4	Ride A White Swan	(Fly Bug 1)	3	1970	0	1970	
* 5	Hot Love	(Fly Bug 6)	1	1971	0	1971	
7	Get It On	(Fly Bug 10)	1	1971	10	1971	(Reprise 1032)
8	Jeepster	(Fly Bug 16)	2	1971	0	1971	
9	Telegram Sam	(T. Rex 101)	1	1972	0	1972	
10	Debora / One Inch Rock (Re-Issue)	(Magnify Echo102)	7	1972	0	1972	
11	Metal Guru	(EMI Marc 1)	1	1972	0	1972	
12	Children Of The Revolution	(EMI Marc 2)	2	1972	0	1972	
13	Solid Gold Easy Action	(EMI Marc 3)	2	1972	0	1972	
14	20th Century Boy	(EMI Marc 4)	3	1973	0	1973	
15	The Groover	(EMI Marc 5)	4	1973	0	1973	
16	Truck On (Tyke)	(EMI Marc 6)	12	1973	0	1973	
17	Teenage Dream	(EMI Marc 7)	13	1974	0	1974	
18	Light Of Love	(EMI Marc 8)	22	1974	0	1974	
19	Zip Gun Boogie	(EMI Marc 9)	41	1974	0	1974	
20	New York City	(EMI Marc 10)	15	1975	0	1975	
21	Dreamy Lady	(EMI Marc 11)	30	1975	0	1975	
22	London Boys	(EMI Marc 13)	40	1976	0	1976	
23	I Love To Boogie	(EMI Marc 14)	13	1976	0	1976	
24	Laser Love	(EMI Marc 15)	41	1976	0	1976	
25	The Soul Of My Suit	(EMI Marc 16)	42	1977	0	1977	
26	Return Of The Electric Warrior (Ep)	(Rarn Mbsf 001)	50	1981	0	1981	
27	You Scare Me To Death	(Cherry RedCherry 29)	51	1981	0	1981	
28	Telegram Sam (Re-Entry)	(T. Rex 101)	69	1982	0	1982	
29	Magarex	(Marc On Waxtanx 1)	72	1985	0	1985	
30	Get It On (Re-Mix)	(Marc On Waxmarc 10)	54	1987	0	1987	
31	20th Century Boy (Re-Issue)	(Marc On Waxmarc 501)	13	1991	0	1991	
	OBITUARY: D: 16 SEP 1977 MARC'S CAR HIT A TREE NEAR PUTNEY, SURREY, ENGLAND						
T'Pau	Mixed Vocal/Instrumental Group from the UK, Lead Singer With The Group Is Carol Decker						
1	Heart And Soul	(Siren Srn 41)	4	1987	4	1987	(Virgin 99466)
2	China In Your Hand	(Siren Srn 64)	1	1987	0	1987	
3	Valentine	(Siren Srn 69)	9	1988	0	1988	
4	Sex Talk (Live)	(Siren Srn 80)	23	1988	0	1988	
5	I Will Be With You	(Siren Srn 87)	14	1988	0	1988	
6	Secret Garden	(Siren Srn 93)	18	1988	0	1988	
7	Road To Our Dream	(Siren Srn 100)	42	1988	0	1988	
8	Only The Lonely	(Siren Srn 107)	28	1989	0	1989	
9	Whenever You Need Me	(Siren Srn 140)	16	1991	0	1991	
10	Walk On Air	(Siren Srn 142)	62	1991	0	1991	
11	Valentine (Re-Issue)	(Virgin Valeg 1)	53	1993	0	1993	
T-Bones	Studio Production By Joe Saraceno, See Also Hamilton, Joe Frank & Reynolds						
1	No Matter What Shape (Your Stomach's In)		0	1966	3	1966	(Liberty 55836)
T-Boz	Female Vocalist from the USA						
1	Touch Myself (From Fled)	(Laface74321422882)	48	1996	40	1996	(Arista 35080)
2	Ghetto Love		0	1997	16	1997	(So So Def 78527)
	HIT 2 IS CREDITED TO DA BRAT FEATURING T-BOZ						

ISSUE	TITLE	UK LBL	UK POS	UK YEAR	US POS	US YEAR	US LBL
T-Connection	Male Vocal/Instrumental Group from the USA						
1	Do What You Wanna Do	(Tk Xc 9109)	11	1977	0	1977	
2	On Fire	(Tk Tkr 6006)	16	1978	0	1978	
3	Let Yourself Go	(Tk Tkr 6024)	52	1978	0	1978	
4	At Midnight	(Tk Tkr 7517)	53	1979	0	1979	
5	Saturday Night	(Tk Tkr 7536)	41	1979	0	1979	
T-Empo	Mixed Vocal/Instrumental Group from the UK						
1	Saturday Night Sunday Morning	(Ffrr Fcd 232)	19	1994	0	1994	
2	The Look Of Love / The Blue Room	(Ffrr Fcd 281)	71	1996	0	1996	
T-Power	Male Producer Mark Royal from the UK						
1	Police State	(Sound Of Underground Tpowcd 001)	63	1996	0	1996	
T. Texas Tyler	Male Country Vocalist, B: David Luke Myrick 20 Jun 1916 In Mena, Arkansas						
! 1	Filopino Baby		0	1945	5	1946	(4 Star 1009)
2	Deck Of Cards		0	1948	21	1948	(4 Star 1228)
	HIT 1 IS CREDITED TO T. TEXAS TYLER & THE OKLAHOMA MELODY BOYS • OBITUARY: D: 28 JAN 1972.						
T.C. Curtis	Male Vocal/Instrumentalist from Jamaica						
1	You Should Have Known Better	(Hot Melt Vs754)	50	1985	0	1985	
T.G. Sheppard	Male Vocalist, Real Name William Neal Browder B: 20 Jul 1942 from Humboldt, Tennessee						
20	I Loved 'em Every One		0	1981	37	1981	(Warner Bros/Curb 49690)
	OTHERS WERE C/W HITS						
T.H.S. - The Horn Section	Mixed Vocal/Instrumental Group from the USA						
1	Lady Shine (Shine On)	(Fourth &Broadway Brw 10)	54	1984	0	1984	
T.S. Monk	Male Vocal/Instrumental Group from the USA						
1	Bon Bon Vie	(Mirage K 11653)	63	1981	0	1981	
2	Candidate For Love	(Mirage K 11648)	58	1981	0	1981	
T.S.D.	Female Vocal Group from the UK						
1	Heart And Soul	(Avex UkAvexcd 21)	69	1996	0	1996	
2	Baby I Love You	(Avex UkAvexcd 34)	64	1996	0	1996	
T.W.A	Male Instrumental/Production Group from the UK						
1	Nasty Girls	(MercuryMercd 441)	51	1995	0	1995	
T99	Male Production/Instrumental Group from Belgium						
1	Anasthasia	(Xl Xls 19)	14	1991	0	1991	
2	Nocturne	(Emphasis6574097)	33	1991	0	1991	
Ta Mara & The Seen	Lead Singer With The Quintet Is Margaret Cox						
1	Everybody Dance		0	1985	24	1985	(A&M 278)
Tab Hunter	Male Vocalist, Real Name Arthur Andrew Kelm B: 11 Jul 1931 In New York City						
* 1	Young Love	(London Hld8380)	1	1957	1	1957	(Dot 15533)
2	99 Ways	(London Hld8410)	5	1957	11	1957	(Dot 15548)
3	(I'll Be With You) In Apple Blossom Time		0	1959	31	1959	(Warner Bros 5032)
4	99 Ways (Re-Entry)	(London Hld8410)	29	1957	0	1957	
Tab Smith & His Orchestra	Male Bandleader/Saxophonist from the USA						
* 1	Because Of You		0	1951	20	1951	(United 104)
	OBITUARY: D: 19 AUG 1971 (AGED 62).						
Tabernacle	Male Instrumental/Production Group from the UK						
1	I Know The Lord	(Good GrooveCdgg1)	62	1995	0	1995	
2	I Know The Lord (Re-Mix)	(Good GrooveCdggx1)	55	1996	0	1996	
Tack Head	Male Rapper from the USA						
1	Dangerous Sex	(Sbk Sbk 7014)	48	1990	0	1990	
Taco	Real Name Taco Ockerse B: 1955 Jakarta, Indonesia						
* 1	Puttin' On The Ritz		0	1983	4	1983	(RCA 13574)
Taffy	Female Vocalist from the UK						
1	I Love My Radio (My Dee Jay's Radio)	(TransglobalType 1)	6	1987	0	1987	
2	Step By Step	(TransglobalType 5)	59	1987	0	1987	
Tag Team	Male Rap Duo Cecil Glenn & Steve Gibson from Atlanta, USA.						
* 1	Whoomp! (There It Is)	(Club ToolsShxcd 1)	34	1994	2	1993	(Life 79500)
2	Addams Family (Whoomp!)	(Atlas Pzcd 305)	53	1994	0	1994	
3	Whoomp! (There It Is) (Re-Mix)	(Club ToolsShxr 1)	48	1994	0	1994	
Tairrie B	Female Rapper from the USA						
1	Murder She Wrote	(MCA 1455)	71	1990	0	1990	

ISSUE	TITLE	UK LBL	UK POS	UK YEAR	US POS	US YEAR	US LBL
Taja Sevelle Female Vocalist from the USA							
1	Love Is Contagious	(Paisley Park W 8257)	7	1988	0	1988	
2	Wouldn't You Love To Love Me	(Paisley Park W 8127)	59	1988	0	1988	
Tak Tix Female Vocalist from the USA							
1	Feel Like Singing	(Am:Pm 5813212)	33	1996	0	1996	
Take That Male Vocal Group: Mark Owen, Gary Barlow, Jason Orange, Howard Donald & Robbie Williams from Manchester, England							
1	Promises	(RCA Pb 45085)	38	1991	0	1991	
2	Once You've Tasted Love	(RCA Pb 45257)	47	1992	0	1992	
3	It Only Takes A Minute	(RCA 74321101007)	7	1992	0	1992	
4	I Found Heaven	(RCA 74321108137)	15	1992	0	1992	
5	A Million Love Songs	(RCA 74321116307)	7	1992	0	1992	
6	Could It Be Magic	(RCA 74321123137)	3	1992	0	1992	
7	Why Can't I Wake Up With You	(RCA 74321133102)	2	1993	0	1993	
8	Pray	(RCA 74321154502)	1	1993	0	1993	
9	Relight My Fire	(RCA 74321167722)	1	1993	0	1993	with Lulu
10	Baby	(RCA 74321182122)	1	1993	0	1993	
11	Everything Changes	(RCA 74321167732)	1	1994	0	1994	
12	Love Ain't Here Anymore	(RCA 74321214832)	3	1994	0	1994	
13	Sure	(RCA 74321236622)	1	1994	0	1994	
14	Love Ain't Here Anymore (Re-Entry)	(RCA 74321214832)	55	1994	0	1994	
15	Back For Good	(RCA 74321271462)	1	1995	7	1995	(Arista 12848)
16	Never Forget	(RCA 74321299572)	1	1995	0	1995	
17	How Deep Is Your Love	(RCA 74321355592)	1	1996	0	1996	
18	How Deep Is Your Love (Re-Entry)	(RCA 74321355592)	71	1996	0	1996	
Talk Talk Male Vocal/Instrumental Group from the UK Lead Singer With The Rock Band was Mark Hollis							
1	Talk Talk	(EMI 5284)	23	1982	0	1982	
2	Today	(EMI 5314)	14	1982	0	1982	
3	Talk Talk (Re-Mix)	(EMI 5352)	52	1982	0	1982	
4	My Foolish Friend	(EMI 5373)	57	1983	0	1983	
5	It's My Life	(EMI 5443)	46	1984	31	1984	(EMI America 8195)
6	Such A Shame	(EMI 5433)	49	1984	0	1984	
7	Dum Dum Girl	(EMI 5480)	74	1984	0	1984	
8	Life's What You Make It	(EMI Emi 5540)	16	1986	0	1986	
9	Living In Another World	(EMI Emi 5551)	48	1986	0	1986	
10	Give It Up	(Parlophone R6131)	59	1986	0	1986	
11	It's My Life (Re-Issue)	(Parlophone R6254)	13	1990	0	1990	
12	Life's What You Make It (Re-Issue)	(Parlophone R6264)	23	1990	0	1990	
Talking Heads Mixed Vocal/Instrumental Group from the USA/UK Lead Singer With The Quartet Is David Byrne							
1	Take Me To The River		0	1978	26	1978	(Sire 1032)
2	Once In A Lifetime	(Sire Sir 4048)	14	1981	0	1981	
3	Houses In Motion	(Sire Sir 4050)	50	1981	0	1981	
4	Burning Down The House		0	1983	9	1983	(Sire 29565)
5	This Must Be The Place	(Sire W 9451)	51	1984	0	1984	
6	Slippery People	(EMI 5504)	68	1984	0	1984	
7	Road To Nowhere	(EMI Emi 5530)	6	1985	0	1985	
8	And She Was	(EMI Emi 5543)	17	1986	0	1986	
9	Wild Wild Life	(EMI Emi 5567)	43	1986	25	1986	(Sire 28629)
10	Radio Head	(EMI Em 1)	52	1987	0	1987	
11	Blind	(EMI Em 68)	59	1988	0	1988	
12	Lifetime Piling Up	(EMI Em 250)	50	1992	0	1992	
Tam White Male Vocalist from the UK							
1	What In The World's Come Over You	(Rak 193)	36	1975	0	1975	
Tami Lynn Female Vocalist from the USA							
1	I'm Gonna Run Away From You	(Mojo 2092 001)	4	1971	0	1971	
2	I'm Gonna Run Away From You (Re-Issue)	(Contemporaries Cs 9026)	36	1975	0	1975	
Tami Show Mixed Vocal/Instrumental Group from Chicago Fronted By Cathy & Clair Massey							
1	The Truth		0	1991	28	1991	(RCA 2694)
Tammi Terrell Female Vocalist, Real Name Thomasina Montgomery 24 Jan 1946 From Phiadelphia							
+ 1	I Can't Believe You Love Me		0	1966	27	1966	(Motown 1086)
+ 2	Come On And See Me		0	1966	25	1966	(Motown 1095)
3	Ain't No Mountain High Enough		0	1967	19	1967	(Tamla 54149)
4	Your Precious Love		0	1967	5	1967	(Tamla 54156)

ISSUE	TITLE	UK LBL	UK POS	UK YEAR	US POS	US YEAR	US LBL
5	If I Could Build My Whole World Around You / If This World Was Mine	(Tamla MotownTmg 635)	41	1968	10	1968	(Tamla 54161)
* 6	Ain't Nothing Like The Real Thing	(Tamla Motown Tmg 655)	34	1968	8	1968	(Tamla 54163)
7	You're All I Need To Get By	(Tamla Motown Tmg 668)	19	1968	7	1968	(Tamla 54169)
8	Keep On Loving Me Honey		0	1968	24	1968	(Tamla 54173)
9	You Ain't Livin' Till You're Lovin'	(Tamla Motown Tmg 681)	21	1969	0	1969	
10	Good Lovin' Ain't Easy To Come By	(Tamla Motown Tmg 697)	26	1969	30	1969	(Tamla 54179)
11	Good Lovin' Ain't Easy To Come By (Re-Entry)	(Tamla Motown Tmg 697)	48	1969	0	1969	
12	What You Gave Me		0	1969	49	1969	(Tamla 54187)
13	Onion Song	(Tamla Motown Tmg 715)	9	1969	50	1970	(Tamla 54192)

OBITUARY: D: 16 MAR 1970 BRAIN TUMOUR.

Tammy Jones   Female Vocalist from the UK

1	Let Me Try Again	(Epic Epc 3211)	5	1975	0	1975	

TRY LISTENING TO THE HIT ON 33 RPM; THERE'S A MAN SINGING

Tammy Payne   Female Vocalist from the UK

1	Take Me Now	(Talkin LoudTlk 12)	55	1991	0	1991	

Tammy Wynette   Female C/W Vocalist, Real Name Virginia Wynette Pugh B: 5 May 1942 from Mississippi

* 8	Stand By Your Man	(Epic Epc 7137)	1	1975	19	1968	(Epic 10398)

REST ARE C/W HITS

Tams   Male Vocal Group from the USA   Names: Charles & Joseph Pope, Robert Smith, Horace Key & Floyd Ashton

1	What Kind Of Fool (Do You Think I Am)		0	1964	9	1964	(ABC-Paramount 10502)
2	Be Young Be Foolish Be Happy	(Stateside Ss2123)	32	1970	0	1970	
3	Hey Girl Don't Bother Me	(Probe Pro 532)	1	1971	0	1971	
4	There Ain't Nothing Like Shaggin'	(Virgin Vs 1029)	21	1987	0	1987	

Tane Cain   Female Vocalist, Wife Of Jonathan Cain from Journey

1	Holdin' On		0	1982	37	1982	(RCA 13287)

Tanita Tikaram   Female Vocalist from the UK

1	Good Tradition	(Wea Yz 196)	10	1988	0	1988	
2	Twist In My Sobriety	(Wea Yz 321)	22	1988	0	1988	
3	Cathedral Song	(Wea Yz 331)	48	1989	0	1989	
4	World Outside Your Window	(Wea Yz 363)	58	1989	0	1989	
5	We Almost Got It Together	(Wea Yz 443)	52	1990	0	1990	
6	Only The Ones We Love	(East West Yz558)	69	1991	0	1991	
7	I Might Be Crying	(East West Yz879cdx)	64	1995	0	1995	

Tanya Blount   Female Vocalist from the USA

1	I'm Gonna Make You Mine	(Polydor Pzcd315)	69	1994	0	1994	

Tanya Donelly   Female Vocalist

1	Pretty Deep	(4ad Bad 7007cd)	55	1997	0	1997	

Tanya Tucker   Female Country Singer, B: 10 Oct 1958 Seminole, Texas

22	Not Fade Away		0	1978	70	1978	(MCA 40976)

Tara Kemp   Singer/Songwriter/Classical Pianist from the USA

* 1	Hold You Tight	(Giant W 0020)	69	1991	3	1991	(Giant 19458)
2	Piece Of My Heart		0	1991	7	1991	(Giant 19364)

Tarriers   Male Vocal/Instrumental Trio from the USA   Names: Bob Carey, Erik Darling & Alan Arkin

1	Cindy, Oh Cindy	(London Hln8340)	26	1956	9	1956	(Glory 247)
2	Banana Boat Song	(Columbia Db3891)	15	1957	4	1956	(Glory 249)

HIT 1 IS CREDITED TO VINCE MARTIN WITH THE TARRIERS • ERIK LEFT AND BECAME A MEMBER OF THE ROOFTOP SINGERS

Tasha Thomas   Female Vocalist from the USA

1	Shoot Me (With Your Love)	(Atlantic LV 4)	59	1979	0	1979	

Tasmin Archer   Female Vocalist From Bradford, England

1	Sleeping Satellite	(EMI Em 233)	1	1992	32	1993	(Sbk 50426)
2	Sleeping Satellite (Re-Entry)	(EMI Em 233)	67	1993	0	1993	
3	In Your Care	(EMI Cdems 260)	16	1993	0	1993	
4	Lords Of The New Church	(EMI Cdems 266)	26	1993	0	1993	
5	Arienne	(EMI Cdems 275)	30	1993	0	1993	
6	Shipbuilding	(EMI Cdems 302)	40	1994	0	1994	
7	One More Good Night With The Boys	(EMI Cdem 401)	45	1996	0	1996	

Tata Vega   Female Vocalist from the USA

1	Get It Up For Love	(Motown Tmg1140)	52	1979	0	1979	

Tatjana   Female Vocalist from Croatia

1	Santa Maria	(Love This Luvthis Cdx4)	40	1996	0	1996	

ISSUE	TITLE	UK LBL	UK POS	UK YEAR	US POS	US YEAR	US LBL
2Tavares	Male Vocal Family Group from the USA: Feliciano, Ralph, Antone, Arthur & Perry Lee Tavares						
1	Check It Out		0	1973	35	1973	(Capitol 3674)
2	Remember What I Told You To Forget / My Ship		0	1975	25	1975	(Capitol 4010)
3	It Only Takes A Minute	(Capitol Tav 2)	46	1986	10	1975	(Capitol 4111)
* 4	Heaven Must Be Missing An Angel	(Capitol Cl15876)	4	1976	15	1976	(Capitol 4270)
5	Don't Take Away The Music	(Capitol Cl15886)	4	1976	34	1976	(Capitol 4348)
6	Mighty Power Of Love	(Capitol Cl15905)	25	1977	0	1977	
7	Whodunit	(Capitol Cl15914)	5	1977	22	1977	(Capitol 4398)
8	One Step Away	(Capitol Cl15930)	16	1977	0	1977	
9	The Ghost Of Love	(Capitol Cl15968)	29	1978	0	1978	
10	More Than A Woman	(Capitol Cl15977)	7	1978	32	1978	(Capitol 4500)
11	Slow Train To Paradise	(Capitol Cl15996)	62	1978	0	1978	
12	A Penny For Your Thoughts		0	1982	33	1982	(RCA 13292)
13	Heaven Must Be Missing An Angel (Re-Issue)	(Capitol Tav 1)	12	1986	0	1986	
Taylor Dayne	Female Vocalist, Real Name Leslie Wundermann B: 3 Jul 1962 Long Island, New York						
* 1	Tell It To My Heart	(Arista 109616)	3	1988	7	1987	(Arista 9612)
2	Prove Your Love	(Arista 109830)	8	1988	7	1988	(Arista 9676)
* 3	I'll Always Love You	(Arista 111536)	41	1988	3	1988	(Arista 9700)
4	Don't Rush Me		0	1988	2	1988	(Arista 9722)
5	With Every Beat Of My Heart	(Arista 112760)	53	1989	5	1989	(Arista 9895)
* 6	Love Will Lead You Back	(Arista 113277)	69	1990	1	1990	(Arista 9938)
7	I'll Be Your Shelter	(Arista 112966)	43	1990	4	1990	(Arista 2005)
8	Heart Of Stone		0	1990	12	1990	(Arista 2057)
9	Can't Get Enough Of Your Love	(Arista74321147852)	14	1993	20	1993	(Arista 12580)
10	I'll Wait	(Arista74321203472)	29	1994	0	1994	
11	Original Sin (Theme From The Shadow)	(Arista74321223462)	63	1995	0	1995	
12	Say A Prayer	(Arista74321324292)	58	1995	0	1995	
13	Tell It To My Heart (Re-Mix)	(Arista74321335962)	23	1996	0	1996	
Tc	Male Production/Instrumental Duo from Italy						
1	Berry	(Union Cityucrt 1)	73	1992	0	1992	
2	Funky Guitar	(Union Cityucrt 13)	40	1992	0	1992	
3	Harmony	(Union Cityucrd 20)	51	1993	0	1993	
Teach-In	Mixed Vocal/Instrumental Group From Holland						
1	Ding-A-Dong	(Polydor 2058570)	13	1975	0	1975	
Team	Male Vocal/Instrumental Group from the UK						
1	Wicki Wacky House Party	(EMI 5519)	55	1985	0	1985	
Teardrop Explodes	Male Vocal/Instrumental Group from the UK						
1	When I Dream	(Mercurytear 1)	47	1980	0	1980	
2	Reward	(Mercurytear 2)	6	1981	0	1981	
3	Treason (It's Just A Story)	(Mercurytear 3)	18	1981	0	1981	
4	Passionate Friend	(Zoo Tear 5)	25	1981	0	1981	
5	Colours Fly Away	(Mercurytear 6)	54	1981	0	1981	
6	Tiny Children	(Mercurytear 7)	44	1982	0	1982	
7	You Disappear From View	(Mercurytear 8)	41	1983	0	1983	
Tears For Fears	Male Vocal/Instrumental Duo from the UK						
1	Mad World	(Mercury Idea 3)	3	1982	0	1982	
2	Change	(Mercury Idea 4)	4	1983	0	1983	
3	Pale Shelter	(Mercury Idea 5)	5	1983	0	1983	
4	The Way You Were	(Mercury Idea 6)	24	1983	0	1983	
5	Mother's Talk	(Mercury Idea 7)	14	1984	27	1986	(Mercury 884638)
* 6	Shout	(Mercury Idea 8)	4	1984	1	1985	(Mercury 880294)
7	Everybody Wants To Rule The World	(Mercury Idea 9)	2	1985	1	1985	(Mercury 880659)
8	Head Over Heels	(Mercury Idea 10)	12	1985	3	1985	(Mercury 880899)
9	Suffer The Children	(Mercury Idea 1)	52	1985	0	1985	
10	Pale Shelter (Re-Issue)	(Mercury Idea 2)	73	1985	0	1985	
11	I Believe (A Soulful Re-Recording)	(Mercury Idea 11)	23	1985	0	1985	
12	Everybody Wants To Rule The World (Re-Entry)	(Mercury Idea 9)	73	1986	0	1986	
13	Everybody Wants To Run The World	(Mercuryrace 1)	5	1986	0	1986	
14	Everybody Wants To Run The World (Re-Entry)	(Mercuryrace 1)	73	1986	0	1986	
15	Sowing The Seeds Of Love	(Mercury Idea 12)	5	1989	2	1989	(Fontana 874710)
16	Woman In Chains	(Fontana Idea13)	26	1990	36	1990	(Fontana 876248)
17	Advice For The Young At Heart	(Fontana Idea14)	36	1990	0	1990	
18	Laid So Low (Tears Roll Down)	(Fontana Idea17)	17	1992	0	1992	

ISSUE	TITLE	UK LBL	UK POS	UK YEAR	US POS	US YEAR	US LBL
19	Woman In Chains (Re-Issue)	(Fontana Idea16)	57	1989	0	1989	
20	Break It Down Again	(Mercuryidecd 18)	20	1993	25	1993	(Mercury 862330)
21	Cold	(Mercuryidecd 19)	72	1993	0	1993	
22	Raoul And The Kings Of Spain	(Epic 6624765)	31	1995	0	1995	
23	God's Mistake	(Epic 6634185)	61	1996	0	1996	

HIT 19 IS CREDITED TO TEARS FOR FEARS FEATURING OLETA ADAMS • NAMES: ROLAND ORZABAL B: 22 AUG 1961 & CURT SMITH B: 24 JUN 1961

Technician 2 Male Production/Instrumental Group from the UK

1	Playing With The Boy	(MCA Mcs 1710)	70	1992	0	1992	

Techniques Male Vocal Group, Jim Moore, Jim Falin, Jim Tinney & Beauford Harold Funk (Buddy Harold)

1	Hey! Little Girl		0	1957	29	1957	(Roulette 4030)

Techno Twins Mixed Vocal Group from the UK

1	Falling In Love Again	(Prt 7p 224)	75	1982	0	1982	
2	Falling In Love Again (Re-Entry)	(Prt 7p 224)	70	1982	0	1982	

Technohead Mixed Vocal/Instrumental/Production Duo from the UK

1	I Wanna Be A Hippy	(Mokum Db	6	1996	0	1996	
2	Happy Birthday	(Mokum Db	18	1996	0	1996	
3	Banana-Na-Na (Dumb Di Dumb)	(Mokum Db	64	1996	0	1996	

SEE ALSO TRICKY DISCO & G.T.O.

Technotronic Male Producer, Real Name Jo Bogaert from Belgium

*	1	Pump Up The Jam	(Swanyard Syr4)	2	1989	2	1989	(Sbk 07311)
*	2	Get Up (Before The Night Is Over)	(Swanyard Syr8)	2	1990	7	1990	(Sbk 07315)
	3	This Beat Is Technotronic	(Swanyard Syr9)	14	1990	0	1990	
	4	Rockin' Over The Beat	(Swanyard Syr14)	9	1990	0	1990	
	5	Megamix	(Swanyard Syr19)	6	1990	0	1990	
	6	Turn It Up	(Swanyard Syd9)	42	1990	0	1990	
	7	Move That Body	(Ars 6568377)	12	1991	0	1991	
	8	Work	(Ars 6573317)	40	1991	0	1991	
	9	Move This		0	1992	6	1992	(Sbk 50400)
	10	Pump Up The Jam (Re-Mix)	(Worx Worxcd004)	36	1996	0	1996	

Ted Heath & His Orchestra Male Orchestra Leader from the UK

1	Vanessa	(Decca F 9983)	11	1953	0	1953	
2	Hot Toddy	(Decca F 10093)	6	1953	0	1953	
3	Dragnet	(Decca F 10176)	12	1953	0	1953	
4	Dragnet (Re-Entry)	(Decca F 10176)	9	1953	0	1953	
5	Dragnet (2nd Re-Entry)	(Decca F 10176)	11	1953	0	1953	
6	Dragnet (3rd Re-Entry)	(Decca F 10176)	11	1954	0	1954	
7	Dragnet (4th Re-Entry)	(Decca F 10176)	12	1954	0	1954	
8	Skin Deep	(Decca F 10246)	9	1954	0	1954	
9	The Faithfull Hussar	(Decca F 10746)	18	1956	0	1956	
10	Swingin' Shepherd Blues	(Decca F 11000)	3	1958	0	1958	
11	Tequila	(Decca F 11003)	21	1958	0	1958	
12	Tom Hark	(Decca F 11025)	24	1958	0	1958	
13	Sucu Sucu	(Decca F 11392)	36	1961	0	1961	
14	Sucu Sucu (Re-Entry)	(Decca F 11392)	47	1961	0	1961	

Ted Nugent B: 13 Dec 1948 Detroit, Involved With Amboy Dukes And Damn Yankees

1	Cat Scratch Fever		0	1977	30	1977	(Epic 50425)

Ted Straeter & His Orchestra Male Bandleader/Singer/Instrumentalist (Piano) from the USA

1	Imagination		0	1940	29	1940	(Columbia 3546)
2	The Most Beautiful Girl In The World		0	1952	27	1952	(MGM 11275)

Ted Weems & His Orchestra Male Orchestra Leader, Real Name Wilfred Theodore Weymes B: 26 Sep 1901 Pitcairn, Pennsylvania

*	2	Somebody Stole My Gal		0	1924	1	1924	(Victor 19212)
*	29	Heartaches		0	1947	1	1947	(Victor 2175)
	30	Violets		0	1947	14	1947	(Mercury 5052)
	31	Peg O' My Heart		0	1947	5	1947	(Mercury 5052)
	32	I Wonder Who's Kissing Her Now		0	1947	2	1947	(Decca 25078)
*	33	Mickey		0	1947	3	1947	(Mercury 5062)
	34	They'll Be Some Changes Made (Re-Issue)		0	1947	28	1947	(Decca 25288)
	35	The Secretary Song		0	1947	20	1947	(Mercury 5081)
	36	Hindustan		0	1948	24	1948	(Mercury 5139)

OBITUARY : D: 7 FEB 1969 IN TULSA, OKLAHOMA, (AGED 72).

Teddi King Female Jazz-Style Vocalist, B: 18 Sep 1929 Boston

1	Mr. Wonderful		0	1956	18	1956	(RCA 6392)

OBITUARY: D: 18 NOV 1977.

ISSUE	TITLE	UK LBL	UK POS	UK YEAR	US POS	US YEAR	US LBL	
Teddy Bears Mixed Vocal Group from the USA								
* 1	To Know Him Is To Love Him	(London Hln8733)	2	1958	1	1958	(Dore 503)	
2	To Know Him Is To Love Him (Re-Issue)	(Lightning Lig9015)	66	1979	0	1979		
	NAMES PHIL SPECTOR, MARSHALL LEIB & ANNETTE KLEINBARD							
	PHIL B: 26 DEC 1940 BRONX							
	HIT 2 WAS BACKED WITH ENDLESS SLEEP (RE-ISSUE) BY JODY REYNOLDS							
	THE HIT WAS INSPIRED BY THE ENGRAVING ON THE GRAVE OF PHIL'S FATHER							
Teddy Pendergrass Male Vocalist, B: 26 Mar 1950 Philadelphia								
1	The Whole Town's Laughing At Me	(Philadelphia International Pir 5116)	44	1977	0	1977		
2	Close The Door	(PhiladelphiaInternationalInt. 3648)	41	1978	25	1978	(PhiladelphiaPir 6713)	
3	Only You	(PhiladelphiaInternational Pir 6713)	41	1978	0	1978		
4	Two Hearts	(20th CenturyTc 2492)	49	1981	40	1981	(20th Century 2492)	
5	Hold Me	(Asylum Ekr 32)	44	1986	0	1986		
6	Joy	(Elektra Ekr75)	58	1988	0	1988		
7	The More I Get The More I Want	(X-Clusive Xclu011cd)	35	1994	0	1994		
8	Don't Keep Wasting My Time		0	1997	90	1997	(Surefire 18002)	
	CAR ACCIDENT LEFT HIM PARTIALLY PARALYSED							
Teddy Phillips & His Orchestra Male Orchestra Leader from the USA								
1	Wishin'		0	1952	29	1952	(King 15156)	
Teddy Riley Male Producer from the USA								
1	Is It Good To You	(MCA Mcs 1611)	53	1992	0	1992		
2	Baby Be Mine	(MCA Mcstd 1772)	37	1993	0	1993		
	HIT 1 IS CREDITED TO TEDDY RILEY FEATURING TAMMY LUCAS • HIT 2 IS CREDITED TO BLACKSTREET FEATURING TEDDY RILEY							
Teddy Walters Vocalist From The USA								
1	Laughing On The Outside (Crying On The Inside)		0	1946	4	1946	(Ara 135)	
Tee Set Vocals With The Dutch Quintet Are From Peter Tetteroo								
* 1	Ma Belle Amie		0	1970	5	1970	(Colossus 107)	
	GROUP SOLD OVER 100,000 IN HOLLAND, THEIR EQUIVALENT TO A MILLION SELLER							
Teegarden & Van Winkle Names David Teegarden & Skip Knape, Drums And Keyboard Duo								
1	God, Love And Rock And Roll		0	1970	22	1970	(Westbound	170)
**Teen `Queens**  `F`emale R&B Duo, Real Names Betty & Rosie Collins from the USA								
1	Eddie My Love		0	1956	14	1956	(Rpm 453)	
Teena Marie Female Vocalist, Real Name Mary Christine Brockert B: 1967 In Santa Monica								
1	I'm A Sucker For Your Love	(Motown Tmg1146)	43	1979	0	1979		
2	Behind The Groove	(Motown Tmg1185)	6	1980	0	1980		
3	I Need Your Lovin'	(Motown Tmg1203)	28	1980	37	1980	(Gordy 7189)	
4	Lovergirl		0	1985	4	1985	(Epic 04619)	
5	Oo La La La	(Epic 651423 7)	74	1988	0	1988		
6	Since Day One	(Epic 656429 7)	69	1990	0	1990		
	HIT 1 IS CREDITED TO TEENA MARIE, CO-LEAD VOCALS RICK JAMES							
Teenage Fanclub Male Vocal/Instrumental Group from the UK								
1	Star Sign	(Creation Cre105)	44	1991	0	1991		
2	The Concept	(Creation Cre111)	51	1991	0	1991		
3	What You Do To Me (Ep)	(Creation Cre115)	31	1992	0	1992		
4	Radio	(Creationcrescd 130)	31	1993	0	1993		
5	Norman 3	(Creationcrescd 142)	50	1993	0	1993		
6	Fallin'	(Epic 6602622)	59	1994	0	1994		
7	Mellow Doubt	(Creationcrescd 175)	34	1995	0	1995		
8	Sparky's Dream	(Creation Cre201)	40	1995	0	1995		
9	Neil Jung	(Creationcrescd 210)	62	1995	0	1995		
10	Have Lost It (Ep)	(Creationcrescd 216)	53	1995	0	1995		
11	Ain't That Enough	(Creationcrescd 228)	17	1997	0	1997		
12	I Don't Want Control Of You	(Creationcrescd 238)	43	1997	0	1997		
	HIT 6 IS CREDITED TO TEENAGE FANCLUB AND DE LA SOUL							
Tekno Too Male Production/Instrumental Duo from the UK								
1	Jet-Star	(D-ZONE DANCE012)	56	1991	0	1991		
Television `Male Vocal/Instrumental Group from the USA								
1	Marquee Moon	(Elektra K12252)	30	1977	0	1977		
2	Prove It	(Elektra K12262)	25	1977	0	1977		
3	Foxhole	(Elektra K12287)	36	1978	0	1978		

ISSUE	TITLE	UK LBL	UK POS	UK YEAR	US POS	US YEAR	US LBL
Telex Male Vocal/Instrumental Duo From Belgium							
1	Rock Around The Clock	(Sire Sir 4020)	34	1979	0	1979	
Telly Savalas Male Actor/Vocalist from the USA							
1	If	(MCA 174)	1	1975	0	1975	
2	You've Lost That Loving Feeling	(MCA 189)	47	1975	0	1964	
Temperance Seven Male Vocal/Instrumental Band from the UK							
1	You're Driving Me Crazy	(Parlophone R4757)	1	1961	0	1961	
2	Pasadena	(Parlophone R4781)	4	1961	0	1961	
3	Hard Hearted Hannah / Chilli Bom Bom	(Parlophone R4823)	28	1961	0	1961	
4	The Charleston	(Parlophone R4851)	22	1962	0	1962	
Temple Of The Dog Male Vocal/Instrumental Group from the USA							
1	Hunger Strike	(A&M Am 0091)	51	1992	0	1992	
Tempos Names Gene Schachter, Mike Lazo, Jim Drake & Tom Minoto							
1	See You In September		0	1959	23	1959	(Climax 102)
Temptations Male Soul Group Formed In Detroit In 1960							
1	Try It Baby		0	1964	15	1964	(Tamla 54095)
+ 1	Dream Come True		0	1962	22	1962	(Gordy 7001)
3	The Way You Do The Things You Do		0	1964	11	1964	(Gordy 7028)
4	I'll Be In Trouble		0	1964	33	1964	(Gordy 7032)
5	Girl (Why You Wanna Make Me Blue)		0	1964	26	1964	(Gordy 7035)
* 6	My Girl	(Stateside Ss378)	43	1965	1	1965	(Gordy 7038)
7	It's Growing	(Tamla Motown Tmg 504)	49	1965	18	1965	(Gordy 7040)
8	It's Growing (Re-Entry)	(Tamla Motown Tmg 504)	45	1965	0	1965	
9	Since I Lost My Baby / You've Got To Earn It		0	1965	17	1965	(Gordy 7043)
* 10	My Baby / Don't Look Back		0	1965	13	1965	(Gordy 7047)
11	Get Ready	(Tamla MotownTmg 688)	10	1969	29	1966	(Gordy 7049)
12	Ain't To Proud To Beg	(Tamla Motown Tmg 565)	21	1966	13	1966	(Gordy 7054)
* 13	Beauty Is Only Skin Deep	(Tamla Motown Tmg 578)	18	1966	3	1966	(Gordy 7055)
14	I Know (I'm Losing You)	(Tamla Motown Tmg 587)	19	1966	8	1966	(Gordy 7057)
15	All I Need		0	1967	8	1967	(Gordy 7061)
16	You're My Everything	(Tamla Motown Tmg 620)	26	1967	6	1967	(Gordy 7063)
17	(Loneliness Made Me Realise) It's You That I Need		0	1967	14	1967	(Gordy 7065)
* 18	I Wish It Would Rain	(Tamla Motown Tmg 641)	45	1968	4	1968	(Gordy 7068)
19	I Could Never Love Another (After Loving You)	(Tamla Motown Tmg 658)	47	1968	13	1968	(Gordy 7072)
20	Please Return Your Love To Me		0	1968	26	1968	(Gordy 7074)
* 21	Cloud Nine	(Tamla Motown Tmg 707)	15	1969	6	1968	(Gordy 7081)
* 22	I'm Gonna Make You Love Me	(Tamla Motown Tmg 685)	3	1969	2	1968	(Motown 1137)
23	The Composer		0	1969	27	1969	(Motown 1146)
24	Run Away Child, Running Wild		0	1969	6	1969	(Gordy 7084)
25	I'll Try Something New		0	1969	25	1969	(Motown 1142)
26	Don't Let The Joneses Get You Down		0	1969	20	1969	(Gordy 7086)
27	I'm Gonna Make You Love Me (Re-Entry)	(Tamla Motown Tmg 685)	49	1969	0	1969	
* 28	I Can't Get Next To You	(Tamla Motown Tmg 722)	13	1970	1	1969	(Gordy 7093)
29	I Second That Emotion	(Tamla Motown Tmg 709)	18	1969	0	1969	
30	Psychdelic Shack	(Tamla MotownTmg 741)	33	1970	7	1970	(Gordy 7096)
31	Why (Must We Fall In Love)	(Tamla Motown Tmg 730)	31	1970	0	1970	
* 32	Ball Of Confusion	(Tamla MotownTmg 749)	7	1970	3	1970	(Gordy 7099)
33	Ungena Za Ulimwengu (Unite The World)		0	1970	33	1970	(Gordy 7102)
34	Ball Of Confusion (Re-Entry)	(Tamla Motown Tmg 749)	48	1970	0	1970	
* 35	Just My Imagination (Running Away With Me)	(Tamla MotownTmg 733)	8	1971	1	1971	(Gordy 7105)
+ 36	It's Summer		0	1971	29	1971	(Gordy 7109)
37	Superstar (Remember How You Got Where You Are)		32	1972	8	1971	(Gordy 7111)
	(Tamla MotownTmg 800)						
38	Take A Look Around	(Tamla MotownTmg 808)	13	1972	30	1972	(Gordy 7115)
* 39	Papa Was A Rollin' Stone	(Tamla MotownTmg 839)	14	1973	1	1972	(Gordy 7121)
40	Masterpiece		0	1983	7	1983	(Gordy 7126)
41	The Plastic Man		0	1973	40	1973	(Gordy 7129)
42	Hey Girl (I Like Your Style)		0	1973	35	1973	(Gordy 7131)
43	Law Of The Land	(Tamla Motown Tmg 866)	41	1973	0	1973	
44	Let Your Hair Down		0	1974	27	1974	(Gordy 7133)
45	Happy People		0	1975	40	1975	(Gordy 7138)
46	Shakey Ground		0	1975	26	1975	(Gordy 7142)
47	Glasshouse		0	1975	37	1975	(Gordy 7144)
48	Standing On The Top (Part 1)	(Tamla Motown Tmg 1263)	53	1982	0	1982	

ISSUE	TITLE	UK LBL	UK POS	UK YEAR	US POS	US YEAR	US LBL
49	Treat Her Like A Lady	(Tamla Motown Tmg 1365)	12	1984	0	1984	
50	Papa Was A Rollin' Stone (Re-Mix)	(Motown Zb41431)	31	1987	0	1987	
51	Look What You Started	(Motown Zb41733)	63	1988	0	1988	
52	All I Want From You	(Motown Zb43233)	71	1989	0	1989	
53	The Motown Song		0	1991	10	1991	(Warner Bros 19322)
54	My Girl (Re-Issue)	(Epic 6576767)	2	1992	0	1992	
55	The Jones'	(Motown Tmg1403)	69	1992	0	1992	

NAMES EDDIE KENDRICKS, PAUL WILLIAMS, MELVIN FRANKLIN, OTIS WILLIAMS & ELBRIDGE BRYANT
PREVIOUS NAMES WERE THE DISTANTS, PRIMES ELGINS • OBITUARY : PAUL D: 17 AUG 1973.

Temptations (2) White Quartet Featuring Larry Curtis, Neil Stevens, Artie Sands & Artie Martin

	TITLE	UK LBL	UK POS	UK YEAR	US POS	US YEAR	US LBL
1	Barbara		0	1960	29	1960	(Goldisc 3001)

10cc Male Vocal/Instrumental Group from the UK

	TITLE	UK LBL	UK POS	UK YEAR	US POS	US YEAR	US LBL
1	Donna	(Uk 6)	2	1972	0	1972	
2	Rubber Bullets	(Uk 36)	1	1973	0	1973	
3	The Dean And I	(Uk 48)	10	1973	0	1973	
4	Wall Street Shuffle	(Uk 69)	10	1974	0	1974	
5	Silly Love	(Uk 77)	24	1974	0	1974	
6	Life Is A Minestrone	(Mercury 6008 010)	7	1975	0	1975	
7	I'm Not In Love	(Mercury 6008 014)	1	1975	2	1975	(Mercury 73678)
8	Art For Arts Sake	(Mercury 6008 017)	5	1975	0	1975	
9	I'm Mandy Fly Me		6	1976	0	1976	
10	People In Love		0	1977	40	1977	(Mercury 73917)
* 11	The Things We Do For Love	(Mercury 6008 022)	6	1976	5	1977	(Mercury 73875)
12	Good Morning Judge	(Mercury 6008 025)	5	1977	0	1977	
13	Dreadlock Holiday	(Mercury 6008 035)	1	1978	0	1978	
14	Runaway	(Mercury Mer 113)	50	1982	0	1982	
15	I'm Not In Love (Re-Recording)	(Avex Uk Avexcd 2)	29	1995	0	1995	

NAMES ERIC STEWART, GRAHAM GOULDMAN, LOL CREME & KEVIN GODLEY

Ten City Male Vocal/Instrumental Group from the USA

	TITLE	UK LBL	UK POS	UK YEAR	US POS	US YEAR	US LBL
1	That's The Way Love Is	(Atlantic A 8963)	8	1989	0	1989	
2	Devotion	(Atlantic A 8916)	29	1989	0	1989	
3	Where Do We Go	(Atlantic A 8864)	60	1989	0	1989	
4	Whatever Makes You Happy	(Atlantic A 7819)	60	1990	0	1990	
5	Only Time Will Tell / My Peace Of Heaven	(East WestAmerica A 8516)	63	1992	0	1997	
* * 6	Fantasy	(Columbia 456595042)		1993	0	1993	

Ten Pole Tudor Male Vocal/Instrumental Group from the UK

	TITLE	UK LBL	UK POS	UK YEAR	US POS	US YEAR	US LBL
1	Who Killed Bambi	(Virgin Vs 256)	6	1979	0	1979	
2	Rock Around The Clock	(Virgin Vs 290)	21	1979	0	1979	
3	Swords Of A Thousand Men	(Stiff Buy 109)	6	1981	0	1981	
4	Wunderbar	(Stiff Buy 120)	16	1981	0	1981	
5	Throw The Baby Out With The Bathwater	(Stiff Buy 129)	49	1981	0	1981	

Ten Sharp Male Vocal/Instrumental Duo From Holland

	TITLE	UK LBL	UK POS	UK YEAR	US POS	US YEAR	US LBL
1	You	(Columbia 106566647)		1992	0	1992	
2	Ain't My Beating Heart	(Columbia 636580947)		1992	0	1992	

10,000 Maniacs Mixed Vocal/Instrumental Group from the USA

	TITLE	UK LBL	UK POS	UK YEAR	US POS	US YEAR	US LBL
1	These Are Days	(Elektra Ekr 156)	58	1992	0	1992	
2	Candy Everybody Wants	(Elektra Ekr 160cd1)	47	1993	0	1993	
3	Because The Night	(Elektra Ekr 175cd)	65	1993	11	1993	(Elektra 64595)

Ten Years After Male Vocal/Instrumental Group from the UK, Names Alvin Lee, Chick Churchill, Leo Lyons & Ric Lee

	TITLE	UK LBL	UK POS	UK YEAR	US POS	US YEAR	US LBL
1	Live Like A Man	(Deram Dm 299)	10	1970	0	1970	
2	I'd Love To Change The World		0	1971	40	1971	(Columbia 45457)

Tennessee Ernie Ford Male Vocalist, Real Name Ernest Jennings Ford B: 13 Feb 1919 On A Farm Outside Bristol, Tennessee.

	TITLE	UK LBL	UK POS	UK YEAR	US POS	US YEAR	US LBL
4	Mule Train		0	1949	9	1949	(Capitol 40258)
6	The Cry Of The Wild Goose		0	1950	15	1950	(Capitol 40280)
7	Ain't Nobody's Business Buy My Own		0	1950	22	1950	(Capitol 1124)
8	I'll Never Be Free		0	1950	3	1950	(Capitol 1124)
* 9	The Shotgun Boogie		0	1950	14	1950	(Capitol 1295)
11	Mister And Mississippi		0	1951	18	1951	(Capitol 1521)
16	The Honeymoon's Over		0	1954	16	1954	(Capitol 2809)
17	Give Me Your Word	(Capitol Cl14005)	1	1955	0	1955	
18	Ballad Of Davy Crockett	(Capitol Cl14506)	3	1956	5	1955	(Capitol 3058)
* 20	Sixteen Tons	(Capitol Cl14500)	1	1956	1	1955	(Capitol 3262)
21	That's All		0	1956	17	1956	(Capitol 3343)

ISSUE	TITLE	UK LBL	UK POS	UK YEAR	US POS	US YEAR	US LBL
22	In The Middle Of An Island		0	1957	23	1957	(Capitol 3762)

UNLISTED HITS WERE C/W • OBITUARY : D: 17 OCT 1991 LIVER COMPLICATIONS.

Terence Trent D'Arby Male Vocalist, B: 15 Mar 1962 New York City

ISSUE	TITLE	UK LBL	UK POS	UK YEAR	US POS	US YEAR	US LBL
1	If You Let Me Stay	(Cbs Trent 1)	7	1987	0	1987	
2	Wishing Well	(Cbs Trent 2)	4	1987	1	1988	(Columbia 07675)
3	Dance Little Sister (Part One)	(Cbs Trent 3)	20	1987	30	1987	(Columbia 08023)
4	Sign Your Name	(Cbs Trent 4)	2	1988	4	1988	(Columbia 079119
5	To Know Someone Deeply Is To Know Someone Softly	(Cbs Trent 6)	55	1990	0	1990	
6	Do You Love Me Like You Say	(Columbia 146590732)		1993	0	1993	
7	Delicate	(Columbia6593312)	14	1993	0	1993	
8	She Kissed Me	(Columbia6595922)	16	1993	0	1993	
9	Let Her Down Easy	(Columbia6598642)	18	1993	0	1993	
10	Holding Onto You	(Columbia6614235)	20	1995	0	1995	
11	Vibrator	(Columbia6622585)	57	1995	0	1995	

HIT 7 IS CREDITED TO TERENCE TRENT D'ARBY FEATURING DES'REE D'ARBY WAS ORIGINALLY SPELLED DARBY

Teresa Brewer Female Vocalist, Real Name Theresa Breuer B: 7 May 1931 Toledo, Ohio

ISSUE	TITLE	UK LBL	UK POS	UK YEAR	US POS	US YEAR	US LBL
* 1	Music! Music! Music!		0	1950	1	1950	(London 30023)
2	Choo'n Gum		0	1950	17	1950	(London 30100)
3	Longing For You		0	1951	23	1951	(London 1086)
4	Gonna Get Along Without Ya Now		0	1952	25	1952	(Coral 60676)
5	You'll Never Get Away		0	1952	17	1952	(Coral 60829)
* 6	Till I Waltz Again With You		0	1952	1	1952	(Coral 60873)
7	Dancin' With Someone (Longin' For You)		0	1953	17	1953	(Coral 60953)
8	Into Each Life Some Rain Must Fall		0	1953	23	1953	(Coral 60994)
* 9	Ricochet (Rick-O-Shay)		0	1953	2	1953	(Coral 61043)
10	Baby Baby Baby		0	1953	12	1953	(Coral 61067)
11	Bell Bottom Blues		0	1954	17	1954	(Coral 61066)
12	Our Heartbreaking Waltz		0	1954	23	1954	(Coral 61066)
13	Jilted		0	1954	6	1954	(Coral 61152)
14	Skinnie Minnie (Fish Tail)		0	1954	22	1954	(Coral 61197)
* 15	Let Me Go Lover		9	1955	6	1954	(Coral 61315)
16	Pledging My Love		0	1955	17	1955	(Coral 61362)
17	Silver Dollar		0	1955	20	1955	(Coral 61394)
18	The Banjo's Back In Town		0	1955	15	1955	(Coral 61448)
* 19	A Tear Fell	(Vogue/Coral Q 72146)	2	1956	5	1956	(Coral 61590)
20	Bo Weevil		0	1956	17	1956	(Coral 61590)
21	A Sweet Old Fashioned Girl	(Vogue/Coral Q 72172)	3	1956	7	1956	(Coral 61636)
22	Mutual Admiration Society		0	1956	21	1956	(Coral 61737)
23	Empty Arms		0	1957	13	1957	(Coral 61805)
24	Nora Malone	(Vogue/Coral Q 72224)	26	1957	0	1957	
25	You Send Me		0	1957	8	1957	(Coral 61898)
26	The Hula Hoop Song		0	1958	38	1958	(Coral 62033)
27	Heavenly Lover		0	1959	40	1959	(Coral 62084)
28	How Do You Know It's Love	(Coral Q 72396)	21	1960	0	1960	
29	Anymore		0	1960	31	1960	(Coral 62219)

HIT 15 IS CREDITED TO TERESA BREWER WITH THE LANCERS

Teri De Sario Female Singer/Songwriter From The Miami

ISSUE	TITLE	UK LBL	UK POS	UK YEAR	US POS	US YEAR	US LBL
1	Ain't Nothin' (Gonna Keep Me From You)	(CasablancaCan 128)	52	1978	0	1978	
* 2	Yes, I'm Ready		0	1979	2	1979	(Casablanca 2227)

HIT 2 IS CREDITED TO TERI DESARIO WITH K.C.

Terra Firma Male Producer Claudio Giussani From Italy

ISSUE	TITLE	UK LBL	UK POS	UK YEAR	US POS	US YEAR	US LBL
1	Floating	(Platipus Plat21cd)	64	1996	0	1996	

Terri Gibbs Female Country Singer, B: 15 Jun 1954 Augusta, Georgia

ISSUE	TITLE	UK LBL	UK POS	UK YEAR	US POS	US YEAR	US LBL
1	Somebody's Knockin'		0	1981	13	1981	(MCA 41309)

Terri Symon Male Vocalist from the UK

ISSUE	TITLE	UK LBL	UK POS	UK YEAR	US POS	US YEAR	US LBL
1	I Want To Know What Love Is	(A&M 5810592)	54	1995	0	1995	

Terri Wells Female Vocalist from the USA

ISSUE	TITLE	UK LBL	UK POS	UK YEAR	US POS	US YEAR	US LBL
1	You Make It Heaven	(PhillywoodPws 111)	53	1983	0	1983	
2	I'll Be Around	(PhillywoodLon 48)	17	1984	0	1984	

Terrorize Male Producer, Real Name Shaun Imrei from the UK

ISSUE	TITLE	UK LBL	UK POS	UK YEAR	US POS	US YEAR	US LBL
1	It's Just A Feeling	(Hamster Ster1)	52	1992	0	1992	
2	Feel The Rhythm	(Hamster12ster 2)	69	1992	0	1992	
3	It's Just A Feeling (Re-Issue)	(Hamster Ster8)	47	1992	0	1992	

ISSUE	TITLE	UK LBL	UK POS	UK YEAR	US POS	US YEAR	US LBL
Terrorvision Male Vocal/Instrumental Group from the UK							
1	American Tv	(Total Vegascdvegas 3)	63	1993	0	1993	
2	New Policy One	(Total VegasCdvegas 4)	42	1993	0	1993	
3	My House	(Total VegasCdvegas 5)	29	1994	0	1994	
4	Oblivion	(Total VegasCdvegas 6)	21	1994	0	1994	
5	Middleman	(Total VegasCdvegas 7)	25	1994	0	1994	
6	Pretend Best Friend	(Total VegasCdvegas 8)	25	1994	0	1994	
7	Alice What's The Matter	(Total VegasCdvegas 9)	24	1994	0	1994	
8	Some People Say	(Total VegasCdvegas 10)	22	1995	0	1995	
9	Perseverance	(Total VegasCdvegas 11)	5	1996	0	1996	
10	Celebrity Hit List	(Total VegasCdvegas 12)	20	1996	0	1996	
11	Bad Actress	(Total VegasCdvegas 13)	10	1996	0	1996	
12	Easy	(Total VegasCdvegas 14)	12	1997	0	1997	
Terry Dactyl & The Dinosaurs Male Vocal/Instrumental Group from the UK							
1	Seaside Shuffle	(Uk 5)	2	1972	0	1972	
2	On A Saturday Night	(Uk 21)	45	1973	0	1973	
Terry Dene Male Vocalist from the UK							
1	A White Sport Coat	(Decca F 10895)	18	1957	0	1957	
2	Start Movin'	(Decca F 10914)	15	1957	0	1957	
3	A White Sport Coat (Re-Entry)	(Decca F 10895)	30	1957	0	1957	
4	Stairway Of Love	(Decca F 11016)	16	1958	0	1958	
Terry Gilkyson & The Easy Riders Names Terry Gilkyson, Frank Miller & Rick Dehr							
* 1	Marianne		0	1957	4	1957	(Columbia 40817)
Terry Hall Male Vocalist from the UK							
1	Missing	(Chrysalis Chs 3381)	75	1989	0	1989	
2	Forever J	(Anxious Anx1024cdx)	67	1994	0	1994	
3	Sense	(Anxious Anx1027cd)	54	1994	0	1994	
4	Chasing Rainbows (Ep)	(Anxious Anx1033cd1)	62	1995	0	1995	
5	Ballad Of A Landlord	(SouthseaBubble Co Cdbubble 1)	50	1997	0	1997	
Terry Jacks Male Vocalist Terry, Hails from Winnipeg, Canada							
* 1	Seasons In The Sun	(Bell 1344)	1	1974	1	1974	(Bell 35432)
2	If You Go Away	(Bell 1362)	8	1974	0	1974	
	ALSO RECORDED WITH HIS WIFE AS THE POPPY FAMILY						
Terry Lightfoot & His New Orleans Jazzmen Vocal/Instrumental (Clarinet) With Male Jazz Band from the UK							
1	True Love	(Columbia Db4696)	33	1961	0	1961	
2	King Kong	(Columbia Scd2165)	29	1961	0	1961	
3	Tavern In The Town	(Columbia Db4822)	49	1962	0	1962	
Terry Neason Female Vocalist from the UK							
1	Lifeboat	(Wea Yz 830)	72	1994	0	1994	
Terry Nelson & C Company Dj/Vocalist From Russellville, Alabama							
* 1	Battle Hymn Of Lt. Calley		0	1971	37	1971	(Plantation 73)
Terry Shand & His Orchestra Male Bandleader/Vocal/Pianist from the USA							
1	I Can't Love You Any More (Any More Than I Do)		0	1940	16	1940	(Decca 3127)
Terry Stafford A 6'3 Male Singer/Sports Athlete From Amarillo, Texas							
* 1	Suspicion	(London Hlu9871)	31	1964	3	1964	(Crusader 101)
2	I'll Touch A Star		0	1964	25	1964	(Crusader 105)
Terry Wogan Male Dj/Vocalist/Talk Show Host From Ireland							
1	Floral Dance	(Philips 6006 592)	21	1978	0	1978	
Tesla Male Vocal/Instrumental Group from the USA							
* 1	Love Song		0	1990	10	1989	(Geffen 22856)
2	Signs	(Geffen Gfs 3)	70	1991	8	1991	(Geffen 19653)
	NAMES JEFF KEITH, TOMMY SKEOCH, TROY LUCCKETTA, BRIAN WHEAT & FRANK HANNON						
Tevin Campbell Male Vocalist From Texas B: 1978							
* 1	Round And Round		0	1991	12	1991	(Paisley P 21740)
* 2	Tell Me What You Want Me To Do	(Qwest W 0102)	63	1992	6	1991	(Qwest 19131)
* 3	Can We Talk		0	1993	9	1993	(Qwest 18346)
4	I'm Ready		0	1994	9	1994	(Qwest 18264)
5	Always Ready		0	1994	20	1994	(Qwest 18260)
6	Back To The World		0	1996	47	1996	(Qwest)

ISSUE	TITLE	UK LBL	UK POS	UK YEAR	US POS	US YEAR	US LBL	
Tex Beneke & His Orchestra Male Bandleader/Saxophonist, Real Name Gordon Beneke from the USA								
1	Hey! Ba-Ba-Re-Bop		0	1946	4	1946	(RCA Victor	1859)
2	The Whiffenpoof Song		0	1946	19	1946	(RCA Victor	1859)
3	It Couldn't Be True (Or Could It?)		0	1946	12	1946	(RCA Victor	1835)
4	Cynthia's In Love		0	1946	15	1946	(RCA Victor	1858)
5	I Know		0	1946	9	1946	(RCA Victor	1914)
6	Give Me Five Minutes More (From Sweethearts Of Sigma		0	1946	4	1946	(RCA Victor	1922)
7	The Woodchuck Song		0	1946	22	1946	(RCA Victor	1951)
8	Passe'		0	1946	9	1946	(RCA Victor	1951)
9	A Gal In Calico		0	1946	6	1946	(RCA Victor	1991)
10	Oh, But I Do (From The Time, Place And The Girl)		0	1947	11	1947	(RCA Victor	1991)
11	Anniversary Song (From The Jolson Story)		0	1947	3	1947	(RCA Victor	2126)
12	My Heart Is A Hobo		0	1947	22	1947	(RCA Victor	2260)
13	As Long As I'm Dreaming		0	1947	21	1947	(RCA Victor	2260)
14	Moolight Whispers		0	1948	26	1948	(RCA Victor	2667)
15	St Louis Blues March		0	1948	5	1948	(RCA Victor	2722)
16	Meadowlands		0	1948	21	1948	(RCA Victor	2898)
17	I Can Dream, Can't I (From Right This Way)		0	1949	12	1949	(RCA 78-3553)	
Male Actor/Vocalist, Real Name Maurice Woodward Ritter B: 12 Jan 1905 Near Murvaul, Texas.								
1	I'm Wasting My Tear On You		0	1944	11	1944	(Capitol 174)	
2	There's A New Moon Over My Shoulder		0	1944	26	1944	(Capitol 174)	
15	High Noon (Do Not Forsake Me)		0	1952	12	1952	(Capitol 2120)	
16	The Bandit		0	1954	30	1954	(Capitol 2916)	
17	The Wayward Wind	(Capitol Cl14581)	8	1956	28	1956	(Capitol 3430)	
18	I Dreamed Of A Hill-Billy Heaven		0	1961	20	1961	(Capitol 4567)	
	REST ARE C/W HITS							
	OBITUARY : D: 3 JAN 1974 HEART ATTACK.							
Tex Williams & The Western Caravan Male Country Singer, B: Sollie Paul Williams, 23 Aug 1917 Near Ramsey, Illinois								
* 2	Smoke! Smoke! Smoke! (That Cigarette)		0	1947	1	1947	(Capitol America 40001)	
5	Don't Telephone, Don't Telegraph, Tell A Woman		0	1948	27	1948	(Capitol America 40081)	
6	Suspicion		0	1948	24	1948	(Capitol America 40108)	
12	Life Gets Tee-Jus, Don't It?		0	1948	27	1948	(Capitol 15271)	
	UNLISTED SONGS ARE C/W HITS							
Texas Mixed Vocal/Instrumental Group from the UK								
1	I Don't Want A Lover	(Mercury Tex1)	8	1989	0	1989		
2	Thrill Has Gone	(Mercury Tex2)	60	1989	0	1989		
3	Everyday Now	(Mercury Tex3)	44	1989	0	1989		
4	Prayer For You	(Mercury Tex4)	73	1989	0	1989		
5	Why Believe In You	(Mercury Tex5)	66	1991	0	1991		
6	In My Heart	(Mercury Tex6)	74	1991	0	1991		
7	Alone With You	(Mercury Tex7)	32	1992	0	1992		
8	Tired Of Being Alone	(Mercury Tex8)	19	1992	0	1992		
9	So Called Friend	(Vertigo Texcd9)	30	1993	0	1993		
10	You Owe It All To Me	(Vetigo Texcd10)	39	1993	0	1993		
11	So In Love With You	(Vertigo Texcd11)	28	1994	0	1994		
12	Say What You Want	(MercuryMerdd 480)	3	1997	0	1997		
13	Halo	(MercuryMercd 482)	10	1997	0	1997		
14	Black Eyed Boy	(MercuryMercd 490)	5	1997	0	1997		
Texas Jim Robertson Male Country Singer from the USA								
1	I'll Be Back In A Year, Little Darlin'		0	1941	21	1941	(Bluebird 8606)	
2	Let Me In		0	1953	24	1953	(RCA Victor	4077)
That Petrol Emotion Male Vocal/Instrumental Group from the UK								
1	Big Decision	(Polydor Tpe 1)	43	1987	0	1987		
2	Dance	(Polydor Tpe 2)	64	1987	0	1987		
3	Genius Move	(Virgin Vs 1002)	65	1987	0	1987		
4	Abandon	(Virgin Vs 1242)	73	1990	0	1990		
5	Hey Venus	(Virgin Vs 1290)	49	1990	0	1990		
6	Tingle	(Virgin Vs 1312)	49	1991	0	1991		
7	Sensitize	(Virgin Vs 1261)	55	1991	0	1991		
The The Male Vocalist, Real Name Matt Johnson With Backing Musicians from the UK								
1	Uncertain Smile	(Epic Epc A 2787)	68	1982	0	1982		
2	This Is The Day	(Epic A 3710)	71	1983	0	1983		
3	Heartland	(Some BizzareTruth 2)	29	1986	0	1986		

ISSUE	TITLE	UK LBL	UK POS	UK YEAR	US POS	US YEAR	US LBL
4	Infected	(Some BizzareTruth 3)	48	1986	0	1986	
5	Slow Train To Dawn	(Some BizzareTense 1)	64	1987	0	1987	
6	Sweet Bird Of Truth	(Epic Tense 2)	55	1987	0	1987	
7	The Beat(En) Generation	(Epic Emu 8)	18	1989	0	1989	
8	Gravitate To Me	(Epic Emu 9)	63	1989	0	1989	
9	Armageddon Days Are Here (Again)	(Epic Emu 10)	70	1989	0	1989	
10	Shades Of Blue (Ep)	(Epic 6557968)	54	1991	0	1991	
11	Dogs Of Lust	(Epic 6584572)	25	1993	0	1993	
12	Slow Emotion Replay	(Epic 6590772)	35	1993	0	1993	
13	Love Is Stronger Than Death	(Epic 6593712)	39	1993	0	1993	
14	Dis-Infected (Ep)	(Epic 6598112)	17	1994	0	1994	
15	I Saw The Light	(Epic 6610912)	31	1995	0	1995	

Theatre Of Hat   Male Vocal/Instrumental Group from the UK

ISSUE	TITLE	UK LBL	UK POS	UK YEAR	US POS	US YEAR	US LBL
1	Do You Believe In The Westworld	(Burning RomeBrr 2)	40	1982	0	1982	
2	The Hop	(Burning RomeBrr 3)	70	1982	0	1982	

Thelma Houston   Female Vocalist from Leyland, Mississippi

ISSUE	TITLE	UK LBL	UK POS	UK YEAR	US POS	US YEAR	US LBL
1	Don't Leave Me This Way	(Motown Tmg1060)	13	1977	1	1977	(Tamla 54278)
2	Saturday Night, Sunday Morning		0	1979	34	1979	(Tamla 54297)
3	If You Feel It	(RCA 77)	48	1981	0	1981	
4	You Used To Hold Me So Tight	(MCA Mca 932)	49	1984	0	1984	
5	Don't Leave Me This Way (Re-Recording)	(Dynamo Dynd001)	35	1995	0	1995	

Them   Male Vocal/Instrumental Group from the UK

ISSUE	TITLE	UK LBL	UK POS	UK YEAR	US POS	US YEAR	US LBL
1	Baby Please Don't Go	(Decca F 12018)	10	1965	93	1965	(Parrot 9727)
2	Here Comes The Night	(Decca F 12094)	2	1965	24	1965	(Parrot 9749)
3	Mystic Eyes		0	1965	33	1965	(Parrot 9796)
4	Baby Please Don't Go (Re-Issue)	(London Lon292)	65	1991	0	1991	

LEAD SINGER WITH THE QUINTET WAS VAN MORRISON • OTHER MEMBERS WERE BILLY HARRISON, ALAN HENDERSON, JOHN MCAULEY & PETER BARDENS
THE GROUP DISBANDED IN 1966

Then Jerico   Male Vocal/Instrumental Group from the UK

ISSUE	TITLE	UK LBL	UK POS	UK YEAR	US POS	US YEAR	US LBL
1	Let Her Fall	(London Lon 97)	65	1987	0	1987	
2	The Motive (Living Without You)	(London Lon145)	18	1987	0	1987	
3	Muscle Deep	(London Lon156)	48	1987	0	1987	
4	Big Area	(London Lon204)	13	1989	0	1989	
5	What Does It Take	(London Lon223)	33	1989	0	1989	
6	Sugar Box	(London Lon235)	22	1989	0	1989	

Theola Kilgore   Gospel-Blues Singer And Hails From Louisiana

ISSUE	TITLE	UK LBL	UK POS	UK YEAR	US POS	US YEAR	US LBL
1	The Love Of My Man		0	1963	21	1963	(Serock 2004)

Therapy   Male Vocal/Instrumental Group from the UK

ISSUE	TITLE	UK LBL	UK POS	UK YEAR	US POS	US YEAR	US LBL
1	Teethgrinder	(A&M Am 0097)	30	1992	0	1992	
2	Shortsharpshock (Ep)	(A&M Amcd 208)	9	1993	0	1993	
3	Face The Strange (Ep)	(A&M 5803052)	18	1993	0	1993	
4	Opal Mantra	(A&M 5803612)	14	1993	0	1993	
5	Nowhere	(A&M 5805052)	18	1994	0	1994	
6	Trigger Inside	(A&M 5805352)	22	1994	0	1994	
7	Die Laughing	(A&M 5805892)	29	1994	0	1994	
8	Innicent X	(Volume Volcd1)	53	1995	0	1995	
9	Stories	(A&M 5811052)	14	1995	0	1995	
10	Loose	(A&M 5811652)	25	1995	0	1995	
11	Diane	(A&M 5812912)	26	1995	0	1995	

These Animal Men   Male Vocal/Instrumental Group from the UK

ISSUE	TITLE	UK LBL	UK POS	UK YEAR	US POS	US YEAR	US LBL
1	This Is The Sound Of Youth	(Hi-Rise Flatscd7)	72	1994	0	1994	
2	Life Support Machine	(Hut Hutcd 76)	62	1997	0	1997	
3	Light Emitting Electrical Wave	(Hut Hutcd 81)	72	1997	0	1997	

They Might Be Giants   Male Vocal/Instrumental Duo from the USA

ISSUE	TITLE	UK LBL	UK POS	UK YEAR	US POS	US YEAR	US LBL
1	Birdhouse In Your Soul	(Elektra Ekr104)	6	1990	0	1990	
2	Instanbul (Not Constantinople)	(Elektra Ekr110)	61	1990	0	1990	

Thin Lizzy   Male Vocal/Instrumental Group from Ireland

ISSUE	TITLE	UK LBL	UK POS	UK YEAR	US POS	US YEAR	US LBL
1	Whiskey In A Jar	(Decca F 13355)	6	1973	0	1973	
2	The Boys Are Back In Town	(Vertigo 6059139)	8	1976	12	1976	(Mercury 73728)
3	Jailbreak	(Vertigo 6059150)	31	1976	0	1976	
4	Don't Believe A Word	(Vertigo Lizzy001)	12	1977	0	1977	
5	Dancing In The Moonlight (It's Caught Me In The Spotlight)	(Vertigo 6059117)	14	1977	0	1977	

ISSUE	TITLE	UK LBL	UK POS	UK YEAR	US POS	US YEAR	US LBL
6	Rosalie-Cowgirl's Song (Medley)	(Vertigo Lizzy 2)	20	1978	0	1978	
7	Waiting For An Alibi	(Vertigo Lizzy003)	9	1979	0	1979	
8	Do Anything You Want To	(Vertigo Lizzy004)	14	1979	0	1979	
9	Sarah	(Vertigo Lizzy 5)	24	1979	0	1979	
10	Chinatown	(Vertigo Lizzy 6)	21	1980	0	1980	
11	Killer On The Loose	(Vertigo Lizzy 7)	10	1980	0	1980	
12	Killers Live (EP)	(Vertigo Lizzy 8)	19	1981	0	1981	
13	Trouble Boys	(Vertigo Lizzy 9)	53	1981	0	1981	
14	Hollywood (Down On Your Luck)	(Vertigo Lizzy10)	53	1982	0	1982	
15	Cold Sweat	(Vertigo Lizzy11)	27	1983	0	1983	
16	Thunder And Lightning	(Vertigo Lizzy12)	39	1983	0	1983	
17	The Sun Goes Down	(Vertigo Lizzy13)	52	1983	0	1983	
18	Dedication	(Vertigo Lizzy14)	35	1991	0	1991	
19	The Boys Are Back In Town (Re-Issue)	(Vertigo Lizzy15)	63	1991	0	1991	

LEAD SINGER WITH THE QUARTET IS PHIL LYNOTT B: 20 AUG 1951 • PHIL WAS THE SON-IN-LAW TO TV PRESENTER LESLIE CROWTHER D: 1996
OBITUARY : LYNOTT D: 4 JAN 1986 DRUG OVERDOSE.

Think Studio Group Formed For The Hit

1	Once You Understand		0	1972	23	1972	(Laurie 3583)

3rd Bass Male Rap Group from the USA

1	The Gas Face	(Def Jam 655627 0)	71	1990	0	1990	
2	Brooklyn-Queens	(Def Jam 655830 7)	61	1990	0	1990	
* 3	Pop Goes The Weasel	(Def Jam 6569547)	64	1991	29	1991	(Def Jam 73728)

Third Dimension (Featuring) Julie Mixed Vocal/Instrumental Group from the UK
Mcdermott

1	Don't Go	(Soundproofmcstd 4082)	34	1996	0	1996	

3rd Party

1	Can U Feel It		0	1997	62	1997	(A&M 582084)

Third World Male Vocal/Instrumental Group from Jamaica

1	Now That We've Found Love	(Island Wip 6457)	10	1978	0	1978	
2	Cool Meditation	(Island Wip 6469)	17	1979	0	1979	
3	Talk To Me	(Island Wip 6496)	56	1979	0	1979	
4	Dancing On The Floor (Hooked On Love)	(Cbs A 1214)	10	1981	0	1981	
5	Try Jah Love	(Cbs A 2063)	47	1982	0	1982	
6	Now That We've Found Love (Re-Issue)	(Island Is 219)	22	1985	0	1985	

Thirst Male Vocal/Instrumental Group from the UK

1	The Enemy Within	(Ten Ten 379)	61	1991	0	1991	

This Island Earth Mixed Vocal/Instrumental Group from the UK

1	See That Glow	(Magnet Mag266)	47	1985	0	1985	

38 Special Southern-Rock Group, Lead Singer With The Sextet Is Donnie Van Zant

	Hold On Loosely		0	1981	27	1981	(A&M 2316)
2	Caught Up In You		0	1982	10	1982	(A&M 2412)
3	You Keep Runnin' Away		0	1982	38	1982	(A&M 2431)
4	Been The One		0	1983	19	1983	(A&M 2594)
5	Back Where You Belong		0	1984	20	1984	(A&M 2615)
6	Teacher Teacher		0	1984	25	1984	(Capitol 5405)
7	Like No Other Night		0	1986	14	1986	(A&M 2831)
8	Second Chance		0	1989	6	1989	(A&M 1273)
9	The Sound Of Your Voice		0	1991	33	1991	(Charisma 98773)

HIT 8 IS CREDITED TO THIRTY EIGHT SPECIAL

This Mortal Coil Mixed Vocal/Instrumental Group from the UK

1	Song To The Siren	(4ad Ad 310)	66	1983	0	1983	
2	Song To The Siren (Re-Entry)	(4ad Ad 310)	75	1983	0	1983	

This Way Up Male Vocal/Instrumental Duo from the UK

1	Tell Me Why	(Virgin Vs 954)	72	1987	0	1987	

This Year's Blonde Mixed Vocal/Instrumental Group from the UK

1	Platinun Pop	(Creole Cr 19)	46	1981	0	1981	
2	Who's That Mix	(Debut Debt3034)	62	1987	0	1987	

Thom Pace Male Vocalist from the USA

1	Maybe	(RSO 34)	14	1979	0	1979	

ISSUE	TITLE	UK LBL	UK POS	UK YEAR	US POS	US YEAR	US LBL
Thomas & Taylor	Mixed Vocal Duo from the USA						
1	You Can't Blame Love	(CooltempoCool 123)	53	1986	0	1986	
Thomas Dolby	Male Vocal/Multi-Instrumentalist, Real Name Thomas Morgan Dolby Robertson B: 14 Oct 1958 Cairo, Egypt						
1	Europa And The Pirate Twins	(Parlophone R6051)	48	1981	0	1981	
2	Windpower	(Venice In PerilVips 103)	31	1982	0	1982	
3	She Blinded Me With Science	(Venice In PerilVips 104)	49	1982	5	1983	(Capitol 5204)
4	She Blinded Me With Science (Re-Entry)	(Venice In PerilVips 104)	56	1983	0	1983	
5	Hyperactive	(ParlophoneOdeon R 6065)	17	1984	0	1984	
6	I Scare Myself	(ParlophoneOdeon R 6067)	46	1984	0	1984	
7	Airhead	(Manhattan Mt38)	53	1988	0	1988	
8	Close But No Cigar	(Virgin Vs 1410)	22	1992	0	1992	
9	I Love You Goodbye	(Virgin Vs 1417)	36	1992	0	1992	
10	Silk Pyjamas	(Virgin Vs 1430)	62	1992	0	1992	
11	Hyperactive (Re-Mix)	(ParlophoneCdemcts 10)	23	1994	0	1994	
Thomas Lang	Male Vocalist from the UK						
1	The Happy Man	(Epic Vow 4)	67	1988	0	1988	
Thomas Wayne With The Delons	Real Name Thomas Wayne Perkins B: 22 Jul 1940 In Battsville, Mississippi						
1	Tragedy		0	1959	5	1959	(Epic 07283)
	OBITUARY : D: 15 AUG 1971 CAR ACCIDENT.						
Thompson Twins	Mixed Vocal/Instrumental Group from the UK/New Zealand, Names: Tom Bailey, Alannah Currie & Joe Leeway (Left In 1986)						
1	Lies	(Arista Arist486)	67	1982	30	1983	(Arista 1024)
2	Love On Your Side	(Arista Arist504)	9	1983	0	1983	
3	We Are Detective	(Arista Arist526)	7	1983	0	1983	
4	Watching	(Arista Twins 1)	33	1983	0	1983	
5	Hold Me Now	(Arista Twins 2)	4	1983	3	1984	(Arista 9164)
6	Doctor! Doctor!	(Arista Twins 3)	3	1984	11	1984	(Arista 9209)
7	You Take Me Up	(Arista Twins 4)	2	1984	0	1984	
8	Sister Of Mercy	(Arista Twins 5)	11	1984	0	1984	
9	Sister Of Mercy (Re-Entry)	(Arista Twins 5)	66	1984	0	1984	
10	Lay Your Hand On Me	(Arista Twins 6)	13	1984	6	1985	(Arista 9396)
11	Don't Mess With Doctor Dream	(Arista Twins 9)	15	1985	0	1985	
12	King For A Day	(Arista Twins 7)	22	1985	8	1986	(Arista 9450)
13	Revolution	(Arista Twins 10)	56	1985	0	1985	
14	Revolution (Re-Entry)	(Arista Twins 10)	75	1986	0	1986	
15	Get That Love	(Arista Twins 12)	68	1987	31	1987	(Arista 9577)
16	Get That Love (Re-Entry)	(Arista Twins 12)	66	1987	0	1987	
17	In The Name Of Love '88	(Arista 111808)	46	1988	0	1988	
18	Sugar Daddy		0	1989	28	1989	(Warner Bros 22819)
19	Come Inside	(Warner BrosW 0058)	56	1991	0	1991	
20	The Saint	(Warner BrosW 0080)	53	1992	0	1992	
Those 2 Girls	Female Vocal Duo from the UK						
1	Wanna Make You Go...Uuh!	(Final Vinyl74321233782)	74	1994	0	1994	
2	All I Want	(Final Vinyl74321254202)	36	1995	0	1995	
Thousand Yard Stare	Male Vocal/Instrumental Group from the UK						
1	Seasonstream (Ep)	(StifledAardvark Aard St)	65	1991	0	1991	
2	Comeuppance	(StifledAardvark Aard 007)	37	1992	0	1992	
3	Spindrift (EP)	(StifledAardvark Aardt 010)	58	1992	0	1992	
4	Version Of Me	(PolydorAardc 012)	57	1993	0	1993	
Thrashing Doves	Male Vocal/Instrumental Group from the UK						
1	Beautiful Imbalance	(A&M Tdove 1)	50	1987	0	1987	
Three Degrees	Female Vocalist from the UK						
1	Maybe		0	1970	29	1970	(Roulette 7079)
* 2	Tsop (The Sound Of Philadelphia)	(Philadelphia International Pir 2289)	22	1974	1	1974	(Phil/Inter 3540)
3	Year Of Decision	(PhiladelphiaInternational Pir 2073)	13	1974	0	1974	
* 4	When Will I See You Again	(PhiladelphiaInternational Pir 2155)	1	1974	2	1974	(Phil/Inter 3550)
5	Get Your Love Back	(PhiladelphiaInternational Pir 2737)	34	1974	0	1974	
6	Take Good Care Of Yourself	(PhiladelphiaInternational Pir 3177)	9	1975	0	1975	
+ 7	I Didn't Know		0	1975	18	1975	(Phil/Inter 3561)
8	Long Lost Lover	(PhiladelphiaInternational Pir 3352)	40	1975	0	1975	
9	Toast Of Love	(Epic Epc 4215)	36	1976	0	1976	
10	Givin' Up Givin' In	(Ariola Aro 130)	10	1978	0	1978	
11	Woman In Love	(Ariola Aro 141)	3	1979	0	1979	
12	The Runner	(Ariola Aro 154)	12	1979	0	1979	

ISSUE	TITLE	UK LBL	UK POS	UK YEAR	US POS	US YEAR	US LBL	
13	The Golden Lady	(Ariola Aro 170)	56	1979	0	1979		
14	Jump The Gun	(Ariola Aro 183)	48	1979	0	1979		
15	My Simple Heart	(Ariola Aro 202)	9	1979	0	1979		
16	The Heaven I Need	(Supreme Supe102)	42	1985	0	1985		

HIT 2 IS CREDITED TO MFSB FEATURING THE THREE DEGREES • ORIGINAL LINE-UP WAS FAYETTE PINKNEY, LINDA TURNER & SHIRLEY PORTER
LINDA & SHIRLEY WERE REPLACED BY VALERIE HOLIDAY & SHEILA FERGUSON

3 Colours Red

1	Nuclear Holiday	(Creation Crescd 250)	22	1997	0	1997	
2	Sixty Mile Smile	(Creation Crescd 254)	20	1997	0	1997	
3	Pure	(Creation Crescd 265)	28	1997	0	1997	
4	Copper Girl	(Creation Crescd 270)	'30	1997	0	1997	

Three Dog Night Male Vocal/Instrumental Group from the UK

	1	Try A Little Tenderness		0	1969	29	1969	(Dunhill 4177)
*	2	One		0	1969	5	1969	(Dunhill 4191)
	3	Easy To Be Hard		0	1969	4	1969	(Dunhill 4203)
	4	Eli's Coming		0	1969	10	1969	(Dunhill 4215)
	5	Celebrate		0	1970	15	1970	(Dunhill 4229)
*	6	Mama Told Me (Not To Come)	(Stateside Ss8052)	3	1970	1	1970	(Dunhill 4239)
	7	Out In The Country		0	1970	15	1970	(Dunhill 4250)
	8	One Man Band		0	1970	19	1970	(Dunhill 4262)
*	9	Joy To The World	(Probe Pro 523)	24	1971	1	1971	(Dunhill 4272)
*	10	Liar		0	1971	7	1971	(Dunhill 4282)
*	11	An Old Fashioned Love Song		0	1971	4	1971	(Dunhill 4294)
	12	Never Been To Spain		0	1972	5	1972	(Dunhill 4299)
	13	The Family Of Man		0	1972	12	1972	(Dunhill 4306)
*	14	Black & White		0	1972	1	1972	(Dunhill 4317)
	15	Pieces Of April		, 0	1972	19	1972	(Dunhill 4331)
*	16	Shambala		0	1973	3	1973	(Dunhill 4352)
	17	Let Me Serenade You		0	1973	17	1973	(Dunhill 4370)
*	18	The Show Must Go On		0	1974	4	1974	(Dunhill 4382)
	19	Sure As I'm Sittin' Here		0	1974	16	1974	(Dunhill 15001)
	20	Play Something Sweet (Brickyard Blues)		0	1974	33	1974	(Dunhill 15013)
	21	'til The World Ends		0	1975	32	1975	(ABC 12114)

LEAD SINGER WITH THE WEST COAST COMBO IS DANNY HUTTON • THEIR NAME IS AN AUSTRALIAN TERM FOR 'EXTREME COLD'

Three Flames Male R&B Trio From New York

1	Open The Door, Richard		0	1947	1	1947	(Columbia 37268)

Three Good Reasons Male Vocal/Instrumental Group from the UK

1	Nowhere Man	(Mercury Mf899)	47	1966	0	1966	

Three Suns Instrumental Trio, Al & Morty Nevins With Artie Dunn From The USA

	1	Long Ago (And Far Away)		0	1944	16	1944	(Hit 7085)	
	2	How Many Hearts Have You Broken?		0	1944	7	1944	(Hit 7092)	
	3	Twilight Time		0	1944	14	1944	(Hit 7092)	
	4	All Of My Life		0	1945	10	1945	(Hit 7126)	
	5	Five Minutes More		0	1946	7	1946	(Majestic 7197)	
	6	Romours Are Flying		0	1946	7	1946	(Majestic 7205)	
	7	Peg O' My Heart		0	1947	1	1947	(RCA Victor | 2272)
	8	I Still Get Jealous		0	1947	21	1947	(RCA Victor | 2469)
	9	I'm Looking Over A Four-Leaf Clover		0	1948	10	1948	(RCA Victor | 2688)
	10	Just For Now		0	1948	24	1948	(RCA Victor | 2946)
	11	You, You, You Are The One		0	1949	21	1949	(RCA Victor | 3322)
	12	Cruising Down The River		0	1949	24	1949	(RCA Victor | 3349)
!	13	Beyond The Sunset		0	1950	7	1950	(RCA Victor | 3599)
	14	Don't Take Your Love From Me		0	1950	21	1950	(RCA Victor | 5347)
	15	The Creep		0	1954	22	1954	(RCA Victor | 5553)
	16	Moonlight And Roses (Bring Memories Of You)		0	1954	24	1954	(RCA Victor5768)	

HIT 13 IS CREDITED TO THE THREE SUNS WITH ROSALIE ALLEN & ELTON BRITT • OBITUARY : MORTY D: 20 JUL 1990 CANCER. ARTIE D: 1989. AL D: 1965.

3t

*	1	Anything	(Epic 6627152)	2	1996	15	1995	(Mjj Music 77913)
	2	24/7	(Epic 6631995)	11	1996	0	1996	
	3	Why	(Epic 6636482)	2	1996	0	1996	

ISSUE	TITLE	UK LBL	UK POS	UK YEAR	US POS	US YEAR	US LBL
Throwing Muses Mixed Vocal/Instrumental Group from the USA							
1	Counting Backwards	(4ad Ad 1001)	70	1991	0	1991	
2	Firepile (Ep)	(4ad Bad 2012)	46	1992	0	1992	
3	Bright Yellow Gun	(4as Bad 4018cd)	51	1994	0	1994	
4	Shark	(4ad Bad 6016cd)	53	1996	0	1996	
Thuli Dumakude Male Vocalist From South Africa							
1	The Funeral (September 25 1977)	(MCA Mca 1228)	75	1988	0	1977	
	FLIP SIDE OF HIT 1 WAS CRY FOR FREEDOM BY GEORGE FENTON & JONAS GWANGWA						
Thunder Male Vocal/Instrumental Group from the USA/Uk							
1	Dirty Love	(EMI Em 126)	32	1990	0	1990	
2	Backstreet Symphony	(EMI Em 137)	25	1990	0	1990	
3	Gimme Some Lovin'	(EMI Em 148)	36	1990	0	1990	
4	She's So Fine	(EMI Em 158)	34	1990	0	1990	
5	Love Walked In	(EMI Em 175)	21	1991	0	1991	
6	Low Life In High Places	(EMI Em 242)	22	1992	0	1992	
7	Everybody Wants Her	(EMI Em 249)	36	1992	0	1992	
8	A Better Man	(EMI Cdbetter)	18	1993	0	1993	
9	Like A Satellite (Ep)	(EMI Dem 272)	28	1993	0	1993	
10	Stand Up	(EMI Cdem 365)	23	1995	0	1995	
11	River Of Pain	(EMI Cdem 367)	31	1995	0	1995	
12	Castles In The Sand	(EMI Cdem 372)	30	1995	0	1995	
13	In A Broken Dream	(EMI Cdem 384)	26	1995	0	1995	
14	Don't Wait Up	(Raw PowerRawx 1020)	27	1997	0	1997	
15	Love Worth Dying For	(Raw PowerRawx 1043)	60	1997	0	1997	
Thunderclap Newman Male Vocal/Instrumental Trio from the UK, Names Andy Newman, Jimmy Mccullock & John Keen							
1	Something In The Air	(Track 604-031)	1	1969	37	1969	(Track 2656)
2	Accidents	(Track 2094 001)	46	1970	0	1970	
	THE GROUP WAS ORIGINALLY PUT TOGETHER BY PETE TOWNSEND • OBITUARY : JIMMY B: 1953, D: 27 SEP 1979.						
Thunderthighs Female Vocal Group from the UK							
1	Central Park Arrest	(Philips 6006 386)	30	1974	0	1974	
Thurston Harris Male Vocalist, B: 11 Jul 1931 Indianapolis							
1	Little Bitty Pretty One		0	1957	6	1957	(Aladdin 3398)
	FIRST RECORDED WITH THE LAMPLIGHTERS IN 1953						
	BACKING VOCALS ON THE HIT ARE BY THE SHARPS						
	OBITUARY :D: 14 APR 1990 HEART ATTACK.						
Tia Carrere Female Vocalist from the USA							
1	Ballroom Blitz	(Reprise W 0105)	26	1992	0	1992	
Tierra Group Led By The Salas Brothers Formed In 1972 From Los Angeles							
1	Together		0	1980	18	1980	(Boardwalk 5702)
Tiffany Female Vocalist, Real Name Tiffany Darwisch B: 20 Oct 1971 Oklahoma							
1	I Think We're Alone Now	(MCA Mca 1211)	1	1987	1	1987	(MCA 53167)
2	Could've Been	(MCA Tiff 2)	4	1988	1	1988	(MCA 53231)
3	I Saw Him Standing There	(MCA Tiff 3)	8	1988	7	1988	(MCA 53285)
4	Feelings Of Forever	(MCA Tiff 4)	52	1988	0	1988	
5	Radio Romance	(MCA Tiff 5)	13	1988	35	1989	(MCA 53623)
6	All This Time	(MCA Tiff 6)	47	1989	6	1988	(MCA 53371)
Tiger Mixed Vocal/Instrumental Group from the UK/Ireland							
1	Race	(Trade 2 Trdcd004)	37	1996	0	1996	
2	My Puppet Pal	(Trade 2 Trdcd005)	62	1996	0	1996	
3	On The Rose	(Trade 2 Trdcd008)	57	1997	0	1997	
Tigertailz Male Vocal/Instrumental Group from the USA							
1	Love Bomb Baby	(Music ForNations Kut 132)	75	1989	0	1989	
2	Heaven	(Music ForNations Kut 137)	71	1991	0	1991	
Tight Fit Mixed Vocal Group from the UK							
1	Back To The Sixties	(Jive Jive 002)	4	1981	0	1981	
2	Back To The Sixties (Part 2)	(Jive Jive 005)	33	1981	0	1981	
3	The Lion Sleeps Tonight	(Jive Jive 9)	1	1982	0	1982	
4	Fantasy Island	(Jive Jive 13)	5	1982	0	1982	
5	Secret Heart	(Jive Jive 20)	41	1982	0	1982	
Tik & Tok Male Vocal Duo from the UK							
1	Cool Running	(Survival Sur016)	69	1983	0	1983	

ISSUE	TITLE	UK LBL		UK POS	UK YEAR	US POS	US YEAR	US LBL
Til Tuesday	Lead Singer With The Quartet Is Almee Mann							
1	Voices Carry			0	1985	8	1985	(Epic 04795)
2	What About Love			0	1986	26	1986	(Epic 06289)
Tilt	Male Instrumental/Production Group from the UK							
1	I Dream	(PerfectoPerf 112cd)		69	1995	0	1995	
2	My Spirit	(PerfectoPerf 139cd)		61	1997	0	1997	
3	Places	(Perfecto	64Perf 149cd)		1997	0	1997	
Tim Dog	Male Rapper from the USA							
1	Bitch With A Perm	(Dis-Stress Discd 1)		49	1994	0	1994	
2	Make Way For The Indian	(Island Cid 586)	29	1995	0	1995		
	HIT 2 IS CREDITED TO APACHE INDIAN AND TIM DOG							
Tim Finn	Male Vocalist From New Zealand							
1	Persuasion	(Capitol 6592482)		43	1993	0	1993	
2	Hit The Ground Running	(Capitol Cdcls694)		50	1993	0	1993	
Tim Hardin	Male Vocalist from the USA							
1	Hang On To A Dream	(Verve Vs 1504)		50	1967	0	1967	
Tim McGraw	Male Country Singer, B: 1 May 1967 In Delhi, Louisiana							
* 1	Indian Outlaw			0	1994	15	1994	(Curb 76920)
* 2	Don't Take That Girl			0	1994	17	1994	(Curb 76925)
3	I Like, I Love It			0	1995	25	1995	(Curb 96961)
4	It's Your Love			0	1997	13	1997	(Curb 73019)
	HIT 4 IS CREDITED TO TIM MCGRAW WITH FAITH HILL							
Timbuk 3	Vocal/Instrumental Duo from the USA, Real Names Pat & Barbara Kooyman Macdonald							
1	The Future So Bright I Gotta Wear Shades	(Irs Irm 126)		21	1987	19	1987	(Irs 52940)
Time	Funk Band From Minneapolis With Lead Singer Morris Day							
1	Jungle Love			0	1985	20	1985	(Warner Bros 29181)
2	The Bird			0	1985	36	1985	(Warner Bros 29094)
* 3	Jerk Out			0	1990	9	1990	(Paisley Park 19750)
Time Frequency	Male Production/Instrumental Group from the UK							
1	Real Love	(Jive Jivet 307)		60	1992	0	1992	
2	New Emotion (Ep)	(InternalAffairs Kgbcd 009)		36	1993	0	1993	
3	The Ultimate High / The Power Zone	(InternalAffairs Kgbd010)		17	1993	0	1993	
4	Real Love (Re-Mix)	(Internal	Affairs Kgbcd 8011)		1993	0	1993	
5	Real Love (Re-Mix) (Re-Entry)	(InternalAffairs Kgbcd 011)		71	1994	0	1994	
6	Such A Phantasy	(InternalAffairs Kgbd 013)		25	1994	0	1994	
7	Dreamscape '94	(InternalAffairs Kgbd 015)		32	1994	0	1994	
Time Of The Mumph	Male Producer Mark Mumford from the UK							
1	Control	(Fresh Frsht		69	1995	0	1995	
Time Uk	Male Vocal/Instrumental Group from the UK							
1	The Cabaret	(RedBus/Aroadia Tim123)		63	1983	0	1983	
Time Zone	Male Vocal/Instrumental Duo from the USA/Uk							
1	World Destruction	(Virgin Vs 743)		44	1985	0	1985	
Timebox	Male Vocal/Instrumental Group from the UK							
1	Beggin'	(Deram Dm 194)		38	1968	0	1968	
Timelords	See Also Klf							
1	Doctorin' The Tardis	(KlfCommunicationS Klf 003)		1	1988	0	1988	
Times Two	Names Johnny Dollar & Shanti Jones From California							
1	Strange But True			0	1988	21	1988	(Reprise 27998)
Timex Social Club	Male Vocal/Instrumental Group from the USA							
1	Rumors	(CooltempoCool 133)		13	1986	8	1986	(Jay 7001)
	LEAD VOCALIST WITH THE GROUP IS MICHAEL MARSHALL							
Timi Yuro	Real Name Rosemarie Timothy Aurro Yuro B: 4 Aug 1940 Chicago							
1	Hurt			0	1961	4	1961	(Liberty 55343)
2	What'a A Matter Baby (Is It Hurting You)			0	1962	12	1962	(Liberty 55469)
3	Make The World Go Away			0	1963	24	1963	(Liberty 55587)
	TIMI LOST HIS VOICE IN 1980, NUMEROUS OPERATIONS TO CORRECT THE PROBLEM							
Timmie 'oh Yeah' Rogers	Male Comedian, B: 4 Jul 1915 Detroit							
1	Back To School Again			0	1957	36	1957	(Cameo 116)

ISSUE	TITLE	UK LBL	UK POS	UK YEAR	US POS	US YEAR	US LBL
Timmy -T-	Real Name Timmy Torres B: 23 Sep 1967 from California						
1	Time After Time		0	1990	40	1990	(Jam City 5003)
* 2	One More Try		0	1991	1	1991	(Quality 15114)
Timmy Thomas Male Vocalist, B: 13 Nov 1944 Evansville, Indiana							
* 1	Why Can't We Live Together	(Mojo 2027 012)	12	1973	3	1972	(Glades 1703)
+ 2	What Can I Tell Her		0	1973	19	1973	(Glades 1717)
3	New York Eyes	(Portrait A 6805)	41	1985	0	1985	
4	Why Can't We Live Together (Re-Mix)	(Tk Tkr 1)	54	1990	0	1990	
	HIT 3 IS CREDITED TO NICOLE WITH TIMMY THOMAS						
Timothy B. Schmit B: 30 Oct 1947 Sacramento							
1	Boys Night Out		0	1987	25	1987	(MCA 53137)
FORMER MEMBER OF POCO 1970-77 AND THE EAGLES 1977-82							
Tin Machine Male Vocal/Instrumental Group from the USA/Uk							
1	Under The God	(EMI-Usa Mt 68)	51	1989	0	1989	
2	Tin Machine / Maggie's Farm (Live)	(EMI-Usa Mt 73)	48	1989	0	1989	
3	You Belong In Rock 'n' Roll	(London Lon305)	33	1991	0	1991	
4	Baby Universal	(London Lon310)	48	1991	0	1991	
	SEE ALSO DAVID BOWIE						
Tin Tin Australian Duo Steve Kipner & Steve Groves Disbanded In 1973							
1	Toast And Marmalade For Tea		0	1971	20	1971	(Atco 6794)
Tin Tin Out Male Instrumental/Production Duo from the UK							
1	The Feeling	(DeepDistraxion Oilycd 029)	32	1994	0	1994	
2	Always	(East West Yz911cd)	14	1995	0	1995	
3	All I Wanna Do	(Vc RecordingsVcrd 15)	31	1997	0	1997	
4	Dance With Me	(Vc Recordings Vcrd 17)	35	1997	0	1997	
HIT 1 IS CREDITED TO TIN TIN OUT FEATURING SWEET TEE							
HIT 2 IS CREDITED TO TIN TIN OUT FEATURING ESPRITU							
HIT 4 IS CREDITED TO TIN TIN OUT FEATURING TONY HADLEY							
Tina Charles Female Vocalist from the UK							
1	I Love To Love	(Cbs 3937)	1	1976	0	1976	
2	Love Me Like A Lover	(Cbs 4237)	28	1976	0	1976	
3	Dance Little Lady Dance	(Cbs 4480)	6	1976	0	1976	
4	Dr. Love	(Cbs 4779)	4	1976	0	1976	
5	Rendezvous	(Cbs 5174)	27	1977	0	1977	
6	Love Bug - Sweets For My Sweets (Medley)	(Cbs 5680)	26	1977	0	1977	
7	I'll Go Where The Music Takes Me	(Cbs 6062)	27	1978	0	1978	
8	I Love To Love (Re-Mix)	(Dmc Deck 1)	67	1986	0	1986	
Tina Moore Female Vocalist							
1	Never Gonna Let You Go	(Delirious74321511052)	7	1997	0	1997	
Tina Turner Female Vocalist, Real Name Anna Mae Bullock B: 26 Nov 1938 from the USA							
1	Let's Stay Together	(Capitol Cl 316)	6	1983	26	1984	(Capitol 5323)
2	Help	(Capitol Cl 325)	40	1984	0	1984	
* 3	What's Love Got To Do With It	(Capitol Cl 334)	3	1984	1	1984	(Capitol 5354)
4	Better Be Good To Me	(Capitol Cl 338)	45	1984	5	1984	(Capitol 5387)
5	Private Dancer	(Capitol Cl 343)	26	1984	7	1985	(Capitol 5433)
6	I Can't Stand The Rain	(Capitol Cl 352)	51	1985	0	1985	
7	Show Some Respect		0	1985	37	1985	(Capitol 5461)
* 8	We Don't Need Another Hero (Thunderdome)	(Capitol Cl 364)	3	1985	2	1985	(Capitol 5491)
9	One Of The Living	(Capitol Cl 376)	55	1985	15	1985	(Capitol 5518)
10	It's Only Love	(A&M Am 285)	29	1985	15	1986	(A&M 2791)
11	Typical Male	(Capitol Cl 419)	33	1986	2	1986	(Capitol 5615)
12	Two People	(Capitol Cl 430)	43	1986	30	1986	(Capitol 5644)
13	What You Get Is What You See	(Capitol Cl 439)	30	1987	13	1987	(Capitol 5668)
14	Break Every Rule	(Capitol Cl 452)	43	1987	0	1987	
15	Tearing Us Apart	(Duck W 8299)	56	1987	0	1987	
16	Addicted To Love	(Capitol Cl 484)	71	1988	0	1988	
17	The Best	(Capitol Cl 543)	5	1989	15	1989	(Capitol 44442)
18	I Don't Want To Lose You	(Capitol Cl 553)	8	1989	0	1989	
19	Steamy Windows	(Capitol Cl 560)	13	1990	39	1990	(Capitol 44473)
20	Look Me In The Heart	(Capitol Cl 584)	31	1990	0	1990	
21	Be Tender With Me Baby	(Capitol Cl 593)	28	1990	0	1990	
22	It Takes Two	(Warner BrosRod 1)	5	1990	0	1990	
23	Nutbush City Limits	(Capitol Cl 630)	23	1991	0	1991	

ISSUE	TITLE	UK LBL	UK POS	UK YEAR	US POS	US YEAR	US LBL
24	Way Of The World	(Capitol Cl 637)	13	1991	0	1991	
25	Love Thing	(Capitol Cl 644)	29	1992	0	1992	
26	I Want You Near Me	(Capitol Cl 659)	22	1992	0	1992	
27	I Don't Wanna Fight	(ParlophoneCdrs 6346)	7	1993	9	1993	(Virgin 12652)
28	Disco Inferno	(ParlophoneCdr 6357)	12	1993	0	1993	
29	Why Must We Wait Until Tonight	(ParlophoneCdr 6366)	16	1993	0	1993	
30	Goldeneye	(ParlophoneCdr 71001)	10	1995	0	1995	
31	Whatever You Want	(ParlophoneCdr 6429)	23	1996	0	1996	
32	On Silent Wings	(ParlophoneCdr 6434)	13	1996	0	1996	
33	Missing You	(ParlophoneCdr 6441)	12	1996	84	1996	(Virgin 38553)
34	Something Beautiful Remains	(ParlophoneCdr 6448)	27	1996	0	1996	
35	In Your Wildest Dreams	(ParlophoneCdr 6451)	32	1996	0	1996	

Tindersticks Male Vocal/Instrumental Group from the UK

1	Kathleen (EP)	(This Way UpWay 2833cd)	61	1994	0	1994	
2	Nore More Affairs	(This Way UpWay 3822)	58	1995	0	1995	
3	Travelling Light	(This Way UpWay 4533)	51	1995	0	1995	
4	Bathtime	(This Way UpWay 6166)	38	1997	0	1997	

Tingo Tango Male Vocal/Instrumental Group from the UK

1	It Is Jazz	(ChampionChamp 250)	68	1990	0	1990	

Tinman Male Producer, Real Name Paul Dakeyne from the UK

1	Eighteen Strings	(Ffrr Fcd 242)	9	1994	0	1994	
2	Gudvibe	(Ffrr Fcd 262)	49	1995	0	1995	

Tiny Hill Orchestra Male Vocalist/Bandleader from the USA

1	Doodle Doo Doo		0	1939	14	1939	(Vocalion 5060)
2	Angry		0	1939	13	1939	(Vocalion 4957)
3	I Get A Kick Outa Corn		0	1940	28	1940	(Vocalion 5469)
4	Five Foot Two, Eyes Of Blue		0	1940	25	1940	(Okeh 5635)
5	The Guy At The End Of The Bar		0	1941	25	1941	(Okeh 5924)
6	How Many Hearts Have You Broken		0	1944	14	1944	(Decca 4447)
7	Hot Rod Race		0	1951	29	1951	(Mercury 5547)
8	Slow-Poke		0	1952	28	1952	(Mercury 5740)

Tiny Tim Male Novelty Singer/Ukulele Player, Real Name Herbert Khaury B: 12 Apr 1930 New York

1	Tip-Toe Thru' The Tulips With Me		0	1968	17	1968	(Reprise 0679)
2	Great Balls Of Fire	(Reprise Rs 20802)	45	1969	0	1969	
! 3	Leave Me Satisfied		0	1988	70	1988	(Nlt 1993)

HE HAD AN UNUSUALLY HIGH VOICE WHICH THE AUDIENCE FOUND DIFFICULT TO TAKE SERIOUS.
OBITUARY : D: 1 DEC 1996. HEART ATTACK (WHILST ON STAGE).

Tippa Irie Male Vocalist from the UK)

1	Hello Darling	(GreensleevesBubb Tippa 4)	22	1986	0	1986	
2	Heartbeat	(GreensleevesBubb Tippa 5)	59	1986	0	1986	
3	Shouting For The Gunners	(London Loncd342)	34	1993	0	1993	
4	Staying Alive '95	(TelstarCdstas 2776)	48	1995	0	1995	

HIT 3 IS CREDITED TO ARSENAL F.A. CUP SQUAD FEATURING TIPPA IRIE AND PETER HUNNIGALE
HIT 4 IS CREDITED TO FEVER FEATURING TIPPA IRIE

Titanic Male Vocal/Instrumental Group from Norway

1	Sultana	(Cbs 5365)	5	1971	0	1971	

Titiyo Female Vocalist from Sweden

1	After The Rain	(Arista 112722)	60	1990	0	1990	
2	Flowers	(Arista 113212)	71	1990	0	1990	
3	Tell Me (I'm Not Dreaming)	(Arista74321185622)	45	1994	0	1994	

Tito Puente Jr. & The Latin Mixed Vocal/Instrumental Group from the USA
Rhythm

1	Oye Como Va	(Media Mcstd40013)	36	1996	0	1996	
2	Oye Como Va (Re-Recording)	(Media Mcstd40120)	56	1997	0	1997	

HITS 1-2 ARE CREDITED TO TITO PUENTE JR. & THE LATIN RHYTHM FEATURING TITO PUENTE, INDIA & CALI ALEMAN

Tito Simon Male Vocalist from Jamaica

1	This Monday Morning Feeling	(Horse Hoss 57)	45	1975	0	1975	

Tlc Female Vocal Group, Tionne Watkins, Lisa Lopes & Rozonda Thomas from Atlanta.

* 1	Ain't 2 Proud 2 Beg	(Arista 115265)	13	1992	6	1992	(Laface 24008)
* 2	Baby-Baby-Baby	(Arista74321111297)	55	1992	2	1992	(Laface 24028)
* 3	What About Your Friends		0	1992	7	1992	(Laface 24025)
4	Hat 2 Da Back		0	1993	30	1993	(Laface 24043)

	ISSUE	TITLE	UK LBL	UK POS	UK YEAR	US POS	US YEAR	US LBL
*	5	Creep	(Arista74321254212)	22	1995	1	1994	(Laface 24082)
*	6	Red Light Special	(Arista74321273662)	18	1995	2	1995	(Laface 24097)
*	7	Waterfalls	(Arista74321298812)	4	1995	1	1995	(Laface 24107)
*	8	Diggin' On You	(Arista74321319252)	18	1995	5	1995	(Laface 24119)
	9	Creep (Re-Issue)	(Arista74321340942)	6	1996	0	1996	

Toad The Wet Sprocket Pop Quartet from Santa Barbara, California

	ISSUE	TITLE	UK LBL	UK POS	UK YEAR	US POS	US YEAR	US LBL
	1	All I Want		0	1992	15	1992	(Columbia 74355)
	2	Walk On The Ocean		0	1992	18	1992	(Columbia 74706)
	3	Fall Down		0	1994	33	1994	(Columbia 77474)

Tobin, Mathews & Co Male Guitarist from Calumet, Illinois

	ISSUE	TITLE	UK LBL	UK POS	UK YEAR	US POS	US YEAR	US LBL
	1	Ruby Duby Du		0	1960	30	1960	(Chief 7022)

Toby Beau Names Balde Silva, Ron Rose, Steve Zipper & Danny Mckenna

	ISSUE	TITLE	UK LBL	UK POS	UK YEAR	US POS	US YEAR	US LBL
	1	My Angel Baby		0	1978	13	1978	(RCA 11250)

Todd Rundgren Male Vocalist, B: 22 Jun 1948 Upper Darby, Pennsylvania

	ISSUE	TITLE	UK LBL	UK POS	UK YEAR	US POS	US YEAR	US LBL
	1	We Gotta Get You A Woman		0	1970	20	1970	(Ampex 31001)
	2	I Saw The Light	(Bearsville K15506)	36	1973	16	1972	(Bearsville 0003)
	3	Hello It's Me		0	1973	5	1973	(Bearsville 0009)
	4	Good Vibrations		0	1976	34	1976	(Bearsville 0309)
	5	Can We Still Be Friends		0	1978	29	1978	(Bearsville 0324)
	6	Loving You's A Dirty Job But Somebody's Gotta Do It	(Cba A 6662)	73	1985	0	1985	

HIT 1 IS CREDITED TO RUNT • HIT 6 IS CREDITED TO BONNIE TYLER GUEST VOCALS TODD RUNDGREN

Todd Terry Project Male Producer from the USA

	ISSUE	TITLE	UK LBL	UK POS	UK YEAR	US POS	US YEAR	US LBL
	1	Weekend	(Sleeping BagSbuk 1t)	28	1988	0	1988	
	2	Weekend (Re-Mix)	(Ore Ag 13cd)	28	1995	0	1995	
	3	Keep On Jumpin'	(ManifestoFescd 11)	8	1996	0	1996	
	4	Something Goin' On	(ManifestoFescd 25)	5	1997	0	1997	

HIT 3 IS CREDITED TO TODD TERRY FEATURING MARTHA WASH AND JOCELYN BROWN HIT 4 IS CREDITED TO TODD TERRY

Together Male Vocal/Instrumental Group from the UK

	ISSUE	TITLE	UK LBL	UK POS	UK YEAR	US POS	US YEAR	US LBL
	1	Hardcore Uproar	(Ffrr F 143)	12	1990	0	1990	

Tokens Male Vocal Group from the USA

	ISSUE	TITLE	UK LBL	UK POS	UK YEAR	US POS	US YEAR	US LBL
*	1	Tonight I Fell In Love		0	1961	15	1961	(Warwick 615)
*	2	The Lion Sleeps Tonight	(RCA 1263)	11	1961	1	1961	(RCA Victor 7954)
	3	I Hear Trumpets Blow		0	1966	30	1966	(B.T. Puppy 518)
	4	Portrait Of My Love		0	1967	36	1967	(Warner Bros 5900)

NAMES NEIL SEDAKA, HANK MEDRESS, EDDIE RABKIN & CYNTHIA ZOLITIN
THEY ORIGINALLY FORMED AS THE LINC-TONES IN 1955 • THE LINE-UP HAS CHANGED MANY TIMES SINCE 1956

Tokyo Ghetto Pussy Male Instrumental/Production Duo from Germany, Also Known As Jam & Spoon

	ISSUE	TITLE	UK LBL	UK POS	UK YEAR	US POS	US YEAR	US LBL
	1	Everybody On The Floor (Pump It)	(Epic 6111132)	26	1995	0	1995	
	2	I Kiss Your Lips	(Epic 6623212)	55	1996	0	1996	

Tol & Tol Male Vocal/Instrumental Duo from Holland

	ISSUE	TITLE	UK LBL	UK POS	UK YEAR	US POS	US YEAR	US LBL
	1	Eleni	(Dover Roj 5)	73	1990	0	1990	

Tom Browne Male Vocalist from the USA

	ISSUE	TITLE	UK LBL	UK POS	UK YEAR	US POS	US YEAR	US LBL
	1	Funkin' For Jamaica (N.Y.)	(Arista Arist357)	10	1980	0	1980	
	2	Thighs High (Grip Your Hips And Move)	(Arist Arist 367)	45	1980	0	1980	
	3	Fungi Mama (Bebopafunkadiscolypso)	(Arista Arist450)	58	1982	0	1982	
	4	Funkin' For Jamaica (Re-Mix)	(Arista 114998)	45	1992	0	1992	

Tom Clay Male Dj At Kgbs-Los Angeles

	ISSUE	TITLE	UK LBL	UK POS	UK YEAR	US POS	US YEAR	US LBL
*	1	What The World Needs Now Is Love - Abraham, Martin And John		0	1971	8	1971	(Mowest 5002)

OBITUARY : D: 22 NOV 1995 (AGED 66).

Tom Cochrane Male Vocalist from Canada

	ISSUE	TITLE	UK LBL	UK POS	UK YEAR	US POS	US YEAR	US LBL
*	1	Life Is A Highway	(Capitol Cl 660)	62	1992	6	1992	(Capitol 44815)

Tom Glazer & The Do-Re-Mi Children's Chorus B: 3 Sep 1914 Philadelphia

	ISSUE	TITLE	UK LBL	UK POS	UK YEAR	US POS	US YEAR	US LBL
	1	On Top Of Spaghetti		0	1963	14	1963	(Kapp 526)

Tom Johnston Tom Hails from California And Was A Member Of The Doobie Brothers

	ISSUE	TITLE	UK LBL	UK POS	UK YEAR	US POS	US YEAR	US LBL
	1	Savannah Nights		0	1980	34	1980	(Warner Bros 49096)

Tom Jones Male Vocalist, Real Name Thomas Jones Woodward B: 7 Jun 1940 In Treforrest, Wales

	ISSUE	TITLE	UK LBL	UK POS	UK YEAR	US POS	US YEAR	US LBL
*	1	It's Not Unusual	(Decca F 12062)	1	1965	10	1965	(Parrot 9737)
	2	Once Upon A Time	(Decca F 12121)	32	1965	0	1965	
*	3	What's New Pussycat	(Decca F 12203)	11	1965	3	1965	(Parrot 9765)
	4	With These Hands	(Decca F 12191)	13	1965	27	1965	(Parrot 9787)
	5	Thunderball	(Decca F 12292)	35	1966	25	1966	(Parrot 9801)

ISSUE	TITLE	UK LBL	UK POS	UK YEAR	US POS	US YEAR	US LBL
6	Once There Was A Time / Not Responsible	(Decca F 12390)	18	1966	0	1966	
7	This And That	(Decca F 12461)	44	1966	0	1966	
* 8	Green Green Grass Of Home	(Decca F 2251)	1	1966	11	1967	(Parrot 40009)
9	Detroit City	(Decca F 22555)	8	1967	27	1967	(Parrot 40012)
10	Funny Familar Forgotten Feelings	(Decca F 12599)	7	1967	0	1967	
11	I'll Never Fall In Love Again	(Decca F 12639)	2	1967	49	1967	(Parrot 40018)
12	I'm Goming Home	(Decca F 12693)	2	1967	0	1967	
* 13	Delilah	(Decca F 12747)	2	1968	15	1968	(Parrot 40025)
14	Help Yourself	(Decca F 12812)	5	1968	35	1968	(Parrot 40029)
15	A Minute Of Your Time	(Decca F 12854)	14	1968	0	1968	
16	Love Me Tonight	(Decca F 12924)	9	1969	13	1969	(Parrot 40038)
* 17	I'll Never Fall In Love Again (Re-Issue)		0	1967	6	1967	(Parrot 40018)
18	Without Love (There Is Nothing)	(Decca F 12990)	10	1969	0	1969	
* 19	Without Love (There Is Nothing) (Re-Entry)	(Decca F 12990)	49	1970	5	1970	(Parrot 40045)
20	Daughter Of Darkness	(Decca F 13013)	5	1970	13	1970	(Parrot 40048)
21	I (Who Have Nothinq)	(Decca F 13061)	16	1970	14	1970	(Parrot 40051)
22	I (Who Have Nothing) (Re-Entry)	(Decca F 13061)	47	1970	0	1970	
23	Can't Stop Loving You		0	1970	25	1970	(Parrot 40056)
* 24	She's A Lady	(Decca F 13113)	13	1971	2	1971	(Parrot 40058)
25	She's A Lady (Re-Entry)	(Decca F 13113)	47	1971	0	1971	
26	Puppet Man	(Decca F 13183)	49	1971	26	1971	(Parrot 40064)
27	Resurrection Shuffle		0	1971	38	1971	(Parrot 40064)
28	Puppet Man (Re-Entry)	(Decca F 13183)	50	1971	0	1971	
29	Till	(Decca F 13236)	2	1971	0	1971	
30	The Young New Mexican Puppeteer	(Decca F 13298)	6	1972	0	1972	
31	Letter To Lucille	(Decca F 13393)	31	1973	0	1973	
32	Something 'bout You Baby I Like	(Decca F 13550)	36	1974	0	1974	
33	Say You'll Stay Until Tomorrow	(EMI 2583)	40	1977	15	1976	(Epic 50308)
49	A Boy From Nowhere	(Epic Ole 1)	2	1987	0	1987	
50	It's Not Unusual (Re-Issue)	(Decca F 103)	17	1987	0	1987	
51	I Was Born To Be Me	(Epic Ole 4)	61	1988	0	1988	
52	Kiss	(China China 11)	5	1988	31	1988	(China 871038)
53	Move Closer	(Jive Jive 203)	49	1989	0	1989	
54	Couldn't Say Goodbye	(Dover Roj 10)	51	1991	0	1991	
55	Carrying A Torch	(Dover Roj 12)	57	1991	0	1991	
56	Delilah (Re-Issue)	(The Hit LabelTom 10)	68	1992	0	1992	
57	All I Need Is Love	(ChildlineChildcd 93)	19	1993	0	1993	
58	If I Only Knew	(Ztt Zang 59cd)	11	1994	0	1994	

UNLISETED HITS ARE C/W • IN 1963 HE FORMED HIS OWN TRIO CALLED THE SENATORS
IN THE EARLY DAYS HE WORKED UNDER THE NAME OF TOMMY SCOTT

Tom Petty & The Heartbreakers Male Vocal/Instrumental Group from the USA

ISSUE	TITLE	UK LBL	UK POS	UK YEAR	US POS	US YEAR	US LBL
1	Anything Thats Rock N' Roll	(Shelter Wip6396)	36	1977	0	1977	
2	American Girl	(Shelter Wip6403)	40	1977	0	1977	
3	Breakdown		0	1978	40	1978	(Shelter 62008)
5	Refugee		0	1980	15	1980	(Backstreet 41169)
6	The Waiting		0	1981	19	1981	(Backstreet 51100)
7	Stop Draggin' My Heart Around	(Wea K 79231)	50	1981	3	1981	(Modern 7336)
8	You Got Lucky		0	1982	20	1982	(Backstreet 52144)
9	Change Of Heart		0	1983	21	1983	(Backstreet 52181)
10	Don't Come Around Here No More	(MCA Mca 9260	50	1985	13	1985	(MCA 52496)
11	Needles And Pins		0	1986	37	1986	(MCA 52772)
12	Jammin' Me		0	1987	18	1987	(MCA 53063)
13	I Won't Back Down	(MCA Mca 1334)	28	1989	12	1989	(MCA 53369)
14	Runnin' Down A Dream	(MCA Mca 1359)	55	1989	23	1989	(MCA 53682)
15	Free Fallin'	(MCA Mca 1381)	64	1989	7	1990	(MCA 53748)
16	Learning To Fly	(MCA Mcs 1555)	46	1991	28	1991	(MCA 54124)
17	Too Good To Be True	(MCA Mcs 1616)	34	1992	0	1992	
18	Something In The Air	(MCA Mcstd 1945)	53	1993	0	1993	
19	Mary Jane's Last Dance	(MCA Mcstd 1966)	52	1994	14	1994	(MCA 54732)
20	You Don't Know How It Feels		0	1994	13	1994	(Warner Bros 18030)
21	Walls (From She's The One)		0	1996	69	1996	(Warner Bros 17593)

NAMES TOM PETTY, MIKE CAMPBELL, BENMONT TENCH, RON BLAIR & STAN LYNCH
TOM WAS B: 20 OCT 1953 GAINESVILLE, FLORIDA

ISSUE	TITLE	UK LBL	UK POS	UK YEAR	US POS	US YEAR	US LBL
Tom Robinson Band Male Vocalist And Instrumental Group from the UK							
1	2-4-6-8 Motorway	(EMI 2715)	5	1977	0	1977	
2	Don't Take No For An Answer	(EMI 2749)	18	1978	0	1978	
3	Up Against The Wall	(EMI 2787)	33	1978	0	1978	
4	Bully For You	(EMI 2916)	68	1979	0	1979	
5	War Baby	(Panic Nic 2)	6	1983	0	1986	
6	Listen To The Radio	(Panic Nic 3)	39	1983	0	1983	
7	Rikki Don't Lose That Number	(Castaway Tr 2)	58	1984	0	1984	
	HITS 5-7 ARE CREDITED TO TOM ROBINSON						
Tom T. Hall Male Vocalist/Country Music Story Teller, B: Thomas Hall 25 May 1936 In Olive Hill, Kentucky							
13	The Year That Clayton Delaney Died		0	1971	42	1971	(Mercury 73221)
22	I Love		0	1974	12	1974	(Mercury 73436)
23	That Song Is Driving Me Crazy		0	1974	63	1974	(Mercury 73488)
25	Sneaky Snake		0	1974	55	1974	(Mercury 73641)
	OTHER HITS ARE C/W						
Tom Tom Club Formed By Chris Frantz & Tina Weymouth As A Studio Project In The Usa							
1	Wordy Rappinghood	(Island Wip 6694)	7	1981	0	1981	
2	Genius Of Love	(Island Wip 6735)	65	1981	31	1982	(Sire 49882)
3	Under The Boardwalk	(Island Wip 6762)	22	1982	0	1982	
Tom Wilson Male Producer from the UK							
1	Technocat	(Pukka Cdpuka4)	33	1995	0	1995	
2	Let Your Body Go	(Clubscenedcsrt 050)	60	1996	0	1996	
	HIT 1 IS CREDITED TO TECHNOCAT FEATURING TOM WILSON						
Tommy Boyce & Bobby Hart Tommy B: 1944, Charlottesville, Virginia, Bobby B: 1944, Phoenix, Arizona							
1	Out And About		0	1967	39	1967	(A&M 858)
* 2	I Wonder What She's Doing Tonight		0	1967	8	1967	(A&M 893)
3	Alice Long (You're Still My Favourite Girlfriend)		0	1968	27	1968	(A&M 948)
Tommy Bruce & The Bruisers Male Vocal/Instrumental Group from the UK							
1	Ain't Misbehavin'	(Columbia Db4453)	3	1960	0	1960	
2	Broken Doll	(Columbia Db4498)	36	1960	0	1960	
3	Babette	(Columbia Db4773)	50	1962	0	1962	
4	Blue Girl	(Parlophone R5042)	31	1963	0	1963	
5	Blue Girl (Re-Entry)	(Parlophone R5042)	47	1963	0	1963	
	HIT 3 IS CREDITED TO TOMMY BRUCE						
Tommy Cooper Male Comedian/Vocalist From Chiswick, West London, England							
1	Don't Jump Of The Roof Dad	(Palette Pg9019)	40	1961	0	1961	
2	Don't Jump Of The Roof Dad (Re-Entry)	(Palette Pg9019)	50	1961	0	1961	
	OBITUARY : A MUCH LOVED COMMEDIAN/MAGICIAN WHO DIED ON STAGE FROM A HEART ATTACK						
Tommy Dee Real Name Thomas Donaldson B: 15 Jul 1936 Virginia							
1	Three Stars		0	1959	11	1959	(Crest 1057)
	THE HIT WAS A TRIBUTE TO BUDDY HOLLY, BIG BOPPER & RITCHIE VALENS • VOCALS BY CAROL KAY & THE TEEN-AIRES						
Tommy Dorsey Orchestra Male Bandleader/Instrumenalist (Trombone), B: 19 Nov 1905, Pennsylvania							
* 23	Marie		0	1937	1	1937	(Victor 25523)
* 66	Boogie Woogie		0	1938	1	1938	(Victor 26054)
* 148	There Are Such Things		0	1942	1	1942	(Victor 27974)
* 149	Boogie Woogie (Re-Entry)		0	1943	5	1943	(Victor 26054)
175	Aren't You Glad You're You? (From The Bells Of St. Mary's)		0	1946	14	1946	(Victor 1728)
176	The Moment I Met You		0	1946	11	1946	(Victor 1761)
177	We'll Gather Lilacs		0	1946	25	1946	(Victor 1809)
178	There's Good Blues Tonight		0	1946	23	1946	(Victor 1842)
179	I Don't Know Why (I Just Do)		0	1946	16	1946	(Victor 1901)
180	How Are Things In Glocca Mora? (From Finian's Rainbow)		0	1947	9	1947	(Victor 2121)
181	It's The Same Old Dream (From It Happened In Brooklyn)		0	1947	21	1947	(Victor 2210)
182	Until		0	1948	4	1948	(Victor 3061)
183	Down By The Station		0	1949	11	1949	(Victor 3317)
184	The Hucklebuck		0	1949	5	1949	(Victor 3427)
185	Again (From Roadhouse)		0	1949	6	1949	(Victor 3427)
186	The Most Beautiful Girl In The World (From Jumbo)		0	1953	21	1953	(Victor 5449)
* 187	Tea For Two Cha Cha	(Brunswick05757)	3	1958	10	1958	(Decca 30704)
	OBITUARY :- D: 26 NOV 1956, CHOKED TO DEATH.						
Tommy Edwards Male Vocalist, B: 17 Feb 1922 Richmond, Virginia							
1	The Morning Side Of The Mountain		0	1951	24	1951	(MGM 10989)

ISSUE	TITLE	UK LBL	UK POS	UK YEAR	US POS	US YEAR	US LBL
2	It's All In The Game		0	1951	18	1951	(MGM 11035)
3	Please, Mr.Sun		0	1952	22	1952	(MGM 11134)
4	You Win Again		0	1952	13	1952	(MGM 11326)
5	A Fool Such As I		0	1953	24	1953	(MGM 11395)
6	Baby, Baby, Baby (From Those Red Heads From Seattle)		0	1953	26	1953	(MGM 11541)
7	Secret Love (From Calamity Jane)		0	1954	28	1954	(MGM 11604)
* 8	It's All In The Game (Re-Issue)	(MGM 989)	1	1958	1	1958	(MGM 12688)
9	Love Is All We Need		0	1958	15	1958	(MGM 12722)
10	Please Mr.Sun (Re-Recording)		0	1959	11	1959	(MGM 12757)
11	The Morning Side Of The Mountain (Re-Recording)		0	1959	27	1959	(MGM 12757)
12	My Melancholy Baby	(MGM 1020)	29	1959	26	1959	(MGM 12794)
13	I Really Don't Want To Know		0	1960	18	1960	(MGM 12890)

OBITUARY : D: 23 OCT 1969 IN HENRICO, VIRGINIA, (AGED 47).

Tommy Facenda B: 10 Nov 1939 Norfolk, Virginia

1	High School U.S.A.		0	1959	28	1959	(Atlantic 51 To 78)

Tommy Hunt Male Vocalist from the USA

1	Crackin' Up	(Spark Srl 1132)	39	1975	0	1975	
2	Loving On The Losing Side	(Spark Srl 1146)	28	1976	0	1976	
3	One Fine Morning	(Spark Srl 1148)	44	1976	0	1976	

Tommy James & The Shondells Male Vocalist, Real Name Thomas Jackson B: 29 Apr 1947 In Dayton, Ohio

* 1	Hanky Panky	(Roulette Rk 7000)	38	1966	1	1966	(Roulette 4686)
2	Say I Am (What I Am)		0	1966	21	1966	(Roulette 4695)
3	It's Only Love		0	1966	31	1966	(Roulette 4710)
* 4	I Think We're Alone Now		0	1967	4	1967	(Roulette 4720)
* 5	Mirage		0	1967	10	1967	(Roulette 4736)
6	I Like The Way		0	1967	25	1967	(Roulette 4756)
7	Gettin' Together		0	1967	18	1967	(Roulette 4762)
* 8	Mony Mony	(Major MinorMm 567)	1	1968	3	1968	(Roulette 7008)
9	Do Something To Me		0	1968	38	1968	(Roulette 7024)
* 10	Crimson And Clover		0	1969	1	1969	(Roulette 7028)
* 11	Sweet Cherry Wine		0	1969	7	1969	(Roulette 7039)
* 12	Crystal Blue Persuasion		0	1969	2	1969	(Roulette 7050)
13	Ball Of Fire		0	1969	19	1969	(Roulette 7060)
14	She		0	1969	23	1969	(Roulette 7066)
15	Draggin' The Line		0	1971	4	1971	(Roulette 7103)
16	I'm Coming Home		0	1971	40	1971	(Roulette 7110)
17	Three Times In Love		0	1980	19	1980	(Millennium 11785)

Tommy Leonetti Male Vocalist, B: 10 Sep 1929 Bergen, New Jersey

| 1 | The Happy Wanderer | | 0 | 1954 | 29 | 1954 | (Capitol 2788) |
| 2 | Free | | 0 | 1956 | 23 | 1956 | (Capitol 3442) |

OBITUARY : D: 15 SEP 1979.

Tommy Mara Male Vocalist from the USA

| 1 | I'll Try | | 0 | 1953 | 28 | 1953 | (Jubilee 6040) |

Tommy Mclain Male Vocalist, From South Louisiana

| 1 | Sweet Dreams | (London Hl10065) | 49 | 1966 | 15 | 1966 | (Msl 197) |

Tommy Page Male Vocalist, B: 24 May 1969 From West Caldwell, New Jersey

| 1 | A Shoulder To Cry On | | 0 | 1989 | 29 | 1989 | (Sire 27645) |
| * 2 | I'll Be Your Everything | (Sire W 9959) | 53 | 1990 | 1 | 1990 | (Sire 19959) |

HIT 2 HAD BACKING VOCALS BY THREE MEMBERS OF NEW KIDS ON THE BLOCK

Tommy Quickly Male Vocalist from the UK

| 1 | Wild Side Of Life | (Pye 7n 15708) | 33 | 1964 | 0 | 1964 | |

Tommy Roe Male Vocalist, Real Name Thomas David Roe B: 9 May 1942 Atlanta, Georgia.

* 1	Sheila	(HMV Pop 1060)	3	1962	1	1962	(ABC ParamounT 10329)
2	Susie Darlin'	(HMV Pop 1092)	37	1962	35	1962	(ABC-ParamounT 10362)
3	The Folk Singer	(HMV Pop 1138)	4	1963	0	1963	
4	Everybody	(HMV Pop 1207)	9	1963	3	1963	(ABC-ParamounT 10478)
5	Everybody (Re-Entry)	(HMV Pop 1207)	49	1963	0	1963	
6	Come On		0	1964	36	1964	(ABC-Paramount 10515)
* 7	Sweet Pea		0	1966	8	1966	(ABC 10762)
8	Hooray For Hazel		0	1966	6	1966	(ABC 10852)
9	It's Now Winters Day		0	1967	23	1967	(ABC 10888)
* 10	Dizzy	(Stateside Ss2143)	1	1969	1	1968	(ABC 11164)
11	Heather Honey	(Stateside Ss2152)	24	1969	29	1969	(ABC 11211)

ISSUE	TITLE	UK LBL	UK POS	UK YEAR	US POS	US YEAR	US LBL
* 12	Jam Up Jelly Tight		0	1970	8	1970	(ABC 11247)
13	Stagger Lee		0	1971	25	1971	(ABC 11307)
Tommy Sands Male Vocalist, B: 27 Aug 1937 Chicago							
* 1	Teen-Age Crush		0	1957	2	1957	(Capitol 3639)
2	Goin' Steady		0	1957	16	1957	(Capitol 3723)
3	Ring My Phone		0	1957	16	1957	(Capitol 3723)
4	Sing Boy Sing		0	1958	24	1958	(Capitol 3867)
5	Old Oaken Bucket	(Capitol Cl15143)	25	1960	0	1960	
Tommy Shaw B: Montgomery, Alabama, Former Lead Guitar With Styx In 1990 Tommy Joined The Damn Yankees							
1	Girls With Guns		0	1984	33	1984	(A&M 2676)
Tommy Steele Male Actor/Vocalist from the UK							
1	Rock With The Caveman	(Decca F 10795)	13	1956	0	1956	
2	Rock With The Caveman (Re-Entry)	(Decca F 10795)	23	1956	0	1956	
3	Singing The Blues	(Decca F 10819)	1	1956	0	1956	
4	Knee Deep In The Blues	(Decca F 10849)	15	1957	0	1957	
5	Singing The Blues (Re-Entry)	(Decca F 10819)	24	1957	0	1957	
6	Butterfingers	(Decca F 10877)	25	1957	0	1957	
7	Butterfingers (Re-Entry)	(Decca F 10877)	8	1957	0	1957	
8	Singing The Blues (2nd Re-Entry)	(Decca F 10819)	29	1957	0	1957	
9	Water Water / Handful Of Songs	(Decca F 10923)	5	1957	0	1957	
10	Shiralee	(Decca F 10896)	11	1957	0	1957	
11	Hey You	(Decca F 10941)	28	1957	0	1957	
12	Water Water / Handful Of Songs (Re-Entry)	(Decca F 10923)	28	1957	0	1957	
13	Nairobi	(Decca F 10991)	3	1958	0	1958	
14	Happy Guitar	(Decca F 10976)	20	1958	0	1958	
15	The Only Man On The Island	(Decca F 11041)	16	1958	0	1958	
16	Come On Let's Go	(Decca F 11072)	10	1958	0	1958	
17	Tallahassee Lassie	(Decca F 11152)	16	1959	0	1959	
18	Give Give Give	(Decca F 11152)	28	1959	0	1959	
19	Tallahassee Lassie (Re-Entry)	(Decca F 11152)	25	1959	0	1959	
20	Little White Bull	(Decca F 11177)	6	1959	0	1959	
21	Little White Bull (Re-Entry)	(Decca F 11177)	30	1960	0	1960	
22	What A Mouth	(Decca F 11245)	5	1960	0	1960	
23	Must Be Santa	(Decca F 11299)	40	1960	0	1960	
24	Writing On The Wall	(Decca F 11372)	30	1961	0	1961	
	HITS 1-12 ARE CREDITED TO TOMMY STEELE & THE STEELMEN						
Tommy Tucker Male Vocalist, Real Name Robert Higginbotham B: 5 Mar 1939 Springfield, Ohio.							
1	Hi-Heel Sneekers	(Pye 7n 25238)	23	1964	11	1964	(Checker 1067)
	OBITUARY: D: 22 JAN 1982 FROM POISONING.						
Tommy Tutone Rock Band From San Francisco With Vocals By Tommy Heath							
1	Angel Say No		0	1980	38	1980	(Columbia 11278)
2	867-5309 / Jenny		0	1982	4	1982	(Columbia 02646)
Tommy Zang Male Vocalist from the USA							
1	Hey Good Lookin'	(Polydor Nh66957)	45	1961	0	1961	
Tone Loc Male Rapper, Real Name Anthony Smith from Los Angeles							
* 1	Wild Thing - Loc'ed After Dark	(Fourth & Broadway Brw 121)	21	1989	2	1988	(Delicious 102)
* 2	Funky Cold Medina - On Fire	(Fourth & Broadway Brw 129)	13	1989	3	1989	(Delicious 104)
3	I Got It Goin' On	(Fourth & Broadway Brw 140)	55	1989	0	1989	
Toney Lee Male Vocalist from the USA							
1	Reach Up	(TMT TMT 2)	64	1983	0	1983	
Tongue 'N' Cheek Mixed Vocal/Instrumental Group from the UK							
1	Nobody (Can Love Me)	(Criminal Bus 6)	59	1988	0	1988	
2	Encore	(Syncopate Sy33)	41	1989	0	1989	
3	Tomorrow	(Syncopate Sy34)	20	1990	0	1990	
4	Nobody	(Syncopate Sy37)	37	1990	0	1990	
5	Forget Me Nots	(Syncopate Sy39)	26	1991	0	1991	
	HIT 1 IS CREDITED TO TONGUE IN CHEEK						
Toni Arden Female Vocalist, Real Name Is Antoinette Aroizzone							
1	I Can Dream, Can't I		0	1949	7	1949	(Columbia 38612)
2	Too Young		0	1951	15	1951	(Columbia 39271)
3	Kiss Of Fire		0	1952	14	1952	(Columbia 39737)
4	I'm Yours		0	1952	24	1952	(Columbia 39737)

ISSUE	TITLE	UK LBL	UK POS	UK YEAR	US POS	US YEAR	US LBL
* 5	Padre		0	1958	13	1958	(Decca 30628)

HIT 1 IS WITH THE HUGO WINTERHALTER'S ORCHESTRA • HITS 2, 3 AND 4 ARE WITH PERCY FAITH'S ORCHESTRA

Toni Basil Female Vocalist/Choreographer/Actress, B: 1950 from Los Angeles

* 1	Mickey	(RadialchoiceTic 4)	2	1982	1	1982	(Chrysalis 2638)
2	Nobody	(RadialchoiceTic 2)	52	1982	0	1982	

Toni Braxton Female Vocalist from the USA

1	Give U My Heart		0	1992	29	1992	(Laface 24026)
2	Love Shoulda Brought You Home	(Laface74321249412)	33	1994	33	1993	(Laface 2035)
* 3	Another Sad Love Song	(Laface74321163502)	51	1993	7	1993	(Laface 24047)
* 4	Breathe Again	(Laface74321185442)	2	1994	3	1993	(Laface 24054)
5	Another Sad Love Song (Re-Entry)	(Laface74321163502)	15	1994	0	1994	
* 6	You Mean The World To Me	(Laface74321214702)	30	1994	7	1994	(Laface 24064)
7	I Belong Yo You		0	1994	28	1994	(Laface 24081)
8	How Many Ways		0	1994	35	1994	(Laface 24081)
* 9	You're Makin' Me High / Let It Flow	(Laface74321395402)	7	1996	1	1996	(Arista 24160)
* 10	Un Break My Heart	(Laface74321410632)	2	1996	1	1996	(Arista 24200)
11	I Don't Want To / I Love Me Some Him	(Laface74321468612)	9	1997	19	1997	(Arista 24229)

HIT 1 IS CREDITED TO BABYFACE FEATURING TONI BRAXTON

Toni Childs Female Vocalist from the USA

1	Don't Walk Away	(A&M Am 462)	53	1989	0	1989	

Toni Fisher (Miss) Female Vocalist, B: 1931 Los Angeles

1	The Big Hurt	(Top Rank Jar261)	30	1960	3	1959	(Signet 275)
2	West Of The Wall		0	1962	37	1962	(Big Top 3097)

Toni Harper & East Beale Sextet Male Child Vocalist from the USA

1	Candy Store Blues		0	1948	22	1948	(Columbia 38229)

Toni Warne Female Vocalist from the UK

1	Ben	(Mint Chew 110)	50	1987	0	1987	

Tonight Male Vocal/Instrumental Group from the UK

1	Drummer Man	(Target Tds 1)	14	1978	0	1978	
2	Money That's Your Problem	(Target Tds 2)	66	1978	0	1978	

Tonja Dantzler Female Vocalist from the USA

1	In And Out Of My Life	(Ffrr Fcd 246)	66	1994	0	1994	

Tony & Joe Real Names Tony Savonne & Joe Saraceno, See Also T-Bones

1	The Freeze		0	1958	33	1958	(Era 1075)

Tony Bellus Real Name Anthony Bellusci B: 17 Apr 1936, Chicago

1	Robbin' The Cradle		0	1959	25	1959	(Ncr 023)

Tony Bennett Male Vocalist, Real Name Anthony Dominick Benedetto B: 13 Aug 1925 In Queens, New York

* 1	Because Of You		0	1951	1	1951	(Columbia 39362)
2	I Won't Cry Anymore		0	1951	12	1951	(Columbia 39362)
* 3	Cold, Cold Heart		0	1951	1	1951	(Columbia 39449)
4	Blue Velvet		0	1951	16	1951	(Columbia 39555)
5	Solitaire		0	1951	17	1951	(Columbia 39555)
6	Here In My Heart		0	1952	15	1952	(Columbia 39745)
7	Have A Good Time		0	1952	16	1952	(Columbia 39764)
8	Stay Where You Are		0	1952	29	1952	(Columbia 39866)
9	Congratulations To Someone		0	1953	20	1953	(Columbia 39910)
10	I'm The King Of Broken Hearts		0	1953	22	1953	(Columbia 39965)
* 11	Rags To Riches		0	1953	1	1953	(Columbia 40048)
12	Stranger In Paradise	(Philips Pb 420)	1	1955	2	1953	(Columbia 40048)
13	Why Does It Have To Be Me?		0	1953	26	1953	(Columbia 40121)
14	There'll Be No Teardrops Tonight		0	1954	7	1954	(Columbia 40169)
15	Please Driver (Once Around The Park Again)		0	1954	29	1954	(Columbia 40213)
17	Cinnamon Sinner		0	1954	8	1954	(Columbia 40272)
18	Not As A Stranger		0	1954	27	1954	(Columbia 40311)
19	Take Me Back Again		0	1954	29	1954	(Columbia 40272)
20	Funny Thing		0	1954	24	1954	(Columbia 40376)
21	Close Your Eyes	(Philips Pb 445)	18	1955	0	1955	
22	Come Next Spring	(Philips Pb 537)	29	1956	0	1956	
23	Can You Find It In Your Heart		0	1956	16	1956	(Columbia 40667)
24	From The Candy Store On The Corner To The Chapel On The Hill		0	1956	7	1956	(Columbia 40726)
25	Happiness Street (Corner Sunshine Square)		0	1956	38	1956	(Columbia 40726)
26	The Autumn Waltz		0	1956	18	1956	(Columbia 40770)

ISSUE	TITLE	UK LBL	UK POS	UK YEAR	US POS	US YEAR	US LBL
27	In The Middle Of An Island - I Am		0	1957	9	1957	(Columbia 40965)
28	Ca, C'est L'amour		0	1957	22	1957	(Columbia 41032)
29	Young And Warm And Wonderful		0	1958	23	1958	(Columbia 41172)
30	Firefly		0	1958	20	1958	(Columbia 41237)
31	Till - Serenata	(Philips Pb 1079)	35	1961	0	1961	
* 32	I Left My Heart In San Francisco		46	1965	19	1962	(Columbia 42332)
33	I Wanna Be Around		0	1963	14	1963	(Columbia 42634)
34	The Good Life	(Cbs Aag 153)	27	1963	18	1963	(Columbia 42779)
35	Who Can I Turn To (When Nobody Needs Me)		0	1964	33	1964	(Columbia 43141)
36	If I Ruled The World	(Cbs 201735)	40	1965	34	1965	(Columbia 43220)
37	I Left My Heart In San Francisco (Re-Entry)	(Cbs 201730)	40	1965	0	1965	
38	I Left My Heart In San Francisco (2nd Re-Entry)	(Cbs 201730)	25	1965	0	1965	
39	The Very Thought Of You	(Cbs 202021)	21	1965	0	1965	

Tony Blackburn Male Dj/Vocalist from the UK

ISSUE	TITLE	UK LBL	UK POS	UK YEAR	US POS	US YEAR	US LBL
1	So Much Love	(MGM 1375)	31	1968	0	1968	
2	It's Only Love	(MGM 1467)	42	1969	0	1969	

Tony Brent Male Vocalist from the UK

ISSUE	TITLE	UK LBL	UK POS	UK YEAR	US POS	US YEAR	US LBL
1	Walkin' To Missouri	(Columbia Db3147)	9	1952	0	1952	
2	Make It Soon	(Columbia Db3187)	9	1953	0	1953	
3	Walkin' To Missouri (Re-Entry)	(Columbia Db3147)	7	1953	0	1953	
4	Got You On My Mind	(Columbia Db3226)	12	1953	0	1953	
5	Make It Soon (Re-Entry)	(Columbia Db3187)	9	1953	0	1953	
6	Cindy Oh Cindy	(Columbia Db3844)	16	1956	0	1956	
7	Cindy Oh Cindy (Re-Entry)	(Columbia Db3844)	30	1957	0	1957	
8	Dark Moon	(Columbia Db3950)	17	1957	0	1957	
9	The Clouds Will Soon Roll By	(Columbia Db4066)	24	1958	0	1958	
10	The Clouds Will Soon Roll By (Re-Entry)	(Columbia Db4066)	20	1958	0	1958	
11	Girl Of My Dreams	(Columbia Db4177)	16	1958	0	1958	
12	Why Should I Be Lonely	(Columbia Db4304)	24	1959	0	1959	

Tony Camillo's Bazuka Male Vocal/Instrumental Group from the USA

ISSUE	TITLE	UK LBL	UK POS	UK YEAR	US POS	US YEAR	US LBL
1	Dynomite (Part 1)	(A&M Ams 7168)	28	1975	0	1975	

Tony Capstick Male Vocalist from the UK, With The Carlton Main/Frickley Colliery Band

ISSUE	TITLE	UK LBL	UK POS	UK YEAR	US POS	US YEAR	US LBL
1	The Sheffield Grinder / Capstick Comes Home	(Dingles Sid 27)	3	1981	0	1981	

Tony Carey Male Vocalist/Instrumentalist (Keyboards), B: 16 Oct 1953, Was With The Groups Rainbow And Planet P

ISSUE	TITLE	UK LBL	UK POS	UK YEAR	US POS	US YEAR	US LBL
1	A Fine Fine Day		0	1984	22	1984	(MCA 52343)
2	The First Day Of Summer		0	1984	33	1984	(MCA 52388)

Tony Christie Male Vocalist Real Name Anthony Fitzgerald B: 25 Apr 1944 In Conisborough, Near Doncaster, Yorkshire,

ISSUE	TITLE	UK LBL	UK POS	UK YEAR	US POS	US YEAR	US LBL
1	Las Vegas	(MCA Mk 5058)	21	1971	0	1971	
2	I Did What I Did For Maria	(MCA Mk 5064)	2	1971	0	1971	
* 3	Is This The Way To Amarillo	(MCA Mks 5073)	18	1971	0	1971	
4	Avenues And Alleyways	(MCA Mks 5101)	37	1973	0	1973	
5	Drive Safely Darlin'	(MCA 219)	35	1976	0	1976	

Tony Clarke Male Actor/Singer/Songwriter, B: New York City

ISSUE	TITLE	UK LBL	UK POS	UK YEAR	US POS	US YEAR	US LBL
1	The Entertainer		0	1965	31	1965	(Chess 1924)

OBITUARY: D: 1970 IN DETROIT.

Tony Crombie & His Rockets Male Vocal/Instrumental Group from the UK, With Tony On Drums

ISSUE	TITLE	UK LBL	UK POS	UK YEAR	US POS	US YEAR	US LBL
1	Teach You To Rock / Short'nin Bread	(Columbia Db3822)	25	1956	0	1956	

Tony De Vit Male Producer from the UK

ISSUE	TITLE	UK LBL	UK POS	UK YEAR	US POS	US YEAR	US LBL
1	Burning Up	(Wea Iconcd 001)	25	1995	0	1995	
2	Hooked	(Labello DanceLad 18cd)	28	1995	0	1995	
3	To The Limit	(X-Plode Bang1cd)	44	1995	0	1995	
4	I'll Be There	(Labello DanceLad 25cd2)	37	1996	0	1996	

HITS 2, 4 ARE CREDITED TO 99TH FLOOR ELEVATORS WITH TONY DE VIT

Tony Di Bart Male Vocalist from the UK

ISSUE	TITLE	UK LBL	UK POS	UK YEAR	US POS	US YEAR	US LBL
1	The Real Thing	(C.C.B. Ccbcd15001)	1	1994	0	1994	
2	Do It	(C.C.B. Ccbcd15003)	21	1994	0	1994	
3	Why Did Ya	(C.C.B. Ccbmc15004)	46	1995	0	1995	
4	Turn Your Love Around	(C.C.B. Ccbcd15006)	66	1996	0	1996	

Tony Etoria Male Vocalist from the UK

ISSUE	TITLE	UK LBL	UK POS	UK YEAR	US POS	US YEAR	US LBL
1	I Can Prove It	(GTO GT 89)	21	1977	0	1977	

ISSUE	TITLE	UK LBL	UK POS	UK YEAR	US POS	US YEAR	US LBL
Tony Ferrino	Male Comedian/Vocalist, Real Name Steve Coughan from the UK						
1	Help Yourself / Bigamy At Christmas	(RCA 74321430302)	42	1996	0	1996	
Tony Hadley	Male Vocalist from the UK						
1	Lost In Your Love	(EMI Em 222)	42	1992	0	1992	
2	For Your Blue Eyes Only	(EMI Em 234)	67	1992	0	1992	
3	The Game Of Love	(EMI Cdem 254)	72	1993	0	1993	
4	Dance With Me	(Vc Recordings Vcrd 17)	35	1997	0	1997	
	HIT 4 IS CREDITED TO TIN TIN OUT FEATURING TONY HADLEY						
Tony Hatch	Male Orchestra Leader from the UK						
1	Out Of This World	(Pye 7n 15460)	50	1962	0	1962	
Tony Jackson & The Vibrations	Male Vocalist With Instrumental Group from the UK						
1	Bye Bye Baby	(Pye 7n 15685)	38	1964	0	1964	
2	(Everything I Do) I Do It For You	(Bell74321193062)	47	1994	0	1994	
	HIT 2 IS CREDITED TO Q FEATURING TONY JACKSON						
Tony Joe White	Male Vocalist, B. 23 Jul 1943 Oak Grove, Louisiana						
1	Polk Salad Annie		0	1969	8	1969	(Monument 1104)
2	Groupy Girl	(MonumentMon 1043)	22	1970	0	1970	
Tony Martin	Male Vocalist, Real Name Alvin Morris Jr B: 25 Dec 1912 Oakland						
* 7	To Each His Own		0	1946	4	1946	(Mercury 3022)
8	Rumours Are Flying		0	1946	9	1946	(Mercury 3032)
9	I'll Dance At Your Wedding		0	1947	23	1947	(RCA Victor 2512)
10	Hooray For Love		0	1948	21	1948	(RCA Victor 2690)
11	Confess		0	1948	25	1948	(RCA Victor 2812)
12	For Every Man There's A Woman (From Casbah)		0	1948	30	1948	(RCA Victor 2689)
13	It's Magic (From Romance On The High Seas)		0	1948	11	1948	(RCA Victor 2862)
14	If You Stub Your Toe On The Moon		0	1949	17	1949	(RCA Victor 3383)
15	Circus		0	1949	24	1949	(RCA Victor 78-3488)
16	There's No Tomorrow (From Two Tickets To Broadway)		0	1949	2	1949	(RCA Victor 78-3582)
17	Marta (Rambling Rose Of The Wildwood)		0	1949	15	1949	(RCA Victor 3598)
18	I Said My Pajamas (And Put On My Prayers)		0	1950	3	1950	(RCA Victor 78-3613)
19	Valencia		0	1950	18	1950	(RCA Victor 3755)
20	La Vie En Rose		0	1950	9	1950	(RCA Victor 3819)
21	Would I Love You (Love You, Love You)		0	1951	19	1951	(RCA Victor4056)
* 22	I Get Ideas		0	1951	3	1951	(RCA Victor 4141)
23	I Apologise		0	1951	20	1951	(RCA Victor 4056)
24	The Musicians		0	1951	24	1951	(RCA Victor 4225)
25	Vanity		0	1951	18	1951	(RCA Victor 4246)
26	Over A Bottle Of Wine		0	1951	17	1951	(RCA Victor 4220)
27	Domino		0	1951	9	1951	(RCA Victor 4343)
28	Kiss Of Fire		0	1952	6	1952	(RCA Victor 4671)
29	Some Day (From The Vagabond King)		0	1952	24	1952	(RCA Victor 4836)
30	Luna Rossa (Blushing Moon)		0	1952	27	1952	(RCA Victor 4836)
31	Dance Of Destiny		0	1952	27	1952	(RCA Victor 5008)
32	April In Portugal (The Whisp'ring Serenade)		0	1953	17	1953	(RCA Victor 5279)
33	Sorta On The Border		0	1953	26	1953	(RCA Victor 5352)
34	Stranger In Paradise		6	1955	1	1954	(RCA Victor 5535)
35	Here		0	1954	4	1954	(RCA Victor 5665)
36	Walk Hand In Hand		2	1956	10	1956	(RCA Victor 6493)
Tony Meehan Combo	Male Instrumental Group from the UK						
1	Song Of Mexico	(Decca F 11801)	39	1964	0	1964	
Tony Merrick	Male Vocalist from the UK						
1	Lady Jane	(Columbia Db7913)	49	1966	0	1966	
Tony Orlando	Male Vocalist, Real Name Michael Anthony Orlando B: 3 Apr 1944 From New York City						
1	Halfway To Paradise		0	1961	39	1961	(Epic 9441)
2	Bless You	(Fontana H 330)	5	1961	15	1961	(Epic 9452)
Tony Osborne Sound	Orchestra from the UK						
1	Man From Madrid	(HMV Pop 827)	50	1961	0	1961	with Joanne Brown
2	The Shepherd's Song	(Philips 6006 266)	46	1973	0	1973	
Tony Pastor & His Orchestra	Male Bandleader/Saxophonist/Singer, Real Name Antonio Pestritto from the USA						
1	Maria Elena		0	1941	9	1941	(Bluebird 11127)
2	Green Eyes		0	1941	21	1941	(Bluebird 11168)

ISSUE	TITLE	UK LBL	UK POS	UK YEAR	US POS	US YEAR	US LBL
3	Twenty-One Dollars A Day-Once A Month		0	1941	25	1941	(Bluebird 11231)
4	That Ain't The Way I Dreamed It		0	1942	21	1942	(Bluebird 11502)
5	Hey, Mabel!		0	1943	20	1943	(Bluebird 0802)
6	Dance With A Dolly (With A Hole In Her Stocking)		0	1944	9	1944	(Bluebird 0827)
7	Bell-Bottom Trousers		0	1945	2	1945	(Victor 1661)
8	Five Salted Peanuts		0	1945	11	1945	(Victor 1661)
9	Please No Squeeza Da Banana		0	1945	13	1945	(Victor 1693)
10	Sioux City Sue		0	1946	10	1946	(Cosmo 471)
11	Red Silk Stockings And Green Perfume		0	1947	8	1947	(Columbia 37330)
12	I Wonder, I Wonder, I Wonder		0	1947	11	1947	(Columbia 37353)
13	The Lasy From Twenty-Nine Palms		0	1947	11	1947	(Columbia 37562)
14	You Started Something		0	1948	16	1948	(Columbia 38297)
15	It's Like Taking Candy From A Baby		0	1949	21	1949	(Columbia 38355)
16	Grieving For You		0	1949	11	1949	(Columbia 38383)
17	A You're Adorabl (The Alphabet Song)		0	1949	12	1949	(Columbia 38449)

OBITUARY : D: 31 OCT 1969 (AGED 62).

Tony Perkins   Male Actor/Vocalist, B: 4 Apr 1932 New York City

1	Moon-Light Swim		0	1957	24	1957	(RCA 7020)

HE WAS FAMOUS FOR HIS ROLE AS NORMAN BATES IN PSYCHO • OBITUARY: D: 12 SEP 1992 AIDS.

Tony Rallo & The Midnight Band   Male Vocal/Instrumental Group from the USA/France

1	Holdin' On	(Calibre Cab150)	34	1980	0	1980	

Tony Rees & The Cottages   Male Vocal Group from the UK

1	Viva El Fulham	(Sonet Son 2059)	46	1975	0	1975	

Tony Rich Project   Male Vocalist from the USA

* 1	Nobody Knows	(Laface74321356422)	4	1996	2	1996	(Arista 24115)
2	Like A Woman	(Laface74321401612)	27	1996	41	1996	(Arista 24175)
3	Leavin'	(Laface74321438382)	52	1996	92	1996	(Arista 24204)

Tony Scott   Male Vocalist from the USA

1	That's How I'm Leaving / The Chief	(ChampionChamp 97)	48	1989	0	1989	
2	Get Into It / Thats How I'm Living (Re-Issue)	(ChampionChamp 232)	63	1990	0	1990	

THE CHIEF WAS ONLY LISTED FROM THE 22 APR 1989

Tony Sheveton   Male Vocalist from the UK

1	Million Drums	(Oriole Cb 1895)	49	1964	0	1964	

Tony Terry   Male Vocalist, B: 12 Mar 1964 Pinehurst, North Carolina

1	Lovey Dovey	(Epic Tony 2)	44	1988	0	1988	
2	With You		0	1991	14	1991	(Epic 73713)

Tony Tribe   Male Vocalist From Jamaica

1	Red Red Wine	(Downtown Dt419)	50	1969	0	1969	
2	Red Red Wine (Re-Entry)	(Downtown Dt419)	46	1969	0	1969	

Tony! Toni! Tone!   R&B-Funk Trio From Oakland, California, Names Dwayne & Raphael Wiggins With Timothy Christian

1	Oakland Stroke	(Wing Wing 7)	50	1990	0	1990	
* 2	Feels Good		0	1990	9	1990	(Wing 877436)
3	It Never Rains (In Southern California)	(Wing Wing 10)	69	1991	34	1991	(Wing 879068)
* 4	If I Had No Loot	(Polydor Pzcd292)	44	1993	7	1993	(Wing 859056)
* 5	Anniversary		0	1993	10	1993	(Wing 859566)
6	(Lay Your Head On My) Pillow		0	1994	31	1994	(Wing 858260)
7	Let's Get Down	(MercuryMercd 485)	33	1997	0	1997	
8	Thinking Of You		0	1997	28	1997	(Mercury 57482)

HIT 7 IS CREDITED TO TONY! TONI! TONE! FEATURING DJ QUIK

Top   Male Vocal/Instrumental Group from the UK

1	Number One Dominator	(Island Is 496)	67	1991	0	1991	

Topol   Male Actor/Vocalist from Israel

1	If I Were A Rich Man	(Cbs 202561)	9	1967	0	1967	

Tori Amos   Female Vocalist from the USA

1	Silent All These Years	(East West Yz618)	51	1991	0	1991	
2	China	(East West Yz7531)	51	1992	0	1992	
3	Winter	(East West A7504)	25	1992	0	1992	
4	Crucify	(East West A7479)	15	1992	0	1992	
5	Silent All These Years (Re-Issue)	(East West 7433)A	26	1992	0	1992	
6	Cornflake Girl	(East West A7281cd)	4	1994	0	1994	
7	Pretty Good Year	(East West A7263cd)	7	1994	0	1994	
8	Past The Mission	(East West Yz7257cd)	31	1994	0	1994	

ISSUE	TITLE	UK LBL	UK POS	UK YEAR	US POS	US YEAR	US LBL
9	God	(East West A7251cd)	44	1994	0	1994	
10	Caught A Lite Sneeze	(East West A5524cd1)	20	1996	0	1996	
11	Talula / Sister Named Desire (Ep)	(East West 8512cd1)A	22	1996	0	1996	
12	Hey Jupiter / Professional Widow	(East West 5494cd)A	20	1996	0	1996	
13	Blue Skies	(PerfectoPerf 130cd1)	26	1996	0	1996	
14	Professional Widow (It's Got To Be Big)	(East West A5450cd)	1	1997	0	1997	
15	Silent All These Tears		0	1997	65	1997	(Atlantic 83001)

HIT 13 IS CREDITED TO BT FEATURING TORI AMOS

Tornados   Male Instrumental Quintet From England, Lead Guitar Is Alan Caddy With George Bellamy, Roger Lavern,
Heinz Burt & Clem Cattini.

* 1	Telstar	(Decca F 11494)	1	1962	1	1962	(London 9561)
2	Globetrotter	(Decca F 11562)	5	1963	0	1963	
3	Robot	(Decca F 11606)	17	1963	0	1963	
4	The Ice Cream Man	(Decca F 11662)	18	1963	0	1963	
5	Dragonfly	(Decca F 11745)	41	1963	0	1963	

Total   Female Vocal Trio, Keisha Spivey, Jakima Raynor & Pan Long From New York City.

* 1	Can't You See	(Tommy BoyTbcd 700)	43	1995	13	1995	(Tommy Boy 7676)
2	No One Else		0	1996	22	1996	(Bad Boy)
3	Kissin' You	(Arista74321404172)	29	1996	12	1996	(Arista 79056)
4	When Boy Meets Girl		0	1996	50	1996	(Arista 79074)
5	Do You Think About Us	(PuffDaddy/Arista 74321458492)	49	1997	0	1997	

HIT 1 IS CREDITED TO TOTAL FEATURING NOTORIOUS B.I.G.

Total Contrast   Male Vocal/Instrumental Duo from the UK

1	Takes A Little Time	(London Lon 71)	17	1985	0	1985	
2	Hit And Run	(London Lon 76)	41	1985	0	1985	
3	The River	(London Lon 83)	44	1986	0	1986	
4	What You Gonna Do About It	(London Lon 95)	63	1986	0	1986	

Toto   Male Vocal/Instrumental Group from the USA

* 1	Hold The Line	(Cbs 6784)	14	1979	5	1978	(Columbia 10830)
2	99		0	1980	26	1980	(Columbia 11173)
3	Rosanna	(Cba A 2079)	12	1983	2	1982	(Columbia 02811)
4	Make Believe		0	1982	30	1982	(Columbia 03143)
* 5	Africa	(Cbs A 2510)	3	1983	1	1982	(Columbia 03335)
6	I Won't Hold You Back	(Cbs A 3392)	37	1983	10	1983	(Columbia 03597)
7	Stranger In Town		0	1984	30	1984	(Columbia 04672)
8	I'll Be Over You		0	1986	11	1986	(Columbia 06280)
9	Without Your Love		0	1987	38	1987	(Columbia 06570)
10	Pamela		0	1988	22	1988	(Columbia 07715)
11	I Will Remember	(Columbia6626552)	64	1995	0	1995	

FORMED IN 1978 WITH LEAD VOCALS BY ROBERT TOTEAUX, AKA BOBBY KIMBALL

Toto Coelo   Female Vocal Group from the UK

1	I Eat Cannibals (Part 1)	(RadialchoiceTic 10)	8	1982	0	1982	
2	Dracula's Tango / Mucho Macho	(RadialchoiceTic 11)	54	1982	0	1982	

Tottenham Hotspur F.C.   Male Soccer Vocalist Team With Vocals/Instumentals From Chas & Dave from the UK.

1	Ossie's Dream (Spurs Are On Their Way To Wembley)	(Rockney Shelf 1)	5	1981	0	1981	
2	Tottenham Tottenham	(Rockney Shelf 2)	19	1982	0	1982	
3	Hot Shot Tottenham	(Rainbow Rbr16)	18	1987	0	1987	
4	When The Year Ends In 1	(A1 A 1324)	44	1991	0	1991	

ALL HITS ARE CREDTIED TO TOTTENHAM HOTSPUR F.A. CUP FINAL SQUAD

Touch Of Soul   Mixed Vocal/Instrumental Group from the UK

1	We Got The Love	(CooltempoCool 204)	46	1990	0	1990	

Tourists   Mixed Vocal/Instrumental Group from the UK

1	Blind Among The Flowers	(Logo Go 350)	52	1979	0	1979	
2	The Loneliest Man In The World	(Logo Go 360)	32	1979	0	1979	
3	I Only Want To Be With You	(Logo Go 370)	4	1979	0	1979	
4	So Good To Be Back Home Again	(Logo Tour 1)	8	1980	0	1980	
5	Don't Say I Told You So	(RCA Tour 2)	40	1980	0	1980	

Tower Of Power   Lenny Williams Was Lead Singer Of This R&B Funk Band, Originally Known As The Motowns

1	You're Still A Young Man		0	1972	29	1972	(Warner Bros 7612)
2	So Very Hard To Go		0	1973	17	1973	(Warner Bros 7687)
3	Don't Change Horses (In The Middle Of A Stream)		0	1974	26	1974	(Warner Bros 7828)

ISSUE	TITLE	UK LBL	UK POS	UK YEAR	US POS	US YEAR	US LBL
Toxic Two Male Production/Instrumental Duo from the USA							
1	Rave Generator	(PWL InternationalPWL 223)	13	1992	0	1992	
Toy Dolls Male Vocal/Instrumental Group from the UK							
1	Nellie The Elephant	(Volume Vol 11)	4	1984	0	1984	
Toyah Female Vocalist from the UK							
1	Four From Toyah (Ep)	(Safari Toy 1)	4	1981	0	1981	
2	I Want To Be Free	(Safari Safe 34)	8	1981	0	1981	
3	Thunder In The Mountain	(Safari Safe 38)	4	1981	0	1981	
4	Four More From Toyah (Ep)	(Safari Toy 2)	14	1981	0	1981	
5	Brave New World	(Safari Safe 45)	21	1982	0	1982	
6	Ieya	(Safari Safe 28)	48	1982	0	1982	
7	Be Proud Be Loud (Be Heard)	(Safari Safe 52)	30	1982	0	1982	
8	Rebel Run	(Safari Safe 56)	24	1983	0	1983	
9	The Vow	(Safari Safe 58)	50	1983	0	1983	
10	Don't Fall In Love	(Portrait A 6160)	22	1985	0	1985	
11	Soul Passing Through Soul	(Portrait A 6359)	57	1985	0	1985	
12	Echo Beach	(Eg Ego 31)	54	1987	0	1987	
Toys Female Vocal Trio from the USA							
* 1	The Lovers Concerto	(Stateside Ss460)	5	1965	2	1965	(Dynovoice 209)
2	Attack	(Stateside Ss483)	36	1966	18	1966	(Dynovoice 214)
	NAMES BARBARA HARRIS, BARBARA PARRITT & JUNE MONTIERO						
Tracey Lee Female Vocalist from the USA							
1	The Theme (It's Party Time)	(Universal Und56133)	51	1997	55	1997	(Bystorm 56114)
Tracey Ullman Female Vocalist, B: 30 Dec 1959 Buckinghamshire, England							
1	Breakaway	(Stiff Buy 168)	4	1983	0	1983	
2	They Don't Know	(Stiff Buy 180)	2	1983	8	1984	(MCA/Stiff 52347)
3	Move Over Darling	(Stiff Buy 195)	8	1983	0	1983	
4	My Guy	(Stiff Buy 197)	23	1984	0	1984	
5	Sunglasses	(Stiff Buy 205)	18	1984	0	1984	
6	Helpless	(Stiff Buy 211)	61	1984	0	1984	
Traci Lords Female Vocalist from the USA							
1	Fallen Angel	(RadioactiveRaxtd 18)	72	1995	0	1995	
Tracie Female Vocalist from the UK							
1	The House That Jack Built	(Respond Kob701)	9	1983	0	1983	
2	Give It Some Emotion	(Respond Kob704)	24	1983	0	1983	
3	Soul's On Fire	(Respond Kob708)	73	1984	0	1984	
4	(I Love You) When You Sleep	(Respond Kob710)	59	1984	0	1984	
5	I Can't Leave You Alone	(Respond Sbs 1)	60	1985	0	1985	
	HIT 5 IS CREDITED TO TRACIE YOUNG						
Tracie Spencer Female Vocalist, B: 1976 In Waterloo, Iowa							
1	This House	(Capitol Cl 612)	65	1991	0	1991	
Tracy Chapman Female Vocalist from the USA							
1	Fast Car	(Elektra Ekr73)	5	1988	6	1988	(Elektra 69412)
2	Crossroads	(Elektra Ekr95)	61	1989	0	1989	
3	Give Me One Reason		0	1996	3	1996	(Electra 64346)
Tracy Spencer Female Vocalist, B: 12 Jul 1976 Waterloo, Iowa							
1	Symptoms Of True Love		0	1988	38	1988	(Capitol 44140)
2	This House		0	1991	3	1991	(Capitol 44652)
Trade Martin B: 19 Nov 1943 Union City, New Jersey							
1	That Stranger Used To Be My Girl		0	1962	28	1962	(Coed 570)
Trade Winds Names Pete Anders & Vinnie Poncia							
1	New York's A Lonely Town		0	1965	32	1965	(Red Bird 020)
	THEY FIRST RECORDED WITH THE VIDELS THEN THE INNOCENCE						
Traffi Male Vocal/Instrumental Group from the UK							
1	Paper Sun	(Island Wip 6002)	5	1967	0	1967	
2	Hole In My Shoe	(Island Wip 6017)	2	1967	0	1967	
3	Here We Go Round The Mulberry Bush	(Island Wip 6025)	8	1967	0	1967	
4	No Face, No Name, No Number	(Island Wip 6030)	40	1968	0	1968	
	NAMES STEVIE WINWOOD, CHRIS WOOD, JIM CAPALDI & DAVE MASON						
Tramaine Female Vocalist from the USA							
1	Fall Down (Spirit Of Love)	(A&M Am 281)	60	1985	0	1985	

ISSUE	TITLE	UK LBL	UK POS	UK YEAR	US POS	US YEAR	US LBL
Trammps	Male Vocal Group from the USA						
1	Zing Went The Strings Of My Heart	(Buddah Bds 405)	29	1974	64	1972	(Buddah 306)
2	Sixty Minute Man	(Buddah Bds 415)	40	1975	0	1975	
3	Hold Back The Night	(Buddah Bds 437)	5	1975	36	1976	(Buddah 507)
4	That's Where The Happy People Go	(Atlantic K 0703)	35	1976	27	1976	(Atlantic 3306)
5	Soul Seachin' Time	(Atlantic K10797)	42	1976	0	1976	
6	Disco Inferno	(Atlantic K10914)	16	1977	0	1977	
7	Disco Inferno (Re-Issue)	(Atlantic K11135)	47	1978	11	1978	(Atlantic 3389)
8	Hold Back The Night	(Network Nwk65)	30	1992	0	1992	
	HIT 8 IS CREDITED TO KWS FEATURING GUEST VOCALS FROM THE TRAMMPS • LEAD SINGER WITH THE GROUP IS JIMMY ELLIS						
Trans-X	Mixed Vocal/Instrumental Group from Canada						
1	Living On Video	(Boiling PointPosp 650)	9	1985	0	1985	
Transformer 2	Mixed Vocal/Instrumental Group From Holland/Belgium						
1	Just Can't Get Enough	(Positiva Cdtiv49)	45	1996	0	1996	
Transvision Vamp	Mixcd Vocal/Instrumental Group from the UK						
1	Tell That Girl To Shut Up	(MCA Tvv 2)	45	1988	0	1988	
2	I Want Your Love	(MCA Tvv 3)	5	1988	0	1988	
3	Revolution Baby	(MCA Tvv 4)	30	1988	0	1988	
4	Sister Moon	(MCA Tvv 5)	41	1988	0	1988	
5	Baby I Don't Care	(MCA Tvv 6)	3	1989	0	1989	
6	The Only One	(MCA Tvv 7)	15	1989	0	1989	
8	Landslide Of Love	(MCA Tvv 8)	14	1989	0	1989	
9	Born To Be Sold	(MCA Tvv 9)	22	1989	0	1989	
10	(I Just Wanna) B With U	(MCA Tvv 10)	30	1991	0	1991	
11	If Looks Could Kill	(MCA Tvv 11)	41	1991	0	1991	
Trash	Male Vocal/Instrumental Group from the UK						
1	Golden Slumbers / Carry That Weight	(Apple 17)	35	1969	0	1969	
Trash Can Sinatras	Male Vocal/Instrumental Group from the UK						
1	Hayfever	(Go!Disc Godcd	98)61	1993	0	1993	
Trashmen	Male Surf-Rock Quintet From Minneapolis						
1	Surfin' Bird		0	1963	4	1963	(Garrett 4002)
2	Bird Dance Beat		0	1964	30	1964	(Garrett 4003)
	NAMES TONY ANDREASON, DAL WINSLOW, BOB REED & STEVE WAHRER • OBITUARY : STEVE B: 1942, D: 21 JAN 1989 THROAT CANCER.						
Traveling Wilburys	Male Vocal/Instrumental Group from the USA/UK						
1	Handle With Care	(Wilbury W 7732)	21	1988	0	1988	
2	End Of The Line	(Wilbury W 7637)	52	1989	0	1989	
3	Nobody's Child	(Wilbury W 9773)	44	1990	0	1990	
Travis & Bob	Real Name Travis Pritchett & Bob Weaver Both From Alabama						
1	Tell Him No		0	1959	8	1959	(Sandy 1017)
Travis Wammack	Works Mainly As A Session Guitarist From Walnut, Mississippi, Raised In Memphis						
1	Scratchy		0	1964	80	1964	(Ara 204)
2	Love Being Your Fool (Shu-Doo-Pa-Poo-Poop)		0	1975	38	1975	(Capricorn 0239)
Tremeloes	Male Vocal/Instrumental Group from the UK Names: Alan Blakely, Dave Munden, Rick West & Len Hawkes						
* 1	Here Comes My Baby	(Cbs 202519)	4	1967	13	1967	(Epic 10139)
* 2	Silence Is Golden	(Cbs 2723)	1	1967	11	1967	(Epic 10184)
* 3	Even The Bad Times Are Good	(Cbs 2930)	4	1967	36	1967	(Epic 10233)
4	Be Mine	(Cbs 3043)	39	1967	0	1967	
5	Suddenly You Love Me	(Cbs 3234)	6	1968	0	1968	
6	Helule Helule	(Cbs 2889)	14	1968	0	1968	
7	My Little Lady	(Cbs 3480)	6	1968	0	1968	
8	I Shall Be Released	(Cbs 3873)	29	1968	0	1968	
9	Hello World	(Cbs 4065)	14	1969	0	1969	
10	Call Me Number One	(Cbs 4582)	2	1969	0	1969	
11	By The Way	(Cbs 4815)	35	1970	0	1970	
12	Me And My Life	(Cbs 5139)	4	1970	0	1970	
13	Hello Buddy	(Cbs 7294)	32	1971	0	1971	
Trevor Walters	Male Vocalist from the UK						
1	Love Me Tonight	(Magnet Mag198)	27	1981	0	1981	
2	Stuck On You	(Sanity Is 002)	9	1984	0	1984	
3	Never Let Her Slip Away	(Polydor Posp716)	73	1984	0	1984	

ISSUE	TITLE	UK LBL	UK POS	UK YEAR	US POS	US YEAR	US LBL
Trey Lorenz Male Vocalist from the USA							
1	Someone To Hold	(Epic 6587857)	65	1992	19	1992	(Epic 74482)
2	I'll Be There	(Columbia6581377)	2	1992	1	1992	(Columbia 74330)
3	Photograph Of Mary	(Epic 6589542)	38	1993	0	1993	
	HIT 2 IS UNCREDITED DUET WITH MARIAH CAREY						
Tri Male Vocal/Instrumental Group from the UK							
1	We Got The Love	(Epic 6623642)	61	1995	0	1995	
Tribal House Male Vocal/Instrumental Group from the USA							
1	Motherland-A-Fri-Ca	(CooltempoCool 198)	57	1990	0	1990	
Tribe Of Toffs Male Vocal/Instrumental Group from the UK							
1	John Kettley (Is A Weatherman)	(CompletelyDifferent Daft 1)	21	1988	0	1988	
Tricia Penrose Female Vocalist from the UK							
1	Where Did Out Love Go	(RCA 74321428152)	71	1996	0	1996	
Trickbaby Female Vocal/Instrumental Group from the UK							
1	Indie-Yarn	(Logic74321423152)	47	1996	0	1996	
Tricky Male Rapper from the UK							
1	Aftermath	(Fourth & Broadway Brcd 288)	69	1994	0	1994	
2	Overcome	(Fourth & Broadway Brcd 304)	34	1995	0	1995	
3	Black Steel	(Fourth & Broadway Brcd 320)	28	1995	0	1995	
4	The Hell (Ep)	(Fourth & Broadway Brcd 326)	12	1995	0	1995	
5	Pumpkin	(Fourth & Broadway Brcd 330)	26	1995	0	1995	
6	Christiansands	(Fourth & Broadway Brcd 340)	36	1996	0	1996	
7	Milk	(Mushroom D 1494)	10	1996	0	1996	
8	Tricky Kid	(Fourth & Broadway Brcd 341)	28	1997	0	1997	
9	Makes Me Wanna Die	(Fourth & Broadway Brcd 348)	29	1997	0	1997	
	HIT 5 IS CREDITED TO GARBAGE FEATURING TRICKY • HIT 7 TO TRICKY VS THE GRAVEDIGGAZ • SEE ALSO STARVING SOULS						
Tricky Disco Mixed Vocal/Instrumental/Production Duo from the UK							
1	Tricky Disco	(Warp Wap 7)	14	1990	0	1990	
2	House Fly	(Warp 7wap 11)	55	1991	0	1991	
Triffids Male Vocal/Instrumental Group From New Zealand							
1	Trick Of The Light	(Island Is 350)	73	1988	0	1988	
Trini Lopez Male Vocalist, Real Name Trinidad Lopez 111 B: 15 May 1937 Dallas.							
* 1	If I Had A Hammer	(Reprise R 20198)	4	1963	3	1963	(Reprise 20198)
2	Kansas City	(Reprise R 20236)	35	1963	23	1963	(Reprise 20236)
3	Lemon Tree		0	1965	20	1965	(Reprise 0336)
4	I'm Comin' Home Cindy	(Reprise R 20455)	28	1966	39	1966	(Reprise 0455)
5	Gonna' Get Along Without Ya Now	(Reprise R 20455)	41	1967	0	1967	
6	Trini Tracks	(RCA 154)	59	1981	0	1981	
Trinidad Oil Company Mixed Vocal/Instrumental Group From Trinidad							
1	The Calendar Song	(Harvest Har5122)	34	1977	0	1977	
Irio Male Vocal/Instrumental Group From Germany							
1	Da Da Da	(Mobile Suitcorporatcorp 5)	2	1982	0	1982	
Triplets Female Vocalists, Real Names Diana, Sylvia & Vicky Villegas							
1	You Don't Have To Go Home Tonight		0	1991	14	1991	(Mercury 878864)
Tripping Daisy Male Vocal/Instrumental Group from the USA							
1	Piranha	(Island Cid 638)	72	1996	0	1996	
Trisha Yearwood Female Vocalist							
1	How Do I Live	(MCA Mcstd48064)	66	1997	0	1997	
Triumph Male Vocal/Instrumental Group from Canada, Names: Rik Emmett, Mike Levine & Gil Moore							
1	Hold On		0	1979	38	1979	(RCA 11569)
2	I Live For The Weekend	(RCA 13)	59	1980	0	1980	
3	Somebody's Out There		0	1986	27	1986	(MCA 52898)
Troggs Male Vocal/Instrumental Group from the UK							
* 1	Wild Thing	(Fontana Tf 689)	2	1966	1	1966	(Atco 6415)
* 2	With A Girl Like You	(Fontana Tf 717)	1	1966	29	1966	(Atco 6415)
3	I Can't Control Myself	(Page One Pof001)	2	1966	0	1966	
4	Anyway That You Want Me	(Page One Pof010)	8	1966	0	1966	
5	Give It To Me	(Page One Pof015)	12	1967	0	1967	
6	Night Of The Long Grass	(Page One Pof022)	17	1967	0	1967	
7	Hi Hi Hazel	(Page One Pof030)	42	1967	0	1967	

ISSUE	TITLE	UK LBL	UK POS	UK YEAR	US POS	US YEAR	US LBL
* 8	Love Is All Around	(Page One Pof040)	5	1967	7	1968	(Fontana 1607)
9	Little Girl	(Page One Pof056)	37	1968	0	1968	
10	Wild Thing	(WeekendCdweek 103)	69	1993	0	1993	

NAMES: REG PRESLEY, CHRIS BRITTON, PETER STAPLES & RONNE BOND • HIT 10 IS CREDITED TO TROGGS AND WOLF

Tronikhouse Male Producer, Real Name Kevin Saunderson from the USA

1	Up Tempo	(Kms Uk Kmsuk	68	1992	0	1992	

Troubadours Du Roi Baudouin Mixed Vocal Group From Zaire

1	Sanctus (Missa Luba)	(Philips Bf 1732)	28	1969	0	1969	
2	Sanctus (Missa Luba) (Re-Entry)	(Philips Bf 1732)	37	1969	0	1969	

Trouble Funk Male Vocal/Instrumental Group from the USA

1	Woman Of Principle	(Fourth &Broadway Brw70)	65	1987	0	1987	

Troy Shondell Male Vocalist, B: 14 May 1944 Fort Wayne, Indiana

* 1	This Time	(London Hlg9432)	22	1961	6	1961	(Liberty 55353)

Truce Female Vocal Group from the UK

1	The Finest	(Big Life Blrd118)	54	1995	0	1995	
2	Celebration Of Life	(Big Life Blrd126)	51	1996	0	1996	

Trudy Richards Female Vocalist from the USA

1	The Breeze (That's Bringin' My Homey Back To Me)		0	1953	19	1953	(Derby 823)

True Faith With Final Cut Mixed Vocal/Instrumental Group from the USA

1	Take Me Away	(Network Nwk20)	51	1991	0	1991	

Trussel Male Vocal/Instrumental Group from the USA

1	Love Injection	(Elektra K12412)	43	1980	0	1980	

Truth (1) Male Vocal/Instrumental Group from the UK

1	Confusion (Hits Us Every Time)	(FormationTruth 1)	22	1983	0	1983	
2	A Step In The Right Direction	(FormationTruth 2)	32	1983	0	1983	
3	No Stone Unturned	(FormationTruth 3)	66	1984	0	1984	

Truth (2) Male Vocal Duo from the UK

1	Girl	(Pye 7n 17035)	27	1966	0	1966	

Tubes Male Vocal/Instrumental Group from the USA

1	White Punks On Dope	(A&M Ams 7323)	28	1977	0	1977	
2	Prime Time	(A&M Ams 7423)	34	1979	0	1979	
3	Don't Want To Wait Anymore	(Capitol Cl 208)	60	1981	35	1981	(Capitol 5007)
4	She's A Beauty		0	1983	10	1983	(Capitol 5217)

LEAD SINGER WITH THE GROUP IS JOHN WALDO B: 17 SEP 1950 OMAHA, NEBRASKA • JOHN WALDO IS NOW KNOWN AS FEE WAYBILL

Tullio De Piscopo Male Vocalist from Italy

1	Stop Bajon (Primavera)	(GreyhoundGrey 9)	58	1987	0	1987	

Tune Rockers Male Instrumental Group from the USA

1	The Green Mosquito		0	1958	44	1958	(United Artists139)

Turbans R&B Quintet Led By Al Banks, Disbanded In 1961

1	When You Dance		0	1956	33	1956	(Herald 458)

Turntable Orchestra Male Vocal/Instrumental Duo from the USA

1	You're Gonna Miss Me	(Republic Lic012)	52	1989	0	1989	

Turtles Male Vocal/Instrumental Group from the USA

1	It Ain't Me Babe		0	1965	8	1965	(White Whale 222)
2	Let Me Be		0	1965	29	1965	(White Whale 224)
3	You Baby		0	1966	20	1966	(White Whale 227)
* 4	Happy Together	(London Hl10115)	12	1967	1	1967	(White Whale 244)
* 5	She'd Rather Be With Me	(London Hlu10135)	4	1967	3	1967	(White Whale 249)
6	You Know What I Mean		0	1967	12	1967	(White Whale 254)
7	She's My Girl		0	1967	14	1967	(White Whale 260)
8	Elenore	(London Hl10223)	7	1968	6	1968	(White Whale 276)
9	You Showed Me		0	1969	6	1969	(White Whale 292)

FORMED AS THE NIGHTRIDERS IN LOS ANGELES IN 1961 LED BY MARK VOLMAN • BECAME THE CROSSFIRES, CHANGED THEIR NAME TO THE TURTLES IN 1965

Tuxedo Junction All Female Disco Group from the USA

1	Chattanooga Choo Choo		0	1978	32	1978	(Butterfly 1205)

Tweets Male Instrumental Group from the UK

1	The Birdie Song (Birdie Dance)	(Prt 7p 219)	2	1981	0	1981	
2	Let's All Sing Like The Birdies Sing	(Prt 7p 226)	44	1981	0	1981	
3	The Birdie Song (Birdie Dance) (Re-Entry)	(PRT 7p 219)	46	1982	0	1982	

ISSUE	TITLE	UK LBL	UK POS	UK YEAR	US POS	US YEAR	US LBL
12 Gauge Male Rapper, Real Name Isiah Pinkney from Augusta, Georgia							
* 1	Dunkie Butt (Please Please Please)		0	1994	2 8	1994	(Danzalot 75373)
Twenty 4 Seven Hits Are Credited To Twenty 4 Seven Featuring Captain Hollywood Project							
1	I Can't Stand It	(Bcm Bcmr 395)	7	1990	0	1990	
2	Are You Dreaming	(Bcm Bcmr	17	1990	0	1990	
Twenty Fingers (Featuring) Gillette Mixed Vocal/Instrumental Group, Charles Babie, Manfred Modr And Female Rapper Sandra Gillette From the USA							
* 1		Short Dick Man (MultiplyCdmult 12)	21	1994	14	1994	(Sos/Zoo 14194)
* 2	Short Short Man (Re-Mix)	(Multiply Cdmulty 7)	11	1995	14	1994	(Sos/Zoo 14194)
3	Lick It	(Zyx Zyx 75908)	48	1995	0	1995	
	HITS 1-2 ARE CREDITED TO 20 FINGERS FEATURING GILLETTE • HIT 3 IS CREDITED TO 20 FINGERS FEATURING ROULA						
Twice As Much Male Vocal Duo from the UK							
1	Sittin' On A Fence	(Immediate Im033)	25	1966	0	1966	
Twiggy Female Actress/Vocalist from the UK							
1	Here I Go Again	(Mercury 6007 100)	17	1976	0	1976	
Twin Hype Male Rap Duo from the USA							
1	Do It To The Crowd	(Profile Prof255)	65	1989	0	1989	
Twinkle Female Vocalist from the UK							
1	Terry	(Decca F 12013)	4	1964	0	1964	
2	Golden Lights	(Decca F 12076)	21	1965	0	1965	
Twisted Sister Male Vocal/Instrumental Group from the USA, Lead Singer Is Dee Snider B: 15 Mar 1955 New York							
1	I Am (I'm Me)	(Atlantic A 9854)	18	1983	0	1983	
2	The Kids Are Back	(Atlantic A 9827)	32	1983	0	1983	
3	You Can't Stop Rock N' Roll	(Atlantic A 9792)	43	1983	0	1983	
4	We're Not Gonna Take It	(Atlantic A 9657)	58	1984	21	1984	(Atlantic 89641)
5	Leader Of The Pack	(Atlantic A 9478)	47	1986	0	1986	
2 Bad Mice Male Production/Instrumental Group from the UK							
1	Hold It Down	(Moving Shadow Shadow 14)	70	1992	0	1992	
2	Hold It Down (Re-Entry)	(Moving Shadow Shadow 14)	48	19920			
3	Bombscare	(Arista 74321397662)	46	1996	0	1996	
Two Cowboys Male Production/Instr6mental Duo From Italy							
1	Everybody Gonfi-Gon	(3 Beat Tabcd221)	7	1994	0	1994	
2 For Joy Male Production/Instrumental Duo from the UK							
1	In A State	(Mercury Mer 333)	61	1990	0	1990	
2	Let The Bass Kick	(All Around The World Globe 102)	67	1991	0	1991	
2 Funky 2 Starring Katherine Dion Mixed Vocal/Instrumental Group from the UK							
1	Brothers And Sisters	(Logic 74321170772)	56	1993	0	1993	
2	Brothers And Sisters (Re-Mix)	(Around The World Cdglobe 138)	36	1996	0	1996	
2 House Male Production/Instrumental Duo from the USA, Names Rafael Vargas & Roger Pauletts							
1	Go Techno	(Atlantic A 7519)	65	1992	0	1992	
2 In A Room Male Vocal Duo from the USA							
1	Somebody In The House Say Yeah!	(Big Life Blr 12)	66	1989	0	1989	
* 2	Wiggle It	(Sbk Sbk 19)	3	1991	15	1990	(Cutting 98887)
3	She's Got Me Going Crazy	(Sbk Sbk 23)	54	1991	0	1991	
4	El Trago (The Drink)	(Positiva Cdtiv 18)	34	1994	0	1994	
5	Ahora Es (Now Is The Time)	(Positiva Cdtiv 32)	43	1995	0	1995	
6	Giddy-Up	(Encore Cdcor 008)	74	1996	0	1996	
2 In A Tank							
1	Boogie Woogie Bugle Boy	Fusion Aldcd1	48	1995	0	1995	
2 In A Tent Male Production/Instrumental Duo from the UK							
1	When I'm Cleaning Windows (Turned Out Nice Again)	(Love This Sponcd 1)	25	1994	0	1994	
2	Boogie Woogie Bugle Boy (Don't Stop)	(Bald Cat Baldcd 1)	48	1995	0	1995	
3	When I'm Cleaning Windows (Turned Out Nice Again) (Re-Entry)	(Love This Sponcd 1)	62	1996	0	1996	
* 3	Dear Mama		0	1995	9	1995	(Interscope 98273)
4	Old School		0	1995	9	1995	(Interscope 98273)
	HIT 1 HAS VOCALS FROM GEORGE FORMBY • HIT 2 IS CREDITED TO 2 IN A TANK						
2 Live Crew Rap Quartet From Miami							
1	Me So Horny		0	1989	26	1989	(Skyywalker 130)
2	Banned In The USA		0	1990	20	1990	(Lluke98915)

ISSUE	TITLE	UK LBL	UK POS	UK YEAR	US POS	US YEAR	US LBL
3	Shake A Lil' Something	0	1996	72	1996	(Lil' Joe 890)	
	HIT 3 IS CREDITED TO LUKE FEATURING 2 LIVE CREW						

2 Mad   Male Vocal/Instrumental Duo from the UK

1	Thinking About Your Body	(Big Life Blr 37)	43	1991	0	1991	

Two Man Sound   Male Vocal/Instrumental Group From Belgium

1	Que Tal America	(Miracle M 1)	46	1979	0	1979	

Two Men, A Drum Machine And A Trumpet   Male Instrumental Duo from the UK

1	I'm Tired Of Getting The Push Around	(London Lon141)	18	1988	0	1988	
2	Heat It Up	(Jive Jive 174)	21	1988	0	1988	
	HIT 2 IS CREDITED TO WEE PAPA GIRL RAPPERS • FEATURING TWO MEN AND A DRUM MACHINE						

Two Nations   Male Vocal/Instrumental Group from the UK

1	That's The Way It Feels	(10 Ten 168)	74	1987	0	1987	

2pac

* 1	I Get Around		0	1993	11	1993	(Interscope 98372)
* 2	Keep Ya Head Up		0	1993	12	1993	(Interscope 98345)
3	California Love	(Island Drwcd 3)	6	1996	6	1996	(Interscope 00000)
* 4	How Do U Want It?	(Island 228546532)	17	1996	1	1996	(Interscope 864652)
5	I Ain't Mad At Cha	(Death Row/Island Drwcd 5)	13	1996	0	1996	
6	Runnin'		0	1997	84	1997	(Solar 70134)
7	Wanted Dead Or Alive	(Def Jam 5744052)	16	1997	0	1997	
8	Runnin' (Re-Entry)		0	1997	81	1997	(Solar 70134)
9	Stop The Gunfight		0	1997	77	1997	(Intersound 9269)

Two People   Male Vocal/Instrumental Group from the UK

1	Heaven	(Polydor Posp844)	63	1987	0	1987	

2wo Third3   Male Vocal/Instrumental Group from the UK

1	Hear Me Calling	(Epic 6600642)	48	1994	0	1994	
2	Ease The Pressure	(Epic 6604782)	45	1994	0	1994	
3	I Want The World	(Epic 6608542)	20	1994	0	1994	
4	I Want To Be Alone	(Epic 6610852)	29	1994	0	1994	

2 Unlimited   Mixed Vocal Duo, Anita Dells B: 25 Dec 1971 & Ray Slijngaard B: 28 Jun 1971 From Amsterdam.

1	Get Ready For This	(PWL Continental PWL 206)	2	1991	0	1991	
2	Twilight Zone	(PWL Continental PWL 211)	2	1992	0	1992	
3	Workaholic	(PWL Continental PWL 228)	4	1992	0	1992	
4	The Magic Friend	(PWL Continental PWL 240)	11	1992	0	1992	
5	No Limit	(PWL Continental Pwcd 256)	1	1993	0	1993	
6	Tribal Dance	(PWL Continental Pwcd 262)	4	1993	0	1993	
7	Faces	(PWL Continental Pwcd 268)	8	1993	0	1993	
8	Maximum Overdrive	(PWL Continental Pwcd 276)	15	1993	0	1993	
9	Let The Beat Control Your Body	(PWL Continental Pwcd 280)	6	1994	0	1994	
10	The Real Thing	(PWL Continental Pwcd 306)	6	1994	0	1994	
11	No One	(PWL Continental Pwcd 306)	17	1994	0	1994	
12	Her I Go	(PWL Continental Pwcd 317)	22	1995	0	1995	
13	Get Ready For This		0	19953	8	1995	(Radikal/Crtq. 15535)
14	Do What's Good For Me	(PWL Continental PWL 322cd1)	16	1995	0	1995	

Two-Ton Baker   Male Band Leader, Real Name Dick Baker from the USA

1	Near You		0	1947	12	1947	(Mercury 5066)
2	I'm A Lonely Little Petunia (In A Onion Patch)		0	1947	21	1947	(Mercury 5066)
	HITS 1 AND 2 ARE CREDITED TO TWO-TON BAKER & HIS MUSIC MAKERS						

Tycoon   Lead Singer With The Sextet was Norman Mershon

1	Such A Woman		0	1979	26	1979	(Arista 0398)

Tygers Of Pan Tang   Male Vocal/Instrumental Group from the UK

1	Hellbound	(MCA 672)	48	1981	0	1981	
2	Love Potion No 9	(MCA 769)	45	1982	0	1982	
3	Rendezvous	(MCA 777)	49	1982	0	1982	
4	Paris By Air	(MCA 790)	63	1982	0	1982	

Tyler Collins   Female R&B Singer, B: Harlem.

1	Girls Nite Out		0	1990	6	1990	(RCA 2630)

Tyme   All-Male Soul Group until the arrival of Gonzalez & Moore from the USA.

* 1	So Much In Love	(CameoParkway P 871)	21	1963	1	1963	(Cameo Parkway 871)
2	Wonderful! Wonderful!		0	1963	7	1963	(Cameo Parkway 884)
3	Somewhere		0	1964	19	1964	(Cameo Parkway 891)
4	People	(Direction 583903)	16	1969	39	1969	(Columbia 44630)

T

666

ISSUE	TITLE	UK LBL	UK POS	UK YEAR	US POS	US YEAR	US LBL
5	You Little Trustmaker	(RCA 2456)	18	1974	12	1974	(RCA 10022)
6	Ms Grace	(RCA 2493)	1	1974	0	1974	
7	God's Gonna Punish You	(RCA 2626)	41	1976	0	1976	

DONALD BANKS, AL BERRY, NORMAN BURNETT, GEORGE HILLIARD & GEORGE WILLIAMS • TERRI GONZALEZ & MELANIE MOORE REPLACED HILLARD & BERRY

Typically Tropical Male Vocal/Instrumental Duo from the UK

1	Barbados	(Gull Guls 14)	1	1975	0	1975	

Tyree Male Producer from the USA

1	Turn Up The Bass	(Ffrr Ffr 24)	12	1989	0	1989	
2	Hardcore Hip House	(Dj International Djin 11)	70	1989	0	1989	
3	Move Your Body	(Cbs 655470 7)	72	1989	0	1989	

HIT 1 IS CREDITED TO TYREE FEATURING KOOL ROCK STEADY • HIT 3 FEATURES J.M.D.

Tyrone Brunson Male Instrumentalist from the USA

1	The Smurf	52	1982	0	1982		

Tyrone Davis B: 4 May 1938 Greenville, Mississippi

*	1	Can I Change My Mind		0	1969	5	1969	(Dakar 602)
	2	Is It Something You've Got		0	1969	34	1969	(Dakar 605)
*	3	Turn Back The Hands Of Time		0	1970	3	1970	(Dakar 616)
+	4	I'll Be Right There		0	1970	8	1970	(Dakar 618)
+	5	Could I Forget You		0	1971	10	1971	(Dakar 623)
	6	There It Is		0	1973	32	1973	(Dajar 4523)
	7	Give It Up (Turn It Loose)		0	1976	38	1976	(Columbia 10388)

Tyrrel Corporation Male Vocal/Instrumental Duo from the UK

1	The Bottle	(Volante Tyr 1)	71	1992	0	1992	
2	Going Home	(Volante Tyr 2)	58	1992	0	1992	
3	Walking With A Stranger / One Day	(Volante Tyr 3)	59	1992	0	1992	
4	You're Not Here	(CooltempoCdcool 292)	42	1994	0	1994	
5	Better Days Ahead	(CooltempoCdcool 303)	29	1995	0	1995	

Tzant Mixed Vocal/Instrumental Duo from the UK

1	Hot And Wet (Believe It)	(Logic74321376832)	36	1996	0	1996	

U

ISSUE	TITLE	UK LBL	UK POS	UK YEAR	US POS	US YEAR	US LBL
U.K. Male Vocal/Instrumental Group from Canada/Spain							
1	Nothing To Lose	(Polydor Posp 55)	67	1979	0	1979	
2	Small Town Boy	(Media Mcstd 40049)	74	1996	0	1996	
U.K. Apachi With Shy FX Male Vocal/Instrumental Duo From The UK							
1	Original Nuttah	(Sound Of Underground Sour 008cd)	39	1994	0	1994	
U-Krew Lead Singer With The Rap Quintet Is Kevin Morse							
1	If U Were Mine		0	1990	24	1990	(Enigma 75051)
	ORIGINALLY FORMED AS THE UNTOUCHABLE KREW IN 1984						
U.K. Mixmasters Male Producer, Real Name Nigel Wright from the UK							
1	The Night Fever Megamix	(Iq Zb 44339)	23	1991	0	1991	
2	Lucky 7 Megamix	(Iq Zb 44731)	43	1991	0	1991	
3	Bare Necessities Megamix	(Connect Zb 35135)	14	1991	0	1991	
U.K. Players Male Vocal/Instrumental Group from the UK							
1	Love's Gonna Get You	(RCA 326)	52	1983	0	1983	
U.K. Subs Male Vocal/Instrumental Group From The UK							
1	Stranglehold	(Gem Gems 5)	26	1979	0	1979	
2	Tomorrow's Girls	(Gem Gems 10)	28	1979	0	1979	
3	She's Not There / Kicks (EP)	(Gem Gems 14)	36	1979	0	1979	
	U.K. Subs						
4	Warhead	(Gem Gems 23)	30	1980	0	1980	
5	Teenage	(Gem Gems 30)	32	1980	0	1980	
6	Party In Paris	(Gem Gems 42)	37	1980	0	1980	
7	Keep On Runnin' (Till You Burn)	(Gem Gems 45)	41	1981	0	1981	
U.S. Bonds See Gary U.S. Bonds							
U2 Male Vocal/Instrumental Group from Ireland							
1	Fire	(Island Wip 6679)	35	1981	0	1981	
2	Gloria	(Island Wip 6733)	55	1981	0	1981	
3	A Celebration	(Island Wip 6770)	47	1982	0	1982	
4	New Year's Day	(Island Uwip 6848)	10	1983	0	1983	
5	Two Hearts Beat As One	(Island IS 109)	18	1983	0	1983	
6	Pride (In The Name Of Love)	(Island IS 202)	3	1984	33	1984	(Island 99704)
7	The Unforgetable Fire	(Island IS 220)	6	1985	0	1985	
8	With Or Without You	(Island IS 319)	4	1987	1	1987	(Island 99469)
9	I Still Haven't Found What I'm Looking For	(Island IS 328)	6	1987	1	1987	(Island 99430)
10	Where The Streets Have No Name	(Island Is 340)	4	1987	13	1987	(Island 99408)
11	In God's Country	(Island 7-99385)	48	1987	0	1987	
12	Desire	(Island Is 400)	1	1988	3 *	1988	(Island 99250)
13	Angel Of Harlem	(Island IS 402)	9	1988	14	1989	(Island 99254)
14	When Love Comes To Town	(Island IS 411)	6	1989	0	1989	
15	All I Want Is You	(Island IS 422)	4	1989	0	1989	
16	The Fly	(Island Is 500)	1	1991	0	1991	
17	Mysterious Ways	(Island IS 509)	13	1991	9	1990	(Island 866188)
18	The Fly (Re-Entry)	(Island IS 500)	62	1992	0	1992	
19	One	(Island IS 515)	7	1992	10	1992	(Island 866533)
20	Even Better Than The Real Thing	(Island Is 525)	12	1992	32	1992	(Island 866977)
21	Even Better Than The Real Thing (Re-Mix)	(Island Real U2)	8	1992	0	1992	
22	Who's Gonna Ride The Wild Horses	(Island Is 550)	14	1992	35	1992	(Island 864521)
23	Stay (Faraway, So Close) / I've Got You Under My Skin	(Island Cid 578)	4	1993	0	1993	

ISSUE	TITLE	UK LBL	UK POS	UK YEAR	US POS	US YEAR	US LBL
24	Hold Me, Thrill Me, Kiss Me, Kill Me	(Island A 7131cd)	2	1995	16	1995	(Island 87131)
25	Discotheque	(Island Cid 649)	1	1997	10	1997	(Island 854774)
26	Staring At The Sun	(Island Cid 658)	3	1997	26	1997	(Island 854972)
27	Discotheque (Re-Entry)	(Island Cid 649)	72	1997	0	1997	
28	Last Night On Earth	(Island Cid 664)	10	1997	0	1997	
29	Last Night On Earth (re-entry)	(Island Cid 664)	68	1997	0	1997	

NAMES: PAUL HEWSON, ADAM CLAYTON, DAVE EVANS & LARRY MULLEN JR.
HIT 23'S FLIP SIDE IS CREDITED TO FRANK SINATRA WITH BONO BUT NOT ALL DISCS HAD THIS FORMAT.
HIT 14 IS CREDITED TO U2 FEATURING B.B. KING SEE ALSO "B.B. KING

U96 Male Producer, Real Name Alex Christiansen from Germany

1	Das Boot	(M&G Mags 28)	18	1992	0	1992	
2	Inside Your Dreams	(Logic 74321209722)	44	1994	0	1994	
3	Club Bizarre	(Urban 5750152)	70	1996	0	1996	

U4EA See New Atlantic

UB40 Male Vocal/Instrumental Group from the UK

	ISSUE	TITLE	UK LBL	UK POS	UK YEAR	US POS	US YEAR	US LBL
	1	King / Food For Thought	(Graduate Grad 6)	4	1980	0	1980	
	2	My Way Of Thinking / I Think It's Going To Rain	(Graduate Grad 8)	6	1980	0	1980	
	3	The Earth Dies Screaming / Dream A Lie	(Graduate Grad 10)	10	1980	0	1980	
	4	Don't Let It Pass You / Don't Slow Down	(Dep International Dep 1)	16	1981	0	1981	
	5	One In Ten	(Dep International Dep 2)	7	1981	0	1981	
	6	I Won't Close My Eyes	(Dep International Dep 3)	32	1982	0	1982	
	7	Love Is All Is All Right	(Dep International Dep 4)	29	1982	0	1982	
	8	So Here I Am	(Dep International Dep 5)	25	1982	0	1982	
	9	I've Got Mine	(Dep International 7 Dep 6)	45	1983	0	1983	
*	10	Red Red Wine	(Dep International 7 Dep 7)	1	1983	34	1984	(A&M 2600)
	11	Please Don't Make Me Cry	(Dep International 7 Dep 8)	10	1983	0	1983	
	12	Many Rivers To Cross	(Dep International 7 Dep 9)	16	1983	0	1983	
	13	Cherry Oh Baby	(Dep International Dep 10)	12	1984	0	1984	
	14	If It Happens Again	(Dep International Dep 11)	9	1984	0	1984	
	15	Riddle Me	(Dep International Dep 15)	59	1984	0	1984	
	16	I Got You Babe	(Dep International Dep 20)	1	1985	28	1985(A&M 2758)	
	17	Don't Break My Heart	(Dep International Dep 22)	3	1985	0	1985	
	18	Sing Our Own Song	(Dep International Dep 23)	5	1986	0	1986	
	19	All I Want To Do	(Dep International Dep 24)	41	1986	0	1986	
	20	Rat In Mi Kitchen	(Dep International Dep 25)	12	1987	0	1987	
	21	Watchdogs	(Dep International Dep 26)	39	1987	0	1987	
	22	Maybe Tomorrow	(Dep International Dep 27)	14	1987	0	1987	
	23	Reckless	(EMI Em 41)	17	1988	0	1988	
	24	Breakfast In Bed	(Dep International Dep 29)	6	1988	0		1988
	25	Where Did I Go Wrong	(Dep International Dep 30)	26	1988	0	1988	
	26	Red Red Wine (Re-Issue)		0	1988	1	1988	(A&M 1244)
	27	I Would Do For You	(Dep International Dep 32)	45	1989	0	1989	
	28	Homely Girl	(Dcp International Dep 33)	6	1989	0	1989	
	29	Here I Am (Come And Take Me)	(Dep International Dep 34)	46	1990	7	1991	(Virgin 99141)
	30	Kingston Town	(Dep International Dep 35)	4	1990	0	1990	
	31	Wear You To The Ball	(Dep International Dep 36)	35	1990	0	1990	
	32	I'll Be Your Baby Tonight	(EMI Em 167) 6 1990	0	1990			
*	33	The Way You Do The Things You Do	(Dep International Dep 38)	49	1991	6	1990	(Virgin 98978)
	34	Impossible Love	(Dep International Dep 37)	47	1990	0	1990	
	35	One In Ten	(Ztt Zang 39)	17	1992	0	1992	
*	36	(I Can't Help) Falling In Love	(Dep International Depdg 40)	1	1993	1	1991	(Virgin 12653)
	37	Higher Ground	(Dep International Depd 41)	8	1993	0	1993	
	38	Bring Me Your Cup	(Dep International Depd 42)	24	1993	0	1993	
	39	C'est La Vie	(Dep International Depd 43)	37	1994	0	1994	
	40	Reggae Music	(Dep International Depdg 44)	28	1994	0	1994	
	41	Until My Dying Day	(Dep International Depdx 45)	15	1995	0	1995	
	42	Tell Me Is It True	(Dep International Depd 48)	14	1997	0	1997	

HITS 16, 24 ARE CREDITED TO UB40 FEATURING CHRISSIE HYNDE • HIT 23 IS CREDITED TO AFRIKA BAMBAATTA WITH UB40 & FAMILY
HIT 32 IS CREDITED TO ROBERT PALMERAND UB40 • HIT 35 IS CREDITED TO 808 STATE VS UB40
LEAD SINGER WITH THE OCTET IS ALI CAMPBELL B: 15 FEB 1959 BIRMINGHAM, ENGLAND.
THEIR NAME IS TAKEN FROM THE DHSS UNEMPLOYMENT BENEFIT FORM

UCC See Urban Cookie Collective

ISSUE	TITLE	UK LBL	UK POS	UK YEAR	US POS	US YEAR	US LBL

Udo Jurgens B: 30 Sep 1934, Klagenfurt, Austria

| * | 1 | Merci Cherie | | 0 | 1966 | 0 | 1966 | |
| | | THE ENGLISH TITLE 'WALK AWAY' WAS A HIT FOR MATT MONRO IN 1964 | | | | | | |

UFO Male Vocal/Instrumental Group from the UK

	1	Only You Can Rock Me	(Chrysalis Chs 2241)	50	1978	0	1978	
	2	Doctor Doctor	(Chrysalis Chs 2287)	35	1979	0	1979	
	3	Shoot Shoot	(Chrysalis Chs 2318)	48	1979	0	1979	
	4	Young Blood	(Chrysalis Chs 2399)	36	1980	0	1980	
	5	Lonely Heart	(Chrysalis Chs 2482)	41	1981	0	1981	
	6	Let It Rain	(Chrysalis Chs 2576)	62	1982	0	1982	
	7	When It's Time To Rock	(Chrysalis Chs 2672)	70	1983	0	1983	

Ugly Kid Joe Male Rock Band From California, Lead Vocals From "Whitfield Crane"

	1	Everything About You	(Mercury Mer 367)	3	1992	9	1992	(Mercury 866632)
	2	Neighbor	(Mercury Mer 374)	28	1992	0	1992	
	3	So Damn Cool	(Mercury Mer 383)	44	1997	0	1997	
	4	Cat's In The Cradle	(Mercury Mercd 385)	7	1993	6 *	1993	(Stardog 864888)
	5	Busy Bee	(Mercury Mercd 389)	39	1993	0	1993	
	6	Milkman's Son	(Mercury Mercd 435)	39	1995	0	1995	

UHF Male Production/Instrumental Group from the USA

| | 1 | UHF/ Everything | (XI Xls 25) | 46 | 1991 | 0 | 1991 | |

Ultimate Kaos Male Vocal Group From The UK

	1	Some Girls	(Wild Card Cardd 12)	9	1994	0	1994	
	2	Some Girls (Re-Entry)	(Wild Card Cardd 12)	67	1996	0	1996	
	3	Hoochie Booty	(Wild Card Cardd 14)	17	1995	0	1995	
	4	Show A Little Love	(Wild Card Cardw 18)	23	1995	0	1995	
	5	Right Here	(Wild Card 5795832)	18	1995	0	1995	
	6	Casanova	(Polydor 5759312)	24	1997	0	1997	

Ultra High Male Vocalist Michael McCloud from the UK

| | 1 | Stay With Me | (MCA Mcstd 40007) | 36 | 1995 | 0 | 1995 | |
| | 2 | Are You Ready For Love | (MCA Mcstd 40039) | 45 | 1996 | 0 | 1996 | |

Ultracynic

| | 2 | Nothing Is Forever (Re-Mix) | (All Around The World Cdglobe 139) | 47 | 1997 | 0 | 1997 | |

Ultra Nate Female Vocalist From The USA

	1	It's Over Now	(Eternal Yz 440)	62	1989	0	1989	
	2	Is It Love	(Eternal Yz 509)	71	1991	0	1991	
	3	Show Me	(Warner Bros W 0219cd)	62	1994	0	1994	
	4	Free	(Am:Pm 5822432)	4	1997	0	1997	

Ultra-Sonic Male Production/Instrumental Duo from the UK

| | 1 | Obsession | (Clubscene Dcsrt 027) | 75 | 1994 | 0 | 1994 | |
| | 2 | Do You Believe In Love | (Clunscene Dcsrt 070) | 47 | 1996 | 0 | 1996 | |

Ultracynic Mixed Vocal/Instrumental Group From The UK

| | 1 | Nothing Is Forever | (380 Pew 2) | 50 | 1992 | 0 | 1992 | |

Ultramarine Male Instrumental Duo from the UK

	1	Kingdom	(Blanco Y Negro Neg 65cd)	46	1993	0	1993	
	2	Barefoot (Ep)	(Blanco Y Negro Neg 67cd)	61	1994	0	1994	
	3	Hymn	(Blanco Y Negro Neg 87cd)	65	1996	0	1996	
		HIT 3 IS CREDITED TO ULTRAMARINE FEATURING DAVID MCALMONT						

Ultravox Male Vocal/Instrumental Group From The UK/Canada

	1	Sleepwalk	(Chrysalis Chs 2441)	29	1980	0	1980	
	2	Passing Strangers	(Chrysalis Chs 2457)	57	1980	0	1980	
	3	Vienna	(Chrysalis Chs 2481)	2	1981	0	1981	
	4	Slow Motion	(Island Wip 6691)	33	1981	0	1981	
	5	All Stood Still	(Chrysalis Chs 2522)	8	1981	0	1981	
	6	The Thin Wall	(Chrysalis Chs 2540)	14	1981	0	1981	
	7	The Voice	(Chrysalis Chs 2559)	16	1981	0	1981	
	8	Reap The Wild Wind	(Chrysalis Chs 2639)	12	1982	0	1982	
	9	Hymn	(Chrysalis Chs 2657)	11	1982	0	1982	
	10	Visions In Blue	(Chrysalis Chs 2676)	15	1983	0	1983	
	11	We Came To Dance	(Chrysalis Vox 1)	18	1983	0	1983	
	12	One Small Day	(Chrysalis Vox 2)	27	1984	0	1984	

ISSUE	TITLE	UK LBL	UK POS	UK YEAR	US POS	US YEAR	US LBL
13	Dancing With Tears In My Eyes	(Chrysalis Uv 1)	3	1984	0	1984	
14	Lament	(Chrysalis Uv 2)	22	1984	0	1984	
15	Dancing With Tears In My Eyes (Re-Entry)	(Chrysalis Uv 1)	74	1984	0	1984	
16	Lament (Re-Entry)	(Chrysalis Uv 2)	73	1984	0	1984	
17	Love's Great Adventure	(Chrysalis Uv 3)	12	1984	0	1984	
18	Same Old Story	(Chrysalis Uv 4)	31	1986	0	1986	
19	All Fall Down	(Chrysalis Uv 5)	30	1986	0	1986	
20	Vienna (Re-Issue)	(Chrysalis Cdchss 3936)	13	1993	0	1993	

Umberto Bindi Male Vocalist From Italy

1	Il Nostro Concerto	(Oriole Cb 1577)	47	1960	0	1960	

Umboza Male Instrumental/Production Duo from the UK

1	Cry India	(Positiva Cdtiv 43)	19	1995	0	1995	
2	Sunshine	(Positiva Cdtiv 47)	14	1996	0	1996	

Una Mae Carlisle Female Pianist/Vocalist from the USA

1	Walking By The River		0	1941	14	1941	(Bluebird 11033)

OBITUARY: D: 1956, (AGED 37).

Unation Mixed Vocal/Instrumental Group from the UK

1	Higher And Higher	(MCA Mcstd 1773)	42	1993	0	1993	
2	Do You Believe In Love	(MCA Mcstd 1976)	75	1993	0	1993	

Uncanny Alliance Mixed Vocal/Instrumental Duo Ffrom the USA

1	I Got My Education	(A&M Am 0128)	39	1992	0	1992	

Undercover Male Vocal/Instrumental Group From The UK

1	Baker Street	(Pwl International Pwl 239)	2	1992	0	1992	
2	Never Let Her Slip Away	(Pwl International Pwl 255)	5	1992	0	1992	
3	I Wanna Stay With You	(Pwl International Pwl 258)	28	1993	0	1993	
4	Lovesick	(Pwl International Pwl 271)	62	1993	0	1993	

HIT 4 IS CREDITED TO UNDERCOVER FEATURING JOHN MATTHEWS

Underground Sunshine Names Jane Little, Chris Connors With Frank & Betty Kohl

1	Birthday		0	1969	26	1969	(Intrepid 75002)

Undertakers Male Vocal/Instrumental Group from the UK

1	Just A Little Bit	(Pye 7n 15607)	49	1964	0	1964	

Undertones Male Vocal/Instrumental Group from the UK

1	Teenage Kicks	(Sire Sir 4007)	31	1978	0	1978	
2	Get Over You	(Sire Sir 4010)	57	1979	0	1979	
3	Jimmy Jimmy	(Sire Sir 4015)	16	1979	0	1979	
4	Here Comes The Summer	(Sire Sir 4022)	34	1979	0	1979	
5	You've Got My Number (Why Don't You Use It?)	(Sire Sir 4024)	32	1979	0	1979	
6	My Perfect Cousin	(Sire Sir 4038)	9	1980	0	1980	
7	Wednesday Week	(Sire Sir 4042)	11	1980	0	1980	
8	It's Going To Happen!	(Ardeck Aros 8)	18	1981	0	1981	
9	Julie Ocean	(Ardeck Ards 9)	41	1981	0	1981	
10	Teenage Kicks (Re-Issue)	(Ardeck Ards 1)	60	1983	0	1983	

Underworld Male Vocal/Instrumental Group from the UK

1	Spikee / Dogman Go	(Junior Boy's Own Jbo 17cd)	63	1993	0	1993	
2	Dark And Long	(Junior Boy's Own Jbo 19cds)	57	1994	0	1994	
3	Born Slippy	(Junior Boy's Own Jbo 29cd)	52	1995	0	1995	
4	Pearl's Girl	(Junior Boy's Own Jbo 38cds1)	24	1996	0	1996	
5	Born Slippy (Re-Mix)	(Junior Boy's Own Jbo 44cds)	2	1996	0	1996	
6	Pearl's Girl (Re-Entry)	(Junior Boy's Own Jbo 45cds1)	22	1996	0	1996	
7	Born Slippy (Re-Mix) (Re-Entry)	(Junior Boy's Own Jbo 44cds)	74	1996	0	1996	

Undisputed Truth Mixed Vocal/Instrumental Group From The USA

1	Smiling Faces Sometimes		0	1971	3	1971	(Gordy 7108)
+ 2	You Make Your Own Heaven And Hell Right Here On Earth		0	1971	24	1971	(Gordy 7112)
3	You + Me = Love	(Warner Bros K 16804)	43	1977	0	1977	

ORIGINAL LINE-UP WAS JOE HARRIS, BRENDA EVANS & BILLIE CALVIN • THERE HAVE BEEN MANY CHANGES AFTER THEIR '71 HITS

Unifics Soul Group Formed In Howard University In Washington D.C.

1	Court Of Love		0	1968	25	1968	(Kapp 935)
2	The Beginning Of My End		0	1969	36	1969	(Kapp 957)

LEAD SINGER WITH THE SOUL GROUP IS AL JOHNSON • OBITUARY: HAL WORTHINGTON D: 20 FEB 1990, MURDERED (SHOT).

Union Male Instrumental Group from Holland with Rugby Team Vocalists from the UK

1	Swing Low (Run With The Ball)	(Columbia 6575317)	16	1991	0	1991	

1HIT IS CREDITED TO UNION" FEATURING THE "ENGLAND WORLD CUP SQUAD

ISSUE	TITLE	UK LBL	UK POS	UK YEAR	US POS	US YEAR	US LBL
Union Gap See Gary Puckett"							
Unique Mixed Vocal/Instrumental Group from the USA							
1	What I Got Is What You Need	(Prelude A 3707)	27	1983	0	1983	
Unique 3 Male Rap/Scratch Group from the UK							
1	The Theme	(10 Ten 285)	61	1989	0	1989	
2	Musical Melody / Weight For The Bass	(10 Ten 298)	29	1990	0	1990	
3	Rhythm Takes Control	(10 Ten 327)	41	1990	0	1990	
4	No More	(10 Ten 387)	7419910	1991			
	HIT 3 IS CREDITED TO UNIQUE 3 FEATURING KARIN						
Unit Four Plus 2 Male Vocal/Instrumental Group from the UK							
1	Green Fields	(Decca F 11821)	48	1964	0	1964	
2	Concrete And Clay	(Decca F 12071)	1	1965	28	1965	(London 9751)
3	You've Never Been In Love Like This Before	(Decca F 12144)	14	1965	0	1965	
4	Baby Never Say Goobye	(Decca F 12333)	49	1966	0	1966	
	LEAD SINGER WITH THE SEXTET IS TOMMY MOELLER						
United Kingdom Symphony Orchestra from the UK							
1	Shades (Theme From The "Crown Paint" Television Advert)	(Food For Thought Yum 108)	68	1985	0	1985	
Unitone Rockers (Featuring) Steel Male Vocal/Instrumental Group from the UK							
1	Children Of The Revolution	(The Hit Label Hlc 4)	60	1993	0	1993	
Unity Mixed Vocal/Instrumental Group from the UK							
1	Unity	(Cardiac Cny 6)	64	1991	0	1991	
Universal							
1	Rock Me Good	(London Loncd 397)	19	1997	0	1997	
29	Last Night On Earth (Re-Entry)	(Island Cid 664)	68	1997	0	1997	
Unjustified See 1300 Drums							
Uno Clio (Featuring) Martine McCutcheon							
1	Are You Man Enough	(Avex UK Avexcd 14)	62	1995	0	1995	
Untouchables Male Vocal/Instrumental Group from the USA							
1	Free Yourself	(Stiff Buy 221)	26	1985	0	1985	
2	I Spy For The FBI	(Stiff Buy 227)	59	1985	0	1985	
Unv Soul Vocal Quartet from Detroit							
1	Something's Goin On	0		1993	29	1993	(Maverick 18564)
Upsetters Male Instrumental Group from Jamaica							
1	Return To Django / Dollar In The Teeth	(Upsetter US 301)	5	1969	0	1969	
Upside Down Male Vocal Group from the UK							
1	Change Your Mind	(World Cdworld 1a)	11	1996	0	1996	
2	Every Time I Fall In Love	(World Cdworld 2a)	18	1996	0	1996	
3	Ever Time I Fall In Love (Re-Entry)	(World Cdworld 2a)	71	1996	0	1996	
4	Never Found A Love Like This Before	(World Cdworld 3a)	19	1996	0	1996	
5	If You Leave Me Now	(World Cdworld 4a)	27	1996	0	1996	
Uptown String Band							
1	I'm Looking Over A Four-Leaf Clover	0		1948	11	1948	(Mercury 5100)
	VOCALS ON HIT ARE BY "JOSEPH GIARDINO"						
Up Yer Ronson (Featuring) Mary Pearce Mixed Vocal/Instrumental Group from the UK							
1	Lost In Love	(Hi-Life/Polydor 5795572)	27	1995	0	1995	
2	Are You Gonna Be There?	(Hi-Life/Polydor 5763272)	27	1996	0	1996	
3	I Will Be Released	(Hi-Life/Polydor 5737352)	32	1997	0	1997	
Urban All Stars Mixed Vocal/Instrumental Group from the UK							
1	It Began In Africa	(Urban Urb 23)	64	1988	0	1988	
Urban Blues Project Male Vocal/Instrumental Group from the USA							
1	Love Don't Live	(Am:Pm 5817932)	55	1996	0	1996	
	HIT IS CREDITED TO URBAN BLUES PROJECT FEATURING "MICHAEL PROCTOR						
Urban Cookie Collective Mixed Vocal/Instrumental Group from the UK							
1	The Key The Secret	(Pulse 8 Cdlose 48)	2	1993	0	1993	
2	Feels Like Heaven	(Pulse 8 Cdlose 55)	5	1993	0	1993	
3	Sail Away	(Pulse 8 Cdlose 56)	18	1994	0	1994	
4	High On Happy Vibe	(Pulse 8 Cdlose 60)	31	1994	0	1994	

ISSUE	TITLE	UK LBL	UK POS	UK YEAR	US POS	US YEAR	US LBL
5	Bring It On Home	(Pulse 8 Cdlose 73)	56	1994	0	1994	
6	Spend The Day	(Pilse 8 Cdlose 85)	59	1995	0	1995	
7	Rest Of My Love	(Pulse 8 Cdlose 93)	67	1995	0	1995	
8	So Beautiful	(Pulse 8 Cdlose 100)	68	1995	0	1995	
9	The Key The Secret (Re-Mix)	(Pulse 8 Cdlose 109)	52	1996	0	1996	
	HIT 9 IS CREDITED TO "UCC"						
Urban Dance Squad Rap Group from Holland with Patrick Remington							
	Deeper Shade Of Soul		0	1991	21	1991	(Arista 2026)
Urban Discharge Mixed Vocal/Instrumental Group from the USA							
1	Wanna Drop A House (On That Bitch)	(MCA Mcstd 40020)	51	1996	0	1996	
Male Production/Instrumental Group from the UK							
1	A Trip To Trumpton	(Faze 2 Faze 5)	6	1992	0	1992	
2	The Feeling	(Faze 2 Faze 10)	67	1992	0	1992	
3	Living In A Fantasy	(Faze 2 Cdfaze 13)	57	1993	0	1993	
Urban Shakedown (Featuring) Micky Finn Male Vocal/Instrumental Group from the UK/Italy							
1	Some Justice	(Urban Shakedown Urbst 1)	23	1992	0	1992	
2	(Urban Shakedown Urbst 2)		59	1992	0	1992	
3	Some Justice	(Urban Shakedown Urbst 3)	49	1995	0	1995	
	HIT 3 IS CREDITED TO "URBAN SHAKEDOWN" FEATURING "BO GENERAL"						
Urban Soul Male Producer, Real Name Roland Clarke From The USA							
1	Alright	(Cooltempo Cool 231)	60	1991	0	1991	
2	Alright (Re-Mix)	(Cooltempo Cool 244)	43	1991	0	1991	
3	Always	(Cooltempo Cool 251)	41	1992	0	1992	
Urban Species Male Vocal/Instrumental Group from the UK							
1	Spiritual Love	(Talkin Loud Tlkcd 45)	35	1994	0	1994	
2	Brother	(Talkin Loud Tlkcd 47)	40	1994	0	1994	
3	Listen	(Talkin Loud Tlkcd 50)	47	1994	0	1994	
	HIT 3 IS CREDITED TO URBAN SPECIES FEATURING MC SOLAAR						
Urge Overkill Male Vocal/Instrumental Group from the USA							
1	Sister Havana	(Geffen Gfstd 51)	67	1993	0	1993	
2	Positive Bleeding	(Geffen Gfstd 57)	61	1993	0	1993	
3	Girl You'll Be A Woman Soon	(Mca Mcstd 2024)	37	1994	0	1994	
Uriah Heep Lead Singer With The Hard-Rock Band Is David Byron							
1	Easy Livin'	0	1972	39	1972	(Mercury 73307)	
Urusei Yatsura							
1	Strategic Hamlets	(Che Che 67cd)	64	1997	0	1997	
2	Fake Fur	(Che Che 70cd)	58	1997	0	1997	
USA For Africa Various major artists got together to raise funds for the people of Africa							
* 1	We Are The World	(Cbs Usaid 1)	1	1985	1	1985	(Columbia 04839)
US3 Male Production/Instrumental Duo from the UK							
1	Riddim	(Blue Note Cdcl 686)	34	1993	0	1993	
* 2	Cantaloop	(Blue Note Cdcl 696)	23	1993	9	1994	(Blue Note 44945)
3	I Got It Goin' On	(Blue Note Cdcl 708)	52	1994	0	1994	
4	Come On Everybody (Get Down)	(Blue Note Cdcl 784)	38	1997	0	1997	
	HIT 1 IS CREDITED TO US3 FEATURING TUKKA YOOT						
	HIT 2 IS CREDITED TO US3 FEATURING KOBIE POWELL" & "RAHSAAN"						
Usher Male Vocalist from the USA							
1	Think Of You	(Laface 74321269252)	70	1995	0	1995	
Usura Mixed Vocal/Instrumental Group from Italy							
1	Open Your Mind	(Deconstruction 74321128042)	7	1993	0	1993	
2	Sweat	(Deconstruction 74321154602)	29	1993	0	1993	
Utah Saints Male Production/Instrumental Duo From The UK							
1	What Can You Do For Me	(Ffrr F 164)	10	1991	0	1991	
2	Something Good	(Ffrr F 187)	4	1992	0	1992	
3	Believe In Me	(Ffrr Fcd 209)	8	1993	0	1993	
4	I Want You	(Ffrr Fcd 213)	25	1993	0	1993	
5	I Still Think Of You	(Ffrr Fcd 225)	32	1994	0	1994	
6	Ohio	(Ffrr Fcd 264)	42	1995	0	1995	
Utopia Names Todd Rundgren, Roger Powell, Kasim Sulton & Willie Wilcox							
1	Set Me Free		0	1980	27	1980	(Bearsville 49180)

ISSUE	TITLE	UK LBL	UK POS	UK YEAR	US POS	US YEAR	US LBL
V.I.M.	Male Production/Instrumental Group from the UK						
1	Maggie's Last Party	(F2 Boz 1)	68	1991	0	1991	
V.I.P.S	Male Vocal/Instrumental Group from the UK						
1	The Quarter Moon	(Gem Gems 39)	55	1980	0	1980	
Val Doonican	Male Vocalist From Ireland						
1	Walk Tall	(Decca F 11982)	3	1964	0	1964	
2	The Special Years	(Decca F 12049)	7	1965	0	1965	
3	I'm Gonna Get There Somehow	(Decca F 12118)	25	1965	0	1965	
4	The Special Years (Re-Entry)	(Decca F 12049)	49	1965	0	1965	
5	Elusive Butterfly	(Decca F 12358)	5	1966	0	1966	
6	What Would I Be	(Decca F 12505)	2	1966	0	1966	
7	Memories Are Made Of This	(Decca F 12566)	11	1967	0	1967	
8	Two Streets	(Decca F 12608)	39	1967	0	1967	
9	If The Whole World Stop Loving	(Pye 7n 17396)	3	1967	0	1967	
10	You're The Only One	(Pye 7n 17465)	37	1968	0	1968	
11	Now	(Pye 7n 17534)	43	1968	0	1968	
12	If I Knew Then What I Know Now	(Pye 7n 17616)	4	1968	0	1968	
13	Ring Of Bright Water	(Pye 7n 17713)	48	1969	0	1969	
14	Morning	(Philips 6006 177)	12	1971	0	1971	
15	Heaven Is My Woman's Love	(Philips 6028 031)	34	1973	0	1973	
16	Heaven Is My Woman's Love (Re-Entry)	(Philips 6028 031)	47	1973	0	1973	
Valentine Brothers	Male Vocal Duo from the USA						
1	Money's Too Tight (To Mention)	(Energy Nrg 1)	73	1983	0	1983	
Valentinos							
+ 1	Lookin' For A Love		0	1962	8	1962	(Sar 132)
Valerie Carr	Female Vocalist, B: 1936 New York						
1	When The Boys Talk About The Girls	(Columbia Db 4131)	29	1958	19	1958	(Roulette 4066)
2	When The Boys Talk About The Girls (Re-Entry)	(Columbia Db 4131)	30	1958	0	1958	
Valerie Landsberg	See Kids From *Fame*						
Valjean	Real Name Valjean Johns. B. 19 Nov 1934 Shattuck, Oklahoma						
1	Theme From "Ben Casey"		0	1962	28	1962	(Carlton 573)
Van Halen	Male Vocal/Instrumental Group from the USA/Holland						
1	You Really Got Me		0	1978	36	1978	(Warner Bros 8515)
2	Dance The Night Away		0	1979	15	1979	(Warner Bros 8823)
3	Runnin' With The Devil	(Warner Bros Hm 10)	52	1980	0	1980	
4	(Oh) Pretty Woman		0	1982	12	1982	(Warner Bros 50003)
5	Dancing In The Street		0	1982	38	1982	(Warner Bros 29986)
* 6	Jump	(Warner Bros W 9384)	7	1984	1	1984	(Warner Bros 29384)
7	I'll Wait		85	1984	13	1984	(Warner Bros 29307)
8	Panama	(Warner Bros W 9273)	61	1984	13	1984	(Warner Bros 29250)
9	Why Can't This Be Love	(Warner Bros W 8740)	8	1986	3	1986	(Warner Bros 28740)
10	Dreams	(Warner Bros W 8642)	62	1986	22	1986	(Warner Bros 28702)
11	Love Walks In		0	1986	22	1986	(Warner Bros 28626)
12	Black And Blue		0	1988	34	1988	(Warner Bros 27891)
13	When It's Love	(Warner Bros W 7816)	28	1988	5	1988	(Warner Bros 27827)
14	Finish What Ya Started		0	1988	13	1988	(Warner Bros 27746)
15	Feels So Good	(Warner Bros W 7565)	63	1989	35	1989	(Warner Bros 27565)
16	Poundcake	(Warner Bros W 0045)	74	1991	0	1991	
17	Top Of The World	(Warner Bros W 0066)	63	1991	27	1991	(Warner Bros 19151)

ISSUE	TITLE	UK LBL	UK POS	UK YEAR	US POS	US YEAR	US LBL
18	Jump (Live)	(Warner Bros W 0155cd)	26	1993	0	1993	
19	Can't Stop Lovin' You	(Warner Bros W 0288cd)	0	1995	30	1995	(Warner Bros 17909)
20	Don't Tell Me	(Warner Bros W 0280cd)	27	1995	0	1995	
21	Can't Stop Lovin' You	(Warner Bros W 0288cd)	33	1995	0	1995	

NAMES: EDDIE & ALEX VAN HALEN, DAVID LEE ROTH, MICHAEL ANTHONY"
HIT 4 WAS ORIGINALLY RELEASED AS 'PRETTY WOMAN'

Van McCoy Male Singer/Songwriter/Producer, B: 6 Jan 1944 Washington D.C.

ISSUE	TITLE	UK LBL	UK POS	UK YEAR	US POS	US YEAR	US LBL
* 1	The Hustle	(Avco 6105 038)	3	1975	1	1975	(Avco 4653)
2	Change With The Times	(Avco 6105 042)	36	1975	0	1975	
3	Soul Cha Cha	(H&L 6105 065)	34	1977	0	1977	
4	The Shuffle	(H&L 6105 076)	4	1977	0	1977	

HIT 1 IS CREDITED TO VAN MCCOY WITH THE SOUL CITY SYMPHONY
OBITUARY: D: 6 JUL 1979 HEART ATTACK.

Van Morrison Male Vocalist, Real Name George Ivan. B: 31 Aug 1945 Belfast, Northern Ireland

ISSUE	TITLE	UK LBL	UK POS	UK YEAR	US POS	US YEAR	US LBL
1	Brown-Eyed Girl		0	1967	10	1967	(Bang 545)
2	Come Running		0	1970	39	1970	(Warner Bros 7383)
3	Domino		0	1970	9	1970	(Warner Bros 7434)
4	Blue Money		0	1971	23	1971	(Warner Bros 7462)
5	Wild Night		0	1971	28	1971	(Warner Bros 7518)
6	Tupelo Honey		0	1972	47	1972	(Warner Bros 7543)
7	Bright Side Of The Road	(Mercury 6001 121)	63	1979	0	1979	
8	Have I Told You Lately	(Polydor Vans 1)	74	1989	0	1989	
9	Whenever God Shines His Light	(Polydor Vans 2)	20	1989	0	1989	
10	Gloria	(Polydor Vancd 11)	31	1993	0	1993	
11	Have I Told You Lately (That I Love You)	(Rca 74321271702)	71	1995	0	1995	
12	Days Like This	(Exile Vancd 12)	65	1995	0	1995	
13	No Religion	(Exile 5775792)	54	1995	0	1995	
14	The Healing Game	(Exile 5733912)	46	1997	0	1997	

HIT 9 IS CREDITED TO VAN MORRISONAND CLIFF RICHARD   HIT 10 IS CREDITED TO VAN MORRISON AND JOHN LEE HOOKER
HIT 11 IS CREDITED TO CHIEFTANS WITH VAN MORRISON

Van Stephenson Singer/Sonwriter from Nashville

ISSUE	TITLE	UK LBL	UK POS	UK YEAR	US POS	US YEAR	US LBL
1	Modern Day Delilah	0		1984	22	1984	(Mcs 52376)

Van Twist Mixed Vocal/Instrumental Group from Belgium/Zaire

ISSUE	TITLE	UK LBL	UK POS	UK YEAR	US POS	US YEAR	US LBL
1	Shaft	(Polydor Posp 729)	57	1985	0	1985	

Vandenberg Names Adrian Vandenberg, Bert Heerink, Dick Kemper & Jos Zoomer

ISSUE	TITLE	UK LBL	UK POS	UK YEAR	US POS	US YEAR	US LBL
1	Burning Heart	0		1983	39	1983	(Atco 99947)

ADRIAN JOINED WHITESNAKE IN 1989

Vanessa-Mae

ISSUE	TITLE	UK LBL	UK POS	UK YEAR	US POS	US YEAR	US LBL
1	Toccata And Fugue	(EMIClassics Mae 8816812)	16	1995	0	1995	
2	Red Hot	(EMICdmae 2)	37	1995	0	1995	
3	Classical Gas	(EMI/Premier Cdem 404)	41	1995	0	1995	
4	I'm A Doun For Lack O'Johnnie	(Emi Premier Cdmae 3)	28	1996	0	1996	

ON THE 26 OCT 1996, HIT 4 WAS CREDITED AS (A LITTLE SCOTTISH FANTASY)

Vanessa Paradis Female Vocalist from France

ISSUE	TITLE	UK LBL	UK POS	UK YEAR	US POS	US YEAR	US LBL
1	Joe Le Taxi	(Fa Productions Posp 902)	3	1988	0	1988	
2	Be My Baby	(Remark Po 235)	6	1992	0	1992	
3	Sunday Mondays	(Remark Pzcd 251)	49	1993	0	1993	
4	Just As Long As You Are There	(Remark Pzcd 272)	57	1993	0	1993	

Vanessa Williams Female Vocalist, B: Tarrytown, New York

ISSUE	TITLE	UK LBL	UK POS	UK YEAR	US POS	US YEAR	US LBL
1	The Right Stuff	(Wing Wing 3)	71	1988	0	1988	
2	Dreamin'	(Wing Wing 4)	74	1989	8	1989	(Wing 871078)
3	The Right Stuff (Re-Mix)	(Wing Winr 3)	62	1989	0	1989	
4	Running Back to You		0	1991	18	1991	(WING 867518)
* 5	Save The Best For Last	(Polydor Po 192)	3	1992	1	1992	(Wing 865136)
6	Just For Tonight		0	1992	26	1992	(Wing 865888)
7	Love Is		0	1993	3	1993	(Giant 18630)
8	The Sweetest Days	(Mercury Mercd 422)	41	1995	18	1994	(Wing 851110)
* 9	Colours Of The Wind	(Walt Disney Wd 7677cd)	21	1995	4	1995	(Hollywood 64001)
10	The Way That You Love	(Mercury Mercd 439)	52	1995	0	1995	
11	Where Do We Go From Here (From *Eraser*)		0	1996	71	1996	(Mercury 578102)

HIT 6 IS CREDITED TO VANESSA WILLIAMS AND BRIAN MCNIGHT

V

675

Vangelis   Male Instrumentalist, Real Name Evangeios Papathanassiou B: 29 Mar 1943 Valos, Greece

ISSUE	TITLE	UK LBL	UK POS	UK YEAR	US POS	US YEAR	US LBL
1	Chariots Of Fire / Titles	(Polydor Posp 246)	12	1981	1	1982	(Polydor 2189)
2	Heaven And Hell, Third Movement	(BBC 1)	48	1981	0	1981	
	(Theme From The BBC-Tv Series, *The Cosmos*)						
3	Chariots Of Fire / Titles (Re-Entry)	(Polydor Posp 246)	41	1982	0	1982	
4	Conquest Of Paradise	(East West Yz 704	60	1992	0	1992	
	TOGETHER WITH DEMIS ROUSSOS HE FORMED APHRODITE'S CHILD						
	SEE ALSO JON & VANGELIS						

Vanilla Fudge   Male Vocal/Instrumental Group from the USA/UK

ISSUE	TITLE	UK LBL	UK POS	UK YEAR	US POS	US YEAR	US LBL
1	You Keep Me Hangin' On	(Atlantic 584 123)	18	1967	67	1967	(Atco 6590)
2	You Keep Me Hangin' On (Re-Entry)		0	1968	6	1968	(Atco 6590)
3	Take Me For A Little While		0	1968	28	1968	(Atco 6616)
	NAMES MARK STEIN, VINNIE MARTELL, TIM BOGERT, ROD STEWART, JEFF BECK & CARMINE APPICE						

Vanilla Ice   Male Rapper, Born Robert Van Winkle B: 31 Oct 1968 Miami Lakes, Florida

ISSUE	TITLE	UK LBL	UK POS	UK YEAR	US POS	US YEAR	US LBL
* 1	Ice Ice Baby	(Sbk Sbk 18)	1	1990	1	1990	(Sbk 07335)
* 2	Play That Funky Music	(Sbk Sbk 20)	10	1991	4	1990	(Sbk 07339)
3	I Love You	(Sbk Sbk 22)	45	1991	0	1991	
4	Rollin' In My 5.0	(Sbk Sbk 27)	27	1991	0	1991	
5	Satisfaction	(Sbk Sbk 29)	22	1991	0	1991	

Vanity Fare   Male Vocal/Instrumental Group from the UK

ISSUE	TITLE	UK LBL	UK POS	UK YEAR	US POS	US YEAR	US LBL
1	I Live For The Sun	(Page One Pof 075)	20	1968	0	1968	
* 2	Early In The Morning	(Page One of 142)	8	1969	12	1969	(Page One 21027)
* 3	Hitchin' A Ride	(Page One Pof 158)	16	1969	5	1970	(Page One 21029)
	NAMES TREVOR BRICE, TONY GOULDEN, BARRY LANDEMAN, DICK ALLIX & TONY JARRETT						

Vapors   Male Vocal/Instrumental Group from the UK

ISSUE	TITLE	UK LBL	UK POS	UK YEAR	US POS	US YEAR	US LBL
1	Turning Japanese	(United Artists Bp 334)	3	1980	36	1980	(Liberty 1364)
2	News At Ten	(United Artists Bp 345)	44	1980	0	1980	
3	Jimmie Jones	(Liberty Bp 401)	44	1981	0	1981	
	LEAD SINGER WITH THE QUARTET IS DAVID FENTON						

Vardis   Male Vocal/Instrumental Group from the UK

ISSUE	TITLE	UK LBL	UK POS	UK YEAR	US POS	US YEAR	US LBL
1	Let's Go	(Logo Var 1)	59	1980	0	1980	

Various Artists (EP, LP, 78s)

ISSUE	TITLE	UK LBL	UK POS	UK YEAR	US POS	US YEAR	US LBL
* 1	Oklahoma! Cast Album		0	1943	9	1943	(Decca 359)
2	Carousel - The Original Soundtrack	(Capitol Lct 6105)	27	1956	0	1956	
3	All Star Hit Parade	(Decca F 10752)	2	1956	0	1956	
4	Carousel - The Original Soundtrack) (Re-Entry)	(Capitol Lct 6105)	26	1956	0	1956	
5	All Star Hit Parade No 2	(Decca F 10915)	15	1957	0	1957	
6	The Food Christmas (EP)	(Food Food 23)	63	1989	0	1989	
7	Further Adventures Of North (EP)	(Deconstrction Pt 43372)	64	1990	0	1990	
8	The Apple (EP)	(Apple App 1)	60	1991	0	1991	
9	Fourplay (EP)	(Xl Xlfp 1)	45	1992	0	1992	
10	The Fred (EP)	(Heavenly Hvn 19)	26	1992	0	1992	
11	Gimme Shelter (EP)	(Food Cdordera 1)	23	1993	0	1993	
12	Subplates Volume 1 (EP)	(Suburban Base Subbase 24cd)	69	1993	0	1993	
13	The Two Tone (EP)	(2 Tone Chstt 31)	30	1993	0	1993	
14	Help (Ep)	(Go! Discs Godcd 135)	51	1995	0	1995	
15	New York Undercover (EP)	(Uptown Mcstd 48002)	39	1996	0	1996	
16	Dangerous Minds (EP)	(MCA Mcstd 48007)	35	1996	0	1996	
17	Espn Presents The Jock Jam		0	1997	50	1997	(Tommy Boy 7780)

Various Artists (Montages)

ISSUE	TITLE	UK LBL	UK POS	UK YEAR	US POS	US YEAR	US LBL
1	Calibre Cuts	(Calibre Cab 502)	75	1980	0	1980	
2	Deep Heat '89	(Deep Heat Deep 10)	12	1989	0	1989	
3	The Brits 1990	(RCA Pb 43565)	2	1990	0	1990	
4	The Sixth Sense	(Deep Heat Deep 12)	49	1990	0	1990	
5	Time To Make The Floor Burn	(Megabass Megax 1)	16	1990	0	1990	

Vaughn Horton & His Polka Debs

ISSUE	TITLE	UK LBL	UK POS	UK YEAR	US POS	US YEAR	US LBL
1	Toolie Oolie Doolie (The Yodel Polka)		0	1948	11	1948	(Continental 1223)

Vaughn Monroe & His Orchestra   Male Vocalist/Bandleader, B: 7 Oct 1911 Akron, Ohio

ISSUE	TITLE	UK LBL	UK POS	UK YEAR	US POS	US YEAR	US LBL
1	There I Go		0	1940	1	1940	(Bluebird 10848)
2	Is It Love Or Is It Conscription		0	1940	26	1940	(Bluebird 10901)
3	So You're The One		0	1941	16	1941	(Bluebird 10901)
4	High On A Windy Hill		0	1941	13	1941	(Bluebird 10976)

ISSUE	TITLE	UK LBL	UK POS	UK YEAR	US POS	US YEAR	US LBL
5	There'll Be Some Changes Made		0	1941	24	1941	(Bluebird 11025)
6	Racing With The Moon		0	1941	25	1941	(Bluebird 11070)
7	G'bye Now		0	1941	12	1941	(Bluebird 11114)
8	The Worm That Loved The Litle Tater Bug		0	1941	22	1941	(Bluebird 11207)
9	Yours		0	1941	16	1941	(Bluebird 11146)
10	If It's You		0	1941	16	1941	(Bluebird 11245)
11	The Shrine Of St. Cecelia		0	1942	21	1942	(Bluebird 11344)
12	Tengerine		0	1942	11	1942	(Bluebird 11433)
13	Three Little Sisters		0	1942	13	1942	(Bluebird 11508)
14	My Devotion		0	1942	1	1942	(Victor 27925)
15	Hip, Hip, Hooray		0	1942	20	1942	(Victor 27925)
16	When The Lights Go On Again (All Over The World)		0	1942	1	1942	(Victor 27945)
17	Let's Get Lost		0	1943	1	1943	(Victor 1524)
18	The Trolley Song		0	1944	4	1944	(Victor 1605)
19	The Very Thought Of You		0	1944	19	1944	(Victor 1605)
20	Rum And Coca-Cola		0	1945	8	1945	(Victor 1637)
21	There! I've Said It Again		0	1945	1 *	1945	(Victor 1637)
22	Something Sentimental		0	1945	12	1945	(Victor 1714)
23	Just A Blue Serge Suit		0	1945	17	1945	(Victor 1725)
24	Fishin' For The Moon		0	1945	17	1947	(Victor 1736)
25	Are These Really Mine?		0	1946	12	1946	(Victor 1736)
26	Let It Snow! Let It Snow! Let It Snow!		0	1945	1	1945	(Victor 1759)
27	Seems Like Old Times		0	1946	7	1946	(Victor 1911)
28	Who Told You That Lie?		0	1945	15	1946	(Victor 1892)
29	It's My Lazy Day		0	1946	16	1946	(Victor 1892)
30	The Things We Did Last Summer		0	1946	13	1946	(Victor 1972)
31	You Can't See The Sun When You're Cryin'		0	1947	21	1947	(RCA Victor 2053)
32	Dreams Are A Dime A Dozen		0	1947	22	1947	(Victor 2226)
33	I Wish I Didn't Love You So		0	1947	2	1947	(RCA Victor 2294)
34	Kokomo, Indiana		0	1947	10	1947	(RCA Victor 2361)
35	You Do		0	1947	5	1947	(RCA Victor 2361)
36	Ballerina		0	1947	1 *	1947	(RCA Victor 2433)
37	How Soon (Will I Be Seeing You)		0	1947	3	1947	(RCA Victor 2523)
38	In A Little Book Shop		0	1947	21	1947	(RCA Victor 2573)
39	Passing Fancy		0	1948	24	1948	(RCA Victor 2573)
40	Matinee		0	1948	20	1948	(RCA Victor 2671)
41	Completely Yours		0	1948	22	1948	(RCA Victor 2712)
42	It's The Sentimental Thing To Do		0	1948	21	1948	(RCA Victor 2748)
43	Melody Time		0	1948	22	1948	(RCA Victor 2785)
44	Blue Shadows On The Trail		0	1948	26	1948	(RCA Victor 2785)
45	What Do I Have To Do (To Make You Love Me)		0	1848	23	1948	(RCA Victor 2811)
46	The Maharajah Of Magador		0	1948	19	1948	(RCA Victor 2851)
47	Cool Water		0	1948	9	1948	(RCA Victor 2923)
48	Ev'rday I Love You (Just A Little Bit More)		0	1948	22	1948	(RCA Victor 2957)
49	In My Dreams		0	1948	20	1948	(RCA VIctor 3133)
50	Red Roses For A Blue Lady		0	1949	3	1949	(RCA Victor 3319)
* 51	Riders In The Sky (A Cowboy Legend)		0	1949	1	1949	(RCA Victor 3411)
52	Someday		0	1949	1	1949	(RCA Victor 78-3510)
53	That Lucky Old Sun (Just Rolls Around Heaven All Day)		0	1949	6	1949	(RCA Victor 78-3531)
54	Vieni Su (Say You Love Me Too)		0	1949	19	1949	(RCA Victor 78-3549)
55	Mule Train		0	1949	10	1949	(RCA Victor 78-3600)
56	Bamboo		0	1950	4	1950	(RCA Victor 78-3627)
57	Thanks, Mister Florist		0	1950	20	1950	(RCA Victor 3773)
58	Sound Off		0	1951	3	1951	(RCA Victor 4113)
59	On Top Of Old Smoky		0	1951	8	1951	(RCA Victor 4114)
60	Old Soldiers Never Die		0	1951	7	1951	(RCA Victor 4146)
61	Meanderin'		0	1951	28	1951	(RCA Victor 4271)
62	Charmaine		0	1952	27	1952	(RCA Victor 4375)
63	Mountain Laurel		0	1952	22	1952	(RCA Victor 4479)
64	Lady Love		0	1952	18	1952	(RCA Victor 4611)
65	Idaho State Fair		0	1952	20	1952	(RCA Victor 4611)
66	Ruby		0	1953	27	1953	(RCA Victor 5286)
67	They Were Doin' The Mambo		0	1954	7	1954	(RCA Victor 5767)
68	Black Denim Trousers And Motorcycle Boots		0	1955	38	1955	(RCA 6260)
69	Don't Go To Strangers		0	1956	38	1956	(RCA 6358)

ISSUE	TITLE	UK LBL	UK POS	UK YEAR	US POS	US YEAR	US LBL
70	In The Middle Of The House		0	1956	11	1956	(RCA 6619)
	OBITUARY: D: 21 MAY 1973 (AGED 61).						

Vegas Male Vocal Instrumental Duo from the UK

ISSUE	TITLE	UK LBL	UK POS	UK YEAR	US POS	US YEAR	US LBL
1	Possessed	(RCA 74321110437)	32	1992	0	1992	
2	She	(RCA 74321124657)	43	1992	0	1992	
3	Walk Into The Wind	(RCA 74321122462)	65	1993	0	1993	

Velvelettes Female Vocal Group from the USA

ISSUE	TITLE	UK LBL	UK POS	UK YEAR	US POS	US YEAR	US LBL
1	Needle In A Haystack		0	1964	45	1964	(V.I.P. 25007)
+ 2	He Was Really Saying Something		0	1965	21	1965	(V.I.P. 25013)
3	These Things Will Keep Me Loving You	(Tamla Motown Tmg 780)	34	1971	0	1971	

Velvets Male Vocal Group from the USA

ISSUE	TITLE	UK LBL	UK POS	UK YEAR	US POS	US YEAR	US LBL
1	That Lucky Old Sun	(London Hlu 9328)	46	1961	0	1961	
2	Tonight (Could Be The Night)	(London Hlu 9372)	50	1961	26	1961	(Monument 441)
	LEAD SINGER WITH THE QUINTET IS VIRGIL JOHNSON						

Velvet Underground Mixed Vocal/Instrumental Group from the USA/UK

ISSUE	TITLE	UK LBL	UK POS	UK YEAR	US POS	US YEAR	US LBL
1	Venus In Furs	(Sire W 0224cd)	71	1994	0	1994	

Vent 414 Male Vocal/Instrumental Group from the UK

ISSUE	TITLE	UK LBL	UK POS	UK YEAR	US POS	US YEAR	US LBL
1	Fixer	(Polydor 5753292)	71	1996	0	1996	

Ventures Male Instrumental Rock And Roll Band from Washington

ISSUE	TITLE	UK LBL	UK POS	UK YEAR	US POS	US YEAR	US LBL
* 1	Walk Don't Run	(Top Rank Jar 417)	8	1960	2	1959	(Dolton 25)
* 2	Perfidia	(London Hlg 9232)	4	1960	15	1960	(Dolton 28)
3	Ram-Bunk-Shush	(London Hlg 9292)	45	1961	29	1961	(Dolton 32)
4	Lullaby Of The Leaves	(London Hlg 9344)	43	1961	0	1961	
5	Walk Don't Run '64		0	1964	8	1964	(Dolton 96)
6	Slaughter On Tenth Avenue		0	1964	35	1964	(Dolton 300)
* 7	Hawaii Five-O		0	1969	4	1969	(Liberty 56068)
	NAMES: NOKIE EDWARDS, BOB BOGIE, HOWIE JOHNSON & DON WILSON						
	HIT 5 IS A DIFFERENT RECORDING TO HIT 1						
	VARIOUS MEMBER CHANGES SINCE 1959						

Vera Lynn Female Vocalist, Real Name Vera Margaret Welsh B: 20 Mar 1919 East Ham, London, England.

ISSUE	TITLE	UK LBL	UK POS	UK YEAR	US POS	US YEAR	US LBL
1	You Can't Be True, Dear		0	1948	9	1948	(London 202)
2	Again (From Roadhouse)		0	1949	23	1949	(London 310)
* 3	Auf Wiedersehen Sweetheart	(Decca F 9927)	10	1952	1	1952	(London 1227)
* 4	Yours (Quiere Me Mucho)		0	1952	7	1952	(London 1261)
5	Forget Me Not	(Decca F 9985)	7	1952	0	1952	
6	Homing Waltz	(Decca F 9959)	9	1952	0	1952	
7	Forget Me Not (Re-Entry)	(Decca F 9959)	5	1952	0	1952	
8	Windsor Waltz	(Decca F 10092)	11	1953	0	1953	
9	We'll Meet Again		0	1954	29	1954	(London 1348)
10	If You Love Me (Really Love Me)		0	1954	21	1954	(London 1412)
11	My Son, My Son	(Decca F 10372)	1	1954	28	1954	(London 1501)
12	Who Are We	(Decca F 10715)	30	1956	0	1956	
13	A House With Love In It	(Decca F 10799)	17	1956	0	1956	
14	The Faithful Hussar (Don't Cry My Love)	(Decca F 10846)	29	1957	0	1957	
15	Travellin' Home	(Decca F 10903)	20	1957	0	1957	
	HIT 11 WAS WITH FRANK WEIR, HIS SAXOPHONE, HIS ORCHESTRA & CHORUS						
	SHE WAS AWARDED THE O.B.E. IN 1969 & MADE DAME VERA LYNN IN 1975						

See Also Frank Weir

Verdelle Smith She Hails From St. Petersburg, Florida

ISSUE	TITLE	UK LBL	UK POS	UK YEAR	US POS	US YEAR	US LBL
1	Tar And Cement	0		1966	38	1966	(Capitol 5632)

Vernon Dalhart Male Opera Tenor, Recorded Under Many Pseudonyms

ISSUE	TITLE	UK LBL	UK POS	UK YEAR	US POS	US YEAR	US LBL
1	Till The Clouds Roll By (From Oh, Boy!)		0	1917	10	1917	(Emerson 7192)
2	Till We Meet Again		0	1919	9	1919	(Edison Amberol 3670)
3	Tuck Me To Sleep (In My Old 'tucky Home)		0	1921	2	1921	(Emerson 18807)
4	Weep No More, My Mammy		0	1922	5	1922	(Columbia 3500)
5	I Want My Mammy		0	1922	10	1922	(Columbia 3520)
6	Dear Old Southland		0	1922	12	1900	(Emerson Amberol 4508)
7	The Pal That I Loved (Stole The Gal I Loved)		0	1924	4	1924	(Okeh 40177)
8	The Wreck Of The Old 97		0	1925	4	1925	(Victor 19427)
* 9	The Prisoner's Song		0	1925	1	1925	(Victor 19427)
10	In The Baggage Coach Ahead		0	1925	14	1925	(Victor 19627)

ISSUE	TITLE	UK LBL	UK POS	UK YEAR	US POS	US YEAR	US LBL
11	The Ledder Edged In Black		0	1925	10	1925	(Brunswick 2900)
* 12	The Prisoner's Song (Re-Entry)		0	1925	1	1925	(Victor 19427)
13	The Death Of Floyd Collins		0	1925	3	1925	(Victor 19779)
14	The Wreck Of The Shenandoah		0	1926	6	1926	(Victor 19779)
15	The Convict And The Rose		0	1926	9	1926	(Victor 19770)
16	The Governor's Pardon		0	1926	8	1926	(Victor 19983)
17	There's A New Star In Heaven Tonight-Rudolph Valentino		0	1926	4	1926	(Columbia 718)
18	The Miami Storm		0	1927	14	1927	(Columbia 15100)
19	The Wreck Of The Number Nine		0	1927	16	1927	(Columbia 15121)
20	The Mississippi Flood		0	1927	17	1927	(Victor 20611)
21	Lindbergh (The Eagle Of The U.S.A.)		0	1927	4	1927	(Columbia 1000)
22	Lucky Lindy		0	1927	11	1927	(Columbia 1000)
23	My Carolina Home		0	1927	7	1927	(Victor 20795)
24	My Blue Ridge Mountain Home		0	1928	7	1928	(Victor 20539)
25	The Memory That Time Cannot Erase		0	1928	19	1928	(Victor 21094)
26	Hallelujah		0	1928	6	1928	(Columbia 15449)
27	Farm Relief Song		0	1929	7	1929	(Columbia 15449)

REAL NAME MARION TRY SLAUGHTER B: 6 APR 1883 JEFFERSON, TEXAS
HIT 2 IS CREDITED TO VERNON DALHART AND GLADY'S RICE • HIT 3 WAS WITH THE CRITERION TRIO
HIT 4 WAS ON THE 'B' SIDE OF AL JOLSON'S HIT 39 • HIT 5 IS CREDITED TO VERNON DALHART AND AL BERNARD
HITS 23, 24, 25 ARE CREDITED TO VERNON DALHART AND CARSON ROBISON • HIT 27 IS CREDITED TO AL CRAVER
OBITUARY : D: 15 SEP 1948.

Vernons Girls   Female Vocal Group from the UK

	TITLE	UK LBL	UK POS	UK YEAR	US POS	US YEAR	US LBL
1	Lover Please	(Decca F 11450)	16	1962	0	1962	
2	Lover Please (Re-Entry) / You Know What I Mean	(Decca F 11450)	39	1962	0	1962	
3	Loco-Motion	(Decca F 11495)	47	1962	0	1962	
4	You Know What I Mean (Re-Entry)	(Decca F 11450)	37	1962	0	1962	
5	You Know What I Mean (2nd Re-Entry)	(Decca F 11450)	50	1962	0	1962	
6	Funny All Over	(Decca F 11549)	31	1963	0	1963	
7	Do The Bird	(Decca F 11629)	50	1963	0	1963	
8	Do The Bird (Re-Entry)	(Decca F 11629)	44	1963	0	1963	

Vernon's Wonderland   Male Producer, Matthias Hoffmann, from Germany

	TITLE	UK LBL	UK POS	UK YEAR	US POS	US YEAR	US LBL
1	Vernon's Wonderland	(Eye-Q Classics Eyecl 004cd)	59	1996	0	1996	

Veronica   See Craig Mack

Versatiles   See 5th Dimension

Veruca Salt   Male Vocal/Instrumental Group from the USA

	TITLE	UK LBL	UK POS	UK YEAR	US POS	US YEAR	US LBL
1	Seether	(Hut Hut 16)	61	1994	0	1994	
2	Seether (Re-Issue)	(Hut Hutcd 29)	73	1994	0	1994	
3	Number One Blind	(Hi-Rise Flatscd 16)	68	1995	0	1995	
4	Volcano Girls	(Outpost Oprcd 22197)	56	1997	0	1997	
5	Benjamin	(Outpost Oprcd 22261)	75	1997	0	1997	

Verve   Male Vocal/Instrumental Group from the UK

	TITLE	UK LBL	UK POS	UK YEAR	US POS	US YEAR	US LBL
1	She's A Superstar	(Hut Hut 16)	66	1992	0	1992	
2	Blue	(Hut Hutcd 29)	69	1993	0	1993	
3	This Is Music	(Hut Hutcd 54)	35	1995	0	1995	
4	On Your Own	(Hut Hutcd 55)	28	1995	0	1995	
5	History	(Hut Hutcd 59)	24	1995	0	1995	
6	Bitter Sweet Symphony	(Hut Hutdg 82)	2	1997	0	1997	
7	The Drugs Don't Work	(Hut Hutdg 88)	1	1997	0	1997	

Verve Pipe   Male Vocal/Instrumental Quintet from the USA

	TITLE	UK LBL	UK POS	UK YEAR	US POS	US YEAR	US LBL
1	The Freshman		0	1997	8	1997	(RCA 64733)

Vesta Williams   Female Vocalist from the USA

	TITLE	UK LBL	UK POS	UK YEAR	US POS	US YEAR	US LBL
1	Once Bitten Twice Shy	(A&M Am 362)	14	1986	0	1986	

Vibrations   Names James Johnson, Richard Owens, Dave Govan, Carlton Fisher & Don Bradley

	TITLE	UK LBL	UK POS	UK YEAR	US POS	US YEAR	US LBL
1	The Watusi		0	1961	25	1961	(Checker 969)
2	My Girl Sloopy		0	1964	26	1964	(Atlantic 2221)

THE GROUP ORIGINALLY RECORDED AS THE JAYHAWKS. SEE ALSO TONY JACKSON

Vibrators   Male Vocal/Instrumental Group from the UK

	TITLE	UK LBL	UK POS	UK YEAR	US POS	US YEAR	US LBL
1	Automatic Lover	(Epic Epc 6137)	35	1978	0	1978	
2	Judy Says (Knock You In The Head)	(Epic Epc 6393)	70	1978	0	1978	

ISSUE	TITLE	UK LBL	UK POS	UK YEAR	US POS	US YEAR	US LBL

Vic Damone Male Vocalist, Real Name Vito Farinola B: 12 Jun 1928 Florida

ISSUE	TITLE	UK LBL	UK POS	UK YEAR	US POS	US YEAR	US LBL
1	I Have But One Heart (O Marinariello)		0	1947	7	1947	(Mercury 5053)
2	You Do (From Mother Wore Tights)		0	1947	7	1947	(Mercury 5056)
3	Thoughtless		0	1948	22	1948	(Mercury 5104)
4	My Fair Lady		0	1948	27	1948	(Mercury 5121)
5	It's Magic (From Romance On The High Seas)		0	1948	24	1948	(Mercury 5138)
6	Say Something Sweet To Your Sweetheart		0	1948	23	1948	(Mercury 5192)
* 7	Again (From Road House)		0	1949	6	1949	(Mercury 5261)
* 8	You're Breaking My Heart		0	1949	1	1949	(Mercury 5271)
9	The Four Winds And The Seven Seas		0	1949	16	1949	(Mercury 5271)
10	My Bolero		0	1949	10	1949	(Mercury 5313)
11	Why Was I Born?		0	1949	20	1949	(Mercury 5326)
12	Sitting By The Window		0	1950	29	1950	(Mercury 5343)
13	God's Country		0	1950	27	1950	(Mercury 5374)
14	Vagabond Shoes		0	1950	17	1950	(Mercury 5429)
15	Tzena, Tzena, Tzena		0	1950	6	1950	(Mercury 5454)
16	Just Say I Love Her		0	1950	13	1950	(Mercury 5474)
17	Can Anyone Explain (No! No! No!)		0	1950	25	1950	(Mercury 5474)
18	Cincinnati Dancing Pig		0	1950	11	1950	(Mercury 5477)
19	My Heart Cries For You		0	1950	4	1950	(Mercury 5563)
20	Music By The Angels		0	1950	18	1950	(Mercury 5563)
21	Tell Me You Love Me		0	1951	21	1951	(Mercury 5572)
22	If		0	1951	28	1951	(Mercury 5565)
23	My Truly, Truly Fair		0	1951	4	1951	(Mercury 5646)
24	Longing For You		0	1951	12	1951	(Mercury 5655)
25	Calla Calla		0	1951	13	1951	(Mercury 5698)
26	Jump Through The Ring		0	1952	22	1952	(Mercury 5785)
27	Here In My Heart		0	1952	8	1952	(Mercury 5858)
28	Take My Heart		0	1952	30	1952	(Mercury 5877)
29	Rosanne		0	1952	23	1952	(Mercury 5877)
30	Sugar		0	1953	13	1953	(Mercury 70054)
31	April In Portugal		0	1953	10	1953	(Mercury 70128)
32	Eternally (From Limelight)		0	1953	12	1953	(Mercury 70186)
33	Ebb Tide		0	1953	10	1943	(Mercury 70216)
34	A Village In Peru		0	1953	30	1953	(Mercury 70269)
35	The Breeze And I		0	1954	21	1954	(Mercury 70287)
36	The Sparrow Sings		0	1954	27	1954	(Mercury 70326)
* 37	On The Street Where You Live	(Philips Pb 819)	1	1958	4	1956	(Columbia 40654)
38	An Affair To Remember (Our Love Affair)	(Philips Pb 745)	29	1957	16	1957	(Columbia 40945)
39	An Affair To Remember (Our Love Affair) (Re-Entry)	(Philips 745)	30	1958	0	1958	
40	The Only Man On The Island	(Philips Pb 837)	24	1958	0	1958	
41	You Were Only Fooling (While I Was Falling In Love)		0	1965	30	1965	(Warner Bros 5616)

HIT 6 IS CREDITED TO VIC DAMONE AND PATTI PAGE

Vic Dana B: 26 Aug 1942 Buffalo, New York

ISSUE	TITLE	UK LBL	UK POS	UK YEAR	US POS	US YEAR	US LBL
1	Shangri-La		0	1964	27	1964	(Dolton 92)
2	Red Roses For A Blue Lady		0	1965	10	1965	(Dolton 304)
3	I Love You Drops		0	1966	30	1966	(Dolton 319)

Vic Reeves Male Vocalist from the UK

ISSUE	TITLE	UK LBL	UK POS	UK YEAR	US POS	US YEAR	US LBL
1	Born Free	(Sense Sigh 710)	6	1991	0	1991	
2	Dizzy	(Sense Sigh 712)	1	1991	0	1991	
3	Abide With Me	(Sense Sigh 713)	47	1991	0	1991	
4	I'm A Believer	(Parlophone Cdr 6412)	3	1995	0	1995	

HIT 1 IS CREDITED TO VIC REEVES & THE ROMAN NUMERALS · HIT 2 IS CREDITED TO VIC REEVES & THE WONDER STUFF
HIT 4 IS CREDITED TO EMF AND REEVES & MORTIMER

Vice Squad Mixed Vocal/Instrumental Group from the UK

ISSUE	TITLE	UK LBL	UK POS	UK YEAR	US POS	US YEAR	US LBL
1	Out Of Reach	(Zonophone Z 26)	68	1982	0	1982	

Vicious Pink Mixed Vocal/Instrumental Duo from the UK

ISSUE	TITLE	UK LBL	UK POS	UK YEAR	US POS	US YEAR	US LBL
1	Cccan't You See	(Parlophone R 6074)	67	1984	0	1984	

Vicki Brown See J.J. Barry

Vicki Lawrence Female Vocalist, B: 26 May 1949 Inglewood, California

ISSUE	TITLE	UK LBL	UK POS	UK YEAR	US POS	US YEAR	US LBL
1	The Night The Lights Went Out In Georgia		0	1972	1 *	1972	(Bell 45303)

V

680

ISSUE	TITLE	UK LBL	UK POS	UK YEAR	US POS	US YEAR	US LBL
Vicki Sue Robinson Female Vocalist, B: 1955 Philadelphia							
1	Turn The Beat Around	0	1976	10	1976	(RCA 10562)	
Vicky D Female Vocalist from the USA							
1	The Beat Is Mine	(Virgin Vs 486)	42	1982	0	1982	
Vicky Leandros Female Vocalist, B: 1950 Greece, Raised In Hamburg, Germany							
* 1	Come What May (Apres Toi)	(Philips 6000 049)	2	1972	0	1972	
2	The Love In Your Eyes	(Philips 6000 081)	48	1972	0	1972	
3	The Love In Your Eyes (Re-Entry)	(Philips 6000 081)	40	1973	0	1973	
4	The Love In Your Eyes (2nd Re-Entry)	(Philips 6000 081)	46	1973	0	1973	
5	When Bouzoukis Played	(Philips 6000 111)	44	1973	0	1973	
6	When Bouzoukis Played (Re-Entry)	(Philips 6000 111)	45	1973	0	1973	
Vicki Young Female Vocalist From The USA							
1	I Love You So Much		0	1953	26	1953	(Capitol 2478)
2	Honey Love		0	1954	25	1954	(Capitol 2865)
Victor E. Lundberg Male News Reader For Wmax, B: 1923, Grand Rapids, Michigan							
* 1	An Open Letter To My Teenage Son		0	1967	10	1967	(Liberty 55996)
Victoria Wilson Female Vocalist							
1	Reach 4 The Melody	(Sony S3 Vwjcd 1)	72	1997	0	1997	
Victor Jory B: 20 Feb 1911, Hit Was Issued On Two 10 Records							
* 1	Tubby The Tuba		0	1946	0	1946	
Victor Lundberg See Victor E. Lundberg							
Victor Simonelli Male Producer from the USA							
1	Feels So Right	(Soundproof/MCA Mcstd 40068)	63	1996	0	1996	
HIT IS CREDITED TO VICTOR SIMONELLI PRESENTS SOLUTION							
Victor Young & His Orchestra Male Violinist/Conductor, B: 8 Aug 1900 Chicago							
1	Gems From The Band Wagon		0	1931	20	1931	(Brunswick 6172)
2	The Last Round-Up		0	1933	3	1933	(Brunswick 6651)
3	Who's Afraid Of The Big Bad Wolf?		0	1933	3	1933	(Brunswick 6651)
4	The Old Spinning Wheel		0	1934	10	1934	(Brunswick 6725)
5	This Little Pig Went To Market		0	1934	6	1934	(Brunswick 6747)
6	Flirtation Walk		0	1934	10	1934	(Decca 279)
7	Mr. And Mrs. Is The Name		0	1934	17	1937	(Decca 279)
8	Ev'ry Day		0	1935	7	1935	(Decca 350)
9	Sweet Music		0	1935	19	1935	(Decca 350)
10	About A Quarter To Nine		0	1935	3	1935	(Decca 418)
11	Way Back Home		0	1935	6	1935	(Decca 452)
12	She's A Latin From Manhattan		0	1935	1	1935	(Decca 418)
13	It Never Dawned On Me		0	1935	18	1935	(Decca 582)
14	Take Me Back To My Boots And Saddle		0	1935	20	1935	(Decca 581)
15	Lights Out		0	1936	13	1936	(Decca 703)
16	It's A Sin To Tell A Lie		0	1936	5	1936	(Decca 751)
17	Will You Remember?		0	1937	14	1937	(Decca 1199)
18	Johnny One-Note		0	1937	17	1937	(Decca 1280)
19	La Vie En Rose		0	1950	27	1950	(Decca 24816)
20	Mona Lisa		0	1950	7	1950	(Decca 27048)
21	The Third Man Theme		0	1950	22	1950	(Decca 27048)
22	My Heart Cries For You		0	1951	29	1951	(Decca 27333)
23	Ruby		0	1953	20	1953	(Decca 28675)
24	Limelight Theme		0	1953	26	1953	(Decca 28735)
25	The High And The Mighty		0	1954	6	1954	(Decca 29203)
26	Main Theme Around The World		0	1957	13	1957	(Decca 30262)
OBITUARY: D: 11 NOV 1956 (AGED 56).							
HIT 26 IS CREDITED TO VICTOR YOUNG & HIS SINGING STRINGS							
Vida Simpson Female Vocalist from the US							
1	Oohhh Baby	(Hi-Life Hicd6)	70	1995	0	1995	
Video Kids Mixed Vocal Duo from Holland							
1	Woodpeckers From Space	(Epic A 6504)	72	1985	0	1985	
Video Symphonic Orchestra from the UK							
1	The Flame Trees Of Thika	(EMI EMI 5222)	42	1981	0	1981	

ISSUE	TITLE	UK LBL	UK POS	UK YEAR	US POS	US YEAR	US LBL
Vienna Philharmonic Orchestra Orchestra From Vienna							
1	Theme From *The Onedin Line*	(Decca F 13259)	15	1971	0	1971	
View From The Hill Mixed Vocal/Instrumental Group from the UK							
1	No Conversation	(EMI EMI 5565)	58	1986	0	1986	
2	I'm No Rebel	(EMI Em 5580)	59	1987	0	1987	
Vik Venus (Alias: Your Main Moon Man) Radio Personality, Real Name Jack Spector From New York.							
1	Moonflight		0	1969	38		1969 (Buddah 118)
	OBITUARY : D: 8 MAR 1994 HEART ATTACK (WHILST ON AIR).						
Vikki Female Vocalist from the UK							
1	Love Is...	(Prt 7p 326)	49	1985	0	1985	
Vikki Carr Female Vocalist, Real Name Florencia Bisenta De Casillas Martinez Cardona B: 19 Jul 1941 El Paso, Texas.							
* 1	It Must Be Him (Seul Sur Son Etoile)	(Liberty Lib 55917)	2	1967	3	1967	(Liberty 55986)
2	There I Go	(Liberty Lbf 15022)	50	1967	0	967	
3	The Lesson		0	1968	34	1968	(Liberty 56012)
4	With Pen In Hand	(Liberty Lbf 15166)	43	1969	35	1969	(Liberty 56092)
5	With Pen In Hand (Re-Entry)	(Liberty Lbf 15166)	39	1969	0	1969	
6	With Pen In Hand (2nd Re-Entry)	(Liberty Lbf 15166)	40	1969	0	1969	
Village People Male Vocal/Instrumental Group from the USA							
1	San Francisco (You've Got Me)	(Djm Djs 10817)	45	1977	0	1977	
* 2	Macho Man		0	1978	25	1978	(Casablanca 922)
* 3	In The Navy	(Mercury 6007 209)	2	1979	4	1979	(Casablanca 973)
* 4	Y.M.C.A.	(Mercury 6007 192)	1	1978	12	1978	(Casablanca 945)
5	Go West	(Mercury 6007 221)	15	1979	0	1979	
6	Can't Stop The Music	(Mercury Mer 16)	11	1980	0	1980	
7	Sex Over The Phone	(Record Shack Soho 34)	59	1985	0	1985	
8	Y.M.C.A. (Re-Mix)	(Bell 74321177182)	12	1993	0	1993	
9	In The Navy (Re-Mix)	(Bell 74321198192)	36	1994	0	1994	
	LEAD SINGER WITH THE GROUP IS VICTOR WILLIS						
Village Stompers Dixieland-Style Band From Greenwich Village, New York							
1	Washington Square		0	1963	2	1963	(Epic 9617)
Vince Guaraldi Trio Male Pianist/Jazz Trio Leader, B: 17 Jul 1932 San Francisco							
1	Cast Your Fate To The Wind		0	1963	22	1963	(Fantasy 563)
	OBITUARY: D: 6 FEB 1976 HEART ATTACK.						
Vince Hill Male Vocalist From The UK							
1	The River's Run Dry	(Piccadilly 7n 35043)	49	1962	0	1962	
2	The River's Run Dry (Re-Entry)	(Piccadilly 7n 35043)	41	1962	0	1962	
3	Take Me To Your Heart Again	(Columbia Db 7781)	13	1966	0	1966	
4	Heartaches	(Columbia Db 7852)	28	1966	0	1966	
5	Merci Cheri	(Columbia Db 7824)	36	1966	0	1966	
6	Edelweiss	(Columbia Db 8127)	2	1967	0	1967	
7	Roses Of Picardy	(Columbia Db 8185)	13	1967	0	1967	
8	Love Letters In The Sand	(Columbia Db 8268)	23	1967	0	1967	
9	Importance Of Your Love	(Columbia Db 8414)	32	1968	0	1968	
10	Doesn't Anybody Know My Name?	(Columbia Db 8515)	50	1969	0	1969	
11	Little Blue Bird	(Columbia Db 8616)	42	1969	0	1969	
12	Look Around	(Columbia Db 8804)	12	1971	0	1971	
Vince Martin Male Vocalist from the US							
1	Cindy Oh Cindy	(London Hln 8340)	26	1956	9	1956	(Glory 247)
	HIT IS CREDITED TO VINCE MARTIN AND THE TARRIERS						
Vince Neil Male Vocalist from the USA							
1	You're Invited (But Your Friend Can't Come)	(Hollywood Hwd 123)	63	1992	0	1992	
Vincent Bell							
* 1	Airport Love Theme (Gwen And Vern)		0	1970	31	1970	(Decca 32659)
Vincent De Moor							
1	Flowtation	(Xl Recordings Xls 89cd)	54	1997	0	1997	
Vince Wayne							
1	Blue Piano		0	1953	29	1953	(Triple A 2506)
Vindaloo Summer Special Mixed Vocal/Instrumental Group From The UK							
1	Rockin' With Rita (Head To Toe)	(Vindaloo Ugh 13)	56	1986	0	1986	

ISSUE	TITLE	UK LBL	UK POS	UK YEAR	US POS	US YEAR	US LBL
Viola Wills Female Vocalist From The USA							
1	Gonna Get Along Without You Now	(Ariola/Hansa Aha 546)	8	1979	0	1979	
2	Both Sides Now / Dare To Dream	(Streetwave Khan 66)	35	1986	0	1986	
Violinski Male Instrumental Group from the UK							
1	Clog Dance	(Jet 136)	17	1979	0	1979	
Vipers Skiffle Group Male Vocal/Instrumental Group from the UK							
1	Don't You Rock Me Daddy-O	(Parlophone R 4261)	10	1957	0	1957	
2	Cumberland Gap	(Parlophone R4289)	10	1957	0	1957	
3	Streamline Train	(Parlophone R 4308)	23	1957	0	1957	
Virtues							
1	Guitar Boogie Shuffle		0	1958	5	1958	(Hunt 324)
	INSTRUMENTAL TRIO FROM PHILADELPHIA						
Virus Male Instrumental/Production Duo from the UK							
1	Sun	(Perfecto Perf 107cd)	62	1995	0	1995	
2	Moon	(Perfecto Perf 134cd)	36	1997	0	1997	
Visage Male Vocal/Instrumental Group from the UK							
1	Fade To Grey	(Polydor Posp 194)	8	1980	0	1980	
2	Mind Of A Toy	(Polydor Posp 236)	13	1981	0	1981	
3	Visage	(Polydor Posp 293)	21	1981	0	1981	
4	Damned Don't Cry	(Polydor Posp 390)	11	1982	0	1982	
5	Night Train	(Polydor Posp 441)	12	1982	0	1982	
6	Pleasure Boys	(Polydor Posp 523)	44	1982	0	1982	
7	Love Glove	(Polydor Posp 691)	54	1984	0	1984	
8	Fade To Grey (Re-Mix)	(Polydor Pzcd 282)	39	1993	0	1993	
Viscounts (1) Male Instrumental Quintet, Names Harry Haller, Joe & Bobby Spievak, Larry Vecchio & Clark Smith from New Jersey.							
1	Harlem Nocturne		0	1959	52	1959	(Madison 123)
2	Harlem Nocturne (Re-Issue)		0	1966	39	1966	(Amy 940)
Viscounts (2) Male Vocal Group from the UK							
1	Shortin' Bread	(Pye 7n 15287)	16	1960	0	1960	
2	Who Put The Bomp	(Pye 7n 15379)	21	1961	0	1961	
Vision Male Vocal/Instrumental Group from the UK							
1	Love Dance	(Mvm Mvm 2886)	74	1983	0	1983	
Vivian Blaine Female Vocalist from the USA							
1	Bushel And A Peck	(Brunswick 05100)	12	1953	0	1953	
Vivienne Mckone Female Vocalist from the UK							
1	Sing (Ooh-Ee-Ohh)	(Ffrr F 183)	47	1992	0	1992	
2	Beware	(Ffrr F 202)	69	1992	0	1992	
Vixen Female Vocal/Instrumental Group from the USA							
1	Edge Of A Broken Heart	(Manhattan Mt 48)	51	1988	26	1988	(EMI-Manhattan 50141)
2	Cryin'	(Manhattan Mt 60)	27	1989	22	1989	(EMI-Manhattan 60167)
3	Love Made Me	(EMI-Usa Mt 66)	36	1989	0	1989	
4	Edge Of A Broken Heart (Re-Entry)	(Manhattan Mt 48)	59	1989	0	1989	
5	How Much Love	(EMI-USA Mt 87)	35	1990	0	1990	
6	Love Is A Killer	(EMI-USA Mt 91)	41	1990	0	1990	
7	Not A Minute Too Soon	(EMI America Mt 93)	37	1991	0	1991	
	NAMES JANET KUEHNEMUND, ROXY PETRUCCI, JANET GARDNER & SHARE PEDERSEN						
Vladimir Cosma Hungarian Orchestra							
1	David's Song (Main Theme From *Kidnapped*)	(Decca Fr 13841)	64	1979	0	1979	
Vocaleers							
+ 1	Is It A Dream		0	1953	8	1953	(Red Robin 114)
Voggue Female Vocal Duo From Canada							
1	Dancin' The Night Away	(Mercury Mer 76)	39	1981	0	1981	
Vogues Vocal Band, Lead Singer Is Bill Burkette. Formed In Pennsylvania							
1	You're The One		0	1965	4	1965	(Co & Ce 229)
2	Five O'Clock World		0	1965	4	1965	(Co & Ce 232)
3	Magic Town		0	1966	21	1966	(Co & Ce 234)
4	The Land Of Milk And Honey		0	1966	29	1966	(Co & Ce 238)
* 5	Turn Around, Look At Me		0	1968	7	1968	(Reprise 0686)
6	My Special Angel		0	1968	7	1968	(Reprise 0766)

ISSUE	TITLE	UK LBL	UK POS	UK YEAR	US POS	US YEAR	US LBL
7	Till		0	1968	27	1968	(Reprise 0788)
8	No, Not Much		0	1969	34	1969	(Reprise 0803)
Voice Of The Beehive Mixed Vocal/Instrumental Group From The USA/UK							
1	I Say Nothing	(London Lon 151)	45	1987	0	1987	
2	I Walk The Earth	(London Lon 169)	42	1988	0	1988	
3	Don't Call Me Baby	(London Lon 175)	15	1988	0	1988	
4	I Say Nothing (Re-Issue)	(London Lon 190)	22	1988	0	1988	
5	I Walk The Earth (Re-Issue)	(London Lon 206)	46	1988	0	1988	
6	Monsters And Angels	(London Lon 302)	17	1991	0	1991	
7	I Think I Love You	(London Lon 308)	25	1991	0	1991	
8	Perfect Place	(London Lon 312)	37	1992	0	1992	
	SEE ALSO GIMME SHELTER (EP), VARIOUS ARTISTS (EP, LP, 78S							
Voices That Care Various Members Assembled To Raise Funds, Led By David Foster							
* 1	Voices That Care		0	1991	11	1991	(Giant 19350)
Volcano Mixed Vocal/Instrumental Group from the UK/Norway							
1	More To Love	(Deconstruction 74321221832)	32	1994	0	1994	
2	That's The Way Love Is	(Exp Expcd 002)	72	1995	0	1995	
	HIT 2 IS CREDITED TO VOLCANO WITH SEAN CARTWRIGHT							
Volumes Lead Singer With The R&B Quintet Is Ed Union							
1	I Love You		0	1962	22	1962	(Chex 1002)
Vonda Sheppard See Dan Hill							
Voxpoppers Vocal Quintet From New York City							
1	Wishing For Your Love		0	1958	18	1958	(Mercury 71282)
Voyage Disco Assembly From UK/France							
1	From East To West / Scots Machine	(GTO GT 224)	13	1978	0	1978	
2	Souvenirs	(GTO GT 241)	56	1978	0	1978	
3	Let's Fly Away	(GTO GT 245)	38	1979	0	1979	
Voyager Male Vocal/Instrumental Group from the UK							
1	Halfway Hotel	(Mountain Voy 001)	33	1979	0	1979	
Vybe Female Vocal Group from the USA							
1	Warm Summer Daze	(Fourth & Broadway Brcd 315)	60	1995	0	1995	

W

ISSUE	TITLE	UK LBL	UK POS	UK YEAR	US POS	US YEAR	US LBL
W.A.S.P.	Male Vocal/Instrumental Group from the USA						
2	95 - Nasty	(Capitol Cl 432)	70	1986	0	1986	
3	Cream Until You Like It	(Capitol Cl 248)	32	1987	0	1987	
4	I Don't Need No Doctor (Live)	(Capitol Cl 469)	31	1987	0	1987	
5	Live Animals (F..K Like A Beast)	(Music For Nations Kut 109)	61	1988	0	1988	
6	Mean Man	(Capitol Cl 521)	21	1989	0	1989	
7	The Real Me	(Capitol Cl 534)	23	1989	0	1989	
8	Forever Free	(Capitol Cl 546)	25	1989	0	1989	
9	Chainsaw Charlie (Murders In The New Morgue)	(Parlophone Rs 6308)	17	1992	0	1992	
10	The Idol	(Parlophone Rpd 614)	41	1992	0	1992	
11	I Am One	(Parlophone 10rg 6324)	56	1992	0	1992	
12	Sunset And Babylon	(Capitol Cdcl 698)	38	1993	0	1993	
Wa Wa Nee	Dance Band from Australia/New Zealand/USA						
1	Sugar Free		0	1987	35	1987	(Epic 07283)
Wadsworth Mansion	Names Steve Jablecki, John Poole, Wayne Gagnon & Mike Jablecki						
1	Sweet Mary		0	1971	7	1971	(Sussex 209)
Wag Ya Tail	Male Vocal/Instrumental Group from the UK						
1	Xpand Ya Mind (Expansions)	(Pwl International Pwl 238)	49	1992	0	1992	
Wah!	Male Vocal/Instrumental Group from the UK						
1	The Story Of The Blues	(Eternal Jf 1)	3	1982	0	1982	
2	Hope (I Wish You'd Believe Me)	(Wea X 9880)	37	1983	0	1983	
3	Come Back	(Beggars Banquet Beg 111)	2	1984	0	1984	
Waikikis	Male Instrumental Group from Belgium						
1	Hawaii Tattoo	(Pye International 7n 25286)	41	1965	33	1965	(Kapp 30)
Wailers	Instrumental Quintet from Washington, Tacoma, Washington, Formed In 1958						
1	Tall Cool One		0	1959	36	1959	(Golden Crest 518)
2	Tall Cool One (Re-Issue)		0	1964	38	1964	(Golden Crest 518)
Waitresses	Female Vocal Group from the UK						
1	Christmas Wrapping	(Zellsland Wip 6821)	45	1982	0	1982	
Waldo De Los Rios	Orchestra from Argentina						
1	Mozart Symphony No.40 In G Minor	(A&M Ams 836)	5	1971	0	1971	
Walker Brothers	Gary, Real Name Gary Leeds B: 3 Sep 1944, Glendale, California						
1	Love Her	(Philips Bf 1409)	20	1965	0	1965	
* 2	Make It Easy On Yourself	(Philips Bf 1428)	1	1965	16	1965	(Smash 2009)
3	My Ship Is Coming In	(Philips Bf 1454)	3	1965	0	1965	
4	The Sun Ain't Gonna Shine Anymore	(Philips Bf 1473)	1	1966	13	1966	(Smash 2032)
5	(Baby) You Don't Have To Tell Me	(Philips Bf 1497)	13	1966	0	1966	
6	Another Tear Falls	(Philips Bf 1514)	12	1966	0	1966	
7	Deadlier Than The Male	(Philips Bf 1537)	34	1966	0	1966	
8	Stay With Me Baby	(Philips Bf 1548)	26	1967	0	1967	
9	Walking In The Rain	(Philips Bf 1576)	26	1967	0	1967	
10	No Regrets	(GTO Gt 42)	7	1976	0	1976	
Wallflowers							
1	One Headlight	(Interscope Ind 95532)	54	1997	0	1997	
Wall Of Sound (Featuring) Gerald Lethan	Male Vocal/Instrumental Group from the USA						
1	Critical (If You Only Knew)	(Positiva Cdtiv 4)	73	1993	0	1993	
Wall Of Voodoo	Male Vocal/Instrumental Group from the USA						
1	Mexico Radio	(Illegal Ils 36)	64	1983	0	1983	

ISSUE	TITLE	UK LBL	UK POS	UK YEAR	US POS	US YEAR	US LBL
Wally Badarou Male Keyboard Instrumentalist from France							
1	Chief Inspector	(Fourth & Broadway Brw 37)	46	1985	0	1985	
Wally Cox Male Comedy Actor/Vocalist from the USA							
1	What A Crazy Guy (Dufo)		0	1953	27	1953	(RCA Victor 5278)
2	There Is A Tavern In The Town		0	1953	24	1953	(RCA Victor 5278)
Wally Jump Jr. & The Criminal Element Male Producer, Real Name Arthur Baker from the USA							
1	Turn Me Loose	(London Lon 126)	60	1987	0	1987	
2	Put The Needle To The Record	(Cooltempo Cool 150)	63	1987	0	1987	
3	Tighten Up - I Just Can't Stop Dancing	(Breakout USA 621)	24	1987	0	1987	
4	Private Party	(Breakout USA 624)	57	1988	0	1988	
5	Everybody (Rap)	(Deconstruction Pb 44701)	30	1990	0	1990	
Walter Beasley Male Vocalist from the USA							
1	I'm So Happy	(Urban Urb 14)	70	1988	0	1988	
Walter Brennan Male Movie Star/Vocalist, B: 25 Jul 1894, Massachusetts							
1	Dutchman's Gold		0	1960	30	1960	(Dot 16066)
2	Old Rivers		38	1962	5	1962	(Liberty 55436)
3	Mama Sang A Song		0	1962	38	1962	(Liberty 55508)
Walter Egan Male Vocalist, B: 12 Jul 1948, Jamaica, New York							
1	Magnet And Steel		0	1978	8	1978	(Columbia 10719)
Walter Murphy & The Big Apple Band Orchestra Leader, B: 1952 New York City							
* 1	A Fifth Of Beethoven	(Private Stock Pvt 59)	28	1976	1	1976	(Private Stock 45073)
Walter Schumann							
2	Ballad Of Davy Crockett		0	1955	14	1955	(RCA 6041)
Walter Wanderley Male Organist/Pianist/Composer, B: 1931 Brazil							
1	Summer Samba (So Nice)		0	1966	26	1966	(Verve 10421)
Wanda Jackson Female Vocalist, B: 20 Oct 1937 In Maud, Oklahoma							
3	Let's Have A Party	(Capitol Cl 15147)	32	1960	37	1960	(Capitol 4397)
4	Mean Mean Man	(Capitol Cl 15176)	46	1961	0	1961	
5	Mean Mean Man (Re-Entry)	(Capitol Cl 15176)	40	1961	0	1961	
6	Right Or Wrong		0	1961	29	1961	(Capitol 4553)
7	In The Middle Of A Heartache		0	1961	27	1961	(Capitol 4635)
Wang Chung Male Vocal/Instrumental Group from the UK Lead Singer With The Group Is Jack Hues							
1	Dance Hall Days	(Geffen A 3837)	21	1984	16	1984	(Geffen 29310)
2	Don't Let Go		0	1984	38	1984	(Geffen 29377)
3	Everybody Have Fun Tonight		0	1986	2	1986	(Geffen 28562)
4	Let's Go!		0	1987	9	1987	(Geffen 28531)
5	Hypnotize Me		0	1987	36	1987	(Geffen 28359)
Wannadies Vocal/Instrumental Group from Sweden							
1	Might Be Stars	(Indolent/RCA Die 003cd1)	51	1995	0	1995	
2	How Does It Feel	(Indolent/RCA Die 004cd1)	53	1996	0	1996	
3	You And Me Song	(Indolent/RCA Die 005cd)	18	1996	0	1996	
4	Someone Somewhere	(Indolent/RCA Dle 006cd)	38	1996	0	1996	
5	Hit	(Indolent/RCA Die 009cd1)	20	1997	0	1997	
6	Shorty	(Indolent/RCA Die 010cd1)	41	1997	0	1997	
War Male Vocal/Instrumental Group from the USA/Canada/Denmark							
* 1	Spill The Wine		0	1970	3	1970	(Mgm 14118)
2	All Day Music		0	1971	35	1971	(United Artists 50815)
* 3	Slippin' Into Darkness		0	1971	16	1971	(United Artists 50867)
* 4	The World Is A Ghetto		0	1973	7	1973	(United Artists 50975)
* 5	The Cisco Kid		0	1973	2	1973	(United Artists 163)
6	Gypsy Man		0	1973	8	1973	(United Artists 281)
7	Me And Baby Brother	(Island Wip 6303)	21	1976	15	1973	(United Artists 350)
8	Ballero (Live)		0	1974	33	1974	(United Artists 432)
* 9	Why Can't We Be Friends		0	1975	6	1975	(United Artists 629)
10	Low Rider	(Island Wip 6267)	12	1976	7	1975	(United Artists 706)
* 11	Summer		0	1976	7	1976	(United Artists 834)
12	Galaxy	(MCA 339)	14	1978	39	1978	(MCA 40820)
13	Hey Senorita	(MCA 359)	40	1978	0	1978	
14	You Got The Power	(RCA 201)	58	1982	0	1982	
15	Groovin'	(Bluebird Br 16)	43	1985	0	1985	
	OBITUARY: MILLER D: 1980 MURDERED						

ISSUE	TITLE	UK LBL	UK POS	UK YEAR	US POS	US YEAR	US LBL
Ward Brothers	Male Vocal/Instrumental Group from the UK						
1	Cross That Bridge	(Siren Siren 37)	32	1986	0	1986	
Warm Sounds	Male Vocal Duo from the UK						
1	Birds And Bees	(Deram Dm 120)	27	1967	0	1967	
Warrant	Male Vocal/Instrumental Group from the USA Lead singer is Jani Lane						
1	Down Boys		0	1989	27	1989	(Columbia 68606)
* 2	Heaven		0	1989	2	1989	(Columbia 68985)
3	Sometimes She Cries		0	1990	20	1990	(Columbia 73095)
4	Cherry Pie	(CBS 6562587	59	1990	10	1990	(Columbia 73510)
5	I Saw Red		0	1991	10	1991	(Columbia 73597)
6	Cherry Pie (Re-Issue)	(Columbia 6566867)	35	1991	0	1991	
Warren G	Male Rapper, Real Name Warren Griggin III from Long Beach, California						
* 1	Regulate	(Death Row A 8290cd)	5	1994	2	1994	(Death Row 98280)
* 2	This DJ	(Ral Ralcd 1)	12	1994	9	1994	(Viol./Ral 853236)
3	This Dj (Re-Entry)	(Ral Ralcd 1)	72	1994	0	1994	
4	Do You See	(Ral Ralcd 3)	29	1995	0	1995	
5	What's Love Got To Do With It (From Supercop)	(Interscope Ind 97008)	2	1996	32	1996	(Interscope 97008)
6	I Shot The Sheriff	(Def Jam/Mercury Defcd 31)	2	1997	20	1997	(Mercury 573564)
7	Smokin' Me Ou	(Def Jam 5744432)	14	1997	0	1997	
Warren Mills	Male Vocalist from Zambia						
1	Sunshine	(Jive Jive 99)	74	1985	0	1985	
Warren Zevon	Male Singer/Songwriter/Pianist, B: 24 Jan 1947 Chicago						
1	Werewolves Of London		0	1978	21	1978	(Asylum 45472)
Was (Not Was)	Male Vocal/Instrumental Brothers Don & Davis Was						
1	Out Comes The Freaks	(Ze/Geffen A 4178)	41	1984	0	1984	
2	Spy In The House Of Love	(Fontana Was 2)	51	1987	16	1988	(Chrysalis 43266)
3	Walk The Dinosaur	(Fontana Was 3)	10	1987	7	1989	(Chrysalis 43331)
4	Spy In The House Of Love (Re-Entry)	(Fontana Was 2	21	1988	0	1988	
5	Out Comes The Freaks Again	(Fontana Was 4)	44	1988	0	1988	
6	Anything Can Happen	(Fontana Was 5)	67	1988	0	1988	
7	Papa Was A Rolling Stone	(Fontana Was 7)	12	1990	0	1990	
8	How The Heart Behaves	(Fontana Was 8)	53	1990	0	1990	
9	Listen Like Thieves	(Fontana Was 10)	58	1992	0	1992	
10	Shake Your Head	(Fontana Was 11)	4	1992	0	1992	
11	Somewhere In America	(Fontana Was 12)	57	1992	0	1992	
	(THERE'S A STREET NAMED AFTER MY DAD) • HIT 5 IS A RE-RECORDING OF HIT 1						
Waterboys	Male Vocal/Instrumental Group from the UK/Ireland						
1	The Whole Of The Moon	(Ensign Eny 520)	26	1985	0	1985	
2	Fisherman's Blues	(Ensign Eny 621)	32	1989	0	1989	
3	And A Bang On The Ear	(Ensign Eny 624)	51	1989	0	1989	
4	The Whole Of The Moon (Re-Issue)	(Ensign Eny 642)	3	1991	0	1991	
5	Fisherman's Blues (Re-Issue)	(Ensign Eny 645)	75	1991	0	1991	
6	The Return Of Pan	(Geffen Gfstd 42	24	1993	0	1993	
7	Glastonbury Song	(Geffen Gfstd 49)	29	1993	0	1993	
Waterfront	Male Vocal/Instrumental Duo, Chris Duffy & Phil Cilla from Cardiff, Wales.						
1	Broken Arrow	(Polydor Won 3)	63	1989	0	1989	
2	Cry	(Polydor Won 1)	17	1989	10	1989	(Polydor 871110)
3	Nature Of Love	(Polydor Won 2)	63	1989	0	1989	
Wavelength	Male Vocalist from the UK						
1	Hurry Home	(Ariola Aro 281)	17	1982	0	1982	
Wax	Male Vocal/Instrumental Duo from the USA/UK						
1	Right Between The Eyes	(RCA Pb 40509)	60	1986	0	1986	
2	Bridge To Your Heart	(RCA Pb 41405)	12	1987	0	1987	
Way Of The West	Male Vocal/Instrumental Group from the UK						
1	Don't Say That's Just For White Boys	(Mercury Mer 66)	54	1981	0	1981	
Way Out West	Male Production/Instrumental Duo from the UK						
1	Ajare	(Deconstruction 74321243802)	52	1994	0	1994	
2	Domination	(Deconstruction 74321342822)	38	1996	0	1996	
3	The Gift	(Deconstruction 74321401912)	15	1996	0	1996	

ISSUE	TITLE	UK LBL	UK POS	UK YEAR	US POS	US YEAR	US LBL
Waylon & Willie							
1	Good Hearted Woman		0	1975	25	1994	(RCA 10529)
2	Mammas Don't Let Your Babies Grow Up To Be Cowboys		0	1978	42	1978	(Rca 11198)
3	I Can't Get Off On You		0	1978	42	1978	(Rca 11198)
4	Just To Satisfy You		0	1982	52	1982	(Rca 13073)
Waylon Jennings Male Vocalist And Former Dj, B: 15 Jun 1937 Littlefield, Texas							
44	Luckenbach, Texas (Back To The Basic Of Love)		0	1977	25	1977	(RCA 10924)
* 56	Theme From The Dukes Of Hazzard (Good Ol'boys)		0	1980	21	1980	(RCA 12067)
Wayne Fontana & The Mindbenders Male Vocal/Instrumental Group from the UK, Glyn Geoffrey Ellis B: 28 Oct 1945 Manchester, Uk							
1	Hello Josephine	(Fontana Tf 404)	46	1963	0	1963	
2	Stop Look And Listen	(Fontana Tf 451)	37	1964	0	1964	
3	Um Um Um Um Um Um	(Fontana Tf 497)	5	1964	0	1964	
* 4	Game Of Love	(Fontana Tf 535)	2	1965	1	1965	(Fontana 1509)
5	It's Just A Little Bit Too Late	(Fontana Tf 579)	20	1965	0	1965	
6	She Needs Love	(Fontana Tf 611)	32	1965	0	1965	
* 8	A Groovy Kind Of Love	(Fontana Tf 644)	2	1966	2	1966	(Fontana 1541)
9	Come On Home	(Fontana Tf 684)	16	1966	0	1966	
10	Can't Live With You (Can't Live Without You)	(Fontana Tf 697)	28	1966	0	1966	
11	Goodbye Bluebird	(Fontana Tf 737	49	1966	0	1966	
12	Ashes To Ashes	(Fontana Tf 731)	14	1966	0	1966	
13	Pamela Pamela	(Fontana Tf 770)	11	1966	0	1966	
14	The Letter	Fontana Tf 869)	42	1967	0	1967	
Wayne Gibson Male Vocalist from the UK							
1	Kelly	(Pye 7n 15680)	48	1964	0	1964	
2	Under My Thumb	(Pye Disco Demand Dds 2001)	17	1974	0	1974	
W.A.S.P							
1	Wild Child	(Capitol Cl 388)	71	1985	0	1985	
Walter Schumann Choral Group from the USA							
1	I See The Moon		0	1953	26	1953	(RCA Victor 5478)
Wayne Marshall Male Vocalist from the UK							
1	Ooh Aah (G-Spot)	(Soultown Soulcds 322)	29	1994	0	1994	
2	Spirit	(Soultown Soulcds 00352)	58	1995	0	1995	
4	G Spot	(MBA Inter 9006)	50	1996	0	1996	
5	Never Knew Love Like This	(Sony S2 6629382)	40	1996	0	1996	
Wayne Newton Male Actor/Singer/Multi-Instrumentalist, B: 3 Apr 1942 Roanoke, Virginia							
1	Danke Schoen		0	1963	13	1963	(Capitol 4989)
2	Red Roses For A Blue Lady		0	1965	23	1965	(Capitol 5366)
* 3	Daddy Don't You Walk So Fast		0	1972	4	1972	(Chelsea 0100)
4	Years		0	1980	35	1980	(Aries II 108)
Wayne Raney Male Country Vocal/Instrumentalist (Harmonica) from the USA							
1	Why Don't You Haul Off And Love Me?		0	1949	22	1949	(King 791)
We Five Lead Singer With The Californian Quintet Is Beverly Bivens							
* 1	You Were On My Mind		0	1965	3	1965	(A&M 770)
2	Let's Get Together		0	1965	31	1965	(A&M 784)
We've Got A Fuzzbox And We're Gonna Use It Female Vocal/Instrumental Group from the UK							
1	Xx Sex / Rules And Regulations	(Vindaloo Ugh 11)	41	1986	0	1986	
2	Love Is The Slug	(Vindaloo Ugh 14)	31	1986	0	1986	
3	What's The Point	(Vindaloo Yz 101)	51	1987	0	1987	
4	International Rescue	(Wea Yz 347)	11	1989	0	1989	
5	Pink Sunshine	(Wea Yz 401)	14	1989	0	1989	
6	Self!	(Wea Yz 408)	24	1989	0	1989	
Weather Girls Female Vocal Duo from the USA							
1	It's Raining Men	(CBS A 2924)	73	1983	0	1983	
2	It's Raining Men (Re-Entry)	(CBS A 2924)	2	1984	0	1984	
Weather Prophets Male Vocal/Instrumental Group from the UK							
1	She Comes From The Rain	(Elevation Acid 1)	62	1987	0	1987	
Weavers Male Folk Group from the USA, With Pete Seeger, Lee Hays, Ronnie Gilbert & Fred Hellerman							
* 1	Tzena, Tzena, Tzena		0	1950	2	1950	(Decca 27077)
2	Goodnight, Irene		0	1950	1	1950	(Decca 27077)
3	The Roving Kind		0	1950	11	1950	(Decca 27332)

ISSUE	TITLE	UK LBL	UK POS	UK YEAR	US POS	US YEAR	US LBL
4	So Long (It's Been Good To Know Ya)		0	1951	4	1951	(Decca 27376)
* 5	On Top Of Old Smoky		0	1951	2	1951	(Decca 27515)
6	Kisses Sweeter Than Wine		0	1951	19	1951	(Decca 27670)
7	When The Saints Go Marching In		0	1951	27	1951	(Decca 27670)
8	Winoweh		0	1952	14	1952	(Decca 27928)
9	Around The Corner (Beneath The Berry Tree)		0	1952	19	1952	(Decca 28054)
10	Midnight Special		0	1952	30	1952	(Decca 28272)
11	Sylvie		0	1954	27	1954	(Decca 28919)

Webb Pierce   Male Country Singer, B: 8 Aug 1921 West Monroe, Louisiana

ISSUE	TITLE	UK LBL	UK POS	UK YEAR	US POS	US YEAR	US LBL
* 15	More And More		0	1954	22	1954	(Decca 29252)
47	I Ain't Never		0	1959	24	1959	(Decca 30923)

Wedding Present   Male Vocal/Instrumental Group from the UK

ISSUE	TITLE	UK LBL	UK POS	UK YEAR	US POS	US YEAR	US LBL
1	Nobody's Twisting Your Arm	(Reception Rec 009)	46	1988	0	1988	
2	Why Are You Being So Reasonable Now	(Reception 011)	42	1988	0	1988	
3	Kennedy	(RCA Pb 43117)	33	1989	0	1989	
4	Brassneck	(RCA Pb 43403)	24	1990	0	1990	
5	3 Songs (EP)	(RCA Pb 44021)	25	1990	0	1990	
6	Dalliance	(RCA Pb 44495)	29	1991	0	1991	
7	Lovenest	(RCA Pt 44750)	58	1991	0	1991	
8	Blue Eyes	(RCA Pb 45185)	26	1992	0	1992	
9	Go-Go Dancer	(RCA Pb 45183)	20	1992	0	1992	
10	Three	(RCA Pb 45181)	14	1992	0	1992	
11	Silver Shorts	(RCA Pb 45311)	14	1992	0	1992	
12	Come Play With Me	(RCA Pb 45313)	10	1992	0	1992	
13	California	(RCA Pb 45315)	16	1992	0	1992	
14	Flying Saucer	(RCA 74321101157)	22	1992	0	1992	
15	Boing!	(RCA 74321101177)	17	1992	0	1992	
16	Love Slave	(RCA 743211101167)	17	1992	0	1992	
17	Sticky	(RCA 74321116917)	17	1992	0	1992	
18	The Queen Of Outer Space	(RCA 74321116927)	23	1992	0	1992	
19	No Christmas	(RCA 74321116937)	25	1992	0	1992	
20	Yeah Yeah Yeah Yeah Yeah	(Island Cid 585)	51	1994	0	1994	
21	It's A Gas	(Island Cid 591)	71	1994	0	1994	
22	2,3, Go	(Cooking Vinyl Frycd 048)	67	1996	0	1996	
23	Montreal	(Cooking Vinyl Frycd 053)	40	1997	0	1997	

Wednesday   Names: Mike O'Neil, Randy Begg, John Dufek & Paul Andrew Smith

ISSUE	TITLE	UK LBL	UK POS	UK YEAR	US POS	US YEAR	US LBL
1	Last Kiss		0	1974	34	1974	(Sussex 507)

Wee Papa Girl Rappers   Female Vocal Duo from the UK

ISSUE	TITLE	UK LBL	UK POS	UK YEAR	US POS	US YEAR	US LBL
1	Faith	(Jive Jive 164)	60	1988	0	1988	
2	Heat It Up	(Jive Jive 174)	21	1988	0	1988	
3	Wee Rule	(Jive Jive 185)	6	1988	0	1988	
4	Soulmate	(Jive Jive 193)	45	1988	0	1988	
5	Blow The House Down	(Jive Jive 197)	65	1989	0	1989	

Weekend   Mixed Multi-National Vocal/Instrumental Group

ISSUE	TITLE	UK LBL	UK POS	UK YEAR	US POS	US YEAR	US LBL
1	Christmas Medley / Auld Lang Syne	(Lifestyle Xy 1)	47	1985	0	1985	

Weezer   Male Vocal/Instrumental Group from the USA

ISSUE	TITLE	UK LBL	UK POS	UK YEAR	US POS	US YEAR	US LBL
1	Undone - The Sweater Song	(Geffen Gfstd 85)	35	1995	0	1995	
2	Buddy Holly	(Geffen Gfstd 88)	12	1995	0	1995	
3	Say It Ain't So	(Geffen Gfstd 95)	37	1995	0	1995	
4	El Scorcho	(Geffen Gfstd 22167)	50	1996	0	1996	

Weird Al Yankovic   Novelty Singer From Los Angeles

ISSUE	TITLE	UK LBL	UK POS	UK YEAR	US POS	US YEAR	US LBL
* 1	Eat It	(Scotti Brothers/Epic A 4257)	36	1984	2	1984	(Rock 'N' Roll 04374)
2	Smells Like Nirvana	(Scotti Brothers Po 219)	58	1992	35	1992	(Scotti Brothers 75314)

Wendell Hall   Male Author/Poet/Composer/Vocalist/Guitarist/Xylophonist, B: 23 Aug 1896 St. George, Kansas

ISSUE	TITLE	UK LBL	UK POS	UK YEAR	US POS	US YEAR	US LBL
* 1	It Ain't Gonna Rain No Mo'		0	1923	1	1923	(Victor 19171)

Wendell Williams   Male Rapper from the USA

ISSUE	TITLE	UK LBL	UK POS	UK YEAR	US POS	US YEAR	US LBL
1	Everybody (Rap)	(Deconstruction Pb 44701)	30	1990	0	1990	
2	So Groovy	(Deconstruction Pb 44567)	74	1991	0	1991	

Wendy & Lisa   Female Vocal Duo from the USA

ISSUE	TITLE	UK LBL	UK POS	UK YEAR	US POS	US YEAR	US LBL
1	Waterfall	(Virgin Vs 999)	66	1987	0	1987	
2	Side Show	(Virgin Vs 1012)	49	1988	0	1988	
3	Are You My Baby	(Virgin Vs 1156)	70	1989	0	1989	
4	Lolly Lolly	(Virgin Vs 1175)	64	1989	0	1989	

ISSUE	TITLE	UK LBL	UK POS	UK YEAR	US POS	US YEAR	US LBL
5	Satisfaction	(Virgin Vs 1194)	27	1989	0	1989	
6	Waterfall (Re-Mix)	(Virgin Vs 1223)	69	1989	0	1989	
7	Strung Out	(Virgin Vs 1272)	44	1990	0	1990	
8	Rainbow Lake	(Virgin Vs 1280)	70	1990	0	1990	
Wendy James Female Vocalist from the UK							
1	The Nameless One	(MCA Mcstd 1732)	34	1993	0	1993	
2	London's Brilliant	(MCA Mcstd 1763)	62	1993	0	1993	
Wendy Moten Female Vocalist from the USA							
1	Come In Out Of The Rain	EMI-Usa Cdmt 105)	8	1994	0	1994	
2	So Close To Love	(EMI-Usa Cdmts 106)	34	1994	0	1994	
Wesson Brothers Male Comedy Duo, Dick & Gene from the USA							
1	All Right Louie, Drop The Gun		0	1949	11	1949	(National 9070)
West Coast Rap All-Stars Hit Was In Benefit For Inner City Youth, Artists Include MC Hammer							
1	We're All In The Same Game		0	1990	35	1990	(Warner Bros 19819)
West End Female Vocal Group from the UK							
1	The Love I Lost	(Pwl Sanctuary Pwcd 253)	3	1993	0	1993	
2	Love Rules	(RCA 74321292702)	44	1995	0	1995	
West Ham United Cup Squad Male Soccer Team Vocalist from the UK							
1	I'm Forever Blowing Bubbles	(Pye 7n 45470)	31	1975	0	1975	
West Street Mob Male Vocal Group from the USA							
1	Break Dancin' / Electric Boogie	(Sugarhill Sh 128)	71	1983	0	1983	
2	Break Dancin' / Electric Boogie (Re-Entry)	(Sugarhill Sh 128)	64	1983	0	1983	
Westbam Male Producer from Germany							
1	Celebration Generation	(Low Spirit Pqcd 5)	48	1994	0	1994	
2	Bam Bam Bam	(Low Spirit Pzcd 329)	57	1994	0	1994	
3	Wizards Of The Sonic	(Urban Pzcd 344)	32	1995	0	1995	
4	Always Music	(Low Spirit 5779152)	51	1996	0	1996	
Westside Connection							
1	Bow Down		0	1996	21	1996	(Priority 53227)
2	Gangstas Make The World Go Round		0	1997	40	1997	(Priority 63264)
Westworld Mixed Vocal/Instrumental Group from the USA/UK							
1	Sonic Boom Boy	(RCA Boom 1)	11	1987	0	1987	
2	Be-Na-Na-Bam-Boo	(RCA Boom 2)	37	1987	0	1987	
3	Where The Action Is	(RCA Boom 3)	54	1987	0	1987	
4	Silvermac	(RCA Boom 4)	42	1987	0	1987	
5	Everything Good Is Bad	(RCA Pb 42243)	72	1988	0	1988	
Wet Wet Wet Male Vocal/Instrumental Group, Marti Pellow, Graeme Clark, Neil Mitchell & Tom Cunningham from Scotland							
1	Wishing I Was Lucky	(Precious Jewel 3)	6	1987	0	1987	
2	Sweet Little Mystery	(Precious Jewel 4)	5	1987	0	1987	
3	Angel Eyes	(Precious Jewel 6)	5	1987	0	1987	
4	Temptation	(Precious Jewel 7)	12	1988	0	1988	
5	With A Little Help From My Friends	(Childline Line 1)	1	1988	0	1988	
6	Sweet Surrender	(Precious Jewel 9)	6	1989	0	1989	
7	Broke Away	(Precious Jewel 10)	19	1989	0	1989	
8	Hold Back The River	(Precious Jewel 11)	31	1990	0	1990	
9	Stay With Me Heartache - I Feel Fine	(Precious Jewel 13)	30	1990	0	1990	
10	Make It Tonight	(Precious Jewel 15)	37	1991	0	1991	
11	Put The Light On	(Precious Jewel 16)	56	1991	0	1991	
12	Goodnight Girl	(Precious Jewel 17)	1	1992	0	1992	
13	More Than Love	(Precious Jewel 18)	19	1992	0	1992	
14	Lip Service (EP)	(Precious Jewel 19)	5	1992	0	1992	
15	Blue For You - This Time (Live)	(Precious Jwlcd 20)	38	1993	0	1993	
16	Shed A Tear	(Precious Jwlcd 21)	22	1993	0	1993	
17	Cold Cold Heart	(Precious Jwlcd 22)	23	1994	0	1994	
18	Love Is All Around	(Precious Jwlcd 23)	1	1994	0	1994	
19	Julia Says	(Precious Jwlcd 24)	3	1995	0	1995	
20	Don't Want To Forgive Me No	(Precious Jelcd 25)	7	1995	0	1995	
21	Somewhere Somehow	(Precious Jwlcd 26)	7	1995	0	1995	
22	She's All On My Mind	(Precious Jwldd 27)	17	1995	0	1995	
23	Morning	(Mercury Jwldd 28)	16	1996	0	1996	
24	If I Never See You Again	(Mercury Jwlcd 29)	3	1997	0	1997	
25	Strange	(Mercury Jwlcd 30)	13	1997	0	1997	

ISSUE	TITLE	UK LBL	UK POS	UK YEAR	US POS	US YEAR	US LBL
26	If I Never See You Again (Re-Entry)	(Mercury Jwlcd 29)	72	1997	0	1997	
27	Strange (Re-Entry)	(Mercury Jwlcd 30)	74	1997	0	1997	
28	Yesterday	(Mercury Jwlcd 31)	4	1997	0	1997	
Wet Willie Rock Band From Alabama With Brothers Jimmy & Jack Hall							
1	Keep On Smillin'		0	1974	10	1974	(Capricorn 0043)
2	Street Corner Serenade		0	1978	30	1978	(Epic 50478)
3	Weekend		0	1979	29	1979	(Epic 50714)
Whale Mixed Vocal/Instrumental Group from Sweden							
1	Hobo Humpin' Slobo Babe	(East West Yz 798cd)	46	1994	0	1994	
2	I'll Do Ya	(Hut Hutdg 51)	53	1995	0	1995	
3	Hobo Humpin' Slobo Babe (Re-Issue)	(Hut Hutcd 64)	15	1995	0	1995	
Wham! Male Vocal Duo from the UK							
1	Young Guns (Got For It)	(Innervision Ivl A2766)	3	1982	0	1982	
2	Wham Rap	(Innervision Ivl A2442)	8	1983	0	1983	
3	Bad Boys	(Innervision A 3143)	2	1983	0	1983	
4	Club Tropicana	(Innervision A 3613)	4	1983	0	1983	
5	Club Fantastic Megamix	(Innervision A 3586)	15	1983	0	1983	
* 6	Wake Me Up Before You Go Go	(Epic A 4440)	1	1984	1	1984	(Columbia 04552)
7	Freedom	(Epic A 4743)	1	1984	3	1985	(Columbia 05409)
* 8	Careless Whispers	(Epic A 4603)	1	1984	1	1984	(Columbia 04691)
9	Last Christmas	(Epic A 4949)	2	1984	0	1984	
* 10	Everything She Wants	(Epic A 4949)	2	1984	1	1985	(Columbia 04840)
11	I'm Your Man	(Epic A 6716)	1	1985	3	1986	(Columbia 05721)
12	Last Christmas (Re-Issue)	(Epic Wham 1)	6	1985	0	1985	
13	The Edge Of Heaven	(Epic Fin 1)	1	1986	10	1986	(Columbia 06182)
14	Where Did Your Heart Go	(Rpic Fin 1)	28	1986	0	1986	
15	Last Christmas (2nd Re-Issue)	(Epic 650269 7)	45	1986	0	1986	
When In Rome Male Vocal/Instrumental Group from the UK Names: Clive Farrington, Andrew Mann & Michael Floreale							
1	The Promise	(10 Ten 244)	58	1989	11	1988	(Virgin 99323)
Whigfield Female Vocalist from Denmark							
1	Saturday Night	(Systematic Syscd 3)	1	1994	0	1994	
2	Another Day	(Systematic Syscd 4)	7	1994	0	1994	
3	Think Of You	(Systematic Syscd 10)	7	1995	0	1995	
4	Close To You	(Systematic Syscd 18)	13	1995	0	1995	
5	Last Christmas / Big Time	(Systematic Syscd 24)	21	1995	0	1995	
Whipping Boy Male Vocal/Instrumental Group from Ireland							
1	We Don't Need Nobody Else	(Columbia 6622207)	51	1995	0	1995	
2	When We Were Young	(Columbia 6628062)	46	1996	0	1996	
3	Twinkle	(Columbia 6632272)	55	1996	0	1996	
Whispers Male Vocal Group from the USA							
* 1	And The Beat Goes On	(Solar So 1)	2	1980	19	1980	(Solar 11894)
2	Lady	(Solar So 4)	55	1980	28	1980	(Solar 11928)
3	My Girl	(Solar So 8)	26	1980	0	1980	
4	It's A Love Thing	(Solar So 16)	9	1981	28	1981	(Solar 12154)
5	I Can Make It Better	(Solar So 19)	44	1981	0	1981	
6	Contagious	(MCA MCA 937)	56	1985	0	1985	
7	And The Beat Goes On (Re-Issue)	(Solar MCA 1126)	45	1987	0	1987	
8	Rock Steady	(Solar MCA 1152)	38	1987	7	1987	(Solar 70006)
9	Special F/X	(Solar MCA 1178)	69	1987	0	1987	
Whistle Rap Trio Formed In 1985 With Garvin Dublin, Brian Faust & Rickford Bennett							
1	(Nothin' Serious) Just Buggin'	(Champion Champ 12)	7	1986	0	1986	
2	Always And Forever		0	1990	35	1990	(Select 2014)
Whistling Jack Smith Real Name Billy Moeller B: 2 Feb 1946 from the UK							
* 1	I Was Kaiser Bill's Batman	(Deram Dm 1120	5	1967	20	1967	(Deram 85005)
White & Torch Male Vocal/Instrumental Duo Roy White & Steve Torch from the UK							
1	Parade	(Chrysalis Chs 2641)	54	1982	0	1982	
White Lion Names Mike Tramp, James Lomenzo, Gref D'angelo & Vito Bratta							
1	Wait		0	1988	8	1988	(Atlantic 89126)
2	When The Children Cry		0	1989	3	1989	(Atlantic 89015)
White Plains Male Vocal Group from the UK							
1	My Baby Loves Lovin'	(Deram Dm 280)	9	1970	13	1970	(Deram 85058)
2	I've Got You On My Mind	(Deram Dm 291)	17	1970	0	1970	
3	Julie Do Ya Love Me	(Deram Dm 315)	8	1970	0	1970	

ISSUE	TITLE	UK LBL	UK POS	UK YEAR	US POS	US YEAR	US LBL
4	When You Are King	(Deram Dm 333)	13	1971	0	1971	
5	Step Into A Dream	(Deram Dm 371)	21	1973	0	1973	
White Town Male Vocalist, Real Name Jyoti Mishara from Derby, Uk							
1	Your Woman (Abort, Retry, Fail)	(Chrysalis Cdchs 5052)	1	1997	25	1997	(Chrysalis 58638)
2	Undressed	(Chrysalis Cdchs 5058)	57	1997	0	1997	
White Zombie Male Vocal/Instrumental Group from the USA							
1	More Human Than Human	(Geffen Gfstd 92)	51	1995	0	1995	
2	Electric Head Part 2 (The Ecstacy)	(Geffen Gfsxd 22140)	31	1996	0	1996	
Whitehead Bros Male Vocal Duo from the USA							
1	Your Love Is A 187	(Motown Tmgcd 1434)	32	1995	0	1995	
2	Forget I Was A 'G'	(Motown Tmgcd 1441)	40	1995	0	1995	
Whiteout Male Vocal/Instrumental Group from the UK							
1	Detroit	(Silvertone Orecd 66)	73	1994	0	1994	
2	Jackie's Racing	(Silvertone Orecd 68)	72	1995	0	1995	
Whitesnake Heavy-Metal Band With Lead Singer David Coverdale							
1	Snake Bite (Ep)	(EMI International Inep 751)	61	1978	0	1978	
2	Long Way From Home	(United Artists Bp 324)	55	1979	0	1979	
3	Fool For Your Loving	(United Artists Bp 352)	13	1980	0	1980	
4	Ready An' Willing	(United Artists Bp 363)	43	1980	0	1980	
5	Ain't No Love In The Heart Of The City	(Sunburst/Liberty Bp 381)	51	1980	0	1980	
6	Don't Break My Heart Again	(Liberty Bp 395)	17	1981	0	1981	
7	Would I Lie To You	(Liberty Pb 399)	37	1981	0	1981	
8	Here I Go Again / Bloody Luxury	(Liberty Bp 416)	34	1982	1	1987	(Geffen 28339)
9	Guilty Of Love	(Liberty Bp 420)	31	1983	0	1983	
10	Give Me More Time	(Liberty Bp 422)	29	1984	0	1984	
11	Standing In The Shadow	(Liberty Bp 423)	62	1984	0	1984	
12	Love Ain't No Stranger	(Liberty Bp 424)	44	1985	0	1985	
13	Still Of The Night	(EMI EMI 5606)	16	1987	0	1987	
14	Is This Love	(EMI Em 3)	9	1987	2	1987	(Geffen 28233)
15	Here I Go Again (Re-Mix)	(EMI Em 35)	9	1987	0	1987	
16	Give Me All Your Love	(EMI Em 23)	18	1988	0	1988	
17	Fool For Your Loving (Re-Recording)	(EMI Em 123)	43	1989	37	1989	(Geffen 22715)
18	The Deeper The Love	(EMI Em 128)	35	1990	28	1990	(Geffen 19951)
19	Now You're Gone	(EMI Em 150)	31	1990	0	1990	
20	Is This Love / Sweet Lady Luck (Re-Issue)	(EMI Cdem 329)	25	1994	0	1994	
21	Too Many Tears	(EMI Cdem 471)	46	1997	0	1997	
Whitney Houston Female Vocalist, B: 9 Aug 1963 Newark, New Jersey, Former Backing Singer For Chaka Khan							
1	You Give Good Love		0	1985	3	1985	(Arista 9274)
2	Saving All My Love For You	(Arista Arist 640)	1	1985	1	1985	(Arista 9381)
3	How Will I Know	(Arista Arist 656)	5	1986	1	1985	(Arista 9434)
4	Hold Me	(Asylum Ekr 32)	44	1986	0	1986	
5	Greatest Love Of All	(Arista Arist 658)	8	1986	1	1986	(Arista 9466)
* 6	I Wanna Dance With Somebody (Who Loves Me)	(Arista Ris 1)	1	1987	1	1987	(Arista 9598)
7	Didn't We Almost Have It All	(Arista Ris 31)	14	1987	1	1987	(Arista 9616)
8	So Emotional	(Arista Rist 43)	5	1987	1	1987	(Arista 9642)
9	Where Do Broken Hearts Go	(Arista 109793)	14	1988	1	1988	(Arista 9674)
10	Love Will Save The Day	(Arista 111516)	10	1988	9	1988	(Arista 9720)
11	One Moment In Time	(Arista 111613)	1	1988	5	1988	(Arista 9743)
12	It Isn't, It Wasn't, It Ain't Never Gonna Be	(Arista 112545)	29	1989	0	1989	
* 13	I'm Your Baby Tonight	(Arista 113594)	5	1990	1	1990	(Arista 2108)
* 14	All The Man That I Need	(Arista 114000)	13	1990	1	1991	(Arista 2156)
15	I'm Your Baby Tonight (Re-Entry)	(Arista 113594)	69	1990	0	1990	
* 16	The Star Spangled Banner (Live)		0	1991	20	1991	(Arista 2207)
17	Miracle		0	1991	9	1991	(Arista 2222)
18	My Name Is Not Susan	(Arista 114510)	29	1991	20	1991	(Arista 12259)
19	I Belong To You	(Arista 114727)	54	1991	0	1991	
* 20	I Will Always Love You	(Arista 74321120657)	1	1992	1	1992	(Arista 12490)
* 21	I'm Every Woman	(Arista 74321131502)	4	1993	4	1993	(Arista 12519)
* 22	I Have Nothing	(Arista 74321146142)	3	1993	4	1993	(Arista 12527)
23	Run To You	(Arista 74321153332)	15	1993	31	1993	(Arista 12570)
24	Queen Of The Night	(Arista 74321169302)	14	1993	0	1993	
25	I Will Always Love You (Re-Entry)	(Arista 74321120652)	25	1993	0	1993	
26	Something In Common	(MCA Mcstd 1957)	16	1994	0	1994	

ISSUE	TITLE	UK LBL	UK POS	UK YEAR	US POS	US YEAR	US LBL
* 27	Exhale (Shoop Shoop)	(Arista 74321332472)	11	1995	1	1996	(Arista 12885)
28	I Believe In You And Me (The Preacher's Wife) (Arista 74321468602)		16	1997	4	1996	(Arista 13293)
29	Count On Me	Arista 74321345842)	12	1996	8	1996	(Arista 00000)
30	Why Does It Hurt So Bad		0	1996	26	1996	(Arista 13213)
31	Step By Step (From Preacher's Wife)	(Arista 74321449332)	13	1996	15	1997	(Arista 13312)

Who Male Vocal/Instrumental Group from the UK, Names: Roger Daltrey, Pete Townshend, John Entwistle & Keith Moon

ISSUE	TITLE	UK LBL	UK POS	UK YEAR	US POS	US YEAR	US LBL
1	I Can't Explain	(Brunswick 05926)	8	1965	93	1965	(Decca 31725)
2	Anyway Anyhow Anywhere	(Brunswick 05935)	10	1965	0	1965	
3	My Generation	(Brunswick 05944)	2	19657	4	1966	(Decca 31877)
4	Substitute	(Reaction 591 001)	5	1966	0	1966	
5	A Legal Matter	(Brunswick 05966)	32	1966	0	1966	
6	I'm A Boy	(Reaction 591 004)	2	1966	0	1966	
7	The Kids Are Alright	(Brunswick 05965)	41	1966	0	1966	
8	The Kids Are Alright (Re-Entry)	(Brunswick 05965)	48	1966	0	1966	
9	Happy Jack	(Reaction 591 010)	3	1966	24	1967	(Decca 32114)
10	Pictures Of Lily	(Track 604 002)	4	1967	51	1967	(Decca 32156)
11	The Last Time / Under My Thumb	(Track 604 006)	44	1967	0	1967	
12	I Can See For Miles	(Track 604 011)	10	1967	9	1967	(Decca 32006)
13	Call Me Lightning	(Track 604 023)	25	1968	40	1968	(Decca 32288)
14	Dogs	(Track 604 023)	25	1968	0	1968	
15	Magic Bus	(Track 604 024)	26	1968	25	1968	(Decca 32362)
16	Pinball Wizard	(Track 604 027)	4	1969	19	1969	(Decca 32465)
17	I'm Free		0	1969	37	1969	(Decca 32519)
18	The Seeker	(Track 604 036)	19	1970	44	1970	(Decca 32670)
19	Summertime Blues	(Track 2094 002)	38	1970	27	1970	(Decca 32708)
20	See Me, Feel Me		0	1970	12	1970	(Decca 32729)
21	Won't Get Fooled Again	(Track 2094 009)	9	1971	15	1971	(Decca 32846)
22	Let's See Action	(Track 2094 012)	16	1971	0	1971	
23	Behind Blue Eyes		0	1971	34	1971	(Decca 32888)
24	Join Together	(Track 2094 102)	9	1972	17	1972	(Decca 32983)
25	Relay	(Track 2094 106)	21	1973	39	1972	(Track 33041)
26	Love Reign O'er Me		0	1973	76	1973	(MCA 40152)
27	5.15	(Track 2094 115)	20	1973	0	1973	
28	The Real Me		0	1974	92	1974	(MCA 40182)
29	Squeeze Box	(Polydor 2121 275)	10	1976	16	1975	(MCA 40475)
30	Substitute (Re-Issue)	(Polydor 2058 803)	7	1976	0	1976	
31	Who Are You	(Polydor Who 1)	18	1978	14	1978	(MCA 40948)
32	Long Live Rock	(Polydor Who 2)	48	1979	0	1979	
33	You Better You Bet	(Polydor Who 4)	9	1981	18	1981	(Warner Bros 49698)
34	Don't Let Go The Goat	(Polydor Who 005)	47	1981	0	1981	
35	Anthena	(Polydor Who 6)	40	1982	28	1982	(Warner Bros 29905)
36	Ready Steady Who (EP)	(Polydor Who 7)	58	1983	0	1983	
37	My Generation (Re-Issue)	(Polydor Posp 907)	68	1988	0	1988	
38	My Generation (2nd Re-Issue)	(Polydor 8546372)	31	1996	0	1996	

OBITUARY: KEITH MOON D: 7 SEP 1978 DRUG OVERDOSE

Whodini Male Rap/Scratch Duo from the USA

ISSUE	TITLE	UK LBL	UK POS	UK YEAR	US POS	US YEAR	US LBL
1	Magic's Wand	(Jive Jive 28)	47	1982	0	1982	
2	Magic's Wand (The Whodini Electric Ep)	(Jive Jive 61)	63	1984	0	1984	

Whooliganz Male Rap Duo from the USA

ISSUE	TITLE	UK LBL	UK POS	UK YEAR	US POS	US YEAR	US LBL
1	Put Your Hanz Up	(Positiva Cdtiv 17)	53	1994	0	1994	

Whoosh

ISSUE	TITLE	UK LBL	UK POS	UK YEAR	US POS	US YEAR	US LBL
1	Whoosh	(Wonderboy/A&M Wboyd 006)	72	1997	0	1997	

Whycliffe Male Vocalist from the UK

ISSUE	TITLE	UK LBL	UK POS	UK YEAR	US POS	US YEAR	US LBL
1	Heaven	(MCA Mcstd 1944)	56	1993	0	1993	
2	One More Time	(MCA Mcstd 1955)	72	1994	0	1994	

Wigan's Chosen Few Instrumental Plus Crowd Vocals from the USA

ISSUE	TITLE	UK LBL	UK POS	UK YEAR	US POS	US YEAR	US LBL
1	Footsee	(Pye Disco Demand Dds 111)	9	1975	0	1975	

Wigan's Ovation Male Vocal/Instrumental Group from the UK

ISSUE	TITLE	UK LBL	UK POS	UK YEAR	US POS	US YEAR	US LBL
1	Skiing In The Snow	(Spart Srl 1122)	12	1975	0	1975	
2	Per-So-Nal-Ly	(Spark Srl 1129)	38	1975	0	1975	
3	Super Love	(Spark Srl 1133)	41	1975	0	1975	

ISSUE	TITLE	UK LBL	UK POS	UK YEAR	US POS	US YEAR	US LBL
Wilbert Harrison Male R&B Vocalist, B: 5 Jan 1929 Charlotte, North Carolina							
* 1	Kansas City		0	1959	1	1959	(Fury 1023)
2	Let's Work Together (Part 1)		0	1970	32	1970	(Sue 11)
Wild Cherry Male Vocal/Instrumental Group from the USA Names Bob Parissi, Mark Avsec, Allen Wentz, Bryan Bassett & Ron Beitle							
* 1	Play That Funcky Music	(Epic Epc 4593)	7	1976	1	1976	(Epic 50225)
Wild Colour Mixed Vocal/Instrumental Group from the UK							
1	Dreams	(Perfecto Perf 105cd)	25	1995	0	1995	
Wild Weekend Male Vocal/Instrumental Group from the UK							
1	Breakin' Up	(Parlophone R 6204)	74	1989	0	1989	
2	Who's Afraid Of The Big Bad Love	(Parlophone R 6249)	70	1990	0	1990	
Wildchild Male Producer Roger Mckenzie from the UK							
1	Legends Of The Dark Black (Part 2)	(Hi-Life Hicd 9)	34	1995	0	1995	
2	Renegade Master (Re-Issue)	(Hi-Life 5771312)	11	1995	0	1995	
3	Jump To My Beat	(Hi-Life 5757372)	30	1996	0	1996	
Wildhearts Male Vocalist from the UK							
1	Tv Tan	(Bronze Yz 784cd)	53	1993	0	1993	
2	Caffeine Bomb	(Bronze Yz 794cd)	31	1994	0	1994	
3	Suckerpunch	(Bronz Yz 828cd)	38	1994	0	1994	
4	If Life Is Like A Love Bank I Want An Overdraft	(East West Yx 874cd)	31	1995	0	1995	
5	I Wanna Go Where The People Go	(East West Yz 923cd)	16	1995	0	1995	
6	Just In Lust	(East West Yz 967cd)	28	1995	0	1995	
7	Sick Of Drugs	(Round Wild 1cd)	14	1996	0	1996	
8	Red Light-Green Light (EP)	(Round Wild 2cd)	30	1996	0	1996	
9	Anthem	Mushroom Mush 6cd)	21	1997	0	1997	
Wilfred Brambell & Harry H. Corbett Male Actor/Vocal Duo from the UK							
1	At The Palace (Parts 1-2)		25	1963	0	1963	
Will Bradley & His Orchestra Male Orchestra Will Downing from the USA							
1	A Love Supreme	(Fourth & Broadway Brw 90)	14	1988	0	1988	
2	In My Dreams	(Fourth & Broadway Brw 104)	34	1988	0	1988	
3	Free	(Fourth & Broadway Brw 112)	58	1988	0	1988	
4	Where Is The Love	(Fourth & Broadway Brw 122)	19	1989	0	1989	
5	Test Of Time	(Fourth & Broadway Brw 146)	67	1989	0	1989	
6	Come Together As One	(Fourth & Broadway Brw 159)	48	1990	0	1990	
7	There's No Living Without You	(Fourth & Broadway Brcd 278)	67	1993	0	1993	
Will Glahe Orchestra Male Orchestra Leader/Instrumentalist (Accordion)							
*1	Beer Barrel Polka		0	1939	1	1939	(Victor V-710)
6	You Can't Be True Dear		0	1948	17	1948	(RCA Victor 1117)
7	Liechtensteiner Polka		0	1957	16	1957	(London 1755)
Will Powers Female Vocalist, Real Name Lyn Goldsmith from the USA							
1	Kissing With Confidence	(Island Is 134)	17	1983	0	1983	
	ADDITIONAL VOCALS ON HIT BY CARLY SIMON						
Will Smith							
1	Men In Black	(Columbia 6648682)	1	1997	0	1997	
Will To Power Mixed Vocal/Instrumental Duo from the USA							
* 1	Baby I Love Your Way - Freebird Medley	(Epic 653094 7)	6	1989	1	1988	(Epic 08034)
2	I'm Not In Love	(Epic 6565377)	29	1990	7	1990	(Epic 73636)
William Bell Male Vocalist, Real Name William Yarborough B: 16 Jul 1939 Memphis							
+ 1	Everybody Loves A Winner		0	1967	18	1967	(Stax 212)
+ 2	A Tribute To A King	(Stax 601 038)	31	1968	16	1968	(Stax 248)
+ 3	Private Number	(Stax 101)	8	1968	17	1968	(Stax 0005)
4	I Forgot To Be Your Lover		0	1968	45	1968	(Stax 0015)
5	Tryin' To Love Two		0	1977	10	1977	(Mercury 73839)
6	Headline News	(Absolute Lute 1)	70	1986	0	1986	
William De Vaughn Male Vocalist/Guitarist From Washington D.C.							
* 1	Be Thankful For What You've Got	(Chelsea 2005 002)	31	1974	4	1974	(Roxbury 0236)
2	Be Thankful For What You've Got	(EMI 5101)	44	1980	0	1980	
William Kapell Male Pianist from the USA							
1	The Eighteenth Variation (Rachmaninoff Rhapsody On A Theme)		0	1953	19	1953	(RCA Victor 4210)

ISSUE	TITLE	UK LBL	UK POS	UK YEAR	US POS	US YEAR	US LBL
William Orbit Male Producer from the UK							
1	Water From A Vine Leaf	(Guerilla Vscdt 1465	59	1993	0	1993	
Willie Collins Male Vocalist from the USA							
1	Where You Gonna Be Tonight	(Capitol Cl 410)	46	1986	0	1986	
Willie Colon Male Vocalist from the USA							
1	Set Fire To Me	(A&M Am 330)	41	1986	0	1986	
Willie Hutch Male Vocalist from the USA							
1	In And Out	(Motown Tmg 1285)	51	1982	0	1982	
2	Keep On Jammin'	(Motown Zb 40173)	73	1985	0	1985	
Willie Mitchell Male Guitarist, B: 1928 Ashland, Mississippi							
1	20-75		0	1964	31	1964	(Hi 2075)
2	Soul Seranade	(London Hlu 10186)	43	1968	23	1968	(Hi 2140)
3	The Champion	(London Hlu 10545)	47	1976	0	1976	
Willie Nelson Male Vocalist, B: 30 Apr 1933 Fort Worth, Texas							
28	Blue Eyes Crying In The Rain		0	1975	21	1975	(Columbia 10176)
30	Good Hearted Woman		0	1975	25	1975	(RCA 10529)
300	On The Road Again (From Honeysuckle Rose)		0	1980	20	1980	(Columbia 11351)
70	Always On My Mind	(CBS A 2511)	49	1982	5	1982	(Columbia 02741)
500	Let It Be Me		0	1982	40	1982	(Columbia 03073)
* 85	To All The Girls I've Loved Before	(CBS A 4252)	17	1984	5	1984	(Columbia 04217)
Wilson Phillips Female Vocal Trio, Sisters Wendy & Carnie Wilson & Chynna Phillips from the USA							
* 1	Hold On	(Sbk Sbk 6)	6	1990	1	1990	(Sbk 07322)
* 2	Release Me	(Sbk Sbk 11)	36	1990	1	1992	(Sbk 07327)
3	Impulsive	(Sbk Sbk 16)	42	1990	4	1990	(Sbk 07337)
4	You're In Love	(Sbk Sbk 25)	29	1991	1	1991	(Sbk 07343)
5	The Dream Is Still Alive		0	1991	12	1991	(Sbk 07356)
6	You Won't See Me Cry	(Sbk Sbk 340	18	1992	20	1992	(Sbk 07385)
7	Give It Up	(Sbk Sbk 36)	36	1992	30	1992	(Sbk 50398)
Wilson Pickett Male Vocalist, B: 18 Mar 1941, Prattville, Alabama							
+ 1	If You Need Me		0	1963	30	1963	(Double-L 713)
2	It's Too Late		0	1963	49	1963	(Double-L 717)
* 3	In The Midnight Hour	(Atlantic At 4036)	12	1965	21	1965	(Atlantic 2289)
4	Don't Fight It	(Atlantic At 4052)	29	1965	53	1965	(Atlantic 2306)
5	634-5789	(Atlantic At 4072)	36	1966	13	1966	(Atlantic 2320)
+ 6	Ninety Nine And A Half		0	1966	13	1966	(Atlantic 2334)
* 7	Land Of A 1000 Dances	(Atlantic 584-039)	22	1966	6	1966	(Atlantic 2348)
* 8	Mustang Sally	(Atlantic 584-066)	28	1966	23	1966	(Atlantic 2365)
9	Everybody Needs Somebody To Love		0	1967	29	1967	(Atlantic 2381)
10	I Found A Love (Part 1)		0	1967	32	1967	(Atlantic 2394)
+ 11	Soul Dance Number Three		0	1967	10	1967	(Atlantic 2412)
* 12	Funky Broadway	(Atlantic 584-130)	43	1967	8	1967	(Atlantic 2430)
13	Stag-O-Lee		0	1968	15	1968	(Atlantic 2448)
14	Jealous Love		0	1968	50	1968	(Atlantic 2484)
15	She's Lookin' Good		0	1968	15	1968	(Atlantic 2504)
16	I'm A Midnight Mover	(Atlantic 584-203)	38	1968	24	1968	(Atlantic 2528)
17	I Found A True Lov		0	1968	42	1968	(Atlantic 2558)
18	A Man And A Half		0	1968	42	1968	(Atlantic 2575)
19	Hey Jude	(Atlantic 584-236)	16	1969	23	1969	(Atlantic 2591)
20	Minnie Skirt Minnie		0	1969	50	1969	(Atlantic 2611)
+ 21	You Keep Me Hanging On		0	1969	16	1969	(Atlantic 2682)
22	Sugar Sugar		0	1970	25	1970	(Atlantic 2722)
23	Engine Number 9		0	1970	14	1970	(Atlantic 2765)
* 24	Don't Let The Green Grass Fool You		0	1971	17	1971	(Atlantic 2781)
* 25	Don't Knock My Love (Part 1)		0	1971	13	1971	(Atlantic 2797)
26	Fire And Water		0	1972	24	1972	(Atlantic 2852)
27	In The Midnight Hour (Re-Recording)	(Motown Zb 41583)	62	1987	0	1987	
Wilton Felder Male Saxophonist from the USA							
1	Inherit The Wind	(MCA 646)	39	1980	0	1980	
2	(No Matter How High I Get) I'll Still Be Lookin' Up	(MCA MCA 919)	63	1985	0	1985	
HITS 1-2 HAS UNCREDITED VOCALS BY BOBBY WOMACK • HIT 2 HAS CO-VOCALS BY ALTRINA GRAYSON							
Wilton Place Street Band The Hit Is A Studio Production In Wilton Place							
1	Disco Lucy (I Love Lucy Theme)		0	1977	24	1977	(Island 078)

ISSUE	TITLE	UK LBL	UK POS	UK YEAR	US POS	US YEAR	US LBL
Win Male Vocal/Instrumental Group from the UK							
1	Super Popoid Groove	(Swamplands Lon 128)	63	1987	0	1987	
Winans Male Vocal Group from the USA							
1	Let My People Go (Part 1)	(Qwest Q 8874)	71	1985	0	1985	
Wind Lead Singer With The Studio Group Is Tony Orlando							
1	Make Believe / Groovin With Mr. Bloe		0	1969	28	1969	(Life 200)
Windjammer Male Vocal/Instrumental Group from the USA							
1	Tossing And Turning	(MCA MCA 897)	18	1984	0	1984	
Windsor Davies & Don Estelle Male Actor/Vocal Duo from the UK							
1	Whispering Grass	(EMI 2290)	1	1975	0	1975	
2	Paper Doll	(EMI 2361)	41	1975	0	1975	
Wing And A Prayer Fife And Drum Corps Mixed Vocal/Instrumental Group from the USA							
1	Baby Face	(Atlantic K 10705)	12	1976	14	1975	(Wing & Prayer 103)
Winger Male Vocal/Instrumental Group from the USA							
1	Seventeen		0	1989	26	1989	(Atlantic 88958)
2	Headed For A Heartbreak		0	1989	19	1989	(Atlantic 88922)
3	Miles Away	(Atlantic A 7802)	56	1991	12	1990	(Atlantic 87824)
Winifred Atwell Female Pianist from the UK							
* 1	Black And White Rag	(Various Labels)	0	1952	0	1952	
2	Britannia Rag	(Decca F 10015)	11	1952	0	1952	
3	Britannia Rag (Re-Entry)	(Decca F 10015)	5	1953	0	1953	
4	Coronation Rag	(Decca F 10110)	12	1953	0	1953	
5	Coronation Rag (Re-Entry)	(Decca F 10110)	5	1953	0	1953	
6	Flirtation Waltz	(Decca F 10161)	12	1953	0	1953	
7	Flirtation Waltz (Re-Entry)	(Decca F 10161)	10	1953	0	1953	
8	Flirtation Waltz (2nd Re-Entry)	(Decca F 10161)	12	1953	0	1953	
* 9	Let's Have A Party	(Philips Pb 213)	2	1953	0	1953	
10	Rachmaninoff's 18th Variation On A Theme By Paganini	(Philips Pb 234)	9	1954	0	1954	
11	Rachmaninoff's 18th Variation ... (Re-Entry)	(Philips Pb 234)	19	1954	0	1954	
* 12	Let's Have Another Party	(Philips Pb 268)	1	1954	0	1954	
13	Let's Have A Party (Re-Entry)	(Philips Pb 213)	14	1954	0	1954	
14	Let's Have A Ding Dong	(Decca F 10634)	3	1955	0	1955	
15	Poor People Of Paris	(Decca F 10681)	1	1956	0	1956	
16	Port Au Prince	(Decca F 10727)	18	1956	0	1956	
17	Left Bank	(Decca F 10762)	14	1956	0	1956	
18	Make It A Party	(Decca F 10796)	7	1956	0	1956	
19	Let's Rock 'N Roll	(Decca F 10852)	28	1957	0	1957	
20	Let's Rock 'N Roll (Re-Entry)	(Decca F 10852)	24	1957	0	1957	
21	Let's Have A Ball	(Decca F 10956)	4	1957	0	1957	
22	Summer Of The Seventeenth Doll	(Decca F 11143)	24	1959	0	1959	
23	Piano Party	(Decca F 11183)	10	1959	0	1959	
Winifred Shaw Female Vocalist from the USA							
1	Lullaby Of Broadway	(United Artists Up 36131)	42	1976	0	1976	
Wink Martindale Male Vocalist/Tv Show Host, Real Name Winston Martindale B: 4 Dec 1933 In Jackson, Tennessee							
* 1	Deck Of Cards	(London Hld 8962)	18	1959	7	1959	(Dot 15968)
2	Deck Of Cards (Re-Entry)	(London Hld 8962)	28	1960	0	1960	
3	Deck Of Cards (2nd Re-Entry)	(London Hld 8962)	45	1960	0	1960	
4	Deck Of Cards (3rd Re-Entry)	(London Hld 8962)	5	1963	0	1963	
5	Deck Of Cards (Re-Issue)	(Dot Dot 109)	22	1973	0	1973	
Winstons Richard Spencer Leads This Soul Septet From Washington D.C.							
* 1	Color Him Father		0	1969	7	1969	(Metromedia 117)
Wire Male Vocal/Instrumental Group from the UK							
1	Outdoor Miner	(Harvest Har 5172)	51	1979	0	1979	
2	Eardrum Buzz	(Mute Mute 87)	68	1989	0	1989	
Wireless							
1	I Need You	(Chrysalis Cdchs 5059)	68	1997	0	1997	
Wizzard Male Vocal/Instrum. Group from the UK, Roy Wood, Rick Price, Bill Hunt, Mike Bernie, Nick Pentelow, Charlie Grima, Keith Smart & Hugh McDowell							
1	Ball Park Incident	(Harvest Har 5062)	1	1972	0	1972	
* 2	See My Baby Jive	(Harvest Har 5070)	1	1973	0	1973	
3	Angel Fingers	(Harvest Har 5076)		1973	0	1973	

ISSUE	TITLE	UK LBL	UK POS	UK YEAR	US POS	US YEAR	US LBL
4	I Wish It Could Be Christmas Everyday	(Harvest Har 5079)	4	1973	0	1973	
5	Rock 'N' Roll Winter	(Warner Bros K 16357)	6	1974	0	1974	
6	This Is The Story Of My Love (Baby)	(Warner Bros K 16434)	34	1974	0	1974	
7	Are You Ready To Rock	(Warner Bros K 16497)	8	1974	0	1974	
8	I Wish It Could Be Christmas (Re-Issue)	(Harvest Har 5173)	41	1981	0	1981	
9	I Wish It Could Be Christmas (Re-Entry)	(Harvest Har 5173)	23	1984	0	1984	

Wolfsbane   Male Vocal/Instrumental Group from the USA

ISSUE	TITLE	UK LBL	UK POS	UK YEAR	US POS	US YEAR	US LBL
1	Ezy	(Def America Defa 11)	68	1991	0	1991	

Womack And Womack   Mixed Vocal Duo from the USA

ISSUE	TITLE	UK LBL	UK POS	UK YEAR	US POS	US YEAR	US LBL
1	Love Wars	(Elektra E 9799)	14	1984	0	1984	
2	Baby I'm Scared Of You	(Elektra E 9733)	72	1984	0	1984	
3	Soul Love - Soul Man	(Manhattan Mt 16)	58	1986	0	1986	
4	Teardrops	(Fourth & Broadway Brw 101)	3	1988	0	1988	
5	Life's Just A Ballgame	(Fourth & Broadway Brw 116)	32	1988	0	1988	
6	Celebrate The World	(Fourth & Broadway Brw 125)	19	1989	0	1989	
7	Secret Star	(Warner Bros W 0222cd)	46	1994	0	1994	

Wombles   Male Producer/Vocalist, Real Name Mike Batt from the UK

ISSUE	TITLE	UK LBL	UK POS	UK YEAR	US POS	US YEAR	US LBL
1	The Wombling Song	(CBS 1794)	4	1974	0	1974	
2	Remember Your A Womble	(CBS 2241)	3	1974	0	1974	
3	Banana Rock	(CBS 2465)	9	1974	0	1974	
4	Minuetto Allegretto	(CBS 2710)	16	1974	0	1974	
5	Wombling Merry Christmas	(CBS 2842)	2	1974	0	1974	
6	Wombling White Tie And Tails	(CBS 3266)	22	1975	0	1975	
7	Super Womble	(CBS 3480)	20	1975	0	1975	
8	Let's Womble To The Party Tonight	(CBS 3794)	34	1975	0	1975	

Wonder Dogs   Canine Vocal Group from the UK

ISSUE	TITLE	UK LBL	UK POS	UK YEAR	US POS	US YEAR	US LBL
1	Ruff Mix	(Flip Flip 001)	31	1982	0	1982	

Wonder Stuff   Male Vocal/Instrumental Group from the UK

ISSUE	TITLE	UK LBL	UK POS	UK YEAR	US POS	US YEAR	US LBL
1	Give Give Give Me More More More	(Polydor Gone 3)	72	1988	0	1988	
2	A Wish Away	(Polydor Gone 4)	43	1988	0	1988	
3	It's Yer Money I'm After Baby	(Polydor Gone 5)	40	1988	0	1988	
4	Who Wants To Be The Disco King	(Far Out Gone 6	28	1989	0	1989	
5	Don't Let Me Down Gently	(Polydor Gone 7)	19	1989	0	1989	
6	Golden Green / Get Together	(Polydor Gone 8)	33	1989	0	1989	
7	Circlesquare	(Polydor Gone 10)	20	1990	0	1990	
8	The Size Of A Cow	(Polydor Gone 11)	5	1991	0	1991	
9	Caught In My Shadow	(Polydor Gone 12)	18	1991	0	1991	
10	Sleep Alone	(Polydor Gone 13)	43	1991	0	1991	
11	Dizzy	(Sense Sigh 712)	1	1991	0	1991	
12	Welcome To The Cheap Seats (EP)	(Polydor Gone 14)	8	1992	0	1992	
13	On The Ropes (EP)	(Polydor Goncd 15)	10	1993	0	1993	
14	Full Of Life (Happy Now)	(Polydor Goncd 16)	28	1993	0	1993	
15	Hot Love Now (EP)	(Polydor Goncd 17)	19	1994	0	1994	
16	Unbearable	(Polydor Goncd 18)	16	1994	0	1994	

Wonders

ISSUE	TITLE	UK LBL	UK POS	UK YEAR	US POS	US YEAR	US LBL
1	That Thing You Do! (From That Thing You Do!)	(Play-Tone/Epic 6640552)	22	1997	1	1996	(Epic 78401)

Woodentops   Male Vocal/Instrumental Group from the UK

ISSUE	TITLE	UK LBL	UK POS	UK YEAR	US POS	US YEAR	US LBL
1	Everyday Living	(Rough Trade Rt 178)	72	1986	0	1986	

Woody Herman Orchestra   Male Instrumentalist (Clarinet & Saxophone)/Orchestra Leader, Real Name Woodrow Wilson Herman B: 16 May 1913 In Milwaukee

ISSUE	TITLE	UK LBL	UK POS	UK YEAR	US POS	US YEAR	US LBL
1	I Double Dare You		0	1937	18	1937	(Decca 1523)
* 2	At The Woodchopper's Ball		0	1939	9	1939	(Decca 2440)
40	Gee, It's Good To Hold You		0	1946	17	1946	(Columbia 36870)
41	Let It Snow, Let It Snow, Let It Snow!		0	1946	7	1946	(Columbia 36909)
42	Everybody Knew But Me		0	1946	11	1946	(Columbia 36909)
43	Atlanta G.A		0	1946	11	1946	(Columbia 36949)
44	Surrender		0	1946	8	1946	(Columbia 36985)
45	Mabel! Mabel!		0	1946	12	1946	(Columbia 36995)
46	Across The Alley From The Alamo		0	1947	12	1947	(Columbia 37289)
47	That's My Desire		0	1947	13	1947	(Columbia 37329)
48	Tallahassee (From Variety Girl)		0	1947	15	1947	(Columbia 37387)
49	Pancho Maximillian Hernandez		0	1947	25	1947	(Columbia 37355)
50	Civilization (Bongo, Bongo, Bongo) (From Angel In The Wings)		0	1947	15	1947	(Columbia 37885)
51	I Told Ya I Love Ya, Now Get Out		0	1948	23	1948	(Columbia 38047)

ISSUE	TITLE	UK LBL	UK POS	UK YEAR	US POS	US YEAR	US LBL
52	Sabre Dance		0	1948	3	1948	(Columbia 38102)
53	Early Autumn		0	1952	28	1952	(Mars 300)

Woolpackers Male Vocal/Instrumental Group/Cast Members Of The English Tv Soap Emmerdale

1	Hillbilly Rock Hillbilly Roll	(RCA 74321425412)	5	1996	0	1996	

Working Week Mixed Vocal/Instrumental Group from the UK

1	Venceremos – We Will Win	(Virgin Vs 684)	64	1984	0	1984	

World Of Twist Male Vocal/Instrumental Group from the UK

1	The Storm	(Circa Yr 55)	42	1990	0	1990	
2	The Storm (Re-Entry)	(Circa Yr 55)	74	1991	0	1991	
3	Sons Of The Stage	(Circa Yr 62)	47	1991	0	1991	
4	Sweets	(Circa Yr 72)	58	1991	0	1991	
5	She's A Rainbow	(Circa Yr 82)	62	1992	0	1992	

World Party Male Vocal/Instrumental Group from the UK/Ireland

1	Ship Of Fools (Save Me From Tomorrow)	(Ensign Eny 606)	42	1987	27	1987	(Chrysalis 43052)
2	Message In The Box	(Ensign Eny 631)	39	1990	0	1990	
3	Way Down Now	(Ensign Eny 634)	66	1990	0	1990	
4	Thank You World	(Ensign Eny 643)	68	1991	0	1991	
5	Is It Like Today	(Ensign Cdeny 658)	19	1993	0	1993	
6	Give It All Away	(Ensign Cdeny 659)	43	1993	0	1993	
7	All I Gave	(Ensign Cdenys 660)	37	1993	0	1993	
8	Beautiful Dream	(Chrysalis Cdchs 5053)	31	1997	0	1997	

World Premiere Male Vocal/Instrumental Group from the USA

1	Share The Night	(Epic A 4133)	64	1984	0	1984	

World Warrior Male Producer, Real Name Simon Harris from the UK

1	Street Fighter Ii	(Living Beat Lbecd 27)	70	1994	0	1994	

World's Famous Supreme Team Male Vocal/Scratch Group from the USA

1	Buffalo Gals	(Charisma Malc 1)	9	1982	0	1982	
2	Hey DJ	(Charisma Team 1)	52	1984	0	1984	
3	Opera House	(Virgin Vs 1273)	75	1990	0	1990	

Worlds Apart Male Vocal Group from the UK

1	Heaven Must Be Missing An Angel	(Arista 74321139362)	29	1993	0	1993	
2	Wonderful World	(Arista 74321153402)	51	1993	0	1993	
3	Everlasting Love	(Bell 74321164802)	20	1993	0	1993	
4	Could It Be I'm Falling In Love	(Bell 74321189952)	15	1994	0	1994	
5	Beggin' To Be Written	(Bell 74321211982)	29	1994	0	1994	

Wreckx-N-Effect Male Rap Group, Markell Riley, Aqil Davidson & Brandon Mitchell from the USA

	1	Juicy	(Motown Zb 43295)	29	1990	0	1990	
*	2	Rump Shaker	(MCA Mcs 1725)	24	1992	2	1992	(MCA 54388)
	3	Wreckx Shop	(MCA Mcstd 1969)	26	1994	0	1994	
	4	Rump Shaker (Re-Issue)	(MCA Mcstd 1989)	40	1994	0	1994	

OBITUARY : D: ALL THREE FROM GUNSHOT WOUNDS IN 1990

Wright Brothers Male Vocalists from the USA

1	If I Give My Heart To You		0	1954	25	1954	(MGM 11776)

WWF Superstars Male Wrestling/Vocalist from the USA/UK

1	Slam Jam	(Arista 74321124887)	4	1992	0	1992	
2	Slam Jam (Re-Entry)	(Arista 74321124887)	75	1993	0	1993	
3	Wrestlemania	(Arista 74321136832)	14	1993	0	1993	
4	USA	(Arista 74321153092)	71	1993	0	1993	

Wu-Tang Clan

1	Triumph	(Loud 74321510212)	46	1997	0	1997	

Wurzels Male Vocal/Instrumental Group from the UK

1	Drink Up Thy Zider	(Columbia Db 8081)	45	1967	0	1967	
2	Combine Harvester (Brand New Key)	(EMI 2450)	1	1976	0	1976	
3	I Am A Cider Drinker (Paloma Blanca)	(EMI 2520)	3	1976	0	1976	
4	Farmer's Bill's Cowman (I Was Kaiser Bill's Batman)	(EMI 2637)	32	1977	0	1977	

Wyclef Jean & The Refugee Allstars

1	We Trying To Stay Alive	(Columbia 6646815)	13	1997	0	1997	

ISSUE	TITLE	UK LBL	UK POS	UK YEAR	US POS	US YEAR	US LBL
X-Press 2	Male Production/Instrumental Group from the UK						
1	London X-Press	(Junior Boy's Own Jbo 12)	59	1993	0	1993	
2	So What!	(Junior Boy's Own Jbo 16cd)	32	1993	0	1993	
3	Rock 2 House / Hip Housin'	(Junior Boy's Own Jbo 21cd)	55	1994	0	1994	
4	The Sound	(Junior Boy's Own Jbo 36)	38	1996	0	1996	
5	Tranz Euro Xpress	(Junior Boy's Own Jbo 42cd)	45	1996	0	1996	
	Hit 3 is Credited To X-Press 2 Featuring Lo-Pro						
X-Ray Spex	Mixed Vocal/Instrumental Group from the UK						
1	The Day The World Turned Day-Glo	(EMI International Int 553)	23	1978	0	1978	
2	Identity	(EMI International Int 563)	24	1978	0	1978	
3	Germ Free Adolescents	(EMI International Int 573)	19	1978	0	1978	
4	Highly Inflammable	(EMI International Int 573)	45	1979	0	1979	
X-Static	Mixed Vocal/Instrumental Group from Italy						
1	I'm Standing (Higher)	(Positiva Cdtiv 25)	41	1995	0	1995	
Xavier	Male Vocal/Instrumental Group from the USA						
1	Work That Sucker To Death / Love Is The One	(Liberty Up 651)	53	1982	0	1982	
Xpansions	Male Producer, Real Name Ritchie Malone from the UK						
1	Elevation	(Arista 113683)	49	1990	0	1990	
2	Move Your Body (Elevation) (Re-Entry)	(Arista 113683)	7	1991	0	1991	
3	What You Want	(Arista 114 246)	55	1991	0	1991	
4	Move Your Body (Re-Mix)	(Arista 74321294982)	14	1995	0	1995	
Xscape	Female Vocal Group from the USA						
1	Just Kickin' It	(Columbia 6598622)	29	1993	2	1993	(So So Def 77119)
* 2	Understanding		0	1994	8	1994	(So So Def 77335)
3	Just Kickin' It (Re-Issue)	(Columbia 6608642)	54	1994	0	1994	
* 4	Feels So Good	(Columbia 6625022)	34	1995	32	1995	(So So Def 77921)
* 5	Who Can I Run To?	(Columbia 6628112)	31	1996	8	1995	(So So Def 78056)
6	Keep On, Keeping On	(East West A 4287cd)	39	1996	10	1996	(Flavour Unit)
7	Do You Want To		0	1996	50	1996	
	Hit 6 Is Credited To Xscape Featuring Mc Lyte						
XTC	Male Vocal/Instrumental Group from the UK						
1	Live Begins At The Hop	(Virgin Vs 259)	54	1979	0	1979	
2	Making Plans For Nigel	(Virgin Vs 282)	17	1979	0	1979	
3	Generals And Majors / Don't Lose Your Temper	(Virgin Vs 365)	32	1980	0	1980	
4	Towers Of London	(Virgin Vs 372)	31	1980	0	1980	
5	Sgt Rock (Is Going To Help Me)	(Virgin Vs 384)	16	1981	0	1981	
6	Senses Working Overtime	(Virgin Vs 462)	10	1982	0	1982	
7	Ball And Chain	(Virgin Vs 482)	58	1982	0	1982	
8	Love On A Farmboy's Wages	(Virgin Vs 613)	50	1983	0	1983	
9	All You Pretty Girls	(Virgin Vs 709)	55	1984	0	1984	
10	Mayor Of Simpleton	(Virgin Vs 1158)	46	1989	0	1989	
11	The Disappointed	(Virgin Vs 1404)	33	1992	0	1992	
12	The Ballad Of Peter Pumpkinhead	(Virgin Vs 1415)	71	1992	0	1992	

Y

ISSUE	TITLE	UK LBL	UK POS	UK YEAR	US POS	US YEAR	US LBL
Y & T	Male Vocal/Instrumental Group from the USA						
1	Mean Streak	(A&M Am 135)	41	1983	0	1983	
Y?N-Vee	Female Vocal Group from the USA						
1	Chocolate	(Ral Ralcd 2)	65	1994	0	1994	
Yannis Markopoulos	Orchestra From Greece						
1	Who Pays The Ferryman	(BBC Resl 51)	11	1968	0	1968	
Yarbrough & Peoples	Mixed Vocal/Instrumental Duo from the USA						
1	Don't Stop The Music	(Mercury Mer 53)	7	1980	1	9 *	1981	(Mercury 76085)
2	Don't Waste Your Time	(Total Experience Xe 501)	60	1984	0	1984	
3	Guilty	(Total Experience Fb 49905)	53	1986	0	1986	
4	I Wouldn't Lie	(Total Experience Fb 49841)	61	1986	0	1986	
	NAMES: CAVIN YARBROUGH & ALISA PEOPLES						
Yardbirds	Male Vocal/Instrumental Group from the UK Names: Keith Relf, Chris Dreja, Paul Samwell-Smith, Anthony Topham & Jim McCarty						
1	Good Morning Little Schoolgirl	(Columbia Db 7391)	44	1964	0	1964	
* 2	For Your Love	(Columbia Db 7499)	3	1965	6	1965	(Epic 9790)
3	Heart Full Of Soul	(Columbia Db 7594)	2	1965	9	1965	(Epic 9823)
4	Evil Hearted You / Still I'm Sad	(Columbia Db 7706)	3	1965	0	1965	
5	I'm A Man		0	1965	17	1965	(Epic 9857)
6	Shapes Of Things	(Columbia Db 7848)	3	1966	11	1966	(Epic 10006)
7	Over Under Sideways Down	(Columbia Db 7928)	10	1966	13	1966	(Epic 10035)
8	Happenings Ten Years Time Ago	(Columbia Db 8024)	43	1966	30	1966	(Epic 10094)
Yazoo	Mixed Vocal/Instrumental Duo From The UK						
1	Only You	(Mute Mute 020)	2	1982	0	1982	
2	Don't Go	(Mute Yaz 001)	3	1982	0	1982	
3	The Other Side Of Love	(Mute Yaz 002)	13	1982	0	1982	
4	Nobody's Diary	(Mute Yaz 003)	3	1983	0	1983	
5	Situation	(Mute Yaz 4)	14	1990	0	1990	
Yazz	Female Vocalist From The UK						
1	Doctorin' The House	(Ahead Of Our Time Ccut 27)	6	1988	0	1988	
2	The Only Way Is Up	(Big Life Blr 4)	1	1988	0	1988	
3	Stand Up For Your Love Rights	(Big Life Blr 5)	2	1988	0	1988	
4	Fine Time	(Big Life Blr 6)	9	1989	0	1989	
5	Where Has All The Love Gone	(Big Life Blr 8)	16	1989	0	1989	
6	Treat Me Good	(Big Life Blr 24)	20	1990	0	1990	
7	One True Woman	(Polydor Po 198)	60	1992	0	1992	
8	How Long	(Polydor Pzcd 252)	31	1993	0	1993	with Aswad
9	Have Mercy	(Polydor Pzcd 309)	42	1994	0	1994	
10	Everybody's Got To Learn Sometime	(Polydor Pzcd 316)	56	1994	0	1994	
11	Good Thing Going	(East West Ew 062cd)	53	1996	0	1996	
12	Never Can Say Goodbye	(East West Ew 081cd)	61	1997	0	1997	
Yell!	Male Vocal Duo from the UK						
1	Instant Replay	(Fanfare Fan 22)	10	1990	0	1990	
Yello	Male Vocal/Instrumental Duo from Switzerland						
1	I Love You	(Stiff Buy 176)	41	1983	0	1983	
2	Lost Again	(Stiff Buy 191)	73	1983	0	1983	
3	Goldrush	(Mercury Mer 218)	54	1986	0	1986	
4	The Rhythm Divine	(Mercury Mer 253)	54	1987	0	1987	
5	The Race	(Mercury Yello 1)	7	1988	0	1988	
6	Tied Up	(Mercury Yello 2)	60	1988	0	1988	
7	Of Course I'm Lying	(Mercury Yello 3)	23	1989	0	1989	

ISSUE	TITLE	UK LBL	UK POS	UK YEAR	US POS	US YEAR	US LBL
8	Blazing Saddles	(Mercury Yello 4)	47	1989	0	1989	
9	Rubberbandman	(Mercury Yello 5)	58	1991	0	1991	
10	Jungle Bill	(Mercury Mer 376)	61	1992	0	1992	
11	The Race (Re-Issue)	(Mercury Mer 382)	55	1992	0	1992	
12	How How	(Mercury Mercd 414)	59	1994	0	1994	

HIT 4 IS CREDITED TO YELLO FEATURING SHIRLEY BASSEY

Yellow Balloon Lead Singer With The Quintet Is Alex Valdez

| 1 | Yellow Balloon | | 0 | 1967 | 25 | 1967 | (Canterbury 508) |

Yellow Dog Male Vocal/Instrumental Group From The Usa/Uk

| 1 | Just One More Night | (Virgin Vs 195) | 8 | 1978 | 0 | 1978 | |
| 2 | Wait Until Midnight | (Virgin Vs 217) | 54 | 1978 | 0 | 1978 | |

Yellow Magic Orchestra Male Instrumental Group From Japan

| 1 | Computer Game (Theme From The Invaders) | (A&M Ams 7502) | 17 | 1980 | 0 | 1980 | |

Yes Male Vocal/Instrumental Group from the UK/South Africa

1	Your Move		0	1971	40	1971	(Atlantic 2819)
2	Roundabout		0	1972	13	1972	(Atlantic 2854)
3	Wonderous Stories	(Atlantic K 10999)	7	1977	0	1977	
4	Going For The One	(Atlantic K 11047)	24	1977	0	1977	
5	Don't Kill The Whale	(Atlantic K 11184)	36	1978	0	1978	
6	Owner Of A Lonely Heart	(Atco B 9817)	28	1983	1	1983	(Atco 99817)
7	Leave It	(Atco B 9787)	56	1984	24	1984	(Atco 99787)
8	Love Will Find A Way	(Atco A 9449)	73	1987	30	1987	(Atco 99449)
9	Rhythm Of Love		0	1988	40	1988	(Atco 99419)

ROCK-GROUP FORMED IN 1968 WITH VOCALS FROM JON ANDERSON
THE GROUP WERE ALL FROM THE UK FOR THE FIRST FIVE HITS

Yin & Yan Male Vocal Duo from the UK

| 1 | If | (EMI 2282) | 25 | 1975 | 0 | 1975 | |

Yo-Yo Female Rapper, Real Name Yolanda Whitaker B: 4 Aug 1971 From Los Angeles

| 1 | You Can't Play With My Yo-Yo | | 0 | 1991 | 36 | 1991 | (Eastwest 98831) |

Yogi Yorgesson & The John Duffy Trio Real Name Harry Stewart Sweden

| * 1 | I Yust Go Nuts At Christmas | | 0 | 1949 | 5 | 1949 | (Capitol 781) |

Yoko Ono Female Vocalist from Japan

| 1 | Walking On Thin Ice | (Geffen K 79202) | 35 | 1981 | 0 | 1981 | |

Yosh (Featuring) Lovedeejay Akemi

| 1 | It's What's Up Front That Counts | (Limbo Limb 46cd) | 69 | 1995 | 0 | 1995 | |
| 3 | The Screamer | (Limbo Limb 54cd) | 38 | 1996 | 0 | 1996 | |

Yothu Yindi Male Vocal/Instrumental Group from Australia

| 1 | Treaty | (Hollywood Hwd 116) | 72 | 1992 | 0 | 1992 | |

Young & Company Mixed Vocal/Instrumental Group from the USA

| 1 | I Like (What You're Doing To Me) | (Excalibur Exc 501) | 0 | 1980 | 0 | 1980 | |

Young & Moody Band Male Vocal/Instrumental Group from the UK

| 1 | Don't Do That | (Bronze Bro 130) | 63 | 1981 | 0 | 1981 | |

Young Black Teenagers

| 1 | Tap The Bottle | (MCA Mcstd 1967) | 39 | 1994 | 0 | 1994 | |

Young Disciples Mixed Vocal/Instrumental Group from the UK/USA

1	Get Yourself Together	(Talkin Loud Tlk 2)	68	1990	0	1990	
2	Apparently Nothin'	(Talkin Loud Tlk 5)	46	1991	0	1991	
3	Apparently Nothin' (Re-Entry)	(Talkin Loud Tlk 5)	13	1991	0	1991	
4	Get Yourself Together (Re-Issue)	(Talkin Loud Tlk 15)	65	1991	0	1991	
5	Young Disciples (EP)	(Talkin Loud Tlk 18)	48	1992	0	1992	

Young Idea Male Vocal Duo from the UK

| 1 | With A Little Help From My Friends | (Columbia Db 8205) | 10 | 1967 | 0 | 1967 | |

Young Mc Male Rapper, Real Name Marvin Young B: 10 May 1967 England

| * 1 | Bust A Move | (Delicious Vinyl Brw 137) | 73 | 1989 | 7 | 1989 | (Delicious Vinyl 105) |
| 2 | Principal's Office | (Delicious Vinyl Brw 161) | 54 | 1990 | 33 | 1990 | (Delicious Vinyl 99137) |

Young Mc

| 3 | That's The Way Love Goes | (Capitol Cl 623) | 65 | 1991 | 0 | 1991 | |

Young-Holt Unlimited Names Eldee Young, Isaac Holt & Don Walker Who Left In 1968

| 1 | Wack Wack | | 0 | 1967 | 40 | 1967 | (Brunswick 55305) |
| * 2 | Soulful Strut | | 0 | 1968 | 3 | 1968 | (Brunswick 55391) |

HIT 1 IS CREDITED TO THE YOUNG HOLT TRIO

ISSUE	TITLE	UK LBL	UK POS	UK YEAR	US POS	US YEAR	US LBL
Youngbloods Names Jesse Colin Young, Jerry Corbitt, Lovell Levinger & Joe Bauer							
1	Get Together		0	1967	62	1967	(RCA 9752)
* 2	Get Together (Re-Issue)		0	1969	5	1969	(RCA 9752)
	YOUNG WAS B: PERRY MILLER 11 NOV 1944						
Youssou N'dour Male Vocalist From Senegal							
1	Shaking The Tree	(Virgin Vs 1167)	61	1969	0	1969	
2	Shaking The Tree (Re-Issue)	(Virgin Vs 1167)	57	1990	0	1990	
3	7 Seconds	(Columbia 6605082)	3	1994	0	1994	
4	7 Seconds (Re-Entry)	(Columbia 6605082)	60	1994	0	1994	
5	Undecided	(Columbia 6609712)	53	1995	0	1995	
Yvonne Elliman Female Vocalist, B: 29 Dec 1951 Honolulu							
1	I Don't Know How To Love Him	(MCA Mmks 5077)	47	1972	28	1971	(Decca 32785)
2	Love Me	(RSO 2090 205)	6	1976	14	1976	(RSO 858)
3	Hello Stranger	(Rso 2090 236)	26	1977	15	1977	(RSO 871)
5	If I Can't Have You	(RSO 2090 266)	4	1978	1	1978	(RSO 884)
6	Love Pains		0	1979	34	1979	(RSO 1007)
Yvonne Fair Female Vocalist from the USA							
1	It Should Have Been Me	(Tamla Motown Tmg 1013)	5	1976	0	1976	
Yvonne Gage Female Vocalist from the USA							
1	Doin' It In A Haunted House	(Epic A 4519)	45	1984	0	1984	
Yvonne Keele See Scott Fitzgerald							
Yogi Yorgesson & The John Duffy Trio							
2	Yingle Bells		0	1949	7	1949	(Capitol 781)
Yosh (Featuring) Lovedeejay Akemi Male Producer From Holland							
2	It's What's Up Front That Counts (Re-Mix)	(Limbo Limb 50cd)	31	1995	0	1995	
Yvette Michele Female Vocalist from the USA							
1	I'm Not Feeling You	(Loud 74321465222)	36	1997	44	1997	(Loud 64789)
Y-Traxx							
1	Mystery Land (EP)	(Ffrr Fcd 292)	63	1997	0	1997	

Z

ISSUE	TITLE	UK LBL	UK POS	UK YEAR	US POS	US YEAR	US LBL
Zager & Evans Male Vocal Duo, Real Names Denny Zager & Rick Evans from the USA							
1	In The Year 2525 (Exordium And Terminus)	RCA 1860)	1	1969	1 *	1969	(RCA 0174)
Zaine Griff Male Vocalist from New Zealand							
1	Tonight	(Automatic K 17547)	54	1980	0	1980	
2	Ashes And Diamonds	(Automatic K 17610)	68	1980	0	1980	
Zapp Male Vocal/Instrumental Group from the USA							
1	It Doesn't Really Matter	(Warner Bros W 8879)	57	1986	0	1986	
2	Computer Love (Part 1)	(Warner Bros W 8805)	64	1986	0	1986	
Zee Female Vocalist from the UK							
1	Dreamtime	(Perfecto Perf 122cd)	31	1996	0	1996	
2	Say My Name	(Perfecto Perf 135cd)	36	1997	0	1997	
Zeitia Massiah Female Vocalist from the UK							
1	I Specialize In Love	(Union City Ucrcd 27)	74	1994	0	1994	
2	This Is The Place	(Virgin Vscdt 1511)	62	1994	0	1994	
	HIT 1 IS CREDITED TO ARIZONA FEATURING ZEITIA						
Zelma Davis See C & C Music Factory							
Zephyrs Male Vocal/Instrumental Group from the UK							
1	She's Lost You	(Columbia Db 7481)	48	1965	0	1965	
Zero B Male Instrumentalist (Keyboards) from the UK							
1	The (EP)	(Ffrreedom Tab 102)	32	1992	0	1992	
2	Reconnection (EP)	(Internal Liecd 6)	54	1993	0	1993	
Zero Vu (Featuring) Lorna B							
1	Feels So Good	(Avex UK Avexcd 53)	69	1997	0	1997	
Zero Zero Male Production/Instrumental Duo from the UK							
1	Zeroxed	(Kickin Kick 9)	71	1991	0	1991	
Zhane Male Vocal Duo from the USA							
1	Hey Mr. Dj	(Epic 6596102)	26	1993	6 *	1993	(Flavor Unit 77177)
2	Hey Mr. Dj (Re-Entry)	(Epic 6596102)	50	1993	0	1993	
3	Groove Thang	(Motown Tmgcd 1423)	34	1994	17	1994	(Motown 2228)
4	Vibe	(Motown Tmgcd 1430)	67	1994	0	1994	
5	Shame	(Jive Jivet 372)	66	1995	28	1994	(Hollywood/Jive 42269)
6	It's A Party	(Elektra Ekr 226cd)	23	1996	0	1996	
7	4 More	(Tommy Boy Tbcd 7779a)	52	1997	0	1997	
8	Request Line	(Motown 8606452)	22	1997	39	1997	(Motown 850614)
9	Crush	(Motown 5716712)	44	1997	0	1997	
	HIT 6 IS CREDITED TO BUSTA RHYMES FEATURING ZHANE						
	HIT 7 IS CREDITED TO DE LA SOUL FEATURING ZHANE						
Zig & Zag Male Puppet Duo From Ireland							
1	Them Girls Them Girls	(RCA 74321251042)	8	1994	0	1994	
2	Them Girls Them Girls (Re-Entry)	(RCA 74321251042)	74	1995	0	1995	
3	Hands Up! Hands Up!	(Arista 74321284392)	21	1995	0	1995	
Ziggy Elman & His Orchestra Male Bandleader/Instrumentalist (Trumpet)							
1	Body And Soul (From Three's A Crowd)		0	1947	25	1947	(MGM 10071)
	D: 26 JUN 1968, (AGED 54)						
	REAL NAME HARRY FINKELMAN, PLAYED WITH BENNY GOODMAN, TOMMY DORSEY AND OTHERS						
Ziggy Marley & The Melody Makers Mixed Vocal/Instrumental Group from Jamaica							
1	Tomorrow People	(Virgin Vs 1049)	22	1988	39	1988	(Virgin 99347)

ISSUE	TITLE	UK LBL	UK POS	UK YEAR	US POS	US YEAR	US LBL
2	Look Who's Dancing	(Virgin America Vus 5)	65	1989	0	1989	

NAMES DAVID 'ZIGGY', SHARON & STEPHEN. THEIR FATHER IS BOB MARLEY

Ziggy Talent Male Saxophonist/Novelty Singer from the USA

1	Please Say Goodnight To The Guy, Irene		0	1950	25	1950	(RCA Victor 3925)

Zion Train Mixed Vocal/Instrumental Group from the UK

1	Rise	(China Wokcd 2085)	61	1996	0	1996	

Zodiac Mindwarp & The Love Reaction Mixed Vocal/Instrumental Group from the UK

1	Prime Mover	(Mercury Zod 1)	18	1987	0	1987	
2	Backseat Education	(Mercury Zod 2)	49	1987	0	1987	
3	Planet Girl	(Mercury Zod 3)	63	1988	0	1988	

Zoe Female Vocalist from the UK

1	Sunshine On A Rainy Day	(M&G Mags 6)	53	1990	0	1990	
2	Sunshine On A Rainy Day (Re-Mix)	(M&G Mags 14)	4	1991	0	1991	
3	Lightning	(M&G Mags 18)	37	1991	0	1991	
4	Holy Days	(M&G Mags 21)	72	1992	0	1992	

Zombies Male Vocal/Instrumental Group from the UK

1	She's Not There	(Decca F 11940)	12	1964	2 *	1964	(Parrot 9675)
2	Tell Her No	(Decca F 12072)	42	1965	6	1965	(Parrot 9723)
3	Time Of The Season		0	1969	3 *	1969	(Date 1628)

Names: Rod Argent, Colin Blunstone, Paul Atkinson & Chris White
The Group Disbanded In 1967, Rod went on to form Argent

Zoo Experience (Featuring) Destry Mixed Vocal/Instrumental Group from the USA/UK

1	Love's Gotta Hold On Me	(Cooltempo Cool 261)	66	1992	0	1992	

Zoot Money & The Big Roll Band Male Instrumental Group from the UK

1	Big Time Operator	(Columbia Db 7975)	25	1966	0	1966	

Zucchero Male Vocal/Guitarist, Real Name Adelmo Fornaciari from Italy

1	Senza Una Donna (Without A Woman)	(London Lon 294)	4	1991	0	1991	
2	Diamante	(London Lon 313)	44	1992	0	1992	
3	Miserere	(London 329)	15	1992	0	1992	

HIT 1 IS CREDITED TO ZUCCHERO AND PAUL YOUNG   HIT 2 IS CREDITED TO ZUCCHERO WITH RANDY CRAWFORD
HIT 3 IS CREDITED TO ZUCCHERO WITH LUCIANO PAVAROTTI
SEE ALSO SEPARATE ENTRIES

ZZ Top Male Vocal/Instrumental Group from the USA

1	Tush		0	1975	20	1975	(London 220)
2	I Thank You		0	1980	34	1980	(Warner Bros 49163)
3	Gimme All Your Lovin'	(Warner Bros W 9693)	61	1983	37	1983	(Warner Bros 29693)
4	Sharp Dressed Man	(Warner Bros W 9576)	53	1983	0	1983	
5	TV Dinners	(Warner Bros W 9334)	67	1984	0	1984	
6	Legs	(Warner Bros W 9272)	16	1985	8	1984	(Warner Bros 29272)
7	Gimme All Your Lovin' (Re-Entry)	(Warner Bros W 9693)	10	1984	0	1984	
8	Sharp Dressed Man (Re-Entry)	(Warner Bros W 9576)	22	1984	0	1984	
9	Summer Holiday (EP)	(Warner Bros W 8946)	51	1985	0	1985	
10	Sleeping Bag	(Warner Bros W 20010	27	1985	8	1985	(Warner Bros 28884)
11	Stages	(Warner Bros W 2002)	43	1986	21	1986	(Warner Bros 28810)
12	Rough Boy	(Warner Bros W 2003)	23	1986	22	1986	(Warner Bros 28733)
13	Velcro Fly	(Warner Bros W 8650)	54	1986	35	1986	(Warner Bros 28650)
14	Doubleback	(Warner Bros W 9812)	29	1990	0	1990	
15	My Head's In Mississippi	(Warner Bros W 0009)	37	1991	0	1991	
16	Viva Las Vegas	(Warner Bros W 0098)	10	1992	0	1992	
17	Rough Boy (Re-Issue)	(Warner Bros W 0111)	49	1992	0	1992	
18	Pincushion	(RCA 74321184732)	15	1994	0	1994	
19	Breakaway	(RCA 74321192282)	60	1994	0	1994	
20	What's Up With That	(RCA 74321394822)	8	1996	0	1996	

NAMES BILLY GIBBONS, DUSTY HILL & FRED BEARD
BILLY WAS LEAD GUITARIST WITH MOVING SIDEWALKS

? & The Mysterians Male Vocal/Instrumental Group from the USA/Mexico. Lead singer of the quintet is Rudy Martinez

* 1	96 Tears	(Cameo Parkway C428)	37	1966	1	1966	(Cameo Parkway 428)
2	I Need Somebody		0	1966	22	1966	(Cameo Parkway 441)